D1078308

Who's Who in Scotland

2016

Carrick Media

Falkirk Community Trust	
LB	
Askews & Holts	
920.0411	£75.00

Published by Carrick Media
89 Mount Pleasant Way, Kilmarnock KA3 1HJ
01563 521839

Copyright 2016 Carrick Media

Printed in Great Britain by Biddles Books Limited

All rights reserved. No part of this publication may be reproduced, stored in a retrieval system or transmitted in any form or by any means, electronic, mechanical, photocopying, recording, or otherwise, without the prior permission of Carrick Media.

British Library Cataloguing-in-Publication Data
A catalogue record for this book is available from the British Library

ISBN 978-0-9933162-2-7

Preface

Welcome to Who's Who in Scotland 2016. This is a very special edition - it marks the 30th anniversary of the book. Firmly established as Scotland's dictionary of contemporary biography, this book first appeared in 1986. It is simultaneously a useful address book, a mine of information, and an essential guide to the establishments of Scotland (academic, ecclesiastical, legal, commercial, professional, political, artistic and literary) as well as to individuals who conform to no known category or establishment. Also, the book can be a source of amusement and miscellaneous interest.

Our thanks to all who responded to our requests for information about themselves, including and especially the hundreds of new entrants, without whose co-operation there would have been no book.

The Editor
Kilmarnock
June 2016

ADVERTISEMENTS

ANIMALS AND WILDLIFE

NORTH ATLANTIC SALMON CONSERVATION ORGANIZATION (NASCO)
11 Rutland Square, Edinburgh EH1 2AS

Tel: 0131 228 2551
Fax: 0131 228 4384
E-mail: hq@nasco.int
Web: www.nasco.int
Contact: Dr. Peter Hutchinson.

NASCO is an international, inter-governmental, treaty organization. It is the only inter-governmental organization with its headquarters in Scotland. NASCO is dedicated to the conservation, restoration, enhancement and rational management of wild Atlantic salmon stocks. NASCO has as its member parties: Canada, Denmark (in respect of the Faroe Islands and Greenland), the European Union, Norway, the Russian Federation, and the United States of America. All international negotiations on any aspect of the conservation of wild Atlantic salmon in the North Atlantic area are organised through NASCO in Scotland. Thirty-six non-Government organizations have observer status to NASCO.

ARTISTIC AND CULTURAL

ROYAL SCOTTISH NATIONAL ORCHESTRA
73 Claremont Street, Glasgow G3 7JB

Tel: 0141 226 3868
Fax: 0141 221 4317
E-mail: admin@rsno.org.uk
Contact: Krishna Thiagarajan, Chief Executive; Dame Susan Bruce, Chair; Peter Oundjian, Music Director.

The Royal Scottish National Orchestra is Scotland's national symphony orchestra performing a wide range of world-class music, supported by innovative community and education work, throughout Scotland and beyond.

SCOTTISH POETRY LIBRARY
5 Crichton's Close, Canongate, Edinburgh EH8 8DT

Tel: 0131 557 2876
E-mail: reception@spl.org.uk
Web: www.scottishpoetrylibrary.org.uk
Contact: Asif Khan, Director; Julie Johnstone, Librarian.

A free reference and lending library for Scotland's poetry in its three languages and for British and international poetry, with a focus on contemporary work. Stock includes books, CDs, magazines, newscuttings and a children's collection and Online catalogue, INSPIRE. Lending is free to the public; also by post. The Library has charitable status: Friends £35 for free postal borrowing, newsletter and to support the work.

SCOTTISH REVIEW ONLINE
Prestwick International Airport, Liberator House, Suite 216, Prestwick KA9 2PT

Tel: 01292 473777
Web: www.scottishreview.net
Contact: Kenneth Roy, Editor; Islay McLeod, Deputy Editor.

Weekly current affairs magazine. Informed commentary on Scottish affairs and the wider world, essays, reportage and biography. Subscribers receive the magazine free of charge by registering on http://www.scottishreview.net

CHARITABLE AND VOLUNTARY

THE ROYAL ENVIRONMENTAL HEALTH INSTITUTE OF SCOTLAND
19 Torphichen Street, Edinburgh EH3 8HX

Tel: 0131 229 2968
Fax: 0131 228 2926
E-mail: contact@rehis.com
Web: www.rehis.com
Contact: Tom Bell, Chief Executive, tb@rehis.com; President, Professor Kofi Aidoo.

The Institute is an independent, self-financing registered Scottish charity whose main objectives are for the benefit of the community to promote the advancement of Environmental Health by:
a. stimulating general interest in and disseminating knowledge concerning Environmental Health;
b. promoting education and training in matters relating to Environmental Health; and
c. maintaining, by examination or otherwise, high standards of professional practice and conduct on the part of Environmental Health Officers in Scotland.
d. Improving and protecting the health and wellbeing of Scotland's people through education, training and qualifications in Environmental Health.

THE ROYAL SOCIETY FOR THE SUPPORT OF WOMEN OF SCOTLAND
14 Rutland Square, Edinburgh EH1 2BD

Tel: 0131 229 2308
E-mail: info@igf.org
Web: www.igf.org
Contact: Dr. Maurice S. Hankey, Chief Executive Officer.

The Society originated in 1847. Applications are considered from ladies who are aged 50 years or over, resident in Scotland, single, widowed, divorced, or formally separated, of good character and require assistance by reason of financial hardship through low incomes and limited capital, age or ill-health. Scottish Charity number: SC016095.

EDUCATION

UNIVERSITIES SCOTLAND
Holyrood Park House, 106 Holyrood Road, Edinburgh EH8 8AS

Tel: 0131 226 1111
E-mail: info@universities-scotland.ac.uk
Web: www.universities-scotland.ac.uk
Contact: Alastair Sim, Director.

"The most effective regional organisation of its kind in the UK" (Commission on Scottish Education). Universities Scotland is the official voice of the Scottish universities and higher education institutions. The Convener (2012-16) is Professor Sir Pete Downes, Principal and Vice-Chancellor, University of Dundee.

THE UNIVERSITY OF EDINBURGH
Old College, South Bridge,
Edinburgh EH8 9YL

Tel: 0131 650 1000
Fax: 0131 650 2147
Web: www.ed.ac.uk
Contact: Professor Sir Timothy O'Shea, Principal, 0131 650 2150; Ms Sarah Smith, University Secretary, 0131 650 2144, university.secretary@ed.ac.uk; Dr Ian Brian Conn, Director of Communications, Marketing and External Affairs, 0131 650 2248, ian.conn@ed.ac.uk

The University of Edinburgh, with some 35,582 students and over 3,992 academic and research staff, is one of the world's leading centres of higher education, devoted to excellence in teaching and research across a broad range of disciplines and professions. It especially values its intellectual and economic relationship with the Scottish community that forms its base and provides a wide range of research, educational, commercial and cultural services.

UNIVERSITY OF ST ANDREWS
College Gate, North Street, St Andrews, Fife KY16 9AJ

Tel: 01334 462525
Fax: 01334 462543
Web: www.st-andrews.ac.uk
Contact: Professor Sally Mapstone, Principal and Vice-Chancellor, 01334 462544, principal@st-andrews.ac.uk; Niall Scott, Director, Corporate Communications, 01334 462244, ns30@st-andrews.ac.uk

Founded in 1413, Scotland's first University and the third oldest in the english-speaking world. World-leading teaching and research in the arts, science, medicine and divinity. One of Europe's most research-intensive seats of learning and among the world's top-rated multi-faculty institutions for teaching quality, research excellence and student satisfaction. Consistently ranked among the UK's top five universities in independent league tables.

FINANCIAL

BANK OF ENGLAND
Agency for Scotland, 177 West George Street, Glasgow G2 2LB

Tel: 0141 221 7972
E-mail: scotland@bankofengland.co.uk
Web: www.bankofengland.co.uk

The Bank of England promotes the good of the people of the United Kingdom by maintaining monetary and financial stability. The primary role of the Agency, which represents the central bank in Scotland, is to report to the Monetary Policy Committee and Financial Policy Committee on business conditions faced by firms based in Scotland.

HEALTH

BRITISH MEDICAL ASSOCIATION (SCOTLAND)
14 Queen Street, Edinburgh EH2 1LL

Tel: 0131 247 3000
Fax: 0131 247 3001
E-mail: bmascotland@bma.org.uk
Contact: Jill Vickerman, Scottish Secretary; Membership Services:
0870 60 60 828; General Enquiries: 0131 247 3000; Press Enquiries:
0131 247 3050/3052.

The British Medical Association in Scotland represents doctors from all branches of medicine. It is a voluntary professional association, independent trade union, scientific and educational body and a publishing house. The BMA and the BMJ Publishing Group, which is one of the most influential medical publishers in the world, produce a wide range of journals, reports and medical books. With a UK membership of 154,541 and 16,204 in Scotland, the BMA is regarded as the voice of the medical profession.

SCOTTISH ASSOCIATION FOR SLEEP APNOEA

Web: www.scottishsleepapnoea.co.uk
Contact: Scott Elliot, Treasurer, 01450 375046.

The Association has three main aims and objectives. These are: to raise awareness both in the general public and in the medical profession regarding the medical condition of sleep apnoea and its symptoms; to raise funds for research into sleep apnoea and the publication of such research; and to provide support to the sufferers of sleep apnoea and their families through volunteers; and where available, by local groups.
Scottish Charity No. SCO23352

HOUSING

BIELD HOUSING & CARE
79 Hopetoun Street, Edinburgh EH7 4QF

Tel: 0131 273 4000
Fax: 0131 557 6327
E-mail: info@bield.co.uk
Web: www.bield.co.uk
Contact: Brian Logan, Chief Executive; Director of Housing Services; Scott Smith, Director of Finance & ICT Services; Jayne Pashley, Director of Human Resources; Charlie Dickson, Director of Care Services; Stuart Dow, Director of Asset Management.

We aim to improve the quality of life of older people by offering a diverse range of housing, care and other services. We are a non profit organisation with charitable status, governed by legislation promoting and regulating registered housing associations. We provide supported housing, community alarm services and home and day care services to approximately 15,000 older people in Scotland.

LAW
(see also LAW FIRMS under "PROFESSIONAL SERVICES")

THE FACULTY OF ADVOCATES
Parliament House, Edinburgh EH1 1RF

Tel: 0131 226 5071
Web: www.advocates.org.uk

The Faculty of Advocates, which has been in existence since at least 1532, is a body of independent lawyers who specialise in the preparation and presentation of cases before the courts and tribunals of Scotland. There are currently more than 450 practising advocates available to take instructions from solicitors throughout Scotland and from a number of professional bodies and individuals by means of a direct access scheme. The Faculty is a democratic body led by its Dean who is elected by a vote of the whole membership. The Faculty operates a rigorous training and education programme and is also responsible for maintaining discipline and standards at the Bar.

SCOTTISH LAW COMMISSION
140 Causewayside, Edinburgh
EH9 1PR

Scottish Law Commission
promoting law reform

Tel: 0131 668 2131
Fax: 0131 662 4900
E-mail: info@scotlawcom.gsi.gov.uk
Web: www.scotlawcom.gov.uk
Contact: The Hon Lord Pentland, Chairman; Malcolm McMillan, Chief Executive; Susan Cutsforth, Office Manager.

The Commission is an independent statutory body established in 1965 which is responsible to Scottish Ministers. Further information about our work can be found at www.scotlawcom.gov.uk.

LOCAL GOVERNMENT

ABERDEENSHIRE COUNCIL
Woodhill House, Westburn Road,
Aberdeen AB16 5GB

Tel: 03456 081208
E-mail: enquiries@aberdeenshire.gov.uk
Web: www.aberdeenshire.gov.uk
Contact: Jim Savege, Chief Executive, 01224 665402.

Aberdeenshire Council is the sixth largest of Scotland's 32 unitary authorities in population (236,260) and the fourth largest in area (6,313 sq km). The area was recently ranked as the best place to live in Scotland, based on a series of factors including, employment, the housing market, environment, education and health.

PROFESSIONAL SERVICES

1. ACCOUNTANTS

GERBER LANDA & GEE, CHARTERED ACCOUNTANTS
Pavilion 1, Finnieston Business Park, Minerva Way, Glasgow G3 8AU

Tel: 0141 221 7446
Fax: 0141 248 2469
E-mail: mail@gerberlandagee.co.uk
Web: www.gerberlandagee.co.uk
Contact: Thomas Hughes, LLB, CA, CTA; Charles Martin, CA, CTA; Harry Seddon, FCCA.

Gerber Landa & Gee is a three Director practice with around 20 employees, which has been in existence for almost 50 years. We have an expertise in every aspect of family business and taxation as well as experience in corporate reconstruction and recovery. We pride ourselves in our staff ethos and training. Our overall aim is to provide a high quality service to all clients supported by confidentiality and integrity.

2. LAW FIRMS

LEDINGHAM CHALMERS LLP
Johnstone House,
52-54 Rose Street,
Aberdeen AB10 1HA

ledingham|chalmers_{LLP}

Tel: 01224 408408
Fax: 01224 408400
E-mail: mail@ledinghamchalmers.com
Web: www.ledinghamchalmers.com
Contact: Jennifer Young, Chairman and Partner; Brian Hay, Chief Executive.

Ledingham Chalmers LLP offers a full range of legal services to businesses, private clients, the insurance and public sectors from its office locations in Aberdeen, Inverness, Edinburgh and Stirling.

TURCAN CONNELL
Princes Exchange,
1 Earl Grey Street,
Edinburgh EH3 9EE

TURCAN CONNELL
LEGAL · WEALTH MANAGEMENT · TAX

Tel: 0131 228 8111
E-mail: enquiries@turcanconnell.com
Web: www.turcanconnell.com

The Turcan Connell Group is a leading firm of legal, wealth management and tax advisers headquartered in Edinburgh with offices in Glasgow and London. The Group offers a comprehensive range of services including our flagship 'Turcan Connell Family Office' to individuals, families and charities, delivered by an interdisciplinary team of lawyers and tax planners, as well as investment and financial planning specialists, through Turcan Connell Asset Management Limited, a wholly owned subsidiary company.

3. REPUTATION MANAGEMENT AND PUBLIC RELATIONS

INDIGO
27 Maritime Street, Leith, Edinburgh EH6 6SE

Tel: 0131 554 1230
E-mail: admin@indigopr.com
Web: www.indigopr.com
Twitter: @IndigoScotland
Facebook: Indigo (PR) Ltd
LinkedIn: Indigo (PR) Ltd

Indigo offers reputation management for companies and individuals through creative, engaging, compelling and effective media relations, public affairs and crisis management.

Our aim is to add value as trusted advisers, working in partnership to ensure the right messages get across to the right people at exactly the right time.

Taking an integrated approach, we deliver innovative media campaigns, thought provoking content, policy solutions and compelling arguments which ultimately influence debate and outcomes.

Ethical, practical and always professional.

PROFESSIONAL AND TRADE ORGANISATIONS

INSTITUTE OF DIRECTORS SCOTLAND
10 Charlotte Square, Edinburgh EH2 4DR

Tel: 0131 557 5488
E-mail: iod.scotland@iod.com
Web: www.iodscotland.com
Contact: Avril Gall.

Providing personal and professional development for directors and senior management, members and non-members, from private, public and third sector organisations. We aim to assist individuals and Boards acquire the skills and knowledge required to fulfil their Corporate Governance and Leadership responsibilities. Our wide variety of courses and workshops run year-round and include the Chartered Director Programme; Role of the Non-Executive Director; Role of the Chair; Role of the Trustee workshops; a variety of Boardroom Skills workshops; a Coaching/Mentoring Service and Board Evaluation & Development Services.

RELIGIOUS

ACTION OF CHURCHES TOGETHER IN SCOTLAND
Jubilee House, Forthside Way, Stirling FK8 1QZ

Tel: 01259 216980
Fax: 01259 215964
E-mail: ecumenical@acts-scotland.org
Web: www.acts-scotland.org

ACTS is Scotland's national ecumenical body. ACTS expresses and resources the ecumenical commitment and action of its member churches. It works in close partnership with companion bodies in Britain and Ireland. ACTS staff team work closely with denominational ecumenical offices at the national level and churches together groups at the local level. ACTS encourages engagement and good relationships among the churches and wider civic society.

CHRISTIAN AID SCOTLAND
Sycamore House,
290 Bath Street,
Glasgow G2 4JR

Tel: 0141 221 7475
Web: www.christianaid.org.uk/scotland
E-mail: glasgow@christian-aid.org
Contact: Sally Foster-Fulton, Head of Christian Aid Scotland.

Christian Aid Scotland is the official agency of the Scottish churches for emergency aid and tackling of global poverty. We support partner organisations who are working to end the injustice of poverty in 46 countries, through both long-term projects and emergency response.

THE CHURCH OF SCOTLAND
121 George Street, Edinburgh EH2 4YN

Tel: 0131 225 5722
Fax: 0131 220 3113
Web: www.churchofscotland.org.uk
Contact: The Principal Clerk of the General Assembly.

The Church of Scotland, part of the one Holy, Catholic and Apostolic Church, is the national church in Scotland, recognised by the State but independent in spiritual matters. Trinitarian in doctrine, Reformed in tradition and Presbyterian in polity, it exists to glorify God, to work for the advancement of Christ's kingdom throughout the world and to provide religious services for the people in Scotland, through parish ministry. It co-operates with other churches in various ecumenical bodies in Scotland and beyond.

CHURCH OF SCOTLAND GUILD
121 George Street, Edinburgh EH2 4YN

Tel: 0131 240 2217
E-mail: guild@churchofscotland.org.uk
E-mail: iwhyte@churchofscotland.org.uk
Web: www.cos-guild.org.uk
The Guild is a component element of the Church of Scotland, Scottish Charity No. SC011353.
Contact: Iain Whyte, General Secretary, iwhyte@cofscotland.org.uk

The Guild is a movement within the Church of Scotland whose aim is "to invite and encourage both women and men to commit their lives to Jesus Christ and to enable them to express their faith in worship, prayer, and action". With around 900 groups across the country, the Guild has raised millions via its Project Partnership Scheme for projects at home and abroad. The Guild is represented on other church councils as well as other ecumenical, national and international bodies.

THE SALVATION ARMY
Scotland Office:
12a Dryden Road, Loanhead,
Midlothian EH20 9LZ

E-mail: Carol.Bailey@salvationarmy.org.uk
Tel: 0131 440 9101
Contact: Lieutenant-Colonel Carol Bailey.

West Scotland Division:
4 Buchanan Court, Cumbernauld Road, Stepps, Glasgow G33 6HZ
Tel: 0141 779 5001 Fax: 0141 779 5011
E-mail: russell.wyles@salvationarmy.org.uk
Contact: Major Russell Wyles.

North Scotland Division:
Deer Road, Woodside, Aberdeen AB24 2BL
Tel: 01224 496001 Fax: 01224 496011
E-mail: Brian.Slinn@salvationarmy.org.uk
Contact: Major Brian Slinn.

East Scotland Division:
12a Dryden Road, Loanhead, Midlothian EH20 9LZ
Contact: Lieutenant-Colonel Carol Bailey.
E-mail: carol.bailey@salvationarmy.org.uk
Tel: 0131 440 9101

The Salvation Army is an integral part of the universal Christian church. Its message is based on the Bible, its motivation is the love of God as revealed in Jesus Christ. Its mission is to proclaim his Gospel, to persuade men and women to become his disciples and to engage in a programme of practical concern for the needs of humanity. Its ministry is offered to all, regardless of race, creed, colour or sex.

SCHOOLS

FETTES COLLEGE
Carrington Road, Edinburgh EH4 1QX

Tel: 0131 311 6701
Fax: 0131 311 6714
E-mail: enquiries@fettes.com
Web: www.fettes.com
Contact: Mr Michael Spens, Headmaster.

Fettes College is one of the UK's pre-eminent co-educational boarding schools with 760 students aged between 7 and 18. Our mission is to develop broadly educated, confident and thoughtful individuals. The hopes and aspirations of each of our students are of central importance to us, and the happy, purposeful environment of Fettes College encourages students to flourish and fully develop the skills and interests they possess.

TRANSPORT

FIRSTGROUP PLC
395 King Street, Aberdeen AB24 5RP

Tel: 01224 650100
Fax: 01224 650149
Web: www.firstgroupplc.com
Contact: Tim O'Toole, Chief Executive; Stuart Butchers, Group Head of Media.

FirstGroup plc is the leading transport operator in the UK and North America and our services help to create strong, vibrant and sustainable local economies. During the last year around 2.4 billion people relied on us to get to work, to education, to visit family and friends and much more and, each day, every one of our 110,000 employees works hard to deliver vitally important services for our passengers.

FirstGroup is one of Britain's largest bus operators with around a fifth of bus services outside London. A fleet of some 6,300 buses carries approximately 1.7 million passengers a day in a huge number of communities including 40 of the UK's largest towns and cities.

FirstGroup is also one of the most experienced rail operators in the UK and the only one to run every sort of railway - long distance, regional, commuter and sleeper operations. We carried more than 280 million passengers in 2014/15. We operate two passenger franchises – Great Western Railway (GWR) and TransPennine Express – and one open access operator, First Hull Trains.

FirstGroup North America is the leader in student transportation, transit contracting and vehicle fleet maintenance services in the United States and Canada.

- First Student is the largest provider of student transportation in North America, with a fleet of approximately 49,000 school buses carrying some six million students every school day across the US and Canada.

- First Transit has 60 years of experience and is one of the largest private sector providers of transportation contract and management services in North America, moving more than 350 million passengers annually.

- Greyhound is the only national provider of scheduled intercity coach services in the US and Canada, providing scheduled passenger services to 3,800 destinations carrying approximately 18 million passengers a year.

Our vision is to provide solutions for an increasingly congested world... keeping people moving and communities prospering.

UNIONS

SCOTTISH TRADES UNION CONGRESS
333 Woodlands Road, Glasgow, G3 6NG

Tel: 0141 337 8100 Fax: 0141 337 8101
E-mail: info@stuc.org.uk
Contact: Grahame Smith, General Secretary.

The STUC is Scotland's umbrella body for trade unions in Scotland. Its purpose is to co-ordinate, develop and articulate the views and policies of the Trade Union Movement in Scotland reflecting the aspirations of trade unionists as workers and citizens.

The STUC represents 596,303 members of 38 affiliated unions. We speak for trade union members across Scotland, and for those that suffer discrimination in the workplace and in society.

Biographies

An A to Z of prominent people in Scotland

A

Abbot, Grant. Head Teacher, Bathgate Academy, since 2012 (formerly Acting Head Teacher). Career: PE and Guidance teacher; Depute Head Teacher, Linlithgow Academy. Address: Bathgate Academy, Edinburgh Road, Bathgate, West Lothian EH48 1LF; T.-01506 653725.

Abercrombie, Ian R., QC, LLB (Hons). Sheriff Principal, South Strathclyde, Dumfries and Galloway, since 2015; formerly Sheriff of Tayside, Central and Fife at Dunfermline; b. 7.7.55, Bulawayo. Educ. Milton High School; Edinburgh University. Recreations: travelling; walking. Address: Sheriff Principal's Chambers, Airdrie Sheriff Court, Graham Street, Airdrie ML6 6EE; T.-01236 751121.

Abernethy, Rt. Hon. Lord (John Alastair Cameron), PC 2005. Senator, College of Justice, 1992-2007; b. 1.2.38, Newcastle-upon-Tyne; m., Elspeth Mary Dunlop Miller; 3 s. Educ. Clergy House School, Khartoum; St. Mary's School, Melrose; Glenalmond College, Perth; Pembroke College, Oxford. National Service, 2nd Lt., RASC, Aldershot and Malta, 1956-58. Called to the Bar, Inner Temple, 1963; admitted Member, Faculty of Advocates, 1966; Advocate-Depute, 1972-75; Standing Junior Counsel to Department of Energy, 1976-79, Scottish Development Department, 1978-79; QC (Scotland), 1979; Vice-Dean, Faculty of Advocates, 1983-92; President, Pensions Appeal Tribunals for Scotland, 1985-92 (Legal Chairman, 1979-85); Chairman, Faculty Services Ltd., 1983-89 (Director, 1979-83); Hon. Fellow, Pembroke College, Oxford, 1993; International Bar Association: Vice Chairman, 1993-94, Chairman, Judges' Forum, 1994-98, Member, Council, Section on Legal Practice, 1998-2002, and Member, Council, Human Rights Institute, 1998-2000 and 2002-05; Trustee, Faculty of Advocates 1985 Charitable Trust, since 1985; Member, Executive Committee, Society for the Welfare and Teaching of the Blind (Edinburgh and South East Scotland), 1979-92; Trustee, Arthur Smith Memorial Trust, 1975-2001, Chairman, 1990-2001; President, Scottish Medico-Legal Society, 1996-2000; Governor, St. Mary's School, Melrose, 1998-2012, Vice-Chairman, 2004-2012; Member, International Legal Assistance Consortium, since 2002; Commissioner, Northern Ireland (Remission of Sentences) Act 1995, since 2008; Trustee, Southern Africa Litigation Centre, 2008-2015; Justice of Appeal, Botswana, since 2009; Judge of Interim Independent Constitutional Dispute Resolution Court, Kenya, 2010. Publications: Medical Negligence: an introduction, 1983; Reproductive Medicine and the Law (ed A A Templeton and D J Cusine, 1990) (Contributor). Club: New, Edinburgh. Recreations: travel; nature conservation; Africana. Address: (b.) 4 Garscube Terrace, Edinburgh EH12 6BQ; T.-0131-337 3460.

Abram, Henry Charles, LLB, WS. Company Director, Tods Murray LLP, 2008-2012; Solicitor, Tods Murray WS, 1973-2008; b. 11.8.51, Glasgow; m., Leslie Anne Hamilton; 2 s.; 1 d. Educ. Merchiston Castle School; Aberdeen University. Articled Tods Murray WS; qualified, 1976; Partner, 1978; Chairman, Management Board, 1994-97; Chairman, 1998-2002. Member, Council of Law Society of Scotland, 1983-86; Chairman of Governors, Merchiston Castle School, 2000-07; Member, High Constables and Guard of Honour of Holyroodhouse; Chairman, Chiene + Tait LLP; Director and Company Secretary, Hunter Real Estate Investment Managers Ltd; Chairman, Cuthbertwhite; Trustee, Lloyds TSB Foundation for Scotland; Trustee, Scottish Civic Trust; Chairman, St Columba's Hospice Rebuild Campaign; Past Member, Audit and Risk Management Committee of The National Trust for Scotland, 2008-2011. Recreations: shooting; stalking; golf; skiing; running. Address: (b) 107 George Street, Edinburgh EH2 3ES; T.-0131-240-0900; e-mail: hcabram@gmail.com

Ace, Jeff. Chief Executive, Dumfries and Galloway NHS Board. Address: (b.) Mid North, Crichton Hall, Dumfries DG1 4TG.

Adam, George. Lord Provost of Aberdeen, since 2012; b. 26.1.57. Educ. Brechin High School; Duncan Jordanstone College of Art, Dundee. Career: worked in the corporate communications sector for more than 30 years, as a designer, event organiser and video producer; Format Communications, Aberdeen (produced programmes and events for a wide range of companies and organisations, including the Oil & Gas and Retail sectors), 1979-90; The Presentation Business, Aberdeen (ran own production company, mainly involved in corporate video and digital imaging projects), 1999-2012; elected member for Hilton, Stockethill and Woodside Ward, since 2007. Lord Lieutenant of Aberdeen, since 2012; Honorary Patron of Aberdeen Performing Arts; Aberdeen's member of the World Energy Cities Partnership; membership of outside bodies includes Commissioner of the Northern Lighthouse Board. Recreations: gardening; visual arts; music; cinema; theatre. Address: Town House, Broad Street, Aberdeen AB10 1LP; T.-01224 522637.

Adam, George. MSP (SNP), Paisley, since 2011; Councillor for Paisley South: Ward 5 in Renfrewshire Council, 2007-2012; m., Stacey. Active with the SNP in Paisley since the 1980s. Worked in the motor industry as a sales manager. Member: Multiple Sclerosis Society of Scotland; Scottish Parliament: full member of the Education Committee; member of the Cross-Party Group on Carers; SPPA Committee; Convener, CPG MS; Patron, SDEF; Political Liaison Officer to the Cabinet Secretary for Education and Lifelong Learning. Recreations: passionate supporter of St Mirren FC, Chair, SMISA (St Mirren Independent Supporters Association); Honorary President, Paisley Pirates. Address: (b.) Scottish Parliament, Edinburgh EH99 1SP; 4 Johnston Street, Paisley PA1 1XG.

Adam, Ian Clark. Non-Executive Director, Britannia Building Society, 1998-2008 (Non-Executive Chairman, 2004-08); b. 2.9.43; m., Betty; 1 d.; 1 s. Educ. Harris Academy. Trainee Accountant, Henderson & Logie, 1962-67; Price Waterhouse: Audit Senior and Assistant Manager (Rio de Janeiro), 1967-70, Manager, Bristol, 1970-76, Partner, Edinburgh, 1976-86, Senior Partner, Scotland, 1986-95; Financial Director, Christian Salvesen plc, 1995-98; Non-Executive Director: Fishers Holdings Ltd, 1996-2004, St. Leonards School, St. Columbas Hospice (Chairman), Edinburgh; Member, Council, Scottish Further and Higher Education Funding Council (2003-2011); Old Master Co of Merchants of the City of Edinburgh; Member, High Constable City of Edinburgh; MICAS 1967. Recreations: reading; golf; travel. Address: Gowanfield, 2 Cammo Road, Edinburgh EH4 8EB; T.-0131 339 6401.

Adams, Professor David, MA, MCD, PhD, FAcSS, FRTPI, FRICS, FRSA. Ian Mactaggart Professor of Property and Urban Studies, University of Glasgow, since 2004; b. 10.9.54, Menston, England; m., Judith Banks; 1 s.; 1 d. Educ. Rossall School; University of Cambridge; University of Liverpool. Planning Assistant, Leeds City Council, 1978-83; Research Assistant, University of Reading, 1983-84; Lecturer, University of Manchester, 1984-93; University of Aberdeen: Senior Lecturer, 1993-95, Reader, 1995-97,

Professor of Land Economy, 1997-2004. Publications: Urban Planning and the Development Process, 1994; Land for Industrial Development (Co-author), 1994; Greenfields, Brownfields and Housing Development (Co-author), 2002; Planning, Public Policy and Property Markets (Co-editor), 2005; Urban Design in the Real Estate Development Process (Co-editor), 2011; Shaping Places: Urban Planning, Design and Development (Co-author), 2013. Recreations: walking; listening to classical music. Address: (b.) Urban Studies, School of Social and Political Sciences, University of Glasgow, 25 Bute Gardens, Glasgow G12 8RS.
E-mail: david.adams@glasgow.ac.uk

Adams, Professor Colin Ean, BSc (Hons), PhD. Professor of Freshwater Ecology, University of Glasgow, since 2009, Director, Scottish Centre for Ecology and The Natural Environment, since 1995; b. 21.06.59, Dumfries; 2 d. Educ. Annan Academy; University of Glasgow. Lecturer in Ecology, University of Glasgow, since 1995; Professor in Freshwater Biology, University of Tromsø, 2006. Member, Science Advisory Committee to Scottish Natural Heritage; Trustee, Loch Lomond Fishery Trust. Recreations: sailing; game shooting. Address: (b.) Scottish Centre for Ecology and Natural Environment, University of Glasgow, Rowardennan, Glasgow G63 0AW; T.-01360 870 271; e-mail: colin.adams@glasgow.ac.uk

Adams, Kaye, MA (Hons). Scottish television presenter; 28.12.62, Falkirk; 2 d. Educ. University of Edinburgh. Started media career as a graduate trainee at Central Television; moved to Scottish Television in 1988, hosted Scottish Women, 1993-99; anchored the ITV talk show Loose Women, 1999-2006, co-anchor, since 2013; regular guest host of Channel 5 panel show The Wright Stuff, 2007-2010; guest co-host of The Hour on STV, 2009; joined BBC Radio Scotland in 2010; guest presenter of Channel 5's LIVE with... programme, since 2011; co-hosted the daytime chat show Sunday Scoop, since 2013. Co-patron of Kindred, a Scottish based charity supporting families of young people with disabilities. Address: BBC Radio Scotland, 40 Pacific Quay, Glasgow G51 1DA; T.-0141 422 6000.

Adams, Sheenagh, MA (Hons). Keeper of the Registers of Scotland, since 2009; b. 31.8.57, Dundee; m., Peter Craig; 2 d. Educ. Harris Academy, Dundee; St. Andrews University. Welfare Rights Officer, Strathclyde Regional Council, 1979-82; Tenant Participation Officer, Clydebank Council and TPAS, 1982-85; Principal Management Officer, Falkirk District Council, 1985-90; Principal, Scottish Office, 1990-99; Secretary, Historic Buildings Council for Scotland, 1995-99; Head, Heritage Policy, Historic Scotland, 1995-99; Head, Voluntary Issues Unit, Scottish Executive, 1999-2002; Director of Heritage Policy, Historic Scotland, 2002-06; Managing Director, Registers of Scotland, 2006-09. Address: (b.) Meadowbank House, 153 London Road, Edinburgh EH8 7AU; e-mail: sheenagh.adams@ros.gov.uk

Adamson, Clare, BSc. MSP (SNP), Motherwell and Wishaw, since 2016 (Central Scotland, 2011-16); b. Motherwell; m., John Adamson; 1 s.; 3 stepchildren. Educ. Glasgow Caledonian University. Career: European Development Manager (IT) at a Glasgow-based software house; worked for four years at the SNP HQ Campaign Unit as Project Manager of the SNP's 'Activate Project'. Active role in the Scottish Accident Prevention Council (Vice Chairman) and the Lanarkshire International Children's Games Organising Committee. Currently serves on the Welfare Reform Committee and Local Government & Regeneration Committee; Member: National Union of Journalists; qualified as a Member of the British Computer Society; Member, National Trust for Scotland; Convener, Parliamentary Cross Party Group on Accident Prevention and Safety Awareness. Recreations: painting; watching live music, especially folk music. Address: (b.) Scottish Parliament, Edinburgh EH99 1SP.

Addison, Alexander, MBE, MB, ChB, FRCGP, DObstRCOG. Senior Partner, Addison, Scott, Kane & Ferguson, 1978-95; Chairman, Lanarkshire LMC, 1989-95; Member, Scottish Committee, BMA, since 1984, and Fellow, BMA, since 1993; Member, RCCC Council, 1996-2000; Medical Officer and Anti-Drugs Officer, RCCC; b. 23.8.30, Kerala; m., Joan Wood; 3 s. Educ. Keith Grammar School; Aberdeen Grammar School; Aberdeen University. House Surgeon and Physician, Woodend General Hospital, Aberdeen, 1954-55; Captain, RAMC; Junior Medical Specialist, Cowglen MH, 1955-58; SHO, Bellshill MH, 1958-59; GP in Douglas and Physician to Lady Home Hospital, 1959-95; Member, West of Scotland Faculty of GP College, 1967-79 and of Scottish Council, 1976-78; Member, Lanarkshire LMC, since 1972, and of AMAC, since 1975; Chairman, Lanarkshire AMAC, 1982-86; Chairman, Scottish Association of General Practitioner Hospitals, 1985-87; Member, Scottish Committee of Medical Commission on Accident Prevention, 1976-98; Member, National Medical Consultative Committee, 1977-83; Honorary Surgeon, St. Andrews Ambulance Association, 1959-89. Recreations: curling; golf; reading. Address: (h.) 7 Addison Drive, Douglas, Lanarkshire ML11 0PZ; T.-01555 851302.

Agnew of Lochnaw, Sir Crispin Hamlyn. 11th Baronet (created 1629); Chief of the Agnews; Advocate 1982; Queen's Counsel (1995); Deputy Social Security Commissioner (2000-08); Deputy Judge of the Upper Tribunal, since 2008; Chairman, Pension Appeal Tribunal, 2002-2012; Unicorn Pursuivant of Arms, 1981-86; Rothesay Herald of Arms, since 1986; Trustee, John Muir Trust, 1989-2005; Chairman, Crofting Law Group; Council, SYHA, 2008-2012 and Board Member, SYHA, 2010-2012; b. 13.5.44, Edinburgh; m., Susan Rachel Strang Steel, PgDip, Careers Adviser; 1 s.; 3 d. Educ. Uppingham School; Royal Military Academy, Sandhurst. Commissioned Royal Highland Fusiliers, 1964, as 2nd Lieutenant; Major, 1977; Retired, 1981. Member: Royal Navy Expedition to East Greenland, 1966; Joint Services Expedition to Elephant Island, Antarctica, 1970-71; Army Nuptse Himal Expedition, 1975; Army Everest Expedition, 1976; Leader: Army East Greenland Expedition, 1968; Joint Services Expedition to Chilean Patagonia, 1972-73; Army Api Himal Expedition, 1980. Publications: Licensing (Scotland) Act 1976 (5th edition 2002) (Co-author); Agricultural Law in Scotland, 1996; Connell on the Agricultural Holdings (Scotland) Acts (Co-author) 1996; Land Obligations, 1999; Crofting Law, 2000; articles in various newspapers and journals. Recreations: mountaineering; sailing and mountain biking. Address: 6 Palmerston Road, Edinburgh EH9 1TN; T.-0131-668 3792.

Agnew, Denis, DipDA, MPhil, PhD; b. 1950, Clydebank; m., Carole (née Rowan); 1 d. (Julie); 1 s. (Julian). Educ. Royal Scottish Academy of Music & Drama; University of Glasgow; Queen Margaret University College, Edinburgh; Leverhulme Scholar (2001). Theatre practitioner (1972-2003) as actor, director & tutor. Published in international Journal of Scottish Theatre; compiled and edited booklet The Hospice: A History of St Margaret of Scotland Hospice, 2015. Chair of Equity Scottish Committee (1999-2003). Elected Councillor, West Dunbartonshire Council, since 2003; elected Leader of Council, 2007; elected Provost and Chair of Council, 2007-2012. Awarded The Knight's Cross of the Order of Merit of The Republic of Poland in August 2013.

Agnew, Ian, MA (Hons) (Cantab). Rector, Perth High School, 1975-92; b. 10.5.32, Newcastle-upon-Tyne; m., Gladys Agnes Heatherill; 1 d. Educ. King's College School, Wimbledon; Pembroke College, Cambridge. Assistant Teacher of Modern Languages, Melville College,

Edinburgh, 1958-63; Assistant Teacher of Modern Languages, then Principal Teacher of Russian, George Heriot's School, Edinburgh, 1964-70; Housemaster, Craigmount Secondary School, Edinburgh, 1970-73; Deputy, Liberton High School, Edinburgh, 1973-75. Non-Executive Director, Perth and Kinross Healthcare NHS Trust, 1994-98; Minute Secretary, Headteachers Association of Scotland, 1979-81; Committee Member, SCCORE; President: Perthshire Musical Festival, 1978-88, Perth Chamber Music Society, 1982-89; Past President, Rotary Club of Perth St. John's; Past Chairman: Barnton and Cramond Conservative Association and West Edinburgh Conservative and Unionist Association; Serving Officer (OStJ), Priory of Scotland of the Most Venerable Order of St. John; Member, Society of High Constables, City of Perth; Governor: Balnacraig School, Perth, 1981-2007, Kilgraston School, 1990-99, Convent of the Sacred Heart, Bridge of Earn; Secretary, Friends of Perth Festival of the Arts, 1996-99; Member, Advisory Group, Perth College Development Trust; Chairman, Friends of St. John's Kirk, Perth, 1996-2008; Past President, Fair City Probus Club, Perth. Recreations: music (opera); reading; tennis; gardening. Address: (h.) Northwood, Heughfield Road, Bridge of Earn, Perthshire PH2 9BH; T.-01738 81 2273; e-mail: I.agnew576@btinternet.com

Agnew, Rosemary. Scottish Information Commissioner, since 2012. Previously Chief Executive, Scottish Legal Complaints Commission (2009-2012). Address: (b.) Kinburn Castle, Doubledykes Road, St. Andrews KY16 9DS; T.-01334 464610.
E-mail: sic@itspublicknowledge.info
Web: itspublicknowledge.info

A'Hearn, Terry. Chief Executive Officer, Scottish Environment Protection Agency, since 2015. Educ. St Bernards; University of Melbourne; London Business School. Senior Policy Officer, Department of Treasury and Finance, Melbourne, Australia, 1989-93; Director, Sustainable Development, Environmental Protection Authority, Melbourne, Australia, 2003-09; Acting CEO, Environment Protection Authority, Melbourne, Australia, 2009-2010; Director, Global Regulatory Innovation, Climate Change & Sustainability Services, WSP Environment & Energy, London, 2010-2012; Board Member, UK Institute of Environmental Management and Assessment, 2012-2014; Chief Executive Officer, Northern Ireland Environment Agency, 2012-2015; Senior Associate (Honorary), Cambridge Institute for Sustainability Leadership (CISL), since 2010. Address: Strathallan House, Castle Business Park, Stirling FK9 4TZ.

Ahmad, Mushtaq, OBE, BA, MA. Lord-Lieutenant for Lanarkshire, since 2010; b. India; 3 s.; 2 d. Educ. Murray College; JI College, Sialkot; University of Punjab; University of Glasgow. Teacher training, Jordanhill College of Education; taught Economics and Modern Studies for 2 years in Scotland; spent 3 years in London heading an East London school's large department, before returning to Lanarkshire working as Specialist Organiser for the largest Adult Basic Education Programme in Scotland for 17 years. Over several years, has served the community in Lanarkshire as a Councillor in Hamilton District and South Lanarkshire Councils, holding a number of posts; also served a term as Provost of South Lanarkshire, 2003-07; voluntary work through the Citizen's Advice Bureau and other bodies.

Ahmed-Sheikh, Tasmina, OBE. MP (SNP), Ochil and South Perthshire, since 2015; SNP Trade and Investment spokesperson and Deputy Shadow Leader of the House in the House of Commons; founder and chair of the Scottish Asian Women's Association; b. 5.10.70, Chelsea; m., Zulfikar Sheikh; 4 c. Educ. University of Edinburgh; University of Strathclyde. Partner, Hamilton Burns (Glasgow law firm). Address: House of Commons, London SW1A 0AA.

Aikman, Gordon, BEM. Motor Neurone Disease campaigner; b. 2.4.85; m., Joe Pike. Educ. Kirkcaldy High School; University of Edinburgh. Former policy and communications adviser, Scottish Labour Party; Director of Research for the Better Together campaign in the Scottish Independence Referendum, 2012-14. Raised over £400,000 for Motor Neurone Disease research. Written about campaigning work and personal journey with Motor Neurone Disease for The Scotsman, Daily Record and The Herald; writes a monthly column in the Scottish edition of The Sunday Times. Won the Judges' Award at the Scottish Politician of the Year awards in November 2014, and Campaigner of the Year in the 2015 ceremony; awarded the Daily Record's Our Heroes Award alongside fellow campaigner Lucy Lintott in 2015; awarded an honorary doctorate by the University of Edinburgh in July 2015; awarded the British Empire Medal 'for services to Motor Neurone Disease Awareness and Research' in the Queen's Birthday Honours List 2015; awarded the Kingdom FM Award at Kingdom FM's annual Local Hero Awards ceremony which celebrates all that's great in Fife, 2015.
E-mail: gordonsfightback@gmail.com

Airlie, Adrienne Anne, BAcc, CA, APFS, MCIE. Chief Executive, Martin Aitken & Co Ltd, since 2013, Senior Partner, 2010-13; Director, Martin Aitken Financial Services Limited, since 2007; b. 3.5.58, Glasgow; m., Campbell Airlie; 2 s.; 2 d. Educ. Notre Dame High School, Glasgow; Glasgow University. Partner and Chartered Accountant, Martin Aitken & Co, 1995-2009. Scottish Convenor, Association of Charity Independent Examiners, since 1997; Charity Committee Member, The Institute of Chartered Accountants of Scotland, since 2008, Council Member, since 2005; Board Member, Scottish Family Business Association (SFBA), since 2009; Board Member, Mercy Corps Scotland, since 2010. Recreations: gym; reading. E-mail: ada@maco.co.uk

Airlie, 13th Earl of (David George Coke Patrick Ogilvy), KT, GCVO, PC, KStJ; b. 17.5.26, London; m., Virginia Fortune Ryan; 3 s.; 3 d. Educ. Eton College. Lieutenant, Scots Guards, 1944; serving 2nd Bn., Germany, 1945; Captain, ADC to High Commissioner and C-in-C Austria, 1947-48; Malaya, 1948-49; resigned commission, 1950; Chairman, Ashdown Investment Trust Ltd., 1968-82; Director, J. Henry Schroder Wagg & Co. Ltd., 1961-84 (Chairman, 1973-77); Chairman, Schroders plc, 1977-84; Scottish and Newcastle Breweries plc, until 1983; Director, Royal Bank of Scotland Group, 1983-93; Director, Royal Bank of Scotland plc, 1991-93; Chairman, General Accident Fire & Life Assurance Corporation plc, 1987-97; Chancellor of the Royal Victorian Order, 1984-97; Trustee, Royal Collection Trust, 1993; Ensign, Queen's Body Guard for Scotland (Royal Company of Archers) (President, Council, since 2001), Captain General, 2004-2011; Chancellor of the Most Noble and Ancient Order of the Thistle, November 13th 2007; Royal Victorian Chain and Chancellor, Royal Victorian Order; former Lord Chamberlain of Queen's Household; Chancellor, University of Abertay, Dundee, 1994-2009; President, National Trust for Scotland, 1997-2002; Hon. President, Scottish Council, The Scout Association; Chairman, Historic Royal Palaces, 1998-2002. Address: (h.) Airlie House, Cortachy, Kirriemuir, Angus DD8 4QJ.

Airlie, Countess of (Virginia Fortune Ryan), DCVO. Lady in Waiting to HM The Queen, since 1973; Chairman, National Galleries of Scotland, 1997-2000; b. 9.2.33,

London; 3 s.; 3 d. Educ. Brearley School, New York City. Commissioner, Royal Fine Arts Commission; Trustee, Tate Gallery, 1983-95; Trustee, National Gallery, London, 1989-95; Member, Industrial Design Panel, British Rail, 1974-91. Founder/Governor, Cobham School; President, Angus Red Cross. Address: (b.) Airlie House, Cortachy, Kirriemuir, Angus DD8 4QJ; T.-01575 540231.

Aitchison, James Douglas, MA (Hons), MEd (Hons). Director, Scotland - Malawi School Improvement Programme, 2005-08 (Adviser to Schools Inspectorate, Uganda, 2003-05); Head Teacher, Boclair Academy, Bearsden, 1991-2002; Head Teacher, Gleniffer High School, Paisley, 1984-91; b. 2.7.47, Glasgow. Educ. High School of Glasgow; Glasgow University; University of Marburg. Teacher, Lycee Faidherbe, Lille; Principal Teacher, Bearsden Academy; Assistant Head Teacher, Gryffe High School, Houston. Recreations: curling; walking; travel. Address: (h.) 44 Keystone Road, Milngavie, Glasgow G62 6QG; T.-0141-956 6693.

Aitken, Fraser Robert, KSJ, MA, BD. Minister at St. Columba Church, Ayr, since 1991; b. 8.1.53, Paisley. Educ. John Neilson Institution, Paisley; University of Glasgow. Assistant Minister, Fairmilehead Parish Church, Edinburgh, 1977-78; Minister at Neilston Parish Church, 1978-84; Minister at Girvan North Parish Church, 1984-91. President, Glasgow-Ayrshire Society; Chaplain, Strathclyde Police 'U' Division; Trustee, Maclaurin Gallery; President, Glasgow-Ayrshire Society; President, Carrick Burns Club; Honorary President, Greenock Burns' Club; Moderator of the Presbytery of Ayr, 1996-97; Convener, The Nominations Committee of The General Assembly, 2000-02; Chaplain, Wellington School, Ayr. Recreations: musical theatre; reading; wining and dining; visiting Vienna and York. Address: (h.) The Manse of St. Columba, 3 Upper Crofts, Alloway, Ayr KA7 4QX; T.-01292 443747; e-mail: frasercolumba@msn.com

Aitken, Hugh, CBE. Director, CBI Scotland, since 2015. Educ. Woodside Secondary School. Career: European Distribution Manager, Digital Equipment Corporation, 1979-1985; European Logistics and Materials Manager, Apollo Computers, 1985-89; Sun Microsystems: Manager, European Logistics and Materials, 1989-1999, Director, European Logistics and Materials, 1992-94, Director of Business Strategy, 1994-95, Director of European Manufacturing, 1995-98, VP European Operations, 1998-2001, VP WW Customer Fulfillment, 2001-05; Chairman, Electronics Scotland, 2000-06; Sun Microsystems: VP WW Customer Fulfillment, 2006-08, Vice President, WW Manufacturing, 2008-09; VP WW Manufacturing, Oracle Corporation, 2009-2010; Microsoft, 2011-2013; President, ASCC INC (Aitken's Supply Chain Consultancy), 2013-2014. Address: CBI Scotland, 160 West George Street, Glasgow G2 2HQ; T.-0141 222 2184. E-mail: hugh.aitken@cbi.org.uk

Aitken, Keith, MA (Hons). Freelance Journalist, Broadcaster and Conference Facilitator, since 1995; b. 31.10.57, Edinburgh; m., Christine Willett; 1 d. Educ. University of Edinburgh. The Scotsman: graduate trainee, 1979-82, Parliamentary Correspondent, 1982-85, Labour Correspondent, 1985-88, Industrial Editor, 1988-92, Economics Editor and Chief Leader Writer, 1992-95; former Columnist: The Scotsman, The Herald, Scotland on Sunday, Holyrood Magazine; Columnist (since 2000), crossword compiler and opera reviewer, Scottish Daily Express; Scotland Correspondent (since 2011), Public Finance. Writer and presenter, discussion programmes and documentaries, BBC Radio Scotland, World Service and Radio 4; Video/DVD writer and presenter, and podcaster;

Trustee, National Mining Museum of Scotland. Visiting Lecturer, Edinburgh Napier University. Awards include Business and Industry Writer of the Year, Scottish Press Awards, 1986 and 1987. Publications: The Bairns o' Adam, 1997; How Scotland's Parliament Will Work, 1999; Understanding Scotland's Parliament, 1999. Recreations: collecting US political memorabilia; reading; theatre and music; gardening; deplorable blues guitar. Address: 25 Bridge Road, Colinton Village, Edinburgh EH13 0LH; T.-07850 115148.
E-mail: keith@kaitken.fsnet.co.uk
Website: www.keithaitken.co.uk

Aitken, Professor Robert Cairns Brown, CBE, MB, ChB, DPM, MD, DSc (Hon), FRCPEdin, FRCPsych. Chairman, Royal Infirmary of Edinburgh NHS Trust, 1994-97; Professor of Rehabilitation Studies, Edinburgh University, 1974-94 (Dean, Faculty of Medicine, 1990-91, Vice-Principal, 1991-94); Honorary Consultant in Rehabilitation Medicine, Lothian Health Board, 1974-94; b. 20.12.33, Dunoon; m., Audrey May Lunn; 1 s.; 1 d. Educ. Dunoon Grammar School; Cargilfield School, Edinburgh; Sedbergh School, Yorkshire; Glasgow University. Institute of Aviation Medicine, RAF, 1959-62; Orpington and Maudsley Hospitals, 1962-66; Senior Lecturer/Consultant Psychiatrist, Royal Infirmary and Royal Edinburgh Hospital, 1967-74. President, International College of Psychosomatic Medicine, 1985-87; Chairman, Napier Polytechnic of Edinburgh Governors, 1983-90; Member, Council for Professions Supplementary to Medicine, 1983-90; Member, General Medical Council, 1991-96; Director, Lothian Health Board, 1991-93; Editor, Journal of Psychosomatic Research, 1979-85; occasional WHO consultant; Foundation Secretary, then President, Society for Research in Rehabilitation, 1981-83; Member, Human Genetics Advisory Commission, 1996-99. Publications: papers on measurement of mood; flying phobia; management of disability. Recreations: people, places and pleasures of Edinburgh, Scotland and beyond. Address: (h.) 11 Succoth Place, Edinburgh EH12 6BJ; T.-0131-337 1550; e-mail: cairns.aitken@ed.ac.uk

Aitken, William Mackie. JP, DL. MSP (Conservative), Glasgow, 1999-2011 (Conservative Justice Spokesman, 2001-03 and 2007-2011; Convener, Justice Committee, 2007-2011; Parliamentary Business Manager and Chief Whip, 2003-07; Housing Spokesman, 1999-2001); b. 15.4.47, Glasgow. Educ. Allan Glen's School, Glasgow. Chairman, Scottish Young Conservatives, 1975-77; Councillor, City of Glasgow, 1976-99: Convenor, City Licensing Committee and Vice-Convenor, Personnel Committee, 1977-79, Leader of the Opposition, City Council, 1980-84 and 1992-96, Bailie of the City, 1980-84, 1988-92, 1996-99; Magistrate, Depute Lord Lieutenant, City of Glasgow. Recreations: football; reading; foreign travel. Address: (h.) 35 Overnewton Square, Glasgow G3 8RW; T.-0141-357 1284.

Aitkenhead, Geoff, BSc, CEng, FICE, MCIWEM. Asset Management Director, Scottish Water, 2002-2015, Executive Director, Capital Investment; Chairman, Scottish Water Solutions, since 2003; b. 26.9.54, Gosforth; 3 d. Educ. Wyndham School, Egremont; University of Newcastle Upon Tyne. Graduate engineer with Northumbrian Water engaged in environmental clean-up of the River Tyne; 3 years in Qatar, Arabian Gulf, with consulting engineers Pencol International on oil export facilities and public health projects; City of Salford, urban sewerage schemes; Borders Regional Council, Capital Planning Manager; East of Scotland Water, Strategic Operations and Customer Service roles; Scottish Water, Director of Asset Management, responsible for Asset Planning, Capital Investment delivery. Former Chairman,

WaterAid Scotland; Past-President, Institution of Water Officers. Recreations: hill walking; motorcycling; travel. Address: (b.) Castle House, 6 Castle Drive, Carnegie Campus, Dunfermline KY11 8GG; T.-01383 848471.

Akers, Fiona Moira, LLB (Hons), DipLP. Partner, Dickson Minto W.S., Solicitors, since 1999, Head of IP/Technology; b. 5.5.65, Paisley; m. Educ. Craigholme School; Edinburgh University. Trained with McGrigor Donald (now Pinsent Masons), Partner, 1997-99. Address: (b.) 16 Charlotte Square, Edinburgh EH2 4DF; T.-0131-225-4455; e-mail: fiona.akers@dmws.com

Alessi, Dario Renato, FRS, FRSE. Principal Investigator, Honorary Professor and Director of the MRC Protein Phosphorylation and Ubiquitylation Unit, University of Dundee, since 2012; b. 23.12.67, Strasbourg, France; 1 s. Educ. European School of Brussels; University of Birmingham. Discovered and characterised PDK1 protein Kinase; discovered and characterised the mechanism of activation and function of the LKB1 tumour suppressor; identified two physiological substrates of the WNK1 and WNK4 Kinase that control blood pressure; described the mechanism by which PKB/AKT enzyme is activated; identified ERM proteins as potential substrates for the LRRK2 Parkinson's Disease Kinase. Colworth Medal, 1999; Eppendorf Young European Investigator Award, 2000; Makdougall Brisbane Prize, 2002; Philip Leverhulme Prize, 2002; Embo Gold Medal, 2005, Francis Crick Prize, 2006; elected Fellow of Royal Society, 2008; elected Fellow of the Academy of Medical Sciences, 2012. Recreations: running; watching football and collecting stamps. Address: MRC Protein Phosphorylation Unit, College of Life Science, University of Dundee, Dundee DD1 5EH; T.-01382 385602.
E-mail: d.r.alessi@dundee.ac.uk

Alexander, Professor Alan, MA, OBE, FRSE. General Secretary, Royal Society of Edinburgh (RSE), since 2013; Chair, Scottish Water, 2002-06 (Chair Designate, 2001-02); Chairman, West of Scotland Water Authority, 1999-2002; Professor of Local and Public Management, Strathclyde University, 1993-2000, now Emeritus Professor (Head, Department of Human Resource Management, 1993-96, Professor of Local Government, 1987-93); Visiting Professor, University of Edinburgh Management School, since 2006; b. 13.12.43, Glasgow; m., Morag MacInnes (Morag Alexander, qv); 1 s.; 1 d. Educ. Possil Secondary School, Glasgow; Albert Secondary School, Glasgow; Glasgow University. Lecturer/Assistant Professor, Political Science, Lakehead University, Ontario, 1966-71; Lecturer in Politics, Reading University, 1971-87. Member of Board, Housing Corporation, 1977-80; Member, Standing Research Committee on Local and Central Government Relations, Joseph Rowntree Memorial Trust, 1988-92; conducted inquiry into relations between Western Isles Islands Council and BCCI, 1991; Director, Scottish Local Authorities Management Centre, 1987-93; Member, Commission on Local Government and the Scottish Parliament, 1998-99; Chair, Glasgow Regeneration Fund, 1998-2001; Trustee, Quarriers, 1995-2000; Trustee, WaterAid, 2001-06; Trustee, David Hume Institute, since 2012; Member, Council, Royal Society of Edinburgh, since 2012; Chair, Scottish Council, Outward Bound, 2012-15; Vice-Chair, Royal Society of Edinburgh enquiry 'Digital Scotland: Spreading the Benefits', 2012-14; Member, Accounts Commission, 2002-08; Member, Economic and Social Research Council, 2003-09. President, Institution of Water Officers, 2005-06; Chair: Postwatch Scotland, 2007-08, Distance Lab Ltd., 2006-2010, RCUK/UUK Review of Full Economic Costing of University Research, 2008-09, Waterwise, 2010-2015, Data Access Committee, Understanding Society, 2010-2015.

Publications: Local Government in Britain since Reorganisation, 1982; The Politics of Local Government in the UK, 1982; L'amministrazione locale in Gran Bretagna, 1984; Borough Government and Politics: Reading, 1835-1985, 1985; Managing the Fragmented Authority, 1994; The Future of DLOs/DSOs in Scotland, 1998; articles in learned journals. Recreations: theatre; cinema; walking; avoiding gardening.

Alexander, Sir Daniel Grian (Danny). Vice-President, Asian Infrastructure Investment Bank, since 2016; MP (Liberal Democrat), Inverness, Nairn, Badenoch and Strathspey, 2005-2015; Chief Secretary to the Treasury, 2010-2015; Secretary of State for Scotland, 2010; b. 15.5.72, Edinburgh; m., Rebecca Hoar; 2 d. Educ. Lochaber High School, Fort William; University of Oxford.

Alexander, Professor David Alan, MA (Hons), CPsychol, PhD, FBPS, FRSM, (Hon) FRCPsych. Emeritus Professor of Mental Health, Robert Gordon University (former Director, Aberdeen Centre for Trauma Research); Principal Adviser, UK Police Services; b. 28.8.43, Ellon. Educ. George Watson's College, Edinburgh; Morgan Academy, Dundee; University of St. Andrews; University of Dundee. MRC Research Scholar; Lecturer, then Senior Lecturer in Mental Health, then Professor of Mental Health, Faculty of Medicine, University of Aberdeen; Visiting Lecturer: FBI Academy, Virginia, USA, Scottish Police College and Pakistan School of Military Intelligence. Associate Member of the Scottish Institute for Policing Research; Founding Member, "Trauma Care" and "Hostage UK". Visiting Professor to universities in USA, Russia, Croatia, Spain, West Indies and Pakistan (Honorary Professor, National University of Sciences and Technology, Pakistan's premier university); The Armed Forces Compensation Scheme, Expert Medical Review Panel (Ministry of Defence); Advisory Committee on Assessment of Terrorists (British Psychological Society). Publications: co-author of three books; numerous professional articles. Recreations: badminton; squash; martial arts. Address: (b.) Aberdeen Centre for Trauma Research, The Robert Gordon University, Garthdee Road, Aberdeen AB10 7QG; e-mail: d.a.alexander@rgu.ac.uk

Alexander, Major-General David Crichton, CB. Commandant, Scottish Police College, 1979-87; b. 28.11.26, Aberdour; m., 1, Diana Joyce (Jane) Fisher (deceased); 2, Elizabeth Patricia Fleming; 1 s.; 1 step-s.; 2 d. Educ. Edinburgh Academy; Staff College, Camberley; Royal College of Defence Studies. Royal Marines, 1944-77 (2nd Lieutenant to Major-General, including Equerry and Acting Treasurer to Duke of Edinburgh); Director-General, English Speaking Union, 1977-79. President, Corps of Commissionaires, 1994-97; Member, Civil Service Final Selection Board, 1978-88; Chairman, Edinburgh Academy, 1985-90; Freeman, City of London; Liveryman, Painter Stainers' Company; Member, Transport Users Consultative Committee for Scotland, 1989-93; President, SSAFA Fife, 1990-94. Recreation: gardening. Address: (h.) Baldinnie, Park Place, Elie KY9 1DH; T.-01333 330882.

Alexander, Douglas, MA (Hons), LLB, DipLP. MP (Labour), Paisley and Renfrewshire South, 2005-2015, Paisley South, 1997-2005; Shadow Foreign Secretary, 2011-15; Shadow Secretary of State for Work and Pensions, 2010-11; Secretary of State for International Development, 2007-10; Secretary of State for Scotland, 2006-07; Secretary of State for Transport, 2006-07; Minister for Europe, 2005-06; Minister for Trade, 2004-05; Minister for the Cabinet Office and Chancellor of the Duchy of Lancaster, 2003-04; Minister of State, Cabinet Office, 2002-2003; Minister of

State, Department of Trade and Industry, e-Commerce and Competitiveness, 2001-02; b. 26.10.67, Glasgow; m., Jacqui Christian. Educ. Park Mains High School, Erskine; University of Edinburgh; University of Pennsylvania. Speechwriter for Dr. Gordon Brown, MP, 1990; Brodies WS, Edinburgh, 1994-96; Solicitor, Digby Brown, Edinburgh, 1996-97. Publication: New Scotland, New Britain, 1999. Recreations: running; angling.

Alexander, Rev. Douglas Niven, MA, BD, DUniv. Minister, Erskine Parish Church, Bishopton, 1970-99, retired; b. 8.4.35, Eaglesham; m., Dr. Joyce O. Garven; 1 s.; 2 d. Educ. Hutchesons' Boys' Grammar School, Glasgow; Glasgow University (President, SRC, 1958); Union Theological Seminary, New York. Assistant Minister, St. Ninian's Church, Greenock, 1961-62; Warden, Iona Community House, Glasgow, 1963-70. Secretary, Scottish Union of Students, 1958; Assessor to Lord Rector, Glasgow University, 1969-71; Chaplain to Erskine Hospital, since 1970; Moderator, Paisley Presbytery, 1984; Mair Memorial Lecturer, Glasgow University, 1987; Chairman, British Churches Committee for Channel 4 TV, 1986-88; Convener, Church of Scotland Board of Communication, 1987-91; Member: Scottish Committee, IBA, 1988-90; National Religious Advisory Committee, IBA, 1988-90; Central Religious Advisory Committee, 1988-92; National Religious Advisory Committee, ITC, 1991-92; Scottish Viewers Consultative Committee, ITC, 1991-92; Member, Church of Scotland Board of Social Responsibility, 1997-2001. Awarded Honorary Degree - Doctor of the University (DUniv), University of Glasgow, June 2007. Recreation: researching ways of salmon poachers! Address: West Morningside, Main Road, Langbank PA14 6XP; T.-01475 540249; e-mail: douglas.alexander@langbank.org

Alexander, Professor Michael Joseph, BA, MA (Oxon). Professor Emeritus of English Literature, St. Andrews University; b. 21.5.41, Wigan; m., 1, Eileen Mary McCall (deceased); 2, Mary Cecilia Sheahan; 1 s.; 2 d. Educ. Downside School; Trinity College, Oxford; Perugia University; Princeton University. Editor, William Collins, London, 1963-65; Lecturer, University of California, 1966-67; Editor, André Deutsch, London, 1967-68; Lecturer: East Anglia University, 1968-69, Stirling University, 1969; Senior Lecturer, 1977; Reader, 1985; Berry Professor of English Literature, St Andrews University, 1985-2003. Publications: Earliest English Poems (Translator), 1966; Beowulf (Translator), 1973; Twelve Poems, 1978; The Poetic Achievement of Ezra Pound, 1979; History of Old English Literature, 1983; Macmillan Anthology of English Literature, 1989; Beowulf (Editor), 1995; Sons of Ezra (Editor), 1995; The Canterbury Tales – The First Fragment (Editor), 1996; The Canterbury Tales: Illustrated Prologue (Editor), 1996; A History of English Literature, 2000; Medievalism: the Middle Ages in Modern England, 2007; Old English Riddles from the Exeter Book (Translator), 2007; The First Poems in English (Translator), 2008; Geoffrey Chaucer, 2012; Reading Shakespeare, 2013. Address: School of English, St. Andrews University, St. Andrews KY16 9AL; T.-01865-741774.
E-mail: michael.j.alex@gmail.com

Alexander, Morag, BA (Hons), OBE. Chair, ELCAP, since 2015; Lay member, General Optical Council, 2007-2014; Scotland Commissioner, Equality and Human Rights Commission, 2007-2010; Convener, Scottish Social Services Council, 2001-07; Director, Equal Opportunities Commission, Scotland, 1992-2001; Trustee, Turning Point Scotland, 2000-07; b. 10.10.43, Kilwinning; m., Professor Alan Alexander (qv); 1 s.; 1 d. Educ. Lourdes Secondary School, Glasgow; Glasgow University; Lakehead University, Ontario. Research Assistant, ASTMS, 1971-73; Editor and Researcher, RIPA, 1973-82; freelance journalist

and consultant, 1982-90; Founding Editor, Women in Europe, 1985-89, and UK Correspondent, Women of Europe, 1987-92; Founding Director, Training 2000 (Scotland) Ltd., Scottish Alliance for Women's Training, 1990-92; Member, Policy Committee, Children in Scotland, Chair, Early Years Advisory Group, 1995-2003; Board Member, Scottish Commission for the Regulation of Care, 2001-07; Member, Board, Partnership for a Parliament, 1997; Member, Scottish Senate, the Windsor Meetings, 1997-2000; Member, Expert Panel on Procedures and Standing Orders, Scottish Parliament, 1997-98; Member, Committee of Inquiry into Student Finance, 1999; Member, Governing Body, Court, Queen Margaret University, 2001-08; Trustee and Board Member, ELCAP, since 2010. Recreations: music; opera; visiting art galleries and museums; walking.
E-mail: morag.alexander@virginmedia.com

Alexander, Wendy, MA (Hons), MA (Econ), MBA. MSP (Labour), Paisley North, 1999-2011; Vice-Principal (International), University of Dundee, since 2015; Associate Dean, Global Business, Degree Programmes and Career Services, London Business School, since 2012; b. 27.6.63, Glasgow; m., Prof. Brian Ashcroft; 1 s.; 1 d. Educ. Park Mains School, Erskine; Pearson College, Canada; Glasgow University; Warwick University; INSEAD, France. Research Officer, Scottish Labour Party, 1988-92; Senior Associate, Booz Allen & Hamilton Int., 1994-97; Special Adviser to Secretary of State for Scotland, 1997-98; Minister for Communities, 1999-2000; Minister for Enterprise and Lifelong Learning, 2000-01; Minister for Enterprise, Transport and Lifelong Learning, 2001-02; Leader, Labour in Scottish Parliament, 2007-08. Visiting Professor, University of Strathclyde, 2002-2012. Address: (b.) Nethergate, Dundee DD1 4HN.

Allan, Alasdair James, MA, PhD. MSP (SNP), Western Isles, since 2007; Minister for Learning, Science and Scotland's Languages, Scottish Government, 2011-16; b. 6.5.71, Edinburgh. Educ. Selkirk High School; University of Glasgow; University of Aberdeen. Senior Vice President, Students Representative Council, Glasgow University, 1991-92; Researcher, SNP Headquarters, 1998-99; Parliamentary Assistant: Michael Russell MSP, 1999-2002, Alex Salmond MP, 2002-03; Policy and Parliamentary Affairs Manager, Carers Scotland, 2003-04; Senior Media Relations Officer, Church of Scotland, 2004-06; Parliamentary Assistant to Angus B MacNeil MP, 2006-07. National Secretary, SNP, 2003-06; Scottish Parliament Local Government and Communities Committee, 2007-2010; former Vice President, Scots Language Society. Recreations: Scottish languages and literature; hill walking; travel; promoting Scottish independence; singing in a Gaelic choir. Address: (b.) 31 Bayhead, Stornoway, Isle of Lewis HS1 0JS: T.-01851 702272; e-mail: alasdair.allan.msp@scottish.parliament.uk

Allan, Angus, BSc (Hons), MBA (2002). Depute Principal, South Lanarkshire College; Board Member, Loch Lomond and the Trossachs National Park Authority; Convener, Environmental Association of Colleges and Universities, since 2015; HM Inspector of Education; b. 28.3.60, Glasgow; m.; 3 s. Educ. Larkhall Academy; Edinburgh University. Lecturer in Agriculture, Kirkley College, Northumberland, 1982-85; farming, Ross-shire, 1985-88; Elmwood College, Cupar, 1988-2001 (latterly as Assistant Principal); Principal, Oatridge Agricultural College, 2001-02. Church of Scotland Elder. Recreation: sailing.

Allan, Charles Maitland, MA, MUniv (Aberdeen). Journalist, Economist and Farmer; b. 19.8.39, Stirling; m., Fiona Vine; 2 s.; 2 d. Educ. Dartington Hall; Aberdeen

University. Lecturer in Economic History, Glasgow University, 1962-63; Lecturer in Economics, St. Andrews University, 1963-65; Lecturer and Senior Lecturer, Strathclyde University, 1965-74; Producer/Presenter, BBC, 1982-86; Managing Editor, Ardo Publishing Co. Publications: Theory of Taxation; Death of a Papermill; Farmer's Diary I, II, III, IV, V; Neeps and Strae; The Truth Tells Twice; Them That Live The Longest. Recreations: cycling; cricket; turning off television sets; World Caber Tossing Champion, 1972. Address: (h.) Whinhill of Ardo, Methlick, Ellon, Aberdeenshire; T.-01651 806 218; e-mail: chas@charlieallan.com

Allan, Gary James Graham, QC, LLB (Hons); b. 21.1.58, Aberdeen; m., Margaret Muriel Glass; 1 s.; 1 d. Educ. Aberdeen Grammar School; University of Aberdeen. Legal apprenticeship, McGrigor Donald & Co., Solicitors, Glasgow and Edinburgh, 1980-82; Hughes Dowdall, Solicitors, Glasgow: Assistant Solicitor, 1982-1986, Partner, 1986-93; Admitted as a Member of the Faculty of Advocates, 1994; Appointed Queen's Counsel, 2007; Senior Advocate Depute (Crown Counsel), 2007-11; Advocate Depute ad hoc, since 2001. Executive Member, Glasgow Bar Association, 1983-93; Member, Management Committee, Castlemilk Law Centre, 1985-87; Local Parliamentary Liaison Officer, Law Society of Scotland, 1986-88; President, Aberdeen Grammar School Former Pupils' Club, 2007-08; Director, Hillhead High School War Memorial Trust Limited, 2000-2012; Director, Casus Omissus: The Aberdeen Law Project, since 2010; Appeal Chair member of the Judicial Panel of the Scottish Football Association, since 2011. Address: (b.) Mackinnon Advocates, Glasgow High Court, 1 Mart Street, Saltmarket, Glasgow G1 5NA; T.-0141 553 4890.

Allan, George Alexander, MA (Hons). Headmaster, Robert Gordon's College, Aberdeen, 1978-96; b. 3.2.36, Edinburgh; m., Anne Violet Veevers; 2 s. Educ. Daniel Stewart's College, Edinburgh; Edinburgh University. Teacher of Classics, Glasgow Academy, 1958-60; Daniel Stewart's College: Teacher of Classics, 1960-63, Head of Classics, 1963-73 (appointed Housemaster, 1967); Schoolmaster Fellow Commoner, Corpus Christi College, Cambridge, 1972; Deputy Headmaster, Robert Gordon's College, 1973-77. Former Chairman and former Secretary, Headmasters' Conference (Scottish Division) (Member, National Committee, 1982 and 1983); Governor, Welbeck College, 1980-89; Council Member, Scottish Council of Independent Schools, 1988-96 and 1997-2002; Director, Edinburgh Academy, 1996-2003; Governor, Longridge Towers School, Berwick-upon-Tweed, 2004-08. Recreations: gardening; music. Address: 5 Abbey View, Kelso, Roxburghshire TD5 8HX.

Allan, James Morrison, FRICS, MCIArb. Chartered Surveyor; b. 1.10.43, Edinburgh; m., Elizabeth Howie Sneddon Jack; 2 s. Educ. George Watson's College; Heriot Watt College. Joined Phillips Knox & Arthur as Apprentice Quantity Surveyor, 1960; qualified ARICS, 1965; FRICS, 1975; retired from partnership, 2004; RICS: Chairman, National Junior Organisation, 1975-76; Chairman, Quantity Surveyors Committee in Scotland, 1988-89; Chairman, RICS in Scotland, 1991-92; Member, RICS Management Board, 1992-95; Chairman, RICS Business Services Ltd., 1997-2003; Honorary Secretary, RICS, 2004-2010; Lay Member of the Regulatory Committee of the Law Society of Scotland, 2011-14. Recreations: family; caravanning and motoring; golf. Address: (h.) 4 Silverston Way, Longniddry, East Lothian EH32 0PF; T.-01875 852377; e-mail: jamesallan@btinternet.com

Allan, Sheriff John Douglas, OBE, BL, DMS. Sheriff of Lothian and Borders at Edinburgh, 2000-08; b. 2.10.41, Edinburgh; m., Helen E.J. Aiton; 1 s.; 1 d. Educ. George Watson's College, Edinburgh; Edinburgh University.

Solicitor in private practice, Edinburgh, 1963-67; Procurator Fiscal Depute, Edinburgh, 1967-71; Solicitor, Crown Office, Edinburgh, 1971-76; Assistant Procurator Fiscal, then Senior Assistant Procurator Fiscal, Glasgow, 1976-79; Solicitor, Crown Office, Edinburgh, 1979-83; Procurator Fiscal for Edinburgh and Regional Procurator Fiscal for Lothians and Borders, 1983-88; Sheriff of Lanark, 1988-2000. Part-time Lecturer in Law, Napier College, Edinburgh, 1963-66; Sheriffs' Association: Secretary, 1991-97, Vice-President, 1997-2000, President, 2000-2002; Chairman, Judicial Commission, General Assembly of the Church of Scotland, 1998-2003, Member, since 2009; Member, Board, Scottish Children's Reporter Administration, 1995-2003 (Deputy Chairman, 2002-03); Regional Vice-President, Commonwealth Magistrates' and Judges' Association, 2003-09 (Council Member, 2000-03, Member, since 2009); Member, Judicial Appointments Board for Scotland, 2002-08; Chairman, Executive Committee of Scottish Council, Scout Association, 2009-2013; Vice President, South East Scotland Regional Scout Council, since 2013; Holder, Scout "Medal of Merit". Recreations: Scouts; youth leadership; walking; Church. Address: 80 Greenbank Crescent, Edinburgh EH10 5SW; T.-0131-447-2593; e-mail: jdouglasallan@lumison.co.uk

Allan, Terrence William, BSc (Eng) (Hons), MEd. Emeritus Head of Computer Education, University of Aberdeen, since Sept. 2010; b. 8.10.47, Forres; m., Linda; 1 s.; 1 d. Educ. Elgin Academy; University of Aberdeen. Lecturer: Aberdeen College of Commerce, 1970-81, Aberdeen College of Education, 1981-88; Northern College: Senior Lecturer and Depute Head of Computer Education Department, 1988-94; Head of Computer Education Department, 1994-2001; University of Aberdeen: Head of Computer Education, 2001-2010. Member of Executive Committee of Scottish Table Tennis Association, 1992-94; Chairman of Disciplinary Committee of Scottish Table Tennis Association, 1993-2002. Recreations: information technologies; photography; jogging; hifi; DIY. Address: (h.) 32 Middleton Circle, Bridge of Don, Aberdeen AB22 8NZ; T.-01224 821448; e-mail: terry@allans.org

Allardyce, Jason, MSc. Editor, The Sunday Times Scotland, since 2012; b. 23.10.71, Greenock; m., Aine; 1 d. Educ. Greenock Academy; Queen Margaret University. Reporter: West Highland Free Press, 1990-95, The Scotsman, 1995-97; Political Correspondent, Scotland on Sunday, 1997-98; Political Reporter, The Times, 1998-99; Assistant Editor, Scotland on Sunday, 1999-2004; The Sunday Times Scotland: Assistant Editor, 2004-06, Associate Editor, 2006-2010, then Political Editor. UK Daily News Journalist of the Year, 1997; Scottish Journalist of the Year, 2003; Scottish Political Journalist of the Year, 2002, 2003, 2004, 2010. Recreations: walking; golf; rescuing spiders. Address: (b.) The Sunday Times, Fifth Floor, Guildhall, 57 Queen Street, Glasgow G1 3EN; T.-0141 4205338; e-mail: jason.allardyce@sunday-times.co.uk

Allen, Martin Angus William, MA, BD (1st Class Hons), ThM. Retired Minister, Chryston Parish Church of Scotland (1977-2007); b. 5.8.42, St. Andrews; m., Ann; 2 s. Educ. St. Andrews University; Edinburgh University; Covenant Seminary, St. Louis, USA. Assistant Education and Training Officer, Scottish Gas Board, 1964-71; Student in Theology, Edinburgh University, 1971-74; Assistant Minister, Church of Scotland, Wester Hailes, Edinburgh, 1974-75; Post Graduate Student, St. Louis, USA, 1975-76. Former Trustee, Rutherford House, Edinburgh - Theological Study Centre; former Trustee and Chairman, Crieff Trust - (Ministers' Fellowship). Recreations: golf; walking; reading. Address: (h.) Lealenge, High Barrwood

Road, Kilsyth G65 0EE; T.-01236 826616; e-mail: annmartinallen@gmail.com

Allfrey, Brigadier H. David, MBE, FRGS. Chief Executive and Producer, The Royal Edinburgh Military Tattoo, since 2011; b. 1959. Commissioned into the Royal Scots Dragoon Guards in 1979, commanded the Regiment, 2000-02, and 51 (Scottish) Brigade, 2007-2010; Colonel of the Regiment, since 2015. Champion for Events and Festivals, Scottish Tourism Alliance. Visiting Professor, Edinburgh Napier University. Address: The Tattoo Office, 1 Cockburn Street, Edinburgh EH1 1QB.

Allison, Barbara. Director of People, Communications & Ministerial Support Directorate, Scottish Government. Previously Director of People, 2009-15, Head of HR, 2008-09, Director of Human Resources, Scottish Prison Service, 2003-08 and held roles in Finance, Manufacturing and Strategy and Corporate Services. Address: (b.) Director of People, Communications & Ministerial Support, St Andrew's House, Regent Road, Edinburgh EH1 3DG; T.-0131 244 4593.

Allison, Charles William, MBChB, FRCA. Consultant Anaesthetist, Stracathro Hospital, Brechin, 1982-2012 (retired); Consultant, Ninewells Hospital, Dundee; Honorary Senior Lecturer, Dundee University; b. 1.7.52, Newport on Tay; m., Elspeth Stratton; 2 d. Educ. Madras College, St. Andrews; Dundee University. Training grades in anaesthesia, Dundee, 1976-81; Clinical Research Fellow, Hospital for Sick Children, Toronto, 1982. Editor, Annals of the Scottish Society of Anaesthetists, 1999-2003; President, NESSA, 2004-05; Secretary, DMGS, since 1982; Dean, Guildry of Brechin, 2007-09; President: Rotary Club of Brechin, 2010-11, Scottish Society of Anaesthetists, 2012-13, Dundee Medical Club, 2012-13. Publications: papers and book chapter. Recreations: golf; curling; photography. Address: Summerbank House, Brechin, Angus DD9 6HL; T.-01356 623624.
E-mail: charlie18h@btinternet.com

Allon, Christina Macleod, BScSocSci, DipCG, CIM, MICG; b. 8.5.53, Stornoway; m., John Paul Allon. Educ. Nicolson Institute, Stornoway and Edinburgh, Napier and Robert Gordon Universities. Careers Adviser in Highland; Management roles within Grampian Regional Council; Chief Executive, Grampian Careers; Director, Careers Scotland (SE); Non Executive on Bòrd na Gàidhlig; Non Executive Director and member of Strategic Board, Scottish Government. Recreations: walking; birdwatching; music; reading. Address: (b.) 2 Beachgate, Inverbervie, Angus DD10 0QZ; e-mail: jpcallon@msn.com

Almaini, Professor A.E.A., BSc (Eng), MSc, PhD. Professor, School of Engineering, Edinburgh Napier University, 1992-2010, Professor Emeritus, since 2010; b. 1.7.45, Baghdad; m., Shirley May; 2 s.; 1 d. Educ. London University; Salford University; Loughborough University. Research Scientist, Scientific Research Foundation, 1970-79; Lecturer, then Senior Lecturer, Napier University, 1980-91. Publications: Electronic Logic Systems (book); over 100 papers published. Recreation: gardening. Address: (b.) School of Engineering, Merchiston Campus, Edinburgh EH10 5DT; e-mail: a.almaini@napier.ac.uk

Alstead, Brigadier (Francis) Allan (Littlejohns), CBE, DL, MPhil, FCILT, FCMI, FCIPD, FInstD, FBISA. Director, Alstead Consulting and Launchsite Ltd, since 2000; Chief Executive, sportscotland (formerly Scottish Sports Council), 1990-2000; Chef de Mission for Scottish Team, Commonwealth Games 2002; Chairman, Mercy Corps Scotland, 2001-08; Board Member, Mercy Corps International, USA, 2001-08; Board Member, CRP (Bosnia), 2005-08; Chairman, Scottish Target Shooting Federation, 2011-15; b. 19.6.35, Glasgow; m., Joy Veronica Edwards; 2 s. Educ. Glasgow Academy; Royal Military Academy, Sandhurst; Royal Naval Staff College; Joint Services Staff College; Edinburgh University; University of Wales, Aberystwyth. Commissioned into King's Own Scottish Borderers, 1955; commanded 1st Bn., KOSB, 1974-76 (Mention in Despatches); Military Assistant to Quarter-Master-General, 1976-79; Instructor, Army Staff College, Camberley, 1979-81; Assistant Chief of Staff, BAOR, 1981-84 (Colonel); Commander, 51st Highland Brigade, 1984-87 (Brigadier); NATO Research Fellow, Edinburgh University, 1987-88; NATO HQ Reinforcement Co-ordinator, 1988-90. Member, Royal Company of Archers (Queen's Bodyguard in Scotland); Deputy Lieutenant, City of Edinburgh; Regimental Trustee, KOSB, 1980-2006; Trustee, KOSB Association, since 2006; Trustee, Youth Sport Trust, 1992-99; Deputy Hon. Colonel, City of Edinburgh Universities OTC, 1990-99; Governor, Moray House College, 1991-97; Governor, Glasgow Academy, 1995-2001; Member, Executive, Scottish Council, Development and Industry, 1995-2008; Member, Lowland RFCA, since 1995; Trustee, Council for the Advancement of Arts, Recreation and Education, 2003-2014; Director and Trustee, Seagull Trust, 1995-2007; Non-Executive Director, JRG Ltd, 1996-2007; Trustee, Erskine Hospital, 2001-2012; Member, General Council, Erskine Hospital, since 2012; Member, Council, National Playing Fields Association, 2001-07; President, SSAFA, Edinburgh, East and Midlothian, 1990-98 and then Edinburgh and Lothians, 2003; FRSA, 1994-2002; Mercy Corps, Humanitarian Hero Award, 2008; DUniv (Glasgow Caledonian), 2009. Publications: Ten in Ten; The Reinforcement of Europe in Crisis and War. Recreations: walking; archery. Address: (h.) 49 Moray Place, Edinburgh EH3 6BQ.

Alston, Dr. David. Chair, NHS Highland, since 2016. Career history: teacher, then organiser for the Workers Education Association in the Highlands; helped establish Cromarty Courthouse Museum and was its Curator/Manager; elected councillor, since 1999, representing the Black Isle. Non-executive member, Highland Council, 2003-2011, appointed Board Member in 2012. Address: NHS Highland, Assynt House/Beechwood Park, Inverness IV2 3BW; T.-01463 717123.

Amner, Neil, LLB (Hons), DipLP, Law. President, Glasgow Chamber of Commerce, since 2016 (Board Member, since 2012); Partner, MacRoberts, since 2015; Director, Glasgow Chamber of Commerce, since 2006. Educ. Glasgow Academy; University of Glasgow. Career: Partner and Head of Infrastructure, Environment & Transport: Biggart Baillie LLP, 1995-2012, DWF Biggart Baillie, 2012-13; Deputy President, Glasgow Chamber of Commerce, 2014-16. Chartered Fellow of Chartered Institute of Logisitics & Transport (UK). Member, European Aviation Law Association; Board Member, European Freight & Logistics Leaders Forum; Member, United Kingdom Environmental Law Association; European Freight & Logistics Leaders Forum. Recognised as leader in fields of transport, environmental and Scottish parliamentary law in both Legal 500 and Chambers directories of the legal profession. Recreations: triathlon; watersports; running; cycling; skiing and five-a-side football. Address: Glasgow Chamber of Commerce, 30 George Square, Glasgow G2 1EQ; T.-0141 204 2121.

Amyes, Professor Sebastian Giles Becket, BSc, MSc, PhD, DSc, Drhc, FRCPath, FIBiol. Professor of Microbial

Chemotherapy, Edinburgh University; b. 6.5.49, Stockton Heath; 1 s.; 1 d. Educ. Cranleigh School; University College, London. Edinburgh University, since 1977; Reader, 1988; Professor, 1992, Head of Medical Microbiology Department, 1997-2000. Royal Pharmaceutical Society annual conference award, 1984; C.L. Oakley lectureship, Pathological Society, 1987; Doctor honoris causa, Semmelweis University, Hungary, 2004; Honorary member of the Hungarian Society of Microbiology, 2007. Recreations: fishing; opera; golf; exploring parts of the world that the tour companies have not yet found. Address: (b.) Molecular Chemotherapy, Centre for Infectious Diseases, Little France, Edinburgh EH16 4SB; T.-0131 242 6652.
E-mail: s.g.b.amyes@ed.ac.uk

Anderson, Professor Annie S., BSc, PhD, SRD, FRCP (Edin). Professor of Public Health Nutrition, Ninewells Medical School, University of Dundee; Director, Centre for Public Health Nutrition Research, since 1996; b. 24.12.57, Torphins; m., Professor Robert Steele. Educ. Cults Academy, Aberdeen; RGIT; University of Aberdeen. Dietitian, Cambridge Area Health Authority, 1979-81; Research Assistant, Medical School, University of Cambridge, 1982-84; Research Dietitian, Grampian Health Board, 1985-86; Postgraduate Research Student, Department of Obstetrics, University of Aberdeen, 1987-91; Research Fellow (Human Nutrition), University of Glasgow, 1991-96; Member, Dundee University Court, 1999-2001; Editor, Journal of Human Nutrition and Dietetics (2001-06); Member, Scientific Advisory Committee on Nutrition, 2001-04, 2004-08, 2009-11; Observer (on behalf of UICC), WCRF/AICR Review Fund, Nutrition and Physical Activity; Chair, MRC Scientific Committee of National Prevention Initiative, since 2012; Workstream Lead on Health and Sustainability for Scottish Government National Food and Drink Policy, 2003-2011; Director, Scottish Cancer Foundation, since 2006; Co Director, Scottish Cancer Prevention Network, since 2008; Policy Adviser: Bowel Cancer UK, since 2006, Bowel Cancer Now, since 2012. Recreation: genealogy. Address: Centre for Research into Cancer Prevention and Screening, Centre for Public Health Nutrition Research, Division of Cancer Research, Level 7, Mailbox 7, Ninewells Medical School, Dundee DD1 9SY; T.-01382 383299; e-mail: a.s.anderson@dundee.ac.uk

Anderson, Dorothy Elizabeth, BSc (Hons), MB, ChB (with Commendation), MRCP(UK), DMRD, FRCR, FRCP(Glas). Consultant Radiologist, Glasgow Royal Infirmary, 1981-2010; Honorary Clinical Lecturer, then Senior Lecturer, Glasgow University, 1982-2010; b. 1950, Glasgow; m., David Anderson; 1 s.; 1 d. Educ. Glasgow High School for Girls; Glasgow University. Pre-registration posts, Stobhill Hospital and Glasgow Royal Infirmary; post-registration year, Respiratory Unit, Knightswood Hospital; trained in radiology, Western Infirmary, Glasgow (Registrar, then Senior Registrar). Recreations: choral singing; walking; reading; history; piano; travel.
E-mail: deanderson@doctors.org.uk

Anderson, Douglas Kinloch, OBE, MA. Chairman, Kinloch Anderson (Holdings) Ltd., Edinburgh, since 1975; Director: Fidelity Special Values PLC; F & C Private Equity Trust PLC; b. 19.2.39, Edinburgh; m., Deirdre Anne; 2 s.; 1 d. Educ. George Watson's Boys College; St. Andrews University. Joined Kinloch Anderson Ltd., 1962 (fifth generation in family business); Assistant on Master's Court, Edinburgh Merchant Company, 1976-79; elected Honorary Member, St. Andrew's Society of Washington DC, 1985; Board Member, Scottish Tourist Board, 1986-92; Member, Edinburgh Festival Council, 1988-90; President, Edinburgh Royal Warrant Holders Association,

1987-88; former Member, Scottish Committee, Institute of Directors; President, Edinburgh Chamber of Commerce, 1988-90; Master, Edinburgh Merchant Company, 1990-92; Deputy Chairman, Edinburgh Marketing Ltd., 1990-92; Director, Lothian and Edinburgh Enterprise Ltd., 1990-95; elected Leith High Constable, 1993, Moderator, 2010; Freeman, City of London; Past President, Royal Warrant Holders Association. Recreations: golf; fishing; watching rugby; travel (non-business). Address: (b.) Commercial Street/Dock Street, Leith, Edinburgh EH6 6EY; T.-0131-555 1355; e-mail: douglaska@kinlochanderson.com

Anderson, Elaine, MB, ChB, FRCSEd, MD. Associate Medical Director, Cancer Services, NHS Lothian, since 2014; Consultant Breast Surgeon, since 1994; b. 19.10.58. Educ. Trinity Academy, Edinburgh; Edinburgh University. Accreditation in general surgery, 1993. Recreations: sailing; gardening; running. Address: (b.) Breast Unit, Western General Hospital, Crewe Road, Edinburgh EH4 2XU; T.-0131 537 1614.
E-mail: elaine.anderson@nhslothian.scot.nhs.uk

Anderson, Gavin John, LLB (Hons), DipLP. Advocate, since 2001; b. 22.8.71, Edinburgh; m., Lynne Ann Montgomery. Educ. St Thomas of Aquin's High Sch., Edinburgh; Aberdeen University. Solicitor, 1995-2000; awarded Faculty of Advocates Scholarship, 2000; admitted to Faculty, 2001; Member Westwater Advocates (www.westwateradvocates.com). Recreations: golf; classic cars. Address: (b.) Advocates' Library, Parliament House, Edinburgh EH1 1RF; T.-0131 226 5071.

Anderson, Iain Buchanan, MA, DipEd, LGSM. Music Presenter/Sports Commentator, BBC, since 1985; m., Marion Elizabeth; 3 s.; 1 d. Educ. Bellahouston Academy, Glasgow; Glasgow University; Guildhall School. Lecturer in Speech and Drama, Jordanhill College, 1967; Arts Editor/Presenter, Radio Clyde, 1974. Former Rugby Correspondent, Scotland on Sunday. Address: (h.) Elmhurst, Station Road, Langbank PA14 6YA; T.-0147 554 0733; e-mail: iain53@btinternet.com

Anderson, Ian Wilson Russell, CBE (2013), MBChB, DSc (Hon), FRCS (Glasgow), FRCS (England), FRCS (Edinburgh), FCEM, FRCP (Glasgow), FRCP (London), FRCPEd, Hon. FACP. Formerly Consultant, Accident and Emergency, Victoria Infirmary, Glasgow; formerly Honorary Clinical Senior Lecturer, University of Glasgow; b. 4.5.51, Prestwick. Educ. Ayr Academy; University of Glasgow. House Officer posts, Glasgow; completed general professional training in surgery, 1980; completed specialist training in accident and emergency medicine and surgery, 1984; Director, Medical and Dental Defence Union of Scotland; Past President, Faculty of Accident and Emergency Medicine; Past President, Royal College of Physicians and Surgeons of Glasgow.

Anderson, Karen. Chair, Architecture and Design Scotland; Founding Partner, Anderson Bell Christie. Educ. Glasgow's Mackintosh School of Architecture. Career: worked on architectural projects, masterplanning and urban and rural design guidance in areas as diverse as Raploch, Stirling; the Isle of Gigha; Argyll and Bute; and North Lanarkshire; formerly part-time lecturer in Architecture, University of Strathclyde. Formerly Convenor of the Saltire Housing Design Awards Panel; former Commissioner of the Royal Fine Art Commission for Scotland; currently Chair, Architecture and Design Scotland and practising architect. Address: (b.) Architecture and Design Scotland, Bakehouse Close, 146 Canongate, Edinburgh EH8 8DD; T.-0131 556 6699.

Anderson, Keith, BA, CA. Chief Corporate Officer, ScottishPower, since 2011; Chief Executive, ScottishPower Renewables, since 1998. Educ. Edinburgh Napier

University; ICAS. Audit Manager, Standard Life, 1991-93; Audit Manager, Insurance, Royal Bank of Scotland, 1993-98; Senior Consultant, Ernst & Young, 1998-2000; Director of Strategy - UK, ScottishPower, 2003-05; Chairman, Wise Group, 2010-12. Appointed to the Board of ScottishPower in 2012. Address: Cathcart Business Park, Spean Street, Glasgow G44 4BE; T.-0141 568 2000.

Anderson, Kenneth, MBChB, MD, FRCP (Glas & Edin). Consultant Physician with special interest in respiratory medicine; b. Glasgow; m., M. Ruth Adamson. Educ. Allan Glen's School; Glasgow University. Visiting Physician, University of Colorado Hospitals, Denver; President, Scottish Thoracic Society, 2016. Recreations: golf at Barassie and St Andrews; gardens. Address: Crosshouse Hospital, Kilmarnock KA2 0BE; T.-01563 577903.

Anderson, Lin. Crime novelist and screenwriter; b. Greenock. Worked in the Nigerian bush for five years during the 1980s, and later wrote an African short story which was broadcast on BBC Radio Four; another of her African stories was published in the 10th Anniversary Macallan/Scotland on Sunday Short Story Collection. Before turning full time to writing, taught maths and computing at George Watson's College, Edinburgh. A film of her screenplay Small Love was shown at London Film Festival and Edinburgh International Film Festival in 2001, and broadcast on Scottish Television in 2001 and 2002. Graduated from the newly founded Screen Academy Scotland, and has further screenplays in production. Member of the Femmes Fatales crime writing trio, together with Alanna Knight and Alex Gray. Co-founder with Alex Gray of Bloody Scotland, Scotland's International Crime Writing Festival; Chair of the Society of Authors in Scotland. Publications: Rhona MacLeod series: Driftnet (2003), Torch (2004), Deadly Code (2005), Blood Red Roses (2005), Dark Flight (2007), Easy Kill (2008), Final Cut (2009), Reborn (2010), Picture Her Dead (2011), Paths of the Dead (2014), The Special Dead, 2015; Patrick de Courvoisier series: The Case of the Black Pearl (2014), The Case of the Missing Madonna (2015); screenplays: Small Love (2001), River Child (2006), The Incredible Lightness of Brian (2006); non-fiction: Braveheart: From Hollywood to Holyrood (2004). Address: Jenny Brown Associates, 33 Argyle Place, Edinburgh EH9 1JT.

Anderson, Lloyd, BSc (Hons) Botany (Imperial College), ARCS, PhD Plant Sciences (Lancaster), Dip. Desert Ecology (Ben Gurion University of the Negev), CBiol., MSBiol. Director, British Council Scotland; Director, British Council Georgia (2011); Deputy Director, British Council Russia (2010); Director, Science, Engineering & Environment, British Council (1998-2011); Secretary to the Science, Engineering & Environment Advisory Committee, British Council (1998-2011); Assistant to the Director, Institute of Terrestrial Ecology, NERC (1995-1998); Senior Scientific Officer, NERC (1991-1995); Section Head, Animal Health Trust (1989-1991); First Secretary, Science & Health, British Council India (1986-1989); Postdoctoral Research Fellow, Edinburgh University (1980-1986). Membership of: Core Officials Group, Global Science and Innovation Forum; International Network, ESRC; Natural Sciences Committee, UK National Commission to UNESCO; Working Group on Access to Scientific Information, UK UNESCO; Area Panel for Latin America and the Caribbean, British Academy; Advisory Council, Institute for the Study of the Americas; Editorial Committee for 'People and Science', British Science Association. Address: (b.) The Tun, 4 Jackson's Entry, Holyrood Road, Edinburgh EH8 8PJ; T.-0131 524 5753; e-mail: lloyd.anderson@britishcouncil.org

Anderson, Professor Michael, OBE, MA, PhD, Dr hc, HonDLitt, FBA, FRSE, FRHistSoc, Hon FFA. Professor (Emeritus, since 2007) of Economic History, University of Edinburgh, since 1979; b. 21.2.42, Woking; m. (1),

Rosemary Elizabeth Kitching; 1 s.; 1 d.; m. (2), Elspeth MacArthur. Educ. Kingston Grammar School; Queens' College, Cambridge. University of Edinburgh: Assistant Lecturer, 1967-69, Lecturer, 1969-75, Reader, 1975-79, Dean of Faculty of Social Sciences, 1985-89, Vice-Principal, 1989-93, and 1997-2000, Acting Principal, 1994, Senior Vice-Principal, 2000-07. Member: Scottish Records Advisory Council, 1984-93, Economic and Social Research Council, 1990-94, Follett Committee on Libraries and Follett Implementation Group, 1993-97, British Library Board, 1994-2003, Council of British Academy, 1995-98, Research Information Network Advisory Board, 2005-2011, National Statistics Centre for Demography Advisory Board, 2006-2012, ONS UK Population Theme Advisory Board, since 2012, HEFCE Research and Innovation Strategic Advisory Committee, 2006-09; Scottish Census Steering Committee, 2009-2011; Curator, Royal Society of Edinburgh, 1997-99; Trustee, National Library of Scotland, 1998-2012, Chairman, 2000-2012; Chairman, Research Support Libraries Programme, 1998-2003. Publications: Family Structure in Nineteenth Century Lancashire, 1971; Approaches to the History of the Western Family, 1981; Population Change in North-Western Europe 1750-1850; many papers on family sociology and history and historical demography. Recreations: natural history; gardening; study of ancient civilisations. Address: (b.) School of History, Classics and Archaeology, Doorway 4, Teviot Place, Edinburgh EH8 9AG.

Anderson, Moira, OBE. Singer; b. Kirkintilloch; m., Dr. Stuart Macdonald. Educ. Ayr Academy; Royal Scottish Academy of Music, Glasgow. Began with Kirkintilloch Junior Choir, aged six; made first radio broadcast for BBC in Scotland, aged eight; was Teacher of Music in Ayr before becoming professional singer; made first professional broadcast, White Heather Club, 1960; has toured overseas, had her own radio and TV series; has introduced Stars on Sunday, ITV; appeared in summer shows, cabaret, pantomime and numerous other stage shows; several Royal Variety performances.

Anderson, Neil Robert, LLB (Hons), DipLP, NP. Partner, Ledingham Chalmers LLP, Solicitors, since 2008; b. 10.5.71, Edinburgh; m., Jill Shaw Andrew. Educ. Dalkeith High School; University of Aberdeen. Trained, Fyfe Ireland WS, Edinburgh, 1994-96; Biggart Baillie, Glasgow: Assistant, 1996-99, Associate, 1999-2003, Partner, 2003-08. Recreations: cinema/film; orchid cultivation; travel to anywhere. Address: (b.) Johnstone House, 52-54 Rose Street, Aberdeen AB10 1HA; T.-01224-408-408; e-mail: neil.anderson@ledinghamchalmers.com

Anderson, Peter David, MA, PhD, FSA Scot, FRHistS, FRSA. Deputy Keeper, National Archives of Scotland (formerly Scottish Record Office), 1993-2009; b. 10.3.47, Greenock; m., Jean Johnstone Smith; 1 d.; 1 s. (deceased). Educ. Hutchesons' Grammar School, Glasgow; Glasgow School of Art; St. Andrews University; Edinburgh University. Teacher of History, Cranhill Secondary School, Glasgow, 1972-73; Research Assistant, Scottish Record Office, 1974-80; Registrar, National Register of Archives (Scotland), 1980-83; Secretary, NRA(S), 1984-85; Conservation Officer, 1985-89; Head, Records Liaison Branch, 1989-93. Chair, International Council on Archives Committee on Archive Buildings and Equipment, 1996-2004; Chair, Society of Archivists, 2005-07; External Examiner, Dundee University Centre for Archive and Information Studies, 2005-09; Secretary, Scottish Oral History Group, 1984-88, Deputy Convener, 1988-2008; Chair, Linlithgow Heritage Trust, since 2008. Publications: Robert Stewart, Earl of Orkney, Lord of Shetland, 1533-93, 1982; Black Patie, 1993; The Stewart Earls of Orkney, 2012; articles on archival and historical subjects. Recreations: drawing and painting; drama. Address: (h.) 74 Burghmuir Court, Linlithgow EH49 7LL; T.-01506-844663.

Anderson, Robert Alexander, MA, BD (Glas), DPhil (Oxon). Minister, Blackburn and Seafield Church, since 1998; b. 3.4.47, Kilwinning; m., Christine Main; 2 step s.; 1 step d. Educ. Kilwinning High School; Irvine Royal Academy; Glasgow University; Hertford College, Oxford. Missionary of The Church of Scotland as Tutor in Theology at St. Paul's United Theological College, Limuru, Kenya, 1980-86; Head of Theology and Philosophy, 1984-86; Dean of Studies, 1982-83 and 1984-85; Minister, Overtown Parish Church, 1986-89; P/T Chaplain, Shotts Prison, 1988-89; Chaplain, Edinburgh University, 1989-94; Development Officer, Carberry Tower, 1994-96. Publications: Intimations of Love Divine, 1996; Stop The World, I Want To Think, 1998; Who Cares Wins, 2000; Changes in Spiritual Freedom in the Church of Scotland, 2005; The Church of Scotland Ministry Disciplinary Proceedings, the New Testament, Natural Justice and Human Rights, 2011; Grains of Gold, 2012, 2nd Edition, 2015. Recreation: golf. Address: (b.) 5 MacDonald Gardens, Blackburn EH47 7RE; T.-01506 652825.

E-mail: robertanderson307@btinternet.com

Anderson, Very Rev. Canon William Rutherfoord Turnbull, MA, FTCL, FLCM, MTh. Formerly Parish Priest, St. Francis R.C. Church, Aberdeen (retired), previously Administrator, St. Mary's R.C. Cathedral, Aberdeen; b. 7.1.31, Glasgow. Educ. George Watson's College, Edinburgh; University of Edinburgh; Sidney Sussex College, Cambridge. Curate, St. David's, Dalkeith, 1960-61; staff, St. Mary's College, Blairs, Aberdeen, 1961-69; Producer, BBC Scotland Religious Department, 1969-77; Spiritual Director, Pontifical Scots College, Rome, 1977-85; staff, St. Mary's College, Blairs, Aberdeen, 1985-86; R.C. Chaplain, University of Aberdeen, 1986-93. Canon, R.C. Diocese of Aberdeen; former Major Scholar, Sidney Sussex College, Cambridge; Poetry Society Gold Medal for verse-speaking, 1980; Preacher of the Year, The Times and College of Preachers, 1996; Warrack Lecturer, Aberdeen University, 1998; Hon. teaching fellow (Latin), Aberdeen University, 2005-2010. Publication: Words and the Word, 2010. Recreations: walking; music and literature. Address: 24 Kirk Manor Court, Cults, Aberdeen AB15 9SF.

Andrew, Hugh, BA (Oxon), FSA Scot. Managing Director, Birlinn Ltd (incorporating John Donald, Polygon, Mercat and Tuckwell Press); Managing Director, Seol Ltd.; Director, Compass Independent Publishing Services; b. 8.4.62. Educ. Glasgow Academy; Magdalen College, Oxford. Set up own publishing company, Birlinn Ltd., 1992; Joint Managing Director, Canongate Books, 1994-99. Chairman, Ossian Trust; Trustee, The Great Tapestry of Scotland. Recreations: reading; music; travel; archaeology; history; islands. Address: (b.) West Newington House, 10 Newington Road, Edinburgh EH9 1QS; T.-0131-668 4371; e-mail: hugh@birlinn.co.uk

Andrew, John Anthony, MA, FRICS, IRRV. Chief Surveyor, Scottish Government, since 1996; b. 10.10.52, Ormskirk; m., Mary MacLeod MacKay; 3 s. Educ. Ormskirk Grammar School; Heanor Grammar School; Downing College, University of Cambridge. Valuation Office, Inland Revenue, Cleveland North, 1976-78; Lecturer in Land Economy, University of Aberdeen, 1978-81; Valuation Office, Inland Revenue, Aberdeen and Dumfries, 1981-89; Principal Estates Surveyor, Scottish Office, 1989-92 and 1994-96; Principal, Scottish Office Agriculture and Fisheries Department, Land Use and Conservation Division, 1992-94. Vice Chairman, RICS in Scotland, 2002; Member: RICS Scotland Board, 1999-2012, RICS Scottish Valuation Professional Group Board; External Examiner, Heriot-Watt University, 1999-2003, Napier University, 2003-08, Aberdeen University, 2007-2011; Member, Editorial Advisory Board, Journal of Facilities Management; Area Coordinator, Compassion UK; Trustee, EMMS International. Address: Scottish Government SPCD: Property Division, 3-G (N) Victoria Quay, Edinburgh EH6 6QQ; T.-0131-244 4521; e-mail: anthony.andrew@scotland.gsi.gov.uk

Andrews, Professor June, FRCN, RMN, RGN, MA (Hons). Director, Dementia Services Development Centre, University of Stirling; former Director, Centre for Change and Innovation, Health Department, Scottish Executive; b. Kilwinning. Educ. Ardrossan Academy; Glasgow University; Nottingham University. NHS nursing and management posts, Nottingham and London; Director of Nursing, Forth Valley Acute Hospitals NHS Trust; Royal College of Nursing: adviser on ethics and Aids, Assistant Director Policy and Research, Scottish Board Secretary. Address: (b.) Department of Applied Social Science, University of Stirling, Stirling FK9 4LA.

Annand, David Andrew, DA, ARBS. Sculptor; b. 30.1.48, Insch, Aberdeenshire; m., Jean; 1 s.; 1 d. Educ. Perth Academy; Duncan of Jordanstone College of Art, Dundee. Lecturer, Sculpture Department, Duncan of Jordanstone College of Art, Dundee, 1972-74; Art Department, St. Saviour's High School, Dundee, 1975-88; full-time sculptor, since 1988; RSA Latimer Award, 1976; RSA Benno Schotz Award, 1978; RSA Ireland Alloys Award, 1982; Scottish Development Agency Dundee Technology Park Competition, 1986, "Deer Leap", Sir Otto Beit Medal, 1986; Royal Botanic Garden, Edinburgh "Ardea Cinerea", 1987; Winner, Almswall Road Sculpture Competition, Irvine Development Corporation, "The Ring", 1989; Winner, Perth High Street Sculpture Competition, Perth Partnership "Nae Day Sae Dark", 1989; Baxters of Speyside "Royal Stag" cast by Powderhall Bronze, 1993; Tranent Massacre Memorial bronze casting by Powderhall Bronze, 1995; Winner, competition to design sculpture for Lord Street, Wrexham, 1995, "Y Bwa" Civic Society Award, 1995; Winner, competition to design sculpture, Ashworth Roundabout, Blackpool, "Helter-skelter", 1995; Strathcarron Hospice composition, 1996; British High Commission, Hong Kong, "Three Cranes in Flight", 1997; Hamilton Town Square "Strongman", 1998; Aberdeen Angus Bull, Alford, 2001; The Declaration of Arbroath, Arbroath, 2001; Civic Pride, Barnet, London, 2001; other commissions completed in 2001 for BT Brentwood and Maidstone Borough Council; Winner of project to create a memorial to the poet Robert Fergusson, 2002; Sir Jimmy Shand Memorial, 2003; completed commissions in Redruth, Poole, Belfast, Mansfield, Hawick, Wirral, Republic of Ireland, 2004-09. Recreations: music; bird watching; wine and food. Address: Pigscrave Cottage, The Wynd, Kilmany, Cupar, Fife KY15 4PT; T.-01382 330 714.
Web: www.davidannand.com

Annandale and Hartfell, 11th Earl of (Patrick Andrew Wentworth Hope Johnstone of Annandale and of That Ilk). Chief, Clan Johnstone; Baron of the Barony of the Lands of the Earldom of Annandale and Hartfell, and of the Lordship of Johnstone; Hereditary Steward, Stewartry of Annandale; Hereditary Keeper, Keys of Lochmaben Castle; Deputy Lieutenant, Dumfriesshire, 1987-92, Vice-Lieutenant, since 1992; b. 19.4.41, Auldgirth, Dumfriesshire; m., Susan Josephine; 1 s.; 1 d. Educ. Stowe School; Royal Agricultural College, Cirencester. Member: Dumfriesshire County Council, 1970-75, Dumfries and Galloway Regional Council, 1975-85, Scottish Valuation Advisory Council, 1982, Solway River Purification Board, 1973-85; Underwriter, Lloyds, London, 1976-2004. Address: (b.) Annandale Estates Office, St. Anns, Lockerbie DG11 1HQ.

Arbuthnott, 17th Viscount of (John Keith Oxley); b. 18.7.50; m.; 1 s.; 2 d. Scottish farmer and businessman. Address: (h.) Kilternan, Arbuthnott, by Laurencekirk, Kincardineshire AB30 1PA.

Arbuthnott, Professor Sir John Peebles, PhD, ScD, FSB, HonFTCD, PRSE, FIIB, FRCPath, HonFRCPSGlasg. Principal and Vice Chancellor, Strathclyde University, 1991-2000; Chairman, Greater Glasgow NHS Board, 2002-07; b. 8.4.39; m., Elinor Rutherford Smillie; 1 s.; 2 d. Educ. Glasgow University; Trinity College, Dublin. Assistant Lecturer, then Lecturer, Department of Bacteriology, Glasgow University, 1960-67; Research Fellow of the Royal Society, 1968-72; Senior Lecturer, Department of Microbiology, then Senior Lecturer, Department of Bacteriology, Glasgow University, 1972-75; Professor of Micriobiology, Trinity College, Dublin, 1976-88; Professor of Microbiology, Nottingham University, 1988-91. Secretary/Treasurer, Carnegie Trust for the Universities of Scotland, 2000-04; Member, Board, Food Standards Agency; Chairman, Scottish Food Advisory Committee, 2000-02; Chairman, National Review of Allocation of Health Resources in Scotland, 1997-99; Chairman, Standing Committee on Resource Allocation to NHS in Scotland, 2001-03; Director, Scottish Science Trust; Chairman, Wolfson Institute of Health, Medicine and the Environment, University of Durham, 2000-07; Chairman, Commission on Voting Systems, Boundaries and Representation in Scotland, 2004-06; President, Scottish Association of Marine Science, 2004-2010; Independent Chair of Review of Clyde Valley Local Authorites; Royal Society of Edinburgh, Council Member, 2007-2010, President, 2011-14; Co-founder of the African Cancer Control Programme, AfrOx, since 2007; Member, External Advisory Group of the Glasgow Centre for Population Health, since 2008; Trustee, Lloyds TSB Foundation for Scotland, since 2009; Chair, Medical and Scientific Advisory Committee of Lamellar Biomedical Ltd, since 2009. Honorary Degrees: DSc: University Lodz, Poland, University Teknologi, Malaysia, Glasgow University, Glasgow Caledonian University, University of Durham, 2007, Napier University, 2013; LLD: Queens University, Belfast, Aberdeen University; DEd, Queen Margaret University College; DUniv, Strathclyde University; Distinguished Fellowship, International Medical University, Malaysia; Open University, 2014. Recreations: bird-watching; photography. Address: (h.) 9 Curlinghall, Largs KA30 8LB.

Archer, Gilbert Baird. Vice Lord-Lieutenant for Tweeddale, since 2008; Chairman, Tods of Orkney Ltd (oatcake and biscuit manufacturers), since 1970; b. 24.8.42, Edinburgh; m., Irene Conn; 2 d. Educ. Melville College. Chairman: John Dickson & Son Ltd, 1985-97, Borders 1996 Ltd, 1996-98; Director, EPS Moulders Ltd, 1985-88, Scottish Council for Development and Industry, 1993-96; Chairman, Leith Chamber of Commerce, 1986-88; President, Edinburgh Chamber of Commerce, 1990-92; Chairman, Association of Scottish Chambers of Commerce, 1993-96; Deputy President, British Chambers of Commerce, 1995-96; Chairman, Edinburgh Common Purpose, 1991-94; Director, Scottish Council of Independent Schools, 1988-91; Member, Council, Governing Bodies Association of Independent Schools, 1988-91; Chairman, St. Columba's Hospice, 1998-2004 (now Vice President); Vice Convenor, George Watson's College, 1978-80; Governor, Fettes College, 1986-90; Napier University, 1991-97; Master: Company of Merchants of the City of Edinburgh, 1997-99, Gunmakers' Company, 2006-07; Moderator, High Constables of Port of Leith, 1990-91; DL Tweeddale, 1994. Recreation: previously flying, now country pursuits. Clubs: Army and Navy, New (Edinburgh). Address: 10 Broughton Place Lane, Edinburgh EH1 3RS; T.-0131-556 4518; Fax: 01856-850213.

Archer, Janet. Chief Executive, Creative Scotland, since 2013. Career history: work in Scotland includes chairing the artist-led organisation, The Work Room; supported the British Council in programming their showcases in Edinburgh and as a former dancer, choreographer, founder and Artistic Director of the Nexus Dance Company, touring into Scotland as well as attending the Scottish Youth Dance Festivals held in Stirling in the 1980's; 16 years with the Newcastle based National Dance Agency, Dance City as Chief Executive and Artistic Director were instrumental to the organisation's growth, and included the project management of a large scale capital development working with a Scottish design team led by Malcolm Fraser Architects; formerly Dance Director, Arts Council England working as part of the national strategy team; has a broad knowledge of the wider arts and creative industries having been involved in developing Arts Council England's 10 year framework for the arts: Achieving Great Art For Everyone; also led the team that delivered the State of the Arts 2012 conference: Artists Shaping the World. Address: Creative Scotland, Waverley Gate, 2-4 Waterloo Place, Edinburgh EH1 3EG; T.-0131 523 0025.

Archer, John William, BA (Hons). Independent film and television producer; b. 19.9.53, Evesham; 4 s. Educ. Dean Close School, Cheltenham; University of Birmingham; University College, Cardiff. Researcher, Nationwide, 1975-77; Director, BBC TV, London: Writers and Places, Global Report, Omnibus; Producer, The Book Programme, Did You See...?; Editor, Saturday Review, A Week of British Art; Head of Music and Arts, BBC Scotland, 1989, including editing Edinburgh Nights; Executive Producer, The Bigger Picture, Billy Connolly's World Tour of Scotland/Australia; producing and directing Stevenson's Travels; BAFTA Award, best programme/ series without a category for Did You See...?, 1983; Chief Executive, Scottish Screen, 1996-2001; Managing Director, Hopscotch Films Ltd., since 2002; Producer, 'Writing Scotland'. Recreations: walking; tree planting; mountain biking; necessary gardening; novels. Address: (b.) Hopscotch Films, Film City Glasgow, 401 Govan Road, Glasgow G51 2QJ; T.-0141-440-6740.
E-mail: john@hopscotchfilms.co.uk

Archibald, George. Chief Executive, Midlothian and East Lothian Chamber of Commerce; Executive Director, The Business Partnership. Address: (b.) Midlothian & East Lothian Chamber of Commerce, Moulsdale House, Edinburgh College, 24D Milton Road East, Edinburgh EH15 2PP; T.-0131 603 5043.

Argondizza, Pauline Hazel, GMusRNCM, PPRNCM, PGDipRNCM. Cellist, Royal Scottish National Orchestra; (former Associate Principal Cellist, Principal Cellist, 1989-2011); b. 10.3.63, Chelmsford; m., Dr. Peter Argondizza; 2 c. Educ. Chelmer Valley High School; Colchester Institute; Royal Northern College of Music; Banff School of Fine Arts, Banff, Alberta, Canada. Co-Principal Cellist, English National Opera Orchestra, 1988. Address: (h.) 0/2, 119 Randolph Road, Broomhill, Glasgow G11 7DS; T.-0141 384 8617; e-mail: pauline.argondizza@btopenworld.com

Argyll, Duke of (Torquhil Ian Campbell); b. 29.5.68. Succeeded to title, 2001. Chief of Clan Campbell.

Arkless, Richard, BA (Hons), LLB. MP (SNP), Dumfries and Galloway, since 2015; b. 1975, Stranraer. Educ. Glasgow Caledonian University, Glasgow; School of Law, University of Strathclyde. Address: House of Commons, London SW1A 0AA.

Armes, Right Rev. Dr. John, BA, MA, PhD. Bishop, Diocese of Edinburgh, since 2012; formerly Dean, Diocese of Edinburgh, 2010-12; Rector, St John the Evangelist Church, Edinburgh, 1998-2012; b. 1955; m., Clare; 4 c. Educ. Cambridge University; University of Manchester; Salisbury–Wells Theological College. Deaconed 1979. Priested 1980. Formerly Area Dean, Rossendale in the Manchester Diocese; priest-in-charge, Goodshaw &

Crawshawbooth, 1994-98; Anglican Chaplain to University of Manchester; Team Vicar and then Team Rector, Parish of Whitworth (University Parish), Convener of Chaplaincy Ecumenical Team, 1986-94; Chaplain, Agriculture and Rural Life in Cumbria (two-thirds time) and Team Vicar in Greystoke Team Ministry, looking after Watermillock Parish, 1982-86. Curate, Walney, Barrow in Furness; Chaplain, Barrow Sixth Form College, 1979-82. Recreations: theatre; cinema; walking; reading novels; watching sport; travel and humour. Address: Diocesan Office, 21a Grosvenor Crescent, Edinburgh EH12 5EL; T.- 0131 538 7044.

Armour, Emeritus Professor Sir James, CBE, BVMS, PhD, HonDU (Stirling), Dr hc Utrecht, Hon. DVM&S (Edin), HonDU (Glasgow), HonFIBiol, FRCVS, FRSE, FMedSci. Dean of Faculties, Glasgow University, 2001-04; Emeritus Professor of Veterinary Parasitology; Vice-Principal (Planning - External Relations), 1991-95; Dean, Faculty of Veterinary Medicine, 1986-90; Chairman, Glasgow Dental Hospital and School NHS Trust, 1995-99; Vice-President, Royal Society of Edinburgh, 1998-2000; b. 17.9.29, Basra, Iraq; m., 1, Irene Morris (deceased); 2, Christine Strickland; 2 s.; 2 d. Educ. Marr College, Troon; Glasgow University. Colonial veterinary service, Nigeria, 1953-60; Research Scientist, Wellcome Ltd., 1960-63; Glasgow University: Research Fellow, 1963-67, Lecturer/Senior Lecturer, 1967-73, Reader, 1973-76. Chairman, Government Committee on Animal Medicines, 1987-95; Chairman, Editorial Board, In Practice (veterinary journal), 1980-90; Chairman, Governing Body, Institute of Animal Health, 1989-97; Member, Governing Body: Moredun Research Institute, Edinburgh, 1997-2006, Institute of Aquaculture, Stirling, 1997-2003; Member, Hannah Foundation Board, since 1998; Trustee, Scottish Science Trust, 1999-2001; Chairman: Moredun Foundation for Animal Health and Welfare, 2000-04, Higher Education Funding Council Research Assessment Panels for Agriculture, Food Science and Veterinary Science, 1999-2001; Member, Royal Society of Edinburgh Inquiry into Foot and Mouth Disease in Scotland, 2001; Chairman, St. Andrews Clinics for Children in Africa, 2000-07, 2008-09, 2009-2010. Awards: RCVS John Henry Steel Medal, Royal Agricultural Society Bledisloe Award, BVA Wooldridge Medal, Pfizer WAAVP Award, BVA Chiron Award; Royal Society of Edinburgh Medal, 2002. Captain, Royal Troon GC, 1990-92, Honorary President, 2007-2010; Member, Hannah Trust, since 2012. Publications: joint author of textbook on veterinary parasitology; editor, two books; 150 scientific articles. Recreation: golf. Address: (h.) 4b Towans Court, Prestwick, Ayrshire; T.-01292 470869.

Armour, Robert Malcolm, OBE, MBA, LLB (Hons), DipLP, WS, NP, FEI. Director, Albion Community Power plc, Nuclear Liabilities Fund Ltd, Eneus Energy Ltd; Senior Counsel, Gowlings UK LLP; Chair, Regenerco Renewable Energy; Smarter Grid Solutions and the Street by Street Solar Programme; Deputy Chair, NuGeneration Limited, since 2015; Non Executive Director, Oil and Gas Authority, since 2015; b. 25.9.59, Edinburgh; m., Anne Ogilvie White. Educ. Daniel Stewart's and Melville College, Edinburgh; Edinburgh University. Solicitor, Haldanes McLaren and Scott, WS, Edinburgh, 1983-86; Partner, Wright, Johnston and MacKenzie, Edinburgh, 1986-90; Scottish Nuclear Limited: Company Secretary, 1990-95, Director, Performance Development, 1993-95; Director, Corporate Affairs, British Energy, 1999-2009; General Counsel and Company Secretary, British Energy plc, 1995-2009; Director, Network Project, EDF Energy, 2009-2010; Past Chair, SCDI (2009-2013); Energy Regulation Commission (2013-14). Recreations: golf; curling. Address: (b.) Smarter Grid Solutions Ltd, 39 Cadogan Street, Glasgow G2 7AB.

Armstrong, Dr Ernest McAlpine, CB, LLD, FRCSEd, FRCPGlas, FRCPEd, FRCGP, FFPH. Chairman,

Alcohol Focus Scotland, since 2011; Chief Medical Officer, Scottish Executive Health Department, 2001-05; b. 3.6.45, Motherwell; m., Dr Katherine Mary Dickson Armstrong; 2 s. Educ. Hamilton Academy; Glasgow University. Lecturer in Pathology, Glasgow University, 1971-74; General Practitioner, Connel, 1975-93; Secretary, British Medical Association, London, 1993-2000. Recreations: music; hill-walking; sailing. Address: (h.) Craiglora, Connel, Argyll PA37 1PH.

Armstrong, Lord (Iain Gillies Armstrong), QC. Senator of the College of Justice, since 2013; b. 26.5.56; m., Deirdre Elizabeth Mary MacKenzie; 1 d.; 1 s. Educ. Inverness Royal Academy; University of Glasgow. Admitted to the Faculty of Advocates in 1986; Clerk of Faculty, 1995-99; Standing Junior Counsel for the Department of Social Security, 1998-2000; appointed Queen's Counsel in 2000; full-time Advocate Depute (Crown Office), 2000-03; Vice-Dean of the Faculty of Advocates, 2008-2013. Member of the Standing Committee on Legal Education in Scotland, 1995-99; Governor of Fettes College, Edinburgh, 1991-2011; Member of the Advisory Panel to the School of Law of the University of Glasgow. Address: (b.) Court of Session, Parliament House, Edinburgh EH1 1RQ; T.- 0131 226 2595.

Arnold, Andy, MA (Hons), DipEd. Artistic Director of Tron Theatre Glasgow, since 2008; Founder and Artistic Director, The Arches, Glasgow (1991-2008); Director, Bloomsbury Theatre, London (1986-89); Artistic Director, Theatre Workshop, Edinburgh, 1980-85; Theatre Director, since 1980; Community Artist and Cartoonist, since 1974; b. Southend-on-Sea. Directing Credits include: The Drawer Boy, Translations, Bailegangaire, Metropolis, The Theatre Cut, Caligari, The Devils, The Crucible, Sexual Perversity in Chicago, Waiting for Godot; The Caretaker, A Midsummer Night's Dream, Juno and the Paycock, Playboy of the Western World, adaptations of Tam O'Shanter and Beowulf, The Battle of Stirling Bridge, Stirling Castle, 1997; Can't Pay; Won't Pay. Two Paper Boat awards; Spirit of Mayfest Award; only Scottish-based artist shortlisted for 1999 Creative Briton Award. Honorary Doctor of Letters, Strathclyde University. Recreations: playing five-a-side football and supporting Hibs.

Arnold, Professor Brian, OBE, BSc, MSc, DipEd. Retired Head of School of Science Education, Northern College, Aberdeen (1997-2000); Honorary Sheriff, 2004; JP (1989-2009); b. 8.7.39, Pontypridd, Wales; m., Sandra Anne; 2 s. Educ. Pontypridd Boys' Grammar; University College of Wales, Aberystwyth. Science Teacher: Bexley Grammar, 1963-64, Wagar High, Montreal, 1964-66; Acting Head of Biology, Wolverhampton Grammar, 1966-68; Lecturer in Biology, 1968-87, Coordinator of Primary Education, 1987-91, Aberdeen College of Education; Development Director, 1991-95, Head of Department of Science and Technology, 1995-97; Course Leader for BA in Professional Development Botswana, 1996-98, Head of School of Science Education, Northern College. Principal Examiner in Biology, 1976-80; Convener of Biology Panel, 1986-92; Convener, Higher Still Biology, 1995-97; Scottish Examination Board. External Examiner, BEd Tech, Edinburgh University, 1996-2000. Address: (h.) 2 South Headlands Crescent, Newtonhill, Stonehaven AB39 3TT.

Arnott, Ian Emslie, DA, DipTP, RSA, RIBA, FRIAS, OStJ. Retired Architect; Chairman, Saltire Society, 2001-04; b. 7.5.29, Galashiels. Educ. Galashiels Academy; Edinburgh College of Art. Flying Officer, RAF, 1955-57; Founding Partner, then Chairman, Campbell and Arnott, 1962-94; External Examiner, Dundee University, 1989-93.

RSA Gold Medal for Architecture, 1981; nine Civic Trust Awards; one RIBA Award; two EAA Awards. Publication: The Hidden Theatres of the Marche, 2013. Recreations: music; painting; reading; resting. Address: The Rink, Gifford, East Lothian EH41 4JD; T.-01620 810278.

Arran, 9th Earl of (Arthur Colum Michael Connolly-Gore); British peer and an elected hereditary member of the House of Lords for the Conservative Party; b. 14.7.38; m., Eleanor van Cutsem; 2 d. Educ. Eton College and Balliol College, Oxford. Served in the Grenadier Guards, gaining the rank of Second Lieutenant; Assistant Manager of the Daily Mail, then Assistant General Manager of the Daily Express and the Sunday Express in the 1970s; formerly a director of Waterstone's; active in the Lords for the Conservatives, serving in several junior ministerial roles. Succeeded as 9th Earl of Arran, 1983.

Arshad, Rowena, EdD (Edin), EdD (Edinburgh Napier University) (Honorary), MEd (Community Education), OBE. Head of the Moray House School of Education; Director, Centre for Education for Racial Equality in Scotland (CERES), since 1994; Senior Lecturer in Equity and Rights; Equal Opportunities Commissioner for Scotland, 2001-07; Member of the Scotland Committee of the Equality and Human Rights Commission; Member (first ever black woman Member), Scottish Trades Union Congress General Council, 1997-2003; b. 27.4.60, Brunei Town, Brunei; m., Malcolm Quarrie Parnell; 1 s.; 1 d. Educ. Methodist Girls School, Penang, West Malaysia; Moray House Institute of Education; Edinburgh University. Education and Campaigns Organiser, Scottish Education and Action for Development, 1985-88; Director, Edinburgh Multicultural Education Centre, 1988-90. Currently, on the board of Her Majesty's Inspectorate of Education; the Scottish Funding Council; Chair of Equality Forward, first equality unit for Scottish Colleges and Universities; Member of the Scottish Advisory Group of the British Council; Member, Editorial Board of the Journal of Race Equality Teaching. Formerly, Chair of the Equality Advisory Group, COPFS (2003-05); Chair of Linknet Mentoring Initiative, Edinburgh (2000-03); Chair of the Widening Access to Council Membership Progress Group (2004-05); first Honorary President of the Institute of Contemporary Scotland; Member of the Independent Committee of Inquiry into Student Finance (Cubie Committee); Member of the Working Party on Guidelines in Sex Education in Scottish Schools (Section 2A); Convenor of the Education Institute of Scotland Anti-Racist Committee; Member, STUC Black Workers Committee; Member of the Race Equality Advisory Forum. Author of numerous chapters to publications on equality; principal writer of the first anti-sectarian education resource for teachers and youth workers in Scotland. Recreations: keen reader of crime novels; border collies and animal issues; international cuisine and baroque music. Address: (b.) CERES, Moray House School of Education, Room 2:13, St. John's Land, School of Education, Holyrood Road, Edinburgh EH8 8AQ; T.-0131 651 6446.

Arthur, Adrian, BL. Hon. Fellow, University of Abertay Dundee; Editor, The Courier, Dundee, 1993-2002; b. 28.9.37, Kirkcaldy; m., Patricia Mill; 1 s.; 2 d. Educ. Harris Academy, Dundee; St. Andrews University. Joined staff of People's Journal; through the editorial ranks of The Courier (Deputy Editor, 1978-93). Recreations: golf; travel; Rotary. Address: (h.) 33 Seaforth Crescent, West Ferry, Dundee DD5 1QD; T.-01382 776842.
E-mail: adrianarthur33@blueyonder.co.uk

Arthur, Alexander James, MA, MLitt, CA. Retired Senior Lecturer, Accountancy, University of Aberdeen; b. 18.8.53, Dingwall, Ross-shire; 4 s.; 1 d. Educ. Tain Royal Academy; Aberdeen University. Mann Judd Gordon, CA, Stornoway, 1978-81; Oil Industry, Aberdeen, 1981-90,

principally Shell UK Exploration and Production and Comex UK Ltd. Director, Mental Health Aberdeen; Court Member (General Council Assessor), University of Aberdeen; Director, Alex. Arthur Ltd. (main business activity: Higher Education Services). Recreation: sailing. Address: (b.) University of Aberdeen Business School, Edward Wright Building, Dunbar Street, Aberdeen AB24 3QY; e-mail: arthur@abdn.ac.uk

Arthur, Lt. General Sir Norman, KCB (1985), CVO (2007). Lord Lieutenant, Stewartry of Kirkcudbright, Dumfries and Galloway Region, 1996-2006; b. 6.3.31, London (but brought up in Ayrshire, of Scottish parents); m., Theresa Mary Hopkinson; 1 s.; 1 d.; 1 s. (deceased); m., Jillian C. Andrews, née Summers. Educ. Eton College; Royal Military Academy, Sandhurst. Commissioned Royal Scots Greys, 1951; commanded Royal Scots Dragoon Guards, 1972-74, 7th Armoured Brigade, 1976-77, 3rd Armoured Division, 1980-82; Director, Personal Services (Army), 1983-85; commanded Army in Scotland, and Governor of Edinburgh Castle, 1985-88; retired, 1988; Honorary Colonel, Royal Scots Dragoon Guards, 1984-92; Col. Comdt. Military Provost Staff Corps, 1983-88; Honorary Colonel, 205 (Scottish) General Hospital, Territorial Army, 1988-93; Colonel, The Scottish Yeomanry, 1992-97; mentioned in Despatches, 1974. Officer, Royal Company of Archers; President, Scottish Conservation Projects Trust, 1989-93; Vice President, Riding for the Disabled Association, Edinburgh and the Borders, 1988-94; Chairman: Army Benevolent Fund, Scotland, 1988-2000, Leonard Cheshire Foundation, SW Scotland, 1994-2000; Member, Committee, Automobile Association, 1990-98; humanitarian aid work, Croatia and Bosnia, 1992-2015; President, Reserve Forces and Cadet Association, Lowlands, 2000-06; Member, British Olympic equestrian team (three-day event), 1960. Recreations: riding; country sports; country life; reading. Address: (h.) Newbarns, Dalbeattie, Kirkcudbrightshire DG5 4PY; T.-01556 630227, and The Garden House, Sparsholt, Winchester, Hants SO21 2NS; T.-01962 776279.

Arthur, Tom. MSP (SNP), Renfrewshire South, since 2016; b. 1985, Paisley. Educ. Cross Arthurlie Primary; Barrhead High School; University of Glasgow. Joined the SNP in 2009. Address: Scottish Parliament, Edinburgh EH99 1SP.

Asher, Catherine Archibald, OBE, BA, RGN, SCM, RNT, DUniv. Former Chairman, National Board for Nursing, Midwifery and Health Visiting for Scotland (1982-95); b. 6.7.33, Edinburgh. Educ. Woodside School, Glasgow; Edinburgh University; Open University. Ward Sister, Glasgow Royal Infirmary, 1956-61; Nurse Teacher, Senior Tutor, Principal Nursing Officer (Teaching), Glasgow Royal Infirmary School of Nursing, 1963-74; Director of Nurse Education, Glasgow Eastern College of Nursing and Midwifery, 1974-91; Acting Principal, Glasgow College of Nursing and Midwifery, 1991-95; Governor, University of Paisley, 1996-2005 (Chairman, Court, 2002-05). Address: (h.) 73 Roman Court, Roman Road, Bearsden, Glasgow G61 2NW.

Asher, Professor R. E., BA, PhD, DLitt, FRSE, FRAS. Professor of Linguistics, Edinburgh University, 1977-93, Professor Emeritus and Honorary Fellow, since 1993; b. 23.7.26, Gringley-on-the-Hill, Nottinghamshire. Educ. King Edward VI Grammar School, Retford; University College London. Assistant, Department of French, University College, London, 1951-53; Lecturer in Linguistics, then Lecturer in Tamil, School of Oriental and African Studies, London, 1953-65; joined Department of Linguistics,

Edinburgh University, 1965; Dean, Faculty of Arts, 1986-89; Member, University Court, 1989-92; Vice-Principal, 1990-93; Curator of Patronage, 1991-93; Director, Centre for Speech Technology Research, 1994. Visiting appointments: Visiting Professor of Linguistics, University of Illinois, Urbana-Champaign, 1967; Visiting Professor of Tamil and Malayalam, Michigan State University, 1968; Visiting Professor of Linguistics, University of Minnesota, 1969; Chaire des Professeurs Etrangers, Collège de France, 1970; Subrahmaniya Bharati Fellow, Tamil University, Thanjavur, 1984-85; Visiting Professor, International Christian University, Tokyo, 1994-95; first occupant of Vaikom Muhammed Basheer Chair, Mahatma Gandhi University, Kottayam, Kerala, 1995-96. Medal, Collège de France, Paris, 1970; Gold Medal, Kerala Sahitya Akademi, India, 1983; Honorary Fellow, Sahitya Akademi (India's National Academy of Letters), 2007; Basheer Puraskaram (Basheer memorial prize), 2010. Publications: A Tamil Prose Reader, 1971; Some Landmarks in the History of Tamil Prose, 1973; Me Grandad 'ad an Elephant! (translation), 1980; Towards a History of Phonetics (Co-Editor), 1981; Tamil, 1982; Studies on Malayalam Language and Literature, 1989; National Myths in Renaissance France: Francus, Samothes and the Druids, 1993; Scavenger's Son (translation), 1993; Atlas of the World's Languages (Co-Editor), 1994; Encyclopedia of Language and Linguistics (Editor-in-Chief), 1994; Concise History of the Language Sciences: from the Sumerians to the Cognitivists (Co-Editor), 1995; Malayalam, 1997; Basheer, Stories of the Freedom Struggle (Editor), 1998; The Novels and Stories of Vaikom Muhammed Basheer, 1999; Colloquial Tamil, 2002; What the Sufi Said (translation), 2002; Wind Flowers: Contemporary Malayalam Short Fiction (Editor and translator), 2004; Pudumaipittan: The Complete Short Stories (translation from Tamil), 2014. Address: (b.) PPLS, University of Edinburgh, Dugald Stewart Building, Edinburgh EH8 9AD.

Aspden, Professor Richard Malcolm, PhD, DSc, FIPEM. Professor of Orthopaedic Science, Aberdeen University, since 2000; b. 23.9.55, Malta; m., Anne Maclean; 3 s.; 2 d. Educ. Bosworth College, Desford; University of York; University of Manchester (postgraduate). Research Associate, University of Manchester; Wellcome Research Fellow: University of Lund, University of Manchester, University of Aberdeen; MRC Senior Fellow, University of Aberdeen. Chairman, Haddo User Group; European Editor, Journal of Back and Musculoskeletal Research; Editorial Consultant, Journal of Biomechanics. Publications: 2 books; 130 research papers. Recreations: woodworking; music; hill-walking. Address: (b.) University of Aberdeen, Division of Applied Medicine, IMS Building, Foresterhill, Aberdeen AB25 2ZD; T.-01224 437445. E-mail: r.aspden@abdn.ac.uk

Atack, Alison Mary, LLB, NP, FRSA, FICS. Partner, Lindsays Property (formerly Kidstons, Solicitors), since 1994; Member, Council, Law Society of Scotland (Past Convener, Professional Conduct Committee; Convener: Professional Practice Committee, Complaints Committee, Competence Committee and Regulatory Committee of Law Society; Member, Education and Training, Remuneration Guarantee Fund and Professional Practice Committees and Audit); b. 23.2.53, Richmond; m., Iain F. Atack; 1 s.; 1 d. Educ. Larbert High School; Glasgow University. Legal training and assistant, Biggart Baillie and Gifford, Glasgow. Formerly: Governor, Jordanhill College of Education. Recreations: hillwalking; skiing; gym; sailing; opera. Address: (b.) 1 Royal Bank Place, Glasgow G1 3AA; T.-0141-943 1188; e-mail: alisonatack@lindsays.co.uk

Atholl, 12th Duke of (Bruce George Ronald Murray); b. 6.4.60, South Africa; m., Charmaine Myrna (née Du Toit); 2 s.; 1 d. Succeeded to the title, 2012. Has the right to raise Europe's only legal private army, named the Atholl Highlanders (a unique privilege granted to his family by Queen Victoria after visiting Blair Atholl in 1844). Educated at Saasveld Forestry College before serving two years' National Service with the South African Infantry Corps. Currently a volunteer member of the Transvaal Scottish Regiment, holding the rank of Lieutenant. Previously managed a tea plantation, then ran a signage business producing signs for commercial buildings. Commissioned into the Atholl Highlanders in 2000, being appointed as Lieutenant Colonel.

Atiyah, Michael Francis, OM, FRS, Hon FRSE, Hon DSc (Oxford, Cambridge, Harvard and others). President, Royal Society of Edinburgh, 2005-08; Honorary Professor, Edinburgh University, since 1997; b. 22.4.29, London; m., Lily Jane Myles Brown; 2 s. Educ. Victoria College, Cairo; Manchester Grammar School; Trinity College, Cambridge. Fellow: Trinity College, Cambridge, 1954-58 and since 1997, Pembroke College, Cambridge, 1958-61; Reader/Professor, Oxford, 1961-69; Professor, Institute for Advanced Study, Princeton, USA, 1969-73; Royal Society Research Professor, Oxford, 1973-90; Master, Trinity College, Cambridge, 1990-97; President, Royal Society, 1990-95; Grand Officer, Legion d'Honneur, 2011. Fields Medal, 1966; Abel Prize, 2004; Collected Works, OUP, 1998, 2004 and 2014. Recreations: music; gardening.

Atkinson, Professor The Rev. David, BSc, PhD, FSB, CBiol, MIEEM, FHEA, FRSA, FRCP (Edin), MISoilSci. Emeritus Professor of Land Resources and former Vice Principal, Scottish Agricultural College; b. 12.9.44, Blyth; m., Elisabeth Ann Cocks (deceased 2012); 1 s.; 2 d. Educ. Newlands County Secondary Modern School; Hull University; Newcastle-upon-Tyne University; Theological Institute of Scottish Episcopal Church (TISEC). East Malling Research Station, Maidstone, 1969-85; Macaulay Institute for Soil Research, 1985-87; Macaulay Land Use Research Institute, 1987-88; Professor of Agriculture, Aberdeen University, and Head, Land Resources Department, Scottish Agricultural College, 1988-93; Deputy Principal (R. & D.) and Dean, Edinburgh Centre, Scottish Agricultural College, 1993-2000, Vice Principal, 2000-04. Honorary Professor, University of Edinburgh, 1994-2006; Visiting Professor, Washington State University, 1983, Michigan State University, 1986, University of Michigan Biological Station, 1987-92; Member, BCPC Council, since 1994, Vice Chairman, 2002-2009, Trustee, since 2009, BCPC Medal, 2001; Member, Advisory Group, Royal College of Physicians (Edinburgh), 2004-2012; Member, Management Board, MRCP, 2005-2011; Member, Scottish Government Food and Drink Forum and Convenor of Committee on Food Affordability, Access and Security, 2008-2010; Chair, ACTS Rural Committee, 2005-2012 and 2014-15, Committee Member, since 2012; Ordained Deacon, 2005; Priest, 2006; Associate Curate, Aberdeen Cathedral, 2005-07; Interim Priest, St Devenick's, Aberdeen, 2007-09; Associate Minister, St. Mary Inverurie with St Anne Kemnay and St Mary Auchindoir, since 2009; Information Officer, Diocese of Aberdeen and Orkney, since 2005; Chair, TISEC Board of Studies, 2007-08; Editor, Northern Light, 2007-2014; Convenor: SEC Church in Society Committee, since 2014, SEC Rural Network, since 2014; Director, Falkland Rural Enterprises Limited, since 2006, Chair, since 2012; Chair, Scottish Pilgrim Routes Forum management committee, since 2012; Board Member, Nourish, 2013. Recreations: discussing organic agriculture and GM issues; music; reading thrillers; quotations. Address: (b.) SAC, Craibstone Estate, Bucksburn, Aberdeen AB21 9YA. E-mail: atkinson390@btinternet.com

Atkinson, Elspeth. Director for Scotland, Wales and Northern Ireland, Macmillan Cancer Support, since 2005.

Address: (b.) Third Floor, 132 Rose Street, Edinburgh EH2 3JD; T.-0131 260 3720.

Atkinson, Michael Kent. Non-executive Director: UK Asset Resolution Ltd (previously Northern Rock plc and Bradford & Bingley plc), since 2008, Bank of Ireland Group, since 2012; b. 19.05.45, Recife, Brazil; m., Eufemia Alexandra; 2 s. Educ. Blundells School, Tiverton, Devon. Joined Bank of London and South America in 1964, later acquired by Lloyds Bank; most of career in executive positions in the Bahamas, Colombia, Ecuador, Panama, Bahrain, Dubai, Paraguay and Argentina before returning to UK in 1989 to be Regional Executive Director, South East Region of Lloyds Bank; became Group Finance Director, Lloyds Bank, later Lloyds TSB, 1994-2002; retired from executive positions but remained as non-executive director, Lloyds TSB until 2003; Coca-Cola HBC SA, 1998-2013; Gemalto NV, 2004-2013; Telent plc (previously Marconi plc), 2002-07; Cookson Group plc, 2003-05; Millicom International Cellular SA, 2007-10; Standard Life plc, 2005-2011. Recreations: tennis and golf (active); enjoys watching football and rugby; enjoys computers; skiing; travelling.

Atkinson, Peter. Chief Executive, Macfarlane Group PLC, since 2003. Career: Procter & Gamble and S.C. Johnson; Senior Executive roles, GKN PLC and its joint venture partners, 1988-2001; successful track record of both business turnarounds and business development with extensive exposure to international business, having worked in the UK, Continental Europe and the USA; responsible for the US automotive and materials handling businesses of Brambles Industries PLC, 2000-03. Non-Executive Director of Speedy Hire PLC, 2004-2011. Address: (b.) Macfarlane Group PLC, 21 Newton Place, Glasgow G3 7PY; T.-0141 333 9666.

Auchincloss, Matthew, MA, LLB, DipLP, Solicitor-Advocate. Director of The Public Defence Solicitors' Office, since 2005; b. 16.10.71, Edinburgh. Educ. Sandhurst School; Linlithgow Academy; University of Glasgow. Admitted as a Solicitor in Scotland, 1997; Partner in Gordon McBain and Company, Solicitors, Edinburgh, 1999; joined Public Defence Solicitors' Office, 2003; joined the College of Justice as a Solicitor with extended rights of audience, 2005. Tutor for Central Law Training. Recreations: music; horse riding. Address: (b.) Public Defence Solicitors' Office, 50 St. Mary's Street, Edinburgh EH1 1SX; T.-0131 557 1222; e-mail: mauchincloss@pdso.org.uk

Audain, Irene, MBE, MA (Hons), MEd, AdvDip (Educ), DipInfoScience. Chief Executive, Scottish Out of School Care Network, since 1993; b. 10.7.56, Glasgow. Educ. University of Glasgow; University of Strathclyde; The Open University. Voluntary sector work: promoting school age childcare, children's rights, has also been involved in promoting equality. Recreation: travel. Address: (b.) Level 2, 100 Wellington Street, Glasgow G2 6DH; T.-0141 564 1284.

Austin, Lloyd, BSc (Hons). Head of Conservation Policy, RSPB Scotland, since 1999; b. 5.10.60, Haddenham; divorced; 1 s.; 2 d. Educ. Peter Symond's School, Winchester; Edinburgh University. Scientific Officer, Department of Environment (NI), 1985-86; Conservation Officer: Cleveland Wildlife Trust, 1986-88, Lincolnshire Wildlife Trust, 1988-90; Conservation Planning Officer (Scotland), RSPB, 1990-99. Trustee, Scottish Environment Link, since 2000, Chair of Trustees, 2004-07; Trustee: Stop Climate Chaos Scotland, since 2006, Fred Edwards Trust,

since 2010. Recreations: natural history; travel; current affairs. Address: (b.) 2 Lochside View, Edinburgh Park, Edinburgh EH12 9DH; T.-0131-317-4100.

B

Bagshaw, Stuart Neville, Dip (Arch). Director/Sole Proprietor, SBA Architects Ltd, since 2009; b. 2.12.48; m., Lesley; 2 s.; 1 d. Educ. Whitcliffe Mount Grammar School; Leicester Polytechnic. Career: Project Architect/Team Leader, Warrington New Town Development Corporation; Senior Architect, Western Isles Council; Director/Sole Proprietor, Stuart Bagshaw & Associates, 1982-2009. RIAS Fellow; RIBA Member; Registered Chartered Architect; Member, Scottish Society of Architect Artists; various awards. Address: (b.) SBA Architects Ltd, Marybank Lodge, Lews Castle Grounds, Isle of Lewis HS2 0DD; T.-01851-70-4889.
E-mail: sbaarchitects@btconnect.com

Baillie, Ian David Hunter, CBE. Non-stipendiary Minister, United Reformed Church; b. 18.12.40, Dundee; m., Margaret McCallum McFarlane; 3 d. Educ. Hutchesons Boys Grammar School. Eight years in life assurance; 35 years in social work; retired as Director of Social Work, Church of Scotland Board of Social Responsibility, 1990-2002; Director, Jeely Piece Club. Recreations: sport (watching); reading. Address: (b.) 17 Williamwood Park West, Netherlee, Glasgow G44 3TE.
E-mail: baillie123@btinternet.com

Baillie, Jackie. MSP (Labour), Dumbarton, since 1999; Shadow Cabinet Secretary for Finance, Constitution and Economy, since 2014; Social Justice, Equalities and Welfare, 2013-2014; Wellbeing and Cities Strategy, 2010-2013; Minister for Social Justice, 2000-01; Deputy Minister for Communities, 1999-2000; b. 15.1.64, Hong Kong; m., Stephen; 1 d. Educ. Glasgow University (part-time: to be completed). Co-ordinator, Gorbals Unemployed Workers Centre, 1987-90; Resource Centre Manager, Strathkelvin District Council, 1990-96; Community Economic Development Manager, East Dunbartonshire Council, 1996-99. Board Member, Volunteer Development Scotland, 1997-99; Chairperson, Scottish Labour Party, 1997-98. Address: (b.) Dumbarton Constituency Office, 11 Castle Street, Dumbarton G82 1QS; T.-01389 734214.

Baillie, Professor John, MA, CA. Visiting Professor of Accountancy: Heriot-Watt University, Edinburgh, 1989-99, University of Glasgow, 1996-2012, University of Edinburgh, 2013; Member, Reporting Panel, Competition Commission, 2002-2011; Chair, Accounts Commission, 2007-2013; Member, Accounts Commission, 2003-07; Chair, Audit Scotland, 2008-2011; Board Member, Audit Scotland, 2003-2013; Member, Local Government Finance Review Committee, 2004-07; m., Annette; 1 s.; 1 d. Educ. Whitehill School. Johnstone-Smith Professor of Accountancy, Glasgow University, 1983-88; Partner, KPMG, 1978-93; Partner, Scott-Moncrieff, 1993-2001. Institute of Chartered Accountants of Scotland: Convenor, Research Committee, 1994-99, member, various technical and professional affairs committees. Recreations: keeping fit; reading; music; golf.

Bain, Aly, MBE. Fiddler; b. 1946, Lerwick. Co-founder, Boys of the Lough, 1972; Soloist; TV and radio anchorman.

Bain, Professor Andrew David, OBE, FRSE; b. 21.3.36, Glasgow; m., Eleanor Riches; 3 s. Educ. Glasgow Academy; Cambridge University. Various posts, Cambridge University, 1959-67; Professor of Economics: Stirling University, 1967-77, Strathclyde University, 1977-84; Group Economic Advisor, Midland Bank, 1984-90. Member: Committee to Review the Functioning of Financial Institutions, 1977-80, Monopolies and Mergers Commission, 1980-81; Visiting Professor, Glasgow University, 1991-97; Board Member, Scottish Enterprise, 1991-97; Chairman of Trustees, Scottish Enterprise Pension Scheme, 1995-2004; Member, Competition Appeals Tribunal, 2000-2011. Publications: The Control of the Money Supply, 1970; The Economics of the Financial System (2nd Edition), 1992.

Bain, Dorothy, QC. Senior Counsel Member, Ampersand stable of advocates at the Faculty of Advocates, Edinburgh, since 2011. Solicitor, Dundas & Wilson CS Edinburgh, Litigation Department; Personal Injury Law, Clinical Negligence Law, Professional Negligence Law, Public and Fatal Accident Inquiries, 1990-94; Called to the Bar, 1994; Advocate Depute, November 2002-December 2003; Senior Advocate Depute, January 2004-2005; Assistant Principal Advocate Depute, January 2006-May 2009. Appointed QC in 2007; Commissioned by the Lord Advocate & Solicitor General to report on and make recommendations in relation to the prosecution of Sexual Crime in Scotland, which in turn resulted in the creation of the National Sex Crimes Unit: February-October 2008; Principal Advocate Depute, June 2009-July 2011; November 2011, nominated to the list of Special Counsel by the Lord President in terms of the Criminal Justice & Licensing (Scotland) Act 2010; Advocacy Skills Instructor on the Advocates training course for Devils. Address: Advocates' Library, Parliament House, Edinburgh EH1 1RF.

Bain, Iain Andrew, MA. Editor and Proprietor, The Nairnshire Telegraph, since 1987; b. 25.2.49, Nairn; m., Maureen Beattie; 3 d. Educ. Nairn Academy; Aberdeen University. Joined The Geographical Magazine, 1974, Editor, 1981-87. Chairman, Nairn Museum Ltd. Recreations: reading; writing; photography; golf. Address: (b.) 10 Leopold Street, Nairn IV12 4BG; T.-01667 453258.

Bain, Marion. Interim Chief Executive, NHS National Services Scotland, since 2016 (Medical Director, since 2009); Honorary Professor, University of Edinburgh, College of Medicine & Veterinary Medicine, since 2012. Experience includes clinical practice, public health medicine and medical management gained from teaching and district general hospitals, Departments of Public Health in health boards, the Scottish Government and NHS National Services Scotland. Fellow of the Faculty of Public Health. Address: National Services Scotland, Area 027, Gyle Square, 1 South Gyle Crescent, Edinburgh EH12 9EB; T.-0131 275 6000.

Bain, Simon. Group Business Correspondent and Personal Finance Editor, Herald & Times Newspapers; joined The Herald, 1997; b. 20.8.51, London; m., Norma; 1 s.; 1 d. Educ. St Paul's School; Christ's College, Cambridge. Reporter, The Scotsman, 1981-88; Business Editor, Scotland on Sunday, 1988-96. UK Regional Press Awards Business Highly Commended, 2011, 2013; 2014; British Press Award winner, 1981; Scottish Press Award winner, 1986, 1992, 1998, 2000, 2007, 2012; Journalist of the Year, 2000; B & B Personal Finance Award winner, 1994, 1998, 2001, 2008; AIC award, 2004-06, 2011, 2013, 2014, 2015. Address: (h.) 32 Craigleith Drive, Edinburgh; T.-07803 970326.

Bain, William, LLB, DipLP, LLM. MP (Labour), Glasgow North East, 2009-2015; b. 29.11.72, Glasgow. Educ. St. Roch's Secondary School, Glasgow; University of Strathclyde. Researcher/Tutor/Sessional Lecturer, The Law School, University of Strathclyde, 1996-2004; Senior Lecturer in Public Law, Law Department, London South Bank University, 2004-09. Member, Tax Law Rewrite Committee, 2010; PPS to Sadiq Khan, Minister of State, Department for Transport; Shadow Transport Minister, 2010; Shadow Food, Agriculture and Fisheries

Minister, 2010-2011; Shadow Scotland Office Minister, 2011-2015. Publications: 'Strategies for the Future' in Bates (ed) 'Devolution to Scotland: The Legal Aspects' (Co-Author), 1997; 'Where Next for Labour' (contributor), 2011. Recreations: reading; films; contemporary music; walking; tennis.

Baird, Professor David Tennent, CBE, BA (Cantab), MB, ChB, MD (hc), DSc, FRCP, FRCOG, FRS(Ed), FMed.Sci. Emeritus Professor of Reproductive Endocrinology, Edinburgh University, since 2000; b. 13.3.35, Glasgow; m. 1, Frances Lichtveld (m. dissolved); 2 s.; m. 2, Anna Frances Glasier. Educ. Aberdeen Grammar School; Aberdeen University; Trinity College, Cambridge; Edinburgh University. After clinical training in endocrinology and obstetrics, spent three years (1965-68) as an MRC travelling Research Fellow at Worcester Foundation for Experimental Biology, Shrewsbury, Mass., USA, conducting research on reproductive endocrinology; Deputy Director, MRC Unit of Reproductive Biology, Edinburgh, 1972-77; Professor of Obstetrics and Gynaecology, Edinburgh University, 1977-85; Medical Research Council Professor of Reproductive Endocrinology, Edinburgh University, 1985-2000; served on a number of national and international committees. Publications: over 400 original papers in peer review journals and four books on reproduction. Recreations: ski mountaineering; music; sport. Address: (b.) Edinburgh University, Simpson Centre for Reproductive Health, 51 Little France Crescent, Edinburgh EH16 4SA; T.-0131-242 6367; e-mail: dtbaird@ed.ac.uk

Baird, Professor James Ireland, BSc (Hons), PhD, MICE, CEng, FCIWM. Director, Caledonian Environment Centre, Glasgow Caledonian University, since 1994; b. 31.10.58, Patna, Ayrshire; m., Janice McLauchlan; 1 s.; 1 d. Educ. James Hamilton Academy, Kilmarnock; University of Glasgow. Research Engineer, British Hydromechanics Research Association; Research and Development Manager, Water Research Centre, Medmenham, Bucks. General Councillor, Institute of Wastes Management. Recreations: tennis; hillwalking.

Baker, Christopher. Director, Scottish National Portrait Gallery, since 2012. Career history: Curator, Christ Church Picture Gallery, Oxford; Deputy Director, Scottish National Gallery, 2003-2012. Enjoys an international reputation as a scholar-curator and has organised some of the Scottish National Gallery's most successful exhibitions, such as The Discovery of Spain (2009) and Turner and Italy (2009). Address: Scottish National Portrait Gallery, 1 Queen Street, Edinburgh EH2 1JD; e-mail: pginfo@nationalgalleries.org

Baker, Claire. MSP (Labour), Scotland Mid and Fife, since 2007; Shadow Cabinet Secretary for Culture, Europe and External Affairs, since 2014; b. 4.3.71, Fife; m., Richard Baker, MSP. Career history: worked in a variety of research and policy posts including Research Officer for the Scottish Parliamentary Labour Group, Research Officer for the trade union Amicus and a similar role for the Royal College of Nursing; Policy Manager for the Scottish Council for Voluntary Organisations. Former Shadow Minister for Education, Scottish Parliament. Address: (b.) Scottish Parliament, Edinburgh EH99 1SP.

Baker, Richard. MSP (Labour), North East Scotland, since 2003; b. 29.5.74, Edinburgh. Educ. Aberdeen University. Address: (b.) Scottish Parliament, Edinburgh EH99 1SP; T.-0131 348 5000.

Baker, Emeritus Professor Thomas Neville, BMet, PhD, DMet (Sheffield), DSc (Strathclyde), DEng (Sheffield), FIM, FInstP, CEng, CPhys. Research Professor, Department of Mechanical and Aerospace Engineering – Metallurgy and Engineering Materials Group, Strathclyde University; b. 11.1.34, Southport; m., Eileen May Allison

(deceased). Educ. King George V School, Southport; Sheffield University. National Service, Royal Corps of Signals; Research Metallurgist, Nelson Research Laboratories, English Electric Co., Stafford, 1958-60; Scientist, Project Leader, Tube Investments Research Laboratories, Hinxton Hall, Cambridge, 1961-64; Department of Metallurgy, Strathclyde University: SRC Research Fellow, 1965, Lecturer, 1966, Senior Lecturer, 1976, Reader, 1983, Professor, 1990, Professor of Metallurgy (1886 Chair), 1992-99, Vice Dean, School of Chemical and Materials Science, 1979-82, Head, Department of Metallurgy, 1986-87, Head, Division of Metallurgy and Engineering Materials, 1988-90; President, University of Strathclyde Staff Club, 1976-77; University of Strathclyde representative as a Governor of the Renfrewshire Educational Trust, 1989-97; Committee Member, Institute of Materials, Minerals and Mining (IoM3) (formerly Institute of Metals), Metal Science Committee, 1980-94, Materials Technology Committee, 1994-96, Process Science and Technology Committee, 1996-99, Integrated Processing and Manufacturing Committee, 1999-2006, High Temperature Materials Committee, since 2007; Chairman of Organizing Committee of Annual Conference on 'Metals and Materials', 1982-92 and conference series on 'Erosion and Wear of High Temperature Materials used in Aerospace and Power Generation', 1998, 2001, 2010, 2015; Member, Council, Scottish Association for Metals, 1975-79 and since 1997, Vice-President, 1999-2000, President, 2001. Awards: IoM3 Vanadium Medal, 2009; IoM3 Tom Colclough Medal & Prize, 2010; Leverhulme Trust Visiting Professorship, 2012. Publications: Yield, Flow and Fracture in Polycrystals (Editor), 1983; Titanium Technology in Microalloyed Steels (Editor); 1997; over 200 learned society publications. Recreations: music; collecting books; creating a garden. Address: (b.) Department of Mechanical and Aerospace Engineering, Strathclyde University, Glasgow; T.-0141-548 3101; (h.) Clovelly, Rowantreehill Road, Kilmacolm PA13 4NW.

Balfour of Burleigh, Lord (Robert Bruce), CEng, FIEE, FRSE, Hon. D Litt (Robert Gordon), Hon. DUniv (Stirling), Hon. FRIAS. Vice Lord-Lieutenant, Clackmannan, 1995-2001; Chancellor, Stirling University, 1988-98; b. 6.1.27, London. Educ. Westminster School, London. Graduate Apprentice, English Electric Company, 1951; various positions in manufacturing mangement; started English Electric's manufacturing operations in India as General Manager of new company in Madras, 1957-64; returned to Liverpool as General Manager; appointed General Manager, D. Napier & Son, before leaving the company in 1968; joined Bank of Scotland as a Director, 1968; Deputy Governor, Bank of Scotland, 1977-91. Forestry Commissioner, 1971-74; Chairman: Scottish Arts Council, 1971-80, Federation of Scottish Bank Employers, 1977-86, The Turing Institute, 1983-92, Scottish Committee, ABSA, 1988-94, United Artists Communications (Scotland) Ltd., until 1996; Director: Scottish Investment Trust plc, 1971-96, Tarmac plc, 1981-90, William Lawson Distillers Ltd., 1984-96, Television Educational Network, 1990-96, Edinburgh Book Festival, 1981-96 (Chairman, 1981-87); Member, British Railways (Scottish) Board, 1982-92; Treasurer: Royal Society of Edinburgh, 1989-94, Royal Scottish Corporation; President, Friends of Vellore; President, Franco-Scottish Society, 1985-96; Life Member and Trustee, 1990-96, John Muir Trust; Trustee, Bletchley Park Trust, 2000-09; Trustee, Radcliffe Trust, 1974-2014.

Balfour of Burleigh, Lady (Janet Morgan), MA, DPhil, FRSAS, Hon LLD (Strathclyde), Hon DLitt (Napier), FRSE, CBE. Member, American Philosophical Society; Chevalier de l'Ordre Grand Ducale de la Couronne de Chêne; Writer; Company Director; b. 5.12.45, Montreal; m., Lord Balfour of Burleigh. Educ. Newbury County Girls'

Grammar School; Oxford University; Sussex University; Harvard University. Member: Central Policy Review Staff, Cabinet Office, 1978-81, Board, British Council, 1989-99; Special Adviser to Director-General, BBC, 1983-86; Chairman: Espirito Ltd, 2010-2014, Cable & Wireless Flexible Resource Ltd., 1993-97; Non-Executive Director: Cable & Wireless, 1988-2004, W.H. Smith, 1989-95, Midlands Electricity, 1990-96, Scottish American Investment Co., 1991-2008, Scottish Oriental Smaller Companies Investment Trust, since 1994, Albion Enterprise VCT plc, since 2007, The Scottish Life Assurance Company, 1995-2001, Nuclear Generation Decommissioning Fund Ltd, 1996-2005, Nuclear Liabilities Fund, since 2005, Nuclear Liabilities Financing Assurance Board, 2008-2015, New Medical Technologies plc, 1997-2004, BPB plc, 2000-05, Stagecoach plc, 2001-2010, Murray International plc, since 2003; Non-Executive Director, NDA Archives Ltd, since 2014; Scottish Medical Research Fund, 1992-94; Member: Scottish Museums Council Development Resource, 1988-97, Ancient Monuments Board for Scotland, 1990-97, Book Trust Scotland, 1992-99, Scottish Economic Council, 1993-95, Scottish Hospitals Endowment Research Trust, 1992-98, Dorothy Burns Charity, 1994-2002; Chairman, Scotland's Book Campaign, 1994-96, Scottish Cultural Resources Access Network, 1995-2004, Scottish Museum of the Year Award, 1999-2004; Trustee: Carnegie Endowment for the Universities of Scotland, since 1993, National Library of Scotland, 2002-2010, Stewart Ivory Foundation, 2001-08, Trusthouse Charitable Foundation, since 2006, The Royal Anniversary Trust, since 2010; Ordre Grand-Ducal de la Couronne de Chêne (Luxembourg), since 2014. Publications: Diaries of a Cabinet Minister 1964-70 by Richard Crossman (4 volumes) (Editor); The Future of Broadcasting, (Co-Editor, 1982); Agatha Christie: a biography, 1984; Edwina Mountbatten: a life of her own, 1991; The Secrets of rue St. Roch, 2004. Recreations: music of JS Bach and Handel; sea bathing; pruning; ice skating out of doors.

Balfour, Ian Leslie Shaw, MA, LLB, BD, PhD, SSC, NP. Solicitor (Consultant, Balfour & Manson) since 1955; b. 16.6.32, Edinburgh; m., Joyce Margaret Ross Pryde; 3 s.; 1 d. Educ. Edinburgh Academy; Edinburgh University. Qualified as Solicitor, 1955; commissioned, RASC, 1955-57; Partner, then Senior Partner, Balfour & Manson, 1959-97; Secretary, Oliver & Son Ltd., 1959-89; Fiscal to Law Society of Scotland, 1981-1997. Baptist Union of Scotland: President, 1976-77, Law Agent, 1964-97, Secretary, Charlotte Baptist Chapel, Edinburgh, 1980-2000, Secretary, Scottish Baptist College, 1983-2003; Secretary, Elba Housing Society Ltd., 1969-92; Council, Society for Computers and Law, 1988-92; Director, Edinburgh Medical Missionary Society; Honorary Vice-President, Lawyers Christian Fellowship, 1997. Publication: Author, "Revival in Rose Street: Charlotte Baptist Chapel, 1808-2008", 2007. Recreations: gardening; home computing; lay preaching (Lecturer in Church History, Edinburgh Faith Mission Bible School and Institute of Biblical Studies, since 2008 and Edinburgh Bible College, since 2013). Joint Auditor, Edinburgh Sheriff Court, since 1991. Address: (h.) 32 Murrayfield Avenue, Edinburgh EH12 6AX; T.-0131-337 2880; e-mail: I_Balfour@msn.com

Balfour, Jeremy. MSP (Scottish Conservative), Lothian Region, since 2016. Educ. Edinburgh Academy; Edinburgh University; London Bible College. Elected to Edinburgh City Council, representing Corstorphine/Murrayfield. Address: Scottish Parliament, Edinburgh EH99 1SP.

Balfour, Robert William, BSc, FRICS. Lord-Lieutenant of Fife, since 2014; b. 25.3.52, Edinburgh; m., Jessica McCrindle; 4 s. (1 deceased). Educ. Eton; Edinburgh University. Managing Partner, Balbirnie Home Farms, since 1991; Management trainee, Ocean Group, 1974-78; Surveyor, Bell-Ingram, Perth, 1978-88; Bidwells Chartered Surveyors, Perth, 1988-94, Associate Partner, 1991; Chairman, RICS RPD (Scotland), 1990-91; Convenor, Scottish Landowners Federation, 1999-2002; Member, Board of Management, Elmwood College, 2000-08; Member, East Area Board, Scottish Natural Heritage, 2003-07, Area Advisor, 2007; Director, Fife Coast and Countryside Trust, since 2003, Chairman, 2007-2015; Chairman, Association of Deer Management Group, 2005-2011; Director, Paths for all Partnership, 2005-2013; Chairman, Kettle Growers Ltd., 2006-2011. General Trustee, Church of Scotland, since 2012; Vice Lord-Lieutenant of Fife, 2013-14; DL (Fife), 1994; Elder, Markinch Parish Church; Member, Royal Company of Archers. Recreations: shooting; skiing; music; arts; travel. Address: (b.) Pitillock Farm, Freuchie KY15 7JQ; T.-01337 857437; e-mail: robertwbalfour@gmail.com

Balfour, William Harold St. Clair. Solicitor (retired); b. 29.8.34, Edinburgh; m., 1, Patricia Waite (m. dissolved); 1 s.; 2 d.; 2, Alice Ingsay McFarlane; 2 step. d. Educ. Hillfield, Ontario; Edinburgh Academy; Edinburgh University. Partner, Balfour & Manson, 1962-98; Clerk to Admission of Notaries Public, 1971-92; Prison Visiting Committee, 1965-70; Chairman, Basic Space Dance Theatre, 1980-86; Friends of Talbot Rice Art Centre, 1982-97, Garvald Trustees, 1980-2004, Wellspring Management, 1990-97, Tekoa Trust, since 1990; Council Member: Scottish Association of Marine Science, 2002-2010, Audit Committee, 2009-2013. Recreations: walking; current affairs; charities. Address: (h.) 11 Nelson Street, Edinburgh EH3 6LF; T.-0131-556 7298.
E-mail: w.whsbalfour@btopenworld.com

Ball, Graham Edmund, FDS RCS (Eng), FDS, RCS (Edin). Consultant in Dental Public Health, South East Scotland Health Board; Clinical Lead for Dentistry, NHS 24; Honorary Senior Lecturer, Bute Medical School, St Andrews University; b. 14.12.53; m., Carolyn Bowyer; 1 s.; 2 d. Educ. King Edward VI School, Southampton; Welsh National School of Medicine. Registrar, Oral Surgery, Portsmouth hospitals, 1979-81; general dental practice, 1984-88; Community Dental Officer, Orkney Health Board, 1988-91; Chief Administrative Dental Officer, Orkney Health Board, 1991-95; Consultant in Dental Public Health, Fife, Borders and Lothian NHS Boards, 1995-2003. Recreations: sailing; walking. Address: (b.) Fife NHS Board, Cameron House, Cameron Bridge, Leven, Fife; T.-01592 226407; e-mail: graham.ball@nhs.net

Ballantyne, Professor Colin Kerr, MA, MSc, PhD, DSc, FRSE, FRSA, FRSGS. Professor in Physical Geography, St. Andrews University, since 1994; b. 7.6.51, Glasgow; m., Rebecca Trengove; 1 s.; 1 d. Educ. Hutchesons' Grammar School; Glasgow University; McMaster University; Edinburgh University. Lecturer in Geography, St. Andrews University, 1980-89, Senior Lecturer in Geography and Geology, 1989-94. Gordon Warwick Award, 1987; Presidents' Medal, Royal Scottish Geographical Society, 1991; Newbigin Prize, Royal Scottish Geographical Society, 1992; Scottish Science Award, Saltire Society, 1996; Wiley Award, British Geomorphological Research Group, 1999; Clough Medal, Edinburgh Geological Society, 2010; Coppock Research Medal, Royal Scottish Geographical Society, 2015; Lyell Medal, Geological Society, 2015. Visiting Professor, UNIS, Svalbard, since 2000; Erskine Fellow, University of Canterbury, New Zealand, 2003 and 2013. Publications: The Quaternary of the Isle of Skye, 1991; The Periglaciation of Great Britain, 1994; Classic

Landforms of the Isle of Skye, 2000; Paraglacial Geomorphology, 2002. Recreations: music; travel; mountaineering; skiing; writing. Address: (h.) Birchwood, Blebo Craigs, Fife KY15 5UF; T.-01334 850567; e-mail: ckb@st-and.ac.uk

Ballantyne, Fiona Catherine, OBE, MA, FCIM. Director, RIO Ltd, since 2014; Director, 4Consulting Ltd., 2001-2011; Member, Board, Queen Margaret University College, Edinburgh, 1995-2005, Vice Chair, 2002-05; Director, The Audience Business Ltd., 1998-2004; Member, Scottish Committee, Institute of Directors, 1996-2006; Member, Audit Committee, Scottish Further and Higher Education Funding Councils, 2000-02; b. 9.7.50, Bristol; m., A. Neil Ballantyne. Educ. Marr College, Troon; Edinburgh University. Former Market Researcher and Market Research Manager; Research and Planning Manager, Thistle Hotels Ltd., 1975-77; Assistant Marketing Manager, Lloyds & Scottish Finance Group, 1977-79; Scottish Development Agency: Marketing Manager, Small Business Division, 1979-84, Head of Small Business Services, 1984-88, Director, Tayside and Fife, 1988-90; Managing Director, Ballantyne Mackay Consultants, 1990-2012; Vice-Chair: BBC Broadcasting Council for Scotland, 1991-96, Duncan of Jordanstone College of Art, 1988-94; Director, Edinburgh Healthcare Trust, 1994-96; Director, The Essentia Group (formerly Network Scotland Ltd.), 1991-2001, Chairman, 1997-2001; Member, Board, Scottish Campaign for Learning, 1997-98; Member, Ofcom Consumer Panel, 2004-2012; Board Member, Museums Galleries Scotland, 2004-2012; Chair, MGS, 2007-2012; Board Member, Edinburgh Printmakers, 2004-08; Trustee: OSCR, since 2008, Love Music Productions Ltd., since 2009; Water Customer Forum, since 2012; Governor, Royal Conservatoire of Scotland, since 2015. Recreations: walking; swimming; gardening; painting. Address: (b.) 15 Palmerston Road, Edinburgh EH9 1TL.

Ballard, Mark, MA (Hons). Assistant Director, Barnardo's Scotland; MSP (Scottish Green Party), Lothian Region, 2003-07; Lord Rector, University of Edinburgh, 2006-09; b. 27.6.71, Leeds; m., Heather Stacey; 2 s.. Educ. Lawnwood Comprehensive, Leeds; Edinburgh University. Worked for European Youth Forest Action, 1994-98; Editor, Reforesting Scotland, 1998-2001; Director, EMBE Environmental Communications, 2002-03. Publication: Scotlands of the Future (Contributor). Recreations: cycling; Indian cookery. Address: (b.) 111, Oxgangs Road North, Edinburgh EH14 1ED; T.-0131 446 7000; e-mail: mark.ballard@barnardos.org.uk

Band, Thomas Mollison, b. 28.3.34, Aberdeen; m., Jean McKenzie Brien (d. 2011); 1 s.; 2 d. Educ. Perth Academy. Principal, Tariff Division, Board of Trade, London, 1969-73; Director (Location of Industry), Department of Industry, Glasgow, 1973-76; Assistant Secretary: (Industrial Policy), Scottish Economic Planning Department, 1976-78, (Housing), Scottish Development Department, 1978-82, (Finance), Scottish Office, 1982-84; Director, Historic Buildings and Monuments, Scottish Development Department, 1984-87; Chief Executive, Scottish Tourist Board, 1987-94; Member, Board of Management, Perth Housing Association, since 1993, Chairman, 2003-09; Chairman: Andersons Enterprises Ltd., 1994-99, Perth Theatre Ltd., 1995-2002, Edinburgh Europa Ltd., 1994-98, Select Line Breaks Ltd., 1995-98; Governor: Edinburgh Telford College, 1990-98, Queen Margaret College, 1995-2002; President, European Bureau Lesser Used Languages (UK), 2003-08; Preses, Scots Language Society, 2004-08. Recreations: gardening; skiing. Address: (h.) Heathfield, Pitcairngreen, Perthshire; T.-01738 583 403.

Banfill, Professor Phillip Frank Gower, BSc, PhD, CSci, CChem, FRSC, MCIOB, FHEA. Professor of Construction Materials, Heriot-Watt University, since 1995; b. 20.3.52,

Worthing; m., Patricia; 1 s.; 1 d. Educ. Lancing College; Southampton University; Liverpool University. Former Lecturer, Liverpool University. Publications: three books; 177 papers. Recreations: choral singing; hill walking; model railways. Address: (b.) School of the Built Environment, Heriot-Watt University, Riccarton, Edinburgh EH14 4AS; T.-0131-451 4648.

Banks, Gordon, BA (Hons). MP (Labour), Ochil and Perthshire South, 2005-2015; Shadow Scotland Office Minister, 2012-2015; Shadow Business Minister, 2010-2011; b. 1955, Acomb, Northumberland; m.; 2 c.

Banks, Lang. Director, WWF Scotland, since 2013. Address: WWF Scotland, The Tun, 4 Jackson's Entry, Holyrood Road, Edinburgh EH8 8PJ; T.-0131 659 9100; web: www.wwfscotland.org.uk

Banks, Professor William McKerrell, BSc, MSc, PhD, CEng, FIMechE, FREng, FRSE. Emeritus Research Professor of Advanced Materials, Strathclyde University (Professor, since 1991); formerly Director, Centre for Advanced Structural Materials; formerly Co-Director, Scottish Polymer Technology Network; President, SCOTETA, 2010-11; Past President and Chairman, Board of Trustees, IMechE; formerly Chairman, Qualifications and Membership Board, IMechE; formerly Chairman, Trustee Board Awards Committee, IMechE; former member, EC (UK) Council (now Engineering Council); former Member, Engineering and Technology Board (now Engineering UK); Past Chairman and Vice Chairman, Engineering Professors' Council; former Director of Research and Training, Faraday Plastics; b. 28.3.43, Irvine; m., Martha Ruthven Hair; 3 s. Educ. Irvine Royal Academy; Strathclyde University. Senior Research Engineer, G. & J. Weir Ltd., 1966-70; Lecturer, Senior Lecturer, Reader, Professor, Strathclyde University, since 1970. Recipient of James Alfred Ewing Medal (Royal Society and ICE), 2007; recipient of James Clayton Prize (IMechE), 2011; 150th Anniversary Gold Medal Award from IMechE, 1998; Member of SQA "Qualifications Design Team" for Technological Studies/Engineering (Rep RSE), 2010-14. Recreations: family; Bible teaching; gardening; travel. Address: (h.) 19 Dunure Drive, Hamilton ML3 9EY; T.-01698 823730.

Bannatyne, Hon. Lord (Iain Peebles). Senator of the College of Justice, since 2008. Address: (b.) Parliament House, 11 Parliament Square, Edinburgh EH1 1RQ.

Bantick, Allan David, OBE. Chairman, Scottish Wildlife Trust, 2008-2014; b. 22.12.39, London; m., Heather Susan; 1 d. Educ. Kingsbury County Grammar School. RAF Physical Education specialising in aircrew survival, mountain rescue and outdoor pursuits, 1957-83; Record Producer, 1984-2005; 1990-: Founder Member: Scottish Badgers, Scottish Beaver Network; Founding Chairman, Boat of Garten Wildlife Group; regular contributor to Radio and TV Wildlife Programmes including Nature's Calendar and Spring Watch. Joined the Council of The Scottish Wildlife Trust in 2005; became a Trustee of The Royal Society of Wildlife Trusts in 2006. Appointed OBE in the 2015 New Years Honours List. Recreations: golf; hill walking. Address: (h.) 23 Craigie Avenue, Boat of Garten, Inverness-shire PH24 3BL; T.-01479 831768. E-mail: allanbantick@yahoo.co.uk

Barbenel, Professor Joseph Cyril, BDS, BSc, MSc, PhD, LDS RCS(Eng), CBiol, FIBiol, CPhys, FInstP, CEng, FIPEM, FEAMBES, FRSE. Emeritus Professor,

Strathclyde University, since 2001; b. 2.1.37, London; m., Lesley Mary Hyde Jowett; 2 s.; 1 d. Educ. Hackney Downs Grammar School, London; London Hospital Medical College; Queen's College, Dundee (St. Andrews University); Strathclyde University. Dental House Surgeon, London Hospital, 1960; National Service, RADC, 1960-61 (Lieutenant, 1960, Captain, 1961); general dental practice, London, 1963; student, University of St Andrews, 1963-67; Lecturer, Department of Dental Prosthetics, Dental School, Dundee, 1967-69; Senior Lecturer, Reader, Professor, Bioengineering Unit, Strathclyde University. Recreations: music; art; theatre. Address: (b.) University of Strathclyde, Centre for Ultrasonic Engineering, 204 George Street, Glasgow G1 1XW; T.-0141-552 4400.
E-mail: j.c.barbenel@strath.ac.uk

Barbour, Professor James Jack, OBE (1992), BA (Jt Hons Politics), CHSM, FRCP (Edin). Chief Executive, Lothian NHS Board, 2001-2012; b. 16.1.53; partner, Julie Barnes; 1 s.; 2 d. Educ. Madras College, St. Andrews; University of Strathclyde. Graduate Management Trainee, NHS in Scotland, 1977-79; Administrator, Greater Glasgow Health Board, 1979-83; EEC Exchange scholarship in Germany, 1981; Unit Administration, Great Ormond Street Group of Hospitals, 1983-86; General Manager: Royal Manchester Children's Hospital, 1986-87; Aberdeen Royal Infirmary, 1987-92; Chief Executive: Aberdeen Royal Hospital NHS Trust, 1992-94; Central Manchester Healthcare NHS Trust, 1994-98; Sheffield Health Authority, 1998-2001. Alumnus, London Business School Development Programme, 1989. Honorary Professor, Queen Margaret University, 2002; University of Strathclyde, 2012; Member of Court, University of Edinburgh, 2006-2012; Burgess, City of Aberdeen, 1992. Recreation: trying to stay fit! E-mail: jamesjackbarbour@gmail.com

Bardell, Hannah. MP (SNP), Livingston, since 2015; Business, Innovation and Skills spokesperson in the House of Commons, since 2015; b. 1984, Craigshill, Livingston. Educ. Broxburn Academy; University of Stirling. Career: SNP election campaign for the Scottish Parliament election, 2007; worked for Alex Salmond and Ian Hudghton MEP for 3 years; joined the US State Department in their Edinburgh Consulate; subsequently worked in the oil and gas industry initially with Subsea 7 and later as Head of Communications & Marketing for the UK, Africa & Norway with Oil & Gas Service company Stork. Address: House of Commons, London SW1A 0AA.

Barkby, Irene, MBA. Director of Nursing, Strategy and Governance, NHS National Services Scotland. Educ. University of the West of Scotland. Career: significant Health Service background having spent over 30 years in a variety of roles including Clinical Practice, Business/Service Management and Professional Leadership; Health Service Director in a Territorial Health Board, since 1999; seconded to the Scottish Government for two years prior to joining NHS National Services Scotland; joined NHS National Services Scotland as Nurse Director in March 2009 and took on the additional responsibilities of Director of Strategy and Planning in December 2011. Address: National Services Scotland, Area 027, Gyle Square, 1 South Gyle Crescent, Edinburgh EH12 9EB; T.-0131 275 6000.

Barker, Emeritus Professor John Reginald, BSc, MSc, PhD, FBIS, FRAS, FRSE. Professor of Electronics (1985-2008), University of Glasgow, since 1985; b. 11.11.42, Stockport; m., Elizabeth Carol Maguire; 2 s.; 1 d. Educ. New Mills Grammar School; University of Edinburgh; University of Durham; University of Warwick. University of Warwick: SRC Personal Research Fellowship, 1969-70, Lecturer in Theoretical Physics, 1970-84, Senior Lecturer, 1984-85; Affiliate Professor, Colorado State University, 1979-83; Distinguished Science Lecturer, Yale University, 1992; Irvine Lectures in Chemistry, St. Andrews, 1994; TV/broadcasting: History of the Microchip, 1982; The Magic Micro Mission, 1983. Member, various SERC/DTI committees, 1987-93: Devices Committee, Electronic Materials Committee, National Committee for Superconductivity, Materials Commission, Molecular Electronics Committee (Chairman, 1990-93). Fellow of the Royal Society of Edinburgh (1990): served as Convenor of the Mathematics section and Convenor of the Electronics and Electrical Engineering Section. Royal Philosophical Society of Glasgow: Council Member (2010-2013), Vice-President (2014-). Nomads Club (2006-). Publications: over 360 scientific papers; Physics of Non-Linear Transport in Semi-conductors (Co-Author), 1979; Granular Nanoelectronics (Co-Author), 1991. Recreations: hill-walking; astronomy; reading; photography. Address: (b.) Rankine Building, School of Engineering, College of Science and Engineering, University of Glasgow, Glasgow G12 8LT; T.-0141 338 6026.
Web site: http://johnreginaldbarker.co.uk.
E-mail: John.Barker@glasgow.ac.uk.

Barley, Nick. Director, Edinburgh International Book Festival, since 2009. Ran his own publishing company, August Publications, before becoming Editor of The List (2003-06); then became Director of The Lighthouse, Scotland's National Centre for Architecture and Design. As Director of the Book Festival he has introduced several innovations including Unbound, a new strand of late night events, a Reader's First Book Award for debut novelists and the 2012 Edinburgh World Writers' Conference. Publications: Lost and Found: critical voices in new British design, 1999; Breathing Cities: the architecture of movement, 2000. Address: (b.) Edinburgh International Book Festival, 5 Charlotte Square, Edinburgh EH2 4DR; T.-0131 718 5666.

Barlow, Nevile Robert Disney, OBE, DL, FRICS. Chartered Surveyor and Farmer; Chairman, Scottish Borders Valuation Appeal Panel, since 1995; b. 3.2.41, Bagshott, Surrey; m., Myfanwy Louise Kerr-Wilson; 3 s. Educ. Winchester College; Royal Agricultural College, Cirencester. Assistant Agent, Bathurst Estate, Cirencester, 1963-95; Resident Sub-Agent, Bletchingdon Park, 1966-67; Head Factor, National Trust for Scotland, 1986-91; Vice-President, Scottish Landowners' Federation, (Convener, 1991-94); Member, Board, East of Scotland Water, 1995-99; Member, East Region Board, Scottish Environmental Protection Agency, 1996-2000. Recreations: shooting; fishing; sailing; rowing. Address: Parkcroft House, Redpath, Earlston TD4 6AD; T.-01896 849267.

Barnard, Professor Alan John, BA, MA, PhD, FBA, FSAScot. Professor of the Anthropology of Southern Africa, Edinburgh University, 2001-2015 (retired); Honorary Consul of Namibia in Scotland, since 2007; b. 22.2.49, Baton Rouge, USA; m., Dr Joy E. Barnard. Educ. New Providence High School; George Washington University; McMaster University; University College London. Junior Lecturer in Social Anthropology, University of Cape Town, 1972-73; Field Research with Bushmen in Botswana, 1974-75 and later; Lecturer in Social Anthropology, University College London, 1976-78; Lecturer in Social Anthropology, 1978-90, Senior Lecturer, 1990-94, Reader, 1994-2001, Edinburgh University. Hon. Secretary, Association of Social Anthropologists, 1985-89. Publications include:

Hunters and Herders of Southern Africa, 1992; Kalahari Bushmen (children's book), 1993; Encyclopaedia of Social and Cultural Anthropology (Co-Editor), 1996; History and Theory in Anthropology, 2000; Social Anthropology, 2000; The Hunter-Gatherer Peoples, 2001; Africa's Indigenous Peoples (Co-Editor), 2001; Self- and Other Images of Hunter-Gatherers (Co-Editor), 2002; Hunter-Gatherers in History (Editor), 2004; Anthropology and the Bushman, 2007; Social Anthropology and Human Origins, 2011; Genesis of Symbolic Thought, 2012; Language in Prehistory, 2016. Recreations: walking; cooking; watercolour painting. Address: (b.) School of Social and Political Science, Edinburgh University, Chrystal Macmillan Building, George Square, Edinburgh EH8 9LD.
E-mail: A.Barnard@ed.ac.uk

Barnes, David. Chief Agricultural Officer for Scotland, since 2015; formerly Deputy Director, Department for Agriculture and Rural Affairs, Scottish Government. Address: (b.) St. Andrew's House, Regent Road, Calton Hill, Edinburgh EH1 3DG.

Barnes, Eddie, MA. Director of Strategy and Communications, Scottish Conservative Party, since 2014; b. 10.6.72, Ormskirk, Lancashire; m., Malini Geeta; 1 s.; 1 d. Educ. St. Bede's Comprehensive, Ormskirk; Glasgow University. Scottish Catholic Observer Reporter, 1997, Editor, 1998-2000; Scottish Daily Mail, Political Reporter, 2000-02, Political Editor, 2002-04; Political Editor, Scotland on Sunday, 2004-2013. Address: Scottish Conervative Central Office, 67 Northumberland Street, Edinburgh EH3 6JG; T.-0131 524 0030.

Barnes, James David Kentish. Director, Dobbies Garden Centres plc, 1994-2006; b. 18.4.30, Cheshire; m., 1, Julie Pinckney; 1 s.; 1 d.; m. 2, Susan Mary Leslie. Educ. Eton College; Royal Military Academy Sandhurst. Commissioned 5th Innis Dragoon Guards, 1948-57. Served Germany, Korea, Middle East. Joined John Waterer Sons & Crisp (Horticulture), 1957. Managing Director, 1968-84; Managing Director (Owner), Dobbie and Co Edinburgh, 1968-94; National Trust for Scotland member of Council and Chairman of Gardening committee, 1996-2000; Chairman, NTS Enterprise Company, 2000-05; Director, Grimsthorpe and Drummond Castle Trust Ltd., since 2005. Recreations: cricket; golf; shooting; fishing; gardening; clubs: cavalry & guards, MCC, Muirfield. Address: (h.) Biggar Park, Biggar, Lanarkshire ML12 6JS.

Barnet, James Paul, MA, LLB. Former Partner, Macbeth Currie & Co., Solicitors; Honorary Sheriff, Tayside Central and Fife, at Dunfermline; former Dean, Dunfermline District Society of Solicitors; b. 20.7.37, Darlington; m., Margaret Smart; 4 s. Educ. Dunfermline High School; Edinburgh University. Admitted as Solicitor, 1961. Council Member, Law Society of Scotland, 1985-88; Captain, Scottish Universities Golfing Society, 1980-81; President, Dunfermline Rotary Club, 1985-86. Recreations: golf (Fife Matchplay Champion, 1968); reading; quoting Dr. Johnson. Address: (h.) 33 Drumsheugh Gardens, Edinburgh EH3 7RN.

Barr, Ian Mason, DA, BA, PGCE. Artist; Educationalist; b. 16.3.46, Glasgow; m., Joan Sinclair; 2 s.; 1 d. Educ. Rutherglen Academy; Glasgow School of Art; University of Strathclyde. Teacher, Strathclyde Regional Council Education Department, 1969-82; National Development Officer, Scottish Curriculum Development Service, 1982-85; Member of Staff, Jordanhill College of Education, 1985-87; Director,

Curriculum Evaluation Advisory Service, 1991-93; Director, Scottish Consultative Council on the Curriculum, 1993-2000; Specialist Adviser in Values Education, UNESCO, 1993-95; Founder, Ian M Barr Consultancy, since 2001. Founder Member, Strathclyde Environmental Education Group, 1975; Member, Secretary of State's Education for Sustainable Development Group, 1997-99; Board Member, Scottish Council for Research in Education, 1998-2003; Founder Member, European Educational Design Group, 1988; Board Member, Centre for Creative Communities, 1998-2000; Chair, Independent Television Commission Education Advisory Committee, 2000-03; Member, Scottish Arts Council Forum on the Arts and Education, 2002-03; Member, Campaign for Drawing Advisory Committee; Trustee, National Galleries of Scotland, 2005-2013; Convener, Art Fund Highland Branch, 2014. Authored and edited several publications on aspects of education and the curriculum; numerous exhibitions in UK and Europe. Recreations: gardening; music; reading; cinema; hill walking; mole catching. Address: Whitefield, Ordhill, Fortrose IV10 8SH; T.-01381 622545; e-mail: ianmbarr@btinternet.com

Barraclough, David Rex, BSc, DSc, FRAS. Chairperson, Enable (formerly Scottish Society for the Mentally Handicapped), 1998-2001; b. 7.3.40, Halifax; m., Christine; 1 s.; 1 d. Educ. Crossley and Porter Boys' School, Halifax; Imperial College, London University. Research Physicist, AEI Ltd., 1962-64; Research Assistant, Bradford University, 1964-68; Geophysicist, British Geological Survey, 1969-2000. Vice-President, Royal Astronomical Society, 1999-2000. Recreations: walking; reading; listening to music. Address: (h.) 49 Liberton Drive, Edinburgh.
E-mail: drbarraclough@hotmail.com

Barrett, John Andrew. MP (Liberal Democrat), Edinburgh West, 2001-10; b. 11.2.54, Hobart, Australia; m., Carol; 1 d. Educ. Forrester High School; Telford College; Napier Polytechnic. Company Director, ABC Productions, 1985-2001; Member, City of Edinburgh Council, 1995-2001; Director, The EDI Group, 1995-99; Board Member, Edinburgh International Film Festival, 1995-2001; Board Member, Lothian and Borders Screen Industry Office, 1998-2001; Member, Edinburgh Filmhouse Board, 1999-2001. Recreations: cinema; travel; music.

Barrie, Andrew, BSc, BD. Minister of Rothesay: Trinity, Church of Scotland, since 2010; m., Sheila. Educ. Muiredge Primary; Uddingston Grammar; Strathclyde University; Aberdeen University. Minister: Lochranza and Pirnmill with Shiskine (Isle of Arran), 1984-2000, Denny: Westpark, 2000-2010. Address: 12 Crichton Road, Rothesay, Isle of Bute PA20 9JR; T.-01700 503010; e-mail: drew.barrie@btinternet.com

Barrie, Ken, BA Hons (Psych), CQSW, PGDip (Alcohol Studies). Senior Lecturer, University of the West of Scotland, since 1987; b. 13.4.52, Edinburgh; m., Nancy Docherty; 1 s. Educ. Royal High School, Edinburgh; Strathclyde University; Edinburgh University; Paisley University. 1975-83: Social Worker, Strathclyde Regional Council; full range of social work tasks; specialism in addiction, Centre for Alcohol and Drug Studies, University of Paisley, since 1983. Run largest Post Graduate Course on Alcohol and Drug Studies in UK. Recreations: swimming; cycling; canoeing. Address: (b.) University of the West of Scotland, High Street, Paisley PA1 2BE; T.-0141 848 3140; e-mail: ken.barrie@uws.ac.uk

Barron, Steve, BSc (Hons). Chief Executive, The Highland Council, since 2013, previously Depute Chief Executive and Director of Housing and Property; m.; 3 s. Educ. Lochardil Primary School; Inverness Royal Academy; Heriot Watt University. Career: 13 years in the health service in Lothian and Highland (Head of Facilities with the former Highland Primary Care Trust); Managing Director of Robertsons Facilities Management, Inverness, for 8 years; joined The Highland Council in 2008. Address: Highland Council Headquarters, Glenurquhart Road, Inverness IV3 5NX; T.-01349 886606.

Barstad, Professor Hans Magnus, Ctheol, Drtheol (Oslo, Norway), DD, The University of Edinburgh. Professor Emeritus of Hebrew Bible/Old Testament, University of Edinburgh, since 2006; Professor of Old Testament, University of Oslo, 1986-2005; b. 7.6.47, Asnes, Norway; m., Wenche; 1 s.; 1 d. Educ. University of Oslo, Norway. Studies in theology, University of Oslo; Assistant Academic Librarian, University Library, Oslo, 1971; Research Fellow (Hebrew Bible, Semitic languages) under the Norwegian Research Council, Oslo, Rome, Oxford, 1976, 1978-79; Academic Librarian and Keeper of Theological Books, University of Oslo, 1980; Fellow, Nordic Council of Ministers, Copenhagen, 1981; appointed Senior Academic Librarian, 1981; received Degree of Dr. theol., University of Oslo, 1982; Fellow, Deutscher Akademischer Austauschdienst, University of Tübingen, 1982; Fellow, Norwegian Ministry of Foreign Affairs, The Hebrew University, Jerusalem, 1983; appointed Keeper of Rare Books and Incunabula, Norwegian National Library, 1984; Visiting Senior Fellow, Oriel College, Oxford, 1992; Chairman of the Board of the Norwegian National Library, 1988-92. Member of the Royal Norwegian Society of Sciences and Letters; Member of the Norwegian Academy of Science and Letters. Secretary General of the Norwegian Academy, 1998-2000. Received the Nansen Award for excellence in research in 2004; Board member, Holberg Foundation, since 2003. Member of numerous international editorial boards. Publications: The Religious Polemics of Amos, 1984; A Way in the Wildnerness, 1989; Det gamle testamente, 1993; The Myth of the Empty Land, 1996; The Babylonian Captivity of the Book of Isaiah, 1997; History and the Hebrew Bible, 2008. Recreation: walking. Address: (b.) New College, Mound Place, Edinburgh EH1 2LX; T.-0131 650 8916; e-mail: h.barstad@ed.ac.uk

Bartlett, Professor Robert John, MA, DPhil, FRHS, FBA, FSA, FRSE. Professor of Mediaeval History, St. Andrews University, since 1992; b. 27.11.50, London; m., Honora Hickey; 1 s.; 1 d. Educ. Battersea Grammar School; Peterhouse, Cambridge; St. John's College, Oxford. Lecturer in History, Edinburgh University, 1980-86; Professor of Medieval History, University of Chicago, 1986-92. Presenter, "Inside the Medieval Mind", BBC4, 2008; "The Normans", BBC2, 2010; "The Plantagenets", BBC2, 2013. Publications: Gerald of Wales 1146-1223, 1982; Trial by Fire and Water: the medieval judicial ordeal, 1986; The Making of Europe, 1993; England under the Norman and Angevin Kings, 2000; Medieval Panorama (Editor), 2001; The Hanged Man: A Story of Miracle, Memory and Colonization in the Middle Ages, 2004; The Natural and the Supernatural in the Middle Ages, 2008; Why can the dead do such great things? Saints and Worshippers from the Martyrs to the Reformation, 2013. Recreations: walking; squash. Address: (b.) Department of Mediaeval History, St. Andrews University, St. Andrews KY16 9AL; T.-01334 463308.

Barton, Professor Geoffrey John, BSc (Manchester), PhD (London). Head of Computational Biology and Professor of Bioinformatics, College of Life Sciences, University of Dundee, since 2001; b. 01.11.60, Glenelg, Australia; m., Julia; 3 s. Educ. Challney High School; Luton VIth Form College; University of Manchester; Birkbeck College, University of London. Imperial Cancer Research Fund Fellow, Lincoln's Inn Fields, London, 1987-89; Royal Society University Research Fellow, Laboratory of Molecular Biophysics, University of Oxford, 1989-97; Research and Development Team Leader and Head of European Macromolecular Structure Database, EMBL European Bioinformatics Institute, Hinxton, Cambridge, 1997-2001. Fellow of the Society of Biology (FSB). 100+ peer reviewed publications. Recreations: family; DIY; playing the flute; swimming. Address: (b.) College of Life Sciences, University of Dundee, Dow Street, Dundee DD1 5EH; T.-01382 385860.
E-mail: g.j.barton@dundee.ac.uk
Web: www.compbio.dundee.ac.uk

Batchelor, Andrea Maria, BSc (Hons), TeachCert, MAppSci. Trustee, National Library of Scotland, 2005-2014; Head of Education (Inclusion), South Lanarkshire Council, 1996-2014; b. 3.11.54, Leeds; m., John Batchelor; 2 s. Educ. Edinburgh University; Jordanhill College; Glasgow University. Strathclyde Regional Council: Psychologist, 1978-83, Lanark Division; Senior Psychologist, 1983-88, Ayr Division; Depute Principal Psychologist, 1988-90, Dunbarton Division; Education Officer, 1990-93, Glasgow Division; Education Officer, 1993-96, Lanark Division. Member of Scottish Executive Action Team for Better Integrated Children's Services, 2000-02; Member, Advisory Council, Learning and Teaching Scotland, 2001-2011. Publication: "For Scotland's Children", 2001. Recreations: yoga; swimming; salsa; reading; travel. Address: (h.) 40 Buchanan Drive, Rutherglen, Glasgow G73 3PE; T.-0141 647 6302.

Batchelor, Louise Mary, BA (Hons). Freelance journalist, conference facilitator and broadcaster, since 2009; Environment Correspondent, BBC Scotland, 1994-2008; b. 23.2.53, Swanage; m., David Batchelor; 2 s. Educ. Dorchester Grammar School; Reading University. Milton Keynes Gazette, 1974; Oxford Mail, 1977; BBC Radio Scotland, 1978; Presenter/Reporter, Reporting Scotland, 1980; Presenter, Newsnight, 1981-82; Presenter, Breakfast News (Scotland), 1982-83; presenter, various programmes, including Voyager, Fringes of Faith; Presenter, Newsroom South East, 1989. Media Natura Award, 1996, for environment reporting; British Environment and Media Award for TV News and Current Affairs coverage of the environment, 2003; Director, Fair Isle Bird Observatory Trust; Member, Steering Group, Portmoak Community Woodlands; Member, Executive Group, Partnership Against Wildlife Crime (PAW) Scotland; Member, Scottish Green Party. Recreations: walking; bird watching; playing cello; swing dancing. Address: The Old Manse, Scotlandwell, Kinross KY13 9HY.
E-mail: louise@louisebatchelor.co.uk

Bateman, Derek Walls. Former Presenter, BBC Radio Scotland (1995-2013); b. 10.5.51, Selkirk; m., 1, Alison Edgar (deceased); 2 d.; 2, Judith Mackay; 1 d. Educ. Selkirk High School; Edinburgh College of Commerce. Scotsman Publications; Glasgow Herald; BBC Scotland; Scotland on Sunday; freelance (Sunday Times, STV). Publication: Unfriendly Games (Co-Author), 1986. Recreation: wine.

Bateman, Meg (Vivienne Margaret), MA (Hons), PhD. Gaelic poet; b. 13.4.59, Edinburgh; 1 s. Educ. Mary Erskine School, Edinburgh; University of Aberdeen. Poetry collections: Orain Ghaoil (1990); Aotromachd is Dàin Eile (Lightness and Other Poems) (1997); Soirbheas/Fair Wind, 2007; (both shortlisted for Scottish Book of the Year Award); Transparencies, 2013; translations of Gaelic poetry published in An Anthology of Scottish Women Poets, Gàir nan Clàrsach (The Harps' Cry); Duanaire na

Sracaire/Songbook of the Pillagers, 2007; The Glendale Bards, 2014. Address: (b.) Sabhal Mòr Ostaig, Sleat, Isle of Skye IV44 8RQ; T.-01471 888310; e-mail: meg.smo@uhi.ac.uk

Bates, Damian, BA (Hons). Editor-in-Chief, Aberdeen Journals, since 2013 and Editor, Press and Journal, since 2011; b. 9.4.69, Blackpool, Lancashire. Educ. Cardinal Allen RC High School, Fleetwood; St. Mary's VIth Form, Blackpool; Reading University. Trainee Reporter; Business Reporter; Deputy Business Editor; Crime Reporter - all Evening Gazette, Middlesbrough; Assistant News Editor; Deputy News Editor - The News, Portsmouth; News Editor; Assistant Editor (News) - Telegraph and Argus, Bradford; Deputy Editor, then Editor, Evening Express, Aberdeen; Visiting Professor, Robert Gordon University. Publication: No More I Love Yous - The Nikki Conroy Story. Address: (b.) AJL, Lang Stracht, Aberdeen; T.-01224 690222.

Batho, Mark Thomas Scott, MA (Hons). Vice Principal (University Services), University of Abertay Dundee; b. 10.6.56, Ashtead, Surrey; m., Vivienne Ann; 2 s.; 1 d. Educ. Glyn Grammar School, Epsom; St Andrews University. Non-Executive Board Member, Royal Scottish National Orchestra; Non-Executive Board Member, Creative Skillset; Non Executive Board Member, Goodison Group in Scotland; Council Member, Scottish Association for Marine Science (SAMS); Session Clerk, St Giles' Cathedral Edinburgh. Address: (b.) University of Abertay Dundee, Bell Street, Dundee DD1 1HG; T.-01382 308014.

Baughan, Mike, OBE, BEd, FEIS. Former Chief Executive, Learning and Teaching Scotland (formerly Scottish Consultative Council on the Curriculum), 2000-2004; b. 11.6.44, Dumfries; m., Anna; 1 s.; 1 d. Educ. St. Joseph's College, Dumfries; Dundee University; Dundee College of Education. RAF; brief career in industrial banking; English Teacher, secondary schools, Dundee, 1975-82; Churchill Fellow, 1977; Adviser in Education, Tayside Regional Council, 1982-87; Rector, Webster's High School, Kirriemuir, 1987-97; Scottish Consultative Council on the Curriculum: Development Fellow, 1997-98, appointed Chief Executive, 1998. Chair/Member, various national education committees; Fellow, Education Institute of Scotland; Past Council Member, Save the Children Scotland; Past Member of Ancient Monuments Board for Scotland; Ex Director and Board Member of Young Enterprise Scotland. Recreations: 6 grandchildren; hill-walking; member of the Munro Society and the Grampian Club; golf; gardening; fishing; theatre; travel. Address: (b.) 6 Shepherd's Road, Newport-on-Tay, Fife DD6 8HJ.

Baxter, Jayne, MSP (Labour), Mid Scotland and Fife, 2012-16. Educ. Edinburgh Napier University. Background in local government with a particular interest in social care, young people, economic development and community planning. Former Member of the Education and Culture Committee, Scottish Parliament.

Baxter, Mary Ross, MBE, MA, LRAM; b. 23.9.27, Glasgow. Educ. Park School, Glasgow; Glasgow University. John Smith & Son, Booksellers, Glasgow, 1952-56; British European Airways, Glasgow Office, 1956-60; Director, National Book League Scotland (now known as Scottish Book Trust), 1960-89; former President, International PEN Scottish Centre; Trustee, The Pushkin Prizes in Scotland. Honorary Member, Scottish Library Association. Recreations: music; books; home-decorating; cooking; gardening. Address: (h.) 18 Crown Terrace, Glasgow G12 9ES; T.-0141-3399554. E-mail: marybaxglasgow@aol.com

Baxter, Neil, MA (Hons). Secretary & Treasurer, The Royal Incorporation of Architects in Scotland, since 2008. Educ. Lenzie Academy; University of Glasgow. Principal,

Neil Baxter Associates, 1988-2008. Address: The Royal Incorporation of Architects in Scotland, 15 Rutland Square, Edinburgh EH1 2BE; T.-0131 229 7545.

Baxter, Peter R., DHE. Curator, Benmore Botanic Garden, since 1995; b. 30.6.58, Irvine; m.; 1 s.; 1 d. Address: (b.) Benmore Botanic Garden, Benmore, Dunoon PA23 8QU; e-mail: p.baxter@rbge.org.uk

Baynham, John William, CBE, Doctor (honoris causa) (Edinburgh), Doctor (honoris causa) (Queen Margaret University College, BSc, PhD, DIC. Chairman, Lothian Health Board, 1990-97; Chairman, Scottish Health Board Chairmen's Group, 1995-97; b. 20.1.29, Blantyre; m., Marie B. Friel (deceased, 2012); 1 d. Educ. Bathgate Academy; Aberdeen University; Imperial College, London. Scottish Agricultural Industries PLC, 1955-87, latterly as Agribusiness Director. Member, Lothian Health Board, 1987-90; Chairman, Board of Governors, Moray House Institute of Education, Heriot Watt University, 1991-95; Governor, Queen Margaret College, 1995-99; Chairman, Salaries Committee, Conference of Scottish Centrally Funded Colleges, 1995-99. Recreations: good food; wine; grandchildren. Address: (h.) 'Rathmullan', 2, Somnerfield Park, Haddington, East Lothian EH41 3RX; T.-01620 825750; e-mail: jonmar29@tiscali.co.uk

Bazarnic, Zoja. Principal Officer, Consulate General Edinburgh, since August 2012; b. Yugoslavia; m., Cliff Bazarnic; 1 d; 1 stepson. Educ. Stanford University. Career: Advertising and Direct Mail Coordinator at Stanford University Press; joined the State Department in 2002 as a political officer; served as a consular officer in Havana, Cuba, 2003-2005, a political officer in Rome, Italy, 2005-2007, and a watch officer in the State Department's 24 hour Operations Center, 2007-2008; seconded to the Multinational Force and Observers peacekeeping organisation in the Sinai as an observer to the Egypt-Israel Treaty of Peace, 2008-09; Senior Political Officer in the Office of European Union and Regional Affairs, 2009-2011; concluded a one-year detail advising U.S. Senator Susan M. Collins of Maine on foreign policy and assistance issues as a Pearson Fellow in June 2012. Recreations: travelling; snorkeling; running; eating Italian food. Address: (b.) 3 Regent Terrace, Edinburgh EH7 5BW; T.-0131 556 8315.

Beamish, Claudia, MSP (Labour and Cooperative), South Scotland, since 2011; Shadow Minister for Environment and Climate Change; b. 9.8.52; m., Michael Derrington; 1 d.; 1 s. Chair of the Scottish Labour Party, 2008-10, former Chair of Socialist Environmental Resources Association; Member of the Cooperative Group of MSPs. Taught part-time in South Lanarkshire Primary Schools and has also run a community theatre company. Awarded the RSPB Environment Politician of the Year in the Nature of Scotland Awards, 2014. Address: (b.) Scottish Parliament, Edinburgh EH99 1SP.
Web: www.claudiabeamish.com.

Beamish, Sally, DMus. Composer; b. 26.8.56, London; 2 s.; 1 d. Educ. Camden School for Girls; Royal Northern College of Music; Staatliche Hochschule für Musik. Viola player until 1989 (SCO, Academy of St. Martin's, Raphael Ensemble); professional composer, since 1990. Resident composer, Swedish and Scottish Chamber Orchestras, 1998-2003; several CDs on BIS label; opera, orchestral, vocal, chamber and solo works. Concertos: Violin, Viola (3), Cello (2), Percussion (2), Accordion, 3 St. Qts. Recreations: walking; reading; writing. Contact Scottish Music Centre.

E-mail: info@scottishmusiccentre.com
Web: www.sallybeamish.com

Beat, Janet Eveline, BMus, MA. Composer; Lecturer, Glasgow University, 1996-2004; Artistic Director and Founder, Soundstrata (electro-acoustic ensemble); Honorary Research Fellow, Music Department, Glasgow University; b. 17.12.37, Streetly. Educ. High School for Girls, Sutton Coldfield; Birmingham University. Freelance Orchestral Player, 1960s; Lecturer: Madeley College of Education, 1965-67, Worcester College of Education, 1967-71, Royal Scottish Academy of Music and Drama, 1972-96; music published by Furore Verlag, Kassel; wrote musical criticism for The Scotsman; G.D. Cunningham Award, 1962; her works have been performed throughout the UK as well as in Switzerland, Germany, Poland, North America, South America, Greece, Australia, Japan, Austria, Portugal, Spain and Africa. Recreations: travel; reading; art. Address: The Gait, Candleriggs, Glasgow G1 1NQ; T.- 0141 552 5222. E-mail: info@scottishmusiccentre.com

Beath, Professor John Arnott, OBE, MA, MPhil, FRSE, FRSA. Emeritus Professor of Economics, St. Andrews University; member, Prison Service Pay Review Body; member, Competition Appeal Tribunal; b. 15.6.44, Thurso; m., Dr. Monika Schroder. Educ. Hillhead High School; St. Andrews, London, Pennsylvania and Cambridge Universities. Research Officer, Department of Applied Economics, Cambridge University; Fellow, Downing College, Cambridge; Lecturer, then Senior Lecturer in Economics, Bristol University. Member, Research Priorities Board, Economic and Social Research Council, 1996-2000; Chair, Conference of Heads of University Departments of Economics, 1997-2003; RAE Panellist, 1996, 2001; Chair, Economic Research Institute of Northern Ireland, 2003-09; Member, Review Body on Doctors' and Dentists' Remuneration, 2003-09; Council member, Economic and Social Research Council, 2009-14; Secretary-General, Royal Economic Society, 2008-15. Publication: The Economic Theory of Product Differentiation. Recreations: gardening; golf; music. Address: (h.) Simonden, Ceres, Cupar KY15 5PP.

Beattie, Alistair Duncan, MD (Hons), FRCPGlas, FRCPLond. Consultant Physician, Southern General Hospital, Glasgow, 1976-2002; Honorary Clinical Lecturer, Glasgow University, 1977-2002; Chairman, Medical and Dental Defence Union of Scotland, 2002-2012; b. 4.4.42, Laurencekirk; m., Gillian Margaret McCutcheon; 3 s.; 2 d. Educ. Paisley Grammar School; Glasgow University. Junior hospital appointments, Royal Infirmary and Western Infirmary, Glasgow, 1965-69; Department of Materia Medica, Glasgow University: Research Fellow, 1969-73, Lecturer, 1973-74; MRC Research Fellow, Royal Free Hospital, London, 1974-75. Chairman, Medical and Dental Defence Union of Scotland. Recreations: golf; music. Address: (h.) Flat 3/2 Lauderdale Mansions, 47 Novar Drive, Glasgow G12 9UB; T.-0141-334 0101.

Beattie, Andrew Watt, LLB (Hons), DipLP, NP. First Scottish Parliamentary Counsel, since 2012; Scottish Parliamentary Counsel, 2008-2012; Depute Scottish Parliamentary Counsel, 1999-2008; b. 16.11.72, Aberdeen; m., Claire Louise. Educ. Elgin Academy; Edinburgh University. Solicitor, Shepherd & Wedderburn, WS, 1995-99. Recreations: hillock-walking; squash; camping. Address: (b.) Office of the Scottish Parliamentary Counsel, Victoria Quay, Edinburgh EH6 6QQ; T.-0131-244 1665.

Beattie, Bryan William, JP, BA, FRSA. Chairman, Eigg Box, since 2014; Chairman and Founder, Tappstory Ltd, since 2015; Expert Adviser to Minister for Tourism, Culture and Sport, 2003-05; Special Adviser to Royal Scottish Academy of Music and Drama, 2005-08; Chairman, Board of Governors, Eden Court Theatre, 1996-2002; Board Member, Scottish Screen, 1998-2003; b. 3.5.60, Dundee; m., Emer Leavy; 3 d.; 1 s. Educ. High School of Dundee; Stirling University. Director, Stirling Festival, 1984-86; Arts Development Officer for Scotland, Scottish Council on Disability, 1986-87; Principal, Creative Services (arts consultancy), since 1992; Director, Big Sky (publisher and event producer), since 2011; Chairman, Scottish Youth Theatre, 1993-99; Councillor, Highland Regional Council, 1994-96, and Highland Council, 1995-99 (Chairman, Cultural and Leisure Services Committee, 1995-99); Board Member, Ross and Cromarty Enterprise, 1996-2002, Vice-Chairman, 1999-2002; Chairman: Feis Rois, 2006-2011, Booth Scotland, 2007-2012; Trustee, Dewar Arts Awards, 2011-2013; Member, University of Highlands and Islands Foundation, 1996-99 and 2008-10; Founder Member, Highlands and Islands Alliance, 1998; author of plays for tv, radio and theatre; Editor, "ImagiNation: Stories of Scotland's Future", 2011; Producer, "The Boy and the Bunnet", "Infinite Scotland", "Scotland Inspired"; broadcaster; columnist, Press and Journal, 1994-2008; occasional acting. Recreations: music; books; sport. Address: (h.) Drumderfit, North Kessock, by Inverness IV1 3ZF; T.-01463 731596.
E-mail: bryan@creativeservicesscotland.co.uk

Beattie, Colin. MSP (SNP), Midlothian North and Musselburgh, since 2011. Originally from Forfar. Has had a career in national and international finance, working in both the UK and overseas. Served as a councillor in Midlothian, 2007-2012. Address: (b.) Scottish Parliament, Edinburgh EH99 1SP.

Beaty, Professor Robert (Bob) Thompson, OBE, BSc (Hons), FREng, FIEE, CEng. Managing Director, GlenCon Ltd., 1996-2007; Chairman, Scottish Enterprise Renfrewshire, 1999-2003; b. 13.10.43, Kilmarnock; m., Anne Veronica; 2 s. Educ. Hamilton Academy; Glasgow University. Hoover Scholar, 1961-65; Test Engineer, Hoover Ltd., Cambuslang, 1965-68; IBM, 1968-96, latterly Director of Personal Computer Manufacturing and Development Site at Greenock. Former Chair of Court, University of the West of Scotland; former Vice-Chairman, Board of Management, James Watt College; Visiting Professor in Product Design, Glasgow University; former Board Member, SIDAB; Honorary Doctorate received from the University of the West of Scotland, 2010. Recreations: cycling; hill-walking; golf; travel; France. Address: (h.) Glenside, 89 Newton Street, Greenock PA16 8SG; T.- 01475 722027/07961 068614.
E-mail: bob.beaty@btopenworld.com

Beaumont, Professor Paul Reid, LLB, LLM, FRSE. Professor of European Union and Private International Law, University of Aberdeen, since 1995 (Head, Law School, 2000-08); b. 27.10.60, Hamilton; m., Marion; 1 s.; 1 d. Educ. Claremont High School, East Kilbride; Glasgow University; Dalhousie University, Canada. University of Aberdeen: Lecturer in Public Law, 1983-91, Senior Lecturer in Public Law, 1992-95. Adviser to UK and Scottish Governments on private international law (1996-2013). Author and editor of several books. Recreations: golf; stamp collecting. Address: School of Law, University of Aberdeen, Aberdeen AB24 3UB; T.-01224 272439; e-mail: p.beaumont@abdn.ac.uk

Beaumont, Professor Phillip Barrington, BEcon (Hons), MEcon, PhD. Professor, School of Business and

Management, Glasgow University, since 1990; b. 13.10.49, Melbourne, Australia; m., Patricia Mary Ann McKinlay; 2 children. Educ. Camberwell High School, Melbourne; Monash University, Melbourne; Glasgow University. Glasgow University: Research Fellow, Lecturer, 1976-84; Senior Lecturer, 1984-86; Reader, 1986-90. Visiting Professor: Massachusetts Institute of Technology, Boston, 1982, McMaster University, 1986, Case Western Reserve University, 1988, Cornell University, 1990. Publications: Bargaining in the Public Sector, 1978; Safety at Work and the Trade Unions, 1981; Job Satisfaction in Public Administration, 1983; The Decline of Trade Union Organization, 1987; Change in Industrial Relations, 1990; Public Sector Industrial Relations, 1991; Human Resource Management, 1993; The Future of Employment Management, 1995. Recreations: tennis; badminton; cricket; shooting; fishing. Address: (b.) The University, Glasgow G12 8QQ; T.-0141-339 8855.

Beaumont, Professor Steven Peter, OBE, MA, PhD, FRSE, FREng, CEng, MIET. Professor of Nanoelectronics, Department of Electronics and Electrical Engineering, Vice Principal Emeritus, University of Glasgow; b. 20.2.52, Norwich; m., Joanne Mary; 1 s.; 2 d. Educ. Norwich School; Corpus Christi College, Cambridge University. Research Fellow, Glasgow University, 1978-83; Barr and Stroud Lecturer in Electronics, Glasgow University, 1983-86, Senior Lecturer, 1986-89, Head of Department of Electronics and Electrical Engineering, 1994-98, Vice Principal (Research & Enterprise), 2005-2014; Director: Institute for System Level Integration, 1999-2004, Intellemetrics Ltd., 1982-90, System Level Integration Ltd, Electronics Scotland, 1998-2004, Photonix Ltd, 2005-2010, Kelvin Nanotechnology Ltd., Thermoelectric Conversion Systems Ltd; Awards Convener, Royal Society of Edinburgh. Recreations: walking; crofting. Address: (h.) 13 Kelvinside Terrace South, Glasgow G20 6DW; T.-0141-330 2112.

Becher, Mark, MA (Hons), PGCE. Headteacher, The Compass School, Haddington, since 1997; b. 11.1.66, Ayr; m., Agnieszka; 1 d. Educ. Queen Margaret Academy, Ayr; University of Dundee; Craigie College of Education; University of Strathclyde. Primary Teacher: The Edinburgh Academy, 1988-93; Primary Teacher/Senior Teacher, The Mary Erskine and Stewart's Melville Junior School, 1993-97. Member, Scottish Council of Independent Schools Governing Board, 2004-2013; Lay Assessor, Scottish Qualification for Headship, since 2010. Recreations: theatre; rugby; hillwalking; golf. Address: (b.) The Compass School, West Road, Haddington EH41 3RD; T.-01620 822642; e-mail: office@thecompassschool.co.uk

Bechhofer, Professor Frank, MA, FRSE. Honorary Fellow, Edinburgh University; b. 10.10.35, Nurnberg, Germany; m., Jean Barbara Conochie; 1 s.; 1 d. Educ. Nottingham High School; Queens' College, Cambridge. Junior Research Officer, Department of Applied Economics, Cambridge University, 1962-65; Edinburgh University: Lecturer in Sociology, 1965-71, Reader in Sociology, 1971-87, Director, Research Centre for Social Sciences, 1984-97, Professor of Social Research, 1988-97. Address: (h.) 51 Barnton Park View, Edinburgh EH4 6HH; T.-0131-339 4083; e-mail: frank@bechhofer.demon.co.uk

Beckett, Rev. David Mackay, BA, BD. Minister, Greyfriars Tolbooth and Highland Kirk, Edinburgh, 1983-2002; b. 22.3.37, Glasgow; m., Rosalie Frances Neal; 2 s. Educ. Glenalmond; Trinity Hall, Cambridge; St. Andrews University. Assistant Minister, Dundee Parish Church (St. Mary's), 1963-66; Minister, Clark Memorial Church, Largs, 1966-83; Moderator, Presbytery of Ardrossan, 1974.

Convener, Committee on Public Worship and Aids to Devotion, General Assembly, 1978-82; President, Church Service Society, 1986-88; Secretary, General Assembly Panel on Doctrine, 1987-95; Moderator, Presbytery of Edinburgh, 1999-2000. Publication: The Lord's Supper, 1984. Address: (h.) 31 (1F1) Sciennes Road, Edinburgh EH9 1NT.

Beckett, John, QC. All-Scotland Floating Sheriff, since 2008; Solicitor General for Scotland, 2006-07. Educ. University of Edinburgh. Elected to the Faculty of Advocates, 1993; Advocate Depute and a Senior Advocate Depute, since 2003; Principal Advocate Depute, 2006. Address: (b.) Scottish Courts, Parliament Square, Edinburgh.

Bedford, Professor Tim, BSc (Hons), MSc, PhD. Associate Deputy Principal (Knowledge Exchange and Research Enhancement), University of Strathclyde, since 2010, Professor of Decision Making and Risk Analysis, since 2001; b. 14.4.60, London. Educ. Oulder Hill, Rochdale; Warwick University. Fellow, Kings College, Cambridge, 1984-87; Lecturer in Probability, Delft University of Technology, Netherlands, 1987-94; Senior Lecturer in Applications of Decision Theory, Delft University of Technology, 1994-2000. Hon Doctorate, Faculté Polytechnique de Mons, Belgium, 2008. Fellow of the Royal Society of Edinburgh; Member, Scottish Funding Council Research & Knowledge Exchange Committee, since 2014; Member, Royal Society of Edinburgh Business Innovation Forum, since 2015. Publication: Probabilistic Risk Analysis: Foundations and Methods. Recreations: jazz music; gardening; family. Address: (b.) Department of Management Science, Sir William Duncan Building, 130 Rottenrow, Glasgow G4 0GE; T.-0141-548 2394.
E-mail: tim.bedford@strath.ac.uk

Beedham, Dr. Christopher, BSc, PhD. Lecturer in German, St. Andrews University, since 1984; b. 29.12.52, Cleethorpes; m., Barbara H. Chruscik; 2 d. Educ. Barton-upon-Humber Grammar School; Salford University; Leipzig University. Research Assistant in Applied Linguistics, University of Aston in Birmingham, 1979-81; Teaching Assistant, English Dept. of the Philological Faculty, Moscow State University, 1982-84. Publications: The Passive Aspect in English, German and Russian, 1982; German Linguistics: An Introduction, 1995; *Langue and Parole* in Synchronic and Diachronic Perspective (Editor), 1999; Language and Meaning, 2005; Rules and Exceptions (Co-Editor), 2014; Letter to Times Higher Education, 3.7.2014. Recreations: 5-a-side football; hill-walking; cycling; jogging; gym; yoga; travel; music. Address: (b.) Dept. of German, School of Modern Languages, University of St. Andrews, St. Andrews, Fife KY16 9PH; T.-01334 463657; e-mail: c.beedham@st-andrews.ac.uk

Beevers, Professor Clifford, OBE, BSc, PhD, MILT, DSc. Professor Emeritus, Heriot Watt University, since 2005, Professor of Mathematics, since 1993; b. 4.9.44, Castleford; m., Elizabeth Ann; 2 d. Educ. Castleford Grammar School; Manchester University. Senior Lecturer, 1985; Director, CALM, 1985; Chairman of the e-Assessment Association, 2006-12, Vice Chairman, 2012-13. Past Chairman, Edinburgh Branch, British Retinitis Pigmentosa Society. Chairman of the Juniper Green Community Council. Recreations: walking; Reading; theatre. Address: (b.) School of Mathematical and Computer Sciences, Heriot Watt University, Riccarton, Edinburgh EH14 4AS; T.-0131-451 3233; e-mail: C.E.Beevers@hw.ac.uk

Begbie, Alexander (Sandy), MBA, FCIBS. Chief Operations Officer, Standard Life plc, since 2012, People and Operations Director, 2010-2012; b. 13.04.66, Edinburgh; 2 d. Educ. Musselburgh Grammar School; Edinburgh University. The Royal Bank of Scotland plc,

1983-2000; Scottish Power plc, 2000-07; Director, Human Resources and Corporate Responsibility, Aegon, 2007-2010. Former Non-Executive Director, Scottish Government; former Chairman of the Scottish Government Remuneration Group. Former Non-Executive Advisory, Wharton Executive Board, Philadelphia, USA; currently Non-Executive Director with KPMG; Chairman, the Board of Career Ready Scotland; Chairman, the Regional Invest in Youth Board, Edinburgh and the Lothians. Recreations: reading; running; travelling. Address: (h.) 2 Belgrave Mews, Edinburgh EH4 3AX.
E-mail: sandy_begbie@standardlife.com

Begg, Dame Anne, DBE, MA. MP (Labour), Aberdeen South, 1997-2015; b. 6.12.55, Forfar. Educ. Brechin High School; University of Aberdeen; Aberdeen College of Education. Teacher of English and History, Webster's High, Kirriemuir, 1978-88; Assistant Principal Teacher, then Principal Teacher of English, Arbroath Academy, 1988-97. Disabled Scot of the Year, 1988. Chair, Work and Pensions Select Committee, 2010-15. Recreations: cinema; theatre; reading.

Begg, Professor Hugh MacKemmie, MA, MA, PhD, DipTP, FRTPI. Consultant Economist and Chartered Planner; Visiting Professor, University of Abertay, Dundee; Associate, Cambridge Economic Associates; b. 25.10.41, Glasgow; m., Jane Elizabeth Harrison; 2 d. Educ. High School of Glasgow; St. Andrews University; University of British Columbia; Dundee University. Lecturer in Political Economy, St. Andrews University; Research Fellow, Tayside Study; Lecturer in Economics, Dundee University; Assistant Director of Planning, Tayside Regional Council; Visiting Professor, Technical University of Nova Scotia; Consultant, UN Regional Development Project, Egypt and Saudi Arabia; Consultant, Scottish Office Industry Department, Scottish Office Agriculture and Forestry Department; Head, School of Town and Regional Planning, Dundee University; Dean of Faculty of Environmental Studies, Dundee University. External Adjudicator, Scottish Enterprise; Convener, The Standards Commission for Scotland; Member, Private Legislation Procedure (Scotland) Extra-Parliamentary Panel; Member, Local Government Boundary Commission for Scotland; Honorary Professor of Economics, University of Abertay Dundee; Reporter, Directorate for Environmental and Planning Appeals; Assessor for Private and Hybrid Bills, Scottish Parliament; Honorary Fellow, Patrick Geddes Institute, Dundee University. Recreations: Scottish history; hill walking; watching rugby; puppy walking for guide dogs for the blind. Address: (h.) 4 The Esplanade, Broughty Ferry, Dundee; T.-01382 779642.
E-mail: hughbegg@blueyonder.co.uk

Begg, Ian McKerron, DA, FRIAS, FSA Scot, FFCS. Architect (retired); Designer; b. 23.6.25, Kirkcaldy; 3 d. Educ. Kirkcaldy High School; Edinburgh College of Art. Partner, Robert Hurd & Partners, 1951-83; Interim Director, Edinburgh New Town Conservation Committee; Interim Director, Edinburgh Old Town Committee for Conservation and Renewal. Honorary Member, Saltire Society. Recreations: travel; supporting Scotland's identity. Address: Ravens'Craig, Plockton, Ross-shire IV52 8UB; T.-01599 544 265; e-mail: ianbegg@ravenscraig.me.uk

Begg, William Kirkwood, OBE. Retired former Chairman and Managing Director, Begg, Cousland Holdings Ltd.; Former Chairman, Begg Cousland & Co. Ltd.; b. 5.2.34; m., Thia St Clair; 2 s.; 1 d. Educ. Glenalmond College. Former Chairman, Scottish Advisory Committee on Telecommunications; former Member, CBI SME Council; former Privy Council Nominee to General Convocation, Strathclyde University; former Director, Weavers' Society of Anderston; Founder Trustee, Dallas Benevolent Fund; Chairman of Trustees, James Paterson Trust; former Director (and former Vice Chairman), The Wise Group;

former Director, Commercially Wise Ltd.; former Director, Merchants' House of Glasgow; former Member, Scottish Industrial Development Advisory Board; former Member, CBI Council for Scotland; former Convener of Trustees, the George Craig Trust Fund. Recreations: sailing; shooting; DIY. Address: (h.) 12 Hughenden Gardens, Glasgow G12 9XW.

Beggs, Professor Jean Duthie, CBE, PhD, BSc, FRS, FRSE. Professor of Molecular Biology, Edinburgh University, since 1999; Royal Society Darwin Trust Research Professor, since 2005; b. 16.4.50, Glasgow; m., Dr Ian Beggs; 2s. Educ. Glasgow High School for Girls; Glasgow University. Post-doctoral Fellow, University of Edinburgh, 1974-77; Post-doctoral Fellow, ARC Plant Breeding Institute, Cambridge, 1977-79; Lecturer, Department of Biochemistry, Imperial College of Science and Technology, London, 1979-85; Royal Society University Research Fellow, Edinburgh University, 1985-89; Royal Society Cephalosporin Fund Senior Research Fellow, University of Edinburgh. 1989-99; Edinburgh University Professorial Research Fellow, 1994-99; Beit Memorial Fellowship, 1976-79; Elected Member, EMBO, 1991; Member various committees of Royal Society (London and Edinburgh), Biochemical Society, RNA Society; Royal Society Gabor Medal, 2003; Biochemical Society Novartis Medal, 2004; University of Edinburgh Chancellor's Award, 2005; Vice President, Royal Society of Edinburgh, 2009-2012. Recreations: walking; skiing; scuba diving. Address: (b.) Institute of Cell Biology, Wellcome Trust Centre for Cell Biology, Edinburgh University, King's Buildings, Mayfield Road, Edinburgh, EH9 3JR; T.-0131-650 5351.

Belch, Professor Jill J. F., MD (Hons), FRCP, FMEdSci, FRSE. Professor and Director of The Institute of Cardiovascular Research; Dean of Research, Medical School, University of Dundee; NHS Tayside R&D Director; b. 22.10.52, Glasgow. Educ. Morrison's Academy, Crieff; University of Glasgow. University of Glasgow and Royal Infirmary: Research Fellow, 1980, Lecturer, 1984; University of Dundee and Ninewells Hospital: Senior Lecturer, 1987, Reader, 1990, Professor, 1996. Publications: over 350 peer-reviewed articles in scientific journals. Recreations: family; skiing. Address: (b.) Division of Cardiovascular and Diabetes Medicine, Medical Research Institute, Ninewells Hospital and Medical School, Dundee DD1 9SY; T.-01382 383092.

Belcher, Professor Claire Alice, BSocSc, MPhil, PhD, FCA. Professor of Law, University of Dundee, since 2000; Non-Executive Director, NHS Education for Scotland, since 2006; b. 11.12.59, Stoke-on-Trent; 2 s.; 3 d. Educ. Congleton County Grammar School for Girls; Keele University; University of Cambridge; University of Manchester. Trained as Chartered Accountant with KPMG (then PMM & Co); University of Keele: Lecturer in Accounting, PhD part-time, Lecturer in Law; Senior Lecturer in Law, University of Dundee. Publishes in the field of corporate governance; Directors' decisions and the law, 2013 (book). Led AHRC network for research on institutional governance. Address: (b.) School of Law, University of Dundee, Dundee DD1 4HN.
E-mail: c.a.belcher@dundee.ac.uk

Belhaven and Stenton, 13th Lord (Robert Anthony Carmichael Hamilton); b. 27.2.27. Succeeded to title, 1961.

Bell, Sheriff Andrew Montgomery, BL. Sheriff of Lothian and Borders, at Edinburgh, 1990-2004 (Sheriff of Glasgow and Strathkelvin, at Glasgow, 1984-90); b. 21.2.40, Edinburgh; m., Ann Margaret Robinson; 1 s.; 1 d. Educ. Royal High School, Edinburgh; Edinburgh University. Solicitor, 1961-74; called to Bar, 1975; Sheriff of South Strathclyde, Dumfries and Galloway, at Hamilton, 1979-84. Address: (h.) 5 York Road, Edinburgh EH5 3EJ; T.-0131-552 3859.

Bell, Christopher Philip, BMus, MMus. Conductor/Chorusmaster; Chorus Director; b. 1.5.61, Belfast. Educ. Royal Belfast Academical Inst.; Edinburgh University. Chorus Master/Director: Edinburgh University Musical Society Choir, 1984-88, Edinburgh Royal Choral Union, 1987-90, Royal Scottish National Orchestra Chorus, 1989-2004, Royal Scottish National Orchestra Junior Chorus, since 1995, Belfast Philharmonic Choir, 2005-2011. Chorus Director, Grant Park Chorus, Chicago, USA, since 2002; Artistic Director: Total Aberdeen Youth Choir, 1992-96, National Youth Choir of Scotland, since 1996, Ulster Youth Choir, 1999-2003, Children's Classic Concerts, 2002-08. Associate Conductor, BBC Scottish Symphony Orchestra, 1987-89; Principal Guest Conductor, State Orchestra of Victoria, Melbourne, 1997-99; Associate Conductor, Ulster Orchestra, since 2009. Guest conductor with various orchestras and choirs annually. Publications: Author, My Voice is Changing; Co-Author: Go for Bronze; Go for Silver, Go for Gold; General Editor, SingBronze, Sing Silver, SingGold. Recordings: Mahler *Symphony no 3*, Chandos; Paray *Joan of Arc Mass*, Reference. Grammy Nomination 1999; Britten Ceremony of Carols (Signum); The Pulitzer Project (Cedille); *Burns Sequence: There's Lilt in the Song*, NYCoS; Holst *The Planets, Naxos;* A Family Christmas (Signum). Scotsman of the Year - Creative Talent, 2001; Charles Groves Prize, 2003. Master of the University (Open Univ, hon) 2009. Address: 2F1/143 Warrender Park Road, Edinburgh EH9 1DT; T.-07712 050295; e-mail: bellman@ednet.co.uk

Bell, Colin John, MA (Hons), HonLLD (Aberdeen). Broadcaster; Journalist; Author; b. 1.4.38, London; m., Caroline Rose Bell; 1 s.; 3 d. Educ. St. Paul's School; King's College, Cambridge. Journalist, The Scotsman, 1960-62 and 1975-78; Journalist/Contributor, London Life, Sunday Times, Sunday Telegraph, Daily Mirror, Sunday Mail, etc.; Lecturer, Morley College, 1965-68; College Supervisor, King's College, Cambridge, 1968-75; Parliamentary candidate (SNP), West Edinburgh, 1979; European Parliamentary candidate (SNP), North East Scotland, 1979; Vice-Chairman, SNP, 1978-84; Campaign Director, Euro Election, 1984; a Senior Fellow, the 21st Century Trust, 1990; Rector, Aberdeen University, 1991-93. Publications: City Fathers, 1969; Boswell's Johnson, 1971; Scotch Whisky, 1985; Radical Alternative (Contributor), 1978; The Times Reports (Series) (Editor); Scotland's Century, 1999; Murder Trail, 2002. Recreations: jazz; Scottish history.

Bell, Professor Derek, BSc, MBChB, MD, FRCP(E), FRCP(L), FRCP(G), FSAM. President, Royal College of Physicians Edinburgh; Professor of Acute Medicine, Imperial College London; Director, NIHR CLAHRC; previously National Clinical Lead, Emergency Services Collaborative (England); National Clinical Lead, Unscheduled Care Collaborative (Scotland); b. 24.3.55, Dundee; m., Sonya R. Lam; 1 s.; 2 d. Educ. Morgan Academy; Edinburgh University. Qualified in medicine, Edinburgh University, 1980; trained in general and respiratory medicine, Royal Infirmary of Edinburgh, until 1988; moved to London and became a Consultant and Clinical Director of Chest Medicine and Intensive Care before returning to Edinburgh, 1996, to develop acute medicine; Past President, Society for Acute

Medicine (UK). Recreation: youth and veteran international hockey player. Address: (h.) 14 Wilton Road, Edinburgh EH16 5JX.
E-mail: d.bell@imperial.ac.uk

Bell, Malcolm John, Cert (Natural Sci), Cert (Fire Investigation) Edin. Convener, Shetland Islands Council, since 2012; Elected Member of Shetland Islands Council for Lerwick North and Bressay (Independent), since 2012; Trustee, Shetland Charitable Trust, since 2012; Chair, NHS Shetland Endowment Committee, since 2012; Member, Northern Community Justice Authority, since 2012; Honorary Sheriff, Sheriffdom of Grampian, Highlands and Islands at Lerwick, since 2010; Non Executive Director, NHS Shetland, since 2010; Trustee, Shetland Citizens Advice Bureau, since 2012; Trustee, The Shetland Trust, since 2012; Chair, Hunter and Morrison Trust, since 2012; ex officio member of Lerwick and Bressay Community Councils, since 2012; b. 10.01.64, Lerwick; m., Moira Simpson; 2 s. Educ. Anderson High School, Lerwick; The Open University; University of Edinburgh. Scottish Police College. Interim General Manager, COPE Ltd, Shetland, 2010-12; Independent Convener, Shetland Adult Protection Committee, 2010-12; Chair, Shetland Community Health and Care Partnership, 2010-12; Police Officer in Northern Constabulary, 1980-2009; promoted Detective Sergeant and Scientific Support Manager for Northern Constabulary, 1996; promoted to Inspector in 2000 and Deputy Area Commander for Shetland; promoted to Chief Inspector and Area Commander Shetland, 2006; appointed Deputy Divisional Commander for Northern Division of Northern Constabulary, 2008; Member: Amnesty International, National Association of Retired Police Officers, Retired Police Officers Association Scotland (RPOAS). Recreations: reading; photography; travel; cooking; cinema. Address: (b.) Town Hall, Lerwick, Shetland ZE1 0HB; T.-01595 744544; e-mail: malcolm.bell@shetland.gov.uk; Twitter: @malcolm_bell

Bell, Patrick Ian, BA (Hons). Partner, Shepherd and Wedderburn LLP, since 2007; b. 22.3.67, Edinburgh; m., Karen Jane (nee White); 2 s.; 1 d. Educ. The Edinburgh Academy; Trinity College, Glenalmond; St. Chad's College, University of Durham; Guildford Law College. Linklaters & Paines, London: Trainee Solicitor, 1991-93, Assistant Solicitor, 1993-95; Assistant Solicitor, Linklaters & Paines, Singapore, 1995-98; Managing Associate, Linklaters & Alliance, London, 1998-2001; Partner: Linklaters, Warsaw, 2001-05, McClure Naismith, Solicitors, 2005-07. Finance Law Specialist with wide banking and capital markets experience; Member: Law Society of England and Wales (1996), Court of Directors, The Edinburgh Academy (2006-2012), Salmon & Trout Association (Scotland) (1993), New Club (2006), Wooden Spoon Society (2007). Recreations: fishing; tennis; skiing; history. Address: (b.) 1 Exchange Crescent, Conference Square, Edinburgh EH3 8UL; T.-0131 473 5355.
E-mail: patrick.bell@shepwedd.co.uk

Bell, Robin, MA, MSc. Writer, Broadcaster and Artist; b. 4.1.45, Dundee; m. (1), Suzette Von Feldau (divorced 1996) (2), Eirwen Bengough (deceased 2014); 2 d.; 5 gc. Educ. Morrison's Academy, Crieff; St. Andrews University; Perugia University, Italy; Union College, New York; Columbia University, New York. Formerly: Director of Information, City University of New York, Regional Opportunity Program; Assistant Professor, John Jay College of Criminal Justice, City University of New York; Member, US Office of Education Task Force in Educational Technology; Audio-Visual Editor, Oxford University Press; Editor, Guidebook series to Ancient Monuments of Scotland; Secretary, Poetry Association of

Scotland. Television and Radio Industries of Scotland Award for Best Radio Feature, 1984; Sony Award, Best British Radio Documentary, 1985; Creative Scotland Award, 2005. Publications: The Invisible Mirror, 1965; Culdee, Culdee, 1966; Collected Poems of James Graham, Marquis of Montrose (Editor), 1970; Sawing Logs, 1980; Strathinver: A Portrait Album 1945-53, 1984; Radio Poems, 1989; The Best of Scottish Poetry (Editor), 1989; Bittersweet Within My Heart: collected poems of Mary Queen of Scots (Translator/Editor), 1992; Scanning the Forth Bridge, 1994; Le Château des Enfants, 2000; Chapeau!, 2001; Civil Warrior, 2002; Tethering a Horse, 2004; How To Tell Lies, 2006; Auchterarder, Strathearn's Royal Burgh, 2008; Behind You, 2011; Ruchill Linn (with music by Gabriel Jackson), 2012; Set On A Hill: A Strategic View Over Scottish History, 2012; Art exhibitions: My River, Your River (following the 2005 Gleneagles G8); Drawing The Tay (Travelling solo exhibition); Strathearn: A Celebration (permanent heritage exhibition at Gleneagles Station), 2015. Address: (h.) The Orchard, Muirton, Auchterarder PH3 1ND.

Bell, Tom, MSc, Ch. EHO FREHIS, MIFEH. Chief Executive, The Royal Environmental Health Institute of Scotland (REHIS), since 2004; b. 15.9.58, Edinburgh; m., Angela; 2 d. Educ. Leith Academy, Edinburgh; Napier College and The University of Edinburgh. Qualified as an Environmental Health Officer, 1980; Corporate Membership of REHIS, 1983; gained MSc in Environmental Health, University of Edinburgh, 1993; Training Adviser to REHIS, 1998, Director of Professional Development to REHIS, 1999; Chartered Environmental Health Officer status gained, 2004, Elected Fellow of REHIS, 2008. Honorary Fellow, The University of Edinburgh, 1994-98; Honorary Member, Malawi Environmental Health Association, 2010; Member of the International Federation of Environmental Health, 2013; Member of The Council, REHIS, 1994-98; Hon. Treasurer, REHIS, 1995-98. Recreations: sport; travel; family life. Address: (b.) 19 Torphichen Street, Edinburgh EH3 8HX; T.-0131 229 2968; e-mail: tb@rehis.com

Bellars, Wendy Ann, MA (Hons) Glas, DipEd, PGCE, MA (Ed Man) De Montfort. Head, Queen Victoria School, Dunblane, since 2007; b. 25.12.60, Glasgow; divorced. Educ. Hillhead High School, Glasgow; University of Glasgow. Teacher of English: Renfrew High School, 1983-85, Gordonstoun School, 1985-88, The King's School, Chester, 1988-95 (also Head of Department); Deputy Head, Bishop's Stortford College, 1995-2000; Principal, St. Leonard's School, 2001-03; Housemistress, Cheltenham Ladies' College, 2003-04; Staff Tutor, The Open University in Scotland, 2005-06. Recreations: reading; theatre; music; walking the dogs. Address: (b.) Queen Victoria School, Dunblane FK15 0JY; T.-0131 310 2901.
E-mail: head@qvs.org.uk

Belton, Professor Valerie, PhD, MA, BSc (Hons). Professor of Management Science, University of Strathclyde, since 1999, Associate Deputy Principal (Education); President, EURO (European Federation of Operational Research Societies), 2009-2010; President, UK Operational Research Society, 2004-06; b. 9.8.56, Rotherham. Educ. Wath upon Dearne School; Durham University; Lancaster University, Cambridge University. Operational Research Analyst, Civil Aviation Authority; Academic, University of Kent, 1984-88; Academic, University of Strathclyde, since 1988. Chair, International Society of Multicriteria Decision Making, 2000-04; Editor, Journal of Multicriteria Decision Analysis; author of a book and many academic articles. Recreations: orienteering; mountain biking. Address: (b.) University of Strathclyde,

Management Science, 40 George Street, Glasgow G1 1QE; T.-0141-548 3615; e-mail: val.belton@strath.ac.uk

Bennett, Professor Mark, BA, PhD, AcSS. Emeritus Professor of Developmental Psychology, University of Dundee, since 2015; b. 12.10.56, Bangkok, Thailand; m., Ann Warren; 1 s. Educ. Farnborough Grammar School; University of Reading; LSE. Lecturer: University of Durham, 1982-85, Roehampton Institute, London, 1985-91, University of Dundee, since 1991, also Reader, then Professor. Editor of the journal Infant & Child Development, 2001-2010; elected to the Academy of Social Sciences, 2006. Major Publications: The Child as Psychologist, 1993; Developmental Psychology: Achievements & Prospects, 1999; The Development of the Social Self (Co-Author), 2004. Recreations: hill-walking; cycling; music. Address: School of Psychology, University of Dundee, Dundee DD1 4HN; T.-01382 384631; e-mail: m.bennett@dundee.ac.uk

Bennett, Robin Alexander George, MA, LLB. Retired solicitor; b. 6.6.40, Edinburgh; m., Mary Funk; 2 d. Educ. Hillhead High School, Glasgow; Glasgow University. Assistant: Harrisons and Crosfield, Malaysia and Brunei, 1965-78, Solicitor, Drummond Johnstone and Grosset, Cupar, 1978-80. Partner: Drummond Cook and Mackintosh, Cupar, 1980-90, Wallace and Bennett, 1990-92, Bennetts, Cupar, 1992-2010. Consultant with Murray Donald Drummond Cook LLP, 2010-11. Chairman, Tranquilliser Addiction Solicitors Group, 1988-90; Founder/Secretary, Scottish TSB Depositors Association, 1986; Chairman, Ceres and District Community Council, 1980-82 and 1993-98; Member of the Executive, then Director, Scottish Legal Action Group, 1980-2011 (Vice Chair, 1989-95); Trustee, The Lady Margaret Skiffington Trust, 2004-2015 (Chair, 2004-2013); Honorary Sheriff, Cupar, 1991-2014. Recreations: hill-walking; water gardening; listening to organ music. Address: (h.) Sandakan, Curling Pond Road, Ceres, Fife KY15 5NB; T.-01334 828452; e-mail: ragbennett@yahoo.com

Bennie, Dr Peter. Chair, BMA Scotland, since 2014; consultant psychiatrist. Educ. Glasgow University Medical School. Trained in hospitals in the west of Scotland before taking up a consultant post in Glasgow in 1997, moving to work in Paisley in 2007; former chairman of the BMA's Representative Body. Address: BMA Scotland, 14 Queen Street, Edinburgh EH2 1LL; T.- 0131 247 3030.

Bennison, Dr Jennifer Marion, MA, MSc, MBBChir, FRCGP. Executive Officer (Quality), Scottish Council, Royal College of General Practitioners, since 2012; Assistant Director of Postgraduate General Practice Education, South East Scotland, 2006-2014; General Practitioner; GP Partner, Rose Garden Medical Centre, Edinburgh, since 1998; b. Essex; divorced; 2 s.; 2 d. Educ. Hertfordshire and Essex High School for Girls; Corpus Christi College, Cambridge; Royal Free Hospital School of Medicine, London. GP Principal, Leith Walk Surgery, Edinburgh, 1993-98; Director, Phased Evaluation Programme, RCGP Scotland, 1999-2002; former Deputy Chairman (Policy), Scottish Council, Royal College of General Practitioners. Recreations: children; walking; singing. Address: (b.) Rose Garden Medical Centre, 4 Mill Lane, Leith, Edinburgh EH6 6TL; T.-0131-554 1274.
E-mail: Jenny.Bennison@lothian.scot.nhs.uk

Bentley, Professor Michael, BA, PhD, FRHistS. Emeritus Professor of Modern History, St Andrews University; b. 12.8.48, Rotherham; 1 s.; 1 d. Educ.

Oakwood School, Rotherham; Sheffield University; St John's College, Cambridge. Lecturer in History, Sheffield University, 1971-95. Publications: The Liberal Mind; Politics without Democracy; Climax of Liberal Politics; Companion to Historiography; Modern Historiography; Lord Salisbury's World; Modernizing England's Past; The Life and Thought of Herbert Butterfield. Recreations: reading; piano. Address: (b.) Christ Church, Oxford OX1 1DP; T.-01865 286077; e-mail: michael.bentley@st-andrews.ac.uk

Berry, Professor Christopher Jon, BA, PhD, FRSE. Honorary Professorial Research Fellow, (Emeritus Professor [Political Theory]), Glasgow University; b. 19.6.46, St. Helens; m., Christine; 2 s. Educ. Upholland Grammar School; Nottingham and LSE. Lecturer, then Senior Lecturer, then Reader, then Professor, Department of Politics, University of Glasgow. Author of 7 books and over 50 other academic publications. Recreation: contemporary literature. Address: (b.) Adam Smith Building, The University, Glasgow G12 8RT; T.-0141 330 5064; e-mail: christopher.berry@glasgow.ac.uk

Berry, David S., BSc (Hons) Phys (Edin). Leader, East Lothian Council, 2007-2010; b. 13.4.48, London. Educ. North Berwick High; University of Edinburgh. Honeywell Information Systems, London, 1971-73; Siemens AG, Munich, Germany, 1973-77; Applied Computer Systems, Sunnyvale, California, 1977-82; Product Planning Manager, AMD, Sunnyvale, California, 1982-88; Marketing Manager, Adaptec, Milpitas, California, 1988-93; Loch Moy Ltd., Database Consultancy, Edinburgh, since 1993; Proprietor, GoForth Tours, since March 2013. Elected Member, East Lothian Council, since 1999. Board Member, SEPA, 2002-09; Convener, Association of Nationalist Councillors, 2005-2010; Member, National Executive, SNP, 2006-2013 (resigned from SNP, March 2013). Nominated Herald Local Politician of the Year, 2010. Recreations: film; history; marine watersports. Address: (b.) East Lothian Council, John Muir House, Haddington EH41 3HA; T.-01620 827821; e-mail: dberry@eastlothian.gov.uk

Berry, William, MA, LLB, DL, WS. Formerly Senior Governor and Chancellor's Assessor, St. Andrews University; Partner and Chairman, Murray Beith Murray, WS, Edinburgh, 1967-2004; Chairman: Scottish Life Assurance Co., Inchcape Family Investments Ltd; Director: Scottish American Investment Co. Plc, Fleming Continental European Investment Trust Plc, Alliance Trust plc, Second Alliance Trust plc, Dawnfresh Holdings Ltd, and other companies; b. 26.9.39, Newport-on-Tay; m., Elizabeth Margery Warner; 2 s. Educ. Ardvreck, Crieff; Eton College; St. Andrews University; Edinburgh University. Interests in farming, forestry, etc. Depute Chairman, Edinburgh Festival Society, 1985-89; Deputy Lieutenant, Fife, 2007-2014; Chairman, New Town Concerts Society Ltd; Trustee/Board Member of many charities and cultural bodies. Performer in three records of Scottish country dance music. Recreations: music; shooting; forestry; conservation. Address: Tayfield House, Newport-on-Tay, Fife DD6 8HA.

Bevan, Professor John Stuart, BSc (Hons), MBChB (Hons), MD, FRCP (Edin). Consultant Physician and Endocrinologist, Aberdeen Royal Infirmary, since 1991; Honorary Senior Clinical Lecturer, Aberdeen University (1991), Honorary Reader in Endocrinology (2006), Honorary Professor in Endocrinology (2009); Member, Clinical Committee, Society for Endocrinology, since 1997; Visiting Endocrinologist to Orkney Islands, since 1994; b. 18.9.53, Portsmouth; m., Sheena Mary; 2 s.; 2 d. Educ.

Portsmouth Northern Grammar School; Dunfermline High School; Edinburgh University. Registrar in Endocrinology, Radcliffe Infirmary, Oxford, 1981-83; Medical Research Council Training Fellow in Endocrinology, Oxford, 1984-86; Senior Registrar in Medicine and Endocrinology, University Hospital of Wales, Cardiff, 1987-90; Associate Editor, Clinical Endocrinology, 1994-2004, Senior Editor, since 2008; Member, Specialist Advisory Committee for Endocrinology and Diabetes, 1998-2002; Council Member, Royal College of Physicians of Edinburgh, 2006-2012; Chair, Scottish Paediatric Endocrinology, Managed Clinical Network, 2010-12. Publications: papers on clinical neuroendocrinology, particularly the treatment of human pituitary tumours. Recreations: cricket; guitar; ornithology. Address: (b.) JJR Macleod Centre for Endocrinology & Diabetes, Aberdeen Royal Infirmary, Foresterhill, Aberdeen AB25 2ZP; T.-01224 554437; e-mail: johnbevan@nhs.net

Beveridge, Stuart Gordon Nicholas, LLB (Hons), DipLP, NP. Partner, Grant Smith Law Practice, since 2001; b. 19.3.68, Edinburgh. Educ. George Heriot's School; Daniel Stewart's and Melville College; Edinburgh University. Traineeship, Campbell Smith and Co., Solicitors, Edinburgh; Legal Adviser, Citizen's Advice Bureau, Edinburgh; Oddbins Wine Merchants; Aberdein Considine and Co., Aberdeen (Partner, 1998-2001). President, Aberdeen Bar Association, 2001-02 (Committee Member, 1995-2003). Recreations: wine; cooking; cinema; failing to finish DIY projects. Address: (b.) Amicable House, 252 Union Street, Aberdeen AB10 1TN; T.-01224 621620.

Bewsher, Colonel Harold Frederick, LVO, OBE. Vice-President, The Atlantic Salmon Trust (Chairman, 1995-2005); Vice Chairman, Association of Deer Management Groups in Scotland, 2001-2012 (Member, Executive Committee, since 1998); Chairman, The Airborne Initiative (Scotland) Ltd., 1995-98; Lieutenant, The Queen's Bodyguard for Scotland (Royal Company of Archers) (Secretary, 1982-94); Captain of Shooting, 2003/06/09, Queen's Prize Winner, 2001, 2006; b. 13.1.29, Glasgow; m., Susan Elizabeth Cruickshank; 2 s. Educ. Merchiston Castle School; Royal Technical College; Glasgow University; Royal Military Academy, Sandhurst. The Royal Scots, 1949-72; Operational Service in Korea, Port Said and Suez, South Arabia, Radfam and Aden, Staff College, 1961, Joint Services Staff College, 1966; DS Staff College, 1967-69, CO Scottish Infantry Training Regiment, 1969-71; Colonel GS Military Operations, MOD, 1971-72. Director-General, Scotch Whisky Association, 1973-94. Chairman, New Club, Edinburgh, 1981-82; Chairman, Scottish Society for the Employment of Ex-Regular Soldiers, Sailors and Airmen, 1973-83; Freeman, City of London, 1992; Liveryman, Worshipful Company of Distillers, 1993. Recreations: outdoors — salmon fishing, field sports, deer stalking. Address: 33 Blacket Place, Edinburgh EH9 1RJ; T.-0131-667 4600.

Bezuidenhout, Rev. Louis Christiaan, MA, DD. Minister, Kinloss and Findhorn Church of Scotland, since 2014; formerly Minister: Church of Scotland, Kirkmichael, Tinwald & Torthorwald; b. 9.7.54. Johannesburg, South Africa; m., Elsie; 1 s.; 1 d. Educ. Hartswater Secondary School, South Africa; University of Pretoria, South Africa. Lecturer, Semitic Languages, University of Pretoria, 1977-78; Minister of Religion, Dutch Reformed Church, South Africa, 1978-84; Senior Lecturer, Semitic Languages, University of Pretoria, 1984-89; Visiting Scholar, University of St. Andrews, 1989-90; Minister of Religion, Stellenbosch, South Africa, 1990-97; Professor and Head of Department of Biblical Studies, Pretoria, 1997-2000. Published 41 scientific and popular scientific articles on Hebrew literature, Akkadian literature and theology.

Recreations: painting; photography. Address: Findhorn Road, Kinloss, Forres, Moray IV36 6TX; T.-01309 690162.

Bezuidenhout, Willem Jacobus, BA, BD, NHED, MEd. Minister, Church of Scotland (Parish of Kirkmichael, Tinwald and Torthorwald), since 2007; b. 14.8.53, Johannesburg, South Africa; m., Hazel; 1 s.; 1 d. Educ. Hartswater High School, South Africa; Pretoria University; Johannesburg University. Ordination as Minister, Dutch Reformed Church, 1977; Senior Liaison Officer, Foreign Office, Namibia, 1989-90; Senior Liaison Officer, State President's Office, Cape Town, South Africa, 1990-92; English Teacher, Vorentoe High School, Johannesburg, 1992-2000; Minister, St Andrews Presbyterian Church, Pretoria, 2000-07. University of Pretoria: Dux Awards: 1976, 1977; University of Johannesburg, 1994: Gold Medal; South African Education Association: Top Student, RSA. Recreations: photography; hiking; volleyball; music; film. Address: (h.) The Manse of Tinwald, Tinwald, Dumfries DG1 3PL; T.-01387 710246.
E-mail: willembezuidenhout@btinternet.com

Bhopal, Professor Raj Singh, CBE, DSc (hon), BSc, MBChB, MD, MPH, FFPH, FRCP (Edin). Bruce and John Usher Chair of Public Health, University of Edinburgh, since 1999 (Head, Division of Community Health Sciences, 2000-03); Honorary Consultant in Public Health Medicine, Lothian Health Board, since 1999; b. 10.4.53, Moga, Punjab, India; m., Roma; 4 s. Educ. University of Edinburgh; University of Glasgow. House Officer/Senior House Officer, medicine and surgery, 1978-82; Trainee GP, 1980; Registrar/Senior Registrar/Lecturer in Public Health Medicine, 1983-88; Senior Lecturer/Honorary Consultant in Public Health Medicine, 1988-91; Professor of Epidemiology and Public Health, University of Newcastle upon Tyne, 1991-99 (Head, Department of Epidemiology and Public Health); Non-Executive Director (Vice-Chairman), Newcastle and North Tyneside Health Authority, 1992-96; Non-Executive Director, Health Education Authority, 1998-99; Chairman, Steering Committee, National Resource Centre on Ethnic Minority Health, 2002-08; Member, MRC Health Services Research and Public Health Board, 1999-2003. Publications: Books: Concepts of Epidemiology, 2002, 2008 (2nd ed); Public Health, Past, Present and Future, 2004; The Epidemic of Coronary Heart Disease in South Asians, 2003; Ethnicity, race and health in multicultural societies, 2007 (second edition in 2014 as Migration, Ethnicity, Race and Health); over 250 papers in journals and chapters in books on Legionnaires' disease, environmental epidemiology, primary care, ethnicity and health, application of epidemiology in public health and health care. Recreations: chess; golf; hill climbing; photography; travel; music; reading. Address: (b.) Centre for Population Health Sciences, University of Edinburgh, College of Medicine and Veterinary Medicine, Teviot Place, Edinburgh EH8 9AG; T.-0131-650 3216; e-mail: raj.bhopal@ed.ac.uk

Biagi, Marco. MSP (SNP), Edinburgh Central, 2011-16; Minister for Local Government and Community Empowerment, 2014-16. Former policy adviser with SNP's parliamentary central staff, supporting all the party's MSPs. Educated at the universities of St Andrews, California (Berkeley), Oxford and Glasgow.

Bibby, Neil. MSP (Labour), West Scotland, since 2011; Chief Whip, since 2014; b. 6.9.83, Paisley. Educ. Glasgow University. Became a local councillor in Renfrewshire in 2007. Former chair of Young Labour UK. Address: (b.) Scottish Parliament, Edinburgh EH99 1SP.

Biberbach, Petra Elke, MSc, FRSA. CEO, PAS, since 2005; Member, Loch Lomond National Park Authority, since 2010, Chair, Planning and Access Committee, since 2014; b. Germany, Nuremburg; 1 s.; 1 d. Educ. Glasgow University. Trustee, Civic Trust, since 2014; Board Member, ACOSVO, since 2014; Trustee, PAS Foundation, since 2015; Board Member, Zero Waste Scotland, since 2014; Panel Member, Review of Planning in Scotland, 2015-16. Recreations: golf coach level 1; gardening; cycling; European cinema; crime; fiction. Address: 3rd Floor, 125 Princes Street, Edinburgh EH2 4AD; T.-07812 103967; e-mail: petra@pas.org.uk

Biddulph, 5th Lord (Anthony Nicholas Colin). Interior Designer and Sporting Manager; b. 8.4.59; m., Hon. Sian Gibson-Watt (divorced); 2 s. Educ. Cheltenham; RAC, Cirencester. Recreations: shooting; design; fishing; skiing; racing; painting. Address: Address: (h.) Makerstoun, Kelso TD5 7PA; T.-01573 460 234; 8 Orbel Street, London SW11 3NZ; T.-020 7228 9865.
E-mail: nickbiddulph@makerstoun.com

Biggart, Thomas Norman, CBE (1984), WS, MA, LLB. Partner, Biggart Baillie & Gifford, Solicitors, Glasgow and Edinburgh, 1959-95; b. 24.1.30; m., Eileen Jean Anne Gemmell; 1 s.; 1 d. Educ. Morrison's Academy, Crieff; Glasgow University. Royal Navy, 1954-56 (Sub-Lt., RNVR). Law Society of Scotland: Council Member, 1977-86; Vice-President, 1981-82; President, 1982-83; President, Business Archives Council, Scotland, 1977-86; Member, Executive, Scottish Council (Development and Industry), 1984-94; Member: Scottish Tertiary Education Advisory Council, 1984-87, Scottish Records Advisory Council, 1985-91; Director: Clydesdale Bank, 1985-97; Independent Insurance Group, 1986-2000 (Chairman, 1989-93); Chairman, Beechwood, Glasgow, 1989-97; Trustee, Scottish Civic Trust, 1989-97; Member, Council on Tribunals (Chairman, Scottish Committee), 1990-98; Honorary Member, American Bar Association, 1982; OStJ, 1968. Recreations: golf; hill-walking. Address: (h.) Gailes, Kilmacolm, Renfrewshire PA13 4LZ; T.-0150 587 2645.

Birch, Robert. Rector, Dalziel High School, Motherwell, since 2011; b. 24.10.61; m., Jane; 3 d. Teacher of Mathematics, 1983-92; Assistant Principal Teacher, 1992-97; Dalziel High School: Principal Teacher, 1997-2001, Assistant/Deputy Head, 2001-06; Head Teacher, Queensferry High School, 2006-2011. Address: (b.) Crawford Street, Motherwell ML1 3AG; T.-01698 274900.

Bird, Professor Colin C., CBE, Drhc (Edin), MBChB, PhD, FRCPath, FRCPE, FRCSE, FRSE, FAMS, Knight's Cross, Order of Merit (Poland) 2006. Dean, Faculty of Medicine, Edinburgh University, 1995-2002; b. 5.3.38, Kirkintilloch; m., Ailsa M. Ross; 2 s.; 1 d. Educ. Lenzie Academy; Glasgow University. McGhie Cancer Research Scholar, Glasgow Royal Infirmary, 1962-64; Lecturer in Pathology: Glasgow University, 1964-67, Aberdeen University, 1967-72; MRC Goldsmiths Travelling Fellow, Chicago, 1970-71; Senior Lecturer in Pathology, Edinburgh University, 1972-75; Professor and Head, Department of Pathology, Leeds University, 1975-86; Professor of Pathology and Head, Department of Pathology, Edinburgh University, 1986-95. Recreations: golf; hill walking; music. Address: (h.) 45 Ann Street, Edinburgh EH4 1PL.

Bird, Jackie, DLitt. Journalist; b. 31.7.62, Bellshill; 1 s.; 1 d. Educ. Earnock High School. Music/Film/Television Editor, Jackie Magazine; Radio News Reporter and Presenter, Radio Clyde; Reporter, Evening Times; Reporter, Sun; Reporter/Presenter, TVS; Presenter: Reporting Scotland, BBC Scotland's Hogmanay Live and Children in Need programmes. Address: (b.) BBC Scotland, 40 Pacific Quay, Glasgow G51 1DZ.

Birley, Tim(othy) Grahame, BSc(Eng), MSc, ACGI, FRTPI, FRSA. Independent adviser on sustainable development and public policy, since 1995; b. 13.3.47, Kent; m., Catherine Anne; 1 s.; 2 d. Educ. Sir Roger Manwood's Grammar School; Imperial College, London University; Edinburgh University. Local government, 1965-

71; academic appointments, 1973-81; Director, Energy and Environment Research, 1982-85; Scottish Office: Inquiry Reporter, 1985-87, Principal Inquiry Reporter, 1987-88, Deputy Director, Scottish Development Department, 1988-90, Head, Rural Affairs Division, 1990-95. Director, Centre for Human Ecology, Edinburgh University, 1995-96; Chair, Project Selection Panel, Millennium Forest for Scotland Trust, 1996-97; Vice-President, APRS, 1998-2003; Facilitator for government, local government, companies, NGOs and community organisations on many aspects of sustainable development and tacking climate change. Author or co-author of numerous reports including Reality Check, 2001/2 (for WWF); Mainstreaming sustainable development in regional regeneration, 2004 (for ESEP); Best Value and sustainable development toolkits for local government, 2006 (for SSN) and for the wider public services (for Scottish Executive); Mourne National Party Working Party report, 2007; Towards a Step Change in Sustainable Development Education in Scottish Schools, 2011 (for WWF). Recreation: family outings. Address: (b.) 6 Malta Terrace, Edinburgh EH4 1HR; T.-0131-332 3499.

Birss, Rev. Alan David, DL, MA (Hons), BD (Hons). Minister, Paisley Abbey, since 1988; Deputy Lieutenant of Renfrewshire, since 2015; b. 5.6.53, Ellon; m., Carol Margaret Pearson; 1 s. Educ. Glenrothes High School; St. Andrews University; Edinburgh University. Assistant Minister, Dundee Parish Church (St. Mary's), 1978-80; Minister, Inverkeithing Parish Church of St. Peter, 1982-88. Past President, Church Service Society; Past President, Scottish Church Society. Address: The Manse of Paisley Abbey, 15 Main Road, Castlehead, Paisley PA2 6AJ; T.-0141-889 3587.
E-mail: alan.birss@paisleyabbey.org.uk

Bisset, David W., FAMS, MCLIP, FSA (Scot), DEAB, FEAB. Secretary, Scottish Esperanto Association, since 1997; b. 8.8.38, Motherwell; m., Jean; 1 s.; 1 d. Educ. Dalziel High, Motherwell; University of Strathclyde. Librarian, Coatbridge Technical College, 1962-72; Head of Library Services, Bell College of Technology, Hamilton, 1972-95. Various positions within the Esperanto Movement in Scotland and Britain; Hon. Vice-President, Hamilton Civic Society. Recreations: cultural tourism; town walking; architectural history. Address: (h.) 47 Airbles Crescent, Motherwell ML1 3AP; T.-01698 263199.

Bisset, Raymond George, OBE. Provost, Aberdeenshire Council, 2003-07 (Convener, 1999-2003); Non-executive member, Aberdeen Harbour Board, 2008-10; Chairman, North East of Scotland Fisheries Partnership, 2000-07; b. 16.8.42, Ellon; m., Heather Bisset. Educ. Inverurie Academy; Aberdeen University; College of Education. Chemistry/Physics Teacher, Ellon Academy, 1963-64; Maths/General Science Teacher, Insch School, 1965-74; Head Teacher: Keithall Primary School, 1975-76; Kintore Primary and Secondary School, 1977-81; Kintore Primary School, 1981-94. Provost, Gordon District Council, 1992-96; Member, North of Scotland Water Authority (NOSWA), 1995-99; Chairman, Gordon Area Tourist Board, 1986-89, 1991-96; Hon. President, University for Children and Communities, 1999-2007; former Chairman, Inverurie and District Round Table; Founder Chairman, North East Scotland Anglers' Federation; former Hon. President, Inverurie Arthritis Society; Member, NHS (Grampian), 2001-07 and since 2009; Chairman, Nestour (VisitScotland), 2005-08; Chair of NHS (Grampian) Clinical Governance Committee, 2002-07; Chair, NHS (Grampian) Patient Focus Public Involvement Committee, 2011-12; Member, Garioch Probus Club; Chair, NHS (Grampian) Endowments Committee, since 2009; Co-Chair, Aberdeenshire Transitional Leadership Group in Adult Health and Social Care, 2013-2016; Chair of Aberdeenshire Integrated Joint Board in Adult Health and Social Care, until 2016; Chair, Aberdeenshire Community Health Partnership, 2013-15;

Member, Aberdeenshire Community Planning Board, since 2013; past Chair, Grampian Houston Association; Member, Garioch Probus Club; Honorary Member, Inverurie Angling Association and Inverurie Cricket Club; former President, Inverurie Angling Association. Recreations: angling; golf; hill walking; reading; amateur writing. Address: (h.) The Schoolhouse, Keithhall, Inverurie, Aberdeenshire AB51 0LX; T.-01467 621015.
E-mail: raymond_bisset@yahoo.co.uk

Bisset, Dr (William) Michael, BSc, MBChB, DCH, MSc, MD, FRCP, FRCPCH. Regional Medical Director, North of Scotland Planning Group, since 2015; Consultant Paediatric Gastroenterologist, since 1992; b. 17.2.56, Edinburgh; m., Amanda Bisset. Educ. George Watson's College, Edinburgh; Edinburgh University; London University. Lecturer in Paediatric Gastroenterology, 1986-92. Address: (b.) Royal Aberdeen Children's Hospital, Westburn Road, Aberdeen AB25 2ZG; T.-01224 554715.

Bisset, Alan. Author and playwright; b. 17.11.75. Educ. Falkirk High School; University of Stirling. After a short spell as a secondary school teacher at Elgin Academy, gained a Masters degree in English from the University of Stirling; wrote his first novel, Boyracers (2001); lectured in creative writing at Bretton Hall College, now part of the University of Leeds, and tutored the creative writing MLitt at the University of Glasgow; became a full-time writer in December 2007, then a playwright shortly after. His various novels and plays have been shortlisted for numerous awards, and in 2011 he was named Glenfiddich Spirit of Scotland writer of the year. In 2012, he became active in the campaign for Scottish independence. Address: A M Heath & Company Limited, Authors' Agents, 6 Warwick Court, Holborn, London WC1R 5DJ.

Bissett, Graeme. Chairman, Macfarlane Group, since 2012. Career: joined the Board of Macfarlane Group in 2004 as a Non-Executive Director; former Finance Director of International Groups and former Partner with Arthur Andersen; currently Chairman, Children 1st and Non-Executive Director of a number of listed and private companies. Member of the Council, Institute of Chartered Accountants of Scotland, became Chair of the Audit Committee in 2004, member of the Nominations Committee and the Remuneration Committee. Address: (b.) 21 Newton Place, Glasgow G3 7PY; T.-0141 333 9666.

Black, Rev. Archibald Tearlach, BSc. Chairman of Council, The Saltire Society, 1997-2001; retired Church of Scotland minister, formerly at Ness Bank Church, Inverness; b. 10.6.37, Edinburgh; m., Bridget Mary Baddeley; 2 s.; 1 d. Elected Member of Council, National Trust for Scotland, 1991-96, 1997-2002 and 2003-08; Chairman, Sorley MacLean Trust, 2000-2011. Recreations: Inverness Gaelic Choir; all the arts; the enjoyment of Scotland's natural and cultural heritage. Address: (h.) 16 Elm Park, Inverness IV2 4WN; T.-01463 230588.
E-mail: a.black236@btinternet.com

Black, Elspeth Catherine, LLB, NP. Solicitor, since 1973; Honorary Sheriff, Dunoon, since 1997; b. 25.10.50, Kilmarnock; m., James Anthony Black; 1 s.; 1 d. Educ. Kilmarnock Academy; Glasgow University. Apprentice, then Assistant, Wright, Johnston and McKenzie, Glasgow, 1971-74; Assistant, Messers Wm. J. Cuthbert and Hogg, Fort William, 1974-75; Assistant, then Partner, Kenneth W. Pendreich and Co. Dunoon, 1975-87; Partner, Elspeth C. Black and Co., Dunoon and Anderson Banks and Co., Oban, Fort William and Balivanich, 1987-98; Partner,

Corrigall Black, Dunoon, since 1998; accredited Child Law Specialist. Recreations: swimming coaching (Chief Coach, Dunoon ASC); running/fitness training. Address: (b.) 20 John Street, Dunoon; T.-01369 704777.

Black, Mhairi. MP (SNP), Paisley and Renfrewshire South, since 2015; b. 12.9.94. Educ. University of Glasgow. Baby of the House and the youngest MP since the Reform Act of 1832. Address: House of Commons, London SW1A 0AA.

Black, Professor Robert, QC, LLB (Hons), LLM, FRSA, FRSE, FFCS, FHEA. Professor of Scots Law, Edinburgh University, since 1981 (Emeritus, since 2005); Temporary Sheriff, 1981-94; b. 12.6.47, Lockerbie. Educ. Lockerbie Academy; Dumfries Academy; Edinburgh University; McGill University, Montreal. Advocate, 1972; Lecturer in Scots Law, Edinburgh University, 1972-75; Senior Legal Officer, Scottish Law Commission, 1975-78; practised at Scottish bar, 1978-81; QC, 1987; General Editor, The Laws of Scotland: Stair Memorial Encyclopaedia, 1988-96 (formerly Deputy and Joint General Editor). Publications: An Introduction to Written Pleading, 1982; Civil Jurisdiction: The New Rules, 1983; various articles on the Lockerbie disaster. Recreation: blogging on Lockerbie: http://lockerbiecase.blogspot.com. Address: (h.) 6/4 Glenogle Road, Edinburgh EH3 5HW; T.-0131-557 3571; 4 Vygie Street, Middelpos 8193, Northern Cape, South Africa; T.-+27 (0)799 308368.
E-mail: rblackqc@gmail.com

Black, Robert William, CBE, MA (Hons, Econ), MSc (Town Planning), MSc (Public Policy), LLD, FRSE, FRSA. Auditor General for Scotland, 2000-2012; b. 6.11.46, Banff; m., Doreen Mary Riach; 3 s.; 1 d. Educ. Robert Gordon's College, Aberdeen; Aberdeen University; Heriot-Watt University; Strathclyde University. Nottinghamshire County Council, 1971-73; City of Glasgow Corporation, 1973-75; Strathclyde Regional Council, 1975-85; Chief Executive: Stirling District Council, 1985-90, Tayside Regional Council, 1990-95; Controller of Audit, Accounts Commission for Scotland, 1995-99. Former Fellow, Royal Statistical Society (resigned in 2012); Hon. Doctor of Law, University of Aberdeen, 2004; Hon. Doctor of Business Administration, Queen Margaret University College, 2006; Fellow of the Royal Society of Edinburgh (FRSE), 2006; Honorary Member of the Chartered Institute of Public Finance; Lay Member of Court, University of Edinburgh, 2012; Public Interest Member, Institute of Chartered Accountants of Scotland (ICAS), 2012; Board Member, The British Library, 2012; Chairman, Scottish Commission on Housing and Wellbeing, since 2013; Fellow of the Royal Society of Arts (FRSA). Recreations: the outdoors and the arts. E-mail: robertwblack@me.com

Black, Professor Sue Margaret, OBE, BSc, PhD, DSc, FRSE, FRAI, FRCPEdin, FRSB, HFRCPSG, CertFA-I. Deputy Principal for Public Engagement, University of Dundee, since 2013; Director of The Centre for Anatomy and Human Identification, University of Dundee, since 2003; Director, Centre for International Forensic Assistance, since 2002; b. 7.5.61, Inverness; m., Tom Black; 3 d. Educ. Inverness Royal Academy; University of Aberdeen. Lecturer in Anatomy, Guy's and St. Thomas' Hospitals, 1986-92; Consultant in Forensic Anthropology, University of Glasgow, 1992-2000; Head of Profession in Kosovo for Foreign and Commonwealth Office, 1999-2000; Director, Centre for International Forensic Assistance; DVI (Disaster Victim Identification) national training programme co-ordinator. Certified Forensic Anthropologist; RAI Medal, 2008; Police Commendation, 2008. Publications:

Developmental Juvenile Osteology, 2000; The Juvenile Skeleton, 2004. Recreation: writer. Address: (b.) Centre for Anatomy and Human Identification, University of Dundee, Dundee DD1 5EH; T.-01382 385776; e-mail: s.m.black@dundee.ac.uk

Blackadder, Elizabeth, DBE, RA, RSA. Artist; Her Majesty's Painter and Limner in Scotland, since 2001; b. 24.9.31, Falkirk. Educ. Falkirk High School; Edinburgh University; Edinburgh College of Art. Lecturer, School of Drawing and Painting, Edinburgh College of Art, 1962-86; first Scottish woman painter elected full member, Royal Academy and Royal Scottish Academy. Honorary Doctorates: Heriot Watt University, University of Strathclyde, University of Edinburgh, University of Aberdeen, University of Glasgow, University of Stirling, University of St. Andrews, University of London.

Blackford, Ian. MP (SNP), Ross, Skye and Lochaber, since 2015; b. 14.5.61; m., Ann. Educ. The Royal High School, Edinburgh. Career: 20 years in the financial industry; analyst with NatWest Securities, before moving to a managerial role; ran Deutsche Bank's operations in Scotland and the Netherlands; formed consultancy business First Seer in 2002; joined the Dutch baking products company CSM in 2005 as an investor relations manager; appointed non-executive chairman of the Edinburgh-based telecommunications firm Commsworld in 2006. Trustee, Golden Charter Trust; formerly chairman of the Glendale Trust; formerly a member of the FlySkye group, campaigning to bring commercial air services back to Skye; formerly National Treasurer of the Scottish National Party. Prominent supporter of Hibs football club. Address: House of Commons, London SW1A 0AA.

Blackie, Professor John Walter Graham, BA (Cantab), LLB (Edin). Professor of Law, Strathclyde University, since 1991, Emeritus, since 2009; Advocate, since 1974; b. 2.10.46, Glasgow; m., Jane Ashman. Educ. Uppingham School; Peterhouse, Cambridge; Harvard; Merton College, Oxford; Edinburgh University. Open Exhibitioner, Peterhouse, Cambridge, 1965-68; St. Andrews Society of New York Scholar, Harvard, 1968-69; practised at Scottish bar, 1974-75; Edinburgh University: Lecturer, 1975-88, Senior Lecturer in Scots Law, 1988-91. Director, Blackie & Son Ltd., publishers, 1970-93. Recreations: music, particularly horn playing; sailing, particularly classic boats. Address: (h.) 23 Russell Place, Edinburgh EH5 3HW.

Blacklock, Telfer George, MA, LLB, DipLP, NP. Partner, Blacklocks Solicitors, since 1992; b. 3.3.58, Edinburgh; m., Mairead; 4 s. Educ. St. Marks, Swaziland; George Heriots, Edinburgh; Edinburgh University. Balfour & Manson, 1982-92. Recreations: golf; bridge; cinema; cooking. Address: (b.) 89 Constitution Street, Edinburgh EH6 7AS; T.-0131 555 7500; e-mail: tgb@blacklocks.co.uk

Blackman, Kirsty. MP (SNP) Aberdeen North, since 2015; b. 1986; m., Luke Blackman; 2 c. Elected to Aberdeen City Council as an SNP councillor in the Hilton/Stockethill ward, in the Aberdeen North constituency in the Aberdeen City Council election, 2007, re-elected in 2012; became Convener of the SNP in Aberdeen City Council. Address: House of Commons, London SW1A 0AA.

Blackmore, Professor Stephen, CBE, BSc, PhD, CBE, FRSE, FLS, FRSB, CBiol. Chair, Darwin Initiative, Darwin Expert Committee, since 2015; Her Majesty's Botanist in Scotland, since 2010; Visiting Professor, Glasgow University, since 1999; Honorary Professor,

University of Edinburgh, since 2003; Honorary Professor, Kunming Institute of Botany, since 2003; Board of Governors, Edinburgh College of Art, 2003-2010; Trustee, Seychelles Islands Foundation, since 1996; Trustee, Little Sparta Trust, 2001-09; Trustee, Botanic Gardens Conservation International, since 2001; b. 30.7.52, Stoke on Trent; m., Patricia Jane Melrose; 1 s.; 1 d. Educ. St George's School, Hong Kong; Reading University. Royal Society Aldabra Research Station, Seychelles, 1976; Lecturer and Head of National Herbarium, University of Malawi, 1977; Palynologist, British Museum (Natural History), 1980; Keeper of Botany, Natural History Museum, 1990; Regius Keeper, Royal Botanic Garden Edinburgh, 1999-2013. Publications: Gardening the Earth, 2009; Green Universe, 2012; author of numerous research papers on plant taxonomy and palynology. Recreations: photography; hill-walking; blues guitar music. Address: (b.) Royal Botanic Garden, 20A Inverleith Row, Edinburgh EH3 5LR; T.-0131-248 2930; e-mail: S.Blackmore@rbge.org.uk

Blackwood, John Grahame, LLB (Hons), DLP, WS. Partner, HBJ Gateley, since 2015; Partner, McClure Naismith, Solicitors, 2000-2015, formerly Head of Banking Unit; b. 21.11.65, Glasgow. Educ. Dundee High School; Aberdeen University. Trainee Solicitor, Alex Morison & Co.; Solicitor, then Director, Bank of Scotland. Recreations: golfing; skiing; sailing. Address: (b.) Exchange Tower, 19 Canning Street, Edinburgh EH3 8EH; T.-0131 228 2400.

Blaikie, Professor Andrew, MA, PhD, FAcSS, FRHistS. Professor of Historical Sociology, University of Aberdeen, since 1999; b. 30.11.56, St. Anne's. Educ. Kirkham Grammar School; Downing College, Cambridge; Queen Mary College, London. Lecturer, Birkbeck College, University of London, 1986-91; Department of Sociology, University of Aberdeen: Lecturer, 1991, Senior Lecturer, 1995, Nuffield Foundation Research Fellow, 1998, Director of Research in Social Sciences and Law, 1999-2001, Head of Sociology, 2002-04; Secretary, Economic and Social History Society of Scotland, 1994-99 and Member of Council, 2010-2014; Executive Committee, British Sociological Association, 1997-2001 (Vice Chair), Member of Council, 2007-2010; Advisory Panel, Centre for Remote and Rural Studies, 2009-2010. Publications: Illegitimacy, Sex and Society, 1994; Ageing and Popular Culture, 1999; The Scots Imagination and Modern Memory, 2010. Recreations: swimming; hillwalking; travel. Address: (h.) 5 Pilot Square, Aberdeen AB11 5DS; T.-01224 588313; e-mail: a.blaikie@abdn.ac.uk

Blair, Anna Dempster, DPE. Writer and Lecturer; b. 12.2.27, Glasgow; m., Matthew Blair; 1 s.; 1 d. Educ. Hutchesons' Girls Grammar School, Glasgow; Dunfermline College. Novels: A Tree in the West; The Rowan on the Ridge; Short Stories: Tales of Ayrshire; Scottish Tales; The Goose Girl of Eriska; Seed Corn; social history: Tea at Miss Cranston's; Croft and Creel; More Tea at Miss Cranston's; Old Giffnock. Recreations: film-making; travel; reading; friendship. Address: (h.) 20 Barrland Drive, Giffnock, Glasgow G46 7QD; T.-0141-638 0676.

Blair, John Samuel Greene, OBE (Mil), TD, TAVRD, KStJ, BA, Hon. DLitt (St. Andrews), ChM, FRCSEdin, FRCP, FICS, D(Obst)RCOG, FSAScot, FRHistS, Diploma in History of Medicine, Society of Apothecaries (Honorary), 2004. Honorary Senior Teacher, Faculty of Medicine, University of Dundee, since 2004; Vice-President, International Society for the History of Medicine, 2000-04; Editorial Manager, International Journal of Medical History, 2002-06; Honorary Reader, History of Medicine and Apothecaries Lecturer, St. Andrews University, 1997-2002 (Senior Lecturer, 1993-97); Honorary Senior Lecturer in Surgery, Dundee University, 1967-90; Apothecaries Lecturer, Worshipful Society of London, since 1991; Member, Editorial Board, Vesalius, since 1994; Member, Organising Committee, International Society for the History of Medicine, Cyprus Congress, 2009; b. 31.12.28, Wormit, Fife; m., Ailsa Jean Bowes, MBE; 2 s.; 1 d. Educ. Dundee High School (Harris Gold Medal for Dux of School, 1946, Intermediate Athletics Champion, 1944, School Golf Champion, 1945, Runner-up, School Athletics Championship, 1946); St. Andrews University (Harkness Scholar, 1946-50). National Service, RAMC, 1952-55 (member of RAMC four-man team finalists in Army Golf Championship, 1954); Tutor, Department of Anatomy, St. Salvator's College, St. Andrews, 1955; surgical and research training, Manchester, Dundee, Cambridge, London, 1957-65; Member, Court of Examiners, Royal College of Surgeons of Edinburgh, 1964-93; Consultant Surgeon, Perth Royal Infirmary, 1965-90; postgraduate Clinical Tutor, Perth, 1966-74; first North American Travelling Fellow, St. Andrews/Dundee Universities, 1971; Secretary, Tayside Area Medical Advisory Committee, 1974-83; Member, Education Advisory Committee, Association of Surgeons, 1984-88; Secretary, Perth and Kinross Division, British Medical Association, 1982-90; Member, Scottish Council and Chairman's Sub-Committee, BMA, 1985-89; Fellow of the BMA, 1990; Chairman, Armed Forces Committee, BMA, 1992-98; President: British Society for the History of Medicine, 1993-95, Scottish Society for the History of Medicine, 1990-93; Captain, Royal Perth Golf Club, 1997-99; British National Delegate, International Society for the History of Medicine, 1999-2001; Honorary Colonel (TA), RAMC; Member, Principal's Council, St Andrews University, 1984-99; Elder, Church of Scotland; Hospitaller, Priory of Scotland, Order of St. John of Jerusalem; Mitchiner Lecturer, Army Medical Services, 1994; Haldane Tait Memorial Lecturer, 1998; Osler Club Lecturer, 1998; Birmingham Medical History Society Lecturer, 1998; Douglas Guthrie Memorial Lecturer, 1998; Brigadier Ian Haywood Lecturer, 1999; Haywood Society Lecturer, 1999; Pybus Society Lecturer, 2001; International Blood Transfusion Society Lecturer, 2004; Invited Speaker, International Congress on High Technology Medicine and Doctor-Patient Relationship, Istanbul, 2006; Invited speaker, Division of Medical Humanities, University of Arkansas, 2007; Annual Osler Oration, 2007. Publications: books on medical history and anatomy including the history of medicine at St. Andrews University, 1987, the centenary history of the RAMC, 1998, The Conscript Doctors – Memories of National Service, 2001 and History of Medicine in Dundee University, 2007. Recreations: golf; travel; bridge. Address: (h.) 143 Glasgow Road, Perth; T.-Perth 623739; e-mail: jgb143@btinternet.com

Blair, Robin Orr, CVO, MA, LLB, WS. Angus Herald Extraordinary; Lord Lyon King of Arms and Secretary, Order of the Thistle, 2001-08. Educ. Rugby School; St. Andrews University; Edinburgh University. Partner, Dundas & Wilson, 1967-97 (Managing Partner, 1976-83 and 1988-91); Partner, Turcan Connell WS, 1997-2000. Purse Bearer to the Lord High Commissioner to General Assembly of Church of Scotland, 1989-2002. Address: 2 Blacket Place, Edinburgh EH9 1RL; T.-0131-667 2906.

Blake, Professor Christopher, CBE, FRSE, MA, PhD. Chairman, Glenrothes Development Corporation, 1987-96; b. 28.4.26; m.; 2 s.; 2 d. Educ. Dollar Academy; St. Andrews University. Royal Navy, 1944-47; teaching posts, 1951-53; Assistant, Edinburgh University, 1953-55; Stewarts & Lloyds Ltd., 1955-60; Lecturer, then Senior Lecturer, St Andrews University, 1960-67; Dundee

University: Senior Lecturer, then Professor of Economics, 1967-74; Bonar Professor of Applied Economics, 1974-88; Director, Alliance Trust plc, 1974-94; Director, William Low & Co. plc, 1980-90 (Chairman, 1985-90). Recreation: golf. Address: (h.) 7 Provost Niven Close, St. Andrews, Fife KY16 9BL.

Blakey, Rev. Ronald Stanton, MA, BD, MTh. Editor, Church of Scotland Year Book, 2000-2011; b. 3.7.38, Glasgow; m., Kathleen Dunbar; 1 s. Educ. Hutchesons' Boys' Grammar School, Glasgow; Glasgow University. Minister: St. Mark's, Kirkconnel, 1963-67; Bellshill West, 1967-72; Jedburgh Old Parish with Edgerston and Ancrum, 1972-81. Member, Roxburgh District Council, 1974-80 (Chairman of Council, 1977-80); Religious Adviser, Border Television, 1973-81; Member, Borders Region Children's Panel, 1974-80; JP, 1974-80; Church of Scotland: Deputy Secretary, Department of Education, 1981-88; Secretary, Assembly Council, 1988-98; Israel Project Secretary, Board of World Mission, 1998-2000. Publication: The Man in the Manse, 1978. Recreation: collecting antiquarian books on Scotland. Address: (h.) 24 Kimmerghame Place, Edinburgh EH4 2GE; T.-0131 343 6352.

Blanchflower, Brian William, BSc (Hons), PGCSE (Distinction). Rector, Dunfermline High School, Fife, since 2007; b. 8.1.56, Belfast; m., Karen Ann Simpson; 1 s.; 1 d. Educ. Dunfermline High School; University of Edinburgh; Moray House College of Education. Teacher of Mathematics and Geography, Inverkeithing High School, 1979-83; Assistant Principal Teacher of Geography, Buckhaven High School, 1983-84; Principal Teacher of Geography, Beath High School, 1984-87; Assistant Rector, 1987-90, Depute Rector, 1990-96, Rector, 1996-2007, Lochgelly High School. Recreations: rugby; hill-walking. Address: (b.) Dunfermline High School, Jennie Rennie's Road, Dunfermline, Fife KY11 3BQ; T.-01383-602402. E-mail: brian.blanchflower@fife.gov.uk

Blaxter, Professor John Harry Savage, MA (Oxon), DSc (Oxon), HonDUniv (Stirling), FRSB, FRSE. Hon. Professor, Stirling University; b. 6.1.29, London; m., Valerie Ann McElligott; 1 s.; 1 d. Educ. Berkhamsted School; Brasenose College, Oxford. SO, then SSO, Marine Laboratory, Aberdeen, 1952-64; Lecturer, Zoology Department, Aberdeen University, 1964-69; PSO, 1969, SPSO, 1974, DCSO, 1985-91, Hon. Research Fellow, 1992-2001, Scottish Marine Biological Association, later Scottish Association for Marine Science, Oban; Hon. Professor, St. Andrews University, 1990-99; President, Fisheries Society of the British Isles, 1992-97 (Beverton Medal, 1998); Individual Achievement Award, American Institute of Fisheries Research Biologists, 1998; Editor, Advances in Marine Biology, 1980-98; Editor, ICES Journal of Marine Science, 1991-97; Member, Editorial Board, Encyclopaedia of Ocean Sciences, 1998-2001; Trustee, Argyll Fisheries Trust, 1999-2010. Recreations: golf; gardening. Address: (h.) Lag-an-Tobair, Old Shore Road, Connel, Oban, Argyll PA37 1PT; T.-01631 710588.

Bloxwich, Janet Elizabeth. Principal Bassoon, Orchestra of Scottish Opera, since 1980; b. 11.4.56, Brentwood; m., Alan J. Warhurst. Educ. Belfairs High School; Southend Technical College; Royal College of Music, London. Two years freelancing in London; on staff at Royal Conservatoire of Scotland, since 1997. Recreations: hillwalking; painting; wood-turning; instrument repairs; cooking. Address: 91 Fotheringay Road, Pollokshields, Glasgow G41 4LH; T.-0141-423 2303.

Blyth, Emeritus Professor Thomas Scott, BSc, DesSc, DSc, CMath, FIMA, FRSE, Corr. Member, Soc.Roy.Sc. Liege. Professor of Pure Mathematics, St Andrews University, since 1977; b. 3.7.38, Newburgh; m., Jane Ellen Christine Pairman; 1 d. Educ. Bell-Baxter High School, Cupar; St Andrews University. NATO Research Scholar, Sorbonne, 1960-63; St Andrews University: Lecturer in Mathematics, 1963-72, Senior Lecturer, 1972-73, Reader, 1973-77; Dean, Faculty of Science, 1994-98; Chairman, British Mathematical Colloquium, 1987; President, Edinburgh Mathematical Society, 1979-80. Publications: more than 130 research papers and ten books. Address (b.) Mathematical Institute, North Haugh, St Andrews KY16 9SS; T.-01334 463684; e-mail: tsb@st-and.ac.uk or tsblyth.prof@btinternet.com

Blythe, Graham, MA. Head of the European Commission Office in Scotland, since 2012; b. 6.7.61; m., Catherine Ross; 1 d.; 1 s. Educ. University of Aberdeen; Leeds; Nice. Career history: University of Bradford, 1987-89; University of Bristol, 1989-93; European Commission Official, since 1993. Address: European Commission, Office in Scotland, 9 Alva Street, Edinburgh EH2 4PH; T.-0131 225 2058. E-mail: graham.blythe@ec.europa.eu

Bogle, Albert Orr. Minister of Church of Scotland, St. Andrew's Parish Bo'ness, since 1981; Moderator of the General Assembly of the Church of Scotland, 2012-13; b. 3.2.49, Glasgow; m., Martha; 1 s.; 1 d. Educ. Woodside Senior Secondary School; Glasgow University; Edinburgh University. Moderator of Falkirk Presbytery, 1993; Founder Chairman, The Vine Trust, 1985; Convener, Church of Scotland's Church Without Walls, 2004; Director of Branches, 1985; Director, Sanctus Media, 2009; Project Director, World Without Walls, 2005. Pioneering the use of media and internet within the structure of the Church of Scotland; helping the Church nationally and internationally to see the benefits of technology to communicate. Publications: Book: Pray Today, 1987; 5 albums of songs - Lamplighter, Run Scared No More, Brave, Cardboard House, Cries In The Dark. Recreations: music; songwriting; walking; film making; writing. Address: St. Andrew's Manse, 11 Erngath Road, Bo'ness; T.-01506 822195; e-mail: albertbogle@mac.com

Bolland, Alexander, QC (Scot),. BD, LLB; b. 21.11.50, Kilmarnock; m., Agnes Hunter Pate Moffat; 1 s.; 2 d. Educ. Kilmarnock Academy; St. Andrews University; Glasgow University. Admitted Faculty of Advocates, 1978; Captain, Army Legal Services, 1978-80; Standing Junior Counsel to Department of Employment in Scotland, 1988-92; QC (Scot), since 1992; Temporary Sheriff, 1988-99. Dental Vocational Appeal Tribunal, since 2011; Judicial Proceedings Panel, Church of Scotland, since 2013. Recreations: Hellenistics; walking; reading. Address: (h.) 60 North Street, St. Andrews, Fife; T.-01334 474599.

Bolton, David John, BSc, FCA. Chief Executive, K3 Business Technology Group plc, since 2014 (CFO, 1998-2014); b. 26.07.51, Brighton; m., Anna-Maija; 2 s. Educ. Lewes Grammar School, Sussex; Southampton University. Qualified as Accountant with Baker Sutton (Ernst & Young) in London; various company and group roles, BTR, 1976-88; Bricom management buyout, 1988-95, then Shorts Vice President after sale of business to Bombardier, 1988-90; Finance Director, Hollas Group plc, 1995-98. Recreations: running; house building.

Bond, Maurice Samuel, BA, MSc, MTh, MEd, PhD, PGCE. Minister of St. Michael's Church, Dumfries, since 1999; Hon. Chaplain, Glasgow University, Crichton Campus, Dumfries, since 2002; Ceremonial Burgh Chaplain to Dumfries Cornet Club, since 1999; b. 25.6.52, Augher, Northern Ireland; 1 s; 1 d. Educ. Limavady High School; Universities of Nottingham, Cambridge, Dublin and Belfast.

Joiner, 1967-71; Teacher, 1978-79; Minister of the Presbyterian Church in Ireland, 1981-91; Minister of the Church of Scotland, Downfield South Church, Dundee, 1991-99. Dumfries and Galloway NHS Medical Research Ethics Committee, 2005-2008; Research Ethics Committee of Glasgow University, Crichton Campus, since 2005. Publications: Reconciliation of Cultures in Reconciling Memories, 1998; Presence: in Theology in Scotland, 1998. Recreation: rugby. Address: St. Michael's Manse, 39 Cardoness Street, Dumfries DG1 3AL; T.-01387 253849; e-mail: mauricebond399@btinternet.com

Bond, Professor Sir Michael R., MD, PhD, FRSE, FRCSEdin, FRCA (Hon), FRCPsych, FRCPSGlas, DPM, DSc (Leics, Hon), DUniv (Glas, Hon). Hon. Fellow, Faculty of Pain Medicine, Royal College of Anaesthetists (2013); Emeritus Professor of Psychological Medicine, Glasgow University; President, International Association for the Study of Pain, 2002-05; b. 15.4.36, Balderton, Nottinghamshire; m., Jane; 1 s.; 1 d. Educ. Magnus Grammar School, Newark; Sheffield University. Professor of Psychological Medicine, Glasgow University, 1973-98 (former Vice-Principal, Glasgow University, former Administrative Dean, Faculty of Medicine); Member, Council, SHEFC, 1992-96; Chair, Joint Medical Advisory Committee for UK Funding Councils, 1992-95; Chairman, Medical Committee, UFC, 1989-92; former Director (former Chairman), Head Injuries Trust for Scotland; former Member, Council, St. Andrews Ambulance Association; Past President, British Pain Society, Interim President, 2009/10; former Director, Prince and Princess of Wales Hospice, Glasgow. Governor, Glasgow High School, Chairman, 2001-06; Trustee, Lloyds TSB Foundation, 1999-2005; Fellow, Royal Society of Arts; Knight Bachelor, 1995; Deacon, Incorporation of Bakers of Glasgow, 2011-12; Late Deacon, 2012-13. Recreations: reading; music; painting (President, Bearsden Art Club, since 2014). Address: (b.) No. 2 The Square, University of Glasgow, University Avenue, Glasgow G12 8QQ; T.-0141-330 3692; e-mail: m.bond@admin.gla.ac.uk

Bondi, Professor Liz, MA, PhD, PGDip (Couns). Professor of Social Geography, University of Edinburgh, since 2001, Head of School of Health in Social Science, 2008-2011; b. 24.06.55, Redhill, Surrey. Educ. Reigate County School; University of Edinburgh; University of Manchester. University of Edinburgh: Demonstrator in Geography, 1985-88, Lecturer, 1988-92, Senior Lecturer, 1992-2001, Co-Director of Counselling Studies, 2004-07. Address: (b.) School of Health in Social Science, University of Edinburgh, Teviot Place, Edinburgh EH8 9AG; T.-0131-650-2529; e-mail: liz.bondi@ed.ac.uk

Bone, Professor Sir (James) Drummond, MA, DLitt, DEd, DUniv (Glas), FRSE. Master, Balliol College, Oxford, since 2011; Chair, Arts and Humanities Research Council, since 2014; Vice-Chancellor, University of Liverpool, 2002-08; Chairman, Advisory Board, Laureate Inc., 2008-2011; b. 11.7.47, Ayr; m., Vivian. Educ. Ayr Academy; Glasgow University; Balliol College, Oxford. Lecturer in English and Comparative Literary Studies, Warwick University; Lecturer, Senior Lecturer, and Professor, English Literature, Glasgow University (Vice-Principal, 1995-99); Principal, Royal Holloway, University of London, 2000-02; President, Universities UK, 2005-07; Honorary Fellow, Royal Holloway, 2004. Knighted, Queen's Birthday Honours, 2008. Academic Editor and Advisory Editor, The Byron Journal; Co-Editor, Romanticism. Recreations: music; skiing; Maseratis. Address: (h.) The Old Manse, Bow of Fife, Cupar, Fife.

Bone, Professor Thomas R., CBE, MA, MEd, PhD, FCCEA, FSES, FRSGS. Professor and Deputy Principal, Strathclyde University, until 1996; b. 2.1.35, Port Glasgow; m., Elizabeth Stewart; 1 s.; 1 d. Educ. Port Glasgow High School; Greenock High School; Glasgow University;

Jordanhill College. Teacher of English, Paisley Grammar School, 1957-62; Lecturer in Education: Jordanhill College, 1962-63, Glasgow University, 1963-67; Jordanhill College: Head of Education Department, 1967-71, Principal, 1972-92. Member, Dunning Committee, 1975-77; Chairman, Educational Advisory Council, 1978-88; Vice-Chairman: Scottish Examination Board, 1977-84; Scottish Tertiary Education Advisory Council, 1984-87; Chairman: Scottish Council for Educational Technology, 1981-87, Standing Conference on Studies in Education, 1982-84, Council for National Academic Awards Board for Organisation and Management, 1983-87, Council for National Academic Awards Committee for Teacher Education, 1987-89, General Teaching Council for Scotland, 1990-91; Member, Complaints Committee, Law Society of Scotland, 1996-2000. Publication: School Inspection in Scotland, 1968; chapters in books and articles in journals. Clubs: Western Gailes Golf; Paisley Burns; Paisley Probus. Recreations: golf; bridge. Address: (h.) 7 Marchbank Gardens, Ralston, Paisley.

Bonnar, Anne Elizabeth, MA, FRSA. Director, Bonnar Keenlyside; arts management consultant; b. 9.10.55, St. Andrews; 2 s.; 2 d. Educ. Dumbarton Academy; Glasgow University; City University, London; Transition Director, Creative Scotland, 2008; Trustee, National Galleries of Scotland, 2002-2010; Director, National Theatre of Scotland, 2004-08; General Manager, Traverse Theatre, 1986-91; Publicity Officer, Citizens' Theatre, Glasgow, 1981-85. Address: (b.) 15 Old Fishmarket Close, Edinburgh EH1 1RN; T.-0131-225 7677; e-mail: anne@b-k.co.uk

Bonnar, David James, OBE, FRSA; b. 20.10.50, Dunfermline; m., Sally Elizabeth Armour; 2 s. Educ. Dunfermline High School. Royal Bank of Scotland, 1968-73; Theatre Royal, Glasgow, 1975-80; Theatre Royal, Newcastle upon Tyne, 1980-84; General Manager, Perth Repertory Theatre, 1984-94; Director (National Lottery), Scottish Arts Council, 1994-99, Artisanat Gallery, 2000-09; Board Member: Foxtrot Theatre Co., 2000-06, craftscotland, 2007-08. Recreations: gardening; opera; architecture. Address: (h.) 12 Queen Street, Perth PH2 0EQ; T.-01738 633424.

Bonomy, Rt. Hon. Lord (Iain Bonomy). Senator of the College of Justice, 1997-2012; permanent judge of the UN International Criminal Tribunal for the Former Yugoslavia, 2004-09; b. 15.1.46, Motherwell; m., Jan; 2 d. Educ. Dalziel High School; University of Glasgow. Apprentice Solicitor, East Kilbride Town Council, 1968-70; Solicitor, Ballantyne & Copland, 1970-83; Advocate, 1984-93; Queen's Counsel, 1993-96; Advocate Depute, 1990-93; Home Advocate Depute, 1993-96. Surveillance Commissioner, 1998-2004 and since 2010; LLD (Strathclyde). Address: (b.) Parliament House, Edinburgh EH1 1RF.

Borley, Lester, CBE, DLitt, FRSGS, FTS; b. 7.4.31, Pontardawe, S. Wales; m., Mary Alison Pearce; 3 d. Educ. Dover County Grammar School; Queen Mary College, University of London. Joined British Travel Association, London, 1955: Assistant to General Manager (USA), New York, 1956-61, Manager, Midwestern States (USA), Chicago, 1961-64, Manager, Australia, 1964-67, Manager, West Germany, Frankfurt, 1967-70; Chief Executive, Scottish Tourist Board, 1970-75; Chief Executive, English Tourist Board, 1975-83; The Director, National Trust for Scotland, 1983-93; Secretary General, Europa Nostra, The Hague, 1992-96; Visiting Lecturer: Edinburgh University/College of Art, Academia Istropolitana, Slovakia, International Cultural Centre, Cracow; Adviser, World Monuments Fund, New York; Past Chairman, Icomos (UK), Cultural Tourism Committee; Past Chairman,

Europa Nostra UK. Recreations: gardening; visiting museums and galleries; reading social history; music. Address: (h.) 4 Belford Place, Edinburgh EH4 3DH; T.-0131-332 2364; e-mail: lesterborley@waitrose.com

Borthwick of that Ilk, Lord (John Hugh Borthwick), DL. 24th Lord Borthwick; Hereditary Falconer to the Kings and Queens of Scotland; b. 14.11.40; m. Adelaide; 2 d. Educ. Gordonstoun; Edinburgh School of Agriculture. Recreations: stalking; wild trout fishing. Club: Edinburgh New Club. Address: (h.) The Garden Flat, Crookston, Heriot, Midlothian EH38 5YS.

Borthwick, Alan Charles, LLB, NP. Partner, Brechin Tindal Oatts, Solicitors, Glasgow and Edinburgh, since 1983, Chairman, since 2014; b. 25.4.57, Glasgow; m., Sheila; 1 d. Educ. Glasgow Academy; Glasgow University. Brechin Robb, Solicitors, 1977-81; joined Tindal Oatts & Rodger, 1981. Member, Council, Law Society of Scotland, 1995-98; Board Member, Children's Hospice Association Scotland, 1993-2005; Trustee of the following charities: Pollock Charitable Trusts; The Baird Trust. Recreations: golf; skiing; garden; family. Address: (b.) 48 St. Vincent Street, Glasgow G2 5HS; T.-0141-221 8012; e-mail: acb@bto.co.uk

Borthwick, Professor George Cooper, CBE, FRSE, CEng, DEng, DBA, BSc (Hons), FIMechE, FIET, CCMI, FRCSEd(Hon), FRCPS(Glas), FRCOG(Hon), FRCOphth (Hon). Chairman, Non Executive Director, Touch Bionics, 2011-2015; Chairman, Surgeons Lodge Ltd., since 2009; former Chairman, Scottish Business in the Community; former Chairman, Tayside Flow Technologies Ltd.; former Chairman, Nova Science Ltd.; former Member, Scottish Higher Education Review Panel; former Chairman, Edinburgh Napier University Court (2008-2012); former Chairman, Mpathy Medical Devices Ltd.; Director, Surgeons' Hall Trust Ltd, since 2005; b. 17.8.44, Glasgow; m., Milly Chalmers Redfern; 2 s.; 1 d. Educ. Lourdes Senior Secondary School, Glasgow; Strathclyde University. Worked for Ethicon for 33 years; former President, Ethicon Europe, former Managing Director, Ethicon Ltd UK, and former Member, Ethicon Global Council. Visiting Professor, Napier University, since 1993; former Chairman, Breast Cancer Institute (2001-2012); former Lay Member, Senate of Surgery of Great Britain and Ireland; former Lay Member, Joint Committee on Higher Surgical Training; former President, European Association of the Surgical Suture Industry; Hon. Fellow, Association of Surgeons of East Africa, since 1995; Hon. Member, James IV Association of Surgeons; Patron, Royal College of Surgeons in Ireland, since 1997; Patron, Royal College of Surgeons of England; Master, Worshipful Company of Needlemakers, 2012-13; Regent, Royal College of Surgeons of Edinburgh, since 2004; Freeman, City of London. Recreations: golf; antiques; art; theatre. Address: (h.) Hillside, 28 St John's Road, Edinburgh EH12 6NZ; T.-0131 334 6945.

Boswell, Philip. MP (SNP), Coatbridge, Chryston and Bellshill, since 2015; b. 23.7.63, Coatbridge; m.; 3 c. Career as a quantity surveyor and contracts engineer in the oil industry. Address: House of Commons, London SW1A 0AA; T.-020 7219 8059.
E-mail: phil.boswell.mp@parliament.uk

Bouchier, Professor Ian Arthur Dennis, CBE, MB, ChB, MD, FRCP, FRCPEdin, FFPHM, Hon. FCP (SAf), FSB, FMedSci, MD h.c., FRSE, FRSA. Professor of Medicine, Edinburgh University, 1986-97 (now Emeritus Professor);

b. 7.9.32, Cape Town, South Africa; m., Patricia Norma Henshilwood; 2 s. Educ. Rondebosch Boys High School; Cape Town University. Instructor in Medicine, School of Medicine, Boston University, 1964; London University: Senior Lecturer in Medicine, 1965; Reader in Medicine, 1970; Professor of Medicine, Dundee University, 1973-86. Member: Court, Dundee University, Council, Royal Society, Edinburgh, Medical Research Council; former Chief Scientist, Scotland; Past President, World Organization of Gastroenterology; former Dean, Faculty of Medicine and Dentistry, Dundee University; Past President, British Society of Gastroenterology. Publications: Clinical Skills (2nd edition), 1982; Gastroenterology (3rd edition), 1982; Gastroenterology: clinical science and practice (2nd edition), 1993. Recreations: music; history of whaling; cooking. Address: (h.) 8A Merchiston Park, Edinburgh EH10 4PN.

Boulton, Professor Geoffrey Stewart, OBE, FRS, FRSE, BSc, PhD, DSc, FGS, Hon D.Technol (Chalmers), Hon D.Science (Heidelberg, Birmingham, Keele). General Secretary, Royal Society of Edinburgh, 2007-2011; Regius Professor Emeritus of Geology and Mineralogy, Edinburgh University, 1986-2008 (Vice-Principal, Edinburgh University, 1999-2008, Provost and Dean, Faculty of Science and Engineering, 1994-99); b. 28.11.40, Stoke-on-Trent; m., Denise Bryers; 2 d. Educ. Longton High School; Birmingham University. Geological Survey of GB, 1962-64; University of Keele, 1964-65; Birmingham University, 1965-67; Water Supply Department, Kenya, 1968; University of East Anglia, 1968-81; Extraordinary Professor, University of Amsterdam, 1981-86. President, Quaternary Research Association, 1991-94; President, British Glaciological Society, 1989-91; President, Geological Society of Edinburgh, 1991-94; Member: Nature Conservancy Council for Scotland Science Board, 1991-92, Natural Environmental Research Council, 1993-98 (Chair, Earth Science and Technology Board, 1993-98), Royal Commission on Environmental Pollution, 1993-2000, Scottish Higher Education Funding Council, 1997-2003, Scottish Association for Marine Science Council, 1998-2003, Royal Society Council, 1997-99 and since 2012, Prime Minister's Council for Science and Technology, 2004-2011; Chair, Scottish Knowledge Transfer Taskforce, 2003-07; Chair, Research Committee, League of European Research Universities, 2003-2009; Scottish Science Advisory Committee, 2002-2008; Chair, Royal Society Science Policy Advisory Group, since 2011; President, Scottish Association for Marine Science, since 2013; Seligman Crystal, International Glaciological Society, 2001; Kirk Bryan Medal, Geological Society of America, 1982; Lyell Medal, The Geological Society, 2006; Tedford Award for Science, Institute for Contemporary Scotland, 2006; Honorary Fellow, International Union for Quaternary Research, 2007; James Croll Medal of the Quaternary Research Association, 2011; Commandeur dans l'Ordre des Palmes Academiques, Government of France; Royal Gold Medal of the Royal Geographical Society, 2014; Chair, Academic Council of the University of Heidelberg, since 2007; Member, Strategic Council of the University of Geneva, since 2009; President, Commission of the International Council for Science & Technology Data, since 2014; UK Polar Medal, 2015. Clubs: New Club, Edinburgh; Arctic Club. Recreations: violin; sailing; mountaineering. Address: (b.) School of Geosciences, University of Edinburgh, Grant Institute, Kings Buildings, West Mains Road, Edinburgh EH9 3JW; e-mail: g.boulton@ed.ac.uk

Bourhill, Peter. Owner, Edinburgh Life magazine. Educ. Leeds University. Address: Edinburgh Life Magazine, PO Box 28948, Gorebridge EH22 9BD; T.-07850 938407.
E-mail: editorial@edinburghlifemagazine.com

Bourne, Patrick. Consul General of Ireland to Scotland, since 2013; b. Dublin, Ireland. Served at Department of Foreign Affairs Dublin, 1990; Embassy of Ireland,

Baghdad, 1990-91; Embassy of Ireland, Tehran, 1991-94; Embassy of Ireland, Copenhagen, 1994-95; Political Division, Dublin, 1995-97 (Deputy Director, Western Balkans); Embassy of Ireland, Canberra (Deputy Head of Mission), 1997-2001; National Forum on Europe, Dublin, 2001-02; Development Cooperation Division, Dublin (Director for Civil Society Programmes), 2002-04; Embassy of Ireland, Delhi (Deputy Head of Mission), 2004-09; Department of Foreign Affairs, Dublin, 2009-2013. Address: Consulate General of Ireland, 16 Randolph Crescent, Edinburgh EH3 7TT; T.-0131 226 7711; e-mail: pat.bourne@dfa.ie

Bowden, Frederick A.W. Chairman, Tullis Russell Group, since 2001; b. 20.1.47, Aberdeen; m., Sheila; 2 s.; 1 d. Educ. Robert Gordon's Institute of Technology. Production Management Trainee, Inveresk Paper Company, 1964-68; held several management positions, Arjo Wiggins Appleton, 1968-91; Operations Director/Managing Director/Chief Executive, Tullis Russell Group, since 1991. Address: (b.) Markinch, Glenrothes KY7 6PB.

Bowen, Sheriff Principal Edward Farquharson, CBE, TD, QC, LLB. Advocate; Sheriff Principal, Lothian and Borders, 2005-2011; Sheriff Principal, Glasgow and Strathkelvin, 1997-2005; Temporary Judge of the Court of Session, 2000-2015; Chairman, Commissioners of Northern Lighthouses, 2003-05; Visiting Professor of Law, University of Strathclyde, 1999-2004; b. 1.5.45, Edinburgh; m., Patricia Margaret Brown; 2 s.; 2 d. Educ. Melville College, Edinburgh; Edinburgh University. Admitted Solicitor, 1968; Advocate, 1970; Standing Junior Counsel, Scottish Education Department, 1976; Advocate Depute, 1979-83; Sheriff of Tayside, Central and Fife, at Dundee, 1983-90; Partner, Thorntons WS, 1990-91; resumed practice at Scottish Bar; QC, 1992; Chairman (Part-time) Industrial Tribunals, 1995-97; Member, Criminal Injuries Compensation Board, 1996-97; Chairman, Independent Review of Sheriff & Jury Procedure, 2009-2010; Governor, Dundee Institute of Technology, 1987-90; Chancellor's Assessor, University of Edinburgh, since 2011; served RAOC TA/TAVR, 1964-80. Recreation: golf. Address: (h) The Old Manse, Lundie, Angus DD2 5NW.

Bowen, Janet, JP. Lord Lieutenant, Ross-shire, since 2007; formerly Chair, Highlands and Islands Volunteer Council of the Red Cross; m., Christopher Bowen; 2 c. Twenty-six years involvement in the voluntary sector, including 20 years serving on the Children's Panel, 5 years with Leonard Cheshire Homes as well as working with Children 1st, the Highland Hospice, WRVS and other charities. Active Member of the "church family" in the local Episcopal church.

Bowie, Allan. President, NFU Scotland, since 2015; m., Christine; 2 s.; 1 d. Farms in North East Fife and Clackmannanshire; former Chairman of the North East Fife branch and served two years as Chairman for East Central region; Vice President, NFU Scotland, 2009-2015. Address: Head Office, Rural Centre - West Mains, Ingliston, Midlothian EH28 8LT; T.-0131 472 4000.

Bowler, David P., BA, MPhil, FSA Scot, MIFA. Director, Alder Archaeology Ltd., since 2009. Educ. McGill University, Montreal; Lincoln College, Oxford. Address: (b.) 55 South Methven Street, Perth PH1 5NX; T.-01738 622393; e-mail: director@alderarchaeology.co.uk

Bowler, Kenneth Charles, BSc, DPhil, ARCS, CPhys, FInstP. Emeritus Professor of Physics, University of Edinburgh, since 2005, Professor of Computational Particle Physics, since 1999; b. 4.10.43, Luton; m., Christine Mary Whalley; 2 d. Educ. Luton Grammar School; Imperial

College London; University of Sussex. Lecturer in Mathematical Physics, University of Edinburgh, 1968, Senior Lecturer in Physics, 1986, Reader in Physics, 1994. Co-founder, Edinburgh Parallel Computing Centre (EPCC); Chair, Research Interest Group, Parkinson's UK Edinburgh Branch, since 2011. Publications: author or co-author of various articles on theoretical and computional physics in refereed journals. Recreations: walking; cycling; tennis; golf; music; cinema. Address: (b.) School of Physics & Astronomy, The University of Edinburgh, James Clerk Maxwell Building, The King's Buildings, Edinburgh EH9 3JZ; T.-0131-650-5233; e-mail: kcb@ph.ed.ac.uk

Bowman, Professor Adrian William, BSc (Hons), DipMathStat, PhD, FRSE. Professor of Statistics, University of Glasgow, since 1995; b. 3.1.55, Ayr; m., Janet Edith Forster; 2 s.; 1 d. Educ. Prestwick Academy; Ayr Academy; University of Glasgow; University of Cambridge. Lecturer in Mathematical Statistics, University of Manchester, 1981-86; University of Glasgow: Lecturer in Statistics, 1986-90, Senior Lecturer in Statistics, 1990-92, Reader in Statistics, 1992-95. Publications: Applied Smoothing Techniques for Data Analysis, (Co-author), 1997; Statistics and Problem Solving (Co-editor), 1999. Recreations: music, particularly singing. Address: (b.) School of Mathematics and Statistics, University of Glasgow, Glasgow G12 8QQ; T.-0141-330 4046. E-mail: adrian.bowman@glasgow.ac.uk

Bowman, (Bernard) Neil, LLB, NP. Formerly Consultant (retired, 2008), previously Senior Partner, Bowman Scottish Lawyers, Solicitors, Dundee and Forfar, 1984-98; b. 11.11.43, Dundee; m. (1967), (Sheriff) Pamela Margaret Munro Wright (divorced 2010); 2 d.; 3 grandsons; m., Karin Boehm (2011). Educ. High School of Dundee where he captained the Cricket XI in 1961 & 1962, the Rugby XV in 1961/2, the Debating Team in 1962 and was CSM in the CCF; Edinburgh University; St. Andrews University. Apprenticeship, Sturrock Morrison & Gilruth, Solicitors, Dundee, 1967-69; admitted Solicitor, 1969; Notary Public, 1970; assumed Partner, Gray Robertson & Wilkie (subsequently Bowman Gray Robertson and Wilkie, now Bowmans) 1971. Secretary: Dundee Institute of Architects, 1970-96, Dundee Building Trades (Employers) Association, 1970-89, Dundee Construction Industry Group Training Association, 1970-93, Tayside Construction Safety Association, 1975-89; Joint Secretary, Local Joint Council for Building Industry, 1970-89, and Local Joint Apprenticeship Committee for the Building Industry, 1970-89; Clerk, Three United Trades of Dundee and to Mason Trade, Wright Trade and Slater Trade of Dundee, 1970-2000; Lord Dean of Guild of Dundee, 1987-90; first Lord President, Court of Deans of Guild of Scotland, 1989; Director, High School of Dundee, 1980-90; Chairman, High School of Dundee Scholarship Fund, 1987-90; Co-opted Member, Law Society of Scotland Committees - Public Relations and Conference, 1982-90, Complaints, 1987-90; Member: Working Party on "Corporate Conveyancing," 1989, School Age Team Sports Enquiry, 1989; Committee Member and National Selector, Scottish Cricket Union, 1974-83; Selector, 1990; President: Scottish Counties Cricket Board, 1981, Scottish Cricket Union, 1989. Recreations: family; cricketophile; travel; golf; music; opera. Addresses: (h.) 96 Dunnichen Avenue, Gowanbank, Forfar, Angus DD8 2EJ and Mullhaven House, St Peter, Barbados BB26004; e-mail: bnb551@gmail.com

Bowman, Phillip. Chairman, The Miller Group, since 2012; former Chief Executive, Smiths Group plc; b. 14.12.52, Melbourne, Australia. Educ. Westminster School; Pembroke College, Cambridge. Price Waterhouse, 1974-78; Gibbs Bright and Co Pty Ltd, Melbourne, 1978-83; Granite Industries, Atlanta, 1983-85; Bass plc, London, 1985-89 (Financial Director, 1991-94, Chief Executive, Retail

Division, 1994-95); Coles Myer Ltd, Melbourne (Financial Director), 1995-96; Chairman, Liberty plc, 1998-2000; Chief Executive, Allied Domecq plc, 1999-2005; Non-Executive Director: BSkyB GP plc, 1994-2003, Berry Bros & Rudd, since 2006, Better Capital Ltd, since 2009; Senior Independent Director, Burberry Group plc, since 2002; Director, Scottish & Newcastle plc, 2006-08; Member, Advisory Board, Alchemy Partners, 2000-09; Chairman, Coral Eurobet Holdings, 2004-05; appointed as Chief Executive of Scottish Power in 2007 and oversaw the sale of the group to Spain's Iberdrola in December 2007. Recreations: scuba diving; entomology; opera; computers; electronics. Address: (b.) Miller House, 2 Lochside View, Edinburgh Park, Edinburgh EH12 9DH; T.-0870 336 5000.

Bownes, Professor Mary, OBE (2006), BSc, DPhil. Vice-Principal (Community Development), University of Edinburgh; b. 14.11.48, Drewsteignton, Devon. Educ. Univ. of Sussex. Career: postdoctoral associate, Univ. of Freiburg and Univ. of California, Irvine, 1973-76; Lecturer in genetics and Developmental Biology, Univ. of Essex, 1976-79; Univ. of Edinburgh, Lecturer in Molecular Biology, 1979-89, Senior Lecturer, 1989-91, Reader 1991-94, Personal Chair in Developmental Biology, since 1994, Associate Dean for Postgraduates Faculty of Science and Engineering, 1997-98, Head, Institute of Cell and Molecular Biology, 1998-2001, Vice-Principal, 2003-2006, Senior Vice-Principal; Member, numerous university committees and groups; Director, Scottish Initiative for Biotechnology Education, since 2002; Member, Editorial Advisory Board, Journal of Embryology and Experimental Morphology/Development, 1982-88; Member, Editorial Board, Insect Molecular Biology, since 1990; Associate Editor, Developmental Biology, 1992-95; Member, Editorial Board, Journal of Endocrinology, since 2000. Author of numerous papers in journals, book chapters and review articles; external examiner, Univ. of Sussex, 1996-2000, Univ. of Oxford, 2001-03, Univ. of York, 2004-06, Univ. of Glasgow, 2005-09, Univ. of Leicester, 2007-09; Chair, Steering Committee, Science and Plants for Schools (SAPS) Biotechnology Scotland Project, 2000-09, Member, 1998-2000; Chair, Board, Edinburgh Centre for Rural Research, 2003-2011 (Member, 1999, Member, Executive Committee, 2000-03); Chair, Strategy Board, BBSRC, 2004-07, Students and Fellowships Strategy Panel, BBSRC, 2004-08; Chair, Young People's Committee, RSE, 2003-2011; Member: Board, Genetics Society, 1980-83, Committee, Br Society for Developmental Biology, 1982-87 (Treasurer, 1984-89), Advisory Board Institute for Science Education Scotland, 2002-03, Advisory Board, MRC, 2002-03, Cell and Molecular Biology Section Committee, RSE, 2004-06, public eng on Educ Committee, RSE, since 2009, Meetings Committee, RSE, 2005-09, Skills Committee 2011 SFC, 2006-09, Board, Highlands and Islands Enterprise, 2008; Member, Executive Committee, RSE, since 2008; Board of Scot Association of Marine Sciences and Chair of Education Committee; CBiol, FIBiol, FRES, FRSE, FRSA 2009. Publications: Metamorphosis (jt ed, 1985); Ecdysone from Metabolism to Regulation of Gene Expression (ed, 1986). Style – Prof Mary Bownes, OBE. Address: (b.) The University of Edinburgh, Charles Stewart House, Room 2.2, 9-16 Chambers Street, Edinburgh EH1 1HT.

Boyack, Sarah. MSP (Labour), Lothian, 2011-16, Edinburgh Central, 1999-2011; Shadow Cabinet Secretary for Environmental Justice, 2015-16. Former lecturer in Planning; Minister for Transport and Environment, 1999-2000; Minister for Transport and Planning, 2000-01; Convener, Environment and Rural Development Committee, 2003-07; Deputy Minister for Environment and Rural Development, 2007; Shadow Cabinet Secretary for Rural Development, Environment and Climate Change, 2007-2011; Shadow Cabinet Secretary for Local Government and Planning, 2011-14; Shadow Cabinet Secretary for Rural Affairs, Food and Environment, 2014-15.

Boyd, Alan Robb, LLB, BA, NP. Director, Public Law, McGrigors LLP (formerly McGrigor Donald), 1997-2010; Consultant, Pinsent Masons LLP, 2010-2014; b. 30.7.53, Glasgow; m., Frances Helen; 2 d. Educ. Irvine Royal Academy; Dundee University. Principal Solicitor, Shetland Islands Council, 1979-81; Principal Solicitor, Glenrothes Development Corporation, 1981-84; Legal Advisor, Irvine Development Corporation, 1984-97. Law Society of Scotland: Member, Council, 1985-97, Convener, Finance Committee, 1992-94, Vice-President, 1994-95, President, 1995-96; President, European Company Lawyers' Association, 1992-94; Convenor, Association for Scottish Public Affairs, 1998-2000. Recreations: golf; reading; gardening; music. Address: (h.) 26, Hannah Wynd, St Quivox, Ayr KA6 5HB; T.-01292 521936.

Boyd of Duncansby, Rt Hon Lord (Colin David Boyd), PC, BA (Econ), LLB. Senator of the College of Justice, since 2012; Life Peer; Lord Advocate, 2000-06; Solicitor General for Scotland, 1997-2000; Member of the Scottish Executive, 1999-2006; Head of Public Law, Dundas & Wilson LLP, 2007-2012; b. 7.6.53, Falkirk; m., Fiona Margaret MacLeod; 2 s.; 1 d. Educ. Wick High School; George Watson's College, Edinburgh; University of Manchester; University of Edinburgh. Solicitor, 1978-82; called to Bar, 1983; Advocate Depute, 1993-95; took Silk, 1995; Solicitor Advocate, 2007-2012; Honorary Fellow, Society of Advanced Legal Studies; Honorary Professor of Law, University of Glasgow, 2007-2012; Member, Commission on Scottish Devolution, 2008-09; Chairman, Northern Lighthouse Heritage Trust, 2008-2012. Publication: The Legal Aspects of Devolution (Contributor), 1997. Recreations: hill-walking; reading; watching rugby. Address: (b.) Court of Session, Parliament House, Parliament Square, Edinburgh EH1 1RQ.

Boyd, Dr Donald MacLeod, MB, ChB, DipTheol. Medical Practitioner; Highlands and Islands Campaign Manager, Scottish Christian Party "Proclaiming Christ's Lordship", 2006-07, Chairman, 2007-2010; Leader, Scottish Christian Party, since 2010; Nomination Officer, Christian Party, since 2013; Chairman, Westhill Community Council, Inverness, 2011-2014; Webmaster, since 2013; Minister, Inverness Free Presbyterian Church of Scotland, 1989-2000 (Clerk, Northern Presbytery, 1991-2000); Church Tutor in Systematic Theology, 1995-2000; b. Glasgow; m., Elizabeth Schouten; 1 s.; 3 d. Educ. Glasgow Academy; Glasgow University. Southern General Hospital, 1978; Stobhill General Hospital, 1979; Vale of Leven Hospital, 1979; ordained Free Presbyterian Church of Scotland, 1983; Clerk of Religion and Morals Committee, 1984-92 and Convener, 1992-94; Deputy to Australia and New Zealand, 1988; Member, Churches Liaison Committee on AIDS, Highland Health Board, 1992-94; Member, Highland Regional Council Education Committee, 1994-96; Moderator of Synod of Free Presbyterian Church of Scotland, 1997-98; Church delegate to the European Court of Human Rights, February 2000. Publications: Popular History of the Origins of the Free Presbyterian Church of Scotland, 1987; "What's that Tune? A Melody Index of Sol-fa Tunes", 2009. Recreations: reading; writing; Street Pastor, since 2007; gardening; walking; photography; British Sign Language; historical research; advanced driving; astrophysics; genealogy. Address: Inverness.

Boyd, Professor Ian L., BSc, PhD, DSc, FRSB, FRSE. Chief Scientific Adviser, Department for Environment, Food and Rural Affairs, since 2012; Professor in

Biology, University of St Andrews, since 2001; Chair, UK Food Research Partnership, since 2013; Chair, Governance Board for UK Climate Projections, since 2015; Director, Sea Mammal Research Unit, 2001-2012; Director, Scottish Oceans Institute, 2009-2012; Chief Executive, SMRU Ltd., 2006-09; Chair, Marine Alliance for Science and Technology for Scotland, 2005-2010; Member, Scottish Science Advisory Council, 2010-2014; b. 9.2.57, Kilmarnock; m., Sheila M.E. Aitken; 1 s.; 2 d. Educ. George Heriot's School, Edinburgh; Aberdeen University; Cambridge University. Churchill Fellow, 1980; Institute of Terrestrial Ecology, Monks Wood, 1982-87; British Antarctic Survey, 1987-2001; Antarctic Service Medal of the United States, 1995; Bruce Medal, Royal Society of Edinburgh, 1995; Honorary Professor, Birmingham University, 1997; Scientific Medal, Zoological Society of London, 1998; Editor-in-Chief, Journal of Zoology, 2006-08; Marsh Award for Marine and Freshwater Conservation, 2006. Member, Council, Hebridean Trust and Seamark Trust; Member, Natural Environment Research Council, since 2013; Member, Biotechnology and Biological Sciences Research Council, since 2013. Publications: seven books; 150 papers. Recreations: walking; photography. Address: (b.) College Gate, North Street, St Andrews University, St Andrews KY16 9AJ; T.-01334 462553.

Boyle, Professor Alan Edward, LLD, MA, BCL. Professor of Public International Law, University of Edinburgh, since 1995; Barrister, since 1977; b. 28.3.53, Belfast; m., Caroline. Educ. Royal Belfast Academical Institution; University of Oxford (Pembroke College). Queen Mary College, University of London, Faculty of Law, 1978-94; University of Texas, School of Law, 1988 and 1994; Paris II and X, 2000-01; LUISS, Rome, 2009; Essex Court Chambers, London, since 2006; General Editor, International and Comparative Law Quarterly, 1998-2006. Publications: International Law and The Environment (Co-author), 2009; The Making of International Law (Co-author), 2007. Recreations: gliding; music; theatre. Address: (b.) School of Law, University of Edinburgh, Old College, South Bridge, Edinburgh EH8 9YL.

Boyle, James, FRSE. Chair, National Library of Scotland; b. 29.3.46; m., Marie; 3 s. Head of BBC Radio Scotland when it was named UK Radio Station of the Year; former Controller of BBC Radio 4; has had several public service posts, including Chair of the Scottish Arts Council and Chair of the Scottish Cultural Commission; founder and first Chair of Edinburgh UNESCO City of Literature; founder of Glasgow UNESCO City of Music. Address: (b.) George IV Bridge, Edinburgh EH1 1EW; T.-0131 623 3700.

Bracadale, The Hon. Lord (Alastair P. Campbell), MA, LLB. Senator of the College of Justice, since 2003; Judge of the Court of Session and High Court of the Justiciary, since 2003; b. 18.9.49, Skye. Educ. George Watson's College; University of Aberdeen. English Teacher, Vale of Leven Academy, Dunbartonshire, 1973-75 before returning to study law at the University of Strathclyde; admitted as a solicitor in 1979 and entered the Procurator Fiscal service as a prosecutor; admitted to the Faculty of Advocates in 1985; called to the English Bar at the Inner Temple in 1990; Advocate Depute, 1990-93; Standing Junior Counsel in Scotland to HM Customs and Excise, 1995; appointed Queen's Counsel, 1995; served as Home Advocate Depute, 1997-98; Member: Criminal Justice Forum, 1996-97; Scottish Criminal Rules Council 1996-98, Criminal Injuries Compensation Board, 1997; Home Advocate Depute (Scotland's senior prosecutor), 1997-1999; Senior Crown Counsel in Lockerbie trial, Camp Van Zeist, the Netherlands, 1999-2001. Address: (b.) Parliament House, 11 Parliament Square, Edinburgh EH1 1RQ.

Brackenridge, Bill. Chairman, Scottish Legal Complaints Commission, since 2013; Chairman, Argyll & Bute Adult Protection Committee, since 2008; Non-Executive Director, The State Hospital, since 2013; b. 12.4.47, Edinburgh; m., Lorna Frances Brackenridge; 1 d.; 1 s. Educ. The High School of Glasgow; Universities of Glasgow & Strathclyde. Career: Market Development Executive, British Airways, 1969-75; Policy Planner, Strathclyde Regional Council, 1975-79; Consultant, later Partner, The Hay Group, 1979-2003. Non-Executive Director, Highlands and Islands Airports Ltd, 1999-2005; Chairman, Scottish Ambulance Service, 2003-09; Non-Executive Director, NHS Highland, 2006-2013. Recreations: gardening; walking; enjoying the sun. Address: (b.) Scottish Legal Complaints Commission, The Stamp Office, 10-14 Waterloo Place, Edinburgh EH1 3EG; T.-0131 201 2188.
E-mail: Bill.Brackenridge@scottishlegalcomplaints.org.uk

Bradley, Very Rev. Dr. Ian Campbell, MA, BD, DPhil. Principal, St. Mary's College, St. Andrews; Minister; Writer and Broadcaster; Reader in Practical Theology and Church History, St. Andrews University; Honorary Church of Scotland Chaplain, St. Andrews University; b. 28.5.50, Berkhamsted; m., Lucy Patricia; 1 s.; 1 d. Educ. Tonbridge School, Kent; New College, Oxford; St. Andrews University. Research Fellow, New College, Oxford, 1971-75; Staff Journalist, The Times, 1976-82; ordained into Church of Scotland, 1990; Head, Religious Broadcasting, BBC Scotland, 1990-91; Lecturer in Practical Theology, Aberdeen University, 1992-99. Vice President: The Sullivan Society, The Stainer Society. Publications: The Call to Seriousness, 1974; William Morris and his World, 1975; The Optimists, 1976; The Penguin Annotated Gilbert & Sullivan, 1980; The Strange Rebirth of Liberal Britain, 1982; Enlightened Entrepreneurs, 1986; The Penguin Book of Hymns, 1989; God is Green, 1990; O Love That Wilt Not Let Me Go, 1990; Marching to the Promised Land, 1992; The Celtic Way, 1993; The Power of Sacrifice, 1995; The Complete Annotated Gilbert and Sullivan, 1996; Columba, Pilgrim and Penitent, 1996; Abide with Me – the World of the Victorian Hymn, 1997; Celtic Christianity: Making Myths and Chasing Dreams, 1999; The Penguin Book of Carols, 1999; Colonies of Heaven: Celtic Models for Today's Church, 2000; God Save the Queen – The Spiritual Dimension of Monarchy, 2002; You've Got to Have a Dream: The Message of the Musical, 2004; Oh Joy! Oh Rapture! The Enduring Phenomenon of Gilbert and Sullivan, 2005; The Daily Telegraph Book of Hymns, 2005; The Daily Telegraph Book of Carols, 2006; Believing in Britain, 2006; Pilgrimage - A cultural and spiritual journey, 2009; Water Music: Music Making in the Spas of Europe and North America, 2010; Grace, Order, Openness and Diversity: Reclaiming Liberal Theology, 2010; God Save the Queen - The Spiritual Heart of Monarchy, 2012; Water: A Spiritual History, 2012; Lost Chords and Christian Soldiers: The Sacred Music of Arthur Sullivan, 2013; Argyll - The Making of a Spiritual Landscape, 2015. Recreations: music; walking; family; spas; tennis; singing. Address: (b.) St Mary's College, South Street, St Andrews KY16 9JU; T.-01334 462840.

Bradshaw, Jeremy Peter. Chair of Molecular Biophysics, University of Edinburgh, since 2008, Assistant Principal (Researcher Development), since 2013, International Dean, College of Medicine and Vet Medicine, since 2009; Visiting Professor, Zhejiang University, China, since 2013; m., Bridget; 2 d. Educ. Loughborough Grammar School; St. Peter's College,

University of Oxford. University Demonstrator, The University of Edinburgh, 1986-89; Lecturer, Royal (Dick) School of Veterinary Studies, 1989-99, Senior Lecturer, 1999-2002; Reader in Preclinical Veterinary Studies, The University of Edinburgh, since 2002. Visiting Professor, Tsukuba University, Japan; Treasurer, UK Council for Graduate Education. Address: (b.) College of Medicine and Veterinary Medicine, The University of Edinburgh, The Chancellor's Building, 47 Little France Crescent, Edinburgh EH16 4SB.

Brady, Adrian J.B, BSc, MB, ChB, MD, FRCP (Glasg), FRCPE, FBHS, FESC, FAHA. Associate Professor and Consultant Cardiologist, Glasgow Royal Infirmary, since 1996; b. 27.5.61, Edinburgh; 1 s.; 2 d. Educ. Edinburgh Academy; Scotus Academy; Edinburgh University. Trained in Cardiology at Hammersmith Hospital and National Heart and Lung Institute, London; Winner, American Heart Association Young Investigator Award, 1993; Winner, British Cardiac Society Young Investigator Award, 1993; Secretary, British Hypertension Society; Chairman, Guidelines Committee, British Cardiovascular Society; Visiting Professor, Mayo Clinic; Faculty Member, American Heart Association. Recreations: skiing; golf; piano. Address: (b.) Cardiology Department, Walton Building, Glasgow Royal Infirmary, Glasgow G4 0SF; T.-0141-211 4727.

Brady, John, BSc Hons (Open), MBA with Distinction. Head of Fundraising, St Andrew's Hospice (Lanarkshire), since 2015; b 10.03.65, Glasgow. Educ. Craigmount High School; Glasgow University; Open University; Strathclyde University. Advertising Sales Manager, Angel Publishing, 1986-91; Financial Adviser, City Financial Partners, 1991-95; Field Sales Executive, Daily Record, 1995-97; Field Sales Executive, The Scotsman, 1997-98; Scottish Manager, British Lung Foundation, 1998-2000; Donor Development Manager, Sense Scotland, 2000-02; Community Investment Programme Manager, BT Scotland, 2002-03; Fundraising and Communications Manager, Alcohol Focus Scotland, 2003-05; Head of Fundraising, Sense Scotland, 2005-10; Director, Business Development, Erskine, 2010-12; Chief Executive Officer, OneKind (formerly Advocates for Animals), 2012-15. Recreations: family; films; football; reading. Address: (b.) St. Andrew's Hospice Ltd, Henderson Street, Airdrie, Lanarkshire ML6 6DJ; T.-01236 766951.

Braid, Sheriff Peter John, LLB (Hons), WS. Sheriff, Edinburgh, since 2015 (formerly Sheriff, Haddington); Solicitor Advocate, 1995-2005; Partner, Morton Fraser, Solicitors, 1985-2005; b. 6.3.58, Edinburgh; m., Heather McIntosh; 2 s. Educ. George Watson's College, Edinburgh; University of Edinburgh. Recreations: golf; bridge; cycling. Address: Sheriff Court House, 27 Chambers Street, Edinburgh EH1 1LB.

Brailsford, Hon. Lord (Sidney) Neil Brailsford. Senator of the Royal College of Justice in Scotland, since 2006; b. 15.8.54, Edinburgh; m., Elaine Nicola Robbie; 3 s. Educ. Daniel Stewart's College, Edinburgh; Stirling University; Edinburgh University. Admitted Scottish Bar, 1981, English Bar, 1990; Standing Junior Counsel, Department of Agriculture and Fisheries, 1987-92; QC, 1994; Advocate Depute, 1999-2000. Treasurer, Faculty of Advocates, 2000; Member, Court, Stirling University, 2001-05; Part-time Chairman, Discipline Committee, Institute of Chartered Accountants of Scotland, 2002-06. Recreations: food; wine; travel; reading; American history and politics; baseball; fishing; supporting Heart of Midlothian Football Club. Address: (b.) Parliament House, Edinburgh EH1 1RF; Kidder Hill Road, Grafton, Vermont 05146, USA.

Brankin, Rhona, Hon. FRIBA. MSP (Labour), Midlothian, 1999-2011; Shadow Cabinet Secretary for Education and Lifelong Learning, 2007-2010; Minister for Communities, 2007; Deputy Minister for Environment and Rural Development, 2005-07; Deputy Minister for Health and Community Care, 2004-05. Educ. Aberdeen University; Northern College. Former teacher and lecturer on special educational needs; Deputy Minister for: Culture and Sport, 1999-2000, for Environment and Rural Development, 2000-01; former Chair, Scottish Labour Party; Honorary Member of Chartered Institute of Library and Information Professionals in Scotland.

Brannan, Fr. Chris. Parish Priest of Banchory, since 2012. Address: Corsee Cottage, 5 High Street, Banchory AB31 5RP; T.-01330 822835; e-mail: fr.chris@deeside-catholics.org.uk

Brannen, Roy. Chief Executive, Transport Scotland, since 2015 (previously Director of Trunk Roads and Bus Operations). Career history: Transport Scotland and Transport Directorate since joining the then Scottish Executive in 1999. Chartered Civil Engineer with over 25 years' experience in highways and transportation and a Fellow of both the Institution of Civil Engineers and the Chartered Institution of Highways and Transportation. Address: Transport Scotland, Buchanan House, 58 Port Dundas Road, Glasgow G4 0HF; T.-0141 2727100.

Bray, Professor Francesca Anne, PhD. Professor of Social Anthropology, University of Edinburgh, since 2005; b. 18.12.48, Cairo, Egypt; m., A.F. Robertson. Educ. Collège Sévigné, Paris; Girton College, Cambridge. Research Associate, East Asian History of Science Library, Cambridge, 1973-82; Leverhulme Research Fellow, Needham Research Institute (formerly East Asian History of Science Library), Cambridge, 1982-84; Chargée de Recherche, Centre National de la Recherche Scientifique (CNRS), Paris, 1985-87; Professor of Anthropology, UCLA, 1988-93; Senior Wellcome Research Fellow, Centre for the History of Science, Technology and Medicine, Manchester University; Professor of Anthropology, University of California Santa Barbara, 1993-2004. Prix Bordin for History, Académie des Inscriptions et Belles-Lettres, Institut Français, for Science and Civilisation in China, Vol. V1 Part 2, Agriculture, 1985; Dexter Prize (Society for the History of Technology) for Technology and Gender. Currently member of Edelstein Committee, Society for the History of Technology; International Scientific Advisory Board, Max Planck Institute for the History of Science. Address: (b.) Social Anthropology, SSPS, Chrystal Macmillan Building, George Square, Edinburgh EH8 9LD; e-mail: francesca.bray@ed.ac.uk

Brechin, George, OBE. Non Executive Director, Health and Safety Executive, since 2013. Educ. University of Glasgow. Career: joined the Department of Health in London in 1972; moved to the NHS in Scotland in 1988, holding three NHS Trust Chief Executive posts before joining NHS Fife; Chief Executive, NHS Fife, 2002-2012; Interim Chief Executive, State Hospitals Board for Scotland, 2014-2015. Companionship of the Institute of Healthcare Management; Vice-Chair, Board of Trustees of the Royal Zoological Society of Scotland; President of Council, Zoological Society of Glasgow and the West of Scotland. Address: Health and Safety Executive, Belford House, 59 Belford Road, Edinburgh EH4 3UE.

Breeze, David John, OBE, BA, PhD, HonDLitt (Glasgow), HonFSA Scot, FRSE, HonMIFA. Chief Inspector of

Ancient Monuments, Scotland, 1989-2005; Head of Special Heritage Projects, Historic Scotland, 2005-09; Visiting Professor, Department of Archaeology, Durham University, since 1993; Honorary Professor, Edinburgh University, since 1996; Honorary Professor, Newcastle University, since 2003; b. 25.7.44, Blackpool; m., Pamela Diane Silvester; 2 s. Educ. Blackpool Grammar School; Durham University. Inspector of Ancient Monuments, Scotland, 1969-88; Principal Inspector of Ancient Monuments, Scotland, 1988-89. Member: International Committee of the Congress of Roman Frontier Studies, since 1983, International Committee on Archaeological Heritage Management, 1997-2009, Council, Society of Antiquaries of London, 1984-86 and 2009-2013, Council, Royal Society of Edinburgh, 1997-2000; Trustee, Senhouse Roman Museum, since 1985; Chairman: 1989, 1999 and 2009 Hadrian's Wall Pilgrimages, British Archaeological Awards, 1993-2009; President: South Shields Archaeological and Historical Society, 1983-85, Society of Antiquaries of Scotland, 1987-90, Society of Antiquaries of Newcastle, 2008-11, Royal Archaeological Institute, 2009-2011, Cumberland and Westmorland Antiquarian and Archaeological Society, 2011-14; Corresponding Member, German Archaeological Institute; Current Archaeology "Archaeologist of the Year 2009"; recipient of the European Archaeological Heritage Prize 2010. Publications: The Building of Hadrian's Wall, The Army of Hadrian's Wall, Hadrian's Wall, and Roman Officers and Frontiers (all Co-author); Roman Scotland: a guide to the visible remains; Roman Scotland: some recent excavations (Editor); The Romans in Scotland (Co-author); The Northern Frontiers of Roman Britain; Roman Forts in Britain; Studies in Scottish Antiquity (Editor); Hadrian's Wall, a souvenir guide; A Queen's Progress, an introduction to the buildings associated with Mary Queen of Scots in Scotland; The Second Augustan Legion in North Britain; Service in the Roman Army (Co-editor); Invaders of Scotland (Co-author); Roman Scotland: Frontier Country; The Stone of Destiny: Symbol of Nationhood (Co-author); Historic Scotland, 5000 Years of Scotland's Heritage; Historic Scotland, People and Places; Stone of Destiny, artefact and icon (Co-editor); The Antonine Wall; Frontiers of the Roman Empire (Co-author); Handbook to the Roman Wall; Roman Frontiers in Britain; Edge of Empire, Rome's Scottish Frontier, The Antonine Wall; Frontiers of the Roman Empire, The European Dimension of a World Heritage Site (Co-editor); The Frontiers of Imperial Rome; The First Souvenirs, Enamelled Vessels from Hadrian's Wall (editor); 200 Years: The Society of Antiquaries of Newcastle upon Tyne, 1813-2013 (editor); Hadrian's Wall: A History of Archaeological Thought; Understanding Roman Frontiers (Co-editor); The Roman Army. Recreations: reading; walking; travel. E-mail: davidbreeze@hotmail.co.uk

Brennan, Ian, BA, FCCA, MBA. Head of Business Analysis, Scottish Housing Regulator, since 2009; Vice Chairman, Cardonald College, since 2011; b. 20.6.59, Glasgow; m., Carolyn; 1 s.; 1 d. Educ. Holyrood, Glasgow; Strathclyde University; Glasgow University. Early career in the utility sector in finance and IT; worked in a variety of audit posts in the public and private sectors, latterly as an IT audit specialist with the Accounts Commission for Scotland in the late 1980's and early 1990's; joined Ayrshire and Arran Health Board as Chief Internal Auditor; left the NHS to join the University of Glasgow, serving as Head of Internal Audit and Head of Management Services; became Risk Manager for the Medical and Dental Defence Union of Scotland (MDDUS). Non Executive Vice-Chairman, Cardonald College, Glasgow (Chair, Audit Committee and Remuneration Committee); within the tertiary education sector, acts as Vice Chair, Governance Development Group; Chair, Council of Higher Education Internal Auditors, 1996-98.

Recreations: squash; tennis; writing. Address: (b.) Highlander House, 58 Waterloo Street, Glasgow G2 7DA; T.-0141 271 3702.
E-mail: ian.brennan@scottishhousingregulator.gsi.gov.uk

Brett Young, Michael Jonathan, DL. Manager, East Sutherland Village Advisory Service, 1986-99; Director: Voluntary Groups, East Sutherland, 1996-99, and since 2001, Highland Advice and Information Network Ltd., 1994-99; Deputy Lieutenant, Sutherland, 1995-2012; Chairman, Voluntary Groups, East Sutherland, 2011-14; b. 18.10.37, Salisbury; m., Helen Dorothy Anne Barker; 2 s. Educ. Dartmouth. Royal Australian Navy, 1956-69; Sales and Marketing Manager, 1969-79; Senior Account Manager, 1979-84. Chairman, PR Committee, Retread Manufacturers Association, 1975-79; Executive Member, Community Organisations Group, Scotland, 1990-93; Chairman: East Sutherland Council of Social Service, 1991-94, East Sutherland Local Community Care Forum, 1993-99; Chairman, SSAFA, Sutherland; Chairman, Dornoch Cricket Club, 1991-2005. Recreations: cricket; naval history; music. Address: (h.) West Shinness Lodge, Lairg, Sutherland; T.-01549 402495.

Brew, David Allan, BA, MSc. Head of Fisheries, Marine Scotland, 2009-2011; b. 19.2.53, Kettering. Educ. Kettering Grammar School; Heriot-Watt University; Strathclyde University; European University Institute, Florence. Administration Trainee and HEO(D), Scottish Office, 1979-81; Administrator, DGV, Commission of the EC, 1981-84; Principal, Scottish Office, Glasgow, 1984-88, Edinburgh, 1988-90; Head: Electricity Privatisation Division, 1990-91, European Funds and Co-ordination Division, 1991-95, Sea Fisheries Division,1995-98; Cabinet Office, Constitution Secretariat, 1998-99; Chief Executive, Institute of Chartered Accountants of Scotland, 2000-03; Scottish Government, Head: Cultural Policy Division, 2004-06, Rural Communities Division, 2006-09. Member, Court, Heriot-Watt University, 1985-91 and 2000-06; Member, AUC, 2004-2011; Board Member: MG Alba, since 2012, Creative Scotland, since 2015, Robert Gordon University, 2012-15; Public Member, Network Rail, 2012-15. Recreations: languages; music; film; gastronomy. Address (h.) 1 Dundas Street, Edinburgh EH3 6QG; T.-0131-556 4692.

Breward, Professor Chris, Principal, Edinburgh College of Art, since 2011; Vice-Principal, University of Edinburgh. Educ. The Courtauld Institute and the Royal College of Art. Taught the history of design, Royal College of Art, 1994-99 before becoming Research Director at the London College of Fashion; moved to the V&A in 2004. Fellow of the Royal Society of Arts and an Honorary Fellow of the Royal College of Art. Trustee of the National Museums of Scotland, Hospitalfield and the Fruitmarket Gallery, Edinburgh. Address: Edinburgh College of Art, The University of Edinburgh, Lauriston Place, Edinburgh EH3 9DF; T.-0131 651 5800.

Bridges, Professor Roy Charles, BA, PhD, FRGS, FRHistS, FFCS. Emeritus Professor of History, Aberdeen University; President, Hakluyt Society, 2002-08; b. 26.9.32, Aylesbury; m., Jill Margaret Lewis; 2 s.; 2 d. Educ. Harrow Weald County Grammar School; Keele University; London University. Lecturer in History, Makerere University, Uganda, 1960-64; joined Aberdeen University, 1964. Council Member, Royal Historical Society, 1995-98; Chairman, Garioch Area, Aberdeenshire Forum of Community Councils, 1999-2005. Publications: Africa in Times Atlas of World Exploration; Compassing the Vaste Globe of the Earth (Co-editor), 1996;

Imperialism, Decolonization and Africa, 1999; People and Places in Newmachar, 2001; Journal of Jacob Wainwright, 2007. Recreations: bookbinding; geology; gardening. Address: (h.) Newmachar House, Newmachar AB21 0RD; T.-01651 863046; e-mail: rbridges@globalnet.co.uk

Briggs, Miles Edward Frank. MSP (Scottish Conservative), Lothian region, since 2016. Educ. Auchtergaven Primary School; Perth Grammar School; Robert Gordon University. Stood as the Conservative candidate in United Kingdom general election, 2010 for the North East Fife constituency, then in the Scottish Parliament election, 2011 for North East Fife. Address: Scottish Parliament, Edinburgh EH99 1SP.

Brink, Professor Stefan, Fil.Dr. Professor, Scandinavian Studies, University of Aberdeen, since 2005. Educ. Uppsala University. Address: (b.) Scandinavian Studies, University of Aberdeen; e-mail: s.brink@abdn.ac.uk

Brittain, Christopher Neil, BSc, MB, ChB, MBA, MRCGP, DRCOG, DipIMC, RCS (Edin.), FRSocMed, FFICS, MInstAC; b. 3.3.49, Birmingham; m., Rosemary; 1 s.; 1 d. Educ. Bishop Vesey's Grammar School, Sutton Coldfield; St. Andrews University; Dundee University; Heriot Watt University. Senior Partner, Anstruther Medical Practice, 1978-97; Co-ordinator for Scotland, Sargent Cancer Care for Children, 1997-99. Executive Director, Scottish Science Trust, 1999-2003; Chairman, British Association of Immediate Care, 1994-97; Director, Resuscitation Council UK, 1995-1997; Member, East Board, Scottish Environment Protection Agency, 2002-07; Board Member, SSERC, 2001-04. Executive Committee, Association for the Protection of Rural Scotland, 2011-14; Trustee, Fife Folk Museum, since 2014. Recreations: the countryside; walking. Address: (h.) The White House, Smithy Brae, Kilrenny, Anstruther, Fife KY10 3JN; T.-01333 310191.

Britton, Professor David, BSc, MSc, PhD, FInstP. Professor of Physics, University of Glasgow, since 2007; Project Leader, GRIDPP (UK Computing for LHC), since 2007; b. 25.2.60, Colwyn Bay; m., Linda Barclay; 1 s.; 1 d. Educ. Rydal School; University of Nottingham; University of Victoria. Research Associate, McGill University, Montreal, Canada, 1989-96; Lecturer, Imperial College London, 1996-2001, Senior Lecturer, 2001-04, Reader of Physics, 2004-07. Member: CMS Experiment, 1996-2006, ATLAS Experiment, since 2007; Project Manager, GRIDPP Project, 2001-07. Recreations: running; sailing. Address: (b.) Kelvin Building, University of Glasgow, Glasgow G12 8QQ; T.-0141 330 5454.
E-mail: david.britton@glasgow.ac.uk

Broadhurst, Paul Anthony, MBChB, MD, FRCP, FESC, FHRS. Consultant Cardiologist, Aberdeen Royal Infirmary, since 2002; Training programme director for cardiology, since 2013; b. 19.12.58, Ashford, Middx; m., Amanda Jayne Powe; 2 s. Educ. Ashford Grammar School; University of Dundee. Research Fellow in Cardiology, Northwick Park Hospital, Harrow, 1987-90; Registrar then Senior Registrar in Cardiology, St. Bartholomew's Hospital, London, 1990-97; Consultant Cardiologist, Borders General Hospital and Royal Infirmary of Edinburgh, 1997-2002. Previous Secretary, Scottish Cardiac Society; Member, Scottish Executive CHD Advisory Committee, since 2010. Publication: Cardiology Explained (Joint Author), 1997. Recreations: fishing; playing the piano; skiing. Address: Department of Cardiology, Aberdeen Royal Infirmary, Foresterhill, Aberdeen AB21 2ZB; T.-01224 559308; e-mail: paul.broadhurst@nhs.net

Broadie, Professor Alexander, MA, PhD, DLitt, DUniv, FRSE. Professor of Logic and Rhetoric, Glasgow University, 1994-2009; Hon. Professorial Research Fellow, since 2009. Educ. Royal High School, Edinburgh; Edinburgh University; Balliol College, Oxford; Glasgow University. Henry Duncan Prize Lecturer in Scottish Studies, Royal Society of Edinburgh, 1990-93; Gifford Lecturer, Aberdeen University, 1994; Patron, Sutherland Trust, 2007; Doctor honoris causa (Blaise Pascal), 2007; Saltire Society Scottish History Book of the Year, 2009; Leader, Leverhulme International Network on 17c Scottish Philosophy, 2010-14. Publications: A Samaritan Philosophy, 1981; George Lokert: Late-Scholastic Logician, 1983; The Circle of John Mair, 1985; Introduction to Medieval Logic, 1987; Notion and Object, 1989; The Tradition of Scottish Philosophy, 1990, rev. edn., 2011; Paul of Venice: Logica Magna, 1990; Robert Kilwardby O.P.: on time and imagination, 1993; Introduction to Medieval Logic (2nd edition), 1993; The Shadow of Scotus, 1995; The Scottish Enlightenment: an anthology, 1997; Why Scottish Philosophy Matters, 2000; The Scottish Enlightenment: The Historical Age of the Historical Nation, 2001; The Cambridge Companion to the Scottish Enlightenment, 2003, Chinese edn., 2010; George Turnbull: Principles of Moral and Christian Philosophy, 2004; Thomas Reid on Logic, Rhetoric and the Fine Arts, 2005; A History of Scottish Philosophy, 2009; Agreeable Connexions: Scottish Enlightenment Links with France, 2012. Address: (b.) University of Glasgow, School of Humanities, Glasgow G12 8QQ; T.-0141-330 4509.

Brock, Deidre, BA. MP (SNP), Edinburgh North and Leith, since 2015; Shadow SNP Spokesperson (Devolved Government Relations), since 2015; Shadow SNP Westminster Group Leader (Scottish Parliament/Scottish Government Liaison), since 2015; b. Western Australia; 2 d. Educ. Curtin University; Western Australian Academy of Performing Arts. Worked for Rob Gibson MSP before being elected as SNP Councillor on the City of Edinburgh Council for the Leith Walk ward in 2007; formerly Convenor of Culture and Leisure; re-elected in the 2012 elections; formerly Deputy Lord Provost of Edinburgh. Select committees in Parliament: Public Accounts Commission, since 2015, Public Accounts Committee, since 2015. Recreations: theatre; netball; cinema; traditional Scottish music and arts. Address: House of Commons, London SW1A 0AA.

Brock, Jackie. Chief Executive, Children in Scotland, since 2012. Career: worked across local government and the third sector; 12 years experience across various posts and departments in the Civil Service and most recently led the major change programme underway in Scottish education, Curriculum for Excellence, as Deputy Director of Learning and Support; has experience across the developments in Scotland's schools including significantly additional support for learning and health and well-being but also in foster, kinship and residential care and youth justice. Address: (b.) Children in Scotland, Princes House, 5 Shandwick Place, Edinburgh EH2 4RG; T.-0131 228 8484.

Brockie, Rev. Colin Glynn Frederick, BSc (Eng), BD, SOSc. Minister, Kilmarnock: Grange, 1978-2007; Clerk to Presbytery of Irvine and Kilmarnock, 1992-2011; Hon. Chaplain, 327 (Kilmarnock) Squadron, Air Training Corps, since 1978; Chaplain, West Scotland Wing, ATC, since 2001; Secretary, Society of Ordained Scientists, since 2013; b. 17.7.42, Westcliff on Sea; m., Barbara Katherine Gordon; 2 s.; 1 d. Educ. Musselburgh Grammar School; Aberdeen Grammar School; University of Aberdeen. Probationary year, Aberdeen: Mastrick, 1967-68; Minister, St. Martin's, Edinburgh, 1968-78. Recreations: billiards; photography; computing. Address: 36 Braehead Court, Kilmarnock,

Ayrshire KA3 7AB.
E-mail: revcol@revcol.demon.co.uk

Brocklebank, Ted. MSP (Conservative), Mid Scotland and Fife, Scottish Parliament, 2003-2011; Shadow Minister for Europe, External Affairs and Culture, 2007-2011; formerly Scottish Conservative Rural Development and Fisheries Spokesman; b. 24.9.42, St. Andrews; 2 s. Educ. Madras College, St. Andrews. D.C. Thomson, Dundee, 1960-63; Freelance Journalist, 1963-65; Scottish TV, 1965-70; Grampian Television: Reporter, 1970-76, Head of News and Current Affairs, 1977-85, Head of Documentaries and Features, 1985-95; M. D., Greyfriars Prods, St. Andrews, 1995-2003. BAFTA Award for What Price Oil?; Radio Industries Club of Scotland Special Award (Documentary) for Tale of Two Cities; Norwegian Amanda award for Oil, eight-part series on world oil business, networked on Channel 4 and throughout USA on PBS; BMA Award for Scotland the Grave. Recreations: Life Member, St. Andrews Preservation Trust; Trustee, Kinburn Trust (St. Andrews) Charitable Trust.

Brodie, Chic, BSc. MSP (SNP), South Scotland, 2011-16. Educ. Morgan Academy, Dundee; University of St Andrews. Has run several companies and been an advisor to small and start-up companies in Scotland. Stood as a Liberal Democrat candidate in the 1992, 1997 and 2001 UK General Elections; then switched parties to the Scottish National Party, standing for them in the 2010 UK general election for Ayr, Carrick and Cumnock and the 2011 Scottish Parliament general election for Ayr.

Brodie of Lethen, Ewen John, CVO. Lord-Lieutenant of Nairnshire, since 1999; b. 16.12.42, Inverness; m., Mariota Menzies; 3 d. Educ. Harrow School. Lt., Grenadier Guards, 1961-64; IBM (UK) Ltd., 1965-74; Director, John Gordon & Son Ltd, 1992-2011; estate management, since 1975; Recreation: country sports. Address: (h.) The Dower House, Lethen, Nairnshire IV12 5PR; T.-01667 452123.

Brodie, James, OBE, FFCS. National Chairman, Victim Support Scotland, 1998-2003; Director, The Ayrshire Hospice, 1987-2008; b. 29.4.38, Elderslie; m., Anne Tweedie; 1 s. Educ. Ayr Academy. Joined Ayrshire Constabulary, 1955, and retired as Superintendent; during career was: Chairman, West of Scotland Security Association; Chairman, Ayrshire and Arran Review Committee on Child Abuse; National Secretary, SASD; Director, Strathclyde Police Crime Prevention courses; Member, National Council, SACRO; Member, Home Office Working Party on vandalism caused by fires; Member, Secretary of State's Working Party on Police Community courses; Member, Executive Committee, Strathclyde Federation of Boys' Clubs; Member, West of Scotland Committee, Institute of Contemporary Scotland; Co-Chairman, Joint Management Committee, 1st Ayr Company, BB; Elder, St Columba Church. Recreations: reading; music; gardening. Address: (h.) 3 Portmark Avenue, Doonbank, Ayr KA7 4DD; T.-01292 443553.

Brodie, Penny, FRSA. Executive Director, Lead Scotland, 2007-2015; b. Calgary, Canada; 1 s.; 1 d. Educ. James Fowler High School; Dundee College. Administrator, Maxwelltown Information Centre, Dundee, 1995-99; Co-ordinator (Programme), Visual Research Centre, Dundee University, 1999-2001; Chief Executive, Perth and Kinross Association of Voluntary Services (PKAVS), 2001-07. Director: Scotland's Garden Trust; Board Member/Chairman, Perth College

UHI, 2004-2014; former Member, Soroptimist International Perth, 2005-2012, having served as Regional Representative, Vice-President, President Elect, President (two terms of office) and Immediate Past President; also having served as Vice-President, President Elect, President and Immediate Past President for Soroptimist International Scotland North Region. Recreations: travel; reading. Address: (h.) Blairgowrie, Perthshire; T.-0131 228 9441.
E-mail: pbrodie8@gmail.com

Brodie, Peter, MA (Oxon), MA (Ed) (Kent), PGCE. Rector, The Glasgow Academy, since 2005; b. 23.5.57, Oxford. Educ. Abingdon School; St. John's College, Oxford. The King's School, Canterbury: Head of English, 1987-94, Housemaster, 1994-2005. Editor of several Longman Study Texts. Recreations: gardens; walking; reading. Address: (b.) Colebrooke Street, Glasgow G12 8HE; T.-0141 342 5485; e-mail: rector@tga.org.uk

Brodie, Rt. Hon Lord (Philip Hope Brodie); QC, LLB, LLM. Senator of the College of Justice in Scotland, since 2002; Chairman, Judicial Studies Committee, 2006-2012; b. 14.7.50; m.; 2 s.; 1 d. Educ. Dollar Academy; Edinburgh University; University of Virginia. Address: Parliament House, Parliament Square, Edinburgh EH1 1RQ.

Broni, David Alexander Thomas, MBA. Account Manager, Scottish Enterprise, since 2002; b. 25.10.57, Glasgow; m., Ann Frances; 1 s.; 1 d. Educ. St. Mungo's Academy. Joined civil service, 1975; Manpower Services Commission, 12 years, Training Agency, 2 years, Scottish Office Industry Department, 2 years; Head of Secretariat, Scottish Enterprise, 4 years; Scottish Development International, 7 years; Chair of Tullochan (2 years); Director, Glasgow Rotary Charities Appeal (3 years); Chair, Scottish Enterprise Staff Charity Fund (5 years); Founder, D2B Adventure. Recreations: adventure racing organiser; swimming; Rotary. Address: (b.) Caspian House, 2 Mariner Court, 8 South Avenue, Clydebank Business Park, Clydebank G81 2NR; T.-0141 951 3009; e-mail: davy.broni@gmail.com

Brooke, (Alexander) Keith, FRAgS. Farmer; b. 11.2.46, Minnigaff; m., Dilys K. Littlejohn; 1 s.; 3 d. Educ. George Watson's College, Edinburgh. President, Blackface Sheep Breeders Association, 1985-86, Hon. President, 1989-90 and since 2007. Awarded Connachan Salver for Services to the Breed by Blackface Sheep Breeders' Association, 2007; Director: Royal Highland and Agricultural Society of Scotland, 1986-93 and since 1994 (formerly Convener, Public Relations and Education Committee, Inaugural Chairman, Royal Highland Education Trust, 1998-2001, Honorary Treasurer and Chief Steward, Press Radio and Television), Animal Diseases Research Association, now Moredun Foundation for Animal Health and Welfare, 1981-96, Wallets Marts PLC, 1989-91, Scottish, English and Welsh Wool Growers Ltd., 1988-95, Wigtownshire Quality Lamb Ltd., 1991-96; Chairman, Blackface Sheep Breeders' Development Board, 1996-99; Member: Council of Awards of Royal Agricultural Societies, since 1997 and RHASS Representative on Scottish Panel; Council, British Rouge de l'Ouest Sheep Society, 1986-97 (Chairman, 1990-92, Treasurer, 1994-97); formerly Chairman of Stewartry Western District Agricultural Club; Chairman of Stewartry District Association of YFCs and Final Chairman of Old South West Area of YFCs; member of winning Scottish International Beef Judging Team, 1966, and member of winning Stewartry Team, 1970 at the Royal Highland Show

Stockjudging Competition for the Glasgow Herald Trophy; member of winning team from Stewartry Western in 1966 Scottish National Beef Judging Competition. Address: (h.) Carscreugh, Glenluce, Newton Stewart DG8 0NU; T.-01581 300334.

Brooke, Hazel, MBE, MA. Executive Director, Scottish Cot Death Trust, 1988-2005; b. 31.7.45, Forfar; m., Anthony Brooke; 2d. Educ. Inverness Royal Academy; Edinburgh University; Strathclyde University. Unilever, London; The Rank Organisation, London; Scottish Council, Development and Industry, Edinburgh; Glasgow University; Member, Merchant's House, Glasgow; Vice Chair of Court, Glasgow Caledonian University. Recreations: reading; wine appreciation; singing. Address: (h.) 9 Campbell Drive, Bearsden G61 4NF; T.-0141-942 7492.

Brookes, Sue. Governor, HM YOI Polmont Prison, since 2012. Address: (b.) Polmont, Brightons, Falkirk FK2 0AB; T.-01324 711558.

Brooks, James, DSc, PhD, MPhil, BTech, FRSC, CChem, FGS, CGeol, CSci. Senior Partner, Brooks Associates Glasgow, since 1986; President, Baptist Union of Scotland, 2002-03; Myron Sturgeon Professor in Geological Sciences, Ohio University, 2003; m., Jan Slack; 1 s. (Daniel); 1 d. (Naomi). Educ. Salt Grammar School, Yorkshire; University of Bradford. Research Scientist, British Petroleum, 1969-75; Senior Research Fellow, Bradford University, 1975-77; Research Associate/Senior Scientist, British National Oil Corporation/Britoil PLC, 1977-86. Visiting Lecturer, Glasgow University, 1978-98; Chairman/Director, Petroleum Geology '86 Limited, 1985-99; Visiting Lecturer, University of Bradford, 2004-2010; Geological Society: Vice President, 1984-87, Secretary, 1987-90; Founder and First Chairman of The Petroleum Group, The Geological Society (1981); AAPG Distinguished Achievement Award for service to petroleum geology, 1993; AAPG Distinguished Lecturer to North America, 1989-90; Geological Society Distinguished Service Award, 1999; Life Member, AAPG, 1990; Man of Achievement, 2005; Honorary Member, AAPG, 2006; Honorary Fellow, Royal Society of Chemistry (2014); UK Government Exchange Scientist to USSR (1971); Royal Society Visiting Scientist to India (1976-77) and to USSR (1991). Chairman, Shawlands Academy School Board, 1992-98; Member of Research Ethics Committee for West of Scotland NHS, 2006-2011; Royal Society of Chemistry Ambassador to Schools; The Geological Society Scrutineer for Chartered Geologist (CGeol) status, since 2007; elected to position of Chair, University of Bradford Alumni, October 2013; Honorary Member, Royal Society of Chemistry (2014); Executive Committee Member, Keir Hardie Society (2015); University of Bradford (Council, 1977-80 and since 2013). Publications: 18 books including: "Origin and Development of Living Systems" and "Origin of Life" (awarded Golden Medallion and Order of Merit); "The Full Spectrum: My Life, Times and Views" (autobiography), 2013; 100 research papers. Recreations: travel; reading; writing; sport (English soccer!); Christian work. Address: (h.) 12 Terringzean View, Cumnock, Ayrshire KA18 1FB; T.-01290 425 645; e-mail: dr.jim.brooks@gmail.com

Brooks, Dr. Naomi, BSc (Hons), PhD. Lecturer (Sport), University of Stirling, since 2012; b. Glasgow. Educ. Shawlands Academy, Glasgow; Ohio University. Post-doctoral Fellow, Human Nutrition Research Centre for Aging, Tufts University, Boston, MA, USA, 2005-06; Post-doctoral Associate, Stellenbosch University, South Africa, 2007-09, Lecturer, 2010-12. Presented invited seminars at universities in the USA and South Africa and given research presentations at various international conferences, one of which achieved the Health and Wellness Award: Best Oral Presentation on Sport at the Physiological Society of Southern Africa, Annual Meeting, 2008. Published numerous research papers in peer-reviewed journals; written chapters for books and spoken at various international conferences. Address: (b.) School of Sport, University of Stirling, Stirling FK9 4LA; T.-01786 466 478; Fax: 01786 466 477; e-mail: n.e.brooks@stir.ac.uk Web: www.stir.ac.uk/sport

Brooks, Stuart. Director and Chief Executive, John Muir Trust. Address: (b.) Tower House, Station Road, Pitlochry, PH16 5AN; T.-01796 484934.

Broun, Janice Anne, BA. Freelance journalist and author; b. 24.3.34, Tipton; m., Canon Claud Broun; 2 s.; 1 d. Educ. Dudley Girls High School; St. Anne's College, Oxford. Publications: Conscience and Captivity: Religion in Eastern Europe, 1988; Prague Winter, 1988; Albania: Religion in a Fortress State, 1989; Bulgaria: Religion Denied, 1989; Romania: Religion in a Hardline State, 1989; six entries in Censorship: A World Encyclopedia, 2002; frequent contributions and book reviews to Keston Institute publications: Religion, State and Society and Frontier. Recreations: swimming; cycling; music; art; history; Tai-chi. Address: Martin Lodge, Ardross Place, Alness, Ross-shire, IV17 0PX; T.-01349 882442. E-mail: janiceandclaudbroun@yahoo.co.uk

Brown, Alan. MP (SNP), Kilmarnock and Loudon, since 2015; b. 12.8.70, Kilmarnock. Educ. Loudon Academy; Glasgow University. Worked in both the public and private sectors, as a Civil engineer. Elected SNP councillor in the 2007 East Ayrshire Council election (Irvine Valley ward); re-elected in 2012; held positions in Housing and Strategic Planning & Resources. Address: House of Commons, London SW1A 0AA.

Brown, Alan David Gillespie, MBChB, FRCOG, FRCSE. Consultant Obstetrician and Gynaecologist, initially at Eastern General Hospital, then at the Royal Infirmary, Edinburgh, 1983-2004; b. 27.5.39, Falkirk; m., Elizabeth Ballantyne; 2 step-s; 1 step-d. Educ. Dalhousie School, Fife; Merchiston Castle School, Edinburgh; Medical Faculty, Edinburgh University. MRC Research Fellowship, Middlesex Hospital, London; appointed Senior Lecturer/Hon. Consultant in O & G, University Hospital of South Manchester, 1975; returned to Edinburgh, 1983. Previously, Hon. Gynaecologist and Vice-Chair, Caledonia Youth; President, Edinburgh Obstetrical Society, 2002-04; Member, Business Committee, General Council, University of Edinburgh, since 2005, Convener, 2009-2012, Regent of the University, since 2012. Publications: over 50 articles and textbook chapters. Recreations: golf; theatre; opera; travel. Address: (h.) Arthur Lodge, Blacket Place, Edinburgh EH9 1RL; T.-0131 667 5163; e-mail: alanbrown179@btinternet.com

Brown, Alastair Nigel, LLB (Hons), PhD. Sheriff of Tayside, Central and Fife at Dundee; b. 3.5.55, Kirkcaldy; m., Dr Susan Brown; 2 s.; 1 d. Educ. Royal Grammar School, Newcastle-upon-Tyne; University of Edinburgh. Solicitor (Scotland), 1979; Member, Procurator Fiscal Service, 1981-2009, including Procurator Fiscal, Dunfermline, 2003 and Advocate Depute, 2003-09; Solicitor (England & Wales), 1992; Advocate - Called to Bar, 2010, practised, 2010-2011. Council of Europe expert on Corruption Law; Trustee, St Thomas' Church, Corstorphine. Publications: "Money Laundering" (2009); Criminal Evidence and Procedure: An Introduction", 3rd ed. (2011); Annotated Statutes: Human Rights Act, 1998; Proceeds of Crime Act, 2002; Extradition Act, 2003; Sexual Offences (Scotland) Act, 2009; Bribery Act, 2010.

Address: (b.) Dundee Sheriff Court, 6, West Bell Street, Dundee DD1 9AD.

Brown, Professor Alice, MA, PhD, CBE, FRSE, FRCP Edin, FRSA, AcSS, Cipfa (Hon). Chair, Scottish Funding Council, since 2013; General Secretary, Royal Society of Edinburgh, 2011-2013; Scottish Public Services Ombudsman, 2002-2009; b. 30.9.46, Edinburgh; m., Alan James Brown; 2 d. Educ. Boroughmuir High School, Edinburgh; Stevenson College, Edinburgh; University of Edinburgh. Lecturer in Economics, University of Stirling, 1984; University of Edinburgh: Lecturer, Departments of Economics, Continuing Education and Politics, 1985-92, Senior Lecturer in Politics, 1992-97, appointed Head of Politics Department, 1995, appointed Head, Planning Unit, 1996, Personal Chair, 1997; Co-Director, Institute of Governance, 1998-2002, Vice Principal, 1999-2002, Professor Emeritus, 2008. Honorary Degree (Doctor of the University), University of Stirling, 2004; Fellow of Stevenson College, Edinburgh, 2006; Honorary Degree (Doctor of Laws), Edinburgh Napier University, 2009; Honorary Degree (Honoris Causa), University of Edinburgh, 2008. Received Special Recognition Award from the Political Studies Association, 2009. Council Member, Administrative Justice and Tribunals Council (AJTC), 2008-2013; Trustee, David Hume Institute; Chair, Lay Advisory Group, Royal College of Physicians of Edinburgh, 2009-2013; Member, Advisory Board, Institute for Advanced Studies in the Humanities, University of Edinburgh, 2011-2013; Member, Scottish Resource Centre Steering Committee, Edinburgh Napier University, 2011-2013. Fellow, Sunningdale Institute, 2008-2012; Executive Member, British and Irish Ombudsman Association (BIOA), 2006-2009; Member, Architects Registration Board, 2006-2009; Member, Committee on Standards in Public Life, 1999-2003; ESRC Research Grants Board and other committees, 1997-2001; Board Member, Scottish Higher Education Funding Council (SHEFC), 1998-2002; Chair, Community Planning Taskforce, 2000-02; Member, Public Sector Finance Taskforce, 2001; Member, Scottish Committee, British Council, 1998-2002; Member, Hansard Society Scotland and other committees, 1998-2002; Member, Advisory Group to the EOC in Scotland, 1995-2002; Member, Advisory Group to the CRE in Scotland, 2003-07; Member, Consultative Steering Group in Scotland, 1997-98; Executive Member, Political Studies Association, 1996-1999; Executive Member, Centre for Scottish Public Policy; Assistant Editor, Scottish Affairs journal, 1992-2002; Co-Editor, The Scottish Government Yearbook, 1989-1991. Hon. Degree, Dlitt, Glasgow Caledonian University, 2012; Hon. Degree, Dr of Social Sciences, Queen's University of Belfast, 2014; Member, Board of Governors, Public Policy, Institute for Wales, since 2014; Member, Strategic Group on Women and Work, Scottish Government, since 2013; Member of Programme Board of Scotland's Futures Forum, since 2016. Publications: The MSC in Scotland (Joint Editor and Contributor) 1989; Restructuring Education in Ireland (Joint Author), 1993; A Major Crisis: The Politics of Economic Policy in Britain in the 1990s (Joint Author), 1996; Gender Equality in Scotland (Joint Author), 1997; Politics and Society in Scotland (Joint Author), 1996 and 1998; The Scottish Electorate (Joint Author), 1999; New Scotland, New Politics (Joint Author), 2001; The Changing Politics of Gender Equality in Britain (Joint Editor), 2002; Author of numerous book chapters, articles, papers and reports. Recreations: reading; music; cooking. Address: Scottish Funding Council, Apex 2, 97 Haymarket Terrace, Edinburgh, Midlothian EH12 5HD; T.-0131 313 6500.

Brown, Professor Alistair J.P., BSc, PhD, DSc, FRSE, FAAM, FSB. Professor of Molecular and Cell Biology, Aberdeen University, since 1998; b. 5.2.55; m., Carolyn Michie; 2 s (Myles and Cameron). Educ. George Watson's College, Edinburgh; University of Aberdeen. Biotechnology Lecturer, Glasgow University, 1983-89; Aberdeen University: Biotechnology Lecturer, 1989-91, Senior Lecturer, 1992-96, Reader, 1996-98. Society for General Microbiology Kathleen Barton-Wright Prize Lecturer, 2002. Recreations: reading; skiing; Scottish rugby; his family. Address: (b.) Institute of Medical Sciences, Foresterhill, Aberdeen AB25 2ZD; T.-01224 437482.

Brown, Andrew Stewart, BArch (Hons), RIBA, ARIAS. Managing Partner, Simpson and Brown Architects, 1977-2009, Consultant, since 2010; b. 7.6.45, Northwood; m., Morven Islay Helen Gibson; 1 s.; 1 d. Educ. Bradfield College, Berkshire; Edinburgh University. Architect with Sir Basil Spence Glover and Ferguson, Edinburgh, 1970-73; Architect with Andrew Renton, Edinburgh, 1973-77; Founding Partner, Simpson and Brown Architects, 1977; Director and Company Secretary, Addyman Associates, Building Research, Building Archaeologists and Archaeologists. Trustee, Scotland's Churches Scheme, 1997-2012; Trustee, Scotland's Churches Trust, 2012-2014; former Chairman, Traverse Theatre, Edinburgh. Recreations: restoring vintage motorcars and older buildings. Address: (h.) 49 Stirling Road, Edinburgh EH5 3JB; T.-(b.) 0131 555 4678.
E-mail: sbrown@simpsonandbrown.co.uk

Brown, Colin. Deputy Director, Office of the Director General Health and Social Care and Chief Executive, NHS Scotland, Scottish Government. Address: (b.) St. Andrews House, Regent Road, Edinburgh EH1 3DG; T.-0131 244 2131.

Brown, Rev. Colin Campbell, BD. Principal Clerk to General Assembly, since 2004; Minister, Darnley United Free Church, Glasgow, since 1979; Moderator, General Assembly, United Free Church of Scotland, 2002; Teacher (part-time) of Religious Education, Williamwood High School, Glasgow, since 1987; b. 30.8.54, Perth; m., Joyce; 1 s. Educ. Perth High School; University of Edinburgh; Moray House College of Education. Convener, United Free Church Youth Committee, 1985-89; Moderator, Presbytery of Glasgow and the West, 1990-91; Convener, Action of Churches Together in Scotland Education Group, 1992-94; Convener, United Free Church Ministry and Home Affairs Committee, 1997-2002; part-time Religious Education Teacher, Renfrew High School, 1980-87. Address: 2 Waukglen Drive, Southpark, Darnley, Glasgow G53 7UG; T.-0141-638 6101.

Brown, Professor David William, MA (Edin/Oxon), PhD (Cantab), DPhil (Oxon), DLitt (Edin), FBA, FRSE. Professor of Theology, Aesthetics and Culture, St. Andrews University, 2007-2015, Wardlaw Professor, 2008-2015, Professor Emeritus, since 2015; b. 1.7.48, Galashiels. Educ. Keil School, Dumbarton; University of Edinburgh; University of Oxford; University of Cambridge. Fellow and Tutor in Theology and Philosophy, Oriel College, Oxford and University Lecturer in Philosophical Theology, Oxford, 1976-90; Van Mildert Professor of Divinity, Durham University and Canon of Durham Cathedral, 1990-2007. Fellow of British Academy, since 2002, Member of its Council (Governing Body), 2008-2012. Publications: The Divine Trinity, 1985; Continental Philosophy and Modern Theology, 1987; Tradition and Imagination, 1999; Discipleship and Imagination, 2000; God and Enchantment of Place, 2004; God and Grace of Body, 2007; God and Mystery in Words, 2008; Divine Humanity, 2011; Durham Cathedral: Community, Fabric and Culture, 2015; 7 other books. Recreation: gardening.
E-mail: dwb21@st-andrews.ac.uk

Brown, Derek. Head of Education, Fife Council, since 2014. Career: Senior Depute, Jordanhill School, then Headteacher, Oldmachar Academy (2009-2014). Address: (b.) Fife Council, Fife House, North Street, Glenrothes, Fife KY7 5LT; T.-0845 155 0000.

Brown, Douglas. Head Teacher, Boclair Academy. Address: Inveroran Drive, Bearsden G61 2PL; T.-0141 955 2358; e-mail: office@boclair.e-dunbarton.sch.uk

Brown, Douglas Carl Jessen, DA (Edin), DMS, MPhil, FRSA, MSDC, MIMGT, AIST, ASIC. Honorary Secretary, Commonwealth Games Council for Scotland, 1999-2011, Hon. Life Vice President, 2011; Member, Board of Management, Scottish Amateur Swimming Association, 1995-2003; b. 2.10.40, Edinburgh; m., Noreen Simpson; 2 s.; 2 d. Educ. High School of Dundee; Edinburgh College of Art; Edinburgh College of Commerce; Open University. Lecturer, then Depute Head, School of Design, Edinburgh College of Art, 1964-86; Director, School of Design, Edinburgh College of Art/Heriot-Watt University, 1986-95 (retired); professional practice in design and making, silversmith and jeweller; Member, Senate, Heriot-Watt University, 1986-95; Secretary, Association of Scottish Schools of Design, 1988-90; Member, Board of Governors, Edinburgh College of Art, 1974-79, 1988-89; teaching and coaching competitive swimming at club and district levels, 1977-89; Administrative Co-ordinator for all aquatic events, Commonwealth Games, 1986; Chairman, Organising Committee, European Swimming Cup, 1988; Technical Co-ordinator, European Junior Swimming and Diving Championships, 1997; Member, Amateur Swimming Federation of Great Britain Committee, 1995-2001. Recreations: reading; photography; travel; boating; fishing. Address: (h.) 29 Hartington Place, Edinburgh EH10 4LF; T.-0131-229 6924.

Brown, Sir Ewan, CBE, MA, LLB, DUniv (Heriot-Watt), CA, FRSE, FCIBS, FRSA, Hon FRZS (Scot). Director: Scottish Financial Enterprise (Chairman), Noble Grossart Holdings Ltd.; Stagecoach Holdings Plc; James Walker (Leith) Ltd (Chairman); b. 23.3.42, Perth; m., Christine; 1 s.; 1 d. Educ. Perth Academy; St. Andrews University. CA apprentice with Peat Marwick Mitchell, 1964-67. Senior Governor of Court, St. Andrews University; Board Member, Entrepreneurial Scotland; Trustee, Royal Scottish Academy Foundation; Deputy Chair, Edinburgh International Festival Society, 2006-2014; Honorary Professor in Finance, Heriot Watt University, 1988-2010; Treasurer, Royal Society of Edinburgh, 2008-12; Trustee, National Youth Orchestras of Scotland, 2006-2011; Member, Council of Assembly, Church of Scotland, 2004-07; Chairman, University Court, Heriot-Watt University, 1996-2002; Master, The Company of Merchants of the City of Edinburgh, 1994-95; Lord Dean of Guild, City of Edinburgh, 1995-97; Council Member: Institute of Chartered Accountants of Scotland, 1988-91, Scottish Business School, 1974-80; previous directorships: Scottish Transport Group, 1983-88, Scottish Development Finance, 1983-93, Harrison Lovegrove Plc, Lloyds Banking Group, 1999-2009, John Wood Group plc, 1983-2006, Pict Petroleum plc, 1973-95, Scottish Widows Bank plc, 1994-97; Trustee, Carnegie Trust for the Universities of Scotland, 1988-2005; Chairman: Lloyds TSB Scotland, 1998-2008, Dunedin Income Growth Investment Trust Plc, 1996-2001, Transport Initiatives Edinburgh Ltd, 2002-06, Scottish Knowledge Plc, 1997-2002; Governor, Edinburgh College of Art, 1986-89; Chair, Creative Scotland 2009 Ltd, 2008-2010. Knighted in 2014 for services to business, public life and philanthropy. Recreations: family; golf; skiing; Scottish art; Mah Jongg. Address: (b.) 48 Queen Street, Edinburgh; T.-0131-226 7011.

Brown, Gavin. MSP (Conservative), Lothian, 2011-16, Lothians, 2007-2011; Shadow Minister for Enterprise, Energy and Tourism, 2007-2011; Shadow Minister for Finance, Employment and Sustainable Growth, 2011-16; b. 4.6.75, Kirkcaldy; m., Hilary Jane Brown (nee Fergus); 1 d.; 2 s. Educ. Fettes College; Strathclyde University. Solicitor, McGrigor Donald, 1998-2002; Director, Speak with Impact Ltd, since 2002. Finance Committee; JCI Most Outstanding Trainer in the World Award, 2004. Recreations: tae kwon-do (1st Degree Black Belt).

Brown, Hamish Macmillan, MBE, D.Litt, D.Uni, Open, FRSGS. Author, Lecturer, Photographer and Mountaineer; b. 13.8.34, Colombo, Sri Lanka. Educ. several schools abroad; Dollar Academy. National Service, RAF, Middle East/East Africa; Assistant, Martyrs' Memorial Church, Paisley; first-ever full-time appointment in outdoor education (Braehead School, Fife); served many years on Scottish Mountain Leadership Board; has led expeditions world-wide for mountaineering, skiing, trekking, canoeing, botanising, etc. Publications: Hamish's Mountain Walk, 1979 (SAC award); Hamish's Groats End Walk, 1981 (Smith's Travel Prize shortlist); Time Gentlemen, Some Collected Poems, 1983; Eye to the Hills, 1982; Five Bird Stories, 1984; Poems of the Scottish Hills (Editor), 1982; Speak to the Hills (Co-Editor), 1985; Travels, 1986; The Great Walking Adventure, 1986; Hamish Brown's Scotland, 1988; Climbing the Corbetts, 1988; Great Walks Scotland (Co-author), 1989; Scotland Coast to Coast, 1990; Walking the Summits of Somerset and Avon, 1991; From the Pennines to the Highlands, 1992; The Bothy Brew & Other Stories, 1993; The Fife Coast, The Last Hundred, 1994; 25 Walks Fife; Seton Gordon's Scotland (anthology); Fort William and Glen Coe Walks, 1996; Compendium: Hamish's Mountain Walks/Climbing the Corbetts, 1997; Fife in Focus, Photographs of the Fife Coast; 25 Walks, Skye and Kintail, 2000; Billy Black's Dog/The Lost Hogmanay (stories), 2002; Travelling Hopefully (poems), 2003; Along the Fife Coastal Path, 2004; Seton Gordon's Scotland (anthology), 2005; Exploring the Edinburgh to Glasgow Canals, 2006; The Mountains Look on Marrakech (Atlas traverse), 2006 (shortlisted for Boardman-Tasker Prize, 2007); A Scottish Graveyard Miscellany, Achnashellach (poems); Seton Gordon's Cairngorms (Anthology), 2009; Hamish's Mountain Walk, 2010; Hamish's Groat's End Walk, 2011; Walking the Mull Hills, 2011; The High Atlas; Peaks and Climbs (200 photographs); The Oldest Post Office in the World and Other Scottish Oddities, 2012; Climbing the Corbetts, 2012; Three Men on the Way Way (West Highland Way), 2013; Tom Weir, An Anthology, 2013; Fantasies, Fables, Fibs and Follies (stories), 2014; Canals Across Scotland, 2015. Recreations: books; music; Morocco; alpine gardening. Address: 8 Links Place, Burntisland, Fife KY3 9DY; T.-01592 873546.

Brown, Professor Ian James Morris, MA (Hons), MLitt, PhD, DipEd, FRSA, FHEA, FFCS. Professor in Drama and Dance, Kingston University, since 2010; Freelance scholar, arts and education consultant, 2002-2010; Playwright, since 1969; b. 28.2.45, Barnet; m., 1, Judith Sidaway; 2, Nicola Axford; 1 s.; 1 d. Educ. Dollar Academy; Edinburgh University; Crewe and Alsager College. Schoolteacher, 1967-69, 1970-71; Lecturer in Drama, Dunfermline College, 1971-76; British Council: Assistant Representative, Scotland, 1976-77, Assistant Regional Director, Istanbul, 1977-78; various posts, Crewe and Alsager College, 1978-86, latterly Leader, BA (Hons) Drama Studies; Programme Director, Alsager Arts Centre, 1980-86; Drama Director, Arts Council of Great Britain, 1986-94; Queen Margaret University College, Edinburgh: Reader, 1994-95, Professor of Drama, 1995-2002, Head, Drama Department, 1996-99, Dean, Arts Faculty, 1999-2002, Director, Scottish Centre for Cultural Management and Policy, 1996-2002. British Theatre Institute: Vice Chairman, 1983-85, Chairman, 1985-87; Member, International Advisory Committee, O'Neill Theatre Center,

1994-2012; Chair, Scottish Society of Playwrights, 1973-75, 1984-87, 1997-99 and 2010-13; Scottish Society of Playwrights Council Member, 1999-2007 and 2009-2010; Chair, Highlands and Islands Theatre Network, 2005-09; President, Association for Scottish Literary Studies, 2010-2015, Publications Convener, since 2015; Cultural Consultant, Rose Theatre, Kingston, 2012-14; Visiting Professor, Centre for the Study of Media and Culture in Small Nations, University of Glamorgan, 2007-13; Honorary Senior Research Fellow (Visiting Professor), Department of Scottish Literature, University of Glasgow, since 2007; plays include Mother Earth, The Bacchae, Carnegie, The Knife, The Fork, New Reekie, Mary, Runners, Mary Queen and the Loch Tower, Joker in the Pack, Beatrice, First Strike, The Scotch Play, Bacchai, Wasting Reality, Margaret, A Great Reckonin; An Act o Love; books include Poems for Joan, 2001, and Journey's Beginning: the Gateway building and company, 2004; General Editor, The Edinburgh History of Scottish Literature, 2007; Joint Series Editor, Edinburgh Companions to Scottish Literature, since 2007 (renamed International Companions, from 2014); Co-Editor, Edinburgh Companion to Twentieth-Century Scottish Literature, 2009; Editor, From Tartan to Tartanry (2010); Co-Editor, International Journal of Scottish Theatre and Screen, since 2010; Editor, Edinburgh Companion to Scottish Drama (2011); Editor, Literary Tourism, the Trossachs and Walter Scott (2012); Co-Editor and contributor, Lion's Milk: Turkish Poems by Scottish Poets, 2012; Scottish Theatre: Diversity, Language, Continuity, 2013; Co-Editor, Roots and Fruits of Scottish Culture: Scottish Identities, History and Contemporary Literature (2014); new book of poems: Collyshangles in the Canopy (2015). Saltire Society: Council member, since 2010, Executive Board member, since 2011, Convenor, since 2014; Vice-Chair, Standing Committee of University Drama Departments, since 2013. Recreations: theatre; sport; travel; cooking. Address: Flat 2/1, 2 Darnley Road, Glasgow G41 4NB.

Brown, J. Craig, CBE, DUniv, BEd (Hons), BA, DA. Non-Executive Director, Aberdeen FC, since 2013, formerly Manager, 2010-2013; Manager, Motherwell FC, 2009-2010; Football Consultant, Derby County FC, 2005-07; International Representative, Fulham FC, 2004-05; Manager, Preston North End, 2001-04; Technical Director and International Team Manager, Scottish FA, 1993-2001; Assistant National Coach and Under 21 Team Manager, 1986-93; Manager, Clyde FC, 1977-86; Assistant Manager, Motherwell FC, 1975-77; b. 1.7.40, Glasgow; 2 s.; 1 d. Educ. Hamilton Academy; Scottish School of Physical Education; Open University. Teacher, Head Teacher, Lecturer in Education, 1962-86; Professional footballer: Rangers F.C., 1958-60, Dundee F.C., 1960-66 (League Champion 1962), Falkirk F.C., 1965-68. FIFA Instructor; AEFCA (Alliance of European Football Coaches' Associations) Vice President; Patron, Scottish Disability Sport; Sports Photographers' Personality of the Year, 1989, 1996; City of Glasgow Sportsperson of the Year, 1997; Bells Manager of the Month on 7 occasions; Clydesdale Bank Premier League Manager of the Month on 4 occasions; Hall of Fame - Scottish Football Association, 2010, Clyde FC, 2012, Strathclyde University, 2013. Publications: Activity Methods in the Middle Years, 1975; Craig Brown, The Autobiography, 1998; The Game of My Life, 2001, 2003. Recreation: golf. Address: (b.) Aberdeen Football Club plc, Pittodrie Stadium, Aberdeen AB15 4BE.

Brown, Rt. Hon. (James) Gordon, PC, MA, PhD, MP. Prime Minister and First Lord of the Treasury, 2007-10; Leader of the Labour Party, 2007-10; Chancellor of the Exchequer, 1997-2007; MP (Labour), Kirkcaldy and Cowdenbeath, 2005-2015, Dunfermline East, 1983-2005; UN Special Envoy for Global Education, since 2012; b.

20.2.51; m., Sarah; 2 s. Educ. Kirkcaldy High School; Edinburgh University. Rector, Edinburgh University, 1972-75; Temporary Lecturer, Edinburgh University, 1976; Lecturer, Glasgow College of Technology, 1976-80; Journalist and Current Affairs Editor, Scottish Television, 1980-83. Contested (Labour) South Edinburgh, 1979; Chairman, Labour Party Scottish Council, 1983-84; Opposition Chief Secretary to the Treasury, 1987; Shadow Minister for Trade and Industry, 1989. Publications: The Red Paper on Scotland (Editor), 1975; The Politics of Nationalism and Devolution (Co-Editor), 1980; Scotland: The Real Divide, 1983; Maxton, 1986; Where There is Greed, 1989; John Smith: Life and Soul of the Party (Co-Author), 1994; Values, Visions and Voices: An Anthology of Socialism (Co-Author), 1994: Maxton: A Biography, 2002; Speeches, 1997-2006, 2006; Moving Britain Forward, Selected Speeches, 1997-2006, 2006; Courage: Eight Portraits, 2007; Wartime Courage, 2008; Beyond the Crash, 2010; My Scotland, Our Britain, 2014. Recreations: reading and writing; football; golf; tennis.

Brown, Janet Marjorie, BSc, PhD, FInstP, FRSE. Chief Executive, Scottish Qualifications Authority, since 2007; b. 31.07.51, Sheffield. Educ. High Storrs Grammar School for Girls, Sheffield; University of Birmingham. Visiting Assistant Professor, University of Illinois, Urbana, IL USA, 1981-84; Member of Technical Staff, Bell Laboratories, AT & T, Murray Hill, NJ USA, 1984-90; Director of Process Architecture & Characterisation, SEMATECH, Austin, TX USA, 1990-93; Director, Reliability & Quality Assurance, Motorola, Austin, TX USA, 1993-97; European Operations Director, Smartcard Division, Motorola, East Kilbride, 1997-98; Director of Operations, Networking Systems Memories, Motorola, Austin TX, 1998-2000; Managing Director, Industries, Scottish Enterprise, Glasgow, 2000-07. Address: (b.) Scottish Qualifications Authority, The Optima Building, 58 Robertson Street, Glasgow G2 8QD; T.-0845 213 5588.
E-mail: janet.brown@sqa.org.uk

Brown, Jenny, MA (Hons). Literary agent; b. 13.5.58, Manchester; m., Alexander Richardson; 4 s. Educ. George Watson's College; Aberdeen University; Open University (Honorary Doctorate), 2015. Assistant Administrator, Edinburgh Festival Fringe Society, 1980-82; Director, Edinburgh Book Festival, 1983-91; Presenter, Scottish Television book programmes, 1989-94; National Co-ordinator, Readiscovery Campaign, 1994-95; Head of Literature, Scottish Arts Council, 1996-2002. Commissioner, Press Complaints Commission, 1993-97; Non-Executive Director, Scottish Television (Regional) Ltd., 1998-2004; Governor, George Watson's College, 1999-2005; Board Member, Edinburgh International Book Festival, since 2003; Company Secretary, Edinburgh UNESCO City of Literature Trust, 2004-07; Chair, Association of Scottish Literary Agents, 2009-11; Chair, Bloody Scotland (Scotland's Crime Writing Festival), since 2010. Address: (b.) 31-35 Marchmont Road, Edinburgh EH9 1HU; e-mail: jenny@jennybrownassociates.com

Brown, Jock (John Winton), MA (Cantab), NP. Consultant, Brodies LLP, Solicitors (formerly Partner); Chairman, Children's University Trust, Scotland; Trustee, Children's University, England; Football Commentator, The Sun Goals; b. 7.5.46, Kilmarnock; m., Ishbel; 3 d. Educ. Hamilton Academy; Cambridge University (Sidney Sussex College). Journalist, The Glasgow Herald, and D.C. Thomson & Co. Ltd. (The Sunday Post), 1967-68; Assistant Secretary, The Scottish Football League, 1968-70; Journalist, D.C. Thomson & Co. Ltd. (The Sunday Post), 1970-73; Ballantyne & Copland, Solicitors, Motherwell (Partner, from 1977), 1973-93; Consultant, Ballantyne & Copland, and Director, Caledonian

Television Ltd., 1993-95; Sports Law Consultant, Harper Macleod, Solicitors, Glasgow, 1995-97; General Manager, Football, Celtic F.C., 1997-98; Partner: Winton Brown, Solicitors, Hamilton, 1999-2005, Bishops Solicitors LLP, Glasgow, 2005-06; Brodies LLP, Glasgow, 2006-2010. Part-Time: Sports Broadcaster, BBC Radio Scotland, 1977-80; Football Commentator: Scottish Television plc, 1980-90, BSkyB, 1989-95, BBC Scotland Television, 1990-97; Current Affairs Radio Broadcaster, Scot FM, 1999-2000; Football Commentator: ITV On Digital, 1999-2001, ntl, 2001-02, Setanta Sports, 2003-09, BT Vision and Scottish Televison, 2009-10; Sky Sports, 2010-2012. Publication: Celtic-Minded, 1999. Recreation: golf. Address: (b.) 2 Blythswood Square, Glasgow G2 4AD; T.-0141-248-4672. E-mail: jock.brown@brodies.com

Brown, John, CBE, MBA. Chairman, NHS Greater Glasgow and Clyde, since 2015. Educ. University of Glasgow. Senior Civil Servant, Central Government, 2000-2013; Member, Lay, Advisory Board, Royal College of Physicians and Surgeons of Glasgow, 2014-15; Company Secretary, Student Loans Company, 2014-15; Managing Director, JJ Brown Consulting Ltd, since 2014. Associate, Chartered Institute of Management Accountants; Fellow, Institute of Leadership & Management; Fellow, Institute of Credit Management; Member, Institute of Chartered Secretaries & Administrators. Address: NHS Greater Glasgow and Clyde, 1055 Great Western Road, Glasgow G12 0XH; T.-0141 201 4444.

Brown, John Caldwell, DA, RSW. Painter; Member, Board, Leith School of Art, 1991-2007; b. 19.10.45, Irvine; m., Elizabeth Ann (deceased); 3 s. Educ. Ardrossan Academy; 1967 David Murray Scholarship, Royal Academy; Glasgow School of Art. RSA Carnegie Travelling Scholarship and GSA Cargill Travelling Scholarship, 1968; Director of Art, Fettes College, 1971-86; Director of Art, Malvern College, 1986-88; Head of Art, Edinburgh Academy, 1988-97; former Lecturer (part-time): Edinburgh College of Art, Leith School of Art; solo exhibitions: GSA, 1970, Moray House, 1989, Torrance Gallery, 1992, Open Eye Gallery, 1996, 1998, 2000, 2002, Duncan Miller Fine Art London, 1996, 1997, 1999, 2000, 2001, 2005, 2007, 2008, 2010, 2013, 2014, John Davies Gallery, 2001, 2003, Richmond Hill Gallery, 2003, 2005, The Scottish Gallery, 2004, 2006, 2009, 2011, 2014, Lemon Street Gallery, 2009, 2011, Rendezvous Gallery, 2010, Stafford Gallery, 2015. James Torrance Award, RGI, 1970; Scottish Arts Club Award SAAC, 1993; Scottish Provident Award, 1993; Heinzel Gallery Award SAAC, 1994; 2010 RSW Council Award; commissioned to make Prestigious Print Edition for Art in Healthcare; Mackintosh Residency in Collioure; Plein-Air Prize PA1; elected Member: Visual Arts Scotland, 1994, Royal Scottish Society of Painters in Watercolour, 1996; Alexander Graham Munro Award, RSW, 2004. Corporate purchase - Aberdeen Assets. Address: (b.) 163B Craigleith Road, Edinburgh EH4 2EB; T.-07816592760.

Brown, Professor John Campbell, BSc, PhD, DSc, FRAS, FRSE, FInstP. Leverhulme Emeritus Research Fellow, 2012-16; Professor Emeritus & Honorary Senior Research Fellow, since 2010; Astronomer Royal for Scotland, since 1995; Professor of Astrophysics, Glasgow University, 1984-96, Regius Chair of Astronomy, 1996-2010; Honorary Professor, Edinburgh University, since 1996, Aberdeen University, since 1997; b. 4.2.47, Dumbarton; m., Dr. Margaret I. Brown; 1 s.; 1 d. Educ. Dumbarton Academy; Glasgow University. Glasgow University Astronomy Department: Research Assistant, 1968-70, Lecturer, 1970-78, Senior Lecturer, 1978-80, Reader, 1980-84; Nuffield Fellow, 1983-84; Kelvin Medallist, 1983-86; Armagh Robinson Medallist, 1998; Institute of Physics Public Awareness of Physics Award, 2002; Royal Astronomical Society Gold Medal (G) 2012; DAAD Fellow, Tubingen University, 1971-72; ESRO/GROC Fellow, Space Research Laboratory, Utrecht, 1973-74; Visitor: Australian National University, 1975, High Altitude Observatory, Colorado, 1977; NASA Associate Professor, Maryland University, 1980; NSF Fellow, University of California at San Diego, 1984; Brittingham Professor, University of Wisconsin, 1987; Visiting Professor: University of Amsterdam, 1999, ETH Zurich, 1999, NASA Goddard SFC, 1999, CNRS Meudon, 1999, University of Alabama, Huntsville, 2003; NASA UC Berkeley, 2006; Marlar Lectureship, Rice U, Texas, 2006; Project Astronomer, Time and Space, Natl. Maritime Museum, 2003-06; Member: SERC Solar System Committee, 1980-83, Council, Royal Astronomical Society, 1984-87, 1990-93 (Vice-President, 1986-87), Council, Royal Society of Edinburgh, 1997-2000, International Astronomical Union, since 1976; President, BAAS Physics Section, 2001. Recreations: cycling; walking; painting; lapidary; conjuring; photography; woodwork. Address: (b.) School of Physics and Astronomy, Glasgow University, Glasgow G12 8QW; T.-0141-330 5182. E-mail: john.brown@glasgow.ac.uk

Brown, John Souter, MA (Hons), FCIPR. Public Relations Consultant; Fellow, Chartered Institute of Public Relations; Accredited PR practitioner; b. 15.10.48, Glasgow; m., Angela McGinn; 1 s.; 1 d. Educ. Kirkcaldy High School; Edinburgh University. Statistics and Information Officer, Lanark County Council, 1970-72; Senior Officer (Research, Planning Publicity), Manchester City Social Services Department, 1972-75; Press Officer, Strathclyde Regional Council, 1975-80; Journalist and Presenter, Scottish Television, 1980-82; Editor, What's Your Problem?, 1982-84; Ways and Means, 1984-86; Senior Producer (Politics), Scottish Television, 1986-91; North of Scotland TV Franchise Team, 1991; Managing Director, Lomond Television, 1992-93; Head of Public Relations, Strathclyde Regional Council, 1993-96; Head of Public Relations and Marketing, Glasgow City Council, 1996-2004; Consultant, Napiershall Formula, since 2015. Chair, Volunteer Centre, Glasgow, 1996-98; Director, Scottish Foundation, 1990-2002; Member, BAFTA Scotland; Member, NUJ; Scotland CIPR Chair, 2004-05; CIPR Council and Board Member, 2008-2012; Chair, CIPR Professional Practices Committee, 2012; National CIPR Treasurer, 2008; Chair, Iprovision CIPR Benevolent Fund, 2010-2015; Awarded Stephen Tallents Medal, 2007; Trustee, Radio Clyde Cash for Kids, 2009-2014; Member, Research Panel, Huddersfield University Centre for Communications and Consultation Research, 2013. Publication: PR and Communication in Local Government and Public Services, 2013 (Co-Author). Address: (h.) 129 Balshagray Avenue, Glasgow G11 7EG; T.-0141 959 4380 or 07881 818474. E-mail: johnbrownpr@gmail.com

Brown, Keith James, MA (Hons). MSP (SNP), Clackmannanshire and Dunblane, since 2011, Ochil, 2007-2011; Cabinet Secretary for Economy, Jobs and Fair Work, since 2016; Cabinet Secretary for Infrastructure, Investment and Cities, 2014-16; Minister for Transport and Veterans, 2012-14; Minister for Housing and Transport, 2011-2012; Minister for Transport and Infrastructure, 2010-2011; Minister for Schools and Skills, 2009-2010; b. 20.12.61, Edinburgh; separated; 2 s.; 1 d. Educ. Tynecastle High School; Dundee University. Royal Marines, 1980-83; local government administrative officer, since 1988. Member, Association of Electoral Administrators. Recreations: astronomy; hill-walking; football. Address: (b.) Scottish Parliament, Edinburgh EH99 1SP.

Brown, Professor Kenneth Alexander, BSc, MSc, PhD, FRSE. Professor of Mathematics, Glasgow University; Vice-President, London Mathematical Society, 1997-99 and since 2009; b. 19.4.51, Ayr; m., Irene M.; 2 s. Educ. Ayr

Academy; Glasgow University; Warwick University. Recreations: reading; running. Address: (b.) School of Mathematics and Statistics, Glasgow University, Glasgow G12 8QW; T.-0141-330 5180.
E-mail: Ken.Brown@glasgow.ac.uk

Brown, Professor Kenneth J., BSc, PhD, FRSE. Professor Emeritus in Mathematics, Heriot-Watt University (Professor, 1993-2007); b. 20.12.45, Torphins; m., Elizabeth Lobban; 1 s.; 2 d. Educ. Banchory Academy; Robert Gordon's College; Aberdeen University; Dundee University. Lecturer in Mathematics, Heriot Watt University, 1970-81, Senior Lecturer, 1981-91, Reader, 1991-93. Publications: 50 papers. Recreations: tennis; theatre; reading; bridge. Address: (h.) 3 Highlea Grove, Balerno, Edinburgh EH14 7HQ; T.-0131-449 5314; e-mail: mthkjb@gmail.com

Brown, R. Iain F, MBE, MA, MEd, ABPsS, ChPsychol, ERC (Hon). Senior Lecturer in Psychology, University of Glasgow (retired); b. 16.1.35, Dundee; m., Catherine G.; 2 d. Educ. Daniel Stewart's College, Edinburgh; St. Andrews University; Edinburgh University; Glasgow University. Education Department, Corporation of Glasgow; Department of Psychological Medicine, Glasgow University; Senior Lecturer, Department of Psychology, University of Glasgow 1968-2000. Honorary Senior Research Fellow, University of Glasgow, until 2005. National Training Advisor, Scottish Council on Alcohol, 1979-94; Member, Executive, Scottish Council on Alcohol, 1980-94 and Alcohol Focus Scotland, 1998-2007; Chairman, Society for the Study of Gambling, London, 1987-92; Founding Chairman, European Association for the Study of Gambling, 1992-95; Chairman, Glasgow Council on Alcohol, 1985-2014, President, since 2014; Founding Chairman, Confederation of Scottish Counselling Agencies, 1989-93; President, Scottish Unitarian Association, 2005-09; Vice-Convener, Scottish Inter Faith Council, 2009-2011; Chairman, Glasgow Anniesland Lib-Dems; Candidate: Glasgow Anniesland (Holyrood) 2000, Motherwell (Westminster) 2001. Various publications, mainly on addictions, in scientific books and journals. Recreations: travel; music. Address: (h.) 13 Kirklee Terrace, Glasgow G12 0TH; T.-0141-339 7815.
E-mail: iain.brown13@gmail.com

Brown, Robert, LLB (Hons). Councillor, Rutherglen South Ward on South Lanarkshire Council, since 2012; MSP (Liberal Democrat), Glasgow, 1999-2011; Spokesperson in Justice and Civil Liberties, 2008-2011; Liberal Democrat Group Business Manager, 2007-08; Convener, Scottish Parliament Education Committee, 2003-05; Deputy Minister for Education and Young People, 2005-07; b. 1947, Newcastle upon Tyne; m.; 1 s.; 1 d. Educ. Gordon Schools, Huntly; Aberdeen University. Solicitor; former Senior Civil Partner, Ross Harper and Murphy; former Glasgow District Councillor (Leader, Lib Dem Group, 1977-92). Address: Council Offices, Beckford Street, Hamilton ML3 0AA; T.-01698 453609.

Brown, Russell Leslie. MP (Labour), Dumfries and Galloway, 2005-2015, Dumfries, 1997-2005; b. 17.9.51, Annan; m., Christine Margaret Calvert; 2 d. Educ. Annan Academy. Employed by ICI for 23 years in variety of positions; Local Councillor, since 1986. Recreations: walking; sport, especially football.

Brown, Sarah Laura, BSc (Hons), PGCE, MA (EdMgmt), PGDipEd and Leadership, SQH. Headteacher, Kinross High School. Address: Loch Leven Community Campus, Muirs KY13 8FQ; T.-01577 867100.
E-mail: kinrosshigh@pkc.gov.uk

Brown, Simon Thomas David, LLB (Hons), DipLP, WS, MCSI, FRSA. Partner and Head of Corporate, Anderson Strathern Solicitors, since 1997; b. 22.4.60, Edinburgh; m.,

Karen Ivory; 2 s.; 1 d. Educ. Royal High School, Edinburgh; Edinburgh University. Dundas and Wilson CS, 1983-89; Partner, Steedman Ramage WS, 1989-97. Director, Publishing Scotland. Recreations: golf; football; family; travel; literature. Address: (b.) 1 Rutland Court, Edinburgh EH3 8EY; T.-0131 270 7700; e-mail: simon.brown@andersonstrathern.co.uk

Brown, Professor Stewart J., BA, MA, PhD, FRHistS, FRSE. Professor of Ecclesiastical History, Edinburgh University, since 1988; Dean, Faculty of Divinity, 2000-04; Head of the School of Divinity, 2010-2013; b. 8.7.51, Illinois; m., Teri B. Hopkins-Brown; 1 s.; 1 d. Educ. University of Illinois; University of Chicago. Fulbright Scholar, Edinburgh University, 1976-78; Whiting Fellow in the Humanities, University of Chicago, 1979-80; Assistant to the Dean, College of Arts & Sciences, and Lecturer in History, Northwestern University, 1980-82; Associate Professor and Assistant Head, Department of History, University of Georgia, 1982-88; Visiting Lecturer, Department of Irish History, University College, Cork, 1986; Editor, Scottish Historical Review, 1993-99. Publications: Thomas Chalmers and the Godly Commonwealth in Scotland, 1982 (awarded Agnes Mure Mackenzie Prize from Saltire Society); Scotland in the Age of the Disruption (Co-author), 1993; William Robertson and the Expansion of Empire (Editor), 1997; Piety and Power in Ireland 1760-1960 (Co-editor), 2000; Scottish Christianity in the Modern World (Co-editor), 2000; The National Churches of England, Ireland and Scotland, 1801-1846, 2001; Cambridge History of Christianity, vol. 7: Enlightenment, Reawakening, and Revolution 1660-1815 (Co-editor), 2006; Providence and Empire: Religion, Politics and Society in the United Kingdom 1815-1917, 2008; The Union of 1707: New Dimensions (Co-editor), 2008; The Oxford Movement: Europe and the Wider World, 1830-1930 (Co-editor), 2012; Religion, Identity and Conflict in Britain: From the Restoration to the Twentieth Century (Co-editor), 2013. Recreations: swimming; hill-walking. Address: (h.) 160 Craigleith Hill Avenue, Edinburgh EH4 2NB; T.-0131-539 2863; e-mail: s.j.brown@ed.ac.uk

Brown, Rev. William David, BD, CQSW. Retired Minister, Murrayfield Parish Church, Edinburgh (2003-2013); Chairman, Children 1st, 2000-09; b.21.8.48, Edinburgh; m., Shirley; 1s.; 1d. Educ. Forrester High School; Edinburgh University; Moray House College. Scottish Office, 1964-70; Royal Scottish Society for the Protection of Cruelty to Children (now Children 1st): Inspector and Project Officer, 1970-78; Development Officer, Scotland. 1978-83; New College studying for BD, 1983-87; Church of Scotland Minister, Carlisle and Longtown. Recreations: reading; walking.

Browne of Ladyton, Rt. Hon. Lord (Desmond Browne), LLB (Hons). Former Labour MP, Kilmarnock and Loudoun (1997-2010); Secretary of State for Defence, 2006-08; Secretary of State for Scotland, 2007-08; Chief Secretary to the Treasury, 2005-06; Minister for Immigration and Citizenship, 2004-05; Minister for Work, 2003-04; Under Secretary of State, Northern Ireland Office, 2001-03; b. 22.3.52; m., Maura; 2 s. Educ. St Michael's Academy, Kilwinning; Glasgow University. Partner, Ross Harper and Murphy, 1980-85; Senior Partner, McCluskey Browne, Kilmarnock, 1985-92; called to the Bar, 1993; Member, Council, Law Society of Scotland, 1988-91; Chair, Children's Rights Group, 1981-86; Member, Sheriff Court Rules Council, 1990-92; Member, Dean's Council, Faculty of Advocates, 1994-97. Recreations: football; swimming; reading. Address: House of Lords, London SW1A 0PW.

Browning, Derek, MA, BD, DMin. Minister, Morningside Parish Church, Edinburgh, since 2001; b. 24.5.62, Edinburgh. Educ. North Berwick High School; Corpus

Christi College, Oxford; St. Mary College, St. Andrews; Princeton Theological Seminary. Minister, Cupar Old Parish Church, 1987-2001; Moderator, Presbytery of St. Andrews, 1996-97; Convener, Prayer and Devotion Committee, Panel on Worship, 2000-04; Convener of Assembly Arrangements Committee and the Business Committee of the General Assembly. Recreations: reading; cooking; croquet; travel; the arts. Address: (h.) 20 Braidburn Crescent, Edinburgh EH10 6EN; T.-0131 447 1617; e-mail: derek.browning@btinternet.com

Browning, Professor George Gordon, MD, ChB, FRCS(Ed.), FRCPS(Glas). Professor of Otolaryngology, Head and Neck Surgery, University of Glasgow, 1991-2002, now Emeritus Professor; Honorary Consultant Otolaryngologist, Glasgow Royal Infirmary, since 1978; Senior Consultant Otologist to British MRC Institute of Hearing Research, 1992-2002; Editor in Chief, Clinical Otolaryngology, 2004-2014; b. 10.1.41, Glasgow; m., Annette; 1 s.; 2 d. Educ. Kelvinside Academy; University of Glasgow. Resident House Surgeon, Western Infirmary, Glasgow, 1964-65; West of Scotland General Surgical Training Scheme, 1965-70; West of Scotland Otorhinolaryngological Training Scheme, 1970-76; MRC Wernher-Piggot Travelling Fellow, Harvard University, 1976-77. President, Otorhinolaryngological Research Society UK, 1992-94; Chairman, British Society of Academics in Otolaryngology, UK, 1995-99; Vice-Chairman, Specialist Advisory Committee in Otolaryngology, 1997-99; President, Section of Otology, Royal Society of Medicine, 1999-2000; Chairman, Academic Board, Royal Society of Medicine, 2001-03 (Vice-Chairman, 2000-01); Vice-President, Royal Society of Medicine, 2005-07; Member, Post-Graduate Examining Boards, FRCS Edinburgh, since 1997, and FRCPS Glasgow, since 1987. Publications: Updated ENT (3rd Edition), 1994; Picture Tests in Otolaryngology (Co-Author), 1998; Clinical Otology and Audiology (2nd Edition), 1998; Otoscopy – A Structured Approach (Co-Author), 1995; Scott Brown's Otolaryngology Head & Neck Surgery (7th Ed., Co-editor), 2008; over 120 scientific articles. Recreations: silversmithing; skiing; swimming. Address: (b.) MRC Institute of Hearing Research, Scottish Section, Glasgow Royal Infirmary, 16 Alexandra Parade, Glasgow G31 2ER; T.-0141-201 8750.

Brownlee, Derek. Director, Corporate Banking Division Scotland, Royal Bank of Scotland, since 2013. MSP (Conservative), South of Scotland, 2005-2011; formerly Conservative Finance Spokesman; Head of Research & Content, Royal Bank of Scotland, 2011-2013; Member of Advisory Board, Reform Scotland, since 2013.

Brownlie, Alistair Rutherford, OBE, MA, LLB, SSC, FCSFS, NP; b. 5.4.24, Edinburgh; m., Martha Barron Mounsey. Educ. George Watson's; Edinburgh University. Served as radio operator in 658 Air O.P. Squadron RAF, Europe and India; apprenticed to J. & R.A. Robertson, WS; qualified Solicitor, 1950; in private practice, until 1995; Member, Committee on Blood Grouping (House of Lords); Solicitor for the poor, 1955-64, in High Court of Justiciary; Secretary, SSC Society, 1970-95, now Archivist; former Member, Council, Law Society of Scotland; Legal Aid Central Committee; Chairman, Legal Aid Committee, Scottish Legal Aid Board, 1986-90; founder Member, Past President, now Hon. Fellow, Chartered Society of Forensic Sciences; Member, Vice-Chairman, Scottish Council of Law Reporting, 1975-97; Chairman, Edinburgh Diabetes Research Trust; Fellow, RSA; Hon. Fellow, Cancer Research UK; Member, 1124 Society of St. Giles; Elder, Church of Scotland and United Reformed Church. Publications: The Universities and Scottish Legal Education; Drink, Drugs and Driving (Co-author); Crime Investigation: art or science (Editor); HM Advocate v Preece - A Judicial Fiasco; autobiography: "The Treasured

Years"; various papers on forensic science, criminal law, legal aid and local history. Recreations: the pen and the mouse. Address: (h.) 8 Braid Mount, Edinburgh; T.-0131-447 4255; e-mail: a.brownlie@icloud.com

Bruce, Adam Robert. WS. Marchmont Herald of Arms at the Court of the Lord Lyon, since 2012; Global Head of Corporate Affairs, Mainstream Renewable Power, since 2008; b. 1968; m., Donna Maria-Sofia Granito Pignatelli di Belmonte; 2 s. Educ. Glenalmond College; Balliol College, Oxford University (MA Hons) (President, Oxford Union, 1989); Edinburgh University (LLB). Formerly a solicitor in private practice (Writer to HM Signet, 2001); Chairman, RenewableUK (2007-2010); Chairman, Offshore Wind Programme Board (2012-2015). Formerly Finlaggan Pursuivant to Clan Donald, and Unicorn Pursuivant at the Court of the Lord Lyon; FRSA; FSA (Scot); OStJ. Address: c/o The Court of the Lord Lyon, HM New Register House, Edinburgh EH1 3YT.

Bruce, Alistair James, LLB, NP. Solicitor; Partner, Director, Lows, Solicitors, Kirkwall, since 1985; b. 4.12.58, Perth; m., Jane; 2 s. Educ. Perth Academy; University of Dundee. Apprenticeship with A.C. Morrison and Richards, Advocates, Aberdeen, 1980-82; Assistant Solicitor, T.P. and J.L. Low, Kirkwall, 1982-85. Member, Council, Law Society of Scotland, 1996-98. Past President, Rotary Club of Kirkwall; Secretary, Orkney Arts Theatre. Recreations: golf; drama; St. Magnus Cathedral Choir. Address: (b.) 5 Broad Street, Kirkwall, Orkney; T.-01856 873151; e-mail: Alistair.bruce@lowsorkney.co.uk

Bruce, David, MA, FRPS, Chevalier de L'Ordre des Arts et des Lettres. Writer and Consultant; Director, Scottish Film Council, 1986-94; b. 10.6.39, Dundee; m., Barbara; 1 s.; 1 d. Educ. Dundee High School; Aberdeen Grammar School; Edinburgh University. Freelance (film), 1963; Assistant Director, Films of Scotland, 1964-66; Director, Edinburgh International Film Festival, 1965-66; Promotions Manager, Mermaid Theatre, London, 1966-67; Executive Officer, British Universities Film Council, 1967-69; joined Scottish Film Council as Assistant Director, 1969; Depute Director, SFC and Scottish Council for Educational Technology, 1977-86. Chairman, Mental Health Film Council, 1982-84; Chairman, Scottish Society for History of Photography, 1983-86 and 2003-2014; Chairman, Association of European Film Institutes, 1990-94; Director, David Octavius Hill Bicentenary Festival, 2002; Glasgow Film Theatre, Chairman, 2002-08; Chairman, Regional Screen Scotland, 2008-2010. Various publications, including Scotland–the movie, 1996. Recreations: movies; music; photo-history. Address: (h.) Rosebank, 150 West Princes Street, Helensburgh G84 8BH.
E-mail: david@bruce150.me.uk

Bruce, Fraser Finlayson, RD, MA (Hons), LLB, FSA(Scot). Regional Chairman, Industrial Tribunals for Scotland 1993-97 (Permanent Chairman, 1982-93); Solicitor, since 1956; b. 10.10.31, Kirkcaldy; m. (1), Joan Gwendolen Hunter (deceased); 2 step-s; m. (2), Violet Margaret Ross MacGregor; 1 step-d. Educ. St. Andrews University. National Service, Royal Navy, 1956-58, commissioned Sub-Lieutenant, RNVR; Legal Assistant: Lanark County Council, 1958-60, Inverness County Council, 1960-66; Depute County Clerk: Argyll County Council, 1966-70, Inverness County Council, 1970-72; County Clerk, Inverness County Council, 1972-75; Joint Director of Law and Administration, Highland Regional Council, 1975-82; Temporary Sheriff, 1984-92. Served RNVR, 1956-76, retiring as Lieutenant-Commander RNR. Recreations: hill walking; reading (in philosophy and naval/military history). Address: (h.) Arlberg, Mossie Road, Grantown-on-Spey PH26 3HW; T.-01479 873969.

Bruce of Bennachie, Baron (Sir Malcolm Gray Bruce), MA, MSc. MP (Liberal Democrat, formerly Liberal), Gordon, 1983-2015; Deputy Leader, Liberal Democrat Party, 2014-15; President, Scottish Liberal Democrats, 2000-2015; Liberal Democrat Shadow Secretary of State for the Department of Trade and Industry, 2003-05; Liberal Democrat Shadow Secretary of State for the Department of the Environment, Food and Rural Affairs, 2001-02; Liberal Democrat Treasury Spokesman, 1995-2000; Chairman, Liberal Democrat Parliamentary Party, 1999-2001; b. 17.11.44, Birkenhead; m., 1, Jane Wilson; 1 s.; 1 d; m., 2, Rosemary Vetterlein; 1 s.; 2 d. Educ. Wrekin College; St. Andrews University; Strathclyde University. Trainee Journalist, Liverpool Daily Post & Echo, 1966-67; Section Buyer, Boots the Chemist, 1968-69; Fashion Retailing Executive, A. Goldberg & Sons, 1969-70; Research and Information Officer, NESDA, 1971-75; Marketing Director, Noroil Publishing, 1975-81; Director, Aberdeen Petroleum Publishing; Editor/Publisher, Aberdeen Petroleum Report, 1981-83; Co-Editor, Scottish Petroleum Annual, 1st and 2nd editions; Called to the Bar (Gray's Inn), 1995. Vice Chairman, Political, Scottish Liberal Party, 1975-84; Rector, Dundee University, 1986-89; Privy Councillor, 2006; Chair, Globe UK - APPG dialogue on climate change, 2004-06; President, Globe International, 2004-06; Vice-Chair, Globe UK, since 2006; Vice-President, Globe International, since 2006; Trustee, RNID, 2004-2010; Honorary National Vice President of National Deaf Children's Society (NDCS). Recreations: reading; music; theatre; hill-walking; cycling; travel. Address: House of Lords, Westminster, London SW1A 0PW.

Bruce, Roderick Lawrence, LLB (Hons). Partner, Dickson Minto WS, 1986-2010; b. 8.3.48, Edinburgh; m., Jane; 1 s.; 3 d. Educ. Boroughmuir School; Edinburgh University. Partner, Dundas and Wilson CS, 1977-86. Recreations: golf; squash; skiing; theatre. Address: (b.) 16 Charlotte Square, Edinburgh EH2 4DF; T.-0131-225 4455; e-mail: roderick.bruce@dmws.com

Bruce, Professor Steve, BA, PhD, FBA, FRSE. Professor of Sociology, Aberdeen University, since 1991; b. 1.4.54, Edinburgh; m., Elizabeth S. Duff; 1 s.; 2 d. Educ. Queen Victoria School, Dunblane; Stirling University. Variously Lecturer, Reader and Professor of Sociology, Queen's University of Belfast, 1978-91. Publications: author of numerous books on religion, and on the Northern Ireland conflict. Recreation: shooting. Address: (b.) Department of Sociology, Aberdeen University, Aberdeen AB24 3QY; T.-01224 272761.

Bruce, Dame Susan, DBE, MPhil, LLB, Dip, FRSA, DUniv. Partner, Aurum Resolution LLP, since 2015; Director, Bruce Consultancy, since 2015; Chief Executive, City of Edinburgh Council, 2011-15; m. Educ. Jordanhill College of Education; University of Strathclyde; JFK School of Government, Harvard. Career: local government, 1976; appointed to the Director role in East Dunbartonshire covering Education, Social Work, Housing and Cultural Services in 2000 and then Chief Executive in 2004; Chief Executive of Aberdeen City Council from 2008 before joining City of Edinburgh Council. First public sector leader to receive the Prince's Ambassador in Scotland Award, 2010 and again in 2011; Scottish Business Insider Public Sector Leader of the Year Award, 2010; HR Network Chief Executive of the Year, 2013; MIPIM UK City Leader of the Year, 2014; Board Chair, RSNO, since 2015. Recreations: the arts; reading; gardening. Address: (b.) 5th Floor, Quartermile Two, 2 Lister Square, Edinburgh EH3 9GL.

Brunt, Professor Peter William, CVO, OBE, MD, FRCP (Lond), FRCP (Edin), FRCS (Edin) (Hon). Consultant Physician, Aberdeen Royal Infirmary, 1970-2001; Clinical Professor of Medicine, Aberdeen University, 1996-2001; Physician to The Queen in Scotland, 1983-2001; non-stipendiary Minister in Episcopal Church of Scotland; Chairman, Alcohol Focus Scotland; Chairman, Medical Council on Alcohol; Vice-President, Royal College of Physicians, Edinburgh, 2005-08; b. 18.1.36, Prestatyn; m., Marina Evelyn Anne Lewis; 3 d. Educ. Manchester Grammar School; King George V School; Liverpool, London, Edinburgh and Johns Hopkins Universities. Recreations: mountaineering; music. Address: (h.) Flat 4, 1, Hillpark Rise, Edinburgh EH4 7BB; T.-0131-312-6687; (h.) The Knotts, Watermillock, Penrith CA11 0JP; e-mail: peterbrunt123@btinternet.com

Bruntisfield, 3rd Baron (Michael John George Warrender); b. 9.1.49; succeeded to title, 2007.

Brunton, Rodger James Horne, DipArch, RIBA, FRIAS, MaPS. Partner, Brunton Design Studio, since 1999; b. 11.7.51, Dundee; m., Sheila; 1 s.; 1 d. Educ. Morgan Academy, Dundee; School of Architecture, Duncan of Jordanstone College of Art. Dundee District Council, 1975-80; Robbie and Wellwood Architects, 1980-85; Brunton Voigt Partnership, 1985-99. Past President, Dundee Institute of Architects; Secretary, Dundee Institute of Architects; Past Chairman, Morgan Academy Former Pupils Association; Past Chairman, School Board, Carnoustie High School; Past Chairman, Carnoustie Centre Action Group. Recreations: after-dinner speaking; amateur operatics. Address: (b.) 95 Dundee Street, Carnoustie DD7 7EW; T.-01241 858153.
E-mail: rodger@bruntondesign.com

Brunton, Sandy, DipY and BM. President, Mull and Iona Chamber of Commerce, since 2001; Convenor, Mull and Iona Community Trust; b. 22.7.59, Oban; m., Jane; 1 s.; 2 d. Educ. Oban High School; James Watt, Greenock; Southampton College of Higher Education. Shipwright/Boatbuilder, Southampton, 1983-86; Retailer and Subpostmaster, Fionnphort, Mull, since 1986. Address: The Ferry Shop, Fionnphort, Isle of Mull PA66 6BL; T.-01681 700470; e-mail: bruntonmull@aol.com

Bruton, Annette. Principal, Edinburgh College, since 2015; Chief Executive, Care Inspectorate, 2012-15; b. East Lothian. Career: trained and worked as a Geography teacher before moving into Learning Support and Special Educational Needs; joined HM Inspectorate of Education in 2001 and was appointed as Chief Inspector in 2005 playing a key role in developing the successful multi-agency child protection inspections; Director of Education, Culture and Sport, Aberdeen City Council, 2009-2011. Address: Edinburgh College, 350 West Granton Road, Edinburgh EH5 1QE.

Bryce, Professor Charles F.A., BSc, PhD, DipEdTech, EurBiol, CBiol, FIBiol, CSci, CChem, FRSC, FHEA. Emeritus Professor at Edinburgh Napier University, since 1983; b. 5.9.47, Lennoxtown; 2 s. Educ. Lenzie Academy; Shawlands Academy; Glasgow University; Max Planck Institute, Berlin. Former Executive Editor, Computer Applications in the Biosciences; Editor of Biotechnology; Vice President, European Federation of Biotechnology (EFB); Member, EFB Task Group on Public Perceptions of Biotechnology; Chairman, EFB Task Group on Education and Mobility; Member, EFB Executive Board; Adviser to the Committee on Science and Technology in Developing Countries (India); former Chairman, UK Deans of Science Committee; Secretary General, European Association for Higher Education in Biotechnology; President, Academic

Board, CSM International, Singapore; actively involved in quality audit and quality assessment in biomedical sciences and forensic science in UK, Eire, Bosnia and Hertzegovina, Australia, Bangladesh and Zambia; Visiting Professor, Zhengzhou University, China; Director, TopoSphere. Recreations: competitive bridge; collecting wine. Address: (b.) 75 Carnbee Avenue, Edinburgh EH16 6GA.

Bryce, Colin Maxwell, DA (Edin), CertEd, FCSD. Artist/Photographer, since 2011; Special Advisor to the Vice Principals, Napier University, 2006-08, Dean, Faculty of Arts and Social Science, 1997-2006; b. 14.9.45, Edinburgh; m., Caroline Joy; 2 s. Educ. Royal High School, Edinburgh; Edinburgh College of Art; Moray House College of Education. Art and Design Teacher, Portobello High School, 1968-75; Head of Art and Design, Wester Hailes Education Centre, 1975-85; Education Advisory Officer/Senior Education Officer/Chief Executive, The Design Council Scotland, 1985-90; Managing Director, Quorum Graphic Design, 1990-91; Head, Department of Design, Napier University, 1992-97. Board Member/Chair, Craigmillar Opportunity Trust, 2001-11; Director/Chair, Creative Edinburgh, 2000-11; Trustee, Scottish Historic Buildings Trust. Recreations: looking and listening. Address: 126 Willowbrae Road, Edinburgh EH8 7HW; e-mail: colinmbryce@mac.com

Bryce, Professor Tom G.K., BSc, MEd, PhD. Emeritus Professor of Education, University of Strathclyde, Professor, since 1993; Vice-Dean (Research), 1997-2002; b. 27.1.46, Glasgow; m., Karen Douglas Stewart; 1 s.; 1 d. Educ. King's Park Secondary School, Glasgow; Glasgow University. Teacher of Physics, Jordanhill College School, 1968-71; P.T. of Physics, King's Park Secondary School, 1971-73; part-time Lecturer in Psychology, Glasgow University, 1972-75; Open University Tutor, 1979-84; Lecturer, 1973, Head of Psychology, 1983, Head, Division of Education and Psychology, 1987-93, Jordanhill College of Education; Head, Department of Educational Studies, University of Strathclyde, 1993-94. Chairman, Editorial Board, Scottish Educational Review, 1988-2002. Publications include: Scottish Education (Co-Editor), 1999 (2nd edition: Post-devolution, 2003; 3rd edition: Beyond Devolution, 2008); 4th edition: Referendum, 2013. Recreations: moutaineering (Munro completer); badminton. Address: (b.) School of Education, Faculty of Humanities and Social Sciences, University of Strathclyde, Lord Hope Building, 141 St James Road, Glasgow G4 0LT; e-mail: t.g.k.bryce@strath.ac.uk

Bryden, Duncan Mackenzie, BSc (Hons), MSocSc, CBiol. Rural Development Consultant, since 2002; Past Convener, Cairngorms National Park Authority; b. 22.01.59, Edinburgh; m., Michelle; 3 s. Educ. Glenalmond College; Edinburgh University; Birmingham University. Visitor Services Manager, Rothiemurchus Estate, Aviemore, 1986-91; Senior Tourism Executive, Highlands and Islands Enterprise, 1991-92; Head of Planning and Research, Ross and Cromarty Enterprise, 1992-94; Director, Tourism and Environment Forum, 1994-2000; Director, Scottish Wildlife Trust, 2000-02. Lecturer, University of The Highlands and Islands; Community Councillor. Recreations: mountaineering; mountain biking; fishing; carpentry. Address: (h.) Sheneval, Tomatin, Inverness IV13 7XY; T.-01808 511777.
E-mail: duncan@brydenassociates.co.uk

Bryden, Professor Ian Gordon, BSc, PhD, CEng, CPhys, FIMechE, FIMarE, FInstP. Vice Principal (Research)/Assistant Principal (Specialist Colleges), University of the Highlands and Islands, since 2013; Chair, Renewable Energy, University of Edinburgh, 2006-2013;

Non Executive Director, European Marine Energy Centre (EMEC), Stromness, Orkney, since 2005; Professor and Dean of Postgraduate Studies, Robert Gordon University, 1996-2006; b. 12.9.58, Dumfries; 2 s.; 1 d. Educ. Lockerbie Academy; University of Edinburgh. Research Assistant, Heriot-Watt University; Research Engineer, BMT Ltd.; Lecturer, Heriot-Watt University; Senior Engineer, ICIT/IOE. Recreations: reading; cycling; music. Address: University of the Highlands and Islands, Executive Office, Ness Walk, Inverness IV3 5SQ.

Buccleuch and Queensberry, Duke of (Richard Walter John Montagu Douglas Scott), KBE, FRSE. Hon. Col., 52nd Lowland, 6th Battalion, The Royal Regiment of Scotland; President, National Trust for Scotland, 2002-2012; b. 14.2.54; m., Lady Elizabeth Kerr; 2 s.; 2 d. Member, Millennium Commission, 1994-2003; Deputy Chairman, Independent Television Commission, 1996-98; President, Royal Scottish Geographical Society, 1999-2005; Member, National Heritage Memorial Fund, 2000-05; President: Royal Blind, since 2008, St Andrew's First Aid, since 2008; Trustee, Royal Collection, since 2011. Address: (h.) Dabton, Thornhill, Dumfriesshire.

Buchan-Hepburn, 7th Baronet of Smeaton-Hepburn (Sir Alastair Buchan-Hepburn), Bart; b. 27.6.31, Hatton, Ceylon; m., Georgina Elizabeth Turner; 1 s.; 3 d. Educ. Charterhouse; St Andrews University; Royal Military Academy, Sandhurst. 1st King's Dragoon Guards, 1952-57; Captain, 1954; ADC to GOC-in-C Malaya, 1954-57; Arthur Guinness and Son Co. Ltd., 1958-86; Director, Broughton Brewery, 1986-2001; Trustee, Dundee Industrial Heritage Trust, 1999-2006; Chief R&A Marshall, Open Championship, 2000 and 2005; Chairman, Valentine Marketing Ltd., 2002-03; Chairman, Valentine Holdings Ltd., 2002-03; Vice-President, Maritime Volunteer Service, 2001-2010; Life Member, St Andrews Preservation Trust; Member, Baronets' Trust, since 1992; Life Member, St Andrews Preservation Trust; Member, Committee, Royal British Legion, St Andrews Branch; Member: Vestry of All Saints Episcopal Church, St. Andrews; New Club, Edinburgh; Royal Scots Club, Edinburgh; Royal and Ancient Golf Club of St. Andrews; 1st Queen's Dragoon Guards Old Comrades Association; Member, The European Commission for the Nobility of Europe (CILANE). Recreations: travels; leading international appeal for the return of James Hepburn 4th Earl of Bothwell's remains to Scotland from Denmark; golf; tennis; shooting; gardening; fishing; reading. Address: (h.) Chagford, 60 Argyle Street, St Andrews KY16 9BU; T.-01334 472161; mobile: 07939139545; e-mail: alastairbh@gmail.com

Buchanan, Cameron R.M. Regional Member of the Scottish Parliament (Conservative), 2013-16; b. Edinburgh; 2 s.; 2 d. Educ. St Edward's School, Oxford; Sorbonne, Paris. Lived and worked in France, Germany and Italy; Managing Director, Harrisons of Edinburgh, 1985-97; Entrepreneur of the Year, 1992; Textile Consultant, since 1997. High Constable of Leith; Hon. Co. Edinburgh Golfers. Recreations: skiing; tennis; golf. T.-0131 220 5775.
E-mail: cameron@cameronbuchanan.com

Buchanan, William Menzies, DA. Head of Fine Art, 1977-90, Acting Director, 1990-91, Deputy Director, 1991-92, Glasgow School of Art; b. 7.10.32, Caroni Estate, Trinidad, West Indies. Educ. Glasgow School of Art. Art Teacher, Glasgow, 1956-61; Exhibitions Officer, then Art Director, Scottish Arts Council, 1961-77; Member, Fine Art Board, Council for National Academic Awards, 1978-81;

Chairman, Stills Gallery, Edinburgh, 1987-92. Publications: Scottish Art Review, 1965, 1967, 1973; Seven Scottish Painters catalogue, IBM New York, 1965; The Glasgow Boys catalogue, 1968; Joan Eardley, 1976; Mr Henry and Mr Hornel Visit Japan catalogue, 1978; Japonisme in Art (Contributor), 1980; A Companion to Scottish Culture (Contributor), 1981; The Stormy Blast catalogue, Stirling University, 1981; The Golden Age of British Photography (Contributor), 1984; The Photographic Collector (Contributor), 1985; Willie Rodger: A Retrospective (Contributor to catalogue), 1986; Scottish Photography Bulletin (Contributor), 1988; History of Photography (Contributor), 1989; Mackintosh's Masterwork (Editor), 1989 (2nd edition, 2004); British Photography in the 19th Century (Contributor), 1989; The Art of the Photographer J. Craig Annan, 1992; Photography 1900 (Contributor), 1993; J. Craig Annan: selected texts and bibliography, 1994; The Dictionary of Art (Contributor), 1995; Woven Image: Contemporary British Tapestry Catalogue (Contributor), 1996; Studies in Photography (Contributor), 1996, 2006; Charles Rennie Mackintosh: Art, Architecture and Design (CD Rom, General Editor), 1997; The Dictionary of Women Artists (Contributor), 1997; Studies in Photography (Contributor), 1997, 2003, 2006; Journal of the Scottish Society for Art History (Contributor), 2001; New Dictionary of National Biography (Contributor), 2004; The Oxford Companion to the Photograph (contributor), 2005. Recreation: gardening. Address: (h.) 20 Laurelhill Place, Stirling FK8 2JH; T.-0178 647 5403.

Buckland, Roger, MA, MBA, MPhil. Emeritus Chair of Finance & Accountancy, University of Aberdeen (Head of Business School, Chair of Accountancy, 1993-2015); b. 22.04.51, Swallownest, England; m., Professor Lorna McKee; 2 d. Educ. Aston High School, South Yorkshire; Selwyn College, University of Cambridge. Research Assistant, University of Aston, 1972-74; Research Fellow, University of York, 1974-78; Lecturer in Finance, University of Aston, 1978-93; Visiting Professor, Bordeaux Business School, 1989-90, Michigan State University, 2011. Address: University of Aberdeen Business School, Edward Wright Building, Dunbar Street, Old Aberdeen AB24 3QY; T.-01224 272206; e-mail: acc040@abdn.ac.uk

Buckland, Professor Stephen T., BSc, MSc, PhD, CStat. Professor of Statistics, St. Andrews University, since 1993 (Director, Centre for Research into Ecological and Environmental Modelling, 1999-2004 and 2009-2014); Co-Director, National Centre for Statistical Ecology, since 2005; b. 28.7.55, Dorchester; 1 d. Educ. Foster's School, Sherborne; Southampton University; Edinburgh University; Aberdeen University. Lecturer in Statistics, Aberdeen University, 1977-85; Senior Scientist, Tuna/Dolphin Program, Inter-American Tropical Tuna Commission, San Diego, 1985-87; Senior Consultant Statistician, Scottish Agricultural Statistics Service, 1988-93, Head, Environmental Modelling Unit, 1991-93. Publications: The Birds of North-East Scotland (Co-editor), 1990; Distance Sampling: estimating abundance of biological populations (Co-author), 1993; Introduction to Distance Sampling (Co-author), 2001; Estimating Animal Abundance (Co-author), 2002; Advanced Distance Sampling (Co-editor), 2004; Modelling Population Dynamics (Co-author), 2014; Distance Sampling: Methods and Applications (Co-author), 2015. Recreations: wildlife photography; natural history; walking; reading. Address: (b.) St. Andrews University, The Observatory, Buchanan Gardens, St. Andrews KY16 9LZ; T.-01334 461841.

Buddle, (Elizabeth) Anne. Collections Adviser, National Galleries of Scotland, since 2015 (Head of Collections Management, 2000-2015, Registrar, 1993-

2000); Portrait of the Nation project, 2009-2011; b. 4.5.51, Chatham, Kent; m., A.V.B. Norman (deceased); 1 s. (from husband's pr. m.). Educ. Christ's Hospital, Hertford. Placers Department, British Museum, 1971; Victoria and Albert Museum, 1972-93: Public Relations, 1972-73, Indian Section, 1973-78, Department of Prints, Drawings and Paintings, 1978-88, Loans Officer, 1988-89, Registrar, 1989-93; Institute of Art and Law Diploma, 2013; NMDC Spoliation Working Group, since 2014. Publications: "Tigers round the Throne", 1990; "The Tiger and The Thistle" (catalogue); (web: www.tigerandthistle.net) and various collection management papers; Scots and Udaipur (in preparation). Recreations: study of church monuments; gardening; 18th-century Scots and India. Address: (b.) National Galleries of Scotland, 75 Belford Road, Edinburgh EH4 3DR; T.-0131-624 6315.
E-mail: abuddle@nationalgalleries.org

Bullock, Michael Peter, MBE, MA, FCILT. Chief Executive, Northern Lighthouse Board, since 2014; b. 7.1.61, Liverpool; m., Clare Diana (nee Fairbairn); 1 s.; 1 d. Educ. Scarisbrick Hall School, Lancashire; Britannia Royal Naval College; Royal College of Defence Studies; Kings College London. Royal Navy, 1980-2014; Commander Logistics, HMS Illustrious, 1998-99; Career Manager, 1999-02; British Defence Staff, Washington DC, 2002-05; Head of Supply Chain Policy, Defence Logistics Organisation, 2005-07; UK Liaison Officer, Directorate of Logistics, United States Joint Staff, Pentagon, 2007-10; Royal College of Defence Studies, 2010-11; Commodore, 2011; Assistant Chief of Staff Logistics and Infrastructure, Navy Command HQ, 2011-14. Recreation: family; classic cars. Address: (b.) 84 George Street, Edinburgh EH2 3DA; T.-0131-473-3112; e-mail: mikeb@nlb.org.uk

Bunch, Antonia Janette, OBE, MA, FCLIP, FSAScot, FRSA. Librarian (retired); b. 13.2.37, Croydon. Educ. Notting Hill and Ealing High School; Strathclyde University. Assistant Librarian, Scottish Office; Librarian, Scottish Health Service Centre; Lecturer, Strathclyde University; Director, Scottish Science Library. Founding Chairman, Association of Scottish Health Sciences Librarians; Member: Standing Committee on Science and Technology Libraries, IFLA, 1987-91, Advisory Committee, British Library Science Reference and Information Service, 1987-96, Advisory Committee on Telematics for the Scottish Parliament, 1996-97; Chairman: Friends of St. Cecilia's Hall and the Russell Collection of Early Keyboard Instruments, 1997-2003; Trustee, Scottish Homeopathic Research and Education Trust, 1998-2008. Publications: Libraries in Hospitals (Co-author), 1969; Hospital and Medical Libraries in Scotland: an Historical and Sociological Study, 1975; Health Care Administration: an Information Sourcebook, 1979; The Temple of Harmony: a new architectural history of St Cecilia's Hall, Edinburgh (Co-author), 2011. Recreations: gardening; music; travelling in Italy. Address: Dove Cottage, Garvald, Haddington, East Lothian EH41 4LL.

Buncle, Tom, BA, MA. Managing Director, Yellow Railroad International Destination Consultancy; b. 25.6.53, Arbroath; m., Janet; 2 s. Educ. Trinity College, Glenalmond; Exeter University; Sheffield University; London Business School. Various overseas posts (North America, Europe, Asia), British Tourist Authority, 1978-91; International Marketing Director, then Chief Executive, Scottish Tourist Board, 1991-2000. Board Member: Scottish Prison Service Risk Monitoring and Audit Committee, 2004-2014; Fellow, UK Tourism Society; Experts' Committee of World Tourism Cities Forum (China); Fellow, UK Tourism Management Institute; National Committee Member, UK Tourism Consultants

Network. Recreations: wind-surfing; scuba diving; cycling; sailing; hill-walking. E-mail: tom@yellowrailroad.com

Bundy, Professor Alan Richard, CBE, BSc, PhD, FRS, FREng, FRSE, FAAAI, FECCAI, FBCS, FIET. Professor, University of Edinburgh; b. 18.5.47, Isleworth; m., D. Josephine A. Maule; 1 d. Educ. Heston Secondary Modern School; Springgrove Grammar School; Leicester University. Tutorial Assistant, Department of Mathematics, Leicester University, 1970-71; University of Edinburgh: Research Fellow, Metamathematics Unit, 1971-74; Lecturer, Department of Artificial Intelligence, 1974-84; Reader, 1984-87; Professorial Fellow, 1987-90; Professor, since 1990. Editorial Board: AJ & Society Journal, Communications of the ACM. IJCAI Donald E. Walker Distinguished Service Award, 2003; IJCAI Research Excellence Award, 2007; CADE Herbrand Award, 2007. Publications: Artificial Intelligence: An Introductory Course, 1978; The Computer Modelling of Mathematical Reasoning, 1983; The Catalogue of Artificial Intelligence Tools, 1984; Rippling: Meta-level Guidance for Mathematical Reasoning. Recreation: walking. Address: (b.) School of Informatics, Edinburgh University, Informatics Forum, Crichton Street, Edinburgh EH8 9AB; T.-0131 650 2716.

Burgess, Margaret. MSP (SNP), Cunninghame South, 2011-16; Minister for Housing and Welfare, 2012-16. Ayrshire born and bred, has served as a Councillor in Dreghorn and as SNP group leader on Cunninghame District Council. Previously worked as the Manager of East Ayrshire Citizens Advice Bureau and as a Director of Citizens Advice Scotland.

Burgess, William George, MA, PhD. Deputy Director, Environmental Quality, Scottish Government; b. 8.5.70, Aberdeen; m., Adrienne Kirk; 1 d. Educ. Keith Grammar School; Churchill College, Cambridge University. Social Work Services Group, Scottish Office, 1994-96; Finance Group, Scottish Office, 1996-97; Referendum Bill Team, Scotland Bill Team, Scotland Act Implementation, 1997-2000; Private Secretary to Deputy First Minister, 2000-02; Head of Sustainable Development Team, Scottish Executive, 2002-04; Deputy Director, Criminal Law and Licensing, Scottish Government, 2004-2010; Deputy Director, Facilities and Estates Services, Scottish Government, 2010-11; Session Clerk, St Andrews and St George's West Church, Edinburgh. Scottish Young Scientist of the Year, 1988; CEGB Prize, Cambridge University, 1991. Recreations: choral music; historical research. Address: (b.) Victoria Quay, Edinburgh EH6 6QQ; T.-0131-244 0240.
E-mail: george.burgess@gov.scot

Burgon, Robert Douglas, BA, MLitt, FPMI, HonFCIPHE, HonFSoPHE. Chief Executive, Scottish & Northern Ireland Plumbing Employers' Federation, since 1988; Secretary and Pensions Manager, Plumbing Pensions (UK) Ltd., since 1988; Past Chairman, World Plumbing Council; Court Assistant, Worshipful Company of Plumbers; b. 3.8.55, Haddington; m., Sheila Georgina Bryson. Educ. North Berwick High School; Heriot Watt University. SNIPEF: Assistant Industrial Relations Officer, 1978, Assistant to the Director, 1979, Secretary, 1983. Recreation: music (church organist). Address: (b.) Bellevue House, 22 Hopetoun Street, Edinburgh EH7 4GH; T.-0131-556 0600.

Burke, Florence. Chief Executive Officer, Music in Hospitals Scotland, since 2016. Development Manager,

CEiS, 1997-2008; Director for Scotland, Carers Trust, 2008-2016. Address: Music in Hospitals, 10 Forth Street, Edinburgh EH1 3LD; T.-0131 556 5848.
E-mail: info@musicinhospitalsscotland.org.uk

Burley, Lindsay, CBE, MBChB, FRCPE, FRCGP, FRSA, MCIArb. Chair, NHS Education for Scotland; Partner, Eskhill & Co; formerly Chief Executive, NHS Borders; b. 2.10.50, Blackpool; m., Robin Burley. Educ. Queen Mary School, Lytham; University of Edinburgh. Lothian Health Board: Consultant Physician, Unit General Manager, Director of Planning and Development. Address: (b.) Eskhill House, 15 Inveresk Village, Musselburgh EH21 7TD; T.-0131 271 4000; e-mail: lindsay@eskhill.com

Burman, Professor Michele Jane, BA, MSc, PhD. Professor of Criminology, University of Glasgow, since 2003; Co-Director, Scottish Centre for Crime and Justice Research (SCCJR), since 2006; b. London; m., Neil Hutton; 2 d. Educ. Springfield Convent, Cape Town; University of Cape Town and University of Edinburgh. Board Member, Ethnic Minority Law Centre; Director, Women's Support Project. Publications: academic articles and papers on gender and justice. Recreations: gardening; cooking; travelling. Address: (b.) Ivy Lodge, 63 Gibson Street, University of Glasgow.
E-mail: michele.burman@glasgow.ac.uk

Burman, Peter Ashley Thomas Insull, MBE, MA, FSA, Dr hc, Brandenburg Technical University, Cottbus, Germany. Director of Conservation & Property Services, The National Trust for Scotland, 2002-07; Professor of Cultural Management, World Heritage Studies, Cottbus University, 2007-2012; Independent Arts and Cultural Heritage Consultant; b. 15.9.44, Solihull. Educ. Kings College, Cambridge; ICCROM, Rome. Assistant Secretary, Deputy Secretary, Secretary (Chief Executive), Church of England, Council for the Care of Churches and the Cathedrals Fabric Commission for England, 1968-90; Director, Centre of Conservation Studies, University of York, 1990-2002; Visiting Professor, Department of Fine Arts, University of Canterbury, Christchurch, New Zealand, 2002. Publications include: Books: Chapels and Churches: Who Cares?, 1977; St. Paul's Cathedral, 1987; 7 book chapters; Refereed articles: Reflections on the Lime Revival, 1995; The Ethics of Using Traditional Building Materials, 1997; The Study and Conservation of Nineteenth Century Wall Paintings, 2003. Esher Award, SPAB. Memberships include: Chairman, Falkland Stewardship Trust; Trustee and Archivist, Hopetoun House; Fabric Advisory Committee, St George's Chapel, Windsor Castle; Historic Environment Strategic Forum (Participation) for Scotland; Companion, Guild of St. George; Garden History Society; Trustee and Board of Guardians, SPAB; Ancient Monuments Society; Georgian Group; Victorian Society; Twentieth Century Society. Recreations: music; playing keyboard instruments and recorders; walking, especially in remote upland areas; reading, especially books relating to the Buddhist Dharma; cooking (attended one of Alastair Little's cookery courses in Umbria). Address: (h.) Brunton House, Brunton Street, Falkland KY15 7BQ; T.-01337 857610; e-mail: peterburman@btinternet.com

Burnet, George Wardlaw, LVO, BA, LLB, WS, KStJ, JP. Lord Lieutenant, Midlothian, 1992-2002; b. 26.12.27, Edinburgh; m., Jane Elena Moncrieff; 2 s.; 1 d. Educ. Edinburgh Academy; Lincoln College, Oxford; Edinburgh University. Senior Partner, Murray Beith & Murray, WS, 1983-91; Chairman, Life Association of Scotland Ltd., 1985-93; Chairman, Caledonian Research Foundation, 1988-99. Captain, Queen's Bodyguard for Scotland (Royal Company of Archers); former Midlothian County Councillor; Elder, Church of Scotland, since 1962; Convenor, Church of Scotland Finance Committee, 1980-83; Hon. Fellow, Royal Incorporation of Architects in

Scotland. Address: (h.) Rose Court, Inveresk, Midlothian EH21 7TD.

Burnett, Alexander, LLB. MSP (Scottish Conservative), Aberdeenshire West, since 2016; b. 30.7.73. Educ. Eton College; Newcastle University. The son of James Comyn Amherst Burnett of Leys and Fiona Mercedes Phillips; 4th great grandson of Nicholas I of Russia on his mother's side. Address: Scottish Parliament, Edinburgh EH99 1SP.

Burnett, Charles John, KStJ, DA, AMA, FSAScot, FHSS, MLitt. Ross Herald of Arms, 1988-2010, Ross Herald Extraordinary, since 2011; Chamberlain, Duff House, Banff, 1997-2004; Curator of Fine Art, Scottish United Services Museum, Edinburgh Castle, 1985-96; President, Heraldry Society of Scotland, 2004-2015, President Emeritus, since 2015; Vice-Patron, Genealogical Society of Queensland, 1986-2010; Chairman, Banff Preservation and Heritage Society, 2002-2010; b. 6.11.40, Sandhaven, by Fraserburgh; m., Aileen E. McIntyre; 2 s.; 1 d. Educ. Fraserburgh Academy; Gray's School of Art, Aberdeen; Aberdeen College of Education; University of Edinburgh. Advertising Department, House of Fraser, Aberdeen, 1963-64; Exhibitions Division, Central Office of Information, 1964-68 (on team which planned British pavilion for World Fair, Montreal, 1967); Assistant Curator, Letchworth Museum and Art Gallery, 1968-71; Head, Design Department, National Museum of Antiquities of Scotland, 1971-85. Heraldic Adviser, Girl Guide Association in Scotland, 1978-2010; Librarian, Priory of the Order of St. John in Scotland, 1987-99; Vice President, Society of Antiquaries of Scotland, 1992-95; Honorary Citizen of Oklahoma, 1989; Chevalier, Orders of St. Maurice and St. Lazarus, 1999; Knight of the Royal Order of Francis I, 2002; President, 27th International Congress of Genealogical and Heraldic Sciences at St. Andrews University, 2006; Chairman, Pitsligo Castle Trust, 2010-2014; Honorary President, The Moray Burial Ground Research Group, since 2012; Member of the Spanish Noble Company of Ballesteros, 2010. Recreations: reading; visiting places of historic interest. Address: (h.) Seaview House, Portsoy, Banffshire AB45 2RS; T.-01261 843378. E-mail: charles@rossherald.co.uk

Burnett, David Anderson, DA (Edin), RIBA, FRIAS. Partner, BPA Architecture (formerly Burnett Pollock Associates), since 1974; b. 9.6.44, Edinburgh; m., Rosemary; 3 s. Educ. George Watson's College, Edinburgh; Edinburgh College of Art. Chamberlin Powell and Bon, London, 1968-70; Casson Conder & Partners, London, 1970-72; Sir Basil Spence Glover and Ferguson, Edinburgh, 1973-74. Recreations: reading; writing; travel. Address: BPA Architecture, 17B Graham Street, Edinburgh EH6 5QN; T.-0131-555 3338. E-mail: dburnett@bpa-architecture.co.uk

Burnett of Leys, James Comyn Amherst. Chief of the Name and Arms of Burnett. Address: Banchory Business Centre, Burn O'Bennie Road, Banchory AB31 5ZU.

Burnett, Robert Gemmill, LLB, SSC, NP. Solicitor, since 1972; Solicitor Advocate, since 1993; Senior Solicitor Advocate, since 2010; b. 18.1.49, Kilmarnock; m., Patricia Margaret Masson; 1 s.; 2 d. Educ. George Heriot's School, Edinburgh; Edinburgh University. Apprentice, then Assistant, then Partner, Drummond Miller WS; Partner, BCKM. Member, Criminal Law Committee, Law Society of Scotland; Member, Criminal Courts Rules Council. Recreations: golf; gardening. Address: (b.) 53 George IV Bridge, Edinburgh; T.-0131-225 3456.

Burnett, Rodney Alister, MB, ChB, FRCP, FRIPHH, FRCPath. Lead Clinician in Pathology, University Department of Pathology, Western Infirmary, Glasgow, 1985-2007 (retired); b. 6.6.47, Congleton; m., Maureen Elizabeth Dunn; 2 d. Educ. Sandbach School; St. Andrews University. Lecturer in Pathology, Glasgow University, 1974-79; Consultant in administrative charge, Department of Pathology, Stobhill Hospital, Glasgow, 1979-85. Specialist Adviser, Royal Institute for Public Health and Hygiene, and Chairman, Board of Education and Examination for Anatomical Pathology Technology, 1994-2012; Vice President, Association of Clinical Pathologists, 2001-03. Address: (h.) 77 Blairbeth Road, Burnside, Glasgow G73 4JD; T.-0141-634 4345.

Burnie, Joan Bryson. Columnist, Daily Record, 1987-2014, formerly Associate Editor; b. 19.12.41, Glasgow; 1 s.; 1 d. Educ. Hutchesons' Girls' Grammar School. Filed pix, Herald; married; had children; freelanced; Contributing Editor, Cosmopolitan, 1977-81; You (Mail on Sunday), 1984-90; "Just Joan", Daily Record, since 1979; hacks around the air waves for BBC Radio 5 and BBC Scotland. Publications: Scotland The Worst; Post Bus Country. Recreations: lunch; walking dogs; gardening.

Burns, Andrew. Leader, The City of Edinburgh Council, since 2012; b. 1965; m.; 1 s. Educ. University of Ulster. Career: professional background in personnel and training, and worked for several years in a variety of personnel and training roles in both manufacturing industry and the service sector; became a Graduate of the Chartered Institute of Personnel and Development (CIPD) in 1990, gaining Full Member status of the CIPD in 2003; first elected to The City of Edinburgh Council in May 1999 and has represented the Fountainbridge/Craiglockhart ward since; previously had responsibility for the transport and education portfolios while in administration. Chair of the Electoral Reform Society, 2008-2011. Recreations: walking; cycling; films; music; reading. Address: (b.) City Chambers, High Street, Edinburgh EH1 1YJ; T.-0131 529 3287. E-mail: leader@edinburgh.gov.uk

Burns, The Hon. Lord (David Burns), QC. Senator of the College of Justice, since 2012. Career: legal assistant in New York and California; admitted to the Faculty of Advocates in 1977; became a Queen's Counsel in 1991; practiced family, personal injury and planning; full-time Advocate Depute, 1989-91; Deputy Commissioner of Social Security; one of the advocates representing Abdelbaset al-Megrahi during the Lockerbie trial (2000-02); served as a temporary judge, 2002-05; became a part-time sheriff in 2007.

Burns, John. Chief Executive, NHS Ayrshire & Arran, since 2012; m.; 2 c. NHS career started at Tayside Health Board in 1983; held several positions throughout Scotland before taking up the post as Chief Executive of Dumfries and Galloway Acute and Maternity Hospitals NHS Trust in 2001; formerly Director of Health Services, then Chief Executive, NHS Dumfries & Galloway. Chaired a range of national work programmes including Financial Shared Services, review of Cervical Cytology Laboratory Services and the Implementation Board for the Managed Services Network for Children and Young People's Cancer.

Burns, Richard Ronald James, MA, LLB, WS. Trustee of the Carnegie Trust for the Universities of Scotland; Director of several investment trust companies; b. 5.5.46, Gourock; m., Catherine Ogilvie Bryson; 2 s.; 2 d. Educ. Trinity College, Glenalmond; Merton College, Oxford; University of Edinburgh. Apprentice Solicitor, W & J Burness WS, 1969-71, Qualified Assistant, 1971-73; Trainee Investment Manager, Baillie Gifford & Co, 1973-77, Partner, 1977-2006 (Joint Senior Partner, 1999-2006). Publications: A Century of Investing (centenary history of Baillie Gifford); The History of Scottish Mortgage Investment Trust PLC.

Recreations: reading; golf; gallery visiting. Address: (h.) 31 Saxe Coburg Place, Edinburgh EH3 5BP; T.-0770 343 9226; e-mail: rburns@iitplc.com

Burnside, David Melville, LLB, NP. Managing Director, Burnside Legal Services (Aberdeen) Ltd, since 2013; Consultant, Burness Paull LLP, 2009-2015; b. 5.3.43, Dumfries; m., Gill; 3 s.; 2 d. Educ. Dumfries Academy; University of Edinburgh. Apprentice Solicitor, Melville & Lindesay W.S., Edinburgh, 1964-67; Assistant Solicitor: National Coal Board Legal Department, 1967-70, Clark & Wallace, Advocates, Aberdeen, 1970-71 (Partner, 1971-89); formed Burnside Advocates (later Burnside Kemp Fraser), 1989 (firm merged with Simpson and Marwick, 2004), thereafter Partner, then Consultant until 2009; acted for families in Chinook, Brent Spar and Cormorant Alpha helicopter crashes and Piper Alpha explosion (joint lead negotiator for Piper Alpha settlement); Member, Personal Injury Panel; Member, Executive Committee, and Scottish Convenor, Association of Personal Injury Lawyers, 1990-96; certified by Law Society of Scotland as an employment law specialist, since 1990; Treasurer, Employment Law Group; Past President: Aberdeen Bar Association, Junior Chamber, Aberdeen; Member, Board of Directors, Legal Defence Union; President, Society of Advocates in Aberdeen, 2000-01 (Treasurer, 1999-2000); Member, Edinburgh Town Council, 1967-70; Chairman, Board of Governors, Albyn School for Girls, 2001-05; Chairman, Organising Committee, Aberdeen FC Centenary, 2003; Board Member, Aberdeen Performing Arts, since November 2014; Free Burgess and Guild Member of Burgh of Aberdeen. Recreations: family; music; theatre; following the Dons; spending time in France. Address: (b.) 31 Albert Terrace, Aberdeen AB10 1XY; T.-01224 636645.

Burnside, John. Writer; b. 19.3.55, Dunfermline. Scottish Arts Council Book Award, 1988, 1991, 1995, 2006; Geoffrey Faber Memorial Prize, 1994; Whitbread Poetry Prize, 2000; Saltire Book of the Year, 2006; Prix Zepter, 2009; The Forward Poetry Prize, 2011; TS Eliot Prize for Poetry, 2011; Petrarca-Preis, 2011; CORINE International Zeit Publishing Literature Award, 2011; Prix Virgin-Lire, 2011. Publications: poetry: The hoop, 1988; Common Knowledge, 1991; Feast Days, 1992; The myth of the twin, 1994; Swimming in the flood, 1995; A Normal Skin, 1997; The Asylum Dance, 2000; The Light Trap, 2002; The Good Neighbour, 2005; Selected Poems, 2006; Gift Songs, 2007; The Hunt in the Forest, 2009; Black Cat Bone, 2011; All One Breath, 2014; fiction: The Dumb House, 1997; The Mercy Boys, 1999; Burning Elvis, 2000; The Locust Room, 2001; Living Nowhere, 2003; The Devil's Footprints, 2007; Glister, 2008; A Summer of Drowning, 2011; memoir: A Lie About My Father, 2006; Waking Up In Toytown, 2010; Something Like Happy, 2013; I Put A Spell On You, 2014. Address: (b.) c/o Rogers, Coleridge and White Ltd, 20 Powis Mews, London W11 1JN.

Burr, Malcolm, LLB (Hons), DipLP, LLM (Hons), NP. Chief Executive, Comhairle nan Eilean Siar, since 2005; b. 24.3.66, Edinburgh; m., Chrissie (nee Kennedy). Educ. George Heriot's School, Edinburgh; Edinburgh University; Cambridge University (Sidney Sussex College). Trainee Solicitor, later Solicitor, Strathclyde Regional Council, Glasgow, 1990-94; Principal Solicitor, Comhairle Nan Eilean, Stornoway, 1994-97; Chief Administrative Officer, 1997-2000, Assistant Chief Executive, 2000-05, Orkney Islands Council; Hon. Sec., Society of Local Authority Chief Executives in Scotland (SOLACE Scotland), 2011-14, Vice Chair, 2014-15; Member of Court, University of the Highlands and Islands. Recreations: current affairs; history; reading; walking; following football and rugby.

Address: (b.) Council Offices, Sandwick Road, Stornoway, Isle of Lewis HS1 2BW; T.-01851 822600; e-mail: m.burr@cne-siar.gov.uk

Burt, John Clark, OBE, MA (Hons), CertEd. Education management consultant, since 2013; Principal, Angus College, 1996-2013; b. 25.4.51, Dunfermline; m., Dory; 1 s.; 1 d. Educ. Dunfermline High School; Edinburgh University; Moray House College. Marketing Economist, Lloyds and Scottish Finance, 1974-76; Lecturer/Senior Lecturer in Economics and Marketing, Fife College, 1976-96. Member, Scottish Welfare to Work Advisory Task Force; Member, East of Scotland European Partnership; Director, FE Development, Scottish Further Education Funding Council (seconded); Chair of "Differences College Make Group", Scottish Executive; awarded OBE for services to Further Education in Scotland, 2006. Recreations: golf; hill-walking; running; Italian language.

Burt, Professor Steven Leslie, BA, PhD, FRSA. Professor of Retail Marketing, University of Stirling, since 1998, Deputy Principal, 2007-2015, Senior Deputy Principal, 2011-2014; b. 23.3.60, Chorley, Lancashire; m., Wendy Hayes; 2 s. Educ. Bolton School; Queen's College, Oxford University; University of Wales; University of Stirling. University of Stirling: Research Fellow, then Lecturer, then Senior Lecturer, 1984-98, Head, Department of Marketing, 1993-95, 2000-03, Director, Institute for Retail Studies, 1993-96, 1999-2003; Visiting Professor, Lund University, Sweden, 2000-2013; Visiting Professor, Queens University, Kingston, Ontario, 2003-04; Visiting Professor, IGR-IAE Universite de Rennes 1, France, 2006-07. President, European Association for Education and Research in Commercial Distribution. Recreation: watching Stirling Albion Football Club. Address: (b.) University of Stirling, Stirling FK9 4LA; T.-01786 467399.
E-mail: s.l.burt@stir.ac.uk

Burton, Anthony Winston, OBE, BA (Hons) Keele. Chairman, Friends of Scottish Opera, since 2012; Board Member, Scottish Opera, since 2012; Council Member, Which?, since 2014; Secretary, The Planning Exchange Foundation, since 2002; Director, Greenbelt Group of Companies, since 2002. Recreations: piano; opera; sailing a vintage wooden yacht; travelling. Address: Scottish Opera, 39 Elmbank Crescent, Glasgow G2 4PT; T.-0141 248 4567.

Bush, Paul Anthony, OBE (2007), BEd, DipSC, FISC. Chief Operating Officer, EventScotland, since 2007; Chair, Commonwealth Games Scotland, since 2015; Chair, East of Scotland Institute of Sport, since 2007; Member, UK Sport Major Events Panel, 2008; b. 11.6.57, Leicester; m., Katriona Christine. Educ. Gateway Sixth Form College, Leicester; Borough Road College; Moray House College. Professional Swimming Coach, Bradford and Leicester; Sports/Swimming Development Officer, Leeds City Council; Technical Director, Amateur Swimming Association; Assistant Head of Development, English Sports Council; Director, Sporting Initiatives Sports Marketing and Media Consultancy. Leicestershire County Swimming Coach; Swimming Team Manager, Olympic, World, European, Commonwealth Games; Chef de Mission, BOA, European Youth Olympics; General Team Manager, Scottish Commonwealth Games Council, Manchester, 2002; Fellow, BISA; General Secretary, British Swimming Coaches Association; Member, English Sports Council Task Force – Young People and Sport; Event Director, World Cyclo Cross Championships, Leeds; school governor; Chef de Mission, Scottish Commonwealth

Game Team, Melbourne, 2006; 2011 Scottish Event Professional of the Year. Recreations: golf; walking the dogs; sport in general; travel. Address: Ochil Paddocks, Burnfoot, Glendevon, nr. Dollar FK14 7JY; e-mail: Paul.Bush@eventscotland.org

Busuttil, Professor Anthony, OBE, MOM, KHS, MD, FRCPath, FRCP (Glasg), FRCPE, FRCS (Edin), DMJ (Path), FBAFM, FFSS, FRSSA, FRSM, FFFLM (Lond). Emeritus Regius Professor of Forensic Medicine, Edinburgh University, since 2006; Past Chairman, European Council for Legal Medicine; Honorary Consultant Pathologist, Edinburgh Universities NHS Trust, since 1976; Clinical Lead, Forensic Medical Examiner Service, NHS Lothian; Forensic Physician, Lothian and Borders Police Force, since 1980; b. 30.12.45, Rabat, Malta; m., Angela; 3 s. Educ. St. Aloysius' College, Malta; Royal University of Malta. Junior posts, Western Infirmary, Glasgow; Lecturer in Pathology, Glasgow University. Address: (h.) 78 Hillpark Avenue, Edinburgh EH4 7AL; T.-0131-336 3241; e-mail: tony@busuttil.demon.co.uk

Bute, 7th Marquess of (John Colum Crichton-Stuart); b. 26.4.58; m.; 1 s.; 3 d. British Formula Three Champion, 1984; Formula One Ferrari Test Driver, 1985; JPS Lotus Grand Prix Driver, 1986; Works Driver for World Champion Sports Prototype Team Silk Cut Jaguar, 1988 (Joint Winner, Le Mans, 1988); Lead Driver for Toyota GB, World Sports Prototype Championship, 1989, 1990.

Butler, Cllr Bill. MSP (Labour), Glasgow Anniesland, 2000-2011; Councillor, Glasgow City Council (Greater Pollok ward), since 2012; m., Patricia Ferguson (qv). Educ. Stirling University; Notre Dame College of Education. English teacher, 20 years; elected Glasgow City Councillor, 1987 (Convener, Policy and Resources (e-Glasgow) Working Group; Vice-Convener, Policy and Resources Committee; Secretary, Labour Group). Address: City Chambers, George Square, Glasgow G2 1DU; T.-0141 287 5735.
E-mail: bill.butler@glasgow.gov.uk

Butlin, Ron, MA, DipAECD. Poet, Novelist, Opera Librettist, Journalist; b. 17.11.49, Edinburgh. Educ. Dumfries Academy; Edinburgh University. Appointed Edinburgh Makar (Poet Laureate), 2008, reappointed, 2011-2014; made Honorary Writing Fellow by Edinburgh University, 2009; Specialist Advisor to Scottish Arts Council, 2009; Writer in Residence, Lothian Region Education Authority, 1979, Edinburgh University, 1981, 1984-85; Scottish/Canadian Writing Exchange Fellow, University of New Brunswick, 1983-84; Writer in Residence for Midlothian, 1989-90; Writer in Residence, Craigmillar Literacy Trust; Novelist in Residence, St. Andrews University, 1998-99. Publications: poetry: Stretto, 1976; Creatures Tamed by Cruelty, 1979; The Exquisite Instrument, 1982 (Scottish Arts Council Book Award); Ragtime in Unfamiliar Bars, 1985 (SAC Book Award, Poetry Book Society recommendation); Histories of Desire 1995; prose: The Tilting Room (short stories), 1983 (SAC Book Award); The Sound of My Voice (novel), 1987; Blending In (play), 1989; Mauritian Voices (Editor), 1996; Night Visits (novel), 1997; When We Jump We Jump High!, 1998; Faraway Pictures (opera), 2000; Our Piece of Good Fortune (poetry), 2002; Vivaldi and the Number 3 (short stories), 2004; Without a Backward Glance - New and Selected Poems, 2005; Good Angel, Bad Angel (Opera), 2005; Belonging (novel), 2006; No More Angels (short stories), 2007; The Perfect Woman (Opera), 2008. Awarded the Prix MillePages, 2004 and the Prix Lucioles, 2005 (both for Best Foreign Novel); The Money Man (Opera), 2010; The Magicians of Edinburgh (poetry), 2012;

Ghost Moon (novel), 2014 (nominated for the International Impac Award, 2016); Wedlock (opera), 2014; The Magicians of Scotland (poetry), 2015; Here Come The Trolls! (verse for children), 2015. Recreations: music; travel. Address: (h.) 7 West Newington Place, Edinburgh EH9 1QT; T.-0131-667 0394.

Butt, Professor John, OBE, MA, PhD, FBA, FRSE, FRCO(CHM), ADCM. Gardiner Professor of Music, University of Glasgow, since 2001; b. 17.11.60, Solihull; m., Sally Cantlay; 4 s.; 1 d. Educ. Solihull School; King's College, University of Cambridge. Temporary Lecturer, University of Aberdeen, 1986-87; Research Fellow, Magdalene College, Cambridge, 1987-89; University Organist and Professor of Music, UC Berkeley, California, 1989-97; University Lecturer and Fellow, King's College Cambridge, 1997-2001. Eleven CD recordings on organ and harpsichord; Director, Dunedin Consort (Edinburgh), three recordings; Gramophone and Midem awards for recording of Handel's Messiah. Publications: five books. Recreations: reading; walking; tai chi. Address: (b.) Music Department, University of Glasgow, 14 University Gardens, Glasgow G12 8QQ; T.-0141-330 4571.
E-mail: j.butt@music.gla.ac.uk

Butterworth, Neil, MA, HonFLCM. Chairman, Scottish Society of Composers, 1991-2003; broadcaster, composer, writer and conductor; b. 4.9.34, Streatham, London; m., Anna Mary Barnes; 3 d. Educ. Rutlish School, Surrey; Nottingham University; London University; Guildhall School of Music, London. Lecturer, Kingston College of Technology, 1960-68; Head, Music Department, Napier College, Edinburgh, 1968-87; Music Critic, Times Educational Supplement, 1983-97. Conductor: Sutton Symphony Orchestra, 1960-64, Glasgow Orchestral Society, 1975-83, 1989-2002; Chairman: Incorporated Society of Musicians, Edinburgh Centre, 1981-86, Inveresk Preservation Society, 1988-95; Churchill Fellowship, 1975. Publications: Haydn, 1976; Dvorak, 1980; Dictionary of American Composers, 1983 (2nd edition, 2005); Aaron Copland, 1984; Vaughan Williams, 1989; Neglected Music, 1991; The American Symphony, 1998; over 300 compositions. Recreations: autographs; collecting books and records; giant jigsaw puzzles. Address: (h.) The Lodge, East High Street, Greenlaw, Berwickshire TD10 6UF; T.-01361 810408.

Byers, Eric. Chief Executive, Fife Chamber of Commerce, since 2014. Over 20 years involved in a broad range of economic development work; worked in senior management positions in Fife since 1985, including five years as Head of Economic Development at Fife Council and has an enormous amount of experience in working with the public, private and voluntary sectors. Address: (b.) Evans Business Centre, 1 Begg Road, John Smith Business Park, Kirkcaldy, Fife KY2 6HD; T.-01592 647740.

Byng, Jamie. Publisher, Canongate Books, since 1994; b. 27.6.69, Winchester; m. (1), Whitney Osborn McVeigh (m. diss.); 1 s.; 1 d.; m. (2), Elizabeth Sheinkman; 1 s.; 1 d. Educ. Winchester College; Edinburgh University. Recreations: tennis; cooking; deejaying; reading; drinking. Address: (b.) 14 High Street, Edinburgh EH1 1TE; T.-0131-557 5111.

Byrne, John. Dramatist and stage designer; b. 1940, Paisley. Plays include: The Slab Boys, Cuttin' A Rug, Still Life (trilogy); Normal Service; Cara Coco; television series: Tutti Frutti; Your Cheatin' Heart. Associate of the Royal Scottish Academy, 2004; Honorary Doctorate: University of Paisley, 1997, Robert Gordon University Gray's School of Art, Aberdeen, 2006, University of Dundee, 2011.

Byrne, Kate (Kathleen) Frances, MA, MSc, PhD, CEng, MBCS, CITP, FRSA. Commissioner, The Royal

Commission on the Ancient and Historical Monuments of Scotland; Research in Computational Linguistics, University of Edinburgh, since 2002; b. 2.12.59, London; m., Peter Emrys Williams. Educ. St. Catherine's, Twickenham; University of Edinburgh. Various posts in the Scottish Office Computer Service, 1985-91; MIS Manager, Heriot-Watt University, 1991-92; Information Systems Manager, RCAHMS, 1992-98; Infrastructure Manager at Tullis Russell Papermakers, 1998-99; Head of Computer Services and Deputy Director of ICT, The National Library of Scotland, 1999-2002. Currently research fellow in the School of Informatics, Edinburgh University. Director of Scran and The Scran Trust; Scottish Government non-executive director, 2010-13; Director of The Wildlife Information Centre, 2012-13; Director of The Scottish Gliding Union, 2005-08; Member of "Walking On Air" (Gliding for the Disabled); Deputy CFI of Scottish Gliding Centre. Recreations: gliding; hill-walking. Address: (h.) 5 Kirkhill Way, Penicuik EH26 8HH; T.-01968 674114; e-mail: k.byrne@ed.ac.uk

Byrne, Laurie, MA (Hons). Headteacher, Holyrood RC Secondary School, Glasgow, since 2012; b. 7.6.56, Glasgow; m., Helen; 1 s.; 1 d. Educ. St. Patrick's High School, Dumbarton; University of Glasgow; Notre Dame College. Teacher of Modern Languages, St. Margaret's HS, Airdrie, 1980-85; Assistant Principal Teacher of Guidance, Holy Cross, Hamilton, 1985-89; Principal Teacher of Guidance, St. Aidan's HS, Wishaw, 1989-96; Assistant Head, Cardinal Newman HS, Bellshill, 1996-2000; Deputy Head, St. Ninian's HS, Giffnock, 2000-04; Head Teacher, St. Maurice's HS, Cumbernauld, 2004-12. Past Chair, Catholic Headteachers' Association of Scotland, 2009-2011; Member of Catholic Education Commission Executive, 2011-2014. Recreations: football; travel. Address: Holyrood RC Secondary School, 100 Dixon Road, Glasgow GU2 8AU.
E-mail: lbyrne@holyrood-sec.glasgow.sch.uk

Byrne, Rosemary, Dip Ed, DipSen. Joint Leader, Solidarity (Scotland); MSP (Solidarity), South of Scotland, 2003-07; b. 3.3.48, Irvine; m., James; 1 s. Educ. Irvine Royal Academy; Craigie College, Ayr. Primary teacher, Ayrshire, 1977-88; Learning Support Teacher, 1988-96; Senior Teacher, North Ayrshire Network Support Team, 1996-99; Principal Teacher, Pupil Support, Ardrossan Academy, 1999-2003. Address: (h.) Williamsfield, Irvine; T.-01294 311105.

C

Cable, Clare. Chief Executive and Nurse Director of The Queen's Nursing Institute Scotland, since 2014. Educ. Sutton High School; University of Southampton. Trained as a children's nurse in Oxford and in 1993 joined the Royal College of Nursing as Research and Development Officer, completing a Masters degree a year later; Director, Quality Improvement Programme, Royal College of Nursing, 2003-2007; Policy Adviser, RCN Scotland, 2007-2014. Address: The Queen's Nursing Institute Scotland, 31 Castle Terrace, Edinburgh EH1 2EL; T.-0131 229 2333; e-mail: office@qnis.org.uk

Cackette, Paul, LLB (Hons), DipLP, NP. Deputy Solicitor to the Scottish Government; b. 26.3.60, Edinburgh; m., Helen Thomson; 1 s.; 2 d. Educ. George Heriot's School, Edinburgh; Edinburgh University. Admitted as a Solicitor, 1985; Solicitor, Kirkcaldy District Council, 1985-88; Office of Solicitor to Secretary of State for Scotland, 1988-99; Office of Solicitor to the Scottish Government, 1999-2003 and since 2008. Recreations: literature; athletics. Address: (b.) Victoria Quay, Edinburgh EH6 6QQ; T.-0131 244 0959.

Caddy, Professor Brian, BSc, PhD, CChem, MRSC, FCSFS. Professor of Forensic Science, Strathclyde University, 1992-99, now Emeritus Professor; b. 26.3.37, Burslem, Stoke-on-Trent; m., Beryl Ashworth; 1 s.; 1 d. Educ. Longton High School, Stoke-on-Trent; Sheffield University. MRC Research Fellow, 1963-66; Strathclyde University: Lecturer in Forensic Science, 1966-77, Senior Lecturer in Forensic Science, 1977-92. Founder Member, European Network of Forensic Science Institutes; President, Forensic Science Society, 1999; Member, Executive Committee, Council for the Registration of Forensic Practitioners, 1999; appointed Commissioner to the Scottish Criminal Cases Review Commission, 2006-2015; Review of the Damilola Taylor case for the Home Secretary, 2007; appointed external verifer for the Council for the Regulation of Forensic Practitioners, 2004, 2006 and 2007. Publications: three books; over 90 papers/articles. Editor, Science and Justice (Forensic Science Society journal), 1993-1999. Recreations: reading; painting; walking the dog; dining with friends; good food and wine. Address: (h.) 5 Kings Park, Torrance, Glasgow G64 4DX; T.-01360 622 358; e-mail: B.Caddy@strath.ac.uk

Cadell of Grange, William Archibald, MA (Cantab), FRIAS, RIBA; b. 9.3.33; m., Mary-Jean Carmichael; 3 s. Educ. Merchiston Castle; Trinity College, Cambridge; Regent Street Polytechnic. Founded William A. Cadell, Architects, 1968, retired 1995; Manager, Grange Estate, 1971-2000; Chairman, Drum Housing Development, 1991-2009; Commissioner, Royal Fine Art Commission for Scotland, 1992-2000; Trustee, Architectural Heritage Fund, 1997-2007. Recreations: gardening; forestry; the arts. Address: Swordie Mains, Linlithgow, West Lothian EH49 7RQ; T.-01506 842946; e-mail: wacadell@gmail.com

Caie, Professor Graham Douglas, CBE, MA, PhD, FEA, FRSA, FRSE, FFCS. Honorary Research Professor, Glasgow University; Vice President, Royal Society of Edinburgh; formerly Clerk of Senate and Vice-Principal, Glasgow University; Emeritus Professor of English Language, Glasgow University, since 1990; Senate Assessor, Glasgow University Court, 1998-2003; b. 3.2.45, Aberdeen; m., Ann Pringle Abbott; 1 s.; 1 d. Educ. Aberdeen Grammar School; Aberdeen University; McMaster University, Canada. Teaching Assistant, McMaster University, 1968-72; Amanuensis and Lektor, Copenhagen University, 1972-90. Chairman, Medieval Centre, Copenhagen University, 1985-90; Visiting Professor: McMaster University, 1985-86, Guelph University, 1989; Associate Fellow, Clare Hall, Cambridge, 1977-78; Court of Queen Margaret University; Member, Scottish Arts Council Advisory Panel; Vice-President, Scottish Texts Society; Secretary, European Society for the Study of English; Trustee and Vice-Chairman, National Library of Scotland; Member, Council, Dictionary of Older Scottish Tongue; Board, Scottish Language Dictionaries; English Panel, AHRC; English Panel, RAE; Board, English Subject Centre (HEA); SQA English Panel. Publications: Medieval Manuscripts in Context; Judgement Day II edition 1, The Theme of Doomsday in Old English Poetry; Beowulf; Bibliography of Junius XI MS; numerous articles. Address: (h.) 12B Upper Glenburn Road, Bearsden, Glasgow G61 4BW; T.-0141-943 1192; e-mail: G.Caie@englang.arts.gla.ac.uk

Caimbeul, Aonghas Phàdraig, MA. Sgrìobhadair; Fearnaidheachd (òraidiche agus craoladair); r. Uibhist-a-Deas; p., Liondsaidh; 1. m.; 5 n. Foghlam: Ard-Sgoil an Obain; Oilthaigh Dhùn Eideann. Treis aig: A' Phàipear Bheag, BBC Rèidio, Grampian Telebhisean; Sgrìobhaiche an t-Sabhail Mhòir, 1990-92; Oraidiche an sin on uairsin; Crìosdaidh; ag obair air nobhal mòr an-dràsda. Air foillseachadh: 2 leabhar bàrdachd; nobhal dheugairean; dà nobhal eile tighinn a-mach am bliadhna. Cuir-seachad: bhith ris an teaghlach agus leughadh Tolstoy. Seòladh: Sabhal Mòr Ostaig, An Teanga, Slèite, an t-Eilein Sgitheanach; F.-01471 844373.

Cairns, Professor Douglas Laidlaw, MA (Hons), PhD, FHEA, MAE. Professor of Classics, University of Edinburgh, since 2004; b. 10.1.61, Glasgow; widowed; 1 s. Educ. Eastbank Academy, Glasgow; University of Glasgow. Temporary Lecturer in Greek, University of St. Andrews, 1986; Lecturer in Classics, University of Otago, New Zealand, 1988-92; Lecturer/Senior Lecturer in Classics: University of Leeds, 1992-99, University of Glasgow, 1999-2004. Research Fellow, Georg-August Universität, Göttingen, 1987-88, 1993-95; Humboldt Universität, Berlin, 2011; Visiting Professor: Kyoto University, 2008, Florida State University, 2012; elected member, Academia Europaea, 2013. Publications: Author of Aidôs: The Psychology and Ethics of Honour and Shame in Ancient Greek Literature, 1993; Bacchylides: Five Epinician Odes, 2010; Sophocles: Antigone, 2016. Recreations: music; travel; cinema; food and wine. Address: (b.) School of History, Classics and Archaeology, University of Edinburgh EH8 9AG; T.-0131 651 1647; e-mail: douglas.cairns@ed.ac.uk

Cairns, Very Rev. John Ballantyne, KCVO, LTh, LLB, DD, LLD. Chaplain, then Extra Chaplain to the Queen, since 1997; Dean of the Chapel Royal, 2006-13; Chaplain, The Queen's Bodyguard for Scotland, Royal Company of Archers, since 2007; Chaplain to the Lieutenancy of Dumbarton, since 1997; Moderator, General Assembly of the Church of Scotland, 1999-2000; General Trustee of Church of Scotland, since 1995; Dean of the Order of St. John, since 2011; b. 15.3.42, London; m., Dr. Elizabeth Emma Bradley; 3 s. Educ. Sutton Valence School, Kent; Bristol University; Edinburgh University. Messrs Richards, Butler & Co., Solicitors, City of London, 1964-68; Administrative Assistant, East Lothian County Council, 1968-69; Assistant Minister, St. Giles, Elgin, 1973-75; Minister, Langholm, Ewes and Westerkirk Parish Churches, 1975-85, also linked with Canonbie, 1981-85; Clerk, Presbytery of Annandale and Eskdale, 1980-82; Minister, Riverside Church, Dumbarton, 1985-2001; Parish Minister, Aberlady and Gullane Parish Churches, 2001-09; Locum Minister, St. Columba's Church, Pont Street, London, 2010-2012; Convener, Maintenance of the Ministry Committee and Joint Convener, Board of Ministry and Mission, Church of Scotland, 1984-88; Chairman, Judicial Commission of General Assembly, 1993-98; Convener, General Assembly Committee on Chaplains to Her Majesty's Forces, 1993-98; Moderator, Presbytery of Dumbarton, 1993-94; Chaplain to Moderator of General Assembly, 1995; Chaplain to Lord High Commissioner (HRH Duke of York), 2007; Divisional Chaplain, Strathclyde Police, 1987-2001; Chairman of Governors, Compass School, 2008-2015; President, Dumbarton Burns Club, 2002; President, Friends of St Andrew's, Jerusalem, 2005-2011; DD University of Aberdeen, 2003; LLD University of Bristol, 2004; KCVO, 2013. Publications: Keeping Fit for Ministry, 1988; Democracy and Unwritten Constitutions, 1989. Recreations: golf; gardening; music; Robert Burns. Address: Bell House, Roxburghe Park, Dunbar, East Lothian EH42 1LR.

Cairns, Professor John William, LLB, PhD, FRSE, FSA Scot. Professor of Civil Law, University of Edinburgh, since 2012; b. 17.8.55, Crieff; partner, Donald Jardine. Educ. Hutchesons' Boys' Grammar School; University of Edinburgh. Lecturer in Jurisprudence, Queen's University of Belfast; Lecturer, Senior Lecturer, Reader, Professor of Legal History (2000-2012), University of Edinburgh; Visiting Professor: Southern Methodist University, Dallas, 1986, Miami, 1988, 1991, 1995. Chairman, Council, The Stair Society; President, Eighteenth-Century Scottish Studies Society, 2006-08. Recent Publications: The Creation of the Ius Commune: From Casus to Regula (Co-Editor), 2010; Beyond Dogmatics: Law and Society in the Roman World (Co-Editor), 2007; The Jury in the History of the Common Law (Co-Editor), 2002; Critical Studies in Ancient Law, Comparative Law and Legal History (Co-Editor), 2001. Recreations: cooking; reading; cinema. Address: (b.) University of Edinburgh, School of Law, Old College, South Bridge, Edinburgh EH8 9YL; T.-0131-650 1000; e-mail: john.cairns@ed.ac.uk

Cairns, Robert, MA, DipEd. Chairman, East of Scotland Water, 1998-2002; Member, City of Edinburgh Council, 1995-2007; b. 16.7.47, Dundee; 2 s. Educ. Morgan Academy; Edinburgh University; Moray House College of Education. Assistant Editor, Scottish National Dictionary, 1969-74; Parliamentary candidate (Labour), North Edinburgh, 1973, February 1974; Teacher, James Gillespie's High School, 1975-96; Member, City of Edinburgh District Council, 1974-95 (Convener, Planning and Development Committee, 1986-95); Board Member, East Regional Board SEPA, 2004-09. Recreation: walking. Address: (h.) Eastergate Cottage, Harrietfield, Logiealmond, Perthshire; T.-01738 880393. E-mail: robert.cairns401@googlemail.com

Cairns, Professor Robert Alan, BSc, PhD, FInstP, FRSE. Emeritus Professor of Applied Mathematics, School of Mathematics and Statistics, St. Andrews University; b. 12.3.45, Glasgow; m., Ann E. Mackay. Educ. Allan Glen's School, Glasgow; Glasgow University. Lecturer in Applied Mathematics, St. Andrews University, 1970-83; Senior Lecturer, 1983-85; Reader, 1985-91; Professor, 1991-2010. Member, SERC Laser Committee, 1990-93; Member, SERC Atomic and Molecular Physics Sub-Committee, 1990-93; Chairman, Plasma Physics Group, Institute of Physics, 1999-2001 (Committee Member, 1981-84); Member, Editorial Board, Plasma Physics, 1983-85; Editor, Journal of Plasma Physics, 1995-2006. Publications: Plasma Physics, 1985; Radiofrequency heating of plasmas, 1991. Recreations: music (listening to and playing recorder and baroque flute); golf; hill-walking. Address: (b.) School of Mathematics and Statistics, St. Andrews University, North Haugh, St. Andrews, Fife KY16 9SS; T.-01334 463707.

Cairns Speitel, Pauline. Senior Editor, Scottish Language Dictionaries. Editor managing the revision of the Concise Scots Dictionary; also manages the Word Collection. Began career in publishing with Chambers in Edinburgh, then spent twenty years with the Scottish National Dictionary Association, as lexicographer on all of their dictionary projects. Directed lexicographical projects with a range of community groups in Scotland. Address: Scottish Language Dictionaries, 25 Buccleuch Place, Edinburgh EH8 9LN; T.-0131 650 4149; e-mail: pcspeitel at scotsdictionaries.org.uk

Caithness, 20th Earl of (Malcolm Ian Sinclair), PC; b. 3.11.48; 1 s.; 1 d. Educ. Marlborough; Royal Agricultural College, Cirencester. Succeeded to title, 1965; Parliamentary Under Secretary of State, Department of Transport, 1985-86; Minister of State, Home Office, 1986-88; Minister of State, Department of the Environment, 1988-89; Paymaster General and Minister of State, HM Treasury, 1989-90; Minister of State, Foreign and Commonwealth Office, 1990-92; Minister of State, Department of Transport, 1992-94; Trustee, Queen Elizabeth Castle of Mey Trust, since 1996; Trustee and Chief Executive, Clan Sinclair Trust, since 1999; elected Member, House of Lords, since 1999.

Calder, Professor Andrew Alexander, MD, FRCS (Edin), FRCP (Glas), FRCP (Edin), FRCOG, HonFCOG (SA). Professor Emeritus and Assistant Principal for Reproductive Health, University of Edinburgh, Professor of Obstetrics and Gynaecology, 1987-2009; Honorary Professor in the School of Medicine, University of St Andrews, since 2012; Chairman, Tenovus Scotland, since 2011; formerly Director, Jennifer Brown Research Laboratory and Tommy's Centre for Fetal and Maternal Health Research, Queen's Medical Research Institute; b. 17.1.45, Aberdeen; m., Valerie Anne Dugard; 1 s.; 2 d. Educ. Glasgow Academy; Glasgow University. Clinical training posts, Glasgow, 1968-72; Research Fellow, Nuffield Department of Obstetrics and Gynaecology, University of Oxford, 1972-75; Lecturer/Senior Lecturer, Obstetrics and Gynaecology, University of Glasgow, 1975-86; Consultant Obstetrician and Gynaecologist: Glasgow Royal Infirmary and Royal Maternity Hospital, 1978-86, Royal Infirmary of Edinburgh and Simpson Centre for Reproductive Health, 1987-2009; British Exchange Professor, University of California, Los Angeles, 1992. Blair Bell Memorial Lecturer, RCOG, 1977; WHO Travelling Fellow, Uruguay, 1985. Recreations: music; golf; curling; history of medicine. Address: Department of Obstetrics and Gynaecology, Royal Infirmary of Edinburgh, Little France, Edinburgh; e-mail: a.a.calder@ed.ac.uk

Calder, Rev. Bryce, MA (with Merit) (Hist), BD (First Class Hons) (OT Stud). Parish Minister, St. David's Memorial Park, since 2001; b. 26.12.66, Bo'ness; m., Helen Calder (nee Miller); 1 s.; 1 d. Educ. Bo'ness Academy; Edinburgh University. Metropolitan Police Officer, 1985-87; Candidate for Church of Scotland Ministry, 1988-93; Assistant Minister of Troon: St. Medan's, 1994; Parish Minister, Buckhaven and Manager, Buckhaven Theatre, 1995-2000. Founder Member, Levenmouth YMCA; Retired Company Director, Cutting Edge Theatre Company; Chairman, Friends of SYCAM (A Charity that supports Children's Aid work in India); Chair of Kirkintilloch and Lenzie ACTS Group; Chair of Friends of St. David's Memorial Park Parish Church; Member of Church of Scotland Safeguarding Committee; recently nominated Convenor of Safeguarding sub group focussing on the safe inclusion in worship of those who present a potential risk to children and vulnerable adults. Recreations: football (supporter of Motherwell FC); bowls; theatre; reading; listening to music; playing Rickenbacker bass guitar; dog walking; reading and reciting Burns poetry. Address: 2 Roman Road, Kirkintilloch, Glasgow G66 1EA; T.-0141-776 1434. E-mail: ministry100@aol.com

Calder, Finlay, OBE; b. 20.8.57, Haddington; m., Elizabeth; 1 s.; 1 d. Educ. Daniel Stewart's and Melville

College. Played rugby for Scotland, 1986-90; captained Scotland, 1989; captained British Isles, 1989.

Calder, George, BA (Hons) (Cantab), LLB; b. 20.12.47; 2 d. Educ. George Watson's College, Edinburgh; Cambridge University; Edinburgh University. Joined Civil Service (Department of Employment), 1971; worked in European Commission (cabinet of George Thomson), 1974-76; Treasury, 1977-79; Manpower Services Commission, 1979-87; Scottish Office/Scottish Government (Head of European Funds and Co-ordination Division, Head of Personnel, Head of Water Services Unit), 1987-99; Head, Scottish Government EU Office, 1999-2004. Recreations: football; military history; book clubs; hill-walking; gardening.

Calder, Jenni, BA, MPhil. Freelance Writer; b. 3.12.41, Chicago, Illinois; 1 s.; 2 d. Educ. Perse School for Girls, Cambridge; Cambridge University; London University. Freelance writer, 1966-78; taught and lectured in Scotland, England, Kenya and USA; Lecturer in English, Nairobi University, 1968-69; successively Education Officer, Head of Publications, Head of Museum of Scotland Publications, National Museums of Scotland, Edinburgh, 1978-2001. Publications: Chronicles of Conscience: a study of George Orwell and Arthur Koestler, 1968; Scott (with Angus Calder), 1969; There Must be a Lone Ranger: the Myth and Reality of the American West, 1974; Women and Marriage in Victorian Fiction, 1976; Brave New World and Nineteen Eighty Four, 1976; Heroes: from Byron to Guevara, 1977; The Victorian Home, 1977; The Victorian Home from Old Photographs, 1979; RLS, A Life Study, 1980; The Robert Louis Stevenson Companion (Editor), 1980; Robert Louis Stevenson and Victorian Scotland (Editor), 1981; The Strange Case of Dr Jekyll and Mr Hyde (Editor), 1979; Kidnapped (Editor), 1981; Catriona (Editor), 1981; The Enterprising Scot (Editor), 1986; Island Landfalls (Editor), 1987; Bonny Fighters: The Story of the Scottish Soldier, 1987; Open Guide to Animal Farm and Nineteen Eighty Four, 1987; The Wealth of a Nation (Editor), 1989; St. Ives, a new ending, 1990; Scotland in Trust, 1990; Treasure Islands (Editor), 1994; Mediterranean (poems, as Jenni Daiches), 1995; Tales of the South Seas (Editor), 1996; The Nine Lives of Naomi Mitchison, 1997; Everyman's Poetry: Robert Louis Stevenson (Editor), 1997; Present Poets anthology, Editor), 1998; Translated Kingdoms (anthology, Editor), 1999; A Beleaguered City and Other Tales of the Seen and the Unseen (Editor), 2000; Scots in Canada, 2003; Not Nebuchadnezzar: In Search of Identities, 2005; Scots in the USA, 2005; Smoke (poems, as Jenni Daiches), 2005; Letters from the Great Wall (fiction, as Jenni Daiches), 2006; Frontier Scots: The Scots Who Won the West, 2009; Lost in the Backwoods: Scots and the North American Wilderness, 2013; Waverley by Walter Scott, adapted for the modern reader, 2014; Forgive (fiction, as Jenni Daiches), 2014. Recreations: music; films; walking the dog. Address: (h.) 31 Station Road, South Queensferry, West Lothian; T.-0131-331 1287.

Calder, Professor Muffy, OBE, BSc, PhD, FRSE, FREng, FBCS. Professor of Formal Methods (Computer Science), Glasgow University, since 1999; Chief Scientific Adviser, Scottish Government, 2012-2014; Vice-Principal, Head of College of Science and Engineering, University of Glasgow, since 2015; b. 21.5.58, Shawinigan, Quebec, Canada; m., David Calder. Educ. Stirling University; St Andrews University. Research Fellow, Edinburgh University and Stirling University, 1983-87; Lecturer/Senior Lecturer, Computing Science, Glasgow University, 1988-99. Recreations: road running; hill-running. Address: (b.) Department of Computer Science, Glasgow University. T.-0141-330 4969.

Calder, Robert Russell, MA. Critic, Philosophical Writer, Historian of Ideas, Poet, Freelance Journalist, Book Reviewer, Performer and Singer; b. 22.4.50, Burnbank. Educ. Hamilton Academy; Glasgow University; Edinburgh University. Co-Editor, Chapman, 1974-76 and 1986-91; Editor, Lines Review, 1976-77; Theatre Critic and Feature Writer, Scot, 1983-86; Staff Writer, Popmatters (Chicago), Journal of Global Culture; Staff writer, All About Jazz. Books: A School of Thinking, 1995; Narcissism, Nihilism, Simplicity (Editor), 1992; poetry: Il Re Giovane, 1976, Ettrick & Annan, 1981; Serapion, 1996; Urlaubsgedichte, 2009. Recreations: music - opera singing; jazz piano. Address: (h.) 23 Glenlee Street, Burnbank, Hamilton ML3 9JB; T.-01698 824244; e-mail: serapion@btinternet.com

Calderwood, Dr Catherine, MA (Cantab), FRCOG, MBChB, FRCP (Edin). Chief Medical Officer, Scottish Government; consultant obstetrician and gynaecologist, NHS Lothian; 3 c. Educ. University of Cambridge; University of Glasgow. Career: national clinical director for maternity and women's health, NHS England; formerly Acting Deputy Chief Medical Officer, Scottish Government. Member of the Royal College of Obstetricians and Gynaecologists; Honorary Fellow of the Royal College of Physicians of Edinburgh. Address: Scottish Government, St. Andrew's House, Regent Road, Edinburgh EH1 3DG.

Calderwood, Robert. Chief Executive, Greater Glasgow and Clyde NHS Board, since 2009. Career history: joined Argyll and Clyde Health Board in 1974 having previously been an NHS Administrative Trainee; became Hospital Administrator for Greenock Royal and Associated Hospitals in 1978; appointed Administrator, Acute Services, for Inverclyde District in 1981; became Deputy Unit Administrator for all acute services within Renfrewshire in 1984; joined Greater Glasgow Health Board in 1985 as Unit Administrator for Western Infirmary/Gartnavel General Hospital Unit; appointed as Director of Property and Strategic Planning at Greater Glasgow Health Board in 1988; became Unit General Manager for the Southern General Hospital Unit in April 1991 and became its first Chief Executive on achieving Trust status in 1993; appointed Chief Executive for both the Southern General Hospital and Victoria Infirmary NHS Trusts in 1997, and appointed Chief Executive of the South Glasgow University Hospitals NHS Trust in 1999; Programme Director for the implementation of the Board's Acute Services Strategy in 2003; appointed as Chief Operating Officer for Greater Glasgow Acute Division; role was expanded to include the acute elements of Clyde in April 2006 when NHS Greater Glasgow and Clyde was formed; key member of NHSGGC's most senior executive team. Address: (b.) J. B. Russell House, Gartnavel Royal Hospital, 1055 Great Western Road, Glasgow G12 0XH.

Caldwell, David Hepburn, MA, PhD, FSA, FSAScot. Former Keeper of Scotland and Europe; Director, Finlaggan Archaeological Project, National Museums of Scotland; President of the Society of Antiquaries of Scotland; Vice-President of the Society for Post-Medieval Archaeology; Director, Fife Cultural Trust; b. 15.12.51, Kilwinning, Ayrshire; m., Margaret Anne McGovern; 1 s.; 2 d. Educ. Ardrossan Academy; Edinburgh University. Joined staff, National Museum of Antiquities, 1973. Publications: The Scottish Armoury, 1979; Scottish Weapons and Fortifications, 1981; Scotland's Wars and Warriors, 1998; Islay, Jura and Colonsay, A Historical Guide, 2001 and 2011; Islay Land of the Lordship, 2008; (Co Author) The Lewis Chessmen Unmasked, 2010; (Co Author) The Lewis Chessmen, New Perspectives, 2014. Recreations: travelling; table tennis; dressmaking. Address: (h.) 3 James Park, Burntisland, Fife KY3 9EW; T.-872175.

Caldwell, Miller H., MA, CQSW, DipSocWk, DipRS, FFCS. Guest Speaker, Writer and Film Script Writer; Camp Manager, Mundihar NWFP Pakistan 2006 Post

Earthquake; former Dumfries and Galloway Authority Reporter; b. 6.10.50, Glasgow; m., Jocelyn M. France; 2d. Educ. Glasgow Academy; London University; Moray House College; Jordanhill College. Fraternal Worker, Ghana, West Africa, Overseas Council, Church of Scotland, 1972-78; Postgraduate student, 1978-80; School Social Worker, Central Regional Council, 1980-83; Kilmarnock and Loudon Reporter, 1983-88; Area Reporter, Kyle and Carrick, Cumnock and Doon Valley, 1988-92; Principal Reporter, Dumfries and Galloway, 1992-95; Regional Reporter, 1995. Past President, Dumfries and Galloway Burns Club (direct descendent of Robert Burns). Currently serving on the committee of the Society of Authors in Scotland; volunteer in the Cinnamon Trust caring for the pets of the terminally ill. Publications: Operation Oboe (Historical Novel); Have You Seen My ...Umm...Memory (Self Help Memory Book); Poet's Progeny (Editor) (A line of descent from the Bard); Ponderings - poems and short stories in large print; Restless Waves (Novel); 7 Point 7 (On the Richter Scale) The Diary of the Camp Manager (Biography); Untied Laces (Autobiography), 2009; Miss Martha Douglas (Novel); The Last Shepherd (Novel); The Parrot's Tale (Novel); Jim's retiring Collection; The Crazy Psychologist; Take the Lead (Biography); childrens books: Lawrence The Lion; The Spotless Dalmation; Chaz The Friendly Crocodile. Recreations: all things West African; piano; clarinet. Address: (h.) Netherholm, Edinburgh Road, Dumfries.
E-mail: netherholm6@yahoo.com
web: www.netherholmpublications.com

Caldwell, Sheila Marion, BA (Hons), Fellow of Royal Geographical Society, ARSGS. Member, Committee, Royal Scottish Geographical Society; b. England; m., Major Robert Caldwell, TD (deceased). Educ. Tunbridge Wells Grammar School; University College, London. Founder/Principal, Yejide Girls' Grammar School, Ibadan, Nigeria; first Principal, Girls' Secondary (Government) School, Lilongwe, Malawi; Depute Head, Mills Grammar School, Framlingham, Suffolk; Head, St. Columba's School, Kilmacolm, 1976-87; Treasurer, Secondary Heads' Association, Scotland, 1984-87. Recreations: travel; art history and architecture; music, opera and ballet; cooking. Address: (h.) 27 Oxford Road, Renfrew PA4 0SJ; T.-0141-886 2296.

Calman, Professor Sir Kenneth Charles, KCB 1996, DL, MD, PhD, FRCP, FRCS, FRSE. Chancellor, University of Glasgow, since 2006; Chairman, National Trust for Scotland, 2010-2015; Chairman, Commission on Scottish Devolution, 2008-09; Vice-Chancellor and Warden, Durham University, 1998-2007; b. 25.12.41, Glasgow; m., Ann; 1 s.; 2 d. Educ. Allan Glen's School, Glasgow; Glasgow University. Lecturer in Surgery, Western Infirmary, Glasgow, 1968-72; MRC Clinical Research Fellow, London, 1972-73; Professor of Oncology, Glasgow University, 1974-84; Dean of Postgraduate Medicine, 1984-89; Chief Medical Officer, Scottish Home and Health Department, 1989-91; Chief Medical Officer, Department of Health, 1991-98. Chairman, Executive Board, World Health Organisation, 1998-99; Deputy Chair, The British Library, 2010-15. Recreations: golf; Scottish literature; gardening; cartoons; sundials. Address: (b.) University of Glasgow G12 8QQ.

Cameron of Lochbroom, Rt. Hon. Lord (Kenneth John Cameron), Life Baron (1984), PC (1984), MA (Oxon), LLB, QC, FRSE, Hon. FRIAS. Senator of the College of Justice, 1989-2003; Chairman, Royal Fine Art Commission for Scotland, 1995-2005; b. 11.6.31, Edinburgh; m., Jean Pamela Murray; 2 d. Educ. Edinburgh Academy; Corpus Christi College, Oxford; Edinburgh University. Advocate, 1958; Queen's Counsel, 1972; President, Pensions Appeal Tribunal for Scotland, 1976; Chairman, Committee of Investigation Under Agricultural Marketing Act 1958, 1980; Advocate Depute, 1981; Lord Advocate, 1984; Hon. Bencher, Lincoln's Inn; Hon. Fellow, Corpus Christi College, Oxford; Hon. Fellow, RIAS; Hon Fellow, RSA. Recreation: fishing. Address: (h.) Stoneyhill House, Musselburgh.

Cameron, Alastair Ian. Chief Executive, Scottish Churches Housing Action, since 1994; b. 3.4.53, Dundee; m., Mary Jane Elton; 2 s.; 1 d. Educ. Glasgow Academy; Lenana School, Nairobi; University of Kent at Canterbury. Neighbourhood Worker, Rochdale Metropolitan Council, 1980-85; Development Worker, Edinburgh Council for the Single Homeless, 1985-92; Housing Strategy Manager, Wester Hailes Partnership, 1992-94. Convener, Rural Housing Scotland; Member, Religious Society of Friends. Recreations: traditional music; cycling; allotment gardening. Address: 3 Esplanade Terrace, Edinburgh EH15 2ES; e-mail: mandolin.alastair@gmail.com

Cameron, Right Rev. Andrew Bruce. Primus of the Scottish Episcopal Church, 2000-06; Bishop of Aberdeen and Orkney, Scottish Episcopal Church, 1992-2006; b. 2.5.41, Glasgow; m., Elaine Cameron; 2 s. Educ. Eastwood Secondary School; Edinburgh Theological College. Curate, Helensburgh and Edinburgh, 1964-70; Chaplain, St. Mary's Cathedral, Edinburgh, 1970-75; Diocesan and Provincial Youth Chaplain, 1969-75; Rector, St. Mary's Church, Dalmahoy, and Anglican Chaplain, Heriot Watt University, 1975-82; Churches Development Officer, Livingston Ecumenical Parish, 1982-88; Rector, St. John's Episcopal Church, Perth, 1988-92; Convener, Mission Board, Scottish Episcopal Church, 1988-92; Resident Scholar, Bruton Parish Church, Williamsburg, USA, 2006-07; Int. Warden, Scottish Churches House, Dunblane, 2008. Recreations: music; theatre; various sports; gardening. Address: (h.) 21/1 Barossa Place, Perth PH1 5HH; T.-01738 441172; e-mail: bruce2541@gmail.com

Cameron, Rev. Charles Millar, BA, BD, PhD. Church of Scotland Minister: St Andrew's Trinity Church, Johnstone, since 2013, Prestongrange Church, Prestonpans, 2012-2013; St Andrew's Church, Dumbarton, 2009-2012; b. 1951, Glasgow; m.; 1 c. Educ. Universities of Stirling and Glasgow. Previous Ministries: Dunfermline; Northern Ireland; Glasgow; Ayrshire. Address: 45 Woodlands Crescent, Johnstone PA5 0AZ.

Cameron, Colin. Freelance Television Producer; Managing Director, Lion Television Scotland, 2004-07; Controller, Network Development, BBC Nations and Regions, 2001-04; b. 30.3.50; m., Christine Main; 2 s. Educ. Glasgow Academy; Duke of York School, Nairobi; Polytechnic of Central London. Journalist, Current Affairs, BBC Scotland, 1973-76; Film Director, That's Life, 1976-77; Producer/Director, Everyman and Heart of the Matter, 1977-85; Editor, Brass Tacks, BBC North, 1985-88; Head of Documentary Features, BBC Television, 1988-91; BBC Scotland: Head of Television, 1991-96, Head of Production, 1997-2000, Head of Network Programmes, 2000-01. Chair, Balfron Community Council, since 2013; Vice Chair, Strathendrick Singers, since 2013; RTS International Current Affairs Award, 1984; UN Association Media Peace Prize, 1984; e-mail: cc@colincameronmedia.com

Cameron, Colin, BL. Retired Solicitor; b. 24.8.33, Lanark; m., Rachel Weir Allison Cameron; 3 s.; 1 d. Educ. Uddingston Grammar School; Glasgow University. Solicitor, Wilson and Morgan, Blantyre, Malawi, 1957-61; Minister of Transport and Communications, Malawi, 1961-64; Solicitor, Allan Black and McCaskie, Elgin, 1964-66; Solicitor to

Cumbernauld and Irvine Development Corporations, 1966-70; own Legal practice in Irvine, 1970-2000. Council Member, Law Society of Scotland, 1976-82; served as VSO Volunteer in Solomon Islands, 1988-90; Hon. Consul to Republic of Malawi, 1994-2010; Member of Scotland/Malawi Partnership, since 2010; Past President, Irvine Rotary Club; Past Secretary, Abbeyfield Irvine and District Society Ltd; Hon. Vice President, Clan Cameron Association; Board Member & Secretary, ANCHO Housing Association, Irvine. Recreations: hill-walking; swimming; music; reading; family. Address: (h.) 4 Dickson Way, Irvine KA12 9JD; T.-01294 313103; e-mail: accameron@btinternet.com

Cameron, David Roderick Simpson, FRIAS, MRTPI, FSA Scot. Retired architect-planner; b. 2.6.41, Inverness; m., Filitsa Boulton; 1 s.; 2 d. Educ. George Watson's College; Edinburgh College of Art; Newcastle University; Leith School of Art. Depute Director of Planning, City of Edinburgh District Council, 1983-96; ECOS Project Manager for revival of Kazimierz in Krakow, 1993-96. Hon. Chieftain, Clan Cameron Association Scotland, since 2012; Chairman: Saltire Society, 1990-95, Patrick Geddes Memorial Trust, 1991-99; Convener, Historic Burghs Association of Scotland, 1993-99; Hon. Secretary, Edinburgh Architectural Association, 1972-75; Membership Secretary, Scottish Society of Architect Artists, 2008-2015; Member, Council, National Trust for Scotland, 1994-99, Grants Council, Scottish Community Foundation, 1996-2006, Council, Cockburn Association, 2003-2012, Mapa Scotland Trust, since 2010. Recreations: art; angling; history; trees. Address: (b.) 4 Dovecot Road, Edinburgh EH12 7LE.

Cameron, Donald Andrew John Cameron. MSP (Scottish Conservative), Highlands and Islands region, since 2016; Shadow Cabinet Secretary for Health and Sport, since 2016. Educ. University of Oxford; City University London. Advocate. Conservative candidate in the Ross, Skye and Lochaber constituency, in the United Kingdom general election, 2010. Address: Scottish Parliament, Edinburgh EH99 1SP.

Cameron of Lochiel, Donald Angus, MA, FCA, DL. 27th Chief of the Clan Cameron; Lord-Lieutenant of Inverness, since 2002; JP, Highland Region, 2002-08; Director, J. Henry Schroder & Co. Limited, 1984-99; President, Highland Society of London, 1994-97; b. 2.8.46; m., Lady Cecil Kerr; 1 s. 3 d. Educ. Harrow; Christ Church, Oxford. 2nd Lieutenant, Queen's Own Cameron Highlanders (TA), 1966-68; Chartered Accountant, 1971. Address: (h.) Achnacarry, Spean Bridge, Inverness-shire.

Cameron, Rt. Rev. Douglas M. Bishop of Argyll and the Isles, 1993-2003; b. 23.3.35, Natal; m., Anne Patricia Purnell; 2 d. Educ. Eastwood Grammar School; Edinburgh Theological College; University of the South, Sewanee, Tennessee. Curate, Christ Church, Falkirk, 1962-65; Priest, Papua New Guinea, 1965-74, Archdeacon, 1972-74; Rector: St. Fillan's and St. Hilda's, Edinburgh, 1974-88, St. Mary's, Dalkeith, and St. Leonard's, Lasswade, 1988-92; Canon and Synod Clerk, Diocese of Edinburgh, 1990-92; Dean of Edinburgh, 1991-92. Recreations: walking; music; cooking. Address: (h.) 23 Craigs Way, Rumford, Falkirk FK2 0EU; T.-01324 714137.

Cameron, Professor Dugald, OBE, DA, FCSD, DSc (hc) (Strathclyde). Former Chairman, Glasgow Prestwick International Airport Consultative Committee (retired); Director, Glasgow School of Art, 1991-99; Visiting Professor, University of Strathclyde, since 1999; Visiting

Professor, Department of Aerospace Engineering, University of Glasgow, since 2000; Companion, Royal Aeronautical Society, 1996; Industrial Design Consultant, since 1965; Hon. President, R. Aero Soc. Prestwick Branch; b. 4.10.39, Glasgow; m., Nancy Inglis. Educ. Glasgow High School; Glasgow School of Art. Industrial Designer, Hard Aluminium Surfaces Ltd., 1962-65; Visiting Lecturer, Glasgow School of Art, 1963-70; Head of Product Design, Glasgow School of Art, 1970-82; Head of Design, 1982-91. Hon. Professor, Glasgow University, 1993-99; Director, Squadron Prints, 1977-2000; Member: Engineering Advisory Committee, Scottish Committee, Council of Industrial Design, since 1966, Industrial Design (Engineering) Panel and 3D Design Board, CNAA, since 1978, Scottish Committee of Higher Education, Design Council; commission RAFVR (T), 1974; Adviser, Railway Heritage Trust, since 2003; Patron: Universities of Glasgow and Strathclyde Air Squadron, 2001. Publications: Glasgow's Own (a history of 602 City of Glasgow Squadron, Royal Auxiliary Air Force), 1987; Glasgow's Airport, 1990; compiler of 'Central to Glasgow', 2006; compiler of 'From the Karoo to the Kelvin', 2010; 'Personal Passions', 2013 - Baird of Bute Award, 2013. Recreations: railways; flying (lapsed private pilot); aviation history (particularly Scottish). Address: (h.) Achnacraig, Skelmorlie, Ayrshire.

Cameron, Brigadier Ewen Duncan, OBE; b. 10.2.35, Bournemouth; m., Joanna Margaret Hay; 2 d. Educ. Wellington College; Royal Military Academy, Sandhurst. Commissioned The Black Watch, 1955; DS, The Staff College, 1972-75; Commanding Officer, 1st Bn., The Black Watch, 1975-78; Commander, Royal Brunei Armed Forces, 1980-82; Indian College of Defence Studies, Delhi, 1983; Divisional Brigadier, Scottish Division, 1984-86; Director of Administration and Personnel, National Trust for Scotland, 1986-98, Deputy Director, 1998-2000. Member, Queen's Bodyguard for Scotland (Royal Company of Archers). Recreations: opera; bridge; bird-watching; travel; golf; gardening. Address: (h.) The Old Manse, Arngask, Glenfarg, Perth PH2 9QA; T.-01577 830394.

Cameron, J. Gordon, MA, LLB, DipLP, WS, NP. Partner, Stuart & Stuart WS, since 1987; b. 15.11.57, Edinburgh; m., Deborah Jane; 1 s.; 1 d. Educ. George Watson's College; Aberdeen University. Joined Stuart & Stuart WS, 1985. Hon. Secretary and Treasurer, Royal Celtic Society. Recreations: hill-running; photography; foreign travel. Address: (b.) 25 Rutland Street, Edinburgh EH1 2RN; T.-0131-228 6449; e-mail: gcameron@stuartandstuart.co.uk

Cameron, John Angus, MBChB, MRCGP, MBA. Medical Director, NHS Dumfries and Galloway, since 2003; b. Bath. Educ. Marlborough College; Edinburgh University. GP, Biggar, 1982-99; Medical Director, Dumfries and Galloway Primary Care Trust, 2001-02. Non Executive Director, Lanarkshire Health Board, 1992-99. Recreations: hill farming; hill-walking. Address: (b.) Crichton Hall, Dumfries DG1 4TG; T.-01387 244001. E-mail: anguscameron@nhs.net

Cameron, John Bell, CBE, FSAC, AIAgricE. Director, South West Trains, since 1995; Chairman, Scottish Beef Council, since 1997; Farmer, since 1961; b. 14.6.39, Edinburgh; m., Margaret Clapperton. Educ. Dollar Academy. Vice President, National Farmers' Union, 1976-79, President, 1979-84; Member, Agricultural Praesidium of EEC, 1979-84; Chairman, EEC Advisory Committee for Sheepmeat, 1982-90; Chairman, World Meats Group, (IFAP), since 1983; Chairman, Board of Governors, Dollar Academy, since 1985; Chairman, United Auctions Ltd., since 1985; President: Scottish Beef Cattle Association, since 2006, National Sheep Association (Scotland), since 2004; Vice President, National Sheep Association, since 2014; Member, Board of Governors, Macaulay Land Use Research Institute, since 1987; Chairman, British Railways (Scottish) Board, 1988-93; Member, British Railways Board, 1988-94; honorary doctorate of technology, Napier University, 1998. Long Service Award, Royal Observer Corps. Recreations: flying; shooting; travelling. Address: (h.) Balbuthie Farm, by Leven, Fife; T.-01333 730210.

Cameron, (John Roderick) Hector, LLB, NP. Solicitor; b. 11.6.47, Glasgow; m., Rosemary Brownlee; 1 s.; 1 d. Educ. High School of Glasgow; Friends School, Wigton; St. Andrews University; Queen's College, Dundee. Admitted Solicitor, 1971; Partner, Bishop, Milne Boyd & Co., 1973; Chairman, Glasgow Junior Chamber of Commerce, 1981; Managing Partner, Bishop & Co., 1985; Partner, Dorman Jeffrey & Co., 1990; Director, Merchants House of Glasgow, 1986; Director, Glasgow Chamber of Commerce, 1987; Partner, Hector Cameron, Solicitor, 1993; Partner, Abercrombie Capital Partners LLP, 2005; Partner, Lancaster Capital, 2010. Recreations: reading; sailing. Address: (b.) 2 Lancaster Crescent, Glasgow G12 0RR.

Cameron, Rev. Dr. John Urquhart, BA, BSc, PhD, BD, ThD. Parish Minister, Broughty Ferry, 1974-2008; b. 10.6.43, Dundee; m., Jill Sjoberg; 1 s.; 1 d. Educ. Falkirk High School; St. Andrews University; Edinburgh University; University of Southern California. Marketing Executive, Beechams, London, 1969-73; Assistant Minister, Wellington Church, Glasgow, 1973-74; Chaplain, Royal Naval Reserve, 1976-81; Marketing Consultant, Pergamon Press, Oxford, 1977-81; Religious Education Department, Dundee High School, 1980-87; Sports Journalist and Travel Writer, Hill Publications, Surrey, 1981-2006; Physics Department, Dundee College of Further Education, 1987-95; Moderator, Presbytery of Dundee, 1993-94; Chaplain, Royal Caledonian Curling Club, 1980-95; Chaplain, Black Watch ACF, 1994-99. National and international honours in both summer and winter sports, 1960-85; sports scholarship, University of Southern California, 1962-64. Recreations: golf; skiing; curling. Address: 10 Howard Place, St. Andrews, Fife KY16 9HL; T.-01334 474 474. E-mail: jucameron43@yahoo.co.uk

Cameron, Sheriff Lewis, MA, LLB. Retired Solicitor; Sheriff of South Strathclyde Dumfries and Galloway at Hamilton, 1994-2002, at Dumfries, 1988-94; b. 12.8.35, Glasgow; m., Sheila Colette Gallacher; 2 s.; 2 d. Educ. St. Aloysius College; Blairs College; St. Sulpice, Paris; Glasgow University. RAF, 1954-56; admitted Solicitor, 1962. Member, Legal Aid Central Committee, 1970-80; Legal Aid Secretary, Airdrie, 1978-87; Chairman, Social Security Appeal Tribunals, 1983-88; Dean, Airdrie Society of Solicitors, 1984-85; Tutor, Strathclyde University, 1981-88; Treasurer, Monklands Victim Support Scheme, 1983-88; Chairman: Dumfries and Galloway Family Conciliation Service, 1988-92, Dumfries and Galloway, Scottish Association for the Study of Delinquency, 1988-92; Member, Scotland Committee, National Children's Homes; Trustee, Oscar Marzaroli Trust; Chairman, PHEW, 1994-2000. E-mail: cameron.lewis@virgin.net

Cameron, Dr. Lisa. MP (SNP), East Kilbride, Strathaven and Lesmahagow, since 2015; m., Mark; 2 d. Educ. Duncanrig Secondary School, East Kilbride; Strathclyde University; Glasgow University. NHS Consultant working with clients who have mental health problems and learning difficulties. Served the public at Hairmyres Hospital, Wishaw General Hospital, Dykebar Hospital and the State Hospital. Expert Witness within the Scottish Court system working in cases of childhood sexual abuse and domestic violence. Ative local Union Representative, campaigning for workers' rights, pay, pensions and issues of discrimination and equality. Address: Room 510, 1 Parliament Street, House of Commons, London SW1A 0AA.

Cameron, Liz, OBE. Chief Executive, Scottish Chambers of Commerce, since 2004. Educ. University of Strathclyde. Personnel & Training Manager, Playtex Limited, 1978-84; Business Support Manager, Inverclyde Enterprise Trust, 1984-88; External Relations/Media Manager, Scottish Council for Development & Industry, 1988-91; Chief Executive, Renfrewshire & West of Scotland Local Employer Network, 1991-96; Chief Executive/Director, Renfrewshire Chamber of Commerce, 1996-2004. Address: (b.) 30 George Square, Glasgow G2 1EQ; T.-0141 204 8316; E-mail: lcameron@scottishchambers.org.uk Web: scottishchambers.org.uk

Cameron, Michael. Chief Executive, Scottish Housing Regulator. Address: (b.) Highlander House, 58 Waterloo Street, Glasgow G2 7DA; T.-0141 305 4187; michael.cameron@scottishhousingregulator.gsi.gov.uk

Cameron, Sandy, CBE. Chair at Sacro, since 2014. Educ. Strathclyde University; Aberdeen University. Social worker in Clackmannanshire, 1973-75; Principal Officer, Research and Planning Fieldwork, 1975-81; Assistant Director of Social Work in Central Region, 1981-87; Director of Social Work, Borders Regional Council, 1987-95; Executive Director, Social Work, South Lanarkshire Council, 1995-2006; Chairman, Parole Board for Scotland, 2006-2013. Chair, Management Board of the Institute for Research and Innovation in Social Services, 2000-2013; Chair of Executive Governance Group, Centre for Youth and Criminal Justice, University of Strathclyde; Panel Member, Independent Jersey Care Inquiry; Trustees, Lloyds TSB Foundation in Scotland; Chairman of the Fred Edwards Trust; Board member, Capability Scotland; Visiting Professor, Strathclyde University, since 1998. Former Secretary and President, Association of Directors of Social Work; former Non-Executive Director, The State Hospitals Board for Scotland. Address: (b.) Sacro, 29 Albany Street, Edinburgh EH1 3QN; T.-0131 624 7250.

Campbell, Aileen, MA Hons (Soc Sci). MSP (SNP), Clydesdale, since 2011, South of Scotland, 2007-2011; Minister for Children and Young People, 2011-16; formerly Minister for Local Government and Planning, 2011; b. 18.5.80, Perth. Educ. Collace PS; Perth Academy; University of Glasgow. Press Officer for Shona Robison MSP and Stewart Hosie MP, 2006-07; PA to Nicola Sturgeon MSP, 2005-06; Editorial Assistant, Scottish Standard, 2005; Editor, Construction Magazine, Keystone, 2004-05. Address: (b.) Kirkton Chambers, 12 Kirkton Street, Carluke ML8 4AB; T.-01555 750249. E-mail: aileen.campbell.msp@scottish.parliament.uk

Campbell of Airds, Alastair Lorne, OStJ. Former Chief Executive, Clan Campbell; Archivist, Inveraray Castle, 1984-97; H.M. Unicorn Pursuivant of Arms, Court of the Lord Lyon, 1986-2008; Islay Herald of Arms Extraordinary, since 2008; b. 11.7.37, London; m., Mary-Ann Campbell-Preston; 3 s.; 1 d. Educ. Eton; R.M.A., Sandhurst. Regular Army, 1955-63 (commissioned Argyll and Sutherland Highlanders); Reid Pye and Campbell, 1963-71 (Managing Director, 1970-71); Waverley Vintners Ltd., 1972-83 (Marketing Director, 1972, Managing Director, 1977). Member: Queen's Bodyguard for Scotland (Royal Company of Archers), Chapter of Scottish Priory, Order of St John; FSA Scot; Patron, Armorial and Heraldry Society of Australasia; Chairman, Advisory Committee on Tartan to the Lord Lyon; Member, Council, National Trust for Scotland, 1996-2001; Honorary Research Fellowship, University of Aberdeen, 1996-2001. Publications: Two Hundred Years — The Highland Society of London; The

Life and Troubled Times of Sir Donald Campbell of Ardnamurchan; The History of Clan Campbell – Vol. I. Recreations: painting; fishing; walking. Address: (h.) Inverawe Barn, Taynuilt, Argyll PA35 1HU; T.-01866 822207.

Campbell, Andrew Robertson, CBE, OBE, DL, FRAGS. Deputy Lord Lieutenant for the Stewartry of Kirkcudbright; Convener/Leader, Dumfries and Galloway Council, 1999-2005; Vice President, COSLA, 2003-07; b. 18.06.44, Castle Douglas; m., Maureen; 1s.; 1d. Educ. Loretto School. Farmer in partnership with wife and son; Past Director, Royal Highland Agricultural Society; Past Scottish Director, NFU Mutual Insurance Society; Past President, Castle Douglas Rotary; Fellow, Royal Agricultural Society; Councillor, Dumfries and Galloway, 1995-2007; Board Member, Dumfries and Galloway Health Board. Recreations: rugby supporter and past player; country sports. Address: (h.) Whitecraigs, Whitepark Road, Castle Douglas DG7 1EX; T.-01556 502183.

Campbell, Bridget. Director, Environment & Forestry, Scottish Government. Address: Victoria Quay, Edinburgh EH6 6QQ; T.-0131-244 5452.

Campbell, Calum, BA (Hons), MBA, RGN, HV. Chief Executive, NHS Lanarkshire, since 2015; b. 7.11.65, Erskine; m., Fidelma; 3 s. Educ. St. John Bosco; Trinity High School; Paisley University; Glasgow Caledonian University. Director of Strategic Change, NHS Grampian, 2001-04; Director of Governance and Delivery, NHS Argyll & Clyde, 2004-06; Acting Chief Executive: Swansea NHS Trust, 2006-08, ABM University NHS Board Wales, 2008-09; Chief Executive, NHS Borders, 2010-2015. Address: (b.) NHS Lanarkshire Headquarters, Kirklands, Fallside Road, Bothwell G71 8BB; T.-01698 858176; e-mail: calum.campbell@lanarkshire.scot.nhs.uk

Campbell, Christopher. Managing Director, Campbells Prime Meat. Address: Campbells Prime Meat Ltd, The Heatherfield, Lathallan, by Linlithgow EH49 6LQ.

Campbell, Christopher Robert James, LLB (Hons). Retired Group General Counsel, The Royal Bank of Scotland Group (2010-2015); b. Edinburgh; m., Kay; 1 s.; 1 d. Educ. Daniel Stewart's and Melville College; University of Edinburgh. Joined Dundas and Wilson, 1980: Assistant Solicitor, 1982, Partner, 1987, Partner in Charge of Glasgow Office, 1991, Managing Partner, 1996; joined RBS in 2005 as Director, Group Legal. Honorary Professor of Commercial Law, University of Glasgow. Recreations: golf; music; football.

Campbell, Professor Colin, BSc, PhD. Chief Executive Officer, The James Hutton Institute, Aberdeen, since 2015. Educ. University of Strathclyde. Post-doctoral researcher, Hill Farming Research Organisation, University of Edinburgh, 1986-87; Science Leader, Macaulay Land Use Research Institute, 1987-2011; Director of Science Excellence, The James Hutton Institute, Aberdeen, 2011-15. Director, James Hutton Institute's Post-Graduate School; Visiting Professor at Soil and Environment Department, Swedish Agricultural Sciences University (SLU), Uppsala, Sweden. Address: The James Hutton Institute, Craigiebuckler, Aberdeen AB15 8QH; T.-0844 928 5428; e-mail: colin.campbell@hutton.ac.uk

Campbell, Colin MacIver, MA (Hons). MSP (SNP), West of Scotland, 1999-2003; SNP Defence Spokesperson, 1995-2003; National Secretary, SNP, 1997-99; b. 31.8.38, Ralston, Paisley; m., Evelyn; 3 s. Educ. Paisley Grammar School; Glasgow University; Jordanhill College of Education. Teacher: Hillhead High School, 1961-63, Paisley Grammar School, 1963-67; Principal Teacher, Greenock Academy, 1967-73; Depute Head Teacher,

Merksworth High, 1973-77; Head Teacher, Westwood Secondary, 1977-89; Tutor (part-time), Strathclyde University Senior Studies Institute, 1995-98. Member, Renfrewshire Council, 1995-99; General Election Candidate: 1987, 1992, 1997; Euro Candidate: 1989, 1994. Elder, Church of Scotland; Former Chairman, Kilbarchan Civic Society and Kilbarchan Community Council; Former Convener, Kilbarchan SNP; Past Convener, Renfrew West SNP; Past Chairman, Kilbarchan Pipe Band, 2009-2011; Member, Lowlands Reserve Forces and Cadets Association, 1997-2003. Publication: co-author, Can't Shoot a Man With a Cold, 2004; author, 'Engine of Destruction. The 51st (Highland) Division in the Great War', 2013. Recreation: military history. Address: (h.) Braeside, Shuttle Street, Kilbarchan PA10 2PR.

Campbell, David Ross, CBE, CMIM, FInstD. Director, The Wise Group of Companies, since 2009; Public Member, Network Rail Ltd, 2009-2015; Chairman, NHS National Services Scotland, 2004-08; Chairman and Director of a number of private companies; Chairman, Health Education Board for Scotland, 1995-2001; b. 27.9.43, Glasgow; m., Moira. Educ. Whitehill Senior Secondary School, Glasgow; James Watt Memorial College, Greenock. Officer, Merchant Navy, 1961-68; Sales Executive, 1968-69; various management positions, George Outram & Co. Ltd., 1969-73; Managing Director, Scottish & Universal Newspapers Ltd., 1974-84; Executive Director, Scottish & Universal Investments Ltd.; Chief Executive, Clyde Cablevision Ltd., 1982-84; Chairman and Chief Executive, West Independent Newspapers Ltd., 1984-94; Chairman, Saltire Holdings Ltd., 1991-93. Past President: Scottish Newspaper Proprietors Association, Glasgow Chamber of Commerce; Liveryman and Freeman, City of London; Regional Chairman, PSYBT. Recreations: golf; theatre; travel; reading. Address: (h.) Summerlea, Summerlea Road, Seamill KA23 9HP.

Campbell, Donald. Writer; b. 25.2.40, Wick; m., Jean Fairgrieve; 1 s. Educ. Boroughmuir High School, Edinburgh. Playwright, essayist, lyricist and poet; stage plays include: The Jesuit, 1976; The Widows of Clyth, 1979; Blackfriars Wynd, 1980; Till All The Seas Run Dry, 1981; Howard's Revenge, 1985; Victorian Values, 1986; The Fisher Boy and the Honest Lass, 1990; The Auld Fella, 1993, Nancy Sleekit, 1994, Glorious Hearts, 1999; also active as writer and director in a number of community projects; script co-ordinator, The Dundee Mysteries, Dundee Rep; poetry includes: Rhymes 'n Reasons, 1972; Blether, 1979; Selected Poems: 1970-1990, 1990; Homage To Rob Donn, 2007; other work includes: A Brighter Sunshine (theatre history), 1983, Playing for Scotland (theatre history), 1996, Joe Corrie - A Legend and His Legacy (theatre history); four television plays, 50 radio programmes, Cities of the Imagination - Edinburgh, 2003 (travel writing). Fellow in Creative Writing, Dundee University, 1987-89; William Soutar Fellow, Perth, 1991-93; Royal Literary Fund Fellow, Napier University, 2000-01; Life Member, Writers Guild of Great Britain, 2005; Hon. Fellow, Association of Scottish Literary Studies, 2010; awards include: three Fringe Firsts; Silver Medal, 1983 New York Radio Festival for A Clydebuilt Man; Radio Industries Club Award for The Miller's Reel, 1987. Address: (h.) 85 Spottiswoode Street, Edinburgh EH9 1BZ; T.-0131-447 2305.

Campbell, Doris Margaret, MD, FRCOG. Honorary Reader, Obstetrics and Gynaecology and Reproductive Physiology, Aberdeen University; b. 24.1.42, Aberdeen; m., Alasdair James Campbell; 1 s.; 1 d. Educ. Aberdeen High School for Girls; Aberdeen University. Resident house officer posts, Aberdeen, 1967-69; Research Fellow, Aberdeen University, 1969-73; Registrar in Obstetrics and Gynaecology, Aberdeen Hospitals, 1973-74; Lecturer in Obstetrics and Gynaecology and Physiology, Aberdeen University, 1974-84. Former Member, Scottish Women's

Hockey Council. Recreations: bridge; badminton; guiding. Address: (h.) 77 Blenheim Place, Aberdeen; T.-01224 639984; e-mail: d.m.campbell@abdn.ac.uk

Campbell, Duncan, BA (Hons), MSc, Chartered MCIPD. Deputy Chief Executive, National Library of Scotland, since 2004; b. 30.11.54, Dunfermline; m., Murdina; 1 d. Educ. Dunfermline High School; Heriot Watt University; University of Strathclyde. Address: (b.) National Library of Scotland, George IV Bridge, Edinburgh EH1 1EW.

Campbell, Edward James, MA, LLB. Managing Director, Campbell's Prime Meat Ltd., 1970-2006; b. 18.3.37, Edinburgh; m., Ellen; 2 s.; 2 d. Educ. Daniel Stewart's College, Edinburgh; Edinburgh University. Worked in family business (Campbell Brothers Ltd); started Campbell's Prime Meat Ltd., 1970. Recreations: reading; cinema; bridge; travel. Address: 6 Easter Belmont Road, Edinburgh EH12 6EX;T.-0131-337 7698; e-mail: ellen_campbell@btinternet.com

Campbell, Fiona, BA (Hons), BMus. Development Manager, Voluntary Arts, since 2013; Vice Convener and Director, Traditional Dance Forum of Scotland (TDFS); b. 9.10.70, Wellington, New Zealand. Educ. Wellington East Girls College; Victoria University of Wellington. Press and Marketing Officer, National Association of Youth Orchestras, 1996-97, 1999; Project Administrator, SEAD, 1998-2000. Convenor & Director, TMSA; Director, Neo Productions; Board Director, Scottish Fiddle Festival. Postgraduate Certificate in Cultural Policy and Management (Heriot Watt University, 2004). Recreations: traditional music, song and dance; musical theatre and opera; reading; craftwork; swimming and historical interests. Address: (b.) 5 Appin Lane, Edinburgh EH14 1JL; T.-07951918366; e-mail: fiona@voluntaryarts.org

Campbell, Hugh Hall, QC, BA (Hons), MA (Oxon), LLB (Hons), FCIArb. Queen's Counsel, since 1983; b. 18.2.44, Glasgow; m., Eleanor Jane Hare; 3 s. Educ. Glasgow Academy; Trinity College, Glenalmond; Exeter College, Oxford; Edinburgh University. Called to Scottish Bar, 1969; Standing Junior Counsel to Admiralty, 1976. Recreations: carnival, wine, music. Address: (h.) 12 Ainslie Place, Edinburgh EH3 6AS; T.-0131-225 2067.

Campbell, Rev. Dr. Iain Donald, MA, BD, MTh, PhD. Minister, Point Free Church, Isle of Lewis, since 2009; Minister, Back Free Church of Scotland, Isle of Lewis, 1995-2009; b. 20.9.63, Stornoway; m., Anne M. Davidson; 2 s.; 1 d. Educ. Nicolson Institute, Stornoway; University of Glasgow; Free Church College. Minister, Snizort Free Church, Isle of Skye, 1988-95; Editor, The Instructor (Free Church of Scotland youth magazine), 1990-96; Editor, The Monthly Record of the Free Church of Scotland, 1996-2000; Review Editor, Scottish Bulletin of Evangelical Theology, since 2003. Publications: In Thy Likeness, 1990; Heart of the Gospel (Editor), 1995; The Doctrine of Sin, 1999; The Gospel According to Ruth, 2003; Heroes and Heretics, 2004; On the First Day of the Week, 2005. Recreations: reading; walking; scootering. Address: Point Free Church, Isle of Lewis HS2 0PX.

Campbell, Iain. Chief Executive, Bòrd na Gàidhlig, since 2015 (formerly Chair). Formerly Senior Project Manager of Soillse, an inter-University partnership project involved in a range of research areas associated with Gaelic language maintenance and revitalisation; experienced senior manager and researcher with Masters Degrees in Regional Economics, Business Administration and Rural Development. Represents Bòrd na Gàidhlig on the Board of MG ALBA. Address: Bòrd na Gàidhlig, Great Glen House, Leachkin Road, Inverness IV3 8NW; T.-01463 225454. E-mail: oifis@gaidhlig.org.uk

Campbell, Professor Ian, MA, PhD. Emeritus Professor of Scottish and Victorian Literature, Edinburgh University (Professor, since 1992); b. 25.8.42. Lausanne, Switzerland. Educ. Lausanne; Findochty; Buckie; Mackie Academy, Stonehaven; Aberdeen University; Edinburgh University. Joined staff, English Department, Edinburgh University, 1967; Visiting Professor, Guelph, Duke, UCLA; Europa Professor, Mainz; Visiting Lecturer, United States, Canada, France, Switzerland, Italy, Japan. Publications: editorial team of Carlyle Letters, numerous books and articles on Scottish and Victorian Literature. Recreations: music; sport. Address: (b.) Department of English, Edinburgh University, 50 George Square, Edinburgh EH8 9LH; Fax: 0131-650 6898; e-mail: Ian.Campbell@ed.ac.uk

Campbell, Sir Ian, CBE, OStJ, VRD, JP. Deputy Chairman, Heath (Scotland) Ltd., 1987-95; Chairman, Select Assured Properties PLC, 1989-96; Director, Hermiston Securities, since 1990; b. 3.2.23, Edinburgh; m., Marion Kirkhope Shiel; 1 d. Educ. Daniel Stewart's College, Edinburgh. Royal Navy, 1942-46; Royal Naval Reserve, 1946-64 (retired with rank of Commander); John Line & Sons, 1948-61 (Area Manager, West of England); Managing Director, MacGregor Wallcoverings Ltd., 1965-77; Finance Director, Scottish Conservative Party, 1977-89. Director, Travel System Ltd., 1987-90; Councillor, City of Edinburgh, 1984-88; Member, Transport Users Consultative Committee for Scotland, 1981-87; Freeman, City of Glasgow, 1991. Recreations: golf; vintage cars; water colour painting. Address: (h.) Merleton, 10 Boswall Road, Edinburgh EH5 3RH; T.-0131-552 4825.

Campbell, Sir Ilay Mark, Bt, MA (Oxon). Director, High Craigton Farming Co.; b. 29.5.27, Edinburgh; m., Margaret Minette Rohais Anderson; 2 d. Educ. Eton; Christ Church, Oxford. Christie's: Scottish Agent, 1968, Joint Scottish Agent, 1973-92; Chairman, Christie's Scotland, 1978-96; Honorary Vice-President, Scotland's Garden Scheme; Trustee: Crarae Gardens Charitable Trust, 1978-2002, Tree Register of the British Isles, 1988-2006; Chairman, Church Buildings Renewal Trust, 1993-98 (Trustee, 1993-2001); Past President, Association for the Protection of Rural Scotland; former Convener, Church of Scotland Committee on Artistic Matters; Member, Historic Buildings Council for Scotland, 1989-98; Member, Gardens Committee, National Trust for Scotland, 1995-2001; former Scottish Representative, National Arts Collection Fund. Recreations: heraldry; genealogy; collecting heraldic bookplates. Address: (h.) Crarae Lodge, Inveraray, Argyll PA32 8YA; T.-01546 886274.

Campbell, John David; QC, Scotland, since 1998; b. 1949, Inverness; 2 s.; 3 d.; m., Kate Knight (2009). Educ. Gordonstoun; Edinburgh University. Former Solicitor, 1972-78, Advocate, since 1981; Barrister, Lincoln's Inn, since 1990; Arbitrator; Chairman, Scottish Historic Buildings Trust, since 2007. Publication: Scottish Planning Encyclopaedia (Contributor), 2001. Recreations: family; music; gardening. Address: (b.) Advocates Library, Parliament House, Edinburgh EH1 1RF. E-mail: jcampbellqc@advocates.org.uk

Campbell, Mary Theresa MacLeod, OBE, BA, CA. Chief Executive Officer, Blas Limited in Edinburgh and Manhattan, since 2002; b. 24.2.59, Glasgow; 2 d.; 2 s. Educ. Lochaber High School; University of Stirling. Ernst and Young, 1980-86; Noble Group Limited, 1986-98; British Linen Bank Ltd., 1998-99. Founding Director, British Linen

Advisers Ltd., 1999-2002; Recreations: literature; theatre; opera; Barra. Address: (b.) Blas Limited, 1 Rutland Square, Edinburgh EH1 2AS.
E-mail: mary@blasltd.com

Campbell, Melfort Andrew, OBE, FRSA. Chairman, Imes Group Ltd., since 1997; b. 6.6.56, Exeter; m., Lucy Nickson; 3 d. Educ. Ampleforth College, York. Director, Imes Ltd; past Chairman, CBI Scotland; Chairman, Atlantic Salmon Trust; Director, Scottish Enterprise; Co Chair, Innovation Scotland. Recreations: fishing; shooting; rugby; tennis. Address: (b.) Old School, Maryculter, Aberdeen AB12 5GN; T.-01224 533533.

Campbell, Morag. Chief Executive, National Youth Choir of Scotland, since 2012. Formerly Assistant Principal (Creative Industries), Stevenson College, Edinburgh. Address: National Youth Choir of Scotland, The Mitchell, North Street, Glasgow G3 7DN; T.-0141 287 2856.

Campbell, Murdo Macdonald, BD (Hons), DipMin. Minister, Brightons Parish Church of Scotland, since 2007; formerly Minister, Carloway, Isle of Lewis, 1997-2007; b. 13.5.60, Stornoway, Isle of Lewis; m., Lorraine Anne Campbell (nee McLeod); 2 s. Educ. Bayble Junior Secondary; Nicolson Institute, Stornoway; Aberdeen University. Probationer, Martins Memorial Church, Stornoway; Elder, St. Columbas Church; Divinity Student Attachment: Ruthrieston South and Ruthrieston West Churches, Aberdeen, Aberdeen Royal Infirmary Chaplaincy; Inducted and Ordained to Carloway Church of Scotland; Chairperson, Carloway Youth Initiative; Convener, Presbytery Parish Appraisal Committee; Chairperson, Carloway School Board; Moderator of Presbytery. Member, Church of Scotland National Mission Committee. Recreations: hill walking. Address: (b.) The Manse, Maddiston Road, Brightons, Falkirk FK2 0JP; T.-01324 712062; e-mail: murdocampbell@hotmail.com

Campbell, Niall Gordon, BA. Under Secretary, Civil and Criminal Law Group, Scottish Executive Justice Department, (formerly Scottish Office Home Department) 1997-2001; b. 9.11.41, Peebles; m., Alison M. Rigg; 3 s. Educ. Edinburgh Academy; Merton College, Oxford. Entered Scottish Office 1964; Assistant Secretary, 1978; various posts in Scottish Education Department and Scottish Development Department; Under Secretary, Social Work Services Group, 1989-97. Member, Parole Board for Scotland, 2003-09; Chairman, SACRO, 2002-07; Chairman, Scottish Association for the Study of Offending, 2001-06; Council of the British Trust for Ornithology, 2006-2011; Company Secretary, Citizens Advice Edinburgh, since 2008. Address: (h.) 15 Warriston Crescent, Edinburgh.

Campbell, Nicholas Andrew Argyll (Nicky), OBE. Scottish radio and television presenter and journalist; b. 10.4.61, Edinburgh; m. (1), Linda Larnach (divorced); m. (2), Tina Ritchie; 4 d. Educ. Edinburgh Academy; University of Aberdeen. Career history: jingle writer, then breakfast show host, Northsound Radio, 1981-85; Capital Radio, London, 1986-87; BBC Radio 1, 1987-97; joined BBC Radio 5 Live in 1997; TV presenter: Wheel of Fortune, 1988-96, Watchdog, 2001-09, co-host, Long Lost Family, since 2011; currently presents both the BBC Radio 5 Live breakfast programme and BBC One's Sunday morning show The Big Questions. Won seven Sony Awards, including a Gold Award in 2007 for the Radio 5 Live Breakfast programme as "Best News and Current Affairs Programme" (with Shelagh Fogarty); received an Honorary Doctorate from the Robert Gordon University,

Aberdeen in 2008; won a Royal Television Society Award for best 'Popular Factual' programme for Long Lost Family in 2013; Television BAFTA award for best "Features Programme" in 2014. Publication: Blue Eyed Son, 2004.

Campbell, (Robert) Mungo (McCready), BA, MPhil, FRSA. Deputy Director, Hunterian Museum & Art Gallery, University of Glasgow, since 1997; b. 8.10.59, Newcastle upon Tyne; m., Teresa Margaret Green; 1 s.; 1 d. Educ. Royal Grammar School, Newcastle upon Tyne; University of Durham; University of Glasgow. Assistant Keeper, National Gallery of Scotland, Edinburgh, 1987-97; Member, Scottish Arts Council Visual Arts Committee, 1998-2003; Board Member: SCRAN, 2004-06, Scottish Museums Council, 2001-07; Chair: VAGA Scotland, 2005-07, The Skateraw Foundation, 2009-2010. Recreations: island life; walking with my children; cooking good food; eating good food. Address: (b.) Hunterian Museum, University of Glasgow, Glasgow G12 8QQ; T.-0141-330 4735.

Campbell, Roderick, BA (Hons), LLM. MSP (SNP), North East Fife, 2011-16; b. 15.6.53, Edinburgh. Educ. Reading School; Exeter University; University of Glasgow; University of Strathclyde. Has a degree in politics and qualified as a solicitor in both England, Wales and Scotland. Formerly a partner in an international law firm based in London. Qualified as an Advocate in 2008.

Campbell, Stewart, BSc, DipSH. Member: Scottish Criminal Cases Review Commission, 2007-2015, Parole Board for Scotland, since 2015; formerly Health and Safety Executive Director, Scotland, 2001-08; b. 9.4.48, Bridge of Allan; m., Susan; 2 s. Educ. McLaren High School, Callander; Glasgow University. Nuffield and Leverhulme Travelling Fellowship, 1983-84; Chair, Friends of Duchess Wood. Publication: Labour Inspection in the European Community. Recreations: golf; hill-walking; genealogy.
E-mail: stewart.campbell18@googlemail.com

Campbell of Pittenweem, Rt. Hon. (Walter) Menzies Campbell, CH (2013), CBE (1987), Kt (2003), PC, QC, MA, LLB, LLD. MP (Liberal Democrat), North East Fife, 1987-2015; Advocate, since 1968; Queen's Counsel, since 1982; Leader, Liberal Democrats, 2006-07; Liberal Democrat Shadow Foreign Secretary, 2001-06; Deputy Leader, Liberal Democrats, 2003-06; Member, Parliamentary Assembly of OSCE, 1992-1997; Leader, UK delegation to the NATO Parliamentary Assembly, 2010-2015; b. 22.5.41, Glasgow; m., Elspeth Mary Urquhart. Educ. Hillhead High School, Glasgow; Glasgow University; Stanford University, California. President, Glasgow University Union, 1964-65; took part in Olympic Games, Tokyo, 1964; AAA 220-yards champion, 1964, 1967; Captain, UK athletics team, 1965, 1966; 1966 Commonwealth Games, Jamaica; UK 100-metres record holder, 1967-74. Advocate Depute, 1977-80; Standing Junior Counsel to the Army in Scotland, 1980-82. Parliamentary candidate (Liberal): Greenock and Port Glasgow, February, 1974, and October, 1974, East Fife, 1979, North East Fife, 1983; Chairman, Scottish Liberal Party, 1975-77; Member, Select Committee on Defence, 1992-99; Party Spokesman on Defence, Foreign Affairs and Sport, until 1997, Foreign Affairs and Defence, 1997-2001; Member: Select Committee on Foreign Affairs, 2008-2015, Parliamentary Committee on Intelligence and Security, 2008-2015, UK Sports Council, 1965-68, Scottish Sports Council, 1971-81; Chairman, Royal Lyceum Theatre, Edinburgh, 1984-87; Member, Broadcasting Council for Scotland, 1984-87. Honorary Degrees. DUniv Glasgow University, 2001; LLD Strathclyde University, 2005; LLD

St. Andrews 2006; Chancellor of St. Andrews University, since 2006. Recreations: all sports; music; theatre.

Campbell, William Kilpatrick, MA (Hons). Director, Mainstream Publishing, since 1978; b. 1.3.51, Glasgow; 2 d. Educ. Kilmarnock Academy; Edinburgh University. Postgraduate research, Universities of Edinburgh and California; world travel, 1975; Publications Manager, Edinburgh University Student Publications, 1976-78. Publications: Alternative Edinburgh (Co-Editor), 1972; Another Edinburgh, 1976. Recreations: soccer; rugby; wine; books; people. E-mail: billcampbell450@gmail.com

Canavan, Dennis, BSc (Hons), DipEd, DUniv, LLD. MSP (Independent), Falkirk West, 1999-2007; b. 8.8.42, Cowdenbeath. Educ. St. Bride's and St. Columba's Schools, Cowdenbeath; Edinburgh University. Principal Teacher of Mathematics, St. Modan's High School, Stirling, 1970-74; Assistant Head, Holyrood High School, Edinburgh, 1974; Leader, Labour Group, Stirling District Council, 1974; MP, West Stirlingshire, 1974-83; MP, Falkirk West, 1983-2000; Chair: Scottish Parliamentary Labour Group, 1980-81, PLP Northern Ireland Committee, 1989-97; Member: Foreign Affairs Select Committee, 1982-97, British–Irish Inter-Parliamentary Body, 1992-2000, International Development Select Committee, 1997-99; Scottish Parliament European and External Relations Committee, 1999-2007; Convener, All-Party Sports Group, Scottish Parliament, 1999-2007; President, then Convener, Ramblers Scotland, 2007-2012, Vice-President, since 2012; Trustee of the Scottish Mining Museum, since 2007; Honorary President, Milton Amateurs Football Club; Honorary Doctorates from University of Strathclyde and University of Stirling. Chair of St. Mary's Primary School Bannockburn Parent Council, 2009-2014; Chair of Falkirk Football Community Foundation, since 2010; Patron of Falkirk & District Association for Mental Health, since 2007; Patron of The Driving Force, Bonnybridge, since 2009; Honorary President of Rivers Forth & Teith Anglers' Association, since 2008; Chair of YesScotland Advisory Board, 2012-2014. Publication: Author of Autobiography, "Let the People Decide", 2009. Recreations: hill-walking; swimming; football (former Scottish Universities football internationalist). Address: Ardsonas, Sauchieburn, Bannockburn FK7 9PZ; T.-01786 812581; e-mail: canavan897@btinternet.com

Canning, Very Rev. Bernard John Canon, FSA Scot. Paisley Diocesan Archivist, since 1983; b. 30.3.32, Derry. Educ. St. Eugene's Boys' School, Derry; St. Columb's College, Derry; St. Kieran's College, Kilkenny. Ordained Priest for the Diocese of Paisley, 1956; Assistant: St. James's, Renfrew, 1956-68, St Fergus', Paisley, 1968-74, St Laurence's, Greenock, 1974-87; Parish Priest: Christ the King, Howwood, and Our Lady of Fatima, Lochwinnoch, 1987-95, St James's, Paisley, 1995-96, St. John the Baptist's, Port Glasgow, 1996-99, St. Thomas's, Neilston, 1999-2007; retired 2007. Hon. Canon, Paisley Cathedral Chapter, 1989, full Member, 2001; Member, Editorial Board, The Parish Magazine & Journal, Glasgow, 1962-74; first Press Officer, Paisley Diocese, 1964-88; Member, Board of Governors, National Catholic Press Office, 1968-87. Publications include: Joy and Hope: St. Fergus', Paisley, 1971; A Building from God: St James's, Renfrew 1877-1977, 1977; Padraig H. Pearse and Scotland, 1979; Irish-born Secular Priests in Scotland 1829-1979, 1979; Adventure in Faith: St Ninian's, Gourock 1880-1980, 1980; The Living Stone: St Aloysius', Springburn 1882-1982, 1982; Instruments of His Work : Little Sisters of the Poor, Greenock 1884-1984, 1984; St. Mungo's, Ladyburn, Greenock 1935-1985, 1985; The Charleston Story: St Charles', Paisley, 1986; Bishops of Ireland 1870-1987, 1987; St. Fillan's, Houston 1841-1991, 1991; St. Mary's, Paisley 1891-1991, 1991; The Poor Sisters of Nazareth &

Derry 1892-1992, 1992; St Colm's Church, Kilmacolm, 1992; Bishop Neil Farren, Bishop of Derry 1893-1980, 1993; St John the Baptist Parish, Port Glasgow, 1846-1996, 1996; Diocese of Paisley, 1947-1997, 2001; The Street That Is Gone But Lives On, 2001; Derry City Cemetery 1853-2003, 2003; Bishop John Keys O'Doherty of Derry, 1889-1907, 2007. Recreation: historical research. Address: (b.) 18 Royal Street, Gourock PA19 1PW; T./Fax: 01475-633687.

Cantlay, Michael Brian, OBE, BA, MBA, DUniv (Stirling). Chair, VisitScotland; Board Member, VisitBritain; CEO, William Glen and Son Ltd; President, William Glen and & Son Inc, San Francisco; Chair, William Glen Canada Ltd, Toronto; b. 2.2.64, Galashiels; m., Linda. Educ. McLaren High School, Callander; Strathclyde University. CEO, "The Whisky Shop", 1992-2004, CEO, Hector Russell Ltd, 1993-2005; Chair, Callander Community Council, 1992-93; Chair, Scottish Enterprise Forth Valley, 1995-2001; Advisory Board Member, Scottish Enterprise, 2000-02; Deputy Chair, VisitScotland, 2001-05; Chair, Forth Valley College, 2005-09; Convener, Loch Lomond and Trossachs National Park Authority, 2006-2010; Non Executive-Director, Highlands and Islands Airports Ltd, 2008-2014. Address: Callandrade, Callander, Perthshire FK17 8HW.

Cantley, Maurice, OBE, BSc, PhD; b. 6.6.37, Cambuslang; m., Rosalind Diana Jones; 2 d. Educ. Bedford Modern and Bristol Grammar; Bristol University. Unilever Ltd., 1961-67; McCann Erickson Advertising, London, 1967-76; Director of Recreation and Tourism, Tayside Regional Council, 1976-82; Head of Tourism, HIDB, 1982-85; Marketing Director, Highlands and Islands Development Board, 1985-91. Director, Highlands and Islands Enterprise, 1991-99; Innovators Counselling and Advisory Service for Scotland, 1999-2012; Hon. Education Officer, Society of Cosmetic Chemists of GB, 1963-66; Chairman, Association of Directors of Recreation, Leisure and Tourism, 1980-82. Recreations: classical music; cycling; crosswords. Address: (h.) Oldshorebeg, Kinlochbervie, Sutherland IV27 4RS.

Caplan, Lady (Joyce Caplan). President, Friends of University Library, Edinburgh, since 2002; Chair, Poetry Association of Scotland, since 2002; Chair, Scottish Poetry Library, 2004-09; m.,1. David Leigh (d. 1970); 2. Lord Caplan (deceased); 1 d. Member of Children's Panel, 1978-81; Governor, Lomond School, Helensburgh, 1985-89; Chairman: Play in Scottish Hospitals, 1990-96, Smiths Place Group, 1992-95, Scottish Play Council, 1992-95; Chair, Children's Classic Concerts, since 2010, Board Member, since 1999; Chair, Snowball Trust, since 2000; Chairman, Couple Counselling Scotland, 1997-2001; Lecturer, Edinburgh University, since 1980; Edinburgh Burns Club Council, 2010; Committee of PEN, 2012 (Scotland); Muriel Spark Society Committee, 2012; Member, the John P. Mackintosh Memorial Committee, since 2013; Patron of the Tagore Centre, since 2015. Recreations: books; music; friends; paintings; poetry. Address: (h.) Nether Liberton House, Old Mill Lane, Edinburgh EH16 5TZ.

Cardownie, Steve. Depute Lord Provost of the City of Edinburgh Council (formerly Deputy Leader); Leader, SNP Group; b. 1.6.53, Leith; m.; 2 s. Educ. Leith Academy; Telford College. Civil service; National Executive Committee Member, CPSA, five years; Councillor, Edinburgh, since 1988; Director, Edinburgh Jazz and Blues Festival; Employment Tribunal Member, since 1981; Member, Culture & Sport Committee and Transport & Environment; Director, Community Football Academy, Spartans FC. Recreations: hill-walking; running; Heart of Midlothian FC; theatre; reading; fine wines and travelling. Address: (b.) City Chambers, High Street, Edinburgh; T.-0131-529 3266.

E-mail: steve.cardownie@edinburgh.gov.uk

Carey, Professor Frank A., BSc, MD, FRCPath. Professor and Consultant Pathologist, since 1995; Clinical Leader, Scottish Pathology Network, since 2005; b. 5.7.61, Cork, Ireland; m., Dr Julie Curran; 1 s.; 1 d. Educ. University College, Cork. Senior House Officer, Cork University Hospital, 1986-87; Registrar in Pathology, Royal Infirmary of Edinburgh, 1987-89; Senior Registrar, Royal Infirmary of Edinburgh, 1989-95; Consultant, Tayside University Hospitals, since 1995. Member, Scottish Council, Royal College of Pathologists. Address: (b.) Department of Pathology, Ninewells Hospital and Medical School, Dundee DD1 9SY; T.-01382 632548.

Carlaw, Jackson. MSP (Scottish Conservative), Eastwood, since 2016 (West Scotland, 2007-2016); Deputy Leader of the Scottish Conservatives and Shadow Cabinet Secretary for Culture, Tourism and External Affairs; b. 12.4.59; m.; 2 s. Educ. Glasgow Academy. Address: (b.) Scottish Parliament, Edinburgh EH99 1SP; Constituency Office: 69 Ayr Road, Newton Mearns, Glasgow G77 6SP.

Carlisle, Elva A.M., MA. National Convener, Church of Scotland Guild, 2000-01; b. 27.5.35, Linlithgow; m., Dr J.M. Carlisle (deceased); 2 s. Educ. Marr College, Troon; Glasgow University. Teacher in Ayrshire and Glasgow until early retirement, 1992; Elder, Church of Scotland. Recreations: reading; doing crosswords; opera; visiting other countries. Address: (h.) 117 Fotheringay Road, Glasgow G41 4LG; T.-0141-423 4554.

Carloway, Rt. Hon. Lord (Colin John MacLean Sutherland), PC 2008. Lord President of the Court of Session, since 2015; Senator of the College of Justice, since 2000; Lord Justice Clerk and President of the Second Division of the Court of Session, 2012-15; b. 20.5.54; m., Jane Alexander Turnbull; 2 s. Educ. Edinburgh Academy; Edinburgh University (LLB Hons). Advocate, 1977; Advocate Depute, 1986-89; QC (Scot), 1990. Treasurer, Faculty of Advocates, 1994-2000. Address: (b.) Parliament House, Edinburgh EH1 1RQ.

Carlyle, Robert, OBE. Actor and Director; b. 14.4.61; m., Anastasia Shirley; 3 c. Trained, RSAMD; Duncan Macrae Memorial Prize for Scots verse. Credits include: (film) The Full Monty, Carla's Song, Trainspotting, Riff Raff (European film of the year), Priest, Plunkett and MacLeane, Ravenous, The Beach, Angela's Ashes, The World Is Not Enough, There's Only One Jimmy Grimble, To End All Wars, 51st State, Once Upon a Time in the Midlands, Black and White, Dead Fish, Marilyn Hotchkiss Ballroom Dancing and Charm School, The Mighty Celt, Eragon, 28 Weeks Later, Flood, Stone of Destiny, The Meat Trade, Summer, I Know You Know, The Tournament; California Solo; The Legend of Barney Thomson; Trainspotting 2; (television) Hitler: The Rise of Evil, 2003; Gunpowder, Treason and Plot, 2004; Class of '76, 2005; Human Trafficking, 2005; Hamish Macbeth (title role), 2005; Born Equal, 2006; The Last Enemy, 2008; 24: Redemption, 2008; Stargate Universe, 2009-2011; Once Upon a Time, since 2011; (theatre) Twelfth Night, Cuttin' A Rug, Othello; (television and theatre) Go Now, Face; as Director of Rain Dog Theatre Company: Wasted, One Flew Over the Cuckoo's Nest (Paper Boat Award), Conquest of the South Pole, Macbeth (Paper Boat Award); Best Actor: Evening Standard Film Awards, 1998; Film Critics' Circle Awards, 1998, Bowmore Whisky/Scottish Screen Awards, 2001, Michael Elliott Awards, 2001; David Puttnam Patrons Award. Patron of School For Life Romania, Charity No. 1062953.

Carmichael, Alexander Morrison (Alistair), MP. Liberal Democrat MP, Orkney and Shetland, since 2001; Deputy Leader, Scottish Liberal Democrats, since 2012; Secretary of State for Scotland, 2013-15; b. 15.7.65; m., Kathryn Jane; 2 s. Educ. Islay High School; Aberdeen University. Hotel manager, 1984-89; Procurator Fiscal Depute, Crown Office, Edinburgh and Aberdeen, 1993-96; solicitor in private practice, 1996-2001. Address: (b.) House of Commons, London SW1A 0AA; e-mail: carmichaela@parliament.uk

Carmichael, (Katharine) Jane, MA (Mod Hist). Former Director of Collections, National Museums of Scotland (2003-2015); b. 12.3.52; m., Adrian Craxton; 1 step son; 2 d.; 2 step daughters. Educ. St. Leonards; St. Andrews; Edinburgh University. Imperial War Museum, 1974-2003: Keeper of Photographic Archive, 1982-95, Director of Collections, 1995-2003. Served various committees of National Museums Directors Conf., since 1995. FRSA, 2000; FSA (Scot). Publications: 1st World War Photographers, 1989; contributed to various journal articles. Recreations: the family; country walking; going to the ballet.

Carmichael of Carmichael (Richard John). 26th Baron of Carmichael, since 1980; 30th Chief of Name and Arms of Carmichael, since 1981; Chartered Accountant; Farmer; b. 1.12.48, Stamford; m., Patricia Margaret Branson; 1 s.; 2 d.; 4 gs.; 1 gd. Educ. Hyton Hill Preparatory School; Kimbolton School; Coventry College of Technology. Audit Senior, Coopers and Lybrand, Tanzania, 1972; Audit Manager, Granger Craig Tunnicliffe, Tauranga, New Zealand, 1974; ACA, 1971; FCA, 1976; Factor/Owner, Carmichael Estate, 1980; Director: Carmichael Heritage Leisure Ltd.; claims family titles: Earldom of Hyndford, Viscountcies of Inglisberry and Nemphlar, and Lordship Carmichael of Carmichael. Member, Standing Council of Scottish Chiefs; New Zealand Orienteering Champion, 1977; International Orienteering Federation Senior Event Advisor, 1996-2016 including World Masters Games 2006 and Race The Castles 2014. Recreations: orienteering; skiing; Clan Carmichael Association. Address: Carmichael House, Carmichael, by Biggar, Lanarkshire ML12 6PG; T.-01899 308336; e-mail: chiefcarm@aol.com; web: www.carmichael.co.uk

Carr, Professor Chris, MA, PhD, DMS, ACMA, CEng, MIMechE. Professor of Corporate Strategy, Edinburgh University, since 1999; b. 13.8.51, Brentwood; m., Jennifer Munro; 1 s.; 1 d. Educ. Harrow; Trinity Hall, University of Cambridge; Warwick University. Early career in industry with British Aerospace, GKN; Lecturer: Buckingham University; Warwick University; Bath University; Senior Lecturer/Associate Research Director, Manchester Business School; Visiting Professor, Moscow State University; Visiting Professor, International Business, Witten-Herdecke University, Germany; teaching/research overseas: Harvard Business School; Zhejiang University; Shenzen University; IIMB, Bangalore; St Petersburg University; Sao Paulo University; HEC; University of Carlos III; Bicocca University; Bilgi University. Publications: Britain's Competitiveness, 1990; Strategic Investment Decisions, 1994; numerous articles in academic journals including the Strategic Management Journal and Sloan Management Review. Recreations: politics; tennis; sailing. Address: (b.) Edinburgh University Management School, 29 Buccleuch Place, Edinburgh EH8 9JS; T.-0131-650 6307; e-mail: Chris.Carr@ed.ac.uk

Carruth, Stewart. Chief Executive, Stirling Council, since 2014. Returning Officer for elections to the Council and the Stirling Parliamentary Constituency for the Scottish, Westminster and European Parliaments and the Loch Lomond and Trossachs National Park. Address: (b.) Old Viewforth, Stirling FK8 2ET; T.-0845 277 7000.

Carruthers, Professor Gerard Charles, BA, MPhil, PhD, FRSE. Francis Hutcheson Professor of Scottish Literature, University of Glasgow, Head of Department, Scottish Literature, 2007-2011; b. 4.7.63, Lennoxtown,

Stirlingshire. Educ. St. Andrew's High School, Clydebank; University of Strathclyde; University of Glasgow. Temporary Lecturer, Department of Scottish Literature, University of Glasgow, 1992-93; Research Fellow, Department of English, University of Aberdeen, 1993-95; Lecturer, Department of English, University of Strathclyde, 1995-2000; Lecturer, then Senior Lecturer, then Reader, then Professor, Department of Scottish Literature, University of Glasgow, since 2000, Co-Director of The Centre for Robert Burns Studies; Convener, 'Burns Scotland' (the National Burns Collection); Member, Abbotsford Library Advisory Committee; Fellow of the Royal Society of Edinburgh, 2013; Visiting Research Fellow, All Souls College, Oxford, 2012; Visiting Professor of English, University of Wyoming, 2011-12; W.Ormiston Roy Memorial Research Fellow, University of South Carolina, 2002; Principal Investigator, major AHRC grant-led project, 'Editing Robert Burns for the 21st Century'; President of the Newman Association of the United Kingdom, 2009-2011. Publications include: General Editor, Oxford University Press Edition of The Works of Robert Burns, since 2008; Scottish Literature, A Critical Guide, 2009; Robert Burns, 2006; Editor: The Edinburgh Companion to Robert Burns, 2009; The Devil To Stage: Five Plays by James Bridie, 2007; Burns: Selected Poems, 2006; Co-Editor: The Burns Encyclopaedia, 2013; The Cambridge Companion to Scottish Literature, 2012; Scotland and the 19th Century World, 2012; Fickle Man: Robert Burns for the 21st Century, 2009; Walter Scott, Reliquiae Trotcosienses, 2004; Beyond Scotland, 2004; English Romanticism and the Celtic World, 2003. Recreations: playing guitar; watching football. Address: Scottish Literature, 7 University Gardens, University of Glasgow; T.-0141 330 4286.

E-mail: gerard.carruthers@glasgow.ac.uk

Carslaw, Michael John Howie, BSc, MBA, PhD. Headmaster, St. Leonards School, St. Andrews, since 2008; b. 15.07.56, Glasgow; m., Nicola; 3 d. Educ. Merchiston Castle School; Universities of Newcastle, Nottingham and London. Career: Asankrangwa Secondary School, Ghana; Wellingborough School, Northamptonshire; Head of Science, City of London Freemen's School; Deputy Head, Ardingly College, West Sussex. Address: (b.) St. Leonards School, St. Andrews, Fife KY16 9QJ.

Carson, Finlay Hamilton, MSP (Scottish Conservative), Galloway and West Dumfries, since 2016; b. Twynholm. Runs IT business. Conservative candidate, UK Parliament, for the Dumfries and Galloway constituency in 2015. Address: Scottish Parliament, Edinburgh EH99 1SP.

Carswell, William Steven, MA, LLB. Chairman, General Trustees of the Church of Scotland, 1999-2003; retired Director, Association for the Relief of Incurables; former Trustee, Ferguson Bequest Fund (retired); b. 13.7.29, Manchester; m., Jean Lang Sharpe; 2 s. Educ. Hutchesons' Boys' Grammar School; Glasgow University. Legal Assistant, Dunbarton County Council, 1953-56; Legal Assistant, Stirling County Council, 1956-59; Partner, McGrigor Donald, 1960-89. Recreations: golf; walking; cycling. Address:(h.) 13 Stratton Drive, Giffnock, Glasgow G46 7AB; T.-0141-638 1286; e-mail: wscarswell@ntlworld.com

Carter, Professor Alan, DPhil (Oxon), MA (Sussex), BA Hons (Kent). Emeritus Professor of Moral Philosophy, University of Glasgow; b. 5.7.52, Lincolnshire. Educ. Monkwearmouth Grammar School; St. Cross College, Oxford. Lecturer in Political Theory, University College Dublin, 1987; Lecturer in Philosophy, Heythrop College, University of London, 1988; Professor of Philosophy and Environmental Studies, University of Colorado at Boulder, 2001; Professor, University of Glasgow, since 2005. Board of Directors of Friends of The Earth Scotland. Publications: 3 books; over 50 articles in academic journals. Recreations: hiking; playing electric guitar; movies. Address: (b.) 69 Oakfield Avenue, Glasgow G12 8LT; T.-0141 330 5692; e-mail: acr@arts.gla.ac.uk

Carter, Professor Sir David Craig, MB, ChB, MD, FRCSEdin, FRCPEdin, FRCSIre (Hon), FACS (Hon), FRCGP (Hon), FCS HIC (Hon), FRACS (Hon), LLD (Hon), FRSEd, FRCGP (Hon), FAcadMedSci, FFPHM, DSc (Hon), LLD (Hon). Chairman, Board for Academic Medicine, Scotland, since 2005; Chairman, Managed Service Network for Neurosurgery in Scotland, 2009-13; Chairman, BMA Board of Science, 2002-05; Vice Principal, Edinburgh University, 2000-02; Member, Scientific Executive Board, Cancer Research UK, 2002-04 (Chairman, Programmes and Projects Committees, 2000-04); Trustee, Cancer Research UK, 2004-07; Vice Chairman, Cancer Research UK, 2005-07; President, British Medical Association, 2001-02; Chief Medical Officer (Scotland), 1996-2000; Surgeon to the Queen in Scotland, 1993-97; b. 1.9.40, Penrith; m., Ilske; 2 s. Educ. St. Andrews University. Lecturer in Clinical Surgery, Edinburgh University, 1969-74; 12-month secondment as Lecturer in Surgery, Makerere University, Kampala, Uganda, 1972; Senior Lecturer in Surgery, Edinburgh University, 1974-79; 12-month secondment as Associate Professor of Surgery, University of California, 1976; St. Mungo Professor of Surgery, Glasgow University, 1979-88; Honorary Consultant, Glasgow Royal Infirmary, 1979-88; Regius Professor of Clinical Surgery, Edinburgh University, 1988-96; Honorary Consultant Surgeon, Edinburgh Royal Infirmary, 1988-96. Former Council Member, Royal College of Surgeons of Edinburgh; former Member, Broadcasting Council for Scotland; former Chairman, Scottish Council for Postgraduate Medical and Dental Education; former Co-editor, British Journal of Surgery; Member, Medical Advisory Committee, Higher Education Funding Council, 1994-97; Non-executive Director, Lothian Health Board, 1994-96; President, Surgical Research Society, Association of Surgeons (Great Britain and Ireland), 1996-97; Vice President, Royal Society of Edinburgh, 2002-08; Chairman: The Health Foundation, 2002-08, Queens Nursing Institute, Scotland, 2002-2010. Moynihan Prize, 1973; James IV Association of Surgeons Travelling Fellow, 1975; Royal Medal, British Medical Association, 2006; Royal Medal, Royal Society of Edinburgh, 2007. Recreation: music. Address: (h.) 19 Buckingham Terrace, Edinburgh EH4 3AD.

Carwood-Edwards, Jean, MEd. Chief Executive, Early Years Scotland, since 2013. Educ. University of Glasgow; Jordanhill College. Career: Head of School of Education, James Watt College of Further and Higher Education, 2002-07; Early Years Team Leader, Learning and Teaching Scotland, 2007-2010; Programme Director and Area Adviser, Education Scotland, 2010-2012. Address: (b.) Granville Street, Glasgow, Lanarkshire G3 7EE; T.-0141 221 4148.

Casely, Gordon, KStJ, FRSA, FSAScot. Journalist and heraldist; Baron-Baillie of Miltonhaven; personal herald to the Chief of Irvine; b. 29.6.43, Glasgow; 1 s. Educ. Hutchesons' Boys' Grammar School. Reporter, D.C. Thomson & Co. Ltd., Dundee, Aberdeen and Elgin, 1966-68; Evening Express, Aberdeen, 1968-73; PRO, Greater Glasgow Passenger Transport Executive, 1973-78; public affairs posts in banking, local government, offshore and energy industries, 1978-95 (Assistant Director, CBI Scotland, 1988-91). Director, Herald Strategy Ltd., since 1999; Founder Member, Heraldry Society of Scotland, 1977; Press Officer, Commonwealth Games Council for Scotland, 1989-93; Member: Scottish Commonwealth Games Team, Auckland, 1990, Guild Burgess of Aberdeen, 1992; Hon. Vice-President, Lonach Highland and Friendly Society, since 1990; Member, Lonach Pipe Band, 2002-10; President, Aberdeen Welsh Society, 1997-98; Governor, Scottish Tartans Authority, 2003-2010. Publications: magazine contributor and obituarist; I Belong To Glasgow (human history of the Subway), 1975; ed. Who Do You Think You Are? (heraldry in modern Scotland), 2006. Recreations: piping; painting; promoting heraldry; pedalling the continents; poking fun at Abellio ScotRail. Address: (h.) Westerton Cottage, Crathes, Kincardineshire AB31 6LA; T.-01330 844753; e-mail: gcasely@herald-strategy.co.uk

Cash, John David, CBE, BSc, MB, ChB, PhD, FRCPath, FRCPGlas, FRCPE, FRCSEdin, FRCP. National Medical and Scientific Director, Scottish National Blood Transfusion Service, 1979-96; Honorary Professor, Department of Medicine, Edinburgh University, 1987-96; Member, Management Board, National Institute of Biological Standards and Control, 1996-2004; Governor, Fettes College, 1997-2003; b. 3.4.36, Reading; m., Angela Mary Thomson; 1 s.; 1 d. Educ. Ashville College, Harrogate; Edinburgh University. Edinburgh and South East Scotland Blood Transfusion Service: Deputy Director, 1969, Regional Director, 1974. President, Royal College of Physicians of Edinburgh, 1994-98. Recreations: fishing; gardening. Address: 1 Otterburn Park, Edinburgh EH14 1JX.

Caskie, Rev. J. Colin, BA, BD. Minister at Rhu and Shandon, 2002-2012; b. 17.8.47, Glasgow; m., Alison McDougall; 2 s.; 1 d. Educ. Knightswood Secondary School; Strathclyde University; Glasgow University. Minister, Penilee: St Andrew, 1977-83; Minister, Carnoustie, 1983-2002; Moderator, Presbytery of Angus, 1995; Chairman, The Duncan Trust, 1992-2002; Vice-Convenor, General Assembly's Board of Stewardship and Finance, 1998-2001, Convenor, 2001-05; Clerk to Presbytery of Dumbarton, 2005-2012; Moderator, Presbytery of Dumbarton, 2011-2012; Clerk to the Presbytery of Perth, since 2015. Recreations: stamp collecting; gardening. Address: (h.) 13 Anderson Drive, Perth PH1 1JZ.

Catterall, Nicola Jane, BA, ACA, FRSA. Chief Operating Officer, National Galleries Scotland, since 2007; Director and Trustee, Dewar Arts Awards; Director and Trustee, National Galleries of Scotland Foundation; Director and Trustee, Glasgow Sculpture Studios; Faculty Advisory Board, Durham University; b. 14.12.58, Holmfirth; 2 d. Educ. George Stephenson High; University of Durham (St. Mary's College). Chartered Accountant, Ernst & Young, 1980-84; various roles in Investment Banking, J.P. Morgan, 1985-98; Investment Management, Standard Life Investments, 1998-2003; Programme Director for Demutualisation of Standard Life, 2003-2006; Director of Finance, National Galleries of Scotland, 2007. Recreations: sculpture; wine. Address: 73 Belford Road, Edinburgh EH4 3DS; T.-0131 624 6202.

Catto, Professor Sir Graeme R.D., Kt, MB, ChB (Hons), MD (Hons), DSc, FRCP, FRCPE, FRCPGlas, FRCGP (Hon), FRSE, FFPM, FMedSci, FRCSE (Hon); FHEA, FAcadMEd. Emeritus Professor of Medicine, Universities of London and Aberdeen, since 2009; Professor of Medicine, University of Aberdeen, 2005-09; Vice-Principal, King's College London, and Dean, Guy's, King's and St. Thomas' Hospitals Medical and Dental Schools, 2000-05; Professor of Medicine, University of London, 2000-05; Pro Vice Chancellor, University of London, 2003-05; President, General Medical Council, 2002-09; Chairman, Robert Gordon's College, 1995-2005; b. 24.4.45, Aberdeen; m., Joan Sievewright; 1 s.; 1 d. Educ. Robert Gordon's College; Aberdeen University. Research Fellow/ Lecturer/Senior Lecturer/Reader in Medicine, Aberdeen University, 1970-88; Harkness Fellow of Commonwealth Fund of New York, 1975-77 (Fellow in Medicine, Harvard Medical School and Peter Bent Brigham Hospital, Boston); Aberdeen University: Professor in Medicine and Therapeutics, 1988-2000, Dean, Faculty of Clinical Medicine, 1992-98, Vice-Principal 1995-2000; Vice Chairman, Aberdeen Royal Hospitals NHS Trust, 1992-99; Chief Scientist, NHS in Scotland, 1997-2000; Member, Scottish Higher Education Funding Council, 1996-2002; Member, General Medical Council, Education and Standard Committees, 1994-2002 (Chairman, Education, 1999-2002); Treasurer, Academy of Medical Sciences, 1998-2001; Governor, PPP Medical Foundation, 2000-02; Member, SE London Strategic Health Authority, 2002-05; Member, Council for the Regulation of Healthcare Professionals; Hon. DSc, St Andrews University, 2003; Hon. LLD, Aberdeen University, 2002; Hon. MD, University of Southampton, 2004; Hon. DSc, Robert Gordon University, 2004; Hon. FRCGP, 2000; Hon. FRCSE, 2002; Fellow, King's College London, 2005; Hon. DSc, University of Kent, 2007; Hon. DSc, South Bank University, 2008; Hon DSc, University of London, 2009; Hon. MD, University of Brighton, 2010; Hon MD, University of Buckingham, 2015; President, College of Medicine, 2010-14; Chairman, Scottish Stem Cell Network, 2008-2011; Chairman, Chairman, Higher Education Better Regulation Group, 2009-2012; President, Association for the Study of Medical Education, 2009-2013; Member, Qatar Council for Healthcare Practitioners; Co-chair, Review Group on Medical and Dental School Intakes in England, 2011-2012; Member, Commission on Assisted Dying, 2010-11; Chairman, Dignity in Dying, since 2012; Chairman, Lathallan School. Recreations: hills and glens. Address: Maryfield, Glenbuchat, Strathdon, Aberdeenshire AB36 8TS; T.-0197 56 41317. E-mail: gcatto@btinternet.com

Catto, Joan, LLB, NP; b. 30.4.46, Aberdeen; m., Sir Graeme Catto; 1 s.; 1 d. Educ. Aberdeen High School for Girls; Aberdeen University. Qualified as a solicitor in 1968; career in Aberdeen (apart from two years in the US); Partner, Burnett & Reid, 1990-2002; Partner, Ledingham Chalmers, 2002-08, Consultant, 2008-10; Chairman, Social Security Appeal Tribunal, 1983-98; Chairman, Child Support Appeal Tribunal, 1998-2002; Founder member, Scottish Family Law Association, 1980-2008; Founder board member, Scottish Children's Reporter Administration, 1992-98; Safeguarder in Sheriff Courts (including 1990s Orkney cases) and Children's Panels, 1980-99; Court reporter, Aberdeen Sheriff Court re contact & custody cases, 1980-2002; Member, Scottish Legal Group of British Agencies for Adoption & Fostering, 1980-2008; listed as a Leader in the field of Family Law, Chambers' Legal Directory, 1995-2005; Vice-Chairman, Grampian Healthcare NHS Trust, 1993-1999; Assessor, Dean of Guild, City of Aberdeen, 1999-2007; Member, Group of Friends, Mither Kirk Project, Aberdeen, 2000-2010; Member, University Court, University of Aberdeen, 2002-10; Convener, formerly Member, Business Committee, University of Aberdeen, 1994-2010; Local Chairman, RSNO Circle, 2004-2012; Chair, Voluntary Service Aberdeen; Member, Board of Friends, Aberdeen Cyrenians (charity for the homeless); Member, fund-raising team, Red Cross, Aberdeen. Recreations: needlework of all kinds; English setters; R&R in Glenbuchat. Address: (h.) 4 Woodend Avenue, Aberdeen AB15 6YL; T.-01224 310509. E-mail: joancatto@btinternet.com

Catto, Simon James Dawson, LLB (Hons), DipLP, NP. Partner, HBJ Gateley Wareing, since 2006; Solicitor-Advocate, since 2007; b. 21.5.72, Aberdeen; m., Caroline; 1 d. Educ. Robert Gordon's College, Aberdeen; Edinburgh University. Ledingham Chalmers, Aberdeen: Trainee

Solicitor, 1995-97, Solicitor, 1997-2002; Partner, Ledingham Chalmers, Edinburgh, 2002-06. Burgess of Guild of The City of Aberdeen. Recreations: music; sport; travel. Address: (b.) Exchange Tower, 19 Canning Street, Edinburgh EH3 8EH; T.-0131 222 9560; e-mail: scatto@hbj-gw.com

Cawdor, 7th Earl of (Colin Robert Vaughan Campbell); b. 30.6.62; m., Lady Isabella Stanhope; 1 s.; 3 d. Succeeded to title, 1993. Educ. Eton; St. Peter's College, Oxford.

Cha, Sang Y., BTh, MTh, FRSA. Parish Minister, St. Mungo's, Alloa, since 2011; b. 2.2.77, Seoul, South Korea. Educ. University of Cambridge, Selwyn College; University of Edinburgh. New College; University of Cambridge, Fitzwilliam College. Coordinated client public relations, logistics and planning in film/TV projects, William Morris Agency, Inc., Beverly Hills, CA, USA, 1999-2000; Vice-President of Talent and Development, JS Entertainment, Inc., Studio City, CA, USA, 2001-2002; instructed English grammar and writing (basic and advanced), Americorps National Service Project, Anchorage, AK, USA, 2002-03; Church of Scotland, Cambridge, Edinburgh, Alloa, since 2006. Maintenance of Jimmy's Night Shelter, Cambridge, 2003-07; University of Cambridge Divinity Faculty Board, 2007-08; Member of the Board of Trustees, Alloa Town Centre Business District, since 2012; Voting Member of the Council, Clackmannanshire Council's Education, Sport and Leisure Committee, since 2012. Recreations: jazz; saxophone; certified bow hunter and archery enthusiast; tennis; staying busy with 2 border collies; love to work with children and the elderly. Address: (b.) 10 Bedford Place, Alloa FK10 1LJ; T.-01259 723004; e-mail: syc@cantab.net

Chalmers, Douglas, MA (Hons), PhD. Caledonian Scholar; Scottish President of University and College Union, since 2015; Senior Lecturer, Department of Social Sciences, Media and Journalism, Glasgow Caledonian University, since 2002; b. 22.6.57, Dundee; m., Mhairi McGowan; 2 s.; 1 d. Educ. Kirkton High School, Dundee; Dundee University. National Organiser, Young Communist League, 1981-83; General Secretary, Young Communist League, 1983-85; Scottish Organiser, Communist Party, 1985-88; Scottish Secretary, Communist Party, 1988-91; Convener, Democratic Left Scotland, 1991-95; Researcher, Glasgow Caledonian University, 1996-2002; Executive Member, Scottish Constitutional Convention, 1989-95; Member, Council, Scottish Civic Forum, 2001-05, Board Member, 2001-05; Member, Broadcasting Council for Scotland, 2005-07, Audience Council Scotland, 2007-2010; Member, University Senate, since 2012; Member, University Council, since 2013. Recreations: politics; community; family; sport; musician; languages. Address: (b.) Glasgow Caledonian University, 70 Cowcaddens Road, Glasgow G4 0BA; T.-0141 331 3350; e-mail: d.chalmers@gcal.ac.uk
http://www.caledonian.ac.uk/cbs/departments/cultural
business/meetthestaff/drdchalmers/
http://www.douglaschalmers.com

Chalmers, Very Rev. John Pearson, BD. Principal Clerk to the General Assembly of the Church of Scotland; Moderator of the General Assembly of the Church of Scotland (2014-2015); Chaplain in Ordinary to HM The Queen; Patron of Donaldson's School; b. 5.6.52, Bothwell; m., Elizabeth; 2 s.; 1 d. Educ. Marr College; Strathclyde University; Glasgow University. Minister, Renton Trinity, 1979-86; Clerk, Dumbarton Presbytery, 1982-86; Minister, Palmerston Place, Edinburgh, 1986-95; Deputy General Secretary, Board of Ministry, Church of Scotland, 1995-2001; Pastoral Adviser and Associate Secretary, Ministries Council, Church of Scotland, 2001-2010. Recreations: golf; bee-keeping. Address: (b.) 121 George Street, Edinburgh EH2 4YN; T.-0131-225 5722.
E-mail: jchalmers@cofscotland.org.uk

Chalmers, Roderick Thomas Alexander, MBChB, FRCSEd, MD, FRCS. Consultant Vascular Surgeon, Royal Infirmary of Edinburgh, since 1998; Honorary Senior Lecturer, Edinburgh University Medical School, since 1998; b. 18.5.63, Edinburgh; m., Clare Elizabeth Chalmers; 1 d. Educ. George Watson's College, Edinburgh; Edinburgh University. House Surgeon/Physician, Royal Infirmary, Edinburgh, 1986-87; Senior House Officer, General Surgery, South-east Scotland, 1987-89; basic surgical training rotation, South-east Scotland, 1989-92; Research Fellow in Vascular Surgery, University of Iowa, 1992-93; career registrar surgery, South-east Scotland, 1993-95; Senior Registrar/Senior Clinical Fellow, St Mary's Hospital, London, 1995-98. Director, Scottish National Service for the Treatment of Thoraco-Abdominal Aneurysms; Convener, Higher Surgical Skills Course, Royal College of Surgeons of Edinburgh. Recreations: mountaineering; golf. Address: (h.) Morar House, Braidwood Bridge, Midlothian EH26 9LW; T.-01968 678225; e-mail: rod.chalmers@luht.scot.nhs.uk

Chambers, Professor Helen Elizabeth, MA, PhD. Emeritus Professor of German, St Andrews University; b. 4.3.47, Glasgow; m., Hugh Rorrison; 2 s. Educ. Hutchesons' Girls' Grammar School, Glasgow; Glasgow University; Freiburg University. Lecturer, then Senior Lecturer in German, Leeds University, 1972-99; Visiting Lecturer in German, Melbourne University, 1998. Publications: Supernatural and Irrational Elements in the Works of Theodor Fontane, 1980; Co-existent Contradictions: Joseph Roth in Retrospect (Editor), 1991; Theodor Fontane: The London Symposium (Co-Editor), 1995; T. Fontane, Effi Briest (Co-Translator), 1995; The Changing Image of Theodor Fontane, 1997; Theodor Fontane and the European Context (Co-Editor), 2001; Violence, Culture and Identity (Editor), 2006; Humor and Irony in Nineteenth-Century German Women's Writing, 2007; T. Fontane, No Way Back (Co-Translator), 2010; Fontane-Studien, 2014. Recreations: theatre; film; travel. Address: (b.) School of Modern Languages, St Andrews University, St Andrews KY16 9PH; T.- 01334 463670.

Chambers, Rev. Samuel John, OBE, BSc. Retired Church of Scotland Minister; b. 3.4.44, Banbridge, Co. Down, Northern Ireland; m., Anne; 2 s.; 1 d. Educ. Banbridge Academy; Annadale Grammar School, Belfast; Queen's University Belfast; Presbyterian College, Belfast. Minister, Presbyterian Church in Ireland, 1972-84, Belfast, Donegal and Comber, Co. Down; Chairman, East Belfast Youth Council, 1972-73; Chief Executive, Relate, Northern Ireland, 1984-98; Chairman, International Commission on Marriage and Interpersonal Relationships, 1994-98; Church of Scotland Minister, Ness Bank Church of Scotland, Inverness, 1998-2009. Contributions to Journal of Sexual and Marital Therapy; presenter 'Thought for the day', Radio Ulster, 1979-98, Radio Scotland, 1998-2009. Recreations: golf; travel; hill walking. Address: (h.) Bannlagan Lodge, 4 Earls Cross Gardens, Dornoch, Sutherland IV25 3NR; T.-01862 811520.

Chandler, Glenn. Playwright and novelist; b. 1949, Edinburgh. Educ. Royal High School, Edinburgh. Written plays for theatre and radio, original screenplays for television and films, television series, and novels.

Moved from Scotland to London and began writing for the Soho Poly, where his early plays were produced; went on to write for BBC Television and Radio, and for Granada Television (including its series Crown Court (TV series)) before creating and writing his own series Taggart for STV Productions (ITV Network). Awards: BAFTA (1991), Taggart (winner of Best Drama Serial Award); Writers' Guild of Great Britain Award (1993) (winner of Best Original Drama Serial); BAFTA (1995), nominated Best TV Writer; BAFTA (1997), Taggart nominated for Best Drama Serial Award. Address: MBA Literary Agents, 62 Grafton Way, London W1T 5DW.

Chaplain, Professor Mark Andrew Joseph, BSc (Hons), PhD, FRSE. Gregory Chair of Mathematics, University of St Andrews, since 2015; b. 1.5.64, Dundee; m., Fiona; 3 s. Educ. St John's RC High School, Dundee; Dundee University. Lecturer, School of Mathematical Sciences, Bath University, 1990-96; Senior Lecturer, Department of Maths, Dundee University, 1996-98; Reader in Mathematical Biology, Dundee University, 1998-2000; former Ivory Chair of Applied Mathematics, Dundee University, Head of Mathematics Division, 2006-2012. Whitehead Prize, London Mathematical Society, 2000; recipient of 2014 Lee Segel Prize from The Society of Mathematical Biology. Publications: On Growth and Form: Spatio-Temporal Pattern Formation in Biology; Polymer and Cell Dynamics: Multiscale modelling and numerical simulations. Recreations: golf; squash; badminton; tennis. Address: (b.) School of Mathematics and Statistics, University of St Andrews, Mathematical Institute, North Haugh, St Andrews KY16 9SS.

Chapman, Douglas. MP (SNP), Dunfermline and West Fife, since 2015. Address: House of Commons, London SW1A 0AA.

Chapman, Professor John N., MA, PhD, FInstP, FIEEE, FRSE. Emeritus Vice Principal and Professor, Physics and Astronomy, Glasgow University, since 2014, formerly Vice Principal and Head of College of Science and Engineering; b. 21.11.47, Sheffield; m., Judith M.; 1 s.; 1 d. Educ. King Edward VII School, Sheffield; St. John's College and Fitzwilliam College, Cambridge. Research Fellow, Fitzwilliam College, Cambridge; Lecturer, Glasgow University. Recreations: photography; walking; tennis. Address: (b.) Kelvin Building, Glasgow University, Glasgow G12 8QQ; T.-0141-330 4462.
E-mail: john.chapman@glasgow.ac.uk

Chapman, Peter John, MSP (Scottish Conservative), North East Scotland region, since 2016; Shadow Cabinet Secretary for Rural Economy and Connectivity, since 2016. Conservative candidate in Banffshire and Buchan Coast in the 2016 Scottish Parliament election. Address: Scottish Parliament, Edinburgh EH99 1SP.

Chapman, Professor Robert, BSc, PhD, CPhys, FInstP. Emeritus Professor of Physics, University of the West of Scotland, since 2011; b. 10.8.41, Holytown; m., Norma Gilchrist Hope; 3 d. Educ. Bellshill Academy; University of Glasgow. UKAEA Research Fellow, AWRE, Aldermaston, and AERE, Harwell, 1966-70; University of Manchester: Lecturer, 1970-75, Senior Lecturer, 1975-87, Reader in Physics, 1987-93; Paisley University: Head, Department of Physics, 1993-96, Head, Department of Electronic Engineering and Physics, 1996-2000, Head, School of Information and Communication Technologies, 2000-03, Acting Vice Principal, Research and Commercialisation,

2004-06. Publications: 200 research papers. Recreations: walking; gardening; listening to music. Address: (b.) University of the West of Scotland, Paisley PA1 2BE; T.-0141-848 3600; e-mail: robert.chapman@uws.ac.uk

Charlesworth, Professor Brian, BA, PhD, FRS, FRSE, Foreign Associate, US National Academy of Sciences. Senior Honorary Professorial Fellow, Edinburgh University, since 2007; b. 29.4.45, Brighton; m., Deborah Maltby; 1 d. Educ. Haberdashers' Aske's Elstree School; Queens' College, Cambridge. Post-doctoral Fellow, University of Chicago, 1969-71; Lecturer, Genetics, University of Liverpool, 1971-74; Lecturer, Biology, Sussex University, 1974-82; Reader in Biology, Sussex University, 1982-84; Professor of Biology, University of Chicago, 1985-92; G.W. Beadle Distinguished Service Professor of Ecology and Evolution, University of Chicago, 1992-97; Royal Society Research Professor, Edinburgh University, 1997-2007. Darwin Medal, The Royal Society, 2000. Publications: Evolution in Age-structured Populations, 1994; co-author, Evolution: A Very Short Introduction, 2003; co-author, Elements of Evolutionary Genetics, 2010. Recreations: walking; listening to classical music. Address: (b.) Institute of Evolutionary Biology, Edinburgh University, The King's Buildings, Edinburgh EH9 3FL; T.-0131-650 5751.

Cherry, Joanna. MP (SNP), Edinburgh South West, since 2015; Justice and Home Affairs spokesperson in the House of Commons; b. 1966. Educ. University of Edinburgh. Worked as a research assistant with the Scottish Law Commission (1990) before practising as a solicitor with the Edinburgh legal firm Brodies until 1995; worked as a part-time tutor in constitutional law, family law and civil court practice at the University of Edinburgh, 1990-1996; admitted as an advocate in 1995, with a particular interest in employment and industrial relations, health and safety, mental health, personal injury and professional negligence; served as a Standing Junior Counsel to the Scottish Government, 2003-2008, and as an Advocate Depute and Senior Advocate Depute, 2008-2011; appointed a Queen's Counsel in 2009; formerly advocate with the Arnot Manderson stable within the Faculty of Advocates. Set up the "Lawyers for Yes" campaign group in 2014. Address: House of Commons, London SW1A 0AA.

Chester, Richard Waugh, MBE, FRAM, GRSM, ARCM. Director, National Youth Orchestras of Scotland, 1987-2007; b. 19.4.43, Hutton Rudby; m., Sarah Chapman-Mortimer; 1 s.; 2 d. Educ. The Friends' School, Great Ayton; Huddersfield College of Technology, Music Dept.; Royal Academy of Music. Flautist: BBC Northern Ireland, 1965-1967; Principal Flute: Royal Scottish National Orchestra, 1967-87; Conductor; Teacher; Adjudicator; Consultant. Trustee: Lochaber Music School; Acting for Charities Trust; Scottish School Orchestra Trust; Dewar Arts Awards; Agar Trust; The Edinburgh Quartet Trust. Recreations: swimming; walking; reading. Address: (h.) Milton of Cardross, Port of Menteith, Stirling FK8 3JY; T.-01877 385634; e-mail: mail@rchester.co.uk

Chestnutt, Glenn Alexander, BA (Hons), DASE, MDiv, ThM, PhD. Minister of St John's Church, Gourock, since 2009; b. 23.01.70, Ballymoney, N. Ireland; m., Hannah; 1 s. Educ. Dalriada Grammar School; University of Ulster; Queen's University of Belfast; Princeton Theological Seminary; University of Edinburgh. PhD Candidate, New College, University of Edinburgh, 2004-08; Probationary Minister, Cramond Kirk (Church of Scotland), 2007-08. Member of Church of Scotland Ministries Council, since 2011; Member of Church of Scotland Theological Forum, since 2013; Member of Church of Scotland Ecumenical Relations Committee, since 2014. Publication: 'Challenging the Stereotype. The Theology of Karl Barth as a Resource for Inter-religious Encounter in a European Context' (Author), 2010. Address: The Manse, 6 Barrhill Road, Gourock PA19 1JX; e-mail: glenn.chestnutt@gmail.com

Chesworth, Air Vice Marshal George Arthur, CB, OBE, DFC. Lord-Lieutenant of Moray, 1994-2005; b. 4.6.30; m.; 1 s. (deceased); 2 d. RAF, 1948-84; Chief Executive, Glasgow Garden Festival, 1985-88. Hon. Colonel, 76th Regiment (V), 1992-97; Hon. Air Commodore, 2622 (Highland) Squadron Royal Auxilliary Air Force, 2004-2010.

Cheyne, George Martin Frazer, BSc, DUniv. Chair, NHS Ayshire & Arran Health Board, since 2012; Chair, Grameen in the UK, since 2011; b. 17.5.44, Ayr; m., Beatrice; 1 s.; 1 d. Educ. Ayr Academy; Strathclyde University. Over 30 years with ICI of which 20 years abroad managing ICI businesses in Dubai, Zambia, Chile, Hong Kong, and Mexico as CEO or MD; Chair of Court, Glasgow Caledonian University, 2005-2011. Past Vice Chair, Lloyds TSB Foundation for Scotland; Past Chair, Ayrshire Council on Alcohol, current Board Member. Recreation: golf. Address: (h.) 65 Gailes Road, Troon KA10 6TB; T.-01292 317442; e-mail: mcheyne17@yahoo.co.uk

Chick, Jonathan Dale, MA (Cantab), MBChB, MPhil, DSc (Edin), FRCPE, FRCPsych. Consultant Psychiatrist, Royal Edinburgh Hospital and Senior Lecturer, Dept. of Psychiatry, Edinburgh University, 1979-2010; Honorary Professor, Queen Margaret University, since 2009; Medical Director, Castle Craig Hospital Scotland; b. 23.4.45, Wallasey; 2 s. Educ. Queen Elizabeth Grammar School, Darlington; Corpus Christi College, Cambridge; Edinburgh University. Posts in Edinburgh teaching hospitals, 1971-76; scientific staff, MRC Unit for Epidemiological Studies in Psychiatry, 1976-79. Chief Editor, Alcohol and Alcoholism; Hon. Life Fellow, Soc. Study Addiction and French Society for Addictology; awarded Royal College of Psychiatrists Research Medal and Prize. Publications: numerous research papers; two books. Recreation: music.

Chillingworth, David Robert, BA (Mod), TCD, MA (Oxon). Bishop of St. Andrews, Dunkeld and Dunblane, since 2005; Primus of the Scottish Episcopal Church, since 2009; b. 23.6.51, Dublin, Ireland; m., Alison; 2 s.; 1 d. Educ. Portora Royal School, Enniskillen; Royal Belfast Academical Institution; Trinity College, Dublin; Oriel College, Oxford; Ripon College, Cuddesdon. Curate Assistant, Holy Trinity, Joanmount, Belfast (Connor), 1976-79; Church of Ireland Youth Officer, 1979-83; Curate Assistant, Bangor Abbey (Down and Dromore), 1983-86; Rector, Seagoe Parish Church, Portadown, 1986-2005; Dean of Dromore, 1995-2002; Archdeacon of Dromore, 2002-05. Recreations: music; sailing; cycling; reading; travel. Address: (b.) 28A Balhousie Street, Perth PH1 5HJ; T.-01738 580426; e-mail: bishop@standrews.anglican.org

Chisholm, Duncan Fraser, OStJ, JP (Retd). Director, Duncan Chisholm & Sons Ltd., Inverness; Director, Inverness City Business Improvement District; Chairman, The Kiltmakers Association of Scotland Ltd., 2000-2014; Justice for Sheriffdom of Grampian, Highlands and Islands, 1989-2011; Member, Order of St. John, since 2003; Member, Inverness St. Columba New Charge Commission of Church of Scotland; Member, The Highland Society of London; Director, Inverness Business Improvement District Ltd., since 2009; b. 14.4.41, Inverness; m., Mary Rebecca MacRae; 1 s.; 1 d. Educ. Inverness High School. Member,

Inverness District Council, 1984-92; Member, Board of Governors, Eden Court Theatre, Inverness, 1984-88; President, Inverness and Highland Chamber of Commerce, 1983-84 (Vice-President, 1982-83); Member, Highland TAVRA Committee, 1988-92; Vice-Chairman, Inverness, Loch Ness and Nairn Tourist Board, 1988-96; President, Clan Chisholm Society, 1978-89; Chairman, Inverness Town Twinning Committee, 1992-98; Member, Management Committee: Highland Export Club, 1998-2008, Inverness Project Board Member, 1997-2007; GSL, Scout Association, since 1969 (Scout Leader, 1960-69); Session Clerk, St. Columba High Church, Inverness, 2001-2010. Recreations: swimming; music; painting. Address: (b.) 47-51 Castle Street, Inverness; T.-01463 234599; e-mail: Duncan@kilts.co.uk

Chisholm, Malcolm. MSP (Labour), Edinburgh North and Leith, 1999-2016; Shadow Minister for Culture and External Affairs, 2007-08 (Minister for Health and Community Care, 2001-04, Minister for Communities, 2004-06); MP (Labour), Edinburgh North and Leith (formerly Edinburgh Leith), 1992-2001; b. 7.3.49; m.; 2 s.; 1 d. Former teacher. Parliamentary Under-Secretary of State, Scottish Office (Minister for Local Government, Housing and Transport) 1997 (resigned over cuts).

Christian, Professor Reginald Frank, MA (Oxon). Professor of Russian and Head of Department, St. Andrews University, 1966-92, now Emeritus Professor; b. 9.8.24, Liverpool; m., Rosalind Iris Napier; 1 s.; 1 d. Educ. Liverpool Institute High School; Queen's College, Oxford. RAF, 1943-46 (aircrew), flying on 231 Sqdn. and 6 Atlantic Ferry Unit (Pilot Officer, 1944); Foreign Office (British Embassy, Moscow), 1949-50; Lecturer and Head of Russian Department, Liverpool University, 1950-55; Senior Lecturer, then Professor of Russian and Head of Department, Birmingham University, 1955-66; Visiting Professor: McGill University, Montreal, 1961-62, Institute of Foreign Languages, Moscow, 1964-65; Dean, Faculty of Arts, St. Andrews University, 1975-78; Member, University Court, 1971-73, 1981-85. President, British Universities Association of Slavists, 1967-70; Member, International Committee of Slavists, 1970-75; Honorary Vice-President, Association of Teachers of Russian; Member, UGC Arts Sub-Committee on Russian Studies. Publications: Russian Syntax (with F.M. Borras), 1959 and 1971; Korolenko's Siberia, 1954; Tolstoy's War and Peace: A Study, 1962; Russian Prose Composition (with F.M. Borras), 1964 and 1974; Tolstoy: A Critical Introduction, 1969; Tolstoy's Letters, edited, translated and annotated, 1978; Tolstoy's Diaries, edited, translated and annotated, 1985 and 1994; Alexis Aladin – The Tragedy of Exile, 1999. Recreations: music; reading. Address: (h.) 48 Lade Braes, St. Andrews, Fife; T.-01334 474407.

Christie, John, MTheol, DipEd. Educational consultant, since 2002; Director of Lifelong Learning, Scottish Borders Council, 2001-02 (Director of Education, 1995-2001); Non-Executive Director, Learning and Teaching Scotland, 2000-04; b. 25.12.53, Edinburgh; m., Katherine; 2 d. Educ. Daniel Stewart's College; St. Andrews University; Edinburgh University; Moray House College of Education. Teacher, 1977-83; Principal Assistant, Stockport MBC, 1983-85; Assistant Director of Education, then Depute Director of Education, Tayside Regional Council, 1985-95. Hon. Treasurer, Association of Directors of Education in Scotland, 1995-2002; Member: Health Education Board for Scotland, 1991-97, Advisory Committee on Scottish Qualification for Headship, since 1999, Scotland Against Drugs Primary School Initiative, COSLA/SEED Group on Value-Added in Schools; Non-Executive Director, Scottish Consultative Council on the Curriculum, 1995-2000. E-mail: jchristie@tinyworld.co.uk

Christie, Very Rev. John Cairns, BSc, BD (Hons), PGCertEd, CBiol, MSB. Moderator of the General Assembly of the Church of Scotland, 2010-2011; Interim Minister, Old Cumnock: Trinity; Kilmacolm: Old Kirk; Arisaig and the Small Isles linked with Mallaig St. Columba's and Knoydart; West Kilbride; Lausanne: St. Andrew; Greenock: Finnart St Paul's; Paisley: Oakshaw Trinity; Church of Scotland Minister, Hyndland Parish Church, Glasgow, 1990-2004; Convener: Church of Scotland Board of Parish Education, 2001-05, Joint Committee for Safety and Protection of Children, 2001-05, Safeguarding Committee, 2005-2010; Teacher, 1972-86; b. 9.7.47, Glasgow; m., (1) Elizabeth McDonald McIntosh (died 1993); 1 d. Elizabeth Margaret; (2) Annette Cooke Carnegie Evans (nee Hamill). Educ. Hermitage School, Helensburgh; University of Strathclyde; Jordanhill College; University of Glasgow. Teacher, Albert Secondary School, Springburn, Glasgow, 1973-76, Assistant Principal Teacher, Guidance, 1976-78; Principal Teacher of Science, Tiree High School, 1978-84; Warden, Dalneigh Hall of Residence, 1984-86; Honours Degree in New Testament and Systematic Theology, University of Glasgow, 1986-90; Probationer Assistant Minister, Mosspark Parish Church, 1989-90. Recreations: hill-walking; reading; radio; tv; DIY; gardening. E-mail: rev.jcc@btinternet.com

Chrystie, Kenneth, LLB (Hons), PhD. Chairman, Hugh Fraser Foundation, since 1987; Director: Murgitroyd plc, Nautricity Ltd., Glasgow Science Centre; Past President, Royal Glasgow Institute of the Fine Arts; b. 24.11.46, Glasgow; m., Mary; 1 s.; 2 d. Educ. Duncanrig Senior Secondary; University of Glasgow; University of Virginia. Joined McClure Naismith, 1968. Publications: contributor to Encyclopedia of Scots Law, Labour Law Handbook and other legal publications. Recreations: golf; curling; tennis. Address: 2 Redlands Road, Glasgow G12 0SJ; T.-0141 339 2757; e-mail: kgchrystie@icloud.com

Churchill, Professor Robin, LLB, LLM, PhD. Professor of International Law, University of Dundee, since 2006; b. 02.02.47, Pulham Market, Norfolk; m., Margaret Churchill (nee Powell); 1 s.; 1 d. Educ. King Edward IV, Norwich; University College London. Research Officer in International Law, British Institute of International and Comparative Law, London, 1970-77; Lecturer, Senior Lecturer, Reader and Professor of Law, Cardiff University, 1977-2006; Visiting Professorial Fellow, University of Wollongong, Australia, 2005-06; Lecturer, University of Tromsø, Norway, 1983-84. Publications: Author of 3 books and over 100 papers on International and EU Law. Recreations: walking; cycling; bird watching; music; campanology. Address: (b.) School of Law, University of Dundee, Scrymgeour Building, Park Place, Dundee DD1 4HN; T.-01382-386795; e-mail: r.r.churchill@dundee.ac.uk

Clancy, Nina. Chief Executive, RSABI (formerly known as the Royal Scottish Argricultural Benevolent Institution), since 2013; Director, Scottish Agricultural Organisation Society Ltd; previously worked with NFU Scotland as Regional Manager for Lothian and Borders; self-employed insurance agent with NFU Mutual and Group Secretary for NFU Scotland based in the Scottish Borders; built up the business to be the largest agency in Scotland, giving her an in depth knowledge of the rural community and rural business. Director of Border Ice Rink Ltd; President, Border Ladies Curling. Address: The Rural Centre, West Mains, Ingliston, Newbridge, Midlothian EH28 8LT; T.-0131 472 4166; e-mail: nina.clancy@rsabi.org.uk

Clancy, Rev. P. Jill, BD, DipMin. Minister of Religion, Annbank linked with Tarbolton Parish Church of Scotland, since 2013; Chaplain at Kilmarnock Prison, since 2013; b.

10.7.70, Irvine; m., Frank J. Clancy. Educ. Kilwinning Academy; Aberdeen University. YTS, Cunningham District Council; Rating Clerk, Northern Ireland Trailers; Distribution Assistant, Caledonian Paper Mill; Minister of Religion, St. John's Church of Scotland, Gourock, 2000-08; Tron St. Mary's Church of Scotland, Balornock, Glasgow, 2008-2013. Recreations: play piano and sing; conducts a Community Choir called 'Songs for All'. Address: (b.) 1 Kirkport, Tarbolton, Ayrshire KA5 5QJ.

Clapham, David Charles, LLB, SSC. Solicitor (Principal, private practice, since 1984); Partner in Claphams Solicitors; Part-time Immigration Judge (formerly Adjudicator), since 2001; Part-time Sheriff, since 2007; Secretary, Glasgow, Argyll and Bute and Dunbartonshire Local Valuation Panel, since 1996; Part-time Tribunal Judge (formerly Part-time Chairman), Social Security Appeal Tribunals, since 1992, and Disability Appeal Tribunals, since 2000; Legal member, Mental Health Tribunal for Scotland, since 2005; Director, Legal Defence Union; Legal Assessor to General Medical Council, since 2010; Legal Assessor to Nursing and Midwifery Council, since 2011; Legal Assessor to General Teaching Council for Scotland, since 2012; b. 16.10.58, Giffnock; m., Debra Clapham; 1 s.; 2 d. Educ. Hutchesons' Boys' Grammar School, Glasgow; University of Strathclyde. Legal apprenticeship, 1979-81; admitted Solicitor, 1981; admitted Notary Public, 1982; founded own legal practice, 1984; part-time Tutor, University of Strathclyde, 1984-92; part-time Lecturer, Glasgow University, 1991-94; Secretary, Strathclyde Region Local Valuation Panel, 1988-96; Glasgow Bar Association: Secretary, 1987-91, Vice President, 1991-92, President, 1992-93; Secretary, Scottish Law Agents Society, 1994-97; Council Member, Royal Faculty of Procurators in Glasgow, 1996-99; Temporary Sheriff, 1998-99. Address: (b.) 1B & 1C Helena House, Clarkston Toll, Glasgow G76 7RA; T.-0141-620-0800.

Clark of Calton, (Baroness M. Lynda Clark), QC, LLB, PhD. Judge of the Court of Session in Scotland, since 2006; Advocate-General for Scotland, 1999-2006; MP (Labour), Edinburgh Pentlands, 1997-2005; Life Peer; Admitted Advocate, 1977; Lecturer in Jurisprudence, Dundee University, 1973-76; Standing Junior Counsel, Department of Energy, 1984-89; called to English Bar, 1988; appointed QC, 1989; contested Fife North East (Labour), 1992. Former Member, Scottish Legal Aid Board and Edinburgh University Court. Address: (b.) House of Lords, London, SW1A 0AA.

Clark, Anita, MA, BA (Hons), FRSA. Head of Dance, Creative Scotland, since 2004; b. 26.11.71, Dunfermline. Educ. Royal Scottish Academy of Music and Drama; London College of Dance; University of Buckinghamshire. Freelance community dance artist, 1992-96; Dance co-ordinator, Glasgow City Council, 1996-97; Education Officer, Birmingham Royal Ballet, 1998-2000; Artistic Director, Citymoves Dancespace, Aberdeen, 2001-04. Lisa Ullmann Fellowship awardee in 2004. Recreations: dance and performing arts. Address: (b.) Creative Scotland, Waverley Gate, 2-4 Waterloo Place, Edinburgh EH1 3EG; T.-0330 333 2000; e-mail: anita.clark@creativescotland.com

Clark, Professor Brian Drummond, BA, MA, MBE. Professor, Environmental Management and Planning, Aberdeen University, since 1994; Committee on Radioactive Waste Management (CORWM), since 2003; b. 22.1.38, Sherborne; m., Edwina Clegg; 1 s.; 2 d. Educ. Ashville College, Harrogate; Liverpool University. Board Member, Scottish Environment Protection Agency (SEPA), 2000-08; Chair, North

Region Board, SEPA and Chair, Planning and Finance Committee, 2000-08; Commission Member, Local Government Boundary Commission Scotland, 2007-13; Governor, Macaulay Land Use Institute, Aberdeen, 2005-11; Governor, The James Hutton Institute, since 2010. UNEP Global 500 Award; Author of 10 books. Recreations: croquet; gardening; Aberdeen FC. Address: (h.) 'Farragon', 513 North Deeside Road, Cults, Aberdeen AB15 9ES; T.-01224 867159; e-mail: briandrummondclark@btinternet.com

Clark, Bryan Malott, FC (Optom). Honorary Sheriff of Grampian Highland and Islands, since 2000; Retired Optometrist; b. 6.10.37, Orkney; m., Sheila Matheson Cusiter; 2 s.; 1 d. Educ. Kirkwall Grammar School; Stow College, Glasgow. Independent Optometrist in Orkney, 1961-2001. Past Orkney AOC Chairman; Past President, Rotary Club of Orkney; Past Chairman, Kirkwall Chamber of Commerce. Recreations: travel; gardening; golf. Address: (h.) Westwood, Berstane Road, Kirkwall, Orkney KW15 1NA; T.-01856 872659.
E-mail: westwoodclark@btinternet

Clark, David Alexander, EurIng, BEng (Hons), CEng, MIET. Managing Director, Dalzell Consulting Ltd, since 2002; b. 01.11.65, Duns; engaged to Judith Miller. Educ. Hamilton Grammar School; University of Strathclyde. Engineer and Manufacturing Manager, British Steel, Corus, 1987-98; Engineering Manager, Operations Development: Allied Distillers Ltd., 1998-2002; Chief Executive, Shetland Islands Council, 2009-2010. Scottish Chairman, Steel & Industrial Managers Association, 1992-98; Director, Allied Domecq First Pension Trust, 2000-02. Recreations: sports cars; Cuban cigars; malt whisky; hi-fi. Address: (h.) 3 Dalzell Castle, Dalzell Estate, Lanarkshire ML1 2SJ; T.-07919 274104; e-mail: david.clark@dalzell.org.uk

Clark, David Findlay, OBE, DL, MA, PhD, CPsychol, FBPsS, ARPS, FFICS. Deputy Lieutenant, Banffshire, 1992-2005; Consulting Clinical Psychologist; former Director, Area Clinical Psychology Services, Grampian Health Board; Clinical Senior Lecturer, Department of Mental Health, Aberdeen University; b. 30.5.30, Aberdeen; m., Janet Ann Stephen; 2 d. Educ. Banff Academy; Aberdeen University. Flying Officer, RAF, 1951-53; Psychologist, Leicester Industrial Rehabilitation Unit, 1953-56; Senior, then Principal Clinical Psychologist, Leicester Area Clinical Psychology Service, and part-time Lecturer, Leicester University and Technical College, 1956-66; WHO short-term Consultant, Sri Lanka, 1977; various lecturing commitments in Canada and USA, since 1968. Honorary Sheriff, Grampian and Highlands; former Governor, Aberdeen College of Education; Member, Grampian Children's Panel, 1970-85; Safeguarder (Social Work Scotland Act, 1969 and Children (Scotland) Act, 1995), 1985-2008; Past Chairman, Clinical Division, British Psychological Society. Publications: Help, Hospitals and the Handicapped, 1984; One Boy's War, 1997; Stand By Your Beds!, 2001; Stand By Your Beds!, 2nd Edition, 2006; Remember Who You Are!, 2007; Chancer, 2007; book chapters and technical and magazine articles. Recreations: photography; reading; writing; chess; guitar playing; painting and drawing; golf. Address: (h.) Glendeveron, 8 Deveron Terrace, Banff AB45 1BB; T.-01261 812624.
E-mail: drdavidfindlayclark@btinternet.com

Clark, Derek John, BMus (Hons), DipMusEd (Hons), DRSAMD. Head of Music, Scottish Opera, since 1997; b. 22.8.55, Glasgow; m., Heather Fryer; 1 d. Educ. Dumbarton Academy; Royal Scottish Academy of Music and Drama; University of Durham; London Opera Centre. Debut as professional accompanist, 1976; joined music staff, Welsh National Opera, 1977, conducting debut 1982; Guest Conductor, Mid Wales Opera, 1989-92; Guest Coach and Conductor, Welsh College of Music, 1990-97; Conductor,

South Wales Opera, 1994-96; Guest Coach at major Conservatoires, National Opera Studio, since 1997; arranger/composer since late 1980s including work for radio and television; musicals for young people; Orchestral Reductions of Operas (Pocket Publications); choral music (Pub: Roberton/Goodmusic). Appointed Musical Director, Dundee Choral Union, 2011. Silver Medallist, Worshipful Company of Musicians, 1976. Recreation: reading. Address: (b.) Scottish Opera, 39 Elmbank Crescent, Glasgow G2 4PT; T.-0141-248 4567.

Clark, Gregor Munro, CB, LLB. Counsel to the Scottish Law Commission, since 2006; b. 18.4.46, Glasgow; m., 1, Jane Maralyn Palmer (deceased); 2, Alexandra Groves Miller or Plumtree; 1 s.; 2 d. Educ. Queen's Park Senior Secondary School, Glasgow; Queen's College, St Andrews University. Admitted Faculty of Advocates, 1972; Lord Advocate's Department, 1974-99 (Assistant Parliamentary Draftsman, then Deputy Parliamentary Draftsman, then Parliamentary Draftsman); Counsel to the Scottish Law Commission, 1995-2000; Scottish Parliamentary Counsel, Scottish Executive, 1999-2002 and 2004-06; Scottish Parliamentary Counsel (UK), 2002-04. Recreation: piano. Address: (b.) Scottish Law Commission, 140, Causewayside, Edinburgh EH9 1PR; T.-0131 662 5219.
E-mail: gregor.clark@scotlawcom.gsi.gov.uk

Clark, Guy Wyndham Nial Hamilton, FCISI, JP. Lord Lieutenant of Renfrewshire, since 2007 (Vice Lord Lieutenant, Renfrewshire, 2002-07, Deputy Lieutenant, 1987-2002); JP Inverclyde, since 1987; b. 28.3.44; m., Brighid Lovell Greene; 2 s.; 1 d. Educ. Eton. Commd. Coldstream Guards, 1962-67; Investment Manager, Murray Johnstone Ltd., Glasgow, 1973-77; Partner, R.C. Greig & Co. (Stockbrokers), Glasgow, 1977-86; Director, Greig, Middleton & Co. Ltd., 1986-97; Managing Director, Murray Johnstone Private Investors Ltd., 1997-2001; Managing Director, Aberdeen Private Investors, 2001-06; Director, Bell Lawrie Investment Management, 2006-08. Member, Executive Committee, Erskine Hospital for Disabled Servicemen, 1986-97; Member, International Stock Exchange, 1983. Chairman, JP Advisory Committee, 1991-2002; President, The Reserve Forces and Cadets Association for the Lowlands of Scotland; Vice President, Erskine Hospital; Patron, Accord Hospice, Paisley; Hon. President, St Columba's School, Kilmacolm; Vice President, Army Cadet Force League (West Lowland); President, Renfrewshire and Inverclyde Branch - SSAFA; Hon. Patron, Glasgow Refrewshire Society. Recreations: gardening and field sports. Address: (h.) Braeton, Inverkip PA16 0DU; T.-01475 520 619; Fax: 01475 521 030.
E-mail: g.clark282@btinternet.com

Clark, Johnston Peter Campbell, LLB, DipLP, NP, MCISI. Managing Partner, Blackadders LLP Solicitors, since 1999; b. 29.10.62, Dundee; m., Sara Elizabeth Philp; 1 s.; 1 d. Educ. High School of Dundee; Aberdeen University. Trainee Solicitor, Blackadder Gilchrist and Robertson, 1984-86; Solicitor, Blackadder Reid Johnston, 1986-88; Partner, Blackadders LLP, since 1988. Past Dean, Faculty of Procurators and Solicitors, Dundee; Secretary, Dundee Disabled Children's Association; past Deacon, Baker Incorporation of Dundee. Recreations: watching football; playing tennis; garden. Address: (b.) 34 Reform Street, Dundee DD1 1RJ; T.-01382 229222; (b.) 5 Rutland Square, Edinburgh EH1 2AX; T.-0131 222 8000.
E-mail: johnston.clark@blackadders.co.uk

Clark, Katy. MP (Labour), North Ayrshire and Arran, 2005-2015; b. 3.7.67, Kilwinning. Educ. University of Aberdeen. Member of Scottish Affairs Committee, 2005-2010; Member of European Scrutiny Committee, 2005-2010; Member of the Procedure Committee, 2005-2010;

Member of Business, Innovation and Skills Committee, 2010-15; Member of Environmental Audit Committee, 2010-15; Member of Speakers' Panel of Chairs, 2010-15.

Clarke, Andrew David, MA, PhD. Emeritus Senior Lecturer, University of Aberdeen, since 2015, appointed Senior Lecturer in New Testament in 1995; b. 3.12.64, Bradford; m., Jane; 2 s.; 1 d. Educ. Dean Close School, Cheltenham; University of Cambridge (Girton College). Research Librarian, Tyndale House, Cambridge, 1990-95; Lecturer, then Senior Lecturer, New Testament, University of Aberdeen, since 1995. Chairman of Tyndale House Council, 2005-12; Trustee of Universities and Colleges Christian Fellowship, 2005-12; Member, Studiorum Novi Testamenti Societas. Publications: A Pauline Theology of Church Leadership, 2008; Serve the Community of the Church: Christians as Leaders and Ministers (First-Century Christians in the Graeco-Roman World), 2000; Secular and Christian Leadership in Corinth: A Socio-Historical and Exegetical Study of 1 Corinthians 1-6, 2nd Edition, 2006. Address: (b.) Divinity and Religious Studies, University of Aberdeen, Aberdeen AB24 3UB.

Clarke, (Christopher) Michael, CBE, BA (Hons), FRSE. Director, Scottish National Gallery, since 2000, Deputy to The Director-General, since 2007; b. 29.8.52, York; m., Deborah Clare Cowling; 2 s.; 1 d. Educ. Felsted School, Essex; Manchester University. Art Assistant, York City Art Gallery, 1973-76; Research Assistant, British Museum, 1976-78; Assistant Keeper in charge of prints, Whitworth Art Gallery, Manchester, 1978-84; Assistant Keeper, National Gallery of Scotland, 1984-87, Keeper, 1987-2000. Visiting Fellow, Yale Center for British Art, 1985; Clark Art Institute, 2004; Chevalier de l'Ordre des Arts et des Lettres, 2004; Fellow of the Royal Society of Edinburgh, 2008; Commander of the British Empire, 2009; Commander of the Order of the Dannebrog, 2012. Publications include: The Tempting Prospect; A Social History of English Watercolours; The Arrogant Connoisseur: Richard Payne Knight (Co-Editor); Lighting Up the Landscape – French Impressionism and its Origins; Corot and the Art of Landscape; Eyewitness Art – Watercolours; Corot, Courbet und die Maler von Barbizon (Co-Editor); Oxford Concise Dictionary of Art Terms; Monet: The Seine and The Sea (Co-author); The Playfair Project. Recreations: listening to music; golf. Address: (b.) Scottish National Gallery, The Mound, Edinburgh EH2 2EL; T.-0131-624 6511.

Clarke, Eric Lionel. MP (Labour), Midlothian, 1992-2001; b. 9.4.33, Edinburgh; m., June; 2 s.; 1 d. Educ. Holy Cross Academy; W.M. Ramsey Technical College; Esk Valley Technical College. Coal miner, 1949-77; General Secretary, NUM Scottish Area, 1977-89; County Councillor, Midlothian, 1962-74; Regional Councillor, Lothian, 1974-78. Recreations: fly fishing; gardening; carpentry. Address: (h.) 32 Mortonhall Park Crescent, Edinburgh; T.-0131-664 8214.

Clarke, John. Headteacher, Berwickshire High School, since 2012. Educ. Ripon, North Yorkshire. Senior Depute, Earlston High School, 2007-2012. Address: (b.) Duns, Berwickshire TD11 3QG; T.-01361 883 710; e-mail: bhs@scotborders.gov.uk

Clarke, Kevin John, BA. Emeritus University Secretary, University of Stirling, since 2012; b. 8.3.52, Reading; m., Linda Susan Stewart; 2 d. Educ. Presentation College, Reading; University of Stirling. Scientific Officer, British Library Lending Division, 1975-77; Administrative Assistant, Loughborough University, 1977-83; Assistant

Registrar, University of Newcastle upon Tyne, 1983-85; Clerk to the Senatus Academicus, 1985-89, Deputy Secretary, 1989-95, University of Aberdeen; University Secretary, University of Stirling, 1995-2012. Recreations: music; hill-walking; cycling. E-mail: kjc1@stir.ac.uk

Clarke, The Rt. Hon. Lord (Matthew Gerard Clarke), PC (2009). Senator of the College of Justice, since 2000. Educ. Holy Cross High School, Hamilton; Glasgow University (MA, LLB). Solicitor, 1972; Lecturer, Depatment of Scots Law, Edinburgh University, 1972-78; admitted, Faculty of Advocates, 1978; QC (Scot), 1989; a Judge, Courts of Appeal of Jersey and Guernsey, 1995-2000; Leader, UK Delegation, Council of the Bars and Law Societies of EC, 1992-96; Hon. Fellow, Europa Institute, Edinburgh University, since 1995.

Clarke, Owen J., CBE. Chairman, Scottish Ambulance Service, 1997-2003; Member, Accounts Commission for Scotland, 2003-09; Non-Executive Member, Programme Board, Scottish Government, 2007-2011; Chairman, Health Department, National Management Performance Committee, 2006-2011; b. 15.3.37, Edinburgh; m., Elizabeth; 2 s.; 1 d. Educ. Portobello High School, Edinburgh. Head of Inland Revenue, North of England, 1988-90; Head of Inland Revenue, Scotland, 1990-97. Trustee, Friends of Craigmillar, 1994-2001. Recreations: golf; hill-walking. Address: (h.) Dyngarth, Redholm Park, North Berwick EH39 4RA; T.-01620 892623.

Clarke, Rt. Hon. Thomas, CBE, JP. Former MP (Labour), Coatbridge and Chryston and Bellshill (formerly Monklands West); Shadow Secretary of State for Scotland, 1992-93; b. 10.1.41, Coatbridge. Educ. Columba High School, Coatbridge; Scottish College of Commerce. Former Assistant Director, Scottish Council for Educational Technology; Provost of Monklands, 1975-82; Past President, Convention of Scottish Local Authorities; MP, Coatbridge and Airdrie, 1982-83; author: Disabled Persons (Services Consultation and Representation) Act, 1986, International Development (Reporting and Transparency) Act, 2006; elected four times to Shadow Cabinet; Minister for Film and Tourism, 1997-98; director, amateur film, Give Us a Goal. Recreations: films; walking; reading.

Clarkson, Graeme Andrew Telford, LLB. Senior Partner, Clarkson Hamilton; b. 6.9.53, Fraserburgh; m., Moira; 3 s. Educ. High School of Dundee; Aberdeen University. Law Apprentice, Allan MacDougall & Co., Edinburgh; Assistant, Ranken & Reid, Edinburgh; Assistant, then Partner, then Senior Partner, Baird & Company. Past Chairman, Kirkcaldy Round Table; former Council Member, Law Society of Scotland; part time Convenor, Mental Health Tribunal for Scotland. Address: (b.) 2 Park Place, Kirkcaldy, Fife KY1 1XL; T.-01592 268608.

Cleland, Ronald John, BA. Member and Vice Convener, Court, University of Strathclyde, since 2008; Non Executive Director, Beatson Cancer Charity; Chair of Board, Audit Scotland, 2011-14; Board Member, NHS Greater Glasgow & Clyde, 1999-2011; Chairman, Prince & Princess of Wales Hospice, 2003-08; Non-executive Director, Scottish Government, 2010; Interim Chair, NHS Western Isles, 2006-07; Chairman, North Glasgow University Hospitals NHS Trust, 1998-2004; Chairman, West Glasgow Hospitals NHS Trust, 1997-98; Vice-Chairman, Yorkhill Hospitals NHS Trust, 1992-97; Non-Executive Adviser, Odgers Berndtson, 2006-2013; Director & Partner, Thomson Partners Ltd, 1987-2006; m., Sheena; 2 s.; 2 d. Educ. Allan Glen's

School; Strathclyde University. Recreations: sporting interests, both actively and as spectator; walking; reading; travel and music.
E-mail: ronnie.cleland@hotmail.com

Clifford, John Gilmore, MA (Oxon), MSc (Edin), FRSA. Honorary Consul of Austria for Scotland; Dean of Consular Corps in Edinburgh and Leith, 2014-2015; m. Elisa Trimby/Clifford, illustrator, engraver, artist, writer, taught at Glasgow School of Art (died 2001); 2 s: Ben, actor, Universities of Glasgow & Augsburg; Royal Conservatoire Scotland; Adam, percussionist/actor, Royal Academy of Music London; Jacques Lecoq Ecole Théâtre Internationale Paris; both also at Edinburgh International and Fringe Festivals. Educ. Henley on Thames Grammar School, Oxfordshire; St Catherine's College Oxford (Mod Langs); Goethe Institut, Germany; Europa Institute; University of Edinburgh, European Legal Studies, EU Environment Law. Hon Consul of Austria for Scotland, 2003; Dean, Consular Corps in Edinburgh and Leith, 2014-2015; Fellow, Royal Society of Art; Business Committee, General Council of University of Edinburgh; Consultant, Austrian Trade Commission and Austrian Cultural Forum; re-discovery in Edinburgh 2007 of ashes of Alfred Adler, Psychoanalyst/Founder Institute for Individual Psychology; historic meeting of Scottish Freudians and Austrian Adlerians Edinburgh, 2011; re-interment, Central Cemetery Vienna, 2011; European and international public affairs: political, cultural and ecological exchange; Quadro Europa, Edinburgh (public affairs as above); Focus Scotland Ltd (delegations, study/cultural/professional programmes); Freudenstadt Symposium (Professor Chris Harvie, former MSP), Universities of Edinburgh & Tübingen; Associate, University of Edinburgh, former Centre for Human Ecology, 1990s; Lothian Regional Councillor, 1994-1996 (esp European Affairs, Environmental Strategy); election campaigns: candidate (Labour) for European Parliament 1999, numerous local/regional elections; Branch Chairman; Council Member, Scottish Civic Forum (Environment/Europe), 2004-08; Community Councillor, Stockbridge/Inverleith, 2006-2011; Projects Director, St Andrew Foundation, public/constitutional affairs - Russia, 1996-2000; Secretary, Scottish Council of Fabian Societies, 1987-1997; Secretary/Chairman, Edinburgh Fabian Society, 1987-1998; Member, sometime Committee Member, European Movement, Scottish Council; Member, Edinburgh Committee, Helsinki Citizens Assembly, 1996-2009; Member/contributor, British-Yugoslav Society, then Scotland - South Slav Society, 1990s; Oyster Club Edinburgh; Chairman, Friends of Demarco Gallery, 1996-2000; Scottish Arts Club; Youth Music Theatre UK; Chairman, Friends of the Lyceum Youth Theatre, 2001-06. Publications/contributions/papers include: Joint translator, Earth Politics - Ernst Ulrich von Weizsäcker: Environmental Politics for the 21st century; Scottish Office report on sub-state legislation in Europe (reference Austria); Scotland's Place in Europe, John Wheatley Centre (CSPP); Freudenstadt Symposium, and papers, Regionalism in Europe, 2010 ongoing; low energy housing seminars, Scottish Parliament; regular renewable energy events, sustainable architecture with wood; seminars and exhibitions. Some interests: architecture; music; theatre and other performing arts; visual arts; cinema; reading and exchange of ideas; psychoanalysis; ecology; world/social affairs, especially Europe/Middle East (and beyond); political thought, cultures and anthropology - the Other: mountain walking; family and friends; conversation and laughter. Address: (h/w) Austrian Consulate & Focus Scotland, 9 Howard Place, Edinburgh EH3 5JZ; T.-0131 558 1124; e-mail: johnclifford@focusscotland.co.uk; mobile: 07968 97 57 83.

Clift, Benedict, BMSc (Hons), MBChB, FRCSEd, FRCSOrth. Consultant Orthopaedic and Trauma Surgeon, Ninewells Hospital, Dundee, since 1995; Honorary Senior Lecturer, Dundee University; b. 22.7.62, Manchester; m., Alison; 1 s.; 2 d. Educ. Cardinal Langley Grammar School; Dundee University. Recreations: jazz; trees; Dante; Homer; classical piano; wrist watches. Address: (b.) Department of Orthopaedic and Trauma Surgery, Ninewells Hospital, Dundee DD1 9SY; T.-01382 660111; e-mail: ben.clift@nhs.net

Clitheroe, Neil, BSc. Global Retail Director, Iberdrola, since 2016; Chief Executive Officer, Retail and Generation, ScottishPower, 2011-16; m.; 1 d. Educ. University of Bath; Copenhagen Business School. Formerly Vice President of customer service for Iberdrola USA, responsible for all customer-facing office and field activities across Iberdrola USA's three operating companies — Central Maine Power, NYSEG and RG&E —which deliver natural gas and electric energy to 2.4 million customers in the North-eastern United States. Completed the Achieving Breakthrough Service program at the Harvard Business School and the Advanced Leadership program at the Wharton School, University of Pennsylvania. Address: (b.) Atlantic Quay, Robertson Street, Glasgow G2 8SP; T.-0141 568 2000.

Clive, Eric McCredie, CBE, MA, LLB, LLM, SJD, Dr hc, FRSE. Honorary Professor, School of Law, Edinburgh University, since 2014; b. 24.7.38, Stranraer; m., Kay McLeman; 2 d. Educ. Stranraer Academy; Stranraer High School; Universities of Edinburgh, Michigan, Virginia. Lecturer, Senior Lecturer, Reader, Professor of Scots Law, Faculty of Law, Edinburgh University, 1962-81; Commissioner, Scottish Law Commission, 1981-99; Visiting Professor, School of Law, Edinburgh University, 1999-2014. Publications: The Law of Husband and Wife in Scotland (4th edition), 1997; Principles, Definitions and Model Rules of European Private Law (co-editor), 2009; legal articles. Address: (h.) 14 York Road, Edinburgh EH5 3EH; T.-0131-552 2875.

Clouting, David Wallis, BDS, MSc, LDSRCS (Eng), DDPH, FFPH. Clinical Director of Community Dental Services, Borders Primary Care NHS Trust, 2000-03, NHS Borders, 2003-2013; b. 29.3.53, London; m., Dr. Margaret M.C. Bacon; 3 s.; 1 d. Educ. Leyton County High School for Boys; University College Hospital Dental School, London; Institute of Dental Surgery, London; Joint Department of Dental Public Health, London Hospital Medical College and University College. Senior Dental Officer for Special Needs, East and North Hertfordshire Health Authorities, 1983-90; Chief Administrative Dental Officer, Borders Health Board, 1990-95; Community Dental Services Manager, Borders Community Health Services NHS Trust, 1995-99. Recreations: amateur radio; cooking; hill walking. Address: (h.) 36 Gallowhill, Peebles EH45 9BG.

Clow, Robert George Menzies. Former Chairman, John Smith & Son (Glasgow) Ltd. (Managing Director (1969-94); b. 27.1.34, Sian, Shensi, North China; m., Katrina M. Watson (divorced). Educ. Eltham College, London. Interned by Japanese as a child; National Service, RAF; trained as a bookseller, Bumpus London; worked in Geneva; joined John Smith & Son (Glasgow), 1960. Founded, with others, The New Glasgow Society, 1965 (Chairman 1967, 1968); worked for 12 years in rehabilitating St. Vincent Crescent, Glasgow, as founder member, St. Vincent Crescent Area Association; Secretary, First Glasgow Housing Association, since 1978; Past Chairman, Heritage Buildings Preservation Trust, currently Trustee. Restored Aiket Castle, 1976-79 (winner of an Europa Nostra Merit Award, 1989); National Trust for Scotland: Member, Council 1978 and 1991, Member, Executive, 1980-90; formerly Executive Member, Committee, Strathclyde Building Preservation Trust, 1986; Architectural Heritage Fund Council of Management, 1989-

2001. Recreations: farming; bee keeping; opera; restoring old houses; swimming; reading on holiday. Address: Millhouse of Aiket by Aiket Castle, Dunlop, Ayrshire; T.-(b.) 015604 84643.

Clugston, Dr. Carol, BSc (Hons), PhD, CMgr, FCMI, FLF. College Secretary/COO, College of Medical, Veterinary & Life Sciences, University of Glasgow, since August 2010; b. 26.10.62, Glasgow; m., Ewan J. Graham; 1 s. Educ. Dumbarton Academy; University of Glasgow. Research Scientist, Cancer Research Campaign, Beatson Laboratories, 1989-94; Nanoelectronics Research Centre Administrator, University of Glasgow, 1994-98; Executive Assistant to Vice-Principal (Research), University of Glasgow, 1998-2000; Secretary to the Faculty of Medicine/Head of Division of Education and Administration, University of Glasgow, 2005-2010. Community Councillor, Stepps & District. Recreations: silversmithing; painting. Address: (b.) MVLS College Office, Wolfson Medical School Building, University of Glasgow, University Avenue, Glasgow G12 8QQ; T.-0141-330-3142; e-mail: carol.clugston@glasgow.ac.uk

Clydesmuir, 3rd Baron (David Ronald Colville); b. 8.4.49; m.; 2 s.; 2 d. Educ. Charterhouse. Succeeded to title, 1996.

Cobbe, Professor Stuart Malcolm, MA, MD, FRCP, FMedSci, FRSE. Professor of Medical Cardiology, Glasgow University, 1985-2008; Consultant Cardiologist (Part-Time), Glasgow Royal Infirmary, since 2008; b. 2.5.48, Watford; m., Patricia Frances; 3 d. Educ. Royal Grammar School, Guildford; Cambridge University. Training in medicine, Cambridge and St. Thomas Hospital, London; qualified, 1972; specialist training in cardiology, National Heart Hospital, London, and John Radcliffe Hospital, Oxford; research work, University of Heidelberg, 1981; Consultant Cardiologist and Senior Lecturer, Oxford, 1982-85. Recreation: cycling. Address: (b.) Department of Medical Cardiology, Walton Building, Royal Infirmary, Glasgow G31 2ER; T.-0141-211 4722.

Coburn, David. Member of the European Parliament for Scotland (United Kingdom Independence Party), since 2014; b. 11.2.59, Glasgow. Educ. High School of Glasgow; University of Leeds. Ran the Lexicon School of English in Kensington in 1993; worked as an art dealer and City of London trader before owning a freight company. Contested the seat of Old Bexley and Sidcup in 2010; also stood in Bexley and Bromley in the 2012 London Assembly election.

Cochrane, Keith, FRSE. Chief Executive, The Weir Group PLC, since 2009; m.; 2 c. Following a number of years with Arthur Andersen, joined Stagecoach Group plc, 1993, appointed Finance Director, 1996 and Group Chief Executive, 2000; joined Scottish Power plc, 2003, became Director of Group Finance; joined The Weir Group as Finance Director, 2006. Chartered Accountant and Member of the Institute of Chartered Accountants of Scotland; Non-Executive Director, Royal Scottish National Orchestra Society Ltd. Recreations: golf; gardening; watching Scotland play rugby. Address: (b.) Head Office, Clydesdale Bank Exchange, 20 Waterloo Street, Glasgow G2 6DB; T.-0141 637 7111.

Cochrane of Cults, 4th Baron (Ralph Henry Vere Cochrane), DL; b. 20.9.26; m.; 2 s.; succeeded to title, 1990. Educ. Eton; King's College, Cambridge.

Cockburn, Professor Forrester, CBE, FRSE, MD, FRCPGlas, FRCPEdin, FRCPCH (Hon), FRCSEd (Hon), DCH. Past Chairman, Yorkhill NHS Trust; Emeritus Professor and Senior Research Fellow, Department of Child Health, Royal Hospital for Sick Children, Yorkhill, Glasgow; formerly Samson Gemmell Professor of Child Health, Glasgow University; b. 13.10.34, Edinburgh; m., Alison Fisher Grieve; 2 s. Educ. Leith Academy; Edinburgh University. Early medical training, Edinburgh Royal Infirmary, Royal Hospital for Sick Children, Edinburgh, and Simpson Memorial Maternity Pavilion, Edinburgh; Research Fellow in Paediatric Metabolic Disease, Boston University; Visiting Professor, San Juan University, Puerto Rico; Nuffield Fellow, Institute for Medical Research, Oxford University; Wellcome Senior Research Fellow, then Senior Lecturer, Department of Child Life and Health, Edinburgh University. Publications: a number of articles and textbooks on paediatric medicine, neonatal medicine, nutrition and metabolic diseases. Recreations: gardening and walking. Address: (b.) 53, Hamilton Drive, Glasgow G12 8DP; T.-0141 339 2973.

Cockburn, Dr. Hermione. British television and radio presenter; Scientific Director, Our Dynamic Earth, since 2014; b. 1973, Sussex; m.; 2 s. Educ. University of Edinburgh. Worked at various academic institutes including a two-year post-doctorate at the School of Earth Sciences at the University of Melbourne; has carried out extensive fieldwork in Antarctica, Australia, and Namibia; helped to establish the education service Our Dynamic Earth; presented BBC's Tomorrow's World and Rough Science; regular presenter of Resource Review on the Teachers' TV channel, 2005-2010. Associate lecturer with the Open University, teaching environmental science in Scotland. Publication: The Fossil Detectives: Discovering Prehistoric Britain (Co-Author), 2008. Address: 112-116 Holyrood Gait, Edinburgh EH8 8AS; T.-0131 550 7800.

Cockhead, Peter, BSc (Econ), MA, MSc, MRTPI, MZIP. Town Planning Adviser to Zambian Government (for VSO); Teaching Fellow in Town and Regional Planning, University of Dundee; Associate, BusinessLab, Aberdeen; b. 1.12.46, Beckenham; m., Diana Douglas; 2 s.; 1 d. Educ. Beckenham Grammar School; London School of Economics; University of Witwatersrand, South Africa; University of Edinburgh. Lecturer: University of Witwatersrand, 1970-71, University of Edinburgh, 1973-74; Consultant: OECD, Paris, 1974, Percy Johnson-Marshall and Associates, Edinburgh, 1974-75; Grampian Regional Council: Assistant Director of Planning, 1975-83, Depute Director of Planning, 1983-90, Regional Planning Manager, 1990-95; Director of Planning and Strategic Development, Aberdeen City Council, 1995-2001; Director, North East Scotland Transport Partnership (NESTRANS), 2002-07. Chairman, Scottish Society of Directors of Planning, 1997-98; Chairman, Scottish Planning Education Forum, 1999-2001; Executive Secretary, North Sea Commission, 1992-95; Member, Scottish Executive Committee, Royal Town Planning Institute, 2009-2011. Recreations: hillwalking; open water swimming; music.
E-mail: peter.cockhead@live.co.uk

Coffey, Willie, MSP (SNP), Kilmarnock and Irvine Valley, since 2011, Kilmarnock and Loudoun, 2007-2011; b. 24.5.58. Educ. University of Strathclyde. Formerly a councillor on East Ayrshire Council; Software Development Manager, then Quality and Risk Manager with Learning and Teaching Scotland. Address: (b.) Scottish Parliament, Edinburgh EH99 1SP.

Cogdell, Professor Richard John, BSc, PhD, FRS, FRSE, FRSA, FSB. Hooker Professor of Botany, Glasgow University, since 1993; b. 4.2.49, Guildford; m., Barbara; 1 s.; 1 d. Educ. Royal Grammar School, Guildford; Bristol University. Post-doctoral research, USA, 1973-75; Botany Department, Glasgow University, 1975-94, now Institute of Molecular, Cell and Systems Biology in the College of Medical, Veterinary and Life Sciences. Member, Board of

104 WHO'S WHO IN SCOTLAND

Governors, Scottish Crop Research Institute, 1997-2005; Chairman, Trustees, Glasgow Macintyre Begonia Trust; Member, Council of the Biochemical Society, 2007-2010; Chairman of the Scientific Advisory Board of the Max Planck Institute for Bioinorganic Chemistry, Mülheim-an-der-Ruhr, 2007-2013; Trustee Director of The Genome Analysis Centre, 2009-2012; President of the International Society for Photosynthesis Research, 2013; Council of BBSRC, 2013. Recreations: cricket; aerobics; Scottish dancing; theatre. Address: (b.) Institute of Molecular, Cell and Systems Biology, GBRC, Glasgow University, Glasgow G12 8QQ; T.-0141-330 4232.
E-mail: Richard.Cogdell@glasgow.ac.uk

Coggins, Professor John Richard, MA, PhD, OBE, FRSE, FRSB. Emeritus Professor of Molecular Enzymology, School of Biology, Glasgow University; b. 15.1.44, Bristol; m., Dr. Lesley F. Watson; 1 s.; 1 d. Educ. Bristol Grammar School; The Queen's College, Oxford; Ottawa University. Post-doctoral Fellow: Biology Department, Brookhaven National Laboratory, New York, 1970-72, Biochemistry Department, Cambridge University, 1972-74; Glasgow University: Lecturer/Senior Lecturer/Professor, Biochemistry Department, 1974-95, Director, Graduate School of Biomedical and Life Sciences, 1995-97, Head, Division of Biochemistry and Molecular Biology, 1997-98, Research Director, Institute of Biomedical and Life Sciences, 1998-2000, Director/Dean, Institute of Biomedical and Life Sciences, 2000-05; Vice-Principal, Life Sciences, Medicine & Veterinary Medicine, 2006-09; Pro Vice-Principal, 2009-10. Biochemical Society: Chair, Molecular Enzymology Group, 1982-85; Chair, Policy Committee, 2004-8; Chair, Portland Press, 2010-13. SERC: Chair, Biophysics & Biochemistry Committee, 1985-88; Managing Director, Biomac Ltd., 1988-94; Member, DTI-Research Councils Biotechnology Joint Advisory Board, 1989-94; AFRC Council, 1991-94; Biochemistry Adviser to UFC, 1989-92; Governing Member, Caledonian Research Foundation, 1994-2007, Chair, 2008-09; Chair, HEFC Biochemistry Research Assessment Panel, 1995-96; Royal Society of Edinburgh: Research Awards Convener, 1999-2002, Vice President (Life Sciences), 2003-06; Chairman, RSE Scotland Foundation, 2009-12; Member, Scottish Science Advisory Committee, 2002-07; Chairman, Heads of University Biological Science Departments, 2003-07; Trustee, Glasgow Science Centre, since 2004; BBSRC Council, 2008-14; RIN Advisory Board, 2005-11; Treasurer, Biosciences Federation, 2007-09; Royal Society of Biology Council, 2009-17. Recreations: gardening; travelling. Address: 5 Chapelton Gardens, Bearsden, Glasgow G61 2DH; T.-0141-942-5082.
E-mail: john.coggins@glasgow.ac.uk

Cohen, Professor Anthony Paul, CBE, BA, MSc (SocSc), PhD, HonDSc (Edin), FRSE. Honorary Professor of Social Anthropology, University of Edinburgh; Emeritus Professor, Queen Margaret University; b. 3.8.46, London; m., Professor Bronwen J. Cohen OBE; 3 s. Educ. Whittlehame College, Brighton; Southampton University. Research Fellow, Memorial University of Newfoundland, 1968-70; Assistant Professor, Queen's University, Kingston, Ontario, 1970-71; Lecturer/Senior Lecturer in Social Anthropology, Manchester University, 1971-89; Professor of Social Anthropology, Edinburgh University, 1989-2003 (Provost of Law and Social Sciences, 1997-2002); Principal and Vice-Chancellor, Queen Margaret University, Edinburgh, 2003-09. Convener, Scottish Forum for Graduate Education, 1996-98; Convener, Universities Scotland Health Committee, 2006-09. Publications: The Management of Myths; The Symbolic Construction of Community; Whalsay: Symbol, Segment and Boundary in a Shetland Island Community; Self Consciousness: an alternative anthropology of identity; Belonging (Editor); Symbolising Boundaries (Editor); Humanising the City?

(Co-Editor); Questions of Consciousness (Co-Editor); Signifying Identities (Editor). Recreations: occasional thinking; music; novels.

Cohen, Lady Patricia Townsend Wade, BSc, PhD. Honorary Professor of Molecular Biology, Dundee University, since 2001; Head of Molecular Biology and Special Appointments Career Scientist, Medical Research Council Protein Phosphorylation Unit, Department of Biochemistry, University of Dundee, 1991-2009; Fellow of the Society of Biology; b. 3.5.44, Worsley, Lancashire; m., Professor Sir Philip Cohen (qv); 1 s.; 1 d. Educ. Bolton School; University College, London. Postdoctoral Research Fellow, Department of Medical Genetics, Washington University, Seattle, USA, 1969-71; Department of Biochemistry, University of Dundee: Science Research Council Fellowship, 1971-72, Research/Teaching Fellow (part-time), 1972-83, Lecturer (part-time), 1983-90, Senior Lecturer, 1990-91, Honorary Reader, 1995. Publications: 160 articles and reviews in scientific journals; Editor, Inhibitors of Protein Kinases and Protein Phosphatases, 2004. Recreations: reading; golf. Address: (h.) Inverbay Bramblings, Invergowrie, Dundee DD2 5DQ; T.-01382 562328; e-mail: p.t.w.cohen@dundee.ac.uk

Cohen, Professor Sir Philip, BSc, PhD, FRS, FRSE, FFMedSci, FAA. Professor of Enzymology, University of Dundee, since 2010; Director of the Scottish Institute for Cell Signalling (SCILLS), 2008-2012; Honorary Director, Medical Research Council Protein Phosphorylation Unit, 1990-2012; Director, Wellcome Trust Biocentre, 1997-2007; b. 22.7.45, London; m., Patricia Townsend Wade (qv); 1 s.; 1 d. Educ. Hendon County Grammar School; University College, London. Science Research Council/NATO postdoctoral Fellow, Department of Biochemistry, University of Washington, 1969-71; Dundee University: Lecturer in Biochemistry, 1971-78, Reader in Biochemistry, 1978-81, Professor of Enzymology, 1981-84; Royal Society Research Professor, 1984-2010. Publications: over 500 papers and reviews, one book. Recreations: bridge; golf; natural history. Address: (h.) Inverbay Bramblings, Invergowrie, Dundee; T.-01382 562328.

Cohen, Professor Stephen Douglas, BSc, PhD. Emeritus Professor, University of Glasgow (formerly Professor of Number Theory, 2002-09); b. 7.1.44, London; m., Yvonne Joy Roulet; 2 d. Educ. Allan Glen's School, Glasgow; University of Glasgow. Department of Mathematics, University of Glasgow: Lecturer, 1968, Senior Lecturer, 1988, Reader, 1992; visiting positions: Research Associate, University of Illinois, 1979, Lecturer, University of Witwatersrand, 1987, Professor, University of Limoges, France, 1994; Member, various editorial boards including: Finite Fields and Their Applications, since 1995, Applicable Algebra, 1996-2008, Glasgow Mathematical Journal, 1986-99 and 2002-07, Proceedings of Edinburgh Mathematical Society, 1991-97. Publications: over 100 articles in mathematics research journals. Recreations: walking; music appreciation, church activities. Address: (b.) Department of Mathematics, University of Glasgow Glasgow G12 8QW; T.-0141-330 6356.
E-mail: sdc@maths.gla.ac.uk

Cohn, Professor Samuel Kline, MA, PhD, FRHistS. Professor of History, Glasgow University, since 1995; b. 1949, Birmingham, Alabama; m., Genevieve Warwick; 2 s. Educ. Indian Springs School; Harvard University. Assistant Professor, Wesleyan University, Connecticut, 1978-79; Assistant Professor, Brandeis University, 1979-86; Associate Professor of History, Brandeis University, 1986-89; Visiting Professor, Brown University, 1990-91; Professor of History, Brandeis University, 1989-95.

Publications include: Women in the Streets: Essays on Sex and Power in the Italian Renaissance, 1996; The Cult of Remembrance and the Black Death: Six Renaissance Cities in Central Italy, 1997; The Black Death and the Transformation of the West (Co-author), 1997; Creating the Florentine State: Peasants and Rebellion, 1348-1434, 1999; The Black Death Transformed: Disease and Culture in Early Renaissance Europe, 2002; Popular Protest in Late Medieval Europe; Lust for Liberty: The Politics of Social Revolt in Medieval Europe, 1200-1425, 2006; Cultures of Plague in Sixteenth-Century Italy, 2009. Recreation: hill-running. Address: (h.) 14 Hamilton Drive, Glasgow; T.-0141-330 4369.

Cole-Hamilton, Alex. MSP (Scottish Liberal Democrat), Edinburgh Western, since 2016. Educ. University of Aberdeen (President of the Students' Association). Liberal Democrat candidate: Scottish Parliament elections in 2003 for Kirkcaldy and 2007 for Stirling; United Kingdom general election in 2005 for Kirkcaldy and Cowdenbeath. Address: Scottish Parliament, Edinburgh EH99 1SP.

Cole-Hamilton, Anni, MA Hons (Eng Lang + Lit) Edin. Principal, Moray Firth Tutorial College, since 1999; Principal, Moray Firth School, 2002-2010; b. 24.9.49, Cupar, Fife; m., Simon Cole-Hamilton; 2 d. Educ. Craigholme, Glasgow; Hutchesons' Grammar, Glasgow; George Watson's, Edinburgh; Edinburgh University. Founder and Principal of Moray Firth School. Founder, Chairman (and worst player) of The Truly Terrible Orchestra, Inverness. Recreations: laughter with friends and family; reading; red wine; walking. Address: (b.) 94 Academy Street, Inverness IV1 1LU; T.-01463 716151; e-mail: ach@mfschool.co.uk

Cole-Hamilton, Professor David John, BSc, PhD, CChem, FRSC, FRSE. Emeritus Professor, University of St Andrews, since 2014, Irvine Professor of Chemistry, 1985-2014; b. 22.5.48, Bovey Tracey; m. (1), Elizabeth Ann Brown (diss. 2008) 2 s.; 2 d.; m. (2), Rosemary Elizabeth Macrae (née Semple). Educ. Haileybury and ISC; Hertford; Edinburgh University. Research Assistant, Temporary Lecturer, Imperial College, 1974-78; Lecturer, Senior Lecturer, Liverpool University, 1978-85. Sir Edward Frankland Fellow, Royal Society of Chemistry, 1984-85; Corday Morgan Medallist, 1983; President: Chemistry Section, British Association for the Advancement of Science, 1995, Chemistry Sectional Committee, Royal Society of Edinburgh, 1993-95; President, Dalton Division, Royal Society of Chemistry, since 2013; Vice President and President Elect, European Association of Chemical and Molecular Sciences (EuCheMs), 2013-14, President, since 2014; Vice President, Royal Society of Chemistry, Dalton Council, 1996-99; Royal Society of Edinburgh Education Committee, since 2012; Museums and Galleries Commission Award for Innovation in Conservation, 1995 (runner-up); Royal Society of Chemistry Award for Organometallic Chemists, 1998; Tilden Lecturer, Royal Society of Chemistry, 2000-2001; Sir Geoffrey Wilkinson Prize Lecturer of the Royal Society of Chemistry, 2005-06; Scientific Editor, Journal of the Chemical Society, Dalton Transactions, 2000-03. Address: (b.) Department of Chemistry, The Purdie Building, St. Andrews, Fife KY16 9ST; T.-01334 463805; e-mail: djc@st-and.ac.uk

Colella, Professor Anton, BA (Hons), DipEd. Chief Executive, Institute of Chartered Accountants of Scotland, since 2006; Chairman, Scottish Council of Independent Schools, since 2010; Chairman, Global Accounting Alliance, since 2011; Chief Executive, Scottish Qualifications Authority, 2003-06 (Director of Qualifications, 2002-03); b. 25.5.61, Glasgow; m., Angela; 2 s.; 2 d. Educ. St Mungo's Academy, Glasgow; Stirling University. Teacher of Religious Education, Holyrood Secondary School, Glasgow, 1983-87; Principal Teacher of Religious Education, St Columba's High School, Gourock, 1987-92, Holyrood Secondary School, 1992-96; Assistant Head Teacher, Holyrood Secondary School, 1996-99; Depute Head Teacher, St Margaret Mary's Secondary, Glasgow, 1999-20001; seconded to Scottish Qualifications Authority, 2001; Board Member: Glasgow College of Nautical Studies, 1998, Quality Assurance Agency Scotland Committee, 2001, Scottish Further Education Unit, 2001, CBI Scotland, 2008, Columba 1400, 2008; Honorary Professor of Education, University of Glasgow, since 2012; Honorary Doctorate, BPP University, since 2014; Board Member, Adam Smith Business School, since 2013. Recreations: family life; music; rugby; eating out. Address: (b.) CA House, 21 Haymarket Yards, Edinburgh EH12 5BH; T.-0131-347 0266; e-mail: acolella@icas.org.uk

Collins, Rev. Catherine E. E., MA (Hons), BD, CertEd, DipCounselling. Parish Minister, Broughty Ferry New Kirk, since 2006; b. 12.11.54, Hastings; m., Rev. David A. Collins; 2 s. Educ. Kelso High School; University of St. Andrews. Teacher of English, Full Time and Temporary in Borders and Renfrewshire, 1977-89; Parish Minister (Job Share), Greyfriars Parish Church, Lanark, 1993-2006. (Past) Moderator of Presbytery; Depute Presbytery Clerk; Convener, Pastoral Support, Church of Scotland's Board of Ministry; currently Trustee, Housing and Loan Fund for Retired Ministers; member, Ministries' Council; Honorary chaplain, University of Abertay. Recreations: gardening; walking; genealogy. Address: (h./b.) 25 Ballinard Gardens, Broughty Ferry, Dundee DD5 1BZ; T.-01382 778874; e-mail: ccollins@broughtynewkirk.com

Collins, Rev. David Arthur, BSc (Hons) Zoology, BD. Parish Minister (Church of Scotland): Auchterhouse linked with Monikie and Newbigging and Murroes and Tealing, since 2009; Auchterhouse linked with Murroes and Tealing, since 2006; b. 15.6.51, Dumbarton; m., Rev. Catherine E.E. Collins; 2 s. Educ. Clydebank High School; University of Glasgow; University of St. Andrews; Jordanhill College. Teacher of Biology, Selkirk High School, 1974-79; Assistant Education Officer, Glasgow Museum Education Service, 1979-88; Education Officer, Dundee Art Galleries and Museums, 1988-89; (BD/Ministry Training, 1989-93); Parish Minister, Lanark: Greyfriars, 1993-2006; Parish Minister, Auchterhouse linked with Murroes and Tealing, 2006-09. Part-time Biology Teaching, Lanark Grammar School, 1998-2006; Church of Scotland National Assessor, since 2010; Church of Scotland Recruitment Task Group Member, since 2011; Moderator, Presbytery of Dundee, 2015-16. Recreations: photography; drawing and painting; reading; swimming; walking. Address: 25 Ballinard Gardens, Broughty Ferry, Dundee DD5 1BZ; T.-01382 778874; e-mail: dcollins@webartz.com

Collins, Dennis Ferguson, MA, LLB, WS, FRPSL. Senior Partner, Carlton Gilruth, Solicitors, Dundee, 1976-93; Honorary Sheriff; b. 26.3.30, Dundee; m., Elspeth Margaret Nicoll; 1 s.; 1 d. Educ. High School of Dundee; St. Andrews University. Solicitor, 1957; Part-time Lecturer in Scots Law, St. Andrews University, then Dundee University, 1960-79; Dean, Faculty of Procurators and Solicitors in Dundee, 1987-89; Agent Consulaire for France in Dundee, 1976-96; Hon. Secretary, Dundee Society for Prevention of Cruelty to Children, 1962-90; Assessor to the Lord Dean of Guild of Dundee, 1989-2011; Clerk to the Guildry Incorporation of Dundee, 1993-2000; Treasurer, Dundee Congregational Church, since 1966; Past President,

Dundee and District Philatelic Society; Past President, Association of Scottish Philatelic Societies; Fellow of the Royal Philatelic Society of London. Recreations: family and local history; Chinese postal history; gardening; travelling in France; reading. Address: (h.) Stirling Lodge, Craigiebarn Road, Dundee DD4 7PL; T.-01382 458070.

Collins, Sir Kenneth Darlingston, BSc (Hons), MSc; b. 12.8.39, Hamilton; m., Georgina Frances Pollard; 1 s.; 1 d. Educ. St. John's Grammar School; Hamilton Academy; Glasgow University; Strathclyde University. Steelworks apprentice, 1956-59; University, 1960-65; Planning Officer, 1965-66; WEA Tutor, 1966-67; Lecturer: Glasgow College of Building, 1967-69, Paisley College of Technology, 1969-79; Member: East Kilbride Town and District Council, 1973-79, Lanark County Council, 1973-75, East Kilbride Development Corporation, 1976-79; Chairman, NE Glasgow Children's Panel, 1974-76; European Parliament: Deputy Leader, Labour Group, 1979-84, Chairman, Environment Committee, 1979-84 and 1989-99 (Vice-Chairman, 1984-87), Socialist Spokesman on Environment, Public Health and Consumer Protection, 1984-89; Member (Labour), European Parliament, 1979-99; Chairman, Scottish Environment Protection Agency, 1999-2007; Ambassador for the National Asthma Campaign, until 2007; Chairman, Advisory Committee, SAGES (Scottish Association of Geosciences, Environment & Society), 2008-2010. Fellow, Royal Scottish Geographical Society; Hon. Fellow, Chartered Institution of Water and Environmental Management; Hon. Fellow, Chartered Institution of Wastes Management; former Board Member, Institute for European Environmental Policy, London; Fellow, Industry and Parliament Trust; former Board Member, Energy Action Scotland; former Member, British Waterways Scotland Group; former Trustee, The Green Foundation; Board Member, Central Scotland Forest Trust, 2001-04 (Chairman, 1998-2001); Former Board Member, Forward Scotland; Chairman, Tak Tent Cancer Support, 1999-2002; former Member, Management Board, European Environment Agency; Honorary Vice President, Environment Protection UK, until 2009; Vice President, Royal Environmental Health Institute of Scotland, until 2009; Vice President: Town and Country Planning Association, The Trading Standards Institute, The Association of Drainage Authorities, until 2009; former Chairman, Health Equality Europe; Member, Advisory Board, ESRC Genomics Policy and Research Forum, until 2005; Member: European Public Affairs Consultancies Association (EPACA) Professional Practices Panel, until 2009, European Commission High Level Group on Competitiveness, Energy and the Environment, 2006-08. Knighthood in 2003 for services to Environmental Protection; Honorary Degree of Doctor, University of Paisley, 2004; Honorary Doctor of Science, University of Glasgow, 2009. Recreations: music; dogs; gardening. Address: (b.) 11 Stuarton Park, East Kilbride G74 4LA; T.-01355 221345; e-mail: ken.collins@blueyonder.co.uk

Collins, Kenneth E., MPhil, PhD, FRCGP. President, Glasgow Jewish Representative Council, 1995-98 and 2004-07 (Hon. President, 1998-2001); Chairman, Scottish Council of Jewish Communities, 1999-2003 and 2007-08; Chairman, Scottish Jewish Archives Centre; b. 23.12.47, Glasgow; m., Irene Taylor; 1 s.; 3 d. Educ. High School of Glasgow; Glasgow University. General medical practitioner in Glasgow, 1978-2007; Medical Officer, Newark Lodge, Glasgow; Research Fellow, Centre for the History of Medicine, Glasgow University; Visiting Professor, Hebrew University of Jerusalem, since 2007. Past Chairman, Glasgow Board of Jewish Education. Publications: Aspects of Scottish Jewry, 1987; Go and Learn: International Story of the Jews and Medicine in Scotland, 1988; Second City Jewry, 1990; Be Well!, Jewish Immigrant Health and Welfare in Glasgow, 1860-1914, 2001; ed., Scotland's

Jews, 2nd Edition, 2008; Narrative editor, Jewish Glasgow, an Illustrated History (2013). Address: (h.) 2/2 11 Kennedy Court, Braidholm Crescent, Giffnock, Glasgow G46 6HH. E-mail: drkcollins@gmail.com

Coltman, Professor Viccy, BA, MA, PhD, FSA (London). Professor of Eighteenth-Century History of Art, University of Edinburgh (Head of History of Art, 2010-13); b. 15.4.72, Leamington Spa. BA, University of Bristol, 1990-93; MA, Courtauld Institute of Art, 1994-95, PhD, 1996-99; appointed Lecturer, History of Art, University of Edinburgh, 2002, Senior Lecturer, 2006. Philip Leverhulme Prize, 2006. Recreation: yoga. Publications: Fabricating the Antique: Neoclassicism in Britain; Classical Sculpture and the Culture of Collecting (Author). Address: (b.) 20 Chambers Street, Edinburgh EH1 1JZ; T.-0131 650 4124; e-mail: viccy.coltman@ed.ac.uk

Coltrane, Robbie, DA. Actor/Director; b. 31.3.50, Glasgow. Educ. Trinity College, Glenalmond; Glasgow School of Art. Film credits: Subway Riders, 1979, Balham Gateway to the South, 1980, Britannia Hospital, 1981, Scrubbers, 1982, Krull, 1982, Ghost Dance, 1983, Chinese Boxes, 1984, The Supergrass, 1984, Defense of the Realm, 1985, Revolution, 1985, Caravaggio, 1985, Absolute Beginners, 1985, Mona Lisa, 1985, Eat the Rich, 1987, The Fruit Machine, 1987, Slipstream, 1988, Bert Rigby, You're a Fool, 1988, Danny Champion of the World, 1988, Let It Ride, 1988, Henry V, 1988, Nuns on the Run, 1989, Perfectly Normal, 1989, Pope Must Die, 1990, Oh What A Night, 1991, Adventures of Huck Finn, 1992, Goldeneye, 1995, Buddy, 1996, Montana, 1997, Frogs for Snakes, 1997, Message in a Bottle, 1998, The World Is Not Enough, 1999, From Hell, 2000, Harry Potter and the Philosopher's Stone, 2001, Harry Potter and the Chamber of Secrets, 2002, Harry Potter and Prisoner of Azkaban, 2003, Harry Potter and the Goblet of Fire, 2004, Ocean's 12, Stormbreaker, 2005, Harry Potter and the Order of the Phoenix, 2006; The Brothers Bloom, 2007; Harry Potter and the Half Blood Prince, 2007; Harry Potter and the Deathly Hallows, 2010; Brave, 2011; Great Expectations, 2011; Arthur Christmas, 2011; Effie, 2014; theatre credits: The Bug, 1976, Mr Joyce is Leaving, 1978, The Slab Boys, 1978, The Transfiguration of Benno Blimpie, 1978, The Loveliest Night of the Year, 1979-80, Dick Whittington, 1979, Snobs and Yobs, 1980, Yr Obedient Servant (one-man show), 1987, Mistero Buffo (one-man show), 1990; television credits include: roles in several The Comic Strip Presents productions, lead role in Tutti Frutti (BBC Scotland), Alive and Kicking, 1991, Coltrane in a Cadillac, 1992, Cracker, 1993, 1994, 1995, Ebbtide, 1996, Coltrane's Planes and Automobiles, 1997, Alice in Wonderland, 1998, The Plan Man, Frazier, 2004, Cracker 9:11, 2005, B Road Britain, 2007, Murderland, 2009; Lead Balloon, 2010; Five Go to Rehab; The Hunt for Tony Blair; Yes Prime Minister; Crackanory. Recreations: vintage cars; sailing; painting; reading; movies. Address: c/o CDA, 167-169 Kensington High Street, London W8 6SH.

Colvin, Professor Calum Munro, DA, MA (RCA), RSA, OBE. Professor of Fine Art Photography, Dundee University, since 2001; artist, since 1985; b. 26.10.61, Glasgow. Educ. North Berwick High School; Duncan of Jordanstone College of Art and Design; Royal College of Art, London. Lecturer in Fine Art, Dundee University, from 1993; Creative Scotland Award, 2000; 13th Higashikawa Overseas Photographer Prize, 1997; has exhibited work internationally since 1986 with work in many collections; recent solo exhibitions include Scottish National Gallery of Modern Art, 1998; Kawasaki City Museum, 1998; UNESCO Headquarters, Paris, 2005; Royal Scottish Academy, 2009; Scottish National Portrait Gallery, 2015. Address: (h.) 1

Duddingston Park South, Edinburgh EH15 3NX; T.-0131-669 0218; m. 0780 327 4694.
E-mail: calumcolvin@me.com

Comiskey, Patricia Bernadette, BSc, MSc, PhD, LLB, DipLP. Advocate, since 2001. Educ. Leicester Polytechnic; University of Minnesota; Edinburgh University. Researcher in Textile Technology, University of Minnesota, 1981-83; Lecturer in Textile Technology, Leicester Polytechnic, 1983-88; Assistant Fabric Technologist, Marks and Spencer, London, 1988-90; Menswear Buyer Manager, Jenners Ltd, Edinburgh, 1990-95; Tutor Law School, University of Edinburgh, 2001-04; Clerk to the Examiners, Faculty of Advocates, 2003-09; Board Member, Stepfamily Scotland, 2005-09; Member, Edinburgh Branch Committee, Royal Overseas League Club, 2007-2010. Member of the Council of The Stair Society, since 2009. Address: (b.) Parliament House, Edinburgh EH1 1RF.
E-mail: patricia.comiskey@advocates.org.uk

Conn, Stewart. Poet and playwright; b. 1936, Glasgow, brought up Kilmarnock. Educ. Glasgow University. Author of numerous stage plays, including The Burning, Herman, The Aquarium, By the Pool, Clay Bull; television work includes The Kite, Bloodhunt; poetry includes In the Kibble Palace, The Luncheon of the Boating Party, At the Aviary, In the Blood; Stolen Light; Distances: a personal evocation of people and places; l'Ànima del Teixidor; Ghosts at Cockcrow; The Loving-Cup; The Breakfast Room; Estuary; The Touch of Time: New & Selected Poems; his production of Carver (by John Purser) won Gold Medal Award, New York, International Radio Festival, 1991; left BBC, 1992; appointed to Edinburgh's poet laureateship, 2002-05. Editor, 100 Favourite Scottish Poems, 2006; 100 Favourite Scottish Love Poems, 2008; Stolen Light shortlisted for Saltire Scottish Book of the Year; The Breakfast Room chosen as 2011 Scottish Mortgage Investment Trust Poetry Book of the Year.
E-mail: stewartconn@btinternet.com

Connaghan, John, CBE. NHS Scotland Chief Operating Officer, Scottish Government, since 2014; Chairman, OPEX Ltd. Educ. Glasgow Caledonian University; Strathclyde University. Career: joined the NHS in the late 1980s, holding Chief Executive positions over a ten year period in three different NHS Trusts in Scotland; led the national effort in reducing waiting times in 2002 and was appointed Director of Health Delivery for Scotland in 2006; took the additional responsibilities as Director for Workforce and performance NHSScotland in 2011; became Acting Director, General Health and Social Care and Chief Executive of the NHS in 2013. Awarded Commander of British Empire, 2015. Address: Scottish Government, St. Andrew's House, Regent Road, Edinburgh EH1 3DG.

Connal, Robert Craig, QC, LLB (Hons), SSC. Solicitor, since 1977; Partner, Pinsent Masons LLP, since 2012; Head of Advocacy (Litigation and Compliance), since 2014; Partner, McGrigors, 1980-2012 (Head of Commercial Litigation, 2002-07); Senior Litigation Partner and UK Head of Advocacy, 2007-2012; Solicitor Advocate: Scotland (civil), 1996, (criminal), 2004, England and Wales, (all courts), 2006; b. 7.7.54, Brentwood; m., Mary Ferguson Bowie; 2 d. Educ. Hamilton Academy; University of Glasgow. Apprentice, Brown, Mair, Gemmill & Hislop, 1975-77; Assistant, McGrigor Donald, 1977-1980. Council Member, Royal Faculty of Procurators in Glasgow, 1995-98; appointed Scotland's first Solicitor Advocate QC, 2002; External Examiner, University of Aberdeen, 2001-05; Convenor, Law Society of Scotland Supreme Courts Training Course (Civil), since 2004; Arbitrator; NITA

Awarded Advocacy Trainer; Registered in the DIFC Court, Dubai; Committee Member, Society of Solicitor Advocates; Vice-Chairman (Scotland), BICBA; Law Society of England and Wales Solicitor Advocate of the Year, 2012. Publications: Contributor, Stair Memorial Encyclopedia; many articles in press and professional journals. Recreations: rugby referee; gardens (but not gardening). Address: (b.) 141 Bothwell Street, Glasgow G2 7EQ; T.-0141-567-8633.

Connarty, Michael, BA, DCE. MP (Labour), Linlithgow and East Falkirk, 2005-2015; Falkirk East, 1992-2005; Board Member, Parliamentary Office of Science and Technology, 1996; Chair, European Scrutiny Select Committee, 2006-2010; Board Chair (unpaid), Scottish National Jazz Orchestra; b. 3.9.47, Coatbridge; m., Margaret Doran; 1 s.; 1 d. Educ. Stirling University; Jordanhill College of Education; Glasgow University. Member, Stirling District Council, 1977-90 (Council Leader, 1980-90); Member, Convention of Scottish Local Authorities, 1980-90 (Depute Labour Leader, 1988-90); Member, Scottish Executive, Labour Party, 1981-92; Vice-Chair, Socialist Educational Association, 1983-85; Council Member, Educational Institute of Scotland, 1984-85; PPS to Tom Clarke, MP, 1987-88; Chair, Labour Party Scottish Local Government Committee, 1988-90; Vice-Chairman, Scottish MAP, 1988-95; Secretary, PLP Science and Technology Comittee, 1992-97; Member, European Directives Committee on Agriculture, Environment and Health and Safety, 1993-96; Chair, Economy, Industry and Energy Committee, Scottish PLP Group, 1993-97; Scottish Co-ordinator, Labour Crime and Drugs Campaign, 1993-97; Scottish Task Force Leader on Skills and Training in Scotland and Youth and Students, 1995-97; Member, Select Committee on the Parliamentary Commissioner for Administration, 1995-97; Chairman, Scottish Parliamentary Labour Party Group, 1998-99; Member of the Humanist Group; Chemical Industry Group - Vice Chair; Haemophilia Group (Chair, 2004-08); Human Trafficking and Modern Day Slavery Group - Vice Chair, since 2011. Recreations: family; hill-walking; reading; music. Address: (b.) 5 Kerse Road, Grangemouth FK3 8HQ; T.-01324 474832.

Connell, Douglas Andrew, LLB, DUniv. Consultant and former Senior Partner, Turcan Connell; Deputy Chairman, Turcan Connell Asset Management Limited; former Chairman, Museums Galleries Scotland; Trustee, Hampshire Cultural Trust; b. 18.05.54, Callander; m., Marjorie Elizabeth; 2 s. Educ. McLaren High School; Edinburgh University. Qualified as a solicitor, 1976; admitted as a Writer to the Signet, 1976; Scottish Arts Council: Member, 1994-97, Chairman, Lottery Committee, 1994-97; Member, Edinburgh Festival Council, 1997-2001; Member, Strategic Historic Environment, 2014-15; Trustee, Historic Scotland Foundation, since 2001; Trustee, Edinburgh International Festival Endowment Fund, 2007-15; Trustee, The Royal Scottish Academy Foundation, 2013-15; Member, Scottish Committee Historic Houses Association, 2000-14; Chairman, Edinburgh International Book Festival, 1991-95; General Editor, Scottish Private Client Law Review, 2003-06; Member, University of St. Andrews Court, 2002-06; Chairman, Governance and Nominations Committee; Chairman, Recognition Committee of Scottish Museums Council, 2007-11; General Council Assessor, Court of University of Edinburgh, 2007-11. Recreations: Venice; travelling and organising. Address: (b.) Princes Exchange, 1 Earl Grey Street, Edinburgh EH3 9EE; T.-0131 228 8111.
E-mail: douglas.connell@turcanconnell.com

Connell, Professor John Muir Cochrane, MBChB, MD, FRCP, FAHA, FRSE, FMedSci. Chair of Board, NHS Tayside, since 2015; Vice Principal, University of Dundee, since 2012; Dean of Medicine, 2009-2012; formerly Professor of Endocrinology, Glasgow

University (1996-2009); Head, Graduate School, Faculty of Medicine, University of Glasgow, 2008-09; Honorary Consultant Physician, Western Infirmary, Glasgow, 1987-2009; b. 10.10.54; m., Dr Lesley Connell; 3 s.; 1 d. Educ. Hutchesons' Grammar School; Glasgow University. Research Fellow, MRC Blood Pressure Unit, Western Infirmary, Glasgow; MRC Travelling Fellow, Howard Florey Institute, Melbourne, 1986-87; Senior Clinical Scientist and Hon. Consultant Phsyician, MRC Blood Pressure Unit, 1987-94; Professor in Medicine, Department of Medicine and Therapeutics, Western Infirmary, 1994-96; Clinical Director, Medicine, West Glasgow, 2006-08. Honorary Secretary, Association of Physicians of Gt. Britain and Ireland, 2001-07; Member, grant-awarding committees, British Heart Foundation, etc; Fellowship Secretary, Royal Society of Edinburgh, since 2014. Clubs: New Club, Edinburgh; New Golf Club, St Andrews. Recreations: family; golf; literature. Address: (b.) Ninewells Hospital and Medical School, University of Dundee DD1 9SY.

Connolly, Billy, CBE. Stand-up comedian; Actor; Television Presenter; b. 24.11.42; m. 1., Iris (m. dissolved) 1 s.; 1 d.; 2, Pamela Stephenson; 3 d. Welder, Clyde shipyards; began show-business career with Gerry Rafferty as The Humblebums; first solo concert, 1971; has toured throughout the world with stand-up comedy shows. Television includes: Androcles and the Lion; Head of the Class; Billy; Billy Connolly's World Tour of Scotland (Scottish BAFTA: Best Entertainment Programme); Down Among the Big Boys (Scottish BAFTA: Best Drama); The Bigger Picture (Scottish BAFTA: Best Arts Programme); The Life and Crimes of Deacon Brodie; Billy Connolly's World Tour of Australia; Return to Nose and Beak (Comic Relief special); Billy Connolly: A Scot in the Arctic; Gentleman's Relish; Billy Connolly's World Tour of England, Ireland and Wales; World Tour of New Zealand; Journey To The Edge of the World; Billy Connolly's Route 66. Films Include: Absolution; Bullshot; Water; The Big Man; Muppet Treasure Island; Mrs Brown; Still Crazy; The Changeling; PAWS; The Debt Collector; The Boondock Saints; The Imposters; Beautiful Joe; An Everlasting Piece; Cletis Tout; Gabriel and Me; The Man Who Sued God; Timeline; The Last Samurai; Lemony Snicket's A Series of Unfortunate Events; Fido; Garfield 2; Gulliver's Travels; Open Season 2. Theatre: The Red Runner; The Beastly Beatitudes of Blathazar B; What About Dick? Videos: Connolly, 1975; Big Banana Feet, 1976; Billy Connolly in Concert, 1978; Billy Connolly Bites Yer Bum Live/Hand Picked By Billy, 1982; The Pick of Billy Connolly, 1982; An Audience With Billy Connolly, 1985; Billy & Albert, 1987; 25 B.C. The Best of 25 Years of Billy Connolly, 1992; World Tour of Scotland, 1994; Live at the Apollo, 1994; Two Bites of Billy Connolly, 1995; A Scot in The Arctic, 1995; Billy Connolly's World Tour of Australia, 1996; Billy Connolly: Two Night Stand, 1997; Billy Connolly: Erect for 30 Years, 1998; Billy Connolly: One Night Stand Down Under and The Best of the Rest, 1999; Billy Connolly Live: The Greatest Hits, 2001; Billy Connolly's World Tour of England, Ireland and Wales, 2002; Billy Connolly Live in Dublin 2002, 2002; Billy Connolly's World Tour of New Zealand, 2004; The Odeon Hammersmith London Live, 2004; Billy Connolly: Live in New York, 2005; Billy Connolly Live: Was it Something I Said?, 2006; Journey To The Edge of the World, 2009; Billy Connolly "The Man" Live in London, 2010. Books Include: Gullible's Travels, 1982; Billy Connolly's World Tour of Australia, 1996; Journey to the Edge of the World, 2009.

Connor, George. Board Member, Parole Board for Scotland, since 2015 (Chief Executive, 2014-15); b. 22.11.57, Glasgow; 1 s.; 1 d. Educ. St Mungo's Academy, Glasgow. Department of Health & Social Security, 1975-89; Ministry of Defence, 1989-2007; Criminal Injuries Compensation Authority, 2007-2012; Scottish Government,

2012-2014. Recreations: reading; live music. Address: (b.) Saughton House, Broomhouse Drive, Edinburgh EH11 3XD; T.-0131 244 3404.
E-mail: george.connor@scotland.gsi.gov.uk

Connor, James Michael, MD, DSc, BSc (Hons), MB, ChB (Hons), FRCP. Former Professor of Medical Genetics and Director, West of Scotland Regional Genetics Service (1987-2011) (Wellcome Trust Senior Lecturer and Honorary Consultant in Medical Genetics, Glasgow University, 1984-87); b. 18.6.51, Grappenhall, England; m., Dr. Rachel A.C. Educ. Lymm Grammar School, Cheshire; Liverpool University. House Officer, Liverpool Royal Infirmary; Resident in Internal Medicine, Johns Hopkins Hospital, USA; University Research Fellow, Liverpool University; Instructor in Internal Medicine, Johns Hopkins Hospital, USA; Consultant in Medical Genetics, Institute of Medical Genetics, Yorkhill, Glasgow. Publications: Essential Medical Genetics (Co-author), 1984 (6th edition, 2011); Principles and Practice of Medical Genetics (Co-Editor), (5th edition, 2007); various articles on aspects of medical genetics. Recreations: mountain biking; sea kayaking and classic cars. Address: (h.) East Collarie Farm, by Fenwick, Ayrshire.

Conroy, Professor James Charles, BEd, MA, PhD. Vice Principal (Internationalisation), University of Glasgow, Professor of Religious and Philosophical Education, since 2004, Fellow of the Academy of Social Sciences, formerly Dean for European Affairs and Strategy (2012-2013); formerly Dean of Faculty of Education (2006-2010); b. 30.04.55, Portadown, Northern Ireland; m., Denise Frances (nee Meagher); 1 s.; 2 d. Educ. St. Patrick's College, Armagh; London (St. Mary's); Lancaster; VU, Amsterdam. Accounts Controller, Chase Bank of Ireland, 1973-76; Development Officer, Adult Education, Westminster Diocese, 1981-83; Teacher and Head of Department of RE, St. Brendan's VIth Form, 1983-87; Senior Lecturer, Education and Theology, St. Mary's College, Twickenham, 1987-90; Director, RE and Pastoral Care, St. Andrew's College, Bearsden, 1990-99; Head of Department of RE, University of Glasgow, 1999-2004. 2007 Board of Directors: Learning and Teaching Scotland; President, Association For Moral Education (based in US), 2007; Chair, Philosophy of Education Society of Great Britain; Chair, Journal of Moral Education Trust. Publications: Does Religious Education Work?, 2013; Catholic Education: Inside-out/Outside-in, 1999, Betwixt and Between: The Liminal Imagination, Education and Democracy, 2004. Recreations: antique furniture; gardening; cooking; family. Address: (b.) Faculty of Education, St. Andrew's Building, 11 Eldon Street, Glasgow G3 6NH; T.-0141 330 3002.
E-mail: james.conroy@glasgow.ac.uk

Constance, Angela. MA (Soc.Sci), MSc (Social Work). MSP (SNP), Almond Valley, since 2011, Livingston, 2007-2011; Cabinet Secretary for Communities, Social Security and Equalities, since 2016; Cabinet Secretary for Education & Lifelong Learning, 2014-16; Cabinet Secretary for Training, Youth & Women's Employment, 2014; Minister for Youth Employment, 2011-2014; Minister for Children and Young People, 2011; Minister for Skills and Lifelong Learning, 2010-11; b. 15.7.70; m., Garry Knox; 1 s. Educ. West Calder High; Boness Academy; Glasgow University; Stirling University. Social Worker, 1997-2007; Social Worker/Mental Health Officer, 2002-07; Social Worker/Mental Health Officer/Practice Teacher, 2005-07. Member, West Lothian Coun., 1997-2007. Recreations: jogging; reading; drawing. Address: (b.) Scottish Parliament, Edinburgh EH99 1SP.
E-mail: angela.constance.msp@scottish.parliament.co.uk

Conti, Most Rev. Mario Joseph, KC* HS, PhL, STL, DD, FRSE, DLitt. Archbishop Emeritus of Glasgow; Archbishop of Glasgow, 2002-2012; Bishop of Aberdeen, 1977-2002; Apostolic Administrator, Paisley, 2004-05; Member,

Pontifical Council for the Promotion of Christian Unity, Rome, 1984-2014; Member, Historic Buildings Council of Scotland, 2000-03; b. 20.3.34, Elgin. Educ. St. Marie's Convent; Springfield School, Elgin; Blairs College, Aberdeen; Pontifical Scots College, Pontifical Gregorian University, Rome. Ordained priest, Rome, 1958; Curate, St. Mary's Cathedral, Aberdeen, 1959-62; Parish Priest, St. Joachim's, Wick and St. Anne's, Thurso, 1962-77. Commendatore, Order of Merit, Italian Republic; President-Treasurer, SCIAF, 1977-85; President, National Liturgy Commission, 1981-85; Member, International Commission for English in the Liturgy, 1978-87; Chairman, Scottish Catholic Heritage Commission, 1980-2014; President, Commission for Christian Doctrine and Unity, 1986-2012; first Convener, Central Council, ACTS, 1990-93; Co-Moderator, Joint Working Group of the World Council of Churches and the Roman Catholic Church, 1996-2006; Head of Catholic Delegation to 8th General Assembly, World Council of Churches, Harare, 1998; a President, Churches Together in Britain and Ireland, 1999-2005; Member, Pontifical Commission for the Cultural Heritage of the Church, 1994-2004; Member, Health Appointments Advisory Council, 1994-2000; Member, Historic Buildings Council for Scotland, 2000-03; Knight Commander of the Holy Sepulchre, 1989; Grand Prior, Scottish Lieutenancy, since 2013; Principal Chaplain to British Association of the Sovereign Military Order of Malta, 1995-2000 and 2005-2015; Conventual Chaplain, Grand Cross, since 2001; (Italian State honour): Grande Ufficiale (1 Classe) dell'Ordine della Stella della Solidarietà Italiana, 2007; DD honoris causa: Aberdeen, 1989, Glasgow, 2010; DLitt, Glasgow Caledonian, 2015. Recreations: music; art. Address: (h.) 40 Newlands Road, Glasgow G43 2JD.
E-mail: mario.conti@rcag.org.uk

Conway, Stephen Andrew, FCMI. Chief Executive, Erskine, since 2011; Director, Strategic Planning and Performance, NHS National Services Scotland, 2007-2011; Chief Executive, NHS Orkney, 2004-07; b. 24.2.57, Otley, Yorkshire; m., Heather; 1 s.; 1 d. Educ. Berkhamsted School. Commissioned in Royal Marines in September 1976, appointments included Signal Officer, Special Boat Service, Adjutant Commando Training Centre, Second in Command, Comacchio Group and Commanding Officer, Royal Marines Reserve Scotland; retired in 2002 as Lieutenant Colonel. National Emergency Planning Officer, NHS Scotland. Recreations: sailing; antique furniture restoration. Address: (h.) 9 Castle Gardens, Drymen, Glasgow G63 0HT; T.-01360 660109.
E-mail: steve.conway@erskine.org.uk

Cook, Rev. James Stanley Stephen Ronald Tweedie, BD, DipPSS. Minister, Hamilton West Parish Church, 1974-2001; b. 18.8.35, Tullibody; m., Jean Douglas Maclachlan; 2 s.; 1 d. Educ. Whitehill Senior Secondary School, Glasgow; St Andrews University. Apprentice quantity surveyor, Glasgow, 1953-54; regular soldier, REME, 1954-57; Assistant Preventive Officer, Waterguard Department, HM Customs and Excise, 1957-61; Officer, HM Customs and Excise, 1961-69; studied for the ministry, 1969-74. Chairman, Cruse (Lanarkshire), 1983-93, 1994-99; Chairman, Cruse – Scotland, 1991-95, Convener, 1999-2001; Member, Council, Cruse UK, 1988-94; Member, National Training Group, Cruse, 1987-94; Member, Action Research for Crippled Child Committee, 1977-94; Substitute Provincial Grand Master, Lanarkshire (Middle Ward), 1983-88; Honorary Provincial Grand Chaplain, since 1989; founder Member, Wishaw Victim Support Scheme, 1985; Member, Hamilton Rotary Club, 1980-2014, President, 1994-95; Member, Hamilton Crime Prevention Panel, 1976-2000, Chairman, 1986-87; Moderator, Presbytery of Hamilton, 1999-2000; Mental Health Chaplain, 1988-2010. Recreations: music; photography; DIY; computer enthusiast. Address: Mansend, 137a Old Manse Road, Netherton, Wishaw ML2 0EW.

Cooke, Anthony John, BA (Hons), MA (Manchester); b. 15.7.43, Salford, Lancashire; m., Judith Margaret; 2 s. Educ. Accrington Grammar School; Manchester University. Teacher, Bishops College, Carriacou, Grenada, West Indies; Lecturer, Dundee College of Commerce; Lecturer/Senior Lecturer, University of Dundee; Consultant, Historic Scotland. Publications: Stanley: From Arkwright Village to Commuter Suburb, 2003; From Popular Enlightenment to Lifelong Learning, 2006; The Rise and Fall of the Scottish Cotton Industry, 1778-1914 (2010); A History of Drinking. The Scottish Pub, since 1700 (2015). Recreations: walking; swimming; choral singing. Address: (h.) 424, Blackness Road, Dundee DD2 1TQ; T.-01382 668476.
E-mail: a_j_cooke@btinternet.com

Cooke, Professor David John, BSc, MSc, PhD, CPsych, FBPsS, FRSE, DUniv. Professor of Forensic Clinical Psychology, Glasgow Caledonian University, since 1992; Head of Forensic Clinical Psychology, Greater Glasgow Community and Mental Health Services NHS Trust, 1984-2007; Glasgow University: Honorary Lecturer, since 1984, Honorary Senior Research Fellow, since 1989, Visiting Professor, 1997-2001; b. 13.7.52, Glasgow; m., Janet Ruth Salter; 2 d. Educ. Larbert High School; St. Andrews University; Newcastle-upon-Tyne University; Glasgow University. Clinical Psychologist, Gartnavel Royal Hospital, 1976-83; Cropwood Fellow, Institute of Criminology, Cambridge University, 1986; Visiting Professor, University of Bergen, since 2006; President, European Association of Psychology and Law, 2009-2012. The Medal of David The Invincible of The Armenian Philosophical Academy, 2012. Recreations: sailing; opera; cooking. Address: (b.) Glasgow Caledonian University, Cowcaddens Road, Glasgow G4 0BA; T.-0141 331 3119.
E-mail: djcooke@rgardens.vianw.co.uk

Cooke, Nicholas Huxley, MA (Oxon), FRSA. Independent sustainability consultant, CLEAR Services Ltd; b. 6.5.44, Godalming, Surrey; m., Anne Landon; 2 s.; 3 d. Educ. Charterhouse School; Worcester College, Oxford. Retail management, London; chartered accountancy training, London; British International Paper, 1972-78; Director (Scotland), British Trust for Conservation Volunteers, 1978-84; Director, Scottish Conservation Projects Trust, 1984-98; Member, Scottish Committee for European Year of the Environment, 1987-88; Policy Committee Member, Scottish Council for Voluntary Organisations, 1992-2002; Board Member: Youthlink Scotland, Falkirk Environment Trust, Dundee Waste and Environment Trust, 1996-99; Member, Scottish Employer Supported Volunteering Group, 1997-2002; Chair, Scottish Committee, Voluntary Sector NTO, 1997-2001, Gowanbank Historic Village Ltd, 2001-04; Director, Rockdust Ltd., 2005-08; Secretary, Scottish Senior Alliance for Volunteering in the Environment (SSAVE), 2001-03; Managing Director, Scottish Organic Producers Association, 2003-05 (Chair, 2002-03); Secretary, Incorporated Glasgow, Stirlingshire and Sons of the Rock Society, since 2007 (Preses, 2003-04); Secretary, Scottish Pilgrim Routes Forum, since 2012; Hon. President, Callander Youth Project Trust (Chair, 2004-09). Recreations: fishing; field entomology; walking; pilgrimage routes. Address: (b.) The Old School House, 23 King Street, Doune, Perthshire FK16 6DN; T.-01786 841809; e-mail: Nick@clearserv.co.uk

Cooper, Professor Christine, BA, MSc, PhD. Professor of Accounting, Strathclyde University, since 1999; b.

16.3.56, London; 1 d. Educ. Crown Woods, Eltham, London; Greenwich University; London School of Economics. Trustee, Association for Accountancy and Business Affairs. Publication: 'Critical Perspectives on Accounting' Journal (Co-Editor). Address: (b.) Department of Accounting and Finance, Strathclyde University, Glasgow G4 0LN; T.-0141-548 3231; e-mail: c.cooper@strath.ac.uk

Cooper, Professor Sally-Ann, BSc, MB, BS, MD, FRCPsych. Professor of Learning Disabilities, Institute of Health and Wellbeing, Glasgow University, since 1999; Honorary Consultant in Learning Disabilities Psychiatry, NHS Greater Glasgow and Clyde, since 1999; b. 28.4.61, Lincoln; m., Mark Guy Venner Anderson. Educ. Medical College of St Bartholomew's Hospital, London. Address: (b.) Institute of Health and Wellbeing, Glasgow University, Academic Centre, Gartnavel Royal Hospital, 1055 Great Western Road, Glasgow G12 0XH; T.-0141-211 3701.

Cooper, Professor Thomas Joshua, BA, MA. Professor of Fine Art, Senior Researcher, Glasgow School of Art, since 2002; artist; b. 19.12.46, San Francisco; m., Catherine Alice Mooney; 2 d. Educ. Arcata High School, CA; University of New Mexico; Humboldt State University. Former Senior Lecturer, Trent Polytechnic, Nottingham; Head of Fine Art Photography, Glasgow School of Art, 1982-2000. Creative Scotland Award, 2005. Recreations: walking; music; wine; film; reading. Address: (b.) Glasgow School of Art, 167 Renfrew Street, Glasgow G3 6RQ; T.-0141 353 4500.

Corbett, Gavin. Policy Adviser, Shelter Scotland, since 2001; Green Cllr. for Fountainbridge/Craiglockhart Ward in Edinburgh, since 2012; b. 9.10.65, Cumnock; partner, Karen Robertson; 2 s. Educ. Cumnock Academy; Glasgow University. Joined Shelter Scotland as campaign worker, 1993-2000. Recreations: climbing hills; cycling; campaigning. Address: (h.) 28 Briarbank Terrace, Edinburgh EH11 1SU; T.-0131-337 5227. E-mail: karenandgavin@blueyonder.co.uk

Cormack, Arthur. CEO of Fèisean nan Gàidheal, since 1992; Director of Macmeanmna Ltd., since 2004; b. 21.4.65, Portree, Isle of Skye; m., Shona (nee Macdonald); 2 s.; 1 d. Educ. Portree High School. Ran R Cormack Clothing (family business), 1985-92; established and ran EISD Music, 1987-2003; founder of Macmeanmna (Gaelic Music Recording Label), 1987; Chairman and Co-founder of AROS Ltd, 1991; Member of Bòrd na Gàidhlig, 2003-2009, Chair, 2009-2012; Gaelic Singer (professional as solo artist), since 1983. Former member of Scottish Arts Council. Recreations: music; graphic design. Address: (b.) Meall House, Portree, Isle of Skye IV51 9BZ; T.-01478 613355; e-mail: arthur@feisean.org

Cormack, James Shearer, LLB (Hons), DipLP. Solicitor, Partner, Pinsent Masons LLP, since 2012; b. 11.11.68, Inverness; m., Emma; 1 s.; 2 d. Educ. Lochaber High School; University of Edinburgh. Trainee Solicitor, then Qualified Assistant, McGrigor Donald, 1991-95; Member, Faculty of Advocates, 1996-2001; Partner, McGrigors LLP, 2001-2012. Recreations: family; cinema; golf. Address: (b.) Pinsent Masons LLP, Princes Exchange, 1 Earl Grey Street, Edinburgh EH3 9AQ; T.-0131 777 7356. E-mail: jim.cormack@pinsentmasons.com

Cormack, Professor Robert John, MA, FRSA, FRSE, DLitt (Cape Breton), Doctor honoris causa (Edin), Fellow (University of the Highlands and Islands). Principal, UHI Millennium Institute, 2001-09; b. 14.12.46, Blantyre; divorced, 2009; m. (2010); 1 s.; 2 d. Educ. Montrose Academy; Aberdeen University; Brown University, USA.

Queen's University of Belfast: Lecturer in Sociology, 1973-87, Senior Lecturer, 1987-92, Reader, 1992-96, Professor, 1996-2001, Head, Department of Sociology and Social Policy, 1991-93, Dean, Faculty of Economics and Social Sciences, 1993-95, Pro-Vice Chancellor, 1995-2001. Member, Court of Queen Margaret University, 2010; Editorial Advisory Board, Widening Participation and Lifelong Learning, since 1999; Trustee, Royal Society of Edinburgh; Trustee, David Hume Institute, since 2015. Publications: numerous books and articles on Northern Ireland including Discrimination and Public Policy in Northern Ireland (Co-author). Address: (b.) 16b Glencairn Crescent, Edinburgh EH12 5BT. E-mail: rjc@fastmail.fm

Cornwell, Professor John Francis, PhD, BSc, DIC, ARCS, FRSE. Emeritus Professor, St. Andrews University, since 2002, Professorial Fellow, since 2009 (Chairman: Theoretical Physics Department, 1978-83, Professor of Theoretical Physics, 1979-2002, Chairman, Physics Department, 1984-85); 2 d. Educ. Imperial College, London. Lecturer in Applied Mathematics, Leeds University, 1961-67; St. Andrews University: Lecturer in Theoretical Physics, 1967-73, Reader, 1973-79. Publications: Group Theory in Physics, three volumes, 1984, 1989; Group Theory and Electronic Energy Bands in Solids, 1969; 62 research papers. Address: (b.) Department of Physics and Astronomy, St. Andrews University, North Haugh, St. Andrews, Fife KY16 9SS; T.-01334 476161.

Cornwell, Professor Keith, BSc, PhD, DEng, FIMechE. Emeritus Professor of Heat Transfer, Heriot Watt University; b. 4.4.42, Abingdon; m., Sheila Joan Mott; 1 s.; 1 d. Educ. City University, London. Research Fellow, Middlesex Polytechnic; Lecturer, Head of Department, Dean of Engineering, Director of Quality, and Head, School of Mathematical and Computing Science, Heriot-Watt University; Head of Heriot Watt Dubai Campus, UAE; Chairman, C-MIST Ltd, 2009-2014. Publications: The Flow of Heat; numerous journal papers. Recreations: classic cars; hillwalking. Address: (h.) Ivanlea, Main Road, Dirleton EH39 5EA; e-mail: cornwellmail@gmail.com

Corrie, John Alexander. Member (Conservative), European Parliament for West Midlands Region, 1999-2004 (for Worcestershire and South Warwickshire, 1994-99); Co-ordinator, Development Committee, 1999-2004; Member, Budgets Committee, 1999-2004; Co-President, ACP/EU Joint Parliamentary Assembly, 1999-2002, now Honorary Life President; Member of North South Forum, 2002-04; Vice-President, Working Group "A", Foreign Affairs and Development, 2002-04; Deligation Leader to Dafur (Sudan), 2004; Election Monitor in Malawi, Congo, Brassaville, Solomon Isles, Madagascar, The Seychelles, Fiji, Peru, Tanzania, Chad and Rawanda, 2002-04; farms family farm in Galloway; b. 1935; m.; 1 s.; 2 d. Educ. Kirkcudbright Academy; George Watson's College, Edinburgh; Lincoln Agricultural College, New Zealand. Commissioned from the ranks of New Zealand Army, 2nd Lieutenant, 1956; Nuffield Farming Scholar, 1972; National Chairman, Scottish Young Conservatives, 1964; MP (Conservative): Bute and North Ayrshire, 1974-83, Cunninghame North, 1983-87; PPS to Secretary of State for Scotland, 1979-81; introduced Private Member's Bill to reduce upper limit on abortion, 1979; Member: European Assembly, 1975-76 and 1977-79, Council of Europe, 1983-87, Western European Union (Defence Committee), 1983-87; Chief Whip, Conservatives in Europe, 1997-99; Senior Instructor, British Wool Board, Agricultural Training Board, 1970-74; elected to Council, Belted Galloway Cattle Society, 1978; Chairman, Scottish Transport Users Consultative Committee, 1988-94; Vice Chairman, Central Transport Consultative Committee, 1988-94; Council

Member, Royal Agricultural Society of England, 1992-2000; Industrial Fellowship with Conoco and Du Pont, USA, 1987; awarded Wilberforce Plaque for Humane Work, 1981; Belted Galloway Judge, Royal Show, 2006; won Supreme Belted Galloway Champion at Royal Highland in 2010; Patron: Kisumu Children's Trust, Kenya, since 2006, DTI Mine Clearing and Development Initiative, since 2006; Hon. Chairman, ICCSD China, since 2006; Vice Chairman, Belted Galloway Society, 2008-2011; Chairman, Belted Galloway Cattle Society, 2011-2014; President, European Sustainable Project Group, 2004-2010; President, Rigget Galloway Cattle Society, 2009-2013; 2012 Lecture on "Democracy Building" in Biskek, Kirgyzstan; observer in Libya in 2012 on war situation. Publications: Forestry in Europe; Fish Farming in Europe; The Importance of Forestry in the World Today; Towards a Community Rural Policy (Co-author). Address: (h.) Park House Tongland, Kirkcudbright DG6 4NE. E-mail: j.corrie126@btinternet.com

Corry, Maurice. MSP (Scottish Conservative), West Scotland region, since 2016; b. 6.60. Former Argyll and Bute councillor, representing Lomond North; stood for the Scottish Parliament in 2016 as the Conservative candidate for Dumbarton. Address: Scottish Parliament, Edinburgh EH99 1SP.

Corsar, The Hon. Dame Mary Drummond, DBE (1993), FRSE, MA; b. 8.7.27, Edinburgh; m., Colonel Charles H.K. Corsar (qv) (deceased, 2011); 2 s.; 2 d. Educ. Westbourne, Glasgow; St. Denis, Edinburgh; Edinburgh University. Chairman, Women's Royal Voluntary Service, 1988-93; Chairman, Scotland, WRVS, 1981-88; Midlothian Girl Guides: Secretary, 1951-66, County Commissioner, 1966-72; Deputy Chief Commissioner, Girl Guides Scotland, 1972-77; Member: Parole Board for Scotland, 1982-89, Executive Committee, Trefoil Centre, 1975-2002, Visiting Committee, Glenochil Detention Centre, 1976-94, Management Committee, Church of Scotland Youth Centre, Carberry, 1976-82; Chairman, Lloyds TSB Foundation Scotland, 1994-97. Recreations: countryside; reading; handicrafts. Address: (h.) Flat 4, 85 South Oswald Road, Edinburgh EH9 2HH; T.-0131 662 0194.

Cosgrove, Rt. Hon. Lady (Hazel Josephine Aronson), CBE, LLD. Senator of the College of Justice in Scotland, 1996-2006; b. 12.1.46, Glasgow; m., John A. Cosgrove; 1 s.; 1 d. Educ. Glasgow High School for Girls; Glasgow University. Advocate at Scottish Bar, 1968-79; Sheriff: Glasgow and Strathkelvin at Glasgow, 1979-83, Lothian and Borders at Edinburgh, 1983-96; Temporary Judge, Court of Session and High Court, 1992-96; Past Chairman, Mental Welfare Commission for Scotland; Past Chairman, Expert Panel on Sex Offending; Past Depute Chairman, Boundaries Commission for Scotland. Recreations: swimming; walking; opera; foreign travel. Address: (b.) Parliament House, Edinburgh EH1 1RQ; T.-0131-225 2595; e-mail: hazelcosgrove@uk2.net

Cosgrove, Stuart, PhD. Journalist and broadcaster; Director of Creative Diversity, Channel Four Television, 2010-2015; b. Perth. Educ. Hull University. Lecturer, film and television; cultural critic; Media Editor, NME; contributor, The Face, The Guardian, The Observer, Arena; regular presenter, The Late Show, BBC TV; joined Channel Four after period as independent producer; appointed Senior Commissioning Editor, then Controller of Arts and Entertainment, before returning to Scotland. Co-host, BBC Radio Scotland's popular comedy football phone-in, Off The Ball; co-host, BBC Scotland's Saturday football results show, Sportscene Results; Head of Programmes (Nations and Regions), Channel Four Television, 1997-2015.

Recreation: supporter of St Johnstone F.C. Address: (b.) BBC Radio Scotland, 40 Pacific Quay, Glasgow G51 1DA.

Coton, Professor Frank Norman, BSc, PhD, CEng, FRAeS, AFAIAA. Professor of Low Speed Aerodynamics, University of Glasgow, since 2003, Dean of Engineering, 2007-09, Vice Principal (Academic and Educational Innovation), since 2010; b. 25.05.63, Dumbarton; m., Caroline; 1 s.; 1 d. Educ. Vale of Leven Academy; University of Glasgow. Production Engineering Apprentice, Rolls Royce Ltd., 1980-84; Glasgow University: Research Assistant, 1987-89, Lecturer, Department of Aerospace Engineering, 1986-89, Senior Lecturer, 1986-2000, Reader, 2000-03. Recreation: travel Address: (b.) Office of the Vice Principal (Academic and Educational Innovation), No. 10 The Square, University of Glasgow, Glasgow G12 8QQ; T.-0141 330 4305; e-mail: frank.coton@glasgow.ac.uk

Coull, Rev. Morris. Interim Moderator, Greenock Westburn Church, since 2012; m., Ann. Career: two years as an assistant at Bearsden South Parish Church on the North side of Glasgow; first charge in New Cumnock Old Parish Church in Ayr Presbytery, 1974-83; joined Hillington Park Parish Church on the south side of Glasgow in 1983; during a sabbatical period in 1993 attached to Peachtree Presbyterian Church in Atlanta, Georgia, USA; linked charge of Allan Park South with the Church of the Holy Rude in Stirling, 1996-2006; retired from full-time ministry, 2006; Locum at Old Gourock and Ashton Parish Church, 2006-08; returned to full-time ministry in 2008; Minister at Skelmorlie and Wemyss Bay Parish Church, 2008-2011; retired from full-time ministry in April 2011; returned to full-time Ministry in 2014 when inducted to Greenock St. Margaret's Church. Involved in taking 144 ministers, elders and their spouses over to Charlotte, North Carolina to see Team Ministry in action in four successful church locations in 2006. Address: 105 Finnart Street, Greenock PA16 8HN; T.-01475 892874.

Coulsfield, Rt. Hon. Lord (John Taylor Cameron), QC, BA, LLB. Senator of the College of Justice, 1987-2002; b. 24.4.34, Dundee; m., Bridget Deirdre Sloan. Educ. Fettes College; Corpus Christi College, Oxford; Edinburgh University. Admitted to Faculty of Advocates, 1960; Queen's Counsel, 1973; Lecturer in Public Law, Edinburgh University, 1960-64; Advocate Depute, 1977-80; Keeper of the Advocates Library, 1977-87; Chairman, Medical Appeal Tribunals, 1985-87; Judge of the Appeal Courts of Jersey and Guernsey, 1986-87; Scottish Judge, Employment Appeal Tribunal, 1992-96; Chairman, Joint Standing Committee on Legal Education, 1997-2003; Trustee, National Library of Scotland, 2000-2010; Judge of Appeal, Botswana, 2005-09; PC, 2000; Hon Fellow, National Library of Scotland, 2012. Address: 17 Moray Place, Edinburgh EH3 6DT; e-mail: coulsfield@aol.com

Couper, Jean, CBE, BSc, MCMI. Chairman, Scottish Criminal Cases Review Commission; Director: K3 Management Consultants Ltd, Catalyst Consulting, The Merchants' House of Glasgow; Chair, Advisory Audit Board, Scottish Parliament Corporate Body; Trustee, Glasgow Medical and Nursing Trust; The Endrick Trust; b. 31.8.53, Kilmarnock; m., John Anderson Couper; 1 s.; 1 d. Educ. Kilmarnock Academy; University of Glasgow. Production Engineer and Foundry Manager, Glacier Metal Co., 1974-79; Materials Manager, Levi Strauss, 1979-81; Management Consultant: Arthur Young, 1982-87, Price Waterhouse, 1987-95; Chairman, Scottish Legal Aid Board, 1998-2006 (Member, 1994-98); Director, Ombudsman Services Ltd (2006-2012); Chair, Aberlour Child Care Trust

(2008-2014); Deputy Chairman, Health Education Board for Scotland, 2000-01 (Member, 1994-2001); Member, Accounts Commission, 2002-08; Member, Police Advisory Board for Scotland, 2002-06; Vice-Chairman, Wise Group, 1988-96; Vice Chairman, Heatwise Glasgow Ltd., 1988-96; National President, Junior Chamber Scotland, 1983; Senator, Junior Chamber International. Recreations: gardening; skiing. Address: Glenesk House, 36 Sherbrooke Avenue, Pollokshields, Glasgow G41 4EP; T.-0141 427 3416; e-mail: jean.couper@k3consultants.co.uk

Cousin, David Alastair Henry, BVMS, MRCVS, DBR. Partner, veterinary practice, Kintyre, 1972-2009; Honorary Sheriff, Campbeltown Sheriff Court, since 1990; b. 19.4.44, Kincardine on Forth; m., Anne Macleod; 1 s.; 1 d. Educ. Balfron High School; Glasgow University; Liverpool University. Veterinary practice, Campbeltown: Veterinary Assistant, 1966, Junior Partner, 1972, Senior Partner, 1982; retired, 2009. Former Commodore, Campbeltown Sailing Club, 1995. Recreations: sailing; shooting; gardening; music. Address: (h.) Southpark, Kilkerran Road, Campbeltown; T.-01586 553108.

Coutts, Alister William, DQS, BA (Hons), MBA (Dist), MSc, PhD, FRICS, FCIOB, FCMI. Senior Partner, Dr Alister W Coutts and Partners LLP, Construction and Management Consultants, since 2011; Associate, Edinburgh Napier University, since 2015; b. 21.12.50, Aberdeen; m., Sheelagh Anne Smith; 1 s.; 2 d. Educ. Robert Gordon's College, Aberdeen; Dundee College of Technology; Open University; University of Hong Kong; Heriot-Watt University. Armour and Partners, Chartered Quantity Surveyors: Assistant Quantity Surveyor, 1969-71, Quantity Surveyor, 1975-76; Senior Quantity Surveyor, Anderson Morgan Associates, Chartered Surveyors, 1976-78; Professional Officer, Public Works Department, Hong Kong Government, 1978-81; Project Co-ordinator, Hong Kong Mass Transit Railway Corporation, 1981-89; Project Management and Development Director, DCI (Holdings) Ltd., 1989-93; Director of Operations, Fife Health Board, 1993-98; Director of Property and Architectural Services and PPP Projects Director, The Highland Council, 1998-2007; Partner, Head of Public Sector Services, Robinson Low Francis LLP, Construction and Property Consultants, 2007-2011; External Examiner in Quantity Surveying and Contract Administration, Edinburgh Napier University, 2008-2012; Visiting Lecturer in Project Finance and Project Risk Management, Edinburgh Napier University, 2012-13. Member, Children's Panel (Grampian), 1976-78. President, Scottish Football Association Referees (Angus and Perthshire), 1994-96. Member, Scottish Council, Royal Institution of Chartered Surveyors, 2005-2011. Recreations: travel; lecturing; academic research; watching soccer. Address: (b.) 29 Lady Nairne Drive, Perth PH1 1RF; T.-01738 565749.

Coutts, Rev. Fred, MA, BD. Healthcare Chaplain, NHS Grampian, 1989-2012 (retired, 2012); Moderator, Presbytery of Aberdeen, 2000-01; Healthcare Chaplaincy Training Officer (Scotland), 1997-2001; b. 13.1.47, Forfar; m., Mary Lawson Fraser Gill; 2 s.; 1 d. Educ. Brechin High School; Dollar Academy; St. Andrews University; Edinburgh University. Assistant Minister, Linwood Parish Church, 1972-74; Minister: Buckie North, 1974-84, Mastrick, Aberdeen, 1984-89. Chairman: Buckie Community Council, 1981-83, Moray Firth Community Radio Association, 1982-83. Recreations: music; photography; computing. Address: Ladebank, 1 Manse Place, Hatton, Peterhead AB24 0UQ; T.-01779 841 320; e-mail: fred.coutts@btinternet.com

Coutts, Herbert, KM, MBE, SBStJ, AMA, FMA, FFCS, FSAScot, Bailie of Dolphinstoun. Director of Culture and Leisure, Edinburgh City Council, 2001-07, retired 2007; b. 9.3.44, Dundee; m., Angela E.M. Smith; 1 s.; 3 d. Educ. Morgan Academy, Dundee. Assistant Keeper of Antiquities and Bygones, Dundee City Museums, 1965-68, Keeper, 1968-71; Superintendent, Edinburgh City Museums, 1971-73, City Curator, Edinburgh City Museums and Art Galleries, 1973-96, Head of Museums and Galleries, 1996-97, Head of Heritage and Arts, 1997-98, Director of Recreation, Edinburgh City Council, 1998-2001. Vice-President, Museum Assistants Group, 1969-70; Member: Government Committee on future of Scotland's National Museums and Galleries, 1979-80; Council, Museums Association, 1977-78, 1987-88; Council, Society of Antiquaries of Scotland, 1981-82; Board, Scottish Museums Council, 1985-88; Museums Adviser, COSLA, 1985-90; Member, Paxton House Trust, 1988-2002 and since 2007; External Examiner, St. Andrews University, 1994-97. Member, Board, Museums Training Institute, 1995-2004; Contested Angus South (Lab), 1970; Trustee, East Lothian Community Development Trust, 1989-2007; Member, Scottish Catholic Heritage Commission, since 2006; Trustee, Scottish Catholic Heritage Collections, since 2011; Trustee, National Galleries of Scotland, 2007-2011; Board Member, Order of Malta Dial-a-Journey Ltd., since 2007, Chairman, since 2011; Chairman, Wheelchair Accessible Vehicle Enterprise Ltd, since 2011; Member, Dunbar Community Council, since 2007; Member, Dunbar Community Development Company, since 2007; Trustee, Battle of Prestonpans (1745) Trust, since 2007; Chairman, Scottish Battlefields Trust, since 2014; major projects include: City of Edinburgh Art Centre, Museum of Childhood extension, People's Story Museum, City Art Centre extension, Scott Monument restoration, Usher Hall restoration and extension. Publications: Ancient Monuments of Tayside; Tayside Before History; Edinburgh: an illustrated history; Huntly House; Lady Stair's House; The Pharaoh's Gold Mask; Gold of the Pharaohs (Editor); Dinosaurs Alive! (Editor); Sweat of the Sun — Gold of Peru (Editor); Golden Warriors of the Ukrainian Steppes (Editor); StarTrek – the exhibition (Editor); Quest for a Pirate (Editor); Gateway to the Silk Road – Relics from the Han to the Tang Dynasties from Xi'an, China (Editor); Faster, Higher, Stronger – The Story of the Olympic Movement (Editor); articles in archaeological and museums journals; Strategy Documents: Towards The New Enlightenment - A Cultural Policy for Edinburgh; Festivals Strategy; Theatre Strategy; Allotments Strategy; A Capital Commitment to Sport-Sport and Physical Recreation Strategy for Edinburgh. Recreations: family; gardening; opera; writing; reading; walking. Address: (h.) Kirkhill House, Queen's Road, Dunbar EH42 1LN; T.-01368 863113; e-mail: coutts826@btinternet.com

Coutts, (Thomas) Gordon, MA, LLB, QC, FCIArb. Queen's Counsel, since 1973; b. 5.7.33, Aberdeen; m., Winifred K. Scott; 1 s.; 1 d. Educ. Aberdeen Grammar School; Aberdeen University. Advocate, 1959; Chairman, Industrial Tribunals, 1972-2003; Chairman, Medical Appeal Tribunals, 1984-2005; Barrister, Lincolns Inn, 1994; Vice President (Scotland), VAT and Duties Tribunals, 1996-2008; Temporary Judge, Court of Session, 1991-2004; Special Commissioner, Income Tax, 1996-2004; Chairman, Financial Services and Markets Tribunal, 2001-08; Chartered Arbitrator. Recreations: travel; stamp collecting. Address: (h.) 6 Heriot Row, Edinburgh.

Cowan, Sheriff Annella Marie, LLB (Hons), MSc. Sheriff of Grampian Highland and Islands at Aberdeen since 1997; b. 14.11.53, Sheffield; m., James Temple Cowan (marriage dissolved). Educ. Elgin Academy; University of Edinburgh. Admitted Solicitor, 1978; Procurator Fiscal Depute, 1978-86; seconded to Scottish Law Commission, 1984-86; admitted Faculty of Advocates, 1987; Sheriff, Tayside Central and Fife at Stirling, 1993. Recreations: equestrianism; foreign travel. Address: Sheriff's Chambers, Sheriff Court, Aberdeen AB10 1WP; T.-01224 648316.

Cowan, Cathie. Chief Executive, NHS Orkney, since 2010. Career history: began NHS career in the 1980s as a nurse in Glasgow and held a number of clinical and managerial posts before taking up role as Director of Nursing in Fife; moved to Fife Health Board as Director of Service Development & Planning, played a key role in service transformation; Director in an integrated health and social care partnership, Glasgow City Council. Deputy Chair, Innovation Partnership Board. Address: NHS Orkney, Balfour Hospital, New Scapa Road, Kirkwall, Orkney KW15 1BH.

Cowan, John Mervyn, TD, MCIBS. Lt. Col. (Retd) RA/TA; b. 13.2.30, Oban; m., Marion Neilson Kidd; 1 s.; 2 d. Educ. Oban High School. National Bank of Scotland, National Commercial Bank of Scotland, Royal Bank of Scotland, 1946-90 (retired); TA commission, 1963; commanded 207 (Scottish) Battery RA(V), 1980-82; J.S.L.O., HQ Scotland, 1982-90; Chairman: The Sandilands Trust, 1993-2011, Royal Artillery Association Scottish Region, 1991-2002 (President, 2002-09), Earl Haig Fund (Scotland), 1993-99, SSAFA West Lothian, 2001-05; Patron, RA Council for Scotland; Trustee, 445 and City of Edinburgh RA Regimental Trusts. Recreations: travel; charitable works; sport. Address: (h.) 39 Kinloch View, Blackness Road, Linlithgow, West Lothian EH49 7HT; T.-01506 671618.

Cowan, Margaret Morton (Lady Cowan), MA. Member, Council, National Trust for Scotland, 1989-94 and 1997-2002; former Member of Executive and of Finance Committee; b. 4.11.33, Newmilns; m., Sir Robert Cowan ; 2 d. Educ. St. George's School for Girls, Edinburgh; Edinburgh University. British Petroleum Company, 1955-59; Teacher, West Midlands Education Authority, 1965-76; Consultant and Lecturer in Use of Language, Hong Kong, 1976-81; Member, Justice of the Peace Committee, Inverness, 1985-2000; Member, Scottish Committee, British Council, 1991-2000; Convener, Highland Festival, 1992-97. Address: (h.) 1 Eyre Crescent, Edinburgh EH3 5ET; T.-0131-556 3379.

Cowan, Ronnie. MP (SNP), Inverclyde, since 2015. Manages IT company; worked with major companies all over the UK and Ireland. Son of Morton and Scotland football goalkeeper Jimmy Cowan. Address: House of Commons, London SW1A 0AA.

Cowie, Alan. Freelance television producer, journalist and broadcaster; Media Training Consultant - Africa, Asia, Middle East, London and Scotland, 2011-16; Digital UK, North of Scotland Liaison, 2008-2010; Head, Current Affairs, Grampian Television, 1998-2000; b. 28.4.48, Aberdeen; m., Evelyn; 2 d. Educ. Aberdeen Grammar School; Central College, London; Jordanhill College of Education, Glasgow. Teacher, Glasgow, 1971-72; Reporter/Presenter, Radio Scotland, 1972-75; joined Grampian Television as News Reporter, 1975; Programme Editor, 1988. Burgess, City of Aberdeen. Recreations: Scottish art; music; fishing; e-mail: alancowietv@aol.com

Cox, Gilbert Kirkwood, CVO, MBE, JP. Lord Lieutenant of Lanarkshire, 2000-2010; Honorary Sheriff, since 2002; Board Member, New Lanarkshire plc; Board Member, Lanarkshire, Prince's Trust, Scotland; Director/Trustee, Airdrie Savings Bank, 1987-2012 (President, 1996-98); retired General Manager Scotland, Associated Perforators & Weavers Ltd.; b. 24.8.35, Chapelhall, Airdrie; m., Marjory Moir Ross Taylor; 2 s.; 1 d. Educ. Airdrie Academy. National Coal Board, 1953-63; David A. McPhail & Sons Ltd., 1963-68; D.A. Monteith Holdings, 1968-71. Chair, Board of Management, Coatbridge College, 1997-2000; founder Member and Past President,

Monklands Rotary Club. Recreations: golf; gardening; walking. Address: (h.) Bedford House, Commonhead Street, Airdrie ML6 6NS; T.-01236 763331.
E-mail: coxgk@btinternet.com

Cox, Roy Frederick, OBE. Chairman, Sense Scotland; Director, Old Mill Chimneys Scotland Ltd, since 2014; b. 4.11.49, Leicester; m., Elizabeth; 1 s.; 1 d. Educ. New Parks Boys School; College of Textiles, Leicester. Engineering apprenticeship, Mellor Bromley; textile mechanical engineer, Corar's. Past President, Clydebank Rotary Club; Member, The Incorporation of Bonnetmakers and Dyers of Glasgow; a Freeman Citizen of Glasgow. Author of Children's book. Recreations: golf; gardening; travelling. Address: Duntiglennan Farm, Farm Road, Duntocher, Clydebank G81 6RS; T.-01389 876061; e-mail: enquiries@scottishchimneys-omh.com

Coyle, Andrew, CMG, BA (Hons), PhD, FKC. President of the Howard League for Penal Reform in Scotland; Emeritus Professor, London University, since 2011; Visiting Professor, Essex University, since 2011; b. 17.6.44, Edinburgh. Educ. Edinburgh University. Scottish Prison Service, including Governor, Greenock, Peterhead and Shotts Prisons, 1973-91; Governor, Brixton Prison, 1991-97; Director, International Centre for Prison Studies and Professor of Prison Studies, Kings College, London University, 1997-2010. Member, Judicial Appointments Board for Scotland, since 2009; Administrative Justice and Tribunals Council, since 2009. T.-020 7842 8505.
E-mail: andrew.coyle@icps.essex.ac.uk

Craig, Ian. Chief Executive Officer, Transport for Edinburgh Ltd, 2013-16; Chief Executive, Lothian Buses, 2013-15; Director, Traveline Scotland Ltd, 2008-2015. Educ. Campbeltown Grammar; Napier University. Commercial Director, ARRIVA Yorkshire Ltd, 2001-03; Director & General Manager, ARRIVA Scotland West Ltd, 2003-06 (3 years, 5 months); Managing Director, Lothian Buses, 2006-2013. Winner, Outstanding Contribution to Public Transport, Scottish Transport Awards 2012; Winner, Edinburgh, Lothians & the Borders Regional Director, Institute of Directors Scotland, Director of the Year Awards, 2011.

Craig, Mary, OBE, FCIBS, FRSA. Strategic Advisor and former Chief Executive, Lloyds TSB Foundation for Scotland (2009-2014); b. Lanarkshire. Career: worked in TSB, 1969-1997, during which she progressed from being a junior teller to a Senior Manager; joined Lloyds TSB Foundation for Scotland in a role working directly with charities in West Central Scotland in 1997, Deputy Chief Executive, 2000-09. Former Chair of Evaluation Support Scotland; involved with many charities, including formal roles, such as The Child and Family Trust (former Chair), and has a leading role in working with Scotland's other charitable funders; former Chair, Scotland's Funders Forum. Address: (b.) Lloyds TSB Foundation for Scotland, Riverside House, 502 Gorgie Road, Edinburgh EH11 3AF; T.-0131 444 4020.

Craig, Susan. Floating Sheriff of Lothian and Borders based at Livingston, since 2013; Solicitor Advocate, since 1994; admitted, Faculty of Advocates, 2015. Educ. University of Aberdeen. Accredited Employment Law Specialist; Litigation partner in Brodies WS until 2001; Partner at Shepherd and Wedderburn until 2003; Employment Judge based in Edinburgh, since 2003; appointed a part-time Sheriff in 2011. Address: Livingston Sheriff Court, Sheriff Court House, The Civic Centre,

Howden South Road, Livingston EH54 6FF; T.-01506 402 400.

Craigie, Cathie. MSP (Labour), Cumbernauld and Kilsyth, 1999-2011; b. 1954, Stirling; m.; 2 c. Councillor, Cumbernauld and Kilsyth District Council, 1984-96 (Council Leader, 1994-96); Member, North Lanarkshire Council, 1995-99; former Chair, Cumbernauld Housing Partnership.

Cramb, Auslan, MA (Hons). Scottish Correspondent, Daily Telegraph since 1994; b. 6.10.56, Dunoon; m., Catriona; 1 s.; 1 d. Educ. Perth Academy; Aberdeen University. Reporter, Press and Journal, 1979-82; Reporter, Press Association, Glasgow, 1982-85; The Herald, Glasgow, 1985-90; Environment Correspondent, The Scotsman, 1990-94. Scottish Specialist Writer of the Year, 1992 and 1993. Publications: Who Owns Scotland Now?, 1996; Fragile Land, 1998. Address: (b.) Daily Telegraph, 5 Coates Crescent, Edinburgh, EH3 7AL.

Cramb, Rev. Erik McLeish, LTh. Former National Co-ordinator, Scottish Churches Industrial Mission; Convener, Church of Scotland Committee on Ecumenical Relations; b. 26.12.39, Glasgow; m., Elizabeth McLean; 2 s.; 3 d. Educ. Woodside Secondary School, Glasgow; Glasgow University and Trinity College. Minister: St. Thomas' Gallowgate, Glasgow, 1973-81, St. Paul's United Church, Kingston, Jamaica, 1981-84, Yoker, Glasgow, 1984-89; Organiser for Tayside, Scottish Churches International Mission, 1989-97. Socialist; Member, Iona Community, 1972-2009; former Chairman, Church Action on Poverty; Hon. Fellow, Al Maktoum Institute. Recreation: supports Partick Thistle. Address: (h.) Flat 35, Braehead, Methven Walk, Dundee DD2 3FJ; T.-01382 526196.
E-mail: erikcramb@blueyonder.co.uk

Cramond, Ronald Duncan, CBE (1987), MA, MPhil, FSA (Scot). Secretary, Intellectual Access Trust, 1995-2012; b. 22.3.27, Leith; m., 1, Constance MacGregor (deceased); 1 s.; 1 d; m., 2, Ann Rayner. Educ. George Heriot's School; Edinburgh University. Commissioned Royal Scots, 1950; entered War Office, 1951; Private Secretary to Parliamentary Under Secretary of State, Scottish Office, 1956; Principal, Department of Health for Scotland, 1957; Mactaggart Fellow, Glasgow University, 1962; Haldane Medallist in Public Administration, 1964; Assistant Secretary, Scottish Development Department, 1966; Under Secretary, 1973; Under Secretary, Department of Agriculture and Fisheries for Scotland, 1977. Deputy Chairman, Highlands and Islands Development Board, 1983-88; Member, Scottish Tourist Board, 1985-88; Trustee: National Museums of Scotland, 1985-96, Cromarty Arts Trust, 1988-91, Bo'ness Heritage Trust, 1989-97, Scottish Civic Trust, 1988-95; Vice President, Architectural Heritage Society of Scotland, 1989-94; Chairman, Scottish Museums Council, 1990-93; Commissioner, Countryside Commission for Scotland, 1988-92; Chairman, Scottish Greenbelt Foundation, 1992-2000. Recreations: reading and researching Scottish history; visiting museums and galleries; testing plastic hips. Address: (h.) 1-8 Dunard Garden, Edinburgh EH9 2HZ.

Cranstoun of That Ilk and Corehouse, David Alexander Somerville, TD, MA, MSc, PhD, DL. Member, Queen's Bodyguard for Scotland (Royal Company of Archers); b. 19.12.43, Washington DC; m., Dr. iur. M.M. Glättli; 2 s. Educ. Winchester College; Trinity College, Oxford. National List Trials Officer, ESCA, 1973; Emeritus Fellow, SAC, 2003. Director, Scottish Quality Cereals; Director, Crop Evaluation Ltd; Member, AHDB Recommended List Project Board; Cereal Specialist, SAC, 1982-2003; Chairman, Scottish Society for Crop Research, 1996-2000; Board Member, Clyde River Purification Board, 1992-96; Member, Clyde Area Advisory Group, 2005-2010; Hon. Director, Lord Roberts Workshops (Edinburgh); Vice President, SSAFA Forces Help (Lanark); Commissioned Queens Own Lowland Yeomanry (TA), 1964, Lt. Col., 1982; Comd District Specialist Training Team, 1988, TA Col. Lowlands, 1990; Hon. Col. Glasgow and Lanarkshire Bn. ACF, 2001-06; Member, Lowland Reserve Forces and Cadets Association, 1969. Recreation: forestry. Address: (h.) Corehouse, Lanark ML11 9TQ.

Craven, Professor Alan James, MA, PhD, FInstP, CPhys, FRMS. Emeritus Professor and Senior Honorary Research Fellow, University of Glasgow, since 2012; b. 18.4.47, St. Helens; m., Rosalind; 1 s.; 1 d. Educ. Prescot Grammar School; Emmanuel College, Cambridge University. Cavendish Laboratory, Cambridge: Research Student, 1969-75, Post-doctoral Research Assistant, 1975-78; Department of Physics and Astronomy, University of Glasgow: Lecturer, 1978-89, Senior Lecturer, 1989-91, Reader in Physics, 1991-98, Professor of Physics, 1998-2012. Address: School of Physics and Astronomy, University of Glasgow, Glasgow G12 8QQ.

Crawford, Barbara Elizabeth, OBE, MA (Hons), PhD. Honorary Reader in Medieval History, St. Andrews University, since 2001; Hon. Director, Strathmartine Centre for Scottish History; b. 5.4.40, Barnsley; m., Robert M.M. Crawford; 1 s. Educ. Queen Margaret's School; St. Andrews University. Carnegie Senior Scholarship, 1968; Temporary Lecturer, Department of History, Aberdeen University, 1969; Lecturer in Medieval History, St. Andrews University, 1972. Elected Fellow, Society of Antiquaries London, 1973; Fellow Society of Antiquaries of Scotland, 1964; Member Norwegian Academy of Science and Letters, 1997; Fellow, Royal Society of Edinburgh, 2001; Leverhulme Research Fellow, 2000-01; President of the Society of Antiquaries of Scotland, 2008-2011; awarded Hon. Professorship, University of the Highlands & Islands. Publications: Scandinavian Scotland, 1987; The Biggings, Papa Stour, Shetland, 1999; The Northern Earldoms: Orkney and Caithness from AD 870-1470, 2013. Recreations: exploring areas of Viking settlement in Scotland and North Atlantic. Address: (b.) The Strathmartine Centre, 2, Kinburn Place, St. Andrews KY16 9DT; T.-01334 478644.
E-mail: bec@strathmartine.demon.co.uk

Crawford, Professor Dorothy H., OBE, MBBS, PhD, MD, DSc, FRCPath, FRSE, FAcadMedSci. Emeritus Professor of Medical Microbiology, University of Edinburgh, since 2010 (Professor, 1997-2010); b. 13.4.45, Glasgow; m., Dr. W.D. Alexander; 2 s. Educ. St. Thomas's Hospital Medical School. Senior Lecturer then Reader, Royal Post-graduate Medical School, London, 1985-90; Professor of Medical Microbiology, London School of Hygiene and Tropical Medicine, 1990-97.

Crawford, Douglas James, LLB, DipLP, NP, CF, WS. Partner in CMS Cameron McKenna LLP; formerly Partner and Founder in the corporate group of Aberdeen office, Dundas & Wilson (1997-2014); b. 28.2.65, Ayr; m., Alison; 1 s.; 2 d. Educ. Belmont Academy, Ayr; Edinburgh University. Trained, Shepherd & Wedderburn WS, 1987-89; Assistant, Associate, Partner, Maclay Murray & Spens, 1989-97. Recreations: golf; winter sports. Address: (b.) 6 Queen's Road, Aberdeen AB14 4ZT; T.-07798 855 290; e-mail: douglas.crawford@cms-cmck.com

Crawford, Professor Elizabeth Bryden, LLB (Hons), PhD. Emeritus Professor of International Private Law, University of Glasgow; b. 20.04.49, Glasgow; m., Robin Crawford; 1 s.; 1 d. Educ. Laurel Bank School, Glasgow; University of Glasgow. Admitted as Solicitor,

1974; successively since 1976, Lecturer, Senior Lecturer, Reader in the Conflict of Laws, Professor, University of Glasgow. Publications include: Crawford & Carruthers, International Private Law: A Scots Perspective, 4th edition, 2015. Recreations: golf; cooking. Address: (b.) School of Law, Stair Building, University of Glasgow, Glasgow G12 8QQ; T.-0141-330 4729; e-mail: e.crawford@law.gla.ac.uk

Crawford, Hugh William Jack, BArch, DipTP, RIBA, FRIAS, FRTPI. Principal, Sir Frank Mears Associates, since 1985; Part-time Inquiry Reporter (Local Plans), Scottish Executive, 1982-2005; b. 19.1.38, Dalry; m., Catherine Mary McIntyre; 1 s.; 2 d. Educ. Dalry High School; University of Strathclyde. Partner, Sir Frank Mears and Partners, 1965-85. Scottish Chairman, Royal Town Planning Institute, 1979, 1980, 1992; Past President, Committee of Liaison for Planning Practitioners in Member Countries of the European Union; President of Honour, European Council of Town Planners, Brussels, since 1985; former National Vice-President, Pedestrians Association; President, Association of Mediators. Recreations: walking; visiting historic buildings and towns; art galleries and museums. Address: (b.) 67 Ferry Gait Drive, Edinburgh EH4 4GJ; T.-0131 531 8455.
E-mail: h.crawford@btinternet.com

Crawford, Professor Robert, MA, DPhil, FRSE, FBA, FEA. Professor of Modern Scottish Literature and Bishop Wardlaw Professor of Poetry, School of English, St. Andrews University, since 1995 (Head of School, 2002-05); Associate Director, St. Andrews Scottish Studies Centre, 1993-2009; Poet and Critic; b. 23.2.59, Bellshill; m., Alice Wales; 1 s.; 1 d. Educ. Hutchesons' Grammar School, Glasgow; Glasgow University; Balliol College, Oxford. Snell Exhibitioner & Carnegie Scholar, Balliol College, Oxford, 1981-84; Elizabeth Wordsworth Junior Research Fellow, St. Hugh's College, Oxford, 1984-87; British Academy Postdoctoral Fellow, Department of English Literature, Glasgow University, 1987-89; Lecturer in Modern Scottish Literature, School of English, St. Andrews University, 1989-95. Former Co-Editor, Verse Magazine; Co-Editor, Scottish Studies Review, 1999-2004. Publications: The Savage and the City in the Work of T.S. Eliot, 1987; A Scottish Assembly, 1990; Sharawaggi (Co-author), 1990; About Edwin Morgan (Co-Editor), 1990; Other Tongues: young Scottish poets in English, Scots and Gaelic (Editor), 1990; The Arts of Alasdair Gray (Co-Editor), 1991; Devolving English Literature, 1992; Talkies, 1992; Reading Douglas Dunn (Co-Editor), 1992; Identifying Poets, 1993; Liz Lochhead's Voices (Co-Editor), 1993; Twentieth Century Literature of Scotland: a selected bibliography, 1995; Talking Verse (Co-Editor), 1995; Masculinity, 1996; Penguin Modern Poets 9 (Co-Author), 1996; Robert Burns and Cultural Authority (Editor), 1997; Launch-site for English Studies: Three Centuries of Literary Studies at the University of St. Andrews (Editor), 1997; Impossibility, 1998; The Scottish Invention of English Literature (Editor), 1998; The Penguin Book of Poetry from Britain and Ireland since 1945 (Co-Editor), 1998; Spirit Machines, 1999; The New Penguin Book of Scottish Verse (Co-Editor), 2000; Scottish Religious Poetry (Co-Editor), 2000; The Modern Poet, 2001; Heaven-Taught Fergusson, 2002; The Tip of My Tongue, 2003; Selected Poems, 2005; The Book of St. Andrews (Editor), 2005; Apollos of the North, 2006; Contemporary Poetry and Contemporary Science, 2006 (Editor); Scotland's Books, 2007; Full Volume, 2008; The Bard, Robert Burns, A Biography, 2009; The Best Laid Schemes (Co-Editor), 2009; New Poems, Chiefly in the Scottish Dialect (Editor), 2009; The Beginning and the End of the World, 2011; Simonides, 2011; On Glasgow and Edinburgh, 2013; Bannockburns: Scottish Independence and Literary Imagination, 1314-2014, 2014; Testament,

2014; Young Eliot, 2015. Recreation: mischief. Address: (b.) School of English, St. Andrews University, St. Andrews, KY16 9AL; T.-01334 476161, Ext. 2666.

Crawford, 29th Earl of, and Balcarres, 12th Earl of (Robert Alexander Lindsay), KT, GCVO, PC. Premier Earl of Scotland; Head of House of Lindsay; b. 5.3.27; m., Ruth Beatrice Meyer; 2 s.; 2 d. Eton; Trinity College, Cambridge. Grenadier Guards, 1945-49; MP (Conservative), Hertford, 1955-74, Welwyn and Hatfield, February to September, 1974; Opposition Front Bench Spokesman on Health and Social Security, 1967-70; Minister of State for Defence, 1970-72; Minister of State for Foreign and Commonwealth Affairs, 1972-74; Chairman, Lombard North Central Bank, 1976-80; Director, National Westminster Bank, 1975-88; Director, Scottish American Investment Co., 1978-88; Vice-Chairman, Sun Alliance & London Insurance Group, 1975-91; President, Rural District Councils Association, 1959-65; Chairman, National Association of Mental Health, 1963-70; Chairman, Historic Buildings Council for Scotland, 1976-83; Chairman, Royal Commission on Ancient and Historical Monuments of Scotland, 1985-95; First Crown Estate Commissioner, 1980-85; former Deputy Lieutenant, Fife; Chairman, National Library of Scotland, 1990-2000; Lord Chamberlain to HM Queen Elizabeth The Queen Mother, 1992-2002. Hon. Fellow, RIAS, NLS. Address: (h.) Balcarres, Colinsburgh, Fife KY9 1HN.

Crawford, Robert Hardie Bruce, JP. MSP (SNP), Stirling, since 2007, Mid Scotland and Fife, 1999-2007; Cabinet Secretary for Parliamentary Business and Government Strategy, 2011-2012; Minister for Parliamentary Business, 2007-2011; Chairman, SNP, 2004-07; Shadow Minister for Parliament, 2003-04; Shadow Minister, Environment and Energy, 2001-03; Shadow Minister, Transport and the Environment, 2000-01; Chief Whip, SNP Scottish Parliamentary Group, 1999-2001; b. 16.2.55, Perth; m., Jacqueline; 3 s. Educ. Kinross High School; Perth High School. Civil servant, Scottish Office, 1974-99; Leader, Perth and Kinross Council, 1995-99; Chairman, Kinross-shire Partnership Ltd., 1997-99; Chairman, Perth and Kinross Recreation Facilities Ltd, 1995-99; Member: Perthshire Tourist Board, Scottish Enterprise Tayside, Perth College, 1995-99. Recreations: golf; watching Dunfermline Athletic. Address: (h.) 12 Douglas Crescent, Kinross; T.-01577 863531.

Crawford, Robin, LLB, CA. Chair, Scottish Government Review of Procurement in Construction, 2012-13; Vice Chairman of Scottish Further and Higher Education Funding Council; Director, Skills Development Scotland Ltd; Member of Court, Strathclyde University, 2007-14; Vice Chairman of Erskine; Director of The Merchants House of Glasgow. Partner, KPMG, 1979-2003; Captain, Glasgow Golf Club, 2008; Chairman, Scottish Business Crime Centre Ltd., 2003-08; Member, Council, CBI Scotland, 2000-06; Governor, then Vice-Chairman, Laurel Bank and Laurel Park Schools, 1998-98; b. 2.10.48, Greenock; m., Elizabeth; 1 s.; 1 d. Educ. Greenock Academy; Glasgow University. Recreations: golf; fly fishing; hillwalking.
E-mail: robert.crawford3@ntlworld.com

Crawford, Ruth, QC, LLB (Hons), DipLP. Admitted Faculty of Advocates, 1993; b. 17.7.65, Glasgow. Educ. Cranley School for Girls; George Heriot's School; Aberdeen University. Standing Junior Counsel to Keeper of the Registers of Scotland, 1998-2002; Second Standing Junior Counsel to Scottish Executive, since 2002. Address: Advocate's Library, Parliament House, Parliament Square, Edinburgh EH1 1RF; T.-0131-226 5071.

Crawley, Angela, BA. MP (SNP), Lanark and Hamilton East, since 2015; SNP Spokesperson for Women and Equalities and Young People and Community Resources; b. Hamilton. Educ. University of Stirling; University of Glasgow. Worked in Brighton for the Educational Travel Group; elected to South Lanarkshire Council for the Hamilton Ward in 2012; National Convenor of the SNP's youth-wing, Young Scots for Independence, since 2014; sits on the National Executive Committee; member of the House of Commons Women and Equalities Committee; former Parliamentary Assistant for a Government Minister and Member of the Scottish Parliament. Address: House of Commons, London SW1A 0AA.

Creally, Eugene P., LLB (Hons), DipLP, PhD. Appointed Queen's Counsel, 2011; Advocate, since 1993; Clerk of Faculty, Faculty of Advocates, 1999-2003; Standing Junior Counsel to Lord Advocate (1998-2005); Counsel to Billy Wright Inquiry; Vice Chairman of Faculty of Advocates Free Legal Services Unit; Member of the Court of Session Rules Council, 2004-2011; Standing Counsel to Advocate General for Scotland, 2009-2012; b. 3.2.61, Dungannon, Co. Tyrone; 1 s. Educ. St Patrick's Academy, Dungannon; Queens University, Belfast; Edinburgh University. Address: (b.) Advocates Library, Parliament House, Edinburgh EH1 1RF; T.-0131-226 5071.

Crerar, Lorne Donald, LLB (Hons), NP, FCIBS. Founding Partner and Chairman, Harper Macleod LLP, since 1987; Chair in Banking Law, University of Glasgow, since 1997; b. 29.07.54, Renfrew. Educ. Kelvinside Academy, Glasgow; Glasgow University. Partner in Mackenzie Robertson & Co, 1979-87. Chairman, Discipline for Scottish Rugby Union, since 1995; International Rugby Board Judicial Officer, since 1995; Chairman, Discipline for European Rugby Cup Limited, since 1999; Chairman, Discipline for 6 Nations Limited, since 1999; Deputy Chairman, Scottish Enterprise Glasgow, 2000-2003; Chairman, Sub-Group Housing Improvement Task Force, 2001-03; Convener, Standards Commission for Scotland, 2003-07; Non Executive Director, Scottish Government Justice Department, until 2011; Independent Member of the Purchasers Information Advisory Group, 2005-08; Chairman, Independent Review of Audit, Inspection, Regulation and Complaints Handling in the Public Sector ("The Crerar Review") (1 July 2006-August 2008). Board Member, Highlands & Islands Enterprise, 2007-2011; Chairman, Highlands & Islands Enterprise, since 2011; Chairman Highlands and Islands Audit Committee, 2011-2012; Advisory Board Member, Scottish Investment Bank, since 2011. On Editorial Board of "World Sports Law Report"; elected "Fellow" of the Chartered Institute of Bankers, June 1999; listed in "Chambers Guide to the Legal Profession" as one of Scotland's very few "Sports Law Experts". Publications: "The Law of Banking in Scotland", 2nd edition, 2007; commissioned author for Stair Memorial Encyclopedia (the leading Scottish Text) for financial institutions, banking and currency (published December 2000); Independent Reviewer of Lending Code, 2010-11 which covers all personal and small business lending in the UK. Recreations: The West Highlands of Scotland and its history; hillwalking; fishing and sailing. Address (b) Harper Macleod LLP, The Ca'd'oro Building, 45 Gordon Street, Glasgow G1 3PE; T.-0414 227-9377.
E-mail: lorne.crerar@harpermacleod.co.uk

Crerar, Paddy. Chief Executive, North British Trust Group, since 2002; Non Executive Director: Highlands and Islands Enterprise, since 2014, VisitScotland, 2009-2015; b. 21.10.68, Oban; m., Sheila. Educ. Rockfield, Oban; George Watson's, Edinburgh. Career: Commercial Union Assurance; North British Trust Group; Founding Director, North British Holidays, British Trust Hotels; Easy Breaks and Crerar Hotels; Founder of Crerar Management Ltd., CEO of Swallow Hotels; owner of Newmains Farm - Pedigree Luing & Highland Cattle. Thistle Award Winner; Trustee of Hospitality Industry Trust Scotland; Chairman, North British Hotels Trust; Director of Mull & Iona Enterprise. Recreations: field sports; sailing and shouting at kids; hockey; rugby. Address: (b.) 1 Queen Charlotte Lane, Edinburgh; T.-0131 561 1203.
E-mail: crerar@crerarhotels.com

Cresswell, Lyell Richard, BMus (Hons), MusM, PhD. Composer; b. 13.10.44, Wellington, New Zealand; m., Catherine Mawson. Educ. Victoria University of Wellington; Toronto University; Aberdeen University. Music Organiser, Chapter Arts Centre, Cardiff; Forman Fellow, Edinburgh University, 1980-82; Canadian Commonwealth scholarship, 1969-70; Dutch Government bursary, 1974-75; Ian Whyte Award, 1978; APRA Silver Scroll, 1979; Cramb Fellow, Glasgow University, 1982-85; Winner, Scottish Arts Council Creative Scotland Award, 2001; Inaugural Elgar Bursary, 2002; Hon. DMus, Victoria University of Wellington, New Zealand, 2002; New Zealand School of Music/Creative New Zealand Composer in Residence, 2006-07; Sounz Contemporary Award, 2011. Address: (h.) 4 Leslie Place, Edinburgh EH4 1NQ; T.-0131-332 9181; e-mail: lcress@talktalk.net

Crewe, Martin Alistair, BSc, PhD, MBA, MSc. Director, Barnardo's Scotland, since 2007; b. 13.07.60, London; m., Jane; 3 s.; 1 d. Educ. Alleyn's School, London; Exeter University; Nottingham-Trent University; Stirling University. Regional Manager, NSPCC, 1989-97; Finance Director, Barnardo's Scotland, 1997-2007. Board Member, Office of The Scottish Charity Regulator (OSCR), 2006-2010; Board Member, Edinburgh College, 2012-2015. Recreation: bringing up children. Address: (b.) 111 Oxgangs Road North, Edinburgh EH14 1ED; T.-0131 446 7000; e-mail: martin.crewe@barnardos.org.uk

Crichton, David. Chair, NHS Health Scotland, since 2015. Over 35 years of experience in economic development, research and consulting, working in the academic, public and private sectors. Chief Executive: Scottish Enterprise Edinburgh and Lothian, 1998-2003, Confederation of Forest Industries, 2005-2007; Global Director of Country and Economic Research in the Economist Intelligence Unit until 2009, and since then has worked as an international development adviser in Afghanistan, Serbia, Tanzania and Montserrat. Board of NHS Lothian, 2004-2007; Director of Harakat, a Non-Governmental Organisation promoting investment reforms in Afghanistan. Address: (b.) Meridan Court, NHS Health Scotland, 5 Cadogan Street, Glasgow G2 6QE; e-mail: healthscotlandchair@nhs.net

Crichton, John Hugh McDiarmid, BMedSci (Hons), BMBS, PhD, FRC Psych, FHEA. Consultant Forensic Psychiatrist, since 2000; Honorary Fellow in Law, since 2000; Honorary Senior Clinical Lecturer, 2011; Chair of the Faculty of Forensic Psychiatry, Royal College of Psychiatrists in Scotland, since 2012; Consultant to the International Committee of the Red Cross, since 2015; Clinical Director, Forensic Medicine and Psychiatry, Psychotherapy and Rehabilitation; Clinical Lead, Forensic Mental Health, NHS Lothian, 2009-2011; Medical Director, Forensic Mental Health Services managed Care Network and State Hospital's Board for Scotland, 2005-06; b. 8.9.66, Edinburgh; m., Dr. Anne-Marie Crichton; 3 d. Educ. Edinburgh Academy; Nottingham University; Trinity Hall, Cambridge. Nightingale Research Scholar, Institute of Criminology, Cambridge University, 1993; Lecturer in Developmental Psychiatry, Cambridge University, 1997;

Lecturer in Forensic Psychiatry, Edinburgh University, 1998. Publications: Psychiatric Patient Violence: Risk and Response, 1995; Homicide, Mental Disorder and the Media, 2015. Recreation: gardening. Address: (b.) Orchard Clinic, Royal Edinburgh Hospital, Edinburgh EH10 5HF; T.-0131-537 5858; e-mail: john.crichton@nhslothian.scot.nhs.uk

Crichton, Robin, Chevalier des Arts et des Lettres. Retired film producer and director; b. 14.5.40, Bournemouth; m., 1, Trish Dorrell, 2, Flora Maxwell Stuart; 3 d. Educ. Sherborne; Paris; Edinburgh. Built Scotland's first independent film studio, 1968; started film training scheme, now Napier University M.A., 1970; founded first animation studio in Scotland; managed first independent outside broadcast unit in Scotland; Founder Member: Scottish ACTT Committee, Scottish Film Archive; former UK Vice-Chair and Scottish Chair, Independent Programme Producers' Association; former Co-ordinator, Working Party, Scottish Screen; co-initiated Annual Co-production Conference; organised Scottish stand at international TV television markets; Churchill Fellowship, 1990 (to study models for Scottish Screen); Co-production Consultant to various European broadcasters and producers; former Project Leader, Eureka Audiovisual Federation; founder Director, Scottish Screen Locations; Consultant Programme Buyer, Gaelic Television Committee; President, L'Association Charles Rennie Mackintosh en Roussillon; Chairman, The King Arthur Trust Association. Publications: On the Trail of King Arthur; Monsieur Mackintosh; Sara; The Curious Case of Santa Claus; Christmas Mouse. Recreations: writing; DIY. Address: Keeper's House, Traquair, by Innerleithen, Peebleshire EH44 6PP; T.-01896 831188.
E-mail: crichton.efp@g.mail.com

Criddle, Byron John, BA (Keele), MA (Leicester). Emeritus Reader in Politics, University of Aberdeen, since 2007; Honorary Research Fellow, Swansea University, since 2007; b. 23.03.42, Stroud, Gloucestershire; m., Professor Janet Askham (deceased); 1 s.; 1 d. Educ. The Judd School, Tonbridge, Kent; University of Keele; University of Leicester. Assistant History Master, Newarke Girls' School, Leicester, 1964-66; Assistant Lecturer in Politics, University of Aberdeen, 1968-69, Lecturer in Politics, 1969-84; Visiting Professor of Political Science, University of Massachusetts, 1984-85; Senior Lecturer in Politics, University of Aberdeen, 1985-95, Reader in Politics, 1995-2007. Publications: Socialists and European Integration: A Study of the French Socialist Party (1969); The French Socialist Party: Resurgence and Victory (Co-Author), 1984; The French Socialist Party: Emergence of a Party of Government (Co-Author), 1988; The French Communist Party in the Fifth Republic (Co-Author), 1994; The Almanac of British Politics (Co-Author), 1996, 1999, 2002, 2005 editions; Parliamentary Profiles (Co-Author), various editions from 1997; contributor since 1983 to Nuffield General Election Studies, most recently The British General Election of 2010, 2010. Recreations: book accumulation: occasional broadcasting; hymnology. Address: (h.) 1 Cardigan Mansions, 19 Richmond Hill, Richmond, Surrey TW10 6RD and 121 Blenheim Place, Aberdeen AB25 2DL; T.-020 8940 4863; e-mail: b.criddle@abdn.ac.uk

Crockart, Mike, BSc (Social Services). MP (Liberal Democrat), Edinburgh West, 2010-2015; m.; 2 s. Educ. Perth High School; Edinburgh University. Career: contested Edinburgh North and Leith, 2005 general election; Convener, Edinburgh West Liberal Democrats, 2009; PPS to Michael Moore as Secretary of State for Scotland until 2010. Member: Joint Committee on Human Rights, 2011-12, Business, Innovation and Skills Select Committee, 2012, Scottish Affairs Select Committee, 2012; Liberal Democrat Parliamentary Party DECC Committee Co-Chair, 2012-2013; Founder of the APPG on Nuisance Calls. Recreations: photography; classical music. Address: (b.) 185 St John's Road, Edinburgh EH12 7SL.

Crofts, Roger Stanley, CBE, BA, MLitt, CertEd, FRSE, FRSGS, FRGS, FIEEM, Hon DSc (St Andrews), Hon DSc (Glasgow); Knight's Cross of the Icelandic Order of the Falcon; Icelandic Soil Conservation Medal. Adviser, lecturer and writer; Chief Executive, Scottish Natural Heritage, 1991-2002; b. 17.1.44, Leicester; m. Lindsay Manson; 1 s.; 1 d. Educ. Hinckley Grammar School; Liverpool University; Leicester University. Research Assistant in Geography: Aberdeen University, 1966-72, University College, London, 1972-74; entered Scottish Office, 1974; Senior Research Officer, 1974-78; Principal Research Officer, 1978-84; Assistant Secretary, Highlands and Tourism Division, Industry Department, 1984-88; Assistant Secretary, Rural Affairs Division, Scottish Development Department, 1988-91. Chairman, IUCN UK Committee, 1999-2002; Chair, World Commission on Protected Areas (Europe), 2001-08; Chairman, Plantlife International, 2007-2010; Chairman, Royal Scottish Geographical Society, since 2014; Board Member: Scottish Agricultural College, 2002-2010, National Trust for Scotland, 2004-09, Fieldfare Ecological Development, Crichton Carbon Centre, 2009-2014, Galloway and Southern Ayrshire Biosphere Reserve; Project Director, Watson Bird Centre and Celebration; Patron, Scottish Association of Geography Teachers; Visiting Professor in Geography and Environment, University of Aberdeen, 1998-2012; Honorary Professor in Geoscience, University of Edinburgh, until 2011. Publications: Co-Author/Editor: 'Land of Mountain and Flood'; 'Scotland's Environment: the Future'; 'Conserving Nature: Scotland and the Wider World'; 'Scotland: The Creation of its Natural Landscape'; 'Ecosystems and Health: a UK Perspective'; 'Healing the Land: Soil Conservation and Land Restoration in Iceland'. Recreations: gardening; choral singing; hill-walking; wildflower photography. Address: (h.) 6 Eskside West, Musselburgh EH21 6HZ; T.-0131-665 0788.

Cromartie, Earl of (John Ruaridh Grant Mackenzie), MIExpE. Land manager, since 1989; Executive Member, Mountaineering Council of Scotland, 1990-2007, and President, 2003-07; Explosives Consultant, since 1979; b. 12.6.48, Inverness; m. (1), Janet; 2 s.; m. (2), Jane Margaret Eve Austin. Educ. Rannoch School; Strathclyde University. Research Geologist, New Quebec, 1970s; Chief of the Clan Mackenzie and as such do (unpaid) visits to USA, Canada, Australia, as unofficial ambassador for Scotland; President, Scottish Mountaineering Club, 2012-2014. Many articles on mountaineering; co-author of guide books on mountaineering. Recreations: mountaineering; geology; art. Address: (h.) Castle Leod, Strathpeffer IV14 9AA; T.-01997 421264.

Crombie, Sir Alexander (Sandy), FFA; b. 08.02.49; m. Margaret; 2 d. Educ. Buckhaven High School. Senior Independent Director, Royal Bank of Scotland Group plc, 2009; Vice Chairman, The Board of Governors of The Royal Conservatoire of Scotland, 2007; President, The Cockburn Association, 2009. Joined Standard Life, 1966; Group Chief Investment Manager, 1996-98; Chief Executive Standard Life Investments, 1998-04; Group Chief Executive, Standard Life, 2004-09. Chairman, Creative Scotland, 2010-15; Chairman, UNESCO City of Literature Trust, 2006-11. Address: (b.) Royal Bank of Scotland, Gogarburn, Edinburgh EH12 1HQ.

Crompton, Professor David William Thomasson, OBE, MA, PhD, ScD, BSc (Open), FRSE, FRSB. Director, St Andrew's Clinics for Children, since 1992; b. 5.12.37, Bolton; m., Effie Mary Marshall; 1 s.; 2 d.

Educ. Bolton School; Sidney Sussex College, University of Cambridge; Fellow, Sidney Sussex College, Cambridge, 1964-85; Lecturer, Parasitology, Cambridge University, 1968-85; Adjunct Professor, Nutritional Sciences, Cornell University, 1981-2004; John Graham Kerr Professor of Zoology, Glasgow University, 1985-2000; Visiting Professor, University of Nebraska, 1982; Chairman, Company of Biologists Ltd., 1994-2000; Scientific Medal, Zoological Society of London, 1977; Member, WHO Expert Committee on Parasitology; Hon. Member: Slovak Society of Parasitologists, 1999, American Society of Parasitologists, 2001, Helminthological Society of Washington, 2002. Honorary Fellow, University of Glasgow, 2005. Publications: author/editor,10 books; Co-editor, Parasitology, 1972- 82; author/co-editor, 250 scientific papers, Recreations: books; gardening. Address: (h.) 101A Clifton Hill, London NW8 0JR; T.-0207 625 1204; e-mail: dwtc@tyndrum.demon.co.uk

Crook, Professor Jonathan Nicholas, BA, MSc (Econ), Hon DBA, FRSE. Professor of Business Economics, University of Edinburgh Business School; Director, Credit Research Centre, Edinburgh University, since 1997; b. 2.5.53, Clevedon; m., Kate Vincent; 2 d. Educ. Cheltenham Grammar School; Lancaster University; University College, Cardiff. Research Assistant, Sheffield University, 1977-79; Lecturer, then Senior Lecturer, then Reader, Department of Business Studies, Edinburgh University, 1979-2002, Head of Management Science and Business Economics Group, 2005-09, Director of Research, since 2014. Joint winner, Goodeve Medal (OR Society). Fellow, Wharton Financial Institutions Center, University of Pennsylvania, USA; External Research Fellow, Centre for Finance, Credit and Macroeconomics, University of Nottingham; Fellow, Royal Society of Edinburgh. Publications: Managerial Economics (Co-author); Economics of Modern Business (Co-author); Credit Scoring and its Applications (Co-author); Credit Scoring and Credit Control (Co-editor); Readings in Credit Scoring (Co-editor); Joint Editor, Journal of the Operations Research Society. Awarded Honorary Doctorate, University of Abertay, 2011. Recreations: singing; walking; enjoying family. Address: (b.) Credit Research Centre, University of Edinburgh Business School, Edinburgh University, 29 Buccleuch Place, Edinburgh EH8 9JS; T.-0131 650 3802; e-mail: j.crook@ed.ac.uk

Cross, Mhairi. Chief Executive, National Mining Museum Scotland, since 2015. Wealth of experience in the cultural sector, spanning over 20 years. Set up the first contemporary art gallery in Falkirk, establishing artist in residence programmes across educational establishments in North Lanarkshire and developing the Arts and Museum Service in Renfrewshire; also successfully developed the visitor experience within Paisley Museum and the educational programme for children and young people. Recreations: cultural activities; canoeing; kayaking; cycling; running; swimming. Address: (b.) Lady Victoria Colliery, Newtongrange, Midlothian EH22 4QN; T.-0131 663 7519.

Cross, Mike. Director, Health and Safety Executive, Scotland and Northern England, since 2014. Address: (b.) Belford House, 59 Belford Road, Edinburgh EH4 3UE.

Cross, Professor Rod, BSc (Econ), BPhil. Professor of Economics, University of Strathclyde, since 1991; Visiting Professor, University of Aix-Marseille, since 2003; b. 27.3.51, Wigan. Educ. Wigan Grammar School; London School of Economics; University of York. Research Assistant, University of Manchester, 1972-74; Temporary Lecturer, Queen Mary College, University of London, 1974-75; Lecturer, University of St. Andrews, 1975-91. Adviser to Governor, Polish National Bank, 1990-92; Occasional Member, H.M. Treasury Academic Panel. Publications: Economic Theory and Policy in the UK, 1982; Unemployment Hysteresis and the Natural Rate Hypothesis (Editor), 1988; The Natural Rate of Unemployment, 1995. Recreations: hillwalking; rugby league and union, fiction. Address: (b.) Department of Economics, University of Strathclyde, Sir William Duncan Building, 130 Rottenrow, Glasgow G4 0GE; T.-0141-548 3855/4555; e-mail: rod.cross@strath.ac.uk

Crotty, Professor Patrick. Professor of Irish and Scottish Literature, University of Aberdeen, since 2005 (Head of School of Language and Literature, 2009-2012); b. 18.04.52, Fermoy, Ireland; 3 s. Educ. St. Colman's College, Fermoy; University College Cork; University of Stirling. Primary Teacher, Lismore, Co. Waterford, Bishopstown, Cork, 1978-86; Senior Lecturer in English, Trinity College, Carmarthen, Wales, 1986-98; Head of English Department, St. Patrick's College, Dublin City University, 1998-2001; Professor of Irish and Scottish Literary History, University of Ulster, 2001-05; Director of Research Institute of Irish and Scottish Studies, University of Aberdeen, 2007-09. Director of Yeats International Summer School, Sligo, 2006-08. Publications: Modern Irish Poetry, 1995; Penguin Book of Irish Verse, 2010; Oxford Companion to English Literature (Associate Editor), 2009. Recreation: music. Address: (b.) Taylor Building, University of Aberdeen, King's College, Aberdeen AB24 3UB; T.-01224 272562. E-mail: p.j.crotty@abdn.ac.uk

Crowe, Sheriff Frank Richard, LLB. Sheriff of Lothian and Borders at Edinburgh, since 2008; Solicitor Advocate; b. 15.3.52, Kirkcaldy; m., Alison Margaret Purdom (separated); partner, The Hon. Lady Scott; 2 d.; 1 s. Educ. Kirkcaldy High School; Royal High School, Edinburgh; University of Dundee. Law Apprentice, North of Scotland Hydro-Electric Board, 1973-75; Procurator Fiscal Depute: Dundee, 1975-78, Glasgow 1978-81; Senior Legal Assistant, Crown Office, 1981-83; Senior Depute Procurator Fiscal, Edinburgh 1983-87; Senior Depute i/c Crown Office Fraud Unit, 1987-88; Assistant Solicitor i/c High Court Unit, Crown Office, 1988-91; Procurator Fiscal, Kirkcaldy, 1991-96; Regional Procurator Fiscal, South Strathclyde, Dumfries and Galloway, 1996-99; Procurator Fiscal, Hamilton, 1996-99; Deputy Crown Agent, Crown Office, 1999-2001; Sheriff of Tayside Central and Fife at Dundee, 2001-04; Director of the Judicial Studies Committee, 2004-08. Member: Management Committee, Lothian Victim Support Scheme, 1983-89, Training Advisory Committee, Victim Support Scotland, 1994-98, Council, Law Society of Scotland, 1996-99, Scottish Executive Stephen Lawrence Steering Group, 1999-2001; Chairman, Advisory Committee, Zone Project Dundee, 2003-04; Consultant to Justice Oversight Commission for Northern Ireland, 2003-06; Member and latterly Chairman of Stockbridge Primary School Board, Edinburgh, 2003-07; Member of Antisocial Behaviour Expert Advisory Group, 2008-09; Member of the Council of the Sheriffs' Association, 2004-2008; contributor to "Sentencing Practice", since 2004; External Examiner in Criminal and Civil Procedure for the Law Diploma at Edinburgh University, 2004-09; Member of Bail Project Board, 2007-2008; Member of Lay Justice Reform Group, 2007-08; Member of Expert Group in Scottish Government Review of Anti-Social Behaviour legislation, 2008-2009; Member of the Criminal Courts Rules Council, since 2008; Member of

Advisory Committee into Research on Drug Treatment and Testing II Orders, 2009-2010; Member of Lothian and Borders Justice of the Peace Training Committee, since 2011; President, The Royal High School FP Club, since 2013; Member, Board of Apex Scotland, since 2013. Publications: Criminal Appeals Chapter in the Stair Encyclopaedia; Co-author of the JSC Bench Book for Justices of the Peace and Legal Advisers' Manual. Recreations: dog walking; racing; music. Address: (b.) Edinburgh Sheriff Court, 27 Chambers Street, Edinburgh EH1 1LB; e-mail: sheriff.frcrowe@scotcourts.gov.uk

Crowe, Victoria Elizabeth, OBE, Drhc, MA (RCA), RSA, RSW. Artist, Painter and Printmaker; b. 8.5.45, Kingston-on-Thames; m., Michael Walton; 1 s. (deceased); 1 d. Educ. Ursuline Convent Grammar School, London; Kingston College of Art; Royal College of Art. Part-time Lecturer, Drawing and Painting, Edinburgh College of Art, 1968-98; solo exhibitions: Scottish Gallery, Edinburgh, 1970, 1973, 1977, 1982, 1995, 1998, 2001, 2004, 2008, 2010, 2012, 2014; Thackeray Gallery, London, 1983, 1985, 1987, 1989, 1991, 1994, 1999, 2001, 2003, 2005, 2007; Bruton Gallery, Bath and Leeds, 1989, 1993, 1998; Plant memory: Royal Scottish Academy, 2007; A Shepherd's Life, retrospective, Scottish National Portrait Gallery, 2000, touring throughout Scotland and to Mercer Art Gallery, Harrogate, and Hatton Art Gallery, Newcastle upon Tyne, 2001-02; Shepherd's Life, 2009 Fleming Collection, London; overview, retrospective solo show, Fine Art Society, London, 2009; solo show, Browse and Darby, London, 2012, 2015; exhibited throughout Europe and USA with Artists for Nature Foundation; significant portrait commissions, NPG, SNPG, universities and public bodies; work in public and private collections, 2003-07; Senior Visiting Scholar, St. Catherine's College, Cambridge University; Honorary doctorate, Aberdeen University, 2009; elected fellow of Royal Society Edinburgh, 2010. Recreation: travel. Address: (b.) c/o Scottish Gallery, 16 Dundas Street, Edinburgh EH3 6HZ.

Crozier, Paul Vincent. Resident Sheriff of Glasgow and Strathkelvin based at Glasgow, since 2013; Solicitor Advocate, since 2002. Educ. Strathclyde University. Admitted as a solicitor in 1985; set up practice in Dumbarton in 1987; sat as a Relief Stipendiary Magistrate, 1993-98; Lecturer in criminal procedure in the Diploma in Legal Practice at Strathclyde University, 1998-2002; appointed as a part-time Sheriff in 2009; Shrieval Convenor of Mental Health Tribunals. Chairman of the Championship Committee of the Scottish Rugby Union, 2011-13. Address: 1 Carlton Place, Glasgow G5 9DA; T.-0141 429 8888.

Cruickshank, Alastair Harvey, LLB, WS, DL. Retired Solicitor and Consultant; b. 10.8.43, Perth; m., Moira E. Pollock (deceased); 2 s. Educ. Perth Academy; Edinburgh University. Apprentice, then Assistant, Shepherd & Wedderburn, WS, Edinburgh, 1964-67; Assistant, then Partner, then Consultant, Condie Mackenzie & Co. (now Condies), 1967-2007. Diocese of Brechin: Registrar, 1974-99, Chancellor, 2000-03; Member, Perth Society of High Constables; Captain, Royal Perth Golfing Society, 2001-2003; Deputy Lieutenant, Perth and Kinross, since 1995. Recreations: hill-walking; sailing; chamber music, opera and classical music generally. Address: 8 Kincarrathie Crescent, Perth PH2 7HH; T.-01738 628484.

Cruickshank, Sheena Carlin, CVO, JP. Lord Lieutenant, County of Clackmannan, 2001-2011; b. 26.3.36, Stirling; m., Alistair Booth Cruickshank; (qv); 2 s.; 1 d. Educ. High School of Stirling. Honorary Sheriff. Recreation: quilting.

Cubie, Sir Andrew, CBE, FRSE, LLD (Edinburgh, Glasgow, Glasgow Caledonian), DUniv (Edinburgh Napier), DBA (QMUC), FRCPS (Glas) (Hon), FCGI, LLB, NP, WS, FRSA. Chair, Leadership Foundation for Higher Education, since 2010; Consultant; b. 24.8.46,

Northallerton; m., Professor Lady Heather Ann Cubie, MBE; 1 s.; 2 d. Educ. Dollar Academy; Edinburgh University. Partner, Fyfe Ireland & Co., WS, 1971; Chairman, Bird Semple Fyfe Ireland WS, 1991-94; non-executive Director, Kinloch Anderson Ltd, Scotland's Futures Forum and Scottish Cancer Foundation. Chairman: Quality Scotland Foundation, Scottish Credit and Qualification Framework, RNLI Scotland, Centre for Healthy Working Lives, Scotland's Garden Trust, the Scottish Chamber Orchestra Foundation and Joint Negotiating Committee of USS; Advisor to The World Bank, Washington; Trustee and Deputy Chairman of RNLI UK and Ireland; sometime Chairman, Northern Lighthouse Board, Education Scotland, Independent Committee of Inquiry into Student Finance (the "Cubie Committee"); Member: Ministerial Action Group on Standards in Scottish Schools and, Independent Commission on Local Government and the Consultative Steering Group on the Scottish Parliament; former Chairman: CBI Scotland, Governing Council, George Watson's College, Edinburgh Napier University, Committee of University Chairs for the UK (CUC); former Trustee of British Council and Chair in Scotland; Chair, VSO. Recreations: sailing; gardening. Address: (b.) 4/4 The Cedars, Edinburgh EH13 0PL. E-mail: andrew@cubie-edinburgh.com

Cubie, Professor Lady Heather Ann, MBE, BSc, MSc, PhD, FRCPath, FRSE. Senior Advisor, University of Edinburgh Global Health Academy; b. 8.12.46, Dunfermline; m., Andrew Cubie; 1 s.; 2 d. Educ. Dunfermline High School; Edinburgh University. Director, Scottish HPV Reference Laboratory, 2008-2012; NHS Lothian R&D Director, 1996-2008; Honorary Professor of Research and Research Management, College of Medicine and Veterinary Medicine, University of Edinburgh, since 2006; Head of Service, Scottish Training Scheme for Clinical Scientists in Microbiology, 1997-2011; Chairman, Association of Clinical Microbiologists, 1999-2002. Publications: in field of Human Papilloma Virus (HPV) and molecular diagnostics in clinical virology. Recreations: gardening; travel; walking. Address: (b.) Global Health Academy, 1 George Square, Edinburgh EH8 9JZ; e-mail: Heather.Cubie@ed.ac.uk

Cullen of Whitekirk, Rt. Hon. Lord (William Douglas Cullen), KT, PC, LLD, DUniv, FRSE, HonFREng, Hon FRCSEd, FRCPEd. Chancellor, University of Abertay Dundee, since 2009; Lord President and Lord Justice General, 2001-05; b. 18.11.35, Edinburgh; m., Rosamond Mary Downer; 2 s.; 2 d. Educ. Dundee High School; St. Andrews University (MA); Edinburgh University (LLB). Called to the Scottish Bar, 1960; QC, 1973; Advocate-Depute, 1977-81; Lord Justice Clerk, 1997-2001; PC, 1997; Life Peer, 2003; Justice of Civil and Commercial Court of Qatar Financial Centre, since 2007; Chairman: Inquiry into the Piper Alpha Disaster, 1988-90, Inquiry into the Shootings at Dunblane Primary School, 1996, Ladbroke Grove Rail Inquiry, 1999-2001, Review of fatal accident inquiry legislation, 2008-09. Member, Royal Commission on the Ancient and Historical Monuments of Scotland, 1987-97; Member, Napier University Court, 1996-2005; Chairman: Cockburn Association, 1984-86, Board of Governors, St. Margaret's School, Edinburgh, 1994-2001; Honorary President, SACRO, since 2000; President, Saltire Society, 2005-2011. Recreations: gardening; natural history. Address: (b.) House of Lords, London SW1A 0PW.

Cumberford, Audrey, BEd (Hons), MBA, FCIM, FCMI. Principal & Chief Executive, West College Scotland, since 2012; Principal and Chief Executive, Reid Kerr College, 2011-2012; Director, Renfrewshire Chamber of Commerce, since 2010; Member of Scottish Funding Council, since 2009; b. 25.07.65, Glasgow. Educ. Uddingston Grammar; Moray House College of Education (Edinburgh University); Open University. Graduate Assistant, Bristol University; Sales Executive with GSK (Glaxo) and Baker Norton Pharmaceuticals; Sales and Marketing Manager in Product Design and Manufacture Sector; Senior Lecturer, Business School, Edinburgh's Telford College; Head of Department, Reid Kerr College. Address: West College Scotland, Waterfront Campus, Custom House Way, Greenock PA15 1EN; T.-01475 724433.

Cumming, Professor Allan David, BSc, MBChB, MD, FRCPE. Professor of Medical Education and Dean of Students, College of Medicine and Veterinary Medicine, University of Edinburgh; b. 12.2.51, Buenos Aires, Argentina; m., Lindsay Cumming (nee Galloway); 1 s.; 1 d. Educ. Nairn Academy; University of Edinburgh. Training posts in medicine/nephrology, 1975-89; Clinical research fellowship, University of Western Ontario, 1984-85; Honorary Consultant Physician, Renal Medicine, Lothian University Hospitals Division, 1998-2012. Now responsible for personal tutor system in medicine and veterinary medicine, University of Edinburgh; research and development in medical education. Chancellor's Award for teaching, University of Edinburgh, 2004; Chair, MEDINE2 Network for Medical Education in Europe. Recreations: golf; curling; music. Address: (b.) Queens Medical Research Institute, 47 Little France Crescent, Edinburgh EH16 4TJ; T.-0131 242 9311.
E-mail: allan.cumming@ed.ac.uk

Cumming, Grant Philip, BSc (Hons), MD, MBChB, FRCOG. Consultant, Obstetrician and Gynaecologist, Dr. Grays Hospital, Elgin, since 2000; Honorary Senior Lecturer, Grampian University Hospitals NHS Trust, since 2000; Honorary Professor, University of the Highlands and Islands; b. 8.5.61, Derby; m., Fiona; 1 s.; 2 d. Educ. George Heriots School, Edinburgh; St. Andrews University; Victoria University, Manchester. Aberdeen Royal Infirmary and Maternity Hospital, 1996-2000. Medical Director, The Menopause and You (CD Rom); Scientific Lead: menopausematters.co.uk, babyfeedingmatters.co.uk, health-e-space.com. Recreations: golf; conjuring. Address: (b.) Dr Grays Hospital, Elgin, Moray; T.-01343 543131; e-mail: grant.cumming@nhs.net

Cumming, Sandy, CBE, BSc (Hons); b. 30.10.52, Dingwall; m., Rosemary; 2 d. Educ. Dingwall Academy; University of Edinburgh. Highlands and Islands Development Board, 1973-1991; Highlands and Islands Enterprise, 1991-2010 (HIE Chief Executive, 2000-2010); Vice Chair, the Scottish Rural College; Trustee, The Robertson Trust; Member, the Accounts Commission; Chair, Cromarty Firth Port Authority. Address: (b.) 15 Cradlehall Meadows, Inverness IV2 5GD; T.-01463 795533; e-mail: sandy.cumming@btopenworld.com

Cunningham, David Kenneth, CBE, BEd, MEd (Hons), DUniv, FRSA, FSQA. Independent Education Consultant; General Secretary, School Leaders Scotland (SLS) (formerly HAS), 2008-2015; Head Teacher, Hillhead High School, Glasgow, 1993-2008; b. 19.4.48, Saltcoats; m., Marion S. Shedden; 2 d. Educ. Ardrossan Academy; Glasgow University; Jordanhill College of Education. Principal Teacher of English, North Kelvinside Secondary, 1976-80; Assistant Head Teacher, Garthamlock Secondary, 1980-82; Adviser in English, Dunbarton Division, 1982-90, Education Officer (Acting), 1989-90; Inspector, Quality Assurance Unit, Strathclyde Regional Council, 1990-93; Examiner, Setter, Principal Examiner, SEB, 1979-90; Member, Board, Glasgow Area, Young Enterprise Scotland; Vice-Chair, Glasgow Board, Young Enterprise Scotland; Director and Vice Chair, National Board, Young Enterprise Scotland; Headteachers Association of Scotland: Executive Member, 1997-2005, Vice President, 2000-01,

President, 2001-02; Member, UCAS Standing Committee, 1997-2007; Director, Notre Dame Centre for Children, Young People and Families, 1999-2012; Associate Assessor, HMI, 1999-2008; Member, New National Qualifications Steering Group, 2001-04; Member, Ministerial Task Group New National Qualifications; Chair, English and Communications Higher Still Revision Group; Chair, revision of Mental Health Higher, 2010; Vice-Chair, Educational Broadcasting Council for Scotland, 2002-07, Chair, since 2007; Member, Minister's Group on Race Relations Amendment Act, 2002; Member, SQA Qualifications Committee, since 2003; Member, Advisory Board of SCHOLAR, since 2005; Member, SFEU Core Skills Advisory Group; Director, DKC Consulting Ltd; Trustee, Scottish Board, Children's University, since 2013; Trustee, ICAS Foundation, since 2014; Adviser to Education Department, Isle of Man government, since 2014; Honorary DUniv. from Heriot Watt University, 2015; Ambassador, Girl Guides, since 2003; Governor, Belmont House School, since 2012, Chair, since 2013; Director, Flying Start Enterprises, 2010-14; co-optee, RSA Scottish committee, 2015. Publication: Reading for 'S' Grade English, 1988. Recreations: various sports; reading; photography; travel; family. Address: (h.) Hillbrae, 154 Glasgow Road, Nerston, East Kilbride, Glasgow G74 4PB; T.-01355 230335.
E-mail: ken.cunningham@ntlworld.com

Cunningham, Emeritus Professor Ian M.M., CBE, FRSE, FSB, FRAgS, Hon. Assoc. RCVS, Bsc, PhD, FRSGS, Dr hc (Edin); b. 30.9.25, Kirknewton; m., Agnes Whitelaw Frew. Educ. Lanark Grammar School; Edinburgh University. Assistant Economist, West of Scotland Agricultural College, 1946-47; Lecturer in Agriculture, Durham School of Agriculture, 1947-50; Lecturer, then Senior Lecturer, Edinburgh University, 1950-68; Director, Hill Farming Research Organisation, 1968-80; Professor of Agriculture, Glasgow University, and Principal, West of Scotland Agricultural College, 1980-87. Former Member: Farm Animal Welfare Council, Hill Farming Advisory Committee, Scotland, Agricultural Food Research Council, Court, University of Edinburgh; Chairman, Board, Macaulay Land Use Research Institute, 1987-95; Chairman, National Trust for Scotland, 1998-2000; former Chairman, Advisory Committee on Sites of Special Scientific Interest; former Governor, Royal Agricultural Society of England; George Hedley Memorial Award for services to the sheep industry; Massey Ferguson Award for services to British agriculture; Sir William Young Award for services to livestock production in Scotland. Address: (h.) 5 The Bridges, Peebles EH45 8BP.

Cunningham, Right Reverend John, JCD, RC. Bishop of Galloway, 2004-2014; b. 22.2.38, Paisley. Educ. St. Mary's Primary, Paisley; St. Mary's College, Blairs, Aberdeen; St. Peter's College, Cardross; Scots College and Gregorian University, Rome. Assistant Priest, Our Lady of Lourdes, Bishopton, 1964-69; Professor of Canon Law, St. Peter's College, Cardross and Newlands (Glasgow), 1967-81; Advocate of the Roman Catholic Scottish National Tribunal, 1970-82; Assistant Priest, St. Columba's, Renfrew, 1974-86; Judicial Vicar, Roman Catholic National Tribunal, 1986-92; Parish Priest, St. Patrick's Greenock, 1992-2004; Nominated Papal Chaplain in 1994; Vicar-General, Diocese of Paisley, 1997-2004; Nominated Prelate of Honour in 1999. Address: 24 Johnston Terrace, Greenock PA16 8BD.

Cunningham, Maggie. Executive and Leadership Coach and Tutor; Chief Executive Officer, Columba 1400, 2013-15; Owner, Perform2Succeed, 2009-2013; Joint Head of Programmes and Services for BBC Scotland, 2005-09; Head of Radio, Scotland, 2000-05; m.; 2 c. Producer, BBC Highland, 1979; freelance journalist, 1982-89; BBC Radio nan Gaidheal: Executive Producer, 1989; Editor, 1992; BBC Scotland: Secretary, 1995, returned to production to set up BBC Scotland's Talent Pool, 1997, Head of Features, Education and Religion, 1999; current Board Member: Scotland Venezuela music project, Sistema Scotland; Member of Court of the University of the West of Scotland.

Cunningham, Roseanna. MSP (SNP), Perthshire South and Kinross-shire, since 2011, Perth, 1999-2011; Cabinet Secretary for the Environment, Climate Change and Land Reform, since 2016; Cabinet Secretary for Fair Work, Skills and Training, 2014-16; Minister for Community Safety and Legal Affairs, 2011-14; Minister for Environment, 2009-2011; SNP Deputy Leader, 2000-04; Shadow Minister for Rural Affairs, Environment, Culture and Sport, 2003-04; Shadow Minister for Justice, 1999-2003; Convener, Rural Affairs and Environment Committee, 2007-09; Convener, Health Committee, 2004-07; Convener, Justice and Home Affairs Committee, 1999-2000; MP (SNP), Perth, 1995-2001; b. 27.7.51, Glasgow. Educ. University of Western Australia. SNP Research Department, 1977-79; law degree, Edinburgh University; Trainee Solicitor, Dumbarton District Council, 1983-84; Solicitor, Dumbarton, 1984-86; Solicitor, Glasgow, 1986-89; called to the Scottish Bar, 1990. Recreations: folk festivals; reading; cinema; cats; novice hill-walker. Address: (b.) Scottish Parliament, Edinburgh EH99 1SP.

Curran, Frances. MSP (SSP), West of Scotland, 2003-07; former Co-chair, Scottish Socialist Party; b. 21.5.61, Glasgow; 1 s. Educ. St Andrews Secondary School, Glasgow.

Curran, James, MBE. Former Chief Executive, Scottish Environment Protection Agency (2012-15). Career History: worked in environmental science and environmental regulation for 30 years; undertaken studies in hydrometeorology, numerical modelling of dispersion in marine waters, and water resources management as well as a spell of direct regulatory enforcement with agricultural and industrial businesses; formerly consultant to the Scottish Office and was for some years the Head of Science, Scottish Environment Protection Agency, then Head of Environmental Strategy; in 2006, co-founded and then ran Entrading, the UK's first comprehensive eco-store and cafe in central Glasgow; Director of Science and Strategy, SEPA, 2009-2011.

Curran, Margaret. MP (Labour), Glasgow East, 2010-2015; MSP (Labour), Glasgow Baillieston, 1999-2011; Shadow Secretary of State for Scotland, 2011-2015; Shadow Minister for Disabilities, 2010-2011; Minister for Parliament, Scottish Executive, 2004-07; Minister for Communities, 2002-04. Educ. Glasgow University. Former Lecturer in Community Education; Deputy Minister for Social Justice, Scottish Executive, 2001.

Currie, Rev. Ian Samuel, MBE, BD. Retired Minister (2010); b. 14.8.43, Glasgow; m., Jennifer; 1 s.; 1 d. Educ. Bellahouston Academy; Trinity College; University of Glasgow; Minister: Blairhill Dundyvan Church, Coatbridge, 1975-80, St John's Church, Paisley, 1980-91, Oakshaw Trinity Church, Paisley, 1991-2005, United Church of Bute, 2005-2010. Chair, Victim Support Scotland, 1993-98; former Director, Wynd Centre, Paisley. Recreation: chess. Address: 15 Northfield Park, Largs, North Ayrshire KA30 8NZ; T.-01475 648783; e-mail: ianscurrie@tiscali.co.uk

Currie, Ken. Painter; b. 1960, North Shields. Educ. Paisley College; Glasgow School of Art. Worked on two films about Glasgow and Clyde shipbuilding, 1983-85; specialises in political realism, including a series of murals for the People's Palace Museum, Glasgow, on the socialist history of the city.

Curtice, Professor John Kevin, MA (Oxon). Professor of Politics, Strathclyde University, since 1998; Senior Research Fellow, ScotCen Social Research, since 2015;

Research Consultant, ScotCen Social Research, 2001-2015; b. 10.12.53, Redruth; m., Lisa; 1 d. Educ. Truro School; Magdalen and Nuffield Colleges, Oxford. Research Fellow, Nuffield College, Oxford; Lecturer in Politics, Liverpool University; Fellow, Netherlands Institute for Advanced Study, 1988-89; Senior Lecturer in Politics, Strathclyde University, 1989-96; Reader in Politics, Strathclyde University, 1997-98. FRSA 1992; FRSE 2004; FAcSS 2013, FBA 2014. Publications include: How Britain Votes; Understanding Political Change; Labour's Last Chance; On Message; New Scotland, New Politics; The Rise of New Labour; New Scotland, New Society; British Social Attitudes; Devolution – Scottish Answers to Scottish Questions?; Has Devolution Delivered?; Has Devolution Worked?; Revolution or Evolution? The 2007 Scottish elections. Recreations: music; gardening. Address: (b.) School of Government and Public Policy, Strathclyde University, 16 Richmond Street, Glasgow G1 1XQ; T.-0141-548 4223.

Curtis, Professor Adam Sebastian Genevieve, MA, PhD, FRSE. Professor of Cell Biology, Glasgow University, 1967-2004; Director, Centre for Cell Engineering, 1996-2004; Emeritus Professor and Hon. Senior Research Fellow, since 2004; President, Tissue and Cell Engineering Society, 2002-03; b. 3.1.34, London; m., Ann Park; 2 d. Educ. Aldenham School; Kings College, Cambridge; University of Edinburgh. University College, London: Honorary Research Assistant, 1957-62, Lecturer in Zoology, 1962-67. Director, Company of Biologists Ltd., 1961-99; Governor, Westbourne School, 1985-90; Council Member, Royal Society of Edinburgh, 1983-86; President, Society of Experimental Biology, 1991-93; Editor, IEEE Transactions in Nanobioscience, 2002-08; FIMM 2008; FBSE 2005; Editor, Scottish Diver magazine, 1978-91, and 1994-97; President, Scottish Sub-Aqua Club, 1972-76. Recreations: sports diving; gardening. Address: (h.) 2 Kirklee Circus, Glasgow G12 0TW; T.-0141-339 2152.

Cuschieri, Professor Sir Alfred, MD, DM (Hon), MD (Hon), ChM, FRSE, FMed Sci, FIBiol, FRCSEng, FRCSEd, FRCSI (Hon), FRCPSGlas (Hon). Co-Director, Institute of Medical Science and Technology, Universities of Dundee and St Andrews; Professor of Surgery, Scuola Superiore S'Anna di Studi Universitari Pisa, since 2003; b. 30.9.38, Malta; m., Dr. M.P. Holley; 3 d. Educ. St. Aloysius College; Royal University of Malta; Liverpool University. Professor and Head of Department of Surgery and Molecular Oncology, Dundee University, 1976-2003; Lecturer/Senior Lecturer/Reader in Surgery, Liverpool University. Previous President, British Association of Surgical Oncology, Academic Departments of Surgery in Europe, International Hepato-biliary Pancreatic Association, European Association of Endoscopic Surgery. Previous Director, Minimal Access Therapy Training Unit for Scotland (MATTUS) and Surgical Skills Unit, Ninewells Hospital & Medical School, University of Dundee. Recreations: fishing; painting; carving; music; gardening. Address: (h.) Denbrae Mill, Strathkinness Low Road, St Andrews, Fife KY16 9TY.

Cusine, Sheriff Douglas James, LLB. Sheriff, Grampian, Highland and Islands at Aberdeen, 2001-2011; All-Scotland Floating Sheriff based at Peterhead, 2000-01; b. 2.9.46, Glasgow; m., Marilyn Calvert Ramsay; 1 s.; 1 d. Educ. Hutchesons' Boys' Grammar School; Glasgow University. Solicitor, 1971, Lecturer in Private Law, Glasgow University, 1974-76; Aberdeen University: Lecturer in Private Law, 1977-82, Senior Lecturer, 1982-90, Professor, Department of Conveyancing and Professional Practice of Law, 1990-2000. Member: Council, Law Society of Scotland, 1988-99, Lord President's Advisory Council on

Messengers-at-Arms and Sheriff Officers, 1989-97; Member, UK Delegation to CCBE, 1997-2000; Member, Council of the Sheriffs Association, 2006-09. Publications: Marine Pollution: Law and Practice (Co-Editor), 1980; Cases and Materials in Commercial Law (Co-Editor), 1987; A Scots Conveyancing Miscellany (Editor), 1987; New Reproductive Techniques: A Legal Perspective, 1988; Law and Practice of Diligence (Co-Author), 1989; Reproductive Medicine and the Law (Co-Editor), 1990; Standard Securities, 1990, 2nd ed., (Co-Author), 2002; Missives (Co-Author), 1993, 2nd ed., 1999; Requirements of Writing (Co-Author), 1995; Servitudes and Rights of Way (Co-Author), 1998; various articles on medico-legal issues and conveyancing. Recreations: swimming; walking; bird-watching. Address: The Brae, Gurney Street, Stonehaven, Kincardineshire AB39 2EB.

Cuthbertson, Rev. Malcolm, BA, BD (Hons). Minister, Mure Memorial Church, since 2010; b. 3.4.56, Glasgow; m., Rena Fennel; 1 s.; 2 d. Educ. Grangemouth High School; Stirling University; Aberdeen University. Probationer Assistant, Crown Court Church, London, 1983-84; Minister, Easterhouse: St. George's and St. Peter's Church of Scotland, 1984-2010. Recreations: eating out; reading theology. Address: Mure Memorial Church, Maxwell Drive, Garrowhill, Glasgow G69 6LS; T.-0141 773 1216.

Cuthell, Rev. Thomas Cuthbertson, MA, BD. Minister Emeritus, St. Cuthbert's Parish Church, Edinburgh, since 2007 (retired); b. 18.2.41, Falkirk. Educ. Bo'ness Academy; University of Edinburgh. Assistant Minister, St. Giles Cathedral, Edinburgh; Minister, North Church, Uphall. Recreations: travel; music; sailing. Address: Flat 10, 2 Kingsburgh Crescent, Edinburgh EH5 1JF.

Cutler, Timothy Robert (Robin), CBE, BSc, DSc. b. 24.7.34, India; m., Ishbel W.M.; 1 s.; 1 d. Educ. Banff Academy; Aberdeen University. Colonial Forest Service, Kenya, 1958-64; New Zealand Government Forestry, 1964-90, latterly Chief Executive, New Zealand Ministry of Forestry; Director General, Forestry Commission, 1990-95. Recreations: golf; travel. Address: 14 Swanston Road, Edinburgh EH10 7BB; T.-0131-445 5437.

Czerkawska, Catherine, MA (Hons); MA (postgraduate). Novelist and Playwright; b. 3.12.55, Leeds; m., Alan Lees; 1 s. Educ. Queen Margaret's Academy, Ayr; St. Michael's Academy, Kilwinning; Edinburgh University; Leeds University. Published two books of poetry (White Boats and a Book of Men); taught EFL in Finland and Poland; thereafter, full-time freelance writer working on novels including The Curiosity Cabinet, 2005, radio, television and stage plays; Pye Award for Best Radio Play, 1980, O Flower of Scotland; Scottish Radio Industries Club Award, 1983, Bonnie Blue Hen; Wormwood, and Quartz produced Traverse Theatre, Edinburgh, 1997 and 2000; God's Islanders, Birlinn, 2006. Novels including The Curiosity Cabinet, Bird of Passage, The Amber Heart, Ice Dancing and The Physic Garden (Saraband 2014). Recreations: antique textiles. Website: www.wordarts.co.uk
E-mail: catherine.czerkawska@gmail.com

D

Dalby, Martin, BMus, ARCM. Composer; freelance music/recording producer; music lecturer; Chairman, Composers' Guild of Great Britain, 1995-98; Founding Director: UK Music (formerly British Music Rights), 1999-2001, British Academy of Composers and Songwriters, 1998-2000; Warden of Performers and Composers Section, ISM (Incorporated Society of Musicians), 2001; Chairman, ISM SW Scotland Centre, 2004-2011; b. 25.4.42, Aberdeen; m., Hilary. Educ. Aberdeen Grammar School; Royal College of Music. Music Producer, BBC Radio 3, 1965-71; Cramb Research Fellow in Composition, Glasgow University, 1971-72; Head of Music, BBC Scotland, 1972-91; Executive Music Producer, BBC Scotland, 1991-93. Recreations: flying; railways; bird-watching; hill-walking. Address: (h.) 23 Muirpark Way, Drymen, Stirlingshire G63 0DX; T.-01360 660427.
E-mail: martindalby@btinternet.com
Website: www.impulse-music.co.uk/dalby/

Dale, Brian Graeme, LLB, WS, NP. Partner, Brooke & Brown, WS, Dunbar, 1974-2014; b. 20.11.46, London; m., Judith Gail de Beaufort Franklin; 4 s.; 2 d. Educ. Bristol Grammar School; Aberdeen University. Diocese of Edinburgh, Scottish Episcopal Church: Treasurer, 1971-2000, Secretary, 1974-90, Registrar, 1974-2001, Chancellor, 2001-07; Registrar and Lay Clerk to the Episcopal Synod. Recreations: music; bridge; singing; family life. Address: (h.) 46 Moray Avenue, Dunbar, East Lothian; T.-01368 864801.

Dale, Professor John Egerton, BSc, PhD, FRSE, FSB. Emeritus Professor of Plant Physiology, Edinburgh University, since 1993; b. 13.2.32, London; m., Jacqueline Joyce Benstock (deceased) 1 s.; 2 d.; m. (2), Kay. Educ. City of London School; Kings College, London. Plant Physiologist, Empire Cotton Growing Corporation, Uganda, 1956-61; Edinburgh University: Lecturer in Botany, then Reader, 1961-85, Professor of Plant Physiology, 1985-93, Head, Division of Biological Sciences, 1990-93. Secretary, Society for Experimental Biology, 1974-79; Secretary General, Federation of European Societies of Plant Physiology, 1978-84; Trustee, Peter Potter Gallery, 1994-99; Institute of Biology: Chairman, Scottish Branch, 2000-2001, Member, Council, since 2000; Scottish Wildlife Trust: Acting Chairman, 2002, Vice Chairman, 1999-2002. Publications: 100 papers on growth of leaves and related topics. Recreations: the arts; travel; gardening. Address: (h.) The Old Bothy, Drem, North Berwick, EH39 5AP; T.-01620 850394.

Dalhousie, Earl of (James Hubert Ramsay), DL, CStJ. Chairman: Jamestown Investments Ltd., Dunedin Smaller Companies Investment Trust plc, Brechin Castle Centre Ltd.; President: Caledonian Club; Vice-Chairman, Game and Wildlife Conservation Trust, 1987-2009; Director, Scottish Woodlands, 1993-2005; b. 17.1.48, London; m., Marilyn; 1 s.; 2 d. Educ. Ampleforth College. Commissioned, Coldstream Guards, 1968-71; Hambros Bank Ltd (Director, 1981); Co-Founder, Jamestown Investments, 1987. Captain, Royal Company of Archers; Vice Lord Lieutenant, County of Angus; Governor, Unicorn Preservation Society, 2001-2013; Hon. Captain, RNR; President, Angus Branch, Order of St John; Board Member, Deer Commission Scotland, 2005-2010; Lord Steward, since 2009. Address: (b.) Dalhousie Estates Office, Brechin DD9 6SG; T.-01356 624566.

Dallas, Garry, BA (Hons), DipTP, MSc. Director, Services to Communities, Clackmannanshire Council, since 2010; b. 15.8.59, Kirkcaldy; m., Ruth. Educ. Glenrothes High School; Strathclyde University; Heriot-Watt University. Planning Officer, Principal Planner, Planning Manager, Property Development Manager, Head of Planning and Property Development, Clackmannan District Council, 1983-95; Executive Director, Development Services, Clackmannanshire Council, 1995-2001, Director, Development and Environmental Services, 2001-09. Founding Director, Alloa Tower Building Preservation Trust. Recreations: motor sports; swimming; golf. Address: (b.) Clackmannanshire Council, Greenfield, Alloa FK10 2AD; T.-01259 452531.

Dalrymple, Sir Hew (Fleetwood) Hamilton-, 10th Bt (created 1697), GCVO, 2001 (KCVO, 1985, CVO, 1974). Lord Lieutenant, East Lothian, 1987-2001; Captain General, Queen's Bodyguard for Scotland (Royal Company of Archers); Gold Stick for Scotland, 1996-2004; b. 9.4.26; m., Lady Anne-Louise Mary Keppel; 4 s. Educ. Ampleforth; Staff College, Camberley, 1957. Commissioned Grenadier Guards, 1944; DAAG HQ 3rd Division, 1958-60; Regimental Adjt., Grenadier Guards, 1960-62; retired, 1962; Vice-Chairman, Scottish & Newcastle Breweries, 1983-86 (Director, 1967-86); Chairman, Scottish American Investment Co., 1985-91 (Director, 1967-94); DL, East Lothian, 1964; JP, 1987. Address: Leuchie, North Berwick, East Lothian; T.-01620 892903.

Dalrymple Hamilton, North John Frederick, OBE, TD, MA (Hons), DL. Farmer and Land Manager; b. 7.5.50, Edinburgh; m., Sally Anne How; 2 s.; 1 d. Educ. Aberdeen University. Scottish and Newcastle Breweries, 1972-82; certificate of farming practice, East of Scotland College of Agriculture, 1982-84; farming of Bargany Farms, since 1984. TA Commission, 1967-95; Officer, Queen's Bodyguard for Scotland; Vice Lieutenant for Ayrshire and Arran; President, RBL(S), Maybole Branch; Chair, Lowland RFCA, 2003-07. Address: (h.) Lovestone, Girvan, Ayrshire KA26 9RF.

Dalyell, Kathleen Mary, DL, MA, FRSAS, OBE. Chairman, Royal Commission on Ancient and Historical Monuments of Scotland, 2000-05; Administrator, The Binns; Director, Heritage Education Trust, 1987-2005; Director, Weslo Housing Association, 1994-2003; Trustee, Carmont Settlement Trust, 1997-2013; Deputy Lieutenant, West Lothian, until 2012; b. 17.11.37, Edinburgh; m., Tam Dalyell; 1 s.; 1 d. Educ. Convent of Sacred Heart, Aberdeen; Edinburgh University; Craiglochart Teacher Training College. Teacher of History, St. Augustine's Secondary School, Glasgow, 1961-62; James Gillespie's High School for Girls, Edinburgh, 1962-63; Member, Historic Buildings Council for Scotland, 1975-87; Member, Lady Provost of Edinburgh's Delegation to China, 1987; Member, National Committee of Architectural Heritage Society for Scotland, 1983-89 (Vice-Chair, 1986-89); Chairman, Bo'ness Heritage Trust, 1988-93; Trustee, Paxton Trust, 1988-92; Member, Ancient Monuments Board for Scotland, 1989-2000; Member, Royal Fine Art Commission for Scotland, 1992-2000; Member, Lord Mackay's Panel on Governance, NTS, 2003; Member, Court of University of Stirling, 2002-08; Trustee, Hopetoun Preservation Trust (2005); Hon. Degree, University of Edinburgh, 2006; Hon. Degree, Stirling University, 2008; Trustee, National Museums of Scotland Charitable Trust. Recreations: reading; travel; hillwalking; chess. Address: The Binns, Linlithgow EH49 7NA; T.-01506 83 4255.

Dalyell, Tam. MP (Labour), Linlithgow (formerly West Lothian), 1962-2005; Father of House of Commons, 2001-05; Weekly Columnist, New Scientist, 1967-2005;

Chairman, All-Party Latin America Group, 1998-2005; Rector, Edinburgh University, 2003-06; President, Scottish Council for Development and Industry, 2004-08; b. 9.8.32, Edinburgh; m., Kathleen Wheatley; 1 s.; 1 d. Educ. Edinburgh Academy; Harecroft; Eton; King's College, Cambridge; Moray House, Edinburgh. National Service, Scots Greys; Teacher, Bo'ness Academy, 1957-61; Deputy Director of Studies, Ship-School Dunera, 1961-62; Member, Public Accounts Committee, 1962-66; PPS to R.H.S. Crossman, 1964-70; Vice-Chairman, Parliamentary Labour Party, 1974-76; Member, European Parliament, 1975-78; Member: National Executive Committee, Labour Party, 1986-87, Advisory Council on Biological Sciences, Edinburgh University; a Vice-President, Research Defence Society; led Parliamentary Delegation to: Libya, 2001, Bolivia, 2000, Peru, 1999, Brazil, 1976. Hon. Doctor of Science, Edinburgh University, 1994; Hon. Doctor, City University, London, 1998; Hon. Doctor, St. Andrews University, 2003; Hon. Doctor, Napier University, Edinburgh, 2004; Hon. Doctor, University of Stirling, 2006; Hon. Doctor, Open University, 2006; Hon. Doctor, Heriot-Watt University, 2011; Hon. President, Classical Association of Scotland, since 2006. Publications: Case for Ship Schools, 1959; Ship-School Dunera, 1961; Devolution: the end of Britain?, 1978; A Science Policy for Britain, 1983; One Man's Falklands, 1983; Misrule, 1987; Dick Crossman: a portrait, 1989; "The Importance of being awkward", Autobiography, 2011. Address: (h.) The Binns, Linlithgow EH49 7NA; T.-01506-834255.

Dane, Graham Charles, BSc, BA, MEd, MCIL, MInstP, CPhys, FEIS. Educational Consultant, occasionally in Africa; formerly Principal Teacher of Physics, St Augustine's High School, Edinburgh, 1983-2010, seconded to International Relations Unit, Scottish Executive Education Department, 2002-03; b. 19.7.50. Educ. Saint Andrews University. Teacher of Science, Merksworth High School, Paisley, 1973-75; Information Scientist, The Electricity Council, London, 1975-77; Teacher of Physics, Forrester High School, Edinburgh, 1978-80; Assistant Principal Teacher of Science, Deans Community High School, Livingston, 1980-83. Elected Member, General Teaching Council for Scotland (Convener, Committee on Exceptional Admission to the Register), 1995-2001; holder of numerous trade union positions over the years, mainly in the EIS; Member of the Board, Scottish Council for Research in Education, 1992-98; Chair, Currie Community Council, 1998-2013; Treasurer, Socialist Educational Association Scotland, 2010-2015; Governor, Donaldson's College, 1996-2005; Trustee of Currie Community Centre; Chair, Management Committee of Currie Community Centre, since 2014; Member of Scottish Committee of WEA, 2009-2012. Recreations: travel; languages; learning new things; meeting people he likes; enjoying the arts; being a grandfather. Address: (h.) 25 Thomson Road, Edinburgh EH14 5HT.

Daniel, Ronald (Ron), OBE, Advanced DipIM, Avon Prizeman, CMCIPD, past CMCMI, past MIQA. National Chairman, Victim Support Scotland, 2003-09; Trustee: Victim Support Scotland, 2009-2010, Voluntary Action Fund Scotland, 2009-2010; Chairman: Voluntary Action Fund Scotland, since 2010, Moving On (Edinburgh) Ltd., 2002-07; b. 22.4.36; m., Cecilia; 2 d. Educ. Dunfermline High School, Lauder; Glenrothes and Kirkcaldy Tech Colleges. Civil Service, 1958-86; Senior Advisor, The Industrial Society, 1986-90; Director, Human Resources, Baillie Gifford, 1990-96; Management Consultant, 1996-2005; Chairman, Institute of Professional Civil Servants, Rosyth, 1967-78; Chairman, Royal Dockyards IPCS Committee, 1975-78. Councillor on Dunfermline Town Council and Fife County Council, 1967-73; Chairman of Health, Planning and Industrial Development Committees,

1969-73; Magistrate, 1969-73; Chairman, Whitley Council, Rosyth, 1975-78; Chairman, Dunfermline Civic Week Committee, 1975-88; Group Chairman, IIM, 1976-79; Chairman, Dunfermline Sound Talking Newspaper for the Blind, 1976-2005; Part time Lecturer in Management and Industrial Relations, 1979-82; Chairman, Victim Support Fife, 1997-2002; Vice Chairman, Victim Support Scotland, 2002-03. Recreations: volunteering; keeping (reasonably) fit; speakers club. Address: 4 Coldingham Place, Dunfermline, Fife KY12 7XL; T.-01383 738730.
E-mail: ron.daniel@btinternet.com

Darling of Roulanish, Baron (Alistair Maclean Darling), PC, LLB. MP (Labour), Edinburgh South West, 2005-2015, Edinburgh Central, 1987-2005; Member, Board of Directors, Morgan Stanley, since 2016; Chair of the Better Together Campaign, 2012-14; Chancellor of the Exchequer, 2007-10; Secretary of State for Trade and Industry, 2006-07; Secretary of State for Transport, 2002-06; Secretary of State for Scotland, 2003-06; Secretary of State for Work and Pensions, 2001-02; b. 28.11.53, London; m., Margaret Vaughan; 1 s.; 1 d. Educ. Loretto School; Aberdeen University. Solicitor, 1978-83; Advocate, since 1984; Member: Lothian Regional Council, 1982-87, Lothian and Borders Police Board, 1982-87; Governor, Napier College, 1985-87; Chief Secretary to the Treasury, 1997-98; Secretary of State for Social Security, 1998-2001.

Darling, Ian Marshall, OBE, FRICS. Member, Lands Tribunal for Scotland, 2004-2013; b. 16.4.45, Perth; m., Kate; 1 s.; 1 d. Educ. Perth Academy; London University (College of Estate Management and Wye College). Partner, Bell Ingram, 1974; Managing Partner, 1987-96; Director, Chesterton Scotland, 1996-2001. Chairman, Royal Institution of Chartered Surveyors in Scotland, 1997-98; Master, Company of Merchants of the City of Edinburgh, 2000-01; Board Member, British Waterways, 2000-06; Chairman, Council, RSPB, 2008-2012; Member, Court of University of Edinburgh, 2003-08. Recreations: nature conservation; ornithology. T.-07766 573059.

Darwent, Rt. Rev. Frederick Charles, LTh (Hon), JP. Bishop of Aberdeen and Orkney, 1978-92; b. 20.4.27, Liverpool; m., 1, Edna Lilian Waugh (deceased); 2 d.; 2, Roma Evelyn Fraser. Educ. Warbreck School, Liverpool; Ormskirk Grammar School; Wells Theological College, Somerset. Followed a banking career, 1943-61; War Service, Far East, 1945-48; ordained Deacon, 1963, Priest, 1964, Diocese of Liverpool; Curate, Pemberton, Wigan, 1963-65; Rector: Strichen, 1965-71, New Pitsligo, 1965-78, Fraserburgh, 1971-78; Canon, St. Andrew's Cathedral, Aberdeen, 1971; Dean of Aberdeen and Orkney, 1973-78. Recreations: amateur stage (acting and production); calligraphy; music. Address: (h.) 107 Osborne Place, Aberdeen AB25 2DD; T.-01224 646497.

Das, Sachinandan, MB, BS, FRCR, DMRT. Director and Chairman, Bharatiya Ashram, Dundee, a multicultural, multiethnic voluntary organisation, since 2007; b. 1.8.44, Cuttack, India; m., Dr. Subhalaxmi; 1 s.; 1 d. Educ. Ravenshaw Collegiate School; SCB Medical College, Cuttack, India; Utkal University. Senior House Officer in Radiotherapy, Plymouth General Hospital, 1969-70; Registrar in Radiotherapy and Oncology, then Senior Registrar, Mersey Regional Centre for Radiotherapy, Liverpool, 1970-77; Consultant in administrative charge, Ninewells Hospital, Dundee, 1987-91, Clinical Director, 1991-98; Regional Postgraduate Education Advisor in Radiotherapy and Oncology, 1987-2002. Member: Standing Scottish Committee, National Medical Consultative Committee, Scottish Paediatric Oncology Group, Joint Radiological Safety Committee, Radiation Hazards Sub-

Committee, Unit Medical and Dental Advisory Committee; Council Member, Scottish Radiological Society, 1987-93; Head, Department of Radiotherapy and Oncology, Dundee University, 1987-2000; Chairman, Tayside Oncology Research Committee, 1987-2007. Recreations: gardening; walking; reading. Address: (h.) Grapevine, 42 Menzieshill Road, Dundee DD2 1PU; T.-Dundee 642915.

Datta, Dipankar, MBBS, FRCPGlas, FRCPLond. Retired Consultant Physician (1975-97); former Honorary Senior Clinical Lecturer and Clinical Sub-Dean, Glasgow University; Founder Director, Scottish Overseas Aid; b. 30.1.33, Chittagong, India; m., Dr. J.B. Datta; 1 s.; 1 d. Educ. Calcutta University. Former Vice Chairman, UN Association, Glasgow; former Chairman, Overseas Doctors' Association, Scottish Division; former Chairman, British Medical Association, Lanarkshire; former Member, Central Executive Committee, Scottish Council, United Nations Association; former Member, Lanarkshire Health Board; former Member, Scottish Council, British Medical Association; former Member, Executive Committee, Scottish Council, Royal Commonwealth Society for the Blind; former Member, Senate, Glasgow University; former Member, General Medical Council; Chairman, South Asia Voluntary Enterprise; former Chairman, Scottish India Forum. Recreations: reading - history, economics and international politics. Address: (h.) 9 Kirkvale Crescent, Newton Mearns, Glasgow G77 5HB; T.-0141-639 1515. E-mail: dipankardatta@hotmail.com

Datta, Pradip Kumar, MBE, MS, FRCS(Edin), FRCS(Eng), FRCS(Ire), FRCS(Glas). Honorary Consultant Surgeon, Caithness General Hospital; b. 14.5.40, Calcutta, India; m., Swati; 1 s. Educ. St. Aloysius High School, Visakhapatnam, India; Andhra University, Visakhapatnam, India. Surgical Registrar: Hope Hospital, Salford, Poole General Hospital, Plymouth General Hospital, Royal Cornwall Hospital, Truro; Senior Surgical Registrar, Whittington Hospital, London; former Honorary Secretary, Royal College of Surgeons of Edinburgh. Visiting Lecturer: University Sains Malaysia, National University of Singapore; Honorary Fellow, College of Surgeons of Sri Lanka, 2012. Recreations: playing squash; tennis; fly-fishing. Address: (h.) Garvyk, 17 Newton Avenue, Wick KW1 5LJ; T.-01955 605050.

Davey, Andrew John, BSc (Hons), DipArch, RIBA, RIAS. Partner, Simpson & Brown Architects of Edinburgh; b. 6.6.52, Exmouth, Devon; m., Christina; 2 s.; 1 d. Educ. Queen Elizabeth's School, Devon; Bartlett School of Architecture; University College London. Publication: joint author, The Care and Conservation of Georgian Houses', 1978 (now in its 4th Edition). Address: (b.) Simpson and Brown Architects, St. Ninian's Manse, Quayside Street, Edinburgh EH6 6EJ; T.-0131 555 4678; e-mail: admin@simpsonandbrown.co.uk

Davidson, Professor Colin William, BSc, DipER, PhD, CEng, HonFIEE. Retired chartered engineer; b. 18.9.34, Edinburgh; m., Ranee M.N. Cleland; 2 d. Educ. George Heriot's School; Edinburgh University. Lecturer, Edinburgh University, 1956-61; Electronics Engineer, Nuclear Enterprises (GB) Ltd., 1961-64; Lecturer, Heriot-Watt College/University, 1964-67; Associate Professor, Chulalongkorn University, Bangkok, 1967-68; Heriot-Watt University: Senior Lecturer, 1968-85, Professor of Electrical Engineering, 1985-88, Dean of Engineering, 1976-79 and 1984-87, Head of Department, 1979-87. Member, Lothian Regional Council, 1990-94; Vice-President, Institution of Electrical Engineers, 1990-93, 1995-98, Honorary Treasurer, 1999-2001; Member, Engineering Council Senate and Board for Engineers'

Regulation, 1996-98; Secretary, West Highland Anchorages and Moorings Association, 2001-05; Secretary, Argyll Community Housing Association, 2005-07; Member, Council, Institution of Engineering and Technology, 2007-2010; Past Chairman, Craignish Community Council; Board Member, Argyll Community Housing Association, since 2014; Freeman, City of London; Liveryman, Worshipful Company of Engineers. Recreations: sailing; CLYC. Address: (h.) Tigh-nan-Eilean, Ardfern PA31 8QN; T.-01852 500532.

Davidson, Professor Donald Allen, BSc, PhD, FRSE. Emeritus Professor of Environmental Science, Stirling University; b. 27.4.45, Lumphanan; m., Caroline E. Brown; 1 s.; 2 d. Educ. Robert Gordon's College, Aberdeen; Aberdeen University; Sheffield University. Lecturer, St. David's University College, Wales, 1971-76; Lecturer, Senior Lecturer, Reader, Strathclyde University, 1976-86; Reader, Stirling University, 1986-91. Editor of journal Earth and Environmental Science Transactions of the Royal Society of Edinburgh. Publications include: The Evaluation of Land Resources, 1992; many papers. Recreations: exploring the countryside; maintaining an old house and garden. Address: (b.) Biological and Environmental Science, Stirling University, Stirling FK9 4LA; T.-01786 823599.

Davidson, Duncan Lewis Watt, BSc (Hons), MB, ChB, FRCPEdin. Chairman, Tweedsmuir Community Company; Consultant in Medical Education, 2002-05; Consultant Neurologist, Tayside; Honorary Senior Lecturer in Medicine, Dundee University, 1976-2002; b. 16.5.40, Kingston, Jamaica; m., Dr. Anne V.M. Maiden; 4 s.; 1 d. Educ. Knox College, Jamaica; Edinburgh University. House Officer, Senior House Officer, Registrar and Senior Registrar posts in medicine and neurology, Edinburgh, 1966-75; Peel Travelling Fellowship, Montreal, 1973-74; MRC clinical scientific staff, MRC Brain Metabolism Unit, Edinburgh, 1975-76. Recreations: gardening; photography. Address: (h.) Oliver, Tweedsmuir, Biggar ML12 6QN; T.-01899 880278.

Davidson, Ian Graham, MA (Hons). MP (Labour and Co-op), Glasgow South West, 2005-2015 (Glasgow Pollok, 1997-2005, Glasgow Govan 1992-97); b. 8.9.50, Jedburgh; m., Morag Mackinnon; 1 s.; 1 d. Educ. Jedburgh Grammar School; Galashiels Academy; Edinburgh University; Jordanhill College of Education. Project Manager, Community Service Volunteers, 1985-92; Councillor, Strathclyde Regional Council, 1978-92 (Chair, Education Committee, 1986-92); former Member, Public Accounts Select Committee; Member, Committee of Selection, 1997-99; Secretary, Trade Union Group of Labour MPs, 1998-2002.

Davidson, Rev. Ian Murray Pollock, MBE, MA, BD. Minister, Allan Park South Church and Church of the Holy Rude, Stirling, 1985-94; Chairman, General Trustees, Church of Scotland, 1994-99; b. 14.3.28, Kirriemuir; m., Isla; 2 s. Educ. Montrose Academy; St. Andrews University. National Service, 1949-51; Minister: Crieff North and West Church (St. Andrew's), 1955-61, Grange Church, Kilmarnock, 1961-67, Cambuslang Old Church, 1967-85; Convener, Maintenance of the Ministry Committee and Board, Church and Ministry Department, 1981-84; General Trustee, 1975-2003. Publications: At the Sign of the Fish (history of Cambuslang Old Parish Church), 1975; A Guide to the Church of the Holy Rude. Recreations: travel; photography; reading; writing. Address: (h.) 13/8 Craigend Park, Edinburgh EH16 5XX; T.-0131-664 0074.

Davidson, Professor Ivor John, MA, PhD, MTh. Professor of Systematic and Historical Theology, since 2009; b. 23.12.67, Glasgow; m., Dr. Julie Elaine Hunter (née); 1 d. Educ. Bradford Grammar School; University of

Glasgow; University of Edinburgh. Part-time Lecturer, University of Glasgow, 1992-94; Temporary Lecturer, University of St Andrews, 1994-96; Lecturer, University of Otago, New Zealand, 1997-99, Senior Lecturer, 2000-04, Professor of Theology, 2005-09; Head of School, Dean of Faculty of Divinity and Principal, St Mary's College, St Andrews, 2010-13. Peer assessor and international academic consultant in Arts and Humanities. Academic awards include Logan Prize (most distinguished graduate in Arts, University of Glasgow); Jeffrey, Cowan, Ramsay Medals, Kenmure Scholarship, Coulter Prize, Scott Scholarship etc. Publications: books include: Ambrose De officiis (2 vols.), 2002; The Birth of the Church, 2004; A Public Faith, 2005; God of Salvation, 2011; numerous articles in learned journals. Peer Assessor in Humanities. Recreations: walking; running; music; reading. Address: (b.) St. Mary's College, St Andrews, Fife KY16 9JU; T.- 01334 462850; e-mail: ijd1@st-andrews.ac.uk

Davidson, Jane. Chief Executive, NHS Borders, since 2015 (previously Deputy Chief Executive, 2012-15). Began career in Lanarkshire, moving to the State Hospitals Board for Scotland, holding the post of Director of Finance; worked as a senior manager in the NHS in Scotland, since 1993; worked with the Scottish Government as Deputy Director of Health Finance; led the modernisation and integration of the health finance division of the Scottish Government Health Directorates with responsibility for the development and implementation of the financial planning strategy and the financial performance management of NHS Boards; appointed Director of Finance, NHS Borders in 2010, then Chief Operating Officer in 2010. Address: NHS Borders, Headquarters, Borders General Hospital, Melrose, Roxburghshire TD6 9BS.

Davidson, John Knight (Jake), OBE, MD, FRCP (Edin), FRCP (Glas), FRCR, (Hon) FACR, (Hon) FRACR. Consultant Radiologist; expert adviser on bone disease in compressed air and diving medicine; b. 17.8.25, Edinburgh; m., Edith E. McKelvie; 2 s.; 1 d. Educ. George Watson's Boys College, Edinburgh; Edinburgh University. Adviser in Bone Disease in Divers MRC, Aberdeen, US Navy, 1970- 92; Non Executive Director, Yorkhill NHS Trust, 1993-95; Member, Council, Medical and Dental Defence Union, 1971-95; Chairman, Health Policy, Council, Scottish Conservative and Unionist Association, 1991-95; Member, BBC Medical Advisory Group, 1988-95; Consultant Radiologist in Administrative Charge, Western Infirmary and Gartnavel General, Glasgow, 1967-90; Royal College of Radiologists: Member, Council, 1974-77, 1984-87, Chairman, Examining Board, 1976-79, Scottish Committee, 1985-89; Member, Council, Royal Glasgow Institute of Fine Arts, 1978-88; Deputy President, Glasgow and Renfrewshire, British Red Cross Society, 1988-93; Honorary Fellow: Royal Australian and New Zealand College of Radiology, 1981, Scottish Radiological Society, 1990, American College of Radiology, 1992, Medical and Dental Defence Union, Scotland, 1995; Honorary Fellow and Medallist, International Skeletal Society, 1995; Rohan Williams Professor, Australasia, 1977; Aggarwal Memorial Oration, India, 1988. Member: Royal and Ancient Golf Club, St Andrews; Pollok GC, Glasgow; Queen Anne Golfing Society; British Golf Collectors Society; Glasgow Art Club; RLS Club; Buchanan Bridge Club, Glasgow. Editor: Jake's Corner, Queen Anne Golfing Society, 1948- 2008, Aseptic Necrosis of Bone and numerous publications. Recreations: golf; water colours; golf history; Robert Louis Stevenson; bridge; meeting people. Address: (h.) 1/1, 15 Beechlands Avenue, Netherlee, Glasgow G44 3YT; T.- 0141-637 0290; e-mail: jaked15b@gmail.com

Davidson, Julie. Writer and journalist; freelance contributor to radio, television, books, newspapers and magazines, since 1981; b. 11.5.43, Motherwell; m., Harry Reid (qv); 1 d. Educ. Aberdeen High School for Girls. Trainee Journalist, D.C. Thomson Ltd., Dundee, 1961-64; Feature Writer and Sub-Editor, Aberdeen Press & Journal, 1964-67; The Scotsman: Feature Writer, 1967-77, Columnist, 1977-81; The Herald: Television Critic, 1981- 95, Columnist, 1995-97. Columnist/Critic of the Year, Scottish Press Awards, 1985; Critic of the Year, Scottish Press Awards, 1988-89-92-94-95; Canada Travel Award, 1992; Travelex Travel Writers Award, 1999; Scottish Thistle Travel Media Award, 1999. Publications: Scots We Ken, 2007; Reflections of Scotland, 2009; Looking for Mrs Livingstone, 2012. Recreations: reading; cinema; walking; travelling; wildlife; lunching.
E-mail: julie.davidson3@virgin.net

Davidson of Glen Clova, Lord (Neil Forbes Davidson), QC, BA, MSc, LLB, LLM, DUniv (Stirling). Advocate General for Scotland, 2006-10; Solicitor General for Scotland, 2000-01; b. 13.9.50; m. Educ. Stirling University; Bradford University; Edinburgh University. Admitted, Faculty of Advocates, 1979; Standing Junior Counsel to Registrar General, 1982, to Department of Health and Social Security, 1988; called to the Bar, Inner Temple, 1990; Director, City Disputes Panel, 1993-2000. Author, Davidson Review on UK Implementation of EU Regulation (2007); Judicial Review in Scotland (1986). Address: Axiom Advocates, Faculty of Advocates, Parliament House, Edinburgh EH1 1RF; T.-0131 226 5071.

Davidson, Professor Peter Robert Keith Andrew, BA, MA, PhD (Cantab), MA. Senior Research Fellow, Campion Hall, University of Oxford, since 2015; Professor of Renaissance Studies, Scholar-Keeper of the University's Collections, Aberdeen University, 2000- 2015; b. 14.5.57, Glasgow; m., Jane Barbara Stevenson. Educ. Clare College, Cambridge; York University. Lecturer, St Andrews University, 1989-90; Universiteit Leiden, 1990-92; Lecturer, Warwick University, 1992- 2000 (Senior Lecturer, 1995, Reader, 1998). Publications; Poems and Translations of Sir Richard Fanshawe; Poetry and Revolution; Early Modern Women's Poetry; The Idea of North; The Collected Poems of S. Robert Southwell S. J.; The Universal Baroque; The Palace of Oblivion; The Triumphs of the Defeated; Winter Light; The Library and Archive Collections of the University of Aberdeen, an introduction and description; Distance and Memory; The Last of the Light. Recreation: casuistry. Address: (b.) 9 (3F2) Antigua Street, Edinburgh EH1 3NH.

Davidson, Professor Roger, MA, CertEd, PhD, FRHistS. Emeritus Professor of Social History; b. 19.7.42, Guildford; m., Mo Townson; 1 s.; 1 d. Educ. King Edward VI School, Chelmsford; St Catharine's College, Cambridge. Teacher in History and Economics, Watford Boys Grammar School, 1965-67; Research Graduate, St Catharine's College, Cambridge, 1967-70; Lecturer, 1970, Senior Lecturer, 1984, Reader, 1996, in Economic and Social History, Edinburgh University. Former Member, Scottish Records Advisory Council. Publications: Whitehall and the Labour Problem in Late-Victorian and Edwardian Britain, 1985; Dangerous Liaisons: A Social History of VD in 20th Century Scotland, 2000; The Sexual State: Sexuality and Scottish Governance 1950-80 (2012). Recreations: bird-watching; reading. Address: (b.) School of History, Classics and Archaeology, University of Edinburgh, William Robertson Wing, Teviot Place, Edinburgh EH8 9AG; e-mail: Roger.Davidson@ed.ac.uk

Davidson, Ruth. MSP (Conservative) Edinburgh Central, since 2016 (Glasgow, 2011-16); Leader of the Scottish

Conservatives, since 2011; b. 10.11.78, Edinburgh. Educ. Buckhaven High School, Fife; University of Edinburgh; University of Glasgow. Career: worked as a presenter, journalist and documentary maker with the BBC and a number of newspapers and radio stations. Address: Scottish Parliament, Edinburgh EH99 1SP.

Davidson, Valerie, BA, IPFA. Deputy Chief Executive, Strathclyde Partnership for Transport (SPT), formerly Assistant Chief Executive; b. 19.10.67, East Kilbride; m., Alasdair Davidson; 1 s. Educ. St. Brides High School; Glasgow College of Technology. Career History: Trainee Accountant, Surrey Borough Council; Systems Auditor (Secondment), Surrey County Council; Contracts Auditor, Surrey Heath Borough Council; Internal Audit Manager, London Borough of Croydon; Depute Director, CIPFA Scotland/Secondment as Competition Consultant; Head of Finance, SPT, then Director of Finance. Consulting Author to Stairs Encyclopedia; contributing Author to CIPFA Publications; Member, LASAAC. Recreations: cooking; golf. Address: (h.) 14 Norwood Drive, Whitecraigs, Glasgow G46 7LS; T.-0777 177 3790.
E-mail: valerie.davidson1@ntlworld.com

Davies, Alan Graham, LLB(Hons), Dip. Legal Practice. Solicitor in private practice since 1983, Partner, since 1987; b. 4.2.59, Perth; m., Fiona; 2 s.; 1 d. Educ. Perth Grammar School; University of Edinburgh. Recreations: golf; football; skiing; tennis. Address: (b.) 25 South Methven Street, Perth; T.-01738 620451.

Davies, Professor Christine Tullis Hunter, OBE, MA, PhD (Cantab), FInstP, FRSE. Professor of Physics, University of Glasgow, since 1999; b. 19.11.59, Clacton, Essex; m., John Davies; 2 d. Educ. Colchester County High School for Girls; Churchill College, University of Cambridge. Postdoctoral Research Associate, Cornell University, 1984-86; SERC Advanced Fellow, Glasgow University, 1987-93; Lecturer, 1993-96; Reader, 1996-99. Fulbright Scholar and Leverhulme Trust Fellow, University of California at Santa Barbara, 1997-98; PRARC Senior Fellow, 2001-04; Royal Society/Leverhulme Trust Senior Fellow, 2008; Rosalind Franklin Award, Royal Society, 2005. STFC Particle Physics Grants Panel (Theory), 2006-09; IOP Council and Chair of Diversity Committee, 2007-2011; RCUK (Wakeham) Committee, 2008; Royal Society Wolfson Research Merit Award, 2012-2017. Recreations: walking; photography. Address: (b.) School of Physics & Astronomy, University of Glasgow, Glasgow G12 8QQ; T.-0141 330 4710; e-mail: christine.davies@glasgow.ac.uk

Davies, Sir Howard John, MA, MS. Chairman, The Royal Bank of Scotland, since 2015; Professor of Practice at the Paris Institute of Political Science (Sciences Po); Chairman of the Phoenix Group; b. 12.2.51; m., Prue Keely; 2 s. Educ. Bowker Vale County Primary School; Manchester Grammar School; Merton College, Oxford University; Stanford Graduate School of Business. Worked at the Treasury and the Foreign and Commonwealth Office, which included a posting of Private Secretary to the British Ambassador to France; McKinsey and Company, 1982-87; Special Advisor to Chancellor of the Exchequer Nigel Lawson, 1985-86; Controller of the Audit Commission, 1987-92; Director General of the Confederation of British Industry, 1992-95; Deputy Governor of the Bank of England, 1995-97; Chairman of the Financial Services Authority, 1997-2003; Director of the London School of Economics and Political Science, 2003-2011. Independent Director of Prudential plc and Chair of the Risk Committee; Member of the Regulatory and Compliance Advisory Board of Millennium Management LLC; Chair of the International Advisory Council of the China Securities Regulatory Commission; Member of the International Advisory Council of the China Banking Regulatory Commission; Council Member of the Asian Bureau of Finance and Economic Research in Singapore. Chair, UK Airports Commission, 2012-15. Writes regularly for The Financial Times, Times Higher Education, Project Syndicate and Management Today. Publications: Chancellors Tales (Co-Author), 2006; Global Financial Regulation: the Essential Guide, 2008; Banking on the Future: the fall and rise of central banking, 2010; The Financial Crisis: Who's to Blame, 2010; Can Financial Markets be Controlled?, 2015. Recreations: supporter of Manchester City Football Club and the Lancashire County Cricket Club; plays cricket for Barnes Common and Powerstock and Hooke cricket clubs. Address: RBS, 36 St Andrew Square, Edinburgh EH2 2YB.

Davies (a.k.a. Glasse-Davies), Professor R. Wayne, MA, PhD, ScD. Chairperson, Snowsport Scotland, since 2014; CEO, Brainwave-Discovery Ltd., Edinburgh, since 2010; Scientific Director, Pathfinder Cell Therapy Inc, since 2010; Hon. Professor, University of Edinburgh, since 2009; Director, Brainwave-Discovery Ltd., since 2007; Director, Age Analytics Ltd., since 2011; Robertson Professor of Biotechnology, Glasgow University, 1989-2009; b. 10.6.44, Cardiff; m., Victoria Glasse; 3 s.; 2 d. Educ. Queen Elizabeth's Hospital, Bristol; St. John's College, Cambridge. Research Fellow, University of Wisconsin, 1968-71; H3 Professor, Universität zu Köln, FRG, 1971-77; Lecturer, University of Essex, 1977-81; Senior Lecturer, UMIST, 1981-83; Vice-President, Scientific and Research Director, Allelix Biopharmaceuticals, Toronto, 1983-89; Neuropa Ltd.: Founding Director, 1996, CEO, 1997-2000; CEO Uman Genomics AB, Sweden, 2001-03. Recreations: poetry and literature; cello; skiing. Address: (b.) University of Edinburgh, Institute of Adaptive and Neural Computation, Informatics Forum, 10 Crichton Street, Edinburgh EH8 9AB.

Davies, Susan, BSc, MSc. Director of Conservation, Scottish Wildlife Trust; Director & Trustee (voluntary), Venture Trust, since 2015. Educ. University of St Andrews; University of Aberdeen. Career history: various positions, Joint Nature Conservation Committee, 1990-99; Scottish Natural Heritage: Director of Operations (North), 2006-2010, Director of Policy & Advice, 2010-13; Director, Langholm Moor Demonstration Project, 2010-13; Deputy Director, Rural & Environment Science & Analytical Services Division (Secondment), Scottish Government, 2013-14; Acting CEO, Scottish Natural Heritage, 2015-16. Member, IUCN UK National Committee; Fellow of Society of Biology (FSB). Address: Scottish Wildlife Trust, Harbourside House, 110 Commercial Street, Edinburgh EH6 6NF.

Davila, Professor James R., BA, MA, PhD. Professor of Early Jewish Studies, University of St Andrews, since 2008; b. 08.08.60, San Diego, Ca., USA. Educ. Crawford High School; UCLA; Harvard University. Visiting Assistant Professor of Jewish Studies, Tulane University, 1988-89, Visiting Assistant Professor of Classics, 1989-91; Assistant Professor of Religion, Central College, 1991-95; Lecturer in Early Jewish Studies, University of St Andrews, 1995-2006; Reader in Early Jewish Studies, University of St Andrews, 2006-08. Member of the editorial team that published Dead Sea Scrolls. Publications: numerous articles and books on ancient Judaism and related matters. Blog: PaleoJudaica (paleojudaica.blogspot.com). Address: (b.) St. Mary's College, University of St Andrews, St Andrews, Fife KY16 9JU; T.-01334 462834; e-mail: jrd4@st-andrews.ac.uk

Davis, Margaret Thomson. Novelist; b. Bathgate; 2 s. Educ. Albert Secondary School. Worked as children's nurse; Red Cross nurse; short story writer; novelist; author of autobiography, The Making of a Novelist; novels include

The Breadmakers, A Baby Might Be Crying, A Sort of Peace, The Prisoner, The Prince and the Tobacco Lords, Roots of Bondage, Scorpion in the Fire, The Dark Side of Pleasure, A Very Civilised Man, Light and Dark, Rag Woman Rich Woman, Daughters and Mothers, Wounds of War, A Woman of Property, A Sense of Belonging, Hold Me Forever, Kiss Me No More, A Kind of Immortality, Burning Ambition, A Darkening of The Heart, A Deadly Deception, Goodmans of Glassford Street, Red Alert, Double Danger, The Kellys of Kelvingrove. Committee Member: International PEN (Scottish Branch); Society of Authors; Lecturer in Creative Writing; Honorary President, Strathkelvin Writers Club. Recreations: reading; travelling; being with friends.

Davis, Ray, DipArch, MSc, DipUD, RIBA, FRIAS. Consultant Architect, McLean Architects; former Managing Director, Davis Duncan Architects; b. 11.2.48, Glasgow; m., Ruth; 3 d. Educ. Aberdeen Grammar School; Robert Gordon University; Heriot Watt University. Alison and Hutcheson and Partners: Architect, Edinburgh Office, 1973-79, Senior Architect and Office Manager, Glasgow, 1979-81; Visiting Lecturer, Planning Department, Mackintosh School, 1979-81; formed Ray Davis Architects and Urban Design Consultants, 1981; part-time Design Tutor, Department of Architecture, Strathclyde University, 1981-86; formed current practice, 1982. Convenor, Baptist Union Property Group, 1997. Recreations: golf; sketching; skiing; church. Address: (b.) 29 Eagle Street, Craighall Business Park, Glasgow G4 9XA; T.-0141 353 2040; e-mail: raydavis@macleanarchitects.co.uk

Davison, Timothy Paul, BA (Hons), MHSM, DipHSM, MBA, MPH. Chief Executive, NHS Lothian, since 2012; b. 4.6.61, Newcastle upon Tyne; m., Fiona Jane Maguire; 1 s. Educ. Kenton School, Newcastle upon Tyne; Stirling University; Glasgow University. Appointments in Stirling Royal Infirmary, Royal Edinburgh Hospital, Glasgow Royal Infirmary, 1984-90; Sector General Manager, Gartnavel Royal Hospital, 1990-91; Unit General Manager, Mental Health Unit, Glasgow, 1991-92, Community and Mental Health Unit, Glasgow, 1992-94; Chief Executive, Greater Glasgow Community and Mental Health Services NHS Trust, 1994-99; Chief Executive, Greater Glasgow Primary Care NHS Trust, 1999-2002; Chief Executive, North Glasgow University Hospitals NHS Trust (subsequently Division), 2002-05; Chief Executive, NHS Lanarkshire, 2005-2012. Recreations: tennis; military and political history. Address: (b.) NHS Lothian, Waverley Gate, 2-4 Waterloo Place, Edinburgh EH1 3EG.

Dawe, Jennifer Ann (Jenny), MA, PhD. Leader, City of Edinburgh Council, 2007-2012; Leader, Liberal Democrat Group, City of Edinburgh Council, 1999-2012; b. 27.4.45, Edinburgh; 4 s. Educ. Trinity Academy; Aberdeen University; Edinburgh University. Former Librarian, Tanzania and Malawi, 1966-80; Tutor, American and Commonwealth History Department, Edinburgh University, 1985-87; Admin and Information Officer, Lothian Community Relations Council, 1988-90; Welfare Rights Officer, Lothian Regional Council, 1990-96; Senior Welfare Rights Officer, East Lothian Council, 1996-2007. City of Edinburgh Councillor, 1997-2012. Recreations: travel; reading; gardening; Hearts supporter.

Dawson, Professor John Alan, BSc, MPhil, PhD, DBA (Hon), FRSE. Professor Emeritus, Universities of Edinburgh and Stirling, since 2009; Professor of Marketing, Edinburgh University, 1990-2009; Professor of Retailing, Stirling University, 2005-09; Visiting Professor: Escuela Superior de Administración y Dirección de Empresas

(ESADE), Barcelona; University of Marketing and Distribution Sciences, Kobe, Japan; b. 19.8.44, Hyde; 1 s.; 1 d. Educ. Lady Manners School, Bakewell; University College, London; Nottingham University. Lecturer, Nottingham University; Lecturer, Senior Lecturer, Reader, St. David's University College, Wales; Fraser of Allander Professor of Distributive Studies, Stirling University; Visiting Lecturer, University of Western Australia; Visiting Research Fellow, Australian National University; Visiting Professor: Florida State University, Chuo University, University of South Africa, University of Marketing and Distribution Sciences, Kobe, Boconni University, Milan, Saitama University, Japan. Chairman, National Museums of Scotland Retailing Ltd, 1997-2002. Publications: Evaluating the Human Environment, 1973; Man and His World, 1975; Computing for Geographers, 1976; Small-Scale Retailing in the UK, 1979; Marketing Environment, 1979; Retail Geography, 1980; Commercial Distribution in Europe, 1982; Teach Yourself Geography, 1983; Shopping Centre Development, 1983; Computer Methods for Geographers, 1985; Retailing in Scoland 2005, 1988; Evolution of European Retailing, 1988; Retailing Environments in Developing Countries, 1990; Competition and Markets, 1992; European Cases in Retailing, 1999; The Inernationalisation of Retailing in Asia, 2003; International Retailing Plans and Strategies in Asia, 2005; Strategic Issues in International Retailing, 2006; The Retailing Reader, 2008; Global Strategies in Retailing, 2013. Recreations: sport; writing. Address: (b.) University of Edinburgh Business School, 29 Buccleuch Place, Edinburgh EH8 9JS; T.-0131-650 3830.

Dawson, Rev. Morag Ann, BD, MTh. Minister of Dalton linked with Hightae linked with St Mungo, since 2011; Minister, Galashiels, 2003-2011; b. 1.11.52, Gorebridge; 1 s.; 1 d. (twins). Educ. Greenhall High School; New College, School of Divinity, University of Edinburgh. Civil Servant (CO), Register House, Edinburgh, 1970-74; Strathclyde Police (HCO), Glasgow, 1974-79; Church of Scotland Minister, since 1999. Young University Institution, Falkirk; P/T Chaplain, Kilmarnock Prison. Recreations: rugby; music; reading; walking. Address: (h.) The Manse, Hightae, Lockerbie DG11 1JL; T.-01387 811 499; e-mail: moragdawson@yahoo.co.uk

Dawson, Peter, MA. Secretary, Royal and Ancient Golf Club of St Andrews, 1999-2015; b. 28.5.48, Aberdeen. Educ. Corpus Christi College, Cambridge.

Dawson, Thomas Christopher, BA (Hons), FSA (Scot). Archaeologist; Managing Director, The SCAPE Trust, since 2001; Research Fellow, University of St Andrews, since 2000; b. Oxford. Educ. University of Leicester. Senior Archaeologist, Museum of London, 1989-91; Archaeological site director with AFAN-sites in Lyon and Haute Savoie, 1992-94; Archaeological supervisor, Elms Farm Project, Essex, 1994; Archaeologist with the Department of Archaeology, Sri Lanka (VSO posting), 1995-98; Project Officer, Excavation of the Chateau de Mayenne, 1999; Director: The Bardsey Island Trust, 2002-08, The SCRAN Trust, since 2010, SCRAN Ltd, since 2010. Commissioner, Royal Commission on the Ancient and Historical Monuments of Scotland; Editor, Coastal Archaeology and Erosion in Scotland (Historic Scotland). Recreations: cycling; travel. Address: (b.) St Katharine's Lodge, St Andrews KY16 9AL; T.-01334 467172; e-mail: tcd@st-andrews.ac.uk

Dawson Scott, Robert, MA, MLitt. Playwright; Head of Engagement, STV (Web Editor, stv.tv); b. 24.7.56; London; 3 d. Educ. Oxford University; Strathclyde University. Formerly Theatre critic, The Times; formerly Head of

Content, scotsman.com. Founder of Critics Awards for Theatre in Scotland (CATS). Recreations: music; hill-walking. Address: (b.) 6 Westercraigs, Glasgow G31 2HZ; T.-0141-554 7106.

Day, Martyn. MP (SNP), Linlithgow and East Falkirk, since 2015; b. 1971, Falkirk. Educ. Linlithgow. Elected to West Lothian Council in the Scottish local elections, 1999 representing the Linlithgow ward; Development and Transport portfolio on the Council Executive, West Lothian Council, 2007-2012; served on over 40 committees and outside bodies; appointed spokesperson for Development and Transport and group whip in 2012. Address: House of Commons, London SW1A 0AA.

Deacon, Professor Susan. MA (Hons), MBA, FRSA. Assistant Principal, External Relations, University of Edinburgh; Non-Executive Director, ScottishPower Ltd, since 2012; Trustee, Edinburgh College Development Trust, 2014-15; Chair, Institute of Directors (IOD) Scotland, since 2015; Non-Executive Director, Lothian Buses Ltd, since 2015; Chair, Edinburgh Festivals Forum, since 2016; b. 2.2.64; 1 s. 1 d. Educ. Musselburgh Grammar School; University of Edinburgh. Chairman (2010-12)/Non-Executive Director (2009-10), ScottishPower Renewables Ltd; Honorary Professor, School of Social and Political Science, University of Edinburgh (2010-12); Early Years Adviser to Scottish Government (2010-11); Professor of Social Change, Queen Margaret University (2007-10); Trustee, Iberdrola Foundation (2009-14); Founding Chairperson, Hibernian Community Foundation (2008-12); Member of the Scottish Parliament (Labour), Edinburgh East & Musselburgh (1999-2007); Minister for Health and Community Care, Scottish Executive (1999-2001); MBA Director of Programmes, Heriot-Watt University (1994-8); research/management positions in local government (1987-1994). Other previous appointments include RSA UK Drugs Commission; Strategic Review of National Trust for Scotland; Traverse Theatre Board; Dewar Arts Awards Trust; Pfizer UK Foundation Board. Address: University of Edinburgh, Charles Stewart House, 9-16 Chambers Street, Edinburgh EH1 1HT.
E-mail: susan.deacon@ed.ac.uk

Dean, (Catherine) Margaret, MA, CVO. Lord Lieutenant of Fife, 1999-2014; b. 16.11.39, Edinburgh; m., Brian Dean; 3 d. Educ. George Watson's Ladies' College; Edinburgh University. Teacher of English; Past Chairman, Dunfermline Heritage Trust. Recreations: bridge; theatre; family (grandchildren); walking. Address: (h.) Viewforth, 121 Rose Street, Dunfermline KY12 0QT; T.-01383 722488.

Dean, Michael, LLB (Hons), DipAdvEurStud (Bruges). Partner, Maclay Murray & Spens LLP, since 1998; Honorary Consul for the Federal Republic of Germany in Glasgow and Port of Glasgow, since 2007; b. 15.01.60, Glasgow; m., Anne; 3 d. Educ. St. Aloysius' College, Glasgow; University of Glasgow; College of Europe, Bruges. Working in the area of European Law and competition law; heads up Maclays' EU Competition and Regulatory practice; heavily involved in export related matters, distribution, public law, procurement law, bribery and ethical compliance programmes, Competition and Markets Authority merger and market inquiries, FCA inquiries and European Commission cartel inquiries. Recreations: tennis; football; running; theatre. Address: (b.) G1, 1 George Square, Glasgow G2 1AL; T.-0330 222 1713; e-mail: michael.dean@mms.co.uk

Deans, Rev. Dr. Graham Douglas Sutherland, MA, BD (Hons), MTh (Oxon), MLitt, DMin, FBS. Minister at Aberdeen: Queen Street, since 2008; b. 15.8.53, Aberdeen; m., Marina Punler. Educ. Mackie Academy, Stonehaven; University of Aberdeen; Westminster College, Oxford; Pittsburgh Theological Seminary; University of St Andrews. Winner of Richard J Rapp Memorial Prize, 2006. Assistant Minister, Craigsbank Parish Church, Corstorphine, 1977-78; Parish Minister: Denbeath with Methilhill, 1978-87, St. Mary's Parish Church, Dumfries, 1987-2002, South Ronaldsay and Burray, 2002-08. Depute Clerk and Treasurer, Presbytery of Kirkcaldy, 1981-87; Chaplain, Randolph Wemyss Memorial Hospital, 1980-87; Moderator, Presbytery of Dumfries and Kirkcudbright, 1994-95; Convener: Committee on Glebes, 1991-92, Committee on Music and Worship, 1993-96, Committee on the Maintenance of the Ministry, 1997-2000 (Vice-Convener, 1991-96), Committee on Ministry, 2000-02; Member: Assembly Committee on Probationers, 1991-97, Maintenance of the Ministry Committee, 1991-98, Board of Ministry, 1998-2002, Ministry Support Committee, 1998-2001, Ministry Development Committee, 2001-02; Trustee, Housing and Loan Fund, 1999-2004; Convener, Business and Finance Committee, Presbytery of Aberdeen, 2011-2014; Member, Executive Committee, Hymn Society of Great Britain and Ireland, 1998-2001, 2002-08 and 2009-2015. Publications: A History of Denbeath Church, 1980; Children's Addresses in the Expository Times, 1983, 1987 and 1988; Presbyterian Praise, 1999; contributions to Bulletin of the Hymn Society; contributor to Christian Hymns (new edition), 2004; contributor to Come Celebrate (Contemporary Hymns), 2009; "Race Shall Thy Works Praise Unto Race": the Development of Metrical Psalmody in Scotland, 2012; contributor to Transactions of the Burgon Society (Volume 13), 2013; contributor to Thanks and Praise, 2015. Recreation: music. Address: 51 Osborne Place, Aberdeen AB25 2BX; T.-01224 646429; e-mail: graham.deans@btopenworld.com

Deans, Joyce Blair, CBE, DUniv, BArch, PPRIAS, RIBA, ACIArb, FRSA. Architect; President, Royal Incorporation of Architects in Scotland, 1991-93 (first woman President); b. 29.1.27, Glasgow; m., John Albert Gibson Deans; 2 s.; 2 d. Educ. Laurel Bank School for Girls; University of Strathclyde. Re-entered profession as Assistant, private practice, 1968; appointed Associate, 1972; established own practice, 1981. Elected Member, Council: Glasgow Institute of Architects, 1975-90 (first woman President, 1986-88); Royal Incorporation of Architects, 1979-95; first female Vice President, Royal Incorporation of Architects in Scotland, 1986-88; Member, Building Standards Advisory Committee, 1987-96; Chairman, BSAC (Research), 1988-96 (first woman); Chairman (first woman), Scottish Construction Industry Group, 1996-2001 (Member, since 1991); Director, Cairn Housing Association, 1988-99; Founder Member, Glasgow West Conservation Trust, 1987-2000; Governor: Laurel Bank School for Girls 1981-99, Board Member, Glasgow School of Art, 1986-98, (Vice Chairman (Estates) 1992-98); Vice Chairman of Court, Strathclyde University, 2000-03 (Member of Court, 1993-2003); elected to Management Council for Learning in Later Life Students' Association, Strathclyde University, 2003; elected President, Learning in Later Life Students' Association, 2004-06; elected Vice President, Royal Institute of British Architects, 1993-95, and 1999-2001; Member: RIBA Council, 1991-2001, Patrick Geddes Award Panel, since 1993; Industrial Assessor (Architecture), SHEFC, 1994-95; External Examiner, Part 3, since 1994; Member, Professors' Advisory Team, University of Strathclyde, since 1993; Member, MSc Management Advisory Board, University of Northumbria at Newcastle, 1997-2003. Founder Member and Chairman, Brookwood Computer Group, 2006; Member, Executive Council of Friends of Loch Lomond and the Trossachs, since 2007, Trustees 'Membership' Chairman, since 2011; Consultant to the Development Group of Bearsden Cross Parish Church, 2007-2010; Member of The Church Board, since 2011. Hon. DUniv (University of Strathclyde), 1996; MBE, 1989; CBE, 1999; awarded Glasgow Institute of Architects Supreme Award, 2009; Author of 'The Time of Our Lives',

2012; lectured widely on 'The Time of Our Lives', since 2012; Member of Judging Panel for RIAS Awards, 2013. Recreations: gardening; golf; walking; reading; theatre. Address: 11 South Erskine Park, Bearsden, Glasgow G61 4NA; T.-0141-942 6795.

Deans, Mungo Effingham, BSc (Econ), LLB. A Judge of the Upper Tribunal and Resident Judge of the First-tier Tribunal, Immigration and Asylum Chamber; Resident Senior Immigration Judge, Asylum and Immigration Tribunal, 2005-2010; Regional Adjudicator, Immigration Appellate Authority, 1996-2005; part-time Legal Member, Immigration Appeal Tribunal, 2000-05; b. 25.5.56, Lytham St. Annes; m., Kathryn Atkinson; 3 s. Educ. Fettes College, Edinburgh; London School of Economics; University of Edinburgh. Admitted as Solicitor, 1981; Lecturer, Department of Law: Napier University, 1981-82, Dundee University, 1983-96; Chairman: Social Security Appeal Tribunals, 1989-99, Disability Appeal Tribunals, 1992-99; Immigration Adjudicator, 1994. Publication: Scots Public Law, 1995. Recreations: Scottish history; fine art. Address: (b.) F-t T, Immigration & Asylum Chamber, 5th Floor, Eagle Building, 215 Bothwell Street, Glasgow G2 7EZ; T.-0300 123 1711.

Deary, Professor Ian John, BSc, PhD, MBChB, FRCPE, FRCPsych, FBA, FRSE, FMedSci. Professor of Differential Psychology, University of Edinburgh, since 1995; Director, University of Edinburgh Centre for Cognitive Ageing and Cognitive Epidemiology; b. 17.5.54, Carluke; m., Ann Marie Barclay; 1 s.; 2 d. Educ. Hamilton Academy; University of Edinburgh. House Officer, Royal Infirmary of Edinburgh, 1983-84; Senior House Officer in Psychiatry, Maudsley Hospital, London, 1984-85; Department of Psychology, University of Edinburgh: Lecturer, 1985-90, Senior Lecturer, 1990-92, Reader, 1992-95. Royal Society-Wolfson Research Merit Award, 2002-07. Publications: Looking Down on Human Intelligence; Intelligence – A Very Short Introduction; Personality Traits (Co-author); A Lifetime of Intelligence (Co-author); editor of two books on personality; over 500 refereed scientific papers, principally on human cognitive ability and cognitive ageing, and personality. Recreations: saxophone; lyric-writing; late Victorian novels; English Romantic composers; cycling; Motherwell F.C. Address: (b.) Department of Psychology, University of Edinburgh, 7 George Square, Edinburgh EH8 9JZ; T.-0131-650 3452; e-mail: I.Deary@ed.ac.uk

Deila, Ronny. Former Manager, Celtic FC (2014-16); b. 21.9.75, Porsgrunn, Norway. Youth career: Urædd; Senior career: Urædd, 1992-93; Odd Grenland, 1993-2004; Viking, 2004-05; Strømsgodset, 2006-2008; Sparta/Bragerøen, 2009-2011; National team: Norway U17, 1992-93; Norway U18, 1994; Norway U21, 1996; Teams managed: Brodd, 2005, Strømsgodset (assistant coach), 2006-2008, Birkebeineren (assistant coach, 2007-08), Strømsgodset, 2008-14 (head coach). Player Honours: Odd Grenland, Norwegian Football Cup, 2000; Managerial Honours: Strømsgodset, Norwegian Football Cup, 2010, Tippeligaen, 2013; Celtic, Scottish League Cup, 2014-15, Scottish Premiership, 2014-15, 2015-16; Individual Honours: Kniksen Award - Coach of the Year: 2013.

Delahunt, Jim, BA. Journalist and Broadcaster; Columnist, Scottish Sun, since 2010; b. 10.5.62, Irvine. Educ. St. Andrews Academy, Saltcoats; Glasgow Caledonian University. Reporter, Kilmarnock Free Press; Reporter, West Sound; Editor, Daily Winner; Night News Editor, Radio Clyde; Sub-Editor, The Sunday Times; Sub-Editor, Reporter then Presenter, Scottish Television, 1990-2006; Presenter, Setanta Sports, 2006-09; Columnist, Sunday Herald, 1999-2010; Sports Editor, Radio Clyde, 2010-2015. Recreations: horse-racing; ex-amateur jockey. E-mail: jjimmydel@aol.com

Delaney, Alastair Gordon. Chief Operating Officer, Education Scotland; b. 27.12.66, St Andrews. Career: Youth Work Manager, Highland Association of Youth Clubs; Community education worker in Central Regional Council; Service Manager in Stirling Council; HM Inspector, 2000-03; HM Assistant Chief Inspector, 2003-2010. Recreations: driving; technology; playing music. Address: (b.) Denholm House, Almondvale Business Park, Almondvale Way, Livingston, West Lothian EH54 6GA; T.-01506 600230. E-mail: alastair.delaney@educationscotland.gsi.gov.uk

Della Sala, Professor Sergio F., MD, PhD, FRSE. Professor of Human Cognitive Neuroscience; Hon. Consultant in Neurology, Edinburgh; b. 23.9.55. Chair of Neuropsychology, Aberdeen; Milan. Senior Neurologist, Milan teaching hospital; Head, Neuropsychology Unit, Veruno, Italy. Address: (b.) University of Edinburgh, 7 George Square, Edinburgh.

Demarco, Professor Richard, CBE, RSW, SSA, Hon. FRIAS, FRSA, DA, Hon. DFA, ACA, Hon. LLD (Dundee). Artist and Writer; Director, Richard Demarco Gallery, 1966-92; b. 9.7.30, Edinburgh; m., Anne Muckle. Educ. Holy Cross Academy, Edinburgh; Edinburgh College of Art. National Service, KOSB and Royal Army Education Corps, 1954-56; Art Master, Scotus Academy, Edinburgh, 1957-67; Vice-Chairman, Board, Traverse Theatre Club, 1963-67; Director, Sean Connery's Scottish International Education Trust, 1972-73; Member: Board of Governors, Carlisle School of Art, 1970-74, Edinburgh Festival Society, 1971-86; Contributing Editor, Studio International, 1982-84; External Assessor, Stourbridge College of Art, 1988-90; Artistic Director, European Youth Parliament, since 1993; Professor of European Cultural Studies, Kingston University, 1993-2000, Emeritus Professor, since 2000; Director, Demarco European Art Foundation, since 1993; Trustee, Kingston-Demarco European Cultural Foundation, 1993-95; Honorary Member, Scottish Arts Club; Elected Member, L'Association International des Critiques D'Art (AICA), 1994. Awards: Gold Order of Merit, Polish People's Republic; Chevalier de L'Ordre des Arts et Lettres; Order of Cavaliere della Reppublica d'Italia; Scottish Arts Council Award for services to Scotland's visual arts, 1975; Medal, International Theatre Institutes of Great Britain and Poland, 1992; Honorary Doctorate, Atlanta College of Art, 1993; Arts Medal, Royal Philosophical Society of Glasgow, 1995; appointed Commander, Military and Hospitaller Order of St. Lazarus of Jerusalem, 1996; Honorary Fellow of the Institute of Contemporary Scotland, 2003; awarded silver 'Gloria Artis' Medal by the Minister of Culture for Poland; awarded Honorary Citizenship of Lodz, Poland, 2007; awarded Honorary Fellow of Edinburgh College of Art, 2007; Honorary President of the Society of Scottish Artists, 2007. Publications: The Road to Meikle Seggie; The Artist as Explorer; A Life in Pictures; Kunst=Kapital: The Adam Smith Lecture, 1995; Honouring Colmcille, 1997; Demarco: On the Road to Meikle Seggie, 2000; The Demarco Collection and Archive: an Introduction, 2009. Recreation: walking "The Road to Meikle Seggie".

Dempsey, Steve BSc, MSc. Retired Headteacher; b. 2.2.54, Dungannon, Co. Tyrone. Educ. Royal School, Dungannon; Edinburgh University; Sheffield University; Moray House College of Education. Teacher of Physics,

Wallace High School, Stirling, 1978-82; Auchmuty High School, Glenrothes: APT Science, 1982-86, PT Physics, 1986-95; Assistant Headteacher, Banff Academy, 1995-2001; Deputy Headteacher, Wick High School, 2001-03; Headteacher, Brechin High School, 2004-2014. Recreations: football; reading.

Denham, Ashten, MSc. MSP (Scottish National Party), Edinburgh Eastern, since 2016. Educ. Keele University; London School of Public Relations; Open University. Career history: PR and Marketing Officer, ScottClem, 1998-2001; Senior Account Executive, Spreckley Partners, 2001-02; Events Executive, Zinc Management, 2002; Account Manager, Rocket PR, 2002-03; Digital Marketing, Tearfund, 2012-13; Head of Campaigns and Advocacy, Common Weal Scotland, 2013-15. Referendum Agent for Scottish Borders, Women For Independence, September 2014. Advocacy, Abolition Scotland, 2013; Events co-ordinator for YES Scottish Borders, 2013-14; Speaker & National Committee Member, Women For Independence, since 2014. Recreations: green building; skiing. Address: Scottish Parliament, Edinburgh EH99 1SP.

Denholm, Alastair Kennedy, DUniv (Glasgow), FUniv (Caledonian), FCIBS, FEI; b. 27.9.36, Glasgow; m., Rosalind Murray Hamilton (deceased). Educ. Hutchesons' (Boys) Grammar School. Clydesdale Bank PLC, 1953-91; Managing Director, Quality Management Advisers (Scotland), 1992-98; Director, The Prince's Scottish Youth Business Trust, 1985-2009; Member, Board, Central College of Commerce, 1991-2003; Governor, Hutchesons' Grammar School, 1996-2011, Chairman of Governors, 2003-2010; Director, Hutchesons' School, Trust and Club 1995 Ltd., 1996-2011; Director, Laurel Park School Co. Ltd., 2001-05; Lord Dean of Guild, Merchants House of Glasgow, 2001-03; Director, Ship Venture Ltd., 2001-09; Hon. President, Chartered Institute of Marketing, since 2003; Lay Member, Audit Registration Committee, Institute of Chartered Accountants of Scotland, 1995-2009; Director, Glasgow Bute Benevolent Society, since 1980; Director, Glasgow Native Benevolent Society, 1991-2008; Governor, Glasgow Caledonian University (including its founding organisation), 1978-95; Deacon, Incorporation of Hammermen, 1988-89; Chairman, Glasgow Junior Chamber of Commerce, 1976-77; President, Association of Deacons of the Fourteen Incorporated Trades of Glasgow, 2003-04; Treasurer, Action for Disaster, 1973-95; Chairman, Chartered Institute of Bankers in Scotland, Glasgow, 1987-88; Director, Glasgow Chamber of Commerce, 1994-97; Treasurer, Williamwood Parish Church of Scotland, 1962-2009, Elder, since 1962; District Governor, Rotary International District 1230, 1999-2000; HOEC Treasurer, Rotary International World Conference 1997, 1996-98; Bridgeton Burns Club: Director, since 2000, Treasurer, since 2007. Recreations: golf; curling; Rotary. Address: (h.) Whitley, 28 Milverton Road, Whitecraigs, Glasgow G46 7JN; T.-0141-638 2939.

Denney, Alan Alexander, National Secretary, Scotland, Prospect (formerly IPMS), since 1990; b. 25.1.57, Stirling; m., Jacqueline May; 2 s.; 1 d. Educ. Plaistow Grammar School; East Ham College of Technology. Civil Service (Department of Trade), 1975-78; Prospect (formerly IPMS) since 1979. Address: (b.) Suite 4, Glenorchy House, 20 Union Street, Edinburgh GH1 3LR; T.-0131 558 5288; e-mail: alan.denney@prospect.org.uk

Dennis, Richard. Head of Accountant in Bankruptcy, since 2015. Career in the Civil Service, both in Scotland and at Whitehall; 15 years at the Scottish Government and 10 years at Whitehall before that. Worked with the European Commission in the Directorate General concerned with Environmental Policy; held a range of finance related posts including a five year spell at the UK HM Treasury; Head of Civil Law Policy, then Head of the Fire and Rescue Division, Scottish Government. Address: Accountant in Bankruptcy, 1 Pennyburn Road, Kilwinning KA13 6SA.

Dennis, Roy, MBE. Wildlife Consultant/Ornithologist; Specialist, species recovery & ecological restoration projects, satellite tracking, UK and overseas; Director, Highland Foundation for Wildlife, since 1996; b. 4.5.40. Educ. Price's School. Migration Research Assistant, UK Bird Observatories, 1958-59; Warden, Lochgarten Osprey Reserve, 1960-63; Warden, Fair Isle Bird Observatory, 1963-70; Highland Officer, RSPB, 1971-87, Regional Officer (North Scotland), 1987-91; Main Board Member, Scottish Natural Heritage, 1992-97; Director, Cairngorms Partnership, 1995-97; Member, Deer Commission for Scotland, 1999-2002; President, Fair Isle Bird Observatory Trust; Honorary President, Scottish Ornithologists' Club; Patron, Trees for Life. Publications: Ospreys and Speyside Wildlife; Birds of Badenoch and Strathspey; Puffins; Ospreys; Peregrine Falcons; Divers; The Loch; Golden Eagles; A Life of Ospreys, 2008. TV presenting, latest Autumnwatch 2011 & Springwatch 2012. Recreations: travel; photography; bird-watching. Address: Half Davoch Cottage, Dunphail, Forres, Moray IV36 2QR; e-mail: roydennis@aol.com; websites: www.roydennis.org; www.raptortrack.org

Denniston, Rev. David William, BD, DipMin. Minister, St. Cuthberts, Edinburgh, since 2008; b. 23.4.56, Glasgow; m., Jane Ross; 2 s.; 1 d. Educ. Hutchesons' Boys Grammar School, Glasgow; University of Glasgow. Minister: Ruchazie Parish Church, Glasgow, 1981-86, Kennoway, Fife, 1986-96; Minister, North Church, Perth, 1996-2008. Recreations: hill-walking; fishing; music. Address: (h.) 34a Murrayfield Road, Edinburgh EH12 6ER; T.-0131 337 6637; e-mail: denniston.david@gmail.com

Dent, John Anthony, MMEd, MD, FHEA, FRCS (Edin). International Relations Officer, AMEE (The Association for Medical Education in Europe), since 2011; Reader in Medical Education and Orthopaedic Surgery, University of Dundee, since 1990; b. 4.3.53, Kendal; m., Frances Jane Wyllie; 1 s.; 1 d. Educ. Haversham Grammar School, Cumbria; University of Dundee. Hand Research Fellow, Princess Margaret Rose Orthopaedic Hospital, Edinburgh; Christine Kleinert Hand Fellow, University of Louisville, Kentucky, USA; co-established Dundee Hand Surgery Service, Ninewells Hospital, Dundee; undergraduate teaching, Clinical Skills Centre; has worked in curriculum development and implementation, University of Dundee Medical School, since 1997; External Examiner: University of Brighton, 1995-98, University of Sunderland, 1998-2001, University of East Anglia, since 2003, University of Hong Kong, since 2010. Member, Examinations Committee, Royal College of Surgeons of Edinburgh, since 1997; Member, National Panel of Specialists for Training in Orthopaedic and Trauma Surgery, 1993-2000; Guest Lecturer: University of Gezira, Sudan, 1996, and to Association of Surgeons of India, Bombay, 1996. Publications: papers on upper limb surgery and medical education; The Musculoskeletal System: Core Topics in the New Curriculum (Co-Author/Editor), 1997; Churchill's Mastery of Medicine: Surgery 2 (Co-Author/Editor), 3rd ed, 2008; A Practical Guide for Medical Teachers (Co-Editor), 3rd ed, 2008. Recreations: heraldry; history; gardens. Address: (b.) Tay Park House, 484 Perth Road, Dundee DD2 1LR; T.-01382 381991.
E-mail: j.a.dent@dundee.ac.uk

Deregowski, Professor Jan Bronislaw, BSc, BA, PhD, DSc, FBPsS, FRSE. Professor of Psychology, Aberdeen University, since 1986 (Reader, 1981-86); b. 1.3.33, Pinsk, Poland; m., Eva Loft Nielsen; 2 s.; 1 d. Educ. London University. Lecturer, then Senior Lecturer, Aberdeen

University, 1969-81. Publications: Illusions, Patterns and Pictures: a cross-cultural perspective; Distortion in Art; Perception and Artistic Style (Co-author). Address: (b.) Department of Psychology, King's College, Old Aberdeen AB24 2UB; T.-Aberdeen 272246.
E-mail: j.b.deregowski@abdn.ac.uk

Devereux, Alan Robert, CBE, DL, CEng, MIEE, CBIM. Chairman, Scottish Ambulance Service NHS Trust, 1995-97; Founder, Quality Scotland Foundation; International Director, Gleneagles PLC, 1990-2001; Director, Scottish Mutual Assurance Society, 1976-2003; Director, Abbey National Life, 1999-2003; Chairman, Mission Aviation Fellowship, since 2004; b. 18.4.33, Frinton-on-Sea; m., 1, Gloria Alma Hair (deceased); 1 s.; 2, Elizabeth Tormey Docherty. Educ. Colchester School; Clacton County High School; Mid Essex Technical College. Marconi's Wireless Telegraph Company: apprentice, 1950-55, Standards Engineer, 1955-56; Technical Production Manager, Halex Division, British Xylonite Company, 1956-58; Technical Sales Manager, SPA Division, Sanitas Trust, 1958-65; General Manager, Dobar Engineering, 1965-67; various managerial posts, Norcros Ltd., 1967-69; Group Managing Director, Scotcros Ltd., 1969-78; Deputy Chairman, Scotcros Ltd., 1978-80. CBI: Chairman, Scotland, 1977-79 (Deputy Chairman, 1975-77), Council Member, 1972-84, Member, President's Advisory Committee, 1979; UK Regional Chairman, 1979; Chairman, Small Industries Council for Rural Areas of Scotland, 1975-77; Member, Scottish Development Agency, 1977-83; Chairman, Scottish Tourist Board, 1980-90; Director, Children's Hospice Association for Scotland; Scottish Free Enterprise Award, 1978; Deputy Lieutenant, Renfrewshire, since 1985. Recreations: walking; charities; clock restoration. Address: (h.) South Fell, 24 Kirkhouse Road, Blanefield, Glasgow G63 9BX; T.-01360 770464.
E-mail: aland@post.almac.co.uk

Devine, Rt. Rev. Joseph, PhD. Bishop Emeritus of Motherwell; b. 7.8.37, Glasgow. Educ. St. Mary's College, Blairs, Aberdeen; St. Peter's College, Cardross; Pontifical Scots College, Rome. Ordained Priest, Glasgow, 1960; Private Secretary to Archbishop of Glasgow, 1964-65; Assistant Priest, St. Robert Bellarmine, Glasgow, 1965-67; St. Joseph's, Helensburgh, 1967-72; on staff, St. Peter's College, Cardross, 1967-74; Assistant Chaplain, Catholic Chaplaincy, Glasgow University, 1974-77; nominated Titular Bishop of Voli, and Auxiliary Bishop to Archbishop of Glasgow, 1977; translated to Diocese of Motherwell, 1983; retired, 2013. Recreations: reading; watching sport. Address: (b.) Bishop's House, 27 Smithycroft, Hamilton ML3 7UL; T.-01698 459129.

Devine, Professor Sir Thomas Martin, Kt, OBE, BA, PhD, DLitt (Strathclyde), Hon DLitt (Queen's Belfast), Hon DLitt (Abertay, Dundee), Hon DUniv (Strathclyde), FRHistS, FSA Scot, FRSE, HonMRIA, FBA, FRSA. Sir William Fraser Professor Emeritus of Scottish History and Palaeography, University of Edinburgh, since 2014, Personal Senior Research Professor in History; Director, Scottish Centre for Diaspora Studies, since 2008; Head, School of History, Classics and Archaeology, University of Edinburgh, 2009-2010; Glucksman Research Professor in Irish and Scottish Studies and Director, Research Institute of Irish and Scottish Studies, Aberdeen University, 1998-2003; Director, Arts and Humanities Research Council, Centre for Irish and Scottish Studies, 2001-05; b. 30.07.46, Motherwell; m., Catherine Mary Lynas; 2 s. of whom 1 deceased; 3 d. Educ. Our Lady's RC High School, Motherwell; Strathclyde University. Strathclyde University: Lecturer, then Senior Lecturer and Reader, Department of History, 1969-88 (Head of Department, 1990-92), Dean, Faculty of Arts and Social Sciences, 1993-94, Deputy Principal, 1994-97, Professor of Scottish History, 1988-98, Director of Research Centre in Scottish History, 1994-98; Visiting Professor, University of Guelph, Canada, 1983 and

1988 (Adjunct Professor in History, since 1988); Adjunct Professor in History, University of North Carolina; Governor, St. Andrews College of Education, 1990-94. Joint Founding Editor with TC Smout, Scottish Economic and Social History, 1980-84. British Academy/Leverhulme Trust Senior Research Fellow, 1992-93; Trustee, National Museums of Scotland, 1995-2002; Member, RAE Panel in History, 1992, 1996; Member, Council, British Academy, 1999-2001; Convener, Irish-Scottish Academic Initiative, 1998-2002; Chair, Joint Working Party, NMS and NTS, Museum of Scottish Country Life, 1999-2003; Member, Advisory Group, Glasgow City of Architecture and Design, 1999; Member, Secretary of State for Scotland's Advisory Committee, Friends of Scotland Initiative, 2001-03; Member, Scottish Council on Archives, 2002-08; Member, Advisory Committee on ESRC Devolution Programme; Member, Research Awards Advisory Committee, The Leverhulme Trust; Trustee, Edinburgh City of Literature, 2005-09; Winner: Senior Hume Brown Prize, 1977, Agnes Mure MacKenzie Prize for Scottish Historical Research, Saltire Society, 1992, Henry Duncan Prize, Royal Society of Edinburgh, 1995; Royal Gold Medal, Royal Society of Edinburgh (RSE), 2001; Hon. Fellowship, University of the West of Scotland, 2005; John Aitkenhead Medal, Institute of Contemporary Scotland, 2006; Member, Academy of Merit, Institute of Contemporary Scotland, 2006; RSE/Beltane Senior Prize for Excellence in Public Engagement across all disciplines (2012); RSE Inaugural Sir Walter Scott Medal for Excellence in the Humanities and Creative Arts (2012); Wallace Prize, American-Scottish Foundation (2015). Publications: The Tobacco Lords, 1975; Lairds and Improvement in Enlightenment Scotland, 1979; Ireland and Scotland 1600-1850 (Co-Editor), 1983; Farm Servants and Labour in Lowland Scotland 1770-1914, 1984; A Scottish Firm in Virginia 1767-77, 1984; People and Society in Scotland 1760-1830 (Co-Editor), 1988; The Great Highland Famine, 1988; Improvement and Enlightenment (Editor), 1989; Conflict and Stability in Scottish Sociey (Editor), 1990; Irish Immigrants and Scottish Society in the Eighteenth and Nineteenth Centuries (Editor), 1991; Scottish Emigration and Scottish Society, 1992; Scottish Elites, 1993; The Transformation of Rural Scotland, 1994; Clanship to Crofters' War, 1994; Industry, Business and Society in Scotland since 1700 (Co-Editor), 1994; Glasgow: I, Beginnings to 1830, 1995; St. Mary's, Hamilton: a social history; Exploring the Scottish Past, 1995; Scotland in the Twentieth Century (Co-Editor), 1996; Eighteenth Century Scotland: New Perspectives (Co-Editor), 1998; The Scottish Nation, 1700-2000, 1999; Celebrating Columba – Irish-Scottish Connections 597-1997 (Co-Editor), 1999; Scotland's Shame? - Bigotry and Sectarianism in Modern Scotland, 2000; Being Scottish – Personal Reflections on Scottish Identity Today, 2002; Scotland's Empire, 1600-1815, 2003; The Transformation of Scotland (Co-Editor), 2005; The Scottish Nation, 1700-2007, 2006; Clearance and Improvement: Land, Power and People in Scotland, 1600-1900, 2006; Scotland and the Union, 1707-2007 (Editor), 2007; To the Ends of the Earth: Scotland's Global Diaspora, 1750-2010, 2011; Scotland and Poland: Historical Connections, 1500-2010 (Co-Editor), 2011; Scotland and the British Empire (Co-Editor), 2011; The Oxford Handbook of Modern Scottish History, 1500-2010 (Co-Editor), 2012; Recovering Scotland's Slavery Past (Editor), 2015; Independence or Union: Scotland's Past and Scotland's Present, 2016. Recreations: grandchildren; walking in and exploring the Hebrides; watching skilful football; travelling in the Mediterranean. Address: (b.) School of History, Classics and Archaeology, William Robertson Wing, Old Medical School, University of Edinburgh, Edinburgh EH8 9AG.
E-mail: t.m.devine@ed.ac.uk

de Vink, Peter Henry John, BComm. Managing Director, Edinburgh Financial and General Holdings Ltd., since 1978; b. 9.10.40, Amsterdam; m., Julia Christine (Krista) Quarles van Ufford (deceased); m., Jean Murray-Lyon (dissolved); 1 d.; 1 s. Educ. Edinburgh University. National Service, Dutch Army, 1961-63; Edinburgh University, 1963-66; Ivory and Sime Investment Managers, 1966-78, latterly as Managing Director; elected Councillor (Independent) in Midlothian, May 2012. Address: (b.) The Office Huntly Cot Temple Midlothian EH23 4TF; T.-0131-225 6661; (h.) Huntly Cot, Temple, Midlothian EH23 4TS; T.-01875 830345; e-mail: PdeV@efgh.co.uk

Dewar, Alan Robert, LLB (Hons). Queen's Counsel, since 2002; Treasurer of the Faculty of Advocates, 2007-2011; Advocate, since 1989; b. 9.12.56, Edinburgh; m., Katherine Margaret Dewar; 1 s.; 2 d. Educ. Lasswade High School, Midlothian; Dundee University. Solicitor in private practice, 1982-88 (Partner in law firm, 1986-88); Writer to the Signet, since 1986; Advocate Depute, 1996-99; Standing Junior Counsel to various Government departments, including Scotland Office, 2000-02. Recreations: golf; football; jazz. Address: (h.) 6 Crawford Road, Edinburgh; T.-0131 667 1810; e-mail: AlanRDewar@aol.com

Dewar, Gordon. Chief Executive, Edinburgh Airport, since 2012. Career: started as a consultant with Halcrow, managing the company's transport business in Scotland; moved to First Group, and was Managing Director of the company's east of Scotland bus operations; became Commercial Director for First Group in Scotland and latterly Commercial Director for First Scotrail; joined Arriva as Commercial Director for the UK regions in 2006, and was appointed as Managing Director of Glasgow Airport (BAA) in 2007; Managing Director, Edinburgh Airport, 2008-2010; Chief Executive, Bahrain International Airport, 2010-12. Address: Edinburgh Airport Limited, EH12 9DN; T.-0844 448 8833.

Dewar-Durie, Andrew Maule, CBE, DL. Chairman, Sea Fish Industry Authority, 2002-07 (Deputy Chairman, 2000-02); b. 13.11.39, Bath; m., Marguerite Kottulinsky; 2 s.; 1 d. Educ. Wellington College. Regular soldier, Argyll and Sutherland Highlanders, 1958-68, retiring with rank of Captain; Export Representative to Senior Export Director, White Horse Distillers, 1968-83; International Sales Director, Long John International, 1983-87; James Burrough Distillers: International Sales Director, 1987-89, Managing Director, 1990; Chief Executive Officer, James Burrough Ltd., 1990-91; Allied Distillers Ltd.: Managing Director, 1991-97, Chairman, 1997-99. Deputy Lieutenant, Dunbartonshire, since 1996; CBI Scotland: Council Member, 1993, Vice Chairman, 1996, Chairman, 1997-99; Non-Executive Director, Britannic Asset Management, 2001-04; Keeper of the Quaich, since 1989, Master, since 1992; Liveryman, Worshipful Company of Distillers, since 1986; Liveryman, Worshipful Company of Fishmongers, since 2009; President, Edinburgh Royal Warrant Holders Association, 1999-2000; Director, Royal Edinburgh Military Tattoo, 2000-2008, Vice Chairman, 2008-2010; Executive Council Member, Erskine Care, 2008-2015; Non-Executive Director, St Andrew's Links Ltd, since 2012. Recreations: rough shooting; theatre; cinema. Address: Finnich Malise, Croftamie, West Stirlingshire G63 0HA; T.-0136 066 0257; e-mail: dewardurie@talktalk.net

Dewhurst, Professor David, BSc, PhD. Professor of e-learning; Director of Learning Technology, College of Medicine and Veterinary Medicine, University of Edinburgh, since 1999, formerly Assistant Principal (e-learning and e-health); b. 27.2.50, Crewe; 2 s. Educ. Crewe County Grammar School; Sheffield University. Lecturer, University of Sheffield; Lecturer/Senior Lecturer, Sheffield Hallam University; Principal Lecturer/Professor of Health Sciences, Leeds Metropolitan University. Address: (b.) Learning Technology Section, College of Medicine and Veterinary Medicine, University of Edinburgh, 15 George Square, Edinburgh EH8 9XD; T.-0131 6511564; e-mail: d.dewhurst@ed.ac.uk

Dey, Graeme, MSP (SNP), Angus South, since 2011. Born in Aberdeen. Joined D C Thomson as a journalist in 1980 and became sports editor of the Dundee Courier. Election agent to Mike Weir MP from 2001. Address: (b.) Scottish Parliament, Edinburgh EH99 1SP.

Dhir, Rani, MBE, BA, DHS, FCIOH, FCIOB, FRSA. Executive Director, Drumchapel Housing Co-operative Ltd, since 1990; concurrently pursues wider interests at National Level in Business and Voluntary Community; currently Non Executive Director, Scottish Legal Aid Board; Trustee, Erskine Hospital; Non Executive Director, Greater Glasgow and Clyde Health Board, 2004-2012; Chair, East Dunbartonshire Community Health Partnerships, 2010-2012; Chair, West Dunbartonshire Community Health Partnership, 2006-2010; Non Executive Director, Communities Scotland, 2001-08; Chair, Communities Scotland Housing Regulation Board for Scotland, 2001-08; Non-Executive Director, Lloyds TSB Scotland, 2000-05; b. Dundee. Educ. Morgan Academy, Dundee. First Degree, BA Business Studies; Post Graduate Diploma, Personnel and Development; Post Graduate Diploma, Housing. Pursued career in housing in Glasgow, in Independent Social Housing Sector; Pioneer in Community Ownership Housing in Scotland. Trustee, PATH (Scotland) Ltd., 2006-2013; Trustee, Ankur Arts, since 2007; Trustee, Lloyds TSB Foundation for Scotland, 1999-2005. Address: (b.) Drumchapel Housing Co-operative Ltd, 4 Kinclaven Avenue, Glasgow G15 7SP; T.-0141 944 4902.
E-mail: enquiries@drumchapelhc.org.uk

Diamond, Professor Sir Ian, FBA, FRSE, FAcSS. Principal and Vice-Chancellor, University of Aberdeen, since 2010. Career History: University of Southampton: Lecturer, 1980, then Senior Lecturer, then Professor, then Dean of Social Sciences, 1997, then Deputy Vice-Chancellor, 2001; former Chief Executive, Economic and Social Research Council (ESRC). Chair, Executive Group of Research Councils UK, 2004-09; Honorary degrees from the Universities of Glasgow and Cardiff. British Council Scotland Advisory Council, 2011. Address: (b.) University of Aberdeen, King's College, Aberdeen AB24 3FX; T.-01224 272000.

Dick, David, OBE, BA (Hons), MLitt, DIC, PhD, CEng, FIET; b. 20.3.29, Edinburgh; m., Muriel Elsie Margaret Buchanan; 5 d. Educ. Boroughmuir School, Edinburgh; Heriot-Watt College, Edinburgh; Imperial College, London; Open University; University of Dundee; Edinburgh Napier University. Electrical Engineer, North of Scotland Hydro-Electric Board, 1951-54; Lecturer, Dundee College of Technology, 1954-60; Head, Department of Electrical Engineering, Coatbridge Technical College, 1960-64; Depute Principal, Napier College of Science and Technology, Edinburgh, 1964-69; Principal, Stevenson College of Further Education, Edinburgh, 1969-87; Managing Director, Clerkington Publishing Co. Ltd., 1997-2003. Manpower Services Commission: Chairman, Lothian District Manpower Committee, 1981-82, Member, Lothian and Borders Area Manpower Board, 1982-85; Member and Chairman, various committees: Scottish Technical Education Council, Scottish Business Education Council, 1969-87; Member and Chairman, Fire Services Examination Board (Scotland), 1968-86; Member, Construction Industry Training Board, 1976-85; Member,

Electrical Engineering Services Committee, CITB, 1976-88; Member, General Convocation, Heriot-Watt University, Edinburgh, 1970-73; Past Chairman, Scottish Committee, Institution of Electronic and Radio Engineers; former Honorary President, Edinburgh and District Spastics Association; Lay Inspector of Fire Services for Scotland, 1994-99; Chairman, IET, SERMS Committee, 2012; Elected Fellow of Stevenson College, Edinburgh, 2009. Publications: Capital Walks in Edinburgh – The New Town, 1994; Street Biographies of the Royal Burgh of Haddington, 1997; Who was Who in the Royal Mile, Edinburgh, 1997; Who was Who in Durban Street Names, 1998; A Scottish Electrical Enlightenment (Editor), 2000; A Millennium of Fame of East Lothian, 2000. Recreations: music (flute); gardening; writing historical biographies; history of Scottish education. Address: (h.) 37 Craiglockhart Loan, Edinburgh EH14 1JR.

Dick, Dennis J. N., MBE, FRSA; b. 1.10.34, Dundee; m., Mary Willis; 1 s. Educ. Gordonstoun; Stirling High School. Journalist, DC Thomson, Dundee, 1956-58; Writer, Weekly Scotsman, Edinburgh, 1958-59; Publicity, BBC Scotland, Edinburgh, 1959-60; PRO (including launch of the station), Grampian TV, Aberdeen, 1961; Journalist and TV Editor, Radio Times, BBC, London, 1961-70; PRO, BBC South and West of England, Bristol, 1970-78; TV Producer/Editor TV Features, BBC West, Bristol, 1978-84; Manager, BBC Aberdeen and Radio and Television Producer, BBC Scotland, 1984-88; Chairman/Managing Director, own TV company, Wildview Productions, Aberdeen/Little Brechin, 1988-93; produced and directed over 200 TV programmes; now retired. Burgess, City of Aberdeen; President, St. Andrews Probus Club, 2002-03; Vice-Chairman, Scottish Wildlife Trust, 2002-05; Representative Member, National Trust for Scotland Council, 2003-07; Chairman, Scottish Wildlife Trust, 2005-08; Chairman, James Aitken Arboretum Committee, 2009-2011. Trustee, Royal Botanic Garden Edinburgh, 2009-2013; Member: Scottish Biodiversity Committee, FCS Perth and Argyll Regional Forestry Forum, 2009-2012; Chair, Tayside Biodiversity Partnership, 2009-2014; Trustee: Perth and Kinross Quality of Life Trust, 2009-2012, Botanics Foundation, 2011-2013. Recreations: working with wildlife; hill walking; gardening; website design; photography; travel. Address: (h.) 8/5 New Cut Rigg, Edinburgh EH6 4QR; T.-0131 467 0210; e-mail: ddick@wildview.info

Dick, Rev. John Hunter Addison, MA, MSc, BD. Parish Minister, Aberdeen: Ferryhill, 1982-2012; Master, Christ's College, University of Aberdeen, 2005-2012; b. 27.12.45, Dunfermline; 3 s. Educ. Dunfermline High School; Edinburgh University. Research Assistant, Department of Geography, Edinburgh University, 1967-70; Senior Tutor, Department of Geography, Queensland University, 1970-78; student of divinity, 1978-81; Assistant Minister, Edinburgh: Fairmilehead, 1981-82. A Burgess of Guild of Aberdeen. Governor, Robert Gordon's College, 1993-2012; Trustee, Aberdeen Educational Endowments Trust, 1998-2012. Recreations: music; painting; walking. Address: 18 Fairfield Road, Kelty KY4 0BY.

Dick, Robert J. W., LLB, CA. Non Executive Director, EPIC - Ediston Property Investment Company, since 2014; b. 10.07.55, Ayr. Educ. Ayr Academy; University of Edinburgh. Whinney Murray (now Ernst & Young), Edinburgh, 1977-80; Price Waterhouse, Hong Kong, 1980-83; Comex Houlder Diving, Aberdeen, 1983-85; CALA Group, Edinburgh, 1985-2008. Address: Ediston Property Investment Company, 39 George Street, Edinburgh EH2 2HN.

Dickinson, Professor Harry Thomas, BA, DipEd, MA, PhD, DLitt, FHA, FHEA, FRHistS, FRSE. Professor of British History, Edinburgh University, 1980-2006, Emeritus Professor, since 2006; Professor of British History, Nanjing University, since 1987; b. 9.3.39, Gateshead; m., Jennifer Elizabeth Galtry; 1 s.; 1 d. Educ. Gateshead Grammar School; Durham University; Newcastle University. Teacher of History, Washington Grammar School, 1961-64; Earl Grey Fellow, Newcastle University, 1964-66; History Department, Edinburgh University: Assistant Lecturer, 1966-68, Lecturer, 1968-73, Reader, 1973-80; Associate Dean (Postgraduate), 1992-96; Convener, Senatus PGS Committee, 1998-2001; Visiting Professor, Nanjing University, China, 1980, 1983, 1985, 1987, 1994 and Peking University in Beijing, 2011; Fulbright Scholar, 1973; Huntington Library Fellowship, 1973; Folger Shakespeare Library Fellowship, 1973; Winston Churchill Fellow, 1980; Leverhulme Award, 1986-87 and 2006-07; Ahmanson Fellowship, UCLA, 1987; Anstey Lecturer, University of Kent, 1989; Douglas Southall Freeman Professor, University of Richmond, Virginia, 1987; Lewis Walpole Library Fellowship (Yale University), 2004; Chairman, Publications Committee, Historical Association, 1991-94; Vice-President, Royal Historical Society, 1991-95, 2003-05; President, Historical Association, 2002-05 (Vice President, 1995-97 and 2005-2014, Deputy President, 1997-98); Member, Humanities Committee, CNAA, 1991-93; National Auditor, Higher Education Quality Council, 1993-95; Team Assessor, History, TQA, SHEFC, 1995-96; Member, Marshall Aid Commonwealth Commission, 1987-96; Member, QAA History Subject Benchmarking Committee, 1998-99; Academic Auditor, QAA, 1997-2001; Academic Reviewer, QAA, 1998-2001; Chair, History Panel, Arts and Humanities Research Council, 2002-06; Member, History Panel, QCA, 2003-2010; Member, Lord Chancellor's Advisory Council on National Records and Archives, 2006-2014; Editor, History, 1993-2000. Publications: Bolingbroke; Walpole and the Whig Supremacy; Liberty and Property; British Radicals and the French Revolution; The Correspondence of Sir James Clavering; Politics and Literature in the 18th Century; The Political Works of Thomas Spence; Caricatures and the Constitution 1760-1832; Britain and the French Revolution; The Politics of the People in Eighteenth-century Britain; Britain and the American Revolution; The Challenge to Westminster (Co-Author); A Companion to Eighteenth-Century Britain; Constitutional Documents of the United Kingdom, 1782-1835; British pamphlets on the American Revolution, 8 vols.; Reactions to Revolutions (Co-Author); Les îles Britanniques et la Révolution Française (Co-Author); Ireland in the Age of Revolution, 1760-1805, 6 vols.; many pamphlets, essays and reviews. Recreations: reading; films. Address: (h.) 44 Viewforth Terrace, Edinburgh EH10 4LJ; T.-0131-229 1379; e-mail: Harry.Dickinson@ed.ac.uk

Dickson, Dr. Belinda Jane, OBE, BEd. Self-employed businesswoman; b. 15.9.59, Glasgow; 2 d. Educ. Bearsden Academy; Dunfermline College. Marketing Telephone Rentals, 1981-87; self-employed, since 1987; Entrepreneur of the Year, 2000; Scottish Businesswoman of the Year, 1999; Member, Board, UK Fashion & Textiles Association; Honorary Degree, Napier University; Doctor of Letters, Caledonia University. Recreations: skiing; squash; swimming; walking. Address: (b.) BJD Design (Belinda Robertson), Fenton Barns, The Law Range, Fenton Barns Retail Village, North Berwick EH39 5BW.
E-mail: belinda@belindarobertson.com

Dickson, Graeme. Director-General, Enterprise, Environment and Innovation, Scottish Government, since 2011. Address: (b.) Scottish Government, St. Andrew's House, Regent Road, Edinburgh EH1 3DG.

Dickson, Professor James Holms, BSc, MA, PhD, FLS, FRSE. Emeritus Professor, since 2002; Professor of Archaeobotany and Plant Systematics, Glasgow University, since 1998 (Reader in Botany, 1993-98); b. 29.4.37, Glasgow; m. Camilla A. Lambert, 1 s.; 1 d. Educ. Bellahouston Academy; University of Glasgow; University of Cambridge. Fellow, Clare College, University of Cambridge, 1963-70; Lecturer then Senior Lecturer in Botany, University of Glasgow, 1970-93. Leader, Trades House of Glasgow Expedition to Papua, New Guinea, 1987; Consultant, Britoil, Glasgow Garden Festival, 1988; currently working on plant remains found with 5,300 year old Tyrolean Iceman, and with 550 year old British Columbian iceman. Neill Medallist, Royal Society of Edinburgh, 1996; twice Past President, Glasgow Natural History Society; Past President, Botanical Society of Scotland; Leverhulme Emeritus Fellow, 2006-07: "Archaeobiology of Ancient Icemen". Northlight Heritage Dickson Laboratory for Bioarchaeology named in honour (shared with the late Camilla Dickson, eminent archaeobotanist), 2012. Publications: five books, including The Changing Flora of Glasgow, Plants and People in Ancient Scotland and Ancient Ice Mummies; many papers on Scottish flora, Ice Age plants, archaeobotany, the Tyrolean Iceman. Address: (b.) Graham Kerr Building, Glasgow University; T.-0141-330 4364.

Dickson, John (Iain) Anderson, BSc, DipArch, RIBA, PPRIAS. Architect; formerly Senior Partner, George Watt & Stewart, Aberdeen; President, Royal Incorporation of Architects in Scotland, 1999-2001; b. 28.5.51, Hamilton; m., Patricia Frances Whyte. Educ. Aberdeen Grammar School; Scott Sutherland School of Architecture, Robert Gordon's Institute of Technology, Aberdeen. Architectural Assistant: Department of Housing and Construction, Darwin, Australia, 1973-74, W.G. Crerar & Partners, Inverness, 1976-77; Architect, George Watt & Stewart, Aberdeen, 1977-80. Chairman, Kincardine and Deeside Area, British Field Sports Society, 1995-98; Senior Under Officer, Aberdeen University Officer Training Corps, 1973; Chairman, RIAS Practice Board, 1995-99; Member, RIBA Council, 1999-2001; Director, Aberdeenshire Housing Partnership, 1999-2004; Member, Scottish Construction Industry Group, 1999-2001; Member, Leadership Group, Scottish Enterprise Forestry Cluster, 2000; Member, Sounding Board, Scottish Executive Review of Scotland's Cities, 2001; Director, RIAS Insurance Services Ltd., 2002-04; Member, Advisory Board, Centre for Timber Engineering, Napier University, 2002-04; Member, Executive RIAS Insurance Services, 2004-2011; Chair, RIBA/RIAS Membership Liaison Group, since 2009; Member, RIAS Council, since 2008; Member, RIAS Education Committee, since 2010; Professional Studies Adviser, Scott Sutherland School of Architecture and the Built Environment, Robert Gordon University, since 2009; Member, RIAS Council, since 2008; Member, RIAS Education Committee, since 2010; Chair, Judging panel, RIAS/RIBA Awards in Scotland, 2015. Recreations: field sports; fishing; shooting; good food; wine. Address: (h.) Kentucky, Banchory, Kincardineshire AB31 4EQ.
E-mail: kentuckybanchory@btinternet.com

Dickson, Malcolm Rae, QPM, MA, DipCrim. Board Member, Scottish Children's Reporter Administration, since 2008; Board Member, Children's Convenor and Tribunal Board, States of Guernsey, since 2013; Joint Secretary, Borders Network of Conservation Groups, since 2014; Landowner, since 2008; b. 5.7.56, Galashiels; m., Anna; 1 s. Educ. Earlston High School; Berwickshire High School; University of St. Andrews; University of Cambridge. Joined Lothian and Borders Police as Graduate Entrant Constable in 1977; served in Uniform, CID and Drugs Squad through ranks to Inspector, then in Planning, East Lothian and Central Edinburgh to Chief Superintendent. Commanded many large public events

including Edinburgh's Millennium Street Party and Open Golf Championship. Later Assistant Chief Constable and Deputy Chief Constable, then the Assistant Inspector of Constabulary for Scotland; responsible for several seminal reports which resulted in improved policing across a range of functions; completed Police career in 2008. Publications: Author of 'The Role of Policing in Modern Scotland' (A Chapter in 'Policing Scotland'), 2nd ed. 2010. Recreations: drawing and painting indifferent pictures; riding; fishing; reading.

Dickson, Sheriff Robert Hamish, LLB, WS, DL. Sheriff of South Strathclyde, Dumfries & Galloway at Airdrie, since 1988; Deputy Lieutenant of Lanarkshire, since 2012; b. 19.10.45, Glasgow; m., Janet Laird Campbell (deceased 2004); 1 s. Educ. Glasgow Academy; Drumtochty Castle; Glenalmond; Glasgow University. Solicitor, Edinburgh, 1969-71, and Glasgow, 1971-86; Partner, Brown Mair Gemmill & Hislop, Solicitors, Glasgow, 1973-86; appointed floating Sheriff of South Strathclyde, Dumfries & Galloway at Hamilton, 1986; President, Sheriffs' Association, 2006-09. Publication: Medical and Dental Negligence, 1997. Recreations: golf; music; reading. Address: (b.) Airdrie Sheriff Court, Airdrie; T.-Airdrie 751121.

Dillon, J. Shaun H., DRSAM (Comp), FSA Scot. Professional Musician; Composer, Oboist and Teacher of Woodwind; b. 30.12.44, Sutton Coldfield. Educ. Berwickshire High School; Fettes College; Royal Scottish Academy of Music; Guildhall School of Music. Studied composition with Frank Spedding and Edmund Rubbra; awarded prize for composition for Leicestershire Schools Orchestra, 1965; commissions from various bodies, including Scottish Amateur Music Association; Instructor of Woodwind: Edinburgh Corporation, 1967-72, Aberdeen Corporation (latterly Grampian Region), 1972-81; Freelance Musician, since 1981; sometime Director of Music, St. Mary's Cathedral, Aberdeen; two suites of Airs and Graces for strings published; Secretary, Association of Instrumental and Vocal Specialists, 1975-78; Scotland and Northern Ireland Region Council member of Musicians Union, since 2005. Recreations: reading, especially history, literature; crosswords; playing flute (badly) in ceilidh bands. Address: (b.) 34 Richmond Street, Aberdeen AB25 4TR; T.-01224 630954.

Dinning, Robert James (Fred), BSc (Eng), MBA, CEng, CEnv, FEI, FIET, FCMI; b. 16.12.52; m., Elizabeth Johnstone. Educ. Kilmarnock Academy; Glasgow University. Formerly Energy and Environment Director of the Scottish Power Group (retired at end of 2005). Main Board Member, Scottish Environment Protection Agency, 2006-2013; Court Member, University of the West of Scotland; Board Member, Sustainable Development Panel (until 2010); Board Member, SAC Commercial Ltd., 2013-15; Board Member, SRUC, since 2015; Chair, Carbon Trust Consultant Accreditation Board; Chair (until 2012), Edinburgh Research Partnership Energy JRI (until 2010); Member, Sustainable Development Panel (until 2010); Member, Church of Scotland Church and Society Council and Convenor of Council sub group on energy and environmental issues (2005-09). Member, Advisory Board, WWF Scotland (until July 2013). Fellow of the Energy Institute and member of its Scottish Committee. Delivered a wide range of lectures and speeches on energy and environment topics affecting the UK and Scotland. Recreations: keen cruising yachtsman (RYA Yachtmaster), kayaker, hillwalker and cyclist. Address: (h.) South Brae, Dunlop, Ayrshire KA3 4BP.

Di Rollo, Alison. Head, National Sexual Crimes Unit, since 2013; Senior Advocate Depute; joined NSCU in 2010, Deputy Head, 2011-13. Address: Crown Office, 25 Chambers Street, Edinburgh EH1 1LA; T.-0844 561 3000.

Di Rollo, Simon Ronald, QC, LLB (Hons). Advocate, since 1987; b. 28.10.61, Edinburgh; m., Alison Margaret Lafferty; 1 s.; 1 d. Educ. Holy Cross Academy; Scotus Academy; Edinburgh University. Admitted to Faculty of Advocates, 1987; Advocate Depute, 1997-2000. Recreations: Italian; cooking; walking; golf. Address: (b.) Advocates' Library, Parliament House, Edinburgh EH1 1RF.

Dixon, Andrew, BSc. Freelance Director, Culture Creativity Place Ltd, since 2013; Chief Executive, Creative Scotland, 2010-13; Programme Director, Hull UK City of Culture, 2013-14; b. 1958. Educ. University of Bradford. Career: administrator and youth projects director of the Major Road Theatre Company; after five years as an arts officer in Local Government moved to Northern Arts, progressing to become its Chief Executive and was a member of the national executive team of Arts Council England for three years; Chief Executive, NewcastleGateshead Initiative, 2005-2010. Alternative Businessman of the year 2005, for his public sector work in North East England; honorary doctorate, Northumbria University, 2008; former member, North East Economic Forum. Address: (b.) 12A Great Stuart Street, Edinburgh EH3 7TN.

Dixon, Dr. Richard, BSc (Hons), MSc (distinction), PhD. Director, Friends of the Earth Scotland, since 2013; b. 22.3.64, Dublin, Ireland. Educ. Exeter School; St. Andrews University; Edinburgh University; Glasgow Caledonian University. Development Officer, CSV Glasgow, 1992-94; Assistant Environmental Policy Officer, Strathclyde Regional Council, 1993-94; Head of Research, Friends of The Earth Scotland, 1994-2002; Head of Policy, WWF Scotland, 2002-05, Director, 2005-2013. Board Member: Stop Climate Chaos Scotland, SNIFFER, SEPA. Recreations: cycling; science fiction; computing. Address: (b.) Thorn House, 5 Rose Street, Edinburgh EH2 2PR; e-mail: rdixon@foe-scotland.org.uk

Dobie, Margaret G.C., OBE, MA, DipSocStud, FFCS. Hon. Vice President, Scottish Association for the Study of Delinquency, 1997-2005; b. Galloway; m., James T.J. Dobie; 3 s. Educ. Benedictine Convent, Dumfries; Dumfries Academy; Edinburgh University. Medical Social Worker; Chair, Dumfries and Galloway Regional Children's Panel, 1971-77; Member, Broadcasting Council for Scotland, 1987-91; Chair, Dumfries and Galloway Children's Panel Advisory Committee, 1982-89; Chair, Children's Panel Advisory Group, 1985-88; Member, Polmont Young Offenders' Institution Visiting Committee, 1992-99; Chair, Dumfries & Galloway Valuation Appeal Panel, 1987-2004. Recreations: travel; tennis; reading. Address: (h.) 6, Mountainhall Park, Dumfries, DG1 4YS T. 01387-254595; e-mail: mgcd3@btinternet.com

Dobie, Rev. Rachel Jean Wayland, LTh. Minister, Broughton, Glenholm, Kilbucho linked with Skirling, linked with Stobo, Drumelzier linked with Tweedsmuir, 1996-2008; b. 17.8.42, Forres; m., Kirkpatrick H. Dobie; 1 s.; 1 d. Educ. Dumfries Academy; Jordanhill College; Edinburgh University. Primary schoolteacher, 1963-80; Auxiliary Minister, Dalbeattie with Urr, 1990-93; Church of Scotland Sunday School Adviser, 1976-86; Reader, 1982-90; Chair, Marriage Guidance, Dumfries, 1984-86; Member, General Assembly Youth Education Committee, 1985-93; Vice-Convener, General Assembly Board of Parish Education 1993-97; Hon. Secretary, Church Service Society, 1997-2003; Moderator, Presbytery of Melrose and Peebles, 2002/03; Member, Mission and Discipleship Council, 2005-09; Contributor to BBC religious broadcasting; President, Church Service Society, 2010-12.

Publication: Time Together, 1981. Recreations: music; fine arts; Address: (h.) 20 Moss Side Crescent, Biggar ML12 6GE; T.-01899 229 244.

Docherty, Martin. MP (SNP), West Dunbartonshire, since 2015; b. 21.1.71. Educ. Glasgow College of Food Technology (now City of Glasgow College); University of Essex; Glasgow School of Art. Worked for a decade for the West Dunbartonshire Community and Volunteering Services; joined the SNP in 1991, and was elected one year later as Scotland's youngest councillor to the-then Clydebank District Council in 1992, at the age of 21; elected to the third seat of the Anderston/City ward of Glasgow City Council in Scottish local elections (2012-15). Address: House of Commons, London SW1A 0AA.

Docherty, Cllr Sadie. Lord Provost and Lord Lieutenant of Glasgow, since 2012; representing Linn Ward (Labour), since 2007; m.; 2 c. Migrated to Scotland in the mid 1950s; formerly Glasgow Council's Executive Member for Communities and Housing; also chaired Policy Development Committees responsible for Sustainability and the Environment, and Children and Families. Address: Glasgow City Council, City Chambers, George Square, Glasgow G2 1DU; T.-0141 287 2000.
E-mail: sadie.docherty@councillors.glasgow.gov.uk

Docherty, Thomas, MP (Labour) Dunfermline and West Fife, 2010-2015; b. 28.1.75; m., Katie McCulloch; 1 s.; 1 d. Educ. Open Univ. Research Assistant to Scott Barrie MSP, 1999-2002; Public Affairs Officer, BNFL, 2002-05; Communications Manager, Network Rail, 2006-07; Account Dir, communications consultancy, 2007-10. Contested (Lab): Tayside N, 2001; S of Scotland, Scottish Parliament, 2003.

Dodd, Marion Elizabeth, MA, BD, LRAM. Minister of Kelso Old and Sprouston Parish Church, 1989-2010 (retired); b. 19.4.41, Stirling. Educ. Glasgow High School; Burgh School/Knowepark Primary School (both in Selkirk); Selkirk High School; Esdaile School, Edinburgh; Edinburgh University. Foreign Office, London (Russian translator), 1962-64; Iron and Steel Institute, London, (Editor, Stahl translated from Russian), 1964-67; BBC Singers, 1967-84; Assistant Minister, Colinton Parish Church, 1987-89 (ordained in July 1988). Member, Board of Parish Education, 1989-94, Board of World Mission, 1994-98, Panel on Worship, 1993-2000 (Music Committee Member); Church Hymnary Revision Committee, 1995-2005; Liturgical Group, 2010-2013; Nomination Committee, 2011-15; Vice-Convener, Panel on Review and Reform, 2005-08; President, Church Service Society, 2004-06; Secretary, Dunkeld Fellowship, since 2009; Moderator, Jedburgh Presbytery, 1993-94 and 2007-08; Locum at Earlston, Lauder, Caddonfoot linked with Galashiels: Trinity, Oxnam (Interim Moderator, 2011-14); Chairperson, Abbeyfield Kelso Society Ltd., 1995-2009; Chairperson, Kelso Churches Together, 1992-93, 1996-97, 2000-01, 2005-06. Musical Director, Kelso Amateur Operatic Society, 1990-93; Musical Director, Roxburgh Singers, since 1996; Musical Director, Choir of Local Voices (cross-Border choir joining together in harmony, rather than conflict), since 2013. Teacher of solo singing. Recreations: music; cooking; travel; reading; interior design. Address: Esdaile, Tweedmount Road, Melrose TD6 9ST; T.-01896 822446; e-mail: mariomndodd@btinternet.com

Dodd, Raymond Henry, PhD, MA, BMus, ARAM. Cellist and Composer; b. 31.3.29; m., Doreen Joyce; 1 s.; 1 d.

Educ. Bryanston School; Royal Academy of Music; Worcester College, Oxford. Music Master, Sedbergh School, 1951-55; Aberdeen University: Lecturer in Music, 1956, Senior Lecturer in Music, 1971-91, Head of Department, 1981-88; Visiting Professor of Music, Wilson College, USA, 1972-73. As a cellist he has performed widely, particularly in Scotland where he is known as a soloist and chamber music player; was for many years a member of the Aberdeen Trio; compositions include orchestral, vocal and chamber music pieces with a number of broadcasts; awarded Szymanowski Medal, Polish Ministry of Art and Culture, 1982. Address: (h.) 14 Giffordgate, Haddington, East Lothian EH41 4AS; T.- 01620 824618.

Dodds, Alistair Bruce, CBE, MA (Hons), MBA, FIPD. Retired Chief Executive, The Highland Council (2007-2013); Member, Board of Trustees, National Galleries of Scotland, since 2014; Member, Board of Directors, Highlands and Islands Enterprise, since 2014; b. 23.8.53, Kelso; 1 d.; m., Ann Clark. Educ. Glenrothes High School; Edinburgh University; Strathclyde University; Dundee University. Assistant Director of Personnel, Fife Regional Council, 1988; Depute Director of Manpower Services, Highland Regional Council, 1991; Director of Personnel Services, The Highland Council, 1995, Director of Corporate Services/Deputy Chief Executive, 1998. Awarded Honorary Fellowship, University of The Highlands and Islands (2014). Recreations: Scottish contemporary art; watching rugby; golf; walking dogs. Address: Highlands and Islands Enterprise, Fraser House, Friar's Lane, Inverness IV1 1BA; T.-01463 234171; e-mail: doddsab@btinternet.com

Doherty (Hon. Lord Doherty) (J. Raymond Doherty). Senator of the College of Justice, since May 2010. LLB (Edinburgh), BCL (Oxon), LLM (Harvard); Advocate, since 1984; QC, since 1997; b. 30.1.58, Stirling; m., Arlene Donaghy; 1 s.; 2 d. Educ. St. Mungo's Primary School, Alloa; St Joseph's College, Dumfries; Edinburgh University; Hertford College, Oxford; Harvard Law School. Standing Junior Counsel to Ministry of Defence (Army), 1990-91; Standing Junior Counsel to Scottish Office Industry Department, 1992-97; Advocate Depute, 1998-2001; Clerk of Faculty, Faculty of Advocates, 1990-95; Joint Editor, Armour on Valuation for Rating, since 1990; Contributor, Stair Memorial Encyclopaedia of the Laws of Scotland; Lands Valuation Appeal Court, since 2011; Upper Tribunal (Tax and Chancery), since 2013; Commercial Judge, since 2014; Chairman of the Competition Appeal Tribunal, since 2015. Address: (b.) Supreme Courts, Parliament House, 11 Parliament Square, Edinburgh EH1 1RQ; T.-0131-225 2595.

Doherty, Una, LLB. Advocate, since 1999; b. Stirling; m., Douglas Fairley. Educ. High School of Stirling; Edinburgh University. Solicitor, 1988-98; Litigation Partner, Balfour and Manson, 1993-98. Address: (b.) Advocates' Library, Parliament House, Edinburgh EH1 1RF; T.-0131-226 5071.

Doig, Ian Peebles, CPFA, FCCA, MAAT. Independent Consultant & Non-Executive Director, since 2004; m., Barbara; 1 d. Educ. Alva Academy; Alloa Academy; Scottish College of Commerce; Strathclyde University. Assistant Director of Finance, Central Regional Council, 1981-86; Director, CIPFA in Scotland, 1986-2004; range of independent consultancy projects, since 2004; SSSC Council Member, 2005-2011; SEPA Board Member, 2006-2013. National Records of Scotland Management Board Member & Chair of Audit & Risk Committee, since 2011; Scottish Court Service Audit Committee Member, 2011-14;

Care Inspectorate Board Member, since 2012; The Scotland Office Audit Committee Member, 2008-2011; Merchiston Community Councillor, since 2005; Board of Trustees Member and Chair of Audit and Risk Committee, National Trust for Scotland, since 2013. Recreations: walking; music; Doig Family Society, Hon. Treasurer. Address: (h./b.) 2E Gillsland Road, Edinburgh EH10 5BW; e-mail: ianpdoig@yahoo.com

Doig, P. Michael R., MA (Hons). B. 2.5.48, Glasgow; m., Catherine; 2 s. Educ. High School of Glasgow; University of Glasgow. Teacher/Assistant Principal Teacher/Principal Teacher of Modern Languages, 1972-81; Assistant Head Teacher, Hermitage Academy, Helensburgh, 1981-85; Depute Head Teacher, Kirkintilloch High School, 1985-92; Head Teacher, Cumbernauld High School, 1992-2000; Head Teacher, Bearsden Academy, 2001-08. President, Headteachers' Association of Scotland, 2003; Elected Member, General Teaching Council Scotland, 2005-08; Panel Practice Adviser, East Dunbartonshire Children's Panel Area Support Team, 2009-2016; Lay Representative, NHS Education for Scotland, 2010-2016. Recreations: music; travel; walking. Address: (h.) 3 Moorfoot Way, Bearsden, Glasgow G61 4RL.
E-mail doigmichael@hotmail.com

Dolezalek, Professor Gero R., Dr. Jur. (Frankfurt). Emeritus Professor of Civil Law, University of Aberdeen (Professor, 2005-09); b. 18.01.43, Poznan, Poland; m., Iva L. Dolezalek; 3 s.; 1 d. Educ. Schools in Austria, West-Berlin, Western Germany; Universities of Kiel, Florence, Frankfurt, Modena. Researcher, Max-Planck-Institut for European Legal History, Frankfurt, 1971-85; Professor, Faculty of Law: Nijmegen, Netherlands, 1985-89, University of Cape Town, South Africa, 1989-95; Senior Researcher, School of Law, University of Aberdeen, 1995-96; Professor, Faculty of Law, University of Leipzig, Germany, 1996-2005. Guest professorships in Belgium, France, Germany, Italy. Publication: Scotland under Jus Commune. Census of manuscripts of Scottish legal literature mainly between 1500 and 1660, Edinburgh 2010 (The Stair Society volumes 55, 56, 57). Address: 17 Heriot Row, Edinburgh EH3 6HP.

Dominiczak, Professor Anna F., OBE, MD, FRCP, FMedSci, FRSE. Regius Professor of Medicine, Vice Principal and Head of College of Medical, Veterinary and Life Sciences, since 2010; Head of Division of Cardiovascular and Medical Sciences, University of Glasgow, 2008-2010; Director, BHF Glasgow Cardiovascular Research Centre, 2001-2010; British Heart Foundation Chair of Cardiovascular Medicine, University of Glasgow, 1998-2010; Honorary Consultant Physician and Endocrinologist, since 1993; b. 26.8.54, Gdansk, Poland; m., Dr. Marek Dominiczak; 1 s. Educ. Copernicus High School, Gdansk; Medical School, Gdansk. Junior House Officer, Glasgow Royal Infirmary, 1982; Senior House Officer (and Registrar) in Medicine, Royal Alexandra Hospital, Paisley, 1983-86; MRC Clinical Scientist and Honorary Registrar (and Senior Registrar), Western Infirmary, Glasgow, 1986-92; British-American Research Fellow and Associate Professor, University of Michigan, Ann Arbor, USA, 1990-91; University of Glasgow: Clinical Lecturer and Honorary Senior Registrar in Medicine and Endocrinology, 1992-93, British Heart Foundation Senior Research Fellow, Senior Lecturer, then Reader in Medicine, 1993-97. Member, MRC Physiological Medicine Board, 2000-04; Member, British Heart Foundation Project Grant Committee, 2000-04; Member, the Wellcome Trust Physiological Sciences Committee, 2005-2008; Secretary, International Society of Hypertension; President, European Society of

Hypertension, 2013-2015; Member, Foundation Leducq Scientific Advisory Committee, 2006-2011, Vice President, 2009-2011; Member of the Council, Royal Society of Edinburgh, 2009-2014; Elected Fellow, American Heart Association, since 1996; Elected Fellow, Academy of Medical Sciences, since 2001; Elected Fellow, Fellowship of the Royal Society of Edinburgh, since 2003; Vice President, Life Sciences, Royal Society of Edinburgh, 2012-2014; Elected Fellow, European Society of Cardiology, since 2008; Editor in Chief, Clinical Science, 2004-2008; Editor in Chief, Hypertension, since 2012; Co-founder and Member of the Board, Stratified Medicine Scotland - Innovation Centre, since 2013. Recreation: modern literature. Address: (b.) College of Medical, Veterinary and Life Sciences, University of Glasgow, Wolfson Medical School Building, University Avenue, Glasgow G12 8QQ; T.-0141 330 2738.
E-mail: anna.dominiczak@glasgow.ac.uk

Don, Nigel, BA, MEng, LLB. MSP (SNP), Angus North and Mearns, 2011-16, North East Scotland, 2007-2011; self-employed musician; b. 16.4.54. Educ. King's College School; Pembroke College, Cambridge; University of London. Thirteen year career as a chemical engineer with Unilever; time out of working to stay at home and raise his children, which allowed his wife to continue working; later became a music teacher and a music publisher; formerly Director, Masterclass Music Ltd; former councillor for Ninewells ward; former SNP Group Convenor on Dundee City Council; elected in May 2007 to the multi-member Lochee ward but resigned as councillor in August 2007 to concentrate on role as MSP. Member: Performing Right Society, Mechanical Copyright Protection Society. Recreations: walking and music; member of the Musicians' Union.

Donald, George Malcolm, RSA, RSW, DA, ATC, MEd. Former Director of Summer School, Centre for Continuing Studies, ECA; current Keeper, Royal Scottish Academy; former Lecturer, Edinburgh College of Art; b. 12.9.43, Ootacamund, South India; 1 s.; 1 d. Educ. Robert Gordon's College; Aberdeen Academy; Edinburgh College of Art; Hornsey College of Art; Edinburgh University. Joined Edinburgh College of Art as Lecturer, 1969; Visiting Lecturer, five Faculties of Art in India, 1979; Visiting Professor: University of Central Florida (Drawing and Anatomy, 1985 to present); Hon. Professor, Al Maktoum Institute, Dundee; Visiting Prof. University of Central Florida (Art Dept) and Florida Interactive Entertainment Academy Orlando, Florida. Strasbourg, 1986, Belgrade, 1987, Sechuan Fine Art Institute, China, 1989, Chinese Academy of Fine Art, 1994, Osaka and Kyoto Universities, Japan, 1999, 2002 and 2007; Visiting Tutor, The Royal Drawing School, London, since 2008; Latimer Award, RSA, 1970; Guthrie Award, RSA, 1973; Scottish Arts Council Bursary, 1973; RSA Gillies Bequest Travel Award to India, 1978, USA, 2003; SAC Travel and Study Award, Indiana, 1981; RSA Gillies Prize, 1982; RSW Mary Marshall Brown Award, 1983; RGI Cargill Award, 1987; Scottish RSW Arts Club Award, 2006, 2013; one man shows: Florida, 1985, Helsinki, 1985, Edinburgh Festival, 1985, 2011; Belgrade, 1987, Florida, 1987, Edinburgh, 1988, 1990, London, 1992-94, Edinburgh 1993, 1994, 1995, 1998, 1999, 2002, 2003, 2005, 2007, 2008, Bohun Gallery, Henley, 2009, 2011, Open Eye Gallery, Edinburgh, 2012, 2015. Address: (h.) Bankhead, by Duns, Berwickshire TD11 3QJ; T.-01361 883014; e-mail: g.donald@surfree.co.uk
web: www.georgedonald.com

Donald, Marion Coats (nee McClure), DipArch (Abdn), MPhil, RIBA, FRIAS; b. 15.5.47, Aberdeen; m.

John Donald; 1 s.; 1 d.; Educ. Aberdeen High School for Girls; Colchester County High School for Girls; Scott Sutherland School of Architecture, RGIT; Scott Sutherland School of Architecture, Robert Gordon University. Student architect, Lyster, Grillet & Harding, Cambridge, 1969-70; Sir Basil Spence, Glover and Ferguson, 1972; Architectural Assistant, SSHA, 1973-74; Architect, Jenkins and Marr, 1974-76; Principal, John and Marion Donald, Chartered Architects, 1976-2006; Professional Studies Advisor, Scott Sutherland School of Architecture, RGU, 2002-2009; retired 2009. Former Chairman, Aberdeen Soroptimist Housing Society Ltd; Elder, Queen's Cross Church 1977-. RIBA Award, 1998; Aberdeenshire Design Award: 2004 (Housing), 2000 (Conservation); Association for Preservation of Scotland Award, 1995; Aberdeen Civic Society Award, 1984; Civic Trust Commendation, 1984. Recreations: family; gardening; music; art and architecture. Address: Forbes Lodge, Strathdon, Aberdeenshire AB36 8YA; T.-01975 651393; e-mail: mariondonald@ifb.co.uk

Donald, Rev. Peter Harry, MA, PhD, BD. Minister, Crown Church, Inverness, since 1998; b. 3.2.62, Edinburgh; m., Brigid Mary McNeill; 1 s.; 1 d. Educ. George Watson's College; Gonville and Caius College, University of Cambridge; University of Edinburgh. Scouloudi Research Fellow, Institute of Historical Research, University of London, 1986-87; Probationer Assistant, St. Michael's Church, Edinburgh, 1990-91; Minister, Leith St. Serf's Parish Church, 1991-98. Member, Faith and Order Commission, 1993-2014. Publication: An Uncounselled King: Charles I and the Scottish Troubles 1637-1641, 1990; God in Society (Co-editor), 2003. Recreations: golf; piano; singing; walking; family. Address: 39 Southside Road, Inverness IV2 4XA; T.-01463 230537.

Donaldson, Rev. Alan. General Director, Baptist Union of Scotland, since 2010. Formerly Senior Pastor, Dumfries Baptist Church. Address: (b.) 48 Speirs Wharf, Glasgow G4 9TH; T.-0141 423 6169.

Donaldson, David, MA, BD, DipEd, DMin. Minister, Manish-Scarista, Isle of Harris, since 2015; b. 6.7.43, Glasgow; m., Jean; 1 s.; 3 d. Educ. Glasgow Academy; Glasgow University; Princeton Theological Seminary. Church of Scotland Missionary in Taiwan, 1969-75; Minister: St. David's, Bathgate, 1975-82, Whitfield, Dundee, 1982-90, Duddingston Kirk, Edinburgh, 1990-2000, St. Andrew's in The Grange, Guernsey, 2000-03, St. Cuthbert's, Clydebank linked with Duntocher Trinity, 2003-2010, Caldwell linked with Dunlop, 2010-2015. Publication: The Scottish Parish System - seen as incarnational. Recreations: badminton; reading. Address: The Manse, Scarista, Isle of Harris HS3 3HX; T.-01859 550200; e-mail: davidandjeandonaldson@gmail.com

Donaldson, Professor Iain Malcolm Lane, BSc, MB, ChB, MA, FRCPE, MRCP. Professor of Neurophysiology, Edinburgh University, 1987-2003; Emeritus Professor, Edinburgh University, since 2003; b. 22.10.37; m.; 1 s. Educ. Edinburgh University. House Physician and Surgeon, Research Fellow, Honorary Lecturer, Honorary Senior Registrar, Departments of Medicine and Surgical Neurology, Edinburgh University, 1962-69; Anglo-French Research Scholarship, University of Paris, 1969-70; Research Officer, University Laboratory of Physiology, Oxford, 1970-79; Fellow and Tutor in Medicine, St. Edmund Hall, Oxford, 1973-79; Professor of Zoology, Hull University, 1979-87; Honorary Librarian, Royal College of Physicians of Edinburgh, since 2000; Emeritus Fellow, St. Edmund Hall, Oxford, since 1979. Recreation: studying the past. Address: (b.) Royal College of Physicians of Edinburgh, 9 Queen Street, Edinburgh EH2 1JQ.

Donaldson, James Andrew, BDS, BA, DFM. Principal in general dental practice; Chairman, Dental Practitioners Association, 2009-2011; President, General Dental Practitioners Association, 2002-05 and 2011-2012; b. 28.2.57, Glasgow; divorced; 1 s.; 3 d. Educ. Coatbridge High School; Dundee University; Open University; Glasgow University. Dental Adviser, British Antarctic Survey, 1986-97; Member: National Council, General Dental Practitioners Association, 1989-2013, Scottish General Dental Services Committee, 1991-93, Aberdeen District Council, 1984-86, Grampian Regional Council, 1986-88; Director, "Open Wide" Dental Courses; contested Liberal Democrat, Aberdeen North, elections to Scottish Parliament, 1999, Westminster election, 2001; Burgess of Guild, City of Aberdeen, 2009. Recreations: golf; skiing; football. Address: (h.) 120 Hamilton Place, Aberdeen AB15 5BB; T.-07721 453802.
E-mail: jimdonaldson1@btinternet.com

Donaldson, Stuart. MP (SNP), West Aberdeenshire and Kincardine, since 2015. Educ. Durris Primary School; Banchory Academy; University of Glasgow. Worked for a Member of the Scottish Parliament in Aberdeenshire; has gained an in-depth knowledge on local issues in the North East including farming and oil & gas, and has been an effective campaigner across West Aberdeenshire & Kincardine. Address: House of Commons, London SW1A 0AA.

Doncaster, Neil, MBA. Chief Executive, Scottish Professional Football League, since 2013; b. 1970, Devon. Educ. Bristol University. Career: qualified as a solicitor and worked for four years for Burges Salmon, solicitors; joined Norwich City in November 1997 as company secretary and solicitor, promoted to Head of Operations in 1999, then Chief Executive, 2001-09. Director of The Football League, 2006-09; elected to The Football Association board as one of two representatives of The Football League, 2008-09; Chief Executive, Scottish Premier League, 2009-2013. MBA from the University of East Anglia, 2008. Address: Hampden Park, Glasgow G42 9DE; T.-0141 620 4140.
Web: www.spfl.co.uk

Donegan, Kate, OBE, BA. Project Executive, SPS Women Offenders Project, Scottish Prison Service, since 2013; b. 21.4.53, Newport on Tay; m., Dr Chris Donegan; 2 s. Educ. Kirkcaldy High School; Stirling University. Assistant Governor: Cornton Vale, 1977-84, Barlinnie Prison, 1984-87; Deputy Governor: Reading Prison, 1987-89; Deputy Governor, Perth Prison, 1989-91; Head, Operational Manpower, Planning Unit, 1991-93; seconded to Staffing Structure Review Team, 1993-94; Deputy Governor, Barlinnie Prison, 1994-95; Deputy Chief Inspector of Prisons, 1995-96; Governor, HM Prison and Institution, Cornton Vale, 1996-2001; Governor, HMP Glenochil, 2001-06; Governor, HMP, Perth, 2006-2010; Deputy Chief Inspector of Prisons, 2010-2011; Governor, HM YOI Polmont, 2011-2012; Governor, HMP and YOI Cornton Vale, 2012-2014. Awarded OBE in Queen's Birthday Honours, June 2014. Recreations: gardening; reading; computing. Address: (b.) Scottish Prison Service Headquarters, Calton House, 5 Redheughs Rigg, Edinburgh EH12 9HW.

Donnachie, Professor Ian, MA, MLitt, PhD, FRHistS, FSA (Scot). Emeritus Professor of History, The Open University in Scotland; b. 18.6.44, Lanark. Educ. Lanark Grammar School; Glasgow University; Strathclyde University. Research Assistant, Galloway Project, Strathclyde University, 1967-68; Lecturer in Social Studies: Napier Polytechnic, 1968-70, Deakin University, Victoria, 1982; Visiting Fellow: Deakin University, Victoria and Sydney University, NSW, 1985; Hon. Lecturer, Dundee University, since 1998; Chair, Friends of New Lanark World Heritage Site. Publications include: A History of the Brewing Industry in Scotland; Industrial Archaeology in the British Isles (jointly); Scottish History 1560-1980 (jointly); That Land of Exiles: Scots in Australia (jointly); Forward! Labour Politics in Scotland 1888-1988 (Co-Editor); A Companion to Scottish History from the Reformation to the Present (jointly); The Manufacture of Scottish History (Co-editor); Historic New Lanark: the Dale and Owen Industrial Community since 1785 (Co-author); Studying Scottish History, Literature and Culture; Modern Scottish History: 1707 to the present (Co-Editor); Robert Owen, Owen of New Lanark and New Harmony; Dictionary of Scottish History (jointly); From Enlightenment to Romanticism Anthologies I-II (Co-editor); Robert Owen, Social Visionary; Birlinn Companion to Scottish History (jointly); Edinburgh Classic Editions. Historic New Lanark. Recreations: walking; countryside.
E-mail: I.Donnachie@open.ac.uk

Donnelly, Dougie, LLB. Presenter/commentator, Premier Sports TV; Golf Channel USA and worldwide coverage of European Tour Golf; sports video writer and director; b. 7.6.53, Glasgow; m., Linda; 3 d. Educ. Hamilton Academy; Strathclyde University. Former Presenter, BBC Television Sport: Grandstand, World Championship snooker, Olympic Games (summer and winter), World Cup, Commonwealth Games, Ryder Cup, golf, Sportscene, Match of the Day; Mid-Morning Show, Album Show, Radio Clyde, 1976-92. Chairman, Commonwealth Games Endowment Fund; after-dinner speaker, conference and seminar host. Recreations: sport; travel; reading; good food and wine. Address: (b.) David John Associates, 6 Victoria Crescent Road, Glasgow G12 9DB; T.-07774 248753.
E-mail: david@davidjohnassociates.co.uk

Donnison, Professor David. Emeritus Professor, Glasgow University, since 1990, Honorary Research Fellow; b. 19.1.26. Lecturer: Manchester University, 1950-53, Toronto University, 1953-55; London School of Economics and Political Science: Reader, 1956-61, Professor, 1961-69; Director, Centre for Environmental Studies, London, 1969-75; Chairman, Supplementary Benefits Commission, 1975-80; Professor of Town and Regional Planning, Glasgow University, 1980-90. Address: Flat 0/1, 17 Cranworth Street, Glasgow G12 8BZ.

Donohoe, Brian H. MP (Labour), Central Ayrshire, 2005-2015, Cunninghame South, 1992-2005; b. 10.9.48, Kilmarnock; m., Christine; 2 s. Educ. Irvine Royal Academy; Kilmarnock Technical College. Secretary, Irvine and District Trades Council, 1973-81; Chair: North Ayrshire and Arran LHC, 1977-79, Cunninghame Industrial Development Committee, 1975-79; former full-time trade union official (NALGO). Recreations: flying model helicopters; gardening. Address: (h.) 5 Greenfield Drive, Irvine, Ayrshire; T.-01294 274419.

Donovan, Professor Robert John, OBE (2007), BSc, PhD, DSc (Hon), CChem, FRSC, FRSE. Emeritus Professor of Chemistry, Edinburgh University (Professor, since 1979); b. 13.7.41, Nantwich; m., Marion Jacubeit; 1 d. Educ. Sandbach School; University College of Wales, Aberystwyth; Cambridge University. Research Fellow, Gonville and Caius College, 1966-70; Edinburgh University: Lecturer in Physical Chemistry, 1970-74, Reader in Chemistry, 1974-79. Member: Physical

Chemistry Panel, Science & Engineering Research Council, 1977-80, Management Committee, SERC Synchrotron Radiation Source, Daresbury, 1977-80, SERC Synchroton Radiation Facility Committee, 1979-84; Chairman, SERC Laser Facility Committee, 1989-92; Member, SERC Science Board, 1989-92; Chairman, Facilities Commission, SERC, 1993-94; Coordinator, STFC, Synchrotron and Free-Electron Laser Science, 2006-09; awarded Corday-Morgan Medal and Prize, Royal Society of Chemistry, 1975; Member: Faraday Council, Royal Society of Chemistry, 1981-83, 1991-93; Vice President, Royal Society of Edinburgh, 1998-2001 (Member, Council, 1996-2001); Member of Council, CCLRC, 2004-06; Tilden Prize, Royal Society of Chemistry, 1995. Recreations: hill-walking; skiing; sail-boarding; cross-country skiing. Address: (b.) School of Chemistry, Edinburgh University, West Mains Road, Edinburgh EH9 3JJ; T.-0131-650 4722; e-mail: R.Donovan@ed.ac.uk

Doran, Frank, LLB (Hons). MP (Labour), Aberdeen North, 2005-2015, Aberdeen Central, 1997-2005; b. 13.4.49; 2 s.; m. (2), Joan Ruddock. Educ. Leith Academy; University of Dundee. Solicitor, 1977-87; MP (Labour), Aberdeen South, 1987-92; Co-ordinator, National Trade Union Political Fund Ballot Campaign, 1993-96.

Dorchester, Martin. Chief Executive, David MacBrayne Ltd, since 2012. Career: Managing Director for Dixons B2B business; ran consultancy business with clients ranging from large private sector businesses to smaller third sector organisations. Address: (b.) Ferry Terminal, Gourock PA19 1QP; T.-01475 650100.

Doris, Bob, MA. MSP (SNP), Glasgow Maryhill and Springburn, since 2016 (Glasgow region, 2007-2016); b. 11.5.73; a. Vale of Leven. Educ. University of Glasgow. Campaign manager to Bill Wilson for the SNP leadership in 2003. Convener, Scottish Parliament's cross party group on Racial Equality in Scotland; formerly convener of the SNP Maryhill Constituency Branch and Glasgow Regional Association SNP (GRA). Has campaigned successfully on a number of issues including free school meals, kinship care payments, extending rail provision in Maryhill and Town Centre Regeneration Fund money for Glasgow. A leading campaigner against the Glasgow Labour Council's closure of 20 primary and nursery schools, and supported the parental occupation of Wyndford and St Gregory's primary schools in Maryhill. Address: (b.) Scottish Parliament, Edinburgh EH99 1SP.

Dornan, James, MSP (SNP), Glasgow Cathcart, since 2011; SNP Deputy Whip, since 2012; b. 17.3.53. Represented the Langside Ward, Glasgow City Council, 2007-2012 (SNP Group Leader until 2011). Address: (b.) Scottish Parliament, Edinburgh EH99 1SP.

Dorrian, Lady Leeona June, QC, LLB. Lord Justice Clerk, since 2016; Senator of the College of Justice, since 2005; b. 16.6.57, Edinburgh. Educ. Cranley Girls' School, Edinburgh; University of Aberdeen. Admitted to the Faculty of Advocates in 1981; Standing Junior Counsel to the Health and Safety Executive and Commission, 1987-1994, Advocate Depute, 1988-91, Standing Junior to the Department of Energy 1991-94; appointed Queen's Counsel, 1994; called to the English Bar in 1991, at the Inner Temple; Member of the Criminal Injuries Compensation Board, 1997-2001; appointed a Temporary Judge of the Court of Session, 2002. Address: (b.) Parliament House, 11 Parliament Square, Edinburgh EH1 1RQ.

Dorward, David Campbell, MA, ARAM. Composer, since 1944; Music Producer, BBC, 1962-91; b. 7.8.33, Dundee; m., Janet Offord; 1 s.; 2 d. Educ. Morgan Academy, Dundee; St. Andrews University; Royal Academy of Music. Teaching, 1960-61; Freelance, 1961-62. Arts Adviser,

Lamp of Lothian Collegiate Trust, 1967-98; Member, Scottish Arts Council, 1972-78; Consultant Director, Performing Right Society, 1985-90; Patron's Fund Award, 1958; Royal Philharmonic Prizewinner, 1958; compositions include five string quartets, two symphonies, four concertos, Tonight Mrs Morrison (one-act opera), A Christmas Carol (musical), and incidental music for TV, radio, film and stage. Recreations: reviving old scores; walking in the country. Address: (h.) Dovecot House, Preston Road, Prestonpans EH32 9JZ; T.-01875 810 512; e-mail: ddorward@btinternet.com

Dougall, Rona. Freelance journalist; presenter, Scotland Tonight on STV, since 2011; m., David Halliday; 2 d. Educ. Edinburgh University. Formerly with Radio Forth; became Scotland correspondent with Sky News (1996-2011). Address: STV, Pacific Quay, Glasgow G51 1PQ.

Douglas, Alan. Journalist and Broadcaster; b. 16.10.51, Dundee; m., Viv Lumsden (qv); 2 d. Educ. Forfar Academy. Local newspapers, 1970-74; BBC Local Radio Reporter and Producer, 1974-78; Reporter/Presenter, BBC TV Scotland, 1978-95; freelance broadcaster and journalist, BBC TV and Radio, corporate and Scottish TV; Director, The Broadcasting Business Ltd (media consultancy), 1989-2013; Director, Scotcars.co.uk (motoring website), 2009-2014; contributor to magazines, websites, newspapers, radio and tv on transport and travel. Former Guild of Motoring Writers' Regional Journalist of the Year. Recreations: cars; driving buses; walking; eating; drinking. Address: (b.) Pink Elephant Communications, Lochinch House, 86 Dumbreck Road, Glasgow G41 4SN.
E-mail: alan.doug@ntlworld.com

Douglas, Muriel Margaret, MBE, CPM, CIPD. Head, NHS Central Register Scotland, since 1995; b. 19.5.46, Edinburgh; m., Peter James Douglas; 1 s. Educ. Tynecastle High; Napier University. Retail, 1961-66; Scottish Office Computer Centre, 1966-70; General Register Office (1971 Census); SOCC - Payroll, 1972-81; Scottish Office Education Department, 1981-89; Personnel, Promotion Boards, 1989-90. Adviser to Privacy Advisory Committee, NHS Central Register Governance Board; Medical Research Management Board for England, Wales and Scotland; Community Health Advisory Group. Recreations: swimming; dancing; reading; walking. Address: (b.) Cairnsmore House, The Crichton, Dumfries DG1 4GW; T.-01387 259 820.
E-mail: muriel.douglas@gro-scotland.gsi.gov.uk

Douglas, Professor Sir Neil James, MD, DSc, FRCP, FRCPE. Emeritus Professor of Respiratory and Sleep Medicine, Edinburgh University; former President, British Sleep Society; Chairman, UK Academy of Medical Royal Colleges, 2009-2012; President, Royal College of Physicians of Edinburgh, 2004-2010; Consultant Physician, since 1983; b. 28.5.49, Edinburgh; m., Dr. Sue Galloway; 1 s.; 1 d. Educ. Dundee High School; Trinity College, Glenalmond; St. Andrews University; Edinburgh University. Lecturer in Medicine, Edinburgh University, 1974-83; MRC Travelling Fellow, University of Colorado, 1980-81. Recreations: fishing; gardening; eating. Address: (b.) Respiratory Medicine, Royal Infirmary, 51 Little France Crescent, Edinburgh EH16 4SA; T.-0131 242 1836.

Douglas-Home, Lady (Lavinia) Caroline, MBE 2010, DL, FSA Scot. Deputy Lieutenant, Berwickshire, 1983-2012; b. 11.10.37 (daughter of Baron Home of the Hirsel, KT, PC). Educ. privately. Woman of the Bedchamber

(Temporary) to Queen Elizabeth the Queen Mother, 1963-65; Lady-In-Waiting (Temporary) to HRH Duchess of Kent, 1966-67; Estate Factor, Douglas and Angus Estates, 1960-95; Trustee, National Museum of Antiquities of Scotland, 1982-85; President, Borders Branch, British Red Cross, 1998-2010, Chairman, Borders Volunteer Council, since 2010; Trustee, Scottish Episcopal Church Nominees, since 1993; Trustee, Scottish Redundant Churches Trust, since 1995; Governor, Longridge Towers School, 1995-2010; President, Berwick Citizens Advice Bureau, 1996-2014. Recreations: fishing; gardening; reading; antiquities. Address: (h.) Heaton Mill House, Cornhill-on-Tweed, Northumberland TD12 4XQ; T.-01890 882303.

Douglas-Scott, Susan, DipCOT, BSc (Hons), MSc (QMUC). Consultant in Health Equality and Social Care Issues and Humanist Celebrant, since 2010; Chair, ILF Scotland, since 2015; Non Executive Board Member, NHS Education for Scotland, since 2010; Chief Executive, The Long Term Conditions Alliance Scotland (LTCAS), 2009-2010; b. 12.9.60, Glasgow; 1 s.; 1 d. Educ. Eastwood High School; Glasgow School of Occupational Therapy; Caledonian University. Occupational therapist, NHS, 1981-82; social work, 1983-87; manager, social work, 1987-92; registration and inspection officer, 1992-98; Head of Service, Sense Scotland, 1998-2000; Director, fpa Scotland, 2000-03; Chief Executive, PHACE Scotland (Promoting Health and Challenging Exclusion), 2003-05; Chief Executive, Epilepsy Scotland, 2005-09. Recreations: yoga; crafts; singing; Reiki; cooking.

Dove, Rev. Giles Wilfred, MA, MPhil, BD, FRSA, FSA Scot. Chaplain and Head of Divinity, Glenalmond College, since 2007; Director of Development, National Library of Scotland, 2005-2007; Non-Stipendiary Curate, St. Mary's Church, Dunblane, 2005-07; b. 25.1.62, Hendon; m., Katherine Ann MacCallum; 2 s.; 1 d. Educ. Winchester College; University of St. Andrews; University of Glasgow. Alumnus Relations Officer, University of St. Andrews, 1988-91, Development Officer, 1992-97; Director of Communications and Development, University of Stirling, 1998-2005. Scottish Episcopal Church: Ordained Priest, 2006, Ordained Deacon, 2005, Convener, Standing Committee, General Synod, 2002-05, Trustee, Pension Fund, 2002-05, Convener, Budget Review Committee, General Synod, 2002-04, Convener, Resources Committee, General Synod, 1999-2002, Member, Board for Ministry, General Synod, 1999-2002; Trustee, Council for Advancement and Support of Education, 1999-2005; Governor, Aberlour Child Care Trust, 2001-04; Vice-Chairman, Board of Management, St. Mary's Episcopal Primary School, Dunblane, 2000-02; Director, Rymonth Housing Society Ltd., 1993-95; Trustee, St. Andrews Preservation Trust Ltd., 1991-94; Freeman of The City of London. Publications: "Alma Matters: A Guide To Alumni Relations"; "Pilgrimage Sites" (in "The Fife Book"); various articles in professional journals. Recreations: choral music; ecclesiastical history; good food and drink; Scottish islands. Address: (h.) The Chaplain's House, Glenalmond College, Perth PH1 3RY; e-mail: gilesdove@glenalmondcollege.co.uk

Dow, Douglas C. J., KStJ, LLB. Chancellor and Registrar, The Priory of Scotland of the Order of St. John; retired solicitor; b. 18.7.43, Johnstone; m., Alice Mackay; 1 s.; 2 d. Educ. Paisley Grammar School; Glasgow University. Partner, Stirling and Gilmour, Solicitors, West Dunbartonshire, 1969-2008. Town Clerk, Burgh of Cove and Kilcreggan, 1967-75. Past President, Helensburgh Rotary Club. Interests: arms and armour; medieval churches; history and art. Recreations: shooting; sailing. Address: (h.) Holyrood, Kilcreggan, Helensburgh G84 0HN; T.-01436 842405.

Dow, Rear-Admiral Douglas Morrison, CB, DL. Chief Executive, The National Trust for Scotland, 1992-97; Deputy Lieutenant, City of Edinburgh, since 1996; b. 1.7.35; m., Felicity Margaret Mona Napier; 2 s.; Educ. George Heriot's School; BRNC Dartmouth. Joined RN, 1952; served Staff of C-in-C Plymouth, 1959-61; HMS Plymouth, 1961-63; RN Supply Sch., 1963-65; Staff of Comdr FEF, 1965-67; HMS Endurance, 1968-70; BRNC Dartmouth, 1970-72; Cdr 1972; Assistant Director, Officer Appointments (S), 1972-74; Sec to Comdr British Navy Staff, Washington, 1974-76; HMS Tiger, 1977-78; NDC Latimer, 1978-79; Captain 1979; CSO(A) to Flag Officer Portsmouth, 1979; Sec to Controller of Navy, 1981; Captain, HMS Cochrane, 1983; Commodore, HMS Centurion, 1985; RCDS, 1988; Rear Admiral, 1989; Director General, Naval Personal Services, 1989-92. Vice-Chairman, George Heriot's Trust, 1996-2009; President, South Queensferry Sea Cadets, 1993-2009; President, Royal Naval Association Edinburgh, since 1994. Recreations: rugby union; fly fishing; shooting; golf; gardening. Address: (h.) Tor Lodge, 1 Eskbank Terrace, Dalkeith, Midlothian EH22 3DE.

Dow, Professor Julian Alexander Thomas, MA PhD, ScD, FRSE. Professor of Molecular and Integrative Physiology, Glasgow University, since 1999 (Chair of Integrative & Systems Biology, 2008-10); b. 1957; m., Shireen-Anne Davies; 3 s.; 2 d. Educ. King's School, Gloucester; St. Catharine's College, University of Cambridge. Glasgow University: Lecturer, 1984-94, Senior Lecturer, 1994-97, Reader, 1997-99; Nuffield Fellow, 1992-94. President's Medal, Society for Experimental Biology, 1992; Member, several committees, BBSRC. Recreations: skiing; diving. Address: (b.) Davidson Building, University of Glasgow, Glasgow G12 8QQ.
E-mail: julian.dow@glasgow.ac.uk

Dow, Professor Sheila Christine, MA (Hons), MA (Econ), PhD. Professor Emeritus in Economics, Stirling University (Professor, 1996-2009, Head of Department, 2002-04); Adjunct Professor of Economics, University of Victoria, Canada, since 2012; b. 16.4.49, Dumfries; m., Professor Alexander Dow; 2 d. Educ. Hawick High School; St. Andrews University; University of Manitoba; McMaster University; Glasgow University. Overseas Office, Bank of England, 1970-72; Economist, then Senior Economist, Department of Finance, Government of Manitoba, 1973-77; Lecturer, then Reader, Department of Economics, Stirling University, 1979-96. Chair, International Network for Economic Method, 2001-02; special advisor to House of Commons Treasury Select Committee, 2001-2010; Director of Stirling Centre for Economic Methodology, 2005-10. Publications: Macroeconomic Thought, 1985; Financial Markets and Regional Economic Development, 1990; Money Matters (Co-author), 1982; Money and the Economic Process, 1993; The Methodology of Macroeconomic Thought, 1996; Economic Methodology: An Inquiry, 2002; A History of Scottish Economic Thought (Co-editor), 2006; Open Economics (Co-editor), 2009; Foundations for New Economic Thinking, 2012. Address: (b.) Division of Economics, Stirling University, Stirling FK9 4LA; T.-01786 467470; e-mail: s.c.dow@stir.ac.uk

Dow, Sylvia, MLitt, ALAM, LRAM, FRSA. Playwright, since 2010; Arts Education Consultant; Head of Education, Scottish Arts Council, 1994-2004; b. 19.7.39, Edinburgh; m., Ronald Dow; 1 s.; 1 d. Educ. James Gillespie's High School for Girls; Edinburgh College of Speech and Drama. Freelance radio actor/presenter, California, 1960-65; Tutor, Edinburgh College of Speech and Drama, 1969-70; Drama Teacher (Head of Drama),

Bo'ness Academy, 1970-85; Education Officer, MacRobert Arts Centre, 1985-93; Arts Co-ordinator, Central Region Education Service, 1993-94. Recreation: arts. E-mail: sylvia.dow@btinternet.com

Downes, Bob, DipTP, BPhil. Chairman, Global Surface Intelligence, since 2012; Chair, CENSIS, Scottish Sensor Innovation Centre, since 2013; Non Executive Director, Scottish Government, since 2014; Director, Network Investment, Openreach, 2009-2011; Scottish Government, non-executive director, since 2014; b. 10.8.51, Belfast; m., Julie McGarvey; 2 s. Educ. Portora Royal School, Enniskillen; Dundee University; Duncan of Jordanstone College of Art, Dundee; BPhil, Open University. Local government, 1976-82; Dundee Project, 1982-84; SDA, 1984-87; Director: North East, SDA, 1987-90, Conran Roche Planning, London, 1990-92; independent consultant, 1992-93; Chief Executive, Dumfries and Galloway Enterprise, 1993-94; Director, Scottish Enterprise, 1994-99; BT Scotland: Director, Economic Development, 1999-2000; Director, e-business Development, 2000-01, National Manager, 2001-02, Director, 2002-05. Advisor, Flax Trust, Belfast, 1994-2001; Director: Wise Group, Glasgow, 1997-2000, Emerging Business Trust, Belfast, 1996-2004, Businesslab, 1996-2003; Director Scotland, Openreach, 2005-09; Member, President's Executive Committee, National Council for Urban Economic Development, Washington D.C., 1996-2001; Member, Advisory Board, The Competitiveness Institute, Barcelona, 1998-99; Director, Big Issue International, 2002-04; Director, Scottish Ensemble, since 2012; Board Member, Scottish Arts Council, 2003-05; Advisory Board Group, DA Group, 2002-05; Glasgow University Adam Smith Business School Advisory Board, since 2005; Scottish Environmental Protection Agency, Deputy Chairman, non-executive director, since 2008; Glasgow School of Art, Trustee, since 2009; Care Visions Group, Advisor, 2010-13; Scotrail Advisory Board, 2008-2013. Recreations: biking; sea kayaking; live music; travelling; films; history; whisky collecting; biographies; Kelvin walkway. Address: (h.) 21 Cleveden Road, Kelvinside, Glasgow G12 0PQ.

Downes, Professor Sir Charles Peter, OBE, FRSE, FMedSci, FRSB, PhD. Principal and Vice-Chancellor, University of Dundee, since 2009; formerly Vice Principal and Head of College of Life Sciences, Prof. of Biochemistry, since 1989; b. 15.10.53, Manchester; m., Dr Elizabeth Naomi; 1 s.; 1 d. Educ. Kings School, Macclesfield; Stockport College of Technology; Birmingham University. Experimental Officer, ICI Pharmaceuticals, 1973-78; MRC Training Fellow, Cambridge, 1981-83; Research Group Leader, ICI Pharm., 1983-85; Cellular Pharmacologist/Senior Cellular Pharmacologist, Smith Kline and French/Smith Kline Beecham, 1985-89. Chairman, The Biochemical Society, 2000-2004. Recreations: golf; previously playing, now spectating, football. Address: (b.) University Executive Office, University of Dundee, Dundee DD1 4HN; T.-01382 385561.
E-mail: c.p.downes@dundee.ac.uk

Downie, Emeritus Professor Robert S., MA, BPhil, FRSE, FRSA. Honorary Professorial Research Fellow, Glasgow University; b. 19.4.33, Glasgow; m., Eileen Dorothea Flynn; 3 d. Educ. High School of Glasgow; Glasgow University; Queen's College, Oxford. Tutor, Worcester College, Oxford, 1958; Glasgow University: Lecturer in Moral Philosophy, 1959, Senior Lecturer, 1968, Professor of Moral Philosophy, 1969 (Stevenson Lecturer in Medical Ethics, 1984-88); Visiting Professor: Syracuse University, New York, 1963-64, Dalhousie University, Nova Scotia, 1976. Publications: Government Action and Morality, 1964; Respect for Persons, 1969; Roles and Values, 1971; Education and Personal Relationships, 1974; Caring and Curing, 1980; Healthy Respect, 1987; Health Promotion: models and values, 1990; The Making of a Doctor, 1992; Francis Hutcheson, 1994; The Healing Arts: an Oxford illustrated anthology, 1994; Palliative Care Ethics, 1996; Medical Ethics, 1996; Clinical Judgement – Evidence in Practice, 2000; The Philosophy of Palliative Care: Critique and Reconstruction, 2006; Bioethics and the Humanities, 2007; End of Life Choices, 2009. Recreation: music. Address: (b.) Department of Philosophy, Glasgow University G12 8QQ; T.-0141-339 1345.
E-mail: Robert.Downie@glasgow.ac.uk

Dowson, William K., BSc, MSc. Agent for Scotland, Bank of England, since 2010; b. 3.3.71, Bridlington; m Sarah Laing; 2 s.; 1 d. Educ. Wycliffe College; University of London. Joined Bank of England, 1995; worked in policy and management roles in Banking, Financial Stability and Markets Directorates, before joining Agency Network. Assessor to the Executive Committee of the SCDI, and an Observer on the Council of CBI Scotland. Recreations: sailing; walking; reading. Address: (b.) Bank of England, Agency for Scotland, 177 West George Street, Glasgow G2 2LB; T. 0141 221 7972; e-mail: scotland@bankofengland.co.uk

Doyle, Rev. David Wallace, MA (Hons), BD (Hons). Retired Minister, St. Mary's Parish Church, Motherwell (1987-2015); b. 12.4.48, Glasgow; m., Alison W. Britton; 1 s.; 1 d. Educ. High School of Glasgow; University of Glasgow; Corpus Christi, University of Cambridge. Assistant Minister, East Kilbride Old Parish Church, 1973-74; Minister, Tulliallan and Kincardine Parish Church, Fife, 1977-87. Recreations: music; gardening.

Doyle, Gemma, MA. MP Labour (Co-op), West Dunbartonshire, 2010-2015; Shadow Minister for Defence, 2010-2015; b. 1981. Educ. Our Lady and St Patrick's High, Dumbarton; Glasgow University. Member: Select Committee on Armed Forces Bill, 2011; Energy and Climate Change, 2010; Administration, 2010; Chair, PLP Departmental Group for Defence, 2010.

Doyle, Roberta, BA. Director of External Affairs, National Theatre of Scotland, since 2007; b. 05.01.60, Glasgow; m., Cemal Ozturk; 1 s. Educ. Notre Dame High, Glasgow; University of Strathclyde. Head of Publicity, Citizens Theatre Company, 1986-90; Director of Marketing, Scottish Ballet, 1990-92; Head of Marketing and Press, Scottish Opera, 1992-2000; Director of Public Affairs, National Galleries of Scotland, 2000-04; Director of External Affairs, Scottish Opera, 2005-07. Tutor on Arts Council England/Theatrical Management Association/Scottish Arts Council/Arts Council Ireland Essentials of Arts Marketing Courses. Member of Scotland Advisory Committee, National Autistic Society; member, British Council UK Cultural Diplomacy Group; Campaign Group member, Culture Counts. Guest lecturer and speaker worldwide on arts and cultural management and policy. Recreations: theatre; opera; riding; Turkish culture and Italian cooking. Address: National Theatre of Scotland, Civic House, 26 Civic Street, Glasgow G4 9RH; T.-0141 221 0970.
E-mail: roberta.doyle@nationaltheatrescotland.com

Driscoll, Professor Stephen T., BA, MSc, PhD. Professor of Archaeology, University of Glasgow, since 2005, Lecturer, Department of Archaeology, since 1992; b. 11.11.58, Monterey, California, USA; m., Katherine S. Forsyth; 3 d. Educ. St. Anselm's Abbey School, Washington, DC; University of Pennsylvania, Philadelphia.

Founding Director of Glasgow Archaeological Research Division (GUARD) - full contract unit, 1989-94; Research Director of GUARD, since 1994; Lecturer in Archaeology, University of Glasgow, 1992-97, Senior Lecturer, 1997-2005. Editor of Scottish Archaeological Journal, since 1998; Vice President, Glasgow Archaeological Society, since 2007. Publications: Excavations at Edinburgh Castle (Co-Author), 1997; Excavations at Glasgow Cathedral, 2002; Alba: Gaelic Kingdom of Scotland, 2002. Recreations: cycling; gaelic language. E-mail: s.driscoll@archaeology.gla.ac.uk

Drummond, Rev. John Whiteford, MA, BD. Retired Minister; b. 27.6.46, Glasgow; m., Barbara S. Grant; 1 s.; 3 d. Educ. Bearsden Academy; University of Glasgow. Probationer Assistant, St. Francis-in-the-East Church, Bridgeton, 1970-71; Ordained Assistant, King's Park Parish Church, Glasgow, 1971-73; Minister: Linwood Parish Church, 1973-86, Rutherglen West Parish Church, 1986-2007, Rutherglen West and Wardlawhill Parish Church, 2007-2011. Recreations: reading; television; family. Address: (h.) 25 Kingsburn Drive, Rutherglen G73 2AN; T.-0141 571 6002.

Drummond, Rev. Norman Walker, CBE, FRSE, DUniv. Chairman, Scottish Commemorations Panel, since 2012; Special Representative for Scotland, UK Advisory Group, World War 1 Commemorations, since 2012; Visiting Professor of Leadership in Education, University of Edinburgh; Chaplain to the Queen in Scotland, since 1993; Non-executive Director, J & J Denholm Ltd, since 2002; Hon Colonel, The Black Watch ACF, since 2014; Chairman, Drummond International, since 1999; Founder and Chairman, Columba 1400, Community and International Leadership Centre, Isle of Skye, since 1997; Chairman, Lloyds TSB Foundation for Scotland, 2003-09; Founder and non-executive Chairman, The Change Partnership Scotland, 1999-2003; Chairman, Community Action Network Scotland, 2001-03; b. 1.4.52, Greenock; m., Lady Elizabeth Kennedy; 3 s.; 2 d. Educ. Merchiston Castle School; Fitzwilliam College, Cambridge; New College, Edinburgh. Chaplain to the Forces, 1976-82; Depot, The Parachute Regiment and Airborne Forces, 1977-78; 1st Bn., The Black Watch (Royal Highland Regiment), 1978-82; Chaplain, Fettes College, 1982-84; Headmaster, Loretto School, 1984-95; Minister, Kilmuir and Stenscholl, Isle of Skye, 1996-98; BBC National Governor and Chairman, Broadcasting Council for Scotland, 1994-99; former Chairman, BBC Children in Need; Member, Queen's Bodyguard for Scotland (Royal Company of Archers); Past President: Victoria League for Overseas Students in Scotland, Edinburgh Bn., Boys' Brigade; former Governor, Gordonstoun School; former Chairman, Aiglon College, Switzerland; former Member, Scottish Committee for Imperial Cancer Research; former Trustee, Foundation for Skin Research; former Member, Scottish Committee, Duke of Edinburgh's Award Scheme; former Member, Court, Heriot-Watt University; former Chairman, Musselburgh and District Council of Social Services. Publications: The First Twenty Five Years (the official history of the Black Watch Kirk Session); Mother's Hands; The Spirit of Success; The Power of Three; Step Back. Recreations: rugby football; cricket; golf; curling; traditional jazz. Address: Drummond International, 35 Drummond Place, Edinburgh EH3 6PW.

Drummond, Robbie, BAcc (Hons), CA. Group Finance Director, David MacBrayne Group Ltd, since 2012; b. 8.6.69, Inverness; m., Amanda Drummond; 2 d. Educ. Morrisons Academy; Glasgow University. Early career spent with KPMG and Pricewaterhousecoopers (Corporate Finance); subsequently held senior finance positions with Thus plc, Invocas plc and HBOS plc. Scottish Council for Development and Industry (Highlands & Islands) Committee Member. Recreations: trail and long distance

running. Address: (h.) 56 Braehead Avenue, Milngavie, East Dunbartonshire G62 6DY; T.-07766021415; e-mail: robbie.drummond@davidmacbrayne.co.uk

Drummond, Sheriff Thomas Anthony Kevin, LLB, QC. Retired Sheriff, Lothian and Borders at Jedburgh, Selkirk and Duns (2000-2013); b. 3.11.43, Howwood, Renfrewshire; m., Margaret Evelyn Broadley; 1 d. (1 d. deceased). Educ. St. Mirin's Academy, Paisley; Blairs College, Aberdeen; Edinburgh University. Admitted, Faculty of Advocates, 1974; Advocate Depute, 1985-90; Member, Firearms Consultative Committee, 1989-97; Member, Criminal Injuries Compensation Board, 1990-96; Home Advocate Depute, 1996-97; Sheriff, Glasgow and Strathkelvin, 1997-2000. Joint Chairman, Institute of Chartered Accountants of Scotland, 1993-2000. Hon. US Deputy Marshal, 1998. Chair, Legislation Regulation and Guidance Committee, PAWS (Partnership for Action against Wildlife Crime Scotland). Publications (legal cartoons): The Law at Work; The Law at Play; Great Defences of Our Time. Recreations: fishing; shooting. Address: (h.) Pomathorn House, Penicuik, Midlothian; T.-01968 674046.
E-mail: kdrummondqc@btinternet.com

Drummond Young, Hon. Lord (James Edward Drummond Young), QC. Senator of the College of Justice in Scotland, since 2001; former Chairman, Scottish Law Commission; b. 1950; m.; 1 d. Educ. Cambridge University; Harvard University; Edinburgh University. Admitted, Faculty of Advocates, 1976. Address: Parliament House, Parliament Square, Edinburgh EH1 1RQ.

Drury, John Kenneth, MBChB, PhD, FRCS. Consultant, General Surgeon, Victoria Infirmary NHS Trust, 1986-2010, (Clinical Director, General Surgery, 1993-99); Registrar for Surgical Examinations, Royal College of Physicians and Surgeons of Glasgow, since 1999; Director, Surgical Examinations, RCPSG, since 2003; Member, Intercollegiate Committee for Basic Surgical Examinations, since 2003; Member, Council, RCPSG, 2003-09; b. 23.1.47; m., Gillian Gilmore; 1 s.; 1 d. Educ. Paisley Grammar School; University of Glasgow. Research Fellow, Department of Physiology, University of Glasgow, 1973-76; West of Scotland Surgical Training Scheme, 1976-86. Committee Member, RNLI; Member: Vascular Society of Great Britain, European Society for Vascular and Endovascular Surgery. Recreations: sailing; golf; local art. Address: (b.) Ross Hall Hospital, Crookston Road, Glasgow G52 3NQ; e-mail:jkdlba@btinternet.com

Drysdale, Professor David Douglas (Dougal), BSc, PhD, MRSC, FIFireE, FSFPE, CEng, FRSE. Professor Emeritus (Fire Safety Engineering), Edinburgh University, since 2004; Chairman, International Association for Fire Safety Science, 2002-05; b. 30.9.39, Dunfermline; m., Judyth McIntyre; 3 s. Educ. Edinburgh Academy; Edinburgh University; Cambridge University. Post-doctoral Fellow, University of Toronto, 1966-67; Research Lecturer, Leeds University, 1967-74; Lecturer, Fire Engineering, Edinburgh University, 1974-92; Visiting Professor, Centre for Fire Safety Studies, Worcester Polytechnic Institute, Mass., USA, 1982; Reader, Fire Safety Engineering, Edinburgh University, 1990-98, Professor, Fire Safety Engineering, 1998-2004; Member of the Buncefield Major Incident Investigation Board, 2006-2009; SFPE Man of the Year (USA), 1983; BRE Fire Research Lecturer, 1995; SFPE Arthur B. Guise Medal for eminent achievement advancing the Science of Fire Protection Engineering, 1995; IAFSS Kawagoe Medal for lifelong career in and contribution to fire safety science, 2002; IFE Rasbash Medal, 2005; International Forum of Fire Research Directors' Sjolin Award for "outstanding career in fire science", 2005; SFPE 2009 D. Peter Lund Award for "significant contribution to the advancement of the profession".

Publications: Introduction to Fire Dynamics, 3rd Edn., 2011; Handbook of Fire Protection Engineering, 4th Edn. (co-ed.), 2008; Fire Safety Journal (ed.), 1988-2009. Recreations: music; hill walking; curling; cycling; coarse golf. Address: (b.) School of Engineering, Edinburgh University, King's Buildings, Edinburgh, EH9 3JN; T.-0131-650 5724.

Drysdale, James Cunison, LLB. Partner, Ledingham Chalmers LLP, specialising in Rural, Private Client and Environmental Law (formerly Partner, Anderson Strathern Solicitors); b. 30.4.56, Edinburgh; m., Fiona Jean nee Duncan Millar; 1 s.; 3 d. Educ. Winchester College; Aberdeen University. Apprentice at Brodies, 1979-81; Assistant Solicitor: Murray Beith and Murray, 1981-83, J & F Anderson, 1983-86. Treasurer and Council Member, UKELA (UK Environment Law Association) until 1 July 2009, having served the full term; Legal Adviser to the Association of Salmon Fishery Boards, for 15 years to 2009; Clerk of the Course Fife Foxhounds Point To Point. Recreations: countryside pursuits. Address: (b.) Suite B1, Stirling Agricultural Centre, Stirling FK9 4RW; e-mail: jim.drysdale@ledinghamchalmers.com

Drysdale, Thomas Henry, LLB, WS. Retired Solicitor; b. 23.11.42, Stirlingshire; m., Caroline Drysdale (nee Shaw); 1 s.; 2 d. Educ. Cargilfield and Glenalmond College; University of Edinburgh (LLB, 1964). Qualified as a Solicitor, 1966; Partner in Shepherd and Wedderburn WS, 1967-99 (Managing Partner, 1988-94); Partner in Olivers WS, 1999-2004; Chairman of Edinburgh Solicitors' Property Centre, 1981-88; Deputy Keeper of HM Signet, 1991-98; Part time Judge of the First Tier, the Tribunals Service, 2003-2013; Honorary Consul for Hungary, 2001-2012. Secretary and Treasurer, The Stair Society (legal history), since 1998; Member, Scottish Tribunals and Administrative Justice Advisory Committee, since 2013; Vice Chairman, Gullane Area Community Council. Recreations: skiing; walking; gardening; reading. Address: 6 The Glebe, Manse Road, Dirleton, East Lothian EH39 5FB; T.-01620 850264.
E-mail: tomdrysdale@btinternet.com

Duckett, Professor Jane. Professor, Edward Caird Chair of Politics and Director of the Scottish Centre for China Research, University of Glasgow, since 1999. Educ. Universities of Leeds and London (SOAS); Nankai University; Fudan University. Lecturer, University of Manchester, 1995-97; Lecturer, University of York, 1997-99. President, British Association for Chinese Studies; International Dean for East Asia, University of Glasgow. Lord Provost of Glasgow Award for Education, 2011. Publications: The Entrepreneurial State in China, 1998; China's Changing Welfare Mix, 2011; The Chinese State's Retreat from Health, 2011. Address: University of Glasgow, R1202 Level 12, Adam Smith Building, Glasgow G12 8RT; e-mail: Jane.Duckett@glasgow.ac.uk

Duffin, Stuart, DA, RE, RSA, SSA. Studio Etcher, Glasgow Print Studio, 1984-1989; Studio Workshop Manager, 1989-2002; Etching Master, since 2002; b. 13.6.59. Educ. Gray's School of Art, Aberdeen. SAC award to study and travel in Italy, 1987; exchange visit to Senej Print Workshop, Moscow, 1992; British Council support to study at the Jerusalem Print Workshop, 1996 and 2012; solo exhibitions: Glasgow Print Studio, 1995, 2001, 2013, Gallery of Jerusalem Print Workshop, 1998; Visiting lecturer tour and exhibition, New Zealand, 2002, 2007-2010. Address: c/o Glasgow Print Studio, Trongate 103, Glasgow G1 5HD.
E-mail: info@stuartduffin.com
Website: www.stuartduffin.com

Duffus, John Henderson, BSc, PhD, DSc, CSci, CBiol, MSB, CChem, FRSC. Adjunct Professor, Chulabhorn Graduate Institute, Bangkok; Consultant, Edinburgh Centre for Toxicology (EdinTox). Educ. Arbroath High School; Edinburgh University; Heriot-Watt University. Research Fellow: Warwick University, 1965-67, Edinburgh University, 1967-70; Lecturer, Heriot-Watt University, 1970-80; Senior Lecturer in Environmental Toxicology, Heriot-Watt University, 1980-97; Hon. Fellow in Public Health Sciences, Edinburgh University, 1997; WHO Consultant, Toxicology and Chemical Safety, since 1981; Member, UK Department of the Environment Advisory Committee on Hazardous Substances, 1991-99; Titular Member, IUPAC Commission on Toxicology, 1991-2001, Chair, 1997-2001; Titular Member, IUPAC Committee on the Teaching of Chemistry, 1999-2001; Member, RSC Committee on Environment, Health and Safety; Member, UK HSE Biocides Consultative Committee, 2001-06; Titular Member, IUPAC Division VII, Chemistry and Human Health Committee, 2004-08; Adjunct Professor, Asian Institute of Technology, 2005; Chair, IUPAC Subcommittee on Toxicology and Risk Assessment, 2001-2015; Scientific Advisor, EC, 2009-2014. Publications: Environmental Toxicology, 1980; Environmental Toxicology and Ecotoxicology, 1986; Magnesium in Mitosis and the Cell Cycle (Co-Author), 1987; Yeast: A Practical Approach (Co-Editor), 1988; The Toxicology of Chemicals, Series 1, Carcinogenicity, Vol III, Vol IV (Co-Editor/Author), 1991-93; Toxic Substances in Crop Plants (Co-Editor/Author), 1991; Cancer and Workplace Chemicals, 1995; IUPAC Glossaries of Terms Used in Toxicology, Pure and Applied Chemistry, 1993-2015; Carcinogenicity of Inorganic Substances (Chief Editor/Author), 1997; Chemical Risk Assessment (Co-Author), 1999; Risk Assessment and Elemental Speciation, 2001, 2003, 2006; Fundamental Toxicology (Co-Editor, Author), 2006; Concepts in Toxicology (Co-Author), 2009; NLM-SOT ToxLearn Multi-Module Toxicology Tutorial (Co-Editor/Author), 2010 continuing; Encyclopedia of Toxicology, 3rd Edition (Contributor), 2014. Awards: US Society of Toxicology Education Award, 2012; Princess Chulabhorn Gold Medal, 2012. Address: (b.) Edinburgh Centre for Toxicology, 43 Mansionhouse Road, Edinburgh EH9 2JD.

Duffy, David, BBS, MA. Chief Executive, Clydesdale Bank PLC, since 2015. Educ. Terenure College; Trinity College Dublin. Career: Goldman Sachs International, 1987-97, served as Business Manager of Information Technology, Head of General Services, Europe, 1988-93, Head of Human Resources, Europe, 1993-97; ING Group, 1998-2006, Global Head of Human Resources and Global Chief Operating Officer, President and Chief Executive Officer of the franchises in the US and Latin America, 2000-06, served at New York as the Head of the Global Wholesale Banking Network, based in Amsterdam, 2004-06; Chief Executive of Corporate and Investment Banking International, Standard International Holdings SA and Standard Bank Group Limited, 2006-2011, established Celtic Advisory International, which provides Capital Raising and Corporate Development Advisory Services to corporate and emerging companies; Chief Executive, Allied Irish Banks, 2011-2015. Advisor for Strategic Corporate Development at Intune Networks. Address: Clydesdale Bank PLC, 30 St Vincent Place, Glasgow G4 0PT.

Dugdale, Kezia, MSP (Labour), Lothian, since 2011; Leader of the Scottish Labour Party, since 2015; b. 28.8.81, Aberdeen. Educ. Harris Academy, Dundee; University of Aberdeen; University of Edinburgh. Worked in public affairs, latterly with the National Union of Students; ran the parliamentary office of Lord Foulkes, 2007-2011; Shadow Cabinet Secretary for Education and Lifelong Learning, 2013-15; Deputy Leader, the Scottish Labour Party, 2014-15. Weekly columnist, Scottish Daily Record. Recreations: going to the cinema; reading Scottish crime novels; enjoying the City of Edinburgh. Address: (b.) Scottish Parliament, Edinburgh EH99 1SP.

Dugmore, Professor Andrew J., PhD, BSc, FGS, FRSA (Scot). Professor of Geosciences, University of Edinburgh, since 2007; Adjunct Professor (Research), City University of New York, USA, since 2002; Adjunct Professor (Research), School of Human Evolution and Social Change, Arizona State University, USA, since 2013; m., Thelma (nee Williamson); 1 s.; 1 d. Educ. Denes High School, Lowestoft; University of Birmingham; University of Aberdeen. Lecturer, Senior Lecturer, University of Edinburgh, 1992-2004, Reader in Tephrochronology, 2004-07. Visiting Lecturer, University of Lund, Sweden, 1997; President's Award, Royal Scottish Geographical Society, 2002. Recreations: hill walking and mountaineering. Address: (b.) Institute of Geography, School of Geosciences, University of Edinburgh, Drummond Street, Edinburgh EH8 9XP; T.-0131 650 8156.
E-mail: andrew.dugmore@ed.ac.uk

Dukes, Professor Paul, BA (Cantab), MA, PhD, FRSE. Professor of History, Aberdeen University, 1964-99, Emeritus Professor, since 1999; b. 5.4.34, Wallington; 1 s.; 1 d. Educ. Wallington County Grammar School; Cambridge University. Advisory Editor, History Today. Publications: several books on aspects of Russian, American, European and world history. Recreations: hill-walking; travel. Address: (b.) History Department, Aberdeen University, Aberdeen; T.-01224 273886; e-mail: p.dukes@abdn.ac.uk

Dumville, Professor David Norman, MA (Cantab), PhD (Edin), HonMA (Pennsylvania). Sixth-Century Professor in History, Palaeography and Celtic, University of Aberdeen, since 2005; Fellow, Girton College, Cambridge, since 1978; b. 5.5.49, Hillingdon, London. Educ. St Nicholas Grammar School, Northwood, Middlesex; Emmanuel College, Cambridge; Ludwig-Maximilian Universität München; University of Edinburgh. Career History: University of Wales Fellow, Department of Welsh, University College of Swansea; Assistant Professor, Department of English, University of Pennsylvania; Lecturer, Reader, then Professor, Department of Anglo-Saxon, Norse and Celtic, University of Cambridge; Sixth-Century Professor in History, Palaeography and Celtic, University of Aberdeen. Honorary Member, Royal Irish Academy. Publications: 15 books, about 150 scholarly articles. Recreations: politics and other arguments. Address: (b.) Department of History, University of Aberdeen, King's College, Old Aberdeen AB24 3FX; T.-01224-272455; e-mail: d.n.dumville@abdn.ac.uk

Dunbar, John Greenwell, OBE, MA, FSA, HonFSA Scot, HonFRIAS. Architectural historian; Secretary, Royal Commission on the Ancient and Historical Monuments of Scotland, 1978-90; b. 1.3.30, London; m., Elizabeth Mill Blyth. Educ. University College School, London; Balliol College, Oxford. joined staff, Royal Commission on the Ancient and Historical Monuments of Scotland, 1953. Publications: The Historic Architecture of Scotland, 1966; Accounts of the Masters of Works, Volume 2 (1616-1649), (Joint Editor), 1982; Sir William Burrell's Northern Tour, 1997; Scottish Royal Palaces, 1999; Buildings of Scotland: Borders, 2006 (Joint Author). Address: (h.) Paties Mill, Carlops, by Penicuik, Midlothian EH26 9NF; T.-01968 660250.

Dunbar, Professor Lennox Robert, DA, RSA. Emeritus Professor of Fine Art, Grays School of Art; Painter and Printmaker; b. 17.5.52, Aberdeen; m., Jan Storie; 2 s.; 1 d. Educ. Aberdeen Grammar School; Grays School of Art. Part-time Lecturer, 1975-82; Etching Technician, Peacock Printmakers, 1978-82; Education Officer, Peacock Printmakers, 1982-86; appointed Lecturer in Painting and Printmaking, Grays School of Art, 1986; Visiting Lecturer, Duncan of Jordanstone College of Art, Dundee, and Newcastle University; Visiting Artist/Tutor, Louisiana State University; College of Santa FE, New Mexico; participated in many group and one-man exhibitions; numerous awards including Latimer Award, 1978, Guthrie Award, 1984, Shell Expro Premier Award, 1991, 1993 and 2006; work in many private and public collections.

Dunbar, Morrison Alexander Rankin, CBE, KCSJ, FRSAMD. Chairman: Royal Scottish Academy of Music and Drama Trust, 1992-2004, Westbourne Music, 1998-2008, Cantilena Festival, Islay, 2002-2011; b. 27.4.29, Glasgow; m., Sally Joan Sutherland; 2 s.; 1 d. Educ. Belmont House; Gresham House. Managing Director, Morrison Dunbar Ltd. Builders, 1957-81. President: Scottish Building Contractors Association, 1968, Scottish Building Employers Federation, 1975, Building Employers Confederation, 1980, Builders Benevolent Institution, 1987; Lord Dean of Guild, Merchants House of Glasgow, 1991-93; Chairman: Epilepsy Association of Scotland, 1990-93, Royal Scottish Academy of Music and Drama, 1987-91, Royal Scottish National Orchestra, 1993-97; Member, Trades House of Glasgow. Recreations: music; art galleries; golf. Address: (h.) 18 Devonshire Terrace Lane, Glasgow G12 9XT; T.-0141-357 1289.

Dunbar-Nasmith, Professor Emeritus Sir James Duncan, Kt (1996), CBE (1976), BA, DA, RIBA, PPRIAS, FRSA, FRSE. Partner, Law and Dunbar-Nasmith, Architects, Edinburgh and Forres 1957-99; b. 15.3.27, Dartmouth. Educ. Lockers Park; Winchester College; Trinity College, Cambridge; Edinburgh College of Art (Hon. Fellow, 1997). Lt., Scots Guards 1945-48; ARIBA, 1954; President: Edinburgh Architectural Association, 1967-69, Royal Incorporation of Architects in Scotland, 1971-73; RIAS Lifetime Achievement Award, 2012; Member, RIBA Council, 1967-73 (Vice-President and Chairman, Board of Architectural Education, 1972-73); Council, ARCUK, 1976-84, Board of Education, 1976-88 (Vice Chairman, 1977); Professor and Head, Department of Architecture, Heriot-Watt University and Edinburgh College of Art, 1978-88; President, Scottish Civic Trust (Chairman, 1995-2003); Vice-President, Europa Nostra, 1997-2005, Hon. Life Member, 2005. Member: Royal Commission on Ancient and Historical Monuments of Scotland, 1972-96, Ancient Monuments Board for Scotland, 1969-82 (interim Chairman, 1972-73), Historic Buildings Council for Scotland, 1966-93; Trustee, Architectural Heritage Fund, Theatres Trust, 1983-95; Deputy Chairman, Edinburgh Festival Society, 1981-85. Recreations: music; theatre; skiing; sailing. Address: (b.) Sandbank, Findhorn, Moray IV36 3YY; T.-0130 9690445.
E-mail: jdnasmith@fastmail.net

Duncan, Arnold Durham, MIPI. Honorary Sheriff, Sheriffdom of Grampian, Highland and Islands at Lerwick, Shetland, since 2003; b. 10.9.46, Lerwick, Shetland. Educ. Scalloway Junior Secondary and Lerwick Central Secondary Schools, Shetland; Scottish Police College: Junior and Senior Divisions, Kincardine, Fife; Central College of Commerce, Glasgow. Appointed Boy Clerk with former Zetland Constabulary, 1962; appointed Constable in Zetland Constabulary, 1966; appointed Detective Constable, with Northern Constabulary, 1973; promoted Detective Sergeant, 1976; appointed Force Liaison officer, with responsibilities for Economic Key Points in area viz.: Dounreay Atomic Reactor, Caithness; Flotta Oil Terminal, Orkney and Sullom Voe Oil Terminal, Shetland, 1980; awarded Police Long Service and Good Conduct Medal, 1989; promoted to Inspector and Deputy Sub Divisional Officer, Shetland Islands Area, 1990; retired

from Police Service, 1996; casual contract with Crown Office and Procurator Fiscal Service, as Precognition Officer/Office Manager, 2001-02; Commission held as Procurator Fiscal Depute at Lerwick, Shetland. Ex Chairman, Scalloway Community Council; Chairman, Scalloway Waterfront Trust; Ex Chairman, Shetland Health Board Independent Review Panel; Elder, Church of Scotland, Tingwall Parish. Recreations: coastal/hill walking; local history; reading; gardening; choir member. Address: "Springbank Lodge", Houl Road, Scalloway, Shetland ZE1 0UA; T.-01595 880419.
E-mail: add90@btinternet.com

Duncan, Atholl. Executive Director, UK and Global, ICAS - the professional body for CAs (ICAS), since 2011; Head of News and Current Affairs, BBC Scotland, 2006-2011. Educ. George Watson's College, Edinburgh; Napier University; Harvard Business School and Cranfield School of Management. Joined DC Thomson in 1982 as a reporter; joined BBC Scotland in 1985 as a researcher and sub-editor; worked on a variety of news and sport programmes including Focal Point, Upfront, Newsnight and Sportscene and produced more than 1,000 editions of Reporting Scotland before becoming Managing Editor for News and Current Affairs in 1996; became Director of Corporate Affairs, Scottish Water in 2003. Non-executive Director: Sportscotland, 2001-09, Hibernian Community Foundation, since 2009, British Horseracing Authority, since 2014. Address: (b.) ICAS, CA House, 21 Haymarket Yards, Edinburgh, EH12 5BH.

Duncan, Elaine Margaret, BSc (Hons) Behavioural Sciences. Chief Executive, Scottish Bible Society, since 2006; b. 29.8.58, Whitehaven, Cumbria. Educ. Whitehaven Grammar School; Huddersfied Polytechnic. Universities and Colleges Christian Fellowship, 1981-95; Scripture Union Scotland, 1995-2006. Address: (b.) 7 Hampton Terrace, Edinburgh EH12 5XU; T.-0131-337-9701; e-mail: elaine.duncan@scottishbiblesociety.org

Duncan, Fiona. Chief Executive, Lloyds TSB Foundation for Scotland, since 2014. Director, THINK Consulting Solutions, 2009-2013; Deputy Chief Executive, Lloyds TSB Foundation for Scotland, 2013-14. Address: Lloyds TSB Foundation for Scotland, Riverside House, 502 Gorgie Road, Edinburgh EH11 3AF; T.-0131 444 4020.

Duncan, The Right Reverend Dr Gregor. Bishop of Glasgow and Galloway, since 2010; b. 11.10.50. Educ. Allan Glen's School; University of Glasgow; Clare College, Cambridge. Studied for the priesthood at Ripon College Cuddesdon; ordained in 1984 and began career as an Assistant Curate at Oakham; Chaplain of Edinburgh Theological College, then Rector of St Columba's, Largs, then St Ninian's, Pollokshields in Glasgow; Dean of Glasgow and Galloway until elevation to the Episcopate in 2010. Consecrated and installed as Bishop of Glasgow and Galloway at St Mary's Cathedral in Glasgow on 23 April 2010. Address: Glasgow & Galloway Diocesan Centre, 5 Vincent Place, Glasgow G1 2DH; T.-0141 221 5720.

Duncan, Ian. Member of the European Parliament for Scotland (Scottish Conservatives), since 2014; Chairman, The English-Speaking Union, since 2014; b. 13.2.73. Educ. Alyth High School; Bristol University; University of St. Andrews. Policy Analyst BP, 1998-99; Deputy Chief Executive/Secretary, Scottish Fishermen's Federation, 1999-2003; Head of Policy & Communication, The Scottish Refugee Council, 2004-2005; Head of EU Office, The Scottish Parliament, 2005-2011; European Officer (secondee), Scotland Europa, 2009. Publications include:

Three-dimensionally mineralized insects and millipedes from the Tertiary of Riversleigh, Queensland, Australia, 1998 (Co-Author). Recreations: oil painting; ipad; art.

Duncan, John. Lord-Lieutenant, Ayrshire and Arran, since 2006; m., Jess; 1 s.; 1 d.; 1 stepdaughter. Joined Renfrew and Bute Constabulary as a Police Cadet in 1959, retiring as Deputy Chief Constable of Strathclyde Police in 2001.

Duncan, William, BSc (Hons), MCIPD, PhD. Chief Executive, Royal Society of Edinburgh, since 1985; Chief Executive, RSE Scotland Foundation, since 1996; Secretary to Trustees, Scottish Science Trust, 1997-98; Trustee of Glasgow Science Centre, since 2010; b. 6.12.50, Edinburgh. Educ. Linlithgow Academy; Edinburgh University. Greater London Council, 1975-78; Lothian Regional Council, 1978-85. Recreations: contemporary music; opera. Address: (b.) 22/26 George Street, Edinburgh EH2 2PQ; T.-0131-240 5000.

Duncan Millar, Ian, MBE, BScAg, MRICS, FRAgS. Chair, Moredun Foundation, since 2012; Farmer, since 1973; b. 1.6.51, Aberfeldy; m., Hazel; 1 s.; 1 d. Educ. Loretto School; Aberdeen University. Trainee Surveyor, Renton Finlayson, 1972-74; running family farms of Tirinie and Wester Tullich, since 1973; Chair, Highland Glen Producers, 1980-90 and 2000-09; Council of Scottish Agricultural Arbiters & Valuers, 2006-13, President, 2008-10; Agricultural Arbitrator, 2006 (ACIARB); Director: National Fallen Stock Cic, 2003-2012, Moredun Research Institute, 2003-2012. Fellow of Royal Agricultural Society, 2003; MBE, 2010; Member, Agricultural Rent Review Working Group, 2012. Recreations: ornithology & wildlife; curling. Address: Tirinie, Aberfeldy, Perthshire PH15 2ND; T.-01887 830394; e-mail: idmtirinie@aol.com

Dundas-Bekker, Althea Enid Philippa; b. 4.11.39, Gorebridge; m., Aedrian Ruprecht Bekker (deceased); 2 d. Business work abroad, in London, and with the National Trust for Scotland; inherited Arniston House, 1970, and restoring ever since. Recreations: Scottish history; Scottish songs; walking dogs. Address: (h.) Arniston House, Gorebridge, Midlothian EH23 4RY; T.-01875 830238.

Dundee, 12th Earl of (Alexander Henry Scrymgeour). Hereditary Royal Standard-Bearer for Scotland; b. 5.6.49; m.; 1 s.; 3 d. Educ. Eton; St. Andrews University. Address: Farm Office, Birkhill, Cupar, Fife.

Dundonald, 15th Earl of (Iain Alexander Douglas Blair); b. 17.2.61; m., Marie Beatrice Louise Russo (divorced, 2011); 2 s.; 1 d. Educ. Wellington College; Royal Agricultural College, Cirencester. Company Director; Hon. Chilean Consul to Scotland; Founder Director, Anglo Scientific and Associated Companies, since 2001. Interests: marine and rural environment; rural housing; Scottish affairs; innovation. Address: Lochnell Castle, Benderloch, Argyll.

Dunion, Kevin Harry, OBE, MA (Hons), MSc, Hon. LLD, FRSA. Honorary Professor and Executive Director, Centre for Freedom of Information, University of Dundee; Commissioner, Standards Commission for Scotland; Panel Member, International Finance Corporation Access to Information Appeals Panel; Board Member, Scottish Legal Complaints Commission; Member, The World Bank Access to Information Appeals Board; Visiting Professor, University of Northumbria; Chairperson, University of St Andrews Students Association Board, 2012-2014; Lord Rector, University of St Andrews, 2008-2011; Scottish Information Commissioner, 2003-2012; Chief Executive, Friends of the Earth Scotland, 1991-2003; Honorary Senior Research Fellow, University of Strathclyde, 1998-2004; b. 20.12.55, Bridge of Allan; m., Linda Dunion (qv); 2 s.; 1 step d. Educ. St Andrew's High School, Kirkcaldy; St Andrews University; Edinburgh University. HM Inspector

of Taxes, 1978-80; Administrator, Edinburgh University Students Association, 1980-84; Scottish Campaigns Manager, Oxfam, 1984-91. Editor, Radical Scotland, 1982-85; Chair: Scottish Education and Action for Development, 1990-92, Friends of the Earth International, 1996-99 (Treasurer, 1993-96); Member: Secretary of State's Advisory Group on Sustainable Development, 1996-99, Scottish Executive Ministerial Group on Sustainable Scotland, 1999-2001, Scottish Executive Cabinet Sub-Committee on Sustainable Scotland, 2001-03, Board, Scottish Natural Heritage, 2000-03, United Nations Environment and Development International Advisory Board, 1999-2002. Publications: Living in the Real World: An International Role for Scotland's Parliament, 1993; Troublemakers: the Struggle for Environmental Justice in Scotland, 2003; The Democracy of War, 2007; Freedom of Information in Scotland in Practice, 2011. Address: (h.) Third Acre, 2 Fairies Road, Perth PH1 1NB.
E-mail: kevindunion@hotmail.com

Dunlop, Alastair Barr, OBE (1989), FRICS. Deputy Chairman, Lothians Ethics of Medical Research Committee, 1984-2004; General Commissioner for Income Tax, 1991-2009; Member, NHS Complaints Panel; Chairman, Paintings in Hospitals Scotland, 1991-2004; b. 27.12.33, Calcutta; m., Catriona C.L.H. MacLaurin; 1 s.; 1 d. Educ. Radley. Member, British Schools Exploring Society Expedition, Arctic Norway, 1950. National Service, 1952-54 (active service, Malaya: 2nd Lt., 1st Bn., RWK); commerce, City of London, 1954-58; agricultural student, 1959-61; Land Agent, Inverness, 1962-71 (Partner, Bingham Hughes & Macpherson); Joint Founding Director, Martin Paterson Associates Ltd., 1971; ecology studies, Edinburgh University, 1973-74. Member, Lothian Health Board, 1983-91 (Vice-Chairman, 1989-91); Scottish Member, RICS Committee for Wilson Report on Financial Institutions, 1973-74; Chairman, Edinburgh and Borders Branch, RICS, 1977; Life Member, Institute of Directors; President and Past President, Edinburgh South Conservative Association; Chairman, South Edinburgh Conservative Association, 1980-84 and 1992-00, Central and South, Scottish Conservative and Unionist Association, 1985-88; Chairman, Edinburgh Branch, World Wildlife Fund, 1982-96; elected Member, Council, National Trust for Scotland, 1992-97. Recreations: golf; reading; fine arts. Address: (h.) 12B Corrennie Drive, Edinburgh EH10 6EG; T.-0131 447 5209.

Dunlop, Eileen. Biographer and Children's Writer; b. 13.10.38, Alloa; m., Antony Kamm (deceased). Educ. Alloa Academy; Moray House College. Publications: Robinsheugh, 1975; A Flute in Mayferry Street, 1976; Fox Farm, 1978; The Maze Stone, 1982 (SAC Book Award); Clementina, 1985 (SAC Book Award); The House on the Hill, 1987 (commended, Carnegie Medal); The Valley of Deer, 1989; Finn's Island, 1991; Tales of St. Columba, 1992; Green Willow's Secret, 1993; Finn's Roman Fort, 1994; Tales of St. Patrick, 1995; Castle Gryffe, 1995; Waters of Life, 1996; The Ghost by the Sea, 1997; Warrior's Bride, 1998; A Royal Ring of Gold, 1999; Ghoul's Den, 1999; The Haunting of Alice Fairlie, 2001; Nicholas Moonlight, 2002; Weerdwood, 2003; Queen Margaret of Scotland, 2005; Robert Louis Stevenson: The Travelling Mind, 2008; Co-author, with Antony Kamm: Scottish Verse to 1800, 1985; A Book of Old Edinburgh, 1983. Recreations: reading; gardening; theatre. Address: (h.) 46 Tarmangie Drive, Dollar FK14 7BP; T.-01259 742007.

Dunlop, Forbes. Chief Executive, Scottish Swimming, since 2013. Career: taught, coached and tutored swimming coach education courses and was part of the team that helped secure the National Swimming Academy at the University of Stirling as a location for one of British Swimming's Intensive Training Centres; held roles at sportscotland, since 2002, including Lead Manager, Achieving Excellence, 2004-09, then Partnership Manager, Achieving Excellence, 2002-04, then Head of Sporting Pathways until 2013. Served on the Board of Directors, recently as Chairman of the British Paralympic Performance Services in the lead into the 2012 Paralympic Games. Address: National Swimming Academy, University of Stirling, Stirling FK9 4LA; T.-01786 466520.

Dunlop, Juliet. Scottish freelance broadcast journalist; Columnist, The Scotsman. Career: Presenter for the BBC, appearing on the BBC News channel, BBC World News and BBC One daytime updates, 2008-2011; fronted the interactive news headlines for the BBC's red button news service; also presented daytime news updates on BBC One; co-anchored STV's overnight coverage of the Scottish Parliamentary elections in May 2011; presenter for STV in East Central Scotland, 2011-2013.

Dunlop, Sheriff William, LLB, QC. Sheriff of North Strathclyde, 1995-2014; Temporary Judge of the Court of Session and the High Court of Justiciary, since 2009; b. 7.3.44, Glasgow; m., Janina Marthe; 1 s.; 2 d. Educ. High School of Glasgow; Glasgow University. Solicitor, 1968-84; called to Scottish Bar, 1985; QC, 2011. Governor, The High School of Glasgow, 1999-2012; Member, Council, Sheriffs' Association, 2001-04; International Rugby Board Match Commissioner for European Cup and Six Nations matches, 1999-2012; Chairman, Scottish Rugby Union Championship Appeals Panel, since 2000. Address: (b.) Glasgow High Court, 1 Mart Street, Glasgow G1 5JT.

Dunn, Professor Douglas Eaglesham, OBE, BA, FRSL, Hon.LLD (Dundee, 1987), Hon.DLitt (Hull, 1995). Emeritus Professor, St Andrews University (Professor, School of English, 1991-2008, Head of School, 1994-99); formerly Director, St Andrews Scottish Studies Institute (1993-2008); b. 23.10.42, Inchinnan. Educ. Renfrew High School; Camphill Senior Secondary School, Paisley; Hull University. Books of poems: Terry Street, 1969, The Happier Life, 1972, Love or Nothing, 1974, Barbarians, 1979, St. Kilda's Parliament, 1981, Elegies, 1985, Selected Poems, 1986, Northlight, 1988, Dante's Drum-Kit, 1993, The Donkey's Ears, 2000, The Year's Afternoon, 2000; New Selected Poems, 2003; Secret Villages (short stories), 1985; Boyfriends and Girlfriends (short stories), 1995; Andromache (translation), 1990; Poll Tax: The Fiscal Fake, 1990; Editor: Choice of Lord Byron's Verse, 1974, The Poetry of Scotland, 1979, A Rumoured City: New Poets from Hull, 1982; Two Decades of Irish Writing: a Critical Survey, 1975; The Essential Browning, 1990; Scotland: an anthology, 1991; Faber Book of Twentieth Century Scottish Poetry, 1992; Oxford Book of Scottish Short Stories, 1995; 20th Century Scottish Poems, 2000; author of plays, and TV films using commentaries in verse. Gregory Award, 1968; Somerset Maugham Award, 1972; Geoffrey Faber Memorial Prize, 1975; Hawthornden Prize, 1982; Whitbread Award for Poetry and Whitbread Book of the Year Award, 1985; Cholmondeley Award, 1989; awarded the Queen's Gold Medal for Poetry, 2013. Honorary Visiting Professor, Dundee University, 1987; Fellow in Creative Writing, St. Andrews University, 1989-91; Honorary Fellow, Humberside College, 1987. Address (b.) School of English, St. Andrews University, St. Andrews KY16 9AL.

Dunnett, Major Graham Thomas, TD, JP. Lord Lieutenant of Caithness, 1995-2004; b. 8.3.29, Wick; m., Catherine Elizabeth Sinclair; 3 s. Educ. Wick High School; Archbishop Holgates Grammar School, York. 1st Seaforth Highlanders, Malaya, 1948-51; 11th

Seaforth Highlanders, Caithness, 1951-71; became 2nd Lieutenant, 1950, Lieut., 1952, Captain, 1956, Major and Coy. Comdr., 1964; Deputy Lieutenant of Caithness, 1975; Vice Lieutenant, 1986. Recreations: gardening; walking; country dancing. Address: Cathel Sheiling, Loch Calder, Thurso KW14 7YH; T.-01847 871220.

Dunnett, Margaret Annie Geddes. Lord Lieutenant of Caithness, since 2004.

Dunning, Claire, BA, DipM, MCIM, MCSD, FCIM, FRSA. Managing Director, Dunning Creating Sparks, since 1996; formerly President, Glasgow Chamber of Commerce; b. 26.08.65, Glasgow; m., Julian Westaby. Educ. Bearsden Academy, Glasgow; Grays School of Art, Aberdeen; Glasgow Central College of Commerce. Management Trainee, Retail Sector, 1988-90; Sales and Marketing in Design Sector, 1990-96. Board Director: The Chartered Institute of Marketing; Glasgow Chamber of Commerce, Scottish Chamber of Commerce. Recreations: the arts; hillwalking; gardening; animals. Address: (b.) Dunning Creating Sparks, 90 Mitchell Street, Glasgow G1 3NQ; T.-0845 055 1350; e-mail: claire@creatingsparks.com

Dupree, Professor Marguerite Wright, BA, MA, DPhil, FRHistS. Honorary Professor (School of Social and Political Sciences), University of Glasgow; b. 18.04.50, Boston, MA, USA; m., Richard Hughes Trainor; 1 s.; 1 d. Educ. Skyline High School, Oakland, California, USA; Mount Holyoke College; Princeton University; University of Oxford. Research Officer, Nuffield College, Oxford, 1977-78; Research Fellow, Emmanuel College, Cambridge, 1978-82; Fellow, Wolfson College, Cambridge, since 1982; University of Glasgow: Research Fellow, 1986-97, Senior Lecturer, 1997-2003, Reader, 2003-06. Publications: Lancashire and Whitehall: the diary of Sir Raymond Streat (Editor), 1987; Family Structure in the Staffordshire Potteries, 1840-1880, 1995; Medical Lives in the Age of Surgical Revolution (Co-Author), 2007. Recreation: tennis. Address: (b.) Centre for the History of Medicine, Department of Economic and Social History, University of Glasgow, Lilybank House, Bute Gardens, Glasgow G12 8RT; T.-0141-330-6072.
E-mail: marguerite.dupree@glasgow.ac.uk

Durie, Roy Ross, FRICS, MIMgt. Consultant, Ryden, Edinburgh; b. 11.5.48, Edinburgh; m., Dorothy; 1 s.; 3 d. Educ. Edinburgh Academy; Britannia Royal Naval College, Dartmouth. Royal Navy Officer (Lt. R.N.), 1966-72; joined Ryden, 1973. Director, Forth Sector Ltd.; Director, Social Firm Development Trust; Elder, St. Giles, Edinburgh. Recreations: walking; swimming; sailing; skiing; golf; rugby. Address: (b.) Ryden, 46 Castle Street, Edinburgh EH2 3BN; T.-0131-225 6612; mobile: 07836 347247; e-mail: roy.durie@ryden.co.uk

Durnin, John. Chief Executive, Pitlochry Festival Theatre, since 2007, Artistic Director, since 2003; b. 7.1.60, Kew, Surrey. Educ. St. Paul's School, London; New College, Oxford. Stage Manager, Forum Theatre, Wythenshawe, 1982-84; Assistant Director, Library Theatre Company, Manchester, 1984-87; Associate Director, Everyman Theatre, Cheltenham, 1987-89; Freelance Director, 1989-91; Artistic Director: Northcott Theatre, Exeter, 1991-98, Theatre Venture, London, 1999-2000, Gatton Community Theatre, Surrey, 2000-03. Recreations: photography; cycling; hill walking; music. Address: (b.) Pitlochry Festival Theatre, Port-na-Craig, Pitlochry PH16 5DR; T.-01796 484600; e-mail: admin@pitlochryfestivaltheatre.com

Durrani, Professor Tariq Salim, OBE, FRSE, FREng, FIEEE, FIET. Research Professor, Department of Electronic and Electrical Engineering, Strathclyde University, since 1982; b. 27.10.43, Amraoti, India; m., Clare Elizabeth; 1 s.; 2 d. Educ. Marie Colaco High School, Karachi; Engineering University, Dacca; Southampton University. Research Fellow, Southampton University, 1970-76; joined academic staff, Strathclyde University, 1976, Chairman, Department of Electronic and Electrical Engineering, 1986-90, Deputy Principal, 1990-91, and 2000-06; Director, Scottish Electronics Technology Group, since 1983; President, IEEE Signal Processing Society, 1993-94; Chair, IEEE Periodicals Council, 1996-98; President, IEEE Engineering Management Society, 2006-07; Vice-Chair, Technical Activities, IEEE Region 8, 2003-06; Director: Glasgow Chamber of Commerce, since 2003, Institute for System Level Integration, 2002-09; Vice President, Royal Society of Edinburgh, 2007-2010; Director, Equality Challenge Unit, 2008-2010; Member, Scottish Funding Council, 2005-09; Director, UK National Commission for UNESCO, since 2011; Vice President, IEEE, 2010-2011; Vice President (International), Royal Society of Edinburgh, since 2012. Publications: six books; over 350 technical research papers. Recreation: playing occasional golf badly. Address: (b.) Department of Electronic and Electrical Engineering, Strathclyde University, Glasgow; T.-0141-548 2540.

Durward, Professor Brian Ross, PhD, MSc, MCSP. Director of Educational Development, NHS Education for Scotland, since 2008; b. 6.10.54, Aberdeen; m., Anne; 1 s.; 1 d. Educ. Glasgow Royal Infirmary; School of Physiotherapy; Strathclyde University. Qualified as a Physiotherapist in 1977 and after working in a number of Glasgow hospitals became Head Physiotherapist at the Institute for Neurological Sciences at the Southern General Hospital, Glasgow. Became a Lecturer in Physiotherapy at Queen Margaret College, Edinburgh in 1985, then Head of Physiotherapy in 1999; Dean of School of Health and Social Care, Glasgow Caledonian University, until 2008. Published extensively in the area of Stroke Rehabilitation. Recreations: fishing; walking. Address: (b.) NHS Education for Scotland (NES), Thistle House, 91 Haymarket Terrace, Edinburgh EH12 5HE; T.-0131-313 8000; e-mail: brian.durward@nes.scot.nhs.uk

Durward, William Farquharson, MB, ChB, FRCP(Edin), FRCP(Glas). Medico-Legal Practice (Expert Witness); Consultant Neurologist, Greater Glasgow and Lanarkshire Health Boards, 1977-2009 (retired); Honorary Clinical Senior Lecturer in Neurology, Glasgow University, since 1978; Director, Cloburn Quarry Co. Ltd.; b. 16.9.44, Kilmarnock; m., Ann Roy Paterson; 1 s.; 1 d. Educ. Kilmarnock Academy; Glasgow University; Boston University. Employed by NHS, 1968-2009; specialist training grades, 1969-77. Recreations: walking; reading; railway conservation; Latin (language and literature); writing letters to newspapers. Address: (h.) Overdale, 20 South Erskine Park, Bearsden, Glasgow G61 4NA; T.-0141-942 3143; e-mail: w.durward@ntlworld.com

Duthie, Peter. Group Chief Executive, Scottish Exhibition + Conference Centre. Address: Exhibition Way, SECC, Glasgow G3 8YW.

Duthie, Sir Robert (Robin) Grieve, CBE (1978), CA, LLD, CBIM, FRSA, FRIAS, DTech (Napier). Chairman, RG Duthie & Co. Ltd., since 1984; b. 2.10.28, Greenock; m., Violetta Noel Maclean; 2 s.; 1 d. Educ. Greenock Academy. Apprentice Chartered Accountant, Thomson Jackson Gourlay and Taylor, CA, 1946-51; joined Blacks of Greenock, 1952; appointed Managing Director, 1962;

Chairman, Black & Edgington, 1972-83. Chairman, Inverkip Society, 1966; Director, Greenock Chamber of Commerce, 1966; Member, Clyde Port Authority, 1971-83 (Chairman, 1977-80); Director, Royal Bank of Scotland plc, 1978-98; Director, British Assets Trust plc, 1977-98; Chairman, Scottish Development Agency, 1979-88; Chairman, Britoil PLC, 1988-90; Vice Chairman, BP Advisory Board Scotland, 1990-2001; Chairman, Neill Clerk Group plc, 1993-98; Director, Greenock Provident Bank, 1969-75 (Chairman, 1975); Director, Devol Engineering Ltd., 1993-2003; Member, Scottish Telecommunications Board, 1972-77; Council Member, Institute of Chartered Accountants of Scotland, 1973-78; Member: East Kilbride Development Corporation, 1976-78, Strathclyde Region Local Valuation Appeal Panel, 1976-83; CBI Tax Liaison Officer for Scotland, 1976-79; Chairman, Made Up Textile Association of Great Britain, 1972; Member: British Institute of Management Scottish Committee, 1976, Glasgow and West of Scotland Committee, Scottish Council (Development and Industry), 1975-79; Chairman, Greenock Club, 1972; Captain, Greenock Cricket Club, 1960-61; Commissioner, Queen Victoria School, Dunblane, 1972-89; Commissioner, Scottish Congregational Ministers Pension Fund, 1973-2003; Member, Scottish Economic Council, 1980-96; Member of Council, Royal Caledonian Curling Club, 1984-88; Treasurer, Greenock West URC, since 1970. Awarded Honorary Degree of Doctor of Laws, Strathclyde University, 1984. Recreation: golf. Address: (h.) Fairhaven, 181 Finnart Street, Greenock, PA16 8JA; T.-01475 722642.

Duxbury, Professor Geoffrey, BSc, PhD, CPhys, FInstP, OSA, FRSE. Emeritus Professor of Physics, Strathclyde University; b. 6.11.42, Blackburn; m., Mary R.; 1 s.; 1 d. Educ. Cheadle Hulme School; Sheffield University. Junior Research Fellow, National Physical Laboratory, 1967-69; Research Assistant, Research Associate, Lecturer in Chemical Physics, Bristol University, 1970-80; Senior Lecturer/Reader, Strathclyde University, 1981-86. Marlow Medal, Faraday Division, Royal Society of Chemistry, 1975; elected to be a Senior Member of the Optical Society of America in 2012. Publication: Infrared Vibration-Rotation Spectroscopy: From Free Radicals to the Infrared Sky, 2000. Address: (b.) Department of Physics, SUPA, Strathclyde University, Glasgow, G4 0NG; T.-0141-548 3271; e-mail: g.duxbury@strath.ac.uk

Dye, Jonathan, BSc (Hons), CA. Head of Finance, Citizens Advice Scotland, since 2013, Head of Financial Governance, 2009-2011; Deputy Chairman, English-Speaking Union of the Commonwealth, since 2011; Chairman, English-Speaking Union, Scotland, 2003-09; Treasurer, Edinburgh City Youth Cafe, 1997-2003; Chartered Accountant, Pricewaterhousecoopers, 1993-2003, National Australia Bank, since 2003; Head of Sarbanes-Oxley Compliance, NAB UK, 2007-09; Governor, English Speaking Union of The Commonwealth, since 2003, Deputy Chairman, since 2011; Member, Security Board, Association of Payment and Clearing Services (APACS), 2004-07; b. 29.5.71, Dundee. Educ. Harris Academy, Dundee; St. Andrews University. Address: ESU, 23 Atholl Crescent, Edinburgh EH3 8HQ.

Dyer, Catherine. Chief Executive, Crown Office & Procurator Fiscal Service (COPFS) (acting as Civil Service Head of the Staff and Legal Advisor to the Lord Advocate on prosecution matters). Formerly Procurator Fiscal at Linlithgow (carried out a major management review of COPFS; joint author of the Pryce-Dyer report, published in Spring 2002, marking the beginning of major modernisation in COPFS); COPFS Head of Change Management from April 2002; led the team implementing the reforms recommended in the Pryce-Dyer report and in 2003 became the first woman to be appointed Procurator Fiscal for Glasgow. After 5 years leading the COPFS largest and busiest office, went on to set up and lead the COPFS Strategy & Delivery Division in May 2008. Solicitor with a private practice background as well as extensive experience as a prosecutor; first woman appointed Crown Agent for Scotland. Address: (b.) Crown Office, 25 Chambers Street, Edinburgh EH1 1LA.

Dysart, 13th Earl of (John Peter Grant of Rothiemurchus), DL. Landowner; b. 22.10.46, Rothiemurchus; m., Philippa; 1 s.; 2 d. Educ. Gordonstoun. Chairman and Director, Scot Trout Limited, 1989-95; Past Chairman, Highland Region, Forestry, Farming and Wildlife Advisory Group; Patron, Highland Hospice; Vice-President, Scottish Landowners' Federation, 1991-2004; Deputy Lieutenant, Districts of Lochaber, Inverness, Badenoch and Strathspey, 1986-2001; Member: Council, National Trust for Scotland, 1990-95, Native Woodlands Advisory Panel to the Forestry Commission, 1993-97, National Access Forum, 1993-99, Cairngorm Partnership, 1995-2003; Chairman, Tourism and Enivronment Task Force, 1995-98; President, Royal Zoological Society of Scotland, 1996-2006. Recreations: skiing; shooting. Address: (b.) Doune of Rothiemurchus, by Aviemore, Inverness-shire PH22 1QP.

E

Eadie, Jim. MSP (SNP), Edinburgh Southern, 2011-16; b. 10.2.68, Glasgow. Educ. Waverley Secondary School; University of Strathclyde. Prior to entering parliament, worked for the Royal College of Nursing and Scottish Television, before becoming head of the Scottish branch of the Association of the British Pharmaceutical Industry in 2002; started healthcare consulting business in 2007.

Eagles, Professor John Mortimer, MBChB, MPhil, FRCPsych. Retired Honorary Professor, Mental Health, Aberdeen University (2007-2011); Consultant Psychiatrist, Royal Cornhill Hospital, Aberdeen, 1985-2011; Honorary Reader, Mental Health, Aberdeen University, 2000-07; b. 21.10.52, Newport-on-Tay; m., Janette Isobel Rorke; 2 d. Educ. Bell-Baxter High School, Cupar; Aberdeen University; Edinburgh University. Resident House Officer posts, Aberdeen, 1977-78; Senior House Officer/Registrar in Psychiatry, Royal Edinburgh Hospital, 1978-82; Lecturer, Department of Mental Health, Aberdeen University, 1982-85; Honorary Senior Lecturer, Department of Mental Health, Aberdeen University, 1985-2000; Psychiatric Tutor for trainee psychiatrists, Aberdeen, 1987-92. Chairman, North-East Regional Postgraduate Medical Education Committee, 1990-95; former Chair, Scottish Division, Royal College of Psychiatrists Undergraduate Student Teaching and Recruitment Group. Recreations: cricket; golf; travel; reading; creative writing. Address: (h.) 41 Binghill Park, Milltimber, Aberdeenshire AB13 0EE.

Eassie, Rt. Hon. Lord (Ronald Mackay). Senator of the College of Justice, 1997-2015; formerly Chairman, the Scottish Law Commission; b. 1945; m.; 1 s. Educ. Berwickshire High School; St. Andrews University; Edinburgh University. Admitted, Faculty of Advocates, 1972; QC, 1986. Address: Parliament House, Parliament Square, Edinburgh EH1 1RQ.

Eastmond, Clifford John, BSc, MD, FRCP, FRCPE, MStJ. Retired Consultant Rheumatologist; previous appointments: Associate Medical Director and Consultant Rheumatologist, NHS Grampian (Clinical Director of Medicine, 1995-99); Clinical Senior Lecturer, Aberdeen University; private practice, Albyn Hospital, Aberdeen; b. 19.1.45, Ashton-under-Lyne; m., Margaret Wadsworth; 2 s.; 1 d. Educ. Audenshaw Grammar School; Edinburgh University. House Officer posts, Edinburgh, one year; moved to Liverpool for further training, subsequently to Rheumatism Unit, Leeds. Elder, Church of Scotland; Past President, Westhill and District Rotary Club; Paul Harris Fellow; Director, Seabank House, Aberdeen, since 2007; Member, Aberdeen and North East Committee of Order of St John. Clubs: Royal Northern and University Club, Aberdeen; The Cairngorm Club. Recreations: skiing; hillwalking; music; shooting. Address: (h.) The Rowans, Skene, Aberdeenshire AB32 6YP; T.-01224 790370.

Easton, Robin Gardner, OBE, MA, DUniv, DipEd. Rector, The High School of Glasgow, 1983-2004; b. 6.10.43, Glasgow; m., Eleanor Mary McIlroy; 1 s.; 1 d. Educ. Kelvinside Academy; Sedbergh School; Christ's College, Cambridge; Wadham College, Oxford. Teacher of French and German, Melville College, Edinburgh, 1966-72; Housemaster and Deputy Head, French Department, Daniel Stewart's and Melville College, 1972-78; Head, Modern Languages, George Watson's College, 1979-83. Elder, Church of Scotland; former Member, Glasgow Children's Panel, Glasgow University Court, Scripture Union Scotland

Board; Glasgow Street Pastor. Recreations: preaching; politics (Scottish Independence); history; hill walking. Address: (h.) 21 Stirling Drive, Bearsden, Glasgow G61 4NU; T.-0141-943 0368.

Ebsworth, J. Headteacher, Alloa Academy. Address: (b.) Bowhouse Road, Alloa, Clackmannanshire. FK10 1DN; T.-01259 214979; e-mail: alloa@edu.clacks.gov.uk

Eddie, Rev. Duncan Campbell, MA (Hons), BD (Hons). Minister, Holburn West, Aberdeen, since 1999; Moderator, Presbytery of Aberdeen, 2015-16; b. 17.2.63, Fraserburgh; m., Dr. Carol Buchanan; 2 s. Educ. Mackie Academy, Stonehaven; Aberdeen University; Edinburgh University. Assistant Minister, Edinburgh, 1990-91; Minister, Old Cumnock: Crichton West linked with St. Ninian's, 1992-99. Recreations: music; reading. Address: 31 Cranford Road, Aberdeen AB10 7NJ.
E-mail: minister@holburnwestchurch.org.uk

Edie, Cllr. Paul. Chair, Care Inspectorate, since 2013; Councillor, City of Edinburgh Council, since 1994. Educ. St Augustine's; Napier University. Career: Non Executive Director, NHS Lothian, 2007-2012; Convenor of Health, Social Care and Housing, City of Edinburgh Council, 2007-2012; Local Community Planning Engagement Officer, East Lothian Council, 2012-2013. Member of the Board, Edinburgh International Film Festival, 2001-2010; Audit Officer, Intellectual Property and Licensing Associate, Assay Technician, Scottish National Blood Transfusion Service, 1988-2007; Health Care Improvement Scotland Board, since 2013; Scottish Social Services Council Member, since 2013. Address: Care Inspectorate, Compass House, 11 Riverside Drive, Dundee DD1 4NY; T.-0845 600 9527; e-mail: enquiries@careinspectorate.com

Edington, Martin G. R., LLB, NP, WS. Sheriff: Linlithgow, since 2003, Livingston, since 2009; b. 28.10.55; m., Susan Jane Phillips; 2 s. Educ. Fettes College; Dundee University. Partner, Turnbull Simson and Sturrock WS, 1983-2001. Recreations: travelling; curling; rugby; cricket. Address: (b.) Civic Centre, Howden Road South, Livingston EH54 6FF.

Edward, Rt. Hon. Sir David Alexander Ogilvy, KCMG, QC, LLD, FRSE; b. 14.11.34, Perth; m., Elizabeth Young McSherry; 2 s.; 2 d. Educ. Sedbergh School; University College, Oxford; University of Edinburgh. National Service, RNVR, 1956-57 (Sub-Lt.); Advocate, 1962; Clerk, Faculty of Advocates, 1967-70, Treasurer, 1970-77; Queen's Counsel, 1974; President, Consultative Committee, Bars and Law Societies of the European Community, 1978-80; Salvesen Professor of European Institutions, University of Edinburgh, 1985-89; Professor Emeritus, 2008; Judge of the Court of First Instance of EC, 1989-92; Judge of the Court of Justice of EC, 1992-2004; Temporary Judge of the Court of Session, 2004-09. Member, Panel of Arbitrators, International Centre for Settlement of Investment Disputes, 1981-89, 2004-; Chairman, Continental Assets Trust plc, 1986-89; Director, Adam & Company plc, 1984-89; Director, Harris Tweed Association Ltd., 1985-89; Specialist Adviser to House of Lords Select Committee on the European Communities, 1985-88; Member: British Council Law Advisory Committee, 1974-88, Scotland Advisory Committee, 2008-2014; Trustee: National Library of Scotland, 1966-95, Industry and Parliament Trust, 1995-2013 (Vice President, since 2013), Carnegie Trust for the Universities of Scotland, 1995-2015 (Chairman, 2003-2015), Hopetoun Foundation, 1992-2010 (Chairman, Hopetoun Preservation Trust, 1988-92); Chairman, Scottish Council of Independent Schools 2005-2010; President,

Franco-Scottish Society, 1996-2015 (Hon. President, since 2015); President, Johnson Society, 1995-96; President, Edinburgh Sir Walter Scott Club, 2001-02; Patron, Scottish European Educational Trust, since 2014; Hon. Bencher, Gray's Inn, 1992; Hon. LLD: Edinburgh University, 1993, Aberdeen University, 1997, Napier University, 1998, Glasgow University, 2003, St Andrews University, 2015; Dr. h.c.: Universitat des Saarlandes, 2001, Westfalische Wilhelms-Universitat Munster, 2001; Doctor of the University (D Univ) honoris causa Surrey, 2003; Knight Commander of the Order of St Michael & St George, 2004 (CMG. 1981); Privy Counsellor, 2005; Officier de l'Ordre de la Légion d'Honneur and Chevalier de l'Ordre des Arts et des Lettres (France) 2012; Fellow of the Royal Society of Edinburgh, 1990 (Royal Medallist, 2005); Convener, International Committee, 2008-2013. Vice-President: British Institute of International and Comparative Law; Member: the Calman Commission on Scottish Devolution, 2008-09, the Commission on a Bill of Rights, 2011-12; Hon. President, Scottish Arbitration Centre, since 2011. Address: (h.) 32 Heriot Row, Edinburgh EH3 6ES; T.- 0131-225 7153; e-mail: david.edward@dileas.net

Edward, Ian, MA, LLB. Solicitor (retired); b. 3.9.35, Aberdeen; m., 1, Marguerite Anne Leiper (deceased); m., 2, Gudrun Clapier; 2 s.; 1 d. Educ. Robert Gordon's College, Aberdeen; University of Aberdeen; Fitzwilliam College, University of Cambridge. HM Colonial Service (District Officer, Northern Rhodesia), 1959-63; C. & P. H. Chalmers, Solicitors, Aberdeen (now Ledingham Chalmers): Legal Assistant, Partner, Senior Partner, Consultant, 1963-2000. Part-time Chairman of Employment Tribunals, 1997-2004; sometime historian, Royal Aberdeen Golf Club. Recreations: hill-walking; golfing; gardening. Address: (h.) 23 St. Fillan's Terrace, Edinburgh EH10 5PJ; T.-0131-447 8353.

Edward, John David, MA (Hons) St Andrews, MPhil (Glasgow). Director/Chief Executive of Scottish Council of Independent Schools, since 2010; b. 22.09.68, Edinburgh; m., Alexandra Angulo Noriega; 1 s.; 1 d. Educ. The Edinburgh Academy; University of St Andrews; University of Glasgow; Università per Stranieri, Siena. European Community Humanitarian Office (ECHO), 1994-95; The European Policy Centre, Brussels, 1995-96; EU Policy Manager, Scotland Europa, Brussels, 1996-2001; Parliamentary Manager, Scottish Enterprise, 2002-03; Head of European Parliament Office in Scotland, Edinburgh, 2003-09. Member: The Steel Commission, 2003-06; Campbell Commission on Home and Community Rule, 2011-2012; Trustee, Scottish European Educational Trust, since 2011; Salzburg Global Fellowship; Scottish Qualifications Authority, Advisory Council. Recreations: Scottish and mini rugby; running; matters European and Colombian. Address: (b.) The Scottish Council of Independent Schools (SCIS), 61 Dublin Street, Edinburgh EH3 6NL; T.-0131 556 2316; e-mail: john@scis.org.uk

Edwards, George Lowden; b. 6.2.39, Kirriemuir; m., Sylvia Izatt; 1 d. Educ. Webster's Seminary, Kirriemuir; Dundee Institute of Technology. Production Engineer, Burroughs Machines Ltd., Cumbernauld, 1961-64; Development Division, Scottish Council (Development and Industry), Edinburgh, 1964-67; General Manager, GR Designs Ltd., Perth, 1967-68; London Director, Scottish Council (Development and Industry), 1968-78; Manager, Public Affairs Scotland, Conoco (UK) Ltd., Aberdeen, 1978-83; Manager, Public Affairs, Conoco (UK) Ltd., London, 1983-85; Head of Corporate Affairs, Clydesdale Bank PLC, 1988-96; Chairman Scotland, GPC International, 1997-2002; Chairman, Association of Professional Political Consultants in Scotland, 1998-2002. Honorary Fellow, University of Abertay, Dundee.

Recreations: music; travel; food and wine. Address: (h.) 11 Almond Court East, Braehead Park, Edinburgh EH4 6AZ; e-mail: george@georgeedwards.org

Edwards, Kevin John, MA, PhD, DSc, FRGS, CGeog, FSA, FSAScot, FRSE, MAE. Professor in Physical Geography, University of Aberdeen, since 2000, Adjunct Chair in Archaeology, since 2007; Adjunct Professor, Graduate School in Anthropology, City University of New York, since 2002; Life Member, Clare Hall, University of Cambridge, since 2012; b. 18.9.49, Dartford; 2 s. Educ. Northfleet Boys' School; Gravesend Grammar School; St. Andrews University; Aberdeen University. Tutorial Fellow in Geography, University of Aberdeen, 1972-75; Lecturer in Environmental Reconstruction and Research Member, Palaeoecology Centre, Queen's University of Belfast, 1975-80; University of Birmingham: Lecturer in Biogeography, 1980-90, Senior Lecturer in Geography, 1990-92, Reader in Palaeoecology, 1992-94; Honorary Research Fellow, Limnological Research Center, University of Minnesota, 1983; Professor of Palaeoecology, Department of Archaeology and Prehistory, University of Sheffield, 1994-2000 (Head of Department, 1996-99); Visiting Researcher, Department of Geography and Geology, University of Copenhagen, 2007-09; Visiting Fellow, Clare Hall and Visiting Scholar, McDonald Institute for Archaeological Research, University of Cambridge, 2011-2012; Christensen Fellow, St Catherine's College, University of Oxford, 2012; 133rd Rhind Lecturer, Society of Antiquaries of Scotland/Royal Society of Edinburgh, 2012. Member, NERC Radiocarbon Dating Laboratory Committees, 1995-2000; Chairman, Oxford University Radiocarbon Accelerator Unit Users' Committee, 1995-2000; Deputy Chairman, SCAPE Trust, 2001-04; Panel Member for Geography, Environmental Studies and Archaeology, UK Research Excellence Framework (REF2014). Publications: Quaternary History of Ireland (Co-Editor), 1985; Scotland: Environment and Archaeology 8000BC-AD1000 (Co-Editor), 1997; Holocene Environments of Prehistoric Britain (Co-Editor), 1999; numerous articles in geography, archaeology, botany and quaternary science. Recreations: reading; family history. Address: (b.) Department of Geography and Environment, University of Aberdeen, Elphinstone Road, Aberdeen AB24 3UF; T.-01224 272346; e-mail: kevin.edwards@abdn.ac.uk

Edwards, Rob (Robert Philip), MA. Environment Editor, Sunday Herald, since 1999; Consultant, New Scientist, since 1994; Freelance Journalist, since 1980; Television Producer, since 1990; Founder Member and Chair, The Ferret (www.theferret.scot), since 2015; b. 13.10.53, Liverpool; m., Fiona Grant Riddoch; 2 d. Educ. Watford Boys Grammar School; Jesus College, University of Cambridge. Organiser, Scottish Campaign to Resist the Atomic Menace, 1977-78; Campaigns Organiser, Shelter (Scotland), 1978-80; Research Assistant to Robin Cook, 1980-83; Freelance Journalist, writing for Social Work Today, The Scotsman, New Statesman, 1980-89; Environment Editor, Scotland on Sunday, 1989-94; Correspondent, The Guardian and Columnist, Edinburgh Evening News, 1989-94; Freelance Journalist, writing for New Scientist, The Sunday Herald, The Guardian etc., since 1994; various media awards. Publications: Co-author of three books, including Still Fighting for Gemma, 1995. Recreations: music; opera; mountains. Address: 53 Nile Grove, Edinburgh EH10 4RE; T.-0131-447 2796; e-mail: rob.edwards@blueyonder.co.uk
Website: www.robedwards.com

Eglinton and Winton, Earl of (Archibald George Montgomerie). Chairman, Edinburgh Investment Trust, 1994-2003. Grieveson Grant, 1957-72 (Partner, from 1964); Gerrard & National, 1972-92 (Managing

Director, from 1972, Deputy Chairman, from 1980); Chairman, Gerrard Vivian Gray, 1989-95. Address: (h.) Balhomie, Cargill, Perth PH2 6DS; T.-01250 883222.

Eilbeck, Professor John Christopher, BA, PhD, FRSE. Professor Emeritus, Department of Mathematics, Heriot-Watt University, since 2010 (Head of Department, 1984-89, Dean of Science, 1998-2001); b. 8.4.45, Whitehaven; 3 s. Educ. Whitehaven Grammar School; Queen's College, Oxford; Lancaster University. Royal Society European Fellow, ICTP, Trieste, 1969-70; Research Assistant, Department of Mathematics, UMIST, Manchester, 1970-73; Heriot-Watt University: Lecturer, Department of Mathematics, 1973-80, Senior Lecturer, 1980-85, Reader, 1985-86; Long-term Visiting Fellow, Center for Nonlinear Studies, Los Alamos National Laboratory, New Mexico, 1983-84; Visiting Fellow, Corpus Christi College, Cambridge, 2001. Publications: Rock Climbing in the Lake District (Co-author), 1975; Solitons and Nonlinear Wave Equations (Co-author), 1982. Recreation: mountaineering. Address: (b.) Department of Mathematics, Heriot-Watt University, Riccarton, Edinburgh EH14 4AS; T.-0131-451 3220.

Elder, Dorothy-Grace. MSP, Glasgow, 1999-2003 (Independent, formerly SNP MSP); newspaper columnist; television scriptwriter and producer (documentaries); Hon. Professor, The Robert Gordon University, Aberdeen, since 2006; m., George Welsh; 1 s.; 2 d. D.C. Thomson newspapers; Glasgow Herald as reporter, investigations writer, news feature writer, leader writer; TV and radio news, BBC Scotland; feature writer and columnist, Scottish Daily News Co-operative; feature writer and columnist, Sunday Mail; productions for Scotland and the network, BBC and Scottish TV. Political Columnist, Scottish Daily Express, since 2002. Honorary President, Glasgow NE Multiple Sclerosis Society; Honorary Patron, No Panic; Oliver Award winning columnist, 1995-96; British Reporter of the Year (Investigations), UK Press Awards, 1996-97; citation, Humanitarian Aid Work, City of Pushkin, Russia, 1998, 1999. E-mail: dg.elder@ntlworld.com

Elgin, 11th Earl of, and Kincardine, 15th Earl of, (Andrew Douglas Alexander Thomas Bruce), KT (1981), DL, JP; 37th Chief of the Name of Bruce; Captain, Queen's Bodyguard for Scotland (Royal Company of Archers); b. 17.2.24; m., Victoria Usher; 3 s.; 2 d. Educ. Eton; Balliol College, Oxford. Lord Lieutenant of Fife, 1987-99; President, Scottish Amicable Life Assurance Society, 1975-94; Chairman, National Savings Committee for Scotland, 1972-78; Member, Scottish Postal Board, 1980-96; Lord High Commissioner, General Assembly, Church of Scotland, 1980-81; Grand Master Mason of Scotland, 1961-65; President, Royal Caledonian Curling Club, 1968-69; President, Boys Brigade (UK), 1963-85; Hon. LLD, Dundee, 1977, Glasgow, 1983. Address: (h.) Broomhall, Dunfermline KY11 3DU; T.-01383 872222; e-mail: elginkincardine@gmail.com

Eliott of Redheugh, Margaret Frances Boswell. Chief of Clan Elliot; Chairman, Elliot Clan Society and Sir Arthur Eliott Memorial Trust; Deputy Lieutenant of Roxburgh, Ettrick & Lauderdale; Member, Standing Council of Scottish Chiefs; Trustee, Boswell Museum & Mausoleum Trust, Boswell Book Festival and the Roxburgh Landward Benevolent Trust; b. 13.11.48; m., 1, Anthony Vaughan-Arbuckle (deceased); 1 s.; 1 d.; 2, Christopher Powell Wilkins. Educ. Hatherop Castle School. Address: Redheugh, Newcastleton, Roxburghshire.

Ellery, Derek George McNicoll, LLB (Hons), DipLP. Partner, DWF LLP; b. 09.05.61, Irvine; m., Linda; 1 s.; 1 d. Educ. Kilmarnock Grammar; Grange Academy, Kilmarnock; Glasgow University. Solicitor, Wilde Sapte, London, 1985-87; Associate, Ashurst Morris Crisp, London, 1987-93; Associate, Semple Fraser, Glasgow,

1993-96, Partner, 1996-97; Partner, Biggart Baillie, Glasgow, since 1997. Company Secretary, Glasgow Opportunities; Trustee, St. Andrew's First Aid. Recreations: golf; cycling. Address: (h.) Brannochlie, 2 Burnside Road, Whitecraigs, Glasgow G46 6TT; T.-0141 639 0288; e-mail: derekgmellery@googlemail.com

Ellington, Marc Floyd, DL. Baron of Towie Barclay; Laird of Gardenstown and Crovie; Deputy Lieutenant, Aberdeenshire; b. 16.12.45; m., Karen Leigh; 2 d. Non Executive Director, Historic Scotland; Trustee, National Galleries of Scotland; Vice-President, Buchan Heritage Society; Partner, Heritage Press (Scotland), Soundcraft Audio; Director: Gardenstown Estates Ltd., Heritage Sound Recordings; Board Member, The Heritage Lottery Fund Scotland, 1998-2004; Chairman, Grampian Region Tourism Task Force, 1992-96; Board Member, British Heritage Commission, 1998-2003; Board Member, Scottish Enterprise Grampian, 1992-96; Member, Historic Buildings Council for Scotland, 1980-98; Communications, Heritage and Tourism Consultant. Recipient: Saltire Award; Civic Trust Award; European Architectural Heritage Award; Officer the Order of St John; Honorary Fellow of the Royal Incorporation of Architects Scotland (2014); FSA. Recreations: sailing; historic architecture; art collecting; music. Address: Towie Barclay Castle, Auchterless, Turriff, Aberdeenshire AB53 8EP; T.-01888 511347.

Elliot, Alison Janet, OBE, MA, MSc, PhD, LLD, DD, DUniv, FRCPEdin, FRSE. Associate Director, Centre for Theology and Public Issues, University of Edinburgh; b. 27.11.48, Edinburgh; m., John Christian Elliot; 1 s.; 1 d. Educ. Bathgate Academy; Edinburgh University; Sussex University. Research Associate, Department of Linguistics, Edinburgh University, 1973-74; Lecturer in Psychology, Lancaster University, 1974-76, Edinburgh University, 1977-85; Convener, Church and Nation Committee, Church of Scotland, 1996-2000; Moderator of the General Assembly of the Church of Scotland, 2004-05; Honorary Fellow, New College, University of Edinburgh; Convener, Scottish Council for Voluntary Organisations (SCVO), 2007-2013. Publications: Child Language, 1981; The Miraculous Everyday, 2005. Recreations: music; cookery. Address: (b.) CTPI, New College, Mound Place, Edinburgh EH1 2LX; e-mail: Alison.Elliot@ed.ac.uk

Elliot, Frances Mary, MB, ChB, MBA, MRCGP. Medical Director, NHS Fife; Deputy Chief Medical Officer, Scottish Government, 2013-2014; Chief Executive, Healthcare Improvement Scotland, 2009-2013; Medical Director, NHS Fife, 2004-09; Non-executive Member, Board, HEBS, 1996-2003; Principal in general practice, 1987-98; b. 13.4.60, Edinburgh; m., John Gordon Elliot. Educ. St. Columba's High School, Dunfermline; Glasgow University; Stirling University. Recreations: walking; photography; bird watching. Address: (b.) NHS Fife, Hayfield House, Hayfield Road, Kirkcaldy, Fife KY2 5AH.

Elliot, Sir Gerald Henry; b. 24.12.23, Edinburgh; m., Margaret Ruth Whale; 2 s.; 1 d. Educ. Marlborough College; New College, Oxford. Indian Army, 1942-46; Christian Salvesen, 1948-88. Chairman: Christian Salvesen PLC, 1981-88, Scottish Provident Institution, 1983-89, Scottish Arts Council, 1980-86, Prince's Scottish Youth Business Trust, 1987-94; Vice Chairman, Scottish Business in the Community, 1987-89; Trustee, National Museums of Scotland, 1987-91; Member of Court, Edinburgh University, 1984-93; Chairman: Scottish Unit Managers Ltd., 1984-88, Martin Currie Unit Trusts, 1988-90; Chairman, Forth Ports Authority, 1973-79; Chairman, Scottish Opera, 1987-92; Chairman of Trustees, David Hume Institute, 1985-95; Chairman, Institute of Directors,

Scottish Division, 1989-92; Trustee and Director, Edinburgh Festival Theatre, 1995-98; Member, Court of Regents, Royal College of Surgeons, 1990-99; President, UN50 Scotland, 1994-95; Fellow, Royal Society of Edinburgh, since 1977; Honorary Consul for Finland in Edinburgh and Leith, 1957-89; Hon. d.h.c., Edinburgh University, 1989; Hon. LLD, Aberdeen University, 1991; KT (1986); Honorary Fellow, New College, Oxford. Address: (b.) 39 Inverleith Place, Edinburgh EH3 5QD; T.-0131-552 6208.

Elliott, Professor Robert F., BA (Oxon), MA, FRSE. Professor of Economics, Aberdeen University (Director, Health Economics Research Unit, 2001-2012); b. Thurlow, Suffolk; m., Susan Elliott Gutteridge; 1 s. Educ. Haverhill Secondary Modern School, Suffolk; Ruskin College and Balliol College, Oxford; Leeds University. Joined Aberdeen University, 1973, as Research Fellow, then Lecturer; Director, Scottish Doctoral Programme in Economics, 1989-99; Member, Training Board, ESRC, 1995-99; Chair of Reviews for, and Consultant to, many public and private sector organisations, including Megaw Committee of Inquiry into Civil Service Pay, the EEC Commission, HM Treasury OECD, HIDB, DETR, and McCrone Committee, Scottish Executive; President, Scottish Economic Society, 2002-05; Commissioner, Low Pay Commission, 2007-2015. Publications: books on Pay in the Public Sector, 1981; Incomes Policies, Inflation and Relative Pay, 1981; Incomes Policy, 1981; Unemployment and Labour Market Efficiency, 1989; Labour Market Analysis, 1990; Public Sector Pay in the EU, 1999; Advances in Health Economics, 2003; Decentralised Pay Setting, 2003. Recreations: music; reading; hill-walking; golf. Address: (h.) 11 Richmondhill Place, Aberdeen AB15 5EN; T.-01224 314901.

Ellis, Tim. Chief Executive, Keeper and Registrar General, National Records of Scotland, since 2013. Career: Head of FOI Unit, Scottish Executive, 2003-06; Senior Manager, Communities Scotland, 2006-08; Deputy Director, Housing Investment, The Scottish Government, 2008-2010; Head of Cabinet and Corporate Secretariat, The Scottish Government, 2011-13. Address: General Register House, 2 Princes Street, Edinburgh EH1 3YY; T.-0131 535 1314.

Elphinstone, 19th Lord (Alexander Mountstuart Elphinstone); b. 15.4.80; m., Nicola Hall; 3 c. Educ. Belhaven Hill School; Eton College; Newcastle University; SOAS, University of London. Succeeded to title, 1994.

Elvidge, Sir John William, KCB, FRSE, BA. Chairman, Edinburgh Airport Limited, since 2012; Permanent Secretary, Scottish Government, 2003-2010; b. 9.2.51, London; m., Maureen Margaret Ann McGinn. Educ. Sir George Monoux School; St Catherine's College, Oxford. Scottish Office, 1973-88; Director of Implementation, Scottish Homes, 1988-89; Scottish Office, 1989-98, latterly as Head of Economic Infrastructure Group, Scottish Office Development Department; Cabinet Office, 1998-99 (Deputy Head of Economic and Domestic Secretariat); Head, Scottish Executive Education Department, 1999-2002; Head, Scottish Executive Finance and Central Services Department, 2002-03. Recreations: reading; theatre; music; film; painting; food; wine; sport; walking. Address: Edinburgh Airport Limited, Edinburgh EH12 9DN; T.-0844 448 8833.

Emberson, Eleanor Avril, BSc, PhD. Chief Executive, Revenue Scotland, since 2015; Head of Revenue Scotland, Scottish Government, 2012-15; Director of Financial Strategy, Scottish Government, 2013-14; Chief Executive, Scottish Court Service, 2004-2012; Head of New Educational Developments Division, Scottish Executive Education Department, 2001-04; b. 14.9.67, Irvine. Educ. Arran High School; St Andrews University. Senior Assistant Statistician, Retail Prices Index, Central Statistical Office, 1993-95; Head, GES Data Unit, HM Treasury, 1995-98; Finance Co-ordinaton Team Leader, Scottish Executive Finance, 1998-99; Head of Curriculum, International and Information Technology Division, Scottish Executive Education Department, 1999-2001. Address: (b.) Victoria Quay, Edinburgh EH6 6QQ; T.-0131 244 7500.

Emberson, Martyn, QFSM, BA (Hons). HM Chief Inspector, Fire Service, Scottish Government, since 2016. Educ. Teesside University; University of Lincoln. Merchant Navy Deck Officer, Bank Line, 1979-83; Assistant Terminal Manager, United States Lines, 1983-84; Fire Officer, Cleveland Fire Brigade, 1984-2003; Nottingham Fire and Rescue Service: Deputy Chief Fire Officer, 2003-06, Chief Fire Officer, 2006-2015. Awarded the Queen's Fire Service Medal for services to the Fire and Rescue Service in 2013. Address: HM Fire Service Inspectorate, St Andrew's House, Regent Road, Edinburgh EH1 3DG.

Emery, Vic. Chair, Zero Waste Scotland, since 2014. Educ. University of Portsmouth. Managing Director, BAE Systems Naval Warship Division, 1997-2008; Non-Executive Board Member, Scottish Enterprise Regional Advisory Board, 2008-2010; Chairman, New Campus Glasgow Project, 2009-2010; Convener, Scottish Police Services Authority, 2009-2012; Chairman of tie and TEL, Edinburgh Trams, 2010-2012; President, Glasgow Chamber of Commerce, 2013-15; Chair, Scottish Police Authority, 2012-15. Trustee, Scottish Maritime Museum, since 2007. Address: Zero Waste Scotland, Ground Floor, Moray House, Forthside Way, Stirling FK8 1QZ; T.-01786 433930.

Emslie, Rt. Hon. Lord; Hon. (George) Nigel (Hannington) Emslie. Senator of the College of Justice in Scotland, 2001-2012 (retired); b. 17.4.47. Admitted, Faculty of Advocates, 1972; QC (Scotland), 1986; Dean, Faculty of Advocates, 1997-2001.

Emslie, Donald Gordon. Executive Chairman, Castle Hotel Management Company; Chairman, Thorpe Hall Leisure Ltd; Chief Executive, SMG plc, July 2006-March 2007; Chief Executive, SMG Television, 1999-July 2006; Managing Director, Broadcasting, Scottish TV, 1997-99; b. 8.5.57; m., Sarah; 2 d. Appointed to SMG plc Board, 1999; Ex Chairman, ITV Council; Ex Chairman, The Royal Lyceum Theatre Company; Ex Chairman, Royal Zoological Society Scotland; Non Executive Director: Scottish Rugby plc, 2008-2012, Scottish Water, since 2008; former Director, joint board, Scottish Arts Council and Scottish Screen Skillset UK; Fellow, Royal Television Society; Fellow, Royal Society of Arts; awarded Honorary Doctorate, DBA, Robert Gordon University Aberdeen, 2010. Address: (b.) 32 Drumsheugh Gardens, Edinburgh EH3 7RN.

Entwistle, Raymond Marvin, FCIB, FCIBS. Chairman, Scoban plc (now Hampden & Co. plc), since 2010; former Chairman, Adam & Company Group (2005-10); Managing Director, Adam & Company Group plc, 1993-2004; b. 12.6.44, Croydon; m., Barbara Joan Hennessy; 2 s.; 1 d. Educ. John Ruskin Grammar School. Several managerial appointments with Lloyds Bank. Governor, Edinburgh College of Art, 1989-99; Chairman, Fruit Market Gallery,

Edinburgh, 1988-2000; Non-executive Director: John Davidson (Holdings) Ltd, 1992-96, JW International Plc., 1995-96, Dunedin Smaller Companies Investment Trust PLC, 1998-2014, I & H Brown Ltd, since 2003; Chairman, Scottish Civic Trust, 2003-2012; Trustee, Victim Support Scotland Campaign Board, since 2008; Trustee, RHS Preservation Trust, since 2015. Recreations: golf; shooting; fishing; antiques.

Erdal, David Edward, MA, MBA, PhD. Trustee, Russell Trust (Chairman, 1985-96); b. 29.3.48, Umtali, Zimbabwe; 1 s.; 1 d. Educ. Glenalmond; Brasenose College, Oxford; Harvard Business School; University of St. Andrews. English Language Teacher, London, 1972-74; Tianjin Foreign Language Institute, People's Republic of China, 1974-76; Tullis Russell Group, 1977-2004 (Director, 1981-2004; Chairman, 1985-96); Baxi Partnership Ltd, 1987-2012 (Director, 1994-2012, Chairman, 1994-99); Childbase CASP Trust, 2007-2013 (Chairman, 2007-2013); Chancellor's Assessor, University of St Andrews, 2010-14. Fellow, Royal Society of Arts. Publication: 'Local Heroes: how Loch Fyne Oysters embraced employee ownership and business success', 2008; 'Beyond the Corporation: Humanity Working', 2011. Recreations: sailing; reading; coastal rowing. Address: (h.) 11 High Street West, Anstruther KY10 3DJ; e-mail: david@erdal.org.uk Web: http://daviderdal.net

Erroll, 24th Earl of (Merlin Sereld Victor Gilbert Hay). Hereditary Lord High Constable of Scotland; Chief of Scottish Clan Hay; b. 20.4.48; m.; 2 s.; 2 d. Educ. Eton; Trinity College, Cambridge. Succeeded to title, 1978.

Erskine, Professor Andrew William, MA, DPhil (Oxon). Professor of Ancient History, University of Edinburgh, since 2007; m., Michelle; 1 s. Educ. Southend High School, Southend-on-Sea; New College, Oxford. Lecturer, University of Birmingham, 1986-89; University of Wales Fellow, 1989-90; Lecturer, University College Dublin, 1990-2002; Alexander Von Humboldt Fellow, University of Munich, 1997-98; Professor of Classics, National University of Ireland Galway, 2002-04; Reader, University of Edinburgh, 2005-07; Leverhulme Research Fellow, 2008-09. Publications: The Hellenistic Stoa: Political Thought and Action, 1990; Troy Between Greece and Rome, 2001; A Companion to the Hellenistic World, 2003; A Companion to Ancient History, 2009; Roman Imperialism, 2010; Form and Function in Roman Oratory, 2010 (Co Author); The Gods of Greece, 2010 (Co Author); Creating a Hellenistic World, 2011 (Co Author); Encyclopedia of Ancient History, 2013 (General Editor). Address: (b.) School of History, Classics and Archaeology, Teviot Place, University of Edinburgh EH8 9AG; e-mail: andrew.erskine@ed.ac.uk

Erskine, Donald Seymour, DL, FRICS; b. 28.5.25, London; m., Catharine Annandale McLelland; 1 s. 4 d. Educ. Wellington College. RA (Airborne), 1943-47 (Captain); Pupil, Drumlanrig Estate, 1947-49; Factor, Country Gentlemen's Association, Edinburgh, 1950-55; Factor to Mr A.L.P.F. Wallace, 1955-61; Factor and Director of Estates, National Trust for Scotland, 1961-89; Member, Queen's Bodyguard for Scotland (Royal Company of Archers); Deputy Lieutenant, Perth and Kinross; General Trustee, Church of Scotland, 1989-2000. Recreations: golf; shooting; singing. Address: (h.) Cleish House, Cleish, Kinrossshire KY13 0LR; T.-01577 850232.

Evans, Alan Thomson, BMedBiol, MD, FRCPath. Consultant and Honorary Senior Lecturer in Pathology, since 1993; b. 20.9.62, Buckhaven; m., Caroline; 1 s.; 1 d. Educ. Buckhaven High School; University of Aberdeen. House Officer, Aberdeen Royal Infirmary, 1986-87; Senior House Officer in Pathology, Ninewells Hospital, Dundee, 1987-88; Lecturer in Pathology, University of Dundee, 1988-90; Senior Registrar in Pathology, Ninewells Hospital, Dundee, 1990-93. Chairman, Panel of Examiners in Dermatopathology, Royal College of Pathologists, 2008-2013; Chair, Specialist Advisory Committee Dermatopathology, Royal College of Pathologists. Recreations: gardening; architectural history; opera. Address: Department of Pathology, Ninewells Hospital and Medical School, Dundee DD1 9SY; T.-01382 632548; e-mail: alan.evans@nhs.net

Evans, Professor Andrew Jonathan, MB, ChB, MRCP, FRCR. Professor of Breast Imaging, Dundee University, since 2009; b. 2.6.61, Birmingham; m., Rosemary Smith; 2 s. Educ. Ysgol Bryn Elian; Birmingham University. Medical SHO, Stafford, 1985-87; Radiology Registrar, Nottingham, 1987-92; Consultant Breast Radiologist, Nottingham, 1992-2009; Director, Nottingham International Breast Education Centre, 2006-09. Chairman, Symposium Mammographicum meetings, 2002 and 2008; Vice Chairman, RCR Breast Group, since 2009. Publications: author of 119 peer reviewed scientific papers; 4 books and 19 book chapters. Recreations: plays French horn; composes classical music. Address: (b.) Mailbox 4, Ninewells Hospital and Medical School, Dundee DD1 9SY; T.-01382 632196; e-mail: a.z.evans@dundee.ac.uk

Evans, Professor Brian Mark, BSc, Dip URP, MSc, MRTPI, FCSD, MIoD, AoU. Professor of Urbanism and Landscape, Glasgow School of Art, since 2015; Head of Urbanism, Mackintosh School of Architecture, Glasgow School of Art, since 2010; Partner, Gillespies, Landscape Architects & Urban Designers, 1989-2015; Board Member: the Academy of Urbanism, 2005-2013, the Nordic Urban Design Association, since 2005; Co Chair, Sheffield Sustainable Development & Design Panel, since 2009; Deputy Chair, Architecture and Design Scotland, 2004-2010; Enabler, Commission for the Built Environment, London, 2003-08; b. 1953, St. Andrews; m., Susan Ann Jones. Educ. Linlithgow Academy; University of Edinburgh; University of Strathclyde. Artistic Professor, Urban Design & Planning, School of Architecture, Chalmers University, Gothenburg, Sweden, 1998-2004; Honorary Professor, Glasgow School of Art, 2008-2012. Publications: Urban Identity (Learning from Place 2, 2011, editor); Space! Place! Life! (Learning from Place 1, 2011, editor); Making Cities Work (Wylie 2004 - urban design advisor); Tomorrow's Architectural Heritage, 1991 (joint author); publications and articles in English, Swedish, Italian, Dutch on urban design and landscape planning. Address: (b.) The Glasgow School of Art, 167 Renfrew Street, Glasgow G3 6RQ; T.-0141 353 4500.

Evans, David Pugh, ARCA, RSA, RSW; paints in Edinburgh; b. 20.11.42, Gwent. Educ. Newbridge Grammar School; Newport College of Art; Royal College of Art. Lecturer, Edinburgh College of Art, 1965-68; Fine Art Fellow, York University, 1968-69; Lecturer, Edinburgh College of Art, 1969-2000; travelled and painted throughout USA, 1975; solo exhibitions: Marjorie Parr Gallery, London; Mercury Gallery, London; York University; Fruitmarket Gallery, Edinburgh; Open Eye Gallery, Edinburgh; Gilbert Parr Gallery, London. Address: (h.) 17 Inverleith Gardens, Edinburgh EH3 5PS; T.-0131-552 2329.

Evans, Professor George William, BA (Oxon), BA, MA, PhD (Berkeley). Professor, School of Economics and Finance, University of St Andrews, since 2007; Professor,

Economics Department, University of Oregon, USA, since 1994; b. 3.4.49, New York; m., Pauline Andrews; 2 s. Educ. University of California, Berkeley; Balliol College, Oxford University. Lecturer, Economics, University of Stirling, 1978-81; Assistant Professor, Stanford University, 1981-87; Lecturer, Senior Lecturer, Reader, Economics, London School of Economics, 1987-92; Professor, Economics, University of Edinburgh, 1993-94. Publications: over 70 papers published in refereed journals; book: Learning and Expectations in Macroeconomics (Co-Author), 2001. Address: (b.) School of Economics and Finance, Castlecliffe, The Scores, University of St Andrews, St Andrews KY16 9AL; T.-01334 462423; e-mail: ge21@st-andrews.ac.uk

Evans, Leslie Elizabeth, BA (Hons) Music. Permanent Secretary to the Scottish Government, since 2015; Director-General, Learning and Justice, Scottish Government, 2010-15, Director-General, Education, 2009-2010, Director, Europe, External Affairs and Culture, DG Economy, 2007-09; Head of Tourism, Culture and Sport, Scottish Executive Education Department, 2006-07; b. 11.12.58; m., Derek George McVay; 1 s. Educ. Liverpool University. Assistant to Director, Greenwich Festival, 1981; Entertainments Officer, London Borough of Greenwich, 1981-83; Arts Co-ordinator, Sheffield CC, 1983-85; Senior Arts Officer, Edinburgh DC, 1985-87; Principal Officer, Stirling CC, 1987-89; City of Edinburgh Council: Assistant Director of Recreation, 1989-99, Strategic Projects Manager, 1999-2000; Scottish Executive: Head: Local Government, Constitution and Governance, 2000-03, Public Service Reform, 2003-05. Member, Scotch Malt Whisky Society. Recreations: the arts; pilates and keeping fit. Address: (b.) Scottish Government, St Andrews House, Regent Road, Edinburgh EH1 3DG.
E-mail: leslie.evans@scotland.gsi.gov.uk

Evans, Mairi, MA. MSP (SNP), Angus North and Mearns, since 2016. Educ. University of Aberdeen. Senior Assistant, National Trust for Scotland, 2002-2010; Councillor, Angus Council, since 2007 (spokesperson on economic development), became convener of infrastructure services, then later the development and enterprise convener. Former Chairwoman of the East of Scotland European Consortium; represented Convention of Scottish Local Authorities (COSLA) on the executive of the Council of European Municipalities and Regions. Address: Scottish Parliament, Edinburgh EH99 1SP.

Everest, Anne, BA (Hons). Head, St George's School for Girls, since 2010. Educ. St Mary's Grammar School, Hull; University of Hull. Career: Deputy Head, Robert Gordon's College, 2002-07; Head, St Margaret's School, Aberdeen, 2007-2010. Address: (b.) Garscube Terrace, Edinburgh EH12 6BG; T.-0131 311 8000.
E-mail: office@st-georges.edin.sch.uk

Everett, Peter, BSc (Hons), SPMB; b. 24.9.31, London; m., Annette Patricia Hyde; 3 s.; 1 d. Educ. George Watson's College; Edinburgh University. Royal Engineers, 1953-55 (2nd Lt.); joined Shell International Petroleum Company, 1955; Managing Director: Brunei Shell Petroleum Co. Ltd., 1979-84, Shell UK Exploration and Production, 1985-89; retired, 1989. Honorary Professor, Heriot Watt University, 1989. Recreation: golf. Address: (h.) Cluain, Castleton Road, Auchterarder, Perthshire PH3 1JW.

Ewart, Michael, BA, DPhil. Director, Scottish International Education Trust, since 2009; Lay Member, Judicial Appointments Board for Scotland, since 2009; b. 9.9.52, Anthorn; m., Dr. Sally Anderson; 1 s.; 1 d.

Educ. St Peter's, Southbourne; Jesus College, Cambridge; York University. 1977: joined Scottish Office: Scottish Education Department, Scottish Home and Health Department, Royal Commission on Legal Services in Scotland; Assistant Private Secretary to Secretary of State for Scotland, 1981-82; Civil Service Fellow in Politics, Glasgow University, 1982-83; Scottish Home and Health Department, Scottish Education Department, 1983-91; Chief Executive, Scottish Court Service, 1991-99; Head of Schools Group, Scottish Executive Education Department, 1999-2002, Head of Department, 2002-07; Chief Executive, Scottish Prison Service, 2007-09. Board Member: Scottish Ballet, 2007-13, Phoenix Futures, Education Scotland; Chair, Phoenix Scotland. Recreations: music; books; climbing; skiing; running; geocaching. Address: (b.) Scottish International Education Trust, c/o Turcan Connell, Princes Exchange, 1 Earl Grey Street, Edinburgh EH3 9EE; e-mail: m.ewart@tesco.net

Ewing, Annabelle, LLB (Hons). MSP (SNP), Cowdenbeath, since 2016 (Mid Scotland and Fife region, 2011-16); SNP MP, Perth, 2001-05; Minister for Youth and Women's Employment in the Scottish Government, 2014-16; b. 20.8.60, Glasgow. Educ. Craigholme School; Glasgow University; Johns Hopkins University; Europa Institute, Amsterdam University. Admitted Solicitor, 1986; Legal Service, EC, 1987; worked for law firms in Brussels, 1987-96; lawyer, EC, 1997; Ewing & Co., Solicitors: Associate, 1998-99, Partner, 1999-2001; Consultant, Leslie Wolfson & Co., Glasgow, 2001-03. Honorary President, SNP Brussels Branch. Recreations: walking; swimming; travel; reading. Address: (b.) Scottish Parliament, Edinburgh EH99 1SP.

Ewing, Fergus. MSP (SNP), Inverness and Nairn, since 2011, Inverness East, Nairn and Lochaber, 1999-2011; Cabinet Secretary for the Rural Economy and Connectivity, since 2016; Minister for Business, Energy and Tourism, 2011-16; Minister for Community Safety, 2007-2011; b. 20.9.57; m., Margaret Ewing (deceased). Educ. Loretto School, Edinburgh; Glasgow University. Solicitor. Recreations: piano; reading; running; hill-walking; former member of local mountain rescue team. Address: (b.) Scottish Parliament, Edinburgh EH99 1SP; T.-01463 713004.

Exley, Mandy. Director, Retina Festivals Ltd, since 2014; former Principal, Edinburgh College; b. 09.10.61; 1 s.; 2 d. Educ. Perth College. Principal, Perth College, 2006-2010; Principal and Chief Executive, Jewel and Esk College, 2010-2012. Chairman, Air Service Training, 2006-2010.

F

Fabiani, Linda. MSP (SNP), East Kilbride, since 2011, Central Scotland, 1999-2011; Minister for Europe, External Affairs and Culture, 2007-09; b. 14.12.56, Glasgow. Educ. Hyndland School, Glasgow; Napier College, Edinburgh; Glasgow University. Various Housing Association posts, 1982-99. Recreations: music; literature; friends. Address: (b.) Scottish Parliament, Edinburgh EH99 1SP.
E-mail: linda.fabiani.msp@scottish.parliament.uk

Fairbairn, The Hon. Mrs Elizabeth, MBE. Trustee, Scottish National War Memorial; President, Clan Mackay Society; Treasurer, Standing Council of Scottish Chiefs; b. 21.6.38; 3 d. Address: 38 Moray Place, Edinburgh EH3 6BT; T.-0131-225 2724.

Fairbairn, Martin MacLean, BCom, CA. Senior Director (Institutions and Corporate Services), Scottish Further and Higher Education Funding Council, since 2009; Interim Chief Officer, Glasgow Colleges' Regional Board, since 2015; b. 20.9.63, Dunfermline; m., Anne Fairbairn (nee Marshall); 2 s.; 1 d. Educ. Queen Anne High, Dunfermline; University of Edinburgh. Auditor, Touche Ross & Co., 1984-93; Director of Finance, Stevenson College Edinburgh, 1993-2000; Deputy Director, FE Funding, Scottish Funding Councils for Further and Higher Education, 2000-04; Director of Governance & Management: Appraisal & policy, Scottish Further and Higher Education Funding Council, 2004-09. Chair, Audit & Risk Committee, Mercy Corps Scotland. Recreations: church organist; youth work; badminton; golf; cycling. Address: (b.) Scottish Funding Council, Apex 2, 97 Haymarket Terrace, Edinburgh EH12 5HD; T.-0131 313 6500; e-mail: mfairbairn@sfc.ac.uk

Fairgrieve, James Hanratty, DA, RSA, RSW. Painter; b. 17.6.44, Prestonpans; m., Margaret D. Ross; 2 s.; 1 d. Educ. Preston Lodge Senior Secondary School; Edinburgh College of Art. Postgraduate study, 1966-67; Travelling Scholarship, Italy, 1968; Senior Lecturer in Drawing and Painting, Edinburgh College of Art, 1968-98; President, SSA, 1978-82; exhibited in Britain and Europe, since 1966. Recreation: angling. Address: (h.) Burnbrae, Gordon, Berwickshire.

Fairlamb, Professor Alan Hutchinson, CBE, MB, ChB, PhD, FLS, FRSE, FMedSci, FRSB. Wellcome Principal Research Fellow, University of Dundee, since 1996, Professor of Biochemistry, since 1996, Head of Division of Biological Chemistry & Drug Discovery, 1996-2012, Co-Director of Drug Discovery Unit, since 2006; b. 30.4.47, Newcastle-upon-Tyne; m., Carolyn Strobos; 1 s.; 2 d. Educ. Hymers College, Hull; Edinburgh University. Surgical and Medical House Officer, Longmore and Western General Hospitals, Edinburgh, 1971-72; Faculty of Medicine Research Scholar, University of Edinburgh, 1972-75; MRC Travelling Fellow, University of Amsterdam, 1975-76; Research Fellow: University of Edinburgh, 1976-80, London School of Hygiene and Tropical Medicine, 1980-81; Assistant Professor, The Rockefeller University, New York, 1981-87; Senior Clinical Lecturer, London School of Hygiene & Tropical Medicine, 1987-90; Professor of Molecular Parasitology and Head, Biochemistry and Chemotherapy Unit, LSHTM, 1990-96. Current committee memberships: Governing Board, Open Lab Foundation; Academy of Medical Sciences Council. Publications: author of more than 200 scientific articles and reviews on biochemistry and chemotherapy of neglected tropical diseases. Recreations: gardening; fishing; photography. Address: (b.) Division of Biological Chemistry & Drug Discovery, School of Life Sciences, Wellcome Trust Biocentre, University of Dundee, Dundee DD1 5EH; T.-01382 345155; Fax: 01382 345542.
E-mail: a.h.fairlamb@dundee.ac.uk

Fairley, Douglas, LLB (Hons). Queen's Counsel, since 2012; b. 20.2.68, Glasgow; m., Una Doherty. Educ. Hutchesons' Grammar School; University of Glasgow. Solicitor, Maclay Murray and Spens, 1992-98; Admitted to the Faculty of Advocates, 1999; Full-time Employment Judge, 2010-2011; Full-time Advocate Depute, 2011-15. Publication: Contempt of Court in Scotland (Co-Author). Recreations: music; tennis; skiing; curling.

Falconer, David. Director, Pain Association Scotland, since 1989; b. Perth; m., Rosanne; 1 s.; 1 d. Educ. Perth High School. HM Forces Royal Core of Signals, 1964-78; Scottish Agriculture Industry, 1978-88; Pain Association Scotland, since 1989. Member, Scottish Cross Party, Chronic Pain; Scottish Advisory Board, Chronic Pain. Recreation: mountaineer. Address: (b.) Pain Association Scotland, Cramond House, Cramond Glebe Road, Edinburgh EH4 6NS; T.-0131 312 7955; e-mail: dfalconer@painassociation.com

Falconer, Professor Kenneth John, MA, PhD (Cantab), FRSE. Professor in Pure Mathematics, St. Andrews University, since 1993; b. 25.1.52, Middlesex; m., Isobel Jessie Nye; 1 s.; 1 d. Educ. Kingston Grammar School; Corpus Christi College, Cambridge. Research Fellow, Corpus Christi College, Cambridge, 1977-80; Lecturer, then Reader, Bristol University, 1980-93; Visiting Professor: Oregon State University, 1985-86; Isaac Newton Institute, Cambridge, 1999, 2011 & 2015, IHES, Paris, 2005-06, Australian National University, Canberra, 2009, East China Normal University, Shanghai, 2010. Publications Secretary, London Mathematical Society, 2006-09. Publications: The Geometry of Fractal Sets; Fractal Geometry — Mathematical Foundations and Applications; Techniques in Fractal Geometry; Fractals: A Very Short Introduction; Unsolved Problems in Geometry (Co-author); 110 papers. Recreations: hill-walking and long distance walking (Long Distance Walkers Association: Chair, 2000-03, Editor of its journal Strider, 1987-92 and 2007-2012). Address: (h.) Lumbo Farmhouse, St. Andrews, Fife; T.-01334 478507; e-mail: kjf@st-and.ac.uk

Falkland, 15th Viscount (Lord Lucius Edward William Plantagenet Cary). Premier Viscount of Scotland on the Roll; b. 8.5.35, London; 2 s.; 3 d. (1 deceased). Educ. Wellington College; Alliance Francaise, Paris. Formerly journalist, theatrical agent, chief executive of international trading company; entered Parliament, 1984 (SDP), 1987 (Liberal Democrats); Deputy Chief Whip, House of Lords, for Liberal Democrats, 1987-2001; Culture, Media, Sport and Tourism Spokesman, 1994-2007; Chairman, House of Lords Works of Art Committee, 2008-2010; joined independent crossbenches, House of Lords, 2012; elected Member, House of Lords, since 1999. Recreations: racing; golf; motor-cycling; cinema. Clubs: Brooks's, Sunningdale Golf. Address: (b.) House of Lords, London SW1; e-mail: lordfalkland@aol.com

Fallick, Professor Anthony Edward, BSc, PhD, FRSE, FRSA. Emeritus Professor, University of Glasgow; Professor of Isotope Geosciences, University of Glasgow, 1996-2012; b. 21.4.50, Chatham. Educ. St. Columba's High School, Greenock; University of Glasgow. Research Fellow:

McMaster University, Canada, 1975-78; University of Cambridge, 1978-80; Research Fellow, Lecturer, Reader, Professor, Scottish Universities Research and Reactor Centre, East Kilbride, 1980-98; Head of Isotope Geosciences Unit, Scottish Universities Research and Reactor Centre, East Kilbride, 1986-99; Director, Scottish Universities Environmental Research Centre, 1998-2007; 1997 Schlumberger Medallist, Mineralogical Society of Great Britain and Ireland; 2001 Richard A. Glenn Award, American Chemical Society; 2004 Coke Medal of the Geological Society of London; 2009/10 Distinguished Lecturer of the Mineralogical Society; 2013 Clough Medallist, Edinburgh Geological Society; Honorary Professor in the Universities of Glasgow, Edinburgh and St. Andrews. Address: (b.) S.U.E.R.C., Rankine Avenue, East Kilbride, Glasgow G75 0QF; T.-013552 23332.
E-mail: t.fallick@suerc.gla.ac.uk

Fannin, A. Lorraine, OBE, BA (Hons), DipEd. Director, BookSource; Trustee, National Library of Scotland, 2001-2014; Board Member, Edinburgh UNESCO City of Literature Trust; Chief Executive, Publishing Scotland, 1987-2008. Educ. Victoria College, Belfast; Queen's University, Belfast; Reading University. Previously Teacher; broadcaster; journalist; children's book supplier, 1979-89. Recreations: galleries; books and friends. Address: (b.) BookSource, 50 Cambuslang Road, Cambuslang, Glasgow G32 8NB; T.-0845 370 0063; Fax: 0845 370 0064.

Faris, Janice Mary, BSc, BD, CertEd. Parish Minister, Innerleithen, Traquair and Walkerburn Church of Scotland, since 2001; b. 16.6.56, Birmingham; m., Paul Samuel Alexander Faris; 1 s.; 1 d.; 2 grandsons. Educ. Wellington Girls High School (Salop); Southampton University; Edinburgh University; Moray House College of Education. Supply Teaching, Belfast, 1978-79; Biology Teacher, Richmond Lodge Girls School, Belfast, 1979-82; Supply Teaching, Biology/RE, West Lothian; Auxiliary Ministry, Armadale Kirk of Calder, Church of Scotland, 1991; Part-Time Hospital Chaplain, St. John's Livingston Parish Ministry, 2001. Church and Society Council. Recreations: knitting; reading; walking; golf. Address: 1 Millwell Park, Innerleithen EH44 6JF; T.-01896 830309; e-mail: revjfaris@hotmail.com

Farley-Sutton, Captain Colin David, RN, DL; b. 20.12.31, Rugby; m., Sheila Wilson Baldwin; 2 s.; 2 d. Educ. Rugby College of Technology and Arts; RN Engineering College, Plymouth; RN College, Greenwich. Royal Navy, 1950-82. President, Caithness Branch, Red Cross, 1991-97. Address: (h.) Shepherd's Cottage, Lynegar, Watten, Caithness KW1 5UP; T.-01955 621697.

Farmer, Professor John Gregory, BSc, PhD, CChem, FRSC, FGS. Professor Emeritus, Edinburgh University, since 2009; b. 18.02.47, Market Bosworth; m., Margaret Ann McClimont; 2 s.; 1 d. Educ. Kilmarnock Academy; Glasgow University. Post-Doctoral Investigator, Woods Hole Oceanographic Institution, Mass., USA, 1972-74; Research Assistant and Fellow, Department of Forensic Medicine and Science, Glasgow University, 1974-86; Lecturer, Senior Lecturer and Reader in Environmental Chemistry, Edinburgh University, 1987-2003; Professor of Environmental Geochemistry, Edinburgh University, 2004-08; Chairman, 8th International Conference on Heavy Metals in the Environment, Edinburgh, 1991; Chairman, 6th International Symposium on Environmental Geochemistry, Edinburgh, 2003; President, Society for Environmental Geochemistry and Health, 2002-05; Executive Editor, Science of the Total Environment, 2002-11. Recreations: cricket; Kilmarnock FC; history; hill walking; wine. Address: (b.) School of Geosciences, Edinburgh University; Crew Building, Alexander Crum Brown Road, Edinburgh EH9 3FF.
E-mail: j.g.farmer@ed.ac.uk

Farmer, Sir Tom, CVO, CBE, KCSG, FRSE, DL. Founder and former Chairman and Chief Executive, Kwik-Fit Holdings PLC (1984-2002); Chancellor, Queen Margaret University, since 2007; b. 10.7.40, Edinburgh; m., Anne Drury Scott; 1 s.; 1 d. Educ. Holy Cross Academy. Founding Chancellor of Queen Margaret University. Address: (b.) Maidencraig House, 192 Queensferry Road, Edinburgh EH4 2BN; T.-0131 315 2830.
E-mail: info@maidencraig.com

Farquharson, Sir Angus, KCVO, OBE, CStJ, MA, FRICS. Lord Lieutenant of Aberdeenshire, 1998-2010; Vice Lord Lieutenant, 1987-98 (DL, 1984); b. 27.3.35, Haydon Bridge; m., Alison Mary Farquharson of Finzean; 2 s.; 1 d. Educ. Trinity College, Glenalmond; Downing College, Cambridge. Chartered Surveyor, Estate Factor, Farmer and Forester; Council Member, Scottish Landowners Federation, 1980-88; Member: Regional Advisory Committee, Forestry Commission, 1980-94; Red Deer Commission, 1986-92; Nature Conservancy Committee for Scotland, 1986-91; Director, DWP Harvesting, 1987-2008; NE Committee, SNH, 1991-94; Hon. President, Deeside Scouts; Elder and General Trustee, Church of Scotland, 1996-2006; Director, Scottish Traditional Skills Training Centre, 2006. Recreations: gardening; shooting; walking; local history; nature conservation. Address: (h.) Glenferrick Lodge, Finzean, Banchory, Aberdeenshire AB31 6NG; T.-01330 850 229.

Farquharson, Kenny (Kenneth James), MA (Hons), DipJour. Columnist and senior writer, The Times, since 2015; b. 8.5.62, Dundee; m., Caron Stoker; 2 s. Educ. Lawside R.C. Academy, Dundee; University of Aberdeen; University College, Cardiff. Industry Reporter, Coventry Evening Telegraph, 1985-88; Scotland on Sunday: Investigative Reporter, 1989-93, Political Editor, 1993-97; Political Editor, Daily Record, 1997-98; Scottish Political Editor, The Sunday Times, 1998-2002; Assistant Editor: The Sunday Times (Scotland), 2002-07, Scotland on Sunday, 2007-09; Deputy Editor, Scotland on Sunday, 2009-2015; Deputy Editor, The Scotsman, 2013-2015. Director, Scottish European Aid, 1993-94; Convenor, Scottish Parliamentary Journalists' Association, 1997-2000. Political Journalist of the Year, 2001, Scottish Press Awards. Publication: Restless Nation (Co-author), 1996. Recreations: cooking; architecture; art; photography.

Farrell, Sheriff James Aloysius, QC, MA, LLB. Sheriff of Lothian and Borders, 1986-2009; b. 14.5.43, Glasgow; m., 1, Jacqueline Allen (divorced); 2 d.; m., 2, Patricia McLaren. Educ. St. Aloysius College; Glasgow University; Dundee University. Admitted to Faculty of Advocates, 1974; Advocate-Depute, 1979-83; Sheriff: Glasgow and Strathkelvin, 1984-85, South Strathclyde, Dumfries and Galloway, 1985-86; 2010 Temporary Sheriff Principal, Glasgow and Strathkelvin; 2010, 2011 Temporary Sheriff Principal, Central, Tayside and Fife; 2012, 2013 Temporary Sheriff Principal, South Strathclyde, Dumfries and Galloway, 2012, 2013 Temporary High Court Judge. Recreations: sailing; cycling; hill-walking. Address: (b.) Sheriff's Chambers, Edinburgh; T.-0131-225 2525.

Farrer, Peter William. Chief Operating Officer, Scottish Water, since 2013; b. 1962, Balerno, Midlothian; m., Caroline; 1 s.; 1 d. Educ. Currie High School, Midlothian; Heriot-Watt University, Edinburgh. Thirty years in water industry in Scotland since graduating in 1984 for Scottish Water and predecessor organisations; Engineering Design & Construction, 1984-96; various operational senior management roles, 1996-2002; General Manager Operations, 2002-2006; General Manager (Tactical Planning & Performing), 2006-08. Chartered Civil Engineer, 1990; MBA, 2001. Recreations: rugby; cycling. Address: (b.) 6 Castle Drive, Carnegie Campus, Dunfermline KY11 8GG; T.-01383 848466; e-mail: peter.farrer@scottishwater.co.uk

Faulds, Ann, BA. Partner, CMS Cameron McKenna LLP (Head of Planning and Transport team), since 2014; former Chairman, Lothian Buses. Elected Member, Strathclyde Partnership for Transport (SPT), since 2012; Board Member, Fife NHS Board, since 2014. Member, Accounts Commission for Scotland, 2003-09; Chair, Edinburgh Chamber of Commerce transport policy group, 2009-2014; Member, Lothian Buses Board, 2010-2014. Publications: Scottish Roads Law; annotated the Transport (Scotland) Act 2001. Address: CMS Cameron McKenna LLP, Saltire Court, 20 Castle Terrace, Edinburgh EH1 2EN; T.-0131 200 7452; e-mail: ann.faulds@cms-cmck.com

Fawcett, Richard, OBE, BA, PhD, FRSE, FSA. Emeritus Professor, School of Art History, University of St Andrews; b. 31.12.46, Hoyland, Yorkshire; m., Susan; 1 s.; 1 d. Educ. Ecclesfield Grammar School; University of East Anglia. Ancient Monuments Inspectorate, Historic Scotland (and its predecessor bodies), since 1974. Publications: books include: "Scottish Architecture 1371-1560", 1994; Scottish Medieval Churches, 2002; "The Architecture of The Scottish Medieval Church", 2011. Recreations: architectural history; music; reading. Address: (h.) 61 Loughborough Road, Kirkcaldy, Fife KY1 3BZ; T.-01592 653911; e-mail: richard.fawcett@hotmail.co.uk

Fearn, Professor David Ross, BSc, PhD, CMath, FIMA, FRSE. Professor of Applied Mathematics, University of Glasgow, since 1993, International Dean for the Americas since 2010, Vice Principal and Acting Head of the College of Science and Engineering, 2014, Dean, Learning and Teaching, College of Science and Engineering (2010-2014), Dean, Faculty of Information and Mathematical Sciences (2004-2010), Head, Department of Mathematics (1997-2003); b. 11.2.54, Dundee; m., Elvira D'Annunzio; 1 s.; 1 d. Educ. Grove Academy, Dundee; University of St. Andrews; University of Newcastle upon Tyne. Research Associate: Florida State University, 1979-80, University of Cambridge, 1980-85; University of Glasgow: Lecturer, 1985-90, Senior Lecturer, 1990-92, Reader, 1992-93. Recreations: walking; gardening; DIY. Address: (b.) University Gardens, Glasgow G12 8QW; T.-0141-330 5417.
E-mail: David.Fearn@glasgow.ac.uk

Fearon, Brian. Chairman, Apex Scotland, since 2013. Educ. Queens University Belfast; University of Sheffield; Middlesex Polytechnic. Joined Central Regional Council Social Work Department in 1980, appointed Director of Social Work (later with housing as Director of Social Services), East Dunbartonshire Council, 1995-2000; served as a member of the Expert Panel on Sex Offenders and the Scottish Community Justice Accreditation Panel; former Convenor of the Criminal Justice Standing Committee and former Secretary of the Association of Directors of Social Work in Scotland; worked, among other places, in Dumfries and Galloway, Western Isles and the University of Edinburgh Criminal Justice Social Work Development Centre; elected member of Clackmannanshire Council, 2003-07, Convenor of Education, then Scrutiny; Interim Chief Executive, Apex Scotland, 2009-2010, Apex Board Member, since 2009. Address: (b.) Apex Scotland, 9 Great Stuart Street, Edinburgh EH3 7TP; T.-0131 220 0130.
E-mail: admin@apexscotland.org.uk

Fee, Kenneth, BL, MA, FRCS. Emeritus Editor, Scots Independent; b. 14.7.31, Glasgow; m., Margery Anne Dougan; 3 s.; 1 d. Educ. Gourock High School; Hamilton Academy; Glasgow University; Strathclyde University. President, Glasgow University SRC and Scottish Union of Students; Editor, Gum, Ygorra and (founding) GU Guardian; sometime in military intelligence; Sub-Editor, Glasgow Herald; former Managing Director, Strathclyde Publishing Group; itinerant teaching; Member, Scottish Executive, NASUWT, 1983-98; various SNP branch, constituency and national offices, since 1973; Editor, Scots Independent, 1985-2004. Publication: How to Grow Fat and Free. Recreations: chess; gastronomy; campaigning. Address: (h.) 18 Cleveden Drive, Rutherglen G73 3SZ; T.-0141 560 1931.

Fee, Mary. MSP (Labour), West Scotland, since 2011; Shadow Cabinet Secretary for Infrastructure, Investments and Cities, since 2014; b. 23.3.54, Edinburgh. Educ. Leith Walk Primary, Edinburgh; Broughton Secondary, Edinburgh. Employment with the Bank of Scotland, 1972-1974; British Telecom, 1974-1984, transferred within British Telecom to their Glasgow offices; joined Tesco in 1990 in Renfrew; Renfrewshire Councillor, 2007-2012. Convenor of the Equal Opportunities Committee, Scottish Parliament, since 2012, substitute member for the Finance Committee; established and convenes the Cross-Party Group on Families Affected by Imprisonment; member of other Cross-Party Groups including Cancer, Epilepsy, Human Trafficking, Mental Health, Middle East and South Asia, Scotch Whisky, Scottish Showmens Guild, Taiwan and Towns and Town Centres. Member, Usdaw (trade union); became a shop steward in 1990; elected onto the Usdaw Executive in 2000 and later became a member of the STUC General Council; served as a member of the Employment Tribunals until 2011. Address: (b.) Scottish Parliament, Edinburgh EH99 1SP.

Fellows, Marion. MP (SNP), Motherwell and Wishaw, since 2015; b. 5.5.49. Educ. Heriot Watt University. Early career in a variety of related roles in both the public and private sectors; subsequently taught in further education, spending 19 years teaching business studies at West Lothian College, where she was an active and senior member of the EIS Trade Union; has lived with her family in Wishaw and Bellshill for 40 years, and has represented Wishaw as a local SNP councillor since 2012. Senior figure in the Yes Motherwell and Wishaw campaign, which won a majority locally in the 2014 Independence Referendum. Address: House of Commons, London SW1A 0AA.

Ferguson, Professor Allister Ian, BSc, MA, PhD, FInstP, FRSE, CPhys, FFCS. Professor of Photonics, Strathclyde University, since 1989; Technical Director, Institute of Photonics, University of Strathclyde, since 1996, Deputy Principal, 2004-2011, Adviser to Principal, since 2012; b. 10.12.51, Aberdeen; m., Kathleen Ann Challenger. Educ. Aberdeen Academy; St. Andrews University. Lindemann Fellow, Stanford University, 1977-79; SERC Research Fellow, St. Andrews, 1979-81; SERC Advanced Fellow, Oxford, 1981-83; Junior Research Fellow, Merton College, Oxford, 1981-83; Lecturer, then Senior Lecturer, Southampton University, 1983-89. Fellow: Royal Society of Edinburgh, since 1993, Institute of Physics, Optical Society of America, Institution of Electrical and Electronics Engineers. Address: (b.) McCance Building, University of Strathclyde, Glasgow G1 1XQ; T.-0141 548 3264.

Ferguson, Iain William Findlay, QC, LLB (Hons), DipLP. Queen's Counsel, since 2000; b. 31.7.61, Edinburgh; m., Valerie Laplanche; 2 s. Educ. Firrhill High School, Edinburgh; Dundee University. Advocate, 1987; Standing Junior Counsel to Ministry of Defence (Army), 1991-98, and to Scottish Development Department (Planning matters), 1998-2000. Recreations: cooking; rugby; cycling. Address: (h.) 16 McLaren Road, Edinburgh EH9 2BN; T.-0131-667 1751.

Ferguson, Michael Anthony John, BSc, PhD, CBE, FRS, FRSE, FMedSci. Regius Professor of Life Sciences, since 2013, Associate Dean for Research Strategy, School of Life Sciences, University of Dundee, since 2007, Professor of Molecular Parasitology, since 1994; b. 6.2.57, Bishop Auckland; m., Dr Lucia Güther; 1 s. Educ. St. Peter's School, York; University of Manchester. Post-doctoral fellow: Rockefeller University, New York, 1982-85, Oxford University, 1985-88; Lecturer, University of Dundee, 1988-91, Reader, 1991-94. Colworth Medal (Biochemical Society), 1991; Wright Medal (British Society for Parasitology), 2006; Royal Society of Edinburgh Royal Medal, 2013. Recreations: travel; astronomy. Address: (b.) School of Life Sciences, University of Dundee, Dundee DD1 5EH; T.-01382 386672; e-mail: m.a.j.ferguson@dundee.ac.uk

Ferguson, Professor Pamela Ruth, LLB (Hons), DipLP, PhD. Professor of Scots Law, University of Dundee, since 2000; b. 7.4.63, Glasgow; m., Dr. Euan W. Macdonald; 1 s. Educ. Bearsden Academy; Glasgow University; Dundee University. Procurator Fiscal Depute/Trainee Solicitor, Crown Office, Edinburgh and Procurator Fiscal's Office, Kirkcaldy, 1986-89; Lecturer, 1989-95; Senior Lecturer, 1995-99. Winner, Dr. John McCormick Prize (jointly); Most Distinguished Law Graduate, 1985; awarded Royal Society of Edinburgh Research Fellowship, 1997. Publication: Co-author of Draft Criminal Code for Scotland. Address: (b.) School of Law, University of Dundee, Dundee DD1 4HN; T.-01382 385189; e-mail: p.r.ferguson@dundee.ac.uk

Ferguson, Patricia. MSP (Labour), Glasgow Maryhill and Springburn, 2011-16, Glasgow Maryhill, 1999-2011; former Minister for Tourism, Culture and Sport; former Deputy Presiding Officer and Minister for Parliamentary Business; b. 1958, Glasgow; m., William G. Butler. Educ. Gartnethill Convent Secondary School, Glasgow.

Ferguson, Ron, MA, BD, ThM. Freelance journalist and author; Minister, St. Magnus Cathedral, Orkney, 1990-2001; former Columnist, The Herald; b. 27.10.39, Dunfermline; m., Cristine Jane Walker; 2 s.; 1 d. Educ. Beath High School, Cowdenbeath; St. Andrews University; Edinburgh University; Duke University. Journalist, Fife and Edinburgh, 1956-63; University, 1963-71; ordained Minister, Church of Scotland, 1972; Minister, Easterhouse, Glasgow, 1971-79; exchange year with United Church of Canada, 1979-80; Deputy Warden, Iona Abbey, 1980-81; Leader, Iona Community, 1981-88. Publications: Geoff: A Life of Geoffrey M. Shaw, 1979; Grace and Dysentery, 1986; Chasing the Wild Goose, 1988; The Whole Earth Shall Cry Glory (Co-Editor), 1985; George MacLeod, 1990; Daily Readings by George MacLeod (Editor), 1991; Black Diamonds and the Blue Brazil, 1993; Technology at the Crossroads, 1994; Love Your Crooked Neighbour, 1998; Donald Dewar Ate My Hamster, 1999; Hitler Was A Vegetarian, 2001; The Reluctant Reformation of Clarence McGonigall, 2003; Fear and Loathing in Lochgelly, 2003; Blue Rinse Dreams and Banoffee Pie, 2005; Mole Under The Fence: Conversations with Roland Walls, 2006; Helicopter Dreams: The Quest for the Holy Grail, 2006; George Mackay Brown: The Wound and the Gift, 2011; plays: Every Blessed Thing, 1993, Orkneyinga, 1997; Ending It All, 2006; poetry: Pushing the Boat Out (Contributor), 1997. Recreation: supporting Cowdenbeath Football Club. Address: (h.) Vinbrek, Orphir, Orkney KW17 2RE; T.-01856 811378.
E-mail: ronbluebrazil@aol.com

Ferguson, Professor Ronald Gillies, MA, BPhil, CertSecEd. Emeritus Professor of Italian, University of St Andrews, since 2014, Professor of Italian, 2004-14, Head of The School of Modern Languages, 2005-09; b. 21.7.49, Birkenshaw, Lanarkshire; m., Annie Ferguson (nee Ballouard); 1 s.; 1 d. Educ. Uddingston Grammar School; University of Glasgow; University of St. Andrews; Jordanhill College of Education. University of Lancaster: Lecturer in Italian, 1979-96, Senior Lecturer in Italian, 1996-97; University of St. Andrews: Senior Lecturer in Italian, 1997-2004, first ever Chair of Italian. Made Cavaliere della Stella della Soldarietà Italiana (one of Italy's highest honours) by the President of Italy for distinction in the fields of Italian Renaissance theatre, Italian identity studies, and Venetian language linguistics and culture, and for making St. Andrews a centre for the study of Italian, 2005; made Fellow of the Ateneo Veneto di Scienze, Lettere ed Arti (one of Italy's foremost learned societies) for distinguished contributions to Venetian language and culture, 2006; made Research Professor, St Andrews, 2010. Publications: Italian False Friends, 1994; The Theatre of Angelo Beolco (Ruzante): Text, Context and Performance, 2000; Italian Identities (ed.), 2002; A Linguistic History of Venice, 2007; Saggi di Lingua e Cultura Veneta, 2013. Recreations: birdwatching; reading. Address: (h.) 3 Muir Gardens, St. Andrews, Fife KY16 9NH; T.-01334 472 383; e-mail: rgf@st-and.ac.uk

Ferguson, William James, OBE, FRAgS. Farmer, since 1954; Director, Hannah Research Institute, since 1995; Vice Lord Lieutenant, Aberdeenshire; Honorary Fellow, SAC, since 1999; Trustee, Aberdeen Endowments Trust, 2002-2012; Chair, Land and Finance Committee, since 2005; b. 3.4.33, Aberdeen; m., Carroll Isobella Milne; 1 s.; 3 d. Educ. Turriff Academy; North of Scotland College of Agriculture. National Service, 1st Bn., Gordon Highlanders, 1952-54, serving in Malaya during the emergency. Former Director, Rowett Research Institute, Aberdeen; former Chairman, Aberdeen Milk Company; former Chairman, North of Scotland College of Agriculture; former Member, Scottish Country Life Museums Trust Ltd.; former Vice Chairman, SAC. Recreations: golf; field sports. Address: (h.) Nether Darley, Fyvie, Turriff, Aberdeenshire AB53 8LH.

Fergusson, Rt. Hon. Alexander Charles Onslow. MSP (Conservative), Galloway and West Dumfries, 2011-16, Galloway and Upper Nithsdale, 2003-2011 (South of Scotland, 1999-2003); Presiding Officer, Scottish Parliament, 2007-2011; b. 8.4.49, Leswalt; m., Jane Merryn Barthold; 3 s. Educ. Eton; West of Scotland Agricultural College. Farm management adviser, 1970-71; farmer, 1971-99; restaurateur, 1981-86. Community Councillor; JP, 1998-99; Deputy Lieutenant of Ayrshire, 1998-99. Recreations: curling; rugby (spectator); cricket. Address: (h.) Grennan, Dalry, Kirkcudbright DG7 3PL; T.-01644 430250.

Fergusson of Kilkerran, Sir Charles, 9th Bt; b. 10.5.31; m., Hon. Amanda Mary Noel-Paton; 2 s.

Fergusson, Professor David Alexander Syme. MA, BD, DPhil, DD, FBA, FRSE. Professor of Divinity, Edinburgh University, since 2000; b. 3.8.56, Glasgow; m., Margot McIndoe; 2 s. Educ. Kelvinside Academy; Glasgow University; Edinburgh University; Oxford University. Assistant Minister, St. Nicholas Church, Lanark, 1983-84; Associate Minister, St. Mungo's Church, Cumbernauld, 1984-86; Lecturer, Edinburgh University, 1986-90; Professor of Systematic Theology, Aberdeen University, 1990-2000. Chaplain to Moderator of the General Assembly, 1989-90; President, Society for the Study of Theology, 2000-02. President, Association of University Departments of Theology and Religious Studies, 2005-8; Principal of New College, from 2008, Vice-Principal, University of Edinburgh, 2009-11; Chaplain-in-Ordinary to HM The Queen in

Scotland, 2015. Publications: Bultmann, 1992; Christ, Church and Society, 1993; The Cosmos and the Creator, 1998; Community, Liberalism and Christian Ethics, 1998; John Macmurray: Critical Perspectives, 2002; Church, State and Civil Society, 2004; Scottish Philosophical Theology, 2007; Faith and Its Critics, 2009; Blackwell Companion to 19th Century Theology, 2010; Cambridge Dictionary of Christian Theology, 2011; Creation, 2014; Christian Theology: 21st Century Challenges, 2015. Recreations: football; golf. Address: 23 Riselaw Crescent, Edinburgh EH10 6HN; T.-0131-447 4022; e-mail: David.Fergusson@ed.ac.uk

Fernie, Professor John, MA, MBA, PhD. Honorary Professor, University of St Andrews; Emeritus Professor of Retail Marketing, Heriot-Watt University, Head of School of Management and Languages, 2002-07 (Head of School of Management, 1999-2002); Director of Institute of Retail Studies, University of Stirling, 1996-98; b. 4.3.48, East Wemyss, Fife; m., Suzanne Ishbel; 1 s.; 1 d. Educ. Buckhaven High School; Dundee University; Edinburgh University; Bradford University. Lecturer/Senior Lecturer, Huddersfield Polytechnic, 1973-88; Senior Lecturer, University of Abertay Dundee, 1988-96; Senior Lecturer/Professor, University of Stirling, 1996-98. Recent books include: Principles of Retailing (co-author) and Logistics and Retail Management (co-author). Recreations: golf; travelling; 5 a side football. Address: (b.) Heriot-Watt University, Edinburgh EH14 4AS; T.-0131-451-3880; e-mail: j.fernie@hw.ac.uk

Ferrell, Professor William Russell, MB, ChB, PhD, FRCP(Glas). Honorary Senior Research Fellow, Institute of Infection Immunity and Inflammation, University of Glasgow; b. 8.3.49, St. Louis, USA; m., Anne Mary Scobie; 3 s. Educ. St. Aloysius College; University of Glasgow. University of Glasgow: Lecturer, Senior Lecturer, Reader in Physiology; Visiting Professor, University of West of Scotland. Recreations: skiing; computing; tennis. Address: (b.) Room 407, Level 4, McGregor Building, University of Glasgow, Glasgow G12 8QQ.

Ferrier, Margaret. MP (SNP), Rutherglen and Hamilton West, since 2015; Shadow SNP Spokesperson, Scotland Office, since 2015; b. 1960, Glasgow. Former commercial sales manager for a manufacturing construction company in Motherwell. Joined the Rutherglen branch of the SNP in Cambuslang in 2011. Member, Scottish Affairs Committee, since 2015. Address: House of Commons, London SW1A 0AA; T.-020 7219 5278.
E-mail: margaret.ferrier.mp@parliament.uk

Fiddes, James Angus Gordon, OBE, DUniv, MA, DipTP, FRICS. Former Consultant Surveyor (retired, 2011); b. 1.3.41, Edinburgh; m., Valerie; 2 d. Educ. George Heriot's School, Edinburgh; Gonville and Caius College, Cambridge; Edinburgh College of Art. Richard Ellis & Son, London and Glasgow, 1964-67; Richard Stanton and Son Pty, Sydney, 1967-68; Kenneth Ryden and Partners, 1969-99 (Partner, 1973, Senior Partner, 1989). Trustee, National Museums of Scotland, until 2010. Recreations: sport; arts. Address: (h.) 178 Mayfield Road, Edinburgh EH9 3AX; T.-0131 667 5534; e-mail: jimfiddes@hotmail.com

Fife, 4th Duke of (David Charles Carnegie); MA (Cantab), MBA. Chairman, Elsick Development Company; Estate Management (the Southesk Estate); b. 3.3.61; m., Caroline Anne Bunting; 3 s. Educ. Eton; Cambridge; Royal Agricultural College, Cirencester; Edinburgh University. Career history: Stockbroker: Cazenove & Co., London, 1982-85, Bell Lawrie, Edinburgh, 1988-89; Chartered Accountant, Reeves & Neylan, Forfar, 1992-96. Honorary President, Angus Show; Vice-Chairman, Historic Houses Association for Scotland; Vice-Chairman, Angus Conservative and Unionist Association; Honorary President, Montrose and District Angling Club; Honoray Patron, The Edinburgh Angus Club. Address: Kinnaird Castle, Brechin, Angus DD9 6TZ.

Findlay, David J., BSc (Hons), MB, ChB, FRCPsych. Retired Consultant Psychiatrist, Tayside Primary Care (1991-2014); part-time Policy Adviser, Care of the Elderly, Scottish Executive Health Department, 1998-2001, Departmental Specialty Adviser in Psychiatry (Old Age), 2001-07; Honorary Senior Lecturer, Department of Psychiatry, Dundee University, since 1991; b. 2.6.54, Duns; m., Patricia; 1 s.; 3 d. Educ. Ayr Academy; Glasgow University. Junior House Officer, 1979-80; Gartnavel Royal Hospital Training Scheme, 1980-83; Lecturer in Psychiatry, Dundee University, 1984-87; Consultant Psychiatrist and Clinical Tutor, Gartnavel Royal Hospital, 1987-91; Royal Dundee Liff Hospital: Service Manager, Old Age Psychiatry, 1993-1996, Clinical Director, Elderly Services, 1996-99; Chair, RCPsych Philosophy Special Interest Group (Scotland), 2002-07; Chair, RCPsych in Scotland Old Age Faculty, 2008-2012. Recreations: chess; reading; films.

Findlay, Donald Russell, QC, LLB (Hons), MPhil, FRSA. Advocate, since 1975; former Lord Rector, St. Andrews University; b. 17.3.51, Cowdenbeath; m., Jennifer E. Borrowman. Educ. Harris Academy, Dundee; Dundee University; Glasgow University. Sometime Lecturer in Commercial Law, Heriot-Watt University. Elected Chairman, Faculty of Advocates Criminal Bar Association, 2010. Recreations: Glasgow Rangers FC; Egyptology; archaeology; wine; ethics; travelling first class; Cowdenbeath FC. Address: (b.) MacKinnon Stable, Glasgow High Court, 1 Mart Street, Saltmarket, Glasgow G1 5NA; e-mail: donaldrfin@aol.com

Findlay, Neil, BA. MSP (Labour), Lothian, since 2011; Shadow Cabinet Secretary of State for Health, 2013-15; b. 6.3.69. Educ. St. Kentigern's Academy, Blackburn; University of Strathclyde. Apprentice bricklayer; worked in the social housing sector; PGCE in secondary education; formerly Company secretary, Fauldhouse Community Development Trust (currently Board Member); formerly West Lothian councillor, and part-time support for learning teacher with Falkirk Council, until 2012. Member, EIS and Unite Trade Union. Address: (b.) Scottish Parliament, Edinburgh EH99 1SP.

Findlay, Richard, CBE. Chair, Creative Scotland, since 2015; Chairman: STV Group plc, 2007-2013; formerly Group Chief Executive, Scottish Radio Holdings plc; Founding Chairman, National Theatre of Scotland, until 2013; b. 5.11.43; m., Elspeth; 2 s.; 1 d. Educ. Royal Scottish Academy of Music and Drama. Chairman of Trustees, RSAMD; Chairman, Broadcasting Service of Saudi Arabia; Central Office of Information. Made a CBE in 2013 for services to Arts and Creative Industries. Recreations: music; golf; theatre. Address: Creative Scotland, Waverley Gate, 2-4 Waterloo Place, Edinburgh EH1 3EG.

Finkelstein, Professor David, BA (Columbia), PhD (Edin), FEA, FRSA. Chair in Continuing Education and Head of the Office of Lifelong Learning, University of Edinburgh, since 2015; b. 5.4.64, Bogota, Colombia; m., Alison Sinclair; 1 s.; 1 d. Educ. Commonwealth High School, San Juan, Puerto Rico; Columbia College, Columbia University; University of Edinburgh. Archivist, National Library of Scotland, 1990-91; British Academy Postdoctoral Research Fellow, Department of English Literature, University of Edinburgh, 1991-94; Napier University, Edinburgh: Lecturer, Print Media, Publishing and Communication Department, 1994-98, Senior Lecturer, Print Media, Publishing and Communication Department, 1998-2000; Queen Margaret University College, Edinburgh: Head of Department, Media and Communication, 2000-03, Acting Head of School (Associate Dean) of Social Sciences, Media and Communication, 2003; Research Professor of Media and Print Culture, Queen Margaret University, Edinburgh, 2003-2012; Dean, School of Humanities, University of Dundee, 2012-2014. Board of Trustees member, National Library of Scotland, 2011-2013; Series co-editor, Journalism Studies: Key Texts, since 2005; Editorial Board, Victorian Periodicals Review, since 2006; Editorial Board, Media History, since 2007; Member of the British Association of Victorian Studies; the Bibliographical Society; the Edinburgh Bibliographical Society; Lifetime Honorary Member, Victorian Studies Association of Western Canada. Publications: over 45 books and articles, including: The Edinburgh History of the Book in Scotland, 1880-2000 (Co-Editor), 2007; An Introduction to Book History (Co-Author), 2005; The House of Blackwood: Author-Publisher Relations in the Victorian Era, 2002; The Book History Reader (Co-Editor), 2001, rev. ed 2006; An Index to Blackwood's Magazine, 1901-1980, 1995. Recreations: running; watching obscure films; reading idiosyncratic novels. Address: (b.) Office of Lifelong Learning, University of Edinburgh, Paterson's Land, Holyrood Road, Edinburgh EH8 8AQ; T.-0131 650 6185; e-mail: d.finkelstein@ed.ac.uk

Finlay, Robert Derek, BA, MA, FInstD, FRSA, MCIM; b. 16.5.32, London; m., Una Ann Grant; 2 s.; 1 d. Educ. Kingston Grammar School; Emmanuel College, Cambridge. Lt., Gordon Highlanders, Malaya, 1950-52; Captain, Gordon Highlanders TA, 1952-61; Mobil Oil Co. UK, 1953-61; Associate, Principal, Director, McKinsey & Co., 1961-79; Managing Director, H.J. Heinz Co. Ltd., 1979-81; Senior Vice-President, Corporate Development, 1981-93, Chief Financial Officer, 1989-92, Area Vice President, 1992-93, World HQ; H.J. Heinz Co., 1981-93; Chair, Dawson International PLC, 1995-98 (non executive Chair, 1998). Member, London Committee, Scottish Council Development and Industry, 1975-2003; Member: Board, US China Business Council, 1983-93, Board, Pittsburgh Public Theatre, 1986-93, US Korea Business Council, 1986-92, Board, Pittsburgh Symphony Society, 1989-93; Vice Chairman, World Affairs Council of Pittsburgh, 1986-93; Chairman, Board of Visitors Center for International Studies, University of Pittsburgh, 1989-93; Governor, Three Rivers Rowing Association, Pittsburgh, since 1982. Publication: 2006 Autobiograpy "Time To Take Her Home - The Life and Times of RDF". Recreations: rowing; music; theatre. Address: (h.) Mains of Grantully, by Aberfeldy, PH15 2EG.

Finlayson, Niall Diarmid Campbell, OBE, MBChB, PhD, PPRCPE, FRCPL, FRCPSG, FRCSE. Consultant Physician, Royal Infirmary of Edinburgh, 1973-2003; President, Royal College of Physicians of Edinburgh, 2001-04; Director of Communications, Royal College of Physicians of Edinburgh, 2004-09; Chief Medical Officer, Bright Grey Insurance, since 2003; Chairman, Life Care (Edinburgh) Ltd, 2005-2015; b. 21.4.39, Georgetown, Guyana; m., Dale Kristin Anderson; 1 s.; 1 d. Educ. Loretto School, Musselburgh; Edinburgh University. Lecturer in Therapeutics, Edinburgh University, 1966-69; Assistant Professor of Medicine, Cornell University Medical College,

New York Hospital, USA, 1970-72. Recreations: history; music. Address: (h.) 10 Queens Crescent, Edinburgh EH9 2AZ; e-mail: niall.finlayson@brightgrey.com

Finn, Anthony, MA (Hons), FEIS (1997), Special FEIS (2010), CBE (2014). Retired Chief Executive, General Teaching Council for Scotland (2008-2013); Honorary Professor of Teacher Education, University of Glasgow; Chair, Scottish College for Educational Leadership; Member, Management Board, Curriculum for Excellence until 2013; Rector, St. Andrew's High School, Kirkcaldy, 1988-2006; formerly Senior Manager, Fife Council Education Service, 2006-08; b. 4.6.51, Irvine; m., Margaret Caldwell. Educ. St. Joseph's Academy, Kilmarnock; Glasgow University. Teacher, Principal Teacher, Assistant Head Teacher, Depute Head Teacher, Acting Head Teacher, St. Andrew's Academy, Saltcoats, 1975-88. Member, SEED Teachers' Agreement Communication Team, 2001-08; Elected Member, General Teaching Council, 1991-2001; Convener, General Teaching Council Education Committee, 1993-2001; Chair, SEED Memorandum Committee, 1991-2001; Member, Executive, Catholic Headteachers' Association Scotland, 2001-06; Member, Catholic Education Commission for Scotland, until 2008; Formerly: Teachers' Representative, National Committee for the Staff Development of Teachers, Member, Advisory Committee, Scottish Qualification for Headship, Governor, Moray House Institute of Education, Assessor, Teacher Education, Scottish Higher Education Funding Council, Chair, Fife Secondary Head Teachers Association. Recreations: sport; travel; literature; current affairs. Address: (h.) 1 Blair Place, Kirkcaldy KY2 5SQ; T.-01592 640109.

Finnie, James Ross, CA. Chair, Food Standards Scotland; Non-executive Member, the Water Industry Commission Scotland; Non-executive Member, NHS Greater Glasgow and Clyde Board; Honorary President, Scottish Environment LINK, 2011-15; Member, The Poverty Truth Commission, 2014-15; b. 11.2.47, Greenock; m., Phyllis Sinclair; 1 s.; 1 d. Educ. Greenock Academy. Member, Executive Committee, Scottish Council (Development and Industry), 1976-87; Chairman, Scottish Liberal Party, 1982-86; Member: Inverclyde District Council, 1977-97, Inverclyde Council, 1995-99; MSP (Liberal Democrat), West of Scotland, 1999-2011; Minister for Rural Affairs, 1999-2000; Minister for Environment and Rural Development, Scottish Executive, 2000-07; Liberal Democrat Shadow Secretary for Health and Well being, 2007-2011; Vice Convener, Health and Sport Committee, 2007-2011. Address: (h.) 91 Octavia Terrace, Greenock PA16 7PY; T.-01475 631495.

Finnie, John. MSP (Independent), Highlands and Islands, since 2012 (SNP, 2011-12). Born and brought up in Lochaber. Served for 30 years in the police. Formerly SNP group leader in Highland Council. Member of the Scottish Green Party, since 2014. Address: (b.) Scottish Parliament, Edinburgh EH99 1SP.

Fisher, Archie, MBE. Folk singer, guitarist, composer, broadcaster; b. 1939, Glasgow. First solo album, 1966; formerly presenter, Travelling Folk, BBC Radio; Artistic Director, Edinburgh International Folk Festival, 1988-92.

Fisher, Gregor. Actor (television, theatre, film). Credits include (BBC TV): Rab C. Nesbitt series (leading role), Naked Video series, Scotch and Wry, Para Handy, Oliver Twist, Empty. Best Actor award, Toronto Festival, for One, Two, Three.

Fitton, Professor John Godfrey, BSc, PhD, FGS, FRSE. Professor of Igneous Petrology, Edinburgh University, since, 1999; b. 1.10.46, Rochdale; m., Dr Christine Ann Fitton; 2 s.; 1 d. Educ. Bury Grammar School; Durham University. Turner and Newall

Research Fellow, Manchester University, 1971-72; Edinburgh University: Lecturer, 1972-89; Senior Lecturer, 1989-94; Reader, 1994-99; served on NERC Research Grants and ODP Committees; Co-Chief Scientist, Ocean Drilling Programme Leg 192, 2000. Publications: Alkaline Igneous Rocks (ed.); Origin and Evolution of the Ontong Java Plateau (ed.); more than 100 refereed papers. Recreations: house restoration; walking; wine; old maps; antiques; gemmology. Address: (b.) School of GeoSciences, Edinburgh University, Grant Institute, West Mains Road, Edinburgh, EH9 3JW; T.-0131-650 8529; e-mail: Godfrey.Fitton@ed.ac.uk

Fitzgerald, Professor Alexander Grant, BSc, PhD, DSc, FRMS, CPhys, FInstP, FRSE. Emeritus Harris Professor of Physics, Dundee University, since 2005; b. 12.10.39, Dundee; m., June; 1 s.; 2 d. Educ. Perth Academy; Harris Academy; St. Andrews University; Cambridge University. Research Fellow, Lawrence Berkeley Laboratory, University of California; Lecturer, Senior Lecturer, Reader, Professor, Dundee University. Publications: 212 conference and journal papers; book: Quantitative Microbeam Analysis (Co-editor). Recreations: swimming; golf. Address: (b.) Department of Physics, Dundee University, Dundee, DD1 4HN; T.-01382 384553.
E-mail: a.g.fitzgerald@dundee.ac.uk

FitzPatrick, Joe. MSP (SNP), Dundee City West, since 2007; Minister for Parliamentary Business, since 2012; b. 1.4.67. Educ. Whitfield High School; Inverness College; Abertay University; Dundee University. Career: worked as an assistant to Shona Robison MSP and Stewart Hosie MP in their Dundee Constituency Office and was a Dundee City Councillor from 1999 serving as SNP group Whip and Finance Spokesperson on Dundee Council; member of all the main Committees during term of office as a Dundee Councillor, 1999-2007, and a member of the Licensing Board, 2003-07; also represented the Council on a number of outside bodies. After election to the Scottish Parliament, became Parliamentary Liaison Officer for Cabinet Secretary for Finance, John Swinney; helped to set up a Cross Party Group on Life Sciences. Address: (b.) Scottish Parliament, Edinburgh EH99 1SP; Constituency Office: 8 Old Glamis Road, Dundee DD3 8HP.

Fitzpatrick, Professor Julie Lydia, OBE, BVMS (Hons), MSc, PhD, DSc, DipECBHM, DipECSRHM, FRAgs, DLSHTM, FIBiol, MRCVS, FRSE. Scientific Director of The Moredun Research Institute and Chief Executive of The Moredun Group, since 2004; b. 1.3.60, Glasgow; m., Dr. Andrew Fitzpatrick; 2 s. Educ. Wellington School, Ayr; University of Glasgow; University of Bristol; University of London. Veterinary Practitioner, Northumberland, 1982-87; Research Assistant, University of Bristol, 1987-88; PhD student, University of Bristol, 1988-92; Lecturer, University of Glasgow Veterinary School, 1993-98; Head of Division of Farm Animal Medicine and Production, 1998; Personal Chair in Farm Animal Medicine, 1999. Awarded the G. Norman Hall medal for research in animal diseases, 2003; President of the Association of Veterinary Readers and Research Workers, 2003-04; Member: Royal College of Veterinary Surgeons Research Committee, 2002-2012, Scottish Science Advisory Committee, 2004-2010, Advisory Committee on Animal Feedstuffs, 2002-07; Director: Edinburgh Centre for Rural Research, since 2004, Moredun Scientific Limited, since 2005; Member: Agricultural Strategy Group for Scotland, 2005-07, Scottish Animal Health and Welfare Advisory Group, since 2005, Veterinary Fellowships Committee, The Wellcome Trust, 2007-2012, International Panel, The Royal Society of Edinburgh, 2007-2010, Sustainable Agriculture Strategy

Panel, Biotechnology and Biological Sciences Research Council, 2008-2011; Chairman, Veterinary Policy Group of the British Veterinary Association, 2004-07; Director, Global Alliance for Livestock Veterinary Medicines, 2007-2012; Fellow of The Royal Agricultural Societies, 2010; Member, BBSRC Food Security Advisory Panel, since 2012; Co-Chair of the Southern African Centre for Infectious Disease Surveillance, since 2011. DSc (Heriot-Watt), 2012; OBE (2014) for services to Animal Medicine and Science; British Veterinary Association Chiran Award, 2014. Recreations: walking; skiing; reading. Address: (b.) Moredun Research Institute, Pentlands Science Park, Bush Loan, Penicuik, nr. Edinburgh EH26 0PZ; T.-0131 445 5111; e-mail: julie.fitzpatrick@moredun.ac.uk

Fitzpatrick, Kieran, LLB (Hons), MSI, TEP. Partner, Mowat Hall Dick Solicitors, since 2005; b. 12.10.63, Belfast. Educ. Queen's University Belfast. Bird Semple, Glasgow, 1994-96; Wright Johnston and Mackenzie, Edinburgh, 1996-2005. Address: (b.) 45 Queen Charlotte Street, Leith, Edinburgh EH6 7HT.
E-mail: kieran.fitzpatrick@mhdlaw.co.uk

Fladmark, Professor Emeritus, Jan Magnus, DA(Edin), DipTP, HonFRIAS. Patron, Largs Viking Festival, since 2007; Professor Emeritus, Robert Gordon University, since 2002; Hon. Fellow, Edinburgh University, since 1971; b. 12.2.37, Romsdal, Norway; m., Caroline Ashton Miller; 1 s.; 3 d. Educ. Gjermundnes Agricultural College; Ulvestads Commercial College; Hamar Cathedral School; Gimlemoen Military College; Edinburgh College of Art. Press Photographer, Sunnmorsposten,1953-55; National Service, Norwegian Army, 1957-58; PSV Conductor, Scottish Omnibuses, 1959-61; Architect, Moira and Moira, 1964-66; Research Fellow, Edinburgh College of Art, 1966-67; Planning Officer, Scottish Office, 1967-70; ODA Programme Director, Edinburgh University, 1970-76; Assistant Director, Countryside Commission for Scotland, 1976-92; Director, Robert Gordon University Heritage Unit, 1992-2002, Professor in Heritage Management, 1993; CEO, The Heyerdahl Institute, Norway, 2000-03; Adviser, Lima Metropolitan Authority, Peru, 1975; Adviser, Mezzogiorno Development Agency, Italy, 1980; Chairman, Royal Town Planning Institute (Scotland), 1981-82; Governor, Edinburgh College of Art, 1982-88; Council Member, Saltire Society, 1984-88; Chairman, Scottish Interagency Liaison Group, 1987-90; Secretary, Advisory Panel on National Parks, 1989-90; Founding Chairman, Countryside Around Towns Forum, 1989-91; Convener, Scottish Forum on the Environment, 1989-92; MOD Environment Committee, 1989-92; Assessor, Loch Lomond Park Authority and Central Scotland Countryside Trust, 1990-92; Trustee, Sir Patrick Geddes Memorial Trust, since 1991; Visiting Lecturer, Chinese Society of Rural Development Planning, Taiwan, 1994; Adviser, Moscow School of Social and Economic Sciences, 1998; Contributor, Indo-UK Colloquium on Conservation and Cultural Tourism, Cochin, 2004; Fellow, Salzburg Seminar in American Studies, 1973; Glenfiddich Living Scotland Award, 1986; Fladmark of that ilk, since 1981. Publications: The Future of Scotland (Contributing-Author), 1977; Buildings of the Scottish Countryside (Co-Author), 1985; Landscapes under stress (Contributing-Author), 1987; Countryside Planning in Practice: The Scottish Experience (Contributing-Author), 1988; The Countryside Around Towns, 1988; The Mountain Areas of Scotland: Conservation and Management (Co-Author), 1990; Tomorrow's Architectural Heritage: Landscape and Buildings in the Countryside (Co-Author), 1991; Heritage: Conservation, Interpretation and Enterprise (Editor), 1993; The SYHA Environmental Charter: Enjoying the Great Outdoors and the Cultural Riches of Scotland (Co-Author), 1994; The Wealth of a Nation: Heritage as a Cultural and

Competitive Asset, 1994; Cultural Tourism (Editor), 1994; Sharing the Earth: Local Identity in Global Culture (Editor), 1995; In Search of Heritage as Pilgrim or Tourist? (Editor), 1998; Heritage and Museums: Shaping National Identity (Editor), 2000; Heritage and Identity: Shaping the Nations of the North (Editor), 2002. Recreation: fighting own ignorance. Address: (b.) Macduff House, 40 High Street, Auchtermuchty, Fife KY14 7AP; T.-07745 221101; e-mail: mfladmark@hotmail.com

Flanagan, Andrew. Chair, Scottish Police Authority, since 2015; Civil Service Commissioner; Chair of the Audit and Risk Committee, NHS Business Services Authority; Chartered Accountant. Career history: Chief Executive of Scotland's biggest media firm, STV (previously SMG), for 10 years until 2006; Chief Executive, NSPCC, the leading UK Children's charity, until 2013. Non-executive appointments: Criminal Injuries Compensation Authority, CIPFA Business Services Ltd. Held a number of senior finance roles in the media, IT and telecommunications sectors. Address: Scottish Police Authority, 1 Pacific Quay, Glasgow G51 1DZ; T.-0141 585 8300.

Flanagan, Caroline Jane, LLB, DipLP, NP. Partner, Ross & Connel, Solicitors, Dunfermline, since 1990; Member, Council, Law Society of Scotland, 1998-2007; President, Law Society of Scotland, 2005/06; b. 12.1.61, Bridge of Allan; m., Roy Flanagan; 1 s.; 1 d. Educ. Dollar Academy; Edinburgh University. Trainee, then Assistant Solicitor, Edinburgh, 1982-87; Assistant, then Partner, Ross and Connel, since 1988; accredited as specialist in family law, since 1996; family law arbitrator; Dean, local Faculty of Solicitors, 1998-2000. Address: (b.) 18 Viewfield Terrace, Dunfermline, KY12 7JH; T.-01383 721156.

Flanagan, Larry. General Secretary, Educational Institute of Scotland (EIS), since 2012. Educ. University of Stirling. Career: Teacher, Blantyre High School; Senior Teacher, Penilee High School; Principal Teacher of English, Hillhead High School, Glasgow, 1996-2013. Former EIS Council representative and Convener of the EIS Education Committee; member of the EIS Executive Committee; represents the EIS on the Scottish Government's Curriculum for Excellence Management Board; former SQA Examiner and served for 8 years as a Councillor on Glasgow District Council, rising to Vice-Chair of Economic Affairs and the Local Management Committee. Address: The Educational Institute of Scotland, 46 Moray Place, Edinburgh EH3 6BH; T.-0131 225 6244.

Flavell, Professor Andy, BSc, PhD. Professor in Plant Genomics, University of Dundee, since 2010; b. 27.03.51, Brentwood; m., Julie; 1 s.; 1 d. Educ. King Edward VIII Grammar, King's Lynn; University of Sheffield. Postdoctoral research: Imperial Cancer Research Fund Laboratories, London, 1975-79, Dana Farber Cancer Centre, Boston, USA, 1979-80, Imperial Cancer Research Fund, Mill Hill Laboratory, London, 1980-83; University of Dundee: Lecturer in Biochemistry, 1983-93, Senior Lecturer in Biochemistry, 1993-2002, Reader in Plant Genetics, 2002-2010. Recreations: cycling; hill walking; slot racing. Address: (b.) Division of Plant Sciences, University of Dundee at SCRI, Invergowrie, Dundee DD2 5DA; e-mail: a.j.flavell@dundee.ac.uk

Fleck, Professor James, MA, BSc, MSc. Honorary Professor, University of Edinburgh Business School (2015); Deputy Director of *Optima*, ESRC and MRC Integrated

PhD studies in optical medical imaging with innovation and entrepreneurship, University of Edinburgh and University of Strathclyde (2014); Editor-in-Chief of the international journal, *Technology Analysis & Strategic Management* (2013); Professor of Innovation Dynamics, Open University, 2005-2013; former Dean, The Open University Faculty of Business and Law (2005-2011); Freeman of The Worshipful Company of Information Technologists; b. 18.7.51, Kano, Nigeria; m., Heather Anne Morrison; 2 s.; 3 d. Educ. Perth Academy; University of Edinburgh; Manchester University. Engineer, MK-Shand, Invergordon, 1974-75; Computer Programmer, CAP Limited, London, 1976; Research Fellow and Lecturer, Technology Policy Unit, University of Aston, 1980-85; Lecturer in Operations Management, Heriot-Watt University, 1985-86; Lecturer, then Senior Lecturer, Department of Business Studies, University of Edinburgh, 1986-96, Chair of Organisation of Industry and Commerce, 1996-2004 (Director, University of Edinburgh Management School, 1996-99). Joseph Lister Lecturer for the Social Sciences, British Association for the Advancement of Science, 1995-96. Publications: Expertise and Innovation – Information Technology Strategies in the Financial Services Sector (Joint Author), 1994; Exploring Expertise (Joint Editor), 1998. Recreations: reading; DIY; windsurfing; eating out. Address: (h.) Grange Park House, 38 Dick Place, Edinburgh EH9 2JB; T.-07753600055.

Fleming, Maurice. Editor, The Scots Magazine, 1974-91; b. Blairgowrie; m., Nanette Dalgleish; 2 s.; 1 d. Educ. Blairgowrie High School. Trained in hotel management before entering journalism; worked on various magazines; has had five full-length plays performed professionally, as well as one-act plays by amateurs; founder Member: Traditional Music and Song Association of Scotland, Scottish Poetry Library; Past Chairman, Blairgowrie, Rattray and District Civic Trust; Past Chairman, Blair in Bloom. Publications: The Scots Magazine — A Celebration of 250 Years (Co-Editor); The Ghost O' Mause and Other Tales and Traditions of East Perthshire; Old Blairgowrie and Rattray; The Real Macbeth and Other Stories from Scottish History; The Sidlaws: Tales, Traditions and Ballads; Not of This World: Creatures of the Supernatural in Scotland; More Old Blairgowrie and Rattray. Recreations: walking; reading; bird-watching; enjoying the countryside; folksong and folklore. Address: (h.) Craigard, Perth Road, Blairgowrie; T.-Blairgowrie 873633.

Fletcher, James Macmillan. Leader, East Renfrewshire Council, since 2004; Director, Scottish Futures Trust, since 2008; b. 27.04.54, Glasgow; m., Alison; 2 d. Educ. Penilee Secondary School; Stow College of Education. Local Government: Councillor, Eastwood District Council, 1988-95; Convener of Education, East Renfrewshire Council, 1995-2004; Professional: Contracts Officer with Ministry of Defence until 1994; Head of Army Pensions Office, 1994-97; Head of Army Pensions Agency, 1997-2001; Head of Tri-Service Pensions Agency with EDS Ltd., 2001-05. Non Executive Director of Scottish Enterprise Renfrewshire, 2000-08. Recreations: watching sport and travel. Address: (h.) 35 Fowlis Drive, Newton Mearns, East Renfrewshire G77 6JL; T.-0141 639 6201.
E-mail: jim.fletcher@eastrenfrewshire.gov.uk

Fletcher, Sheriff Michael John, LLB. Sheriff of Tayside Central and Fife at Perth, 2000-2014 (retired); b. 5.12.45, Dundee; m., Kathryn Mary; 2 s. Educ. High School of Dundee; St. Andrews University. Partner, Ross Strachan & Co., 1970-88; Partner, Miller Hendry (Hendry and Fenton), 1988-94; Part-time Lecturer in Civil and Criminal Procedure, University of Dundee, 1974-94; Legal Aid Reporter, 1978-94; Temporary Sheriff, 1991-94; Sheriff of South Strathclyde Dumfries & Galloway at Dumfries, 1994-99; Sheriff of Lothian and Borders at Edinburgh,

1999-2000; Editor, Scottish Civil Law Reports, since 1999; Member, Sheriff Court Rules Council, 2001-2010; President, Sheriffs' Association, 2009-2011, formerly Vice President; Member, Judicial Studies Committee, 2006-2012; Council Member, Commonwealth Magistrates and Judges Association, 2009-2012, Regional Vice President, since 2012. Publication: Delictual Damages (Co-Author). Recreations: golf; gardening; travel; fine wines; learning Japanese language.

Fletcher, Professor Roger, MA, PhD, FIMA, FRSE, FRS. Professor of Optimization, Department of Mathematics, Dundee University, 1984-2005; Professor Emeritus, since 2005; Honorary Professor, University of Edinburgh, since 2005; b. 29.1.39, Huddersfield; m., Mary Marjorie Taylor; 2 d. Educ. Huddersfield College; Cambridge University; Leeds University. Lecturer, Leeds University, 1963-69; Principal Research Fellow, then Principal Scientific Officer, AERE Harwell, 1969-73; Senior Research Fellow, then Senior Lecturer, then Reader, Dundee University, 1973-84. Publications: Practical Methods of Optimization, 2nd edition, 1987. numerous others. Recreations: hill-walking; music; bridge. Address: (h.) 43 Errol Road, Invergowrie, Dundee DD2 5BX; T.-01382 562452.

Flint, Professor David, TD, MA, BL, D.Univ, CA. Professor of Accountancy, Glasgow University, 1964-85 (Vice-Principal, 1981-85); b. 24.2.19, Glasgow; m., Dorothy Mary Maclachlan Jardine; 2 s.; 1 d. Educ. High School of Glasgow; Glasgow University. Royal Signals, 1939-46 (Major; mentioned in Despatches); Partner, Mann Judd Gordon & Company, Chartered Accountants, Glasgow, 1951-71; Lecturer (part-time), Glasgow University, 1950-60; Hon. Pres., Glasgow Chartered Accountants Student Society, 1959-60; Dean, Faculty of Law, 1971-73. Council Member, Scottish Business School, 1971-77; Institute of Chartered Accountants of Scotland: President, 1975-76, Vice-President, 1973-75, Convener, Research Advisory Committee, 1974-75 and 1977-84, Convener, Working Party on Future Policy, 1976-79, Convener, Public Sector Committee, 1987-89, Convener, Taxation Review and Research Sub-Committee, 1960-64; Lifetime Achievement Award, 2013; Trustee, Scottish Chartered Accountants Trust for Education, 1981-87; Member: Management Training and Development Committee, Central Training Council, 1966-70, Management and Industrial Relations Committee, Social Science Research Council, 1970-72 and 1978-80, Social Sciences Panel, Scottish Universities Council on Entrance, 1968-72; Chairman, Association of University Teachers of Accounting, 1969; Member, Company Law Committee, Law Society of Scotland, 1976-85; Scottish Economic Society: Treasurer, 1954-62, Vice-President, 1977-88; Member, Commission for Local Authority Accounts in Scotland, 1978-80; President, European Accounting Association, 1983-84; Hon. Professor of Accountancy, Stirling University, 1988-91; British Accounting Association Lifetime Achievement Award, 2004. Publications: A true and fair view in company accounts, 1982; Philosophy and Principles of Auditing, 1988. Recreation: golf.

Flint, Professor Harry James, BSc, PhD. Head, Gut Health Division, Rowett Institute of Nutrition and Health, since 1999; Personal Chair in Microbiology, University of Aberdeen, since 2008, Professor, since 2003; b. 5.1.51, London; m. Irene; 1 s.; 2 d. Educ. Abingdon School, Abingdon, Oxfordshire; Edinburgh University. PhD in Genetics, University of Edinburgh, 1972-76; Lecturer in Genetics, University of Nottingham, 1976-80; Lecturer in Biology, University of The West Indies (Barbados), 1980-82; Research Fellow, University of Edinburgh (Dept. of Genetics),

1982-85; Research Scientist, Rowett Research Institute, Aberdeen, 1985-99. Member, UK Advisory Committee on Novel Foods and Processes; Associate Editor, "Microbiology". Publications: Author of 125 primary research papers, 14 reviews and 28 book chapters. Recreations: music; countryside; natural history; history. Address: (b.) Rowett Institute of Nutrition and Health, University of Aberdeen, Greenburn Road, Bucksburn, Aberdeen AB21 9SB; T.-01224 716651; e-mail: h.flint@abdn.ac.uk

Flood, Peter. Rector, Perth High School, since 2012; b. 1961. Former Headteacher, Loudoun Academy, 2009-2012. Recreations: playing the flute; fencing. Address: (b.) Oakbank Road, Perth PH1 1HB; T.-01738 628271.

Flowerdew, Stuart Alan, LLB(Hons), DipLP, NP. Solicitor; Partner, AFJ Solicitors, since 2014; Director, Flowerdew Solicitors Ltd, 2010-2014; Secretary and Treasurer, Faculty of Solicitors in Peterhead and Fraserburgh, 1993-2010; Chairman, Victim Support, Aberdeenshire, 2000-04; b. 5.2.67, Kings Lynn; m., Natalie Anne Lamb; 1 d. Educ. Forres Academy; University of Dundee. Trainee/Assistant, Miller Hendry, Perth, 1989-92; Assistant: Stewart and Watson, Peterhead, 1992-94; Masson & Glennie, Peterhead, 1994-96; Associate, John MacRitchie & Co., SSC, Peterhead, 1997-1999; Partner, Flowerdew Allan, Solicitors, Peterhead, 1999-2010. Recreation: cricket. Address: (b.) 2 Kirk Street, Peterhead; T.-01779 481717; (h.) Braemount, 27 Balmoor Terrace, Peterhead; T.-01779 473117. E-mail: flowerdewsolicitors@hotmail.co.uk

Flyn, Derek, LLB, WS, FSAScot. Solicitor (retired), former partner, Macleod and MacCallum, Inverness (1978-2008); b. 22.8.45, Edinburgh; m., Fiona Mairi Macmillan; 2 s.; 1 d. Educ. Broughton School, Edinburgh; Dundee University. Scottish Court Service, 1962-72 (Sheriff Clerk Depute at Portree, 1967-70); President, Scottish Law Agents Society, 1999-2000; Vice-Chairman, Crofting Law Group, 1994-2004; Chairman, Riding for the Disabled (Highland Group), 2007-2012; Chairman, Scottish Crofting Federation, 2012-2014. Publications: Crofting Law (Co-author), 1990; Green's Annotated Crofters Act (Co-author), 1993 and 2010; Countryside Law in Scotland (Contributor), 2000; Stair Encyclopaedia (Contributor), 2009; First specialist in crofting law accredited by Law Society of Scotland, 1993; Scottish Life and Society (Contributor), 2012. Recreations: music; walking; Ross County FC. Address: (h.) Croyardhill, Beauly IV4 7EX. E-mail: dflyn28mt@outlook.com

Foggie, Janet Patricia, MA, BD, PhD. Minister, St Andrew's Parish Church, since 2009; Chairperson, St Andrews Family Support Project, since 2010; b. 9.4.71, Greenock; m., Dr Alan R. Macdonald; 2 s.; 1 d. Educ. Greenock Academy; Universities of Edinburgh and St Andrews. Post-doctoral research post: Browne Downie Research Fellowship, St Mary's College, University of St Andrews, 2000-01; Assistant Minister, Hope Park Church, St Andrews, Fife, 2001-03; Hospital Chaplain to the Royal Victoria Hospital, Dundee (Part time), 2003-04; Mental Health Care Chaplain/Spiritual Care Provider, Dundee, NHS Tayside, 2004-09; Seconded to NHS Education for Scotland, 2007-2008; Joint Editor, Scottish Journal of Healthcare Chaplaincy, 2006-2011. Publications: Academic: Urban Religion in Renaissance Scotland: The Dominican Order 1450-1560, 2003; Capabilities and Competences for Healthcare Chaplains (Joint Author), 2008; various articles; Fiction: 'The News Steps' in Doris Lumsden's Heart Shaped Bed and

Other Stories, 2004. Recreations: reading; sewing; gardening; cooking and eating. Address: 2 King Street, Dundee. E-mail: rev.foggie@btinternet.com

Foley, John. Chief Executive Officer, Scottish Police Authority, since 2014; formerly Interim Chief Executive Officer (5 months). Previously held several high profile positions within both the public and private sector and across a wide range of industries; former CEO of City Building and held a number of directorships within the UK publishing group, Trinity Mirror; formerly executive and non-executive director with over forty companies and has also successfully run own business; former director of Glasgow Opportunities; previously a member of the influencer groups of Glasgow Chamber of Commerce and the Scottish Council for Development of Industry; UK qualified Chartered Management Accountant and past president of CIMA in Scotland; Chartered Global Management Accountant; Fellow of the Institute of Directors in the UK; member of the Scottish Justice Board. Extensive experience of all aspects of media; writer and conference speaker. Address: Scottish Police Authority, 1 Pacific Quay, Glasgow G51 1DZ; T.-0141 585 8300.

Follett, Professor Georgina Louise Patricia, OBE, MDes, FRSA, FCSD. Deputy Principal for Knowledge Exchange in the Creative Arts, University of Dundee; Director, Knowledge Exchange Hub Design in Action, Duncan of Jordanstone College of Art and Design, University of Dundee; b. 16.7.49, London; m., Adrian Franklin; 1 s.; 1 d. Educ. Channing School; Royal College of Art. Course Leader, Sir John Cass College, 1979-88; Acting Head, Gray's School of Art, 1988-1993; Jeweller (exhibitions include one woman show, Jewellery Gallery, Victoria and Albert Museum). Recreations: gardening; drawing; reading. Address: Design in Action, Matthew Building, DJCAD, University of Dundee, DD1 4HT; T.-01382 385202.

Foot, Professor Hugh Corrie, BA, PhD, FBPsS. Emeritus Professor of Psychology, Strathclyde University, since 1992, b. 7.6.41, Northwood, Middx; m., Daryl M.; 1 s.; 1 d. Educ. Durham University; Queen's College, Dundee. Research Fellow, Dundee University, 1965-68; University of Wales Institute of Science and Technology: Lecturer, 1968-77, Senior Lecturer, 1977-88; Reader, University of Wales College of Cardiff, 1989-91. Recreations: gardening; hill walking. Address: Department of Psychology, Strathclyde University, 40 George Street, Glasgow, G1 1QE.

Forbes, Professor Charles Douglas, DSc, MD, MB, ChB, FRCP, FRCPGlas, FRCPEdin, FRSA, FRSE. Emeritus Professor of Medicine, Dundee University; former Honorary Consultant Physician, Dundee Teaching Hospitals NHS Trust; b. 9.10.38, Glasgow; m., Janette MacDonald Robertson; 2 s. Educ. High School of Glasgow; Glasgow University. Assistant Lecturer in Materia Medica, Glasgow University; Lecturer in Medicine, Makerere, Uganda; Registrar in Medicine, Glasgow Royal Infirmary; Reader in Medicine, Glasgow University; Fellow, American Heart Association; Fullbright Fellow; Director, Regional Haemophilia Centre, Glasgow. Recreation: gardening. Address: (h.) East Chattan, 108 Hepburn Gardens, St. Andrews KY16 9LT; T.-01334 472428.

Forbes, Very Rev. Dr. Graham John Thomson, CBE (2004). Provost, St Mary's Cathedral Edinburgh, since 1990; b. 10.6.51; m., Jane; 3 s. Educ. George Heriot's School, Edinburgh; University of Aberdeen; University of Edinburgh; Edinburgh Theological College. Curate, Old St Paul's Edinburgh, 1976-82; Provost: St. Ninian's Cathedral, Perth, 1982-90; Non-Executive Director, Radio Tay, 1986-90; Founder, Canongate Youth Project, Edinburgh; President, Lothian Association of Youth Clubs, since 1986; HM (lay) Inspector of Constabulary for Scotland, 1995-98; Chairman: Scottish Executive MMR Expert Group, 2001-02, Scottish Criminal Cases Review Commission, 2002; Director, Theological Institute of the Scottish Episcopal Church, 2002-04; Member: Scottish Community Education Council, 1981-87, Children's Panel Advisory Committee, Tayside, 1986-90, Parole Board for Scotland, 1990-95, Scottish Consumer Council, 1995-98, GMC, since 1996, Clinical Standards Board for Scotland, 1999-2005, Historic Buildings Council for Scotland, 2000-02, Scottish Council, Royal College of Anaesthetists, 2001-04; former Chairman, Scottish Criminal Cases Review Commission. Recreations: fly fishing; running. Address: St. Mary's Cathedral Edinburgh, 8 Lansdowne Crescent, Edinburgh EH12 5EQ; T.-0131 225 2978; e-mail: provost@cathedral.net

Forbes, Kate. MSP (SNP), Skye, Lochaber and Badenoch, since 2016. Educ. Dingwall Academy; University of Cambridge. Campaigned with the SNP to address the gender gap around employment in the Highlands. Address: Scottish Parliament, Edinburgh EH99 1SP.

Forbes, 23rd Lord (Malcolm Nigel Forbes); b. 1946. Succeeded to title, 2013.

Forbes, Ronald Douglas, RSA, RGI. Artist; Leverhulme Artist in Residence, Scottish Crop Research Institute, Dundee, 2006-09; Visiting Professor, University of Abertay Dundee, since 2003; Head of Painting, Duncan of Jordanstone College of Art, 1995-2001; b. 22.3.47, Braco; m., Sheena Henderson Bell; 1 s.; 2 d. Educ. Morrison's Academy, Crieff; Edinburgh College of Art. Leverhulme Senior Art Fellow, Strathclyde University, 1973-74; Head of Painting, Crawford School of Art, Cork, Ireland, 1974-78; Artist in Residence, Livingston, 1978-80; Scottish Arts Council Studio Residence Bursary, Amsterdam, 1980; Lecturer, Glasgow School of Art, 1979-83; Director, Master Fine Art postgraduate studies, Duncan of Jordanstone College of Art, University of Dundee, 1983-95; Artist in Residence, University of Tasmania Hobart Centre for the Arts. First Prize, first Scottish Young Contemporary Exhibition, 1967; BBC Scope Film Prize, 1975; RSA Guthrie Award, 1979; Scottish Arts Council Award for Film-making, 1979; Highland Society of London Award, Royal Scottish Academy, 1996; elected RGI (Royal Glasgow Institute of the Fine Arts), 2013. Recreations: cinema; theatre; gardening. Address: (h.) 13 Fort Street, Dundee DD2 1BS; T.-01382 641498.
E-mail: ronnieforbes@blueyonder.co.uk
Website: www.ronald-forbes.com

Ford, Professor Ian, BSc, PhD, FRCP (Glas), FRCP (Edin), FRSE. Professor of Biostatistics and Director, Robertson Centre for Biostatistics, Glasgow University, since 1991, Director, Glasgow Clinical Trials Unit, since 2007, Dean, Faculty of Information and Mathematical Sciences, 2000-04; b. 4.2.51, Glasgow; m., Carole Louise Ford; 1 s. Educ. Hamilton Academy; Glasgow University. Visiting Lecturer, University of Wisconsin, Madison, 1976-77; Lecturer, then Senior Lecturer, Reader, Personal Professor and Professor, Glasgow University, since 1977. Publications: 300 papers. Recreations: gardening; travel. Address: (b.) Robertson Centre for Biostatistics, Boyd Orr Building, Glasgow University, Glasgow; T.-0141-330 4744.

Ford, John Noel Patrick, KStJ, FInstD. Retired (1992) as Chairman, Scotland and Northern Ireland, and Marketing Director, OCS Group Ltd; Director/Administrator, Scottish Civic Trust, 1993-2004; b. 18.12.35, Surbiton; m., Roslyn Madeleine Penfold; 2 s.; 2 d. Educ. Tiffin School, Kingston on Thames. Chancellor, The Priory of Scotland of the

166 WHO'S WHO IN SCOTLAND

Order of St. John, 2002-2011. Deacon, Incorporation of Masons of Glasgow, 1985-86; Deacon Convener, Trades House of Glasgow, 1991-92; Regional Chairman, Glasgow, Princes Scottish Youth Business Trust, 1993-2001; Chairman, Glasgow Committee, Order of St. John, 1993-2002; Trustee, New Lanark Conservation Trust, 1994-2009; Governor, Hutchesons' Educational Trust, 1986-2001; Member, Council, Europa Nostra, 1999-2005; General Commissioner of Inland Revenue, Glasgow North, 1993-2009. Recreations: golf and sport in general; gardening. Address: (h.) South Lodge, Ballindalloch, Balfron G63 0RQ; T.-01360 440347.

Ford of Cunningham (Baroness Margaret Ford). Chairman, STV Plc, since 2013. Over 20 years experience as a non-Executive Director and Chairman of private and listed companies and extensive experience of working with Government; currently Chairman of Barchester Healthcare Limited, the private healthcare provider; Chairman of the Olympic Park Legacy Company, 2009-2012. Appointed to the House of Lords in 2006 and sits as an Independent Peer. Address: STV, Pacific Quay, Glasgow G51 1PQ; T.-0141 300 3704.

Forman, Robert Crawford Banks, MBE, LLB, LLM, WS. Partner, Blackadders LLP; b. 30.3.48, UK; widower; 1 s.; 1 d. Educ. Royal High School; Edinburgh University. Past Moderator of The Society of High Constables of Edinburgh; Chairman, The Scottish Conservative Party; Chairman, East Scotland Salvation Army Advisory Board. Recreations: golf; reading; boating. Address: (b.) 5 Rutland Square, Edinburgh EH1 2AX; T.-0131 222 8111; e-mail: robert.forman@blackadders.co.uk

Forrest, Professor Sir (Andrew) Patrick (McEwen), Kt (1986), BSc, MD, ChM, FRCS, FRCSEdin, FRCSGlas, FRCPEd, DSc (Hon), LLD (Hon), MD (Hon), FACS (Hon), FRACS (Hon), FRCSCan (Hon), FRCR (Hon), FFPH (Hon), FIBiol, FRSE. Professor Emeritus, Edinburgh University; b. 25.3.23, Mount Vernon, Lanarkshire; m., 1. Margaret Beryl Hall (deceased); 1s.; 1d.; 2. Margaret Anne Steward; 1 d. Educ. Dundee High School; St. Andrews University. House Surgeon, Dundee Royal Infirmary; Surgeon Lieutenant, RNVR; Mayo Foundation Fellow; Lecturer and Senior Lecturer, Glasgow University; Professor of Surgery, Welsh National School of Medicine; Regius Professor of Clinical Surgery, Edinburgh University; Visiting Scientist, National Cancer Institute, USA; Associate Dean of Clinical Studies, International Medical College, Malaysia; Chief Scientist (part-time), Scottish Home and Health Department, 1981-87; Chairman, Working Group, Breast Cancer Screening, 1985-86; President: Surgical Research Society, 1974-76, Association of Surgeons of Great Britain and Ireland, 1988-89; Lister Medal, Royal College of Surgeons of England, 1987; Member, Kirk Session, St. Giles Cathedral, 1999-2003. Publications: Prognostic Factors in Breast Cancer (Co-author), 1968; Principles and Practice of Surgery (Co-author), 1985; Breast Cancer: the decision to screen, 1990. Address: (h.) 19 St. Thomas Road, Edinburgh EH9 2LR; T.-0131-667 3203.

Forrest, Archie, RGI. Artist; b. 1950, Glasgow. Educ. Glasgow School of Art. Taught at Glasgow School of Art, 1978-85; works in the Glasgow School/Scottish Colourist tradition with still life, figure and landscape subjects (often France or Italy) of brilliant colour and bravura handling underpinned by fine drawing and sense of form; also a sculptor of considerable merit. Shows with great success in London and in Edinburgh. Member of the Royal Glasgow Institute of Fine Arts, since 1988 and regular exhibitor there and at the Royal Scottish Academy, since 1975; won numerous awards for both his paintings and sculpture. Example of his work can be found in private and corporate collections worldwide. Address: 2 Cleveden Crescent, Glasgow G12 0PD.

Forrester, Rev. Professor Duncan Baillie, MA (Hons), BD, DPhil, HonDTheol (Iceland), HonDD (Glasgow and St. Andrews). Dean, Faculty of Divinity, New College, Edinburgh, 1996-00 (Principal, 1986-96), Professor of Christian Ethics and Practical Theology, 1978-2001, Director, Centre for Theology and Public Issues, 1984-2000; Church of Scotland Minister; b. 10.11.33, Edinburgh; m., Rev. Margaret McDonald; 1 s.; 1 d. Educ. Madras College, St. Andrews; St. Andrews University; Chicago University; Edinburgh University. Part-time Assistant in Politics, Edinburgh University, 1957-58; Assistant Minister, Hillside Church, Edinburgh, and Leader of St. James Mission, 1960-61; as Church of Scotland Missionary, Lecturer and then Professor of Politics, Madras Christian College, Tambaram, South India, 1962-70; ordained Presbyter, Church of South India, 1962; part-time Lecturer in Politics, Edinburgh University, 1966-67; Chaplain and Lecturer in Politics, Sussex University, 1970-78; Member, WCC Faith and Order Commission, 1983-96; President: Society for Study of Theology, 1991-93, Society for Study of Christian Ethics, 1991-94, Church Service Society, 1999-2001; Member, Nuffield Council on Bioethics, 1995-2002; Vice-President, Council on Christian Approaches to Defence and Disarmament; Templeton UK Award, 1999. FRSE, 2007. Publications: Caste & Christianity, 1980; Encounter with God (Co-author), 1983; Studies in the History of Worship in Scotland (Co-Editor), 1984; Christianity and the Future of Welfare, 1985; Theology and Politics, 1988; Just Sharing (Co-author), 1988; Beliefs, Values and Policies, 1989; Worship Now Book II (Co-editor), 1989; Theology and Practice (Editor), 1990; The True Church and Morality, 1997; Christian Justice and Public Policy, 1997; Truthful Action: Explorations in Practical Theology, 2000; On Human Worth: A Christian Vindication of Equality, 2001; Apocalypse Now? Reflections on Faith in a Time of Terror, 2005; Theological Fragments - Explorations in Unsystematic Theology, 2005; Worship and Liturgy in Context (Co-Author), 2009; Living and Loving the Mystery, 2010; Forrester on Christian and Practical Theology, 2010. Recreations: hill-walking; reading; listening to music. Address: (h.) 25 Kingsburgh Road, Edinburgh, EH12 6DZ; T.-0131-337 5646.

Forrester, Ian Stewart, QC, MA, LLB, LLD, MCL. Honorary Professor, Glasgow University; UK Judge of the General Court of the European Court of Justice in Luxembourg, since 2015; Member, Dean's Advisory Board, Tulane University Law School, since 2006; b. 13.1.45, Glasgow; m., Sandra Anne Therese Keegan; 2 s. Educ. Kelvinside Academy, Glasgow; Glasgow University; Tulane University of Louisiana. Admitted to Faculty of Advocates, 1972; admitted to Bar of State of NY, 1977; Queen's Counsel (Scotland), 1988; called to Bar, Middle Temple, 1996; Bencher, 2012; Maclay, Murray & Spens, 1968-69; Davis Polk & Wardwell, 1969-72; Cleary Gottlieb Steen & Hamilton, 1972-81; established independent chambers, Brussels, 1981; Co-Founder, Forrester & Norall, 1981 (Forrester Norall & Sutton, 1989; White & Case/Forrester Norall & Sutton, 1998), practising before European Commission and Courts. Chairman, British Conservative Association, Belgium, 1982-86; Arbitrator, Court of Arbitration for Sport, since 2012; author of numerous papers on European law; Elder, St. Andrew's Church of Scotland, Brussels. Recreations: politics; wine; cooking; restoring old houses.

Forrester, Professor John V., MD (Hons), FRCS(Ed), FRCOphth, FRCS(G), FRCP(Ed), FMedSci, FRSE, FIBiol, FARVO. Emeritus Professor; Professor of Ocular Immunology, University of Western Australia, since 2012; Cockburn Professor of Ophthalmology, since 1984; Raine Visiting Professor, University of Western Australia; b. 11.9.46, Glasgow; m., Anne Gray; 2 s.; 2 d. Educ. St. Aloysius College, Glasgow; Glasgow University. Various hospital appointments, Glasgow, 1971-78; MRC Travelling Fellow, Columbia University, New York, 1976-77;

Consultant Ophthalmologist, Southern General Hospital, 1979-83. Editor, British Journal of Ophthalmology, 1992-2000; Spinoza Professor, University of Amsterdam, 1997; Master, Oxford Ophthalmological Congress, 2000-02; President, European Association for Vision and Eye Research, 2002. Awards: McKenzie Medal 2006; Doyne Medal, 2007; Adjunct Professor, Ophthalmology, University of Western Australia, 2009; Recipient, Alcon Award, 2011; Mildred Weisenfeld Award, 2012; Donders Medal, 2012; Bowman Lectures and Medal, 2012. Address: (b.) Immunology and Infection, Institute of Medical Sciences, Aberdeen University, Aberdeen AB25 2ZD; T.-01224 553782.

Forrester, Rev. Margaret Rae, MA, BD. b. 23.11.37, Edinburgh; m., Duncan B. Forrester; 1 s.; 1 d. Educ. George Watson's Ladies' College; Edinburgh University and New College. Assistant Pastor, Tambaram, Madras; Minister, Telscombe Cliffs URC, Sussex; Assistant Minister, St. George's West, Edinburgh; Chaplain, Napier College, Edinburgh; Minister, St. Michael's, Edinburgh, 1980-2003; Convener, Board of World Mission and Unity, Church of Scotland, 1992-96; Moderator, Presbytery of Edinburgh, 2000-01. Publications: Touch and Go, 2002; The Cat Who Decided, 2007; My Cat Mac, 2010; Mac's Christmas Star, 2012. Recreation: gardening. Address: 25 Kingsburgh Road, Edinburgh EH12 6DZ; T.-0131-337 5646; e-mail: margaret@rosskeen.org.uk

Forsyth of Drumlean, Rt. Hon. Lord (Michael Bruce Forsyth), PC, Kt, MA. Life Peer; MP (Conservative), Stirling, 1983-97; Non-Executive Director: J & J Denholm Ltd, Secure Trust Bank; Chairman, Safor Ltd; Deputy Chairman, J.P. Morgan UK, 2002-05; Secretary of State for Scotland, 1995-97; b. 16.10.54, Montrose; m., Susan Jane; 1 s.; 2 d. Educ. Arbroath High School; St. Andrews University. National Chairman, Federation of Conservative Students, 1976; Member, Westminster City Council, 1978-83; Member, Select Committee on Scottish Affairs; Parliamentary Private Secretary to the Foreign Secretary, 1986-87; Chairman, Scottish Conservative Party, 1989-90; Parliamentary Under Secretary of State and Minister of State, Scottish Office, 1987-92; Minister of State, Department of Employment, 1992-94; Minister of State, Home Office, 1994-95; Parliamentarian of Year, 1996; Member, Select Committee on Monetary Policy, House of Lords; Member, Joint Committee of both Houses of Parliament on future of House of Lords; Director, Robert Fleming International Ltd., 1997-2000; Vice Chairman, Investment Europe, J P Morgan Chase, 2001-2002; Member, Development Board, National Portrait Gallery, 1999-2003; Patron, Craighalbert Centre for Children with Motor Impairments; Patron, CINI (UK); House of Lords: Economic Affairs Select Committee, Barnett Formula Select Committee. Recreations: fly fishing; mountaineering; astronomy; gardening; art; steam engines; skiing. Address: House of Lords, London SW1A 0PW.

Forsyth of that Ilk, Alistair Charles William, JP, KHS, FSCA, FSA Scot, FInstPet, CStJ. Baron of Ethie; Chief of the Name and Clan of Forsyth; b. 7.12.29; m., Ann Hughes; 4 s. Educ. St. Paul's School; Queen Mary College, London. Company Director; CStJ, 1982; KHS, 1992; Freeman of the City of London; Liveryman of the Scriveners Company. Recreations: Scottish antiquities.

Forsyth of that Ilk Younger, Alistair James Menteith, OStJ, MTheol, LLB, DipLP, ACII, FSAScot. Advocate, since 1995; b. 21.12.60, Calcutta; m., Isabelle Richer. Educ. Fettes College; St. Andrews University; Buckingham University; Edinburgh University; Inns of Court School of Law. Executive, publishing and insurance, 1983-86; called to English Bar, Inner Temple, 1990, Member, Lincolns Inn, 1991; employed Lindsays WS, 1992-94; qualified as Solicitor and Notary Public, 1993. Lt., Ayrshire (Earl of

Carrick's Own) Yeomanry Sqn., Queen's Own Yeomanry, 1983-88, Inns of Court and City Yeomanry, 1988-90; Member, Committee, Heraldry Society of Scotland, 1983-86; Secretary, Angus Branch, Order of St. John, 1983-86; Liveryman of the Worshipful Company of Scriveners, 2009; Freeman of the City of London, 2009; Member, Company of Merchants of the City of Edinburgh, 2010. Recreations: heraldry; genealogy; history; wine. Address: Dundrennan, Horsemarket, Falkland, Fife KY15 7BG; T.-01337 858735.

Forsyth, Bill. Film Director and Script Writer; b. 1946, Glasgow. Films include: Gregory's Girl, 1981, Local Hero, 1983, Comfort and Joy, 1984, Housekeeping, 1988, Breaking In, 1990, Being Human, 1993; Gregory's Two Girls, 1999. BAFTA Awards: Best Screenplay, 1982, Best Director, 1983.

Forsyth, Janice, MA (Hons). Broadcaster; b. Glasgow. Educ. Glasgow High School for Girls; Glasgow University. Presenter, The Culture Studio; TV includes: Filmnight (C4), Don't Look Down, NB and Festival Cinema (all Scottish); writes a weekly blog for HeraldScotland. Board Member, Giant Productions. Recreations: cinema; travel; theatre.

Forsyth, Roderick Hugh (Roddy). Journalist; Director, SPFL Trust, since 2013; b. 22.9.53, Lennoxtown; m., Marian Charlotte Reilly; 2 d. Educ. Allan Glen's School, Glasgow. Journalist, D.C. Thomson & Co., 1972-74; Scottish Daily News, 1975; Editor, Carnoustie Times, 1976-77; Editor, What's On in Glasgow, 1978-79; Editor, Clyde Guide, 1979-80; Journalist, Glasgow Herald, 1980-81; Sunday Standard, 1982-83; freelance, since 1983; Scottish Football Correspondent: The Times, 1988-93, Daily and Sunday Telegraph, since 1993, BBC Radio Sport, since 1983, RTE Ireland, since 1988, Ireland on Sunday, since 1996. President, Scottish Football Writers' Association, 2010-13; Director, SPL Trust, 2012-13. Publications: The Only Game, 1990; Fields of Green, 1996; Blue and True, 1996.

Forsythe, Professor John L.R., MD, FRCSEd, FRCSEng, MBBS, FEBS, FRCP (Ed). Consultant transplant surgeon, since 1995; Honorary Professor, University of Edinburgh; b. 27.2.58, Co. Antrim; m., Lorna; 1 s.; 2 d. Educ. Belfast Royal Academy; University of Newcastle upon Tyne. Consultant in General Surgery, Newcastle upon Tyne, 1992-95; Consultant Transplant Surgeon, Royal Infirmary of Edinburgh, since 1995; Chairman, Scottish Transplant Group; President, British Transplantation Society, 2005-07; Non-Executive Board Member, NHS Blood and Transplant, 2005-2013; Lead Clinician for Organ Donation and Transplantation (Scotland); Chairman, Advisory Committee on Safety of Blood, Tissues and Organs (UK Advisory Group); Secretary, European Society of Organ Transplantation; President, European Society of Organ Transplantation. Honorary degree awarded, 2013. Address: (b.) Transplant Unit, Royal Infirmary of Edinburgh, 51 Little France Crescent, Old Dalkeith Road, Edinburgh EH16 4SU; T.-0131 242 1715; e-mail: john.forsythe@nhslothian.scot.nhs.uk

Forteviot, 4th Baron (Sir John James Evelyn Dewar Bart). Member, Queen's Bodyguard for Scotland (Royal Company of Archers); b. 5.4.38. Educ. Eton. Black Watch (RHR), 1956-58.

Forty, Professor Arthur John, CBE, BSc, PhD, DSc, LLD, DUniv, DSc (Hon. Warwick), FRSE. Principal and Vice-Chancellor, Stirling University, 1986-94; b. 4.11.28, Shrivenham; m., Alicia Blanche Hart Gough; 1 s. Educ. Headlands School, Swindon; Bristol University. RAF, 1953-56; Senior Scientist, Tube Investments Ltd., 1956-58;

Lecturer, Bristol University, 1958-64; founding Professor of Physics, Warwick University, 1964-86; Pro-Vice-Chancellor, Warwick Univ., 1970-86; Member, Physics and Materials Science Committees, SERC, 1970-74; Member: UGC, 1982-86 (Vice-Chairman, 1985-86), Computer Board, Universities and Research Councils, 1982-85 (Chairman, 1988-91); Chairman, Committee of Scottish University Principals, 1990-92; Member, British Library Board, 1987-94; Chairman, Information Systems Committee, UFC, 1991-92; Hon. Fellow and Chairman, EPCC, Edinburgh University, 1994-97; Member, Board of Trustees, National Library of Scotland, 1995-2001; Member, Academic Advisory Board, University of the Highlands and Islands, since 1999; author of "Forty Report" on future facilities for advanced research computing. Recreations: dinghy sailing; gardening. Address: (h.) Port Mor, St. Fillans, Perthshire PH6 2NF.

Foster, Angiolina, CBE, MA (Hons), DMS, MCMI. Interim Chief Executive, NHS 24, since 2016; Chief Executive, Healthcare Improvement Scotland, 2014-16; b. 1.2.56, Kirkcaldy; m., Michael Foster; 1 s.; 1 d. Educ. Glasgow University. Housing Officer, Glasgow City Council, 1979-85; Edinburgh District Council: Chief Housing Benefits Officer, 1985-87, Depute Director of Housing, 1987-96; Senior Depute Director of Housing, City of Edinburgh Council, 1996-2001; Director of Regulation and Housing, Communities Scotland, 2001-02; Acting Chief Executive, Glasgow Housing Association (Secondment), 2002-03; Chief Executive, Communities Scotland, 2003-07; Director of Health and Social Care Integration, Scottish Government, 2011-14. Recreations: cycling; hill walking. Address: NHS 24, Caledonia House, Fifty Pitches Road, Cardonald Park, Glasgow G51 4EB.

Foster, John, CBE, FRICS, FRTPI, RIBA, ARIAS, FRSA; b. 13.8.20, Glasgow; m., Daphne Househam; 1 s.; 1 d. Educ. Whitehill School, Glasgow; Royal Technical College, Glasgow. Surveyor with private firm in Glasgow, 1937; Air Ministry during War; Assistant Planning Officer: Kirkcudbright County Council, 1945-47, Holland Joint Planning Committee, Lincolnshire, 1947-48; Deputy County Planning Officer, Holland County Council, 1948-52; Deputy Planning Officer, Peak Park Planning Board, 1952-54; Director, Peak District National Park Board, 1954-68; Director, Countryside Commission for Scotland, 1968-85. Hon. Vice-President, Ramblers Association Scotland (President, 1994-2000); Hon. Fellow, Royal Scottish Geographical Society; Hon. Member and Past Vice Chairman, Commission on National Parks and Protected Areas, World Conservation Union; Fred Packard International Parks Award, 1992; Hon. Member, European Federation of Nature and National Parks; Vice President, Scottish Council for National Parks (President, 2005-08); Vice-President, Association for the Protection of Rural Scotland (APRS); Vice-Chairman, Heritage Unit Advisory Board, Robert Gordon University, Aberdeen, 1992-2001; Life Member, National Trust for Scotland; George Waterston Memorial Award, 1991; Hon. Fellow, Robert Gordon University. Fellow, Royal Society of Arts; Life Member, Royal Commonwealth Society; Hon. Member, St Kilda Club. Recreations: walking; photography; philately; reading. Address: (h.) Birchover, Ferntower Road, Crieff PH7 3DH; T.-01764 652336.

Foster, Professor John Odell, MA, PhD. Emeritus Professor of Social Sciences, University of the West of Scotland; b. 21.10.40, Hertford; m., Renee Prendergast; 1 d. Educ. Guildford Grammar School; St. Catherine's College, Cambridge. Postdoctoral Research Fellow, St. Catherine's College, Cambridge, 1965-68; Lecturer in Politics, Strathclyde University, 1966-81. International Secretary, Communist Party of Britain (Scottish Secretary, 1988-

2000). Publications: Class Struggle and the Industrial Revolution, 1974; Politics of the UCS Work-In, 1986; Track Record: the Caterpillar Occupation, 1988; Paying for the Piper (Co-author), 1996. Recreation: hill-walking. Address: (h.) 845 Govan Road, Glasgow G51.

Foster-Fulton, Rev. Sally. Head of Christian Aid Scotland, since 2016; b. 1964. Previously Associate Minister, Dunblane Cathedral. Convener, Church and Society Council, 2012-16. Address: Christian Aid Scotland, First Floor, Sycamore House, 290 Bath Street, Glasgow G2 4JR; T.-0141 221 7475; e-mail: sfoster-fulton@christian-aid.org

Foulds, Emeritus Professor Wallace Stewart, CBE, MD, ChM, FRCS, FRCSGlas, DO, Hon. FRCOphth, Hon. DSc (Strathclyde), Hon. FRANZCO, Hon. FCMSA. Emeritus Professor of Ophthalmology, Glasgow University; Consultant in Medico-Legal Practice; Senior Consultant, Singapore Eye Research Institute; b. 26.4.24, London; m., Margaret Holmes Walls; 1 s.; 2 d. Educ. George Watson's Boys College, Edinburgh; Paisley Grammar School; Glasgow University. RAF Medical Branch, 1946-49; training posts, Moorfields Eye Hospital, London, 1952-54; Research Fellow, Institute of Ophthalmology, London University, and Senior Registrar, University College Hospital, London, 1954-58; Consultant Ophthalmologist, Addenbrookes Hospital, Cambridge, 1958-64; Tennent Professor, Glasgow University, 1964-89; Honorary Lecturer, Cambridge University and Research Fellow, London University, 1958-64; Past President: Ophthalmological Society of UK, Faculty of Ophthalmologists; Past Chairman, Association for Eye Research; Founder President, Royal College of Ophthalmologists; Hon. Fellow, Royal Society of Medicine; Hon. Fellow, Medical and Dental Defence Union of Scotland. Recreations: sailing; DIY; natural history. Address: Kinnoul Place, 68 Dowanside Road, Glasgow G12 9DL; T.-0141-334 2463.
E-mail: wallace@wsfoulds.demon.co.uk

Foulis, Alan Keith, BSc, MD, FRCPath, FRCP(Ed). Former Consultant Pathologist, Southern General Hospital, Glasgow (retired, 2015); Honorary Clinical Professor, Glasgow University, since 2010; b. 25.5.50, Glasgow; m., (1) Anne Don Martin (deceased); 1 s.; 1 d.; m., (2) Doreen P. Dobson. Educ. Glasgow Academy; Glasgow University. Trained in pathology, Western Infirmary, Glasgow, following brief flirtation with surgery at Aberdeen Royal Infirmary; C.L. Oakley Lecturer, Pathological Society, Oxford, 1987; Bellahouston Medal, Glasgow University, 1987; R.D. Lawrence Lecturer, British Diabetic Association, Manchester, 1989. Publications: research papers on diseases of the pancreas and colon. Recreations: singing; walking; cycling; reading; natural history. Address: (h.) 7 Heathfield Drive, Milngavie, Glasgow; T.-0141-956 3092.

Foulis, Sheriff Lindsay David Robertson, LLB (Hons). Sheriff at Perth, since 2001; Honorary Professor in Scots Law, Dundee University, since 2001; b. 20.4.56, Dundee; m., Ellenore; 2 s.; 1 d. Educ. High School of Dundee; Edinburgh University. Legal apprenticeship, Balfour and Manson, Edinburgh, 1978-80; Legal Assistant, Fred Tyler; Assistant, Reid Johnston Bell and Henderson, 1981; became Partner, 1984; appointed an all-Scotland Floating Sheriff, 2000. Part-time Lecturer, Dundee University, 1994-2000; Member, Sheriff Court Rules Council, 1996-2000; Temporary Sheriff, 1998-99. Publication: Civil Court Practice materials (Co-author). Recreations: sport; now mainly golf (badly); music. Address: Sheriff's Chambers, Sheriff Court House, Tay Street, Perth PH2 8NL; T.-01738 620546; e-mail: Sheriff.LDRFoulis@scotcourts.gov.uk

Foulis, Michael Bruce, BSc (Hons), FRGS. Visiting Professor, Humanities and Social Sciences, Strathclyde

University, 2015; b. 23.8.56, Kilmarnock; m., Gillian Tyson; 1 s.; 1 d. Educ. Kilmarnock Academy; Edinburgh University. Joined Scottish Office, 1978; Private Secretary to Parliamentary Under Secretary of State, 1987-89; seconded to Scottish Financial Enterprise as Assistant Director, 1989-92; Private Secretary to Secretary of State for Scotland, 1993-95; seconded to Cabinet Office as Deputy Head, Devolution Team, Constitution Secretariat, 1997-98; Head of Group, Scottish Education and Industry Department, 1998-99; Head of Economic Development, Enterprise and Lifelong Learning Department, 1999-2001; Head of Environment Group, Environment and Rural Affairs Department, 2001-05; on secondment to Scottish Resources Group working on Corporate Strategy, 2006-07; Director for Housing and Regeneration, Scottish Government, 2007-2010; Director for Strategy and Performance, 2011; Director for Children and Families, 2011-2015. Board Member of Children 1st, 2002-08; Board Member of WASPS (Workshop and Artists Studio Provision (Scotland) Limited), 2008-2011. Recreations: appreciating lithographs; moderate exercise. Address: (b.) University of Strathclyde, Lord Hope Building, 141 St James Road, Glasgow G4 0LT; T.-0141 444 8513.

E-mail: mike.foulis@strath.ac.uk

Foulkes of Cumnock, Rt. Hon. Lord (George Foulkes), PC, JP, BSc (Labour), Lothians, 2007-2011; MP (Labour and Co-operative), Carrick, Cumnock and Doon Valley, 1979-2005; b. 21.1.42, Oswestry; m., Elizabeth Anna; 2 s.; 1 d. Educ. Keith Grammar School; Haberdashers' Aske's School; Edinburgh University. Opposition Spokesman on Foreign Affairs, 1984-92, Defence, 1992-93, Overseas Development, 1994-97; Parliamentary Under-Secretary of State, Department for International Development; 1997-2001; Minister of State for Scotland, 2001-02. President, Scottish Union of Students, 1964-66; Director: European League for Economic Co-operation, 1967-68, Enterprise Youth, 1968-73, Age Concern Scotland, 1973-79; Chairman: Lothian Region Education Committee, 1974-79, Education Committee, COSLA, 1975-79; Rector's Assessor, Edinburgh University, 1968-71; Treasurer, Parliamentarians for Global Action; Chair, Labour Movement for Europe in Scotland; Member: Joint Committee on National Security Strategy, 2010-2013, Lords EU Select Committee, 2011-2015, Lords EU Sub Committee on Foreign Policy, Defence and International Development and Trade, 2011-2015; President, Caribbean Council, since 2011; Member, Board of Directors of Westminster Foundation for Democracy, 2007-2013; Trustee (Vice-Chair), Age Scotland, since 2014; Treasurer, The Climate Parliament Lords Liaison Committee, since 2015. Recreations: boating; watching football (Heart of Midlothian and Ayr United). Address: (h.) 18 Barony Terrace, Edinburgh EH12 8RE.

Fourman, Professor Michael Paul, BSc, MSc, DPhil, FBCS, CITP. Professor, Computer Systems, The University of Edinburgh, since 1988; b. 12.09.50, Oxford; divorced; 2 s.; 1 d. Educ. Allerton Grange, Leeds; Bristol University; Linacre, Oxford. Assistant Professor, Clark University, Worcester, Mass., 1976-77; J.F. Ritt Assistant Professor, Columbia University, NYC, 1977-82; Fellow, University of Cambridge, 1979-80; Reader, Brunel University, London, 1986-87, Professor, Formal Systems, 1987-88; Technical Director, Abstract Hardware Ltd., Uxbridge, 1986-96. Recreations: cooking; sailing. Address: (b.) University of Edinburgh, School of Informatics, Appleton Tower, Crichton Street, Edinburgh EH8 9LE; T.-0131 650 2690.

E-mail: michael.fourman@ed.ac.uk

Fowkes, Professor Francis Gerald Reid, MB, ChB, PhD, FRCPE, FFPH. Emeritus Professor of Epidemiology,

Edinburgh University, since 2011; Director, Wolfson Unit for Prevention of Peripheral Vascular Diseases, 1989-2011; Hon. Consultant, Public Health Medicine, 1985-2011; b. 9.5.46, Falkirk; 1 s.; 1 d. Educ. George Watson's College, Edinburgh; Edinburgh University. Senior Lecturer, University of Wales, 1980-85; Reader/Professor, Edinburgh University, since 1985. Address: (b.) Centre for Population Health Sciences, Edinburgh University, Teviot Place, Edinburgh EH8 9AG; T.-0131-650 3220.

Fowlie, Anna. Chief Executive, Scottish Social Services Council, since 2009. Educ. Edinburgh University and Napier Polytechnic. Career history: worked for 18 years in HR in local authorities; worked within the Employers' Organisation in COSLA, across all local government negotiating bodies; became Team Leader for Children and Young People in COSLA, lobbying on behalf of local government on all policy issues relating to education and children's services with a lead role on the social services workforce; headed up the Scottish Government team improving outcomes for Looked After Children; worked closely with local authorities and other services to raise awareness and aspiration for children and young people in public care. Chartered Member of the Chartered Institute of Personnel and Development; Fellow of the RSA. Address: (b.) Compass House, 11 Riverside Drive, Dundee DD1 4NY.

Fowlis, Angela, DCE. Age Scotland Training Department, since 2014; Director, Scottish Pre-Retirement Council, 2000-2014; b. 1.1.48, Dunfermline. Educ. Kings Park Secondary, Glasgow; Jordanhill College of Education. Primary/nursery Teacher, 1968-76; Lecturer, Langside College, 1976-95; Head of Department, Langside College, 1995-98. Recreations: singing; gardening; golf; badminton.

Fox, Colin Anthony. MSP (Scottish Socialist Party), Lothians, 2003-07; Joint National Spokesperson, Scottish Socialist Party, since 2008, National Convener, 2005-08; b. 17.6.59, Motherwell; 1 s.; 1 d. Educ. Our Lady's High School, Motherwell; Bell College, Hamilton. Spent 20 years as a (socialist) political organiser; SSP Lothians Convenor, 1998-2003. Publication: Motherwell is Won for Moscow. Recreations: reading; walking; golf; sports. Address: 24/3 Ivanhoe Crescent, Edinburgh EH16 6AN; T.-0131-348 6389.

Fox, Professor Keith Alexander Arthur, BSc (Hons), MB, ChB, FRCP, FESC, FMedSci. Duke of Edinburgh Professor of Cardiology, Edinburgh University, since 1989; Honorary Consultant Cardiologist, Royal Infirmary of Edinburgh, 1989-2012; President of the British Cardiovascular Society, 2009-2012; Chair, Scientific Programme of the European Society of Cardiology, 2012-2014; President, ASH (Action on Smoking and Health) Scotland, since 2011; b. 27.8.49, Salisbury, Rhodesia; m., Aileen E.M.; 1 s.; 1 d. Educ. Falcon College; Edinburgh University. Assistant Professor of Medicine, Washington University School of Medicine, 1980-85; Senior Lecturer in Cardiology and Consultant Cardiologist, University Hospital of Wales College of Medicine, 1985-89. Author of more than 600 Medical and Scientific publications. Address: (b.) University of Edinburgh, Chancellor's Building, 49 Little France Crescent, Edinburgh EH16 4SB; T.-0131 242 6378.

Foxley, Michael Ewen, MRCS, LRCP, DA. Leader of The Highland Council, 2008-2012; GP in Fort William, 1980-2010; b. 22.09.48, London; m., Mairead MacRae;

2 s. Educ. Harrow County Boys Grammar School; Middlesex Hospital Medical School, London University. Anaesthetics, then Training for General Practice; Highland Regional Councillor, 1986-96 (Vice-Chair of Planning); Highland Councillor, since 1995 (Fort William and Ardnamurchan); Chair of Land and Environment, 1995-2003; Vice Convener, 2003-07. Chair, West Highland College; Chair, Highlands and Islands Regional FE Board; Member, UHI Court; Director, Mallaig Harbour Authority; Board Member, NHS Highland; Director, community owned land trust. Recreations: hill walking; fishing; crofting. Address: (h.) Dun Famh, 2, Achaphubil, by Fort William PH33 7AL; T.-01397 772 775.
E-mail: michael.foxley@whc.uhi.ac.uk

Frame, Kate, LLB, DipLP, NP. Police Investigations & Review Commissioner (Commissioner) since 2014; extensive experience as a Prosecutor including a Procurator Fiscal Depute, Kilmarnock, 1986-1994; Principal Depute to Crown Office, 1994-2002; District Procurator Fiscal for Aberdeen and Interim Area Procurator Fiscal for Grampian, 2002-2008; Head of International Corporation Unit, Crown Office, 2008-2011; Head of the Criminal Allegations Against the Police Division, Crown Office, 2011-2014. First woman to be appointed as the independent Police Investigations & Review Commissioner. Address: Hamilton House, Hamilton Business Park, Caird Park, Hamilton, ML3 0QA; T.-01698 542900.

France, Professor (Emeritus) Peter, MA, PhD, FBA, FRSE. Professor of French, Edinburgh University, 1980-90, Endowment Fellow, 1990-2000; b. 19.10.35, Londonderry; m., Siân Reynolds; 3 d. Educ. Bradford Grammar School; Magdalen College, Oxford. Fellow, Magdalen College, Oxford, 1960-63; Lecturer, then Reader in French, Sussex University, 1963-80; French Editor, Modern Language Review, 1979-85; President: British Comparative Literature Association, 1992-98, International Society for the History of Rhetoric, 1993-95. Chevalier de la Légion d' Honneur, 2001. Publications: Racine's Rhetoric, 1965; Rhetoric and Truth in France, 1972; Poets of Modern Russia, 1982; Diderot, 1982; Rousseau: Confessions, 1987; Politeness and its Discontents, 1992; New Oxford Companion to Literature in French, 1995; Translator: An Anthology of Chuvash Poetry, 1991, Gennady Aygi: Selected Poems, 1997; Poems of Osip Mandelstam, 2014; Yevgeny Baratynsky: Half-Light, 2015; Oxford Guide to Literature in English Translation, 2000; Mapping Lives: the uses of biography, 2002; General Editor, Oxford History of Literary Translation in English, since 2005; After Lermontov: Translations for the Bicentenary. Address: (b.) 10 Dryden Place, Edinburgh EH9 1RP; T.-0131-667 1177.

Franceschild, Donna, BA. TV Scriptwriter, since 1990; playwight, since 1979; b. 22.11.53, Illinois; partner, Richard Golding; 1 s. Educ. University of California, Los Angeles. TV credits include: The Key, Eureka Street, A Mug's Game, Takin' Over the Asylum, And the Cow Jumped Over the Moon, Bobbin' and Weavin', The Necklace; theatre credits include: And the Cow Jumped Over the Moon, The Sunshine Cafe, Rebel!, Songs for Stray Cats and Other Living Creatures; Tap Dance on a Telephone Line; Mutiny on the M1, Diaries, The Soap Opera, The Cleaning Lady; film credit: Donovan Quick. Creative Writing Fellow, Universities of Glasgow and Strathclyde. Recreation: hill-walking.

Franchi, Leandro, MA, LLB. Partner, Franchi Law LLP; formerly Partner with Franchi Finnieston, Solicitors; Honorary Consul for Italy, since 1991; b. 5.6.60, Paisley; m., Gillian Elaine; 1 s.; 2 d. Educ. St Aloysius College, Glasgow; Dundee University; Glasgow University. Address: (b.) Queens House, 19 St. Vincent Place, Glasgow G1 2DT; T.-0141 225-3811.
E-mail: leandro@franchilaw.co.uk

Franchi, (Sarah) Jane. Reporter/Presenter, BBC Scotland, 1979-2003; b. 15.10.50, Calcutta; m., Alan Franchi. Educ. Benenden School; Edinburgh College of Commerce. Reporter, Aberdeen Journals, 1970; Press and Publicity Officer, Grampian TV, 1971-79. Recreations: swimming; football (spectating!); embroidery; theatre. Address: (h.) 9 Osborne Place, Aberdeen AB25 2BX; T.-01224 645883.

Francis, Alphonse. Founder and Trustee, Hope-Human Development & Welfare Association. Address: (b.) 9 Catacol Grove, Lindseyfield, East Kilbride, Glasgow G75 9FD; T.-44 7850645602; e-mail: afrancis@hope-hdwa.co.uk

Francis, Eileen, MPhil, MRCSLT, FRSA; b. 2.3.40, Tynemouth; m., John Francis; 2 d. Educ. Church High School, Newcastle upon Tyne; Kingdon Ward School of Speech Therapy, London. Speech and language therapist, Cardiff Hospitals, 1962; Lecturer, Moray House Institute of Education, 1971; Senior Lecturer, 1988; Vector, consultancy and training, 1992; Chair, Scottish Institute of Human Relations, 2005-2011. Recreations: community networks; Virginia Woolf Society. Address: (h.) 49 Gilmour Road, Edinburgh EH16 5HU; T.-0131 667 3996.

Francis, John Michael, BSc, ARCS, PhD, DIC, FRSGS, FRZSS, FRSE. Governing Board, UNESCO Centre for Water Law, Policy and Science, University of Dundee, since 2008; Deputy Chair, UNESCO Scotland; former Convener, United Nations Association - Edinburgh; Trustee, The RSE Scotland Foundation, 2004-07; Steering Group Scottish Sustainable Development Forum, 2004-12; Consultant to UNESCO; Chair, UK National Commission for UNESCO, 2000-03; Honorary Fellow, University of Edinburgh, 2000-10; b. 1.5.39, London; m., Eileen; 2 d. Educ. Gowerton Grammar School, near Swansea; Imperial College of Science and Technology, London University. CEGB Berkeley Nuclear Laboratories, 1963-70; Director, Society, Religion and Technology Project, Church of Scotland, 1970-74; Senior Research Fellow, Heriot-Watt University, 1974-76; Principal, Scottish Development Department, 1976-81; Assistant Secretary, Scottish Office, 1981-84, and 1992-95; Director – Scotland, Nature Conservancy Council, 1984-92, then Chief Executive, Nature Conservancy Council for Scotland; Senior Policy Adviser, Home Department, Scottish Office, 1995-99. Consultant, World Council of Churches, 1971-83; Chairman, SRT Project, Church of Scotland, 1979-94; Member: Oil Development Council for Scotland, 1973-76, Advisory Committee for Scotland, Nature Conservancy Council, 1973-76, Council, National Trust for Scotland, 1984-92; Chairman, Edinburgh Forum, 1986-92; Professional Member, World Future Society, Washington DC, 1992-2002; Member: John Muir Trust, 1994-2009, British Association for the Advancement of Science; UK Representative, Millennium Project, United Nations University; Trustee, Society, Religion and Technology Project Trust, 1998-2007; Member, SUPRA, since 1999; Chairman, Sector Committee, Sustainable Development, Peace and Human Rights; UK National Commission for UNESCO, 1999-2003; Member, Church and Society Council, Church of Scotland, 2005-2012; Member Emeritus, SRT Committee, since 2013. Publications: Scotland in Turmoil, 1972; Changing Directions, 1973; Facing Up to Nuclear Power, 1976; The Future as an

Academic Discipline, 1975; The Future of Scotland, 1977; North Sea Oil and the Environment (Jointly), 1992; 'Conserving Nature: Scotland and the Wider World' (jointly), 2005; contributions to scientific journals. Recreations: theatre; hill-walking; ecumenical travels. Address: (h.) 49 Gilmour Road, Newington, Edinburgh EH16 5NU; T.-0131-667 3996.

Francis, Michelle Ruth, BSc (Hons), MSc. Director, Sustainability Catalyst Ltd, since 2012; Freelance Sustainability and Environmental Consultant, since 2005; Main Board Member, Scottish Natural Heritage, 2005-2011; b. 19.1.71, Braintree; m., James Francis; 2 s. Educ. Wallace Hall Academy, Thornhill; Marr College, Troon; University of Aberdeen; Napier University. Environmental Scientist, RSK Environment, Aberdeen, 1993-95; Environment Manager, Railtrack Scotland, Glasgow, 1995-98; Head of Environment, Railtrack/Network Rail, London, 1998-2004. Member: The Scottish Environment Protection Agency Board, since 2014, The Wild Fisheries Review Panel, 2014. Address: (h./b.) Glenhead Cottage, Dunblane FK15 9PD; T.-01786 822581; e-mail: michelle@francis-hq.co.uk

Franklin, Lesley. Head of Junior School, George Heriot's School, since 2013. Career: joined George Heriot's School as a Class Teacher in 1995; member of the Junior School Management Team, since 1999; formerly Assistant Headteacher/Depute with responsibility for the Upper Primary; Deputy Head of the Junior School, 2004-2012. Serves on the panel of Associate Assessors with HMIe. Address: George Heriot's School, Lauriston Place, Edinburgh EH3 9EQ; T.-0131 229 7263.

Franks, Peter, AGSM. Principal Trumpet, Scottish Chamber Orchestra, since 1984; Trumpet Teacher, Royal Conservatoire of Scotland, since 1989; b. 22.4.58, Aylesbury; m., Maureen Hilary Rutter; 1 s.; 1 d. Educ. Aylesbury Grammar School; Guildhall School of Music and Drama. Sub-principal Trumpet, Scottish Chamber Orchestra, 1981-84. Address: 29 West Bankton Place, Murieston West, Livingston EH54 9ED; T.-01506 415514.

Fransman, Professor Martin, BA, MA, PhD. Professor of Economics, University of Edinburgh, since 1996; Director, Institute for Japanese-European Technology Studies, since 1988; b. 17.4.48, Johannesburg; m., Tamar Ludwin; 1 s.; 2 d. Educ. University of the Witwatersrand; University of Sussex. Lecturer: University of Swaziland, 1971-77, University of London, 1977-78; University of Edinburgh: Lecturer, 1978-86, Reader, 1987-96. Publications: The Market and Beyond, 1990 (Masayoshi Ohira Prize, 1991); Japan's Computer and Communications Industry, 1995; Visions of Innovation, 1999; Telecoms in the Internet Age, 2002 (Wadsworth Prize, 2003). Recreations: hill-walking; foreign travel; music; cinema. Address: (b.) Institute for Japanese-European Technology Studies, University of Edinburgh, Old Surgeons' Hall, High School Yards, Edinburgh EH1 1LZ; T.-0131-650 2450; e-mail: M.Fransman@ed.ac.uk

Fraser, Alan William, MA (Hons). Business Adviser; b. 17.12.51, Lennoxtown; m., Joan; 1 d.; 2 s. Educ. Daniel Stewart's College; Banff Academy; Aberdeen University. Entered Scottish Office, 1973; Assistant Secretary to Inquiry into UK Prison Services, 1978-79; Private Secretary to Minister of State, 1979-81; Manager, Scottish Office Efficiency Unit, 1985-88; Head, Industrial Policy and Technology Division, SOID, 1988-91; Principal Private Secretary to Secretary of State for Scotland, 1991-93; Head, Enterprise and Tourism Division, Scottish Office Education and Industry Department, 1993-99; Director of Personnel, Scottish Executive, 1999-2000; Director for Civil Service Reform, 2000-01; Head of 21st Century Government Unit, Scottish Executive, 2001-05. Business Adviser, since 2005; Board Member, Cruse Bereavement Care Scotland, from 2006, Chairman, 2008-13; Secretary, Lothian Sea Kayak Club, since 2008. Recreations: hill-walking; skiing; sea kayaking. Address: (h.) 10, Laverockbank Terrace, Edinburgh EH5 3BJ; T.-0131-552-1994.
E-mail: alanwilliamfraser@blueyonder.co.uk

Fraser, Andrew Kerr, MB, ChB, MPH, FRCP, FFPH. Director of Public Health Science, NHS Health Scotland, since 2012; b. 10.12.58, Edinburgh; m.; 3 s.; 1 d. Educ. George Watson's College; Aberdeen University; Glasgow University. Medical Director, National Services Division, NHS in Scotland; Director of Public Health, Highland Health Board; Deputy Chief Medical Officer, Scottish Executive; Director of Health and Care, Scottish Prison Service. Recreations: music; mountain walking. Address: (b.) Meridian Court, 5 Cadogan Street, Glasgow G2 6QE.

Fraser, Sir Charles Annand, KCVO, WS, DL. Partner, W. & J. Burness, 1956-92 (retired); former Chairman, Adam and Company PLC; former Director: British Assets Trust PLC, Scottish Television PLC, Scottish Business in the Community, Stakis PLC; b. 16.10.28, Humbie, East Lothian; m., Ann Scott-Kerr; 4 s. Educ. Hamilton Academy; Edinburgh University. Purse Bearer to Lord High Commissioner to General Assembly of Church of Scotland, 1969-88; served on Court, Heriot-Watt University, 1972-78; Council Member, Law Society of Scotland, 1966-72; Chairman, Lothian & Edinburgh Enterprise, 1991-94. Publications: Pipe music; The Shepherd House Garden. Recreations: gardening; skiing; piping. Address: (h.) Shepherd House, Inveresk, Midlothian; T.-0131-665 2570.

Fraser, James Edward, CB, MA (Aberdeen), BA (Cantab), FSA Scot. Assistant Local Government Boundary Commissioner for Scotland, 1997-2011; Secretary of Commissions for Scotland, 1992-94; b. 16.12.31, Aberdeen; m., Patricia Louise Stewart; 2 s. Educ. Aberdeen Grammar School; Aberdeen University; Christ's College, Cambridge. Royal Artillery, 1953-55 (Staff Captain, "Q", Tel-El-Kebir, 1954-55); Assistant Principal, Scottish Home Department, 1957-60; Private Secretary to Permanent Under-Secretary of State, Scottish Office, 1960-62; Private Secretary to Parliamentary Under-Secretary of State, Scottish Office, 1962; Principal, 1962-69: SHHD, 1962-64, Cabinet Office, 1964-66, HM Treasury, 1966-68, SHHD, 1968-69; Assistant Secretary: SHHD, 1970-76, Scottish Office Finance Division, 1976; Under Secretary, Local Government Finance Group, Scottish Office, 1976-81, Scottish Home and Health Department, 1981-91. President: Scottish Hellenic Society, Edinburgh and Eastern Scotland, 1987-93, Aberdeen Grammar School Former Pupils' Club, 1997-98 (Hon. Vice-President, since 1998). Recreations: reading; music; walking; Greece, ancient and modern. Address: (h.) 59 Murrayfield Gardens, Edinburgh EH12 6DH; T.-0131-337 2274.

Fraser, James Mackenzie, CBE, MA, MEd. Former Principal & Vice-Chancellor, University of the Highlands and Islands (2011-13); Principal, UHI Millennium Institute (UHI), 2009-2011, Deputy Principal, 2007-09, Secretary, 2002-09; b. 29.07.48, Poolewe; m., Janet Sinclair (deceased); 1 d.; m., Sheila; 1 s.; 1 d. Educ. Plockton High School; University of Edinburgh; University of Stirling. Lecturer, Inverness Technical College, 1971-77; Assistant Registrar, University of Stirling, 1977-87; College Secretary, Queen Margaret College, Edinburgh, 1987-89; Secretary, University of Paisley, 1989-2002. Chair, Board of Trustees, Free Church of Scotland; Director, Free Church Nominees Company, Edinburgh; Chair, Highland Community Care Forum; Clerk to the Free Presbytery of Inverness, Lochaber & Ross. Recreations: music;

genealogy; cinema. T.-01463 741729.
E-mail: james@jamesmfraser.com

Fraser, Lindsey M., BA (Hons), PGCE. Partner, Fraser Ross Associates, literary agency; b. 15.8.61, Edinburgh. Educ. George Watson's College; York University; Froebel Institute, London. Manager, Heffers Children's Bookshop, Cambridge, 1986-91; Executive Director, Scottish Book Trust, 1991-2002. Sir Stanley Unwin Travelling Fellowship, 1989. Address: (b.) 6 Wellington Place, Edinburgh EH6 7EQ; T.-0131-553 2759; e-mail: lindsey.fraser@tiscali.co.uk; web: www.fraserross.co.uk

Fraser, Lady Marion Anne, LT, MA, LRAM, ARCM, LLD, DUniv (Stirling). Chair: Board, Christian Aid, 1990-97; Honorary President, Scottish International Piano Competition, 1999-2007 (Chairman, 1995-99); Chair, Scottish Association of Mental Health, 1995-99; b. 17.10.32, Glasgow; m., Sir William Kerr Fraser; 3 s.; 1 d. Educ. Hutchesons' Girls' Grammar School; University of Glasgow; RSAMD. Lord High Commissioner to General Assembly of the Church of Scotland, 1994; Her Majesty's High Commissioner to the General Assembly of the Church of Scotland, 1995. Formerly Director: RGI, Scottish Opera, Laurel Bank School; Founder Chairman, Friends of the RSA; Chairman, Palcrafts Hadeel, 2003-07; Director, St. Mary's Music School; Trustee, Scottish Churches Architectural Heritage Trust; President, Scotland's Churches' Scheme, 1997-2009; Member, Sponsoring Group, Churches' Enquiry into Unemployment and the Future of Work, 1995-97; Trustee, Lamp of Lothian Collegiate Trust, 1996-2005; President, Scottish Churches Trust, 2012-16. Recreations: family and friends; people and places. Address: (h.) Broadwood, Edinburgh Road, Gifford, East Lothian EH41 4JE; T.-01620 810 319.

Fraser, Murdo Mackenzie, LLB, DipLP. MSP (Conservative), Mid-Scotland and Fife, since 2001; Convener, Scottish Parliament Economy, Energy and Tourism Committee, since 2011; Scottish Conservative Spokesperson on Finance, Economy, Energy & Tourism; Deputy Leader, Scottish Conservatives, 2005-2011; b. 5.9.65, Inverness; m., Emma Jarvis; 1 s.; 1 d. Educ. Inverness Royal Academy; University of Aberdeen. Solicitor, Ross Harper and Murphy and Ketchen and Stevens, WS, Edinburgh, 1989-2001. Chairman, Scottish Young Conservatives, 1989-91, National Young Conservatives, 1991-92; Parliamentary Candidate: East Lothian, 1997, North Tayside, 1999, 2001, 2003, 2007, Perthshire North, 2011. Publications: The Blue Book (2007); The Rivals: Montrose and Argyll and the Struggle for Scotland (2015). Recreations: climbing; classic cars; travel; Scottish history. Address: Scottish Parliament, Edinburgh EH99 1SP; T.-0131-348 5293; e-mail: murdo.fraser.msp@scottish.parliament.uk

Fraser, Sheriff Simon William Hetherington, LLB. Sheriff of North Strathclyde at Dumbarton, 1989-2014; b. 2.4.51, Carlisle; m., Sheena Janet (marr. diss.); m. (2), Fiona; 1 d. Educ. Glasgow Academy; Glasgow University. Solicitor, 1973; Partner, Flowers & Co., Solicitors, Glasgow, 1976-89; Temporary Sheriff, 1987-89. Glasgow Bar Association: Secretary, 1977-79, President, 1981-82; Council member, Sheriffs' Association, 2007-2010. Recreations: watching cricket, and Partick Thistle.

Fraser, Professor William Hamish, MA, DPhil, DUniv, FRHistS. Professor Emeritus, Strathclyde University; b. 30.6.41, Eln; m., Helen Tuach; 1 d. Educ. Keith Grammar School; Aberdeen University; Sussex University. Formerly Professor of History and Dean of Arts and Social Studies,

Strathclyde University. Associate Editor, Dictionary of Nineteenth Century Journalism. Publications: Trade Unions and Society 1850-1880, 1973; Workers and Employers, 1981; The Coming of the Mass Market, 1982; Conflict and Class: Scottish Workers 1700-1838, 1988; People and Society in Scotland 1830-1914, 1990; Glasgow 1830-1914 (Co-editor), 1996; Alexander Campbell and the Search for Socialism, 1996; A History of British Trade Unionism, 1700-1998, 1999; Scottish Popular Politics, 2000; Aberdeen: A New History (Co-Editor), 2000; Dr John Taylor, Chartist, 2006; British Trade Unions 1707-1918, 2007; Britain since 1707 (Co-Author), 2010; Chartism in Scotland, 2010; The Wars of Archibald Forbes, 2015. Recreations: travel; golf. Address: (h.) Braehead, Culvardie, Nethy Bridge PH25 3DH; T.-01479 821291; e-mail: hamishf@btinternet.com

Fraser, Sir William Kerr, GCB (1984), LLD, FRSE. Chancellor, Glasgow University, 1996-2006; b. 18.3.29; m., Lady Marion Fraser, LT (qv); 3 s.; 1 d. Educ. Eastwood Secondary School; Glasgow University. RAF, 1952-55; various posts in Scottish Office, 1955-88, including Permanent Under Secretary of State, 1978-88; Principal and Vice Chancellor, Glasgow University, 1988-95. Chairman, Royal Commission on the Ancient and Historical Monuments of Scotland, 1995-2000. Address: (h.) Broadwood, Edinburgh Road, Gifford, East Lothian EH41 4JE; T.-01620 810 319.

Frater, John W.B., MA. Secretary and Finance Director, Keep Scotland Beautiful, since 2005; b. 12.5.58, Irvine; m., Caroline E. Mackenzie. Educ. Loudoun Academy; Dundee University. Recreations: reading; gardening; wine; pottering around locomotive sheds. Address: (b.) Glendevon House, Castle Business Park, Stirling FK9 4TZ; T.-01786 471333.

Frazer, Rev. Richard Ernest, BA, BD, DMin(Prin), SubChStJ. Minister, Greyfriars Tolbooth and Highland Kirk, Edinburgh, since 2003; Minister, St. Machar's Cathedral, Old Aberdeen, 1993-2003; b. 20.11.57, Stirling; m., Katherine Tullis Sinclair; 2 s.; 1 d. Educ. Doncaster Grammar School; University of Newcastle upon Tyne; University of Edinburgh; Princeton Theological Seminary. Assistant Minister, St. Giles Cathedral, Edinburgh, 1985-87; Minister, Schoharie, Breakabeen, N. Bleheim, New York, USA, 1987-88; Minister, Cargill-Burrelton with Collace, 1988-93. Publication: A Collace Miscellany: a History of the Parish of Collace (Co-Editor and Contributor), 1992. Recreations: family; walking; squash; slow food. Address: (b.) Greyfriars Kirk, Greyfriars Place, Edinburgh EH1 2QQ; T.-0131 225 1900.

Freeland, Lindsay. Chief Executive, South Lanarkshire Council, since 2011. Address: (b.) Council Offices, Almada Street, Hamilton ML3 0AA; T.-01698 454208.

Freeman, Jeane, OBE. MSP (SNP), Carrick, Cumnock and Doon Valley, since 2016; Director, Freeman Associates, since 2005; b. 28.09.53, Ayr. Educ. Ayr Academy; Caledonian and Glasgow Universities. Saatchi & Saatchi; BBC, 1983-87; Director, Apex Scotland, 1987-2000; Senior Civil Servant, 2000-01; Principal Policy Adviser, First Minister, 2001-05. Board Member: Golden Jubilee National Hospital (Chair, since 2011), Scottish Police Authority, since 2013, Judicial Appointments Board for Scotland, 2011-15; Parole Board for Scotland, 2006-2011. Address: Scottish Parliament, Edinburgh EH99 1SP; T.-07774 128755.

French, William Allan, DL, BSc, MSc, CEng, FIMMM, FIET. Depute Lieutenant, Stirling and Falkirk Districts, since 1994; b. 30.12.41, Falkirk; m., Joyce; 2 d. Educ. George Watson's College, Edinburgh; Strathclyde University. Scientific Officer, UKAEA, Dounreay; Production Manager, British Aluminium Co. Ltd., Falkirk;

Lecturer, Napier College, Edinburgh; Head, Department of Industrial Engineering, Falkirk College of Technology; Associate Principal, Falkirk College of Further and Higher Education, 1986-99. Director, Careers Central Ltd., 1995-99; Secretary, Forth Valley Area Scout Association, 1990-2008; District Scout Commissioner, 1990-2008; Board member, Lochgoilhead Scout Centre; founder Area Chairman, Central Scotland Round Table; Past President, Larbert Rotary Club. Recreations: golf; bridge; scouting; rotary; music. Address: (h.) 26 Broomhill Avenue, Larbert FK5 3EH; T.-01324 556850.
E-mail: allanfrench69@gmail.com

Frew, Rosemary, MA, BD (Hons). Minister, Abbotshall Parish Church, Kirkcaldy, since 2005; b. 2.10.61, Glasgow; m., David J A Frew; 1 s.; 1 d. Educ. Linlithgow Academy; Edinburgh University. Assistant Minister, Markinch Parish Church, 1986-87; Minister, Largo and Newburn Parish Church linked with Largo, St. David's Parish Church, 1988-2005. Vice-Convener, Mission and Discipleship Council, Church of Scotland, 2005-07; Clerk to the Presbytery of Kirkcaldy. Recreations: ski-ing; cycling; reading. Address: (work and home) The Abbotshall Manse, 83 Milton Road, Kirkcaldy, Fife KY1 1TP; T.-01592 260315; e-mail: rosiefrew@blueyonder.co.uk

Friedrich, Karin, MA, PhD, FRHistS. Professor of Early Modern European History, School of Divinity, History and Philosophy, University of Aberdeen, since 2004; School of Slavonic and East European Studies, University College London, 1995-2004; b. 12.06.63, Munich, Germany; m., Prof. Robert I. Frost; 1 s.; 1 d. Educ. University of Munich; Georgetown University, Washington DC. Fellow, Royal Historical Society. Publications: The Other Prussia. Poland, Prussia and Liberty, 1569-1772, 2000, Polish trans. 2006 (Orbis Prize in 2001 by American Association for the Advancement of Slavic Studies); ed., Festivals in Germany and Europe: New Approaches to European Festival Culture, 2000; ed., Citizenship and Identity in a Multinational Commonwealth. Poland-Lithuania in Context, 1500-1750, 2008; The Cultivation of Monarchy and the Rise of Berlin. Brandenburg-Prussia 1700 (Co-Author), 2010; Brandenburg-Prussia, 1450-1806. The Rise of a Composite State, 2011. Recreations: flute; skiing; tennis; reading; mountaineering. Address: (b.) Crombie Annexe, Meston Walk, Aberdeen AB24 3FX; T.-01224 272451.

Frier, Professor Brian Murray, BSc (Hons), MD, FRCP (Edin), FRCP (Glas). Consultant Physician, Royal Infirmary, Edinburgh, 1987-2012; Honorary Professor of Diabetes, The Queen's Medical Research Institute, Edinburgh University, since 2001; b. Edinburgh; m., Dr. Isobel M. Wilson; 1 d. Educ. George Heriot's School, Edinburgh; Edinburgh University. Research Fellow in Diabetes and Metabolism, Cornell University Medical Centre, The New York Hospital, 1976-77; Senior Medical Registrar, Royal Infirmary, Edinburgh, 1978-82; Consultant Physician, Western Infirmary and Gartnavel General Hospital, Glasgow, 1982-87. Chairman, Honorary Advisory Panel for Driving and Diabetes to Secretary of State for Transport, 2001-2012; Chairman, Chief Scientist Office Committee for Diabetes Research in Scotland, 2003-06; R.D. Lawrence Lecturer, 1986, Banting Memorial Lecturer, 2009, Diabetes UK; Somogyi Award, Hungarian Diabetes Association, 2004; Governor, George Heriot's Trust, Edinburgh, 1987-94; Vice-President, Royal College of Physicians of Edinburgh, 2008-2012. Publications: Books - Hypoglycaemia and Diabetes: clinical and physiological aspects, 1993; Hypoglycaemia in Clinical Diabetes, 1999, 2nd Edition, 2007, 3rd Edition, 2014; Insulin Therapy: A Pocket Guide, 2013; papers and reviews on diabetes and hypoglycaemia. Recreations: appreciation of the arts; ancient and modern history. Address: (h.) 100 Morningside Drive, Edinburgh EH10 5NT; T.-0131-447 1653.
E-mail: brian.frier@ed.ac.uk

Frith, Professor Simon, BA, MA, PhD, FBA. Tovey Professor of Music, Edinburgh University, since 2006; Professor of Film and Media, Stirling University, 1999-2005; Director, ESRC Media Economics and Media Culture Programme, 1995-2000; b. 25.6.46, England. Educ. Leys School, Cambridge; Balliol College, University of Oxford; University of California, Berkeley. Lecturer, then Senior Lecturer in Sociology, University of Warwick, 1972-87; Director, John Logie Baird Centre, 1987-99, and Professor of English Studies, 1988-99, University of Strathclyde; Rock Critic, Sunday Times, 1982-86; Pop Critic, Observer, 1987-91; Chair of Judges, Mercury Music Prize. Publications: Sound Effects, 1981; Art into Pop, 1987; Music for Pleasure, 1988; Performing Rites, 1996; Music and Copyright, 2004; Taking Popular Music Seriously, 2006. Recreations: music; reading; walking. Address: (b.) Department of Music, University of Edinburgh, Alison House, 12 Nicolson Square, Edinburgh EH8 9DF; T.-0131-650-2426.

Frost, David, CMG. Chief Executive, Scotch Whisky Association, since 2014; b. 1965, Derby; m.; 2 c. Educ. Nottingham High School; St. John's College, Oxford. Career: KPMG, 1990-92, qualified with the Association of Taxation Technicians, receiving the Ivison Medal for outstanding results in personal taxation; Foreign and Commonwealth Office specialist in European issues, trade and global economic affairs, and multilateral diplomacy; most recent overseas posting was as HM Ambassador to Denmark (2006-08); has also served at the British Embassy in Paris, the UK Permanent Representation to the EU in Brussels, the UK Mission to the UN in New York, and the British High Commission in Nicosia; has worked extensively on European Affairs, including as a Director for the EU during the UK's last EU Presidency, and as Director for Strategy and Policy Planning in the Foreign Office, 2008-2010; on loan to the Department for Business, Innovation and Skills serving 3 years as Director for Europe, Trade, and International Affairs, Britain's most senior trade policy official; left the Diplomatic Service at the end of 2013. Recreations: detective fiction and ghost stories; Richard Wagner; football. Address: The Scotch Whisky Association, 20 Atholl Crescent, Edinburgh EH3 8HF; T.-0131 2229200.

Frost, Professor Robert Ian, MA (Hons) St. Andrews, PhD (London), FRHistS. Burnett Fletcher Chair in History, University of Aberdeen, since 2013, Professor of Early Modern History, 2004-2013, Head of The School of Divinity, History and Philosophy, 2004-09; b. 20.06.58, Edinburgh; m., Dr. Karlin Friedrich; 1 s.; 1 d. Educ. George Watson's College, Edinburgh; St. Andrews; School of Slavonic and East European Studies, University of London; Jagiellonian University, Cracow, Poland. School Teacher, Charterhouse, 1984-87; University Teacher, King's College London, 1987-2004, Reader in Early Modern History, History Department, 2001-04. Council of the Royal Historical Society, 2004-08; British Academy Wolfson Foundation Research Professor, 2009-2012. Publications: Author of: After The Deluge: Poland-Lithuania and the Second Northern War, 1655-1660, 1993; The Northern Wars: War, State and Society in North Eastern Europe, 1558-1721, 2000. Recreations: skiing; golf; opera; guitar. Address: (h.) 50 Forest Road, Aberdeen AB15 4BP; T.-01224 322824.
E-mail: robert.frost@abdn.ac.uk

Frutin, Bernard Derek, MBE, FRSA. Inventor; Executive Chairman, Rocep Group of Companies; Director, Gizmo Packaging Ltd; b. 7.2.44, Glasgow; m., 1, Victoria Dykes (divorced); m., 2, Karen Smith; 1 s.; 4 d. Educ. Kelvinside Academy, Glasgow. Winner of nine international innovator awards since 1989, including John Logie Baird and British

Institute of Packaging Environmental Awards; Innovator of the Year, 1989 (Institute of Packaging); Finalist, 1992 Prince of Wales Award; Institute of Packaging Starpack Award for TEC Innovation, 2001. Recreations: sailing; fine food; listening to music. Address: (b.) Rocep Lusol Holdings Ltd., Suite 2, Floor 1, Merlin House, Mossland Road, Hillington, Glasgow GS2 4XZ; T.-0141-885 2222.

Fry, Professor Stephen C., BSc, PhD, FRSE. Professor of Plant Biochemistry, Edinburgh University, since 1995; b. 26.11.53, Sheffield; m., Verena Ryffel; 3 d. Educ. Thornbridge School, Sheffield; Leicester University. Postdoctoral Research Fellow, Cambridge University, 1978-79; Royal Society Rosenheim Research Fellow, Cambridge University, 1979-82; Senior Research Associate, University of Colorado, 1982-83; Lecturer in Botany, then Reader in Plant Biochemistry, Edinburgh University, 1983-95. President's Medal, Society for Experimental Biology, 1988. Publications: The Growing Plant Cell Wall: Chemical and Metabolic Analysis, 1988; 68 review articles; 194 research papers. Recreations: hill-walking; paper chromatography. Address: (b.) The Edinburgh Cell Wall Group, Institute of Molecular Plant Sciences, School of Biological Sciences, Edinburgh University, King's Buildings, Mayfield Road, Edinburgh EH9 3JH; T.-0131-650 5320; e-mail: S.Fry@ed.ac.uk

Fulton, Rev. John Oswald, BSc, BD. General Secretary, United Free Church of Scotland, since 1994; Moderator, General Assembly, United Free Church, 2000-01; b. 9.7.53, Glasgow; m., Margaret P.; 1 d. Educ. Clydebank High School; Glasgow University. Ordained as minister, 1977; Minister, Croftfoot U.F. Church, Glasgow, 1977-94. Recreations: reading; gardening; photography. Address: (b.) 11 Newton Place, Glasgow G3 7PR; T.-0141-332 3435; e-mail: office@ufcos.org.uk

Furley, Professor Peter Anthony, MA, DPhil. Professor Emeritus and Senior Honorary Professorial Fellow, Tropical Biogeography, University of Edinburgh, since 2002; b. 5.8.35, Gravesend; m., Margaret Brenda Dunlop; 1 s.; 3 d. Educ. Gravesend Grammar School; Brasenose College, Oxford University. Tutor, Oxford; University of Edinburgh: Lecturer, 1962, Senior Lecturer, 1975; Professor of Ecology, University of Brasilia, Brazil, 1976; Reader in Tropical Biogeography and Soils, 1989; Professor of Biogeography, 1997-2001. Publications: Diagnóstico geo-sócio-econômico da região Centro-Oeste do Brasil (1977) ed.; Geography of the Biosphere, 1983; Biogeography and Development in the Humid Tropics (1988) ed.; Nature and Dynamics of Forest–Savanna Boundaries, 1992; The Forest Frontier – Brazilian Roraima, 1994; Ecological and Environmental Research in Belize (three volumes), 2001-02; Fragility and Resilience of Amazonian Soils; Human impact on Amazonia: the role of traditional ecological knowledge in conservation and development, 2006; Tropical Savannas and seasonally dry forests: vegetation and environment (2007) ed.; Environmental and human determinates of vegetation distribution in the Hadhramaut region, Yemen, 2010. Recreations: travel; smallholder farming in Andalucia. Address: Institute of Geography, School of Geoscience, University of Edinburgh, Drummond Street, Edinburgh EH8 9XP; T.-0131-650 2517/2523. E-mail: paf@geo.ed.ac.uk

Furlong, Professor Andy, BSc, PhD, DLitt, FAcSS. Professor of Social Inclusion and Education and Dean of Research, College of Social Sciences, Glasgow University, since 2000; b. 12.5.56, Liverpool; 4 s.; 1 d. Educ. University of Leicester. Research Fellow, University of Edinburgh; Lecturer then Senior Lecturer, University of Strathclyde; Senior Lecturer then Reader, University of Glasgow. Editor, Journal of Youth Studies. Address: (b.) School of Education, University of Glasgow, Glasgow G3 6NH; T.-0141-330 4667.
E-mail: andy.furlong@glasgow.ac.uk

Furnell, Professor James R.G., MA (Hons), DCP, PhD, LLB, DipLP, FBPsS. Advocate (called to Scottish Bar, 1993); Chartered Clinical and Forensic Psychologist; b. 20.2.46, London; m., Lesley Anne Ross; 1 s.; 1 d. Educ. Leighton Park Society of Friends School, Reading; Aberdeen University; Glasgow University; Stirling University; Dundee University. Clinical Psychologist, Royal Hospital for Sick Children, Glasgow, 1970-72; Forth Valley Health Board: Senior Clinical Psychologist, 1972-80, Consultant Clinical Psychologist (Child Health), 1980-98. Member: National Consultative Committee of Scientists in Professions Allied to Medicine, 1984-87 (Secretary, Clinical Psychology Sub-Committee), Forth Valley Health Board, 1984-87; Chairman, Division of Clinical Psychology, British Psychological Society, 1988-89; Visiting Professor, Caledonian University, since 1996. Recreations: flying; cross-country skiing. Address: (h.) Glensherup House, Glendevon, by Dollar, Perthshire FK14 7JY.

Furness, Professor Raymond Stephen, BA, MA, PhD. Formerly Professor of German, St. Andrews University, now Emeritus Professor; b. 25.10.33, Builth Wells; m., Janice Fairey; 1 s.; 2 d. Educ. Welwyn Garden City Grammar School; University College, Swansea. Royal Artillery and Intelligence Corps; Modern Languages Department, University of Manchester Institute of Science and Technology; Department of German, Manchester University. Publications: Expressionism; Literary History of Germany 1890-1945; Wagner and Literature; A Companion to Twentieth Century German Literature; An Introduction to German Literature 1871-1990 (Co-Author); The Dedalus Book of German Decadence; Zarathustra's Children: On Heligoland (novel); Wagner. Recreation: claret. Address: (h.) The Dirdale, Boarhills, St. Andrews KY16 8PP; T.-01334 880469.

Furness, Col. Simon John, MBE (2012), OstJ, DL. Landowner; Vice Lord Lieutenant, Berwickshire, 1990-2009; b. 18.8.36, Ayton. Educ. Charterhouse; RMA, Sandhurst. Commissioned Durham Light Infantry, 1956, 2nd Lt.; served Far East, UK, Germany; active service, Borneo, MID Northern Ireland, 1972; retired, 1978; Deputy Colonel (Durham) The Light Infantry, 1989-93. Member, Executive, National Trust for Scotland, 1986-96; Chairman: Berwickshire Civic Society, 1996-2005, Eyemouth Museum Trust, 1981-2005, Eyemouth Harbour Trust, 2003-06; Trustee, Gunsgreen House Trust, since 2003, Chairman, 2011-2015. Recreations: field sports; gardening. Address: The Garden House, Netherbyres, Eyemouth, Berwickshire TD14 5SE; T.-01890 750337.

Fyfe, Maria, BA (Hons). Politician; MP, Glasgow Maryhill, 1987-2001; Member, Scottish Labour Party Policy Forum, since 2009; Member, Labour Party National Policy Forum, 2010-2015; b. 25.11.38, Glasgow; m., James (deceased); 2 s. Educ. Notre Dame High School, Glasgow; Strathclyde University. Glasgow District Councillor, 1980-87; Senior Lecturer, Central College of Commerce, 1977-87; Member, Scottish Executive Committee, Labour Party, 1981-87; Opposition Spokesperson on Women, 1988-91; Scottish Affairs Spokesperson, 1992-95; Chair, Scottish All-Party Parliamentary Group on Children, 1996-99; Chair, Labour Departmental Committee on International Development, 1997-2001; Member, Council of Europe,

1997-2001; Member, British-Irish Parliamentary Body, 1997-2001; Honorary Doctorate, University of Glasgow, 2002; Vice Chair, Glasgow Housing Association, 2002-06. Chair, Remember Mary Barbour Association. Publications: "A Problem Like Maria", 2014; Women Saying No, 2014 (Editor). Address: 10 Ascot Avenue, Glasgow G12 0AX.

Fyfe, Professor Nicholas Robert, MA, PhD (Cantab). Director, Scottish Institute for Policing Research, since 2006; Professor of Human Geography, Dundee University, since 2006; b. 17.10.62, London; m., Gillian Fyfe; 2 s. Educ. Haberdashers' Aske's Hatcham Boys' School; Sidney Sussex College, University of Cambridge. Junior Research Fellow, Sidney Sussex College, Cambridge, 1989-90; Lecturer, Senior Lecturer, University of Strathclyde, 1990-2000; Senior Lecturer, then Reader, University of Dundee, from 2000. Fellow of The Scottish Police College; Fellow of The Royal Geographical Society. Publications: Crime, Policing and Place: essays in Environmental Criminology (Co-Editor), 1992; Images of the Street: planning, identity and control in public space, 1998; Protecting intimidated witnesses, 2001; The Urban Geography Reader (Co-Author), 2005; Centralizing forces? Comparative perspectives on police reform in northern and western Europe (Co-Editor), 2013. Recreations: golf; gardening; travel. Address: (b.) Scottish Institute for Policing Research, School of The Environment, University of Dundee DD1 4HN; T.-01382 384425; e-mail: n.r.fyfe@dundee.ac.uk

G

Gailey, Yvonne. Chief Executive, Risk Management Authority, since 2009. Social work background, working from 1979 to 2001 in Renfrewshire Council as a social work practitioner and criminal justice manager, and throughout her career has demonstrated a commitment to evidence-based practice; five years in training and consultancy, involved in introducing risk assessment tools and effective practice initiatives in Scotland's youth and criminal justice sectors, then 3 years as Director of Operations and Development, Risk Management Authority. Address: (b.) St. James House, 25 St. James Street, Paisley PA3 2HQ.

Galán, Ignacio. Chairman, Scottish Power, since 2007; b. 1950; 4 c. Educ. ICAI (Madrid); ICADE (Madrid); Escuela de Organización Industrial (Madrid). Career: various positions in Grupo Tudor, 1972-1991; Director, Industria de Turbo Propulsores, 1991-1995; Managing Director, Airtel Movil (today Vodafone Spain), 1995-2001; joined Iberdrola as Executive Vice-Chairman and Managing Director, 2001. Visiting Professor, University of Strathclyde, since 2011. Address: (b.) Scottish Power plc, 1 Atlantic Quay, Glasgow G2 8SP.

Galbraith, Rev. Douglas. MA, BD, BMus, MPhil, ARSCM, PhD. Editor, The Church of Scotland Yearbook, since 2011; Convener, Action of Churches Together in Scotland; b. 1940.

Galbraith, Professor Roderick Allister McDonald, BSc, PhD (Cantab), CEng, MRAeS, FRSE. Honorary Senior Research Fellow, School of Engineering, Glasgow University; b. 4.8.47, Lowmoor, England; m., Lynn Margaret Fraser. Educ. Greenock High School; James Watt Memorial College; Paisley College of Technology; Cambridge University. Apprentice Draughtsman/Engineer, Scott's Shipbuilding & Engineering Co. Ltd., 1964-72; Department of Aerospace Engineering, Glasgow University: joined 1975; Reader, 1989, Professor, 1992. Publications: over 100 reports and publications on aerodynamics. Recreations: sailing; walking. Address: (b.) School of Engineering, Glasgow University, Glasgow G12 8QQ; T.-0141-330 5295.

Galea, Paul, MD (Malta), DCH, FRCP (Glas), FRCPCH. Formerly Consultant Paediatrician, Royal Hospital for Sick Children, Yorkhill, Glasgow (retired, 2012); previously Consultant Neonatologist, Royal Maternity Hospital, Glasgow; b. 8.10.50, Rabat, Malta; m., Irene. Educ. Royal University of Malta. Recreations: gardening; DIY, classical music. Address: (h.) 30 Garngaber Avenue, Lenzie, Glasgow G66 4LL; T.-0141-776 6031.
Home e-mail: paul.galea31@btinternet.com

Gallacher, Professor James W. (Jim), MA (Hons), MSc. Emeritus Professor of Lifelong Learning, Glasgow Caledonian University; Council Member, Scottish Further and Higher Education Funding Council, 2005-2010; b. 23.12.46, Glasgow; m., Pauline; 2 s. Educ. St. Ninians School, Kirkintilloch, Glasgow; Glasgow University; London School of Economics; London University. Research Associate, Edinburgh University, 1971-73; Lecturer, Senior Lecturer, Reader, then Professor, Glasgow Caledonian University (and its predecessor institutions), since 1973. In addition to teaching on a range of full-time and part-time degrees, has worked closely with further

education colleges in developing links between further and higher education in Scotland. Established the Centre for Research in Lifelong Learning (jointly with Professor Michael Osborne, University of Stirling) in 1999. This was the first research centre in Scotland to undertake policy orientated work in the field of lifelong learning. Recent and current research includes: further education and social inclusion; further education/higher education links; widening access to further and higher education; work based learning; Modern Apprenticeships; credit and qualification frameworks; the student experience in mass higher education. Member of Scottish Funding Council for Further and Higher Education (SFC); Chair of SFC Learning and Teaching Forum; Member, National Forum for Lifelong Learning; Vice Chair, Universities Association for Lifelong Learning (UALL); Adviser to Scottish Parliament's Enterprise and Lifelong Learning Committee for their inquiry into lifelong learning. Publications: numerous articles, reports and books on basis of research, including: 'Researching Widening Access to Lifelong Learning: Issues and Approaches in International Research', 2004; A Contested Landscape: International Perspectives on Diversity in Mass Higher Education, 2005; 'Learning Outside the Academy', 2006. Recreations: reading; hillwalking. Address: (b.) Centre for Research in Lifelong Learning, Glasgow Caledonian University, 6 Rose Street, Glasgow G3 6RB; T.-0141 273 1339/47; e-mail: jwga@gcal.ac.uk

Gallagher, James D. (Jim), CB, FRSE. Associate Member, Nuffield College, Oxford; Visiting Professor, University of Glasgow; Director, Reassure Ltd, Admin Re UK Services Ltd, Guardian Assurance Ltd; Chair, With Profits Committee, Police Mutual Assurance Society; Member, With Profits Committee, Royal London Assurance; Non Executive Director, Scottish Catholic International Aid Fund; Council Member, Law Society of Scotland; b. Glasgow; m., Una Gallagher (nee Green); 1 s.; 2 d. Educ. St. Aloysius College, Glasgow; Glasgow University; Edinburgh University. Scottish Office, Admin Trainee, 1976; Private Secretary to Minister for Home Affairs etc., 1979; various policy posts, 1981-86; Secretary, Scottish Office Management Group, 1986; Head, Urban Policy, 1988; Private Secretary to successive Secretaries of State, 1989-91; Director, HR, Scottish Prison Service, 1991-95; Head, Local Government and Europe Group, Scottish Office, 1996-99; Economic and Domestic Secretariat, Cabinet Office, 1999; No 10 Policy Unit, 2000; Head, Scottish Executive Justice Department, 2001-05; School of Law, University of Glasgow, 2005-07; Director General, Devolution, Cabinet Office, No 10 Policy Unit, 2007-2010; Secretary, (Calman) Commission on Scottish Devolution, 2008-09; Director, Scottish Mutual, Abbey National, Life Assurance, 1996-2006; Chair, Scottish Provident Supervisory Committee, 2001-08; Non Executive Director, Lothian and Borders Police, 2006-2012.

Gallagher, Sister Maire T., CBE, MA (Hons), MEd, FScotVec, DCE, FSQA. Retired Headteacher; Sister of Notre Dame Religious Congregation, since 1959; b. 27.5.33, Glasgow. Educ. Notre Dame High School, Glasgow; Glasgow University; Notre Dame College of Education. Principal Teacher of History, Notre Dame High School, Glasgow; Lecturer in Secondary Education, Notre Dame College of Education; Headteacher, Notre Dame High School, Dumbarton, 1974-87; Chairman, Scottish Consultative Council on the Curriculum, 1987-91 (Member, Consultative Committee on the Curriculum, since 1976). Member, Executive, Secondary Heads Association (Scottish Branch), 1976-83; Coordinator, Christian Life Movement Groups, West of Scotland; Convener, Action of Churches Together in Scotland, 1999-2002 (Member, Central

Council, 1990-99); Fellow, Scottish Qualifications Authority, 1997; Member, Glasgow Churches Together, since 2004. Recreations: reading; dress-making; bird-watching. Address: (h.) Sisters of Notre Dame, 2/2 90 Beith Street, Glasgow G11 6DQ; T.-0141 357 4576.

Gallagher, Susan. Acting Chief Executive, Victim Support Scotland, since 2014. Over 22 years' experience in the UK voluntary sector in supporting a wide range of victims of crime; leads the strategic development of organisational policy and practice and contributes to driving forward the legislative and political agenda for victims of crime in Scotland; has given evidence to Parliament on many occasions and sits on Governmental and National working Groups shaping victims legislation and strategic policy opportunities; developed the first framework for improving the assessment of victims needs in the aftermath of crime based upon relevant research and practical experiences. Implemented the first VSS responses to supporting people in the aftermath of murder to the development of services to help people affected by crimes committed by young people. Many years spent working at pan-European level on a variety of joint projects with sister victim agencies across Europe; Chair, Victims Organisations Collaboration Forum Scotland; qualified social worker. Address: Victim Support Scotland, 15-23 Hardwell Close, Edinburgh EH8 9RX; T.-0345 603 9213.

Galley, Professor Helen Frances, ONC, HNC, FIMLS, PhD, FBS, FRCA. Professor of Anaesthesia and Intensive Care, University of Aberdeen, since 2010; Editor, British Journal of Anaesthesia, since 2008; Chair, North East Scotland Research Ethics Service; b. 13.01.62, Nottingham; m.; 1 s.; 1 d. Educ. King James' School, Knaresborough; University of Leeds. Research Fellow, University of Leeds, 1989-95; University of Aberdeen: Lecturer, 1995-2002, Senior Lecturer, 2002-09. Sir Humphrey Davy Award, 2002; Grants Officer, Anaesthetic Research Society, since 2007; Member of Senate, University of Aberdeen, since 2010. Recreations: horse riding; playing flute; jewellery making. Address: (h.) Overton of Auchnagatt, Ellon AB41 8TJ; T.-01224 437363.
E-mail: h.f.galley@abdn.ac.uk

Galloway, Janice. Writer; b. 2.12.56, Saltcoats. Educ. Ardrossan Academy; Glasgow University. Variety of paid and unpaid work, including 10 years' teaching English in Ayrshire; music criticism for Glasgow Herald, The Observer, Scotland on Sunday; fiction writing, including collections of short stories and novels; Co-Editor, New Writing Scotland, 1990-92; Editor, The Scotsman and Orange Short Story Collection, 2005; Times Literary Supplement Research Fellow to the British Library, 1999. Publications: The Trick Is To Keep Breathing, 1990; Blood, 1991; Foreign Parts, 1994; Where You Find It, 1996; Pipelines, 2000; Clara, 2002; Boy Book See, 2002; Rosengarten, 2004; This is Not About Me, 2008 (Autobiography) (winner of the Scottish Mortgage Trust Book of the Year (non-fiction) 2009); All Made Up, 2011 (won Best Scottish Book of the Year 2012, Mortgage Trust); Jellyfish, 2015. Staged work: The Trick is to Keep Breathing; Fall. Song cycle: Clara; Monster, for orchestra and voices. Opera: Monster (Co-Writer).

Galloway, Rev. Kathy, DD, BD, DPS. Former Head of Christian Aid Scotland (2009-2016); b. 6.8.52, Dumfries. Educ. Boroughmuir High School, Edinburgh; Glasgow University. Assistant Minister, Muirhouse Parish Church, Edinburgh, 1976-79; Co-ordinator, Edinburgh Peace and Justice Centre, 1980-83; Warden, Iona Abbey, 1983-88; freelance theological consultant, editor and writer, 1989-99; Linkworker for Scotland, Church Action on Poverty, 2000-02; Leader, The Iona Community, 2002-09. Patron, Student Christian Movement. Publications include: Talking to the Bones; A Story to Live By; Walking in Darkness and Light; Sharing the Blessing; Living by the Rule. Address: (h.) 20 Hamilton Park Avenue, Glasgow G12 8DU.

Galloway, 13th Earl of (Randolph Keith Reginald Stewart); b. 14.10.28; m.; succeeded to title, 1978. Educ. Harrow. Address: Senwick House, Brighouse Bay, Borgue, Kirkcudbrightshire, DG6 4TP.

Gamble, Alan James, LLB(Hons), LLM, Advocate. Judge, Upper Tribunal (Administrative Appeals Chamber), Edinburgh, since 2008; Convenor, Mental Health Tribunal for Scotland, since 2005; Deputy Social Security and Child Support Commissioner for Northern Ireland, since 2011; b. 29.4.51, Glasgow; m., Elizabeth Waugh; 2 s.; 1 d. Educ. High School of Glasgow; University of Glasgow; Harvard Law School, USA. Law Apprentice, 1974-76; admitted to Faculty of Advocates, 1978; Lecturer, then Senior Lecturer in Law, University of Glasgow, 1976-93; District Chairman, Tribunals Service, Glasgow, 1993-2008; Deputy Social Security and Child Support Commissioner, Edinburgh, 1994-2008; Social Security and Child Support Commissioner, Edinburgh, 2008. Bible Teacher, Christian Brethren Assemblies; Trustee, Interlink, and other charitable trusts; Dr J. McCormick Prize, 1972; Harkness Fellow, 1972-74. Publications: Contributor, Stair Memorial Encyclopedia; articles in legal journals and Christian periodicals. Recreations: reading; hill-walking. Address: (b.) George House, 126 George Street, Edinburgh EH2 4HH; T.-0131-271-4310.

Gammell, Geraldine, MA, CA. Trustee, The Golden Charter Trust; former Director, The Prince's Trust - Scotland. Educ. Stirling University; Glasgow University. Co-founder and Director, Dundas Commercial Property Funds I and II, 2002-2006; Partner, Springfords Chartered Accountants, 1993-2002; Manager, Business Services, KPMG, 1990-93; Lecturer in Business Finance and Accounting, Napier University and Edinburgh University, 1986-90; Financial Controller/Company Secretary, Ash Gupta Advertising, 1984-86; CA Apprentice, Audit Senior, Management Consultant, Thomson McLintock, 1978-83. Other non-executive Director Appointments: Lothian University Hospitals NHS Trust, 1999-2004; Sick Children's NHS Trust, 1995-99; Traverse Theatre Ltd., 1997-2001. Institute of Chartered Accountants, 1978-81; Chartered Accountant, 1981. Address: The Golden Charter Trust, Canniesburn Gate, 10 Canniesburn Drive, Glasgow G61 1BF; T.-0800 111 4514.

Gammie, Professor Elizabeth, DipM, BA, CA, PhD. Professor of Accountancy, Robert Gordon University, since 2000; b. 20.12.61, Dundee; m., Robert Peter; 1 s.; 1 d. Educ. High School of Dundee; Robert Gordon University. Qualified as CA, 1986, with Ernst and Whinney; became a Lecturer, 1989. Member, ICAS Foundation; Trustee, RDA Aberdeen; Trustee, City Moves; Member, IoD, Examination Board, Institute of Directors; Member, IAESB, International Accounting Education Standards Board. Recreation: equestrianism. Address: (h.) Bogfon Cottage, Maryculter, Aberdeen AB12 5GR; T.-01224 735403.

Garden, Malcolm, LLB, NP. Sheriff of Grampian, Highlands and Islands at Aberdeen, since 2008, at Peterhead, 2001-08; b. 7.8.52, Aberdeen; m., Sandra Moles;

2 s.; 1 d. Educ. Robert Gordon's College, Aberdeen; University of Aberdeen. Apprentice, then Assistant Solicitor, Watt and Cumine, Aberdeen, 1973-76; Clark and Wallace, Aberdeen: Assistant Solicitor, 1976-79, Partner, 1979-2001; Temporary Sheriff, 1994-98; Part Time Sheriff, 2000-01. Part Time Tutor, University of Aberdeen, 1980-85; Member, Aberdeen and North East Legal Aid Committee, 1980-85; Reporter to Scottish Legal Aid Board, 1984-86; Member: Law Society of Scotland, since 1976, Society of Advocates in Aberdeen, since 1978. Recreations: family; golf; football; tennis. Address: Sheriff Court House, Castle Street, Aberdeen.
E-mail: sheriffm.garden@scotcourts.gov.uk

Garden, Michael, MA. Chief Executive, Judicial Appointments Board for Scotland, since 2012. Educ. Perth High School; University of Edinburgh. Career: The Scottish Government: Policy Manager (Health, Agriculture, Job Dispersal), 2000-07, SEARS Frontline Delivery Project Manager, 2007-2011. Address: Thistle House, 91 Haymarket Terrace, Edinburgh EH12 5HD.

Garden, Professor Olivier James, CBE, BSc, MBChB, MD, FRCS (RCPSG), FRCS (Ed), FRCP (Ed), FRACS (Hon), FRCPSCan (Hon), FRSE, FACS (Hon), FRCS (Hon), FCSHK (Hon), FRCSI (Hon). Regius Professor of Clinical Surgery, Edinburgh University, since 2000; Dean International, since 2015; Head, School of Clinical Sciences and Community Health, 2002-06; Director of MSc in Surgical Sciences, since 2007; Director of ChM in General Surgery, since 2011; b. 13.11.53, Carluke; m., Amanda; 1 s.; 1 d. Educ. Lanark Grammar School; Edinburgh University. Lecturer, Glasgow University, 1985-88; Chef de Clinique, Unite de Chirurgie Hepatobiliare et Digestif, Villejuif, France, 1986-87; Senior Lecturer, Edinburgh University, 1988-97; Professor of Hepatobiliary Surgery, Edinburgh University, 1997-2000; Honorary Consultant Surgeon, Royal Infirmary of Edinburgh, since 1988; Director, Scottish Liver Transplant Unit, 1992-2005; President, Association of Upper G1 Surgeons of Great Britain and Ireland, 2002-04; Honorary Company Secretary, British Journal of Surgery Society Ltd., 2003-2012; Surgeon to the Queen in Scotland, since 2004; President, International Hepato-Pancreato-Biliary Association, 2012-2014; Chairman, British Journal of Surgery Society Ltd., since 2012; Vice Chairman, Edinburgh World Heritage Trust, since 2015. Recreations: golf; skiing. Address: (b.) Clinical Surgery, Royal Infirmary of Edinburgh, 51 Little France Crescent, Edinburgh; T.-0131 242 3614; e-mail: ojgarden@ed.ac.uk

Gardiner, Iain Derek, FRICS. Chartered Surveyor, since 1957; Senior Partner, Souter & Jaffrey, Chartered Surveyors, 1986-95; b. 22.12.33, Glasgow; m., Kathleen Elizabeth Johnson; 2 s.; 1 d. Educ. Hutcheson's Grammar School, Glasgow; Royal Technical College, Glasgow. Trainee and Assistant Quantity Surveyor, John H. Allan & Sons, Glasgow, 1950-57; National Service, Royal Engineers, 1957-59; Souter & Jaffrey, Inverness: Quantity Surveyor, 1959-63, Partner, 1963-86. Past Chairman, Royal Institution of Chartered Surveyors in Scotland; Chairman: Inverness Area, RICS in Scotland, 1969-70, Quantity Surveyors Committee, RICS in Scotland, 1989-90, Friends of Eden Court Theatre, 1981-82; Chairman, Inverness Area Scout Council, 1993-2009. Recreations: swimming; travel; cookery; Scouting. Address: (h.) 77 Stratherrick Road, Inverness IV2 4LL; T.-01463 235607.

Gardiner, John Ronald, BL, WS. Consultant, Brodies WS, Solicitors, 2001-04 (Senior Partner, 1992-2001, Partner, 1964-2001); b. 25.10.38, Rangoon; m., Aileen Mary Montgomery; 1 s.; 1 s. (deceased); 1 d. Educ. Fettes College; University of Edinburgh. Admitted Solicitor, 1963; admitted Writer to the Signet, 1964; Partner, Brodie Cuthbertson & Watson W.S. (thereafter Brodies W.S.), 1964; Notary Public, 1966-2007. Governor, Fettes Trust, 1986-96; Member, Rent Assessment Panel for Scotland, 1973-97; River Tweed Commissioner, since 2007; Hon. Secretary: Standing Council of Scottish Chiefs, 1970-72, Salmon and Trout Association (Scottish Branch), 1971-84. Recreations: fishing; shooting; golf; gardening. Address: (h.) 55 Fountainhall Road, Edinburgh EH9 2LH; T.-0131-667 5604.

Gardiner, Lindsay. Regional Leader, PwC in Scotland, since 2012; m.; 2 c. Over 20 years experience of auditing and advising retail financial services and major listed companies, working in a number of locations including San Francisco in the US; joined Pwc in 1989: admitted to partnership in 1999, Head of Financial Services in Scotland, 2005-2010, Head, Audit and Assurance practice, Scotland, 2010-2012. Recreations: golfing; walking; gardening. Address: (b.) PwC, 4th Floor, Atria One, 144 Morrison Street, Edinburgh EH3 8EX; T.-0131 260 4036.

Gardner, Angela Joy, BSc (Hons). Independent Public Affairs Consultant, AJ Enterprises, since 1994; b. 16.9.62, Wolverhampton; m., Andrew Ronald Gardner; 2 d. Educ. Codsall High School; UMIST. BP Chemicals Ltd., South Wales and Grangemouth, 1984-90; BP Schools Link Officer, 1985-90; Senior Public Affairs Officer, BP, 1990-94. Member, General Teaching Council for Scotland, 1990-98; Member, Scottish Examination Board, 1991-94; Member, Scottish Qualifications Authority Engineering Advisory Group, 1999-2003; Associate, Centre for Studies in Enterprise, Career Development and Work, Strathclyde University, 2003-07; Member, Goodison Group in Scotland; Professional Member, Society for Editors and Proofreaders; publish Informed Scotland - learning and skills digest. Address: (h.) 72 Craigcrook Road, Edinburgh EH4 3PN; T.-0131-336 5164.
E-mail: angela.gardner@ajenterprises.co.uk
Web: www.ajenterprises.co.uk

Gardner, Caroline Jane, MBA, CPFA. Auditor General for Scotland, since 2012; b. 1.5.63, London; m. Paul. Educ. University of Aston; University of Warwick; Open University. Wolverhampton MBC, 1985-88; District Audit, 1988-92; Audit Commission, 1992-95; Accounts Commission, 1995-2000; President, CIPFA, 2006-07; Audit Scotland, 2000-11; DFID/Turks and Caicos Islands Government, 2010-11; Member of the International Ethics Standards Board for Accountants (IESBA), 2009-2015; Member of Public Sector Audit Appointments Ltd (PSAA) Board, since 2014; Chair of Public Sector Audit Appointments Ltd Audit Committee, since 2015. Address: (b.) 102 West Port, Edinburgh EH3 9DN; T.-0131 625 1617; e-mail: cgardner@audit-scotland.gov.uk

Garland, Harry Mitchell, MBE, CQSW, FBIM. Retired Chairman, Secretary of State's Advisory Committee on Scotland's Travelling People (1987-95); b. 7.7.28, Aberdeen; m., Phyllis Sandison; 1 s.; 1 d. Educ. Rockwell Academy, Dundee; Robert Gordon's College, Aberdeen; Moray House College, Edinburgh. Probation Officer/Senior Probation Officer/Principal Probation Officer, 1958-69; Depute Director of Social Work, Aberdeen and Kincardine Counties, 1969-73; Director of Social Work: Paisley Burgh, 1973-74, Western Isles, 1974-78, Central Region, 1978-86. Chairman, National Association of Probation Officers in Scotland, 1968-69; President, Association of Directors of Social Work, 1983; Member, Forth Valley Health Board, 1986-90. Recreations: voluntary work; church; golf;

walking. Address: (h.) 7 Cromarty View, Nairn IV12 4HX; T.-01667 453684; e-mail: harryandphyllis@btinternet.com

Garner, John Angus McVicar, MB, ChB, DRCOG, DCH, FRCGP. Principal in general practice, since 1980; British Medical Association: former Chairman, Scottish Council; Vice Chairman, Medical and Dental Defence Union of Scotland; BMA Pension Fund Trustee; Lead Assessor, General Medical Council; b. 4.9.50, London; m., Catherine Lizbeth; 1 s.; 1 d. Educ. Eltham College; Edinburgh University. Lothian Local Medical Committee: Secretary, 1986-89, Chairman, 1991-92; Member: General Medical Services Committee, 1989-2001, National Standing Advisory Committee, 1989-95; Past Chairman, Scottish General Medical Services Committee; former Treasurer, General Medical Services Defence Fund Ltd. Recreations: amphibians and photographing fungi. Address: (h.)1, Drylaw Avenue, Edinburgh EH4 2DD; T.-07702269515. E-mail: johngarne@aol.com

Garrod, Professor Simon Christopher, MA, PhD, FRSE. Professor of Cognitive Psychology, Glasgow University, since 1990; b. 19.11.47, London; 1 s.; 1 d. Educ. Bradfield College, Berks; Oxford University; Princeton University. Lecturer, Senior Lecturer, Reader in Psychology, Glasgow University, 1975-90; Visiting Research Fellow, Max Plank Institute, 1980; Residential Fellow, Netherlands Institute for Advanced Study, 1988. Publications: Understanding Written Language; Language Processing; Saying, Seeing and Acting. Recreations: fishing; hill-walking; sailing. Address: (b.) Institute of Neuroscience and Psychology, Glasgow University, 58 Hillhead Street, Glasgow G12 8QT; T.-0141-330 5033; e-mail: simon@psy.gla.ac.uk

Gartland, Professor Kevan Michael Andrew, BSc (Hons), PhD, FRSB. Special Advisor, since 2011 and Professor of Biological Sciences, Glasgow Caledonian University, since 2005; Hon. Professor, Health Technology and Information, Hong Kong Polytechnic University; m., Jill Susan Gartland; 1 d. Educ. St Philip's Grammar School, Edgbaston; Leeds University; Nottingham University. Research Assistant, Plant Genetic Manipulation Group, Nottingham University, 1982-85; British Technology Group Research Fellow, Plant Genetic Manipulation Group, 1985-86; Lecturer, Plant Molecular Biology, De Montfort University, Leicester, 1986-92; Special Lecturer, Biotechnology, Open Learning, Greenwich University, 1992-96; University of Abertay Dundee: Senior Lecturer, Plant Biotechnology, 1992-95; Leader, Biological Sciences Division, 1995-98; Associate Head, Molecular and Life Sciences, 1996-2001; Division Leader, Molecular and Life Sciences, School of Science and Engineering, 1998-2005; Personal Chair, Biological Sciences, 1999. Founding Director, Abertay Centre for the Environment (ACE), 2002-05; Chair, Higher Education Academy, Biosciences Subject Centre Advisory Board, 2007-12; Member, Heads of University Biological Sciences Executive Committee, 1997-2004; Chair: Biochemical Society Education Committee, 2004-08, Composting Association Scotland; Member: Biochemical Society Executive Committee and Trustees, 2004-08, Board of Directors of Institute of Forest Biotechnology, North Carolina, USA, 2001-09; Director and Chief Executive, Glasgow Caledonian University Company Ltd; Director, Glasgow Caledonian University Academy Company Ltd., 2007-2011; Dean of Life Sciences, Glasgow Caledonian University, 2005-2011; Member, Heads of University Centres of BioMedical Sciences Executive Committee, 2010-2016. Recreations: country living; gentle walking; visiting interesting places. Address: (b.) Room B0.03, Glasgow Caledonian University, Glasgow G4 0BA; T.-0141-331-3120. E-mail: Kevan.Gartland@gcu.ac.uk

Gaul, Cllr Iain. Leader, Angus Council, since 2012; represents Kirriemuir & Dean Ward (SNP). Address: (b.) 46 Prior Road, Forfar DD8 3DT; T.-01307 464698.

Gebbie, George C., LLB (Hons). Advocate, since 1987; b. 27.1.58, Motherwell; m., Anne Gebbie-Oiben; 1 s.; 1 d. Educ. Dalziel High School, Motherwell; Aberdeen University. Legal apprentice to Crown Agent, 1979-81; Procurator Fiscal Depute, Glasgow, 1981-83; Solicitor in private practice, Glasgow, 1983-87. SNP candidate, East Kilbride, 1997 General Election. Recreation: socialising with friends. Address: (b.) Advocates' Library, Edinburgh, EH1 1RF; T.-0131-226 5071.

Geddes, Keith, CBE. Policy Director, Pagoda Public Relations, since 1999; b. 8.8.52, Selkirk. Educ. Galashiels Academy; Edinburgh University; Heriot Watt University. Housing Rights Worker, Shelter, 1977-84; Chair, Lothian Region Education Committee, 1987-90; Leader, Lothian Regional Council, 1990-96; Past President, Convention of Scottish Local Authorities; Leader, City of Edinburgh Council, 1996-99. Board Member: Scottish Natural Heritage, 2000-09, Accounts Commission, 2002-08, Greenspace Scotland, 2002-2010; Chair, Central Scotland Green Network Trust, since 2010. Recreations: golf; cricket; hill-walking. Address: (h.) 12 Woodmill Terrace, Dunfermline, Fife KY11 4SR; T.-01383 623947.

Geekie, Rhondda. Leader of East Dunbartonshire Council, since 2007; Councillor, since 1995; b. 18.7.49, Dundee; m., Allan; 2 s.; 1 d. Educ. St. Michael's Secondary. Dental Surgery Assistant; Optical Assistant. Chair, Silver Birch Scotland (Ltd); Director, EDCAB; Victim Support Area Committee. Recreations: reading; walking. Address: 59 Iona Way, Kirkintilloch, Glasgow G66 3QB; e-mail: rhonddageekie@hotmail.com

Gemmell, Professor Curtis Glen, BSc, PhD, MIBiol, FRCPath. Honorary Senior Research Fellow, School of Medicine, College of Medical, Veterinary and Life Sciences, Glasgow University; Research Professor, University of Strathclyde; Director, In Vivo Simulations Ltd; formerly Director, Scottish MRSA Reference Laboratory and Honorary Bacteriologist, Greater Glasgow Health Board; formerly Professor of Microbial Infection, Medical School, University of St Andrews (2006-2010); b. 26.8.41, Beith, Ayrshire; m., Anne Margaret; 2 d. Educ. Spier's School, Beith; Glasgow University. Glasgow University: Assistant Lecturer, 1966-68, Lecturer, 1968-69; Paisley College of Technology: Lecturer, 1969-71, Senior Lecturer, 1971-76; Glasgow University: Senior Lecturer, 1976-90, Reader, 1990-2000; Professor of Bacterial Infection and Epidemiology, Medical School, 2000-06. Visiting Associate Professor, University of Minnesota, Minneapolis, 1979-80. Recreations: gardening; golf. Address: (h.) Sunninghill, 19 Lawmarnock Crescent, Bridge of Weir PA11 3AS; T.-Bridge of Weir 613350.

Gemmell, Rev. David Rankin, MA, BD. Minister, Ayr Auld Kirk, since 1999; b. 27.2.63, Girvan; m., Helen; 1 s.; 1 d. Educ. Carrick Academy; University of Glasgow. Assistant Minister, Girvan North Church, 1990-91; Minister, Fenwick Parish Church, 1991-99. Chaplain to Ayr Academy, Kyle Academy, Holmston Primary, Southcraig Special Needs School, Ayr College: Parent Council, Ayr Academy; Trustee, McLaurin Gallery; Church Rep on south Ayrshire Council Leadership Panel. Recreations: ex SRU rugby referee; single figure handicap golfer. Address: (h.) 58 Monument Road, Ayr KA7 2UB; T.-01292 262580; e-mail: drgemmell@hotmail.com

Gemmell, Gavin John Norman, CBE, DUniv, CA. Chairman: NetThings; Director: Archangel Informal Investments, Ateeda, St. Mary's Music School; b. 7.9.41, Edinburgh; m., Kathleen Fiona Drysdale; 1 s.; 2 d. Educ. George Watson's College. Qualified CA, 1964; joined Baillie, Gifford & Co., 1964; retired as Senior Partner, 2001; Chairman: Scottish Widows Group, 2001-07, Standing Committee, Scottish Episcopal Church, 1997-2002; Director, Lloyds TSB Group, 2001-07; Trustee, National Galleries of Scotland, 1999-2007; Chairman, Court, Heriot Watt University, 2002-08; Honorary doctorate, Heriot-Watt University, 2009. Recreations: golf; foreign travel. Address: (h.) 14 Midmar Gardens, Edinburgh EH10 6DZ; T.-0131-466 6367.
E-mail: gavingemmell@blueyonder.co.uk

Gemmell, William Ruthven, LLB, WS. Partner, Murray Beith Murray; Solicitor in Scotland and England and Wales; Chief Executive, Murray Asset Management Limited; Director, Wealth Management Association and other companies; b. 4.4.57; m. Fiona Elizabeth Watson; 1 s.; 1 d. Educ. Loretto; Edinburgh University (Law); Aberdeen University (Accountancy). Murray Beith Murray, since 1985; Law Society of Scotland: President, 2006-07, Vice President, 2005-06; Council Member of the Institute of Chartered Accountants of Scotland, 2007-2011; Financial Services Tribunal, 1993-2002, Financial Services Authority Small Business Practitioner Panel, 1999-2007 (Chairman, 2004-06); Financial Services Practitioner Panel, 2004-06; Financial Services and Markets Tribunal, 2001-2010; VAT and Duties Tribunal, 2002-09; Judge, First-tier Tribunal (Tax Chamber), since 2009; Member, Upper Tribunal (Tax and Chancery Chamber), since 2010; Head of the UK Delegation to the Council of European Bars and Law Societies, 2010-13; A Vice President of the Council of European Bars and Law Societies, since 2014. Address: (b.) 3 Glenfinlas Street, Edinburgh EH3 6AQ; T.-0131 225 1200; e-mail: ruthven.gemmell@murraybeith.co.uk

Gerstenberg, Frank Eric, MA (Cantab), PGCE. Principal, George Watson's College, Edinburgh, 1985-2001; b. 23.2.41, Balfron; m., Valerie MacLellan; 1 s.; 2 d. Educ. Trinity College, Glenalmond; Clare College, Cambridge; London University. Assistant Master, Kelly College, Tavistock, 1963-67; Housemaster and Head of History, Millfield School, 1967-74; Headmaster, Oswestry School, 1974-85. Chairman of Governing Council, Glenalmond College, 2005-2011; Governor, The Compass School, Haddington and Loretto School, Musselburgh. Recreations: skiing; sailing; travelling; music; journalism; golf. Address: (h.) 9, Waverley North, East Links Road, Gullane EH31 2AF; T.-01620 842805; e-mail: f.e.g@btinternet.com

Gethins, Stephen. MP (SNP), North East Fife, since 2015; SNP Spokesperson on Europe at Westminster; b. 1976. Educ. Perth Academy; University of Dundee; University of Antwerp; University of Kent. Career in the political and international NGO sector; has worked in peace-building, arms control and democratisation in the Caucasus and Balkans; worked with the NGO Links, based in Tbilisi, with a focus on the conflicts surrounding the breakaway entities in the South Caucasus such as South Ossetia, Abkhazia and Nagorno-Karabakh; worked for Saferworld on arms control and peace-building in the former Soviet Union and Balkans; involved in a range of democratisation projects across the former Soviet Union and Western Balkans. Former Special Adviser to Scotland's First Minister, advising on European and International Affairs as well as Rural Affairs, Energy and Climate Change; also a Political Advisor with the Committee of the Regions in the European Union, worked with local authorities from across Europe; helped Scottish organisations gain influence and funding in the EU at Scotland Europa; involved in the US Government's International Visitor Leadership Programme which analysed 'US Foreign Policy Challenges' in 2011. Member of the House of Commons Foreign Affairs Committee. Address: House of Commons, London SW1A 0AA.

Gibb, George Frederick Cullen, MA, LLB. Formerly Consultant to Messrs Marshall Wilson, Solicitors, Falkirk (1997-2009); Honorary Sheriff at Falkirk, since 1987; b. 19.3.33, Edinburgh; m., Inga Mary Grieve; 1 s.; 2 d. Educ. George Heriot's School, Edinburgh; Edinburgh University. Messrs Marshall Wilson, Solicitors: Partner, 1964, Senior Partner, 1990. Recreations: golf; music; bowls; reading. Address: (h.) 17 Shirra's Brae Road, Stirling FK7 0AY; T.-01786 463235; e-mail: george@gibb43.freeserve.co.uk

Gibbs, Professor Robert, BA. Emeritus Professor of Pre-Humanist Art History, University of Glasgow, since 2011 (Professor, 2006-2011); b. 02.07.46, London. Educ. Ealing Grammar School for Boys; Courtauld Institute, University of London. Research Assistant to Sir Nicolas Pevsner for The Buildings of England: Dorset, Birkbeck College, University of London, 1968-69; University of Glasgow: Lecturer, then Senior Lecturer, from 1991, then Reader, 2001-06, Department of History of Art. Publications: The Life and Career of Lippo di Dalmasio, 2010; Illuminating the Law: Medieval Legal Manuscripts in Cambridge Collections (Co-Author), 2001; The Development of the Illustration of Legal Manuscripts by Bolognese Illuminators between 1250 and 1298, Juristische Buchproduktion im Mittelalter, 1998; Landscape as Property: Bolognese Law Manuscripts and the Development of Landscape Painting, Atti del Congresso della Societa di Storia della Miniatura, 1992; L'Occhio di Tomaso, Treviso, 1981; Tomaso da Modena: Painting in Emilia and the March of Treviso, 1340-80, 1989; In search of Ambrogio Lorenzetti's Allegory of Justice in the Good Commune, 1999; also written on 19th century design. Recreations: music of all genres except 'Light Music'; popular science and evolution. Address: (b.) Department of History of Art, University of Glasgow, Glasgow G12 8QQ; T.-0141 649 1575.
E-mail: robert.gibbs@glasgow.ac.uk

Gibbs, Stephen Cokayne, OBE. Director, Allt Goblach LLP, since 2012; b. 18.7.29, Hertingfordbury, England; m., Lavinia Bacon; 2 s.; 1 d. Educ. Eton College. Served with KRRC (60th Rifles), 1947-49; TA, service with QVR (TA), 1951-63: Lt., 1951, Captain, 1956, Major, 1958; Port Line Ltd., 1949-62: Assistant Manager, 1957, London Manager, 1959; Charles Barker PLC, 1962-87: Director, 1962, Deputy Chairman, 1982-87. Director, Swallow Group PLC, 1970-99; National Trust for Scotland: Member, Executive, 1986-2000 and Council, 1991-96; Member: TUCC for Scotland, 1992-97, Deer Commission for Scotland, 1993-2000; Chairman: Association of Deer Management Groups, 1994-2005, Scottish Venison Partnership, since 2008, Scottish Quality Wild Venison, since 2006. Recreations: stalking; shooting; fishing. Address: The Estate Office, Dougarie, Isle of Arran KA27 8EB; T.-01770 840259.

Gibby, Mary, OBE, BSc, PhD, FRSE. FRSA, Director of Science, Royal Botanic Garden Edinburgh, 2000-2012; Member, Scientific Advisory Committee, Scottish Natural Heritage, 2001-07; Honorary Professor, University of Edinburgh; b. Doncaster; 1 d. Educ. Leeds University; Liverpool University. British Museum (Natural History), 1974-2000. Member, Advisory Committee, Chelsea Physic Garden; Darwin Expert Committee, Defra; RSPB Scottish Committee. Recreations: hill-walking; canals; narrow boats. Address: (b.) Royal Botanic Garden Edinburgh, 20A Inverleith Row, Edinburgh EH3 5LR; e-mail: m.gibby@rbge.ac.uk

Gibson, Alexander John Michael, CBE, ARAgS. Former Chair, Board of Council, Scottish Association for Marine Science (2008-2014); Member, Court of The University of the Highlands and Islands, since 2009, Board, Local Better

Regulation Office, 2007-2010; Chair: Macaulay Land Use Research Institute, 2006-2011, Quality Meat Scotland, Cattle & Sheep Standard Setting Body, 2007-2011, Scottish Salmon Producers Organisation, 2006-08; President, Highland Cattle Society, 1986-88; Scottish Landowners Federation, 1996-2002; Chair: Highland Region, 1996-99, Agricultural Committee, 1995-2000 (Vice Convenor, 2000-02); Founder Board Member, Food Standards Agency, 2000-06; Member, Meat Hygiene Advisory Committee, 2001-04; Chair, Scottish Food Advisory Committee, 2002-06. Fieldsman, Highland Cattle Society, since 1978; Scottish Food Champion, 2001-04; Member, Scottish Food & Health Council, 2005-07. B. 6.6.52, Glasgow; m., Susan Clare Bowser; 1 s.; 1 d. Educ. Gordonstoun. Recreations: field sports; skiing; walking; sailing; cattle breeding. Address: Edinvale, Dallas, Moray IV36 2RW; T.-01343 890 265; e-mail: michael@edinvale.com

Gibson, Edgar Matheson, MBE, TD, DL, DA. Vice Lord Lieutenant, Orkney, 2007-2011; Deputy Lieutenant, Orkney, 1976-2007; Honorary Sheriff, Grampian, Highlands and Islands, since 1992; full-time professional artist since 1990; b. 1.11.34, Kirkwall; m., Jean McCarrick; 2 s.; 2 d. Educ. Kirkwall Grammar School; Gray's College of Art, Aberdeen. National Service, 1958-60; TA and TAVR service to 1985 with Lovat Scouts, reaching Lt. Col.; Battalion Second in Command, 2/51 Highland Volunteers, 1973-76; Joint Services Liaison Officer for Orkney, 1980-85; Cadet Commandant, Orkney Lovat Scouts ACF, 1979-86, Honorary Colonel, 1986-2004; Member, Orkney Health Board, 1991-99; Chairman, Italian Chapel Preservation Committee, since 2006 (Member, since 1976); Trustee, T.A. Military Museum, Weyland, since 1983; Hon. President: Society of Friends of St. Magnus Cathedral, since 1994, Orkney Craftsmen's Guild, 1997-2002 (Chairman, 1962-82); President, Orkney Branch, SSFA and FHS, 1997-2013 (Chairman, 1990-97); Chairman: St. Magnus Cathedral Fair Committee, 1982-2004, Northern Area, Highland TA&VR Association, 1987-93. Recreation: whisky tasting. Address: (h.) Transcona, New Scapa Road, Kirkwall, Orkney; T.-0185687 2849.

Gibson, J.N. Alastair, MD, FRCS (Edin), FRCS (Orth). Consultant Spinal Surgeon, Lothian University Hospitals, since 1993; Honorary Senior Lecturer, University of Edinburgh; b. 21.10.54, Bellshill; m., Laurie-Ann; 2 s.; 1 d. Educ. King Edward VII Grammar School, Sheffield; Royal London Hospital Medical College, London. House Surgeon, London Hospital, 1978-79; Surgical Registrar, Ninewells Hospital, Dundee, 1981-83; Clinical Research Fellow, University of Dundee, 1984-86; University of Edinburgh: Lecturer, 1986-91, Senior Lecturer, 1993-97; Spinal Fellow, Royal North Shore Hospital, Sydney, 1992; Visiting Scholar, University of Sydney, 1992; Visiting Surgeon, Spire Murrayfield Hospital, Edinburgh, since 1998; Council Member, The Royal College of Surgeons of Edinburgh, 2012-17; Member, The Edinburgh Merchant Company; Member, British Association of Spine Surgeons; European Spine Society; International Society for the Study of the Lumbar Spine, New York Academy of Sciences; Consultant, joimax GmbH. Publications: contributor to books and professional journals; Patent: cervical disc replacement prosthesis. Recreations: Member, Mortonhall GC, Lamlash GC, Arran YC; Past President, Thistle LTC. Address: Department of Orthopaedic Surgery, The New Royal Infirmary of Edinburgh, Little France, Edinburgh EH16 4SU; T.-0131-242-3471.
E-mail: j.n.a.gibson@blueyonder.co.uk
web: www.gibsonspine.eu

Gibson, Rev. James McAlpine, TD. Minister, Bothwell Parish Church, since 1989; Minister of Religion (Church of Scotland), since 1977; b. 31.3.48, Edinburgh; m., Doreen Margaret (McCracken); 1 s.; 1 d. Educ. Daniel Stewart's College, Edinburgh; University of Glasgow. Assistant Minister, Paisley Abbey, 1977-78; Minister, Grangemouth Old Parish Church, 1978-89; Territorial Army Chaplain (Royal Army Chaplains Dept.), 1984-2004, First Gulf War (1991) and Bosnia/Croatia (1999-2000), 1986-2004; Moderator of The Presbytery of Hamilton, 2004-05; appointed Chaplain in Ordinary to HM The Queen in Scotland and installed as Member of The Chapel Royal in Scotland, 2004. Territorial Decoration, 2001; Convener of The Board of National Mission of The General Assembly of The Church of Scotland, 2000-04; Convener of Committee on Chaplains to HM Forces for Church of Scotland, 2006-2010; President of the Church of Scotland Chaplains' Association, 2013-14. Recreations: family; travel; theatre; music. Address: (h.) 4 Manse Avenue, Bothwell, Glasgow G71 8PQ; T.-01698 853189.
E-mail: jamesmgibson@msn.com

Gibson, Kenneth. MSP (SNP), Cunninghame North, since 2007; b. 8.9.61, Paisley. Career: SNP councillor in Glasgow for Mosspark, 1992-99; Leader of the Opposition, Glasgow City Council, 1998-99; MSP, Scottish Parliament, 1999-2003; Shadow Cabinet front bencher, 1997-2003; SNP Local Government Convenor, 1997-99 (responsible for writing and producing the SNP manifesto and co-ordinating the campaign for the 1999 local government elections); Convener, Scottish Parliament's Finance Committee, since 2011. Address: (b.) Scottish Parliament, Edinburgh EH99 1SP.

Gibson, Patricia, BA (Hons). MP (SNP), North Ayrshire and Arran, since 2015. Educ. University of Glasgow. Career: Teacher of English for over 20 years in Glasgow, Lanarkshire and East Renfrewshire; served as SNP Education Spokesperson on Glasgow City Council for 5 years, representing Glasgow Pollok Ward as a councillor (2007-2012). Address: House of Commons, London SW1A 0AA.

Gibson, Robert McKay, MA (Hons). MSP (SNP), Caithness, Sutherland and Ross, 2011-2016, Highlands and Islands, 2003-2011; b. 16.10.45, Glasgow; divorced. Educ. High School of Glasgow; University of Dundee. Executive Officer, Civil Service, 1965-68; Teacher (geography and modern studies), 1973-74; Assistant Principal Teacher, Guidance, 1974-77; Principal Teacher, Guidance, 1977-95; writer and musician, since 1995. Recreations: organic gardening; hill-walking; traditional music. Address: (h.) Tir nan Oran, 8 Culcairn Road, Evanton, Ross-shire IV16 9YT; T.-01349 830388.

Gifford, Professor Thomas Douglas MacPharlain, MA, PhD, FRSE. Emeritus Professor and Senior Research Fellow, University of Glasgow; Honorary Librarian of Abbotsford (Walter Scott's Library), since 1993; b. 14.7.40; m., Anne Tait Gifford; 3 d. Educ. Hillhead High School; University of Glasgow; Baliol College, University of Oxford. Lecturer then Senior Lecturer, University of Strathclyde, 1967-86; University of Glasgow: Senior Lecturer, 1986, Reader, 1990, Professor and Chair of Scottish Literature, 1995. Hon. Librarian, Scott's Library, Abbotsford, since 1993. Publications: James Hogg; Neil Gunn and Lewis Grassic Gibbon; History of Scottish Literature – The Nineteenth Century (Editor), 1988; History of Scottish Women's Writing (Co-editor) 1998; Scottish Literature in English and Scots (Co-editor), 2002. Address: (h.) 9 Shielhill, Ayr KA7 4SY; T.-01292 443360.

Gilbert, George, DA, RSW. Painter; Partner, Courtyard Gallery, 1994-2001; many solo and group shows in

Glasgow and Edinburgh; b. 12.9.39, Glasgow; m., Lesley Johnston; 3 s. Educ. Victoria Drive Secondary School, Glasgow; Glasgow School of Art. Teacher of Art, Aberdeenshire, Glasgow, Fife, 1963-89; painter (exhibited widely), since 1963. Elected: RSW, 1973 (Council Member, 1994-98); SAAC, 1991, PAI, 1992. Artstore Award, 1992; Gillies Award (RSW), 1993; RSPSG Award (RGI), 2006; Strathearn Award (RGI), 2007; RSW Council Award, 2007; Scottish Drawing Competition, 2009 (Art Store Award); Scottish Arts Club Award (RSW), 2011; Armour Memorial Award, Paisley Art Institute, 2013. Recreations: walking; reading; music; the arts. Address: 33 Nethergate North, Crail, Fife KY10 3TL.

Giles, Cecilia Elspeth, CBE, MA. Member, Rail Users Consultative Committee for Scotland, 1989-97; b. Dumfries. Educ. Queen Margaret's School, Yorkshire; Edinburgh University. Administrative staff, Khartoum University, 1956-57; joined Administrative staff, Edinburgh University, 1957; Assistant Secretary, Edinburgh University, 1972-87; Committee of Vice-Chancellors and Principals' Administrative Training Officer (seconded part-time), 1983-85. President, Edinburgh University Graduates' Association, 1989-91, Member, Executive Committee and Editorial Committee, since 1987, Hon. President, since 2004; Member, Business Committee, General Council, Edinburgh University, 1988-93, Convener, Constitutional Sub-Committee, 1991-93; Member, Church of Scotland Board of Stewardship and Finance, 1986-93, Vice Convener 1990-93; Member, Church of Scotland Assembly Council, 1993-96; Awarded Government recognition for Intelligence Work at Bletchley Park during WW2, 2009. Publication: Scotland for the Tourist (Co-author). Recreations: entertaining friends, family and godchildren; theatre. Address: (b.) Graduates' Association, 24 Buccleuch Place, Edinburgh EH8 9LN.

Gill, Rt. Hon. Lord (Brian Gill), MA, LLB, PhD, Hon. LLD (Glas), Hon.LLD (Strathclyde), Hon.LLD (St. Andrews), Hon.LLD (Edinburgh), Hon.LLD (Abertay), Hon D.Acad. (RSAMD), FRSE, FRSAMD, KSG. Lord Justice General of Scotland and Lord President of the Court of Session, 2012-2015; Senator of the College of Justice in Scotland, 1994-2015; Lord Justice Clerk, 2001-2012; Vice President, Royal Conservatoire of Scotland and former Chairman, Royal Scottish Academy of Music and Drama; Chairman, Royal School of Church Music; b. 25.2.42; m.; 5 s.; 1 d. Educ. St. Aloysius College; Glasgow University; Edinburgh University. Advocate, 1967; Advocate-Depute, 1977-79; Standing Junior Counsel: Foreign and Commonwealth Office (Scotland), 1974-77, Home Office (Scotland), 1979-81, Scottish Education Department, 1979-81; QC, 1981; called to the Bar, Lincoln's Inn, 1991; Bencher, 2002. Keeper, Advocates' Library, 1987-94; Chairman, Scottish Law Commission, 1996-2001; Chairman, Scottish Civil Courts Review, 2007-09. Address: (b.) c/o Lord President's Office, Court of Session, Edinburgh EH1 1RQ; e-mail: lord.bgill@gmail.com

Gill, Professor Evelyn Margaret, OBE, FRSE, FSB, BSc, PhD, BA. Professor of Integrated Land Use, University of Aberdeen, since 2006, seconded (10%) to DFID as a Senior Research Fellow, since 2009; seconded to the World Bank as Chair of the International Science and Partnership Council of the CGIAR (60%), since 2014; b. 10.1.51, Edinburgh. Educ. Mary Erskine School for Girls; Edinburgh University; Massey University, New Zealand; Open University. Researcher, Forage Intake, AFRC Grassland Research Institute, 1976-89; Overseas Development Administration, 1979-81; Natural Resources Institute, Kent, 1989-96; Chief Executive, Natural Resources International Ltd., 1996-2000; Chief Executive and Director of Research,

Macaulay Land Use Research Institute, Aberdeen, 2000-06. Chief Scientific Adviser, Scottish Government Environment and Rural Affairs, 2006-2011. Recreations: hill walking; reading. Address: (b.) ACES, 23 St Machar Drive, Aberdeen AB24 3UU; T.-07703131373. E-mail: m.gill@abdn.ac.uk

Gill, Kerry James Graham. Journalist; retired Scottish Daily Express Political Editor; b. 29.4.47, Newcastle; m., Andrea Kevan; 2 d. Educ. Durham School; Warwick University. Westminster Press, 1969-71; Evening Post, 1971-72; The Journal, 1972-77; The Scotsman, 1977-87 (Reporter and Glasgow Editor); The Observer, 1979-87; The Times, 1987-93; Daily Record, 1994; joined Scottish Daily Express in 1996 (Assistant Editor, Executive Editor, Editor, Political Editor). Recreations: modern French history; gardening; reading. Address: (h.) Spout Burn, Main Street, Fintry, Stirlingshire; T.-01360 860427.

Gillan, David Stewart, BSc, MDiv, PhD. Minister, St. Michael's Parish Church, Linlithgow, since 2004; Moderator, West Lothian Presbytery, 2014-15; Vice-Convener, World Mission Council, Church of Scotland, 2009-2011; b. 1.10.58, Newfoundland, Canada; m., Sarah Ormerod; 1 d.; 1 s. Educ. Sydney Mines High School, Nova, Scotia; Universities of Edinburgh, Toronto and Mount Allison. Interim Minister, Morija, Lesotho, 1986-87; Minister, Village Main Parish, Johannesburg, South Africa, 1987-98 (including Alexandra, Tembisa, Katlehong and Atteridgeville); Researcher, Commission on the Restitution of Land Rights, South Africa, 1997-98; Executive Director, Churches Council on Theological Education in Canada, 1999-2004. Publication: Book edited, "Church, Land and Poverty", Johannesburg, 1998. Chairperson, Commission on Faith and Witness, Canadian Council of Churches; Lieutenant Governor's Medal, NS, 75. Recreations: writing; Celtic music; guitar (with Sarah, fiddle). Address: (h.) St. Michael's Manse, Kirkgate, Linlithgow, West Lothian EH49 7AL; T.-01506 842195; e-mail: stewart@stmichaels-parish.org.uk

Gillespie, Adrian, BAcc, MBA. Managing Director of Operations (Growth Companies, Innovation and Infrastructure), Scottish Enterprise. Educ. Glasgow University; University of Strathclyde. Career: ten years in commercial and financial management positions within Marks and Spencer plc; Senior Director of Energy and Low Carbon Technologies for Scottish Enterprise with responsibility for working with industry to establish and deliver clear priorities for investment and growth, with a particular focus on offshore energy. Active Board Member, Aberdeen City & Shire Economic Future (ACSEF); member of Scotland's 2020 Climate Change Main Group. Address: Scottish Enterprise, Atrium Court, 50 Waterloo Street, Glasgow G2 6HQ.

Gillespie, Dr. Gary. Chief Economist, Scottish Government, since 2011. Joined the Scottish Government in 2000 from the Fraser of Allander Institute at the University of Strathclyde; appointed to the Senior Civil Services in 2006 and has provided economic advice in a range of policy areas over this time including Health, Enterprise and Finance. Honorary Professor, Glasgow Caledonian University, since 2011; Visiting Professor, University of Strathclyde. Address: Room 4N-01, St. Andrew's House, Edinburgh EH1 3DG.

Gillespie, Professor Thomas Alastair, BA, PhD, Hon DSc (Heriot Watt), FRSE. Emeritus Professor of Mathematics, University of Edinburgh (Professor, since 1997); b. 15.2.45,

Torrance; m., Judith Anne Nelmes; 2 s.; 1 d. Educ. Glasgow Academy; University of Cambridge; University of Edinburgh. Lecturer, 1968-87, Senior Lecturer, 1987-92, Reader in Mathematics, 1992-97, University of Edinburgh; Visiting Professor, Indiana University, 1973-74, 1983-84. Recreations: gardening; making music; hill walking. Address: (b.) School of Mathematics, James Clerk Maxwell Building, Edinburgh EH9 3FD; T.-0131 667 8792.

Gillies, Anne Lorne, MA, PhD, PGCE, LRAM, Drhc. Singer and Writer; Partner, Brìgh Productions, since 2000; b. 21.10.44, Stirling; 1 s.; 2 d. Educ. Oban High School; Edinburgh University; London University; Jordanhill College of Education; Glasgow University. Singer: TV, radio, concert recital, theatre, recording; writer: scripts, children's books, novels, articles, autobiography, songs and 'Songs of Gaelic Scotland', awarded Ratcliff Prize, 2006, for major contribution to the study of folklore in UK and Ireland; education/community development: teacher, resource development; National Education Officer, Comunn na Gaidhlig, 1988-90; Arts Development Officer, Govan Initiative Ltd., 1991-93; Producer and Writer, Scottish Television 1993-95; Lecturer in Gaelic, University of Strathclyde, 1995-98. Awarded Rotary's Paul Harris Fellowship, 2003; Elected Speaker of Year 2005 by Association Speakers' Clubs of Great Britain; Honorary Fellow: University of Highlands and Islands, Royal Incorporation of Architects in Scotland, Association for Scottish Literary Studies; Scottish Government's Ambassador for Gaelic, 2009-2010; Inducted into Scottish Traditional Music Hall of Fame, 2012. Recreations: multiple granny-hood and married bliss. Address: (h.) 33 Stewarton Road, Dunlop, Ayrshire KA3 4DQ.
E-mail: anne@brigh.co.uk

Gillies, Crawford Scott, LLB, ACA, MBA. Chairman, Control Risks Group Ltd., since 2006; Director, Standard Life plc, since 2007; Director, Barclays plc, since 2014; Director, SSE plc, since 2015; b. 5.56, Scotland; m., Alison; 3 s. Educ. Perth Academy; Edinburgh University; Harvard University. Bain and Company, 1983-2008; Touch EMAS Ltd, 2006-2011; Hammonds, 2005-09; Scottish Enterprise plc, 2009-2015; Mitie PLC, 2012-2015. Recreation: trees. Address: 101 George Street, Edinburgh EH2 3ES.

Gillies, Norman Neil Nicolson, OBE, BA, Dr.hc (Aberdeen), DUniv (Open University), FRSA; b. 1.3.47, Flodigarry, Isle of Skye; m., Jean Brown Nixon; 1 s.; 2 d. Educ. Portree High School; Strathclyde University; Open University. College Secretary, Sabhal Mor Ostaig, 1983-88; Director, Sabhal Mor Ostaig, 1988-2008; Director of Development, Clan Donald Lands Trust, 2009-2012; Director: Skye and Lochalsh Enterprise Ltd., 1990-99; Chief, Gaelic Society of Inverness, 2000; Honorary Professor in Contemporary Highland Studies, Aberdeen University, 2002; Professor Emeritus, UHI Millennium Institute, 2009; Chair of the Board of Governors of West Highland College, 2009-2011; Member of the Board of Governors of the Royal Conservatoire of Scotland; Chair, Atlas Arts; Board Member, Urras Fhlòdaigearraidh. Recreations: reading; broadcasting; family. Address: (h.) Innis Ard, Ardvasar, Isle of Skye IV45 8RU; T.-01471 844 281; e-mail: tormod281@btinternet.com

Gillies, Professor Pamela, CBE, BSc, PGCE, MEd, MMedSci, PhD, FRSA, FFPH, FAcSS, Hon FRCPS (Glas), FRSE. Principal and Vice-Chancellor, Glasgow Caledonian University, since 2006; b. 13.02.53, Dundee. Educ. University of Aberdeen; University of Nottingham. Founding Trustee, Grameen Scotland Foundation; Member, Board of Trustees of the British Council, 2008-2014; Member, Scottish Poverty and Truth Commission; Elected

Fellow of the Royal Society of Edinburgh 2015 and of the Faculty of Public Health, Royal College of Physicians of London in 2002; Academician of the Academy for Social Sciences in 2005; Honorary Fellow, Royal College of Physicians of Glasgow, 2007; Fellow of RSA, 1996; Harkness Fellow, Commonwealth Fund of New York, 1992-93; Visiting Professor and Scholar, Cabot House, Harvard University; Board Member, Scottish Institute for Excellence in Social Work (SIESWE), 2006-08; Trustee, Carnegie Trust for the Universities of Scotland. Publications: over 100 academic journals and government reports on health promotion; cross cultural perspectives on HIV/AIDS, sexuality and health; partnership responses to health improvement and community development responses to inequalities in health, focusing on the potential of social action for health. Recreations: tennis; gardening; Glamis Castle Musicale; opera. Address: (b.) Glasgow Caledonian University, Cowcaddens Road, Glasgow G4 0BA; T.-0141 3313113; e-mail: Pamela.Gillies@gcu.ac.uk

Gillies, Rt. Rev. Robert Arthur, BD, PhD. Bishop of Aberdeen and Orkney, since 2007; b. 21.10.51, Cleethorpes; m., Elizabeth; 3 s. Educ. Barton-upon-Humber Grammar School; Edinburgh University; St. Andrews University. Medical Laboratory Technician, 1968-72; Curate: Christ Church, Falkirk, 1977-80, Christ Church Morningside, and Chaplain, Napier College, 1980-84; Chaplain, Dundee University, 1984-90. Hon. Lecturer, Department of Philosophy, Dundee University, 1985-95; Rector, St. Andrew's Episcopal Church, St. Andrews, 1991-2007. Publications: A Way for Healing, 1995; Informing Faith, 1996; Healing: Broader and Deeper, 1998; New Language of Faith, 2001; Where Earth and Heaven Meet, 2005; Sounds Before The Cross, 2007; Three Days in Holy Week, 2014. Recreation: family. Address: St. Clement's Church House, Mastrick Drive, Aberdeen AB16 6UF.

Gillies, Valerie, MA, MLitt, FSAScot. Poet; b. 4.6.48, Edmonton, Canada; m., William Gillies; 1 s.; 2 d. Educ. Edinburgh University; University of Mysore, S. India. Writer in Residence, Duncan of Jordanstone College of Art and Dundee District Libraries; Writer in Residence, East Lothian and Midlothian District Libraries; Writer in Residence, Edinburgh University; Royal Literary Fellow, Queen Margaret University, 2010-2012; Senior Arts Worker (Hospital Arts), Artlink; Creative Scotland Award, 2005; The Edinburgh Makar; Associate of Harvard University. Publications: Each Bright Eye; Bed of Stone; Tweed Journey; The Chanter's Tune; The Ringing Rock; St. Kilda Song; Men and Beasts; The Lightning Tree; The Spring Teller; The Cream of the Well: New and Selected Poems. Recreations: whippet-racing; field-walking; tai chi; swimming. Address: (h.) 67 Braid Avenue, Edinburgh EH10 6ED; T.-0131-447 2876.
E-mail: valeriegillies@hotmail.com

Gillies, Professor William, MA (Edin), MA (Oxon), Hon. D.Litt. (Ulster). Professor of Celtic, Edinburgh University, 1979-2009; Visiting Professor, Harvard University, 2009-10, 2013-15; b. 15.9.42, Stirling; m., Valerie; 1 s.; 2 d. Educ. Oban High School; Edinburgh University; Corpus Christi College, Oxford; Dublin University. Dublin Institute for Advanced Studies, 1969-70; Lecturer, Edinburgh University, 1970-79; Director, SLD Ltd.; Fellow, Royal Society of Edinburgh, 1990; Fellow, Royal Historical Society, 2002. Recreations: walking; gardening; music; Taoist tai chi. Address: (h.) 67 Braid Avenue, Edinburgh EH10 6ED.

Gillis, Richard, OStJ. Solicitor, since 1975; Managing Director, family investment companies, since 2001; b. 22.4.50, Dundee; m., Ruth J. P. Garden. Educ. High School of Dundee. Solicitor, Greater London Council, 1975-77; Archer & Wilcock, Nairobi, Kenya, 1977-80; Shoosmiths, 1980-81; Assistant to the Secretary, TI Group plc, 1981-85; Secretary, ABB Transportation Holdings Ltd (British Rail Engineering Ltd until privatisation) & Trustee, Company Pension Schemes, 1985-95; Clerk to the Council and Company Secretary, University of Derby, 1995-2002. Secretary, Justice report on perjury; Director, then Vice-Chairman, Crewe Development Agency, 1992-95; CBI East Midlands Regional Council, 1993-95; Chairman, Property Committee, Derbyshire Council of the Order of St. John, 1994-2003; Trustee, Priory of England and the Islands of the Order of St. John and Trustee, St. John Ambulance, 1999-2003; Chairman, Audit Committee and Priory Regulations Committee, Regional Member of Priory Chapter, 1999-2005; Honorary Life Member, Court of the University of Derby, 2003; Court of Assistants, Worshipful Company of Basketmakers, 2004-13, Upper Warden, 2012-13. Recreations: Freemasonry; historical films; music; Clubs: Athenæum, New (Edinburgh); Blairgowrie Golf. Address: (h.) Nether Kinfauns, Church Road, Kinfauns, Perth PH2 7LD; T.-01738-860886.

Gillon, Karen Macdonald. MSP (Labour), Clydesdale, 1999-2011; formerly Shadow Minister for Rural Development; b. 18.8.67, Edinburgh; m., James Gillon; 2 s.; 1 d. Educ. Jedburgh Grammar School; Birmingham University. Youth Worker, Terminal One Youth Centre, Blantyre, 1991-94; Community Education Worker, North Lanarkshire Council, 1994-97; PA to Rt. Hon. Helen Liddell, MP, 1997-99. Recreations: sport; music; flower arranging; reading; cooking. Address: (b.) 7 Wellgate, Lanark ML11 9DS; T.-01555 660526.

Gilloran, Professor Alan James. MA PhD. Deputy Principal, Queen Margaret University, Edinburgh, since 1996; Sociologist; b. 7.6.56, Edinburgh; m., Barbara; 1 s.; 1 d. Educ. Daniel Stewart's College, Edinburgh; University of Edinburgh. Researcher, Wester Hailes Representative Council; Research Assistant, Moray House; Research Fellow, University of Edinburgh; Lecturer in Sociology and Social Policy, University of Stirling. Member, Care Development Group on Free Personal Care for Elderly People; Vice Chair, East Lothian Partnership. Publications: academic articles; book chapters; five funded research reports into dementia and mental health. Recreations: badminton; wine; travel. Address: (b.) Queen Margaret University, Craighall, Edinburgh EH21 6UU; T.-0131-474 0000; e-mail: agilloran@qmu.ac.uk

Gilmore, Sheila. MP (Labour), Edinburgh East, 2010-15; Parliamentary Private Secretary to: Michael Dugher, 2013-15, Angela Eagle, 2013-15, Jon Trickett, 2011-13; b. 1.10.49, Aberdeen; m., Brian Gilmore; 3 s.; 1 d. Educ. George Watson's College, Edinburgh; University of Kent at Canterbury; Edinburgh University. Career history: Legal Advisory Officer, Scottish Consumer Council; private law practice in Edinburgh focusing on family law; elected in an Edinburgh District Council by-election for Moredun ward in 1991; Election agent to Nigel Griffiths MP, 1992-2005; Convenor for Housing, 1999-2007; candidate, Scottish Parliament constituency of Edinburgh Pentlands, 2007 Scottish Parliament elections. Member, Select Committee on Political and Constitutional Reform, 2010-15; Chair PLP Departmental Group for Work and Pensions, 2011-15; Member, DWP Select Committee, 2011-15. Recreations: cycling; reading.

Gilmore, Professor William C., LLB, LLM, MA, PhD. Emeritus Professor, International Criminal Law, Edinburgh University, since 2012, Professor, 1996-2012,

Dean and Head of the School of Law, 2004-07; Director, CIMA, Cayman Islands, since 2006; Scientific Expert (Legal), MONEYVAL, Strasbourg, since 1997; b. 31.3.51, Nassau, Bahamas; m., Dr Patricia Shepherd; 1 s.; 1 d. Educ. St Joseph's College, Dumfries; Edinburgh University; University of London; Carlton University. Lecturer, Law, University of West Indies, Barbados, 1973-75; Commonwealth Projects Officer, IILED, Washington D.C., 1977-79; Lecturer/Senior Lecturer/Reader, Faculty of Law, Edinburgh University, 1979-96; Assistant Director, Legal Division/Head, Commercial Crime Unit, Commonwealth Secretariat, Marlborough House, London, 1991-93. Publications include: Dirty Money, 4th ed. 2011; Newfoundland and Dominion Status, 1988; The Grenada Intervention, 1984. Recreations: travel; fishing. Address: (b.) Old College, South Bridge, Edinburgh EH8 9YL.

Gilmour, John Andrew George, MA, LLB, NP. Solicitor; Marketing Consultant; Honorary Sheriff at Dumbarton, since 1991; b. 17.11.37, Balloch; m., Roma Aileen; 3 d. Educ. Morrison's Academy, Crieff; Edinburgh University. Consultant, McArthur Stanton; President, Strathclyde Junior Chamber of Commerce, 1973; Director, Dumbarton Enterprise Trust, 1985-2000; Dean, Faculty of Dunbartonshire Solicitors, 1988-90; Law Society accredited Liquor Licensing Specialist, 1993; President, Helensburgh and Lomond Chamber of Commerce, 2003-2007. Recreations: sport; music; gastronomy. T.-01436 672212.

Gilmour, Simon, MA (Hons), PhD, FSA, FSA Scot, MCIfA. Director of The Society of Antiquaries of Scotland, since 2007; b. 12.06.70, Dundee; m. Dr. Rebecca Jones; 1 d.; 1 s. Educ. Alford Academy; University of Edinburgh. Department of Archaeology Tutor, University of Edinburgh, 1999-2001; numerous excavations and other archaeological projects in Scotland and abroad, since 1996; Aerial Survey Liaison Officer, Royal Commission on The Ancient and Historical Monuments of Scotland, 2001-05; Project Manager in the construction industry, 2005-07. Elected Vice President of The Council for Scottish Archaeology, 2004-2010; elected Hon. Secretary of The Council for Scottish Archaeology, 2001-04; Honorary Fellow of The University of Edinburgh, 2001-04, and 2008-2011; Visiting Fellow of the University Campus Suffolk School of Business, Leadership and Enterprise, since 2013; elected Vice Chair, Built Environment Forum Scotland, 2010-2015. Recreations: skiing; eating out; cinema; archaeology. Address: (b.) Society of Antiquaries of Scotland, c/o National Museums Scotland, Chambers Street, Edinburgh EH1 1JF; T.-0131 247 4115.
E-mail: director@socantscot.org

Gilruth, Jenny. MSP (SNP), Mid Fife and Glenrothes, since 2016. Educ. Madras College, St Andrews; University of Glasgow. Former teacher of Modern Studies and high school head of department. Address: Scottish Parliament, Edinburgh EH99 1SP.

Gimblett, Sheriff Margaret, MA. Sheriff at Dunoon, 1999-2005, part-time Sheriff, 2005-09 (retired); b. 24.9.39, Perth; m., Iain; 1 s.; 1 d. Educ. St. Leonards, St. Andrews; University of Edinburgh; University of Glasgow. Retail Management, John Lewis Partnership, London, until 1970; Partner, Russel and Aitken, Solicitors, 1972-95; Temporary Sheriff, 1994-95; Sheriff, Glasgow and Strathkelvin, 1995-99; Sheriff, Dunoon, 1999-2005; part-time Sheriff, 2005-09; Churchill Fellow. Recreation: gardening. Address: (h.) Croftcat Lodge, Grandtully PH15 2QS.

Gimingham, Professor Charles Henry, OBE, BA, PhD, ScD, FRSE, FIBiol. Regius Professor of Botany, Aberdeen University, 1981-88; b. 28.4.23, Leamington; m., Elizabeth Caroline Baird; 3 d. Educ. Gresham's School, Holt, Norfolk; Emmanuel College, Cambridge. Research Assistant, Imperial College, London, 1944-45; Department of Botany, Aberdeen University: Assistant, 1946-48, Lecturer, 1948-61, Senior Lecturer, 1961-64, Reader, 1964-69, Professor, since 1969, Head of Department, 1981-88; Member: Scottish Committee of Nature Conservancy, 1966-69, Scottish Advisory Committee, Nature Conservancy Council, 1970-80, Countryside Commission for Scotland, 1980-92; President, Botanical Society of Edinburgh, 1982-84; Vice-Chairman, NE Regional Board, Nature Conservancy Council for Scotland, 1991-92; Member: NE Regional Board, SNH, 1992-96, Science Advisory Committee, SNH, 1996-99, Board of Management, Hill Farming Research Organisation, 1981-87, Governing Body, Aberdeen College of Education, 1979-87, Council of Management, Macaulay Institute for Soil Research, 1983-87, Board of Management, Macaulay Land Use Research Institute, 1987- 90; British Ecological Society: Joint Secretary, 1956-61, Vice-President, 1962-64, Joint Editor, Journal of Ecology, 1975-78, President, 1986-87; Patron, Institute of Ecology and Environmental Management, 2000-; Founding Fellow, Institute of Contemporary Scotland, 2000; President, The Heather Trust, 2004-07. Publications: Ecology of Heathlands, 1972; Introduction to Heathland Ecology, 1975; Lowland Heathland Management Handbook, 1992; The Ecology, Land Use and Conservation of the Cairngorms, 2002. Recreations: hill-walking; photography; history and culture of Japan. Address: (h.) 9 Florence Court, 402 North Deeside Road, Cults, Aberdeen AB15 9TD.

Girdwood, David Greenshields, DL, BSc, MEd, SQH. Rector, St. Columba's School, Kilmacolm, since 2002; b. 14.10.57, Tillicoultry; m., Lisa; 2 d. Educ. Alva Academy; St. Andrews University; Jordanhill College; Stirling University; Edinburgh University. Lornshill Academy: Teacher of Chemistry, 1979-85, Assistant Principal of Science, 1985-87; Daniel Stewart's and Melville College: Principal Teacher of Chemistry and Head of Science, 1987-96, Head of Upper School, 1996-2002. Associate Assessor, HMI, 1999-2002; Deputy Lord Lieutenant of Renfrewshire, since 2009; Member of the Erskine Stewart's Melville Governing Council, since 2006. Recreations: rugby; walking. Address: (b.) Duchal Road, Kilmacolm, Renfrewshire PA13 4AU; T.-01505 872238; e-mail: secretary@st-columbas.org

Girvin, Professor Brian, BA, MA, PhD, FRHS. Professor of Comparative Politics, University of Glasgow, since 2000; b. 16.7.50, Cork; partner, Rona Fitzgerald; 1 s. Educ. Sullivan's Quay CBS, Cork; University College, Cork. Temporary Lecturer, National Institute for Higher Education, Limerick, 1978-82; University College, Cork: Temporary Teaching Assistant, 1983-86, Director of European Studies, 1986-88, Lecturer in Modern History, 1986-95; Senior Lecturer in Politics, University of Glasgow, 1995-2000. Member of PEN Scotland. Publications: Politics and Society in Contemporary Ireland (Co-Editor), 1986; The Transformation of Contemporary Conservatism (Editor), 1988; Between Two Worlds: Politics and Economy in Independent Ireland, 1989; The Right in the Twentieth Century: Conservatism and Democracy, 1994; The Green Pool Negotiations and the Origins of the Common Agricultural Policy (Co-Editor), 1995; Ireland and the Second World War: Politics, Society and Remembrance (Co-Editor), 2000; From Union to Union: Nationalism, Democracy and Religion in Ireland since 1800, 2002; The Lemass Era (Co-Editor), 2005; The Emergency: Neutral Ireland, 1939-45, 2006; Continuity, Change and Crisis in Ireland, since the 1960s (Co-Editor), 2008; Continuity and Change in Contemporary Ireland (Co-Editor), 2010. Recreation: mountaineering; cooking; archaeology and photography; film; music; books. Address: School of Political and Social Sciences, University of Glasgow G12 8RT; T.-0141-330 5353. E-mail: brian.girvin@glasgow.ac.uk

Glasby, Michael Arthur, BM, BCh, MA, MSc (Oxon), MA (Cantab), MTh, PhD, MD, DSc (Edin), BD (Lond), FRCP (Edin), FRCS (Edin), FRCS (Eng). Honorary Fellow, University of Edinburgh; Consulting Neurophysiologist, Scottish National Spinal Deformity Centre, Royal Hospital for Sick Children, Edinburgh; b. 29.10.48, Nottingham; m., Celia M.E. Robinson. Educ. High Pavement Grammar School, Nottingham; Christ Church, Oxford; Oxford Medical School. Senior Scholar and Assistant Tutor in Physiology, Christ Church, Oxford, 1971-76; Cardiac Surgeon, Harefield Hospital Transplant Trust, 1981-83; Fellow and Lecturer in Anatomy, New Hall, Cambridge, 1983-87; Lecturer in Anatomy, Royal College of Surgeons of England, 1984-87; joined Edinburgh University as Lecturer, 1987; Reader in Anatomy, 1992-97; Reader in Experimental Neurology, 1997-2004. Editor, anatomy textbook for surgeons and physiology textbook for surgeons; numerous articles. Recreations: Classical and Semitic languages; The Ancient Near East; music; beekeeping; wine; golf. Address: (h.) 3 Cluny Drive, Morningside, Edinburgh EH10 6DN; T.-0131 447 3836; e-mail: michael.glasby@ed.ac.uk

Glasgow, 10th Earl of (Patrick Robin Archibald Boyle), DL. Television Director/Producer; b. 30.7.39; m., Isabel Mary James; 1 s.; 1 d. Educ. Eton; Paris University. Sub.-Lt., RNR, 1959-60; Producer/Director, Yorkshire TV, 1968-70; freelance Film Producer, since 1971; created Kelburn Country Centre (leisure park), 1977, and now manages this and Kelburn Estate; Deputy Lieutenant, Ayrshire; Lib Dem Peer, House of Lords. Address (b.) Kelburn Castle, Fairlie, Ayrshire KA29 0BE; T.-01475 568685; e-mail: admin@kelburncountrycentre.com

Glasier, Anna, OBE, MB, ChB, BSc, FRCOG, MD, DSc, FFPRHC. Director, Lothian Primary Care NHS Trust Family Planning and Well Woman Services, 1990-2010; Honorary Professor: Edinburgh University, University of London; Consultant Gynaecologist, Lothian Health Board, since 1989; Lead Clinician for Sexual Health in NHS Lothian; b. 16.4.50, Salisbury; m., Dr. David T. Baird. Educ. Lord Digby's School, Sherborne. Clinical Research Scientist, Medical Research Council Centre for Reproductive Biology, Edinburgh, 1989-90. Recreation: ski mountaineering.

Glass, Douglas James Allan, LVO, MB, ChB. General Practice Associate in Braemar, since 2013; Apothecary to HM Household, Balmoral, since 1988; Partner in farm (D.L. Glass), since 1982; b. 8.10.53, Dinnet, Aboyne; m., Alison; 1 s.; 4 d. Educ. Aboyne Academy; Banchory Academy; Aberdeen University. Junior House Officer, 1977-78; Senior House Officer, 1978-79; General Practitioner Trainee, 1979-80; General Practice, Australia and New Zealand, 1980-81; General Practice Principal, Peterhead, 1981-87; General Practitioner, Ballater, 1987-2013. Elder, Glenmuick Church, Ballater, since 1988. Recreations: dry stane dyking; golf; snooker; football. Address: (h.) Deecastle, Dinnet, Aboyne, Aberdeenshire; T.-013398 85217.

Glen, Eric Stanger, MB, ChB, FRCSGlas, FRCSEdin. Professore Visitatore, Università degli Studi di Pavia; Consultant Urological Surgeon, Walton Urological Teaching and Research Centre, Southern General Hospital, Glasgow, 1972-99; b. 20.10.34, Glasgow; m., Dr. Patricia. Educ. Airdrie Academy; Glasgow University. Pre-Consultant posts, Western and Victoria Infirmaries, Glasgow; Ship Surgeon, Royal Fleet Auxiliary. Formerly Medical Director, Continence Resource Centre and Helpline for Scotland; Past Chairman, Greater Glasgow Area Medical Committee; Founder and Honorary Member,

International Continence Society; former Honorary Clinical Senior Lecturer, Glasgow University; former Member, Surgical Examination Panel, Royal College of Physicians and Surgeons of Glasgow; Founder, Urological Computing Society; Honorary Co-Chairman, 41st Annual Meeting of the International Continence Society (ICS), 29 August - 2 September, 2011; Lifetime Achievement Award, International Continence Society, Beijing, October 2012. Publications: Co-Editor, ICS History Book "The First 40 Years 1971-2010, 2011; chapters in books; papers on urodynamics, urology and computing. Recreations: travel; writing; computer applications. Address: (h.) 9 St. John's Road, Pollokshields, Glasgow G41 5RJ; T.-0141-423 0759. E-mail: ericnetherlee@btinternet.com

Glen, Marlyn. MSP (Lab), North East Scotland, 2003-2011; b. 30.9.51, Dundee; widowed; 1 s.; 1 d. Educ. Kirkton High School, Dundee; St. Andrews University; Dundee University; Open University. Former teacher.

Glenarthur, 4th Baron (Simon Mark Arthur), Bt, DL. DL, Aberdeenshire, since 1987; Director: Millennium Chemicals Inc., 1996-2004, Medical Defence Union, 2002-06, Audax Global Sàrl, since 2003; a Governor, Nuffield Health, 2000-09; b. 7.10.44; m.; 1 s.; 1 d. Educ. Eton. Retired Major, 10th Royal Hussars (PWO); Helicopter Captain, British Airways, 1976-82; a Lord in Waiting, 1982-83; Parliamentary Under Secretary of State: Department of Health and Social Security, 1983-85, Home Office, 1985-86; Minister of State: Scottish Office, 1986-87, Foreign and Commonwealth Office, 1987-89; Consultant: British Aerospace PLC, 1989-99, Hanson PLC, 1989-99, Imperial Tobacco Ltd., 1996-98; Deputy Chairman, Hanson Pacific Ltd., 1994-97; Chairman, St. Mary's Hospital, Paddington, NHS Trust, 1991-98, British Helicopter Advisory Board, 1992-2004, European Helicopter Association, 1996-2003; President: National Council for Civil Protection, 1991-2003, British Helicopter Association, since 2004; Member (Captain), Queen's Bodyguard for Scotland (Royal Company of Archers); Scottish Patron, The Butler Trust, 1994-2014; Trustee, Royal College of Organists, since 2014; Non-executive Director, Audax Global S.a.r.l, since 2005; a Commissioner, Royal Hospital Chelsea, 2001-07; Honorary Colonel, 306 Hospital Support Medical Regiment (Volunteers), 2001-2011; Honorary Air Commodore, 612 (County of Aberdeen) Squadron, Royal Auxiliary Air Force, 2004-2014; Chairman, National Employer Advisory Board for the Reserves of the Armed Forces, 2002-09; Governor: King Edward VII Hospital (Sister Agnes), 2010-2013 (Chairman of Council, 2012-2013), Sutton's Hospital in Charterhouse, since 2011. Address: (b.) Northbrae Farmhouse, Crathes, Banchory AB31 6JQ; T.-01330 844467; e-mail: glenarthur@northbrae.co.uk

Glennie, Lord (Angus James Scott), MA (Hons). Senator of the College of Justice, since 2005; Principal Commercial Judge, since 2008; m., Patricia Jean Phelan. Educ. Sherborne School, Dorset; Trinity Hall, University of Cambridge. Called to the Bar at Lincoln's Inn, 1974; appointed a Bencher, 2007; worked mainly in commercial and international arbitration whilst at the English Bar, before the Commercial Court and Court of Appeal; took silk there in 1991, and the following year was admitted to the Faculty of Advocates; practised mostly in commercial law, but also worked in other areas, such as judicial review and reparation; appointed Queen's Counsel in Scotland in 1998; worked originally as an Intellectual Property Judge; became a Commercial Judge in 2007. Address: (b.) Parliament House, 11 Parliament Square, Edinburgh EH1 1RQ.

Glennie, John, OBE. Non Executive member, Healthcare Improvement Scotland (Chief Executive, 2013-14); b. 1949. Career: joined local health board as a trainee accountant in 1966, and worked in the NHS ever since; became a Director

of Finance and Deputy Chief Executive with Central Manchester Healthcare Trust before moving to the Borders to take charge of Borders General Hospital NHS Trust in 1995; Chief Executive, NHS Borders, 2003-09. Address: Healthcare Improvement Scotland, Gyle Square, 1 South Gyle Crescent, Edinburgh EH12 9EB; T.-0131 623 4300.

Gloag, Ann, OBE. Non-Executive Director, Stagecoach Group plc (Managing Director, 1986-94, Executive Director, 1986-2000); b. 10.12.42. Educ. Perth High School. Nursing, 1960-80; Founding Partner, Stagecoach, 1980. Address: (b.) Stagecoach Group, 10 Dunkeld Road, Perth PH1 5TW.

Glover, Dame Anne, DBE, FRS, FRSE, FASM. Scottish biologist and academic; Vice Principal, External Affairs and Dean for Europe, University of Aberdeen (Personal Chair of Molecular and Cell Biology); b. 19.4.56. Educ. High School of Dundee; University of Edinburgh; King's College, Cambridge. Career history: first ever Chief Scientific Adviser for Scotland, 2006-2011; former Joint Chair of the Scottish Science Advisory Committee and served on the Scottish Council of Economic Advisers; Chief Scientific Adviser to the President of the European Commission, 2012-14. Honorary positions at the Macaulay and Rowett Institutes and the University of New South Wales, Sydney; Council member of the Natural Environment Research Council, 2001-11. Recognised in 2008 as a Woman of Outstanding Achievement by the UK Resource Centre for Women in Science, Engineering and Technology. Assessed as the 19th most powerful woman in the United Kingdom by Woman's Hour on BBC Radio 4 (February 2013). Honorary Doctorate from Heriot-Watt University, 2013. Address: King's College, Aberdeen AB24 3FX; T.-01224 273736. E-mail: L.a.glover@abdn.ac.uk

Glover, Rev. Robert Lindsay, BMus, BD, MTh, ARCO. C of S Minister (retired) & Organist; b. 21.7.45, Watford; m., Elizabeth Mary Brown; 2 s.; 2 d. Educ. Langholm Academy; Dumfries Academy; Glasgow University. Minister: Newton Parish, near Dalkeith, 1971-76, St. Vigeans Parish, Arbroath, 1976-85, Knox's, Arbroath, 1982-85, St. George's West, Edinburgh, 1985-97, Cockenzie and Port Seton: Chalmers Memorial, 1997-2010. Recreations: music (organ, piano accompaniment, listening); supporting Heart of Midlothian F.C.; reading; travel. Address: 12 Seton Wynd, Port Seton, Prestonpans, East Lothian EH32 0TY; e-mail: rlglover@btinternet.com

Glover, Sue, MA. Writer; b. 1.3.43, Edinburgh; divorced; 2 s. Educ. St. George's School, Edinburgh; Montpellier University; Edinburgh University. Original drama and other scriptwriting for radio, television and theatre; theatre productions include: The Seal Wife, Edinburgh Festival, 1980; An Island in Largo, Byre Theatre, 1981; The Bubble Boy, Glasgow Tron, 1981; The Straw Chair, Traverse Theatre, 1988; Bondagers, Traverse Theatre, 1991 (winner, 1990 LWT Plays on Stage Award); Sacred Hearts, 1994; Artist Unknown, 1996; Shetland Saga, Traverse Theatre, 2000; Blow-outs, Wrecks and Almanacs, 2002; Marilyn en Chantée, 2007; Bear on a Chain, 2010; Marilyn, 2011, Citizens Theatre and Royal Lyceum Theatre; television work includes: The Spaver Connection; Mme Montand and Mrs Miller; Dear Life; televised version of The Bubble Boy won a silver medal, New York Film and Television Festival, and a merit, Chicago International Film Festival, 1983. Publications: The Bubble Boy: You Don't Know You're Born, 1991; Bondagers (Made in Scotland), 1995; Bondagers and The Straw Chair, 1997; Shetland Saga, 2000; The Seal Wife, 2008; Artist Unknown, 2008; Sacred Hearts, 2009; The Bubble Boy, 2009. Recreations: house and garden. Address: (b.) Charles Walker, United Agents, 130 Shaftesbury Avenue, London W1D 5EU.

Godman, Trish. MSP (Labour), West Renfrewshire, 1999-2011; Deputy Presiding Officer, 2003-2011; former Convener, Local Government Committee; b. 1939; m.; 3 s. Educ. St Gerard's Senior Secondary School; Jordanhill College. Former Regional Councillor; former Member, Glasgow City Council. Recreations: allotment holder; music; dancing; reading; cinema.

Gold, Lex, CBE; b. 14.12.40, Rigside; m., Eleanor; 1 s.; 1 d. Educ. Lanark Grammar School. Sub-Editor, Daily Record; professional footballer; joined Civil Service, Glasgow, 1960; Inland Revenue, two years, Civil Service Department, four years, Home Office, 21 years, Training Agency, three years; former Managing Director, Scottish Enterprise; former Director, CBI Scotland; former Director, Scottish Chambers of Commerce; former Chairman, Hibernian Football Club Ltd.; former Chairman, Lanarkshire NHS Board; former Director, Caledonian MacBrayne; former Chairman, Scottish Premier League.

Golden, Maurice, BA, MPhil, LLM. MSP (Scottish Conservative), West Scotland region, since 2016; Shadow Cabinet Secretary for Environment, Climate Change and Land Reform, since 2016. Educ. High School of Dundee; Routt High School; University of Dundee. Career history: Internship, Murray Darling River Basin Commission, 2004; Guest Lecturer, University of Dundee, 2005-07; Director, Golden's Limited, 1998-2007; Campaign Manager, Waste Aware Scotland, 2005-09; Transmission Policy Analyst, Ofgem, 2009-11; appointed Circular Economy Programme Manager, Zero Waste Scotland in 2011. Address: Scottish Parliament, Edinburgh EH99 1SP.

Goldie, Baroness Annabel MacNicoll, DL, LLB. MSP (Conservative), West of Scotland, 1999-2016; Leader, Scottish Conservative Party, 2005-2011; former Convener, Justice 2 Committee; Deputy Lord Lieutenant, Renfrewshire, since 1993; Partner, Donaldson, Alexander, Russell and Haddow (formerly Dickson Haddow and Co.), 1978-2006; b. 27.2.50, Glasgow. Educ. Greenock Academy; Strathclyde University. Admitted Solicitor, 1974; Scottish Conservative Party: Deputy Chairman, 1995-97, Chairman, March-July 1997, Deputy Chairman, 1997-98, Deputy Leader, 1998-2005. Elder, Church of Scotland; Member, West of Scotland Advisory Board, Salvation Army; Honorary Fellow, Strathclyde University; became a Life Peeress in the House of Lords, 2013. Recreations: bird watching; cycling; listening to music.

Gomatam, Professor Jagannathan, BSc, MSc, PhD. Emeritus Professor of Applied Mathematics, Glasgow Caledonian University, Professor, since 1990; b. 20.8.40, India; m., Jean McGregor. Educ. University of Madras; Syracuse University. Research Assistant, Physics Department, then Instructor, Mathematics Department, Syracuse University, 1966-70; Post-Doctoral Research Fellow, Physics Department, Syracuse University, 1970-71; Research Scholar, School of Theoretical Physics, Dublin Institute for Advanced Studies, 1971-73; Lecturer/Reader, Glasgow Caledonian University, 1973-90. Senior Visitor, Mathematical Institute, Oxford University, 1986-87; re-elected to Peer Review College, EPSRC, 2010-2013; Visiting Professor, Strathclyde University, 2007-2013. Address: (b.) School of Engineering and Built Environment, Glasgow Caledonian University, 70 Cowcaddens Road, Glasgow G4 0BA.

Gondzio, Professor Jacek. Professor of Optimization, Edinburgh University, since 2005; b. 01.01.60, Skrzynki, Poland; m., Joanna Karpinska-Gondzio; 1 s. Educ. Warsaw University of Technology. Polish Academy of Sciences, Poland: Research Assistant, 1983-89, Assistant Professor, 1989-98; Research Fellow: Universite Paris Dauphine, France, 1990-91, University of Geneva, Switzerland, 1993-98; Lecturer, Edinburgh University, 1998-2000, Reader, 2000-05. Address: (b.) School of Mathematics, Edinburgh University, King's Buildings, Edinburgh EH9 3JZ; T.-0131 650 8574; e-mail: j.gondzio@ed.ac.uk

Good, Professor Anthony, BSc, PhD (Edin), PhD (Dunelm). Head, School of Social and Political Science, University of Edinburgh, 2006-09, Professor Emeritus in Social Anthropology, since 2009; b. 15.12.41, Congleton, Cheshire; m., Alison; 2 d. Educ. Kings School, Macclesfield; University of Edinburgh; University of Durham. Postdoctoral Research Fellow in Chemistry, University of Alberta, Canada, 1967-69; SRC Postdoctoral Fellow in Chemistry, University of Cambridge, 1969-70; Commonwealth Educational Co-operation Scheme Senior Lecturer in Chemistry, University of Peradeniya, Sri Lanka, 1970-72; Research Fellow in Chemistry, City University, London, 1973-74; SSRC Conversion Fellow in Anthropology, University of Durham, 1974-77; Lecturer in Sociology, University of East Anglia, 1978-79; Lecturer in Social Anthropology: University of Manchester, 1979-80, University of Edinburgh, 1980-91, Senior Lecturer, 1991-2004; Senior Social Development Adviser to the Joint Funding Scheme, Department for International Development, 1987-99. Member, Scottish Advisory Council, Immigration Advisory Service, 2002-08. Publications: Research Practices in the Study of Kinship (Co-Author), 1984; The Female Bridegroom: A Comparative Study of Life-Crisis Rituals in South India and Sri Lanka, 1991; Worship and the Ceremonial Economy of a Royal South Indian Temple, 2004; Anthropology and Expertise in the Asylum Courts, 2007. Address: (b.) School of Social and Political Science, University of Edinburgh, Edinburgh EH8 9LD; T.-0131-650-3941; e-mail: a.good@ed.ac.uk

Goodman, Professor Anthony Eric, MA (Oxon), BLitt (Oxon). Professor of Medieval and Renaissance History, Edinburgh University, 1993-2001, Professor Emeritus, since 2001; b. 21.7.36, London; m., Jacqueline; 1 d. Educ. Selhurst Grammar School, Croydon; Magdalen College, Oxford. Joined staff, Edinburgh University, 1961. Secretary, Edinburgh Branch, Historical Association, since 1975. Publications: The Loyal Conspiracy, 1971; A History of England from Edward II to James I, 1977; The Wars of the Roses, 1981; A Traveller's Guide to Medieval Britain (Co-author), 1986; The New Monarchy, 1471-1534, 1988; John of Gaunt, 1992; Margery Kempe and Her World, 2002; The Wars of the Roses. The Soldiers' Experience (2005). Address: (h.) 23 Kirkhill Gardens, Edinburgh EH16 5DF; T.-0131-667 5988.
E-mail: jackie.goodman1@btinternet.com

Goodwin, Frederick Anderson, DUniv, LLB, CA, FCIBS, FCIB, LLD, FRSE. Former Group Chief Executive, Royal Bank of Scotland Group plc (2000-09); former Senior Adviser, RMJM (2010); b. 17.8.58, Paisley; m. Educ. Glasgow University. Touche Ross: joined, 1979; Partner, 1988; Chief Operating Officer, BCCI Worldwide Liquidation, 1992-95; Deputy Chief Executive, Clydesdale Bank Plc, 1995; Chief Executive/Director, Clydesdale Bank, 1996; Chief Executive/Director, Clydesdale Bank and Yorkshire Bank Plc, 1997-98; Deputy Chief Executive, Royal Bank of Scotland, Plc, 1998-2000. Recreations: golf; cars.

Gordon of Strathblane, Lord (James Stuart Gordon), CBE, DLitt., DUniv, MA (Hons). Chairman, Scottish Radio Holdings, 1996-2005; Director, Johnston Press plc, 1996-

2007, The AIM Trust plc, 1996-2003, Active Capital Trust plc, since 2003; Chairman, RAJAR, 2003-06; Member, BP Scottish Advisory Board, 1990-2003; b. 17.5.36, Glasgow; m., Anne Stevenson; 2 s.; 1 d. Educ. St. Aloysius College, Glasgow; Glasgow University (President of the Union, 1958-59). Political Editor, STV, 1965-73; Managing Director, Radio Clyde, 1973-96; Chief Executive, Scottish Radio Holdings, 1991-96. Member, Court, Glasgow University, 1984-97; Chairman, Advisory Group on Listed Sports Events on Television, 1997-98; Chairman, Scottish Tourist Board, 1998-2001; Trustee, National Galleries of Scotland, 1998-2001; Member, Review Panel on the Future Funding of the BBC; Winner, Observer Mace Debating Tournament, 1957; Sony Special Award for Services to Radio, 1984. Chairman, Scottish Exhibition Centre, 1983-89; Member, Scottish Development Agency, 1981-90. Recreations: his children; genealogy; golf. Address: (b.) House of Lords, London SW1A 0PW.

Gordon, Charlie. MSP (Labour), Glasgow Cathcart, 2005-2011; 3 s. Councillor, Strathclyde Regional Council, 1987-96; Vice Convenor, Roads and Transport (SRC), 1990-94; Convenor, Roads and Transport (SRC), 1994-96; Councillor, Glasgow City Council, 1995-2005; Convenor, Roads (GCC), 1995-96; Chair, Strathclyde Passenger Transport, 1996-99; Deputy Leader, Glasgow City Council, 1997-99, Leader, 1999-2005.

Gordon, Donald Neil, MA, LLB, WS, NP, TEP. Partner, Blackadders (formerly Carltons) Solicitors, 1979-2013 (retired); Senior Tutor, Diploma in Legal Practice, University of Dundee, 1994-2014; Dean, Faculty of Procurators and Solicitors in Dundee, 1999-2001; b. 30.3.51, Aberdeen; m., Alison Mary Whyte; 1 s.; 1 d. Educ. Robert Gordon's College, Aberdeen; University of Aberdeen; University of Edinburgh. Law Apprenticeship, Edinburgh, 1973-75; Assistant Solicitor, Carlton & Reid, Dundee, 1975-79. WS, 1975; Notary Public, 1975; Chairman, Dundee Citizens Advice Bureau, 1996-2001; Honorary French Consul, Dundee, since 1996; President, Abertay Rotary Club, 2001-02; President, Dundee Orchestral Society, 2003-08; Past Chairman, High School of Dundee Parents Association; Director, High School of Dundee, since 2008; joint Editor, Green's Practical Styles (Wills), 2005; Scottish Tutor, STEP, until 2015. Recreations: music; gardening; Rotary.

Gordon, Emeritus Professor George, MA (Hons), PhD, FRSGS, FBAASc, FRSA, FFCS, FRGS. Director of Academic Practice, Strathclyde University, 1987-2005, Professor of Academic Practice, 1991-2005; b. 14.11.39, Edinburgh; m., Jane Taylor Collins; 2 d. Educ. George Heriot's School; Edinburgh University. Edinburgh University: Vans Dunlop Scholar, 1962-64, Demonstrator, 1964-65; Strathclyde University: Assistant Lecturer, 1965-66, Lecturer, 1966-80, Dean, Faculty of Arts and Social Studies, 1984-87; served on SUCE and SCE Geography Panels, SCOVACT, and General Teaching Council for Scotland; Chairman, Council, Royal Scottish Geographical Society, 1999-2005; Hon. Treasurer, Society for Research into Higher Education, 2002-06, Chair of Council, 2007-09; Board of Directors, The Higher Education Academy, 2004-05; Honorary Auditor, Australian Universities Quality Agency, 2002-05; Vice President, British Association for the Advancement of Science, 1991-97; former Member, General Assembly of Open University; Strathclyde University: Member, Senate 1984-2002, Member, Court, 1984-87, 2000-02; Governor, Jordanhill College of Education, 1982-93 (Chairman, 1987-93). Publications: Regional Cities of the UK 1890-1980 (Editor), 1986; Perspectives of the Scottish City (Editor), 1985; The Making of Scottish Geography (Co-Author), 1984; Urban Geography (Co-Author), 1981; Scottish Urban History (Co-Editor), 1983; Settlement Geography (Co-Author), 1983; Academic and Professional Identities (Co-Editor), 2009; Enhancing Quality in Higher Education (Co-Editor), 2013. Recreations: theatre-going; watching sport. Address: (b.) Learning Enhancement, Strathclyde University, 50 George Street, Glasgow.

Gordon, Sir Gerald Henry, CBE, QC, MA, LLB, PhD, LLD, HonFRSE. Sheriff of Glasgow and Strathkelvin, 1978-99; Temporary Judge, Court of Session and High Court of Justiciary, 1992-2004; b. 17.6.29, Glasgow; m., Marjorie Joseph; 1 s.; 2 d. Educ. Queen's Park Senior Secondary School; Glasgow University. Advocate, 1953; Procurator Fiscal Depute, Edinburgh, 1960-65; Edinburgh University: Head, Department of Criminal Law and Criminology, 1965-72, Personal Professor of Criminal Law, 1969-72, Dean, Faculty of Law, 1970-73, Professor of Scots Law, 1972-76; Sheriff of South Strathclyde, Dumfries and Galloway, at Hamilton, 1976-77; Member: Interdepartmental Committee on Scottish Criminal Procedure, 1970-77, Committee on Criminal Appeals and Miscarriages of Justice, 1995-96, Scottish Criminal Cases Review Commission, 1999-2008. Publications: Criminal Law of Scotland, 1967, 1978; Renton & Brown's Criminal Procedure (Editor), 1972, 1983, 1996. Recreations: Jewish studies; coffee conversation; crosswords.

Gordon, Laura. Head Teacher, Alness Academy, since 2014. Career: Teacher of Chemistry, Dingwall Academy; Assistant Principal Teacher of Chemistry, Lochgilphead High School; Principal Teacher of Chemistry, Glenrothes High School; Qualification Development Consultant with the Scottish Qualification Authority; Depute Head Teacher, Dingwall Academy, 2010-2013. Address: Dalmore, Alness IV17 0UY; T.-01349 882614.

Gormley, Phil, QPM, BA. Chief Constable, Police Scotland, since 2016; b. 1957, Glasgow. Educ. University of Gloucestershire; University of Cambridge. Constable, Thames Valley Police, 1985-99, Superintendent and Commander with responsibility for the Southern Oxfordshire area, 1999-2003; Commander Specialist Operations, Metropolitan Police, 2003-07, organised the merger of the Anti-Terrorist Branch and Special Branch into what would become the Counter Terrorism Command in 2006; Deputy Chief Constable, West Midlands Police, 2007-2010; Chief Constable, Norfolk Constabulary, 2010-13; Deputy Director General, National Crime Agency (NCA), 2013-15. Address: Police Scotland, PO Box 21629, Stirling FK7 1EN.

Goudie, Professor Andrew William, CB, FRSE, PhD, MA, BA (Econ), BA (Maths). Special Adviser to the Principal and Visiting Professor, University of Strathclyde, since 2011; Director-General Economy and Chief Economic Adviser, Scottish Government, 2007-2011, Chief Economic Adviser, 1999-2011, and Head of Finance and Central Services Department, 2003-07; b. 3.3.55, London; m., Christine Goudie; 2 s.; 2 d. Educ. Haberdashers' Aske's School, Elstree; Queens' College, University of Cambridge. University of Cambridge, 1978-85: Research Officer, Department of Applied Economics, Research Fellow, Queens' College, Fellow and Director of Studies, Robinson College; Senior Economist, The World Bank, Washington DC, 1985-90; Senior Economic Adviser, Scottish Office, 1990-95; Principal Economist, OECD, Paris, 1995-96; Chief Economist, DFID (formerly ODA), London, 1996-99; Doctor of Letters, University of Strathclyde, 2003. Publications: articles in learned journals. Address: (b.) University of Strathclyde, 16 Richmond Street, Glasgow G1 1XQ; T.-0141 552 4400; e-mail: goudie_a@hotmail.com

Grace, Adrian, MBA. Chief Executive, Aegon UK since 2011. Educ. Ossett School; Henley Business School. Career history: Leeds Permanent Building Society, 1979-84; Mercantile Credit, 1984-2001; Managing Director of the

Small Business Division, Sage Group PLC, 2001-04; Chief Executive, Barclays Insurance, 2004-07; Managing Director, SME banking, Lloyds TSB, 2007-09; Group Business Development Director, Aegon, 2009-11. Member of the Global Management Board for Aegon N.V., since February 2012; non-executive director of Scottish Financial Enterprise (SFE). Address: Aegon, Edinburgh Park, Edinburgh EH12 9SE; T.-0131 549 5054.

Grace, Professor John, BSc, PhD, FIBiol, FRSE. Emeritus Professor of Environmental Biology, Edinburgh University, Professor, since 1992; Head, School of Geosciences, 2002-03; Head, Institute of Ecology and Resource Management, 2000-02; Head, Institute of Atmospheric and Environmental Sciences, 2003-08; b. 19.9.45, Northampton; m., Elizabeth Ashworth; 2 s.; 1 d. Educ. Bletchley Grammar School; Sheffield University. Lecturer, then Reader in Ecology, Edinburgh University, 1970-92. Co-Editor, Functional Ecology, 1986-99; Technical Editor, International Society for Biometeorology, 1983-98; Member, Terrestrial Life Sciences Committee, Natural Environment Research Council, 1986-89; President, British Ecological Society, 2002-03; Chairman, Botanical Society of Scotland, since 2012; Member, Scottish Forestry Trust, since 2013; BES Award, 2007; Marsh Award, 2009. Publications: Plant Response to Wind, 1977; Plants and their Atmospheric Environment (Co-Editor), 1981; Plant-atmosphere Relationships, 1983. Recreations: hill-walking; cycling; fishing; bridge; allotments. Address: (h.) 25 Craiglea Drive, Edinburgh EH10 5PB; T.-0131-447 3030; e-mail: jgrace@ed.ac.uk

Grace, Paul Henry, BSc, FFA. Director, Scottish Equitable Policyholders Trust Ltd., 1998-2012; Director and Honorary Treasurer, Victim Support Scotland Ltd., 1998-2004; Chairman, National Provident Life Fund Supervisory Board, 2000-2010; Member, Scottish Life Fund Supervisory Committee, 2001-2012; b. 25.9.38, Bletchley; m., Aileen Anderson; 1 d. Educ. Bedford Modern School; St. Andrews University. Joined Scottish Equitable as Actuarial Trainee, 1960; joined Zurich Life Assurance Co. as Actuary and Life Manager, 1965; rejoined Scottish Equitable as Actuary, 1980-93; Deputy Chief Executive, 1985-93, Director, 1987-93; Managing Director and Actuary, Scottish Equitable Policyholders Trust Ltd., 1994-98. President, Faculty of Actuaries, 1996-98; Director, Student Loans Company Ltd., 1999-2002; Chairman, Groupe Consultatif Actuariel Europeen, 2004-05. Publication: Introduction to Life Assurance, 1988. Recreation: gardening. Address: 8 March Pines, Edinburgh EH4 3PF; T.-0131 312 6357.

Grady, Patrick. MP (SNP), Glasgow North, since 2015; SNP Westminster Spokesperson on International Development, since 2015; b. 5.2.80, Edinburgh. Educ. Inverness Royal Academy; University of Strathclyde. Advocacy Manager, Scottish Catholic International Aid Fund, 2011-15; lived and worked in London and Malawi. Joined the SNP in 1997, aged 17 and headed the "Yes" campaign in the Kelvin area of Glasgow during the 2014 referendum on Scottish independence. Member of the House of Commons Procedure Committee. Address: House of Commons, London SW1A 0AA.

Graham, Rev. Alasdair Giffen, BD, Dip. Ministry. Minister, Arbroath West Kirk, since 1990; Part-time Chaplain, Arbroath Infirmary; b. 20.4.54, Lanark; m., Joan Janet Forsyth; 1 d. Educ. Gordon Schools, Huntly; Kirkcaldy High School; University of Glasgow. Probationary Assistant, Mastrick Church, Aberdeen, 1980-81; Minister, Redgorton and Stanley Churches, Perthshire, 1981-86; Chaplain, HM Prison, Perth, 1982-86; Minister, St Margaret's Church, Arbroath, 1986-90. District Scout Chaplain; Chaplain, Angus Training Group. Recreations: time with family; walking; reading. Address: (h.) 1 Charles Avenue, Arbroath DD11 2EY; T.-01241 872244.

Graham, Professor David I., MB, ChB, PhD, FRCPath, FRCPS, FMedSci, FRSE. Emeritus Professor; b. 20.7.39, Glasgow; m., Joyce; 1 s.; 1 d. Educ. Penarth County Grammar School; Welsh National School of Medicine, Cardiff. Registrar, Western Infirmary, Glasgow, 1965-68; Lecturer, Department of Neuropathology, Glasgow, 1968-72; Fogarty Fellow, Laboratory of Neuropathology, Philadelphia, 1972-74; Senior Lecturer, Glasgow, 1974-83; Professor of Neuropathology, Glasgow University, 1983-2005; retired. Publications: several books; 300 papers. Recreations: hill-walking; music. Address: (b.) 44 Sycamore Avenue, Lenzie, Kirkintilloch, East Dunbartonshire G66 4NY.
E-mail: neuropathology44@yahoo.co.uk

Graham, (Lord) Donald, FCIBS, BSc, MBA. Director: Children's Music Foundation, since 1995, LCDK Limited, since 2008, Property Developers, 1992-2010; b. 28.10.56, Salisbury, Southern Rhodesia; m., Bridie; 1 s.; 3 d. Educ. St. Andrews College, South Africa; St. Andrews University; INSEAD. Recreations: piping; music; golf. Address: (b.) Children's Music Foundation, 46A Fortrose Street, Glasgow G11 5LP.

Graham, Elspeth Forbes, MA, PhD. Professor of Geography, St Andrews University, since 2012; Co-director, ESRC Centre for Population Change, since 2010; Head of School of Geography and Geosciences, 2004-08; Member, Local Government Boundary Commission for Scotland, 1994-2004; Member, Boundary Commission for Scotland, 1999-2010; b. 7.2.50, Edinburgh; 1 s.; 1 d. Educ. George Watson's Ladies College, Edinburgh; St Andrews University; Durham University. Visiting Lecturer, University of Minnesota, 1979-80; Visiting Senior Research Fellow, National University of Singapore, 2004 and 2008. Publications: Postmodernism and the Social Sciences (Co-editor), 1992; The Geography of Health Inequalities in the Developed World (Co-editor), 2004; research papers on population policies and issues, including low fertility in Scotland and Singapore, and child health and migrant parents in South-East Asia. Recreations: Celtic music and literature; local history. Address: (b.) Department of Geography and Sustainable Development, University of St Andrews KY16 9AL; T.-01334 463908.

Graham, George, QPM. Board Member, Scottish Police Authority, since 2015; Her Majesty's Inspector of Constabulary (HMIC) for Scotland, 2013-14; Chief Constable, Northern Constabulary, 2011-13; b. Dumfries. Joined Dumfries and Galloway Constabulary in 1982; stationed at Dumfries and Locharbriggs; held the position of Chief Superintendent, Head of Operations, until promotion to Deputy Chief Constable, 2006. Represented the Force on the Association of Chief Police Officers Scotland (ACPOS) General Policing Business Area, Crime Business Area, Professional Standards Business Area and Information Management Business Area, gaining a specific portfolio responsibility for Public Interface. Address: Scottish Police Authority, 1 Pacific Quay, Glasgow G51 1DZ.

Graham, Professor Neil Bonnette, BSc, PhD, CChem, FRSC, FIM, FRSE. Professor in Chemical Technology, Strathclyde University, 1973-97; Emeritus Professor in Chemistry, since 1997; b. 23.5.33, Liverpool; 1 s.; 3 d. Educ. Alsop High School, Liverpool; Liverpool University. Research Chemist, Research Scientist, Canadian Industries Ltd., MacMasterville PQ, Canada, 1956-67; Assistant Group Head, then Group Head, Polymer Chemistry, ICI, Runcorn, Cheshire. Member: Advisory Committee on Dental and Surgical Materials, 1980-86; Expert Advisor to the Secretary of State on Active Medical Implants, since 1993; sometime member of various committees, Society of Chemical Industry, Royal Society of Chemistry and Plastics and Rubber Institute; Founder and Technical Director, Polysystems Ltd., 1980-90; Founder and Chairman: Smart Tech Ltd., since 2000, Ocutec Ltd., since 2001; Trustee,

James Clerk Maxwell Trust; Trustee, MacKinnon McNeill Trust. Recreations: music; walking; sailing. Address: (b.) Smart Tech Ltd., Unit M12, 143 Charles Street, Glasgow G21 2QA; T.-0141 942 0484.
E-mail: neilbgraham@msn.com

Graham, Norma, QPM, DipAppCrim & PolMgmt (Cantab). Chief Constable, Fife Constabulary, 2008-2012; b. 19.08.62, Musselburgh; m., Malcolm Graham. Educ. Musselburgh Grammar School. Extensive policing experience in broad range of operational and corporate roles in Edinburgh and the Lothians between 1981 and 2002; notable posts include: Head of Force Drugs Squad; National role with HMIC - inspection of all Scottish forces and services; Divisional Commander for North East Edinburgh; Detective Chief Superintendent, Head of Crime Investigations; Assistant Chief Constable, Central Scotland Police, 2002-05; Deputy Chief Constable, Fife Constabulary, 2005-08. Chair, ACPOS Operational Policing Business Area; first woman Chief Constable in Scotland.

Graham, Lieutenant General Sir Peter, KCB, CBE, HondDLitt. Vice Patron, Gordon Highlanders Museum; Chairman, Regimental Trust Fund, The Gordon Highlanders, 1986-2004; Chairman, The Gordon Highlanders Museum Management Committee, 1994-2003; Chairman, Gordon Highlanders Museum Appeal, 1993-98 and 2002-06; b. 14.3.37; m., Dr Alison Mary Morren, MB, ChB, MRCGP; 3 s. Educ. Fyvie Village School, Aberdeenshire; Hall School, Hampstead; St. Paul's School, London, 1955-56; RMA Sandhurst. Commissioned The Gordon Highlanders, 1956; regimental appointments, Dover, Germany, Scotland, Kenya, 1957-62; HQ Highland Brigade, 1962-63; Adjutant 1 Gordons, Kenya, Edinburgh, Borneo (Despatches), 1963-66; Staff Captain, HQ 1 Br Corps, 1966-67; Australian Staff College, 1968; Company Commander, 1 Gordons, Germany, 1969-70; Brigade Maj., HQ 39 Brigade, Northern Ireland, 1970-72 (MBE); 2nd i/c, 1 Gordons, Ulster, Singapore, 1972-74; Military Assistant to Adjutant General MoD, 1974-75; CO, 1 Gordons, Scotland, Ulster, Chester, 1976-78 (OBE); COS, HQ 3 Armoured Division, Germany, 1978-82; Comd UDR, Ulster (Despatches), 1982-84; Canadian National Defence College, Kingston, 1984-85; Deputy Military Secretary, MoD, 1985-87; GOC Eastern District, 1987-89; Commandant RMA, Sandhurst, 1989-91; GOC Army in Scotland and Governor, Edinburgh Castle, 1991-93. Colonel, The Gordon Highlanders, 1986-94; Chairman, Gordon Highlanders Museum, 1994-2003; Member, Royal Company of Archers, since 1985. Burgess of Guild, City of Aberdeen, 1994; HonDLitt, Robert Gordon University, 1996; Hon. Firemaster, Grampian Fire and Rescue Services, 2010-13; Member, NE Scotland Coord Committee, Better Together, 2013-14. Publication: The Gordon Highlanders Pipe Music Collection (Co-author), 1983 and 1985. Recreations: hill-walking; reading; pipe music; gardening under my wife's directions; amusing grandchildren; military history. Address: (b.) c/o The Gordon Highlanders Musuem, Viewfield Road, Aberdeen AB15 7XH; T.-01224 311200.

Graham, Riddell, BSc. Director of Partnerships, VisitScotland; Chief Executive, Scottish Borders Tourist Board, 1996-2005, Director, 1990-96; b. 13.2.54, Galashiels; 1 s. Educ. Galashiels Academy; Edinburgh University. Borders Regional Council, 1976-83, latterly as Assistant Tourist Officer; joined Scottish Borders Tourist Board, 1983, as Assistant Director of Tourism. Recreations: good food and wine; watching rugby. Address: (b.) Visit Scotland, Ocean Point One, 94 Ocean Drive, Edinburgh EH6 6JH; T.-0131 472 2208.
E-mail: riddell.graham@visitscotland.com

Graham, Rev. William Peter, MA, BD. Ministerial Assistant, Greenbank Parish Church, Edinburgh, since

2009; b. 24.11.43, Edinburgh; m., Isabel Arnot Brown; 2 s. Educ. George Watson's College, Edinburgh; Edinburgh University. Assistant Minister, Dundee (St. Mary's) Parish Church, 1966-68; Minister, Chirnside Parish Church, 1968-93, Bonkyl & Preston, 1973-93, Edrom-Allanton, 1978-93; Clerk, Edinburgh Presbytery, 1993-2008; Clerk, Duns Presbytery, 1982-93; Convener, General Assembly's Nomination Committee, 1990-93, Board of Communication, 2003-05; Vice-Convener: Committee on Education for Ministry, 1996-98, Board of Ministry, 1998-99, Board of Communication, 1999-2002; Governor, George Watson's College, 1998-2008; General Secretary, Old Edinburgh Club, since 2013. Recreations: golf; bowls; theatre; reading; mah jong. Address: (h.) 23/6 East Comiston, Edinburgh EH10 6RZ.

Grahame, Christine, MA, LLB, DipEd, DipLLP. MSP (SNP), Midlothian South, Tweeddale and Lauderdale, since 2011, South of Scotland, 1999-2011 (Convener: Justice Committee, Justice sub-committee on policing); b. 9.9.44, Burton-on-Trent; 2 s. Educ. Boroughmuir School; Edinburgh University. Secondary teacher, 1966-82; solicitor, 1987-99. 1999-2012: Convener, Justice, Health and Sport; Shadow Minister, Social Justice; Convener, Cross-Party Group on Animal Welfare. Recreations: gardening; drinking malt whisky; cats; black and white movies. Address: Scottish Parliament, Edinburgh EH99 1SP; T.-0131-348 5729.
E-mail: christine.grahame.msp@scottish.parliament.uk

Grahame, David Currie, OBE, MA (Hons). Chief Executive, LINC Scotland, since 1993; b. 10.12.53, Hawick. Educ. Langholm Academy; Lockerbie Academy; St. Andrews University. Founding Director, LINC Scotland; Board Member, World Business Angels Association, Brussels; Advisory Board, SU2P Scotland-Stanford Partnership. Recreations: music; classic cinema; food and wine. Address: (b.) Queens House, 19 St. Vincent Place, Glasgow G1 2DT.
E-mail: david_grahame@lincscot.co.uk

Grant, Sir Ian David, CBE, DL, FRAgS; b. 28.7.43, Dundee; m., Eileen May Louisa Yule; 3 d. Educ. Strathallan School; East of Scotland College of Agriculture. Chairman, EEC Cereals Working Party, 1982-88 and International Federation of Agricultural Producers, Grains Committee, 1984-90; Board Member, Scottish Hydro-Electric, 1992-98, Scottish and Southern Energy PLC, 1998-2003 (Deputy Chairman, 2000-03); President, NFU of Scotland, 1984-90; Director: East of Scotland Farmers Ltd., 1978-2002, NFU Mutual Insurance Society Ltd., 1990-2008 (Deputy Chairman, 2003-08), Clydesdale Bank PLC, 1989-97; Member: Scottish Council, CBI, 1984-96, Board, British Tourist Authority, 1990-98, Scottish Economic Council, 1993-97; Chairman: Scottish Tourist Board, 1990-98 (Member, 1988-90), Cairngorms Partnership, 1998-2003, Crown Estate, 2002-09 (Commissioner, 1996-2009); Scottish Exhibition Centre, 2002-2013; Vice President, Royal Smithfield Club; Honorary Doctorate, Business Administration, Napier University; Trustee: NFU Mutual Charitable Trust, since 2009, Castle Mey Trust, since 2010. Recreations: travel; gardening; music. Address: (h.) Leal House, Alyth PH11 8JQ. Tel.: 01828 632695.

Grant, Major James Macalpine Gregor, TD, NDA, MRAC. Landowner and Farmer, since 1961; b. 18.2.38, Nakuru, Kenya; m., Sara Marjory, DL; 3 d. Educ. Eton; Royal Agricultural College, Cirencester. National Service, Queen's Own Cameron Highlanders, 1957-58; TA with 4/5th Queen's Own Cameron Highlanders; Volunteers with 51st Highland Volunteers. Member, Royal Company of Archers, Queen's Bodyguard for Scotland. Address: Roskill House, Munlochy, Ross-shire IV8 8AB; T.-01463 811207.

Grant, Jane. Chief Executive, NHS Forth Valley, since 2013. Joined the NHS in 1983 as a Management Services

Officer within Highland Health Board; worked in Stobhill Hospital as Deputy Administrator; moved to Lanarkshire Health Board as Hospital Administrator within Hairmyres Hospital in the early 1990's; undertook a variety of posts associated with planning, information and contracting within Lanarkshire, culminating in appointment as General Manager of Hairmyres Hospital in 1999; moved back to Glasgow in 2000 to become the General Manager for Surgery in North Glasgow and from April 2005 acted as Chief Executive within the North Glasgow Division; appointed as Director of Surgery and Anaesthetics for NHS Greater Glasgow and Clyde in early 2006 and became the Board's Chief Operating Officer in 2009. Address: Forth Valley Royal Hospital, Stirling Road, Larbert FK5 4WR.

Grant, Liz. Provost of Perth and Kinross, since 2012; b. Kolkata, India. Educ. variety of schools both in Scotland and abroad, latterly the Loreto Convent, an international school in Darjeeling and Morgan Academy, Dundee. Career: spent 35 years in the National Health Service in a variety of posts including Nursing Sister, Clinical Nurse Teacher and Senior Nurse for Continuing Education, at a number of Tayside hospitals; elected to Perth & Kinross Council to serve as an elected member for Blairgowrie and the Glens prior to the multi member Ward system in 2007; served as Convener of the Lifelong Learning Committee for 5 years, the service with the largest budget in the Council. Recreations: a keen all round sports person; reading; walking; gardening. Address: (b.) Rossearn, Perth Road, Blairgowrie PH10 6EJ; T.-01738 475014; e-mail: eagrant@pkc.gov.uk

Grant, Peter. MP (SNP), Glenrothes, since 2015; b. 1961, Lanarkshire; m., Fiona. Professional qualification in public sector finance. Councillor in Glenrothes since 1992; served for 5 years as leader of Fife Council; leader of the SNP group. Strong track record as a local political campaigner, from the anti poll tax campaign of the 1980's to the recent campaign against Labour's school closure programme. Keen amateur musician and a past president of Leslie Bowling Club. Address: House of Commons, London SW1A 0AA.

Grant, Professor Peter Mitchell, OBE, PhD, FIEE, FIEEE, FRSE, FREng. Emeritus Professor; Regius Professor of Engineering, Edinburgh University, 2007-09 (Professor of Electronic Signal Processing, 1987-2007, Head, School of Engineering and Electronics, 2002-08, Head, Department of Electronics and Electrical Engineering, 1999-2002); b. 20.6.44, St. Andrews; m., Marjory Renz; 2 d. Educ. Strathallan School; Heriot-Watt University; Edinburgh University. Two Honorary DEng degrees from Heriot-Watt and Napier Universities, 2007. Publications: Digital Communications (Co-author, 3rd edition) 2009; Digital Signal Processing (Co-author, 2nd edition), 2002. Winner, the Institution of Electrical Engineers Faraday Medal, 2004. Address: (b.) School of Engineering, Edinburgh University, Edinburgh EH9 3JL; T.-0131-651 7125.

Grant, Rhoda, BSc (SocSci), MSP (Labour), Highlands and Islands, since 2007; b. 26.6.63, Stornoway; m., Christopher Mark. Educ. Plockton High School; Open University. Address: (b.) Scottish Parliament, Edinburgh EH99 1SP; Constituency Office: Regional Office, PO Box 5717, Inverness IV1 1YT; T.-01463 716299; e-mail: rhoda.grant.msp@scottish.parliament.uk

Grant, Dr Robert, MBChB, MD, FRCP(Glas), FRCP(Edin). Consultant Neurologist, since 1991; Department of Clinical Neurosciences, Western General Hospital, Edinburgh; b. 19.4.57, Greenock; m., L. Joy C. Grant; 2 s.; 3 d. Educ. Greenock Academy; Glasgow University. Lead Clinician, Scottish Adult Neuro-Oncology Network; Past President, European Association for Neuro-Oncology. Recreations: rugby;

karate; golf. Address: Western General Hospital, Crewe Road South, Edinburgh EH4 2XU.

Grant Peterkin, Major General Anthony Peter, CB, OBE, BA. Army Officer, 1967-2004; Serjeant at Arms, House of Commons, 2004-07; Landowner; b. 6.7.47, London; m., Joanna Young; 1 s.; 1 d. Educ. Ampleforth College; University of Durham; University of Madras. Commissioned into Queen's Own Highlanders, 1967: service in Middle East, Germany, Northern Ireland, Belize, Hong Kong and India; ADC to CGS; Command of 1st Bn. Queen's Own Highlanders, Belize and Germany, 1987-89; Higher Command and Staff Course, Camberley, 1991; Military Adviser to UN Mission, Iraq and Kuwait, 1991; Commander, 24 Airmobile Brigade, 1993-94; Royal College of Defence Studies, 1995; Army Director of Manning and Career Management, 1996-98; Managing Director, OSCE Mission in Kosovo, 1999; GOC, 5 Division, 2000; Military Secretary and Chief Executive, Army Personnel Centre, Glasgow, 2000-04. Recreation: travelling off the beaten track in Indochina. Address: (h.) Grange Hall, Forres, Morayshire; T.-01309 672742.

Gray, Alasdair. Artist and Writer; b. 28.12.34, Glasgow; m., Morag McAlpine; 1 s. Educ. Whitehill Senior Secondary School; Glasgow Art School. Part-time Art Teacher, 1958-62; Scene Painter, 1963-64; has since lived by drawing, painting, writing; Associate Professor of Creative Writing: Glasgow University, Strathclyde University, 2001-03; mural painter in Oran Mor Arts and Leisure Centre, Glasgow, since 2003; Glasgow People's Palace and The Collins Gallery, Strathclyde University have collections of his paintings; extant murals: Palacerigg nature reserve, Cumbernauld; Ubiquitous Chip restaurant, Glasgow; Abbots House local history museum, Dunfermline; completion of Hillhead subway station mural, 2012; retrospective exhibition, Glasgow Municipal Art Gallery, (to come, 2014-15); retrospective exhibition of Fictional Art, Kelvingrove Art Gallery, 2014. Publications: novels: Lanark; 1982 Janine; The Fall of Kelvin Walker; Something Leather; McGrotty and Ludmilla; A History Maker; Poor Things; Mavis Belfrage; Old Men in Love, 2007; other books: Old Negatives (a life in four verse sequences); short story collections: Unlikely Stories, Mostly; Lean Tales (this last also containing work by Jim Kelman and Agnes Owens); Ten Tales Tall and True; Five Glasgow Artists (an exhibition catalogue); Saltire Self-Portrait No. 4; Why Scots Should Rule Scotland (1992 and 1997), Working Legs, a play for people without them; The Book of Prefaces, 2000; Sixteen Occasional Poems; The Ends of Our Tethers: 13 sorry stories, 2003; Fleck: A verse play, 2008; A Gray Playbook, 2009; Collected Verses, 2010; A Life in Pictures (pictorial autobiography), 2011; Every Short Story, 1951-2012, 2012; Of Me and Others - Personal Essays, 2013. Recreations: reading; talking to friends; drinking; walking.

Gray, Alistair B., BA, CA. Chairman, Hammars Hill Energy Limited, since 2006; Founder, Alistair Gray Chartered Accountant, since 1984; Managing Director, Ortak Jewellery Limited, 1990-2014; Board Member, Highlands and Islands Enterprise, 1997-2004; b. 14.6.58, Kirkwall, Orkney; m., Linda; 3 s.; 1 d. Educ. Kirkwall Grammar School; Heriot-Watt University. Chartered Accountant, Arthur Young, Edinburgh, 1979-84. Address: Hatston, Kirkwall, Orkney KW15 1RW; T.-01856 872224.

Gray, Lord (Andrew Godfrey Diarmid Stuart Campbell-Gray); b. 3.9.64. Address: (h.) Airds Bay, Taynuilt, Argyll.

Gray, Henry Withers, MD, FRCP (Lond), FRCP (Glas), FRCR. Retired Consultant Physician in Medicine and Nuclear Medicine; b. 25.3.43, Glasgow; m., Mary Elizabeth Shaw MBE; 1 s.; 2 d. Educ. Rutherglen Academy; University of Glasgow. Lecturer in Medicine, Glasgow

Royal Infirmary, 1969-77; Research Fellow, Johns Hopkins Medical Institutions, USA, 1974-76; retired Medical Adviser to University of Strathclyde. Publications: chapters in 10 books; 103 articles. Recreations: swimming; guitar; photography; garden; Scottish small pipes. Address: (h.) 4 Winton Park, East Kilbride, Glasgow G75 8QW; T.-01355 229525; e-mail: harry.gray@blueyonder.co.uk

Gray, Iain Cumming, BSc Hons (Physics), CertEd. MSP (Labour), East Lothian, since 2007; Shadow Cabinet Spokesperson for Opportunity, since 2015; Shadow Cabinet Secretary for Education and Lifelong Learning, 2014-15; Shadow Cabinet Secretary for Finance, 2013-14; Leader of Labour in The Scottish Parliament, 2008-2011; Shadow First Minister, 2008-2011; b. 7.6.57, Edinburgh; m., Gillianne; 1 d.; 2 step d. Educ. George Watson's; Inverness Royal Academy; Edinburgh University; Moray House College. Teacher: Gracemount High; Escola Basica Chokwe, Mozambique; Inveralmond High; Campaigns Manager, Oxfam in Scotland; MSP, Edinburgh Pentlands, 1999-2003; Scottish Labour: Deputy Minister for: Community Care 1999-2000, Justice, 2000-01; Minister for: Social Justice, 2001-02, Enterprise, Transport and Lifelong Learning, 2002-03; Special Adviser to Alistair Darling (Secretary of State for Scotland), 2003-06; Shadow Minister for Enterprise, Energy and Tourism, 2007; Shadow Cabinet Secretary for Finance and Sustainable Growth 2007-08. Address: (b.) Scottish Parliament, Edinburgh EH99 1SP; T.-0131 348 5000.

Gray, J.N. David, BA. Principal, The Erskine Stewart's Melville Schools, Edinburgh, since 2000; b. 30.4.55, Inverness; m.; 1 s.; 2 d. Educ. Fettes College; Bristol University. Teacher of English, Henbury School, Bristol, 1978-80; Partner, Key Language School, Athens, 1980-85; Teacher, English and Modern Greek, Dulwich College, London, 1985-88; Head of English, Leeds Grammar School, 1988-92; Headmaster, Pocklington School, East Yorks, 1992-2000. Recreations: running; swimming; golf; cricket; music. Address: (b.) Queensferry Road, Edinburgh EH4 3EZ; T.-0131 311 1000; e-mail: principal@esms.org.uk

Gray, James Allan, MB, ChB, FRCPEdin, FSA Scot. Principal Medical Officer, Scottish Widows' Fund, Edinburgh, 1990-97; b. 24.3.35, Bristol; m., Jennifer Margaret Newton Hunter; 1 s. (deceased); 2 d. Educ. St. Paul's School, London; Edinburgh University. Short Service Commission, RAF Medical Branch, 1960-63; Research Fellow and Registrar posts, Edinburgh, 1965-67; Registrar, Bristol Royal Infirmary, 1967-68; Senior Registrar, Royal Free Hospital (Department of Infectious Diseases), London, 1968-69; Consultant in Communicable Diseases, City Hospital, Edinburgh, 1969-95; Assistant Director of Studies (Medicine), Edinburgh Post-Graduate Board, 1976-84; Honorary Senior Lecturer, Department of Medicine, Edinburgh University, 1992-95; Fellow, Royal Medical Society (Senior President, 1958-59); President, British Society for the Study of Infection, 1989-91; Founder Editor, Res Medica, 1957-58; Assistant Editor, Journal of Infection, 1979-86. Publications: Antibacterial Drugs Today (Co-author), 1983; Infectious Diseases (Co-author), 1984, 1992, new edition 1998; Edinburgh City Hospital, 1999. Recreations: hill-walking; pottery collecting; volunteer, National Museums Scotland, since 2005. Address: (h.) Salisbury Heights, 31/6 Salisbury Road, Edinburgh EH16 5AA; T.-0131-667-4124.

Gray, Professor James Robertson, OBE, BSc, FRSGS, DipActMaths, FFA, FIMA, CMath, FSS, FFCS. Professor and Head, Department of Actuarial Mathematics and Statistics, Heriot-Watt University, 1971-89 (now Emeritus);

b. 21.2.26, Dundee; m., Catherine McAulay Towner. Educ. High School of Dundee; Edinburgh University. Actuarial Trainee, Scottish Life Assurance Company, 1947-49; St. Andrews University: Lecturer in Mathematics, 1949-50, Lecturer in Statistics, 1950-62, Senior Lecturer in Statistics (also Head of Department), 1962-71, Member of University Court and Finance Committee; Heriot-Watt University: established first Department of Actuarial Science in UK; Dean, Faculty of Science, 1978-81, Member of University Court and Finance Committee; Council Member, Faculty of Actuaries, 1969-87 (Vice President, 1983-87); Vice-Chairman, Scottish Examination Board, 1984-90 (Convener of Examinations Committee, 1982-90); former Council Member, Royal Scottish Geographical Society and former Convener, Lecture Committee; former Vice-Chairman, Scottish Universities Council on Entrance; Past Chairman: Scottish Branch, Institute of Mathematics and Its Applications, Edinburgh Branch, Royal Statistical Society; Past President, Murrayfield-Cramond Rotary Club; Past President, Murrayfield-Cramond Probus Club; Past Captain, Senior Section of Royal Burgess Golfing Society; Statistical Consultant to Law Society of Scotland, 1978-89; Member: Royal Burgess Golfing Society. Publication: "Probability", University Mathematical Texts, 1967. Recreations: golf; hill-walking; bridge; music; Probus. Address: (h.) Green Gables, 9 Cammo Gardens, Edinburgh EH4 8EJ; T.-0131-339 3330.

Gray, Muriel, BA (Hons). Broadcaster; b. 30.8.58, Glasgow. Educ. Glasgow School of Art. Worked as an illustrator; then as a designer with National Museum of Antiquities; was member of rock band, The Family Von Trapp; had own show with Radio Forth; was frequent presenter on Radio 1; co-presented The Tube, Channel 4; had own arts programme, The Works, Tyne Tees; own music programme, Studio 1, Border TV; presented Casebook Scotland, BBC Scotland; Frocks on the Box, Thames TV; Acropolis Now, ITV; presented The Media Show, Channel 4; Co-Producer and Presenter, Walkie Talkie, Channel 4; currently the first female chair of the board of governors, Glasgow School of Art; first woman Rector, Edinburgh University; Producer/ Presenter/Director, The Munro Show, Scottish TV; Producer/Presenter, Art is Dead...Long Live TV!, Channel Four; The Golden Cagoule, BBC; Ride On. Publications: The First Fifty, 1991; The Trickster (novel), 1994; Furnace (novel), 1997; The Ancient, 2001; Kelvingrove: portal to the world, 2006. Recreation: being in the Scottish Highlands — gets grumpy and miserable if can't be up a mountain every few weeks. Address: (b.) St. Georges Studios, 93-97 St. Georges Road, Glasgow G3 6JA.

Gray, Neil Charles, BA. MP (SNP), Airdrie & Shotts, since 2015; SNP Spokesperson for Fair Work & Employment, since 2015; b. 1986, Orkney. Educ. Kirkwall Grammar School; University of Stirling. Employed as a producer and reporter with BBC Radio Orkney, 2003-08; press and research intern for the SNP parliamentary group at the Scottish Parliament for several months before being appointed as constituency office manager for Alex Neil MSP until election to Parliament. Address: House of Commons, London SW1A 0AA.

Gray, Paul. Director General, Health and Social Care, Scottish Government, since 2013; Chief Executive, NHS Scotland, since 2013; Director General, Governance & Communities, Scottish Government, 2010-2013. Joined the Scottish Government in 1979; appointed to the post of Director General Rural Affairs, Environment and Services at the Scottish Government in July 2009; previous post, up to July 2009, was as the Scottish Government's Director of Change and Corporate Services; previously Director of Primary and Community Care - having joined Health in

October 2005; held the role of Director of eHealth simultaneously; prior to that he was the Scottish Executive Director for Social Justice, covering Social Inclusion, Equalities and Voluntary Issues, from October 2003, and before that, he was the Scottish Executive Director of Information and Communications Technology. Career has covered such diverse areas as Criminal Injuries Compensation, fisheries quota management and licensing, and work with Her Majesty's Inspectorate of Education. Address: (b.) DGHSC Co-ordination, Room 1E.16, St Andrew's House, Edinburgh EH1 3DG; T.-0131 244 2790.

Gray, Peter, LLB (Hons). Queen's Counsel, since 2002; b. 7.11.59, Inverness; m., Bridget; 1 s.; 2 d. Educ. Fettes College, Edinburgh; Southampton University. Called to Bar of England and Wales, 1983; Admitted to Faculty of Advocates, 1992; Advocate Depute, 1998-2000. Address: (b.) Compass Chambers, Advocates Library, Parliament House, Edinburgh EH1 1RF; T.-0131-2265071.
E-mail: peter.gray@compasschambers.com

Gray, Professor Peter Michael David, MA, DPhil, FBCS. Professor Emeritus (formerly Professor, Department of Computing Science, Aberdeen University, 1989-2005); b. 1940, Abingdon; m., Doreen F. Ross; 1 s.; 1 d. Educ. Abingdon School; Queens' College, Cambridge; Jesus College, Oxford. Systems Analyst, Plessey Co., Poole, 1966-68; Research Fellow, Aberdeen University, 1968-72; Lecturer in Computing Science, Aberdeen University, 1972-84; Visiting Associate Professor, University of Western Ontario, 1985; Senior Lecturer, 1985-89. Reader, Church of Scotland. Publication: Logic, Algebra and Databases. Recreations: gardening; croquet. Address: 165 Countesswells Road, Aberdeen AB15 7RA; T.-01224 318172.

Gray, Professor Robert Hugh, MBE, BSc (Econ), MA (Econ), PhD, FCA, FCCA, FAcSS. Retired Professor of Social and Environmental Accounting, St. Andrews University; b. 1.4.52, Manchester; 2 s. Educ. De La Salle College, Salford; Hull University. Manchester University; Glasgow University. Qualified as accountant with KPMG Peat Marwick, 1976; Lecturer, Lancashire Polytechnic, UCNW Bangor, University of East Anglia; Mathew Professor of Accounting and Information Systems, Dundee University, 1990-2000; Professor of Accounting, Glasgow University, 2000-04; Editor, Social and Environmental Accounting, 1992-2009; Director, Centre for Social and Environmental Accounting Research, 1991-2012. Publications: over 300 articles; various books including Accounting for the Environment; The Greening of Accountancy; Accounting and Accountability. Recreations: sailing; rock music. Address: 14 Balgove Road, Gauldry, Newport-on-Tay, Fife DD6 8SH.

Greatrex, Tom, BSc. MP (Labour and Co-operative), Rutherglen and Hamilton West, 2010-2015; Shadow Energy Minister, 2011-2015; b. 30.9.74, Kent; m.; Laura; 2 d. Educ. Judd School, Tonbridge; London School of Economics. Career history: worked as a researcher to Opposition Chief Whip Donald Dewar, prior to the 1997 General Election, remaining in the role after Nick Brown took over as Chief Whip, later moving with him to the Ministry of Agriculture, Fisheries and Food in 1998; left this role in 1999 to work as a GMB Union official for five years; moved to Scotland in 2004 to take on a role as a chief officer at East Dunbartonshire Council, then worked as Director of Corporate Affairs for NHS 24, 2006-07; latterly worked as a policy adviser for Scottish Secretaries Douglas Alexander, Des Browne and Jim Murphy; Shadow Minister for Scotland, 2010-2011. Recreations: Fulham FC; cinema.

Green, Alexander M. S., MTheol (Hons), LLB, LLM, MLitt, FSA (Scot). Director, The Law Agency (Scotland) Ltd., since 2006; Solicitor; Employment Judge (England & Wales); Judge, First Tier Immigration and Asylum Chamber; Procurator Fiscal to The Court of the Lord Lyon; b. 31.12.63, Worcester; m., Sophy M Green or Thomson; 1 d.; 2 gs.; 1 gd. Educ. Dyson Perrins CE High School; St. Andrews University; University of Aberdeen. Article Clerk, Cameron Markby Hewitt, 1991-93; CMS Cameron McKenna LLP: Assistant Solicitor, 1993-2000, Partner, 2000-06. Clubs: The New Club. Societies: The Heraldry Society of Scotland, The White Lion Society. Board of Management, The Instant Neighbour Charity; Free Burgess and Guild Member, The Burgh of Aberdeen; Liveryman of the Worshipful Company of Scriveners of the City of London; Freeman of the City of London. Recreations: history; literature; heraldry; fly fishing; cycling. Address: (b.) 43 Cairnfield Place, Aberdeen AB15 5LX; T.-01224 639712; e-mail: alex@the-lawagency.com

Green, David Russell, OBE, MA (Hons). Director, Scottish Agricultural College Commercial (SACC) Ltd, since 2008; Partner, Stac Pollaidh Self Catering, since 1990; b. 13.6.51, Aberdeen; m., Sheila; 1 s.; 3 d. Educ. Glasgow University. Career: Convener, Highland Council, 1999-2003; Chairman, Crofters Commission, 2002-2006; Scotland Committee Member, Big Lottery Fund, 2006-2014; Chairman, Cairngorms National Park Authority, 2006-2012; formerly Chairman, Scottish Government - Instrumental Music Group (IMG) (2012/13); former Chairman (2015), Scottish Government Music Education Strategy Group (MESG); formerly Chairman, Scottish Government - Instrumental Music Implementation Group (IMIG). Marketing consultant; trainee chartered accountant; hotelier; snowplough driver; fully diversified crofter. Address: (h & b.) Stac Pollaidh Self Catering, Achnahaird, Achiltibuie, Ullapool IV26 2YT; T.-01854 622340; (m.) 07747 007144.
E-mail: dgachiltibuie@hotmail.co.uk

Green, Professor Roger Philip Hywel, MA, BLitt. Professor of Humanity (Latin), University of Glasgow, 1995-2008 (retired); b. 14.6.43, High Wycombe; m., Anne Mary Perry; 1 s.; 1 d. Educ. Royal Grammar School, High Wycombe; Balliol College, University of Oxford. University of St. Andrews: Assistant Lecturer, 1967-70, Lecturer, 1970-92, Senior Lecturer, 1992-94, Reader, 1994-95. Former Secretary, International Association of Neo-Latin Studies. Publications include: The Works of Ausonius, 1991; Augustine on Christian Teaching, 1997; Latin Epics of the New Testament, 2006; George Buchanan: Poetic Paraphrase of Psalms of David, 2011. Recreations: walking; cycling; rail travel; birdwatching; gardening; music; architecture. Address: (b.) Department of Classics, University of Glasgow, Glasgow G12 8QQ; T.-0141-330 5256.

Greene, Jamie. MSP (Scottish Conservative), West Scotland region, since 2016; b. Greenock. Educ. St John's Primary, Port Glasgow; St Stephen's High School, Port Glasgow. Career history: worked for a spell at IBM in Greenock as a call centre analyst before moving to a career in radio - working in advertising sales; moved to London and trained as a TV producer working for many years on a number of productions for TV channels including the BBC and other commercial broadcasters, often using French and Spanish language skills to work and live overseas including stints in Spain, France and Australia; became a commercial manager with a private media company which launched dozens of new television channels, both in the UK and overseas; also helped set up the foundations of the UK's local TV network; became an executive at Viacom - the owners of MTV, Paramount and Nickelodeon as Director of Business Development; former Head of UK Sales at a US television software company. Conservative candidate for North Ayrshire and Arran, United Kingdom general election in 2015; Conservative candidate for the Cunninghame North constituency in the 2016 Scottish Parliament election. Qualified TESOL/TEFL English language teacher; holds a PADI Scuba diving qualification and a sailing skipper licence. Recreations: amateur silversmith; garden; golf; sailing; travel. Address: Scottish Parliament, Edinburgh EH99 1SP.

Greening, Professor Andrew Peter, BSc, MBChB, FRCPE. Professor of Pulmonary Disease, University of Edinburgh; Consultant Physician, Western General Hospital, Edinburgh, 1984-2013; b. 10.10.48, London; m., Rosemary Jean Renwick; 2 s. Educ. George Watson's College, Edinburgh; University of Edinburgh. House Officer and Senior House Officer posts, Edinburgh, 1973-75; Registrar, Senior Registrar, MRC Training Fellow posts, St. Bartholomew's and Hammersmith Hospitals and Royal Postgraduate Medical School, London, 1975-82. Director, Scottish Adult Cystic Fibrosis Service, Western General Hospital, Edinburgh, 1992-2005; Lead Clinician, Respiratory Medicine, Lothian Health, 2005-09; Associate Editor, Thorax and Respiratory Medicine; Member, Grants Committees: Chest, Heart and Stroke Association, British Lung Foundation (Chair), Cystic Fibrosis Trust. International Lecturer on asthma and cystic fibrosis; Member, Scottish, British, European and American Thoracic Societies; President, Scottish Thoracic Society, 2008-2010; President, British Thoracic Society, 2011-2012.

Greenman, Professor Jonathan Vaughan, BA, MA, PhD. Emeritus Professor, Department of Computing Science and Mathematics, Stirling University, since 2002, Professor of Mathematics and Its Applications, 1990-2002; b. 3.3.39, Cardiff; m., Barbara Phyllis; 2 s. Educ. Kingston Grammar School; Cambridge University. Harkness Scholar, University of California, Berkeley; Department of Physics, MIT; Stanford Research Institute, California; Department of Mathematics, Essex University; Tutor, Open University; Senior Analyst, Corporate Planning, British Petroleum plc; Industry Analyst, Centre for Global Energy Studies. Recreations: cinema; walking; travel. Address: (b.) Department of Computing Science and Mathematics, Stirling University, Stirling, FK9 4LA; T.-01786 467460; e-mail: j.v.greenman@stir.ac.uk

Greenwood, Professor Justin, BA (Hons), PhD. Professor of European Public Policy, Robert Gordon University, Aberdeen, since 1996; Visiting Professor, College of Europe; b. 17.5.60, Windlesham. Educ. Newton Abbot Grammar School; Nottingham University. Editorial Advisory Board, Journal of Public Affairs, Interest Groups & Advocacy; Chair, Economic and Social Research Advanced Quantitative Methods Stipend Panel, 2009-10; Trainer, Diplomatic Training Path, European Commission; Trade Association Forum, Final Judging Awards panel. Publications: Book: Interest Representation in the EU, 2011; The Challenge of Change in EU Business Associations (Editor), 2003; Inside the EU Business Associations, 2002; The Effectiveness of EU Business Associations (Editor), 2001; Social Partnership in the European Union (Co-Editor), 2001; Representing Interests in the European Union, 1997; Organised Interests in the New Global Order (Co-Editor) 1999; Collective Action in the European Union: Interest and the New Politics of Associability (Co-Editor) 1997; European Casebook on Business Alliances (Editor) 1995; Organised Interests and the European Community, (jointly), 1992. Address: (b.) Robert Gordon University, Garthdee Road, Aberdeen, AB10 7QE; T.-01224 263406.

Greer, Ross. MSP (Green Party), West of Scotland region, since 2016; b. 1.6.94. Educ. Bearsden Academy; University of Strathclyde. Communities Coordinator, Yes Scotland, Scottish independence referendum, 2014. Scottish Green candidate in the East Dunbartonshire constituency in the United Kingdom general election, 2015; became the Scottish Greens' party spokesman on Europe and external affairs. Youngest ever MSP, elected at the age of 21. Address: Scottish Parliament, Edinburgh EH99 1SP.

Gregor, Dr. Anna, CBE, FRCR, FRCP. Retired Medical Practitioner, since 2008; b. 13.8.48, Prague, Czechoslovakia; m., Neil P. Magee; 2 s. Educ. Royal Free Hospital School of Medicine. Postgraduate Training, Royal Marsden and Brompton Hospitals London, 1973-80; Imperial Cancer Research Fellow, University of Edinburgh, 1980-83; Consultant Clinical Oncologist, Glasgow, 1983-87; Senior Lecturer, Oncology, University of Edinburgh, 1987-97; Consultant Clinical Oncologist, Edinburgh, 1997-2008; Clinical Director SCAN, Macmillan Lead Cancer Clinician, NHS Lothian, Lead Cancer Clinician, Scottish Government, 2001-06; Associate Medical Director, NHS Lothian. Trustee, National Museums of Scotland; Member of Court, Queen Margaret University, Edinburgh. Recreations: cooking; music; travel. Address: (h.) 45 Spylaw Bank Road, Edinburgh EH13 0JF; T.-0131 441 6360; e-mail: annagregor@doctors.net.uk

Gregory, Rear Admiral Michael, OBE. Lord-Lieutenant, Dunbartonshire, since 2008; b. 15.12.45. Wide ranging career in the Royal Navy spanning 36 years (most of this time spent in the Submarine Service with three Submarine Commands followed by Command of a Frigate), then Assistant Director Naval Staff Duties in the MOD Whitehall and Naval and Defence Attaché (Policy) in Washington DC; finished career as Flag Officer, Scotland, Northern England and Northern Ireland; on retirement from the Royal Navy, became CEO of two Industry Support Organisations. Brigadier in the Royal Company of Archers, Queen's Body Guard for Scotland.

Greig, Rev. Alan, BSc, BD. Interim Minister, Dunfermline: Gillespie Memorial Parish Church; Convener, Church of Scotland Council of Assembly, 2008-2012; b. 19.11.51, Helensburgh; m., Ruth D. Evans; 2 s. Educ. Coatbridge High School; University of Strathclyde; University of Edinburgh. Probationer Minister, Northfield Parish, Aberdeen, 1976-77; Minister, Hurlford Reid Memorial Church, Ayrshire, 1977-83; Church of Scotland Missionary working with United Church of Zambia, 1983-92; Minister, Kintore Parish Church, 1992-2013. Recreations: swimming; cycling and walking. Address: 1 Dunnydeer Place, Insch, Aberdeenshire AB52 6HP; e-mail: greig@kincarr.free-online.co.uk

Greig, David. Scottish playwright; Artistic Director, Edinburgh's Royal Lyceum Theatre, since 2016; b. 1969; m.; 2 c. Educ. Bristol University. Work has been performed at all of the major theatres in Britain, including the Traverse Theatre, Royal Court Theatre, Royal National Theatre and the Royal Shakespeare Company, and been produced around the world. After university, in 1990, co-founded Suspect Culture Theatre Company with Graham Eatough and Nick Powell in Glasgow; wrote texts for almost all of their shows until 2004, including Timeless (1997), Mainstream (1999), Candide 2000 (2000), Casanova (2001), Lament (2002), and 8000m (2004); stand-alone plays, from Stalinland (1992) performed at the major theatres; the Traverse produced Europe (1995), The Architect (1996, made into a film of the same title in 2006), Outlying Islands (2002), Damascus (2007) and Midsummer (a play with songs by Gordon McIntyre, 2008); produced around 50 plays, texts, adaptations, translations and libretti in the first two decades of his career. Address: Royal

Lyceum Theatre, 30B Grindlay Street, Edinburgh EH3 9AX; T.-0131 248 4800.

Greig, G. Andrew, MA. Author; b. 23.9.51, Bannockburn; m., Lesley Glaister. Educ. Waid Academy, Anstruther; Edinburgh University. Full-time writer, since 1979; Writer-in-Residence, Glasgow University, 1979-81; Scottish-Canadian Exchange Fellow, 1981-82; Writer-in-Residence, Edinburgh University, 1993-94; climbed on Himalayan expeditions. Publications: six volumes of poetry including This Life, This Life: New and Selected Poems; Found At Sea; two mountaineering books; novels: Electric Brae, Return of John Macnab; When They Lay Bare; That Summer; In Another Light; Romanno Bridge; Fair Helen; non-fiction: Preferred Lies; At the Loch of the Green Corrie. Recreations: music; hills; golf. Website: andrew-greig.weebly.com

Greig, Kenneth Muir, MA, PhD. Rector, Hutchesons' Grammar School, Glasgow, since 2005; b. 30.3.60, Edinburgh; m., Josephine; 1 s.; 1 d. Educ. George Heriot's School, Edinburgh; Worcester College, Oxford; University of Edinburgh. Exploration Geologist, British Petroleum, 1984-87; Mathematics Teacher and Housemaster, Christ's Hospital, 1987-93; Head of Mathematics and Director of Studies, Dollar Academy, 1993-2000; Headmaster, Pangbourne College, 2000-05. Recreations: natural science; watching sport; beachcombing. Address: (b.) Beaton Road, Glasgow G41 4NW; T.-0141 423 2933; e-mail: rector@hutchesons.org

Greig, Martin, LLB (Hons). Convenor, Grampian Joint Police Board, 2007-2012; Member, Aberdeen City Council (Lib Dem), since 2003; Chair, Aberdeen Community Safety Partnership, since 2003; Director and Chairman, Aberdeen Forward Ltd.; Director of Friends of Hazlehead Ltd; b. Aberdeen. Educ. University of Glasgow. Vice-Convenor, Grampian Joint Police Board, 2003-07. Church of Scotland Elder. Address: (b.) Town House, Broad Street, Aberdeen AB10 1FY; T.-01224-522000.
E-mail: mgreig@aberdeencity.gov.uk

Grice, Paul Edward, BSc. Clerk and Chief Executive, Scottish Parliament, since 1999; b. 13.10.61; m.; 2 d. Department of Transport, 1985-87; Department of Environment, 1987-92; joined Scottish Office, 1992 (latterly Head of Division, Constitution Group: Referendum, Scotland Bill, then Director of Implementation); Member, Stirling University Court, 2005-2013; Secretary, Scotland's Futures Forum, 2005-2013; Hon. Fellow, Royal Incorporation of Architects in Scotland, 2006; Member, Economic and Social Research Council, 2009-2015; Trustee, Bank of Scotland Foundation, since 2011; Member, Edinburgh International Festival Board, since 2013. Address: Scottish Parliament, Edinburgh EH99 1SP.

Grier, Scott, OBE, MA, CA, FCIT. President, Loganair Limited; Director, The Glasgow Distilling Company Ltd, since 2014; b. 7.3.41, Kilmacolm; m., Frieda Gardiner; 2 s. Educ. Greenock High School; Glasgow University. Apprenticed, Grahams Rintoul & Co., 1962-66; Accountant, Ardrossan Harbour Company Ltd./Clydeport, from 1967; various posts, Loganair, since 1976; Director: Glasgow Chamber of Commerce, 1990-98, Caledonian MacBrayne Limited, 1996-2006; Chairman, Scottish Tanning Industries Ltd., 1997-2003; Governor, Scottish Sports Aid, 1993-2004; Member, Scottish Tourist Board, 1992-98. Publication: Loganair, A Scottish Survivor, 1962-2012. Recreations: golf; philately; gardening. Address: (h.) Lagavulin, 15 Corsehill Drive, West Kilbride KA23 9HU; T.-01294 823138.

Grieve, Professor Andrew Robert, OBE, DDS, BDS, FDS RCSEd. Professor of Conservative Dentistry, 1980-99, Dean of Dentistry, 1993-97, Dundee University; Consultant in Restorative Dentistry, Tayside Health Board, 1980-99; b. 23.5.39, Stirling; m., Frances M. Ritchie; 2 d. Educ. Perth Academy; St. Andrews University. Junior hospital appointments and general dental practice, 1961-63; Lecturer in Operative Dental Surgery and Dental Therapeutics, St. Andrews University, 1963-65; Lecturer in Conservative Dentistry, Birmingham University, 1965; appointed Senior Lecturer and Consultant in Restorative Dentistry, Birmingham Area Health Authority (Teaching), 1975. Member, Dental Council, Royal College of Surgeons of Edinburgh, 1983-88; President: British Society for Restorative Dentistry, 1986-87 (Honorary Fellow, 2000); President: Royal Odonto-Chirurgical Society of Scotland, 1994-95 (Council Member, 1985-88); Chairman, Tayside Area Dental Advisory Committee, 1987-90; Member, General Dental Council, 1989-99 (Chairman, Legislation Committee, 1994-99); Trustee, Armitstead Lecture Trust, 2003-2011; Member and Trustee, Tayside Pre-Retirement Council, 2003-2014 (Chairman, 2010-2014). Recreations: furniture making; hill-walking; travel. Address: (h.) Ravensfield, 20 Albany Road, Broughty Ferry, Dundee.

Griffin, Mark. MSP (Labour), Central Scotland, since 2011; Shadow Minister for Transport and Veterans, 2013-14; Scottish Labour Spokesman for Sport, 2012-2013; North Lanarkshire Councillor, 2008-2012; b. 19.10.85; m., Stephanie. Educ. University of Strathclyde. Worked in the engineering industry; formerly a serving soldier in the British Territorial Army (TA). Sits on the Scottish Parliament's Infrastructure and Capital Investments Committee and is a member of a number of Cross-Party Parliamentary Groups, including the Cross Party Groups on Deafness, Sport and Industrial Communities. Is in the process of putting a British Sign Language (BSL) (Scotland) Bill through Parliament, through work with the CPG on Deafness; became one of the first MSPs elected in 2011 to put forward plans for a Private Members Bill. Became not only the youngest MSP of the current Parliament, but the youngest in the history of the Parliament upon his election at the age of 25. Address: (b.) Scottish Parliament, Edinburgh EH99 1SP.

Griffiths, Professor Anne Marjorie Ord, LLB (Edin), PhD. Professor, School of Law, Edinburgh University, Personal Chair in Anthropology of Law, since 2004; first female professor of law at Edinburgh University in 297 years; b. 30.12.53, Edinburgh; m., Edwin N. Wilmsen. Educ. St George's School for Girls, Edinburgh; University of Edinburgh; University of London. Apprentice with Messrs Dundas & Wilson, Edinburgh, 1978-1980; Admitted as solicitor in Scotland, 1980; appointed to the University of Edinburgh as a Lecturer in 1980; Lecturer in Law, 1980-1992; Senior Lecturer in Law, 1992-1999; Reader in Law, 1999-2004; Professor, Personal Chair in Anthropology of Law 2004; Distinguished Visiting Professor, Faculty of Law, University of Toronto, 2008; International Institute for the Sociology of Law, Oñati – Gipuzkoa, Spain, 2008 and 2007; Max Planck Institute for Social Anthropology, Halle/Saale, Germany, Visiting Fellow 2005, 2006, 2007, 2008; Centre for Socio-Legal Studies, University of Oxford; Visiting Fellow at International Law & Society Summer Institute, 2005, The University of Texas at Austin; Visiting Professor of Law, 1996, 1998, 2000, 2002, 2004, University of Zimbabwe; Visiting Professor, Southern and Eastern African Regional Centre for Women's Law (SEARCWL-UZ) 2003, 2005, 2007, University of Malaya; Edinburgh University Gender Studies Link Coordinator, 2001; University of Witwatersrand, South African Human Sciences Research Council Research Fellow, 1993, Kenyatta University; Edinburgh University Gender Studies Link Coordinator, 1993; Cornell University, Visiting Associate Professor of Law, 1988; Wolfson College, Oxford, Visiting

Scholar, Center for Socio-Legal Studies, 1985; American Bar Foundation, Chicago, and Northwestern University, African Studies Dept., Research Scholar, 1990-1991; ESRC Research Fellowship, Botswana, 1982. Consultant to UN study on Informal Justice, 2008/9; Special Advisor to International Council on Human Rights Policy, Geneva. Publications include: In the Shadow of Marriage: Gender and Justice in an African Community, 1997; Family Law (Scotland) (Co-Author), 1997, revised second edition in 2006; Mobile People, Mobile Law: Expanding Legal Relations in a Contracting World (Co-Editor), 2005; 'Using Ethnography as a Tool in Legal Research: An Anthropological Perspective', in Theory and Method in Socio-Legal Research in 2005; and 'Localising the Global: Rights of Participation in the Scottish Children's Hearings System and Hearing Children in Children's Hearings', (Co-Author), 2000 and 2005. President, Commission on Legal Pluralism, 2003-2009, Board Member, since 1989; Assistant Editor, Journal of Legal Pluralism and Unofficial Law, (1996-current); Editorial Board, Social Justice, Anthropology, Peace and Human Rights (2004-current); Advisory Board, International Journal of Human Development (2001-current); Editorial Board, Critical African Studies, newly established (2008); e-journal at Edin.Univ.; African Studies Association, UK Executive Member; Centre of African Studies Committee, Edin. Univ. Recreations: theatre; music, especially opera; yoga; cooking. Address: (b.) School of Law, Edinburgh University, Old College, South Bridge, Edinburgh EH8 9YL; T.-0131 650 2057; e-mail: Anne.Griffiths@ed.ac.uk

Griffiths, Keith Michael, LLB, WS. Trustee, The National Trust for Scotland, since 2011; b. 1956, Edinburgh; m., Fiona Smart WS. Educ. Acomb, Oxgangs & South Morningside Primaries; George Watson's College; University of Edinburgh. Apprentice Solicitor and Solicitor, W & J Burness WS, 1977-82; Solicitor, Steedman Ramage WS, 1982-96, Partner from 1984; Partner, Brodies WS, 1996-2005; Trustee and Honorary Treasurer, The John Muir Trust, 2001-08; Member of Council, The National Trust for Scotland, 2006-2011, and of Audit & Risk Management Committee, since 2007; Trustee, The Scottish Rights of Way & Access Society, 2005-11; Trustee, WS Dependants' Annuity Fund, 2001-07; Trustee, The Royal Scottish Geographical Society, 2012-14. Recreations: hill-walking; golf; cycling; music; theatre. Address: (b.) The National Trust for Scotland, Hermiston Quay, 5 Cultins Road, Edinburgh EH11 4DF.

Griffiths, Martin, LLB (Hons), CA. Chief Executive, Stagecoach Group PLC, since 2013, previously Finance Director (2000-2013). Career: former Chairman of the Group of Scottish Finance Directors and a former Director of Troy Income & Growth Trust plc, Trainline Holdings Limited, RoadKing Infrastructure (HK) Limited and Citybus (HK) Limited. Former Senior Independent Non-Executive Director of Robert Walters plc; Young Scottish Finance Director of the year in 2004. Co-Chairman, Virgin Rail Group Holdings Limited; Non-Executive Director, AG Barr plc; Chairman, Rail Delivery Group Limited. Address: Stagecoach Group Head Office, 10 Dunkeld Road, Perth PH1 5TW; T.-01738 442111.

Griffiths, Rev. Melvyn J. Minister, Maryculter Trinity Church of Scotland. Address: The Manse, Kirkton, Maryculter AB12 5FS; T.-01224 730150.

Griffiths, Professor Peter Denham, CBE, BSc, MD, LRCP, MRCS, FRCPath, FRCP(Edin), FCMI, FRSA. Emeritus Professor of Biochemical Medicine, Dundee University (Vice-Principal, 1979-85, Dean of Medicine and Dentistry, 1985-89); Director and Trustee, Scottish Hospitals Endowment Research Trust, 1994-98; b. 16.6.27, Southampton; m., Joy Burgess; 3 s.; 1 d. Educ. King Edward VI School, Southampton; Guy's Hospital, London University. House appointments, Guy's Hospital, 1956-57; Junior Lecturer in Physiology, Guy's Hospital, 1957-58; Registrar and Senior Registrar, Guy's and Lewisham Hospitals, 1958-64; Consultant Pathologist, Harlow Hospitals Group, 1964-66; Senior Lecturer in Clinical Chemistry/Honorary Consultant, St. Andrews University, then Dundee University, 1966-68. Member, General Medical Council, 1986-93; President, 1987-89, and sometime Chairman of Council, Association of Clinical Biochemists; Tayside Health Board: Honorary Consultant, 1966-89, Member, 1977-85; former Director, Dundee Repertory Theatre. Recreations: music; domestic activities. Address: (h.) 52 Albany Road, West Ferry, Dundee DD5 1NW; T.-01382 776772.

Griggs, Professor Russel, OBE. Non-Executive Director, Audit Scotland; b. Edinburgh. Educ. Heriot Watt University. Non executive positions in the private, public and third sector; Chair of the Audit Committee of VisitScotland, a Board member of Scottish Enterprise, and a Non Executive Director of the Scottish Government; appointed as the independent external reviewer to the five clearing banks in the UK in 2011. Honorary Professor of the University of Glasgow; awarded an honorary doctorate by the university in 2002 for services to the industry and to the university; former Associate Professor of Boston University, and former member of the board of the Business School at Georgia Southern University. Address: Audit Scotland, 4th Floor, Athenaeum Building, 8 Nelson Mandela Place, Glasgow, Lanarkshire G2 1BT; T.-0845 146 1010.

Grimmond, Iain William, BAcc (Hons), CA. Former General Treasurer, Church of Scotland (2005-2016); former Director of Finance, Erskine Hospital for Disabled Ex-Servicemen and Women (1981-2004); b. 8.8.55, Girvan; m., Marjory Anne Gordon Chisholm; 1 s.; 2 d. Educ. Hutchesons' Boys Grammar School; Glasgow University. Trainee CA, Ernst & Whinney, Glasgow, 1976-79; Assistant Treasurer, Erskine Hospital, 1979-81. Elder, Giffnock South Parish Church. Recreations: golf; football; reading. Address: (h.) 9 Wemyss Avenue, Crookfur, Newton Mearns, Glasgow G77 6AR; T.-0141-639 4894.

Grimmond, Steve, MA, MBA, FRSA. Chief Executive, Fife Council, since 2013; b. 12.6.63, Dundee; m., Audrey Krawec; 1 s.; 1 d. Educ. Craigie High School, Dundee; Dundee University. Dundee District Council: Special Projects Officer, Principal Officer, Area Renewal; Corporate Planning Officer; Policy Planning Manager, Chief Executive's Department, Dundee City Council; Area Manager, Aberdeenshire Council; Director, Arts and Heritage, Dundee City Council; Director, Leisure and Arts, Dundee City Council; Director, Creative Scotland; Executive Director, Environment, Enterprise and Communities, Fife Council. Recreations: football; visual arts; power boating. Address: (b.) Fife House, Glenrothes KY7 5LT; T.-03451 555555 ext. 444143.
E-mail: steven.grimmond@fife.gov.uk

Grimstone, Sir Gerry, MA, MSc. Chairman: Standard Life plc, since 2007, Candover Investments plc, 2006-2011, The CityUK, since 2012; Deputy Chairman, Barclays, since 2016; b. 27.8.49, London; 1 s.; 2 d. Educ. Whitgift School; Merton College, Oxford University. UK Civil Service, latterly HM Treasury, 1972-86; Schroders Investment

Banking (London, Hong Kong, New York), 1986-2000; various public and private boards, since 2000. Address: (b.) Standard Life plc, 30 Lothian Road, Edinburgh EH1 2DH; T.-0131 245 2151.

Grinyer, Professor John Raymond, MSc, FCA. Emeritus Professor of Accountancy and Business Finance, Dundee University (Deputy Principal, 1997-2000, Dean, Faculty of Law, 1984-85, 1991-1993, Head, Department of Accountancy and Business Finance, 1976-90); b. 3.3.35, London; m., Shirley Florence Marshall; 1 s.; 2 d. Educ. Central Park Secondary Modern School, London; London School of Economics. London Electricity Board, 1950-53; National Service, RAMC, 1953-55; Halifax Building Society, 1955-56; Martin Redhead & Co., Accountants, 1956-60; Hope Agar & Co., Chartered Accountants, 1960-62; Kemp Chatteris & Co., Chartered Accountants, 1962-63; Lecturer, Harlow Technical College, 1963-66; City of London Polytechnic, 1966-71; Cranfield School of Management, 1971-76; Chairman, British Accounting Association, 1980-81 and 1990, and Scottish Representative, 1984-93. Elder, St. Stephens and West Church, Broughty Ferry. Recreations: golf; Member: Royal Tay Yacht Club, Broughty Golf Club. Address: (h.) 81 Dundee Road, Broughty Ferry, Dundee DD5 1LZ; T.-Dundee 775743.

Grinyer, Professor Peter Hugh, MA (Oxon), PhD. Emeritus Professor, St. Andrews University, since 1993; b. 3.3.35, London; m., Sylvia Joyce Boraston; 2 s. Educ. Balliol College, Oxford; London School of Economics. Senior Managerial Trainee, Unilever Ltd., 1957-59; Personal Assistant to Managing Director, E.R. Holloway Ltd., 1959-61; Lecturer and Senior Lecturer, Hendon College of Technology, 1961-64; Lecturer, The City University, London, 1965-69; The City University Business School: Senior Lecturer and Co-ordinator of Research, 1969-72, Reader, 1972-74, Professor of Business Strategy, 1974-79; Esmee Fairbairn Professor of Economics (Finance and Investment), St. Andrews University, 1979-93; Chairman, Department of Economics, 1979-85; Vice-Principal, 1985-87 (Acting Principal, 1986); Chairman, Department of Management, 1987-89; Chairman: St. Andrews Management Institute, 1989-96, St. Andrews Strategic Management Ltd.; Member, Sub-Committee on Management and Business Studies, University Grants Committee, 1979-85; Consultant to NEDO on Sharpbenders Project, 1984-86; Visiting Professor, New York University, 1992, 1996-98; Visiting Professor, Imperial College, London, 2002-04; Non-Executive Director: Glenrothes Enterprise Trust, 1983-86, John Brown plc, 1984-86, Don Bros. Buist plc (subsequently Don and Low (Holdings) Ltd.) 1985-91, Ellis and Goldstein plc, 1987-88; Chairman (non-executive), McIlroy Coates, 1991-95; Member, Scottish Legal Aid Board, 1992-2000; Member, Appeal Panel, Competition Commission, 2000-03; Member, Competition Appeals Tribunal, 2003-2011; Erskine Fellow, University of Canterbury, New Zealand, 1994. Recreations: mountain walking; golf; listening to music. Address: (b.) 60 Buchanan Gardens, St. Andrews KY16 9LX; T.-01334 472966.

Groeneveld, Eva. Head of Public Affairs (Scotland), Which?, since 2015. Account Executive, Ranelagh International Ltd, 2006-07; WWF-UK: Senior Public Affairs Officer, 2007-2010, Public Affairs Manager (Scotland), 2010-2015. Address: (b.) Which? Scotland, 10 York Place, Edinburgh EH1 3EP; T.-0131 523 1341.

Grossart, Sir Angus McFarlane McLeod, CBE, QC, DL, LLD, DBA, DLitt, FRSE, FSA (Scot). Merchant Banker; Chairman and Managing Director, Noble Grossart; formerly chairman or director of numerous publicly listed companies in Scotland, London, the USA and Canada; The Fine Art Society (Chairman); Scotland International (Chairman); Lyon & Turnbull (Chairman); Edinburgh Partners (Chairman); Scottish Futures Trust (Chairman); Wright Health Group (Chairman); Charlotte Street Partners (Chairman); Ronson Capital Partners (Vice Chairman); b. 6.4.37, Glasgow; m., Gay Kerr Dodd; 1 d. Educ. Glasgow Academy; Glasgow University. CA, 1962; Advocate, Scottish Bar, 1963-69; Managing Director, Noble Grossart Ltd., since 1969; formerly a member, trustee or director of numerous public or charitable bodies; Chairman of Trustees, National Galleries of Scotland, 1988-97; Trustee and Deputy Chairman, National Heritage Memorial Fund, 1999-2005; Chairman of Trustees, National Museums of Scotland, 2006-2012; Chairman, Burrell Renaissance, since 2012; Trustee, Glasgow Life, since 2008; Trustee, The High Steward of Scotland's Dumfries House Trust; Chairman, Restoration of St Giles Cathedral, Edinburgh; Chairman, Edinburgh International Cultural Summit Foundation. Recreations: golf; decorative arts; historic architecture. Address: (b.) 48 Queen Street, Edinburgh EH2 3NR; T.-0131-226 7011.

Grosset, Alan George, MA, LLB, WS. Retired Solicitor; formerly Partner, Alex Morison & Co., W.S.; b. 18.1.42, Edinburgh; 1 s.; 1 d. Educ. Royal High School, Edinburgh; Edinburgh University. Law Society of Scotland "Troubleshooter" from inception of scheme, until 1987; Council Member, W.S. Society, 1998-2000; President, Scottish Lawn Tennis Association, 1983-84; Council Member, Lawn Tennis Association, 1980-89; first Chairman, Scottish Sports Association, 1984-90; Vice-Chairman, Scottish Sports Council, 1994-2002 (Member since 1984); Captain, Duddingston Golf Club, 1992-94; Chairman, Confederation of British Sport, 2002-04; Director, Sports Dispute Resolution Panel Ltd., 1997-2008; Depute Clerk, NHS Scotland Tribunal, 2005-2012; Public Interest Member, ICAS Insolvency Permit Committee, 2005-2014. Recreations: golf; tennis.

Groundwater, William, MB, ChB, FRCSEd; b. 20.8.36, Kirkwall, Orkney; m., Sheila M. Williamson; 1 s. Educ. Kirkwall Grammar School; Stromness Academy; Edinburgh University. MB, ChB, Edinburgh University, 1960; FRSCEd, 1966; General Surgical Practice, Thunder Bay, Ontario, 1971-73; Consultant General Surgeon, Balfour Hospital, Kirkwall, Orkney, 1973-99 (retired). Past President, Rotary Club of Orkney; Honorary Sheriff, Sheriffdom of Grampian, Highlands and Islands. Recreations: reading; bookbinding. Address: (h.) Clowigar, Scapa, St. Ola, Orkney KW15 1SD; T.-01856-872965.
E-mail: clowigar@aol.com

Grubb, Rev. Dr. George, BA, BD, BPhil, DMin. Lord Lieutenant and Lord Provost, City of Edinburgh, 2007-2012; b. 1935; m., Elizabeth; 1 s.; 1 d. Educ. James Gillespie's Boys School and Royal High School; University of Edinburgh; Open University. Scottish Schools Junior half mile Champion 1954; Royal High School half mile record holder. National Service in Royal Army Ordinance Corps for two years; Ordained Minister in 1962 in Stoke-on-Trent; Squadron Leader Chaplain in Royal Air Force 1962-70; served in Cosford then three years in Nicosia, Cyprus (during that time touring Tehran, Aden, Malta and Tripoli); Parish Minister at Craigsbank Parish Church 1971-2001. Served on various Committees of the Edinburgh Presbytery and was Moderator; served as Minister in residence at Eden Seminary in St Louis, USA. During one sabbatical leave went to the United Theological College in Zambia. Elected as Councillor for Queensferry in 1999. Chairperson of the Liberal Democrat Group, 2000-07. Recreations: jogging, running, reading and family.

Gruer, Professor Laurence David, OBE, BSc (Hons), MB, ChB, MD, MPH, FFPH, MRCP (UK), FRSA. Honorary Professor of Public Health, Universities of Edinburgh and Glasgow; b. 6.7.53, Aberdeen; m., Nana (deceased); 1 s.; 2 d. Educ. Robert Gordon's College; George Watson's College; University of Edinburgh; University of Glasgow. Edinburgh Medical School, 1972-78; UK hospital medical posts, 1978-83; Medical laboratory research, Lyon, France, 1983-85; Public Health specialist training, Glasgow, 1985-89; Consultant, Public Health Medicine, Greater Glasgow Health Board, 1989-2001; Honorary Senior Clinical Lecturer, University of Glasgow, 1989-2012; Director, HIV and Addictions Resource Centre, Glasgow, 1990-97; Consultant in Public Health Medicine, Public Health Institute of Scotland, 2001-03; Director, Scottish Public Health Specialist Training Programme, 2002-04; Director, Public Health Science, NHS Health Scotland, 2003-2012. Member, UK Advisory Council on the Misuse of Drugs, 1996-2006; OBE, Services to Public Health, 2000; Member, Scottish Committees for AIDS, Drug Misuse, Alcohol Tobacco; Chair, Scottish Committees on Smoking Prevention, Tobacco Control Research. Publications: over 150 reports, chapters in books and papers in journals on HIV and AIDS, drug misuse, tobacco control, health inequalities, ethnicity and health, obesity and infections. Recreations: cooking; cycling; free-style swimming; music; French and Spanish; photography.
E-mail: gruer.health@gmail.com

Gunn, Alexander MacLean, MA, BD; b. 26.2.43, Inverness; m., Ruth T.S.; 1 s.; 1 d. Educ. Edinburgh Academy; Beauly; Dingwall Academy; Edinburgh University and New College. Parish Minister: Wick St. Andrews and Thrumster, 1967-73; Member, Caithness Education Committee, 1968-73; Parish Minister, Glasgow St. David's Knightswood, 1973-86; Minister, Aberfeldy with Amulree and Strathbraan with Dull and Weem, 1986-2006; Convener: Church of Scotland Rural Working Group, 1988-90, General Assembly's Presbytery Development Committee, 1990-92, General Assembly's Mission and Evangelism Resource Committee, 1992-95; Interim Convener, Board of National Mission, 1996; Convener, Regional Committee, Scripture Union Scotland, 1998-2005. Chairman, Breadalbane Academy School Board, 1989-92 and 1996-2002; Lay Member, Education Scotland; Street Pastor; Director, Ascension Trust Scotland; National Chaplain to Workplace Chaplaincy Scotland. Address: "Navarone", 12 Cornhill Road, Perth PH1 1LR; T.-01738-443216; e-mail: sandygunn@btinternet.com

Gusterson, Professor Barry Austin, PhD, FRCPath. Professor of Pathology, Glasgow University, since 2000, Head, Division of Cancer Sciences and Molecular Pathology, since 2002; b. 24.10.46, Colchester; m., Ann Josephine Davies; 1 s.; 2 d. Educ. St Bartholomew's Hospital, London. Senior Clinical Scientist and Consultant, Ludwig Institute of Cancer Research, London, 1983-86; Consultant in Histopathology, Royal Marsden Hospital, 1984; Professor of Histopathology and Chairman, Section on Cell Biology and Experimental Pathology, Institute of Cancer Research, London University, 1986-2000; Founding Director, Toby Robins Breast Cancer Research Centre, London, 1998. Director, Pathology, International Breast Cancer Study Group, Berne, 1995; Oakley Lecturer, Pathological Society of Great Britain and Ireland, 1986; Chairman, Pathology Group, Organisation of European Cancer Institutes, Geneva, 1992-96. Recreations: antique English glass and furniture; gardening; walking; reading. Address: (b.) Department of Pathology, Western Infirmary, Glasgow, G11 6NT; T.-0141-211 2233.

Gwilt, George David, MA, FFA, FBCS, CITP; b. 11.11.27, Edinburgh; m., Ann Sylvester (deceased); 3 s. Educ. Sedbergh; St. John's College, Cambridge. Standard Life, 1949-88, latterly as Managing Director; Director: European Assets Trust NV, 1979-2000, Scottish Mortgage & Trust plc, 1983-98, Hodgson Martin Ltd., 1989-2000, Edinburgh Festival Society Ltd., 1989-95; President, Faculty of Actuaries, 1981-83; Trustee, South of Scotland TSB, 1966-83; Member: Younger Committee on Privacy, 1970-72, Monopolies and Mergers Commission, 1983-87; Convener, Scottish Poetry Library, 1988-2000. Recreations: flute playing; squash. Address: (h.) 39 Oxgangs Road, Edinburgh EH10 7BE; T.-0131-445 1266.

H

Haas, Professor Harald, PhD. Professor (Chair of Mobile Communications), University of Edinburgh, since 2010; b. 15.03.68, Neustadt/Aisch, Germany; m., Sybille Haas; 1 s.; 1 d. Educ. University of Applied Sciences, Nürnberg; University of Edinburgh, College of Science and Engineering. Engineer (Heinz-Nixdorf scholar), Siemens AG, Bombay, India, 1995; Engineer, Siemens AG/Semiconductor Division (now Infineon), Munich, Germany, 1995-97; Consultant, Nokia Networks, Nokia/Oulu, 1999-2000; Research Associate, Department of Electronics & Electrical Engineering/Signals and Systems Group, University of Edinburgh, 1999-2001; Project Manager, Siemens AG/Information & Communication Mobile Networks, Munich, Germany, 2001-02; Associate Professor of Electrical Engineering, School of Engineering and Science, Jacobs University Bremen, 2002-07; Lecturer, School of Engineering, Institute of Digital Communications (IDCOM), University of Edinburgh, 2007-08, Reader, 2008-2010; Chief Scientific Officer, pureLiFi Ltd, since 2012. Publications: Next Generation Mobile Access Technologies: Implementing TDD (Co-Author), 2008; Principles of Impaired and Visible Light Communications (Co-Author), 2015. Address: (b.) The King's Buildings, The University of Edinburgh, Mayfield Road, Edinburgh EH9 3JL; T.-0131 650 5591; e-mail: h.haas@ed.ac.uk

Hadden, William A., BSc, BAO, BCh, MB, FRCSEd and Orth. Consultant Orthopaedic Surgeon, since 1984; b. 23.5.46, Northern Ireland; 3 s. Educ. Methodist College, Belfast; Portadown College, Co. Armagh; Queen's University, Belfast. Surgical training, Northern Ireland, Edinburgh, Dundee, Christchurch (New Zealand). Recreations: golf; squash. Address: (b.) Perth Royal Infirmary, Perth PH1 1NX; T.-01738 473698.

Haddington, 13th Earl of (John George Baillie-Hamilton); b. 21.12.41; m.; 1 s.; 2 d. Succeeded to title, 1986. Educ. Ampleforth. Address: Mellerstain, Gordon, Berwickshire, TD3 6LG.

Haddock, Graham, MBChB, MD, FRCS (Glas), FRCS (Edin), FRCS (Paed). Consultant Paediatric Surgeon, since 1995; Clinical Director of Surgery, 2000-03; b. 7.8.60, Greenock. Educ. Notre Dame High School, Greenock; Glasgow University. Trained in adult general surgery, Glasgow and Edinburgh, in paediatric surgery, Royal Hospital for Sick Children, Yorkhill, Royal Hospital for Sick Children, Edinburgh, and Hospital for Sick Children, Toronto. Chair, JCST Quality Assurance Committee; Honorary Clinical Associate Professor, University of Glasgow; Deputy Head of Admissions, University of Glasgow Medical School. Former Chairman, Specialist Advisory Committee for Paediatric Surgery of The Joint Committee for Surgical Training (JCST), 2009-2012. Formerly National (UK) Commissioner for Explorer Scouts (The Scout Association), 2001-06; Depute Chief Commissioner for Scotland (Programme), 2008-2010; Chief Commissioner for Scotland; former UK Trustee (The Scout Association), 2007-2013. Address: (b.) Department of Paediatric Surgery, Royal Hospital for Sick Children, Yorkhill, Glasgow G3 8SJ; T.-0141-201 0289.

Haddow, Anne Melville, DipEd, BA (Hons), AdvDipEd (Open), MA (Ed), PhD. Board Member, The Care Inspectorate, since 2006; b. 16.03.52, Stirling; m., Robert Haddow; 2 d. Educ. Alloa Academy; Callender Park, College of Education, Falkirk; The Open University; Strathclyde University; Glasgow University. Primary School Teacher, 1974-77; Fieldworker for Centre for Health and Social Research, 1994-2001. Former Vice Chair, Fife Princess Royal Trust for Carers; former Member, The Scottish Social Services Council; article in Social Work Education, Vol.28, No.7, October 2009 - The Caring Experience. Recreations: embroidery; cookery. Address: (h.) 9 Glengarry Court, Glenrothes, Fife KY7 6NN; T.-01592 745140. E-mail: robert.haddow@lineone.net

Haddow, Christopher, QC, LLB (Hons); b. 15.5.47, Edinburgh; m., Kathleen; 3 s. Educ. George Watson's College; Edinburgh University. Admitted to Faculty of Advocates, 1971; Queen's Counsel, 1985. Former Member, Secretary of State's Valuation Advisory Council and of Scottish Valuation and Rating Council; Joint Editor, Armour on Valuation for Rating, since 1990. Recreations: hockey; walking; classic cars. Address: (h.) Abbot's Croft House, North Berwick EH39 5NG.

Haggart, Mary Elizabeth, OBE; b. 8.4.24, Leicester; m., Rt. Rev. A.I.M. Haggart (deceased). Educ. Wyggeston Grammar School for Girls, Leicester; Leicester Royal Infirmary and Children's Hospital. Leicester Royal Infirmary: Staff Nurse, 1947-48, Night Sister, 1948-50, Ward Sister, 1950-56, Night Superintendent, 1956-58, Assistant Matron, 1958-61; Assistant Matron, Brook General Hospital, London, 1962-64; Matron, Dundee Royal Infirmary and Matron Designate, Ninewells Hospital, Dundee, 1964-68; Chief Nursing Officer, Board of Managements, Dundee General Hospitals and Ninewells Hospital, 1968-73; Chief Area Nursing Officer, Tayside Health Board, 1974-82; President, Scottish Association of Nurse Administrators, 1972-77; Member: Scottish Board, Royal College of Nursing, 1965-70, General Nursing Council for Scotland, 1965-70 and 1978-82; Chairman, Scottish Board of Nursing Midwifery and Health Visiting, 1980-83; Member: Standing Nursing and Midwifery Committee, 1971-74 (Vice Chairman, 1973-74), Action on Smoking and Health Scotland, 1978-82 (Chairman, Working Party, Smoking and Nurses); Governor, Dundee College of Technology, 1978-82; Honorary Lecturer, Department of Community Medicine, Dundee University and Medical School, 1980-82; Member: Management Committee, Carstairs State Hospital, 1982-92, United Kingdom Central Council for Nursing Midwifery and Health Visiting, 1980-82, Scottish Hospital Endowments Research Trust, 1986-96. Recreations: walking; music; travel. Address: (h.) 14/2 St. Margaret's Place, Edinburgh EH9 1AY.

Haggerty, Lara. Library Manager and Keeper, Innerpeffray Library (Scotland's oldest free Public Lending Library, founded 1680). Address: (b.) Crieff, Perthshire PH7 3RF; T.-01764 652819.

Hair, Professor Graham Barry, MMus, PhD. Composer; Emeritus Professor of Music, Honorary Research Fellow, School of Engineering, Glasgow University; b. 27.2.43, Geelong, Australia; m., Dr Greta Mary Hair. Educ. Geelong College, Australia; Melbourne University; Sheffield University. Senior Lecturer, Latrobe University, 1975-80; Head, School of Composition, Sydney Conservatorium of Music, 1980-90; has had many commissions, performances, CD recordings, broadcasts and musical works published. Address: (h.) 45 St. Vincent Crescent, Glasgow G3 8NG; T.-0141-221 4933; e-mail: graham.hair@virgin.net

Haites, Professor Neva, OBE, MB, ChB, PhD, FRCP, FRCPath, FMedSci. Professor in Medical Genetics, Vice-Principal for Development, Honorary Consultant in Clinical Genetics, University of Aberdeen; b. 4.6.47, Brisbane, Australia; m., Roy; 2 d. Educ. Somerville House, Brisbane; Queensland University; University of Aberdeen. Formerly: Lead Clinician, North of Scotland Cancer Network, Member, National Screening Committee, Head of Service in Medical Genetics. Address: College Office, Medical School, University of Aberdeen, Foresterhill, Aberdeen; T.-01224 559241; e-mail: n.haites@abdn.ac.uk

Hajivassiliou, Constantinos, BSc (Hons), MBChB, MD, FRCS (Edin), FRCS (Glas), FRCS (Paed), MD, FEBPS, FRCPCH, FRSA. Paediatric/Neonatal Surgeon (Consultant), Royal Hospital for Sick Children, Glasgow, since 1998; Wellcome Trust Senior Lecturer, Glasgow University, since 1999; b. 27.4.61, Nicosia; m., Eva; 2 d. Educ. Edinburgh University. House Officer, then Senior House Officer, 1986-89; Registrar, West of Scotland Rotation, 1989-92; Senior Registrar/Lecturer, Yorkhill and Glasgow University, 1992-98. Lord Moynihan Prize, Association of Surgeons of Great Britain and Ireland, 1995; many other prizes. Recreations: radio amateur; diving; flying; fishing; cooking. Address: (b.) Department of Paediatric Surgery, Royal Hospital for Sick Children, Yorkhill, Glasgow G3 8SJ; T.-0141-201 0852.

Haldane of Gleneagles, James Martin, MA, BA, DUniv (Stirling), CA, FRSA. 28th Laird of Gleneagles; Director: Investors Capital Trust PLC, 1995-2010 (Chairman, since 2004); (Stace Barr Angerstein PLC, 1997-2004), Shires Income plc, 1996-2008 (Chairman, 2003-08); former Chairman, Chiene & Tait, CA (Partner, 1989-2001); former Deputy Chairman, Scottish Life Assurance Co. (Director, 1990-2001); Chairman, Queen's Hall (Edinburgh) Ltd., 1987-2001; Chairman, Scottish Opera Endowment Trust, since 2010; b. 18.9.41, Edinburgh; m., Petronella Victoria Scarlett; 1 s.; 2 d. Educ. Winchester College; Magdalen College, Oxford. Partner, Arthur Young, 1970-89. Chairman, Scottish Chamber Orchestra, 1978-85; Chairman, Craighead Investments PLC, 1982-90; Trustee, D'Oyly Carte Opera Trust, 1985-92 and since 2012; Treasurer, Queen's Bodyguard for Scotland (Royal Company of Archers), 1992-2001; Member: Council, Edinburgh Festival Society, 1985-89, Northern and Scottish Board, Legal and General Assurance Co., 1984-87, Council, National Trust for Scotland, 1992-97, Court, Stirling University, 1997-2005; Chairman of Governors, Innerpeffray Library, 1994-2006. Recreations: music; golf. Address: (h.) Gleneagles, Auchterarder PH3 1PJ; T.-01764 682 388; (b.) 01764 682535.
E-mail: haldane@gleneagles.org

Haldane, Professor John Joseph, BA, PGCE, BA, PhD, Hon LLD, Hon DLitt, FRSA, FRSE, KCHS. J. Newton Rayzor Sr Distinguished Professor of Philosophy, Baylor University, Texas, USA, since 2015; Professor of Philosophy, St. Andrews University, since 1994; Director, Centre for Ethics, Philosophy and Public Affairs; b. 19.2.54, London; m., Hilda Marie Budas; 2 s.; 2 d. Educ. St. Aloysius College, Glasgow; Wimbledon School of Art; London University. Art Master, St. Joseph's Grammar School, Abbey Wood, 1976-79; Lecturer in Moral Philosophy, St. Andrews University, 1983-90, Reader, 1990-94; Stanton Lecturer, University of Cambridge, 1999-2002; Royden Davis Professor of Humanities, Georgetown University, 2001-02; Gifford Lecturer, University of Aberdeen, 2004; Joseph Lecturer, Gregorian University, Rome, 2004; Visiting Professor, Institute for the Psychological Sciences, Virginia, USA, 2005-08; Consultor to Pontifical Council for Culture, Vatican, since 2005; Senior Fellow, Witherspoon Institute Princeton, since 2007; McDonald Lecturer, University of Oxford, 2011; Renwick Fellow, University of Notre Dame, 2013-14; Permanent Fellow, Center for Ethics and Culture, University of Notre Dame, since 2014; Chairman, Royal Institute of Philosophy; Vice President (Scotland), Catholic Union; Member, Editorial Board: American Journal of Jurisprudence, Cambridge Studies in Philosophy, Ethical Perspectives, Journal of Philosophy of Education, Philosophical Explorations, Philosophical Quarterly; Contributor: The Scotsman, The Tablet, Modern Painters etc; and to BBC radio and television, and National Public Radio, USA. Address: (b.) Department of Philosophy, University of St Andrews, St Andrews KY16 9AL; T.-01334 462488; e-mail: jjh1@st-and.ac.uk

Halden, Derek, BSc (Hons), MEng, CEng, FCILT, FRSA, FICE. Director, DHC Ltd., Transport Planning Consultancy, since 1996; Editor, Scottish Transport Review, since 2004; b. 3.10.60, Irvine; m., Deborah; 1 s.; 1 d. Educ. Glasgow High School; Merchiston Castle School; University of Aberdeen; University of Glasgow. Jamieson, Mackay and Partners, Transport Planning Consultants, Glasgow and Sir William Halcrow and Partners, 1982-86; Civil Service - Scottish Office Road and Bridge Projects, Transport Policy, Research, and Transport Research Laboratory, 1987-96. Honorary Research Fellow, University of Aberdeen, since 2003; Committee Member: European Transport Conference, since 2003, Scottish Transport Studies Group, since 1995 (Chair, since 2007); Chair, Chartered Institute of Logistics and Transport Scotland (2011-2013). Recreations: tennis; squash; hill walking; guitar. Address: Longview, Kames, Tighnabruaich PA21 2AB; e-mail: derek@dhc1.co.uk

Halford-MacLeod, Col. Ret. Aubrey Philip Lydiat, MA (Hons). Late Black Watch (RHR); retired Army Officer, retired University and Schools Liaison Officer (Scotland), Recruiting and Liaison, Scotland; former President of the Queich Curling Club; President of the Highland Brigade Curling Club; President of the Fife Branch of the Black Watch Association; Member of the Fife Branch of Friends of Scottish Opera; Hon. Sec., SSPCK; b. 28.4.42, Baghdad; m., Alison Halford-MacLeod (nee Brown) DL; 2 s.; 1 d. Educ. Winchester College; RMA Sandhurst; Magdalen College, Oxford. Commissioned into Black Watch, 1962; Lt., 1964; Capt., 1968; Maj., 1975; Lt. Col., 1985; appointed Commanding Officer, Glasgow and Strathclyde Universities OTC, 1985; Chief of Staff, The Scottish Division, 1988; UK Liaison Officer (as Colonel), US European Command Stuttgart, 1991; SO1 G1 Action and Support Team (Demob Cell), Army HQ Scotland, 1992; Commandant, The Black Watch ACF Battalion, 1993. Recreations: walking the dogs; shooting; fishing; opera; model soldiers; curling; country dancing. Address: (h.) The Old Manse, 28 Skene Street, Strathmiglo KY14 7QL; T.-01337 860715/868930.
E-mail: philip_h@madasafish.com

Halfpenny, Lynne J., BA, DRLP, MISPAL, FFCS. Director of Culture, City of Edinburgh Council, since 2015, Head of Culture and Sport, 2007-2015, Head of Museums and Arts, Culture and Leisure Department, 2002-06; Board Member, Museums Galleries Scotland, since 2006; with Edinburgh Arts Development team, 1989-2002; Board Member, Eastgate Theatre, Peebles, 2010-2012; b. 18.12.63, Aberdeen; m., Bob; 1 s.; 1 d. Educ. Waid Academy; Queen Margaret University College; Dunfermline College of Physical Education. Arts Promotion Officer, Renfrew District Council, 1987-89; freelance arts and events manager, 1985-89. Address: (b.) The City of Edinburgh Council, Waverley Court, 4 East Market Street, Edinburgh EH8 8BG; e-mail: lynne.halfpenny@edinburgh.gov.uk

Hall, Professor Christopher, MA, DPhil, DSc, CEng, FRSC, FIMMM, FREng, FRSE. Emeritus Professor and Professorial Fellow, University of Edinburgh, since 2010, Professor of Materials, 1999-2010, Director,

Centre for Materials Science and Engineering, 1999-2010, Director of Research, School of Engineering and Electronics, 2002-08; b. 31.12.44, Henley-on-Thames; m., Sheila McKelvey (deceased); 1 d.; 1 s. Educ. Royal Belfast Academical Institution; Trinity College, Oxford. Lecturer, Building Engineering, UMIST, 1972-83; Head, Rock and Fluid Physics, Schlumberger Cambridge Research, 1983-88; Head, Chemical Technology, Dowell Schlumberger, St Etienne, France, 1988-89; Scientific Advisor, Schlumberger Cambridge Research, 1990-99; Visiting Fellow, Princeton Materials Institute, Princeton University, USA, 1998; Visiting Professor, University of Manchester, since 1994; Senior Member, Robinson College, Cambridge; Royal Society Mercer Senior Award for Innovation, 2001; Fellow, Royal Academy of Engineering; Fellow, Royal Society of Edinburgh. Address: (h.) 36 Mayfield Terrace, Edinburgh, EH9 1RZ; T.-0131-662 9285.
E-mail: Christopher.Hall@ed.ac.uk

Hall, Professor Denis, BSc, MPhil, PhD, MBA, FInstP, FIEE, FIEEE, FOSA, FRSE, CEng. Professor of Photonics, Department of Physics, Heriot-Watt University, since 1987, former Deputy Principal (Research) (1998-2007); b. 1.8.42, Cardiff; m., Pauline; 2 c. Educ. Manchester University; St Bartholomew's Hospital Medical College; Case Western Research University, Cleveland, Ohio, USA. Senior Research Scientist, Avco Everett Research Laboratory, Boston, 1972-74; Principal Scientific Officer, Royal Signals and Radar Establishment, 1974-79; Senior Lecturer/Reader in Applied Laser Physics, Hull University, 1979-87. Chairman, Quantum Electronics Group Committee, Institute of Physics, 1991-94; Chairman, Quantum Electronics and Optics Division, European Physical Society, 1998-2000. Publications: 150 in journals; 200 papers at conferences. Address: (b.) Department of Physics, Heriot-Watt University, Edinburgh EH14 4AS; T.-0131-451 3081.

Hall, Professor Graham Stanley, BSc, PhD, FRSE, FRAS. Professor Emeritus, University of Aberdeen, since 2011 (Professor of Mathematics, 1996-2011); b. 5.9.46, Warrington; 1 s.; 1 d. Educ. Boteler Grammar School, Warrington; University of Newcastle upon Tyne (Earl Grey Memorial Fellow, 1971-73); Lecturer in Mathematics, University of Aberdeen, since 1973 (Senior Lecturer, 1982, Reader, 1990, Head of Department, 1992-95). Over 200 invited lectures worldwide. Publications: over 160 articles in research journals; General Relativity (Co-Editor), 1996; Recent Developments in Mathematical Relativity (Co-Editor), 2012; book: Symmetries and Curvature; Structure in General Relativity (Author), 2004. Recreations: music (piano); reading; astronomy; sport. Address: (b.) Institute of Mathematics, University of Aberdeen, Aberdeen AB24 3UE; T.-01224 272748; e-mail: g.hall@abdn.ac.uk

Hall, Peter Lindsay, MA, BA (Hons). Director, SCVO, 2008-2011; Director, Orkney CAB, since 2009; b. 13.08.53, Manchester; m., Vera. Educ. Open University. Director and Chair (2005-08), Voluntary Action Orkney, 2003-09; Director and Chair, Gable End Theatre Company, since 2001; Director, The Island of Hoy Development Trust, since 2004; Secretary, Longhope Lifeboat Museum Trust, since 2003; Director and Chair, Employability Orkney, 2006-2014; Director, Hoy Energy Company, since 2009 (all unpaid). Works for the Criminal Justice Section in Orkney. Recreations: writing absurdist plays and pantomines - amateur acting. Address: Seaview, Melsetter, Longhope, Orkney KW16 3NQ; T.-01856 791200.
E-mail: lindsayhall309@gmail.com

Hall, Richard, FCILT. Managing Director, Lothian Buses, since 2016. Career history: 6 years with Stagecoach and 3 years with Veolia Transport in Wales; joined Arriva in 2010, working in the west of Scotland and Glasgow before involvement with the transportation delivery for the 2012 Olympics and the Maltese operation; former Managing Director for RATP in London (responsible for leading over 3700 people, across 11 operating sites, operating contracted bus services for TfL as well as a developing commercial bus and coach operation launched in 2015). Recreations: mountain biking; skiing; keen walker. Address: Lothian Buses, Annandale Street, Edinburgh EH7 4AZ.

Hall, Stewart Martin, FRICS, FAAV, ACIArb, ARAgS. Chartered Surveyor; Managing Director, Davidson & Robertson Rural, since 2005; b. 6.11.70, Cumbria; m., Isla; 1 s.; 2 d. Educ. Cockermouth School; Harper Adams University College. Davidson & Robertson Rural, since 1991; Chairman, RICS matrics Scotland, 2005; Hon. Treasurer, RICS Scotland, 2005-08; President of Scottish Agricultural Arbiters & Valuers Association, 2012-2014; Hon. Director, Royal Highland and Agricultural Society for Scotland; Director, Kirknewton Community Development Trust. Recreation: curling. Address: (b.) Riccarton Mains, Currie, Midlothian EH14 4AR; T.-0131 449 6212.

Hall, Tim. Chairman, Lloyds TSB Foundation for Scotland, since 2014. Career spanning 26 years at Martin Currie, managed charitable funds and UK income trusts; went on to develop the global client service offering for Martin Currie and to help build institutional relationships with core consultants in the UK; managed the investment team, 2004-2010; both a main board director and executive team member; joined Lloyds Foundation's Board of Trustees in October 2011; served as Vice Chairman, 2013-14; member of the Foundation's Investment Committee and Nominations & Remuneration Committee; Chairman, Martin Currie Charitable Foundation; formerly non-executive charity investment consultant to Turcan Connell; maintains strong links with the Princes Trust in its fundraising, and has supported the Prince's Scottish Youth Business Trust as a panel member; also been a project member for Pilotlight Scotland in its work to help smaller charities in Scotland; Trustee to a number of private charitable trusts; Chairman of the Martin Currie Pension Fund; Chair, Board of Governors, Kilgraston School. Address: Lloyds TSB Foundation for Scotland, Riverside House, 502 Gorgie Road, Edinburgh EH11 3AF; T.-0131 444 4020.

Hall, (William) Douglas, OBE (1985), BA, FMA, DUniv (Stirling, 2009); b. 9.10.26, London; m.1, Helen Elizabeth Ellis (m. diss.); 1 s.; 1 d.; 2, Matilda Mary Mitchell. Educ. University College School, Hampstead; University College and Courtauld Institute of Art, London University. Served in Intelligence Corps, 1945-48 (Middle East); on staff of Manchester City Art Galleries 1953-61 (Deputy Director, 1959-61); Keeper, Scottish National Gallery of Modern Art, 1961-86; Awarded Gloria Artis Medal, Polish Ministry of Culture, 2008. Publications: numerous shorter texts; books include William Johnstone, 1980; Alan Davie, with Michael Tucker, Lund Humphries 1992; Haig the Painter, Atelier Books 2003; Art in Exile: Polish Painters in Post-war Britain, Sansom and Company, 2008 (Polish edition pending). Recreations: music; enjoying old age. Address: (h.) Wellgate, Morebattle, Kelso TD5 8QN; T.-01573 440687.

Halliday, David James Finlay, LLB (Hons), DipLP, NP, WS. Partner, Halliday Campbell WS, since 2009; b. 25.7.62, Dunfermline; m., Rona Dougall; 2 d. Educ. High School of Dundee; University of Edinburgh. Qualified as Solicitor, 1988; Assistant Solicitor, Edinburgh, 1989-92; Partner, Orr MacQueen, Solicitors, 1992-99; Partner and Head of Litigation, Boyds Solicitors LLP, 1999-2007;

Partner, HBJ Gateley Wareing (Scotland) LLP, 2007-09. Recreations: music; current affairs; cycling; family. Address: (b.) 7 Tweeddale Court, 14 High Street, Edinburgh EH1 1TE; T.-0131 557 9008.
E-mail: david.halliday@hallidaycampbell.com

Halliday, Dr John Dixon, BA (Hons), PhD. Rector, High School of Dundee, since 2008; Headmaster, Albyn School, 2002-08; b. 24.6.55, Wantage, Berkshire; m., Anna Salvesen; 2 s.; 1 d. Educ. Abingdon School; Exeter University; Robinson College, Cambridge. Lecturer in English, Universitat Passau, Germany; freelance translator; Head of German, Merchiston Castle School; Head of Modern Languages, Housemaster and Director of Middle School, Sedbergh School; Headmaster, Rannoch School; Teacher of Modern Languages, Dollar Academy. Recreations: music – singing, viola; sport; reading. Address: (b.) High School of Dundee, Euclid Crescent, Dundee DD1 1HU; T.-01382 202921.
E-mail: enquiries@highschoolofdundee.org.uk

Halliday, Rt. Rev. Robert Taylor, MA, BD. Bishop of Brechin, 1990-96; b. 7.5.32, Glasgow; m., Dr. Gena M. Chadwin (deceased 2013); 1 d. Educ. High School of Glasgow; Glasgow University; Trinity College, Glasgow; Episcopal Theological College, Edinburgh. Deacon, 1957; Priest, 1958; Assistant Curate, St. Andrew's, St. Andrews, 1957-60, St. Margaret's, Newlands, Glasgow, 1960-63; Rector, Holy Cross, Davidson's Mains, Edinburgh, 1963-83; External Lecturer in New Testament, Episcopal Theological College, Edinburgh, 1963-74; Canon, St. Mary's Cathedral, Edinburgh, 1973-83; Rector, St. Andrew's, St. Andrews, 1983-90; Tutor in Biblical Studies, St. Andrews University, 1984-90; Post-retiral ministry, Christ Church, Morningside, Edinburgh, 1997-2009; St Peter's, Lutton Place, Edinburgh, since 2009. Recreations: walking; reading; visiting gardens and art exhibitions. Address: 28 Forbes Road, Edinburgh EH10 4ED; T.-0131-221 1490.

Halliday, Roger. Chief Statistician, Scottish Government, since 2011. Educ. St. Andrews University. Career: joined the Department of Social Security as an assistant statistician; worked for spells at the Department of Health in England and in a number of statistical and policy making roles at the Scottish Government before leaving in 2005; worked in the Department of Health in England as a policy analyst managing evidence for decision making across NHS issues. Address: Scottish Government, St. Andrew's House, Regent Road, Edinburgh EH1 3DG.

Halling, Professor Peter James, BA, PhD, FRSE. Robertson Professor of Bioprocess Technology, Strathclyde University, since 1996; b. 30.3.51, London. Educ. Calday Grammar School; Churchill College, Cambridge; Bristol University. Postdoctoral Fellow, University College, London, 1975-78; Research Scientist, Unilever Research, Bedford, 1978-83; Professor of Biocatalyst Science, Strathclyde University, 1990-96. Recreation: orienteering. Address: (h.) 34 Montague Street, Glasgow G4 9HX; T.-0141-552 4400.

Halliwell, Professor Francis Stephen, MA, DPhil (Oxon), FBA, FRSE. Professor of Greek, University of St. Andrews, since 1995; b. 18.10.53, Wigan; m., Helen Ruth Gainford (divorced); 2 s. Educ. St. Francis Xavier's, Liverpool; Worcester College, University of Oxford. Lecturer in Classics and Drama, Westfield College, London, 1980-82; Fellow in Classics, Corpus Christi College, University of Cambridge, 1982-84; Lecturer, Senior Lecturer, Reader in Classics, University of Birmingham, 1984-95; Visiting

Professor in Classics, University of Chicago, 1990; Visiting Faculty Fellow, University of California at Riverside, 1993; Visiting Professor in Aesthetics, University of Rome, 1998; H. L. Hooker Distinguished Visiting Professor, McMaster University, 2009; Chaire Cardinal Mercier, Catholic University of Louvain, 2010; Townsend Visiting Professor, Cornell University, 2012. Winner of Premio Europeo d'Estetica 2008, Criticos Prize 2008. Publications: nine books and 90 articles on Greek literature and philosophy, including Aristophanes, Plato and Aristotle. Recreation: music. Address: (b.) School of Classics, Swallowgate, University of St. Andrews, St. Andrews KY16 9AL; T.-01334 462617; e-mail: fsh@st-and.ac.uk

Hallsworth, Fred, BAcc, CA. Founder and Principal, The Hallsworth Partnership, since 2005; NED and Chair of Audit Committee, Scottish Enterprise, 2004-2010; Chairman, Forth Dimension Displays Limited, 2007-2011; NED and Chair of Audit Committee, Central Marketing Agency (Scotland) Limited, since 2007; NED, Point 35 Microstructures Limited, since 2006; NED, Elonics Limited, 2006-2010; NED and Vice-Chairman, Microvisk Technologies Limited, since 2006; NED Golden Charter Limited, 2009-2011; NED, Metaforic Limited, since 2009; Advisory Board Member, Lane Clarke & Peacock LLP, since 2009; b. 03.05.53, Paisley; m., Nicola; 2 s.; 3 d. Educ. St. Mirins Academy; University of Glasgow. Audit Manager: Andersen Brussels, 1981, Andersen Scotland, 1982-88; Head of Audit, Andersen Cambridge, 1994-98; Head of Corporate Finance, Andersen Cambridge, 1988-95; Managing Partner, Andersen Cambridge, 1995-98; Membership of Partnership Council, Andersen UK, 1999-2002; Managing Partner, Andersen Scotland, 1998-2002; Senior Client Service Partner and Head of TMC Deloitte Scotland, 2002-05. Board Member, Scottish Institute for Enterprise, 1999-2008; Chairman, The Kelvin Institute, 2005-08; Council Member: CBI Scotland, 1999-2004, CBI Eastern Region, 1994-98; Co-founder and Board Member, The Cambridge Network, 1996-2002; Board Member, University of Cambridge Finance Committee, 1996-98. Recreations: golf; tennis; gym. Address: (h./b.) The Garden Wing, Houston House, Kirk Road, Houston, Renfrewshire PA6 7AR; T.-07889 721321; e-mail: fred@fredhallsworth.com

Hally, Paul William. Partner and Chairman, Shepherd and Wedderburn LLP (Partner, since 1987). Legal Member, ICAS Business Policy Committee. Address: (b.) 1 Exchange Crescent, Conference Square, Edinburgh EH3 8UL; T.-0131 473 5183; e-mail: paul.hally@shepwedd.co.uk

Halpin, Tom. Chief Executive, Sacro, since 2009. Joined Strathclyde Police in 1979; later appointed Head of CID operations across the force and Divisional Commander for north Glasgow and East Dunbartonshire; Lothian and Borders Police; Assistant Chief Constable, 2005, then Deputy Chief Constable, 2006-09, Temporary Chief Constable, 2008. Awarded Queen's Police Medal, 2008 Birthday Honours List; Chartered Director and Fellow of Institute of Directors; Lay Governor and Member of University Court, Glasgow Caledonian University, since 2011; Trustee, Lloyds TSB Foundation, since 2014. Address: (b.) 29 Albany Street, Edinburgh EH1 3QN; T.-0131 624 7270.

Hamblen, Professor David Lawrence, CBE, MB, BS, PhD, DSc (Hon), FRCS, FRCSEdin, FRCSGlas. Chairman, Greater Glasgow NHS Board, 1997-2002; Emeritus Professor of Orthopaedic Surgery, Glasgow University; Hon. Consultant Orthopaedic Surgeon to Army in Scotland,

1976-99; b. 31.8.34, London; m., Gillian; 1 s.; 2 d. Educ. Roan School, Greenwich; London University. The London Hospital, 1963-66; Teaching Fellow in Orthopaedics, Harvard Medical School/Massachusetts General Hospital, 1966-67; Lecturer in Orthopaedics, Nuffield Orthopaedic Centre, Oxford, 1967-68; Senior Lecturer in Orthopaedics/Honorary Consultant, Edinburgh University/South East Regional Hospital Board, 1968-72; Professor of Orthopaedic Surgery, Glasgow University; 1972-99. Honorary Consultant in Orthopaedic Surgery, Greater Glasgow Health Board, 1972-99; Visiting Professor to National Centre for Training and Education in Prosthetics and Orthotics, Strathclyde University, 1981-2008; Member, Chief Scientist Committee and Chairman, Committee for Research on Equipment for Disabled, 1983-90; Chairman, Journal of Bone and Joint Surgery, 1995-2002 (Member, Editorial Board, 1978-82 and 1985-89); Secretary and Treasurer, JBJS Council of Management, 1992-95; Member, Physiological Systems Board, Medical Research Council, 1983-88; President, British Orthopaedic Association, 1990-91 (Chairman, Education Sub-Committee, 1986-89); Non-Executive Director, West Glasgow Hospitals University NHS Trust, 1994-97; Interim Board Member, Medical Devices in Scotland, 2001-02; Council Member, St. Andrews Ambulance Association, 1998-2013; Consulting Medical Editor, Orthopaedics Today International, 2002-2010. Publications: Outline of Fractures (Co-Author), (12th edition, 2007); Outline of Orthopaedics (Co-Author), (14th edition, 2010). Recreations: golf; curling. Address: (h.) 3 Russell Drive, Bearsden, Glasgow G61 3BB.

Hamblin, Janet, BSc (Maths), CA (ICAS), ICAEW. Non Executive Director and Chair of Audit and Risk Committee, Scottish Government, since 2014. Educ. St Hilary's School; Edinburgh University; Heriot Watt University. Career history: Senior Manager, PwC, 1980-96; Director, Business in the Community, 2000-14; Charities, Housing Associations and Education Audit Partner, RSM UK, since 1997. Recreations: golf; curling; theatre; foreign travel; dance. Address: Scottish Government, St. Andrew's House, Regent Road, Edinburgh EH1 3DG; T.-0300 244 4000.

Hamilton, 16th Duke of (Alexander Douglas-Hamilton). Hereditary Keeper of the Palace of Holyroodhouse; b. 31.3.78; m., Sophie Ann Rutherford; 2 s. Educ. Keil School, Dumbarton; Gordonstoun. Styled Marquess of Douglas and Clydesdale from birth until the 5th of June 2010; currently styled His Grace The Duke of Hamilton and Brandon.

Hamilton, Rt. Hon. Lord (Arthur Campbell Hamilton), BA (Oxon), LLB (Edin). Lord Justice General of Scotland and Lord President of the Court of Session, 2005-2012; b. 10.6.42, Glasgow; m., Christine Ann; 1 d. Educ. High School of Glasgow; Glasgow University. Worcester College, Oxford; Edinburgh University. Advocate, 1968; Standing Junior Counsel to Scottish Development Department, 1975-78, Inland Revenue (Scotland), 1978-82; Queen's Counsel, 1982; Advocate Depute, 1982-85; Judge of the Courts of Appeal of Jersey and of Guernsey, 1988-95; President, Pensions Appeal Tribunals for Scotland, 1992-95; Senator of the College of Justice, 1995-2005. Hon. Fellow, Worcester College, Oxford, 2003; Hon. Bencher, Inner Temple, 2006; Member, supplementary panel of the Supreme Court of the United Kingdom and judge of the Court of Appeal of Botswana (both part time, from 2012); Judge of the Qatar International Court (part time, June 2015). Recreations: music; history. Address: 8 Heriot Row, Edinburgh EH3 6HU; T.-0131-556-4663.

Hamilton, Rev. Dr Alan James, LLB, BD, DipLP, PhD. Minister, Killermont Parish Church, Bearsden, since 2003;

b. 14.8.63, Glasgow; m., Hazel; 3 s. Educ. Williamwood High School; Eastwood High School; Glasgow University; Edinburgh University. Solicitor, 1987; Advocate, 1990. Address: 8 Clathic Avenue, Bearsden, Glasgow G61 2HF; T.-0141 942 0021; e-mail: ajh63@o2.co.uk

Hamilton, David. Labour MP, Midlothian, 2001-2015; b. 24.10.50, Dalkeith; m., Jean; 2 d. Educ. Dalkeith High School. Former coal miner, landscape gardener, training officer, training manager, chief executive, and local councillor. Recreations: films; five grandchildren.

Hamilton, Ian Robertson, QC (Scot), BL, LLD (Hon); b. 13.9.25, Paisley; m., Jeannette Patricia Mairi Stewart; 1 s.; 1 s., 2 d. by pr. m. Educ. John Neilson School, Paisley; Allan Glen's School, Glasgow; Glasgow University; Edinburgh University. RAFVR, 1944-48; called to Scottish Bar, 1954, and to Albertan Bar, 1982; Founder, Castle Wynd Printers, Edinburgh, 1955; Advocate Depute, 1962; Director of Civil Litigation, Republic of Zambia, 1964-66; Hon. Sheriff of Lanarkshire, 1967; retired from practice to work for National Trust for Scotland and later to farm in Argyll, 1969; returned to practice, 1974; Sheriff of Glasgow and Strathkelvin, May-December, 1984; returned to practice. Chief Pilot, Scottish Parachute Club, 1979-90; Student President, Heriot-Watt University, 1990-96; Rector, Aberdeen University, 1994-96; Honorary Member, Sir William Wallace Free Colliers of Scotland, 1997. University of Aberdeen, 1997: LLD (Hon), Hon Research Fellow; Sorley Lifetime Achievement Award, 2008; Law Awards, Scotland 2009 Lifetime Achievement. Publications: No Stone Unturned, 1952; The Tinkers of the World, 1957 (Foyle award-winning play); A Touch of Treason, 1990; The Taking of the Stone of Destiny, 1991, reprinted as Stone of Destiny, 2008 (film of same name released in Scotland, 2008 and world wide, 2009); A Touch More Treason, 1993; From Amento Boothill (e-book), 2011. Recreation: being grumpy. Address: (h.) Lochnaheithe, North Connel, Argyll PA37 1QX; T.-01631 710 427.

Hamilton, Rev. Ian William Finlay, BD, LTH, ALCM, AVCM. Minister Emeritus, Nairn Old Parish Church, 1986-2012; b. 29.11.46, Glasgow; m., Margaret McLaren Moss; 1 s.; 2 d. Educ. Victoria Drive Senior Secondary School, Glasgow; University of Glasgow and Trinity College. Employed in banking, then music publishing; ordained, Alloa North Parish Church, 1978. Moderator, Presbytery of Inverness, 1990-91; Member: General Assembly Parish Re-appraisal Committee, 1994-97; former Member, General Assembly Maintenance of the Ministry Committee; Chaplain to the Moderator of the General Assembly of the Church of Scotland, 2005/06; has participated in several pulpit exchanges to Churches in the USA; Presenter, Reflections (Grampian TV), Crossfire (Moray Firth Radio). Publications: Reflections from the Manse Window; Second Thoughts; They're Playing My Song; Take Four!; I'm Trying to Connect You!; From Pen to Parish; A Century of Christian Witness; several children's talks published in The Expository Times; regular contributor to Manse Window page in People's Friend. Recreations: music (piano and organ); writing; broadcasting on radio and television. Address: (h.) "Mossneuk", 5 Windsor Gardens, St Andrews, Fife KY16 8XL; T.-(h.) 01334 477745.
E-mail: reviwfh@btinternet.com

Hamilton, Dr Mark Patrick Rogers, MBChB, MD, FRCOG. Consultant Gynaecologist, Aberdeen Maternity Hospital; Honorary Senior Lecturer, Aberdeen University; b. 24.4.55, Glasgow; m., Susan Elizabeth Duckworth; 1 s.; 1 d. Educ. High School of Glasgow; Glasgow University. Lecturer, National University of

Singapore, 1985-87; Senior Registrar, Glasgow Royal Infirmary, 1987-90. Member, British Fertility Society Committee, since 1995 (Treasurer, 2001-05, Chair, 2006-08). Address: (b.) Aberdeen Maternity Hospital, Foresterhill, Aberdeen AB25 2ZD; T.-01224 553504.

Hamilton, Rachael. MSP (Scottish Conservative), South Scotland region, since 2016; m.; 3 c. Conservative candidate for the East Lothian constituency in the 2016 Scottish Parliament election. Runs The Buccleuch Arms, St Boswells. Address: Scottish Parliament, Edinburgh EH99 1SP.

Hamilton, Thomas Hunter, BEd, BA (Hons), MEd. Director of Education, Registration and Professional Learning, The General Teaching Council Scotland, since 2006; b. 6.8.55, Ayr; m., Margaret. Educ. Ayr Academy; Craigie College of Education; University of Strathclyde. Teacher of English, Belmont Academy, Ayr, then Cumnock Academy; Principal Teacher of English, Doon Academy, Dalmellington; Lecturer, Senior Lecturer, Associate Head of School/Associate Dean, School of Education, Craigie College/University of Paisley (now University of the West of Scotland); Professional Officer, General Teaching Council Scotland. Recreation: golf. Address: (b.) General Teaching Council Scotland, Clerwood House, 96 Clermiston Road, Edinburgh EH12 6UT; T.-0131 314 6051; e-mail: tom.hamilton@gtcs.org.uk

Hamilton, Trisha. Communications Officer Scotland, UNISON Scotland. Address: (b.) UNISON House, 14 West Campbell Street, Glagow G2 6RX; T.-0141 342 2877; e-mail: t.hamilton@unison.co.uk

Hamilton, William Francis Forbes, BCom, CA, DL. Chairman, Macrae & Dick Ltd., since 1994; b. 19.4.40; m., Anne Davison MB.BS; 1 s. Educ. Inverness Royal Academy; Edinburgh University. McLay, McAlister & McGibbin, CA, Glasgow, 1961-68; Macrae & Dick Ltd.: Company Secretary, 1968-80, Finance Director, 1971-80, Managing Director, 1980-94; Chairman, Menzies BMW, since 1988; Member, BL Cars Distributor Council, 1977-78; Member, Highland Committee, Scottish Council Development and Industry, 1971-2006; Director, Highlands and Islands Airports Ltd., 1995-2001; Member, Highland Committee, Police Dependants' Trust, 1998-2004; Director: Highland Hospice, 1992-95, Highland Hospice Trading Co., 1995-2006, Fresson Trust; DL, since 2000, Vice Lord Lieutenant, since 2002. Recreations: sailing; travel. Address: Craigrory, North Kessock, Inverness IV1 3XH; T.-01463 668802.
E-mail: wfhamilton@macraeanddick.co.uk

Hammond, Charles. Chief Executive Officer, Forth Ports Limited. Address: (b.) Registered Office: 1 Prince of Wales Dock, Edinburgh EH6 7DX; T.-0131 555 8700.

Hampson, Christopher. Chief Executive/Artistic Director, Scottish Ballet, since 2015, Artistic Director, since 2012; b. 31.3.73. Educ. Royal Ballet School. English National Ballet (ENB), until 1999, created numerous award-winning works, including Double Concerto (Critics' Circle National Dance Award and TMA Theatre Award), Perpetuum Mobile, Country Garden, Concerto Grosso, Trapèze and The Nutcracker. Romeo and Juliet, created for the Royal New Zealand Ballet (RNZB), was nominated for a Laurence Olivier Award (Best New Production). Created Sinfonietta Giocosa for the Atlanta Ballet (USA) in 2006 and after a

New York tour it received its UK premiere with ENB in 2007; created Cinderella for RNZB in 2007, which was subsequently hailed as Best New Production by the New Zealand Herald and televised by TVNZ in 2009. Work has toured Australia, China, the USA and throughout Europe; most recent commissions are Dear Norman (Royal Ballet, 2009); Sextet (Ballet Black/ROH2, 2010); Silhouette (RNZB, 2010), Rite of Spring (Atlanta Ballet, 2011) and Storyville (Ballet Black/ROH2, 2012 and National Dance Award nominated). Co-founder of the International Ballet Masterclasses in Prague and has been a guest teacher for English National Ballet, Royal Swedish Ballet, Royal New Zealand Ballet, Hong Kong Ballet, Atlanta Ballet, Bonachela Dance Company, Matthew Bourne's New Adventures and the Genée International Ballet Competition; work now forms part of the Solo Seal Award for the Royal Academy of Dance. Address: Scottish Ballet, Tramway, 25 Albert Drive, Glasgow G41 2PE; T.-0141 331 2931.

Hancock, Professor Peter J. B., PhD, MSc, MA. Professor of Psychology, University of Stirling, since 2007; b. 1958, UK; m., Clare Allan; 2 s. Educ. Leighton Park School, Reading; Trinity College, Oxford. Synthetic chemist, computer programmer, systems manager, Amersham International plc, 1980-87; University of Stirling: Research Fellow, 1987-95, Lecturer, Psychology, 1995, Senior Lecturer, 2002. Recreation: photography. Address: (b.) Psychology, School of Natural Sciences, University of Stirling, Stirling FK9 4LA; T.-01786 467675; e-mail: p.j.b.hancock@stir.ac.uk

Hanlon, Professor Philip, BSc, MD, MRCGP, FRCP, FFPHM, MPH. Professor of Public Health, Glasgow University, since 1999; b. 24.6.54, British North Borneo; m., Lesley; 1 s.; 1 d. Educ. Uddingston Grammar School; Glasgow University. Research Scientist, Medical Research Council, The Gamba, 1984-87; Consultant in Public Health Medicine and Director of Health Promotion, Greater Glasgow Health Board, 1988-93; Medical Director, Royal Alexandra Hospital, Paisley, 1993-94; Senior Lecturer in Public Health, Glasgow University, since 1999; Director, Public Health Institute of Scotland, 2001-03. Recreations: cycling; walking; reading; spending time with family. Address: (b.) Public Health, University of Glasgow, 1 Lilybank Garden G12 8RZ. T.-0141 330 5641.
E-mail: phil.hanlon@glasgow.ac.uk

Hannaford, Professor Philip Christopher, MD, MBChB, FRCGP, FFPH, FFRSH, DRCOG, DCH. NHS Grampian Professor of Primary Care, since 1997; Vice Principal, Research and Knowledge Exchange, University of Aberdeen, 2011-14, Vice Principal (Digital Strategy) and Head of College of Life Sciences and Medicine, since 2014; Guardian, RCGP Oral Contraception Study, since 2001; Director, Institute of Applied Health Sciences, University of Aberdeen, 2002-2011; b. 1.7.58, London; m., Dr. Anne Carol Gilchrist; 1 s.; 1 d. Educ. Aberdeen Grammar School; Aberdeen University. GP training, Sheffield, 1982-85; research training posts, RCGP Manchester Research Unit, 1986-94; Principal, general practice, Manchester, 1986-92; Director, RCGP Manchester Research Unit, 1994-97. Publications: Evidence Guided Prescribing of the Pill (Co-editor); over 220 contributions on contraception, cardiovascular disease, primary care epidemiology, HRT in scientific journals. Recreations: family; walking; music. Address: (b.) Academic Primary Care, Polwarth Building, Foresterhill, Aberdeen AB25 2ZD; T.-01224 437211.

Hanson, Professor William Stewart, BA, PhD, FSA, FSA Scot. Professor of Roman Archaeology, Glasgow University, since 2000 (Head, Department of Archaeology, 1999-2005); b. 1950, Doncaster; m., Lesley Macinnes; 1 d. Educ. Gravesend Grammar School; Manchester University.

Glasgow University: Lecturer in Archaeology, 1975; Senior Lecturer in Archaeology, 1990-2000. Chairman: Scottish Field School of Archaeology, 1982-89, Scottish Archaeological Link, 1990-96; Council for British Archaeology: Member, Executive Committee, 1989-98, Vice-President, 1995-98; President, Council for Scottish Archaeology, 1989-96; Director, large-scale archaeological excavations at several sites in Scotland and northern England, including complete excavation of the Roman Fort at Elginhaugh, Dalkeith; recipient, Glenfiddich Living Scotland Award, 1987. Publications include: Agricola and the conquest of the north; Elginhaugh: a Flavian fort and its annexe; A Roman frontier fort in Scotland: Elginhaugh; Rome's north-west frontier: the Antonine Wall (Co-Author); Scottish archaeology: new perceptions; Roman Dacia: the making of a provincial society (Co-Editor); Archaeology from Historical Aerial and Satellite Archives (Co-Editor); The Army and Frontiers of Rome (Editor); numerous papers and articles. Recreations: tennis; film; karate. Address: (h.) 10 Royal Gardens, Stirling FK8 2RJ; T.-01786 465506.

Hardcastle, Professor Emeritus William John, BA, MA, PhD, Hon DSc, FBA, FRSE, Hon FRCSLT. Director, Speech Science Research Centre, 2004-09; Dean of Research, Queen Margaret University, 1999-2004; Professor of Speech Sciences, since 1993; Dean of Health Sciences, 1999-2002; b. 28.9.43, Brisbane; m., Francesca; 2 s.; 1 d. Educ. Brisbane Grammar School; University of Queensland; Edinburgh University. Lecturer, Institut für Phonetik, Universität Kiel, 1973-74; Lecturer, then Reader, then Professor, Department of Linguistic Science, Reading University, 1974-93; Director, Scottish Centre for Research into Speech Disability, 1997-2003. President, International Clinical Phonetics and Linguistics Association, 1991-2000; Convenor, Scottish Universities Research Policy Consortium, 2001. Publications include: Physiology of Speech Production; Disorders of Fluency and their Effects on Communication (Co-Author); Speech Production and Speech Modelling (Co-Editor); Handbook of Phonetic Sciences (Co-Editor); Co-articulation: Theory, Data and Techniques (Co-Editor). Recreations: hill-walking; badminton; gardening; golf. Address: (b.) Queen Margaret University, Queen Margaret University Drive, Musselburgh, East Lothian EH21 6UU; T.-0131-4740000.

Hardie, Rt. Hon The Lord (Andrew Rutherford Hardie), PC, QC (Scot); b. 8.1.46, Alloa; m., Catherine Storrar Elgin; 2 s.; 1 d. Educ. St. Modan's High School, Stirling; Edinburgh University. Enrolled Solicitor, 1971; Member, Faculty of Advocates, 1973; Advocate Depute, 1979-83; Dean, Faculty of Advocates, 1994-97; Lord Advocate, 1997-2000; created Life Peer and Privy Counsellor, 1997; Senator of the College of Justice, 2000-2012. Address: (b.) House of Lords, Westminster, London SW1A 0PW; e-mail: hardiera@parliament.uk

Hardie, David, LLB Hons, WS, NP. Non-Executive Director, Murray International Trust PLC, since 2014; Non-Executive Chairman: WN Lindsay Ltd, since 2014, Keppie Design, since 2015; b. 17.9.54, Glasgow; m., Fiona Mairi Willox; 3 s. Greenock High School; University of Dundee. Apprentice Solicitor, Dundas & Wilson, 1976-78, Solicitor, 1978-83, Head of former Corporate Department and latterly Head of Corporate Finance, 1987-97, Interim Managing Partner and Head of Corporate Finance, 1997-98, Head of Corporate, 1998-2004, Senior Corporate Partner, since 2003, Head of Knowledge & Learning, 2005-06, Chairman, 2009-12, Partner, 1983-2014. Notary Public; Member of The Society of Writers to Her Majesty's Signet; Head of

Venture Philanthropy at Inspiring Scotland (charity), since 2008. Address: Inspiring Scotland, Riverside House, 502 Gorgie Road, Edinburgh EH11 3AF; T.-0131 442 8760.
E-mail: davidh@inspiringscotland.org.uk

Hardie, Donald Graeme, CVO, KStJ, TD, JP, FIMMM. Director, Hardie Polymers Ltd., 1976-2001; b. 23.1.36, Glasgow; m. (1961) 1, Rosalind Allan Ker (divorced 1995); 2 s.; m. (1999) 2, Sheena McQueen. Educ. Blairmore and Merchiston Castle. Commissioned 41st Field Regiment RA, 1955; Battery Commander 277 (Argyll & Sutherland Highlanders) Regiment RA (TA), 1966; Commanding Officer GSVOTC, 1973; TA Col. Lowlands, 1976; TA Col. DES, 1980; TA Col. Scotland, 1985; ACF Brigadier Scotland, 1987; Hon. Colonel Commandant, Royal Regiment of Artillery, 2003-07 (retired); Vice President, NAA, since 2003. UTR Management Trainee, 1956-59; F.W. Allan & Ker, Shipbrokers, 1960-61; J. & G. Hardie & Co. Ltd., 1961-2001 (former Chairman); Director, Gilbert Plastics Ltd., 1973-76; Director, Ronaash Ltd., 1988-99; Director, Preston Associates (Europe) Ltd., 2002-04; Managing Director, Preston Stretchform Ltd., 2004-2011. Lord Lieutenant, Dunbartonshire, 1990-2007; Hon. Col. 105 Regiment RA(V), 1992-99; Hon. Col. Glasgow & Lanarkshire ACF, 1991-2000; Keeper, Dumbarton Castle, since 1996; Chairman, RA Council of Scotland, 1993-2000; former Chieftain, Loch Lomond Games (retired, 2009); former Trustee, Tullochan Trust (retired, 2011). Recreations: skiing; sailing; shooting; fishing. Address: (h.) East Lodge, Arden, Dunbartonshire G83 8RD; e-mail: donald.hardie@btopenworld.com

Hardie, Fraser. Partner, Blackadders Solicitors, since 2015; Consultant, Lindsays, 2013-2015; b. 4.4.59. Educ. Aberdeen University. Address: (b.) 5 Rutland Square, Edinburgh, Midlothian EH1 2AX; T.-0131 222 8000.

Hardie, William Dunbar, MBE, MA, BA, MUniv. Writer and Entertainer; b. 4.1.31, Aberdeen; m., Margaret Elizabeth Simpson; 1 s.; 1 d. Educ. Robert Gordon's College, Aberdeen; Aberdeen University; Sidney Sussex College, Cambridge. Administrative Assistant, then Assistant Secretary, NE Regional Hospital Board; District Administrator, North District, Grampian Health Board; Secretary, Grampian Health Board, 1976-83. Co-Writer and performer, Scotland The What? (comedy revue); Writer, Dod'n'Bunty column, Aberdeen Evening Express, 1983-2003; Awarded Freedom of the City of Aberdeen (along with Scotland the What? colleagues George Donald and Stephen Robertson), 2008. Recreations: reading; TV-watching; film and theatre-going; sport; avid and totally biased follower of Aberdeen's football team, Scotland's rugby team, and England's cricket team. Address: (h.) 50 Gray Street, Aberdeen AB10 6JE; T.-01224 310591; e-mail: hardie543@btinternet.com

Harding, Professor Dennis William, MA, DPhil, FRSE. Abercromby Professor of Archaeology, University of Edinburgh, 1977-2007; b. 11.4.40. Educ. Keble College, University of Oxford. Assistant Keeper, Department of Antiquities, Ashmolean Museum, University of Oxford, 1965; Lecturer in Celtic Archaeology, University of Durham, 1966 (Senior Lecturer, 1975); Dean, Faculty of Arts, 1983-86, Vice-Principal, 1988-91, University of Edinburgh. Member, S.A.A.S. Studentships Committee, 1982-2001 (Chairman, 1997-2001). Address: (h.) Hilltop Cottage, Hill Road, Gullane, East Lothian EH31 2BE.

Hargreave, Timothy Bruce, MB, MS, FRCSEdin, FRCS, FEB (Urol), FRCP(Ed). Senior Fellow, Department of

Surgery, University of Edinburgh, Medical School, Little France, Edinburgh; b. 23.3.44, Lytham; m., Molly; 2 d. Educ. Harrow; University College Hospital, London University. Senior Registrar: Western Infirmary, Glasgow, University College Hospital, London; Co-Chair, Technical Advisory Group on Devices and Innovations for Male Circumcision, Department of HIV, WHO Geneva; former Consultant Urologist and Renal Transplant Surgeon, Western General Hospital, Edinburgh; Medical Officer, Paray Mission Hospital, Lesotho; former Chair, Science and Ethics Review Group, Human Reproduction Programme, WHO Geneva. Publications: Diagnosis and Management of Renal and Urinary Disease; Male Infertility (Editor); Practical Urological Endoscopy; The Management of Male Infertility; Andrology for the Clinician (Joint Editor), English Edition, 2006, French Edition, 2008, Russian Edition, 2011. Recreation: skiing. Address: (h.) 20 Cumin Place, Edinburgh.

Harkess, Ronald Dobson, OBE, BSc, MS, PhD, NDA, CBiol, MRSB, FRAgS, FRSA, FFCS. Emeritus Fellow, Scottish Rural University College; Agricultural Scientist and Consultant; b. 11.7.33, Edinburgh; m., Jean Cuthbert Drennan (deceased); 2 d. Educ. Royal High School, Edinburgh; Edinburgh University; Cornell University. Senior Fison Research Fellow, Nottingham University, 1959-62; Assistant Grassland Adviser, West of Scotland Agricultural College, Ayr, 1962-72; Senior Agronomist, 1972-86; Technical Secretary, Council, Scottish Agricultural Colleges, 1986-90, Company Secretary, 1987-90; Company Secretary, Scottish Agricultural College, 1990-91; Assistant Principal, Scottish Agricultural College, 1991-93. Past President, Scotia Agricultural Club; Secretary, Perth Amateur Radio Group, since 1993; Past President, Tay Probus. Recreations: amateur radio; philately; gardening. Address: (h.) Friarton Bank, Rhynd Road, Perth PH2 8PT; T.-01738 643435.

Harkness, Very Rev. James, KCVO, CB, OBE, KStJ (2012), MA, DD, FRSA. Extra Chaplain to the Queen, since 2006; Dean of the Chapel Royal in Scotland, 1996-2006; Moderator, General Assembly of the Church of Scotland, 1995-96; Dean of the Order of St. John in Scotland, 2005-2011; President: Royal British Legion, Scotland, 2001-06, Earl Haig Fund Scotland, 2001-06, The Officers' Association, Scotland, 2001-06; Member, Board, Mercy Corps Scotland, 2001-09; b. 20.10.35, Thornhill; m., Elizabeth Anne; 1 s.; 1 d. Educ. Dumfries Academy; Edinburgh University. Assistant Minister, North Morningside Parish Church, 1959-61; Chaplain: KOSB, 1961-65, Queen's Own Highlanders, 1965-69; Singapore, 1969-70; Deputy Warden, RAChD, 1970-74; Senior Chaplain, Northern Ireland, 1974-75; 4th Division, 1975-78; Staff Chaplain, HQ BAOR, 1978-80; Assistant Chaplain General, Scotland, 1980-81; Senior Chaplain, 1st British Corps, 1981-82; BAOR, 1982-84; Deputy Chaplain General, 1985-86; Chaplain General to the Forces, 1987-95. QHC, 1982-95; General Trustee, Church of Scotland, 1996-2011; Chairman, Carberry Board, 1997-2000; Member, Committee on Chaplains to HM Forces, 1997-2005; Member, Board of World Mission, 1997-2000; President, Army Cadet Force Association Scotland, 1996-2004; President, Society of Friends of St. Andrew's, Jerusalem, 1998-2005. Hon. Chaplain to BLESMA, 1995-2002; Governor, Fettes College, 1999-2009; Trustee, Scottish National War Memorial, 2003-2015. Recreations: walking; reading; watching sport. Address: (h.) 13 Saxe-Coburg Place, Edinburgh EH3 5BR; T.-0131-343 1297.

Harlen, Professor Wynne, OBE, MA (Oxon), MA (Bristol), PhD. Director, Scottish Council for Research in Education, 1990-99; Visiting Professor: Liverpool University, 1990-99, University of Bristol, since 1999; Project Director, University of Cambridge, 2003-06; b. 12.1.37, Swindon; 1 s.; 1 d. Educ. Pate's Grammar School for Girls, Cheltenham; St. Hilda's College, Oxford; Bristol University. Teacher/Lecturer, 1958-66; Research Associate, Bristol University School of Education, 1966-73; Research Fellow, Project Director, Reading University, 1973-77; Research Fellow, Centre for Science Education, King's College, London, 1977-84; Sidney Jones Professor of Science Education, Liverpool University, 1985-90; Director, Scottish Council for Research in Education, 1990-99. Chair, Children in Scotland Early Years Forum, 1991-95; Member, Secretary of State's Working Party on the Development of the National Curriculum in Science, 1987-88; President, British Educational Research Association, 1993-94; Chair, OECD Science Expert Group, 1997-2003; Fellow, Educational Institute of Scotland, 2000; Fellow, Scottish Council for Research in Education, 2002; Member, Interacademies Working Group on IBSE, 2005-2012; Member, International Advisory Board of the global IAP Science Education Programme; President, Association for Science Education, 2009; Chair, Working Group of the Royal Society for SRN report on Science and mathematics Education 5-13. Awarded the OBE for services to education in 1991 and given a special award for distinguished service to science education by the (ASE) in 2001. In 2008 she was a winner of the international Purkwa prize for science education; honoured by the Mexican Ministry of Education in 2011. Publications: 43 books, and contributions to 54 others; 180 papers. Recreations: concerts; opera; bee-keeping. Address: Haymount Coach House, Bridgend, Duns, Berwickshire TD11 3DJ; T.-01361 884710.

Harley, Professor Simon Leigh, BSc (Hons), MA (Oxon), PhD, FRSE. Professor of Lower Crustal Processes, Edinburgh University, since 1997; b. 2.7.56, Sydney, Australia; m., Anne Elizabeth; 3 s.; 1 d. Educ. Punchbowl Boys' High School; University of New South Wales; University of Tasmania. Post-doctoral Research Assistant, ETH-Zentrum, Zurich, 1981-83; Lecturer: Oxford University/Fellow St Edmund Hall, 1983-88; Edinburgh University, 1988-92; Reader, Edinburgh University, 1992-97. Member: Sciennes School Board, 1992-96, Australian National Antarctic Research Expeditions (ANARE), 1979-80, 1982-83, 1987-88, 1992-93 and 2006-07; Polar Medal, 2002; Member, CoRWM, since 2007; Mineralogical Society Schlumberger Medal, 2015. Recreations: hill walking; skiing; cycling. Address: (h.) 15 Moston Terrace, Newington, Edinburgh EH9 2DE; T.-0131-650 4839; e-mail: Simon.Harley@ed.ac.uk

Harper, Emma. MSP (SNP), South Scotland region, since 2016; b. Stranraer. Former Clinical Nurse Educator, Dumfries and Galloway Royal Infirmary. SNP candidate for Dumfriesshire, Clydesdale & Tweeddale in the 2015 UK Parliament election. Address: Scottish Parliament, Edinburgh EH99 1SP.

Harper, Professor John, PhD, FRSC. Deputy Principal and Vice-Chancellor, Robert Gordon University, previously Assistant Principal/Dean of the Faculty of Health and Social Care; b. Wick; m; 4 c. Educ. University of Aberdeen. Career: Lecturer in Chemistry at the former Robert Gordon Institute of Technology and subsequently progressed to Senior-Lectureship and then Head of School of Applied Sciences; member of a number of national committees associated with institutional quality assurance, quality enhancement and widening participation; former member of the Health Professions Council; current member of the Board of Management of North East Scotland College and

School Council for St Margaret's School for Girls, Aberdeen. Recreations: enjoys following a range of sports with active participation now being restricted to playing golf! Address: (b.) Robert Gordon University, Garthdee Road, Aberdeen AB10 7QB.

Harper, Robin C. M., MA, DipGC, FRSA, FEIS, FRSSA. MSP, Lothians, 1999-2011; Co-Convener, Scottish Green Party, 2004-08; Chairman, Scottish Wildlife Trust, since 2014; b. 4.8.40, Thurso; m., Jenny Helen Carter Brown. Educ. St. Marylebone Grammar School; Elgin Academy; Aberdeen University. Teacher Braehead School, Fife, 1964-68; Education Officer, Kenya, 1968-70; Assistant Principal Teacher, Boroughmuir High School, 1972-99; Musical Director, Theatre Workshop, Edinburgh, 1972-75; President, Edinburgh Classical Guitar Society, 1980-90; Member, Lothian Children's Panel, 1985-88; Member, Lothian Health Council, 1993-97; President, EIS Edinburgh Local Association, 1990-91; elected Rector: University of Edinburgh, 2000-03, Aberdeen University, 2005-08; Patron, FTC Theatre; former Convener, CPG (Cross Party Group): Children and Young People, Architecture and the Built Environment, Renewable Energy and Energy Efficiency; Member, Petitions Committee; Elected Trustee, National Trust for Scotland, 2011; Elected Trustee, Scottish Wildlife Trust, 2011; Ambassador, Play Scotland, since 2011; Co-Patron, Edinburgh & Lothians Greenspace Trust, since 2011; Patron, Scottish Ecological Design Association, since 2011; Trustee, Dundee Students Association, 2012-14; Chair of Board of Trustees, Communicado Theatre Company, 2011-13; Patron: South Edinburgh Older People's Arts Festival, since 2012, Savoy Opera Theatre, since 2001, Forth Children's Theatre Company, since 1990. Recreations: music; walking; travel; theatre; growing oak trees. Address: Scottish Wildlife Trust, Harbourside House, 110 Commercial Street, Edinburgh EH6 6NF; T.-0131 312 7765.

Harries, Professor Jill Diana, MA, DPhil, FRSE (2010), FRHistS. Emeritus Professor of Ancient History, St Andrews University (Professor, 1997-2014, Head of School, Greek, Latin and Ancient History, 2000-03); b. 20.5.50, London. Educ. Bromley High School GPDST; Somerville College, Oxford. Kennedy Scholar, 1973-74; Lecturer in Ancient History, St Andrews University, 1976-95; Senior Lecturer, 1995-97; Visiting Fellow, All Souls College, Oxford, 1996-97; Leverhulme Fellow, 1996-97; Bird Exchange Fellow, Emory, Atlanta, 2003; Member of Council, St Leonard's School, St Andrews, 1998-2000. Publications: Religious Conflict in Fourth Century Rome, 1983; The Theodusian Code (Editor), 1993; Sidonius Apollinaris and the Fall of Rome, 1994; Law and Empire in Late Antiquity, 1998; Cicero and the Jurists, 2006; Law and Crime in the Roman World, 2007; Imperial Rome AD 284-363: The New Empire (2012). Recreations: travel; hillwalking. Address: (b.) School of Classics, St Salvator's College, St Andrews KY16 9AL; T.-01334 462600.

Harrington, Mhairi Jayne, MSc, PGEd. Principal and Chief Executive, West Lothian College, since 2008; b. 27.10.57, Glasgow; 1 d. Forrester Secondary School, Edinburgh; Callender Park College of Education; Strathclyde University; Open University. Career History: Primary School Teacher, Lothian Regional Council; Youth Worker, then Community Development Officer, Strathclyde Regional Council; West Lothian College: Lecturer of Social Care, Head of Social Care, Head of Community Studies, until 2001, Assistant Principal, 2001-08. Associate Assessor for HMIE (8 years); Board Member, Scotland's Learning Partnership. Recreations: walking; reading. Address: (b.) Almondvale Crescent, Livingston, West Lothian EH54 7EP; T.-01506 427802.
E-mail: mharrington@west-lothian.ac.uk

Harris, Alison. MSP (Scottish Conservative), Central Scotland region, since 2016; b. 23.7.65. Chartered accountant. Conservative candidate (Falkirk constituency) for the 2015 United Kingdom general election; Falkirk West constituency candidate for the 2016 Scottish Parliament election. Address: Scottish Parliament, Edinburgh EH99 1SP.

Harris, Rev. John William Forsyth, MA; b. 10.3.42, Hampshire; m., Ellen Lesley Kirkpatrick Lamont; 1 s.; 2 d. Educ. Merchant Taylors' School, London; St. Andrews University; New College, Edinburgh. Ordained Assistant, St. Mary's, Haddington, 1967-70; Minister: St. Andrew's, Irvine, 1970-77, St. Mary's, Motherwell, 1977-87, Bearsden South, 1987-2006, Bearsden Cross, 2006-2012. Convener: Scottish Churches' Christian Aid Committee, 1986-90, Scottish Christian Aid Committee, 1990-98, Scottish Television's Religious Advisory Committee, 1990-98, Jubilee Scotland, 2001-06, Scottish Palestinian Forum West of Scotland Committee, 2005-07; Vice-Convener, Board of World Mission, 1996-99; Member: Jubilee 2000 Scottish Coalition Steering Group, 1997-2000, Board of Christian Aid, 1990-98, Executive, Church and Nation Committee, 1985-91, Executive, Scottish Churches Council, 1986-90, Make Poverty History Scottish Coalition Steering Group, 2005. Moderator, Dumbarton Presbytery, 1994-95. Fencing Blue, St. Andrews and Edinburgh; Scottish Fencing Team, 1963-66; Scottish Sabre Champion, 1965. Recreations: enjoying grandchildren; Beardie walking and holiday home in Kintyre. Address: 68, Mitre Road, Jordanhill, Glasgow G14 9LL; T.-0141 321 1061; e-mail: jwfh@sky.com

Harris, Julie Elizabeth, LLB (Hons), DipLP, NP. Solicitor Advocate; b. 10.12.71, Farnborough, Kent. Educ. John Paul Academy, Glasgow; Strathclyde University. Joined Allan McDougall & Co, SSC, as trainee Solicitor, 1994; Qualified Solicitor, since 1996. Address: (b.) 3 Coates Crescent, Edinburgh EH3 7AL; T.-0131-225 2121.

Harris, Ray Richard, BSc (Hons), PhD, ARCS, FSS. Chair, Quality Committee, Scottish Credit & Qualifications Framework Partnership; b. 9.5.48, Carshalton, Surrey. Educ. Imperial College, London; Fitzwilliam College, Cambridge. Lecturer, Mathematical Statistics, Exeter University; Principal Lecturer, Applied Statistics, Sheffield City Polytechnic; Professor of Applied Statistics, University of Central Lancashire; Assistant Principal, Academic Development, University of Abertay Dundee; Depute Principal, Perth College; Principal, Stevenson College, Edinburgh; Principal & Chief Executive, Edinburgh's Telford College and Chief Executive, Scotland's Colleges. Recreations: modern literature and playing the guitar badly. Address: (b.) SCQFP, 39 St Vincent Place, Glasgow G1 2ER.

Harris, Stewart. Chief Executive, sportscotland, since 2005. Previously held positions at sportscotland as Acting Chief Executive and Director of Widening Opportunities (responsible for developing the School Sport Co-ordinator Programme and Active Schools Network, which is playing a key part in increasing physical activity levels of children in schools across Scotland); 12 years as a PE teacher. Lifelong involvement with basketball in Scotland as a board member, club and international coach for 25 years at both Scottish and Great Britain students level, as well as extensive experience of working with local authorities. Address: (b.) Doges, Templeton on the Green, 62 Templeton Street, Glasgow G40 1DA; T.-0141 534 6500.

Harris, Tom. Labour MP, Glasgow South, 2005-2015; Glasgow Cathcart, 2001-05; Shadow Minister for the

Environment, Food and Rural Affairs, 2012-13; b. 20.2.64, Irvine; m.; 3 s. Educ. Garnock Academy; Napier College. Reporter, East Kilbride News/Paisley Daily Express, 1986-90; Press Officer, Labour Party in Scotland, 1990-92; Press Officer, Strathclyde Regional Council, 1993-96; Senior Media Officer, Glasgow City Council, 1996; Public Relations Manager, East Ayrshire Council, 1996-98; Chief Public Relations Officer, SPTE, 1998-2001; Parliamentary Private Secretary to Rt. Hon. John Spellar MP, 2004-05; Parliamentary Private Secretary to Rt. Hon. Patricia Hewitt MP, 2005-06; Parliamentary Under Secretary of State for Transport, 2006-08. Recreations: tennis; astronomy; cinema; hill-walking.

Harrison, Professor Andrew, BA, MA, DPhil (Oxon), CChem, MRSC, FRSE. Professor of Solid State Chemistry, Edinburgh University, since 1999; b. 3.10.59, Oxford; m., Alison Ironside-Smith; 3 d. Educ. Newcastle-under-Lyme High School; St John's College, Oxford. Fereday Fellow, St John's College, Oxford, 1985-88; Research Fellow, McMaster University, Canada, 1988-89; Royal Society University Research Fellow, 1990-92; Reader, Department of Chemistry, Edinburgh University, 1996; Nuffield Research Fellow, 1997-98; Eminent Visiting Professor, Riken, Japan, 2000-2003; Director, Institut Laue-Langevin, Grenoble, Seconded from Edinburgh University, since 2006. Recreations: cycling on and off-road; skiing; music of almost every variety; eating and drinking. Address: (b.) Institut Laue-Langevin 6, Rue Jules Horowitz, BP-156-38042, Grenoble Cedex 9, France; T.-0033 47620 7100; e-mail: harrison@ill.eu

Harrison, Professor Bryan Desmond, CBE, BSc, PhD, Hon. DAgricFor, FRS, FRSE. Emeritus Professor of Plant Virology, Dundee University, since 1997 (Professor of Plant Virology, 1991-96); b. 16.6.31, Purley, Surrey; m., Elizabeth Ann Latham-Warde; 2 s.; 1 d. Educ. Whitgift School, Croydon; Reading University. Agricultural Research Council Postgraduate Research Student, 1952-54; Scientific Officer, Scottish Horticultural Research Institute, 1954-57; Senior and Principal Scientific Officer, Rothamsted Experimental Station, 1957-66; Scottish Horticultural Research Institute/Scottish Crop Research Institute: Principal Scientific Officer, 1966, Senior Principal Scientific Officer (Individual Merit), 1969, Deputy Chief Scientific Officer (Individual Merit), 1981; Head, Virology Department, 1966-91; Foreign Associate, US National Academy of Sciences; Honorary Professor, Department of Biochemistry and Microbiology, St. Andrews University, 1987-99; Honorary Research Fellow, The James Hutton Institute, since 1991; Honorary Visiting Professor, Dundee University, 1987-91; Honorary Visiting Professor, Zhejiang University, China, since 2001; Past President, Association of Applied Biologists; Honorary Member: Association of Applied Biologists, Phytopathological Society of Japan, Society for General Microbiology. Recreation: gardening. Address: (b.) The James Hutton Institute, Invergowrie, Dundee DD2 5DA; e-mail: BryanHarrison@Hutton.ac.uk

Harrison, Professor David James, BSc, MBChB, MD, FRCPath, FRCPE, FRCSE. Director of Laboratory Medicine, NHS Lothian, since 2009; John Reid Chair of Pathology, University of St Andrews, since 2012; Director, Edinburgh Breakthrough Breast Cancer Research Unit, 2007-2012; Director, University of Edinburgh Cancer Research Centre and Cancer Research UK Clinical Cancer Centre, 2005-08; Adjunct Professor of Medicinal Chemistry, University of Florida, Gainesville, 2003; Adjunct Professor of Pathology and Forensic Education, University of Canberra, 2004; b. 24.3.59, Belfast; m., Jane; 2 d. Educ. Campbell College, Belfast; Edinburgh University. House Surgeon to

Professor Sir Patrick Forrest, Royal Infirmary of Edinburgh, 1983-84, and House Physician to Professor J S Robson, 1984; University Department of Pathology, Edinburgh: Registrar and Senior House Officer, 1984-86, Lecturer, Honorary Registrar, 1986-87; Lecturer, Honorary Senior Lecturer, 1987-91, Senior Lecturer, 1991-97 and Honorary Consultant, Lothian University Hospitals Division, since 1991. Chairman of 1 healthcare charity. Address: (b.) Director's Office, Laboratory Medicine, Royal Infirmary of Edinburgh, 51 Little France Crescent, Edinburgh EH16 4SA.
E-mail: david.harrison@st-andrews.ac.uk

Hart, Rt. Rev. Monsignor Daniel J., PhL, STL, MA(Hons), Dip Ed. Retired Parish Priest, St. Helen's Langside, Glasgow (1984-2007); Domestic Prelate to His Holiness The Pope; b. 29.5.32, Shenfield. Educ. St. Patrick's High School, Dumbarton; Blairs College, Aberdeen; Pontifical Gregorian University, Rome; University of Glasgow. Principal Teacher of History, Blairs College, Aberdeen, 1961-69; Notre Dame College of Education, 1969-81: Lecturer in Religious Education, Lecturer, In-Service Department, Director, Postgraduate Secondary Course; Director, Papal Visit to Scotland, 1981-82; Director, Religious Education Centre, Archdiocese of Glasgow, 1981-83; Catholic Church Representative, Strathclyde Regional Education Committee, 1983-84; Chairman, Children's Panel Advisory Committee for Strathclyde, 1977-84 (Vice-Chairman, National Advisory Committee, 1977-84); Judge, Scottish Catholic Inter-Diocesan Tribunal, since 1989; Member, Archdiocese of Glasgow Finance Council, 1986-90; Vice-Chairman, Archdiocesan Council of Priests, 1982-84 and 1998-2005; Member, Board of Governors, St. Andrew's College of Education, 1991-99; Member, Merger Committee, St. Andrew's College of Education and University of Glasgow, 1997-99; Chairman, Glasgow Archdiocesan Pilgrimage Committee, 2003-2010. Recreations: golf; photography; swimming; travel. Address: 33 Sanderling View, 1 Barassie Street, Troon KA10 6LU.

Hart, John Francis, MA, LLB. Solicitor; b. 18.10.38, Clydebank; m., Winefride; 3 s. Educ. St Aloysius College; Glasgow University. Solicitor, since 1962; former Lecturer, Glasgow University. Board Member, Mainstay Trust Ltd. Recreations: golf; reading; opera. Address: (h.) 9A Crosbie Road, Troon KA10 6HE; T.-01292 311987.

Hart, Morag Mary, MBE, JP, DL, RGN, RSCN. Deputy Lieutenant, Dunbartonshire, since 1989; Director, Scotsell Ltd., 1982-2007; b. 19.4.39, Glasgow; m., Tom Hart; 1 d.; 1 s. Educ. Westbourne School for Girls, Glasgow. Sick Children's Hospital, Glasgow, 1956-59; Western General Hospital, Edinburgh, 1960-62. County Commissioner, Girlguiding Dunbartonshire, 1982-90; Chairman, Dunbartonshire Area Scout Council, 1994-2004; Member, The Guide Association Council for Scotland, 1982-2000. Justice of the Peace for East Dunbartonshire Commission Area, 1992-2009; President of Girlguiding Dunbartonshire, since 2009. Recreations: reading; gardening; walking. Address: (h.) 18 Campbell Drive, Bearsden, Glasgow G61 4NE; T.-0141-942 1216.

Hart, Professor Robert Albert, BA (Hons), MA, FRSE. Emeritus Professor, Stirling University, since 2014 (Professor of Economics, 1986-2014); b. 7.1.46, Hartlepool; m., Shirley; 3 d. Educ. Hartlepool Grammar School; Liverpool University. Economics Lecturer, Aberdeen University, 1969-73, Leeds University, 1974-75; Senior Lecturer, Strathclyde University, 1976-80; Senior Research Fellow, Science Centre, Berlin, 1980-86; Head, School of

Management, Stirling University, 1991-94. Recreations: walking; reading; drinking beer. Address: (b.) Department of Economics, Stirling University, Stirling FK9 4LA; T.-01786 467471; e-mail: r.a.hart@stir.ac.uk

Hart, Professor Susan Jane Ritchie, BA (Hons), PhD, DipMRS, FRSE. Professor of Marketing, Strathclyde University, since 1998, Associate Deputy Principal; b. 18.7.60, Edinburgh; 1 s.; 1 d. Educ. Bearsden Academy; Strathclyde University. Lecturer, Department of Marketing, Strathclyde University, 1987-92; Professor of Marketing, Heriot-Watt University, 1993-95; Professor of Marketing, Stirling University, 1995-98; Dean, Strathclyde Business School, 2008-2015; University of Strathclyde Executive Dean, Internationalisation, 2011-2015. Editor, Journal of Marketing Management, 2000-2010; Member, AACSB International Board of Directors; Fellow of the Royal Society of Edinburgh (RSE); Fellow of the Chartered Institute of Marketing; Fellow of the Leadership Trust; elected member of the International Board of Directors of AACSB; Board Member, Yorkhill Children's Charity, since 2012. Publications: Marketing Changes, 2003; New Product Development, 1996; Product Strategy and Management, 2007. Recreations: cycling; skiing. Address: (b.) University of Strathclyde, 199 Cathedral Street, Glasgow G4 0GE.

Hart, Thomas, MA, LLB. Editor, Scottish Transport Review, 1998-2004; President, Scottish Association for Public Transport, 2013-15; Lecturer, Department of Economic and Social History, Glasgow University, 1965-98; b. 15.11.39, Kilmarnock; m., Ellen Elizabeth Jones; 2 s. Educ. Spiers School, Beith; Glasgow University. Writer and Consultant on transport and environmental issues; Founder Member of Scottish Transport Studies Group (Secretary, 1984-94, Chair, 1994-2004); Founder Member, Scottish Railway Development Association (Secretary, 1962-67, Vice Chairman, 1967-72); Chairman, Scottish Association for Public Transport, 1972-76; Member, Board, TRANS*form* Scotland, 1997-2011; Member, SPT (Strathclyde Partnership for Transport), since 2006. Publication: Chapters on 'Surface Transport for the 20th Century in Transport and Communications' in K. Veitch (Editor), Vol. 8, Scottish Life and Society, December, 2009; 50 Years of Scottish Transport Campaigns - From Beeching to High Speed Rail, 1962-2012, 2012 (Co-Author). Recreations: walking; travel; gardening. Address: (h.) Birchfield, 81A Kings Road, Beith, Ayrshire KA15 2BN; T.-01505 502164; e-mail: thstsg@btinternet.com

Harte, Professor Ben, BA, MA, PhD (Cantab), FRSE. Professor Emeritus and Senior Honorary Professorial Fellow, University of Edinburgh; b. 30.5.41, Blackpool; m., Angela Elizabeth; 1 s.; 2 d. Educ. Salford Grammar School; Trinity College, Cambridge University. Lecturer/Reader, Edinburgh University, 1965-91; Professor, University of Edinburgh, 1992-2007; Guest Research Investigator, Carnegie Institution of Washington, 1974-75; Visiting Associate Professor, Yale University, 1982; Visiting Research Fellow, University of Cape Town, 1990; JSPS Research Fellow, Ehime University, Japan, 1999; President of the Mineralogical Society of Great Britain and Ireland, 2006-08. Address: (b.) School of GeoSciences, Grant Institute, King's Buildings, Edinburgh EH9 3JW; T.-0131-651 7220; e-mail: ben.harte@ed.ac.uk

Harte, Chris. Chief Executive, Morton Fraser, since 2013 (Partner, since 1999). Member of Morton Fraser's managing board, since 2005, joined as a trainee in 1994. Address: Morton Fraser, Quartermile Two, 2 Lister Square, Edinburgh EH3 9GL; T.-0131 247 1000.

Hartley, Keith Scott, BA, MA. Deputy Director, Scottish National Gallery of Modern Art; b. 27.1.49, Evesham. Educ. Prince Henry's Grammar School, Evesham; St. Catherine's College, University of Oxford; Courtauld Institute, University of London; Freie Universität, W. Berlin. Curator of numerous exhibitions, and author of corresponding catalogues, including: Scottish Art Since 1900, 1989; Otto Dix, Tate Gallery, 1992; The Romantic Spirit in German Art 1790-1990, 1994; Andy Warhol, 2007; Douglas Gordon; Gerhard Richter, 2008; Peter Doig, 2013. Recreations: travel; reading. Address: (b.) Scottish National Gallery of Modern Art, Belford Road, Edinburgh EH4 3DR; T.-0131-624 6251.

Harvey, Professor Alan L., BSc, PhD, MBA, CBiol, FIBiol. Emeritus Professor in Pharmacology, University of Strathclyde; Director, Strathclyde Innovations in Drug Research, 1988-2010; b. 23.6.50, Glasgow. Educ. Hutchesons', Glasgow; Strathclyde University. Lecturer in Physiology and Pharmacology, Strathclyde University, 1974-83; Senior Lecturer, 1983-86. British Pharmacological Society Sandoz Prize, 1983; Redi Award, International Society on Toxicology, 2000; British Pharmaceutical Conference Science Award, 1983. Publications: Toxicon (Editor); Advances in Drug Discovery Techniques, 1998; Natural Product Pharmaceuticals, 2001. Address: (b.) Institute of Pharmacy and Biomedical Sciences, Strathclyde University, Glasgow G4 0NR; T.-0141-553 4155.

Harvey, Liam. Headmaster, St. Mary's School, Melrose. Address: (b.) St. Mary's School, Abbey Park, Melrose TD6 9LN; T.-01896 822517. E-mail: office@stmarysmelrose.org.uk

Harvey, Rev. William John, BA (Hons), BD (Hons). Moderator, Glasgow Presbytery, 1998-99; b. 17.5.37, Glasgow; m., Isabel Mary Douglas; 2 s.; 2 d. Educ. Fettes College, Edinburgh; Oxford University; Glasgow University. National Service, Argyll & Sutherland Highlanders, 1956-58; Ordained Assistant, Govan Old Parish Church, 1964-66; Member, Gorbals Group Ministry, 1963-71; Minister, Laurieston-Renwick Parish Church, Glasgow, 1968-71; Warden, Iona Abbey, 1971-76; Minister: Raploch Parish Church, Stirling, 1976-81, Govan Old Parish Church, 1981-88; Leader, The Iona Community, 1988-95. Member, Church of Scotland Committee on Church and Nation, 1978-86; Kerr Lecturer, Glasgow University, 1987; Team Member, The Craighead Institute of Life and Faith, Glasgow, 1995-2000; Interim Minister, Board of Ministry, The Church of Scotland, 2000-03. Honorary Doctorate of Divinity, Glasgow University, 2012. Recreations: reading; history; bread and wine-making; sea-bird watching. Address: (h.) 501 Shields Road, Glasgow G41 2RF; T.-0141-429 3774. E-mail: jonmol@phonecoop.coop

Harvie, Professor Christopher Thomas, MA Hons (Edin), PhD (Edin). MSP (SNP), Mid Scotland and Fife, 2007-2011; Professor (Hon.) of History, Strathclyde, since 1995; b. 21.9.44, Motherwell; m., Virginia Roundell (deceased); 1 d. Educ. St. Boswells Primary School; Kelso High School; Royal High School, Edinburgh; Edinburgh University. Tutor, Edinburgh University, 1966-69; Lecturer/Senior Lecturer in History, Open University, 1969-80; appointed Professor of British Studies, Eberhard-Karls Universitaet, Tuebingen in 1980; Visiting Fellow, Merton and Nuffield Colleges, Oxford, Strathclyde and Edinburgh; Hon. Professor: Strathclyde University, since 1999, Aberystwyth, since 1996. Founder, Freudenstadt Colloquium, 1991; Co-Chair, Baden-Wuerttemberg Colloquium, 1996; Hon. President, Scottish Association for Public Transport, since 2002. Candidate (SNP) for Kirkcaldy (Scottish Parliament), 2007. 'Free Spirit of the Year' in Herald's Scottish Political Awards, 2008. Publications: The Lights of Liberalism, 1860-86, 1976; Scotland and Nationalism, 1976, 4 eds by 2004; No

Gods and Precious Few Heroes, 4 eds by 2000; The Centre of Things: British Political Fiction, 1991; Cultural Weapons: Scotland and Europe, 1992; The Rise of Regional Europe, 1993, 2nd ed. 2006; The Road to Home Rule (Co-Author), 1999; Travelling Scot, 1999; Scotland: a Short History, 2002; Scotland's Transport, 2001; Mending Scotland, 2004; A Floating Commonwealth: Politics, Technology and Culture on the West Coast, 1860-1930, 2008; Broonland, 2010; Scotland the Brief, 2010; International Men: Liberals in European Politics, 2010; essays; articles; reviews. Recreations: any human activity except sport (but principally painting, music, travel).
Websites: www.uni-tuebingen.de/intelligent-mr-toad/ and www.chrisharvie.co.uk

Harvie, Patrick. MSP (Green), Glasgow, since 2003; co-convenor of the Scottish Green Party; b. 18.3.73. Educ. Dumbarton Academy; Manchester Metropolitan University. Address: (b.) Scottish Parliament, Edinburgh EH99 1SP; T.-0131 348 6363.

Haslam, Shona, MA (PolStud). Programme Manager, Peeblesshire Youth Trust, since 2015; National Director, Asthma UK Scotland, 2007-2015; b. 6.9.74, Kirkcaldy, Fife; m., Marc Haslam; 2 s. Educ. Peebles High School; Aberdeen University. Parliamentary Officer, Evangelical Alliance, 1996-2003; Public Affairs Manager, Asthma UK Scotland, 2003-07. Recreations: walking; family; church; cooking. Address: (b.) Peeblesshire Youth Trust, Rowan Court, Cavalry Park, Peebles EH45 9BU; T.-07957 383 663.

Hassan, Gerry, MA (Hons). Writer, commentator, researcher and policy analyst; b. 21.3.64, Dundee; m. Rosemary Catherine Ilett. Educ. Rockwell High School, Dundee; Glasgow University; University of the West of Scotland. Previously Director of Scottish think tank and held various senior posts in the voluntary sector and business organisations. Senior Research Fellow, Demos; Honorary Fellow, Glasgow Caledonian University; Associate Editor, Renewal. Organiser, Changin Scotland: weekends of politics, culture and ideas at The Ceilidh Place, since 2002. Facilitator, event organiser and campaigner. Publications: A Guide to the Scottish Parliament (Editor), 1999; A Different Future: A Moderniser's Guide to Scotland (Co-Editor), 1999; The New Scottish Politics (Co-Editor), 2000; The Almanac of Scottish Politics (Co-Author), 2001; Tomorrow's Scotland (Co-Editor), 2002; Anatomy of the New Scotland (Co-Editor), 2002; Staying Human: Respect, Values and Social Justice (Co-Author), 2003; The Scottish Labour Party: History, Institutions and Ideas (Editor), 2004; The Political Guide to Modern Scotland (Co-Author), 2004; Scotland 2020: Hopeful Stories for a Northern Nation (Co-Editor), 2005; After Blair: Politics after the New Labour Decade (Editor), 2006; The Dreaming City: Glasgow 2020 and the Power of Mass Imagination (Co-Author), 2007; The Modern SNP: From Protest to Power (Editor), 2009; Radical Scotland: Arguments for Self-Determination (Co-Editor), 2011; Imagination: Stories of Scotland's Future (Co-Editor), 2011; The Strange Death of Labour Scotland (Co-Author), 2012. Recreations: listening and collecting music; Frank Sinatra; watching non-SPL football. Website: www.gerryhassan.com
E-mail: gerry.hassan@virgin.net

Hastings, Gavin, OBE, DUniv (Paisley). Former rugby player; b. 1962, Edinburgh. Educ. George Watson's College, Edinburgh; Paisley University; Cambridge University. 61 Scotland Caps, 1986-95 (20 as Captain); 3 World Cups, 1987, 1991, 1995; 2 British Lions Tours: 1989, Australia, 3 Tests, 1993, New Zealand (Captain), 3 Tests.

Haughey, Clare. MSP (SNP), Rutherglen, since 2016. Former Clinical Nurse Manager with the Perinatal Mental Health Service and specialised in working with mothers who are pregnant or have a baby under one; active trade unionist and a divisional convenor in UNISON; former Trustee of Maternal Mental Health Scotland, a mental health charity. Joined the SNP in 2015 and acted as a team leader during the General Election; social convenor on the SNP's executive committee, since 2016. Address: Scottish Parliament, Edinburgh EH99 1SP.
E-mail: clareforrutherglen@gmail.com

Haughey of Hutchesontown, Baron (William Haughey), OBE (2003). Ex-Chairman, Scottish Enterprise Glasgow; Joint Owner and Executive Chairman, City Refrigeration Holdings (UK) Ltd, since 1985; Non-Executive Director, Dunedin Enterprise (no longer part of Dunedin); b. 2.7.56, Glasgow; m., Susan nee Moore; 1 s. Educ. Holyrood Senior Secondary School, Glasgow; Springburn College, Glasgow. Engineering Supervisor, Turner Refrigeration Ltd, 1973-83; Head of Engineering, UAE UTS Carrier, 1983-85; Charter Member, Duke of Edinburgh Awards Scheme; Member, Growth Fund Panel, Prince's Scottish Youth Business Trust; Patron, CSV; Entrepreneur of the Year, Entrepreneurial Exchange, 2000 (finalist 1999); Business to Business section and Masterclass winner, Ernst & Young Awards, 2000; Refrigeration Industry Business of the Year, 2000; Lanarkshire Business of the Year, 2002; Business Man of the Year, Award Insider Publications, 2003; Bighearted Business Person of the Year, 2004; Excellence in Public Service Award, 2004; Business Award, Great Scot 2005 Awards, Sunday Mail, 2005; Loving Cup from Lord Provost of Glasgow for charity work, 2001; Hon DTech, Glasgow Caledonian University. 2005; St Mungo Medal (awarded to the citizen of Glasgow who has worked tirelessly to promote and enhance the wellbeing of its less fortunate citizens, and at the same time adding to the reputation of Glasgow the Caring City), December 2006. Recreations: golf; reading; football. Address: (b.) City Refrigeration Holdings (UK) Ltd, 17 Lawmoor Street, Glasgow G5 0US; T.-0141-418 9117.
E-mail: willie.haughey@city-holdings.co.uk

Hawkins, Anthony Donald, CBE, BSc, PhD, FSA Scot, FRSE. Director, Loughine Ltd; Associate Professor, Environmental Research Institute; Director, Fisheries Research for Scotland, 1987-2002; Honorary Professor, Aberdeen University; b. 25.3.42, Dorset; m., Susan Mary; 1 s. Educ. Poole Grammar School; Bristol University. Entered Scottish Office as Scientific Officer, Marine Laboratory, Aberdeen, 1965; Senior Scientific Officer, 1969, Principal Scientific Officer, 1972, Senior Principal Scientific Officer, 1978, Deputy Chief Scientific Officer, 1983; Deputy Director of Fisheries Research for Scotland, 1983; conducts research into behaviour and physiology of fish; awarded A.B. Wood Medal, Institute of Acoustics, 1978; Chairman, North Sea Commission Fisheries Partnership; a Director of the newly formed Aquatic Noise Trust. Publications: books on fish physiology, effects of underwater sound on aquatic life, and aquarium systems. Recreations: reading; angling; soccer; breeding whippets. Address: Kincraig, Blairs, Aberdeen; T.-01224 868984.
E-mail: a.hawkins@btconnect.com

Hawkins, Nigel. Founder and former Chief Executive, John Muir Trust; b. 12.9.46, Dundee. Educ. Madras College, St Andrews. Founder, John Muir Trust, 1982

(Trustee, 1984-96, Director (CEO), 1996-2009); Creator, Dundee City of Discovery Campaign, 1985; Chairman, Prospect PR Ltd., 1985-2006; Co-Founder, The Knoydart Foundation, 1983 (Director, 1998-2003); Director, North Harris Trust, 2003-08; Director, Assynt Foundation, 2005-08; Deputy Chairman and Director, Dundee Science Centre Trust, 1998-2004; Director, Sensation Ltd., 1999-2004; Trustee, Dundee Science Centre Endowment Fund, since 2005; Univ. of Abertay Dundee: Fellow, 1998, Member, Court, 1999-2012, Deputy Chairman, Court, 2006-09, Chairman of Court, 2009-2012; President, Dundee and Tayside Chamber of Commerce and Industry, 1997-98; Board Member, North of Scotland Water Authority, 1998-2002. Recreations: mountaineering; cycling; running; good food; Italy. Address: (b.) 1 Auchterhouse Park, Auchterhouse, by Dundee DD3 0QU; T.-01382 320252; e-mail: nigelrobinhawkins@btinternet.com

Hawkins, Paul, MBA. Chief Executive, NHS Fife, since 2015. Educ. Ashridge Business School. Career: Director of Operations (Planned Care), Barnet and Chase Farm Hospitals NHS Trust; Chief Operating Officer, Hywel Dda University Health Board, Wales. Address: NHS Fife, Hayfield Road, Kirkcaldy, Fife KY2 5AH.

Hawley, Dr Graham. Headmaster, Loretto School, since 2014; m., Rachel; 2 c. Educ. Mill Hill School; Durham University. Worked for the National Rivers Authority in Exeter; moved to Scotland and investigated the water quality of the major lochs along the west coast; returned to Devon to complete a Postgraduate Certificate in Education; Assistant Master, Ardingly College, West Sussex, 1996-2000, Housemaster, 2000-04; Deputy Headmaster, Warwick School, 2004-08; Headmaster, Kelly College, Devon, 2008-2014. Recreations: golf; walking; occasional fly-fishing. Address: Loretto School, Linkfield Road, Musselburgh, East Lothian EH21 7RE; T.-0131 653 4444.

Hawthorn, Patricia. Chairman, Scottish Renewables, since 2015; Partner, Shepherd and Wedderburn, since 2007. Working on consenting wind farms both on and offshore in Scotland and offshore in UK waters. Member of RenewableUK's consents and licensing group. Address: Scottish Renewables, 6th Floor, 46 Bath Street, Glasgow G2 1HG; T.-0141 353 4980.

Hay, Alasdair George, QFSM. Chief Officer, Scottish Fire and Rescue Service, since 2013; b. 24.12.61, Edinburgh. Educ. University of Abertay Dundee; Dundee College. Firefighter with Essex County Fire and Rescue Service, 1983-92; senior instructor at the Scottish Fire Services College, 1992-94; joined Tayside Fire and Rescue in 1994, achieved the rank of Deputy Chief Fire Officer by 2009; seconded to the Scottish Fire and Rescue Services Advisory Unit, 2011-12; Acting Chief Fire Officer, Tayside Fire and Rescue, 2012-13. Recipient of the Queen Elizabeth II Golden Jubilee Medal, the Queen Elizabeth II Diamond Jubilee Medal and the Fire Brigade Long Service and Good Conduct Medal. Address: Scottish Fire and Rescue Service Headquarters, Westburn Drive, Cambuslang G72 1AA; T.-0141 646 4501.

Hay, Ken. Chief Executive, Centre for the Moving Image, since 2011. Chief Executive, EM Media, Nottingham, 2001-05; Chief Executive, Scottish Screen, 2005-2011. Address: (b.) Centre for the Moving Image, 88 Lothian Road, Edinburgh EH3 9BZ; T.-0131 228 6382.

Hay, Robert King Miller, BSc, MSc, PhD, FRSB, FSA Scot. Writer and Editor; Archivist, Lismore Museum; Visiting Professor, Swedish University of Agricultural Sciences, Uppsala, 2005-07; Director, Scottish Agricultural Science Agency, 1990-2004; Honorary Fellow of SAC (Scottish Agricultural College), since 2004; b. 19.8.46, Edinburgh; m., Dorothea Harden Vinycomb; 2 s.; 1 d. Educ. Forres Academy, Moray; Aberdeen University; University of East Anglia. AFRC Research Fellow, Edinburgh University, 1971-74; Lecturer in Crop Production: University of Malawi, 1974-76, Edinburgh University, 1976-77; Lecturer in Environmental Sciences, Lancaster University, 1977-82; Leverhulme European Fellow, Agricultural University of Norway, 1981; Head of Plant Sciences, Scottish Agricultural College, Ayr, 1982-90; British Council Research Fellow, University of Western Australia, 1989; Visiting Scientist, McGill University, Montreal, 1997. Publications: Environmental Physiology of Plants, 1981, 1987, 2002; Chemistry for Agriculture and Ecology; The Physiology of Crop Yield, 1989, 2006; Volatile Oil Crops (Ed); Science Policies in Europe: Unity and Diversity (Ed); Lochnavando No More: The Life and Death of a Moray Farming Community, 1750-1850; Lismore: The Great Garden; How an Island Lost its People; contributions to the Compendium of Scottish Ethnology and the Review of Scottish Culture; Annals of Botany (Editor), 1995-2006; 60 scientific papers. Recreations: walking; museum curating; community singing. Address: (h.) Park Steading, Isle of Lismore, Oban PA34 5UN; T.-01631 760 393.
E-mail: dot.bob@btopenworld.com

Haydon, Professor Daniel Thomas, BSc, PhD. Professor of Population Ecology and Epidemiology, University of Glasgow, since 2007; b. 10.06.65, Cambridge; m., Dr. Barbara Mable (common-law). Educ. Perse School, Cambridge; University of Southampton; University of Texas at Austin. Post-doctoral research assistant at University of Oxford, 1992-96, University of British Columbia, 1996-98, University of Edinburgh, 1998-2001, University of Guelph, 2001-04; Lecturer, University of Glasgow, 2004-07. Scientific Medal (Zoological Society of London, 2005); British Lichen Society. Recreations: mountaineering; hill-walking; photography. Address: (b.) Graham Kerr Building, University of Glasgow, Glasgow G12 8QQ; T.-0141 330 6637; e-mail: d.haydon@bio.gla.ac.uk

Haywood, Brent William, LLB, BA, Dip Forensic Medicine. Solicitor Advocate and Mediator, Partner in Lindsay Solicitors; b. 14.8.65, Riverton, New Zealand; m., Heather; 2 sons, Gregor and Jonty. Educ. Southland Boys' High School, New Zealand; Otago University, Dunedin, New Zealand. Writer to Her Majesty's Signet (W.S.); Chair of Business Matters; Director, The Signet Accreditation Limited. Recreations: ultra distance running; straplining; cycling; kayaking; ukulele; member of Jelly Appreciation Society and Keeper of Gallus gallus domesticus. Address: (b.) Caledonian Exchange, 19A Canning Street, Edinburgh EH3 8HE; e-mail: brenthaywood@lindsays.co.uk

Hazel, Dr George McLean, OBE, BSc, MSc, PhD, CEng, MICE, FCIT, FIHT. Director, George Hazel Consultancy Ltd; Chairman, MRC McLean Hazel, 2005-2012, McLean Hazel Ltd., 2001-05; b. 27.1.49, Dunfermline; m., Fiona Isabella Gault; 1 s.; 2 d. Educ. Dunfermline High School; Heriot-Watt University; Cranfield Institute of Technology. Transportation Engineer: City of Edinburgh Corporation, 5 years, Lothian Regional Council, 4 years; Lecturer, Senior Lecturer, Head of Dept., and first Professor of Transport in Scotland, Napier College/Polytechnic/University, 11 years; Director, Oscar Faber TPA, three years; Director of Transportation, Lothian Regional Council, three years; Director of City Development, City of Edinburgh Council, 1996-99. Member, Secretary of State for Scotland's Advisory Group on Sustainable Development; Chair, Urban

Design Alliance, 2004/06; Member, Secretary of State's Steering (2004) Group on National Road User Charging; Advisor to the Commission for Integrated Transport, Lorry Road User Charging Committee of Transport, 2000; Chairman, Edinburgh and East of Scotland Association, Institution of Civil Engineers; President, Institution of Highways and Transportation, 2003-04; International Advisor to the Queensland State Government, Australia; Adjunct Professor, Queensland University of Technology, Brisbane; Chair, Advisory Board, Transport Research Institute, Edinburgh Napier University, since 2011; Awarded Officer of the British Empire (OBE) for services to transport, 2006. Publication: "Making Cities Work" (Author), 2004. Recreations: golf; gardening; travel; music; vintage cars. Address: (h.) 30/3 Easter Steil, Edinburgh EH10 5XE; e-mail: george@georgehazel.com

Hearne, John Michael, BMus, MMus, DMus. Publisher (Longship Music); Freelance Composer; Conductor and Copyist; b. 19.9.37, Reading; m., Margaret Gillespie Jarvie. Educ. Torquay Grammar School; St. Luke's College, Exeter; University College of Wales, Aberystwyth. Teaching, Rugeley, Staffordshire, 1959-60; Warehouseman/ Driver, Torquay, 1961-64; Teaching: Tonlistarskoli Borgarfjardar, Iceland, 1968-69, UCW Aberystwyth, 1969-70; Lecturer, Aberdeen College of Education, 1970-87. Composer, vocal, instrumental and incidental music: BBC commission for BBCSSO, 1990 (trumpet concerto); McEwen Commission, Glasgow University, 1979; A Legend of Margaret, commissioned to celebrate 150th anniversary of St. Margaret's School, Aberdeen, 1996; Into Uncharted Seas, commissioned to commemorate centenary of launch of Discovery on Antarctic expedition; The Ben – a Cantata for Bennachie, commissioned by Gordon Forum for the Arts, 2001; Member, John Currie Singers, 1973-2003; Awarded Radio Forth Trophy, 1985, for most outstanding work on Edinburgh Festival Fringe; joint winner, Gregynog Composers' Award for Wales, 1992. Chorus Manager, Aberdeen International Youth Festival, since 1978; Chairman: Scottish Music Advisory Committee, BBC, 1986-90, Gordon Forum for the Arts, 1991-94; Conductor, Stonehaven and District Choral Society; Past Chairman, Scottish Society of Composers; former Member, Board, National Youth Choir of Scotland; Winner, Gregynog Composers' Award for Wales, 1998; Conductor, Inverurie Choral Society, 1998-2003; Warden, Performers and Composers Section, Incorporated Society of Musicians, 1999; former Member, Board, Enterprise Music Scotland (-2011); Member, Management Committee, Aberdeen "Sound" Festival; Winner, Caledonian Hilton Audience Prize, Waverley Care carol competition, 2010. Recreations: motoring and travel (1954 Daimler Roadster, 1991 SAAB 900 Aero). Address: (h.) Smidskot, Fawells, Keith-Hall, Inverurie AB51 OLN; T.-01651 882 274; website: www.impulse-music.co.uk/hearne.htm

Hecht, George. Honorary Chairman, Jewish Care Scotland, since 2013. Owner, 2gether group, since 2007; Director & Shareholder, George Hecht & Associates Ltd, since 2009. Address: (b.) The Walton Community Care Centre, May Terrace, Giffnock G46 6LD; T.-0141 620 1800; e-mail: admin@jcarescott.org.uk

Hedderwick, Mairi Crawford, DA (Edin). Illustrator, Writer and Public Speaker; b. 2.5.39, Gourock; 1 s.; 1 d. Educ. St. Columba's School, Kilmacolm; Edinburgh College of Art; Jordanhill College of Education. Publications: for children: Katie Morag series, A Walk with Grannie; The Utterly Otterleys; for adults: An Eye on the Hebrides, Highland Journey; Sea Change; Shetland Rambles; The Last Laird of Coll. Hon. Doctorate, Stirling University. Recreations: a day outside ending round a table with friends, food and wine.

Heddle, Steven, BSc, PhD. Convener, Orkney Islands Council, since 2012; represents Kirkwall East ward; b.

Kirkwall; m.; 1 s. Educ. Aberdeen and Edinburgh Universities. Career: worked in R&D and engineering; former IT specialist with Highlands and Islands Enterprise (HIE); previously chair of the authority's education committee; runs a business and technical consultancy, often working with HIE Orkney. Recreations: listening to music; keen football supporter; badminton; sailing; cycling. Address: (b.) Newington, Holm Road, Kirkwall KW15 1PY; T.-01856 877119.

Heenan, Rev. William. BA, MTh. Minister, St Columba's Old Parish Church, Stornoway, since 2012. Address: Stornoway, Na h-Eileanan an Iar; T.-01851 700820.

Heggie, Dr Douglas Cameron, MA, PhD, FRAS, FRSE; b. 7.2.47, Edinburgh; m., Linda Jane Tennent; 2 d. Educ. George Heriot's School, Edinburgh; Trinity College, Cambridge. Research Fellow, Trinity College, Cambridge, 1972-76; Lecturer in Mathematics, Edinburgh University, 1975-85, Reader, 1985-94, Professor of Mathematical Astronomy, 1994-2012, Professor Emeritus, since 2012. Council Member, Royal Astronomical Society, 1982-85; President, Commission 37, International Astronomical Union, 1985-88; Member, Board of Editors, Monthly Notices of the RAS, since 1994. Publications: Megalithic Science; The Gravitational Million-Body Problem; scientific papers on dynamical astronomy. Recreations: family life; walking; music. Address: (b.) Edinburgh University, School of Mathematics, King's Buildings, Edinburgh EH9 3FD; T.-0131 650 5904. E-mail: d.c.heggie@ed.ac.uk

Heller, Martin Fuller Vernon, FRSAMD. Actor, since 1947; Artistic Director, Prime Productions; b. 20.2.27, Manchester; m., Joyce Allan; 2 s.; 4 d. Educ. Rondebosch Boys High School, Cape Town; Central School of Speech Training and Dramatic Art, London. Compass Players, 1948-52; repertory seasons and/or individual productions at following Scottish theatres: St. Andrews Byre, Edinburgh Gateway, Glasgow Citizens' (eight seasons), Edinburgh Royal Lyceum, Edinburgh Traverse, Dundee Repertory, Perth Repertory, Pitlochry Festival; Founder/Artistic Director, Prime Productions, 1985-2014; extensive television and radio work; Member: Scottish Arts Council, 1975-82 (latterly Chairman, Drama Committee); Governor, Pitlochry Festival Theatre (retired 2005); Governor, Royal Scottish Academy of Music and Drama, 1982-94. Recreations: politics; history; listening to music. Address: (h.) 54 Hermiston Village, Currie, Midlothian EH14 4AQ; T.-0131-449 4055.

Hemphill, Greg. Actor, comedian and movie producer (best known for appearances in Still Game and Chewin' the Fat); b. 14.12.69, Glasgow; m., Julie Wilson Nimmo; 2 s. Educ. University of Glasgow. Rector, University of Glasgow, 2001-04.

Henderson, Dr. Callum. Honorary Consul of Rwanda to Scotland, since 2013; Director, Comfort Rwanda, since 1999. Educ. High School of Dundee; University of Edinburgh. Pastor, Elim Pentecostal Church, 1990-98; Leader, Free for Life, 2002-03; Manager of youth homeless units, Bethany Christian Trust, 2003-06; Chair, Rwanda Scotland Alliance, 2009-2013. Publication: Beauty From Ashes, 2007. Address: 82 Arden Grove, Kilsyth, North Lanarkshire G65 9NU; T.-01236 827251; e-mail: callum@comfortrwanda.org.uk

Henderson, Donald Cameron. Head of Scottish Government Children's Rights and Wellbeing Division, since 2015; b. 1961, Shropshire; m., Catherine Louise Fox; 1 s.; 1 d. Educ. Lenzie Academy. Scottish Office, 1981-1999; seconded to FCO, 1984-85; MAFF, 1992-93; Scottish Executive/Government, since 1999; Cabinet Office, 1999-2002; Head of Teachers Division, 2002-07; Interim Chief Executive of Skills Development Scotland, 2007-08; EU Director and Head of Scottish Government Office in Brussels, 2008-11; Head of Public Health Division, 2011-15. Recreations: family; reading; walking. Address: Scottish Government, Victoria Quay, Edinburgh EH6 6QQ.

Henderson, John Gunn, BA, FRSA. Former Chief Executive, Colleges Scotland (2011-2014); Deputy Director, Scotland Office, 2007-2011; Head, International Division, Scottish Executive, 2003-07; Euro 2008 Bid Director, Scottish Football Association (on secondment from the Scottish Executive), 2001-03; b. 29.5.53, Edinburgh; m., Karen; 1 s.; 2 d. Educ. Broughton Secondary, Edinburgh; Open University. Scottish Development Department, 1970-78; Department of Agriculture and Fisheries for Scotland, 1978-85; Scottish Development Department, Trunk Roads Division, 1985-88; Scottish Office Education and Industry Department, 1988-97 (Head, Further Education Funding Unit, 1992-97); Assistant Director of Finance and Head, Private Finance Unit, 1997-2001. Recreations: reading; gardening; beachcombing.

Henderson, Meg. Author, Journalist and Scriptwriter; b. 1948, Glasgow; m., Rab; 1 s.; 2 d. Educ. Garnethill Convent Secondary School (reluctantly). Chief Cardiology Technician, Western Infirmary and Royal Infirmary, Glasgow; VSO, India; spent years fostering children; has worked for the broadsheets, Daily Mail, BBC, Channel 4. Publications: Finding Peggy, 1994; The Holy City, 1997; Bloody Mary, 1998; Chasing Angels, 2000; The Last Wanderer, 2002; Second Sight, 2004; Daisy's Wars, 2005; A Scent of Bluebells, 2006; Ruby, 2010. Recreations: reading, history, walking, radio, peace and quiet, golf, tennis, F1 racing (without having the slightest aptitude for any of them); shouting at politicians on television (or wherever encountered). Address: c/o Karen Duffy, Flamingo Publicity, HarperCollins Publishers, 77-85 Fulham Palace Road, London W6 8JB.

Henderson, Major Sir Richard Yates, KCVO, TD, JP, BA (Oxon), LLB. Lord Lieutenant, Ayrshire and Arran, 1991-2006; b. 7.7.31, Nitshill; m., Frances Elizabeth Chrystal; 3 s. (inc. 1 s. dec.); 1 d. Educ. Rugby; Hertford College, Oxford; Glasgow University. Royal Scots Greys, 1950-52; TA Ayrshire (ECO) Yeomanry, 1953-69 (Major); Deputy Lieutenant, Ayrshire and Arran, 1970-90; Partner, Mitchells Roberton, Solicitors, 1958-90, Consultant, 1991-92. Ensign, Queen's Bodyguard for Scotland (Royal Company of Archers); President, Lowland TAVRA, 1996-2000; Hon. Colonel, Ayrshire Yeomanry Sqn., Scottish Yeomanry, 1992-97; Honorary Sheriff, South Strathclyde Dumfries and Galloway at Ayr, since 1997. Recreations: shooting; tennis; golf. Address: (h.) Blairston, by Ayr, KA7 4EF; T.-01292 441601.

Henderson-Howat, David Barclay, BSc, MA, MBA, FICFor. President, Institute of Chartered Foresters; b. 23.1.54, Trinidad; m., Jean Buchanan-Smith; 1 s.; 3 d. Educ. Abingdon School; University of Edinburgh; Magdalene College, University of Cambridge; University of Strathclyde. Scottish Office, 1976-79; Personal Assistant to Chief Executive, Scottish Development Agency, 1979-80; Harvesting and Marketing Manager, Thetford Forest, 1980-84; Forest Manager, Shiselweni Forest, Swaziland, 1984-86; Forest District Manager, Aberfoyle, Perthshire, 1986-90; Forestry Commission Headquarters, 1990-96; Chief Conservator, Forestry Commission Scotland, 1996-2003; United Nations Forum on Forests, New York, 2003-05; Head of Agriculture Division, Rural Directorate, Scottish Government, 2005-08; Acting Director, Forestry

Commission England, 2010-11; Deputy Director, Forestry Commission Scotland, 2012-13; consultancy work for UN Forum on Forests and FAO, since 2013; Elder, Kirkurd and Newlands Church. Recreations: walking; sailing. Address: (h.) Stoneyknowe, West Linton, Peeblesshire EH46 7BY; T.-01968 660677; e-mail: hendersonhowat@gmail.com

Hendry, Drew. MP (SNP), Inverness, Nairn, Badenoch and Strathspey, since 2015; SNP Transport spokesperson in the House of Commons; Leader, Highland Council, 2012-15; SNP Group Leader, 2011-15; represented Aird and Loch Ness ward (SNP), 2007-2015; m.; 4 c. Former Director with a multinational appliance manufacturer and has long experience in Retail, including online, from the shop floor to senior management; founded a company, Teclan, in Inverness, which offers services for company websites. Former Board Member of the Cairngorms National Park; Member: COHI, H & I Convener's Group, Scottish Cities Alliance - Leadership Group, Inverness Campus - Partnership Forum; Chair: Advisory Board, Caithness and North Sutherland Regeneration Partnership (CNSRP), Highland Public Services Partnership Board (HPSP), since 2012. SNP Group Leader, COSLA. Chair, Highlands & Islands of Scotland European Partnership (HIEP), since 2012; Vice-President and Sole UK representative to the European Union Political Bureau of the Committee of the Regions (CPMR); COSLA European Representative; Honorary Consul to Romania for the Highlands and Islands, since 2012. Director, Teclan Ltd, Inverness; Member, Institute of Directors. Recreations: enjoys walking the dogs in the Highland countryside; reading; films; football. Address: House of Commons, London SW1A 0AA.

Hendry, Dr. Joy McLaggan, MA (Hons), DipEd, DLitt (Hon) (Edin). Editor, Chapman Magazine, since 1972; Writer; b. 3.2.53, Perth; m., Ian Montgomery. Educ. Perth Academy; Edinburgh University. Former teacher; Co-Editor, Chapman, 1972-76, Sole Editor, since 1976; Deputy Convener, Scottish Poetry Library Association, 1983-88; Convener, Committee for the Advancement of Scottish Literature in Schools; Member AdCas; Scottish National Theatre Steering Committee; Campaign for a Scottish Assembly; Member, Drama Committee, Scottish Arts Council; Chair, Scottish Actors Studio, 1993-2000; Member, Literature Forum for Scotland; Member, Scottish Parliament Scots Language Cross-Party Group; Lecturer in drama, Queen Margaret University College, 2000-04; Lecturer in periodical journalism, Napier University, 2000-04; poet and playwright; gives lectures and talks and performances of poetry and song; radio critic, The Scotsman, 1988-97; theatre reviewer; Writer-in-Residence, Stirling District Council, 1991-93. Hon DLitt, University of Edinburgh, 2005. Publications: Scots: The Way Forward; Poems and Pictures by Wendy Wood (Editor); The Land for the People (Co-Editor); Critical Essays on Sorley MacLean (Co-Editor); Critical Essays on Norman MacCaig (Co-Editor); autobiographical essay in Spirits of the Age: Scottish Self Portraits (Saltire Society); Gang Doun wi a Sang (play); radio: The Wa' at the Warld's End, Radio 3 (play); A Many-Faceted Thing (Memory), Radio 4 (major 4-part series). Recreations: going to theatre; cinema; reading; dogs and animal welfare. Address: 4 Broughton Place, Edinburgh EH1 3RX; T.-0131-557 2207. E-mail: joyhendry@blueyonder.co.uk

Hendry, Stephen, MBE. Former professional snooker player; b. 13.1.69; 2 s. Youngest-ever Scottish Amateur Champion (aged 15); has won 74 professional titles worldwide; youngest player to attain No. 1 ranking; youngest player to win World Championship, 1990; World Champion seven times; UK Champion, five times; Masters Champion, six times.

Hendry, Stuart, LLB (Hons), LLM, NP. Partner, MBM Commercial LLP, since 2005; b. 12.1.73, Aberdeen. Murray Beith Murray WS: Solicitor, 1999-2003, Associate

Partner, 2003-05. Address: (b.) 5th Floor, 7 Castle Street, Edinburgh EH2 3AH; T.-0131 226 8203; e-mail: stuart.hendry@mbmcommercial.co.uk

Henley, Professor John Sebastian, BSc (Eng), PhD. Emeritus Professor of International Management, University of Edinburgh Business School; b. 5.4.43, Malvern; m., Sarah J. Sieley; 2 d. Educ. King Edward's School, Birmingham; University College, London; London School of Economics. Personnel Officer, Glaxo Laboratories, 1966-68; Lecturer, Industrial Relations Department, London School of Economics, 1968-72; Lecturer, Faculty of Commerce, University of Nairobi, 1972-75; joined Department of Business Studies, University of Edinburgh, 1975. Publications: co-author of three books; editor of two books; author of over 50 academic papers. Recreations: gardening; theatre; opera; sailing. Address: (b.) University of Edinburgh Business School, 29 Buccleuch Place, Edinburgh EH8 9JY; T.-07812154772; e-mail: J.Henley@ed.ac.uk

Henry, Hugh. MSP (Labour), Renfrewshire South, 2011-16, Paisley South, 1999-2011; former Shadow Cabinet Secretary for Justice; b. 1952, Glasgow; m.; 1 s.; 2 d. Educ. St Mirin's Academy, Paisley; University of Glasgow; Jordanhill College of Education, Glasgow. Career history: worked as an accountant with IBM UK Ltd; teacher and welfare rights officer with Strathclyde Regional Council; local councillor, 1984-99, including 4 years as leader of Renfrewshire Council (1995-99); was appointed Deputy Minister for Health and Community Care in the Scottish Executive in 2001, and moved to become Deputy Minister for Social Justice in 2002; was appointed Deputy Minister for Justice after the Scottish Parliamentary Election, 2003, and became Minister for Education in 2006; retained the education brief in opposition after the 2007 election. Former Convener, European Committee. Scottish Politician of the Year in 2010, for his performance as Convenor of the Public Affairs Committee.

Henton, Margaret Patricia, BSc, CGeol, FGS, FCIWEM, FCIWM, FRSE. Non Executive Director, Board Member, The Coal Authority, since 2010; Board Member, Royal Botanic Garden Edinburgh, since 2011; b. 30.10.49, Edinburgh; m., Richard Henton; 1 s.; 1 d. Educ. George Watson's College; University of Manchester. Clyde River Purification Board, 1972-75; National Coal Board, 1975; Inspector, Forth River Purification Board, 1975-78, Hydrogeologist, 1978-83; Manager, Scotland, Aspinwall & Co., 1983-89; Director, Scotland and Northern Ireland, Aspinwall & Co., 1989-95; Director, Environmental Strategy, Scottish Environment Protection Agency, 1995-2000; Chief Executive, SEPA, 2000-02; Director of Business and Environment, Environment Agency, 2005-2010. Past President, Chartered Institute of Water and Environmental Management, 1996/7; Chair, Independent Regulatory Challenge Panel, HSE; Trustee, Institute for European Environmental Policy; Council Member, Geological Society of London; former Council Member, RSPB; Board Member, UK Carbon Capture and Storage Research Centre, since 2012. Recreations: travel; hill walking; birdwatching; gardens.
E-mail: t.henton@btopenworld.com

Hepburn, James Douglas, MSP (SNP), Cumbernauld and Kilsyth, since 2011, Central Scotland, 2007-2011; Minister for Sport, Health Improvement and Mental Health, Scottish Government, 2014-16; b. 21.5.79, Glasgow; m., Julie Shackleton. Educ. Hyndland Secondary, Glasgow; University of Glasgow. Recreations: football; reading; cinema. Address: (b.) Scottish Parliament, Edinburgh EH99 1SP; T.-0131 3486573.
E-mail: jamie.hepburn.msp@scottish.parliament.uk

Herald, Sheriff John Pearson, LLB, SSC. Sheriff of North Strathclyde at Greenock and Rothesay, 1992-2012 (retired);

b. 12.7.46, Glasgow; m., Catriona; 1 d. Educ. Hillhead High School, Glasgow; Glasgow University. Partner, Carlton Gilruth, Solicitors, Dundee, 1970-91; Depute Town Clerk, Newport-on-Tay, 1970-75; Member, Angus Legal Aid Committee, 1970-79, Secretary, 1979-87; Member, Legal Aid Central Committee, 1981-87; Temporary Sheriff, 1984-91; part-time Chairman, Industrial Tribunals, 1984-91. Chairman, Dundee Citizens Advice Bureau, 1972-79 and 1982-91; President, Rotary Club of North Fife, 1989. Recreations: football; reading.
E-mail: j.p.herald@talk21.com

Herdman, John Macmillan, MA (Hons), PhD (Cantab), DipTh. Writer, since 1963; b. 20.7.41, Edinburgh; m., Mary Ellen Watson. Educ. Merchiston Castle School, Edinburgh; Magdalene College, Cambridge. Creative Writing Fellow, Edinburgh University, 1977-79; Scottish Arts Council bursaries, 1976, 1982, 1998, 2004; Scottish Arts Council Book Awards, 1978 and 1993; Hawthornden Writer's Fellowship, 1989 and 1995; William Soutar Fellowship, 1990-91. Publications: Descent, 1968; A Truth Lover, 1973; Memoirs of My Aunt Minnie/ Clapperton, 1974; Pagan's Pilgrimage, 1978; Stories Short and Tall, 1979; Voice Without Restraint: Bob Dylan's Lyrics and Their Background, 1982; Three Novellas, 1987; The Double in Nineteenth Century Fiction, 1990; Imelda and Other Stories, 1993; Ghostwriting, 1996; Cruising (play), 1997; Poets, Pubs, Polls and Pillar Boxes, 1999; Four Tales, 2000; The Sinister Cabaret, 2001; Triptych, 2004; My Wife's Lovers, 2007; Some Renaissance Culture Wars, 2010; Another Country, 2013. Recreations: reading; walking; listening to music. Address: (h.) 25/8 Ashwood Gait, Edinburgh EH12 8PE; T.-0131-334-4106.

Herries, Amanda J. D, MA. Decorative Arts Writer and Lecturer; b. 1.2.55, Belfast, Northern Ireland; formerly married to William Young-Herries; 3 s. Educ. Christ's Hospital; Newnham College, Cambridge. Curator at The Museum of London (10 years); Residence in Japan (7 years), Lecturing, Advising Arts Companies and Museums; NADFAS Lecturer (range of approximately 12 subjects); Board of Trustees, National Trust for Scotland; Catalogue Co-ordinator, Southern Scotland, Public Catalogue Foundation. Chairman of former arts and fundraising committees in Tokyo and London; Committee Member, Kirkudbright 2000 supporting provision of Art Exhibitions in Kirkcudbright. Recreations: gardening; opera; theatre; exhibitions. Address: (h./b) Herriesdale House, Haugh of Urr, Stewartry of Kirkcudbright DG7 3JZ; T.-07801 537018; e-mail: amandaherries@gmail.com

Hewitt, Professor David S., MA, PhD, FRSE, FEA, FASLS, Professor Emeritus, formerly Regius Chalmers Professor of English Literature, Aberdeen University; b. 22.4.42, Hawick; m., Angela Catherine Williams; 1 s.; 1 d. Educ. Melrose Grammar School; George Watson's College, Edinburgh; Edinburgh University; Aberdeen University. Aberdeen University: Assistant Lecturer in English, 1964, Lecturer, 1968, Senior Lecturer, 1982, Professor in Scottish Literature, 1994; Treasurer, Association for Scottish Literary Studies, 1973-96; Editor-in-Chief, Edinburgh Edition of the Waverley Novels, complete in 30 vols, 1993-2012; President, Edinburgh Sir Walter Scott Club, 1988-89; Honorary Member, Association for Scottish Literary Studies, 1996; Managing Editor, New Writing Scotland, 1983-86; Managing Editor, The Clarendon Edition of the works of Charles Dickens, since 2014. Publications: Scott on Himself (Editor), 1982; Literature of the North (contributor), 1983; Scott and His Influence, 1984; Longer Scottish Poems, Vol. 2 1650-1830, 1987; Scott in Carnival, 1993; The Antiquary, 1995; Northern Visions, 1996; The Edinburgh Edition of the Waverley Novels: A Guide for

Editors, 1996; Redgauntlet, 1997; The Heart of Mid-Lothian, 2003; Rob Roy, 2008; The Betrothed (2009); The Talisman (2009); Woodstock (2009). Address: 21 Ferryhill Place, Aberdeen AB11 7SE; T.-01224 580834; e-mail: david.hewitt@abdn.ac.uk

Hewitt, Gavin Wallace, CMG, MA. Formerly Chief Executive, The Scotch Whisky Association (2003-2013); President, European Spirits Organisation, 2010-2013; Member, Convocation of Heriot Watt University, 2005-2011; Member, Executive Group of Scotland Food & Drink, 2008-2013; Member, Executive of SCDI, 2003-2013; Member of CBI Trade Association Council, 2003-2013; b. 19.10.44, Hawick; 2 s.; 2 d. Educ. George Watson's College, Edinburgh; University of Edinburgh. Ministry of Transport, 1967; seconded to HM Diplomatic Service, and posted to serve overseas at Brussels for negotiation of EC entry, 1970; HM Diplomatic Service with service at home and overseas, 1972, culminating in HM Ambassador to Croatia, 1994-97; HM Ambassador to Finland, 1997-2000; HM Ambassador to Belgium, 2001-2003; Member, International Advisory Board, Scotland Asia Institute, since 2013; Global Scot, since 2001; Keeper of the Quaich, 2009. Address: (h.) 27 Chester Street, Edinburgh EH3 7EN; T.-07720842722; e-mail: gavinhewitt2@googlemail.com

Hewitt, Very Rev. William Currie, BD, DipPS. Minister, Westburn Church, Greenock, 1994-2012; Minister, Elderslie Kirk, 1978-2012; b. 6.4.51, Kilmarnock; m., Moira Elizabeth MacLeod; 2 s.; 1 d. Educ. Kilmarnock Academy; Glasgow University. Moderator, Greenock Presbytery, 1996-97; Moderator, Greenock and Paisley Presbytery, 2003-04; Business Convener, Moderator, General Assembly of the Church of Scotland, 2009-2010. Past President: Innerkip Society, Johnstone Rotary; Paul Harris Award (Greenock Rotary). Recreations: golf; Burns.

Heycock, Professor Caroline Bridget, MA, PhD. Professor of Syntax, University of Edinburgh, since 2007; b. 22.11.60, Folkestone; m., Robert Sandler. Educ. St. Columba's School; King's College, Cambridge University; University of Pennsylvania. Assistant Professor: Oakland University, USA, 1991-92, Yale University, USA, 1992-94; University of Edinburgh: Lecturer, 1994-99, Reader, 1999-2007. Editor, Journal of Linguistics. Recreations: walking; cycling. Address: (b.) Linguistics and English Language, University of Edinburgh, Edinburgh; T.-0131 650 3961.

Heys, Professor Steven Darryll, BMedBiol, MB, ChB, MD, PhD, FRCS(Glas), FRCS(Ed), FRCS(Eng), FHEA. Professor of Surgical Oncology, University of Aberdeen, since 1999; Consultant Surgeon, Aberdeen Royal Infirmary, since 1992; Honorary Research Fellow, Rowett Research Institute, since 1992; b. 5.7.56, Accrington; m., Margaret Susan Proctor; 2 s.; 1 d. Educ. St. Mary's College, Blackburn; Aberdeen University Medical School. House Officer/SHO, Surgery, Aberdeen Royal Infirmary, 1981-84; Registrar, Grampian Health Board, 1984-87; Wellcome Research Training Fellow, Rowett Research Institute, 1987-89; Lecturer in Surgery, Aberdeen University, 1989-92; Senior Lecturer, 1992-96, Reader, 1996-99. Examiner in Surgery, Royal College of Surgeons of Glasgow; External Examiner in Surgery, Royal College of Surgeons of England; External Examiner, Universities of London, Dundee, Belfast; Quality Assurance Team Leader, Postgraduate Medical Education Training Board; Quality Assurance Basic Medical Education and Quality Assurance of Postgraduate Education, General Medical Council.

Publications: numerous scientific papers on aspects of breast cancer, oncology, nutrition and metabolism; book chapters on nutrition, metabolism, oncology; author of 3 books focusing on the history of medicine related to the Great War, 1914-18. Recreations: history; piping; flying; cycling. Address: (b.) University of Aberdeen, School of Medicine & Dentistry, Polwarth Building, Foresterhill, Aberdeen AB25 2ZD.

Heywood, Peter. Director, The Living Tradition Ltd., publisher, since 1993; b. 4.10.49, Manchester; m., Heather; 3 d. Educ. Heywood Grammar School. Long involvement with traditional music; founded The Tradition Bearers, recording traditional musicians, 1999; founded Common Ground on the Hill, Scotland, 2001. Recreations: traditional music; hill-walking. Address: (b.) The Living Tradition, PO Box 1026, Kilmarnock KA2 0LG; T.-01563 571220.
E-mail: pete@thetraditionbearers.com

Higgins, Professor James, MA (Glasgow), L-ès-L (Lyons), PhD (Liverpool), FBA. Emeritus Professor, Latin American Literature, University of Liverpool, since 2004; Honorary Research Fellow in Hispanic Studies, University of Stirling, 2006-2012; b. 28.05.39, Bellshill; m., Kirstine Anne Atwell; 2 s. (1 deceased). Educ. Our Lady's High School, Motherwell; University of Glasgow; University of Lyons. University of Liverpool: Assistant Lecturer in Latin American Studies, 1964-67, Lecturer, 1967-73, Senior Lecturer, 1973-83, Reader, 1983-88, Professor of Latin American Literature, 1988-2004, Head of Department of Hispanic Studies, 1980-82, 1988-97. Visiting Professor: University of Pittsburgh, 1968, University of Waterloo, 1974, University of West Indies, 1979, University of Wisconsin, 1990; Doctor Honoris Causa, University of San Marcos, Lima, 1984; Commander of the Orden al Mérito del Perú, 1988; Corresponding Fellow of the Academia Peruana de la Lengua, 2002. Publications include: César Vallejo en su poesía, 1990; Cambio social y constantes humanas. La narrativa corta de Ribeyro, 1991; Hitos de la poesía peruana, 1993; Myths of the Emergent. Social Mobility in Contemporary Peruvian Fiction, 1994; The Literary Representation of Peru, 2002; ed., Heterogeneidad y Literatura en el Perú, 2003; Lima. A Cultural and Literary History, 2005; Historia de la literatura peruana, 2006; John Barbour's 'The Bruce'. A Free Translation in Verse, 2013; The Emancipation of Peru: British Eyewitness Accounts, 2014. Recreations: reading; walking; gardening; classical music; Scottish literature; travel; whisky. Address: (h.) 6 Carlton House, 15 Snowdon Place, Stirling FK8 2NR; T.-01786 470 641; e-mail: jameshig0@gmail.com

Higgins, John, MBE. Professional snooker player; b. 18.5.75, Wishaw, North Lanarkshire; m., Denise; 2 s.; 1 d. Four time World Champion winning in 1998, 2007, 2009 and 2011. Has won 46 tournaments worldwide. Lives in Wishaw, Lanarkshire.

Higgs, Professor Peter Ware, CH, FRS, FRSE, HonFInstP, DSc (Hon). Professor of Theoretical Physics, Edinburgh University, 1980-96; b. 29.5.29, Newcastle-upon-Tyne; m., Jo Ann Williamson; 2 s. Educ. Cotham Grammar School, Bristol; King's College, London. Postdoctoral Fellow, Edinburgh University, 1954-56, and London University, 1956-58; Lecturer in Mathematics, University College, London, 1958-60; Lecturer in Mathematical Physics, then Reader, Edinburgh University, 1960-80. Hughes Medal, Royal Society, 1981; Rutherford Medal, Institute of Physics, 1984; James Scott Prize, Royal Society of Edinburgh, 1993; Paul Dirac Medal and Prize,

Institute of Physics, 1997; High Energy and Particle Physics Prize, European Physical Society, 1997; Royal Medal, Royal Society of Edinburgh, 2000; Wolf Prize, 2004; Oskar Klein Medal, Royal Swedish Academy of Sciences, 2009; Sakurai Prize, American Physical Society, 2010; Nonino Prize, 2013; Prince of Asturias Prize, 2013; Nobel Prize, 2013; Galileo Galilei Award, 2014; Copley Medal, Royal Society, 2015. Recreations: music; walking; swimming. Address: (h.) 2 Darnaway Street, Edinburgh EH3 6BG; T.- 0131-225 7060.

Highfield, Ashley, FRSA. Chief Executive, Johnston Press plc, since 2011. Educ. City University Business School; Chartered Information Engineer. Career History: Coopers and Lybrand Management Consultancy; Managing Director, Flextech (now Virgin Media) Interactive; Director of New Media and Technology at the BBC, responsible for the launch of the BBC's iPlayer and Editor in Chief of BBC Online; CEO of Project Kangaroo, the video-on-demand BBC/ITV/C4 joint venture; Vice President of Microsoft, responsible for the UK Consumer and Online business, including the UK's largest content portal MSN. Address: Johnston Press plc, Head Office, 108 Holyrood Road, Edinburgh EH8 8AS; T.-0131 225 3361.

Hill, Professor Malcolm, PhD. Research Professor, University of Strathclyde; formerly Professor for the Child and Society and Professor of Social Work, University of Glasgow; b. 18.9.46, London; m., Dr. Wan Ying Hill; 1 s.; 1 d. Educ. Latymer Upper School, Hammersmith; St. Edmund Hall, Oxford; University of London; University of Edinburgh. Social Worker, 1968-79; Researcher, 1979-84; Lecturer, 1985-93; Senior Lecturer, 1993-96. Publications: books on adoption, child care, youth crime, foster care, middle childhood, children and society. Recreations: bridge; gardening; swimming. Address: 66 Oakfield Avenue, Glasgow G12 8LS.

Hill, Professor William George, OBE, BSc, MS, PhD, DSc, DSc (hc), Dhc, FRSE, FRS. Emeritus Professor of Animal Genetics, Edinburgh University, since 2003; Professor of Animal Genetics, 1983-2003; b. 7.8.40, Hemel Hempstead; m., C. Rosemary Austin; 1 s.; 2 d. Educ. St. Albans School; London University; University of California; Iowa State University; Edinburgh University. Edinburgh University: Assistant Lecturer, 1965-67, Lecturer, 1967-74, Reader, 1974-83, Head, Department of Genetics, 1989-90, Institute of Cell, Animal and Population Biology, 1990-93, and Division of Biological Sciences, 1993-98, Dean and Provost, Faculty of Science and Engineering, 1999-2002. Visiting Research Associate, Iowa State University, 1967-68-69-72; Visiting Professor: University of Minnesota, 1966, Iowa State University, 1978, North Carolina State University, 1979, 1985-2005; Consultant Geneticist: Cotswold Pig Development Co., 1965-99, Holstein Friesian Society, 1978-98; Editor, Genetics Research, 1996-2012; Editor-in-Chief, Proceedings Royal Society B, 2005-08; Member: AFRC Animals Research Grant Board, 1986-92, Director's Advisory Group, AFRC Animal Breeding Research Organisation, 1982-86, AFRC Institute of Animal Physiology and Genetics Research, 1986-93, Governing Council, Roslin Institute, 1994-2002, Council, Royal Society, 1993-94, Commonwealth Scholarships Commission, 1998-2004 (Deputy Chair, 2002-04), RAE Panel, 1996, 2001 (Chairman); British Society of Animal Science: Vice-President, 1997-99, President, 1999-00; Genetics Society: Vice President, 2004-08. Recreations: farming; bridge. Address: (h.) 4 Gordon Terrace, Edinburgh EH16 5QH; T.-0131-667 3680; e-mail: w.g.hill@ed.ac.uk

Hillhouse, Sir (Robert) Russell, KCB, FRSE; b. 23.4.38, Glasgow; m., Alison Fraser; 2 d. Educ. Hutchesons' Grammar School, Glasgow; Glasgow University. Entered Home Civil Service as Assistant Principal, Scottish Education Department, 1962; Principal, 1966; HM Treasury, 1971; Assistant Secretary, Scottish Office, 1974; Scottish Home and Health Department, 1977; Principal Finance Officer, Scottish Office, 1980; Under-Secretary, Scottish Education Department, 1985; Secretary, 1987; Permanent Under-Secretary of State, Scottish Office, 1988-98. Director: Bank of Scotland, 1998-2001, Scottish Provident Institution, 1999-2001; Governor, Royal Scottish Academy of Music and Drama, 2000-08; Chairman, Edinburgh Competition Festival Association, 2010-14. Recreations: making music. Address: 12 Russell Place, Edinburgh EH5 3HH; e-mail: rhillhouse@blueyonder.co.uk

Hillier, Professor Stephen Gilbert, OBE, BSc, MSc, PhD, DSc, FRCPath, FRCOG. Professor (Emeritus), Edinburgh University, since 2014; Vice Principal - International, 2008-14; Honorary Consultant Clinical Scientist, NHS Lothian; Professor, MRC Centre for Reproductive Health, Edinburgh University, since 1994; Editor-in-Chief, Journal of Endocrinology, 2000-05; Editor-in-Chief, Molecular Human Reproduction, 2007-2012; b. 16.1.49, Hillingdon; m., Haideh; 2 d. Educ. Hayes County Grammar School; Leeds University; Welsh National School of Medicine. Postdoctoral Research Fellow, National Institutes of Health, USA, 1976-78; Research Scientist, University of Leiden, 1978-82; Senior Lecturer: Reproductive Biochemistry, RPMS, London University, 1982-85, Department of Obstetrics and Gynaecology, Edinburgh University, 1985-94. Member: Interim Licensing Authority for Human Fertilisation and Embryology, 1987-91, Human Fertilisation and Embryology Authority, 1990-96; 1991 Society for Endocrinology Medal; 2004 British Fertility Society Patrick Steptoe Medal; 2006 Society for Endocrinology Jubilee Medal. Publications: Ovarian Endocrinology, 1991; Scientific Essentials of Reproductive Medicine, 1996. Recreation: fly-fishing. Address: (b.) Edinburgh University Centre for Reproductive Health, Queen's Medical Research Institute, 47 Little France Crescent, Edinburgh EH16 4TJ; T.-0131-242 6635; e-mail: s.hillier@ed.ac.uk

Hillman, Professor John Richard, BSc, PhD, HonDSc, CBiol, FSB, FLS, FCMI, FIHort, FRSA, FRSE, FRAgS. Consultant in agriculture and industrial biotechnology; Director, Scottish Crop Research Institute, 1986-2005; Visiting Professor, Dundee University, Edinburgh University and Glasgow University; Founder and Deputy Chairman, Mylnefield Research Services Ltd., 1989-2005; Director, Mylnefield Trust and Mylnefield Holdings Ltd., 2000-05; b. 21.7.44, Farnborough, Kent; m., Sandra Kathleen Palmer; 2 s. Educ. Chislehurst and Sidcup Grammar School; University of Wales. Assistant Lecturer, 1968, and Lecturer, 1969, Physiology and Environmental Studies, Nottingham University; Lecturer, 1971, Senior Lecturer, 1977, Reader, 1980, Professor and Head of Botany, 1982, Glasgow University; Chairman, Agriculture, Natural Resources and Environment Sector Panel, UK Technology Foresight Programme, 1994-95, Agriculture, Horticulture and Forestry Sector Panel, 1995-97; Member, Court, University of Abertay, Dundee, 1997-2005; Member, Board, BioIndustry Association; Chair, Industrial Biotechnology Group, 1996-2005; Member, Scottish Higher Education Funding Council Research and Knowledge Transfer Committee; Honorary Research Fellow of Scottish Crop Research Institute, 2005-2011; Honorary Research Fellow of James Hutton Institute; Angus, Dundee and Perth Employer Support Committee for Reservists; Regulation Working Group, NFU Scotland; Bawden Jubilee Lecturer, 1993; Chairman, Angus Conservative & Unionist Association, 2008-2010; Advisor to the Arab Academy of Sciences, since 2002; British Potato Industry Award, 1999; World Potato Congress 2000 Industry Award; Dr Hardie Memorial Prize; Scottish Horticultural Medal, 2003. Recreations: landscaping;

building renovations; horology; reading. Address: (b.) James Hutton Institute, Invergowrie, Dundee DD2 5DA; T.-01382 562731.

Hillston, Jane, FRSE, PhD, MSc, BA, FBCS. Chair, Quantitative Modelling, University of Edinburgh, since 2006; Director of the Laboratory for Foundations of Computer Science (2011-2014); b. 14.11.63, Manchester; m., Stephen Gilmore; 2 d. Educ. Fallowfield High School for Girls, Manchester; University of York; Lehigh University, USA; University of Edinburgh. Business Analyst, Logical Financial Software Ltd, 1987-88; Research Assistant: Kingston Business School, Kingston University, 1988-89, Department of Computer Science, University of Edinburgh, 1989-91; PhD in Computer Science, 1994; EPSRC Postdoctoral fellowship, 1994-95; Distinguished Dissertation Award from the British Computer Society and the Council of Professors and Heads of Computing, 1995; Lecturer, Department of Computer Science, University of Edinburgh, 1995-2001, Reader, School of Informatics, 2001-06; Roger Needham Award, 2005; Elected Fellow of the British Computer Society; Elected Fellow, RSE, 2007; EPSRC Advanced Research Fellow, 2005-2010. Member, Learned Society and Knowledge Services Board and the Learned Society Awards Committee of the British Computer Society, 2006-09; Chair of the judging panel of the BCS/CPHC Distinguished Dissertation competition (2007-09); Member: Board of Informatics Europe, 2014-2017, UK Computing Research Committee, EPSRC College of Peers, B4 Sectional Committee of the RSE, 2008-2012. Address: (b.) School of Informatics, University of Edinburgh, The Informatics Forum, 10 Crichton Street, Edinburgh EH8 9AB; T.-0131 650 5199; e-mail: jane.hillston@ed.ac.uk

Hilton, Cara. MSP (Labour), Dunfermline, 2013-16; m., Simon; 3 c. Daughter of former Labour MSP Cathy Peattie.

Hinds, Lesley. Lord Lieutenant and Lord Provost, City of Edinburgh, 2003-07; elected for the Inverleith Ward of the City of Edinburgh Council, May 2012 for 5 years; elected Convener of Transport and Environment Committee, May 2012; Chair, Transport for Edinburgh Board; b. 3.8.56, Dundee; m., Martin; 1s.; 2d. Educ. Kirkton High School, Dundee; Dundee College of Education. Teacher, Deans Primary School, 1977-80; Chair, Health Scotland, 2001-07; Labour Councillor, Edinburgh DC, 1984-96 (Leader, 1993-96); City of Edinburgh Council, since 1996; Past Chair: Edinburgh International Festival Society; Edinburgh Military Tattoo Ltd; N Edinburgh Area Renewal (NEAR); Director: N Edinburgh Arts; former Chair, Edinburgh International Conference Centre. Recreations: theatre; dance; swimming; travel. Address: (b.) City Chambers, High Street, Edinburgh EH1 1YJ; T.-0131 529 3235. E-mail: lesley.hinds@edinburgh.gov.uk

Hine, Professor Harry Morrison, MA, DPhil (Oxon). Scotstarvit Professor of Humanity, St. Andrews University, 1985-2008 (Emeritus); b. 19.6.48, Portsmouth; m., Rosalind Mary Ford; 1 s.; 1 d. Educ. King Edward's School, Birmingham; Corpus Christi College, Oxford. P.S. Allen Junior Research Fellow, Corpus Christi College, 1972-75; Lecturer in Humanity, Edinburgh University, 1975-85. Editor (Joint), The Classical Review, 1987-93. Publications: An Edition with Commentary of Seneca, Natural Questions, Book Two, 1981; Studies in the Text of Seneca's Naturales Quaestiones, 1996; L. Annaei Senecae Naturales Quaestiones (Editor), 1996; Seneca, Medea, Translation and commentary, 2000; Seneca, Natural Questions, Translation, 2010. Recreations: walking; reading. Address: (h.) 33 Drumcarrow Road, St. Andrews, Fife KY16 8SE; e-mail: hmh@st-and.ac.uk

Hirst, Sir Michael William, LLB, CA, FRSA, MCIPR, DLitt (2004), FRCP (Edin), 2012. Chairman, Scottish Conservative and Unionist Party, 1993-97; b. 2.1.46, Glasgow; m., Naomi Ferguson Wilson; 1 s.; 2 d. Educ. Glasgow Academy; Glasgow University. Partner, Peat Marwick Mitchell & Co., Chartered Accountants, until 1983; Chairman: Pagoda Public Relations Ltd., since 2000, Millstream Associates Ltd., since 2001; Director of and Consultant to various companies; contested: Central Dunbartonshire, February and October, 1974, East Dunbartonshire, 1979; MP (Conservative), Strathkelvin and Bearsden, 1983-87; Member, Select Committee on Scottish Affairs, 1983-87; Parliamentary Private Secretary, Department of Energy, 1985-87; Vice-Chairman, Scottish Conservative Party, 1987-89; Chairman, Scottish Conservative Candidates Association, 1978-81; Member, Court, Glasgow Caledonian University, 1992-98; Member, Council of the Imperial Society of Knights Bachelor and Chairman, Scottish Division, since 2002; President, Scottish Conservative and Unionist Association, 1989-1992; Chairman, Diabetes UK, 2001-06, Vice President, since 2006; Vice-President, International Diabetes Federation, 2006-09, President-Elect, 2009-2012, Global President, since 2012; Chairman, The Park School Educational Trust, 1993-2010; Chairman, Friends of Kippen Kirk Trust, since 2003; Director, Children's Hospice Association Scotland, 1995-2005; Director, Erskine Hospital, Erskine, 1980-2011; Elder, Kippen Parish Church. Recreations: golf; hill-walking; skiing. Address: (h.) Glentirran, Kippen, Stirlingshire FK8 3DY.
Email: michael.hirst@pagodapr.com; smh@glentirran.co.uk

Hitchman, Professor Michael L., BSc, DPhil, CSci, CChem, FRSC, FRSA, FRSE. Emeritus Professor, University of Strathclyde, since 2004; Young Professor of Chemistry, Strathclyde University, 1984-2004; b. 17.8.41, Woburn, Bedfordshire; 1 s.; 2 d; m., Dr. Migeun Park; 2 step d. Educ. Stratton Grammar School, Biggleswade; Queen Mary College and King's College, London University; University College, Oxford. Assistant Lecturer in Chemistry, Leicester Regional College of Technology, 1963-65; Junior Research Fellow, Wolfson College, Oxford, 1968-70; ICI Postdoctoral Research Fellow, Physical Chemistry Laboratory, Oxford University, 1968-70; Chief Scientist, Orbisphere Corporation, Geneva, 1970-73; Staff Scientist, Laboratories RCA Ltd., Zurich, 1973-79; Lecturer, then Senior Lecturer, Salford University, 1979-84; Strathclyde University: Chairman, Department of Pure and Applied Chemistry, 1986-89, Vice-Dean, Faculty of Science, 1989-92; Honorary Professor, Taiyuan University of Technology, China, since 1994; Visiting Professor, University of West of Scotland, since 2006. Royal Society of Chemistry: Chairman, Electro-analytical Group, 1985-88, Treasurer, Electrochemistry Group, 1984-90; Member, Chemistry and Semiconductor Committees, Science and Engineering Research Council; Member, since 1985, Chairman, 1989-92, International Advisory Board, EUROCVD; Director, Innovative Coating Technologies Ltd.; Director, Jinju Consultancies Ltd.; Medal and Prize, British Vacuum Council, 1993. Editor, Chemical Vapor Deposition, since 1995. Publications: Ring-disk Electrodes (Co-Author), 1971; Measurement of Dissolved Oxygen, 1978; Chemical Vapor Deposition (Co-Editor), 1993; Chemical Vapour Deposition: Precursors, Processes and Applications (Co-editor), 2008. Recreations: humour; cooking; eating; rambling; losing weight.

Hockley, Rear Admiral Chris, CBE. Chief Executive, The MacRobert Trust, since 2014; b. 24.8.59. Educ. Dulwich College; Royal Naval Engineering College Manadon. Defence Logistics Organisation/Director

Supportability & Logistics, MoD/Royal navy, 2005-07; Naval Base Commander Clyde, UK Ministry of Defence, 2007-2011; Deputy Director, Defence Support Review, Ministry of Defence of UK, 2011; Rear Admiral - FOSNNI, FORF, FORes, Ministry of Defence, 2011-14; Chairman, Marine Engineering Advisory Panel, Royal Navy, 2012-14; Rear Admiral, Royal Navy, 1977-2014. Address: The MacRobert Trust, Cromar, Tarland, Aberdeenshire AB34 4UD; T.-013398 81444.

Hodge, Robin Mackenzie, OBE, BA (Hons). Publisher, The List magazine, since 1985; b. Edinburgh. Educ. Edinburgh Academy; Clifton College, Bristol; Durham University. Certificat Europeen en Administration de Projects Culturels (Bruxelles). Production Director, Canongate Publishing Ltd., 1981-84; restoration of 16th-century buildings around Tweeddale Court, Edinburgh Old Town, 1981-88; founded The List, 1985; Chairman, PPA Scotland, 2002-04. OBE (New Year Honours 2012). Address: (b.) 14 High Street, Edinburgh EH1 1TE; T.-0131-550 3050.

Hogg, Lt. Col. Colin Grant Ogilvie, OBE, DL. King's Own Scottish Borderers (KOSB), 1962-2008; Regimental Secretary, 1991-2008; b. 6.12.43, Glasgow; m., Cynthia Rose Mackenzie; 2 d. Educ. St. Mary's Preparatory School; Merchiston Castle School. Commissioned into KOSB, 1965; service with 1st Battalion in Aden, Hong Kong, Borneo, BAOR, Berlin, Northern Ireland; Deputy Assistant Adjutant General, HQ of 1st Armoured Division, Germany, 1981-83; on directing staff, Royal Military Academy, Sandhurst, 1983-84; Commanding Officer, 2nd Battalion, 52 Lowland Volunteers, 1985-88; SOI, Foot Guards and Infantry Manning and Records Office, 1988-91; retired from active list, 1991; Honorary Colonel of the Lothian and Border Army Cadet Force, 1997-2006. Member, Queen's Bodyguard for Scotland, since 1986; Member, Ancient Order of Mosstroopers; Chairman, Borders Branch, SSAFA Forces Help, 1993-2010, National Vice President, since 2010, Member, National Council, 2000-06; Board Member, South of Scotland Youth Awards Trust, since 1994, Trustee and Chairman, since 2010; Chairman, Roxburgh and Berwickshire Conservative and Unionist Association, 1995-98; Governor: Oxenfoord Castle School, 1986-93, St. Mary's School, Melrose, 1994-98; President, Jedburgh Branch, Royal British Legion Scotland, 2005-2012; Member, National Council, Royal British Legion Scotland, 1998-2004; Trustee, Poppyscotland (Earl Haig Fund Scotland), 2000-2011; Member, Poppyscotland Scottish Advisory Committee to the Royal British Legion, since 2011; Honorary Director, Lord Roberts Workshops; Chairman, South of Scotland Youth Awards Trust, since 2012; Deputy Lieutenant, Roxburgh, Ettrick and Lauderdale, since 1995; appointed to the Church of Scotland Committee on Chaplains to HM Forces, 2015. Recreations: field sports and equestrian events. Address: (h.) Mounthooly, Jedburgh TD8 6TJ.

Holden, Catherine Ann, BA. Director of External Relations, National Museums Scotland, since 2004; b. 26.9.64, Blackburn. Educ. Droitwich High School; Oxford University. Brand Manager, Rank Hovis McDougall, 1987-90; Marketing Manager, National Theatre, 1990-94; Head of Marketing, Tate, 1994-2001; Head of Communications, Natural History Museum, 2001-04. Arts Marketing Association Board Member, 1998-2001; Edinburgh Art Festival Board Member, 2004-2015; Fruitmarket Gallery Board Member, since 2009; Craft Scotland Board Member, since 2015. Recreations: visual art and contemporary craft; horse riding. Address: (b.) National Museums Scotland, Chambers Street, Edinburgh EH1 1JF; T.-0131 247 4332.

Holloway, James Essex, BA (Hons), CBE. Director, Scottish National Portrait Gallery, 1997-2012; b. 24.11.48, London. Educ. Marlborough College; Courtauld Institute, London University. Assistant Keeper, National Gallery of Scotland; Assistant Keeper, National Museum of Wales; Deputy Keeper, Scottish National Portrait Gallery. Trustee, Hopetoun House, Abbotsford House, Fleming Collection, Historic Scotland Foundation; Honorary Curator, National Trust for Scotland. Recreations: India; motorbikes; French Horn. Address: (h.) 20 India Street, Edinburgh EH3 6HB.

Holloway, Rt. Rev. Richard Frederick, BD, STM, DUniv (Strathclyde), DD (Aberdeen), DLitt (Napier), DD (Glasgow), FRSE, DUniv (OU), LLD (Dundee), 2009, DUniv (Stirling), 2010. Gresham Professor of Divinity, 1997-2001; Bishop of Edinburgh, 1986-2000; Primus of the Scottish Episcopal Church, 1992-2000; Chair, SAC, since 2005; Chair, Scottish Screen, since 2007; Chair, Creative Scotland Joint Board, 2007-2010; Chair, Sistema Scotland, since 2005; b. 26.11.33; m., Jean Elizabeth Kennedy; 1 s.; 2 d. Educ. Kelham Theological College; Edinburgh Theological College; Union Theological Seminary, New York. Curate, St. Ninian's, Glasgow, 1959-63; Priest-in-charge, St. Margaret and St. Mungo's, Glasgow, 1963-68; Rector, Old St. Paul's, Edinburgh, 1968-80; Rector, Church of the Advent, Boston, Mass, 1980-84; Vicar, St. Mary Magdalen's, Oxford, 1984-86. Doctor of The Royal Conservatoire of Scotland, 2012. Recreations: long-distance walking; reading; going to the cinema; listening to music. Address: (h.) 6 Blantyre Terrace, Edinburgh EH10 5AE. E-mail: richard@docholloway.org.uk

Holmes, Andrew Mayhew, MSc, MICE. Trustee, National Museums of Scotland, since 2009; Chairman, Highland Perthshire Ltd, since 2010; b. 20.6.47, Haltwhistle, Northumberland; m., Catherine; 3 s.; 1 d. Educ. Millom School; Universities of Leeds and Newcastle. Civil Engineer, various posts, NE England and Scotland, 1968-98; Director of City Development, City of Edinburgh Council, 1998-2005. Member, Mobility and Access Committee for Scotland; Board Member, Hill-Adamson Project (National Photography Centre); Board Member, Historic Environment Scotland, since 2015. Recreations: gardening; hill-walking; exploring Italy. Address: (h.) 'Strathtummel', Lower Oakfield, Pitlochry, Perthshire PH16 5DS; T.-01796 473 400. E-mail: a.m.holmes@btinternet.com

Holmes, George Dennis, CB (1979), FRSE, FICfor; b. 9.11.26, Conwy; m., Sheila Rosemary; 3 d. Educ. John Bright's School, Llandudno; University of Wales, Bangor. Forestry Commission, 1948-86 (Director General, 1976-86). Recreations: fishing; golf. Address: (h.) 7 Cammo Road, Barnton, Edinburgh EH4 8EF; T.-0131-339 7474.

Holmes, Professor Megan Christine, BSc, PhD. Professor of Molecular Neuroendocrinology, University of Edinburgh; m., Dr Ferenc A. Antoni; 3 s. Educ. Stourbridge Girls' High School; London University. Exchange Fellow, Royal Society, London, and Hungarian Academy of Sciences, Budapest, at Institute of Experimental Medicine, Budapest, 1982-83; Fogarty Visiting Fellow, Endocrinology and Reproduction Research Branch, National Institute of Child Health, Bethesda, 1983-85; Department of Medicine, Western General Hospital, Edinburgh: Wellcome Postdoctoral Fellowship, 1992-94, Wellcome Career Development Fellowship, 1995-98. Recreation: hill-walking. Address: (b.) Endocrine Unit, Centre for Cardiovascular Sciences, Queen's Medical Research Institute, Little France, Edinburgh EH16 4TJ; T.-0131 242 6737.

Holmes, Professor Peter Henry, OBE, BVMS, PhD, DUniv (hc), DSc (hc), FRCVS, FRSE. Emeritus Professor of Veterinary Physiology, University of Glasgow, Professor, 1982-2008 (retired); formerly Pro Vice-Principal, Vice-Principal, 1997-2005; b. 6.6.42, Cottingham, Yorkshire; m., Ruth Helen; 2 d. Educ. Beverley Grammar School, Yorkshire; University of Glasgow. Joined staff of University of Glasgow Veterinary School, Department of Veterinary Physiology, 1966. Member, Court, University of Glasgow, 1991-95; served on committees of ODA (DfID), BVA, UFAW; Chairman, WHO Strategic & Technical Advisory Group (STAG) for Neglected Tropical Diseases. Recreations: hillwalking; golf; cycling. Address: (b.) 2, Barclay Drive, Helensburgh G84 9RD.

Holmes, Stephen Ralph, MA (Cantab), MTh, PhD. Senior Lecturer in Theology, University of St Andrews, since 2009; b. 8.9.69, Belper; m., Heather Clare (nee Taylor); 3 d. Educ. Dover Grammar School for Boys; Peterhouse, Cambridge; Spurgeon's College, London; King's College London. Minister, West Wickham & Shirley Baptist Church, 1996-98; Research Fellow, Spurgeon's College, 1996-99; Lecturer in Christian Doctrine, King's College London, 1998-2004; Lecturer in Theology, University of St Andrews, 2005-09. Accredited minister, Baptist Union of Scotland; Council member: Evangelical Alliance UK, Scottish Bible Society; published numerous books on topics in Christian theology at academic and popular level; numerous articles in learned journals; Editor, *International Journal of Systematic Theology*. Address: (b.) St. Mary's College, St Andrews KY16 9JU; T.-01334 462838; e-mail: sh80@st-andrews.ac.uk

Holroyd, Nicholas Weddall, BCL (Oxon), LLB, TEP, FSA Scot. Advocate, since 1992; b. 11.3.64, Edinburgh. Educ. Christ Church, Oxford University; University of Edinburgh, Thow Scholarship in Jurisprudence. Trainee, Dundas and Wilson, CS, 1989-91; "devilling" for the Bar, 1991-92; part-time Tutor, Edinburgh University, 1993-2001; Part-time Tutor, University of Glasgow, 2013-2015; Clerk to Faculty of Advocates Law Reform Committee, 1996; Member of Faculty Council, 2004-07; Contributor, Greens' Litigation Styles, since 1996; Contributor, Tolley's Pension Dispute Procedures and Remedies; Committee Member, Society of Trust and Estate Practitioners (Scotland), 2007-2013; Member, Society of Trust and Estate Practitioners EU Committee, 2012-2015; Chairman, Trust Bar, since 2015. Recreation: golf. Address: Advocates Library, Old Parliament House, Edinburgh EH1 1RF; T.-0131-226 5071.

Holton, Yvonne, BA (Hons), FGA, DGA, FRSA. Dingwall Pursuivant, Herald Painter in Scotland; b. 2.7.59, Aberdeen; m., Derek Holton. Educ. St. Margaret's School for Girls, Aberdeen; Edinburgh College of Art. Book Illustrator and Silversmith. Heraldic Artist appointed to The Court of The Lord Lyon in 1990. Recreations: gemmologist; gardening. Address: 11 Mayburn Terrace, Loanhead, Midlothian EH20 9EH; e-mail: yholton@freeuk.com

Home, Earl of (David Alexander Cospatrick Douglas-Home), KT, CVO, CBE. Chairman, Grosvenor Group Ltd., 2007-2010; Chairman, Coutts & Co. Ltd, since 2000; Chairman, Coutts & Co., 1999-2013; b. 20.11.43, Coldstream; m., Jane Margaret Williams-Wynne; 1 s.; 2 d. Educ. Eton; Christ Church, Oxford. Joined Morgan Grenfell & Co. Limited, 1966; appointed Director, 1974 (retired, 1999); Chairman, Morgan Grenfell (Scotland) Ltd., 1986 (resigned 1999); ECGD: Member, Export Advisory Council, 1988-93; Member, Projects Committee, 1989-93; Member, Advisory Board, National Forest, 1991-94; Chairman, CEGELEC Controls Ltd., 1991-94; Council Member, Glenalmond School, since 1995; Conservative Front-Bench

Spokesman on Trade, Industry and Finance, 1997-98; appointed Director, Coutts & Co., 1999; Trustee, The Grosvenor Estate, 1993-2010; Chairman, MAN Ltd., 2000-09; Director, Dubai Financial Services Authority, 2005-2012. Recreations: outdoor sports. Address: (b.) Coutts & Co., 440 Strand, London WC2R 0QS; T.-020 7753 1000.

Home Robertson, John David. MSP (Labour), East Lothian, 1999-2007 (Convenor, Holyrood Progress Group, 2000-04, Scottish Executive Depute Minister for Rural Affairs, 1999-2000, former Member, Communities Committee, Scottish Parliament); MP (Labour), East Lothian, 1983-2001 (Berwick & East Lothian, 1978-83); b. 5.12.48, Edinburgh; m., Catherine Brewster; 2 s. Educ. Ampleforth College; West of Scotland Agricultural College. Farmer; Member: Berwickshire District Council, 1974-78, Borders Health Board, 1975-78; Chairman, Eastern Borders Citizens' Advice Bureau, 1976-78; Member, Select Committee on Scottish Affairs, 1979-83; Chairman, Scottish Group of Labour MPs, 1983; Scottish Labour Whip, 1983-84; Opposition Front Bench Spokesman on Agriculture, 1984-87, on Scotland, 1987-88, on Agriculture, 1988-90; Member, Select Committee on Defence, 1990-97; Member, British-Irish Parliamentary Body, 1993-99; Parliamentary Private Secretary to Dr Jack Cunningham, 1997-99; established Paxton Trust, 1988; Edinburgh Direct Aid convoys to Bosnia, 1994 and 1995 (HGV driver); Observer, elections in Sarajevo, 1996.

Honeyman, Greig, LLB (Hons), NP, WS. Partner, Shepherd and Wedderburn LLP, since 2014; b. 1.10.55, Kirkcaldy; m., Alison; 1 s.; 1 d. Educ. Dunfermline High School; University of Edinburgh. Apprenticeship, W. & J. Burness, WS, 1977-79; enrolled as a Solicitor, 1979; Solicitor, Socttish Special Housing Association, 1979-81; Admitted as Notary Public, 1983; Admitted to the WS Society, 1984; Partner: McNiven & Co., 1981-85, Honeyman & Mackie, 1985-90, Bird Semple Fyfe Ireland - (de-merger 1994), later Fyfe Ireland WS, 1990-2005, later Fyfe Ireland LLP merged with Tods Murray, 2012, merged with Shepherd and Wedderburn, 2014. Recreations: gardening; rugby spectating. Address: (b.) 1 Exchange Crescent, Edinburgh EH3 8UL.
E-mail: greig.honeyman@shepwedd.co.uk

Hood, James. MP (Labour), Clydesdale, 1987-2005, Lanark and Hamilton East, 2005-2015; b. 16.5.48, Lesmahagow; m., Marion; 1 s.; 1 d. Educ. Lesmahagow High School; Nottingham University; WEA. Local councillor, 1973-87; official of NUM, 1973-87; Leader, Nottingham striking miners, 1984-85; Chairman, Miners' Parliamentary Group, 1991-92; former Chairman, All-Party Group on ME; former Chairman, European Legislation Select Committee (1992-98); former Chairman, European Scrutiny Committee (1998-2006); Member, UK Delegation to NATO Parliamentary Assembly, 2007-2010; Member, Western European Union (WEU), 2007-2010; former Convenor, Scottish Labour Group of MPs Home Affairs Committee; sponsor of four Private Members' Bills on under-age drinking, Bill on ME, and Bill on school transport safety.

Hood, Very Rev. Lorna, MA, BD, DD. Minister, Renfrew North Parish Church, since 1979; Honorary Chaplain to the Queen in Scotland, since 2008; Moderator of the General Assembly of the Church of Scotland, 2013-14; b. Irvine, 1953; m., Peter; 2 c. Educ. Kilmarnock Academy; University of Glasgow. Ordained by the Church of Scotland's Presbytery of Edinburgh in 1978 whilst serving as Assistant Minister at St Ninian's Church in Corstorphine, Edinburgh. Assessed as one of the 100 most powerful women in the United Kingdom by Woman's Hour on BBC Radio 4 in February 2013. Honorary Degree of Doctor of Divinity awarded by Glasgow University, December 2014. Address: Alexandra Drive, Renfrew PA4 8UB.

Hook, Professor Andrew Dunnet, MA, PhD, FRSE, FBA. Bradley Professor of English Literature, Glasgow University, 1979-98; b. 21.12.32, Wick; m., Judith Ann (deceased); 2 s.; (1 deceased); 1 d. (deceased). Educ. Wick High School; Daniel Stewart's College, Edinburgh; Edinburgh University; Manchester University; Princeton University. Edinburgh University: Assistant Lecturer in English Literature, 1961-63, Lecturer in American Literature, 1963-70; Senior Lecturer in English, Aberdeen University, 1970-79; Chairman, Committee for Humanities and Member, Committee for Academic Affairs, CNAA, 1987-92; Chairman: Scottish Universities Council on Entrance English Panel, 1986-92, Universities and Colleges Admissions Service English Panel, since 1995; Member: Scottish Examination Board, 1984-92, Scottish Qualifications Authority English Panel, 1996-99; President, Eighteenth-Century Scottish Studies Society, 1990-92. Publications: Scotland and America 1750-1835, 1975, second edition, 2008; American Literature in Context 1865-1900, 1983; Scott's Waverley (Editor), 1971; Charlotte Brontë's Shirley (Editor, with Judith Hook), 1974; Dos Passos: A Collection of Critical Essays (Editor), 1974; The History of Scottish Literature II, 1660-1800 (Editor), 1987; Scott Fitzgerald, 1992; The Glasgow Enlightenment (Co-Editor), 1995; From Goosecreek to Gandercleugh, 1999; Scott's The Fair Maid of Perth (Co-Editor), 1999; F. Scott Fitzgerald: A Literary Life, 2002; Francis Jeffrey's American Journal: New York to Washington 1813 (Co-editor), 2011; Eliza Oddy, A Mississippi Diary: From St Paul, Minnesota to Alton, Illinois, October 1894 to May 1895 (Editor), 2013. Recreations: theatre; opera; catching up on reading. Address: 5 Rosslyn Terrace, Glasgow G12 9NB; e-mail: nassau@palio2.vianw.co.uk

Hooper, Ian Ross, BA; b. 26.5.49, Edinburgh; m., Julie Ellen Vaughan; 1 d.; 1 s. Educ. Hornchurch Grammar School, Essex; Faculty of Fine Arts, University of East Anglia. Department of the Environment, 1973-89; English Heritage, 1984-85; Depute Director and Museum of Scotland Project Director, National Museums of Scotland, 1989-99; Head of Economy and Industry Division, Scotland Office, 1999-2003; Head of Natural Resources Division, Scottish Government, 2003-2011. Recreations: art, music, mountains. Address: 3 Inverleith Row, Edinburgh EH3 5LP.

Hope of Craighead, Rt. Hon. Lord (James Arthur David Hope), KT, PC, FRSE. HM Lord High Commissioner to the General Assembly of the Church of Scotland, 2015-2016; Convener, Crossbench Peers, since 2015; Chief Justice, Abu Dhabi: Global Market Courts, since 2015; Deputy President of the Supreme Court of the United Kingdom, 2009-2013; Chancellor, Strathclyde University, 1998-2013; b. 27.6.38, Edinburgh; m., Katharine Mary Kerr; 2 (twin) s.; 1 d. Educ. Edinburgh Academy; Rugby School; St. John's College, Cambridge (BA); Edinburgh University (LLB); Hon. LLD, Aberdeen (1991), Strathclyde (1993), Edinburgh (1995), Glasgow (2013); DUniv, Strathclyde (2014), BPP University (London), Abertay; Fellow, Strathclyde, 2000. National Service, Seaforth Highlanders, 1957-59; admitted Faculty of Advocates, 1965; Standing Junior Counsel to Inland Revenue, 1974-78; QC, 1978; Advocate Depute, 1978-82; Chairman, Medical Appeal Tribunal, 1985-86; Legal Chairman, Pensions Appeal Tribunal, 1985-86; Dean, Faculty of Advocates, 1986-89; A Senator of the College of Justice, Lord Justice General of Scotland, and Lord President of the Court of Session, 1989-96; A Lord of Appeal in Ordinary, 1996-2009. President, The Stair Society, 1993-2013; President, Commonwealth Magistrates' and Judges' Association, 2003-06; Hon. Professor of Law, Aberdeen, 1994; David Kelbie Award, 2007; Fellow, WS Society, 2011; Baron (Life Peer), 1995. Publications: Gloag and Henderson's Introduction to Scots Law (Joint Editor, 7th edition, Assistant Editor, 8th and 9th editions, Contributor, 11th edition); Armour on Valuation for Rating (Joint Editor, 4th and 5th editions); (Contributor) Stair Memorial Encyclopaedia of Scots Law and Court of Session Practice. Address: (h.) 34 India Street, Edinburgh EH3 6HB; T.-0131-225 8245.
E-mail: hopejad@parliament.uk

Hope, Graham. Chief Executive, West Lothian Council, since 2010; b. 1966; m.; 2 c. Held a number of posts within West Lothian Council since joining in 1996. Address: (b.) West Lothian Council, West Lothian Civic Centre, Howden South Road, Livingston, West Lothian, EH54 6FF.

Hopkins, Professor David James, PhD, MA (Dist), PGCE (Dist), BA (Hons). Professor of Art History, University of Glasgow; b. 29.08.55, Derby; 1 s. Formerly Lecturer at Universities of Edinburgh, St. Andrews and Edinburgh College of Art; from 2000 has been Senior Lecturer, Reader and now Professor, Glasgow University. Publications: books include: 'Marcel Duchamp and Max Ernst', 1998; After Modern Art: 1945-2000, 2000; Dada and Surrealism, 2003; Neo-Avant-Garde, 2006; Dada's Boys: Masculinity after Duchamp, 2007; Virgin Microbe: Essays on Dada, 2014. Exhibition Curation: includes: Dada's Boys, Fruitmarket Gallery, Edinburgh, 2006; Childish Things, Fruitmarket Gallery, Edinburgh, 2010-2011. Address: (b.) Department of Art History, University of Glasgow G12 8QH.

Horner, Professor Robert Malcolm Wigglesworth, CEng, BSc, PhD, FRSE, FICE, Hon. FRIAS. Professor Emeritus, Dundee University, since 2006, Professor of Engineering Management, 1986-2006, Vice Principal, 2012, Deputy Principal, 2002-06, and Director, Enterprise Management, 2000-06 (Chair, School of Engineering and Physical Sciences, 1997-99); b. 27.7.42, Bury; m., Beverley Anne Wesley; 1 s.; 1 d. Educ. The Bolton School; University College, London. Civil Engineer, Taylor Woodrow Construction Ltd., 1966-77; Lecturer, Senior Lecturer, Head, Department of Civil Engineering, Dundee University, 1977-91; Managing Director, International Maintenance Management, 1996-97. Founder Chairman, Dundee Branch, Opening Windows on Engineering; Winner, CIOB Ian Murray Leslie Award, 1980 and 1984; Atlantic Power and Gas Ltd.: Non-executive Director, 1991-97, Director, Research and Development, 1993-97; Chairman: Winton Caledonian Ltd., 1995-97, Whole Life Consultants Ltd., since 2004; Director, Dundee Rep., 1991-2003; Director, Scottish Institute for Enterprise, 1999-2005; Director, Objective 3 Partnership, 2000-03 (Vice Chairman, 2002-03); Member, Council, National Conference of University Professors, 1989-93; Director, Scottish International Resource Project, 1994-95; Member: Technology Foresight Construction Sector Panel, 1994-98, British Council Advisory Committee on Science, Engineering and the Environment, 1994-2005; Member, Construction Futures Technical Reference Group, since 2005 (Chair, 2011-2014); Director, Scottish Enterprise Tayside, 2003-08, Chair, 2005-08; Member, Tayside and Central Scotland Transport Planning Partnership Executive, 2006-2010; Director, Citizens Advice Bureau, Dundee, 1993-2003; Chairman, Friends of St. Paul's Cathedral, 1993-95; Non-Executive Director, CXR Bioscience, since 2008; Member, Construction Industry Training Board Council, since 2015. Recreations: rotary; gardening. Address: (h.) Westfield Cottage, 11 Westfield Place, Dundee DD1 4JU; T.-01382 225933.

Hosie, Stewart. MP (SNP), Dundee East, since 2005; Deputy Leader, SNP, 2014-16; Shadow SNP Westminster Group Leader (Economy), since 2015; b. 1963, Dundee; m., Shona Robison; 1 d. Educ. Carnoustie High School; University of Abertay. Career history: IT systems; SNP Youth Convener, 1986-89; SNP National Secretary, 1999-

2003; Organisation Convener, 2003-05; UK Parliament: contested 1992 and 1997 general elections in Kirkcaldy; SNP Spokesperson for Women, 2005-07, Home Affairs, 2005-07, Economy 2005-2010, Shadow Chief Whip (Commons), 2007-2010; Shadow SNP Spokesperson (Treasury), 2010-2015; SNP Deputy Westminster Leader, since 2010; SNP Chief Whip, 2010-2015. Member, Select Committees on: Members Estimate, since 2015, House of Commons Commission, since 2015, Treasury, 2010-2015. Recreations: football; hill-walking; rugby. Address: (b.) House of Commons, London SW1A 0AA; e-mail: hosies@parliament.uk

Hossack, Dr. William Strachan, MB, ChB, DObstRCOG, Cert. Aviation Medicine; b. 10.9.29, Macduff; m., Catherine Sellar (widower); 1 s.; 1 d. Educ. Banff Academy; Aberdeen University. House Officer, Aberdeen Maternity Hospital and City Hospital, Aberdeen; Junior Specialist Obstetrics, RAF Hospital, St. Athan; GP, Banff, Visiting M.O., Chalmers Hospital and Ladysbridge Hospital, Banff; authorised Medical Examiner (PPL), Civil Aviation Authority. Hon. Medical Adviser, RNLI Macduff; Chairman, Banffshire Hospitals Board; Honorary Sheriff, Grampian Region; General Comissioner, Inland Revenue; Chairman, Martin Trust. Recreations: music; choral singing; watercolour painting; amateur radio. Address: (h.) Kincraig, 39 Skene Street, Macduff, Aberdeenshire AB44 1RP; T.-01261 832099.

Hough, Professor James, OBE, BSc, PhD, FRS, FRSE, FAPS, FInstP, FRAS. Professor of Experimental Physics, Glasgow University, since 1986; emeritus holder of the Kelvin Chair of Natural Philosophy; Director, Institute for Gravitational Research, 2000-09; Member, PPARC Council, 2005-07; Chair, PPARC (now STFC) Education and Training Committee, 2006-2010; Member, ESF Physical and Engineering Science Committee, since 2010; Member, Scottish Science Advisors Council, since 2010; Chief Executive, Scottish Universities Physics Alliance, since 2011; Member, Council, Institute of Physics, since 2011; Chair, Education Committee, Institute of Physics in Scotland, since 2011; Member, Executive Committee, European Physical Society, since 2012; b. 6.8.45, Glasgow; m., Anne Park McNab (deceased); 1 s.; 1 d. Educ. High School of Glasgow; Glasgow University. Glasgow University: Lecturer in Natural Philosophy, 1972, Senior Lecturer, 1983; Visiting Fellow, JILA, University of Colorado, 1983; Max Planck Research Prize, 1991; Duddell Prize, IOP, 2004; PPARC Senior Fellowship, 1997-2000. Publications: 230 refereed publications in learned journals; 60 contributions in books/conference reports. Address: (b.) Department of Physics and Astronomy, University of Glasgow, Glasgow G12 8QQ; T.-0141-330 4706; e-mail: j.hough@physics.gla.ac.uk

Housden, Stuart David, OBE, BSc (Hons) (Zoology). Director, RSPB Scotland, since 1994; Member, UK Board of RSPB; b. 24.6.53, Croydon; m., Catherine Juliet Wilkin; 3 d. Educ. Selhurst Grammar School; Royal Holloway College, London University. Freshwater biologist, Thames Water, 1976; RSPB: Species Investigation Officer, 1977-79, Parliamentary Officer, 1979-82, Manager — Government Unit, 1982-85, Head, Conservation Planning Department, 1985-90, Head, Conservation Planning, 1990-93. Member, Cairngorms Partnership Board, 1995-97; Member, ScottishPower Environment Forum, since 1999; Director, Scottish Government's Rural Development Council, Scottish Biodiversity Group; Churchill Fellow, 1992. Public speaker. Publications: Important Bird Areas in the UK (Co-Editor); numerous articles. Recreations: ornithology; travel; rugby football; work. Address: (b.) RSPB, 2 Lochside View, Edinburgh Park, Edinburgh EH12 9DH. Follow on twitter@StuartHousden.

House, Sir Stephen, QPM. Former Chief Constable, Police Scotland (2012-2015); b. 1957, Glasgow. Career: joined Sussex Police in 1981; served in uniform operational posts in that force and also on transfer in Northamptonshire Police and West Yorkshire Police, 1981-88; joined Staffordshire Police as an Assistant Chief Constable in 1998; led initially in Territorial Policing and latterly in Crime and Operations; joined the Metropolitan Police Service as a Deputy Assistant Commissioner in 2001; appointed to Assistant Commissioner, serving first in Central Operations and then in Specialist Crime; Chief Constable of Strathclyde Police, 2007-2012. Knighted in the Queen's Birthday Honours in recognition for his services to law and order, June 2013. Awarded the Queen's Police Medal in 2005.

Houslay, Professor Miles Douglas, BSc, PhD, FRSE, FRSB, FRSA, FIBiol, CBiol, FMedSci. Director and Chief Scientific Officer, Mironid Ltd; Managing Director, BioGryffe Consulting Ltd.; Professor of Pharmacology (part time), University of Strathclyde, 2011-2015; Professor of Pharmacological Innovation, King's College London (part time); Emeritus Professor, Glasgow University, since 2011; Gardiner Professor of Biochemistry, Glasgow University, 1984-2011; b. 25.6.50, Wolverhampton; m., Rhian Mair; 2 s.; 1 d. Educ. Grammar School, Brewood, Stafford; University College, Cardiff; King's College, Cambridge; Cambridge University. ICI Research Fellow and Fellow, Queens' College, Cambridge, 1974-76; Lecturer, then Reader in Biochemistry, UMIST, 1976-82; Selby Fellow, Australian Academy of Science, 1984; Colworth Medal, Biochemical Society of Great Britain, 1984; Honorary Research Fellow, California Metabolic Research Foundation, since 1981; Editor in Chief, Cellular Signalling, 1984-2014; Deputy Chairman, Biochemical Journal, 1984-89; Editorial Board, Biochimica Biophysica Acta; Member: Committee, Biochemical Society, 1982-85, Research Committee, British Diabetic Association, 1986-91; Chairman, Grant Committee A, Cell and Disorders Board, Medical Research Council, 1989-92; Member: Scientific and Medical Grant Committee, Scottish Home and Health Department, 1991-94, Advisory Board for External Appointments, London University, 1990-92, HEFC RAE Basic Medical and Dental Sciences Panel, since 1996, Wellcome Trust BMB Grant Panel, 1996-2000; Chairman, British Heart Foundation Project Grant Panel; Member, British Heart Foundation Chairs and Programme Grant Panel, 1997-2000; Trustee, British Heart Foundation, 1997-2001; 1998 Founder Fellow, Academy of Medical Sciences; Burroughs-Wellcome Visiting Professor, USA, 2001; Joshua Lederberg Society Prize, Celgene Corp, USA, 2012; Consultant, various pharmaceutical companies in UK, Europe, Asia and USA; co-founder, Biotheryx, inc. Publications: Dynamics of Biological Membranes; over 440 scientific papers. Address: (b.) BioGryffe Consulting Ltd., Torrey Pines, Prieston Road, Bridge of Weir PA11 3AJ. E-mail: miles.houslay@glasgow.ac.uk

Housley, Edward, MB, ChB, FRCPEdin, FRCP. Retired Medical Specialist, Armed Forces Scotland (1975-2007); Consultant Physician to the Army in Scotland, 1995-2006; retired Consultant Physician, Edinburgh Royal Infirmary; b. 10.1.34, Chester, USA; 1 d. Educ. Mundella Grammar School, Nottingham; Birmingham University. Postgraduate training, Department of Medicine, Birmingham University and McGill University, Montreal; former Honorary Senior Lecturer, Department of Medicine, Edinburgh University. Recreation: crossword puzzles. Address: (h.) 6 Kew Terrace, Edinburgh EH12 5JE. E-mail: edhousley@btinternet.com

Houston, Alexander Stewart, BSc (Hons), PhD, FIPEM. Honorary Professor, University of Stirling, since 2007; Medical Imaging Consultant, Hermes Medical Solutions, since 2004; b. 16.06.44, Glasgow; m., Roberta Ann; 1 s.; 2 d. Educ. Woodside Senior Secondary School, Glasgow; University of Glasgow; University of Edinburgh. Research Assistant, University of Dundee, 1971-75; Clinical

Scientist: Royal Naval Hospital Haslar, 1975-2001, Portsmouth Hospitals NHS Trust, 2001-04; Visiting Professor, University of Portsmouth, 2004-07. Norman Veall Medal, 2001. Recreations: astronomy; audio-visual; bridge; photography; songwriting; watching Partick Thistle. Address: (b.) Department of Psychology, University of Stirling FK9 4LA; T.-01786-467640.
E-mail: alex.houston@stir.ac.uk

Houston, Anne C., OBE, CQSW, FRSA. Independent Chair, North Ayrshire Child Protection Committee, since 2014; former Chief Executive, Children 1st (2007-2014); Director, ChildLine Scotland, 1994-2007 and Deputy Chief Executive, Childline UK, 2003-07; b. 28.8.54, Glasgow. Educ. Bishopbriggs High School; Strathclyde University. Social Worker, Intermediate Treatment Officer, Team Leader, Southampton Social Services Department, 1980-86; Project Manager/Tutor, Richmond Fellowship, Glasgow, 1986-90; Counselling Manager, Childline Scotland, 1990-94. Trustee of Cattanach Charitable Trust; Board Member, Care Inspectorate, since 2014; Chair, Scottish Child Protection Committee Chairs Forum, since 2015. Received Honorary Doctorate from University of West of Scotland, June 2015. Recreations: reading; music; swimming; gardening; animals; food and wine with friends; travel. Address: 20 Bellshaugh Lane, Glasgow G12 0PE; T.-07809609571; e-mail: anne@achouston.plus.com

Houston, Brian. Chair, Lothian NHS Board, since 2013; b. 1948, Edinburgh; 4 c. Career: financial and management accounting roles before later running two medium-sized companies as General Manager; has worked as a management consultant specialising in strategy development, planning and implementation of major change programmes for clients in all industries and geographies; also worked as a consultant focussing on board level advice and support in strategy and change management. Served as a Non-Executive Chairman and Director of several private companies and spent eight years on the board of Visit Scotland; Director of Hibernian Football Club. Recreations: hillwalking; cycling; running. Address: Edinburgh and Lothians Health Foundation, 2nd Floor, Waverley Gate, 2-4 Waterloo Place, Edinburgh EH1 3EG; T.-0131 465 5850.

Houston, Graham. Chairman, Scottish Qualifications Authority, since 2009. Experienced, qualified management coach throughout the private and public sectors. Formerly Scottish Director of the Work Foundation (formerly the Industrial Society), then established own consultancy. Elected Councillor, Stirling Council, since 2007; appointed to Board, Scottish Police Authority, 2012. Address: Scottish Qualifications Authority, The Optima Building, 58 Robertson Street, Glasgow G2 8DQ.

Houston, Professor Robert Allan, MA, PhD, FRHS, MAE, FRSE. Professor of Modern History, University of St Andrews, since 1995; b. 27.9.54, Hamilton; m., Dr Veronica Anne O'Halloran. Educ. Edinburgh Academy; University of St Andrews; University of Cambridge. Research Fellow, Clare College, Cambridge, 1981-83; University of St Andrews: Lecturer in Modern History, 1983-93, Reader in Modern History, 1993-95. Visiting Professor, Faculteit der Historische en Kunstwetenschappen, Erasmus University Rotterdam, 1994; Leverhulme Research Fellowship, 1996-97; "Distinguished Visiting Scholar", Department of History, University of Adelaide, 1996. Publications include: Conflict and identity in the history of Scotland and Ireland from the seventeenth to the twentieth century (Co-Editor), 1995; Social change in the age of Enlightenment: Edinburgh, 1660-1760, 1994; Madness and society in eighteenth-century Scotland, 2000; Autism in history. The case of Hugh Blair of Borgue (Co-Author), 2000; The New Penguin History of Scotland (Co-Editor), 2001; Scotland: a very short introduction, 2008; Punishing the dead? Suicide, lordship and community in Britain, 1500-1830, 2010. Recreations: scuba diving; yoga;

tai chi; cooking; travel. Address: University of St Andrews, St Katherine's Lodge, The Scores, St Andrews KY16 9AR.

Howard, Dr Grahame Charles William, BSc (Hons), MBBS, MD, FRCP(Ed), FRCR. Consultant Clinical Oncologist and Honorary Senior Lecturer, Edinburgh University, 1987-2011; Clinical Director, Edinburgh Cancer Centre, 1999-2005; Clinical Director, Cancer Services, 2005-07; b. 15.5.53, London; 3 s. Educ. King Edward VI School, Norwich; St Thomas' Hospital Medical School, London University. Registrar in Oncology, Royal Free Hospital, London; Senior Registrar, Addenbrookes Hospital, Cambridge; appointed Consultant Oncologist, Edinburgh Cancer Centre, 1987; Head of Radiotherapy then Clinical Director, 1999-2005; Chair, Lothian Cancer Planning and Implementation Group, since 2006; several commitments to Royal College of Radiologists; previously Vice-Chair, Scottish Intercollegiate Guideline Network and Chair, Cancer subgroup, until 2007; Chair, Oncology Section, S.E. Scotland Urological Oncology Group, until 2007; Scottish Government Health Department Speciality Adviser for Clinical Oncology. Assistant Editor, Clinical Oncology. Publications: author of scientific papers; writer and author of novels, "The Tales of Dod", 2010, "Spoz and Friends, Tales of a London Medical Student", 2013; "The Euthanasia Protocol", 2015. Recreations: music; sailing; reading. Address: (h.) 4 Ormelie Terrace, Joppa, Edinburgh EH15.

Howat, Rev. Angus John, MA. Minister, Campbeltown, Tarbert and Islay Free Church, 1996-2009; Assistant Clerk, General Assembly, Free Church of Scotland, 1998-2015; Moderator, General Assembly, Free Church of Scotland, 2013; b. 5.8.44, Monifieth; m., Irene Agnes Gardner Bickerton; 3 d. Educ. Daniel Stewart's College, Edinburgh; Edinburgh University; Strathclyde University; Free Church College. Assistant Librarian, Ayr Public Library, 1966-71; Depute County Librarian, Moray and Nairn, 1971-75; Principal Librarian, Moray District Council at Elgin, 1975-85; Temporary Assistant Librarian, Free Church College, 1988-90; Minister, Campbeltown Free Church, 1990-96. Publication: Churches of Moray (Joint Author). Recreations: family history; walking. Address: 57 Garvine Road, Coylton, Ayr KA6 6NZ; T.-01292 570 136.

Howat, Eileen. Chief Executive, South Ayrshire Council, since 2013. Formerly Executive Director - Resources, Governance and Organisation, South Ayrshire Council. Address: South Ayrshire Council, County Buildings, Wellington Square, Ayr KA7 1DR

Howatson, William, MA (Hons). Freelance journalist and columnist, since 1996; b. 22.1.53, Dumfries; m., Hazel Symington Paton; 2 d. Educ. Lockerbie Academy; Edinburgh University. Press and Journal: Agricultural Editor, 1984-96, Leader Writer, 1990-96. Chairman, Guild of Agricultural Journalists, 1995; Member, Scottish Water and Sewerage Customers Council, 1995-99; Member, Angus College Board of Management, since 1996 (Chairman, 2003-06, Vice Chairman, since 2006); Member, Health Education Board for Scotland, 1997-2003; Vice Chair, NHS Health Scotland, 2003-05; Member, East Areas Board, Scottish Natural Heritage, 1997-2003 (Deputy Chairman, 2000-03); Non Executive Director, Angus NHS Trust, 1998; Governor, Macaulay Land Use Research Institute, 1998-2003; Member, Aberdeenshire Council, since 1999; Chairman, North of Scotland Agriculture Advisory Committee, since 2003; Director, Ash Scotland, 2006-08; Board Member, Scottish Environment Protection Agency, 1999-2005 (Chairman, East Regional Board, 2003-

05); Member, East Regional Board, 2006-08; Member, Rail Passenger Committee for Scotland, 2001-03; Member, Esk District Salmon Fishery Board, 2003-07; Provost, Aberdeenshire Council, 2007-12; Chairman, North East of Scotland Fisheries Development Partnership, 2007-12; Member, Grampian Health Board, 2007-11, Chairman, 2011-14; Chairman, Aberdeen City Community Health Partnership, 2009-2012. Columnist of the Year, Bank of Scotland Press Awards, 1992; Fellow of the Royal Agricultural Societies. Publication: Farm Servants and Labour in Lowland Scotland, 1770-1914 (Contributor). Recreations: gardening; hillwalking; reading; Scottish history. Address: (h.) Stone of Morphie, Hillside, Montrose; T.-01674 830746; e-mail: billhowatson@btinternet.com

Howe, Professor Christine Joyce, BA, PhD, CPsychol, AFBPS. Professor of Education, University of Cambridge, since 2006; b. 21.11.48, Birmingham; m., William Robertson; 1 s.; 1 d. Educ. King Edward VI Camp Hill School for Girls; Sussex University; Cambridge University. Career in teaching and research since 1976. Publications: Learning Language in a Conversational Context, 1983; Language Learning, 1993; Group and Interactive Learning, 1994; Conceptual Structure in Childhood and Adolescence, 1998; Gender and Classroom Interaction, 1997; Peer Groups and Children's Development, 2010; Educational Dialogues - Understanding and Promoting Productive Interaction, 2010. Recreations: bridge; tennis; cycling; hillwalking; theatre; film; politics.

Howells, Laurence. Chief Executive, Scottish Funding Council, since 2014; previously a Senior Director responsible for skills, research and knowledge exchange. Educ. Southampton University. Career: worked for the British Library both in Yorkshire and in London, in a number of administrative and policy roles; worked for the London Borough of Waltham Forest as Assistant Education Officer responsible for the Borough's education budget; joined the Scottish Higher Education Funding Council (a predecessor body to SFC) in 1994. Address: (b.) Apex 2, 97 Haymarket Terrace, Edinburgh EH12 5HD; T.-0131 313 6500.

Howie, Andrew Law, CBE, FRAgrS. Chairman: Howie Animal Feed Ltd., 2001-04, Robert Howie & Sons, 1982-2001, Scottish Milk Ltd., 1994-95; b. 14.4.24, Dunlop; m., Joan Duncan; 2 s.; 2 d. Educ. Glasgow Academy. Joined Robert Howie & Sons, 1941; War Service, RN; became Director, 1965; President, Scottish Compound Feed Manufacturers, 1968-70 and 1983-85; President, Compound Animal Feed Manufacturers National Association, 1971-72; Director, Scottish Corn Trade, 1976-78; Vice-President/Feed, UK Agricultural Supply Trade Association, 1980-81; Chairman, Scottish Council, UKASTA, 1985-87; Director, Scottish Milk Marketing Board, 1980-94 (Chairman, 1982-94); Member, CBI Scottish Council, 1989-95. Recreations: golf; gardening; wood-turning. Address: (h.) Newmill House, Dunlop, Kilmarnock KA3 4BQ; T.-01560 484936.

Howie, Professor John Garvie Robertson, CBE, MD, PhD, Hon DSc, FRCPE, FRCGP, FMedSci. Professor of General Practice, Edinburgh University, 1980-2000; b. 23.1.37, Glasgow; m., Elizabeth Margaret Donald; 2 s.; 1 d. Educ. High School of Glasgow; Glasgow University. Registrar, Laboratory Medicine, Western Infirmary, Glasgow, 1962-66; General Practitioner, Glasgow, 1966-70; Lecturer/Senior Lecturer in General Practice, Aberdeen University, 1970-80; Member: Biomedical Research Committee, SHHD, 1977-81, Health Services Research Committee, SHHD, 1982-86, Chief Scientist Committeee, SHHD, 1987-97, Committee on the Review of Medicines,

1986-91. Publications: Research in General Practice; A Day in the Life of Academic General Practice; Academic General Practice in the UK Medical Schools, 1948-2000. Recreations: golf; gardening; music. Address: (h.) 4 Ravelrig Park, Balerno, Midlothian EH14 7DL; T.-0131-449 6305; e-mail: john.howie23@btinternet.com

Howe, Pauline, OBE. Chief Executive, Scottish Ambulance Service Board, since 2009. Career history: CSL Group in London, working mainly with the Health and Local Government Sectors; qualified as an accountant in 1990, winning the Richard Emmott Memorial Prize for Best Performance in the Case Study Paper; returned to Scotland and joined the NHS in Glasgow as Project Accountant with the Glasgow Royal Infirmary Unit, joined the South Glasgow Unit in 1992 as Deputy Director of Finance and helped in its NHS Trust formation; seconded to the Scottish Executive Health Department as Head of Trust Finance in 1996, and later that year joined the State Hospitals Board for Scotland as Finance and Planning Director; joined the Scottish Ambulance Service as Finance Director in March 2000, also taking responsibility for Information and Communications Technology, Fleet Services, Procurement, Planning and Performance management and Risk Management; took on the role of Chief Operating Officer in 2006, becoming Acting Chief Executive in May 2008. Awarded an OBE in the 2015 New Year's honours for services to Scottish Ambulance Service and NHS Scotland. Address: Scottish Ambulance Service Board, National Headquarters, Tipperlinn Road, Edinburgh EH10 5UU.

Howson, Peter, OBE. Painter; b. 1958, London; m., 1 d. Moved to Glasgow, 1962; attended Glasgow School of Art, 1975-77; spent a short period in the Scottish infantry, travelling in Europe; returned to Glasgow School of Art, 1979-81, studying under Sandy Moffat; Artist in Residence, St Andrews and part-time Tutor, Glasgow School of Art, 1985; commissioned by Imperial War Museum to visit Bosnia as war artist, 1993. Address: c/o Flowers East, 82 Kingsland Road, London E2 8DP.

Hoy, Sir Chris, kt (2009), MBE (2005), BSc (Hons). Former Scottish track cyclist; b. 23.3.76; m., Sarra; 1 s. Educ. George Watson's College; University of St. Andrews; Moray House, University of Edinburgh. Multiple world champion and Olympic Games gold and silver medal winner (3 gold medals in 2008 and 2 gold medals in 2012). Britain's most successful Olympian in terms of gold medals and the most successful Olympic male cyclist of all time. Awarded honorary doctorates from Edinburgh University (2005); Heriot-Watt University (2005) and University of St Andrews (2009).

Ho-Yen, Darrel Orlando, BMSc (Hons), MBChB, MD, FRCPath, FRCP, DSc. Board Member, Sight Action, since 2013; former Consultant Microbiologist, Raigmore Hospital, Inverness (1987-2011), Head of Microbiology, 1994-2011; Director: Scottish Toxoplasma Reference Laboratory, 1987-2011, National Lyme Borreliosis Testing, 2001-2011; Honorary Clinical Senior Lecturer, Aberdeen University, 1987-2011; b. 1.5.48; 2 s. Educ. Dundee University. Ninewells Hospital and Medical School, Dundee, 1974-83; Regional Virus Laboratory, Ruchill Hospital, Glasgow, 1983-87. Publications: Better Recovery from Viral Illnesses; Diseases of Infection (Co-Author); Unwind; Human Toxoplasmosis (Co-Author); Climbing Out; Ticks (Co-author); Scientist's Quest; The Science of Laboratory Diagnosis (Section Editor); Ticks, Your Pets, Your Family and You (Co-Author). Address: (b.) Sight Action, Beechwood House, 69-71 Old Perth Road, Inverness IV2 3JH.

Hubbuck, Professor John Reginald, BA (Cantab), MA, DPhil (Oxon), FRSE, FRSA, CMath, FIMA. Emeritus Professor of Mathematics, Aberdeen University; b. 3.5.41, Girvan; m., Anne Neilson; 1 s.; 1 d. Educ. Manchester

Grammar School; Queens' College, Cambridge; Pembroke College, Oxford. Fellow: Gonville and Caius College, Cambridge, 1970-72, Magdalen College, Oxford, 1972-78; President, Edinburgh Mathematical Society, 1985-86. Recreation: hill-walking. Address: (h.) 8 Fonthill Terrace, Aberdeen AB11 7UR; T.-01224 588738; e-mail: j.hubbuck@abdn.ac.uk

Hudghton, Ian. Member of the European Parliament (SNP), since 1998; m., Lily; 1 s.; 1 d. Ran family home decorating business, 20 years; former Member, EU's Committee of the Regions; elected to Angus District Council, 1986 (Housing Convener, eight years); Depute SNP Group Leader and Property Convener, Tayside Regional Council, 1994-96; elected to Angus Council, 1995 (Leader, 1996-98); President, Scottish National Party, since 2005; President, European Free Alliance, 2004-09. Address: (b.) 8 Old Glamis Road, Dundee DD3 8HP; e-mail: ian.hudghton@europarl.europa.eu

Hudson, Barbara Jean, BA (Hons). Dip. App.Soc.Studies. Director BAAF (Adoption and Fostering) Scotland, since 1998; b. Scunthorpe. Educ. King Edward VI Grammar School, Louth; Manchester University; Leeds University. VSO, Nigeria, 1972; Social Work Department, Norwich hospitals, 1973-75; Leeds Social Services Department, 1976-86; Bradford Social Services, 1986-98. Recreations: walking; opera; theatre; friends. Address: (b.) 113 Rose Street, Edinburgh EH2 3DT; T.-0131 226 9270; e-mail: scotland@baaf.org.uk

Hudson, Rev. Eric Vallance, LTh. Retired Minister, Westerton Parish Church, Bearsden (1990-2007); b. 22.2.42, Glasgow; 1 s.; 1 d; m. (2), Anne Morrison. Educ. Paisley Grammar School; Wollongong High School, NSW; Christ's College, Aberdeen and Aberdeen University. Sub-Editor, D.C. Thomson & Co. Ltd., Dundee, 1961-66; Student Assistant, West Kirk of St. Nicholas, Aberdeen, 1966-69; Senior Assistant Minister, New Kilpatrick Parish Church, Bearsden, 1971-73; Minister, Kintore Parish Church, 1973-78; Religious Programmes Officer, Scottish Television, 1978-89; Convener, Association of Bearsden Churches, 1997-99; Convener, Religious Advisory Committee, Radio Clyde, 2004-05; Moderator, Dumbarton Presbytery, 1998-99; President, Westerton Male Voice Choir, since 2011; Director, The Glasgow Highland Club, 2012-2014. Address: 2 Murrayfield Drive, Bearsden, Glasgow G61 1JE; e-mail: evhudson@hotmail.co.uk

Hudson, Professor John Geoffrey Henry, MA (Oxon), MA (Toronto), DPhil, FRHistS, FRSE. Professor of Legal History, University of St Andrews, since 2003; b. 7.5.62, Romford; m., Lise Alexandra McAslan Hudson; 2 d. Educ. Brentwood School; Worcester College, Oxford. Career history: Junior Research Fellow, Worcester College, Oxford; Scouloudi Research Fellow, Institute of Historical Research, University of London; Lecturer in Mediaeval History, University of St Andrews, Reader in Mediaeval History, Professor of Legal History, Director of Institute of Legal and Constitutional Research; William W. Cook, Global Law Professor, University of Michigan Law School. Council Member, Selden Society. Publication: Oxford History of The Laws of England, II: 871-1216, 2012; Recreations: squash; running; music; literature. Address: Department of Mediaeval History, 71 South Street, St Andrews, Fife KY16 9QW; T.-01334 462888; e-mail: jghh@st-andrews.ac.uk

Hughes of Woodside, Lord (Robert Hughes). Life Peer; MP (Labour), Aberdeen North, 1970-97; b. 3.1.32; m.; 2 s.; 3 d. Educ. Powis Secondary School, Aberdeen; Robert

Gordon's College, Aberdeen; Benoni High School, Transvaal; Pietermaritzburg Technical College, Natal. Engineering apprenticeship, South African Rubber Company, Natal, 1949-54; draughtsman, C.F. Wilson & Co., Aberdeen, 1954-70; Member, Aberdeen City Council, 1962-71; Chairman, Aberdeen City Labour Party, 1961-69; Member, Select Committee on Scottish Affairs, 1971; Opposition Junior Spokesman on Scottish Affairs, 1972-74; Parliamentary Under Secretary of State, Scottish Office, 1974-75; Chairman, Select Committee on Scottish Affairs, 1981; Opposition Junior Spokesman on Transport, 1981-83; Opposition Principal Spokesman on Agriculture, 1984-85, on Transport, 1985-87; Member, General Medical Council, 1976-79; Chairman: Anti Apartheid Movement, 1976-94, Action for Southern Africa (ACTSA), 1994-99 (Honorary President, since 1990); Vice-Convenor, Scottish Group, Labour MPs, 1989; Convenor, Scottish Group of Labour MPs, 1990-91; Member, Select Committee on Scottish Affairs, 1992-97; South African National Order 'Grand Companion of OR Tambo', conferred 2004; Trustee, Canon Collins Education Trust for Southern Africa, 1997-2004. Address: (b.) House of Lords, London.

Hughes, Dale William Alexander, LLB (Hons), DipLP. Advocate, since 1993; b. 21.1.67, Glasgow; m., Sally Jane Henderson (deceased); 2 s.; 1 d. Educ. Kirkcaldy High School; George Watson's College, Edinburgh; Aberdeen University; Edinburgh University. Solicitor, 1990-93. Tutor, University of Edinburgh. Recreations: travel; arts; sport. Address: (b.) Advocates Library, Edinburgh.

Hughes, Derek Walter, BSc, BD (Hons), DipEd. Parish Minister, Dalziel St. Andrew's Parish Church, Motherwell, since 1996; b. 27.4.60, Motherwell; m., Elizabeth; 2 d; 1 s.; 1 grandson. Educ. Garrion Academy, Wishaw; Stirling University; Edinburgh University. Teacher of Chemistry, Berwickshire High School, Duns, 1981-86; Parish Minister, Townhead Parish Church, Coatbridge, 1990-96. Recreations: reading; travel. Address: Church Manse, 4 Pollock Street, Motherwell ML1 1LP; T.-01698 263 414; M.-07984 019 903; e-mail: derekthecleric@btinternet.com

Hughes, Professor Gordon. Chairman, Water Industry Commission for Scotland, since 2011. Academic career in the UK, then Senior Adviser on energy and environmental policy at the World Bank until 2001; subsequently worked in the private sector; currently a part-time Professor of Economics at the University of Edinburgh teaching courses in the Economics of Natural Resources and Public Economics. Specialised in the fields of public policy, taxation and applied econometrics; experience covers extensive work in the fields of energy and environmental economics, the regulation of utilities, the design and implementation of tax systems, the functioning of labour and housing markets, and the appraisal of projects. Published many papers in applied econometrics dealing with issues of pensions, labour markets, taxation, and energy policies. Address: The Water Industry Commission for Scotland, First Floor, Moray House, Forthside Way, Stirling FK8 1QZ; T.-01786 430200.

Hughes, Jonathan, BA (Hons), MSc (Hons). Global Councillor, International Union for Conservation of Nature, since 2012; Chief Executive, Scottish Wildlife Trust, since 2014; b. Wrexham, North Wales; engaged to Emmi Hartikainen; 2s.; 1d. Educ. University of Wales; University of Florence (Italy). Council Member, London Wildlife Trust, 1997-98; Woodland and Forestry Policy, Woodland Trust, 1998-2004; Policy Advisor, Forestry Commission England, 2004-2006; Head of Policy, Scottish Wildlife Trust, 2006-09. Board Member, Architecture and Design

Scotland; Academician, Academy of Urbanism; Chair, Postcode Heroes Trust; Co-Founder, World Forum on Natural Capital; Honorary Fellowship, University of Edinburgh, 2015. Address: 110 Commercial Street, Leith, Edinburgh EH6 6NF.

Hughes, Professor Michael David. Emeritus Professor of Management, University of Aberdeen Business School; b. 8.2.47, London; m., Ewa Maria Helinska-Hughes; 1 s.; 2 d. Educ. Farnborough Grammar School; Brunel University. Address: (b.) University of Aberdeen Business School, Edward Wright Building, Aberdeen AB24 3QY; T.-01224 272167.

Hughes, Dr. Peter Travers, OBE (1993), FREng, FIMMM. Chairman, Primary Engineer Programmes; President, Robert Burns World Federation, since 2015; b. 24.12.46; m. (1) 2 s.; m. (2) 1 s.; m. (3). Educ. Wishaw High School; Technical College, Coatbridge; Strathclyde University; Dundee University. Trainee Metallurgist, Clyde Alloy (latterly British Steel), Foundry Metallurgist rising to Foundry Manager, North British Steel Group, 1968-76; General Manager, Lake and Elliot Essex, 1976-80 (Director, 1977-80); Managing Director, National Steel Foundry (1914) Ltd. (subsidiary of Lake and Elliot), 1980-83; initiated MBO forming Glencast Ltd., 1983 (company sold to NACO Inc Illinois USA, 1994); Chairman and Managing Director, Glencast Ltd, 1983-98 (winners Queen's Award for Technological Achievement 1990); Chief Executive, Scottish Engineering, 1998-2012 (President, 1993); Chairman: Steel Castings Research and Trade Association, 1988-92 (Chairman, Research Committee, 1985-88), DTI Steering Committee on UK Development of Solidification Simulation Programmes for Castings, 1988-89; guest lecturer at various conferences UK and abroad; UK President, Institute of British Foundrymen, 1994-95 (President, Scottish Branch, 1984-85); former Chairman, Scottish Steel Founders' Association; former Governor and Member, Court, University of Abertay (formerly Dundee Institute of Technology); Member, Court, University of Strathclyde; Chairman, Board, New Park Preparatory School, 1998-2001; elder, Church of Scotland, 1976; Hon Dr: University of Paisley, 2001; University of Strathclyde, 2006, Napier University, 2006; Fellow, University of Abertay, 2001; FIMgt 1986; FIBF 1988; FIM 1993; CEng 1994; FREng 1995; DMS, University of Strathclyde, 1976; MBA, University of Dundee, 1991; elected Fellow of The Royal Society of Edinburgh (FRSE), 2013. Recreations: soccer; golf; tennis; curling; music; church; after dinner speaking. Address: (h.) West Coldstream Farm, Carluke, Lanarkshire ML8 4QX.
E-mail: peterthughes@btinternet.com

Hughes, Rhona Grace, MD, FRCOG, FRCPE. Consultant Obstetrician, since 1996; Honorary Senior Lecturer, since 1996; b. 29.1.58, Portsmouth; m., Tommy Hepburn; 2 s.; 1 d. Educ. Craigmount High School, Edinburgh; Edinburgh University. House Officer in Medicine and Surgery, 1983-84; Senior House Officer in Obstetrics and Gynaecology, 1984-85; Research Fellow in Virology and Gynaecology, 1985-87; Registrar in Obstetrics and Gynaecology, 1987-90; Senior Registrar, 1990-96 (job share). Recreations: hill-walking; travel; literature; family. Address: (b.) New Royal Infirmary, Little France, Edinburgh; T.-0131 242 2524; e-mail: rhona.hughes@luht.scot.nhs.uk

Hughes, Thomas George, LLB. Sheriff, since 2004; b. 2.1.55, Glasgow; m., Janice; 1 s.; 1 d. Educ. St. Mirin's Academy, Paisley; Strathclyde University. Solicitor, 1979-2004. Recreations: sport; reading. Address: (b.) Sheriff Court House, 6 West Bell Street, Dundee; T.-01382 229961; e-mail: sheriffthughes@scotcourts.gov.uk

Hughes Hallett, Professor Andrew Jonathan, BA (Hons), MSc (Econ), DPhil, FRSA, FRSE. Professor of Economics, George Mason University (USA) and St. Andrews University; council of economic advisers to the Scottish Government; member, Scottish Fiscal Council; advisor for economic affairs to the European Parliament; formerly Professor of Economics, Strathclyde University; Fellow, Royal Society of Edinburgh, since 2000; Research Fellow, Centre for Economic Policy Research, since 1985; Consultant to World Bank, European Commission, UN, IMF, since 1986; Professor and Fulbright Fellow, Princeton University, 1992-94; Jean Monet Professor, since 1996; b. 1.11.47, London; m., Claudia; 2 s.; 1 d. Educ. Radley College; Warwick University; LSE; Oxford University. Lecturer in Economics, Bristol University, 1973-77; Associate Professor, Erasmus University, Rotterdam, 1977-85; David Dale Professor, Newcastle University, 1985-89. Publications: seven books; 250 papers on economic policy and international economics. Address: (b.) 41 Clerk Street, Edinburgh EH8 9JQ; T.-0131-662-4819.
E-mail: ahugheshallett@yahoo.com

Hughes Hallett, David John, FRICS. Consultant; Main Board Member, Scottish Environment Protection Agency, 1995-2002; Board Member, Loch Lomond and the Trossachs National Park Authority, 2002-2010 (Deputy Convener, 2006-2009); Member, East Areas Board of Scottish Natural Heritage, 2005-2008, Local Adviser for SNH, 2008-2012; Panel Member, Waterwatch Scotland, 2006-2009; Board Member, OSCR (Office of the Scottish Charity Regulator), since 2008; Lay Member, Audit Registration Committee, Institute of Chartered Accountants in Scotland, 2008-2014; Member, Registration and Conduct Committee, Scottish Social Services Council, since 2010; Independent Board Member, Public Prosecution Service, Northern Ireland, since 2011; Member of Adjudicating Panels, General Teaching Council for Scotland, since 2012; Member of the Private Rented Housing Panel and Homeowner Housing Panel, since 2012; b. 19.6.47, Dunfermline; m., Anne Mary Wright; 2 s.; 1 d. Educ. Fettes College; Reading University. Chartered Surveyor, rural practice, 1966-76; Land Use Adviser, then Director, Scottish Landowners' Federation, 1976-89. Chairman, Royal Institution of Chartered Surveyors in Scotland, 1988-89; Director, Scottish Wildlife Trust, 1989-98; Member, Policy Committee, Scottish Council for Voluntary Organisations, 1997-2002. Recreations: sailing; sea kayaking; cycling; singing. Address: (h.) The Old School, Back Latch, Ceres, Fife KY15 5NT.
E-mail: david@hugheshallett.co.uk

Hughson, A.V. Mark, MD, MB, ChB, FRCPsych, DPM. Honorary Consultant Psychiatrist, NHS Greater Glasgow and Clyde, 2009-2013; Consultant Psychiatrist, Leverndale Hospital, Glasgow, 1990-2008; Honorary Clinical Senior Lecturer, Glasgow University, since 1991; b. 12.3.47, Edinburgh; m., Joan Scally; 2 s. Educ. George Watson's College, Edinburgh; Glasgow University. Publications: papers on psycho-oncology and other topics. Recreations: playing the organ (not too badly); skiing (badly). Address: (h.) 1 Cleveden Gardens, Glasgow G12 0PU; T.-0141-334 2473.

Hulbert, Dr. John Kenneth Macdonald, MB, CHB, MD. FRSGS, OStJ. Provost of Perth and Kinross, 2007-2012; Councillor, Perth and Kinross, 1995-2012; b. 24.03.39, Madras, S. India; m., Sara née Dobie; 1 s.; 2 d. Educ. Madras College, St. Andrews; Edinburgh University. Knight's Cross of the Order of Merit of the Republic of

Poland. Honorary Fellow of the Royal Scottish Geographical Society, University Lecturer, 1965-72; General Practitioner, 1972-2003. Publication: Perth: A Comprehensive Guide for Locals and Visitors (Author). Recreations: gardening; bee-keeping; walking. Address: (h.) "Wayside", 6 Castle Road, Longforgan, Perthshire DD2 5HA; T.-01382 360294.

Hume, James (Jim) Robert, DipAg, MBA. MSP (Liberal Democrat), South of Scotland, 2007-2016; b. 4.11.62; m., Lynne; 2 s.; 1 d. Educ. Yarrow Primary; Selkirk High School; East of Scotland College of Agriculture; University of Edinburgh. Farming, Partner in "John Hume and Son", since 1988; Councillor, Galashiels and District Ward, Scottish Borders, since 2007; Director, NFUS (National Farmers Union of Scotland), 2004-06 and 2007; Chair of Borders Foundation for Rural Sustainability, 2000-06; Director, Scottish Enterprise Borders, 2002-07. Trustee, Borders Forest Trust, 2000-06. Publication: Co-Author, "Shepherds" by Walter Elliot. Recreations: amateur radio; gardening. Address: (h.) Sundhope Burn, Yarrow, Selkirk TD7 5NF; T.-0131 348 6702.

Hume, John Robert, OBE, BSc, ARCST, FSA Scot, Hon FRIAS, Hon FRSGS, FIESIS. Honorary Professor: Faculty of Arts, University of Glasgow, since 1998, School of History, University of St. Andrews, since 1999; Honorary Life President, Seagull Trust, since 1994 (Chairman, 1978-93); Honorary Vice-President, Association for Industrial Archaeology; Honorary Vice-President, Scottish Railway Preservation Society, since 2000 (Chairman, 1967-76); b. 26.2.39, Glasgow; m., Catherine Hope Macnab; 4 s. Educ. Hutchesons' Boys' Grammar School; Glasgow University; Royal College of Science and Technology. Assistant Lecturer, Lecturer, Senior Lecturer in Economic History, Strathclyde University, 1964-91; Chief Inspector of Historic Buildings, Historic Scotland, 1993-99. Member, Inland Waterways Amenity Advisory Council, 1974-2001; Director, Scottish Industrial Archaeology Survey, 1978-84; Member, Ancient Monuments Board for Scotland, 1981-84; Member, Committee on Artistic Matters, Church of Scotland (Convener, 2003-08); Member, Mission and Discipleship Council, Church of Scotland, 2006-08; Member, Emerging Ministries Task Group, Church of Scotland, 2006-2010; Advisory Member, General Trustees, Church of Scotland; Chairman, Scottish Stained Glass Symposium; Trustee: Scottish Maritime Museum, 1983-98 and since 2009, The Waterways Trust, 2000-2012, Scotland's Churches Scheme, 2000-2012, Scotland's Churches Trust, since 2012; Member, Industrial Archaeology Sub-Committee, English Heritage, 1985-2002; Chair, Royal Commission on the Ancient and Historical Monuments of Scotland, 2005-2015; Chairman, Govan Heritage Trust, since 2015; Patron, Glasgow City Heritage Trust, since 2015. Publications: The Industrial Archaeology of Glasgow; The Industrial Archaeology of Scotland; Dumfries and Galloway, an illustrated architectural guide; Vernacular Buildings of Ayrshire; Wigtownshire Vernacular Buildings; Scotland's Best Churches; West Lothian Churches: an Introduction; The Church Buildings of Ayrshire; as Co-Author: Workshop of the British Empire: Engineering and Shipbuilding in the West of Scotland; Beardmore: the History of a Scottish Industrial Giant; The Making of Scotch Whisky; A Bed of Nails: a History of P. MacCallum & Sons Ltd.; Shipbuilders to the World: a History of Harland and Wolff; Steam Entertainment; Historic Industrial Scenes: Scotland; Industrial History in Pictures: Scotland; Glasgow's Railway Stations; Industry and Transport in Scottish Museums. Recreations: photography; reading; drawing. Address: (h.) 28 Partickhill Road, Glasgow G11 5BP.

Hume, Professor Robert, BSc, MBChB, PhD, FRCP(Edin), FRCPCH. Professor of Developmental Medicine, Dundee University; Consultant Paediatrician, Tayside Universities NHS Trust; b. 5.4.47, Edinburgh; m.,

Shaena Finlayson Blair; 2 d. Educ. Dalkeith High School; Edinburgh University. MRC Fellow, Department of Biochemistry, Edinburgh University, 1975-78; Lecturer, Department of Child Life and Health, Edinburgh University, 1978-80; Senior Lecturer, Department of Child Life and Health, Edinburgh University. Address: (b.) Maternal and Child Health Sciences, Ninewells Hospital and Medical School, Dundee DD1 9SY; T.-01382 660111.

Humes, Professor Walter Malcolm, MA, MEd, PhD, FCS. Retired academic, writer; Visiting Professor of Education, University of Stirling; b. 10.12.45, Newton Mearns. Educ. Eastwood Senior Secondary School; University of Aberdeen; University of Dundee; University of Glasgow. Teacher of English, London and Renfrewshire, 1968-74; Lecturer in English, Notre Dame College, Glasgow, 1974-76; Lecturer in Education, University of Glasgow, 1976-94; Director of Professional Studies, St. Andrew's College, 1994-99; Head of Educational Studies: University of Glasgow, 1999-2000, University of Strathclyde, 2001-04; Professor of Education, University of Aberdeen, 2004-06; University of the West of Scotland, 2006-2010. Editor, Scottish Educational Review, 1990-94. Publications: Scottish Culture and Scottish Education 1800-1980 (Co-editor), 1983; The Leadership Class in Scottish Education, 1986; The Management of Educational Policy: Scottish Perspectives (Co-editor), 1994; Scottish Education (Co-editor), 1999 (2nd edition, 2003, 3rd edition, 2008, 4th edition, 2013); chapters in books and articles in journals on a wide range of educational topics. Recreations: literature; music; swimming. Address: (b.) University of Stirling, Stirling FK9 4LA; e-mail: walter.humes@stir.ac.uk

Humphrey, James Malcolm Marcus, CBE, DL, OStJ, MA. Member, Aberdeenshire Council, 1995-2012 (Member, Grampian Regional Council, 1974-94); Leader, Conservative Group, 1999-2012; Deputy Lieutenant, Aberdeenshire, since 1989; Chairman, North East Scotland Preservation Trust, since 2005; b. 1.5.38, Montreal, Canada; m., Sabrina Margaret Pooley; 2 s.; 2 d. Educ. Eton College; Oxford University. Conservative Parliamentary candidate, North Aberdeen, 1966, Kincardine and Deeside, 1991; Council Member, National Farmers Union of Scotland, 1968-73; Member, Aberdeen County Council, 1970-75 (Chairman of Finance, 1973-75); Grampian Regional Council, 1974-94 (Chairman of Finance, 1974-78, Leader, Conservative Group); Member, Aberdeenshire Council, 1995-2012; Deputy Provost, 2007-2012; Member, Cairngorms National Park Authority Board, 2004-2012; Grand Master Mason of Scotland, 1983-88; former Chairman, Clinterty Agricultural College Council; Member, Queen's Bodyguard for Scotland (Royal Company of Archers); Chairman, North of Scotland Board, Eagle Star Group, 1973-91; Non-Executive Director, Grampian Healthcare NHS Trust, 1993-99; Alternate Member, European Committee of the Regions, 1994-2002; Chairman of the Court of the Convention of The Baronage of Scotland, since 2007; Director: Cairngorms Outdoor Access Trust, 2007-2013, Upper Deeside Access Trust, 2003-07. Recreations: shooting; fishing; photography. Address: (h.) Rhu-Na-Haven, Aboyne, Aberdeenshire.

Humphris, Gerald Michael, BSc (Hons), MClinPsychol, PhD, FRCP (Edin). Chair of Health Psychology, University of St Andrews, since 2003; Honorary Consultant Clinical Psychologist, NHS Lothian, since 2005; b. 18.9.54, Kingston, Surrey; 2 d. Educ. Rutlish Grammar, Merton, London; University of Reading. BSc (Hons), University of Reading, 1973-76; PhD, University of London, 1984; University of Liverpool: MClin in Psychology, 1985, Lecturer/Senior Lecturer, 1991-2001; Reader, University of Manchester, 2001-03. Member: Steering Group of The European

Association for Communication in Healthcare, British Psychological Society (Divisions: Health and Clinical). Recreation: gardening. Address: (b.) Medical School, University of St Andrews, Medical and Biological Sciences Building, North Haugh, St Andrews KY16 9TF; T.-01334 463565; e-mail: gmh4@st-and.ac.uk

Hunter, Andrew Reid, BA (Hons), PGCE. Headmaster, Merchiston Castle School, Edinburgh, since 1998; b. 28.9.58, Nairobi, Kenya; m., Barbara G.; 2 s.; 1 d. Educ. Kenton College, Nairobi; Aldenham School, Elstree; University of Manchester; St. Luke's College, Exeter. Westbrook Hay Preparatory School, 1978-79; Worksop College, 1983-91 (Housemaster, 1987-91); Bradfield College, 1991-98 (Housemaster, 1992-98). Former Chairman, Public Schools Hockey Festival, Oxford; Committee Member, Public Schools Lawn Tennis Association; Governor: Ardvreck Prep School, Crieff; Excelsior Academy, Newcastle. Recreations: reading; attending theatre; former men's county player, tennis, squash and hockey. Address: Castle Gates, Merchiston Castle School, Colinton, Edinburgh EH13 0PU; T.-0131-312 2202.

Hunter, Bobby. Lord-Lieutenant, Shetland, since 2011; b. 1949; m., Mabel; 3 c; 5 grandchildren. Educ. Lerwick; Strathclyde University. Career History: early employment in shipbuilding and marine electrical equipment supply; after periods with Shetland Islands Council and the fish processing industry, returned to marine engineering and supplies until taking early retirement in 2006. Director appointments on behalf of Shetland council's economic development unit, and is a prominent member in the Althing debating society and the Windfarm Supporters Group.

Hunter, Colin M., OBE, MB, ChB, FRCP(Ed), FRCGP, FIHM(Hon). Chair of Trustees, Royal College of General Practitioners, since 2012; Chair, QOF Independent Advisory Committee, National Institute Clinical Excellence; b. 28.4.58, Stirling. Educ. High School of Stirling; Aberdeen University. Principal in general practice, Skene Medical Group, 1986; Honorary Senior Lecturer, Aberdeen University, 1988; Hon. Secretary, N.E. Scotland Faculty, RCGP, 1989-96; first member, RCGP in Scotland, to attain Fellowship of Royal College by Assessment, 1993; Sally Irvine Lecture, Glasgow, 1996; Ian Murray - Scott Lecture, 2003; Chairman, Scottish Council, Royal College of General Practitioners, 1996-2000; National Co-ordinator Primary Care, NHS Education for Scotland, 1999-2005; Hon. Treasurer, Royal College of General Practitioners, 2003-2012. Recreations: hill-walking; singing. Address: The Langdales, 1 Craigston Gardens, Westhill, Aberdeen AB32 6NL; T.-01224 742594; e-mail: colin.hunter@nhs.net

Hunter, David Ian, FRICS. Honorary Swedish Consul to Glasgow, since 2003; Managing Director, Hunter Advisers, since 2005; b. 01.10.53, Glasgow; m., Anna; 2 d. Educ. Eastwood High School, Glasgow. Appentice Surveyor, James Barr & Son, 1972-78; Assistant Surveyor, ultimately Property Director, Scottish Amicable, 1978-96; Managing Director: Argyll Property Asset Manager, 1996-2001, Aberdeen Property Investors, 2001-04. Board Member, British Property Federation (Past President); Member, Bank of England Property Forum. Recreations: field sports; golf; walking. Address: (b.) 185 St. Vincent Street, Glasgow G2 5QD; T.-0141 204 4041.

E-mail: david@hunteradvisers.co.uk

Hunter, George Alexander, OBE (1980), KStJ, KLJ. Founder Governor, Scottish Sports Aid Foundation (1980-

2014); Member, Edinburgh City Council, 1992-2006; b. 24.2.26, Edinburgh; m., Eileen Elizabeth. Educ. George Watson's College, Edinburgh. Served with Cameronians, seconded to 17th Dogara Regiment, Indian Army, 1944-47 (Captain); Lawson Donaldson Seeds Ltd., 1942-82 (Director, 15 years); Honorary Consul for Malta; Secretary, Scottish Amateur Rowing Association, 1948-78 (President, 1978-84); Commonwealth Games Council for Scotland: Treasurer, 1962-78, Secretary, 1978-99; Adviser, Sports Aid Foundation, since 1979; Member, Scottish Sports Council, 1976-84 (Chairman, Games and Sports Committee, 1976-84); Chairman, Scottish Standing Conference for Sport, 1977-84; Secretary, Order of St. John Edinburgh and South East Branch, 1987-2011; Edinburgh Citizen of the Year, 2011. Address: (h.) 1 Craiglockhart Crescent, Edinburgh EH14 1EZ; T.-0131-443 2533.

Hunter, Graham Cran, MA, LLB, MUniv (Hon). Solicitor and part-time University Lecturer (retired); b. 4.10.36, Huntly; m. Janet Catherine Matheson; 3 s. Educ. Gordon Schools, Huntly; Fettes College, Edinburgh; University of Aberdeen. Legal Assistant, Edmonds and Ledingham, Aberdeen 1958-61; Anderson MacArthur & Co., Stornoway, 1961-62; Anderson, Shaw & Gilbert, Inverness, 1962-63; Legal Assistant, Partner, Consultant, Edmonds and Ledingham, (later Ledingham Chalmers) Aberdeen, 1963-2001. Territorial Army, 1959-72, Captain, RA, TA; Part-time Lecturer in School of Law, University of Aberdeen, 1980-2002; Secretary and Treasurer of the Financial Board of Christ's College, Aberdeen, 1972-2001 and Board Member, 2001-2015. Clerk and Assessor to the Seven Incorporated Trades of Aberdeen, 1976-2002; Business Manager of Scotland the What? 1969-96; Hon. Vice-President, Lonach Highland and Friendly Society, since 1996; Trustee, Aberdeen International Youth Festival, 1996-2008; Member of the Board of the National Youth Orchestras of Scotland, 2006-2011. Treasurer, and thereafter Chair, of the Friends of Aberdeen University Library, 1998-2013; Rector's Assessor at the University of Aberdeen to Stephen Robertson, 2008-2011 and Dr Maitland Mackie, 2011-2014; Member of Court, University of Aberdeen, 2008-2014; Member of the Business Committee of the General Council of the University of Aberdeen, since 2015. Presently, Honorary Archival Assistant, University of Aberdeen. Recreations: supports Aberdeen Football Club fervently; plays golf inadequately; escapes to the Western Isles frequently. Address: (h) 62 North Deeside Road, Bieldside, Aberdeen AB15 9DT.

Hunter, James, CBE, FRSE, MA (Hons), PhD. Writer and Historian; Emeritus Professor of History, University of the Highlands and Islands; former Chairman, Highlands and Islands Enterprise; b. 22.5.48, Duror, Argyll; m., Evelyn; 1 s.; 1 d. Educ. Duror Primary School; Oban High School; Aberdeen University; Edinburgh University. Former Director, Scottish Crofters Union; former Chairman, Skye and Lochalsh Enterprise; former Member, Broadcasting Council for Scotland; former Member, Board of Scottish Natural Heritage. Publications: The Making of the Crofting Community, 1976; Skye: The Island, 1986; The Claim of Crofting, 1991; Scottish Highlanders: A People and their Place, 1992; A Dance Called America: The Scottish Highlands, the United States and Canada, 1994; On the Other Side of Sorrow: Nature and People in the Scottish Highlands, 1995; Glencoe and the Indians, 1996; Last of the Free: A Millennial History of the Highlands and Islands of Scotland, 1999; Culloden and the Last Clansman, 2001; Scottish Exodus: Travels Among a Worldwide Clan, 2005; From the Low Tide of the Sea to the Highest Mountain Tops: Community Ownership in the Highlands and Islands, 2012; Set Adrift Upon The World: The Sutherland Clearances, 2015. Address: (b.) 19 Mansefield Park, Kirkhill, Inverness IV5 7ND; T.-01463 831228.

E-mail: jameshunter22548@btinternet.com

Hunter, Professor John Angus Alexander, OBE, BA, MD, FRCPEdin. Professor Emeritus of Dermatology, University of Edinburgh, since 2000; Grant Professor of Dermatology, Edinburgh University, 1981-99; b. 16.6.39, Edinburgh; m., Ruth Mary Farrow; 1 s.; 2 d. Educ. Loretto School; Pembroke College, Cambridge; Edinburgh University. Research Fellow, Institute of Dermatology, London, 1967; Registrar, Department of Dermatology, Edinburgh Royal Infirmary, 1968-70; Exchange Research Fellow, Department of Dermatology, Minnesota University, 1968; Lecturer, Department of Dermatology, Edinburgh University, 1970-74; Consultant Dermatologist, Lothian Health Board, 1974-80; Member: Executive Committee of Investigative Group, British Association of Dermatologists, 1974-76; Executive Committee, British Association of Dermatologists, 1977-79; Secretary, Scottish Dermatological Society, 1980-82; Specialist Advisory Committee, (Dermatology), Joint Committee on Higher Medical Training, 1980-87 (Chairman, 1986-90); Medical Appeal Tribunal, 1981-99; Scottish Committee for Hospital Medical Services, 1983-85; President: Section of Dermatology, Royal Society of Medicine, 1993-94, Scottish Dermatological Society, 1994-97, British Association of Detmatologists, 1998-99. Publications: Common Diseases of the Skin (Co-author); Clinical Dermatology, 1st, 2nd, 3rd and 4th edition (Co-author); Skin Signs in Clinical Medicine (Co-author); Davidson's Principles and Practice of Medicine, 18th, 19th and 20th edition (Co-editor); Davidson's Clinical Cases, 1st and 2nd edition (Co-editor). Recreations: music; gardening; golf. Address: (h.) Sandy Lodge, Nisbet Road, Gullane EH31 2BQ; T.-01620-842-220.

Hunter, Kirk John, MA (Hons), ACIS. Scotland Director and Company Secretary, Dairy UK, since 2010; b. 1.12.54, Glasgow; m., June Wilson. Educ. George Heriots School; Dundee University. Graduate Trainee, SSEB, 1977-79; Trade Association Executive, Thomson McLintock, Glasgow, 1980-83; Commercial Officer, Metal Trades Confederation, London and Glasgow, 1983-86; Peat Marwick McLintock, Glasgow, 1986-89; Company Secretary, Scottish Dairy Association, 1989-2001; Chief Executive, Food Trade Association Management Ltd., 2001-2010. Recreations: sailing; cycling. Address: (h.) 18 Ravelston Road, Bearsden, Glasgow G61 1AW; T.-0141-942 3799.

Hunter, Sir Laurence Colvin, Kt, MA, DPhil, FRSE, FRSA, DUniv (Paisley). Professor of Applied Economics, Glasgow University, 1970-2003, Emeritus Professor, since 2003; b. 8.8.34, Glasgow; m., Evelyn Margaret Green; 3 s.; 1 d. Educ. Hillhead High School, Glasgow; Glasgow University; University College, Oxford. Assistant Lecturer, Manchester University, 1958-59; 2nd Lt., RAEC, 1959-61; Walgreen Postdoctoral Fellow, University of Chicago, 1961-62; joined Glasgow University as Lecturer, 1962; Vice-Principal, 1982-86; Director: External Relations, 1987-90, Business School 1996-99. Council Member, ACAS, 1974-86; Chairman, Police Negotiating Board, 1986-2000; Council Member, Economic and Social Research Council, 1989-92; Editor, Scottish Journal of Political Economy, 1966-97; President, Scottish Economic Society, 1993-96; Treasurer, Royal Society of Edinburgh, 1999-2004. Recreations: golf; painting; curling. Address: (h.) 7 Boclair Crescent, Bearsden, Glasgow G61 2AG; T.-0141-563 7135.

Hunter, Neil. Principal Reporter/Chief Executive Officer, Scottish Children's Reporter Administration, since 2011. Educ. University of Glasgow; Glasgow Caledonian University; Strathclyde University; 1 d. Career: involved in the management of support services for young homeless people in Glasgow and later established one of Scotland's first substance misuse services for children and young people in Springburn, North Glasgow; led the Addictions Partnership for the City of Glasgow; Director of West Glasgow Community Health and Care Partnership (CHCP), until 2010. Address: (b.) Scottish Children's Reporter Administration, Ochil House, Springkerse Business Park Stirling FK7 7XE; T.-0300 200 1555.

Hunter, Peter Matheson, BSc, MPhil, LLB. Legal Officer and Regional Organiser, UNISON Scotland; Lay Member, Employment Appeal Tribunal, since 2000; Member, Addaction Scottish Council; Member, Scottish Consumer Council, 2003-06; b. 11.12.65, Aberdeen. Educ. Cults Academy; Edinburgh University; Glasgow University; Strathclyde University. Scottish Low Pay Unit, 1992, Director, 1999-2001. Lay Member, Employment Tribunal, 1995-2000. Voluntary work in recovery communities. Recreation: Aberdeen FC. Address: (b.) 14 West Campbell Street, Glasgow G2 6RX; T.-0845 355 0845.

Hunter, R. Douglas, LLB (Hons). Partner, Real Estate/Commercial Property, CMS Cameron McKenna LLP, since 2014, formerly Dundas & Wilson CS LLP (1998-2014); b. 8.5.65, Glasgow; m., Lesley; 2 s. Educ. Kelvinside Academy, Glasgow; University of Glasgow. Joined Dundas & Wilson CS as Trainee, 1988. Member, British Council of Offices; British Property Federation; Scottish Property Federation; Founder Member, The Property Standardisation Group. Recreations: golf; rugby (watching); hill walking. Address: (b.) Saltire Court, 20 Castle Terrace, Edinburgh EH1 2EN; T.-0131-200 7437; e-mail: douglas.hunter@cms-cmck.com

Hunter, Sir Thomas Blane, Kt (2005), BA. Entrepreneur; Chairman: West Coast Capital, since 1998, Hunter Foundation, since 1998; Chief Executive Officer, Sports Division, 1984-98. b. 6.5.61, Irvine; m., Marion McKillop; 2 s.; 1 d. Educ. Cumnock Academy; University of Strathclyde. Address: Marathon House, Olympic Business Park, Drybridge Road, Dundonald KA2 9AE; T.-01563 852226.

Hunter Blair, Sir Patrick, Bt, FICFor, BScFor; b. 12.5.58, Dumfries; m., Marguerite; 3 s.; 2 d. Educ. The Edinburgh Academy; The University of Aberdeen. Former Director of Policy and Standards for the Forest Service in Northern Ireland; returned to Scotland in 2005 and owned and managed a small estate in south Ayrshire. Fellow of the Institute of Chartered Foresters; Director, Ayrshire Woodfuels; Director, Scotland's Finest Woodlands; Chair, South Scotland Forestry Forum; Chairman, River Girvan District Salmon Fishery Board. Director, Straiton Village Co-operative; Trustee, Ayrshire Rivers Trust; Vice-President, Royal Scottish Forestry Society; former Board Member, Scottish Natural Heritage. Recreations: family; food; forestry and fishing.

Huntly, Marquess of (Granville Charles Gomer). Chief, House of Gordon, since 1988; b. 4.2.44, Aberdeen; m., 1, Jane Gibb; m., 2, Catheryn Kindersley; 1 s.; 3 d. Educ. Gordonstoun School; Institute of Commercial Management. Chairman: Hintlesham Holdings Ltd., Cock O' The North Liqueur Co. Ltd.; Director, Ampton Investments Ltd.; President, Institute of Financial Accountants, 1989-2000; Chief, Aboyne Highland Games. Recreations: country sports. Address: Aboyne Castle, Aberdeenshire AB34 5JP; T.-01339 887 778.

Hurtado, Professor Larry Weir, BA, MA, PhD, FRSE. Emeritus Professor of New Testament Language, Literature and Theology, University of Edinburgh, since 2011 (Professor 1996-2011), former Head of School of Divinity, former Director of the Centre for the Study of Christian Origins; b. 29.12.43, Kansas City; m., Shannon Hunter; 1 s.; 2 d. Educ. Case Western Reserve University. Pastor, North Shore Assembly of God, Illinois, 1971-75; Assistant

Professor of New Testament, Regent College, Vancouver BC, 1975-78; Professor of Religion, University of Manitoba, Winnipeg, 1978-96. Address: (b.) New College, Mound Place, Edinburgh EH1 2LX; T.-0131-650 8920.

Hutcheon, William Robbie. Editor, Courier and Advertiser, Dundee, 2002-2011; b. 19.1.52, Aberdeen; m., Margo; 1 s.; 2 d. Educ. Aberdeen Academy. Reporter (D.C. Thomson Office in Aberdeen), 1969-70; Sports Sub-Editor, Sports Editor, Chief Sub-Editor, Night News Editor, Deputy Editor, Editor, since 1970, with Courier and Advertiser. Chairman, Editors' Committee, Scottish Daily Newspaper Society, 2007-08. Recreations: sport; travel; music; computing. Address: (h.) 42 Ferndale Drive, Broughty Ferry, Dundee DD5 3DF; T.-01382 774552; e-mail: hutcheon642@btinternet.com

Hutchinson, Peter, PhD, FIFM. Secretary of the inter-governmental North Atlantic Salmon Conservation Organization (NASCO), since 1 July 2013; b. 26.5.56, Glasgow; m., Jane MacKellaig; 1 s.; 1 d. Educ. Queen Elizabeth's Grammar School, Blackburn; Edinburgh University. Assistant Secretary (1986-2012) and Interim Secretary (2012-13), North Atlantic Salmon Conservation Organization (Chairman, Scientific Committee, 1992-2013); Project Co-ordinator, Surface Water Acidification; Research Biologist, Institute of Terrestrial Ecology, Edinburgh University; Member, Consular Corps in Edinburgh and Leith, since 1991. Recreations: golf; squash; rugby union; angling. Address: (h.) 3 St. Ronan's Terrace, Morningside, Edinburgh.
E-mail: peter@phutchinson.net

Hutchison, David, MA, MLitt. Academic and writer; Honorary Professor in Media Policy, Glasgow Caledonian University; Acting Director, Scottish Centre of Journalism Studies, 2003-04; Visiting Professor, Brock University, Canada, 2004; b. 24.9.44, West Kilbride; m., Pauleen Frew; 2 d. Educ. Ardrossan Academy; Glasgow University. Tutor/Organiser, WEA (West of Scotland), 1966-69; Teacher, Reid Kerr College, Paisley, 1969-71; various posts, Glasgow College of Technology/Glasgow Caledonian University, since 1971; Member, West Kilbride District Council, 1970-75 (Chairman, 1972-75); Governor, Scottish Film Council, 1987-95; Member, General Advisory Council, BBC, 1988-96; Board Member, Regional Screen Scotland, 2008-14 (Chair, 2010-14); author of plays, Deadline, Pitlochry Festival Theatre, 1980; Too Long the Heart, Siege Perilous, Edinburgh, 2013; The Blood is Strong, Finborough Theatre, London, 2013. Publications: The Modern Scottish Theatre, 1977; Headlines (Editor), 1978; Media Policy, 1998; The Media in Scotland (Co-Editor), 2008; Centres and Peripheries: Metropolitan and Non-Metropolitan Journalism (Co-Editor), 2011; various articles/chapters. Recreations: walking; the arts; golf. Address: (b.) Caledonian University, Cowcaddens Road, Glasgow G4 0BA; T.-01294 823321.
E-mail: dbhutchison@btinternet.com

Hutchison, Professor James D., PhD, FRCSEd, FRCSGlas, FFSTEd. Regius Professor of Surgery, University of Aberdeen, since 2000; Sir Harry Platt Professor of Orthopaedics, University of Aberdeen, since 1995; Honorary Consultant Orthopaedic Surgeon, NHS Grampian since 1991; b. 8.10.55, Dundee; m., Kate Douglas; 2 s.; 1 d. Educ. High School of Dundee; University of Dundee. Lecturer in Orthopaedics, Edinburgh and Aberdeen, 1986-91; Senior Lecturer, Aberdeen, 1991-95. Past Chairman, Scottish Committee for Orthopaedics and Trauma; previously Specialty Advisor in Orthopaedics to CMO and SGHD; Chairman, Scottish Orthopaedic Services Development Group for Scottish Government

Health Department; Vice-President (2012-15), Chairman of Heritage and Museums Committee and Fellow of the Faculty of Surgical Trainers of Royal College of Surgeons of Edinburgh; Past President, Aberdeen Medico Chirurgical Society (2005-06); Chair, Board of Governors, Robert Gordon's College, Aberdeen, since 2013. Clubs: Royal Northern & University Club, Aesculapian Club, Harveian Society, Moynihan Chirurgical Club. Recreations: family; dogs; curling; shooting; golf; art. Address: Department of Surgery, Medical School, Polwarth Building, Foresterhill, Aberdeen AB25 2ZD; T.-01224 437849; e-mail: j.d.hutchison@abdn.ac.uk

Hutchison, John Charles, MBE, JP, BSc (Hons), CEng, FICE, FIES; b. 23.7.47, Edinburgh; m., Christine Laidlaw; 1 s.; 2 d. Educ. Leith Academy; Heriot-Watt University. Early career erecting steel structures and bridges with Redpath Dorman Long; road construction on Skye and maintenance of roads, bridges, ferries, piers and jetties for Highland Regional Council, Lochaber, 1975-96 as Divisional Engineer; Highland Council, 1996-2007, Lochaber Area Manager. Honorary Sheriff and Justice of the Peace; Chair, Isle of Eigg Heritage Trust; Chair, Scottish Rural Action; Chairman, John Muir Trust, 2009-14; Vice Convener, Mod Lochabair, 2007; Director of Clanranald Castle Tioram Trust, Nevis Partnership and Community Land Scotland; Chairman, West Highland Museum, West Highland College UHI. Recreations: singing; mountaineering and reading. Address: Taigh na Coille, Badabrie, Fort William PH33 7LX; T.-01397 772252.

Hutchison, Sir Peter Craft, Bt, CBE, FRSE. Formerly Chairman, Hutchison & Craft Ltd., Insurance Brokers; b. 5.6.35, London; m., Virginia Colville; 1 s. Educ. Eton; Magdalene College, Cambridge. National Service, Royal Scots Greys (2nd Lt.); Northern Assurance Co. (London); Director of various companies; Past Chairman, Ailsa Shipbuilding Co. Ltd.; Director, Stakis plc, 1979-91; Board Member, Scottish Tourist Board, 1981-87; Vice Chairman, British Waterways Board, 1988-97; Chairman, Board of Trustees, Royal Botanic Garden, Edinburgh, 1985-94; Chairman, Loch Lomond and Trossachs Working Party, 1991-93; Chairman, Forestry Commission, 1994-2001; Deputy Convenor, Board Member, Loch Lomond and the Trossachs National Park Authority, 2002-2010. Deacon, Incorporation of Hammermen of Glasgow, 1984-85. Publication: Seeds of Adventure (Co-Author), 2008. Recreations: plant hunting; gardening; calligraphy. Address: (h.) Broich, Kippen, Stirlingshire FK8 3EN; T.-01786 870317.

Hutt, Stephen M. Former Chief Executive, Royal Highland and Agricultural Society of Scotland (2011-2016).

Hutton, Alasdair Henry, OBE, TD, MStJ. Writer and Narrator, Royal Edinburgh Military Tattoo and other public events, concerts, videos and audio guides, since 1992; b. 19.5.40, London; 2 s. Educ. Dollar Academy; Brisbane State High School. Journalist, The Age, Melbourne, 1959-61, Aberdeen Journals, 1962-64; Broadcaster, BBC, 1964-79; Member, European Parliament, 1979-89; Convener, Scottish Borders Council, 2003-12 (Councillor, Kelso, 2002-12); Member, Queen's Bodyguard for Scotland (Royal Company of Archers); former 2ic, 15th (Scottish Volunteer) Bn., The Parachute Regiment; Elder, Kelso North Church of Scotland; President, Kelso Branch, Royal British Legion Scotland; President, Border Area, Legion Scotland; Member and former Chairman & Vice President, John Buchan Society; Life Member, Edinburgh Sir Walter Scott Club, since 1994 (Chairman, 2013); Patron, ROKPA; Patron, Kelso Ladies' Association; Reader, Borders

Talking Newspaper, since 1997, Patron, 2008; Patron, Borders Independent Advocacy Service, since 2001; Chairman, Disease Prevention Organisation, 1990-2013; River Tweed Commissioner, 2004-2013; Member, Veterans Advisory and Pensions Committee, East of Scotland, 2012-2015; Founder Member, The Robert Burns Guild of Speakers, 2012; Honorary Colonel, Lothian and Borders Battalion, Army Cadet Force, 2006-09; Friend of Abbotsford, since 2010; President, Kelso Farmers Market, 2006-12; Chairman, Kelso Carers Initiative Trust, 2006-12; Chairman, Order of St John, SE Scotland Area; Fellow, Industry and Parliament Trust. Author "15 Para 1947-1993", 1997; "The Tattoo Fox", 2013; "The Tattoo Fox Makes New Friends", 2014. Address: 4 Broomlands Court, Kelso TD5 7SR; T.-01573 224369; Mobile: 07753625734.
E-mail: alasdairhutton@yahoo.co.uk
web: www.alasdairhutton.co.uk

Hutton, Graeme, BSc (Hons), DipArch, RIBA, FRIAS. Professor of Architecture, University of Dundee, since 2002; Practising Architect, since 1990; b. 2.6.64, Shrewsbury; m., Julie; 1 s.; 2 d. Educ. Carnoustie High School; Robert Gordon University. Partner, Hutton Rattray Architects, 1992-96; Design Architect, RMJM Scotland Ltd., 1996-99; University of Dundee, since 1999; Design Consultant, LJRH Architects Dundee, since 2000. RIAS Education Committee. Recreations: photography; music. Address: (h.) 50 Forfar Road, Dundee DD4 7BA; T.-01382 520316; e-mail: the.huttons@blueyonder.co.uk

Hutton, Professor Neil, MA, PhD. Professor of Criminal Justice, University of Strathclyde, b. 20.12.53, Dundee; m., Michele Burman; 2 d. Educ. High School of Dundee; Edinburgh University. Research Fellow: University of Dundee, 1981-83, University of Edinburgh, 1984-87, Victoria University of Wellington, NZ, 1987-90; joined University of Strathclyde in 1990 as Lecturer, then became Senior Lecturer. Member: Sentencing Commission for Scotland, 2003-06. Recreations: cooking; golf. Address: (b.) McCance Building, Richmond Street, Glasgow G1 1XQ; T.-0141-552 4400; e-mail: n.hutton@strath.ac.uk

Hutton, William Riddell, BDS. Dentist, 1961-2001; Honorary Sheriff, since 1996; b. 22.10.38, Glasgow; m., Patricia Margaret Burns; 1 s.; 1 d. Educ. Hamilton Academy; Glasgow University Dental School. International Grenfell Association, Newfoundland and Labrador, 1961-64; General Practice, Lanark, 1964-2001; Member, Secretary and Chairman, Lanarkshire Local Dental Committee, 1964-94; Member and Chairman, Lanarkshire Area Dental Committee, 1975-94; Lord Cornet, Lanark, 1984. Recreations: music; golf; hillwalking; travel. Address: (h.) St. Anthony, 9 Braedale Road, Lanark ML11 7AW; T.-01555 662927.
E-mail: william.hutton@homecall.co.uk

Huyton, Harry, BSc, MSc. Director, OneKind, since 2015. Educ. Durham University; Imperial College London. Operations Coach, DialogueDirect, 2001-03; Research Assistant, IEEP, 2003; Policy Officer, RSPB, 2004-07; Senior Adviser, Environment Agency, 2008-2010; Head of Climate Change Policy & Campaigns, RSPB, 2010-2015; Programme Manager, Cambridge Institute for Sustainability Leadership (CISL), 2015. Address: OneKind, 50 Montrose Terrace, Edinburgh EH7 5DL; T.-0131 661 9734.
E-mail: info@onekind.org

Hvide, Professor Hans Krogh, MSc, PhD. Professor of Economics and Finance, University of Aberdeen, since 2006, SIRE Professor, since 2007; b. 26.09.68, Bergen, Norway; m., Siri Brekke; 2 s.; 1 d. Educ. Norwegian School of Economics and Business; London School of Economics. Associate Professor, Department of Finance and Management Science, NHH, 2002-06; Visiting Associate Professor, MIT/Sloan School, 2005; Professor, Norwegian School of Economics and Business (NHH), 2007. Post-doc at Tel-Aviv University, Research Affiliate, CEPR and IZA. Recreations: tennis; hiking; skiing; reading. Address: (b.) Edward Wright Building, Dunbar Street, Old Aberdeen AB24 3QY; T.-01224 273 411; e-mail: hans.hvide@gmail.com

Hyslop, Fiona J., MA (Hons). MSP (SNP), Linlithgow, since 2011, Lothians, 1999-2011; Cabinet Secretary for Culture, Europe and External Affairs, since 2014; Cabinet Secretary for Culture and External Affairs, 2011-2014; Minister for Culture and External Affairs, 2009-2011; Cabinet Secretary for Education and Lifelong Learning, 2007-2009; b. 1.8.64, Irvine; m.; 2 s.; 1 d. Educ. Ayr Academy; Glasgow University. Standard Life, 1986-99, various sales and marketing positions, latterly Marketing Manager. Recreations: swimming; cinema. Address: (b.) Scottish Parliament, Edinburgh EH99 1SP; T.-0131-348 5921.

I

Ibbotson, Sally Helen, BSc (Hons), MD, MBChB (Hons), FRCP (Edin). Clinical Senior Lecturer in Photobiology, Honorary Consultant Dermatologist, University of Dundee, Ninewells Hospital and Medical School, since 1998; b. 18.2.62, Newcastle upon Tyne. Educ. Central Newcastle High School for Girls; University of Leeds. House Physician and House Surgeon, Leeds General Infirmary and St. James' University Hospital, 1986-87; Teaching Fellow in Medicine, Leeds General Infirmary, 1987-89; Research Fellow, University of Leeds, 1989-92; Royal Victoria Infirmary, Newcastle upon Tyne: Registrar in Dermatology, 1992-94, Senior Registrar in Dermatology, 1994-98; Research Fellow, Harvard University, Boston, USA, 1996-97. Address: (b.) Photobiology Unit, Dermatology Department, University of Dundee, Ninewells Hospital and Medical School, Dundee DD1 9SY; T.-01382 6383499; e-mail: s.h.ibbotson@dundee.ac.uk

Ingle, Professor Stephen James, BA, MA (Econ), DipEd, PhD. Emeritus Professor of Politics, Stirling University; b. 6.11.40, Ripon; m., Margaret Anne; 2 s.; 1 d. Educ. The Roan School, London; Sheffield University; Wellington University, NZ. Commonwealth Scholar, 1964-67; Lecturer in Politics, Hull University, 1967-80; Senior Lecturer, 1980-91; Head of Department, 1985-90. Secretary, Political Studies Association, 1988-89; Member, East Yorkshire Health Authority, 1985-90; Visiting Research Fellow, Victoria University of Wellington, 1993; Academic Fellow of the Open Society Institute, 2006-08; panel member and assessor, Arts and Humanities Research Council, 2009-14; research assessor for the Carnegie Trust, since 2014. Publications: Socialist Thought in Imaginative Literature, 1979; Parliament and Health Policy, 1981; British Party System, 1987, 1989, 1999, 2008; George Orwell: a political life, 1993; Narratives of British Socialism, 2002; The Social and Political Thought of George Orwell: A Reappraisal, 2006. Recreations: theatre; reading; music; hill-walking. Address: (b.) Department of Politics, Stirling University, Stirling FK9 4LA; T.-01786 467568.
E-mail: s.j.ingle@stir.ac.uk

Inglis, Professor Emeritus James Alistair Macfarlane, CBE (1984), MA, LLB. Emeritus Professor, Glasgow University; Professor of Conveyancing, Glasgow University, 1979-93; Professor of Professional Legal Practice, Glasgow University, 1984-93; Partner, McClure, Naismith, Solicitors, Glasgow, 1956-93; Honorary Member, Court of Patrons, Royal College of Physicians and Surgeons of Glasgow, since 1995; b. 24.12.28, Kilmarnock; m., Mary Elizabeth Howie (deceased); 2 s.; 3 d. Educ. Kilmarnock Academy; Fettes College; St. Andrews University; Glasgow University. Qualified as Solicitor, 1952; Member: Board of Management, Victoria and Leverndale Hospitals, 1964-74, Greater Glasgow Health Board, 1975-83; President, Rent Assessment Panel for Scotland, 1976-87; Chairman, Glasgow Hospitals Auxiliary Association, 1985-2001; Dean, Royal Faculty of Procurators in Glasgow, 1989-92; Convener, Ad Hoc Committee, Church of Scotland, into Legal Services of Church, 1978-79; Session Clerk, Caldwell Parish Church, since 1963; General Trustee, Church of Scotland, 1994-2004. Address: (h.) Crioch, Uplawmoor, Glasgow; T.-01505 850315.

Inglis, John, PRSW, RGI, HAWI, FSA Scot, DA. Painter and Lecturer; b. 27.7.53, Glasgow; m., Heather; 2 s.; 2 d. Educ. Hillhead High School; Gray's School of Art. Travelling scholarships to Italy, 1976; Member, Dundee Group, 1979-84; one-man exhibitions: Aberdeen, 1976 and 1977; Glasgow, 1980; Skipton, 1981; Aberdeen Hospitals, 1989; Alloa Museum, 1989; Smith Art Gallery, Stirling, 1993; Illinois, USA, 1997. Scottish Arts Council Award, 1981; RSA Keith Prize, 1975; SAC Bursary, 1982; RSA Meyer Oppenheim Prize, 1982; RSW EIS Award, 1987; SAC Grant, 1988; May Marshall Brown Award, 1994, 2000; Paisley Art Institute Bessie Scott Award, 2007; Bet Low Trust Award, 2013; Elected Honorary Member, Australian Watercolour Institute, 2010. Address: (h.) 84 Burnhead Road, Larbert; e-mail: j.inglis@hotmail.co.uk

Ingold, Professor Timothy, PhD, FBA, FRSE. Professor of Social Anthropology, University of Aberdeen, since 1999; b. 1.11.48, Sevenoaks; m., Anna Kaarina; 3 s.; 1 d. Educ. Leighton Park School; Churchill College, Cambridge University. University of Manchester: Lecturer, Department of Social Anthropology, 1974-85, Senior Lecturer, 1985-90, Professor, 1990-95, Max Gluckman Professor of Social Anthropology, 1995-99; Visiting Professor: University of Helsinki, 1986, University of Tromsø, 1996-2000. Royal Anthropological Institute Rivers Memorial Medal, 1989; Award of Jean-Marie Delwart Foundation, Belgian Academy of Sciences, 1994; Retzius Medal, Swedish Society for Anthropology and Geography, 2004; Royal Anthropological Institute Huxley Memorial Medal, 2014; Knight, First Class, of the Order of the White Rose of Finland, 2014; Honorary Doctorate in Philosophy, Leuphana, University, Lüneburg, 2015. Publications: The Skolt Lapps Today, 1976; Hunters, Pastoralists and Ranchers, 1980; Evolution and Social Life, 1986; The Appropriation of Nature, 1986; What Is An Animal? (Editor), 1988; Tools, Language and Cognition in Human Evolution (Co-Editor), 1993; Companion Encyclopedia of Anthropology: humanity, culture and social life (Editor), 1994; Key Debates in Anthropology (Editor), 1996; The Perception of the Environment, 2000; Creativity and Cultural Improvisation (Co-Editor), 2007; Lines: a brief history, 2007; Ways of Walking (Co-Editor), 2008; Being Alive, 2011; Redrawing Anthropology (Editor), 2011; Imagining Landscapes (Co-Editor), 2012; Biosocial Becomings (Co-Editor), 2013; Making, 2013; Making and Growing (Co-Editor), 2014; The Life of Lines, 2015. Recreation: music. Address: (b.) Department of Anthropology, University of Aberdeen, Aberdeen AB24 3QY; T.-01224 274350; e-mail: tim.ingold@abdn.ac.uk

Ingram, Rt. Hon. Adam. MP (Labour), East Kilbride, 1987-2010; Minister of State for the Armed Forces, 2001-07; b. 1.2.47, Glasgow; m., Maureen McMahon. Educ. Cranhill Secondary School. Programmer/analyst, 1965-1970; systems analyst, 1970-77; trade union official, 1977-87; Councillor, East Kilbride District Council, 1980-87 (Leader of the Council, 1984-87); PPS to Neil Kinnock, Leader of the Opposition, 1988-92; Labour Opposition Spokesperson on Social Security, 1993-95, Science and Technology, 1995-97; Minister of State for Northern Ireland, 1997-2001; Head of Study Team on Defence Role in Counter-Terrorism and Resilience, 2007-08. Recreations: fishing; cooking; reading.

Ingram, Adam Hamilton, BA (Hons). MSP (SNP), Carrick, Cumnock and Doon Valley, 2011-16, South of Scotland, 1999-2011; Minister for Children and Early Years, 2007-2011; b. 1.5.51, Kilmarnock; m., Gerry; 3 s.; 1 d. Educ. Kilmarnock Academy; Paisley College. Manager, A.H. Ingram & Son, Bakers, 1971-76; Senior Economic Assistant, Manpower Services Commission, 1985-86; Researcher and Lecturer, Paisley College, 1987-88; economic development consultant, 1989-99. Recreation: golf.

Ingram, Professor David Stanley, OBE, VMH, BSc, PhD (Hull), MA, ScD (Cantab), HonDUniv (Open), FLS, FRSB, FCIHort, FRSGS (Hon), FRCPEd, FRSE. Honorary Professor, University of Edinburgh, since 1991; Honorary Secretary, RSE Dining Club, 2006-2012; Honorary

Professor, Lancaster Environment Centre, Lancaster University, since 2007; Honorary Professorial Fellow, School of Social and Political Sciences, Edinburgh University, since 2012; Visiting Professor, Glyndŵr University, since 2012; Honorary Professor in Botany, Glasgow University, 1991-2010; Programme Convenor, Royal Society of Edinburgh, 2005-2010; Senior Visiting Fellow, ESRC Genomics Forum, University of Edinburgh, 2006-2013; Independent Member and Deputy Chairman, Joint Nature Conservation Committee, 2001-08; Master, St. Catherine's College, Cambridge, 2000-06; Regius Keeper (Director), Royal Botanic Garden, Edinburgh, 1990-98; Fellow: Royal Society of Biology, Chartered Institute of Horticulture and Royal College of Physicians, Edinburgh; Honorary Fellow: Royal Botanic Garden, Edinburgh, since 1998, Royal Scottish Geographical Society, since 1998, Downing College, Cambridge, since 2001, Myerscough College, since 2001, Worcester College, Oxford, since 2003, St. Catherine's College, Cambridge, since 2006, Ruskin Foundation, since 2014; Honorary Member, British Society for Plant Pathology, since 2008; Companion, Guild of St George, since 2015; b. 10.10.41, Birmingham; m., Alison; 2 s. Educ. Yardley Grammar School, Birmingham; Hull University; Cambridge University. Research Fellow, Glasgow University, 1966-68, Cambridge University, 1968-69; Senior Scientific Officer, Unit of Development Botany, Cambridge, 1969-74; Lecturer, then Reader in Plant Pathology, Botany Department, Cambridge University, 1974-90; Fellow (also Tutor, Dean and Director of Studies in Biology), Downing College, Cambridge, 1974-90; Honorary Professor of Horticulture, Royal Horticultural Society, 1995-2000; President, International Congress of Plant Pathology, 1998; President, British Society for Plant Pathology, 1998; Chairman, Advisory Committee to the Darwin Initiative for the Survival of the Species, 1999-2005; Awarded Victoria Medal of Honour, Royal Horticultural Society, 2004; Member, Board, Scottish Natural Heritage, 1999-2000; author of several books and many papers in learned journals on botany, plant pathology, horticulture, conservation and the history of art. Recreations: gardening; entertaining grandchildren; music; ceramics. Address: Royal Society of Edinburgh, 22-26 George Street, Edinburgh EH2 2PQ.

Ingram, Hugh Albert Pugh, BA (Cantab), PhD (Dunelm); b. 29.4.37, Rugby; m., Dr. Ruth Hunter; 1 s.; 1 d. Educ. Lawrence Sheriff School, Rugby; Rugby School; Emmanuel College, Cambridge; Hatfield College, Durham. Demonstrator in Botany, University College of North Wales, Bangor, 1963-64; Staff Tutor in Natural Science, Department of Extra-Mural Studies, Bristol University, 1964-65; Lecturer, then Senior Lecturer in Botany (Ecology), Dundee University, 1966-97; Editor, Journal of Applied Ecology, 1991-97; Member: Executive Committee, Scottish Field Studies Association, 1989-99, Museums and Galleries Commission Working Party on the non-national museums of Scotland, 1984-86; Trustee, National Museums of Scotland, 1987-94; Chairman, Scottish Wildlife Trust, 1996-99 (Vice-Chairman, Conservation and Science, 1982-87); Royal Society for Nature Conservation: Scottish Trustee, 2000-01, Trustee, 2003, Christopher Cadbury Medal, 2001. Publications: scientific research papers on hydrological aspects of the ecology of peat bogs and other mires. Recreations: music (clarinet, piano); literature; rural history; hill-walking; botanic gardens. Address: Johnstonfield, Dunbog, Cupar, Fife KY14 6JG. E-mail: h.a.p.ingram@dunbog.org.uk

Ingram, Professor Malcolm David, BSc, PhD, DSc. Emeritus Professor of Chemistry, Aberdeen University; m., Lorna Hardman; 1 s.; 1 d. Educ. Oldershaw Grammar School; Liverpool University. Career at Aberdeen University. Chairman, Aberdeen and North of Scotland Section, Royal Society of Chemistry, 1990-93; Humboldt Research Award Winner, 2002; Editor, Physics and Chemistry of Glasses, 1998-2008; Honorary Fellow of the Society of Glass Technology. Publications: 200 in scientific journals. Recreations: gardening; foreign travel. Address: (b.) Department of Chemistry, Aberdeen University, Aberdeen AB24 2UE; T.-01224 272943.

Innes, David, MEd. Headteacher Harlaw Academy, since 2013. Educ. Hazlehead Academy; University of Aberdeen. Address: (b.) 18-20 Albyn Place, Aberdeen AB10 1RG; T.-01224 589251.

Innes, Emeritus Professor John, BCom, PhD, CA, FCMA. Professor of Accountancy, University of Dundee, 1991-01, now Professor Emeritus; b. 11.7.50, Edinburgh; m., Ina. Educ. George Watson's College; University of Edinburgh. Student Accountant and Staff Auditor, KPMG, 1972-75; International Operational Auditor, Uniroyal Inc., 1975-78; Lecturer and Senior Lecturer in Accounting, University of Edinburgh, 1978-91; Canon Foundation Visiting Research Fellow, 1992-93; Visiting Professor, University of Nantes, 1997-99. Publication: various books including Handbook of Management Accounting, 2004. Recreation: tennis. Address: School of Business, University of Dundee, Dundee DD1 4HN; T.-01382 344193; e-mail: j.innes@dundee.ac.uk

Innes of Edingight, Sir Malcolm Rognvald, KCVO, MA, LLB, WS, KStJ. Lord Lyon King of Arms and Secretary to Order of the Thistle, 1981-2001; b. 25.5.38, Edinburgh; m., Joan Hay; 3 s. Educ. Edinburgh Academy; Edinburgh University. Carrick Pursuivant, 1958; Marchmont Herald, 1971; Lyon Clerk and Keeper of the Record, 1966; Member, Queen's Bodyguard for Scotland (Royal Company of Archers). Recreation: reading. Address: 33/6 Kinnear Road, Edinburgh EH3 5PG; T.-0131 552 4924.

Innes, Norman Lindsay, OBE, BSc, PhD, DSc, FRSE. Agricultural Research Consultant; b. 3.5.34, Kirriemuir; m., Marjory Niven Farquhar, MA; 1 s.; 1 d. Educ. Websters Seminary, Kirriemuir; Aberdeen University; Cambridge University. Senior Cotton Breeder: Sudan, 1958-66, Uganda, 1966-71; Head, Cotton Research Unit, Uganda, 1972; National Vegetable Research Station, Wellesbourne: Head, Plant Breeding Section, 1973-84, Deputy Director, 1977-84; Scottish Crop Research Institute: Deputy Director, 1986-94, Head, Plant Breeding Division, 1984-89; Honorary Lecturer, then Honorary Professor, Birmingham University, 1973-84; Member, Board of European Association of Plant Breeders, 1981-86; Chairman, British Association of Plant Breeders, 1982-84; Governing Board Member, International Crops Research Institute for Semi-Arid Tropics, India, 1982-88; Honorary Professor, Dundee University, 1988-95; Honorary Research Professor: Scottish Crop Research Institute, 1994-2011, James Hutton Institute, since 2011; Governing Board Member, International Potato Centre, Peru, 1988-95, Chairman, 1991-95; Vice-President, Association of Applied Biologists, 1990-92, President, 1993-94; Governing Council Member, 1996-2001, Chairman, 1997-2000, International Centre of Insect Physiology and Ecology, Kenya; Member, Board of Trustees, West Africa Rice Development Association, Côte d'Ivoire, 1998-2004, Chairman, 2000-03; Member, Oxfam Council of Trustees, 1982-85; Book Review Editor, Experimental Agriculture, 1996-2012. Recreations: photography; travel. Address: (b.) James Hutton Institute, Invergowrie, Dundee DD2 5DA; T.-01382 562731; e-mail: minnes1960@aol.com

Innes, Cllr Willie. Leader, East Lothian Council, since 2012; represents Preston/Seton/Gosford (Labour). Address: (b.) John Muir House, Haddington EH41 3EN; T.-01620 827007; e-mail:winnes@eastlothian.gov.uk

Inverarity, James Alexander (Sandy), CBE, FRSA, FRAgS, CA. Farmer and Landowner; Chairman: Scottish Agricultural College, 1990-98, Scottish Agricultural Securities Corporation, plc, since 1987; President, Scottish

Farm and Countryside Educational Trust, 1990-98; b. 17.9.35; m., Jean (deceased); 1 s.; 2 d; m. (2), Frances. Educ. Loretto School. President, National Farmers Union of Scotland, 1970-71; Member: Eggs Authority, 1971-74, Farm Animal Welfare Council, 1978-88, Panel of Agricultural Arbiters, 1983-2007, Governing Body, Scottish Crop Research Institute, 1984-97, Dairy Produce Quota Tribunal for Scotland, 1984-85; Director, United Oilseed Producers Ltd., 1985-97 (Chairman, 1987-97). Recreations: shooting; curling. Address: Cransley, Fowlis, Dundee DD2 5NP; T.-01382 580327.

Ireland, Professor Elizabeth. Chair, NHS National Services Scotland, since 2013 (Non-Executive on the board, since 2007 and Vice-Chair in 2012). Career history: University of Stirling: developed partnerships across healthcare and academia to promote learning and the transfer of knowledge - especially regarding qualitative approaches to learning from and improving people's experiences of care; leadership roles at board, regional and national levels, culminating in 4 years (2008-12) as national clinical lead for Palliative and End of Life Care for the Scottish Government; national clinical leadership support to the Better Together programme. Honorary Chair, School of Management, University of Stirling; Vice-Chair, NHS chairs. Address: NHS National Services Scotland, Area 074E, Gyle Square, Edinburgh EH12 9EB.

Ireland, W. Seith S., LLB (Hons). Sheriff at Paisley Sheriff Court, since 2014; formerly Sheriff at Kilmarnock Sheriff Court, 2003-2014; b. 5.4.56, Glasgow; m., Elizabeth. Educ. The High School of Glasgow; University of Glasgow. President: Student Representative Council, University of Glasgow, 1977-78, Glasgow Bar Association, 1993-94; Member, Council of Law Society of Scotland, 1995-98; Convener, Law Society Devolution Committee, 1997-98; Member, Business Committee, General Council of University of Glasgow, 2005-09; Admitted Solicitor, 1982; Assistant: Ross Harper and Murphy, 1982-85, Jim Friel & Co, 1985-86; Principal, Ireland & Co Solicitors, Glasgow, 1986-2003. Member, Council of the Sheriffs' Association, 2009-2013, Honorary Secretary and Treasurer, 2010-2012; Board Member, Phoenix Futures Scotland, since 2013; Member, Council of Scottish Association for the Study of Offending (SASO), since 2013. Recreations: golf; theatre; cooking. Address: (b.) Sheriffs' Chambers, Sheriff Court House, St James Street, Paisley PA3 1HW; e-mail: sheriffwsireland@scotcourts.gov.uk

Irons, Norman MacFarlane, CBE, DL, DLitt, DUniv, Hon. FRCS Ed, CEng, MIMechE, MCIBSE, Knight of The Order of the Dannebrog, Denmark, 2008. Lord Provost and Lord Lieutenant of the City of Edinburgh, 1992-96; Partner, Building Services Consulting Engineers, since 1993; Royal Danish Consul, Edinburgh and Leith, 2000-2011; Consul of Hungary in Scotland, since 2013; b. 4.1.41, Glasgow; m., Anne Buckley; 1 s.; 1 d. Held various posts as Consulting Engineer; founded own practice, 1983. SNP Member, City of Edinburgh District Council, 1976-96; President, Edinburgh Leith and District Battalion, Boys' Brigade, 1998-2003; Dean of Consular Corps, Edinburgh and Leith, 2010-11. Recreation: rugby football. Address: (h.) 141 Saughtonhall Drive, Edinburgh EH12 5TS; T.-0131-337 6154; e-mail: n.irons@ironsfoulner.co.uk

Ironside, Leonard, CBE, JP, FRSA. Member, Aberdeen City Council, since 1995 (elected Councillor, since 1982; currently Convener of Social Care and Wellbeing Committee; Council Leader, 1999-2003; Convener, Social Work Committee); Chairman, Horizon Rehabilitation Centre, 1997-2004; former Director, Grampian Food Resource Centre Ltd; North of Scotland Area Manager, Parkinsons Disease Society, since 2003; Patron, Grampian Special Olympics for Handicapped; Commonwealth Professional Wrestling Champion, since 1981; Athletics Coach, Bon Accord (Special Needs); former Member,

Board, Robert Gordon University, 1999-2008; Feature Writer - Freelance, Aberdeen Independent Newspapers; Member, Board, NHS Grampian, 2001-03; Board Member: North East Sensory Services, since 2013, Alcohol Support Ltd, since 2014; b. Aberdeen; m., Wendy; 2 d. Educ. Hilton Academy, Aberdeen. Member, Grampian Regional Council, 1982-96; Inspector, contributions agency, DHSS, since 1990; formerly Chairman and Founder Member, Grampian Initiative; won Commonwealth Professional Wrestling Championship at Middleweight, 1979; lost Championship, 1981; regained title, 1981; gained European Lightweight title, 1985, relinquished title, 1989; Grampian Ambassador for services to industry, 1996; awarded Scottish Sports Council Rosebowl for services to disabled sports; former Director: Grampian Enterprise Ltd., Scottish Sub-Sea Technology Group; Chair, Aberdeen International Youth Festival, since 2014; Member: Grampian Racial Equality Commission, Aberdeen Sports Council; former Director, Voluntary Service, Aberdeen; Audio Describer for Visually Impaired, since 2014; former Area Manager, Parkinson's Disease Society (retired 2015); Board Member, Aberdeen Exhibition and Conference Centre, since 2007; Member, Granite City Chorus. Publication: When You're Ready Boys - Take Hold: My Grappling Story. Recreations: yoga teacher; also plays tennis, squash, badminton; cycling; after-dinner speaking. Address: (h.) 42 Hillside Terrace, Portlethen, Kincardineshire; T.-01224 780929. E-mail: lironside@aberdeencity.gov.uk

Irvine of Drum, (David Charles Irvine), ACIB. 26th Laird of Drum and Chief of the name Irvine of Drum, since 1992; b. 20.1.39, Birkenhead, Merseyside; m., Carolyn Colbeck; 2 s.; 1 d. Educ. Radley College. Member, Standing Council of Scottish Chiefs; Member, The Convention of the Baronage of Scotland. Recreations: family history; golf; gardening. Clubs: New Club, Edinburgh. Address: (h.) Holly Leaf Cottage, Inchmarlo, Banchory, Kincardineshire; T.-01330-823702; e-mail: drum26@btinternet.com

Irvine of Lairg, Baron (Alexander Andrew Mackay Irvine), PC. Lord High Chancellor of Great Britain, 1997-2003; b. 23.6.40; m. Alison Mary; 2 s. Educ. Inverness Royal Academy; Hutchesons' Boys' Grammar School, Glasgow; Glasgow University; Christ's College, Cambridge. Called to the Bar, Inner Temple, 1967; Bencher, 1985; QC, 1978; a Recorder, 1985-88; Deputy High Court Judge, 1987-97; Lecturer, LSE, 1965-69; Contested (Labour), Hendon North, 1970; elevated to the Peerage, 1987; Opposition Spokesman on Legal and Home Affairs, 1987-92; Shadow Lord Chancellor, House of Lords, 1992-97; Joint President: Industry and Parliamentary Trust, since 1997, British American Parliamentary Group, since 1997, IPU, since 1997, CPA, since 1997; President, Magistrates' Association; Church Commissioner; Trustee: John Smith Memorial Trust, 1992-97, and since 2003, Whitechapel Art Gallery, since 1990, Hunterian Collection, since 1997; Member, Committee, Friends of the Slade, since 1990; Honorary Bencher, Inn of Court of NI, 1998; Fellow, US College of Trial Lawyers, 1998; Honorary Fellow, Society for Advanced Legal Studies, 1997; Honorary Member, Polish Bar, 2000; Knight Commander of the Order of Merit of the Republic of Poland (with Star); Hon. LLD, Glasgow, 1997; Honorary Fellow, London School of Economics, 2001; Dr *hc*, Siena, 2000; Honorary Fellow, Christ's College, Cambridge, 1996; Visiting Professor, University College London, 2004. Recreations: cinema; theatre; collecting paintings; travel. Address: House of Lords SW1A 0PW.

Irvine, Bob. Deputy Director, Climate Change, Greener Scotland and Water, Scottish Government. Address: (b.) St. Andrew's House, Regent Road, Edinburgh EH1 3DG.

Irvine, Fiona, BA (BusEcon). Director, Rainbow HR Ltd; formerly Director of Business Change, Phones 4u; HR

Director, First ScotRail, 2006-09; b. 24.9.69, Johnstone; m., Brian; 2 d. Educ. Paisley Grammar School; Paisley University. Training and Development Assistant, Keyline Business Merchants, 1989-92; Staff Manager, Sainsbury Homebase, 1992; HR Business Partner, Royal Bank of Scotland, 1993-2002; Senior Human Capital Consultant, PWC, 2002; Lloyds TSB: Head of HR, 2003-04, Head of Reward, 2004-05. HR Director of the Year, HR Network Scotland. Address: (b.) Rainbow HR Ltd, 14 Marchbank Gardens, Paisley PA1 3JD; T.-07739 447 369.

Irving, Gordon, MA (Hons). Writer, Journalist and Broadcaster; b. 4.12.18, Annan; m., Elizabeth Dickie (deceased). Educ. Dumfries Academy; Edinburgh University. Staff Journalist, Daily Record, Edinburgh and Glasgow; Reuters' News Agency, London; TV Guide, Scotland; The Viewer, Scotland; Freelance Writer/Journalist, since 1964; Travel Correspondent, UK and overseas media; Scotland Correspondent, Variety, New York. Publications: Great Scot! (biography of Sir Harry Lauder); The Good Auld Days; The Solway Smugglers; The Wit of the Scots; The Wit of Robert Burns; The Devil on Wheels; Brush Up Your Scotland; Annie Laurie; Take No Notice and Take No More Notice! (World's Funniest Signs); The First 200 Years (Story of Dumfries and Galloway Royal Infirmary); 90 Glorious Years (Story of the King's Theatre, Glasgow); "When You're Ready Boys", 2012; television script: Standing Room Only (The Scottish Music Hall). Recreations: making video films of personal travels; collecting trivia; researching Scottish music-hall history; fighting snobs and bumbling bureaucrats; reading all the Sunday broadsheets; surfing the World Wide Web on Internet. Address: (h.) 36 Whittingehame Court, Glasgow G12 OBG; T.-0141-357 2265; e-mail: g.irving1@sky.com

Ivory, Sir Brian Gammell, CBE, MA (Cantab), CA, FRSA, FRSE. Chairman, Marathon Asset Management LLP, since 2011; Chairman, Arcus European Infrastructure Fund LLP, since 2010; Chairman, The Scottish American Investment Company PLC, since 2001; Deputy Chairman, Shawbrook Bank Ltd, since 2011; Chairman, The National Galleries of Scotland, 2000-09; Director, Bank of Scotland, 1998-2007; Director, HBOS plc, 2001-07; b. 10.4.49, Edinburgh; m., Oona Mairi MacPhie Bell-Macdonald (see Oona Mairi MacPhie Ivory); 1 s.; 1 d. Educ. Eton College; Magdalene College, Cambridge. CA apprentice, Thomson McLintock, 1971-75; joined Highland Distillers, 1976, became Director, 1978, Managing Director, 1988, Group Chief Executive, 1994-97, Chairman, 1997-99; Chairman, Macallan Distillers Ltd., 1997-99; Director, Orpar SA, 2003-13; Director, Remy Cointreau SA, since 1991; Chairman, Retec Digital plc, 2006-2013; Chair, Governance and Nominations Committee, St Andrews University, since 2007; Director: Insight Investment Management Ltd., since 2003, Marathon Asset Management LLP, since 2007; Director, Media 5 Solutions Limited, since 2014; Member, Scottish Arts Council, 1983-92 (Vice-Chairman, 1988-92); Member, Arts Council of GB, 1988-92; Chairman, The National Piping Centre, since 1996; Chairman, Great Steward of Scotland's Dumfries House Trust, since 2011; CIMgt, 1997; Paolozzi Gold Medal 2009. Member, Queen's Bodyguard for Scotland (Royal Company of Archers); FRSA 1993; FRSE 2001. Freeman, City of London, 1996. Recreations: the arts; farming; hill-walking. Address: (b.) 12 Ann Street, Edinburgh EH4 1PJ.

Ivory, Lady Oona Mairi MacPhie, DL, MA (Cantab), ARCM, FRSA. Former Chairman, Scottish Ballet; Governor, Royal Conservatoire of Scotland; Trustee, The Piping Trust; Deputy Chairman, The National Piping Centre; Director, The Glasgow International Piping Festival; Director, Enitar Ltd; Trustee, the Sri Lanka Music Trust. Professional Musician; Deputy Lieutenant, City of Edinburgh; b. 21.7.54, Ayr; m., Sir Brian Gammell Ivory (qv); 1 s.; 1 d. Educ. King's College, Cambridge; Royal Scottish Academy of Music and Drama; Royal Academy of Music. Recreations: visual and performing arts; wild places; sailing. Address: (b.) 12 Ann Street, Edinburgh EH4 1PJ.

Izod, Professor (Kenneth) John, BA (Hons), PhD, FRSA, FFCS. Emeritus Professor, since 2011; Professor of Screen Analysis, Stirling University, since 1998 (Dean, Faculty of Arts, 1995-98; Senior Lecturer, Department of Film and Media Studies, 1978-98); Head, Department of Film and Media Studies, 2005-07; b. 4.3.40, Shepperton; m., Irene Chew Geok Keng (divorced 1994); 1 s.; 1 d.; m., Kathleen Morison. Educ. Prince Edward School, Harare City, Zimbabwe; Leeds University. Clerk articled to Chartered Accountant, 1958-63; Projectionist, mobile cinema unit, 1963; Lecturer in English, New University of Ulster, 1969-78; former Governor, Scottish Film Council; Chairman, Stirling Film Theatre, 1982-89 and 1991-92; Principal Investigator, Arts and Humanities Research Council funded project 'The Cinema Authorship of Lindsay Anderson', 2007-10; Co-Investigator, Arts and Humanities Research Council funded project 'British Silent Cinema and the Transition to Sound', 2014-2017. Publications: Reading the Screen, 1984; Hollywood and the Box Office 1895-1986, 1988; The Films of Nicolas Roeg, 1991; Introduction to Television Documentary (Co-Author); Myth, Mind and the Screen, 2001; Screen, Culture, Psyche, 2006; Lindsay Anderson: Cinema Authorship (Co-Author), 2012; Cinema as Therapy: Grief and Transformational Film (Co-Author). Address: (b.) Communications, Media and Culture, University, Stirling FK9 4LA; T.-01786 467520. E-mail: k.j.izod@stir.ac.uk

J

Jack, Alister William. Chairman, Edinburgh Self Storage Ltd, since 2006; Chairman, Galloway Woodlands Ltd, since 2012; Partner, Courance Farms & Dairy; Chairman, Alligator Self Storage Ltd., 2007-2014; Managing Director, Armadillo Self Storage Ltd., 2003-07; b. 7.7.63, Dumfries; m., Ann Hodgson; 1 s.; 2 d. Educ. Trinity College, Glenalmond. Knight Frank, 1983-86; Managing Director, Aardvark Self Storage Limited, 1995-2002; Director, Field and Lawn (Marquees) Ltd., since 1986; Non-Executive Director, James Gordon (Engineers) Ltd., 2003-08; Chairman, Fulling Mill Limited, since 2013; Member, Executive Board, Scottish Conservative Party, 1997-2001; Parliamentary Candidate, Tweeddale, Ettrick and Lauderdale, 1997 General Election; Vice Chairman, Scottish Conservative and Unionist Party, 1997-2001 (Scottish Conservative Party Spokesman on Industry and Economic Affairs, 1996-99); Chairman, River Annan Trust; Chairman, River Annan District Salmon Fishery Board; Member, Queen's Body Guard for Scotland, Royal Company of Archers; Winner, Leith Enterprise Award, 1989; Finalist, The New Venturers 1990. Recreations: fishing; shooting; farming. Address: 140 Balgreen Road, Edinburgh EH12 5XQ; (Office) T.-0131 337 7277.

Jack, James Alexander Penrice, BSc (Hons), BArch, BD, DMin, RIBA, ARIAS. Minister of Duddingston, since 2001; b. 10.12.60, Bellshill; m., Rev. Elizabeth Margaret Henderson. Educ. Dalziel High School; University of Strathclyde; University of Glasgow; Princeton Theological Seminary. Pentland & Baker (Architects) Toronto, Canada, 1981-82; Estates & Buildings Division, University of Strathclyde, 1983-85; Student Placement at parish of Rogart, Sutherland, 1986-87; Probationary Assistant, Dundee Parish (St. Mary's), 1988-89; Minister of Abernyte *linked with* Inchture & Kinnaird *linked with* Longforgan, 1989-2001. Senior Chaplain at HM Prison Castle Huntly, 1989-2001; Trustee of Prison Fellowship Scotland, 1992-2001; General Trustee of the Church of Scotland, since 1995 (appointed Chairman, 2010-2014); Member of Board of Practice and Procedure, 1999-2006; Trustee of Richmond's Hope, since 2008. Publications: author of "Summer in a Highland Parish", article, 1986; co-author, "And You Visited Me", 1993; "Understanding a ministry to Prison Officers" in "Theology Scotland", 2003; "The Reverend John Thomson of Duddingston", 2005. Recreations: genealogy; painting and visiting Edinburgh. Address: (b.) The Manse of Duddingston, 5 Old Church Lane, Edinburgh EH15 3PX; T.-0131 661 4240.

Jack, Lorna, CA, MA. Chief Executive, Law Society of Scotland, since 2009. Educ. Aberdeen University; Harvard Business School; Institute of Chartered Accountants of Scotland. Former: President Americas, Scottish Development International, CEO/chief operating officer for Scottish Enterprise Forth Valley, Head of Global Companies Research Project, Scottish Enterprise, Head of National Food Industry Team, Scottish Enterprise; Non-Executive Board Member of Highlands and Islands Airports Limited and Chair of their Audit Committee; Trustee and Treasurer of the McConnell International Foundation; Trustee of Fiscal Affairs Scotland. Recreations: skiing; travel; reading; music. Address: (b.) 26 Drumsheugh Gardens, Edinburgh EH3 7YR; T-0131-226 7411.

Jack, Professor Ronald Dyce Sadler, MA, PhD, DLitt, FEA, FRSE, FFCS. Emeritus Professor of Scottish and Medieval Literature, Edinburgh University; b. 3.4.41, Ayr; m., Kirsty Nicolson; 2 d. Educ. Ayr Academy; Glasgow University; Edinburgh University. Department of English Literature: Assistant Lecturer, 1965, Lecturer, 1968, Reader, 1978, Professor, 1987, Professor Emeritus 2004, Professorial Fellow University of Glasgow 2006. Associate Dean, Faculty of Arts, 1971-73; Visiting Professor, Virginia University, 1973-74; Director, Universities Central Council on Admissions, 1988-94 (Member, 1973-76); Pierpont Morgan Scholar, British Academy, 1976; Advising Editor: Scotia, 1980-96, Scottish Literary Journal, 1996-2000, Scottish Studies Review, since 2000; Member, Scottish Universities Council on Entrance, since 1981; Governor, Newbattle Abbey College, 1984-89; Beinecke Fellow, Yale, 1992; Visiting Professor, Strathclyde University, 1993; Lynn Woods Neag Distinguished Visiting Professor of British Literature, University of Connecticut, 1998; Joint Director, Bibliography of Scottish Literature in Translation, since 2000; W. Ormiston Roy Fellow, University of South Carolina, 2003; Convenor, Patients Council, Royal Edinburgh Hospital, Edinburgh, 2010. Publications: Robert MacLellan's Jamie the Saxt (Co-Editor), 1970; Scottish Prose 1550-1700, 1972; The Italian Influence on Scottish Literature, 1972; A Choice of Scottish Verse 1560-1660, 1978; The Art of Robert Burns (Co-Author), 1982; Sir Thomas Urquhart, The Jewel (Co-Author), 1984; Alexander Montgomerie, 1985; Scottish Literature's Debt to Italy, 1986, 2nd ed. 2010; The History of Scottish Literature, Volume 1, 1988; Patterns of Divine Comedy, 1989; The Road to the Never Land, 1991; Of Lion and of Unicorn, 1993; The Poems of William Dunbar, 1997; The Mercat Anthology of Early Scottish Literature (Co-Editor), 1997 (revised edition, 2000); New Oxford Dictionary of National Biography (Assoc. Ed.) 2004; Scotland in Europe (Co-Editor), 2006; Myths and the Myth Maker: A Literary Account of J.M. Barrie's Formative Years, 2010; The Earliest Dramas of J.M. Barrie, 2013; Changing Lives, vol. 2 (ed), 2015. Address: (b.) 54, Buckstone Road, Edinburgh EH10 6UN.

Jackson, Ian, MBE, MA. Director for Scotland, General Dental Council, since 2009; b. 30.3.54, Perth; m., Susan (Arthur); 2 s.; 1 d. Educ. Perth Academy; Edinburgh University. Northern Foods, Hull, 1976-78; John Bartholomew & Son, Edinburgh, 1978-80; Lloyds and Scottish Finance, Edinburgh, 1980-81; Self Employed, 1981-82; BT PLC, 1982-2008 (range of roles in sales, business management, recruitment and consultancy). Member, Perth and Kinross Council Lifelong Learning Committee, since 1999; Member, General Teaching Council Scotland, since 2005; Lay Member, Education Scotland, since 1986; Member, Perth College UHI Board, since 2012; Member, Society of High Constables of the City of Perth, since 2011; MBE for services to Education, 2005. Recreations: rugby; walking; industrial archaeology. Address: (h.) 9 Muirend Road, Perth PH1 1JS; T.-01738 639393; e-mail: i.jackson@btinternet.com

Jackson, Jack, OBE, BSc (Hons), PhD, CBiol, FRSB, FRSE; b. 31.5.44, Ayr; m., Sheilah Margaret Fulton; 1 s.; 3 d. Educ. Ayr Academy; Glasgow University; Jordanhill College of Education. Demonstrator, Zoology Department, Glasgow University, 1966-69; Lecturer in Zoology, West of Scotland Agricultural College, 1969-72; Assistant Teacher of Biology, Cathkin High School, 1972-73; Principal Teacher of Biology, Ayr Academy, 1973-83. Senior Examiner and Setter, Scottish Examination Board, 1978-83; Director, Board, Scottish Youth Theatre, 1979-82; Member: Scottish Council, Institute of Biology, 1980-83, School Board, Balerno High School, 1989-99; former Assistant Chief Inspector of Schools with responsibility for science subjects. Visiting Professor, Department of Curricular Studies, University of Strathclyde, since 2007. Lay Examiner, Royal College of Surgeons of Edinburgh, since 2008. Recreations: family life; gardening; hill-walking;

conservation. Address: (h.) 9 Newlands, Kirknewton, West Lothian EH27 8LR; T.-01506 884993; e-mail: profjackjackson@btinternet.com

Jakimciw, Tony, OBE, MA, PGCE. Chairman, Borders College, since 2014; b. 28.6.51, Consett; m., Alice; 1 s.; 1 d. Educ. Hookergate Grammar School; Edinburgh University; Leicester University. Lecturer in Communications, Gateshead College, 1975-84; Senior Lecturer/Director of Development, Hartlepool College, 1984-88; Vice Principal, Carlisle College, 1989-99; Principal, Dumfries and Galloway College, 1999-2012. Member, JISC Advance Board; Chair, JISC RSC UK Steering Group. Recreations: family life; cooking; reading; walking. Address: Borders College, Scottish Borders Campus, Nether Road, Galashiels TD1 3HE.

Jameson, Brigadier Melville Stewart, CBE. Lord Lieutenant for Perth and Kinross; b. 17.7.44, Clunie; m., Sarah Amy Walker Munro; 2 s. Educ. Glenalmond; RMA, Sandhurst. Commissioned into Royal Scots Greys, 1965; served with regiment in Germany, Northern Ireland, Cyprus, Middle East and Edinburgh (where, in 1971, regiment amalgamated with 3rd Carabiniers to form Royal Scots Dragoon Guards); following tour as Chief of Staff 52 Lowland Brigade, commanded Royal Scots Dragoon Guards, 1986-88, at Tidworth; posted as Instructor to Joint Service Defence College Greenwich; Colonel PB17 on Military Secretary's staff, Ministry of Defence; Command, 51 Highland Brigade, 1994-96 based in Perth; Producer and Chief Executive, Edinburgh Military Tattoo, 1995-2007. Officer, Royal Company of Archers; Colonel, The Royal Scots Dragoon Guards. Recreations: shooting; gardening; polo; music (Highland bagpipes). Address: (b.) Home HQ, Royal Scots Dragoon Guards, The Castle, Edinburgh EH1 2YT.

Jamie, Professor Kathleen, MA. Writer; University of Stirling's first appointed Professor of Creative Writing; formerly part-time Lecturer in Creative Writing, School of English, University of St. Andrews; b. 13.5.62, Johnstone. Educ. Currie High School; Edinburgh University. Publications: The Way We Live; The Autonomous Region; The Queen of Sheba; The Golden Peak; The Tree House (won the 2004 Forward Poetry Prize and Scottish Arts Council Book of Year award, 2005); Findings, 2005; Waterlight: selected poems, 2007; Sightlines, 2012 (won the 2014 John Burroughs Medal and the 2014 Orion Book Award); The Overhaul, 2012 (won the 2012 Costa poetry award).

Jamieson, Cathy, BA (Hons), CQSW. Managing Director, Care Visions Residential, since 2015; MP (Labour), Kilmarnock and Loudon, 2010-2015; former Shadow Economic Secretary to the Treasury, UK Government; MSP (Labour and Co-operative), Carrick, Cumnock and Doon Valley, 1999-2011; Minister for Education and Young People, Scottish Executive, 2001-03; former Minister for Justice; b. 3.11.56, Kilmarnock; m., Ian Sharpe; 1 s. Educ. James Hamilton Academy, Kilmarnock; Glasgow Art School; Glasgow University; Goldsmiths College, London; Caledonian University. Professional qualification in art therapy; later trained in social work; Senior IT Worker, Strathclyde Region; Principal Officer, Who Cares? Scotland, developing policy and legislation for young people in care; Member, inquiry team which investigated child abuse in Edinburgh children's homes. Recreation: football (Kilmarnock supporter). Address: Care Visions Residential, Stirling Office, Bremner House, Castle Business Park, Stirling FK9 4TF; T.-01576 204 939.

Jamieson, Charles Reginald Wingate, DA (Glasgow), MFA, PAI, PPAI. Artist, since 1976; Actor, since 1976; b. 12.03.52, Rutherglen; m., Sally Ann Muir. Educ. Hutcheson's Boys Grammar School, Glasgow; Glasgow School of Art; Texas Christian University, Fort Worth, Texas. Borderline Theatre, 1977-79; acted in many TV and Film Productions - Blake's Seven, Goodnight and Godbless, Wheels, Bad Boys; Repertory Theatre with Swansea Grand Theatre; acted in Take The High Road (five years in the 1980's), Scottish Television; also appeared in '2000 Acres of Sky', 'Taggart', 'Still Game', The Angels' Share (Director, Ken Loach), 'River City', BBC Scotland, 2012. Exhibited paintings widely across the country with solo shows: The Dryden Street Gallery, 1984; Gallerie Marie, London, 1990, Duncan Miller Fine Arts, Hampstead, 2000, Panter & Hall, Mayfair, 2001, Duncan R Miller Fine Arts, St. James's, 2003, The Richmond Hill Gallery, Richmond, Surrey, 2004, Duncan R Miller Fine Arts, St. James's, 2006, Mansfield Park Gallery, Glasgow, 2007, The Richmond Hill Gallery, Richmond Hill, Surrey, 2007, Panter & Hall in The Lennox Gallery, Fulham, 2009; The Richmond Hill Gallery, 2009, 2010; The Brownston Gallery, Modbury, Devon, 2012; solo show with The Stafford Gallery in conjunction with Wimbledon Fine Art, 2013; solo show with The Doubt Fire Gallery, 2013; solo show with The Brownston Gallery, Modbury, Devon, 2015; paintings in collections across the world. Member of the organising committee and Chair of Judging of The Aspect Prize from its conception in 2002 until 2010. Awards: Sculpture Prize, Scottish Young Contemporaries, 1972; Norden Scholarship, 1974; GSA Travelling Scholarship, 1974; William Bowie Award, 1999; Richmond Hill Gallery Award, 2004; Diploma of the Paisley Art Institute, 2005; Richmond Hill Gallery Award, 2007. Paisley Art Institute: President, 2004-07, Member of Committee, 2000-07; Committee Member, Dunlop and Lugton Regeneration Group, 1999-2002. Publication: 'Glasgow', 2009 (book of photographs). Recreations: gardening; travel; cooking; reading; films. Address: (h.) The Steading, 41 Lugton Road, Dunlop, Ayrshire KA3 4DL; T.-01560 482419. E-mail: jamieson.charles@btinternet.com

Jamieson, George, LLB (Hons), DipLP. Solicitor (Scotland, since 1985, England and Wales, since 2002); b. 21.8.61, Paisley. Educ. Paisley Grammar School; Strathclyde University. Trainee Solicitor, Hart, Abercrombie, Caldwell and Co., Paisley, 1984-86; Walker Laird, Paisley: Assistant Solicitor, 1986-89, Partner, 1990-2001; Consultant, Pattison and Sim, Paisley, 2001-08. Part-time Immigration Adjudicator, 2002-05; Immigration Judge, 2005-09; Part Time Sheriff, 2006-09; Council Member, Paisley Sheriff Court District, Law Society of Scotland, 1997-2005; Sheriff of South Strathclyde, Dumfries and Galloway at Dumfries, since 2009. Publications: Parental Responsibilities and Rights, 1995; Summary Applications and Suspensions, 2000; Scottish Family Law Legislation (Editor), 2002; Family Law Agreements, 2005. Address: (h.) 19 Keswick Road, Dumfries DG1 3FF; e-mail: georgegjst@aol.com

Jamieson, Gordon. Chief Executive, NHS Western Isles, since 2008; b. Castle Douglas. First came to the Western Isles in September 2006 as part of a Ministerial Support Team; former Nurse Director/Director of Patient Safety, NHS Dumfries and Galloway; joined NHS Western Isles in February 2008 as Nurse Director/Chief Operating Officer. Significant experience of working in the NHS, including almost 20 years at Executive Board level. Address: (b.) 37 South Beach Street, Stornoway, Isle of Lewis HS1 2BB; T.-01851 702997; e-mail: gordon.jamieson@nhs.net

Jamieson, Rev. Gordon David, MA, BD. Church of Scotland Minister; b. 1.3.49, Glasgow; m., Annette; 1 s.; 1 d. Educ. Hamilton Academy; Edinburgh University. Assistant Minister, Tron Moredun, Edinburgh, 1973-74; Minister: Schaw Kirk, Drongan, 1974-79, Elie Parish Church, linked with Kilconquhar and Colinsburgh Parish

Church, 1979-86, Barnhill St. Margaret's Parish Church, Dundee, 1986-2000, Head of Stewardship, 2000-2012. Address: (h.) 41 Goldpark Place, Livingston EH54 6LW; T.-01506 412020; e-mail: gdj1949@talktalk.net

Jamieson, William, BA (Econ), FRSA. Editor, Scot-Buzz, The Website for Business; Freelance Writer and Speaker; Director, Policy Institute, 2000-08; former Executive Editor, The Scotsman, 2000-2012; b. 9.6.45, Newmilns; m., Elaine Margaret Muller; 1 s. Educ. Hurst Grange School, Stirling; Sedbergh School, Yorkshire; Manchester University. Economics Correspondent, Thomson Regionals, 1973-77; City Reporter, Daily Express, 1978; City Editor, Thomson Regionals, 1979-86; Deputy City Editor, Today, 1986; Sunday Telegraph: Deputy City Editor, 1986-95, Economics Editor, 1995-2000. Publications: Goldstrike, 1989; Britain Beyond Europe, 1994; UBS Guide to Emerging Markets (Editor), 1996; Illustrated Guide to the British Economy, 1998; Illustrated Guide to the Scottish Economy (Editor), 1999; Scotland's Ten Tomorrows (Editor), 2006. Business Journalist of the Year and overall Journalist of the Year, 2009, Scottish Media Awards. Recreation: reading other people's newspapers. Address: (h.) Inveregle, Lochearnhead FK19 8PR; T.-07771 800 557.

Jardine, Professor Alan George. Professor of Renal Medicine, University of Glasgow, since 2006, Head of the School of Medicine, since 2013, Head of the Undergraduate Medical School, 2011-14; President, Royal Medico-Chirurgical Society of Glasgow, 2015-16; Consultant Physician, Western Infirmary, Glasgow, 1996-2015; Consultant Physician, Queen Elizabeth University Hospital, Glasgow, since 2015; b. 27.08.60, Thurso; m., Catherine Pickering; 1 s.; 2 d. Educ. Bearsden Academy; University of Glasgow. MRC Clinical Scientist, 1987-90; MRC Blood Pressure Unit, Registrar in Nephrology, 1990-92, then Lecturer in Medicine and Senior Registrar in Medicine, Inverness and Aberdeen, 1992-93, joined University of Glasgow in 1994 as Lecturer, became Senior Lecturer, then Reader in Renal Medicine. Articles on renal, transplant and cardiovascular medicine. Recreations: golf and the outdoors. Address: 7 Cleveden Crescent, Glasgow G12 0PD; T.-0141 357 4062.
E-mail: alan.jardine@glasgow.ac.uk

Jardine, Ian William, BSc, PhD. Chief Executive, Scottish Natural Heritage, since 2002; b. 22.5.59, Edinburgh; m., Anne Daniel; 3 s. Educ. Royal High School, Edinburgh; Durham University; Leeds University. Joined Scottish Office, 1984; worked in various departments, including Scottish Development and Industry Departments; Private Secretary to Ian Lang MP; involved in setting-up of urban partnership initiatives and management of Castlemilk Partnership; Scottish Natural Heritage: joined 1992, former Director of Strategy and Operations (East), 1997-2002; President, Eurosite, 2007-2010; Seconded to European Commission, DG Environment, 2015. Recreations: acting; gardening; natural history. Address: (b.) Great Glen House, Leachkin Road, Inverness IV3 8NW; T.-01463 725001.

Jardine, Stephen. Runs Taste Communications; former Scottish television presenter; co-presenter, STV's The Hour, 2009-2011; regular Columnist for The Scotsman and Daily Record; b. 1963, Dumfries. Joined Radio Tay as a reporter before joining Scottish Television (now STV Central) to work on Scotland Today; former presenter, Scotland Today's East news opt-out, and anchored the main bulletin on Friday night, until December 2007; formerly a regular stand-in presenter/producer of the programme's online video blog, (Not) The Real MacKay; left STV to become GMTV's Scotland Correspondent, 1993-99; moved to Paris as Europe Correspondent, and also presented on GMTV; rejoined STV in 1999 as host of the station's Millennium Hogmanay Show live from the centre of Edinburgh, then moved onto presenting the afternoon talk show Room at the Top and his own evening chat show Tonight at the Top; also presented a number of current affairs programmes for the station, such as Seven Days, Wheel Nuts, Sunday Live and the channel's coverage of The State Opening of the Scottish Parliament; also fronted feature programmes for STV including Drivetime, Summer Discovery, Rich, Gifted & Scots and The Talent; presented a Saturday morning show on Talk 107 until February 2007; presented STV's daily magazine programme, The Five Thirty Show, broadcasting across the station's Northern and Central regions, 2008-09; Columnist for Edinburgh Evening News, 2006-09. Address: (b.) Taste Communications, 93-95 Hanover Street, Edinburgh EH2 1DJ.

Jarvie, Professor Grant, BEd, MA, PhD, PhD (Hon). Professor of Sport, Director of Academy of Sport, University of Edinburgh, since 2012; Senior Management Group and Visiting Professor, University of Toronto, Canada, 2012-13; 2015-16; Vice-Principal, University of Stirling, 2005-2012; Head of School, Arts and Humanities, University of Stirling, 2010-11, Chair of Sport and Vice Principal responsible for Sport, 1997-2012; Honorary Professor, University of Warsaw; Honorary Doctorate, National University Taiwan, 2009; Ministerial Adviser to Scottish Government on both Education and Sport; adviser to a number of governments (United Kingdom, Montenegro, Romania, Portugal, Monaco, Malaysia, and Kenya) on key matters of policy and development; past and present Board Membership includes Sportscotland, Quality Assurance Agency, UNESCO, Prince Albert Foundation; b. 7.11.55, Motherwell. Educ. School, Edinburgh; University of Exeter; Queen's University (Canada); University of Leicester. Recreations: squash; hillwalking. Address: 3 Baberton Mains Cottages, Edinburgh EH14 5AB; T.-07729500769; grantjarvie1@gmail.com

Jasper, Professor David, MA (Cantab), MA (Oxon), PhD (Dunelm), BD (Oxon), DD (Oxon), TEOL.DR (Uppsala-HC), FRSA, FRSE. Clergyman; Professor of Literature and Theology, University of Glasgow, since 1998; Changjiang Chair Professor, Renmin University of China, Beijing, since 2009; b. 1.8.51, Stockton-on-Tees, since 2009; m., Dr. Alison E. Jasper; 3 d. Educ. Dulwich College; Cambridge (Jesus); Oxford (Keble); Durham. Curate, Buckingham Parish Church, England, 1976-79; Chaplain, Fellow, Hatfield College, Durham University, 1979-87; Principal, St. Chad's College, Durham University, 1988-91; Senior Lecturer, Reader, Professor, University of Glasgow, 1991-2012. Elected Fellow of Royal Society of Edinburgh, since 2006. Publications include: The Sacred Desert, 2004; The Sacred Body, 2009; The Sacred Community, 2012. Recreations: reading; music. Address: (h.) 124 Old Manse Road, Wishaw ML2 0EP; T.-01698 373286; e-mail: david.jasper@glasgow.ac.uk

Jauhar, Pramod, MBBS, DPM, FRCPsych, FRCP(Glas). Visiting Psychiatrist, Priory Hospital Glasgow, since 2006; previously Consultant Psychiatrist, Greater Glasgow and Clyde, 1981-2006, and Honorary Clinical Senior Lecturer, University of Glasgow, 1981-2006. Currently: Medical Panellist, Mental Health Tribunal for Scotland, since 2005; Medical Member, Pensions Appeals Tribunal, since 2007. Previously: HM Medical Commissioner (part-time), Mental Welfare Commissions for Scotland, 1998-2006; Clinical Director, Alcohol and Drug Services, Greater Glasgow, 1995-2003; Clinical Director, Mental Health - Medicines Resource Management, Greater Glasgow, 2003-06; Governor, University Court, Glasgow Caledonian University, 2001-07. Recreations: golf; travel. Address: 7 Dalziel Drive, Glasgow G41 4JA.

Jeeves, Professor Malcolm Alexander, CBE, MA, PhD (Cantab), Hon. DSc (Edin), Hon. DSc (St. And.), Hon. DUniv (Stir.), FBPsS, FMedSci, FRSE, PPRSE. Professor of Psychology, St. Andrews University, 1969-93, Emeritus Professor, since 1993; President, Royal Society of

Edinburgh, 1996-99 (Vice-President, 1990-93); b. 16.11.26, Stamford, England; m., Ruth Elisabeth Hartridge; 2 d. Educ. Stamford School; St. John's College, Cambridge University. Lt., 1st Bn., Sherwood Foresters, BAOR, 1945-48; Exhibitioner, St. John's College, Cambridge, 1948-52; research and teaching, Cambridge and Harvard Universities, 1952-56; Lecturer, Leeds University, 1956-59; Professor and Head, Department of Psychology, Adelaide University, 1959-69 (Dean, Faculty of Arts, 1963-64); Member: Council, SERC, 1985-89, Neuroscience and Mental Health Board, MRC, 1985-89, Council, Royal Society of Edinburgh, 1985-88 (Vice President, 1990-93); Director, Medical Research Council Cognitive Neuroscience Research Group, 1983-88; Vice-Principal, St. Andrews University, 1981-85; Chairman, Executive Committee, International Neuropsychological Symposium, 1986-91; Editor-in-Chief, Neuropsychologia, 1990-93; Cairns Memorial Lecturer, Australia, 1986; New College Lecturer, University of NSW, 1987; Drummond Lectures, Stirling University, 2001. Honorary Sheriff, Fife, since 1986. Publications: Analysis of Structural Learning (Co-Author); Psychology Survey No. 3 (Editor); Experimental Psychology: An introduction for biologists; The Effects of Structural Relations upon Transfer (Co-Author); Thinking in Structures (Co-Author); Behavioural Science and Christianity (Editor); Free to be Different (Co-Author); Psychology and Christianity: The View Both Ways; The Scientific Enterprise and Christian Faith; Psychology: Through the eyes of faith (Co-Author); Mind Fields; Human Nature at the Millennium; Science, Life and Christian Belief (Co-author); From Cells to Souls – and Beyond (Editor and Contributor); Human Nature (Editor and Contributor); Neuroscience, Psychology and Religion (Co-Author); Rethinking Human Nature (Editor and Contributor); Minds, Brains, Souls and Gods (Author); The Emergence of Human Personhood: A Quantum Leap? (Editor and Contributor). Recreations: walking; music; fishing. Address: (b.) School of Psychology and Neuroscience, St. Andrews University, St. Andrews KY16 9JU; T.-01334 462072.

Jeffrey, Rev. Kenneth Samuel, BA, BD, PhD. Minister, The Parish Church of Cupar Old and St Michael of Tarvit, 2002-2014; Coordinator of the Centre for Ministry Studies, University of Aberdeen, since 2014; b. 30.09.69, Dundonald, Northern Ireland; m., Linda; 3 s.; 1 d. Educ. Sullivan Upper School, Holywood, Co. Down; Stirling University; Aberdeen University. Teacher, Livingstonia Secondary School, Malawi, 1992-94; Assistant Minister, Rubislaw Parish Church, Aberdeen, 2000-02. Publications: 'When The Lord Walks The Land - The 1858-62 Revival in the North East of Scotland', 2002; contributed to several other books. Recreations: walking; reading; supporting Manchester United. Address: (h.) The North Steading, Dalgairn, Cupar, Fife KY15 4PH; T.-01334 653196. E-mail: ksjeffrey@btopenworld.com

Jeffreys-Jones, Professor Rhodri, BA (Wales), PhD (Cantab). Emeritus Professor of American History and Senior Honorary Professorial Fellow, Edinburgh University (Chair of History 2001-03); b. 28.7.42, Carmarthen; m., Mary Fenton; 2 d. by pr. m. Educ. Ysgol Ardudwy; University of Aberystwyth; Cambridge University; Michigan University; Harvard University. Tutor: Harvard, 1965-66, Fitzwilliam College, Cambridge, 1966-67; Assistant Lecturer, Lecturer, Senior Lecturer, Reader, Professor, Edinburgh University, 1967-2008; Fellow, Charles Warren Center for the Study of American History, Harvard, 1971-72; Canadian Commonwealth Visiting Fellow and Visiting Professor, University of Toronto, 1993; Hon. President, Scottish Association for the Study of America. Publications: Violence and Reform in American History; American Espionage: From Secret Service to CIA; Eagle Against Empire: American Opposition to European Imperialism 1914-82 (Editor); The Growth of Federal Power in American History (Joint Editor); The CIA and American Democracy; North American Spies (Joint Editor); Changing Differences: Women and the Shaping of American Foreign Policy, 1917-1994; Eternal Vigilance? – 50 years of the CIA (Joint Editor); Peace Now! American Society and the Ending of the Vietnam War; American-British-Canadian Intelligence Relations 1939-2000 (Joint Editor); Cloak and Dollar – A History of American Secret Intelligence; The FBI: A History; In Spies We Trust: The Story of Western Intelligence; The American Left: Its Impact on Politics and Society, since 1900 (Neustadt Prize, 2013). Recreations: snooker; vegetable gardening. Address: (b.) History/School of History, Classics and Archaeology, Edinburgh University, Doorway 4, William Robertson Wing, Teviot Place, Edinburgh EH8 9AG; e-mail: R. Jeffreys-Jones@ed.ac.uk

Jenkins, Blair, OBE (2010), MA (Hons). Chief Executive, Yes Scotland campaign, 2012-2014; Chairman, Scottish Broadcasting Commission, 2007-08; Chairman, Scottish Digital Network Panel, 2010-11; Visiting Professor in Journalism, Strathclyde University, 2010-2012; Governor, Glasgow School of Art, 2008-2012; former Head of News and Current Affairs, BBC Scotland (2000-06); b. 8.1.57, Elgin; m., Carol Sinclair; 3 d. Educ. Elgin Academy; Edinburgh University. Reporter, Aberdeen Evening Express, 1974-76; student, 1976-80; Producer, BBC Television News, London, 1981-84; Producer, Reporting Scotland, BBC Scotland, 1984-86; Scottish Television: Producer, Scotland Today, 1986-90, Head of News, 1990-93, Head of Regional Broadcasting, 1993-94, Director of Broadcasting, 1994-97; Media Consultant, 1998-2000. Young Journalist of the Year, Scottish Press Awards, 1977; Chairman, BAFTA Scotland, 1998-2004; Fellow, Carnegie UK Trust, 2011-13. Address: (h.) 9 Fotheringay Road, Glasgow G41 4LZ; T.-0141 424 3118. E-mail: blairjenkins@btinternet.com

Jessamine, Rev. Alistair Lindsay, MA, BD. Minister of Dunfermline Abbey, 1991-2011; b. 17.6.49, Hill of Beath; m., Eleanor Moore. Educ. Beath High School, Cowdenbeath; University of Edinburgh. Assistant Minister, Newlands South Parish Church, Glasgow, 1978-79; Minister, Rankin Parish Church, Strathaven linked with Chapelton, 1979-91; Chaplain: HM Prison, Dungavel, 1979-91, RAF Pitreavie Castle, 1991-95; Moderator, Presbytery of Dunfermline, 1993-94. Recreations: travel; cooking; golf. Address: 11 Gallowhill Farm Cottages, Strathaven ML10 6BZ; T.-01357 520934.

Jiwa, Shainool, PhD. Head, Constituency Studies Research at The Institute of Ismaili Studies, London; Court Member, Edinburgh Napier University, since 2012; Commissioner, Mental Welfare Commission for Scotland, 1998-2002; Chief Examiner, International Baccalaureate Organization, 2002-09; Associate Assessor with Her Majesty's Inspectorate for Education, Scotland, since 2003; m., Shahnavaz Jiwa; 1 s. (Adil); 1 d. (Nabila). Educ. McGill University, Montreal (MA); Edinburgh University (PhD). Began career as Lecturer in Islamic History, Edinburgh University, 1989-91; embarked on career in community development, training and practising as a counsellor; leading role in setting up a range of community-based services for minority ethnic women in Edinburgh, 1991-99; volunteer counsellor, Edinburgh Association for Mental Health, 1996-98; voluntary involvement with Ismaili Muslim community in UK, since 1979. Publications: Towards a Shii Mediterranean Empire, 2009; Founder of Cairo, 2013. Recreations: swimming; reading; walks.

Johnson, Professor Christopher William, MA, MSc, DPhil, CEng, FBCS. Professor, Computing Science, Glasgow University, since 1996 (Head of Computing Science, since 2014); b. 15.4.65, Edinburgh; m., Fionnuala Muireann; 4 s. Educ. Verulam School, St. Albans; Trinity College, Cambridge. Lecturer in Computing Science, University of York, 1991-94; Senior Lecturer in Computing

Science, University of Glasgow, 1994-97. Secretary, IFIP Working Group 13.5 (Human Error and Systems Development). Winner, 2002 NASA/ICASE Fellowship; 2003 award, International Systems Safety Society. Publications: over 200 papers and articles. Recreation: running. Address: (b.) Department of Computing Science, University of Glasgow, Glasgow G12 8QQ; T.-0141-330 6053.

Johnson, Daniel. MSP (Labour), Edinburgh Southern, since 2016; m.; 2 d. Educ. Bonaly Primary School; Daniel Stewart's and Melville College; University of St Andrews; University of Strathclyde. Ran a group of five shops in Edinburgh's City Centre, bringing a strong business experience; the first independent retailer in Edinburgh to become an accredited Living Wage employer. Address: Scottish Parliament, Edinburgh EH99 1SP.
E-mail: daniel.johnson.msp@scottish.parliament.uk

Johnston, Frederick Patrick Mair, CBE, FRSA, MA. Chairman, Johnston Press plc (formerly F. Johnston & Co. Ltd.), 1973-2001, Non-Executive Director, 2001-2010; Director, Lloyds TSB Scotland plc, 1996-2003; Director, Scottish Mortgage & Trust plc, 1991-2002; b. 15.9.35, Edinburgh; m., Elizabeth Ann Jones; 2 s. Educ. Morrison's Academy, Crieff; Lancing College, Sussex; New College, Oxford. Editorial Department, Liverpool Daily Post and Echo, 1959; Assistant Secretary, The Times Publishing Co. Ltd., 1960; Company Secretary, F. Johnston & Co. Ltd., 1969. Chairman, Central Scotland Manpower Committee, 1976-83; Member, Press Council, 1974-88; President, Scottish Newspaper Proprietors' Association, 1976-78; Treasurer, Society of Master Printers of Scotland, 1981-86; President, The Newspaper Society, 1989-90; Chairman, Edinburgh International Book Festival, 1996-2001; Director, Press Association Ltd., 1997-2001. Recreations: reading; travelling.

Johnston, Geoffrey Edward Forshaw, LLB, CA. Chairman, Roses Charitable Trust; Vice Chairman, Scottish Friendly Assurance Society Ltd., 2006-2010 (retired); Managing Director, Arbuckle, Smith and Company, 1972-99; Chairman, Scottish Chambers of Commerce, 1996-2000; b. 20.6.40, Burton-Wirral, England; m., Elizabeth Anne Lockhart; 2 d. Educ. Loretto School, Musselburgh; University of St. Andrews. Wilson Stirling & Co. CA, 1959-65; Arbuckle Smith Group, since 1965: Director, 1968, management buy-out, 1984. Honorary Consul for Belgium, Scotland West and Northern Islands, 1989-95; National Chairman, British International Freight Association, 1990-91; President, Glasgow Chamber of Commerce, 1994-95; Member, Scottish Valuation and Rating Council, 1981-2001; Chairman, Central College of Commerce, 1999-2005. Recreations: sailing; skiing; hillwalking; golf. Address: (h.) Upper Dunard, Station Road, Rhu, Dunbartonshire G84 8LW; T.-01436 820563.

Johnston, George Bonar, DA, RSW. Artist; b. 14.6.33, Edinburgh; m., Margaret (deceased); 1 s.; 1 d. Educ. Bathgate Academy; Edinburgh College of Art. Teacher, 1955-56; Army Officer, 1956-58; Teacher, 1958-59; Lecturer, 1959-66; Art Adviser, Tayside Region, 1966-91. Paintings in private and public collections in Scotland, England, France, North America, Canada. Recreations: fly fishing; reading. Address: 10 Collingwood Crescent, Barnhill, Dundee DD5 2SX; T.-01382 779857.

Johnston, Grenville Shaw, OBE, OStJ, TD, KCSG, CA. Chartered Accountant, since 1968; President, Institute of Chartered Accountants of Scotland, 2000-01; Vice Lord Lieutenant of Moray, 1996-2005, Lord Lieutenant, since 2005; Territorial Army Officer, 1964-89 (Lt. Col.); b. 28.1.45, Nairn; m., Marylyn Jean Picken; 2 d. Educ. Blairmore School; Fettes College. Qualified in Edinburgh with Scott Moncrieff Thomson & Sheills; Thomson

McLintock & Co., Glasgow, 1968-70; joined family firm, W.D. Johnston & Carmichael, Elgin, 1970, Senior Partner, 1975-2001, Consultant, 2001-05 (retired). Commanding Officer, 2nd 51st Highland Volunteers, 1983-86; Hon. Col., 3rd Highland Volunteers, 1997-99; Knight Commander, Order of St. Gregory, 1982, for work for Pluscarden Abbey; OBE for services to Territorial Army; appointed an Officer of the Order of St John, 2011; Chairman, Grampian Committee, Royal Jubilee Trusts, 1982-91; Member, Cairngorm Mountain Trust Ltd.; Trustee and Council Member: Queens Own Highlanders, The Highlanders, 1996-2013; Trustee, National Museums of Scotland, 1998-2006; Director: Cairngorm Mountain Ltd., since 1999 (Chairman, 1999-2014), Highlands and Islands Airports Ltd, 2001-08, (Chairman, since 2009); Caledonian Maritime Assets Ltd, Chairman, 2006-2014; President, Highland Reserve Forces and Cadets Association, 2007-2012; Honorary Member, Elgin Rotary Club, since 2008. Recreations: shooting; fishing; skiing; singing (tenor); curling. Address: (h.) Spynie Kirk House, Spynie, By Elgin, Moray IV30 8XJ.

Johnston, Professor Ian Alistair, BSc, PhD, FRSE. Chandos Professor of Physiology, since 1997; Director, the Scottish Oceans Institute, University of St Andrews, since 2012; CEO and Co-founder, Xelect Ltd., since 2013; Director, Gatty Marine Laboratory, 1985-2008; b. 13.4.49, Barking, Essex. Educ. Addey and Stanhope Grammar School, London; Hull University. NERC Postdoctoral Research Fellow, Bristol University, 1973-75; Lecturer in Physiology, St. Andrews University, 1976-84; Reader, 1984-85; Visiting Senior Lecturer, Department of Veterinary Physiology, Nairobi University, 1981; Visiting Scientist, British Antarctic Survey base, Signy Island, South Orkneys, 1983-84; Council Member, NERC, 1995-2000; Chairman, NERC Marine Science and Technology Board; awarded Scientific Medal, Zoological Society of London; President, Society for Experimental Biology, 2007-09. Recreations: photography; walking; reading. Address: (b.) School of Biology, St. Andrews University, St. Andrews KY16 8LB; T.-01334 463440.

Johnston, Professor Marie, BSc, PhD, DipClinPsych, FBPsS, CPsychol, FRSE, FMedSci, ACSS. Emeritus Professor in Psychology, Aberdeen University; b. 6.7.44, Aberdeen; m., Derek Johnston. Educ. High School for Girls, Aberdeen; Aberdeen University; Hull University. Research Officer, Oxford University, 1971-77; Lecturer, Senior Lecturer, Reader, Royal Free Hospital School of Medicine, 1977-90; Reader, Professor of Psychology, St. Andrews University, 1990-2003; Honorary Clinical Psychologist, Tayside and Fife Health Boards, since 1991; first Chair, Section of Health Psychology, British Psychological Society; Past President, European Health Psychology Society. Recreation: gardening. Address: (b.) School of Psychology, Aberdeen University, King's College, Aberdeen AB24 2UB.

Johnston, Paul. Director General Learning & Justice, Scottish Government, since 2015. Qualified lawyer and joined the Scottish Government Legal Directorate in May 2000; appointed to the Senior Civil Service in October 2007, carrying out a number of roles before being appointed to Director level as Head of the Advocate General's Office in April 2011; Director for Safer Communities, Scottish Government (responsibility for Police, Fire, Resilience, Defence, Security, Drugs Policy and Community Safety), 2013-15. Address: Scottish Government, St. Andrew's House, Regent Road, Edinburgh EH1 3DG.

Johnston, Peter Joseph Barrett Andrew, DipC of Ed. Leader, West Lothian SNP Group; Leader, West Lothian Council, 2007-2012; COSLA Spokesperson, Health and Wellbeing, since 2012; Non Executive Director: NHS Lothian, since 2010, HIS, since 2011; b. 10.3.51, Dundee; m., Christine; 2 d. Educ. Lawside Academy; Calendar Park

College of Education. Teacher, 1978-85; West Lothian District Council: Councillor, 1985-92, Leader, 1992-96; Councillor, West Lothian Council, since 1995. Chairman, Open Door Accomodation Project, 1986-2001. Recreations: golf; watching Dundee United. Address: (b.) Civic Centre, Almondvale, Boulevard, Livingston EH54 6FF; T.-01501 732060.

E-mail: peter.johnston@westlothian.gov.uk

Johnston, Peter William, MA, LLB. Convener, Risk Management Authority, since 2008; Adviser, accounting and auditing regulation and related legislation, since 2003; b. 08.02.43, Peebles; m., Patricia S. Johnston (Macdonald); 1 s.; 1 d. Educ. Larbert High School; University of Glasgow. Career History: Partner, MacArthur & Co Solicitors, Inverness; Procurator Fiscal Service, Assistant Solicitor, Crown Office; Chief Executive: The Institute of Chartered Accountants of Scotland, International Federation of Accountants. Trustee, Friends of Duff House, Banff; Treasurer, St. Andrew's SE Church, Banff; Treasurer, Friends of Chalmers Hospital, Banff. Recreations: grandchildren; music; languages; walking; swimming. Address: 13 Scotstown, Banff, Aberdeenshire AB45 1LA; T.-01261 818762/815549; e-mail: peter@13scotstoun.co.uk

Johnston, Robin Alexander, BSc, MB, BCh, BAO, MD, FRCSEd, FRCSGlas. Consultant Neurosurgeon, since 1985 (of Queen Elizabeth National Spinal Injury Unit, 1992-2009); retired from Clinical Practice, 2009; currently teaching; b. 30.3.49, Belfast; m., Ann. Educ. Belfast Royal Academy; Queens University, Belfast. Various surgical posts, UK, 1974-77; neurosurgical training, Belfast, Dallas, Glasgow, 1977-85. Address: (b.) Institute of Neurological Sciences, Southern General Hospital, Glasgow.

Johnstone, Alex. MSP (Conservative), North East Scotland, since 1999; Party Spokesman on Transport, Infrastructure and Housing; b. 31.7.61, Stonehaven; m. Linda; 1 s; 1 d. Educ. Mackie Academy, Stonehaven. Career history: dairy and arable farmer; candidate, West Aberdeenshire and Kincardine constituency, 2005 General Election. Address: (b.) Scottish Parliament, Edinburgh EH99 1SP; T.-0131-348 5649.

Johnstone, Alison. MSP (Green), Lothian, since 2011; b. 11.10.65, Edinburgh; m.; 1 d. Educ. St. Augustine's High School, Edinburgh. Assistant to Robin Harper, 1999-2011; Councillor for the Meadows/Morningside ward for the City of Edinburgh Council, 2007-2012; joint convenor of the Scottish Green Party, 2007-08. Board of Directors, Scottish Athletics. A former East of Scotland athletics champion. Address: (b.) Scottish Parliament, Edinburgh EH99 1SP.

Johnstone, Professor Eve Cordelia, CBE, MB, ChB, MD (Glas) 1976, FRCP, FRCPsych, FMedSci, FRSE, DPM, Hon MD (Edin) 2014. Emeritus Professor of Psychiatry and Honorary Assistant Principal, University of Edinburgh for Mental Health Research and Development; formerly Professor of Psychiatry and Head, Department of Psychiatry; b. 1.9.44, Glasgow. Educ. Park School, Glasgow; University of Glasgow. Junior posts in Glasgow hospitals; Lecturer in Psychological Medicine, University of Glasgow, 1972-74; Member of Scientific Staff, Medical Research Council, Clinical Research Centre, Northwick Park, 1974-89. Member of Council, Medical Research Council, 1997-2002; Chairman, MRC Neurosciences Board, 1999-2002. Publications: eight books on psychiatric illness; over 400 papers on biological psychiatry. Address: (b.) Royal Edinburgh Hospital, Morningside Park, Edinburgh.

Johnstone, Rev. Mark Edward, DL, MA, BD. Minister of Religion, St. Mary's Manse, Kirkintilloch, since 2000; Deputy Lieutenant of Dunbartonshire; b. 28.5.68, Glasgow; m., Audrey Gail Cameron; 2 s.; 1 d. Educ. Kingsridge Secondary, Drumchapel; University of Glasgow; Trinity College. Parish Minister, Denny, Falkirk; Chaplain to Strathcarron Hospice, Bellsdyke Psychiatric Hospital; Minister In Charge, Northminster United Church, Toronto, Canada; Parish Minister, St. Mary's, Kirkintilloch; Convener, Eldership Working Party/Membership. Convener, Education and Nurture task group; Convener, Mission and Discipleship; Chairman, Board of Directors of Lodging House Mission. Recreations: gym; conjouring; dog walking; fishing. Address: (h.) The Manse, 60 Union Street, Kirkintilloch G66 1DH; T.-0141-776-1252.

E-mail: mark.johnstone2@ntlworld.com

Johnstone, Sir Raymond, CBE, BA, CA; b. 27.10.29, London; m., Susan Sara; 5 step s.; 2 step d. Educ. Eton; Trinity College, Cambridge. Investment Analyst, Robert Fleming & Co. Ltd., London, 1955-60; Partner (CA), Brown, Fleming & Murray (later Whinney Murray & Co.), 1960-68; Director, Shipping Industrial Holdings Ltd., 1964-73; Chairman, Murray Johnstone Ltd., 1984-91 (Managing Director, 1968-88); Director: Scottish Amicable Life Assurance Society, 1971-97 (Chairman, 1983-85); Dominion Insurance Co. Ltd., 1973-95 (Chairman, 1978-95); Scottish Financial Enterprise, 1986-91 (Chairman, 1989-91); Summit Group PLC (Chairman, 1989-98); Murray Income PLC, 1989-99; Murray International PLC, 1989-2005; Murray Global Markets PLC, 1989-2000; Murray Ventures PLC, 1984-99; Murray Enterprise PLC, 1989-00; Chairman, Forestry Commission, 1989-94; Chairman, 1982-86, Hon. President, 1986-97, Scottish Opera; Chairman, Patrons of the National Galleries of Scotland, 1995-2003, Chairman, 1995-99; Chairman, Historic Buildings Council for Scotland, 1995-2002; Chairman, The Nuclear Trust, 1996-2003; Director, The Nuclear Trust, 1996-2007; Director, The Nuclear Liabilities Fund Ltd., 1996-2007; Director, RJ KILN PLC, 1995-2002; Chairman, Atrium Underwriting PLC (formerly Lomond Underwriting plc), 1993-2003. Recreations: fishing; shooting; opera; farming. Address: (h.) 32 Ann Street, Edinburgh EH4 1PJ.

Johnstone, Professor William, BD, MA (Hons), DLitt. Professor of Hebrew and Semitic Languages, Aberdeen University, 1980-2001, Emeritus Professor, since 2001; Minister, Church of Scotland, since 1963; b. 6.5.36, Glasgow; m., Elizabeth M. Ward; 1 s.; 1 d. Educ. Hamilton Academy; Glasgow University; Marburg University. Lecturer in Hebrew and Semitic Languages, Aberdeen University, 1962-72, Senior Lecturer, 1972-80, Dean, Faculty of Divinity, 1983-87; President, Society for Old Testament Study, 1990. Recreation: alternative work. Address: (h.) 9/5 Mount Alvernia, Edinburgh EH16 6AW.

Jones, Alan, BEd, MEd. Leisure consultant, since 2002; Director of Cultural and Leisure Services, Highland Council, 1987-2002; Member, Board, Sportscotland; b. 14.7.56, Bathgate; m., Lesley; 2 d. Educ. St Mary's Academy, Bathgate; Jordanhill College, Glasgow; Glasgow University; Stirling University. Lecturer, Physical Recreation, Stirling University, 1978-81; Sports Officer, Stirling District Council, 1981-86; Community and Leisure Manager, Clackmannan District Council, 1986-87; Director of Leisure and Recreation, Inverness District Council, 1987-95. Set up project to "Green" Inverness; winner, Queen Mother's Birthday Award. Recreations: Member, Physical Activity Task Force; golf; ski-ing. Address: 62 Boswell Road, Inverness IV2 3EJ; T.-01463 718715; e-mail: alanjonesassociates@btopenworld.com

Jones, Andrew Paul Stirling, MA (Hons) Med. Hist; b. 26.06.58, Cheam; m., Maryjaine Jones; 1 s.; 1 d. Educ. Haileybury; St. Andrews University. Media Buyer: J. Walter Thomson Ltd, 1980-82; Hall Advertising Ltd, 1983-84; Media Director: Struthers Advertising Ltd, 1984-89, The Bridge (Rex Stewart) Ltd, 1989-93; Managing Director: FB Media Direction Ltd, 1993-99;

Client Services Director/Commercial Director: Feather Brooksbank Ltd, 2000-2002; Director: Barkers Advertising Ltd, 2003-04; Founding Partner: Cloudline Consulting Ltd, 2005-07; Member: Dunbartonshire Economic Forum, 2007-08; Ofcom Advisory Committee, 2008-11; LINC Scotland, 2007-11; Media Consultant, since 2007; Member, Parole Board for Scotland, 2007-2014; Member, Scottish Solicitors' Discipline Tribunal, since 2008; Panel Chair: Children's Panel, 2007-2014; Board Director, Alternatives, 2012-2014; Member, BBC Audience Council, since 2012; Justice of the Peace Advisory Committee Member, since 2014. Recreations: rugby; golf; skiing; hill walking; music. T.-07736 486378.
E-mail: aj@lomondadventures.com

Jones, Bernadette. Headteacher, St. Joseph's College, Dumfries, since 2008. Address: (b.) Craigs Road, Dumfries DG1 4UU.

Jones, Professor Colin Anthony, BA (Hons), MA. Professor of Estate Management, Heriot-Watt University, since 1998; b. 13.1.49, Wallasey; m., Fiona Jones; 2 d. Educ. Price's School, Fareham, Hants; Wallasey Grammar School; York University; Manchester University. Research associate, Manchester University; Lecturer, Applied Economics, Glasgow University, 1975-80; Department of Land Economics, Paisley University, 1980-98; Member, UK Board, Shelter, 1978-84, and 1990-2007. Publication: The Right to Buy. Address: (b.) School of Energy, Geoscience, Infrastructure and Society, Heriot-Watt University, Riccarton, Edinburgh, EH14 4AS; T.-0131-451 4628; e-mail: c.a.jones@hw.ac.uk

Jones, Professor Hamlyn Gordon, MA (Cantab), PhD, FCIHort. Emeritus Professor, University of Dundee, since 2009, Professor of Plant Ecology, 1997-2009; Adjunct Professor in School of Plant Biology, University of Western Australia, since 2013; Honorary Research Professor, Scottish Crop Research Institute, Dundee, 1998-2011; m., Amanda Jane Corry; 2 d. Educ. St. Lawrence College, Ramsgate; St. John's College, University of Cambridge; Australian National University, Canberra. Research Fellow, St. John's College, Cambridge, 1973-76; Researcher, Plant Breeding Institute, Cambridge, 1972-76; Lecturer in Ecology, University of Glasgow, 1977-78; Leader of Stress Physiology Group, East Malling Research Station, Kent, 1978-88; Director, Crop Science Research and Head of Station, Horticulture Research International, Wellesbourne, Warwick, 1988-97; Special Professor, University of Nottingham, 1991-97; Honorary Professor, University of Birmingham, 1995-98. Member, Scientific Advisory Committee, Scottish Natural Heritage, 2005-2011. Publications: Plants and Microclimate, 1983/1992/2013; Remote Sensing of Vegetation (Co-Author), 2010; joint editor of five other books. Recreations: squash; tennis; mountains; lounging. Address: (b.) Plant Sciences Division, School of Life Sciences, University of Dundee at JHI, Invergowrie, Dundee DD2 5DA; T.-0844 928528.

Jones, Heather A., MA, MBA. Chief Executive Officer, Scottish Aquaculture Innovation Centre, since 2014; b. 23.11.66, Irvine. Educ. Withington Girls' School, Manchester; University of Edinburgh. Policy Officer (Fast Stream), Housing, Rural Affairs and Constitutional Issues, 1989-92; Private Secretary to Lord James Douglas-Hamilton, Under Secretary of State, Scottish Office, 1992-94; Principal, Scottish Office, Sea Fisheries Division, 1994-97; Manager, Locate in Scotland, Houston, Texas, USA, 1997-2000; Cabinet Secretariat, Scottish Executive, 2000-01, Deputy Director, Lifelong Learning, 2001-04, Deputy

Director, Education, 2004-05; Secondment, University of Glasgow, 2006; Deputy Director, Food Policy, Scottish Government, 2007; Deputy Director, Marine Scotland, 2008-2010; Deputy Director, International Division, 2010-2014; Deputy Director, Scottish Government, 2001-2014. Recreations: cooking; eating; travelling. Address: (b.) Scion House, Stirling University Innovation Park, Stirling FK9 4NF; T.-01786 448333.

Jones, Emeritus Professor Huw, BA, MA. Emeritus Professor of Geography, Dundee University; b. Llanidloes; 2 s. Educ. Newtown Boys Grammar School, Powys; University College of Wales, Aberystwyth. Address: (b.) 73 Portree Avenue, Broughty Ferry, Dundee DD5 3EG; T.-01382-738513; e-mail: huwrjones@yahoo.co.uk

Jones, Right Revd. Idris, BA, DMin. Episcopal Bishop of Glasgow and Galloway, 1998-2009; Primus, Scottish Episcopal Church, 2006-09 (retired); National Spiritual Director, Cursillo UK, 2011-14; b. 1943. Educ. University College St. David, Lampeter; New College, Edinburgh; Edinburgh Theological College. Deacon, 1967; Priest, 1968; Curate, St. Mary's, Stafford, 1967-70; Precentor, St. Paul's Cathedral, Dundee, 1970-73; Priest-in-Charge, St. Hugh's, Gosforth, Newcastle, 1973-80; Chaplain, St. Nicholas Hospital, 1975-80; Rector, St. Mary's and St. Peter's, Montrose with St. David's, Inverbervie, 1980-89; Anglican Chaplain, Dundee University and Priest-in-Charge, All Souls, Invergowrie, 1989-92; Canon, St. Paul's Cathedral, Dundee, 1984-92; Rector, Holy Trinity, Ayr, 1992-98; Director, Pastoral Studies, TISEC, 1995-99; President, Rotary Club of Queens Park, 2003; Deacon, Incorporation of Skinners and Glovers, 2007; Hon. Fellow, University of Wales, 2007; President, Glasgow XIII, 2005, Member; Collector, Trades House of Glasgow, 2012-13; Director, Merchant House of Glasgow, 2011; Hon. Fellow, University of Wales, 2006; Deacon Convenor of The Trades of Glasgow, 2014-15. Address: 27 Donald Wynd, Largs KA30 8TH.

Jones, John Owain Ab Ifor, OSrJ, MA, BD, FSAScot. Minister, United Church of Bute (C. of S.), since 2011; b. 16.5.57, St. Asaph, Flintshire; m., Carolyn; 1 s.; 1 d. Educ. Ysgol Syr Hugh Owen, Caernarfon; University of St Andrews. Minister, Tywyn and District Congregational Churches, Tywn, Merionethshire, 1981-87; Lecturer (Part Time), Hebrew and Old Testament, United Theological College, Aberystwyth, and Aberystwyth-Lampeter School of Theology, University of Wales, 1983-87; Assistant, then Associate Minister, Mearns Parish Church, 1987-90; Minister, Arnsheen Barrhill linked with Colmonell Parish Church, 1990-98; Minister, Langside Parish Church, 1998-2002; Minister, Kilbarchan East Church, 2002-2011. Contributor: "Thought for the Day", Radio Scotland (and Radio Cymru equivalent), Radio 4 Daily Service; Convener, Zimbabwe Twinning Committee, Presbytery of Greenock and Paisley, 2005-10. Recreations: reading; music (especially post romantic and twentieth century); astronomy. Address: (h.) UCB Manse, 10 Bishop Terrace, Rothesay PA20 9HF; T.-01700 504502; e-mail: johnowainjones@hotmail.com

Jones, Mervyn David, BSc, MPhil. Partner, Maple Jones and various Public and Private Sector Boards, since 2003; Council Member, Scottish Funding Council, 2003-08; b. 28.11.56, Poole; m., Pauline; 2 s.; 1 d. Educ. Poole Grammar School; Wales and Reading Universities. Research Demonstratorship, University of Reading, 1978-81; Trading, BP Oil International, London and New York, 1981-91; commercial and restructuring management roles, BP Brussels and BP Grangemouth. Chairman, Aquamarine Power Limited, 2007-2012; various CSR Projects (MFIF,

ACE); Director: SMRU Ltd, Greenrock ESCO; Member, SFC Research and Knowledge Transfer Committee; Chair, SFC Knowledge Transfer Group; Member of Court, University of St. Andrews; Chairman, UZ Arts; Chairman, Surface Active Solutions Group, 2013; Chairman, Converge Challenge, 2012-13; Scottish Non-Executive Director of Year, 2009; UK Director of the Year for Environmental Leadership, 2010. Recreations: fishing; golf; skiing; rugby; baroque music; opera; gardening. Address: (h.) 31/10 Ocean Drive, Edinburgh EH6 6JL; T.-0131 554 5680 (business); e-mail: mervyn@maplejones.co.uk

Jones, Professor Peter (Howard), MA, FRSE, FRSA, FSA Scot. Director, Foundation for Advanced Studies in the Humanities, 1997-2002; Member, Spoliation Advisory Panel, since 2000; Professor of Philosophy, University of Edinburgh, 1984-98, Professor Emeritus, since 1998; Director, Institute for Advanced Studies in the Humanities, 1986-2000; b. 1935, London; m., Elizabeth Jean Roberton (deceased); 2 d. Educ. Highgate School; Queens' College, Cambridge. Regional Officer, The British Council, London, 1960-61; Research Scholar, University of Cambridge, 1961-63; Assistant Lecturer in Philosophy, Nottingham University, 1963-64; University of Edinburgh: Lecturer in Philosophy, 1964-77, Reader, 1977-84; Visiting Professor of Philosophy: University of Rochester, New York, 1969-70, Dartmouth College, New Hampshire, 1973, 1983, Carleton College, Minnesota, 1974, Oklahoma University, 1978, Baylor University, 1978, University of Malta, 1993, Belarusian State University, 1997, Jagiellonian University, Cracow, since 2001; Distinguished Foreign Scholar, Mid-America State Universities, 1978; Visiting Fellow, Humanities Research Centre, Australian National University, 1984, 2002; Calgary Institute for the Humanities, 1992; Lothian Lecturer, 1993; Gifford Lecturer, University of Aberdeen, 1994-95; Loemker Lecturer, Emory University, 1996; Trustee: National Museums of Scotland, 1987-99 (Chairman, Museum of Scotland Client Committee, 1991-99), University of Edinburgh Development Trust, 1990-98, Morrison's Academy, Crieff, 1984-98, Fettes College, 1995-2005, Scots at War Trust, Policy Institute, 1999-2008, MBI; Member: Court, University of Edinburgh, 1987-90, Council, Royal Society of Edinburgh, 1992-95, UNESCO forum on Tolerance, Tblisi, 1995, UNESCO dialogue on Europe and Islam, since 1997; Founder Member, The Hume Society, 1974. Publications: Philosophy and the Novel, 1975; Hume's Sentiments, 1982; A Hotbed of Genius, 1986; Philosophy and Science in the Scottish Enlightenment, 1988; The Science of Man in the Scottish Enlightenment, 1989; Adam Smith Reviewed, 1992; James Hutton, Investigation of the Principles of Knowledge, 1999; The Enlightenment World, 2004; Lord Kames: Elements of Criticism, 2005; The Reception of David Hume in Europe, 2005; Ove Arup - Masterbuilder of the Twentieth Century, 2006. Recreations: opera; chamber music; the arts; architecture.

Jones, Rev. William Gerald, MA, BD, ThM. Minister, Kirkmichael with Straiton St. Cuthbert's, since 1985; b. 2.11.56, Irvine; m., Janet Blackstock. Educ. Dalry High School; Garnock Academy, Kilbirnie; Glasgow University; St. Andrews University; Princeton Theological Seminary, Princeton, New Jersey. Assistant Minister, Glasgow Cathedral, 1983-85. Freeman Citizen of Glasgow, 1984; Member, Incorporation of Gardeners of Glasgow, 1984; Moderator, Presbytery of Ayr, 1997-98; Member: General Assembly Panel on Worship, 1987-91, Council, Church Service Society, 1986-98, Committee to Nominate the Moderator of the General Assembly, 1988-92 and 1998-2003, Committee on Artistic Matters, 2000-01; Societas Liturgica, since 1989; Officer and Assistant Chaplain, Order of St. Lazarus of Jerusalem, 1995; Ayr Presbytery Representative, Ayrshire Regional Council of the Scottish Episcopal Church, since 2002; Convener, Administration Committee, Presbytery of Ayr, 1988-91, 2005-08, 2008-09, 2013-14 and 2015-16 (Vice-Convener, 1986-88, 2004-05 and 2014-15); various times Member, Ayr Presbytery Business Committee; Member: Society for Liturgical Study, since 1995; Society for the Study of Theology, since 2000; Council, Scottish Church Society, 2000-06 (Secretary, since 2004, and Editorial Committee member, since 2006); Society for the Study of Christian Ethics, 2003-12; Ayr Presbytery Vacancy Procedure Committee, since 2012 (Acting Convener, 2015-16); Volunteer Worker, Kirkmichael Community Shop, 2010-13; Honorary Chaplain, York Minster, since 2001; Member, The Priory of Scotland of The Order of St. John of Jerusalem, 2006; Life Member, St. John Ayrshire and Arran; Life Member, Ayrshire Archaeological and Natural History Society; broadcaster, West Sound Radio, 1998-2012; Convener, Selection Committee to appoint Associate Presbytery Clerk, 2008-09; Member, Dalmellington Parish Church Support Group, 2007-12; Member, Planning Group, and Co-organiser, Ayr Presbytery Rural Church Conference, 2015 and 2016; Adviser to the (Church of Scotland) Committee on Church Art and Architecture; Chairman, Straiton McCandlish Hall Committee, since 2009; Honorary Patron, Kirkmichael and Water of Girvan Curling Club, since 2013. Represented the Dean of the Chapel Royal in Scotland at the ecumenical service held at Crossraguel Abbey in June 1987 to mark the 800th anniversary of Carrick becoming an independent part of Scotland. Publications: Prayers for the Chapel Royal in Scotland, 1989; Worshipping Together (Contributor), 1991; Common Order (Contributor), 1994; The Times Book of Prayers (Contributor), 1997; A Lenten Meditation (Scottish Church Society), 2005; Sharing the Past: Shaping the Future (Co-editor), 2009; Holy Common Sense: David H.C. Read Remembered (forthcoming); articles on learned and other subjects. Recreations: music; books; writing; country life. Address: The Manse, Kirkmichael, Maybole, Ayrshire KA19 7PJ; T.-01655 750286.

Joseph, Robert William, CBE, MUniv, BSc (Hons). Administrator/Chief Executive, The MacRobert Trust, 2004-2014; b. 6.10.49, Perth; m., Janet Joseph (nee Keighley); 1 s.; 1 d. Educ. Archbishop Holgate's Grammar School, York; Enfield College of Technology; Middlesex University. Entered Civil Service from University, 1972; commissioned into The Royal Air Force as a General Duties/Navigator, 1973; General Duties Aerosystems Course, Royal Air Force College, Cranwell, 1980; Royal Naval Staff College, Greenwich, 1987; Command of Two Front-Line Nimrod MR2 Squadrons, 1992-94; Officer Commanding Royal Air Force Kinloss, Moray, 1994-96; Joint Services Command and Staff College Higher Command and Staff Course, 2000; senior appointment in Nato Supreme Allied Command Headquarters, Virginia, USA, 2000-02; Nato Senior Officers' Course, Rome, 2002. UK staff appointments, 2002-04; retired in Rank of Air Commodore, 2004. Recreations: golf; walking; gardening.

Jowitt, Professor Paul William, CBE, PhD, DIC, BSc(Eng), FCGI, CEng, FREng, FICE, FIPENZ, FRSA, FRSE. Professor of Civil Engineering Systems, Heriot-Watt University, since 1987; Editor, Civil Engineering and Environmental Systems, since 1985; b. 3.8.50, Doncaster. Educ. Maltby Grammar School; Imperial College. Lecturer in Civil Engineering, Imperial College 1974-86 (Warden, Falmouth Hall, 1980-86); Director, Tynemarch Systems Engineering Ltd., 1984-91 (Chairman, 1984-86); Head, Civil Engineering Department, Heriot-Watt University, 1989-91, Head, Civil and Offshore Engineering, 1991-99. Director, Scottish Institute of Sustainable Technology, 1999-2013; Member, East of Scotland Water Authority, 1999-2002; Member, Scottish Water, 2002-08; Board Member, United Utilities Water, 2009-2011; President,

Institution of Civil Engineers, 2009-2010; President, Commonwealth Engineers Council, since 2011. Recreations: painting; Morgan 3-wheelers; Canal narrow boats; digging an allotment. Address: (h.) 14 Belford Mews, Edinburgh EH4 3BT; T.-0131-225 7583; e-mail: p.w.jowitt@hw.ac.uk

Joyce, Eric. BA, MA, MBA, PGCE. MP (Independent), Falkirk, 2012-2015; Labour MP (Falkirk), 2005-2012, Falkirk West, 2000-05; b. 13.10.60, Perth; m.; 2 c. Soldier, Black Watch, 1978-81; Officer, Adjutant General's Corps, 1987-99; Public Affairs Officer, Commission for Racial Equality, 1999-2000. Executive Member, Fabian Society, 1998-2006, Chair, 2004-05; Member, Camelon Labour Club; former Scottish judo champion. Address: (b.) 37 Church Walk, Denny FK6 6DF.

Judge, Professor David. BA, PhD, FRSA. Emeritus Professor of Politics, University of Strathclyde, since 2013; b. 22.5.50, Sheffield; m., Lorraine; 1 s.; 1 d. Educ. Westfield School; Exeter University; Sheffield University. Lecturer, Paisley College, 1974-88; University of Strathclyde: Lecturer, 1988-90, Senior Lecturer, 1990-91, Reader, 1991-94, Professor, 1994-2013, Head of Department, 1994-97, 2004-2010, Head of School, 2011; Fulbright Fellow and Visiting Professor, University of Houston, USA, 1993-94; Visiting Professor, College of Europe, Bruges, 2004-07. Publications: Backbench Specialisation in the House of Commons, 1981; The Politics of Parliamentary Reform (Editor), 1983; The Politics of Industrial Closure (Joint Editor), 1987; Parliament and Industry, 1990; A Green Dimension for the European Community (Editor), 1993; The Parliamentary State, 1993; Theories of Urban Politics (Co-Editor), 1995; Representation: Theory and Practice in Britain, 1999; The European Parliament (Co-Author), 2003, 2nd edn. 2008; Political Institutions in the UK, 2005; Democratic Incongruities: Representative Democracy in Britain, 2014. Recreation: breathing. Address: (b.) School of Government and Public Policy, University of Strathclyde, Glasgow G1 1XQ; T.-0141-548 2365; e-mail: d.judge@strath.ac.uk

Judson, Jane-Claire. Director, Diabetes UK Scotland. Address: (b.) Venlaw, 349 Bath Street, Glasgow G2 4AA.

Jung, Roland Tadeusz, BA, MA, MB, BChir, MD, MRCS, LRCP, MRCP, FRCPEdin, FRCPLond. Consultant Physician (Specialist in Endocrinology and Diabetes), 1982-2008 (retired); Chief Scientist, Scottish Executive Health Department, 2001-07; Honorary Professor, Dundee University; Chairman, Scottish Hospital Endowments Research Trust, 2000-01; Senior Distinction Advisor (Eastern Region) for Scottish Advisory Committee on Distinction Awards, 2003-08; Member and Chair, Programme Management Group, Rowett Institute of Nutrition and Health, Aberdeen University, 2006-12; Visiting Professor, University of Southampton, since 2009. Educ. St. Anselm's College, Wirral; Pembroke College, Cambridge; St. Thomas Hospital and Medical School, London. MRC Clinical Scientific Officer, Dunn Nutrition Unit, Cambridge, and Honorary Senior Registrar, Addenbrooke's Hospital, Cambridge, 1977-79; Senior Registrar in Endocrinology and Diabetes, Royal Postgraduate Medical School, Hammersmith Hospital, London, 1980-82; Clinical Director of General Medicine, Dundee Teaching Hospitals Trust, 1991-94; Director of R and D, Tayside NHS Consortium, 1997-2001. Honour by University of Dundee: The Newton-Jung Diabetes Lecture, November 2012, 2013, 2014, 2015. Publication: Endocrine Problems in Oncology (Co-Editor), 1984; Colour Atlas of Obesity, 1990. Recreations: gardening; 'paved' walking; volunteer day coordinator with National Trust.

Junor, Gordon James, LLB (Hons). Advocate, since 1993; b. 18.1.56, Stannington, Northumberland. Educ. King Edward VI Grammar School, Morpeth; Edinburgh University. Solicitor, local government, 1982-92. Consulting Editor, Reparation Bulletin. Publication: Scottish Older Client Law Service (Housing and Residential Care). Recreation: hillwalking. Address: Freelands, 9 Taits Hill, Selkirk TD7 4LZ; T.-01750 22121. E-mail: gordonjjunor@hotmail.co.uk

Juster, Professor Neal Peter, BSc, PhD, CEng, FIMechE, FRSA. Senior Vice Principal and Deputy Vice Chancellor, University of Glasgow, since 2013, formerly Vice-Principal (Strategy and Resources), 2007-2013; b. 10.9.61, Carshalton; m., Sandra; 1 s.; 1 d. Educ. Emanuel School; University of Leeds. Royal Navy Engineering Officer (Under Training), 1980-84; University of Leeds: Lecturer in Computer Aided Engineering, Department of Mechanical Engineering, 1988-94, Senior Lecturer, Department of Mechanical Engineering, 1994-97; University of Strathclyde: Head of The Department of Design, Manufacturing and Engineering Management, 1997-2002, Dean of The Faculty of Engineering, 2002-06, Pro Vice-Principal, 2006-07, Professor, Computer Aided Engineering, 1997-2007. Member, Academic Standards Committee, Institution of Mechanical Engineers; Trustee: University of Glasgow Trust, University of Glasgow Pension Fund; Chair of Glasgow University Holding Ltd. Recreation: cycling. Address: (b.) Room 243, The Cloisters, Gilbert Scott Building, University of Glasgow, University Avenue, Glasgow G12 8QQ; T.-0141 330 6363; e-mail: neal.juster@glasgow.ac.uk

K

Kane, Patrick Mark, MA (Hons). Writer and Broadcaster; b. 10.3.64, Glasgow; m., Joan McAlpine (divorced); 2 d. Educ. St. Ambrose RC Secondary, Coatbridge; Glasgow University. Worked in London as a freelance writer; returned to Scotland to start professional music career with brother Gregory; achieved Top 10 and Top 20 singles and albums successes with Hue and Cry, 1987-89; TV arts presenter; former Rector, Glasgow University. Publication: The Play Ethic: A Manifesto for a Different Way of Living, 2004.

Kay, Professor Christian Janet, MA, AM, DipGenLing, DLitt. Professor Emeritus of English Language, Glasgow University (Professor, 1996-2005) (retired); Honorary Professorial Research Fellow; b. 4.4.40, Edinburgh. Educ. Mary Erskine School; Edinburgh University; Mount Holyoke College. Lecturer, Glasgow University, 1979-89; Senior Lecturer, Glasgow University, 1989-96. Publications: A Thesaurus of Old English (Co-editor), 1995; Lexicology, Semantics and Lexicography (Co-editor), 2000; Lexis and Texts in Early English (Co-editor), 2001; Proceedings of the 12th International Conference on English Historical Linguistics, 2 vols (Co-editor), 2004; Categorization in the History of English (Co-editor), 2004; Perspectives on the Older Scottish Tongue (Co-editor), 2005; Progress in Colour Studies: Language and Culture (Co-editor), 2006; Historical Thesaurus of the Oxford English Dictionary (Co-editor), 2009; New Directions in Colour Studies (Co-editor), 2011; Colour Studies: A broad spectrum (Co-editor), 2014; English Historical Semantics (Co-author), 2015. Recreation: music. Address: (b.) Glasgow University, Glasgow, G12 8QQ.
E-mail: christian.kay@glasgow.ac.uk

Kay, Jackie, MBE, FRSE. Scottish poet and novelist; Scots Makar - the National Poet for Scotland, since 2016; Professor of Creative Writing, Newcastle University; Cultural Fellow, Glasgow Caledonian University; b. 9.11.61, Edinburgh. Educ. Stirling University. First book of poetry, The Adoption Papers, published in 1991, won the Saltire Scottish First Book Award.

Kay, Stefan George, OBE, BSc, Hon DUniv, CEng, FIMechE, CCMI, FRSA. Managing Director, Inveresk PLC, 1989-2001; Director: Dunedin Enterprise Investment Trust PLC, 1995-2004; Servisan Ltd., since 2002, Power Textiles Ltd, since 2012, Rosie Kay Dance Company Ltd., since 2006, Logistics in Forest Transport Ltd., 2006-09; Director/Trustee, Scottish Railway Preservation Society, since 2001 (Chair, 2001-05); Chair of Trustees, Heriot-Watt University Students' Union, since 2010; b. 25.7.44, Peebles; m., Helen Eugenia; 2 d. Educ. Holy Cross Academy; Heriot-Watt University. Thames Board Ltd., 1967-73; Dexter Ltd., Berwickshire, 1973-78; St. Regis Paper Co. Ltd., Berkshire and Devon, 1979-88. Past President, Paper Federation of Great Britain; Paper Industry Gold Medal, 1996; Chairman, Environment Committee, Confederation of European Paper Industries, 1998-2000; Director of Campus Services, Scottish Borders Campus, Heriot Watt University, 2003-09; Chair, Leadership Committee, Scottish Forest Industries Cluster, 2002-08; Forest Industries Adviser, Heliex Power Ltd, 2012-2015; Liveryman, Worshipful Company of Stationers and Newspaper Makers. Recreations: steam railways; classical music; science fiction and historical literature. Address: (h.) 7 King's Cramond, Edinburgh EH4 6RL; T.-0131-336 5506.
E-mail: sgk@stefankay.abelgratis.co.uk

Kay, William (Billy), MA. Freelance Broadcaster/Writer/Producer; Director, Odyssey Productions; b. 24.9.51, Galston, Ayrshire; m., Maria João de Almeida da Cruz Dinis; 1 s.; 2 d. Educ. Galston High School; Kilmarnock Academy; Edinburgh University. Producer, Odyssey series, Radio Scotland; produced about 240 documentaries on diverse aspects of working-class oral history; Writer/Presenter, TV documentaries, including Miners, BBC Scotland; Presenter, Kay's Originals, Scottish TV. Commandeur d'Honneur, Commanderie du Bontemps de Médoc et des Graves; won Australasian Academy of Broadcast Arts and Sciences Pater award, 1987, 1988; Medallist, International Radio Festival of New York, 1990-92; Sloan Prize for writing in Scots, 1992; Wine Guild of UK 1994 Houghton Award, for Fresche Fragrant Clairettis; Winner: Heritage Society Award, 1995, Wines of France Award, 1996. Awarded Honorary Degree: Doctor of The University of The West of Scotland (DUniv), 2009. Received the Oliver Award from the Scots Independent newspaper in 2010 and made Honorary Preses of the Scots Language Society; Honorary Fellow of The Association for Scottish Literary Studies, since 2015. Publications: Odyssey: Voices from Scotland's Recent Past (Editor); Odyssey: The Second Collection (Editor); Knee Deep in Claret: A Celebration of Wine and Scotland (Co-author); Made in Scotland (poetry); Jute (play for radio); Scots — The Mither Tongue; They Fairly Mak Ye Work (for Dundee Repertory Theatre); Lucky's Strike (play for radio); The Dundee Book; The Scottish World. Recreations: wine; novels; languages; films; fitba, both Scotland and Dundee United. Address: (h.) 72 Tay Street, Newport on Tay, Fife DD6 8AP; e-mail: billykay@sol.co.uk
web: www.billykay.co.uk

Kayne, Steven Barry, BSc, PhD, MBA, LLM, MSc (Med Sci), FRPharmS, FCPP, FIPMI, DAgVetPharm, FFHom, MPS(NZ), FNZCP. Consultant Homoeopathic and Veterinary Pharmacist; book publisher; b. 8.6.44, Cheltenham Spa; m., Sorelle; 2 s. Educ. Westcliff High School; Aston University; Strathclyde University; Glasgow University; University of Wales. Lecturer; Honorary Lecturer, University of Strathclyde School of Pharmacy; Honorary Consultant Pharmacist, Glasgow Homeopathic Hospital; Pharmacy Dean to UK Faculty of Homoeopathy, 1998-2003; Member: Scottish Executive, Royal Pharmaceutical Society of Great Britain, 2000-07, Academic Board, UK Faculty of Homoeopathy, 1999-2003, Government Advisory Board on Homoeopathic Registration, 1993-2008, Herbal Medicines Advisory Committee, 2007-2011, Veterinary Products Committee of Veterinary Medicines Directorate, 2005-13; Governor and Hon. Treasurer, College of Pharmacy Practice, 2002-2010. Publication: Homoeopathic Pharmacy, 1997 (2nd edn 2005); People are Pets (Co-author), 1998; Complementary Therapies for Pharmacists, 2001; Veterinary Pharmacy (Co-editor), 2003; Pharmacy Business Management (Editor), 2004; Sports Medicine for Pharmacists (Editor), 2005; Pocket Companion Homeopathic Prescribing (Joint Author), 2007; Homeopathic Practice (Editor), 2008; Complementary and Alternative Medicine (Editor), 2008; Traditional Medicine - A global perspective (2010); An Introduction to Veterinary Medicine (2011); 450 papers and articles. Recreations: walking in Spey Valley; watching rugby; photography. Address: (b.) 20 Main Street, Busby, Glasgow G76 8DU; T.-0141 644 4344.
E-mail: steven.kayne@strath.ac.uk

Keane, Sheriff Francis Joseph, PhL, LLB. Sheriff of Tayside, Central and Fife, at Kirkcaldy, 1998-2004; b. 5.1.36, Broxburn; m., Lucia Corio Morrison; 2 s.; 1 d. Educ. Blairs College, Aberdeen; Gregorian University, Rome; Edinburgh University. Partner, McCluskey, Keane & Co., 1959; Procurator Fiscal Depute, Perth, 1961, Edinburgh, 1963; Senior PF Depute, Edinburgh, 1971; Senior Legal

Assistant, Crown Office, Edinburgh, 1972; Procurator Fiscal, Airdrie, 1976; Regional Procurator Fiscal, South Strathclyde, Dumfries and Galloway, 1980; Sheriff of Glasgow and Strathkelvin, 1984-93; Sheriff of Lothians and Borders, 1993-98; President, Procurators Fiscal Society, 1982-84. Recreations: music; tennis; walking; painting. Address: (h.) 1/1 West Cherrybank, Stanley Road, Edinburgh EH6 4SW.

Kearney, Catherine, BA (Hons), MEd, PGDip, PGDipLib, MCLIP. Director, CILIPS (Chartered Institute of Library and Information Professionals), since 2013. Educ. University of Glasgow. Career: Library Assistant, Glasgow District Libraries, 1976-80; School Librarian, Craigbank Secondary School, Librarian in Charge, Govan High School, 1984-89; Tutor and Library and Information Services Manager, John Wheatley College, 1989-95; Director of Library and Learning Services, Glasgow College of Building of Printing (now City of Glasgow College), 1995-2003; Assistant Director, Scottish Library and Information Council (SLIC), 2003-2013 (Board member, since 1995). Address: (b.) CILIPS, 126 West Regent Street, Glasgow G2 2RQ; T.-0141 222 5785.

Kearns, Professor Ade J., BA (Hons). Professor of Urban Studies, University of Glasgow, since 2000; b. 11.10.59, Luton; 1 s.; 1 d. Educ. Cardinal Newman RC Secondary, Luton; Sidney Sussex College, Cambridge University. Research, Shelter; Senior Housing Investment Analyst, Housing Corporation; University of Glasgow: Research Fellow, Lecturer, Senior Lecturer; Deputy Director, ESRC Centre for Housing Research and Urban Studies; Acting Director, ESRC Cities Research Programme; Co-Director, ESRC Centre for Neighbourhood Research, 2001-05; Director, ESRC/ODPM Postgraduate Research Programme, 2003-06; Principal Investigator, The Gowell Programme, since 2005. Editor, two special issues, Urban Studies journal. Recreations: reading contemporary fiction; listening to music, especially pop and jazz; city and country walking. Address: Department of Urban Studies, 25-29 Bute Gardens, University of Glasgow, Glasgow G12 8RS; T.-0141-330 5049; e-mail: a.j.kearns@socsci.gla.ac.uk

Keating, Professor Michael James, MA, PhD, FRSE, AcSS, FBA, MAE. Professor of Politics, Aberdeen University, since 1999; b. 2.2.50, Hartlepool; m., Patricia Ann; 1 s. Educ. St Aidan's Grammar School, Sunderland; Oxford University; Glasgow College of Technology. Part-time Lecturer, Glasgow College of Technology, 1972-75; Senior Research Officer, Essex University, 1975-76; Lecturer, North Staffs Polytechnic, 1976-79; Lecturer/Senior Lecturer, Strathclyde University, 1979-88; Professor of Political Science, University of Western Ontario, 1988-99; Professor, European University Institute, Florence, 2000-10. Publications include: The Politics of Modern Europe; Nations against the State, the new politics of nationalism in Quebec, Catalonia and Scotland; The Government of Scotland; The Independence of Scotland; Rescaling the European State. Recreations: sailing; hill-walking; traditional music; reading. Address: (h.) 27 Dundas Street, Edinburgh EH3 6QQ.

Keeble, Professor Neil Howard, BA, DPhil, DLitt, FRSE, FRHistS, FEA. Professor Emeritus of English, Stirling University, since 2011; b. 7.8.44, London; m., Jenny Bowers; 2 s.; 1 d. Educ. Bancroft's School, Woodford Green; St. David's College, Lampeter; Pembroke College, Oxford. Foreign Lektor, Department of English, University of Aarhus, Denmark, 1969-72; Lecturer in English, Aarhus, 1972-74; Stirling University: Lecturer in English, 1974-88, Reader in English, 1988-95, Professor of English, 1995-2001, Head, Department of English Studies, 1997-2000, Deputy Principal, 2001-03 and Senior Deputy Principal, 2003-2010; Honorary Fellow, University of Wales, Lampeter, 2000. Publications: Richard Baxter: Puritan Man

of Letters, 1982; The Literary Culture of Nonconformity in later seventeenth-century England, 1987; The Autobiography of Richard Baxter (Editor), 1974; The Pilgrim's Progress (Editor), 1984; John Bunyan: Conventicle and Parnassus (Editor), 1988; A Handbook of English and Celtic Studies in the United Kingdom and the Republic of Ireland (Editor), 1988; The Cultural Identity of Seventeenth-Century Woman (Editor), 1994; Lucy Hutchinson, Memoirs of the Life of Colonel Hutchinson (Editor), 1995; Cambridge Companion to Writing of the English Revolution (Editor), 2001; John Bunyan: Reading Dissenting Writing (Editor), 2002; Calendar of the Correspondence of Richard Baxter (Co-Compiler), 1991; Daniel Defoe, Memoirs of the Church of Scotland (Editor), 2002; The Restoration: England in the 1660s, 2002; Andrew Marvell, Remarks upon a Late Disingenuous Discourse (Editor), 2003; Daniel Defoe, Memoirs of a Cavalier (Editor), 2008; John Milton, Vernacular Regicide and Republican Writings (Co-Editor), 2013; 'Settling the Peace of the Church': 1662 Revisited (Editor), 2014. Recreations: books and book-collecting; films; Andalucia. Address: (h.) 21 Alexander Drive, Bridge of Allan FK9 4QB; e-mail: n.h.keeble@stir.ac.uk

Keel, Aileen, CBE, MB, ChB, FRCP(G), FRCP(E), FRCPath, MFPH, FRCS(E), FRCGP. Director, Innovative Healthcare Delivery Programme, Farr Institute, University of Edinburgh; Honorary Consultant Haematologist, Edinburgh Royal Infirmary; b. 23.8.52, Glasgow; m., Paul Dwyer (deceased); 1 s. Educ. Glasgow University. Postgraduate training in general medicine and haematology, 1976-87; practised haematology at consultant level in both NHS and private sector in London, 1987-92, including period as Director of Pathology, Cromwell Hospital; Senior Medical Officer, Scottish Office Department of Health, 1992-98; Principal Medical Officer, 1999; Deputy Chief Medical Officer, 1999-2015. Member of a number of medical advisory committees in Scotland and UK. Recreations: arts in general; music in particular, especially opera; keeping fit; current affairs; Member of Art in Healthcare and Scottish Arts Club. Address: (b.) St. Andrew's House, Edinburgh EH1 3DG.

Keeling, Dr Jean Winifred, FRCPath, FRCPEd, FRCPCH. Retired; formerly Consultant Paediatric Pathologist, Royal Hospital for Sick Children, Edinburgh (1989-2005); Honorary Senior Lecturer, Pathology, Edinburgh University, since 1990; b. 13.3.40, Doncaster; m., 1, Anthony Millier; 1 s.; 1 d.; 2, Frederick Walker. Educ. Pontefract and District Girls' School; Royal Free Hospital School, London University. Lecturer in Morbid Anatomy, Institute of Child Health, London University; Consultant Paediatric Pathologist, John Radcliffe Hospital, Oxford; Hon. Clinical Lecturer, Oxford University; Member, Royal Liverpool Children's Inquiry; Past President, Paediatric Pathology Society; Past President, International Paediatric Pathology Association. Publications: Fetal Pathology; Fetal and Neonatal Pathology (Editor); Paediatric Forensic Medicine and Pathology (Joint Editor); papers on fetal and paediatric pathology. Recreations: walking; cooking. Address: (h.) 9 Forres Street, Edinburgh EH3 6BJ; T.-0131 225 9673; e-mail: jeanwkeeling@aol.com

Keen of Elie, Baron (Richard Sanderson Keen), LLB (Hons). Advocate General for Scotland and Minister of State, since 2015; Queen's Counsel, 1993; Chairman, Scottish Conservative and Unionist Party, 2014-2015; Dean of The Faculty of Advocates, 2007-2014; b. 29.03.54, Rustington, Sussex; m., Jane; 1 s.; 1 d. Educ. Dollar Academy; University of Edinburgh. Admitted to the Faculty of Advocates, 1980; Standing Counsel to the DTI, 1986-93; Elected Treasurer of the Faculty of Advocates, 2006. Member of the Bar of England and Wales, 2009. Bencher of the Honourable Society of the Middle Temple,

2010. Recreations: golf; skiing; shooting. Clubs: Hon. Co. Edinburgh Golfers; Golf House Elie; New Club (Edin). Address: (b.) Dover House, 66 Whitehall, London SW1A 2AU; e-mail: rsk@rskeenqc.com

Keir, Colin. MSP (SNP), Edinburgh Western, 2011-16; b. 9.12.59, Edinburgh. Elected Member of City of Edinburgh Council (Drum Brae/Gyle Ward), 2007-2012. Spent 16 years in the office equipment trade and 13 years working with Lothian Buses. Former convener of the regulatory committee of the City of Edinburgh Council. Former Scottish Schools 5000m Champion; former Scottish schools cross-country international.

Kelly, Dame Barbara Mary, CBE, DL, LLD, DipEd. Chairman, The Robertson Trust; Chairman, Peter Pan Moat Brae Trust; Past Convener, Millennium Forest for Scotland Trust; Past Trustee, Royal Botanic Garden Edinburgh; Past Convenor, Crichton Foundation; Partner in farming enterprise; Deputy Lieutenant, Dumfriesshire; former Chairman, Dumfries and Galloway Arts Festival; b. 27.2.40, Dalbeattie; m., Kenneth A. Kelly; 1 s.; 2 d. Educ. Dalbeattie High School; Kirkcudbright Academy; Moray House College. Past Member, Scottish Board BP plc; Past Director, Scottish Post Office Board; Past Chairman, Scottish Consumer Council; former Member: Scottish Economic Council, National Consumer Council, Scottish Enterprise Board, Scottish Tourist Board, Priorities Board, MAFF, Board, Scottish Natural Heritage (and former Chair, West Areas Board), Broadcasting Council for Scotland; former Vice-Chairman, SWRI; Duke of Edinburgh's Award: former Chairman, Scottish Advisory Committee and former Member, UK Advisory Panel; former EOC Commissioner for Scotland; Past Chairman, Dumfries and Galloway Area Manpower Board, Manpower Services Commission; former Director, Clydesdale Bank plc; Past President, Rural Forum; former Chairwoman, Architects' Registration Board. Hon Degrees: University of Strathclyde, 1995; Aberdeen, 1997; Glasgow, 2002; Bell College, 2005; Queen Margaret University, 2005; University of the West of Scotland, 2010; Freeman City of London, 2002. Recreations: painting; music. Address: (h.) Barncleugh, Irongray, Dumfries DG2 9SE; T.-01387 730210.

Kelly, Daniel, QC, LLB (Hons), CertAdvEurStud. Sheriff of South Strathclyde, Dumfries and Galloway, since 2011; b. 22.1.58, Dunfermline; m., Christine Marie MacLeod; 3 s.; 1 d. Educ. Edinburgh University; College of Europe, Bruges. Apprenticeship, Dundas and Wilson CS, 1979-81; Solicitor, Brodies WS, and Tutor in European Institutions, Edinburgh University, 1982-83; Solicitor, Community Law Office, Brussels, 1983-84; Procurator Fiscal Depute, 1984-90; Advocate, since 1991; Temporary Sheriff, 1997-99; Part-time Sheriff, 2005-2011. Editor: Scots Law Times, Sheriff Court Reports, since 1992. Queen's Counsel, since 2007. Publication: Criminal Sentences, 1993. Recreations: swimming; cycling; golf. Address: (b.) Sheriff Court House, 4 Beckford Street, Hamilton ML3 0BT.

Kelly, James. MSP (Labour), Glasgow region, since 2016 (Glasgow Rutherglen, 2007-2016); Scottish Labour Parliamentary Business Manager, since 2014, election co-ordinator for 2016; b. 23.10.63; m., Alexa; 2 d. Served as the election agent for the former Rutherglen and Hamilton West MP Tommy McAvoy at the 1997, 2001, and 2005 general elections; also Chair of the Rutherglen and Hamilton West Constituency Labour Party; background in computing and finance; chartered accountant; worked as a Business Analyst in East Kilbride prior to election in 2007. Served on the Finance Committee and as a Labour Whip

upon entering Parliament; served as the Co-Convener of the Cross-Party Group in the Scottish Parliament on Co-operatives and the deputy Convenor of the Cross-Party Group on Sport; member of the Justice Committee and Shadow Minister for Community Safety, 2008-2011. Address: (b.) Scottish Parliament, Edinburgh EH99 1SP; Constituency Office: 51 Stonelaw Road, Rutherglen, South Lanarkshire G73 3TN.

Kelly, Col. John L., MBE. Director, SecuriGroup, since 2011; soldier, organiser, geographer and noted public speaker. Retired in 2011 after a distinguished 40 year career with the British Army; formerly Joint Regional Liaison Officer for Scotland, in which capacity he was the Military enabling Officer when the Civilian Community required Military Assistance, be it for fire, floods, foot and mouth, severe weather and counter terrorism related matters; commissioned into the Royal Highland Fusiliers (Princess Margaret's own Glasgow and Ayrshire Regiment) and has served across the world principally in the UK, Northern Ireland, Canada, Germany, Belize, Brunei and Berlin; has held a variety of appointments including Chief of Staff of the Ulster Defence Regiment, Commanding Officer of 2nd Battalion 51st Highland Volunteers and Deputy Project Manager in the Procurement Executive. Formerly Deacon Convener of the Trades House in Glasgow. Grand Baillie of the Scottish Jurisdiction of the Order of St Lazurus, the international Christian order of chivalry, since 2011. Address: The Bent, Gartocharn, Dunbartonshire G83 8SB.

Kelly, Professor John Shearer, BSc, MB, ChB, PhD, MA, FRSE, FRCPE, FMedSci, FBPS (Hon). Emeritus Professor of Pharmacology, University of Edinburgh, since 2002; Director, Fujisawa Institute of Neuroscience, 1992-2002; Deputy Editor, Journal of the Royal College of Physicians, Edinburgh, 2002-09; b. 3.3.37, Edinburgh; m., E. Anne Wilkin; 1 s.; 1 d. Educ. George Heriot's School, Edinburgh; University of Edinburgh. House Physician, Western General Hospital, Edinburgh, 1962; House Surgeon, Royal Hospital for Sick Children, Edinburgh, 1963; University of Edinburgh, Department of Pharmacology: Assistant Lecturer, 1963-65, Lecturer, 1965-68; McGill University, Canada: Wellcome Post-doctoral Fellow, Department of Research in Anaesthesia, 1967-68, Canadian Medical Research Council Scholar and Assistant Professor, Departments of Research in Anaesthesia and Physiology, 1968-71; IBRO Research Fellow, University of Geneva, 1970; MRC Scientific Staff, Department of Pharmacology, Cambridge, 1971-79; Fellow of King's College, Cambridge and Lecturer in Pharmacology and Neurobiology, 1976-79; Professor and Chairman, Pharmacology, St. George's Hospital Medical School, London, 1979-85; Professor of Pharmacology, Edinburgh University, 1985-2002; Founding Editor, 1978 and Editor in Chief of the Journal of Neuroscience Methods, 1978-99; Editor of the Journal of the Royal College of Physicians Edinburgh, 2001-09. Publications: 132 papers on neuroscience; 59 book chapters; 216 abstracts. Recreations: classical music; Scottish Malt Whisky Society; Scottish restaurants; Scottish outdoors. Address: (b.) Tamarack, 11 Redhall Bank Road, Edinburgh EH14 2LY; e-mail: j.s.kelly@ed.ac.uk

Kelly, Lorraine, OBE. Television presenter, journalist and actress; b. 30.11.59, Glasgow; m., Steve Smith; 1 d. Educ. Claremont High School, East Kilbride. Career: East Kilbride News; joined BBC Scotland as a researcher in 1983; moved to TV-am as an on-screen reporter covering Scottish news in 1984; co-presented TV-am's Summer Sunday programme in 1989; became a main presenter of Good Morning Britain in 1990; helped launch GMTV in January 1993, and presented a range of programmes, including the main breakfast show; presented GMTV with

Lorraine, 1994-2010; presenter, Lorraine (ITV Breakfast), since 2010. Writes weekly columns for The Sun and The Sunday Post. Address: Roar Global Ltd, 34-35 Eastcastle Street, London W1W 8DW; T.-020 7462 9060.

Kelly, Michael, CBE (1983), OStJ, JP, BSc(Econ), PhD, LLD, DL, FCIM, Knight's Star Order of Merit Poland. Public Relations Consultant, since 1984; Honorary Vice-President, Children 1st, since 1996 (Chairman, Royal Scottish Society for the Prevention of Cruelty to Children, 1987-96); Columnist: Scotsman, Evening Times; Broadcaster, Radio Clyde; Member, Economic and Social Research Council's Advisory Committee, since 2000; Chair, Glasgow Central Constituency Labour Party, since 2005; b. 1.11.40, Glasgow; m., Zita Harkins; 1 s.; 2 d. Educ. St. Joseph's College, Dumfries. Assistant Lecturer in Economics, Aberdeen University, 1965-67; Lecturer in Economics, Strathclyde University, 1967-80; Lord Provost of Glasgow, 1980-84; Rector, Glasgow University, 1984-87; Member, National Arts Collection Fund, 1990-96; Secretary, Scottish Industry Forum, 1995-2000; Scottish Convener, Socialist Civil Liberties Association, since 2002; British Tourist Authority Medal for services to tourism, 1984; Robert Burns Award from University of Old Dominion, Virginia, for services to Scottish culture, 1984; Scot of the Year, 1983; Radio Scotland News Quiz Champion, 1986, 1987; Radio Scotland Christmas Quiz Champion, 1987; Honorary Mayor of Tombstone, Arizona; Kentucky Colonel, 1983; Committee Member, Pollok Golf Club, since 2009. Publications: Paradise Lost: the struggle for Celtic's soul, 1994; London Lines: the capital by underground, 1996. Recreations: golf; skiing. Address: (b.) 50 Aytoun Road, Pollokshields, Glasgow G41 5HE; e-mail: kellymkelly1@aol.com

Kelly, Neil Joseph, LLB (Distinction), DipLP, NP, WS, HonRICS, HonFRIAS, ACIArb. Solicitor, since 1984; Partner, MacRoberts, Solicitors, since 1991, Head of Construction, since 2003, Chairman, 2011-2014; b. 28.6.61, Bellshill; m., Alison Jane (Whyte); 2 s.; 1 d. Educ. St. Patrick's High School; Aberdeen University. Qualified in all forms of dispute resolution mechanisms with particular focus on construction industry. Editor, Scottish Construction Law Review, 2003-08; Contributor, MacRoberts on Scottish Construction Contracts; Convener, Adjudication Society (Scottish Region); Chairman of Chartered Institute of Arbitrators (Scottish Branch). Recreations: travel; opera; classical music. Address: (b.) 30 Semple Street, Edinburgh EH3 8BL; T.-0131-229-5046.
E-mail: neil.kelly@macroberts.com

Kelly, Owen Dennis, OBE, MA (Hons) Chinese, DipSocPol (Edin). Chief Executive, Scottish Financial Enterprise, since 2008; b. 17.7.63, Redhill, Surrey; m., Michelle Anderson; 1 s. 2 d. Educ. John Fisher School, Purley, Surrey; University of Edinburgh. HM Customs and Excise, 1987; Scottish Office, 1988-99; Private Secretary to Minister for Home Affairs and Environment, 1990-92; Locate in Scotland, Director, Japan (Tokyo), 1994-96; Scottish Government, 1999-2008; Principal Private Secretary to First Minister of Scotland, 2003-05; Director of Communications and International, Scottish Government, 2005-07. Made Officer of the British Empire (OBE) in New Year's Honours List, 2014. Recreations: reading; cooking; walking the dog; guitar. Address: (b.) 24 Melville Street, Edinburgh EH3 7NS; T.-0131 247 7700; e-mail: okelly@sfe.org.uk

Kelly, Patrick Joseph, BSc. Author of 'Scotland's Radical Exports'; Non-Executive Director, Scottish Water, 2003-2013; Non-Executive Director, NHS 24, 2001-07; b. 26.10.50, Glasgow; 1 s.; 3 d. Educ. St. Mungo's Academy, Glasgow; Glasgow University. Civil Engineer, Central Regional Council, 1973-86; became active in local government union Nalgo and was elected to National Executive, 1979-86; Scottish Secretary, Society of Civil and Public Servants, 1986-99; former Member and President (1998), General Council, STUC; since 1999, working on various Boards in the public sector, including Civil Service Appeal Board; Board Member, Scottish Enterprise, Edinburgh and Lothian, 1991-2000; Management Committee, War on Want (charity); Anti-apartheid Scottish Committee. Publication: Scotland's Radical Exports, 2011. Recreations: golf; watching football; reading; walking. E-mail: pat1950@btinternet.com

Kelly, Sally Ann. Chief Executive, Aberlour Child Care Trust, since 2014. Qualified as a social worker in 1990; promoted to management post in 1996; has worked in a number of Scottish local authorities in middle and senior management positions; moved to the third sector to take up position as Head of Operations with Barnardo's Scotland in 2008, then temporary role of Acting Director; Senior Manager for the National 3rd Sector GIRFEC Project, 2013-14. Member, Scottish Government Early Years Taskforce; involved in supporting the implementation of the Early Years Collaborative through role as the National Champion for 1-3 year olds. Address: Aberlour Child Care Trust, 36 Park Terrace, Stirling FK8 2JR; T.-01786 450335.

Kelman, James. Novelist; b. 1946, Glasgow. Works include: The Busconductor Hines; A Chancer; Greyhound for Breakfast; A Disaffection; How Late It Was How Late (Booker Prize, 1994); The Good Times (Scotland on Sunday/Glenfiddich Spirit of Scotland Award and the Stakis Prize for Scottish Writer of the Year, 1998); Translated Accounts, 2001; And the Judges Said... (essays), 2002; You have to be careful in the Land of the Free, 2004; Kieron Smith, Boy, 2008 (won Scotland's most prestigious literary award the Saltire Society's Book of the Year award, 2008); If It is Your Life, 2010; Mo Said She Was Quirky, 2012; A Lean Third, 2014. Address: c/o Rogers, Coleridge and White, 20 Powis Mews, London W11 1JN.

Kelsey, Rachael Joy Christina, LLB, DipLP, NP. Founding Partner, Sheehan Kelsey Oswald, Family Law Specialists. Educ. Culloden Academy, Inverness; Edinburgh University. Accredited as Specialist in Family Law and Family Mediator by Law Society of Scotland; FLAGS Family Law Arbitrator; Chair, Director and Trustee, Family Mediation Lothian; Secretary, International Academy of Matrimonial Lawyers; Treasurer, CALM (Comprehensive Accredited Lawyer Mediators); Treasurer, Family Law Association, 2003-05; Chair, Family Law Association, 2005-06. Recreations: wine; gardening; children; boxing. Address: (b.) 93 George Street, Edinburgh EH2 3ES; T.-0131 243 2583; e-mail: rachael.kelsey@sko-family.co.uk

Kemp, Peter, MA, PhD. Trustee, National Library of Scotland, 2002-2013; Diocesan Secretary, Diocese of Argyll and The Isles, since 2009; b. 22.4.44, Maidstone; m., Joan nee Woodyear-Smith; 2 s.; 1 d. Educ. Maidstone Grammar School; Gonville & Caius College, Cambridge. Lecturer, University of Lancaster, 1970-71; IT Officer, University of Cambridge, 1971-76; Fellow, Gonville & Caius College, 1972-76; Head of User Services, University of Newcastle, 1976-82; Associate Professor, University of Delaware, USA, 1982-83; Director, Computing Service:

University of Reading, 1983-87, University of Glasgow, 1987-97; Director of Information Services/University Librarian, University of Stirling, 1997-2008; Director, Numerical Algorithms Group Ltd., 1984-2005; Company Secretary, North Argyll Carers Centre, since 2009. Recreations: sailing; walking; travel; Church. Address: (h.) Lerags Minch, Lerags, Oban PA34 4SE; T.-01631 566963; e-mail: peter.kemp@cantab.net

Kennedy, Alison Louise, BA (Hons). Writer; b. 22.10.65, Dundee. Educ. High School of Dundee; Warwick University. Community Arts Worker, 1988-89; Writer in Residence, Project Ability, 1989-94; Writer in Residence, Hamilton/East Kilbride Social Work Department, 1990-92; fiction critic for Scotsman, etc.; Booker Prize Judge, 1996; five S.A.C. book awards; Saltire Best First Book Award; 2 Saltire Best Book Awards; John Llewellyn Rees/Mail on Sunday Prize; listed, Granta/Sunday Times Best of Young British Novelists; Encore Award; Festival Fringe First; Social Work Today Award; Premio Napoli; Lannan Award for Literature; Austrian State Prize for European Literature; Costa Prize. Honorary Degree, Glasgow University. Publications: Night Geometry and the Garscadden Trains; Looking for the Possible Dance; Now That You're Back; So I Am Glad; Original Bliss; The Life and Death of Colonel Blimp (essay); Everything you Need; On Bull Fighting (non-fiction); Indelible Acts; Paradise; Day; What Becomes; The Blue Book (novel); All The Rage (short stories); The Audition (play); Stella Does Tricks (film); Delicate (performance piece); True (performance piece); Like an Angel (radio play); Confessions of a Medium (radio play); Love Love Love Like The Beatles (radio play); That I should Rise (radio play); On writing (essays); All The Rage (short stories). Recreations: cinema; banjo; Tai Chi.
E-mail: alkenn@talktalk.net

Kennedy, Professor Angus Johnston, MA, PhD, Commandeur et Officier dans l'Ordre des Palmes Academiques; Chevalier dans L'Ordre des Arts et des Lettres. Stevenson Professor of French Language and Literature, Glasgow University; b. 9.8.40, Port Charlotte; m., Marjory McCulloch Shearer; 2 d. Educ. Bearsden Academy; Glasgow University. Glasgow University: Assistant Lecturer in French, 1965, then Lecturer, Senior Lecturer, Reader; former Secretary, British Branch, International Arthurian Society. Publications: books on Christine de Pizan. Address: (b.) French Department, Glasgow University, Glasgow.
E-mail: Angus.Kennedy@glasgow.ac.uk

Kennedy, Professor Gavin, BA, MSc, PhD, (Hon) DLitt. Professor Emeritus, Heriot-Watt University; Fellow, Adam Smith Institute; b. 20.2.40, Collingham, Yorkshire; m., Rita; 2 d.; Patricia Anne; 1 s.; 2 d. Educ. London Nautical School; Strathclyde University. Lecturer: Danbury Management Centre, 1969-71, Brunel University, 1971-73, National Defence College, Latimer, 1972-74; Senior Lecturer in Economics, Strathclyde University, 1973-83; Professor: Defence Finance, Heriot-Watt University, 1983-86, Edinburgh Business School, 1987-2005. Publications: Military in the Third World, 1974; Economics of Defence, 1975; Bligh, 1978 (Yorkshire Post Book of the Year, 1979); Death of Captain Cook, 1978; Burden Sharing in NATO, 1979; Mathematics for Innumerate Economists, 1982; Defence Economics, 1983; Invitation to Statistics, 1983; Everything is Negotiable, 1984, 4th edition, 2009; Negotiate Anywhere, 1985; Macro Economics, 1985; Superdeal, 1985; The Economist Pocket Negotiator, 1987, 5th edition, 2008; Captain Bligh: the man and his mutinies, 1988; Do We Have A Deal?, 1991; Simulations for Training Negotiators, 1993; The Perfect Negotiation, 1993; Negotiation, 1994; Local Pay Bargaining, 1995; The Negotiate Trainer's Manual, 1996; Kennedy on Negotiation, 1997; The New Negotiating Edge, 1998; Profitable Negotiation, 1999; Influencing, 1999; Adam Smith's Lost Legacy, 2005; Strategic Negotiation, 2005; Adam Smith: a moral philosopher and his political economy, 2008; 2nd edition, 2010. Recreation: reading. Address: (h.) 15 Suffolk Road, Edinburgh EH16 5NR; T.-0131 466 8535; Mobile: 07801 65 73 65.
E-mail: gavink9@gmail.com
Web: www.adamsmithslostlegacy.blogspot.co.uk 2005-15.

Kennedy, Rev. Gordon, BSc, BD, MTh. Minister, Craiglockhart Parish Church, Edinburgh, since 2012; Church of Scotland Minister, Portpatrick linked with Stranraer St. Ninian's, 2000-2012; b. 15.9.63, England. Educ. Crookston Castle Secondary; University of Strathclyde; University of Glasgow. Graduate Civil Engineer, Strathclyde Regional Council, 1985-89; Probationer Assistant, Bearsden North Parish Church, 1992-93; Minister, New Cumnock Parish Church, Ayrshire, 1993-2000. 2005 Master of Theology, University of Glasgow. Address: 20 Craiglockhart Quadrant, Edinburgh, Midlothian EH14 1HD.
E-mail: gordonkennedy@craiglockhartchurch.org

Kennedy, Gordon Philip, MA (Hons), MPhil, MBA, MRTPI, MIED. Director, Clearbluewater 2.0 Ltd., economic development consultants; Chairman, Arches Theatre Company, Glasgow, since 2009; Director, Ashton Properties Ltd; Deputy Chief Executive, Scottish Enterprise Glasgow, 2001-08; b. 30.5.57, Glasgow. Educ. St. Mungo's Academy; Glasgow University; Strathclyde University. Planning Assistant, Clydebank District Council, 1982-85; Industrial Economist, Scottish Development Agency, 1985-91; Glasgow Development Agency: Head of Strategic Projects, 1991, Head of Corporate Strategy, 1991-93; Director, Corporate Development, Glasgow Development Agency, 1993-99; Deputy Chief Executive, Scottish Enterprise Glasgow, 1999-2001. Member, Board, Glasgow Council for Voluntary Services. Recreations: cinema; theatre; eating out. Address: (b.) 35 Caird Drive, Glasgow G11 5DX; T.-0141-334-7075.
E-mail: g.kennedy174@btinternet.com

Kennedy, Professor Malcolm William, BSc, PhD. Professor of Natural History, University of Glasgow, since 2008. Educ. Hutchesons Grammar School, Glasgow; University of Glasgow. Scientific Staff, Division of Immunology, National Institute for Medical Research, London, 1979-83; Welcolme Trust University Award Lecturer, University of Glasgow, 1983-90; Senior Lecturer, 1990-91; Reader, 1991-96; Professor of Infection Biology, 1996. Pfizer Academic Award, 1995; Wright Medal of the British Society for Parasitology, 2000. Address: (b.) Graham Kerr Building, University of Glasgow, Glasgow G12 8QQ; T.-0141-330-5819.
E-mail: malcolm.kennedy@glasgow.ac.uk

Kennedy, Professor Peter Graham Edward, CBE (2010), MB, BS, MPhil, MLitt, PhD, MD, DSc, FRCPath, FRCPLond, FRCPGlas, FRSE, FMedSci. Burton Professor of Neurology and Head of Department, Glasgow University, since 1987; Consultant Neurologist, Institute of Neurological Sciences, Southern General Hospital, Glasgow, since 1986; b. 28.3.51, London; m., Catherine Ann; 1 s.; 1 d. Educ. University College School, London; University College, London; University College Medical School. Medical Registrar, University College Hospital, 1977-78; Hon. Research Assistant, MRC Neuroimmunology Project, University College, London, 1978-80; Research Fellow, Institute of Virology, Glasgow University, 1981;

Registrar and Senior Registrar, National Hospital for Nervous Diseases, London, 1981-84; Assistant Professor of Neurology, Johns Hopkins University School of Medicine, 1985; "New Blood" Senior Lecturer in Neurology and Virology, Glasgow University, 1986-87. BUPA Medical Foundation "Doctor of the Year" Research Award, 1990; Linacre Medal and Lectureship, Royal College of Physicians of London, 1991; T.S. Srinivasan Endowment Lecturer and Gold Medal, 1993; Fogarty International Scholar, NIH, USA, 1993-94 (Fogarty Medal); Distinguished Service Award (2010), International Society for Neurovirology; Senior Associate Editor, Journal of Neurovirology; Member: Medical Research Advisory Committee, Multiple Sclerosis Society, 1987-98, Association of Physicians Great Britain and Ireland, Association of British Neurologists; Fellow of the Academy of Medical Sciences; President, International Society for Neurovirology, 2004-2010; Sir James Black Medal (Senior Prize Life Sciences), Royal Society of Edinburgh, 2014. Publications: Infectious Diseases of the Nervous System (Co-Editor), 2000; numerous papers on neurology, neurovirology, neurobiology and sleeping sickness; The Fatal Sleep, 2007. Recreations: reading and writing; music; astronomy; tennis; walking in the country; philosophy. Address: (b.) Institute of Neurological Sciences, Southern General Hospital, Glasgow G51; T.-0141-201 2474.

Kennedy, Professor Robert Alan, BA, PhD, FBPsS, FRSE. Emeritus Professor of Psychology, University of Dundee (Professor, since 1972); Chercheur Associé, Laboratoire de Psychologie et Neurosciences Cognitives, CNRS, Paris-V, since 2006; b. 1.10.39, Stourbridge; m., Elizabeth Wanda; 1 d. Educ. King Edward VI Grammar School, Stourbridge. Senior Tutor then Lecturer in Psychology, University of Melbourne, 1963-65; Lecturer in Psychology: Queen's College, University of St. Andrews, University of Dundee, 1965-72; Senior Lecturer in Psychology, University of Dundee, 1972. Member, Psychology Committee, Social Science Research Council (UK), 1980-82; Committee Member, Experimental Psychology Society, 1984-88; Member, Scientific Affairs Board, British Psychological Society, 1986-88; Member, MRC Neuropsychology Sub-committee, 1982-89; Editorial Board: Acta Psychologica, 1980-88, Psychological Research, 1978-88; Founder Member, European Conference on Eye Movements, since 1980; Convener, Scottish Group of Professors of Psychology, 1985-91; Governor, Dundee College of Education, 1974-78; Member of Court, University of Dundee, 1976-80 and 1990-99; Convener, University Research Committee, 1994-97; Member, Council, Royal Society of Edinburgh, 1999-2001; Honorary Member, Experimental Psychology Society, 2009. Publications: Studies in Long-Term Memory (Co-author); The Psychology of Reading; Reading as a Perceptual Process (Editor); Eye Movements and Information Processing During Reading (Co-editor). Recreations: hill-walking; playing the piano. Address: (b.) Psychology Department, University of Dundee, Dundee DD1 4HN; T.-01382 344622.

Kenway, Professor Richard Donovan, OBE, FRSE, BSc, DPhil, CPhys, FInstP, FLSW. Tait Professor of Mathematical Physics, Edinburgh University, since 1994; b. 8.5.54, Cardiff; m., Anna Kenway; 1 s.; 2 d. Educ. Stanwell School, Penarth; Exeter University; Oxford University. Research Associate, Brown University, 1978-80; Post-doctoral Fellow, Los Alamos National Laboratory, 1980-82; Edinburgh University: Post-doctoral Fellow, 1982-83; Lecturer, 1983-90; Reader, 1990-94; Director of Edinburgh Parallel Computing Centre, 1993-97; Head, Department of Physics and Astronomy, 1997-2000; Chairman, Edinburgh Parallel Computing Centre, since 1997; Chairman, UK National e-Science Centre, 2001-2011;

PPARC Senior Research Fellow, 2001-04; Assistant Principal, 2002-05; Vice Principal, since 2005; Head, School of Physics and Astronomy, 2008-2011; Member, National and International Peer Review and Research Strategy Committees. Publications: co-authored one book; co-edited two books; 145 papers on theoretical particle physics and high performance computing. Recreations: munroing; running. Address: (b.) School of Physics and Astronomy, Edinburgh University, James Clerk Maxwell Building, Peter Guthrie Tait Road, Edinburgh EH9 3FD; T.-0131-650 5245; e-mail: r.d.kenway@ed.ac.uk

Kerevan, George, MA (Hons). MP (SNP), East Lothian, since 2015; Journalist; co-organizer of the Prestwick World Festival of Flight; former Chief Executive, What If Productions (Television) Ltd.; Associate Editor, The Scotsman, 2000-09; b. 28.9.49, Glasgow. Educ. Kingsridge Secondary School, Drumchapel; Glasgow University. Academic posts, Napier University, 1975-2000; freelance journalist and broadcaster, since 1980; Creative Director, Alba Communications Ltd., 2005-06; TV director, producer and script writer, Lamancha Productions Ltd., 1989-2000; Chair, Edinburgh Technology Transfer Centre, 1985-92; Board, Edinburgh Co-operative Development Agency, 1987-92; Chair, EDI Ltd., 1988-95; Board, Edinburgh Venture Trust, 1988-93; Board, Capital Enterprise Trust, 1993-94; Chairman, New Edinburgh Ltd., 1989-95; Board, Lothian and Edinburgh Enterprise Trust, 1989-96; Chair, Edinburgh and Lothians Tourist Board, 1992-95; Board, Traverse Theatre, 1980-84; Council, Edinburgh International Festival, 1984-92; Board, Assembly Productions, 1984-88; Board, Royal Lyceum Theatre, 1984-88; Board, Edinburgh Old Town Trust, 1984-90; Board, 7:84 Theatre Company, 1986-88; Board, Edinburgh International Film Festival, 1988-94; Chair, Edinburgh International Science Festival, 1989-95; Chair, Edinburgh Film House, 1989-94; Board, Boxcar Films, 1993; Chair, Manifesto International Festival of Architecture, 1995; elected Member, Edinburgh District Council, 1984-96 (Convenor, Economic Development Committee, 1986-95); Vice-Convenor, Economic Affairs Committee, COSLA, 1988-90; Board, John Wheatley Centre for Public Policy Research, 1988-93; SNP National Council, 1996-98; SNP environment spokesperson, 1996-98; SNP Parliamentary Candidate for Edinburgh East, 2010 General Election. Recreations: cooking; cats; cinema. Address: (h.) Brunstane House (South Wing), Brunstane Road South, Edinburgh EH15 2NQ; T.-0131-669 8234.

Kernohan, Robert Deans, OBE, MA, FFCS. Journalist, Writer and occasional Broadcaster; b. 9.1.31, Mount Vernon, Lanarkshire; m., Margaret Buchanan Bannerman; 4 s. Educ. Whitehill School, Glasgow; Glasgow University; Balliol College, Oxford. RAF, 1955-57; Editorial Staff, Glasgow Herald, 1957-67 (Chief Leader Writer, 1962-65, Assistant Editor, 1965-66, London Editor, 1966-67); Director-General, Scottish Conservative Central Office, 1967-71; Freelance Journalist and Broadcaster, 1972; Editor, Life and Work, The Record of the Church of Scotland, 1972-90. Chairman, Federation of Conservative Students, 1954-55; Conservative Parliamentary candidate, 1955, 1959, 1964; Member: Newspaper Panel, Monopolies and Mergers Commission (subsequently Competition Commission), 1987-99, Ancient Monuments Board for Scotland, 1990-97, Broadcasting Standards Council, 1994-97, Broadcasting Standards Commission, 1997-99; Chairman, Scottish Christian Conservative Forum, 1991-97; HM Inspector of Constabulary for Scotland (Lay Inspector), 1992-95; Director, Handsel Press Ltd, 1996-2003; Institute of Contemporary Scotland Magnus Magnusson Medal, 2011; Elder, Cramond Kirk, Edinburgh; Honorary President, Scottish Church Theology Society, 1994. Publications: Scotland's Life and Work, 1979;

William Barclay, The Plain Uncommon Man, 1980; Thoughts through the Year, 1985; Our Church, 1985; The Protestant Future, 1991; The Road to Zion, 1995; The Realm of Reform (Editor), 1999; John Buchan in a Nutshell, 2000; An Alliance across the Alps, 2005; numerous contributions to collective works, reviews (notably Scottish Review and Contemporary Review) and reference books, including New Dictionary of National Biography. Recreations: rugby-watching; reminiscence; painting; pontification; patriarchy. Address: (h.) 5/1 Rocheid Park, Edinburgh EH4 1RP; T.-0131-332 7851.

Kerr, Andrew, CertEd, ILAM, MBA. Chief Executive, City of Edinburgh Council, since 2015. Educ. Borough Road College; Loughborough University; Cardiff Business School; Harvard, MIT, Stanford and Berkeley Haas - British Telecom. Area Leisure Officer, Falkirk District Council, 1982-87; Principal Officer, Cardiff City Council, 1987-90; Head of Participation, Sports Council for Wales, 1990-96; Head of Lifelong Learning and Leisure, Caerphilly County Borough Council, 1996-2000; Lead Inspector, Audit Commission, 2000-02; Director, Leisure and Culture, Birmingham City Council, 2002-04; President, ILAM, 2004-05; Director, Performance Improvement, Birmingham City Council, 2004-05; Chief Executive: North Tyneside Council, 2005-2010, Wiltshire Council, 2010-11; Board Member and Trustee, Wiltshire and Swindon Community Foundation, 2010-13; Chief Operating Officer, Cardiff Council, 2012-13; Owner, Kerr Strategic Consultancy Ltd, 2011-15; Chief Executive, Cornwall Council, 2013-15. Former bronze medal-winning 400m sprinter, and represented Great Britain in international athletics. Address: City of Edinburgh Council, Waverley Court, 4 East Market Street, Edinburgh EH8 8BG; T.-0131 200 2300; e-mail: chief.executive@edinburgh.gov.uk

Kerr, Andrew Palmer. Chief Executive Officer, Sense Scotland, since 2011; former MSP (Labour), East Kilbride (1999-2011); Shadow Cabinet Secretary for Finance and Sustainable Growth, 2007-2011; Minister for Health and Community Care, 2004-07; Minister for Finance and Public Services, Scottish Executive, 2001-04; b. 17.3.62, East Kilbride; m., Susan; 3 d. Educ. Claremont High School; Glasgow College. Research Officer, Strathkelvin District Council, 1987-90; Achieving Quality Consultancy, 1990-93; Glasgow City Council, 1993-99. Address: (b.) 43 Middlesex Street, Kinning Park Glasgow G41 1EE; T.-0141 429 0294.

Kerr, Calum. MP (SNP), Berwickshire, Roxburgh and Selkirk, since 2015; SNP Environment and Rural Affairs spokesperson in the House of Commons, since 2015; b. 5.4.72; m.; 3 c. Educ. St Andrews University. Worked in sales for IT companies including Avaya. Chair of Yes Scottish Borders in the run-up to the referendum. Recreations: rugby; family; malt whisky. Address: House of Commons, London SW1A 0AA.

Kerr, Sheriff Joan, MA (Hons), LLB. Sheriff, Glasgow and Strathkelvin, since 2015. Admitted as a solicitor in 1991; solicitor, then partner, HBM Sayers, 1994-2008; appointed as a Stipendiary Magistrate in 2008 and Part Time Sheriff in 2011. Address: Glasgow Sheriff Court, Sheriff Clerk's Office, Sheriff Court House, 1 Carlton Place, Glasgow G5 9DA; T.-0141 429 8888.

Kerr, Liam. MSP (Scottish Conservative), North East Scotland region, since 2016. Conservative candidate in Aberdeen Donside in the 2016 Scottish Parliament election. Address: Scottish Parliament, Edinburgh EH99 1SP.

Kerr, Norman. Director and Company Secretary, Energy Action Scotland, since 2005. Car Industry, Engineer, 1971-81; Heatwise Glasgow (now The Wise Group), Insulation

Supervisor then Production Unit Manager, 1984-96; Development Manager and Deputy Director, Energy Action Scotland, 1996-2005. Trustee: National Energy Action, Scottish Power's Energy People Trust, Aberdeen Heat and Power Company. Address: (b.) Energy Action Scotland, Suite 4A, Ingram House, 227 Ingram Street, Glasgow G1 1DA; T.-0141 226 3064.
E-mail: norman.kerr@eas.org.uk

Kerr, Rev. Mgr. Philip John, PhB, STL. Parish Priest, St Patrick's, Edinburgh, since 2014; Vicar General, Archdiocese of St. Andrews and Edinburgh, since 2000; b. 23.4.56, Edinburgh. Educ. Holy Cross Academy; St. Augustine's High School, Edinburgh; Scots College and Gregorian University, Rome. Assistant Priest, St. Francis Xavier's, Falkirk, 1980-82; Lecturer in Systematic Theology, St. Andrew's College, Drygrange, 1982-86; Vice-Rector and Lecturer in Systematic Theology, Gillis College, Edinburgh, 1986-93; Lecturer in Systematic Theology, Scotus College, Bearsden, 1993-96; R.C. Chaplain, Stirling University, 1993-99; Parish Priest: Sacred Heart, Cowie, 1993-99, Our Lady and St. Ninian, Bannockburn, 1996-99, St. Francis Xavier, Falkirk, 1999-2014. Recreations: classical music; theatre; walking. Address: St Patrick's, 5 South Gray's Close, Edinburgh EH1 1TQ.

Kerr, Tom, ChEng, FIMarE. Provost of West Lothian, since 2007; Councillor, Linlithgow, since 1992; b. 22.07.46, Linlithgow; m., Marion; 1 s.; 1 d. Educ. Linlithgow Academy; Glasgow College of Nautical Studies. Engineer Cadet - Chief Engineer (BP Tanker Co. Ltd), 1962-76; Senior Lecturer: Glasgow College of Nautical Studies, 1976-84, Jeddah, Saudi Arabia (Gray MacKenzie) Inchcape Group; self employed marine consultant, 1988-2009; elected councillor - Linlithgow, 1992-2009. Royal Society of Arts and Institute of Marine Engineers Silver Medal Winner, 1976; various local government committees and local voluntary groups. Recreations: cricket; reading and travel. Address: (b.) West Lothian Council, West Lothian Civic Centre, Howden South Road, Livingston EH54 6FF; T.-01506 281728.

Kerr, William Revill, LLB, PhD, MBA, MSc, FCIS, FCIM, FIH. General Manager, The Glasgow Academy, since 2003; b. 26.4.48, East Kilbride; m. Educ. Duncanrig Senior Secondary School, East Kilbride; Glasgow University; Strathclyde University; Glasgow Caledonian University. Former Secretary, Malin Housing Association, 1988-2003; Chair, Scottish Enterprise Ayrshire, 2000-03; Advisory Board Member, Scottish Enterprise, 2001-02; Ambassador, Princes Scottish Youth Business Trust, 2000-07. Local Enterprise Company Chairs Group, 2000-03; Director, Scottish Enterprise Ayrshire, 1998-2003; Director, Investors in People, Scotland, 2000-02; Director, Ayrshire Development Loan Fund, 2000-02; Director, Business Excellence Ayrshire, 1998-2000; Director, Springboard, 1998-2000; Member, Scottish Disability Consulting Group, 1999-2000; Member, Scottish Qualifications Authority SVQ Advisory Board, 1998-2000; Chairman, Ayrshire and Arran Tourism Industries Forum, 1993-2000; Vice-Chairman, Scotland Committee, British Hospitality Association, 2001; Panel Member, Investors in People, 1997-2001. Publication: Tourism, Public Policy and the Strategic Management of Failure, 2003. Recreations: sport; writing; cycling; old books. Address: (h.) 111 Blackhill Drive, The Grange, Summerston, Glasgow G23 5NN; (b.) The Glasgow Academy, Colebrook Street, Glasgow G12 8HE; T.-0141 334 8558; e-mail: bill.kerr@tga.org.uk

Kesting, Very. Rev. Dr. Sheilagh Margaret. Moderator of The General Assembly of The Church of Scotland, 2007-08; Secretary, Ecumenical Relations, Church of Scotland, since 1993; b. 10.6.53, Stornoway. Educ. Nicolson Institute; Edinburgh University. Parish Minister: Overtown,

Lanarkshire, 1980-86, St. Andrews High, Musselburgh, 1986-93. Recreations: gardening; photography; embroidery. Address: (b.) Church of Scotland Offices, 121 George Street, Edinburgh EH2 4YN; T.-0131 225 5722; e-mail: skesting@cofscotland.org.uk

Kettle, Ann Julia, OBE, MA, FSA, FRHistS, FRSA; b. 2.8.39, Orpington. Educ. Lewes Grammar School; St. Hugh's College, Oxford. University of St. Andrews: Hebdomadar, 1991-94, Dean of Arts, 1998-2002; President, Association of University Teachers (Scotland), 1994-96; Member, Scottish (Garrick) Committee of National (Dearing) Committee of Inquiry into Higher Education, 1996-97; Member, Scottish Higher Education Funding Council, 1997-2000; Trustee, Arts and Humanities Research Board, 2001-05; Trustee, Newbattle Abbey College, since 2012; Chair, Board of Governors, Newbattle Abbey College, 2004-2010. Address: Sunset View, Ellice Place, St. Andrews KY16 9HU; T.-01334 473057; e-mail: ajk@st-andrews.ac.uk

Kidd, Bill. MSP (SNP), Glasgow Anniesland, since 2011, Glasgow, 2007-2011; Scottish Government Chief Whip; Co-President, Parliamentarians for Nuclear Non-Proliferation and Disarmament; b. 24.7.56. SNP candidate at the 1987 general election at Glasgow Hillhead; left the SNP to become a founder member of the Scottish Socialist Party (unrelated to the current party of that name); stood for the group at the Glasgow Central by-election, 1989, but later rejoined the SNP; SNP candidate at Cunninghame South in the 2001 general election; SNP candidate for Glasgow Anniesland at the 2003 and 2007 Scottish Parliament elections. Past Convenor of the SNP's Glasgow Regional Association. Address: (b.) Scottish Parliament, Edinburgh EH99 1SP.

Kidd, David Hamilton, LLB, LLM, WS. Solicitor Advocate, 1994-2013; b. 21.9.49, Edinburgh. Educ. Edinburgh Academy; Edinburgh University. Recreations: cycling; skiing; hill-walking.

Kidd, Mary Helen (May), JP, MA. World President, Associated Country Women of The World, 2010-2013; Deputy World President, Associated Country Women of The World, 2007-2010; Area President (Europe and the Mediterranean), Associated Country Women of the World, 2001-07; former Member, Advisory Board and Council, Scottish Agricultural College; m., Neil M.L. Kidd; 2 s. Educ. Brechin High School; Edinburgh University. Partner in family farming business; former Member: MAFF Consumer Panel, Scottish Consumer Council, Women's National Commission; National Chairman, Scottish Women's Rural Institutes, 1993-96. Recreations: playing piano and organ; creative writing. Address: (h.) Holemill of Kirkbuddo, Forfar, Angus DD8 2NQ.

Kilshaw, David Andrew George, OBE. Solicitor, since 1979; Chairman, Borders Health Board, 1993-2001; b. 18.3.53, Glencoe; 3 s. Educ. Keil School, Dumbarton. Traineeship, Brunton Miller, Solicitors, Glasgow, 1975-80; Solicitor, Borders Regional Council, 1980-83; Partner, Cullen Kilshaw Solicitors, Galashiels, Melrose, Peebles and Kelso, since 1983; Chair: Borders Solicitors Property Centre, since 2000, Border Reivers Professional Rugby Team Board, 2006. Recreation: golf. Address: (b.) 23 Northgate, Peebles; T.-01721 723999.

Kinclaven, Lord (Alexander Featherstonhaugh Wylie), QC, LLB, FCIArb. Lawyer; Member of the Scottish Bar, since 1978; b. 2.6.51, Perth; m., Gail Elizabeth Watson Duncan; 2 d. Educ. Edinburgh University. Qualified Solicitor in Scotland, 1976; called to Scottish Bar, 1978; Standing Junior Counsel to Accountant of Court, 1986-89; Advocate Depute, 1989-92; called to English Bar, 1990; QC (Scot), 1991. Part-time Joint Chairman, Discipline Committee, Institute of Chartered Accountants of Scotland,

1994-2005; Member, Scottish Legal Aid Board, 1994-2002; part-time Sheriff, 2000-05; part-time Chairman, Police Appeals Tribunal, 2001-05; Member, Scottish Criminal Cases Review Commission, 2004-05; Senator of the College of Justice, since 2005; Convener, Children in Scotland, since 2012. Address: (b.) Parliament House, Edinburgh EH1 1RQ.

King, Emeritus Professor Bernard, CBE, MSc, PhD, CCMI, CBiol, FSB. Principal and Vice-Chancellor, University of Abertay, Dundee, 1992-2011; b. 4.5.46, Dublin; m., Maura Antoinette Collinge; 2 d. Educ. Synge St. Christian Brothers School, Dublin; College of Technology, Dublin; University of Aston in Birmingham. Research Fellow, University of Aston, 1972-76; Dundee Institute of Technology, 1976-91: Lecturer, Senior Lecturer, Head, Department of Molecular and Life Sciences, Dean, Faculty of Science; Assistant Principal, Robert Gordon Institute of Technology/Robert Gordon University, 1991-92. Governor, Board, Unicorn Preservation Society; Board of Higher Education Academy, 2007-2010; Vice-Chair, Universities Scotland, 2006-2010; Convenor, Universities Scotland and Vice-President, Universities UK, 2010-2011. Recreations: reading; music; sailing. Address: (h.) 11 Dalhousie Place, Arbroath, DD11 2BT; T.-01382 308012.

King, Professor David Neden, MA, DPhil, CertEd. Emeritus Professor of Economics, Stirling University, since 2009; b. 10.04.45, Birmingham; m., Victoria Susan Robinson; 2 s. Educ. Gresham's School, Norfolk; Magdalen College, Oxford; York University. Consultant Economist, Royal Commission on the Constitution, 1971-72; Economics Master and Head of Economics, Winchester College, 1972-78; Lecturer, Stirling University, 1978-87; Economics Adviser, Department of the Environment, 1987-88; Senior Lecturer, Stirling University, 1987-2002, Professor of Public Economics, 2002-09. Conductor, Stirling University Choir, 1990-2009. Consultant to OECD and the World Bank. Publications: Financial and Economic Aspects of Regionalism and Separatism, 1973; Taxes on Immovable Property, 1983; Fiscal Tiers: the Economics of Multi-level Government, 1984; An Introduction to National Income Accounting, 1984; Banking and Money, 1987; The Complete Works of Robert and James Adam, 1991; Financial Claims and Derivatives, 1999; Unbuilt Adam, 2001; Economics, 2012. Recreations: architecture; music. Address: (b.) Division of Economics, Stirling University, Stirling FK9 4LA; T.-01786 467475. E-mail: d.n.king@stir.ac.uk

King, Elspeth Russell, MA, FMA, DUniv. Director, Smith Art Gallery and Museum, Stirling, since 1994; b. 29.3.49, Lochore, Fife. Educ. Beath High School; St. Andrews University; Leicester University. Curator, People's Palace, Glasgow, 1974-91, with responsibility for building up the social history collections for the city of Glasgow; Director, Dunfermline Heritage Trust, 1991-94; responsible for restoration of, and new displays in, Abbot House. Honorary Doctorate, Stirling University, 2005; Fletcher Award, Saltire Society, 2006. Publications include: The Thenew Factor: the hidden history of women in Glasgow, 1993; Blind Harry's Wallace by Hamilton of Gilbertfield (Editor), 1998; Stirling Girls, 2003; The Face of Wallace, 2005; A History of Stirling in 100 Objects, 2011. Address: (b.) Stirling Smith Art Gallery and Museum, Dumbarton Road, Stirling FK8 2RQ; T.-01786 471917. E-mail: museum@smithartgalleryandmuseum.co.uk

King, Dr. Steve, MBE. Composer/Music Educationalist; Director of Music, Heriot-Watt University, since 1998; Viola Player, Scottish Chamber Orchestra, since 1984; b.

4.12.56, Waltham Cross; 2 s. Educ. Queen Eleanor Grammar School; Royal Northern College of Music. Address: (h.) 8 Hopeward Mews, Dalgety Bay KY11 9TB.

Kingarth, Rt. Hon. Lord (Hon. Derek Emslie). Senator of the College of Justice, since 1997; b. 21.6.49. Educ. Cambridge University; Edinburgh University. Advocate, 1974; Advocate Depute 1985-1988. Address: Parliament Square, Edinburgh EH1 1RQ.

Kinghorn, Carol. Lord Lieutenant of Kincardineshire, since 2007; b. Aberdeen; m., Roderick; 4 c. Educ. Aberdeen; St Andrews. Qualified physiotherapist, spent a number of years working for Westminster Healthcare; worked for the area Red Cross, formerly trustee of the Crombie Trust (a charitable trust for elderly ladies); regional committee member of the Soldiers, Sailors, Airmen and Families Association; active member of a number of local and regional sports clubs and arts societies.

Kinnaird, Alison, MBE, MA, FGE. Glass Engraver and Artist; Clarsach Player; b. 30.4.49, Edinburgh; m., Robin Morton; 1 s.; 1 d. Educ. George Watson's Ladies College; Edinburgh University. Freelance glass artist, since 1971; exhibitions in Edinburgh, 1978, 1981, 1985, in London, 1988, 1995; work in many public and private collections; professional musician, since 1970; has produced three LPs as well as film and TV music; served on Council, Scottish Craft Centre, 1974-76; Council, SSWA, 1975-76; Member: BBC Scottish Music Advisory Committee, 1981-84, BBC Broadcasting Council for Scotland, 1984-88, SAC Crafts Commitee, 1993-96; awarded: SDA/CCC Craft Fellowship, 1980, Glass-Sellers of London Award, 1987, Creative Scotland Award, 2002. Recreations: children; cooking; garden. Address: (h.) Shillinghill, Temple, Midlothian EH23 4SH; T.-01875 830328.

Kinniburgh, Ian. Chairman: NHS Shetland, since 2009, NHS Orkney, since 2015. Career history: Shetlands Islands Council: Senior Environmental Health Officer, 1989-92, Divisional Manager, 1992-95, Head of Infrastructure, 1995-99; Owner and Managing Director, 60 North Recycling Ltd, 2000-2011. Appointed non-executive member of the Board of NHS Shetland in 2003; former Trustee of the Shetland Charitable Trust; currently a Trustee of the Shetland Recreational Trust and Shetland Amenity Trust; Chair, Shetland Partnership Board. Address: NHS Orkney, Garden House, New Scapa Road, Kirkwall, Orkney KW15 1BQ; T.-01856 888000.

Kinnoull, 16th Earl of (Charles William Harley Hay); b. 20.12.62. Educ. Eton College; Christ Church, Oxford. Qualified barrister; worked for insurance provider Hiscox for 25 years; also farms in Perthshire. Succeeded to title, 2013.

Kinross, Lord (Christopher Patrick Balfour), LLB, WS. Solicitor, 1975-2009 (retired); b. 1.10.49, Edinburgh; m., Susan Jane Pitman (divorced); m. (2), Catherine Taylor LLB; 2 s. Educ. Eton College; Edinburgh University. Member, Royal Company of Archers, Queen's Bodyguard for Scotland. Recreations: off-road motorsport; shooting.

Kinsman, Stewart Hayes, OBE, BSc, FRICS. Chief Executive, Hanover (Scotland) Housing Association Ltd., 1979-2007; Chairman, Edinburgh Flood Prevention Group, 2000-06; b. 18.9.43, Burntisland, Fife; 1 s.; 1 d. Educ. Kirkcaldy High School; Heriot-Watt University. Chartered Surveyor, 1966-71; Estates and Buildings Officer, Stirling University, 1971-76; Regional Manager, Hanover Housing Association (GB), 1976-79. Chairman, Scottish Federation of Housing Associations, 1998-2001. Recreations: sailing; wines; digital photography; natural history. Address: (h.) 14 Dryburn Brae, West Linton EH46 7JG; T.-01968 660 198; e-mail: stewartkinsman@btinternet.com

Kintore, 14th Earl of (James William Falconer Keith); b. 1976. Succeeded to title, 2004.

Kirby, Mike. Scottish Secretary, UNISON Scotland. Address: (b.) UNISON House, 14 West Campbell Street, Glasgow G2 6RX; T.-0845 355 0845; e-mail: m.kirby@unison.co.uk

Kirk, David, MA, BM, BCh, DM, FRCS (Eng), FRCS-RCPS (Glas), FRCS (Edin); b. 26.5.43, Bradford; m., Gillian Mary Wroot; 1 s.; 2 d. Educ. King Edwards School, Birmingham; Balliol College, Oxford; Oxford University Clinical Medical School. Resident House Physician and House Surgeon, Radcliffe Infirmary, Oxford; University Demonstrator, Oxford; clinical surgical posts, Oxford and Bristol; Arris and Gale Lecturer, Royal College of Surgeons (England), 1980-81; rotating surgical Registrar appointment, Sheffield; academic surgical research, Sheffield University; Senior Registrar in General Surgery, then in Urology, Bristol; Honorary Clinical Lecturer, Glasgow University, 1984-95; Consultant Urological Surgeon, NHS Greater Glasgow, 1982-2005; Honorary Professor, Glasgow University, 1995-2005; Examiner in Surgery, Royal College of Physicians and Surgeons of Glasgow, 1983-2011; Assessor for IMRCS (Intercollegiate Membership of Royal College of Surgeons) Examinations, 2011-14; Lead Assessor, 2012-14; College representative on IMRCS Quality Assurance Committee, 2008-2014. Secretary/Treasurer, 1983-85, Chairman, 1985-88, Scottish Urological Oncology Group; Council Member: Urology Section, Royal Society of Medicine, 1984-87, British Association of Urological Surgeons, 1988-91; Chairman: Prostate Forum, 1991-94, Intercollegiate Board in Urology, 1994-97; Specialist Adviser in Urology, National Medical Advisory Committee (Scottish Executive), 1996-2004; Member, Specialist Advisory Committee in Urology, Joint Committee on Higher Surgical Training, 1999-2004; President, Scottish Urology Society, 2004-06; Chair, Forth Valley Branch, Cruse Bereavement Care Scotland, 2004-07; Performance Assessor, General Medical Council, 2006-2010; Clinical Adviser, Healthcare Commission, 2007-09; Society of Friends, Dunblane Cathedral: Trustee, since 2014, Council Member, 2006-09 and 2011-14, Convener of Projects Committee, 2014; Trustee, Dunblane Cathedral Trust, 2004-2010; Joint Convener, Pastoral Care Group, Dunblane Cathedral, 2014. Publications: Understanding Prostate Disorders (author); Managing Prostate Disease (author); International Handbook of Prostate Cancer (editor); book chapters and original papers on urological cancer and other topics; annual articles on the history of The Society of Friends of Dunblane Cathedral: Journal of Society of Friends, 2011-2014. Recreations: skiing; hillwalking; classical music. Address: (h.) 1 The Biggins, Keir, Dunblane FK15 9NX; T.-01786 820291; e-mail: david_kirk@tiscali.co.uk

Kirk, Professor Gordon, OBE, MA, MEd, PhD, DUniv, FRSA. Vice-Principal, University of Edinburgh, 2002-03 (Dean, Faculty of Education, 1998-2002); Vice-Convener, General Teaching Council, 1992-2001; Academic Secretary, Universities' Council for the Education of Teachers, 2002-2015; b. 8.5.38, Dunfermline; m., Jane D. Murdoch; 1 s.; 1 d. Educ. Camphill Secondary School, Paisley; Glasgow University. Lecturer in Education, Aberdeen University, 1965-74; Head, Education

Department, Jordanhill College of Education, 1974-81; Principal, Moray House Institute of Education, 1981-98. Member, Munn Committee on the Curriculum of the Secondary School, 1974-77; Chairman: Educational Broadcasting Council, Scotland, 1985-91, Scottish Council for Research in Education, 1984-92; Member: General Teaching Council for Scotland, 1984-2002, Consultative Committee on the Curriculum, 1984-91, Council for National Academic Awards, 1979-93; Vice-Convener, Committee of Scottish Higher Principals, 1993-94. Publications: Scottish Education Looks Ahead (Assistant Editor), 1969; Curriculum and Assessment in the Scottish Secondary School, 1982; Moray House and Professional Education (Editor), 1985; The Core Curriculum, 1986; Teacher Education and Professional Development, 1988; Handbook of Educational Ideas and Practices (Associate Editor), 1990; Scottish Education and the European Community (Editor), 1992; 5-14: Scotland's National Curriculum (Editor), 1994; Moray House and Change in Higher Education (Editor), 1995; Professional Issues in Education series (Co-Editor); Enhancing Quality in Teacher Education, 2000; Moray House and the Road to Merger, 2002; The Chartered Teacher (Co-author), 2004. Recreations: baseball; golf; bridge. Address: (h.) Craigroyston, Broadgait, Gullane, East Lothian; T.-01620 843299; e-mail: gordon.kirk8@btopenworld.com

Kirk, Professor James, MA, PhD, DLitt, FRHistS, FRSE. Professor of Scottish History, Glasgow University, 1999-2005; Hon. Professorial Research Fellow in Ecclesiastical History, School of Divinity, University of Glasgow, 2006-09; b. 18.10.44, Falkirk; m., Dr. Daphne Waters. Educ. Stirling High School; Edinburgh University. Lecturer in Scottish History, Glasgow University, 1972-89, Senior Lecturer, 1989-90, Reader, 1990-99. David Berry Prize, Royal Historical Society, 1973; Wolfson Award, 1977; Hume Brown Senior Prize in Scottish History, 1977; British Academy Major Research Awards, 1989-96; ESRC Research Award, 1993-95. President, Scottish Church History Society, 1989-92; Hon. Secretary: Scottish Record Society, since 1973, Scottish Society for Reformation History, 1980-90; Scottish Section Editor, Royal Historical Society, Annual Bibliography of British and Irish History; an Associate Editor, The New Dictionary of National Biography, 1998. Publications: The University of Glasgow 1451-1577, 1977; Records of the Synod of Lothian and Tweeddale, 1977; The Second Book of Discipline, 1980; Stirling Presbytery Records, 1981; Visitation of the Diocese of Dunblane, 1984; Patterns of Reform, 1989; Humanism and Reform, 1991; The Books of Assumption of the Thirds of Benefices: Scottish Ecclesiastical Rentals at the Reformation, 1995; Scotland's History (Editor), 1995; The Medieval Church in Scotland (Editor), 1995; Her Majesty's Historiographer, 1996; Calendar of Scottish Supplications to Rome 1447-1471, vol. 5 (Editor), 1997; The Church in the Highlands (Editor), 1998; The Scottish Churches, Politics and the Union Parliament (Editor), 2001; Contributor to: The Renaissance and Reformation in Scotland, 1983; Voluntary Religion, 1986; The Seventeenth Century in the Highlands, 1986; Scotland Revisited, 1991; Encyclopedia of the Reformed Faith, 1992, Dictionary of Scottish Church History and Theology, 1993, The Oxford Encyclopedia of the Reformation, 1996; John Knox and the British Reformations, 1999; The New Dictionary of National Biography, 2004; Caindel Alban: Fèill-sgrìobhainn do Dhòmhnall E. Meek, 2008. Recreations: living in Wester Ross; viticulture. Address: (h.) Woodlea, Dunmore, Stirlingshire FK2 8LY; T.-01324 831240; e-mail: james@kirk11.fsnet.co.uk

Kirkhill, Lord (John Farquharson Smith); b. 7.5.30; m.; 1 step d. Lord Provost of Aberdeen, 1971-75; Minister of State, Scottish Office, 1975-78; Chairman, North of Scotland Hydro-Electric Board, 1979-82; Delegate, Parliamentary Assembly, Council of Europe, and W.E.U., 1987-2000 (Chairman, Committee on Legal Affairs and Human Rights, 1991-95); Hon LLD, Aberdeen University, 1974.

Kirkwood of Kirkhope, Lord (Archy Kirkwood), Kt, BSc; b. 22.4.46, Glasgow; m., Rosemary Chester; 1 s.; 1 d. Educ. Cranhill School; Heriot-Watt University. Solicitor; Aide to Sir David Steel, 1971-75, 1977-78; MP (Liberal Democrat), Roxburgh and Berwickshire, 1983-2005; Liberal Spokesman on Health and Social Services, and on Social Security, 1985-87; Alliance Spokesman on Overseas Development, 1987; Liberal Scottish Whip, 1987-88; Social and Liberal Democrat Convener on Welfare, Health and Education, 1988-89; Liberal Democrat Deputy Chief Whip, and Spokesman on Welfare and Social Security, 1989-92, Community Care, 1994-97; Chief Whip, 1993-97; Chairman, Work and Pensions Select Committee (formerly Social Security Select Committee), 1997-2005. Former Trustee, Joseph Rowntree Reform Trust; former Governor, Westminster Foundation for Democracy. Recreations: music; photography. Address: (b.) House of Lords, London SW1A 0PW.

Kirkwood, Susan, BSc, MSc, MBA; b. 18.5.50, Edinburgh. Educ. James Gillespie's High School, Edinburgh; Edinburgh University; Durham University; INSEAD. Exploration Geophysicist, 1973-83; Business Analyst, 1985-94; Company Director, since 1994. JP. Address: (h.) 78 Cairnfield Place, Aberdeen; T.-01224 630979.

Kitchen, John Philip, MA, BMus, PhD (Cantab), FRCO, LRAM. Senior Lecturer in Music, Edinburgh University, 1987-2014; Concert Organist, Harpsichordist, Pianist; Edinburgh City Organist, since 2002; b. 27.10.50, Airdrie. Educ. Coatbridge High School; Glasgow University; Cambridge University. Lecturer in Music, St. Andrews University, 1976-87; Harpsichordist/Organist, Scottish Early Music Consort, 1977-98; BBC and commercial recordings; music reviewer; Director of Music, Old St. Paul's Episcopal Church, Edinburgh. Recreations: more music; entertaining. Address: (b.) Reid School of Music, Alison House, 12 Nicolson Square, Edinburgh EH8 9DF. E-mail: J.Kitchen@ed.ac.uk

Knapman, David John, MPhil. Rector, Dollar Academy, since 2010; b. 1961; m. Brigitte; 2 s. Educ. Morrison's Academy; Exeter University. Mathematics Teacher, Housemaster, Bramdean School, 1985-91; Deputy Head, The Mall School, 1991-99; Head of Year, Assistant Head, Deputy Head, Hampton School, 1999-2010. Hon. Secretary, Tennis Central Scotland; Trustee, HMC Projects in Central and Eastern Europe. Recreations: reading; music; tennis; cricket. Address: Dollar Academy, Dollar FK14 7DU; T.-01259 742511.

Knight, Alanna, MBE, FSA Scot. Novelist; b. Co. Durham; m., Alistair Knight; 2 s. Educ. Jesmond High School. Writing career began, 1965; novels: Legend of the Loch, 1969 (RNA First Novel Award), The October Witch, 1971, This Outward Angel, 1971, Castle Clodha, 1972, Lament for Lost Lovers, 1972, The White Rose, 1974, A Stranger Came By, 1974, The Wicked Wynsleys, 1977; historical novels: The Passionate Kindness, 1974, A Drink for the Bridge, 1976, The Black Duchess, 1980, Castle of Foxes, 1981, Colla's Children, 1982, The Clan, 1985; Estella, 1986; detective novels: Enter Second Murderer, 1988, Blood Line, 1989, Deadly Beloved, 1989, Killing Cousins, 1990, A Quiet Death, 1991, To Kill A Queen, 1992; The Evil that Men Do, 1993, The Missing Duchess, 1994, Inspector Faro and the Edinburgh Mysteries, 1994, The Bull Slayers, 1995; Murder by Appointment, 1996; Inspector Faro's Second Casebook, 1996; The Coffin Lane Murders, 1998; The Final Enemy, 2002; Unholy Trinity, 2004; crime novels: the Sweet Cheat Gone, 1992, This

Outward Angel, 1994; Angel Eyes, 1997; The Royal Park Murder, 1998; The Monster in the Loch, 1998; Dead Beckoning, 1999; The Inspector's Daughter, 2000; The Dagger in the Crown, 2001; Dangerous Pursuits, 2002; An Orkney Murder, 2003; Ghost Walk, 2004; The Gowrie Conspiracy, 2003; Faro and the Royals, 2004; The Stuart Sapphire, 2005; Destroying Angel, 2007; Murder in Paradise, 2008; Quest for a Killer, 2010; The Seal King Murders, 2011; Murders Most Foul, 2013; Deadly Legacy, 2012; The Balmoral Incident, 2014; Akin to Murder, 2015; plays: The Private Life of R.L.S., 1973, Girl on an Empty Swing, 1977; Some Day I'll Find You, 1987; Inspector Faro Investigates, 2001; as Margaret Hope: The Queen's Captain, 1978; The Shadow Queen, 1979; Hostage Most Royal, 1979; Perilous Voyage, 1983; non-fiction: The Robert Louis Stevenson Treasury, 1985; RLS in the South Seas, 1986, Bright Ring of Words (Co-Editor), 1994; true crime: Close and Deadly, 2002; Burke & Hare, 2007; radio short stories, plays and documentaries. Hon. President, Scottish Association of Writers and Edinburgh's Writers' Club. Recreations: walking; reading; painting. Address: (h.) 24 March Hall Crescent, Edinburgh EH16 5HL; T.-0131-667 5230; e-mail: alanna.knight@virgin.net
Website: www.alannaknight.com; Amazon Kindle ebooks

Knops, Professor Robin John, BSc, PhD, Hon.DSc, FRSE. Emeritus Professor of Mathematics, Heriot-Watt University; b. 30.12.32, London; m., Margaret; 4 s.; 2 d. Educ. Nottingham University. Nottingham University: Assistant Lecturer in Mathematics, 1956-59, Lecturer in Mathematics, 1959-62; Newcastle-upon-Tyne University: Lecturer in Applied Mathematics, 1962-68, Reader in Continuum Mechanics, 1968-71; Professor of Mathematics, Heriot-Watt University, Edinburgh, 1971-98 (Head, Department of Mathematics, 1971-83; Dean of Science, 1984-87, Vice Principal, 1988-95; Special Adviser to the Principal, 1995-97). Visiting Professor: Cornell University, 1967 and 1968; University of California, Berkeley, 1968; Pisa University, 1974; École Polytechnique Federale Lausanne, Switzerland, 1980; Royal Society of Edinburgh: Council Member, 1982-92, Executive Committee Member, 1982-92, Meetings Secretary, 1982-87, Chief Executive Editor, Proceedings A, 1982-87, Curator, 1987-92; President: Edinburgh Mathematical Society, 1974-75, International Society for the Interaction of Mechanics and Mathematics, President, 1991-95 (Vice-President, 1995-99); Editor, Applied Mathematics and Mathematical Computation, 1990-2002; Convener, Executive Committee, International Centre for Mathematical Sciences, Edinburgh, 1996-99; Leverhulme Emeritus Fellowship, 2000-02. Publications: Uniqueness Theories in Linear Elasticity (Co-author), 1971; Theory of Elastic Stability (Co-author), 1973. Recreations: walking; reading. Address: (b.) School of Mathematical and Computer Sciences, Colin Maclaurin Building, Heriot-Watt University, Edinburgh EH14 4AS; T.-0131-451 3363; e-mail: r.j.knops@hw.ac.uk

Knottenbelt, Professor Clare Margaret, BVSc, MSc, DSAM, MRCUS. Professor of Small Animal Medicine and Oncology, University of Glasgow, since 2010; b. 5.2.70, Edinburgh; m., David Henderson; 2 d. Educ. Arundel School, Harare, Zimbabwe; Bristol University. Veterinary Surgeon, Yorkshire, 1994-95; Petsavers Resident in Small Animal Medicine, University of Edinburgh, 1995-99; Lecturer in Small Animal Medicine, Glasgow University, 2000-06, Senior Clinician in Small Animal Medicine and Oncology, 2006-2010. Address: (b.) Small Animal Clinical Sciences, School of Vet Medicine, College of MVLS, University of Glasgow; T.-0141 330 5706.
E-mail: clare.knottenbelt@glasgow.ac.uk

Knowles, David Ian, DipHRIM, MIHM. Director, Practitioner and Counter Fraud Services, NHS Scotland, since 2008; b. 16.9.61, Edinburgh; m., Margaret; 1 s.; 1 d. Educ. Gracemount High School. Medical and Health Management throughout Edinburgh, since 1980; moved to National Services Scotland working in Information, 1997; took up post in practitioner services, 2008. Member, various work related committees; Church Elder. Recreations: photography; reading; Times crossword. Address: (b.) Scottish Health Service Centre, Crewe Road South, Edinburgh EH4 2LF.

Knox, James Richard Dunsmuir, MA, MBA, FSA (Scot). Director, Fleming-Wyfold Art Foundation, since 2015; Author; b. 18.10.52, Kilwinning; m., Caroline Angela Owen; 1 s.; 1 d. Educ. Eton College; Trinity College, Cambridge; INSEAD, Fountainbleau; Institute of Business Administration. Feature Writer, The Antique Collector; Associate Publisher, Ebury Press, 1975-78; Associate Publisher, Illustrated News Group, 1980-82; Publisher, The Spectator, 1982-92; Founder, Art for Work, 1992-2005; Managing Director, The Art Newspaper, 2005-2015. Trusteeships: The National Trust for Scotland; Chairman: The Boswell Trust, Ayr Renaissance. Publications: Trinity Foot Beagles, 1978; Robert Byron, 2004; The Genius of Osbert Lancaster, 2008; Curator, The Genius of Osbert Lancaster, 2008; The Wallace Collection; Scottish Country Houses, 2012. Recreations: visual arts; architecture. Address: (h.) Martnaham Lodge, Ayr KA6 6ES.

Knox, Lesley Mary, MA (Cantab). NED and Chair, Remuneration Committee, Centrica Plc, since 2012; SAB Miller Plc (NED), since 2011; Trustee, National Galleries of Scotland, since 2011; Chair, DDL Ltd. (V and A at Dundee), since 2010; Chairman, Grosvenor Group Ltd., since 2011; b. 19.9.53, Johannesburg, South Africa; m., Brian Knox; 1 d. Educ. St. Denis, Edinburgh; Cheltenham Ladies College; Cambridge University. Slaughter and May (qualified as Solicitor), 1976-79; Shearman and Sterling New York (qualified as Attorney), 1979-80; Kleinwort Benson, Corporate Finance Division, 1981-91 (became Director in 1986); Head of Institutional Asset Management, Kleinwort Investment, 1991-96; NED, Bank of Scotland, 1993-2001; NED, Scottish Provident, 1995-2001; British Linen Bank, 1997-99 (became Governor in 1998); wholly Non Executive of a number of companies. Recreations: family; contemporary arts and crafts; opera. Address: (h.) 10A Circus Lane, Edinburgh EH3 6SU; T.-07768 046 422.

Knox, Liz, DA (Edin), PAI, PPAI. Painter, since 1971; President, Paisley Art Institute, 2007-2010; b. 20.01.45, Glasgow; m., Peter Whittle; 2 s. Educ. Hillhead High School, Glasgow and John Neilson, Paisley; Edinburgh College of Art. Art Teacher, Secondary Education, 1971-73; bringing up sons and lecturing part time, 1973-83; Lecturing in Fine Art for Further Education, 1983-2003 (part of this period, member of Advisory Panel, Gray's School of Art, Aberdeen and wrote entire HND Environmental Art validated by SQA, 2001); painting part time, from 1971; full time painter, since 2003 (exhibiting Britain including Edinburgh, Glasgow and London, also France and Netherlands, since 2003). Member, committee of Paisley Art Institute, since 1997; Member of Council, The Glasgow Art Club, 2006-07; Vice President, Paisley Art Institute, 2004-07; Member of Council, The Royal Glasgow Institute of the Arts, since 2010; Assessor, Scottish Drawing Competition, 2007, 2009; Assessor, Aspect Prize, 2010, 2011; Retrospective, Maclaurin Galleries, Ayr, 2012; "Emphatic Interpretations", in collaboration with musician Ben Whittle (First Family Riot) in MacGyver, Westermarkt, Amsterdam, 2015; work held in many private and corporate collections internationally. Selected solo Exhibitions include Calton Gallery, Edinburgh, Duncan Campbell Fine Art, London, Catto Gallery, Hampstead and St. Mary's Episcopal Cathedral, Glasgow. Work selected for book cover by Bloodaxe Books. Awards include: The Concept Gallery Award, 2013; Winner of The Aspect prize, 2003; The Bessie Scott Award at PAI, 2004; The Diploma of Paisley Art Institute, "PAI", 2005; The University of Paisley (now University of The West of Scotland) Award, 2006; The Blythswood Square Quaich at Glasgow Society of Women Artists, 2007; the Arnold Clark Award, 2010. Recreations: music; photography; books; travel. Address: (h.) Jesmond, High Street, Neilston, Glasgow G78 3HJ; T.-0141 587 5559. E-mail: lizknox1@ntlworld.com; web: www.lizknox.com

Kubie, Professor Jorge, BSc (Eng), PhD, DSc(Eng), CEng, FIMechE. Professor of Mechanical Engineering, Napier University, Edinburgh, since 1997 (former Head, School of Engineering); b. 13.6.47, Prague; m., Amanda Jane Kubie; 4d. Educ. Czech Technical University; University College London; Aston University. Research and technical posts in the electricity supply industry, 1974-90; Professor, Mechanical Engineering, Middlesex University, London, 1990-97; Member, Board of Management, Borders College, 2000-02. Address: (b.) School of Engineering, Napier University, Edinburgh, EH10 5DT; T.-0131-455 2595.

Kuenssberg, Nicholas Christopher, OBE, DUniv, BA (Hons) (Oxon), FCIS, FIoD, CCMI, FRSA. Chairman: Social Investment Scotland, since 2013, Klik2learn Ltd, since 2013, mLED Ltd., since 2010, Scott & Fyfe Ltd., since 2009, Canmore Partnership Ltd., since 1999; Honorary Professor, University of Glasgow, since 2008; Trustee, Pitlochry Festival Theatre, since 2010; b. 28.10.42, Edinburgh; m., Sally Robertson; 1 s.; 2 d. Educ. Edinburgh Academy; Wadham College, Oxford. Director, J. & P. Coats Ltd., 1978-91; Chairman, Dynacast International Ltd, 1978-91; Director, Coats Patons plc, 1985-91; Director, Coats Viyella plc, 1986-91; Managing Director, Dawson International plc, 1994-95 (Managing Director, Premier Brands, 1991-94); Non-executive Director: Bank of Scotland West of Scotland Board, 1984-88, ScottishPower plc, 1984-97, Standard Life Assurance Company, 1988-99, Baxi Partnership Ltd., 1996-99, Chamberlin and Hill plc, 1999-2006, Amino Technologies plc, 2004-07; Chairman: GAP Group Ltd., 1996-2005, Stoddard International PLC, 1997-2000, David A. Hall Ltd., 1996-98, iomart Group plc, 2000-08, Keronite plc, 2004-07, eTourism Ltd., 2007-08, Scotland the Brand, 2002-04, ScotlandIS, 2001-03, Institute of Directors, Scotland, 1997-99, Association for Management Education and Training in Scotland, 1996-98; Governor, Queen's College, 1988-91; Visiting Professor, Strathclyde Business School, 1988-91; Trustee, David Hume Institute, 1994-2008; Member, Advisory Group to Secretary of State on Sustainable Development, 1996-99; Member, Scottish Legal Aid Board, 1996-2004; Member, Scottish Environment Protection Agency, 1997-2007 (Deputy Chairman, 2003-07); Member, British Council, Scottish Committee, 1999-2008; Board Member, Citizens Theatre, Glasgow, 2000-03; Chairman, Glasgow School of Art, 2003-2010, QAA Scotland, 2007-2010; Public Interest Member, Council of Institute of Chartered Accountants of Scotland, 2008-2011. Editor, Argument amongst Friends: twenty five years of sceptical enquiry and The David Hume Institute: The first decade. Recreations: languages; opera; travel; sport. Address: (b.) 6 Cleveden Drive, Glasgow G12 0SE; e-mail: horizon@sol.co.uk

Kuenssberg, Sally, CBE, BA, DipAdEd, FRSA; b. 30.7.43, Edinburgh; m., Nicholas; 1 s.; 2 d. Educ. St Leonard's School; University of Oxford. Language Teaching, Europe and South America, 1966-78; Partner, Heatherbank Press, Milngavie, 1981-90; Children's Panel Training Organiser, Department of Adult and Continuing Education, University of Glasgow, 1990-95; Chairman, Scottish Children's Reporter Administration, 1995-2002; Chair, Yorkhill NHS Trust, 2001-04; Member, NHS Greater Glasgow and Clyde Health Board, 2001-07; Trustee, Save The Children, 2003-2011.

Kunkler, Professor Ian Hubert, MA, MB, BChir, DMRT, FRCR, FRCPE, FRSA. Consultant and Honorary Professor in Clinical Oncology, Western General Hospital, University of Edinburgh; b. Wilmslow; m., Alison Jane; 1 s. Educ. Clifton College, Bristol; Magdalene College, Cambridge; St Bartholomew's Hospital, London. President, London Medical Group, 1976-77; House Officer, 1978-79; Senior House Officer, Nottingham City Hospital, 1979-81; Registrar and Senior Registrar, Clinical Oncology, Western General Hospital, Edinburgh; French Government and EEC Research Fellow, Institut Gustave Roussy, Paris, 1986-87; Consultant and Hon. Lecturer in Clinical Oncology, Weston Park Hospital, Sheffield, 1988-92; Honorary Reader, University of Edinburgh, 2006. President, British Oncological Association, 2000-02; Founder and Trustee, Clerk Maxwell Cancer Research Fund, 1998-2004; Member, IAEA international quality assurance group for radiotherapy, since 2005; International adviser in radiotherapy, Institut National du Cancer, France; 2006 British Oncological Association, Excellence in Oncology Team of The Year; Chief Investigator, MRC SUPREMO breast cancer trial. Publications: Walter and Miller's Textbook of Radiotherapy, 1993, 2002; various papers on breast cancer, radiotherapy and telemedicine. Address: (b.) Department of Clinical Oncology, Western General Hospital, Edinburgh EH4 2XU; T.-0131-537-2214; Fax: 0131-537-1470; e-mail: i.kunkler@ed.ac.uk

Kyle, James, CBE, DSc, MCh, FRCS. Chairman, Raigmore Hospital NHS Trust, Inverness, 1993-97; b. 26.3.25, Ballymena, Northern Ireland; m., Dorothy Elizabeth Galbraith; 2 d. Educ. Ballymena Academy; Queen's University, Belfast. Scholarship to Mayo Clinic, USA, 1950; Tutor in Surgery, Royal Victoria Hospital, Belfast, 1952; Lecturer in Surgery, Liverpool University, 1957; Senior Lecturer in Surgery, Aberdeen University, 1959-60, and Consultant Surgeon, Aberdeen Royal Infirmary, 1959-89. Member, Grampian Health Board, 1973-77, Chairman, 1989-93; Chairman, Raigmore Hospital NHS Trust, Inverness, 1993-97; Chairman, Scottish Committee for Hospital Medical Services, 1976-79; elected Member, General Medical Council, 1979-94; Chairman: Scottish Joint Consultants Committee, 1984-89, Representative Body, British Medical Association, 1984-87; President, Aberdeen Medico-Chirurgical Society, 1989-90; British Council Lecturer, SE Asia and South America, 1963-85; Examiner: Belfast, Dublin, Dundee, Edinburgh, Sydney, University of West Indies; Burgess of Aberdeen. Patron: Royal Scottish National Orchestra, Scottish Opera. Publications: Peptic Ulcer; Pye's Surgical Handicraft; Crohn's Disease; Scientific Foundations of Surgery. Recreations: Fellow, Royal Philatelic Society, London; Fellow, Royal Astronomical Society, London; licensed radio amateur, GM4 CHX. Address: (h.) 7 Fasaich, Strath, Gairloch IV21 2DH; T.-01445 712398.

Kyle, Peter McLeod, MBChB, FRCS(Edin), FRCS(Glas), FRCOphth. Consultant Ophthalmologist, Southern General Hospital NHS Trust, 1982-2010 (Clinical Director of Ophthalmology, 1995-2000); Honorary Clinical Senior Lecturer, Glasgow University, 1985-2010; Member, Medical Appeal Tribunals, Scotland, since 1986; Member, Criminal Injuries Compensation Tribunal, since 2009; Member, General Medical Council Fitness to Practice Panel, since 2010; Member, General Optical Council, 1998-2009; Member, General Optical Council Education Committee and Working Group, since 1998; b. 19.8.51,

Rutherglen; m., Valerie Anne Steele; 1 s.; 2 d. Educ. High School of Glasgow; Glasgow University. Lecturer in Ophthalmology, Glasgow University, 1980-84. Convener, Ophthalmology Sub-committee, Royal College of Physicians and Surgeons of Glasgow; Member, Opthalmology Specialist Advisory Board, Royal College of Surgeons of Edinburgh; Deacon, Incorporation of Barbers of Glasgow, 1998-99. Recreations: walking; skiing. Address: (h.) The Stables, Earlsferry, Fife; T.-01333 330647.

Kynoch, George Alexander Bryson, OBE, BSc. Non-Executive Chairman: Red Squirrel Wine Ltd, since 2014, Muir Matheson Ltd., 1998-2007, London Marine Group Ltd., 1997-2004, Benson Group Ltd., 1998-2005, The TEP Exchange Group PLC, 2006-09, RDF Group PLC, 2003-06, TOLUNA PLC, 2005-2011; Non-Executive Director: Talent Group PLC, 2003-2014, TECC-IS PLC, 2003-05; Non Executive Chairman: OCZ Technology Group Inc., 2006-09, Mercury Group PLC, 2007-08, ITWP Acquisitions Ltd, since 2011; Deputy Chairman, The Scottish Conservative and Unionist Party, 2008-2012; MP (Conservative), Kincardine and Deeside, 1992-97; b. 7.10.46, Keith; m. (1), Dr. Rosslyn Margaret McDevitt (deceased); 1 s.; 1 d.; m. (2), Dorothy Anne Stiven. Educ. Cargilfield School, Edinburgh; Glenalmond College, Perth; Bristol University. Plant Engineer, ICI Ltd., Nobel Division, 1968-71; G. and G. Kynoch PLC, 1971-92, latterly as Group Executive Director; Parliamentary Under Secretary of State for Scotland – Minister for Industry and Local Government, 1995-97; Non-Executive Director: Kynoch Group PLC, Aardvark Clear Mine Ltd., 1992-95, PSL Holdings Ltd., 1998, Silvertech International plc, 1997-2000, Midmar Energy Ltd., 1998-99, Premisys Technologies PLC, 1998-2001, Jetcam International Holdings Ltd., 1998-2003; Member, Aberdeen and District Milk Marketing Board, 1988-92; Director, Moray Badenoch and Strathspey Local Enterprise Co. Ltd., 1991-92; Chairman, Scottish Woollen Publicity Council, 1983-90; President, Scottish Woollen Industry, 1990-91; Vice Chairman, Northern Area, Scottish Conservative and Unionist Association, 1991-92; Deputy Chairman, Carlton Club, since 2012. Recreations: golf; travel.

L

Lacy, Very Rev. Dr. David William, BA, BD, DLitt. Minister, Kay Park Parish Church, Kilmarnock, since 1989; Moderator of the General Assembly of the Church of Scotland, 2005-06; b. 26.4.52, Inverness; m., Joan Stewart Roberston; 1 s.; 1 d. Educ. Aberdeen Grammar School; High School of Glasgow; University of Strathclyde; University of Glasgow and Trinity College. Assistant Minister, St. George's West, Edinburgh, 1975-77; Minister, Knightswood: St. Margaret's, Glasgow, 1977-89. Depute Lieutenant of Ayrshire and Arran, since 2013. Recreations: sailing; snooker; choral singing. Address: 52 London Road, Kilmarnock, Ayrshire KA3 7AJ; T.-01563 523113.

Laing, Alasdair North Grant, OBE, FRAgS. Director, PDG Helicopters Ltd, 1975-2015; Chairman, Association of District Fishery Boards; b. 30.12.49, Forres; m., Lucy Ann Anthea Low; 2 s.; 1 d. Educ. Belhaven Hill; Eton College; Royal Agricultural Collge, Cirencester. Trustee, Macaulay Development Trust; President, Royal Highland and Agricultural Society of Scotland, 2004/05; Director, Scottish Agricultural College, 1995-2003; Vice Convenor, Scottish Landowners Federation, 2000-04. Recreations: walking; fishing; stalking. Address: (b.) Logie Estate Office, Forres, Moray IV36 2QN; T.-01667 458900; e-mail: alaing@logie.co.uk

Laing, David Kemlo, LLB. Consultant, Ledingham Chalmers LLP; b. 17.6.53, Aberdeen; m., Marina Maclean; 2 d. Educ. Robert Gordon's College, Aberdeen; University of Edinburgh. Clark and Wallace, Aberdeen, 1974-76; C. & P. H. Chalmers, Aberdeen, 1976-78, Partner, 1978-90; Partner, Ledingham Chalmers, 1991-2013, Chairman, 2000-2011. Vice President, Scottish Bible Society; Trustee, Workplace Chaplaincy Scotland. Address: (b.) 68-70 George Street, Edinburgh EH2 2LR; T.-0131 200 1000. E-mail: david.laing@ledinghamchalmers.com

Laing, Malcolm Donald, MA, LLB, NP. Partner, Ledingham Chalmers LLP, Solicitors; b. 28.11.55, Aberdeen. Educ. Robert Gordon's College; Aberdeen University. Morton Fraser & Milligan, Edinburgh, 1978-82; C. & P.H. Chalmers, 1982-90 (Partner, 1985). Deputy Chair, Cornerstone Community Care; Member of Aberdeen Harbour Board. Recreations: travel; mountaineering; music. Address: (b.) Johnstone House, 52-54 Rose Street, Aberdeen AB15 8JL; T.-01224 408511. E-mail: malcolm.laing@ledinghamchalmers.com

Laing, The Hon. Mark Hector, MA. Chairman, Nairn's Oatcakes Ltd., since 1996; Member of Court, Queen Margaret University; b. 22.2.51, London; m., Susanna Crawford; 1 s.; 2 d. Educ. Eton College; Cambridge University. United Biscuits p.l.c., 1972-96: Factory Director, Glasgow, 1985; Production Director, McVities, 1988; Managing Director, Simmers Biscuits, 1990; Trustee, Robertson Trust. Recreations: walking; gardening; fishing; shooting; photography. Address: (b.) Nairn's Oatcakes Ltd., 90 Peffermill Road, Edinburgh EH16 5UU; T.-0131-620 7000; e-mail: mark@nairns-oatcakes.com

Lally, Patrick James, DL, LLD, KLJ, HRGI, FRSA, OStJ, HONFRIAS. Rt. Hon. Lord Provost of the City of Glasgow and Lord Lieutenant, City of Glasgow, 1996-1999; Deputy Lieutenant, Glasgow; Commandeur, Ordre National du Merite (France); Chairman, Greater Glasgow and Clyde Valley Tourist Board, 1996-99; Director, Glasgow Cultural Enterprises, 1988-99; Justice of the Peace, 1971-2007; b. Glasgow; m., Margaret Beckett McGuire (deceased); 2 s. Elected, Corporation of Glasgow, 1966-75 (Deputy Leader, 1972-75); elected, City of Glasgow Council, 1975-77, and 1980-96; City Treasurer, 1984-86; Leader, City of Glasgow District Council, 1986-92 and 1994-96; Chairman, Greater Glasgow Tourist Board, 1989-96; President, Glasgow International Jazz Festival; Hon. Director, Chinese Peoples Association for Friendship with Foreign Countries; Hon. Member, Royal Glasgow Institute of Fine Arts; Hon. Member, Rotary International; Hon. Citizen, Dalian, China; Hon. Member, Royal Faculty of Procurators in Glasgow; Knight, Order of St. Lazarus; Member, Merchants House of Glasgow; Member, Incorporation of Tailors, Glasgow; Member, Incorporation of Gardeners, Glasgow; Chairman, Scottish Senior Citizens Unity Party; President, Glasgow South East Health Forum; Honorary Fellow, Royal Incorporation of Architects in Scotland; awarded Scottish Tourist Board Silver Thistle Award, 1999. Recreations: enjoying the arts; reading; watching TV; football. Address: 2 Tanera Avenue, Glasgow G44 5BU.

Lamb, Caroline. Chief Executive, NHS Education for Scotland, since 2015. Educ. King's College London. Trained as a Chartered Accountant with KPMG, working with clients including Castle Cement, Citibank, Nestle and the International Committee of the Red Cross in Geneva. Qualified as a Chartered Accountant, then moved to Scotland and became Director of Finance, Edinvar Housing Association; Director of Finance, then University Secretary and Director of Operations, University of Abertay Dundee; joined NHS Education for Scotland in 2004 as Director of Finance and Corporate Resources and Deputy Chief Executive. Trustee of Circle, a Scottish Charity working with families affected by parental substance abuse and imprisonment; Non Executive Director of Tabula Rasa, a Scottish Dance Company. Address: NHS Education for Scotland, Westport 102, West Port, Edinburgh EH3 9DN. E-mail: caroline.lamb@nes.scot.nhs.uk

Lambert, Marc, MA (Hons). Chief Executive, Scottish Book Trust, since 2002. Educ. Uppingham School, Leicestershire; University of Edinburgh. Sales Representative, Penguin Books, 1990-95; Interpretation Officer, The Fruitmarket Gallery, 1995-2000; Assistant Director, Edinburgh International Book Festival, 2000-02. Address: (b.) Sandeman House, Trunk's Close, 55 High Street, Edinburgh EH1 1SR; T.-0131 524 0160.

Lambie, David, BSc (Hons), DipEd, FEIS. Retired MP (Labour), Cunninghame South (1970-92); b. 13.7.25, Saltcoats; m., Netta Merrie; 1 s.; 4 d. Educ. Ardrossan Academy; Glasgow University; Geneva University. Teacher, Glasgow Corporation, 1950-70. Secretary, All Party Committee for Energy Studies, 1980-92; chaired Select Committee on Scottish Affairs, 1981-87; UK Member, Council of Europe and Western European Union, 1987-92; Chairman, PLP Aviation Committee, 1988-92; Chairman, Saltcoats Labour Party, 1992-96. Recreation: watching junior football. Address: (h.) 11 Ivanhoe Drive, Saltcoats, Ayrshire KA21 6LS; T.-01294 464843.

Lamont, D. Murray, BA, MHCIMA (Dip), MSIM, ACIM. Honorary Sheriff, Wick; Hotelier; Company Director; Proprietor: Mackays Hotel Wick, Bin Ends, The Fine Wine Shops, since 1995; b. 1.9.57, Wick, Caithness; 1 d. Educ. Wick High School; Abertay University. Purchased and developed Mackays Hotel; started and developed Bin Ends, The Fine Wine Shops; started and developing, Ebenezer Leisure Ltd. Chairman, Wick Branch RNLI; Director: The Highland

Tourism Operators Group, The Scottish Licensed Trade Benevolent Society. T.-01955 602678; e-mail: murray@mackayshotel.co.uk

Lamont, Johann, MA (Hons). MSP (Labour), Glasgow region, since 2016 (Glasgow Pollok, 1999-2016); Leader, Scottish Labour Party, 2011-14; Deputy Leader of The Labour Party in The Scottish Parliament, 2008-2011; Deputy Minister for Justice, 2006-07; Deputy Minister for Communities, 2004-06; Convener, Communities Committee, 2001-04 (former Deputy Convener, Local Government Committee); b. 1957, Glasgow; m.; 1 s.; 1 d. Educ. Woodside Secondary School; Glasgow University; Jordanhill College of Education; Strathclyde University. Former teacher. Address: (b.) Scottish Parliament, Edinburgh EH99 1SP; T.-0131-348 5846.

Lamont, John. MSP (Conservative), Ettrick, Roxburgh and Berwickshire, since 2011, Roxburgh and Berwickshire, 2007-2011; Shadow Cabinet Secretary for Justice, 2010-2011; Chief Whip and Business Manager, since 2011; b. 15.4.76, Irvine. Educ. Kilwinning Academy, Ayrshire; Glasgow University. Solicitor: Brodies, 2005-07, Freshfields, London, 2000-04, Bristows, London, 2004-05. Recreations: running; swimming; cycling; cooking; ironman triathlons. Address: (h.) 63 High Street, Coldstream TD12 4DL; (b.) 25 High Street, Hawick TD9 9BU; Scottish Parliament, Edinburgh EH99 1SP; T.-0131 348 6533 or 01450 375948.
E-mail: john.lamont.msp@scottish.parliament.uk

Lamont-Brown, Raymond, JP, MA, FSA Scot. Author and Broadcaster; Lecturer, Centre for External Services, St. Andrews University, 1978-98, Centre for Continuing Education, Dundee University, 1988-98; Founder, Japan Research Projects, since 1965; b. 20.9.39, Horsforth, Leeds; m., Dr. Elizabeth Moira McGregor. Educ. Wheelwright Grammar School, Dewsbury; Bradford Technical College; SOAS; Nihon Daigaku, Japan. Honorary Secretary/Treasurer, Society of Authors in Scotland, 1982-89; Past President, St. Andrews Rotary Club; Vice-Chairman, St. Andrews Community Council, 1988-91; Chairman, Arthritis Care Liaison Committee (Central, Fife and Tayside), 1991-97; Member, Council, Arthritis Care, 1991-97. Publications: 60 published books, including Discovering Fife; Phantoms of the Sea; The Life and Times of Berwick-upon-Tweed; The Life and Times of St. Andrews; Royal Murder Mysteries; Scottish Epitaphs; Scottish Superstitions; Scottish Traditions and Festivals; Famous Scots; Scottish Witchcraft; Around St. Andrews; Scottish Folklore; Kamikaze: Japan's Suicide Samurai; Scotland of 100 Years Ago; Kempeitai: Japan's Dreaded Military Police; Edward VII's Last Loves; Tutor to the Dragon Emperor; John Brown; Royal Poxes and Potions; Ships from Hell; Fife in History and Legend; Villages of Fife; Humphry Davy; Andrew Carnegie; St Andrews: City by the Northern Sea; How Fat Was Henry VIII? Address: (h.) 76T Strathern Road, Broughty Ferry, Dundee DD5 1PH; T.-01382 732032.

Lancaster, Colin, LLB, MSc, PhD. Chief Executive, Scottish Legal Aid Board, since 2015. Educ. University of Edinburgh. Deputy Chief Executive and Director of Policy and Development, Scottish Legal Aid Board, 2014-15. Address: The Scottish Legal Aid Board, Thistle House, 91 Haymarket Terrace, Edinburgh EH12 5HE; T.-0131 226 7061.

Lander, Ronald, OBE, BSc, FIET, FScotvec, FSQA. Chairman, Extra Mile Studios Ltd, since April 2013; Chairman and Managing Director, Scotlander Ltd (formerly plc), 1985-2011; Director: Logical Innovations Ltd., 2001-2010, Pyramid Research and Development Ltd., 2000-06, Young Enterprise Scotland, 1998-2001; Director and Chairman, Armadale Tech. Ltd., 2007-2010; b. 5.8.42, Glasgow; m., Elizabeth Stirling; 2 s. Educ. Allan Glen's School; Glasgow University. Chairman and Managing Director, Lander Grayburn & Co. Limited, 1970-83; Deputy Managing Director, Lander Alarm Company (Scotland) Limited, 1975-79; Managing Director, Lander Alarms Limited and Lander Alarms (Scotland) Limited, 1979-85; Chairman, Lander & Jess Limited, 1983-87; Director, Centre for Entrepreneurial Development, Glasgow University, 1985-88; Chairman, Newstel Information Ltd., 1998-99; Member, CBI Scottish Council, 1977-83, 1984-90 and 1992-98; (founding) Chairman, CBI Scotland's Smaller Firms' Working Group, 1977-80; founding Chairman, Entrepreneurial Exchange, 1995-96; founder Member, CBI Industrial Policy Committee, London, 1978-86; Chairman, CBI Scotland Smaller Firms' Committee, 1993-95; Chairman, Scottish Fire Prevention Council, 1979-80; Member, Glasgow University Appointments Committee, since 1979; CBI Representative, Home Office/CBI/TUC Joint Committee on Prison Industries, 1980-87; Industrial Member, Understanding British Industry, Scotland, 1981-89; Member, Council, Scottish Business School, 1982-87; Director, British Security Industry Association Council, 1984-85; Governor, Scottish Sports Aid Foundation, 1985-88; Member: Kincraig Committee (review of parole system and related matters), 1987-89, Manpower Services Committee for Scotland (later the Training Agency), 1987-88; founder Chairman, Local Employer Network (LENS) Scottish Co-ordinating Committee, 1987; Chairman, CBI Scotland Education and Training Committee, 1987-89; Director, SCOTVEC, 1987-93; Member, CBI Business/Education Task Force (the Cadbury Report), 1988; Member, Scottish Consultative Council on the Curriculum, 1988-91; Vice-Convener, Scottish Education/Industry Committee, 1988-91; Founder Member, Glasgow Action, 1985-91; Member, Secretary of State for Scotland's Crime Prevention Committee, 1984-87; Companion IEE, 1986; Board Member, Glasgow Development Agency, 1991-99; Visiting/Honorary Professor, Glasgow University, 1991-2007; National Judge, National Training Awards, 1989-92; Board Member, Glasgow Science Centre, 1999-2007; Director, Picardy Media Group Plc, 1998-2001.
E-mail: regx@ronlander.com

Lang of Monkton, Baron (Ian Bruce Lang), DL, PC, OStJ, BA. Life Peer; Deputy Lieutenant, Ayrshire and Arran, since 1998; President of the Board of Trade, 1995-97; Company Directorships including: Chairman, Marsh & McLennan Companies Inc., Director, Charlemagne Capital Ltd.; Chairman, Patrons of the National Galleries of Scotland, 1999-2006; b. 27.6.40, Glasgow; m., Sandra Caroline Montgomerie; 2 d. Educ. Lathallan School; Rugby School; Sidney Sussex College, Cambridge. MP (Conservative) Galloway and Upper Nithsdale, 1983-97 (Galloway, 1979-83); Member, Select Committee on Scottish Affairs, 1979-81; Trustee, Glasgow Savings Bank and West of Scotland TSB, 1969-82; Scottish Whip, 1981-83; Lord Commissioner of HM Treasury, 1983-86; Vice-Chairman, Scottish Conservative Party, 1983-87; Parliamentary Under Secretary of State, Scottish Office, 1986-87, and at Department of Employment, 1986; Minister of State, Scottish Office, 1987-90; Secretary of State for Scotland, 1990-95. Chairman, The Prime Minister's Advisory Committee on Business Appointments, 2009-2014; Member, House of Lords Select Committee on the Constitution, 2000-05 and since 2012, Chairman, since 2014; Member, Special Committee on the Barnett Formula, 2009; Member, Queen's Bodyguard for Scotland (Royal Company of Archers), since 1974; Governor, Rugby School, 1997-2007; President, Association for the Protection of Rural Scotland, 1998-2001; Hon. President, St. Columba's School, Kilmacolm, 1999-2008. Publication:

Blue Remembered Years, 2002. Address (b.) House of Lords, Westminster, London SW1A 0PW.

Lang, Dr Brian Andrew, MA. PhD. Chairman, Edinburgh World Heritage Trust, since 2015; Chairman, RSNO, 2008-2015; Principal and Vice-Chancellor, St Andrews University, 2001-08; b. 2.12.45; 2 s.; 1 d.; m., Tari. Educ. Royal High School, Edinburgh; Edinburgh University. Social anthropology research, Kenya, 1969-70; Lecturer, Social Anthropology, Aarhus University, 1971-75; Scientific Staff, SSRC, 1976-79; Secretary, Historic Buildings Council for Scotland, 1979-80; Secretary, National Heritage Memorial Fund, 1980-87; Director, Public Affairs, National Trust, 1987-91; Chief Executive and Deputy Chairman, British Library, 1991-2000; Chairman, European National Libraries Forum, 1993-2000; Chair, Heritage Image Partnership, 2000-02; Board Member, Scottish Enterprise Fife, 2003-08; Dr hc, University of Edinburgh, 2008; Hon LLD, University of St. Andrews, 2008; Member: Library and Information Services Council (England), 1991-94, Library and Information Commission, 1995-2000, Council, St. Leonards School, St Andrews, 2001-08; FRSE, 2006; Visiting Professor, Napier University, Edinburgh, since 1999; Visiting Scholar, Getty Institute, Los Angeles, California, 2000; Pforzheimer Lecture, University of Texas, 1998; Trustee: 21st Century Learning Initiative, 1995-99, Hopetoun House Preservation Trust, 2001-05; Deputy Chair, National Heritage Memorial Fund, 2005-2011; Member, Council, National Trust for Scotland, 2001-04; President, Institute of Information Scientists, 1993-94 (Hon. Fellow, 1994); Hon. FLA, 1997; Chairman of Trustees, Newbattle Abbey College, 2004-08; Member: Committee for Scotland, Heritage Lottery Fund, 2004-2011 (Chair, 2005-2011), Cultural Commission, 2004-05; Trustee, National Museums of Scotland, since 2014. Publications: numerous articles and contributions to professional journals. Recreations: music; museums and galleries; pottering. Address: (b.) 4 Manor Place, Edinburgh EH3 7DD; T.-0131 260 9617; e-mail: brian@lang-uk.com

Lang, Professor Chim, MD, FRCP, FRCPE. Professor of Cardiology, University of Dundee, since 2004; Consultant Cardiologist, Ninewells Hospital and Medical School, Dundee, since 2004; b. 12.10.60, Kuala Lumpur, Malaysia; m., Anna-Maria Choy; 2 s.; 1 d. Educ. Kingswood School, Bath; University of Dundee. Lecturer, University of Dundee, 1990-93; Merck International Fellow in Clinical Pharmacology, Vanderbilt University, USA, 1993-96; Professor of Medicine and Deputy Dean, University of Malaya, 1996-2004. Fulbright Scholar, Columbia University, USA, 2001-02; Editor-in-Chief, Cardiovascular Therapeutics; Associate-Editor, Heart; Associate Editor, Clinical Science. Recreations: travel; reading. Address: (b.) Division of Cardiovascular and Diabetes Medicine, Ninewells Hospital and Medical School, Dundee DD1 9SY; T.-01382 383283; e-mail: c.c.lang@dundee.ac.uk

Lang, Stephen, MBChB, FRCPath. Consultant Histopathologist, Ninewells Hospital, Dundee, since 1990; Clinical Leader, Pathology, NHS Tayside, 2013-15; Honorary Senior Lecturer in Histopathology, University of Dundee, since 1990; Associate, General Medical Council; b. 19.9.58, Glasgow; m., Dorothy; 2 s.; 1 d. Educ. Holy Cross High School, Hamilton; Glasgow University. RAF Medical Officer, 1982-87 (RAF Leuchars, 1982-83, RAF Halton, 1983-87); Lecturer/Honorary Senior Registrar in Histopathology, St. Bartholomew's Hospital and The Hospital for Sick Children, Great Ormond Street, London, 1987-90. Recreations: football; golf; cinema; theatre. Address: 56 Wyvis Road, Broughty Ferry, Dundee DD5 3SU; T.-01382 800886; e-mail: stephen.lang@nhs.net

Lang, Tari. Corporate, Reputation and Leadership Adviser, The Lang Consultancy, since 2008; b. 18.06.51,

Prague, Czech; 1 s.; 1 d.; m., Dr. Brian Lang. Educ. St. Theresa, Jakarta, Indonesia; Roehampton Institute (London University). Managing Director, The Rowland Company, 1988-95; UK CEO, Edelman Public Relations Worldwide, 1995-2002; Founder Partner, ReputationInc, 2002-08. Board of National Theatre of Scotland; Edinburgh International Festival; Board of Trustees, National Galleries of Scotland; Nominations Council, Women of Achievement, London. Recreations: cinema; theatre; music; travelling. Address: 4 Manor Place, Edinburgh EH3 7DD; T.-0131 260 9617; e-mail: tari@lang-uk.com

Langley, Crawford James, LLB (Hons), BD, DPA, ACIS, NP. Senior Depute Returning Officer, Aberdeen Constituencies, since 1996; Corporate Director for Legal and Democratic Services, Aberdeen City Council, 2002-06 (Director of Legal and Corporate Services, 1995-2002); Advocate in Aberdeen; b. 21.11.51, Glasgow; m., Janette Law Hamilton (deceased); m. (2), Judith Cripps. Educ. Bellahouston Academy, Glasgow; Glasgow University. Legal apprentice, Corporation of Glasgow, 1973-75; various legal posts, Strathclyde Regional Council, 1975-89, Principal Solicitor, 1984-89; Depute Director of Law and Administration, Tayside Regional Council, 1989-91; Director of Law and Administration, Tayside Regional Council, 1991-95. Recreation: travel. Address: (h.) "Canouan", Eassie, Angus DD8 1SG.
E-mail: c.j.langley@btinternet.com

Lascarides, Professor Alex, BSc, PhD. Professor, University of Edinburgh, since 2010; b. 2.9.63, London. Educ. NHEHS; University of Durham; University of Edinburgh. Address: (b.) School of Informatics, University of Edinburgh, 10 Crichton Street, Edinburgh EH8 9AB.

Lauder-Frost, Gregory MacLennan Scholey, BA (Hons) Modern History (Oxon), PhD (London). Director, Focus Inc Ltd., 2006-2014, Company Secretary, 1996-2005; Editor, The Scottish Genealogist, 2004-07; Clerk to Foulden Mordington & Lamberton Community Council, 2002-2011, elected councillor since 2010, Chairman, since 2012; b. 8.8.51; m. (1); Joanna Margaret nee Pecka, 1981, London (div. 1987); 1 d.; m. (2); Sarah-Jane nee Gladstone, 1998, London; 2 d. Educ. Oxford; Sydney; London. Certified Public Accountant, 1975, Certificate in Business Management, Oxford Centre for Management Studies, Oxon, 1976. Manager/auditor for EMI Ltd., 1975-76; administration, Westminster Hospital, 1977; Executive Officer, Medical Research Council, 1978; senior administrator (finance), NHS, 1979-92; Company Director, Korostovetz (Russia) Ltd., 1991-93; Company Director, UK Books (Export) Ltd., 1992-95; Company Secretary, Mediterranean Entertainments Ltd., 1994-96. Fellow, Royal Commonwealth Society, 1971-2008; Fellow, Society of Antiquaries (Scotland), since 1989; Member, Society of Genealogists, London, since 1977; Life Member (2003), Order of the Crown of Charlemagne; Member: The Freedom Association, 1976-80, The Primrose League, 1977-93; Life Member (Jan. 1977), The International Monarchist League, and subsequently its Publications Officer, 1987-92 and Secretary-General, 1990-91; Member, 1977-92, Conservative Monday Club, and subsequently Secretary (1987) & Chairman (1988-92) of its Foreign Affairs Committee, & Club Political Secretary (1989-92); Ward Secretary & Executive Council Member of the Chelsea Conservative Association, 1977-84; Member (1986-88) and Patron & Executive Council Member (1988-92) Roxburgh & Berwickshire Conservative Association; Member (1981-) & of the Governing Council (since Feb. 2002, Chairman, since 2015), Scottish Genealogy Society, Edinburgh; Member, Ministerial Vacancy Committee, St. Columba's Church of Scotland, 2000; Governor (1985-92), RNLI's Shoreline group; Member, Travellers Club, London, 1988-92; Vice-President, The Western Goals Institute, 1989-2000; Vice President, The Traditional

Britain Group, since 2001; Member: Borders Family History Society, since 1994 (Council, 2004-2012, Acting Editor, 2005-06, Honorary Secretary, since 2013), Council, Berwickshire Civic Society, 2001-2013 (Vice-Chairman, 2011-13), The Architectural Heritage Society of Scotland, The Scottish Record Society (Hon. Treasurer, 2011-14), The Scottish Heraldry Society, The Royal Stuart Society, The Church Society, The Foundation for Medieval Genealogy, since 2002, The Harleian Society, The Swinton Circle, The Conservative Democratic Alliance (Founder Member), 2002-08, United Kingdom Independence Party (UKIP), 2003-2013; Chairman, the Friends of Chirnside Surgery, Berwickshire (2010). Publications: Editor and contributor, Harry Lauder in the Limelight by William Wallace, 1988; major articles in numerous journals and magazines including European Dawn, The Monarchist League Newsletter, The Scottish Genealogist, The Borders Family History Society Magazine, East Lothian Life, and The Double Tressure; several genealogical articles on the famous Electric Scotland website. TV appearances: BBC's Newsnight (opposing Labour MP Alice Mahon's support for Communist insurgents in Central America), 1990, with Enoch Powell (on the EU etc.), 1990; RTV (on Ulster problems); Sky TV News (on the monarchy's hopes in Russia), 1990; Central TV Live (on the media), Birmingham 1990, BBC's Kilroy (on working mothers), 1991; BBC's Bookmark programme Dostoevsky's Travels, 1991; Channel 4's White Tribe debate, 2000; BBC's Weakest Link, 2003; BBC Scotland's Something About Harry (Lauder), 2005; BBC's Newsnight, 2013; BBC Radio 5, 2013. Recreations: riding; walking; reading; classical music; travel; historical and political writing. Clubs: The Lansdowne, Mayfair, W1. Address: The Old School House, Mordington, Berwickshire TD15 1XA; T.-01289 386779; e-mail: lauderfrost@btinternet.com

Laurie, Thomas, OBE, FRICS. Proprietor, Laurie Consultancy Group; former Trustee, Scottish Civic Trust; Trustee, Glasgow City Heritage Trust; b. 11.11.38, Wishaw; m., Jennifer Rose Dunthorne; 1 s.; 2 d. Educ. Hamilton Academy; Glasgow Technical College. Partner, Robert H. Soper & Co., Cumbernauld, 1964-77; Sole Principal, Thomas Laurie Associates, Cumbernauld and Glasgow, 1977-90; Senior Partner, Keillor Laurie Martin Partnership, 1990-2000. Founder Member, Cumbernauld Theatre Group, 1961; Board Member: Cottage Theatre, Cumbernauld, 1964-72, Traverse Theatre, 1972-76 (Chairman); Co-founded the Glasgow Theatre Group (later to become the Tron Theatre); former Chairman, WASPS; Trustee of the Church Buildings Renewal Trust; Vice Chairman, St. Andrews In The Square Trust (Glasgow Centre for Scottish Culture), since 2000; Member: Drama Panel, Scottish Arts Council, 1973-82, SAC, 1976-82; Director of Source2, new restaurant complex at Hughenden, Glasgow; Chairman, Clutha Trust. Singing tutor at Scottish Music School in Barga, Tuscany. Recreations: traditional singing; all forms of art appreciation; hill-walking. Address: (h.) 19B Hughenden Gardens, Glasgow G12 9XZ; T.-0141-338 6822.

Law, Chris. MP (SNP), Dundee West, since 2015. Trained as a French Chef and then went on to University where he received a degree in Cultural and Social Anthropology; operated a tourism business providing tours of the Himalayas on 1950's motorcycles; operated a business as a financial advisor in Dundee for the past 10 years. Address: House of Commons, London SW1A 0AA.

Law, Professor Derek, MA, DUniv, FLA, FInfSc, FKC, FRSE, FCLIP. Emeritus Professor, University of Strathclyde; b. 19.6.47, Arbroath; m., Jacqueline Anne; 2 d. Educ. Arbroath High School, George Watson's College, Edinburgh; University of Glasgow. Assistant Librarian, St.

Andrews University, 1970-77; Sub Librarian, Edinburgh University, 1977-81; Librarian, Erskine Medical Library, 1981-83; Director of Automation, Edinburgh University Library, 1983-84; King's College, London: Librarian, 1984-93, Director of Information Services, 1993-98; Librarian and Head of Information Resource Directorate, University of Strathclyde, 1998-2008; former Chair, JISC Advance. Barnard Prize for Informatics, 1993; IFLA Medal, 2003. Hon. Doctorate, University of Paris. Publications: Royal Navy in World War Two; The Battle of the Atlantic; Networking and the Future of Libraries; Digital Libraries. Address: (b.) Alexander Turnbull Building, 155 George Street, Glasgow G1 1RD; T.-0141-548 4997; e-mail: d.law@strath.ac.uk

Law, Professor Robin C. C., BA, PhD, FRHS, FBA, FRSE. Emeritus Professor of African History, University of Stirling; b. 7.8.44, Chester. Educ. Southend-on-Sea High School; Balliol College, University of Oxford; Centre of West African Studies, Birmingham. Research Assistant in African History, University of Lagos, Nigeria, 1966-69; Research Fellow in West African History, University of Birmingham, 1970-72; University of Stirling: Lecturer in History, 1972-78, Senior Lecturer, 1978-83, Reader, 1983-93, Professor, 1993-2009. Editor, Journal of African History, 1974-82, 1991-95; Series Editor, Hakluyt Society, 1998-2003. Publications: The Oyo Empire c.1600-c.1836, 1977; The Horse in West African History, 1980; The Slave Coast of West Africa, 1550-1750, 1991; The Kingdom of Allada, 1997; The Biography of Mahommah Gardo Baquaqua (Co-author), 2001; Ouidah: The social history of a West African slaving 'port', 1727-1892, 2004. Address: (b.) School of Arts and Humanities, University of Stirling, Stirling FK9 4LA; e-mail: r.c.c.law@stir.ac.uk

Lawrence, Professor Andrew, BSc, PhD, FRAS, FRSE. Regius Professor of Astronomy, Edinburgh University, since 1994, Head of Physics, 2004-08; b. 23.4.54, Margate; partner, Debbie Ann Capel; 3 s.; 1 d. Educ. Chatham House Grammar School, Ramsgate; Edinburgh University; Leicester University. Exchange Scientist, Massachusetts Institute of Technology, 1980-81; Senior Research Fellow, Royal Greenwich Observatory, 1981-84; Research Assistant, then SERC Advanced Fellow, School of Mathematical Sciences, Queen Mary College, London, 1984-89; Lecturer, Physics Department, Queen Mary and Westfield College, London, 1989-94. Visiting Physicist, Stanford, 2008-09. Publications: over 100 in learned journals. Recreations: painting electrons and teasing publishers; acting. Address: (b.) Institute for Astronomy, Edinburgh University, Royal Observatory, Blackford Hill, Edinburgh.

Lawrie, Kenneth, MBA, MA (Econ). Chief Executive, Midlothian Council, since 2009. Educ. St Andrews University; Strathclyde University. Held senior positions with Dartford Borough Council and Scottish Borders Council. Address: (b.) 2 Midlothian House, 40-46 Buccleuch Street, Dalkeith EH22 1DJ; T.-0131 270 7500.

Lawrie, Nigel Gilbert, OBE, BSc, PhD. Formerly Head of Service, Department of Education Services, Inverclyde Council (retired); b. 2.6.47, Edinburgh; m., Janet Clark Warnock; 1 d. Educ. Bearsden Academy; Strathclyde University. Chemistry Teacher, Hermitage Academy, Helensburgh, 1972-75; Principal Teacher of Chemistry, Dunoon Grammar School, 1975-81; Assistant Head Teacher, Garnock Academy, 1981-84; Depute Head Teacher, Castlehead High School, Paisley, 1984-85; Head Teacher, Port Glasgow High School, 1985-2004. President, Headteachers' Association of Scotland, 1998-99; Member: Scottish Examination Board, 1994-97, Board, SCOTVEC,

1995-97, Board, SQA, 1997-99. Recreations: reading; gardening; football; golf. Address: (h.) 6 Cunningham Drive, Largs, Ayrshire.

Lawrie, Paul, MBE, OBE. Professional golfer; b.1.1.69, Aberdeen; m., Marian; 2 s. Assistant, Banchory; turned professional, 1986; Winner, UAP Under 25s Championship, 1992; Winner, Open Golf Championship, 1999. Honorary law doctorate, Robert Gordon University; Honorary Life Member, European Tour. Recreations: snooker; Aberdeen Football Club; cars.

Lawson, Isobel, FFCS. Director/Company Secretary, Stepping Stones for Families, since 1988; Board Member, Childcare First Paisley Partnership; Member, Scottish Government's Early Years Task Force subgroup; b. Paisley; 2 d. Training and consultancy, voluntary sector childcare/education development. Address: (b.) Studio 3003A, Mile End Mill, Paisley PA1 1JS.

Lawson, John Philip, MBE, BSc, FEIS. Honorary President, Scottish Youth Hostels Association, since 2001 (Chairman, 1980-2001); Headteacher, St. Joseph's School, Linlithgow, 1974-94; b. 19.8.37, Bathgate; m., Diana Mary Neal. Educ. St. Mary's Academy, Bathgate; Edinburgh University; Moray House College of Education. Teacher, West Lothian, 1962-94; held various offices in the Educational Institute of Scotland, including President, West Lothian Local Association and Chairman, Lothian Regional Executive; Member, West Lothian Children's Panel, 1972-81; Member, SYHA National Executive, since 1966; Vice-Chairman, SYHA, 1975-80; awarded: Richard Schirrmann Medal by German Youth Hostels Association, 1988, Gezel van de Rugzak, Flemish Youth Hostels Association, 1993; a Director, Scottish Rights of Way Society Ltd., since 1979; a Director, Gatliff Hebridean Hostels Trust, since 1988, Hon. Treasurer, since 2006; President, West Lothian Headteachers Association, 1986-88; President, Federation of Youth Hostels Associations in the European Community, 1990-2001; Vice-President and Board Member, International Youth Hostel Federation, 1994-2002; Member, The Gatliff Trust, since 2003; Vice President, Scottish Rights of Way and Access Society, since 2009. Recreations: hill-walking; travel; music; reading. Address: (h.) Ledmore, Carnbee, Anstruther KY10 2RU; T.-01333 720312.

Lawson, Lilian Keddie, OBE, BSc (Hons), MBA. Formerly Director, Scottish Council on Deafness (2000-2014); b. 23.2.49, Pittenweem; m., John McDonald Young (deceased); 2 d. Educ. Donaldson's School, Edinburgh; Mary Hare Grammar School, Newbury; Edinburgh University; Strathclyde University. Administrative Assistant, progressing to Head of Administration, British Deaf Association, 1981-92; Manager, Sign Language Interpreting Services, Strathclyde Regional Council, 1992-93; Director, RNID Scotland, 1993-2000. Publication: Words in Hand (Co-Author), 1984. Recreations: gardening; genealogy; travel; her children.

Lawson, Peter A., LLB (Hons), DipLP. Partner, Burness Paull LLP, since 2001; b. 20.7.70, Edinburgh; m., Andrea; 2 d.; 1 s. Educ. Dunfermline High School; Edinburgh University. Trainee, Burness LLP, 1994-96, Assistant, 1996-98; Associate, Freshfields Bruckhaus Deringer, 1998-2001. Recreation: sport. Address: (b.) 50 Lothian Road, Edinburgh EH3 9WJ; T.-0131 473 6108.
E-mail: peter.lawson@burnesspaull.com

Lawson, Peter John, LLB, NP. Chairman, Scottish Opera; Solicitor; Partner, Hill Brown, Glasgow, since 1990; b. 25.3.58, Visakapatnam, India. Educ. Glasgow University. Director, Raindog TV Ltd; Director, NVA Europe; Chairman, St Peter's Kilmahew Ltd (arts organisation spearheading the restoration and development of the former St Peter's Seminary and grounds in Cardross); former Committee Member, BAFTA Scotland. Recreations: theatre; travel. Address: (b.) Hill Brown, 3 Newton Place, Glasgow G3 7PU; T.-0141-332 3265.
E-mail: plawson@hillbrown.co.uk

Laybourn, Professor Peter John Robert, MA (Cantab), PhD, FIET, FRSE. Professor of Electronic Engineering, Glasgow University, since 1985, now Emeritus; b. 30.7.42, London; m., Ann Elizabeth Chandler; 2 d. Educ. William Hulme's Grammar School; Bristol Grammar School; Clare College, Cambridge. Research Assistant, Leeds University, 1963-66; Research Fellow, Southampton University, 1966-71; Lecturer, then Senior Lecturer, then Reader, Glasgow University, 1971-85. Recreations: sailing; boat-building; tree collecting. Address: (h.) Gregory Green, Gregory Lane, St Andrews; T.-013344 72520.

Layden, Patrick John, QC, TD, LLB (Hons). Commissioner, Scottish Law Commission, 2008-2014; Deputy Solicitor, Scottish Government Legal Directorate, 2003-08; Legal Secretary to the Lord Advocate, 1999-2003; b. 27.6.49, Edinburgh; m., Patricia Mary Bonnar; 3 s.; 1 d. Educ. Holy Cross Academy, Edinburgh; University of Edinburgh. Scottish Bar, 1973-77; Junior Legal Secretary/Assistant Parliamentary Counsel, Lord Advocate's Department, 1977-83; Assistant Legal Secretary and Scottish Parliamentary Counsel, 1983-99. University of Edinburgh OTC, 1967-71; 2/52 Lowland Vol., 1971-77; 1/51 Highland Vol., 1977-81 (O.C., London Scottish, 1978-81); O.C., 73 Ord. Co. (V), 1981-84. Recreations: walking; reading.

Lazarowicz, Mark, MA, LLB, DipLP. MP, Edinburgh North and Leith, 2001-2015 (Member, Environmental Audit Committee, 2005-2015; previously Member of Scottish Affairs; Environmental, Food and Rural Affairs; Modernisation; Regulatory Reform Committees); Shadow Minister for International Development, 2010-2011; Advocate; b. 8.8.53. Educ. St. Andrews University; Edinburgh University. Member, Edinburgh District Council, 1980-96: Leader of the Council, 1986-93, Chairperson, Labour Group, 1993-94; Member, City of Edinburgh Council, 1999-2001 (Executive Member for Transport, 2000-01, Convenor, Transportation Committee, 1999-2000); Deputy Leader, COSLA Labour Group, 1990-93; Vice-Chairperson, 1988-89, Chairperson, 1989-90, Scottish Labour Party; Founder Member and Board Member, Centre for Scottish Public Policy, 1990-2009; Chairperson, Edinburgh International Conference Centre Ltd., 1992-93; Chairperson, Edinburgh Tourist Board, 1993-94.

Lea, Judith Verna, LLB, DipL, MBA, MSc. Clerk to the Scottish Solicitors Discipline Tribunal, since 2001; Immigration Judge, since 2001; b. 7.1.60, Exeter; m.; 2 s.; 1 d. Educ. Bridge of Don Academy, Aberdeen; Aberdeen University; Dundee University; Napier University. Trainee Solicitor and Solicitor in Private Practice; Senior Legal Assistant with North East Fife District Council; District Court Manager and Legal Adviser with Dundee City Council. Address: (b.) Unit 3.5, The Granary Business Centre, Cupar, Fife KY15 5YQ; T.-01334 659088; e-mail: enquiries@ssdt.org.uk

Lederer, Peter J., CBE. Chairman, Gleneagles Hotels Limited, 2007-2014, Managing Director and General Manager, 1984-2007; Chairman: VisitScotland, 2001-2010, One and All Foundation, Hamilton & Inches Ltd, Taste Communications; Chairman of Trustees, International Futures Foundation; Non-Executive Director: Baxters Food Group Ltd, Pod Global Solutions Ltd; Chairman,

Applecrate Limited; b. 30.11.50; m., Marilyn Ruth MacPhail. Four Seasons Hotels, Canada, 1972-79; Vice President, Wood Wilkings Ltd., Toronto, 1979-81; General Manager, Plaza Group of Hotels, Toronto, 1981-83. Patron, Hospitality Industry Trust Scotland; Freeman, City of London; FHCIMA; Master Innholder; Liveryman, Worshipful Company of Innholders. Address: (b.) 18, Great Stuart Street, Edinburgh EH3 7TN.

Ledingham, Professor Iain McAllan, MSc (Hons), MD (Hons), FRCS (Ed), FRCP (Ed, Glas), FInstBiol, FCCM, DMI (RCSEd), FFICM, FRSE. Professor Emeritus of Medical Education, University of Dundee; formerly Consultant, Middle East Affairs, Royal College of Surgeons of Edinburgh; Special Adviser, University of Durham; b. 26.2.35, Glasgow; m., Eileen; 3 s. Educ. King's Park Senior Secondary, Glasgow; Central School, Aberdeen; University of Glasgow. Early training in surgery/trauma/intensive care; MRC Senior Research Fellow in hyperbaric medicine; first UK Professor of Intensive Care Medicine, University of Glasgow, 1980; Chair, Intensive Therapy Unit, Western Infirmary, Glasgow, 1985; Foundation Chair, Department of Emergency and Critical Care Medicine, Faculty of Medicine and Health Sciences, United Arab Emirates University, 1988 (Dean, FMHS, 1989). First President, Intensive Care Society, UK; President: European Shock Society, European Society of Intensive Care Medicine; Bellahouston Medal, University of Glasgow; La Médaille de la Ville de Paris; The College Medal (RCSEd). Recreations: jogging; hill-walking; music; reading; tree propagation; woodworking; occasional bad golf. Address: Kir Royale, Westown, by Errol, Perthshire PH2 7SU; T.-01821 670210; e-mail: iml@scotpad.co.uk

Lee, John Richard, MA, PhD. Professor of Digital Media, University of Edinburgh; b. 10.01.58, St. Alban's; m., Rosemary Fawcett; 2 s.; 4 d. Educ. Lochaber High School; University of Edinburgh. Research Associate/Part-time Lecturer, University of Edinburgh, 1985; Lecturer, 1993; Senior Lecturer, 1997; Personal Chair in Digital Media, 2010. Joint appointment in Architecture (now Edinburgh College of Art) and Informatics; Director, Edinburgh Computer-Aided Architectural Design Research Unit (EdCAAD), from 1991; Deputy Director, Human Communication Research Centre, since 1993. Recreations: music; sailing. Address: (b.) School of Informatics, Informatics Forum, 10 Crichton Street, Edinburgh EH8 9AB; T.-0131 650 4420; e-mail J.Lee@ed.ac.uk

Lee, Laura Elizabeth, RGN, MSC, DipN. Chief Executive, Maggie's Cancer Caring Centres, since 1996; b. 15.10.66, Whitbank, South Africa; m., Hani Gabra; 2 s.; 1 d. Educ. Peterhead Academy; Birmingham University. Qualified RGN, 1987; various posts in nursing in cancer care in Edinburgh and London, 1987-91; clinical nurse specialist, Edinburgh Breast Unit, 1991-96. Recreations: reading; running; swimming. Address: (b.) The Stables, Western General Hospital, Crewe Road, Edinburgh, EH4 2XG; T.-0131-537 2456.

Legge, Graham, BEd, MEd. Retired Rector, Aberdeen Grammar School (2004-2015); b. 9.4.56, Buckie. Educ. Buckie High School; Aberdeen University. Teacher of Modern Studies, Speyside High School; Teacher of Geography, Northfield Academy; Assistant Principal Teacher, Hilton Academy; Principal Teacher, Geography, The Gordon Schools, Huntly; Assistant Rector, Aboyne Academy; Depute Rector, Banchory Academy; Rector, Kemnay Academy, 1998-2004. Recreations: hill-walking; travel; gardening.

Leigh, Professor Irene May, CBE (2012), OBE (2006), FRSE, DSc, FRCP, FMedSci. Professor, Cellular and Molecular Medicine, College of Medicine, Dentistry and Nursing, University of Dundee; b. 25.4.47, Liverpool; m. (1), P N Leigh; m. (2), JE Kernthaler; 1 s.; 3 d. Educ. Merchant Taylors' School for Girls, Great Crosby; London Hospital Medical College. Consultant Dermatologist, London Hospital, 1983-2006; Professor of Dermatology, 1989-99, Professor of Cellular and Molecular Medicine, 1999-2006, Research Dean, Barts and London School of Medicine and Dentistry, 1997-2002; Director, CRUK Skin Tumour Laboratory, since 1989; Vice Principal and Head of College of Medicine, Dentistry and Nursing, University of Dundee, 2006-2011. Recreations: grandchildren; music. Address: (b.) Clinical Research Centre, College of Medicine, Dentistry and Nursing, Ninewells Hospital and Medical School, Dundee DD1 9SY.
E-mail: i.m.leigh@dundee.ac.uk

Leighton, Sir John, MA (Hons) Edin, MA, FRSE. Director-General, National Galleries of Scotland, since 2006; b. 22.2.59, Belfast; m., Gillian Keay; 1 s.; 1 d. Educ. Portora Royal School, Enniskillen; University of Edinburgh; Edinburgh College of Art; Courtauld Institute. Lecturer and Tutor, Department of Humanities, Edinburgh College of Art, 1983-86; Curator, 19th-Century Paintings, National Gallery, London, 1986-96; Director, Van Gogh Museum, Amsterdam, 1997-2006. Board Member, De Pont Museum for Contemporary Art, Tilburg, since 1998; Trustee, Mauritshuis, The Hague. Appointed Chevalier in the French Ordre des Arts et des Lettres; numerous exhibitions organised. Publications include (Books and Exhibition Catalogues): Co-Author, Signac 1863-1935, 2001; The Van Gogh Museum: A portrait, 2003; Co-Author, Manet and the Sea, 2003; 100 Masterpieces from the National Galleries of Scotland, 2015. Address: (b.) National Galleries of Scotland, 73 Belford Road, Edinburgh EH4 3DS.

Leighton-Beck, Dr Linda Bryce, PhD, DRM, FHEA, MSc, BEd (Hons). Head of Social Inclusion, Public Health, NHS Grampian, since 2003; Honorary Senior Lecturer, Centre of Academic Primary Care, University of Aberdeen, since 2001; b. 23.5.53, Greenock; m., David; 2 d. Educ. Greenock Academy; Aberdeen University; Purdue University; Dunfermline College of Physical Education (now University of Edinburgh). Teacher of P.E., Strathclyde Regional Council, 1975; Lecturer, Dunfermline College of Physical Education; Assistant Director of Leisure Services, East Lothian District Council; Researcher, Scottish Council for Research in Education; Executive Manager, North of Scotland Health Services Research Network, Aberdeen University; Education Manager (North-North East), Scottish Council for Postgraduate Medical and Dental Education (now NHS Education Scotland); Health Improvement Programme Manager, NHS Grampian. Non-Executive Director, Sportscotland, 2000-08; Member, Board of Directors, Aberdeen Foyer, 2001-09. Recreations: running; badminton; music; cooking. Address: (b.) NHS Grampian, Summerfield House, 2 Eday Road, Aberdeen; T.-01224 558743; e-mail: linda.leighton-beck@nhs.net

Leiper, Joseph, OBE, DL, MA, DipEd, ACII. Rector, Oldmachar Academy, 1984-2004; b. 13.8.41, Aberdeen; m., Moira Taylor; 2d. Educ. Aberdeen Grammar School; Aberdeen University. English Teacher: Robert Gordon's College, 1972-73; Bankhead Academy, 1973-75; Principal Teacher, English, Bankhead Academy, 1975-80; Assistant Rector, 1980-82; Depute Rector, Ellon Academy, 1982-84; Chairman, Aberdeen University Business Committee, General Council, 2000-06; appointed to Court, Aberdeen University, General Council Court Assessor, 2000-08; appointed as Deputy Lieutenant of Aberdeen City, 2005; appointed as part-time Associate Teaching Fellow in the School of Education, University of Aberdeen, 2005-07; appointed Burgess of Guild of Aberdeen City, 2005. Recreations: sailing; reading; walking. Address: (h.) 5 Fairview Place, Bridge of Don, Aberdeen AB22 8ZJ.

Leishman, Brian Archibald Scott, MBE. Regimental Trustee, The Cameronians (Scottish Rifles); b. 16.9.36; 1 s.; 1 d. Educ. Fettes College. Retired Regular Army Officer; commissioned The Cameronians (Scottish Rifles); re-badged on disbandment in 1968 The King's Own Scottish Borderers, service in the Arabian Gulf, East Africa and Europe; Italian Staff College, 1971-73; Assistant Defence Attache, British Embassy, Rome, 1974-76; Edinburgh Military Tattoo, 1977, Business Manager, 1978-98. Scottish Tourist Board Silver Thistle Award, 1996; Box Office Management International (New York) Lifetime Achievement Award, 1997; variously, Event Consultancy and Organisation, Editor, Regimental Journal, The Cameronians (Scottish Rifles), 1983-2004; European co-ordinator, International Ticketing Association (New York), 1998-2003; Board Member, Edinburgh Military Tattoo Ltd/Edinburgh Military Tattoo (Charities) Ltd; Founder Member, Edinburgh Capital Group (Edinburgh Entertains), Ticketing Consultant XIII Commonwealth Games Edinburgh, 1986; Chairman, Edinburgh International Jazz and Blues Festival; Board Member, Edinburgh Tourist Board and Edinburgh and Lothians Tourist Board; Member, Advisory Board, International Festival and Events Association (Europe). Recreations: music; photography. Address: (h.) 61 Northumberland Street, Edinburgh EH3 6JQ; T.-0131 557 0187.
E-mail: Brianleishman@blueyonder.co.uk

Leishman, Marista Muriel, MA. Former Director, The Insite Consultancy for Management and Training; b. 10.4.32, Beaconsfield; m., Murray Leishman; 1 s.; 3 d. Educ. St. George's School, Ascot; St. Andrews University. First Head of Education, National Trust for Scotland, 1979-86; writer: memoir of Sir Jamie Stormonth Darling; (2006); memoir: 'My Father: Reith of the BBC'; 'Clydebuilt' on shipbuilding and commercial development on the River Clyde under Great Grandfather George Reith. Recreations: music; painting; writing; hill-walking. Address: (h.) Lettoch Beag, Killiecrankie PH16 5LR; T.-01796 473 120.

Leitch, Angela. Chief Executive, East Lothian Council, since 2011. Over 25 years experience in local government having started career in human resource management and then gaining experience in a range of services, taking up increasingly senior roles at the same time. Headed up West Lothian Council's corporate support services and change management programmes, developing new models of service delivery in conjunction with partner organisations such as health and the police; Head of Service, the City of Edinburgh Council, responsible for city-wide services and the development of an innovative new neighbourhood management and governance arrangement; Chief Executive, Clackmannanshire Council, 2009-2011. Address: East Lothian Council, John Muir House, Haddington EH41 3HA; T.-01620 827222.

Leitch, Ian, CBE. Chair, Audit Scotland, since 2015; Board Member, Scottish Legal Complaints Commission, since 2014; b. 1949. Career: served as a Depute Chief Executive and council solicitor to a unitary authority in local government; Scottish Parliament: former Director of Resources and Governance, former Assistant Clerk/Chief Executive. Former Justice of the Peace. Address: Audit Scotland, Head Office, 4th Floor, 102 West Port, Edinburgh EH3 9DN; T.-0131 625 1500.

Lenihan, Christine, FRSA. Former Chairman, Lloyds TSB Foundation for Scotland (2009-2014); joined the Foundation's Board of Trustees in June 2005; appointed to the Board of Trustees of Elizabeth Finn Care in 2012;

Member, ESRC advisory group on the Future of Scotland. Career began in the pharmaceutical industry, then started own businesses; the first of which was in 1983; a founder of Cabal Communications (a London based magazine publishing company) in 1998. Served as a University Governor and held a number of non executive directorships, including as Chairman of the Scottish University for Industry, Chairman of NHS24 and Chairman of the Scottish NHS Confederation.
E-mail: christine.lenihan@dial.pipex.com

Lenman, Professor Bruce Philip, MA (Aberdeen), MLitt, LittD (Cantab), FRHistSoc, FRSE. Emeritus Professor of Modern History, St. Andrews University, since 2003 (formerly Professor of Modern History); Honorary Professor, University of Dundee, since 2004; b. 9.4.38, Aberdeen. Educ. Aberdeen Grammar School; Aberdeen University; St. John's College, Cambridge. Assistant Professor, Victoria University, Canada, 1963; Lecturer in Imperial and Commonwealth History, Queen's College, Dundee (St. Andrews University), 1963-67; Lecturer, Dundee University, 1967-72; United College, St. Andrews: Lecturer, Department of Modern History, 1972-78, Senior Lecturer, 1978-83; British Academy Fellow, Newberry Library, Chicago, 1982; John Carter Brown Library Fellow, Brown University, Providence, RI, 1984; Harrison Professor, College of William & Mary, VA, 1988-89; Mayers Fellow, Huntington Library, CA, 1997; Hill Fellow, 2004; Bird Professor, Emory University, Atlanta, GA, 1998. Publications: Esk to Tweed, 1975; An Economic History of Modern Scotland 1660-1976, 1977 (Scottish Arts Council Award); The Jacobite Risings in Britain 1689-1746, 1980 (Scottish Arts Council Award); Scotland 1746-1832, 1981; The Jacobite Clans of the Great Glen 1650-1784, 1984; The Jacobite Cause, 1986; The Jacobite Threat (Co-Author), 1990; The Eclipse of Parliament, 1992; England's Colonial Wars, 2000; Britain's Colonial Wars, 2001; Enlightenment and Change, 2009; Editor, Chambers Dictionary of World History, 1993, 3rd ed., 2005; Military Engineers and the Early Modern State, 2013. Recreations: golf; curling; swimming. Address: (h.) Flat 4, 55 Victoria Place, Stirling FK8 2QT; T.-01786-446090.
E-mail: bruceplenman@yahoo.co.uk

Lennon, Professor Justin John, BSc (Hons), MPhil, PhD. Assistant Vice Principal, Glasgow School for Business and Society, since 2015, Vice Dean, since 2012; Professor of Travel and Tourism Business Development, Glasgow Caledonian University, since 1999, Head of Department, Business Management, since 2011; Specialist Policy Advisor, Visit Scotland, since 2005; Non Executive Director, Historic Scotland, since 2007; b. 19.6.61, Birmingham; m., Joanne Lesley; 2 s.; 1 d. Educ. Central Grammar School, Birmingham; Strathclyde University; Oxford Brookes University. Hotel Management, 1983-94; Hotel and Tourism Consultancy, 1992-97; University of Strathclyde, 1995-98. Director, Scottish Tourism Forum, 2005-08; Board Member, Canadian Tourism Commission European Marketing Group, since 2005. Author of 7 books (Dark Tourism, Tourism Statistics, Benchmarking National Tourism Organisations); over 100 journal articles. Address: (b.) Moffat Centre, Travel and Tourism, Glasgow Caledonian University, Glasgow G4 0BA; T.-0141 331 8400; e-mail: jjle@gcu.ac.uk

Lennon, Cllr Monica, BA (Hons). MSP (Labour), Central region, since 2016. Educ. John Ogilvie High School; University of Strathclyde. Career history: Operator, Motorola, 1999-2001; Graduate Planner, Keppie Design, 2001; Planning Officer, South Lanarkshire Council, 2001-07; Senior Planner, Atkins, 2007; Project Manager, Kier Homes Limited, 2008;

Senior Planner, The Scottish Government, 2008-09; Planning Consultant, MLA Planning and Development, 2008-2011; Chair, Lanarkshire Business Group, 2011-12; Planning Consultant, Knight Frank, 2011-12; External Engagement and Fundraiser, Scottish Labour Party, 2015; Councillor and Depute Chair, Housing and Technical Resources Committee, South Lanarkshire Council, since 2012, represents Hamilton North and East. 2012 Finalist, UK Young Planner of the Year, Royal Town Planning Institute. Address: Scottish Parliament, Edinburgh EH99 1SP.

Leonard, Richard. MSP (Labour), Central Scotland region, since 2016. Labour candidate in the Carrick, Cumnock and Doon Valley constituency for the Scottish Parliament election in 2011. Address: Scottish Parliament, Edinburgh EH99 1SP.

Leonard, Tom. B. 22.8.44, Glasgow; m., Sonya; 2 s. Educ. Lourdes Secondary, Glasgow; Glasgow University. Writer in Residence, Paisley Library, 1986-89; Glasgow University, 1991; Bell College, Hamilton, 1993-95; Professor, Creative Writing, Glasgow University, 2001-09. Publications: Intimate Voices: Poems 1965-83; access to the silence: Reports from the Present; Places of the Mind: The Life of James Thomson ("B.V."); (ed.) Radical Renfrew: Poetry from the French Revolution to the First World War; Outside the Narrative: Poems, 1965-2009; Definite Articles: Prose 1973-2012; (trans.) Brecht: Mother Courage and her Children. Address: 56 Eldon Street, Glasgow G3 6NJ; e-mail: mail@tomleonard.co.uk
web: www.tomleonard.co.uk

Leslie, Sheriff Desmond. Sheriff at Ayr. Served Legal apprenticeship with JNO Shaughnessy Quigley and McColl, Glasgow, 1980-1982; qualified as a solicitor in 1982 working with Lambie & Co, Glasgow as assistant and partner until 2005; appointed Part-time Sheriff in 2005 and appointed full-time as All-Scotland Floating Sheriff in 2006; Resident Sheriff in Ayr, since 2010. Address: Sheriff Court House, Wellington Square, Ayr KA7 1EE; T.-01292 292200.

Leslie Melville, The Hon. Mrs Ruth Jacquelyn, MBE, OstJ. Provost of Angus, 2007-2012 (retired); Independent Councillor, 1989-92 and 1995-2012; b. 7.4.41, Aberdeen; m., The Hon Ronald Jocelyn Leslie Melville (widowed); 4 s. (1 son deceased); 1 d. Educ. Stoneywood Primary School; Inverurie Academy; School for the Blind, Edinburgh. Founder and Vice Chair, Brechin Youth Project (The Attic); District Organiser for Angus, WRVS; Member, then Chair of Tayside Health Council; Founder/Chair, Bel-Aid (Scotland working for The Belarussian Victims of Chernobyl); Founder of The Friends of Stracathro Hospital; Founder/Chair, Brechin Arts Festival; Campaigner for the Saving of Stracathro Hospital; former Non Executive Director, Tayside Health Board (retired); Minister, Esk Congregational Church. Address: 34 Park Road, Brechin, Angus DD9 7AP; T.-01356 625259; m.-07730 884308. E-mail: ruthlm1941@gmail.com

Lessels, Norman, CBE, CA; b. 2.9.38, Edinburgh; m., Christine Stevenson Hitchman; 1 s. Educ. Edinburgh Academy. Partner, Ernst & Whinney, until 1980; Partner, Chiene & Tait, CA, until 1998. President, Institute of Chartered Accountants of Scotland, 1987-88; former Director: Standard Life Assurance Company (Chairman, 1988-98), Bank of Scotland, Cairn Energy, Robert Wiseman Dairies PLC. Recreations: golf; music; bridge. Address: (h.) 15 India Street, Edinburgh EH3 6HA; T.-0131-225 5596.

Levein, Craig William. National Coach, Scottish Football Association, 2009-2012; Director of Football, Heart of Midlothian FC, since 2014; b. 22.10.64, Dunfermline.

Senior Clubs played: Cowdenbeath, 1981-83, Heart of Midlothian, 1983-95. Sixteen appearances for National Team, 1990-94. Teams managed: Cowdenbeath, 1997-2000, Heart of Midlothian, 2000-04, Leicester City, 2004-06, Raith Rovers, 2006, Dundee United, 2006-09.

Leven, Marian Forbes, RSA, RSW. Artist; b. 25.3.44, Edinburgh; m., Will Maclean; 2 s.; 1 d. Educ. Bell-Baxter School, Cupar; Gray's School of Art, Aberdeen. Exhibited RSA, RSW, RGI, SSA, AAS; work in private and public collections; Winner, Noble Grossart Painting Prize, 1997; 2013 Winner, Saltire Society Award, Art in Architecture, with Will Maclean. Address: (h.) Bellevue, 18 Dougall Street, Tayport, Fife DD6 9JD.

Leven and Melville, Earl of (Alexander Ian Leslie-Melville); b. 29.11.84. Succeeded to title, 2012. Educ. Gordonstoun. Address: Glenferness House, Nairn IV12 5UP.

Levick, Jemima. Artistic Director and Chief Executive, Stellar Quines Theatre·Company, since 2016. Educ. Queen Margaret University. Artistic Director, Dundee Rep Theatre, 2015-2016, Joint Artistic Director, 2013-2015, Associate Director, 2009-2013. Nominated for a number of theatre awards and won a best director Critics' Award for Theatre in Scotland (CATS) for work on the 2009 Rep production of The Elephant Man. Address: (b.) 30b Grindlay Street, Edinburgh EH3 9AX; T.-0131 229 3851.

Levinthal, Terrence Scott, BES, DipUD, FSAScot. Non Executive Director, Built Environment Forum Scotland, since 2000; Director of Conservation Services and Projects, National Trust for Scotland, 2010-2016; Director, Scottish Civic Trust, 1999-2010 (Technical Director, 1999-2002); Board Member, Loch Lomond and the Trossachs National Park Authority, 2002-2010; b. 9.12.61, Winnipeg. Educ. University of Waterloo; Heriot-Watt/Edinburgh College of Art. Investigator, Royal Fine Art Commission for Scotland, 1988-92; Secretary, The Cockburn Association (Edinburgh Civic Trust), 1992-99. Recreations: hill-walking; skiing; cycling and other outdoor pursuits; the arts; woodworking. Address: 2a/2 Albany Street, Edinburgh EH1 3QB.

Lewis, Bryan David, BA (Hons) Classics, HDipEd (Hons). Headmaster, The Mary Erskine and Stewart's Melville Junior School, since 1989; Vice Principal, The Erskine Stewart's Melville Schools, since 1995; b. 16.2.50, Dublin, Ireland; m., Susan; 3 d. Educ. Dublin High School; Trinity College, Dublin. Taught Classics in Dublin High School, 1973-74; Classics Teacher, Stewart's Melville College, 1974-77, Housemaster, 1977-80, Head of Classics, 1980-89, Assistant Head, 1987-89. Publication: 'Stewart's Melville: The First 10 Years' (Co-Author), 1984. Recreations: sport of all kinds, especially rugby and golf; walking; musical theatre. Address: (b.) Queensferry Road, Edinburgh EH4 3EZ; T.-07776140417; e-mail: bryan.d.lewis@btinternet.com

Lewis, Sheriff Marysia, LLB. Sheriff Principal, Tayside, Central and Fife, since 2015. Educ. University of Strathclyde. Apprenticeship at Dunlop Gordon & Smythe, 1979-81; Solicitor: Monklands District Council, 1981-83, City of Aberdeen District Council, 1983-87; Solicitor, then partner, Ledingham Chalmers LLP (formerly Edmonds & Ledingham), 1987-2008. Appointed part-time sheriff in 2006, then sheriff in 2008. Address: Perth Sheriff Court, Tay Street, Perth PH2 8NL; T.-01738 620546.

Lewis, Sian, MA, DPhil (Oxon). Senior Lecturer in Ancient History, University of St. Andrews, since 2004, Pro-Dean for Postgraduates (Arts), since 2007; b. 30.06.66, Bridgend, Mid Glamorgan. Educ. St. Clare's Convent Grammar School, Porthcawl; University College, Oxford. Teaching Fellow, Trinity College, Dublin, 1991-92; College Tutor, University of Oxford, 1992-94; Tutorial Fellow,

University of Wales Swansea, 1994-96; Lecturer in Ancient History, University of Wales Cardiff, 1996-2004. Publications: News and Society in the Greek Polis, 1996; The Athenian Woman: an iconographic handbook, 2002; Ancient Tyranny (ed), 2006; Greek Tyranny, 2009. Recreations: magic: The Gathering; science fiction; running. Address: (b.) School of Classics, University of St. Andrews, St. Andrews, Fife KY16 9AL; T.-01334 462600; e-mail: sl50@st-andrews.ac.uk

Liddell, Colin, OBE. Director, Friarbank Management Services; b. 28.8.47, Falkirk; m, Sheena Wood Mackay. Educ. Denny High School. Journalist, Johnston Newspaper Group, 1964-69; Editor, Linlithgow Journal & Gazette, 1968-69; Journalist, Scotsman Publications, 1969-1977; Senior Press Officer, Scottish Development Agency, 1977-82; PR Director, then Chief Executive, Charles Barker Scotland, 1982-86; Corporate Affairs Director, United Distillers, 1986-93; Corporate Communications Director, ScottishPower plc, 1993-95; Director, Liddell Thomson Consultancy, 1995-2011; Director, Billcliffe Gallery, 1996; Director, Spreng & Co, 2008; Director, Falkirk FC, since 2014; Vice Chairman, Falkirk FC 1998-2004; Member, CBI Scotland Council, 2002-09 and 2012-14; Board Member, Scottish Enterprise Glasgow, 1999-2002, Scottish Ballet, 1990-95, Royal Scottish National Orchestra, 1995-98, Quality Scotland Foundation, 1991-94. Recreations: golf; gardening; football.

Liddell, Colin, BA, LLB, WS. Chairman, Pitlochry Festival Theatre; Trustee: Pitlochry Highland Games, Dunard Fund and Royal High School Preservation Trust. Educ. Cargilfield School and Fettes College, Edinburgh; Oxford and Edinburgh Universities; accredited specialist in Charity Law. Career: qualified as a solicitor in 1979; J. & H. Mitchell W.S. of Pitlochry, Senior Partner, since 1996; Chairman or Trustee of a number of other charities and community organisations. Publications: Author of Pitlochry: Heritage of a Highland District, 1993; Pitlochry: A History, 2008. Recreations: skiing; walking the hills; writing. Address: J & H Mitchell WS, Atholl Road, Pitlochry PH16 5BU.

Liddell, David, BSc (Hons), CQSW. Director, Scottish Drugs Forum, since 1993; b. 1957; 3 s.; 1 d. Educ. Riddlesdown High School; Sheffield University; Edinburgh University. Bristol Cyrenians, 1978; Dublin Simon Community, 1979; Biochemist: Queen Charlotte's Hospital, London, 1980, Temple Street Children's Hospital, Dublin, 1980; Dublin Committee for Travelling People, 1981-82; Fieldworker, Standing Conference on Drug Abuse, 1985-86; Co-ordinator, Scottish Drugs Forum, 1986-93. Member, Ministerial Drug Task Force, 1994; currently Member: Scottish Advisory Committee on Drug Misuse. Publications: Drug Problems in Edinburgh (Co-author), 1987; Understanding Drug Problems in Scotland (Co-author), 1998; Understanding Drug Issues in Scotland (Co-author), 2000. Recreations: landscape gardening; camping; hostelling; allotment; chauffeur. Address: (b.) 5 Waterloo Street, Glasgow G2 6AY; T.-0141-221 1175; e-mail: dave@sdf.org.uk

Liddell of Coatdyke, Baroness (Helen Lawrie Liddell). Chairman, G3 (Good Governance Group), since 2014; b. 6.12.50; m., Alistair; 1 s.; 1 d. Educ. St. Patrick's High School, Coatbridge; University of Strathclyde. Career: contested East Fife in October 1974; former BBC Scotland economics journalist, 1976-77; General Secretary of Labour Party in Scotland, 1977-86; public affairs director of Scottish Daily Record, 1986-93; Chief Executive, Business Ventures, 1993-94; MP (Labour), Monklands East, 1994-97, Airdrie and Shotts, 1997-2005; Cabinet Minister as Secretary of State for Scotland, 2001-03; British High Commissioner to Australia, 2005-2009. Address: House of Lords, London SW8 5BB.

Liddle, Gordon Wright McFarlane, LLB, DipLP. Sheriff: All-Scotland Sheriff Personal Injury Court, since 2015, Edinburgh, since 2004, All Scotland, since 2000; b. 19.4.51, Glasgow; 1 s.; 1 d. Educ. University of Edinburgh. Called to Scottish Bar, 1988. Temporary Sheriff, 1998. Address: (b.) Sheriff's Chambers, Sheriff Court House, 27 Chambers Street, Edinburgh EH1 1LB; T.-0131 225 2525.

Lilley, Professor David Malcolm James, FRS, FRSE, FRSC. Professor of Molecular Biology, Dundee University, since 1989; b. 28.5.48, Colchester; m., Patricia Mary; 2 d. Educ. Gilberd School, Colchester; Durham University. Joined Biochemistry Department, Dundee University, 1981; awarded: Colworth Medal by Biochemical Society, 1982, Gold Medal of G. Mendel, Czech Academy of Sciences, 1994, Gold Medal of V. Prelog in Stereochemistry, ETH, Zurich; Royal Society of Chemistry Award in RNA and Ribozyme Chemistry; Royal Society of Chemistry Interdisciplinary Award. Publications: 360 scientific papers. Recreations: foreign languages; running; skiing. Address: (b.) School of Life Sciences, Dundee University, Dundee DD1 5EH; T.-01382 344243. E-mail: d.m.j.lilley@dundee.ac.uk

Lindhorst, Gordon John S., LLB (Hons), DipLP, LLM. MSP (Scottish Conservative), Lothian region, since 2016; Advocate, since 1995; Barrister at law, of the Middle Temple, since 2008. Educ. University of Edinburgh; University of Glasgow; Universität Heidelberg. Admitted as Solicitor, 1991; Notary Public, 1992. Legal Reporter: Scots Law Times, 1995-2000, Session Cases, since 2016. Recreations: hillwalking; cabinet making; music. Address: Scottish Parliament, Edinburgh EH99 1SP.

Lindsay, 16th Earl of (James Randolph Lindesay-Bethune), MA, PhD. President, National Trust for Scotland, since 2012; Chairman, Frelish Energy, 2011-13; Chairman, Greenfield Holdings, 2009-2011; Chairman, Scottish Quality Salmon, 1998-2006; Chairman, United Kingdom Accreditation Service, since 2002; Managing Director, Marine Stewardship Council International, 2001-05; Chairman, RSPB Scotland, 1998-2003; Council Member, RSPB UK, 1998-2003; Vice President, RSPB Scotland, since 2004; Board Member, Cairngorms Partnership, 1998-2002; Non-Executive Director, UA (Scotland) plc, 1998-2005; Member, Scottish Power Environment Forum, 1998-2002; President, International Tree Foundation, 1995-2005, Vice President, since 2005; Chairman, Genesis Quality Assurance, 2001-02; Chairman, Elmwood College, 2001-09; Chairman, BPI Pension Scheme Trustees, since 2009; Non-Executive Director, Scottish Resources Group Ltd., 2001-2013; Non-Executive Director, SAC Ltd. (now SRUC), since 2005, Chairman, since 2007; Non-Executive Director, BPI plc, 2006-2015; Member, Select Committee on the EU: Financial Affairs Sub-Committee, since 2015; Member, Better Regulation Commission and Risk & Regulation Advisory Council, 2006-10, Deputy Chairman, from 2007; President, Royal Scottish Geographical Society, 2005-2012, currently Vice President; Chairman, Moorland Forum, since 2007; Associate Director, National Non-Food Crops Centre, since 2007; b. 19.11.55; m., Diana Mary Chamberlayne-Macdonald. Educ. Eton; Edinburgh University; University of California, Davis. Lord in Waiting (Government Whip), 1995; Parliamentary Under Secretary of State, Scottish Office, 1995-97; Member, Secretary of State's Advisory Group on Sustainable Development, 1998-99; Member, Select Committee on European Community Affairs:

Environment, Public Health and Consumer Protection Sub-Committee, 1997-99; Member, UK Round Table on Sustainable Development Sub-Group, 1998-2000; Chairman, Assured British Meat Ltd., 1997-2001; President, Royal Highland Agricultural Society of Scotland (RHASS), 2005-06; Member, Commission on Scottish Devolution, 2008-09; Green Ribbon political award, 1995. Address: (h.) Lahill, Upper Largo, Fife KY8 6JE.

Lindsay, Gerald, BAcc, CA. Managing Director, Hansel Foundation; b. 12.2.64, Glasgow; 2 d. Educ. Marr College, Troon; University of Glasgow; ICAS (Institute of Chartered Accountants of Scotland). Auditor, to management level, Downie Wilson CA, Glasgow, 1985-97; Finance Manager, St Andrew's Ambulance Association, 1997-2000; Finance Director, Hansel, 2000-2011. Recreations: fitness; sports; travel. Address: Broadmeadows, Symington, Ayrshire KA1 5PU; T.-01563 830340.
E-mail: gerry.lindsay@hansel.org.uk

Lindsay, Mark Stanley Hunter, LLB (Hons), DipLP. Advocate, since 1995; Standing Counsel to Home Secretary, 2000-2012; b. 17.5.69, Maybole; m., Rosemary; 2 s.; 1 d. Educ. Carrick Academy, Maybole; University of Glasgow. Energy Consultant, Jacek Mawkowski Associates, Boston, Mass., USA; Congressional Intern, Capitol Hill, Washington DC; Articled Clerk, Macallister Mazengarb, Wellington, NZ; Trainee Solicitor, Tods Murray, WS, Edinburgh; Solicitor, Scottish Office. Recreations: hillwalking; squash; classic cars; American history. Address: Advocates' Library, Parliament House, Edinburgh EH1 1RF; T.-0131-226 5071; (h.) 0131-467 1451; e-mail: MshLindsay@aol.com

Lindsay, Ranald Bruce, LLB(Hons), DipLP, NP. Solicitor-Advocate, since 1993; Solicitor, since 1986; b. 18.3.62, Bellshill; m.; 3 s.; 1 d. Educ. Wishaw High; University of Glasgow. Trained with Bishop & Co., Glasgow, 1984-86; qualified as first Solicitor Advocate in both civil and criminal law, 1993; established own practice, 1994; elected Law Society of Scotland Council Member for Dumfries, 2005-09; Convenor, Law Society of Scotland Access to Justice Committee, 2006-09; Dean, Faculty of Procurators of Dumfriesshire, 2009-2014; qualified light aircraft pilot, 2012. Recreations: reading; films; history; flying; getting away from it all. Address: (b.) Lindsay Solicitors, 75 Buccleuch Street, Dumfries DG1 2AB; T.-01387 259236.

Lingard, Joan Amelia, MBE. Author; b. 23.4.32, Edinburgh; 3 d. Educ. Bloomfield Collegiate School, Belfast; Moray House College of Education, Edinburgh. Member, Scottish Arts Council, 1980-85; Chair, Society of Authors in Scotland, 1980-84; a Director, Edinburgh Book Festival, 1994-98; Hon. Vice-President, Scottish PEN, since 2001; first novel published, 1963; has also written plays for TV, including 18-part series, Maggie, adapted from quartet of teenage books; novels: Liam's Daughter, 1963; The Prevailing Wind, 1964; The Tide Comes In, 1966; The Headmaster, 1967; A Sort of Freedom, 1968; The Lord on our Side, 1970; The Second Flowering of Emily Mountjoy, 1979; Greenyards, 1981; Sisters By Rite, 1984; Reasonable Doubts, 1986; The Women's House, 1989; After Colette, 1993; Dreams of Love and Modest Glory, 1995; The Kiss, 2002; Encarnita's Journey, 2005; After You've Gone, 2007; 40 children's books; Awards: ZDF Preis der Leseratten, W. Germany, for The Twelfth Day of July, 1986; Buxtehuder Bulle, W. Germany for Across the Barricades, 1987; Scottish Arts Council awards for After Colette, 1994, Tom and the Tree House, 1998; Tug of War shortlisted for 1989 Carnegie Medal, 1989 Federation of Children's Book Groups Award, 1989

Sheffield Book Award, runner-up for 1990 Lancashire Children's Book Club of the Year; MBE for Services to Children's Literature, 1999; shortlisted, Scottish Royal Mail Awards for The Sign of The Black Dagger, 2006; nominated for the Astrid Lingren Award, 2006; shortlisted for the Scottish Royal Mail Award, West Sussex Children's Book Award and The Lancashire School Librarian Award 2009 for 'The Eleventh Orphan'; The Chancery Lane Conspiracy, 2010. Recreations: reading; walking; travelling. Address: (b.) David Higham Associates, 5-8 Lower John Street, Golden Square, London W1R 4HA.

Lingard, Robin Anthony, MA, FTS; b. 19.7.41, Enfield; m., Margaret; 2 d. Educ. Felsted School; Emmanuel College, Cambridge. Joined Ministry of Aviation, 1963; Private Secretary to Joint Parliamentary Secretary, Ministry of Technology, 1966-68; appointments, Department of Industry, DTI, etc., to 1984; Head, Enterprise Unit, Cabinet Office, 1984-85; Head, Small Firms and Tourism Division, Department of Employment, 1985-87; full-time Board Member, Highlands and Islands Development Board, 1988-91; Director of Training and Social Development, Highlands and Islands Enterprise, 1991-93; Project Director, University of the Highlands and Islands Project, 1993-97. Member, Scottish Tourist Board, 1988-92; Chairman, Prince's Trust Committee for Highlands, Western Isles and Orkney; Member, Management Board, Prince's Trust and Royal Jubilee Trusts, 1989-95; Chairman, Youth Link Scotland, 1997-2000; Chairman, BBC Scotland Children in Need and Appeals Advisory Committee, 1999-2004; Chairman, Fusion Scotland, 2002-05; Chairman, Sustainable Development Research Centre, 2004-09; Chairman, Highland Community Care Forum, 2007-09; DUniv (Open), 1999; Hon. Fellow, UHI Millennium Institute, 2006. Recreations: watching birds; walking; reading; aviation history. Address: (h.) Kinnairdie House, Dingwall IV15 9LL; T.-01349 861044.

Linklater of Butterstone, Baroness (Veronica Linklater). Life Peer, since 1997; Founder and President, The New School, Butterstone, since 1991; President, Society of Friends of Dunkeld Cathedral, since 1989; Trustee, Esmée Fairbairn Foundation, since 1991; b. 15.4.43, Meikleour, Perthshire; m., Magnus Duncan Linklater (qv); 2 s.; 1 d. Educ. Cranborne Chase; Sorbonne; University of Sussex; University of London. Child Care Officer, London Borough of Tower Hamlets, 1967-68; Co-Founder, Visitors Centre, Pentonville Prison, 1971-77; Governor, three Islington schools, 1970-85; Prison Reform Trust Winchester Prison Project, 1981-82; Butler Trust: Founder, Administrator, Consultant, 1983-87, Trustee, 1987-2001, Vice President, since 2001; JP, Inner London, 1985-88; Co-ordinator, Trustee, Vice Chairman, Pushkin Prizes (Scotland), since 1989; Member, Children's Panel, Edinburgh South, 1989-97; Committee Member, Gulliver Award for the Performing Arts in Scotland, 1990-96; Patron, Sutherland Trust, 1993-2003; Trustee, Young Musicians Trust, 1993-97; Candidate (Liberal Democrat), Perth & Kinross By-Election, 1995; Director, Maggie Keswick Jencks Cancer Caring Centres Trust, 1997-2004; Foundation Patron, Queen Margaret University College, since 1998; Member, Beattie Committee on Post School Provision for Young People with Special Needs, 1998-99; Patron, The Airborne Initiative, 1998-2004; Trustee, Development Trust, University of the Highlands and Islands, 1999-2001; Secretary, Scottish Peers Association, 2000-07; Trustee, The Lyle Charitable Trust, since 2001; Chancellor's Assessor, Napier University Court, 2001-04; Patron, Family and Parenting Institute, since 2002; Patron, Support in Mind, Scotland (formerly National Schizophrenia Fellowship, Scotland), since 2000; Patron, The Probation Boards Association; Appeal Patron, Hopetoun House Preservation Trust, 2001; Member, Advisory Board, The Beacon Fellowship Charitable Trust, since 2003; Member,

Scottish Committee, Barnardo's, 2001-04; Patron, Research Autism, since 2004; Patron, The Calyx, Scotland's Garden Trust, 2004-08; Advisor, Koestler Awards Trust, since 2004; Chairman, House of Lords All Party Parliamentary Group on Offender Learning & Skills, 2005-06; Patron, Action for Prisoners' Families, since 2005; Council Member, The Winston Churchill Memorial Trust; Patron, Home Start Perth, since 2006; Patron, Push, since 2007; President, Crime Reduction Initiative, 2007-2010; Patron, University of St Andrews Medical Campaign Committee, since 2007; President, SOVA, since 2009; Patron, Tacade, 2009-2012; Patron, Epilepsy Scotland, since 2009; Patron, Contact a Family, 2011. Hon. Degree, Queen Margaret University College, Edinburgh. Recreations: music; theatre; gardening. Address: (h.) 71 (1F2) Cumberland Street, Edinburgh EH3 6RD; T.-0131 5589616; e-mail: magnus.linklater1@gmail.com

Linklater, Emeritus Professor Karl Alexander, BVM&S, PhD, CBiol, FIBiol, FRAgS, FRCVS, FRSE. Principal, Scottish Agricultural College, 1999-2002, Emeritus Professor, since 2002; Professor of Agriculture, University of Glasgow, 1999-2002; a Director, The Moredun Foundation, 1991-2009; Director, Vet CPD, 1992-98; Director, the British Veterinary Association, 2003-06; Honorary Fellow, University of Edinburgh, 1998-2010; b. 1.9.39, Stromness, Orkney; m., Margaret; 1 s.; 1 d. Educ. Robert Gordon's College, Aberdeen; Edinburgh University. General veterinary practice, Tarland, Aberdeenshire, 1962-66; North of Scotland College of Agriculture, Aberdeen, 1966-67; Royal (Dick) School of Veterinary Studies, Edinburgh University, 1967-73; East of Scotland College of Agriculture, St. Boswells, 1973-86; Director, SAC Veterinary Services, 1986-97; Vice Principal, SAC, 1997-99; Member, Veterinary Products Committee, 1990-2001; President: Sheep Veterinary Society, 1983-85, British Veterinary Association, 1996-97, Association of Veterinary Teachers and Research Workers (Scotland), 1988-90, Scottish Branch, British Veterinary Association, 1992-94, Scottish Metropolitan Division, BVA, 1979-80; Alan Baldry Award, 1982. Recreations: sport; gardening; sheep breeding. Address: (h.) Bridge Park, Old Bridge Road, Selkirk TD7 4LG; T.-01750 20571.
E-mail: k.linklater@btopenworld.com

Linklater, Magnus Duncan, CBE. Journalist; Columnist for The Times; President, The Saltire Society, since 2011; Chairman, The Little Sparta Trust, since 2000; Chairman, Horsecross Arts Company (Perth Theatre and Concert Hall), since 2013; b. 21.2.42, Harray, Orkney; m., Veronica Lyle; 2 s.; 1 d. Educ. Eton College; Cambridge University. Reporter, Daily Express, Manchester, 1965-66; London Evening Standard: Diary Reporter, 1966-67, Editor, Londoner's Diary, 1967-69; Sunday Times: Editor, Spectrum, 1969-72, Editor, Colour Magazine, 1972-75, News Editor/Features Editor, 1975-83; Managing Editor, The Observer, 1983-86; Editor, London Daily News, 1986-87; Editor, The Scotsman, 1988-94; Chairman, Edinburgh Book Festival, 1994-96; Chairman, Scottish Arts Council, 1996-2001; Presenter, Eye to Eye, Radio Scotland, 1994-97; Columnist, The Times and Scotland on Sunday; Member, National Cultural Strategy Review Group, 1999-2000. Publications: Hoax: the Howard Hughes-Clifford Irving Affair (Co-Author); Jeremy Thorpe: A Secret Life (Co-Author); The Falklands War (with Sunday Times Insight team); Massacre — the story of Glencoe; The Fourth Reich — Klaus Barbie and the Neo-Fascist Connection (Co-Author); Not With Honour — the inside story of the Westland Affair (Co-Author); For King and Conscience — John Graham of Claverhouse, Viscount Dundee (Co-Author); Anatomy of Scotland (Co-Editor); Highland Wilderness; People in a Landscape; Edinburgh (Co-Author). Fellow, Royal Society of Edinburgh; Honorary Doctor of Arts, Napier University; Honorary

Doctor of Law, Aberdeen University; Honorary Doctor of Letters: Glasgow University, Queen Margaret University. Recreations: book-collecting; fishing. Address: (h.) 71 Cumberland Street, Edinburgh EH3 6RD; T.-0131-558 9616; e-mail: magnus.linklater@blueyonder.co.uk

Linkston, Alex, CBE. Chair, Forth Valley NHS Board, since 2012. Former Chief Executive of West Lothian Council. Awarded Quality Scotland's Leadership Award in 2007; Prince's Trust Scottish Volunteer of the Year in 2009. Chair, Youth Link Scotland; Vice Chair of West Lothian College; member of the Scottish Council of the Prince's Trust. Address: (b.) Carseview House, Castle Business Park, Stirling FK9 4SW; T.-01786 463031.

Linlithgow, 4th Marquess of (Adrian John Charles Hope); b. 1.7.46; divorced; 1 s.; 1 d.; 2 s. by pr. m.; succeeded to title, 1987. Educ. Eton. Stockbroker. Address: Philpstoun House, Linlithgow, West Lothian EH49 7NB.

Lishman, Professor Joyce, MA (Oxon), PhD, DipSW, first female Chair in the Robert Gordon University. Emeritus Professor; formerly Head, School of Applied Social Studies, Robert Gordon University (retired); m., Dr. J.R. Lishman; 1 s.; 1 d. Educ. Normanton Girls High School; St. Hilda's College, Oxford University; Edinburgh University; Aberdeen University. Social Worker/Senior Social Worker, Department of Child and Family Psychiatry, Edinburgh; Research Assistant/Research Fellow, Aberdeen University; Editor, Research Highlights Series; Malcolm Sargent Social Worker, Royal Aberdeen Children's Hospital; Lead Assessor, Quality Assessment of Social Work, 1995-96; Trustee, Lloyds TSB (Scotland), 2003-09; Chair, Partnership Drugs Initiative, Lloyds TSB Foundation for Scotland, 2005-08; Director, Inspiring Scotland, 2009. Publications: Handbook for Practice Learning in Social Work and Social Care: Knowledge and Theory; Communication in Social Work; Evaluation and Social Work Practice; Research Highlights in Social Work series - 2011 (General Editor); currently Director of VSA, Aberlour and a Council Member on the SSSC. Address: 458 King Street, Aberdeen AB24 3DE.

Lister-Kaye, Sir John, 8th Bt. of Grange, OBE, DUniv, DSc. Naturalist, Author, Lecturer; Member, International Committee, World Wilderness Foundation, since 1984; Vice President, Association for the Preservation of Rural Scotland, since 1998; President, Scottish Wildlife Trust, 1996-2001; Vice President, RSPB, 2006; b. 8.5.46; m., 1, Lady Sorrel Deirdre Bentinck; 1 s.; 2 d.; 2, Lucinda Anne Law; 1 d. Educ. Allhallows School. Founded Field Studies Centre, Highlands, 1970; founder Director, Aigas Trust, 1979; Director, AigasQuest Ltd., 1997; Director, Ninovus Estates Ltd., 1999; Director, Naturedays Ltd., 2006; Chairman, Scottish Committee, RSPB, 1985-92; Member, Committee for Scotland, NCC, 1989-90; NW Regional Chairman, Scottish Natural Heritage, 1992-96; Honorary Doctorate, University of Stirling, 1995; Honorary Doctorate, St. Andrews University, 2005. Publications: The White Island, 1972; Seal Cull, 1979; The Seeing Eye, 1980; One for Sorrow, 1994; Ill Fares the Land, 1995; Song of the Rolling Earth, 2003; Nature's Child, 2004; At The Water's Edge, 2010; Gods of the Morning, 2015. Address: (h.) House of Aigas, Beauly, Inverness-shire IV4 7AD; e-mail: jlk@aigas.co.uk

Lithgow, Sir William (James), 2nd Bt. of Ormsary, DL, LLD, CEng, FRINA, CIM. Farmer; Director, Lithgows Ltd, since 1956, Chairman, 1959-84, 1988-99; b. 10.5.34; m., 1, Valerie Helen Scott (deceased); 2, Mary Claire Hill; 2 s.; 1 d. Educ. Winchester College. Chairman, Hunterston

Development Company Limited, 1987-2008 (Director, since 1971); Chairman, Scott Lithgow Drydocks Ltd., 1967-78; Vice-Chairman, Scott Lithgow Ltd., 1968-78; Chairman, Western Ferries (Argyll) Ltd., 1972-85; Director, Bank of Scotland, 1962-86; Founder, Landcatch Ltd., 1979. Member: British Committee, Det Norske Veritas, 1966-92, Greenock District Hospital Board, 1961-66, General Board (Royal Society Nominee), Nat. Physical Lab., 1963-66; Honorary President, Students Association, and Member, Court, Strathclyde University, 1964-69; Member: Executive Committee, Scottish Council Development and Industry, 1969-85, Scottish Regional Council, CBI, 1969-76, Clyde Port Authority, 1969-71, West Central Scotland Plan Steering Committee, 1970-74, Board, National Ports Council, 1971-78, Scottish Milk Marketing Board, 1979-83; Chairman, Iona Cathedral Trustees Management Board, 1979-83; Council Member, Winston Churchill Memorial Trust, 1979-83; Member, Queen's Body Guard for Scotland (Royal Company of Archers), 1964; Fellow, Scottish Council Development and Industry; Honorary Vice President: Inverclyde Battalion Boys' Brigade, Mid-Argyll Agricultural Society. Recreations: rural life; invention; photography. Address: (b.) Ormsary Estate Office, Lochgilphead, Argyll PA31 8PE; T.-01880 770700.

Little, Professor Gavin Forbes Macleod, LLB (Hons), PhD (Edin), DipLP, Solicitor. Professor of Public Law, University of Stirling, since 2004; b. 21.01.64, Glasgow; m., Tikus Amanda; 2 s.; 1 d. Educ. The High School of Glasgow; The University of Edinburgh. Lecturer in Law, University of Dundee, 1988-93; Trainee Solicitor, 1994-96; Lecturer in Law, University of Stirling, 1996-2001, Senior Lecturer in Law, 2001-04, Head of the Department of Accounting, Finance and Law, 2002-05, Founding Head of The School of Law, 2005-07, Head of the Division of Law and Philosophy, 2012. Recreations: cycling; hillwalking. Address: (b.) The School of Law, University of Stirling, Stirling FK9 4LA; T.-01786 467301; e-mail: g.f.m.little@stir.ac.uk

Little, Paul. Principal and Chief Executive, City of Glasgow College. Address: (b.) 60 North Hanover Street, Glasgow G1 2BP.

Littlejohn, Professor David, BSc, PhD, CChem, FRSC, FRSE. Professor of Analytical Chemistry, Strathclyde University, since 1988; b. 1.5.53, Glasgow; m., Lesley Shaw MacDonald; 1 d. Educ. Duncanrig Secondary School, East Kilbride; Strathclyde University. Technical Officer, ICI Petrochemicals Division, Wilton, Middlesborough, 1978-80; Lecturer/Senior Lecturer in Chemistry, Strathclyde University, 1981-88; Head of Department, 2005-2010; Associate Deputy Principal (Research and Knowledge Exchange), 2010-2014; Executive Dean of Science, since 2014. Awarded 15th SAC Silver Medal by Royal Society of Chemistry, 1987; Theophilus Redwood Lectureship, 2001; Royal Society of Chemistry Award in Chemical Analysis and Instrumentation, 2005; joint Editor in Chief, Talanta, International Journal of Pure and Applied Analytical Chemistry, 1989-91. Publications: 210 research papers, 10 reviews, 1 book; 6 book chapters. Address: (b.) Department of Pure and Applied Chemistry, Strathclyde University, 295 Cathedral Street, Glasgow G1 1XL; T.-0141 548 2067; e-mail: d.littlejohn@strath.ac.uk

Littlejohn, Doris, BL, DUniv, CBE. Former President, Employment Tribunals (Scotland); b. 19.3.35, Glasgow; m., Robert (deceased); 3 d. Educ. Queen's Park School, Glasgow; University of Glasgow. Solicitor in private practice in Stirling until 1977. Former Chairman of Court, University of Stirling; former Member: Lord Chancellor's Panel on Review of Tribunals, Review Panel on Retention

of Organs after Post Mortems, Human Genetics Advisory Commission, Broadcasting Council for Scotland, General Advisory Committee, BBC. Address: Suilven, 125 Henderson Street, Bridge of Allan FK9 4RQ; T.-01786 832032.

Littlejohn, Robert King, MA (Aberdeen), MA (Sussex), FFCS. Retired; b. 17.3.46, Aberdeen; m., Anna; 1 s.; 2 d. Educ. Morrison's Academy, Crieff; Aberdeen University; Moray House College; Sussex University. Administrative (Education) Officer, RAF, 1969-96 including: Directorate of Air Staff Briefing and Co-ordination, 1987-90; Officer Commanding Administration Wing, RAF Leeming, 1990-93; Head of RAF Resettlement Service, 1993-96; retired in rank of Wing Commander; Registrar, Royal College of Physicians and Surgeons of Glasgow, 1996-2005; Regional SaBRE Campaign Director, Lowland Reserve Forces' and Cadets' Association, 2006-2011. Recreations: golf; hillwalking; opera; Aberdeen FC; Glasgow Warriors. Address: (h.) 8 Auchencruive, Milngavie, Glasgow G62 6EE; e-mail: robertklittlejohn@gmail.com

Livingston, Professor Kay, BEd, MEd, PhD, FRSA. Professor of Educational Research, Policy and Practice, University of Glasgow, since 2007, Research in Teacher Education; b. Girvan; m.; 1 s. Educ. University of Glasgow. Teacher, 1978-87; Lecturer, Craigie College of Education, Ayr, 1987-92; Secondment to Socrates Technical Assistance in European Commission, Brussels, 1997; Senior Lecturer, Coordinator of International Education, University of Paisley, 1993-2001; Director of the Quality in Education Centre (QIE) and Reader in Education, University of Strathclyde, 2001-05; Professor of Education and Director of Scottish Teachers for a New Era, University of Aberdeen, 2005-07; Secondment to Learning and Teaching Scotland (LTS) as Director of International, Research and Innovation and Member of the Corporate Management Team, 2007-2011; Secondment to Education Scotland as Director of International, Research and Innovation and Member of the Corporate Management Group, 2011-12. Editor, European Journal of Teacher Education and Curriculum Journal; Member of UK National Commission UNESCO Scotland Committee; Member of European Union Group on Professional Development of Teachers; Chair of the Commonwealth Games Legacy for Learning Group. Recreations: running; skiing; hill walking; reading.

Livingstone, Andrew Hugh, BSc (Hons), DipEd. Director, Colm Consultants; Education Officer, The Stewart Ivory Foundation; Rector, St. Columba's School, Kilmacolm, 1987-2002; b. 7.12.44, Campbeltown; m., 1, Christine Margaret Henderson (deceased), 2, Alison Brown Reid; 1 s.; 1 d. Educ. Campbeltown Grammar School; University of Aberdeen; University of Glasgow; Jordanhill College of Education. High School of Glasgow, 1968-70; Principal Teacher, Mathematics, Paisley Grammar School, 1970-79; Assistant Rector, Williamwood High School, 1979-83; Depute Rector, Paisley Grammar School, 1987. Recreations: golf; bridge; walking; skiing. Address: (h.) Nithsdale, Lyle Road, Kilmacolm; T.-01505 872404; e-mail: livingstoneah@btinternet.com

Livingstone, Bill (William). Former Editorial Director, Forth Weekly Press, a division of Clyde & Forth Press; Trustee, Carnegie Dunfermline and Hero Fund Trusts, 1992-2014 (Chairman, 2010-2012); Trustee, Carnegie United Kingdom Trust, 2002-2014; b. 23.7.44, Dunfermline; m., Margaret Stark; 2 s.; 2 d. Educ. Dunfermline High School. Entire career with Dunfermline Press Group: Editor, Dunfermline Press, 1984-96. Chairman, Guild of Editors (Scotland), 1994-96. Address:

11 St. Margaret Wynd, Dunfermline KY12 0UT; T.-01383 726182.

Livingstone, Ian Lang, CBE, BL, NP. Chairman: Lanarkshire Health Board, 1993-2002, Lanarkshire Development Agency, 1991-2000, New Lanarkshire Ltd., until 2015; Consultant Solicitor, since 1989; Chairman, Kingdom FM Ltd., since 2008; Chairman, Scottish Local Authorities Remuneration Committee, 2004-2013; Deputy Lord Lieutenant for Lanarkshire, 2008-2013; b. 23.2.38, Hamilton; m., Diane; 2 s. Educ. Hamilton Academy; Glasgow University. Qualified as Solicitor, 1960; Partner, Senior Partner, Ballantyne & Copland, Solicitors, Motherwell, 1962-86, Consultant, until 2014; Chairman and Director, family property investment and development company, since 1987. Former Chairman, Motherwell Football Club; Chairman, Board, Motherwell College, 1989-97; Member, Dalziel High School Board; Chairman, David Livingstone Memorial Trust; Elder, St. Mary's Parish Church, Motherwell; Honorary President, Lanarkshire Chamber of Commerce, since 2006; awarded Doctorate, The University of the West of Scotland, 2008. Recreations: walking; football; music. Address: (h.) 223 Manse Road, Motherwell ML1 2PY; T.-01698 253750.

Livingstone, Jamie. Head of Oxfam Scotland, since 2013. Former print and broadcast journalist, including Political Correspondent on STV News; joined Oxfam in 2011 as Campaigns and Communications Manager, overseeing Oxfam's campaigns, media output and supporter communications in Scotland. Address: Oxfam Scotland, 10 Bothwell Street, Glasgow G2 6LU; T.-0141 285 8854; e-mail: jlivingstone@oxfam.org.uk

Livingstone, Marilyn. MSP (Labour), Kirkcaldy, 1999-2011; b. 1952, Kirkcaldy. Educ. Viewforth Secondary School; Fife College. Fife College of Further and Higher Education: Head of Section – Administration and Consumer Studies, Youth Training Manager, Head of Business School. Member, Kirkcaldy District Council, four years; Member, Fife Council, five years (Chair, Vocational Education and Training Committee, Chair, Fife Vocational and Training Strategy, Member, New Deal Steering Group).

Llewellin, Magnus. Editor-in-Chief, Herald & Times, since 2013 (formerly Deputy Editor); b. 1965; 2 c. Career: joined Edinburgh Evening News in 1990, then the Daily Record, then The Scotsman and Business AM. Currently chairs the judging panel of the Scottish Politician of the Year Awards and is a committee member of the Journalists' Charity in Scotland. Recreations: hillwalking; running; travel. Address: (b.) Newsquest (Herald and Times) Ltd, 200 Renfield Street, Glasgow G2 3QB; T.-0141 302 7005.

Llewellyn, Howard Neil, BA (Hons) Law, Barrister. Immigration Judge, 2006-13; Chair, MAPPA SOG Practice Group, Tayside MAPPA, since 2014; Chief Officer of the Tayside Community Justice Authority, since 2010; Member of the Adoption Panel, Action for Children, since 2016; Member, Parole Board For Scotland, 2003-2010; Independent Chair of Significant Case Reviews (Child Protection), since 2008; b. 29.12.54, London; m., Rosemary; 1 s.; 1 d. Educ. Chingford County High School; The Inns of Court School of Law. Career History: Called to the Bar, 1982; Pupillage; Assistant Justices Clerk; County and Crown Prosecutor; Director of Legal Services, Cambridgeshire Constabulary. The Standards Commission for Scotland; Member, The Highland Children's Panel, 2002-08. Recreation: family life. Address: (h.) Inchstelly House, Alves, Elgin, Morayshire IV80 8UY; T.-07787 525903; e-mail: howardllewellyn@hotmail.co.uk

Lloyd, Ivor Graham, BA, MLib. Retired Depute Principal, University of Abertay Dundee (2005-09); b. 28.10.50, Edinburgh; m., Rosemary; 1 s.; 1 d. Educ. Ainslie Park Secondary School, Edinburgh; University of Strathclyde;

University of Wales. Assistant Librarian, Kirkcaldy Technical College, 1975-76; Subject Librarian, Duncan of Jordanstone College of Art, 1976-84; Depute Chief Librarian, Dundee College of Technology, 1984-89; Chief Librarian, University of Abertay Dundee, 1989-96, Head of Information Services, 1996-2005. Former President and Hon. Member, CILIPS. Recreations: golf; gardening.

Lloyd-Jones, Glyn Robin, MA, BA. Author and Novelist; President, Scottish PEN International, 1997-2000; b. 5.10.34, London; m., Sallie Hollocombe; 1 s.; 2 d. Educ. Blundell's School, Tiverton; Selwyn College, Cambridge University; Jordanhill College of Education. Teaching in Scottish secondary schools; Director, Curriculum Development Centre, Clydebank; English-Speaking Union Thyne Travel Scholarship to America, 1974; President, Scottish Association of Writers, 1981-86; Adviser, Education Department, Dunbartonshire, 1972-89; Co-ordinator, Scottish Forum for Development Education in Schools, 1996-99; radio drama: Ice in Wonderland, 1992 (winner, Radio Times new drama script award); Rainmaker, 1995. Publications: children's: Where the Forest and the Garden Meet, 1980; Red Fox Running, 2007; novels: Lord of the Dance (Winner, BBC/Arrow First Novel Competition, 1983); The Dreamhouse, 1985; Fallen Angels, 1992; education books: Assessment: From Principles to Action, 1985; How to Produce Better Worksheets, 1985; non-fiction: Argonauts of the Western Isles, 1989; Fallen Pieces of the Moon, 2006; The Sunlit Summit, 2013; The Sweet Especial Scene, 2014. Recreations: mountaineering; sea-kayaking; photography; chess. Address: (h.) 26 East Clyde Street, Helensburgh G84 7PG; T.-01436 672010; e-mail: robinlj34@gmail.com

Loasby, Professor Brian John, MA, MLitt, DUniv, FBA, FRSE. Emeritus and Honorary Professor of Economics, University of Stirling, since 1984; b. 02.08.30, Kettering; m., Judith Ann (Robinson); 2 d. Educ. Kettering Grammar School; Emmanuel College, Cambridge. Assistant in Political Economy, University of Aberdeen, 1955-58; Bournville Research Fellow, University of Birmingham, 1958-61; Tutor in Management Studies, University of Bristol, 1961-67; Lecturer in Economics, University of Stirling, 1967-68, Senior Lecturer in Economics, 1968-71, Professor of Management Economics, 1971-84. Publications: The Swindon Project, 1973; Choice, Complexity and Ignorance, 1976; The Mind and Method of The Economist, 1989; Equilibrium and Evolution, 1991; Knowledge, Institutions and Evolution in Economics, 1999 - Schumpeter Prize, 2000; articles and book chapters. Address: (b.) Division of Economics, University of Stirling, Stirling FK9 4LA; T.-01786 472124. E-mail: b.j.loasby@stir.ac.uk

Lochhead, Liz. Poet and Playwright; Scots Makar, 2011-2016; b. 1947, Motherwell. Educ. Glasgow School of Art. Combined teaching art and writing for eight years; became full-time writer after selection as first holder, Scottish/Canadian Writers' Exchange Fellowship, 1978; former Writer in Residence, Tattenhall Centre, Chester. Publications include: Memo for Spring, Islands, Grimm Sisters, Dreaming of Frankenstein, True Confessions; plays include: Blood and Ice, Dracula, Same Difference, Sweet Nothings, Now and Then, True Confessions, Mary Queen of Scots Got Her Head Chopped Off, The Big Picture, Perfect Days, Good Things, Educating Agnes, Liz Lochhead: Five Plays; poetry includes: The Colour of Black and White: Poems 1984-2003, 2003.

Lochhead, Richard Neilson, BA (Hons). MSP (SNP), Moray, since 2006, North East of Scotland, 1999-2006; Cabinet Secretary for Rural Affairs and the

Environment, 2007-2016; b. 24.5.69, Paisley; m.; 2 s. Educ. Williamwood High School, Clarkston; Stirling University. Financial trainee, South of Scotland Electricity Board, 1987-89; Economic Development Officer, Dundee City Council, 1998-99; Office Manager for Alex Salmond, 1994-98. Recreations: cinema; travel; reading fiction and history non-fiction; watching Elgin City, Aberdeen and Scotland football teams; listening to music, cycling & the countryside. Address: (b.) 9 Wards Road, Elgin, Moray IV30 1NL; T.-01343 551111.
E-mail: richard.lochhead.msp@scottish.parliament.uk

Locke, Alasdair James Dougall, MA. Chairman, First Property Group plc, since 2000; b. 29.8.53, Aldershot; m., Kathleen Anne; 2 s. Educ. Uppingham School, Rutland; Wadham College, Oxford University. Assistant Vice President: Citibank N. A., 1974-78, Oceanic Finance Corporation, 1978-81; Vice President, American Express Leasing Corporation, 1981-83; Director, Henry Ansbacher and Co., Ltd., 1983-87; Deputy Chairman, Kelt Energy PLC, 1987-91; Executive Chairman, Abbot Group PLC, 2000-09. Former Member, OSO Advisory Board. Recreations: shooting; golf; skiing. Address: (b.) Minto Drive, Altens, Aberdeen AB12 3LW; T.-01224 299600.

Lockhart of the Lee, Angus Hew, b. 17.8.46, Dunsyre; m., Susan Elizabeth Normand; 1 s.; 1 d. Educ. Rannoch School, Perthshire; North of Scotland College of Agriculture. Recognised as Chief of the Name Lockhart, 1957; Owner and Manager, Lee and Carnwath Estates; Member, Standing Council of Scottish Chiefs. Recreation: shooting. Address: (h.) Newholm, Dunsyre, Lanark ML11 8NQ; T.-01968 682254.

Lockhart, Brian Alexander, BL. Formerly Sheriff Principal, South Strathclyde, Dumfries and Galloway (2005-2015); b. 1.10.42, Ayr; m., Christine Ross Clark; 2 s.; 2 d. Educ. Glasgow Academy; Glasgow University. Partner, Robertson Chalmers and Auld, Solicitors, 1967-79; Sheriff, North Strathclyde, at Paisley, 1979-81; Sheriff, Glasgow and Strathkelvin, 1981-2005; President, Sheriffs' Association, 2003-05; Member, Parole Board for Scotland, 1997-2003; Temporary High Court Judge, 2008-2015; Appeal Sheriff, since 2015. Recreations: fishing; golf; family. Address: (h.) 18 Hamilton Avenue, Glasgow G41; T.-0141-427 1921.

Lockhart, Brian Robert Watson. MA (Hons), DipEd. Headmaster, Robert Gordon's College, Aberdeen, 1996-2004; b. 19.7.44, Edinburgh; m., Fiona Anne Sheddon; 1 s.; 2 d. Educ. George Heriot's School, Edinburgh; Aberdeen University; Moray House; University of Edinburgh. Teacher of History and Economic History, George Heriot's School, 1968-72; Principal Teacher of History, 1972-81; Deputy Rector, High School of Glasgow, 1981-96. Headteachers' Association of Scotland: Member, Council, 1988-2003, Member, Executive, 1989-94; Chair, Universities and Colleges Admissions Service Scottish Standing Committee, 1998-2000 and 2002-03; Member, Higher Still Implementation Group, 1998-2001; Member, Headmasters Conference Universities Committee, 1998-2003; Secretary, HMC (Scottish Division), 2003; Chairman, HMC (Scottish Division), 2004; Member, Business Committee, Aberdeen University, 1999-2011, Vice-Convener, 2006-2010; Member, Council, St. Margaret's School for Girls, Aberdeen, 2004-13; Member, Board of Voluntary Service Aberdeen (VSA), 2004-2011; Member, Board of Hutchesons' Educational Trust, Glasgow, 2005-12, Convenor, Education Committee, 2012-13; Trustee, Robert Nicol Trust, since 2006, Governor, since 2013; Member, Audit Committee, Aberdeen University, 2007-13; Member, Court of University of Aberdeen, 2008-12; Member, University Learning and Teaching Committee, 2010-12; Member, University Remuneration Committee, 2010-12; Convenor, University Student Affairs Committee, 2010-12; Member, University Staff Promotion Committee,

2012; Member, Friends of Aberdeen University Library (FAUL), since 2013; Member, Board of Governors, Lathallan School, since 2013. Publications: Jinglin' Geordie's Legacy, 2003; Robert Gordon's Legacy, 2007; "The Town School": A History of the High School of Glasgow, 2010; "Bon Record": A History of Aberdeen Grammar School, 2012; 'A Great Educational Tradition': A History of Hutchesons' Grammar School, 2015. Recreations: education history research; reading biographies; sport; films; politics. Address: (h.) 80 Gray Street, Aberdeen AB10 6JE; T.-01224 315776.
E-mail: brian.lockhart1@btinternet.com

Lockhart, Dean. MSP (Scottish Conservative), Mid Scotland and Fife region, since 2016; Shadow Cabinet Secretary for Economy, Jobs and Fair Work, since 2016. Career history: Asia-based international lawyer and business adviser for 20 years: Linklaters, London/Singapore, 1992-96, Linklaters, Tokyo, 1997-98, First Secretary (Privatisation), Diplomat, British Embassy, Manila, 1999-2000, Partner, Linklaters, Singapore, 2001-02, Partner, Linklaters, Hong Kong, 2002-06, Partner Linklaters, Singapore, 2007-2015. Conservative candidate for Stirling in the Scottish Parliament election, 2016. Address: Scottish Parliament, Edinburgh EH99 1SP; e-mail: dean.lockhart@scottishconservatives.com

Lockhead, Sir Muir, OBE, DHC. Chairman, National Trust for Scotland, since 2014; Chief Executive, UK transport group FirstGroup, 1995-2010; b. 25.4.45, County Durham; m.; 4 c. Educ. West Cornforth Secondary Modern School. Apprentice mechanic in a bus garage in Darlington, then management trainee with Tarmac; appointed Chief Engineer of Glasgow City Transport in 1979; joined Grampian Regional Transport in 1985 as General Manager, and went on to lead the successful employee buy-out as GRT Group plc. Awarded an Officer of the Order of the British Empire (OBE) in 1996 for services to the bus industry; past President of the Confederation of Passenger Transport; knighted in the 2008 Birthday Honours. Awarded a Doctorate honoris causa (DHC) in 2009 by the University of Aberdeen; awarded the VisitScotland Silver Thistle Award for outstanding services to the tourism industry in Scotland in 2010. Chairman of the Scottish Rugby Union, since 2011 Address: The National Trust for Scotland, Hermiston Quay, 5 Cultins Road, Edinburgh EH11 4DF; T.-0131 458 0200.

Lockley, Stephen Randolph, BSc, CEng, MICE, FILT, MIHT, DipTE. Transport Consultant, since 1997; b. 19.6.43, Manchester; m., Angela; 2 d. Educ. Morecambe Grammar School; Manchester University. Highway and Planning Engineer, Lancashire County Council, 1964-72; Transportation and Planning Engineer, Lanarkshire County Council, 1972-75; Strathclyde Regional Council: Principal Engineer (Transportation), 1975-77, Depute Director of Policy Planning, 1977-80, Principal Executive Officer, 1980-86; Director General, Strathclyde Passenger Transport Executive, 1986-97. Address: 64 Townhead Street, Strathaven, Lanarkshire ML10 6DJ; T.-01357 529395.

Logan, Brian James, BCom (Hons), CPFA. Chief Executive, Bield Housing & Care, since 2010; b. 5.7.71, Edinburgh. Educ. Ross High School, Tranent; University of Edinburgh. Career History: Trainee Accountant, Edinburgh District Council, 1993-96; Accountant, City of Edinburgh Council, 1996-2001; Senior Finance Manager, Hanover (Scotland) Housing Association, 2001-05; Director of Financial Services, Bield Housing & Care, 2005-2010. Address: 79 Hopetoun Street, Edinburgh; T.-0131 273 4000; e-mail: b.logan@bield.co.uk

Logan, Elaine, MA (Edin), PGCE. Headteacher, Glenalmond College, since 2015. Educ. Edinburgh University. Career: began teaching career at Viewforth High School in Kirkcaldy where she taught English for 3

years before taking up the position of English and Drama teacher at Dollar Academy; successfully completed Post Graduate Certificates in Counselling (Moray House, University of Edinburgh) and in Pupil Support and Guidance (Northern College, University of Dundee); became Housemistress of Holm House, Loretto School in September 2001 and continued in this post for 5 years, became Assistant Head - Day Pupils and Pastoral Coordinator, then Acting Head; became the first member of staff in a Scottish school to take up the Senior Management post of 'Director of Compliance, Inspections and Child Protection' in 2009. Teaches English, Drama and Theatre Studies. Address: Glenalmond College, Glenalmond, Perth PH1 3RY.

Logan, Fiona. Chief Operating Officer, Insights, since 2015; former Vice President for Europe, Insights (2015); Chief Executive, Loch Lomond and The Trossachs National Park Authority, 2008-2015. Educ. Strathclyde University Business School. Career History: Greenpeace in New Zealand; major blue chip companies including Uniliver and IBM New Zealand, where she continued her professional development at both Macquarie University in Sydney and Harvard Business School; Marketing Director of IBM New Zealand before she turned 30; after 10 years overseas came back to the UK to run her own successful management consultancy. Address: Insights, Terra Nova, 3 Explorer Road, Dundee DD2 1EG; T.-01382 908050.

Logan, Hugh. Principal, Fife College, since 2013. Previously Principal of Motherwell College; held a variety of posts in colleges as well as working in industry and secondary education. Address: (b.) Pittsburgh Road, Dunfermline, Fife KY11 8DY; T.-0844 248 0115.

Logan, Stephen Douglas, BSc, PhD, LLD (Hon). Chairman, NHS Grampian, since 2015; b. 16.10.50, Glasgow; m., Anne; 2 s. Educ. Annan Academy, Dumfriesshire; University of St. Andrews. Medical Research Council Fellow, Senior Lecturer and Professor of Neuroscience, University of Birmingham; Professor of Neuroscience, University of Aberdeen, 1994-96, Head of Department of Biomedical Sciences, 1996-98, became Vice-Principal and Dean of The Faculty of Medicine and Medical Sciences in 1998. Chairman, Grampian University Hospitals NHS Trust, 2002-04, Vice-Chairman, 1998-2002; Member, NHS Grampian Board, 2002-04; Member, SHEFC, 2003; Head of College of Life Sciences and Medicine, 2003; Senior Vice-Principal, University of Aberdeen, 2004-2015. Board Member, Aberdeen University Research & Industrial Services Ltd (AURIS Ltd), Rowett Research Institute Ltd, TauRx Pharmaceuticals Ltd, Aberdeen Sports Village. Over 100 research publications. Recreations: rugby; golf; reading. Address: (b.) NHS Grampian, Somerfield House, Eday Road, Aberdeen AB24 3FX; T.-01224 558624; e-mail: stephen.logan@NHS.net

Logan, Tracey. Chief Executive, Scottish Borders Council, since 2011. Career: various local authorities and a number of years in the private sector with BAA; Head of Human Resources for the joint venture company CSD which brought together services for Suffolk County Council and Mid Suffolk District Council, delivered in partnership with BT; Scottish Borders Council: Head of Human Resources, 2006-08, Director of Resources, 2008-2011. Address: Scottish Borders Council, Council Headquarters, Newtown St. Boswells, Melrose TD6 0SA; T.-0300 100 1800.

Logan, Rt. Rev. Vincent, DipRE. Bishop Emeritus of Dunkeld; Bishop of Dunkeld, 1981-2012; b. 30.6.41,

Bathgate. Educ. Blairs College, Aberdeen; St. Andrew's College, Drygrange. Ordained Priest, 1964; Assistant Priest, St. Margaret's, Edinburgh, 1964-66; Corpus Christi College, London, 1966-67; Chaplain, St. Joseph's Hospital, Rosewell, Midlothian, 1966-67; Adviser in Religious Education, Archdiocese of St. Andrews and Edinburgh, 1967; Parish Priest, St. Mary's, Ratho, 1977-81; Vicar Episcopal for Education, Edinburgh, 1978. Address: Croghmore, 10 Arnhall Drive, Dundee DD2 1LU.

Logie, Professor Robert Howie, BSc, PhD, CPyschol, FBPsS, FRSA, FRSE. Professor of Human Cognitive Neuroscience, Edinburgh University, since 2004; Anderson Professor of Psychology, Aberdeen University, 1998-2003 (Head, Department of Psychology, 1997-2002); b. 23.3.54, Ajmer, India; m., Elizabeth; 2 s. Educ. Aberdeen Academy; Aberdeen University; University College, London. Researcher, MRC Applied Psychology Unit, Cambridge, 1980-86; Aberdeen University: Lecturer in Psychology, 1987, Senior Lecturer, 1992, Personal Professor, 1995. Publications: over 250 including 15 authored or edited books, notably Visuo Spatial Working Memory, 1995; Cognitive Neuroscience of Working Memory, 2007; Working Memory and Ageing, 2015; Dorothy Hodgkin Lecturer, British Association for the Advancement of Science, 1995. Editor, Quarterly Journal of Experimental Psychology, 2002-05; Chair, Psychonomic Society, 2015; Chair, European Research Council Advanced Grants Panel SH4, 2015-16.

Long, Dr. Ian, MA, BA, AKC, PhD. Headmaster, Albyn School, Aberdeen, since 2008. Educ. Birkbeck College, University of London; King's College London, University of London. Career: Head of Sixth, Brentwood School, 1996-99; Second Deputy Head, City of London Freemen's School, 1999-2008. Address: (b.) 17-23 Queen's Road, Aberdeen AB10 4PB; T.-01224 322408.

Longmore, Marco, MA (Edin), FRSA. Rector, Edinburgh Academy, since 2008. Educ. Edinburgh University; Moray House College. Career: History and Modern Studies teacher, then Year Head, George Heriot's School, Edinburgh; completed the Scottish Qualification for Headship through the University of Edinburgh; Senior Deputy Head, Alleyn's School, London, 2005-08. Address: (b.) 42 Henderson Row, Edinburgh EH3 5BL; T.-0131 556 4603; e-mail: rectorsoffice@edinburghacademy.org.uk

Lord, Geoffrey, OBE, MA, AIB, FRSA; b. 24.2.28, Rochdale; m., Jean; 1 s.; 1 d. Educ. Rochdale Grammar School; Bradford University. Midland Bank Ltd., 1946-58; Greater Manchester Probation and After-Care Service, 1958-76 (Deputy Chief Probation Officer, 1974-76); Secretary and Treasurer, Carnegie UK Trust, 1977-93; former Vice-President, Selcare Trust; former Chairman, Pollock Memorial Missionary Trust; Founder of Artlink (Edinburgh & The Lothians), The ADAPT Trust, 1989 (Trustee, 1989-2007), The Unemployed Voluntary Action Fund, (Chairman, 1990-95); former Trustee, PlayRight Scotland Trust, 1998-2005. Former Trustee and Chairman, HomeStart UK; Past President, Centre for Environmental Interpretation; Council Member, National Youth Orchestras of Scotland, 1998-2013; Trustee, Edinburgh Voluntary Organisations Trusts, 1997-2015 (Secretary, 1997-2009), Murrayfield Dementia Project, 2006-2013, Faith in Older People Trust (FIOP), 2007-2012, BSS (Broadcasting Support Services), 2008-2015; Honorary Fellow, Manchester Metropolitan University, 1987. Publications: The Arts and Disabilities, 1981; Interpretation of the Environment, 1984; Access for Disabled People to Arts Premises - The Journey Sequence (Co-author), 2004; Cathedrals for the Curious: An Introduction to Cathedrals,

Minsters and Abbeys in Britain, 2011. Recreations: the arts; philately; walking; enjoying life. Address: (h.) 9 Craigleith View, Edinburgh.

Lord, Jonathan Christopher, MA. Director, RSAC Motorsport Ltd and consultant; Secretary, The Glasgow Art Club; b. 29.4.53, Alverstoke; 1 s. Educ. Dollar Academy; St. Andrews University. Ministry of Defence (Naval), 1975-76; Royal Scottish Automobile Club, 1976-2006; Member, British Motor Sports Council, 1991-2003; MSA Rallies Committee, 1982-2003; Administrator, The McGlashan Charitable Trust, 2008-15; FIA Observer for International Rallies; MSA Steward; Clerk of the Course, RSAC International Scottish Rally, since 1982 and other international rallies; Secretary to the Vestry, St. Bride's Episcopal Church, Glasgow, since 1991. Recreations: music (especially choral singing); cricket; motor sport; following Dunfermline Athletic FC. Address: (h.) 11 Melrose Gardens, Glasgow G20 6RB; T.-0141-946 5045; e-mail: jcl30@btinternet.com

Lorimer, A. Ross, CBE, MD, DUniv (Glasgow), FMedSci, FRCP. Retired. Previously President, Royal College of Physicians and Surgeons of Glasgow (2000-03); Honorary Professor, Glasgow University; Consultant Physician and Cardiologist, Glasgow Royal Infirmary; b. 5.5.37, Bellshill; m., Fiona Marshall; 3 s. Educ. Uddingston Grammar School; High School of Glasgow; Glasgow University. Recreations: reading; walking. Address: 12, Uddingston Road, Bothwell G71 8PH.

Lorimer, Thomas Aitken (Ken), BEd, MInstAM, FCMI. Director and Chief Executive, Hansel Foundation, 1998-2012; Director and Chief Executive, Hansel Alliance, 1998-2012; b. 17.5.54, Mauchline; 2 d. Educ. Belmont Academy, Ayr; Ayr Academy; Ayr College; Craigie College of Education; Strathclyde University. Joined Ayr County Council, 1971, transferred to Strathclyde Regional Council, 1975, held administrative and public relations appointments with both; Hansel Village: General Administrator, 1985; General Manager, 1992. Member, Scottish Committee, Association for Real Change (ARC); Founding Fellow of the Institute of Contemporary Scotland. Recreations: music; theatre/cinema; literature. E-mail: Kenlorimer@ymail.com

Lothian, Marquis of (Rt. Hon. Michael Andrew Foster Jude Kerr Ancram), PC, DL, QC. Advocate; MP (Conservative), Devizes, 1992-2010; Deputy Leader of the Opposition and Shadow Foreign Seretary, 2001-05; Shadow Defence Secretary, 2005; former Chairman, Conservative Party; Member, Intelligence and Security Committee, since 2006; b. 7.7.45; m.; 2 d. Educ. Ampleforth; Christ Church, Oxford; Edinburgh University. MP: Berwickshire and East Lothian, 1974, Edinburgh South, 1979-87; Parliamentary Under Secretary of State, Scottish Office, 1993-94; Minister of State, Northern Ireland Office, 1994-97; Chairman, Conservative Party in Scotland, 1980-83. Created Life Peer, 2010; DL, Roxburgh District; Freeman of the City of Gibraltar, 2011; Freedom of Devizes, 2011; Chairman, Global Strategy Forum, since 2006; Chairman, MEC, since 2013. Address: (b.) House of Lords, London SW1A 0PW.

Loudon, Alasdair John, LLB, NP, WS. Partner, Turcan Connell, Solicitors, Edinburgh, since 2001; b. 7.4.56, Edinburgh; 2 s.; 1 d. Educ. Edinburgh Academy; Dundee University. Apprentice, Tods, Murray and Jamieson, WS, 1978-80; Qualified Assistant, Warner & Co., 1980-82, Partner, 1982-92; founded Loudons WS, 1992, Senior Partner, until 2001; accredited as specialist in family law; accredited FLAGS arbitrator; formerly Member, Sheriff Court Rules Council for Scotland; President, Edinburgh Bar

Association, 1996-98. Fellow of International Academy of Matrimonial Lawyers. Recreations: golf (Honourable Company of Edinburgh Golfers; Bruntsfield Links, Luffness New and Royal Wimbledon); football (Heart of Midlothian supporter). Address: (b.) Princes Exchange, 1 Earl Grey Street, Edinburgh EH3 9EE; e-mail: alasdair.loudon@turcanconnell.com

Loudon, John Alexander, LLB, SSC. Retired accredited specialist in Liquor Licensing (Betting and Gaming) Law; Convenor of the City of Edinburgh Licensing Forum; b. 5.12.49, Edinburgh; m., Alison Jane Bruce Laird; 2 s. Educ. Edinburgh Academy; Dundee University. Apprenticeship, Tindal, Oatts and Roger, Solicitors, Glasgow. Former Member, Council, Law Society of Scotland; Past President, SSC Society. Recreations: shooting; skiing. Address: (b.) 6c Essex Road, Edinburgh EH4 6LG.

Loudon, Sally, BA (Hons). Chief Executive, Argyll and Bute Council, since 2008; b. 06.12.65, Edinburgh; 1 s.; 2 d. Educ. Musselburgh Grammar School; University of Ulster. Business and Performance Manager, Midlothian Council, 2005-07, Head of Performance and HR, 2007-08. Address: (b.) Chief Executive's Office, Kilmory, Lochgilphead, Argyll and Bute PA31 8RT; T.-01546 604350; e-mail: sally.loudon@argyll-bute.gov.uk

Loudon, William Euan Buchanan (Euan), CBE, FCMI. Chief Executive, St Andrews Links Trust, since 2011; b. 12.3.56, Lanarkshire; m., Penny. Educ. Uddingston Grammar School and RMA Sandhurst. Commissioned into The Royal Highland Fusiliers, 1975; served at regimental duty with the Commando Training Centre in Devon, before attending the Army Staff College in 1988; Chief of Staff 7 Armoured Brigade, 1988-91; appointed OBE after Operation GRANBY, 1991; Military Assistant to Chief of the General Staff, 1993-94; Chief Operations Officer of the UN Military Observer Mission to Croatia, Bosnia, Montenegro, Macedonia and the remainder of the former Yugoslavia; Commanding Officer, 1st Battalion, The Royal Highland Fusiliers, 1995-97; Colonel, Army Personnel Centre, Glasgow, 1997-99; commanded 39 Infantry Brigade, 1999-2001; Chief of Staff and Commander Force Troops, HQNI, 2001-03; General Officer Commanding 2nd Division and Governor of Edinburgh Castle, 2004-07. Appointed CBE, 2004; Graduate of Higher Command and Staff Course and attended the Royal College of Defence Studies, January-March 2004; Chief Executive, Royal Edinburgh Military Tattoo, 2007-2011. Recreations: golf; shooting and conservation; farming; fishing; Scottish Contemporary Art.

Lovat, 16th Lord (Simon Fraser); b. 13.2.77. Educ. Harrow; Edinburgh University. Succeeded to title, 1995.

Lovatt, Charles, MA, MBA, FRSA. Company Director: LI Components Ltd, since 1985, Cacophony Ltd, since 1986; Senior Teaching Fellow, University of St Andrews; b. 1955, Liverpool; 2 d. Educ. Ratcliffe College; Dundee University; Edinburgh University. University of Dundee: Graduates' Council Business Committee, since 2005. Formerly member of: Education Scotland, 2011-2012 (External Member Audit), HMIe, 2010-2011 (External Member Audit), National Library of Scotland, 2009-2014 (Trustee and Board Member, Chair of Audit Committee), Arts Trust of Scotland, 2006-2010 (Trustee), Scottish Arts Council, 2006-2010 (Member of Council & Joint Board), Elmwood College, 2005-2012 (Board of Management, Chair of Quality Assurance Committee & Interim Chair of Audit Committee), Scottish Screen, 2005-2010 (Chair of Investment Committee). Recreations: hill walking; mountain biking; photography.

Love, Professor James, BA, MSc, PhD. Professor of Economics, Adam Smith Business School, University of Glasgow, 2013-2016 (former Head of School); Emeritus

Professor of Economics, formerly Deputy Principal, University of Strathclyde, Vice Principal, 2006-08, Pro Vice-Principal, 2004-06; b. 31.7.48, Dunfermline; m., Jane Lindores Scott; 2 d. Educ. Beath High School; Strathclyde University. Lecturer, Haile Sellassie 1 University, 1971-74; Lecturer, Strathclyde University, 1974-79; Lecturer, Ghana University, 1979-80; Senior Lecturer, University of Lund, 1980-81; Senior Research Fellow, Fraser of Allander Institute, 1984-86; Lecturer, Senior Lecturer, Reader, Strathclyde University, 1986-95; Head, Department of Economics, and Vice-Dean (Research), Strathclyde Business School, 1994-99, Dean, 1999-2004. Chairman, Board of Trustees, SOLAS. Recreations: sport; particularly the (mis)fortunes of Aberdeen FC and Cowdenbeath FC.

Love, Robert Malcolm, MA (Hons), FRSAMD. Independent Producer; Former Head of Drama, Scottish Television; b. 9.1.37, Paisley. Educ. Paisley Grammar School; Glasgow University; Washington University, St. Louis. Actor and Director, various repertory companies, including Nottingham Playhouse, 1962-65; Producer, Thames TV, 1966-75, including Public Eye, Van Der Valk; freelance Producer, 1976-79, including Thames TV, LWT, Seacastle Film Productions, Scottish TV. Awards including: Commonwealth Festival, New York TV and Film Festival, Chicago Film Festival, BAFTA Scotland, nominated for International Emmy, New York, 1982; productions for Scottish include Taggart, High Road, Doctor Finlay, McCallum, The Steamie, Machair. Governor, RSAMD, 1994-2002; Drama Chair, Scottish Arts Council, 1994-99; Chair, Beckett Time Festival, 2000; opera productions include Tosca, Susanna's Secret, Scott at the Opera; Director, Scottish International Piano Competition, 2001-2010. Recreations: literature; music; theatre; travel.

Love, Professor Sandy, BVMS, PhD. Chair, Equine Clinical Studies, University of Glasgow, since 1997; b. 14.3.60, Paisley. Educ. Kelvinside Academy; University of Glasgow. Private practice, Wetherby, Yorkshire 1982-84; Junior Fellow in Veterinary Surgery, University of Bristol, 1984-86; Horserace Betting Levy Board Research Scholar, 1986-87; Lecturer, Equine Medicine, University of Glasgow, 1987-97. Past President, British Equine Veterinary Association; Aberdeen Angus cattle breeder; British Horseracing Authority Racecourse Steward at Ayr, Hamilton Park and Perth. Recreation: racehorse owner. Address: Meikle Burntshields, Kilbarchan PA10 2PD; T.-01505 702642; e-mail: s.love69@btinternet.com

Lovelace, 5th Earl of (Peter Axel William Locke King); b. 26.11.51; m., Kathleen Anne Smolders; succeeded to title, 1964. Address: Ralia, 8 Aultnaskiach Road, Culduthel, Inverness IV2 4BB.

Lovell, Deborah Anne, LLB (Hons), DipLP. Partner, Anderson Strathern, Solicitors, since 2004; b. 28.12.72, Kirkcaldy. Educ. Balwearie High School, Kirkcaldy; Aberdeen University; Edinburgh University. Trainee, Campbell Smith WS, 1995-97; Assistant, McKay & Norwell, Solicitors, 1997-98; Assistant Solictor, Shepherd and Wedderburn, Solicitors, 1998-2002; Anderson Strathern, Solicitors, since 2002. Notary Public; Member, Law Society of Scotland Conveyancing Committee; Member, BCSC; Member, SPF Property Tax Group; Member, The WS Society Knowledge Services Committee; Tutor in Property on The University of Edinburgh Diploma in Legal Practice; Tutor on WS Society/Glasgow School of Law Professional Competence Course; voted a "Rising Star" in the World of Commercial Real Estate by Property Executive Magazine; Member, The Anderson Strathern Team which won The Scott & Co. Specialist Client Team

of The Year Award at The Scottish Legal Awards, 2006 for Property Work on The Stirling-Alloa Kincardine Railway Act. Recreations: horse riding; reading; ski-ing. Address: Anderson Strathern, 1 Rutland Court, Edinburgh EH3 8EY; T.-0131 270 7700.
E-mail: deborah.lovell@andersonstrathern.co.uk

Low, Alistair James, BSc, FFA. Director, Cruden Investments; b. 2.8.42, Dundee; m., Shona Wallace; 2 s.; 1 d. Educ. Dundee High School; St. Andrews University. Recreations: golf; skiing; bridge. Address: (h.) Thornfield, Erskine Loan, Gullane, East Lothian.

Lowder, George, OBE, LLB, MA, QCVS. Chief Executive, Transport for Edinburgh, since 2015; b. Edinburgh. Educ. Cranfield University; University of Aberdeen; University of Strathclyde. Commander and Operations Director, Defence/Army, 1981-2004; Commanding Officer, Army/Defence, 2004-2006; Head of Strategic Planning, United States Department of Defense, 2006; Deputy Director, Strategy, Plans and Policy, UK Ministry of Defence - Defence Intelligence, 2006-09; Head, Security Sector Reform, US Department of State, 2009-2010; Commander of The Army in Scotland, 2010-12; Head of Defence Intelligence Operations, UK Ministry of Defence, 2012-15; Senior Executive, Ministry of Defence, 2012-15. Deputy Colonel and Trustee, The Royal Regiment of Scotland, since 2010; Trustee, The Royal Scots (The Royal Regiment), since 2004; Trustee, Bridge of Don and Glencorse Trust, October 2013. Commendation, Operation Granby, May 1991; Bronze Star, USA, 2006. Recreations: keen skier and golfer. Address: (b.) Annandale Street, Edinburgh EH7 4AZ; T.-0131 554 4494.

Lowe, Professor Gordon Douglas Ogilvie, DSc, MB, ChB, MD, FRCPEdin, FRCPGlas, FRCPLond, FFPH. Emeritus Professor, Glasgow University; b. 2.1.49, London; m., Ann Harvie; 1 s.; 1 d. Educ. Dundee High School; St. Andrews University. House Officer, Royal Infirmary and Maryfield Hospital, Dundee, 1972-73; Senior House Officer, City Hospital, Nottingham, 1973-74; Registrar, Royal Infirmary, Glasgow, 1974-77; Lecturer, Glasgow University, 1978-85, Senior Lecturer, 1985-92, Reader, 1992-93, Professor of Vascular Medicine, 1993-2009. Former Assessor, RCPEdin.; Chairman, SIGN, 2002-07; Past President, British Society for Haemostasis and Thrombosis. Publications: editor of books and author of publications on thrombosis and bleeding disorders. Recreations: travel; railways; gardening. Address: (b.) Room 2.44, New Lister Building, Royal Infirmary, 10 Alexandra Parade, Glasgow G31 2ER; T.-0141-201-8517.

Lowe, Dr. Janet, CBE, BA (Hons), MBA, EdD, DEd, FRSE. Member, Scottish Further and Higher Education Funding Council, 2005-2013; b. 27.9.50, South Normanton; m., Donald Thomas Stewart. Educ. Swanwick Hall Grammar School; Hull University; Dundee University; Stirling University. Immigration Officer, Home Office, 1973-76; Personnel Assistant, Hull University, 1976-80; Administrator, Lothian Region Social Work Department, 1980-82; Napier University: Examinations Officer, Personnel Officer, Assistant Academic Registrar, 1982-88; Secretary and Registrar, Duncan of Jordanstone College of Art, 1988-93; Lauder College: Depute Principal, 1993-96, Principal, 1996-2005. Member: Local Government Finance Review Committee, 2004-06, Board of Management, Scottish Further Education Unit, 1993-2001, Court, Heriot-Watt University, 1999-2005, Court, Dundee University, 2005-2013, Board, Scottish Enterprise, 1998-2004, Board, Skills Development Scotland, 2008-2013; President, Rotary Club of Dunfermline Carnegie, 2008-09; US-UK Fulbright Commissioner, 2009-2012; Honorary Professor, Stirling

University, 2010-2015; Elected Fellow of The Royal Society of Edinburgh, 2010; Trustee, Carnegie Trust for the Universities of Scotland, 2006-2015. Recreations: travel; photography; gardening. Address: 42 Gamekeepers Road, Kinnesswood, Kinross KY13 9JR; T.-01592 840277; e-mail: janetlowe@aol.com

Lowther, Gordon William, BSc, DipRCPath. Head of Service - Genetics, Consultant Clinical Cytogeneticist, Institute of Medical Genetics, Glasgow, since 1997; b. 5.12.55, Newcastle upon Tyne. Educ. Dame Allans Boys School; Sheffield University. Clinical Cytogeneticist, Centre for Human Genetics, Sheffield, 1979-87; Principal Cytogeneticist, then Consultant Clinical Cytogeneticist, Medical Genetics Glasgow. Member, Association for Clinical Genetic Science. Address: (b.) West of Scotland Regional Genetic Services, Laboratory Medicine, Southern General Hospital, 1345 Govan Road, Glasgow GS1 4TF; T.-0141 354 9298.

Ludlam, Professor Christopher A., BSc (Hons), MB, ChB, PhD, FRCP, FRCPath. Emeritus Professor of Haematology and Coagulation Medicine, University of Edinburgh; formerly Consultant Haematologist, Edinburgh Royal Infirmary, 1980-2011; Director, Edinburgh Haemophilia and Thrombosis Centre, 1980-2011; b. 6.6.46, Edinburgh. Educ. Edinburgh University. MRC Research Fellow, 1972-75; Senior Registrar in Haematology, University Hospital of Wales, Cardiff, 1975-78; Lecturer in Haematology, University of Wales, 1979. Address: (b.) School of Clinical Sciences and Community Health, University of Edinburgh, 47 Little France Crescent, Edinburgh; T.-0131 667-6232.
E-mail: Christopher.Ludlam@ed.ac.uk

Lugton, (Charles) Michael Arber, MA. Convener, Administration Board, Scottish Episcopal Church, 2010-15; Member, Business Committee, General Council, University of Edinburgh, 2010-15; Chief Executive, Scottish Law Commission, 2005-08; b. 5.4.51, South Africa; m. Joyce Graham; 2 s. Educ. St. John's College, Johannesburg; the Edinburgh Academy; University of Edinburgh. Joined Scottish Office in 1973; Private Secretary to Permanent Under Secretary of State, 1976-78; Principal Private Secretary to successive Secretaries of State, 1995-97; Head of Constitution and Legal Services Group, Scottish Executive, 2004-05. Recreation: South Africa.

Luke, Garry Alec, PhD (Aberdeen), MBA (Heriot-Watt), MSc (Aberdeen), BSc (Aberdeen), MA (St Andrews), FRSB. Research Scientist; b. 19.2.54, Aberdeen; m., Jane Knowles Murray. Educ. Mackie Academy, Stonehaven; University of St Andrews. Research Scientist, Department of Obstetrics and Gynaecology, University of Aberdeen, 1983-89; Research Fellow, Glasgow Dental Hospital and School, University of Glasgow, 1989-90, University of St Andrews, since 1990. Listed in Who's Who in the World, since 2003; Who's Who in Science and Engineering, since 2007 and biographical dictionaries (Dictionary of International Biography, 2004, Cambridge Blue Book, 2005/06). Peer reviewed publications in numerous scientific journals/books. Recreations: natural history; walking; mediaeval history. Address: (h.) 5 Carr Crescent, Crail, Anstruther, Fife KY10 3XR; (b.) Centre for Biomolecular Sciences, University of St Andrews, Fife KY16 9ST; T.-01334 463415; e-mail: gal@st-andrews.ac.uk

Lumsden, Professor Keith Grant, MA, PhD, FRSE. Professor and Director, Edinburgh Business School, Heriot-Watt University; b. 7.1.35, Bathgate; m. (1), Jean Baillie MacDonald; 1 s.; m. (2), Ruth Edith Reid, 2008. Educ. Bathgate Academy; Edinburgh University; Stanford University, California. Instructor, Department of Economics, then Assistant Professor, Graduate School of Business, Stanford University, 1960-67; Research Associate, Stanford Research Institute, 1965-71; Director, Stanford University Conference: NDTE, 1966, RREE, 1968; Associate Professor, Graduate School of Business, Stanford University, 1968-75; Visiting Professor of Economics, Heriot-Watt University, 1969-70; Director: Economics Education Project, 1969-74, Behavioral Research Laboratories, 1970-72, Capital Preservation Fund Inc., 1971-75, Nielsen Engineering Research Inc., 1972-75; Member, American Economic Association Committee on Economic Education, 1978-81; Academic Director, Sea Transport Executive Programme (STEP), since 1979; Professor of Economics, Advanced Management College, Stanford University, since 1971; Affiliate Professor of Economics, INSEAD, France; Member: Economics Education 14-16 Project, Manchester University, Advisory Council, David Hume Institute, 1984-99, Board of Directors, Hewlett Packard Ltd., 1982-92; Henry Villard Award, Economics America, 1994. Publications: The Free Enterprise System, 1963; The Gross National Product, 1964; International Trade, 1965; Microeconomics: A Programmed Book, 1966; Macroeconomics: A Programmed Book, 1966; New Developments in the Teaching of Economics (Editor), 1967; Excess Demand and Excess Supply in World Tramp Shipping Markets, 1968; Recent Research in Economics Education (Editor), 1970; Basic Economics: Theory and Cases, 1973; Efficiency in Universities: The La Paz Papers (Editor), 1974; Economics Education in the United Kingdom, 1980; Economics: a distance learning study programme, 1991. Recreations: golf; deep sea sports fishing. Address: (h.) 40 Lauder Road, Edinburgh EH9 1UE.

Lumsden, Vivien Dale Victoria, DSD, CDS. Journalist and Television and Radio Presenter, since 1984; Media Consultant, The Broadcasting Business; b. 22.11.52, Edinburgh; m., Alan Douglas (qv); 1 s.; 1 d. Educ. James Gillespie's High School for Girls, Edinburgh; RSAMD. Full-time mother, 1975-82; AA Traffic News Reporter, 1982-84; BBC Scotland: Breakfast Newsreader, 1984-85, Reporting Scotland Presenter, 1985-89, Garden Party, 1988; joined Scottish TV as Presenter, Scotland Today, 1989; also presented chat show, Telethon, BAFTA Awards, Business Game, Home Show; Member of the fundraising committee for Cancer Support Scotland. Recreations: acting; cooking; writing; wine; food; travel; grandchildren! Address: (b.) Pink Elephant Communications, Lochinch House, Dumbreck Road, Glasgow G41 4SN.
E-mail: viv.lumsden@ntlworld.com

Lunan, Charles Burnett, MD, FRCOG, FRCS. Consultant Obstetrician, Princess Royal Maternity, Glasgow, 1977-2005; Consultant Gynaecologist, Royal Infirmary, Glasgow, 1977-2005; b. London; m., Helen Russell Ferrie; 2 s.; 1 d. Educ. High School of Glasgow; Glasgow University. Lecturer, Obstetrics and Gynaecology, Aberdeen University, 1973-75; Senior Lecturer, University of Nairobi, 1975-77; WHO Consultant, Family Planning Programme, Bangladesh, 1984-85. Treasurer, 1982-90, Vice-President, 1990-91, President, Royal Medico-Chirurgical Society of Glasgow, 1991-92; Secretary, Glasgow Obstetrical and Gynaecological Society, 1978-82, Vice President, 1998-2002, President, 2002-04. Recreations: gardening; photography; hill-walking. Address: (h.) Little Newhall, Kinrossie, Perthshire PH2 6HP.

Lunn, John Alexander, LLB (Hons), DipLP, NP. Partner, Morton Fraser LLP, since 2002, Solicitor, since 1988; b.

23.2.64, Haddington; m., Joan; 2 s. Educ. Knox Academy, Haddington; Edinburgh University. Traineeship with East Lothian District Council, 1986-88. Recreations: karate; golf; skiing. Address: (b.) Quartermile Two, 2 Lister Square, Edinburgh EH3 9GL; T.-0131 247 1066.
E-mail: john.lunn@morton-fraser.com

Lunney, James Thomas, LLB, BA (Hons), NP. District Tribunal Judge, Scotland, First-Tier Tribunal, Social Entitlement Chamber; Deputy Judge, Upper Tribunal; District Chairman, The Appeals Service, 1999-2008; Full-time Chairman, Independent Tribunal Service, 1995-99; b. 24.7.54, Glasgow; m., Patricia Anne Lunney, BDS, BA; 2 d. Educ. St. Mirin's Academy, Paisley; Strathclyde University. Apprentice to Pattison & Sim, Solicitors, Paisley, 1979-81; Assistant, 1981-83, Partner, 1983-95; part-time Chairman, Independent Tribunal Service, 1992-95. Recreations: golf; reading; tennis; skiing; motor-cycling. Address: (b.) Wellington House, 134-136 Wellington Street, Glasgow G2 2XL.

Luscombe, Rt. Rev. Lawrence Edward, ChStJ, MA, MPhil, PhD, LLD, DLitt, CA, FRSA, FSA Scot. Primus of the Scottish Episcopal Church, 1985-90, and Bishop of Brechin, 1975-90; a Trustee of the Scottish Episcopal Church, since 1985; b. 10.11.24; m., Dr. Doris Morgan (deceased); 1 d. Educ. Kelham College; King's College, London; Dundee University. Indian Army, 1942-47; Major; Chartered Accountant, 1952; Partner, Galbraith Dunlop & Co. (later Watson and Galbraith), CA, 1953-63; Curate, St. Margaret's, Glasgow, 1963-66; Rector, St. Barnabas', Paisley, 1966-71; Provost, St. Paul's Cathedral, Dundee, 1971-75. Honorary Canon, Trinity Cathedral, Davenport, Iowa, since 1983; Member, Education Committee, Renfrew County Council, 1967-71; Chairman, Governing Body: Glenalmond College, 1986-94; President, Old Glenalmond Club, 1998-2007; Chairman, Governing Body, Edinburgh Theological College, 1985-90; Governor: Lathallan School, 1982-2000, Dundee College of Education, 1982-87; Chairman, Inter-Anglican Finance Committee, 1989-93; Member, Tayside Health Board, 1989-93; Honorary Research Fellow, Dundee University, since 1993; Member, Court of Corporation of the Sons of the Clergy, 1985-99. Address: (h.) Woodville, Kirkton of Tealing, by Dundee DD4 0RD; T.-01382 380331.

Lusk, Dr. Christine (Chris), PhD (St. Andrews), BSc (Edin), CQSW, DipSW, PTA. Director of Student Services, University of St. Andrews, since 2006; b. 04.06.59, Glasgow; m., Andy Neil; 2 s.; 2 d. Educ. Madras College; Universities of Edinburgh, Dundee and St. Andrews. Social Worker in Childcare, NAI Investigations and Homefinding work, 1981-92; University of St. Andrews: Welfare Adviser, Students' Association, 1992-97, Assistant Hebdomadar, 1997-2001, Director of Student Support, 2001-06. Research Interests and publications on the cultural interaction between the diverse student and ancient higher education. Recreations: hill-walking; music; cinema; running; kick-boxing; family. Address: (b.) The ASC (Advice and Support Centre), 79 North Street, St Andrews, Fife KY16 9AL; T.-01334-462020.
E-mail: clusk@st-andrews.ac.uk

Lyall, Professor Fiona, BSc, PhD, MBA, MRCPath. Professor of Maternal and Fetal Health, Yorkhill Hospital, Glasgow, since 2003; b. Johnstone. Educ. Uddingston Grammar Secondary School; University of Glasgow. British Heart Foundation Fellow, MRC Blood Pressure Unit, Glasgow, 1990-92; Obstetrics and Gynaecology, University of Glasgow: Lecturer, 1992-97, Senior Lecturer, 1997-2001, Reader, 2001-02. Member of Medical Advisory Committee for "Tommys The Baby Charity".

Publicaton: Pre-Eclampsia: Etiology and Clinical Practice, 2007. Recreations: aerobics instructor; ski instructor; own horse and dogs. Address: (b.) Institute of Medical Genetics, Yorkhill, Glasgow G3 8SJ; T.-0141 201 0657; e-mail: fionalyall@btinternet.com

Lyall, Fiona Jane, MBE, DL, MB, ChB, DPH. Family Doctor, Laurencekirk, since 1959; Director, Grampian Television PLC, since 1980; Non-Executive Director: Aberdeen Royal Hospitals NHS Trust, since 1992, Templehill Community Council, since 1990; Deputy Lieutenant, Kincardineshire, since 1985; b. 13.4.31, Inverness; m., Dr. Alan Richards Lyall; 1 s.; 1 d. Educ. Inverness Royal Academy; Aberdeen University. Former Member, Laurencekirk Burgh Council; former Kincardine County and Grampian Regional Councillor; Member: Grampian Health Board, 1974, and Kincardine & Deeside Health Council, 1974, Children's Panel Advisory Committee, 1974, Grampian Valuation Appeals Committee, Prince's and Royal Jubilee Trust for Grampian; Treasurer, Action Research for Crippled Child; Trustee, Kincardineshire Silver Jubilee Trust, since 1985. Recreations: skiing; riding; golf. Address: Melrose Bank, Laurencekirk AB30 1FJ; T.-01561 377220; e-mail: fionalyall@btinternet.com

Lyall, Ian James Graeme, MA, LLB, NP. Partner (Property Finance), Pinsent Masons, since 2012 (McGrigors, Solicitors, Edinburgh, 1987-2012); b. 25.4.55, Glasgow; m., Pamela Lyall (nee Coats); 2 s.; 2 d. Educ. Greenock Academy; Aberdeen University. McGrigors, Glasgow Office, Trainee/Apprentice, 1978-80; Assistant Solicitor: McGrigors, Glasgow Office, 1980-84, Baker & McKenzie, London, 1984-86; Head of Real Estate, McGrigors, 1997-2000. Deputy Chairman, EMMS Nazareth (Scottish Charity owning and operating a hospital and school of nursing in Nazareth, Israel). Recreations: skiing; church; motorcycling; family. Address: (h.) 16 Nile Grove, Morningside, Edinburgh EH10 4RF; T.-0131 777 7033; e-mail: ian.lyall@pinsentmasons.com

Lyall, Michael Hodge, MB, ChB, ChM, FRCSEdin. Consultant Surgeon, Tayside University Hospitals NHS Trust, 1975-2006, Medical Director, 2001-06; Honorary Senior Lecturer, Dundee University, since 1975; b. 5.12.41, Methilhill, Fife; m., Catherine B. Jarvie; 3 s. Educ. Buckhaven High School; St. Andrews University. Past President, North Fife Rotary Club; Paul Harris Fellow. Recreation: digital photography. Address: 1 Vernonholme, Riverside Drive, Dundee DD2 1QJ.
E-mail: mhlyall@aol.com

Lyell, 3rd Baron (Charles Lyell), Bt. Elected Member, House of Lords, since 1999; Parliamentary Under-Secretary of State, Northern Ireland Office, 1984-89; b. 27.3.39. Educ. Eton; Christ Church, Oxford. Scots Guards, 1957-59; CA; Opposition Whip, 1974-79; Government Whip, 1979-84; Member, Queen's Bodyguard for Scotland (Royal Company of Archers); DL, Angus, 1988. Address: (h.) Kinnordy House, Kirriemuir, Angus.

Lyle, David Angus, MA, LLB, SSC. Consultant, Solicitor, and Chartered Company Secretary, in private practice, 1993-2010 (retired 2010); b. 7.9.40; m. (1) (1969), Dorothy Ann Clark (marr. diss. 2004); 1 s.; 3 d.; m. (2) (2007), Joyce Simpson (nee Walton). Educ. George Watson's College, Edinburgh; Edinburgh University. Account Executive, Advertising Agencies, London; Indentured, Edinburgh Corporation; Solicitor, Lloyds and Scottish Finance Ltd., Edinburgh; Depute County Clerk, East Lothian County Council; Director of Administration and Law, Dumfries and

Galloway Regional Council; Agency Secretary, Scottish Development Agency; Director/Company Secretary, Scottish Enterprise. Recreations: travel; golf; rambling; munro-bagging. Address: (h.) 56 Strathspey Drive, Grantown-on-Spey, Morayshire PH26 3EY; T.-01479 873814.

Lyle, Kaliani. Scotland Commissioner, Equality and Human Rights Commission. Leads the Scotland Committee which is involved in working strategically with the Scottish Government, Local Authorities, UK Government and Parliament to ensure equality and human rights are at the heart of all work carried out. Career: first race relations officer, Edinburgh District Council, 1989-92; CEO of Scottish Refugee Council, 1995-98; CEO of Citizens Advice Scotland, 1998-2010. Current and previous involvement: Board Member, OSCR; member of Christie Commission on Future delivery of public services in Scotland, Sentencing Commission, McFadden Commission on Charity Law Reform, and Lord Provost Commission on Social Inclusion. Received the Alastair Hetherington Award for humanitarian service by the Institute of Contemporary Scotland in 2007. Address: (b.) EHRC, 151 West George Street, Glasgow G2 2JJ; T.-0141 228 5910.

Lyle, Richard. MSP (SNP), Uddingston and Bellshill, since 2016 (Central Scotland region, 2011-16); b. 12.6.50, Bothwellhaugh, Lanarkshire. Educ. Lawmuir School; Bellshill Academy. Joined the SNP at the age of 16; served as local councillor in Motherwell and North Lanarkshire Council, since 1976; SNP group leader, 1976-95 and North Lanarkshire Council Leader, 1995-2011; COSLA, 2007-2009. Address: (b.) Scottish Parliament, Edinburgh EH99 1SP.

Lynch, Margaret, MA (Hons). Former Chief Executive, Citizens Advice Scotland (2012-2016). Educ. Glasgow University. Career: Development Officer, Technical Services Agency, 1983-87; Director, Labour Communications Ltd, 1987-90; Development Officer, Greater Easterhouse Initiative, 1990-91; Researcher, Scottish Low Pay Unit, 1991-92; Corporate Policy Officer, Central Regional Council, 1991-92; Chief Executive, War on Want, 1995-98; Head of Overseas Programmes, Scottish Catholic International Aid Fund (SCIAF), 2000-07; Quality Matters Co-ordinator, Scottish Council for Voluntary Organisations (SCVO), 2009-10; Director, Scottish Mediation Network, 2010-12. Board Member, Conforti Institute.

Lynch, Professor Michael, MA, PhD, FRHistS, FSAScot. Sir William Fraser Professor of Scottish History, University of Edinburgh, 1992-2005; Chairman, Ancient Monuments Board for Scotland, 1996-2002; President, Society of Antiquaries of Scotland, 1996-99; Trustee, National Museums of Scotland, 2002-05; b. 15.6.46, Aberdeen. Educ. Aberdeen Grammar School; University of Aberdeen; University of London. Lecturer, Department of History, University College, Bangor, 1971-79; Department of Scottish History, University of Edinburgh: Lecturer, 1979-88, Senior Lecturer, 1988-92. Chairman, Historical Association Committee for Scotland, since 1992; Editor, The Innes Review, 1984-92. Publications: Edinburgh and the Reformation, 1981 (SAC Literary Award); The Early Modern Town in Scotland, 1986; The Scottish Medieval Town, 1987; Mary Stewart: Queen in Three Kingdoms, 1988; Scotland: A New History, 1991 (SAC Literary Award); The Reign of James VI, 2000; The Oxford Companion to Scottish History, 2001; Aberdeen before 1800: A New History, 2002; The University of Edinburgh: An Illustrated History, 2003.

Lyon, Catherine E., BA, MA, FCS. Justice of the Peace, Glasgow District, 1996-2003; Bailie, City of Glasgow, 1999-2003; Member, Glasgow City Council, 1995-2003, Conservative Group Leader, 1997-1999; b.

Scotland; m., Andrew. Educ. International Christian University. Japan International Cultural Institute; Teacher of English as a Foreign Language; Freelance interpreter. Constituency Chairman: Pollok Conservative Association, 1982-86, Govan Conservative Association, 1995-2002; Strathclyde Regional Councillor, 1990-95; Chairman, Scottish Conservative Councillors Association, 1998-2002; Depute Chairman, Tory Reform Group (Scotland), 1996-2004; Member, Strathclyde Fire Board, 1996-2003; Patron, Hutchesons' Hospital, 1996-2003; Trustee, Hutchesons' Educational Trust and Member, Board of Governors, Hutchesons' Grammar School, 1997-2007; Member, Institute of Linguists (Scotland); Ambassador for Girl Guiding (Scotland). Recreations: art; history; music; theatre; literature; antiques; food and wine; gardens; architecture; my animals. T.-0141 427 0040.

Lyon, George. Former Member, European Parliament (Liberal Democrat, 2009-2014); b. 16.7.56; m. (divorced); 3 d. Educ. Rothesay Academy; Nuffield Scholar. Founder and owner of farming business, 1994-2009; Director, Scottish Quality Beef and Lamb Association, 1996-97; MSP (Lib Dem), Argyll & Bute, 1999-2007. Member, National Farmers Union of Scotland (held every office including President); Past Chairman, Port Bannatyne School Board; FRAgS. Recreations: swimming; football; skiing; reading.

Lyon, Inglis E. Chief Executive, Highlands and Islands Airports Ltd, since 2005. Address: (b.) Head Office, Inverness Airport, Inverness IV2 7JB.

Mac/Mc

McAdam, Douglas, BSc. Chief Executive, Scottish Land & Estates, since 2006; b. 13.10.66, Haddington, East Lothian; m., Diah; 1 d. Educ. George Watsons College; Dollar Academy; St. Andrews University. General Management Career with John Swire & Sons based in the Far East, 1988-98; General Management with Thames Water (running their Scottish based operations), 1998-2006. Recreations: classic cars; mountain biking; field sports. Address: (b.) Stuart House, Eskmills Business Park, Musselburgh.
E-mail: douglas.mcadam@scottishlandandestates.co.uk

McAllion, John, MA (Hons). MSP, Dundee East, 1999-2003 (Labour); Board Member, Scottish Fair Trade Forum; b. 13.2.48, Glasgow; m., Susan Jean; 2 s. Educ. St. Augustine's Secondary, Glasgow; St. Andrews University. Secondary, Dundee, 1973-78, Social Studies, Balgowan List D School, Dundee, 1978-82; Research Assistant to Bob McTaggart, MP, 1982-86; Regional Councillor, 1984-87; Convener, Tayside Regional Council, 1986-87; Member, Scottish Executive, Labour Party, 1986-88; Senior Vice Chairperson, Dundee Labour Party, 1986, 1987; MP (Labour), Dundee East, 1987-2001. Member, Scottish Socialist Party. Recreations: football; reading; music. Address: (h.) 3 Haldane Street, Dundee DD3 0HP; e-mail: johnmccallion@yahoo.co.uk

McAllister, Eleanor, OBE, HonFRIAS, FRSA, MA, MSc. Consultant in Regeneration; Managing Director, Clydebank Re-built, 2002-2012; b. 08.12.53, Glasgow; 2 d. Educ. Notre Dame High School; Glasgow and Strathclyde. Director, Glasgow Building Preservation Trust, 1984-91; Depute Head, Strathclyde Partnership Office, SRC, 1992-96; Depute Director, Glasgow 1999 Festival Company, 1996-99; Head of Economic and Social Initiatives, Glasgow City Council, 1999-2002. Governor, Glasgow School of Art; Member, Heritage Lottery Fund Scotland Committee. Address: (b.) 10 Vancouver Road, Glasgow G14 9HJ; T.-0141 533 2589; e-mail: ellie53@ntlworld.com

McAlpine, Joan, MA (Hons). MSP (SNP), South Scotland, since 2011; Columnist, Daily Record, since 2012; b. 28.1.64, Gourock; m., Pat Kane (qv) (divorced); 2 d. Educ. St. Columba's RC Comprehensive, Greenock; James Watt College, Greenock; Glasgow University; City University, London. Reporter, Greenock Telegraph, The Scotsman; Reporter, Feature Writer, Columnist, The Scotsman, 1992-95; Feature Writer and Columnist, Daily Record, 1995; Columnist and Feature Writer, then Deputy Editor (News), Sunday Times, 1996-2000; Editor, Sunday Times Scotland, 2000-01; Deputy Editor, The Herald, 2001-06; formerly Columnist, The Scotsman. Journalist of the Year, Scottish Press Awards, 1999; Feature Writer of the Year, Scottish Press Awards, 1999. Publication: A Time to Rage (Co-author with Tommy Sheridan), 1994. Recreations: family; listening to R&B; visiting Islay; Scotland. Address: (b.) Scottish Parliament, Edinburgh EH99 1SP.

McAndrew, Nicolas, CA. Chairman: Martin Currie Enhanced Income Investment Trust PLC, 1998-2005, Beauly District Fishery Board, 2003-2012; Director, Liverpool Victoria Friendly Society, 1996-2005; b. 9.12.34, London; 2 s.; 1 d. Educ. Winchester College. National Service (The Black Watch) commission, 1953-55; articled clerk, Peat Marwick Mitchell, 1955-61; qualified CA, 1961; S.G. Warburg & Co. Ltd., Merchant Bankers, 1962-78; became Chairman, Warburg Investment Management Ltd., and Director, Mercury Securities Ltd.; Managing Director, N.M. Rothschild & Sons Ltd., Merchant Bankers, 1979-88; Chairman: Murray Johnstone Ltd., 1992-99, Derby Trust PLC, 1999-2003. Master, Worshipful Company of Grocers, 1978-79; Board Member: Highlands and Islands Enterprise, 1993-97, North of Scotland Water Authority, 1995-2002. Recreations: fishing; shooting. Address: (h.) Ard-na-Coille, Ruisaurie, by Beauly, Inverness-shire IV4 7AJ; T.-01463 782524.

McAra-McWilliam, Professor Irene, MA, FRSA. Professor of Design, Head of School of Design, The Glasgow School of Art, since 2005; Consultant to industry and government, since 2001; b. 4.2.54, Dufftown; m., Angus McAra. Educ. Mortlach Senior Secondary School; University of Aberdeen. Director of Design Research, Philips Electronics, The Netherlands, 1992-2001; Advisor to European Commission, 1995-2001; Professor of Design Research, University of Technology, Eindhoven, The Netherlands, 2003-05; Professor of Interaction Design and Head of Department, Royal College of Art, London, 2001-04. FRSA; FRCA. Address: (b.) The Glasgow School of Art, 167 Renfrew Street, Glasgow G3 6RQ; T.-0141-353-4589; e-mail: i.mcara-mcwilliam@gsa.ac.uk

McArdle, David Anthony, LLB, PhD. Senior Lecturer, School of Law, Stirling University, since 2005; b. 03.09.67, Chesterfield; partner, Charity Smith; 2 s.; 1 d. Educ. Chesterfield School; University of Wales Aberystwyth; Manchester Metropolitan University. Research Assistant, Manchester Metropolitan University, 1993-97; Research Fellow, De Montfort, Middlesex University, 1997-2001; Lecturer, Robert Gordon University, 2002-05. Several books and numerous articles on legal issues in sport; advice work for various national and international sports bodies and local authorities. Recreations: running; cycling; hillwalking. Address: (b.) School of Law, University of Stirling, Stirling FK9 4LA; T.-01786 467285; e-mail: d.a.mcardle@stir.ac.uk

McArdle, Professor Harry John, BSc (Hons), PhD. Professor, in Biomedical Sciences, University of Aberdeen, since 2000; Honorary Professor in Biological Sciences, University of Nottingham, since 2006; Fellow of Royal Society of Medicine, since 2011; b. 4.1.53, Glasgow; m., Karen Ann. Educ. St. Augustine School, Edinburgh; St. Andrews University. Raines Research Fellow, University of Western Australia; Senior Scientist, Murdoch Institute for Research into Birth Defects, Melbourne, Australia, 1985-90; Lecturer/Senior Lecturer, Department of Child Health, University of Dundee, 1990-96. Recreations: hillwalking; horse riding; skiing. Address: (b.) Rowett Institute of Nutrition and Health, Bucksburn, Aberdeen AB21 9SB; T.-01224 716628; e-mail: h.mcardle@abdn.ac.uk

McArdle, Karen Ann, MA (Hons), MEd, DPhil. Reader, Director of Research and Knowledge Exchange, School of Education, University of Aberdeen, since 2003; b. 16.03.58, Leeds; m., Harry John McArdle. Educ. Harrogate Grammar School; St. Andrews University; La Trobe University; University of West of England. Training and Development Officer, RYMC Training and Development Service, 1981-84; University of Western Australia: Graduate Research Assistant, 1984-85, Extension Officer, 1985-86; Manager, Special Projects, Melbourne College of Textiles, 1986-89; Senior Research Consultant, State Training Board, Australia, 1989-90; Executive Officer, Fife Regional Council, 1990-94; Northern College of Education: Lecturer, 1994-96, Programme Director, 1996-2003. Recreations: horse riding; hillwalking; reading. Address: (b.) University of Aberdeen, King's College Campus, Aberdeen AB24 5UA; T.-01224 274654; e-mail: k.a.mcardle@abdn.ac.uk

Macarthur, Edith, MBE. Actress; b. Ardrossan, Ayrshire. Educ. Ardrossan Academy. Began career, 1948, with Wilson Barrett Company, then Perth Repertory, Gateway Theatre Company, Citizens' Theatre, Glasgow, Bristol Old Vic, Royal Shakespeare Company, Ochtertyre Theatre, Royal Lyceum Theatre Company, West End; television work includes The Borderers, Sunset Song, Weir of Hermiston, Sutherland's Law, Take the High Road, Dr. Finlay, Hamish Macbeth; Taggart; Golden Wedding; nominated for Scottish BAFTA award in The Long Roads, 1993; recent stage appearances: solo-performance play, Marie of Scotland, Jamie the Saxt and The Thrie Estates for the Scottish Theatre Company at Edinburgh Festivals and Warsaw International Festival, 1986, Judith Bliss in Hay Fever, Royal Lyceum Theatre, 1987, Charley's Aunt, Death of a Salesman, Royal Lyceum, 1988, Daphne Laureola, Pygmalion, Pride and Prejudice, Pitlochry Festival Theatre, 1988; The Cherry Orchard, Royal Lyceum, 1989; The Cherry Orchard, The Circle, Arsenic and Old Lace, Pitlochry, 1990; Driving Miss Daisy, Perth, 1991; Cinderella, Glasgow and Edinburgh, 1990, 1991; Good, Glasgow and Edinburgh, 1992; Long Day's Journey into Night, Dundee, 1994 (TMA/Martini Best Actress nomination); The Prime of Miss Jean Brodie, London, 1994-95; The Flou'ers o' Edinburgh; On Golden Pond; Long Day's Journey into Night, Pitlochry Festival Theatre, and tour, 1996; Widows, Traverse Theatre, and tour, 1997. Recreations: music; books.

MacArthur, Elspeth, MA. Member, Board of Management, John Wheatley College, since 2007; Lay Member, Judicial Appointments Board for Scotland, since 2007; Director/Trustee, Scottish Community Development Centre, since 2009; Lay Member, Employment Tribunals Scotland, since 2010; b. 4.2.51, St. Andrews; m., Prof. Michael Anderson. Educ. Madras College; University of Aberdeen; University of Strathclyde. Personnel Assistant, Remploy Ltd, 1975-81; Senior Personnel Officer and Deputy Head of Personnel, British Standards Institution, 1981-91; Assistant/Deputy Director of Personnel, University of Edinburgh, 1991-98, Director of Human Resources, 1998-2007. Scottish HR Director of the Year (not for profit), 2003; Chair, Universities Personnel Association (UK), 2005-07. Address: (b.) Judicial Appointments Board for Scotland, 38-39 Drumsheugh Gardens, Edinburgh EH3 7SW.
E-mail: elspethmacarthur@btinternet.com

McArthur, Liam, MA (Hons). MSP (Liberal Democrat), Orkney, since 2007; b. 8.8.67; m.; 2 s. Educ. Kirkwall Grammar School, Orkney; Edinburgh University. Researcher, Jim Wallace MP, House of Commons, 1990-92; Trainee, European Commission (External Affairs directorate), 1992-93; Account Executive, various EU public affairs consultancies, 1993-96; Associate Director, APCO and APCO Europe, 1996-2002; Special Adviser to Deputy First Minister, Jim Wallace MSP, 2002-05; Director, Greenhaus communications, 2005-06; self employed political consultant, 2006-07. Member: Finance Committee, 2007-08, Rural Affairs & Environment Committee, 2008-2011, Education & Culture Committee, since 2011, Scottish Parliament Corporate Body, Advisory Audit Committee. Address: (b.) Scottish Parliament, Edinburgh EH99 1SP; T.-0131 348 5815; Constituency Office: 14 Palace Road, Kirkwall, Orkney KW15 1PA; T.-01856 876541.
E-mail: liam.mcarthur.msp@scottish.parliament.uk

MacAskill, Kenny, LLB (Hons). MSP (SNP), Edinburgh Eastern, 2011-2016, Edinburgh East and Musselburgh, 2007-2011, Lothians, 1999-2007; Cabinet Secretary for Justice, 2007-2014; Shadow Justice Minister, 2004-07; b. 1958, Edinburgh; m.; 2 s. Educ. Linlithgow Academy; Edinburgh University. Former Solicitor. Former member of the SNP's National Executive Committee and has served as National Treasurer and Vice Convener of Policy.

McAteer, Dympna, MB, BCh, BAO, FRCP, MRad, FRCR. Consultant Radiologist, since 1999; b. 7.11.65, Letterkenny. Educ. Loreto College, Milford; Trinity College Dublin. Junior House Officer, Altnagelvin Hospital, Derry, 1989-90; Medical Senior House Officer, Royal Victoria Hospital, Belfast, 1990-92; Medical Registrar, Belfast City and Whiteabbey Hospitals, 1992-94; Radiology Registrar, Aberdeen Royal Infirmary, 1994-99. Recreations: squash; running; skiing. Address: Department of Radiology, Aberdeen Royal Infirmary, Foresterhill, Aberdeen AB25 2ZN; T.-01224 681818, Ext. 52178; e-mail: d.mcateer@abdn.ac.uk

McAteer, Ian. Chair of the Board, Project Scotland; Group Chairman of The Union, one of the UK's leading regional marketing agencies. Career: Barrister-at-law; former Director, Saatchi & Saatchi London; No.2 at Faulds Advertising for three years before setting up The Union in 1996 with three partners; Fellow, IPA and the Marketing Society; Governor, Merchiston Castle School. Address: Project Scotland, 20 Hopetoun Street, Edinburgh EH7 4GH; T.-0131 226 0700.

MacAulay, Professor Emeritus Donald, MA, BA, DipGenLing. Professor of Celtic, Glasgow University, 1991-96; b. 21.5.30, Isle of Lewis; m., Ella Murray Sangster; 1 s.; 1 d. Educ. Nicolson Institute, Stornoway; Aberdeen University; Cambridge University. Lecturer in English Language, Edinburgh University, 1957-60; Lecturer in Irish and Scottish Gaelic, Trinity College, Dublin, 1960-63; Lecturer in Applied Linguistics, Edinburgh University, 1963-67; Senior Lecturer in Celtic, then Reader in Celtic, Aberdeen University, 1967-91. Publications: Seobhrach as a' Chlaich; Nua-bhardachd Ghaidhlig; The Celtic Languages. Recreations: poetry; living. Address: (b.) 5 Meggetland Terrace, Edinburgh EH14 1AN; T.-0131-443 1823.

MacAulay, Fred. Comedian; Television and Radio Presenter. Former Presenter, The Fred MacAulay Show, BBC Radio Scotland; television includes: Presenter, Life According to Fred; Co-host, New Year Live; Co-host, series and World Cup special, McCoist and MacAulay; Co-host, The 11 O'Clock Show; Team Captain, The Best Show in the World...Probably; Team Captain, Bring Me the Head of Light Entertainment; Team Captain, A Game of Two Halves; Presenter, Comedy Rules; Presenter, Now You See It; theatre: Bad and Crazy in a Jam.

McAveety, Frank (Francis), BA (Hons). Leader of Glasgow City Council, since 2015; Member, Glasgow City Council (elected to represent Ward 19 (Shettleston) at the 2012 Council elections); MSP (Labour and Co-Op.), Glasgow Shettleston, 1999-2011; Minister of Tourism, Culture and Sport, 2003-04; Deputy Minister of Health and Community Care, 2002-03; Deputy Minister for Local Government, 1999-2000; b. 27.7.62, Glasgow; m., Anita Mitchell; 1 s.; 1 d. Educ. All Saints Secondary School, Glasgow; Strathclyde University; St. Andrew's College, Bearsden. Councillor, Glasgow District Council, 1988-96; Leader, Glasgow City Council, 1997-99, Councillor, 1995-99. Board Member, Scottish Youth Theatre. Recreations: labour history; record collecting; football. Address: (h.) 156 Glenbuck Avenue, Robroyston, Glasgow G33 1LW.

McAvoy of Rutherglen, Baron (Thomas McLaughlin), PC. Senior Labour Whip, Labour Spokesperson on: Scotland, Northern Ireland, since 2013; former Government Whip, Treasurer of Her Majesty's Household and Government's Deputy Chief Whip (2008-10); MP (Labour and Co-operative), Glasgow Rutherglen, 1987-2010; b.

14.12.43, Rutherglen; m., Eleanor Kerr; 4 s. Member, Strathclyde Regional Council, 1982-87; Opposition Whip, 1990-93.

McBryde, Professor William Wilson, LLB, PhD, LLD, FRSE. Professor of Commercial Law, Edinburgh University, 1999-2005, Emeritus Professor, since 2005; b. 6.7.45, Perth; 1 s; 2 d. Educ. Perth Academy; Edinburgh University. Apprentice and Assistant, Morton, Smart, Macdonald & Milligan, WS, Edinburgh, 1967-70; Court Procurator, Biggart, Lumsden & Co., Glasgow, 1970-72; Lecturer in Private Law, Glasgow University, 1972-76; Member, Scottish Law Commission Working Party on Contract Law, 1975-2000; Senior Lecturer in Private Law, Aberdeen University, 1976-87; Professor of Scots Law, Dundee University, 1987-99 (Deputy and Vice Principal, 1991-94); Visiting Professor, L'Université de Paris V, 2000-05; Van der Grinten Professor of Commercial Law, University of Nijmegen, 2002-07. Specialist Parliamentary Adviser to House of Lords Select Committee on the European Communities, 1980-83; Member: Scottish Consumer Council, 1984-87, Scottish Advisory Committee on Arbitration, since 1986, Member, DTI Working Party on Rights in Security over Moveables, since 1994, Member, International Working Group on Principles of Insolvency Law, since 2000; Director, Scottish Universities' Law Institute, 1989-95; Honorary Sheriff, Tayside, Central and Fife, at Dundee, since 1991. Recreations: walking; photography. Address: 5 Darris Road, Inverness IV2 4DH.

McCabe, Alan. Editor, Aberdeen Evening Express, since 2011. Educ. Portlethen Academy. Joined Aberdeen Journals as a trainee reporter in 1996; formerly Assistant Editor, then Deputy Editor, Aberdeen Evening Express. Address: Aberdeen Journals Ltd, Lang Stracht, Mastrick Aberdeen AB15 6DF.

McCabe, Stephen, BA (Hons). Leader of Inverclyde Council, since 2007; Assistant Chief Executive of Govan Housing Association Ltd., 1997-2014; b. 25.04.64, Port Glasgow; m., Lesley-Anne McCabe; 3 s.; 1 d. Educ. St. Stephen's High School, Port Glasgow; University of Strathclyde. Trainee Accountant, Inverclyde District Council, 1986-91; Finance Officer, Paisley South Housing Association, 1991-97; Elected Member: Inverclyde District Council, 1992-96, Inverclyde Council, since 1999. Chair, Inverclyde Alliance, since 2007. Recreation: Celtic supporter. Address: (h.) 10 Victoria Gardens, Kilmacolm PA13 4HL; T.-01505 871368; e-mail: stephen.mccabe@inverclyde.gov.uk

McCafferty, Rev. Allan, BSc, BD (Hons). Minister, St Andrews: Hope Park and Martyrs linked with Strathkinness, since 2011; b. 19.1.67, Motherwell. Educ. Garrion Academy, Wishaw; Glasgow University; Edinburgh University. Probationer Minister, Holy Trinity Church, Bridge of Allan, 1991-93; Minister, Kirkwall East Church, 1993-2011. Recreations: choral singing; hill-walking; bowling. Address: 20 Priory Gardens, St Andrews, Fife KY16 8XX; T.-01334 478287.

McCaig, Callum, MA (Hons). MP (SNP), Aberdeen South, since 2015; SNP Energy and Climate Change spokesperson in the House of Commons, since 2015; b. 6.1.85, Aberdeen. Educ. Edinburgh University. Former Parliamentary Assistant to SNP MSP Maureen Watt; first elected to Aberdeen City Council in 2007; became Leader of the SNP group on the council in 2011, then Deputy Council Leader, then Leader of the Council (2011-12); one of the youngest council leaders in all of the United Kingdom at the age of 26; re-elected as a councillor in 2012, remained the group leader of an enlarged SNP delegation. Address: House of Commons, London SW1A 0AA.

McCaig, Professor Colin Darnley, BSc, PhD, FRSE. Regius Professor of Physiology, University of Aberdeen, since 2002; b. 26.6.53, Galashiels; 1 s.; 2 d. Educ. The High School of Glasgow; University of Edinburgh; Glasgow University. Beit Memorial Fellow, University of Edinburgh, 1983-86; Wellcome University Award Lecturer, University of Aberdeen, 1988-2002, Head of School of Medical Sciences, 2003-2015. Address: (b.) Institute of Medical Sciences, University of Aberdeen, Aberdeen AB25 2ZD; e-mail: c.mccaig@abdn.ac.uk

McCall, Stuart. Former Manager, Rangers FC (2015); b. 10.6.64, Leeds; 2 s.; 2 d. Youth career: Pudsey Juniors; Holbeck; Farsley Celtic; Bradford City, 1980-82; Senior career: Bradford City, 1982-88; Everton, 1988-91; Rangers, 1991-98; Bradford City, 1998-2002; Sheffield United, 2002-05; National team: Scotland U21, 1988-90; Scotland, 1990-98; Teams managed: Bradford City, 2000 (caretaker); Bradford City, 2007-2010; Motherwell, 2010-14. Player Honours: Bradford City, English Third Division, 1984-85, English First Division promotion, 1998-99; Rangers, Scottish Premier Division, 1991-92, 1992-93, 1993-94, 1994-95, 1995-96, 1996-97, Scottish Cup, 1992, 1993, 1996, Scottish League Cup, 1993, 1994; Managerial Honours: Motherwell, Lanarkshire Cup, 2010-11, 2012-13, 2013-14; Individual Honours: PFA Team of the Year, Second Division: 1987, 1988, Third Division: 1985; Manager of the Month: July and August 2011, October 2011; SPL Manager of the Season, 2012-13.

McCall Smith, Professor Alexander, CBE, LLB, PhD, FRSE, FRCP(E) (Hon), DIuris (hc), DLitt (hc), LLD (hc), DSc (hc), LittD (hc). Advocate; Professor Emeritus, Faculty of Law, Edinburgh University; Author; Member, International Bioethics Commission, UNESCO, 1998-2004; Vice Chairman, Human Genetics Commission, 2000-04; b. 24.8.48, Zimbabwe; m., Dr. Elizabeth Parry; 2 d. Publications: (non-fiction): Law and Medical Ethics (Co-Author); Butterworth's Medico-Legal Encyclopaedia (Co-Author); Scots Criminal Law (Co-Author); The Duty to Rescue (Co-Author); The Criminal Law of Botswana; Forensic Aspects of Sleep (Co-Author); Errors, Medicine and the Law (Co-Author); Justice and the Prosecution of Old Crimes (Co-Author); fiction: Children of Wax; The Girl who Married a Lion; Heavenly Date; Dream Angus; La's Orchestra Saves The World; Trains and Lovers; The No. 1 Ladies' Detective Agency; Tears of the Giraffe; Morality for Beautiful Girls; The Kalahari Typing School for Men; The Full Cupboard of Life; In The Company of Cheerful Ladies (Saga Prize for wit, 2003); The Miracle at Speedy Motors; The Good Husband of Zebra Drive; Blue Shoes and Happiness; Portuguese Irregular Verbs; The Finer Points of Sausage Dogs; At the Villa of Reduced Circumstances; Unusual Uses for Olive Oil; The Sunday Philosophy Club; Friends, Lovers, Chocolate; The Right Attitude to Rain; The Comfort of Saturdays; The Lost Art of Gratitude; The Charming Quirks of Others; The Forgotten Affairs of Youth; 44 Scotland Street; Espresso Tales; The World According to Bertie; The Unbearable Lightness of Scones; The Importance of Being Seven; Bertie Plays the Blues; Corduroy Mansions; The Dog Who Came in from the Cold; A Conspiracy of Friends; The Saturday Big Tent Wedding Party; The Uncommon Appeal of Clouds; Sunshine on Scotland Street; Bertie's Guide to Life and Mothers; The Handsome Man's Deluxe Café, 2014; Fatty O'Leary's Dinner Party, 2014; What W H Auden can do for you, 2013; The Forever Girl, 2014; A Work of Beauty: Alexander McCall Smith's Edinburgh, 2014; Emma: A Modern Retelling, 2014; The Woman Who Walked in Sunshine, 2015; The Novel Habits of Happiness,

2015; The Revolving Door of Life, 2015; numerous books for children. Author of The Year, 2004, British Book Awards Booksellers' Association Waterstones; Walpole Award for Excellence, 2005; Guiseppe Acerbi Literary Prize, Italy, 2010; Duke LEAF Award for Environmental Achievement, 2013; Burke Medal, Trinity College, Dublin, 2012; Presidential Award of Botswana, 2011; Bollinger Everyman Wodehouse Prize for Comic Fiction, 2015; Fellow of Royal Society of Literature. Recreation: sailing and boats. Address: (b.) c/o David Higham Associates Ltd, 7th Floor, Waverley House, 7-12 Noel Street, London W1F 8GQ.

MacCallum, Emeritus Professor James Richard, BSc, PhD, DSc, CChem, FRSC, FRSE. Professor of Polymer Chemistry, St. Andrews University, now Emeritus Professor (Vice-Principal, 1992-96; Pro-Principal, 1997); b. 3.5.36, Kilmartin; m., Eleanor Margaret Thomson; 2 s.; 1 d. Educ. Dumfries Academy; Glasgow University. Technical Officer, ICI Fibres Division, 1961-62; ICI Research Fellow, Aberdeen University, 1962-63; Lecturer, St. Andrews University, 1964; Dean of Science, 1987; Master, United College, 1988-92; Vice-Principal, 1992-96; Pro-Principal, 1996-97. Recreation: golf. Address: (h.) 9 Cairnsden Gardens, St. Andrews, Fife; T.-01334 473152.

McCann, James Aloysius, MA, LLB. Solicitor and Notary Public; a founding Director, Legal Defence Union in Scotland, 1987, Chairman, since 1990; Consultant, FMC Solicitors; b. 14.8.39, Glasgow; m., Jane Marlow; 3 s.; 1 d. Educ. St. Mungo's Academy, Glasgow; Glasgow University. Former Member, Legal Aid Central Committee; Dean, Faculty of Dunbartonshire Solicitors, 1986-88; Convenor for Law Society PQLE Advocacy Training Courses, 1983-91; Senior Tutor (Professional Legal Practice), Glasgow University, 1981-91; Member, Law Society of Scotland Legal Aid Committee, 1987-97; Reporter, Scottish Legal Aid Board (Co-opted Member, Criminal Applications Committee, 1987-93); appointed Honorary Sheriff at Dumbarton, 1990; Temporary Sheriff, 1991-99. Recreations: sailing; chess; music; golf. Address: (b.) 499 Kilbowie Road, Clydebank G81 2AX.

McCann, Michael. MP (Labour), East Kilbride, Strathaven and Lesmahagow, 2010-2015; m., Tracy Thomson; 1 s.; 1 d. Educ. St Brides High School; St Andrews High School. Secretary, East Kilbride, Strathaven and Lesmahagow CLP, 2004-2010; elected member, Civil and Public Services Association, 1982-92; Scottish Officer, Civil and Public Services Association (CPSA), 1992-98; Deputy Scottish Secretary, Public and Commercial Services Union (PCS), 1998-2008. Member, Labour Party, since 1987; Member, GMB, since 1992. Recreations: golf; music.

McCarter, Ann Iestyn, SRN. Chair, Scottish Redundant Churches Trust, 2000-2013; Past Convener: Board of Practice and Procedure, and Business Committee, General Assembly of the Church of Scotland; Session Clerk, Newbattle Church, Dalkeith, 1994-2005; b. 9.5.41, Glamorgan, S. Wales; m., Iain McCarter; 1 s.; 3 d. Educ. Cheltenham Ladies' College; Western General Hospital, Edinburgh; Guy's Hospital, London. Staff Nurse/Sister, Roodlands Hospital, Haddington. Church of Scotland: Past Member: Board of Social Responsibility, Assembly Council, Board of National Mission; Special Commission looking at Livingston Ecumenical Experiment; Past President, Dalkeith Branch, British Red Cross Society (awarded Badge of Honour). Recreations: choral singing; dress-making; sailing; gardening. Address: (h.) 5 Westfield Grove, Eskbank, Dalkeith EH22 3JH; T.-0131-663 3896.

McCarter, Keith Ian. Sculptor; b. 15.3.36; m., Brenda Maude Edith; 1 s.; 1 d. Educ. The Royal High School of Edinburgh; Edinburgh College of Art. National Service, RA, 1954-56; sculptor: primarily involved in architectural and landscaped situations; numerous commissions including: Ordnance Survey HQ Southampton, 1967, Lagos Nigeria, 1974, Wingate Centre City of London, 1980, Goodmans Yard City of London, 1982, 1020 19th Street Washington DC, 1983, American Express Bank City of London, 1984, Guy's Hospital NCC London, 1986, Royal Executive Park NY, 1986, Evelyn Gardens London, 1987, London Docklands 1988, Midland Bank London, 1989, Vogans Mill London, 1989, Moody Gardens Galveston Texas USA (with Sir Geoffrey Jellicoe), Abbey Road London 1991, Monks Cross York, 1992, John Menzies HQ Edinburgh, 1995, Aldermanbury Bradford, 1998, F I Group Edinburgh, 1999; Monks Cross Technology Park, York, 2001; Norfolk & Norwich University Hospital, 2002; Riverside Greenock, 2008; works in private collections world-wide. Sir Otto Beit medal RBS, 1993; FRSA 1970; ARBS 1991. Appointed Art Strategy Consultant by NGP for their Edinburgh waterfront development masterplanned by Foster and Partners; exhibits at Cyril Gerber Fine Art Gallery, Glasgow and Open Eye Gallery, Edinburgh. Recreations: music; literature; beachcombing. Clubs: Farmers', Melrose RFC. Address: (h.) 10 Coopersknowe Crescent, Galashiels TD1 2DS; T.-01896 751112; e-mail: keith@keith-mccarter.com; web: keith-mccarter.com

McCarthy, James, BSc, FRZSS (Hon). Lecturer and writer; b. 6.5.36, Dundee; m.; 2 s.; 1 d. Educ. Harris Academy, Dundee; Aberdeen University; University of East Africa, Kampala. Military Service, 1954-56 (Royal Marines, commissioned Black Watch, seconded King's African Rifles); Leverhulme Scholar, Makerere College, Kampala, 1959-61; Assistant Conservator of Forests, Tanzania, and Lecturer in Forest Ecology, Forest Training School, 1961-63; Deputy Regional Officer (North England), Nature Conservancy, 1963-69; Deputy Director (Scotland), Nature Conservancy Council, 1975-91; Churchill Fellow, USA, 1976; Nuffield/ Leverhulme Fellow, 1988. Recreation: cross-country skiing. Address: (h.) 6a Ettrick Road, Edinburgh; T.-0131-229 1916; e-mail: mccarthy-james4@sky.com

McCarthy, Shona. Chief Executive, Edinburgh Festival Fringe Society, since 2016; Director, Shona McCarthy Consulting, since 2014. Educ. University of Ulster Coleraine. Director, Foyle Film Festival, 1995-98; Chief Executive, Cinemagic, 1991-2001; Chief Executive, Imagine Belfast 2008, 2001-02; Executive Director, Rubyblue Ltd, 2002-09; Director, British Council Northern Ireland, 2009-2011; Chief Executive, Culture Company 2013, 2011-2014. Recreations: film and film-making; hill-walking; badminton; music and literature; travel. Address: Edinburgh Festival Fringe Society, 180 High Street, Edinburgh EH1 1QS; T.-0131 226 0026.
E-mail: shonamccarthyconsulting@gmail.com

McCausland, Professor W. David, BSc (Econ), MSc (Econ), PhD, SFHEA. Professor of Economics, University of Aberdeen, since 1995; b. Sheffield. Educ. Universities of Hull, Warwick, Keele. Associate of Higher Education Academy's Economics Network. Address: (b.) University of Aberdeen Business School, Old Aberdeen AB24 3QY; T.-01224 272180; e-mail: d.mccausland@abdn.ac.uk

McClatchie, Colin James Stewart, BSc (Econ), FRSE. Vice President, Scottish Opera, since 2015; Chairman, Prescient, since 2007; Member, Global Irish Network, since 2010; b. 1.1.49, Belfast; m., Claire McConaghy; 2 d. Educ. Coleraine Academical Institution; Queen's University,

Belfast. Senior management positions, Thomson Regional Newspapers, Belfast, Newcastle, Reading, Edinburgh, 1971-84; Circulation/Marketing Director, Scottish Daily Record and Sunday Mail Ltd., 1984-94 (and Managing Director, Maxwell Free Newspapers Ltd., 1990-93); Marketing Consultant, 1995. General Manager, News International Newspapers (Scotland) Ltd., 1995-2004; Managing Director, Scotland & Ireland, News International Newspapers, 2004-07; Chairman, St Columba's School, Kilmacolm, 2011-15; Chairman, Scottish Opera, 2008-2014 (Vice-Chairman, 2004-07, Director, 2003-2014); Chairman, Saints & Sinners, 2009-2011; Chairman, Glasgow UNESCO City of Music, 2008-12; Non-Executive Director, Scottish Enterprise, 2004-09 (Chairman, Nomination and Remuneration Committees), Beattie Communications, 2007-08, Dunfermline Press Group, 2007-08; Chairman, The Kemsley Agency, 2008-10. Life Vice President, Newspaper Press Fund (Chairman, West of Scotland District, 1998-2000); Chairman, Institute of Directors, Scotland, 2002-04 (Chairman, West of Scotland Branch, 2001-02); Director, Scottish Networks International, 2001-03; Director, Scottish Enterprise Glasgow, 2002-04; Chairman, Scottish Society of Epicureans, 2002-04; President, Queens University Association Scotland, 2003-05. Clubs: Saints & Sinners, since 2001; Founder Member, Edinburgh Oyster, 2003. Recreations: family; golf; cooking; opera; theatre.
E-mail: colin@mcclatchie.co.uk

McClellan, John Forrest, MA, Hon. FDIT; b. 15.8.32, Glasgow; m., Eva Maria Pressel; 3 s.; 1 d. Educ. Aberdeen Grammar School; Aberdeen University. 2nd Lt., Gordon Highlanders and Nigeria Regiment, Royal West African Frontier Force, 1954-56; entered Civil Service, 1956; Assistant Principal, Scottish Office, 1956-59; Private Secretary to Permanent Under Secretary of State, Scottish Office, 1959-60; Principal, Scottish Office, 1960-68; Civil Service Fellow, Glasgow University, 1968-69; Assistant Secretary, Scottish Office, 1969-77; Under Secretary, Scottish Office, 1977-85; Director, Scottish International Education Trust, 1986-2001. Member, Management Committee, Hanover (Scotland) Housing Association, 1986-2007. Publication: Then A Soldier (novel), 1991. Recreations: gardening; walking. Address: (h.) 7 Cumin Place, Edinburgh EH9 2JX; T.-0131 667 8446.

McClelland, John Ferguson, CBE, FRSE. Chairman, Skills Development Scotland; Member: Public Services Reform Board; Deputy Chair, Public Procurement Reform Board; Chairman, NQC Ltd.; Chairman, Hub Southwest Ltd; Chairman, Vicast Ltd; b. 27.3.45, Glasgow; m., Alice; 1 d. Educ. North Kelvinside School; Glasgow College. South of Scotland Electricity Board, 1963-68; IBM Corporation, 1968-95: European Director of Operations, 1980, European Manufacturing Controller, 1983, Director of Manufacturing, Greenock, 1987, Director of UK Manufacturing, 1992, Vice President, Worldwide Manufacturing, 1994; Digital Corporation, 1995-98, V.P. Worldwide Manufacturing; Global Chief Industrial Officer, and Board Member, Philips B.V., 1998-99; 3 Com Corporation, 1999-2003: Senior Vice President, Worldwide Operations, 1999-2001, President, Business Networks Company, 2001-03; former Chairman: Judging Panel, Quality Scotland Excellence Award, Renfrewshire Enterprise Company, CBI UK Technology and Innovation Committee, Rangers FC PLC, Scottish Further and Higher Education Council. Conducted Review of Public Procurement in Scotland, 2006; Public Sector ICT in Scotland, 2011; Public Procurement in Wales, 2012. Recreations: golf; football.

McClements, David Elliott, LLB (Hons), DipLP. Partner, Russel and Aitken, Solicitors, Denny, since 1998; b.

25.6.67, Kilmarnock; m., Louise; 2 d. Educ. Falkirk High School, University of Edinburgh. Russel and Aitken, Denny, 1990-92, and since 1995; Sandeman and Co., Falkirk, 1992-93; John G. Gray and Co., Edinburgh, 1993-95. Member, Council, Law Society of Scotland, 2001-12, Treasurer, 2009-12; Chair, Falkirk District Association for Mental Health, since 2010; Member, Council, Alzheimer Scotland – Action on Dementia. Publication: Scottish Older Client Law Service (Contributor). Recreations: golf; Boys' Brigade. Address: (h.) 81 Stevenson Avenue, Polmont FK2 0GU; e-mail: de.mcclements@virgin.net

McClure, David. Rector, Madras College, St Andrews. Formerly Head Teacher, Buckhaven High School. Chair, Fife's Curriculum for Excellence steering group; represents Fife at a national level. Address: South Street, St Andrews, Fife KY16 9EJ; T.-01334 659402.

McClure, J. Derrick, MBE, MA, MLitt. Retired Senior Lecturer, Aberdeen University (rtd. 2009); b. 20.7.44, Ayr; m., Ann Celeste nee Bolinger; 3 s. Educ. Ayr Academy; Glasgow University; Edinburgh University. Lektor in Englische Phonetik, University of Tübingen, Germany, 1968-69; Chargé de Cours en Linguistique, University of Ottawa, Canada, 1970-72; English Department, Aberdeen University: Lecturer, 1972-90, Senior Lecturer, 1990-2009 (part-time, 2007-09). Chairman, Forum for Research in the Languages of Scotland and Ulster, 1991-2009; Chairman, Scottish Government's Ministerial Advisory Group on the Scots Language, 2009-2010; Member: Scottish Dictionaries Joint Council, Association for Scottish Literary Studies Language and International Committees, Bibliography of Scottish Literature in Translation Committee. Publications: Why Scots Matters, Language, Poetry and Nationhood (author); Doric. The Dialect of North-East Scotland; numerous articles on Scottish language and literature; translations of Gaelic and other poetry. Recreations: native American history; Japanese language and literature; amateur musical theatre. Address: (b.) School of Language and Literature, University of Aberdeen, Old Aberdeen AB24 2UB; T.-01224-272625.
E-mail: j.d.mcclure@abdn.ac.uk

McClure, Judith, CBE, MA (Oxon), DPhil, FSAScot. Head, St. George's School, Edinburgh, 1994-2009; Chairman, Scottish Region, 1995-98, and Member, Council, Girls' Schools Association; b. 22.12.45, Stockton; m., Dr. Roger Collins. Educ. Newlands Grammar School, Middlesbrough; Somerville College, Oxford. Sir Maurice Powicke Research Fellow, Lady Margaret Hall, Oxford, 1976-77; Lecturer in Medieval Latin and Medieval History, Liverpool University, 1977-79; Lecturer in History, Oxford University (Jesus, Somerville and Worcester Colleges), 1979-81; Teacher and Head of Department in History and Politics, School of St. Helen & St. Katherine, Abingdon, 1981-84; Assistant Head, Kingswood School, Bath, 1984-87; Head, Royal School, Bath, 1987-93. Member: Court, University of Bath, 1989-92, General Convocation, Heriot Watt University, 1994-2011, Court, Heriot Watt University, 2003-2013, Board of Governors, Clifton Hall School, 1994-99, Governing Body, Scottish Council of Independent Schools, 1995-2007, Management Committee, 1998-2007 (Chairman, Management Committee, 2001-07), Board, Scottish Qualifications Authority, 1999-2000, Board, Merchiston Castle School, 1999-2005, Ministerial Strategy Committee on Continuing Professional Development, 2000-03 (Chairman, Leadership and Management Sub-group, 2001-03); Trustee, Hopetoun House, 1997-2002; Convener, Scottish Educational Leadership Management and Administration Society, 2003-09; Member, Judicial Studies Committee, 2006-2013; Chair, Advisory Board of the Scottish Council for Studies in School Administration (SCSSA), Moray House School of Education, since 2012;

Member, China Planning Group, Scottish Government, since 2006; Convener, Scotland-China Educational Network, since 2006; Member, Advisory Board, Confucius Institute for Scotland, University of Edinburgh, since 2007 and Confucius Institute Ambassador for the teaching of Chinese in Scottish Schools, since 2010; Member of the Education Committee of the Royal Society of Edinburgh, 2009-2013; Member, Commission on School Reform, 2012; Judicial Institute Advisory Council, 2013-2016; Scottish International Education Trust, since 2013; Secretary of the Cross Party Group on China at the Scottish Parliament, since 2013; Member of the UK Committee of The 48 Group Club (The Icebreakers), since 2014; Member of the Management Committee of The Scottish Churches' China Group, 2014-15; Chairman of the Advisory Board of the Scottish Centre for Studies in School Administration (SCSSA), since 2012; Honorary DUniv, Heriot-Watt University, June 2014. Publication: Bede: The Ecclesiastical History (Co-author), 1994. Recreations: reading; using a computer; travelling. Address: 12A Ravelston Park, Edinburgh EH4 3DX.

McCluskey, Baron (John Herbert McCluskey), LLD (Dundee). Former Senator of the College of Justice in Scotland; Life Peer, since 1976; b. 12.6.29, Glasgow; m., Ruth Friedland; 2 s.; 1 d. Educ. St. Bede's Grammar School, Manchester; Holy Cross Academy, Edinburgh; Edinburgh University; MA, LLB. Admitted Faculty of Advocates, 1955; Standing Junior Counsel to Ministry of Power (Scotland), 1963; Advocate-Depute, 1964-71; QC (Scot), 1967; Chairman, Medical Appeal Tribunals for Scotland, 1972-74; Sheriff Principal of Dumfries and Galloway, 1973-74; Solicitor General for Scotland, 1974-79. Chairman, Scottish Association for Mental Health, 1985-94; Independent Chairman: Scottish Football League Compensation Tribunal, SFA Appeals Tribunal; Chair, Age Concern (Scotland), 2000-01; Reith Lecturer, BBC, 1986; LLD (Dundee), 1989; Chairman, John Smith Memorial Trust, 1997-2004; Chair, Scottish Government's panel reviewing the UK Supreme Court's jurisdiction over Scottish human rights matters, 2011; Chair, Expert Group of Scottish Government on Leveson in Scotland, 2012/13; Editor, Butterworth's Scottish Criminal Law and Practice series. Publications: Law, Justice and Democracy, 1987; Criminal Appeals, 1992. Recreations: tennis; pianoforte. Address: (b.) House of Lords, Westminster, London SW1A 0PW.

McCluskey, Mary, DCE. Artistic Director (Chief Executive), Scottish Youth Theatre, since 1992; freelance Theatre Director/Drama Tutor, since 1985; b. 16.9.54, Glasgow. Educ. West Senior High School, Garden City, Michigan, USA; Hamilton College of Education; Royal Scottish Academy of Music and Drama. President, Hamilton College of Education SRC, 1975-76; Teacher, Glenlee Primary, Hamilton, 1976-79; Assistant Stage Manager, Dundee Repertory Theatre, 1980-81; YOP Supervisor, Community Projects Agency (East End), 1981-83; YTS Training Officer, Community Projects Agency (South East), 1983-85; Associate Director, Scottish Youth Theatre, 1989-91; Education Officer, Royal Shakespeare Company, 1991-92. Member, BAFTA. Adapted: Wee MacGreegor, Wee MacGreegor Enlists, Medea, Hamlet, Macbeth, The Glory; Jury's Prize for Direction and Pedagogy, Rainbow Festival, St. Petersburg (for Born Bad). Recreations: theatre; films; books; visiting historic sites. Address: (b.) Scottish Youth Theatre, The Old Sheriff Court, 105 Brunswick Street, Glasgow G1 1TF; T.-0141 552 3988.

E-mail: marymccluskey@scottishyouththeatre.org

McClymont, Gregg. MP (Labour), Cumbernauld, Kilsyth and Kirkintilloch East, 2010-2015. Tutorial Fellow, St Hugh's College, Oxford, 2007-10. Visiting Fellow, Nuffield College, Oxford, since 2014. Address: (b.) Lennox House, Cumbernauld G67 1LL.

McCoist, Alistair (Ally) Murdoch, MBE. Manager, Glasgow Rangers, 2011-14, Assistant Manager, 2007-2011; former footballer: Glasgow Rangers F.C., Kilmarnock F.C.; b. 24.9.62, Bellshill; m.; 5 s. Educ. Hunter High School. Debut for St. Johnstone aged 16; signed for Sunderland, 1981; joined Rangers, 1983; became club's leading goal-scorer, August 1997 (421 goals); 61 caps for Scotland, since 1986; Member, Scotland squad, 1990 World Cup Finals, 1992 and 1996 European Championships; former contributor to Question of Sport, BBC TV; ITV football pundit. Scottish Sports Personality of the Year, 1992; Scottish Sports Writers' Player of the Year, 1992. Recreations: reading autobiographies; listening to music. Address: (b.) 16 Royal Terrace, Glasgow G3 7NY.

McColgan, Elizabeth; b. 24.5.64, Dundee; m., Peter Conor McColgan (separated); 2 s.; 1 d. Educ. University of Alabama. Commonwealth Games Gold medallist (10,000 metres), 1986; Silver medallist, World Cross-Country Championships, 1987; Olympic Games Silver medallist (10,000 metres), 1988; Silver medallist, World Indoor Championships, 1989; Gold medallist (10,000 metres) and Bronze medallist (3,000 metres), Commonwealth Games, 1990; World 10,000 Meters Champion (Track), 1991; New York Marathon Winner, 1991; Tokyo Marathon Winner, 1992; London Marathon Winner, 1996; world records: 5,000, 10,000, half marathon on roads.

MacColl, Anne, MA Hons (Glas). Non Executive Director: Social Enterprise Academy, since 2016, CEFAS, since 2016, Glasgow Caledonian University School for Business and Society, since 2014; Associate Director, University of Stirling, since 2015; Chief Executive, Scottish Development International (SDI), 2011-15. Educ. Glasgow University; Strathclyde Graduate Business School (MBA). Career history: lived and worked for two years in Madrid and for 3 years near Toulouse, France, as a management consultant to the French Chambers of Commerce network, and as part of a national private Spanish consultancy, Soluziona; Regional Head for Southern Europe for SDI; Operations Director for the EMEA (Europe, Middle East and Africa) region of SDI (managed SDI's overseas sales & marketing efforts and worked with teams directly to both attract inward investors and support Scottish companies to successfully trade internationally). Strong interest in developing international education links for Scotland. Address: Social Enterprise Academy, Edinburgh Office, Thorn House, 5 Rose Street, Edinburgh EH2 2PR; T.-0131 243 2670.

McColl, James Hamilton, MBE, NDH, SDH, SHM, FRAgS, (Hon) FSAC. Freelance Horticulturalist; b. 19.9.35, Kilmarnock; m., Billie; 1 s.; 1 d. Educ. Kilmarnock Academy; West of Scotland Agricultural College. Staff Member, WSAC, Auchincruive, Ayr, 1956-59; Assistant Head Gardener, Reading University Botanic Garden, 1959-61; Horticultural Adviser/Lecturer, Shropshire Education Authority, 1961-67; Horticultural Adviser: MAFF, Leicestershire, Northants and Rutland, 1967-73; North of Scotland College of Agriculture, 1973-78; Manager of Morrison Bowmore Distillers Ltd (formerly Stanley P Morrison) Innovative Waste Energy Re-Cycling Project at Glengarioch Distillery, Oldmeldrum, 1978-88; featured in the British Pavilion at World Fair, Knoxville, USA (1982) and at the Glasgow Garden Festival (1988); former PRO, Morrison Bowmore Distillers Ltd.; Co-Presenter, The Beechgrove Garden, since inception in 1978; Chairman, Gardening Scotland, 2005-09; Board Member, The Calyx.

Recreations: music; rugby. Address: (h.) Ayrshire Cottage, 45 King Street, Oldmeldrum AB51 0EQ; T.-01651 873955.

McComasky, Julie. Head of Human Resources, First ScotRail. Over 20 years experience in HR both as a learning and development specialist and as a generalist managing change and cultural shift in a complex industry; previous roles have included Head of Learning and Development at ScotRail and Head of HR, Scotland for FirstGroup with responsibility for both the rail and bus divisions within Scotland; played a key part in setting up the ScotRail Training Academy in 2006, which is now regarded as a centre for excellence for learning and development within the rail industry; key achievements have included working in partnership with the rail unions to develop and implement the award winning "Earn as You Learn" a literacy, numeracy and IT programme and the introduction of a Modern Apprenticeship in Customer Service (this programme was awarded the "Best Business Newcomer" award at the 2011 Scottish Apprenticeship Awards). Member: Scottish Advisory Board of People 1st, Chartered Institute of Personnel and Development. Address: First ScotRail, Atrium Court, 50 Waterloo Street, Glasgow G2 6HQ.

McComb, Professor (William) David, BSc, MSc, PhD. Emeritus Professor of Physics, Edinburgh University, since 2006; b. 31.10.40, Belfast; m., Doyleen M. McLeod; 3 d. Educ. Methodist College, Belfast; Queens University, Belfast; Manchester University. Senior Scientific Officer, Theoretical Physics Division, AERE, Harwell; Edinburgh University: Lecturer in Engineering Science, Lecturer in Physics, Reader in Physics, Professor of Statistical Physics. Guest Professor, The Technical University of Delft, 1997; Visiting Fellow, Wolfson College, Cambridge, 1999; Senior Honorary Professorial Fellow, Edinburgh University, 2008; Leverhulme Emeritus Fellow, 2007-09. Publications: The Physics of Fluid Turbulence, 1990; Dynamics and Relativity, 1999; Renormalization Methods: a guide for beginners, 2003; Homogeneous isotropic turbulence: phenomenology, renormalization and statistical closures, 2014. Recreations: reading; gardening; listening to music. Address: (b.) School of Physics, King's Buildings, Edinburgh University, Edinburgh.

McConnell, Bridget Mary, CBE, EdD, MA (Hons), DIA, MEd, FRSA, FFCS. Chief Executive, Culture and Sport Glasgow, since 2007; Executive Director, Culture and Sport, Glasgow City Council, 2005-07, Director, Cultural and Leisure Services, 1998-2005; b. 28.5.58, Lennoxtown; m., Jack Wilson McConnell (qv); 1 s.; 1 d. Educ. St. Patrick's High School, Kilsyth; Our Lady's High School, Cumbernauld; St. Andrews University; Dundee College of Commerce; Stirling University. Curator, Doorstep Gallery, Fife Regional Council, 1983-84; Arts Officer, Stirling District Council, 1984-88; Principal Arts Officer, The Arts in Fife, Fife Regional Council, 1988-96; Service Manager, Community Services, Fife Council, 1996-98. Conference Co-ordinator, Fourth International Conference in Adult Education and the Arts, St. Andrews, 1995; External Verifier, SCOTVEC Arts and Leisure Management Courses, 1990-97; Member, Board, Workshop and Artists Studio Provision Scotland (WASPS) Ltd, 1985-90; Chair, Scottish Youth Dance Festival, 1993-96 (Founder Member, 1988); Chair, Scottish Local Authority Arts Officers Group, 1993-96 (Founder Member, 1991); Vice Chair, Scottish Arts Lobby (SALVO), 1995-97; Member, Scottish Arts Council Combined Arts Committee, 1988-94; Arts Adviser to COSLA, 1997-2001; Member, Scottish Executive, National Culture Strategy Focus Group, 1999-2000; Member, Scottish Executive, Social Inclusion Task Group, 1999-2000; Board Member, RSAMD, 2001-07, Vice Chair, 2007-13; Member, Heritage Lottery Fund Committee, 2004-2010; Awards: British/American Arts Association/University of Minnesota Fellowship, 1987. Awarded Doctor Honoris Causa in July 2008 from Aberdeen University; Doctor of Literature Honoris Causa (DLit), St. Andrews University, 2008; Honorary Doctorate: Royal Conservatoire of Scotland, 2013, University of Glasgow, 2014. Awarded CBE for services to Culture in the 2015 New Years Honours List. Publications: Modernising Britain: Creative Futures (Co-Author), 1997; conference papers on arts and adult education. Recreations: walking; playing piano; swimming; reading. Address: (b.) 220 High Street, Glasgow G4 0QW; T.-0141-287 5058.
E-mail: bridget.mcconnell@glasgowlife.org.uk

McConnell, Colin. Chief Executive, Scottish Prison Service, since 2012. Began career in the Scottish Prison Service as a prison officer before joining the Assistant Governor training programme; Assistant Governor, Glenochil Prison, 1986-1989; spent three years as Management Development Officer at the Scottish Prison Service College before moving to HM Prison Service for England & Wales in 1992; formerly Director General of the Northern Ireland Prison Service. Address: Scottish Prison Service Headquarters, Calton House, 5 Redheughs Rigg, Edinburgh EH12 9HW; T.-0131 244 8745.

McConnell of Glenscorrodale, Rt. Hon. Lord (Jack Wilson McConnell), BSc, DipEd, DUniv. MSP (Labour), Motherwell and Wishaw, 1999-2011; First Minister of Scotland, 2001-07 (Minister for Education, Europe and External Affairs, 2000-2001, Minister for Finance, 1999-2000); b. 30.6.60, Irvine; m., Bridget (qv); 1 s.; 1 d. Educ. Arran High School; Stirling University. Mathematics Teacher, Lornshill Academy, 1983-92; General Secretary, Scottish Labour Party, 1992-98; Chief Executive, Public Affairs Europe Limited, 1998. Member, Stirling District Council, 1984-93, Council Leader, 1990-92, Treasurer, 1988-92, Chair, Leisure and Recreation Committee, 1986-87, Equal Opportunities Committee, 1986-90; Member, European Committee of the Regions, 2001-07; President, 1980-82, Hon. President, 1984-85 and 1991-93, Stirling University Students Association; Executive Member, Scottish Constitutional Convention, 1990-98; Deputy President, NUS Scotland, 1982-83; Chair, Board of Directors, Stirling Windows Ltd., 1988-92; Member, Labour Party Scottish Executive Committee, 1989-92; Parliamentary candidate, Perth and Kinross, 1987. President, European Legislative Regions, 2004; Prime Minister's Special Representative for Peacebuilding, 2008-2010; Chair, Clyde Cash for Kids, 2011; Advisory Board, Institute for Cultural Diplomacy, since 2009; UK/Japan 21st Century Group Board, since 2010; Fellow, UK/China Icebreakers, 2007; Patron, Diana Awards, 2011; Patron, Positive Women, 2011; Chair: APPG on the Sustainable Development Goals; SSE Sustainable Development Fund; Advisory Board, PricewaterhouseCoopers (PwC); Ambassador, Action for Children UK; Professorial Fellow, Stirling University (2014); Vice President, UNICEF UK (2014); Chairperson, McConnell International Foundation (2013). Publication: Proposals for Scottish Democracy, 1989. Recreations: golf; gardening; cinema; music. Address: House of Lords, London SW1A 0PW.

McCorkindale, Rev. Donald George Bruce, BD, DipMin. Church of Scotland Minister at Strontian linked with Morvern linked with Ardgour and Kingairloch, since 2011; Chaplain to the Moderator of the General Assembly, 2011-2012; b. 27.12.63, Glasgow; m., Lesley Rona (Page); 2 s.; 1 d. Educ. Kelvinside Academy, Glasgow; St. Andrews University. Minister, Bonnybridge St. Helens Church, 1992-2000; Dalgety Parish Church, 2000-2011. Publication: The Millennium Challenge, 2000. Address: (h.) The Manse, 2 The Meadows, Strontian PH36 4HZ; T.-01967 402234; e-mail: donald.mccorkindale@live.com

McCormac, Professor Gerry. Principal and Vice Chancellor, University of Stirling, since 2010. Career: University of Michigan: worked on the NASA Dynamics Explorer satellite programme and subsequently became

Director of the high-precision carbon dating facility at Queen's University Belfast; Pro-Vice Chancellor, Queen's University Belfast, 2001-2010 (responsibility for Academic and Financial Planning, Economic Development and External Affairs). Served on the Northern Ireland (NI) Committee of the Institute of Directors, the NI Economic Development Forum, the NI Science and Industry Panel (MATRIX) and the boards of both the NI Science Park and Business in the Community; formerly a Director and Chair of the Management Board of Queen's University's commercialisation company, QUBIS. Currently a member of Universities Scotland, Universities UK, the Carnegie Trust for the Universities of Scotland Executive Committee, the Universities and Colleges Employers' Association (UCEA) Scottish Committee, the United States/Northern Ireland Economic Development Working Group and a board member of Invest Northern Ireland; Fellow of the Society of Antiquaries, the Higher Education Academy and the Royal Society of Arts, Commerce and Manufacturers. Address: (b.) University of Stirling FK9 4LA; T.-01786 473171.

McCormack, Angela Janet. Director/Company Secretary, Voluntary Action - East Renfrewshire, since 2007; Board Member, Consumer Focus Scotland, since 2008; b. 13.09.71, Busby. Educ. Mearns Castle High School; University of The West of Scotland. The Royal Bank of Scotland PLC, 1990-2003; Voluntary Action - East Renfrewshire, 2003; Disabled Persons Housing Service, East Renfrewshire, 2003-05; Postwatch Scotland, 2004-08; Stepping Stones for Families, 2005-09. WSI - West Lowland Battalion Army Cadet Force; Lieutenant, Girls Brigade; MS Society Scottish Council Member, 2011. Recreations: Paisley Philharmonic Choir. Address: (h.) 49 Langcraigs Drive, Glenburn, Paisley PA2 8JP; e-mail: angela.mccormack@ntlworld.com

McCormick, John, FRSE, MA, MEd. Electoral Commissioner, since 2008; m., Jean Frances Gibbons; 1 s.; 1 d. Educ. St. Michael's Academy, Irvine; University of Glasgow. Teacher, St. Gregory's Secondary School, Glasgow, 1968-70; Education Officer, BBC School Broadcasting Council, 1970-75; Senior Education Officer, Scotland, 1975-82; Sec., and Head of Information, BBC Scotland, 1982-87; The Sec. of the BBC, 1987-92; Controller of BBC Scotland, 1992-2004. Chairman, Edinburgh International Film Festival, 1996-2008; Chairman, Scottish Qualifications Authority, 2004-2008; Member, Lay Advisory Committee, Royal College of Physicians, Edinburgh, 2010-2014; Member, Board, Scottish Screen, 1997-2005 (Vice-Chairman, 2004-05); Member, Board, Skillset, 2002-04; Member, Glasgow Science Centre Charitable Trust, 1999-2005; Member, Board, Scottish Opera, since 2005 (Vice-Chair, since 2008); Member, Board, Glasgow School of Art, 2004-07; Member, Board, Royal Scottish Academy of Music and Dance, 2003-08; Non-executive Director, Lloyds TSB Scotland, 2007-09; Director, Irvine Bay Urban Regeneration Company, 2007-2013; Member, Court, University of Strathclyde, 1996-2002; Independent Director, Glasgow Life, since 2013. FRTS 1998; FRSE 2003. Hon. DLitt (Robert Gordon University, Aberdeen), 1997; Hon. LLD (Strathclyde), 1999; DUniv: Glasgow, 1999; Paisley, 2003. Recreation: newspapers. Address: (b.) The Electoral Commission, Lothian Chambers, 59-63 George IV Bridge, Edinburgh EH1 1RN.

McCormick, John William Penfold, BSc, PhD. Chairman, Scottish Association for Public Transport, since 1988; Information Technology Manager, Weir Pumps Ltd., 1979-2003; I.T. and transport consultant; Strategy Officer, Friends of West Highland Lines; President, Rotary Club of Helensburgh, 2012/2013; Director, Transform Scotland,

since 2011; b. 9.6.46, Renfrew; m., Linda M.L.; 1 d. Educ. Paisley Grammar School; Glasgow University. Research Fellow, Glasgow University, 1971-74; computer management, since 1975. Recreations: hill-walking; transport; music. Address: (b.) 11 Queens Crescent, Glasgow G4 9BL; T.-07760 381 729.
E-mail: mail@sapt.org.uk

McCourt, Arthur David, CBE, BSc (Hons). Chief Executive, Highland Council, 1995-2007; b. 11.7.47, Newburgh, Fife; m., Jan; 1 d. Educ. Bell-Baxter High School, Cupar; Edinburgh College of Art; Heriot-Watt University. Various posts with Northumberland County Council, Central Regional Council, Stirling District Council; Assistant Chief Executive, Tayside Regional Council, 1990-93. Recreation: mountaineering. Address: (b.) Westcroft, Lentran, Inverness IV3 8RN; T.-01463 831762; e-mail: arthur.m@btinternet.com

McCowan, David James, BAcc (Hons), FPC. Director of James Cargill Ltd (Financial Services), since 2002; Board Member (Elected), Loch Lomond and Trossachs National Park Authority, since 2010; b. 2.6.75, Glasgow; divorced. Educ. Loretto School, Musselburgh; University of Abertay, Dundee. Pensions and Investment Consultant, Norwich Union, 1997-2001; Director of Rochester International Ltd, since 2010. President, Helensburgh Tennis Club, 2011; Director, Balloch Community Interest Council. Recreations: tennis; golf; waterskiing; skiing. Address: Auchendennan Farm, Arden, Alexandria, Dunbartonshire G83 8RB; T.-01389 710 000.
E-mail: davidjcmccowan@gmail.com

McCracken, Gordon Angus, BD, CertMin, DMin (Prin). Church of Scotland Interim Minister, since 2005; Mediator, since 2010; b. 8.7.56, Glasgow; m., Jessie Malcolm. Educ. Woodside Senior Secondary, Glasgow; University of Glasgow; Princeton Theological Seminary, N. J. Church of Scotland - Parish Minister, Whitburn South, 1988-2002; Parish Minister, Kilwinning Abbey, 2002-05. Served on West Lothian Council Education Committee, 1996-2002. Publications: Bygone Days of Yore, 1990; Whitburne - A Historie O' Its Auld Parioch Kirk, 2000. Address: (h.) 17 Northfield Meadows, Longridge, Bathgate, West Lothian; T.-0791 8600 720; e-mail: gordonangus@btinternet.com

McCreadie, Robert Anderson, QC, LLB, PhD, Advocate; b. 17.8.48, St. Andrews. Educ. Madras College, St. Andrews; Edinburgh University; Christ's College, Cambridge. Lecturer, Dundee University, 1974-78, Edinburgh University, 1978-93; called to Scottish Bar, 1992; Standing Junior Counsel, Department of Transport, 1994-95, Scottish Home and Health Department, 1995-99, Home Affairs and Justice Department, 1999-2000, Advocate Depute, 2000-02; Standing Junior Counsel to Advocate General for Scotland, 2002-03; Queen's Counsel, 2003; part-time Sheriff, 2003-04; Sheriff of Tayside Central and Fife at Perth, 2004-2013. Recreations: music; Scottish history; walking. Address: (h.) 40 Marchmont Crescent, Edinburgh EH9 1HG; T.-0131-667 1383.

McCrone, Iain Alistair, CBE (1987), SDA, ARAgS. Farmer and Company Director; b. 29.3.34, Glasgow; m., Yvonne Findlay (div.); 4 d. Educ. Glasgow Academy; Trinity College, Glenalmond; West of Scotland Agricultural College. Farming on own account, since 1956; Managing Director, McCrone Farmers Ltd., since 1958; began fish farming, 1968; Director: Highland Trout Co. (now Marine Harvest McConnell), 1968-97, Otter Ferry Salmon Ltd., since 1974; Member: Fife Regional Council, 1978-82; Parliamentary candidate (Conservative), Central Fife, 1979,

Council, National Farmers Union of Scotland, 1977-82; Board, Glenrothes Development Corporation, 1980-96; Fife Health Board, 1983-91; Chairman, Oxford Farming Conference, 1988; Chairman, The Farmers Club, 2001; Nuffield Farming Scholar, 1966; President, Scottish Conservative and Unionist Association, 1985-87. Recreations: golf; rugby (spectator). Address: (h.) Cardsknolls, Markinch, Fife KY7 6LP; T.-01337 830267; e-mail: iain.mccrone@btconnect.com

McCrone, Professor Robert Gavin Loudon, CB, MA, MSc, PhD, Hon.LLD, FRSE, Hon FRSGS. General Secretary, Royal Society of Edinburgh, 2005-07 (Vice President, 2002-05); Hon. Fellow of the Europa Institute, since 1992, Edinburgh University; Commissioner, Parliamentary Boundary Commission for Scotland, 1999-2005; Trustee, Scottish Opera Endowment Trust, 1998-2011; b. 2.2.33, Ayr; m., 1, Alexandra Bruce Waddell (deceased); 2 s.; 1 d.; m., 2, Olive Pettigrew Moon (née McNaught); 2 step-d. Educ. St. Catharine's College, Cambridge; University of Wales; Glasgow University. National Service with RASC, 1952-54; Fisons Ltd., 1959-60; Lecturer in Economics, Glasgow University, 1960-65; Fellow, Brasenose College, Oxford, 1965-70; Consultant, UNESCO, 1964; Member, NEDC Working Party on Agricultural Policy, 1967-68; Adviser, House of Commons Select Committee on Scottish Affairs, 1969-70; Chief Economic Adviser, Scottish Office, 1970-92; Under Secretary, 1972-80; Secretary, Industry Department for Scotland, 1980-87; Secretary, Scottish Office Environment Department, 1987-92; Professor, Centre for Housing Research, University of Glasgow, 1992-94; Visiting Professor, Edinburgh University Management School, 1994-2005. Member: Economic and Social Research Council, 1986-89, Council, Royal Economic Society, 1977-82, Council, Scottish Economic Society, 1982-91, Board, Scottish Opera, 1992-98, Advisory Committee, Inquiry into Implementation of Constitutional Reform, 1995-97, National Review of Resources Allocation in the NHS in Scotland, 1998-2000, Board, Queen's Hall, 1998-2002; Deputy Chairman: Royal Infirmary of Edinburgh NHS Trust, 1994-99, Lothian University Hospitals' Trust, 1999-2001; Chairman, Committee of Inquiry into Professional Conditions of Service for Teachers, 1999-2000; Vice Chairman: Royal Society of Edinburgh Inquiry into Foot and Mouth Disease in Scotland, 2001-02, Royal Society of Edinburgh Inquiry into the Crisis in the Scottish Fishing Industry, 2003; Chairman, Royal Society of Edinburgh's Inquiry into the Future of Scotland's Hill & Island Areas, 2007-08. Publications: The Economics of Subsidising Agriculture, 1962; Scotland's Economic Progress 1951-60, 1963; Regional Policy in Britain, 1969; Scotland's Future, 1969; Housing Policy in Britain and Europe (Co-Author), 1995; European Monetary Union and Regional Development, 1997; Scottish Independence: Weighing Up the Economics, 2013, second enlarged edition, 2014. Recreations: music; walking. Address: (b.) 11A Lauder Road, Edinburgh EH9 2EN; T.-0131 667 4766.

McCrorie, Professor James Roderick, BSc, MA, PhD. Professor of Economics and Finance, St. Andrews University, since 2007, Head of School of Economics and Finance, 2010-14; Greenock. Educ. Greenock Academy; St. Andrews University; Essex University. Lecturer in Economics: Essex University, 1995-97 and 1999-2000, London School of Economics, 1997-99, Queen Mary University of London, 2000-03; Lecturer in Econometrics, Essex University, 2003-05; Reader in Economics, Leicester University, 2005-07; Visiting Fellow, CentER, Tilburg University, 2004; Associate Fellow, CORE, Université catholique de Louvain, 2007-08; Research Affiliate, Scottish Institute for Research in Economics, since 2007; External Fellow, Essex Centre for Financial Econometrics, Essex University, since 2014;

Director, Centre for Dynamic Macroeconomic Analysis, St Andrews University, since 2015 (research affiliate, since 2007); Centre for Dynamic Macroeconomic Analysis, St. Andrews University, since 2007; Part-Time Lecturer, New York University in London, 2002-06; Teaching Fellow, University College London, 2006-07; Guest Teacher, London School of Economics, 2011; Academic Assessor, Civil Service Selection Board, since 2003. Recreations: mountaineering; Clyde and West Highland Steamers; music and choral singing; Scotch Malt Whisky. Address: (b.) School of Economics and Finance, University of St. Andrews, St. Salvator's College, St. Andrews KY16 9AR; T.-01334 462482; e-mail: mccrorie@st-andrews.ac.uk

McCulloch, Andrew Grant, LLB, BSc (Soc Sci). Sheriff at Kirkcaldy; b. 10.2.52, Edinburgh; m.; 1 s.; 1 d. Educ. Glasgow Academy; Edinburgh University. Trained, then Assistant, Drummond Miller WS, 1974-79; Partner, 1979-2004; Member, Council, Law Society of Scotland, 1987-98, President, 1996-97; Solicitor Advocate, since 1992; Temporary Sheriff, 1992-99; part-time Sheriff, 2003-04. President, Grange Sports Club, 1990-92. Recreations: golf; cricket; wine. Address: (b.) Sheriff Court House, Kirkcaldy.

McCulloch, Ian, DA, RSA. Painter and Printmaker; b. 4.3.35, Glasgow; m., Margery Palmer; 2 s. Educ. Eastbank Academy; Glasgow School of Art. Elected Member, Society of Scottish Artists, 1964; elected Associate, Royal Scottish Academy, 1989; elected Academician, Royal Scottish Academy, 2005; paintings in many private and public collections; numerous one-man and group exhibitions; 1st prize, Stirling Smith Biennial, 1985; winner, Glasgow International Concert Hall Mural Competition, 1989-90; most recent solo exhibition, RSA Edinburgh, 2007; Collins Gallery, Glasgow, 2009. E-mail: mpm@waitrose.com

McCulloch, Professor James, BSc, PhD. Emeritus Professor of Neuropharmacology, Edinburgh University, since 2013; b. 7.4.51; m., Mailis Christina; 2 s. Educ. Spiers School, Beith; Glasgow University. Glasgow University: Lecturer, 1978-86, Reader, 1986-88, Professor, 1988-2002. Editor, Journal of Cerebral Blood Flow and Metabolism, 1997-2003; Past President, International Society of Cerebral Blood Flow and Metabolism. Publications: four books; 250 scientific papers. Recreations: golf; skiing. Address: (h.) Craigdene, Lochwinnoch Road, Kilmacolm PA13 4DZ; e-mail: Jamesmcculloch7@sky.com

McCulloch, Revd. James Donald, BD, MIOP, MIP3, FSA Scot. Minister of Hurlford Church, since 1996; b. 11.4.51, Coatbridge; m., Ann Johnston; 2 d. Educ. Coatbridge High School (Senior Secondary); University of Glasgow, Trinity College. Winner, Marcus Dods Prize in Advanced Ordinary New Testament Studies, 1995. Newspaper and Commercial Hot Metal Compositor, Baird & Hamilton, then Scottish & Universal Newspapers Hamilton, 1969-91; Glasgow College of Building and Printing: Printing Technician's Certificate, 1974, Winner of Andrew Holmes Memorial Scholarship, 1975; Assistant Minister, Bothwell Parish Church; Past Moderator, Presbytery of Irvine and Kilmarnock (2004-05); Editor of Scottish Church Society Report. Recreations: gymnasium; reading (non-fiction). Address: (h.) Hurlford Church Manse, 12 Main Road, Crookedholm, Kilmarnock, East Ayrshire KA3 6JT; T.-01563 535673.

McCulloch, James Macdonald, BA, MRTPI. Formerly Principal, James McCulloch Consulting; formerly Member, Law Society of Scotland Planning Law Specialist Accreditation Panel; Director for Planning and

Environmental Appeals and Chief Reporter, Scottish Government; b. 1948, Dorchester; m., Jennifer Anne Hay; 3 s.; 2 gsons. Educ. Hardye's School, Dorchester; Lanchester Polytechnic, Coventry. Planning Assistant, Coventry Corporation, 1971-73; Senior Planner and Principal Planner, Scottish Development Department, 1973-84; Reporter then Principal Reporter then Deputy Chief Reporter, 1984-2002. Recreations: walking; eating; the people, landscapes and language of Spain; motorcycling. E-mail: james.mcculloch100@gmail.com

McCulloch, John David, DL. Deputy Lieutenant, Midlothian, since 1992; Clerk to Church of Scotland Presbytery of Lothian, since 1994; b. 5.4.37, Edinburgh; m., Cicely Blackett; 2 s.; 2 d. Educ. Belhaven Hill, Dunbar; Marlborough College. Address: (h.) 20 Tipperwell Way, Penicuik EH26 8QP; T.-01968 672943.

McCulloch, Margaret. MSP (Labour), Central Scotland, 2011-16; b. 9.5.52, Glasgow; m., Ian. Educ. Glasgow Caledonian University. Formerly an independent training consultant; own business based in East Kilbride; formerly an External Verifier with the Scottish Qualifications Authority; worked at the University of Strathclyde for 17 years as a training executive.

McCulloch, Margery Palmer, BA, MLitt, PhD, LRAM. Literary scholar; m., Ian McCulloch; 2 s. Educ. Hamilton Academy; London University; Glasgow University. Publications include: The Novels of Neil M. Gunn: a critical study, 1987; Edwin Muir: poet, critic and novelist, 1993; Lewis Grassic Gibbon: A Centenary Celebration, 2003; Modernism and Nationalism: Literature and Society in Scotland, 1918-1939, 2004; Scottish Modernism and Its Contexts 1918-1959, 2009; Edinburgh Companion to Hugh MacDiarmid, 2011; Scottish and International Modernisms, 2011. Recreation: music. Address: (h.) 51 Victoria Road, Lenzie G66 5AP; e-mail: mpm@waitrose.com

McCulloch, Stewart, OBE. Chairman, Crimestoppers Scotland (2001-07); Chairman, Inverclyde Globetrotters (inaugural year 2010) (remaining active patron); b. 30.12.40, Strathaven, Lanarkshire; m., Janice Ruth (radiographer); 1 s.; 1 d. Educ. Allan Glen's School, Glasgow. Junior reporter, Glasgow Eastern Standard, 1958-60; Reporter, Head of Bureau, Scottish Daily Express, 1960-74; Writer/Deputy News Editor, Scottish Sunday Express, 1974-80; Director/purchasing and promotions, McCulloch Associates (restaurants), 1980-82; Diarist, 'Mr Glasgow', Glasgow Evening Times, 1982-83; Associate, Scottish Television's weekly 'What's Your Problem?' consumer slot, 1983-86; Planning Editor, News, Sport and Current Affairs, STV, 1986-97; Head of Media Relations, Rosyth, 2000; Lecturer, Media Studies, since 2001. Recreations: keep fit; modern history; travel. Address: (h.) 15, Levan Point, Cloch Road, Gourock PA19 1BL; T.-01475 630629 or 07768911895 (m).
E-mail: mccullochmedia@btinternet.com

McCulloch, Stuart James, BSc, MEd, DipEd, MLitt. Former Headmaster, Belmont House School (1999-2005); b. 26.12.50, Melfort; m., (1) Anne Elizabeth (deceased); (2) Maureen Collison; 2 s.; 1 d. Educ. Queen Mary College, London; Stirling University; Glasgow University. Head of Geography, Stewart's Melville, Edinburgh, 1973-92; Deputy Head, Beaconhurst School, 1992-98. Local Historian. Publication: A Scion of Heroes (Author). Recreations: most things, especially bagpipes and books. Address: (h.) Auld Manse, 28 Main Street, New Abbey DG2 8BY; T.-01387 850398.
E-mail: maculafailte@yahoo.co.uk

McCunn, Archibald Eddington, OBE, BSc (Hons), CEng, MIMechE, FCMI; b. 27.5.27, Motherwell; m., Olive Isobel Johnston; 1 s.; 1 d. Educ. Dalziel High School; Strathclyde University. Engineering Management, Colvilles Ltd. BSC,

1952-64; Senior Consultant, Inbucon/AIC, 1964-67; Divisional Chairman, Stenhouse Industries, 1967-71; Divisional Chairman/Consultant, Grampian Holdings plc, 1971-89; Board Member, Highlands and Islands Development Board, 1985-89; Director: A.E. McCunn Consultants Ltd., 1985-95; Chairman, Craftpoint Ltd., 1986-91; Director, McConnell Salmon Ltd., 1990-94; Vice Chairman and Trustee, Argyll and Bute Countryside Trust, 1990-95; Hon. Vice-President, Scottish Salmon Growers Association, 1990-95; Board Member: State Hospital, 1992-96, Scottish Natural Heritage (South West), 1992-97; Board Member, Scottish Greenbelt Foundation, 1992-99; Elder, Church of Scotland, since 1949. Recreations: painting; music; writing; gardening. Address: (h.) 2 McIntosh Way, Motherwell ML1 3BB; T.-01698 253500; e-mail: archiemccunn@blueyonder.co.uk

McDaid, Professor Seamus, CBE, CA, MBA. Formerly Principal and Vice-Chancellor, University of the West of Scotland (formerly Paisley University) (2005-2013); Convener, Universities Scotland, 2011-2012; Vice President, UUK, 2011-2012; b. 23.7.52, Glasgow; m., Alice; 2 d. Educ. St. Mungo's Academy; Glasgow University; Strathclyde University. Qualified as CA, 1974; trained with Wylie & Bisset, CA; worked for Coopers & Lybrand; joined Glasgow College as Lecturer, 1976; Senior Lecturer, 1980, Head, Department of Finance and Accounting, 1987; Dean, Faculty of Business, Glasgow Caledonian University, 1992; Vice Principal, University of Paisley, 1997-2005. Recreations: football; badminton.

MacDermid, Yvonne Jean, OBE, DPA, DCA, DTM. Chief Executive, Money Advice Scotland, since 1997; b. Glasgow. Educ. Woodside Senior Secondary School; Glasgow Caledonian University; Stow College; Central College of Commerce. Local government service, 1975-97; police and trading standards; former Member, Scottish Consumer Council; past Member, Financial Services Authority Independent Consumer Panel; Member, UK Money Advice Trust Partnership; Member, Cross Party Working Group on Poinding and Warrant Sales; Member, Scottish Government Debt Action Forum and Repossessions Sub Group; Member, Protected Trust Deeds Working Group (chaired by the Accountant in Bankruptcy); Non-Executive Board Member, Accountant in Bankruptcy. Publications: A Guide to Money Advice in Scotland (Co-Author), 2nd and 3rd editions; Managing Debt. Regular speaker and contributor/broadcaster in respect of consumer issues relating to credit and debt; Winner of the Martin Williams Award (Credit Today Awards 2013). Recreations: opera; swimming; entertaining; gardening; reading. Address: (b.) Suite 410, The Pentagon Centre, 36 Washington Street, Glasgow G3 8AZ; T.-0141-572 0238. E-mail: y.macdermid@moneyadvicescotland.org.uk

McDevitt, Emeritus Professor Denis Gordon, DSc, MD, FRCP, FRCPI, FRCPEd, FFPM, FRSE. Professor of Clinical Pharmacology, Dundee University Medical School, 1984-2002, now Emeritus Professor (Dean, Faculty of Medicine, Dentistry and Nursing, 1994-97); Honorary Consultant Physician, Tayside Universities Hospitals Trust, 1984-2002; Civil Consultant in Clinical Pharmacology, RAF, 1987-2002; Member, General Medical Council, 1996-2003 (Treasurer, 2001-03); b. 17.11.37, Belfast; m., Anne McKee; 2 s.; 1 d. Educ. Campbell College, Belfast; Queen's University, Belfast. Assistant Professor of Medicine and Consultant Physician, Christian Medical College, Ludhiana, North India, 1968-71; Senior Lecturer in Clinical Pharmacology and Consultant Physician, Queen's University Medical School, 1971-76; Merck International Fellow in Clinical Pharmacology, Vanderbilt University, Nashville, Tennessee, 1974-75; Reader in Clinical Pharmacology, Queen's University Medical School, 1976-

78; Professor of Clinical Pharmacology, Queen's University of Belfast and Consultant Physician, Belfast Teaching Hospitals, 1978-83. Chairman, Clinical Section, British Pharmacological Society, 1985-88 (Secretary, 1978-82); Member, Medicines Commission, 1986-95; President, Association of Physicians of Great Britain and Ireland, 1987-88; Member, Council, Royal College of Physicians of Edinburgh, 2003-08; Member, Board, Faculty of Pharmaceutical Physicians, 2003-08. Recreations: golf; classical music. Address: (h.) 10 Ogilvie Road, Broughty Ferry, Dundee DD5 1LU.

Macdonald, 8th Baron, (Godfrey James Macdonald of Macdonald). Chief of the Name and Arms of Macdonald; b. 28.11.47; m., Claire Catlow; 1 s.; 3 d. Address: (h.) Kinloch Lodge, Isle of Skye.

Macdonald of Tradeston, Rt. Hon. Lord (Gus Macdonald), CBE. Prime Minister's Advisory Committee on Business Appointments, 2009-13; House of Lords Select Committees on Economic Affairs, 2004-2008; Communications, 2008-2012; Digital Skills, 2014-15; Chairman, All Party Parliamentary Humanist Group, 2005-2010; Court Member, Sussex University, 2009-2011; Chancellor, Glasgow Caledonian University, 2007-2012; Senior Advisor, Macquarie Group Ltd., since 2004; Non Executive Director, Scottish Power, 2009-2015; Advisory Board, OECD International Transport Forum, 2009-13; Patron, Dystonia Society, since 2006; Minister for the Cabinet Office and Chancellor of Duchy of Lancaster, 2001-03; Minister for Transport, Department of Environment, Transport and the Regions, 1999-2001; Minister for Business and Industry, Scottish Office, 1998-99; b. 20.8.40, Larkhall; m., Teen; 2 d. Educ. Allan Glen's School, Glasgow. Marine engineer, Stephens, Linthouse, 1955-62; Circulation Manager, Tribune, 1964-65; Journalist, The Scotsman, 1965-67; Television producer/presenter, Granada, 1967-85; C4 Viewers Ombudsman, Right to Reply, 1982-88; Scottish Television: Director of Programmes, 1986-90, Managing Director, 1990-96; Chairman, Scottish Television, subsequently Scottish Media Group plc, 1996-98; Scottish Business Elite Awards: Business Leader of the Year, Chairman of the Year, 1997; founder Chairman, Edinburgh International Telvision Festival, 1976; Chairman, Edinburgh International Film Festival, 1993-96; Governor, National Film and Television School, 1986-97; Visiting Professor, Film and Media, Stirling University, 1986-98; Member, Boards: Scottish Enterprise, 1998, Bank of Scotland, 1998, Scottish Screen, 1997, British Film Institute, 1997-98; Chairman, Cairngorms Partnership, 1997-98; Chairman, Taylor and Francis Group plc, 1997-98. Recreations: words; music; pictures; sports. Address: (b.) House of Lords, London SW1A 0PW.

McDonald, The Very Reverend Alan Douglas, LLB, BD, MTH, DLitt (honoris causa), DD (honoris causa). Parish Minister, St, Leonard's and Cameron, St. Andrews, since 1998; b. 06.03.51, Glasgow; m., Dr Judith McDonald (nee Allen); 1 s.; 1 d. Educ. Glasgow Academy; Strathclyde University; Edinburgh University; St. Andrews University. Legal Apprentice, Biggart Baillie & Gifford, 1972-74; Solicitor, Farquharson Craig, 1974-75; Community Minister, Pilton, Edinburgh, 1979-83; Minister, Holburn Central, Aberdeen, 1983-98; Convener, Church and Nation Committee, 2000-04; Moderator of the General Assembly of the Church of Scotland, 2006-07. Presenter of Thought for the Day, BBC Radio Scotland. Recreations: running; walking; golf; music; poetry; travel; football. Address: (h.) 1 Cairnhill Gardens, St. Andrews KY16 8QY; T.-01334 472793. E-mail: alan.d.mcdonald@talk21.com

McDonald, Very Rev. Dr. Alexander, BA, DUniv (Open), CMIWS. Moderator of the General Assembly, Church of Scotland, 1997-98; b. 5.11.37, Bishopbriggs; m., Essdale Helen McLeod; 2 s.; 1 d. Educ. Bishopbriggs Higher Grade

School; Whitehill Senior Secondary School, Glasgow; Glasgow University and Trinity College. RAF, 1954-56; Management in timber trade: 1952-54, 1956-58; motor trade, 1958-62; student, 1962-68; Minister: St. David's Bathgate, 1968-74, St. Mark's, Old Hall, Paisley, 1974-88; General Secretary, Church of Scotland, Board of Ministry, 1988-2002; Honorary National Vice President of Boys' Brigade, 2008; Honorary President of the Paisley and District Battalion of the Boys' Brigade; wide range of involvement with Boys' Brigade in Scotland, ACCORD, Christian Aid and many others; regular broadcaster. Recreations: reading; walking; fishing. Address: Room 21, McKellar House, Erskine Home, Bishopton PA7 5PU; T.-0141-560 1937; e-mail: amcdpai@gmail.com

MacDonald, Allan, MA. Chief Executive, mneTV, since 1989; Director, purpleTV, since 2012; Chairman, Producers Alliance for Cinema and Television (PACT), Scotland, 2002-07; b. 11.6.53, Eriskay; m., Marion Margaret; 1 d. Educ. St. Vincent's College, Langbank; Blairs College, Aberdeen; Glasgow University. Senior Producer, BBC Highland, Inverness; Senior Producer/Manager, BBC Radio Nan Eilean, Stornoway; Manager, BBC Highland, Inverness; Television Producer, BBC Scotland, Glasgow; Head of Gaelic Television, Grampian TV, 1992-94. Member, Board of Management, Lews Castle College, 1992-95; Skillset National Board for Scotland, 2006-12; Founding Fellow of Institute of Contemporary Scotland. Address: (h.) 39 Hughenden Gardens, Hyndland, Glasgow G12 9YH; e-mail: allan@mnetv.tv

MacDonald, Angus. MSP (SNP), Falkirk East, since 2011; Parliamentary Liaison Officer to Richard Lochhead, Cabinet Secretary for Rural Affairs, Climate Change and the Environment and Dr Aileen MacLeod, Minister for the Environment; Convener of the Cross Party Group on Gaelic. Became the youngest JP in the country, and a Falkirk councillor, in 1992. Studied at the College of Estate Management and had a career in agriculture. Chairman of Mod 2008 in Falkirk. Address: (b.) Scottish Parliament, Edinburgh EH99 1SP.

Macdonald, Angus David, MA (Hons) (Cantab), DipEd. Retired Headmaster, Lomond School, Helensburgh (1986-2009); b. 9.10.50, Edinburgh; m., Isabelle Marjory Ross; 2 d. Educ. Portsmouth Grammar School; Cambridge University; Edinburgh University. Assistant Teacher, Alloa Academy, 1972-73; Assistant Teacher, Edinburgh Academy, 1973-82 (Exchange Teacher, King's School, Parramatta, NSW, 1978-79); George Watson's College, Edinburgh: Principal Teacher of Geography, 1982, Deputy Principal, 1982-86. Chairman, Hovinais High School Charitable Trust. Recreations: outdoor recreation; gardening. Address: Shenavail Farm, Camserney, nr. Aberfeldy, Perthshire PH15 2JF; T.-01887 820728.

Macdonald, Professor Angus John, BSc (Hons), PhD, FSA (Scot), HonFRSGS. Writer on architecture; Head, School of Arts, Culture and Environment, University of Edinburgh, 2002-07 (Senior Lecturer, Department of Architecture, 1988-2002, Head of Department of Architecture, 1996-99, Head of Environmental Studies Planning Unit, 1998-2002); b. 17.1.45, Edinburgh; m., Patricia Clare Mazoura Morrow Scott. Educ. George Heriot's School, Edinburgh; University of Edinburgh. Partner, Aerographica, since 1986; Commissioner, Royal Commission on the Ancient and Historical Monuments of Scotland, 1999-2009; Member, Board of Governors, Edinburgh College of Art, 2003-08. Publications: Wind Loading on Buildings, 1975; Above Edinburgh, 1989; The Highlands and Islands of Scotland, 1989; Granite and Green, 1992; Structure and Architecture, 1994; Structural

Design for Architecture, 1997; Anthony Hunt, 2000; Hebrides: an aerial view of a cultural landscape, 2010 (Co-Author); Routledge Companion of Architectural Design and Practice, 2015 (Contributor). Recreations: hillwalking; music. Address: Department of Architecture, University of Edinburgh, 20 Chambers Street, Edinburgh EH1 1JZ; T.-0131-650 2309; e-mail: angus.macdonald@ed.ac.uk

MacDonald, Calum Sutherland, Corporate member of the Chartered Institution of Wastes Management. Executive Director, Scottish Environment Protection Agency, since 2004; b. 18.7.54, Glasgow; m., Nancy; 1 s.; 2 d. Educ. Allan Glen's School, Glasgow; Glasgow College of Food Technology. Glasgow City Council; Environmental Health Department Student Sanitary Inspector; Environmental Health Officer; Senior Environmental Health Officer; Pollution Control Manager; Principal Environmental Health Officer, 1973-96; Scottish Environment Protection Agency, Divisional Manager West; Environmental Regulation and Improvement Manager, Highlands, Islands and Grampian; Environmental Development Manager; Acting Director of Strategic Planning, 1996-2004. Honorary Vice President, Environmental Protection UK; Member, Zero Waste Scotland Programme Board, Board of Metropolitan Glasgow Strategic Drainage Partnership and Executive Committee of Scottish Council Development and Industry. Founder member and Chairman of Helping Hands Associates, a charitable association helping good causes in Scotland and beyond. Address: (b.) Scottish Environment Protection Agency, Strathallan House, Castle Business Park, Stirling FK9 4TR; T.-01786 452 438; e-mail: calum.macdonald@sepa.org.uk

Macdonald, Professor David Iain Macpherson, BSc, PhD, CGeol, FGS, FRGS, Polar Medal. Professor of Petroleum Geology, University of Aberdeen, since 1999; Head of School of Geosciences, 2005-2010; b. 31.5.53, Bridge of Allan; m., Dr. Christine Mousley; 2 d. Educ. High School of Stirling; University of Glasgow; University of Cambridge. Geologist, British Antarctic Survey, Cambridge, 1975-80; Post Doctoral Fellow, University of Keele, 1980-82; Geologist, BP Petroleum Development, London, 1982-84; Senior Sedimentologist, British Antarctic Survey, 1984-93; Director, Cambridge Arctic Shelf Programme, 1993-99. Publications: Sedimentation, Tectonics and Eustasy, 1991; more than 60 scientific papers. Recreations: hillwalking; reading. Address: (b.) University of Aberdeen, School of Geosciences, Meston Building, Aberdeen AB24 3UE; T.-01224 273451; e-mail: d.macdonald@abdn.ac.uk

MacDonald, Donald. Managing Director, Aros, since 1992; b. 1.3.61, Uig, Isle-of-Skye; m., Sine Ghilleasbuig; 1 s.; 1 d. Educ. Napier University, Edinburgh. Management, Mount Royal Hotel, Edinburgh; returned to his native Skye to manage Co Chomunn Stafainn (community co-operative); Managerial role on the estate of Sir Iain Noble in south Skye in 1986 where he served on the board of Fearann Eilean Iarmain, managing Hotel Eilean Iarmain as well as a whisky company, Praban na Linne; in 1988, invested in the partnership of Tulloch Castle in Dingwall to create hotel and conference centre; Managing Director, Tulloch Castle until 1991, when he relocated to Skye; Co-founder Aros Centre in Portree, which opened in 1993 as a Visitor and Heritage Centre; in 1998 the Centre was further developed to include a purpose built theatre/cinema with conference facilities. Former Board Member, Skye and Lochlash Enterprise, acting as Chair of the Audit Committee; became Chairman, Comunn na Gàidhlig (Gaelic Development Agency), 2008-2011; became Chairman, National Gaelic Arts Agency, 2010; served on the board of Highlands and Islands Enterprise, since 2010 and sits on their Risk and Assurance Committee; Co-

founder, Urras an Taobh Sear (Staffin Community Trust), 1994 (currently Chair). Recreations: keen crofter; raising sheep; growing vegetables and soft fruits; keeping bees; an elder of the Church of Scotland and a precentor of Gaelic psalms. Address: (b.) Glaic A'Lochain, 3 Glasphein, Staffin, Skye IV51 9JZ; T.-01470 562 325; e-mail: donaldsine@aol.com

Macdonald, Very Rev. Finlay Angus John, MA, BD, PhD, DD. Former Principal Clerk, General Assembly of the Church of Scotland (retired, 2010); Moderator, General Assembly, Church of Scotland, 2002-03; Extra Chaplain to HM the Queen; b. 1.7.45, Watford; m., Elizabeth Mary Stuart; 2 s. Educ. Dundee High School; St. Andrews University. Assistant Minister, Bo'ness Old Kirk, 1970-71; Minister, Menstrie Parish Church, 1971-77; Junior Clerk and Treasurer, Stirling and Dunblane Presbytery, 1973-77; Minister, Jordanhill Parish Church, Glasgow, 1977-96; Convener, General Assembly Board of Practice and Procedure, 1988-92; Convener, General Assembly Business Committee, 1989-92; Depute Clerk, General Assembly, 1993-96. Fellow of University of Strathclyde; Member, Scottish Inter Faith Council, 2005-08; Co-Leader, Scottish Inter Faith Pilgrimage to Israel/Palestine, 2008. Publications: Confidence in a Changing Church, 2004; Luke Paul, 2012; Luke Paul and the Mosque, 2013. Recreations: music; hill-walking; reading; gardening. Address: (h.) 8 St Ronan's Way, Innerleithen, Peeblesshire EH44 6RG; T.-01896 831631.
E-mail: finlay_macdonald@btinternet.com

MacDonald, Gordon. MSP (SNP), Edinburgh Pentlands, since 2011; b. 2.1.60, Glasgow. Educ. Cumbernauld High School; Central College of Commerce; Glasgow College of Technology. Management accountant for Lothian Buses, 1989-2011. Address: (b.) Scottish Parliament, Edinburgh EH99 1SP.

McDonald, Sheriff Iona Sara, MA, LLB, NP. Solicitor, since 1980; Sheriff of North Strathclyde at Kilmarnock and Paisley, since 2002; Deputy Lieutenant of Ayrshire and Arran, since 2013; All Scotland Sheriff (floating), 2000-02; former Partner, Mathie Morton Black and Buchanan, Ayr; former Temporary Sheriff (all Scotland jurisdiction); b. 18.11.54; m., Colin Neale McDonald; 1 s.; 1 d. Educ. Cumnock Academy; Glasgow University. Apprentice Solicitor, Cannon Orpin and Co., Glasgow, 1978-80; joined Mathie Morton Black and Buchanan, Ayr, 1980. Safeguarder; Reporter to the Court and Curator Ad Litem in adoption hearings.

McDonald, Emeritus Professor Janet B.I., MA, FRSE, FRSAMD. Professor of Drama, Glasgow University, 1979-2005 (Head, Department of Theatre, Film and Television Studies, 2001-04; b. 28.7.41, Netherlee, Renfrewshire; m., Ian James McDonald; 1 d. Educ. Hutchesons' Girls' Grammar School; Glasgow University. Member: Governing Body, Royal Scottish Academy of Music and Drama, 1979-94, Academic Council, 1994-2002, Board, Citizens' Theatre, 1979-82 (Chair, 1991-2005); Member, Glasgow University Court, 1991-94; Council Member, Royal Society of Edinburgh, 1994-97, Vice-President, 2005-08; Chairman: Drama and Theatre Board, Council for National Academic Awards, 1981-85, Standing Committee of University Departments of Drama, 1982-85, Drama Committee, Scottish Arts Council, 1985-88; Chair, Creative and Performing Arts Committee, CNAA, 1989-91; Member, RAE Drama Panel, 1988, 1992; Member, Performing Arts Advisory Group, Scottish Qualifications Authority, 1999-2002; Member, Music and Performing Arts Research Committee, Arts and Humanities Research Board, 2000 (Chair, 2001-04), Board Member, 2002-04; Director,

Merchants House, Glasgow, 2002-08; Dean of Faculties, Glasgow University, since 2007; Council Member, Royal Philosophical Society, since 2010; Royal Glasgow Institute, since 2013. Address: (h.) 61 Hamilton Drive, Glasgow G12 8DP; T.-0141 339 0013; e-mail: chaika05@aol.com

McDonald, Professor Sir James, BSc, MSc, PhD, FREng, FRSE. Principal and Vice Chancellor, University of Strathclyde, since 2009; Rolls-Royce Chair in Electrical Systems. Educ. University of Strathclyde. Actively involved in energy research and advising government, industry and commerce and holds a number of public posts including: Co-Chair with First Minister, Scottish Energy Advisory Board; Chairman, Scottish Research Partnership in Engineering; Chairman, Energy Technology Partnership; Director, Scottish Enterprise; Chairman, Saltire Prize Technical Advisory Board; Chairman, Glasgow Economic Commission; Chairman, Glasgow Sustainable City Initiative; Co-Chair, Energy Economics and Grid Advisory Group; Member, UKTI Energy Excellence Board; Chairman, Board of Glasgow Science Centre; Higher Education Advisor, Robertson Trust Scholarship Scheme. Address: (b.) 16 Richmond Street, Glasgow G1 1XQ; T.-0141 548 2485.

McDonald, Janis. Chief Officer, Scottish Council on Deafness, since 2014. Educ. St Mungo's, Alloa; University of Aberdeen. Chief Executive Officer: Renfrewshire CVS, 2004-11, Voluntary Action Lochaber, 2011-13. Addictions Counsellor, GCA & RCA Trust, 1978-92. Address: Scottish Council on Deafness, Central Chambers Suite 62 (1st Floor), 93 Hope Street, Glasgow G2 6LD; T.-0141 248 2474.

MacDonald, Jim, MPhil (Town Planning), DipMgmt. Chief Executive, Architecture and Design Scotland. Educ. Edinburgh University; UCL, London. Career: worked with Glasgow City Council, North Lanarkshire Council and the City of Westminster Council; joined A+DS from Historic Scotland. Address: (b.) Architecture and Design Scotland, Bakehouse Close, 146 Canongate, Edinburgh EH8 8DD; T.-0131 556 6699.

MacDonald, John Neil, BA. Director for Scotland, Community Transport Association, since 2006; Chief Executive, Royal Scottish Agricultural Benevolent Institution, 2002-06; b. 8.1.60, Daliburgh, South Uist. Educ. St. Vincent's College, Langbank; Blairs College, Aberdeen; Nicolson Institute, Stornoway, Napier College; Strathclyde University. Contracts Supervisor, SGB plc, 1984-86; Sales Executive: Mannesmann Kienzle, 1986-88; Decision Data Computer (GB) Ltd., 1988-89; Sales and Marketing Consultant, Sequel UK Ltd., 1989-91; Development Officer, Scottish Council for Voluntary Organisations, 1991-2002. Recreations: football; literature; cinema. Address (b.) Community Transport Association, 21 Walker Street, Edinburgh EH3 7HX; T.-0131 220 0052; e-mail: johnm@ctauk.org

McDonald, Mark, MA, MLitt. MSP (SNP), Aberdeen Donside, since 2013, North East Scotland, 2011-2013; b. Inverurie. Educ. Dyce Primary School; Dyce Academy; University of Dundee; University of Aberdeen. Parliamentary Researcher to MSPs Richard Lochhead, Maureen Watt, and Nigel Don, 2003-2011; elected to Aberdeen City Council in 2007 at the age of 26, representing the Dyce/Buckburn/Danestone ward; SNP candidate, Aberdeen by-election, 2004; SNP candidate for Aberdeen South in the 2010 UK general election. Address: (b.) Scottish Parliament, Edinburgh EH99 1SP.

Macdonald, Rev. Mhorag, MA (Hons), BD (Hons). Minister of Cambusnethan Parish Church, since 1989; Moderator, Hamilton Presbytery, 2006-07; b. 6.4.53, Lagos, Nigeria. Educ. Dumbarton Academy; Glasgow University. Secondary Teacher (Modern Languages), Boclair Academy,

Bearsden, 1978-83 (Exchange Teacher, Soultz, Haut Rhin, France, 1981-82); Principal Teacher (Modern Languages), Grovepark, Greenock, 1983-85; Probationer Minister, Bishopton Erskine Church, 1988-89; Ordained and Inducted to Cambusnethan North Parish Church as Parish Minister in 1989. Part-Time Chaplain, Wishaw General; Chaplain, Cambusnethan Primary and Coltness High; Advisor to Board of MADE4U in ML2. Recreations: gardening; walking dog; sudoku, music; photography. Address: (h. and b.) 350 Kirk Road, Wishaw ML2 8LH; T.-01698 381305; e-mail: mhoragmacdonald@btinternet.com

McDonald, Rev. Moira, MA, BD. Minister of Corstorphine Old Parish Church, Edinburgh, since 2005; b. 6.1.69, Elderslie; m., Ian Gates; 1 s.; 1 d. Educ. Renfrew High School; University of Dundee; University of Edinburgh. Minister of Musselburgh: St. Clement's and St. Ninian's Parish Church, 1997-2005. Recreations: gardening; cycling; reading; keeping chickens; playing the piano. Address: (h.) 23 Manse Road, Edinburgh EH12 7SW.
E-mail: moira-mc@live.co.uk

Macdonald, Professor Murdo, MA, PhD, LCAD, FRSA, FSA Scot, HRSA. Chair of History of Scottish Art, University of Dundee, since 1997; b. 25.1.55, Edinburgh. Educ. Hammersmith College of Art, Edinburgh University. Commissioning editor, Polygon Books, 1982-94; art school and university lecturing, 1986-90; art critic (mainly for The Scotsman) 1987-1992; Editor, Edinburgh Review, 1990-1994; Lecturer and Adviser in Scottish Studies, Centre for Continuing Education, University of Edinburgh, 1990-97. Trustee, Sir Patrick Geddes Memorial Trust, 1996-2011, Associate from 2011. Publications: papers and chapters on visual thinking in Scotland in particular re: Patrick Geddes, Highland/Gàidhealtachd Art, Ossian, Burns, Celtic Revival; Scottish Art, 2000. Recreation: hill-walking. Address: Duncan of Jordanstone College of Art and Design, University of Dundee, Dundee DD1 4HT; T.-01382 345287; e-mail: mjsmacdonald@dundee.ac.uk

MacDonald, Neil, FInstP, FEI, MIWM, MIIM. Chairman, Martin Aerospace Ltd., since 2005; Proprietor, Leaders Management and Investment, since 1995; b. 13.12.45, Bracadale, Isle of Skye; m., Marion Storrie Ruthven Wilson; 1 s.; 1 d. Educ. Biggar High School; Coatbridge Technical College; Hartford Graduate Centre. Design Engineer, Marshall and Anderson Ltd., 1961-69; Manufacturing Director: Gray Tool (UK) Ltd., 1969-79, Gray Tool (Europe) Ltd., 1979-83; General Manager, North America, Gray Tool Co. Inc., 1983-85; Managing Director: Sealand Industries PLC, 1985-91, Vickers Shipbuilding (USEL) Offshore, 1991-96; Chairman: Seaboard Lloyd Ltd., 1994-96, Edinburgh Petroleum Services, 1995-2004. Past Chairman: Scottish Enterprise Lanarkshire, Cumbernauld Area Enterprise Trust, East Kilbride Enterprise Trust, Hamilton Group Engineering Centre; Past Member: Lloyds Register of Shipping Scottish Committee, Offshore Engineering Technology Board, Scottish Oil and Gas Innovation Forum, Scottish Enterprise Energy Advisory Board, Scottish Industrial Development Advisory Board, Scottish Enterprise Investment Advisory Board; Founder Member, Institute of Petroleum West of Scotland Branch. Recreations: family; motor sport; the countryside. Address: (b.) Parkboro, 133 Hyndford Road, Lanark ML11 9BB; T.-01555 666908.
E-mail: neil.macdonald1@btconnect.com

MacDonald, Norman Hamilton, FRSA, FSAScot. Historian and Archivist, Clan Donald Society of Edinburgh (President, 1993-2002 and since 2007); Historian to the High Council of Clan Donald, since 2000; b. 4.3.33,

Edinburgh; m., Morag Young McKenzie. Educ. Royal High School, Edinburgh. RAF, 1953-55; accountancy, 1955-63; S.E. Regional Hospital Board, 1963-67; Edinburgh Corporation, later Edinburgh District Council, 1967-91 (retired); Chairman, The 1745 Association, 1991-97; President, Edinburgh Gaelic Choir, 1995-97. Editor, Clan Donald Magazine. Publications: histories of MacDonalds of Glengarry and Keppoch; two cassette recordings of Gaelic and Scots songs; Keppoch (1971); Glengarry (1979, 1995); Clanranald, 2008. Address: (h.) Ceapach, 8 Ethel Terrace, Edinburgh EH10 5NB: T.-0131-447 3970.

Macdonald, Peter Cameron, SDA. Farmer, 1961-96; Director, J. Dickson & Son, Gunmakers, 1968-99, Chairman, 1997-99; b. 14.12.37, Edinburgh; m., Barbara Helen Drimmie Ballantyne (deceased); 2 step-s. Educ. Loretto; East of Scotland College of Agriculture. Vice-President, Scottish Landowners' Federation, 1990-2001 (Convener, 1985-88; Council Member, 1976-2001); Council Member, Blackface Sheepbreeders Association, 1970-74; Member, Forth River Purification Board, 1979-87; Director, Royal Highland and Agricultural Society of Scotland, 1985; Deputy Lieutenant, West Lothian, 1987-2012. Recreations: fishing; shooting; golf. Address: Farmhouse, Waterheads, Eddleston, Peeblesshire EH45 8QX; T.-01721 730229.
E-mail: pmacdonald63@hotmail.com

Macdonald, Peter James, BD. Leader, The Iona Community, since 2009; b. 22.03.58, Dumbarton; m., Lesley Anne Orr; 2 s. Educ. Vale of Leven Academy; University of Glasgow; University of Edinburgh. Career History: National Young Adult Adviser, Church of Scotland; Parish Minister: Kirkcaldy: Torban Church; Parish Minister, Edinburgh: St George's West Church. Recreations: cinema; theatre; reading; walking; sport. Address: (b.) The Iona Community, Savoy House, 140 Sauchiehall Street, Glasgow G2 3DH; T.-0141 332 6343; e-mail: peter.macdonald@iona.org.uk

Macdonald, (Roderick) Lewis, MA, PhD. MSP (Labour), North East Scotland, since 2011, Aberdeen Central, 1999-2011; Shadow Minister for Energy, since 2015; Member, Scottish Labour Public Services and Wealth Creation Team; Opposition Chief Whip, 2013-2015; Shadow Cabinet Secretary for Justice, 2011-2013; Shadow Cabinet Secretary for Infrastructure and Capital Investment, 2011; Shadow Minister for Energy, Enterprise and Tourism, 2007-2011; Deputy Minister for Health and Community Care, 2005-07; for Environment and Rural Development, 2004-05; Deputy Minister for Enterprise and Lifelong Learning, 2003-04; for Enterprise, Transport and Lifelong Learning, 2001-03; for Transport and Planning, 2001; Convener, Holyrood Progress Group, 2000-01; b. 1.1.57, Stornoway; m., Sandra Inkster; 2 d. Educ. Inverurie Academy; Aberdeen University. Research and teaching posts outwith politics, 1983-87, 1992-93; Parliamentary Researcher, office of Frank Doran MP, 1987-92; Shadow Cabinet Adviser to Tom Clarke MP, 1993-97; Member, Labour Party Scottish Executive Committee, 1997-99; Parliamentary candidate, Moray, 1997; Parliamentary Researcher, office of Frank Doran MP, 1997-99. Member, Management Committee, Aberdeen Citizens' Advice Bureau, 1997-99; Member, Grampian Regional Equality Council. Recreations: history; sports and games; the countryside. Address: (b.) 80 Rosemount Place, Aberdeen AB25 2XN; T.-01224-646333; Fax: 01224 645450.
E-mail: Lewis.Macdonald.msp@scottish.parliament.uk

MacDonald, Professor Ronald, BA, MA (Econ), PhD, OBE. Research Professor of Macroeconomics and International Finance, Glasgow University, since 2006; b. 23.4.55, Glasgow; m., Catriona Smith. Educ. Falkirk High School; Heriot Watt University; Manchester University.

Midland Bank Fellow in Monetary Economics, Loughborough University, 1982-84; Lecturer in Economics, Aberdeen University, 1984-88; Senior Lecturer, 1988-89; Robert Fleming Professor of Finance and Investment, Dundee University, 1989-93; Professor of International Finance, Strathclyde University, 1993-2004; Bonar MacFie Professor of Economics, Glasgow University, 2005-06, Adam Smith Professor of Political Economy, 2006-2015. Visiting Professor: Queen's University, Canada, 1988, University of New South Wales, Australia, 1989, European University Institute, Florence, 1998 and 2000, University Cergy-Pontoise, 1999, Centre for Economic Studies, 1999, Reserve Bank of New Zealand, 2000; Visiting Scholar, Monetary Authority of Singapore, 2003; Visiting Economist, African Department, International Monetary Fund, Washington DC, 2003; Visiting Scholar, Central Bank of Norway, 2003; Member, European Monetary Forum, since 1994; Visiting Scholar, International Monetary Fund, Washington DC, since 1991; Research Fellow, CESIFO, Munich, since 2000; International Fellow of Kiel Institute for World Economics; Consultant to the European Commission and European Central Bank; Monetary Adviser, IMF, 2012; FRSE, 2002-2014. Publications: Floating Exchange Rates; Exchange Rate Modelling; Exchange Rate Economics: Theories and Evidence; International Money: theory evidence and institutions (Co-Author); The Political Economy of Financing Scottish Government: Considering a New Constitutional Settlement; nine co-edited books; over 140 refereed journal articles; 37 articles in edited books; over 11,000 citations recorded on Google Scholar; fine art landscape photography. Co-owner, An t-Eilean Photographic Gallery, Portree. Recreations: music; abstract art; windsurfing; boating; cycling. Address: (b.) Department of Economics, Adam Smith Business School, Gilbert Scott Building, Glasgow University, Glasgow G12 8QQ; T.-0141-330-1988.
E-mail: ronald.macdonald@glasgow.ac.uk

McDonald, Sheena Elizabeth, MA, HC, DLitt. Journalist and broadcaster. Address: (b.) Curtis Brown, 28/9 Haymarket, London SW1Y 4SP.
E-mail: se.mcdonald@virgin.net

MacDonald, Professor Simon Gavin George, MA, PhD, FInstP, FRSE; b. 5.9.23, Beauly, Inverness-shire; m., Eva Leonie Austerlitz; 1 s.; 1 d. Educ. George Heriot's, Edinburgh; Edinburgh University. Junior Scientific Officer, Royal Aircraft Establishment, Farnborough, 1943-46; Lecturer in Physics, St. Andrews University, 1948-57; Senior Lecturer in Physics: University College of the West Indies, 1957-62, St. Andrews University, 1962-67; Dundee University: Senior Lecturer in Physics, 1967-73, Professor of Physics, 1973-88, Dean of Science, 1970-73, Vice-Principal, 1974-79, Head, Department of Physics, 1979-85; Chairman, Statistics Committee, Universities Central Council on Admissions, 1989-93; Member, Scottish Universities Council on Entrance, 1969-82 (Vice-Convener, 1973-77, Convener, 1977-82); Chairman, Technical Committee, UCCA, 1979-83; Deputy Chairman, UCCA, 1983-89; Chairman, Board of Directors, Dundee Repertory Theatre, 1975-89. Publications: Problems and Solutions in General Physics; Physics for Biology and Premedical Students; Physics for the Life and Health Sciences; Death is my Mistress; The Crime Committee; My Frail Blood; Publish and be Dead; Swallow Them Up; Dishing The Dirt; A Family Affair; Playing Away; Bloody and Invisible Hand; The Truth In Masquerade; I Spy, I Die; Bow At A Venture; Passport to Perdition; The Plaintive Numbers; The Root of all Evil; Pay the Price; The Forsyth Saga; Murder at the Museum; The Second Forsyth Saga; Mysteries of Space and Time; Murder of an Unknown; The Long Arm; A Further Forsyth Saga, Amorphous; Double Jeopardy; Rendezvous with Death: A Forsyth Duo. Recreations:

bridge; golf; fiction writing. Address: (h.) 7A Windmill Road, St Andrews KY16 9JJ; T.-01334 478014; e-mail: simon.macdonald1@virgin.net

McDonald, Stewart. MP (SNP), Glasgow South, since 2015; b. 24.8.86, Castlemilk, Glasgow. Educ. Govan High School. Career in retail management; holiday rep in Tenerife; parliamentary case worker for Anne McLaughlin MSP, then case worker for James Dornan MSP in 2011. Address: House of Commons, London SW1A 0AA.

McDonald, Stuart. MP (SNP), Cumbernauld, Kilsyth and Kirkintilloch East, since 2015; SNP Spokesperson on Immigration, Asylum and Border Control, since 2015; b. 1978. Educ. Kilsyth Academy; University of Edinburgh. Legal Trainee, Simpson and Marwick Solicitors, 2001-03; Solicitor, NHS Scotland's Central Legal Office, 2003-05; Human Rights Solicitor, Immigration Advisory Service (IAS), 2005-09; Senior Researcher, Scottish Parliament, 2009-2013; Senior Researcher for the pro-independence Scottish independence referendum campaign Yes Scotland, 2013-14; Parliamentary and Public Affairs Officer for the Coalition for Racial Equality and Rights, a Glasgow-based charity, 2015. Member of the House of Commons Home Affairs Select Committee. Address: House of Commons, London SW1A 0AA.

Macdonald, Very Rev. Susan. Dean, Diocese of Edinburgh, since 2012; Rector of Christ Church, Morningside, since 2007; b. 1951. Career: Theological Institute of the Scottish Episcopal Church, 1993-96; Deaconed, 1996; Priested, 1997; Assistant Curate, St John's, Jedburgh, 1996-98; Priest, St Peter, Galashiels, 1998-2001; Priest-in-Charge, Gordon Chapel, Fochabers, 2001-04; Mission 21 Co-ordinator Diocese of Moray, Ross & Caithness, 2001-04; Canon, St Andrew's Cathedral, Inverness, 2003-04; Mission & Ministry Officer, Aberdeen & Orkney, 2005-2007. Address: The Diocese of Edinburgh, 21a Grosvenor Crescent, Edinburgh EH12 5EL; T.-0131 5387033; e-mail: dean@dioceseofedinburgh.org

Macdonell, Hamish Alasdair, BA (Hons). Political commentator and parliamentary reporter; Company Director, Holyrood News, since 2009; b. 5.1.68, Inverness; m., Louisa Mary Buller; 2 s. Educ. Fettes College, Edinburgh; University of York. Reporter, Yorkshire Evening Press, 1990-94; freelance journalist, Africa and Australia, 1994-95; Press Association: Parliamentary Reporter, 1995-97, Scottish Political Editor, 1997-98; Political Editor, Scottish Daily Mail, 1998-2001; Scottish Political Editor, The Scotsman, 2001-09; Founding Member, Caledonian Mercury, 2009-2013; Co Founder, Scottish Speakers, 2013-2015. Recreations: golf; rugby; jazz. Address: 11, East Hermitage Place, Edinburgh EH6 8AA; T.-0131-557 0380.
E-mail: hamishmacdonell@fsmail.net

McDonnell, Michael Anthony, BD, DipTheol, DipCE, Hon MAIRSO. Director, Road Safety Scotland (formerly Scottish Road Safety Campaign), since 2004; b. 13.5.55, Bellshill; m., Rosemary Boyle; 1 s. Educ. St. Patrick's High School, Coatbridge; Hamilton College of Education; St. Andrew's College Drygrange; Chesters College, Glasgow. Strathclyde Regional Council, 1976-81, 1982-83, 1988-90, latterly as Road Safety Training Officer; Royal Society for the Protection of Accidents (ROSPA), 1990-2004. Recreations: football; cinema. Address: (b.) Fourth Floor, Pentland House, 47 Robb's Loan, Edinburgh EH14 1TY.
E-mail: michael.mcdonnell@transportscotland.gsi.gov.uk

MacDougall, James Taylor, CBE; b. 14.5.30, Perth; m., Fiona; 1 d. Educ. Perth Academy; St. Andrews University (University College, Dundee). Admitted as a Solicitor, 1953; National Service, commissioned Royal Armoured Corps (3 Royal Tank Regiment), 1953-55; private practice/local government, 1955-59; Procurator

Fiscal Depute at Dumfries, 1959-69; Procurator Fiscal: at Elgin, 1969-76, at Dumfries, 1976-93 (including Kirkcudbright, 1987-93); Honorary Sheriff at Dumfries, since 1995. Recreations: fishing; shooting; colour photography. Address: (h.) Wheatyards, Torthorwald, Dumfries DG1 3QE; T.-01387 750683.

Macdougall, Rev. Malcolm McAllister (Calum), BD, DChrEd, MTh. Minister, Eddleston linked with Peebles Old Parish Church, since 2001; b. 20.3.52, Greenock; m., Janet MacVicar; 1 s.; 1 d. Educ. Greenock Academy; Kelvinside Academy; University of Edinburgh. Worked in Rope and Canvas Industry and in Banking before entering The Church of Scotland Ministry; served as Probationary Assistant Minister, Greenbank Parish Church, Edinburgh, 1980-81; Minister, St James' Parish Church, Portobello, 1981-2001. Former member: General Assembly's Committee on Church and Nation, General Assembly's Committee on Education; former Chairman, Edinburgh Hospital Broadcasting Service; Chairman, Edinburgh and District Churches Council on Local Broadcasting. Recreations: walking; music; broadcasting. Address: (h.) 7 Clement Gunn Square, Peebles EH45 8LW; T.-01721 720568; e-mail: calum.macdougall@btopenworld.com

McDougall, Margaret. MSP (Labour), West Scotland, 2011-16; b. 23.1.49. Previously represented the Kilwinning South Ward on North Ayrshire Council.

McDougall, Peter. Screenwriter; b. 1947, Greenock. Television and film work includes: Just Another Saturday, 1974 (Prix Italia); Elephant's Graveyard, 1976; Just A Boy's Game, 1979; Shoot for the Sun, 1985; Down Where The Buffalo Go, 1988; Down Among The Big Boys, 1993.

MacDougall, Robert Hugh, MB, ChB, DMRT, FRCS, FRCR, FRCPEdin. Formerly Bute Professor and Dean of Medicine, School of Medicine, University of St. Andrews; Honorary Consultant Clinical Oncologist, Edinburgh Cancer Centre, Western General Hospital, Edinburgh; b. 9.8.49, Dundee; m., Moira Jean Gray; 1 s.; 2 d. Educ. High School of Dundee; St. Andrews University; Edinburgh University. Demonstrator in Anatomy, St. Andrews University; Registrar in Surgery, Aberdeen Royal Infirmary; Lecturer in Clinical Oncology, Edinburgh University; Consultant Radiotherapist and Oncologist, Tayside Health Board; Clinical Director, Department of Clinical Oncology, Western General Hospitals, Edinburgh. Recreation: reading. Address: (b.) 21 Belgrave Crescent, Edinburgh EH4 3AN.

McDowall, Stuart, CBE, MA. Local Government Boundary Commissioner for Scotland, 1982-99; b. 19.4.26, Liverpool; m., Margaret B.W. Gyle (deceased); 3 s. Educ. Liverpool Institute; St. Andrews University. Royal Air Force, 1944-47; Lecturer then Senior Lecturer in Economics, St. Andrews University, 1961-91; Deputy Chairman, Central Arbitration Committee, 1976-96; Master, United College of St. Salvator and St. Leonard, St. Andrews University, 1976-80; Member: Monopolies and Mergers Commission, 1985-90, Restrictive Practices Court, 1993-96; Chairman, Fife Healthcare NHS Trust, 1994-96; Secretary, Scottish Economic Society, 1970-76. Recreations: golf; gardening; music. Address: (h.) 10 Woodburn Terrace, St. Andrews, Fife KY16 8BA; T.-01334 473247.

McEachran, Colin Neil, QC, MA, LLB, JD. QC, since 1981; b. 14.1.40, Glasgow; m., Katherine Charlotte; 2 d. Educ. Glenalmond College; Merton College, Oxford;

Glasgow University; University of Chicago. Advocate, since 1968; Advocate Depute, 1974-77; QC, 1981; Member, Scottish Legal Aid Board, 1990-98; President, Pension Appeal Tribunal Scotland, 1994-2013; Chairman, Commonwealth Games Council for Scotland, 1995-99. Recreations: target shooting; golf; hill-walking. Address: 13 Saxe Coburg Place, Edinburgh; T.-0131-332 6820; e-mail: colinmce@btconnect.com

McEwan, Hon. Lord (Robin Gilmour McEwan), QC, LLB, PhD. Senator of the College of Justice, 2000-08; b. 12.12.43, Glasgow; m., Sheena McIntyre; 2 d. Educ. Paisley Grammar School; Glasgow University. Faulds Fellow in Law, Glasgow University, 1965-68; admitted to Faculty of Advocates, 1967; Standing Junior Counsel, Department of Energy, 1974-76; Advocate Depute, 1976-79; Chairman, Industrial Tribunals, 1981; Sheriff of Lanark, 1982-88, of Ayr, 1988-2000; Member, Scottish Legal Aid Board, 1989-96; Temporary Judge, Court of Session and High Court of Justiciary, 1991-99; Member, Gill Committee on Scottish Civil Courts Review, since 2007; Deputy Chairman, Boundaries Commission for Scotland, since 2007. Publications: Pleading in Court, 1980; A Casebook on Damages (Co-author), 1983; Contributor to Stair Memorial Encyclopaedia of the Laws of Scotland, 1986.

McEwan, Angus Maywood, BA (Hons), RSW, RWS. Artist; Lecturer (part-time) in Art and Design, Dundee College, since 1997; b. 19.7.63, Dundee; m., Wendy Ann Bell McEwan; 3 s. Educ. Carnoustie High School; Duncan of Jordanstone College of Art. Elizabeth Greenshields Foundation Award, Canada, 1987, 1990; RSA Latimer Award, 1995; scholarship to China, 1996; RSW Prize, 1999; Alexander Graham Munro Award; RSW Prize, 2001; Glasgow Arts Club Fellowship; RSA Diana King/ Scottish Gallery Prize, 2002; John Gray Award; RSW Prize, 2004; John Blockley Prize, Royal Institute of Painters in Watercolours (RI), 2005; 2nd Prize, Kaupthing Singer and Friedlander Watercolour Competition; Bronze Award, Shenzhen International Watercolor Biennial, 2013; elected Member of International Guild of Realism, USA; elected Associate Member of The Royal Watercolour Society (RWS), 2009; solo exhibitions: Riverside Gallery, Stonehaven, 1990, Tolquhon Gallery, Aberdeenshire, 1992, Gallery 41, Edinburgh, 1994, Royal Scottish Academy, 1996, Leith Gallery, 1997, Le Mur Vivant Fine Art, London, 1997, Leith Gallery, 2000, Open Eye Gallery, Edinburgh, 2002; Glasgow Arts Club, 2002; solo shows: Open Eye Gallery, 2004, 2006, 2008, 2010; Queens Gallery, 2005; Art of the Real Exhibitions, USA, England, Scotland, China, 2012; many mixed and group exhibitions; work in public and private collections. Recreations: art; photography; reading; playing with children; enjoying life. Address: (h.) 7 Glenleven Drive, Wormit, Newport on Tay, Fife DD6 8NA; T.-01382 542314; e-mail: art@angusmcewan.com Website: www.angusmcewan.com Blogsite: www.artmcewan.blogspot.com

MacEwan, Rev. Donald. Chaplain, St Andrews University, since 2011; m., Maya. Educ. Aberdeen University; Edinburgh University. Career: taught English in Japan for two years; later appointed to an assistantship in Elgin, then obtained PhD in Dublin; Church of Scotland Minister in Largoward and St Monans, 2001-2011. Address: The Chaplaincy Centre, Mansefield, University of St Andrews, 3 St Mary's Place, St Andrews, Fife KY16 9UY; T.-01334 46 2866.

McEwan, Leslie J., JP, MA, DipSA, DipSW. Director of Social Work, City of Edinburgh Council, 1996-2003 (retired); b. 26.2.46; m., Catherine; 2 s. Educ. St Andrews

University; Dundee University; Edinburgh University. Midlothian, East Lothian and Peebles: Child Care Officer, Children's Department, 1967-69, Social Worker, 1969-71, Senior Social Worker, 1971-74, Social Work Advisor, 1974-75; Lothian Regional Council: Divisional Director of Social Work, Midlothian, 1975-80, West Lothian, 1980-85, Depute Director of Social Work, 1985-90, Senior Depute Director of Social Work, 1990-95; Director of Social Work, 1995-96. Associate Consultant, Care and Health, 2004-09; Chair, Fair Charity Edinburgh; Member, Board, MYPAS Charity, Midlothian; Woodturner Volunteer, Grassmarket Community Project. Recreations: fly-fishing; golf; woodturning; choral singing.

McEwan, Ross. Chief Executive, The Royal Bank of Scotland (RBS), since 2013; b. 1957; m., Stephanie; 2 d. Educ. Hastings Boys' High School, New Zealand; Massey University; Harvard. National Mutual New Zealand, 1986-96; Chief Executive, Axa New Zealand, 1996-2002; CEO of First NZ Securities; Executive General Manager with responsibility for the branch network, contact centres and third party mortgage brokers, Commonwealth Bank of Australia, 2003-07; Group Executive, for Retail Banking Services 2007-2012; joined RBS in 2012 as Head of Retail Banking. Address: RBS, 36 St Andrew Square, Edinburgh EH2 2YB; T.-0131 556 8555.
E-mail: Ross.McEwan@rbs.com

McEwan, Roy James, OBE, BSc (Econ), DAARL, FRSA. Chief Executive, Scottish Chamber Orchestra, since 1993; Member, Scottish Arts Council, 2003-07; Chairman, Glasgow Grows Audiences, 2004-2010; b. 12.5.51, Dumfries. Educ. Dumfries High School; Carlisle Grammar School; London School of Economics; Polytechnic of Central London. House Manager, St. George's Theatre, London, 1977-78; Manager, Whitechapel Art Gallery, 1978-79; Administrator, then Director, MacRobert Arts Centre, Stirling, 1979-91; Director of Arts Development, North West Arts Board, Manchester, 1991-93. Chairman, Federation of Scottish Theatres, 1988-91; Scottish Arts Council: Member, Drama Committee, 1991, Member, Combined Arts Committee, 1993-99; Member, Board, Association of British Orchestras, 1993-2003 and since 2014; Member, Board, Scottish Music Information Centre, 1994-2000; Member, Board, Traverse Theatre, since 2012. Address: (b.) 4 Royal Terrace, Edinburgh EH7 5AB.

McEwen, Professor James, MB, ChB, FRCP (Glasgow, Edinburgh, London), FFPH, FFOM, FDSRCS, DIH, FMedSci, HonDSc. Emeritus Professor, Glasgow University, since 2001; Chair, UK Register for Public Health Specialists, 2003-09; Chair, Advisory Group, Health Protection Scotland, 2005-2013; Professor of Public Health, Glasgow University, 1999-2001; Henry Mechan Professor of Public Health, 1989-99; Consultant in Public Health Medicine, Greater Glasgow Health Board; b. 6.2.40, Stirling; m., Elizabeth May Archibald; 1 s.; 1 d. Educ. Dollar Academy; St. Andrews University. Lecturer in Industrial Medicine, Dundee University; Senior Lecturer in Community Medicine, Nottingham University; Chief Medical Officer, The Health Education Council; Professor of Community Medicine, King's College, University of London. President, Faculty of Public Health Medicine, Royal Colleges of Physicians UK, 1998-2001; Chair, Governors of Dollar Academy, since 2014. Recreations: church; gardening. Address: (b.) Auchanachie, Ruthven, Huntly, Aberdeenshire AB54 4SS; T.-01466 760742; e-mail: j.mcewen@tiscali.co.uk

McFadden, Jean Alexandra, CBE, JP, DL, MA, LLB. Member, Garscadden/Scotstounhill Ward, Glasgow City Council, 2007-2012, Chair, Finance, Policy Development and Scrutiny Committee, 2007-09, Executive Member for Corporate Governance, 2009-2010, Executive Member for Education, 2010-2012, Convener, Labour Group, 1995-2012, Convener, Strathclyde Joint Police Board, 2003-07; Senior Lecturer in Law, Strathclyde University, 1992-2006, Visiting Lecturer, since 2006; b. 26.11.41, Glasgow; m., John (deceased). Educ. Hyndland Secondary School; Glasgow University; Strathclyde University. Principal Teacher of Classics, Glasgow and Strathclyde schools, 1967-86; entered local government as Member, Cowcaddens Ward, Glasgow Corporation, 1971; Glasgow District Council: Member, Scotstoun Ward, 1984, Chairman, Manpower Committee, 1974-77, Leader, Labour Group, 1979-86, and 1992-94, Leader, Council, 1979-86, and 1992-94, Treasurer, 1986-92, Convener, 1995-96, Convener, Social Strategy Committee, 1996-99; Vice Lord Lieutenant, City of Glasgow, 1980-92, Deputy Lord Lieutenant, since 1992; President, COSLA, 1990-92; Convener, Scottish Local Government Information Unit, 1984-2003; Member, Board, Scottish Development Agency, 1989-91, GDA, 1992-2000; Chairman, Mayfest, 1983-97; Member, Secretary of State's Health Appointments Advisory Committee, 1994-2000; Convener, West of Scotland Archaeological Joint Committee, 1996-2012; Chair, Charity Law Review Commission in Scotland, 2000-01; Member, Ancient Monuments Board for Scotland, 2000-03; Executive Board Member, Royal Glasgow Institute of the Fine Arts, 2007, President, since 2014; Member, Board of Legal Services Agency, since 1992, Company Secretary, 2012-14, Convener of the Board, since 2014. Recreations: theatre; walking; golf; West Highland terriers. Address: (h.) 16 Lansdowne Crescent, Glasgow G20 6NG; T.-0141-334 3522.

MacFadyen, Alasdair Lorne, LLB. Sheriff, South Strathclyde, Dumfries and Galloway, since 2012; Sheriff, Grampian Highland and Islands at Dingwall, Inverness and Portree, 2002-2012; Appeal Sheriff, since 2015; b. 18.9.55, Glasgow; m., Lynne Ballantyne; 2 d. Educ. High School of Glasgow; Glasgow University. Qualified as Scottish Solicitor, 1978; practised as Solicitor in Private Practice, Edinburgh, Glasgow and Inverness, 1978-2001; Temporary Sheriff, 1995-2000; Part-Time Chairman, Employment Tribunals (Scotland), 2000-01; Part-Time Sheriff, 2000-01; All Scotland Floating Sheriff, based in Aberdeen, 2001-02. Recreations: sailing in Tall Ships; music; cycling. Address: (b.) 4 Beckford Street, Hamilton ML3 0BT; T.-01698 282957.

McFadyen, Jock, BA, MA. Contemporary British painter; b. 1950, Paisley; m. (1), Carol Hambleton; 1 s; m. (2), Susie Honeyman; 1 d.; 1 s. Educ. Glasgow School of Art; Chelsea School of Art. Taught one day a week at the Slade School of Art, 1980-2005; created The Grey Gallery in 2005. Appointed Artist in Residence at the National Gallery, London in 1981; commissioned by the Artistic Records Committee of The Imperial War Museum to record events surrounding the dismantling of the Berlin Wall in 1991; commissioned to design the set and costumes for Sir Kenneth MacMillan's last ballet The Judas Tree at the Royal Opera House, Covent Garden in 1992. Over 40 solo exhibitions; work is held by 30 public collections as well as private and corporate collections in Britain and abroad; elected a Royal Academician of the Royal Academy of Arts in 2012. E-mail: info@jockmcfadyen.com

McFadyen, Norman, CBE, FSA Scot, LLB. Sheriff of Lothian & Borders at Edinburgh, since 2015; b. 24.06.55, Glasgow; m., Pauline Brown; 1 s. Educ. High School of Glasgow; University of Glasgow. Procurator Fiscal Depute, Airdrie, Glasgow and Crown Office, 1978-88; Head of Fraud and Specialist Services, Crown Office, 1988-94; Deputy Crown Agent, 1994-98; Regional Procurator

Fiscal for Lothian and Borders, 1999-2002; Crown Agent Designate, 2002-03; Crown Agent and Chief Executive, 2004-2010; Sheriff of South Strathclyde, Dumfries and Galloway, 2010-2015. Co-Chair, High Court Reform Programme Board, 2004-07; Director, International Society for the Reform of Criminal Law, since 2008; Member, Sentencing Council for Scotland, since 2015. Recreations: walking; swimming. Address: (b.) Sheriff's Chambers, Sheriff Court House, 27 Chambers Street, Edinburgh EH1 1LB; T.-0131 225 2525.

McFall of Alcluith, Baron (John McFall), BSc (Hons), BA, MBA. Life Peer; MP (Labour), Dumbarton, 1987-2010; Chairman, Treasury Committee, 2001-10; Parliamentary Under Secretary of State, Northern Ireland Office, 1998-99; served on: Information Committee, Parliamentary and Scientific Committee, Executive Committee – Parliamentary Group for Energy Studies, British/Italian Group, British/Peru Group, Retail Industry Group, Roads Study Group, Scotch Whisky Group, Parliamentary and Scientific Committee; formerly Opposition Whip with responsibility for Foreign Affairs, Defence and Trade and Industry (resigned post at time of Gulf War); former Deputy Shadow Secretary of State for Scotland; Scottish Whip, 1997-98. Honorary Doctorates from the universities of Glasgow, Strathclyde, Stirling, the West of Scotland and London. Recreations: jogging; reading; golf. Address: House of Lords, Westminster, London SW1A 0PW.

McFarlane, Jim, DipTP. Chairman, Lothian Buses, since 2016, Interim General Manager. Educ. Glasgow School of Art. Scottish Enterprise: Senior Director, Business Transformation, 2001-03, Chief Executive of SE, Edinburgh and Lothian, 2003-07 (led the project teams that established the Edinburgh International Conference Centre and Exchange Financial District, Our Dynamic Earth and the Edinburgh Festival Theatre), Managing Director, Operations, 2007-2015. Significant involvement in the development and implementation of numerous landmark projects including the Edinburgh BioQuarter and The Scottish Centre for Regenerative Medicine. Degree of Doctor Honoris Causa for Leadership to Scottish Enterprise. Address: Lothian Buses, Annandale Street, Edinburgh EH7 4AZ.

Macfarlane of Bearsden, Lord, (Norman Somerville Macfarlane), KT (1996), Kt (1983), DL, FRSE. Life Peer; Honorary Life President, Macfarlane Group PLC (Chairman, 1973-98, Managing Director, 1973-90, Honorary Life President, 1999, Macfarlane Group (Clansman PLC); Honorary Life President, United Distillers (Chairman, 1987-96); Honorary Life President, Diageo (Scotland) Ltd.; Lord High Commissioner, General Assembly of Church of Scotland, 1992, 1993, 1997; b. 5.3.26; m., Marguerite Mary Campbell; 1 s.; 4 d. Educ. High School of Glasgow. Commissioned, Royal Artillery, 1945, served Palestine, 1945-47; founded N.S. Macfarlane & Co. Ltd., 1949 (became Macfarlane Group (Clansman) PLC, 1973); Underwriting Member of Lloyd's, 1978-97; Chairman: The Fine Art Society PLC, 1976-98 (Honorary Life President, 1998), American Trust PLC, 1984-97 (Director, since 1980), Guinness PLC, 1987-89 (Joint Deputy Chairman, 1989-92); Director: Clydesdale Bank PLC, 1980-96 (Deputy Chairman, 1993-96), General Accident Fire and Life Assurance Corporation plc, 1984-96, Edinburgh Fund Managers plc, 1980-98, Glasgow Chamber of Commerce, 1976-79; Member: Council, CBI Scotland, 1975-81, Board, Scottish Development Agency, 1979-87; Chairman, Glasgow Development Agency, 1985-92; Vice Chairman, Scottish Ballet, 1983-87 (Director, 1975-87), Hon. President, since 2001; Director, Scottish National Orchestra, 1977-82; President, Royal Glasgow Institute of the Fine Arts, 1976-87; Member, Royal Fine Art Commission for Scotland, 1980-82; Scottish Patron, National Art Collection Fund, since 1978; Governor, Glasgow School of Art, 1976-87, Hon. President, since 2001; Trustee: National Heritage Memorial Fund, 1984-97, National Galleries of Scotland, 1986-97; Director, Third Eye Centre, 1978-81; Hon. President, Charles Rennie Mackintosh Society, since 1988; Hon. President, High School of Glasgow, since 1992 (Chairman of Governors, 1979-92); Member, Court, Glasgow University, 1979-87; Regent, RCSE, since 1997; President: Stationers' Association of GB and Ireland, 1965, Company of Stationers of Glasgow, 1968-70, Glasgow High School Club, 1970-72; Patron, Scottish Licensed Trade Association, since 1992; Honorary Patron, Queen's Park FC; Vice President, Professional Golfers Association; KT, 1996; DL, Dunbartonshire, 1993, CIMgt, 1996, HRSA, 1987, HRGI, 1987, Hon. FRIAS, 1984, FRSE, 1991, Hon.FScotvec, 1991, Hon. FRCPS Glas., 1992, Hon. Fellow, Glasgow School of Art, 1993; Hon. LLD: Strathclyde, 1986, Glasgow, 1988, Glasgow Caledonian, 1993, Aberdeen, 1995; DUniv., Stirling, 1992; Dr (hc), Edinburgh, 1992; Glasgow St. Mungo Award, 2005; Hon. President, Tenovus Scotland, 2006; Hon. Life Member, Scottish Football League, 2006; Director, Culture and Sport Glasgow, since 2007; Chairman, Roger Billcliffe Gallery; Freeman of Dumfries and Galloway, 2006; Freeman of the City of Glasgow, 2007. Recreations: golf; cricket; theatre; art. Address: (b.) Macfarlane Group PLC, Clansman House, 21 Newton Place, Glasgow G3 7PY; (h.) 50 Manse Road, Bearsden, Glasgow G61 3PN.

Macfarlane, Professor Peter Wilson, CBE, DSc, FBCS, FRCPE(Glasg), FESCE, FRSE. Emeritus Professor; Prof. of Electrocardiology, Glasgow University, 1995-2010; Chairman, 40th International Congress on Electrocardiology, Glasgow, 2013; b. 8.11.42, Glasgow; m., Irene Grace Muir; 2 s. Educ. Hyndland Senior Secondary School, Glasgow; Glasgow University. Glasgow University: Assistant Lecturer in Medical Cardiology, 1967, Lecturer, 1970, Senior Lecturer, 1974, Reader, 1980, Professor, 1991, Hon. Senior Research Fellow, since 2010; President, 5th International Congress on Electrocardiology, Glasgow, 1978; Chairman, 15th and 18th Annual Conferences, International Society of Computerized Electrocardiology, 1990, 1993 (Vice President, since 2014); President: International Society of Electrocardiology, 2007-09, Computing in Cardiology, 2008-14. Author/Editor, 14 books. Recreations: supporting Ayr United; running half-marathons. Address: (h.) 12 Barrcraig Road, Bridge of Weir PA11 3HG; T.-01505 614443.

MacFarlane, Emeritus Professor Thomas Wallace, DDS, DSc, FRSE, FDSRCSEdin, FRCPath, FDSRCPSGlas. Professor of Oral Microbiology, Glasgow University, 1991-2001; Honorary Consultant in Oral Microbiology; Dean of the Dental School, 1995-2000; b. 12.12.42, Glasgow; m., Nancy McEwan Fyfe; 1 s. Educ. Hyndland Senior Secondary School; Glasgow University. Assistant Lecturer, Dental Histology and Pathology, 1966-69; trained in Medical Microbiology and Histopathology, Glasgow Royal Infirmary; Lecturer in Oral Medicine and Pathology, 1969-77; organised and ran the diagnostic service in Oral Microbiology, Glasgow Dental Hospital and School; Senior Lecturer in Oral Medicine and Pathology and Consultant in Oral Microbiology, 1977; Reader in Oral Medicine and Pathology, 1984-91; Head, Department of Oral Sciences, 1992-95. Recreations: music; reading; painting; walking. Address: 5B Mare Park, Muirton, Auchterarder PH3 1LW; T.-01764 664 356.

McGarry, Professor Gerald William. MBChB, MD, FRCS(ORLHNS). Consultant Otolaryngologist, Head and Neck Surgeon, since 1995; Honorary Senior Lecturer, University of Glasgow; Professor of Surgical Studies, RCSEd; b. 30.1.62, Glasgow; m., Carol; 3 s. Educ. St. Augustine Secondary School, Glasgow; Glasgow University. Senior Registrar in Otolaryngology: Glasgow Rotational Scheme, 1992, Royal Brisbane Hospital, Australia, 1993; Locum Consultant Otolaryngologist, Glasgow Royal Infirmary, 1994. Former Vice President, Royal Society of Medicine Section of Laryngology; former Member, Medical Appeals Tribunal; Founder, Scottish Sinus Surgery Group. Publications: Picture Tests in ENT, 1999; Endoscopic Dissection of the Nose and Paranasal Sinuses; papers on rhinology and head and neck cancer; textbook editor and contributor. Recreation: mountaineering. Address: Department of Otolaryngology, Royal Infirmary, Glasgow G31 2ER; T.-0141-211 1660.

McGarry, Natalie. MP (Glasgow East): Independent, since 2015, SNP, 2015; b. 1981, Inverkeithing. Educ. University of Aberdeen. Former convener of the SNP's Glasgow Region Association; co-founder of the Women for Independence group in 2012. Address: House of Commons, London SW1A 0AA.

McGee, Right Reverend Brian. Bishop of Argyll and Isles, since 2016; b. 8.10.65, Greenock. Educ. St Joseph's Primary School, Greenock; Holy Cross Primary School, Greenock; St. Vincent's College, Langbank; St. Mary's College, Blairs; studied for the priesthood at St Patrick's College, Thurles, County Tipperary, 1983-89; Sarum College, Salisbury (Master of Arts degree in Christian Spirituality). Ordained in 1989 as a priest for the Diocese of Paisley by Bishop John Mone; Assistant Priest, St Charles Borromeo Parish, Paisley, 1989-1995; Assistant Priest, Holy Family Parish, Port Glasgow, 1995-1997; Parish Priest, St Joseph's Parish, Clarkston, 1997-2007; Spiritual Director, Scotus College, National Seminary, 2007-2009; Parish Priest, Holy Family Parish, Port Glasgow, 2009-2015. Vicar General of the Diocese of Paisley, since 2014. Address: Diocesan Office, Bishop's House, Esplanade, Oban, Argyll PA34 5AB; T.-01631 567436.

McGee, John. Managing Director, The Crichton Trust, since 2015; b. Edinburgh. Educ. St Catherine's Primary; Holyrood High School, Edinburgh. Sales & Marketing Manager, Wallace Brown Limited, 1983-92; Managing Director, Georgeson Group, 1992-2000; Sales & Marketing Director, Morris Furniture Group, 2000-04; Managing Director, Georgeson Group (Constructive Workspace), formally Axis Interiors, 2004-09; SC Collective UK, 2009-2015. Awarded for 'Outstanding achievements to innovation and workplace performance' in 2005; received prestigious awards and recognitions by the British Council for Offices (BOC) for the innovation, sustainability and creativity elements of project delivery for eight corporate organisations and public sector clients in the UK. Address: The Crichton Trust, Grierson House, Bankend Road, Dumfries DG1 4ZE; T.-01387 247544.

McGeorge, James, BSc, PhD, CBiol, FRBS. University Secretary, University of Dundee, since 2009; b. 16.10.68, Derby; m., Dr. Helen Ruth McGeorge; 1 d. Educ. Bemrose School, Derby; University of Liverpool; University of Stirling. Research Fellow, University of Stirling, 1994-96; University of Abertay Dundee: Executive Assistant, then Assistant Secretary, then Deputy Secretary, then Academic Secretary and Registrar, 1996-2005; Director of Strategic Planning and Governance, then Deputy Secretary, University of Stirling, 2005-09. Member, Audit Committee, Universities & Colleges Admissions Service (UCAS); Member, Universities and Colleges Employers Association Scottish Committee. Recreations: sport; distance running;

food and drink. Address: (b.) University Executive Office, University of Dundee, Dundee DD1 4HN; T.-01382 384006; e-mail: j.mcgeorge@dundee.ac.uk

McGeough, Professor Joseph Anthony, FRSE, FREng, BSc, PhD, DSc, CEng, FIMechE, FCIRP. Regius Professor of Engineering, Edinburgh University, 1983-2005; Emeritus Professor, since 2005; Honorary Professorial Fellow, 2007-2016; Honorary Professor, Nanjing Aeronautical and Astronautical University, China, since 1991; Visiting Professor: University Federico II of Naples, 1994, Glasgow Caledonian University, 1997-2003, Tokyo University of Agriculture and Technology, 2004, Monash University, 2005; b. 29.5.40, Kilwinning; m., Brenda Nicholson; 2 s.; 1 d. Educ. St. Michael's College; Glasgow University; Aberdeen University. Research Demonstrator, Leicester University, 1966; Senior Research Fellow, Queensland University, Australia, 1967; Research Metallurgist, International Research and Development Co. Ltd., Newcastle-upon-Tyne, 1968-69; Senior Research Fellow, Strathclyde University, 1969-72; Lecturer in Engineering, Aberdeen University, 1972-77 (Senior Lecturer, 1977-80, Reader, 1980-83). Member, Council, IMechE, 2000-03, Trustee, Board, 2004-2010, Vice-President, 2006-2010; Member of Council, CIRP, 2006-08, Fellow, since 1987; Chairman, CIRP UK, 2000-03; Editor, Journal of Processing of Advanced Materials, 1991-94; CIRP Editor, Journal of Materials Processing Technology, 1991-2006; Editor, Proceedings of International Conference on Computer-Aided Production Engineering, since 1986; President, Colinton Parish Church Library Society, 2009-2012. Publications: Principles of Electrochemical Machining, 1974; Advanced Methods of Machining, 1988; Micromachining of Engineering Materials (Editor), 2001; Engineering of Human Joint Replacements, 2013. Recreations: gardening; golf.
E-mail: j.a.mcgeough@ed.ac.uk

McGettrick, Emeritus Professor Andrew David, BSc, PhD, FRSE, FIEE, FBCS, CEng. Emeritus Professor, Strathclyde University (formerly Professor of Computer Science, formerly Head, Computer and Information Sciences Department, Head, Computer Science Department, 1996-2001); b. 15.5.44, Glasgow; m., Sheila Margaret Girot; 5 s.; 1 d. Educ. St. Aloysius College, Glasgow; Glasgow University; Cambridge University. Lecturer, then Reader, then Professor, Strathclyde University, since 1969; Editor, Addison Wesley's International Computer Science series; Chairman, IEE Safety Critical Systems Committee; Chairman, UK Computer Science Professors Conference, 1991-93; Vice-President, British Computer Society, since 2004; Chair, Education Board and Education Council of US Association for Computing Machinery (ACM). Publications: four books as author, three books edited. Recreations: running; golf; squash. Address: (b.) Strathclyde University, Glasgow G1 1XH; T.-0141-548 3589.

McGhie, Hon. Lord (James Marshall), QC, LLB (Hons). Chairman, Scottish Land Court; President, Lands Tribunal for Scotland, 1996-2014; Court of Session (part-time), since 2012; b. 15.10.44, Perth; m., Ann M. Cockburn; 1 s.; 1 d. Educ. Perth Academy; Edinburgh University. Scots Bar, 1969; QC, 1983; Advocate-Depute, 1983-86; part-time Chairman, Medical Appeal Tribunals, 1987-92; Member, Criminal Injuries Compensation Board, 1992-96. Address: (b.) Parliament House, High Street, Edinburgh; T.-0131 226 5071.

McGhie, Duncan Clark, CA. Chairman, Scottish Ballet and Scottish Opera, 1999-2004; b. 6.12.44, Newton Mearns, Renfrewshire; m., Una G. Carmichael; 1 s.; 1 d.

Educ. George Watson's College; Institute of Chartered Accountants. CA apprenticeship, 1962-67; Financial Controller, Scottish Division, British Steel Corporation, 1967-78; Group Finance Director, Wm. Collins Publishers, 1978-84; Partner, Coopers and Lybrand (latterly Pricewaterhouse Coopers), 1984-2000. Elder, Church of Scotland; Member, Inland Waterways Advisory Council, 2006-2012. Recreations: golf; music; walking. Address: (b.) 65 Corrour Road, Newlands, Glasgow, G43 2ED; T.-0141-632 4502; e-mail: dcmcghie@outlook.com

McGibbon, David Campbell, FIOD, FCMA, CCMA, DipMS. Chairman, David MacBrayne Group Limited, since 2012 (Deputy Chairman, since 2008); Non-Executive Director and Chair, The Audit Committee; Chair, The Scottish Group, The National Association of Pension Funds (NAPF), since 2011; Vice-Chair, NAPF Regions Board and Member of NAPF Investment Council; Non-Executive Director and Chair, The Audit Committee, Historic Scotland, 2005-2011, Independent Chair, The Audit Committee, since 2012; Independent Chair, The Audit Committee, Historic Environment Scotland (HES), since 2015; b. 03.12.47, Airdrie; m., Anne Gillon Ferguson; 2 d. Educ. Coatbridge High School. Various Accountancy posts with Spillers Ltd., 1968-72 and Scottish & Newcastle Breweries, 1972-77; joined Grampian Holdings plc, 1978, Group Financial Controller, 1978-83, Group Finance Director, 1983-97, Group Finance Director and Company Secretary, 1997-2002; Non-Executive Director, Paladin Resources plc, 1993-2001. Chairman, Group of Scottish Finance Directors, 1993-95; Chairman, London Stock Exchange, Scottish Council, 1998-2001; Chairman of Trustees, Caledonian MacBrayne Pension Fund, since 2006. Recreations: golf (Glasgow Golf Club); reading and travel. Address: (b.) David MacBrayne Ltd, Ferry Terminal, Gourock PA19 1QP.
E-mail: david.mcgibbon@davidmacbrayne.co.uk

McGiffen, Diane, MA, MSc. Chief Operating Officer, Audit Scotland, since 2010, Director of Corporate Services, 2000-2010; b. 24.8.63, Cumbernauld; m., Ross Thomson; 1 s. Educ. Greenfaulds High School, Cumbernauld; Glasgow University; Edinburgh University. Hansard, House of Commons, 1986-89; Edinburgh District Council, 1989-91; COSLA, 1991-92; Wester Hailes Partnership, 1992-96; Accounts Commission, 1996-2000. Address: (b.) 102 West Port, Edinburgh EH3 9DN; T.-0131 625 1608; e-mail: dmcgiffen@audit-scotland.gov.uk

MacGillivray, Alan, MA, DipEd. Educational writer, since 1987; President, Association for Scottish Literary Studies, 2002-06; b. 5.6.35, Kirkcaldy; m., Isobel McCorkindale; 2 s.; 1 d. (deceased). Educ. Dumfries Academy; Edinburgh University. Teacher of English, 1958-67: Ardrossan Academy, Annan Academy, Inverness Royal Academy; Principal Teacher of English, Anderson High School, Lerwick, 1967-72; Lecturer/Senior Lecturer in English, Jordanhill College of Education, Glasgow, 1973-87; Honorary Lecturer in Scottish Literature, University of Strathclyde, 1987-2003. Director, Jordanhill Scottish Literature and Language Project, 1980-82. Publications: The Ring of Words (Joint Editor), 1970; Teaching Scottish Literature (Editor), 1997; Scottish Literature in English and Scots (Joint Editor), 2002; study guides on George Mackay Brown and Iain Banks; Kindly Clouds (Poems), 2005; The Bountiful Loch (Poems), 2007; the saga of fnc gull (Poem), 2009; An Altitude Within (Poems), 2010; RB Cunninghame Graham - Collected Stories and Sketches (Joint Editor), 2011-12; articles, teaching materials, short stories, etc. Recreations: reading; verse writing; walking. Address: (h.) 482 Clarkston Road, Glasgow G44 3QE; T.-0141-571 7562.

McGillivray, Rev. (Alexander) Gordon, MA, BD, STM; b. 22.9.23, Edinburgh; m., Winifred Jean Porter; 2 s.; 2 d. Educ. George Watson's Boys' College, Edinburgh;

Edinburgh University; Union Theological Seminary, New York. Royal Artillery, 1942-45; Assistant Minister, St. Cuthbert's Parish Church, Edinburgh; Minister: Waterbeck Church, 1951-58, Nairn High Church, 1958-73; Clerk, Presbytery of Edinburgh, 1973-93; Clerk, General Assembly of Church of Scotland, 1971-94, retired. Editor, Church of Scotland Yearbook, 1996-99. Recreation: theatre. Address: 36 Larchfield Neuk, Balerno, Midlothian EH14 7NL; T.-0131-449 3901.

McGinty, Cllr John. Leader, West Lothian Council, since 2012. Chair of the Council Executive; a member of the Education Executive; Vice Chair of the Audit and Governance Committee; member of the Performance Committee; Chair of the Employee Appeals Committee; Chair of the Miscellaneous Appeals Committee; Chair of the Avoidance of Disputes Committee; Chair of the Senior Officer Appointment Committee; a member of West Lothian Advisory Committee; a member of the Social Work Complaints Review Committee; West Lothian Council Planning Committee; Vice Chair of Bathgate Local Area Committee; a member of the Joint Consultative Group; Joint Consultative Group (Teaching Staff); Chair of Partnership and Resources Policy Development and Scrutiny Panel (PDSP); member of the Education PDSP; Vice Chair of the Health and Care PDSP; and a member of the Services for the Community PDSP. Address: West Lothian Council, West Lothian Civic Centre, Howden South Road, Livingston, West Lothian EH54 6FF.
E-mail: john.mcginty@westlothian.gov.uk

McGlinchey, Scott, BA, DipM, FRSA, FIOD. Director, Exception Ltd., since 2005; b. 1961, Edinburgh; m.; 3 s. Educ. Royal High School; Napier University. ICL/Fujitsu Services, 1988-2002; positions include General Manager, Managing Director; Newell & Budge Chief Operating Officer, 2002-04. Past Non Exec. Directorships; Young Scot, Edinburgh Chamber of Commerce. Founding Member, Generation Science. Past Member: Scottish Executive Digital Task Force, Modernising Government Reference Group, CBI Council. Recreations: rugby; music.
E-mail: scott.mcglinchey@exceptionuk.com

McGlynn, Rt. Rev. Abbot Emeritus (James Aloysius) Donald, OCSO, STL, SLJ. Monk, Order of Cistercians of Strict Observance, since 1952; Abbot of Nunraw, 1952-2003 (Emeritus); b. 13.8.34, Glasgow. Educ. Holyrood School, Glasgow; St. Bernardine's School, Buckinghamshire; Gregorian University, Rome. President: Scottish Council of Major Religious Superiors, 1974-77, British Isles Regional Council of Cistercian Abbeys, 1980-84; Chairman, Union of Monastic Superiors, 1985-89; Official Roman Catholic Visitor to the General Assembly, Church of Scotland, 1976 and 1985; Commandeur Ecclesiastique, Military & Hospitaller Order of St. Lazarus of Jerusalem, 1985; Chief Akaoluchukwu Nsugbe, Anambra State, Nigeria; Patron, Haddington Pilgrimage of St. Mary & the Three Kings. Address: Sancta Maria Abbey, Nunraw, Garvald, Haddington EH41 4LW; T.-0162 083 0223; e-mail: nunrawdonald@yahoo.com
Web: www.nunraw.org.uk

McGorum, Professor Bruce Campbell, BSc, BVMS, PhD, CEIM, DECEIM, MRCVS. Professor of Equine Medicine, University of Edinburgh since 2002; b. 9.3.61, Dunfermline; m., Isabel Maria McGorum; 3 d. Educ. Queen Anne High School; University of Edinburgh. Veterinary Practitioner, Buckinghamshire, 1985-87; University of Edinburgh: Horserace Betting Levy Board Resident in Equine Studies, 1987-90, Lecturer, then Senior Lecturer, Easter Bush Veterinary Centre, 1990-98, RSE/SOEID

Support Research Fellow, 1998-99, Senior Lecturer, 1999-2002. 2004 Animal Health Trust Veterinary Achievement Award. Recreations: outdoor sports. Address: (b.) Easter Bush Veterinary Centre, Easter Bush, Roslin, Midlothian EH25 9RG; T.-0131-650-6230.
E-mail: bruce.mcgorum@ed.ac.uk

McGovern, James. MP (Labour), Dundee West, 2005-2015; b. 17.11.56; m., Norma Ward; 1 s.; 1 d. Educ. Lawside Roman Catholic Academy, Dundee; Telford College, Edinburgh. Trade union official; PPS to Pat McFadden as Minister of State, Department for Business, Enterprise and Regulatory Reform, 2007-08. Member, Select Committee on Scottish Affairs, 2005-2015. Recreations: reading; gym; watching football.

McGowan, Professor David Alexander, MDS, PhD, FDSRCS, FFDRCSI, FDSRCPSG, FDSRCS (Edin). Professor of Oral Surgery, Glasgow University, 1977-99, Emeritus Professor, since 1999 (Dean of Dental Education, 1990-95); Consultant Oral Surgeon, Greater Glasgow Health Board, 1977-99; b. 18.6.39, Portadown, Co. Armagh; m., Margaret Vera Macaulay; 1 s.; 2 d. Educ. Portadown College; Queen's University, Belfast. Oral surgery training, Belfast and Aberdeen, 1961-67; Lecturer in Dental Surgery, Queen's University, Belfast, 1968; Lecturer, then Senior Lecturer and Deputy Head, Oral and Maxillofacial Surgery, London Hospital Medical College, 1968-77. Postgraduate Adviser in Dentistry, Glasgow University, 1977-90; Chairman, Dental Committee, Scottish Council for Postgraduate Medical Education, 1980-90; Dean, Dental Faculty, and Member of College Council, Royal College of Physicians and Surgeons of Glasgow, 1989-92; Member and Vice-Chairman of Executive, General Dental Council, 1989-99; Member, Court, Glasgow University, 1995-99; Chairman, National Dental Advisory Committee, 1996-99; Member, EC Advisory Committee on Training of Dental Practitioners, 1993-2001; former Council Member, British Association of Oral and Maxillofacial Surgeons; Founder Editor 'Dental History Magazine', 2007-12. Recreations: photography; painting; music. Address: Glenderry, 114 West King Street, Helensburgh G84 8DQ.
E-mail: dmmcgowan@btinternet.com

McGowan, Sheriff John, LLB. Sheriff of South Strathclyde, Dumfries and Galloway at Ayr, 2000-2012; b. 15.1.44, Kilmarnock; m., Elise Smith; 2 s. Educ. St. Joseph's Academy, Kilmarnock; Glasgow University. Admitted Solicitor, 1967; partner in Black Hay & Co, Solicitors, Ayr, 1970-93; Temporary Sheriff, 1986-93; Sheriff of Glasgow and Strathkelvin, 1993-2000. Council Member, Law Society of Scotland, 1982-85. Recreations: golf; choral singing; listening to music. Address: (h.) 20 Auchendoon Crescent, Ayr KA7 4AS; T.-01292 260139.

McGowan, Kenneth John, LLB (Hons). Sheriff, Lothian and Borders at Edinburgh, since 2015; b. 27.4.58, Irvine; m., Nancy; 3 s. Educ. Prestwick Academy; University of Edinburgh. Admitted as Solicitor, 1982; Admitted as Solicitor Advocate, 1998; Employment Judge, 2003-2011; Part Time Sheriff, 2006-2011; Sheriff, Tayside Central and Fife at Stirling, 2011-2015. Recreations: cooking; skiing; travelling. Address: (b.) Sheriff Court House, 27 Chambers Street, Edinburgh EH1 1LB.

McGrath, Professor John Christie (Ian), BSc, PhD. Regius Professor of Physiology, Glasgow University, 1991-2012; Professor Emeritus and Senior Honorary Research Fellow, Glasgow University, since 2012; Senior Principal Research Fellow, Neuroscience Australia, Sydney

NSW, since 2009; Chairman, The Physiological Society, 2006-08; b. 8.3.49, Johnstone; m., Wilma Nicol (deceased); 1 s.; 1 d. Educ. John Neilson Institution, Paisley; Glasgow University. Glasgow University: Research Fellow in Pharmacology and Anaesthesia, 1973-75, Lecturer, 1975-83, Senior Lecturer, 1983-88, Reader, 1988-89, Titular Professor, 1989-91; Co-Director, Clinical Research Initiative in Heart Failure, 1994-2000; Head of Division, Department of Neuroscience and Biomedical Systems, Institute of Biomedical and Life Sciences, 1991-93, 1997-2004; Head of Division of Integrated Biology, 2008-2010. Sandoz Prizewinner, British Pharmacological Society, 1980; JR Vane Medal Winner, British Pharmacological Society, 2011; Pfizer Award for Biology, 1983; Senior Editor, British Journal of Pharmacology, 2001-07, Editor in Chief, since 2009. Fellow of British Pharmacological Society, since 2004; Fellow of Society of Biology, since 2013; Honorary Member of Australian Society for Clinical and Experimental Pharmacology and Therapeutics, since 2013; Honorary Professor, University of Sydney Medical School, since 2013. Recreations: running; politics; travel. Address: (b.) West Medical Building, Glasgow University, Glasgow; T.-0141-330 4483.
E-mail: i.mcgrath@bio.gla.ac.uk

McGregor, Rev. Alistair Gerald Crichton, QC, BD, BA, LLB, WS. Former Minister, North Leith Parish Church, Edinburgh (1987-2002); Temporary Sheriff, 1984-87; b. 15.10.37, Sevenoaks, Kent; m., Margaret Dick Lees or McGregor; 2 s.; 1 d. Educ. Charterhouse; Pembroke College, Oxford; Edinburgh University. Solicitor; Advocate; QC; former Standing Junior Counsel to Queen's and Lord Treasurer's Remembrancer, to Scottish Home and Health Department and to Scottish Development Department; Past Chairman, Discipline Committee, Potato Marketing Board; former Clerk, Rules Council, Court of Session; former Tutor in Scots Law, Edinburgh University; former Chairman, Family Care; former Director, Apex (Scotland) Ltd; former Governor, Loretto School; Chairman, Palcrafts (UK) Ltd; former Governor, Dean Orphanage Trust; former Chairman, Drug Prevention Group; former General Trustee of Church of Scotland. Publication: Obscenity (Co-Author). Recreations: squash; tennis; swimming; travel; cinema. Address: (h.) 22 Primrose Bank Road, Edinburgh EH5; T.-0131-551 2802.

McGregor, Bill, MA, MEd. General Secretary, School Leaders Scotland, 2004-08; b. 14.2.44, Kilmarnock; m., Elspeth Barbara Greene; 1 s.; 1 d. Educ. Kilmarnock Academy; Glasgow University. Teacher, Assistant Rector, Depute Rector, Mainholm Academy, Ayr, 1968-89; Rector, James Hamilton Academy, Kilmarnock, 1989-2004. Member, National Executive, Headteachers' Association of Scotland (Convener, Public and Parliamentary Committee); President, Irvine Burns Club, 2010-11; Director, Irvine Burns Club, since 2012. Publications: bus histories. Recreations: photography (transport); writing. Address: (h.) 25 Blackburn Drive, Ayr KA7 2XW; T.-01292 282043; e-mail: valayrmac@btinternet.com

MacGregor, Professor Bryan Duncan, BSc, MSc, PhD, DipSurv, CertHE, MRTPI, MRICS. MacRobert Professor of Land Economy, Aberdeen University, since 1990, Dean of Social Science and Law, 2002-03, Vice-Principal and Head, College of Arts and Social Sciences, 2003-08, Vice-Principal for Curriculum Reform, then for Special Projects, 2008-11, Vice-Principal and Head of College of Physical Sciences, since 2011; b. 16.10.53, Inverness; m., Nicola; 2 twin d. Educ. Inverness Royal Academy; Edinburgh University; Heriot Watt University; Cambridge University; College of Estate Management; Sabhal Mòr Ostaig (Gaelic College). Lecturer, Department of Land Management, Reading University, 1981-84; Lecturer, Department of

Town and Regional Planning, Glasgow University, 1984-87; Deputy, then Property Research Manager, Prudential Portfolio Managers, 1987-90. Recreations: Gaelic; hill-walking; football; literature; music; thinking. Address: (b.) Fraser Noble Building, King's College, University of Aberdeen, Aberdeen AB24 3UE; T.-01224 273161.

Macgregor, Dr Donald Finlay, BSc, MBChB, FRCP(Edin), FRCPCH. Consultant Paediatrician (Hon. Senior Lecturer), Tayside University Hospitals, Dundee, since 1996; b. 22.9.56, Bridge of Allan; m., Elspeth Mary McLeod; 1 s.; 3 d. Educ. Falkirk High School; St Andrews University; Manchester University. Senior House Officer, 1984; Registrar, 1984-88; Provincial Paediatrician, Eastern Highlands, Papua New Guinea, 1986-88; Fellow, University of British Columbia, Vancouver, 1988-90; Clinical Fellow, BC Children's Hospital, Vancouver, 1988-90; Senior Registrar, Royal Hospital for Sick Children, Edinburgh, 1990-92; Consultant Paediatrician, Lancaster and Kendal Hospitals, 1992-96. Secretary, Scottish Paediatric Society; Regional Advisor, Royal College of Paediatrics and Child Health. Recreations: family; outdoor pursuits; Third World issues. Address: (h.) Bon Accord, 2 Viewlands Road, Perth PH1 1BH; T.-01738 625796.

MacGregor, Fulton. MSP (Scottish National Party), Coatbridge and Chryston, since 2016. Educ. Coatbridge High School; University of Strathclyde; University of Edinburgh. Elected to North Lanarkshire Council, Coatbridge North and Glenboig ward in 2012. Address: Scottish Parliament, Edinburgh EH99 1SP.

MacGregor of MacGregor, Major Sir Malcolm; b. 1959. Chief of Clan Gregor, since 2003.

McGregor, Iain. Honorary Secretary, SABRE (Scotland Against being Ruled By Europe); b. 19.3.37, Stirling. Educ. Selkirk High School; Kelso High School. Army Service, REME; International Trade Exhibitions Publicist, London; Editor, BIPS International Photo-Feature Agency; Journalist, Fleet Street and provinces; Writer and Lecturer in Journalism, Asia, Europe, North America; Founding Director, Institute for Christian Media (Canada); Editor, The Patriot for Scotland; Editor and Publisher, Social Credit International. Recreations: local history; travel; music; theatre; film; books. Address: (h.) 8 Baileyfield Road, Edinburgh EH15 1DL; T.-0131-669 5275.

Macgregor, Jimmie, MBE, DA, FRZSS. Scottish folksinger and broadcaster; b. 10.3.30, Glasgow. Educ. Springbank Academy; Glasgow School of Art. Forefront of British folk revival for more than 20 years; countless radio and TV appearances, tours in Britain and abroad; more than 20 albums recorded; own daily radio programme, Macgregor's Gathering, for more than 10 years; regular TV series on long-distance walks; various books on folk song and the outdoors; has written theme music for TV and radio, illustrated books; gives regular lectures and slide shows; Life Member: RSPB, Scottish Wildlife Trust, Friends of Loch Lomond, John Muir Trust; President, Friends of River Kelvin; Vice-President, Scottish Conservation Projects and Scottish Youth Hostels Association; twice Scot of the Year. Recreations: collecting paintings, pottery, glass, furniture; the outdoors; wildlife; hill-walking; theatre; art; music; antiques; old cars; anything and everything Scottish.

McGregor, John Alexander Stephen, FRICS. Fund Manager, since 2005; Chartered Surveyor, since 1975;

Honorary Consul for Latvia in Scotland; b. 10.02.51, Leith, Edinburgh; m., Elizabeth; 1 s.; 1 d. Educ. Daniel Stewarts College; Northern Polytechnic London. Donaldsons Chartered Surveyors, 1974-76; Leavers, 1977; John Taylor and Partners, 1978; Hartley Cowley & Co., 1979-93; McGregor Chartered Surveyors, 1993-2008; Caledonian Trust plc, 1984-91; Port Dundas Properties and Developments Ltd, 1997-2003; Kintail Properties Ltd, since 1980; St. Wenceslas Ltd, since 1994. Knight of The Hospitaller Order of St. Lazarus; President, the Arctic Club, 2014. Recreations: hill walking; stalking; fishing; the Arctic. Address: (b.) 17 Rutland Street, Edinburgh EH1 2AE; T.-0131-228-3344.

E-mail: jmcgregor@hunterreim.com

McGregor, Margaret Morrice, MA, JP, DL. Director, McGregor Connexions, since 1998; Co-ordinator, British Thyroid Foundation, since 2004; b. 22.10.42, Aberdeen; m., Michael McGregor; 2 s.; 2 step d. Educ. Aberdeen Academy; Aberdeen University. Member, Edinburgh District Council, 1987-96 (Chair, Women's Committee, 1988-96, Licensing Board, 1992-96); Chair, Equal Opportunities Committee, COSLA, 1992-96; Member, City of Edinburgh Council, 1996-99 (Chair, Women's Committee, 1996-99); Depute Lord Provost, 1996-99; Chair, Zero Tolerance Charitable Trust, 1999-2008; Chair, Scottish Refugee Council, 1995-2000; Vice-President, Darfur Training Committee (UNA Edinburgh), 2008-2010. Recreations: campaigning (human rights, prison reform, animal welfare); reading; sailing. Address: (h.) 17 Greenpark, Liberton, Edinburgh EH17 7TA; T.-0131-664 7223.

E-mail: m2mcgregor@aol.com

McGrigor, Sir James Angus Roderick Neil, Bt. MSP (Conservative), Highlands and Islands, 1999-2016; b. 19.10.49, London; m.; 1 s.; 5 d. Educ. Eton; Neuchatel University, Switzerland. Traveller, shipping agent, stockbroker, fish farmer, hill farmer; Conservative candidate, Western Isles, 1997; Euro candidate, Scottish list, 1999; Chairman, Loch Awe Improvement Association; Member, Atlantic Salmon Trust Council; Created Kentucky Colonel, 2010; Member, Royal Company of Archers. Recreations: music; films; fishing; literature. Address: (h.) Ardchonnel, by Dalmally, Argyll PA33 1BW; T.-0131 348 5616.

E-mail: jamiemcgrigor@outlook.com

McGuiness, David Newell, DipEM, FIET, MCMI. Managing Director, Electrical Contractors' Association of Scotland (SELECT), since 2004; The Director, Scottish Joint Industry Board, since 2004; Director: Scottish Electrical Contractors' Insurance Ltd., since 2004, Electrical Engineering Training Foundation, Electrical Safety Council; Trustee, Scottish Electrical Charitable Training Trust, since 2004; ITB Pension Scheme; b. 25.6.59, Banbridge, Northern Ireland; m., Dr Dianne Elizabeth, nee Marshall. Educ. Banbridge Academy; Ulster Polytechnic; Strathclyde University. Recreations: golf; cycling; reading; wine. Address: (b.) The Walled Garden, Bush Estate, Midlothian EH26 0SB; T.-0131 445 5577.

McGuire, Rt. Hon. Dame Anne, PC, MA (Hons). Former MP (Labour), Stirling (1997-2015); b. 26.5.49, Glasgow; m., Len McGuire, CA; 1 s.; 1 d. Educ. Our Lady and St. Francis School, Glasgow; University of Glasgow; Notre Dame College of Education. Development Officer, Community Service Volunteers, 1984-88; National Officer, CSV, 1988-93; Depute Director, Scottish Council for Voluntary Organisations, 1993-97. Assistant Government Whip (Scotland), 1998-2001; Lord Commissioner, HM Treasury (Government Whip), 2001-02; Parliamentary

Under Secretary of State (Scotland Office), 2002-05; Parliamentary Under Secretary of State (Minister for Disabled People), Department of Work and Pensions, 2005-08; Advisor to Cabinet Office on Voluntary Sector, 2008-09. Member of Public Accounts Committee, 2010-2015; PPS to Rt Hon Ed Milliband MP, 2010-11; Shadow Minister for Disabled People, 2011-13; former Chair, All Party Disability Group; former Chair, All Party Group on Wood Panel Industry. Address: (b.) 22 Viewfield Street, Stirling FK8 1UA; T.-01786 446515.

McGuire, Edward, ARCM, ARAM. Composer; b. 15.2.48, Glasgow. Educ. St. Cuthbert's Primary and St. Augustine's Secondary School, Glasgow; Junior Department, RSAMD; Royal Academy of Music, London; State Academy of Music, Stockholm. Won National Young Composers Competition, 1969; Rant selected as test piece for 1978 Carl Flesch International Violin Competition; Proms debut, 1982, when Source performed by BBC SSO; String Quartet chosen for 40th Anniversary Concert, SPNM, Barbican, 1983; featured composer, Park Lane Group series, Purcell Room, 1993, Bath International Guitar Festival, 1996, International Viola Congress, 1998; frequent commissions and broadcasts including Euphoria (EIF/Fires of London), Songs of New Beginnings (Paragon Ensemble), Quintet II (Lontano), Peter Pan (Scottish Ballet), A Glasgow Symphony (NYOS), The Loving of Etain (Paragon Opera), Trombone Concerto (Aix-en-Provence Festival), Encores en Suite (BBC SSO, 2010), Overture Homage to Glasgow (RTO, 2012), plays flute with and writes for Whistlebinkies folk group, CDs include Albannach (Greentrax), 2006, plays bamboo flute with Chinese music group, Harmony Ensemble. His CDs on Delphian Recordings, 'Entangled Fortunes' (2015) and 'Music for Flute, Guitar and Piano' (2006), have both received 'Editor's Choice' in Gramophone Magazine. Recipient of British Composer Award, 2003 and Creative Scotland Award, 2004; Chair, Scottish Region Musicians' Union, since 2003; Chair, Scottish Campaign Against Euro Federalism, since 2001; Vice President, Scotland China Association, since 2008; writes for Workers magazine. Address: c/o Scottish Music Centre, City Hall, Candleriggs, Glasgow G1 1NQ.

Website: www.scottishmusiccentre.com/edward_mcguire

Maguire, Ruth. MSP (SNP), Cunninghame South, since 2016. Educ. Millburn Academy; Sabhal Mòr Ostaig. Career history: Sales and Marketing Manager, Praban Na Linne, 1994-96; Account Manager/Customer Service Team Leader, Compaq, 1997-2001; Sales (Acquisition SME), Integral Arm, 2005-06; Mentor - New Deal Clients, Glasgow Mentoring Network, 2010-11; Ùlpan Gaelic Tutor, 2011; Therapist - Reflexology and Hypnotherapy, Ruth Maguire Reflexology, 2004-2012; SNP Councillor, North Ayrshire Council (elected in 2012); Cabinet Member for Finance and Corporate Support, North Ayrshire Council, (appointed in 2013). Cunninghame South Women's Officer, SNP, 2014-15; Cunninghame South Political Education Officer, SNP, 2014. Daughter of John Finnie, Scottish Green MSP. Address: Scottish Parliament, Edinburgh EH99 1SP.

McInnes, Alison, OBE, FRSA. MSP (Scottish Liberal Democrat), North East Scotland, 2007-2016; former spokesperson for Justice and former Business Manager in the Scottish Parliament; b. 17.7.57; m.; 2 c. Educ. Irvine Royal Academy; McLaren High School, Callendar; University of Glasgow. Career history: 1992-1995: Councillor, Gordon District Council; 1995-2007: Councillor, Aberdeenshire Council; Chair, Infrastructure Services Committee; Chair, Nestrans - the Regional Transport Partnership for North East Scotland; Scottish Liberal Democrat spokesperson on Transport, Local Government and Climate Change, 2007-2011; spokesperson on Health and Justice, 2011-2012. Formerly non-executive director with Scottish Enterprise; formerly Chair, Sustainable Development Group, North Sea Commission; formerly member, Area Board for Scottish National Heritage. Fellow of the Royal Society of Arts; made an OBE in June 2013.

Macinnes, Professor Allan Iain, MA, PhD, FRHistS, FRSA, FRSE, FFCS. Emeritus Professor of History, University of Strathclyde; b. 26.11.49, Inverness; m., Tine Wanning. Educ. Oban High School; University of St. Andrews; University of Glasgow. University of Glasgow: Lecturer in Scottish History, 1973-89, Senior Lecturer in Scottish History, 1989-93, Director, Postgraduate School of Scottish Studies, 1992-93; Burnett-Fletcher Professor of History, University of Aberdeen, 1993-2007; Professor of Early Modern History, University of Strathclyde, 2007-2014. Visiting Professor in British History, University of Chicago, 2003; Chair, Scottish Land Commission, 1996-99; Joint Founder (Chair, Steering Committee), Northern European Historical Research Network, 1997-2002. Research Fellow of the Huntington Library, San Marino, California, 1993, 2002, 2005 and 2012; Ecole des Hautes Etudes en Sciences Sociales, Paris, 2005; Frank Watson Prize in Scottish History, University of Guelph, 1997. Publications: Charles I and the Making of the Covenanting Movement, 1625-41, 1991; Clanship, Commerce and the House of Stuart, 1603-1788, 1996; The British Revolution, 1629-1660, 2004; Union & Empire: The Making of the United Kingdom in 1707, 2007; The British Confederate: Archibald Campbell, Marquess of Argyll, c.1607-1661, 2011. Recreations: supporting Hibernian; gardening with a touch of zen; hillwalking; listening to music – especially jazz; drinking malt whisky. Address: Laingseat Farmhouse, Potterton, Aberdeenshire AB23 8UE.
E-mail: allan.macinnes@strath.ac.uk

McInnes, Professor Colin Robert, MBE, DSc, CEng, FInstP, FREng, FRSE. James Watt Chair, Professor of Engineering Science, School of Engineering, University of Glasgow, since 2014; b. 12.2.68, Glasgow; m., Dr. Karen McLaughlin; 3 s. Educ. Knightswood Secondary School; University of Glasgow. Department of Aerospace Engineering, University of Glasgow: Lecturer, 1991-96, Reader, 1996-99, Professor of Space Systems Engineering, 1999-2004; University of Strathclyde, Professor of Engineering Science, 2004-2014. Royal Society of Edinburgh Bruce Preller Prize Lecture, 1998; Royal Society of Edinburgh Makdougall-Brisbane Prize, 2006; Royal Aeronautical Society Pardoe Space Award, 2000; Philip Leverhulme Prize, 2001; Royal Aeronautical Society Ackroyd Stuart Prize, 2004; Association of Space Explorers Leonov Medal, 2007; Royal Society of Edinburgh Kelvin Prize, 2012; Royal Society Wolfson Research Merit Award, 2015. Publications: Solar Sailing, 1999; around 150 journal papers. Recreations: photography; hillwalking; history of science. Address: School of Engineering, University of Glasgow, Glasgow G12 8QQ; T.-0141-330 8511.
E-mail: colin.mcinnes@glasgow.ac.uk

MacInnes, Hamish, OBE, BEM, DUniv. Writer and Designer; b. 7.7.30, Gatehouse of Fleet. Educ. Gatehouse of Fleet. Mountaineer with numerous expeditions to Himalayas, Amazon and other parts of the world; Deputy Leader, 1975 Everest SW Face Expedition; film Producer/Advisor/safety expert, with Zinnemann, Connery, Eastwood, Putnam, etc.; Advisor, BBC TV live outside broadcasts on climbing; Co-founder, Snow & Avalanche Foundation of Scotland; author of 29 books on travel and adventure, including two autobiographies, fiction and International Mountain Rescue Handbook; designed the first all-metal ice axe, Terrordactyl ice climbing tools, the MacInnes stretchers; Founder, Search and Rescue Dog Association; Honorary Member: Scottish Mountaineering Club, Alpine Club, 2009; former President, Alpine Climbing Group; world authority on mountain rescue;

Doctor of Laws (Hons), Glasgow University; Hon. DSc: Heriot Watt University, Aberdeen University; Doctor of the University, University of Stirling, 1997; Doctor of Laws, University of Dundee, 2004; Member, Scottish Sporting Hall of Fame; The Scottish Award for Excellence in Mountain Culture; President, Guide Dogs Adventure Group; Founder and former Leader, Glencoe Mountain Rescue Team. Recreations: as above. Address: (h.) Glencoe, Argyll; T.-01855 811258.

McInnes, Emeritus Professor William McKenzie, MSc, PhD, CA. Professor of Accounting, Stirling University, 1994-2007; (Head, Department of Accounting, Finance and Law, 1995-98, Vice-Dean, Faculty of Management, 1996-97); b. 24.5.42, Hawick; m., Christine Mary; 1 s.; 1 d. Educ. George Watsons College, Edinburgh; Durham University; Glasgow University. Management Accountant, IBM (UK) Ltd., 1966-68; Lecturer, Kirkcaldy Technical College, 1968-70; Audit Senior, Coopers and Lybrand, Bermuda, 1970-72; Senior Lecturer, Newcastle upon Tyne Polytechnic, 1974-76; Lecturer, then Senior Lecturer, Strathclyde University, 1976-91; Director of Research, Institute of Chartered Accountants of Scotland, 1992-93; SHEFC Team Leader for Quality Assessment of Finance and Accounting, 1995-96; Elder, Cadder Parish Church, since 1984. General Trustee of the Church of Scotland, since 2012. Publications: author or co-author of a number of research papers and reports on accounting and related topics. Recreations: golf; music. Address: (h.) 14 Gleneagles Gardens, Bishopbriggs, Glasgow G64 3EF; T.-0141 772 2639; e-mail: mcinnesbill@hotmail.com

McIntosh, Cllr Bill. Leader, South Ayrshire Council, since 2010; m., Wilma; 1 s.; 1 d. Career in the banking industry; early retirement in 1988 in order to set up McIntosh Management which provided business advice for small and medium sized enterprises; first elected as a Councillor for the Troon East ward in May 1999; has been active in the local community for a number of years as a member of the Troon Business Association and, prior to his election to South Ayrshire Council in 1999, as a Troon community councillor; elected leader of South Ayrshire Council's Conservative and Unionist Group on Monday 25 January 2010. Member of the Chartered Institute of Bankers in Scotland (MCIBS). Recreations: reading; gardening; golf. Address: County Buildings, Wellington Square, Ayr KA7 1DR; T.-01292 612390.

McIntosh, Gordon, BSc, CAS. Director, Enterprise, Planning and Infrastructure, Aberdeen City Council; b. 10.8.56; 2 s.; 1 d. Educ. Keith Grammar School; Glasgow University; Aberdeen University. KPMG (Thomson McLintock), Chartered Accountants, 1979-84; Grampian Regional Council, 1984-96; Director of Economic Development, Aberdeen City Council. Past Chairman, Scottish Local Authorities Economic Development Officers; Past Chairman, Aberdeen and St. John Mountain Rescue Association; Past President, Junior Chamber. Recreations: mountaineering; sailing; kayaking; angling; golf. Address: (b.) Aberdeen City Council, Business Hub 12, 2nd Floor West, Marischal College, Broad Street, Aberdeen AB10 1AB; T.-01224 522941.

Macintosh, Kenneth Donald, MA. MSP (Labour), West Scotland region, since 2016 (Eastwood, 1999-2016); Presiding Officer of the Scottish Parliament, since 2016; b. 15.1.62, Inverness; m., Claire Kinloch Anderson; 2 s.; 4 d. Educ. Royal High School, Edinburgh; Edinburgh University. Joined BBC, 1987; worked in News and Current Affairs, including Breakfast News, Breakfast with Frost, Nine O'Clock News; left as Senior Broadcast Journalist, 1999.

Recreations: reading; music; sport – football, golf, tennis. Address: (b.) Suite 4/5, 1 Spiersbridge Way, Thornliebank G46 8NG.

McIntosh, Sir Neil, CBE, DL, FIPM, ACIS, FRSA. Civil Service Commissioner, 2008-2013; New Zealand Honorary Consul for Scotland, since 2013; Trustee, National Library of Scotland, since 2013; Chairman, Audit Committee of Scottish Public Service Ombudsman Service, 2007-2011; Member, UK Electoral Commission, 2001-08; Chairman, Judicial Appointments Board for Scotland, 2001-08; Independent Expert Adviser to N. Ireland Executive Review of Public Administration, 2002-06; Trustee, National Museums of Scotland, 2000-08; Member, BBC Audience Council for Scotland, 2007-2012; Returning Officer, Greater Manchester Transport Referendum, 2008; Member, Independent Budget Review Panel, 2010; b. 30.1.40, Glasgow; m., Marie; 1 s.; 2 d. Educ. King's Park School, Glasgow. Industry and local government, 1957-69; Director of Personnel, Inverness County/Highland Region, 1969-85; Chief Executive: Dumfries and Galloway Region, 1985-92, Strathclyde Region, 1992-96; various public service duties, since 1996, including: Counting Officer, Scottish Parliament Referendum, Chairman, Commission on Local Government and the Scottish Parliament, Crown Agent's Adviser, Shanghai Municipal Government, Convener, Scottish Council for Voluntary Organisations, 1995-2001. Hon. Doctorate, Syracuse University, and Hon. Doctorate, Glasgow Caledonian University. Recreations: bottle collecting; dry stane dyking.

Macintyre, Iain Melfort Campbell, MB, ChB, MD, FRCSE, FRCPE, FSA (Scot). President, British Society for the History of Medicine, since 2015; Apothecaries' Lecturer in History of Medicine, University of Edinburgh. Formerly Consultant Surgeon, Edinburgh; Surgeon to the Queen in Scotland, 1997-2004; Vice President, Royal College of Surgeons of Edinburgh, 2003-2006; Chairman, Edinburgh Postgraduate Board for Medicine, 1995-2000; b. 23.6.44, Glasgow; m., Tessa Lorna Mary Millar; 3 d. Educ. Daniel Stewart's College, Edinburgh; Edinburgh University. Lecturer in Surgery, Edinburgh University, 1974-78; Visiting Professor, University of Natal, 1978-79; Council of Europe Travelling Fellow, 1986; Honorary Secretary, Royal College of Surgeons of Edinburgh, 2001-03; Member National Medical Advisory Committee, 1992-95.

McIntyre, Rev. Mgr. John Canon, MA (Hons), STL, PhL, DipEd. Retired Parish Priest, St. Bridget's, Baillieston (1995-2015); b. 12.11.37, Airdrie. Educ. St. Aloysius College, Glasgow; Gregorian University, Rome; Glasgow University; Jordanhill College of Education. Ordained to priesthood, Rome, 1961; Assistant, St. Monica's, Coatbridge, 1962-63; student, 1963-68; staff, St. Vincent's College, Langbank, 1968-69, St. Mary's College, Blairs, Aberdeen, 1969-86 (Rector, 1985-86); Parish Priest, St. Bride's, East Kilbride, 1986-89; Rector, Scots College, Rome, 1989-95. Bradley Medal, Glasgow University, 1967. Publications: Scotland and the Holy See (Editor), 1982; The Scots College, Rome 1600–2000 (Co-Author), 2000. Recreations: English literature; bird-watching; history.

Macintyre, Lorn, BA (Hons), PhD. Freelance Writer; b. 7.9.42, Taynuilt, Argyll; m., Mary. Educ. Stirling University; Glasgow University. Novelist and Short Story Writer; publications include Cruel in the Shadow, The Blind Bend, Empty Footsteps and The Broken Lyre in Chronicles of Invernevis Series; Tobermory Days and Tobermory Tales, Maclay Days (short stories); Adoring Venus (novel); Miss Esther Scott's Fancy (short stories).

Recreations: Scottish country dancing; nightjars; the paranormal. Address: (h.) Priormuir, by St. Andrews, Fife; T.-01334 476428; e-mail: lorn.macintyre@btinternet.com

Macintyre, Professor Dame Sally, DBE, FRSE, BA, MSc, PhD, HonDSc. Emeritus Professor, University of Glasgow; b. 27.2.49, Edinburgh; m., Dr Guy Muhlemann. Educ. Durham, London and Aberdeen Universities. Research Fellow, Aberdeen University, 1971-75; Researcher, MRC Medical Sociology Unit, Aberdeen, 1975-83; Director, MRC Medical Sociology Unit, Glasgow, 1983-98; Director, MRC Social and Public Health Sciences Unit, Glasgow, 1998-2008; Hon Director, MRC/CSO Social and Public Health Sciences Unit, Glasgow, 2008-2013; Director, Institute of Health and Wellbeing, Glasgow University, 2011-14. Foundation Fellow, Academy of Medical Sciences. Recreations: skiing; hill-walking; climbing.

Maciver, Rev. James, MA, BD, DipTheol. Principal Clerk of Assembly, Free Church of Scotland, since 2000; Moderator of 2011 General Assembly; Minister, Knock Free Church, Isle of Lewis, since 1997; b. 9.4.54, Stornoway; m., Donna Mary; 2 s.; 1 d. Educ. Nicolson Institute, Stornoway; Glagsow University; Free Church College, Edinburgh; London University. Minister, East Kilbride Free Church, 1987-97; Clerk to Southern Synod, 1990-95; Visiting Lecturer, Glasgow Bible College, 1989-95. Chairman, Bethesda Nursing Home and Hospice, 1998-2002. Recreations: reading; classical music; Gaelic music; golf. Address: (b.) Free Church Manse, Garrabost, Isle of Lewis; T.-01851 870207.

Maciver, John Angus, LLB (Hons) (First Class), DipLP. Partner, Pinsent Masons LLP (formerly McGrigors LLP), since 2008; b. 17.1.73, Inverness. Educ. Currie High School, Edinburgh; University of Edinburgh. McGrigor Donald, Glasgow and Edinburgh, 1997-2002; Clifford Chance, London, 2002-04; DLA Piper, 2004-08. Recreations: golf; skiing; travel. Address: (b.) Princes Exchange, 1 Earl Grey Street, Edinburgh EH3 9AQ; e-mail: john.maciver@pinsentmasons.com

MacIver, Professor Matthew M., CBE, MA, MEd, Dhc (Abdn), DEd (Edin), FUHI, FEIS, FRSA. UK representative on Committee of Experts of the European Charter for Regional or Minority Languages, since 2013; Chairman, Court, University of Highlands and Islands, 2009-2014; Chief Executive/Registrar, General Teaching Council for Scotland, 2001-08; Chair, Bòrd na Gàidhlig, 2006-08; Chairman, Highlands and Islands Educational Trust, since 1994; Honorary Professor of Gaelic Education, University of the Highlands and Islands; Governor, George Watson's College, Edinburgh, since 2009; Committee member, Scottish Association of Churchill Fellows, 2009-2014; Member, BBC's Audience Council for Scotland, since 2011; b. 5.7.46, Isle of Lewis; m., Katrina; 1 s.; 1 d. Educ. Nicolson Institute, Stornoway; Edinburgh University; Moray House College. History Teacher, 1969-72; Principal Teacher of History, Craigmount High School, 1972-80; Assistant Rector, Royal High School, 1980-83; Depute Head Teacher, Balerno High School, 1983-86; Rector, Fortrose Academy, 1986-89; Rector, Royal High School, Edinburgh, 1989-98; Depute Registrar (Education), General Teaching Council for Scotland, 1998-2001. Chairman, Comataidh Craolaidh Gaidhlig (Gaelic Broadcasting Committee), 1996-2001; Member for Scotland on the Ofcom Content Board, 2003-06; Winston Churchill Travelling Fellowship, 1998. Address: (h.) 21 Durham Road, Edinburgh EH15 1NY; T.-0131-669 5029.

MacIver, Netta, OBE. Chief Executive, Scottish Children's Reporter Administration, 2008-2011. Over 30 years' experience of working in Scotland's social care sector, including working with families and children affected by serious physical or sexual abuse; previously

Chief Executive, Turning Point Scotland; also a qualified social worker, and spent her earlier career in Strathclyde in a specialist unit providing services to families where children had been seriously physically or sexually abused; Assistant Director of Social Work for Comhairle nan Eilean in the 1980s before returning to Strathclyde to work with drug and alcohol services and developing the region's strategic response to HIV/AIDS in collaboration with local health boards; joined Turning Point in 1995 as Development Director. Awarded an OBE in 2001 for her work with women offenders and drug misusers.

Mackay of Clashfern, Lord (James Peter Hymers), Baron (1979), PC (1979), KT (1999), FRSE, Hon. FRICE, FRCOG, FRCPE, FRCSE, FLIOT. Lord Clerk Register, since 2007; Lord High Commissioner to the General Assembly of the Church of Scotland, 2005 and 2006; Lord High Chancellor of Great Britain, 1987-97; Chancellor, Heriot Watt University, 1991-2005; b. 2.7.27, Edinburgh; m., Elizabeth Gunn Hymers; 1 s.; 2 d. Educ. George Heriot's School, Edinburgh; Edinburgh University (MA Hons). Lecturer in Mathematics, St. Andrews University, 1948-50; Major Scholar, Trinity College, Cambridge, in Mathematics, 1947, taken up, 1950; Senior Scholar, 1951; BA (Cantab), 1952; LLB Edinburgh (with distinction), 1955; admitted, Faculty of Advocates, 1955; QC (Scot), 1965; Standing Junior Counsel to: Queen's and Lord Treasurer's Remembrancer, Scottish Home and Health Department, Commissioners of Inland Revenue in Scotland; Sheriff Principal, Renfrew and Argyll, 1972-74; Vice-Dean, Faculty of Advocates, 1973-76; Dean, 1976-79; Lord Advocate of Scotland, 1979-84; a Senator of the College of Justice in Scotland, 1984-85; a Lord of Appeal in Ordinary, 1985-87. Part-time Member, Scottish Law Commission, 1976-79; Hon. Master of the Bench, Inner Temple, 1979; Fellow, International Academy of Trial Lawyers, 1979; Fellow, Institute of Taxation, 1981; Director, Stenhouse Holdings Ltd., 1976-77; Member, Insurance Brokers' Registration Council, 1977-79; a Commissioner of Northern Lighthouses, 1975-84; Hon. LLD: Edinburgh, 1983, Dundee, 1983, Strathclyde, 1985, Aberdeen, 1987, Cambridge, 1989, Birmingham, 1990, University of India Law School, 1994, Glasgow 1994, Bath, 1996, Leicester University, 1996, De Montfort, 1999; Hon. DCL: Newcastle, 1990, Oxford, 1998, Robert Gordon, 2000; Hon. Doctor of Laws, College of William and Mary, 1989; Hon. Fellow, Institution of Civil Engineers, 1988; Hon. Fellow, Trinity College, Cambridge, 1989; Hon. Fellow, Girton College, Cambridge, 1989; Hon. Fellow, Royal College of Surgeons, Edinburgh, 1989; Hon. Fellow, Royal College of Physicians of Edinburgh, 1990; Hon. Fellow, Royal College of Obstetricians and Gynaecologists, 1996; Fellow, American College of Trial Lawyers, 1990. Recreations: walking; travel. Address: House of Lords, London, SW1A 0PW.

Mackay of Drumadoon, Rt. Hon. Lord (Donald Sage Mackay), PC, LLB, LLM (University of Edinburgh), LLM (University of Virginia); Senator of the College of Justice in Scotland, 2000-2013; b. 30.1.46, Aberdeen; m., Lesley; 1 s.; 2 d. Educ. George Watson's Boys' College, Edinburgh; Edinburgh University; University of Virginia. Solicitor, 1971-76; called to Scottish Bar, 1976; QC, 1987; Advocate Depute, 1982-85; Member, Criminal Injuries Compensation Board, 1989-95; Solicitor-General for Scotland, 1995; Lord Advocate, 1995-97; created Life Peer, 1995; Opposition Spokesman on Scotland and Constitutional Affairs, House of Lords, 1997-2000; Crossbencher in House of Lords, since 2013. Recreation: Isle of Arran. Address: (h.) 39 Hermitage Gardens, Edinburgh EH10 6AZ; T.- 0131-447 1412.

Mackay, Angus Victor Peck, OBE, MA, BSc (Pharm), PhD (Cantab), MB, ChB, FRCPsych, FRCP (Ed), TPsych. Physician Superintendent and Clinical Director, Lomond and Argyll Mental Health Service, 1980-2004; Honorary Professor in Psychological Medicine, Glasgow University, since 1980; Member, Faculty of Neuroscience, University of Edinburgh; Chairman, Health Technology Board for Scotland, 2000-2014; Member, Panel of Experts for the European Medicines Evaluation Agency; Psychiatric Representative, Committee on Safety of Medicines, DHSS; Chairman of the Secretary of State's Independent Scrutiny Panel on Health Services along the Clyde, 2005-06; Member, Commission on Human Medicines, 2004-06; Board Member (Department of Health, London), 2004-2014; Chairman, Advisory Board on the Registration of Homeopathic Products, since 2014; Member of the Mental Health Tribunal for Scotland, since 2015; b. 4.3.43, Edinburgh; m., Elspeth M.W. Norris; 2 s.; 2 d. Educ. George Heriot's School, Edinburgh; Edinburgh University; Churchill and Trinity Colleges, Cambridge. MRC Research Fellow, Cambridge; Member, senior clinical staff, MRC Neurochemical Pharmacology Unit, Cambridge, with appointment as Lector in Pharmacology, Trinity College (latterly, Deputy Director of Unit). Deputy Chairman, Health Services Research Committee of the Chief Scientist for Scotland; Chairman: Scottish Working Group on Mental Illness, Research and Clinical Section of Royal College of Psychiatrists (Scotland), National Mental Health Reference Group; Member: Research Committee, Mental Health Foundation, Scottish Executive, Royal College of Psychiatrists, NHS Policy Board for Scotland; Honorary Senior Lecturer, Department of Psychology, University of St. Andrews; Medical Director, Argyll and Bute NHS Trust. Recreations: rowing; sailing; rhododendrons. Address: (h.) Tigh an Rudha, Ardrishaig, Argyll; T.-01546 603272.

MacKay, Colin, CBE, BSc, MB, ChB, FRCSEng, FRCSEd, FRCSGlas. Chairman, Board of Governors, UHI Millennium Institute, 2001-09; b. 8.11.36, Glasgow; m., Dr Helen MacKay; 1 s.; 2 d. Educ. Hillhead High School; Glasgow University. Surgical training, Western Infirmary, Glasgow, 1961-69; MRC Travelling Fellowship, Boston University, 1969-70; Senior Lecturer in Surgery, Glasgow University, 1970-82; Consultant Surgeon, Western Infirmary/ Gartnavel General Hospital, Glasgow, 1982-96; Royal College of Physicians and Surgeons of Glasgow: Hon. Treasurer, 1976-86, Vice-President Surgical, 1992-94, Visitor, 1996-97, President, 1997-2000; President, Moynihan Chirurgical Club, 1995-96. Publications: Textbook of Surgical Physiology, 1978, 1988; various publications in medical journals. Recreations: travel; walking. Address: (h.) 73 Buchanan Drive, Bearsden, Glasgow G61 2EP; T.-0141-942 8759; and 4 Lawers Place, Aberfeldy.

McKay, Sheriff Colin Graham, MA, LLB. Retired Sheriff of North Strathclyde at Kilmarnock (2001-07); b. 20.1.42, Bearsden; m., Sandra Anne Coli; 1 s.; 1 d. Educ. St Aloysius College; Clongowes Wood College; Glasgow University. Solicitor, 1966-90; Temporary Sheriff, 1986-90; Sheriff, since 1990; part-time Sheriff, since 2007.

MacKay, Colin Hinshelwood, MA (Hons), FSA Scot. Partner, Colin MacKay Associates; Broadcaster and Writer; b. 27.8.44, Glasgow; m., Olive E.B. Brownlie; 2 s. Educ. Kelvinside Academy, Glasgow; Glasgow University; Jordanhill College of Education. Reporter/Presenter: Border Television Ltd., 1967-70, Grampian Television Ltd., 1970-73; Political Editor, Scottish Television PLC, 1973-92 (Presenter, Ways and Means, 1973-86), Parliamentary Lobby Correspondent, 1985-95; recent programmes include: A Life in Question, People and Power, Politics Tonight, Scotland at Ten, and Sunday Morning with Colin MacKay (BBC Radio Scotland); Talk-In Sunday (Radio Clyde); Westminster File (Border TV); Eikon (Scottish TV); General Assembly (BBC TV/Radio); contributions to BBC World Service, Radio 4, Radio 5 Live; ITV Commentator: Papal Visit to Scotland, 1982, CBI

Conference, Glasgow, 1983. Winner, Observer Mace, 1967 (British Universities Debating Championship); Member, two-man British Universities Canadian Debating Tour, 1967; Commonwealth Relations Trust Bursary to Canada, 1981; Member, Scottish Arts Council, 1988-94; BT Scottish Radio News Broadcaster of the Year, 1997. Publications: Kelvinside Academy: 1878-1978, 1978; The Scottish Dimension in Central and Eastern Canada, 1981. Recreations: music (especially opera); reading; writing. E-mail: colin.mackay@hotmail.co.uk

McKay, Colin Ian, LLB (Hons), DipLP, MPhil. Chief Executive, Mental Welfare Commission, since 2014; b. Scotland; m., Allison Brisbane; 2 s.; 1 d. Educ. North Berwick High School; Edinburgh University; Glasgow University. Solicitor in Private Practice, 1984-86; Solicitor, Lothian Regional Council, 1986-88; Legal and Policy Adviser, Enable (Scottish Society for the Mentally Handicapped), 1989-98; Civil Servant, 1999-2014 (Secretary, Millan Committee on Mental Health Law and Maclean Committee on Violent and Sexual Offenders, 2001-03, Head of Mental Health Bill Team, 2003-04, Member, latterly Acting Head, Strategy and Delivery Unit, 2004, Head, Efficient Government Unit, 2005-07, Head of Public Service Reform Development Division, Scottish Executive, 2007-13, Head of Legal System Division, Head of Strategy Unit, Scottish Government, 2013). Commissioner, Mental Welfare Commission for Scotland, 1996-98. Address: (b.) Mental Welfare Commission, Thistle House, 91 Haymarket Terrace, Edinburgh EH12 5HE; e-mail: colin.mckay@mwcscot.org.uk

Mackay, David James, FCILT. Former Chairman, Lothian Buses plc (resigned, 2010); Chairman, tie Ltd. (Transport Initiatives Edinburgh), 2008-2010 (resigned); Chairman, TEL Ltd., 2006-2010 (resigned); Chairman, Malcolm Group, 2003-05; Chairman, Executive Board, Scottish Rugby Union, 2003-05; Hon. Colonel, Scottish Transport Regiment, 2004-2011 (retired); Chief Executive, John Menzies PLC, 1997-2003; Deputy Chairman, Portland Media Group UK Ltd., 2007-09; Chairman, Glasgow Hawks Sports Trust, 2009-2012; b. 20.5.43, St. Andrews; m., Jane; 1 s.; 1 d. Educ. Kirkcaldy High School; Bradford University; Edinburgh University; Companion, Institute of Management, 1998; FCIT, 1993. Recreations: golf; walking; vintage cars. Address: (h.) 4 East Harbour Road, Charlestown, Fife KY11 3EA.

Mackay, David William, OBE, DUniv, FIBiol, ChEnv, FIWEM, ChBiol, FIFM. Board Member, Scottish Natural Heritage, 2007-13; Environmental Management Consultant, since 2001; b. 06.04.36, Stirling; m., Maureen (deceased 2004). Educ. High School of Stirling; Universities of Glasgow, Strathclyde and Paisley. Fisheries Research, Civil Service, Pitlochry, 1959-66; Clyde River Purification Board, Biologist, Marine Survey Officer, 1966-79; Government of Hong Kong, Principal Environment Protection Officer, 1979-81; Clyde River Purification Board, Depute Director, 1981-89; Ove Arup and Partners, Head of Environment, Hong Kong, 1989-91; North East River Purification Board, General Manager, 1991-96; Scottish Environment Protection Agency, Director, North Region, 1996-2001; EnviroCentre plc, Chairman, 2001-07. Author of around 100 scientific papers. Winston Churchill Fellowship, 1970; Consultant to World Health Organisation, 1975-85; Visiting Professor, Stirling and Strathclyde Universities; former President, Scottish Anglers National Association and Chairman, Seatrout Group. Recreations: growing native Scottish woodland; fishing; shooting; scuba diving. Address: (h.) Succoth Farm, Glass, Huntly, Aberdeenshire AB54 4YL; T.-01466 700-224; e-mail: david-mackay2@sky.com

Mackay, Derek, MSP (SNP), Renfrewshire North and West, since 2011; Cabinet Secretary for Finance and the Constitution, since 2016; Minister for Transport and Islands, 2014-16; b. 30.7.77; 2 s. Leader of Renfrewshire Council, 2007-2011; Minister for Local Government and Planning, Scottish Government, 2011-14. Address: (b.) Scottish Parliament, Edinburgh EH99 1SP.

Mackay, Donald George, MA PhD; b. 25.11.29; m. (1), Elizabeth Ailsa Barr (deceased); 2 s.; 1 d.; m. (2), Catherine Anne McDonald (deceased). Educ. Morgan Academy, Dundee; St. Andrews University; Aberdeen University. Assistant Principal, Scottish Home Department, 1953; Secretary, Royal Commission on Local Government in Scotland, 1966-69; Assistant Secretary, Scottish Development and Agriculture Departments, 1969-83; Under Secretary, Scottish Agriculture and Environment Departments, 1983-88. Member, Scottish Agricultural Wages Board, 1991-97. Publications: Forestry as a Land Use in Scotland, in Rural Land Use: Scotland and Ireland, 1994; Scotland's Rural Land Use Agencies, 1995. Recreation: hill walking; photography; music. Address: (h.) 25 Melville Street, Perth PH1 5PY; T.-01738 621274.

MacKay, Professor Sir Donald Iain, MA, FRSE, FRSGS. Former Chairman, Scottish Mortgage Investment Trust; former Director, Edinburgh New Income Trust; Honorary Professor, Heriot-Watt University, since 1982; b. 27.2.37, Kobe, Japan; m., Diana Marjory Raffan; 1 s.; 2 d. Educ. Dollar Academy; Aberdeen University. Professor of Political Economy, Aberdeen University, 1971-76; Professor of Economics, Heriot-Watt University, 1976-82; Chairman, Scottish Enterprise, 1993-97; Chairman, Picola plc, 1985-2001; Chairman, Grampian Holdings and Malcolm Group, 1998-2003; Vice President, Scottish Association of Public Transport; Governor, National Institute of Economic and Social Research. Recreations: tennis; bridge. Address: (h.) Newfield, 14 Gamekeepers Road, Edinburgh; T.-0131-336 1936. E-mail: sirdonaldmackay@yahoo.co.uk

Mackay, Ian Munro, BCom, CA. Principal, Mackay & Co. Chartered Accountants, 1979-2015; Honorary Sheriff, Dornoch Sheriff Court, 1985-2014; b. 14.9.47, Brora; m., Maureen; 2 s.; 2 d. (1 d. deceased). Educ. Golspie High School; Edinburgh University. Trained as CA in Edinburgh, qualifying in 1973; has worked in the profession since, spending three years in United Arab Emirates, returning to UK in 1979 to set up own practice. Secretary, Dornoch Curling Club, since 1984; President, Ross-shire Curling Province, since 2014; Past President, Sutherland Curling Province; Member, Scots centenary curling tour to Canada, 2003, winning back Strathcona Cup; competitor in World Left Handed Curling Championships, 2008-2013; married to the only left handed World Curling champion from outwith North America in the 40 year history of the Championships (2012). Recreations: curling; local history; holidays in Scotland, France or USA; garden; golf; following most sports. Address: (h.) 4 Sutherland Road, Dornoch, Sutherland; T.-01862 810333. E-mail: ian@ianmackay.plus.com

MacKay, John. Broadcast journalist, television presenter and producer; presenter, STV News at Six and Scotland Tonight; b. 13.9.65. Educ. Penilee Secondary School; University of Glasgow. Began journalism career with The Sunday Post before joining BBC Scotland in 1987 as a reporter, presenter and producer; joined Scottish Television in 1994 as a reporter and presenter for Scotland Today. Publications: The Road Dance, 2002; Heartland, 2004; The Last of the Line, 2006. Address: STV, Pacific Quay, Glasgow G51 1PQ.

Mackay, John, TD, MA, FRSGS, FInstD; b. 14.9.36, St. Andrews; m., Barbara Wallace; 1 s.; 2 d. Educ. Madras College; Dunfermline High School; Kirkcaldy High School; Edinburgh University. Lieutenant, 1st East Anglian Regiment, 1959-63; Territorial Army, 1964-86: Colonel, Royal Engineers (Postal and Courier); Royal Mail, 1963-96:

Director, Philately, 1979-84, Chairman, Scottish Post Office Board, 1988, Operations Director, UK, 1991-92, Director and General Manager, Scotland and Northern Ireland, 1986-96; Chairman, Earl Haig Fund Scotland, 1999-2004. President, Lord's Taverners Scotland, 1994-98; Chairman: Scottish Premier Rugby Limited, 1996-97, Scottish Business in the Community Executive Council, 1995-98, Scotland the Brand Judging Panel, 1998-2002, Edinburgh Common Purpose, 1995-96; Member: Committee, Army Benevolent Fund Scotland, 1988-98, Board, Quality Scotland, 1991-98, Board, Scottish Business in the Community, 1993-98, Quality Assessment Committee, Scottish Higher Education Funding Council, 1994-96; Chairman, Lowland Employers Liaison Committee, 2001-03; Founder Member, The Breakaways Golf Club; Elder, Dean Parish Church. Recreations: golf; watching cricket and rugby; military and European history; Battlefields 19th Century German Art. Address: (h.) Kinrymont, 8 Damside, Dean Village, Edinburgh EH4 3BB; T.-0131-226 2512; e-mail: johnandbarbaramackay@btinternet.com

Mackay, John Angus, OBE, MA, MSc. Former Chief Executive, Bòrd na Gàidhlig; former Director, Gaelic Media Service; former Member: Bòrd na Gàidhlig, An Lanntair, Scottish Arts Council, Highlands and Islands Enterprise; former Chair: NHS Western Isles Board, An Lanntair, Sabhal Mòr Ostaig, The Columba Initiative, BBC Gaelic Advisory Committee; b. 24.6.48, Shader, Isle of Lewis; m., Maria. Educ. Nicolson Institute; University of Aberdeen; University of Stirling; Jordanhill College. Sales Rep, D.C. Thomson, Aberdeen, 1971-72; English teacher, Glasgow, 1973-77; Co-operative Development Officer, Highlands and Islands Development Board, 1977-80; Investigating Officer and Senior Development Manager, Highland and Islands Development Board, 1980-84; Chief Executive, Communn na Gaidhlig, 1985-91. Recreations: books; skiing; swimming. Address: (h.) Druimard Arnol, Isle of Lewis H52 9DB; T.-01851 710479.

McKay, Rev. Johnston Reid, MA (Glasgow), BA (Cantab), PhD (Edin). Barony St. John's Church, Ardrossan, 2002-08; Clerk to the Presbytery of Ardrossan, 2003-2010; Kilwinning Old Parish Church, 2008-2010; b. 2.5.42, Glasgow. Educ. High School of Glasgow; Glasgow University; Cambridge University. Assistant Minister, St. Giles' Cathedral, 1967-71; Church Correspondent, Glasgow Herald, 1968-70; Minister, Bellahouston Steven Parish Church, 1971-78; Governor, Paisley College; Minister, Paisley Abbey, 1978-87; Saltcoats St Cuthbert's Parish Church, 2011-2012; Senior Producer, Religious Programmes, BBC Scotland, 1987-99; Editor, Religious Programmes, BBC Scotland, 1999-2002. Editor, The Bush (newspaper of Glasgow Presbytery), 1975-78; Chairman, Scottish Religious Advisory Committee, BBC, 1981-86; Stanley Mair Lecturer on Preaching, Glasgow University, 1995; Trustee, Baird Trust, since 1999; Wallace Lecturer, 2000; Chalmers Lecturer, 2010-12; Visiting Fellow of New College, University of Edinburgh, 2010-2011; Theological Forum of the General Assembly, since 2015; Member of Scottish PEN. Publications: From Sleep and From Damnation (with James Miller), 1970; Essays in Honour of William Barclay (Joint Editor), 1976; Through Wood and Nails, 1982; This Small Pool, 1996; The Very Thing, 2001; Glimpses of Hope – God Beyond Ground Zero, 2002; Netting Citizens (ed), 2004; A Touch Personal, 2005; Christian Faith and the Welfare of the City - Essays for Alison Elliot (Ed), 2008; The Kirk and the Kingdom - A century of tension in Scottish Social Theology, 2011; Scots Worship, Lent, Holy Week, Easter, 2013 (Ed); Scots Worship, Advent, Christmas, Epiphany, 2014 (Ed). Recreations: walking; gardening. Address: 15 Montgomerie Avenue, Fairlie KA29 0EE; T.-01475 568802. E-mail: johnston.mckay@btopenworld.com

McKay, Kenneth, BSc, PGCE, CPhys, MInstP. Depute Head Teacher, Eyemouth High School; Member of Board of Scottish Qualifications Authority, since 2009; b. 11.08.64, Greenock; m., Patricia; 3 d. Educ. Notre Dame High School, Greenock; University of Glasgow. Graduate Civil Engineer, James Williamson and Partners, 1985-88; Teacher of Physics, Gracemount High School, 1989-92; Senior Teacher, Holy Rood High School, 1992-97; Principal Teacher of Physics, The Royal High School, 1997-2001; Deputy Head Teacher, Preston Lodge High School, 2001-09; Head Teacher, Galashiels Academy, 2009-2014. Vice-Convenor, SQA Qualifications Committee. Publication: "Materials Matter", A Teaching Resource For Standard Grade Science (Co-Author). Address: 17 Briery Bank, Haddington, East Lothian EH41 4AB; e-mail: kenny.mckay@scotborders.gov.uk

Mackay, Kenneth James, MA, BD. Minister of St Nicholas Sighthill Church, Inverness, 1976-2007; b. 14.9.41, Inverness; m., Janet; 1 s.; 1 d. Educ. Fortrose Academy; Aberdeen University. Minister of Church of Scotland, Maryfield - Victoria St., Dundee, 1971-76. Member, Botanical Society of Scotland. Recreations: hill-walking; golf. Address: (h.) 46 Chuckethall Road, Livingston EH54 8FB; T.-01506 410 884.

McKay, Linda, MBE. Non-Executive Director, The Scottish Government; b. 27.5.51, Dunfermline. Educ. Aberdeen High School for Girls; Aberdeen University; Universite de Haute-Bretagne; Scottish School of Further Education, Jordanhill. Assistant Principal, Dundee College of Further Education, 1990-93; Deputy Principal, Glenrothes College, 1993-99; Principal and Chief Executive, Falkirk College of Further and Higher Education, 1999-2005; Principal, Forth Valley College, 2005-2013 (led an innovative and highly successful institution through merger, regionalisation and the delivery of an award winning £60 million estates development). Served as a Board Member of the Enterprise Network, Scottish Enterprise Forth Valley and subsequently on the Regional Advisory Board for Edinburgh; former Member of the Leadership Group of Chemical Sciences Scotland; former Member of the Scottish Funding Council Skills Committee (led a national project on workforce development); appointed to the Board of the Scottish Qualifications Committee in 2000 (charged with restoring public confidence in the Scottish examination system and in this role chaired the SQA Advisory Committee and the SQA Qualifications Committee); worked closely with the Police Service as a member of the Police Advisory Board for Scotland, a Governor of the Scottish Police College and Chair of the Police Scotland Examination Board. Currently Vice Chair of the Wood Commission; re-elected as Convener of the Loch Lomond and Trossachs National Park Authority. Address: Scottish Government, St. Andrew's House, Regent Road, Edinburgh EH1 3DG; T.-0131 244 2636.

MacKay, Professor Norman, CBE, MD, FRCP(Glas), FRCP(Edin), FRCS(Edin), FRCGP, FCPSP, FACP(Hon), FRACP(Hon), FAMS, FAMM, FRCS(Eng), FRCS(I), FRCP(I), FCPSBangl., FCCP(Hon). Dean of Postgraduate Medicine and Professor of Postgraduate Medical Education, Glasgow University, 1989-2001; Consultant Physician, Victoria Infirmary, Glasgow, 1974-89; Member, General Medical Council, 1999-2003; b. 15.9.36, Glasgow; m., Grace Violet McCaffer; 2 s.; 2 d. Educ. Govan High School; Glasgow University. Honorary Secretary: Royal College of Physicians and Surgeons of Glasgow, 1973-83, Standing Joint Committee, Scottish Royal Colleges, 1978-82, Conference of Royal Colleges and Faculties in Scotland, 1982-91; Speciality Adviser in Medicine, West of Scotland Committee of Postgraduate Medical Education, 1982-89; President, Royal Medico-Chirurgical Society of Glasgow,

1982-83; Member, Area Medical Committee, Greater Glasgow Health Board, 1987-89; President, Southern Medical Society, 1989-90; President, Royal College of Physicians and Surgeons of Glasgow, 1994-97; Member, Specialist Training Authority, 1999-2001. Address: (h.) 5 Edenhall Grove, Glasgow G77 5TS; T.-0141-616 2831.

Mackay, Peter, CB. Chairman, Local Government Boundary Commission for Scotland, 2007-2013; Trustee, Cairngorms Outdoor Access Trust, 2009-2013; b. 6.7.40, Arbroath; m., Sarah Holdich; 1 s.; 2 d. Educ. Glasgow High School; St. Andrews University. Teacher, New South Wales, Australia, 1962-63; Private Secretary to Secretaries of State for Scotland, 1973-75; Director for Scotland, Manpower Services Commission, 1983-85; on secondment from Scottish Office to Department of Employment, London, 1985; Under Secretary, Scottish Education Department (Further and Higher Education, Arts and Sport), 1987-89; Secretary and Chief Executive, Scottish Office Industry Department, 1990-95; Executive Director, Advanced Management Programme in Scotland, 1995-97; former Member, Board, Business Banking Division, Bank of Scotland; Member, Competition Commission (formerly Monopolies and Mergers Commission), 1996-2002; Member, Board, Scottish Natural Heritage, 1997-2003; Member, Court, Napier University, 1995-2004; Commissioner, Northern Lighthouse Board, 1999-2008, (Chairman, 2005-07); Chairman, Pacific Horizon Investment Trust, 2004-2010; Chairman, Northern Lighthouse Heritage Trust, since 2013. Recreations: Scotland; high altitudes and latitudes; sea canoeing; sculling. Address: (h.) Silverwood, Dunachton Road, Kincraig, Kingussie PH21 1QE.
E-mail: strathbogie@btinternet.com

Mackay, Rona. MSP (SNP), Strathkelvin and Bearsden, since 2016; m., Ian Mackay. Career: journalist and author; worked as a Parliamentary assistant to Gil Paterson, the SNP MSP for Milngavie and Clydebank. Address: Scottish Parliament, Edinburgh EH99 1SP.

Mackay, Rev. William Morton, MA (Hons), DipEd, DipTh, FCS, FRSGS, FRGS, AFAPC, MACE. Moderator, General Assembly of Free Church of Scotland, 2001; Part-time Lecturer in Church History, Free Church of Scotland College, Edinburgh, 1998-2005; Free Church of Scotland: Clerk of Public Questions, Religion and Morals Committee, 1999-2002, Chairman, International Missions Board, 2002-07; b. 26.3.34, Dundee; m., Catherine; 2 s.; 1 d. Educ. Morgan Academy, Dundee; Queen's College, Dundee; University of St. Andrews; Dundee College of Education; Free Church of Scotland College, Edinburgh. Teacher, Buckhaven High School, Fife, 1959-61; ordained, 1961; Teacher, Colegio San Andres, Lima, Peru, 1961-65, Headmaster, 1966-78; Teacher, Lothian Regional Council, 1978-85; Principal, Presbyterian Ladies' College, Burwood, Victoria, Australia, 1986-97. Diploma of Honour, Government of Peru, for services to education. Royal Scottish Geographical Society: Member of Council, 2003-06 and 2007-2010; Vice Chairman and Treasurer of the Edinburgh Centre; Clan Mackay Society: Member of Council. Publication: Thomas Chalmers: A Short Appreciation, 1980. Recreations: music; photography; cricket; rugby; reading; walking. Address: 53 Lauderdale Street, Edinburgh EH9 1DE.

McKechin, Ann, LLB, DipLP. Labour MP, Glasgow North, 2005-2015, Glasgow Maryhill, 2001-05; Solicitor; Member, Business, Innovation and Skills Select Committee, 2011-15; Shadow Secretary of State for Scotland, 2010-11; Parliamentary Under Secretary of State, Scotland Office, 2008-10; b. 22.4.61, Johnstone. Educ. Paisley Grammar School; Strathclyde University. Partner, Pacitti Jones, Solicitors, 1990-2000. Recreations: films; art history; dance. E-mail: mckechina@gmail.com

McKechnie, Anne Elizabeth, MA, MSc, CPsychol. Consultant Forensic Clinical Psychologist, NHS Greater Glasgow and Clyde, since 2014; b. 21.06.62, Aberdeen; 1 s.; 1 d. Educ. Linlithgow Academy; Aberdeen University. Clinical Psychologist: East Berkshire Health Authority, 1986-89, Parkhead Hospital, Glasgow Health Trust, 1989-91, Douglas Inch Centre, 1991-99. Member: Victim Support Scotland Training Advisory Group, 1991-93 and 1993-95, Mental Health Act Scotland Implementation Group, 2004. Commissioner on Time To Be Heard Pilot Forum, 2010. Recreations: drawing; gardening; cooking; walking. Address: (b.) 16 Bruce Road, Pollokshields G41 5EJ.
E-mail: anne.carpenter@ggc.scot.nhs.uk

McKee, Graham Hamilton, BSc, BPhil. Projects Director, University of Dundee; b. 11.9.51; m., Pilar; 1 s.; 2 d. Educ. Hutchesons' Grammar School, Glasgow; Glasgow University; Newcastle-upon-Tyne University. Assistant Planner, Burnley Borough Council, 1975-77; Scottish Development Agency, 1977-91, latterly as Regional Manager; Scottish Enterprise Tayside: Director Economic Development, 1991-93, Chief Executive, 1994-2001; Senior Director, Scottish Enterprise, 2001-05. Recreation: family. Address: (b.) University of Dundee, Dundee DD1 4HN; T.-01382 385557; e-mail: g.h.mckee@dundee.ac.uk

McKee, Ian, MBE, MBChB, DObst, RCOG, FSOMW. MSP (SNP), Lothians, 2007-2011; b. 2.4.40, South Shields; m., Penelope Ann; 1 s. and 1 stepson; 2 d. and 1 stepdaughter. Educ. Fettes College; Edinburgh University. House Officer: Ingham Infirmary, South Shields, 1965-66, Royal Infirmary Edinburgh, 1966; Medical Officer, Royal Air Force, 1966-71; General Practitioner, Sighthill and Wester Hailes Health Centres, Edinburgh, 1971-2006; Managing Director, Hermiston Publications, 1980-2000. Member, Company of Merchants, City of Edinburgh, since 1982; Burgess of Edinburgh, since 2007. Recreations: hill walking; music.

McKee, Ivan, BSc, BEng. MSP (SNP), Glasgow Provan, since 2016; b. 9.63, Helensburgh, Dunbartonshire. Educ. University of Strathclyde; Newcastle University. Career history: worked for a variety of manufacturing companies following 2 years of voluntary service in Bangladesh with VSO; set up an international manufacturing consultancy business in 2005; invested in, and successfully turned around, a number of manufacturing businesses including the rescue of Dunfermline based Simclar from Administration, 2009-2015; significant international experience having managed businesses in Scotland, England, Poland, Finland, Croatia and Bosnia. Director of Business for Scotland during the Scottish Independence Referendum; Trustee of the charity CEI which supports educational and health projects in rural Bangladesh; former Director of The Common Weal. Address: Scottish Parliament, Edinburgh EH99 1SP.

McKee, Professor (James Clark St. Clair) Sean, BSc, MA, PhD, DSc, FIMA, CMath, FRSE. Research Professor, Strathclyde University, since 2010; b. 1.7.45, Belfast. Educ. George Watson's College, Edinburgh; St. Andrews University; Dundee University; Oxford University. NCR Research Fellow, 1970-72; Lecturer in Numerical Analysis, Southampton University, 1972-75; Fellow, Hertford College, Oxford, 1975-86; Professor of Industrial Mathematics, Strathclyde University, and Consultant

Mathematician, Unilever Research, 1986-88; Professor of Mathematics, Strathclyde University, 1988-2010, Research Professor, since 2010. Homenagem (University of São Paulo), 2003; ICMC Medal of Honour (University of São Paulo), 2009; Homenagem (State University of São Paulo), 2014; Member, Council, ECMI, 1986-2006; Convener of the Informatics, Mathematics and Statistics Sector Committee of the Royal Society of Edinburgh, 2002-06. Founding Fellow, Institute of Contemporary Scotland. Publications: 200 papers; Industrial Numerical Analysis (Co-Editor), 1986; Vector and Parallel Computing (Co-Editor), 1989; Artificial Intelligence in Mathematics (Co-Editor), 1994. Recreations: climbing Munros; golf; theatre; gardening. Address: (b.) Department of Mathematics and Statistics, Strathclyde University, Glasgow G1 1XH; T.-0141-548-3671; e-mail: s.mckee@strath.ac.uk

McKellar, Keith A. J. Chair, West College Scotland, since 2014; Director, Colleges Scotland, since 2014; Chairman, Ardgowan University Teaching Hospice Greenock, since 2014; Chief Executive Officer, Scottish Health Innovations Ltd and NHS Research Scotland Central Management, since 2013; b. 29.6.68, Ayrshire; m., Catriona (nee Geddes); 2 s.; 1 d. Career history: Chief Executive Officer, Pharmaimaging Group Ltd, 2000-05; Authored Review of the Scottish Venison Industry, Deer Commission Scotland, 2009; Non-executive Director, Blackford Analysis Ltd, 2009-12; Vice-Chairman, 2012, Chairman, 2012-13, Board of Management, Stow College, Glasgow; Chief Executive Officer, Hannah Research Institute, 2005-2013; Director, Journal of Dairy Research, 2006-2015. Recreations: history; painting; cycling. Address: 14 Old Station Wynd, Troon KA10 6RR.
E-mail: kajmckellar@aol.com

McKellar, Peter Archibald, LLB (Hons). Senior Managing Partner and Chief Investment Officer, SL Capital Partners LLP, since 1999; b. 28.5.65, Glasgow; m., Karen Emery; 2 s. Educ. Daniel Stewart's and Melville College, Edinburgh; Edinburgh University. J.P. Morgan, Investment Bank, New York and London, 1986-88; EFT Group PLC, Corporate Finance Division, 1988-89; London and Edinburgh Trust plc, 1989-90; Co-Founder, Barry McKellar Ltd., 1990-95; Group Finance Director, Clydeport plc, 1995-98; Group Finance Director, Donside Paper Company Limited, 1998-99; Non-Executive Chairman, Red Lemon Studios Ltd, 1998-99; Governor, Cargilfield School, 2002-2011. Recreations: golf; shooting; swimming. Address: (b.) 1 George Street, Edinburgh EH2 2LL; T.-0131-245 8368.

McKelvie, Christina. MSP (SNP), Hamilton, Larkhall and Stonehouse, since 2011, Central Scotland, 2007-2011; b. 4.3.68, Glasgow; 2 s. Educ. St. Leonards Secondary; Nautical College; Anniesland College, Cardonald; St. Andrews University. Eastern College of Nursing, 1986-87; Glasgow City Council Social Work Department, 1988-2007: Day Service Officer, Depute Manager, Learning and Development Officer. Unison Steward; Community Council; Garrowhill Action Partnership; Convenor, European and External Relations Committee, Scottish Parliament; Co-Convenor, Cross Party Group on Men's Violence against Women; Co-Convenor of the CPG on Human Trafficking; Member, Welfare Reform Committee. Recreations: hillwalking; painting; reading; politics. Address: (b.) Scottish Parliament, Holyrood Road, Edinburgh EH99 1SP; T.-0131 348 6680.
E-mail: christina.mckelvie.msp@scottish.parliament.uk

McKenna, Rosemary, CBE, DCE. MP (Labour), Cumbernauld and Kilsyth, until 2010; b. 8.5.41, Kilmacolm; m., James Stephen McKenna; 3 s.; 1 d. Educ. St. Augustine's Secondary School, Glasgow; St. Andrew's College, Bearsden. Taught in various primary schools, 1974-93; Leader of Council, Cumbernauld and Kilsyth, 1984-88, Provost 1988-92, Leader of Council, 1992-94;

former Member, North Lanarkshire Council; former Policy Board Member: Local Government Management Board, Local Government International Bureau; former Member, Board, Scottish Enterprise; former Member, Executive, Scottish Constitutional Convention; Chair, Scottish Libraries and Information Council, 1993-98; PPS to John Battle, MP, 1998-2000, to Brian Wilson, MP, 2000-01; President, Convention of Scottish Local Authorities, 1994-96. Recreations: reading; cooking.

McKenna, Revd. Scott S., BA, BD (Hons), MTh, MPhil. Minister, Edinburgh: Mayfield Salisbury Church, since 2000; b. 3.2.66, Dunfermline; m., Shelagh M. Laird; 1 s. Educ. Kirkton High School, Dundee; St. Mary's College, University of St. Andrews. Accountant; Probationer Minister, Wellington Church, Glasgow, 1992-93; Minister, Viewpark Parish Church, Uddingston, 1994-2000. Member, Panel on Worship, General Assembly, 1994-98; Member, World Mission Council, General Assembly, 2005-08. Address: (b.) 26 Seton Place, Edinburgh EH9 2JT; T.-0131-667 1286; e-mail: scottsmckenna@aol.com

McKenna, Professor Stephen James, BSc (Hons), MSc, PhD. Professor (Personal Chair of Computer Vision), University of Dundee, since 2008; b. 03.01.69; m., Collette; 3 s.; 1 d. Educ. University of Edinburgh; University of Dundee. Research Fellow, Technopolis Csata, Italy, 1994-95; Post-Doctoral Researcher, Queen Mary College, University of London, 1995-98; Visiting Researcher, George Mason University, USA, 1999; Lecturer, Applied Computing, University of Dundee, 1998-2004, Senior Lecturer, Computing, 2004-07. Publications: Co-Author, Dynamic Vision, 2000; Associate Editor for Journal "Machine Vision & Applications". Recreation: guitar. Address: (b.) School of Computing, University of Dundee DD1 4HN; T.-01382 384732.
E-mail: stephen@computing.dundee.ac.uk

MacKenzie, Angus Alexander, OBE, CA. Chartered Accountant, since 1955; b. 1.3.31, Nairn; m., Catherine; 1 d. Educ. Inverness Royal Academy; Edinburgh University. National Service, RAF, 1955-57; in private practice as CA Assistant in Edinburgh, 1957-59; in private practice in Inverness, since 1959. Recreations: shooting; stalking; hill-walking; gardening. Address: (h.) Apartment 9, Lentran House, Inverness IV3 8RL; T.-01463 831088.

Mackenzie, Professor Ann Logan, MA. E. Allison Peers Professorial Research Fellow, Glasgow University, since 2006; Ivy McClelland Research Professor of Spanish, Glasgow University, since 1995; General Editor, Bulletin of Spanish Studies (1923-), since 1992; b. Greenock. Educ. Greenock Academy; Glasgow University. Lecturer, Senior Lecturer, Reader, Liverpool University, 1968-95. Publications: books and articles on the theatre and literature of 17th-century Spain and on the history of British Hispanism. Recreations: theatre; walking the dogs; house improvements. Address: (b.) Hetherington Building, Bute Gardens, Glasgow University, Glasgow G12 8RS; T.-0141-330 5665.
E-mail: Ann.Mackenzie@glasgow.ac.uk

Mackenzie, Colin, BA, DipSW, CQEW. Retired Chief Executive, Aberdeenshire Council (2008-2015). Educ. Forfar Academy; Strathclyde University; Glasgow University. Trainee Social Worker, Dundee City Corp, 1973-75; Child Care Specialist, 1975-77, Area Team Leader, 1977-82, Tayside Regional Council; Social Work Manager, 1982-85, Divisional Officer, 1985-96, Grampian Regional Council; Head of Service, 1996-2000, Director of Housing and Social Work, 2000-08, Aberdeenshire

Council. Member, 21st Century Review of Social Work, 2004-05, Pres., ADSW, 2005-06. Non Executive Member, Scottish Prison Service Board, 2007-08. Joint Improvement Partnership Board, 2013. Joint Chair, Health and Social Care Delivery Group, 2012-15; Non Executive Director, North East Scotland Preservation Trust.

Mackenzie, Sheriff Colin Scott, DL, BL, FSA Scot. Sheriff of Grampian Highland and Islands, at Lerwick and Kirkwall, 1992-2003; part-time Sheriff, 2004-08; Hon. Sheriff of Grampian, Highland and Islands, since 2009; b. 7.7.38, Stornoway; m., Christeen E.D. MacLauchlan. Educ. Nicolson Institute; Fettes College; Edinburgh University. Procurator Fiscal, Stornoway, 1969-92; Burgh Prosecutor, Stornoway, 1971-75; JP Fiscal, 1971-75; Deputy Lieutenant, 1975-2013 and Clerk to Lieutenancy of the Western Isles, 1975-92; Vice Lord Lieutenant of Islands Area, Western Isles, 1984-92; Founder President, Stornoway Flying Club, 1970; Founding Dean, Western Isles Faculty of Solicitors; elected Council Member, Law Society of Scotland, 1985-92; Convener, Criminal Law Committee, 1991-92; Council Member, Sheriffs' Association, 2002-03; Elder, Church of Scotland, since 1985; Member, Board of Social Responsibility, Church of Scotland, 1990-96; Convener, Assembly Study Group on Young People and the Media, 1991-93; Judicial Commission of General Assembly, Church of Scotland, since 2011. President, Stornoway Rotary Club, 1977; President, Isle of Lewis Probus Club, 2010; President, Lewis Pipe Band; Chairman, Queen's Own Highlanders Association (Lewis Branch), 2009-2014; Chairman, Urras Eaglais Na H-Aoidhe, since 2014. Publications: author of article on Lieutenancy, Stair Memorial Encyclopaedia of Law of Scotland, 1987; The Last Warrior Band, 2000; Shetland, Orkney and Western Isles, Personal Reflections, 2010; St Columba's Ui Church (History of), 2012. Recreation: fishing. Address: (h.) Park House, Matheson Road, Stornoway, Lewis.
E-mail: colinsmackenzie@btinternet.com

MacKenzie, Professor Donald, BSc, PhD, FRSE, FBA. Professor of Sociology, University of Edinburgh, since 1992; b. 3.5.50, Inverness; m., Caroline Bamford; 1s.; 1 d. Educ. Golspie High School; University of Edinburgh. University of Edinburgh: Lecturer in Sociology, 1975-88, Reader in Sociology, 1988-92. Visiting Professor of the History of Science, Harvard University, 1997. Co-winner, U.S. Navy Prize in Naval History, 1989; American Sociological Association Merton Award, 1993 and 2003, Zelizer Prize, 2005 and 2008 and Granovetter Award, 2012; Society for Social Studies of Science Fleck Prize, 1993 and 2003. Publication: Material Markets, 2008. Recreations: cycling; walking; chess. Address: (b.) School of Social and Political Science, George Square, Edinburgh EH8 9LD; T.-0131-650 3980.

Mackenzie, Donnie. Rector, Fortrose Academy, since 2011; m; 2 c. Educ. Mulbuie Primary School; Dingwall Academy; Aberdeen University. Taught at Alness Academy, then Invergordon Academy; joined Fortrose Academy in 1984 as Head of Physics, involved with Physics and Science educational development at both national level and for the local authority; entered senior management at the school in 1997, formerly Depute Head Teacher. Recreations: skiing; plays bridge at local and national level; Ross County supporter. Address: Academy Street, Fortrose IV10 8TW; T.-01381 620310.

Mackenzie, Elizabeth Alice, MA (Post-Grad), CertEd., AMBDA. Educational Consultant (Dyslexia); Member of Management Team, Transition Dyslexia; b. 10.9.41, Glasgow; m., Ian Mackenzie (deceased); 1 s.; 1 d. Educ. St Columba's, Kilmacolm; Laurel Bank, Glasgow; St George's, Edinburgh; Froebel Educational Institute, Roehampton; Kingston University. Primary teacher in London and Scottish schools, 1963-68; Adviser on Children's Religious Programmes, ABC TV, 1965-68; research into children's books for ABC TV, 1968-70; Senior Teacher, Dyslexia Institute, Glasgow, 1989-92; Principal, Dyslexia Institute Scotland, 1992-2004. Management Team, "Dyslexia At Transition", Parents Transition Support Materials and DVD-Rom for Secondary Schools, 2004-07; Member, Scottish Dyslexia Forum, 1996-2004; Project Team, "Count Me In: Responding to Dyslexia", pack of materials for Scottish Primary Schools, 2002-04; Course Director, Dyslexia Institute Teacher Training Course, 1994-98; Course Tutor, Post Graduate Course in Dyslexia and Literacy, York University, 2003-04; Self Esteem Research Project (Glasgow/Paisley Universities), 2003-04. Publications: Dimensions of Dyslexia, Volume I (Contributor); Dyslexia and the Young Offender (paper). Recreations: cooking; design; watching seals. Address: (h.) The Glebe, Southwick, by Dumfries, Dumfries and Galloway DG2 8AR; T.-01387 780276.

Mackenzie, Fiona I., MA (Hons), MBA, CIHM (Dip). Self Employed Consultant; formerly Chief Executive, NHS Board Forth Valley (2001-2013); b. 19.7.58, Edinburgh. Educ. Eastwood High School, Glasgow; University of St. Andrews; Hull University. NHS Graduate Trainee, 1980-82; Hospital Administrator, West Lothian, 1982-84; Operational Manager, Royal Edinburgh Hospital, 1986-89; Assistant Unit General Manager, Mental Health Unit, Lothian Health Board, 1989-91; Acute Services Manager, Monklands Hospital, Lanarkshire Health Board; Director of Planning, Monklands and Bellshill NHS Trust, 1993-96; Chief Executive, Highland Communities NHS Trust, 1996-99; Chief Executive, Highland Primary Care NHS Trust, 1999-2001. Awarded Companionship of the Institute of Health Management, 2009; Board Member, Scottish Futures Trust; appointed Honorary Professor, Stirling University, 2010; crofter. Recreations: sport; cooking. Address: Toscaig, Applecross, Ross-shire IV54 8LY; e-mail: fionatoscaig@btinternet.com

McKenzie, Iain. MP (Labour), Inverclyde, 2011-15; b. 4.4.59, Greenock. Former employee of IBM; elected to Inverclyde Council (Leader of the Council, 2011).

McKenzie, John Murchison, LLB, MCLIP. Chief Executive and Faculty Librarian, Royal Faculty of Procurators in Glasgow, since 2002; b. 7.8.71, Lakhnadon, M. P., India; m., Eleanor; 1 s.; 1 d. Educ. Hebron School, TN, India; High School of Glasgow; Dundee University; Strathclyde University. Legal Librarian, Glasgow City Council, 2000-02. Recreations: football; reading; crafts. Address: (b.) Royal Faculty of Procurators in Glasgow, 12 Nelson Mandela Place, Glasgow G2 1BT; T.-0141 332 3593; e-mail: jmckenzie@rfpg.org

MacKenzie, Ken. Member, Scottish Food Commission, since 2015; formerly Chairman, Scottish Retail Consortium (2006-2014); formerly Member, the Executive of the Scottish Grocers' Federation; formerly Vice-Chair of Skillsmart, the UK retail sector skills council; formerly Chief Officer, Scottish Co-op; formerly Chairman of Caravan Scotland, formerly the National Grocers' Benevolent Fund.

MacKenzie, Kenneth John, CB, MA, AM. Chairman, Historic Scotland Foundation, 2001-2011; Chairman, Edinburgh City Centre Churches Together, 2010-2012; Honorary Professor, Department of Politics and International Relations, University of Aberdeen, 2001-04; Member, National Board of Christian Aid, 2005-08; Member, British Waterways Scotland Group, 2002-07; Associate Consultant, Public Administration International, 2002-08; b. 1.5.43, Glasgow; m., Irene Mary Hogarth; 1 s.; 1 d. Educ. Birkenhead School, Cheshire; Pembroke College, Oxford; Stanford University, California. Assistant Principal, Scottish Home and Health Department, 1965-70;

Private Secretary to Joint Parliamentary Under Secretary of State, Scottish Office, 1969-70; Principal: General Register Office, 1970, Regional Development Division, Scottish Office, 1970-73, Scottish Education Department, 1973-77; Civil Service Fellow: Downing College, Cambridge, 1972, Department of Politics, University of Glasgow, 1974-75; Principal Private Secretary to Secretary of State for Scotland, 1977-79; Assistant Secretary: Scottish Economic Planning Department, 1979-83, Scottish Office Finance Division, 1983-85; Principal Finance Officer, Scottish Office, 1985-88; Under Secretary, Scottish Home and Health Department, 1988-91; Scottish Office, Agriculture and Fisheries Department: Under Secretary, 1991-92, Secretary, 1992-95; Head Economic and Domestic Secretariat, Cabinet Office, 1995-97; Head, Constitution Secretariat, Cabinet Office, 1997-98; Secretary and Head of Department, Scottish Executive Development Department, 1998-2001. Member, Agriculture and Food Research Council, 1992-94; Member, Biotechnology and Biological Sciences Research Council, 1994-95; Quinquennial Reviewer for Court Service, Lord Chancellor's Department, 2001-02. Recreations: amateur dramatics (Member, Edinburgh Makars); church activities (Elder, St Cuthbert's Parish Church, Edinburgh). Address: (h.) 23C/1 Ravelston Park, Edinburgh EH4 3DX; T.-0131 315 2113; e-mail: kenneth@voltaire.plus.com

MacKenzie, Madeleine, LLB (Hons), DipLP. Scottish Parliamentary Counsel, since 2002; b. 27.8.63, Inverness; d. of William Gordon MacKenzie and the late Veronica Dorothy Rachel MacKenzie. Educ. Inverness High School; Aberdeen University. Solicitor in private practice, 1986-90; Assistant, then Depute Scottish Parliamentary Counsel, 1990-2002. Recreations: reading; bridge; music. Clubs: Athenaeum, New; Scottish Arts. Address: (b.) Office of the Scottish Parliamentary Counsel, Victoria Quay, Edinburgh EH6 6QQ; T.-0131-244 1667.
E-mail: madeleine.mackenzie@scotland.gsi.gov.uk

MacKenzie, Mike. MSP (SNP), Highlands and Islands, 2011-16; b. 18.11.58, Oban; m., Lynn. Brought up in Glasgow and lived in Argyll from 1980. Ran a building business on Easdale until 2011. Founding director of Eilean Eisdeal, a community development company in Argyll. Stepped in to save the local pub and restaurant on Easdale when it was in danger of closing.

Mackenzie, Professor Robin Kenneth; BSc, MSc, PhD, CEng, FIOA, FRSA. Vice Principal, Edinburgh Napier University, 2007-12; b. 28.8.44, Edinburgh; m., Georgina Fiona; 3 s. Educ. Trinity Academy; Heriot-Watt University, Edinburgh University; MIT (USA). Research Fellow, Massachusetts Institute of Technology, 1970-72; Lecturer/Senior Lecturer, Heriot-Watt University, 1973-85; Reader in Acoustics, Heriot-Watt University, 1985-90; Royal Society Industrial Fellow, 1990-93; Professor of Acoustics, Sheffield Hallam University, 1993-95; Cruden Fellowship, National Science Foundation Fellowship (USA); Tyndall Medal, Institute of Acoustics, 1980; Queen's Anniversary Prize, 2009; Chairman of various ISO and BSI committees on sound insulation. Publications; Auditorium Acoustics, 1974. Recreations: tennis; golf; chess; skiing. Address: (b.) Edinburgh Napier University, 42 Colinton Road, Edinburgh EH10 5BT; T.-0131-455 5140; e-mail: r.mackenzie@napier.ac.uk

Mackenzie, Simon James, MB, ChB, FRCA. Divisional Medical Director, NHS Lothian, since 2007; Consultant, Intensive Care, Royal Infirmary of Edinburgh, since 1995; Honorary Senior Clinical Lecturer, University of Edinburgh; b. 29.12.60, Edinburgh; m., Nesta; 2 s.; 1 d. Educ. Daniel Stewarts and Melville College; University of Edinburgh. Former Consultant, Western General Hospital, Edinburgh. President, Scottish Intensive Care Society. Publications: papers on intensive care medicine. Recreations: sailing; reading. Address: (b.) Lauriston Rooms, Royal Infirmary, Little France, Edinburgh; T.-0131 242 3306.

McKenzie Smith, Ian, CBE, OBE, PPRSA, PPRSW, RGI, FMA, FRSA, FRSE, FSAScot, FSS, HRA, HRHA, HRUA, HRWA, LLD, DArt, DA, PG Dip (Grays School of Art). Artist (painter); b. 3.8.35; m., Mary Rodger Fotheringham; 2 s.; 1 d. Educ. Robert Gordon's College, Aberdeen; Gray's School of Art, Aberdeen; Hospitalfield College of Art, Arbroath; Aberdeen College of Education. Teacher of Art, 1960-63; Education Officer, Council of Industrial Design, Scottish Committee, 1963-68; Director, Aberdeen Art Gallery and Museums, 1968-89; City Arts and Recreation Officer, City of Aberdeen, 1989-96. Awards: SED Travelling Scholarship (France/Italy); Institute of Contemporary Prints Award, 1969; RSA Guthrie Award, 1971; RSA Sir William Gillies Award, 1980; EUS Thyne Scholarship, 1980; RSW May Marshall Brown Award, 1980; RSW Sir William Gillies Award, 2008; Arts and Business Scotland Award, 2011. Work in permanent collections: Scottish National Gallery of Modern Art, Scottish Arts Council, Arts Council of Northern Ireland, Contemporary Art Society, Aberdeen Art Gallery and Museums, Glasgow Art Gallery and Museums, Abbot Hall Art Gallery, Kendal, Hunterian Museum, Glasgow, Nuffield Foundation, Carnegie Trust, Strathclyde Education Authority, Lothian Education Authority, Royal Scottish Academy, Department of the Environment, City Art Centre, Edinburgh, Perth Art Gallery, IBM, Robert Fleming Holdings, Deutsche Bank, Grampian Hospital Art Trust, The Robert Gordon University, Stirling University, Angus Council; Member, Scottish Arts Council, 1970-77; Member, Scottish Museums Council, 1980-87; Member, Committee of Enquiry into the Economic Situation of the Visual Artist, Gulbenkian Foundation, 1978; Arts Advisor, COSLA, 1977-84; Member, Aberdeen University Museums Committee, 1970-96, and Music Committee, 1970-96; Honorary Member, Friends of Aberdeen Art Gallery and Museums, since 2000; Honorary Member, Peacock Printmakers, since 1993; Trustee: Third Eye Centre, 1966-70, Glasgow Arts Centre, 1966-68, Alba Magazine, 1977-80, WASPS (Scotland), 1973-77, Painters Workshop (Scotland), 1975-89, John Kinross Fund, 1990-2007, Alexander Naysmith Fund, 1990-2007, Spalding Fund, 1990-2007, Sir William Gillies Fund, 1990-2007, Hospitalfield Trust, 1990-2007 (Chair, 2003-07), RSA Enterprise, 1972-2007; Member, ICOM International Exhibitions Committee, 1986-96; Member, Advisory Council on the Export of Works of Art, 1991-2007; Member, Re:Source AIL Panel, 2000-01; External Assessor, Glasgow School of Art, 1982-86, Duncan of Jordanstone College of Art, Dundee, 1986-90, SAC Gifting Scheme, 1997; Assessor: Ruth Davidson Memorial Trust, Morrison Portrait Award, Salvesen Art Trust, Noble Grossart Award, RGU Collections Forum, since 2000; President, RSW, 1988-98; President, Royal Scottish Academy, 1998-2007; Deputy President, RSA, 1990-91; Treasurer, 1990, Secretary, 1991-98; Governor, Edinburgh College of Art, 1976-88 (Chair, Andrew Grant Committee, 1977-88); Governor, The Robert Gordon University, 1989-95; Member, Advisory Board, Robert Gordon University Heritage Unit, 1993-95; Member, Board, Scottish Sculpture Workshop, 1976-2000; Aberdeen Maritime Museum Appeal, 1981-98; Member, National Heritage Scottish Group, 1977-99; National Trust for Scotland: Member, Curatorial Committee, 1991-2001, Member of Council, 1995-99, Member, Buildings Committee, 1998-2000; Commissioner, Museums and Galleries Commission, 1997-2000; Trustee, National Galleries of Scotland, 1999-2007;

Vice President, NADFAS, 2000-07; Chairman, Marguerite McBey Trust, since 2000; Member, Aberdeen Art Gallery Alexander Macdonald Committee, since 2000; Trustee, Royal Scottish Academy Foundation, since 2015. Clubs: Royal Northern and University, Scottish Arts, Royal Overseas League. Address: (h.) Heron House, Angus DD10 9TJ; T.-01674 675898.
E-mail: i.mckenziesmith@btinternet.com

McKeown, James Patrick, LLB, DipLP, NP. Solicitor; b. 17.3.59, Coatbridge; m., Pamela Mary; 2 s.; 1 d. Educ. Aberdeen University. Assistant, Esslemont & Cameron, Aberdeen, 1983-85; Company Secretary, Sysdrill Ltd., 1985-86; Assistant, C. & D. Mactaggart, 1986, appointed Partner, 1987. Judge, Social Security Chamber, Tribunal Service; Vice-Chairman, Scottish Liberal Democrats, Argyll and Bute, 1990-97; former Vice President, Scottish Young Lawyers Association. Recreations: politics; travel. Address: (b.) Castlehill, Campbeltown, Argyll PA28 6AR; T.-01586 552317.

McKerrell of Hillhouse, Charles James Mure, OStJ, FSA Scot. Matriculated Arms 1973, Court of the Lord Lyon, and recognised by interlocutor of the Lord Lyon as Head of the Name and Family. Tartans:- McKerrell of Hillhouse recorded Court of the Lord Lyon, 25 June 1982; McKerrell of Hillhouse (Dress) recorded Court of the Lord Lyon, 2002. Recognised by the Chief Herald of Ireland as 15th Head of the Name, 1975; b. 23.1.51; m., May Weston Cochrane, née White. Educ. Cranleigh. Guardian of the Nobiliary Fraternity of the Nia Naisc, Knight of St Micheil of the Wing (Granted by HRH The Duke of Braganza), Hereditary Companion of the Royal House of O'Conor; GCLJ, Knight Grand Cross of St. Antioche; Kentucky Colonel; Hon. ADC to the Governor of Kentucky; Board Member, EU Commissioner Society of Scottish Armigers; Honorary Captain, Canadian Bush Pilots; Freeman, City of London; Council Member, Royal Celtic Society; Life Member, Royal Stuart Society; representative on Scottish Clans and Families Forum; Councillor of the Community Council of the Royal Burgh of Lochmaben. Address: (h.) Magdalene House, Lochmaben, Dumfries DG11 1PD; T.-01387 810439.
E-mail: mckerrellofhillhouse@btinternet.com

McKerrow, Maureen Grant. President, Scottish Licensed Trade Association, 2001-03; b. 7.12.54, Dumfries; m., Gordon McKerrow; 2 s. Educ. Dumfries Academy. Technician, 1972-78; Director, Globe Inn Ltd., 1977-79; Managing Director, Globe Inn Ltd., since 1999; Chairman, Scottish Ladies Golf Association, 1992; Member, Nicholson Committee on Licensing Reform, 2001. Recreations: curling; golf; art; Robert Burns. Address: (b.) Globe Inn Ltd., 56 High Street, Dumfries DG1 2JA; T.-01387 252335.

MacKessack-Leitch, Hilda Jane Marshall. Deputy Lieutenant, Moray, since 1993; Chairman, Moray and Banff Support Group of NOS (National Osteoporosis Society); b. 4.9.40, Rothes; m., 1, Dr. Ernest V. C. Dawson (deceased); 2, David C. MacKessack-Leitch (deceased); 2 s. Educ. Elgin Academy. Past County Commissioner, The Guide Association, Moray; Past Chairman, Cancer Research Campaign Committee, Elgin and District; Elgin Local Organiser, WRVS, 1976-2000; County President, Girl Guiding Moray, Girl Guiding Scotland, 2014. Recreations: cooking; walking; reading; music. Address: (h.) Sillerton, 61 Mayne Road, Elgin, Moray IV30 1PD; T.-01343 544711.

McKie, Alastair John. Partner, Head of Planning and Environment, Anderson Strathern, since 1998; b. 15.6.62, Ipswich, Suffolk; m., Dr. Margaret Mitchell; 1 d. Educ. Lornshill Academy, Alloa; Dundee University. Qualified as a Solicitor, 1987; elected Legal Associate, Royal Town Planning Institute; Accredited as Specialist in Planning Law, Law Society of Scotland; Writer to Her Majesty's Signet. Recreations: hill walking; fishing; tennis; dogs. Address: (b.) 1 Rutland Court, Edinburgh EH3 8EY; T.-0131 625 7257.
E-mail: alastair.mckie@andersonstrathern.co.uk

McKie, Professor Linda, BA (Hons), MSc, PhD. Professor of Sociology, Head of School of Applied Social Sciences, Durham University; Research Professor in Sociology, Glasgow Caledonian University, 1999-2012; Associate Director, Centre for Research on Families and Relationships, since 2001; Senior Professorial Fellow, Hanken School of Economics, Helsinki, 2004-2010; b. 29.9.56, Belfast; 1 d. Educ. Richmond Lodge; University of Ulster; University of Bath; University of Durham. Lecturer: University of Teesside, 1986-88, University of Glasgow, 1989; Head of Intelligence Unit, Equal Opportunities Commission, Manchester, 1990; Head of Sociology and Social Policy, Queen Margaret University College, 1991-93; Senior Lecturer, Department of General Practice and Primary Care, University of Aberdeen, 1993-99. Elected Fellow, Academy of Social Sciences, 2004; Member of Council, Erskine Veterans Charity; Elected Trustee, British Sociological Association. Publications: fifteen books and over 120 papers on organisations, work and care, health and evaluation, and gender and violence. Recreations: gym training; travel; food and wine. Address: Flat 7, 73 Lothian Road, Edinburgh EH3 9AW.

McKiernan, Professor Peter, BA, MA, CABS, FBAM, FEURAM, FAcSS, FGLA, FCIS, FRSA, MM. Dean of Faculty of Management and Governance, Murdoch University, Perth, Australia and Professor of Management, University of Strathclyde; b. 28.12.53, Accrington; 1 s.; 1 d. Educ. Preston Catholic College; Lancaster University; Surrey University. Former F.D. of mechanical engineering company; Lecturer in Management, University of St Andrews; Senior Lecturer in Strategic Management, Warwick University; Professor of Strategic Management, University of St Andrews, 1992-2010; Head of School of Management, University of St Andrews, 2004-2010; Chairman and President, British Academy of Management, 2001-06; Vice President and President, European Academy of Management, 2001-2010; Executive Board of Association of Business Schools, since 2009 and made Companion in 2008; Chair, Board of Governors, Madras College, 1999-2008; Chair, Board of Governors, West Lothian College, since 2009; Executive Board Member, Scotland's Colleges since 2011; Appointed Chair of West Lothian Region College, 2012; Awarded CEEMAN Institutional Champion Award, 2012. Publications: Sharpbenders; Strategies of Growth; Inside Fortress Europe; Historical Evolution of Strategic Management; Omani Management Cultures; Scenarios for Scotland; Strategic Leadership. Recreations: sailing; poetry. Address: Strathclyde Business School, University of Strathclyde, 99 Cathedral Street, Glasgow.

McKillop, Professor James Hugh, BSc, MB, ChB, PhD, FRCP, FRCR, FMedSci, Hon FAcadMEd, Hon. Doctorate (Orebro). Muirhead Professor of Medicine, Glasgow University, 1989-2011 (Associate Dean for Medical Education, 2000-03 and Head of Undergraduate Medical Education, 2003-06, Deputy Dean of Medicine, 2007-2010, Deputy Head of School of Medicine 2010-11); Honorary Consultant Physician, NHS Greater Glasgow, 1982-2011; b. 20.6.48, Glasgow; m., Caroline A. Oakley; 2 d. Educ. St. Aloysius' College, Glasgow; Glasgow University. Hall Fellow in Medicine, then Lecturer in Medicine, Glasgow University, 1974-82; Postdoctoral Fellow, Stanford University Medical Center, California, 1979 and 1980; Senior Lecturer in Medicine, Glasgow University, 1982-89. Harkness Fellowship, Commonwealth Fund of New York,

1979-80; Robert Reid Newall Award, Stanford University, 1980; Honorary Treasurer, Scottish Society of Experimental Medicine, 1982-87; Honorary Secretary, British Nuclear Cardiology Group, 1982-87; Council Member, British Nuclear Medicine Society, 1985-94 (Hon. Secretary, 1988-90, President, 1990-92); Editor, Nuclear Medicine Communications, 1989-98; Congress President, European Association of Nuclear Medicine, 1997, Member, Executive Committee, 1995-98, Chairman, Education Committee, 1998-2001, Member, Strategy Committee, 1999-2008; Chairman, Administration of Radioactive Substances Advisory Committee, Department of Health, 1996-2004 (Vice Chairman, 1989-95); Member, National Medical Advisory Committee, 1995-98; Specialty Adviser on Nuclear Medicine, SODOH, 1998-2007; Vice-President, Nuclear Medicine Section, Union Europeene Medecines Specialistes; Member, Scottish Medical and Scientific Advisory Committee, 1999-2001, Chairman, 2001-07; Team Leader for GMC Quality Assurance of Basic Medical Education, 2003-2008; Member, GMC, since 2009 and Chair, Undergraduate Board, 2009-2012; Chairman, Medical Advisory Group, NHS Education for Scotland, 2004-2011; Chairman, Scottish Deans' Medical Curriculum Group, 2005-09; Chair, Expert Advisory Panel, British Polio Fellowship, 2008-2012; Member, Caribbean Accreditation Authority for Medicine, 2010-2014, Member, Advisory Committee, since 2014; Vestry Secretary, St Mary's Episcopal Cathedral, Glasgow, since 2011; Chair, Audit and Risk Committee, since 2015. Recreations: music (especially opera); history; football. Address: (h.) Flat 1, 6 Kirklee Gate, Glasgow G12 0SZ.
E-mail: jim.mckillop@glasgow.ac.uk

McKillop, Stewart, MA (Hons), DipAcc, DipEd. Principal, South Lanarkshire College, East Kilbride, since 2001; b. 16.10.55, Glasgow. Educ. Glasgow University. Associate Principal, James Watt College of Further and Higher Education, 1991-2001. Address: (b.) 1 College Way, East Kilbride G75 0NE; T.-01355-807604.
E-mail: angelamartin@slc.ac.uk

McKinlay, Alastair. Rector, Inverness Royal Academy, since 2010. Educ. Campbeltown Grammar School; Jordanhill College. Teacher of Physical Education, Tain Royal Academy, 1982-1988, Principal Teacher of Physical Education, from 1988, Acting Assistant Rector, April-July 1997 and March 1998-February 1999, Depute Rector, 1999-2010. Recreations: basketball; sailing; golf; walking. Address: (b.) Inverness Royal Academy, Culduthel Road, Inverness IV2 6RE; T.-01463 222884.

MacKinnon, Donalda. Head of Programmes and Services for BBC Scotland, since 2005; responsible for all of BBC Scotland's output in and from Scotland on TV, Radio and Online. Address: (b.) BBC Scotland, 40 Pacific Quay, Glasgow G51 1DA.

MacKinnon, Kenneth, BSc (Econ), PGCE, AcadDipEd, MA (Educ), PhD. Board Member/Director, Bòrd na Gàidhlig, 2004-2014; b. 26.8.33, Poplar, London; m., Rosalie Butler; 1 s.; 1 d. Educ. Westcliff High School for Boys; University of London, LSE, Institute of Education. Teacher/Lecturer in Essex secondary schools and technical colleges, 1956-74; Senior/Principal Lecturer/Reader in Sociology of Education at Hatfield Polytechnic 1974-92; Visiting Professor and Reader Emeritus in Sociology of Language at University of Hertfordshire from 1992; Honorary Research Fellow in Celtic, University of Edinburgh, 1991-2004; Honorary Professor in Language Policy and Planning, University of Aberdeen, since 2004; Associate Lecturer in Social Science, Education and Language Studies, The Open University, since 1970. Numerous research studies and publications on Gaelic and other lesser-used language communities, sociology and demography of language, from 1972. Member,

Ministerial Advisory Group on Gaelic (MAGOG), 2000-2002, MG, Alba (Gaelic Media Services), 2008-11. National Records of Scotland: Scottish Census Steering Committee; Population and Migration Statistics (PAMS), 2009-2014. Publications: The Lion's Tongue, 1974; Language Education and Social Processes in a Gaelic Community, 1977; Gaelic - a Past and Future Prospect 1991; An Independent Academic Study on Cornish, 2000. Recreations: caravanning; countryside; traditional music. Address (b.) Ivy Cottage, Ferintosh, The Black Isle, by Dingwall, Ross-shire IV7 8HX; T.-01349 863460; e-mail: ken@ferintosh.org

Mackintosh, Simon, MA, LLB, WS. Chairman, Turcan Connell; Consultant, Macphie of Glenbervie Ltd.; b. Wisbech; m., Catriona; 2 s.; 1 d. Educ. Edinburgh Academy; Glenalmond; Magdalene College, Cambridge University; Edinburgh University. W. & J. Burness: Apprentice, 1980-82, Assistant Solicitor, 1982-85; secondment, Boodle Hatfield, 1983; Partner, W. & J. Burness, 1985-97. Former Convener, Tax Law Committee, Law Society of Scotland; Member, International Academy of Estate and Trust Law; Past Chairman, Scottish Episcopal Church Pension Trustees; Board Member, Edinburgh Book Festival, 1996-2001; Past Chairman, Court of Directors of The Edinburgh Academy; Committee of Charity Law Association; Collector, WS Dependants' Annuity Fund. Recreations: gardening; golf; rugby. Address: (b.) Princes Exchange, 1 Earl Grey Street, Edinburgh EH3 9EE; T.-0131-228 8111.

MacLaren of MacLaren, Donald. Chief of Clan Labhran of Balquhidder and Strathearn; b. 1954; m., Maida Jane Aitchison; 3 s. 2 d. Educ. Dragon School, Oxford; Trinity College, Glenalmond; Edinburgh University. Joined the Foreign and Commonwealth Office in 1978; after postings in Berlin, Moscow, Havana, Caracas and Kiev, served in Tbilisi, Georgia as Her Majesty's Ambassador; left the FCO in 2008 and now runs a partnership teaching people to speak persuasively called Perfect Pitch. Succeeded his father as Chief in 1966; twenty-fifth head of the Clan since Labhran, name-forefather of the Clan eight hundred years ago; descended from King Lorn Mor of the fifth century. Address: Kirkton Farm, Balquhidder, Lochearnhead, Perthshire.

McLaren, Duncan Bruce, MB, BS, BSc, FRCR, FRCP (Edin). Consultant Clinical Oncologist, Western General Hospital, Edinburgh, since 1998; b. 20.3.65, Redditch; m., Dr. Pamela McLaren; 2 d. Educ. Finham Park School; St. Mary's Hospital Medical School, London. Specialist in urological cancer; Member, National Cancer Studies Groups in Prostate and Bladder Cancer; Lead, Scottish Cancer Trials Network, SE Scotland GU Trials Group. Recreations: avid sportsman – former rugby player, now keen squash player and golfer. Address: (b.) Edinburgh Cancer Centre, Western General Hospital, Edinburgh EH4 2XU; T.-0131-537 2215.
E-mail: duncan.mclaren@luht.scot.nhs.uk

MacLaren, Iain Ferguson, MB, ChB, FRCSEdin, FRCS, FRCP Edin. Consultant Surgeon, Royal Infirmary, Edinburgh, 1974-92; b. 28.9.27, Edinburgh; m., Dr. Fiona Barbara Heptonstall; 1 s.; 1 d. Educ. Edinburgh Academy; Fettes College; Edinburgh University. Captain, RAMC, Egypt, 1950-52; Surgical Registrar, Royal Hospital for Sick Children, Edinburgh, 1956-58; Senior Surgical Registrar, Royal Infirmary, 1959-63 and 1964-67; Fellow in Surgical Research, Hahnemann Medical College and Hospital, Philadelphia, 1963-64; Consultant Surgeon, Deaconess Hospital, Edinburgh, 1967-85; Vice-President, Royal College of Surgeons of Edinburgh, 1983-86 (Council

Member, 1977-83 and 1987-94); Fellow, Royal Medical Society (Honorary Treasurer, 1979-85); Chairman, Royal Medical Society Trust, 1985-2003; Honorary Pipe-Major, Royal Scottish Pipers' Society, 1959-62; Honorary Secretary: Harveian Society of Edinburgh, 1968-87, Aesculapian Club, 1978-2004; Hon. Secretary, Royal College of Surgeons of Edinburgh, 1972-77; Secretary, Edinburgh University General Council, 1993-97; Chairman: Professional and Linguistic Assessments Board, General Medical Council, 1996-99, Clan MacLaren Society, 1968-91; Chieftain, Clan Labhran, 1991; President, Edinburgh University Graduates' Association, 1999-2002. Recreations: music; the study of military history; all aspects of Scottish culture. Address: (h.) 3 Minto Street, Edinburgh EH9 1RG; T.-0131-667 3487.

McLaren, Jim. Chairman, Quality Meat Scotland, since 2011. Farmer. Address: (b.) The Rural Centre, Ingliston, Newbridge EH28 8NZ; T.-0131 472 4040.

McLarty, Rev. Russell, BD, MA, BArch. Interim Minister, Parish Church of The Holy Trinity, St Andrews, since 2016; Storyteller, since 1995; b. 1956, Ayr. Educ. The Royal High School, Edinburgh; University of Edinburgh; University of Glasgow. The Church of Scotland: Parish Minister, St, Paul's Glasgow (Blackhill, Provanmill & Royston), 1985-2006, Interim Minister, 2006-2011; Coordinator, Chance To Thrive Pilot Project (Priority Areas of The Church of Scotland), since 2011. Directory Member of Scottish Storytelling Forum; Activities and Societies: Ministry in Church of Scotland, storytelling, architecture. Receations: storytelling; placemaking; mediation; group development. Address: Parish Church of The Holy Trinity, South Street, St Andrews, Fife KY16 9UH; T.-01334 478317; e-mail: holytrinitystandrews@gmail.com

McLatchie, Cameron, CBE, LLB. Chairman, British Polythene Industries, since 2003, formerly Scott & Robertson PLC, 1988-2003; b. 18.2.47, Paisley; m., Helen Leslie Mackie; 2 s.; 1 d. Educ. Boroughmuir School, Edinburgh; Largs High School; Ardrossan Academy; Glasgow University. Whinney Murray & Co., Glasgow, 1968-70; Thomas Boag & Co. Ltd., Greenock, 1970-75; Chairman and Managing Director, Anaplast Ltd., Irvine, 1975-83; this company purchased by Scott & Robertson. Deputy Chairman, Scottish Enterprise, 1997-2000; Non-Executive Director, Royal Bank of Scotland Group PLC, 1998-2002. Recreations: bridge; golf. Address: (b.) 96 Port Glasgow Road, Greenock; T.-01475 501000.

McLaughlan, Ian, FCMI, BA, DipVAMP, DipHE, CertILM. Chief Executive, Youth Scotland, since 2013; Chief Executive, Scottish Pre-school Play Association, 2001-2013; b. 31.8.54, Motherwell; m., Ann; 2 s. Educ. Canterbury of Kent University; City of London University Business School. Boys' Brigade Scotland: Training Development Officer, 1988-96, National Director, 1996-2001. Recreations: cycling; walking; reading. Address: (b.) Balfour House, 19 Bonnington Grove, Edinburgh EH6 4BL; T.-0131 554 2561.

McLaughlin, Anne. MP (SNP), Glasgow North East, since 2015; b. 8.3.66. Educ. Port Glasgow High School; Royal Scottish Academy of Music and Drama; University of Glasgow. Researcher for the MSP Bob Doris; championed the cause of English language skills in Glasgow schoolchildren; SNP campaign co-ordinator when John Mason won the Glasgow East by-election, 2008; former member of the Public Audit and Public Petitions parliamentary committees (2009–2011); MSP, Scottish Parliament (Glasgow), 2009-2011. Address: House of Commons, London SW1A 0AA.

McLaughlin, Gerald. Chief Executive, NHS Health Scotland, since 2010. Career: worked for 20 years as a local authority social work manager, then Glasgow's principal child protection officer; Assistant Director, Royal National Institute for the Blind, Scotland, 1998-2000; Director, British Red Cross, 2000-2010. Formerly non executive member, Board of NHS Greater Glasgow and Clyde, 2004-2010. Address: (b.) Meridian Court, 5 Cadogan Street, Glasgow G2 6QE.

MacLaverty, Bernard. Writer; b. 14.9.42, Belfast; m., Madeline McGuckin; 1 s.; 3 d. Educ. St Malachy's College, Belfast; Queen's University, Belfast. Moved from Belfast to Scotland, 1975; has been a medical laboratory technician, a mature student, a teacher of English and, for two years in the mid-1980s, Writer-in-Residence at Aberdeen University; has been a Guest Writer for short periods at Liverpool John Moore's University of Augsburg and Iowa State University; Member, Aosdana in Ireland; has published five collections of short stories and four novels; has witten versions of his fiction for other media, including radio plays, television plays, screenplays and libretti. Publications: Secrets and Other Stories, 1977; Lamb, 1980; A Time to Dance and other Stories, 1982; Cal, 1983; The Great Profundo and Other Stories, 1987; Walking the Dog and Other Stories, 1994; Grace Notes, 1997; The Anatomy School, 2001; Matters of Life & Death and other stories, 2006; Collected Stories, 2013.

Maclay, Baron (Joseph Paton Maclay), 3rd Baron; Bt. Deputy Lieutenant, Renfrewshire, 1986-2008; Director, Altnamara Shipping Plc, 1994-2002; Chairman, Northern Lighthouse Board, 2001-03 (Commissioner, 1996-2003, Vice Chairman, 2000-01); Chairman, Scottish Maritime Museum, 1998-2005; Chairman, Scottish Nautical Welfare Society, 2002-04; b. 11.4.42; m., Elizabeth Anne Buchanan; 2 s.; 1 d. Educ. Winchester; Sorbonne. Managing Director: Denholm Maclay Co. Ltd., 1970-83, Denholm Maclay (Offshore) Ltd., Triport Ferries (Management) Ltd., 1975-83; Deputy Managing Director, Denholm Ship Management Ltd., 1982-83; Director: Milton Shipping Co. Ltd., 1970-83, Marine Shipping Mutual Insurance Company, 1982-83; President, Hanover Shipping Inc., 1982-83; Director: British Steamship Short Trades Association, 1978-83, North of England Protection and Indemnity Association, 1976-83; Chairman, Scottish Branch, British Sailors Society, 1979-81; Vice-President, Glasgow Shipowners & Shipbrokers Benevolent Association, 1982-83 and 1997-98; President, Glasgow Shipowners and Shipbrokers Benevolent Association, 1998-99; Director, Denholm Ship Management (Holdings) Ltd., 1991-93; Group Marketing Executive, Acomarit Group, 1993-99; Trustee: Cattanach Charitable Trust, 1991-2011 (Chairman, 2009-2011), Western Isles Fisheries Trust, 2004-06, Western Isles Salmon Fisheries Board, 2004-06. Address: (h.) Duchal, Kilmacolm, Renfrewshire PA13 4RS.

MacLean, Rt. Hon. Lord (Ranald Norman Munro MacLean), BA, LLB, LLM, PC, LLD, FSA(Scot), FRSE. Senator of the College of Justice, 1990-2005; Queen's Counsel, since 1977; b. 18.12.38, Aberdeen; m., Pamela Ross (m. dissolved); 2 s.; 1 d. Educ. Inverness Royal Academy; Fettes College, Edinburgh; Cambridge University; Edinburgh University; Yale University. Advocate, 1964; Advocate Depute, 1972-75; Advocate Depute (Home), 1979-82; Chairman, The Cockburn Association (Edinburgh Civic Trust), 1988-96; Member, Secretary of State for Scotland's Criminal Justice Forum, 1996-2000; Member, Parole Board for Scotland, 1998-2000; Chairman, Committee on Serious Violent and Sexual Offenders, 1999-2000; Member, Scottish Judicial Appointments Board, 2002-05; Chairman: Sentencing Commission for Scotland, 2003-05, The Billy Wright Inquiry (Banbridge, Northern Ireland), 2004-2010, The Vale of Leven Hospital Inquiry, 2009-2014; Surveillance

Commissioner, since 2010; Chairman of Governors, Fettes College, 1996-2006. Recreations: hill-walking; swimming. Address: (h.) 67/3 Grange Loan, Edinburgh EH9 2EG.

MacLean, A. Duncan, LLB, DipLP, NP, WS. Partner, Brodies LLP, since 2004 (specialist in shipping and transport); b. 19.2.66, Inverness; m., Esther; 2 d. Educ. Achtercairn Secondary; Dingwall Academy; Edinburgh University. Admitted as Solicitor, 1988; Trained, Guild & Guild, WS, Edinburgh; Solicitor, Brodies, WS, 1989-94; Associate, Henderson Boyd Jackson, Edinburgh, 1994, then Partner, 1996. Trustee, Cherish Watoto, Kenya; Member: British Maritime Law Association, Forum of Insurance Lawyers. Recreations: family; church; sport; the outdoors. Address: (b.) 15 Atholl Crescent, Edinburgh EH3 8HA.

McLean, Catriona Mary, MB, BS, MRCP, FRCR. Consultant Clinical Oncologist, Western General Hospital, Edinburgh, since 1996; b. 30.3.62, Kampala, Uganda; m., Cliff Culley; 1 s.; 1 d. Educ. Sutton High School GPDST; St. Bartholomew's Medical College, London. Address: (b.) Department of Clinical Oncology, Western General Hospital, Edinburgh; T.-0131-537 1000.

Maclean of Dunconnel, Sir Charles (Edward), Bt; b. 31.10.46; m.; 4 d. Educ. Eton; New College, Oxford. Publications: The Wolf Children; The Watcher; Island on the Edge of the World; Scottish Country; Romantic Scotland; The Silence. Address: (h.) Strachur House, Cairndow, Argyll PA27 8BX.

Maclean, Christian. Editor, Floris Books, since 1976; b. 14.2.50, Edinburgh; m., Astrid; 2 s.; 1 d. Educ. Rudolf Steiner School. Address: (b.) 15 Harrison Gardens, Edinburgh; T.-0131-337 2372.

MacLean, Colin R., BSc (Hons), DipEd, MSc. Former Director of Financial Strategy, Scottish Government (2011-13); b. 22.5.51, Dundee; m., Ilse; 2 s.; 1 d. Educ. Forfar Academy; Edinburgh University. Teacher of Mathematics, Edinburgh, 1973-79; Education Adviser (Microelectronics/Computing), Lothian Regional Council, 1980-85; HM Inspector of Schools, 1985-96; Chief Statistician, Scottish Office, 1996-99; HM Depute Senior Chief Inspector of Schools, 1999-2000; Depute Head, Schools Group, 2000-02 (National Exam Co-ordinator, 2001); Director, Children, Young People and Social Care, Scottish Government, 2002-08; Director of Learning, Scottish Government, 2008-2011. Board Member, Streetwork UK; Chair, Partnership Commission for Childcare Reform; Volunteer with Cyrenians Fare Share Programme at Edinburgh Cyrenians; Member of Court and Chair of Audit and Risk Committee, Heriot-Watt University; Trustee of Barnardo's. Recreations: gardening; music; travel. Address: (b.) Streetwork, 2 New Street, Edinburgh EH8 8BH; T.-0131 556 9756.

McLean, Colin William, MA, MBA, FIA, FSIP, FCSI. Managing Director, SVM Asset Management, since 1990; b. 1.10.52. Educ. Jordanhill College School, Glasgow; Glasgow University; Deputy General Manager, FS Assurance, 1974-86; Chief Investment Officer, Scottish Provident, 1986-88; Managing Director, Templeton International, 1988-90; Honorary Professor, Heriot-Watt University Edinburgh; Board Member, CFA Institute. Address: (b.) SVM Asset Management Ltd, 7 Castle Street, Edinburgh EH2 3AH; T.-0131-226 6699.

MacLean, Elizabeth Anne, OBE, MA, Convener, Mobility and Access Committee, Transport Scotland, since 2009; b. 3.9.41, Falkirk; m., Alan Shute; 1 s. Educ. Beacon School, Bridge of Allan; University of London. Civil Servant, MOD and DHSS, 1964-73; Trade Union Officer, National Union of Civil and Public Servants, 1973-90; Assessor, Commissioner for Public Appointments Scotland, 2001-07; Board Member, Cairngorms National Park Authority, 2003-2010. Board Member and Chair, Albyn Housing Society, 1997-2007; Trustee, RNIB Scotland, 2002-2012; Committee Member: Sight Action Highlands & Islands, 1996-2012, Inclusive Cairngorms, since 2003 (Chair, since 2012). Recreations: reading; cooking; music (listening). Address: 8 Strathspey Gardens, Grantown on Spey PH26 3GZ; T.-01479 872812.

MacLean, Eoghainn Charles McEwen, LLB (Private Law Hons), DipLP. Advocate, since 1995; b. 17.4.66, Port of Aden; 2 s. Educ. High School of Glasgow; Glasgow University. Solicitor, McClure Naismith, 1991-93; Solicitor, McGrigor Donald, 1993-94; devil, 1994-95; called to Scots Bar, 1995; Member, Ampersand Stable of Advocates (see ampersandstable.com). Address: (h.) 4 Athole Gardens, Glasgow G12 9AY; T.-0141 560 2003.
E-mail: eoghainn.maclean@advocates.org.uk

Maclean, Iain Farquhar, LLB (Hons), LLM, MSc, DipLP. Advocate. Educ. Portree High School; University of Aberdeen; Emmanuel College, Cambridge; University of Edinburgh. Trainee Solicitor, Brodies WS, 1990-92; Legal Assistant to the Lord President, Court of Session, 1992-93; admitted, Faculty of Advocates, 1994. Contributor, Greens Annotated Rules of the Court of Session. Address: (b.) Advocates' Library, Parliament House, Edinburgh EH1 1RF; T.-0131-226 5071.

McLean, Jack, DA, MSIAD. Freelance Writer and Broadcaster; b. 10.8.46, Irvine. Educ. Allan Glen's School; Edinburgh College of Art; Jordanhill College. Art Teacher in Glasgow for many years; The Scotsman, 1977-81; Glasgow Herald, 1981-97; The Scotsman, 1997-98; Scotland on Sunday, 1997-99; Sports Columnist, Scottish Daily Mail, 1999-2000; Columnist: The Herald, 2000-06, The Scottish Review, since 2006, other publicatons; Radio Clyde, 1982-85; BBC Scotland Art Critic and Adviser, 1991-95; Presenter, The Jack McLean Talk Show, Scottish Television. Columnist of the Year, British Press Awards, 1985; Recipient of several Scottish Press Awards. Publications: The Bedside Urban Voltaire; More Bedside Urban Voltaire; The Sporting Urban Voltaire; City of Glasgow; Hopeless But Not Serious; Earthquake; The Compendium of Nosh, 2006. Recreations: smoking; poverty; dressing; cooking.

MacLean, James Gordon Bruce, MBChB, FRCS. Consultant Orthopaedic Surgeon, Perth Royal Infirmary and Ninewells Hospital, Dundee, since 1994; Honorary Lecturer, Dundee University, since 1994; b. 17.5.58, Carlisle; m., Susan Jane Roberts; 2 s.; 2 d. Educ. Merchiston Castle School, Edinburgh; Dundee University Medical School. Basic surgical training, Norfolk and Norwich Hospitals; specialist orthopaedic training, St Bartholomew's Hospital, Great Ormond Street, Stanmore; Research Fellow/Junior Consultant, University of Capetown; Regional Children's Orthopaedic Surgeon, Tayside. Recreations: hill-walking; rugby; racquet sports; boating. Address: (b.) Orthopaedic Department, Perth Royal Infirmary, Perth PH1 1NX; T.-01738 623311.

Maclean, John. Chair, Audit Scotland, 2014-2015 (retired). Held non-executive directorships at the Bank of Scotland (former chair of the audit committee), HBOS plc, the Bank of Western Australia and asset management company SVM Global (chaired the audit committee); chair of Audit Scotland's Audit Committee until September 2014, and previously an independent, non-executive director of the Audit Scotland Board. Currently a member and deputy chair of Court, Glasgow Caledonian University.

Maclean of Duart, Major The Hon. Sir Lachlan, DL. Major, Scots Guards retired; 28th Chief of Clan Maclean; b. 25.8.42.

MacLean, Rev. Marjory Anne, LLB, BD, PhD, post-nominal VR, RNR. Minister, Abernyte linked with Inchture and Kinnaird linked with Longforgan Parish Churches, since 2011; Royal Naval Reserve Chaplain, since 2004; b. 11.6.62, Forfar. Educ. Forfar Academy; Edinburgh University. Trainee Solicitor, T.P. & J.L. Low, Kirkwall, 1985-87; Probationer, then Assistant Minister, Fairmilehead Parish Church, Edinburgh, 1990-92; Minister, Stromness Parish Church, 1992-98; Depute Secretary, Legal Questions Committee, and Depute Clerk, General Assembly of Church of Scotland, 1996-2010; Acting Principal Clerk, 2002-03 and 2009; Vice-Convener, Church of Scotland Ministries Council, since 2014. Address: The Manse, Longforgan, Dundee.

McLean, Miller Roy, MA, LLB, WS, NP, FCIBS, FIB. Chairman, Adam and Company PLC, since 2010; Group General Counsel, and Group Secretary, The Royal Bank of Scotland Group plc, 2003-2010; Director, Adam and Company PLC; Director, Ulster Bank; Chairman, Royal Bank of Scotland Pension Trustee Ltd; Chairman, Whitehall and Industry Group; Trustee, Industry and Parliament Trust; b. 4.12.49, Scotland; m., Anne Charlotte Gourlay; 1 s.; 1 d. Educ. Vale of Leven Academy; Glasgow University; Edinburgh University. The Royal Bank of Scotland Group plc: Assistant Secretary, 1982-83, Secretary, 1983-88; The Royal Bank of Scotland plc: Secretary, 1985-88, Group Secretary, 1988-90, Assistant Director, Legal and Administration, 1990-91, Director, Legal and Regulatory Affairs, 1991-94; Director, Group Legal and Regulatory Affairs and Group Secretary, 1994-2003. Recreations: golf; gardening; reading; music. Address: (b.) 25 St Andrew Square, Edinburgh EH2 1AF; T.-0131 225 8484.

Maclean, Rob. Television presenter, sports commentator and sports writer; b. 26.11.58, Inverness; m., Pauline; 1 s.; 1 d. Educ. Invergordon Academy. Began career with the Highland News Group in Inverness; worked for an Aberdeen news agency, 1979-81; Northsound Radio for 6 years; BBC Scotland's flagship evening news programme Reporting Scotland, 1986-88; Scotland Today on STV, 1988-90; reporter for both Reporting Scotland and Sportscene, BBC Scotland, 1990-2004; main anchorman for live coverage of Scottish Premier League matches, Setanta Sports, 2004-09; main anchor of STV's UEFA Champions League coverage, 2010; commentator and reporter for BBC Radio Scotland; Presenter, Sportscene, BBC, since 2010. Recreations: playing football; golf; skiing; music; movies. Address: BBC Scotland, 40 Pacific Quay, Glasgow G51 1DA.

McLean, Una, MBE. Actress; b. 1930, Strathaven. Trained, Royal Scottish Academy of Music and Drama; professional debut, Byre, St. Andrews, 1955; pantomime debut, Mother Goose, 1958; joined Citizens' Theatre, Glasgow, 1959; appeared in Five Past Eight revue, 1960s; many television appearances.

Maclean, Emeritus Professor William James, MBE (2006), DA, RSA, RSE, RGI, RSW. Emeritus Professor of Visual Arts, University of Dundee, since 2002, formerly Professor of Fine Art, Duncan of Jordanstone College,

University of Dundee; b. 12.10.41, Inverness; m., Marian Forbes Leven; 2 s.; 1 d. Educ. Inverness Royal Academy; HMS Conway; Grays School of Art, Aberdeen. Postgraduate and Travel Scholarship, Scottish Education Trust Award, Visual Arts Bursary, Scottish Arts Council; Benno Schotz Prize; one-man exhibitions in Rome, Glasgow, Edinburgh and London; group exhibitions in Britain, Europe and North America; represented in private and public collections including Arts Council, British Museum, Scottish National Gallery of Modern Art, Fitzwilliam Museum, Cambridge, and Scottish museum collections. Hon. DLitt, St. Andrews University; Hon. Fellowship UHI (Univ. of Highlands), 2008; Hon. DLitt, University of Aberdeen, 2009; Fellow of Royal Society of Edinburgh (RSE). Address: (h.) Bellevue, 18 Dougall Street, Tayport, Fife.

MacLeary, Alistair Ronald, MSc, DipTP, FRICS, FRTPI, FRSA. Honorary Fellow, Commonwealth Association of Surveying and Land Economy; Honorary Professor, Heriot-Watt University, 2003-09; Member, Administrative Justice and Tribunals Council and Chairman of its Scottish Committee, 2007-09; Member, Council on Tribunals and Chairman of its Scottish Committee, 2005-07; Member, Lands Tribunal for Scotland, 1989-2005; MacRobert Professor of Land Economy, Aberdeen University, 1976-89 (Dean, Faculty of Law, 1982-85); b. 12.1.40, Glasgow; m., Claire Leonard; 1 s.; 1 d. Educ. Inverness Royal Academy; College of Estate Management; Heriot-Watt University; Strathclyde University. Assistant Surveyor, Gerald Eve & Co., Chartered Surveyors, 1962-65; Assistant to Director, Murrayfield Real Estate Co. Ltd., 1965-67; Assistant Surveyor and Town Planner/Partner, Wright & Partners, 1967-76; seconded to Department of the Environment, London, 1971-73; Member: Committee of Inquiry into the Acquisition and Occupancy of Agricultural Land, 1977-79, Home Grown Timber Advisory Committee, Forestry Commission, 1981-87; Chairman, Board of Education, Commonwealth Association of Surveying and Land Economy, 1981-90; President, Planning and Development Division, Royal Institution of Chartered Surveyors, 1984-85; Editor, Land Development Studies, 1986-90; Member, Natural Environment Research Council, 1988-91. Recreations: shooting; golf. Address: (h.) St. Helen's, St. Andrew's Road, Ceres, Fife KY15 5NQ; T.-01334 828862.

McLeish, Rt. Hon. Henry Baird, PC. MP (Labour), Fife Central, 1987-2001; MSP (Labour), Central Fife, 1999-2003; First Minister of Scotland, 2000-01, Minister for Enterprise and Learning, 1999-2000; Consultant, J. Chandler & Co.; b. 15.6.48; m.; 1 s.; 1 step-s.; 1 d.; 1 step-d. Educ. Buckhaven High School, Methil; Heriot-Watt University. Former Research Officer and Planning Officer in local government; former Member, Kirkcaldy District Council and Fife Regional Council (Leader, 1982-87); Scottish Front Bench Spokesman for Education and Employment, 1988-89, for Employment and Training, 1989-92; Shadow Scottish Minister of State, 1992-94; Shadow Minister of Transport, 1994-95; Shadow Minister for Health, 1995-97; Minister of State, Scottish Office (Minister for Home Affairs, Local Government and Devolution), 1997-99. Visiting Professor: University of Arkansas, University of Denver; Visiting Lecturer, US Airforce Academy, Colarado. Honorary Fellow: Edinburgh University; Cambridge Land Institute at Fitzwilliam College, Cambridge. Publications: Scotland First: truth and consequences, 2004; Global Scots: Making It in the Modern World (Co-Author), 2006; Wherever the Saltire Flies (Co-Author), 2006; Scotland: The Road Divides (Co-Author), 2007. Recreations: reading; history; life and work of Robert Burns; malt whisky; Highlands and Islands. Address: 49 George Street, Cellardyke, Fife KY10 3AS.

McLellan, Very Rev. Andrew Rankin Cowie, CBE, MA, BD, STM, DD. HM Chief Inspector of Prisons for Scotland, 2002-09; Minister, St. Andrew's and St. George's,

Edinburgh, 1986-2002; Moderator, General Assembly, Church of Scotland, 2000; b. 16.6.44, Glasgow; m., Irene L. Meek; 2 s. Educ. Kilmarnock Academy; Madras College, St. Andrews; St. Andrews University; Glasgow University; Union Theological Seminary, New York. Assistant Minister, St. George's West, Edinburgh, 1969-71; Minister: Cartsburn Augustine, Greenock, 1971-80, Viewfield, Stirling, 1980-86; Member, Inverclyde District Council, 1977-80; Tutor, Glasgow University, 1978-82; Chaplain, HM Prison, Stirling, 1982-85; Convener, Church and Nation Committee, General Assembly, 1992-96; Chairman, Scottish Religious Advisory Committee, BBC, 1996-2001; Moderator, Church and Society Forum, Churches Together in Britain and Ireland, 1999-2002; Convener, Parish Development Fund, General Assembly, 2002-06; Director, Scottish Television, 2003-07. Warrack Lecturer on Preaching, 2000; Unitas Award, Union Seminary, 2008; Convener, World Mission Council, General Assembly, 2010-2014; Boys' Brigade Chaplain, UK and Ireland; Convener, McLellan Commission on Safeguarding in the Catholic Church in Scotland. Publications: Preaching for these People, 1997; Gentle and Passionate, 2001. Recreations: sport; travel; books; gardening. Address: (h.) 4 Liggars Place, Dunfermline KY12 7XZ.

McLellan, Douglas Richard, MD, FRCPath, FRCP (Glas), DipFM. Consultant, Victoria Infirmary/Southern General Hospital, Glasgow, since 1989; Honorary Senior Lecturer, Glasgow University, since 1989; b. 13.6.55, Glasgow; m., Caitriona; 3 s. Educ. High School of Glasgow; Glasgow University. Registrar in Pathology, Southern General Hospital, Glasgow, 1978-81; Honorary Senior Registrar in Neuropathology (MRC Head Injury Project), Institute of Neurological Sciences, Glasgow, 1981-84; Senior Registrar in Pathology, Western Infirmary, Glasgow, 1984-89. Recreations: bibliomania; Celtology. Address: (h.) 8 Calderwood Road, Newlands, Glasgow G43 2RP.

Maclellan, Professor Euphemia (Effie), FLCM, LGSM, CertPrimEd, DipRSA, BA (Hons), PhD, CPsychol, FHEA, CSci, AFBPsS. Research Professor of Education, School of Education, since 2010; Professor of Education, Department of Educational and Professional Studies, University of Strathclyde, 2005-09, Emeritus Professor, since 2009, Vice Dean (Research), 2005-09, Reader, Department of Educational Studies, since 2002; b. 09.09.47, Glasgow; m., Alasdair James Graham. Educ. Strathbungo Senior Secondary. Class Teacher, Primary Education, Glasgow, 1967-68; Assistant Teacher, in Residential Education, Argyll, 1968-73; Head Teacher, in Residential Education, Argyll, 1973-77; Class Teacher and Assistant Head Teacher in Primary Education, Glasgow (taught at all stages of the school), 1977-88; Lecturer, Department of Educational Studies, University of Strathclyde, 1988-96; Associate Lecturer, Open University, 1992-99; Senior Lecturer, Department of Educational Studies, University of Strathclyde, 1996-2002. Member: European Association for Research on Learning and Instruction, British Psychological Society, General Teaching Council (Scotland). Many publications in peer-reviewed journals. Address: (b.) School of Education, University of Strathclyde, Lord Hope Building, Glasgow G4 0LT; T.-0141 444 8064; e-mail: e.maclellan@strath.ac.uk

McLellan, Gavin. Director of Marketing, Fundraising & External Affairs, Aberlour - Scotland's Charity, since 2014; b. 1970. Educ. Park Mains High School (1987); University of Paisley (BSc Land Economics, 1994). Career: Head of Christian Aid Scotland, 2005-09; Director, Riverside Museum Appeal, 2009-2011; Head of Development, Culture & Sport Glasgow, 2009-2011; Head of Fundraising (Scotland), Maggie's Cancer Caring Centres, 2011-14. Rotating Chair, Disaster Emergency Committee Scotland, GCAP Scotland; Director, Stop Climate Chaos Scotland; Trustee, Natural Change Foundation, since 2013; Member, Royal Institution of Chartered Surveyors (1996). Address: Aberlour Child Care Trust, 36 Park Terrace, Stirling FK8 2JR.

McLellan, John Crawford, BA. Director, The Scottish Newspaper Society, since 2013; b. 8.2.62, Glasgow; m., Patricia; 2 s.; 1 d. Educ. Hutchesons' Grammar School; Stirling University; Preston Polytechnic. Chester Observer, 1984-86; NW Evening Mail, 1987-90; The Journal, Newcastle, 1990-93; Edinburgh Evening News, 1993-2001 (Editor, 1997-2001 and 2004-09); Editor, Scotland on Sunday, 2002-04; Editor, The Scotsman, 2009-2012; Director of Communications, Scottish Conservative Party, 2012-2013. Former Commissioner, Press Complaints Commission; former Member, Defence, Press and Broadcasting Advisory Committee; Honorary Professor, University of Stirling Media Studies Department. Recreations: rugby; football; music. Address: (b.) 21 Lansdowne Crescent, Edinburgh EH12 5EH; T.-0131 535 1064.

MacLennan, Gordon, BSc, DipMS. Chief Executive, Strathclyde Partnership for Transport, since 2010, Deputy Chief Executive, 2006-2010; b. 9.8.49, Johnstone; m., Mhairi S. Rodger; 1 s.; 1 d. Educ. Renfrew High School; Strathclyde University. Manufacturing Director, John Brown Engineering, 1985-96; Manufacturing Director, Alexanders, 1996-97; Chairman & Director, Anderson Precision Gears, 1997-98; Chief Executive, Business Ventures Ltd., 1998-2001; Senior Director, Business Growth, Scottish Enterprise Glasgow, 2001-06; Assistant Chief Executive, Operations, Strathclyde Partnership for Transport, 2006-2010. Director of Clydebank Economic Development Company, 1992-96; Non-Executive Director, Trafalgar House Construction (Regions) Limited, 1993-95; Deacon of the Incorporation of Hammermen of Glasgow, 1997-98 (Rolls Royce, Premier Apprentice Award, 1969, Incorporation of Hammermen, Prince Philip Prize, 1971). Director, Millar Motors Limited, since 1997; Chairman, Carrick Care Homes, 2000-04; Director, GDA Investments Limited, 2002-06; Trustee of the Scottish Enterprise Pension Scheme, 2003-06; Director, Targeting Innovation, 2003-06; Chairman, Glasgow Exports Ltd, 2004-06; Director, Strathclyde University Incubator Limited, 2005-06; Trustee, Trades House of Glasgow, since 2007; Board Member, Gaelic Media Service, 2008-2012. Recreations: business strategy; Isle of Lewis, its people and culture. Address: (b.) Consort House, 12 West George Street, Glasgow G2 1HN; T.-0141 333 3100.
E-mail: garenin@gmail.com

McLennan, John Alan, DipArch (Glas), RIBA, FRIAS, FASI, MCIArb, MAPS, MAPM, FCIOB. Director, The McLennan Partnership Ltd.; b. 29.3.50, Rutherglen; m., Jemima; 1 d. Educ. Rutherglen Academy; Glasgow University. Past President, Glasgow Institute of Architects; Past Deacon, The Incorporation of Masons of Glasgow and The Incorporation of Tailors of Rutherglen; Past President of The Bridgeton Burns Club. Recreations: bowling; gardening. Address: Burnside House, Beech Avenue, High Burnside, Glasgow G73 4RJ; T.-0141-631 3322.
E-mail: alan.mclennan@mclarchitects.co.uk

Maclennan of Rogart, Rt. Hon. Lord (Robert Adam Ross Maclennan), PC. Liberal Democrat Spokesman on Cabinet Office and Scotland, House of Lords, since 2005; MP (Lib. Dem.), Caithness, Sutherland and Easter Ross, 1999-2001 (MP, Caithness and Sutherland, 1966-99); Barrister-at-Law; b. 26.6.36, Glasgow; m., Helen Cutter

Noyes; 2 s.; 1 d. Educ. Glasgow Academy; Balliol College, Oxford; Trinity College, Cambridge; Columbia University, New York. Parliamentary Private Secretary to Secretary of State for Commonwealth Affairs, 1967; Opposition Spokesman on Scottish Affairs and Defence, 1970; Parliamentary Under-Secretary of State, Department of Prices and Consumer Protection, 1974-79; Opposition Spokesman on Foreign Affairs, 1979; Member, Public Accounts Committee, 1979-99; Founder Member, SDP, 1981; Parliamentary Spokesman on Agriculture, 1981, Home Affairs, 1983, Economic Affairs, 1987; elected Leader, SDP, 1987; President, Liberal Democrats, 1994-98; Lib Dem Spokesman on Home Affairs and Arts, 1988-94, Constitutional Affairs and Culture, 1994-2001, and on Europe, 2001-05; Alternate Member, Convention on Future of Europe, 2002-03; Liberal Democrat Lords Spokesman on Cabinet Office and Constitution, since 2006. Recreations: music; theatre; visual arts. Address: (b.) House of Lords, London SW1A 0PW; T.-020 7219 4133.

McLeod, Dr Aileen. MSP (SNP), South Scotland, 2011-16; Minister for Environment, Climate Change and Land Reform, 2014-16; b. 24.8.71, East Kilbride. Educ. Edinburgh University; University of Central Lancashire. Joined the SNP in 2004 on leaving post in the Scottish Parliament; spent 5 years living in Brussels and working as Head of Policy for Alyn Smith MEP; returned home in 2009 to fight the European Parliamentary elections for the SNP; Parliamentary Assistant to Michael Russell MSP, 2009-2011.

MacLeod, Alasdair Fraser, MA (Hons). Head of Editorial Standards and Compliance, BBC Scotland, since 2009; b. 11.1.64, Inverness; m., Catriona Murray; 1 s.; 2 d. Educ. Millburn Academy, Inverness; Glasgow University. BBC Scotland: trainee journalist, Radio Nan Gaidheal, 1986; Researcher, Gaelic television, 1987; Producer, Radio Nan Gaidheal, 1988; Producer, Radio Scotland, 1990; Senior Producer, Radio Scotland, 1993; Editor, weekly programmes, News and Current Affairs, 1994; Editor, Scottish Parliamentary Unit, 1999; Executive Editor, Political Programmes, 2004; Executive Editor, News Programmes, 2007. Address: (b.) BBC Scotland, Pacific Quay, Glasgow G51 1DA.

MacLeod, Donald Roderick, LLB, QC, DipFMS. Queen's Counsel (in Practice at The Scottish Bar), since 2005; Advocate (in Practice at The Scottish Bar), since 1978; b. 24.09.48, Inverness; m., Susan Mary (nee Fulton); 2 d. Educ. High School of Stirling; University of Glasgow. Solicitor, 1973-78; Advocate, 1978-2005; sometime Temporary Sheriff. Labour Parliamentary Candidate, Kinross and W. Perthshire, 1979; Elder, Greenbank Church of Scotland; Member of Board, Scottish Medico-Legal Society; Hon. Secretary, Faculty of Advocates Criminal Bar Association; currently writing book on Firearms Law. Recreations: angling; tying classic salmon flies; music; opera; walking. Address: Advocates Library, Parliament House, Edinburgh; T.-0131-260-5607.

McLeod, Fiona. MSP (SNP), Strathkelvin and Bearsden, 2011-16; Acting Minister for Children and Young People, 2014-15; b. 3.12.57; m.; 1 s. Graduated in medieval and modern history at Glasgow University. A chartered librarian, has worked in education and the health service. SNP regional list member of the Scottish Parliament, 1999-2003.

MacLeod, Professor Iain Alasdair, BSc, PhD, CEng, FIES, FICE, FIStructE. Professor Emeritus; Professor of Structural Engineering, Strathclyde University, 1981-2004;

b. 4.5.39, Glasgow; m., Barbara Jean Booth; 1 s.; 1 d. Educ. Lenzie Academy; Glasgow University. Design Engineer, Crouch and Hogg, Glasgow, 1960-62; Assistant Lecturer in Civil Engineering, Glasgow University, 1962-66; Design Engineer, H.A. Simons Ltd., Vancouver, 1966-67; Structural Engineer, Portland Cement Association, Illinois, 1968-69; Lecturer in Civil Engineering, Glasgow University, 1969-73; Professor and Head, Department of Civil Engineering, Paisley College of Technology, 1973-81; Chairman, Scottish Branch, Institution of Structural Engineers, 1985-86; Vice-President, Institution of Structural Engineers, 1989-90; Member, Standing Committee on Structural Safety, 1989-97; President, Institution of Engineers and Shipbuilders in Scotland, 2012-14. Recreations: hill walking; sailing. Address: (b.) Department of Civil Engineering, Strathclyde University, 75 Montrose Street, Glasgow G1 1XJ.

McLeod, Ian, DA, RSW. Artist; Tutor in Drawing and Painting (part-time), Glenrothes College, 1994-2004; retired; b. 27.6.39, Port Glasgow; m., Mary N. B. Rintoul; 1 s.; 1 d. Educ. Kirkcaldy High School; Burntisland Secondary School; Edinburgh College of Art; Regent Road Institute for Adult Education; Moray House Institute of Education. Welder, Burntisland Shipbuilding Co., Fife, 1954-61; Teacher of Art, Auchmuty High School, Fife, 1967-90; 10 one-man exhibitions; various Scottish Arts Council exhibitions including: Scottish Realism: Bellany, Crozier, Gillon, McLeod and Moffat, 1971, Facts and Fantasy, 1972, Expressionism in Scottish Painting, 1977; over 50 group exhibitions; work in private and public collections. Elected: SSA, 1968, GLA, 1978, RSW, 1996. Recreations: people; books; all kinds of music, especially popular 30s and 40s; left-wing politics; detesting New Labour; hoping for an independent Scotland in his lifetime; gentle hillwalking. Address: (h.) 33 Craigkennochie Terrace, Burntisland, Fife KY3 9EN; T.-01592 873440; e-mail: ianmcleodrsw@aol.com

Macleod, Iseabail Campbell, MA. Editorial Consultant, Scottish Language Dictionaries Ltd., since 2002; b. 27.5.36, Glasgow. Educ. Clydebank High School; Lenzie Academy; Glasgow University. Teacher, 1958-64; Editorial Assistant, Europa Publications, 1965-66; Editor of bilingual dictionaries, Collins, Glasgow, 1966-74; Dictionaries Editor, Editorial Director, W. & R. Chambers, Edinburgh, 1974-77; freelance editor, since 1977; Editorial Director, Scottish National Dictionary Association Ltd., 1986-2002. Publications: Pocket Guide to Scottish Words, 1986, 2nd edition, 2006; Mrs. McLintock's Receipts for Cookery and Pastry-Work (editor), 1986; Glasgow The Official Guide, 1987; Pocket Scots Dictionary (Co-Editor), 1988; Scots Thesaurus (Co-Editor), 1990; Concise English-Scots Dictionary (Co-Editor), 1993; Scots School Dictionary (Co-Editor), 1996; Edinburgh Pocket Guide, 1996; Ilustrated Encyclopedia of Scotland (General Editor), 2004; New Supplement to Scottish National Dictionary (Co-Editor), 2005; About Scotland: People, Places, Heritage (General Editor), 2007; Scotland in Definition: A History of Scottish Dictionaries (Co-Editor), 2012; Scots: Studies in its Literature and Language (Co-Editor), 2013. Recreations: hill-walking; cooking; languages; music. Address: (h.) 11 Scotland Street, Edinburgh EH3 6PU; T.-0131-556 5683; e-mail: i.macleod@tinyworld.co.uk

MacLeod, Professor James Summers, BA, LLM, CA, FTII. Honorary Professor, Department of Accountancy, Edinburgh University, since 1984; b. 3.8.41, Dumfries; m., (1.) Sheila Stromier (deceased); (2.) Rosemary Hoy; 2 s.; 1 d. Educ. Dumfries Academy; Glasgow University. Lecturer, Edinburgh University, 1965-68; Lecturer, Heriot Watt University, 1968-71; joined Arthur Young (now Ernst & Young), 1971; Partner, Ernst & Young, Edinburgh, 1973-

98; Director, British Assets Trust PLC, Scottish Investment Trust PLC and other companies, 1998-2015. Publications: Taxation of Insurance Business (Co-author), 4th edition, 1998; 250 papers. Recreations: bridge; music; reading. Address: (h.) 50 New Swanston, Edinburgh; T.-0131-445 4748.

MacLeod of MacLeod, Hugh. 30th Chief of Clan MacLeod; b. 24.07.73, London; m., Frederique Feder; 1 s. Succeeded to title, 2007. Address: (h.) Dunvegan Castle, Isle of Skye IV55 8WF; T.-01470 521 206.

MacLeod, Rev. John. Moderator of General Assembly of the Free Church of Scotland (Continuing), 2006; Principal Clerk of Assembly, Free Church of Scotland (Continuing), since 2000; Minister, Tarbat Free Church, Portmahomack, since 1978; b. 14.5.48, Fearn; m., Joy Morrison; 7 s.; 2 d. Educ. Tain Royal Academy; Aberdeen University. Pensions Legal Department, Standard Life Assurance, 1969-71; Missioner to Aberdeen students, 1974-75; Highland Church, Vancouver, 1976; Supply Preacher, Toronto, Detroit and Prince Edward Island, 1976-78; Clerk to Training of Ministry Committee, Free Church of Scotland, 1985-2001. Recreations: squeezing quarts into pint pots and getting blood out of stones. Address: Free Church Manse, Portmahomack, Tain; T.-0845 1297055; e-mail: principalclerk@fccontinuing.org

Macleod, John Francis Matheson, MA, LLB, NP. Solicitor in Inverness, 1959-94; b. 24.1.32, Inverness; m., Alexandra Catherine (deceased); 1 s. Educ. Inverness Royal Academy; George Watson's College; Edinburgh University. Solicitor, Fife County Council, 1957-59; in private practice, 1959-94; Parliamentary candidate (Liberal): Moray and Nairn, 1964, Western Isles, 1966; Chairman, Highland Region, Scottish Liberal Party, until 1978; former Vice-Chairman, Broadcasting Council for Scotland; Dean, Faculty of Solicitors of the Highlands, 1988-91; Chairman, Crofters Commission, 1978-86; Member, Council, Law Society of Scotland, 1988-92; Chairman of Council, Gaelic Society of Inverness, 1996-97, Chief for 2005; Chairman, National Trust for Scotland's Culloden Advisory Panel, 2006-2011. Address: (h.) Bona Lodge, Aldourie, Inverness; T.-01463 751327.

MacLeod, John Murray, MA (Hons). Journalist; Writer at Large: Columnist, The Scotsman, 1990-92; Columnist, The Herald, 1991-2002; Columnist, Scottish Daily Mail, since 2002; b. 15.4.66, Kilmallie, Inverness-shire. Educ. Jordanhill College School, Glasgow; James Gillespie's High School, Edinburgh; Edinburgh University. Freelance journalist and writer, since 1988; Scottish Journalist of the Year, 1991; Young Scottish Journalist of the Year, 1991, 1992; Runner-up, Columnist of the Year, 1992, 2008; Runner-up, Feature Writer of the Year, 1996; nominations for Columnist of the Year, 1999, 2001 and 2003; Columnist of the Year, UK Press Gazette Regional Newspaper Awards, 1996. Publications: No Great Mischief If You Fall – The Highland Experience, 1993; Highlanders – A History of the Gaels, 1996; Dynasty – The Stuarts 1560-1807, 1999; Banner in the West - A Spiritual History of Lewis and Harris, 2008; When I Heard The Bell - The Loss of the Iolaire, 2009; Banner in the West, 2010; River of Fire, 2010; None Dare Oppose, 2011. Recreations: walking; cooking; gawking at car ferries. Address: (h.) Drover's Rest, Marybank, Isle of Lewis HS2 0DG; T.-mobile 07776-236-337; 01851-700-275.
E-mail: jm.macleod@btinternet.com

MacLeod, Lorne Buchanan, BA, CA. Chairman, Community Land Scotland, since 2015; Chartered Accountant; b. 13.4.63, Oban. Educ. Oban High School; University of Strathclyde. Ernst and Whinney, Inverness, 1983-87; Highlands and Islands Development Board, 1987-92; Chief Executive, Skye and Lochalsh Enterprise, 1992-98; Director of Strengthening Communities, Highlands and

Islands Enterprise, 1998-2000. Director, Comunn na Gaidhlig, 1998-2000; Director, Highlands and Islands Screen Services Ltd., 1998-2000; Board Member, Community Fund, 2001-03. Council Member, Scottish Further Education Funding Council, 2001-05; Director: Isle of Gigha Heritage Trust, 2002-08, Oban War and Peace Museum, 2003-07; Chairman, Highlands & Islands Community Energy Company, 2004-08; Director: Gigha Renewable Energy Ltd., 2004-08, Jansvans Limited, since 2001, Canan Limited, 2006-11, Cal Mac Ferries Limited, 2006-2012, David MacBrayne Limited, 2006-2012, South Uist Estates, 2007-2012, Northlink Ferries Ltd. 2009-11, Community Land Scotland, since 2014; Winston Churchill Travelling Fellowship, 1997. Recreations: hillwalking; gardening. Address: Orasaig, Crannaig-a-Mhinister, Oban, Argyll PA34 4LU; e-mail: lorne.macleod@btconnect.com

McLeod, Professor Malcolm Donald, CBE, MA, BLitt (Oxon), FRSE, FSA Scot. Vice-Principal, Advancement, University of Glasgow, 1999-2005, Pro Vice-Principal, 2005-06; Trustee, The Hunterian Museum, London, since 1998; b. 19.5.41, Edinburgh; 2 s.; 1 d. Educ. Birkenhead School; Hertford and Exeter Colleges, Oxford. Research Assistant, Institute of Social Anthropology, Oxford, 1964-65; Lecturer, Sociology Department, University of Ghana, 1967-69; Assistant Curator, Museum of Archaeology and Ethnology, Cambridge, 1969-74; College Lecturer and Director of Studies, Magdalene and Girton Colleges, Cambridge, 1969-74; Fellow, Magdalene College, 1972-74; Keeper of Ethnography, British Museum, 1974-90; Director, Hunterian Museum and Art Gallery, Glasgow University, 1990-99; Honorary Lecturer, Department of Anthropology, UCL, 1976-81; Honorary Lecturer, Department of Archaeology, University of Glasgow, 1992-2006; Chairman, Scottish Museums Council, 1996-2001; Curator, The Royal Society of Edinburgh, 1999-2002; Chairman, Caledonian Foundation Inc., USA, 2003-07; Trustee, National Museum of Scotland, 2005-2013; Trustee, Borders Sculpture Park, since 2013. Publications: The Asante, 1981; Treasures of African Art, 1981; Ethnic Sculpture (Co-author), 1985; Jacob Epstein Collector (Co-author), 1989; Peter Manuel, Serial Killer (Co-author), 2009. Address: (h.) The Schoolhouse, Oxnam, Jedburgh TD8 6NB.

Macleod, Mary Elizabeth, LLB (Hons), DipLP, NP. Depute Solicitor of the Church of Scotland, since 1995; b. 23.12.63, Stornoway. Educ. Nicolson Institute, Stornoway; Edinburgh University. Trainee Solicitor, Anderson, Shaw and Gilbert, Inverness, 1986-88; Assistant: Morton, Fraser and Milligan, WS, Edinburgh, 1988-90, Skene, Edwards and Garson, W. S., Edinburgh, 1990-92, Campbell Smith, Edinburgh, 1992-95. Recreations: travel; music; reading. Address: (b.) 121 George Street, Edinburgh EH2 4YN; T.-0131-225 5722.

MacLeod, Sheriff Principal Norman Donald, QC, MA, LLB. Sheriff Principal of Glasgow and Strathkelvin, 1986-97; b. 6.3.32, Perth; m., Ursula Jane Bromley; 2 s.; 2 d. Educ. Mill Hill School; George Watson's Boys College; Edinburgh University; Hertford College, Oxford. Called to the Bar, 1956; District Officer and Crown Counsel, Colonial Service, East Africa, 1957-63; at the Bar, 1963-67; Sheriff at Glasgow, 1967-86; Commissioner, Northern Lighthouse Board, 1986-97 (Chairman, 1990-91); Visiting Professor of Law, Strathclyde University, 1986-97; Honorary Sheriff, North Strathclyde. Recreations: reading; gardening; music; photography. Address: (h.) 23 Lochhead Avenue, Lochwinnoch, Renfrewshire PA12 4AW; T.-01505 843340; e-mail: nandj@normanandjane.plus.com

McLeod, Olivia. Director of Children and Families, Scottish Government, since 2015; m.; 2 d. Career: policy adviser in the Number 10 Policy Unit; Home Office representative to the British Embassy in Washington; Head of Crime Reduction for the London Borough of Tower

Hamlets; voluntary sector work, establishing the Private Equity Foundation; Deputy Director, Care and Justice, Scottish Government; Director of Early Years and Childcare, Department for Education, Whitehall. Address: Scottish Government, Victoria Quay, Edinburgh EH6 6QQ; T.-0300 244 4000.

MacLeod, Peter, MCIBS. Retired Banker; Honorary Sheriff of North Strathclyde at Oban, since 1988; b. 9.6.33, Ruaig, Isle of Tiree; m., Jean MacDonald Buchanan; 2 s. Educ. Oban High School. Served as Captain, Royal Signals, AER; joined Royal Bank of Scotland, 1949; Bank Manager, Tobermory, Kinlochleven, Wick, Oban. Past Commodore and Trustee, Royal Highland Yacht Club; Past Chairman and Founder Treasurer, Oban Round Table; Founder Chairman, West Highland Anchorages and Moorings Association; President, Oban & Lorne Strathspey & Reel Society. Publication: History of Royal Highland Yacht Club, 1881-1999. Recreations: sailing; island wandering; impromptu ceilidhs; beachcombing. Address: (h.) The Wheelhouse, Ganavan, Oban, Argyll; T.-01631 563577.

MacLeod, Roderick Alexander Randle, BA, MBA, BD, DMin. Minister, Strath & Sleat, Isle of Skye, since 2015; formerly Minister, Parish Church of The Holy Trinity, St. Andrews (2004-2015); b. 16.2.65, Edinburgh; m., Annice (nee MacDonald); 1 s.; 2 d. Educ. Fettes College; Universities of Cambridge, Edinburgh, St. Andrews, Aberdeen and Pittsburgh Theological Seminary. Army: Short Service Limited Commission (SSLC), Queens Own Highlanders; Teaching: Schoolmaster, Loretto School, Musselburgh; Church: Assistant Minister, Portree, Isle of Skye; Parish Minister, Bracadale, Isle of Skye; Navy Chaplain, 40 Commando; Commando Training Centre; Royal Marines, Poole; Parish Minister, Holy Trinity, St. Andrews. Recreations: bagpipes; outdoor pursuits; travel. Address: Church of Scotland Manse, 6 Upper Breakish, Isle of Skye IV42 8PY; e-mail: rorymofg@gmail.com

MacLeod, Roderick John, BSc. Principal, The National Piping Centre, since 1996; b. 26.8.62, Johnstone; m., Margaret. Educ. Eastwood High School; University of Strathclyde. Mathematics Teacher, Cleveden Secondary School, Glasgow, 1983-93; Assistant Principal, Mathematics, Dalziel High School, Motherwell, 1993-96. Winner, Highland Society of London gold medals; winner, piping, National Mod; Editor, Piping Today. Publication: The Highland Bagpipe Tutor Book (Editor). Address: (h.) 12 Medrox Gardens, Condorrat, Cumbernauld; T.-0141 353 0220; e-mail: rmacleod@thepipingcentre.co.uk

Macleod, Rev. William, BSc, ThM. Minister, Knightswood Free Church (Continuing), since 2006; Principal, Free Church Seminary, 2002-2014; Editor, Free Church Witness; b. 2.11.51, Stornoway; m., Marion; 2 s.; 1 d. Educ. Aberdeen University; Free Church College; Westminster Seminary. Minister: Partick Free Church, Glasgow, 1976-93; Portree Free Church, 1993-2006. Editor, Free Church Foundations, 1997-2000; former Chairman, Portree High School Board. Recreations: gardening; fishing; reading. Address: (h.) 25 Branklyn Crescent, Academy Park, Glasgow G13 1GJ; T.-0141 959 0292; e-mail: william@themacleods.org.uk

McLusky, Donald S., BSc, PhD. Senior Lecturer in Marine Biology, Stirling University, 1977-2003; Editor, Estuarine Coastal and Shelf Science, 2000-2010; b. 27.6.45, Harrogate; m., Ruth Alicia Donald; 1 s.; 2 d. Educ. Latymer Upper School, London; Aberdeen University; Stirling University. Stirling University: Assistant Lecturer, 1968-70, Lecturer, 1970-77, Head of Department of Biological Sciences, 1985 and 1992-98. Member, Council, Scottish Marine Biological Association, 1976-82, and 1985-91; Member, Scientific Advisory Committee, Scottish Natural Heritage, 1999-2005; Trustee, Estuarine and Coastal Sciences Association; Chair, Central Scotland Valuation Appeal Committee. Publications: Ecology of Estuaries, 1971; The Estuarine Ecosystem, 2004; The Natural Environment of the Estuary and Firth of Forth, 1987; The Estuaries of Central Scotland, 1997; Central Scotland, Land, Wildlife, People, 1993; The Freshwaters of Scotland, 1994; Treatise on Estuarine and Coastal Science, 2011. Recreations: nature; walking; swimming; travel. Address: (h.) Ardoch Cottage, Strathyre, Callander FK18 8NF; T.-01877 384309; e-mail: d.mclusky@btinternet.com

McMahon, Hugh Robertson, MA (Hons), FEIS. Member (Labour), European Parliament, Strathclyde West, 1984-99; Scottish Political Editor, World-Parliamentarian Magazine, since 1999; Lecturer/Consultant, James Watt College, 1999-2011 (retired); Lecturer, Politics, University of Edinburgh, 2003-2010; Visiting Professor, Brookdale CC, New Jersey, 2001; b. 17.6.38, Saltcoats; m., Helen Paterson Grant; 1 s.; 1 d. Educ. Stevenson High School; Ardrossan Academy; Glasgow University. Schoolteacher in Ayrshire (Largs High, Stevenston High, Irvine Royal Academy, Mainholm Academy); Assistant Head, Ravenspark Academy, 1971-84. Vice-Chair, EP Social Affairs, Employment and Working Environment Committee, 1992-94; Member, Social Affairs, Fisheries and Transport Committees; Chair, EP Delegation with Norway, 1989-92; Member: Delegation with Czechoslovakia, EIS, NUJ, GMB; Delegation with Hungary, 1994-96. Scottish Parliament Cross Party Group, Poland, since 2013; Chair, Paisley First Steering Group, 2011-15. Recreation: golf. Address: (b.) 9 Low Road, Castlehead, Paisley PA2 6AQ.

MacMahon, Rev. Janet P.H., BD, MSc, LCST, LLCM. Chaplain, Erskine Care Homes, Bishopton, 2010-11; Minister of Kilmaronock-Gartocharn Parish Church, 2006-09; Minister, Castlemilk West Parish Church, 2002-06; b. 31.5.44, Glasgow; m., Professor M.K.C. MacMahon (qv); 1 s.; 1 d. Educ. Glasgow High School for Girls; Glasgow University; Glasgow School of Speech Therapy. Senior Speech Therapist, 1965-80; Chief Speech Therapist, Greater Glasgow Health Board, 1980-82; Senior Speech Therapist, Capability Scotland, 1983-85; Assistant Minister, Cairns Church, Milngavie, and Govan Old Church, 1989-90; Research and Development Officer in special educational needs, Department of Education, Church of Scotland, 1990-92; Chaplaincy Co-ordinator, Southern General Hospital, Glasgow, 1992-2002. Publications include: Walk in God's Ways, 1993. Recreations: reading crime novels; watching TV soaps. Address: (h.) 14 Hillfoot Drive, Bearsden, Glasgow G61 3QQ; T.-0141-942 8611; e-mail: janetmacmahon@yahoo.co.uk

McMahon, Professor Malcolm Iain, BSc, PhD, DSc, FInstP. Professor of High Pressure Physics, The University of Edinburgh, since 2007; b. 13.01.65, Dundee. Educ. Carnoustie High School; The University of Edinburgh. Postdoctoral Research Associate, University of Edinburgh, 1990-96; Royal Society University Research Fellow: University of Liverpool, 1996-98, University of Edinburgh, 1998-2003; Reader in Physics, University of Edinburgh, 2002-07. Recreations: hillwalking; whisky appreciation. Address: (b.) School of Physics, The University of Edinburgh, Mayfield Road, Edinburgh EH9 3JZ; T.-0131 650 5956; e-mail: mim@ph.ed.ac.uk

McMahon, Michael, BA (Hons). MSP (Labour), Uddingston and Bellshill, 2011-16, Hamilton North and Bellshill, 1999-2011; Shadow Cabinet Secretary for Local

Government & Planning, 2009-2016; Convener, Public Petitions Committee, Scottish Parliament, 2003-07; Shadow Deputy Minister for Parliament and Labour Chief Whip, since 2007; Shadow Cabinet Secretary for Parliamentary Business, 2007-09; m.; 1 s.; 2 d. Educ. Our Lady's High School, Motherwell. Worked as a welder before leaving to go to university; then pursued a career in social and political research.

MacMahon, Professor Michael Kenneth Cowan, BA, PhD, DipLing, FBAAP, FRSA. Professor Emeritus of Phonetics, Glasgow University; b. 7.8.43, Winchester; m., Rev. Janet P.H. MacMahon (qv); 1 s.; 1 d. Educ. Hymers College, Hull; Durham University; Göttingen University; Glasgow University; Reading University. Lecturer in Phonetics and Linguistics, Jordanhill College, Glasgow, 1966-72; Lecturer in Linguistics and Phonetics, 1972-83, Lecturer in English Language, 1983-87, Senior Lecturer in English Language, 1987-97, Professor of Phonetics, 1997-2008, Glasgow University. Senate Assessor to the University Court, 1995-99. Governor, Hutchesons' Educational Trust, 2003-08; Treasurer, International Phonetic Association, 2003-08; President, Henry Sweet Society for the History of Linguistic Ideas, 2008-; Archivist and Secretary, British Association of Academic Phoneticians, 1978-2012. Publications: numerous. Recreations: researching and playing the flute; singing. Address: (h.) 7 Raeswood Gate, The Larches, Glasgow G53 7HF; e-mail: mike.macmahon@glasgow.ac.uk

McMahon, Siobhan. MSP (Labour), Central Scotland, 2011-16; b. 4.7.84. Graduated from Glasgow Caledonian University with a degree in politics. Worked for the Labour group in the Scottish Parliament and was a research assistant to Jim Murphy MP and Ken Macintosh MSP.

McManus, Professor John, DSc, PhD, ARCS, DIC, FRSE, FRSGS, CGeol. Professor of Geology, St. Andrews University, 1993-2001, now Emeritus Professor (Reader, 1988-93); Honorary Director, Tay Estuary Research Centre, 1979-92; b. 5.6.38, Harwich; m., J. Barbara Beveridge (deceased 2007); 2 s.; 1 d. Educ. Harwich County High School; Imperial College, London University. Assistant, then Lecturer, St. Andrews University, 1964-67; Lecturer, Senior Lecturer, Reader, Dundee University, 1967-88; UNESCO Representative, International Commission on Continental Erosion, 1980-84 and 1986; Member: Scottish Natural Heritage East Areas Board and Scientific Advisory Committee, 1992-99, Secretary of State's Committee on Waste Discharges into the Marine Environment; President, Estuarine and Brackish Water Sciences Association, 1995-98; Member, Executive, European Union for Coastal Conservation, 1997-2000; Member, Scottish Environment Protection Agency East Region Board, 2000-07; Member, Eden Estuary Nature Reserve Management Committee; former Treasurer, British Sedimentological Research Group; Consultant on Coastal Erosion and Protection to four Regional Councils; Honorary Fellow, Royal Scottish Geographical Society, since 2001; Trustee, Fife Folk Museum, 2011. Publications: Mining between Ceres and St Andrews, 2010; History of Coal Mining in the East Neuk of Fife, 2016; Executive Editor, Transactions of the Royal Society of Edinburgh, Earth Sciences, 1988-95; Associate Editor, Continental Shelf Research. President: Cupar Choral Association, 1968-78, Cupar Amateur Opera, 1979-91. Recreations: music; East Fife Male Voice Choir; Fife Folk Museum. Address: (b.) School of Geography and Geology, Irvine Building, St. Andrews University, St. Andrews, Fife KY16 9AL; e-mail: jm@st-andrews.ac.uk

McManus, Very Rev. Mathew Francis. Parish Priest, St. Peter-in-Chains, Ardrossan, since 2004; b. 22.9.40, Rutherglen. Educ. Sacred Heart High School, Girvan; St. Andrew's College, Drygrange, Melrose. Assistant Priest, St. Margaret's, Ayr, 1965-76; Chaplain: Ayr County Hospital, 1967-76, Queen Margaret Academy, Ayr, 1968-

79; Member, Strathclyde Childrens Panel Advisory Committee, 1970-75; Parish Priest: New Cumnock, Kirkconnel and Sanquhar, 1976-81, Kirkcudbright, 1981-88, St. Winin's, Kilwinning, 1988-2004; Chairman: Dumfries and Galloway Local Health Council, 1983-87, Castle Douglas Dumfries District CAB, 1984-87, Stewartry Council of Volunary Service, 1985-88; Member: Stewartry School Council, 1985-87, Scottish Consumer Council, 1983-90; Convenor, Association of Scottish Local Health Councils, 1983-92; Complaints Reporter, Law Society of Scotland, 1985-87; Secretary, Association of Vocations Directors of Scotland, 1987-96; Member, Ayrshire and Arran Health Council, 1988-97; Non-Executive Director, Ayrshire and Arran Health Board, 1997-2001; Member, Ayrshire and Arran Health Council, 2001-07; Chair, Ayrshire and Arran Research Ethics Committee, 2001-2010; Member: Scotland Research Ethics Committee, since 2005, North Ayrshire Education Committee, since 1998; Founding Member, Chair, Minerva Housing Association, 1990-2008; Member: National Appeals Panel (Pharmacy), since 1997; Lay Partner, Health Professions Council, 2001-04; Custody Visitor, Police Service Scotland, since 2001; Chair, Interim School Board; new Denominational school for North Ayrshire; Member, CHI Group of Scottish Health Service, since 2008; appointed Canon of the Galloway Diocese, 2009; Member, St. Matthew's Academy Parent Council, since 2005; Member, West of Scotland Research Ethics Service, since 2010. Address: St. Peter's, 1 South Crescent Road, Ardrossan KA22 8DU; T.-01294 464063; mob: 07711 888244; e-mail: mattmcmanus@btconnect.com

McMenamin, Frances Jane, QC, BA, LLB, DUniv. Queen's Counsel, since 1998; b. 21.5.51, Glasgow; m., Ian McCarry. Educ. Notre Dame High School, Glasgow; Strathclyde University. Legal apprenticeship, Hughes, Dowdall & Co., Solicitors, Glasgow, 1974-76; Procurator Fiscal Depute, 1976-84; devilling at Scottish Bar, 1984-85; admitted, Faculty of Advocates, 1985; Junior Counsel practising in criminal law, 1985-98; Temporary Sheriff, 1991-97; Advocate Depute, 1997-2000; criminal defence work, since 2000; Visiting Lecturer, Scottish Police College, Tulliallan, since 1991. Member, Strathclyde University Law School Advisory Panel, since 2000; Director of Faculty Services Ltd., 2003-07; Member of Management Committee of Faculty of Advocates Free Legal Advice Unit, 2005-09; Member of Court, Strathclyde University, 2005-09; Vice Chairperson, Faculty of Advocates Criminal Bar Association, 2007-08; Member, Scottish Criminal Cases Review Commission, since 2010. Awarded Honorary Doctorate, University of Strathclyde, May 2009; appointed Member of Lord Bonomy's Post-Corroboration Review Group, 2014; Member, The Merchants House of Glasgow, since 2015. Recreations: golf; exercise classes; Argentinian tango; reading; travelling with her husband. Address: (h.) 59 Hamilton Drive, Glasgow G12 8DP; T.-0141-339 0519; (b.) Advocates Library, Parliament House, Edinburgh EH1 1RF; T.-0131-226 5071.

McMicking, Major David John, LVO, MSc. Consultant, Human Resources/Sporting, since 1986; b. 29.4.39, Jerusalem; m., Janetta; 1 s.; 1 d. Educ. Eton; RMA, Sandhurst; Strathclyde University. Career soldier, Black Watch, rising to rank of Major; left Army, 1973; executive positions, John Menzies Holdings Ltd., 1973-86; family farming interests, since 1996. Formerly Extra Equerry, Queen Elizabeth The Queen Mother; Chairman, Officers Association Scotland; Director, Earl Haig Fund Scotland, 1997-2000; Secretary, Friends of St. Andrew's, Jerusalem, 1994-2007. Recreation: field sports. Address: (b.) Drumknock, Kilry, Blairgowrie PH11 8HR; T.-01575 560731.

McMillan, Alan Charles, MA (Hons), LLB, DipLP, LLM (Dist), NP. Partner, Commercial Dispute Resolution, Burness LLP, since 2005; b. 5.12.64, Hamilton; m., Isla; 2

s.; 1 d. Educ. Garrion Academy; University of Edinburgh. Teacher of English as a Foreign Language, for Business Purposes in Spain, Thailand and Scotland, 1987-91; Trainee Solicitor, MacRoberts, 1995-96; Solicitor, Dundas & Wilson CS, 1996-2005. Co-Editor, "Dilapidations in Scotland" (2nd ed.); Chair, Property Litigation Association (Scotland); CEDR - accredited Mediator. Recreations: reading; cycling; music; languages. Address: (h.) 28 Inverleith Row, Edinburgh EH3 5QH; T.-0131-473-6141 (day); e-mail: alan.mcmillan@burness.co.uk

McMillan, Amanda. Chief Executive, AGS Airports Ltd. (United Kingdom-based owner of Aberdeen, Glasgow and Southampton Airports), since 2014. Address: (b.) St Andrew's Drive, Paisley PA3 2ST.

MacMillan of MacMillan and Knap, George Gordon, MA (Cantab). Chief of Clan MacMillan; b. 20.6.30, London; m., (Cecilia) Jane Spurgin (deceased 2005); 2 s. Educ. Aysgarth School; Eton; Trinity College, Cambridge. Schoolmaster, Wellington College, 1953-63; Lecturer, Trinity College, Toronto, 1963-64; Lecturer, Bede College, Durham, 1965-74. Resides in small historic house with gardens and woods open to the public. Address: (h.) Applehouse, Finlaystone, Langbank, Renfrewshire PA14 6TJ; T.-01475 540285; e-mail: chief@clanmacmillan.org

Macmillan, Very Rev. Gilleasbuig Iain, MA, BD. Minister, St. Giles', The High Kirk of Edinburgh, 1973-2013; Chaplain to the Queen in Scotland, since 1979; Dean of the Order of the Thistle, since 1989.

Macmillan, Gordon, MA (Hons). Head of News, Scotland, STV, since 2004. Educ. Perth Academy; University of Aberdeen. BBC News: Graduate News Trainee, 1982-83, Producer, 1983-87; BBC: Producer, BBC Scotland, 1987-90, Editor, Television News, 1990-95, Chief Assistant to MD, Regional Broadcasting, 1995-96; Senior Programme Editor, CNN, 1996-99. Address: (b.) STV, Pacific Quay, Glasgow G51 1PQ.

Macmillan, Sheriff Iain Alexander, CBE, LLD, BL. Sheriff of South Strathclyde, Dumfries and Galloway, at Hamilton, 1981-92; b. 14.11.23, Oban; m., Edith Janet McAulay; 2 s.; 1 d. Educ. Oban High School; Glasgow University; Scottish Commercial College. RAF (France, Germany, India), 1944-47; Solicitor (Sturrock & Co., Kilmarnock), 1952-81; Council Member, Law Society of Scotland, 1964-79 (President, 1976-77); Trustee, Glasgow Art Club, since 2005. Publication: I Had It From My Father. Recreation: music. Address: (h.) 2 Castle Drive, Kilmarnock, Ayrshire; T.-01563 525864; e-mail: mick.millan@virgin.net

McMillan, Sir Iain (Macleod), Kt, CBE, FCIB, FCIBS, FAIA, CCMI, FRSA, FSQA. Retired Director, CBI Scotland (1995-2014); Chairman, Scottish Business Education Coalition, 2002-07; Vice Chairman, Scottish Qualifications Authority (Chairman, International and Commercial Committee), 2004-06, Member, Board, 1997-2006; Non-Executive Director, Scottish Ambulance Service (Chairman, Audit Committee, 2000-08); Chairman, Scottish North American Business Council (Member, Board, since 1999); Member, Board, British American Business Council; Member, Executive Committee, British American Business Council; Member, Advisory Committee, Scottish Economic Policy Network (scotecon), 2002-07; Chairman, Advisory Board, University of Strathclyde Business School; Member, Advisory Board, Scottish Co-investment Fund, 2003-08; Member, Advisory Board, Scottish Enterprise Investments, 2008-2010; Chairman, The Industrial Mission Trust (Trustee, 2008-2013); Trustee, The Teaching Awards Trust, 2007-2013; Member, Commission on Scottish Devolution, 2008-09; Selected Air Member, Lowland Reserve Forces' and Cadets' Association; Member, Literacy Commission, 2008-2010; Trustee, The Carnegie Trust for the Universities of Scotland; Honorary Air Commodore, 602 (City of Glasgow) Squadron, Royal Auxiliary Air Force; Member, Scottish Advisory Committee SkillForce; Chairman, Independent Commission for Competitive and Fair Taxation in Scotland, 2015-2016; Chairman, Work Place Chaplaincy Scotland, 2014-2016; b. 25.4.51, Glasgow; m., Giuseppina; 3 s. Educ. Bearsden Academy. Trainee Banker, 1970-76; Manager, TSB Group plc, 1976-89; Liaison Officer for Scotland and Northern England, The Royal Jubilee and Prince's Trusts (secondment), 1984-85; Senior Manager, TSB Group plc, 1989-93; Assistant Director, CBI Scotland, 1993-95. Member, Scottish Advisory Board, Equal Opportunities Commission, 1995-2001; Chairman, Higher Still Employment and Training Group, 1997-2000; Member, Scottish Executive's Committee of Review into the Careers Service, 1999-2000; Member, Board, Young Enterprise Scotland, 1999-2003. Publications: Manufacturing Matters (Co-Author), 1994; The Challenge for Government in Scotland (Principal Author), 1996; Scottish Manufacturing: a shared vision (Co-Author), 1997; Business and Parliaments – Partners for Prosperity (Co-Author), 1998; Towards a Prosperous Scotland (Co-Author), 1999; Scotland's Economy: an agenda for growth (Co-Author), 2003; The Scottish Economy: The Priority of Priorities (Co-Author), 2006; Energising the Scottish Economy: a Business Agenda for Reform and Recovery, 2010. Recreations: reading; walking. Address: 11 Pirleyhill Gardens, Falkirk, Stirlingshire FK1 5NB.

Macmillan, James Loy, CBE, BMus, PhD. Composer and Conductor; Composer/Conductor, BBC Philharmonic, 2000-09; Affiliate Composer, Scottish Chamber Orchestra, since 1990; part-time Teacher, Royal Scottish Academy of Music and Drama, since 1989; Visiting Composer, Philharmonia, since 1991; Visiting Professor, University of Strathclyde, since 1997; b. 16.7.59, Kilwinning; m., Lynne; 2 d.; 1 s. Educ. Cumnock Academy; Edinburgh University; Durham University. Principal compositions: The Confession of Isobel Gowdie, London Proms, 1990; Busqueda, Edinburgh International Festival, with Diana Rigg, 1990; featured composer, Musica Nova, 1990, Huddersfield Contemporary Music Festival, 1991; Veni, Veni, Emmanuel, percussion concerto for Evelyn Glennie, London Proms, 1992; Visitatio Sepulchri, one act opera, Mayfest, 1993; Ines de Castro, for Scottish Opera, Edinburgh International Festival, 1996; The World's Ransoming, for orchestra and cor anglaise, 1996; Cello Concerto, 1996; Symphony: Vigil, 1997; featured composer, Edinburgh International Festival, 1993; recording of Tryst and The Confession of Isobel Gowdie by BBC SSO won Gramophone Award, contemporary music category, 1993; Seven Last Words, BBC TV, 1994; Raising Sparks, 1997, for chamber ensemble; String Quartet: Why Is This Night Different?, 1988; featured composer, Raising Sparks Festival, South Bank Centre, London, 1997 (South Bank Show Award for Classical Music, 1997); Evening Standard Classical Music Award, 1997 for Outstanding Artistic Achievement for Symphony: Vigil and Raising Sparks Festival; Quickening, 1998; Mass, 2000; Cello Sonata no2 dedicated to Julian Lloyd Webber; The Birds of Rhiannon, 2001; O Bone Jesu, 2001; Piano concerto No.2, 2003; A Scotch Bestiary, 2004; Sundogs, 2006; The Sacrifice, 2007; St John Passion, 2008; Violin Concerto, 2010; Oboe Concerto, 2010. Honorary Fellow, Blackfriars Hall, University of Oxford; Patron: St Mary's Music School, Edinburgh, London Oratory School Schola Cantorum. DUniv, (Paisley); DLitt (University of Strathclyde); FRASMD; HonFRIAS.

Macmillan, Emeritus Professor (John) Duncan, MA, PhD, LID, FRSA, FRSE, HRSA. Emeritus Professor of the History of Scottish Art, Edinburgh University; Curator, Talbot Rice Gallery, Edinburgh University, 1979-2004; Hon. Curator, Royal Society of Edinburgh, 2008-2012; Art

Critic, The Scotsman; b. 7.3.39, Beaconsfield; m., Vivien Rosemary Hinkley; 2 d. Educ. Gordonstoun School; St. Andrews University; London University; Edinburgh University. Lecturer, then Senior Lecturer, then Reader, then Professor, Department of Fine Art, Edinburgh University. Recreation: walking. Address: (h.) 20 Nelson Street, Edinburgh; T.-0131-556 7100.

Macmillan, John Ernest Newall, LLB, NP. Employment Partner, MacRoberts Dundee, since 2013; Managing Partner, MacRoberts Glasgow, 1998-2005; b. 27.9.56, Kilmarnock; m., Caroline Elizabeth; 2 s.; 2 d. Educ. Merchiston Castle School, Edinburgh; Dundee University. Apprenticeship, Bird Semple and Crawford Herron, Glasgow, 1978-80; Solicitor, J. and J. Sturrock & Co., Kilmarnock, 1980-82; Solicitor, MacRoberts Glasgow, 1982-86, Partner (Litigation and Employment), since 1986 (moved to Dundee in 2013), Managing Partner, 1998-2005 and since 2014; Board Member, EELA. Former Captain, Kilmarnock (Barassie) Golf Club. Recreations: golf; skiing; bridge; travel. Address: (b.) 5 West Victoria Dock Street, Dundee DD1 3JT.

E-mail: john.macmillan@macroberts.com

McMillan, Joyce Margaret, MA (Hons), DipEd, DLitt. h.c. (Queen Margaret Univ. College). Journalist and Arts Critic; Theatre Critic and Columnist, The Scotsman, since 1998; b. 29.8.52, Paisley. Educ. Paisley Grammar School; St. Andrews University; Edinburgh University. Theatre Reviewer, BBC Radio Scotland and The Scotsman, 1979-81; Theatre Critic, Sunday Standard, 1981-83; Radio Critic, The Herald, 1983-95; Scottish Theatre Critic, The Guardian, 1984-93; Scotland on Sunday: Social/Political Columnist, 1989-97, Theatre Critic, 1993-97; Arts/Political Columnist, The Herald, 1997-98. Chair, NUJ Freelance Branch, Edinburgh; Member, National Executive Committee, NUJ, London; Member, Consultative Steering Group on the Scottish Parliament, 1998-99; Member, Scottish National Theatre Working Group, 2000-01; Chair, Hansard Society Working Group, Scotland; Visiting Professor, Drama and Creative Industries, Queen Margaret University, Edinburgh, since 2006. Publications: The Traverse Story, 1963-88, 1988; Charter for the Arts in Scotland, 1992. Recreations: food; drink; films; music; talking politics. Address: 8 East London Street, Edinburgh, EH7 4BH; T.-0131-557 1726.

McMillan, Malcolm. Chief Executive, Scottish Law Commission, since 2008; b. 27.3.55, Ayr; m., Mary Clare Campbell; 3 d. Educ. Royal High School, Edinburgh; University of Edinburgh. Admitted as Solicitor in 1979; Legal Assistant, Argyll and Bute District Council, 1979-80; Legal Adviser in the Office of Solicitor to the Secretary of State for Scotland, 1982-99; Deputy Legal Secretary to the Lord Advocate, 1999-2003; Divisional Solicitor for the Rural Affairs Division in the Scottish Government Legal Directorate, 2003-08. Recreations: walking; swimming. Address: (b.) Scottish Law Commission, 140 Causewayside, Edinburgh EH9 1PR; T.-0131 668 2131; e-mail: malcolm.mcmillan@scotlawcom.gsi.gov.uk

Macmillan, Cllr Mark. Leader, Renfrewshire Council, since 2012; represents Paisley South West (Labour). Board membership: Renfrewshire Council, Education Policy Board, Emergencies Board, Leadership Board, Paisley South Local Area Committee, Sport, Leisure & Culture Policy Board. T.-0300 300 1286.

E-mail: cllr.mark.macmillan@renfrewshire.gov.uk

McMillan, Michael Dale, BSc, LLB, NP, FFCS. Consultant, Burnett & Reid LLP, Solicitors, Aberdeen (formerly Managing Partner); Senior Tutor, The University of Aberdeen Law School, since 2000; b. 15.2.44, Edinburgh; m., Isobel Ross Mackie; 2 s.; 1 d. Educ. Edinburgh Academy; Edinburgh University. Partner, Macdonalds Sergeants, Solicitors, East Kilbride and

Glasgow, 1971-92; Secretary: East Kilbride Chamber of Commerce, 1971-86, East Kilbride Chamber of Trade, 1971-92; Board Member, East Kilbride Development Corporation, 1979-84; Secretary, Pilgrim Legal Users' Group, 1985-92; Captain, East Kilbride Golf Club, 1979; Chairman, Strathaven Academy School Board, 1991-92; President, East Kilbride Burns Club, 1989-91; Captain, Inchmarlo Golf Club (Banchory), 1997-99; President, Deeside Musical Society, 1998-2000 and 2007-08 and Treasurer, since 2004; Burgess of Guild, City of Aberdeen. Recreations: golf; sailing; gardening. Address: (h.) Belnies, Strachan, Banchory, Aberdeenshire AB31 6LU; T.-01330 850249.

E-mail: mike.mcmillan@me.com

McMillan, Stuart, MBA, BA (Hons). MSP (SNP), Greenock and Inverclyde, since 2016 (West of Scotland region, 2007-2016); b. 6.5.72, Barrow-in-Furness; m., Alexandra; 2 d. Educ. Port Glasgow High School; University of Abertay, Dundee. Supply Analyst, IBM UK Ltd., Greenock, 1998-2000; Parliamentary Researcher, SNP Whips Office, Westminster, London, 2000-03; Office Manager, Bruce McFee MSP, Scottish Parliament, 2003-07. Recreations: play bagpipes; sport; travel. Address: (b.) Scottish Parliament, Edinburgh EH99 1SP; e-mail: stuart.mcmillan.msp@scottish.parliament.uk; Constituency Office: 4 Argyle Street, Greenock PA15 1XA; T.-01475 720930.

McMillan, Professor Thomas Murray, BSc, MAppSci, PhD, FBPsS. Professor of Clinical Neuropsychology, Glasgow University, since 1999; Adviser to Greater Glasgow Health Board, since 1999; b. 7.3.54, Prestwick; m., Sarah Louise Wilson; 1 d. Educ. Prestwick High School; Ayr Academy; Aberdeen University; London University; Glasgow University. Lecturer in Clinical Psychology, Institute of Psychiatry, London; Head of Clinical Neuropsychology, St George's Healthcare, London; Professor of Clinical Psychology, Surrey University. Publications include: Handbook of Neurological Rehabilitation; Neurobehavioural Disability and Social Handicap. Recreations: cross-country running. Address: (b.) Mental Health and Wellbeing, University of Glasgow, Gartnavel Royal Hospital, Glasgow, G12 0XH; T.-0141-211 0354.

McMillan, William Alister, BL. Solicitor, since 1955; b. 19.1.34, Ayr; m., Elizabeth Anne; 3 d. Educ. Strathallan; Glasgow University. Clerk of the Peace, County of Ayr, 1974-75; Honorary Sheriff, Ayr; Hon. Governor, Strathallan School; Hon. President, Ayr RFC. Recreations: sailing; golf. Address: (h.) Afton Lodge, Mossblown, by Ayr; T.-01292 520 710.

Macmillan Douglas, Angus William, OBE, BA. Director, Douglas Gorham Consultancy Ltd., since 2008; former Director, National Support Services, NHS Scotland; National Director, Scottish Blood Transfusion Service, 1997-2004; b. 18.11.46, Edinburgh; m., Rosemary-Jane Meynell; 2 d. Educ. Blairmore School; Wellington College; Ealing Business School; INSEAD. Assistant UK Co-ordinator, British Petroleum International, 1981-84; Business Manager, BP Information Systems, 1984-85; European Developments Manager, BP Gas International, 1985-88; Managing Director, East Africa Trading, British Petroleum, 1988-91; Head of Political Affairs, British Petroleum Group, 1991-96. Representative, East African Trade Organisation, 1988-91; Member, Energy Policy Committee, CBI, 1992-96; Member, Management Committee, Industry and Parliament Trust, 1992-96; Director, European Blood Alliance, 1998-2007;

Chairman, Angus Conservative Association, 2004-08; Chairman, UK Forum of Blood Services, 2001-04; Member, Royal Company of Archers (Queen's Bodyguard for Scotland); Governor, Kilgraston School, 1999-2005; Member, Scottish Conservative Policy Advisory Group; Member, Court, Abertay University; Chairman, New Club, since 2014; Member, Better Together Funding Board and Adviser to Better Together Campaign, 2014. Recreations: family; tennis; walking. Address: (b.) Brigton, Douglastown, by Forfar DD8 1TP; T.-01307-820-215.

McMurdo, Professor Marion Elizabeth Taylor, MBChB, MD, FRCPEdin, FRCPGlas, FRCPLond. Professor of Ageing and Health, University of Dundee, since 1997; Honorary Consultant, Medicine for the Elderly, Tayside Primary Care Trust, since 1997; b. Glasgow; m., Dr. Grant L. Hutchison. Educ. Marr College, Troon; University of Dundee. Deputy Medical Director, Drug Development (Scotland) Ltd., 1984-86; Lecturer in Geriatric Medicine, University of Dundee, 1986-88, Senior Lecturer/Reader in Ageing and Health; External Tutor to International Institute on Ageing, since 1997; Chair, UK NIHR ageing research network, 2009-2015. Recreations: golf; photography; cycling. Address: Ageing and Health, Mail Box 1, Ninewells Hospital and Medical School, Dundee DD1 9SY; T.-01382 383086.

McMurray, Professor John J.V., BSc (Hons), MBChB (Hons), MD, FRCP (Edin and Glas), FESC, FACC, FAHA, FRSE, FMedSci. Professor of Medical Cardiology, Glasgow University, since 1999; Honorary Consultant Cardiologist; Western Infirmary, Glasgow, 1995-2015; Queen Elizabeth University Hospital, Glasgow, since 2015; b. 17.12.58, Enniskillen, Co. Fermanagh; m., Christine; 5 s.; 1 d. Educ. St Patrick's College, Knock, Belfast; Manchester University. Consultant Cardiologist, Western General Hospital, Edinburgh, 1993-95. Publications: 700 medical and scientific papers; 15 books. Recreations: reading; travelling; Celtic FC. Address: (b.) British Heart Foundation Cardiovascular Research Centre, University of Glasgow G12 8TA; T.-0141-211 6311 and T.-0141 330 3479; Fax: 0141 330 6955.
E-mail: john.mcmurray@glasgow.ac.uk

Macnab of Macnab, James William Archibald. 24th Chief, Clan Macnab; b. 1963. Succeeded to title, 2013.

Macnair, Charles Neville, QC, LLB. Queen's Counsel, since 2002; Sheriff of Tayside, Central and Fife at Cupar, since 2009; Sheriff (floating), Tayside Central and Fife at Dunfermline, 2006-2009; b. 18.3.55, London; m., Patricia Anne Dinning; 2 d. Educ. Bryanston School; Aberdeen University. Commissioned, Queen's Own Highlanders, 1977-80; Solicitor, 1982-87; admitted, Faculty of Advocates, 1988; Part time Sheriff, 2005-06. Recreations: sailing; reading. Address: Sheriff Court House, County Buildings, St Catherine Street, Cupar KY15 4LX.

Macnair, William Peter Cameron, BA (Hons), MPhil, FRSA. Rhetorician, since 1993; Managing Director, Black Isle Communications Ltd., since 1996; Director of Operations, Burnwynd History and Art Ltd., since 2003; b. 19.1.46, Edinburgh; m., Charlotte Teresa (nee Doyle); 3 s. Educ. Charterhouse; London and St. Andrews. Army Officer Commissioned April 1971, Queens Own Highlanders; served Northern Ireland, Belize and Germany, left September 1992, Lieutenant Colonel. Scottish Parliamentary Candidate, Shettleston, 2007. High Constable of Edinburgh; Director, Order of Malta

Dial-A-Journey; Chairman, Gayfield Association; Secretary, Cuidich 'n Righ Club; Consul for Hashemite Kingdom of Jordan in Scotland. Recreations: reading; watercolours; walking. Address: (h.) 11 Windsor Street, Edinburgh EH7 5LA; T.-0131 478 0760; e-mail: willie@rhetoric.co.uk

McNairney, John. Chief Planner for the Scottish Government, since 2012. Career: practiced as a chartered town planner in local government, planning consultancy and, most recently, in central government over the last 30 years; joined the Scottish Office at devolution initially leading a range of planning and transport policy developments and subsequently implementation of the Scottish Executive's Freedom of Information legislation; appointed Assistant Chief Planner (2005) supporting development of the Planning (Scotland) Act and subsequently its implementation, the Delivering Planning Reform Agenda and the development of Scotland's ePlanning programme. Address: (b.) Victoria Quay, Edinburgh EH6 6QQ.
E-mail: John.McNairney@scotland.gsi.gov.uk

McNally, John. MP (SNP), Falkirk, since 2015; m., Sandra; 2 c. Elected with a vote of 34,831, a majority of 19,701 over his nearest rival (the largest vote for a Scottish MP in the 2015 General Election, the largest majority for a Scottish MP in the 2015 General Election, and the highest amount of votes polled for any SNP candidate in any election in the history of the party). Elected to Falkirk council in 2005, after winning the Herbertshire by-election. Address: House of Commons, London SW1A 0AA.

Macnaughton, Rev. (Gordon) Fraser (Hay), MA, BD, DipCPC. Minister, St. Magnus Cathedral, Kirkwall, Orkney, since 2002; b. 27.3.58, Glasgow; m., Carole; 2 d. Educ. Glasgow Academy; Glasgow University; Edinburgh University. Assistant, Newlands South Church, Glasgow, 1981-85; Minister, Fenwick Parish Church, 1985-91; Chaplain, Dundee University, 1991-97; Parish Minister, Killermont Parish Church, Bearsden, 1997-2002. Coach to Scottish Universities Rugby XV, 1995-97. Recreations: rugby; bird-watching; conservation issues; history; volleyball; cycling; seafishing. Address: (h.) Cathedral Manse, Berstane Road, Kirkwall, Orkney KW15 1NA; T.-01856 873312; e-mail: macnaughton187@btinternet.com

McNaughton, James Leslie, LLB. Retired Solicitor; Safeguarder with Aberdeenshire Council, since 1996; Member, Grampian Valuation Panel; Honorary Sheriff at Banff, since 2005; b. 8.12.43, Aberdeen; m., Pauline nee Booth; 1 s.; 1 d. Educ. Robert Gordon's College, Aberdeen; Aberdeen University. Assistant, then Partner with Stewart and Watson, Solicitors, Banff, Turriff and elsewhere; retired. Past President: Rotary Club of Banff, Society of Solicitors of Banffshire, Banff Town and County Club. Recreations: golf; reading; walking; good food and wine. Address: (h.) 16 Campbell Street, Banff AB45 1JR; T.-01261-812349; e-mail: mcnaughton206@btinternet.com

McNaughton, John Ewen, OBE, FRAgS. Retired Justice of the Peace. Past Member, Scottish Beef Council; Chairman, Forth Valley Countryside Initiative, 1999-2003; b. 28.5.33, Edinburgh; m., Jananne Ogilvie Honeyman; 2 s.; 2 d. Educ. Cargilfield; Loretto. Born and bred a hill sheep farmer; after a short spell in America, began farming at Inverlochlarig with father; served on Council, NFU of Scotland; Chairman, Scotch Quality Beef & Lamb Association, 1981-97; Vice President, Royal Highland and

Agricultural Society of Scotland, 1997-98; Member: British Wool Marketing Board, 1975-2000, Panel of Agricultural Arbiters, 1973-98, Red Deer Commission, 1975-92; Elder, Church of Scotland. Recreations: woodworking; gardening. Address: Inverlochlarig, Balquhidder, Lochearnhead, Perthshire FK19 8PH; T.-01877 384 232; e-mail: john@inverlochlarig.com

Macnaughton, Professor Sir Malcolm Campbell, MD, LLD, FRCPGlas, FRCOG, FFFP, FRSE, FSLCOG (Hon.), FACOG (Hon.), FRCA (Hon.), FRACOG (Hon.). Professor of Obstetrics and Gynaecology, Glasgow University, 1970-90; b. 4.4.25, Glasgow; m., Margaret-Ann Galt; 2 s.; 3 d. Educ. Glasgow Academy; Glasgow University. RAMC, 1949-51; Lecturer in Obstetrics and Gynaecology, Aberdeen University, 1957-61; Senior Lecturer, St. Andrews University, 1961-66; Consultant, Eastern Regional, 1966-70. President: RCOG, 1984-87, British Fertility Society, 1993-95. Recreations: walking; fishing. Address: (h.) 9 Glenburn Road, Bearsden, Glasgow GL1 4PT; T.-0141-942-1909.

MacNeacail, Aonghas. Writer (poetry, journalism, scriptwriting for TV, film and radio, librettoes); b. 7.6.42, Uig, Isle of Skye; m., Gerda Stevenson (qv); 1 s. Educ. Portree High School; Glasgow University. Writing fellowships: Sabhal Mor Ostaig, 1977-79, An Comunn Gaidhealach, 1979-81, Ross and Cromarty District Council, 1988-90, Glasgow and Strathclyde Universities, 1993-95, Sabhal Mor Ostaig, 1995-98; tours to Ireland, Germany, North America, Japan, Israel, etc.; opera librettoes for Alasdair Nicolson and William Sweeney; songs for Capercaillie, Phil Cunningham; art with Simon Fraser, Kenny Munro, Diane MacLean; short-listed, Paul Hamlyn Foundation Award for Poets, 1997; Stakis Award, Scottish Writer of the Year, 1997. Publications: books: An Seachnadh, 1986; Rock-Water, 1990; Oideachadh Ceart, 1996; Laoidh an Donais òig ('hymn to a young demon'), 2007; poems widely anthologised. Recreations: newsprint; red wine; thinking about walking.

McNee, Sir David Blackstock, Kt, QPM, FBIM, FRSA, KStJ. Non-Executive Director and Adviser to a number of public limited companies; b. 23.3.25; m., 1, Isabella Clayton Hopkins (deceased); 1 d.; 2, Lilian Bissland Bogie Campbell. Educ. Woodside Senior Secondary School, Glasgow. Joined City of Glasgow Police, 1946; Deputy Chief Constable, Dunbartonshire Constabulary, 1968; Chief Constable: City of Glasgow Police, 1971-75, Strathclyde Police, 1975-77; Commissioner, Metropolitan Police, 1977-82. Honorary Vice-President, Boys' Brigade, since 1980; Vice-President, London Federation of Boys Clubs, since 1982; Patron, Scottish Motor Neurone Association, 1982-97; President, National Bible Society of Scotland, 1983-96; Freeman, City of London, 1977; President, Glasgow City Committee, Cancer Relief, 1987-92. Recreations: fishing; golf; music.

MacNee, Professor William, MB, ChB, MD(Hons), FRCP(Glas), FRCP(Edin). Professor of Respiratory and Environmental Medicine, Edinburgh University; Visiting Professor, Department of Biological Sciences, Napier University; Honorary Consultant Physician, Lothian Health Board, since 1987; Clinical Director, Respiratory Medicine Unit, 1992-98; Clinical Director, Respiratory Medicine, Lothian University Hospitals NHS Trust, 1998-2005; b. 18.12.50, Glasgow; m., Edna Marina Kingsley; 1 s.; 1 d. Educ. Coatbridge High School; Glasgow University. House Physician/House Surgeon, Glasgow and Paisley, 1975-76; SHO/Registrar in Medicine, Western Infirmary/Gartnavel Hospitals, Glasgow, 1976-79; Registrar in Respiratory Medicine, City Hospital, Edinburgh, 1979-80; MRC Research Fellow/Honorary Registrar, Department of Respiratory Medicine, Royal Infirmary, Edinburgh, 1980-82; Lecturer, Department of Respiratory Medicine, City Hospital, Edinburgh, 1982-83; Senior Registrar, Respiratory Medicine/Medicine, Lothian Health Board, 1983-87; MRC Research Fellow, University of British Columbia, Vancouver, 1985-86; Senior Lecturer in Respiratory Medicine, 1987-93; Reader in Medicine, Edinburgh University, 1993-97; Head, Cardiovascular-Thoracic Service, Royal Infirmary of Edinburgh, 1998-99. Council Member, Scottish Thoracic Society, 1990-93; Hon. Secretary, British Lung Foundation (Scotland); Chairman, British Lung Foundation Scientific Committee, 1997-2000; Chairman, European Respiratory Society Scientific Programme Committee, 1999-2003; Congress Chair, European Respiratory Society, 2003-04; President, European Respiratory Society, 2006-07; Council Member, Royal College of Physicians of Edinburgh, since 2001; Vice President, British Lung Foundation, since 2005. Publications: scientific papers, reviews and books on respiratory medicine topics. Recreations: music; sport. Address: (b.) ELEGI Colt Research, MRC/uoE Centre for Inflammation Research, Level 2, The Queen's Medical Research Institute, 47 Little France Crescent, Edinburgh EH16 4TJ; T.-0131 242 6583; e-mail: w.macnee@ed.ac.uk

MacNeil, Angus, BEng, PGCE. MP (SNP), Na h-Eileanan An Iar, since 2005; Deputy Foreign Affairs Spokesperson, SNP, since 2015, Spokesperson for Transport, 2005-2015; 3 d. Educ. Castlebay Secondary School, Isle of Barra; Nicolson Institute, Stornoway, Isle of Lewis; Strathclyde University; Jordanhill College. Career history: Teacher; Convener, Lochaber branch SNP, 1999; SNP Spokesperson for: Environment, 2005-07; Fishing, 2005-10, Food and Rural Affairs, 2005-10, Work and Pensions, 2007-08; contested Inverness East, Nairn and Lochaber, 2001 general election. Chair, Energy and Climate Change Select Committee; Member, Scottish Affairs Committee, 2005-09. Recreations: football; sailing; fishing. Address: (b.) House of Commons, London SW1A 0AA.

McNeil, Duncan. MSP (Labour), Greenock and Inverclyde, 1999-2016; b. 7.9.50, Greenock. Career history: worked as a boilermaker at Scott Lithgow, initially as an apprentice, 1965-79; after working as a co-ordinator for the Unemployed Workers Centres in Glasgow, became a full-time official in the GMB Union in 1981 and later a Regional Organiser; for six years prior to his election from his current constituency, in May 1999, he was on the Labour Party's Scottish Executive Committee. Served on the Enterprise and Lifelong Learning Committee for 15 months and went on to became Labour's Chief Whip; elected to the Scottish Parliamentary Corporate Body in December 2001. Following re-election in May 2003, became Chair of the Scottish Parliamentary Labour Party.

McNeil, Lynne. Editor, Life and Work, since 2002; b. 19.12.67, Dunfermline; m., Charles Craig Robin McNeil; 1 d. Educ. Inverkeithing High School; Napier College, Edinburgh. East Lothian Courier, 1986-89; United News Service, Edinburgh, 1989-94; Telegraph and Argus, Bradford, 1994; Railtrack North East, 1994; Greenock Telegraph, 1994-95; The Herald, 1995-2002. Recreations: reading; swimming. Address: (b.) 121 George Street, Edinburgh EH2 4YN; T.-0131 225 5722; e-mail: lrobertson@lifeandwork.org

McNeil, Neil. Headteacher, Glenwood High School, Glenrothes. Address: (b.) South Parks Road, Glenrothes, KY6 1JX; T.-01592 583404.

McNeil, Neil, MB, ChB, DPH, DPA, FFCM, FFPH, MREHIS. Consultant in Public Health Medicine/Director of Community Medicine/Unit Medical Officer/District Medical Officer, Lanarkshire Health Board, 1976-92; Honorary Senior Clinical Lecturer/Honorary Clinical

Lecturer, Department of Public Health, Glasgow University, 1976-92; b. 4.6.31, Glasgow; m., Florence Ward Butterworth; 2 s.; 1 d. Educ. Govan High School; Glasgow University. SHO, Senior Resident, House Physician and House Surgeon, Western Infirmary, Glasgow, 1956-58; Hall Fellow, Glasgow University, 1958-60; Registrar, Western Infirmary, Glasgow, 1960-61; Divisional Medical Officer of Health, City of Glasgow, 1962-65; Principal Lecturer in Health Education and Medical Officer, Jordanhill College, Glasgow, 1965-68; Medical Officer of Health, North-East Hampshire, and Honorary Consultant, Aldershot, 1968-69; Medical Officer, Scottish Home and Health Department, 1969-73; Honorary Lecturer, Departments of Materia Medica and Community Medicine, Glasgow University, 1973-74; Consultant Epidemiologist, Communicable Diseases (Scotland) Unit, Ruchill Hospital, 1973-74; Senior Medical Officer, Scottish Home and Health Department, 1974-76. Dr. MacKinlay Prize in Public Health and Preventive Medicine, Glasgow University, 1962. Publications on community medicine, environmental medicine, public health, immunisation and infectious disease control. Recreations: tennis; photography; natural history; Gaelic language and culture; Scottish history and archaeology. Address: (h.) Claddach, 25 Waterfoot Road, Newton Mearns, Glasgow G77 5RU.

Macneil of Bara, Roderick 'Rory' Wilson. Chief of Clan Niall and 27th of Barra; b. 22.10.54; m., Sau Ming. Succeeded to title, 2010. Lives at Kisimul Castle, Isle of Barra.

McNeill, James Walker, QC. Advocate, since 1978; a Judge of the Courts of Appeal of Jersey and Guernsey, since 2006; b. 16.2.52, Dunoon; m., Katherine Lawrence McDowall; 2 s.; 1 d. Educ. Dunoon Grammar School; Sidney Sussex College, Cambridge; Edinburgh University. QC, 1991; Standing Junior Counsel, Department of Transport in Scotland, 1984-88, Inland Revenue, 1988-91. Member of Council, Commonwealth Law Association, 2005-2011; Session Clerk, St. Andrew's and St. George's Parish Church, Edinburgh, 1999-2003; Chair of Music Committee, Scottish International Piano Competition, 2004-2011; Member, Judicial Appointments Board for Scotland, since 2012; Trustee and Secretary, Edinburgh City Centre Churches Together, since 2012; Chair, Disciplinary Appointments Committee of the Institute and Faculty of Actuaries, since 2013. Recreations: music; travel. Address: (b.) Advocates' Library, Parliament House, Edinburgh EH1 1RF; T.-0131-226 5071.

McNeill, Patricia Anne, FRSA. Consultant specialising in transforming learning, business and people. Formerly Project Manager, Blend2Learn (2006-09); b. 03.08.48, Duns, Berwickshire; 2 s. Educ. Berwickshire High School. Career History: Head of Student Services, Queen Margaret College; Training and Media Manager, Integrated Micro Applications Ltd. (INMAP); Commercial Manager, Centre for Software Engineering, Stirling Univ.; Managing Dir., Talkback Training Ltd., 1987-2005. Expert Advisor/Evaluator, European Learning Programmes (Leonardo & Erasmus). Address: Cheeklaw Brae House, Station Road, Duns, Berwickshire TD11 3HS; T.-07939 023211; e-mail: annemcneill38@gmail.com

McNeill, Pauline, LLB. MSP (Lab), Glasgow Kelvin, since 2016 and 1999-2011; Director, McNeill & Stone, since 2015; b. 12.9.62, Paisley; m., William Joseph Cahill. Educ. Our Lady's High School, Cumbernauld; Strathclyde University. President, National Union of Students (Scotland), 1986-88; Regional Organiser, GMB, 1988-99. Recreations: music; films; guitar;

singing. Address: Scottish Parliament, Edinburgh EH99 1SP.

McNeill, Professor (Robert) John, BA (Hons), MSc, LLM, MPhil. Independent Member (Service Complaints Panel), MoD, since 2008; former Police Investigations & Review Commissioner (Commissioner) (PIRC), 2013-2014; Police Complaints Commissioner for Scotland (Commissioner), 2009-2013; Probation Board for Northern Ireland (PBNI), 2006-2012; Honorary Professor, Glasgow Caledonian University, since 2010; Visiting Professor, University of Ulster, since 2011; Visiting Professor, University of Chester, since 2011; Honorary Professor, Queen Margaret University, Edinburgh, since 2011; Honorary Professor at Sheffield University's School of Law, 2014-16; b. 7.7.1945, Belfast; m., Margaret Alison McCartney; 1 s.; 2 d. Educ. Annandale Grammar; Queen's University Belfast; Open University; University of Edinburgh; University of Strathclyde. Various administrative posts, Northern Ireland, 1968-72; Probation and Aftercare Officer, Northern Ireland Probation Service, 1972-73; Governor, Northern Ireland Prison Service, 1973-80; Governor, Scottish Prison Service, 1980-85; Chief Executive and Company Secretary, previously Depute Director, SACRO, 1985-96; Deputy Director, Acting Director, Scottish Prison Service, 1996-2005. Numerous Board positions in national and international Non-Governmental Organisations, 1980-2005; Board Member, Risk Management Authority Scotland, 2004-08; Independent Member, Parole Board for England and Wales, 2005-08; Independent Member, Civil Nuclear Police Authority, 2005-09; Commissioner, Scottish Human Rights Commission, 2008-09; Cropwood Fellowship, University of Cambridge, 1985; previously Fellow of the Institute of Directors, Fellow of the Chartered Institute of Management; various publications on criminal justice issues. Recreations: fly fishing and shooting. T.-07738447272.
E-mail: consultmcneill@gmail.com

McNeilly, Professor Alan S., BSc, PhD, DSc, FSB, FRSE. Program Leader, MRC Centre for Reproductive Health, Edinburgh University, since 2011; Honorary Professor, University of Edinburgh, since 1994; b. 10.2.47, Birmingham; m., Judy; 1 s.; 3 d. Educ. Handsworth Grammar School, Birmingham; Nottingham University; Reading University; Edinburgh University. Research Lecturer, Department of Reproductive Medicine, St. Bartholomew's Hospital, London, 1971-75; Visiting Professor, University of Manitoba, Canada, 1975-76; Research Scientist, MRC Reproductive Biology Unit, Edinburgh, 1976-2011, Deputy Director, 1986-2008. Editor-in-Chief, Journal of Endocrinology, 1995-2000; Member, Home Office APC, 1998-2006; Chairman: Society for Reproduction and Fertility, 1999-2005, Science Committee Society for Endocrinology, 2008-2012. Fellow of Royal Society of Edinburgh, 1995; Fellow of Society of Biology, 2010; Member Faculty of 1000, since 2010; Society for Endocrinology Dale Medallist, 2008; Society for Reproduction and Fertility Marshall Medallist, 2008. Recreations: walking; golf; orienteering; bee-keeping; gardening. Address: (b.) MRC, CRH, The Queen's Medical Research Institute, 47 Little France Crescent, Edinburgh EH16 4TJ; T.-0131-242 6162; e-mail: a.mcneilly@ed.ac.uk

Macnicol, Malcolm Fraser, MBChB, BSc (Hons), FRCS, MCh, FRCP, FRCSEd (Orth), DipSportsMed. Consultant Orthopaedic Surgeon: Royal Hospital for Sick Children and Royal Infirmary, Edinburgh, 1979-2007, Spire Murrayfield Hospital, Edinburgh, since 1984; Senior Orthopaedic Lecturer, Edinburgh

University, 1979-2005; b. 18.3.43; m., Anne Morag; 2 s.; 1 d. Educ. Royal High School, Edinburgh; Edinburgh University. Research Fellow, Stanford and Harvard Universities; Lecturer in Orthopaedic Surgery, Edinburgh, 1976-78; Senior Lecturer, Perth, W. Australia, 1978-79; UK European Travelling Orthopaedic Fellow, 1981; ABC Travelling Fellow, 1982; Member, Council of Management, Journal of Bone and Joint Surgery, 1998-2002; Treasurer, Royal College of Surgeons, Edinburgh, 1987-90; President, British Orthopaedic Association, 2001-2002; Chairman, BOA Medicolegal Subcommittee, 1999-2003; Honorary Medical Adviser to the Scottish Rugby Union, 2004-08; Patron, Scottish Post-Polio Network, since 2005. Publications: 6 books; 156 professional papers. Recreations: painting; tennis. Address: (h.) Redhouse, 1 South Gillsland Road, Edinburgh EH10 5DE; T.-0131-447 2694; (b.) 0131 536 1000.

McNulty, Des, BA. Deputy Director, Policy Scotland, College of Social Sciences, University of Glasgow; Knowledge Exchange and Outreach Manager, Urban Big Data Centre; MSP (Labour), Clydebank and Milngavie, 1999-2011; formerly Shadow Education Minister; b. 28.7.52, Stockport; m.; 2 s. Educ. St. Bede's College Manchester; University of York; University of Glasgow. Senior Lecturer in Sociology, Glasgow Caledonian University; Director of Strategic Planning, Glasgow Caledonian University; Member, Strathclyde Regional Council, 1990-96; Member, Glasgow City Council, 1995-99; Member of Court, University of Glasgow, 1994-99; Assessor to Board, Scottish Opera, 1996-99; Chair, Glasgow Healthy City Partnership, 1995-99; Chair, Glasgow 1999 Festival of Architecture and Design; Non Executive Director, Greater Glasgow Health Board, 1998-99; Board Member, The Wise Group.

McOwan, Rennie, DUniv, FSA Scot. Writer and Broadcaster; b. Stirling; m., Agnes Mooney; 3 s.; 1 d. Educ. Alva Academy. Reporter, Stirling Journal; Sub-Editor, Kemsley Newspapers, Daily Record; Public Relations, Roman Catholic Church; Sub-Editor, Features Writer, Scotsman Publications; Assistant Publicity Secretary, National Trust for Scotland; Scottish Book Trust Lecturer under Writers in Schools and Writers in Public schemes; former Guest Lecturer, Film and Media Studies, Stirling University (retired); Contributor to newspapers and magazines in Britain and overseas; radio and TV scripts and research; Outdoor Writers Guild Golden Eagle award for access campaigning and writing about Scottish subjects, 1997; Provost of Stirling's Civic Award (Arts and Culture), 1998; Honorary Doctorate, University of Stirling, 1996. Publications: Light on Dumyat; The White Stag Adventure; The Day the Mountain Moved; Jewels On The Move; Robert Burns for Beginners; St. Andrew for Beginners; Magic Mountains; Walks in the Trossachs and the Rob Roy Country; The Green Hills; Kilchurn Castle: a history; Loch Lomond and The Trossachs; contributed to: Walking in Scotland; Poetry of the Scottish Hills; Speak to the Hills; Wild Walks; The Story of Scotland; Discover Scotland; Great Walks, Scotland; Classic Coastal Walks of Britain; On Foot Through History. Recreations: mountaineering; Scottish history and literature. Address: 7 Williamfield Avenue, Stirling FK7 9AH; T.-01786 461316; e-mail: tmcowan@btinternet.com

McPhee, George, MBE, BMus, FRCO, DipMusEd, RSAM, Hon. FRSCM, Hon. FGCM. Visiting Professor of Organ, St. Andrews University; Chairman, Paisley International Organ Festival; Organist and Master of the Choristers, Paisley Abbey, since 1963; b. 10.11.37, Glasgow; m., Margaret Ann Scotland; 1 s.; 2 d. Educ. Woodside Senior Secondary School, Glasgow; Royal Scottish Academy of Music and Drama; Edinburgh University. Studied organ with Herrick Bunney and Fernando Germani; Assistant Organist, St. Giles' Cathedral, 1959-63; joined staff, RSAMD, 1963; Conductor, Scottish Chamber Choir, 1971-75; Conductor, Kilmarnock and District Choral Union, 1975-84; since 1971, has completed 12 recital tours of the United States and Canada; has been both Soloist and Conductor with Scottish National Orchestra; numerous recordings and broadcasts; has taken part in numerous music festivals as Soloist; Adjudicator; Examiner, Associated Board, Royal Schools of Music; Special Commissioner, Royal School of Church Music; President, Incorporated Society of Musicians, 1999-2000; Silver Medal, Worshipful Company of Musicians; Honorary Doctorate, University of Paisley; Vice President, Royal College of Organists. Recreations: golf; walking. Address: (h.) 17 Main Road, Castlehead, Paisley PA2 6AJ; T.-0141-889 3528; e-mail: profmcphee@aol.com

McPhee, Susan Anne, LLB, BA. Director of External Affairs, Citizens Advice Scotland, since 2010 (former Acting Chief Executive); former Member, Scottish Legal Aid Board (2005-2012); Member, Scottish Government Debt Action Forum; b. 3.3.59, Edinburgh; m., Gordon Annand; 2 s. Educ. James Gillespie's High School; Aberdeen University; Open University. Edinburgh City Council, 1979-81; Solicitor with Messrs Lindsay and Kirk, Advocates in Aberdeen, 1981-90; Legal Services Adviser, Citizens Advice Scotland, 1990-98; Head of Social Policy and Public Affairs of Citizens Advice Scotland, 1998-2010. Member of: Scottish Parliament Working Group on Replacement for Poinding and Warrant Sales, Scottish Executive Debt Relief Working Group, Cross Party Cross Parliamentary Group on Tackling Debt; elected member of SCVO Policy Forum, since 2012. Recreations: music; films; junk jewellery. Address: (b.) 2 Powderhall Road, Edinburgh EH7 4GB; T.-0131 550 1000; e-mail: susan.mcphee@cas.org.uk

Macpherson, Archie. Sports broadcaster and journalist. Former headmaster; football commentator, BBC Scotland, until 1990; reported Olympic Games, 1984 and 1988, for BBC network; commentator, Scottish Television, since 1988; author of: Action Replays, 1991, Blue and Green, 1989, 'Jock Stein' Definitive Biography, 2004; 'Flower of Scotland?', 2005; 'A Game of Two Halves', 2009; Undefeated: The Life and Times of Jimmy Johnstone, 2010; 'Silent Thunder', 2014 (novel). E-mail: archie613@btinternet.com

Macpherson, Ben, BA, LLB. MSP (SNP), Edinburgh Northern and Leith, since 2016. Educ. University of York; University of Edinburgh; The Open University. Career history: Data Processor, Standard Life, 2002-03; Volunteer English Teacher, Projects Abroad, 2003; Peace One Day: Campaigner, 2004, Intern, 2005; Intern, Citigate Public Affairs (now Grayling), 2006; Clerical Assistant, James Gillespie's High School, 2008-09; Intern, Scottish Parliament, 2009-2010; Marketing/Public Affairs Assistant, Aquamarine Power, 2010; Voluntary Public Affairs Advisor, Campaign for Fair Access to the Legal Profession, 2012-13; Brodies LLP: Trainee Solicitor, 2013-15, Solicitor, 2015-16. Member of British delegation, Jung Königswinter Conference, July 2013. Recreations: current affairs; economics; political philosophy; political activism; running; football; playing guitar; travel. Address: Scottish Parliament, Edinburgh EH99 1SP.

McPherson, Elaine, MA (Hons), MBA. Chief Executive, Clackmannanshire Council, since 2011; b. Stirling. Worked for the Council for 22 years, starting as a Policy Officer and rising to Head of Service, first in the Education service and then at the corporate centre as Head of Strategy & Customer Services; previously worked for Central Regional Council and Fife Regional Council. Address: Clackmannanshire Council, Greenfield, Alloa, Clackmannanshire FK10 2AD; T.-01259 450000.

McPherson, Malcolm Henry, LLB, WS. Solicitor; Senior Partner of international law firm, HBJ Gateley; b. 22.5.54, Edinburgh; 1 s.; 3 d. Educ. George Watson's College, Edinburgh; Edinburgh University. Apprentice, Henderson & Jackson, WS, 1975-77; Partner, since 1978; Vice-chairman, Scottish Solicitors' Discipline Tribunal; Member, Judicial Panel of Scottish Football Association; Chairman, Space Solutions Scotland. Recreations: field sports; sailing; golf. Address: (b.) Exchange Tower, 19 Canning Street, Edinburgh EH3 8EH; T.-0131-228 2400; e-mail: mmcpherson@hbjgateley.com

Macpherson, Peter, FRCP, FRCR, DTCD, FLS. Emeritus Consultant Neuroradiologist, Institute of Neurological Sciences; President: British Society of Neuroradiologists, 1990-92, Botanical Society of the British Isles, 1991-93; b. 10.10.25, Inveraray; m., Agnes Cochrane Davidson; 4 d. Educ. Inveraray Grammar School; Keil School, Dumbarton; Anderson College, Glasgow. House Surgeon, Royal Infirmary, Stirling; Junior Hospital Medical Officer, Robroyston Hospital, Glasgow; Chest Physician, Argyll; Registrar/Senior Registrar, Western Infirmary, Glasgow. Commodore, Oban Sailing Club, 1958-60; President, Glasgow Natural History Society, 1979-81 and 1983-86; Honorary Secretary, Botanical Society of the British Isles, Committee for Scotland, 1977-95, Chairman, 1995-99; Plant Recorder for Lanarkshire, since 1978; Elder, Church of Scotland, since 1957. Recreations: natural history; sailing. Address: (h.) Ben Alder, 15 Lubnaig Road, Glasgow; T.-0141-632 0723.

MacPherson, Professor Robin David, BA (Hons), MLitt, FRSA. Chair, Creative Industries, University of Highlands and Islands, since 2015; Director, Screen Academy Scotland, 2006-2015; Director, Institute for Creative Industries, Edinburgh Napier University, 2010-15; b. 24.12.59, Glasgow; 1 d. Educ. Garthamlock Secondary, Glasgow; Stirling University. Freelance Photographer, Writer and Bookseller, 1980-89; Producer/Director of Documentary, Current Affairs and Drama for Edinburgh Film Workshop Trust, 1989-97; Independent Television Producer/Managing Director, Asylum Pictures Ltd., Edinburgh, since 1997; Development Executive, Scottish Screen, 1999-2002; Napier University, since 2002 (Lecturer, then Senior Lecturer, then Professor). BAFTA (UK) Nomination 1996, for Channel 4 Drama 'The Butterfly Man'; Vice Chair, Producers Association for Cinema and Television in Scotland, 1997-99; Trustee, Edinburgh Television Trust, 1993-99; Board Member, Creative Scotland, 2010-15; Board Member, Creative Edinburgh, 2011-15. Recreation: hillwalking. Address: Shetland College, Gremista, Lerwick, Shetland ZE1 0PX; T.-01595 771323; e-mail: robin.macpherson@uhi.ac.uk

Macpherson, Shonaig, CBE, LLB (Hons), FRSE. Solicitor, DUniv (Gla). Chairman, National Trust for Scotland, 2005-2010; Chairman, ITI Scotland Limited, 2003-09; Chairman, SCDI, 2004-09; Senior Partner, McGrigors, 2002-04; b. 29.9.58. Educ. University of Sheffield; College of Law, Chester. Articled Clerk, Norton Rose, London, 1982-85; qualified as Solicitor (England), 1984; Solicitor in Corporate/Commercial Department, Knapp Fisher, London, 1985-87; Assistant Company Secretary, Storehouse PLC, 1987; in-house lawyer, Harrods Ltd., and associated companies, 1987-89; Partner, Calow Easton, London 1989-91; Partner, McGrigor Donald,

London and Edinburgh, 1991; qualified as Solicitor (Scotland), 1992; Managing Partner, McGrigor Donald, Edinburgh, 1996; appointed Senior Partner (Scotland), McGrigor, 2002-04. Non-executive Member, Scottish Executive Management Group, 2001-07; President, Edinburgh Chamber of Commerce and Enterprise, 2002-04; Visiting Professor, Department of Mechanical Engineering, Heriot Watt University; Chairman, Scottish Council for Development and Industry, 2004-09; Chairman, Scottish Council Foundation, 2004-09; Director and Secretary, Edinburgh International Film Festival, 2001-09; Director, Young Enterprise Scotland, 2001-04; Deputy President, British Chambers of Commerce, 2004-06; Director, Edinburgh International Conference Centre Limited, 2004-2014 (retired); Chairman, Princes Scottish Youth Business Trust Limited, 2005-2012 (retired); Director, Braveheart Investment Group plc, 2006-08; Trustee, The Princes's Trust Council, 2007-2010; Vice Chairman, The Robertson Trust, since 2004; Governor, Edinburgh College of Art, 2000-2011; Vice Chairman, The Royal Edinburgh Military Tattoo Ltd., 2007-2015; Council Member, The Open University, since 2009; Member of Court, Heriot Watt University, 2009-2015; Chairman, Royal Lyceum Theatre, Edinburgh, since 2012; Member, Commission on Scottish Devolution (Calman Commission), 2009-2010; Trustee, Dunedin Consort, since 2012; Chairman, Macpherson Coaches Ltd, 2012-13 (retired); Member, Joint Managerial Board of Scotland Office and Office of Advocate General; Trustee, Euan's Guide Limited, since 2015; Governor, Royal Conservatoire of Scotland, since 2015. Recreations: film; music; reading. Address: (b.) Lochcote, Linlithgow EH49 6QE; e-mail: shonaigm@btconnect.com

Macpherson, Professor Stuart Gowans, OBE, MB, ChB, FRCS(Glas), FRCP(Edin), FRCS(Edin), FRCS(England), FRCGP, FAcadMEd (Hon). Professor Emeritus, Postgraduate Medical Education, University of Edinburgh; b. 11.7.45, Glasgow; m., Norma Elizabeth Carslaw; 2 s.; 1 d. Educ. Alan Glen's School, Glasgow; University of Glasgow. Formerly Senior Lecturer in Surgery, University of Glasgow and Consultant General Surgeon. Sat on Scottish and UK national committees on postgraduate medical education; formerly Chair, Postgraduate Medical Education and Training Board. Recreations: travelling; family; golf. Address: 33/4 Blackford Road, Edinburgh EH9 2DT; T.-0131 668 4574.
E-mail: macphersonsg@gmail.com

Macpherson of Cluny (and Blairgowrie), The Honourable Sir William, KB (1983), TD, MA. 27th Hereditary Chief of the Clan Macpherson (Cluny-Macpherson); b. 1.4.26; m., Sheila McDonald Brodie (deceased 2003); 2 s. (1 son deceased, 2007); 1 d. Educ. Summer Fields, Oxford; Wellington College; Trinity College, Oxford (Hon. Fellow, 1991). Scots Guards, 1944-47 (Captain); 21st Special Air Service Regiment (TA), 1951-65 (Lt.-Col. Commanding, 1962-65); Honorary Colonel, 21st SAS, 1983-91. Called to the Bar, Inner Temple, 1952; Queen's Counsel, 1971-83; Recorder of the Crown Court, 1972-83; Member, Senate and Bar Council, 1979-83; Bencher, Inner Temple, 1978; Judge of the High Court of Justice (of England and Wales), Queen's Bench Division, 1983-96; Honorary Member, Northern Circuit, since 1987. Member, Queen's Bodyguard for Scotland (Royal Company of Archers), since 1976, Brigadier, 1989, Ensign, 2002, Lieutenant, 2003-06; Vice President, Royal Scottish Corporation, until 2006; President, Highland Society of London, 1991-94; Hon. LLD, Dundee University, 1999. Recreations: golf; fishing; rugby football; archery. Address: (h.) Newton Castle, Blairgowrie, Perthshire PH10 6SU.

MacQuarrie, John Kenneth (Ken), MA (Eng/Hist), DipEd. Director, BBC Scotland, since 2004; b. 5.6.52, Tobermory; m., Angela Sparks; 1 s.; 2 d. Educ. Oban High School; Edinburgh University; Moray House College of

Education. Joined BBC Scotland as Researcher, 1975; Radio Producer, BBC Highland, 1976; Producer, Television, 1979; Head of Gaelic, 1988; Head of Gaelic and Features, 1992; Head of Broadcast, 1997; Head of Programmes and Scottish Services, 2000. Board Member, Gaelic Media Service, 2004-08; Vice Chair, Celtic Film and Television Association, 1986-93; Founder Member, Scottish Screen Forum; Former Governor, Scottish Film Council. Recreations: sailing; reading; walking. Address: (b.) BBC Scotland, 40 Pacific Quay, Glasgow G51 1DA; T.-0141 422 6100; e-mail: ken.macquarrie@bbc.co.uk

McQueen, Eric. Chief Executive, Scottish Courts and Tribunals Service, since 2013. Address: (b.) Saughton House, Broomhouse Drive, Edinburgh EH11 3XD; T.-0131 444 3300.

MacQueen, Professor Hector Lewis, LLB (Hons), PhD, FRSE, FBA. Professor of Private Law, Edinburgh University, since 1994; Dean of Law, 1999-2003; Dean of Research, College of Humanities and Social Science, 2004-08; Scottish Law Commissioner, since 2009; b. 13.6.56, Ely; m., Frances Mary Young; 2 s.; 1 d. Educ. George Heriot's School, Edinburgh; Edinburgh University. Lecturer, Senior Lecturer, Reader, all in Law, Edinburgh University, 1979-94; Director, David Hume Institute, Edinburgh, 1991-99; Visiting Professor, Cornell University, 1991; Visiting Professor, Utrecht University, 1997; Distinguished International Professor, Stetson University College of Law, Florida, USA, 2007-09; Secretary, Scottish Historical Review, 1986-99; Editor, Hume Papers on Public Policy, 1993-99; Editor, Edinburgh Law Review, 1996-2001; Editor, Scots Law News (www.law.ed.ac.uk/sln), since 1996; Scottish Representative, European Contract Commission, 1995-2001; Member, Co-ordinating Committee, Study Group towards a European Civil Code, 1999-2008; Literary Director, Stair Society, since 1999; Chair, Scottish Records Advisory Council, 2001-08; Member, DTI Intellectual Property Advisory Committee, 2003-05; Ministry of Justice (UK) Advisory Panel on Public Sector Information, 2004-11; Director, AHRC Research Centre for Studies in Intellectual Property and Information Technology Law, Edinburgh University, 2002-07; Vice-President (Humanities), Royal Society of Edinburgh, 2008-2011; Chair, Scottish Medievalists Conference, 2007-2011; Chair of Trustees, The David Hume Institute, 2012-2015; President, Society of Legal Scholars, 2012-13. Publications: Common Law and Feudal Society in Medieval Scotland; Studying Scots Law; Copyright, Competition and Industrial Design; Contract Law in Scotland (Co-Author); Unjustified Enrichment Law Basics; Contemporary Intellectual Property: Law and Policy (Co-Author). Recreations: Scotland; cricket; walking – sometimes with golf clubs, sometimes with a camera; reading. Address: (b.) Scottish Law Commission, 140 Causewayside, Edinburgh EH9 1PR; T.-0131 668 2131. E-mail: hector.macqueen@scotlawcom.gsi.gov.uk

MacQueen, Professor Emeritus Jack (John), MA (Glasgow), MA (Cantab), Hon DLitt, FRAS, FRSE. Professor Emeritus, Edinburgh University, since 1988; b. 13.2.29, Springboig; m., Winifred W. MacWalter; 3 s. Educ. Hutchesons' Boys Grammar School; Glasgow University; Christ's College, Cambridge. RAF, 1954-56 (Pilot Officer, Flying Officer); Assistant Professor of English, Washington University, St. Louis, Missouri, 1956-59; Edinburgh University: Lecturer in Medieval English and Scottish Literature, 1959-63, Masson Professor of Medieval and Renaissance Literature, 1963-72; Director, School of Scottish Studies, 1969-88; Professor of Scottish Literature and Oral Tradition, 1972-88; Endowment Fellow, 1988-92. Publications: St. Nynia, 1961, 1990, 2005; Robert Henryson, 1967; Ballattis of Luve, 1970; Allegory, 1970;

Progress and Poetry, 1982; Numerology, 1985; Rise of the Historical Novel, 1989; Scotichronicon III and IV (with W. MacQueen), 1989; Scotichronicon I and II (with W. MacQueen), 1993; Scotichronicon V and VI (with W. MacQueen and D.E.R. Watt), 1995; Place-Names in the Rhinns of Galloway and Luce Valley, 2002; Complete and Full with Numbers, 2006; Place-Names of the Wigtownshire Moors and Machars, 2008; Archibald Pitcairne: The Latin Poems (with W. MacQueen), 2009; Archibald Pitcairne: The Phanaticks, 2012; Archibald Pitcairne: Tollerators and con-Tollerators, 2015; Oxford Book of Scottish Verse (with T. Scott), 1966; A Choice of Scottish Verse 1470-1570 (with W. MacQueen), 1972; Humanism in Renaissance Scotland (Co-Author), 1990. Recreations: walking; occasional archaeology; music; astronomy. Address: (h.) Slewdonan, Damnaglaur, Drummore, Stranraer DG9 9QN. E-mail: jackmacqueen@gmail.com

McQueen, James Donaldson Wright, MA, PhD, ARSGS. Food Industry Analyst and Map Publisher; b. 14.2.37, Dumfries; m., Jean Evelyn Brown; 2 s.; 1 d. Educ. King's Park School, Glasgow; Glasgow University. Assistant Lecturer, Department of Geography, Glasgow University, 1960-61; Milk Marketing Board Executive, 1961-89 (England & Wales, 1961-62, Scotland, 1963-89); Deputy Managing Director, Scottish Milk Marketing Board, 1985-89; Chief Executive, Scottish Dairy Trade Federation (latterly Scottish Dairy Association), 1989-95; UK representative on the Board of the European Dairy Association (EDA), Brussels, 1990-95; Adviser on Milk Industry Matters to the States of Jersey, 2003-07; Chairman, Milk Price Review Panel, States of Guernsey, 2007; Honorary Research Fellow, School of Geographical and Earth Sciences, University of Glasgow, 1999-2011. Address: Ormlie, 53 Kingston Road, Bishopton, Renfrewshire PA7 5BA; e-mail: mcqueen@agri-food.co.uk

MacQueen, Norrie, BA, MSc (Econ), DPhil. Honorary Research Fellow, School of International Relations, University of St Andrews; Fellow, Scottish Global Forum; b. 11.4.50, Glasgow; m., Betsy (nee King); 1 d. Educ. Shawlands Academy; University of Ulster; London School of Economics. Ministry of Education, Mozambique, 1977-79; Research Officer, Glasgow University, 1980-83; Senior Lecturer, University of Papua New Guinea, 1986-90; Research Fellow, Australian National University, 1990; Reader, University of Sunderland, 1990-96; Dundee University, 1996-2012 (Senior Lecturer, Head of Department of Politics, 1998-2005); United Nations Electoral Officer, Timor-Leste, 2012. Publications: The Decolonization of Portuguese Africa, 1997; United Nations Peacekeeping in Africa, 2002; Peacekeeping and the International System, 2006; European Security after Iraq, 2006 (Joint Editor); Colonialism, 2007; The United Nations: a Beginner's Guide, 2010; The United Nations, Peace Operations and the Cold War, 2011; Humanitarian Intervention and the United Nations, 2011; The Oxford Handbook of United Nation Peacekeeping Operations, 2015 (Joint Editor). Recreations: hillwalking; cycling; music. Address: 6 Glenalmond Terrace, Perth PH2 0AU; e-mail: norriemacqueen@yahoo.co.uk

McQuillan, Kathleen T., OBE, BA, LLB, Solicitor. Independent Assessor for Public Appointments, since 2012; Vice-Chair, Parole Board for Scotland, 2009-2011; Legal Convenor, Mental Health Tribunal for Scotland, since 2007; b. Glasgow; m., James McQuillan; 1 s. Educ. Bellarmine Secondary School; University of Strathclyde. Admitted as Solicitor in 1981; Solicitor in practice specialising in criminal law, 1981-89; Authority's Advocate, Criminal Injuries Compensation Authority, 1989-2002; Solicitor to the Board, Strathclyde Joint Police Board, 2003-04;

Member, Parole Board for Scotland, 2004-2011 and since 2014. Recreations: cinema; reading; music; current affairs.

MacRae, Alan. President, Scottish Football Association, since 2015. Joined Cove Rangers as a player in 1979, became Chairman (1984-1999), leading the Aberdeenshire club from the amateurs, to the ranks of the Juniors and eventually to the Highland League; appointed President, Cove Rangers (1999), then Honorary President until 2007; appointed Council Member, Scottish Football Association in 1993 before becoming 1st Vice President, served as 2nd Vice-President. Member of Professional Game Board. Address: Scottish Football Association Ltd, Hampden Park, Glasgow G42 9AY; T.-0141 616 6000.
E-mail: info@scottishfa.co.uk

MacRae, Donald J. R., OBE, BSc (Hons), MBA, FCIBS, FRSE, FRAgS. Chief Economist, Lloyds Banking Group Scotland; former Director, Lloyds TSB Scotland plc; Board Member, Highlands and Islands Enterprise; Past Board Member, Scottish Enterprise; b. 12.8.54, Inverness; m., Anne de Diesbach; 1 s.; 1 d. Educ. Fortrose Academy; Edinburgh University. Economist/Analyst, Imperial Chemical Industries, 1979-82; Project Manager, Farmplan Computer Systems, 1982-84; Lecturer, University of Newcastle upon Tyne, 1984-86; TSB Bank Scotland plc: Manager, 1986-90, Senior Manager, 1990-98, Chief Manager, Strategy and Development, 1998-2001. Member, Advisory Board, Interface; Member, Rural Development Council; Past Member, Scottish Government: Purchasers Information Advisory Group, Economists Advisory Group; Member: Economic Statistics Advisory Group, Economists Advisory Group, Committee of Inquiry on Crofting; Trustee, David Hume Institute; Visiting Professor, University of Abertay Dundee; former Member of Court, University of Highlands and Islands; Member of Court, Royal Conservatoire of Scotland; Member, Skills Committee of Skills Development Scotland and Scottish Funding Council. Recreations: music; film; theatre; vintage tractors. Address: (b.) The Mound, Edinburgh EH1 1YZ; T.-0131 243 5447.

McSherry, Sheriff John Craig Cunningham, LLB (Hons). Advocate; part-time Sheriff, 2000-03; All-Scotland Floating Sheriff, 2003-06; resident Sheriff at Dunfermline, since 2006; b. 21.10.49, Irvine; m., Elaine Beattie; 2 s. Educ. Ardrossan Academy; Glasgow University. Senior Partner, McSherry Halliday, Solicitors, 1983-92. Chairman, Largs and Saltcoats Citizens Advice Bureaux, 1976-83; Council Member, Law Society of Scotland, 1982-85; part-time Immigration Appeals Adjudicator, 2001-03. Recreations: country pursuits; skiing; music; bridge; golf. Address: (h.) 2 Heriot Row, Edinburgh EH3 6HU; T.-0131-556 8289; e-mail: jccmcs@hotmail.com

McTaggart, Anne. MSP (Labour), Glasgow, 2011-16; former Shadow Minister for Democracy; m.; 3 c. Educ. Chryston High School, North Lanarkshire; University of Strathclyde. Former Councillor in the Drumchapel/Anniesland ward of Glasgow City Council (2009-2012); previously social worker and local chair of the local primary school's parents council. Member of the Glasgow Labour Women's Forum and the Co-operative Party.

MacTaggart, Kenneth Dugald, BA (Hons), PhD. Managing Director, Alba Consult Ltd, since 2001; b. 15.4.53, Glasgow; m., Caroline McNicholas; 2 d. Educ. Allan Glen's School, Glasgow; Glasgow University; Paisley College; Aston University. Economic Research, Aston University, 1976-80; Editor, Export Times, London

1980-84; Editor, Property International, London and Bahrain, 1984-87; Director, Inc. Publications, London, 1987-88; Senior Economist, HIDB, 1988-91; Chief Economist, then Director of Strategy, then Head of Knowledge, Highlands & Islands Enterprise, 1991-2001; Managing Director, Alba Consult, economic development, since 2001; Development Economics Consultant, Upper Quartile, since 2009. Co-editor, NASA Apollo 11 Flight Journal. Civilian Service Medal (Afghanistan), 2012. Recreations: hill-walking; piano; astronomy. Address: (h.) The Sutors, 28 Broadstone Park, Inverness IV2 3LA; T.-01463 233717; e-mail: ken@wyvis.com

McVicar, William, RD*, CA. Past Chairman of Trustees, Church of Scotland Housing and Loan Fund for Retired Ministers and Widows and Widowers of Ministers, 1983-2008 (Trustee, 1976-2008); Retired Chartered Accountant; b. 29.6.32, Rutherglen; m., Doreen Ann; 1 s.; 1 d. Educ. George Heriot's School, Edinburgh. Royal Navy, 1950-52; RNVR/RNR, 1955-86 (retired list, Commander RNR); Admitted ICAS, 1958 (T.C. Garden & Co., CA, Edinburgh); Partner, T.C. Garden & Co., CA, Edinburgh, 1962-79; Partner, Coopers and Lybrand, 1979-91. Recreations: travel; food and wine; gardening; grand-children. Address: (h.) The Ley, Innerleithen, Peeblesshire EH44 6NL; T.-01896 830 240.
E-mail: williammcvicar@btinternet.com

MacWalter, Ronald Siller, BMSc (Hons), MB, ChB (Hons), MD, MRCP(UK); FRCP(Edin); FRCP (Glas). Consultant Physician in Stroke Medicine and General Medicine, Ninewells Hospital, Dundee, since 1997; Consultant Physician in Medicine for the Elderly, Royal Victoria Hospital, Dundee, 1986-97; Honorary Reader in Medicine, Dundee University, Ninewells Hospital, Dundee, since 1986; Honorary Associate Professor of Medicine, Kigezi International School of Medicine, Cambridge, 2001-04; b. 14.12.53, Broughty Ferry; m., Sheila Margaret Nicoll; 2 s. Educ. Harris Academy, Dundee; Dundee University; University of Florida. Registrar in Medicine and Haematology, Department of Clinical Pharmacology, Ninewells Hospital, Dundee; Senior Registrar in General Medicine and Geriatric Medicine, Nuffield Department of Medicine, John Radcliffe Hospital, Oxford. Publication: Secondary Prevention of Stroke; Managing Stroke and TIAs in Practice; Aids to Clinical Examination; papers on stroke.

Macwhirter, Ian. Scottish political commentator; Rector, Edinburgh University, 2009-2012. Educ. University of Edinburgh; b. London; 3 c. Career: worked for the BBC for almost 20 years, becoming Scottish political correspondent in 1987, then from 1989 as a member of the Westminster press contingent; worked at both the UK Parliament and Scottish Parliament, presenting the BBC2 programmes "Westminster Live" and "Scrutiny"; writes weekly columns for The Herald and Sunday Herald; returned to Scotland to help launch the Sunday Herald in 1999; presented the Scottish Parliament magazine programme "Holyrood Live"; writes for the Guardian Unlimited website and the New Statesman. Recreation: hill walking. Address: (b.) The Herald, 200 Renfield Street, Glasgow G2 3PR.

McWilliam, Rev. Thomas Mathieson, MA, BD. Retired Minister; Clerk, Presbytery of Ross, 2000-09; b. 12.11.39, Glasgow; m., Patricia Jane Godfrey; 1 s.; 1 d. Educ. Eastwood Secondary School; Glasgow University; New College, Edinburgh. Assistant Minister, Auld Kirk of Ayr, 1964-66; Minister: Dundee St. David's North, 1966-72, East Kilbride Greenhills, 1972-80, Lylesland Parish Church, Paisley, 1980-97, Contin Parish, 1997-2003. Convener, Youth Education Committee, General Assembly,

1980-84; Moderator, Paisley Presbytery, 1985-86; Convener, Board of Practice and Procedure, General Assembly, 1992-96. Recreations: walking; reading; gardening; bowling. Address: (h.) Flat 3, 13 Culduthel Road, Inverness IV2 4AG; T.-01463 718981.

M

Maan, Bashir Ahmed, CBE, JP, DL, MSc. President, Scottish Council of Voluntary Organisations, 2001-06; President, National Association of British Pakistanis, 1999-2007; Chair, Scottish Police Authorities Forum, 2000-03; b. 22.10.26, Maan, Pakistan; 1 s.; 3 d. Educ. D.B. High School, Quila Didar Singh; Punjab University; Strathclyde University. Involved in the struggle for creation of Pakistan as a student, 1943-47; organised rehabilitation of refugees from India in Maan and surrounding areas, 1947-48; emigrated to UK and settled in Glasgow, 1953; Founder Secretary, Glasgow Pakistan Social and Cultural Society, 1955-65 (President, 1966-69); Member, Executive Committee, Glasgow City Labour Party, 1969-70; Vice-Chairman, Glasgow Community Relations Council, 1970-75; Member, Glasgow Corporation, 1970-75 (Magistrate, City of Glasgow, 1971-74; Vice-Chairman, then Chairman, Police Committee, 1971-75); Member, National Road Safety Committee, 1971-74 and Scottish Accident Prevention Committee, 1971-75; Member, BBC Immigrant Programmes Advisory Committee, 1972-80; Convenor, Pakistan Bill Action Committee, 1973; contested East Fife Parliamentary seat, February 1974; President, Standing Conference of Pakistani Organisations in UK and Eire, 1974-77; Police Judge, City of Glasgow, 1974-75; Member: City of Glasgow District Council, 1975-84, Glasgow City Council, 1995-2003; Bailie, City of Glasgow, 1980-84 and 1996-99; Deputy Chairman, Commission for Racial Equality, 1977-80; Member, Scottish Gas Consumers Council, 1978-81; Member, Greater Glasgow Health Board, 1981-92; Deputy Lieutenant, Glasgow, since 1982; Hon. Research Fellow, Glasgow University, 1988-91; Hon. Fellow, Glasgow Caledonian University, 2003-08; Founder Chairman, Scottish Pakistani Association, 1984-91, and 1994-2000; Judge, City of Glasgow District Courts, 1968-97; Chairman, Strathclyde Community Relations Council, 1986-93 and 1994-96; Member, BBC General Advisory Council, 1992-95; a Governor, Jordanhill College of Further Education, 1987-91; Chairman, Mosque Committee, Islamic Centre, Glasgow, 1986-91; Convener, Strathclyde Joint Police Board, 1999-2003; Member: Police Advisory Board Scotland, 1999-2003, Muslim Council of Britain, 1998-2008; Chair, Council of Ethnic Minority Organisations Scotland (CEMVO), 2003-2011; Trustee, Ethnic Minority Foundation (EMF), 2003-08; Trustee, British Muslim Research Centre (BMRC), 2002-08; President, Islamic Centre, Glasgow, 2007-2010; LLD, University of Strathclyde, 1999; DUniv, Glasgow, 2001; DLitt (Glasgow Caledonian), 2002. Publication: The New Scots, 1992; The Thistle and The Crescent, 2008; Muslims in Scotland, 2015. Recreations: golf; reading. Address: (h.) 8 Riverview Gardens, Glasgow G51 8EL; T.-0141-429 7689.

Magee, Jane Deborah, MA (St Andrews), MA (London), PGCE (Dundee). Director, English Language Teaching (ELT), University of St. Andrews, since 2006; b. 26.07.51, Glasgow; m., Stephen Magee; 2 s.; 1 d. Educ. Park School, Glasgow; St. Andrews; Institute of Education, University of London. Legal Executive, London, 1977-79; Librarian, University of London, 1974-75; Teacher: Scotland, 1975-77, Markopoulo, Greece, 1979-80; Management Accountant: Schlumberger, London, 1982-84, Schlumberger, China, 1985-86; Administrator, Beijing Normal University, 1987-89; Programme Director, ELT, St. Andrews, 1996-2006. Recreations: photography; (slow) walking; swimming; gardening; running; travelling. Address: (b.) University of St. Andrews, ELT, Kinnessburn, Kennedy Gardens, St. Andrews, Fife KY16 9DJ; T.-01334-462255; e-mail: jane.magee@st-andrews.ac.uk

Magee, Stephen Robert, MA, PGCE, MSc. Chair, Board of Governors, Fife College, since 2014; Vice Principal,

University of St. Andrews, 2003-2014; b. 19.4.53, Glasgow; m., Jane; 2 s.; 1 d. Educ. Marr College, Troon; Universities of St. Andrews, London and Edinburgh. Management Trainee, Williams and Glyns Bank, 1976; Teacher, Frontistirion Klavas, 1979; Lecturer, Waltham Forest College, 1981; Senior Lecturer, Beijing Foreign Studies University, 1985; University of St. Andrews: Director, ELT, 1989, Director, Admissions, 1996-2003. Publications: Seventy Five Years Since Saussure: Magee et al. Editors (Beijing), 1988; Introducing Linguistics: Liu, Magee and Wang (Beijing), 1989. Recreations: spectating and travelling. Address: Fife College, Pittsburgh Road, Dunfermline KY11 8DY.

Magnusson, Sally Anne, MA (Hons). Presenter, Reporting Scotland, BBC, since 1998; Presenter, Hard Cash, BBC, 2000-02; Reporter, 4 X 4 Reports, 2001-03; Presenter, Britain's Secret Shame, 2003-04; Presenter, Songs of Praise, BBC, since 1983; Presenter, Daily Politics, BBC; Reporter, Panorama, BBC1; Presenter, Tracing Your Roots, Radio 4; Presenter, Sally on Sunday, Radio Scotland; b. 11.10.55, Glasgow; m., Norman Stone; 4 s.; 1 d. Educ. Laurel Bank School; Edinburgh University. Reporter, The Scotsman, 1979-81; News/Feature Writer, Sunday Standard, 1981-83; Reporter, Current Account, BBC Scotland, 1983, Presenter, Sixty Minutes, BBC, 1983-84; Presenter, London Plus, BBC, 1984-85; Presenter, Breakfast News (formerly Breakfast Time), BBC, 1985-99. Awards: Feature Writer of the Year, 1982; Royal Television Society, 2004; Institute of Contemporary Scotland, 2007. Publications: The Flying Scotsman, 1981; Clemo - A Love Story, 1984; A Shout in the Street, 1990; Family Life, 1999; Dreaming of Iceland, 2004; Glorious Things, 2004; Life of Pee, 2010; Horace and the Haggis Hunter, 2012.

Mahmood, Tahir Ahmed, CBE, MBBS, BSc, MD, FRCOG, FRCP (Ireland), MFFP, MBA (HCM), FACOG (Hon), FRCP (Edin). Consultant Obstetrician and Gynaecologist, Victoria Hospital, Kirkcaldy, since 1990; Clinical Senior Lecturer, Obstetrics and Gynaecology, Aberdeen University, since 1990; Senior Lecturer, School of Biological and Medical Sciences, St. Andrews University, since 1995; Clinical Senior Lecturer, University of Edinburgh, since 1996; Teaching Sub Dean, Medical School, Dundee, 2001-2012; Director, Women and Children's Health Directorate, Fife Acute NHS Hospitals Trust, 1998-2006; Member, BMA Scottish Council, 1996-2003; b. 7.10.53, Pakistan; m., Aasia Bashir; 2 s. Educ. King Edward Medical College, Lahore, Punjab University. Member, Scottish Hospital Staffing Review Committee, sub-speciality of obstetrics and gynaecology, 1986-88; Member, Minimal Invasive Surgery Subgroup and Clinical Resource Management, Procurement Group for Acute Unit, Fife, 1991-92; Ethicon RCOG Travelling Fellowship, 1991; Member, Senate, Aberdeen University, 1992-2000; Hon. Secretary, Northern Obstetrical and Gynaecological Society, 1993-98, Chairman, 1999-2012; Member, Area Medical Committee, Fife, 1993-98, Chairman, 1995-98; Member, Council, Royal College of Obstetricians and Gynaecologists (RCOG), 1994-2000, and 2002-2010, and of Scottish Committee, RCOG, 1994-2000, and 2002-2010; Honorary Secretary, Scottish Committee, RCOG, 2004-07; Chairman, Hospital Recognition Committee of the RCOG, 2005-07; Vice President, Royal College of Obstetricians and Gynaecologists, 2007-2010; Member, Council of European Board and College of Obstetrics and Gynaecology (EBCOG), since 2008, Chair Task force to develop Standards of care in Europe, since 2010 and President Elect, EBCOG (2011-2014); Medical Advisor, Jennifer Brown Research Fund Fife Appeal, 2004-2011. National Lead, Heavy Menstrual Bleeding Audit based at Office of Research and Clinical Audit, RCOG, 2010-14; President, Edinburgh Obstetrical Society, 2012-2014; Life Trustee, Lindsay Stewart Foundation R & D Centre -

RCOG, London, since 2010. Publications: Models of Care in Woman's Health and Maternity Services-RCOG Publications (Co-Author), 2009-2010; Clinical Obstetrics and Gynaecology - Best Practice and Research: Abortion and Post Abortion Care (Guest Editor), 2010; Obesity: A ticking time bomb for reproductive health (Co-Editor), 2012. Recreations: reading; history; walking. Address: (b.) Victoria Hospital, Hayfield Road, Kirkcaldy, Fife; T.-01592 643355.

Mahoney, Professor Craig, BEd, MA, PhD, TTC, CPsychol. Principal and Vice-Chancellor, University of the West of Scotland, since 2013; b. Tasmania, Educ. Tasmanian College of Advanced Education (now the University of Tasmania); Birmingham University; The Queen's University of Belfast. Career: founding Dean of the School of Sport, Performing Arts and Leisure, Wolverhampton University; Deputy Vice-Chancellor, Northumbria University; Chief Executive, Higher Education Academy, 2010-2013. Served as a reviewer for the Quality Assurance Agency in England and since 1995 has been on numerous committees and validation panels in UK Higher Education; part of a panel to produce a new quality benchmark for Hospitality, Leisure, Sport and Tourism in 2008; has held a variety of external examination engagements (at subject, programme and PhD level) to confirm standards and oversee the assurance of quality in UK Higher Education; past Chair of the British Association of Sport and Exercise Sciences (BASES); makes regular TV and radio appearances for the BBC, ITV and Sky; frequent contributions to newspapers and magazine articles on topics ranging across education, performance and undercover reporting; previously Deputy Chair of the South Tyneside NHS Trust; member of the JISC Advance Board; independent Governor at Tyne Met FE College; Non Executive Director, Plus Resource Development International Board. Published widely in the areas of children's fitness, health, sport, exercise, performance and education and sport psychology. Recreations: travel; music; sport; spending time with family. Address: (b.) Paisley Campus, Paisley PA1 2BE; T.-0141 8483000.

Main, Very Rev. Professor Alan, TD, MA, BD, STM, PhD, DD. Professor of Practical Theology, Christ's College, Aberdeen, 1980-2001; Moderator, General Assembly, Church of Scotland, 1998-99; b. 31.3.36, Aberdeen; m., Anne Louise Swanson; 2 d. Educ. Robert Gordon's College, Aberdeen; University of Aberdeen; Union Theological Seminary, New York. Minister, Chapel of Garioch Parish, Aberdeenshire, 1963-70; Chaplain, University of Aberdeen, 1970-80; Chaplain, 153(H) Artillery Support Regiment, RCT(V), 1970-92; Provost, Faculty of Divinity, Aberdeen University, 1990-93; Master, Christ's College, Aberdeen, 1992-2001. Moderator: Garioch Presbytery, 1969-70, Aberdeen Presbytery, 1984-85; Convener, Board of World Mission, 2000-02; Adviser in Religious Broadcasting, Grampian Television, 1976-86; Chairman: Grampian Marriage Guidance, 1977-80, Cruse, 1981-84; Patron, Seven Incorporated Trades of Aberdeen, 2000-2013; Minister, St. Andrews Scots Kirk, Colombo, 2002-03; Convener, Israel Centres, 2003-04; President, The Boys' Brigade, 2005-07. Recreations: music; golf. Address: (h.) Kirkfield, Barthol Chapel, Inverurie AB51 8TD.

Main, Professor Brian G.M., BSc, MBA, MA, PhD, FRSE. Professor of Business Economics, Edinburgh University, since 1991; Director, David Hume Institute, 1995-2005; b. 24.8.47, St. Andrews; m., June Lambert; 2 s.; 1 d. Educ. Buckhaven High School; St. Andrews University; University of California, Berkeley. Lecturer, then Reader in Economics, Edinburgh University, 1976-87; Professor of Economics and Chairman, Department of Economics, St. Andrews University, 1987-91. Recreation: fishing. Address: (b.) University of Edinburgh Business School, 29 Buccleuch Place, Edinburgh EH8 9JS; T.-0131-650 8360; e-mail: Brian.Main@ed.ac.uk

Main, Carol, BLD, MBE, BA. Director, Live Music Now Scotland and International Development, since 1984; Founding Director, National Association of Youth Orchestras, 1979-2003; Classical Music Editor, The List, since 1985; b. 21.12.58, Kirkcaldy; 1 d. Educ. Kirkcaldy High School; Edinburgh University. Freelance music critic; radio broadcaster. Board Director: Association of British Orchestras, Traditional Music Forum; Governor: Royal Conservatoire of Scotland. Previous Board Directorships include: Enterprise Music Scotland (Chair), Voluntary Arts Scotland (Vice-Chair). Hebrides Ensemble (Chair, 2004-2011), Enterprise Music Scotland (Chair, 1999-2001), St Mary's Music School, Edinburgh Festival Fringe Society, 1986-2005. Address: (b.) 14 Lennox Street, Edinburgh EH4 1QA; T.-0131 332 2110; e-mail: carol.main@gmail.com

Main, Professor Ian Graham, BSc, MSc, PhD, FRSE. Professor of Seismology and Rock Physics, University of Edinburgh, since 2000; Director of Research, School of Geosciences; Member: the Research Advisory Forum of the Scottish Energy Technology Partnership (ETP); the Scottish Regional Advisory Group for Enhanced Learning and Research for Humanitarian Assistance (ELRHA); b. 8.9.57, Aberdeen; m., 1. Anthea Stephen (divorced); 1 d.; m., 2. Melanie Miller; 1 d. Educ. Ross High School, Tranent, East Lothian; University of St. Andrews; University of Durham; University of Edinburgh. Lecturer in Geophysics, University of Reading, 1985-89; Lecturer, then Reader in Seismology and Rock Physics, University of Edinburgh, 1989-2000; Visiting Professor: École Normale Supérieure, Paris, 1999, University of Bologna, 2000; Head of the Earth Sciences research group, School of Geosciences, 2003-07; Director, Joint Research Institute in Subsurface Science and Engineering (Ecosse), 2007-09; Member: International Seismological Centre Governing Council, 1988-2013, Royal Society of Edinburgh Sectional Committee on Chemistry and Earth Sciences, 2009-2012, International Commission on Earthquake Forecasting for civil protection, 2010-2011; Member, The HEFCE Research Excellence Framework (REF) Panel on Earth Systems and Environmental Sciences, 2013-14; Moderator, Nature debate on earthquake prediction, 1999; Awards: Bullerwell Lecturer in Geophysics, 1997, Elected Fellow, Royal Society of Edinburgh, 2009, Royal Society of Edinburgh Research Fellowship, 2010, Louis Néel medal of the European Geosciences Union, 2014. Recreations: writing and performing folk music; running (very slowly). Address: (b.) School of Geosciences, University of Edinburgh, West Mains Road, Edinburgh EH9 3JW; T.-0131-650 4911; e-mail: ian.main@ed.ac.uk

Mair, Alexander, MBE (1967). Governor, Robert Gordon's College, Aberdeen, 1988-2002; b. 5.11.22, Echt; m., Margaret Isobel. Educ. Skene Central School; School of Accountancy, Glasgow. Company Secretary, Grampian TV, 1961-70; appointed Director, 1967; Director and Chief Executive, 1970-87. President: Junior Chamber, Aberdeen, 1960-61, Aberdeen Chamber of Commerce, 1989-91; Chairman: Aberdeen International Football Festival, 1988-91, Oil Industry Community Fund, 1993-2001, RGIT Limited, 1989-98. Recreations: golf; skiing; gardening. Address: (h.) Ravenswood, 66 Rubislaw Den South, Aberdeen AB15 4AY; T.-01224 317619.

Mair, Alistair S.F., MBE, DL, LLD, BSc, BA, FRSA. Managing Director, Caithness Glass Ltd., 1977-98; Chairman, 1991-98; b. 20.7.35, Drumblade; m., 1, Anne Garrow (deceased); 2, Mary Bolton; 4 s.; 1 d. Educ. New

Machar School; Robert Gordon's College, Aberdeen; Aberdeen University; Open University. Rolls Royce, Glasgow, 1957-71: graduate apprentice, PA to General Manager, Production Control Manager, Product Centre Manager; RAF, 1960-62 (short-service commission, Technical Branch); Managing Director, Caithness Glass Ltd., 1971-75; Marketing Director, Worcester Royal Porcelain Co., 1975-76. Non-Executive Director: Grampian Television, 1986-2001, Crieff Hydro Ltd., 1994-2003 (Chairman, 1996-2003), Murray VCT 3 PLC, 1997-2005; Governor, Morrison's Academy, Crieff, 1985-2006 (Chairman, 1996-2006); Commissioner, Queen Victoria School, Dunblane, 1992-97; Member, Aberdeen University Court, 1993-2010, Convener, Finance and Estates Committee, 1998-2003, Chancellor's Assessor, Senior Lay Member, and Vice Chairman, 2000-2010; Member, UHI Board, 2008-2013; Chairman, Scottish Committee of University Chairmen, 2001-07; Chairman, CBI Scotland, 1989-91, and Member, CBI Council, 1985-97; President, British Glass Manufacturers Confederation 1997, 1998; Chairman, Crieff Auxiliary Association (Richmond House), 1993-99; Honorary President, Duke of Edinburgh Award, Perth and Kinross, since 1993; Chairman, Perth, Ochil and South Perthshire Conservative and Unionist Associations, 1999-2009. Recreations: reading; history; gardening; walking; current affairs. Address: (h.) Woodend, Madderty, Crieff PH7 3PA; T.-01764 683210.

Mair, Christopher John Montgomerie Alpine, FICS. Honorary Consul for Norway, since 1963; C. A. Mair (Shipping) Ltd., since 1987; Shipping Agent and Broker, since 1956; b. 10.06.39, The Hague, Netherlands; m., Janette Louise; 2 d. Educ. Cranleigh. R. L. Alpine & Co. Ltd., 1956-87. Honorary Vice Consul for Denmark, since 1966. Recreations: swimming; golf. Address: (h.) 32 Caldwell Road, West Kilbride KA23 9LF. Address: (b.) Winton Buildings, Ardrossan KA22 8BY; T.-01294 605284; e-mail: chris@mairshipping.co.uk

Mair, Colin David Robertson, MA, CertEd. Rector, The High School of Glasgow, 2004-2015; b. 4.8.53, Edinburgh. Educ. Kelvinside Academy; St. Andrews University; Glasgow University; Jordanhill College. The High School of Glasgow: Teacher of Latin, 1976-79, Head of Rugby, 1977-88, Head of Latin, 1979-85, Bannerman Housemaster, 1982-85, Assistant Rector, 1985-96, Deputy Rector, 1996-2004; General Convocation of the University of Strathclyde, 2009-2010. Commonweal Committee, Trades House of Glasgow, 2004-06; awarded the SQA Fellowship Award 2014; Member, UCAS Scottish Standing Group, 2003-2015; Member, School Leaders Scotland Council, 1997-2013; received Scottish Cricket Writers Award, 1993 "for services to cricket". Recreations: cricket; golf; rugby; walking; watching Partick Thistle. Address: (h.) 17 Ladywood, Milngavie, Glasgow G62 8BE; T.-0141 956 5792.

Maitland, Peter Salisbury, BSc, PhD, FRSE. Independent Consultant in Freshwater Ecology, since 1986; Visiting Professor, Glasgow University, since 1997; Founder, Scottish Freshwater Group; b. 8.12.37, Glasgow; m., Kathleen Ramsay; 1 s.; 2 d. Educ. Bearsden Academy; Glasgow University. Lecturer in Zoology, Glasgow University, 1959-67; Senior Scientific Officer, Nature Conservancy, 1967-70; Principal Scientific Officer, Institute of Terrestrial Ecology, 1970-86; Senior Lecturer in Ecology, St. Andrews University, 1978-82. Royal Society of Edinburgh Fellowship, 1980; Neill Medal, 1993; Freshwater Biological Association Fellowship, 1996; Zoological Society of London's Marsh Wildlife Award for Conservation, 1999; Fishery Society of the British Isles: Beverton Medal, 2009. Publications: 12 books; 260 scientific papers. Recreations: wildlife conservation; fish-keeping; gardening; walking; music. Address: (h.) Nether Sunnyside, Gladshot, Haddington EH41 4NR; T.-01620 823691.

Maitland-Carew, The Hon. Gerald Edward Ian, DL. Lord Lieutenant, Roxburgh, Ettrick and Lauderdale, since 2007; b. 28.12.41, Dublin; m., Rosalind Averil Speke (1972); 2 s. (Edward, 1976 and Peter, 1978); 1 d. (Emma, 1974). Educ. Harrow School. Army Officer, 15/19 The Kings Royal Hussars, 1960-72; looked after family estates, since 1972; Lieutenant, Royal Company of Archers; Chairman, Lauderdale Hunt, 1980-2000; Chairman, Lauderdale and Galawater Branch, Royal British Legion Scotland; Deputy Lieutenant, Ettrick and Lauderdale and Roxburgh, 1989; elected Member, Jockey Club, 1987; Member, Border Area, TA Committee; Chairman, International League for the Protection of Horses, 1999-2007; Vice President, World Horse Welfare, since 2007; President, Gurkha Welfare Trust of Scotland, since 2003; President, Border Rifle League, 1994; Chairman, Gurkha Welfare Trust of Scotland, 1996-2003. Recreation: shooting; horse riding; horse racing. Address: (h.) The Garden House, Thirlestane Castle, Lauder, Berwickshire TD2 6PD; T.-07971196351.
E-mail: maitland-carew@thirlestanecastle.co.uk

Maizels, Professor Rick, BSc, PhD, FRSE. Professor of Zoology, Edinburgh University, since 1995; b. 14.5.53, London. Educ. University College London. MRC Scientific Staff, NIMR, Mill Hill, 1979-83; Lecturer, Reader and Professor, Department of Biology, Imperial College, London, 1983-95. Address: (b.) Ashworth Laboratories, Edinburgh University EH9 3JT; T.-0131-650 5511.

Malcolm, Hon. Lord (Colin Campbell), LLB (Hons); b. 1.10.53; m., Fiona Anderson. Senator of the College of Justice, since 2007. Educ. Grove Academy, Broughty Ferry; School of Law, University of Dundee. Admitted to the Faculty of Advocates in 1977; Lecturer, School of Law, University of Edinburgh, 1977-79; Standing Junior Counsel to the Scottish Development Department, 1984-1990, appointed Queen's Counsel in 1990; elected Vice-Dean of the Faculty of Advocates in 1997, Dean of the Faculty, 2001-04; part-time member of the Mental Welfare Commission for Scotland, 1997-2001; one of the first members of the Judicial Appointments Board for Scotland on its establishment in 2002, serving until 2005; appointed to the Bench of the Supreme Courts of Scotland in 2007, succeeding Lord Wheatley in the Outer House of the Court of Session; took the judicial title, Lord Malcolm; served as a judge of the Commercial Court of the Court of Session; appointed to the Second Division of the Inner House in 2014; appointed a member of the Privy Council of the United Kingdom in 2015; sworn a member of the Council on 19 March 2015. Address: (b.) Parliament House, 11 Parliament Square, Edinburgh EH1 1RQ.

Malden, Reginald John, FMA, MPhil; b. 5.12.44. Educ. Durham School; University of York. FSA Scot, 1963; FMA, 1982. Linlithgow Pursuivant Extraordinary, 1994 & 2010; appointed Unicorn Pursuivant, 2012. Editor (1979-87), Chairman (1987-1991), Vice President (1991-2015), President, since 2015 and Fellow of the Heraldry Society of Scotland. Worked in Local Government Museums & Galleries, 1963-2001, before becoming Director of the Paxton Trust, 2002-09. Secretary, York Philosophical Society (1970-76), York Archaeological and Yorkshire Architectural Society (1970-76); Secretary, British Association for the Advancement of Science (Section H Anthropology & Archaeology) (1978-81). Chairman, Dalrymple Donaldson Fund (1995-2005). Published prize winning books of photographic history; written and lectured widely on local history and heraldry. Articles in The Double Tressure; The York Historian; Archaeologia Aeliana &c. Publications: Let Paisley Flourish (1991); Let Durham Flourish (1996); The Monastery & Abbey of Paisley

(2000); The Dunvegan Armorial (2006); Floreat Dunelmia - 600 years of Durham School (2014); We Shall Go Not Forth Again (2015); currently collaborating with his wife Eilean in the preparation of a pre-1672 Armorial, Ordinary and Gazetteer Scottish coats of arms. Lives in Berwickshire.

Malik, Hanzala, BSc. MSP (Labour), Glasgow, 2011-16; Member, Glasgow City Council, 1995-2012; Bailie; b. 26.11.56, Glasgow; m., Haleema Sadia; 1 s.; 1 d. Educ. University of the West of Scotland. Manager, Dhool Farms Ltd, 1982-87; Financial Consultant, 1987-88; Director, Azad Video, 1988-92. Chair, Board, West of Scotland Regional Equality Council. Recreations: badminton; charity work; community work; cooking; philately; swimming.

Mallinson, Edward John Harold, LLM, MPharm, FRPharmS, HonMFPH. Formerly Consultant in Pharmaceutical Public Health (Chief Administrative Pharmaceutical Officer), NHS Lanarkshire, 1984-2010; b. 15.3.50, Bingley; m., Diana Gray; 2 d. Educ. Bradford Grammar School; Bradford University; Cardiff Law School. Honorary Treasurer, Scottish Medico-Legal Society; Secretary and Treasurer, Pharmacy Law and Ethics Association; Staff Pharmacist (Ward Pharmacy Services), Bradford Royal Infirmary, 1973-78; District Pharmaceutical Officer, Perth and Kinross District, 1978-83. Secretary, Scottish Specialists in Pharmaceutical Public Health (formerly Scottish Chief Administrative Pharmaceutical Officers' Group), 1988-90, 1996, and 1999-2001 (Chairman, 1990-92, and 1997-98); Member, Scottish Executive, Royal Pharmaceutical Society of Great Britain, 2000-02 (Hon. Secretary, Bradford & District Branch, 1978, Hon. Secretary, Dundee & Eastern Scottish Branch, 1979-83, Hon. Secretary and Treasurer, Lanarkshire Branch, 1984-2004, Chairman, 2006-08); Charter Silver Medallist, 2001; Member, RPSGB Disciplinary Committee, 2007-2010; Member, GPhC Fitness to Practise Committee, since 2010; Member of Council, Royal Society of Health, 1992-96, and 2004-11, Honorary Treasurer, 1996; Vice Chairman and Secretary, Pharmaceutical Group, Royal Society of Health, 1986-89; Chairman, Strathclyde Police/Lanarkshire Health Board Drug Liaison Committee, 1985-91; Member, General Synod, Scottish Episcopal Church, 1986-95; Honorary Treasurer, Comunn Gaidhlig na h-Eaglais Easbaigich; Honorary Treasurer, Affirming Apostolic Order, 1993-98; Secretary, Lanarkshire Branch, British Institute of Management, 1989-91 (Chairman, 1991-94); Social Secretary, Heraldry Society of Scotland, since 2005; Treasurer, Scottish Medico Legal Society. Recreations: genealogy; Gaelic language and culture; heraldry; photography; cooking. Address: (h.) Malden, North Dean Park Avenue, Bothwell, Glasgow G71 8HH; e-mail: e.mallinson@talktalk.net

Malone, Bernadette, CBE, MA, DipEd, MBA. Chief Executive, Perth and Kinross Council, since 2003; b. Dundee; m. Educ. Lawside Academy; Dundee University. Clerk to the Lord Lieutenancy, Perth and Kinross. Address: (b.) 2 High Street, Perth PH1 5PH; T.-01738 475001; e-mail: bmalone@pkc.gov.uk

Mann, Professor David George, BSc, BA, PhD, DSc. Senior Principal Research Scientist, Royal Botanic Garden, Edinburgh, since 1996; b. 25.2.53, Romford, Essex; m. (1), Lynn Barbara (divorced); 1 s.; 1 d. (2) Rosa Trobajo. Educ. Brentwood School; Bristol University; Edinburgh College of Art. Edinburgh University: Demonstrator, 1978-81, Lecturer, 1981-90, Director of Studies, 1989-90; Deputy Regius Keeper (Deputy Director), Royal Botanic Garden, Edinburgh, 1990-96. G.W. Prescott Award, 1991, 1997. Publications: editor/author of 170 papers and books. Recreations: classical piano; printmaking and painting.

Address: (b.) Royal Botanic Garden, Inverleith Row, Edinburgh EH3 5LR; T.-0131-552 7171; e-mail: d.mann@rbge.org.uk

Manning, Professor Aubrey William George, OBE, BSc, DPhil, CBiol, FSB, FRZSS, FRSE, Dr (h c) (Toulouse), DUniv (Open), HonDSc (St. Andrews), HonMA (Worcs), HonDSc (Edin), HonFGS. Professor of Natural History, Division of Biological Sciences, Edinburgh University, 1973-97, Professor Emeritus, since 1997; b. 24.4.30, London; m.; 3 s., inc. 2 by pr. m. Educ. Strode's School, Egham; University College, London; Merton College, Oxford. Research, 1951-54; National Service, Royal Artillery, 1954-56; Lecturer, then Reader in Zoology, Edinburgh University, 1956-73; Secretary-General, International Ethological Committee, 1971-79; President: Association for the Study of Animal Behaviour, 1981-84, Biology Section, British Association for the Advancement of Science, 1993; Member: Scottish Advisory Committee, Nature Conservancy Council, 1982-89, Advisory Committee on Science, NCC, 1985-89; Chairman of Council, Scottish Wildlife Trust, 1990-96; Trustee, National Museums of Scotland, 1997-2005; President, Royal Society of Wildlife Trusts, 2006-2010; Goodwill Ambassador, UN International Year of Planet Earth, 2008-09; Association for the Study of Animal Behaviour Medal, 1998; 2011 RSE Beltane Senior Prize for Public Engagement; Member, Wellcome Trust Population Studies Panel, 1996-99; Patron, Population Matters; Dobzhansky Memorial Award, Behavioural Genetics Association, 1996; Zoological Society of London Silver Medal, 2003; RSPB Lifetime Achievement Award, 2013; Presenter: Earth Story series, BBC2, 1998, Talking Landscapes series, BBC 2, 2001, Landscape Mysteries series, BBC2, 2003, Unearthing Mysteries series, Radio 4, 1999-2006; The Sound of Life, 2004; The Rules of Life, 2005. Publication: An Introduction to Animal Behaviour, 6th edition (Co-Author), 2012; research papers in biological journals. Recreations: woodland conservation; walking; architecture. Address: (h.) The Old Hall, Ormiston, East Lothian EH35 5NJ; T.-01875 340536; e-mail: jaherrmanning@aol.com

Mansfield and Mansfield, 9th Earl of (Alexander David Mungo Murray); b. 17.10.56; m., Sophia Mary Veronica Ashbrooke; 1 s.; 3 d. Succeeded to title, 2015. Address: Estate Office, Scone Palace, Perth PH2 6BD.

Manson, Alexander Reid, CBE, SDA, FRAgS. Farmer; General Commissioner of Income Tax, 1991-2006; b. 2.9.31, Oldmeldrum; m., Ethel Mary Philip; 1 s.; 2 d. Educ. Robert Gordon's College; North of Scotland College of Agriculture. Member, Oldmeldrum Town Council, 1960-65; founder Chairman, Aberdeen Beef and Calf Ltd., 1962; Past President, Scottish Agricultural Organisation Society Ltd.; Chairman, Buchan Meat Producers Ltd., 1982-92; Member, Meat and Livestock Commission, 1986-95; Past President, Federation of Agricultural Cooperatives; Member, Williams Committee of Enquiry, 1989; Member, EU Beef Advisory Committee, 1986-96; Director, National Animal Data Centre, 1992-95; Chairman, Oldmeldrum Heritage Society, since 2000. Recreations: history; bird-watching. Address: (h.) Kempswood, Oldmeldrum, Inverurie AB51 ODN; T.-01651 872226.

Mapstone, Sally Louise, DPhil. Honorary President, Scottish Text Society, since 2012; Fellow and Tutor in English, St. Hilda's College, Oxford, since 1989; Pro-Vice Chancellor (Education), University of Oxford, since 2010; Principal, University of St Andrews (appointed from September 2016); b., Hillingdon, Middlesex; m., Martin Griffiths. Educ. Vyners Grammar School, Ickenham, Middlesex; Wadham College, Oxford University. Editor,

Weidenfeld & Nicolson Publishers, London, 1978-81; Junior Research Fellow, St. Hilda's College, Oxford, 1984-86; Lecturer and Supernumerary Fellow, St. Hilda's College, Oxford, 1986-89; Junior Proctor, Oxford University, 2006-07. Publications: author and editor of 7 books on older Scots literature, and numerous articles on the same subject. Recreations: reading and running. Address: (b.) 25 Buccleuch Place, Edinburgh EH8 9LN; T.-01865 276 860; e-mail: sally.mapstone@st-hildas.ox.ac.uk

Mar and Kellie, Earl of (James Thorne Erskine). Estate Worker; Scottish Liberal Democrat Life Peer, sitting as Lord Erskine of Alloa Tower (Liberal Democrat Spokesman on Scotland, 2001-04, Member, House of Lords Select Committee on the Constitution, 2001-04); Liberal Democrat Assistant Whip, 2002-07 and 2009-2010; Assistant Transport Spokesman, 2004-2013; b. 10.3.49, Edinburgh; m., Mary Irene; 1 step s.; 3 step d.; 1 step d. deceased. Educ. Eton; Moray House College of Education; Inverness College. Community Service Volunteer, York, 1967-68; Youth and Community Worker, Craigmillar, 1971-73; Social Worker, Sheffield, 1973-76, Grampian Region, 1976-78; Social Worker, Prison Social Worker, Community Service Supervisor, Highland Region, 1979-87; Builder, Kincardine, 1990-92; Project Worker, SACRO, Falkirk, 1992-93; Royal Auxiliary Air Force Regiment, 1979-85; Royal Naval Auxiliary Service, 1985-88; Chairman, Strathclyde Tram Inquiry, 1996; Parliamentary Commissioner, Burrell Collection (Lending) Inquiry, 1997; Member, House of Lords Select Committee on Religious Offences, 2002-03; Member, House of Lords administration and works committee, 2004-08; campaigning for a Dominion with UN, NATO and EU Member status, since 2004; Member, Independence Convention, since 2005; Member, House of Lords ad hoc Committee for the Barnett Formula, 2008-09; Member, Joint Committee on Statutory Investments, 2008-2013. Recreations: canoeing; hill-walking; boat building; Alloa Tower. Address: Hilton Farm, Alloa FK10 3PS.

Maran, Emeritus Professor Arnold George Dominic, MB, ChB, MD, FRCS, FACS, FRCP, FRCS (Eng), FDS (Hon), DSc (Hon). Former Professor of Otolaryngology, Edinburgh University, now Emeritus Professor; Past President, Royal College of Surgeons; Consultant Surgeon, Royal Infirmary and City Hospital, Edinburgh, since 1974; b. 16.6.36, Edinburgh; m., Anna; 1 s.; 1 d. Educ. Daniel Stewart's College; Edinburgh University; University of Iowa. Fifteen Visiting Professorships to foreign universities; Honorary Fellowship, Royal College of Surgeons of South Africa, Royal College of Surgeons of Hong Kong, Royal College of Physicians of Edinburgh, Royal College of Surgeons of England, Royal College of Physicians and Surgeons of Glasgow, Royal Society of Medicine. Order of Gorka Dakshina Bahu, Nepal. Publications: six surgical textbooks and 160 scientific papers; The Voice Doctor (Book Guild 2006); The Mafia: Inside The Dark Heart (Mainstream 2008); Golf at the North Pole (FastPrint 2014). Recreations: golf; playing piano; writing; living in Italy. Address: (h.) 2 Orchard Brae, Edinburgh EH4 1NZ; T.-0131-332 0055.

Marcella, Professor Rita Christina, MA (Hons), DipLib, DipEd, PhD, FCMI, FCILIP. Dean, Aberdeen Business School, Robert Gordon University, since 2004, Professor of Corporate Communication, since 2002; b. 10.7.56, Fraserburgh; m., Philip Marcella; 1 s.; 1 d. Educ. Peterhead Academy; Aberdeen University; Robert Gordon University. Librarian, RGIT, 1983-86; Lecturer, Robert Gordon University, 1986-94; Senior Lecturer, 1994-97; Depute Head of School, Robert Gordon University, 1998-2001; Head of School, Northumbria University, 2001-02. Committee Member: Scottish Council for Development and

Industry (SCDI) North East, Grampian Racial Equality Council; Arts and Humanities Research Council Panel Member. Research into health and safety management and the use of the internet in election campaigns. Recreations: reading; visiting Italy. Address: (b.) Aberdeen Business School, Robert Gordon University, Garthdee Road, Aberdeen AB10 7QE; T.-01224 263904; e-mail: r.c.marcella@rgu.ac.uk

Marjoribanks, John Logan, MA (Cantab). Local Government Political Restrictions Exemptions Adjudicator for Scotland, 2007-2015; Chairman, Gavinton, Fogo & Polwarth Community Council, 2012-14; Chairman, Local Government Boundaries Commission for Scotland, 2000-07; Member, Committee of Management, Berwickshire Housing Association, 2001-07; Member, East Regional Board, Scottish Environment Protection Agency, 2002-05; Member, Board of Governors, Macaulay Land Use Research Institute, Aberdeen, 2004-07; b. 21.8.44, Nicosia, Cyprus; m., Andrea Ruth; 1 s.; 2 d. Educ. Merchiston Castle School, Edinburgh; St. John's College, Cambridge. Scottish Agricultural Industries Ltd., 1965-73; Overseas Development Ministry, on secondment to Government of Zambia, Department of Agriculture, 1973-78; Commonwealth Development Corporation (now CDC Group plc), 1979-2000: latterly Director, Public Affairs. Recreations: heraldry; bridge. Address: (h.) Eden House, Gavinton, Duns TD11 3QS; T.-01361 884523.

Markland, John A., CBE, MA, PhD, Hon. Dr.h.c, ACIS. Member of Court, University of Edinburgh, 2001-2011, Convener of Audit Committee, 2003-06, Vice Convener of Court, 2006-2011; Trustee, Gannochy Trust, since 2009; Member, Scotland Advisory Group, The Woodland Trust; Chairman, Scottish Leadership Foundation, 2001-08; Board Member, Horsecross Arts Ltd., 2007-2013; President, Old Boltonians Association, 2006-07; b. 17.5.48, Bolton; m., Muriel Harris; 4 d. Educ. Bolton School; Dundee University. Demographer, Somerset County Council, 1974-76; Senior Professional Assistant, Tayside Regional Council, 1976-79; Personal Assistant to Chief Executive, then Assistant Chief Executive, then Chief Executive, Fife Regional Council, 1979-95; Chief Executive, Fife Council, 1995-99; Chairman, Scottish Natural Heritage, 1999-2006. Vice Chairman, then Chairman, Environmental Campaigns, 2000-06; Chairman: Forward Scotland, 1996-2000, Society of Local Authority Chief Executives (Scotland), 1993-95, Secretary of State for Scotland's Advisory Group on Sustainable Development, 1998-99. Recreation: trying to keep fit. Address: 3, St. Leonard's Bank, Perth PH2 8EB; T.-01738 441798.

Marnoch, The Rt. Hon. Lord (Michael Stewart Rae Bruce), MA, LLB, LLD (Aberdeen). Senator of the College of Justice, 1990-2005 (retired); b. 26.7.38; m., Alison Stewart; 2 d. Educ.; Loretto; Aberdeen University. Advocate, 1963; QC, 1975; Sworn of the Privy Council, 2001; Standing Counsel to Department of Agriculture and Fisheries for Scotland, 1973; to Highlands and Islands Development Board, 1973; Advocate-Depute, 1983-86; Member, Criminal Injuries Compensation Board, 1986-89. Chairman for Scotland, Salmon and Trout Association, 1989-94. Recreations: golf; fishing. Address: (b.) Parliament House, Edinburgh; T.-0131-225 2595.

Marquis, Alistair Forbes, MBE, BA, MEd, DipCE, FCollP. Appointed a Member of the British Empire by HM The Queen, Jan. 2011 for services to education, young people and the community. International Educational Consultant, working for The World Bank and an Educational Trust. Board Member of Council of Management of Couple Counselling Lothian, 2011-16. HM

Inspector/Assistant Chief Inspector/Chief Inspector, 1989-2011; b. 13.01.50, Glasgow; m.; 1 d. Educ. Queen's Park Senior Secondary School; Jordanhill College, Glasgow; Open University; Edinburgh University. Assistant Teacher, Leithland Primary School, Glasgow, 1971-77; Depute Head Teacher, Dedridge Primary School, West Lothian, 1977-79; Head Teacher, Bankton Primary School, West Lothian, 1979-89. Member, Scottish Committee on Special Educational Needs, 1985-88; Scottish Government representative on the European Evaluation in Education Network, 2006-11; Chairman, Lanthorn Community Complex Management Committee, Livingston, 1979-82; SFA Football Referee, 1972-2016; Church of Scotland Elder, 1985-2016 and National Safeguarding Committee, 2005-08, elected Vice-Chairman, Livingston Ecumenical Parish, 2006-16; Captain, 5th Livingston Company of The Boys' Brigade, 1979-89, Chairman of the Scotland Committee of The Boys' Brigade, 1991-2000; Elected Representative, UK Brigade Executive for East Lowland Area, 1989-2000; Scottish Member, UK Management Committee, 1991-99; President, West Lothian Battalion, 2000-04 and 2007-11, Hon Vice-President, 2011-15; Hon Vice-President, The Scout Association, The Scottish Council, 1996-2000. Member, Rotary International; Past President of the RC of Whitburn; Assistant District Governor (D1020), 2010-12, District Governor Nominee, 2012-13, District Governor Elect, 2013-14, District Governor, 2014-15 and Immediate Past District Governor, 2015-16. Recreations: gardening; reading; walking; football refereeing; foreign holidays.
E-mail: afmarquis@blueyonder.co.uk

Marr, Colin. Theatre Director, Eden Court Theatre, since 1997; b. 3.4.66, Glasgow; m., Nicky; 2 d. Educ. Hutcheson's Grammar School; University of Edinburgh; Open University. Hall Manager, Queen's Hall, Edinburgh, 1988-92; Theatre and Commercial Manager, Traverse Theatre, Edinburgh, 1992-97. Address: (b.) Bishop's Road, Inverness IV3 5SA; T.-01463 239841.

Marr, Douglas, CBE, MA, MEd. Writer, Commentator and Educationalist; Her Majesty's Inspector of Education (HMIE) (part-time), 2004-2011; Principal Consultant, Acorn Consulting (Scotland), since 2004; School Management and Curriculum Co-ordinator, Aberdeenshire Education and Recreation, 2002-04; Senior Teaching Fellow, University of Aberdeen, School of Education, 2004-06; b. 7.2.47, Aberdeen; m., Alison; 1 d. Educ. Aberdeen Grammar School; University of Aberdeen. Teacher of History, Hilton Academy, Aberdeen, 1970-71; Assistant Principal Teacher of History, Aberdeen Grammar School, 1971-76; Principal Teacher of History, Hilton Academy, Aberdeen, 1976-81; Assistant Rector, Kemnay Academy, 1981-84; Depute Rector, The Gordon Schools, Huntly, 1984-87; Headteacher: Hilton Academy, 1987-88, St. Machar Academy, Aberdeen, 1988-95; Rector, Banchory Academy, 1995-2002. Member, Business Management Committee, University of Aberdeen, 2001-06; Member, Aberdeen University Court, 2002-06. Publication: Leisure Education and Young People's Leisure (Co-Author), 1988. Recreations: squash; suffering at the hands (and feet) of Aberdeen F. C.; Member, Leicestershire County Cricket Club; walking; gardening. Address: (h.) Oak Lodge, Alford, Aberdeenshire AB33 8DH; T.-019755 63062; e-mail: douglas.marr@alford.co.uk

Marra, Jenny. MSP (Labour), North East Scotland, since 2011; Shadow Cabinet Secretary for Health, Wellbeing and Sport, since 2014; former Shadow Minister for Youth Employment; b. 6.11.77, Dundee. Studied history at St Andrews University, won a scholarship to Emory University, Atlanta. Returned to her home town and became head of press at Dundee University. Worked for Labour MEPs in Brussels and Strasbourg. Took a Scots law degree. Address: (b.) Scottish Parliament, Edinburgh EH99 1SP.

Marrian, Ian Frederic Young, MA, CA. Accountancy Education Advisor; b. 15.11.43, Kilwinning; m., Moira Selina McSwan; 1 s.; 2 d. Educ. Royal Belfast Academical Institution; Queens University, Belfast; Edinburgh University. Qualified as CA, 1969; Deloitte Haskins & Sells: audit practice, Rome, 1969-72, London, 1972-73, Audit Partner, Edinburgh, 1973-78, Technical Partner, London, 1978-81; Chief Executive and Secretary, Institute of Chartered Accountants of Scotland, 2003-04. Chairman, Paxton Trust. Recreations: gardening in the grand scale; wines. Address: (h.) Walled Garden, Bowerhouse, Dunbar EH42 1RE; T.-01368-862293.
E-mail: ian@ianmarrian.co.uk

Marsack, Robyn Louise, BA, BPhil, DPhil. Director, Scottish Poetry Library, since 2000; b. 30.1.53, Wellington, New Zealand; m., Stuart Airlie; 1 d. Educ. Wellington Girls' College; Victoria University, Wellington; Oxford University. Junior Research Fellow, Wolfson College, Oxford, 1979-82; Editor, Carcanet Press, 1982-86; freelance editor, translator and writer, 1987-99. Member, Scottish Arts Council Literature Committee, 1994-99, Chair, Grants to Publishers Panel, 1996-99; Member, Society of Authors Committee of Management, 2001-04; Member, Board of Directors, Carcanet Press, since 2005; Chair, Literature Forum for Scotland, 2010-12. Recent publications: co-edited Twenty Contemporary New Zealand Poets, 2009; co-edited After Lermontov: translations for the bicentenary, 2014; edited Fall in Ghosts: selected war prose by Edmund Blunden, 2014; translations include The Way of the World by Nicolas Bouvier, 1992, 2007; The Scorpion-Fish by Nicolas Bouvier, reissued 2014. Recreations: reading, reading, reading. Address: (b.) Scottish Poetry Library, 5 Crichton's Close, Canongate, Edinburgh EH8 8DT; T.-0131-557 2876.
E-mail: robyn.marsack@spl.org.uk

Marsh, Professor John Haig, BA, MEng, PhD, CEng, FREng, FIET, FOSA, FInstP, FRSA, FIEEE, FRSE, FFCS. Head of School of Engineering, University of Glasgow, since 2010; Professor of Optoelectronic Systems, University of Glasgow, since 1996; Founder and Chief Technical Officer, Intense Ltd, 2000-2011; b. 15.4.56, Edinburgh; m., Anabel Christine Mitchell. Educ. Glasgow Academy; Cambridge University; Liverpool University; Sheffield University. University of Sheffield: Research Fellow, 1980-83, Research Scientist, 1983-86; Department of Electronics and Electrical Engineering, University of Glasgow: Lecturer, 1986-90, Senior Lecturer, 1990-94, Reader, 1994-96. Director, NATO Advanced Study Institute, Glasgow, 1990; Founding Chair, Scottish Chapter, IEEE/LEOS, 1996-98; Vice President, LEOS, 1999-2001 and 2003-05; President, 2008-09 of IEEE Photonics Society (IEEE LEOS, prior to February 2009); elected Member, Board of Governors, 2001-03. Awarded LEOS Engineering Achievement, 2006 (jointly with A.C. Bryce); LEOS Distinguished Service Award, 2006; Member, Board of Governors, IEEE Technology Management Council, 2012-13. Publications: Waveguide Optoelectronics (Co-editor); more than 500 papers, book chapters and patents. Recreations: walking; cooking; music; malt whisky. Address: (b.) School of Engineering, James Watt Building South, University of Glasgow, Glasgow G12 8QQ; e-mail: john.marsh@glasgow.ac.uk

Marshall, Leon McGregor, CA. Senior Partner, Stevenson & Kyles, CA, Glasgow, since 1995; Member, Church of Scotland World Mission Council, 2005-2013 (Vice-Convener, 2006-09); Moderator, Presbytery of

Greenock, 2002-03; Session Clerk, Kilmacolm Old Kirk, since 1997; b. 10.6.50, Glasgow; m., 1, Barbara Anne McLean (deceased); 2 s.; 1 d.; 2, Judith Margaret Miller (deceased); 3, Barbara Anne Orr. Educ. High School of Glasgow; Glasgow University (as part of CA training). Joined Stevenson & Kyles as a student, 1967; qualified CA, 1972 (joint winner, ICAS Gold Medal); made Partner, 1974. Treasurer, St Enoch's Hogganfield Church, Glasgow, 1973-80; Treasurer, Kilmacolm Old Kirk, 1984-97; Convener, Church of Scotland Central Services Committee, 2001-05; Member, Board of Stewardship and Finance, General Assembly, Church of Scotland, 1990-2001 (Convener, 1997-2001; Convener, Budget and Allocation Committee, 1993-97); Reader, Church of Scotland, since 1987. Recreations: reading; travel; watching football. Address: (b.) 25 Sandyford Place, Glasgow G3 7NG; T.-0141-248 3856; e-mail: lm@stevenson-kyles.co.uk

Marshall, Professor Mary Tara, OBE, MA, DSA, DASS, FRSE. Former Director, Dementia Services Development Centre, Stirling University; b. 13.6.45, Darjeeling, India. Educ. Mary Erskine School for Girls; Edinburgh University; London School of Economics; Liverpool University. Child Care Officer, London Borough of Lambeth, 1967-69; Social Worker, Personal Service Society, Liverpool, 1970-74; Research Organiser, Age Concern, Liverpool, 1974-75; Lecturer in Social Studies, Liverpool University, 1975-83; Director, Age Concern Scotland, 1983-89. Former Member, Royal Commission on Long-term Care of the Elderly; Hon. DEd, Queen Margaret University College; Hon. Degree of Doctor of Science in Social Science, University of Edinburgh, 2004; Hon DUniv, University of Stirling, 2006; Fellow of the Royal Society of Edinburgh; Fellow of the British Society of Gerontology; 2008 British Geriatrics Society medal for the relief of suffering of older people; 2010 RC of Psych, Faculty of Old Age Psych: Lifetime achievement award. Sessional Inspector with Care Inspectorate, 2007-2015; Senior Consultant, Dementia Centre, HammondCare. Publications: The State of Art in Dementia Care, 1997; Food Glorious Food, perspectives on food and dementia, 2003; Perspectives on Rehabilitation and Dementia, 2005 (Ed); Walking not Wandering, 2006 (Ed) (Co-Author); Social Work and people with dementia (Co-author), 2006; Time for dementia (Co-Ed), 2010; Designing balconies, roof terraces and roof gardens for people with dementia, 2010; Transforming the quality of life for people with dementia through contact with the natural world (Co-Editor), 2011; Designing outdoor spaces for people with dementia, University of Stirling/Hammond Care (Co-Editor), 2012; Designing mental health units for older people, 2014; Creating culturally appropriate outside spaces and experiences for people with dementia (Co-Author), 2014. Recreations: photography; bird-watching. Address: (h.) 24 Buckingham Terrace, Edinburgh EH4 3AE; T.-0131 343 1732.

Marshall, Professor William James, BA, M-ès-L, DPhil, MA. Professor of Comparative Literary and Cultural Studies, University of Stirling, since 2008; Director of Institute of Modern Languages Research, School of Advanced Study, University of London, 2011-2014; b. 21.2.57, Newcastle Upon Tyne. Educ. Gosforth High School; Westfield College, University of London; Université de Paris-X Nanterre; University of Oxford; Polytechnic of Central London. Lecteur, Université de Paris-X Nanterre, 1978-79; Lecturer, Sunderland Polytechnic, 1982-83; Lecturer, University of Liverpool, 1983-84; Lecturer/Senior Lecturer/Reader, Southampton University, 1984-2000; Professor of Modern French Studies, Glasgow University, 2000-08. Publications: Victor Serge the Uses of Dissent, 1992; Guy Hocquenghem, 1996; Quebec National Cinema, 2000;

Musicals Hollywood and Beyond (co-ed.) 2000; France and the Americas: Culture, Politics and History (ed.), 2005; Montreal-Glasgow (ed.), 2005; André Téchiné, 2007; The French Atlantic: Travels in Culture and History, 2009. Address: (b.) School of Arts and Humanities, University of Stirling, Stirling FKG 4LA; T.-01786 467536; e-mail: w.j.marshall@stir.ac.uk

Martin, Aoife, BA (mod), MBA. Registrar of Companies for Scotland, since 2015. Educ. Trinity College, Dublin; University of Edinburgh; University of Wales, Bangor. Economist, Sea Fish Industry Authority, 2001-04; Fisheries Manager, Deepwater, Ministry of Fisheries, 2004-2011; Director, Spatial Forestry and Land Management, Ministry for Primary Industries, New Zealand, 2011-15. Address: Registrar of Companies (Scotland), 4th Floor, Edinburgh Quay 2, 139 Fountainbridge, Edinburgh EH3 9FF. E-mail: enquiries@companies-house.gov.uk

Martin, David. Chief Executive, Dundee City Council. Address: (b.) 21 City Square, Dundee DD1 3BD; T.-01382 434201; e-mail: david.martin@dundeecity.gov.uk

Martin, David McLeod, DA, RSW, RGI. Painter; b. 30.12.22, Glasgow; m., Isobel Agnes Fowlie Smith (deceased); 4 s. Educ. Govan High School; Glasgow School of Art; Jordanhill College of Education. RAF, 1942-46. Principal Teacher, Hamilton Grammar School, 1973-83; retired early to paint full-time; exhibits regularly in Scotland; exhibited RA, 1984; numerous group shows; one man shows, Glasgow, Edinburgh, Perth, Greenock, Newcastle, Stenton, London; John Martin Gallery, London, 2008, 2010, 2012, 2013, 2014 and 2015; Lemon Street Gallery, Truro, 2007, 2009, 2011, 2014 and 2015; The Richmond Hill Gallery, London, 2011; mixed shows: New York Art Fair, 1998 and 2002, Johannesburg, 1999; featured artist, Perth festival, 1999; 2004: John Martin Gallery, London, The Albany Gallery, Edgar Modern Gallery, Bath, 2015, Lemon Street Gallery, Truro, Richmond Hill Gallery, London; Smithy Gallery, Blanefield, 2005; 2006/07: The Everard Reid Gallery, Johannesburg; "Lalique", Madison Avenue, New York; The Chelsea Gallery, Palo Alto, California; London Art Fair with Lemon Street Gallery, 2013; Richmond Hill, 2012; Purple Gallery, Birmingham, 2011/12/13/15/16; The Roger Billcliffe Gallery, Glasgow, 1998, 2001, 2003, 2005, 2007, 2009, 2011, 2014 and 2015; John Davies Gallery, 2007. Former Vice President, RSW. Address: (h.) The Old Schoolhouse, 53 Gilmour Street, Eaglesham, Glasgow G76 0LG.

Martin, David Weir, BA (Econ), MA. Vice-President, European Parliament, 1989-2004, Member (Labour) for Lothians, 1984-99, Senior Member for Scotland, since 1999; b. 26.8.54, Edinburgh; 1 s.; 1 d. Educ. Liberton High School; Heriot-Watt University; Leicester University. Worked as stockbroker's assistant and animal rights campaigner; became Lothian Regional Councillor, 1982; Rapporteur; Intergovernmental Conferences; The EU's Aid for Trade; Economic Relations with Korea. Publications: Bringing Common Sense to the Common Market — A Left Agenda for Europe; European Union and the Democratic Deficit; Europe — An Ever Closer Union; Towards a Wider, Deeper, Federal Europe; Maastricht in a Minute; 1996 and all that; A Partnership Democracy for Europe. Recreations: soccer; reading. Address: (b.) Midlothian Innovation Centre, Pentlandfield, Roslin, Midlothian EH25 9RE.

Martin, Donald. Head of Publishing, D.C. Thomson & Co. Ltd., since 2015. Formerly Editor: The Sunday Post and

The Weekly News, and Editor-in-Chief of newspapers, D.C. Thomson & Co. Ltd and Aberdeen Journals Ltd., (2010–2015), The Herald (2008-2010), Evening Times, Aberdeen Evening Express and North West Evening Mail. Past President of the UK Society of Editors and former Chairman of the Scottish Newspaper Society. Address: (b.) 80 Kingsway East, Dundee DD4 8SL; T.-01382 223131.

Martin, Gillian. MSP (SNP), Aberdeenshire East, since 2016; m.; 2 c. Educ. Ellon Academy. Career history: worked as a lecturer for 15 years in TV production; lecturer at North East Scotland College; became politically active during the Scottish independence referendum; helped found Women for Independence (WFI), on the WFI executive, as the member for North East. Address: Scottish Parliament, Edinburgh EH99 1SP.

Martin, Graham Dunstan, MA, BLitt, GradCertEd. Writer; Senior Lecturer, Edinburgh University, 1982-2000; b. 21.10.32, Leeds; m., 1, Ryllis Daniel; 2 s.; 1 d.; 2, Anne Crombie; 2 s. Educ. Leeds Grammar School; Oriel College and Linacre College, Oxford. Schoolteacher, 1956-65; Assistant Lecturer, then Lecturer, in French, Edinburgh University, 1965-82. Publications: (philosophy) Language, Truth and Poetry, 1975; The Architecture of Experience 1981, Shadows in the Cave, 1990; Inquiry into Speculative Fiction, 2003; Does it Matter?, 2005; Living on Purpose, 2008; (novels) Giftwish, 1980; Catchfire, 1981; The Soul Master, 1984; Time-Slip, 1986; The Dream Wall, 1987; Half a Glass of Moonshine, 1988; (pamphlets) Invention of Whisky; Little Richard and the Snake-Charmers; poems and poetry translations including Jules Laforgue, 1998; Blog: Soul Reasons. Recreations: music; jazz; walking; good food; the Celtic past. Address: 21 Mayfield Terrace, Edinburgh EH9 1RY; T.-0131-667 8160; e-mail: gdunstanmartin@btinternet.com

Martin, Rev. Iver, BSc, DipTheol. Principal, Edinburgh Theological Seminary; b. 29.6.57, Grantown on Spey; m., Mairi Isabel Macdonald; 2 s.; 4 d. Educ. Camphill High School, Paisley; Robert Gordon's Institute of Technology; Free Church College. National Semiconductor (UK) Ltd.: Graduate Process Engineer, 1980, Senior Engineer, 1983; European Process Engineer, Lam Research Corporation Ltd., 1985; European Product and Sales Engineer, Silicon Glen Technology, 1987-90; own company, Solus (UK) Ltd., 1990-92; Assistant Minister, Stornoway Free Church, 1995-97; Minister, Bon Accord Free Church, Aberdeen, 1997-2003; Minister, Stornoway Free Church of Scotland, 2003-2015. Recreations: reading; music. Address: ETS, 15 North Bank Street, Edinburgh EH1 2LS; T.-0131 718 4133; e-mail: iverm@aol.com

Martin, Rev. James, MA, BD, DD. Minister, High Carntyne, Glasgow, 1954-87; b. 21.1.21, Motherwell; m., Marion Gordon Greig; 2 d. Educ. Dalziel High School, Motherwell; Glasgow University. Minister, Newmilns West Church, 1946-54; Convener, Publications Committee, General Assembly, 1978-83 and Board of Communications, 1983-87; Bruce Lecturer, Trinity College, 1960-64. Publications: Did Jesus Rise from the Dead?; The Reliability of the Gospels; Letters of Caiaphas to Annas; Suffering Man, Loving God; The Road to the Aisle; People in the Jesus Story; A Plain Man in the Holy Land; Listening to the Bible; William Barclay: A Personal Memoir; My Friend Bobby; It's You, Minister; It's My Belief; Travels in the Holy Land; God-Collared; William Barclay in a Nutshell; You Can't Be Serious; A Parish Minister's Hats; More About Bobby; Grit for the Road of Life; Seen From My Manse Window; More Grit for Life's Road; More Views from My Manse Window; Manse Memories; People, Places and Puzzles of the New Testament;

More Manse Memories; Tales From My Ministry; More Tales From My Ministry. Recreations: football; conversation. Address: 9 Magnolia Street, Wishaw; T.-01698 385825.

Martin, Jim. Scottish Public Services Ombudsman. Address: (b.) 4 Melville Street, Edinburgh EH3 7NS.

Martin, Louise, CBE. Chair, sportscotland, since 2008 (previously served two terms on the Board, 1997-2005). Immediate Past Chair of the Commonwealth Games Scotland (CGS) and has a long and ongoing association with the Games as a competitor, team manager and administrator. First elected as a board member of CGS in 1995 (Chair, 1999-2007); Commonwealth Games Federation Honorary Secretary, since 2011 (the first woman to hold a position on their Executive Board); Chair of the Commonwealth Advisory Board on Sport; responsible for the introduction of the Commonwealth Youth Games to the international sporting calendar, the Commonwealth Sports Development Conference and the development of the Commonwealth Sports Awards; led the successful bid for the 2014 Commonwealth Games which resulted in Glasgow being awarded the Games in November 2007 and was appointed as Vice Chair of the Organising Committee. Board Member, UK Sport and Chair of the Scottish Sports Hall of Fame Committee. Address: sportscotland, Headquarters, Doges, Templeton on the Green, 62 Templeton Street, Glasgow G40 1DA; T.-0141 534 6500

Martin of Springburn, Rt. Hon. Lord (Michael John Martin). Speaker of the House of Commons, 2000-09 (Deputy Speaker, 1997-2000); MP (Labour, then Speaker), Glasgow Springburn, 1979-2005; Glasgow (North East), 2005-09; b. 3.7.45, Glasgow; m., Mary McLay; 1 s.; 1 d. Educ. St. Patrick's Boys' School, Glasgow. Member, Glasgow Corporation, 1973-74, and of Glasgow District Council, 1974-79. Member, Speaker's Panel of Chairmen, since 1987; Chairman, Scottish Grand Committee, 1987-97. Fellow, Parliament and Industry Trust; Member, College of Piping; Union: Unite Union. Recreations: hill-walking; local history; piping; Forth and Clyde Canal enthusiast. Address: (h.) 27 Smeaton Drive, Glasgow G64 3BF.

Martin, Paul. MSP (Labour), Glasgow Provan, 2011-16, Glasgow Springburn, 1999-2011; b. 1967, Glasgow; m., Marie. Educ. All Saints RC Secondary. Career: served an apprenticeship in the construction industry, then became a construction manager; at the age of 26, became a Glasgow District Councillor following a Council By-Election in December 1993; formerly Vice-Convenor of the Glasgow District Council Economic and Development Committee, Convenor of the North Area Committee and Convenor of the Youth Committee; served as the Parliamentary aide to the Lord Advocate, 2001-07; Labour's shadow minister for Justice, 2007-09; promoted to the shadow cabinet in November 2009 as Labour's business manager; appointed Labour's shadow spokesman on community safety in 2007; appointed Business Manager for Labour in the Scottish Parliament in 2009, sitting on the Business Bureau of the Scottish Parliament. Recreations: golf; football (in goals); playing keyboard.

Martin, Robert (Roy) Logan, QC, LLB. Advocate, since 1976; Barrister, since 1990; Judge of the Court of Appeal of Jersey and Guernsey, since 2013; b. 31.7.50, Glasgow; m., Fiona Frances Neil; 1 s.; 2 d. Educ. Paisley Grammar School; Glasgow University. Solicitor, 1973-76; admitted to Faculty of Advocates, 1976; Member, Sheriff Courts Rules Council, 1981-84; Standing Junior Counsel, Department of

Employment (Scotland), 1983-84; Advocate-Depute, 1984-87; admitted to Bar of New South Wales, 1987; Queen's Counsel, 1988; called to the Bar, Lincoln's Inn, 1990; Queen's Counsel (England and Wales), 2008; admitted to Bar of Northern Ireland, 2010; Chairman (part-time), Industrial Tribunals, 1990-96; Chairman, Scottish Planning, Local Government and Environmental Bar Group, 1991-96; Chairman, Police Appeals Tribunal, since 1997; Vice-Dean, Faculty of Advocates, 2001-04; Dean, Faculty of Advocates, 2004-07; Co-Chair, Forum for Barristers and Advocates, 2002-06; Co-Chair, International Council for Advocates and Barristers, 2004-08; Trustee, National Library of Scotland, 2004-07; Member, Judicial Appointments Board for Scotland, 2007-2010; Honorary Member, Australian Bar Association, 2008; Bencher, Middle Temple, 2011; Honorary Professor, University of Glasgow, since 2006; Affiliate, Royal Incorporation of Architects in Scotland, 1995; HonFRIAS, 2009; Honorary Secretary, The Wagering Club, 1982-91; Governor, Loretto School, 2002-2012, Chairman, 2007-2012; Trustee, Royal College of Obstetricians and Gynaecologists, since 2013. Recreations: shooting; skiing; modern architecture; vintage motor cars. Address: (h.) Kilduff House, Athelstaneford, East Lothian EH39 5BD; T.-01620 880202.

Martin, Ross, BSc (Hons), PGCE. Chief Executive, Scottish Council for Development and Industry, since 2014; Adviser at Commission on School Reform, since 2012; Adviser at Business Improvement Districts Scotland, 2011-13; Founding Partner, Adopt an Intern Ltd, since 2010; Director, TPS, 2005-2013. Educ. Moray House College; Heriot-Watt University. Elected Member, Lothian Regional Council, 1990-96; Chair, Lothian & Borders Police Authority, 1991-96; Convener of Education Authority, West Lothian Council, 1995-1999; Deputy Leader, West Lothian Council, 1995-1999; Director, Networks Central Ltd, 1999-2003; Director, Scottish Forum for Modern Government, RGU, 2003-2006; Policy Director, Centre for Scottish Public Policy, 2006-2013; Adviser, Scotland's Towns Partnership, 2012-13. Member, Heriot Watt University Court, 1986-96; Board Member, Scottish Police College, 1992-95; High School Teacher, Fife Council, 1989-93; Board Member, West Lothian College, 1990-1992; Student President, Heriot-Watt University, 1986-88. Address: (b.) 1 Cadogan Square, Cadogan Street, Glasgow G2 7HF; T.-0141 243 2667.

Martin, Professor William, BSc, PhD. Professor of Cardiovascular Pharmacology, University of Glasgow, since 1995; Head of Division of Neuroscience and Biomedical Systems, 2004-08; Senate Assessor on University Court, 2010-2013; b. 12.7.55, Glasgow; m., Anne Marie McCartney; 1 s.; 1 d. Educ. Glenwood Secondary; University of Glasgow. Post-doctoral Research Fellow, Babraham, Cambridge, 1980-83; Post-doctoral Research Fellow, State University of New York, 1983-85; Lecturer, Department of Cardiology, University of Wales College of Medicine, 1985-87; External Examiner: National University of Ireland, 2009-14, University College Dublin, 2002-07, University of Nottingham, 2002-07, King's College London, 2006-2010. Institute for Scientific Information Highly Cited Researcher Award in Pharmacology, 2002; Elected Fellow of the British Pharmacological Society, 2012. Recreations: hill-walking; ballroom dancing; keeping fit. Address: (b.) School of Life Sciences, College of Medical, Veterinary & Life Sciences, University of Glasgow, Glasgow G12 8QQ; T.-0141-330 4489; e-mail: William.Martin@glasgow.ac.uk

Marwick, George Robert, SDA, CVO. Lord Lieutenant for Orkney, 1997-2007 (Vice Lieutenant, 1995, Deputy Lieutenant, 1976); Chairman, Swannay Farms Ltd., 1972-2010; Chairman, Campbeltown Creamery (Holdings) Ltd., 1974-90; Honorary Sheriff, Grampian Highlands and Islands, since 2000; b. 27.2.32, Edinburgh; m., 1, Hanne Jensen; 3 d.; 2, Norma Gerrard. Educ. Port Regis; Bryanston; Edinburgh School of Agriculture. Councillor, local government, 1968-78; Vice-Convener, Orkney County Council, 1970-74, Convener, Orkney Islands Council, 1974-78; Chairman, North of Scotland Water Board, 1970-73; Member, Scottish Agricultural Consultative Panel, 1972-98 (formerly Winter Keep Panel, 1964-72); Director, North Eastern Farmers Ltd., 1968-98;, Member: Countryside Commission for Scotland, 1978-86, Council, National Trust for Scotland, 1979-84. Recreations: shooting; motor sport. Address: (h.) Whitewisp, Orchil Road, Auchterarder, Perthshire; T.-01764 662381.

Marwick, Rt. Hon. Tricia. MSP, Mid Fife and Glenrothes, 2011-16, Central Fife, 2007-2011, Mid-Scotland and Fife, 1999-2007; Presiding Officer, Scottish Parliament, 2011-16 (resigned membership of the Scottish National Party to be independent of any party); b. 5.11.53, Cowdenbeath; m., Frank; 1 s.; 1 d. Public Affairs Office, Shelter Scotland, 1992-99. Recreations: reading; watching sport.

Mason, Dr. Christopher, MBE, MA, PhD. Member, Glasgow City Council, 1995-2012; President, Clyde Maritime Trust (Chairman, 1991-2012); b. 8.3.41, Hexham; m., 1, Stephanie Maycock, 2, Marie Blair Reid; 2 d. Educ. Marlborough College; Magdalene College, University of Cambridge. Lecturer in Politics, University of Glasgow, 1966-93; Temporary First Secretary, Foreign and Commonwealth Office, 1971-73; Member, Strathclyde Regional Council, 1982-96 (Liberal Democrat Group Leader, 1986-96); Chairman, Scottish Liberal Party, 1987-88; founded Clyde Maritime Trust, 1991. Publication: The Effective Management of Resources – The International Politics of the North Sea, 1979; various articles. Recreations: sailing; gardening; holidays.

Mason, Professor Sir David Kean, CBE, BDS, MD, FRCS, FDS, FRCPath, FRSE, Hon. DSc, Hon. DChD, Hon. LLD, Hon. FFD, Hon. FDS, Hon. FRCS. President, General Dental Council, 1989-94; b. 5.11.28, Paisley; m., Judith Armstrong; 2 s.; 1 d. Educ. Paisley Grammar School; Glasgow Academy; St. Andrews University; Glasgow University. RAF Dental Branch, 1952-54; Registrar in Oral Surgery, Dundee, 1954-56; Senior Lecturer in Dental Surgery and Pathology, Glasgow University, 1964-67; Professor of Oral Medicine, Glasgow University, 1967-92 (Dean of Dental Education, 1980-90); Chairman, National Dental Consultative Committee, 1976-80; Member: Medicines Commission, 1976-80, Dental Committee, MRC, 1973-83, Physiological Systems Board, MRC, 1976-80, GDC, 1976-93, Dental Strategy Review Group, 1980-81, Dental Review Working Party, UGC, 1986-87, WHO Expert Committee on Oral Health, 1991-98; Convener, Dental Council, RCPSGlas, 1977-80; John Tomes Prize, RCS England, 1979; Colyer Prize RCS England, 1993; Honorary Member, British Dental Association, 1993; Honorary Member, American Dental Association, 1994. Publications: Salivary Glands in Health and Disease (Co-Author); Introduction to Oral Medicine (Co-Author); Self Assessment: Manuals I and II (Co-Editor); Oral Manifestations of Systemic Disease. Recreations: golf; tennis; gardening; enjoying the pleasure of the countryside. Address: (h.) Cherry Tree Cottage, Houston Road, Kilmacolm, Renfrewshire; T.-Kilmacolm 2001.

Mason, John. MSP (SNP), Glasgow Shettleston, since 2011; MP (SNP), Glasgow East, 2008-10. Trained as an accountant in Glasgow, then worked for housing associations, nursing homes, and with a charity in London; spent 3 years in Nepal with an NGO representing churches from all over the world. Elected as the Councillor for the Garrowhill ward in 1998 at a by-election and held the seat in 1999 and 2003. Led the SNP Group on the Council, from 1999 and was elected in 2007 as Councillor of Baillieston. Address: 888 Shettleston Road, Glasgow G32 7XN.

Mason, John Kenneth, CBE, BA (Oxon), MPhil. Director, Economic Development Directorate, Scottish Government; b. 26.6.56, Chichester; m., Alison Margaret Cruickshanks; 1 s.; 2 d. Educ. Chichester High School; Hertford College, Oxford; University College, London. Kent County Council; Department of Environment; Scottish Office; Registers of Scotland; Director of Climate Change and Water Industry Directorates, Scottish Government; Principal Private Secretary to the First Minister, Scottish Executive, Head of Tourism, Culture and Sport Group. Director of Scottish Swimming. Recreations: photography; gardening. Address: (b.) St Andrew's House, Edinburgh EH1 3DG; T.-0131-244 0779; e-mail: john.mason@scotland.gsi.gov.uk

Mason, Professor Emeritus John Kenyon French, CBE, MD, LLD, FRCPath, FRCP(Ed), DMJ, FRSE. Regius Professor of Forensic Medicine, Edinburgh University, 1973-85; Honorary Fellow, Faculty of Law, Edinburgh University, 1985-2012; b. 19.12.19, Lahore; m., Elizabeth Latham (deceased); 2 s. Educ. Downside School; Cambridge University; St. Bartholomew's Hospital. Regular Officer, Medical Branch, RAF, following War Service; Consultant in charge, RAF Department of Aviation and Forensic Pathology, 1957-73. President, British Association in Forensic Medicine, 1981-83; Swiney Prize in Jurisprudence, 1978. Publication: Forensic Medicine for Lawyers, 4th edition; Law and Medical Ethics, 9th edition (Co-Author); Medico-legal Aspects of Reproduction and Parenthood, 2nd edition; Legal and Ethical Aspects of Healthcare (Co-author); The Troubled Pregnancy. Address: (h.) 66 Craiglea Drive, Edinburgh EH10 5PF; T.-0131-447 2301; e-mail: Ken.Mason@ed.ac.uk

Mason, Professor Roger A., MA, PhD, FRHistS. Professor of Scottish History, University of St Andrews, since 2005; Director, St Andrews Institute of Scottish Historical Research, since 2007; b. 29.07.54, Aberdeen; m., Ellen Colingsworth. Educ. Rannoch School; Edinburgh University. Lecturer, then Reader, St Andrews University, from 1983. Extensive publications in Scottish History; former Editor 'Scottish Historical Review'; President, Scottish History Society, 2013-16. Recreations: reading; walking the dog. Address: (b.) School of History, University of St Andrews, St Andrews, Fife KY16 9AL; T.-01334 462882; e-mail: ram@st-andrews.ac.uk

Massie, Allan Johnstone, CBE, BA, FRSL. Author and Journalist; b. 16.10.38, Singapore; m., Alison Langlands; 2 s.; 1 d. Educ. Drumtochty Castle; Trinity College, Glenalmond; Trinity College, Cambridge. Schoolmaster, Drumtochty Castle, 1960-71; taught EFL, 1972-75; Creative Writing Fellow, Edinburgh University, 1982-84, Glasgow and Strathclyde Universities, 1985-86; Editor, New Edinburgh Review, 1982-84; Fiction Reviewer, The Scotsman, since 1975; Television Critic, Sunday Standard, 1981-83 (Fraser of Allander Award, Critic of the Year, 1982); Sports Columnist, Glasgow Herald, 1985-88; Columnist: Daily Mail, The Scotsman, Sunday Times; contributor to The Spectator, the Literary Review and The Independent. Publications: (novels): Change and Decay in all around I see; The Last Peacock; The Death of Men (Scottish Arts Council Book Award); One Night in Winter; Augustus; A Question of Loyalties; The Sins of the Father;

Tiberius; The Hanging Tree; Shadows of Empire; Caesar; These Enchanted Woods; The Ragged Lion; King David; Antony; Nero's Heirs; The Evening of the World; Arthur the King; Caligula; Charlemagne and Roland; Surviving; Death in Bordeaux (non-fiction): Colette; How Should Health Services be Financed?: A Patient's View; Muriel Spark; Ill Met by Gaslight; Five Edinburgh Murders; The Caesars; A Portrait of Scottish Rugby; The Royal Stuarts: A History of the Family That Shaped Britain; 101 Great Scots; Byron's Travels; Glasgow: Portraits of a City; Edinburgh; The Novel Today: A Critical Guide to the British Novel, 1970-89; The Thistle and the Rose: Six Centuries of Love and Hate Between the Scots and the English (as Editor): Edinburgh and the Borders in Verse (radio play): Quintet in October (plays): The Minstrel and the Shirra; First-Class Passengers. Recreations: reading; watching rugby; cricket; racing; walking the dogs. Address: (h.) Thirladean House, Selkirk TD7 5LU; T.-Selkirk 20393.

Masters, Christopher, CBE, BSc (Hons), PhD, AKC, FRSE; b. 2.5.47, Northallerton; m., Gillian Mary Hodson; 2 d. Educ. Richmond School; King's College, London; Leeds University. Shell Research BV/Shell Chemicals UK Ltd., 1971-77; joined Christian Salvesen as Business Development Manager, 1979; transferred to Christian Salvesen Inc., USA, 1982, as Director of Planning; Managing Director, Christian Salvesen Seafoods, 1983-85; Managing Director, Industrial Services Division, 1985-89; a Director, Christian Salvesen PLC, 1987-97; Chief Executive, Christian Salvesen PLC, 1989-97; Executive Chairman, Aggreko plc, 1997-2002; Chairman: Babtie Group Ltd., 2002-04, Voxar Ltd., 2002-04, SMG plc, 2004-07, Sagentia Group plc, 2006-2010, Energy Assets Group plc, since 2012, Young Enterprise Scotland, 1994-97, Quality Assessment Committee of Higher Education Funding Council, 1991-95; Vice Chairman, Scottish Opera, 1996-99; Member, Scottish Higher Education Funding Council, 1995-2005, Chairman, 1998-2005; Chairman, Festival City Theatres Trust, 2002-2013; Independent Co-Chairman, Scottish Science Advisory Council, since 2011; Non-Executive Director: British Assets Trust, 1989-2009, Scottish Widows, 1991-2000, Scottish Chamber Orchestra Trust, 1993-2012, John Wood Group PLC, 2002-2012, The Alliance Trust PLC, 2002-2012, The Crown Agents, since 2005, Speedy Hire plc, since 2011; Murgitroyd Group PLC, since 2015; Master, The Merchant Company of Edinburgh, 2007-09; Lord Dean of Guild of the City of Edinburgh, 2009-2011; Member of Court of Edinburgh University, since 2011; Honorary Degrees: Strathclyde University and St. Andrews University, 2006, University of Abertay Dundee and Edinburgh University, 2007. Recreations: wines; music. Address: (h.) 12 Braid Avenue, Edinburgh EH10 6EE; T.-0131-447 0812; cm@chrismasters.co.uk

Masterton, Professor Gordon Grier Thomson, OBE, DTech, DEng, BSc, BA, MSc, DIC, FREng, FRSE, FICE, FIStructE, FIES. Professor of Future Infrastructure, Edinburgh University, since 2015; Vice President, Jacobs, 2004-2014; President, The Institution of Civil Engineers, 2005-06; President, Institution of Engineers and Shipbuilders in Scotland, 2010-12; Founder of Scottish Engineering Hall of Fame, 2011; b. 9.6.54, Charlestown, Fife; m., Lynda Christine Jeffries; 1 s.; 1 d. Educ. Dunfermline High School; University of Edinburgh; Imperial College London; Open University. Babtie Shaw & Morton, 1976; Director, Babtie Group Ltd., 1993; Director, Babtie International Ltd., 1993; Director, Babtie Malaysia, 1995 (based in Kuala Lumpur); Managing Director, Facilities Business, 2002, Environment Business, 2004; UK Government Project Representative for Crossrail Project, London, 2009-2013. Visiting Professor: University of Paisley, 2001-05, Glasgow Caledonian University, since 2011, Edinburgh University, since 2012; Member, Smeatonian Society, since 2004; Chairman, Construction

Industry Council, Scotland, 2002-04, Chairman, Construction Industry Council UK, 2010-12; Royal Commissioner on the Ancient and Historical Monuments of Scotland, 2003-2015, Vice-Chairman, 2010-2015; Member, Historic Scotland/RCAHMS Transition Advisory Board, 2013-15; Court Assistant, Worshipful Company of Engineers, since 2012; Member of Master Court, Incorporation of Hammermen of Glasgow, since 2015; Chairman, Scottish Lime Centre Trust, 2007-09; President, Glasgow Grand Opera Society, 1991-94; Honorary Doctorate: Caledonian University, 2007, Heriot-Watt University, 2012; TV appearances as presenter in 'Life After People', The History Channel, 2008, and two subsequent series and as himself in Unbuilt Britain, BBC, 2014; Thomas Telford: The Man who Built Britain, BBC, 2007; Canals: The Making of a Nation, BBC, 2015. Recreations: opera; engineering history; skiing; genealogy. Address: Corrievreck, Montrose Terrace, Bridge of Weir, Renfrewshire PA11 3DH; T.-01505 613503; e-mail: themastertons@btinternet.com

Mather, Jim. Chairman of Homes for Scotland; Visiting Professor at Heriot-Watt and Strathclyde Universities; MSP (SNP), Argyll & Bute, 2007-11, Highlands and Islands, 2003-07; Minister for Enterprise, Energy and Tourism, 2007-11; b 6.3.47; m.; 1 s.; 1 d. Educ. Paisley Grammar School; Greenock High School; Glasgow University. Chartered Accountant. Address: 13 Sutherland Avenue, Pollokshields, Glasgow G41 4JJ.

Matheson, Alexander (Sandy), CVO, OBE, FRPharmS, JP. Lord Lieutenant, Western Isles Area, since 2001; Chairman, Highlands and Islands Airports Ltd., 2001-07; Chairman, Harris Tweed Authority, 2001-07; b. 16.11.41, Stornoway; m., Irene Mary Davidson, BSc, MSc; 2 s.; 2 d. Educ. Nicolson Institute, Stornoway; Robert Gordon's Institute of Technology, Aberdeen. Chairman, Stornoway Pier and Harbour Commission, 1991-2001 (Member, 1968-2010); Member, Stornoway Trust Estate, 1967-2009 (Chairman, 1971-81); Chairman: Stornoway Branch, RNLI (1974-81 and 1994-2004), Western Isles Development Fund, 1972-98, Western Isles Health Board, 1993-2001 (Member, 1973-2001); Member, Stornoway Town Council, 1967-75; Provost of Stornoway, 1971-75; Member: Ross and Cromarty County Council, 1967-75, Western Isles Islands Council, 1974-94 (Chairman, Development Services, 1974-80, Vice-Convener, 1980-82, Convener, 1982-90); President, Islands Commission of the Conference of Peripheral Maritime Regions of Europe, 1987-91 and 1993-94; Honorary Sheriff, since 1972; Chairman, Roderick Smith Ltd., Stornoway; Founding Chairman, Hebridean Men's Cancer Support Group, 2007-2012. Address: (h.) 33 Newton Street, Stornoway, Isle of Lewis; T.-01851 702082.

Matheson, Angus Macrae, MA, LLB. Solicitor and Notary Public; Partner, Burnett & Reid, Solicitors, since 1979; b. 25.9.51, Inverness; m., Paula Louise Taylor; 4 s.; 1 d. Educ. Inverness Royal Academy; University of Aberdeen. Apprentice, 1974-76; Assistant, 1976-79. Past President, Gordonian Rugby Club; Past Chairman, Seafield Club. Recreations: rugby; golf; music; wine; touring Scotland. Address: (b.) 15 Golden Square, Aberdeen AB10 1WF; T.-01224 644 333; e-mail: ammatheson@burnett-reid.co.uk

Matheson, Ann, OBE, MA, MLitt, PhD, Hon. DLitt (St And), Drhc (Edin); b. 5.7.40, Wester Ross; m., T. Russell Walker. Educ. Dingwall Academy; St Andrews University; Edinburgh University. Ferranti Ltd., 1962-64; Teaching in Finland, 1964-67; National Library of Scotland: Assistant Keeper, 1972-83, Keeper, 1983-2000. Chairman, Literature Committee, Scottish Arts Council, 1997-2003; Chairman, Consortium of European Research Libraries; Chairman, NEWSPLAN 2000; Chairman, Literature Alliance Scotland; Chairman, Sabhal Mòr Ostaig Library Advisory Committee; Secretary, General Council, University of Edinburgh; Saltire Society Literary Panel; Secretary General, Ligue des Bibliothèques Européennes de Recherche; Trustee and Secretary, Scottish Poetry Library. Fletcher of Saltoun Award (Arts and Humanities), 2014; Professor h.c., Sofia, 2015. Publications: Theories of Rhetoric, 1995; Gaelic Union Catalogue (Co-Editor) 1984; For the Encouragement of Learning, (Co-Editor), 1989. Recreations: literature; travel. Address: Yewbank, 52 Liberton Brae, Edinburgh, EH16 6AF; T.-0131-629 9109; e-mail: a.matheson@tinyworld.co.uk

Matheson, Gordon, CBE, MA, FCIPD, FRSA. Visiting Professor, University of Strathclyde, since 2016; former Leader, Glasgow City Council (2010-2015), Member, 1999-2016, previously City Treasurer and Chair of Education; Scottish Local Politician of the Year, 2012 and 2014, Herald Awards; Member, Scottish Labour Party wider Shadow Cabinet; b. 1.11.66, Glasgow; Civil Partner: Stephen Wallace. Educ. University of Glasgow; University of Strathclyde. Former Member, Board: Royal Scottish National Orchestra, Scottish Low Pay Unit, Strathclyde University Court, Glasgow City Marketing Bureau (Chair), 2010-2015, Glasgow 2014 Commonwealth Games Strategic Group, Strathclyde Pension Fund, Strathclyde Police. Awarded CBE in HM The Queen's New Year Honours for Services to Local Government and the Community. Has run Great Scottish Run and New York Marathon.

Matheson, John Alexander, CBE, BA, MBA, CPFA. Director of Health Finance, eHealth and Analytics in the Health and Social Care Directorate of Scottish Government, since 2008; Past Chairman, Scottish Branch and President (2015), Chartered Institute of Public Finance and Accountancy; Member, Board of Management, Edinburgh's Telford College, 1998-2007; Chair, Audit Committee, Edinburgh Marketing, since 2012; b. 23.6.55, Dingwall; m., Judi; 1 s.; 1 d. Educ. Invergordon Academy; Heriot-Watt University; Edinburgh University. Finance Director, Edinburgh Healthcare NHS Trust, 1994-99; Finance Director, NHS Lothian, 2000-08. Finance Director of the Year, 2004 (non profit sector). Recreation: hill-walking; golf. T.-0131-244 3464.

Matheson, Michael, BSc, BA, Dip. Applied Soc Sci. MSP (SNP), Falkirk West, since 2007, Central Scotland, 1999-2007; Cabinet Secretary for Justice, since 2014; Minister for Public Health, 2011-14; Member: Health and Sport Committee, 2007-2011, Justice and Home Affairs Committee, 2000-01, Justice 1 Committee, 2001-2004, Enterprise and Culture Committee, since 2004; Vice Convener: Cross Party Group on Sport, 2007-2011, European and External Relations Committee, 2009-2010, Cross Party Group on Cuba; Co-Convenor, Cross Party Group on Malawi; End of Life Assistance Committee, June 2010 - December 2010; b. 8.9.70, Glasgow. Educ. John Bosco Secondary School; Queen Margaret College, Edinburgh; Open University. Community Occupational Therapist: Highland Regional Council, Social Work Department, 1991-93, Stirling Council, Social Work Department, 1993-99. Member, Ochils Mountain Rescue Team. Recreation: mountaineering. Address: (b.) 15A East Bridge Street, Falkirk FK1 1YD; T.-01324 629271.

Mathewson, Sir George Ross, CBE, BSc, PhD, MBA, LLD (Dundee), LLD (St. Andrews), DUniv (Glasgow), Dr.hc (Edinburgh), FCIBS, CEng, MIEE, CCMI. Chairman, Royal Bank of Scotland Group plc, 2001-06; Non-Executive Director, Stagecoach Group, since 2006; President, International Monetary Conference, 2005-06; Director: Scottish Investment Trust Ltd., 1981-2009; b.

14.5.40, Dunfermline; m., Sheila Alexandra Graham Bennett; 2 s. Educ. Perth Academy; St. Andrews University; Canisius College, Buffalo, New York. Assistant Lecturer, St. Andrews University, 1964-67; Systems Engineer (various positions), Bell Aerospace, Buffalo, New York, 1967-72; ICFC: Executive in Edinburgh Area Office, 1972-81, Area Manager, 1974-79, Director and Assistant General Manager, 1979-81; Chief Executive, Scottish Development Agency, 1981-87; Royal Bank of Scotland Group plc: joined as Director, Strategic Planning and Development, 1987, Group Chief Executive, 1992-2000, Executive Deputy Chairman, 2000-2001; National Business Lifetime Achievement Award, 2003. Chairman: Royal Botanic Garden Edinburgh Campaign Board, Wood Mackenzie Ltd., since 2007, Council of Economic Advisers to the Scottish Government, since 2007, Trustee Board, Royal Botanic Gardens, since 2007. Recreations: tennis; skiing; gardening; rugby; golf; business; shooting. E-mail: merklands.house@virgin.net

Mathieson, Fiona McDougall, BEd, BD, PGCommEd, MTh. Minister, Carrick Knowe Parish, Edinburgh, since 2001; b. 28.12.62, Lennoxtown; m., Angus Mathieson. Educ. Mearns Castle High; Williamwood Secondary; Jordanhill College; Glasgow University; Edinburgh University; Heriot Watt University. Career History: Assistant Minister, Greenbank Edinburgh; Church of Scotland National Youth Adviser; Chaplain to The University of Glasgow. Director, Corstorphine Dementia Project. Recreations: food; wine and friends. Address: 21 Traquair Park West, Corstorphine, Edinburgh EH12 7AN; T.-0131-334-9774; e-mail: fiona.mathieson@ukgateway.net

Mathieson, John George, CBE, TD, DL, BL. Retired Solicitor; Chairman, Thorntons, WS, Tayside, 1990-97; b. 15.6.32, Argyll; m., Shirley Bidder (deceased); 1 s.; 1 d. Educ. George Watson's College, Edinburgh; Glasgow University. Territorial Army, 1951-86: Commanding Officer The Highland Regiment RA, TA Colonel for Highlands, Honorary Colonel 105 Regiment RA(TA), Chairman, Highlands TA Association; ADC TA, the Queen, 1975-80. Scottish Director, Woolwich Building Society, 1975-96; Chairman: Independent Tribunal Service, 1992-2004, Arbroath Branch, Royal British Legion, Scotland and Earl Haig Fund, Scottish Solicitors Discipline Tribunal, 1986-92, Royal Artillery Council for Scotland, Dundee SSAFA, 2002, Lloyds TSB Foundation Scotland, 1999-2002, SSAFA Dundee, 2002-07; Deputy Lieutenant, Angus, 1977; Honorary President, Angus Bn., Boys' Brigade; Elder, Colliston Parish Church. Recreations: shooting; golf; gardening. Address: (h.) Willanyards, Colliston, Arbroath, Angus; T.-01241 890286.

Matthew, Alan Stuart, LLB. Solicitor, since 1980; b. 9.12.56, Dundee; 2 d. Educ. Morgan Academy, Dundee; University of Dundee. Apprentice Solicitor, J. R. Stevenson and Marshall, Dunfermline, 1978-80; Solicitor: Thorntons & Dickies, Dundee, 1980-82, Clark Oliver, Arbroath and Forfar, 1982-84, Messrs Burns Veal and Gillan (later Burns Veal), Dundee, 1984-85; Partner: Burns Veal, 1985-98, Partner, Miller Hendry (incorporating Burns Veal), since 1998. Director, Solicitors Financial Services Ltd., 1990-2000; Member, Council, Law Society of Scotland, 1997-2009; Member, Council, Faculty of Solicitors and Procurators in Dundee, 1997-2009. Recreations: rugby; hillwalking; after dinner speaking. Address: (b.) 13 Ward Road, Dundee DD1 1LU; T.-01382 200000.

Matthews, Baird, BL. Solicitor in private practice, 1950-2003; Honorary Sheriff, Kirkcudbright and Stranraer; b. 19.1.25, Newton Stewart; m., Mary Thomson Hope; 2 s.; 1 d. Educ. Douglas Ewart High School; Edinburgh University. Commissioned, Royal Scots Fusiliers, 1944; demobilised as Captain, 1st Bn., 1947; Partner, A. B. & A. Matthews, Solicitors, Newton Stewart; Clerk to General Commissioners of Income Tax, Stranraer and Newton Stewart Districts, 1952; Burgh Prosecutor, Newton Stewart, 1968; Depute Procurator Fiscal for Wigtownshire, 1970; Chairman, Board of Local Directors, General Accident Fire and Life Assurance Corporation, 1988; Director, Newcastle Building Society (Scottish Board), 1991; Dean of Faculty of Stewartry of Kirkcudbright Solicitors, 1979; Dean of Faculty of Solicitors of the District of Wigtown, 1983; Chairman, Appeals Tribunal; President, Newton Stewart Golf Club. Recreations: golf; travel; conversation. Address: (h.) Marchbank, Newton Stewart; T.-01671 403143; e-mail: baird.matthews@gmail.com

Matthews, the Hon. Lord (Hugh Matthews). Senator of the College of Justice, since 2007; b. 4.12.53, Port Glasgow; m., Lindsay Mary Auld Wilson. Educ. St Joseph's Academy, Kilmarnock; Glasgow University. Admitted to Faculty of Advocates, 1979; Standing Junior Counsel, Department of Employment, 1984-88; Advocate Depute, 1988-93; QC, 1992; Temporary Sheriff, 1992-97; Sheriff of Glasgow and Strathkelvin, 1997-2007; Temporary Judge, 2004-07. Recreations: sport; music; looking after animals; ancient history; science fiction and astronomy. E-mail: lordmatthews@scotcourts.gov.uk

Matthews, Professor John Burr Lumley, MA, DPhil, FRSE, FRSA, FFCS. Honorary Professor, University of Stirling, 1984-99; Honorary Fellow, Scottish Association for Marine Science; b. 23.4.35, Isleworth; m., Jane Rosemary Goldsmith; 1 s.; 2 d. Educ. Warwick School; St. John's College, Oxford University. Research Scientist, Oceanographic Laboratory, Edinburgh, 1961-67; Senior Lecturer, later Professor, Department of Marine Biology, University of Bergen, Norway, 1967-84; Visiting Professor, University of British Columbia, Canada, 1977-78; Deputy Director, Dunstaffnage Marine Laboratory, 1984-88; Director, NERC Dunstaffnage Marine Laboratory and Scottish Association for Marine Science, 1988-94; Secretary, The Scottish Association for Marine Science, 1988-99. Deputy Chairman, South West Regional Board, Scottish Natural Heritage, 1994-97; Secretary, International Association for Biological Oceanography, 1994-2003; Trustee, Oban Hospice Ltd., 1999-2006; Patron, Hebridean Whale & Dolphin Trust, since 2009 (Trustee, 1999-2001, Chairman, 2001-08); Trustee, NADAIR Trust, 2003-07. Recreations: walking; gardening; family history; pethau cymreig. Address: (h.) The Well, 18 Manse Road, Milnathort, Perth and Kinross KY13 9YQ; T.-01577 861066; e-mail: matthews.oban@tiscali.co.uk

Maver, Professor Thomas Watt, BSc (Hons), PhD, HonFRIAS. Research Professor, Mackintosh School of Architecture, Glasgow School of Art; Emeritus Professor of Computer Aided Design, Department of Architecture and Director of the Graduate School, Strathclyde University, 1982-2003 (Head of Department, 1983-85, 1988-91, Vice-Dean, Faculty of Engineering, 1993-2002); b. 10.3.38, Glasgow; m., Avril Elizabeth Cuthbertson; 2 d. Educ. Eastwood Secondary School; Glasgow University. Special Research Fellow, Engineering Faculty, Glasgow University, 1961-67; Strathclyde University: Research Fellow, School of Architecture, 1967-70, Director, Architecture and Building Aids Computer Unit, Strathclyde, since 1970; Visiting Professor: Technical University Eindhoven, Universiti Sains Malaysia, University of Rome (La Sapienza); Past Chairman and first Honorary Fellow of the Design Research Society; CIBSE Bronze Medal, 1966; Royal Society Esso Gold Medal, 1989; Distinguished Service Awards: BEPAC, eCAADe, SIGRADIA, IBPSA and ACADIA; Founder, CAAD Futures and eCAADe. Recreation: maintaining a remote 17th century farmhouse within Galloway forest park. Address: (h.) 8 Kew Terrace,

Glasgow G12 0TD; T.-0141-339 7185.
E-mail: t.w.maver@strath.ac.uk

Mavor, Prof. John, BSc, MPhil, PhD, DSc (Eng), FREng, FRSE, FIEEE. Vice-President (Physical Science and Engineering), Royal Society of Edinburgh, 2004-Sept. 2007; Principal and Vice-Chancellor, Napier University, 1994-2002; b. 18.7.42; m., Susan Christina Colton; 2 d. Educ. City University, London; London University; Edinburgh University. AEI Research Labs, London, 1964-65; Texas Instruments Ltd, Bedford, 1968-70; Emihus Microcomponents, Glenrothes, 1970-71; University of Edinburgh: Lecturer, 1971, Reader, 1979, Lothian Chair of Microelectronics, 1980, Head of Department of Electrical Engineering, 1984-89, Professor of Electrical Engineering, 1986-94, Dean, 1989-94, and Provost, 1992-94, Faculty of Science and Engineering. Hon. DSc, Greenwich, 1998, City, 1998. Publications: MOST Integrated Circuit Engineering, 1973; Introduction to MOS LSI Design, 1983; over 150 technical papers in professional electronics journals. Recreations: gardening; walking; steam railways. Address: 8 Heriot Row, Edinburgh EH3 6HU.

Maxwell, Donald, MA, DMus(Hon), FRWCMD, FLeedsCM. Professional Singer; b. 12.12.48, Perth; 1 d. Educ. Perth Academy; Edinburgh University. Former Teacher of Geography; since 1976, professional Singer with British opera companies and orchestras; Principal Baritone, Scottish Opera, 1978-82; Principal Baritone, Welsh National Opera, 1982-85; guest appearances, BBC Proms, Edinburgh Festival, Royal Opera House, London, Vienna, Paris, Milan, Tokyo, New York, Amsterdam, Salzburg, Buenos Aires – notably as Falstaff; Director, National Opera Studio, 2001-08; Head of Opera, RWCMD, 2004-09; comedy – The Music Box with Linda Ormiston. Recreation: railways. Address: (b.) Music International, 13 Ardilaun Road, Highbury, London N5 2QR; T.-020 7359 5183; e-mail: donmaxpen@hotmail.com

Maxwell, Ingval, OBE, DA (Dun), RIBA, FRIAS, CAABC, ACA, FSA Scot. International Consultant in Architectural Conservation, since 2008; Director, Technical Conservation Research and Education, Historic Scotland, 1993-2008; b. 28.5.44, Penpont; m., Susan Isabel Maclean; 1 s.; 1 d. Educ. Dumfries Academy; Duncan of Jordanstone College of Art, Dundee. Joined Ministry of Public Buildings and Works as Architect, 1969; Area Architect, then Principal Architect, Ancient Monuments Branch, 1972-85; Assistant Director of Works, Historic Scotland, 1985-93; Architectural Advisor, Ancient Monuments Board for Scotland, 1993-2003; Architectural Advisor, Historic Buildings Council for Scotland, 1993-2003; RIBA Research Award, 1970-71; RIAS Thomas Ross Award, 1988; Chairman, Scottish Vernacular Buildings Working Group, 1990-94; Chairman, Scottish Conservation Forum in Training and Education, 1994-2008; Convenor, Scottish Stone Liaison Group, 1997-2007; Member, RIAS Conservation Committee; Member, European Commission COST Action C5, 1996-2000; Chairman, European Science Foundation COST Action C17, 2002-06; Member, European Construction Technology Platform - Focus Area Cultural Heritage, 2006-08; Member, Architects Accredited in Building Conservation, since 1999; Member, ICOMOS UK Executive Committee, 1995-2006; Member, ICOMOS International Scientific Committee on Stone, since 2000; Member, UCL Centre for Historic Buildings, Collections and Sites Academic Advisory Committee, 2001-08; Member, UK and Ireland Blue Shield Organisation, 2001; Member, AHRC EPSRC Science and Heritage Advisory Committee, 2008-2014; Trustee, Charles Wallace India Trust, 2003-2013; Trustee, Council on Training in Architectural Conservation, since 2008; Chairman, COTAC, since 2013; UNESCO/ICOMOS World Heritage Official, 2008-2013; RIBA Conservation Accreditation Steering Group Member, since 2009; Adviser, EC FP7 Cultural Heritage Identity Card, 2009-2013; Member, Advisory Board, Learn Direct and Build, since 2010; External Examiner, Faculty of Arts, University of Plymouth, 2010-2013; RIBA Conservation Training Course Leader, 2011-2013; Director, CyArk Europe, since 2013; Member, Historic Environment Forum, Heritage Skills Task Group, since 2013. Publications: Building Materials of the Scottish Farmstead, 1996; Conservation of Historic Graveyards Guide for Practitioners (Co-Author), 2001; Stone in Scotland (Co-Author), 2006; INFORM - Masonry Decay, 2005, Fire Safety, 2005, Repairing Scottish State Roofs, 2006, Repointing Rubble Stonework, 2007, Cleaning Sandstone, 2007; COST Action C17 "Fire Loss to Historic Buildings" Final Report (3 vols) (Editor), 2007; COST Action C17 "Fire Loss to Historic Buildings" Conference Proceedings (4 vols) (Editor), 2007; Stone in Context Conference Proceedings (Editor), 2008; Integrating Digital Technologies in Support of Historic Building Information Modelling: BIM4C (Author), 2014; Fire and Flood in the Built Environment: Keeping the threat at Bay (2 vols) (Author), 2015. Recreations: photography; astronomy; aircraft; buildings. Address: (h.) 135 Mayfield Road, Edinburgh EH9 3AN.

Maxwell, Professor Simon, MD, PhD, FRCP, FRCPE, FBPharmacolSci, FHEA. Consultant Physician, Western General Hospital, Edinburgh, since 1998; Senior Lecturer, Edinburgh University, since 1998; b. 14.2.62, Edinburgh; m., 1 s. Educ. Nottingham High School; Birmingham University. Lecturer in Medicine, Birmingham Medical School, 1990-96; Senior Lecturer in Medicine, Leicester Medical School. Chairman, Scottish Medical Academic Staff Committee, BMA; Vice-President, British Pharmacological Society; Chairman, Lothian University Hospitals Drug and Therapeutics Committee. Address: (b.) Clinical Pharmacology Unit, University of Edinburgh, Clinical Research Centre, Western General Hospital, Edinburgh EH4 2XU; T.-0131 537 1826; e-mail: s.maxwell@ed.ac.uk

Maxwell, Stewart, MSP, BA (Hons). MSP (SNP), West of Scotland, 2003-2016; Minister for Communities and Sport, 2007-09; SNP Parliamentary Group Secretary, 2003-07; b. 24.12.63, Glasgow; m., Mary; 1 d. Educ. King's Park Secondary School; Glasgow College of Technology. Strathclyde Fire Brigade: Industrial Training Manager, 1993-94; Senior Admin Officer, 1994-2000; Management Information System Project Manager, 2000-03. SNP Deputy Health Spokesperson, 2004-06; SNP Spokesperson on Sport, Culture and Media, 2006-07; Honorary Vice President, Royal Environmental Health Institute of Scotland, since 2006. Recreations: reading; swimming; golf; scuba diving; photography; watching rugby; eating out.

Maxwell, Dr. William (Bill), MA (Hons), MAppSci, PhD, CPsychol, FRSA. Chief Executive, Education Scotland; b. 14.11.57, Edinburgh; m., Margaret; 2 d. Educ. High School of Dundee; University College Oxford; Glasgow University; Edinburgh University. Area Principal Psychologist, Grampian Council, 1992-94; HM Inspector of Schools, 1994-2002; HM Chief Inspector of Education, 2002-06; Head of Education, Information and Analytical Services, Scottish Government, 2006-08; HM Chief Inspector of Education and Training in Wales, 2008-2010; HM Senior Chief Inspector of Education (Scotland), 2010-11; Transitional Chief Inspector, Education Scotland, July 2011 to December 2011. Recreations: climbing and mountaineering; cycling and the arts. Address: (b.) Denholm House, Almondvale House, Almondvale Business Park, Livingston EH54 6GA; T.-01506 600366.

Maxwell-Irving, Alastair Michael Tivey, BSc, CEng, MIEE, MIMgt, FSA, FSAScot, Antiquarian and Archaeologist; b. 1.10.35, Witham, Essex; m., Esther Mary Hamilton, MA, LLB. Educ. Lancing College; London University; Oxford University (1975); Stirling University (1992). General Electric Company, 1957; English Electric Company, 1960; Assistant Factor, Annandale Estates, 1966; Weir Pumps Ltd., 1970-91; founder Member and Secretary, 1975-78, Central Scotland Branch, British Institute of Management. Contributor, Burke's Landed Gentry, 1963-2001; Nigel Tranter Memorial Award, 2003; Trustee, Bonshaw Preservation Trust, 2007. Publications: Genealogy of the Irvings of Dumfries, 1965; The Irvings of Bonshaw, 1968; The Irvings of Dumfries, 1968; Lochwood Castle, 1968; Early Firearms and their Influence on the Military and Domestic Architecture of the Borders, 1974; Cramalt Tower: Historical Survey and Excavations, 1977-79, 1982; Borthwick Castle: Excavations 1979, 1982; Andrew Dunlop (Clockmakers' Company 1701-32), 1984; Hoddom Castle: A Reappraisal of its Architecture and Place in History, 1989; Lochwood Castle, 1990; The Castles of Buittle, 1991; Lockerbie Tower, 1992; Torthorwald Castle, 1993; Scottish Yetts and Window Grilles, 1994; The Tower-Houses of Kirtleside, 1997; Kenmure Castle, 1997; The Border Towers of Scotland: their history and architecture – The West March, 2000; The Maxwells of Caerlaverock (in Lordship and Architecture in Medieval and Renaissance Scotland), 2005; Family Memoirs, 2007 and 2008; Reginald Tivey: A Celebration of his Art, 2011; The Border Towers of Scotland 2, 2014. Recreations: architecture and history of the Border towers of Scotland; archaeology; family history and genealogy; Florence and the art and architecture of Tuscany; horology; heraldry; photography; gardening. Address: (h.) Telford House, Blairlogie, Stirling FK9 5PX. E-mail: a.maxwellirving@gmail.com

May, Douglas James, LLB. Queen's Counsel, since 1989; b. 7.5.46, Edinburgh. Educ. George Heriot's; Edinburgh University. Advocate, 1971; Temporary Sheriff, 1990-99; Social Security Commissioner, Child Support Commissioner, 1993-2008; Judge of the Upper Tribunal, Administrative Appeals Chamber, since 2008; Member of Tribunal Procedure Committee, 2008-2015; Parliamentary candidate (Conservative), Edinburgh East, 1974, Glasgow Cathcart, 1983. Recreations: golf (Captain: Scotland Universities Golfing Society, 1990-91, Merchants of Edinburgh Golf Club, 1997-99); photography (ARPS, 1997, FRPS, 2002, President, Edinburgh Photographic Society, 1996-99); Chairman, Conceptual Contemporary Panel of Royal Photographic Society distinction awards, 2010; travel.

May, Malcolm Stuart, BA, BD, STM, CQSW. Chief Officer, Dundee Voluntary Action, 1979-2002 (retired); b. 9.9.40, Isle of Shapinsay, Orkney; m., Alison Wood; 1 s.; 1 d. Educ. Kilmarnock Academy; The Gordon Schools, Huntly; Hamilton Academy; Queen's University, Belfast; Glasgow University; Union Theological Seminary, New York. Assistant Minister, The Old Kirk, West Pilton, Edinburgh, 1966-68; staff, Iona Community, Glasgow, 1968-72; social work training, 1972-73; Training Officer, Scottish Council for Voluntary Organisations, 1973-78. Member, Board of Management, Dundee College, 1989-2003; Non-Executive Director, Tayside Health Board, 1994-98. Recreations: reading; choral singing (member of Bearsden Choir); hill-walking; woodwork. Address: (h.) 37 Campsie Drive, Milngavie G62 8HX. E-mail: malcolm.may@btopenworld.com

Mayhew, Dr. Peter Watts, BSc, PhD. Senior Conservation Manager, RSPB, since 1990; b. 30.6.59, Glasgow; 2 d. Educ. Hutchesons' Grammar, Glasgow; Glasgow University. Research Ornithologist, 1980-83; Head of Conservation, British Association for Shooting and Conservation, 1984-89. Board Member, Deer Commission for Scotland, 2005-10; Member, Scottish Natural Heritage Deer Panel, 2010-2013; Chair, Capercaillie Biodiversity Action Plan Group. Chair, Cairngorms, Speyside, Deer Management Group. Recreations: mountaineering; sailing; bird ringing. Address: (b.) RSPB, Etive House, Beechwood Park, Inverness IV2 3BW; T.-01463 228809. E-mail: pete.mayhew@rspb.org.uk

Mays, Deborah Clare, MA (Hons), PhD, IHBC, FRSA, FSA (Scot), Hon FRIAS. CEO, The Heritage Place, since 2014; Director, Berwickshire Housing Association Enterprise, since 2014; Director and Assistant Secretary, Royal Incorporation of Architects in Scotland, 2012-14, and Chief Executive Officer, Scottish Building Contract Committee, 2012-14; b. 10.8.62, Redhill, Surrey; m., Dr Sean O'Reilly; 2 d. Educ. Lavant House School; University of St Andrews. Historic Scotland: Inspector of Historic Buildings, listing and casework, also Assessor to the Historic Buildings Council, then Project Manager, Modernisation, then Deputy Chief Inspector, latterly Director of Policy and Outreach. Secretary, Society of Architectural Historians of Great Britain; Editor of 3 books; full list of published articles; lectures. Recreations: culture; architecture. Address: (b.) The Heritage Place, 115 Henderson Row, Edinburgh EH3 5BB; T.-07794 705163.

Mazda, Dr. Xerxes. Director of Collections, National Museums Scotland, since 2015. Educ. University of Cambridge. Head of Collections Access, Science Museum, London, 1992-2005; Head of Learning, Volunteers and Audiences, The British Museum, 2005-2013; Deputy Director, Engagement, Royal Ontario Museum, 2013-15. Address: National Museum of Scotland, Chambers Street, Edinburgh EH1 1JF; T.-0300 123 6789.

Mead, Elaine. Chief Executive, NHS Highland, since 2011. Career: clinical background having previously been a diagnostic radiographer; Director of Operations and Deputy Chief Executive of the West Dorset General Hospitals NHS Trust, then Chief Operating Officer with NHS Highland, 2005-2010. Address: (b.) NHS Highland, Assynt House, Beechwood Park, Inverness IV2 3HG.

Meek, Professor Donald Eachann MacDonald, MA (Cantab), MA, PhD, DLitt (Glas), FRHistS. Hon. Fellow of the Association for Scottish Literary Studies; FRSE, 2003-2013; Professor of Scottish and Gaelic Studies, Edinburgh University, 2002-08; Chairman, Gaelic Books Council, 2002-04; b. 16.5.49, Glasgow, brought up in Tiree; m., Rachel Jane Rogers; 2 d. Educ. Oban High School; Glasgow University; Emmanuel College, Cambridge. Lecturer, Senior Lecturer and Reader in Celtic, Edinburgh University, 1979-92; Professor of Celtic, Aberdeen University, 1993-2001. Assistant Editor, Historical Dictionary of Scottish Gaelic, Glasgow University, 1973-79; Honorary Secretary, Gaelic Society of Glasgow, 1974-79; Member, Gaelic Advisory Committee to Broadcasting Council for Scotland, 1976-78 and of Gaelic Panel, National Bible Society of Scotland, 1978-2008; President, Edinburgh and Lothians Baptist Association, 1992-93; Clerk and Treasurer, Board of Celtic Studies (Scotland), 1994-2009; Chief, Gaelic Society of Inverness, 1998, 1999; Chairman, Ministerial Advisory Group on Gaelic, Scottish Executive, 2001-02; Editor, Gaelic Bible, 1992 edition and later revisions; a General Editor, Dictionary of Scottish Church History and Theology, 1993; President, Scottish Church History Society, 2001-04; President, Scottish Gaelic

Texts Society, since 2011. Publications: books include Mairi Mhor nan Oran, 1977, second edition 1998; The Campbell Collection of Gaelic Proverbs and Proverbial Sayings, 1978; Island Harvest: A History of Tiree Baptist Church, 1988; Sunshine and Shadow: the story of the Baptists of Mull, 1991; A Mind for Mission: essays (Editor), 1992; Tuath is Tighearna: Poetry of the Clearances and the Land Agitation (Editor), 1995; The Quest for Celtic Christianity, 2000; Caran an t-Saoghail: Anthology of Nineteenth-century Gaelic Poetry, 2003; The Kingdom of MacBrayne (Co-Author), 2006, second edition, 2008; Gaelic Prose Writings of the Rev. T. M. Murchison (Editor), 2010; Steamships to St Kilda, 2010; Mo La Gu Seo, Gaelic autobiography of T. M. Murchison (Editor), 2011; From Comet to CalMac: Two Hundred Years of Hebridean and Clyde Shipping (Co-author), 2011; Laoidhean Spioradail Dhùghaill Bhochanain (Editor), 2015; Scottish Gaelic Studies, vols. 18, 19, 20, 21 (Editor); Gath, Vol. I - 4 (Co-editor); endless articles on Gaelic and Highland themes. Recreations: boat-building; art; photography; getting to know the Highlands; watching CalMac; filling the wastepaper basket. Address: (h.) 18 Cricket Place, Brightons, Falkirk FK2 0HZ.

Mehta, Phiroze Sorabji, BSc (Hons), BSc(Eng), MSc, CEng, FIMechE, FRSA, FHEA. Senior Lecturer in CAD, 1986-2005, AHOD Creative Technologies Division, 2001-02 (retired), Glasgow Caledonian University; b. 9.10.44, Bombay; m., Margaret Jane Bowie; 2 s.; 1 d. Whessoe Ltd.: Design Engineer, 1970-75, Senior Design Engineer, 1975-78; Senior Design Engineer, Nuclear Design Department, Babcock Power Ltd., 1978-84; Senior Lecturer in Engineering Design, University of Central England, Birmingham, 1984-86; Glasgow Caledonian University, 1986-2005. SQA Chief Moderator Manufacture; Institution of Mechanical Engineers: Fellow, Professional Interview Panel, Past Chairman, Glasgow Panel; Past Chairman, IMechE Scottish Committee; Past President, Ayr & Prestwick Lions Club; Board Member, Scottish Qualifications Authority Board, 1999-2000; Member, National Qualifications Committee, 1999-2000; Director, SPTC, 1998-2000. Recreations: theatre; concerts; music. Address: (h.) 12 St. Leonards Road, Ayr KA7 2PT.

Meighan, Stephen, BSc, LLB. Chairman, Victim Support Scotland, since 2014; b. 1958. Educ. Mungo's Academy; University of Glasgow. Career history: worked for 15 years in the Ministry of Defence in Whitehall, London; Royal Navy Department and the Central Staff Department dealing with political relationships in the Americas and with the garrisons in Belize and the Falkland Islands; Private Secretary to Government Ministers and Senior Officials; specialist recruitment programmes; the marketing of defence equipment in the Far East; Chief Financial Officer for the British Government in the Al Yamamah Saudi Arabia defence contract; also worked in the Ministry of Defence Operation Rooms throughout the Gulf War in 1990-91 and the Yugoslavian hostage crisis in 1992; joined British Aerospace at the beginning of 1998, working in the South African programme involving the sale of some 40 frontline aircraft in the South African Airforce; following British Aerospace's merger with GEC Marconi in 2000, became Managing Director of the Asia-Pacific region, responsible for the UK business export for all company activities in the Far East until 2009; extensive business experience covers activities in the US, including JV work with Boeing, Europe, the Middle and Far East; has worked in many successful programmes, notably in Saudi Arabia, Japan, South Korea, Malaysia and Thailand; lived in Kuala Lumpur, 2006-2009; returned to Scotland in 2009 for family reasons; worked advising small companies on working in the Far East, both as a paid consultant and on a pro bono basis, in property development and was a full time student for two years; Chair of the Policy and Strategy Committee, Victim Support Scotland, 2010-14. Address: Victim Support Scotland, 15/23 Hardwell Close, Edinburgh EH8 9RX; T.-0131 668 4486.

Meldrum, Angus Alexander, BSc, DIA. Director, Crerar Hotel Group Ltd., since 1999; The Patron, Benevolent Society of The Licensed Trade of Scotland, since 2005; Chairman, Thistle Pub Company 3 plc, 2006-2013; Director, An Lochran (Glasgow Gaelic Arts Agency) Ltd., 2006-2013; Group Chairman, Belhaven Brewery Group plc, 2004-05 (Director, 2002-05); Managing Director, Tennent Caledonian Breweries Ltd., 1992-2001 (Director, since 1981); Chairman, Chrysalis Radio/Arrow Glasgow Ltd., 2003-04; b. 7.11.45, Stornoway; m., Anne-Marie; 1 s. Educ. Bayble School, Lewis; Kingussie High School; Edinburgh University; Bath University Management School. Joined Bass plc, London, 1971; Market Analyst and Group Product Manager, Bass Brewers Ltd., 1971-78; Marketing Manager, Tennent Caledonian Breweries Ltd., 1978-81; Marketing Director, Tennent Caledonian Breweries Ltd., 1981-90; Marketing Director, Bass Brewers (Scotland and Ireland), 1981-90; Brands Marketing Director (UK and International), Bass Brewers Ltd., Burton-on-Trent, 1990-92; Director, Bass Ireland Ltd., 1981-95; Director, Tennents Ireland Ltd. (Dublin), 1981-95; Director, Bass Export Ltd., 1990-94; Director, Maclay's Brewery & Co. plc, Alloa, 1992-2002; Managing Director, J.G. Thomson Ltd. (Wines and Spirits Merchants), 1992-2001; President, Brewers Association of Scotland, 1992-94; Council Member, UK Brewers Society, 1992-94; Millennium Chairman, Scottish Licensed Trade Association, 1999-2000; Freeman, City of Glasgow, since 1982; Keeper of the Quaich, since 1992; Baron d'Honneur de Confrerie des Compagnons Goustevin de Normandie, since 2001; Scottish Licensed Trade Lifetime Achievement Award, 2001; Scottish Advertising Industry Awards 2007 Special 21st Anniversary Award of Scotland's Best Marketeer Ever. Recreations: fishing; shooting; rugby; football; shinty; Scottish music; Gaelic culture. Address: (b.) Lochgreen Consultants, Lochgreen, Gryffe Road, Kilmacolm, Renfrewshire PA13 4BA; T.-01505 872609.

Meldrum, Dr Hamish. Former Chairman of the British Medical Association (2007-12); b. 1948, Edinburgh. Educ. Stirling High School; Edinburgh University. Career history: general medicine; senior housing officer and registrar in Torbay, Devon; moved into general practice in the late 1970s, joining a surgery in Bridlington, East Yorkshire (stayed for more than 30 years); first became involved with the BMA after joining the local medical committee for East Yorkshire; joined the BMA GPs' Committee in 1991; part of the GPC team that negotiated the new GP contract; Deputy Chairman of the GPC, 1999-2004, Chairman, 2004-2007; currently a non-executive director of the BMJ publishing group and a member of the audit committee of the Royal College of General Practitioners. Fellow of the Royal College of General Practitioners and of the Royal College of Physicians of Edinburgh. Address: Royal College of General Practitioners, 25 Queen Street, Edinburgh EH2 1JX; T.-020 3188 7730.

Meldrum, James, MA (Hons), FRSA; b. 9.8.52, Kirkintilloch. Educ. Lenzie Academy; Glasgow University. Administration Trainee/HEO (Admin), Scottish Office, 1973-79; Principal grade posts, Scottish Economic Planning Department, Scottish Development Department, Scottish Office Personnel Division, 1979-86; Deputy Director, Scottish Courts Administration, 1986-91; Head, Investment Assistance Division, Scottish Office Industry Department, 1991-94; Registrar General for Scotland, 1994-99; Director of Administrative Services, Scottish Executive, 1999-2002; Director of Business Management and Area Business Manager, Glasgow, Crown Office and Procurator Fiscal

Service, 2002-03; Keeper of the Registers of Scotland, 2003-2009. Address: (h.) 5 Roman Road, Kirkintilloch, Glasgow G66 1EE; T.-0141 776 7071.
E-mail: jim.meldrum1@btinternet.com

Mennie, William Patrick, BL, NP, IAC, MCSI. Partner, Grigor & Young, Solicitors, Elgin and Forres, 1964-2004 (Senior Partner, from 1984); Consultant, 2004-08; b. 11.10.37, Elgin; m., Patricia Leslie Bogie; 2 s.; 1 d. Educ. Elgin Academy; Edinburgh University. Solicitor, 1960; Honorary Sheriff at Elgin, since 1993; accredited by Law Society of Scotland as a specialist in agricultural law, 1993-2013; Secretary, Malt Distillers Association of Scotland, 1970-2003. Recreations: game shooting and fishing. Address: (h.) Innesmill, Urquhart, Elgin; T.-01343 842643.

Menzies, Rt. Hon. Lord (Duncan A.Y. Menzies). Senator of the College of Justice, since 2001; appointed to the Inner House, 2012; sworn of the Privy Council, 2012; b. 28.8.53, Edinburgh; m., Hilary Weston; 2 s. Educ. Edinburgh Academy; Cargilfield; Glenalmond (scholar); Wadham College, Oxford (scholar); Edinburgh University. Advocate, 1978; Standing Junior Counsel to The Admiralty, 1984-91; Queen's Counsel, 1991; accredited mediator, 1992; Temporary Sheriff, 1996-97; Advocate Depute, 1998-2000; Home Advocate Depute, 1998-2000; Chairman, Scottish Planning, Local Government and Environmental Bar Group, 1997-2001; Member, Faculty Council, 1997-2001; Parliamentary Candidate, Midlothian, 1983, Edinburgh Leith, 1987; founder, Scottish Wine Society; 2012: Maître de la Commanderie de Bordeaux à Edimbourg; Honorary Bencher of the Inner Temple, 2013. Recreations: shooting; golf; wines; planting trees. Address: (b.) Court of Session, Parliament House, Edinburgh; T.-0131-225 2595.

Merrylees, Andrew, RSA, BArch, DipTP, RIBA, FRIAS, FCSD, FRSA. Honorary Professor of Architecture, University of Dundee; b. 13.10.33, Newmains; m., Maie Crawford; 2 s.; 1 d. Educ. Wishaw High School; University of Strathclyde. Sir Basil Spence, Glover and Ferguson: joined 1957, Associate, 1968, Partner, 1972; set up Andrew Merrylees Associates, 1985 (now retired). Member: Advisory Council for the Arts in Scotland. RIBA Bronze Medal; Saltire Award; Civic Trust Award; Art in Architecture Award; RSA Gold Medal; SCONUL Award; RIAS Lifetime Achievement Award. Recreations: architecture; painting; cooking. Address: (b.) 32 Ravelston Garden, Edinburgh EH4 3LE; T.-0131 337 9019; e-mail: amerrylees@btinternet.com
web: www.andrewmerrylees.com

Middleton, David Fraser, CBE, MA. Chief Executive, Historic Environment Scotland, since 2015; b. 23.6.56, Paisley; m., Diane Lamberton; 1 d. Educ. Paisley Grammar School; Glasgow University. Joined Scottish Office as Administration Trainee, 1978; Private Secretary to Minister of State, Scottish Office, 1982-84; seconded to Cabinet Office, 1984; Principal, Scottish Office Finance Group, 1984-89; Director of Strategy, Whitfield Urban Partnership, 1989-91; Assistant Secretary, Housing, 1991-96; Assistant Secretary, 1996-97, Roads; Head of Personnel, 1997-99; Head of Local Government, Europe and External Relations Group, Department of Finance and Central Services, Scottish Executive, 1999-2002; Head of Food and Agriculture Group, Environment and Rural Affairs Department, Scottish Executive, 2002-06; Special Projects Officer, UHI (Millennium Institute), 2006-07 (on loan from Scottish Executive); Head of Scotland Office, Ministry of Justice, 2007-09; Chief Executive, Transport Scotland, Scottish Government, 2009-2015. Recreation: golf (Royal Musselburgh Golf Club). Address: Historic

Environment Scotland, Longmore House, Salisbury Place, Edinburgh EH9 1SH; T.-0131 668 8600.

Middleton, Jeremy Richard Hunter, LLB, BD. Former Parish Minister, Davidson's Mains Parish Church (1988-2015); b. 19.3.53, Kilbarchan; m., Susan (nee Hay); 3 s. Educ. Craigflower Preparatory School, Charterhouse; Old College, New College, Edinburgh. Address: Innean Mor, Southend PA28 6RF; T.-01586 830439.

Milburn, Professor George Henry William, PhD, CChem, FRSC, FBIM, Dr (h.c.). Retired: Reseach Adviser/Research Professor, Napier University, 1998-99, Head, Department of Applied Chemical and Physical Sciences, 1973-98; Adjunct Professor, University of South Florida, 2000; Consultant, Lahti Polytechnic, Finland, 1998-2001; b. 25.11.34, Wallasey; 1 s.; 1 d. Educ. Wallasey Grammar School; Leeds University. Short service commission, Royal Corps of Signals, 1959-63; Staff Demonstrator, Leeds University, 1963-66; Research Fellow, Sydney University, 1967-68; Senior Scientific Officer, Agricultural Research Council, 1968-69; Lecturer, Plymouth Polytechnic, 1969-70; Senior Lecturer, Sheffield Polytechnic, 1970-73.Convener, Committee of Scottish University Heads of Chemistry Departments, 1994-97; Honorary Doctorate, Technical University, Budapest, 1988; Silver Star Laureate, Poland, 1996. Publications: more than 50 scientific publications including a textbook on crystal structure analysis. Recreations: golf; bridge; photography; guitar playing; drawing; painting. Address: (h.) 14 Station Court, North Berwick, East Lothian EH39 4DA; T.-01620 248217; e-mail: harry@milburnh.fsnet.co.uk

Millan, Professor Charles Gordon, MA, PhD, FRSA, Officier Dans L'Ordre Des Palmes Académiques. Independent Higher Education Professional; Professor of French, Strathclyde University, 1991-2009; b. 25.9.46, Kirkcaldy; m., Margaret Anne Robbie; 1 s.; 1 d. Educ. Kirkcaldy High; Merrywood Grammar, Bristol; Edinburgh University. Temporary Lecturer, Edinburgh University, 1970-71; Teacher, Broughton High School, 1972-76; Strathclyde University, since 1976, Director, Languages for Business Unit, since 1990 (Languages for Export Award, 1994 and 2001), Chairman, Department of Modern Languages, 1994-98 and 2000-06, Vice-Dean, Faculty of Arts and Social Sciences, 1995-98; Chair, University Council of Modern Languages (ScotCom), 2001-07. Publications include: Pierre Louÿs ou le Culte de l'Amitié, 1979; Stéphane Mallarmé, Poésies (jointly), 1983; A Throw of the Dice: The Life of Stéphane Mallarmé, 1994; Documents Mallarmé, new series, I, 1998, II, 2000, III, 2003, IV, 2005; Situating Mallarmé, (Co-editor), 2000; Les Mardis de Stéphane Mallarmé, 2008; Pierre Louÿs-Georges Louis, correspondance croisée 1890-1917, 4 vols, 2015; Founding Editor, Les Cahiers Stéphane Mallarmé; Founding Editor, Les Etudes Stéphane Mallarmé. Recreations: cinema; reading. Address: (h.) 32 Broughton Place, Edinburgh EH1 3RT; T.-0131 556 0907.

Millar, Professor Alan, MA, PhD, FRSE. Emeritus Professor of Philosophy, Stirling University; b. 14.12.47, Edinburgh; m., Rose-Mary Marchand; 1 s. Educ. Edinburgh University; Cambridge University. Stirling University: Lecturer in Philosophy, 1971, Senior Lecturer, 1991, Head, Department of Philosophy, 1988-94, 2003-06. Awarded Mind Association Research Fellowship, 1996-97; Visiting Fellow, Clare Hall, Cambridge, 1997; elected Fellow of the Royal Society of Edinburgh, 2005; Member, Editorial Board, Philosophical Quarterly, since 2002; Member, the Executive and Council of the Royal Institute of Philosophy, since 2009; Vice-President, Mind Association, 2013-14; President, Mind Association, 2014-15. Publications:

Reasons and Experience, 1991; Reason and Nature (Co-Editor), 2002; Understanding People, 2004; Epistemic Value (Co-Editor), 2009; Social Epistemology (Co-Editor), 2010; The Nature and Value of Knowledge (Co-Author), 2010; articles in the philosophy of mind, epistemology, philosophy of religion, history of ethics. Recreations: reading; walking; films; cooking. Address: (b.) Stirling University, Stirling FK9 4LA; T.-01786 467555; e-mail: alan.millar@stir.ac.uk

Millar, Ann Rangeley, MA (Hons), MSc, FAcSS. Assistant Director, Scottish Further and Higher Education Funding Council (from 2004); Deputy Chief Researcher, Office of Chief Researcher, Scottish Executive Social Research, from 1993; b. 23.1.50, Yorkshire; m., Donald Iain Lamont Millar; 1 s. Educ. Perth Academy; Aberdeen University; Edinburgh University. Scottish Development Department: Research Officer, Population Research, 1973-75, Senior Research Officer, Urban Regeneration Research, 1976-78; Scottish Home and Health Department: Senior Research Officer, Criminological Research, 1979-86, Principal Research Officer, 1987-90, Principal Research Officer, Civil Law Research, 1991-93. Member, Economic and Social Research Council's Strategic Research Board, 2004-08. Recreations: travel; architecture. Address: (b.) Donaldson House, 97 Haymarket Terrace, Edinburgh EH12 5HD; e-mail: annmillar@sfc.uc.uk

Millar, Catriona, BA Hons (Fine Art). Artist - Figurative Painter, since 2005; b. 23.01.56, Milngavie; m., Roddy Phillips; 2 s. Educ. Douglas Academy, Milngavie; Gray's School of Art, Aberdeen. Exhibited at Royal Scottish Academy, Edinburgh, March 2005; Degree Show at Gray's School of Art, June 2005; First Solo Exhibition at Dundas St. Gallery, Edinburgh, October 2006; Solo Exhibitions at Riverside Gallery, Stonehaven, 2006-09; Queens Gallery, Dundee, 2010; Rendezvous Gallery, Aberdeen, 2011; Tolquhon Gallery, Tarves, 2012; exhibited at: Art at Five, Brighton, 2012; Fairfax Gallery, Royal Tunbridge Wells, 2012. Works exhibited across the UK; works in private and public collections in UK, Europe, America and Far East. Paintings collected in recipe books: Fun with Spinach, The Handsome Chip and Life of Pie. Recreations: walking; music; theatre; the lake district.
E-mail: catriona@catrionamillar.com

Millar, Jamie, LLB, NP. Group Legal Counsel, Arnold Clark, since 2014; Consultant, Lindsays, since 2014 (Partner, 2010-2014); Past President, Law Society of Scotland, since 2011; b. 05.02.49, Dunfermline; m., Diane; 2 s.; 1 d. Educ. Kirkcaldy High School; Edinburgh University. Apprentice Solicitor, Tindal Oatts and Rodger, 1971-73, Assistant Solicitor, 1973-75, Partner, 1975-86; Partner, Bishop and Robertson Chalmers, 1986-99; Partner, Morison Bishop, 1999-2002; Chairman, Bishops Solicitors LLP, 2002-06; Partner, Brodies LLP, 2006-09. Recreations: hill-walking; theatre; travel. Address: (b.) 43 Allison Street, Glasgow G42 8NJ.

Millar, Paul. Consul-General of the Czech Republic (Honorary), since 1996; b. 30.4.33, Brno, Czech Republic; m., Paula; 1 d. Educ. Mendel University, Brno. Agricultural advisory service; veterinary research; teaching, school of agriculture; Commonwealth Bureau of Animal Breeding and Genetics; Britbreed Ltd.; Fullwood CS. Publications: Mendelian Inheritance in Goats; Mendelian Inheritance in Cattle. Recreations: golf; gardening. Address: Consulate General of the Czech Republic, 12A Riselaw Crescent, Edinburgh EH10 6HL.
E-mail: paul.millar@blueyonder.co.uk

Miller, Professor Alan, BSc, PhD, CPhys, FInstP, FRSE, FIEEE (USA), FOSA (USA). Chief Executive Officer, Scottish Universities Physics Alliance (SUPA), University of Glasgow, since May 2015, and Emeritus Professor of Physics, Heriot-Watt University, since January 2015;

Trustee and Board Member, Royal Zoological Society of Scotland (RZSS), since May 2015; Deputy Principal (Research and Knowledge Transfer) and Professor of Physics, Heriot-Watt University, 2009-14; Fellowship Secretary and Council Member, 2011-14, and Research Awards Convenor, 2008-11, Royal Society of Edinburgh (RSE); Vice-Principal (Research), 2003-09, Head of School of Physics and Astronomy, 1997-2003, Professor of Semiconductor Physics, 1993-2009, University of St Andrews; Professor of Physics and Electrical Engineering, University of Central Florida, USA, 1989-93; Senior Principal Scientific Officer, Royal Signals and Radar Establishment, Malvern, 1981-89; Visiting Assistant Professor of Physics, North Texas University, 1979-81; Research Fellow, Heriot-Watt University, 1974-79; b. 5.6.49, Dunfermline; m. Susan Linklater; 3 d. Educ. Woodmill High School; Gibraltar Grammar School; University of Edinburgh; University of Bath. Past Editor, Optical & Quantum Electronics (Chapman & Hall); Past Editor, Cambridge Studies in Modern Optics (series of monographs, CUP); Past Chair, Institute of Physics Semiconductor Group; Past Chair; Committee of Scottish Professors of Physics; Past Chair, Scottish Chapter, IEEE Lasers and Electro-Optics Society; Past Chair, Royal Society of Edinburgh Physics Committee. Publications: Nonlinear Optics in Signal Processing (Editor); Nonlinear Optical Materials and Devices for Applications in Information Technology (Editor); Laser Sources and Applications (Editor); Semiconductor Quantum Optoelectronics: From Quantum Physics to Smart Devices (Editor); Ultrafast Photonics (Editor); 200 journal research papers. Recreations: music and grandchildren. Address: Kelvin Building, University of Glasgow, Glasgow G12 8QQ; T.-0141-330-8790.
E-mail: Alan.Miller@supa.ac.uk

Miller, Alan Douglas, LLB (Hons), DipLP. Sheriff, Sheriffdom of Glasgow and Strathkelvin at Glasgow; b. 30.11.59, Edinburgh; m., Alison; 1 s.; 2 d. Educ. Stewart's/Melville College, Edinburgh; Edinburgh University. Children's Reporter, Strathclyde, 1985-90; Regional Children's Reporter, Dumfries and Galloway, 1990-95; Principal Reporter, Scottish Children's Reporter Administration, 1995-2005; Part-time Sheriff, convener of various tribunals and youth justice consultant, 2005-2010; floating Sheriff, Sheriffdom of South Strathclyde, Dumfries and Galloway, 2010-2011. Company Secretary, Linlithgow Young People's Project; Associate Member, Iona Community; Elder, Church of Scotland. Recreations: music; walking; cycling; reading; family. Address: (b.) Sheriff Courthouse, 1 Carlton Place, Glasgow G5 9DA; T.-0141-429-8888; e-mail: sheriffamiller@scotcourts.gov.uk

Miller, Alexandra, MA, MSc. Head of Communications & Enterprise, National Library of Scotland, since 2012, Director of Customer Services, Development & External Relations, 2011-12; b. Scotland; m., Colin Balfour. Educ. University of St. Andrews; Napier University. Communications posts with Spider Systems, Glasgow City Council, KPMG, the Scottish Arts Council, the Scottish Health Service and the Civil Service, 1975-91; Director of Corporate Affairs, Telewest plc, 1991-97; Director of Consultancy, Clearview Strategy, 1997-2004. Member, Chartered Institute of Marketing and the Chartered Institute of Public Relations; Member, BBC Broadcasting Council for Scotland, 2002-06; Member, BBC Audience Council Scotland, 2006-07; Member, Executive Committee, Scottish Council for Development and Industry (SCDI), since 2004. Address: (b.) National Library of Scotland, George IV Bridge, Edinburgh EH1 1EW; T.-0131 623 3700; e-mail: a.miller@nls.uk

Miller, Professor Andrew, CBE, MA, BSc, PhD, DUniv (Stirling, Open University), FRSE. Principal and Vice-Chancellor, University of Stirling, 1994-2001; Emeritus Professor, since 2001; General Secretary, Royal Society of

Edinburgh, 2001-05; Secretary and Treasurer, Carnegie Trust for the Universities of Scotland, 2004-2013; b. 15.2.36, Kelty, Fife; m., Rosemary S.H. Fyvie; 1 s.; 1 d. Educ. Beath High School; Edinburgh University. Assistant Lecturer in Chemistry, Edinburgh University, 1960-62; Postdoctoral Fellow, CSIRO, Melbourne, and Tutor in Chemistry, Ormond College, Melbourne University, 1962-65; Staff Scientist, MRC Laboratory of Molecular Biology, Cambridge, 1965-66; Lecturer in Molecular Biophysics, Oxford University and (from 1967) Fellow, Wolfson College, 1966-83 (Honorary Fellow, since 1995); on secondment as first Head, European Molecular Biology Laboratory, Grenoble Antenne, France, 1975-80; Professor of Biochemistry, Edinburgh University, 1984-94; Vice-Dean of Medicine, Edinburgh University, 1991-93; Vice-Principal, Edinburgh University, 1993-94. Committee Member: British Biophysical Society, 1972-74, SERC Synchrotron Radiation Facility Committee, 1979-82, Biological Sciences Committee, 1982-85, Neutron Beam Research Committee, 1982-85; Council Member, Institut Laue-Langevin, 1981-85; Member: MRC Joint Dental Committee, 1984-86, UGC Biological Sciences Committee, 1985-89; (part-time) Director of Research, European Synchrotron Radiation Facility, Grenoble, 1986-91; Member: Advisory Board, AFRC Food Research Institute, 1985, UFC Advisory Groups on Biological Sciences and Pre-clinical Medicine, 1989, Scientific Council, Grenoble University, 1989; Director, Scottish Knowledge plc, 1997-2002; Member, Minister of Education's Action Group on Standards in Scottish Schools, 1997-99; Member, Council, Royal Society of Edinburgh, since 1997 (Convener, International Committee, 1999-2001, Chairman, RSE Scotland Foundation, 2005-09, Bicentennial Medal, 2008); Member, UNESCO UK Science Committee, 2002-03; Adviser to Wellcome Trust on UK–French Synchrotron, 1999-2000; Member, Scottish Executive Science Strategy Group, 1999-2000; Interim Chief Executive, Cancer Research UK, 2001-02; Chairman, International Centre for Mathematical Sciences, Edinburgh, 2001-05; Member, Council, Open University, 2001-05; Deputy Chairman, Scottish Food Advisory Committee, 2003-05; Board Member, Food Standards Agency, 2003-05. Publications: Minerals in Biology (Co-Editor), 1986; over 180 research papers. Address: 5 Blackford Hill Grove, Edinburgh EH9 3HA.

Miller, Sheriff Colin Brown, LLB. Sheriff for South Strathclyde, Dumfries and Galloway, 1991-2010, retired and then re-employed Sheriff, 2010; b. 4.10.46, Paisley; m., Joan Elizabeth Blyth; 3 s. Educ. Paisley Grammar School; Glasgow University. Partner, McFadyen & Semple, Solicitors, Paisley, 1971-91; Council Member, Law Society of Scotland, 1983-91 (Convener, Conveyancing Committee, 1986-89; Convener, Judicial Procedure Committee, 1989-91; Chairman, Working Party on Rights of Audience in Supreme Courts, 1990-91); Dean, Faculty of Procurators in Paisley, 1991. Recreations: walking; photography; travel; railways; ships. Address: (b.) c/o Ayr Sheriff Court, Wellington Square, Ayr; T.-01292 268474.

Miller, Sir Donald John, FREng, FRSE, BSc(Eng), DSc, DUniv, FIMechE, FIEE; b. 9.2.27, London; m., Fay G. Herriot; 1 s.; 2 d. Educ. Banchory Academy; Aberdeen University. Metropolitan-Vickers, 1947-53; British Electricity Authority, 1953-55; Preece Cardew & Rider (Consulting Engineers), 1955-66; Chief Engineer, North of Scotland Hydro-Electric Board, 1966-74; South of Scotland Electricity Board: Director of Engineering, 1974, appointed Deputy Chairman, 1979; Chairman, Scottish Power, 1982-92. Chairman, Power Division, IEE, 1977. Recreations: reading; gardening; walking; sailing. Address: (h.) Puldohran, Gryffe Road, Kilmacolm, Renfrewshire; T.-01505 873988.

Miller, Gordon, BSc. Retired Rector, Blairgowrie High School (2007-2013); b. 10.10.57, Glasgow; m., Julie Elizabeth; 1 s.; 1 d. Educ. High School of Glasgow; Strathclyde University. Assistant Teacher, Lochend Secondary School, Glasgow, 1980-85; Assistant Principal Teacher and Principal Teacher of Guidance, Lochgilphead High School, 1985-92; Assistant Rector, Carluke High School, 1992-96; Depute Rector, Crieff High School, 1996-99; Rector, Mearns Academy, 1999-2007. Council member, School Leaders Scotland, 2000-06 and 2008-2011, Treasurer, 2003-06. Recreations: golf; hill-walking. Address: Kirriemuir, Angus.

Miller, Ian. Leader, Perth & Kinross Council since 2007; b. 31.7.49, Perth; m., Angela; 1 s.; 1 d. Educ. Craigend Primary School; Perth High School. SNP Councillor Career: first elected to Perth and Kinross District Council in May 1995; held the post of Convener of Development Control Committee; re-elected in 1999 and again in 2003; elected as Leader of the SNP Group in 1999; became Leader of the Council in May 2007; elected as one of the 4 councillors in the multi member ward of Strathmore in 2007 and again in 2012; Chair, Community Planning Partnership, Perth & Kinross Council, since 2007. Heavily involved in the Alyth community attending the Halls Association, Gala Committee, Community Council. Recreations: gardening; traditional Scottish music. Address: (b) Perth & Kinross Council, The Atrium, 137 Glover Street, Perth PH2 0LQ; T-01738 475018; e-mail: imiller@pkc.gov.uk

Miller, Sheriff Ian Harper Lawson, MA, LLB. Sheriff of Glasgow and Strathkelvin at Glasgow, since 2001; b. 16.1.54, Aberdeen; m., Sheila Matthews Howie; 1 s.; 3 d. Educ. Robert Gordon's College, Aberdeen; Aberdeen University. Admitted as a Solicitor, 1980; Partner, Burnett & Reid, Solicitors, Aberdeen, 1986-91; Advocate, 1992; Sheriff of Grampian, Highland and Islands at Aberdeen, 1998-2001. Recreations: reading; music. Address: (b.) Sheriff's Chambers, Sheriff Court of Glasgow and Strathkelvin, 1 Carlton Place, Glasgow G5 9DA; T.-0141-429 8888.

Miller, Rev. Ian Hunter, BA, BD. Retired Minister at Bonhill (1975-2012); b. 30.5.44, Johnstone; m., Joan Elizabeth Parr; 2 s. Educ. Johnstone High School; Glasgow University; Open University. Travel agent, latterly Branch Manager, A.T. Mays, 1962-69; Assistant Minister, Renfrew Old Kirk, 1974-75. Freeman of Dumbarton. Moderator, Dumbarton Presbytery, 1985-87; Past Chairman, Lomond and Argyll Division, NHS Argyll and Clyde; Past Chairman, West Dunbartonshire Health and Social Justice Committee. Board of Tullochan Trust. Recreations: golf; badminton; music; drama and public speaking. Address: Derand, Queen Street, Alexandria G830AS; T.-01389 753039; e-mail: revianmiller@btinternet.com

Miller, Ian James, OBE, MA, LLB. Chairman, Mental Welfare Commission for Scotland, 2000-08; Member, National Appeal Panel for Entry to Health Boards' Pharmaceutical Lists, 1997-2008; Governor, Morrison's Academy, Crieff, 1998-2002; Member, Business Committee, University of Edinburgh General Council, 2001-05; Director, Edinburgh Healthcare NHS Trust, 1995-99; Trustee, Lothian Primary Care NHS Trust, 1999-2000; Member: Police Complaints Commissioner for Scotland Advisory Panel, 2008-2010, Executive Committee, Edinburgh Headway Group, 2008-2010; Trustee, Edinburgh Napier University Development Trust; b. 21.10.38, Fraserburgh; m., Sheila Mary Hourston; 1 s.; 2 d. Educ. Fraserburgh Academy; Aberdeen University; Edinburgh University. Private legal practice, 1963-68; Senior Legal Assistant, Inverness County Council, 1968-70; Depute County Clerk, then County Clerk, Ross and Cromarty

County Council, 1970-75; Chief Executive, Inverness District Council, 1975-77; Director of Law and Administration, Grampian Regional Council, 1977-84; Director, Kildonnan Investments Ltd., Aberdeen, 1984-87; Secretary and Academic Registrar, Napier University, Edinburgh, 1987-99. Recreations: golf; curling; bridge. Address: (h.) 80 Craiglockhart Road, Edinburgh EH14 1EP.

Miller, James, CBE (1986), MA, CBIM. Chairman, 1970-99, Managing Director, 1970-91, The Miller Group Ltd. (formerly James Miller & Partners); Chairman, Royal Scottish National Orchestra, 1997-2002; b. 1.9.34, Edinburgh; m., 1, Kathleen Dewar (deceased); 2, Iris Lloyd-Webb; 1 s.; 3 d. Educ. Edinburgh Academy; Harrow School; Balliol College, Oxford. National Service, Royal Engineers. James Miller & Partners Ltd.: joined, 1958, appointed Director, 1960; Scottish Representative, Advisory Committee to the Meteorological Services, 1980-92; Chairman, Federation of Civil Engineering Contractors, 1985-86, President, 1990-93; Director, British Linen Bank Ltd., 1983-99 (Chairman, 1997-99); Member, Scottish Advisory Board, British Petroleum, 1990-2001; Director, Bank of Scotland, 1993-2000; Deacon Convener, Incorporated Trades of Edinburgh, 1974-77; President, Edinburgh Chamber of Commerce, 1981-83; Assistant, 1982-85, Treasurer, 1990-92, Master, 1992-94, Merchant Company of Edinburgh; Chairman, Court, Heriot-Watt University, 1990-96. Recreation: shooting. Address: (h.) Alderwood, 49 Craigcrook Road, Edinburgh EH4 3PH; T.-0131-332 2222.

Miller, Professor James Alexander, PhD, MBA, BSc (Hons), RN, FRSM. Director, The Open University in Scotland, 2010-2015; Deputy Vice-Chancellor, Glasgow Caledonian University, since 2015; Chief Executive, Royal College of Physicians and Surgeons of Glasgow, 2005-August 2010; b. 11.3.64, Bridge of Allan; m., Winnie Miller (nee Dekonski); 1 s.; 1 d. Educ. Alloa Academy; University of Edinburgh; Napier University; Abertay University. Student Nurse, North Lothian College of Nursing and Midwifery, 1983-86; various clinical and senior nurse roles in Edinburgh, 1986-92; West Lothian NHS Trust: Deputy Director of Nursing, 1992-94, Nurse Manager, 1994-98, General Manager, 1998-2001; General Manager, NHS Greater Glasgow, 2001-05. Non-executive roles: Lay Governor, Glasgow Caledonian University, since 2006; Trustee, British Geriatric Society, since 2012. Publications: a number of peer reviewed manuscripts in journals. Recreations: golf; reading; music. Address: (h.) Tweeniehills, 33 Sandholes Road, Brookfield, Renfrewshire PA5 8UY; T.-01505 336057; e-mail: jamesm31@aol.com

Miller, James David Frederick, CBE, DUniv (Stirling, Paisley), MA (Cantab). Chairman, Wolverhampton and Dudley Breweries PLC, 1992-2001; Director: J & P Coats Ltd, Coats Patons PLC, Coats Viyella PLC, 1980-91; Chairman, Fairbridge Scotland, 1998-2006; Vice-Chairman, Forth Valley Enterprise, 1996-2003; Director, J. and J. Denholm Ltd., 1997-2005; Chairman, Clackmannan College of FE, 2004-06; b. 5.1.35, Wolverhampton; m., Saffrey Blackett Oxley; 3 s. (1 deceased); 1 d. Educ. The Edinburgh Academy; Emmanuel College, Cambridge; London School of Economics. National Service, Argyll and Sutherland Highlanders (commissioned South Staffords); Council Member, Outward Bound Limited, 1985-95; Vice-Chairman, Royal Scottish National Orchestra; Director, Edinburgh Academy, 1985; Commissioner, Queen Victoria School, 1987-97; Governor, Scottish College of Textiles, 1989; Director, Edinburgh Military Tattoo Ltd., 1990-2000; Director, Scottish Life Assurance Company, 1995-2001; Chairman, Court, Stirling University, 1992-99; Chairman, SCOTVEC, 1992-96; Chairman, Scottish Examinations Board, 1994-96; Chairman, SQA (Scottish Qualifications Authority), 1996-2000. Recreations: gardening; golf; walking. Address: (h.) Blairuskin Lodge, Kinlochard, Aberfoyle, by Stirling FK8 3TP; T.-01877 387 249; e-mail: J.D.F.M@btinternet.com

Miller, Keith Manson, CBE, D (Eng), BSc (Hons), DipMS, FCIOB, FRICS. Retired Chief Executive, Miller Group (1994-2015); b. 19.3.49, Edinburgh. Educ. Loretto; Heriot-Watt University; Glasgow University. Recreations: sailing; skiing.

Miller, Professor Kenneth, LLB, LLM, PhD. Professor Emeritus, Strathclyde University (former Vice Principal); b. 11.12.51, Paisley; m., Margaret Macleod. Educ. Paisley Grammar School; Strathclyde University; Queen's University, Canada. Lecturer in Law, then Senior Lecturer, Strathclyde University, 1975-91; Deputy General Editor, Stair Memorial Encyclopaedia of the Laws of Scotland, 1990-96; Editor, Juridical Review, 2000-08; Deputy Chair, Central Arbitration Committee. Publications: Employment Law in Scotland (Co-Author); Law of Health and Safety at Work in Scotland; Employment Law – A Student Guide. Recreations: reading; golf; walking. Address: (b.) McCance Building, Strathclyde University, 16 Richmond Street, Glasgow G1 1XQ; T.-0141-552 4400; e-mail: kenneth.miller@strath.ac.uk

Miller, May, MA. Board Member, Creative Scotland, since 2012; Deputy Chair, BAFTA Scotland, since 2011; b. Dumbarton; m., Alan Mitchinson; 1 s.; 1 d. Educ. Clydebank High School; Glasgow University. Creative Director, Arts and Factual, BBC Scotland; Creative Director, Mentorn (Scotland); Head of Talkback Thames (Scotland). Board Member, Glasgow City Heritage Trust; RTS Member. Recreations: film; tv; music; art. E-mail: may.miller@hotmail.com

Miller, Nigel. Chairman, Livestock Health Scotland, since 2015; President, NFU Scotland, 2011-2015, formerly Vice-President (2007-2011). Member, Board: Scotland's Rural College (SRUC), SAC Commercial Ltd, Moredun Research Institute, Pentland Science Park. Address: Scotland's Rural College (SRUC), Peter Wilson Building, Kings Buildings, West Mains Road, Edinburgh EH9 3JG; T.-0131 535 4000.

Miller, Sir Ronald Andrew Baird, CBE (1985), BSc, CA, DSc, DUniv. Chairman, Edinburgh Napier University Development Trust; b. 13.5.37, Edinburgh. Former Chairman, Dawson International PLC; former Chairman, Court, Edinburgh Napier University.

Miller, Professor William L., MA, PhD, FBA, FRSA, FRSE. Emeritus Professor of Politics, Glasgow University (Professor, since 1985); b. 12.8.43, Glasgow; m., Fiona Thomson; 2 s.; 1 d. Educ. Aberdeen Grammar School; Royal High School, Edinburgh; Edinburgh University; Newcastle University. Formerly Lecturer, Senior Lecturer and Professor, Strathclyde University; Visiting Professor, Virginia Tech., Blacksburg, Virginia, 1983-84; also taught at Universities of Essex and Cologne; frequent Contributor to Press and TV; Member, Editorial Board: Electoral Studies. Publications: Electoral Dynamics, 1977; The End of British Politics?, 1981; The Survey Method in the Social and Political Sciences, 1983; Elections and Voters, 1987; The Quality of Local Democracy, 1988; How Voters Change, 1990; Media and Voters, 1991; Alternatives to Freedom, 1995; Political Culture in Contemporary Britain, 1996; Values and Political Change in Postcommunist Europe, 1998; Models of Local Governance, 2000; A Culture of Corruption? 2001; Anglo-Scottish Relations from 1900 to Devolution and Beyond, 2005; Multicultural Nationalism: Islamophobia, Anglophobia and Devolution, 2006; The Open Economy and its Enemies - Public Opinion in East Asia and Eastern Europe, 2006. Address: (b.) Department of Politics, Glasgow University G12 8RT; T.-0141-330 5980.

Millican, Douglas, Bcom, CA, AMCT. Chief Executive, Scottish Water, since 2013, Finance and Regulation Director, 2007-2013, Finance Director, 2002-07; b. 13.9.64, Edinburgh; m., Jane; 2 s.; 1 d. Educ. Edinburgh Academy; Edinburgh University. Price Waterhouse, 1986-91, 1993-96; East of Scotland Water: Financial Controller, 1996-2002; Commercial Director, 2000-02. Recreations: Church; skiing; cycling. Address: (b.) Scottish Water, Castle House, 6 Castle Drive, Dunfermline, Fife KY11 8GG; T.-01383 848465; e-mail: douglas.millican@scottishwater.co.uk

Milligan, Eric. Chair, Licensing Board, since 2012; Convener, Lothian and Borders Police Board, 2003-07; Lord Provost and Lord Lieutenant, City of Edinburgh, 1996-2003; b. 27.1.51, Edinburgh; m., Janis. Educ. Tynecastle High School; Napier College of Commerce and Technology. Former printer; Member (Labour), Edinburgh District Council, 1974-78; Lothian Regional Councillor, 1978-96 (Chairman, Finance Committee, 1980-82, 1986-90, Convener, 1990-96); President, COSLA, 1988-90; City of Edinburgh Councillor, since 1995 (Convener, 1995-96); JP, Edinburgh, 1996; awarded Chevalier, Ordre National du Mérite, 1996; Honorary Degree: Doctor of Business Administration, Napier University, 1999; Honorary Fellow, Royal College of Surgeons of Edinburgh, 2000; Honorary Degree: Doctor of the University, Heriot-Watt University, 2004. Address: (b.) City Chambers, High Street, Edinburgh EH1 1YJ; T-0131 200 2000.

Milligan, Janey Louise, LLM, FRICS, FCIArb, MAICA. Managing Director, Construction Dispute Resolution, since 1997; Chairman, Royal Institution of Chartered Surveyors, 2007-08; b. 27.05.60, Glasgow; m., Andrew Milligan; 2 d. Educ. Kilsyth Academy; Glasgow College of Building & Printing; University of Strathclyde. Director of Quantity Surveying, UNICK Architects, 1986-93; Lecturer, Glasgow Caledonian University, 1993-97. Non Executive Member, RICS UK and Ireland World Regional Board (UK & I WRB), 2010-2014; Director, Scottish Arbitration Centre, since 2011; Treasurer, Airdrie Clarkston Parish Church of Scotland, since 2008. Recreations: swimming; photography; golf; reading. Address: (b.) 291 Springhill Parkway, Glasgow Business Park, Glasgow G69 6GA; T.-0141 773 3377; e-mail: jlm@cdr.uk.com

Mills, Harold Hernshaw, CB, BSc, PhD. Chairman: Caledonian MacBrayne Ltd., 1999-2006, Edinburgh World Heritage Trust, 1999-2006, Land Trust, until 2014 (Board Member, 1998-2015); Board Member: Northlink Orkney and Shetland Ferries Ltd., 2002-09, Northlink Ferries Ltd., 2006-09; Trustee and Director, Scottish Maritime Museum; Board Member, Edinburgh City Centre Partnership Company, 2002-06; Trustee: The City of Adelaide Charitable Trust, The Waterways Trust, 2012-13, The Scottish Waterways Trust, 2012-14; b. 2.3.38, Greenock; m., Marion Elizabeth Beattie. Educ. Greenock High School; Glasgow University. Cancer Research Scientist, Roswell Park Memorial Institute, Buffalo, New York, 1962-64; Lecturer, Chemistry Department, Glasgow University, 1964-69; Greenock Town Council, 1965-69, Hon. Treasurer, 1967-69; Principal, Scottish Home and Health Department, 1970-76; Assistant Secretary: Scottish Office, 1976-81, Privy Council Office, 1981-83, Scottish Development Department, 1983-84; Under Secretary, Scottish Development Department, 1984-88; Principal

Finance Officer, Scottish Office, 1988-92; Secretary, Scottish Office Environment Department, 1992-95; Secretary and Head of Department, Scottish Office Development Department, 1995-98. Governor, Queen Margaret University College, 1998-2004; Director, Home in Scotland, 1998-2004 (Chairman, 2000-04); Director, Home Group, 2000-04; Director, Home Housing Trust, 2000-04. Address (h.) 21 Hatton Place, Edinburgh EH9 1UB.

Mills, Ian Thomas, BSc, MPhil. Arts/Education Consultant; b. 20.5.48, Hamilton; m., Margaret; 2 d. Educ. Dalziel High School, Motherwell; Glasgow University; Strathclyde University. Chemistry Teacher, Dalziel High School, Motherwell, 1970-75; Senior Housemaster, Lanark Grammar School, 1975-78; Assistant Head Teacher, then Depute Head Teacher, Carluke High School, 1978-85; Area Education Officer, Perth and Kinross, 1985-91; Assistant Director of Education, Tayside Regional Council, 1991-95; Director of Education and Leisure Services, East Dunbartonshire Council, 1995-2000; General Manager, National Youth Choir of Scotland, 2001-07; Head of Principal's Office, Royal Conservatoire of Scotland (formerly RSAMD), 2007-2014. Administrator, Scottish International Piano Competition; Chairman, Drake Music Scotland Board; Member, Children's Classic Concerts Board. Recreations: music; family-based activities; Rotary (District Governor, 2010-11). Address: 28 Kirkhouse Road, Blanefield G63 9BX; T.-07814989155; e-mail: ian@ian-mills.co.uk

Mills, Peter Rodney, BSc, MD, FRCP, FACP. Consultant Physician and Gastroenterologist, Western Infirmary, Glasgow, since 1988; b. 27.12.48, St. Albans; m., Hazel; 1 s.; 1 d. Educ. St. George's School, Harpenden; University of St. Andrews. Senior Registrar in Medicine/Gastroenterology, Royal Infirmary, Glasgow, 1979; Visiting Assistant Professor, Yale University School of Medicine, 1983; Associate Professor, Division of Gastroenterology, Medical College of Virginia, 1985; Honorary Professor, University of Glasgow, 2010; Director of Medical Examinations, Royal College of Physicians and Surgeons of Glasgow, 2000-06; Chairman, Board for SCE in Gastroenterology, 2007-2012; President, Scottish Society of Gastroenterology, 2007-2010. Publications: 165 papers in gastroenterology and liver journals. Recreations: golf; hillwalking. Address: (h.) 19 Kirklee Road, Glasgow G12 0RQ; T.-0141-339 8206.
E-mail: p.r.mills@clinmed.gla.ac.uk

Mills, Simon James, MA (Cantab). Head of College, Robert Gordon's College, since 2014; b. 28.4.69, Dundee; m., Ruth; 2 s.; 1 d. Educ. Glenalmond College; Pembroke College, Cambridge. BP Oil, Sales and Marketing, Herts, 1991-93; Geography Teacher, Blundell's School, Devon, 1993-97; Head of Geography and Housemaster, Stamford School, Lincs, 1997-2005; Second Master, The Portsmouth Grammar School, Hants, 2005-09; Headmaster, Lomond School, 2009-2014. Recreations: skiing; golf; running; cycling; windsurfing; sailing. Address: (b.) Robert Gordon's College, Schoolhill, Aberdeen AB10 1FE; T.-01224 646346; e-mail: s.mills@rgc.aberdeen.sch.uk
web: www.rgc.aberdeen.sch.uk

Milne, James Smith, CBE, DL, DBA (Hon), DHC. Chairman and Managing Director, Balmoral Group Holdings Ltd., since 1980; b. 26.12.40, Aberdeen; m., Gillian; 2 s.; 2 d. Burgess of Guild, City of Aberdeen; Deputy Lieutenant, City of Aberdeen; Member of the North-east Committee and Fellow of the Scottish Council for Development and Industry; Chairman of Friends of ANCHOR ARI.

Milne, Professor Lorna Catherine, MA, PhD, Chevalier dans l'Ordre des Palmes Académiques. Professor of French, University of St. Andrews, since 2006, Dean of Arts, 2006-09, Vice-Principal (Proctor), since 2011; b.

19.08.59, Stirling. Educ. Dollar Academy; St. Andrews; Auckland (New Zealand). HM Diplomatic Service, London and East Berlin, 1983-87; Doctoral Studies, 1987-91; Lecturer: Aston University, 1991-96, St. Andrews University, 1996-2001, Senior Lecturer, 2001-06. Publications: Author: L'Evangile Selon Michel, 1994, Patrick Chamoiseau: Espaces d'une ecriture antillaise, 2006; numerous scholarly articles and edited volumes. Address: (b.) University of St. Andrews, St. Andrews, Fife KY16 9AH; T.-01334 462588.
E-mail: lcm2@st-andrews.ac.uk

Milne, Nanette Lilian Margaret, OBE, MBChB, FFARCS. MSP (Conservative), North East region, 2003-2016; former Conservative Spokesman on Public Health; Spokesman on Environment, 2007-2010; Spokesman on Health and Community Care, 2005-07; b. 27.4.42, Aberdeen; m., Dr. Alan D. Milne; 1 s.; 1 d. Educ. Aberdeen High School for Girls; University of Aberdeen. Various hospital posts (to registrar grade), 1965-73; career break, 1973-78; part-time medical research, 1978-92. Vice-chairman, Scottish Conservative Party, 1988-92; Aberdeen City Councillor, 1988-99; Director, Grampian Enterprise Ltd., 1992-98; Trustee, Aberdeen International Youth Festival; Member, Aberdeen University Court, 1996-2005. Recreations: the countryside (hill-walking, etc); skiing; golf; gardening.

Milne, Simon Stephen, MBE, BSc, FRGS. Regius Keeper, Royal Botanic Garden Edinburgh, since 2014; Chief Executive, Scottish Wildlife Trust, 2004-2014; b. 30.1.59, Dundee; m., Françoise (né Sevaux); 1 s.; 2 d. Educ. University of St Andrews; Royal Naval College, Greenwich. Commissioned into Royal Marines, 1976; retired from Royal Marines in Rank of Lieutenant Colonel, 2000; Director, Sir Harold Hillier Gardens and Arboretum, 2000-04; Member, Scottish Biodiversity Committee, National Reintroductions Forum; Honorary Professor, University of Edinburgh (2010); Member, Her Majesty's Body Guard of the Honourable Corps of Gentlemen at Arms (appointed 2011). Address: Royal Botanic Garden Edinburgh, 20A Inverleith Row, Edinburgh EH3 5LR.

Milne, Stewart, CBE. Chairman of Aberdeen F.C., since 1998; b. 1950. Founded the Aberdeen-based Stewart Milne Group in 1975, a housebuilding contractor; started off his business renovating bathrooms. Scottish Entrepreneur of the Year award, 2005; Commander of the Order of the British Empire (CBE) in 1998 for services to the house building industry in Scotland. Honorary Chairman, Cornton Football Club, since 2009. Address: Aberdeen Football Club plc, Pittodrie Stadium, Pittodrie Street, Aberdeen AB24 5QH.

Milton, Ian Murray. Chairman, Milton Hotels Ltd.; Director, Nevis Range Development Company PLC; b. 25.7.45, Glasgow; m., Ann; 1 s.; 3 d. Educ. Lochaber High School; Scottish Hotel School, Glasgow. Began Milton Hotels with brother, 1965. Recreations: golf; skiing; computing. Address: (b.) Milton Hotels Ltd., 1 RFL House, Anderson Street, Dunblane FK15 6AJ; T.-01786 820090; e-mail: ian.milton@miltonhotels.com

Minke, Kim, MA. Director of The Danish Cultural Institute, 2009-2015; b. 5.3.50, Denmark; m., Conny Minke; 1 s.; 1 d. Educ. University of Copenhagen (DK). Assistant Lecturer, University of Copenhagen, 1973-75; Assistant Professor, Institute of Press Research, Aarhus (DK), 1975-82; Head of Department, Danish School of Journalism, Aarhus (DK), 1982-94, Director, 1994-2007,

Lecturer, 2007-09; Director of "Free and Independent Press in Mongolia Project", 1992-2000; Editor of "Ejour" (internet magazine), 2001-07. Publications: several books and articles in Danish, English and French on the media; recent books: "Aviskrigen" (2008) and "Danske Medier" (2009).

Misra, Prem Chandra, BSc, MBBS, DPM (RCP&S, Edin and Glas), MRCPsych, FRCPsych. Consultant Psychiatrist; Professor; b. 24.7.41, Lucknow, India; m., Sandhya; 1 s.; 2 d. Educ. KK Degree College and King George's Medical College, Lucknow, India; Lucknow University. Rotating Intern, King George's Medical College Hospital, Lucknow, 1967; Demonstrator, Department of Human Physiology, Lucknow University, 1967; Resident Senior House Officer, General Medicine and Geriatrics, Wigan and Leigh Group of Hospitals, 1968-69; Resident House Surgeon, General Surgery, Wigan Royal Infirmary, 1968-69; Resident House Physician, General Medicine, Whelley Hospital, Wigan, 1969-70; Resident Senior House Officer in Psychiatry, then Resident Registrar in Psychiatry, Bolton District General Hospital, 1970-73; Senior Psychiatric Registrar (Midland Area Consultant Training Scheme), Hollymoor Hospital, Birmingham, 1973-76; Consultant Psychiatrist, Solihull Area Health Authority, 1976; appointed Consultant Psychiatrist, Glasgow Royal Infirmary and Duke Street Hospital, 1976-2005; Consultant in Charge, Acorn Street Day Hospital, 1979-87; Deputy Physician Superintendent, Gartloch and Parkhead Hospitals, Glasgow, 1984-92. President, Indian Association of Strathclyde, since 1981; Member, Executive Committee: Strathclyde Community Relations Council, 1981-85, Scottish Council for Racial Equality, 1982-84; Member: Social and Welfare Committee, CRC, for Ethnic Groups and Vietnam Refugees, 1982-84, Board of Directors, Scottish Refugee Council, 1994-2000; Secretary, Division of Psychiatry, Eastern District of Glasgow, 1980-94; President, British Society of Medical and Dental Hypnosis (Scotland), 1987-89; Governor, Glasgow Caledonian University, 1998-2005; Lead Consultant of Royal College of Psychiatrists for Transcultural Psychiatry in Scotland; Member: Executive Committee, British Society of Research on Sex Education, International Scientific Committee on Sexuality and Handicap, International Advisory Board of Israel Society of Clinical and Experimental Hypnosis, International Committee of Sexologists, Society for the Advancement of Sexual Health; Executive Committee Member, European Society of Hypnosis; Justice of the Peace, 1980-2007; awarded Ludwika Bierkoskigo Medal by Polish Medical Association for "outstanding contributions in the prevention and treatment of disabilities"; "Robert Burns Award" by Indian Writers Association of Scotland; "Merit Award" by Greater Glasgow Health Council; and "Award of an Honour" by the Asian Federation of Sexology Mumbai, India; "Lifetime Achievement in Medicine Award" - Association of Indian Organisations West Scotland, 2009. Publications: Modern Trends in Hypnosis; research papers. E-mail: prof.p.misra@gmail.co.uk

Mitchell, Rev. Alexander Bell, DipTechEd, BD. Retired Minister, St. Blane's Church, Dunblane (2003-2014); b. 28.6.49, Baillieston; m., Elizabeth Brodie; 1 s.; 2 d. Educ. Uddingston Grammar School; New College, Edinburgh. Assistant Minister, Dunblane Cathedral, 1979-81; Minister, St Leonard's Church, Dunfermline, 1981-2003. Recreations: golf; hill-walking. Address: 24 Hebridean Gardens, Crieff PH7 3BP; T.-01764 652241.
E-mail: alex.mitchell6@btopenworld.com

Mitchell, Alison. Headteacher, Rosshall Academy. Address: 131 Crookston Road, Crookston, Glasgow G52 3PD; T.-0141 582 0200.

Mitchell, Dr. David Scott, MSc, IHBC, ICME. Acting Chief Executive, Historic Environment Scotland, since 2016, Director of Conservation, 2010-16, Director of

Technical Conservation Group, 2008-2016; b. 28.1.70; m., Lesley; 2 s.; 1 d. Educ. High School of Stirling; Strathclyde University; Edinburgh University. Career History: Director, Heritage Engineering, Industrial Heritage Co. Ltd, Head of Conservation Resources. Director, The Centre for Digital Documentation and Visualisation, The Scottish Ironwork Foundation; Scouts Scotland Trustee. Recreations: scouting; photography. Address: (b.) Historic Environment Scotland, Longmore House, Salisbury Place, Edinburgh EH9 1SH; T.-0131 668 8929; e-mail: david.mitchell33@outlook.com

Mitchell, David William, CBE. Hon. President, Scottish Conservative and Unionist Party, 2004-2010; Chairman, Scottish Conservative and Unionist Party, 2001-04; b. 4.1.33, Glasgow; m., Lynda Katherine Marion Guy; 1 d. Educ. Merchiston Castle School. Cmmnd (NS), RSF, 1950; Member, Board, Western General Hospital, 1965-72; President, Timber Trades Benevolent Society of UK, 1974; Member, Scottish Council, CBI, 1979-85; Director, Mallinson-Denny (Scotland), 1977-90; Hunter Timber Scotland, 1990-92; Joint Managing Director, M. & N. Norman (Timber) Ltd., 1992-96 (Non-Executive, 1996-98); President: Scottish Timber Trade Association, 1980-82, Scottish Conservative and Unionist Association, 1981-83; Member: Scottish Council (Development and Industry), 1984-95, Board of Cumbernauld New Town, 1985-97 (Chairman, 1987-97), Board of Management, Craighalbert Centre for Children with Motor Impairment, 1992-96; Treasurer, Scottish Conservative Party, 1990-93 and 1998-2001. Clubs: Royal & Ancient Golf; Prestwick Golf; Queens Park FC. Recreations: fishing; shooting; golf. Address: Old Mill House, Symington, Ayrshire KA1 5QL; T.-01563 830851; e-mail: david.mitchell43@virgin.net

Mitchell, Rev. Duncan Ross, BA (Hons), BD (Hons). Retired Minister, St. Andrews Church, West Kilbride; b. 5.5.42, Boddam, Aberdeenshire; m., Sandra Brown; 2 s.; 1 d. Educ. Hyndland Senior Secondary School, Glasgow; Strathclyde University; Glasgow University. Worked in insurance industry, four years; Minister, Craigmailen UF Church, Bo'ness, 1972-80; Convener, Assembly Youth Committee, UF Church, 1974-79; Member: Scottish Joint Committee on Religious Education, 1974-79, Multilateral Conversation in Scotland, 1976-79, Board of Social Responsibility, Church of Scotland, 1983-86; Ardrossan Presbytery: Convener, World Mission and Unity, 1984-88, Convener, Stewardship and Finance, 1988-91, Convener, Superintendence Committee, 1994-97; Convener, General Assembly Board of World Mission and Unity's Local Involvements Committee, and Executive Member of the Board, 1987-92; Church of Scotland Delegate to Council of Churches for Britain and Ireland Assembly; Moderator, Ardrossan Presbytery, 1992-93. Recreations: supporting Partick Thistle and writing. Address: 11 Dunbar Gardens, Saltcoats; T.-01294 474375.
E-mail: revrossmitchell@gmail.com

Mitchell, George Edward, CBE. Former Governor, Bank of Scotland; Chairman, The Malcolm Group; b. 7.4.50, Edinburgh; m., Agnes; 3 d. Educ. Forrester High School, Edinburgh. Bank of Scotland, since 1966. Recreations: football; tennis; family.

Mitchell, Gordon K., DA, RSA, RSW, RGI. Artist; b. 16.11.52, Edinburgh; m., Deirdre; 1 s.; 3 d. Educ. Royal High School; Edinburgh College of Art. Former Art Teacher (Deputy Headmaster, St. Serf's School, 1986-89); elected: SSA, 1977, SAAC, 1990 (President, 1993-96), RSW, 1996, ARSA, 1998, RGI, 1998, RSA, 2005. Served on council of SSA, SAAC, RSW, SABA, RSA; Vice President of the RSA, 2006-2009; President of The Scottish

Artists Benevolent Association (SABA), since 2014; Inverarity One to One Travel Award, RGI; Artist Convener, RGI, 2001-06; President of The Scottish Arts Club, 2008-2010; exhibited widely at home and abroad; work in public and private collections. Prizes and awards include: RSA Student Prize; Borders Biennial Competition; Scottish Drawing Competition; Mayfest Award; William Gillies Award; Scottish Amicable Prize; Scottish Provident Award; Whyte and Mackay Award; Dunfermline Building Society Award; RSA J. Murray Thompson Award; RSA Maude Gemmel Hutchison Award x3; Royal Bank of Scotland Award, RGI. Recreations: current affairs; golf. Address: (h.) 6 Learmonth Terrace, Edinburgh EH4 1PQ; T.-0131 332 3588; e-mail: gordon@gordonmitchell.co.uk
website: www.gordonmitchell.co.uk

Mitchell, Iain Grant, QC, LLB (Hons), FSA Scot, FRSA, FFCS. Queen's Counsel, since 1992; Barrister (Middle Temple), since 2012; Chairman, Surveillance Working Party, CCBE, since 2015; United Kingdom Representative, IT Committee, CCBE, since 2011; Temporary Sheriff, 1992-97; Joint Editor, International Free and Open Source Software Law Review; Honorary Lecturer, Institut für Informations-, Telekommunikations- und Medienrecht, Westfälische Wilhelms-Universität, Münster; b. 15.11.51, Edinburgh. Educ. Perth Academy; Edinburgh University. Called to Scottish Bar, 1976; Conservative candidate, Falkirk West, General Election, 1983, Kirkcaldy, General Election, 1987, Cumbernauld and Kilsyth, General Election, 1992, Dunfermline East, General Election, 1997, Edinburgh North and Leith, General Election, 2001, Dundee East, Scottish Parliament Election, 1999, Scotland, European Election, 1999, Falkirk West, Scottish Parliament Election, 2002; Honorary Secretary, Scottish Conservative and Unionist Association, 1993-98, Scottish Conservative and Unionist Party, 1998-2001; Chairman, North Queensferry Community Council; Chairman, North Queensferry Community Trust; Chairman, North Queensferry Arts Trust; Reader, Church of Scotland; Member, Church of Scotland Church & Society Council; Chairman, Trust for an International Opera Theatre of Scotland; Chairman, Scottish Baroque Ensemble Ltd., 1999-2001; Member: Executive Committee of European Movement (Scottish Council), Committee, Perth Civic Trust, 1999-2002; Chairman, Perthshire Public Arts Trust; Trustee, Forth Bridge Memorial Public Arts Trust; Board Member, Capella Nova; Board Member, Animotion Art (London) Ltd; Chairman, Scottish Society for Computers and Law; Member, IT Panel of the Bar Council of England and Wales; Joint Editor, e-law Review. Publications: contributor to "Electronic Evidence", 3rd edition, 2012; "Open Source Software - Law Policy and Practice", 2013. Burgess of the City of Edinburgh; Freeman, City of London; Liveryman, Worshipful Company of Information Technologists. Recreations: music and the arts; photography; cinema; walking; history; travel; writing; finding enough hours in the day. Address: (b.) Advocates Library, Parliament House, High Street, Edinburgh; T.-0131-226 5071.

Mitchell, Ian, BSc (Hons), MSc (Distinction). Deputy Director, Learning and Schools, Scottish Government, since 2011; Deputy Director, Environmental Quality, Scottish Government, 2010; Deputy Director, Public Bodies Policy, Scottish Government, 2007-2010; Director of Regeneration, Communities Scotland, 2003-07; b. 11.10.63, Dumfries; spouse, Elizabeth Riach; 1 s. Educ. Dumfries Academy; Heriot Watt University; Napier University. Senior Economic Policy Officer, Corporate Policy, Fife Council, 1990-99; Senior Civil Servant, Scottish Government (Enterprise Networks; Local Government Constitution and Governance; Public Service Reform; Environment; Education; Health and Social Care), 1999-2015; Board Member, Community Enterprise in Scotland. Former Member, Community Planning Task Force/Implementation

Group. Recreations: cycling; hill walking; travel writing. Address: (b.) Directorate Health and Social Care, Scottish Government, Room GE: 07, St Andrews House, Edinburgh EH1 3DG.

Mitchell, Sheriff James Kenneth, LLB. Sheriff of Glasgow and Strathkelvin, since 1985; b. 30.4.49, Glasgow; m., Frances Kane; 1 s. Educ. Paisley Grammar School; Glasgow University. Solicitor, 1972-78; Partner, Ross Harper and Murphy, 1975-78; admitted Faculty of Advocates, 1979. Council Member, Sheriffs' Association, 1998-2001; Member, Glasgow Sheriff Court Standing Advisory Committee, 1997-2000; Member, National Council, Victim Support Scotland, 2001-03; Member, Judicial Studies Committee, 2005-2011; Member, Glasgow and Strathkelvin J. P. Training Committee, 2008-2010; Member, Glasgow and Strathkelvin JP Advisory Committee, since 2010; Member, Judicial Studies Committee Jury Manual Committee, 2006-2012, Judicial Institute for Scotland Jury Manual Committee, since 2013. Recreations: family; friends; football; films; fun. Address: (b.) Sheriff's Chambers, 1 Carlton Place, Glasgow G5 9DA; T.-0141-429 8888.

Mitchell, (Janet) Margaret. Member (C), Central Scotland, Scottish Parliament, since 2003; Scottish Conservative Justice Spokesperson, since 2013; b. 15.11.52, d. of late John Aitken Fleming and of Margaret McRae Fleming (nee Anderson); m. (1978), Henry Thomson Mitchell. Educ. Coatbridge High School; Hamilton Teacher Training College (DipEd); Open University (BA); Strathclyde University (LLB: DipLLP), Jordanhill College (Dip Media Studies); Primary School Teacher, Airdrie and Bothwell, 1974-93; Mem. and Cons. Gp. Leader, Hamilton DC, 1988-96; Non-Exec. Dir., Stonehouse and Hairmyres NHS Trust, 1993-97; Special Adviser to David McLetchie, MSP and James Douglas-Hamilton, MSP, 1999-2002; Scottish Cons. Justice Spokesman, 2003-07; Convener, Scottish Parliamentary Equal Opportunities Committee, 2007-2011; Scottish Cons. Local Government and Planning Spokesman, 2011-13; Member, Commonwealth Parliamentary Association Scotland Branch Executive, since May 2011; Convener, Cross Party Groups on Dyslexia; Adult Survivors of Childhood Sexual Abuse; The Caribbean; Co-Convener of The CPG on Taiwan; Mem., Scottish Cons. Party Exec., 2002-03; Hon. Mem., Board of Advisers, ThinkScotland.org; Arthritis Link Volunteers, since 2004. Clubs: The New Club, Edinburgh Recreations: music; cycling; photography. Address: Huntly Lodge, Fairfield Place, Bothwell G71 8RP; Scottish Parliament, Edinburgh EH99 1SP.
E-mail: margaret.mitchell.msp@scottish.parliament.uk

Mitchell, Joan, MA (Edin), MA (Manitoba), PhD (Glasgow). Scottish Natural Heritage Board, 2007-2013; b. 17.12.42, Carsluith; m., Steve; 2 s. Educ. Douglas Ewart High School; University of Edinburgh; University of Manitoba; University of Glasgow. Lecturer in Geography, University of Glasgow, 1966-71; self employed Farmer, since 1972; elected Member, Dumfries and Galloway (Regional) Council, 1994-2007; EU Committee of The Regions, 1997-2001. Trustee, Cree Valley Community Woodlands; Member, FC NFLS Evaluation Panel; Chair, Galloway & Southern Ayrshire Biosphere Partnership Board. Recreations: hill walking (Chair, Newton Stewart Walking Festival). Address: (h./b.) Bagbie, Newton Stewart, Carsluith, Dumfries and Galloway DG8 7DU; e-mail: joan@bagbie.co.uk

Mitchell, John, BSc. Head Teacher, Kilsyth Academy, 1985-2005; Non-Executive Trustee of Lanarkshire Acute Hospitals Trust, 2001-04; Board Member, Learning Teaching Scotland, 2002-06; Board Member, SQA, 2006-2010; b. 4.1.45, Kirkintilloch; m., Irene; 1 s.; 1 d. Educ. Lenzie Academy; Glasgow University; Jordanhill College. Teacher, North Kelvinside Secondary, Glasgow, 1968-70; Physics Teacher, Balfron High School, 1970-72; Bishopbriggs High School, 1972-79; Assistant Head Teacher, Kilsyth Academy, 1979-84; Depute Head Teacher, Knightswood Secondary, 1984-85. President, HAS, 1996. Address: (h.) 10 Blair Drive, Milton of Campsie; T.- 01360 310477; john@jamitchell.co.uk

Mitchell, John, QPM. Director of Investigations, Police Investigations & Review Commissioner (PIRC) (formerly named Police Complaints Commissioner for Scotland (PCCS)), since 2012. Former Detective Chief Superintendent and head of CID at Strathclyde Police responsible for strategic overview and operational delivery of investigations into some of the most high profile crimes committed in the Strathclyde Police area. As part of Operation Rubicon, was responsible for the strategic oversight of the investigation considering phone hacking, data protection offences and allegations of perjury relating to offences that may have been committed within the jurisdiction of the Lord Advocate for Scotland. Awarded the Queen's Police Medal in the Queen's Birthday Honours 2012. Address: Police Investigations & Review Commissioner, Hamilton House, Hamilton Business Park, Caird Park, Hamilton ML3 0QA. T: 01698 542900.

Mitchell, (John) Angus (Macbeth), CB, CVO, MC, LLD(Hon), (Dundee), DUniv (Stirling). b. 25.8.24, Ootacamund, India; m., Ann Williamson; 2 s.; 2 d. Educ. Marlborough College; Brasenose College, Oxford. Royal Armoured Corps (Captain), 1943-46; Scottish Office, 1949-84; Principal Private Secretary to Secretary of State for Scotland, 1958-59; Under Secretary, Social Work Services Group, 1969-74; Secretary, Scottish Education Department, 1976-84. Order of Orange-Nassau, 1946; Chairman, Scottish Marriage Guidance Council, 1965-69; Vice-Convener, Scottish Council of Voluntary Organisations, 1986-91; Member, Commission for Local Authority Accounts in Scotland, 1985-89; Chairman of Court, Stirling University, 1984-92; Chairman, Scottish Action on Dementia, 1986-94; Member, Historic Buildings Council for Scotland, 1988-94; Trustee, Dementia Services Development Trust, 1988-2000. Publications: Scottish Office Ministers 1885-1985; Procedures for the Reorganisation of Schools in England, 1986; Monumental Inscriptions in SW Midlothian, 2004. Recreations: old Penguins; gravestones; family history. Address: (h.) Saint Margaret's Care Home, 5 East Suffolk Road, Edinburgh EH16 5PU; e-mail: 31kinnear@googlemail.com

Mitchell, John Logan, QC, LLB (Hons). Queen's Counsel, since 1987; Advocate Depute, 1981-85; b. 23.6.47, Dumfries; m., Christine Brownlee Thomson; 1 s.; 1 d. Educ. Royal High School, Edinburgh; Edinburgh University. Called to Bar, 1974; Standing Junior Counsel to Forestry Commission; Standing Junior Counsel, Department of Agriculture and Fisheries. Past President, Royal High School F.P. Club. Recreations: running; golf. Address: (h.) 17 Braid Farm Road, Edinburgh; T.-0131-447 8099.

Mitchison, Neil, MA, MBCS, CITP, CEng. Research Manager, Risk Analyst and Broadcaster; b. 02.05.51; m., Aideen O'Malley; 3 s.; 2 d. Educ. Edinburgh Academy; Trinity College, Cambridge; Edinburgh University. Research Fellow, University of Sussex, 1978-79; Radio Producer, Presenter, and Journalist, BBC Highland, 1980-84; Computer Analyst and Research Project Manager, European Commission, 1985-93; Consultant Editor, Europe, BBC TV, 1993-94; Program Manager, Major

Accident Hazards Bureau, European Commission, 1994-2002, Research Action Leader in Cyber Security, 2005-06, European Commission Representative in Scotland, 2006-2012, Research Manager, 2012-14. Vice President, Commission Scientifique "Risques Accidentels", INERIS (F), 1999-2006; President, Association for Go in Italy, 1999-2005; Parliamentary Candidate (Lib Dem), 1989, 1992, 1997 and 1999. Publications: Identity Theft - a discussion paper, 2004; Accident Scenarios and Emergency Response, 1999; Guidelines on a Major Accident Prevention Policy and Safety Management System, 1998; Safety and Runaway Reactions, 1997; Safety Management Systems in the Process Industry, 1994.

Moffat, Alistair Murray, MA (Hons), MPhil, FRSA. Rector, University of St Andrews, 2011-2014; Journalist; Film Maker; b. 16.6.50, Kelso; m., Lindsay Thomas; 1 s.; 2 d. Educ. Kelso High School; St. Andrews University; Edinburgh University; London University. Ran Edinburgh Festival Fringe, 1976-81; Arts Correspondent/Producer/Controller of Features/Director of Programmes, Scottish Television; Managing Director, Scottish Television Enterprises. Publications: The Edinburgh Fringe, 1978; Kelsae — A History of Kelso from Earliest Times, 1985; Remembering Charles Rennie Mackintosh, 1989; Arthur and the Lost Kingdoms, 1999; The Sea Kingdoms, 2001; The Borders, 2002; Homing, 2003; Heartland Images of the Scottish Borders, 2004; Before Scotland, 2005; Tyneside, 2005; East Lothian, 2006; "The Reivers", 2007; "Fife", 2007; "The Wall", 2008; "Edinburgh", 2008; "Tuscany. A History", 2009; The Faded Map, 2010; The Scots: A Genetic Journey, 2011; The British: A Genetic Journey, 2013; The Great Tapestry of Scotland, 2013; The Great Tapestry of Scotland: The Making of a Masterpiece, 2013; Hawick, A History From Earliest Times, 2014; Bannockburn, 2014; Scotland: A History from Earliest Times, 2015. Recreations: sleeping; supporting Kelso RFC. Address: (h.) The Henhouse, Selkirk TD7 5EY.

Moffat, Anne, RMN. Labour MP, East Lothian, 2001-10; b. 30.3.58, Dunfermline; m.; 1 s. Educ. Woodmill High School. Nursing sister; NEC, Cohse and Unison; former National President, Unison; former Ashford Borough Councillor; former Chair of Organisation, Labour Party; formerly on Labour Party NEC.

Moffat, Rev. Richard. Minister, Girvan North Parish Church, since 2013; b. Glasgow, 1953. Worked in the Presbyterian Church of Canada, based in the southwest of the country at Kelowna, British Columbia, 1993-2013. Address: Girvan North Parish Church, 12a Montgomerie Street, Girvan KA26 9HE; T.-01465 712 672.

Moffett, Ian Weatherston, LLB (Hons), WS, NP. Retired Solicitor; b. 25.4.50, Edinburgh; m., Jinty; 3 s. Educ. George Watsons Boys College, Edinburgh; Edinburgh University. Partner in Dundas & Wilson, 1977-2005; Partner, Anderson Strathern, 2005-2010; Consultant, Anderson Strathern, 2010-2013; Non Executive Director, Registers of Scotland, 2007-2012; Chair, LawWorks Scotland, the pro bono legal charity, 2011-2015; Chair, Kingussie Community Development Company; Chair, Badenoch Heritage; Director, Cairngorm Outdoor Access Trust. Recreations: family; walking and country pursuits; golf; collecting books relating to Scottish History (particularly Speyside and Edinburgh). Address: St Giles, Acres Road, Kingussie, Inverness-shire PH21 1LA; T.-01540 661 414; e-mail: ianwmoffett@hotmail.com

Mohamed, Judith. Head, Oldmachar Academy, since 2014. Educ. Rainey Endowed School, Magherafelt;

University of Stirling. Aberdeen City Council: Strategic Officer - seconded, 2013; Deputy Head Teacher, 2008-2014. Address: Jesmond Drive, Bridge of Don, Aberdeen AB22 8UR; T.-01224 820887.

Moignant, Professor Elizabeth Ann, MA, DPhil, FSA, FRSE. Professor of Classical Art and Archaeology, University of Glasgow, 2000-2011, now Professor Emerita; Director, Institute for Art History, University of Glasgow, 1998-2004; Dean, Faculty of Arts, 2005-09; b. 3.1.51, Poole; m., A.E. Yearling; 1 step-s.; 1 step-d. Educ. King's High School for Girls, Warwick; St. Hugh's College, Hertford College, Oxford University. Temporary Lecturer in Classics, University of Newcastle-upon-Tyne, 1977-78; University of Glasgow: Lecturer in Greek, 1978-92, Senior Lecturer in Classics, 1992-2000. Publications: Corpus Vasorum Antiquorum; Great Britain Fascicles 16 (National Museum of Scotland), 1989; 18 Glasgow Collections, 1997; 22 (Aberdeen University), 2006; Greek Vases, an Introduction, 2006; Knossos, The North Cemetery, 1996. Recreations: music; collecting contemporary decorative art; crime fiction. Address: Classics, School of Humanities, University of Glasgow, Glasgow G12 8QQ; T.-0141 330 7361; e-mail: elizabeth.moignant@glasgow.ac.uk

Moir, Grant. Chief Executive Officer, Cairngorms National Park Authority, since 2013. Educ. Aberdeen University. Career: Rural Affairs Department of the Scottish Executive; formerly Director of Conservation and Visitor Experience, Loch Lomond and the Trossachs National Park Authority. Address: (b.) 14 The Square, Grantown on Spey PH26 3HG; T.-01479 873535.

Moir, Mark Duncan, LLB, DipLP. Advocate, since 2000; b. 11.9.64, Edinburgh. Educ. Boroughmuir High School; Edinburgh University. Royal Air Force Police, 1983-92; Strathclyde Police, 1992-93. Address: (h.) Park Circus, Glasgow.

Mole, George Alexander (Sandy). Chairman: Scottish Borders Produce, since 2004, Coastal Grains Ltd., 1998-2009; President, National Farmers Union of Scotland, 1996-97; b. 7.6.43, Duns; m., Jean Mitchell; 1 s.; 2 d. Educ. St. Mary's, Melrose; Merchiston Castle. NFU of Scotland: President, Mid and East Berwick; Chairman, AFRC Cereal Consultative; Convener, Cereals Committee; Member: EEC Commission Cereals Advisory Committee, Home Grown Cereals Authority R. & D. Committee, Institute of Brewing Cereal Publicity. Recreations: golf; shooting. Address: 11 Welltower Park, Ayton, Eyemouth TD14 5RR.

Mollison, Professor Denis, ScD. Professor of Applied Probability, Heriot-Watt University, 1986-2003, Professor Emeritus, since 2003; Chairman, Hebridean Whale and Dolphin Trust, since 2013 (Trustee, since 1999); Trustee, John Muir Trust, 1986-2007 and 2008-13 (Co-Founder, 1983); b. 28.6.45, Carshalton; m., Jennifer Hutton; 1 s.; 3 d. Educ. Westminster School; Trinity College, Cambridge. Research Fellow, King's College, Cambridge, 1969; Lecturer in Statistics, Heriot-Watt University, 1973. Elected Member of Council, National Trust for Scotland, 1979-84, 1999-2004 and 2005-2010; Chairman, Mountain Bothies Association, 1978-94; Convener, Scottish Green Liberal Democrats, since 2001. Publications: research papers on epidemics, ecology and wave energy. Address: (h.) The Laigh House, Inveresk, Musselburgh EH21 7TD; T.-0131-665 2055; e-mail: denis.mollison@gmail.com

Monaghan, Carol, BSc (Hons). MP (SNP), Glasgow North West, since 2015; m., Feargal Dalton; 1 s; 2 d. Educ.

Strathclyde University. Trained as a teacher, gaining a PGCE in Physics and Mathematics; worked in many Glasgow schools, including 14 years at Hyndland Secondary (Head of Physics and Head of Science); spent two years as a Glasgow University lecturer training future teachers; SQA consultant (involved in developing physics qualifications at a national level). Address: 500 Dumbarton Road, Glasgow G11 6SL.

Monaghan, Professor Pat, FRSE. Professor of Animal Ecology, University of Glasgow, since 1997. Address: Environmental and Evolutionary Biology, Graham Kerr Building, University of Glasgow, Glasgow G12 8QQ; T.-0141-330 5968; e-mail: p.monaghan@bio.gla.ac.uk

Monaghan, Dr Paul. MP (SNP), Caithness, Sutherland and Easter Ross, since 2015; b. 1966, Montrose; m.; 1 d. Educ. Inverness Royal Academy; University of Stirling. Joined the Scottish National Party in 1994 and has held various roles within their Wester Ross branch. Board Member, UHI North Highland College; Director, Highland Homeless Trust; Director, Inverness MS Therapy Centre; Director, 'Food for Families' based in Invergordon; Member, SSE Fairburn Windfarm Community Fund; founding member of the North Highland College Foundation. Graduate Member, British Psychological Society; Fellow, Institute of Leadership and Management. Address: House of Commons, London SW1A 0AA.

Monckton, Professor Darren George, BSc, PhD. Professor of Human Genetics, University of Glasgow, since 2005; b. 28.8.66, Eastleigh. Educ. Wyvern Comprehensive, Fair Oak; University of Bath; University of Leicester. Postdoctoral Research Assistant, University of Leicester, 1992-93; Postdoctoral Research Fellow; Baylor College of Medicine, Houston, Texas, USA, 1993-95, UTMD Anderson Cancer Center, Houston, Texas, USA, 1995-96; University of Glasgow: Lecturer in Genetics, 1996-2000, Reader in Genetics, 2000-05. Muscular Dystrophy Association Neuromuscular Disease Research Fellow, 1993; Muscular Dystrophy Association Sammy Davis Jr. Neuromuscular Disease Named Research Fellow, 1994-96; Lister Institute Research Fellow, 1998-2003; Genetical Society Balfour Lecturer, 1999; Member of the Lister Institute of Preventive Medicine, since 2005; Leverhume Research Fellow, 2007-08; Tenovus (Scotland) Medal Lecturer, 2008; Scientific Meetings Officer for the UK Genetics Society, 2002-06; Chairman of the 4th International Myotonic Dystrophy Consortium Meeting, 2003. More than 50 journal articles, and book chapters published; more than 100 invited seminars and conference presentations. Recreations: fishing; football; wildlife and photography. Address: (b.) Institute of Molecular, Cell and Systems Biology, University of Glasgow, Glasgow G12 8QQ; T.-0141 330 6213; e-mail: d.monckton@bio.gla.ac.uk

Mone, Rt. Rev. John Aloysius. Bishop Emeritus of Paisley; formerly Titular Bishop of Abercorn and Auxiliary Bishop of Glasgow; b. 22.6.29, Glasgow. Educ. Holyrood Secondary School; Seminaire St. Sulpice and Institut Catholique, Paris. Ordained Priest, 1952; Assistant: St. Ninian's, Knightswood, Glasgow, 1952-75, Our Lady and St. George, Glasgow, 1975-79; Parish Priest, St. Joseph's, Tollcross, Glasgow, 1979-84; Auxiliary Bishop in Glasgow, 1984-88; Bishop of Paisley, 1988-2004. Scottish President, Scottish Catholic Marriage Care; Chairman, Scottish Catholic International Aid Fund, 1975-77; President, Paisley Family Society; President, National Justice and Peace Commission, 1987-2004; President, National Social Care Commission, 1996-2004; President/Treasurer, Scottish Catholic International Aid Fund, 1985-2004. Accredited Skill Level One, British Sign Language, July 2007.

Recreations: golf; piano. Address: 30 Esplanade, Greenock PA16 7RU.

Mone of Mayfair, Baroness (Michelle Mone), OBE. Founder and Co-Owner, MJM International Ltd., inventor of the Ultimo bra; b. 1972, Glasgow; m., Michael (divorced 2013); 3 c. Career: modelling in Glasgow, then Labatts Brewers; started MJM International Ltd in 1996. World Young Business Achiever, 2000; winner of 'Business Woman of the Year' at the Corporate Elite Awards, 2000. Address: (b.) MJM International Ltd, 8 Redwood Crescent, Peel Park, East Kilbride, Glasgow G74 5PA; T.-0845 812 0202.

Monro, Stuart Kinnaird, OBE, BSc, PhD, DUniv, DSc, CGeol, FGS, FHEA, FRSSA, FSAScot, FRSGS, FRSE. Scientific Director, Our Dynamic Earth, 1996-2014; Honorary Professor in the School of Geosciences, University of Edinburgh, since 2008; Scientific Director, Scottish Consortium for Rural Research, since 2009; b. 3.3.47, Aberdeen; m., Shiela Monro, nee Wallace; 3 s.; 1 d. Educ. Aberdeen Academy; University of Aberdeen; University of Edinburgh. Appointed as Geologist to British Geological Survey (then, Institute of Geological Sciences), 1970; retired as Principal Geologist, 2004. President: Edinburgh Geological Society, 2005-07 and 2016, Westmorland Geological Society, 1994-2005, Royal Scottish Society of Arts, 2002-05 and 2014; Honorary Fellow, College of Science and Engineering, Edinburgh University, 2005-08, co-opted member of Edinburgh University Court, 2007-2014 and Vice Convener, 2011-2014; Member of St Andrews University Court, 2014; Independent Co-Chair, Scottish Science Advisory Council, 2007-09; Trustee, National Museums of Scotland, 2005-2012; Non-executive Director of the Edinburgh International Science Festival; Honorary Geological Advisor to the John Muir Trust; Open University Tutor in Earth Sciences, 1982-2009; OBE for Services to Science, 2006; Distinguished Service Award, Geological Society of London, 2009; Honorary doctorates: Open University, Heriot-Watt University, Edinburgh University; Honorary Fellowship, Royal Scottish Geographical Society. Recreations: reading; travel; hill walking. Address: (h.) 34 Swanston Grove, Edinburgh EH10 7BW; T.-0131 445 4619; e-mail: stuart.monro@dynamicearth.co.uk/

Monteith, Brian. Policy Director, ThinkScotland.org; Chairman, English-Speaking Union Scotland; Communications Director, Global Britain (think tank); Columnist, Edinburgh Evening News; MSP (Independent), Mid-Scotland and Fife, 1999-2007; former Conservative Spokesman on Finance, Local Government and Public Services (2003-05); Spokesman on Education, Arts, Culture and Sport, 1999-2003; divorced; 2 s.; m., Jacqueline Anderson. International Public relations consultant; former National Chairman, Scottish Young Conservatives and Federation of Conservative Students; National Co-ordinator, No, No Campaign, Scottish devolution referendum.

Montgomerie, Colin, OBE (2005), MBE (1998); Professional golfer; b. 23.6.63; m. (1), Eimear, née Wilson (m dis 2006); 2 d.; 1 s.; m. (2), Gaynor Knowles (divorced 2016). Amateur victories: Scottish Amateur Stroke-play Championship 1985, Scottish Amateur Championship 1987; tournament victories since turning professional in 1987: Portuguese Open 1989, Scandinavian Masters 1991, 1999 and 2001, Dutch Open 1993, Volvo Masters 1993 and 2002, Spanish Open 1994, English Open 1994, German Open 1994 and 1995, Trophee Lancome 1995, Alfred Dunhill Cup 1995, Dubai Desert Classic 1996, Irish Open 1996, 1997 and 2001, European Masters 1996, Sun City Million

Dollar Challenge 1996, European Grand Prix 1997, King Hassan II Trophy 1997, World Cup (Individual) 1997, Andersen Consulting World Champion 1997, PGA Championship 1998, 1999 and 2000, German Masters 1998, British Masters 1998, Benson and Hedges International Open 1999, Standard Life Loch Lomond Invitational 1999, Int Open Munich 1999, World Matchplay Championships Wentworth 1999, French Open Paris 2000, Skins Game USA 2000, Ericsson Australian Masters 2001, TCL Classic 2002, Macau Open 2003, Caltex Masters presented by Carlsberg, Singapore 2004, Dunhill Links Championship 2005, UBS Hong Kong Open 2006, European Open Ireland 2007; US Open: third 1992, second 1994, 1997 and 2006; second, The Open, 2005; US PGA 1995 (second); Tournament Players Championship 1996 (second); team memb: Eisenhower Trophy (amateur) 1984 and 1986, Walker Cup (amateur) 1985 and 1987, Alfred Dunhill Cup 1988, 1991, 1992, 1993, 1994, 1995 (winners), 1996, 1997, 1998, 1999 and 2000, World Cup 1988, 1991, 1992, 1993, 1997, 1998, 1999 and 2007 (winners), Ryder Cup 1991, 1993, 1995 (winners), 1997 (winners), 1999, 2002 (winners), 2004 (winners) and 2006 (winners), UBS Cup 2003 and 2004; Henry Cotton Rookie of the Year 1988, winner European Order of Merit 1993, 1994, 1995, 1996, 1997, 1998, 1999 and 2005. Non playing Captain, European Ryder Cup Team, 2010 (winners). Publication: The Real Monty: The Thinking Man's Guide To Golf. Recreations: motor cars; music; DIY. Address: (b.) IMG (London), McCormack House, Hogarth Business Park, Burlington Lane, Chiswick, London W4 2TH.

Montgomery, Cllr Adam. Provost, Midlothian Council, 2007-2012; Labour Councillor for Penicuik Ward, since 1996; Labour Group Leader and Opposition Spokesperson for Recreation and Leisure; b. 05.11.50, Irvine, Ayrshire; m., Karen; 2 s.; 1 d. Educ. Dalkeith High School. Career History: Cost Clerk, Midlothian County Council; Housing Officer, National Coal Board; Area Housing Officer, City of Edinburgh Council. Founder Member, Danderhall Community Council; Nalgo Branch Secretary, City of Edinburgh and Scottish Council positions. Recreations: football - Kilmarnock supporter and member, Scotland Supporters Club; reading; writing poetry; music; theatre. Address: (b.) Midlothian Council, Midlothian House, Dalkeith EH22 1DJ; T.-0131 271 3085.
E-mail: adam.montgomery@midlothian.gov.uk

Montgomery, Sir (Basil Henry) David, 9th Bt, JP, DL. Lord Lieutenant, Perth and Kinross, 1995-2006; Chairman, Forestry Commission, 1979-89; b. 20.3.31.

Montgomery, Iona Allison Eleanor, BA (Hons), RSW. Artist; Lecturer (part-time): Edinburgh College of Art, since 1997, Grays School of Art, since 1994; b. 14.4.65, Glasgow. Educ. Boclair Academy; Glasgow School of Art; Tamarind Institute, University of New Mexico. Exhibited widely in UK, Europe, USA and Japan, since 1989; solo exhibitions in UK, Europe, USA; work in numerous public collections; Alexander Graham Munro Award, RSW, 1990; Lauder Award, 1991, Lady Artists Club Trust Award, 1992, Cross Trust Bursary, 1994, Glasgow District Council Bursary, 1995; elected, RSW, 1991. Recreations: walking; music; film; travel. Address: (h.) 13 Avon Avenue, Bearsden, Glasgow G61 2PS.

Montgomery, John, LLB (Hons). Sheriff at Ayr, since 2005; Solicitor, since 1976; b. 17.9.51, Kilwinning; m., Susan Wilson Templeton; 1 s.; 3 d. Educ. Ardrossan Academy; Glasgow University. Partner in Carruthers Curdie Sturrock & Co. Solicitors, Kilmarnock, 1980-2003; Temporary Sheriff, 1995-2000; Part-time Sheriff, 2000-03; Floating Sheriff, 2003-05. Recreations: gardening; walking;

travel. Address: (b.) Sheriff Court, Wellington Square, Ayr KA7 1DR.

Montgomery, Lindsay, CBE. Board Member, Keep Scotland Beautiful; former Chief Executive, Scottish Legal Aid Board (1999-2015). Wide background in the public sector including having been a Director of Scottish Natural Heritage and held posts in HM Treasury and Export Credit Guarantee Department. Chairman, Non Departmental Public Bodies Chief Executives' Forum; Chairman, Central Government Procurement Supervisory Board; Board Member, and latterly, Deputy Chair, OSCR (Office of the Scottish Charity Regulator), 2004-2014. Address: Keep Scotland Beautiful, Glendevon House, The Castle Business Park, Stirling FK9 4TZ; T.-01786 471333; e-mail: board@keepscotlandbeautiful.org

Montgomery, Steve. Managing Director of First Rail at Firstgroup plc, since 2015. Former Passenger Service Manager for the Glasgow Queen Street, Edinburgh and North of Scotland areas in 1997; held various senior posts before becoming Operations and Safety Director when FirstGroup took over the franchise in 2004. Address: (b.) 395 King Street, Aberdeen AB24 5RP.

Montrose, 8th Duke of (James Graham), OStJ. Captain, Queen's Bodyguard for Scotland, 2006-2015. Member, since 1965; Member, House of Lords, since 1996, elected Hereditary Peer, 1999, Conservative Opposition Whip, 2001-2010; Opposition Spokesman for Scottish Affairs, 2001-2010; b. 6.4.35, Salisbury, Rhodesia; m., Catherine Elizabeth MacDonell Young; 2 s.; 1 d. Educ. Loretto. Farmer/Landowner; Member of Council, National Farmers Union of Scotland, 1981-86; Vice Chairman, Loch Lomond and Trossachs Working Party, 1991-93; President, Royal Highland and Agricultural Society, 1997-98; Chairman, Buchanan Community Council, 1982-93; President, National Sheep Association, since 2011. Address: (b.) Montrose Estates Ltd., Buchanan Castle, Drymen, Glasgow G63 0AG; T.-01360 660307.

Moonie, Helen. Provost, South Ayrshire, since 2012; represents Ward 2, Prestwick (Labour). Address: South Ayrshire Council, Council Headquarters, County Buildings, Wellington Square, Ayr KA7 1DR; T.-01292 612289.
E-mail: helen.moonie@south-ayrshire.gov.uk

Moore, Douglas Thomas, Cert. Christian Studies (Glasgow). Auxiliary Minister, since 2003 (current placement: Coylton and Drongan Parish Church); Flight Information Services Officer, since 1995 (retired, 2011); b. 24.7.54, Glasgow; m., Margaret Lindsay; 2 s. Educ. Shawlands Academy. Air Traffic Control, since 1972 (retired, 2011); Reader, Church of Scotland, since 1998. Chaplain and President, Monkton and Prestwick Branch, British Legion; President, Prestwick Speechmasters. Recreations: family; gardening; photography. Address: (h.) 9 Midton Avenue, Prestwick, Ayrshire KA9 1PU; T.-01292 671352; e-mail: douglastmoore@hotmail.com

Moore, George, QC, LLB (Hons). Solicitor and Solicitor Advocate; formerly Senior Partner, HBM Sayers (currently consultant); b. 7.11.47, Kilmarnock; m., Ann Beattie; 2 s.; 1 d. Educ. High School of Glasgow; Glasgow University. Former Member, Glasgow and North Argyll Legal Aid Committee; former Reporter to Scottish Legal Aid Board; former part-time Chairman, Industrial Tribunals in Scotland; former Member, Sheriff Court Rules Council, 1987. Recreations: tennis; golf; boating. Address: (b.) 13 Bath Street, Glasgow G2 1HY; T.-0141-353 2121.

Moore, Professor Johanna D., BS, MS, PhD, FRSE, FBCS, CITP. Professor, School of Informatics, Edinburgh University, since 1998, Head of School of Informatics, since 2014; b. 16.7.57, USA; m., Dr N. Goddard; 2 s. Educ. University of California at Los Angeles (UCLA). Graduate Research Assistant, then Teaching Assistant/Teaching Fellow, UCLA; University of Pittsburgh: Research Scientist, Learning Research and Development Centre, 1990-98, Assistant Professor of Computer Science and Intelligent Systems, 1990-96, Associate Professor of Linguistics, 1996-98, Associate Professor of Computer Science and Intelligent Systems, 1996-98, Director, Intelligent Systems Program, 1996-98. President, Association for Computational Linguistics, 2004; Chair, Cognitive Science Society, 2007-08; Associate Editor, Speech Communication; Associate Editor, Cognitive Science. Publication: Participating in Explanatory Dialogues: Interpreting and Responding to Questions in Context, 1995. Address: (b.) School of Informatics, Edinburgh University, 10 Crichton Street, Edinburgh EH8 9AB; T.-0131-651 1336.

Moore, Michael, MA, CA. Senior Adviser on Devolution, PwC, since 2016; Chairman, Borders Book Festival, since 2015; Trustee/Director, The Tweed Foundation, since 2015; MP (Liberal Democrat), Berwickshire, Roxburgh and Selkirk, 2005-2015, Tweeddale, Ettrick and Lauderdale, 1997-2005; Representative on the Smith Commission on Devolution, 2014; European Business Adviser to the Deputy Prime Minister, 2013-15; Secretary of State for Scotland, 2010-2013; UK Spokesman on Transport, 1999-2001, Spokesman on Scotland, 2001, Deputy Foreign Affairs Spokesman, 2001-05, Defence Spokesman, 2005-06, Foreign Affairs Spokesman, 2006-07; Deputy Leader, Scottish Liberal Democrats, 2002-2010; International Development Spokesman, 2007-2010; Scotland and Northern Ireland Spokesman, 2008-2009; b. 3.6.65; m., Alison Louise Hughes; 1 d. Educ. Strathallan School; Jedburgh Grammar School; Edinburgh University. Manager, Corporate Finance practice, Coopers and Lybrand. Member, House of Commons Scottish Select Committee, 1997-99; Governor and Vice Chairman, Westminster Foundation for Democracy, 2002-05; Council Member, Royal Institute of International Affairs, 2004-2010; Parliamentary Visiting Fellow, St. Antony's College, Oxford, 2003-04; Governor, The Ditchley Foundation, since 2010. Recreations: jazz; films; walking; rugby. Address: Borders Book Festival, Harmony House, St Mary's Road, Melrose TD6 9LJ.

Moos, Khursheed Francis, OBE, MB, BS, BDS, FRCSEdin, FDS RCS (Eng, Edin), FDS RCPS (Glas). Consultant Oral and Maxillofacial Surgeon (retired); Honorary Professor, Glasgow University; b. 1.11.34, London; m., Katharine Addison; 2 s.; 1 d. Educ. Dulwich College; Guy's Hospital, London; Westminster Hospital. National Service, RADC, Lt., 1959, Capt., 1960; Registrar in Oral Surgery, Mount Vernon Hospital, Middlesex, 1966-67; Senior Registrar, Oral Surgery, University of Wales, Cardiff, 1967-69; Consultant Oral Surgeon, S. Warwicks and Coventry Hospitals, 1969-74; Consultant Oral and Maxillofacial Surgeon, Canniesburn Hospital, Glasgow, 1974-99; Dean, Dental Faculty, Royal College of Physicians and Surgeons of Glasgow, 1992-95; Chairman, Intercollegiate Examination Board in oral and maxillofacial surgery, 1995-98; Civilian Consultant to Royal Navy, 1976-2010; President: Cranio-facial Society of Great Britain, 1994-95, British Association of Oral and Maxillofacial Surgeons, 1991-92; Down Surgical Prize, 1988; Colyer Medal, Royal College of Surgeons of England, 1997; Indian Medical Association (UK): Chairman, Board of Directors, 1999-2000, President, 1998-99; Honorary Senior Research Fellow, Glasgow University, since 1999. Publications include contributions to books and various papers. Recreations: music; natural history; philately; Eastern philosophy; gardening. Address: (h.) 43 Colquhoun Street, Helensburgh G84 9JW; T.-01436 673232; e-mail: kmoos@udcf.gla.ac.uk

Moray, Earl of (John Douglas Stuart); b. 29.8.66. Succeeded to the title, 21st Earl of Moray, 2011. Address: (h.) Darnaway Castle, Forres, Moray.

Morgan, Alasdair, MA, BA. Electoral Commissioner, since 2014; MSP (SNP), South of Scotland, 2003-2011; MSP (SNP), Galloway and Upper Nithsdale, 1999-2003; MP (SNP), Galloway and Upper Nithsdale, 1997-2001; Deputy Presiding Officer, Scottish Parliament, 2007-2011; b. 21.4.45, Aberfeldy; m., Anne Gilfillan; 2 d. Educ. Breadalbane Academy, Aberfeldy; Glasgow University. SNP: National Treasurer, 1983-90, Senior Vice-Convener, 1990-91, Depute Leader, 1990-91, National Secretary, 1992-97, Vice President, 1997-2004. Recreation: hillwalking.

Morgan, Angela Rosalie, BA (Hons), CQSW, MSc (Econ). Chief Executive, Includem, since 2007; b. 28.02.58, Isleworth; m., John Short. Educ. Basingstoke High School for Girls; Sussex University; University of London. Resettlement Officer, MIND London, 1985-88; Scottish Association for Mental Health, 1988-2002 (latterly Deputy CE). Recreations: reading; walking; birdwatching. Address: (b.) Includem, Unit 6, Academy Office Park, Gower Street, Glasgow G51 1PT; T.-0141 427 0523; e-mail: angela.morgan@includem.co.uk

Morgan, Diane, MA, BA, MUniv. Writer, historian. Educ. Aberdeen High School for Girls; Aberdeen University; Cambridge University. Law Lecturer, RGIT; Founding Editor/Publisher, Leopard, 1974-88. Aberdeen Civic Society Award, 1982 and 2000. Publications: The Aberdeen Series: Footdee, 1993, Round About Mounthooly, 1995, The Spital, 1996, The Spital Lands: From Sunnyside to Pittodrie, 1997, Old Aberdeen, Vol. 1, 2000; A Monumental Business, 2001; The Woodside Story, 2003; Lost Aberdeen, 2004; Lost Aberdeen: The Outskirts, 2007; The Granite Mile, 2008; Lost Aberdeen: The Freedom Lands, 2009; Aberdeen's Union Terrace Gardens: War and Peace in the Denburn Valley, 2015. Recreations: book collecting; travel; local history. Address: (b.) 'The Braes' 36 Ferryhill Place, Aberdeen AB11 7SE.

Morgan, Mary, BSc, MSc. Director of the Scottish National Blood Transfusion Service (SNBTS), since 2012. Educ. Boclair Academy; Western College of Nursing and Midwifery, Glasgow; Stow College, Glasgow; Glasgow Caledonian University; Kings College London. Career: Nursing Manager, Medical Directorate, NHS Argyll & Clyde, November 1996-April 2000; Directorate Manager, Medicine, NHS Argyll & Clyde, April 2000-March 2003; Acting Hospital Manager, Royal Alexandra Hospital, March 2003-March 2004; Service General Manager, NHS Argyll and Clyde, April 2004-May 2006; General Manager, Emergency Care & Medicine, NHS Greater Glasgow and Clyde, April 2006-August 2008; Director, Health Protection Scotland, NHS National Services Scotland, September 2008-January 2012. Address: Head Office: Scottish National Blood Transfusion Service, 21 Ellen's Glen Road, Liberton, Edinburgh EH17 7QT; T.-0131 536 5700.

Morgan, Professor Peter John, BSc, PhD, FIBiol, ChBiol, FRSE. Vice-Principal, University of Aberdeen and Director, Rowett Institute of Nutrition and Health, since 2008; b. 23.2.56, Armthorpe, Yorkshire; m., Professor Denise Kelly; 1s.; 1d. Educ. Aylesbury Grammar School; Queen Mary College, London; University of Aberdeen; Imperial College, London. Recreations: music (classical and jazz); swimming. Address: (b.) Rowett Institute of Nutrition and Health, University of Aberdeen, Greenburn Road, Bucksburn, Aberdeen AB21 9SB; T.-01224 438663.

Morison, Hugh, CBE, MA, DipEd. Chief Executive, Scotch Whisky Association, 1994-2003; b. 22.11.43, Bognor Regis; m.; 2 d. Educ. Chichester High School for Boys; St. Catherine's College, Oxford. Assistant Principal, Scottish Home and Health Department, 1966-69; Private Secretary to Minister of State, Scottish Office, 1969-70; Principal: Scottish Education Department, 1971-73, Scottish Economic Planning Department, 1973-79 (seconded to Offshore Supplies Office, Department of Energy, 1974-75); Assistant Secretary, Scottish Economic Planning Department, 1979-82; Gwilym Gibbon Research Fellow, Nuffield College, Oxford, 1982-83; Assistant Secretary, Scottish Development Department, 1983-84; Under Secretary, Scottish Home and Health Department, 1984-88, Scottish Office Industry Department, 1988-93; Non-Executive Director, Weir Group PLC, 1988-93; Member, Health Appointments Advisory Committee (Scotland), 1995-2000; Member, Executive Committee, Barony Housing Association, 1996-2010, Convenor, 2005-09; Chairman, Scottish Business and Biodiversity Group, 1999-2003; President, Confédération Européenne des Producteurs de Spiritueux, 2001-03; Chairman, Letterfearn Moorings Association, since 2001; Governor, UHI Millennium Institute, subsequently University of the Highlands and Islands, 2004-2013; Non-Executive Director, Praban na Linne Ltd., 2005-06. Publications: The Regeneration of Local Economies, 1987; Dauphine (Co-Author), 1991; The Feelgood Fallacy, 2008. Recreations: sailing; archaeology; literature; playing the euphonium.

Morrice, Graeme. MP (Labour), Livingston, 2010-2015; b. 23.2.59, Edinburgh. Educ. Broxburn Academy; Napier University. Parliamentary Private Secretary to Harriet Harman MP (Shadow Deputy Prime Minister); Councillor, West Lothian, 1987-2012. Recreations: music; art; literature. Address: (h.) 9 Tarbert Drive, Murieston, Livingston EH54 9GZ; T.-01506 793305.

Morrice, Katherine Anne. Elected Member, East Ayrshire Council, since 2007, Spokesperson for Community Wellbeing, since 2007; b. 29.07.52, Edinburgh; 1 s. Educ. Tynecastle High School, Edinburgh; Stevenson College, Edinburgh. Research Officer, Hannah Research Institute, Ayr, 1986-2006. COSLA Appointment: Trustee of National Library of Scotland; Council Appointment: Trustee of Cumnock and Doon Valley Minerals Trust; Member of West of Scotland Archaeology Service; Member of Board of Shire Housing Association; Council Appointment: Director of Yipworld.com. Recreations: reading; cinema; music. Address: (b.) East Ayrshire Council, Council HQ, London Road, Kilmarnock KA3 7BU; T.-01563 576519; e-mail: kathy.morrice@east-ayrshire.gov.uk

Morris of Balgonie & Eddergoll, Stuart Gordon Cathal, OStJ, DHM, FRSA, FSA Scot. Director, Balgonie Castle Enterprises, since 1985; Historian, Armorist and writer; b. 17.04.65, Aberfeldy, Perthshire; m., Kelly Hollie-Whittaker. Educ. Bell Baxter High School; Elmwood College; Napier College; University of Birmingham. Director, Theobald-Hicks, Morris & Gifford, 2001-06. Matriculated Arms (Morris of Balgonie & Eddergoll, quartered with Stuart, formerly of Langlees), Court of the Lord Lyon, Tartan, Morris of Balgonie, 1987; Member, Officer (2011) of the Venerable Order of St John of Jerusalem, 2003; Commander of the Order of Polonia Restituta, 1990; Companion of the Order of Malta, 2007; 2010 Grand Cross of The Order of The Eagle of Georgia; Rector for Scotland for the Order of the Eagle of Georgia, 2011; Cross of Merit 2nd Class, Red Cross of the Republic of San Marino, 2012; Member, Military Order of the Stars and Bars, 2012; Freeman of the City of London, 2001; Liveryman, Worshipful Company of Meadmakers, 1982; Grand Officer, Order of St Agatha, Republic of San Marino, 2012; FSA Scot, 1983; FRSA, 1990; Hon. Colonel, Commonwealth of Kentucky, 1999; Hon. Lieutenant Colonel and ADC. to the Governor of the State of Georgia, 1991; Founder Member: Heraldry Society of Scotland, Scottish Castles Association (Membership Secretary, 1996-2010, Secretary, 1998-2003, Chairman, 2003-05, Vice-Chairman, since 2005); Member of the Stewart Society (Council, 1998-2006 and since 2010); Chairman, Central Fife Group of the Order of St John, 2007-08, Chairman, since 2008, Fife Area Chairman, since 2015; Royal Celtic Society (Member of Council, 2009); HRFCA, since 2015; Member, Sons of Confederate Veterans, 2012; Vice-Chairman, Markinch Heritage Group, 2007-2011; Diploma of Honour, St. Andrew Association, Austria, 1994; Advance the Colors Award, Sons of Confederate Veterans, 2001; awarded 10th Anniversary Medal of the Albert Schweitzer Society of Austria, 1994; Founder, Tay Rail Bridge Disaster Memorial Trust, 2010. Club: Royal Scots Club, Edinburgh. Recreations: heraldry; genealogy; history; history of highland dress; castles; portrait painting; archery. Address: Balgonie Castle, by Markinch, Fife KY7 6HQ; T.-01592 750 119; e-mail: sbalgonie@yahoo.co.uk; web: www.balgoniecastle.co.uk

Morris, Alistair Lindsay, LLB, DipLP, WS NP. Solicitor; Chief Executive, Pagan Osborne Ltd; b. 30.7.58, Dunfermline; m., Sandra Willins; 2 s. Educ. Queen Anne High School, Dunfermline; Aberdeen University. Council Member, Law Society of Scotland, since 1992 (Member, Management Board, Vice President, 2013/14, President, 2014/15); Legal Member, Judicial Appointments Board for Scotland, 2015-19. Recreations: golf; motor sport; football; rugby. Address: (b.) 12 St. Catherine Street, Cupar, Fife KY15 4HH; T.-01334 653777.

Morris, Professor Andrew David, MBChB, MSc, MD, FRCPEdin, FRCPGlas, FRSE, FMedSci. Honorary Professor, University of Dundee; Professor of Medicine, Director of the Usher Institute of Population Health Sciences and Informatics and Vice Principal, Data Science, University of Edinburgh, since 2014; Dean of Medicine, University of Dundee, 2012-14; Chief Scientist, Scottish Government Health Department, since 2012; Chair, Scottish Diabetes Group (lead clinician for diabetes in Scotland), 2002-06; b. 7.10.64; m., Elspeth Claire; 2 d.; 1 s. Educ. Robert Gordon's College, Aberdeen; Glasgow University. Undergraduate and research training, Glasgow University; since 1995, has co-ordinated the DARTS initiative (clinical network for people with diabetes in Tayside); Chair, Royal College of Edinburgh Diabetes Registry, 1998-2002; Chair, Health Technology Board for Scotland Topic Specific Group, 2001-2002; Member, Modernisation Board, NHS in Scotland, 2000-01; Member, Scottish Health Change Panel, 2002-05; Governor, Health Foundation, since 2008; Co-founder, Aridhia Informatics, 2007; Saltire Society Scottish Science Award, 2005. Recreations: golf; squash; family life. Address: (b.) School of Medicine, Ninewells Hospital and Medical School, Dundee DD1 9SY; T.-01382 638028.

Morris, Professor Christopher David, BA, DipEd, MIFA, FSA, FSA Scot, FRHistS, FRSA, FRSE. Professor of Archaeology, Glasgow University, 1990-2006, Vice-

Principal, 2000-06; Chair in Archaeology, UHI Millennium Institute, 2007-09; Interim Director, Conservation Services, Projects and Policy, National Trust for Scotland, 2009-2010; b. 14.4.46, Preston. Educ. Queen Elizabeth's Grammar School, Blackburn; Durham University; Oxford University. Assistant Lecturer, Hockerill College of Education, Bishops Stortford, 1968-72; Lecturer, then Senior Lecturer in Archaeology, 1972-88, Reader in Viking Archaeology, 1989-90, Durham University. Member, Ancient Monuments Board for Scotland, 1990-2001; Royal Commissioner, Ancient and Historical Monuments of Scotland, 2000-09, Vice-Chair, 2006-09. Recreations: classical music and opera; singing and choirs; jazz; theatre; dog walking; ski-ing; fun runs. Address: (b.) Lynamer, Tulloch, Nethy Bridge PH25 3EF.
E-mail: chris@cdmorris.co.uk

Morris, Professor Eleanor Smith, AB Arch Sci (Hons) (Harvard/Radcliffe), MCP (U Penn), PhD (Edinburgh) AICP, RTPI. Town Planning Consultant, Director, Governing Board, Commonwealth Human Ecology Council, London, 1997-2014; Chair, CHEC Executive Committee (2008-2010); Visiting Professor, Urban Planning and Sustainable Development, Clemson University, South Carolina, USA, 2003; NGO Delegate, 2009, UN Commission Human Settlements (Habitat), Nairobi, Kenya; NGO Delegate, UN World Urban Forum, Barcelona, Spain, 2004; 8th, 11th and 12th Commission on Sustainable Development, UN, New York, 1999, 2003 and 2004; Habitat (+5) UN General Assembly (UNGASS), 2001; Pre-Commonwealth Heads of Government Meeting, Edinburgh, 1997, Durban, S.A. 1999; Abuja, Nigeria, 2003, Trinidad, 2009; Rapporteur, 16th Session UN Commission Human Settlements (Habitat), Nairobi, Kenya, 1997; b. 14.11.35, Washington, D.C.,; dau of Hon. Lawrence M C Smith and Eleanor Houston Smith; m. James Shepherd Morris, RSA, FRIBA (deceased); 2 s.; 1 d. Educ. National Cathedral School for Girls, Washington, D.C.; Germantown Friends School, (Cum laude) Philadelphia, Pa. Academic Director Emerita, Centre for the Study of Environmental Change and Sustainability, Institute of Ecology and Resource Management, Edinburgh University, 1996-99; Faculty Lecturer, Centre for Human Ecology, 1990-1995; Lecturer/Course Director, Department of Urban Design and Regional Planning, 1967-90; Lecturer/Course Administrator, Department of Architecture, 1960-67. Planning Practice in Philadelphia City Planning Commission, New Jersey State Planning Board, London County Council; Past Chairman, Royal Town Planning Institute, Scotland, 1986-1987; Member, Council, Royal Town Planning Institute, London, 1982, 1986-87; Member, Executive Committee, RTPI Scottish Branch, 1977-94; Member, Board, Environment Show, Glasgow Garden Festival, 1988-92; Member, Board Link Housing Association, 1987-1995; Member, Council, Executive, Building and American Liaison Committees, National Trust for Scotland, 1992-2004; Trustee, Schuylkill Center for Environmental Education, Philadelphia, 1995-2001; 2003-2009; Co-Chair, Friends of the Schuylkill Nature Center, since 2009; Member, National Advisory Board, National Museum for Women in Arts, Washington DC, since 1989; Member, Lothian Committee, National Art Collections Fund, 1993-2001. Publications include: "Down with Eco-Towns! Up with ECO Communities. A Review of the 2009-2010 Eco Town Proposals in Britain" (Springer, 2011); James Morris Architect and Landscape Architect, 1931-2006 (Royal Scottish Academy, 2007); British Town Planning and Urban Design: Principles and Practices (Longman, 1997); "Berlin, London or Paris - A New Capital for Europe" (Routledge, 1994). Recreation: piano sailing. Address: Woodcote Park, Fala and Soutra, Midlothian EH37 5TG; T.-01875-833-684; e-mail: emorrischec@yahoo.co.uk

Morris, Sheriff John C., QC, LLB. All Scotland Floating Sheriff, attached to Edinburgh, since 2014; b. 11.4.52. Educ. Allan Glen's School, Glasgow; Strathclyde University. Solicitor, 1975-85; called to Scottish Bar, 1985; Advocate Depute, 1989-92; called to English Bar, 1990; Temporary Sheriff, 1993-98; took silk, Scottish Bar, 1996. Chairman, Advocates Criminal Law Group, 1996-98; Member, Temporary Sheriffs Association Committee, 1994-98; Appointed Temporary Judge, 2008; appointed Sheriff's Appeal Court, 2015. Recreations: golf; bird-watching; walking; wine. Address: (b.) Edinburgh Sheriff Court, Chambers Street, Edinburgh.

Morris, Professor Richard Graham Michael, MA, DPhil, FRSE, FMedSci, CBE, FRS. Neuroscience, Edinburgh University, (Professor, since 1993, Reader, 1989-93); b. 27.6.48, Worthing; divorced; 2 d. 1 s. Educ. St. Albans, Washington DC; Marlborough College; Cambridge University; Sussex University. Addison Wheeler Fellow, Durham University, 1973-75; SSO, British Museum (Natural History), 1975-77; Researcher, BBC Television, 1977; Lecturer, St. Andrews University, 1977-86; MRC University Research Fellow, 1983-86. Member, MRC Neurosciences Grants Committee, 1981-85, MRC Neurosciences Board, 1993-98, Innovation Panel, 1997-2001, Strategy Development Group, 2000-04; Hon. Secretary, Experimental Psychological Society, 1985-89; Chairman: Brain Research Association, 1990-94, Sectional Committee for Medicine and Biomedical Sciences, Royal Society of Edinburgh, 1995-97; Member, Council, European Neuroscience Association, 1994-98; Member, Council, Royal Society of Edinburgh, Scottish Science Advisory Committee; President, Federation of European Neuroscience Societies, 2006-08; Fellow, Royal Society, Royal Society of Edinburgh, Academy of Medical Sciences, American Academy of Arts and Sciences, American Association for Advancement of Science and Norwegian Academy of Science and Letters; Prizes: Zotterman Medal (Sweden), 1999; Outstanding Contribution to British Neuroscience, 2002; EJN Award, 2004; Santiago Grisolia Award, 2007; Fondation IPSEN Prize, 2013; Royal Medal, Royal Society of Edinburgh, 2014; Chairman, Department of Neuroscience, Edinburgh University, 1998-2002; Head of Neurosciences and Mental Health, The Wellcome Trust, 2007-2010; Royal Society/Wolfson Professor of Neuroscience, 2006-2011. Publications: academic papers and books. Recreation: sailing. Address: (b.) Centre for Cognitive and Neural Systems, Neuroscience, Edinburgh University, 1 George Square, Edinburgh EH8 9JZ; T.-0131-650 3518/3520; e-mail: r.g.m.morris@ed.ac.uk

Morris, Professor Robert John, BA, DPhil. Emeritus Professor of Economic and Social History, Edinburgh University, since 1993; b. 12.10.43, Sheffield; m., Barbara; 1 s.; 1 d. Educ. Acklam Hall, Middlesbrough; Keble and Nuffield Colleges, Oxford. Lecturer, Senior Lecturer, then Professor, Economic and Social History, Edinburgh University, from 1968. Editor, Book of the Old Edinburgh Club; Founding Editor, History and Computing; Patron, Thoresby Society, Leeds; President, Scottish Economic and Social History Society; President, European Urban History Association, 2000-02. Recreation: planting apple trees. Address: (b.) William Robertson Wing, Teviot Place, Edinburgh EH8 9AG.

Morrison, Sir Alexander Fraser, CBE, FRSA, BSc, CEng, FICE, MIHT, FScotvec, FCIOB. Director, Morrison Construction Group Plc, 1970-2001 (Chairman, 1984-2000); Deputy Chairman, Clydesdale Bank Plc, 1999-2004 (Director, 1994-99); b. 20.3.48, Dingwall; m., Patricia Janice Murphy; 1 s.; 2 d. Educ. Tain Royal Academy; Edinburgh University. National Federation of Civil Engineering Contractors: Chairman, 1993-94, Vice President, 1994-96; Chairman, Highlands and Islands

Enterprise, 1992-98; Vice President, Royal Highland and Agricultural Society of Scotland, 1995-96; Chairman, University of the Highlands and Islands Project, 1997-2000; Director, Aberforth Split Level Trust plc, 1991-2003; Director, Chief Executives Organisation, 2003-2013 and International President, 2009/10; Chairman, Teasses Capital Ltd., since 2003; Chairman, Ramco Holdings Ltd., 2005-2013; Chairman, American Patrons of the National Library and Galleries of Scotland, since 2010; winner, 1991 Scottish Business Achievement Award; Hon. Doctor of Technology: Napier University, 1995, Glasgow Caledonian University, 1997; Honorary Doctor, Open University, 2000; Chairman, Council, St. Leonard's School, St Andrews, 1999-2007. Recreations: rugby; golf; skiing; opera; the countryside; theatre; art. Address: (b.) Teasses House, Ceres, Leven, Fife KY8 5PG.

Morrison, Rt. Rev. Angus, MA, BD, PhD. Minister, Parish of Orwell and Portmoak, Kinross-shire; Moderator of the General Assembly of the Church of Scotland, 2015-16; Chaplain to the Queen in Scotland, since 2006; b. 30.8.53, Oban; m., Marion Jane Matheson; 3 s.; 1 d. Educ. Oban High School; Glasgow University; London University; Edinburgh University. Minister, Free Presbyterian Church of Scotland Oban Congregation, 1979-86, Edinburgh Congregation, 1986-89; Moderator, Southern Presbytery, Free Presbyterian Church, 1987-88; Minister, Associated Presbyterian Churches, Edinburgh, 1989-2000; Moderator, APC General Assembly, 1998-99; Minister, St. Columba's Old Parish Church, Stornoway, 2000-2011; Convener, Church of Scotland Mission and Discipleship Council, 2005-2009. Contributor, Dictionary of Scottish Church History and Theology, 1993; Contributor, New Dictionary of National Biography; Contributor, Dizionario di Teologia Evangelica, 2007; Editor, Tolerance and Truth. The Spirit of the Age or the Spirit of God?, 2007; Moderator, Presbytery of Lewis, 2003-04; Chaplain to the Lord High Commissioner to the General Assembly of the Church of Scotland, 2005, 2006; Visiting Scholar, Princeton Theological Seminary, July-October 2009. Recreations: reading; walking; music. Address: (h.) 41 Auld Mart Road, Milnathort, Kinross KY13 9FR.
E-mail: angusmorrison3@gmail.com

Morrison, Colin Andrew, BA, MEd, DipM, FCIM, CertEd, FCIBS. Deputy Chief Executive and Director of Education, Chartered Institute of Bankers in Scotland; b. 14.10.61, Ellon; m., Stella Ross Ingram. Educ. Peterhead Academy; Robert Gordon's Institute of Technology; Aberdeen College of Education; Edinburgh University. Former Outdoor Pursuits Instructor and F.E. Lecturer/Senior Lecturer; Head of Business Studies, Stevenson College, 1990-91. Recreations: dinghy sailing; skiing. Address: (b.) 38b Drumsheugh Gardens, Edinburgh EH3 7SW; T.-0131-473 7777.

Morrison, James, RSA, RSW, DA, DUniv (Stirling). Painter in oil and watercolour; b. 11.4.32, Glasgow; m., Dorothy McCormack; 1 s.; 1 d. Educ. Hillhead High School; Glasgow School of Art. Taught part-time, 1955-58; won Torrance Memorial Prize, RGI, 1958; Visiting Artist, Hospitalfield, 1962-63; Council Member, SSA, 1964-67; staff, Duncan of Jordanstone College of Art, 1965-87; won Arts Council Travelling Scholarship to Greece, 1968; painting in various regions of France, 1976-82; numerous one-man exhibitions since 1956, in Scotland, London, Italy, France, West Germany, Canada; four works in private collection of Duke of Edinburgh and numerous other works in public and private collections; several group exhibitions since 1980 in UK and Europe; regular series of expeditions to paint in Africa (Botswana) and Canadian and Greenland High Arctic, since 1990. Publications: Aff the Squerr; Paris in Winter. Recreation: playing in a chamber music group.

Address: (h.) Craigview House, Usan, Montrose, Angus; T.-Montrose 672639.

Morrison, John Lowrie, OBE. Scottish contemporary artist; b. 1948, Maryhill, Glasgow. Educ. Dowanhill Primary School; Glasgow; Hyndland Prep School, Glasgow; Hyndland Secondary School, Glasgow; Glasgow School of Art. Founded the Jolomo Award in 2007 - the prestigious annual award for Scottish Landscape Painting (the largest arts award in Scotland and the UK's largest privately funded arts award with a prize currently of £25,000 for the winner, and £35,000 for all the prizes). Appointed Officer of the Order of the British Empire (OBE) in the 2011 New Year Honours for services to art and charity in Scotland. Address: Jolomo Ltd, The Jolomo Studio, Tigh-na-Barnashalg, Tayvallich, by Lochgilphead, Argyll PA31 8PN; T.-01546 870303.
E-mail: jolomo@thejolomostudio.com

Morrison, Katrina Croft, MA (Hons), MBA, MTS. Senior International Tourism Manager, Scottish Enterprise, various roles, since 1993; Trustee, Royal Botanic Garden Edinburgh, 2005-2013; b. 18.12.59, Aberdeen; m., Colin McLean; 1 s.; 1 d. Educ. Dollar Academy; Aberdeen University. Manager, Blackwell Retail Ltd., 1983-93; Course Tutor, Booksellers Association, 1989-2002. Member, Business Committee of General Council of Aberdeen University, 1985-2000. Recreations: traditional music and dance; gardening; silversmithing.

Morrison, Neil. Head Teacher, Portlethen Academy, since 2012. Address: Bruntland Road, Portlethen AB12 4QL; T.-01224 782174.

Morrison, Sheriff Nigel Murray Paton, QC. Sheriff of Lothian and Borders at Edinburgh, since 1996; Appeal Sheriff, since 2015; Temporary judge of the Court of Session and High Court, since 2013; b. 18.3.48, Paisley. Educ. Rannoch School. Called to the Bar of England and Wales, Inner Temple, 1972; admitted to Scottish Bar, 1975; Assistant Editor, Session Cases, 1976-82; Assistant Clerk, Rules Council, 1978-84; Clerk of Faculty, Faculty of Advocates, 1979-86; Standing Junior Counsel to Scottish Development Department (Planning), 1982-86; Temporary Sheriff, 1982-96; Chairman, Social Security Appeal Tribunals, 1982-91; Second (formerly Junior) Counsel to the Lord President of the Court of Session, 1984-89; First Counsel to the Lord President, 1989-96; Counsel to Secretary of State under Private Legislation Procedure (Scotland) Act 1936, 1986-96; QC, 1988; Chairman, Medical Appeal Tribunals, 1991-96; Trustee, National Library of Scotland, 1989-98; Director of Judicial Studies, 2000-04; Vice-President, Sheriffs' Association, 2009-2011, President, 2011-13. Publications: Green's Annotated Rules of the Court of Session (Principal Editor); Stair Memorial Encyclopaedia of the Laws of Scotland (Contributor); Sentencing Practice (Editor). Recreations: music; riding; Scottish country dancing; being taken by his dogs for walks. Address: 27 Chambers Street, Edinburgh EH1 1LB; T.-0131-225 2525.

Morrison, Peter, MA, LLB. Singer (Baritone) entertainer and former solicitor; b. 14.8.40, Greenock; m., Irene McGrow; 1 s.; 1 d. Educ. Greenock Academy; Glasgow University. Local Authority (Paisley and Clydebank) legal departments, 1965-68; Private legal practice with Torrance Baird and Allan, Solicitors, Glasgow, 1968-77; own legal practice, 1977-96; consultant with Paton Farrell Solicitors, 1996-2000; now an associate with Adie Hunter, Solicitors, Glasgow; 1958 - singing pupil of Cecil Cope and then Marjorie Blakeston; Choral Scholar with Glasgow

University Chapel Choir for 5 years; toured English Cathedrals, 1964/65 with choir; principal singer with University Cecilian Society for 6 years and also the University Choral society; started broadcasting with BBC in 1961 as a group singer and later as soloist; auditioned as soloist for BBC in 1967 and solo broadcasts and recitals thereafter; founder member of the John Currie Singers in 1968; first television series for BBC Scotland, 1971, continuing until 1979 and including Show of the North, Castles in the Air, Songs of Scotland, Something to Sing About (for BBC 2), This is Peter Morrison, 1977; other work includes Hogmanay shows, Friday Night is Music Night (radio), 1976-97, concerts in Royal Festival Hall, Albert Hall, Fairfield Halls, The Barbican Centre; television series for Channel 4 (Top Cs and Tiaras), STV and Grampian; innumerable theatre and concert performances in UK and abroad; continues to promote and perform in concert and theatre shows around the country; entertained the Royal Family at public occasions and private parties; many commercial CD recordings; immediate past President, Scottish Showbusiness Benevolent Fund; past Honorary President, Glasgow Phoenix Choir; Honorary President, Arran Music and Drama Club. Still producing and performing in shows, often with son Richard and daughter Jackie, throughout Scotland (Rodgers and Hammerstein Gala nights, Broadway and Beyond Vol. 1 and Vol. 2, The Nearly New Year Show and numerous variety shows). Recreations: golf; watching rugby, cricket and football; loves working with his children on stage whenever possible; along with wife Irene in thrall to his four grandchildren Peter, Robin, Henrietta and Bertie. E-mail: peterdmorrison@talktalk.net
web: www.petermorrison.net

Morrison, Steve. Scottish television producer; Rector, University of Edinburgh, since 2015; b. 3.3.47, Glasgow. Educ. University of Edinburgh; National Film and Television School. Career: radio producer with BBC Scotland; joined Granada Television in 1974; formed Granada Film before becoming Director of Programmes, then Chief Executive (2001); co-founded independent TV production and distribution company all3media in 2003, becoming non-executive chairman in 2013. Advisory board of the Edinburgh College of Art. Production credits include My Left Foot, The Field and Jack and Sarah. Instrumental in the formation of the campaign group Third World First, which went on to become the anti-poverty organisation People and Planet. First student to run for Rector of the University of Edimburgh in 1969. Address: University of Edinburgh, Old College, South Bridge, Edinburgh EH8 9YL; T.-0131 650 1000.

Morrow, Dr Joseph John, KStJ, QC, DL. Lord Lyon King of Arms, since 2014. Labour councillor for the Maryfield ward until 2009 (held the positions of Convenor of the Economic Development Committee, Convenor of the Dundee Waterfront Development Board, and was Depute Lord Provost); Her Majesty's Commissioner for the Mental Welfare Commission for Scotland (1999-2006); First-tier Tribunal Judge (Immigration and Asylum Chamber) (2002-2013); appointed President of the Mental Health Tribunal for Scotland in 2008; appointed as Vice Lord Lieutenant of the City of Dundee in 2009; President of the Additional Support Needs Tribunals for Scotland (2010-2014); Member, Faculty of Advocates and took silk, 2015. Incumbent of the Chapel of Glamis Castle; former Chancellor of the Diocese of Brechin; Honorary Canon of St Paul's Cathedral, Dundee; the 108th Grand Master of the Grand Lodge of Scotland, 2004-05; appointed Commander of the Venerable Order of St John in 2012; promoted to the rank of Knight in 2015. Recreations: ecclesiastical history; rearing rare breed sheep. Address: Court of The Lord Lyon, HM New Register House, West Register Street, Edinburgh EH1 3YT; T.-0131 556 7255.

Morrow, Martin Thomas, LLB (Hons), DipLP, NP. Solicitor Advocate; b. 2.7.64, Glasgow; m., Amanda Catherine; 1 s.; 2 d. Educ. St. Aloysius College, Glasgow; University of Strathclyde. Ian McCarry Solicitors, Glasgow, 1986-88; Levy, McRae, Solicitors, Glasgow, 1988-89; Blackadder, McMonagle, Solicitors, Falkirk, 1990-92; Principal, Milligan Telford and Morrow, Solicitors, since 1992. Member, Council, Law Society of Scotland, 1997-2001. Recreations:, golf; tennis. Address: 1 Cockburn Street, Falkirk FK1 1DJ; T.-01324 633221.

Morton, Rev. Alasdair J., MA, BD, DipEd, DipRE, FEIS. Minister, Bowden linked with Newtown St. Boswells, 1991-2000; b. 8.6.34, Inverness; m., Gillian M. Richards; 2 s.; 2 d. Educ. Bell-Baxter School, Cupar; St. Andrews University; Hartford Theological Seminary. District Missionary/Minister, Zambia (Northern Rhodesia), 1960-65; Chaplain and Religious Education Lecturer, Malcolm Moffat Teachers' College, Serenje, Zambia, 1966-67; Principal, David Livingstone Teachers' College, Livingstone, Zambia, 1968-72; Minister, Greyfriars Parish Church, Dumfries, 1973-77; General Secretary, Department of Education, Church of Scotland, 1977-91. Recreations: choral singing; gardening. Address: 16 St Leonard's Road, Forres IV36 1DW; e-mail: alasgilmor@hotmail.co.uk

Morton, Alasdair Matthew, BAcc (Hons), CA. Head of Fraud Optimisation, UK Retail, Royal Bank of Scotland, since 2005; Trustee, National Galleries of Scotland, since 2007; b. 12.8.72, Falkirk. Partner, Dr Andrew John Farrall. Educ. Prestwick Academy; University of Glasgow. Career: KPMG (Glasgow), 1994-97; Arthur Andersen (London), 1997-99; KPMG (Edinburgh), 1999-2005; Royal Bank of Scotland Group (Edinburgh), since 2005. National Galleries of Scotland: Trustee; Chair, Audit and Risk Committee; Remuneration Committee member. Recreations: travel; art; opera; gym; cycling. Address: (b.) Business House B, Ground Floor, Royal Bank of Scotland Group, Gogarburn, Edinburgh EH12 1HQ; T.-07747 843 894.
E-mail: alasdairmorton@hotmail.com

Morton, Rev. Andrew Reyburn, MA, BD, DD; b. 24.5.28, Kilmarnock; m., Marion Armstrong Chadwin; 2 s.; 2 d. Educ. Kilmarnock Academy; Glasgow University; Edinburgh University; Bonn University. Scottish Secretary, Student Christian Movement, 1953-56; Minister, Moncreiff Parish, East Kilbride, 1956-64; Chaplain, Edinburgh University, 1964-70; Warden, Wolfson Hall and Co-ordinating Warden, Halls of Residence, Glasgow University, 1970-74; Social Responsibility Secretary and, latterly, Secretary, Division of Community Affairs and Assistant General Secretary, British Council of Churches, 1974-81; Secretary, Inter-Church Relations Committee and Assistant Secretary, Overseas Council, subsequently Assistant Secretary, Board of World Mission and Unity, Church of Scotland, 1982-88; Deputy General Secretary, Board of World Mission and Unity, Church of Scotland, 1988-93; Secretary, Committee on Church and Nation, Church of Scotland, 1994-97; Associate Director, Centre for Theology and Public Issues, University of Edinburgh, 1994-2001; Alumni Officer, School of Divinity, University of Edinburgh, 1997-2010. Recreation: walking. Address: (h.) 7a Laverockbank Terrace, Edinburgh EH5 3BJ; T.-0131-538 7049; e-mail: morton@ootbox.com

Morton, J. Gavin, CA CTA. Senior Private Client Partner, Chiene & Tait CA, since 2014, Partner, since 1985. (b.) 61 Dublin Street, Edinburgh EH3 6NL; T.-0131 558 5800; web: www.chiene.co.uk

Morton, Earl of (John Stewart Sholto Douglas). Scottish peer and landowner; Partner of Dalmahoy Farms Ltd; b. 17.1.52; m., Amanda Kirsten Mitchell; 3 c. Educ. Dunrobin Castle; North of Scotland Agricultural College. Farming at Backbridge, Malmesbury, 1974-77;

Director of Dalmahoy Country Club, 1978. Address: Dalmahoy Estate Office, Kirknewton, Midlothian EH27 8EB; T.-0131-333 1331.

Morton, 'Uel (Samuel). Chief Executive, Quality Meat Scotland, since 2006. Formerly with United Farmers. Address: (b.) The Rural Centre, Ingliston, Newbridge EH28 8NZ; T.-0131 472 4040; e-mail: info@qmscotland.co.uk

Mosson, Alexander Francis, KHS. Lord Provost of the City of Glasgow, 1999-2003; b. 27.8.40, Glasgow; m., Maureen; 4 s.; 3 d. Educ. St Patrick's Primary School; St Patrick's Junior Secondary School; St Mungo's Academy. Served apprenticeship, Barclay Curles boiler shop and Alexander Stephen shipyard, Linthouse, as a plater; worked in insulating industry; then employed as an Industrial Appeals Organiser with British Red Cross Society, Scottish Branch; elected Councillor, 1984; former Deputy Lord Provost; former Vice Convener and Convener, Protective Services Committee; former Vice Convener of Personnel. Officer, Order of St. John, since 2000; Hon. Fellow of the Royal College of Physicians and Surgeons, 2003; Order of St. Christopher of Barga, 2004; Knight of the Holy Sepulchre of Jerusalem, September 2005; Freeman of the City of Bethlehem, 2004; Deputy Lord Lieutenant, 2004. Hon. LLD, Glasgow; Hon. LLD, Glasgow Caledonian; Hon. LLD, Strathclyde. Recreations: reading Scottish and Irish history; painting; watching football. Address: (h.) 1 Danes Drive, Glasgow G14 9HZ; T.-0141954 3360.

Mounfield, J. Hilary, OBE, MA (Hons), FRSA. Convenor, Dementia Services Development Trust, 2008-2014; Ambassador, Scottish Epilepsy Centre; Chair, Art in Healthcare; Non-Executive Director, National Waiting Times Centre NHS Board, 2003-11; Convenor, Scottish Arts Club, 2008-11; Chief Executive, Epilepsy Scotland, 1995-2005; Chair, European Committee of the International Bureau for Epilepsy, 2001-05; International Ambassador for Epilepsy; b. 19.7.41, Edinburgh; 2 s.; 1 d. Educ. Boroughmuir School; Edinburgh University. Research, Scottish Development Department and Ministry of Housing, 1963-66; teaching, London, 1973-84; fund-raising for charities, 1984-91; Appeals Director, Penumbra, 1991-95. Chair: ICFM, Scotland, 1993-95, Bighearted Scotland, 1993-96, Joint Epilepsy Council, 1998-2001; Convenor, ACOSVO, 1997-2000; Chair, Voluntary Health Scotland, 2000-03; Founding Fellow, Institute of Contemporary Scotland. Recreations: reading; art; travel. E-mail: hilary.mounfield@blueyonder.co.uk

Mountain, Edward Brian Stanford. MSP (Scottish Conservative), Highlands and Islands region, since 2016; b. 1961. Caithness, Sutherland and Ross constituency candidate in the 2011 Scottish Parliament election; Inverness, Nairn, Badenoch and Strathspey constituency candidate in the 2015 United Kingdom general election; Inverness and Nairn constituency candidate in the 2016 Scottish Parliament election. Address: Scottish Parliament, Edinburgh EH99 1SP.
E-mail: edward.mountain.msp@scottish.parliament.uk

Moutinho, Professor Luiz, BA, MA, PhD, FCIM. Professor of BioMarketing and Futures Research, DCU Business School, Dublin City University, Ireland; formerly Professor of Marketing and former Director, Doctoral Programme, Glasgow University Adam Smith Business School (1999-2015); b. 29.1.49, Lisbon. Held posts at: Cardiff Business School; University of Wales (Cardiff); Cleveland State University, Ohio; Northern Arizona University; California State University;

Director, Doctoral Programmes, Confederation of Scottish Business Schools, 1987-89; Professor of Marketing, since 1989; appointed to Foundation Chair of Marketing, Glasgow University, 1996. Publications: 27 books, most recently The Routledge Companion to the Future of Marketing, 2014. Address: (h.) Cragdarroch, Shore Road, Cove, G84 0NU; T.-01436 842851.

Muir, Eunice Elizabeth, RN, RM, ADM, MBA, FCMI. Clinical eHealth Lead (NMAHP's), The Scottish Government, since 2012; Chairman, St. Vincent's Hospice Howwood, since 2013; b. 24.1.57, Greenock; m., Dr Kenneth C. Muir. Educ. Greenock High School; Glasgow Caledonian University. Apprentice Tracer/Draughtsman, John G Kincaid & Co. Ltd, Greenock/Springburn College of Engineering, Glasgow, 1973-1976; Student Nurse, Inverclyde College of Nursing, 1976-1979; Student Midwife, University Hospital of Wales, Cardiff, 1979-1980; Staff Midwife, Paisley Maternity Hospital, 1980-1981; Labour Suite Midwifery Sister, Paisley Maternity Hospital, 1981-1990; Clinical Manager, Royal Alexandra Hospital, 1991-1994; Head of Midwifery/Service Manager, Royal Alexandra Hospital, 1994-1998; Deputy Director of Nursing, Quality & Planning, Falkirk & District Royal Infirmary, 1998-1999; Deputy Director of Nursing & Planning, Forth Valley Acute Hospitals NHS Trust, 1999-2000; Clinical Lead/Risk Management Executive, CNORIS, SEHD/Willis, 2000-2002; Deputy Director of Nursing & Operations, NHS 24, 2002-2004; Executive Nurse Director, NHS 24 2004-2006; Professional Adviser, NHS Scotland Maternity Telehealth Project (secondment) SEHD/NES, 2006-2007; Interim Nurse Director (secondment), Acute Division, NHSGGC, 2007-2008; Executive Nurse Director, NHS 24, 2008-2012. Director and Vice Chair, Cruse Bereavement Care Scotland, 2003-09; Director, St. Vincent's Hospice, Renfrewshire, since 2009. Recreations: golf; gym; reading; music. Address: (h.) Nithsdale, Bridge of Weir, Renfrewshire PA11 3AN; T.-07803 609492; e-mail: eemuir@icloud.com

Muir, Kenneth Blair, MA (Hons), DipEd, FRSGS. Chief Executive, General Teaching Council for Scotland, since 2013; Strategic Director (School Years) and Director of Inspection, Education Scotland, 2012/13; b. 12.3.55, Dunoon. Educ. Dunoon Grammar School; Glasgow University. Teacher of Geography, Principal Teacher of Geography, Ayr Division, 1978-88; Social Subjects Staff Tutor, 1988-90; Adviser in Social Subjects, Fife, 1990-95; HM Inspector of Education based in Dundee, 1995-2003; HM Assistant Chief Inspector initially responsible for Secondary Schools and latterly Colleges, 2003-05; former HM Chief Inspector of Education: initially responsible for Pre-School Centres and Independent Schools (2005-09); responsible for Secondary Schools, Colleges, Teacher Education and Inspection of Prison Education, 2009-12. Recreations: golf; orienteering; hill walking. Address: (b.) Clerwood House, 96 Clermiston Road, Edinburgh EH12 6UT; T.-0131 314 6000.
E-mail: ken.muir@gtcs.org.uk

Muir, Robert Douglas, MA (Hons), ACIB. HIE Area Manager, Lochaber, Skye and Wester Ross; b. 28.8.54, Irvine; m., Nanette Thomson Buchanan; 2 s. Educ. Ardrossan Academy; Glasgow University; Tübingen Universität. Recreations: history; travel; languages; music; following the fortunes of Kilmarnock F. C. Address: (b.) King's House, The Green, Portree, Isle of Skye IV51 9BS; T.-01478 612841; e-mail: robert.muir@hient.co.uk

Muir Wood, Professor David, MA, PhD, FREng, FRSE, FICE. Professor of Geotechnical Engineering, University of Dundee, 2009-2014, Emeritus Professor, since 2014;

Emeritus Professor of Civil Engineering, University of Bristol, since 2009; Professor affilierad i geoteknik, Chalmers tekniska högskola, Gothenburg, Sweden, since 2014; b. 17.3.49, Folkestone; m., Helen Rosamond Piddington; 2 s. Educ. Royal Grammar School, High Wycombe; Peterhouse, Cambridge. 1973-75: William Stone Research Fellow, Peterhouse, Cambridge; 1975: Royal Society Research Fellow, Norwegian Geotechnical Institute, Oslo; 1975-87: Fellow, Emmanuel College, Cambridge; 1975-78: University Demonstrator, Soil mechanics, Cambridge University Engineering Department; 1978: Geotechnical engineer, Scott, Wilson, Kirkpatrick and Partners, Hong Kong; 1978-87: University Lecturer, Soil mechanics, Cambridge University Engineering Department; 1983: Associate, Geotechnical Consulting Group; 1986: Visiting Research Associate, University of Colorado, Boulder; 1987-95: Cormack Prof. of Civil Engineering, Univ. of Glasgow; 1995-96: Royal Society Industry Fellow, Babtie Group, Glasgow; 1995-2009: Prof. of Civil Engineering, Univ. of Bristol; 1997-2002: Head, Department of Civil Engineering, Univ. of Bristol; 2000: MTS Visiting Prof. of Geomechanics, Univ. of Minnesota; 2003: Foundation for Industrial Science Visiting Prof., Institute for Industrial Science, University of Tokyo; 2003-07: Dean, Faculty of Engineering, University of Bristol; 2008: Japan Society for Promotion of Science Visiting Professor, Nagoya Institute of Technology; Visiting Professor, Politecnico di Milano, 2014; Martin Fahey Visiting Professor, Centre for Offshore Foundation Systems, University of Western Australia, Perth, 2013. Elder, Cairns Church of Scotland, Milngavie, 1993-1998; Elder, Church of Scotland, Monikie & Newbigging, Murroes & Tealing, 2011; Rex Moir Prize (1969); Archibald Denny Prize (1970); British Geotechnical Society Prize (1978); 20th Bjerrum Lecturer, Oslo (2005); Poulos Lecturer, Sydney (2010); 19th Prague Geotechnical Lecturer (2011); Associate Editor, Canadian Geotechnical Journal; Member, Smeatonian Society of Civil Engineers; Senior Fellow, Technical University, Dresden, 2015. Publications: Books: 'Pressuremeter testing' (Co-Author), 1987; 'Soil behaviour and critical state soil mechanics', 1990; 'Piled foundations in weak rock' (Co-Author), 1999; 'Geotechnical modelling', 2004; 'Soil mechanics: a one-dimensional introduction', 2009; 'Civil engineering: a very short introduction', 2012. Recreations: music; opera; singing; travel; photography. Address: (h.) Kirklands, Kirkton of Monikie, Broughty Ferry, Angus DD5 3QN; T.-01382 370685; e-mail: muirwood@talk21.com

Mulholland, Professor Clive, BSc, PhD, CSci, FIBMS, SFHEA, FRSA. Principal and Vice Chancellor, University of the Highlands and Islands, since 2014. Educ. Ulster University. Career in the scientific civil service before moving to the NHS and the university sector; Director of Lifelong Learning, University of Ulster, 2000-07; Deputy Vice Chancellor, University of Glamorgan, 2007-2013; Deputy Vice Chancellor (Research & Student Experience), University of South Wales, 2007-2014. Address: University of the Highlands and Islands, Executive Office, Ness Walk, Inverness IV3 5SQ; T.-01463 279215. E-mail: clive.mulholland@uhi.ac.uk

Mulholland, Francis, PC, QC, LLB (Hons), MBA, DipLP, NP, LLD (Hon). Lord Advocate, since 2011; Solicitor General for Scotland, 2007-2011; b. 18.4.59, Coatbridge; m., Marie Elizabeth. Educ. Columba High School, Coatbridge; Aberdeen University; Edinburgh University. Trainee, Bird Semple & Crawford Herron, Solicitors, Glasgow, 1982-84; Procurator Fiscal Depute: Greenock, 1984-87, Glasgow, 1987-91; Solicitor, Crown Office, Edinburgh, 1991-96; Procurator Fiscal Depute, Edinburgh, 1996; Advocate Depute, 1997-99; Assistant Procurator Fiscal, Edinburgh, 1999-2002; Procurator Fiscal, Edinburgh, 2002-03; Senior Advocate Depute, 2003-06;

Area Procurator Fiscal, Lothian and Borders, 2006-07. Member of the Privy Council, since 2011; LLD (Honorary), University of Aberdeen, June 2013. Recreations: football; golf; military history. Address: (b.) Crown Office, 25 Chambers Street, Edinburgh.

Mullen, Ian M., OBE, BSc, MRPharmS, DL. Chairman, East Central Hub Co., since 2012; Consultant on healthcare and pharmaceutical issues; accredited executive coach; self-employed community pharmacist, since 1971; Chair, Forth Valley NHS Board, 2002-2012; Deputy Lieutenant, Stirling and Falkirk; b. 11.5.46, Stirling; m., Veronica Drummond; 2 s.; 1 d. Educ. St. Modan's High School, Stirling; Heriot-Watt University. Registered MPS, 1970; Chairman, Pharmaceutical General Council (Scotland), 1986-88; Vice-Chairman, National Pharmaceutical Consultative Committee, 1987-89; Member, UK Advisory Committee on Borderline Substances, 1986-89; Vice-Chairman, Forth Valley Health Board, 1989-91; Director, Common Services Agency of the NHS in Scotland, 1991-94, Vice-Chairman, 1993; Director, Central Scotland Chamber of Commerce, 1990-93; Chairman: St. Andrew's School Board, 1990-93, Falkirk and District Royal Infirmary NHS Trust, 1993-99, Scottish NHS Trust Chairmen's Group, 1998-2000, Forth Valley Acute Hospitals NHS Trust, 1999-2002, Scottish NHS Chairmen's Group, 2000-02, Scottish Health Matters (Communications Group), Urban Life Properties Ltd, since 2003, Serco Health Advisory Board UK & Europe, 2012-13; Serco Non-Executive (Scotland). Recreations: walking; golf; watching football. Address: (b.) Robertson House, Castle Business Park, Stirling FK9 4TZ; T.-01786 431627.

Mullen, Professor Thomas John, LLB (Hons), Glasgow, LLM (Harvard). Professor of Law, School of Law, University of Glasgow, since 2004; b. 26.01.59, Glasgow; m., Christine Hamilton; 1 s.; 1 d. Educ. St. Aloysius College, Glasgow; University of Glasgow; Harvard Law School. Legal Apprentice, Hughes Dowdall & Co, Glasgow, 1981-83; Solicitor (Scotland), since 1984; University of Glasgow: Lecturer in Public Law, 1983-92, Senior Lecturer in Public Law, 1992-2003. Special Adviser to House of Commons Select Committee on Scottish Affairs, 1996-97. Publications: Judicial Review in Scotland (Co-Author), 1996; Public Law in Scotland, eds (Co-Author), 2006. Recreations: reading; running; tennis; cooking. Address: (b.) School of Law, University of Glasgow G12 8QQ; T.-0141 330 4179; e-mail: tom.mullen@glasgow.ac.uk

Mulligan, Margaret Mary, BA (Hons). MSP (Labour), Linlithgow, 1999-2011; Shadow Minister for Housing and Communities, 2008-2011; Deputy Minister for Communities, 2003-04; Convenor, Education, Culture and Sport Committee, 1999-2001; b. 12.2.60, Liverpool; m., John; 2 s.; 1 d. Educ. Notre Dame High School; Manchester University. Retail and personnel management, 1981-86; Councillor, Edinburgh District Council, 1988-95 (Chair of Housing, 1992-97); Councillor, City of Edinburgh Council, 1995-99. Recreations: music; theatre; reading.

Mullin, Roger, MA (Hons). MP (SNP), Kirkcaldy and Cowdenbeath, since 2015; m., Barbara. Educ. University of Edinburgh. Honorary Professor, University of Stirling (teaches postgraduates Applied Decision Theory, The Political Environment, and Organisation Change); undertaken 27 international assignments for the United Nations and governments in many parts of the world; former columnist for The Times Educational Supplement Scotland; freelanced as an education consultant; wide range of publications in the fields of Decision Making, Education, Leadership and Politics; former SNP Vice Convener. Address: House of Commons, London SW1A 0AA.

Mumford, Colin John, BMedSci, DM, FRCP(E), DIMCRCS(Ed). Consultant Neurologist, Western General Hospital, Edinburgh and Royal Infirmary of Edinburgh, since 1996; b. 24.11.59, Liverpool. Educ. St. Margaret's High School, Liverpool; Nottingham University Medical School. Senior House Officer in Medicine, Newcastle upon Tyne teaching hospitals; Registrar in Neurology, Queen's Medical Centre, Nottingham and National Hospital for Neurology, London; Research Fellow, University of Cambridge; Senior Registrar in Neurology, Edinburgh teaching hospitals. Recreations: hillwalking; motorcycling. Address: (b.) Department of Clinical Neurosciences, Western General Hospital, Edinburgh EH4 2XU; T.-0131-537 1169.

Mundell, Rt. Hon. David Gordon, LLB (Hons), MBA. MP (Conservative), Dumfriesshire, Clydesdale and Tweeddale, since 2005; Secretary of State for Scotland, since 2015; Parliamentary Under-Secretary of State for Scotland, 2010-2015; Chairman, Scottish Conservative and Unionist Party, 2007-08 and since 2011; Shadow Secretary of State for Scotland, 2005-10; MSP (C), South of Scotland, 1999-2005; b. 27.5.62, Dumfries; m., Lynda Carmichael (divorced); 2 s.; 1 d. Educ. Lockerbie Academy; Edinburgh University; Strathclyde University. Trainee Solicitor, Tindal Oatts, Glasgow, 1987-87; Solicitor, Maxwell Waddell, Glasgow, 1987-89; Commercial Lawyer, Biggart Baillie, Glasgow, 1989-91; Group Legal Adviser Scotland, BT, 1991-98; Head of National Affairs, BT Scotland, 1998-99. Recreations: family pursuits; travel. Address: House of Commons, London SW1A 0AA; T.-020 7219 4895.
E-mail: david@davidmundell.com

Mundell, John Weir. Chief Executive, Inverclyde Council, since 2006; formerly Corporate Director – Environment, East Dunbartonshire Council; b. Edinburgh; m., Karen; 3 s. Educ. Currie High School; Heriot-Watt University. Entered local government, 1974 (City of Edinburgh Corporation, then Commercial Manager, Lothian Regional Council); Head of Central Contracts, Central Regional Council, 1994-95. Recreations: karate; farming. Address: (b.) Municipal Buildings, Greenock PA15 1LY; T.-01475 712701.

Mundell, Oliver. MSP (Scottish Conservative), Dumfriesshire, since 2016; m., Catherine. Educ. Moffat Academy; University of Edinburgh. Career history: worked for multinational oil and gas firm Royal Dutch Shell; senior parliamentary aide to Geoffrey Cox QC MP in the UK Parliament; co-ordinated the local Better Together campaign across Dumfries and Galloway on behalf of the Conservative Party in the run up to the Independence Referendum; played a key role in a number of local election campaigns. Recreations: keen swimmer and enjoys relaxing in front of a good film. Address: Scottish Parliament, Edinburgh EH99 1SP.

Munn, Professor Pamela, OBE, AcSS, MA, MLitt, CertEd. Emeritus Professor of Curriculum Research, University of Edinburgh, since 2010; formerly Dean, Moray House School of Education; b. 31.3.49, Glasgow; m., Graham Hamilton Munn. Educ. Hermitage School, Helensburgh; Aberdeen University. Teacher of History, 1972-78; Research Fellow, Stirling University, 1979-84; Lecturer in Applied Research in Education, York University, 1984-86; Senior Research Officer, then Depute Director, Scottish Council for Research in Education, 1986-94; Professor of Curriculum Research, Moray House Institute of Education, 1994-98. Member, Scottish Consultative Council on the Curriculum; Fellowship, CIDREE, 1996; SCRE Silver Medal, 1984; Fellowship, SCRE, 2002; Fellow, Society for Educational Studies, 2012; Chair, Education for Citizenship Review Group; Member, Discipline Task Group, Review of Initial Teacher Education Group; President, British Educational Research Association, 2007-09; Honorary Member, SERA, 2012; Convenor, Appeal Board, GTCS, since 2012. Publications: The Changing Face of Education 14-16; Education in Scotland: policy and practice from pre-school to secondary, 1997; Parents and Schools: customers, managers or partners?, 1993; Alternatives to Exclusion from School, 2000. Recreations: hill-walking; gardening; reading, especially crime fiction. Address: (b.) Simon Laurie House, School of Education, University of Edinburgh, Holyrood Road, Edinburgh EH8 8AQ; T.-0131-651 6357.

Munro of Foulis, Hector William, MRICS. 31st Chief of Clan Munro; b. 20.2.50; m., Sarah Duckworth; 1 s.; 2 d. Educ. Oratory School; Royal Agricultural College, Cirencester. Farmer and Chartered Surveyor. Address: (h.) Foulis Mains, Evanton, Ross-shire.

Munro, Professor Colin Roy, BA, LLB. Emeritus Professor, scholar and teacher; Professor of Constitutional Law, Edinburgh University, 1990-2009 (Dean, Faculty of Law, 1992-94); b. 17.5.49, Aberdeen; m., Ruth Elizabeth Pratt; 1 s.; 1 d. Educ. Aberdeen Grammar School; Aberdeen University. Lecturer in Law, Birmingham University, 1971-72, Durham University, 1972-80; Senior Lecturer in Law, then Reader in Law, Essex University, 1980-85; Professor of Law, Manchester University, 1985-90; Chief Examiner, London University LLB (External) Degree, 1991-97; Member, Consultative Council, British Board of Film Classification, 2000-2011; Member, Advertising Advisory Committee, 2005-09. Publications: Television, Censorship and the Law; Studies in Constitutional Law; Devolution and the Scotland Bill (Co-author); The Scotland Act 1998 (Co-author). Recreations: sport; cinema and theatre; real ale. Address: (b.) School of Law, Old College, South Bridge, Edinburgh EH8 9YL.

Munro, Professor David Mackenzie, MBE, BSc, PhD, FRGS, FRSA, FSAScot. Geographical Consultant; Member, Scientific and Technical Committee, Prince Albert II of Monaco Foundation, since 2009; Patron, Wild Camel Protection Foundation, since 2008; Honorary President, Kinross-shire Civic Trust, since 2007; Director and Secretary, Royal Scottish Geographical Society, 1996-2008; Honorary Professor, Dundee University, since 2007; Member, Council, National Trust for Scotland, 1995-2008; Chairman, Permanent Committee on Geographical Names for British Official Use, 1999-2009; Chairman, UK Division of United Nations Group of Experts on Geographical Names, 1999-2009; b. 28.5.50, Glasgow. Educ. Daniel Stewart's College; Edinburgh Academy; Edinburgh University. Research Associate, then Research Fellow, Edinburgh University, 1979-96; Leader/Co Leader, Edinburgh University expeditions to Central America, 1981, 1986, 1988, 1991. Chairman, Michael Bruce Trust; Honorary President, Jules Verne Film Festival, Paris, 2001; Vice-President, 8th UN Conference on the Standardization of Geographical Names, 2002; Scotia Centenary Medal, 2005; Chairman, South Georgia Heritage Trust, 2006; Business Committee, General Council, University of Edinburgh, since 2012. Publications: Chambers World Gazetteer (Editor); Oxford Dictionary of the World (Editor); Gazetteer of the Baltic States; A World Record of Major Conflict Areas; Loch Leven and the River Leven – a

Landscape Transformed; Consultant, Times Atlas of the World; Scotland: an Encyclopedia of Places and Landscapes; numerous articles and reports on land use in Central America. Recreations: walking; travel; exploring landscapes. Address: (h.) Rose Cottage, The Cobbles, Kinnesswood, Kinross KY13 9HL; T.-01592-840-203; e-mail: davidmunro@kinaskit.co.uk

Munro, Rev. David Peacock, MA, BD, STM. Minister, Bearsden North Church, 1967-96; Clerk, Presbytery of Dumbarton, 1986-2005; b. 7.9.29, Paisley; m., Jessie Scott McPherson; 3 d. Educ. Paisley Grammar School; Glasgow University; Union Theological Seminary, New York. Minister, Aberluthnott Parish Church, 1953-56, Castlehill Church, Ayr, 1956-67. Vice-Convener, General Assembly Council, 1988-90, Convener, 1990-95; Moderator, Dumbarton Presbytery, 1978-79; Chairman, General Assembly Board of Education, 1974-79; Convener, General Assembly Education Committee, 1981-85. Recreations: golf; gardening. Address: (h.) 14 Birch Road, Killearn, Glasgow G63 9SQ; T.-01360 550098.

Munro, Donnie, DA. Director of Development, Sabhal Mòr Ostaig; former guitarist and lead singer, Runrig; b. 2.8.53, Skye; m.; 3 children. Former Art Teacher, Inverness and Edinburgh; Rector, Edinburgh University, 1991-94; contested (Labour) Ross, Skye and Inverness West, 1999. Dr. HC, Edinburgh, 1994. Most recent solo album, Heart of America, won Album of the Year in the Scottish TradMusic Awards 2006.

Munro, Ian, BA (Hons) Zoology, PGCE (Biol), FSB. Rector, Kelvinside Academy, since 2016; b. 1981. Educ. George Heriot's School; Royal Zoological Society of Scotland; University of Edinburgh; University of Cambridge. Teacher of Biology: George Heriot's School, 2005, Gordonstoun School, 2006; George Heriot's School: Director of Rowing & Teacher of Biology, 2006-2010, Head of Extracurricular Activities, Head of Year & International Service Coordinator, 2007-2010; Head of Biology, Gordonstoun School, 2010-2013; Deputy Headmaster, Shiplake College, 2013-16. The world's youngest HMC school rector. Address: Kelvinside Academy, 33 Kirklee Road, Glasgow G12 0SW; T.-0141 357 3376.

Munro, Jean Mary, BA (Hons), PhD. Vice President, Society of Antiquaries of Scotland, 2002-05; Chairman, Council, Scottish History Society, 1989-93; b. 2.12.23; m., Robert William Munro. Educ. London University; Edinburgh University. WRNS, 1944-47; freelance historical researcher; Member, Council, National Trust for Scotland, 1964-69 and 1987-92 (Executive, 1968-80); Chairman, Council, Scottish Genealogy Society, 1983-86 (Vice-President, since 1987); Chairman, Council, Scottish Local History Forum, 1984-88. Publications (as Jean Dunlop): the British Fisheries Society; the Clan Chisholm; the Clan Mackenzie; the Clan Gordon; the Scotts; the Clan Mackintosh; (as Jean Munro): ed texts for the Scottish Record Society; (with R.W. Munro): Tain through the Centuries; The Scrimgeours; The Acts of the Lords of the Isles. Recreations: reading; walking. Address: (h.) 15a Mansionhouse Road, Edinburgh EH9 1TZ; T.-0131-667 4601.

Munro, Rev. John P.L., MA, BD, PhD. Mediator; Minister, Kinross Parish Church, 1998-2008; b. 11.5.47, Edinburgh; m., Pat Lawson; 1 s.; 1 d. Educ. Edinburgh Academy; Christ's College, Cambridge; Edinburgh University. Church of Scotland Chaplain, Stirling University, 1977-82; Lecturer, St. Paul's Theological

College, Kenya, 1982-85; Minister, St. Vigeans and Knox's Church, Arbroath, 1986-90; Assistant Secretary, Church of Scotland Department of World Mission, 1990-98. Secretary, Guntrip Trust; Trustee, Bridge Pastoral Foundation. Recreations: music. Address: (h.) 5 Marchmont Crescent, Edinburgh EH9 1HN; T.-0131 623 0198.
E-mail: jplmunro@yahoo.co.uk

Munro, Rev. John Robert, DSD, BD. Minister, Edinburgh: Fairmilehead, since 1992; b. 23.11.48, Glasgow; m., Lillian Primrose; 1 d. Educ. Whitehill Senior Secondary, Glasgow; Royal Scottish Academy of Music and Drama, Edinburgh University. Assistant Minister, Palmerston Place, Edinburgh, 1975-76; Minister, St. Bernard's, Stockbridge, Edinburgh, 1976-92 (Chairman of Stockbridge House for the Elderly). Various General Assembly Committees, 1978-2005; Ponton House Trust Presbytery Publicity Secretary; Chairman of the Ponton House Trust; freelance broadcaster and Presbytery Publicity Secretary. Recreations: golf and fine art. Address: (b.) 6 Braid Crescent, Edinburgh EH10 6AU; T.-0131 446 9363; e-mail: revjohnmunro@hotmail.com

Munro, Neil Kenneth, MA (Hons.) Managing Editor, Times Educational Supplement Scotland, since 2011; b. 18.3.52, Stornoway; m., Eilish; 2 s. Educ. Nicolson Institute, Stornoway; Edinburgh University. Editor, West Highland Free Press, 1974-75; Reporter, Depute Editor, Times Educational Supplement Scotland, 1975-2001, Editor, 2001-2011. Recreations: cycling; swimming; reading. E-mail: neil.munro@tess.co.uk

Munro, Nicola Susan, CB, BA. Board Member, Consumer Futures Scotland, since 2008; Board Member, Scottish Refugee Council, since 2008; b. 11.01.48, Hitchin; m., Graeme Munro; 1 s.; 1 d. Educ. Harrogate Grammar School; Warwick University. Scottish Office posts dealing with health, civil and criminal justice, museums, special needs and human resources, 1970-85; Head of Specialist Hospital Services and Food Division, Scottish Office, 1985-89; Head of Urban Regeneration and Local Economic Development, 1989-92; Head of Curriculum, Testing and Careers Division, 1992-95; Head of Public Health Policy Unit, Scottish Executive, 1995-2000; Head of Environment Group, Scottish Executive, 2000-01; Head of Scottish Development Department, Scottish Government, 2001-07. Consumer Advisory Panel, Office of Rail Regulator, Member; Board Member, Scottish Wildlife Trust. Recreations: travel; family; theatre and art. T.-0131 556 3201; e-mail: gandnmunro@hotmail.com

Muqit, Miratul Mohamid Khan, MB, ChB (Hons). Scottish clinical neurologist and scientist, University of Dundee; b. 12.10.73, Glasgow. Educ. University of Edinburgh; University College London; Harvard University. Completed general medical training at the Hammersmith Hospital and hospitals affiliated to Imperial College London; trained as a neurologist at several London hospitals, including King's College Hospital, the National Hospital for Neurology and Neurosurgery, Royal London Hospital, St Barts and Homerton Hospital, Charing Cross Hospital and Hurstwood Park Neurological Centre; trained in movement disorders with Andrew Lees and Khailash Bhatia at the National Hospital. Awarded a Wellcome Trust Intermediate Clinical Fellowship in 2008; appointed Consultant Neurologist at Ninewells Hospital in Dundee in 2011; received a Wellcome Trust Senior Clinical Fellowship to continue research in 2013; scientist at the University of Dundee's Medical Research Council Protein Phosphorylation and Ubiquitylation Unit; main subspecialist interests are Parkinson's disease and related movement disorders; major interest in inherited forms of

Parkinson's disease. Awarded the 2013 Linacre Medal and Prize Lecture of the Royal College of Physicians. Address: Medical Research Council Protein Phosphorylation and Ubiquitylation Unit, University of Dundee, Sir James Black Centre, School of Life Sciences, Dundee DD1 5EH; T.- 01382 388377; e-mail: m.muqit@dundee.ac.uk

Murdoch, Professor Brian Oliver, BA, PhD, LittD, FRHistS, AMusTCL. Professor of German, Stirling University, since 1991; Emeritus, 2007; b. 26.6.44, London; m., Ursula Irene Riffer; 1 s.; 1 d. Educ. Sir George Monoux Grammar School, London; Exeter University; Jesus College, Cambridge. Lecturer in German, Glasgow University; Assistant/Associate Professor of German, University of Illinois; Lecturer/Senior Lecturer in German, Stirling University; Visiting Fellow, Trinity Hall, Cambridge, 1989; Visiting Fellow and Waynflete Lecturer, Magdalen College, Oxford, 1994; Hulsean Lecturer in Divinity, University of Cambridge, 1997-98; Speaker's Lecturer in Biblical Studies, and Visiting Fellow of Oriel College, University of Oxford, 2000-02; author of a number of books and articles on medieval German and Celtic literature, also on literature of the World Wars. Recreations: jazz; numismatics; books. Address: 4 St James Orchard, Stirling FK9 5NQ.

Murdoch, Helen Elliot, MBA, FCIH, MRICS, ACIPD. Chief Executive, Hanover (Scotland) Housing Association Ltd., since 2007; Director, Housing & Care Services, 1995-2007; m., John Murdoch; 1 s. Professional Housing Management Trainee and other senior posts with SSHA (Scottish Special Housing Association), 1974-85; Area Housing Manager, Dunfermline District Council, 1985-95. Chartered Surveyor; Member, various Scottish Government Working Parties; particular interest and experience in Strategic Management, Management of Change and Organisational Culture. Recreations: running; hill-walking; art. Address: 95 McDonald Road, Edinburgh EH7 4NS; T.- 0131 557 7420 (office); e-mail: hmurdoch@hsha.org.uk

Murdoch, Iain Campbell, MA, LLB, DipEd, BD. Minister, Cambusnethan Old and Morningside Parish Church, Wishaw, since 1995; b. 16.10.50, Glasgow; m., Elizabeth Gibson; 1 s.; 1 d. Educ. Larchfield School, Helensburgh; Haileybury College, Hertford; Trinity College, Oxford; University of Edinburgh. Legal Apprentice, Simpson & Marwick WS, 1973-74; Economics Teacher, Brighton College, 1976-77; PT History, Keil School, 1977-79; Principal Teacher, General Studies, Rossall School, Fleetwood, 1979-89; Assistant Minister, Duddingston Kirk, Edinburgh, 1992-94; Founder Member and Present Advisor, MADE4U in ML2 (a charitable company making a difference in Wishaw). Parliamentary Candidate, SDP/Liberal Alliance, Wyre, 1983 and 1987; successful petitioner to Scottish Parliament, 2001-03; Member, Church of Scotland Church and Society Council, 2010-14. Recreations: hill walking; being a grandad. Address: (h.) 22, Coronation Street, Wishaw ML2 8LF; T.-01698-384235.

Murdoch, Professor Jim, MA, LLM. Professor of Public Law, Glasgow University, since 1998, International Dean for Student Mobility; b. 26.6.55, Hamilton. Educ. Strathaven Academy; Hutcheson's Grammar School; Glasgow University; University of California at Berkeley; Open University. Solicitor; Glasgow University: Lecturer; Senior Lecturer; Visiting Professor: University of Mainz; University of Hamburg; University of Freiburg; University of Paris Ouest; Council of Europe, Strasbourg: Professor Stagiere; long term consultant; Pro Merito medal, Council of Europe,

2012. Publications: Reed and Murdoch, Human Rights Law in Scotland (3rd Edition), 2011; The Protection of Liberty and Security of Person (2nd Edition), 2002; The Treatment of Prisoners: European Standards, 2006. Recreations; hill walking; foreign travel. Address: (b.) School of Law, Glasgow University, Glasgow G12; T.- 0141-330 4178.

Murdoch, Kirk, LLB, NP. Partner and Chairman (Scotland and Northern Ireland), Pinsent Masons LLP, since 2012; Senior Partner, and Real Estate Partner, McGrigors, Solicitors, since 2004; b. 7.3.55, Ayr; 2 s.; 1 d. Educ. Ayr Academy; Edinburgh University. McGrigor Donald: Apprentice, 1976, Legal Assistant, Partner, Real Estate, 1982, Head of Real Estate, 1992-97, Managing Partner, 1997-2002, Managing Partner Scotland and Real Estate Partner, 2002-04. Member, SCDI Executive Committee; Non Executive Chairman, Irvine Bay Developments Ltd; Non Executive Director, Ayr Renaissance LLP; Non Executive Director, Beatson Institute; Member, Scottish Business Board. Recreations: golf; rugby. Address: (b.) 141 Bothwell Street, Glasgow G2 7EQ; T.- 0141 567 8400.
E-mail: kirk.murdoch@pinsentmasons.com

Mure, Kenneth Nisbet, QC. Advocate, Scotland, since 1975; Barrister, Grays Inn, since 1990; Fellow, Chartered Institute of Taxation, since 1981; Judge, Tax and Chancery and C.I.C. Tribunals; b. 11.4.47, Glasgow. Educ. Cumbernauld JS School; Glasgow High School; Glasgow University. Address: (b.) Advocates' Library, Edinburgh.

Murison, Alison. Head Teacher, Aberdeen Grammar School, since 2015. First female Head Teacher in the school's 759 year history. Former Head Teacher, Hazelhead Academy (2009-2015). Address: Aberdeen Grammar School, Skene Street, Aberdeen AB10 1HT; T.-01224 642299.

Murning, Lt. Col. Ian Henry, TD, LLB (Hons), LLM, DPA, FRICS, MInstRE. Principal, Murning Associates, Chartered Surveyors and Property Consultants, since 1994; Visiting Professor, Edinburgh Napier University, Faculty of Engineering, Computing and Creative Industries, since 2012; Honorary Secretary, Royal Institution of Chartered Surveyors in Scotland, 2006-2012; Member, Investigation and Professional Conduct Enforcement Committee, Institute of Chartered Accountants of Scotland, 2007-2013; Member, Scottish Funding Council for Further and Higher Education, 2005-2011; Member, Scottish Further Education Funding Council, 2003-05; Member, Homeowners Housing Panel, since 2012; Member, Private Rented Housing Panel, since 2012; Chairman, Capital Investment Committee, Scottish Funding Council, 2003-09; Programme Director, Napier University, 1994-2007; b. 24.12.43, Chapelhall; m., Seona Jean Meiklejon; 1 s.; 2 d. Educ. Dalziel High School; Glasgow University; College of Estate Management; London University; Edinburgh University. Valuer, Stirling Valuation Office, Highlands and Islands; Office of Chief Valuer (Scotland); District Valuer, Dumfries and Galloway, 1988-94. Chairman, Royal Institution of Chartered Surveyors in Scotland, 1995-96; Member, General Council, Royal Institution of Chartered Surveyors, 1994-96; Commander, Royal Engineers (National Defence), Army HQ Scotland, 1991-95; Commander, District Specialist Training Team, Army HQ Scotland, 1996-97; served with 52(L) Div/Dist Engrs (TA), 1963-67, Royal Monmouthshire Royal Engineers (Militia), 1967-68, 71 (Scottish) Engineer Regt (V), 1968-74; 12 Engr Bde, 1984-86; Member: Society of High Constables of Edinburgh, 1993-2012, Merchant Company of Edinburgh, 1995; Freeman,

Honourable Company of Air Pilots, 2014; Military Member, The Reserve Forces and Cadets Association for the Lowlands of Scotland, 1997; Governor, George Watson's College, 2000-09; Chairman, UNIFI Scotland, 2009-2012. Chairman, Scottish Civil Service Flying Club, since 2009; Director and Secretary, RAF Leuchars Flying Club, 2011-2014. Address: (b.) 21 Redhall House Avenue, Edinburgh EH14 1JJ; T.-0131-443 8839.
E-mail: ianmurning@hotmail.com

Murphy, Andrew, MA. Group Productivity Director, John Lewis Partnership, since 2015; Chairman, Scottish Retail Consortium, since 2014; Retail Director, John Lewis plc, 2010-15; Chairman, UK China Visa Alliance, 2013-15; Director, London First, 2013-15; m. Educ. University of Aberdeen; Northwestern University - Kellogg School of Management. Chairman, Aberdeen City Centre Association, 2004-05; Non Executive Director, Edinburgh Leisure, 2005-07; Chairman, Essential Edinburgh, 2006-08; Advisory Board Member: Scottish Retail Consortium, 2005-09, Cooperative Development Scotland, 2007-09; Managing Director, Aberdeen & Edinburgh, John Lewis, 2004-09; Director, Operations Development, John Lewis, 2009-2010; Member, Commission for the Future of Local Government, 2012. Address: Scottish Retail Consortium, Box 112, 12 Southbridge, Edinburgh EH1 1DD; T.-07880 039 743.

Murphy, Jim. MP (Labour), East Renfrewshire (formerly Eastwood), 1997-2015; Leader of the Scottish Labour Party, 2014-15; Shadow Secretary of State for International Development, 2013-14; Shadow Defence Secretary, 2010-13; Secretary of State for Scotland, 2008-10; Minister for Europe, 2007-08; b. 23.8.67, Glasgow; m.; 3 c. Educ. Bellarmine Secondary School, Glasgow; Milnerton High School, Cape Town. National President, National Union of Students, 1994-96; Special Projects Manager, Scottish Labour Party, 1996-97; PPS to Helen Liddell (Secretary of State for Scotland), 2001-02; Assistant Government Whip, 2002-05; Parliamentary Secretary, Cabinet Office, 2005-06; Minister of State for Employment and Welfare Reform, 2006-07. Recreations: football; cinema; reading.

Murphy, Peter Alexander, MA, MEd. Rector, Whitfield High School, Dundee, 1976-93; b. 5.10.32, Aberdeen; m., Margaret Christie; 3 s.; 1 d. Educ. Aberdeen Grammar School; Aberdeen University. Assistant Principal Teacher of English, Aberdeen Grammar School, 1963-65; Principal Teacher of English, Summerhill Academy, Aberdeen, 1965-71; Head Teacher, Logie Secondary School, Dundee, 1971-76; Labour Councillor (Carnoustie & District), Angus Council, 1999-2012 and Depute Provost of Angus, 2007-2012. Publications: Life and Times of Logie School (Co-Author); The Life of R.F. MacKenzie (A Prophet without Honour), 1999. Address: Ashlea, 44 Burnside Street, Carnoustie, Angus DD7 7HL.

Murphy, Sheriff Sean Francis, QC, MA (Hons), LLB, DipLP, PGCE. Sheriff of Glasgow and Strathkelvin, since 2007; b. 17.07.58, Glasgow; m., Honor; 1 s.; 2 d. Educ. St Aloysius College, Glasgow; University of St Andrews; Strathclyde University; Christ's and Notre Dame College of Education, Liverpool. Assistant Master of History, St Edmund Campion Upper School, Oxford, 1981-83 and St. Augustine's Upper School, Oxford, 1983-86; Messrs Ross Harper and Murphy, Glasgow: Trainee Solicitor, 1989-91, Court Assistant Solicitor, 1991; Visiting Lecturer in Law, Glasgow College of Technology, 1988-90; Advocate, 1992; Advocate Depute, 1991-2001; Standing Junior Counsel to the Scottish Executive, 2001-03; QC, 2003; Senior Advocate Depute, 2003-07. Secretary, Faculty of Advocates Criminal Lawyers Group, 1997-99; Committee Member, Scottish Medico-Legal Council, since 2006; Chairman, Glenmarnock Wheelers CC, 1994-2004. Recreations: cycling; reading; listening to radio drama and sitting patiently at Firhill. Address: (b.) Sheriff Court of Glasgow and Strathkelvin, 1 Carlton Place, Glasgow G5 9DA; T.-0141 429 8888.
E-mail: sheriffsmurphy@scotcourts.gov.uk

Murray, Rt. Hon. Lord (Ronald King Murray), PC (1974), MA, LLB, Dr.h.c.(Edin). Senator of the College of Justice in Scotland, 1979-95; b. 15.6.22; m., Sheila Winifred Gamlin. Educ. George Watson's College; Edinburgh University; Jesus College, Oxford (Honorary Fellow, 1999). Advocate, 1953; QC, 1967; MP (Leith), 1970-79; Lord Advocate, 1974-79. Assessor, Edinburgh University Court, 1981-93 (Vice-Chairman, 1990-93). Recreations: sailing; astronomy. Address: (h.) 1 Inverleith Grove, Edinburgh EH3 5PB; T.-0131-551 5330.

Murray, Athol Laverick, PhD, MA, LLB, FRHistS, FSA Scot. Chairman, Scottish Records Association, 1997-2000; Vice-President, Society of Antiquaries of Scotland, 1989-92; Keeper of the Records of Scotland, 1985-90; b. 8.11.30, Tynemouth; m., Irene Joyce Cairns; 1 s.; 1 d. Educ. Lancaster Royal Grammar School; Jesus College, Cambridge; Edinburgh University. Research Assistant, Foreign Office, 1953; Scottish Record Office: Assistant Keeper, 1953-83, Deputy Keeper, 1983-84. Recreations: historical research; bowling. Address: (h.) 33 Inverleith Gardens, Edinburgh EH3 5PR; T.-0131-552 4465; e-mail: atholmurray@hotmail.com

Murray, (Bridget) Jane, BA (Oxon), MA, PhD. Commissioner, Royal Commission on the Ancient and Historical Monuments of Scotland, 1999-2009; Chair, The Whithorn Trust, 2005-08; b. 25.7.37, Tunbridge Wells; m., John Murray, QC (Lord Dervaird); 3 s. Educ. Royal Tunbridge Wells County Grammar School for Girls; St Hugh's College, Oxford; Edinburgh University. Involved in various archaeological projects and organisations. Recreations: gardening; walking; architecture. Address: (h.) 4 Moray Place, Edinburgh EH3 6DS; T.-0131-225 1881.

Murray, Sir David Edward (KT 2007). Chairman, Murray Capital Limited; Founder, The Murray Foundation, 1997; Queen's Award for Voluntary Service, November 2006; b. 14.10.51, Ayr; 2 s. Educ. Fettes College; Broughton High School. Young Scottish Businessman of the Year, 1984; Hon. Doctorate, Heriot-Watt University, 1986; Hon. Doctorate, University of Edinburgh, 2008; Chairman, UK 2000 (Scotland), 1987; Governor, Clifton Hall School, 1987. Recreations: sports sponsorship; collecting and producing wine, Chevalier du Tastevin - Clos de Vougeot, November 2006. Address: (b.) 26 Charlotte Square, Edinburgh EH2 4ET.

Murray, Diana Mary, MA (Cantab), FSA, FSAScot, MIFA, IoD. Senior Executive, Historic Environment Scotland, since 2015; former Chief Executive, Royal Commission on the Ancient and Historical Monuments of Scotland (RCAHMS) (2004-2015) and Historic Scotland (2013-2015); Honorary Fellow of the School of History, Classics and Archaeology, Edinburgh University; b. 14.9.52, Birmingham; m., Robin F. Murray; 2 d. Educ. King Edward VI Camp Hill School for Girls, Birmingham; New Hall, Cambridge. RCAHMS: Research Assistant, 1976-83, Head of Recording Section, 1983-90, Curator, Archaeology Record, 1990-95, Curator Depute, National Monuments Record of Scotland (NMRS), 1995-2004.

Chairman, Institute of Field Archaeologists, 1995-96; Board Member: National Trust for Scotland, 2008-2014, Scottish Waterways Trust, Scottish Seabird Centre, Royal Botanic Gardens of Edinburgh; Board Trustee: Arts and Business Scotland, since 2016, Scottish International Education Trust, since 2015. Recreations: choral singing; gardening. Address: (b) HES, John Sinclair House, 16 Bernard Terrace, Edinburgh EH8 9NX; T.-0131 662 1456; e-mail: diana.murray@rcahms.gov.uk

Murray, Duncan Law, LLB (Hons). Sheriff Principal, North Strathclyde, since 2014; part time Sheriff, 2006-2014; b. 5.5.59; m., Ianthe Elizabeth Lee Craig; 2 s.; 1 d. Educ. Aberdeen Grammar School; Aberdeen University. Robson McLean Paterson: apprentice, 1980-82; Assistant, 1982-85; Partner, Robson McLean, 1985-2002; Partner, Morton Fraser, 2002-2014. President, Law Society of Scotland, 2004-05. Recreations: golf; ski-ing; hill-walking; family. Club: Luffness New Golf.

Murray, Elaine Kildare, BSc (Hons), PhD. MSP (Labour), Dumfriesshire, 2011-16, Dumfries, 1999-2011; former Shadow Minister, Community Safety & Legal Affairs; former Vice Convenor, Justice Committee; Shadow Minister for Housing and Transport, 2011-13; Shadow Minister for Environment, 2008-2011; Shadow Minister for Enterprise, 2007-08; Vice Convener, Finance Committee, 2007-08; Deputy Minister for Tourism, Culture and Sport, 2001-03; b. 22.12.54, Hitchin, Herts; m., Jeff Leaver; 2 s.; 1 d. Educ. Mary Erskine School, Edinburgh; Edinburgh University; Cambridge University. Postdoctoral Research Fellow: Cavendish Laboratory, Cambridge, Royal Free Hospital, London; Senior Scientific Officer, Institute of Food Research, Reading; Associate Lecturer, Open University in Scotland. Recreations: family activities; reading; cooking; music.

Murray, Elma. Chief Executive, North Ayrshire Council. Address: (b.) Cunninghame House, Irvine KA12 8EE; T.-01294 324 124.

Murray, Professor Gordon Cameron, BSc, BArch, MCIArb, RIBA, RTPI, PPRIAS. Partner, Ryder Architecture, since 2012; Director, GMA Ryder, since 2012; Founding Principal, Gordon Murray Architects, 2010-12; Professor of Architecture, University of Strathclyde, since 2007; b. 26.7.52; m., Sharon Boyle; 2 d. Educ. University of Strathclyde. Assistant Architect: Richard Moira, Betty Moira & James Wann, 1974; Department of Architecture and Related Services, 1975-77; Project Architect, Sinclair and Watt Architects, 1977-79; Partner: Cunningham Glass Murray Architects, 1987-92; Glass Murray Architects, 1992-99; gm and ad architects, 1999-2010. External Examiner, University of Ulster, 2004/09; University of Bath, since 2012. President: Glasgow Inst. of Architects, 1998-2000; RIAS, 2003-05. Member, Board, Lighthouse Trust, 2003-09. Chair, Technologies Excellence Group - Curriculum for Excellence, 2009-10; Chair, Standing Council of Heads of UK Schools of Architecture, 2010-12. Publications: James Miller, Architect: a monograph, 1990; Challenging Contextualism: the work of gm and ad architects, 2002; Curious Rationalism, 2006; To Have and to Hold: Future of a Contested Landscape, 2012; Venice Biennale, 2012. Recreations: cinema; art; saxophone; jazz; travel. Address: (b.) 221 West George Street, Glasgow G2 2ND; T.-0141 285 0230.
E-mail: gmurray@ryderarchitecture.com
(www.ryderarchitecture.com)

Murray, Gordon Lindsay Kevan. Partner, Murray Snell WS, Solicitors; Secretary, Royal Scottish National Orchestra Society Ltd.; Director, 1990-93, Secretary and Treasurer, The RSNO Foundation; b. 23.5.53, Glasgow; m., Susan Patricia; 1 s.; 3 d. Educ. Lenzie Academy;

Edinburgh University. Address: (b.) 40 Castle Street, Edinburgh EH2 3BN; T.-0131-625 6625.
E-mail: mail@murraysnell.com

Murray, Sheriff Gregor Kenneth, LLP, DipLP. Sheriff, Forfar Sheriff Court, since 2011; b. 8.9.64, Dundee; m., Jane; 1 d. Educ. Morgan Academy, Dundee; University of Dundee. Partner: Carltons, Dundee, 1990-99, Blackadders, Dundee, 1999-2004, RSB Macdonald, Dundee, 2004-2011; Lecturer and Course Leader, Civil Procedure Course, University of Dundee, 2000-2011. Recreations: golf; Dundee United; reading; cookery. Address: Sheriff Courthouse, Market Street, Forfar.

Murray, Ian. MP (Labour), Edinburgh South, since 2010; Shadow Secretary of State for Scotland, since 2015; b. 10.8.76. Educ. Dumbryden Primary School; Wester Hailes Education Centre; University of Edinburgh. Worked at the Royal Blind, then pensions management; joined Edinburgh-based internet television station (Worldart.com) helping to build a new online TV station; set-up 100 mph Events Ltd (event management business); elected to Liberton Council in 2003, represented the larger Liberton/Gilmerton ward, 2007-2010; Shadow Minister for Employment Relations, Consumer and Postal Affairs, 2011-2013; Shadow Minister for Trade & Investment (including Employment Relations and Postal Affairs), 2013-15. Address: (b.) House of Commons, London SW1A 0AA.

Murray, Professor Isobel (Mary), MA, PhD. Writer and Critic; Honorary Research Professor in Modern Scottish Literature, Aberdeen University; Fellow, Association of Scottish Literary Studies; Associate Editor, Oxford Dictionary of National Biography; b. 14.2.39, Alloa; m., Bob Tait. Educ. Dollar Academy; Edinburgh University. Assistant Lecturer, Lecturer, Senior Lecturer, Reader, Professor, Department of English, Aberdeen University; books include several editions of Oscar Wilde (most recently Oscar Wilde: The Major Works, 2000), introductions to new editions of J. MacDougall Hay's Gillespie, Ian MacPherson's Shepherds' Calendar, Robin Jenkins' Guests of War, Iain Crichton Smith's Consider the Lilies, George MacKay Brown's Magnus, and Jessie Kesson's Where the Apple Ripens; edited, Beyond This Limit: Selected Shorter Fiction of Naomi Mitchison; A Girl Must Live: stories and poems by Naomi Mitchison; Ten Modern Scottish Novels (with Bob Tait), 1984; Scottish Writers Talking, 1996; Somewhere Beyond: A Jessie Kesson Companion; published Jessie Kesson: Writing Her Life, 2000 (National Library of Scotland/Saltire Society Research Book of the Year); Scottish Writers Talking 2, 2002; Scottish Writers Talking 3, 2006; Scottish Writers Talking 4, 2008; Jessie Kesson: A Country Dweller's Years, from 2008; Series Editor, Naomi Mitchison Library: Introductions to: When We Become Men, Travel Light, The Conquered, Anna Comnena, Cleopatra's People, The Bull Calves, We Have Been Warned, The Delicate Fire, 2012; Scottish Novels of the Second World War. Address: (b.) 5 St Machar Place, Old Aberdeen, Aberdeen AB24 3SF; T.-Aberdeen 491938; e-mail: imurray@abdn.ac.uk

Murray, Rev. John James, DipTH. Minister, Free Church of Scotland (Continuing); b. 11.9.34, Dornoch; m., Cynthia MacPhee; 1 s.; 1 d. Educ. Dornoch Academy; Edinburgh University; Free Church College. Caledonian Insurance Company, 1955-59; Assistant Editor, Banner of Truth Trust, 1960-73; Minister: Free High Church, Oban, 1978-89, St. Columba's Free Church, Edinburgh, 1989-2000, Edinburgh Free Church (Continuing), 2000-02 (retired 2002). Moderator, General Assembly, Free Church of Scotland (Continuing), 2003. Publications: Behind a Frowning Providence, 1990; The Life and Writings of John

Marshall, 2005; Catch the Vision, 2007; 1560: The Greatest Year in Scotland's History, 2010; Life of John Knox, 2011; A God Centred Vision for Church and Nation, 2014. Address: (h.) 7 Greenacres Way, Glasgow G53 7BG; T.-0141-620 3983; e-mail: johnmurray@fccontinuing.org

Murray, Leonard G., JP (Retd), BL, SSC, KCJSJ, KCHS. Retired Solicitor (formerly Senior Partner of Levy & McRae, Glasgow). After-dinner speaker; Scottish Wit of the Year 2012; Dean of the Guild of Robert Burns Speakers; Ambassador to Glasgow Caledonian University; Honorary President of Greenock Burns Club. Author "The Pleader"; member of the Committee of Justice For Megrahi. Recreations: golf; bowls. Address: 19 Ladywood, Milngavie G62 8BE; 0141 563 9624; 07836 707031; len.murray@ntlworld.com; www.lenmurray.co.uk

Murray, Peter, LLB (Hons), DipLP. Partner, Ledingham Chalmers LLP, since 2002, Board Member, since 2012; b. 27.10.71, Edinburgh; m., Alison; 2 d.; 1 s. Educ. Easthampstead Park; Dunfermline High; Aberdeen University. Trainee Solicitor, Clark & Wallace, Solicitors, 1994-97; Solicitor/Associate, Ledingham Chalmers, Solicitors, 1997-2002. Deputy Chairman, Albyn School, Aberdeen; Burgess of The City of Aberdeen; Notary Public; Registrar to the Episcopal Diocese of Aberdeen and Orkney; Advocate in Aberdeen; Council Member, Moray Chamber of Commerce; Columnist, Energy Voice. Recreation: family. Club: The Royal Northern and University Club. Address: (b.) Johnstone House, 52-54 Rose Street, Aberdeen AB10 1HA; T.-01224 408445. E-mail: peter.murray@ledinghamchalmers.com

Murray, Robert John, MSc, MCIBS. Planning Convener, Angus Council, since 2012; Vice President, COSLA, 2007-2012; Leader, Angus Council, 1998-2007 (Deputy Leader, 1995-98); b. 3.2.51, Montrose; 1 s.; 1 d. Educ. Montrose Academy; University of Abertay, Dundee. Member, Tayside Regional Council, 1994-96; Board Member, NOSWA; Non Executive Director, Improvement Service, since 2008. Recreations: cycling; walking. Address: (h.) 8 Beechgrove, Monifieth DD5 4TE. E-mail: cllrmurray@angus.gov.uk

Murray, Roderick Macpherson, BA (Hons). Director, An Lanntair, since 1985, Head of Visual Arts and Literature; b. 31.3.56, Coll, Isle of Lewis. Educ. Back Junior Secondary School; Nicolson Institute, Stornoway; Glasgow School of Art. Recreations: cycling; chess; arts. Address: (b.) An Lanntair, Kenneth Street, Stornoway, Isle of Lewis HS1 2DS; T.-01851 703307; e-mail: roddy@lanntair.com

Murray, Professor T. Stuart, MD, PhD, FRCGP, FRCPGlas. West of Scotland Director of Postgraduate General Practice Education, 1985-2011; Professor of General Practice, University of Glasgow, 1992-2011 (retired); b. 22.7.43, Muirkirk, Ayrshire; m., Anne Smith; 1 s.; 2 d. Educ. Muirkirk Junior Secondary School; Cumnock Academy; University of Glasgow. Early training in cardiology; entered general practice, 1971; Senior Lecturer in General Practice, 1977. Publication: Modified Essay Questions for the MRCGP Examination; Guide to Postgraduate Medical Education (Co-author). Recreations: travel; reading; sport. Address: (h.) 61 Braeside Avenue, Milngavie, Glasgow G62 6NN; T.-0141-956-1981; e-mail: t.smurray@btinternet.com

Murray, Thomas Kenneth, WS. Partner, Gillespie MacAndrew LLP Solicitors, since 1983; b. 25.6.58, Edinburgh; m., Sophie Mackenzie; 3 d. Educ. Sedbergh School; Dundee University. Purse Bearer to Lord High Commissioner to Church of Scotland, since 2003; Deacon, Incorporation of Goldsmiths of the City of Edinburgh; Director, Mercy Corps; Trustee, The Scottish National War Memorial. Recreations: fishing; golf. Address: 5 Atholl Crescent, Edinburgh EH3 8EJ; T.-0131 260 7501; e-mail: tom.murray@gillespiemacandrew.co.uk

Murray-Smith, Professor David James, MSc, PhD, DSc, CEng, FIET. Emeritus Professor and Honorary Senior Research Fellow, Glasgow University; b. 20.10.41, Aberdeen; m., Effie Smith; 2 s. Educ. Aberdeen Grammar School; Aberdeen University; Glasgow University. Engineer, Inertial Systems Department, Ferranti Ltd., Edinburgh, 1964-65; Glasgow University: Assistant, Department of Electrical Engineering, 1965-67, Lecturer, 1967-77, Senior Lecturer, 1977-83, Reader, 1983-85, Professor of Engineering Systems and Control, 1985-2005, Dean, Faculty of Engineering, 1997-2001. Past Chairman, United Kingdom Simulation Council. Recreations: hill-walking; photography; strong interest in railways. Address: (b.) School of Engineering, Rankine Building, University of Glasgow, Glasgow G12 8QQ; T.-0141-942 2864; e-mail: david.murray-smith@glasgow.ac.uk

Murray-Smith, Professor Roderick, BEng, PhD. Professor of Computing Science, University of Glasgow, since 1999; b. 03.04.69, Glasgow; m., Sophie; 2 s. Educ. Bearsden Academy; University of Strathclyde. Research Engineer, Daimler Benz Research, Berlin, Germany, 1990-97; Visiting Researcher, MIT, 1994-5; Research Fellow, Technical University of Denmark, 1997-99; Senior Researcher, Hamilton Institute, NUIM Ireland, 2002-2008; Seconded to Nokia Denmark, 2008-2009; Director of SICSA (The Scottish Informatics and Computer Science Alliance), 2012-2014. Publications: 3 edited books and a wide range of scientific papers. Address: School of Computing Science, University of Glasgow; T.-0141 330 4984; e-mail: Roderick.Murray-Smith@glasgow.ac.uk

Murrell, Peter T. Chief Executive, Scottish National Party, since 2001; b. 8.12.64, Edinburgh; m., Nicola Sturgeon. Educ. Craigmount High School, Edinburgh. Publicity Officer, Church of Scotland, 1984-87; Parliamentary Assistant to: Alex Salmond, MP, 1987-94, Allan Macartney, MEP, 1994-98; Head of Office, Ian Hudghton, MEP, 1998-99; Parliamentary Co-ordinator, SNP Westminster Group, 2000-01. Recreations: golf; cooking; gardening. Address: (b.) 3 Jackson's Entry, Edinburgh EH8 8PJ; T.-0131-525 8907. E-mail: peter.murrell@snp.org
twitter.com/PeterMurrell; facebook.com/PeterMurrellSNP

Muscatelli, Professor Vito Antonio, MA (Hons) (Logan Prize), PhD, FRSE, AcSS, FRSA, Hon LLD (McGill). Principal and Vice-Chancellor, University of Glasgow, since 2009, Daniel Jack Professor of Political Economy, Department of Economics, 1992-2007, Vice Principal (Strategy and Advancement), 2004-07; Principal and Vice-Chancellor, Heriot-Watt University, 2007-09; b. 1.1.62, Bari, Italy; m., Elaine Flood; 1 s.; 1 d. Educ. High School of Glasgow; Glasgow University. Lecturer, Senior Lecturer, Glasgow University, 1984-92, Dean, Faculty of Social Sciences, 2000-04; Visiting Professor: University of Parma (Italy), 1989, Catholic University, Milan, 1991, 1997, University of Bari (Italy), 1995-2004; Editor, Scottish Journal of Political Economy, 1989-2003; Member, Editorial Advisory Board, International Review of Economics and Business, 1995-2001; Member, Advisory Panel of Economic Consultants to the Secretary of State for Scotland, 1998-2000; Research Fellow, CES-info Research Institute Munich, since 1999; Special Adviser, House of

Commons Treasury Select Committee, 2007-10; HEFCE RAE Panel, 2001, 2008; Member, Council, Royal Economic Society, 2002-06; Member, ESRC Research Grants Board, 2002-07; Convener, Universities Scotland and Vice-President, Universities UK, 2008-2010; Member, Financial Services Advisory Board for Scotland, 2009-2011; Member of Board, Scottish Funding Council, since 2012; Director, UK National Centre for Universities and Business, 2012-13; Hon. Fellow, Societa Italiana Degli Economisti, 1996; Fellow, Royal Society of Edinburgh, 2003; Academician, Learned Societies in the Social Sciences, 2004; Knight Commander (Commendatore), Republic of Italy, 2009. Director: High School of Glasgow Board, since 2000, Russell Group of Universities, since 2009, Universitas 21 Group of Universities, since 2009; Board, Glasgow City Marketing Bureau, since 2009; Trustee, Council for the Advancement and Support of Education (Europe), since 2013; Chair, Glasgow & Clyde Valley Commission on Urban Economic Growth, since 2015; Honorary President, David Hume Institute, since 2015; Director, Beatson Institute, since 2015; Member, Scottish Government's Council of Economic Advisers, since 2015; Director, Universities Superannuation Scheme Board, since 2015. Publications: Macroeconomic Theory and Stabilisation Policy (Co-author), 1988; Economic and Political Institutions in Economic Policy (Editor of volume), 1996; Monetary Policy, Fiscal Policies and Labour Markets: Macroeconomic Policymaking in the EMU, 2004; articles in journals. Recreations: music; literature; football; strategic games. Address: University of Glasgow, Glasgow G12 8QQ; T.-0141 330 5995; e-mail: principal@glasgow.ac.uk

Musson, John Nicholas Whitaker, MA (Oxon); b. 2.10.27; m., Ann Preist (deceased 2004); 1 s.; 3 d. Educ. Clifton College; Brasenose College, Oxford. Served as Guardsman and Lt., Lancashire Fusiliers, 1945-48; HM Colonial Administrative Service (later Overseas Civil Service) 1951-59 (District Officer and Instructor, Institute of Administration, N. Nigeria); British Petroleum Co., London, 1959-61; Assistant Master and Housemaster, Canford School, Dorset, 1961-72; Warden, Glenalmond College, 1972-87; Scottish Division Chairman, Headmasters' Conference, 1981-83; Scottish Director, Independent Schools Careers Organisation, 1987-93; Governor, George Watson's College, Edinburgh, 1989-98; Governor, Clifton College, Bristol, since 1989; Director and Trustee, Scottish European Aid and Mercy Corps Europe, 1996-2000; Country Director, Bosnia/Herzegovina, for Mercy Corps/Scottish European Aid, 1998-99; Vice Chairman, Mercy Corps, Europe, 2000-07. Recreations: travel; art; music; Egyptology; rugby. Address: (h.) 47 Spylaw Road, Edinburgh EH10 5BP.

Myles, Bob. Leader, Angus Council, 2007-2012; Councillor for Brechin and Edzell, since 1999, and represents the Council on Police, Fire & Tayside Contracts Joint Boards; b. 9.2.54; m., Agnes; 3 d. Educ. Brechin High School; Edinburgh University. Livestock Farmer. Board and Committee member of SNFU, 1998-2009, and past Angus Branch President; President, Edzell Curling Club; past President of North and South Esk Province, 1999-2000; Committee Member, Angus and Fettercairn shows; Member: Edzell Drama Club, Edzell Burns Club; past Chairman and Member, Brechin Round Table. Address: (h.) Dalbog, Edzell, Brechin DD9 7UU; T.-01356 648265; e-mail: cllrmyles@angus.gov.uk

Myles, David Fairlie, CBE. Hill Farmer; Member, Angus District Council, 1984-96; b. 30.5.25, Cortachy, Kirriemuir; m., Janet I. Gall (deceased); 2 s.; 2 d. Educ. Brechin High School. Auctioneer's clerk, 1941-43; Royal Marines, 1943-46; Tenant Hill Farmer, since 1946; Director of auction company, 1963-81; Member, Transport Users Consultative Committee for Scotland, 1973-79; Council Member, NFU of Scotland, 1970-79 (Convener, Organisation and Publicity Committee, 1976-79); Member, Meat Promotion Executive, MLC, 1975-79; Chairman, North Angus and Mearns Constituency Conservative Party, 1971-74; MP (Conservative), Banff, 1979-83; Joint Secretary, Backbench Conservative Agriculture Committee, 1979-83; Secretary, Backbench Conservative European Committee, 1980-83; Member: Select Committee on Agriculture and Select Committee on European Legislation, 1979-83, North of Scotland Hydro-Electric Board, 1985-89, Angus Tourist Board, 1984-92, Potato Marketing Board, 1988-97; Dean, Guildry of Brechin, 1993-94; Lord President, Court of Deans of Scotland, 1995-96; Session Clerk, Edzell-Lethnot Parish Church, 1996-2002; Elder, Edzell-Lethnot Parish Church. Recreations: curling; traditional Scottish fiddle music; works of Robert Burns. Address: (h.) The Gorse, Dunlappie Road, Edzell, Brechin DD9 7UB; T.-01356 648207.

Myskow, Lyndsey Morag, BSc, MB, ChB, DCH, DFFP. Principal in General Practice, since 1984; Honorary Senior Lecturer, Department of General Practice, University of Edinburgh, since 1999; Associate Specialist in Psychosexual Medicine, Royal Infirmary, since 2005; b. 28.10.55, Ilford, Essex; m., Derrick Wrenn. Educ. Linlithgow Academy; Edinburgh University Medical School. Recreations: cooking; exercise; cats. Address: (h.) 8 Magdala Crescent, Edinburgh EH12 5BE; T.-0131-337 1043; e-mail: lyndsey.myskow@lothian.scot.nhs.uk

N

Nagl, Hazel Anna, RSW, RGI, PAI. Artist/Painter (still life and landscape painter with a special interest in the Scottish garden); b. 2.11.53, Glasgow; m., James Geoffrey Keanie; 1 d. Educ. Glasgow School of Art. Exhibits on a regular basis throughout Scotland; RSW, 1988; PAI, 1995; SAAC 1994; RGI Stone Prize, 1987 and 1990; RGI Mackinlay Award, 1994; RGI Eastwood Publications Award, 1994; SAAC Prize, 1994; PAI Prize 1996 and 1998; 1st Prize, Laing Competition, 1999; RGI, 2000; Alexander Graham Award; RSW, 2010; Convener, RGI, since 2012. Address: (h.) Lawmarnock House, Troon Drive, Bridge of Weir PA11 3HF.

Nairn, Nicholas Cameron Abel. Known as Nick Nairn. Current occupation: Chef; Food Consultant; TV chef; TV presenter; writer of cook books; proprietor and teacher at both Nick Nairn Cook Schools (one in Port of Menteith, one in Aberdeen) (www.nicknairn.com); proprietor and consultant at Nick Nairn Consulting (www.nicknairn.com) which operates Kailyard restaurant by Nick Nairn at Doubletree Hilton Dunblane Hydro. He has Nick Nairn food range, including shortbread biscuits, oatcakes, breakfast cereals and bread products sold in Scottish supermarkets, including Morrisons. Honours: 2007 Honorary Doctorate from Stirling University for outstanding contribution to Scottish cuisine and promoting healthy eating, plus multiple food awards including 2003 Fellowship to the Master Chefs of Great Britain; Glenfiddich Spirit of Scotland Awards 2000 for contribution to Food & Drink; 1996 Scottish Chef of the Year; 1991 Michelin star at Braeval Restaurant; 1986 Scottish Field/Bollinger Newcomer of the Year. Books: Nick has published 10 cook books of his own and collaborated on many others. These include: Nick Nairn Cook School Book, 2008; Fish 'n' Tips, 2006; Nick Nairn's Top 100 Chicken Recipes, 2004; Great British Menu, 2006; New Scottish Cookery, 2002; Nick Nairn's Top 100 Salmon Recipes, 2002; Island Harvest, 1998; Wild Harvest I and II, 1996/7. Television: Nick appears regularly on Saturday Kitchen, Landward, The One Show, This Morning. Other television: Paul & Nick's Big Food Trip, 2 series, 2012/13; series 3, 2015; 2010 Channel 4, co-presenter, Iron Chef UK; 2009 ITV, presenter, Taste The Nation; 2009 BBC2, presenter, Eating In The Sun; 2009 BBC2, Put Your Menu Where Your Mouth Is; 2009 onwards: BBC1, The One Show, presenter of one-off specials; 2007 BBC2, represented Scotland, Great British Menu; 2007-present, BBC2 Scotland co-presenter, Landward; 2007-present, BBC1 presenter and contributor, Saturday Kitchen; 2006 BBC2, finalist for Scotland, Great British Menu; 2003 BBC Scotland presenter, Nick Nairn And The Dinner Ladies; 2003 Actor, Scottish Executive Healthy Eating advertising campaign; 2002 BBC1, presenter So You Think You're A Good Driver?; Foodfest 2001, TV advertising campaign; 2001 BBC2, presenter Kitchen Invaders; 2000 BBC radio Scotland, presenter Cooking With History; 2000 Carlton TV presenter, Back To Basics with Nick Nairn; 1998 ITV presenter, GMTV Christmas Cooking with Nick Nairn; 1998-present, BBC1 presenter, Celebrity Ready Steady Cook; 1997 BBC1, Island Harvest; 1996 BBC2, Wild Harvest 2 with Nick Nairn; 1996-98 BBC2 Presenter, Who'll Do The Pudding; Weakest Link, Chefs TV Blunders, Beechgrove Garden, This Morning and Good Food Live; Masterchef, Light lunch and Carlton Daily, appearances on Friends Like These, Celebrity; regular contributor to Food and Drink, Masterchef, Junior, from 1996; BBC2 presenter, Ready Steady Cook, 1996-2010; BBC2, Wild Harvest with Nick Nairn, 1996. B. 12.1.59, Stirling. Educ. Mclaren High School, Callander; Merchant Navy 1976-83. Became chef, self-taught. Previous restaurants: Braeval, Aberfoyle, 1986; Nairns, Glasgow 1997. Recreations: cycling; hill-walking; eating out; travel. Nick is married with 2 children. Address:

(b.) Nick Nairn Enterprise, Nick Nairn Cook School, Port of Menteith, Stirling FK8 3JZ; T.-01877 389 900. E-mail: info@nicknairncookschool.com

Nanjiani, Shereen, MA (Hons). Presenter, BBC Radio Scotland, since 2006; Journalist, Scottish Television, 1983-2006; b. 4.10.61, Elderslie. Educ. John Neilson High School, Paisley; Glasgow University. Joined STV as a trainee journalist, 1983; moved to reporting two years later; became presenter of Scotland Today, 1985; presented election programmes; presented, Secret Scotland documentary series; presented Scottish Politician of the Year Awards.

Napier, Brian William, MA, LLB, PhD, QC. Advocate (and barrister at the English bar), since 1996; Queen's Counsel, since 2002; b. 09.01.49, Dublin, Republic of Ireland; m., Elizabeth. Educ. George Watson's College, Edinburgh; University of Edinburgh; University of Cambridge. Lecturer and Teacher of Law, Queens' College, Cambridge, 1974-89; Professor of Law, Queen Mary College, University of London, 1989-96. Recreations: walking; music. Address: (b.) c/o Faculty of Advocates, Edinburgh EH1 1RF.

Napier, 15th Lord, 6th Baron Ettrick (Francis David Charles Napier); b. 3.11.62; m., Zara Jane McCalmon; 2 c. Clan Chief of Clan Napier; 12th baronet of Nova Scotia. Succeeded to the title, 2012.

Napier, Sheriff Graeme. Sheriff, Grampian, Highlands and Islands at Aberdeen. Address: Sheriff Court House, Castle Street, Aberdeen AB10 1WP.

Nash, Professor Anthony Aubrey, BSc, MSc, PhD, FMedSci, FRSE. Professor of Veterinary Pathology, Edinburgh University, since 1994; Group Leader and Director, Centre for Infectious Diseases, Roslin Institute; b. 6.3.49, Coalville; m., Marion Ellen Bazeley; 4 d. Educ. Nenbridge Secondary Modern School; Queen Elizabeth College, London University. Lecturer, Department of Pathology, Cambridge University, 1984; Visiting Investigator, Scripps Research Institute, La Jolla, USA, 1989; Professor and Head, Department of Veterinary Pathology, Edinburgh University, since 1994; Director, Centre for Infectious Diseases, Edinburgh University. Eleanor Roosevelt Cancer Fellowship, 1989-90. Recreations: family; gardening; football. Address: (b.) The Roslin Institute, University of Edinburgh, Easter Bush, Edinburgh EH25 9RG; T.-0131 651 9177; e-mail: tony.nash@ed.ac.uk

Nash, Derek Andrew, LLB, DipLegPrac, NP, WS. Partner, Lindsays WS, Solicitors, since 2003; b. 18.12.64, Glasgow; m., Anne; 1 s.; 1 d. Educ. Daniel Stewart's and Melville College, Edinburgh; University of Edinburgh. Training, Balfour and Manson, Solicitors, 1987-89; Orr MacQueen WS: Assistant, 1990-92, Associate, 1992-95, Partner, 1995-99; Partner, Skene Edwards WS, 1999-2003. Trustee, Heralds Trust. Recreations: golf; family; church; books; film. Address: (b.) Caledonian Exchange, 19A Canning Street, Edinburgh EH3 8HE; T.-0131 656 5734; e-mail: dan@lindsays.co.uk

Nash, Pamela. MP (Labour), Airdrie and Shotts, 2010-2015; b. 24.6.84, Airdrie. Educ. St Margaret's School, Airdrie; Glasgow University. Formerly constituency assistant for John Reid and subsequently his parliamentary assistant for 3 years.

Nash, Victoria Jane, BSc, PhD. Director for Scotland, Ofcom (Office of Communications), since 2004; b. 17.6.57, Northampton; m., Robin Campbell; 2 step d. Educ. Cheadle Hulme School; Oxford Polytechnic; Stirling University. Senior Research Officer, Scottish Office Education Department, 1982-83; Project Co-ordinator, Scottish

Council for Educational Technology, 1983-85; Policy Analyst, then Assistant Chief Executive, then Chief Executive, Fife Regional Council, 1985-96; Director, Scottish Water and Sewerage Customers Council, 1996-99; Chief Executive, East Dunbartonshire Council, 1999-2004. Board Member: Scottish Opera, 2001-05, Scottish Ballet, 2001-09, NHS Forth Valley, 2006-2014 (Vice-Chairman, since 2011). Recreations: singing; swimming; cats; bird watching. Address: (b.) 39 St Vincent Place, Glasgow G1 2ER; T.-0141 229 7400.
E-mail: vicki.nash@ofcom.org.uk

Naylor, (Charles) John, OBE, MA, CCMI, FRSA. Chair, Office of the Scottish Charity Regulator, 2006-2011; b. 17.8.43, Newcastle upon Tyne; m., Margery Thomson; 2 s. Educ. Royal Grammar School, Newcastle upon Tyne; Haberdashers' Aske's School, Elstree; Clare College, Cambridge University. Director, YMCA National Centre, Lakeside, Cumbria, 1975-80; National Council of YMCAs: Deputy Secretary, 1980-82, National Secretary, 1982-93; Chief Executive, Carnegie United Kingdom Trust, 1993-2003. Member and Chairman, YMCA European and World Committees, 1976-92; Chair, Association of Heads of Outdoor Education Centres, 1979-80; Chair, MSC and DES Working Party on Residential Experience and Unemployment, 1980-81; Member, National Advisory Council for Youth Service, 1985-88; Vice-Chairman, National Council for Voluntary Youth Services, 1985-88; Founding Convener, Scottish Grant-making Trusts' Group, 1994-97; Chairman, Brathay Exploration Group, 1995-2000, Trustee, 2000-06; Group Scout Leader, 82nd Inverleith (Cramond) Scouts, 1996-2003; Member, Development Grants Board, Scout Association (UK), since 2002, Chairman, 2005-2010; Member, Scottish Charity Law Review Commission, 2000-01; Big Lottery Fund (BLF) UK Board Member, 2004-06; Medical Research Scotland Board Member, 2005-2014; Chair, BLF Community Fund Scotland Committee; Chairman, BLF Scotland Young Peoples Fund; Treasurer and Trustee, The Tomorrow Project, 2002-2013; Chair, RSA Scotland, 2012-2014; President, YMCA Scotland, since 2012; Member, UK Scout Council, 2005-2010; Chair, Strange Town Youth Theatre Company, since 2011; Board Member: Foundation Scotland, since 2011, National Trust for Scotland Audit and Risk Management Committee, since 2011; Elder, Cramond Kirk, since 1998. Publications: Guide to Scottish Grant-making Trusts; Writing Better Fund Raising Applications (Contributor); Charity Law and Change: British and German Perspectives (Contributor); contributions to other books and periodicals. Address: (b.) Orchard House, 25B Cramond Glebe Road, Edinburgh EH4 6NT; T.-0131 312 8956.

Neil, Alex., MA (Hons). MSP (SNP), Airdrie and Shotts, since 2011, Central Scotland, 1999-2011; Cabinet Secretary for Social Justice, Communities and Pensioners' Rights, 2014-16; Cabinet Secretary for Health and Wellbeing, 2012-14; Cabinet Secretary for Infrastructure and Capital Investment, 2011-12; Minister for Housing and Communities, 2009-2011; (former Deputy Convener, European and External Relations Committee; former Member, Finance Committee; former Member, Regional Congress of the Council of Europe; former Convener, Enterprise and Culture Committee, 2004-07, former Chairman, Enterprise and Lifelong Learning Committee, 2000-03); Economic Consultant; b. 22.8.51, Irvine; m., Isabella Kerr; 1 s. Educ. Dalmellington High School; Ayr Academy; Dundee University. Scottish Research Officer, Labour Party, 1975; General Secretary, Scottish Labour Party (SLP), 1976; Marketing Manager, 1979-83; Director: Cumnock and Doon Enterprise Trust, 1983-87, Prince's Scottish Youth Business Trust, 1987-89; Chairman, Network Scotland Ltd., 1987-93; Policy Vice-Convener, Scottish National Party, 1994-2000. Recreations: family; reading; gardening; travel. Address: (h.) 26 Overmills Road, Ayr KA7 3LQ; T.-01292 286675.

Neil, Andrew Ferguson, MA (Hons), FRSA. Publisher, The Scotsman, Scotland on Sunday, Edinburgh Evening News, Scotsman.com, 1996-2006; Chief Executive: The Business, 1999-2008; Chairman: The Spectator, since 2004, Spectator Business, 2008-2010, Apollo, since 2004, handbag.com, 2004-06; Presenter: This Week with Andrew Neil, BBC1, The Sunday Politics, BBC1, The Daily Politics, BBC2, Straight Talk, BBC News Channel, 2006-2010; Chairman: World Media Rights, since 2005, ITP Dubai, since 2006, Peters, Fraser and Dunlop, 2008-2010; Lord Rector, University of St. Andrews, 1999-2002; b. 21.5.49. Educ. Paisley Grammar School; Glasgow University. Conservative Research Department, 1971-72; Correspondent in Belfast, London, Washington, New York, for The Economist, 1973-82,UK Editor, London, 1982-83; Editor, Sunday Times, 1983-94; Executive Chairman, Sky TV, 1988-90; Executive Editor, Fox News, New York, 1994; author of Full Disclosure (autobiography). Address: (b.) Glenburn Enterprises, Flat 3, 53 Onslow Gardens, London SW7 3QF; T.-020 7581 1655.
E-mail: afneil@icloud.com

Neil, John, OBE. Honorary President, The Boys' Brigade UK & Republic of Ireland, since 2005; b. 19.04.35, Coatbridge; m., Nancy McCreadie Henry (deceased); 1 s.; 1 d. Educ. Airdrie Academy; Coatbridge Albert Secondary. Structural Engineering Industry, Wm. Bain & Co. Ltd., Coatbridge, 1951-61; Military Service, RAF Regiment, Egypt & Iraq, 1953-55; various professional positions, The Boys' Brigade: Secretary for Leadership Training (Scotland and Ireland), 1961-79; Chief Executive, Glasgow Battalion, 1979-2000; Brigade President, United Kingdom & Republic of Ireland, 2003-05; Ambassadorial BB Tours to New Zealand, Hong Kong, Ghana, South Africa, Thailand, China and Australia. National Youth Agency for Scotland (YouthLink Scotland): Representative Member, 1997-98, Vice-Chairman, 1998-2001, Chairman to Board of Directors, 2001-05; various positions in The Church of Scotland including Elder, Hamilton Old Parish Church, since 1975, Treasurer and Finance Convener, 1988-98; Chairman, National Audit Committee and Vice-Convener, General Assembly Central Coordinating Committee, 2001-05. Fundraiser & Financial Adviser to major Youth Development Projects, since 1967; Fundraising Advisor to The Boys' Brigade Hong Kong, since 2011; Musical Director & Organist, Lanarkshire Churches, since 1970; Member, The Duke of Edinburgh's Award Committee for Scotland, 1984-88; Founding Trustee (& Secretary), The Sir James Robertson Charitable Trust, 1994-2012; Trustee, Netherton Amateur Athletic Association Sports Trust, 1994-2000; Honorary Life Member, St Andrews Ambulance Association Scotland, since 1994; Holder of The Lord Provost of Glasgow Gold Medal "for Public Service" 2000; Tax Commissioner for Lanark Division, 2001-05; Chairman, Parliamentary Cross Party Conference on Anti-Social Behaviour Bill, 2002; Member, The Merchants House of Glasgow, since 2002; Chairman to Board of Trustees, Search for Truth Charitable Trust, 2007-09; Initiator and Patron, Glasgow Stedfast Association, 2008-2015; National President and Chairman, Federation of Stedfast Associations United Kingdom and Republic of Ireland, 2013-2015. Publications: series of educational work books for young people, on Overseas Mission; Brigade Song Book; Text Books on specialised B.B. subjects; Historic Millennium Directory of The Old Parish Church of Hamilton, 2000. Recreations: golf; music; reading; spectator sports; overseas travel. Address: (h.) 150 Silvertonhill Avenue, Hamilton, South Lanarkshire ML3 7PP; T.-01698 335462; e-mail: jneilbb@blueyonder.co.uk

Neilson, Margaret Marion, MA (Hons), LLB, DipLP. Resident Sheriff in Inverness; formerly Part-time Sheriff, Part-time Employment Judge, Part-time Immigration Judge, Part-time Judge of the Social Entitlement Chamber, Partner,

Balfour & Manson; b. Falkirk. Educ. Mary Erskine School, Edinburgh; Edinburgh University. Recreations: scuba diving; travel; hillwalking.

Neilson, Mike. Director for Digital, Scottish Government, since 2012; previously Acting Director General for Enterprise and Environment. Worked for the UK Treasury, the UK Permanent Representation in Brussels and for the European Commission before moving to the Scottish Government; has worked on a wide range of public policy issues from financial regulation to environmental policy and has experience of public sector structural reform, particularly in the water, housing and marine sectors. Address: (b.) Scottish Government, Victoria Quay, Edinburgh EH6 5QQ.

Nelson, Donald Bruce, BSc, MBA, PhD, FCMI. Registrar, College of Science and Engineering, University of Edinburgh, since 2009; b. 9.8.58, Stranraer; m., Christine Diane Thorburn; 1 s.; 1 d. Educ. Stranraer Academy; University of Glasgow; University of Edinburgh. HM Inspector of Taxes, 1983-84; University of Edinburgh: various administrative posts, 1984-98, Director of Planning, 1998-2003, Director of Planning and Deputy Secretary, 2003-04, Academic Registrar and Deputy Secretary, 2004-09; Director, Edinburgh University Press, 2001-03. Director, FloWave TT Ltd; Director, SSTRIC Ltd; Chairman, Edinburgh South Liberal Association, 1986-88; Treasurer, Edinburgh South Liberal Democrats, 1988-91; Member, The Association of University Teachers Administrative Staff Committee, 1991-97/Chairperson, 1994-97; Member, Association of University Administrators Board of Trustees, 2003-12; Vice-Chair and Chair-Elect, 2005-06/Chair, 2006-08, Treasurer, 2010-12; Member, Higher Education Senior Managers Forum, 2006-08; Non-Executive Board Member, Student Awards Agency Scotland, 2007-13; Member of Court, University of the Highlands and Islands, 2011-14. Awarded Robbie Ewen Fellowship for University Administrators, 1997. Recreations: reading; listening to classical music; Stranraer Football Club; wilfing. Address: (h.) 47 Beauchamp Road, Edinburgh EH16 6LU; T.-0131-664 3020; e-mail: d.b.nelson@ed.ac.uk

Nelson, (Peter) Frederick, BSc, CEng, MIEE. Senior Consultant, Electrical Engineering, Atkins Power Generation; b. 2.9.52, Glasgow; m., (Caroline) Ann; 3 s. Educ. John Neilson; Strathclyde University. President, Scottish Canoe Association, 1980-90; Member, Commonwealth Games Council for Scotland, since 1982; Chairman, Scottish Sports Association, 1990-96; Member, Scottish Sports Council, 1990-98; Chairman, Scottish Outdoor Recreation Network, 2000-06; Elder, Davidson's Mains Parish Church. Recreations: kayaking; cycling; DIY. Address: (h.) 11 Barnton Park Place, Edinburgh EH4 6ET.

Ness, James Iain, LLB, NP. Solicitor; Deputy Registrar, Law Society of Scotland, since 2008; b. 5.7.57, Johannesburg; m., Anne; 1 s.; 1 d. Educ. Robert Gordon's, Aberdeen; Edinburgh University. Apprenticed, Connell & Connell, Edinburgh; Assistant, then Partner, then Senior Partner, Austins. Past President, Rotary Club of Dalbeattie. Recreation: skiing. Address: (b.) 26 Drumsheugh Gardens, Edinburgh; T.-0131 226 7411.

Neville, Richard. Editor, Courier and Advertiser, Dundee, since 2011. Career History: Edinburgh Evening News; Daily Record and The Press, York, then The Scotsman as News Editor and then Deputy Editor, then Editor, Business AM, 2000-2002, then Deputy Editor of the Press and Journal, Aberdeen, 2003-2011. Address: The Courier, 80 Kingsway East, Dundee DD4 8SL; T.-01382 223131; e-mail: editor@thecourier.co.uk

Newell, Emeritus Professor Alan F., MBE, BSc, PhD, FIEE, CEng, FBCS, FRSE, ILTM, HonFCSLT. NCR Professor of Electronics and Microcomputer Systems, Dundee University, since 1980; Director, Dundee University Microcomputer Centre, since 1980; (Head, Department of Applied Computing, 1997-2002, Deputy Principal, 1993-95); Academic Leader, Queen Mother Research Centre for Information Technology to support older people, 2003-06; b. 1.3.41, Birmingham; m., Margaret; 1 s.; 2 d. Educ. St. Philip's Grammar School; Birmingham University. Research Engineer, Standard Telecommunication Laboratories; Lecturer, Department of Electronics, Southampton University. Recreations: family life; skiing; sailing. Address: (b.) School of Computing, Dundee University, Dundee, DD1 4HN; T.-01382 388085.

Newlands, Gavin. MP (SNP), Paisley and Renfrewshire North, since 2015; b. 2.2.80, Paisley; m., Lynn; 2 d. Educ. St James' Primary School; Trinity High School; James Watt College. Member of the SNP for 25 years, joining the youth wing of the party in 1992, getting involved during the campaigns against the poll tax; became a local community council councillor for Renfrew in 2011 and has supported many local causes, including a West of Scotland-based foodbank. Member of Paisley Rugby Club for 16 years, serving as club captain for 3 years. Address: House of Commons, London SW1A 0AA.

Newlands, James Nichol, HNC, DipTechEd. Honorary Sheriff at Selkirk, since 1999; b. 20.11.37, Selkirk; m., Esther; 1 s.; 1 d. Educ. Selkirk High School; Napier University; Moray House College. Engineering Apprenticeship, 1952-58; National Service, KOSB, 1958-60; Engineering Industry, 1960-67; Lecturer, Galashiels College of FE, 1967-69; Teacher Training, Moray House, 1969-71; Teacher of Technical Education, Galashiels Academy, 1971-86; Principal Teacher of Technical Education, Selkirk High School, 1986-96; retired, 1996; Selkirk Provost, 1997-2001. Deacon of The Selkirk Incorporation of Hammermen, 1983-89, now a Life Member; served as a Reader on "The Borders Talking Newspaper" for 12 years, one of the founding members but now retired. Delivered the Address at The Redeswire Stone, Carter Bar, 2002; gave The Flodden Oration on Flodden Hill, 1999; delivered The Melrose Oration in Melrose Abbey, 2003; also The Trysten Tree Address in Kelso, 2004; appointed as a case worker for Military Charity SSAFA in 2002 - ongoing. Publications: author of "The History of The Selkirk Hammermen"; co-author of "The Flower of The Forest". Recreation: rugby supporter (captained Selkirk RFC, 1960-61). Address: (h.) 5 Mavis Bank, Selkirk TD7 4EA; T.-01750 20492.

Newman, Professor Simon Peter, BA, MA, MA, PhD, FRSA, FRHistS. Sir Denis Brogan Professor of American Studies, University of Glasgow, since 2002; b. 8.7.60, Basildon; m., Marina Moskowitz. Educ. St. Joseph's College, Ipswich; University of Nottingham; University of Wisconsin; Princeton University. Assistant Professor of History, Northern Illinois University, 1991-97; Mellon Postdoctoral Fellow in the Humanities, University of Pennsylvania, 1994-95; Senior Lecturer in History, University of Glasgow, 1997-2002; Director, Andrew Hook Centre for American Studies, University of Glasgow, 1997-2002; Chairman, British Association for American Studies, since 2004. Philip A. Rollins Fellowship in History, Princeton University, 1989-90; Mellon Postdoctoral

Fellowship in the Humanities, University of Pennsylvania, 1994-95; Resident Fellowship, Rockefeller Study and Conference Center, Bellagio, Italy, 1998; Coca Cola Fellowship, International Center for Jefferson Studies, Monticelle, Virginia, 2000; Member, Executive Committee, British Association for American Studies, 1999-2006; Chair, Scottish Association for the Study of America, 2001-03; former Chairman, British Association for American Studies. Publications: Vue D'Amérique: La Révolution Française Jugée Par Les Américains (Co-editor), 1989; Parades and the Politics of the Street: Festive Culture in the Early American Republic, 1997; Embodied History: The Lives of the Poor in Early Philadelphia, 2003. Clubs: Reform Club. Recreations: long distance and cross country running; cooking. Address: (b.) Modern History, 1 University Gardens, University of Glasgow, Glasgow G12 8QQ; T.-0141-330 3585; e-mail:spn@arts.gla.ac.uk

Ni, Professor Xiongwei, BSc, PhD, CEng, FIChemE, Professor of Process and Reaction Engineering, Heriot-Watt University, since 1999; b. 22.2.60, Beijing, China; m., Wendy Margaret Hogg; 1s.; 1d. Educ. Yan-Ting Primary and High School, Sichuan China; Chong-Qing University, Sichuan; Leeds University. Research Fellow, Edinburgh University, 1986-89; Research Associate, Cambridge University, 1989-91; Lecturer, Teeside University, 1991-94; Strathclyde University: Lecturer, 1994-96; Senior Lecturer, 1996-97; Senior Lecturer, Heriot-Watt University, 1997-99; Foxwell Memorial Award, Institute of Energy, 1985. Recreations: tennis; badminton; golf; bridge. Address: (b.) School of Engineering and Physical Sciences, Heriot-Watt University, Edinburgh, EH14 4AS; T.-0131-451 3781; e-mail: X.Ni@hw.ac.uk

Nicholls, Brian, BSc (Econ). Senior Business Consultant, Scottish Enterprise, 1991-98; Director, Scottish Opera, 1993-99; b. 21.9.28, London; m., Mary Elizabeth Harley; 1 s.; 2 d. Educ. Haberdashers' Aske's School; London University; Harvard Business School. George Wimpey Ltd., 1951-55; Constructors John Brown Ltd., 1955-75; Director, CJB Projects Ltd., 1972-75; Director, CJB Pipelines Ltd., 1974-75; Deputy Chairman, CJB Mohandessi Iran Ltd., 1974-75; Industrial Adviser to Secretary of State for Trade, 1975-78; Director: John Brown Engineering Ltd., 1978-91, John Brown Engineering Gas Turbines Ltd., 1978-91, Rugby Power Company Ltd., 1990-91; Vice President, John Brown Power Ltd., 1987-90; Member: Council, British Railway Export Group, 1976-78, British Overseas Trade Board, 1978; Vice President, Scottish Council Development and Industry, 1991-98; Fellow, Scottish Council Development and Industry, 1998. Publications: Columnist for Jazz Journal, 1952-58; Editor: Jazz News, 1957-59. Deputy Chairman, National Jazz Federation, 1954-59. Recreations: music; reading; walking. Address: (h.) Blairlogie Park, Blairlogie, by Stirling FK9 5PY; T.-01259 761497.

Nicholson, Professor Keith, BSc (Hons), MSc, PhD, Chem, CISA, CISM, MIoD, FAAG, FRSC. Independent Technology Strategy and Security Advisor & CEO, Skaill Advisory Services, since 2000; b. Lochiver; m. Angela. Educ. Kelvin; Univ. Manchester; Univ. Strathclyde. Non-executive Board Member, Scottish Natural Heritage, since 2010; Chair, Audit & Risk Committee, Scottish Natural Heritage, since 2012; Non-executive Board Member, Scottish Environmental Protection Agency, since 2011; Member, Audit Committee, SEPA, since 2011; Non-executive Board Member, Scottish Higher and Further Education Funding Council, since 2012; Member, Audit Committee, Scottish Higher and Further Education Funding Council, since 2012; Member, Research & Knowledge Exchange Committee, Scottish Higher and Further

Education Funding Council, since 2012; Member & Chair, Revenue Scotland, since 2015; Technology Advisor, Scottish Government, since 2008; Member, Scottish Government Cyber Security Advisory Board, since 2011; Hon. Fellow, Univ. Paisley, 2002-07; CEO, TP Group, 1991-2000; Professor of Energy & Environmental Engineering, University of Aalborg, Denmark, 1999-2000; Professor of Energy & The Environment, Robert Gordon University, Aberdeen, 1991-99; A. Professor, Geochemistry, Geothermal Energy Institute, University of Auckland, New Zealand, 1987-1991; CEO, Envirosurveys, Auckland, New Zealand, 1987-1990. Publications: Doing Business on the Internet, 1993; Geothermal Fluids: Chemistry & Exploration Techniques, 1993, 2011; Skye: The Complete Visitors Guide (Co-author), 1994; Geothermal Energy, 1987 (Ed); Geothermal Energy, 1989 (Ed); Manganese Mineralisation (Ed), 1997; Energy & the Environment (Ed), 1999; over 150 scientific papers and reports. Best Business Award, 1993; winning medallist, IoD IT Director, 2002. Recreations: wildlife; hill-walking; photography; golf; archaeology; antiquarian books; malt whisky. Address: (b.) Scottish Natural Heritage, Great Glen House, Leachkin Road, Inverness IV3 8NW. E-mail: knicholson@knicholson.co.uk

Nicholson, Peter Alexander, LLB (Hons). Editor, Journal of the Law Society of Scotland, since 2004; Deputy Editor, 2003-04; Managing Editor, W. Green, The Scottish Law Publisher, 1989-2003; General Editor, Scots Law Times, 1985-2003; Scottish Editor, Current Law, 1985-96; General Editor, Greens Weekly Digest, 1986-2003; b. 22.5.58, Stirling; m., Morag Ann Fraser; 1 s.; 3 d. Educ. St. David's RC High School, Dalkeith; Edinburgh University. Admitted as Solicitor, 1981. Reporter, Client Relations Office, Law Society of Scotland, 2005-2012. Lay Minister of the Eucharist. Recreations: choral singing; gardening; keeping fit. Address: (h.) 32 Buckstone Loan, Edinburgh EH10 6UD; T.-0131-445 1570.

Nickson of Renagour, Lord (David Wigley Nickson), KBE (1987), CBE (1981), DL, CBIM, FRSE. Life Peer (1994); Chancellor, Glasgow Caledonian University, 1993-2002; Vice Lieutenant, Stirling and Falkirk, 1997-2004 (Deputy Lieutenant, 1982-97); b. 27.11.29, Eton; m., Helen Louise Cockcraft (deceased 2012); 3 d.; m. (2), Eira Drysdale, 2013. Educ. Eton College; Royal Military Academy, Sandhurst. Commissioned, Coldstream Guards, 1949-54; William Collins: joined, 1954, Director, 1961-85, Joint Managing Director, 1967, Vice-Chairman, 1976-83, Group Managing Director, 1979-82; Director: Scottish United Investors plc, 1970-83, General Accident plc, 1971-98 (Deputy Chairman, 1993-98), Scottish & Newcastle Breweries plc, 1981-95 (Chairman, 1983-89), Radio Clyde Ltd., 1982-85, National Australia Bank Ltd., 1991-96, National Australian Group (UK) Ltd., 1993-98, Hambros PLC, 1989-98; Chairman, Clydesdale Bank, 1991-98 (Director, 1981-98); Chairman, Pan Books, 1982-83; Chairman, Scottish Enterprise, 1990-93 (SDA, 1988-90); President, CBI, 1986-88; Chairman, CBI in Scotland, 1979-81; Chairman, Countryside Commission for Scotland, 1983-86; Member: Scottish Industrial Development Advisory Board, 1975-80, Scottish Committee, Design Council, 1978-81, Scottish Economic Council, 1980-95, National Economic Development Council, 1985-88; Chairman, Atlantic Salmon Trust, 1988-95; Chairman, Senior Salaries Review Body, 1989-95; President, Association of District Salmon Fisheries Board, 1996-2012; Chairman, Secretary of State for Scotland's Scottish Salmon Strategy Task Force, 1995-97; Chairman, Scottish Advisory Committee, Imperial Cancer Research Fund, 1994-2001; Trustee: Princes Youth Business Trust, 1987-90, Princess Royal's Trust for Carers, 1990-94; Captain of Queen's Bodyguard for Scotland (Royal Company of Archers); D.Univ, Stirling,

1986; Hon. DBA Napier Polytechnic, 1990; Honorary Fellow, Paisley College, 1992; Honorary Freeman, Fishmongers Company, 1999, Honorary Freeman, City of London, 1999. Recreations: fishing; bird-watching; the countryside. Address: (h.) The River House, Doune, Perthshire FK16 6DA; T.-01786 841614.

Nicol, Rev. Douglas Alexander Oag, MA, BD (Hons). Minister of Hobkirk and Southdean linked with Ruberslaw; b. 5.4.48, Dunfermline; m., Anne Wilson Gillespie; 2 s.; 1 d. Educ. Kirkcaldy High School; Edinburgh University; Glasgow University. Assistant Warden, St. Ninian's Centre, Crieff, 1972-76; Minister, Lochside, Dumfries, 1976-82; Minister, St. Columba, Kilmacolm, 1982-91. Chairman, Board of Directors, National Bible Society of Scotland, 1984-87; Convener, Board of National Mission, Church of Scotland, 1990-91; General Secretary, Church of Scotland Board of National Mission, 1991-2005; Secretary, Church of Scotland Mission and Discipleship Council, 2005-2009. Recreations: family life and family history; travel; athletics. Address: The Manse, Denholm TD9 8NB; T.-01450 870268; e-mail: daon@lineone.net

Nicoll, Alan John, LLB, NP. Senior Partner, Laurie and Company Solicitors LLP, since 2002; b. 28.7.55, Aberdeen; m., Carole Jane Burtt; 2 s.; 2 d. Educ. Robert Gordon's College; University of Aberdeen. Served Apprenticeship at AC Morrison & Richards, 1976-78; Employed as Solicitor, Edmonds & Ledingham, 1978-80; Employed by John Laurie & Co, 1980-81, became a Partner in 1981. Recreations: tennis; golf; skiing; hillwalking; cycling. Address: (b.) 17 Victoria Street, Aberdeen AB10 1UU; T.-01224 645085; e-mail: alan@laurieandco.co.uk

Nicoll, Andrew Ramsay, MA (Hons), MPhil, GradDipARM, RMARA. Development Manager, Scran, RCAHMS, since 2014; Archivist, Society of Helpers of the Holy Souls, British Province, since 2013; Outreach Officer, ScotlandsPlaces, Royal Commission on the Ancient and Historical Monuments of Scotland, 2013-2014; Keeper of The Scottish Catholic Archives, 2003-2012; b. 2.5.78, Dundee. Educ. Forfar Academy; University of Dundee; University College London. Treasurer, Scottish Catholic Historical Association, since 2010; Director and Trustee, Archives and Records Association, United Kingdom and Ireland, 2009-2012. Address: (b.) RCAHMS, John Sinclair House, 16 Bernard Terrace, Edinburgh EH8 9NX; T.-0131 662 1456.

Nicolson, Professor Donald James, BA, LLB, PhD. Professor of Law, Strathclyde University, since 2001; b. 1.6.61, Cape Town. Educ. Fish Hoek High School; University of Cape Town; Cambridge University. Temporary Lecturer, University of Cape Town, 1984; Lecturer, Reading University, 1989-92; Lecturer, Bristol University, 1992-2000. Publications: Professional Legal Ethics: Critical Interrogations, 1999; Feminist Perspectives on Criminal Law, 2000. Recreations: skiing; surfing; cycling; jazz; literature. Address: (b.) School of Law, Strathclyde University, 173 Stenhouse Building, 173 Cathedral Street, Glasgow G64 0RQ; T.-0141-548 3978.

Nicolson, John, MA (Hons). MP (SNP), East Dunbartonshire, since 2015; SNP spokesperson on Culture, Media and Sport in the House of Commons; b. 1961, Glasgow. Educ. University of Glasgow; Harvard University. Joined the BBC in 1987; reported for a variety of heavyweight BBC programmes including On the Record, Panorama, Assignment, The Late Show, and numerous live general election, European election, and budget programmes; reporter on Newsnight for three years, presented Watchdog Healthcheck on BBC1 and the BBC's Breakfast News; studio presenter for the BBC on 11 September 2001 as the Twin Towers collapsed, anchoring live on BBC News 24 and BBC1 - a broadcast which won the BBC a Foreign Press Association award for best breaking news coverage; moved to ITV and presented Live with John Nicolson, a three-hour morning news magazine on the ITV News Channel; guest reported on Holiday; presented radio show on LBC 97.3 and has been a panellist on Radio 4's long running comedy show The News Quiz; regular contributor to the Cumulus Media Networks radio programme The John Batchelor Show. Writes extensively about architecture and design, as well as politics and travel. Address: House of Commons, London SW1A 0AA.

Nicolson, John Alick (Jan); b. 26.9.45, Inverness; m., Effie; 1 s. Educ. Portree High School. Chairman, Skye and Lochalsh Enterprise, 1991-96; Board Member, Highlands and Islands Enterprise, 1996-98; Chairman, Hi-Screen Ltd., 1997-98; Director: Jansvans Ltd., Isle of Skye Renewables; Director, Mica UK Ltd.; President, Rotary Club of Portree and District, 2010; Founder Member and Past Chairman, Isle of Skye Round Table; Rotary Paul Harris Fellow (PHF), 2012. Recreations: collecting vintage vehicles. Address: (h.) Almondbank, Viewfield Road, Portree, Isle of Skye IV51 9EU; T.-01478 612696.

Nimmo, The Very Rev. Dr. Alexander Emsley, BD, MPhil, PhD, FSA (Scot). Dean of Aberdeen & Orkney, since 2008; Rector of St Margaret's, Aberdeen, since 1990; b. 28.02.53, Glasgow. Educ. University of Aberdeen; University of Edinburgh. Precentor, Inverness Cathedral, 1978-81; Priest-in-Charge, St. Peter's Stornoway, 1981-83, Rector, 1984; Rector, All Saints' Edinburgh, 1984-90. Chairman, 1745 Association, 2011 (Friends of St Machar's Cathedral); Chairman, 1745 Association, 2011-2014. Publications: contributor to Dictionary of Scottish Church History and Theology, 1993; After Columba, After Calvin, 1999 (contributor); A Life Less Ordinary: The Life of Fr John Comper, 2003; contributor to Sir Thomas Urquhart of Cromarty, 2011; occasional papers; The Aberdeen Doctors, 2011; contributor to Living with Jacobitism, 1690-1788, 2014. Address: St. Margaret of Scotland, Gallowgate, Aberdeen AB25 1EA; T.-01224-644969.

Nimmo, Rev. Peter William, BD, ThM. Minister of Old High St. Stephen's Church of Scotland, Inverness, since 2004; b. 19.1.66, Dumbarton; m., Katharina; 1 s.; 1 d. Educ. Vale of Leven Academy, Alexandria; Glasgow University; Princeton Theological Seminary, NJ, USA (Fulbright Scholar). Associate Minister, Currie Kirk, Edinburgh, 1996-98; Minister of High Carntyne Parish Church, Glasgow, 1998-2004. Member: Parish Development Fund Committee, 2005-07, Iona Community Board, 1999-2003; Church and Society Council and Society, Religion and Technology Committee, since 2013; Chair, Waverley Care Highland and Argyll and Bute Advisory Group, 2010-12; Member of the Council of the Church Service Society, since 2014. Address: 24 Damfield Road, Inverness IV2 3HU; T.-01463 250802; e-mail: peternimmo@minister.com

Nimmo Smith, Rt. Hon. Lord (William Austin Nimmo Smith), BA, LLB. Senator of the College of Justice, 1996-2009 (retired); b. 6.11.42, Edinburgh; m., Dr. Jennifer Nimmo Smith; 1 s.; 1 d. Educ. Eton; Balliol College, Oxford; Edinburgh University. Advocate, 1969; Standing Junior Counsel, Department of Employment, 1977-82; QC, 1982; Advocate Depute, 1983-86; Chairman, Medical Appeal Tribunals and Vaccine Damage Tribunals, 1986-91; part-time Member, Scottish Law Commission, 1988-96; Temporary Judge, Court of Session, 1995-96; Outer House, Court of Session, 1996-2005; Inner House, First Division, Court of Session, 2005-09; Privy Counsellor, 2005; Chairman of Council, Cockburn Association (Edinburgh

Civic Trust), 1996-2001. Recreations: mountaineering; music. Address: (b.) Parliament House, Edinburgh EH1 1RQ.

Nisbet, James Barry Consitt, LLB. Stipendiary Magistrate, Glasgow, 1984-2007 (retired); b. 26.7.42, Forfar; m., Elizabeth McKenzie; 2 d. Educ. Forfar Academy; Edinburgh University. Legal Assistant, Warden Bruce & Co., WS, Edinburgh, 1967-68; Legal Assistant, then Junior Depute Town Clerk, then Depute Town Clerk, Perth City Council, 1968-75; Senior Depute Director of Administration, Perth and Kinross District Council, 1975-84. Head Server, St. Ninian's Episcopal Cathedral, Perth; Past Secretary-General, Scottish Guild of Servers. Recreations: transport, especially railways and tramways; archaeology; music; foreign travel; genealogy. Address: (b.) 12 Pitcullen Terrace, Perth PH2 7EQ.

Nish, David. Former Chief Executive, Standard Life plc (2010-2015); b. 5.5.60, Glasgow; m., Caroline; 1 s.; 1 d. Educ. Paisley Grammar School; Glasgow University. Price Waterhouse: Graduate Trainee to Senior Manager, 1981-93, Partner, 1993-97; Deputy Finance Director, Scottish Power, 1997-99, Finance Director, 1999-2005, Executive Director, Infrastructure Division, 2005; Finance Director, Standard Life plc, 2006-2010. Recreations: cycling; travel; family; watching sport.

Noakes, Rab. Director, Neon Productions Limited, since 1995; b. 13.5.47, St. Andrews; m., Stephanie Pordage. Educ. Bell Baxter Senior High School, Cupar, Fife. Minor Civil Service career in the MPNI working in Glasgow, Alloa and London, 1963-67; various labouring jobs including Flying Carpet Servicer, Guardbridge Paper Mill, 1967-69; in 1969 a summer of music residency in Denmark kick-started the ability to make a living from performing, writing, production and recording which continues to this day (15 albums and many songs recorded); in 1987 a contract with BBC culminated in the position of Head of Entertainment at BBC Radio Scotland; since setting up Neon Productions in 1995 thousands of hours have been provided for broadcast on radio and TV including a weekly show, Brand New Country, for BBC Radio Scotland; the company is also a record company and engages in music publishing. Council Member, SAC; Executive Committee, MU. Address: (b.) Studio Two, 19 Marine Crescent, Glasgow G51 1HD; T.-0141 429 6366.
E-mail: mail@go2neon.com

Noble, R. Ross, MBE, MA, FSA (Scot). Museum Curator, 1973-2003 (retired); Member, Scottish Committee of Heritage Lottery Fund, 2009-2015; Member, UNESCO Scotland Committee Network, since 2008; Member, Historic Environment Advisory Council for Scotland, 2003-09; b. 9.6.42, Ayr; m., Jean; 1 s.; 1 d. Educ. Ardrossan Academy; Aberdeen University. Travelling Curator, Scottish Country Life Museums Trust, 1973-76; Curator, Highland Folk Museum and Regional (later Highland) Curator for the local authority's Museum Service, 1976-2003. Elected Fellow, Society of Antiquaries of Scotland, since 1982; Convenor, Scottish Country Life Museums Trust, 2000-07; Elected Director, Newtonmore Community Woodland and Development Trust, 2003-09; Member: Museums Association, Scottish Vernacular Buildings Working Group, British Regional Furniture Society, Scottish History Society; Member and Past President, Society for Folk Life Studies; Member, United Nations Association UK (UNA-UK), since 2012. Publications include: The Cultural Impact of the Highland Clearances, BBC History On-Line, 2001; Earth Buildings in the Central Highlands: Research and Reconstruction. Medieval or Later Rural Settlements: 10 Years On, 2003; "Highland Vernacular Furniture and Context" in Furniture and Fittings in the Traditional Scottish Home, Scottish Vernacular Buildings Working Group, 2007. Recreations: walking; swimming; sailing; painting. Address: (h.) "Creageiro", Church Terrace, Newtonmore PH20 1DT; T.-01540 673392; e-mail: rrossnoble@btinternet.com

Noble, Sir Timothy Peter, Bt, MA, MBA. Chairman, Spark Energy Ltd; Director, International Correspndence Schools Ltd; b. 21.12.43; m., Elizabeth Mary Aitken; 2 s.; 1 d. Educ. University College, Oxford; Gray's Inn, London; INSEAD, Fontainebleau. Recreations: skiing; tennis; golf; music; bridge; wine; astronomy; poetry. Clubs: Bruntsfield, Summit. Address: (h.) Ardnahane, Barnton Avenue, Edinburgh; T.-0131-336 3565.

Nolan, Andrea. Principal, Edinburgh Napier University, since 2013. Educ. Trinity College Dublin. Career: veterinary practice; Researcher, Universities of Cambridge, Bristol and the Technical University, Munich; joined the University of Glasgow in 1989 as Lecturer and rose to become Professor of Veterinary Pharmacology and Dean of the Faculty of Veterinary Medicine; joined the Senior Management Group as Vice Principal for Learning & Teaching in 2004; Senior Vice-Principal & Deputy Vice Chancellor, 2009-2013. Address: (b.) Sighthill Campus, Sighthill Court, Edinburgh EH11 4BN.

Nolan, Fr William. Bishop of Galloway, since 2014; b. 26.1.54. Educ. Cathedral Primary School, Motherwell; St Patrick's Primary School, Craigneuk; St Vincent's College, Langbank; St Mary's College, Blairs. Completed studies for ordination at the Pontifical Scots College, Rome, 1971-78, earning a Licence in Sacred Theology from the Gregorian University in June 1978; ordained priest for the Diocese of Motherwell on 30 June 1977 in St Bernadette's Church, Motherwell; subsequently held the following pastoral assignments: Assistant Priest, Our Lady of Lourdes, East Kilbride, 1978-1980; Assistant Priest, St. David's, Plains, 1980-1983; Assistant Priest, St Bridget's, Baillieston, 1990-1994; Parish Priest, Our Lady of Lourdes, East Kilbride, 1994-2014. Served as Vice-Rector of the Scots College in Rome, 1983-90; appointed Administrator of St John Ogilvie parish, Blantyre in November 2013 and Vicar General of the Motherwell Diocese in June 2014. Address: Diocesan and Pastoral Office, Candida Casa, 8 Corsehill Road, Ayr KA7 2ST; T.-01292 266750.

Normand, Andrew Campbell, LLB (Hons), DipLP. Partner, DAC Beachcroft Scotland LLP; b. 4.12.62, Perth; m., Sheila; 3 s.; 1 d. Educ. Perth High School; Edinburgh University. Traineeship, Nightingale and Bell SSC, 1985-87; Assistant Solicitor, Gray Muirhead WS, 1991-96; Partner, HBJ Gateley Wareing (formerly Henderson Boyd Jackson), 1996-2008. WS Society; Director, Scottish National Jazz Orchestra. Recreations: jazz; piano. Address: (b.) 24 Dublin Street, Edinburgh EH1 3PP; T.-0131 524 7797.
E-mail: cnormand@dacbeachcroft.com

Normand, Sheriff Andrew Christie, CB, MA, LLB, LLM, SSC, FSAScot. Sheriff at Glasgow, since 2003; Crown Agent for Scotland, 1996-2003; b. 7.2.48, Edinburgh; m., Barbara Jean Smith; 2 d. Educ. George Watson's College, Edinburgh; Edinburgh University; Queen's University, Kingston, Ontario.

Norrie, Professor Kenneth McKenzie, LLB, DLP, PhD, FRSE. Professor, University of Strathclyde; b. 23.6.59, Dundee. Educ. Kirkton High School, Dundee; University of

Dundee; University of Aberdeen. Lecturer in Law: University of Dundee, 1982-83, University of Aberdeen, 1983-90; Gastprofessor, Universität Regensburg, Germany, 1990; Senior Lecturer in Law, University of Strathclyde, 1990-95; Visiting Professor, University of Sydney, Australia, 1997; Visiting Professor, Victoria University of Wellington, 2008. Publications: Parent and Child; Defamation; Trusts; Children's Hearings. Recreations: gardening; travel. Address: (b.) Law School, University of Strathclyde, Graham Hills Building, 50 George Street, Glasgow G1 1BA; T.-0141-548 3393.

Norris, Richard, BA (Hons). Director, Scottish Health Council, since 2005; b. 01.04.59, Luton; m., Morag; 2 d. Educ. Branston School, Lincolnshire; City of London Polytechnic. Chief Executive, Centre for Public Policy, 1993-97; Director of Policy, Scottish Association for Mental Health, 1997-2005. Address: (b.) Delta House, 50 West Nile Street, Glasgow G1 2NF; T.-0141 241 6308. E-mail: richard.norris@scottishhealthcouncil.org

Northesk, 15th Earl of (Patrick Charles Carnegy); b. 23.9.40. Music and theatre critic. Educ. Trinity Hall, Cambridge. Written a number of books on Richard Wagner, including one on the subject of his operas that took 40 years to write; also written about stage and theatre, both as an author and critic, and has appeared on radio programmes such as Radio 3's CD Review. Succeeded to title, 2010.

Northrop, Alasdair, BA (Hons). Tourist guide and professional writer; Owner, Caledonia Tours, since 2016; Editor, Scottish Business Insider, 2000-2016; b. 23.5.57, Chalfont-St-Giles; 1 s. Educ. Leamington College for Boys; Middlesex Polytechnic. Reporter, Heart of England Newspapers, 1978-83; Sub Editor, Southern Evening Echo, Southampton, 1983-85; Deputy Editor, North Western Evening Mail, Barrow-in-Furness, 1985-89; Business Editor, Western Daily Press, Bristol, 1989-94; Business Editor, Manchester Evening News, 1994-2000. BT Business Journalist of the Year, 1996; BT North West Business Journalist of the Year, 1996. Recreations: theatre; music; walking; swimming; badminton; travelling.

Nutton, Richard William, MB, BS, MD, FRCS. Consultant Orthopaedic Surgeon, since 1987; Honorary Senior Lecturer, since 1989; b. 16.11.51, Halifax; m., Theresa Mary Turney; 2 s.; 1 d. Educ. Sedbergh School; Newcastle upon Tyne University. Special interest in knee and shoulder surgery; Honorary Medical Adviser to the Scottish Rugby Union; Governor, Merchiston Castle School, Edinburgh. Recreations: fishing; shooting; golf; skiing; cycling. Address: (b.) Royal Infirmary of Edinburgh, Little France, Edinburgh; T.-0131-242 3493.

O

Ó Baoill, Professor Colm, MA, PhD. Professor of Celtic, Aberdeen University, since 1996; b. 22.9.38, Armagh, Ireland; 3 d. Educ. St. Patrick's College, Armagh; Queen's University of Belfast. Assistant Lecturer, Queen's University of Belfast, 1962; Aberdeen University: Lecturer, 1966, Senior Lecturer, 1980, retired 2003. Chief, Gaelic Society, Inverness, 1993. Address: (h.) 19 King's Crescent, Old Aberdeen AB24 3HJ; T.-01224 637064; e-mail: c.oboyle@abdn.ac.uk

O'Brien, Professor James Paul, MA (Hons), MEd, PhD, DipEdTech, FRSA, FIPDA. Professor Emeritus; Dean, Moray House School of Education, Edinburgh University, 2007-09 (retired); b. 23.4.50, Stirling; m., Elaine Margaret Kathleen Smith; 1 d. Educ. St. Mirin's Academy, Paisley; Glasgow University. Teacher, 1973-85; Lecturer, St. Andrew's College of Education, 1985-88, Director, 1988-93, Assistant Principal, 1992-93; Vice-Principal, Moray House Institute, 1993-98; Vice-Dean, Moray House School of Education, 1998-2007. Recreations: soccer; music; reading. Address: (b.) Holyrood Campus, Holyrood Road, Edinburgh EH8 8AQ; T.-0131-651 6357.

O'Brien, His Eminence Keith Michael Patrick Cardinal, KM, GCHS, BSc, DipEd, DD, LLD. Archbishop Emeritus of St. Andrews and Edinburgh; b. 17.3.38, Ballycastle, Northern Ireland. Educ. Saint Patrick's, Dumbarton; Holy Cross Academy, Edinburgh; Edinburgh University; St. Andrew's College, Drygrange; Moray House College of Education. Teacher, St. Columba's High School, Fife; Assistant Priest, Kilsyth, then Bathgate; Spiritual Director, St. Andrew's College, Drygrange; Rector, Blairs College, Aberdeen; ordained Archbishop by Cardinal Gray, 1985; retired, 2013. Created Cardinal by Pope John Paul II on 21 October 2003; 2004: awarded Honorary Doctor of Laws, University of St. Francis Xavier, Antigonish, Nova Scotia; Honorary Doctor of Divinity, University of St. Andrews; Honorary Doctor of Divinity, University of Edinburgh. Recreations: music; walking.

O'Brien, Susan, BA (Hons), BPhil, LLB. Chair of the Historical Child Abuse Inquiry, Scotland, since 2015; Queen's Counsel, since 1998; Advocate, since 1987; b. 13.8.52, Edinburgh; m., Professor Peter Ross; 2 d. Educ. St George's School for Girls, Edinburgh; York University; Edinburgh University. Admitted Solicitor, 1980; Assistant Solicitor, Shepherd and Wedderburn, WS, 1980-86; Standing Junior Counsel to Registrar General, 1991, and to Home Office, 1992-97, and to Keeper of the Registers, 1998; Temporary Sheriff, 1995-99; fee paid Employment Judge, Employment Tribunals, since 2000; Member of Investigatory Powers Tribunal, since 2009; fee paid Chairman of Pensions Appeal Tribunals for Scotland, since 2012; Reporter to Scottish Legal Aid Board, 1999-2005; Chair, Caleb Ness Inquiry for Edinburgh and The Lothians Child Protection Committee, 2003; Chairman, Faculty Services Ltd., (and office bearer in the Faculty of Advocates), 2005-07. Address: (b.) Advocates' Library, Parliament Square, Edinburgh EH1 1RQ; T.-0131-226 5071.

O'Carroll, Derek, LLB (Hons), DipLP. Appointed Sheriff in 2010, based at Airdrie; called to Bar, 2000; part-time Chairman, Social Security Appeals Tribunal, 1999-2007; part-time Chairman, Private Rented Housing Panel for Scotland, 2007-2010; part-time Chairman, Rent Assessment Panel for Scotland, 2002-07; part-time Chairman, Mental Health Tribunal for Scotland, 2005-2010; part-time Sheriff, 2006-2010; b. 20.1.60, St Albans. Educ. Cults Academy, Aberdeen; Edinburgh University. Citizens Rights Office, Edinburgh, 1982-85; Castlemilk Law Centre, Glasgow, 1985; Uludag University, Turkey, 1985-88; Transfert, Paris, 1988-90; Legal Services Agency, Glasgow, 1990-94; Govan Law Centre, Glasgow, 1995-99. Member, Scottish Legal Aid Board, 1998-2002; Convener, Scottish Legal Action Group, 2001-04; Director, Faculty Services Ltd., 2003-07; Member, Council of Faculty of Advocates, 2005-08; Member, Council of the Sheriffs' Association, 2011-2014; Honorary Secretary and Treasurer, Sheriffs' Association, since 2015; Director, Thistle Foundation, 2005-07. Recreations: good food and wine; swimming; pool; keep-fit; travel.
E-mail: sheriffdocarroll@scotcourts.gov.uk

O'Donnell, Annemarie. Chief Executive, Glasgow City Council, since 2014; m.; 2 c. Joined Glasgow District Council from a legal practice in the east end of Glasgow in 1991; worked as a solicitor and then senior solicitor in a team focusing on construction, housing and planning; promoted to Chief Solicitor - leading the council's work on commercial contracts, procurement, planning and environmental law (1996-2003); appointed Assistant Head of Legal and Administrative Services, a new post with responsibility for the running of elections - along with committee services, registrars, litigation, licensing and corporate law; two-year secondment as Depute Director of Social Work Services (played a key role in steering the service through a significant programme of service reform); returned to Corporate Services in 2007, serving as Assistant Director and Head of External Governance; Executive Director of Corporate Services, 2011-2014. Member of the Law Society of Scotland. Address: City Chambers, Glasgow G2 1DU; T.-0141 287 4552.
E-mail: annemarie.o'donnell@glasgow.gov.uk

O'Donnell, Fiona. MP (Labour), East Lothian, 2010-15; b. 27.1.60, Nanaimo, Vancouver Island, Canada; 3 s.; 1 d. Educ. Lochaber High School; University of Glasgow. Member, Select Committee on Scottish Affairs, 2010-2011; Shadow Minister for Fisheries and the Natural Environment, 2011-2012; Member, Select Committee on International Development, 2012-15; Member, GMB.

O'Donnell, Mark, MA (Hons), MSc. Chief Executive, Chest Heart & Stroke Scotland, since 2015. Educ. Portobello High School; University of Edinburgh; Open University. Development Officer, Drugs and Alcohol, West Lothian Council, 2000-02; Director of Projects & Service Development, ASH Scotland, 2002-06; Head of Planning, Performance & Estates (General Manager), Scottish Ambulance Service, 2006-09; Director of Planning & Equalities (maternity cover secondment), NHS Health Scotland, 2009; Scottish Government: National Smoking Cessation Co-ordinator (Secondment), 2010-11, Acting Policy Director Health & Social Care (Secondment), 2013-14, Deputy Director Health & Social Care (Secondment), 2011-14; Director, MS Society Scotland, 2014-15. Board Member/Vice Chair, Scottish Drugs Forum, 2000-04; Scottish Advisory Board Member, Marie Curie UK, 2009-12; Board Member, Health and Social Care Alliance Scotland, 2015; Trustee, SCVO (Scottish Council for Voluntary Organisations), since 2014; Chair, Liberton Primary School Association, 2012-14. Address: Chest Heart & Stroke Scotland, Head Office, Third Floor, Rosebery House, 9 Haymarket Terrace, Edinburgh EH12 5EZ; T.-0131 225 6963; e-mail: admin@chss.org.uk

O'Donovan, Professor Oliver Michael Timothy, MA, DPhil, FBA, FRSE. Emeritus Professor, University of Edinburgh, since 2012 (Professor, Christian Ethics and Practical Theology, 2006-2012); Honorary Professor, University of St Andrews, since 2013; b. 28.06.45,

Edgware, Middlesex; m., Joan Elizabeth Lockwood; 2 s. Educ. University College School, Hampstead; Balliol College, Oxford. Lecturer, Wycliffe Hall, Oxford, 1972-77; Assistant Professor, Wycliffe College, Toronto, 1977-82; Regius Professor of Moral and Pastoral Theology and Canon of Christ Church, Oxford, 1982-2006. Publications: Author: Resurrection and Moral Order, The Desire of The Nations, The Ways of Judgment, The Church in Crisis, The Word in Small Boats, Self, World and Time; Finding and Seeking. Address: 6a Comely Park, Dunfermline KY12 7HU; e-mail: oliver.odonovan@ed.ac.uk

O'Dwyer, Dana, MA (Hons), MCC, PG Cert Com Educ, MInstLM. Chief Executive, Capability Scotland, since 2011; previously Chief Executive, The Mungo Foundation; m., Prof. James Thomson. Career: worked as an Assistant Director of Planning and Community Care with Greater Glasgow Health Board and for two local authorities and a homeless charity. Board Member of the Coalition of Care and Support Providers in Scotland (CCPS). Address: Capability Scotland, 11 Ellersly Road, Edinburgh EH12 6HY; T.-0131 347 1001.

O'Dwyer, Professor Patrick Joseph, MCh, FRCSI, FRCSGlas. Professor of Surgery, Glasgow University, since 1998; Consultant Surgeon, Gartnavel General Hospital and Queen Elizabeth University Hospital, Glasgow, since 1990; b. 24.7.52, Newport, Ireland; m., Cindy; 4 s.; 1 d. Educ. Newport Vocational School; University College Cork. Trainee in Surgery, University Hospital, Cork, 1979-83; Research Fellow, Harvard Medical School, 1983-84; Clinical Fellow, Ohio State University, 1984-86; Lecturer in Surgery, University College Dublin, 1986-90; Senior Lecturer and Reader in Surgery, Glasgow University, 1990-98. Publications: 150 papers in journals. Recreations: music; hill-walking. Address: University Department of Surgery, Western Infirmary, Glasgow G11 6NT; T.-0141-211 2804.

Ogg, Derek Andrew, LLB, FFCS. Formerly Head, National Sexual Crimes Unit, Crown Office, Edinburgh (2009-2011); formerly Assistant Principal Advocate Depute, Crown Office; former Senior Advocate Depute; Queen's Counsel, since 1999; Advocate, since 1989; b. 19.9.54, Dunfermline. Educ. Dunfermline High School; Edinburgh University. Solicitor in private practice, 1980-89. Chairman, Institute of Chartered Accountants of Scotland Discipline Tribunal, 2000-2007; Chairman, Scottish AIDS Monitor Charitable Trust, 1983-94; Trustee, Waverly Care Trust (proprietors of Scotland's AIDS Hospice), 1990-2002. Member, Royal Philosophical Society of Glasgow. Recreations: hill-walking; classic cars; reading; music; occasional radio and TV commentator. Address: (h.) 18 Lanark Street, Glasgow G1 5PY; T.-0141-572 4843.
E-mail: derekandrewogg@hotmail.com

Ogilvie, Campbell. Former President, Scottish Football Association (2011-2015). Career history: appointed General Secretary, Rangers F.C. in 1978 and later became a director until 2005; Operations Director, Heart of Midlothian, 2005-08, appointed Managing Director in 2008; Treasurer, now second vice-president of the Scottish Football Association, 2003-2007, first vice-president, 2007-2011.

Ogilvy, Sir Francis (Gilbert Arthur), 14th Bt, MRICS. Chartered Surveyor; b. 22.4.69; m., Dorothy Margaret Stein; 3 s.; 1 d. Educ. Edinburgh Academy; Glenalmond College; Royal Agricultural College, Cirencester; BSc (Hons) (Reading). Address: (h.) Winton House, Pencaitland, East Lothian EH34 5AT.

Ogle, Geoff. Chief Executive Officer, Food Standards Scotland (FSS), since 2015; Interim Director, Food Standards Agency in Scotland (FSA), June 2014 - March 2015. Civil servant, since 1984 and during this time has undertaken a variety of posts including Private Secretary to the Child Support Agency (CSA), Chief Executive and both Head of External Relations and Head of Internal Communications in the CSA; moved in 2002 to the Department for Work and Pensions (DWP) as a pension Centre Manager and then Head of the International Pension Centre; joined the Food Standards Agency in 2008, posts included Senior Investigating officer during the horsemeat incident and FSA's Acting Director in Wales.

O'Grady, Sheriff Michael Gerard, QC, MA, LLB. Sheriff, Lothian and Borders, since 2007; Sheriff, Glasgow and Strathkelvin at Glasgow, 2000-07; b. 19.8.54, Glasgow. Educ. St. Patrick's High School, Dumbarton; University of Glasgow. Solicitor, private practice (Ross Harper and Murphy, and Gordon McBain and O'Grady), 1977-88; called to the Bar, 1988; Advocate Depute, 1993-97; Standing Junior to Foreign and Commonwealth Office, 1997-98, QC, 1998; Temporary Judge, since 2004. Recreations: reading; music; guitar; travel. Address: (b.) Sheriffs' Chambers, Sheriff Court, Edinburgh.

Ogston, Professor Derek, CBE, MA, MD, PhD, DSc, MLitt, FRCPEdin, FRCP, FGB, FRSE, FRSA, BTh, Hon. LLD, DTM+H. Professor of Medicine, Aberdeen University, 1983-97 (Dean, Faculty of Medicine, 1984-87; Vice-Principal, 1987-97); Member, Court, Aberdeen University, 1998-2002; b. 31.5.32, Aberdeen; m., Cecilia Marie; 1 s.; 2 d. Educ. King's College School, Wimbledon; Aberdeen University. Aberdeen University: Lecturer in Medicine, 1962-69, Senior Lecturer in Medicine, 1969-75, MRC Travelling Fellow, 1967-68, Reader in Medicine, 1975-76, Regius Professor of Physiology, 1977-83. Member, Grampian Health Board, 1991-97 (Vice-Chairman, 1993-97); Member, General Medical Council, 1985-94. Publications: Haemostasis: Biochemistry, Physiology and Pathology (Joint Editor), 1977; The Physiology of Hemostasis, 1983; Antifibrinolytic Drugs: Chemistry, Pharmacology and Clinical Usage, 1984; Venous Thrombosis: Causation and Prediction, 1987; Life and Works of George Smith, RSA, 2000; George Leslie Hunter, 2002; Working Children (jointly), 2003; Leslie Hunter: Paintings of France and Italy, 2004; Children at School (jointly), 2005; King's College Aberdeen (jointly), 2009; Stichill Parish: Past and Present (jointly), 2009. Recreations: music; history of art; wildlife. Address: (h.) 64 Rubislaw Den South, Aberdeen AB15 4AY; T.-01224 316587.

O'Hagan, Professor David, BSc, PhD, DSc, CChem, FRSC, FRSE. Professor and Head of Organic Chemistry, University of St. Andrews, since 2000; b. 29.9.61, Glasgow; m., Anne; 3 d. Educ. Holyrood Secondary School, Glasgow; Glasgow University; Southampton University. Postdoctoral research, Ohio State University, 1985-86; University of Durham: Demonstrator, 1986-88, Lecturer in Chemistry, 1988-99, Professor of Organic Chemistry, 1999-2000. Chairman, Editorial Board, Natural Product Reports, and Journal of Fluorine Chemistry; Chairman, RSC Fluorine Subject Group. Publication: The Polyketide Metabolites, 1991. Recreations: golf; walking; gardening. Address: Millbank Park, 51 Millbank, Cupar, Fife KY15 5EA; T.-01334 650708; e-mail: dol@st-andrews.ac.uk

O'Hara, Brendan. MP (SNP), Argyll and Bute, since 2015; SNP Defence spokesperson in the House of Commons, since 2015; b. 27.4.63, Glasgow. Educ. St. Andrew's Secondary, Carntyne. Educ. Strathclyde

University. Successful career as a TV producer; wrote, produced and directed the "Road To Referendum" documentary series which was broadcast on STV in 2013 and was subsequently nominated for a BAFTA Scotland award in the Current Affairs category; worked for STV, Sky Sports and the BBC. Credits include Comedy Connections and Movie Connections (BBC1), The Football Years (STV) and Scotland's Greatest Album (STV). Currently working on the second series of David Hayman's very successful series following in the footsteps of Tom Weir. Address: House of Commons, London SW1A 0AA.

Oldfather, Irene, BA (Hons), MSc. Director, Health and Social Care Alliance, since 2011; MSP (Lab), Cunninghame South, 1999-2011; former Chair, Scottish Parliament European Committee, 2002-2011; Member, European Committee of Regions, 1997-2011; former Chair, Cross Party Group on Alzheimers; former Member, Cross Party Group on Tobacco Control; b. Glasgow. Educ. Strathclyde University; University of Arizona. Researcher, Dumbarton Council on Alcohol, 1976-77; Lecturer, University of Arizona, 1977-78; Research Officer, Strathclyde Regional Council, 1978-79; various posts, Glasgow District Council Housing Department, 1979-90; Political Researcher, 1990-98; writer and broadcaster on European affairs, 1994-98; part-time Lecturer, Paisley University, 1996-98; Councillor, North Ayrshire, 1995-99; UK Member, European Economic and Social Committee (EESC), since 2015.

Oliver, Professor Christopher William, BSc, MBBS, FRCS (Tr&Orth), FRCP, DMI, RCSEd, MD, FFSTEd. Consultant Trauma and Orthopaedic Surgeon, Royal Infirmary of Edinburgh, since 1997; Honorary Professor, Physical Activity for Health, University of Edinburgh, since 2015; b. 5.1.60, London; m., Josephine Hilton; 2 d. Educ. Romford Technical High School, London; University College Hospital, London. Basic surgical training, London and Harrow, 1985-89; Orthopaedic Registrar, York, Leeds, Harrogate, 1989-92; Research Fellow, Spinal Science, Middlesbrough, 1992-94; Senior Registrar, Oswestry and Stoke-on-Trent, 1994-96; Trauma Fellow, Harborview Hospital, Seattle, USA, 1996; Consultant Trauma Surgeon, John Radcliffe Hospital, Oxford, 1996-97. Member, Council, Royal College of Surgeons of Edinburgh, 2002-12; Convener of Examinations, RCSEd, 2006-08; Chairman, Intercollegiate Committee for Basic Surgical Examinations, 2008-2011. Recreations: cycling; whitewater and sea kayaking; computers. Address: (b.) F6341, New Royal Infirmary Edinburgh, Old Dalkeith Road, Edinburgh EH16 4SU; T.-0131-242 3402.
Web: orthodoc.aaos.org/chrisoliver/
E-mail: cwoliver@btopenworld.com

Oliver, Professor Nick, MA, PhD. Professor of Management, University of Edinburgh Business School, since 2000, Head of School, 2007-2012; b. 03.08.58, Carlisle. Educ. Austin Friars School, Carlisle; University of Edinburgh. Lecturer in Organisational Behaviour, Cardiff Business School, University of Wales, Cardiff, 1985-92; University of Cambridge: Lecturer in Management Studies, Judge Business School, 1992-97, Reader in Management Studies, 1997-2000. Member: Academy of Management, European Operations Management Association. Publications: The Japanization of British Industry (Co-Author), 1988; The Japanization of British Industry: Developments in the 1990s (Co-Author), 1992. Recreations: skiing; windsurfing; running; canoeing; sailing; cycling and motorcycling. Address: (b.) University of Edinburgh Business School, University of Edinburgh, 29 Buccleuch

Place, Edinburgh EH8 9JS; T.-0131 651 3198.
E-mail: nick.oliver@ed.ac.uk

Ó Maolalaigh, Professor Roibeard, BA, MA, PhD. Professor of Gaelic, University of Glasgow, since 2005, Vice-Principal and Head of the College of Arts, since 2015, Head of Department, Department of Celtic, 2007-2011, Head of School of Humanities, 2012-14, Holder of the first ever established Chair of Gaelic, since 2010; b. 05.07.66, Dublin, Ireland; m., Margaret Macleod; 4 s. Educ. Drimnagh Castle, CBS; University College, Dublin; University of Edinburgh. Career History: Lecturer, Department of Celtic, University of Edinburgh; Assistant Professor and Bibliographer, School of Celtic Studies, Dublin Institute for Advanced Studies. Chairman, Gaelic Books Council, 2005-2010. Address: (b.) Department of Celtic and Gaelic, University of Glasgow G12 8QQ; T.-0141-330-4222.
E-mail: roibeard.omaolalaigh@glasgow.ac.uk

O'Neill, John, MA (Hons). Rector, The High School of Glasgow, since 2015. Educ. The University of Glasgow. Teacher of History, Politics and Religion, St Thomas More School, 1988-89; Teacher of History & Modern Studies, Glasgow City Council, 1989-92; Teacher of History & Politics & House Tutor (Rogerson West), Merchiston Castle School, 1992-97; Teacher of History/Modern Studies and Assistant Housemaster, The Glasgow Academy, 1997-2000; House Master, Rogerson West House, Merchiston Castle School, 2000-02; Head of Sixth Form and Housemaster, Merchiston Castle School, 2002-04; Senior Deputy Rector, The High School of Glasgow, 2004-15. Address: (b.) 637 Crow Road, Glasgow G13 1PL; T.-0141 954 9628.

O'Neill of Clackmannan, Lord (Martin (John) O'Neill), BA (Econ). MP (Labour), Ochil, 1997-2005 (Clackmannan, 1983-97, East Stirlingshire and Clackmannan, 1979-83); b. 6.1.45; m., Elaine Samuel; 2 s. Educ. Trinity Academy, Edinburgh; trades union and evening classes; Heriot-Watt University; Moray House College of Education. President, Scottish Union of Students, 1970-71; school teacher, 1974-79; Tutor, Open University, 1976-79. Member, Select Committee, Scottish Affairs, 1979-80; Opposition Spokesman, Scottish Affairs, 1980-84; Opposition Spokesman on Defence, 1984-88; Shadow Defence Secretary, 1988-92; Shadow Spokesman on Energy, 1992-95; Chairman, Trade and Industry Select Committee, 1995-2005; Chairman, Nuclear Industry Association, 2007-11. Honorary degree, Heriot-Watt University, 2011. Recreations: watching football; reading; listening to jazz; cinema. Address: (b.) House of Lords, London SW1; e-mail: oneillm@parliament.uk

O'Neill, Mark William Robert, BA Hons, HDipEd, FMA, PhD. Director of Policy and Research, Glasgow Life (formerly Culture and Sport Glasgow), since 2010, Head of Arts and Museums, since 2007; b. 10.11.56. Educ. University College, Cork; Leicester University; Getty Leadership Inst. Curator, Springburn Museum, 1985-90; Glasgow Museums, since 1990; Keeper of Social History, 1990-92; Senior Curator of History, 1992-97; Head, Curatorial Services, 1997-98; Head, Glasgow Museums, 1998-2005, Head of Arts and Museums, since 2005. Publications: numerous articles on philosophy and practice of museums. Recreations: classical music; fiction; psychology. Address: (b.) Glasgow Life, 220 High Street, G4 0QW; T.-0141 287 0446.
E-mail: mark.o'neill@glasgowlife.org.uk

Ord, Peter John, CVO, BSc (Hon Ag), FBA, FRICS, FRAgS. Chartered Surveyor; b. 18.5.47, Edinburgh University; London University (Wye College). Hamilton and Kinneil Estates, 1971-74; Factor of Strathmore Estates and Strathmore English Estates, 1974-95; Arthur Young McLelland Moors/Ernst and Young, 1974-90; Resident

Factor of Balmoral Estate, 1995-2009; Consultant with Bell Ingram, since 2009. Chairman, The Cairngorms Outdoor Access Trust (formerly The Upper Deeside Access Trust), since 1998; Governor/Board Member, Gordonstoun School, 2001-2014; Trustee, Invercauld Estate, Braemar, since 2014; Trustee, The National Trust for Scotland, since 2013; Director, Shielbridge Ltd; Member, Sheil Fisheries Sub-Board; Member, University of Dundee Botanic Gardens Trust Steering Group; Elder, Glamis Parish Church. Formerly Chairman, The Rural Practice Division of The Royal Institution of Chartered Surveyors in Scotland; formerly Chairman, Angus Tourist Board. Former memberships: Board member, Angus College of Further Education; Board member, The River Dee Trust; Member, Glamis Community Council; member, The Cairngorms Outdoor Access Forum; Council member, Scottish National Ski Council (Snowsport Scotland); member, Executive Council of the Scottish Sports Association. Recreations: skiing; sailing; fishing; shooting; curling; Scottish Country Dancing. Address: (h.) The Mill, Milton of Ogilvie, Glamis, Forfar, Angus DD8 1UN; T.-01307 840719; e-mail: pordbnc@aol.com

O'Regan, Noel, BMus, MSc, DPhil. Reader, Music, University of Edinburgh, since 2015; b. 27.12.49, Roscommon, Ireland. Educ. Gormanston College; University College Galway; University College Cork; Oxford University. Research Chemist, Pfizer Corporation, 1974-78; Teacher, Christian Brothers College, Cork, 1978-80; Lecturer in Music, University of Lancaster, 1984-85, University of Edinburgh, 1985-96; Senior Lecturer, University of Edinburgh, 1996-2015. Chairman, Georgian Concert Society; Director, Edinburgh Renaissance Singers. Recreations: music; films; hillwalking; travelling. Address: (h.) 14 Rankeillor Street, Edinburgh EH8 9HY; T.-0131 667 7853; e-mail: n.o.regan@ed.ac.uk

O'Reilly, Denis St. John, MSc, MD, FRCP (Glas), FRCPath. Formerly Consultant Clinical Biochemist, Royal Infirmary, Glasgow (1984-2012); Director, The Scottish Trace Element and Micronutrient Reference Laboratory; b. 30.3.51, Cork; m., Margaret M.P. Lucey; 2 s.; 1 d. Educ. Presentation Brothers College, Cork; University College, Cork; Birmingham University. Registrar, Queen Elizabeth Medical Centre, Birmingham, 1976-78; Senior Registrar, Bristol Royal Infirmary, 1978-84; Ainsworth Scholar-Research Fellow, Norsk Hydro Institute for Cancer Research, Oslo, 1982. Address: (h.) 47 Strathblane Road, Milngavie G62 8HA.

Ormiston, Linda, OBE (2001), MA, DRSAMD, Hon. DMus (St. Andrews). Singer — Mezzo Soprano; teaches singing on The Musical Theatre Course at The Dance School of Scotland in Glasgow and on the Music Theatre post graduate course at the RSAMD; b. 15.1.48, Motherwell. Educ. Dalziel High School, Motherwell; Glasgow University; Royal Scottish Academy of Music and Drama; London Opera Centre. Has sung all over Britain, France, Belgium, Italy, Germany, Austria, Holland and Yugoslavia; has sung regularly at Scottish Opera, Opera North, and Glyndebourne; also well-known in lighter vein and as a member of The Music Box; recordings include Noyes Fludde, HMS Pinafore and Ruddigore with New Sadlers Wells Opera and Tell Me Pretty Maiden; has appeared at New York, Vancouver, Monte Carlo, Brussels and Tokyo; debut, Frankfurt Opera, 1993; debut, Salzburg Festival, 1994; debut, English National Opera, 1995. Recreations: playing the piano; skating; golf. Address: The Dance School of Scotland, Knightswood Secondary School, 60 Knightswood Road, Glasgow G13 2XD.

Ormond, Rupert Frank Guy, BA, MA, PhD. Director, Marine Conservation International; Hon. Professor, Heriot-Watt University, Edinburgh; Secretary, International Coral Reef Society; Director, University Marine Biological Station Millport, 1999-2006; Senior Lecturer, London University, 1999-2006; Visiting Professor, Glasgow University, 2000-07; Chief Scientist, Save Our Seas Foundation, 2007-2011; b. 1.6.46, Bristol; m., Mauvis ne Gore; 2 s.; 1 d. Educ. Clifton College, Bristol; Peterhouse, Cambridge. Lecturer/Senior Lecturer, Biology Department, 1974-99, Director, Tropical Marine Research Unit, 1982-99, York University. District Councillor, Ryedale District Council, 1987-96; Council, WWF Scotland, 2000-06, Scottish Natural Heritage Scientific Advisory Committee, 2000-04. Publications include: Red Sea Coral Reefs (Co-author); Marine Biodiversity (Co-author). Recreations: natural history; travel; classical music. Address: (h.) 37 Main Street, Newton, West Lothian EH52 6QE.

O'Rourke, Daniel (Donny), MA, MPhil. Poet, journalist, film-maker, broadcaster, and teacher; b. 5.7.59, Port Glasgow. Educ. St. Mirin's Academy, Paisley; Glasgow University; Pembroke College, Cambridge. Vice President, European Youth Council, 1983-85; Chairman, Scottish Youth Council, 1982-84; Producer, BBC TV and Radio Scotland, 1984-86; Reporter, Scottish Television, 1986-87; Producer, 1987-92, Head of Arts, 1992-93, Head of Arts and Documentaries, 1993-94; Executive Producer, BBC Scotland, 1994-95; folk music reviewer, The Herald and New Statesman, 1985-90; Creative Writing Fellow, Glasgow University and Strathclyde University, 1995-97; Head of English and Media Studies, Department of Adult and Continuing Education, Glasgow University, 1996-98; Poet in Residence, Edinburgh International Book Festival, 1999; Columnist, Sunday Herald, 1999; Member, Manpower Services Commission Youth Training Board, 1982-84; Member, Scottish Community Education Council, 1981-84; Chairman of Judges, Scottish Writer of the Year Award, 1996, 1997; Director, Tron Theatre Company, 1993-95; Member, Editorial Board, "11/9"; Artistic Director, Reacquaintance Robert Burns in Glasgow (year-long celebration), 2000; theatre: The Kerrera Saga (with George Wyllie), 1998, On Your Nerve, A Wake for Frank O'Hara, 1996. Major 'special recognition' Scottish Arts Council Award, 2008, 2009; Swiss Scots exchange fellow, Bern. 2008; shortlisted for National Library of Scotland pamphlet prize for 'One Light Burning'; Dave Whyte CD of his setting of these songs launched, March 2009. Publications: Second City, 1991; Rooming Houses of America, 1993; Dream State, the new Scottish poets, 1994; chapter in Burns Now, 1994; Eftirs/Afters, 1996; The Waist Band and Other Poems, 1997; Modern Music, 1997; Ae Fond Kiss, 1999; Across the Water, 2000 (Co-Editor); New Writing Scotland anthologies – Some Kind of Embrace, 1997; The Glory Signs, 1998; Friends and Kangaroos, 1999; The Cleft in my Heart, 2008; Blame Yesterday, 2008; Still Waiting To Be Wise (CD, with Dave Whyte), 1999; On A Roll, 2001; poems in various anthologies and textbooks. Recreations: Italian food; playing guitar; Irish literature; Americana. Address: (h.) 63 Barrington Drive, Glasgow G4 9ES.

E-mail: donny.orourke@btinternet.com

Orr, Joanne, BA (Hons), DipIndArch, MA, MBA. Chief Executive Officer, Museums Galleries Scotland, since 2004. Getty Foundation Museum Leadership Institute, 2010. Founding Chair, UNESCO Scotland. Address: Waverley Gate, 2-4 Waterloo Place, Edinburgh EH1 3EG.

Orr, John Douglas, CBE, MB, ChB, MBA, FRCSEd, FRCP (Edin). Consultant Paediatric Surgeon, Royal Hospital for Sick Children, Edinburgh, 1984-2009; b. 11.7.45, Edinburgh; m., Elizabeth Erica Yvonne Miklinska; 2 s.; 1 d. Educ. George Heriot's School, Edinburgh; High School, Dundee; University of St. Andrews; Stirling University. Formerly Medical Director, The Royal Hospital for Sick Children, Edinburgh and Associate Medical Director, University Hospitals Division - NHS Lothian.

President, Royal College of Surgeons of Edinburgh, 2006-09. Recreations: golf; gardening. Address: (b.) Royal College of Surgeons of Edinburgh, Nicolson Street, Edinburgh EH8 9DW; T.-0131-527 1600; e-mail: PastPresident@rcsed.ac.uk

Orr-Ewing, Duncan Charles, BA, MRICS. Head of Species and Land Management, RSPB Scotland, since 1999; b. 19.01.64, Redhill; m., Caroline Louise; 1 d. Educ. Dr Challoner's Grammar School, Amersham, Bucks; Durham University. Chartered Surveyor, Humberts, Hatfield, Herts, 1986-91; Project Officer for Red Kite Reintroduction, RSPB Scotland, Inverness, 1991-94; Conservation Officer, Central Scotland, RSPB Scotland, Glasgow, 1994-99; Head of Species and Land Management, RSPB Scotland, Edinburgh, 1999-2011. Member of Scotland's Moorland Forum; Chair, Link Deer Task Force; Director of Langholm Demonstration Project; Member, Central Scotland and Tayside Raptor Study Groups and Scottish Ornithologist's Club. Recreations: birdwatching; bird ringing; foreign travel. Address: (b.) RSPB Scotland, 2 Lochside View, Edinburgh EH12 9DH; T.-0131 317 4100; e-mail: duncan.orr-ewing@rspb.org.uk

Orr Ewing, Major Edward Stuart, DL, JP, CVO. Lord Lieutenant, Wigtown, 1989-2006; b. 28.9.31, London; m., 1, F.A.B. Farquhar (m. dissolved); 2, Diana Mary Waters; 1 s.; 2 d. Educ. Sherborne; RMCS, Shrivenham. Black Watch RHR, 1950-69 (Major); Farmer and Landowner, since 1964. Recreations: country sports; skiing; sailing; painting.

Osborne, Rt. Hon. Lord (Kenneth Hilton Osborne), QC (Scot). Senator of the College of Justice, 1990-2011; b. 9.7.37. Advocate, 1962; QC, 1976; Chairman, Local Government Boundary Commission, 1990-2000.

Osborne, Sandra, MSc. MP (Labour), Ayr, Carrick and Cumnock, 2005-2015, Ayr, 1997-2005; b. 23.2.56; m., Alastair; 2 d. Educ. Camphill Senior Secondary School, Paisley; Anniesland College; Jordanhill College; Strathclyde University. Former community worker.

Osborne, Stephen Peter, BA, MSc, PhD. Vice Convener, Scottish Council for Voluntary Organisations (SCVO), since 2011; Professor of Public Management, University of Edinburgh, since 2006; b. 25.9.53, Birmingham; m., Kathleen; 3 s.; 2 d. Educ. Solihull School; Universities of Sussex, Bath and Birmingham. Social Worker, 1976-85; Social Work Manager, 1985-90; Lecturer/Professor, University of Aston, 1990-2006; Associate Dean for Quality, University of Edinburgh, 2012-2013; Deputy Dean of University of Edinburgh Business School, since 2013. Recreations: cycling; music; reading; walking. Address: (b.) University of Edinburgh Business School, 29 Buccleuch Place, Edinburgh; T.-07848979975. E-mail: stephen.osborne@ed.ac.uk

O'Shea, Professor Sir Timothy Michael Martin, PhD, BSc. Principal and Vice-Chancellor, University of Edinburgh, since 2002; b. 28.3.49; m., Professor Eileen Scanlon; 2 s.; 2 d. Educ. Royal Liberty School, Havering; Sussex University; Leeds University. Open University: Founder, Computer Assisted Learning Research Group, 1978, Lecturer, 1980-82, Senior Lecturer, 1983-87, Institute of Educational Technology, Professor of IT and Education, 1987-97, Pro-Vice-Chancellor for QA and Research, 1994-97, Master, Birkbeck College and Professor of Information and Communication Technologies, 1998-2002, Provost, Gresham College, 2000-02, Pro-Vice-Chancellor, 2001-02, University of London. Address: University of Edinburgh, Old College, South Bridge, Edinburgh EH8 9YL.

Osler, Douglas Alexander, CB, KSG, MA (Hons). HM Senior Chief Inspector and Chief Executive, HM Inspectorate of Education, Scottish Executive, 1996-2002; b. 11.10.42, Edinburgh; m., Wendy I. Cochrane; 1 s.; 1 d.

Educ. Royal High School, Edinburgh; Edinburgh University; Moray House College of Education. Teacher of History/Careers Master, Liberton Secondary School, Edinburgh, 1965-68; Principal Teacher of History, Dunfermline High School, 1968-74. English Speaking Union Fellowship to USA, 1966; International Leadership Visitor Program to USA, 1989; President, Standing International Conference of Inspectorates, 1999-2002; Visiting Professor, University of Strathclyde, 2003-05; Interim Scottish Prisons Complaints Commissioner, 2003; Chair, Statutory Inquiry, Northern Ireland, 2004; led inquiry into Scottish Court Service, 2005; Chairman of Commissioners, South Eastern Education and Library Board, Northern Ireland, 2006-2010; Chairman, Royal Blind Asylum and School, 2008-2014; Member, Scottish Committee of SkillForce; Trustee, Scottish Schools Pipes and Drums Trust; Past President, Rotary Club of Edinburgh. Book reviewer, Scotsman newspaper. Publications: Queen Margaret of Scotland; Sources for Modern Studies, Volumes 1 and 2.

Osowska, Francesca, OBE, MA (Econ), MA (EuroEcon). Director for the Scotland Office, The UK Government, since 2015. Educ. Cumbria; Cambridge University; College of Europe in Bruges. Career history: joined the civil service as an economist in 1993 (Employment Department in Sheffield); after brief stints in London and Brussels, moved to Edinburgh in 1997 as a government economist with the then Scottish Office; joined the Scottish Office education department in 1998 before going on to hold posts in the education and justice departments of the Scottish Executive and was appointed Head of Sport at the Scottish Executive/Government; Principal Private Secretary to the First Minister, 2007-09; Director for Culture, External Affairs and Tourism, Scottish Government, 2009-2010, Director for Housing, Regeneration and the Commonwealth Games, 2010-2013, Director for the Commonwealth Games and Sport, 2013-14. Address: Scotland Office, 1 Melville Crescent, Edinburgh EH3 7HW; T.-0131 244 9022.

O'Sullivan, Very Reverend Monsignor Canon Basil, JCL. Parish Priest, Holy Family, Dunblane, since 1988; appointed Chaplain to His Holiness Benedict XVI, October 2008; b. 1932, Fishguard. Educ. St. Finbarr's College, Cork; All Hallow's College, Dublin; Pontifical University of St. Gregory, Rome. Assistant Priest: St. Joseph's, Dundee, 1959-63, St. Andrew's Cathedral, Dundee, 1963-70; R.C. Chaplain, Dundee University, 1964-70; Parish Priest: St. John Vianney's, Alva, 1970-74, St. Columba's, Dundee, 1974-88. Canon of Dunkeld Chapter, since 1992. Judge of The Scottish Catholic Tribunal; formerly Administrator, Diocese of Dunkeld. Recreations: reading; gardening; walking. Address: (h.) St. Clare's, Claredon Place, Dunblane FK15 9HB; T.-01786 822146.

Oswald, Cllr Helen. Provost, Angus Council, since 2012; Councillor (SNP), Carnoustie, Angus, since 2007; b. 30.1.47, Dundee; m., Ed Oswald; 2 d. Educ. Rockwell High School, Dundee; Angus College, Arbroath. Councillor, Sidlaw East and Ashludie, Angus, 1999-2007. Board Member, Scottish National War Memorial; Member, Carnoustie Rotary Club; Chair, Angus Educational Trust; Member, Carnoustie Fairtrade Group; Director, Carnoustie Golf Link Management Committee Ltd. Recreations: family; reading. Address: (b.) 7 The Cross, Forfar, Angus DD8 1BX; T.-01307 473000. E-mail: provost@angus.gov.uk

Oswald, Rev. John, BSc, BD, PhD. Retired Interim Minister; b. 10.10.47, Glasgow; m., Barbara R.; 1 s. Educ. Kelvinside Academy; Edinburgh University. Management posts, Nickerson Seed Specialists; Managing Director, David Bell Ltd., Penicuik; candidate for ministry; Assistant Minister, Eddleston linked with Peebles Old; Minister, Lorne and Lowland Parish Church, Campbeltown; Minister, Muthill with Trinity Gask and Kinkell. Recreations: golf;

gardening; reading. Address: 1 Woodlands Meadow, Rosemount, Blairgowrie PH10 6GZ.

Oswald, Kirsten. MP (SNP), East Renfrewshire, since 2015; b. Dundee; m.; 2 s. Educ. Carnoustie High School; Glasgow University. Senior Human Resources professional; became active in the Scottish National Party during the 2014 Scottish independence referendum, serving on the committee of the local Women for Independence group with responsibility for local food bank collections. Ran community social media sites. Recreation: keen Dundee United fan. Address: House of Commons, London SW1A 0AA.

O'Toole, Tim, CBE, JD, BA. Chief Executive, FirstGroup plc, since 2010; b. 1955; m., Patricia; 1 s.; 1 d. Educ. University of Pittsburgh School of Law; LaSalle University in Philadelphia, PA. Career: in-house lawyer for Consolidated Rail Corporation (CRC), acting as lead counsel in litigation that facilitated the deregulation of the US railroad network, became Vice President & General Counsel and continued to oversee much of the company's capital transactions, which led later to a move into finance as the company's VP & Treasurer and subsequently Senior VP & Chief Financial Officer, then President and CEO; recruited to London Underground in 2003 to oversee its rebuilding after years of neglect and in the face of record demand; Managing Director, London Underground, until 2009; appointed to the Board of FirstGroup as a Non-Executive Director, May 2009 and subsequently appointed Chief Operating Officer and Deputy Chief Executive Officer, June 2010. Non-Executive Director of CSX Corporation, a freight transportation company in North America. Honorary Doctorate of Letters, LaSalle University in Philadelphia, PA. Involved with charity work throughout career, most notably as a pro bono advocate for abused children in the Philadelphia Family Court for over 15 years. Recreations: golf; member of Merion Golf Club and Royal Aberdeen. Address: (b.) FirstGroup plc, 395 King Street, Aberdeen AB24 5RP; T.-01224 650100.

Ouston, Hugh Anfield, MA (Hons), DipEd. Head of College, Robert Gordon's College, Aberdeen, 2004-2014; b. 4.4.52, Dundee; m., Yvonne; 2 s.; 2 d. Educ. Glenalmond College; Christ Church, University of Oxford. Teacher of History, North Berwick High School, 1977-84; Head of History, Beeslack High School, 1984-92; Assistant Head, Dunbar Grammar School, 1992-97; Deputy Principal, George Watson's College, 1997-2004. Recreations: birdwatching; gardening; hill walking; sailing; poetry. Address: (h.) Pitscaff House, Newburgh, Aberdeenshire AB41 6AQ; E-mail: hughouston@gmail.com

Owen, John P., BSc, MA, FRSC, CChem, PGCE. Headmaster, Beaconhurst School, Bridge of Allan, Stirling, since 2012; b. 27.8.57, Plymouth; m., Elizabeth; 2 s. Educ. Plymouth College; University of Bath; University of the West of England. Head of Chemistry, Glenalmond College, 1999-2007; Housemaster, Reid's House, 2002-07, Sub Warden, 2007-2012. Fellow, Royal Society of Chemistry and Chartered Chemist. Past President, British Association of International Mountain Leaders. Member, Scottish Canoe Association, British Association Snowsport Instructors, Tayside Mountain Rescue Team. Recreations: mountaineering; canoeing; orienteering; cycling; reading. Address: 52 Kenilworth Road, Bridge of Allan, Stirling FK9 4RR; T.-01786 832146.
E-mail: headmaster@beaconhurst.com

P

Pacione, Professor Michael, MA, PhD, DSc, FRSGS. Professor of Geography, Strathclyde University, since 1990; b. 14.10.47, Dundee; m., Christine Hopper; 1 s.; 1 d. Educ. Lawside Academy, Dundee; Dundee University. Lecturer in Geography, Queens University, Belfast, 1973-75; Lecturer, Senior Lecturer, Reader, Strathclyde University, Glasgow, 1975-89; Visiting Professor, University of Guelph, 1984, and University of Vienna, 1995. Publications: 25 books and more than 140 academic research papers. Recreations: travel; photography; scuba diving. Address: (b.) Department of Geography, Strathclyde University, 50 Richmond Street, Glasgow G1 1XH; T.-0141-548 3793.
E-mail: m.pacione@strath.ac.uk

Pack, Professor Donald Cecil, CBE, MA, DSc, HonD Univ. Strathclyde (2014), CMath, FIMA, FEIS, FRSE. Emeritus Professor, Strathclyde University, since 1986; b. 14.4.20, Higham Ferrers; m., Constance Mary Gillam (deceased); 2 s.; 1 d. Educ. Higham Ferrers Primary School; Wellingborough School; New College, Oxford. Ordnance Board, Cambridge, 1941-43; Armament Research Department, Ministry of Supply, Fort Halstead, 1943-46; Lecturer in Mathematics, Queen's College Dundee, St. Andrews University, 1947-52; Visiting Research Associate, Maryland University, 1951-52; Lecturer in Mathematics, Manchester University, 1952-53; Professor of Mathematics, Strathclyde University, 1953-82 (Vice-Principal, 1968-72); Honorary Professor, 1982-86; Member, various Government scientific boards and committees, 1952-84; Consultant, DERA Fort Halstead, Ministry of Defence, 1984-2001; Member, Defence Scientific Advisory Council, 1975-80; DERA Visiting Fellow, 1999; first Hon. Member, European Consortium for Mathematics in Industry, 1988; Chairman, Scottish Certificate of Education Examination Board, 1969-77; Chairman, Committee of Inquiry into Truancy and Indiscipline in Scottish Schools, 1974-77 ("Pack Report" published by HMSO, 1977); Hon. President, National Youth Orchestra of Scotland (Chairman, Steering Committee, 1978, Chairman, 1978-88); Member, Scottish Arts Council, 1980-85; Member, UK Committee for European Music Year 1985 and Chairman, Scotland Advisory Committee, 1983-86; Member: General Teaching Council for Scotland, 1966-73, Dunbartonshire Education Committee, 1960-66; Governor, Hamilton College of Education, 1976-81; Council Member, Royal Society of Edinburgh, 1960-63; a Founder, Hon. Treasurer and Council Member, Institute of Mathematics and its Applications, 1964-72; Member: International Advisory Committee on Rarefied Gas Dynamics Symposia, 1976-88, British National Committee for Theoretical Mechanics, 1973-78, Council, Gesellschaft fuer angewandte Mathematik und Mechanik, 1977-83; Guest Professor: Technische Universitaet, Berlin, 1967, Bologna University and Politecnico di Milano, 1980, Technische Hochschule, Darmstadt, 1981; other visiting appointments, Warsaw University, 1977, Kaiserslautern University, 1980 and 1984. Past President: Edinburgh Mathematical Society, Glasgow Mathematical Association; Honorary President, Milngavie Music Club, 1994-2010, President, 1983-93. Recreations: music; gardening. Address: (h.) 18 Buchanan Drive, Bearsden, Glasgow G61 2EW; T.-0141-942 5764.

Pagan, Graeme Henry, MBE, BL, WS. Solicitor, Hosack & Sutherland, Oban, 1960-2007; Member, Solicitors Discipline Tribunal, 1995-2006; Honorary Sheriff of North Strathclyde at Oban, since 1988; b. 20.3.36, Cupar; m., Heather; 1 s.; 2 d. Educ. New Park, St. Andrews; Bedford School; Edinburgh University. Part-time Procurator Fiscal, Oban, 1970-79; Regional Organiser, Shelter Campaign for the Homeless, 1968-75; Chairman, Oban Housing Association, 1971-98; Founder Member, Oban Abbeyfield Society; Founder of Solicitors charitable ventures Will Aid and Will Relief Scotland; Convener, Argyll & Bute Scottish Liberal Democrats, 1991-2000; Joint Convenor, Oban Concern for Palestine; Director of Charitable Companies, Mary's Meals and Will Relief Scotland; Director, Oban Hospice, 2000-2010; Trustee, The Oban Charitable Trust; Local Treasurer, Yes Lorn and The Isles for the 2014 referendum; Lifetime Achievement Award, Law Awards of Scotland, 2006. Publication: Memoirs: Once Bitten Twice Fined, 2004; bereavement book "Don't Mention The Coal Scuttle" (Co-Author). Recreations: family; jazz; malt whisky; wandering in the Highlands on foot and bike. Address: (h.) Neaveton, Oban, Argyll; T.-01631 563737.

Page, Professor Alan Chisholm, LLB, PhD. Professor of Public Law, Dundee University, since 1985; b. 7.4.52, Broughty Ferry; m., Sheila Duffus; 1 s.; 1 d. Educ. Grove Academy; Edinburgh University. Lecturer in Law, University College, Cardiff, 1975-80; Senior Lecturer in Law, Dundee University, 1980-85; Head, Department of Law, 1980-95, 2005-06; Dean, School of Law, 2006-2015; Dean, Faculty of Law, 1986-89; Deputy Principal, Research Governance, 2011-15. Publications: Constitutional Law of Scotland; The Executive in the Constitution; Investor Protection; Legislation. Recreation: mountaineering. Address: (h.) Westlands, Westfield Road, Cupar, Fife KY15 5DR.

Paget, Elspeth Mary, LLB (Hons), DipLP, TEP. Partner, Gillespie MacAndrew LLP, since 2005; b. 1960, Glasgow; 2 c. Educ. Wellington School, Ayr; University of Edinburgh. Traineeship with Alex Morison & Co., 1982-84; Assistant with AC Bennett & Fairweather WS, 1984-89; Partner, Bennett and Robertson, 1989-2005; Tutor in Private Client Course of The Diploma in Legal Practice, University of Edinburgh, 2002-06; Member, The Society of Trust and Estate Practitioners (STEP), since 2007; holds STEP Advanced Certificate in International Succession and Probate (2013); Full Professional Member, Solicitors for the Elderly. Address: (b.) 5 Atholl Crescent, Edinburgh EH3 8EJ; T.-0131 225 1677.
E-mail: elspeth.paget@gillespie.macandrew.co.uk

Paisley of Westerlea, The Much Hon. Duncan Wilson, FRSA, FSA Scot. Succeeded as 16th Head of the Name; 5th Laird of the Barony of Westerlea (15th May 1993); Ambassador (Overseas), Capability Scotland, 1993-2006; Patron, Westerlea School, Edinburgh, 1993-2006; Patron, Kagyu Samye Ling Monastery and Tibetan Centre, Eskdalemuir; b. 30.8.48, Woodcote; m., Jane Crichton Rankin; 3 d. Educ. Cannock House School; Westwood. Regular Army, 1966-90 (Gordon Highlanders, RAOC) General List; King's Own Scottish Borderers, 1990-95; attended Barony College of Agriculture, 1991-92; Regional Liaison Officer, Scottish Landowners' Federation, 1992-93; The Guild of Master Craftsmen: Assessment Officer (S.W. Scotland), 1993-96; Regional Manager and Trainer (W), 1996-2000; Chief Assessor (Scotland), since 2000; Director, Westerlea Trading; PPC, The Referendum Party, 1996-97; President, Scottish Tartans Society, 1997-2001; Director, Register of All Publicly known Tartans, 1997-2001; Hon. Col. Legion of Frontiersmen, 2001-04; Freeman of Glasgow; Member, Incorporation of Weavers, Glasgow; Member, Incorporation of Weavers, Edinburgh; Member, Heraldry Society of Scotland; Member, Royal Celtic Society and Royal Scots Club; formerly Captain, Balgonie Castle (1992-2013). Recreations: hill-walking; Scottish domestic architecture; family history; gardening. Address: (h.) Ardtalla, Kirkburn, Slamannan, Stirlingshire FK1 3AE; T./Fax: 01324 851535; Mob: 07739 749038; e-mail: paisleyofwesterlee@ad.co.uk

Palfreyman, Professor John, BSc, DPhil, FIWSc. Former Head of the School of Contemporary Sciences, University of Abertay Dundee (now retired); BioScientist; b. 30.7.51, Potters Bar; 2 d. Educ. Stationers' Company's School; London and Sussex Universities. Research Biochemist, Royal Infirmary Glasgow; Research Fellow, MRC Institute of Virology, Glasgow; University of Abertay Dundee. Member, Coupar Angus Community Council; Board Member: Forward Coupar Angus, Windfall Community Development Trust. Recreations: theatre; photography; hill walking (Munro bagging); cycling. Address: The Neuk, Caddam Road, Coupar, Angus, Perthshire PH13 9EF; e-mail: palfreyman85@gmail.com

Palmer, Professor Tracy, BSc, PhD, FRSE (2009), FSB (2010). Professor of Molecular Microbiology, University of Dundee, since 2007, Head of Molecular Microbiology, since 2009; b. 8.5.67, Sheffield; m., Frank Sargent; 2 s. Educ. Stocksbridge High School; University of Birmingham. Postdoctoral Research Assistant, University of Dundee, 1992-93, University Research Fellow, 1993-96; Royal Society University Research Fellow, John Innes Centre, Norwich, 1996-2004, MRC Senior Non-Clinical Research Fellow, 2004-07; MRC Senior Non-Clinical Research Fellow, University of Dundee, 2007-09; Professor of Molecular Microbiology, John Innes Centre, Norwich, 2005-07. The Fleming Prize, 2002. Address: (b.) Division of Molecular Microbiology, College of Life Sciences, University of Dundee, Dundee DD1 5EH; T.-01382 386 464; e-mail: t.palmer@dundee.ac.uk

Park, Ian Michael Scott, CBE, MA, LLB. Partner, Paull & Williamsons, Advocates, Aberdeen, 1961-91, Consultant thereafter; Member: Criminal Injuries Compensation Board, 1983-2000, Criminal Injuries Compensation Appeals Panel, 1996-2002; b. 7.4.38, Aberdeen; m., Elizabeth M.L. Struthers, BL, MBE; 2 s. Educ. Aberdeen Grammar School; Aberdeen University. Assistant to and subsequently Partner in Paull & Williamsons; Member, Society of Advocates in Aberdeen, since 1962, Treasurer, 1991-92, President, 1992-93; Sometime part-time Assistant, Department of Public Law, Aberdeen University; President, Law Society of Scotland, 1980-81 (Council Member, 1974-85); Chairman, Aberdeen Citizens Advice Bureau, until 1988; Secretary, Aberdeen Granite Association, 1962-84; Temporary Sheriff, 1976-84; Honorary Sheriff at Aberdeen, since 1996; part-time Chairman, Medical Appeals Tribunals, until 1996; frequent broadcaster on legal topics. Retired following diagnosis of Parkinsons Disease. Address: (h.) 46 Rubislaw Den South, Aberdeen AB15 4AY; T.-01224 313799.

Park, John William. MSP (Labour), Mid Scotland and Fife, 2007-2012; b. 14.9.73; 2 d. Educ. Woodmill High School; Blacklaw Primary (both Dunfermline); Adam Smith College, Kirkcaldy; Carnegie College, Dunfermline. Rosyth Dockyard: Electrical Fitter, 1989-98, Trade Union Convenor, 1998-2001; AEEU, formerly AMICUS, now UNITE: Research Officer, 2001-02, National Industrial Campaigns Officer, 2002-03; Head of Employee Relations, Babcock Naval Services, 2003-04; Assistant Secretary, STUC, 2004-07.

Park, Neil Ferguson, BSc, MBA. Partner, 25i Plus LLP; Secretary/Treasurer, Lothians Golf Association; Council Member, Tantallon Golf Club; b. 26.9.62, Gosport; m., Judith Frances; 1 s.; 1 d. Educ. Daniel Stewart's and Melville College, Edinburgh; Aberdeen University; Edinburgh University. Recreations: golf; triathlons; road-running; writing. Address: (b.) 43 Hopetoun Terrace, Gullane, East Lothian EH31 2DD.

Parker, Cameron Holdsworth, CVO, OBE, DL, BSc. Lord Lieutenant of Renfrewshire, 1998-2007; b. 14.4.32, Dundee; m., Marlyne Honeyman; 3 s. Educ. Morrison's Academy, Crieff; Glasgow University. Managing Director,

latterly also Chairman, John G. Kincaid & Co. Ltd., Greenock, 1967-80; Chairman and Chief Executive, Scott Lithgow Ltd., Port Glasgow, 1980-83; Board Member, British Shipbuilders, 1977-80, 1981-83; Chief Executive, Prosper Enginering Ltd., Irvine, 1983-84; Managing Director, Lithgows Limited, 1984-92, Vice-Chairman, 1992-97. Freeman, City of London; Liveryman, Worshipful Company of Shipwrights; Member, Council, CBI Scotland, 1986-92; Member, Argyll and Clyde Health Board, 1991-95; Board Member, Scottish Homes, 1992-96; Director, Clyde Shaw Ltd., 1992-94; Honorary President, Accord Hospice, 1998-2007; President, SSAFA Forces Help, Renfrewshire, 1998-2007; DUniv University of Paisley, 2003. Recreation: golf; gardening. Address: (h.) Heath House, Kilmacolm, Renfrewshire PA13 4PE; T.-01505 873197.

Parker, Colin. Chief Executive, Aberdeen Harbour Board, since 2006; b. 5.10.57, Manchester; m., Victoria Louise Walker; 2 d.; 1 s. Educ. HMS Conway Merchant Navy School; Liverpool Polytechnic. Merchant Navy Cadet and Officer, 1974-87; Aberdeen Harbour Board: Vessel Traffic Services Officer, 1987-90, Assistant Harbour Master, 1990-94, Harbour Master, 1994-2006. Chairman, SCDI's NE Committee; Chair, British Ports Association, 2012-14; Chairman, Scottish Ports Committee of British Ports Association, 2002-06. Recreations: golf; walking; photography. Address: Harbour Office, 16 Regent Quay, Aberdeen AB11 5SS; T.-01224 597000.

Parker, David, BSc. Leader of Scottish Borders Council, since 2003; b. 28.1.74, Manchester; m., Ruth; 1 s. (Angus, b. 2009). Educ. Heriot-Watt University. Freelance IT Consultant, 1995-98; elected Local Government Councillor, since 1995; Special Needs Technology Adviser, Heriot-Watt University, 1998-2002; Depute Leader, Scottish Borders Council, 2002-03. Leader of Independent Members within Convention of Scottish Local Authorities, since 2007. Recreations: walking; cycling; cooking; wine appreciation. Address: (b.) Council Headquarters, Newtown St. Boswells, Melrose TD6 0SA; T.-01835 826571; e-mail: dparker@scotborders.gov.uk

Parkinson, Frederick Alexander Ian. Honorary Consul for Netherlands, 1998-2012; Deputy Lieutenant, Kincardineshire; Chairman, Grampian Valuation Panel, since 1997; b. 12.10.41, Royston; m., Ann Delyth; 1 s.; 2 d. Educ. Sutton Valence, Kent; Hatfield Polytechnic. Articled Clerk, Chartered Accountants, 1958-62; Officer, Royal Navy, 1963-79; Projects Manager, Software Company, 1980-83; MD, Profit Through Partnership Ltd., 1983-98. Chairman, Aberdeen CAB, 1993-2004; Member, Grampian Valuation Committee and Panel, since 1983; Ridder van Oranje-Nassau, 2012. Recreation: sailing. Address: Banchory Devenick, Kincardineshire.

Parks, Rowan Wesley, MB, BCh, BAO, MD, FRCSI, FRCS(Edin). Professor of Surgical Sciences, University of Edinburgh, since 2010; Honorary Consultant Surgeon, Royal Infirmary of Edinburgh, since 1999; b. 5.3.66, Belfast; m., Janet Margaret; 2 s.; 2 d. Educ. Royal Belfast Academical Institution; Queen's University, Belfast. Research Fellow, Queen's University, Belfast, 1994-96; Higher Surgical Trainee, Northern Ireland, 1996-98; Clinical Fellow, Edinburgh, 1998-99. Moynihan Medal, Association of Surgeons of Great Britain and Ireland; Millin Lecturer and Medal, Royal College of Surgeons of Ireland. Recreation: boating. Address: Department of Clinical Surgery, Royal Infirmary of Edinburgh, Edinburgh EH16 4SA; T.-0131 242 3616; e-mail: R.W.Parks@ed.ac.uk

Parr, Professor John Brian, BSc (Econ), MA, PhD, AcSS. Professor of Regional and Urban Economics, Glasgow University, since 1989; b. 18.3.41, Epsom; m., Pamela Jean Harkins; 2 d. Educ. Henry Thornton School; London University; University of Washington. Instructor,

University of Washington, 1966; Assistant Professor/Associate Professor, University of Pennsylvania, 1967-75; joined Glasgow University as Lecturer, 1975. Fellow of the Academy of Social Sciences; Fellow of Regional Science Association International; Associate Editor, Journal of Regional Science, since 1979; Member, Board of Management, Urban Studies, since 1981; Member, Editorial Board, Review of Urban and Regional Development Studies, since 1995; Chairman, British-Irish Section, Regional Science Association International, 1981-85. Publications: various journal articles on urban and regional analysis; Christaller Central Place Structures (Co-Author); Regional Policy: Past Experience and New Directions (Co-Editor); Analysis of Regional Structure: Essays in Honour of August Lösch (Co-Editor); Market Centers and Retail Location (Co-Author). Address: (b.) School of Social and Political Sciences, Glasgow University, Glasgow G12 8QQ; T.-0141-330 2000, Ext. 4724/4121; e-mail: John.Parr@glasgow.ac.uk

Parr, Nick. Chief Executive, Dundee Rep Theatre and Scottish Dance Theatre, since 2015. Worked in theatres across the UK, including Nottingham Theatre Royal, Derby Assembly Rooms, Liverpool Empire and Edinburgh Playhouse; Venues Manager, North Lanarkshire Council; Head of Marketing and Press, Scottish Ballet, 2000-04; Venues Manager, Motherwell Concert Hall and Theatre, 2004-2011 (oversaw the £6 million refurbishment of Motherwell Concert Hall and Theatre and the start of a £3-million refurbishment to Airdrie Town Hall); Commercial Director, Festival and King's Theatres, Edinburgh, 2011-15. Deputy Chair, Quarter Primary School Parent Council, 2010-12; Chair, Braidwood Primary School Parent Council, 2012-14; Board Member, Culture Republic, since 2015. Address: Dundee Rep Theatre, Tay Square, Dundee DD1 1PB; T.-01382 227684.

Parr, Rose Marie, BSc (Hons), FRPharmS, PhD. Chief Pharmaceutical Officer for Scotland, since 2015. Educ. University of Strathclyde; University of Glasgow. Career history: registration in 1982, then hospital pharmacist with Lanarkshire Health Board; became Director of Pharmacy in 1993 at the Scottish Centre for Pharmacy Postgraduate Education (SCPPE) which would later become the Scottish Centre for Post Qualification Education; became the Director of Pharmacy of NHS Education for Scotland (NES) in 2002, when several healthcare education organisations joined to form a single national body. Appointed as an Honorary Reader, Robert Gordon University in Aberdeen in 2004; Visiting Professor, University of Strathclyde in Glasgow. Elected the first Chair of the Scottish Pharmacy Board of the Royal Pharmaceutical Society of Great Britain (RPSGB) in 2007. Address: Scottish Government, St Andrew's House, Regent Road, Edinburgh EH1 3DG.

Parratt, David Richmond, LLB (Hons), PhD, DipLP, DipICArb, FCIArb, FRHistS, FSALS, FSA Scot, FCS, FRSA. Director of Training and Education at the Faculty of Advocates, since 2012; Advocate, since 1999; Barrister of Lincoln's Inn, since 2009; Mediator and Arbitrator; b. 13.2.70, Dundee; m., Margaret Sarah Thomson. Educ. Glasgow Academy; High School of Dundee; Aberdeen University; Edinburgh University. Solicitor, 1995-99; Tutor, Faculty of Law, Edinburgh University, 1996-98; Honorary Lecturer, Centre for Energy, Petroleum and Mineral Law and Policy (CEPMLP), University of Dundee; Honorary Research Fellow, School of Law, University of Dundee; CEDR Accredited Mediator; Called to the Scottish Bar, 1999; Called to the Bar of Dubai International Finance Centre, 2007; Called to the English Bar, 2009; Supporting Member, London Maritime Arbitration Association; Member: LCIA, BIICL; Freeman, The Worshipful

Company of Arbitrators, London; Clerksroom, London; Terra Firma Chambers, Edinburgh. Publications: "The Development and Use of Written Pleadings in Scots Civil Procedure" (Stair Society); various articles on Scottish Legal History, Civil Procedure and International Arbitration. Recreations: golf; skiing; antiquarian books. Address: (b.) Advocates' Library, Parliament House, Edinburgh EH1 1RF; T.-0131 226 5071; e-mail: dparratt@hotmail.com

Parratt, Emeritus Professor James Roy, MSc, PhD, DSc, MD (h.c.), DSc (med), FRCPath, DipRelStudies (Cantab), FRPharmS, FESC, FISHR, FIBiol, FRSE. Professor Emeritus, Strathclyde University, since 1998; b. 19.8.33, London; m., Pamela Joan Lyndon Marels; 2 s.; 1 d. Educ. St. Clement Danes Holborn Estate Grammar School; London University. Spent nine years in Nigeria as Head of Pharmacology, Nigerian School of Pharmacy, then in Physiology, University Medical School, Ibadan; joined Strathclyde University, 1967; appointed Reader, 1970; Personal Professor, Department of Physiology and Pharmacology, 1975-83; Professor of Cardiovascular Pharmacology, 1983-98; Research Professor, 2001-06; Head, Department of Physiology and Pharmacology, 1986-90; Honorary Research Professor, Albert Szent-Gyorgy: Medical Faculty, University of Szeged, Hungary, since 1998; Chairman, Cardiac Muscle Research Group (now British Society for Cardiovascular Research), 1980-83; Vice President, European Shock Society, 1995-98; Gold Medal, Szeged University, 1975; Honorary Member, Hungarian Pharmacological Society, 1983; Honorary Doctorate, Albert Szent-Gyorgi Medical University, Hungary, 1989; Gold J.E. Purkyne Honorary Medal, Academy of Sciences of Czech Republic, 1995; Honorary Fellow, British Pharmacological Society, 2015; Fellow, International Academy of Cardiovascular Sciences (Lifetime Achievement Award, 2014); Sodalem honoris causa, Slovak Medical and Cardiological Societies, 1997; Honorary Member, Czech Cardiological Society, 1998; Honorary Citizen of the City of Winnipeg, 2001; Chairman, Universities and Colleges Christian Fellowship, 1984-90; Chairman, Interserve Scotland, 2000-03; Leverhulme Trust Emeritus Fellow, 2001-03; Szent-Gyorgyi Fellow, Hungarian State Government, 2002-03; former Vice-Chairman, Scripture Union; Past Chairman, SUM Fellowship; Lay Preacher, Baptist Unions of Scotland and Great Britain; Honorary President, Baptist Lay Preachers Association of Scotland, 1985-90; former Member, Board of Ministry, Baptist Union of Scotland. Recreations: music; piano playing; making jam; Scottish islands. Address: (h.) 10 St. Germains, Bearsden, Glasgow G61 2RS; T.-0141-942 7164; e-mail: pimjam.parratt@btinternet.com

Parsons, Ruth. Former Chief Executive, Historic Scotland (2010-12); previously Director of Local Government, the Third Sector and Public Service reform in Scottish Government (2005-09); b. Fife; 1 s. Director of Large Business Group, HM Customs & Excise, 2001-05; HM Customs & Excise, 1983-2005; worked with Cabinet Office supporting Public Service Reform Agenda, Improving Leadership Capacity of Leading Change in the Senior Civil Service. Recreations: enjoying historic sites across Scotland; football; travelling; reading.

Patel of Dunkeld, Baron (Narendra Babubhai Patel). Chancellor, University of Dundee, since 2006; b. 1938, Tanzania; m., Dr. Helen Dally; 2 s.; 1 d. Educ. Harrow High School; St. Andrews University. Previously President, Royal College of Obstetrics and Gynaecologists; previously Chairman: Academy of Medicine, Royal College; Clinical Standards Board, Scotland, Quality Improvement Scotland; currently Chairman: National Patient Safety Agency, Stem Cell Oversight Committee, UK National Stem Cell

Network; Member, Science and Technology Committee, since 1999; Patron of several charities; Fellow, Academy of Medical Science, Royal Society of Edinburgh; Hon. Dr. and Hon. Fellow, Universities and Colleges. Author of numerous publications on maternal/foetal medicine, epidemiology, obstetrics and gynaecology. E-mail: patel_naren@hotmail.com

Paterson, Aileen. Scottish writer and illustrator; best known for the series of children's books about Maisie the kitten; b. 30.11.34, Burntisland; m.; 6 c. Educ. Burntisland Primary School; Kirkcaldy High School; Edinburgh Art College. Career history: ran a solo pottery studio in Dublin during the 1950s and was an art teacher for 18 years; also made lifesize ragdolls, painted and became a craftworker; began writing Maisie books in 1982.

Paterson, Professor Alan Alexander, OBE, LLB (Hons), DPhil (Oxon), FRSA, FRSE. Solicitor. Professor of Law, Strathclyde University, since 1984; b. 5.6.47, Edinburgh; m., Alison Jane Ross Lowdon; 2 s.; 1 d. Educ. Edinburgh Academy; Edinburgh University; Pembroke College, Oxford. Research Associate, Oxford Centre for Socio-Legal Studies, 1972-73; Lecturer, Law Faculty, Edinburgh University, 1973-84; Visiting Professor, University of New Mexico Law School, 1982, 1986. Former Chairman: Committee of Heads of University Law Schools of the UK, Scottish Legal Action Group and British and Irish Legal Education and Technology Association; Chairman, Legal Services Group, Citizens Advice Scotland; Vice-Chair, Joint Standing Conference on Legal Education in Scotland; former Member, Council, Law Society of Scotland; past President, Society of Legal Scholars; Member, Judicial Appointments Board, 2002-08; Member, Scottish Legal Complaints Commission, 2008-2011. Publications: Lawyers and the Public Good, 2012; The Law Lords, 1982; The Legal System of Scotland (Co-author), 1993; Law, Practice and Conduct for Solicitors (Co-author), 2006; Paths to Justice Scotland (Co-Author), 2001. Address: (b.) Centre for Professional Legal Studies, Strathclyde University Law School, Graham Hills Building, Level 7, 50 George Street, Glasgow G1 1BA.
E-mail: prof.alan.paterson@strath.ac.uk

Paterson, Alex. Chief Executive, Highlands and Islands Enterprise, since 2010. Educ. University of Strathclyde; University of Bath. Career History: Industrial marketing with Esso Chemicals and Volvo; joined the Scottish Development Agency, and on the formation of Scottish Enterprise, became Head of Small Business Development in Renfrewshire Enterprise; Managing Director of a consultancy and training organisation based in Glasgow and operating throughout the UK; joined HIE, 2001 as Director of Developing Skills, became Director of Regional Competitiveness, 2008. Address: (b.) Highlands and Islands Enterprise, Fraser House, Friar's Lane, Inverness IV1 1RN; T.-01463 244 210.
E-mail: alex.paterson@hient.co.uk

Paterson, Calum, BA, MBA, CA, FRSE. Managing Partner, Scottish Equity Partners, since 2000; b. 13.4.63, Edinburgh; m., Amanda McLean. Educ. Linlithgow Academy; University of Strathclyde. Ernst and Young, 1985-88; Scottish Development Agency, 1988-91; Scottish Enterprise, 1991-2000. Recreation: various sports. Address: (b.) 17 Blythswood Square, Glasgow G2 4AD; T.-0141-273 4000.

Paterson, Professor David Maxwell, BSc, PhD. Executive Director of the Marine Alliance for Science and Technology for Scotland (MASTS), University of St. Andrews; Royal Society University Research Fellow; Professor, Coastal Ecology, since 2000; b. 16.6.58, Dalry; m., Marie; 2 d. Educ. Royal High School, Edinburgh; University of Glasgow; University of Bath. Royal Society Research Fellow, University of Bristol, 1988; University of St. Andrews: Lecturer, 1993, Reader in Environmental Biology, 1996; Council of the Scottish Association for Marine Science (SAMS). Publications: 130 peer reviewed publications; Editor, Marine Biodiversity; 4 edited books including "Marine Biodiversity and Ecosystem Functioning". Recreations: natural history; music; squash; family. Address: (h.) 22 Pinkerton Road, Crail, Fife KY10 3UB; T.-01333 450047; e-mail: d.paterson@st-and.ac.uk

Paterson, Dianne Elizabeth, LLB, NP. Managing Partner, Russel + Aitken, Solicitors, Edinburgh, since 2006, Partner, since 1985; Non Executive Director of ESPC, 2001-07; b. 8.1.58, Dundee; m., Dr. John W. Paterson. Educ. High School of Dundee; University of Aberdeen. Apprenticeship (Legal) with Robson McLean and Paterson, Solicitors, 1979-81; Solicitor with Russel + Aitken, since 1981. Credited for opening a property shop in The Royal Infirmary of Edinburgh (1988-2000); responsible for the launch of the 'Russel + Aitken Design Award'. Recreations: appreciation of art; sculpture; opera; classical music. Address: (h.) 18 Clarendon Crescent, Edinburgh EH4 1PU; T.-0131 228 5500; (b.) 27 Rutland Square, Edinburgh EH1 2BU.
E-mail: dianne.paterson@russelaitken.com

Paterson, Gil. MSP (SNP), Clydebank and Milngavie, since 2011, West of Scotland, 2007-2011 (Convener of Standards, Procedures and Public Appointments Committee); b. 11.11.42, Glasgow. Educ. Possilpark Secondary School. Career history: Gil's Motor Factors (own business); served as a Scottish National Party (SNP) councillor in Strathclyde Regional Council and sat on the SNP's National Executive Committee; MSP, Central Scotland, Scottish Parliament, 1999-2003 (sat on Local Government and Procedures committees in the Parliament); returned to running his business but stayed active in the SNP, becoming the party's Vice-Convenor in charge of Fundraising. Elected as the SNP Group Convener; member of Justice Committee and member of Standards, Procedures and Public Appointments Committee. Address: (b.) Scottish Parliament, Edinburgh EH99 1SP; Constituency Office: Unit 16, Clyde Street Business Centre, Clydebank G81 1PF.

Paterson, Rev. John Love, MA, BD, STM. Minister Emeritus, St. Michael's Parish Church, Linlithgow, since 2003 (Minister, 1977-2003); Chaplain to The Queen, since 1996; b. 6.5.38, Ayr; m. Educ. Ayr Academy; Glasgow University; Edinburgh University; Union Theological Seminary, New York. Minister: Presbyterian Church of East Africa, 1964-72, St. Andrew's, Nairobi, 1968-72; Chaplain, Stirling University, 1973-77. Moderator, West Lothian Presbytery, 1985. Recreations: gardening; Rotary. Address: 22 Waterfront Way, Stirling FK9 5GH; T.-01786 447165.

Paterson, Lewis, BSc, SQH. Acting Principal, Wester Hailes Education Centre, since 2015. Educ. Kilmarnock Academy; Glasgow Caledonian University; University of Paisley; Glasgow University; University of Edinburgh. Curriculum Leader of Numeracy and ICT, McLaren High School, 2002-06; Deputy Head Teacher, Currie Community High School, 2006-12; Acting Head Teacher, Gracemount High School, 2012; Depute Rector, Trinity Academy, Edinburgh, 2012-14, Acting Rector, 2014, Depute Rector, 2014-15. Address: Wester Hailes Education Centre, 5 Murrayburn Drive, Edinburgh EH14 2SU; T.-0131 442 2201; e-mail: admin@whec.edin.sch.uk

Paterson, Ross. Chief Executive, Scottish Public Pensions Agency. Address: (b.) 7 Tweedside Park, Tweedbank, Galashiels TD1 3TE; T.-01896 893 232.

Paterson, Steven. MP (SNP), Stirling, since 2015; b. 1975, Stirling. Educ. Cambusbarron Primary School; Stirling High School; Robert Gordon University; Stirling University. Appointed as media and communications manager to the SNP MSP Bruce Crawford in 2006; elected to Stirling Council in 2007 for the Stirling East ward, re-elected in 2012, appointed deputy SNP group leader in 2013. Address: House of Commons, London SW1A 0AA.

Paterson, Wilma, DRSAM. Freelance Composer/Music Critic/Travel Writer; b. 23.4.44, Dundee; 1 s.; 1 d. Educ. Harris Academy; Royal Scottish Academy of Music. Composition study with Luigi Dallapiccola in Florence; writes chamber and incidental music; contributes to: Odyssey, Heritage, The Scotsman, The Herald, The Sunday Times, Essentially America, Sunday Herald, etc. Publications: A Country Cup; Was Byron Anorexic?; Shoestring Gourmet; A Fountain of Gardens: Flowers and Herbs of the Bible; Lord Byron's Relish; Salmon & Women: The Feminine Angle; Songs of Scotland (Illustrated by Alasdair Gray). Address: 88 Ashburton Road, Glasgow G12 0LZ.
E-mail: williepaterson9@icloud.com

Paterson-Brown, Simon, MB BS, MPhil, MS, FRCS(Ed), FRCS Eng, FCS (HK). Consultant General Surgeon, Royal Infirmary, Edinburgh, since 1994; Past President, Association of Upper Gastrointestinal Surgeons of Great Britain and Ireland; b. 6.2.58, Edinburgh; m., Dr Sheila Finnerty; 3 d. Educ. Trinity College, Glenalmond; St. Mary's Hospital Medical School, London. Senior Lecturer in Surgery, St. Mary's Hospital, London, 1993-94. Council Member, RCS (Ed). Publications: Aids to Anatomy; Guide to Practical Procedures in Medicine and Surgery; Principles and Practice of Surgical Laparoscopy (Editor); Core Topics in General and Emergency Surgery (Editor); Hamilton Bailey's Emergency Surgery (Editor); "A Companion to Specialist Surgical Practice" (Series Editor) (8 volume series). Recreations: music; skiing; golf; running. Address: Department of Surgery, Royal Infirmary, Edinburgh EH16 4SA; T.-0131 242 3595.

Paton, Alasdair Chalmers, BSc, CEng. Chief Executive, Scottish Environment Protection Agency, 1995-2000; Retired Company Director; b. 28.11.44, Paisley; m., Zona G. Gill; 1 s.; 1 d. Educ. John Neilson Institution, Paisley; Glasgow University. Assistant Engineer, Clyde Port Authority, 1967-71; Assistant Engineer, DAFS, 1971-72; Senior Engineer, SDD, 1972-77; Engineer, Public Works Department, Hong Kong Government, 1977-80; Senior Engineer, then Principal Engineer, SDD, 1980-87; Deputy Chief Engineer, 1987-91; Director and Chief Engineer, Engineering, Water and Waste Directorate, Scottish Office Environment Department, 1991-95. Recreations: Rotary; sailing; golf. Address: (h.) Oriel House, Academy Square, Limekilns, Fife KY11 3HN; T.-01383 872218.

Paton, Hon. Lady (Ann Paton). Senator of the College of Justice, since 2000; b. 1952, Glasgow; m., Dr James Y. Paton. Educ. Laurel Bank School, Glasgow; Glasgow University (MA, LLB). Advocate, 1977; Standing Junior Counsel: Queen's and Lord Treasurer's Remembrancer, 1979, Office of Fair Trading in Scotland, 1981; QC (Scot), 1990; Advocate Depute, 1992-94. Director, Scottish Council of Law Reporting, 1995-2000; Member, Criminal Injuries Compensation Board, 1995-2000. Recreations: sailing; music; art. Address: (b.) Parliament House, Edinburgh, EH1 1RQ.

Paton, Rev. Anne Shaw, BA, BD. Minister, East Kilbride Old Parish Church, since 2001; b. 10.11.63, Glasgow; m.,

Thomas Moan; 2 s. Educ. Vale of Leven Academy; Jordanhill College of Education; Glasgow University. Primary School Teacher, West Dunbartonshire. Address: 40 Maxwell Drive, The Village, East Kilbride G74 4HJ; T.-01355 220732; e-mail: annepaton@fsmail.net

Paton, Dr. James Y., BSc, MBChB, MD, DCH, FRCPH, FRCP. Hon. Consultant Respiratory Paediatrician, Royal Hospital for Sick Children, Glasgow, since 2001; Reader, Paediatric Respiratory Medicine, University of Glasgow, since 2001; b. 8.12.51, Glasgow; m., Ann Paton. Educ. Jordanhill College School; Glasgow University. Publications: chapters and articles on Paediatric Respiratory Disease. Recreations: cycling; sailing; hill walking; music. Address: (b.) Department of Child Health, RHSC, Yorkhill, Glasgow G3; T.-0141-201 0238; e-mail: james.paton@glasgow.ac.uk

Paton, Laura, LLB, LLM. Lead Inspector, HM Inspectorate of Contabulary for Scotland (HMICS), since 2013. Educ. University of Glasgow; Glasgow Graduate School of Law. Policy Officer, Children 1st, 2004-05; Policy Development, Scotland's Commissioner for Children and Young People, 2005-09; Senior Policy Officer & National Preventive Mechanism Co-ordinator, HM Inspectorate of Prisons, 2009-13. Address: HM Inspectorate of Constabulary for Scotland (HMICS), 1st Floor West, St Andrew's House, Regent Road, Edinburgh EH1 3DG; T.-0131 244 5614.

Patterson, Lindy Ann, QC, LLB (Hons), WS, FCIArb, FCIES. Partner, CMS Cameron McKenna; b. 12.9.58, Berwick-upon-Tweed. Educ. Eyemouth High School; Edinburgh University. Honorary Member, Royal Institution of Chartered Surveyors; FIDIC President's List of Dispute Adjudicators; Convenor of Construction Accreditation Panel, Law Society of Scotland; contributor to Diploma in Legal Practice, University of Edinburgh; Freeman of Worshipful Company of Arbitrators. Recreations: hill-walking; travel. Address: (b.) Saltire Court, Castle Terrace, Edinburgh.

Pattison, Rev. Kenneth John, MA, BD, STM. Retired Minister; b. 22.4.41, Glasgow; m., Susan Jennifer Brierley Jenkins; 1 s.; 2 d. Educ. Lenzie Academy; Glasgow University; Union Theological Seminary, New York. Minister, Church of Central Africa Presbyterian, Malawi, 1967-77; Minister, Park Parish Church, Ardrossan, 1977-84; Chaplain, Glasgow Royal Infirmary, 1984-90; Associate Minister, St. Andrew's and St. George's, Edinburgh, 1990-96; Minister, Kilmuir and Logie Easter Parish Church, Ross-shire, 1996-2004. Convener, Chaplaincies Committee, Church of Scotland, 1993-96. Recreations: gardening; family history. Address: (h.) 2 Castle Way, St. Madoes, Perthshire PH2 7NY; T.-01738 860340.

Patton, John. National Development Officer, Scottish League of Credit Unions, 2000-07; National President, Educational Institute of Scotland, 1999-2000; b. Derry, 1942; m., Elizabeth Scott; 3 c. Educ. St Columb's College; St Mary's University College, Belfast; University of Delaware. Taught English in Northern Ireland, 1964-71; Press Officer, civil rights movement in Derry, 1968-70; taught in West Lothian, 1971-73; Zambia, 1973-76, Central Region, since 1976; Headteacher, Banchory Primary School, Tullibody, 1985-90, Craigbank Primary School, Sauchie, 1990-2000. Occasional contributor to BBC, Herald and Scotsman on micro-finance and educational issues; fluent Irish Gaelic speaker. Recreations: Scottish and

Irish traditional music; photography.
E-mail: john.patton@phototilly.eu

Pattullo, Sir (David) Bruce, Kt, CBE, BA, Hon. LLD (Aberdeen), DUniv (Stirling), Hon. DBA (Strathclyde), FRSE, FCIB (Scot). Governor, Bank of Scotland, 1991-98; Director (Non-Executive): British Linen Bank, 1977-98, Bank of Wales PLC, 1986-98, NWS Bank, 1986-98; b. 2.1.38, Edinburgh; m., Fiona Jane Nicholson; 3 s.; 1 d. Educ. Belhaven Hill School; Rugby; Hertford College, Oxford. National Service commission, Royal Scots (seconded to West Africa); joined Bank of Scotland, 1961; winner, first prize, Institute of Bankers in Scotland, 1964; Bank of Scotland: Manager, Investment Services Department, 1967-71, Deputy Manager, Bank of Scotland Finance Co. Ltd., 1971-73, Chief Executive, Group Merchant Banking Activities, 1973-78, Deputy Treasurer, 1978, Treasurer and General Manager, 1979-88, Director, 1980-98, Group Chief Executive and a Deputy Governor, Bank of Scotland, 1988-91. Chairman, Committee of Scottish Clearing Bankers, 1981-83 and 1987-89; Director, Standard Life Assurance Co., 1985-96; President, Institute of Bankers in Scotland, 1990-92. Recreations: tennis; hill-walking. Address: (h.) 6 Cammo Road, Edinburgh EH4 8EB.

Paul, Jeanette McIntosh, BSc, BArch (Hons), RIBA, ARIAS. Associate Dean of Learning and Teaching, Duncan of Jordanstone College of Art and Teaching, University of Dundee (Head of Learning and Teaching, 2010-2014, Head of Postgraduate Studies, 2007-2010, Head of School of Design, 2004-07); b. 27.10.56, Giffnock; m., Roderick. Educ. St. Denis School, Edinburgh; Duncan of Jordanstone College, University of Dundee. Assistant Architect, Sir Basil Spence Glover of Ferguson, Edinburgh, 1982-85; Project Architect, Andrew Merrylees Associates, Edinburgh, 1985-87; Senior Architect, Wilson of Wolmersley, Perth, 1987-88; University of Dundee: Lecturer in Interior and Environmental Design, 1988-2002, Senior Lecturer and Deputy Head, School of Design, 2002-04. President, Dundee Institute of Architects, 1999-2001; Board of Directors for WASPS (Workshop of Artists' Studio Provision Scotland Ltd.), since 1999; Joint Winner of The Scottish Design Award 2000 for best commercial/product design. Recreations: travelling; reading; dancing. Address: (b.) Duncan of Jordanstone College, Perth Road, Dundee DD1 4HT; T.-01382 345290. E-mail: j.m.paul@dundee.ac.uk

Pawley, Emeritus Professor G. Stuart, MA, PhD, FRSE, FRS. Professor of Computational Physics, Edinburgh University, 1985-2002, Emeritus Professor, since 2002; b. 22.6.37, Ilford; m., Anthea Jean Miller; 2 s.; 1 d. Educ. Bolton School, Corpus Christi College, Cambridge. Lecturer, Edinburgh University, 1964; Reader, 1970; Personal Chair, 1985; Guest Professor, Aarhus University, Denmark, 1969-70. Recreations: choral singing; mountain walking; rock gardening. Address: (b.) Acres of Keillour, Perth PH1 3RA.

Paxton, Professor Roland Arthur, MBE, MSc, PhD, HonDEng, CEng, FICE, FRSE, AMCST. Chairman, Institution of Civil Engineers Panel for Historical Engineering Works, 1990-2003, Member Scotland, since 1975; Chairman, Historic Bridge and Infrastructure Awards Panel, England and Wales, 1998-2007; Commissioner, Royal Commission on the Ancient and Historical Monuments of Scotland, 1992-2002; Hon. Professor, School of the Built Environment, Heriot-Watt University, since 1994; b. 29.6.32, Altrincham; m., Ann; 2 d. Educ. Altrincham Grammar School; Manchester College of Science and Technology; Heriot-Watt University.

Cartographical surveyor, Ordnance Survey, 1949-55; National Service Royal Artillery, 1951-53; Civil Engineer, Corporations of Sale, Manchester, Leicester, Edinburgh, and Lothian Regional Council, retiring as Senior Principal Engineer, 1959-90; Hon. Senior Research Fellow, Heriot Watt University, 1990-94. Chairman, Forth Bridges Visitor Centre Trust, 1997-2012; Secretary and Director, Laigh Milton Viaduct Conservation Project, 1992-99; Trustee, James Clerk Maxwell Foundation, since 1999; President, Edinburgh Bibliographical Society, 1992-95, Member, since 1966; Winner, Institution of Civil Engineers' Garth Watson Medal, 1999 and Carr Prize, 2001; Lecturer Award, Philadelphia Association for Preservation Technology International, 2000; American Society of Civil Engineers' History and Heritage Award, 2003; Appreciation Award, 2013; author of books and papers on technical innovation, conservation of structures, Telford, Rennie, the Stevensons and historical engineering; organiser, historical engineering plaques; contributor to BBC radio and TV news and documentaries. Address: (b.) School of Energy, Geoscience, Infrastructure and Society, Heriot-Watt University, Edinburgh EH14 4AS; T.-0131-449 5111.

Peacock, Andrew John, BSc, MPhil, MD, FRCP. Honorary Professor, Glasgow University, since 2003; Consultant Physician (Respiratory), West Glasgow Hospitals, since 1990; Director, Scottish Pulmonary Vascular Unit; b. 13.11.49, Montreal; m., Jila Pezeshgi; 1 s.; 2 d. Educ. Westminster School; St. Bartholomew's Hospital Medical College, London University; Caius College, Cambridge University. Senior House Officer, St. Bartholomew's, Addenbrookes and Queen Square Hospitals; Registrar, Brompton Hospital; Senior Registrar, Southampton Hospitals; Research Fellow, University of Colorado; Visiting Scientist, National Heart and Lung Institute, London. Physiologist, 1993 British Expedition to Everest. Publication: Pulmonary Circulation: a handbook for clinicians. Recreations: anything to do with mountains; wine; tennis; golf. Address: (b.) Scottish Pulmonary Vascular Unit, Regional Heart and Lung Centre, Golden Jubilee National Hospital, Glasgow G81 4HX; T.-0141-951-5497.

Peacock, Professor John Andrew, MA, PhD, FRS, FRSE. Professor of Cosmology, Edinburgh University, since 1998; b. 27.3.56, Shaftesbury; m., Heather; 1 s.; 2 d. Educ. Cedars School, Leighton Buzzard; Jesus College, Cambridge. Research Astronomer, Royal Observatory, Edinburgh, 1981-92; Head of Research, Royal Observatory, Edinburgh, 1992-98; UK representative, Anglo-Australian Telescope Board, 1995-2000; Head of Institute for Astronomy, 2007-13. Winner of Shaw Prize in Astronomy, 2014. Publications: Cosmological Physics, 1999. Recreations: playing classical clarinet; hill walking. Address: (b.) Institute for Astronomy, Edinburgh University, Royal Observatory, Edinburgh, EH9 3HJ; T.-0131-668 8100; e-mail: jap@roe.ac.uk

Peacock, Peter James, CBE. Policy Director, Community Land Scotland; Chair, Customer Forum for Water in Scotland; Member, RSPB Scottish Committee; Ofcom Advisory Committee for Scotland; MSP (Labour) Highlands and Islands, 1999-2011; former Member, Rural Affairs and Environment Committee and Standards Committee; Scotland Bill Committee; formerly Minister for Education and Young People and variously, Minister with responsibility for: Finance, EU Structure Funds, Public Service Reform, Local Government, Gaelic, Children and Education, 1999-2006; b. 27.2.52, Edinburgh; 2 s. Educ. Hawick High School; Jordanhill College of Education, Glasgow. Community Worker, Orkney Islands, 1973-75; former Area Officer, Highlands, Islands, Grampian,

Scottish Association of Citizens Advice Bureaux; Member, Highland Regional Council, 1982-96; former Leader and Convener, Highland Council (1995-99); formerly: Member, Highlands and Islands Convention, Honorary President, Scottish Library Association, Board Member, Centre for Highlands and Islands Policy Studies, Member, Scottish Natural Heritage, Non-Executive Director, Scottish Post Office Board, Member, Highland Area Committee, SCDI, Chairman, Scottish Library and Information Council, Vice-President, COSLA; Member, European Committee of the Regions, 1993-99; Chair, Commonwealth Education Ministers Conference, 2003; former Training, Organisation and Policy Consultant; Co-author, Vice-Chairman, subsequently Chairman of successful applicant group for Independent Local Radio franchise, Moray Firth. Recreations: ornithology; golf; watching rugby union. Address: (h.) 'Birchwood', IV2 7QR; T.-01667 460190.

Peaker, Professor Malcolm, FRS, DSc, HonDSc, PhD, FZS, FIBiol, FRSE. Director, Hannah Research Institute, Ayr, 1981-2003; Hannah Professor, Glasgow University, 1981-2003; b. 21.8.43, Stapleford, Nottingham; m., Stephanie Jane Large; 3 s. Educ. Henry Mellish Grammar School, Nottingham; Sheffield University, BSc Zoology; DSc; University of Hong Kong, SRC NATO Scholar; PhD. ARC Institute of Animal Physiology, 1968-78; Head, Department of Physiology, Hannah Research Institute, 1978-81. Chairman, London Zoo Board, 1992-93; Vice-President, Zoological Society of London, 1992-94; Member, Editorial Board: Journal of Dairy Science, 1975-78, International Zoo Yearbook, 1978-82, Journal of Endocrinology, 1981-91; Editor, British Journal of Herpetology, 1977-81; Munro Kerr Lecture, 1997; Raine Distinguished Visitor, University of Western Australia, 1998; 10th Edinburgh Centre for Rural Research/Royal Society of Edinburgh/Institute of Biology Annual Lecture, 2000; Distinguished Lecturer, University of Hong Kong 2002; Chairman, British Nutrition Foundation, 2002-04, Governor, since 1997; Member, Rank Prize Funds Advisory Committee on Nutrition, since 1997. Publications: Salt Glands in Birds and Reptiles, 1975; Avian Physiology (Editor), 1975; Comparative Aspects of Lactation (Editor), 1977; Physiological Strategies in Lactation (Co-Editor), 1984; Intercellular Signalling in the Mammary Gland (Editor), 1995; Biological Signalling and the Mammary Gland (Editor), 1997; papers. Recreations: vertebrate zoology; natural history; golf; grumbling about bureaucrats. Address: (b.) 13 Upper Crofts, Alloway, Ayr KA7 4QX.

Pearson of Rannoch, Lord (Malcolm Everard MacLaren Pearson). Life Peer; Leader, United Kingdom Independence Party (UKIP), since 2010; b. 20.7.42; m.; 3 d. Chairman, PWS Holdings plc; founded Rannoch Trust, 1984. Hon. President, RESCARE (National Society for Mentally Handicapped People in Residential Care), since 1994; Hon. President, The Register of Chinese Herbal Medicine, since 1998. Hon. LLD, CNAA.

Pearson, Graeme. MSP (Labour), South Scotland, 2011-16; Shadow Cabinet Secretary for Justice, 2013-16; b. 1.4.50. A police officer for 38 years, ending his career as director-general of the Scottish Crime and Drug Enforcement Agency. Was responsible for the introduction of the first Scottish CCTV system in Airdrie in the 1980s. A graduate of Glasgow University, now works there as an honorary professor.

Pearson, Iain Clark, FCIBS. Consultant, The Royal Faculty of Procurators in Glasgow; retired senior banker; b. 13.5.45, Kilmarnock; m., Margaret McMillan; 1 s.; 1 d. Educ. Cumnock Academy. The Royal Bank of Scotland PLC: Senior Manager, Chester, 1986-89, Senior Manager,

Glasgow West George Street, 1989-93, Regional Retail Director (Glasgow and West of Scotland), 1993-95, Local Director (Corporate Banking), Glasgow and West of Scotland, 1995-98. 2005 President, New Cumnock Burns Club; 1989 President, Chartered Institute of Bankers, Chester and North Wales. Recreations: football; golf (St. Nicholas, Prestwick); reading. Address: (h.) 8, Bellevale Avenue, Ayr KA7 2RP; T.-01292 264236; e-mail: icpearson@btinternet.com

Pearson, Robbie. Acting Chief Executive, Healthcare Improvement Scotland, since 2016. Educ. University of St Andrews. Director of Planning and Performance, NHS Borders, 2003-2010; Acting Deputy Director/Head of Healthcare Planning, Scottish Government, 2010-2012; Deputy Chief Executive/Director of Scrutiny and Assurance, Healthcare Improvement Scotland, since 2012. Address: Edinburgh Office, Gyle Square, 1 South Gyle Crescent, Edinburgh EH12 9EB; T.-0131 623 4300.

Peat, Jeremy Alastair, OBE, BA, MSc, FRSE, FRSA. Director, David Hume Institute, 2005-2014; monthly columnist, The Herald, since 2005; Board Member, Scottish Enterprise, since 2011, Chair, Economic Policy Committee; Board of Governors, BBC, 2005-06; Panel member: Competition Commission, 2005-2014, Competition and Markets Authority, since 2014; National Trustee for Scotland and Board Member, BBC Trust, 2007-2010; Chair, BBC Pension Trust, 2005-2011; Panel Member, Competition and Markets Authority; Visiting Professor, University of Strathclyde's International Public Policy Institute; Board Member, Signet Accreditation Society; Trustee, Royal Zoological Society of Scotland, since 2010, Chair of Trustees, since 2012; formerly Member, Church of Scotland Commission on the Purposes of Economic Activity; Group Chief Economist, Royal Bank of Scotland, 1993-2005; formerly Vice Chair, Scottish Higher Education Funding Council; Honorary Professor, Heriot-Watt University; Honorary Doctor of Law, Aberdeen University; Honorary Doctor of Letters, Heriot Watt University; Fellow, Industry and Parliament Trust; Fellow, Chartered Institute of Bankers for Scotland; b. 20.3.45, Haywards Heath; m., Philippa Ann; 2 d. Educ. St. Paul's School, London; Bristol University; University College London. Economic Assistant/Economic Adviser, Ministry of Overseas Development, 1969-77; Economic Adviser, Manpower Services Commission, 1978-80; Head, Employment Policy Unit, Ministry of Finance and Development Planning, Government of Botswana, 1980-84; Economic Adviser, HM Treasury, 1984-85; Senior Economic Adviser, Scottish Office, 1985-93. Fellow of the Royal College of Physicians in Edinburgh (2015). Recreations: walking; reading; listening to music; golf.

Peattie, Cathy. MSP (Labour), Falkirk East, 1999-2011; former Deputy Convener, Transport Infrastructure and Climate Change Committee; former Convener, cross-party groups on: Carers; Culture and Media; Men's Violence against Women and Children. Former Convenor, Council of Voluntary Service Scotland; former Chair, Scottish Labour Women's Committee.

Peden, Professor George Cameron, MA, DPhil, FRHistS, FRSE. Emeritus Professor of History, Stirling University, since 2008; b. 16.2.43, Dundee; m., Alison Mary White; 3 s. Educ. Grove Academy, Broughty Ferry; Dundee University; Brasenose College, Oxford. Sub-Editor, Dundee Evening Telegraph, 1960-68; mature student, 1968-75; Tutorial Assistant, Department of Modern History, Dundee University, 1975-76; Temporary Lecturer, School of History, Leeds University, 1976-77; Lecturer in Economic and Social History, then Reader in Economic History,

Bristol University, 1977-90; Professor of History, Stirling University, 1990-2008; Visiting Fellow: All Souls College, Oxford, 1988-89, St. Catherine's College, Oxford, 2002. Publications: British Rearmament and the Treasury 1932-39, 1979; British Economic and Social Policy: Lloyd George to Margaret Thatcher, 1985; Keynes, The Treasury and British Economic Policy, 1988; The Treasury and British Public Policy, 1906-1959, 2000; Keynes and his Critics: Treasury Responses to the Keynesian Revolution, 1925-46 (Editor), 2004; The Transformation of Scotland: The Economy, since 1700 (Co-Editor), 2005; Arms, Economics and British Strategy: From Dreadnoughts to Hydrogen Bombs, 2007. Recreation: hill-walking. Address: (h.) Ardvurich, Leny Feus, Callander FK17 8AS; T.-01877 30488; e-mail: george.peden@stir.ac.uk

Peebles, Don. Head of CIPFA (Chartered Institute of Public Finance and Accountancy) Scotland, since 2013. Qualified accountant; background in local authority finance; former Policy & Technical Officer, Audit Scotland; joined CIPFA in 2002, led on CIPFA's work on local taxation, 2002-04, Policy & Technical Manager, 2004-2013, became CIPFA's Head of Devolved Government in 2014; led on the Institute's work on the Scottish referendum; appointed as the budget adviser to the Welsh Assembly's Finance Committee for the 2015/16 budget process. Address: CIPFA Scotland, 160 Dundee Street, Edinburgh EH11 1DQ; T.-0131 221 8640; e-mail: scotland@cipfa.org

Peggie, Robert Galloway Emslie, CBE, DUniv, FCCA. Chairman, Board, Edinburgh College of Art, 1998-99; Chairman, Local Government Staff Commission for Scotland, 1994-97; b. 5.1.29, Bo'ness; 1 s.; 1 d. Educ. Lasswade High School. Trainee Accountant, 1946-52; Accountant in industry, 1952-57; Edinburgh Corporation, 1957-72: O. and M. Officer, Assistant City Chamberlain, Deputy City Chamberlain, Reorganisation Steering Committee; Chief Executive, Lothian Regional Council, 1974-86; Commissioner (Ombudsman) for Local Administration in Scotland, 1986-94. Former Member, Court, Heriot-Watt University (Convener, Finance Committee); Governor, Edinburgh College of Art; former Trustee, Lloyds TSB Foundation. Recreation: golf. Address: 9A Napier Road, Edinburgh EH10 5AZ; T.-0131-229 6775.

Pelan, John David, BA (Hons). Director, Scottish Civic Trust, since 2010; b. 18.5.64, Belfast; m., Jane Ogden-Smith. Educ. St Mary's CBS Belfast; Trinity College Dublin. Formerly Director of Communications and Depute Secretary, Royal Incorporation of Architects in Scotland, 1993-2006; Director John Pelan Associates, since 2006. Editor, Prospect Magazine, 1999-2001. Recreations: literature; photography. Address: (b.) Scottish Civic Trust, The Tobacco Merchants House, 42 Miller Street, Glasgow G1 1DT; T.-0141-221 1466.
E-mail: john.pelan@scottishcivictrust.org.uk

Pelham Burn, Angus Maitland, LLD, JP, DL. Director, Bank of Scotland, 1977-2000, Chairman, North of Scotland Board, 1973-2001; Chairman, Aberdeen Airport Consultative Committee, 1986-2006; Director, Dana Petroleum plc, 1999-2008; b. 13.12.31, London; m., Anne; 4 d. Educ. Harrow; North of Scotland College of Agriculture. Hudson's Bay Company, 1951-58; Wolf Bounty Officer (Ontario), 1956-59; Company Director, since 1958; Chairman, Scottish Provident, 1995-98; Chairman, Aberdeen Asset Management PLC (formerly, Aberdeen Trust PLC), 1992-2000; Director, Abtrust Scotland Investment Company, 1989-96; Member, Kincardine County Council, 1967-75 (Vice Convener, 1973-75); Member, Grampian Regional Council, 1974-94;

Member, Accounts Commission for Scotland, 1980-94 (Deputy Chairman, 1987-94); Member, Gordon Highlander Museum Committee, 1994-2009; Director, Aberdeen Association for Prevention of Cruelty to Animals, 1975-95 (Chairman, 1984-89); former Chairman, Order of St. John (Aberdeen) Ltd.; Council Member, Winston Churchill Memorial Trust, 1984-94; Member, Queen's Bodyguard for Scotland (Royal Company of Archers), 1968-2009; Vice Lord Lieutenant, Kincardineshire, 1978-99, Deputy Lieutenant, since 1999; Governor, Lathallan School, 2001-04; Honorary Degree of Doctor of Law, (Robert Gordon University), 1996; Patron, Knockando Woolmill Trust, since 2012. Recreations: gardening; wildlife photography. Address: The Kennels Cottage, Dess, Aboyne, Aberdeenshire AB34 5AY.
E-mail: snow.bunting2@gmail.com

Pelly, Frances, RSA. Sculptor; b. 21.7.47, Edinburgh. Educ. Morrison's Academy, Crieff; Duncan of Jordanstone College of Art, Dundee. Part-time lecturing, Dundee, 1974-78; full-time lecturing, Grays School of Art, Aberdeen, 1979-83. Recreations: riding; wildlife; gardening. Address: Quoyblackie, Rendall, Orkney KW17 2HA; T.-01856 751464.

Peltenburg, Emeritus Professor Edgar, BA, PhD, FSA, FRSE. Emeritus Professor of Archaeology, Edinburgh University, since 2008, Professor, 1993-2008; Director, Lemba Archaeological Research Centre, Cyprus, since 1985; b. 28.5.42, Montreal; 3 s.; 1 d. Educ. D'Arcy McGee, Montreal; Birmingham University. Lecturer in Archaeology and Resident Staff Tutor in Argyll, Glasgow University, 1969-78; Edinburgh University: Lecturer in Near Eastern Archaeology, 1978-88, Reader in Archaeology, 1988-93. Member of many committees, including The Council for British Research in the Levant. Publications include: Euphrates River Valley Settlement. The Carchemish Sector in The Third Millennium BC, 2007. Address: (b.) School of History, Classics and Archaeology, University of Edinburgh, Doorway 4, Teviot Place, Edinburgh EH8 9AG; T.-0131-650 2379; e-mail: e.peltenburg@ed.ac.uk

Pender, Sheriff David James, LLB (Hons). Sheriff of North Strathclyde, since 1995; b. 7.9.49, Glasgow; m., Elizabeth; 2 s.; 2 d. Educ. Queen's Park Senior Secondary School, Glasgow; Edinburgh University. Partner, MacArthur Stewart, Solicitors, Oban, 1977. Recreations: reading; travel; bridge. Address: (b.) Sheriff Courthouse, St. James Street, Paisley; T.-0141-887 5291.

Pender, Professor Gareth, BSc, PhD, CEng, FREng, FRSE, FICE, FCIWEM. Professor of Environmental Engineering, Heriot-Watt University, since 2000, Head of School; b. 24.1.60, Helensburgh; m., Isobel McNaught Connell; 2 s. Educ. Vale of Leven Academy; University of Strathclyde. Civil Engineer, Crouch and Hogg, Consulting Engineers, 1984-89; Lecturer, University of Glasgow, 1989-2000. Recreations: golf; skiing. Address: (b.) School of the Built Environment, Heriot-Watt University, Edinburgh EH14 4AS; T.-0131-451 3312; e-mail: g.pender@hw.ac.uk

Penman, Derek, QPM, LLB (Hons), MIoD. HM Inspector of Constabulary for Scotland, since 2014. Educ. Glasgow University. Career: joined Central Scotland Police in 1982 as a cadet before becoming a Constable in 1984; had a varied career, rising through the ranks before being appointed as Temporary Assistant Chief Constable in 2007. Following completion of the UK Strategic Command Course in 2008, was appointed as Assistant Chief Constable with Grampian Police; Deputy Chief Constable, Central Scotland Police, 2011, temporary Chief Constable, 2011-13; Assistant Chief Constable, Local Policing North, 2013-14. Awarded QPM in the 2014 Queen's Birthday Honours; Honorary Colonel with Angus and Dundee Battalion of Army Cadet Force; Member of the Institute of Directors. Address: HM Inspectorate of Constabulary for Scotland (HMICS), 1st Floor West, St Andrew's House, Regent Road, Edinburgh EH1 3DG; T.-0131 244 5614.

Penman, Ian Douglas, BSc (Hons), MD, FRCP(Edin). Consultant Gastroenterologist, Western General Hospital, Edinburgh, since 1997; part-time Senior Lecturer, University of Edinburgh, since 1997; b. 2.2.64, Ayr; m., Jacqueline Patricia Kellaway; 1 s.; 1 d. Educ. Ayr Academy; University of Glasgow. Advanced Fellow, Medical University, South Carolina, USA, 1997-98. T.-0131-537 1758; e-mail: ian.penman@luht.scot.nhs.uk

Pennington, Professor (Thomas) Hugh, CBE, MB BS, PhD, Hon. DSc (Lancaster, Strathclyde, Aberdeen, Hull, Harper Adams), FRCPath, FRCPEdin, FRSA, FMedSci, FRSE. Professor of Bacteriology Emeritus, University of Aberdeen; b. 19.4.38, Edgware, Middlesex; m., Carolyn Ingram Beattie; 2 d. Educ. Lancaster Royal Grammar School; St. Thomas's Hospital Medical School, London University. House appointments, St. Thomas's Hospital, 1962-63; Assistant Lecturer in Medical Microbiology, St. Thomas's Hospital Medical School, 1963-67; Postdoctoral Fellow, University of Wisconsin (Madison), 1967-68; Lecturer then Senior Lecturer in Virology, University of Glasgow, 1969-79; Dean of Medicine University of Aberdeen, 1987-92; Professor of Bacteriology, Aberdeen University, 1979-2003; Governor, Rowett Research Institute, 1980-88, and 1996-2003; Member, Board of Directors, Moredun Research Institute, 2002-06; Chair, Expert Group on 1996 E.coli Outbreak in Central Scotland; Member: BBC Broadcasting Council for Scotland, 2000-05 (Vice Chair, 2003-05); Member, Scottish Food Advisory Committee of the Food Standards Agency, 2000-05; Member, Advisory Council of Campaign for Science and Engineering in the UK; Member, Technical Advisory Group, World Food Program, 2002-07; President, Society for General Microbiology, 2003-06; Chair, Public Inquiry into 2005 South Wales E. coli Outbreak; Caroline Walker Trust Consumer Advocate Award, 1997; Royal Institute of Public Health John Kershaw Memorial Prize, 1998; Thomas Graham Medal, Royal Glasgow Philosophical Society, 2001; Observer Food Monthly Hall of Fame Winner, 2005; Royal Scottish Society of Arts, Silver Medal, 2001, Keith Prize, 2006; Burgess of Guild, City of Aberdeen, 2002; Joseph Lister Medal, Society of Chemical Industry, 2009; Royal Environmental Health Institute of Scotland, Award for Meritorious Endeavours in Environmental Health, 2010. Publications: When Food Kills, 2003; papers, articles and book chapters on viruses and bacteria, particularly their molecular epidemiology, and on food safety; contributor, London Review of Books; Editorial Consultant, The Lancet. Recreations: collecting books; dipterology. Address: (b.) 13 Carlton Place, Aberdeen AB15 4BR; e-mail: mmb036@abdn.ac.uk

Penrose, Rt. Hon. Lord (George William Penrose), PC, MA, LLB, LLD, DUniv, CA, FRSE. Senator of the College of Justice, 1990-2005; b. 2.6.38, Port Glasgow; m., Wendy Margaret Ralph Cooper; 1 s.; 2 d. Educ. Port Glasgow High School; Greenock High School; University of Glasgow. Advocate, 1964; QC, 1978; Procurator to General Assembly of the Church of Scotland, 1984-90; Advocate Depute, 1987-88; Home Advocate Depute, 1989-90; Judge (1990), First Division, Inner House, Court of Session, 2001-05; PC, 2001; Equitable Life Inquiry Reporter, 2004; Chairman of Court, Heriot-Watt University, since 2008;

Reporter, The Penrose Inquiry into blood infection. Recreation: walking.

Pentland, John. MSP (Labour), Motherwell and Wishaw, 2011-16. Born in Motherwell, worked as a welder and spent 28 years with the British Steel Corporation. Elected to Motherwell Council in 1992. PA to Frank Roy MP from 1997 and chair of North Lanarkshire Municipal Bank for 14 years.

Pentland, Hon. Lord (Paul B. Cullen), LLB (Hons), QC. Chairman, Scottish Law Commission, since 2014; Senator of the College of Justice, since 2008; Queen's Counsel, since 1995; b. 11.3.57, Gosforth; m., Joyce Nicol; 2 s.; 1 d. Educ. St Augustine's High School, Edinburgh; Edinburgh University. Clerk, Faculty of Advocates, 1986-91; Standing Junior Counsel, Department of the Environment in Scotland, 1988-91; Advocate Depute, 1992-95; Solicitor General for Scotland, 1995-97; Consultative Steering Group on the Scottish Parliament, 1998-99. Recreations: tennis; bridge. Address: (b.) Supreme Court, Parliament House, Edinburgh EH1 1RQ; T.-0131 225 2595.

Peppé, William Lawrence Tosco, OBE, JP, DL; b. 25.11.37, India; m., Deirdre Eva Preston Wakefield; 3 s. Educ. Wellington College; King's College, Cambridge. Naval Officer, 1955-91 – Commander. Vice Lord Lieutenant, Ross and Cromarty, Skye and Lochalsh, 2005-2012; Hon. Sheriff, Portree and Lochmaddy Courts, 2007; Chairman, Skye and Lochalsh Access Forum, 2007-2010. Recreation: country. Address: Glendrynoch Lodge, Carbost, Isle of Skye IV47 8SX; T.-01478 640218; e-mail: peppe@glendrynoch.co.uk

Pepper, Simon Richard, OBE, BSc, MSc, LLD. Rector, University of St. Andrews, 2005-08; Director, WWF Scotland, 1985-2005; Member, Forestry Commission National Committee for Scotland, 2003-09; Member, Cabinet Sub-committee on Sustainable Scotland, 2004-07; Member, Deer Commission for Scotland, 2005-2010; Chairman, Climate Challenge Fund Panel, 2008-2012; Board Member, Scottish Natural Heritage, since 2010; Member, Heritage Lottery Fund Scottish Committee, since 2011; b. 27.9.47, Worthing; m., Morag; 2 s.; 3 d. Educ. Aberdeen University; University College London. FAO Quelea Project, Chad, Central Africa, 1972-73; Country Parks Officer, Essex County Council, 1973-79; Director, Cultullich Holiday Courses, Aberfeldy, 1979-85. Vice Convenor, Millennium Forest for Scotland, 1995-2001; Member, Secretary of State's Advisory Group on Sustainable Development, 1994-99. Rowing blue, Aberdeen University, Scottish Champion VIIIs, 1971; British University Champion Pairs, 1971. Recreations: enjoying the wild; managing sheep and native woodland of 42 hectare holding. Address: (h.) Upper Brae of Cultullich, Aberfeldy PH15 2EN.

Percy, Professor John Pitkeathly (Ian), CBE, LLD, CA, FRSA. Chairman, John Menzies Pensions, since 2007, Trustee; former Senior Partner, Grant Thornton, London and Scotland; Chairman: Queen Margaret University, 2004-2010, CALA Group Ltd, 2000-2011; Deputy Chairman, The Weir Group PLC, 1996-2010; Scottish Provident, 1993-2001; President of the Foundation for Governance Research and Education; former Chairman: The Accounts Commission, Audit Scotland, Kiln PLC (retired 2005), Companies House (retired 2006); b. 16.1.42, Southport; m., Sheila; 2 d. Educ. Edinburgh Academy; Edinburgh University. Managing Partner, Grant Thornton, London, 1981-88; Honorary Professor of Accounting, Aberdeen

University, 1988. Freeman, City of London; Member, British Academy of Experts; Elder, St. Cuthbert's Church of Scotland; President, Institute of Chartered Accountants of Scotland, 1990-91; Trustee, National Trust for Scotland, since 2011, Deputy Chairman, until 2015. Recreations: golf; fishing. Address: (h.) 4 Westbank, Easter Park Drive, Edinburgh EH4 6SL.

Perman, Ray., BA Hons (Mod Hist), MBA. Director, David Hume Institute; Chairman, The James Hutton Institute. Author of HUBRIS: How HBOS wrecked the best bank in Britain (2012); The Man Who Gave Away His Island, A Life of John Lorne Campbell of Canna, 2010. Chairman, Access to Finance Expert Group, Department Business, Innovation & Skills, 2005-2013; b. 1947, London; m., Fay Young; 3 s. Educ. University of St. Andrews; Open University; University of Edinburgh. Journalist: The Times, the Financial Times; Deputy Editor, the Sunday Standard, 1969-83; Insider Publications Ltd: Managing Director, 1983-94, Chairman, 1994-96, Director, 1996-99; Development Director, Caledonian Publishing plc, 1994-96; Director, GJWS Ltd, 1997-99; Chief Executive, Scottish Financial Enterprise, 1999-2003. Chairman, Inner Ear Ltd, since 2000; Member of the Court, Heriot-Watt University, 2003-09; Board Member, Scottish Enterprise, 2004-09; Chairman, Social Investment Scotland, 2001-09; Chairman, Good Practice Ltd, 2005-2013. Trustee, Botanics Foundation, 2008-2011; Trustee, Poorboy Theatre Company; Chairman of Worldwide Fund for Nature (WWF) Scottish Advisory Council, 1998-2004; Member of the UK Board of Trustees of the WWF, 2001-04. Trustee of the Stewart Ivory Foundation, 2001-08. Recreations: painting; playing the blues; planting trees. Address: 14 East Claremont Street, Edinburgh EH7 4JP; T.-0131 556 4646; mobile: 07971 164315; e-mail: ray@rayperman.com

Perrie, Walter, MA, MPhil. Poet; b. 5.6.49, Lanarkshire. Educ. Hamilton Academy; Edinburgh and Stirling Universities. Publications: Books: Poem on a Winter Night, 1976; A Lamentation for the Children (SAC book award 1978), 1978; By Moon and Sun, 1980; Out of Conflict: Essays on Literature and Ideas, 1982; Concerning the Dragon (Poems), 1984; Roads that Move: a Journey through eastern Europe, 1991; From Milady's Wood and Other Poems, 1997; Caravanserai (poems), 2004; Decagon: Selected Poems, 1995-2005 (selected and edited with an introduction by John Herdman), 2005; Rhapsody of the Red Cliff (Poems), 2005; As Far as Thales: Beginning Philosophy, 2006; The King of France is Bald: Philosophy and Meaning, 2007; Twelve Fables of La Fontaine Made Owre intil Scots, 2007; Lyrics & Tales in Twa Tongues, 2010; First Fragments for an Unknown Lover (poem), 2012; Editing: Co Founding editor of Chapman, 1969-75; Guest editor, double issue of Lines Review on Canadian Literature, 1986; Managing editor, Margin, an international quarterly of the arts, 1986-91; presently Joint Editor of Fras Scottish literary journal, since 2004. Fellowships: Scottish-Canadian exchange fellowship, 1984-85 (based at UBC Vancouver); University of Stirling writer-in-residence, 1991; Strathkelvin District creative writing fellow, 1992-93. Address: (h.) 10 Croft Place, Dunning, Perthshire PH2 0SB.

Perry, John Scott (Jack), CBE, BSc (Pure Sci), DL. Chairman: Scottish Aquaculture Innovation Centre, since 2014, ICG-Longbow Senior Secured UK Property Debt Investments Limited, since 2012; Non Executive Director, European Assets Trust NV, since 2014; Treasurer and Member of Court, University of Strathclyde, since 2011; Chairman, Board of Directors, Hospice Developments Limited, since 2012; b. 23.11.54; m., Lydia; 1 s.; 2 d. Educ. Glasgow University; Strathclyde University. CA (ICAS), 1979; Certified Public Accountant (USA), 1985; Ernst & Young, 1976-2003: Managing Partner, Glasgow, 1995-

2003; Regional Industry Leader, Technol. Communications and Entertainment, Scotland and NI, 1999-2003; Chairman, CBI Scotland, 2001-03 (Member, Council, since 1996); Chief Executive, Scottish Enterprise, 2004-09; Non-Executive Director, Robert Wiseman Dairies, 2010-2012. Chairman: Craigholme School, 2000-07, TMRI Limited, since 2007; Member, Barclays Wealth Advisory Committee, 2010-2014. Former Member, Ministerial Task Force on Economic Forums. Honorary Doctorate in Business Administration, Edinburgh Napier University, 2010, University of Abertay Dundee, 2011. Recreations: golf; skiing; reading; current affairs. Clubs: Glasgow Academical; Royal and Ancient Golf; Western Gailes Golf. Address: Scottish Aquaculture Innovation Centre, Scion House, Stirling University Innovation Park, Stirling FK9 4NF.

Perth, 9th Earl of (John Eric Drummond), BA, MBA; b. 7.7.35. Educ. Downside School; Trinity College, Cambridge; Harvard University. Succeeded to title, 2002.

Pertwee, Professor Roger Guy, MA, DPhil, DSc. Professor of Neuropharmacology, University of Aberdeen, since 1999; Director of Pharmacology, GW Pharmaceuticals, since 2002; b. 21.9.42, Wembley; m., Teresa Bronagh; 1 s. Educ. Eastbourne College; Christ Church, Oxford. International Cannabinoid Research Society: International Secretary, since 1992, President, 1997-98 and 2007-08; First Chairman, International Association for Cannabinoid Medicines, 2005-07; Honorary Senior Research Fellow, Rowett Research Institute, since 1992; Visiting Professor, University of Hertfordshire, since 2000; Co-chairman of the Subcommittee on Cannabinoid Receptors of the International Union of Basic and Clinical Pharmacology (IUPHAR), since 2001; Mechoulam Award for Outstanding Contributions to Cannabinoid Research, 2002. Author of numerous papers on cannabinoids (http://isihighlycited.com/). British Pharmacological Society's Wellcome Gold Medal for Outstanding Contributions to Pharmacology (based mainly on research achievements, 2011). Honorary Fellowship of the British Pharmacological Society, 2013; International Association for Cannabinoid Medicines' Special Award for Major Contributions to the Re-introduction of Cannabis as a Medicine, 2013. Address: School of Medical Sciences, Institute of Medical Sciences, University of Aberdeen, Foresterhill, Aberdeen AB25 2ZD; T.-01224 437404; e-mail: rgp@abdn.ac.uk

Peterkin, Tom, MA Hons (Econ). Political Editor, Scotsman/Scotland on Sunday, since 2014. Educ. Clifton Hall, Midlothian; Glenalmond College, Perthshire; University of Edinburgh. Daily Telegraph: Scottish Political Correspondent, 2001-05, Ireland Correspondent, 2005-08, Correspndent based in London, 2008; Scottish Political Editor, Scotland on Sunday/Scotsman, 2008-2014. Recreations: golf; piping; skiing. Address: The Scotsman and Scotland on Sunday, Orchard Brae House, 30 Queensferry Road, Edinburgh EH4 2HS; T.-0131 311 7311; e-mail: tpeterkin@scotsman.com

Peterson, Eric Spence, LLB, DipLP, NP. Solicitor, since 1983; Honorary Sheriff, since 2010; b. 20.06.60, Lerwick; m., Moira Anne Stewart; 1 s.; 1 d. Educ. Anderson High School, Lerwick; Aberdeen University; Dundee University. Partner, Tait & Peterson, Solicitors & Estate Agents, Lerwick, since 1984; Secretary, Shetland Trust, since 2002; Accredited as a Specialist in Crofting Law by Law Society of Scotland, 2006-2011. Deacon, Lerwick Baptist Church; Member, Gideons International in the British Isles. Recreations: cycling; reading; occasional trout fishing. Address: (b.) Bank of Scotland Buildings, Lerwick,

Shetland; T.-01595 693010; e-mail: eric.peterson@tait-peterson.co.uk

Pethrick, Professor Richard Arthur, BSc, PhD, DSc, FRSC, FRSE, FIMMM. Emeritus Professor, University of Strathclyde, since 2008, appointed Professor in Chemistry in 1983 (Head of Department, 1992-2005); b. 26.10.42; m., Joan Knowles Hume; 1 s. Educ. North Gloucestershire College, Cheltenham; London University; Salford University. Editor: British Polymer Journal, Polymer Yearbook, Polymer International, International Journal of Polymer Materials; Journal of Adhesion Science and Technology; Member, Polymer Committee, European Science Foundation; Member, Committee, MACRO Group, 1979-84; Member, SERC Polymer Materials Committee, since 1994. Address: (b.) Department of Pure and Applied Chemistry, University of Strathclyde, Thomas Graham Building, Cathedral Street, Glasgow G1 1XL.

Petrie, Murray, FRICS; b. 8.6.46, Keith; m., Jennifer; 3 s. Educ. High School of Dundee. Consultant Chartered Surveyor. Former Vice Chair, NHS Tayside; former Director, Maggie Centre (Dundee). Former Chairman, Tayside Primary Care NHS Trust, 1999-2004; former Chair, Perth and Kinross Health and Social Care Co-operative. Recreations: rugby; golf; travelling. Address: (h.) Craigard, 6 Guthrie Terrace, Barnhill, Dundee DD5 2QX; T.-01382 776180.

Pettegree, Professor Andrew David Mark, FRHS. Professor of Modern History, St Andrews University, since 1998, Head of School of History; b. 16.9.57, Rhyl; m., Jane Ryan; 2 d. Educ. Oundle School; Oxford University (BA Hons). Schmidt Scholarship, 1980 (MA, DPhil, 1983); research scholarship, University of Hamburg, 1982-84; Research Fellow, Peterhouse, Cambridge; became Lecturer, St Andrews University, 1986; Reader, 1994; Director, St Andrews Reformation Studies Institute, 1993; Literary Director, Royal Historical Society, 1998. Publications include: Foreign Protestant Communities in Sixteenth Century London; Emden and the Dutch Revolt. Exile and the Development of Reformed Protestantism, 1992; The Early Reformation in Europe, 1992; Calvinism in Europe, 1540-1610 (Co-Editor); The Reformation of the Parishes. The Ministry and the Reformation in Town and Country, 1993; Calvinism in Europe, 1540-1620 (Co-Editor); Marian Protestantism. Six Studies, 1996; The Reformation World, 2000; Europe in the Sixteenth Century, 2001. Recreations: golf; tennis. Address: (b.) Reformation Institute, 69 South Street, St Andrews KY16 9AL; T.-01334 462903.

Pettigrew, Colin William, LLB (Hons). Sheriff of North Strathclyde at Paisley, since 2002; President, The Sheriffs Association, since 2015; b. 19.6.57, Glasgow; m., Linda; 1 s.; 1 d. Educ. The High School of Glasgow; The University of Glasgow. Assistant Court Solicitor, McClure, Naismith, Brodie and Co., Glasgow, 1980-82; Litigation Partner, Borland Johnston and Orr, Glasgow, then Borland Montgomerie Keyden, Glasgow, also TJ & WA Dykes, Hamilton, 1982-2002; Temporary Sheriff, 1999; Part Time Sheriff, 2001-02. Church of Scotland Elder, since 1983. Recreations: golf; travel; gardening and watching sport. Address: (b.) Sheriff Court House, St. James Street, Paisley; T.-0141-887-5291.

Phelps, Professor Alan David Reginald, MA, DPhil, CPhys, MIEEE, FInstP, Fellow APS, FRSE. Professor, Physics, Strathclyde University, since 1993 (Head of Department, 1998-2001); b. 2.6.44, Basingstoke; m., Susan Helen Marshall; 1 d. Educ. Haverfordwest Grammar School; King's College, Cambridge; University College,

Oxford. Research Associate, National Academy of Sciences (USA), 1972-73; Research Officer, Oxford University, 1973-78; Lecturer, then Senior Lecturer, then Reader in Physics, Strathclyde University, 1978-93, Deputy Head of Department, 1993-98 and 2004-09. Chairman, Plasma Physics Group, Institute of Physics, 1995-97. Publications: 500 research papers and reports. Recreations: hill-walking; country pursuits. Address: (b.) Department of Physics, John Anderson Building, Strathclyde University, Glasgow G4 0NG; T.-0141-548 3166; e-mail: a.d.r.phelps@strath.ac.uk

Philip, Rt. Hon. Lord (Alexander Morrison). Senator of the College of Justice, 1996-2007; b. 3.8.42, Aberdeen; m., Shona Mary Macrae (m. diss. 2013); 3 s. Educ. Glasgow High School; St. Andrews University; Glasgow University. Solicitor, 1967-72; Advocate, 1973; Advocate Depute, 1982-85; QC, 1984; Chairman, Medical Appeal Tribunals, 1988-92; Chairman, Scottish Land Court, 1993-96; President, Lands Tribunal for Scotland, 1993-96; Privy Counsellor, 2005. Recreations: piping; golf.

Phillips, Hamish Andrew, BSc, MB, BChir, MRCP(UK), MSc, FRCR, MD. Consultant Clinical Oncologist, Edinburgh Cancer Centre, since 1999; Honorary Clinical Senior Lecturer, University of Edinburgh, since 2002; b. 30.3.62, Hitchin, Herts; m., Nicola Clare Chapman; 1 s.; 2 d. Educ. Fettes College; University of St. Andrews; Trinity Hall, University of Cambridge. SHO in Medicine, Dundee and Leicester; Registrar, Research Registrar then Senior Registrar, Department of Clinical Oncology, Western General Hospital, Edinburgh. Recreations: golf; walking; cooking. Address: (b.) Department of Clinical Oncology, Edinburgh Cancer Centre, Western General Hospital, Edinburgh.

Phillips, Roddy, FRSA. Writer, since 1976; Creative Director of The Agency, since 2006; b. 15.11.57, Aberdeen; m., Catriona Millar; 2 s. Educ. Aberdeen Grammar School; Grays School of Art. Illustrator, Portrait Artist, 1976-85; Graphic Designer, Shell UK, 1976-79; Graphic Designer, Aberdeen Journals, 1980-85; Creative Director and TV Commercials Director, since 1985; weekly columnist of the Press & Journal, since 1996; co-founder of The Agency; Arts Critic of The Press & Journal, since 1987. Publication: The Familiar, 2009. Recreations: playing the guitar; classical music; walking; reading. E-mail: info@roddyphillips.com; web: roddyphillips.com

Phillips-Davies, Alistair. Chief Executive, SSE plc (formerly Scottish and Southern Energy plc), since 2013. Career: joined Southern Electric in 1997; joined the SSE Board as Energy Supply Director in 2002, Deputy Chief Executive, 2012-13 (Board-level responsibility for Generation, Energy Trading, Electricity and Gas Supply, Energy Efficiency, Customer Service, Sales, Marketing and Energy Services). Address: (b.) Inveralmond House, 200 Dunkeld Road, Perth PH1 3AQ.

Pia, Paul Dominic, LL.B. (Hons), WS, NP. Director of PaulPia Ltd: providing directorships, trusteeships and board advisorships, since 2010; b. 29.3.47, Edinburgh; m. Dr Anne Christine Argent; 3 d. Educ. Holy Cross Academy, Edinburgh; Universities of Edinburgh and Perugia; law apprentice Lindsays WS 1968-70; admitted as solicitor and member of Society of Writers to HM Signet 1971; solicitor, Burness LLP (formerly W & J Burness)1970 and partner, latterly senior corporate partner from 1974 to 2010; Associate Member, American Bar Association; Fellow of Institute of Directors and member of Corporate Governance Unit, 2003-04; Director of Scottish North American Business Council, 2000-04 and Trustee of Dewar Arts Awards, 2002-07; Chairman of Japan Society of Scotland, 1996-2000 and of Big Issue Foundation Scotland, 2000-08; Chairman of Moira Anderson Foundation, since 2010; Chairman of various pensions schemes including Baxters Food Group Pension Scheme and Royal Zoo of Scotland

Pension Scheme. Publications : Care Diligence and Skill (handbook for directors); Recreations: hill-walking; travel; foreign languages and oriental culture. Address: (b & h) 34/8 Rattray Grove, Edinburgh EH10 5TZ; T.-0131 447 5122; e-mail: paul@paulpia.com

Pickard, Willis Ritchie Sturrock, MA, LLD, DEd, FSA Scot; b. 21.5.41, Dunfermline; m., Ann Marie nee MacNeil; 2 d. Educ. Daniel Stewart's College; St. Andrews University. The Scotsman: Sub-editor, 1963-72, Leader writer, 1967-72, Features Editor, 1972-77; Editor, Times Educational Supplement Scotland, 1977-2001. Liberal Candidate, East Fife, 1970, 1974. Member, Scottish Arts Council; Chairman, Book Trust Scotland; Rector, Aberdeen University, 1988-90; former Chairman, Scottish Liberal Club; Trustee, National Library of Scotland, 2006-14; former Chairman, Theatre Objektiv; committee member of European Movement in Scotland; Chairman, Liberal International in Scotland; Fellow, Scottish Vocational Education Council. Publication: 'The Member for Scotland: a life of Duncan McLaren' (2011). Recreations: reading; history research. Address: (h.) 13 Lockharton Gardens, Edinburgh EH14 1AU; T.-0131 443 7755.

Pickering, Professor Martin John, BA, PhD, FRSE. Professor of The Psychology of Language and Communication, University of Edinburgh, since 2003; b. 02.06.66, London; m., Elizabeth; 1 s.; 2 d. Educ. City of London School; University of Durham; University of Edinburgh. Science and Engineering Research Council Postdoctoral Fellow, 1990-92; British Academy Postdoctoral Fellow, 1992-95; Glasgow University: Lecturer, 1995-99, Reader, 1999; Reader, Edinburgh University, 2000-03; British Academy Research Readership, 2005-07. Broadbent Lecturer, British Psychological Society, 2006. Publications: Associate Editor, Psychological Science, since 2007; over 70 journal papers. Recreation: entertaining my children. Address: (b.) Department of Psychology, University of Edinburgh, 7 George Square, Edinburgh EH8 9JZ; T.-0131 650 3447; e-mail: martin.pickering@ed.ac.uk

Pickett, Professor James, BSc (Econ), MLit. Professor Emeritus, Strathclyde University, since 1995; b. 7.6.29, Greenock; m., Janet Clelland; 1 s.; 3 d. Educ. Greenock Academy; School of Economics, Dundee; Edinburgh University; Glasgow University; University of Paris. Statistician, Dominion Bureau of Statistics, Canada, 1957-59; Lecturer, Senior Lecturer, Professor and Director, Livingstone Institute of Overseas Development, Strathclyde University, 1961-95; Visiting Professor, University of Saskatchewan, 1962-63; Special Economic Adviser, UN Economic Commision for Africa, 1965-68; Economic Adviser, African Development Bank, 1987-89; UN Chief Economic Adviser to Ethiopian Government, 1992-95; Consultant to British, Canadian and Ghanian Governments, UN, OECD; author and editor, seven books and numerous papers; FRSA; sometime President, Scottish Union of Students. Recreations: hill-walking; listening to music; photography; computing; long-suffering support of Greenock Morton F.C. Address: (h.) 18/4 Harbourside, Kip Village, Inverkip PA16 0BF; T.-01475 529519; e-mail: james.pickett77@btinternet.com

Pieri, Frank, LLB. Sheriff of South Strathclyde, Dumfries and Galloway, since 2005; b. 10.8.54, Glasgow; m., Dorothy Telfer; 2 d. Educ. St. Aloysius College, Glasgow; Glasgow University. Solicitor, 1976-93; Advocate at Scottish Bar, since 1994; Full Time Immigration Adjudicator, 2000-04; Part Time Sheriff, 2004. Council Member: Scottish Law Agents Society, 1991-93, Council of Immigration Judges, 2003. Recreations: ambling;

American crime fiction; Partick Thistle; opera. Address: (b.) Airdrie Sheriff Court, Graham Street, Airdrie ML6 6EE; T.-01236 751121.

Pighills, (Christopher) David, MA. Former Chairman, Pitlochry Festival Theatre; Board Member, New Park Educational Trust, since 2007; former Chairman, Board of Governors, Strathallan School; b. 27.11.37, Bradford. Educ. Rydal School; Cambridge University. Fettes College, 1960-75; Headmaster, Strathallan School, 1975-93. Recreations: shooting; gardening; golf. Address: 3 John Coupar Court, St Andrews KY16 9EB; T.-01334-477264.
E-mail: david.pighillso1@gmail.com

Pignatelli, Frank, CBE, MA, MEd, DEd, DUniv, CCMI, FSQA, FICPD, FScotvec, FRSA, FCIPD, FSC. Pro bono adviser/mentor to individuals and charitable/voluntary/not-for-profit organisations, since 2007; b. 22.12.46, Glasgow; m., Rosetta Anne; 1 s.; 1 d. Educ. St. Mungo's Academy, Glasgow; University of Glasgow. Teacher, head of modern languages, assistant head teacher, 1970-1978; member of directorate Strathclyde education department, 1978-1988; Executive Director of Education, Strathclyde Regional Council, 1988-96; Group Director, Human Resources, Associated Newspapers, London, 1996-97; Chairman and Managing Director, Executive Support and Development Consultancy, 1997-99; Chief Executive Officer, SUfI Ltd., 1999-2006; Visiting Professor, University of Glasgow: School of Education, 1993, Business School, 1997; Independent Adviser to Secretary of State for Scotland on appointments to public bodies, 1996-1999; Chairman: Scottish Management and Enterprise Council, 1999-2002, Strategic Review group on e-learning, 2004-2005, Scottish Parliament Futures Forum Project Board, 2007-08. E-mail frank@pignatelli.co.uk

Pike, (Kathryn) Lorna, MA (Hons). Project Co-ordinator, Faclair na Gàidhlig, since 2003; b. 8.8.56, Fort William. Educ. Lochaber High School, Fort William; Edinburgh University. Editor, Concise Scots Dictionary, 1979-83; Dictionary of the Older Scottish Tongue: Assistant Editor, 1984-86, Editor, 1986-2001; Editor, Scottish National Dictionary Association, 2001-02; Research Officer, Feasibility Study, Institute for the Languages of Scotland, 2001-02; Senior Editor, Scottish Language Dictionaries, 2002-04. Recreations: riding; photography; handicrafts. Address: (b.) Faclair na Gàidhlig, Fàs, Sabhal Mòr Ostaig, Sleat, Isle of Skye IV44 8RQ; T.-01471 888 273.

Pilcher, Rosamunde, OBE. Author; b. 22.9.24, Lelant, Cornwall. Began publishing short stories in Woman and Home, 1945; since then has published hundreds of short stories. Novels include Sleeping Tiger, Under Gemini, Wild Mountain Thyme, The Carousel, Voices in Summer, The Shell Seekers, September, The Blue Bedroom, Flowers in the Rain, Coming Home, Winter Solstice; play: The Dashing White Sergeant. Address: (h.) Penrowan, Longforgan, Perthshire; T.- Dundee 360393.

Pippard, Professor Martin John, BSc, MB, ChB, FRCPath, FRCP. Emeritus Professor of Haematology, Dundee University; b. 16.1.48, London; m., Grace Elizabeth; 2 s.; 1 d. Educ. Buckhurst Hill County High School; Birmingham University. House Physician and House Surgeon, 1972-73; Senior Medical House Officer, 1973-75; Research Fellow, Nuffield Department of Clinical Medicine, Oxford, 1975-78; MRC Travelling Research Fellow, University of Washington, Seattle, 1978-80; Wellcome Trust Research Fellow and Clinical Lecturer, Nuffield Department of Clinical Medicine, 1980-83; Consultant Haematologist, MRC Clinical Research Centre

and Northwick Park Hospital, 1983-88; Professor of Haematology and Honorary Consultant Haematologist, Ninewells Hospital and Medical School, Dundee, 1989-2009, Dean of Medical School, 2006-2009. Recreations: gardening; hill-walking.
E-mail: mjpippard@doctors.org.uk

Pirone, Julie. Director of External Relations, Scotland, Northern Ireland, North and East England, Royal Mail Group. Address: (b.) Tallents House, 21 South Gyle Crescent, Edinburgh EH12 9PB; T.-0131 316 7440.

Pitcaithly, Mary, OBE, LLB, NP. Chief Executive, Falkirk Council, since 1998; b. 17.7.56, Falkirk; 1 d. Educ. Falkirk High; Edinburgh University. Depute Director, Law and Administration, Falkirk District Council, 1989-95; Assistant Chief Executive, Falkirk Council, 1995-98. Address: (b.) Municipal Buildings, Falkirk; T.-01324 506002.

Pittock, Professor Murray, MA, DPhil, DLitt, FEA, FHEA, FRSA, FRHistS, FSAScot, FASLS, FRSE. Bradley Professor of English Literature, Pro Vice-Principal, University of Glasgow; formerly Professor of Scottish and Romantic Literature, Manchester University, 2003-07; Professor in Literature, Strathclyde University, 1996-2003; b. 5.1.62; m., Anne Grace Thornton Martin; 2 d. Educ. Aberdeen Grammar School; Glasgow University; Balliol College, Oxford (Snell Exhibitioner). Lecturer, then Reader, Edinburgh University, 1989-96. Associate Editor, New Dictionary of National Biography; Convener, International Association for the Study of Scottish Literatures; Director, Ossian Monument Trust; Trustee, Jacobite Studies Trust; Royal Society of Edinburgh BP Humanities Research Prize, 1992-94; British Academy Chatterton Lecturer in Poetry, 2002; Visiting appointments: Auburn, Charles University, Prague, NYU, Notre Dame; Trinity College Dublin, Yale. Publications: The Invention of Scotland, 1991, 2014; Spectrum of Decadence, 1993, 2014; Poetry and Jacobite Politics in Eighteenth-Century Britain and Ireland, 1994; Inventing and Resisting Britain, 1997; Jacobitism, 1998; Celtic Identity and the British Image, 1999; Scottish Nationality, 2001; A New History of Scotland, 2003; The Edinburgh History of Scottish Literature (co-editor), 2006; The Reception of Sir Walter Scott in Europe, 2007; James Boswell, 2007; Scottish and Irish Romanticism, 2008; The Myth of The Jacobite Clans: The Jacobite Army in 1745, 2009; The Edinburgh Companion to Scottish Romanticism, 2011; Robert Burns in Global Culture, 2011; Material Culture and Sedition, 2013; The Road to Independence? Scotland in the Balance, 2014; The Reception of Robert Burns in Europe, 2014. Address: (b.) 7 University Gardens, Glasgow G12 8QH; e-mail: Murray.pittock@glasgow.ac.uk

Placido, Professor Francis, BSc, PhD, FInstP, FSAS, FION. Professor, University of the West of Scotland, since 1999; b. 29.9.46, Dalkeith; m., Dorothy Charlotte Torrance; 2 d. Educ. Dalkeith High School; University of Edinburgh. Demonstrator, University of Edinburgh, 1972-77; Paisley College of Technology: Lecturer, 1977-89, Reader in Physics, 1989-99. John Logie Baird Award for Innovation, 1998. Recreations: food and wine; painting. Address: (b.) Thin Film Centre, University of the West of Scotland, High Street, Paisley PA1 2BE; T.-0141-848 3610; e-mail: frank.placido@uws.ac.uk

Pollock, Sheriff Alexander, MA (Oxon), LLB. Sheriff of Grampian, Highland and Islands, at Inverness, 2005-09; b. 21.7.44, Glasgow; m., Verena Francesca Gertraud Alice Ursula Critchley; 1 s.; 1 d. Educ. Rutherglen Academy; Glasgow Academy; Brasenose College, Oxford; Edinburgh University; University for Foreigners, Perugia. Partner, Bonar Mackenzie & Kermack, WS, 1971-73; called to Scottish Bar, 1973; Conservative candidate: West Lothian, General Election, February 1974, Moray and Nairn, General Election, October 1974; MP, Moray and Nairn, 1979-83, Moray, 1983-87; Parliamentary Private Secretary to Secretary of State for Scotland, 1982-86; PPS to Secretary of State for Defence, 1986-87; Advocate Depute, 1990-91; Sheriff (Floating) of Tayside, Central and Fife, at Stirling, 1991-93; Sheriff of Grampian, Highland and Islands, at Aberdeen and Stonehaven, 1993-2001; Sheriff of Grampian, Highland and Islands, at Inverness and Portree, 2001-05. Member, Queen's Bodyguard for Scotland (Royal Company of Archers), since 1984. Recreations: walking; music. Address: (h.) Drumdarrach, Forres, Moray.

Pollock, Linda Catherine, BSc, PhD, MBA, RGN, DistrictNursingCert, RMN. Associate with Dementia Development Centre, University of Stirling, since 2012; Scottish Legal Complaints Commissioner, 2008-2011; Accounts Commission Board Member, since 2009; ENABLE Scotland Board Member, since 2012; Chair, Pain Concern Advisory Board, since 2010; Board Non-Executive Director, Care Inspectorate for Scotland, since 2014; b. 26.11.53, Ayr. Educ. Boroughmuir Senior Secondary; Alloway Primary; Edinburgh University; Aberdeen University; Robert Gordons University. General District and Psychiatric Nursing; teaching and research roles before opting for a management career in NHS; Director of Nursing from 1989; Mental Welfare Commissioner (1997-2005), and specialised in Community and Primary Care before retiring; worked as Nurse Adviser in Nurse Prescribing, to the Chief Nurse in Scotland; worked with Nursing Regulator (NMC) until 2012, and has been doing research with a charity The Queen's Nursing Institute of Scotland (Trustee, since 2014). Publications: numerous articles in professional journals and chapters in nursing books; author, "Community Psychiatric Nursing: Myth and Reality", 1989. Recreations: bridge; Scottish Country Dancing; skiing. E-mail: linda.pollock5@btinternet.com

Pollock, Thomas Alexander Jackson, BArch, RIBA, FRIAS. Senior Partner, The Pollock Hammond Partnership, Architects; b. 7.10.48, Newbridge, Midlothian; m., Clare Gregory; 1 d. Educ. George Watson's College, Edinburgh; Middlebury College, Vermont, USA; University of Edinburgh. Michael Laird and Partners, Edinburgh, 1973-78; William A. Cadell Architects, Linlithgow, 1978-91 (Partner, 1982-91); Pollock Hammond Partnership, since 1991. Member, Conservation Committee, RIAS; Member, Cases Panel, Architectural Heritage Society of Scotland; Trustee, Clan Menzies Charitable Trust; former Chairman, Linlithgow Festival Trust. Recreations: travel; antiques; the arts. Address: (h.) Beinn Castle House, 293 High Street, Linlithgow EH49 7AT; T.-01506 844417; e-mail: mail@pollockhammondarchitects.co.uk

Polson, Michael Buchanan, LLB (Hons), DipLP, MBA. Director, Scottish Financial Enterprise, since 2011; b. 8.7.64, Edinburgh; m., Alison; 1 s.; 2 d. Educ. Anderson High School, Shetland; University of Edinburgh; Edinburgh University Management School. Trainee, Dundas & Wilson, 1987-89, Assistant, 1989-90; Associate, Ashurst, 1990; Senior Solicitor, Dundas & Wilson, 1991-92, Associate, 1992-95, Head of Clients and Sectors, 2010-12, Partner, 1995-2012. Recreations: most sports including golf, tennis and football. Address: (b.) Scottish Financial Enterprise, 24 Melville Street, Edinburgh EH3 7NS; T.-0131 247 7700.

Ponsonby, Bernard Joseph. Political Editor, STV, since 2000, Reporter/Presenter, since 1990; b. Glasgow. Educ.

Trinity High School, Rutherglen; Strathclyde University. Researcher to Rt. Hon. Dr Dickson Mabon, 1987; Press Officer, Scottish Liberal Democrats, 1988-89; party's first Parliamentary candidate, Glasgow Govan, 1988; PR and Media Consultant, freelance Reporter for BBC Radio Scotland, 1989-90; Principal Presenter of political, election, and by-election programmes, Scottish Television, 1994-2004; presented Platform, since 1996, Scottish Voices, Scottish Questions, Trial by Night; Producer of political documentaries: The Salmond Years (2000), The Dewar Years (2001) and The Road to Holyrood (2004). Publication: Donald Dewar: Scotland's first First Minister (contributor). Recreations: golf; Celtic Football Club. Address: (b.) STV, Pacific Quay, Glasgow G51 1PQ; e-mail: bernard.ponsonby@stv.tv

Poole, Anna I., MA, MSt, QC. Part-time judge; b. 11.8.70, Craigtoun; m.; 1 d.; 1 s. Educ. Madras College, St Andrews; Oxford University. Qualified as a Solicitor of the Supreme Court of England and Wales, 1996; then as a Scottish Solicitor with Brodies, 1997; called to Scottish Bar, 1998; First Standing Junior Counsel to the Scottish Government, 2010-2012; QC, 2012; part-time judge of the First-tier Tribunal, 2014; Chancellor of the Diocese of Argyll and the Isles. Recreations: music; walking; travel; reading.

Poole, Sheriff Isobel Anne, OBE, LLB. Part Time Sheriff, 2007-2011 (retired); Sheriff of Lothian and Borders (retired 2007); b. 9.12.41, Oxford. Educ. Oxford High School for Girls (GDST); Edinburgh University. Advocate. Chair, The Edinburgh Sir Walter Scott Club, 2005-07. Recreations: country; arts; gardens; friends. Address: (b.) Sheriffs' Chambers, Sheriff Court, Edinburgh.

Poon, Professor Wilson, MA (Cantab), PhD (Cantab), FInstP, CPhys, FRSE. Professor of Condensed Matter Physics, Edinburgh University, since 1999, Director of Research, School of Physics & Astronomy, since 2006; Engineering and Physical Sciences Research Council (EPSRC) Senior Research Fellow, 2007-2012; b. 1962, Hong Kong; m., Heidi Lau; 1 s.; 1 d. Educ. St Paul's Co-educational College, Hong Kong; Rugby School; Peterhouse and St. John's College, Cambridge. Research Fellow, St Edmund's College, Cambridge, 1986-88; Lecturer, Department of Applied Physics, Portsmouth Polytechnic, 1989; Edinburgh University: Lecturer, 1990-97; Senior Lecturer, 1997-99. Member, Liturgy Committee, Scottish Episcopal Church, since 2012. Recreation: piano. Address: (b.) School of Physics & Astronomy, Edinburgh University, Mayfield Road, Edinburgh, EH9 3JZ; T.-0131-650 5297; e-mail: w.poon@ed.ac.uk

Porteous, Brian William, BSc (Hons), FISPA, DipRM. Director of Porteous Leisure, since 2010; b. 6.2.51, Falkirk; m., Shena; 3 s. Educ. Falkirk High School; St. Andrews University; Moray House College of Education; Loughborough University; Aberdeen University. Joined Scottish Sports Council as Development Officer, 1979, appointed Director of Operations, 1989; Depute Director, Cultural and Leisure Services and Parks and Recreation, Glasgow City Council, 1994-2001; Director of Culture, Sport and Lifestyle, Genesis Consulting, 2001-09. Honorary Secretary, British Orienteering Federation, 1974-76; President, Scottish Orienteering Association, 1996-2000; Board Member, SportsCoach UK, 2002-06; Vice President, International Orienteering Federation, 2004-2012; President, International Orienteering Federation, since 2012. Publication: Orienteering, 1979. Recreations: golf; orienteering; amateur opera/musicals; caravanning. Address: (h.) Kildene, Westfield Road, Cupar KY15 5DS.

Porter, Ann. Chief Executive, Fife Society for the Blind, since 2014. Address: Fife Sensory Impairment Centre, Wilson Avenue, Kirkcaldy, Fife KY2 5EF; T.-01592 644979.

Pounder, Professor Derrick John, MB, ChB, FRCPA, FCFP. Professor of Forensic Medicine, Dundee University, since 1987; b. 25.2.49, Pontypridd; m., Georgina Kelly; 1 s.; 2 d. Educ. Pontypridd Boys' Grammar; Birmingham University. Senior Lecturer (Forensic Pathology), University of Adelaide; Deputy Chief Medical Examiner, Edmonton, Alberta, and Associate Professor, Universities of Alberta and Calgary, 1985-87. Board Member, UN Voluntary Fund for Victims of Torture, 2005-11; Freeman of Llantrisant; Member, Bonnetmakers of Dundee. Recreations: photography; medieval architecture; almost lost causes. Address: (b.) Department of Forensic Medicine, Dundee University, Dundee DD1 4HN; T.-01382 388020; e-mail: d.j.pounder@dundee.ac.uk

Prag, Thomas Gregory Andrew, MA, FCMI. Elected to Highland Council as Liberal Democrat, 2007; b. 2.1.47, London; m., Angela; 3 s. Educ. Westminster School; Brasenose College, Oxford. Joined BBC, 1968, as Studio Manager; Producer, BBC Radio Oxford; Programme Organiser, BBC Radio Highland; first Chief Executive, Moray Firth Radio, 1981, then Managing Director, then Chairman until 2001. Past President, Inverness and District Chamber of Commerce; Fellow, Radio Academy; Board Member, Eden Court Theatre. Vice Chairman, Highland Opportunity Ltd; Board Member, Eden Court Theatre, Inverness Airport Business Park and Highlanders Museum; Non Executive Director, iMedia Associates Ltd; Chairman of an NGO - Media Support Partnership; Vice Chairman, HITRANS; Hon Fellowship, University of the Highlands and Islands. Recreations: good intentions towards restoration of 1950 Daimler; keeping clock collection wound; family; growing vegetables; chasing deer off vegetables; Inverness Choral ('cracking' tenor) Truly Terrible Orchestra (scraping fiddler). Address: Windrush, Easter Muckovie, Inverness IV2 5BN; e-mail: thomas@prags.co.uk

Prentice, Alex, QC. Principal Crown Counsel, since 2011. Career: qualified as a solicitor in 1983 and as a Solicitor Advocate in 1994; practised as a defence solicitor for 21 years; became the first Solicitor Advocate from outwith the Crown Office and Procurator Fiscal Service to be appointed as an Advocate Depute in 2004; appointed as a Senior Advocate Depute in 2006 and became a QC in 2007. Prosecuted a number of significant cases including the shotgun murder at the "Marmion" public house in Edinburgh, the murder of Jolanta Bledaite and HM Advocate v Sheridan and Sheridan. In 2012 he twice secured a murder conviction without a body in the murder of Suzanne Pilley and the retrial in the murder of Arlene Fraser. Address: Crown Office, 25 Chambers Street, Edinburgh EH1 1LA; T.-0131 226 2626.

Prentice-Hyers, Rev. David, BA, MDiv. Minister, Troon Old Parish Church, since 2013. Address: Ayr Street, Troon KA10 6EB; T.-01292 313520.

Prest, Richard. Editor, Sunday Post and Weekly News. Address: (b.) D. C. Thomson & Co Ltd, 80 Kingsway East, Dundee DD4 8SL; T.-01382 223131. E-mail: rprest@dcthomson.co.uk

Preston, Ian Mathieson Hamilton, CBE, BSc, PhD, FEng, MInstP, FIEE, Hon. FCIWEM. Chartered Engineer; b. 18.7.32, Bournemouth; m., Sheila Hope Pringle; 2 s. Educ. Kilmarnock Academy; Glasgow University. University Assistant Lecturer, 1957-59; joined SSEB as Assistant Reactor Physicist, 1959; various appointments until Chief Engineer, Generation Design and Construction Division,

1972; Director General, Central Electricity Generating Board, Generation Development and Construction Division, 1977-83; Deputy Chairman, South of Scotland Electricity Board, 1983-90; Chief Executive, Scottish Power, 1990-95. Non-Executive Director: Deutsche (Scotland), 1996-2002, Hub Power Co. (Pakistan), 1995-99, Kot Addu Power Co. (Pakistan), 1996-99, Mining Scotland Ltd., 1995-98, East of Scotland Water Authority (Chairman), 1995-98; Chairman, Motherwell Bridge Holdings, 1995-2001; President, Scottish Council Development and Industry, 1997-2000. Address: 10 Cameron Crescent, Carmunnock, Glasgow G76 9DX.

Price, Professor David Brendan, BA (Hons), MBBChir, MA, DRCOG, FPCert, MRCGP. General Practice Airways Group Professor of Primary Care Respiratory Medicine, since 2000; b. 28.10.60, Slough; m., Dr Daryl Freeman; 2 s.; 2 d. Educ. Slough Grammar School; University of Cambridge. Paediatric Registrar, Australia, 1988-89; GP, 1999-2000; Chairman, Norwich Vocational Training Scheme, 1990-95; Director, Thorpe Respiratory Research, since 1998; Research Director, General Practice Airways Group, since 2000. Recreations: skiing; scuba diving; horse riding. Address: Department of General Practice and Primary Care, University of Aberdeen, Westburn Road, Aberdeen AB25 2AY; e-mail: d.price@abdn.ac.uk

Price, Professor Martin Francis, PhD, MSc, BSc (Sp. Hons). Director, Centre for Mountain Studies, Perth College, University of the Highlands and Islands, since 2000; Chairholder, UNESCO Chair in Sustainable Mountain Development, since 2009; Visiting Professor, University of Bergen, Norway, since 2014; Professor, since 2005; b. 26.4.57, London; m., Randi Kvinge. Educ. St. Pauls School, London; University of Colorado at Boulder; University of Calgary; University of Sheffield. Scientific Associate, Geographisches Institut, Universität, Bern, Switzerland, 1985-86; Postdoctoral fellow, Environmental and Societal Impacts Group and Advanced Study Program, National Center for Atmospheric Research, Boulder, USA, 1988-91; Scientific director, International Centre for Alpine Environments, Le Bourget-du-Lac, France, 1991; Research scientist, Environmental Change Unit, University of Oxford, England, 1992-95; Programme leader, Mountain Regions and Conservation Programme, Environmental Change Institute, University of Oxford, England, 1995-2000. Numerous awards including King Albert Mountain Award, 2012, and Nobel Peace Prize (as Principal Lead Author, Inter-governmental Panel on Climate Change), 2007. Vice-President, Euromontana. Publications include: "Mountain Area Research and Management: Integrated Approaches" (Editor), 2007; "Lairds, Land and Sustainability: Scottish Perspectives on Upland Management" (Editor), 2013; "Mountains: A Very Short Introduction", 2015. Address: Perth College UHI, Crieff Road, Perth PH1 2NX; T.-01738-877217; e-mail: martin.price@perth.uhi.ac.uk

Price, Professor Nicholas Charles, MA, DPhil (Oxon). Honorary Senior Research Fellow, School of Life Sciences, Glasgow University (Professor of Protein Science, since 2000); b. 12.8.46, Stafford; m., Margaret Hazel Price; 1s.; 2d. Educ. King Edward VI Grammar School, Stafford; Merton College, Oxford; St John's College, Oxford. Stirling University: Lecturer, 1974-77; Senior Lecturer, 1977 -88; Reader, 1988-94; Professor of Biochemistry, 1994-2000. Publications: 3 books; 200 papers. Recreations: running; fundraising. Address: (b.) Joseph Black Building, Glasgow University, G12; T.-0141-330 2889.

Pride, Professor Stephen James, BSc, PhD, FRSE. Honorary Research Fellow, Glasgow University, since 2011 (Professor of Mathematics, 1987-2011); b. 8.1.49, Melbourne. Educ. Hampton High School, Melbourne; Monash University, Melbourne; Australian National University, Canberra. Research Fellow, Open University, 1974-78; Temporary Lecturer in Mathematics, King's College, London University, 1978-79; Lecturer in Mathematics, Glasgow University, 1979-87. Member, Editorial Board, London Mathematical Society, 1989-99; Member, Editorial Board, Semigroup Forum, 2004-2014; Member, Editorial Board, International Electronic Journal of Algebra, 2006-2014; Member, Editorial Board, Glasgow Mathematical Journal, 2008-2014; Member, Mathematics College, Engineering and Physical Sciences Research Council, 1997-99; Member, Commonwealth Scholarship Commission Panel of Advisers, 2001-06. Publications: more than 82 articles on algebra (mainly group theory, semigroup theory and theoretical computer science). Recreations: cycling; travelling; cinema; music. Address: (b.) School of Mathematics and Statistics, University of Glasgow, University Gardens, Glasgow G12 8QW; e-mail: Stephen.Pride@glasgow.ac.uk

Priest, Professor Eric Ronald, BSc, MSc, PhD, DSc, FRSE, FRS. Wardlaw Professor, since 2002, Gregory Professor of Mathematics, St. Andrews University, since 1997, formerly Professor of Theoretical Solar Physics; b. 7.11.43, Birmingham; m., Clare Wilson; 3 s.; 1 d. Educ. King Edward VI School, Birmingham; Nottingham University; Leeds University. St. Andrews University: Lecturer in Applied Mathematics, 1968, Reader, 1977; SERC Senior Fellow, 1992-97. Elected Member, Norwegian Academy of Sciences and Letters, 1994; Chair, PPARC Astronomy Committee, 1998-2001; Chair, RSE Mathematics Committee, 1996-1998; Member, HEFC Research Assessment Exercise Committee, 1992, 1996, 2007; Chair, RSE Physics Committee, 2007-2010; Hale Prize, American Astronomical Society, 2002; Gold Medal of Royal Astronomical Society, 2009; Payne-Gaposchkin medal and prize, Institute of Physics, 2009; Honorary DSc (St Andrews), 2014. Recreations: bridge; walking; singing; swingnastics; children. Address: (b.) Mathematics and Statistics Department, St. Andrews University, St. Andrews KY16 9SS; T.-01334 463709.

Pringle, Alastair. National Director (Scotland), Equality and Human Rights Commission, since 2012. Career: former Head of Patient Focus and Equalities in the Scottish Government Health and Social Care Directorate. Member of the Scotland Committee of the EHRC; has worked extensively in the field of equalities and in tackling discrimination, predominantly in the health sector, and in the design, development and delivery of public services; led on the implementation of health policy on a range of issues including patients' rights, patient information and equalities strategy and policy for both the Health & Wellbeing portfolio of the Scottish Government and for NHS Scotland. Address: (b.) 151 West George Street, Glasgow G2 2JJ; T.-0141 228 5910.

Prior, Alan, BSc (Hons), MLitt, MRTPI. Academic Head of Professional Services Implementation, Heriot-Watt University; Acting Head, School of Life Sciences, Heriot-Watt University, 2009-11; Dean, Arts, Humanities and Social Sciences, Heriot-Watt University, 2004-07, Deputy Head, School of the Built Environment, Heriot-Watt University, 2002-09; b. 21.12.51, Edinburgh; m., Brenda; 2 d. Educ. Portobello High School, Edinburgh; Heriot-Watt University; Glasgow University. Assistant Planning Officer, Perth and Kinross District Council, 1975-77; Senior/Principal Planning Officer, East Kilbride District Council, 1977-85; Lecturer/Senior Lecturer, Edinburgh College of Art, 1985-95; Head, School of Planning and Housing, Edinburgh College of Art, 1996-2002. Publication: joint editor, "Introduction to Planning Practice", 2000. Recreation: hill walking. Address: (b.)

Heriot-Watt University, Edinburgh EH14 4AS; e-mail: a.prior@hw.ac.uk

Prior, Colin. Landscape Photographer: b. Glasgow 1958; m., Geraldine; 2 c. Shoots internationally; clients include, British Airways, Bowmore Whisky, Calmac, Visit Scotland; personal projects include a four-year exploration of Pakistan's Karakoram Mountains and a study of wild bird habitats; runs exclusive photographic workshops in Scotland and overseas; Fellow of the Royal Photographic Society. Publications: Highland Wilderness, Constable; Scotland - The Wild Places, Constable, Living Tribes, Constable, The World's Wild Places, Constable, Scotland's Finest Landscapes, Constable. Exhibitions: The Scottish Visual Experience, Linhof Gallery, London; Land's End, Museum of Education, Glasgow; The World's Wild Places, OXO Tower Gallery, London. Address: Colin Prior Limited, 4 Princes Gate, Bothwell, Glasgow G71 8SP; T. 01698 816333; e-mail: colin@colinprior.co.uk

Pritchard, Professor Duncan Henry, BA, MLitt, PhD. Professor of Philosophy, University of Edinburgh, since 2007; b. 30.01.74, Wolverhampton; m., Mandi; 2 s. Educ. University of St. Andrews. University of Stirling: Lecturer, 2000-02, Leverhulme Fellow, 2002-04, Reader, 2004-06, Professor, 2006-07. Publications: books include: Epistemic Luck; What Is This Thing Called Knowledge? Prizes include a 2007 Philip Leverhulme Prize. Address: (b.) Department of Philosophy, University of Edinburgh, Edinburgh EH8 9JX; T.-0131-651 1734; e-mail: duncan.pritchard@ed.ac.uk

Pritchard, Kenneth William, OBE, BL, WS. Secretary, Law Society of Scotland, 1976-97; Temporary Sheriff, 1995-99, Part-time Sheriff, 2000-03; b. 14.11.33, London; Honorary Sheriff, Dundee; m., Gretta Murray; 2 s.; 1 d. Educ. Dundee High School; Fettes College; St. Andrews University. National Service, Argyll and Sutherland Highlanders, 1955-57; 2nd Lt., 1956; TA, 1957-62 (Captain); joined J. & J. Scrimgeour, Solicitors, Dundee, 1957; Captain, DHSFPRFC, 1959-62; Senior Partner, 1970-76; Member: Sheriff Court Rules Council, 1973-76, Lord Dunpark's Committee considering Reparation upon Criminal Conviction, 1973-77; Hon. Visiting Professor, Law School, Strathclyde University; Hon. Member, Law Institute of Victoria, 1985; Hon. Member, Law Society of New Zealand, 1987; Hon. Member, Faculty of Procurators and Solicitors in Dundee; Member, University Court of Dundee, 1989-93; President, Dundee High School Old Boys Club, 1975-76. Recreation: golf. Address: (h.) 22/4 Kinellan Road, Edinburgh EH12 6ES; T.-0131-337 4294; e-mail: kw.pritchard@btinternet.com

Pritsepov, Andrey A. Consul General of the Russian Federation in Edinburgh, since 2014. Diplomatic rank: Envoy Extraordinary and Minister Plenipotentiary of the Second Class; b. 1960, Russia. Educ. Moscow State Institute of International Relations (MGIMO), 1977-82; various diplomatic positions at the Ministry for Foreign Affairs, Moscow, and Diplomatic Missions in Norway and Denmark, 1982-2004; Senior Counsellor, Embassy of Russia, the United Kingdom, 2004-09; Deputy Director, Second European Department, Ministry of Foreign Affairs of Russia, Moscow, 2009-2014. Address: (b.) 58 Melville Street, Edinburgh EH3 7HF; T.-0131 225 70 98; 0131 220 69 75; e-mail: edinburgh@mid.ru

Prosser, (Leslie) Charles, DFA, DAEd. Secretary, Royal Fine Art Commission For Scotland, 1976-2005; b. 27.10.39, Harrogate; m., Coral; 1 s.; 2 d. Educ. Bath Academy of Art at Corsham Court; Slade School of Fine Art, London University. Assistant Lecturer in Fine Art, Blackpool School of Art, 1962-64; Fine Art research, Royal Academy, Stockholm, 1964-65; Lecturer in Fine Art, Leeds/Jacob Kramer College of Art, 1965-76; research in Art Education, Leeds University, 1974-75. Leverhulme European Arts Research Award, 1964; FRSA, 1997; Hon. FRIAS, 1997, Hon. MRTPI, 2002. Recreation: appreciating the art of planning our surroundings. Address: (h.) 28 Mayfield Terrace, Edinburgh EH9 1RZ; T.-0131-668 1141.

Proudfoot, Edwina Valmai Windram, MA, DipEd, FSA, FSA Scot, MIFA. Archaeologist; Director, St. Andrews Heritage Services, since 1988; Honorary Research Fellow, St. Andrews University, 1985-97; b. 9.3.35, Dover; m., Professor V. Bruce Proudfoot (qv); 2 s. Educ. Invergordon Academy; Inverness Royal Academy; Edinburgh University. Lecturer (including Adult Education) in Archaeology, since 1959; director of excavations, numerous projects; Editor, Discovery and Excavation in Scotland, 1977-90; President, Council for Scottish Archaeology, 1983-89; Founder, first Chairman, Tayside and Fife Archaeological Committee, 1975-82; Member, Ancient Monuments Board for Scotland, 1986-97; Chairman, St. Andrews Preservation Trust, 1988-93; Council Member, National Trust for Scotland, 1984-89, 1989-93, 1993-97, 1999-2004; Chairman, NTS Central, Fife and Tayside Regional Commitee, 1998-2000; Member, Executive Committee, NTS, 1994-2004; Honorary Vice-President, Buteshire Natural History Society, since 1999; Chairman, E. Fife Members Centre, NTS, 2000-04; Chairman, Scottish Church Heritage Research, since 2000; Director, Places of Worship in Scotland Project; Founding Chairman, St Andrews Heritage Trust, 2010; Member, Scottish Episcopal Church Buildings Committee, since 2011. Recreations: gardening; music; walking. Address: 12 Wardlaw Gardens, St. Andrews, KY16 9DW; T.-01334 473293.

Proudfoot, Professor V. Bruce, OBE, BA, PhD, FSA, FRSE, FRSGS, FSA Scot. Vice-President, Royal Scottish Geographical Society, since 1993; Emeritus Professor of Geography, St. Andrews University; b. 24.9.30, Belfast; m., Edwina Valmai Windram Field; 2 s. Educ. Royal Belfast Academical Institution; Queen's University, Belfast. Research Officer, Nuffield Quaternary Research Unit, Queen's University, Belfast, 1954-58; Lecturer in Geography: Queen's University, Belfast, 1958-59, Durham University, 1959-67; Hatfield College, Durham: Tutor, 1960-63, Librarian, 1963-65; Visiting Fellow, University of Auckland and Commonwealth Visiting Fellow, Australia, 1966; Alberta University, Edmonton: Associate Professor, 1967-70, Professor, 1970-74; Co-ordinator, Socio-Economic Opportunity Studies and Staff Consultant, Alberta Human Resources Research Council, 1971-72; Professor of Geography, St. Andrews University, 1974-93. Royal Society of Edinburgh: Convener, Earth Sciences Committee, 1983-85, Vice-President, 1985-88, Convener, Grants Committee, 1988-91, General Secretary, 1991-96, Bicentenary Medal, 1997; Chairman, Society for Landscape Studies, 1979-83; Vice-President, Society of Antiquaries of Scotland, 1982-85; President, Section H, BAAS, 1985; Chairman, Rural Geography Study Group, Institute of British Geographers, 1980-84; Chairman of Council, 1993-99, Chairman of Dundee Centre, 1993-99, Royal Scottish Geographical Society; Hon. President, Scottish Association of Geography Teachers, 1982-84; Trustee, National Museum of Antiquities of Scotland, 1982-85; Hon. Treasurer, East Fife Members' Centre, National Trust for Scotland, 2002-08; Convener, Saltire Society Science Award Panel, 2003-2012, Member, 1994-2003; Hon. Treasurer: Scottish Church Heritage Research, since 2010, St. Andrews Heritage Trust, since 2010. Recreation: gardening. Address: (h.) Westgate, 12 Wardlaw Gardens, St. Andrews KY16 9DW; T.-01334 473293.

Provan, James Lyal Clark. Member, South East Region, European Parliament, 1999-2004, Member, South Downs

West, 1994-99, Member (Conservative), European Parliament, NE Scotland, 1979-89; Vice President, European Parliament, 1999-2004; Chairman, EP Tourism Group, 1997-2004; Chairman, EP Conciliation Committee with Council of Ministers, 1999-2003; Chairman, Rowett Research Institute, Aberdeen, 1991-99 (Board Member, 1990-2005); Non-Executive Director, CNH Global N.V. and New Holland (Holdings), N.V., 1994-2007; Farmer; b. 19.12.36, Glenfarg, Perthshire; m., Roweena Adele Lewis; 2 s.; 1 d. Educ. Ardvreck School, Crieff; Oundle School, Northants; Royal Agricultural College, Cirencester. National Farmers Union of Scotland: Area President, Kinross, 1965, Fife and Kinross, 1971; Tayside Regional Councillor, 1978-81; Member, Tay River Purification Board, 1978-81; European Democratic (Conservative) Spokesman on Agriculture and Fisheries, 1981-87; Questor of European Parliament, 1987-89; former Executive Director, Scottish Financial Enterprise (1990-93); Chairman, McIntosh of Dyce Ltd., McIntosh Donald Ltd., 1989-94; Member, Agriculture and Food Research Council, 1990-94; Member, Lloyds of London, since 1984. Recreations: country pursuits; sailing; flying; politics; agriculture. Address: Summerfield, Glenfarg, Perthshire PH2 9QD; e-mail: jlcprovan@aol.com

Pryce, Jonathan. Director for Agriculture, Food and Rural Communities, Scottish Government. Address: (b.) Scottish Government, Agriculture, Food and Rural Communities, Saughton House, Edinburgh EH11 3XD; T.-0131 244 6688.

Purcell, Steven John, JP. Leader, Glasgow City Council, 2005-2010; b. 19.9.72, Glasgow. Educ. St Thomas Aquinas Secondary School. Glasgow City Council, 1995-2010; Convener, Property Services, 1997-99; Convener, Development and Regeneration Services, 1999-2003; Convener, Education Services Committee, 2003-2005. Recreations: history; music; football.

Purdie, Allister. Governor, HMP & YOI Cornton Vale, since 2013. Joined the Scottish Prison Service in November 1988 starting at Shotts Prison in Lanarkshire, having worked ten years in a family business; moved to Perth Prison in April 1999 as a Unit Manager; HM Prison Edinburgh, 2001-04; HM Prison Barlinnie, 2004-09, Head of Operations and Residential, then Deputy Governor; Scottish Prison Service Headquarters, Senior Operational Advisor leading in the design and build of the new prisons at HM Prison Low Moss and HM Prison Grampian, 2009-2011; Deputy Governor, HM Prison and Young Offenders, Cornton Vale, Stirling, 2011-13. Address: Cornton Road, Stirling FK9 5NU.

Purser, John Whitley, MA, PhD, DHC (Aberdeen). Composer and Lecturer; Poet, Playwright, Musicologist, and Broadcaster; b. 10.2.42, Glasgow; 1 s.; 1 d. Educ. Fettes College; Glasgow University; Royal Scottish Academy of Music and Drama. Manager, Scottish Music Information Centre, 1985-87; Researcher, Sabhal Mòr Ostaig, since 2006; compositions include two operas, numerous orchestral and chamber works; four books of poetry, The Counting Stick, A Share of the Wind, Amoretti and There Is No Night; six radio plays and two radio series, A Change of Tune and Scotland's Music; music history: Is the Red Light On?, Scotland's Music; Erik Chisholm, Scottish Modernist, 1904-1965; literary criticism: The Literary Works of Jack B. Yeats; awards: McVitie Scottish Writer of the Year, 1992; Glenfiddich Living Scotland Award, 1991; Giles Cooper Award, 1992; New York International Radio Festival Gold Medal, 1992; Sony Gold Medal, 1993; Oliver Brown Award, 1993; Scottish Heritage Award, 1993; Hon. Life Member, Saltire Society, 1993; Scottish Traditional Music Awards, 2007; Services to

Industry. Recreations: numerous. Address: (b.) 3 Drinan, Elgol, Isle of Skye IV49 9BG; T.-01471 866262.

Purvis of Tweed (Baron Jeremy Purvis). MSP (Liberal Democrat), Tweeddale, Ettrick and Lauderdale, 2003-2011; b. 15.1.74, Berwick-upon-Tweed. Educ. Berwick-upon-Tweed High School; Brunel University. Research Assistant to Sir David Steel, 1993; Parliamentary Assistant: Liberal International, 1994, ELDR Group, European Parliament, 1995; Personal Assistant to Sir David Steel, subsequently Lord Steel of Aikwood, 1996-1998; GJW Scotland, 1998-2001; Company Director, McEwan Purvis, 2001-03. Member, Finance Committee, Scottish Parliament, 2003-05, Justice 2 Committee, 2005-07, Education, Lifelong Learning and Culture Committee, 2007-08, Finance Committee, 2008-2011. Director, Keep Scotland Beautiful, 2013.

Purvis, John Robert, CBE, MA (Hons). Member for Scotland, European Parliament, 1999-2009 (Member, Industry, Research and Energy Committee; Vice-Chairman, Economic and Monetary Affairs Committee); International Business Consultant (Managing Partner, Purvis & Co.), 1973-2008; Director, European Utilities Trust PLC, 1994-2007; Chairman, Kingdom FM Radio Ltd., 1997-2008, Director, 1997-2013; Chairman, Belgrave Capital Management Ltd., since 1999; Chairman, Financial Future, Brussels, since 2009; b. 6.7.38, St. Andrews; m., Louise Spears Durham; 1 s.; 2 d. Educ. Glenalmond; St. Andrews University. 2nd Lt., Scots Guards, 1956-58; First National City Bank (Citibank NA), London, New York City, Milan, 1962-69; Treasurer, Noble Grossart Ltd., Edinburgh, 1969-73; Director and Secretary, Brigton Farms Ltd., 1969-86; Managing Director, Founder, Owner, Gilmerton Management Services Ltd., 1973-92; Director: James River UK Holdings Ltd., 1984-95, Jamont NV, 1994-95; Member, European Parliament, Mid Scotland and Fife, 1979-84 (Deputy Chief Whip, Group Spokesman on Monetary Affairs, Energy, Research and Technology; Vice Chairman, European Parliament Delegation to the Gulf States); Chairman, IBA Scottish Advisory Committee, 1985-89; Member for Scotland, IBA, 1985-89; Member of Council, St. Leonards School, St. Andrews, 1981-89; Chairman, Economic Affairs Committee, Scottish Conservative and Unionist Association, 1986-97, Vice-President of Association, 1987-89; Member, Scottish Advisory Committee on Telecommunications, 1990-97; Director: Curtis Fine Papers Ltd., 1995-2001, Crown Vantage Ltd., 1995-2001. Recreations: Italy and Scotland. Address: PO Box 29222, St. Andrews KY16 8WL; T.-01334 475830.

Pusey, Professor Peter Nicholas, MA, PhD, FRS, FRSE. Emeritus Professor of Physics, Edinburgh University, Senior Honorary Research Fellow; b. 30.12.42, Oxford; m., Elizabeth Nind; 2 d. Educ. St Edward's School, Oxford; Cambridge University; University of Pittsburgh, USA. Post-doctoral Fellow, IBM, New York, 1969-72; Royal Signals and Radar Establishment (now QinetiQ), Malvern, 1972-91 (Grade 6 from 1980); Head, Department of Physics and Astronomy, Edinburgh University, 1994-97 and 2000-03. Publications: numerous in scientific literature. Address: (b.) School of Physics, Edinburgh University, Mayfield Road, Edinburgh, EH9 3JZ, T.-0131-650 5255; e-mail: pusey@ed.ac.uk

Pyle, Derek Colin Wilson, LLB (Hons), NP, WS. Sheriff Principal of Grampian, Highland and Islands, since 2012; Sheriff of Dundee, 2008-2012; Sheriff of Grampian, Highland and Islands at Inverness, 2005-08; Sheriff of Tayside Central and Fife, 2000-05; b. 15.10.52, Cambridge; m., Jean Blackwood Baillie; 5 s.; 1

d. Educ. Royal High School, Edinburgh; Edinburgh University. Solicitor, since 1976; Partner, Wilson Pyle & Co., WS, 1980-89; Partner, Henderson Boyd Jackson, WS, 1989-99; Solicitor Advocate, since 1994. Formerly Fiscal to Law Society of Scotland; former Council Member, WS Society. Recreations: golf; hill-walking; painting house. Address: (b.) Sheriff Court House, The Castle, Inverness IV2 3EG.

Q

Quar, Iris. Director, The Scottish Child Law Centre; b. 1960. Qualified solicitor with a background in family law practice and extensive experience in advising on child law issues. Trustee and member of the management committee of the Still Birth and Neonatal Death Society Lothians (SANDS), an organisation which supports the bereaved families of stillborn babies and babies who die shortly after birth. Address: Scottish Child Law Centre, 54 East Crosscauseway, Edinburgh EH8 9HD; T.-0131 667 6333; e-mail: iris@sclc.org.uk

Quartson-Mochrie, Judith Alice Araba Siripiwa, BA (Hons), BArch (Hons), ARB. Architect; m., Neil A. Mochrie; 1 s. Educ. King James' School, Knaresborough; Newcastle University. Christian Hauvette Architecte, Paris 1988; Baasner Möller of Langwald, Berlin, 1992; Troughton McAslan, 1994; Foster & Partners, London, 1996; Architect, Associate, Communications Director, Gareth Hoskins Architects, Glasgow, 1998; Jens Bergmark Architects, Edinburgh, 2011. Royal Commissioner for the Royal Commission on the Ancient and Historical Monuments of Scotland, 2010-2015. Recreations: photography; illustration; yoga.
E-mail: jude.qm@googlemail.com

Quayle, Robert Brisco Macgregor, MA. Commissioner, Northern Lighthouse Board, 2004-2013; Chairman, Isle of Man Steam Packet Company, since 2008; b. 06.04.50, Birmingham; m., Deborah Clare Pullinger; 3 s.; 2 d. Educ. Monkton Combe School; Selwyn College, Cambridge. English Solicitor, since 1974; Clerk of Tynwald and Secretary of House of Keys, Isle of Man, 1976-87; Consultant, since 1987; Director of Isle of Man Steam Packet Company, Ellan Vannin Fuels Ltd, WH Ireland (IOM) Ltd and various other companies. Recreations: Anglican Lay Reader; classic cars; music. Address: Mullen Beg, Patrick, Isle of Man IM5 3AW; T.-01624-842912.
E-mail: rqmann@manx.net

Queensberry, 12th Marquess of (David Harrington Angus Douglas); b. 19.12.29. Educ. Eton. Professor of Ceramics, Royal College of Art, 1959-83; succeeded to title, 1954.

Quigley, Elizabeth, MA (Hons). Correspondent, BBC Scotland, since 1999; b. 30.10.71, Glasgow; m., John Swinney MSP. Educ. Lenzie Academy; St Andrews University. Reporter, The Scotsman, 1995-96; Reporter, Scotland on Sunday, 1996-97; Scottish Daily Mail, from 1997: Political Reporter/Features Editor/Feature Writer. Address: (b.) BBC Scotland, The Tun, Holyrood Road, Edinburgh EH8 8PJ; T.-0131-248 4215.

Quinault, Francis Charles, BSc, PhD, FRSAMD. Retired Director of Learning and Teaching Quality, St. Andrews University (formerly Hebdomadar, Assistant Principal for External Affairs and Senior Lecturer in Psychology); formerly Chairman, Byre Theatre; b. 8.5.43, London; m., Wendy Ann Horton; 1 s.; 2 d. Educ. Dulwich College; St.

Catharine's College, Cambridge; Bristol University. Ford Foundation Scholar, Oslo University, 1969-70. Member, National Committee for the Training of University Teachers, 1981-87; Academic Board, RSAMD, 2004-07; Hon. Treasurer, The Kate Kennedy Trust; Past President, St. Andrews Business Club; former Chairman, University of St. Andrews Students' Association; Director, The Canadian Robert T. Jones Jr Scholarship Foundation; Member, Quality Board for Higher Education in Iceland; Director, Fife Cultural Trust; Trustee, New Park Educational Trust. Recreations: acting; singing; hill-walking; learning languages. Address: 5 Hope Street, St. Andrews KY16 9HJ; T.-01334 474560; e-mail: fcq@st-and.ac.uk

Quinn, Andrea, BEng (Hons). Managing Director, Geelox Ltd; Chief Executive Officer, Scottish Police Services Authority (SPSA), 2010-13; Head of Environment, City of Edinburgh Council, 2006-2010; b. 27.4.70, Widnes, Cheshire. Educ. St. Josephs RC High School; Bolton Institute of Higher Education (now the University of Bolton). Career: Trainee Technician, Halton Borough Council (1989); United Utilities (1998). Member, Wastewater Board (2004); as a member of Water UK, represented the company nationally on matters of policy and internationally on a variety of sustainability and research projects.
T.-07545 197693; e-mail: andrea@geelox.co.uk

Quirk, Norman Linton, CA, CLJ. Partner, Hebridean Sea School, since 2011; Chairman, Comar since 2011; Deputy Chair, Mull Theatre, 2010-2011; Executive Director, Mull Theatre, 2008-2010; Chairman, Scottish Chambers of Commerce, 2007-2009; Managing Director, SAGA 105.2 fm, 2004-07; Executive Director, Scottish Ballet, 2000-2004, Vice Chairman and Managing Director, 1998-2000; Partner, Quirk & Co., business and management consultancy, 1991-2011; President, Glasgow Chamber of Commerce, 2006-08; Director: David MacBrayne Ltd., Caledonian MacBrayne Ltd., NorthLink Ferries Ltd, 2008-2013; b. 28.7.47, Glasgow; m., Lesley Helen Quirk (qv); 2 s.; 2 step-s. Educ. Dulwich College. Apprentice CA, 1965-71; Accountant/Office Manager, Thom Decorators, Coatbridge, 1971-74; Chief Accountant, Radio Clyde, Glasgow, 1974-84; Assistant Director, Institute of CAs of Scotland, 1985-87; Regional Controller, Joint Monitoring Unit, 1988-91; Managing Director, Scot FM, 1996. Chairman, Independent Radio Group of Scotland, 1996-2000; President, Glasgow Chamber of Commerce, 2006-08; Director, Scottish Chamber of Commerce, 2006; Community Councillor, Strathard Ward, 2000-06; Member, Incorporation of Hammermen; Director and Treasurer, Scottish Society for Autism; Director, Mull Theatre; Lord's Taverner; Commander, Order of St Lazarus of Jerusalem. Recreations: scuba diving; working with arts organisations. Address: (h.) Ardsorn, Raeric Road, Tobermory, Isle of Mull PA75 6PU; T.-01688-301223; e-mail: norman@quirk.co.uk

R

Radcliffe, Nicholas John, BSc (Double Hons), PhD. Director, Stochastic Solutions Limited, since 2007; Visiting Professor, Maths and Statistics, Edinburgh University, since 1995; b. 31.07.65, London; m., Morag Radcliffe; 1 s. Educ. Sir Frederic Osborn School; Univ. of Sussex; Edinburgh Univ. Manager, Information Systems Group, Edinburgh Parallel Computing Centre, University of Edinburgh, 1990-95; Technical Director, Quadstone Limited, 1995-2007; Advisor: Scottish Equity Partners, 2000-2010, Fluidinfo Limited, since 2006. Publications: Sustainability: A Systems Approach (Co-Author), 1996; Getting Started with Fluidinfo (CoAuthor), O'Reilly Media, 2012. Blogs: The Scientific Marketer (http://scientificmarketer.com), About Tag (http://blog.abouttag.com). Recreations: guitar/music; literature; film; golf. E-mail: njr@stochasticsolutions.com

Rae, Barbara Davis, CBE, RA, RSA, RSW, RGI, RE, FRCA, FRSE, Hon. D.Art, Hon. D.Litt. Painter and Printmaker; b. Falkirk; 1 s. Educ. Morrisons Academy, Crieff; Edinburgh College of Art. Elected RSW, 1975; President, SSA, 1983; works purchased by international private and commercial collectors; elected RSA, 1992; elected RA, 1996; study visit, Arizona Desert, 1998; doctorate, St Andrews University and Napier University; various solo exhibitions in Royal Academy, London, Edinburgh International Arts Festival and internationally including Norway, USA and Mexico; work in many public collections. Hon. Fellowship, Royal College of Art, London; Hon. DLitt, Aberdeen University, 2003; Hon. DLitt, University of St. Andrews, 2008; Fellow, Royal Society of Edinburgh, 2011. Recreation: travel. Contact: Royal Academy of Arts, London.

Rae, The Honourable Lady Rae (Rita Emilia Anna Rae), QC, LLB (Hons). Senator of the College of Justice, since 2014; Sheriff of Glasgow and Strathkelvin, 1997-2013. Educ. St. Patrick's High School, Coatbridge; Edinburgh University. Apprentice, Biggart, Lumsden & Co., Glasgow, 1972-74; Assistant Solicitor: Balfour & Manson, Edinburgh, 1974, Biggart, Baillie & Gifford, Glasgow, 1974-76; Solicitor and Partner, Ross Harper & Murphy, Glasgow, 1976-81; Former Tutor, Advocacy and Pleading, Strathclyde University; Advocate, 1982; Queen's Counsel, 1992. Temporary High Court Judge, 2004-2013; Member, Sentencing Commission for Scotland, 2003-06; Vice Chair, Parole Board for Scotland, 2005-07, Member, since 2001; 2010 Member of Legal 40, University of Glasgow Law School; Member, National Strategic Advisory Group on Violence Reduction, since 2011; 2010 Director, Conforti Institute, Coatbridge; Member, Sacro; Life Member, Scottish Association for the Study of Offending, Chair, Glasgow Branch, 2002-2014. Recreations: piano; theatre; driving; walking; opera; music; Italy; gardening.

Rae, Simon Scott, LLB (Hons), DipLP, NP. Managing Partner and Head of Corporate, DLA Piper Scotland (Partner), since 2004; b. 28.12.72, Edinburgh. Educ. George Watson's College, Edinburgh; Strathclyde University, Glasgow. Dundas & Wilson CS, Edinburgh, 1995-98; Clifford Chance, London, 1998-2004. Address: (b.) Rutland Square, Edinburgh (c/o DLA Piper); T.-0131-242-5085; e-mail: simon.rae@dlapiper.com

Raeburn, James B., OBE, FCIS. Director, Scottish Print Employers Federation and Scottish Newspaper Publishers' Association, 1984-2007; Director, Scottish Daily Newspaper Society, 1996-2010; Director, Scottish Newspaper Society, 2010-12; b. 18.3.47, Jedburgh; m., Rosemary Bisset; 2 d. Educ. Hawick High School. Edinburgh Corporation, 1964-69; Roxburgh County Council, 1969-71; Electrical Contractors' Association of Scotland, 1972-83 (Secretary, 1975-83). Director: Press Standards Board of Finance Ltd., 1990-2013 (Secretary and Treasurer, 2003-2013), Advertising Standards Board of Finance Ltd., 1990-2013, National Council for the Training of Journalists, 1993-2006, Publishing National Training Organisation Ltd., 2000-03; Moderator, The Society of High Constables of Edinburgh, 2015. Recreation: golf. Address: (h.) 44 Duddingston Road West, Edinburgh EH15 3PS.

Raeburn, Sheriff Susan Adiel Ogilvie, LLB, QC. Sheriff of Grampian, Highland and Islands at Elgin, 2011-2015; b. 23.4.54, Ellon. Educ. St. Margaret's School for Girls, Aberdeen; Edinburgh University. Admitted, Faculty of Advocates, 1977; took silk, 1991; part-time Chairman, Social Security Appeal Tribunals, 1986-91; Temporary Sheriff, 1988-92; part-time Chairman, Medical Appeal Tribunals, 1992-93; Reporter to Scottish Legal Aid Board, 1990-93; Sheriff of Glasgow and Strathkelvin, 1993-2011.

Rafferty, Andrew Gordon, BVMS, MRCVS, CertSHP, CertCHP. Principal, Mixed Veterinary Practice, since 1990; b. 18.02.55, Grantown-on-Spey; m., Carol; 4 s. Educ. Edinburgh Academy; Edinburgh University. Grantown Mixed Practice, 1977-81; Castle Douglas Mixed Practice, 1981-89; Grantown-on-Spey Mixed Practice, since 1989. Farmer. Recreations: outdoor sports. Address: Strathspey Veterinary Centre, Forest Road, Grantown-On-Spey, Morayshire PH26 3JJ; T.-01479 872252.

Rafferty, John, LLB (Hons), FSI. Honorary Consul for Canada in Scotland; Chairman, Burness, 1997-2004 (Partner, since 1977); b. 30.6.51, St Andrews. Educ. Edinburgh Academy; Edinburgh University. Burness: Apprentice Solicitor, 1973-75; Assistant Solicitor, 1975-77. Recreations: gardening; hill-walking; countryside. Address: (b.) Consulate of Canada, 5 St. Margaret's Road, Edinburgh EH9 1AZ; T.-07702 359916.

Raistrick, Evlyn, MA. Chairman, Scottish Hockey Union, 1992-96; Tournament Director: Atlanta Olympics, 1996, Commonwealth Games, Manchester, 2002; b. 13.8.42, Edinburgh; m., David William; 3 s. Educ. Boroughmuir School; Edinburgh University. Maths Teacher, Liberton High, 1964-72. Member, Scottish Sports Council, 1993-2001; Vice-Chairman, Executive, Scottish Sports Association, 1993-2001. Recreations: hockey; squash; golf. Address: (h.) Orchard House, Longniddry, East Lothian EH32 0PG.

Ralston, Professor Ian Beith McLaren, OBE, MA, PhD, DLitt, FRSE, FSA, FSA Scot, MCIfA. Head of School of History, Classics and Archaeology, Edinburgh University, since 2013; Abercromby Professor of Prehistoric Archaeology, since 2012; Chair, CFA Archaeology Ltd., since 2000; Vice-President, Society of Antiquaries of Scotland, 2007-2010; Chair, Standing Committee for Archaeology in the Universities, 2007-2010; b. 11.11.50, Edinburgh; m., Sandra Webb; 1 s.; 1 d. Educ. Edinburgh Academy; Edinburgh University. Aberdeen University: Research Fellow in Archaeology, 1974-77, Lecturer in Geography/Archaeology, 1977-85; University of Edinburgh: Lecturer in Archaeology, 1985-90, Senior Lecturer, 1990-98, Personal Chair, 1998-2012. Honorary Chair, Institute of Field Archaeologists, 1991-92; Chair, Scottish Archaeological Finds Allocation Panel, 2004-2011;

President, Council for Scottish Archaeology, 1996-2000. Publications: Archaeological Resource Management in the United Kingdom – an introduction (Co-editor), 2 edn., 2006; The Archaeology of Britain – an Introduction from the Upper Palaeolithic to the Industrial Revolution (Co-editor), 2 edn 2009; Scotland after the Ice Age (Co-editor), 2003; Celtic Fortifications (2006); Angus: archaeology and early history (Co-Author), 2008; books on French archaeology; exhibition catalogues; papers. Recreations: walking; watching St. Johnstone. Address: (b.) William Robertson Wing, Old Medical School, Teviot Place, Edinburgh EH8 9AG; T.-0131-650 2370; e-mail: ian.ralston@ed.ac.uk; web: www.ianralston.co.uk

Ralston, Professor Stuart Hamilton, MBChB, MRCP(UK), MD, FRCP(Glas), FRCP(Edin), FMedSci, FRSE. Professor of Rheumatology, University of Edinburgh; Chair of the Commission on Human Medicines (CHM), since 2013; b. 24.10.55, Glasgow; m., Janet Thomson; 2 s.; 2 d. Educ. Allan Glen's School, Glasgow; Glasgow University. Junior House Officer, Glasgow Royal Infirmary, 1978-79; Senior House Officer, Falkirk and District Royal Infirmary and Aberdeen Teaching Hospitals, 1979-81; Registrar, General Medicine, Glasgow Royal Infirmary, 1981-84; Senior Registrar, Glasgow Royal Infirmary and Southern General Hospital, Glasgow, 1984-87; Locum Consultant Physician, Stobhill Hospital, Glasgow, 1989; Wellcome Senior Research Fellow and Honorary Consultant Physician, Northern General Hospital, Edinburgh, 1989-91; Senior Lecturer, Medicine and Therapeutics, Aberdeen University and Honorary Consultant Physician, Aberdeen Royal Hospitals NHS Trust, 1991-94, Reader, 1994-99; Director, Institute of Medical Science, University of Aberdeen; Professor of Medicine and Bone Metabolism, University of Aberdeen, 1999-2005. President, European Calcified Tissues Society, 1997-2005; Board Member, International Bone and Mineral Society, since 2001; Examiner, Royal College of Physicians of Edinburgh, since 1996; Scientific Advisor to: National Association for Relief of Paget's Disease, since 1997, National Osteoporosis Society, since 1997. Recreations: mountaineering; snowboarding. Address: (b.) Rheumatic Diseases Unit, Western General Hospital, Edinburgh EH4 2XU. E-mail: stuart.ralston@ed.ac.uk

Ramage, Alan W., CBE. Formerly Keeper of the Registers of Scotland; b. 4.12.43, Edinburgh; m., Fiona Lesslie. Educ. Boroughmuir School, Edinburgh; Edinburgh University. Recreations: keeping fit; reading; dog walking. Address: (h.) 12 St Fillan's Terrace, Edinburgh EH10 4NH; T.-0131 447 8463.

Rampling, Professor Roy, PhD, MSc, BSc, DIC, ARCS, MBBS, FRCR, FRCP. Professor of Neuro-Oncology, University of Glasgow, since 2000; b. 13.9.46, Malta; m., Susan Bonham-Carter; 2 s.; 1 d. Educ. Clacton County High School; Imperial College, London; University College, London. University of Glasgow: Senior Lecturer, Radiation Oncology, 1987-97, Reader, 1997-2000. Address: Beatson Oncology Centre, Western Infirmary, Glasgow G11 6NT; T.-0141-211 2627; e-mail: r.rampling@udcf.gla.ac.uk

Ramsay, Rev. (Alexander) Malcolm, BA, LLB, DipMin. Mission Partner of Church of Scotland serving in Nepal; b. 4.3.57, Livingstone, N. Rhodesia (now Zambia); m., Cati Balfour Paul; 1 d.; 1 s. Educ. Merchiston Castle School, Edinburgh; St. John's College, Cambridge; Edinburgh University. Solicitor, 1982-83; ordained Minister of Church of Scotland, 1986; Parish Minister of Bargrennan linked with Monigaff, Wigtownshire, 1987-93; Mission Partner of Church of Scotland teaching Theology in Presbyterian Church of Guatemala, 1994-98; Parish

Minister of Pitlochry, Perthshire, 1998-2011; Mission Partner of Church of Scotland serving in Pastoral Care and Support to United Mission to Nepal, since 2012. Recreations: cycling; poetry. Address: (b.) c/o World Mission Council, Church of Scotland, 121 George Street, Edinburgh EH2 4YN.

Ramsay, Major General Charles Alexander, CB, OBE; b. 12.10.36, North Berwick; m. (1967), Hon. Mary MacAndrew; 2 s.; 2 d. Educ. Eton; Sandhurst. Commissioned Royal Scots Greys, 1956; Staff College, Canada, 1967-68; Commanded Royal Scots Dragoon Guards, 1977-79; Commander 12th Armoured Brigade, 1980-82; Dep DMO MOD, 1983-84; GOC Eastern District, 1984-87; Director General, Army Organisation and Territorial Army, 1987-89; Chairman, Cockburns of Leith Ltd., 1993-2004; Director, John Menzies Plc, 1990-2004, Grey Horse Properties Ltd., Edinburgh Military Tattoo Ltd., 1991-2007; Colonel, The Royal Scots Dragoon Guards, 1992-98; Member, Royal Company of Archers (Queen's Bodyguard for Scotland). Recreations: field sports; equitation; travel. Address: (h.) Pittlesheugh, Greenlaw, Berwickshire TD10 6UL; T.-01890 840678.

Ramsay, Peter John, MCIBS, PMA. Non-Executive Director, National Waiting Times Centre, Golden Jubilee National Hospital, 2003-2011; Stakeholder Director, ABC Schools Ltd, since 2005; b. 13.01.55, Edinburgh; divorced; 1 s.; 2 d. Educ. Gordonstoun School. Former Chair, Gordonstoun Association (retired, 2015). Recreations: rugby (watching); swimming; walking; dogs. Address: (h.) 27 Kildonan Drive, Helensburgh G84 9SB; T.-01436 675414; e-mail: peter.ramsay6@btinternet.com

Randall, Rev. David James, MA, BD, ThM. Minister, Church of Scotland, Macduff, 1971-2010; retired May 2010; b. 5.6.45, Edinburgh; m., Nan Wardlaw; 3 s.; 1 d.; 6 grandchildren. Educ. George Heriot's School; Edinburgh University; Princeton Theological Seminary. Recreations: jogging; reading; swimming. Address: 5 Applehill Gardens, Wellbank, Broughty Ferry, DD5 3UG; T.01382-351812. E-mail: djrandall479@btinternet.com

Randall, Rev. David Steven, BA, BD. Minister, Falkirk Free Church, since 2014; Minister, Loudoun Parish Church, Newmilns, 2009-2014; Minister, Bo'ness Old Kirk (Church of Scotland), 2003-09; b. 28.1.71, Edinburgh; m., Linnea; 2 s.; 2 d. Educ. Banff Academy; Robert Gordon University; University of Aberdeen. Provision of Accounting Services to North Sea Oil Industry, Andersen Consulting (now known as Accenture), 1993-99; Parish Minister, The Church of Scotland, since 2002. Recreations: football; running; current affairs; reading. Address: Falkirk Free Church, Beaumont Drive, Carron, Falkirk FK2 8SN; e-mail: dsrandall@sky.com

Randall, John Norman, BA, MPhil. Trustee, The Islands Book Trust, 2002-2015; b. 1.8.45, Bromley, Kent; 1 s.; 1 d. Educ. Bromley Grammar School; Bristol University; Glasgow University. Department of Economic Affairs; Scottish Office - Assistant Secretary, 1985-99; Registrar General for Scotland, 1999-2003. Recreations: hill-walking; island history. Address: (h.) 31 Lemreway, South Lochs, Isle of Lewis; T.-01851 880365.

Rankin, Professor Andrew C., BSc, MBChB, MD, MRCP, FRCP. Professor, Medical Cardiology, University of Glasgow, since 2006; Reader, Glasgow Royal Infirmary, 2002-06; b. 15.6.52, Larkhall; m., Clare Fitzsimons; 3 s. Educ. Hamilton Academy; Glasgow

University. Registrar, Medical Cardiology, 1980; Lecturer, 1984, then Senior Lecturer, 1993, Medical Cardiology. Hon. Consultant Cardiologist, Glasgow Royal Infirmary, since 1993. Address; (b.) Department of Medical Cardiology, Glasgow Royal Infirmary, Glasgow; T.-0141-211 4833.

Rankin, Professor David W.H., MA, PhD, FRSC, FRSE. Director, Kevock Garden Plants, since 2010; Professor of Structural Chemistry, Edinburgh University, 1989-2010; b. 8.6.45, Birkenhead; m., Stella M. Thomas; 3 s.; 1 d. Educ. Birkenhead School; King's College, Cambridge. Edinburgh University: ICI Research Fellow, 1969, Demonstrator, 1971, Lecturer, 1973, Reader, 1980, Professor, 1989. Publication: Structural Methods in Molecular Inorganic Chemistry. Address: (b.) 16 Kevock Road, Lasswade EH18 1HT.

Rankin, Ian, OBE, FRSE. Novelist; b. 1960, Fife; m.; 2 s. Educ. Edinburgh University. Has been employed as grape-picker, swine-herd, taxman, alcohol researcher, hi-fi journalist and punk musician; creator of the Inspector Rebus novels; first Rebus novel, Knots and Crosses, 1987; this series now translated into 25 languages; elected Hawthornden Fellow; former winner, Chandler-Fulbright Award; two CWA "Daggers"; 1997 CWA Macallan Gold Dagger for fiction for Black and Blue; Mystery Writers of America Edgar Award for best novel: Resurrection Men, 2005; ITV3 Crime Thriller Award for Author of the Year, for Exit Music, 2008; awarded the CWA Cartier Diamond Dagger for lifetime's achievement in crime writing; 1999 Alumnus of the Year, Edinburgh University; Honorary Doctorate: University of Abertay Dundee, University of St. Andrews, University of Edinburgh; University of Hull. Address: c/o Curtis Brown Ltd, Haymarket House, 28-29 Haymarket, London SW1Y 4SP.

Rapport, Professor Nigel Julian, BA, MA, PhD, FRSA, FRSE. Professor of Anthropological and Philosophical Studies, St. Andrews University, since 1996; Head of School of Philosophy, Anthropology, Film & Music, since 2014; b. 8.11.56, Cardiff; m., Elizabeth J.A. Munro; 1 s.; 1 d. Educ. Clifton College, Bristol; Cambridge University; Manchester University. Research Fellow and Associate, Institute of Social and Economic Research, Memorial University of Newfoundland, 1983-87; Lecturer, Blaustein Institute for Desert Research, Ben-Gurion University of the Negev, Israel, 1988; Lecturer, Department of Social Anthropology, Manchester University, 1989; joined St. Andrews University as Lecturer, 1993. Hon. Secretary, Association of Social Anthropologists of the UK and Commonwealth, 1994-98; President, Anthropology and Archaeology Section, British Association for the Advancement of Science, 2000-01; Canada Research Chair in Globalization, Citizenship and Justice, 2004-07; 1996 Royal Society of Edinburgh prize lectureship in the humanities, 1996; Royal Anthropological Institute, Curl Essay Prize, 1996; Royal Anthropological Institute, Rivers Memorial Medal, 2012. Publications: Talking Violence: an anthropological interpretation of conversation in the city, 1987; Diverse World-Views in an English Village, 1993; The Prose and the Passion: anthropology, literature and the writing of E.M. Forster, 1994; Questions of Consciousness (Co-editor), 1995; Transcendent Individual, towards a literary and liberal anthropology, 1997; Migrants of Identity: Perceptions of Home in a World of Movement (Co-editor), 1998; Social and Cultural Anthropology: The Key Concepts, 2000; British Subjects – An Anthropology of Britain (Editor), 2002; The Trouble With Community – Anthropological Reflections on Movement, Identity and Collectivity, 2002; I am Dynamite: an alternative anthropology of power, 2003; Science, Democracy and The Open Society (Editor), 2006; Of Orderlies and Men:

Hospital Porters Achieving Wellness at Work, 2009; Human Nature as Capacity - Beyond Discourse and Classification (Editor), 2010; Reveries of Home - Nostalgia, Authenticity and the Performance of Place (Co-Editor), 2010; Community, Cosmopolitanism and the Problem of Human Commonality, 2012; Anyone - the Cosmopolitan Subject of Anthropology, 2012. Recreations: travel; sport; literature. Address: (b.) Department of Social Anthropology, St. Andrews University, St. Andrews KY16 9AL; T.-01334 462977.

Raven, Hugh J. E. Non-Executive Director, Ardtornish Estate Company (former Managing Director); Chair, Environmental Funders' Network (the umbrella organisation of philanthropists giving to environmental causes); Chair, Marine Conservation Society; Trustee, the John Ellerman Foundation; Trustee, the West Highland Coastal Trust; Trustee, the Corrour Trust; b. 20.4.61, London; m., Jane Stuart-Smith; 2 d. Educ. various schools; Harper Adams Agricultural College; University of Kent at Canterbury. Policy Strategist for the British Overseas Aid Group (a coalition of Oxfam, Christian Aid, Save the Children (UK), CAFOD and ActionAid), 1996; Convenor of the UK Government Green Globe Task Force, 1997-99; Advisor on Rural Policy to Environment Minister Michael Meacher MP, 1999-2000. Director of Ardtornish Estate, Morvern, Argyll, since 1996. Councillor, Royal Borough of Kensington and Chelsea, 1990-94; Member of the BBC Rural and Agricultural Affairs Advisory Committee, 1994-97; Member of the UK Executive Committee of the British American Project, 1996-98; Trustee of the Soil Association, 1992-99; Chair of SERA, the environmental affiliate of the Labour Party, 1997-99; Chair, Lochaber and District Fisheries Trust, 1995-2002; Trustee of the Royal Society for the Protection of Birds, 1997-2002; 1999, 2001 and 2003: Parliamentary Candidate, Scottish Labour Party, Argyll and Bute; Member, UK Sustainable Development Commission, 2004-10; Member of Board, Scottish Natural Heritage, 2004-07; Environment Adviser, Esmee Fairbairn Foundation, 2000-2010; Director, Soil Association Scotland, 2006-2011. Recreations: walking; fishing; sailing; reading. Address: (h.) Kinlochaline Castle, Morvern, Oban, Argyll PA80 5UZ; e-mail: hugh@ardtornish.co.uk

Reay, Professor David Sean, BSc, PhD. Professor of Carbon Management, University of Edinburgh, since 2008; Climate Change Scientist, Author and Advisor, since 1994; b. 02.12.72, Fleet; m., Sarah Louise; 2 d. Educ. Alun School, Mold, N. Wales; University of Liverpool; University of Essex. Senior Research Officer, University of Essex, 1998-2001; Post-Doctoral Research Fellow, University of Edinburgh, 2001-04 and 2004-05, Natural Environment Research Council Fellow, 2005-08, Lecturer in Carbon Management, 2008-09. Natural Environment Research Council Fellowship; British Council Scotland Advisory Committee, since 2009. Publication: Author of: 'Climate Change Begins at Home, 'Your Planet Needs You', 'Methane and Climate Change'. Recreations: writing stories; running; gardening. Address: (b.) School of Geosciences, University of Edinburgh, Edinburgh EH8 9XP; T.-0131 6507723; e-mail: david.reay@ed.ac.uk

Reay, 15th Lord (Aeneas Simon Mackay); b. 1965. Succeeded to title, 2013.

Reed, The Rt. Hon. Lord (Robert John Reed), PC 2008. Justice of the Supreme Court, since 2012; b. 7.9.56, Edinburgh; m., Jane Mylne; 2 d. Educ. George Watson's College, Edinburgh; Edinburgh University (LLB, 1st class Hons); Balliol College, Oxford (DPhil). Admitted to Scottish Bar, 1983; Standing Junior Counsel: Scottish Education Department, 1988-89, Scottish Office Home and Health Department, 1989-95; called to English Bar, 1991; QC, 1995; Advocate Depute, 1996-98; Judge of the Outer House of the Court of Session, 1998-2008; Principal

Commercial Judge, 2006-08; Judge of the Inner House, 2008-2012; ad hoc Judge of the European Court of Human Rights, 1999; Expert Adviser, EU/Council of Europe Joint Initiative with Turkey, 2002-04; Member, Advisory Board, British Institute of International and Comparative Law, 2001-05, Trustee, since 2015; Chairman, Franco-British Judicial Co-operation Committee, 2005-2012; President, EU Forum of Judges for the Environment, 2006-07, Vice-President, 2008-09; Member, UN Task Force on Access to Justice, 2006-08; Convener, Children in Scotland, 2006-2012; Member, Advisory Board, Oxford Institute of European and Comparative Law, since 2014; Bencher of Inner Temple, since 2012; Hon. Professor, University of Glasgow, since 2006; Visitor, Balliol College, Oxford, since 2011; Hon LLD, Glasgow University, 2013; FRSE, 2015. Recreation: music. Address: (b.) Supreme Court of the United Kingdom, Parliament Square, London SW1P 3BD.

Reed, Professor Peter, BA, RIBA, FRIAS, FSAScot. Emeritus Professor, Strathclyde University; b. 31.1.33, Hayes, Middlesex; m., Keow Chim Lim; 2 d. Educ. Southall Grammar School; Manchester University (State Scholar); Open University. Commissioned Officer, RAF, 1960-61; Assistant Lecturer, University of Hong Kong, 1961-64; Architect in practice, Malaysia, 1964-70; joined Strathclyde University Department of Architecture and Building Science as Lecturer, 1970; Professor of Architecture, 1986; Dean, Faculty of Engineering, 1988-90; Vice-Principal Elect, 1990-92; Vice-Principal, 1992-94. Secretary, Kilsyth Civic Trust, 1975-80; Chairman, Kilsyth Community Council, 1975-78; GIA Council, 1982-84; ARCUK Board of Education, 1985-95; Governor, Glasgow School of Art, 1982-94; Glasgow West Conservation Trust, 1990-2000, Convener, 1996-2000; Chairman, Council, Charles Rennie Mackintosh Society, 1991-94. Publications include Glasgow: The Forming of the City (Editor). Recreation: classical music. Address: 67 Dowanside Road, Glasgow G12 9DL; T.-0141-334 1356.

Reekie, Peter, MEng, MICE. Deputy Chief Executive, Scottish Futures Trust, since 2009; b. 14.09.71, Manchester; m., Nikki Temple; 2 d. Educ. Stockport Grammar School; University of Oxford, Hertford College. Allot and Lomax (now Jacobs) Consulting Engineers, 1994-2000; PricewaterhouseCoopers (Consulting and Corporate Finance at The Public Private Interface), 2000-09. Member, RSE Young Academy of Scotland. Recreations: young family and the great Scottish outdoors. Address: (b.) Scottish Futures Trust, 11-15 Thistle Street, Edinburgh EH2 1DF; T.-0131 510 0802.

E-mail: peter.reekie@scottishfuturestrust.org.uk

Reeks, David Robin, MBE, TD, DL, BSc (Eng). Vice Lord Lieutenant of Lanarkshire, 2002-2010; b. 15.6.35, Parkstone; m., Kathleen Veronica Stephens; 1 s.; 1 d. Educ. Canford School; London University. Rig Engineer, UKAEA Dounreay, 1962-67; Senior Engineer, SSEB, 1967-90; Reactor Thermal Performance Engineer, Scottish Nuclear Ltd., 1990-94. Committee Member and Volunteer Convoy Leader, Edinburgh Direct Aid to Bosnia; TA Royal Engineers/Royal Corps of Transport, 1962-90. Recreations: hill-walking; Scottish country dancing. Address: 3 Cedar Place, Strathaven, Lanarkshire ML10 6DW; T.-01357 521695; e-mail: d.reeks@talktalk.net

Rees, Alan Tait, MBE, MA (Cantab), CQSW; b. 4.8.31, Shanghai, China; m., Alison Margaret; 2 s.; 2 d. Educ. Kingswood School, Bath; Gonville and Caius College, Cambridge; London School of Economics; University College, Swansea. Community Development Officer, Tanzania; Lecturer in Youth and Community Studies,

Moray House College; Organising Secretary, Board for Information in Youth and Community Service, Scotland; Senior Community Development Officer, Council of Social Service for Wales; Assistant Director, Edinburgh Voluntary Organisations' Council, retired 1993; Chair, Scotland Yard Adventure Centre, Edinburgh, 1986-98; Chair, Handicabs (Lothian), 1997-2001; Secretary, Scottish Accessible Transport Alliance (retired 2012); Member, Mobility and Access Committee for Scotland, 2002-08; Founder and Board Member (1998-2000), Play Scotland; Secretary, Scottish Branch, International Play Association, 1994-2007. Recreations: gardening and painting. Address: (h.) 20 Seaforth Drive, Edinburgh EH4 2BZ; T.-0131-315 3006.

Rees, Professor Jonathan, BMedSci, MBBS, FRCP, FRCPE, FMedSci. Grant Chair of Dermatology, University of Edinburgh, since 2000; b. 10.10.57, Cardiff; 2 d. Educ. St. Illtyd's College, Cardiff. Trained in internal medicine, Newcastle upon Tyne; trained in dermatology, Vienna and Newcastle-upon-Tyne; trained in molecular genetics, Newcastle-upon-Tyne and Strasbourg; Professor of Dermatology, University of Newcastle, 1992-2000. President, European Society for Dermatology Research. Recreation: rugby. Address: (b.) Department of Dermatology, University of Edinburgh, Lauriston Building, Lauriston Place, Edinburgh EH3 9HA; T.-0131-536 2041; e-mail: jonathan.rees@ed.ac.uk

Reese, Professor Jason Meredith, DPhil, FInstP, FIMechE, FRSE, FREng. Regius Professor of Engineering, University of Edinburgh, since 2013; Weir Professor of Thermodynamics and Fluid Mechanics, University of Strathclyde, 2003-2013, Head of Department, Mechanical & Aerospace Engineering Department, 2011-2013; b. 24.6.67, London; 1 d; m., Dr Alexandra Shepard. Educ. St. Paul's School, London; Imperial College, London; University of Oxford. Lecturer in Engineering, University of Aberdeen, 1996-2000; Lecturer in Mechanical Engineering and ExxonMobil Fellow, King's College London, 2001-03; Co-Founder, Brinker Technology Ltd., Aberdeen (pipeline leak sealing and detection company), 2002. Philip Leverhulme Prize for Engineering, The Leverhulme Trust (2003); 36th Bruce Preller Prize Lectureship, Royal Society of Edinburgh (2004); MacRobert Award Finalist, Royal Academy of Engineering (2006). Member, Scottish Science Advisory Council, since 2012. Recreations: playing the piano; conversation; Byzantine history. Clubs: Oxford Union, Western Club (Glasgow). Address: (b.) School of Engineering, University of Edinburgh, The King's Buildings, Edinburgh EH9 3JL.

Reeve, Bill, BSc (Hons) Dunelm, MBA, CEng, FIMechE. Commercial Director, Transport Scotland, since 2005; b. 22.08.64, Redruth; m., Helen Redican; 2 s. Educ. Hove County Grammar; Brighton, Hove and Sussex VIth Form College; St. Chad's College, Durham; Strathclyde Graduate Business School. Career History: Rolling Stock Maintenance Engineer, British Rail, then Rail Freight Investment Manager; Rail Freight Business Development Manager, EWS Ltd.; Director, Project Sponsorship, Strategic Rail Authority. Past Chairman, Railway Division of Institution of Mechanical Engineers. Recreations: time with family; sailing; international rail travel. Address: (b.) Buchanan House, 58 Port Dundas Road, Glasgow G4 0HF; T.-0141 272 7420.

E-mail: bill.reeve@transportscotland.gsi.gov.uk

Reeves, Philip Thomas Langford, RSA, PPRSW, RE, RGI, ARCA. Artist; b. 7.7.31, Cheltenham; m., Christine

MacLaren (deceased); 1 d. Educ. Naunton Park School, Cheltenham; Cheltenham School of Art; Royal College of Art, London. Lecturer in Graphic Design, Glasgow School of Art, 1954-70, Head of Printmaking, 1970-91; Founder Member: Edinburgh Printmakers, 1967, Glasgow Print Studio, 1972. Address: (h.) 13 Hamilton Drive, Glasgow G12 8DN; T.-0141-339 0720.

Regan, Stewart. Chief Executive, Scottish Football Association, since 2010; b. County Durham. Career history: worked in the brewing industry for 16 years, employed by John Smith, Bass and latterly Coors; worked for Yorkshire County Cricket Club for over four years as chief executive during which time a new Pavilion was created with local authority and educational partner support. Address: The Scottish Football Association Ltd, Hampden Park, Glasgow G42 9AY.

Rehman, Satwat. Director, One Parent Families Scotland, since 2011. Career history: set up and ran the employability charity Skillnet, bringing together employers and job-seekers from ethnic minorities; ten years at Camden London Borough Council, latterly as Deputy Head of Integrated Early Years Services. Address: (b.) Headquarters, 13 Gayfield Square, Edinburgh EH1 3NX; T.-0131 556 3899; e-mail: info@opfs.org.uk

Reid, Alan, MP. Liberal Democrat MP, Argyll and Bute, 2001-2015; b. 7.8.54. Educ. Prestwick Academy; Ayr Academy; Strathclyde University. Maths Teacher, 1976-77; Computer Programmer, 1977-85; Computer Project Manager, Glasgow University, 1985-2001.

Reid, Professor Colin Turriff, MA, LLB, FRSA. Professor of Environmental Law, Dundee University, since 1995 and Dean of the Faculty of Law and Accountancy, 2004-06; b. 10.6.58, Aberdeen; m., M. Anne Palin; 2 d. Educ. Robert Gordon's College, Aberdeen; University College, Oxford; Gonville and Caius College, Cambridge. Lecturer in Public Law, Aberdeen University, 1980-90; Senior Lecturer in Law, Dundee University, 1991-95. Publications: Nature Conservation Law; Environmental Law in Scotland (Editor); A Guide to the Scotland Act 1998 (Co-Author). Recreations: cricket; hockey. Address: (b.) School of Law, Dundee University, Dundee DD1 4HN; T.-01382 384461.

Reid, Derek Donald, MA. Chairman, Harris Tweed Textiles Ltd; various directorships of small companies; Visiting Professor of Tourism, Abertay University, since 2000; b. 30.11.44, Aberdeen; m., Janice Anne Reid; 1 s.; 1 d. Educ. Inverurie Academy; Aberdeen University; Robert Gordon University. Cadbury-Schweppes, 1968-85 (latterly Divisional Director); founding Director/Owner, Premier Brands, 1985-90; Chief Executive, Scottish Tourist Board, 1994-96. Former Deputy Chairman, Sea Fish Industry Authority; former Deputy Chairman: Scotland The Brand; Honorary Doctorate, Business Administration, Robert Gordon University. Recreations: golf; fishing; modern art; fine food/wine. Address: Broomhill, Kinclaven, Stanley, Perth PH1 4QL; T.-01250-883209.
E-mail: dd.reid30@btinternet.com

Reid, Donald Bremner, MA, LLB. Chairman, Mitchells Roberton, since 1997; b. 1.3.51, Glasgow; m., Moira Ruth Wilson; 2 s. Educ. Jordanhill College School; University of Glasgow. Solicitor, 1975; Mitchells Johnston Hill and Hoggan: joined 1976, Partner, 1978, firm amalgamated to form Mitchells Roberton, 1985; Tutor, then Senior Tutor

and Lecturer (part-time), University of Glasgow, 1980-99; Expert Witness. Secretary, Children 1st, Glasgow, 1979-99. Recreations: theatre; reading; drinking coffee and reading newspapers; France. Address: (b.) George House, 36 North Hanover Street, Glasgow G1 2AD; T.-0141-552 3422; e-mail: dbr@mitchells-roberton.co.uk

Reid, Eliane. Operations Manager, Research Into Results Ltd, University of Edinburgh, since 2015; b. 10.8.65, Forfar, Angus. Educ. Forfar Academy; University of Derby. Scottish Natural Heritage: Team Leader with the Chief Scientist Directorate in the Nature Conservancy Council, 1990-97, Strategic Manager, 1997-2000, Head of Projects and Partnerships, 2000-05. Currently work with Scottish, UK and European Governments and organisations involving volunteers; currently supporting the 2014 Commonwealth Games, young people's employability skills through volunteering, environmental organisations in their volunteer involvement and working with BIG Lottery Scotland on several innovative projects. Trustee, the Clinical Genetics Endowment Fund with the University of Dundee and NHS Tayside; Assistant Chief Executive, Volunteer Development Scotland, 1985-2014. Published various academic papers and book chapters between 1992-2000 on technical mapping techniques for environmental conservation. Recreations: sport; socialising with friends/family and travel to destinations which are unusual! Address: (b.) Research Into Results Ltd, University of Edinburgh, Old College, South Bridge, Edinburgh EH8 9YL.

Reid, Elspeth M., MA (Hons), MA, DipArchAdmin, RMARA. Archivist, Falkirk Archives, since 1992; Commissioner, RCAHMS, 2008-2015. Educ. St Andrews; Guelph; University College London. Address: (b.) Falkirk Archives, Callendar House, Callendar Park, Falkirk FK1 1YR.

Reid, Professor Gavin Clydesdale, MA, MSc, PhD, FRSA, FFCS, Hon. DBA (Abertay, 2010), DLitt (Aberdeen, 2012). Professor of Business Management and Strategy, Head of School, Dundee Business School, University of Abertay, since 2014; Professor of Economics, St. Andrews University, 1991-2013; Founder/Director, Centre for Research into Industry, Enterprise, Finance and the Firm (CRIEFF), 1991-2013; Visiting Professor in Accounting and Finance, University of Strathclyde, since 2007; Member, Competition Appeal Tribunal, since 2011; Honorary Professor of Economics, University of St Andrews, since 2013; b. 25.8.46, Glasgow; m., Dr. Julia A. Smith; 2 s.; 4 d. Educ. Lyndhurst Prep School; Frimley and Camberley Grammar School; Aberdeen University (Stephen Scholar); Southampton University (SSRC Student); Edinburgh University. Lecturer, Senior Lecturer, Reader in Economics, Edinburgh University, 1971-91; Visiting Associate Professor: Queen's University, Ontario, 1981-82, Denver University, Colorado, 1984; Visiting Scholar, Darwin College, Cambridge, 1987-88; Visiting Professor, University of Nice, 1990; Leverhulme Trust Research Fellowship, 1989-90; Nuffield Foundation Social Science Research Fellowship, 1997-98; Professor of Enterprise and Innovation, University of the West of Scotland Business School, 2013-14. Editorial Board: Scottish Journal of Political Economy, 1986-98, Small Business Economics, since 1997, Venture Capital, 1998-2008; Member, Council, Scottish Economic Society, 1990-2002, President, 1999-2002; Research Fellow, EIM Business and Policy Research, Rotterdam, since 2002; Chairman, ESRC Network of Industrial Economists, 1997-2001; Member, Economic Council, Britain in Europe, 2002-04; Chair, Scottish Institute for Enterprise Research Forum, 2002-03; National Conference of University Professors, President, 2003-06, Vice-President, 2002-03, Member,

Council, since 1999; President, Institute of Contemporary Scotland, 2005-06; Chairman, ESRC Seminars in Accounting, Finance and Economics, 2006-08; Advisor, Centre for Business Research, Judge Business School, University of Cambridge, since 2009. Publications: The Kinked Demand Curve Analysis of Oligopoly, 1981; Theories of Industrial Organization, 1987; The Small Entrepreneurial Firm (Co-author), 1988; Classical Economic Growth, 1989; Small Business Enterprise, 1993; Profiles in Small Business (Co-author), 1993; Venture Capital Investment, 1998; Information System Development in the Small Firm (Co-author), 2000; The Foundations of Small Business Enterprise, 2007; Risk Appraisal and Venture Capital in High Technology New Ventures (Co-Author), 2008. Recreations: music; reading; running; badminton; poetry. Address: (h.) 23 South Street, St. Andrews KY16 9QS; T.-01334 472932.

Reid, The Rt Hon. Sir George, MA, PC (2004), kt (2012), FRSE (2015). Lord-Lieutenant of Clackmannanshire, 2011-2014; Lord High Commissioner, 2008 and 2009; UK Electoral Commissioner, 2010-2014; Chair, Independent Remuneration Board of National Assembly for Wales, 2010-2014; Director of Strategic Review of Northern Ireland Assembly, 2007-09 and of National Trust for Scotland, 2009-2010; Visiting Professor at Universities of Glasgow and Stirling, since 2007; MSP (Elected SNP, but no political allegiance as Presiding Officer), Ochil, 2003-07; Presiding Officer and Convener of Parliamentary Bureau and Corporate Body, Scottish Parliament, 2003-07; MSP (SNP), Mid-Scotland and Fife, and Deputy Presiding Officer, 1999-2003; b. 4.6.39, Tullibody; m., Daphne Ann; 2 d. Educ. Dollar Academy; St Andrews University. Reporter, Daily Express; Reporter, Scottish Television; Producer, Granada Television; Head of News and Current Affairs, Scottish Television; Presenter, BBC; Director of Public Affairs, International Red Cross. MP, Clackmannan and East Stirlingshire, 1974-79; Member, Parliamentary Assembly of the Council of Europe, 1975-79; Trustee, Glasgow Life and Edinburgh International Tattoo, 2007-2014; Independent Adviser, Scottish Ministerial Code, 2008-2011; Professorial Fellow, University of Stirling and London Academy of Diplomacy, since 2014. Honorary doctorates, Universities of St. Andrews, Queen Margaret, Edinburgh, Stirling and Glasgow.

Reid, Harry William, BA (Hons), Dr hc (Edinburgh), DUniv (Glasgow), FRSA. Writer; former Editor, The Herald; b. 23.9.47, Glasgow; m., Julie Davidson (qv); 1 d. Educ. Aberdeen Grammar School; Fettes College; Oxford University. The Scotsman: Education Correspondent, 1973-77, Features Editor, 1977-81; Sports Editor, Sunday Standard, 1981-82; Executive Editor, Glasgow Herald, 1982-83, Deputy Editor, 1983-97; Chairman, Scottish Editors' Committee, 1999-2001. Visiting Fellow, Faculty of Divinity, Edinburgh University, 2001-02; Governor, Fettes College, 2002-2012; Columnist, The Herald, 2004-2014; Oliver Brown Award, 2007. Publications: Dear Country: a quest for England, 1992; Outside Verdict: An Old Kirk in a New Scotland, 2002; The Final Whistle? Scottish Football: The Best and Worst of Times, 2005; Deadline: The Story of the Scottish Press, 2006; The Independence Book (Co-Ed), 2008; Reformation: The Dangerous Birth of the Modern World, 2009. Recreations: reading; walking; supporting Aberdeen Football Club. Address: 12 Comely Bank, Edinburgh EH4 1AN; T.-0131-332 6690; e-mail: harry.reid@virgin.net

Reid, Heather M.M., OBE, BSc (Hons), MSc, CPhys, MInstP, FRMS. Science Education Consultant; former Weather Forecaster, Met Office; BBC Scotland Weather Forecaster, 1994-2009; b. 6.7.69, Paisley. Educ. Camphill High School, Paisley; Edinburgh University. Joined Met Office to work in satellite image research; became forecaster at Glasgow Weather Centre; known as "Heather the Weather" to viewers. Past-Chair, Institute of Physics in Scotland, 1999-2001; active involvement in Edinburgh Science Festival, Techfest, and promoting the public understanding of science; member of the science and engineering education advisory group set up by the Scottish Government. Recreations: apart from lecturing and giving talks in spare time – watch cricket; hill-walking.

Reid, Iain, LLB. Finance Director, Sunergos Innovations; former Interim Chief Executive, The National Trust for Scotland (2015) (Finance Director, 2010-2015). Educ. University of Edinburgh. Company Secretary, Scottish Widows, 1995-2001; Finance Director, Sopra Group, 2001-07; Global CFO, Axway Software, 2007-08; Finance Director, Grant Management, 2008-09; Director, Reid & Co, 2009-2010. Address: Sunergos Innovations, 47 Little France Crescent, Edinburgh EH16 4TJ; T.-0131 242 9444.

Reid, Professor J.S. Grant, BSc, PhD. Professor of Plant Biochemistry, Stirling University, 1994-2003, now Emeritus; b. 27.3.42, Huntly; m., Mary E. Edwards; 1 s.; 2 d. Educ. Gordon Schools, Huntly; Aberdeen University. Lecturer, University of Fribourg, Switzerland, 1970-73; Lecturer in Biochemistry, Stirling University, 1974-78; Visiting Associate Professor, University of Calgary, 1977-78; Senior Lecturer, then Reader, Stirling University, 1978-94; Visiting Professor, Unilever Research Laboratories, Netherlands, 1988. Address: (b.) School of Biological and Environmental Sciences, Stirling University, Stirling FK9 4LA; T.-01786 461138; e-mail: j.s.g.reid@stir.ac.uk

Reid, James Gordon, LLB (Hons), FCIArb. Queen's Counsel (Scotland), since 1993; Chairman (Part-time), VAT and Duties Tribunals, 1997-2009; Deputy Special Commissioner for Income Tax, 1997-2009; Tribunal Judge (Part-time), First-tier Tribunal (Tax Chamber), since 2009; Deputy Judge of the Upper Tribunal (Tax and Chancery Chamber), since 2009; Temporary Judge of the Court of Session, since 2002; b. 24.7.52, Edinburgh; m., Hannah Hogg Hopkins; 2 s.; 1 d. Educ. Melville College, Edinburgh; Edinburgh University. Solicitor, 1976-80; Advocate, 1980-93; Standing Junior Counsel, Scottish Office Environment Department, 1986-93; admitted as Barrister, Inner Temple, 1991. Recreation: classical guitar. Address: (h.) Blebo House, by St. Andrews, Fife KY15 5TZ.

Reid of Cardowan, Rt. Hon. Lord (John Reid), PC, PhD. MP (Labour), Airdrie and Shotts, 2005-10, Hamilton North and Bellshill, 1997-2005, Motherwell North, 1987-97; Secretary of State for the Home Department, 2006-07; b. 8.5.47, Bellshill; m., 1, Catherine McGowan (deceased), 2, Carine Adler; 2 s. Educ. St. Patrick's Senior Secondary School, Coatbridge; Stirling University. Scottish Research Officer, Labour Party, 1979-83; Political Adviser to Rt. Hon. Neil Kinnock, 1983-85; Scottish Organiser, Trade Unionists for Labour, 1986-87; Armed Forces Minister, 1997-98; Minister of Transport, 1998-99; Secretary of State for Scotland, 1999-2001; Secretary of State for Northern Ireland, 2001-02; Party Chair and Minister without Portfolio, 2001-02; Leader of the Commons and President of the Council, 2002-03; Secretary of State for Health, 2003-05; Secretary of State for Defence, 2005-06. Hon. Prof., University College London; Chair, Institute for Security and Resilience Studies; Senior Advisor, The Chertaff Group; Chairman, Celtic Football Club, 2007-2011. Publication: Cyber Doctrine: Towards a framework for learning resilience (Co-Author), 2011. Recreations:

football; crossword puzzles. Special interests: defence; security; cyber. Address: House of Lords, London SW1A 0PW.

Reid, Karen. Chief Executive, Care Inspectorate, since 2015. Head of Corporate Services, IRISS - Institute for Research and Innovation in Social Services, 2006-09; Director of Operations, SCSWIS, 2009-2012; Director of Strategic Development/Depute Chief Executive, SCSWIS/Care Inspectorate, 2012-15. Holds formal qualifications in accountancy, communications/public relations and project management. Address: Care Inspectorate, Compass House, 11 Riverside Drive, Dundee DD1 4NY; T.-0345 600 9527.

Reid, Professor Kenneth Gilbert Cameron, CBE (2005), MA, LLB, WS, FRSE, FBA (2008). Professor of Scots Law, Edinburgh University, since 2008, Professor of Property Law, 1994-2008; Director, Edinburgh Centre for Private Law, 2009-2012; Law Commissioner for Scotland, 1995-2005; b. 25.3.54, Glasgow; m., Elspeth Christie; 2 s.; 1 d. Educ. Loretto; St. John's College, Cambridge; Edinburgh University. Admitted as a Solicitor, 1980; Lecturer in Law, Edinburgh University, 1980. Author of numerous books and papers on the law of property. Recreation: classical music. Address: (b.) School of Law, Old College, South Bridge, Edinburgh EH8 9YL; T.-0131-650 2015.

Reid, Melanie Frances, MA (Hons). Writer and Columnist, The Times, since 2007; Writer, Spinal Column in The Times Magazine, since 2010; Senior Assistant Editor and Columnist, The Herald, 2001-07; b. 13.4.57, Barnet; m., Clifford Martin; 1 s.; divorced; m., David McNeil. Educ. Ormskirk Grammar School; Edinburgh University. The Scotsman: Graduate Trainee, 1980-82, Woman's Editor, 1983-87; Sunday Mail: Woman's Editor, 1987-2000, Associate Editor, 2000; Columnist, The Express, 2000. Member, Carnegie Commission for Rural Community Development, 2004-07. Journalist and Columnist of the Year 2010, Scottish Press Awards; Columnist of the Year, 2011, UK Press Awards; Co-writer (with Sally Beamish) of musical piece Spinal Chords 2012 for the orchestra of the Age of Enlightenment; Honorary Degree from Stirling University, 2014. Recreation: staying cheerful. Address: (b.) The Times, 1 London Bridge Street, London SE1 9GF. E-mail: melanie.reid@thetimes.co.uk

Reid, Dame Seona Elizabeth, CBE, BA, HonDArt, HonDLitt, FRSA. Director, Glasgow School of Art, 1999-2013; Honorary Professor; b. 21.1.50, Paisley. Educ. Park School, Glasgow; Strathclyde University; Liverpool University. Business Manager, Theatre Royal, Lincoln, 1972-73; Press Officer, Northern Dance Theatre, Manchester, 1973-76; PRO, Ballet Rambert, London, 1976-79; freelance arts consultant, 1979-81; Director, Shape, London, 1981-87; Assistant Director, Greater London Arts, 1987-90; Director, Scottish Arts Council, 1990-99; April 2011: Deputy Chair, National Heritage Memorial Fund and Chair of Scottish Committee of Heritage Lottery Fund; Scottish Commissioner, US-UK Fulbright Commission. Board Member, Cove Park; Universities Scotland Executive Committee. Recreations: walking; travel; the arts.

Reid, Simon H. Croghan, BA, HDipEd. Principal, Gordonstoun School, since 2011; b. 19.10.61, Johannesburg, South Africa; m., Michele C. Reid; 1 s.; 1 d. Educ. Hilton College, Natal; University of Witwatersrand, South Africa. Teacher of English: Brentwood School, Essex, 1986-88, Stowe School, Buckinghamshire, 1988-93;

Housemaster and English Teacher, Christ's Hospital, West Sussex, 1993-2004; Deputy Head, Worksop College, Nottinghamshire, 2004-2011. Recreations: reading; skiing; landscape photography. Address: (b.) Gordonstoun, Duffus, Elgin, Moray IV30 5RF; T.-01343 837807. E-mail: reids@gordonstoun.org.uk

Reid, Sir William Kennedy, KCB, MA, LLD (Aberdeen and Reading), FRCPEd, FRSE; b. 15.2.31, Aberdeen; m., Ann Campbell; 2 s.; 1 d. Educ. Robert Gordon's College; George Watson's College; Edinburgh University; Trinity College, Cambridge. Civil Servant, 1956-89, Department of Education and Science, Cabinet Office, Scottish Office; Member, Council on Tribunals and Its Scottish Committee, 1990-96; Member, Commission for Local Administration in England, 1990-96; Member, Commission for Local Administration in Wales, 1990-96. A Director, International Ombudsman Institute, 1992-96; Parliamentary Commissioner for Administration (Ombudsman), 1990-97; Health Service Commissioner for England, Scotland, Wales, 1990-97; Chairman, Mental Welfare Commission for Scotland, 1997-2000; Chairman, Advisory Committee on Distinction Awards, 1997-2000; Queen Elizabeth the Queen Mother Fellow, Nuffield Trust, 1998; Chairman of Council, St. George's School for Girls, 1997-2003; Chairman, Edinburgh Competition Festival Association, 2007-2010; Chairman, Scottish Churches Architectural Heritage Trust, 2011-2012; Hon. D. Litt (Napier), 1998; Hon. FRCSEd, 2002. Recreations: verse; hill-walking. Address: (h.) Darroch House, 9/1 East Suffolk Park, Edinburgh EH16 5PL.

Reilly, Kerry. National General Secretary/Chief Executive, YMCA Scotland, since 2015. Educ. The Open University; Northern College of Education; Edinburgh Napier University; University of Leeds. Programme Secretary, Dumfries YMCA, 1992-93; Youth Worker, Bellshill & Mossend YMCA, 1995-98; Youth Work Development Officer, YMCA Scotland, 1998-2006; Chair of YMCA Europe Festival 2013, 2010-13; YMCA Manager, YMCA Edinburgh, 2007-2014. Address: YMCA Scotland, James Love House, 11 Rutland Street, Edinburgh EH1 2DQ; T.-0131 228 1464.

Reith, David Stewart, LLB, NP, WS. Chairman, Lindsays, Solicitors, Edinburgh, Glasgow and Dundee, since 1976; b. 15.4.51, Edinburgh; m., Elizabeth Julia Hawkins; 1 s.; 1 d. Educ. Edinburgh Academy; Fettes College; Aberdeen University. Scottish Legal Awards Partner of the Year, 2007. Director: LifeCare (Edinburgh), Lindsays Ltd., Lindsays Financial Planning LLP; Secretary: Edinburgh and Lothians Greenspace Trust, Ponton House Trust, Queensberry House Trust, Scottish Seabird Centre, Mavisbank House Trust; Sir Henry Wade's Pilmuir Trust; Clerk, Incorporation of Cordiners. Recreations: cycling; French conversation; detective novels; wine. Address: (h.) Woodside House, Gladsmuir, East Lothian EH33 2AL.

Reith, Sheriff Fiona Lennox, LLB, QC, FSA Scot. Sheriff of Lothian and Borders at Edinburgh, since 2007; Specialist Sheriff, National Personal Injury Court, since 2015; b. 17.7.55, Ipswich. Educ. Perth Academy; Aberdeen University. Solicitor, Edinburgh, 1979-82; devilled, 1982-83; admitted to Faculty of Advocates, 1983; Standing Junior Counsel in Scotland to Home Office, 1989-92; Advocate-Depute, 1992-95; Standing Junior Counsel, Scottish Office Environment Department, 1995-96; QC, 1996; Sheriff of Tayside, Central and Fife, at Perth, 1999-2000; Sheriff of Glasgow and Strathkelvin, 2000-07. Member, Scottish Legal Aid Board Civil Legal Aid Sub-Committee and Supreme Court Reporter, 1989-92; Member, Sheriff

Court Rules Council, 1989-93; External Examiner in Professional Conduct, Faculty of Advocates, 2000-06; Member, Council of Sheriffs Association, 2003-06 and 2009-2011; Member, Criminal Courts' Rules Council, 2004-2011; Member, Parole Board for Scotland, 2005-07, Vice-Chairman, 2008-09; Member, Lord Coulsfield's Civil Justice Advisory Group, 2004-05 (Report in relation to the Civil Justice System in Scotland, published November 2005). Recreations: walking; theatre; good food and wine; travel. Address: (b.) Sheriff's Chambers, Edinburgh Sheriff Court, 27 Chambers Street, Edinburgh EH1 1LB; T.-0131-225 2525.

Reith, Professor Gerda, MA (Hons), PhD. Professor of Social Science, University of Glasgow, since 2010; b. 24.5.69, Aberdeen; m., Andy Furlong; 2 s.; 1 d. Educ. Lossiemouth High School; Glasgow University. Glasgow University: Research Fellow, 1996-98, Lecturer and Senior Lecturer, 1998-2010. Chair, Research Panel - Responsible Gambling Strategy Board, since 2008. Publications: The Age of Chance: Gambling in Western Culture, 1999 (winner of The Philip Abrams Prize); Gambling - Who Wins? Who Loses? (2002). Address: School of Social and Political Sciences, Adam Smith Building, University of Glasgow, Glasgow G12 8RT; T.-0141 330 3849.
E-mail: gerda.reith@glasgow.ac.uk

Rennie, Allan. Managing Director, Media Scotland (Daily Record and Sunday Mail, Scottish & Universal Newspapers), since 2014, Editor-in-Chief, 2012-2014; b. 5.7.60, Stirling. Educ. Kilsyth Academy. Springburn Times; Johnstone Gazette; Stirling Observer; The Sun; Evening News, Daily Record; Editor, Sunday Mail, 2000-09; Editorial Director, Trinity Mirror, 2009-2012. Recreation: running. Address: One Central Quay, Glasgow G3 8DA; T.-0141-309 3000.

Rennie, Archibald Louden, CB, LLD, FDSRCS (Eng), BSc; b. 4.6.24, Guardbridge, Fife; m., Kathleen Harkess; 4 s. Educ. Madras College, St Andrews; St Andrews University. Experimental Officer, Minesweeping Research Division, 1944-47; joined Department of Health for Scotland, 1947; Private Secretary to Secretary of State for Scotland, 1962-63; Assistant Secretary, Scottish Home and Health Department, 1963-69; Registrar General for Scotland, 1969-73; Under Secretary, Scottish Economic Planning Department, 1973-77; Secretary, Scottish Home and Health Department, 1977-84. Vice-Chairman, Advisory Committee on Distinction Awards, 1985-94; Chancellor's Assessor, St. Andrews University, 1985-89; Member, Scottish Records Advisory Council, 1985-93; Member, Council on Tribunals, and its Scottish Committee, 1987-88; Trustee, Lockerbie Air Disaster Appeal, 1988-91; Chairman, Disciplined Services Pay Review Committee, Hong Kong, 1988; Chairman, Blacket Association, 1971-73; Commodore, Elie and Earlsferry S.C., 1992-94; Chairman, Elie Harbour Trust, 1993-99; Chairman, Elie and the Royal Burgh of Earlsferry Community Council, 2001-03. Publications: Fringe of Gold: The East Neuk through Nine Millennia; The Harbours of Elie Bay: A History. Recreations: Firth-watching; local history; reading; conversation. Address: (h.) The Laigh House, 6A South Street, Elie, Fife KY9 1DN; T.-01333 330741.

Rennie, Colin. Manager for Scotland, Fields in Trust (FIT), formerly National Playing Fields Association (NPFA), since 2005; b. 1956, Montrose, Angus; m., Alyson; 2 s. Educ. Dundee College; Kingsway Technical College. Career History: Westminster Parliamentary Adviser; Chairman: North of Scotland Water Authority,

Dundee Partnership; Convenor, Economic Development, Dundee City Council; Journalist; Architectural Draughtsman. Former SET Board Member; former Dundee and Angus Tourist Board Member. Recreations: hill walking; fly fishing; visiting historic buildings; sport. Address: (b.) Dewar House, Staffa Place, Dundee DD2 3SX; T.-01382 817427.
E-mail: colin.rennie@fieldsintrust.org

Rennie, Professor Robert, LLB, PhD, FRSA. Partner, Harper MacLeod Solicitors, Glasgow, since 2001; Emeritus Professor, since 2014 (Professor of Conveyancing, Glasgow University, 1993-2014); b. 30.6.47, Glasgow; m., Catherine Mary McGregor; 1 s.; 3 d. Educ. Lenzie Academy; Glasgow University. Apprentice then Legal Assistant, Bishop Milne Boyd & Co., Solicitors, Glasgow; joined Ballantyne & Copland as Legal Assistant, 1971, Partner, 1972-2001; Past Convener, Law Society of Scotland Conveyancing Committee. Recreation: classical music. Address: (b.) Harper MacLeod, The Ca'd'oro, 45 Gordon Street, Glasgow G1 3PE.

Rennie, Willie. MSP (Liberal Democrat), North East Fife, since 2016 (Mid Scotland and Fife region, 2011-16); Leader, Scottish Liberal Democrats, since 2011; MP (Liberal Democrat), Dunfermline and Fife West, 2006-10; b. 29.9.67; m., Janet; 2 s. Educ. Paisley College. Chief Executive, Scottish Liberal Democrats and the Party's Chief of Staff, Scottish Parliament, 1997-2001; formerly adviser to Fife's Lib Dem Council Group; self-employed consultant, 2001-03; Account Director, McEwan Purvis, 2003-06. Recreations: road running; hill running. Address: (b.) Scottish Parliament, Edinburgh EH99 1SP.

Renshaw, Professor Eric, BSc, ARCS, DipStats, MPhil, PhD, CStat, FRSE. Emeritus Professor of Statistics, Strathclyde University (Professor, since 1991); b. 25.7.45, Preston; m., Anne Renshaw. Educ. Arnold School, Blackpool; Imperial College, London; Manchester University; Sussex University; Edinburgh University. Lecturer, then Senior Lecturer in Statistics, Edinburgh University, 1969-91. Publication: Modelling Biological Populations in Space and Time; Stochastic Population Processes. Recreations: skiing; golf; hill-walking; mandolin; photography. Address (h.) 42 Leadervale Road, Edinburgh EH16 6PA; T.-0131 664 2370; e-mail: e.renshaw@strath.ac.uk

Renwick, Professor John Peter, MA, PhD, DLitt, FRHistS, FRSE, Commandeur des Palmes Académiques. John Orr Professor of French, Edinburgh University, 1980-2006; Director, Centre de Recherches Francophones Belges, 1995-2010; Research Fellow, The Voltaire Foundation, University of Oxford, since 2008; b. 25.5.39, Gillingham; m., Claudette Gorse; 1 s.; 1 d. Educ. Gillingham Grammar School; St. Bartholomew's Grammar School, Newbury; St. Catherine's College, Oxford; Sorbonne; British Institute in Paris (Leverhulme Research Scholar). Assistant Lecturer, then Lecturer, Glasgow University, 1964-66; Fellow, Churchill College, Cambridge, 1966-72; Maitre de Conférences Associé, Départment de Francais, Université de Clermont-Ferrand, 1970-71, 1972-74; Professor of French, New University of Ulster, 1974-80 (Pro-Vice-Chancellor, 1978-80); Member, Editorial Committee, The Complete Works of Voltaire; Member, Executive Committee, Voltaire Foundation; Member, Editorial Committee, Moralia (Paris); General Secretary, Society of the Friends of the Institut Français d'Ecosse; President, Comité Consultatif, Institut Français d'Ecosse, 1996-2010; Médaille de la Ville de Bort. Publications: La destinée posthume de Jean-Francois Marmontel, 1972; Marmontel, Mémoires, 1972; Marmontel, Voltaire and the Belisaire affair, 1974; Marmontel, Correspondence, 1974; Catalogue de la bibliotheque de Jean-Baptiste Massillon, 1977; Voltaire et Morangies, ou les Lumieres l'ont échappé belle, 1982; Chamfort devant la posterité, 1986; Catalogue de la Bibliotheque du Comte D'Espinchal, 1988; Language and Rhetoric of the French Revolution, 1990; Voltaire, La Guerre Civile de Genève, 1990; Catalogue de la Bibliotheque du College de L'Oratoire de Riom 1619-1792, 1997; Voltaire, Brutus, 1998; Voltaire, Les Guèbres, 1999; Voltaire, Traité sur la Tolérance, 1999 and 2000; L'Invitation au Voyage (Studies in Honour of Peter France), 2000; Jean-Francois Marmontel (1723-1799): Dix études, 2001; Voltaire, Histoire du parlement de Paris, 2005; Voltaire, Essai sur les Probabilités en fait de Justice; Nouvelles Probabilités, 2006; 60@ifecosse, 2006; Marmontel, Mémoires, new edition, revised and considerably expanded, 2008; General editor (and contributor: twelve critical editions), vols. 75A-75B, Oeuvres complètes de Voltaire, 2009; General editor (and contributor), Voltaire, la tolérance et la justice, 2010; Co-Director and contributor of the critical edition of the Essai sur les moeurs (Oeuvres complètes de Voltaire, vols. 21-27 (vol. 22, 2009: vol. 23, 2010: vol. 24, 2011: vol. 25, 2012: vol. 26A, 2013: vol. 26B, 2014: vol. 26C, 2015). Address: (b.) 50 George Square, Edinburgh EH8 5LH.

Reoch, Torquil, MA. Retired Broadcasting Journalist; Producer, BBC Newsnight Scotland, 1999-2014; b. 17.6.54, Glasgow; m., Christine; 1 s.; 2 d.; 2 g-s.; 1 g-d. Educ. George Watson's College, Edinburgh; Edinburgh University; Glasgow University. News Trainee, BBC London, 1979; Reporter, BBC Radio Scotland, 1980; Scotland Correspondent, TV-am, 1983; News Producer, BBC Scotland, 1985; Producer, European Business Channel, Zurich, 1989; Editor, Good Morning Scotland, 1991; News Operations Editor, BBC Scotland, 1997. Recreation: family. T.-07850 715100.
E-mail: torquil@reoch.eu

Reynolds, Professor Siân, BA, MA, PhD, Officier dans l'ordre des Palmes académiques, Fellow of the Learned Society of Wales. Professor (now emerita) of French, Stirling University, since 1990; Honorary Visiting Professor, University of Nottingham, 2015-18; Translator; b. 28.7.40, Cardiff; m., Peter France; 3 d. Educ. Howell's School, Llandaff; St. Anne's College, Oxford; University of Paris VII. Lecturer and Senior Lecturer, Sussex University, 1974-89; Lecturer, Edinburgh University, 1989-90; President, UK Association for the Study of Modern and Contemporary France, 1993-99; Chair, Scottish Working People's History Trust. Publications: Women, State and Revolution (Editor); Britannica's Typesetters; France Between the Wars, gender and politics; Contemporary French Cultural Studies (Joint Editor), 2000; co-editor, The Biographical Dictionary of Scottish Women, 2006; Paris-Edinburgh, 2007; Marriage and Revolution, 2012 (winner, R.H. Gapper Book Prize 2013); translations include F. Braudel, The Mediterranean and novels by crime writers, Fred Vargas and Georges Simenon. Four times co-winner of CWA International Dagger, 2006, 2007, 2009, 2013. Recreation: going to the pictures. Address: (h.) 10 Dryden Place, Edinburgh EH9 1RP.
E-mail: sian.reynolds@stir.ac.uk

Rhodes, Professor Neil Patrick Pawson, MA, DPhil. Professor of English Literature and Cultural History, University of St. Andrews; b. 30.05.53, Carlisle; m., Shirley McKay; 1 s.; 1 d. Educ. Uppingham School; St. Catherine's College, Oxford. Visiting Professor, University of Granada; General Editor, MHRA Tudor and Stuart Translations. Publications include: English Renaissance Translation Theory, 2013; Shakespeare and the Origins of English, 2007; The Renaissance Computer, 2000. Address:

(h.) 36 Marketgate, Crail, Fife; e-mail: nppr@st-andrews.ac.uk

Riach, Alan, BA (Cambridge), PhD (Glasgow). Professor and Chair, Department of Scottish Literature, University of Glasgow, since 2006; Head of Department, 2001-07; President, Association for Scottish Literary Studies, 2006-2010; b. 1.8.57, Airdrie; m., Rae; 2 s. Educ. Gravesend School for Boys, Gravesend, Kent; Churchill College, University of Cambridge, 1976-79: BA; Department of Scottish Literature, University of Glasgow, 1979-85: PhD. Freelance writing and teaching, Scotland, 1985-86; Post-Doctoral Research Fellow, Lecturer, Senior Lecturer, Associate Professor of English, University of Waikato, Hamilton, New Zealand, 1986-2000; Pro-Dean, Faculty of Arts and Social Sciences, University of Waikato, Hamilton, New Zealand, 2000. Many appearances on radio and television in New Zealand, Australia and Scotland. Publications: Representing Scotland in Literature, Popular Culture and Iconography, 2005; Hugh MacDiarmid's Epic Poetry, 1991; The Poetry of Hugh MacDiarmid, 1999; Hugh MacDiarmid: The Collected Works (General Editor), since 1992 (15 volumes published to 2009); The Radical Imagination: Lectures and Talks by Wilson Harris (Co-Editor); Scotlands: Poets and the Nation (Co-Editor); Arts of Resistance: Poets, Portraits and Landscapes of Modern Scotland (Co-Author); contributions to over 20 books and numerous contributions to journals; books of poetry: For What It Is (Co-Author), 1988; This Folding Map (Poems 1978-1988), 1990; An Open Return, 1991; First and Last Songs, 1995; From the Vision of Hell: An Extract of Dante, 1998, Clearances, 2001; Homecoming: New Poems 2001-09, 2009; contributor to other books of poetry. Address: (b.) Department of Scottish Literature, University of Glasgow, 7 University Gardens, Glasgow G12 8QH; T.-0141-330 6144.
E-mail: Alan.Riach@glasgow.ac.uk

Rice, Professor Sir C. Duncan, MA, PhD, FRSE, FRHistS, FRSA. Principal and Vice-Chancellor, Aberdeen University, 1996-2010; b. 20.10.42, Aberdeen; m., Susan Ilene (qv); 2 s.; 1 d. Educ. Aberdeen University; Edinburgh University. Lecturer, Aberdeen University, 1966-69; Assistant Professor of History, then Associate Professor of History, Yale University, New Haven, 1970-79; Professor of History, Hamilton College, Clinton, New York, 1979-85; Professor of History, Dean of Faculty of Arts and Sciences, New York University, 1985-94 (Vice-Chancellor, 1991-96). Board Member: Heritage Lottery Fund Committee for Scotland; Chairman, CASE Europe. Publications: The Rise and Fall of Black Slavery; The Scots Abolitionists 1831-1961; various articles and reviews. Recreations: studio ceramics; contemporary literature.

Rice, Susan, CBE, BA, MLitt, DBA (Hon), DHC (Hon), DLitt (Hon), DUniv (Hon), LLD (Hon), Chartered Banker, FCIBS, CCMI, FRSA, RRCSE, FRSE. Chair, Scottish Water, since 2015; Chairman, Scottish Fiscal Commission, since 2014; Managing Director, Lloyds Banking Group Scotland, 2009-2015; Chairman, Chief Executive, Lloyds TSB Scotland plc, 2002-09; b. 7.3.46, Rhode Island, USA; m., Professor Sir C. Duncan Rice (qv); 2 s.; 1 d. Educ. Wellesley College, Mass., USA; Aberdeen University. Hon. Degrees: Robert Gordon University, Edinburgh University, Heriot-Watt University, Paisley University, Glasgow University, Queen Margaret University, Aberdeen University. Dean, Yale University, 1973-79; Staff Aide to President, Hamilton College, 1980-81; Dean of Students, Colgate University, 1981-86; Senior Vice President and Division Head, Natwest Bancorp, 1986-96; Head, Branch Banking, then Managing Director, Personal Banking, Bank of Scotland, 1997-2000. Chair: Edinburgh International Book Festival, Edinburgh Festivals Forum, Governor's

Patrons of the National Galleries of Scotland, 2020 Climate Group, Committee of Scottish Clearing Banks, Centre for Social Justice Research in Scotland; Non-Executive Director: Court of the Bank of England, SSE plc, J Sainsbury's plc, North American Income Trust, Big Society Capital plc, Banking Standards Board, Charity Bank, National Centre for University and Business (NCUB). President: Scottish Council for Development and Industry; Advisor: First Minister's Council of Economic Advisors. Regent, Royal College of Surgeons, Edinburgh. Recreations: opera; modern art; hill-walking; fly fishing. Address: (b.) Scottish Water, Castle House, 6 Castle Drive, Dunfermline KY11 8GG.
E-mail: susan.rice@scottishwater.co.uk

Richards, Professor David, MA (Cantab), MA (Lond), PhD (Cantab). Emeritus Professor of English Studies, University of Stirling; Visiting Professor, Division of English, NTU, Singapore; b. 15.09.53, Oldham; m., Susan; 1 s.; 1 d. Educ. Manchester Grammar School; Churchill College, Cambridge University. Lecturer, University of Birmingham, 1981-83; Senior Lecturer, University of Leeds, 1983-2002; Founding Director, The Ferguson Centre, Open University, 2002-06. Publication: Masks of Difference: Cultural Representations in Literature, Anthropology and Art, 1995. Recreations: art; sailing; travel. Address: (b.) Department of English Studies, University of Stirling, Stirling; T.-01786 467502; e-mail: david.richards@stir.ac.uk

Richards, Professor Randolph Harvey, CBE, MA, VetMB, PhD, MRCVS, FRSM, FIBiol, FRAgS, FRSE. Vice-Chairman, Moredun Foundation, since 2014; Director, Institute of Aquaculture, University of Stirling, 1996-2009; Roberts Morris Bray Professor of Aquatic Veterinary Studies, since 1991; Veterinary Adviser, Scottish Salmon Producers' Organisation, since 2006; Veterinary Adviser, Scottish Quality Salmon, 1999-2006 (Veterinary Adviser, Scottish Salmon Growers' Association, 1986-99); b. 4.3.48, London; m., Jennifer Halley; 1 d. Educ. Grove Park Grammar School, Wrexham; Jesus College, Cambridge University; University of Stirling. University of Stirling: Deputy Director, Unit of Aquatic Pathobiology, 1976-79, Deputy Director, Institute of Aquaculture, 1979-96. Member, Veterinary Products Committee, Medicines Commission, 1992-2000. Publications: numerous papers on fish pathology in learned journals. Recreations: fine wine and food; shooting. Address: University of Stirling, Stirling FK9 4LA; T.-01786 467904; e-mail: r.h.richards@stir.ac.uk

Richardson, Emeritus Professor John Stuart, MA, DPhil, FRSE. Professor of Classics, Edinburgh University, 1987-2002, Emeritus Professor, since 2002; Dean, Faculty of Arts, and Provost, Faculty Group of Arts, Divinity and Music, 1992-97; Hon. Professor, Durham University, since 2003; Hon. Vice-President, Society for the Promotion of Roman Studies, since 2012, President, 1998-2001; b. 4.2.46, Ilkley; m., (1) Patricia Helen Robotham (deceased); (2) Joan McArthur Taylor; 2 s. Educ. Berkhamsted School; Trinity College, Oxford. Lecturer in Ancient History, Exeter College, Oxford, 1969-72, St. Andrews University, 1972-87; Priest, Scottish Episcopal Church, since 1980; Anglican Chaplain, St. Andrews University, 1980-87; Team Priest, St. Columba's, Edinburgh, since 1987; Honorary Canon, St. Mary's Cathedral, Edinburgh, since 2000. Publications: Roman Provincial Administration, 1976; Hispaniae, 1986; The Romans in Spain, 1996; Appian: The Wars of the Romans in Iberia, 2000; The Language of Empire, 2008; Augustan Rome 44 BC to AD 14, 2012; papers on ancient history. Recreation: choral singing. Address: (h.) 29 Merchiston Avenue, Edinburgh EH10 4PH; T.-0131-228 3094; e-mail: j.richardson@ed.ac.uk

Richardson, Neil, OBE, QPM. Deputy Chief Constable, Police Scotland, 2012-2016. Career: joined Lothian and Borders Police in 1985: served in operational posts such as Community Safety, Firearms, Divisional Operations, and CID, including a secondment to the Scottish Crime and Drug Enforcement Agency (SCDEA), promoted to Assistant Chief Constable for Territorial Policing (2006-08); joined Strathclyde Police as Deputy Chief Constable in 2008 with responsibility for matters including professional standards, complaints and discipline, organisational development, health and safety, change management and overseeing Force programmes and projects; appointed Transformation Director of the National Police Reform Programme in 2011, with responsibility for driving the reform of Scottish Policing through to Day One of the new service to its ultimate end state. Awarded the Queen's Police Medal in 2011.

Richardson, Professor Neville Vincent, BA, DPhil, FRSC, FInstP, FRSE. Master of the United College and Professor of Physical Chemistry, University of St. Andrews, since 1998; b. 25.2.50, Tadcaster; m., Jennifer Margaret; 2 step-s.; 2 step-d. Educ. Oglethorpe Grammar School, Tadcaster; Jesus College University of Oxford. SRC Research Fellow, Chemistry Department, University of Birmingham, 1974-77; Research Assistant, Fritz-Haber Institute, Max Planck Society, 1974-77; University of Liverpool: Lecturer, Chemistry Department, 1979, Senior Lecturer, 1984, Professor, 1988, Director, Surface Science, IRC. Marlow Medal, Royal Society of Chemistry, 1984; British Vacuum Society Medal, 1996; Surface and Colloid Chemistry Prize, RSC, 2003. Recreations: hillwalking; rock and ice climbing; skiing; squash. Address: School of Chemistry, North Haugh, University of St. Andrews, St. Andrews, Fife KY16 9ST; T.-01334 462395; e-mail: nvr@st-and.ac.uk

Riches, Christopher Gabriel, BSc. Publishing Consultant, Riches Editorial Services, since 2006; Project Editor, The Times Good University Guide, since 2006; b. 25.3.52, Oxford; m., Catherine Mary Gaunt; 3 s. Educ. Marlborough College; Manchester University. Copy Editor, Penguin Books, 1973-74; Oxford University Press: Science Education Editor, 1974-76, Publishing Manager, Hong Kong, 1976-81, Reference Editor, 1981-88; Publishing Manager, Collins Reference, Glasgow, 1989-94, Editorial Director, 1994-2006. Council Member, Scottish Publishers' Association, 1995-2003; Hon. Secretary, St. Mary's Episcopal Church, Aberfoyle, 1994-98; Chair, School Board, Killearn Primary School, 1997-99; Member, Killearn Community Council, 2008-09. Publications: Britain the Facts (5 vols), 2008; The History of The Beano (Editor), 2008; The Broons Days Oot, 2009; Oxford Dictionary of Political Biography, 2009, 2013; The Broons Gairdenin' Wisdoms, 2009; Oor Wullie's Dungarees Book for Boys, 2010; The Times Atlas of Britain, 2010; The Times Atlas of London, 2011; The Art and History of The Dandy (editor), 2012; Royal Canadian Geographical Society Atlas of Canada, 2014; Oxford Guide to Countries of the World, 2016; Oxford Dictionary of Contemporary World History, 2016. Recreations: book collecting; gardening; walking. Address: (h.) Achadhu House, Main Street, Killearn G63 9RJ; T.-01360 550544; e-mail: christopher@riches-edit.co.uk

Richmond, John Kennedy, JP, DL. Chairman, Glasgow Airport Consultative Committee, since 1979; b. 23.4.37, Glasgow; m., Elizabeth Margaret; 1 s.; 1 d. Educ. King's Park Secondary School. Conservative Member, Glasgow Corporation, 1963-75; Member, Glasgow District Council, 1975-84; Deputy Lord Provost, 1977-80; Conservative Group Leader, 1975-77. Recreations: tennis; music; travel. Address: (h.) 32 Lochhead Avenue, Lochwinnoch,

Renfrewshire PA12 4AW; T.-01505 843 193; e-mail: richmond32@tiscali.co.uk

Rickman, David Edwin, BCom (Hons). Executive Director of Rules and Equipment Standards, The R & A, since 1996; b. 9.10.64, St. Andrews; m., Jennifer Mary Cameron; 3 d. Educ. Madras College, St. Andrews; Edinburgh University. Joined R. & A. staff, 1987; appointed Assistant Secretary (Rules), 1990. Recreations: sport, especially golf and cycling. Address: (b.) c/o The R & A, St. Andrews, Fife KY16 9JD; T.-01334 460000.

Riddell-Webster, Major-General Michael Lawrence, CBE, DSO. Governor, Edinburgh Castle, since 2015. Educ. Harrow School; Heriot-Watt University. British Army: commissioned into the Black Watch in 1983; served in the former Republic of Yugoslavia (awarded the Queen's Commendation for Valuable Service in 2001), Commanding Officer, 1st Battalion The Black Watch, 2000-03, Deputy Director Equipment Capability Ground Manoeuvre, 2003-05, Commander 39 Infantry Brigade, 2005-07, Director Army Division, Joint Services Command and Staff College, 2007-08; UK Ministry of Defence: Head of Capability (Ground Manoeuvre), 2008-2011, Member at the Royal College of Defence Studies, 2011-12; Director, College of Management and Technology, Defence Academy, Swindon, 2012-14; Student on Energy MSc, Heriot-Watt University, since 2014. Address: (b.) Historic Environment Scotland, Longmore House, Salisbury Place, Edinburgh EH9 1SH.

Riddle, Gordon Stewart, MA. Principal and Chief Ranger, Culzean Country Park, 1976-2001 (Property Manager, Culzean Country Park, 2001-05, Country Park and Conservation Manager, 2004-05); retired; b. 2.10.47, Kelso; m., Rosemary Robb; 1 s.; 1 d. Educ. Kelso High School; Edinburgh University; Moray House College of Education. Biology and History Teacher, Lasswade High School, 1970-71; National Ranger Training Course, 1971-72; Ranger and Depute Principal, Culzean Country Park, 1972-75; National Park Service (USA) Training Course, 1978; Winston Churchill Travelling Fellowship, USA, 1981. Member, Royal Society for the Protection of Birds, Scottish Committee, 1995-99; Chairman, South Strathclyde Raptor Study Group, since 1994. 2005 George Waterstone Memorial Award for services to the National Trust for Scotland; Member, the Scottish Raptor Monitoring Group representing the Scottish Ornithologists' Club; 2010 Donald & Jeff Watson Raptor Award; 2010-2012 Chairman, Ayrshire Branch, Scottish Ornithologists Club. Publications: The Kestrel; Seasons with the Kestrel; Kestrels for Company. Recreations: sport; gardening; birds of prey; photography; hill-walking; music; writing. Address: (h.) Roselea, 5 Maybole Road, Kirkmichael, Ayrshire KA19 7PQ; T.-01655 750335; e-mail: gordon@riddle-kestrel.com; web: www.riddle-kestrel.com

Riddler, Gordon Peterkin, BSc, MBA, CEng, FIMMM. Board Member, Cairngorms National Park Authority, since 2010; b. 12.5.44, Aberdeen; m., Janet Elizabeth; 1 s.; 1 d. Educ. Robert Gordon's College, Aberdeen; Aberdeen University; Strathclyde University. Senior Management and Executive Posts with Gold Fields Ltd., Rio Tinto plc, British Geological Survey, 1970-98; Director, Mineral Industry Research Organisation, 1998-2006; Executive Director on Boards of Minmet plc, Kimcor plc, Tiger Resource Finance plc, Maghreb Minerals plc, 2002-08; community organisations in various capacities, since 2008. FIMMM Futers Gold Medal for outstanding service to the international minerals industry; Trustee, Victoria and Albert Halls (Ballater) Trust; Treasurer, Ballater Highland Games Limited. Recreations: hill walking; golf; reading; gardening.

Address: (b.) Cairngorms National Park Authority, 14 The Square, Grantown on Spey PH26 3HG; (h.) 20 Pannanich Road, Invercauld Park, Ballater, Aberdeenshire AB35 5PA; T.-07711 609 351.

Riddoch, Lesley, BA (Hons). Managing Director, Feisty Ltd. (an independent radio podcast and tv production company); columnist for The Scotsman; b. 21.2.60, Wolverhampton; m., Chris Smith May. Educ. High School of Glasgow; Wadham College, Oxford; University College, Cardiff. Sabbatical President, Oxford University Students Union, 1980; Reporter, BBC Radio Scotland, 1985-88; Co-Presenter, Head On, 1988-90; Presenter, Speaking Out, 1990-94; The Scotsman: Assistant Editor, 1994-96, Associate Editor, 1996-97; Speaker, The People's Parliament, Channel 4, 1994-98; Presenter, You and Yours, BBC Radio 4, 1996-98; Presenter, Midnight Hour, BBC2, 1996-98; Presenter, Channel 4's Powerhouse, 1997-98; Presenter, Lesley Riddoch Programme, BBC Radio Scotland, 1999-2005. Founder and Director, Harpies and Quines (feminist magazine); Trustee, Isle of Eigg Trust, since 1993; Founder and Director, Worldwoman. Norman McEwen Award, 1992; Cosmopolitan Woman of the Year (Communications), 1992; Plain English Award, 1993; Sony Broadcaster of the Year, Silver Award, 2000, 2001. Recreations: playing pool; walking. E-mail: lesley@feistyproductions.co.uk

Rifkind, Rt. Hon Sir Malcolm Leslie, KCMG, QC, LLB, MSc. Secretary of State for Foreign and Commonwealth Affairs, 1995-97; Secretary of State for Defence, 1992-95; Secretary of State for Transport, 1990-92; Secretary of State for Scotland, 1986-90; MP (Conservative), Edinburgh Pentlands, 1974-97, Kensington and Chelsea, 2005-2010, Kensington, 2010-2015; President, Edinburgh University Development Trust, since 2002; director of several companies; b. 21.6.46, Edinburgh; m., Edith Amalia Steinberg; 1 s.; 1 d. Educ. George Watson's College, Edinburgh; Edinburgh University. Assistant Lecturer, University of Rhodesia, 1967-68; called to Scottish Bar, 1970; Opposition Front-Bench Spokesman on Scottish Affairs, 1975-76; Member, Select Committee on European Secondary Legislation, 1975-76; Chairman, Scottish Conservatives' Devolution Committee, 1976; Chairman, Intelligence and Security Committee, since 2010; Joint Secretary, Conservative Parliamentary Foreign and Commonwealth Affairs Committee, 1977-79; Member, Select Committee on Overseas Development, 1978-79; Parliamentary Under-Secretary of State, Scottish Office, 1979-82; Parliamentary Under-Secretary of State, Foreign and Commonwealth Office, 1982-83; Minister of State, Foreign and Commonwealth Office, 1983-86; Member, Queen's Bodyguard for Scotland (Royal Company of Archers); Member, Commonwealth Eminent Person Group, 2010.

Rigg, David, MA (Hons). Chair, Board of Governors, Clydebank College, 2009-2010; Secretary to Court, University of the West of Scotland, 2008-09; University Secretary: University of Paisley, 2002-07, University of the West of Scotland, 2007; b. 15.3.48, Insch; m., Margaret Taylor Mechie; 1 s.; 1 d. Educ. Daniel Stewart's College, Edinburgh; West Calder High School; Dundee University. British Gas, 1971-73; Administrative Assistant, Strathclyde University, 1973-79; Assistant Secretary, Paisley College, 1979-87; Registrar and Depute Secretary, University of Paisley, 1987-2002. Recreations: Argyll; travel; theatre; Hibernian Football Club.

Rimell, Gregor. Highland Councillor, since 2003; Cairngorms National Park Board, since 2003; b. 30.9.44, Clatterbridge; m., Patricia. Educ. Haberdashers' Aske's,

London. Subpostmaster, Kingussie, 1992-2010. Address: (h.) Broomlea, Newtonmore PH20 1AT; T.-01540 673430.
E-mail: gregor.rimell.cllr@highland.gov.uk

Rimer, Jennifer, BMusHons, LRAM, DipEd, FFCS, Hon.ARAM (2009 Award). Headteacher, St. Mary's Music School, Edinburgh, since 1996; SQA Examiner, Setter and Marker, since 1978; b. Kirkcaldy; m., David Rimer; 3 d. Educ. Buckhaven High School; Edinburgh University. Music Teacher, Newcastle, 1970-72; Principal Music Teacher, Lothian Region, 1972-77; St. Mary's Music School: Piano Teacher/Academic Music Teacher, 1982-93; Head of Guidance, Careers and Academic Music, 1993-95. Member, School Leaders Scotland (formerly HAS); Governor, George Heriot's School; former Director, Edinburgh Youth Orchestra; Director, National Youth Orchestras of Scotland (2008). Recreations: family; reading; theatre; art; concerts; youth orchestras; piano; tennis; yoga; walking. Address: (b.) St. Mary's Music School, Coates Hall, 25 Grosvenor Crescent, Edinburgh EH12 5EL; T.-0131-538 7766; e-mail: info@st-marys-music-school.co.uk

Rintoul, Archie B., BA (Hons), MRICS. Chief Valuer Scotland. Address: (b.) Chief Valuer Scotland, 50 Frederick Street, Edinburgh EH2 ING; T.-03000 506251.

Rintoul, Gordon, CBE, BSc, MSc, PhD, AMA. Director, National Museums of Scotland, since 2002; b. 29.5.55, Glasgow; m., Stephanie; 1 s. Educ. Allan Glen's School, Glasgow; University of Edinburgh; University of Manchester. Curator, Colour Museum, Bradford, 1984-87; Director, Catalyst, The Museum of the Chemical Industry, Widnes, 1987-98; Chief Executive, Sheffield Galleries and Museums Trust, 1998-2002. Member, National Museum Directors Conference; Public Engagement with Science Advisory Group, College of Science and Engineering, since 2004; Honorary Professor, University of Edinburgh; Honorary Degree of Doctor honoris causa, University of Edinburgh; Honorary Degree, Doctor of the University (HonDUniv), Napier University. Recreations: running; reading; travelling. Address: (b.) Chambers Street, Edinburgh EH1 1JF; T.-0131-247 4260; e-mail: g.rintoul@nms.ac.uk

Ritchie, Anna, OBE, BA, PhD, FSA, Hon FSA Scot. Freelance archaeologist; b. 28.9.43, London; m., Graham Ritchie; 1 s.; 1 d. Educ. Woking Grammar School for Girls; University of Wales; Edinburgh University. Excavations on Neolithic, Pictish and Viking sites in Orkney; archaeological research and writing; Vice-President, Society of Antiquaries of London, 1988-92; President, Society of Antiquaries of Scotland, 1990-93; Trustee: National Museums of Scotland, 1993-2003, British Museum, 1999-2004. Address: (h.) 11/13 Powderhall Rigg, Edinburgh EH7 4GG; T.-0131 556 1128.

Ritchie, Cameron, LLB. Past President, Law Society of Scotland (2012-2013), Vice President, 2010-2011; Area Procurator Fiscal, Fife, 2002-2010; Procurator Fiscal, Stirling and Alloa, 1996-2002; Solicitor Advocate; b. 25.9.52, Paisley; m., Hazel; 2 s. Educ. John Neilson Institution, Paisley; Glasgow University. Apprentice Solicitor, Wright and Crawford, Paisley, 1972-74; Procurator Fiscal Depute, Ayr, 1974-75, Glasgow, 1975-88; Senior Procurator Fiscal Depute, Hamilton, 1988-93; Assistant Procurator Fiscal, Dundee, 1993-96. Recreations: golf; rugby; watching cricket; military history. Address: (b.) LSS, 26 Drumsheugh Gardens, Edinburgh; T.-0131 226 7411.

Ritchie, Professor David Scarth, MA (Cantab), FRSE. Trustee, James Clerk Maxwell Foundation; Trustee, Clerk Maxwell Cancer Research Fund; m., 1 Heather McLennan (deceased); 2 s.; 2 d.; 2, Astrid Ilfra Chalmers Watson.

Educ. Edinburgh Academy; Cambridge University; Royal Naval College, Greenwich. Lt., Royal Navy, 1944-47; Technical Director, Barr & Stroud Ltd., 1969-85; Chairman, Scottish Education Department survey on industrial liasion in Central Institutions, 1985-88. Governor, Paisley University, 1984-95; Visiting Professor in Management of Technological Innovation, Strathclyde University, 1986-94. Address: (h.) 9 St. Bernards Row, Edinburgh EH4 1HW; T.-0131 343 1036; e-mail: admin@clerkmaxwellfoundation.org

Ritchie, Gordon James Nixon, LLB, NP. Honorary Sheriff of Grampian Highland and Islands at Stonehaven, since 2004; Partner, Connons of Stonehaven, Solicitors, since 1980; Clerk to the Lieutenancy of Kincardineshire, since 1996; b. 2.5.52, Aberdeen; m., Isobel; 2 s.; 2 d. Educ. Mackie Academy; Aberdeen University. Director, Aberdeen Solicitors Property Centre, since 1998. Founder and Secretary, Stonehaven Heritage Society; Editor, Stonehaven of Old, Vols. 1 & 2. Recreations: rallying; motor sport; local history. Address: (h.) Brewlaw, Catterline, Stonehaven, Kincardineshire AB39 2TY; T.-01569 762971.

Ritchie, Grant, MA (Hons), ProfCert. Principal, Dundee and Angus College, since 2015 (previously Depute Principal). Educ. Harris Academy, Dundee; Jordanhill College; University of Aberdeen; Leicester University. Lecturer, Dundee College of Commerce, 1985-88; Section Head, Media & Communications, 1993-96; Depute Principal, Dundee College, 2008-11; Project Director, Creative Loop, since 2006. Member of SQA's Advisory Committee; former Member, Skillset Board for Scotland; chair of a number of groups and organisations locally including the Prince's Trust Board for Tayside and the Bahratiya Ashram multi cultural organisation. Address: Kingsway Campus, Old Glamis Road, Dundee DD5 1NY; T.-0300 123 1010; e-mail: enquiry@dundeeandangus.ac.uk

Ritchie, Ian Cleland, CBE, FREng, FRSE, FBCS, CEng, BSc. Chairman: iomart plc, since 2008, CAS, since 2004, Caspian Learning, 2007-2011, Our Dynamic Earth, since 2010; Independent Co-Chair, Scottish Science Advisory Council, 2009-11. Board Director, Digital Bridges Ltd., 2000-07; Director: Scottish Enterprise, 2000-05, Scottish Funding Council, 2002-07; b. 29.6.50, Edinburgh; m., Barbara Allan Cowie (deceased); 1 s.; 1 d. Educ. West Calder High School; Heriot-Watt University. Development Manager, ICL, 1973-82; Founder and CEO, Office Workstations Ltd., Edinburgh and Seattle, 1984-92; Chair: Voxar, 1995-2002, VIS, 1995-2000, Orbital Software PLC, 1995-2001, Active Navigation Ltd., 1997-2003, Interactive University, 2001-2005, Sonaptic Ltd., 2002-06, Connect, 2006-2008, Scapa Ltd., 2006-10; Director: Particle Physics and Astronomy Research Council, 1999-2002, Epic Group PLC, 1999-2005, Sonaptic Ltd., 2003-06, Channel Four Television Corp, 2000-05, Our Dynamic Earth, since 2004, GO Group, 2008-2012, Edinburgh International Film Festival, 2002-10, Edinburgh International Science Festival, since 2003; Chair, Scottish Software Federation, 1988-89; President: British Computer Society, 1998-99, RCSEd, 2012-2015; Trustee: Bletchley Park, 2000-2009, SCRAN, 1996-2005, National Museums of Scotland, 2002-10, Saltire Foundation, since 2009, Nominet Trust, since 2008; Member, Scottish Funding Council, 2002-07; Chairman: Red Fox Medic Ltd, since 2012; Blipfoto Ltd, since 2012; Cogbooks Ltd, since 2012. Recreations: travel; theatre; arts; web browsing. Address: Coppertop, Green Lane, Lasswade EH18 1HE; T.-0131 663 9486.
M.-07973 214024; e-mail: IRitchie@coppertop.co.uk

Ritchie, Ian Kristensen, MB, ChB, FRCS (Ed), FRCSEd (Orth). Consultant Orthopaedic Surgeon, Forth Valley Acute Hospitals Trust, since 1992; President, The Royal College of Surgeons of Edinburgh, 2012-2015; b. 2.1.53, Annebk, Syria; m., Alyson; 3 d. Educ. Gordon Schools,

Huntly; University of Aberdeen. Medical Officer, Royal Navy, 1978-83; surgical and orthopaedic training, Aberdeen Royal Infirmary, 1983-91; Postgraduate Tutor, Stirling Royal Infirmary, 1999-2003. Member, Council, Royal College of Surgeons of Edinburgh, 2000-05, 2006-2010; Lead Clinician, Orthopaedic Dept., Forth Valley, 2007; Vice President, RCSEd, 2009-2012. Recreations: hillwalking; reading. Address: (b.) Department of Trauma and Orthopaedic Surgery, Forth Valley Royal Hospital, Larbert FK5 4WR; T.-01324 566817.
E-mail: ian.ritchie@nhs.net

Ritchie, John Douglas, CA. Consultant, Jeffrey Crawford incorporating Barstow and Miller, since 2014; Principal, Barstow and Millar, CA, 2002-2014; b. 9.10.52, Edinburgh; m., Joan Moira. Educ. George Watson's College. Barstow & Millar, CA, 1971-85 (Partner, 1978-85); Partner, Pannell Kerr Forster, 1985-98 (Chairman, Edinburgh office, 1993-97). Member, National Board for Nursing, Midwifery and Health Visiting for Scotland, 1988-93, Hon. Consultant, 1993-97; Partner, Whitelaw Wells, 1998-2002; Member, Board, Viewpoint Housing Association, 1991-2000, and 2002-09; Trustee, Viewpoint Trust, 1991-2008; Trustee, New Lanark Trust, since 2008; Director: New Lanark Mill Hotel Ltd, since 2008, New Lanark Trading Ltd., 2008-2013; President, Rotary Club of Braids, 1991-92; Member, Morningside Christian Council, 1985-92; Member, Church of Scotland Board of Parish Education, 1994-99; Treasurer, Scottish Churches Open College, 1995-99; Member, Merchant Company of the City of Edinburgh, since 1985, Assistant, Master's Court, 1998-2001; Trustee, Merchant Company Widows' Fund, 1997-2002; Member, Board of Management, Edinburgh's Telford College, 1998-2001; Trustee, Bequest Fund for Ministers in Outlying Districts of the Church of Scotland, since 1994; Director, Association of Independent Accountants in Scotland, 1999-2002 (Chairman, 2001-02); Director, Scottish Love in Action, 2001-2011; Secretary and Treasurer, Douglas Hay Trust, since 2000; Governor, Melville College Trust, 2001-2012; Trustee, The Merchant Company Retirement Benefits Scheme, 2005-2012; Director, Jamaica Education Support, 2005-2012; Treasurer, Challenger Children's Fund, 2006-09; Member, New College Financial Board, since 2007; Trustee, The Nurses Memorial to King Edward VII in Scotland Scottish Committee, since 2012; Treasurer, Greenbank Parish Church, since 2016. Address: (b.) Midlothian Innovation Centre, Pentlandfield, Roslin, Midlothian EH25 9RE.

Ritchie, Professor Sir Lewis Duthie, kt (2011), OBE (2001), FRSE, BSc, MSc, MBChB, MD, FRCPEdin, FRCPGlas (Hon), FRCGP, FFPH, FBCS, CEng (Computer Science), CITP, DRCOG, FRSA, MREHIS. James Mackenzie Professor of General Practice, University of Aberdeen, since 1992; Honorary Professor of Primary Care and Public Health, University of the Highlands and Islands (UHI), since 2014; Honorary Professor of General Practice, University of Edinburgh, since 2015; b. 26.6.52, Fraserburgh; m., Heather. Educ. Fraserburgh Academy; University of Aberdeen; University of Edinburgh. General practitioner vocational training, 1979-82; public health medicine vocational training, 1982-87; Lecturer in General Practice, University of Aberdeen, 1984-92; Consultant/Honorary Consultant in Public Health Medicine, NHS Grampian, 1987-2012 and since 2014; Principal General Practitioner, Peterhead Health Centre and Community Hospital, 1984-2012; Director of Public Health, NHS Grampian, 2012-14. Chair/member of a number of national governmental advisory committees; former chair, Scottish Medical and Scientific Advisory Committee (SMASAC) and Biomedical and Therapeutics Research Committee (BTRC), Scottish Government; Chair, Independent Review of Primary Care Out of Hours Services in Scotland, 2015; Chair, Queen's Nursing Institute

Scotland (QNIS), since 2015; Chair, Institute of Remote Health Care, since 2014. Publications: Computers in Primary Care; Community Hospitals in Scotland: Promoting Progress; Developing Primary Care in Scotland; Meningococcal C Immunisation Programme in Scotland; Promoting Professionalism and Excellence in Scottish Medicine; Securing the Future of GP Academic Careers in Scotland; Improving the Seasonal Influenza Vaccination Programme in Scotland; Establishing Effective Therapeutic Partnerships; Pulling Together: Transforming Urgent Care for the People of Scotland; papers on computers, cardiovascular disease, cancer, community hospitals, community pharmacy and immunisation. Awards: John Perry Prize, British Computer Society, 1991; Ian Stokoe Award, Royal College of General Practitioners UK, 1992; Blackwell Prize, University of Aberdeen, 1995; Richard Scott Lecture, 2007, University of Edinburgh; Eric Elder Medal, Royal New Zealand College of General Practitioners, 2007; Provost Medal, Royal College of General Practitioners North East Scotland Faculty, 2010; James Mackenzie Lecture and Medal, Royal College of General Practitioners UK, 2010; Stock Memorial Lecture, Association of Port Health Authorities, 2012; Fulton Lecture, Royal College of General Practitioners, West of Scotland Faculty, 2012; DARE Lecture, Faculty of Public Health UK, 2014. Recreations: church; dog walking; classical music; art appreciation; military/naval history; RNLI/civilian gallantry. Address: (h.) Cramond, 79 Strichen Road, Fraserburgh AB43 9QJ; T.-01346 510191; e-mail: l.d.ritchie@abdn.ac.uk

Ritchie, Murray. Scottish Political Editor, The Herald, 1997-2004; b. 5.9.41, Dumfries; m.; 1 s.; 2 d. Educ. High School of Glasgow. Scottish Farmer, 1958-60; Dumfries and Galloway Standard, 1960-65; Scottish Daily Record, 1965-67; East African Standard, 1967-71; joined Glasgow Herald, 1971. Journalist of the Year, Fraser Press Awards, 1980. Publication: Scotland Reclaimed, 2000.

Roads, Elizabeth Ann, LVO, OStJ, FSA, FSA Scot, FHSS, FRHSC, AIH, LLB. Lyon Clerk and Keeper of the Records, since 1986; Snawdoun Herald of Arms, since 2010; Carrick Pursuivant of Arms, 1992-2010; Secretary of the Order of the Thistle, since 2014; b. 5.7.51; m., Christopher George William Roads; 2 s.; 1 d. Educ. Lansdowne House School, Edinburgh; Cambridge College of Technology; Study Centre for Fine Art, London; Edinburgh Napier University. Christie's, Art Auctioneers, 1971-74; Court of the Lord Lyon, since 1975; temporarily Linlithgow Pursuivant Extraordinary, 1987. Recreations: history; reading; countryside activities. Address: (b.) Court of the Lord Lyon, HM New Register House, Edinburgh EH1 3YT; T.-0131-556 7255.

Robb, Professor Emeritus Alan, DA, MA, RCA. Artist and Professor of Fine Art, Duncan of Jordanstone College of Art, Dundee (retired, 2007); Head, School of Fine Art, 1983-2003; b. 24.2.46, Glasgow; m., Cynthia J. Neilson; 1 s.; 1 d. Educ. Robert Gordon's College, Aberdeen; Grays School of Art; Royal College of Art. Assistant Art Master, Oundle School, 1972-75; Crawford School of Art, Cork: Lecturer in Painting, 1975-78, Head of Painting, 1978-80, Head of Fine Art, 1980-83. Member, Fine Art Panel, CNAA, 1985-87; Specialist Advisor, CNAA, 1987-89; Director, Wasps, 1984-94; Director, Art in Partnership, 1987-92; Director, British Health Care Arts Centre, 1988-93; Member, SHEFC Research Advisory Group, 1993-98; Advisor to Commonwealth Commission, 1998-2006; Member, Steering Group, National Association for Fine Art Education, 1988-2005; Lead Assessor for Fine Art, SHEFC Quality Assessment, 1995-96; first one-man exhibition, New 57 Gallery, 1973; Arts Council touring two-man exhibition, 1978-79; regularly exhibits in Scotland at the

Royal Scottish Academy; solo exhibitions: In the Mind's Eye, 1996, True Knowledge, East West Gallery, London, 1997-99, The House of Miracles, East West, 2005, Open Eye Gallery, Edinburgh, 2010, A Painted World, a retrospective, The Macmanus Galleries Dundee, 2012. Publications: Irish Contemporary Art, 1980; In the Mind's Eye, 1996; I Live Now, Academic Gallery, Utrecht, 1999; East-West London; The House of Miracles (author, Euan McArthur), 2005; Ayermanana Cuenca, Spain, 2006. Address: (b.) Duncan of Jordanstone College of Art, University of Dundee, Perth Road, Dundee DD1 4HT.

Robb, David. Chief Executive, Office of the Scottish Charity Regulator, since 2011. Formerly Head of Public Service Reform and Efficiency, Scottish Government. Address: (b.) 2nd Floor, Quadrant House, 9 Riverside Drive, Dundee DD1 4NY.

Robb, Cllr James. Former Leader, Argyll and Bute Council (2013); represents Helensburgh Central (SNP). Chair, Helensburgh Public Realm Improvements Group; CHORD Programme Management Board; Lead Councillor for Strategic Finance, Governance, Law, Improvement and Human Resources. Member: Convention of the Highlands and Islands Conference of Peripheral Maritime Regions; West of Scotland European Forum (substitute member); Loch Lomond and the Trossachs National Park Authority Board; COSLA Convention of Scottish Local Authorities. Address: (b.) 27 Redclyffe Gardens, Helensburgh G84 9JJ; T.-01436 676980; e-mail: James.Robb@argyll-bute.gov.uk

Robbins, Cllr Mike. Provost of Stirling Council, since 2012; represents Dunblane and Bridge of Allan ward; m., Jayne; 2 c. Career history: trained as a housing manager and held posts with local authorities in both England and Scotland; self-employed management consultant and work has included a number of commissions in East Africa as a technical advisor to the governments of Kenya and Zambia; trained as an internal consultant with the Civil Service College and has worked in most central government departments, training senior managers in leadership and management development. Associate of a leading negotiations consultancy and has delivered training solutions to a number of FTSE 100 companies. Recreation: golf. Address: Stirling Council, Old Viewforth, Stirling FK8 2ET; T.-01786 233115.

Roberton, Esther A., BA. Chair, NHS 24, since 2015; Non Executive Director: Scottish Government, since 2014, Scottish Ambulance Service, since 2014; b. 24.6.56, Kirkcaldy; m., William J. Roberton; 2 s. Educ. Buckhaven High School; Edinburgh University. Played a leading role in the campaign to secure and shape Scotland's Parliament, 1994-99; Chair, NHS Fife, 2000-04; Chair, Scottish Further Education Funding Council, 1999-2005; Member, Press Complaints Commission, 2007-2014; Chair, Sacro, 2010-2014. E-mail: esther@roberton.uk.com

Roberts, Professor Bernard, BSc, PhD, FRAS, FRSE. Professor of Solar Magnetohydrodynamics, since 1994; Emeritus Professor, since 2010; b. 19.2.46, Cork; m., Margaret Patricia Cartlidge; 4 s. Educ. Bletchley Secondary Modern and Bletchley Grammar Schools; Hull University; Sheffield University. Lecturer in Applied Mathematics, St. Andrews University, 1971-87, Reader, 1987-94. Chairman, UK Solar Physics Community, 1992-98; Member, Theory Research Assessment Panel, UK Particle Physics and Astronomy Research Council, 1998-2001, Member, Solar System Science Advisory Panel, 2001-03. Saltire Science Award (Saltire Society), 1997; Chapman Medal of the Royal Astronomical Society, 2010. Recreation: hill-walking. Address: (b.) Mathematical Institute, St. Andrews University, St. Andrews KY16 9SS; T.-01334 463716.

Roberts, James Graeme, MA, PhD, FRSA. Professor Emeritus, Aberdeen University; b. 7.11.42, Glasgow; m., Elizabeth Watson Milo Tucker; 2 s.; 2 d. Educ. Hutchesons' Boys' Grammar School, Glasgow; St. Andrews University; Aberdeen University. Aberdeen University: Assistant Lecturer in English, 1964, Lecturer in English, 1968, Senior Lecturer, 1985, Head, Department of English, 1993, Dean of Arts and Divinity and Vice Principal, 1996-2001, Member, University Court, 1981-89, 1995-2005, Vice Principal (Teaching and Learning), 2001-05. Senior Associate (Higher Education Academy), 2006-2010; Chair, Aberdeen Performing Arts, 2002-2012; Chair, Scottish Museums Council, 2001-07; Convener, Church of Scotland Committee on Church Art and Architecture, 2012-16; Elder, Ferryhill Parish Church, Aberdeen. Recreations: walking; swimming; music. Address: (h.) 17 Devanha Gardens, Aberdeen AB11 7UU; T.-01224 582217; e-mail: j.g.roberts@abdn.ac.uk

Roberts, Rev. Maurice Jonathon, BA, BD. Minister: Ayr Free Church of Scotland, 1974-94, Inverness Greyfriars Free Church of Scotland, 1994-99, Inverness (Westhill) Free Church of Scotland (Continuing), 2000-2010 (retired since 2011); Editor, The Banner of Truth, 1988-2003; b. 8.3.38, Timperley; m., Alexandra Macleod; 1 d. Educ. Lymm Grammar School; Durham University; London University; Free Church College, Edinburgh. Schoolteacher. Publications: The Thought of God; Sanctification and Glorification; In Deep Valley of Truth (Korean language); The Christian's High Calling; Great God of Wonders; Can We Know God?; Union and Communion with Christ; The Happiness of Heaven; The Mysteries of God; Finding Peace with God; What Does it Mean to Love God?. Recreations: reading; walking. Address: 5 Muirfield Park, Inverness IV2 4HA.

Roberts, Ralph M. H., BSc. Chief Executive, NHS Shetland, since 2011; b. 1.9.64, Canterbury; m., Mhairi Mackinnon; 3 d. Educ. The Kings School, Canterbury; Oxford Polytechnic. Volunteer Teacher, Kenya, 1982-83; Local Government Officer, 1987-89; NHS Management Trainee, 1989-91; NHS Manager, NHS Lothian and NHS Borders, 1991-2000; NHS Director, NHS Borders, 2000-2010. Recreations: theatre; music; golf; football; rugby. Address: (b.) NHS Shetland, Upper Floor, Montfield, Burgh Road, Lerwick, Shetland ZE1 0LA.

Roberts, Professor Richard Henry, BA (Lancaster), MA and BD (Cantab), PhD (Edin), DiplLCM. Professor Emeritus of Religious Studies, Lancaster University, since 2002; Visiting Emeritus Professor, University of Stirling, since 2002; b. 06.03.46, Manchester; m., Audrey (deceased); 1 s. Educ. William Hulme's Grammar School, Manchester; Universities of Lancaster, Cambridge, Edinburgh and Tübingen. Lecturer in Theology and Religious Studies, University of Leeds, 1975-76; Lecturer in Systematic Theology, University of Durham, 1976-89; Maurice B. Reckitt Research Fellow, University of Lancaster, 1988-91; Professor of Divinity, University of St. Andrews, 1991-95; Professor of Religious Studies, Lancaster University, 1995-2002. Pastoral and Spiritual Care Committee of the Church of Scotland; Member of the Church of the Holy Rude, Stirling. Publications: Hope and its Hieroglyph: A Critical Decipherment of Ernst Bloch's 'Principal of Hope', 1990; A Theology on Its Way: Essays on Karl Barth, 1992; The Recovery of Rhetoric: Persuasive Discourse and Disciplinarity in the Human Sciences (Co-Author), 1993; Religion and the Transformations of Capitalism: Comparative Responses, 1995; Nature Religion

Today: Paganism in the Modern World (Co-Author), 1998; Time and Value (Co-Author), 1998; Religion, Theology and the Human Sciences, 2001/02. Recreations: mountain walking; singing and music (violoncello and flute). Address: (b.) Languages and Cultures, Pathfoot Building, University of Stirling, Stirling FK9 4LA; T.-07707 066921; e-mail: r.h.roberts@stir.ac.uk

Robertson of Port Ellen, Rt. Hon. Lord (George Islay MacNeill Robertson), KT, GCMG, HonFRSE, FRSA, MA, PC. Deputy Chairman, TNK-BP, 2006-2013; Secretary-General, NATO, 1999-2003; b. 12.4.46, Port Ellen, Islay; m., Sandra Wallace; 2 s.; 1 d. Educ. Dunoon Grammar School; Dundee University. Tayside Study Economics Group, 1968-69; Scottish Organiser, General, Municipal, Boilermakers Union, 1969-78; Chairman, Scottish Labour Party, 1977-78; Member, Scottish Executive, Labour Party, 1973-79, 1993-97; MP, Hamilton, 1978-97, Hamilton South, 1997-99; PPS to Secretary of State for Social Services, 1979; Opposition Spokesman on Scottish Affairs, 1979-80, on Defence, 1980-81, on Foreign and Commonwealth Affairs, 1981-93, on Scottish Affairs, 1993-97; Principal Spokesman on Europe, 1984-93; Member, Shadow Cabinet, 1993-97; Shadow Scottish Secretary, 1993-97; Secretary of State for Defence, 1997-99. Member of Board, Scottish Development Agency, 1976-78; Board of Governors, Scottish Police College, 1975-78; Vice Chairman, British Council, 1985-93; President, Royal Institute of International Affairs, 2001-2011; Elder Brother, Trinity House, since 2002. Chairman, John Smith Memorial Trust, 2004-08; Chancellor, Order of St Michael and St George, since 2011; Board, Western Ferries (Clyde), since 2006; Board, Weir Group plc, 2004-2015; Adviser, The Cohen Group (USA), since 2004; Chairman, Ditchley Foundation, since 2009. Hon LLD (Dundee), 2000; Hon DSc (Cranfield), 2000; Hon LLD (Bradford), 2000; Hon LLD (St Andrews); DUniv (Paisley), 2006; Hon Doct (Baku State University, Azerbaijan), 2001; Hon. Regt. Colonel, London Scottish Regiment, 2000; Hon. FRSE, 2003; GCMG (2004); KT (2004); LRPS (2009); Patron, Glasgow Islay Association, since 2003. Publication: 'Islay and Jura - Photographs', Birlinn, 2006. Recreations: family; photography; golf. Address: (b.) House of Lords, London SW1A 0PW.

Robertson, Professor A. G. Boyd, MA, Hon DEd, FASLS. Principal of Sabhal Mòr Ostaig, Isle of Skye, since 2009; b. 14.06.49, Lennoxtown; m., Sheila Finlayson; 3 s. Educ. Paible Secondary, North Uist; Portree High, Skye; Aberdeen University; Aberdeen College of Education. Career History: Teacher of Gaelic, then Principal Teacher of Gaelic, Oban High School; Lecturer, Jordanhill College of Education; University of Strathclyde: Senior Lecturer in Gaelic, Reader in Gaelic and Head of Language Education. Honorary Doctor of Education, University of Edinburgh, 2014; Fellow of the Association of Scottish Literary Studies (ASLS), 2012. Publications: Ty Complete Gaelic (Co-Author); Ty Essential Gaelic Dictionary (Co-Author); Ty Speak Gaelic with Confidence (Co-Author). Recreations: photography; fishing; reading; walking. Address: (b.) Sabhal Mòr Ostaig, Slèite, An t-Eilean Sgitheanach, Isle of Skye IV44 8RQ; T.-01471 888200; e-mail: br.smo@uhi.ac.uk

Robertson, Professor Alastair Harry Forbes, BS, MA, PhD, FRSE. Professor of Geology, Edinburgh University, since 1996; b. 6.12.49, Edinburgh; m., Gillian Mary Robertson; 1 s.; 1 d. Educ. Edinburgh Academy; Edinburgh University; Leicester University. Demonstrator, Cambridge University, 1974-76; Lecturer in Oceanography, Edinburgh University. 1977-85; Academic Visitor, Stanford University. USA, 1985- 86;

Reader, Geology and the International Ocean Discovery Program, Edinburgh University, 1986-96. Publications: numerous scientific papers and edited volumes mainly concerning the geology of the Eastern Mediterranean region. Recreations; outdoor activities; mountain walking; travel; music. Address: (b.) Grant Institute, James Hutton Road, Edinburgh EH9 3FL.
E-mail: alastair.robertson@ed.ac.uk

Robertson, Andrew Ogilvie, OBE, LLB. Glasgow's Carers' Champion, since 2015; former Chairman, Greater Glasgow and Clyde NHS Board; Partner, T.C. Young, Solicitors, 1968-2006; Secretary, Erskine Hospital, 1976-2002, Vice Chairman, 2006-2011, Chairman, 2011; Secretary, Princess Royal Trust for Carers, 1990-2006, Trustee, 2006-2012; Carers Trust, Vice Chairman, 2012; Chairman, Lintel Trust (formerly Scottish Housing Association Charitable Trust), 1991-2007; Director, Scottish Building Society, 1994-2008, Chairman, 2003-06; Chairman, Greater Glasgow Primary Care NHS Trust, 1999-2004; Vice Chairman, Greater Glasgow and Clyde NHS Board, 2004-07; Governor, Sedbergh School, 2000-08; Trustee, Music in Hospitals, since 2007; Trustee, Scotcash, 2007-2011 (Chairman, 2009); Director, Special Olympics, National Summer Games Glasgow 2005 Ltd.; b. 30.6.43, Glasgow; m., Sheila Sturton; 2 s. Educ. Glasgow Academy; Sedbergh School; Edinburgh University. Director, Merchants House of Glasgow, 1978-2006; Secretary, Clydeside Federation of Community Based Housing Associations, 1978-93; Secretary, The Briggait Company Ltd., 1982-88; Director, Glasgow Chamber of Commerce, 1982-93; Chairman, Post Office Users Council for Scotland, 1988-99; Chairman, Greater Glasgow Community and Mental Health Services NHS Trust, 1994-97; Chairman, Glasgow Royal Infirmary University NHS Trust, 1997-99. Recreations: climbing; swimming; sailing; fishing.

Robertson, Angus, MP (SNP), Moray, since 2001; SNP Group Leader in Westminster; b. 28.9.69, London. Educ. Broughton High School; University of Aberdeen. News Editor, Austrian Broadcasting Corporation, 1991-99; Reporter, BBC Austria, 1992-99; Contributor: National Public Radio, USA, Radio Telefis Eireann, Ireland, Deutsche Welle, Germany; Consultant, Communication Skills International, 1994-2001. Member: Privy Council, Intelligence and Security Committee. Recreations: sport (football, rugby, skiing, playing golf badly); films; travel; music; books; history; socialising. Address: (b.) 9 Wards Road, Elgin, Moray IV30 1NL; T.-01343 551111; e-mail: angus.robertson.mp@parliament.uk

Robertson, Dennis. MSP (SNP), Aberdeenshire West, 2011-16; b. 14.8.56, Aberdeen; m., Anne. Educ. Royal Blind School, Edinburgh; Langside College. Registered blind at the age of 11. Qualified in social work and has worked in both the statutory and voluntary sectors.

Robertson, Derek. Chief Executive Officer, Keep Scotland Beautiful, since 2011; Chairman, UK & Ireland Environment Quality Alliance, since 2012; President, Clean Europe Network & European Litter Prevention Association, since 2014. Educ. Strathclyde University. Career: local government; joined the Third Sector in the late 80s; spent the last 20 years in a variety of senior management and leadership roles; worked in service areas that include the environment, regeneration, sustainable development, education, leisure, community development, health and social care, children's services, youth work, and charity fundraising. Board Member, Scotland's 2020 Climate Change Group, since 2011. Address: Keep Scotland Beautiful, First Floor,

Strathallan House, Castle Business Park, Stirling FK9 4TZ.

Robertson, Professor Edmund Frederick, BSc, MSc, PhD, FRSE. Professor Emeritus of Mathematics, St. Andrews University, since 2008; b. 1.6.43, St. Andrews; m., Helena Francesca; 2 s. Educ. Madras College, St. Andrews; St. Andrews University; Warwick University. Lecturer in Pure Mathematics, Senior Lecturer, then Professor of Mathematics, 1968-2008, St. Andrews University. Vice Chairman, Chairman, then Vice Chairman, since 1986, Madras College Endowment Trust; Member, Scottish Mathematical Council, 1997-2004; EPSRC Peer Review College, 1997-2010; Governor, Morrison's Academy, 1999-2006; Chairman, GAP Council, 2003-2009; Chairman, British Mathematical Colloquium Scientific Committee, 2005-2008. Partnership Award, 1992; European Academic Software Award, 1994; American Computational Engineering and Science Award, 1995; Scientific American web site award, 2002; MERLOT award, 2002; "Signum Pro Scientia Absoluta Vera" award, 2008; Comenius Medal, Societas Comeniana Hungarica, 2012. Publications: 26 books; 150 papers. Recreations: history of mathematics; computers; family. Address: (b.) Mathematical Institute, North Haugh, St. Andrews KY16 9SS; T.-01334 463702.

Robertson, Iain Alasdair, CBE, LLB. Chairman, Keep Scotland Beautiful, since 2012; Chairman, Scottish Legal Aid Board, since 2006; Chairman, Coal Liabilities Strategy Board, since 2006; b. 30.10.49, Perth; m., Judith Helen Stevenson; 2 s.; 1 d. Educ. Perth Academy; Aberdeen University. Qualified as a Solicitor, 1973; service at home and abroad with British Petroleum, 1975-90, latterly as BP America's Director of Acquisitions; Chief Executive, Highlands and Islands Enterprise, 1990-2000. Board Member, Scottish Tourist Board, 1993-95; Board Member, Locate in Scotland Supervisory Board, 1992-2000; Board Member, Cairngorm Partnership, 1998-2000; Director, Quality Scotland, 1999-2000; Director, Development and Strategy, AWG plc, 2000-03; Member, Accounts Commission, 2003-2010; Independent Member, BIS Legal Services Group Board, 2004-2011; Independent Member, HMRC Solicitor's Office Strategic Management Group, 2009-2013. Recreations: skiing; sailing; music.

Robertson, James, PhD. Writer; runs an independent publishing company, Kettillonia, and is a co-founder and general editor of the Scots language imprint Itchy Coo, which produces books in Scots for children and young people; b. 1958. Educ. Glenalmond College; Edinburgh University; University of Pennsylvania in Philadelphia. Worked in a variety of jobs after leaving university, mainly in the book trade; a publisher's sales rep and later worked for Waterstone's Booksellers, first as a bookseller in Edinburgh and later as assistant manager of the Glasgow branch; first writer in residence at Hugh MacDiarmid's house outside Biggar, Lanarkshire, 1993-95. Author of several short story and poetry collections, and has published five novels: The Fanatic, 2000; Joseph Knight, 2003; The Testament of Gideon Mack, 2006; And the Land Lay Still, 2010 and The Professor of Truth, 2013. Address: (b.) c/o United Agents LLP, 12-26 Lexington Street, London W1F 0LE.

Robertson, James Ian Summers, FRSE, MD, FRCPLond, FRCPGlas, BSc, MB, BS (Lond), FAHA, CBiol, FIBiol, MD (Hons. Causa) Free Univ. of Brussels, BA (Manc). Board Member, Scottish Opera, 1999-2008; b. 5.3.28, Welbeck; m., Maureen Patricia; 1 s.; 2 d. Educ. Queen Elizabeth's Grammar School, Mansfield; St Mary's Hospital Medical School, London University. Senior Lecturer and Hon. Consultant Physician, St Mary's Hospital, London, 1964-67; Member of staff, MRC, and Hon. Consultant Physician, Western Infirmary, Glasgow, 1967-87; Senior Consultant, Cardiovascular Medicine, Janssen Research Foundation, Belgium, 1987-94; Visiting Professor of Medicine, Prince of Wales Hospital, Hong Kong, 1988-93; Past President, International Society of Hypertension; former Chairman, Scientific Council on Hypertension, International Society and Federation of Cardiology; Foundation President, British Hypertension Society; former Adviser, Cardiovascular Diseases, World Health Organisation; Cheadle Gold Medal, 1954; Jodh Gold Medal, 1979; Hall Lecturer, Cardiac Society, Australia and New Zealand, 1976; Corcoran Lecturer, American Heart Association, 1978; MSD International Award, 1980; Robert Tigerstedt Award, 1980; William Harvey Lecturer, 1983; Scott Heron Lecturer, Queen's University of Belfast, 1984; Franz Gross Memorial Lecturer, International Society of Hypertension, 1984; Distinguished Member Award, International Society of Hypertension, 2006; Honorary Fellowships: Cardiac Society of Australia and New Zealand; Portuguese Cardiac Society; Mexican Hypertension Society; Southern African Hypertension Society; Polish Cardiac Society; Venezuelan Society of Pharmacology; Taiwan Society of Internal Medicine; Chilean Society of Cardiology. Publications: articles on cardiology, hypertension, endocrinology, music criticism; books on hypertension, endocrinology and music. Recreations: literature; opera; cricket. Address: (h.) Apt. 9/1, 205 Albion Street, Glasgow G1 1RU; T.-0141-552-4880; e-mail: jisrwelbeckmerchant@btinternet.com

Robertson, James Roy, LVO, MBE, BSc, MBChB, FRCGP, FRCP. Principal, General Practice, Muirhouse Medical Group, since 1980; Professor, School of Clinical Sciences, University of Edinburgh; Apothecary to the Royal Household at Palace of Holyroodhouse; b. 15.3.51, Edinburgh; m., Elizabeth; 3 s. Educ. Merchiston Castle School, Edinburgh; University of Edinburgh. Chairman and Member, various national governmental committees and working parties on drug abuse issues, HIV and AIDS and alcohol problems; author of papers on these subjects. Publication: Management of Drug Users in the Community (Editor), 1998. Recreations: outdoor activities; travel; family. Address: Molecular, Genetic and Population Health Sciences, University of Edinburgh, Medical School, Teviot Place, Edinburgh EH8 9AG.
E-mail: roy.robertson@ed.ac.uk

Robertson, John. MP (Labour), Glasgow North West, 2005-2015, Glasgow Anniesland, 2000-05; PPS to Secretary of State for Work and Pensions, Yvette Cooper, 2009-2010; PPS to Treasury Secretary, Yvette Cooper, 2008-09; b. 17.4.52, Glasgow; m.; 3 c. Educ. Stow College, Glasgow. Before entering Parliament, worked for 31 years with BT as telephone engineer and local customer manager.

Robertson, John Graeme, CBiol, FRSB, FCMI, FLS, FRGS, FRSA. Director, Global Islands Network, since 2002; b. 15.8.54, Edinburgh; m., Anne Christie; 1 s.; 1 d. Educ. Scotus Academy, Edinburgh. Career History: Co-ordinator, Edinburgh Environment Centre; Director, Friends of the Earth Scotland; Director, Habitat Scotland; Manager, Scottish Islands Network; Editor, Islander Magazine; Chief Executive, Island Web Consortium. Secretary, International Small Islands Studies Association; Editorial Board Member, Island Studies Journal; Chairman, Small Islands Film Trust. Churchill Fellow, 1996; English Speaking Union William Thyne Scholar, 1999; Honorary Research Fellow, Scottish Centre for Island Studies, University of the West of Scotland, 2009-2012; Research Associate, Institute of Island Studies, University of Prince Edward Island,

Canada, 2015-2019. Recreations: birding; exercising dogs; fishing; philately of the Falkland Islands & Tristan da Cunha; travel to islands worldwide. Address: Struan House, Knockintorran, North Uist, Western Isles HS6 5ED; e-mail: graeme@globalislands.net

Robertson, Professor Pamela, BA (Hons), FRSA, FRSE. Senior Curator, Hunterian Art Gallery, and Professor of Mackintosh Studies, Glasgow University. Educ. St George's School for Girls, Edinburgh; University College, London. Member, Historic Buildings Council for Scotland, 1998-2002; Chair, C.R. Mackintosh Society, 2003-06; Member, Reviewing Committee for the Export of Works of Art, 2003-2010; Governor, Glasgow School of Art, 2006-2010; winner, Iris Foundation Award for outstanding contributions to the decorative arts, Bard University, New York, 1997. Publications include: C.R. Mackintosh: the architectural papers, 1990; C.R. Mackintosh: Art is the Flower, 1994; The Chronycle, 2001; Doves and Dreams: The Art of Frances Macdonald and J. Herbert McNair, 2006; Mackintosh Architecture: Context, Making and Meaning (www.mackintosh-architecture.gla.ac.uk), 2014. Recreations: good food and wine; good company. Address: (b.) Hunterian Art Gallery, Glasgow University, Glasgow G12 8QQ; T.-0141-330 5431. E-mail: pamela.robertson@glasgow.ac.uk

Robertson, Professor Peter Kenneth John, BSc (Hons), DPhil, DSc, CSci, CChem, FRSC, CEng, FEI, FICI. Vice-Principal and Pro Vice-Chancellor (Research and Academic Support Services), Robert Gordon University, since 2006; b. 5.6.64, Belfast; m., Dr Jeanette Robertson; 2 s. Educ. Royal Belfast Academical Institution; University of Ulster. Research Officer, Faraday Centre, Carlow, Ireland, 1989-90; Lecturer, Carlow Regional College, Ireland, 1990-91; Higher Scientific Officer, Industrial Research and Technology Unit, 1991-95; Lecturer, School of Applied Sciences, Robert Gordon University, 1995-2000, Professor of Energy and Environmental Engineering, 2000-06. Non-Executive Director, Satrosphere Science Centre; Member, Energy Institute's Accreditation Panel, since 2009; Member, Universities Scotland Research and Commercialisation Committee, since 2006; Member, Northern Ireland Water Council, 2003-2007; Chairman, Scottish Committee of the Royal Society of Chemistry's Analytical Division, 2004-2006; Member, Editorial Board, International Journal of Photoenergy, since 2006; Chairman, Aberdeen and North of Scotland Branch of the British Association for the Advancement of Science, 2000-09. Recreations: hill-walking; photography. Address: (b.) Robert Gordon University, Schoolhill, Aberdeen AB10 1FR; T.-01224 263750.

Robertson, Raymond Scott, MA. Director of Public Affairs, Halogen Communications, since 2002; Chairman, Scottish Conservative and Unionist Party, 1997-2001; b. 11.12.59, Hamilton. Educ. Garrion Academy, Wishaw; University of Glasgow; Jordanhill College of Education. Teacher of History and Modern Studies; MP, Aberdeen South, 1992-97; PPS, Northern Ireland Office, 1993-95; Minister for Education, Housing, Fisheries and Sport, Scottish Office, 1995-97. Recreations: watching football; reading; travelling.

Robertson, William Nelson, CBE, MA, FCII. Member, Advisory Board, Scottish Amicable, 1997-2003; b. 14.12.33, Berwick upon Tweed; m., Sheila Catherine; 2 d. Educ. Berwick Grammar School; Edinburgh University. Joined General Accident, 1958: Deputy Chief General Manager, 1989-90, Group Chief Executive, 1990-95,

Director, 1984-95. Board Member, Association of British Insurers, 1991-95; Director: Morrison Construction, 1995-2001, Scottish Community Foundation, 1996-99, Edinburgh New Tiger Investment Trust, 1996-2001, Alliance Trust, 1996-2002, Second Alliance Trust, 1996-2002. Member, Court, University of Abertay, Dundee, 1996-99. Recreations: hill-walking; gardening.

Robins, John F. Secretary and Campaigns Consultant, Animal Concern, since 1988; Managing Director, Ethical Promotions Ltd., since 1988; Secretary, Save Our Seals Fund, since 1996; Secretary, Animal Concern Advice Line, since 2001; b. 2.1.57, Glasgow; m., Mary E.; 1 s.; 1 d. (deceased). Educ. St. Ninian's High School. Co-ordinator, Glasgow Energy Group, 1978-80; Company Secretary, Scottish Anti-Vivisection Society, since 1981; Ecology Party activist and candidate, 1978-81; Delegate, Anti-Nuclear Campaign, 1978-81; Vice-Chair, Friends of the Earth (Scotland) Ltd., 1981-82; Co-ordinator, Scottish Animal Rights Network, 1983-91; Founder and Co-ordinator, Save Scotland's Seals Fund, 1988-96. Recreation: catching up on lost sleep. Address: (b.) P.O. Box 5178, Dumbarton G82 5YJ; T.-01389 841111; e-mail: animals@jfrobins.force9.co.uk

Robinson, Mike, BA (Hons). Chief Executive, Royal Scottish Geographical Society (RSGS), since 2008; m.; 3 s. Educ. University of Stirling. Board Member, Stop Climate Chaos Scotland; Scottish Environment Link; 2020 Group. Recreations: squash; mountaineering; environment; cutting carbon footprint. Address: (b.) RSGS, 15-19 North Port, Perth PH1 5LU.

Robinson, Professor Olivia F., MA, PhD, FRSE, FRHistS. Professor Emeritus, University of Glasgow, since 2004; b. 22.11.38, Dublin, Ireland. Educ. Newton Manor, Swanage, Dorset; Lady Margaret Hall, Oxford University; Westfield, London University. Successively Lecturer, Senior Lecturer, Reader and Professor in Roman Law in The Law School of Glasgow University; Rice Visiting Professor in the University of Kansas, 1995. Publications: Ancient Rome: City Planning and Administration, 1992; The Criminal Law of Ancient Rome, 1995; Penal Practice and Penal Policy in Ancient Rome, 2007; Sir George Mackenzie's The Laws and Customs of Scotland in Matters Criminal, 2012. Recreations: fishing; skiing; wine. Address: (b.) School of Law, University of Glasgow, Glasgow G12 8QQ; T.-(h.) 0141 339 4115; e-mail: ofr@law.gla.ac.uk

Robison, Shona. MSP (SNP), Dundee City East, since 2003; MSP (SNP), North East Scotland, 1999-2003; Cabinet Secretary for Health and Sport, Scottish Government, since 2014, Cabinet Secretary for Commonwealth Games, Sport, Equalities and Pensioners' Rights, 2014, Minister for Commonwealth Games and Sport, 2011-2014; Minister for Public Health and Sport, 2007-2011; formerly Shadow Minister for Health; b. 26.5.66, Redcar; m., Stewart Hosie; 1 d. Educ. Alva Academy; Glasgow University; Jordanhill College. Admin Officer, 1989-90; Community Worker, 1990-93; Home Care Organiser, 1993-97. Recreation: hill-walking. Address: (b.) 8 Old Glamis Road, Dundee DD3 8HP; T.-01382 623200.
E-mail: shona.robison.msp@scottish.parliament.uk
Web: www.shonarobison.com

Robson, Euan Macfarlane, BA, MSc. Chairman, Water Engine Technologies Ltd, since 2014; Convener, Borders Citizens Advice Consortium, since 2012; Associate, Caledonia Public Affairs Ltd, since 2008; Chief Executive,

Scottish Sustainable Energy Foundation, 2007-08; former Scottish Manager, Gas Consumers' Council; b. 17.2.54, Northumberland; m., Valerie; 2 d. Educ. Trinity College, Glenalmond; Newcastle-upon-Tyne University; Strathclyde University. Teacher, 1976-79; Deputy Secretary, Gas Consumers' Northern Council, 1981-86. Member, Northumberland County Council, 1981-89; Honorary Alderman, Northumberland CC, since 1989; Liberal/SDP Alliance candidate, Hexham, 1983, 1987; Liberal Democrat Scottish Parliamentary spokesman on: Rural Affairs, 1998-99, Justice and Home Affairs, 1999-2001; MSP for Roxburgh and Berwickshire, 1999-2007; Deputy Minister for Parliamentary Business, 2001-03; Deputy Minister for Education and Young People, 2003-05; Convener, Scottish Liberal Democrat Parliamentary Party, 2005-07. River Tweed Commissioner, 1995-2001; author.

Robson, Godfrey, CB (2002), MA. Director, TSB Banking Group plc, since 2015; Director, Lloyds TSB Scotland, 2001-2013; Chairman, Frontline Consultants, 2003-2013; b. 5.11.46; m. Agnes Robson nee Wight (marr. diss.); 1 s. Educ. St. Joseph's College, Dumfries; Edinburgh University. Scottish Office Civil Servant, 1970-2002, Under Secretary, Economic and Industrial Affairs, 1993-2000, Director of Health Policy, 2000-02; Founding Chairman, National Jubilee Hospital, Clydebank, 2002-03; Director and Trustee, Caledonia Youth, 2003-12; Senior Policy Advisor, ICAP, Washington DC, since 2004. Recreations: walking; travel by other means; reading history. Address: 50 East Trinity Road, Edinburgh EH5 3EN; T.-0131 552 9519; Chemin sous Baye, 84110 Vaison la Romaine, France; T.-04 90 37 18 32; e-mail: godfreyrobson@aol.com

Rochford, Professor Gerard, BA, BSc. Psychotherapist; published poet; editor; b. 17.12.32, Dorking; m., Anne Prime (dec.); 3 s.; 7 d. Educ. Worcester Royal Grammar School; Hull University; Oxford University. Medical Research Council, 1960-63; Lecturer in Psychology: Aberdeen University, 1963-67, Hong Kong University, 1967-70; Lecturer/Senior Lecturer, 1970-78, Professor of Social Work Studies, 1978-88, Aberdeen University. Member, Scottish Association of Psychoanalytical Psychotherapists. One of 20 Best Scottish Poems, 2006, Scottish Poetry Library; www.scottishreview.net Makar, since 2011; latest publications: 'Failing Light', 2011; 'Of Love and Water', 2011; 'Morning Crossword' (with Esther Green - artist), 2013. Recreations: family; friends. Address: (h.) 47 Waverley Place, Aberdeen; T.-01224 644873.
E-mail: gerardrochford@btinternet.com

Roddick, Jeanne Nixon, BD (Hons). Minister of Greenbank Parish Church, Glasgow, since 2003; b. 16.05.55, Lennoxtown; m., Graham; 1 s.; 2 d. Educ. Bellahouston Academy; Glasgow University. Address: Greenbank Manse, 38 Eaglesham Road, Clarkston, Glasgow G76 7DJ; T.-0141 644 1395.
E-mail: jeanne.roddick@ntlworld.com

Rodger, Professor Albert Alexander, FREng, DSc (Hon), BSc (Eng), PhD, CEng, FICE, FGS. Vice Principal (External Affairs), University of Aberdeen, 2011-14; Visiting Professor, University of Strathclyde, 2015-17; Emeritus Professor, University of Aberdeen, Vice Principal and Head of College of Physical Sciences, 2003-2011; Board Member, Scottish Further and Higher Education Funding Council, since 2009; Chair of Research and Knowledge Exchange Committee, Scottish Further and Higher Education Funding Council, since 2010; Director of the National Subsea Research Institute, since 2009; Professor of Civil Engineering, Aberdeen University, since 1997 (Dean, Faculty of Science and Engineering, 2001-03);

b. 12.5.51, Greenock; m., Jane Helen; 2 d. Educ. Aberdeen University. Project Engineer, Cementation Research Ltd., London, 1977-79; Aberdeen University: Lecturer in Engineering, 1979-89, Senior Lecturer, 1989-95, Personal Professor, 1995-97. Winner: Award for Excellence, Aberdeen University, 1994; 1997 National John Logie Baird Award for Innovation; Halcrow Premium, Institution of Civil Engineers, 1997; Design Council Millennium Product Award, 1999; Silver Medal, Royal Academy of Engineering, 2000; Fellow of The Royal Academy of Engineering, 2010. Recreations: history of church architecture; photography; swimming. Address: 7 Mill Lade Wynd, Aberdeen AB22 8QN.
E-mail: a.a.rodger@abdn.ac.uk

Rodger, Professor Richard, MA, PhD, AcSS. Professor of Economic and Social History, University of Edinburgh, since 2007; b. 01.10.47, Norfolk. Educ. University of Edinburgh. Lecturer in Economic History, University of Liverpool, 1972-79; Lecturer and Senior Lecturer in Economic and Social History, University of Leicester, 1979-99; Associate Professor of History, University of Kansas, 1982-83, 1987; Visiting Research Fellow, Center for the Humanities, University of Kanas, 1986-87; Director, Centre for Urban History, 1999-2006; Project Director, East Midlands Oral History Archive, 2000-07; Professor of Urban History, University of Leicester, 1999-2007. Awards: Elected Member, Academy of Social Sciences, 2004, Frank Watson Prize for Best Book in Scottish History, 2001-02, Plain English Society Crystal Mark for Software Made Simple series of books. Publications: 16 books including The Transformation of Edinburgh: Land, Property and Trust in the Nineteenth Century, 2001; pbk 2004; Housing the People: the 'Colonies' of Edinburgh, 1860-1950, 1999; Testimonies of the City: Identity, Community and Change in a Contemporary Urban World (Co-Author), 2007; Housing in Urban Britain, 1780-1914, 1995; Cities of Ideas: Civil Society and Urban Governance in Britain 1800-2000 (Co-Author), 2004. Recreations: cricket; long-distance paths; landscapes. Address: (b.) School of History, Classics and Archaeology, University of Edinburgh, Edinburgh EH8 9JY.

Rodger, Willie, RSA, RGI, DA (Glas), DUniv (Stirling). Artist in lino and woodcuts; b. 3.3.30, Kirkintilloch; m., Anne Charmian Henry; 2 s.; 2 d. Educ. Lenzie Academy; Glasgow School of Art. Visualiser, London advertising agency, 1953-54; Art Teacher, Lenzie Academy, 1955-68; Head, Art Department, Clydebank High School, 1968-87. Artist in Residence, Sussex University, 1971; Scottish Historical Playing Cards, 1975; Saltire Awards for Art in Architecture, 1984-89; work in permanent collections in Scotland and England; commissions: Enamel Mural Exhibition Station, Glasgow; illustrations and mural, Dallas Dhu Distillery, Forres; design, Stained Glass Windows, St Mary's Parish Church, Kirkintilloch; Street Banners, 200 anniversary, Union Street, Aberdeen; edition of Lino Cut Prints, P&O Ferries; illustrations, Finding Alba, Scottish Television; lino cut illustrations for The Colour of Black and White by Liz Lochhead, 2003; Images in Bronze for Kirkintilloch Town Trail, 2004; Exhibition, Willie Rodger & Family, 40th Anniversary of Stirling University, 2007. Publications: Scottish Historical Playing Cards; The Field of Thistles (Illustrator); Willie Rodger, Open Eye Gallery. Recreations: gardening; jazz. Address: Stenton, 16 Bellevue Road, Kirkintilloch, Glasgow G66 1AP; T.-0141-776 2116.

Rodgers, Brendan. Manager, Celtic FC, since 2016; b. 26.1.73, Carnlough, Northern Ireland. Senior career: Ballymena United, 1987-90; Reading, 1990-93; Newport, 1993-94; Witney Town, 1994-95; Newbury Town, 1995-96. Teams managed: Chelsea (youth), 2004-08; Watford, 2008-09; Reading, 2009; Swansea City, 2010-12; Liverpool,

2012-15. Address: Celtic FC, Celtic Park, Glasgow G40 3RE.

Rodney, Philip Emanuel, LLB. Chairman, Burness Paull LLP, since 2012; b. 21.08.53, Glasgow; m., Cherie Lindy Rodney; 3 s. Educ. High School of Glasgow; University of Strathclyde. Career: Law Apprentice, McGrigor Donald; Assistant Solicitor, then Partner, Alexander Stone & Co; Partner, then Chairman, Burness LLP. Governor, Hutcheson's Education Trust. Recreations: family; travel; photography; fast cars and loud music. Address: (b.) 120 Bothwell Street, Glasgow G2 7JL; T.-0141 273 6760; e-mail: philip.rodney@burnesspaull.com

Roe, Professor Nicholas Hugh, MA (Oxon), DPhil (Oxon), FEA, FRSE. Professor of English Literature, St. Andrews University, since 1996; b. 14.12.55, Fareham; m., Dr. Susan Jane Stabler; 1 s. Educ. Royal Grammar School, High Wycombe; Trinity College, Oxford. Lecturer in English, Queen's University of Belfast, 1982-85; St. Andrews University: Lecturer in English, 1985-94, Reader in English, 1994-96; Visiting Professor, University of Sao Paulo, 1989; Leverhulme Research Fellow, 1994-95; Visiting Professor, University of Malta, since 2014; Keats-Shelley Association of America Distinguished Scholar, 2014; Director, Coleridge Conference, 1994-2010; Trustee, Keats-Shelley Memorial Association, 1997-2015; Chair, Wordsworth Conference Foundation; Chair, Keats House Foundation, London; Editor, Romanticism (journal); Keats-Shelley Review (journal), 2008-2015; Founder and Director, St. Andrews Poetry Festival ('StAnza'), 1986-92. Publications: Coleridge's Imagination, 1985; Wordsworth and Coleridge, The Radical Years, 1988; The Politics of Nature, 1992; Selected Poetry of William Wordsworth, 1992; Keats and History, 1995; Selected Poems of John Keats, 1995; John Keats and the Culture of Dissent, 1997; Samuel Taylor Coleridge and the Sciences of Life, 2001; Leigh Hunt: Life, Poetics, Politics, 2003; Fiery Heart: The First Life of Leigh Hunt, 2005; English Romantic Writers and the West Country, 2010; John Keats. A New Life, 2012. Address: (b.) School of English, St. Andrews University, St. Andrews KY16 9AL; T.-01334 476161.

Roe, William Deas, CBE, DUniv (Open), BSc, FRSA, FRI. Chair, British Council Scotland, since 2015; Chair, Edinburgh World Heritage, 2012-2015; Non-Executive Board Member, Department for Work and Pensions, 2011-2015; Principal, William Roe Associates, since 1992; b. 9.7.47, Perth. Educ. St Modan's High School, Stirling; University of Edinburgh. Assistant Director, Scottish Council for Voluntary Organisations; Councillor, Edinburgh City and Lothian Region, 1978-84; Board Member, Training and Development Corporation, Maine, USA; National Champion, National Endowment for Science, Technology and Arts (NESTA), 2005-2010; Chair, Highlands and Islands Enterprise, 2004-2012; Leader, Independent Review of Social Work Services in Scotland, 2005-2007; Leader, Independent Review of Post-16 Education and Vocational Training in Scotland, 2010-2011. Interests: sustainable development; organic gardening; renewable energy; community ownership of assets; creativity and design. Recreations: hill-walking; cycling; skiing; visual arts; music. Address: (h.) Duirinish Lodge, Duirinish, Kyle of Lochalsh IV40 8BE; T.-07771 930880; e-mail: willyroe@gmail.com

Roffe, Melvyn Westley, BA, FRSA, FCOpt (Hon). Principal, George Watson's College, Edinburgh, since 2014; b. 15.6.64, Derby; m., Catherine Stratford; 1 s.; 1 d. Educ. The Noel-Baker School, Derby; University of York; University of Durham. Assistant Master, Oundle School, Northants, 1986-93; Monmouth School: Head of English, 1993-97, Director of Studies, 1997-2001; Headmaster, Old Swinford Hospital, Stourbridge, 2001-07; Principal, Wymondham College, Norfolk, 2007-2014. Parliamentary Candidate (Lib Dem), Corby, 1992; Mayor of Oundle, 1993; Lay Member of the Council of the College of Optometrists, 2001-04; Chairman: State Boarding Schools' Association, 2004-06; Chairman: Boarding Schools' Association, 2008-09; Governor and Trustee, The Thetford Academy, 2010-2013; Member, Corporation, City College Norwich, 2009-2013; Honorary Fellow, College of Optometrists, 2009. Recreations: historic transport; cultural pursuits. Address: Colinton Road, Edinburgh EH10 5EG; T.-0131 446 6000; e-mail: principal@gwc.org.uk

Rogers, David A., MA, PhD. Strategy and Constitution Director, Scottish Government, since 2012. Educ. University of Oxford; University of Cambridge. Address: (b.) Scottish Government, St Andrew's House, Regent Road, Edinburgh EH1 3DG; T.-0131-244 5210. E-mail: david.rogers@scotland.gsi.gov.uk

Rogers, Ian Hart. Chief Executive, Scottish Decorators Federation, since 1999; b. 11.6.52, Glasgow; m., Helen; 2 s. Educ. Bearsden Academy; Clydebank College. Began career with Daily Record and Sunday Mail Ltd.; became Sales Manager/Director of roofing and housebuilding company; joined Scottish Building Employers Federation as HQ Secretary. Director, SCORE; Member, Scottish Advisory Committee, ConstructionSkills; Trustee, Scottish Painting and Decorating Apprenticeship Council (SPADAC). Recreations: golf; walking; reading. Address: (b.) Castlecraig Business Park, Players Road, Stirling FK7 7SH; T.-01786 448838; Fax: 01786 450451; e-mail: info@scottishdecorators.co.uk

Rolfe, Mervyn James, CBE, DL, OStJ, MEd, MSc. Chair, ESEP Ltd., 2000-2014; Convener, Scottish Police Services Authority, 2006-08; Chief Executive, Dundee and Tayside Chamber of Commerce, 2002-06; Depute Leader and Convener, Economic Development Committee, Dundee City Council, 1999-2003; Associate Lecturer, University of Abertay, Dundee, since 2000; b. 31.7.47, Wisbech; m., Christine; 1 s. Educ. Buckhaven High School; Dundee University; University of Abertay Dundee. Civil servant, until 1983; Co-ordinator, Dundee Resources Centre for the Unemployed, 1983-87; Vice-Chair, Dundee Trades Council, 1981-82; Leader, Labour Group, Tayside Regional Council, 1994-96; Convener, Tayside Education Committee, 1986-94; Lord Provost and Lord Lieutenant of Dundee, 1996-99; Member, Executive Committee, COSLA, 1990-96; Governor, Dundee (latterly Northern) College of Education, 1986-94; Member, Dundee University Court, 1986-2000; Member, Scottish Community Education Council, 1986-88; Member, General Teaching Council, 1986-95; Member, Dundee Heritage Trust, 1986-99; Executive Member, Campaign for a Scottish Assembly, 1989-91; Member, Scottish Committee for Staff Development in Education, 1987-91; Board Member, Scottish Enterprise Tayside, 1991-96, and 1999-2003; Member, Scottish ESF Objective 3 Monitoring Committee, 1999-2002; Chair, Dundee City Developments Ltd., 1999-2003; Chair, East of Scotland European Consortium, 2000-03; Chair, Instep Initiatives Ltd., 2003-06; Member, City of Discovery Campaign, 1996-2006 (Chair, 1996-2002); Vice-Chair, Unicorn Preservation Society, 2002-2014; Board Member, Angus and Dundee Tourist Board, 1999-2005; Director, Destination Dundee, since 2005; Director, Maggie's Centre Dundee, 2000-04, Chair, 2004-08; Director, Tayside Council on Alcohol, 2007-11; Member, Dundee Partnership Forum, 2000-06; Honorary Fellow, University of Abertay, Dundee; Honorary Colonel 2 (City of Dundee), Signal squadron (v), 2003-2010; Justice of the Peace, 1988-2008. Recreations: reading; travel. Address: (h.) 17 Mains Terrace, Dundee; T.-01382 450073. E-mail: mervynrolfe@aol.com

Rolfe, William David Ian, PhD, FRSE, FGS, FMA. Keeper of Geology, National Museums of Scotland, 1986-96; b. 24.1.36; m., Julia Mary Margaret Rayer; 2 d. Educ. Royal Liberty Grammar School, Romford; Birmingham University. Geology Curator, University Lecturer, then Senior Lecturer in Geology, Hunterian Museum, Glasgow University, 1962-81; Deputy Director, 1981-86; Keeper of Geology, National Museums of Scotland, 1986-96. President, Geological Society of Glasgow, 1973-76; Editor, Scottish Journal of Geology, 1967-72; President, Edinburgh Geological Society, 1989-91; President, Palaeontological Association, 1992-94; President, Society for the History of Natural History, 1996-99. Recreations: visual arts; walking; music. Address: 4A Randolph Crescent, Edinburgh, EH3 7TH; T.-0131-226 2094.

Rolland, Dr. Lawrence Anderson Lyon, DA, PPRIBA, PPRIAS, FRSE, FRSA. President, Royal Incorporation of Architects in Scotland, 1979-81; President, Royal Institute of British Architects, 1985-87; retired Senior Partner, Hurd Rolland Partnership; General Trustee, Church of Scotland, since 1979; Chairman, Court, University of Dundee, 1998-2004, Chancellor's Assessor, 2005-2010; former Member, Architects Registration Board, London, and Chairman, Education and Practise Advisory Group; Member, Board, NTS, 2005-2011; b. 6.11.37, Leven; m., Mairi Melville; 2 s.; 2 d. Educ. George Watson's Boys College; Duncan of Jordanstone College of Art. Entered father's practice, 1959; joined partnership with Ian Begg bringing L. A. Rolland and Partners and Robert Hurd and Partners together as one partnership; Architect for: The Queen's Hall, Edinburgh; restoration and redesign of Bank of Scotland Head Office (original architect: Sibbald, Reid and Creighton, 1805 and later Bryce, 1870); much housing in Fife's royal burghs; British Golf Museum, St Andrews; General Accident Life Assurance, York; Minshull Street Crown Courts, Manchester; redesign of council chamber GMC; winner of more than 20 awards and commendations from Saltire Society, Stone Federation, Concrete Society, Civic Trust, Europa Nostra, R.I.B.A. and Times Conservation Award. Founder Chairman, Scottish Construction Industry Group, 1979-81; Member, Building EDC NEDC, 1982-88; Chairman, Board of Governors, Duncan of Jordanstone College of Art, 1993-94. Recreations: music; fishing. Address: (h.) Blinkbonny Cottage, Newburn, Fife KY8 6JF; e-mail: rolland@newburn.org.uk

Rollo, 14th Lord (David Eric Howard Rollo); b. 1943. Succeeded to title, 1997.

Rorke, Professor John, CBE, PhD, BSc, DEng, CEng, FIMechE, FRSE. Professor Emeritus, formerly Professor of Mechanical Engineering, Heriot-Watt University, 1980-88, and Vice-Principal, 1984-88; b. 2.9.23, Dumbarton; m., Jane Craig Buchanan; 2 d. Educ. Dumbarton Academy; Royal Technical College, Glasgow. Lecturer, Strathclyde University, 1946-51; Assistant to Engineering Director, Alexander Stephen & Sons Ltd., 1951-56; Technical Manager, then General Manager and Engineering Director, William Denny & Bros. Ltd., 1956-63; Technical Director, then Sales Director, Managing Director and Chairman, Brown Bros. & Co. Ltd. and Chairman, John Hastie of Greenock Ltd., 1963-78; Managing Director, Vickers Offshore Group, 1978 (Director of Planning, Vickers PLC, 1979-80). President, Institution of Engineers and Shipbuilders in Scotland, 1985-87; Chairman, Institute of Offshore Engineering Group, 1990-94. Recreations: bridge;

golf. Address: (h.) Flat 23, Lyle Court, 25 Barnton Grove, Edinburgh EH4 6EZ; T.-0131 339 6515. E-mail: jackandjeanerorke@btinternet.com

Rosborough, Linda, BSc, PhD. Director, Marine Scotland, Scottish Government; Head, Common Agricultural Policy Management Division, Scottish Government, 2002-08. Former Lecturer in planning and environmental studies; former advisor to Environment Committee, House of Commons. Address: (b.) Scottish Government, Marine Scotland, Area 1B South, Victoria Quay, Edinburgh EH6 6QQ; T.-0131-244-6944.

Rose, Dilys Lindsay, BA. Writer of fiction, poetry, drama, librettos, since 1980; Teacher, Creative Writing, University of Edinburgh, since 2001; b. 7.2.54, Glasgow; 2 d. Educ. University of Edinburgh. Publications include: fiction: Our Lady of the Pickpockets, Red Tides, War Dolls, Pest Maiden; Lord of Illusions; Pelmanism; poetry: Beauty is a Dangerous Thing, Madame Doubtfire's Dilemma, Lure; When I Wear My Leopard Hat; Bodywork; Twinset. Winner, first Macallan/Scotland on Sunday short story competition, 1991; Hawthornden Fellow; RLS Memorial Award recipient, 1997; Society of Authors Travel Award; Canongate Prizewinner, 2000; UNESCO/World City of Literature Exchange Fellow, 2006; McCash poetry winner, 2006; Leverhulme Research Fellow, 2009. Address: University of Edinburgh, Room 2.03, 2nd Floor, 12 Buccleuch Place, Edinburgh.

Rose, Kenneth Charles, LLP (Hons), DipLP. Solicitor, Partner, CMS Cameron McKenna LLP, since 2014, Dundas & Wilson CS LLP, 1995-2014; b. 23.10.63, Montrose; m., Aileen; 1 s. Educ. Kelso High School; University of Edinburgh. Dundas & Wilson: Trainee, 1986-88, Assistant/Associate, 1988-95. Recreations: music; keep fit; football; rugby. Address: CMS Cameron McKenna LLP, Saltire Court, 20 Castle Terrace, Edinburgh EH1 2EN; T.-0131 200 7348; e-mail: kenneth.rose@cms-cmck.com

Rose, Professor Richard, BA, DPhil, FBA. Director and Professor of Public Policy, Centre for the Study of Public Policy, Strathclyde University, since 2012; b. 9.4.33; m., Rosemary J.; 2 s.; 1 d. Educ. Clayton High School, Missouri, USA; Johns Hopkins University; London School of Economics; Lincoln and Nuffield Colleges, Oxford University. Political public relations, Mississippi Valley, 1954-55; Reporter, St. Louis Post-Dispatch, 1955-57; Lecturer in Government, Manchester University, 1961-66; Professor of Politics, Strathclyde University; Director, Centre for the Study of Public Policy, 1980-2005 and since 2012; Sixth Century Professor, University of Aberdeen, 2005-2011; Consultant Psephologist, The Times, Independent Television, Daily Telegraph, STV, UTV, etc., since 1964; Scientific Adviser, Paul Lazarsfeld Society, Vienna, since 1991; American SSRC Fellow, Stanford University, 1967; Visiting Lecturer in Political Sociology, Cambridge University, 1967; Director, ISSC European Summer School, 1973; Secretary, Committee on Political Sociology, International Sociological Association, 1970-85; Founding Member, European Consortium for Political Research, 1970; Member: US/UK Fulbright Commission, 1971-75, Eisenhower Fellowship Programme, 1971; Guggenheim Foundation Fellow, 1974; Visiting Scholar: Woodrow Wilson International Centre, Washington DC, 1974, Brookings Institution, Washington DC, 1976, American Enterprise Institute, Washington, 1980, Fiscal Affairs Department, IMF, Washington, 1984; Visiting Professor, European University Institute, Florence, 1977, 1978 and since 2010; Visitor, Japan Foundation, 1984; Hinkley Professor, Johns Hopkins University, 1987; Guest Professor, Wissenschaftszentrum, Berlin, 1988-90, 2005-09 and since 2015, Central European University, Prague, 1992-95, Max Planck Institute, Berlin, 1996; Ransone Lecturer, University of Alabama, 1990; Consultant Chairman, NI Constitutional Convention, 1976; Home Office Working Party on Electoral Register, 1975-77; Co-Founder, British Politics Group, 1974; Convenor, Work Group on UK Politics, Political Studies Association, 1976-88; Member, Council, International Political Science Association, 1976-82; Keynote Speaker, Australian Institute of Political Science, Canberra, 1978; Technical Consultant: OECD, World Bank, Council of Europe, International IDEA UN agencies; Member, National Endowment for Democracy International Forum, since 1997; Member, Transparency International Research Advisory Panel, since 1998; Advisor, House of Commons Public Administration Committee, 2003; Director, ESRC Research Programme, Growth of Government, 1982-86; Honorary Vice President, Political Studies Association, UK, 1986; Editor, Journal of Public Policy, 1985-2011; Foreign Member, Finnish Academy of Science and Letters, 1985; Fellow of the British Academy, 1992; Fellow, American Academy of Arts and Sciences, 1994; Robert Marjolin AMEX Prize in International Economics, 1992; Lasswell Award for Lifetime Achievement in Public Policy, USA, 1999; Political Studies Association Award for Lifetime Achievement, 2000; Lifetime Achievement Award, Comparative Study of Electoral Systems, 2008; Dogan Foundation for European Political Sociology, 2009; Sir Isaiah Berlin Award for Lifetime Achievement, 2009; Honorary doctorate, Orebru University, Sweden, 2005; European University Institute, 2010. Publications: The British General Election of 1959 (Co-author), 1960; Must Labour Lose? (Co-author), 1960; Politics in England, 1964; Studies in British Politics (Editor), 1966; Influencing Voters, 1967; Policy Making in Britain (Editor), 1969; People in Politics, 1970; European Politics (Joint Editor), 1971; Governing Without Consensus — An Irish Perspective, 1971; International Almanack of Electoral History (Co-author), 1974; Electoral Behaviour — A Comparative Handbook (Editor), 1974; Lessons From America (Editor), 1974; The Problem of Party Government, 1974; The Management of Urban Change in Britain and Germany (Editor), 1974; Northern Ireland — A Time of Choice, 1976; Managing Presidential Objectives, 1976; The Dynamics of Public Policy (Editor), 1976; New Trends in British Politics (Joint Editor), 1977; Comparing Public Policies (Joint Editor), 1977; What is Governing? — Purpose and Policy in Washington, 1978; Elections Without Choice (Joint Editor), 1978; Can Government Go Bankrupt? (Co-author), 1978; Britain — Progress and Decline (Joint Editor), 1980; Do Parties Make a Difference?, 1980; Challenge to Governance (Editor), 1980; Electoral Participation (Editor), 1980; Presidents and Prime Ministers (Joint Editor), 1980; Understanding the United Kingdom, 1982; United Kingdom Facts (Co-author), 1982; The Territorial Dimension in United Kingdom Politics (Joint Editor), 1982; Fiscal Stress in Cities (Joint Editor), 1982; Understanding Big Government, 1984; The Nationwide Competition for Votes (Co-author), 1984; Public Employment in Western Nations, 1985; Voters Begin to Choose (Co-author), 1986; Patterns of Parliamentary Legislation (Co-author), 1986; The Welfare State East and West (Joint Editor), 1986; Ministers and Ministries, 1987; Taxation By Political Inertia (Co-author), 1987; The Post-Modern President — The White House Meets the World, 1988; Ordinary People in Public Policy, 1989; Training Without Trainers? (Co-author), 1990; The Loyalty of Voters (Co-author), 1990; Lesson-Drawing in Public Policy, 1993; Inheritance before Choice, 1994; What Is Europe?, 1996; How Russia Votes (Co-author), 1997; Democracy and its Alternatives (Co-author), 1998; A Society Transformed: Hungary in Time-Space Perspective, (Co-author), 1999; The International Encyclopedia of Elections (Editor), 2000; Prime Minister in a Shrinking World, 2001; Elections Without Order: Russia's Challenge to Vladimir Putin (Co-author), 2002); Elections and Parties in New European Democracies (Co-author), 2003 (translations in 17 languages), 2nd edition, 2009; Learning from Comparative Public Policy, 2005; Russia Transformed (Co-author), 2006; Parties and Elections in New European Democracies (Co-author), 2009; Understanding Post-Communist Transformation, 2009; Popular Support for an Undemocratic Regime (Co-Author), 2011; Representing Europeans: a Pragmatic Approach, 2013; Learning about Politics in Time and Space, 2014 (translations in 17 languages); Paying Bribes for Public Services (Co-Author), 2015. Recreations: architecture (historical, Europe; modern, America); music; writing. Address: (h.) 1 East Abercromby Street, Helensburgh G84 7SP; (b.) CSPP, McCance Building, University of Strathclyde, Glasgow G1 1XQ.

Rosebery, 7th Earl of (Neil Archibald Primrose), DL; b. 11.2.29; m., Alison Mary Deirdre Reid; 1 s.; 4 d. Educ. Stowe; New College, Oxford. Succeeded to title, 1974. Address: (h.) Dalmeny House, South Queensferry, West Lothian.

Rosie, Elaine, BA, MIoH. Business Manager, Blackwood Housing & Care, since 2014; Director, Elaine Rosie Associates Ltd., 2008-2014; Associate, SOLACE Enterprises, 2010-2014; Scottish Legal Aid Board Member, 2005-2012; b. 6.9.62; m., Paul Grice; 2 d. Educ. James Gillespie's High School; Stirling University. Management Trainee, City of Edinburgh Council Housing Dept., 1984-86; London and Quadrant Housing Trust: Housing Officer, 1986-87, Special Projects Officer, 1987-88, Senior Development Officer, 1989-91; Senior Development Officer, Whiteinch and Scotstoun Housing Association, 1991-92; Depute Director, Shelter Scotland, 1992-2000; Scottish Homelessness Advisory Service Manager, 2000-04; Homepoint National Advisory Committee, 1993-2006; Training and Development Manager, Shelter Scotland, 2004-06; Inspector, The Scottish Housing Regulator, 2006-08. Recreations: hill walking; reading; swimming; dancing. E-mail: rosie_elaine@yahoo.co.uk

Rosie, George. Freelance Writer and Broadcaster; b. 27.2.41, Edinburgh; m., Elizabeth Ann Burness; 2 s.; 1 d. Educ. Trinity Academy, Edinburgh; Edinburgh School of Architecture. Editor, Interior Design magazine, 1966-68; freelance magazine writer, 1968-76; Scottish Affairs Correspondent, Sunday Times, 1976-86; Reporter, Channel 4 TV series Down the Line, 1986-87, Scottish Eye, 1988; Reporter/Writer, The Englishing of Scotland, 1988, Selling Scotland, 1989; Scotching the Myth, 1990; Losing the Heid, 1991; Independence Day, 1996; Secret Scotland, 1997-98, Our Friends in the South, 1998; After Lockerbie (BAFTA Best Documentary winner, 1999); Our Friends in the South, 2000; Chief Braveheart, 2005; Editor, Observer Scotland, 1988-89; award winner, RSPB birds and countryside awards, 1988. Publications: British in Vietnam, 1970; Cromarty, 1975; The Ludwig Initiative, 1978; Hugh Miller, 1982; The Directory of International Terrorism, 1986; as contributor: Headlines, the Media in Scotland, 1978; Death's Enemy, the Pilgrimage of Victor Frankenstein, 2001 (fiction); Curious Scotland, 2004; Tyneside, 2005; Flight of the Titan, 2010; Scottish Government Yearbook, 1982; Scotland, Multinationals and the Third World, 1982; World Offshore Oil and Gas Industry Report, 1987; stage plays: The Blasphemer, 1990; Carlucco and the Queen of Hearts, 1991 (winner, Fringe First, The Independent Theatre Award); It Had To Be You, 1994; radio plays: The Parsi, 1992; Postcards from Shannon, 2000. Recreation: hill-walking. Address: (h.) 70 Comiston Drive, Edinburgh EH10 5QS; T.-0131-447 9660.

Ross, Rt. Hon. Lord (Donald MacArthur Ross), PC, MA, LLB. Lord Justice Clerk and President of the Second

Division of the Court of Session, 1985-97; a Senator of the College of Justice, 1977-97; Chairman, Judicial Studies Committee, Scotland, 1997-2001; Lord High Commissioner to the General Assembly of the Church of Scotland, 1990 and 1991; b. 29.3.27, Dundee; m., Dorothy Margaret Annand (d. 2004); 2 d. Educ. High School of Dundee; Edinburgh University. Advocate, 1952; QC, 1964; Vice-Dean, Faculty of Advocates, 1967-73; Dean of Faculty, 1973-76; Sheriff Principal of Ayr and Bute, 1972-73; Member, Scottish Committee, Council of Tribunals, 1970-76; Member, Committee on Privacy, 1970; Deputy Chairman, Boundary Commission for Scotland, 1977-85; Member, Court, Heriot-Watt University, 1978-90, Chairman, 1984-90; Member, Parole Board for Scotland, 1997-2002; Vice President, Royal Society of Edinburgh, 1999-2002 (Member, Council, 1997-99). Hon. LLD, Edinburgh, Dundee, Abertay Dundee, Aberdeen; Hon. DUniv, Heriot-Watt; FRSE. Recreation: gardening; walking; travel. Address: (h.) 7/1 Tipperlinn Road, Edinburgh EH10 5ET; T.-0131 447 6771; e-mail: RosD33@aol.com

Ross, Dr. Alastair Robertson, CStJ, DA, PGDip, RSA, RGI, FRBS, FSA Scot, FRSA, MBIM, Hon. FRIAS, DArts, PAI. Baron-Bailie of Easter Moncrieffe, since 1974; Artist; Lecturer in Fine Art, Duncan of Jordanstone College, University of Dundee, 1994-2003; b. 8.8.41, Perth; m., Kathryn Margaret Greig Wilson; 1 d. Educ. St. Mary's Episcopal School, Dunblane; McLaren High School, Callander; Duncan of Jordanstone College of Art, Dundee; Greek National Academy of Fine Art, Athens. SED Postgraduate Scholarship, 1965-66; Dickson Prize for Sculpture, 1962; Holokrome (Dundee) Sculpture Prize and Commission, 1962; SED Travelling Scholarship to Amsterdam, 1963; Royal Scottish Academy Chalmers Bursary, 1964; Royal Scottish Academy Carnegie Travelling Scholarship, 1965; Duncan of Drumfork Scholarship to Italy and Greece, 1965; Member, Society of Portrait Sculptors, 1966; award winner, Paris Salon, 1967; Medaille de Bronze, Societe des Artistes Francais, 1968; Elected Associate of the Royal Society of British Sculptors, 1968; Professional Member, Society of Scottish Artists, 1969; Visiting Lecturer, Glasgow School of Art, 1974; Lecturer in Fine Art, Duncan of Jordanstone College of Art, Dundee, 1966-94; Honorary Lecturer, Dundee University, 1969-94; Visiting Lecturer, University of Texas, Arlington, USA, 1996; Medaille D'Argent and elected Membre Associe, Societe des Artistes Francais, 1970; Scottish Representative and Member, Council, Royal Society of British Sculptors, 1972-92; Elected Fellow of the Royal Society of British Sculptors, 1975; Member, Fife St John Executive Committee, 1979-2010 (SBStJ 1979, OStJ 1984, CStJ 1997); Member, Priory Council, Priory of Scotland 1996-2004; Elected Associate of Royal Scottish Academy, 1980; Sir Otto Beit Medal, Royal Society of British Sculptors, 1988; Member, RSA Alexander Naysmith Fund Committee, 1986-89; Member, RSA Spalding Fund Committee, 1986-89; Member, RSA Kinross Fund Committee, 1994-97 and 2005-09; Freeman, City of London, 1989; Sir William Gillies Bequest Award, Royal Scottish Academy for Art History research in Vienna, 1989; Council Member, Society of Scottish Artists, 1972-75; Comm. Bronze relief panel for Royal Calcutta Golf Club; Vice President, Royal Society of British Sculptors, 1988-90; RIAS Dundee Institute of Architects Architectural Awards Panel, 1988-2000; Council Member, British School at Rome, 1990-96; Invited Tutor, School of Scottish Artists in Malta, 1991-93; Hon. Fellow, Royal Incorporation of Architects in Scotland, 1992; Member, Board of Directors, Workshop and Artists' Studio Provision Scotland Ltd., 1997-2004; Council Member, Royal Scottish Academy, 1998-2001; commissioned to design and sculpt Spirit of Scotland Awards, since 1998; exhibited work widely in UK and abroad; work in: Scottish Arts Council Collection; Perth Art Gallery and Museum; Dundee Education Authority Collection; Dundee Art Gallery and Museum;

Collection of Royal Scottish Academy; Collection of the Lamp of Lothian Collegiate Centre, Haddington, East Lothian; University of Abertay Dundee; University of St Andrews; University of Dundee; University of Stirling; Glasgow Caledonian University; Royal Incorporation of Architects in Scotland Headquarters Collection, Edinburgh; Royal Burgh of St Andrews; City Chambers Dundee; Blackness Primary School, Dundee (Dundee Public Arts Scheme); Collection of Paisley Art Institute; Paisley Musuem & Art Galleries; P & O Steam Navigation Company; Superliner "Aurora"; St Leonard's School, St Andrews, Fife; Court of the Lord Lyon HM New Register House, Edinburgh; Rank Xerox HQ, Bucks; RC Diocese of Dunkeld; private collections in France, Austria, Switzerland, Egypt, USA, Norway, Bahamas, Canada, Portugal, India, UK; awarded Personal Civic Reception by City of Dundee, 1999; Publication Award, Carnegie Trust for the Universities of Scotland, 1999-2000; Member, Saltire Society Arts and Crafts in Architecture Awards Adjudication Panel, 2001-05; Member, Board of Trustees, St Andrews Fund for Scots Heraldry, since 2001; Royal Scottish Academy representative, Trust for St. John's Kirk of Perth, 2001-05; Hon. Doctorate of Arts, University of Abertay Dundee, 2003; Elected RGI, 2004; Hon. Life Member, Perthshire Art Association, 2005; External Assessor to the JD Fergusson Arts Awards Trust for the Trust's 2006 Travel Award, 2005; Member, Montrose Heritage Trust Sculpture Commission Adjudication Panel, 2005; Royal Scottish Academician, 2005; Member, RSA General Purposes Committee, 2005-09; Elected Librarian of the Royal Scottish Academy, 2005-09; Awarded Reid Kerr College Sculpture Prize of Paisley Art Institute, 2006; Invited Distinguished Guest Artist, Brechin Arts Festival, 2006; Member, Board of Patrons, University of Abertay Dundee Foundation, since 2006; Hon. Life Member, Paisley Art Institute, 2007; Awarded Reid Kerr College Sculpture Prize of Paisley Art Institute, 2008; Assessor, 2009 Scottish Drawing Competition; Paisley Art Institute Glasgow Art Club Fellowship Award, 2010; Awarded Diploma of Paisley Art Institute (PAI), 2010; Appointed Hon. Vice President, Paisley Art Institute, 2010; Admitted Burgess of the City of Dundee, 2011; presented Masterclass at Glasgow Caledonian University, 2012; Elected Member of Council, Scottish Artists' Benevolent Association, 2012; Guest Lecturer, University of Stirling, 2013; Guest Lecturer to the Burgesses of the City of Dundee, 2013. Recreations: genealogy; heraldry; travel. Address: (h.) Ravenscourt, 28 Albany Terrace, Dundee, DD3 6HS; T.-01382 224235; e-mail: a.r.ross@arross.co.uk; web: www.arross.co.uk or www.arross.com

Ross, Alexander (Sandy), LLB, CYCW. Chief Executive, Murrayfield Media, since 2007; Managing Director, International Development, STV, 2004-07; Managing Director, Scottish Television, 2000-04; b. 17.4.48, Grangemouth; m., Alison Fraser; 2 s.; 1 d. Educ. Grangemouth High School; Edinburgh University; Moray House College. Apprentice lawyer, 1971-73; Lecturer, Paisley College, 1974-75; Producer, Granada TV, 1978-86; Controller, Arts and Entertainment, Scottish Television, 1986-95; Deputy Chief Executive, Scottish Television Enterprises, 1995-97; Controller Regional Production, Scottish Media Group, 1997-2000. Member, Edinburgh Town Council, 1971-74; Member, Edinburgh District Council, 1974-78; President, Moray House Students Union, 1976; Chair, Salford Conference on Media; Member, BAFTA; Director, Assembly Theatre. Recreations: golf; music; reading; watching football; member, Glen Golf Club, Haunted Major Golf Society, Prestonfield Golf Club, Edinburgh Corporation Golf Club. Address: (h.) 10 Campbell Avenue, Edinburgh EH12 6DS; T.-0131-539 1192; mobile: 07803 970 107.
E-mail: sandy.ross@murrayfieldmedia.com

Ross, Commodore Angus, BA, MSc, FCILT. Chairman, Scottish Association for Marine Science, since 2014; m.,

Irene; 2 d. Career history: Programme Management experience in the Ministry of Defence, both strategic (the Navy's long term capability programme) and tactical (delivering information systems); served at sea as the Logistics Officer in HMS Illustrious, HMS London and HMS Galatea, and also served aboard HMS Fearless during the Falklands campaign; served in the Royal Navy for 36 years; Director, Royal Navy Logistics in the Fleet Headquarters, then Operations Director in the service personnel and veteran's agency responsible for human resources, payroll and pensions to all Armed Forces personnel; retired form the Royal Navy in 2010. Consultant in the defence and maritime industries; set up a not for profit business to assist small to medium businesses to work with the Government. Joined the Council of the Scottish Association for Marine Science as Non-Executive Chairman of the audit committee in 2011; member of Court, University of the Highlands and Islands, since 2014; Elder in the Church of Scotland; member of the Merchants House of Glasgow; member, committee of the Highland Reserve Forces' and Cadets' Association. Recreations: yacht skipper; shoots target rifle; climbs mountains; coastal shipping. Address: Scottish Association for Marine Science, Scottish Marine Institute, Oban, Argyll PA37 1QA; T.-01631 559000.

Ross, David Craib Hinshaw, LLB (Hons). Convener, Court of the University of Glasgow, since 2010; Member, Advisory Board of Interface, since 2009; Chair, Committee of Scottish University Chairs, since 2013; Partner, Biggart Baillie, Solicitors, 1977-2009, Chairman and Senior Partner, 2001-2008; Director, Glasgow Chamber of Commerce, 1996-2008, President, 2002; Chairman, Scottish Chambers of Commerce, 2003-07; Director, APUC Ltd., 2007-2015; b. 14.1.48, Glasgow; m., Elizabeth Clark; 2 s.; 1 d. Educ. Kelvinside Academy, Glasgow; Trinity College, Glenalmond; University of Glasgow. Maclay Murray and Spens: Apprenticeship, 1970-72, Assistant, 1972-75; Assistant, Biggart Baillie and Gifford, 1975-77, Head of Corporate, 1997-2001. Director, Scottish Council Development and Industry, 2003-07; Director, British Chambers of Commerce, 2003-07; Chairman, Euro-American Lawyers Group, 1997-2002; Director, Loganair Ltd., 2009-2012, Secretary, 1997-2012. Recreations: rhododendrons; windsurfing. Address: (h.) Eastfield, 10 Ledcameroch Road, Bearsden, Glasgow G61 4AB; T.-0141-942 2569.

Ross, Douglas. MSP (Scottish Conservative), Highlands and Islands region, since 2016; Shadow Cabinet Secretary for Justice, since 2016. Career history: elected to Moray council in 2007 (resigned in 2009); elected to Moray council (2012-14), representing the Fochabers-Lhanbryde ward; Conservative candidate in the Moray constituency in the 2010 and 2015 elections. Football referee, who has officiated as an assistant in the Scottish Premiership and in international play; one of the referees chosen for the 2015 Scottish Cup Final, assisting Willie Collum. Address: Scottish Parliament, Edinburgh EH99 1SP.

Ross, Gail Elizabeth. MSP (SNP), Caithness, Sutherland and Ross, since 2016; elected SNP Councillor, Highland Council in 2011; m.; 1 s. Educ. Wick High School. Confectioner, MacDonald's Bakery, 1988-2000; Marketing Manager, Grey Coast Theatre Company, 2001-03; Advertising Field Sales, The Scotsman, 2003-05; Sales Co-ordinator, Football Aid, 2005-06; Dispenser, Boots, 2006-07; appointed Office Manager, The Scottish Parliament in 2007. Board Member, North Highland College. Address: Scottish Parliament, Edinburgh EH99 1SP.

Ross, Helen Elizabeth, BA, MA (Oxon), PhD (Cantab), FBPsS, CPsychol, FRSE. Honorary Reader, Stirling University, since 1994; b. 2.12.35, London. Educ. South Hampstead High School; Somerville College, Oxford; Newnham College, Cambridge. Assistant Mistress, schools in London and Oxfordshire, 1959-61; Research Assistant and student, Psychological Laboratory, Cambridge University, 1961-65; Lecturer in Psychology: Hull University, 1965-68, Stirling University, 1969-72; Senior Lecturer in Psychology, Stirling University, 1972-83; Research Fellow, DFVLR Institute for Aerospace Medicine, Bonn, 1980-81; Leverhulme Fellowship, 1983-84; Reader in Psychology, Stirling University, 1983-94; Honorary Reader, Stirling University, since 1994. Member, S.E. Regional Board, Nature Conservancy Council for Scotland, 1991-92; Fellowship Secretary, Royal Society of Edinburgh, 1994-97. Publications: Behaviour and Perception in Strange Environments, 1974; E.H. Weber: The Sense of Touch (Co-translator), 1978; E.H. Weber on the Tactile Senses (Co-translator), 1996; The Mystery of the Moon Illusion (Co-author), 2002. Recreations: Gaelic (Diploma, UHI, 2013); hill-walking; compleat Munroist, 1998; traditional music; concertina; smallpipes. Address: (b.) Department of Psychology, Stirling University, Stirling FK9 4LA; T.-01786 467647; e-mail: h.e.ross@stir.ac.uk

Ross, Ian, OBE, FICFor, FRSA. Chairman, Scottish Natural Heritage, since 2014. Educ. Aberdeen University. Formerly Highland Councillor for 13 years; past chair of the Highland Council's Planning, Environment and Development Committee; led on a number of significant strategic developments, including the Council's Highland-wide Local Development Plan and the Onshore Wind Farm Strategy; has been active on sustainability and community engagement issues within both the Highland Council and Scottish forestry; over 30 years of experience of working within the wider Scottish land use sector; extensive experience of working with public sector bodies in best value reviews and the development of improved governance processes. Address: Scottish Natural Heritage, Great Glen House, Leachkin Road, Inverness IV3 6NW; T.-01463 725000.

Ross, Dr John Alexander, CBE, DVMS, FRAgS, LL. Lord Lieutenant of Wigtown, since 2015; Chairman, Dumfries and Galloway NHS Board, 2001-08; Chairman, Moredun Research Institute, 2002-04; Chairman, Moredun Foundation, 2004-2012; Commissioner, The Northern Lighthouse Board, since 2008; Chairman, Programme Board for Prison Healthcare, 2009-2012; Deputy Lieutenant of Wigtown, since 2009; Chairman, Care Farming Scotland, since 2011; Vice-President, Royal Highland Agricultural Society, 2012; b. 19.2.45, Stranraer; m., Alison Jean Darling; 2 s.; 1 d. Educ. George Watson's College, Edinburgh. NFU of Scotland: Convener, Hill Farming Sub-Committee, 1984-90, Wigtown Area President, 1985-86, Convener, Livestock Committee, 1987-90, Vice-President, 1986-90, President, 1990-96. Chairman, Stranraer School Council, 1980-89; Session Clerk, Portpatrick Parish Church, 1975-80; Director, Animal Diseases Research Association; Commissioner, Meat and Livestock Commission, 1996-2002; Chairman, Dumfries and Galloway Health Board, 1997-2000; Chairman, Dumfries and Galloway Primary Care NHS Trust, 2000-01; Director, NFU Mutual Insurance Society, 1996-2012. Fellow of Scottish Agricultural College, 2011; Hon. Doctor of Veterinary Medicine and Surgery (DVMS), 2013. Recreations: golf; curling. Address: Auchenree Cottage, Portpatrick, Stranraer DG9 8TN.
E-mail: auchenree@outlook.com

Ross, Kenneth Alexander, LLB (Hons). Sheriff of South Strathclyde, Dumfries and Galloway at Dumfries, 2000-2014; President, Law Society of Scotland, 1994-95 (Vice-President, 1993-94); b. 21.4.49; m., Morag Laidlaw; 1 s.; 1 d. Educ. Hutchesons' Grammar School, Glasgow; Edinburgh University. President, Edinburgh University Union, 1970-71. Partner, Gillespie, Gifford & Brown (formerly McGowans), Solicitors, Dumfries, 1975-97; Temporary Sheriff, 1987-97; Sheriff of Lothian and Borders at Linlithgow, 1997-2000. Member, Scottish Legal Aid Board, 2004-09; Member, Judicial Appointments Board for Scotland, 2008-12; Member, Council, Law Society of Scotland, 1987-96. Contested General Elections (C): Kilmarnock, Feb. 1974, Galloway, Oct. 1974. Recreations: gardening; golf; curling; walking. Address: Slate Row, Auchencairn, Castle Douglas, Kirkcudbrightshire DG7 1QL.

Ross, Rev. Professor Kenneth Rankin, BA, BD (Hons), PhD. Parish Minister, Netherlorn, since 2010; b. 31.5.58, Glasgow; m., Hester Ferguson Carmichael; 3 s. Educ. Kelvinside Academy, Glasgow; Edinburgh University. Ordained, 1982; Parish Minister, Unst, Shetland, 1982-88; Mission Partner, Board of World Mission, seconded to University of Malawi as Lecturer and latterly Professor of Theology, 1988-98; General Secretary, Church of Scotland Board of World Mission, 1998-2009; Member, International Association for Mission Studies, since 1999; Honorary Secretary, Jubilee Scotland, 2000-2010; Chair, Scotland Malawi Partnership, since 2010; Advisor, World Council of Churches, since 2012; Series Editor, Edinburgh Companions to Global Christianity, since 2014; Moderator, Presbytery of Argyll, 2015-16. Publications: Church and Creed in Scotland, 1988; Gospel Ferment in Malawi, 1995; Here Comes Your King! Christ, Church and Nation in Malawi, 1998; Following Jesus and Fighting HIV/Aids, 2002; Edinburgh 2010; Springboard for Mission, 2009; Atlas of Global Christianity, 1910-2010, 2009; Mission Spirituality and Authentic Discipleship, 2013; Malawi and Scotland: Together in the Talking Place, since 1859, 2013; Roots and Fruits: Retrieving Scotland's Missionary Story, 2014. Recreations: hill-walking; reading; gardening; photography. Address: The Manse, Kilmelford, Oban, Argyll PA34 4XA; T.-01852 200565.
E-mail: kennethr.ross@btinternet.com

Ross, Rev. Matthew Zachary, LLB, BD, MTh, FSAScot. General Secretary, Action of Churches Together in Scotland (ACTS), since 2014; Minister, Parish Churches of Cockpen and Carrington linked with Lasswade and Rosewell, 2009-2014; Church of Scotland Minister, since 1998; b. 15.11.67, Dundee; m., Kristina M. Herbold; 1 d. Educ. Westminster School; University of Edinburgh; University of Glasgow. Research Assistant, House of Commons, 1990-91; Political Researcher, Scottish Liberal Democrats, 1992-93; Researcher, P.S. Public Affairs Consultants Ltd., Edinburgh, 1993-94; Probationer for the ministry, Duddingston Kirk, Edinburgh, 1996-98; Minister, Ceres and Springfield Parish Church, 1998-2003; Acting Depute Clerk, General Assembly of the Church of Scotland, 2002-03; Executive Secretary, Church and Society Commission of the Conference of European Churches, Brussels, Belgium, 2003-2009; Moderator, Church of Scotland Presbytery of Europe, 2009; Vice Convener, Appeals Committee of the Commission of Assembly, 2013-2014; Member, Church & Society Council and Ecumenical Relations Committee of the Church of Scotland, 2009-2014; Convener, World Mission Committee of Lothian Presbytery, 2010-2013; Secretary, Scottish Church Society, 1999-2004; Member, Board of Practice and Procedure and Legal Questions Committee of the Church of Scotland, 1999-2003; Convener, World Mission Committee of the Presbytery of St Andrews, 2000-03; Member, Policy Committee, Centre for Theology and Public Issues, University of Edinburgh, 1996-99. Recreations: history; architecture; travel (especially by rail); sharing laughter with friends. Address: (b.) ACTS, Jubilee House, Forthside Way, Stirling FK8 1QZ.

Ross, Neil Kilgour, MA, LLB. Partner, Grigor & Young, Solicitors, since 1989; b. 17.5.54, Sutton Coldfield; m.,

Kathleen Rae; 1 d. Educ. Inverurie Academy; Aberdeen University. Legal apprentice, Western Isles Islands Council, 1977-79; Legal Assistant, Angus District Council, 1979-82; Depute Director of Legal Services, Clerk of the Peace and Clerk to the Licensing Board, Western Isles Islands Council, 1982-85. Director, Moray Council on Addictions; Director, Moray Property Searchers Ltd.; contributor, Stair Memorial Encyclopedia; Member, Council, Law Society of Scotland, 1994-2003. Recreations: wine; gardening; cricket. Address: (b.) 1 North Street, Elgin IV30 1UA; T.-01343 544077; e-mail: neil@grigor-young.co.uk

Ross, Nicholas Julian, ARCM. Section Principal Clarinet, Orchestra of Scottish Opera; b. 29.1.55, Orsett; divorced; 1 s.; 1 d. Educ. Oakham School; Royal Academy of Music, London. Freelance, two years; joined Scottish Opera as 2nd Clarinet, 1980; appointed Principal Clarinet, 1992. Recreation: cycling. Address: (h.) 22 Eskdale Street, Glasgow G42 8UD; T.-0141-423 1262.
E-mail: nross_clarinet@hotmail.co.uk

Ross, Thomas Leonard, LLB, DipLP. Advocate, since 2000; b. 25.10.63, Glasgow; m., Alison Mary Laurie; 2 d. Educ. Penilee Secondary, Glasgow; Strathclyde University. Admitted as Solicitor, 1985; Solicitor Advocate, 1998; admitted to Bar, 2000. President, Glasgow Bar Association, 1995; Board Member, Legal Defence Union, 1996-97; Criminal Editor, Scolag, 1994-95; Vice Chair, Faculty of Advocates Criminal Bar Association, 2012-14; President, Scottish Criminal Bar Association, since 2015. Address: (h.) 7 Buchlyvie Road, Ralston, Renfrewshire PA1 3AD; T.-0141-810 4161.
E-mail: thomasleonardross@btinternet.com

Ross, Lt-Col. Sir (Walter Hugh) Malcolm, GCVO 2005, (CVO 1994, KCVO, 1999), OBE (1988), DL (2003), JP (2006), KStJ 2009 (CStJ 2007). Chairman, Westminster Group plc, since 2007; Master of the Household to TRH The Prince of Wales and The Duchess of Cornwall, 2006-08; Extra Equerry to HM The Queen, since 1988; HM Lord-Lt Stewartry of Kirkcudbright, since 2006; Member, Queen's Body Guard for Scotland, Royal Company of Archers, since 1981; Brigadier, 2003; Ensign, 2012; b. 27.10.43; m., Susan; 2 d.; 1 s. Educ. Eton; RMA Sandhurst. Scots Guards, 1964-87; Management Auditor, The Royal Household, 1987-89; Secretary, Central Chancery of The Orders of Knighthood, 1989-90; Comptroller, Lord Chamberlain's Office, 1991-2006 (Assistant Comptroller, 1987-90). Freeman, City of London, 1994; Prior of the Order of St John in Scotland, 2009-2015. Address: Netherhall, Bridge-of-Dee, Castle Douglas, Kirkcudbrightshire DG7 2AA.

Ross, William Charles Cameron, DPhil, BTech (Hons), PGCE, MInstP, CPhys. Principal, Orkney College, since 2002; b. 26.1.60, Woking, Surrey; m., Sonia; 3 s. Educ. Winston Churchill School, Woking, Surrey; Universities of Bradford, Leeds, York. Career History: Thornton Upper School, Bradford; Batley High School for Boys; Bradford College; Bournville College, Birmingham. Address: (b.) Orkney College, East Road, Kirkwall, Orkney KW15 1LX; T.-01856 569000; e-mail: bill.ross@orkney.uhi.ac.uk

Rothes, 22nd Earl of (James Malcolm David Leslie); b. 1958. Succeeded to title, 2005.

Roughead, Malcolm, OBE. Chief Executive, VisitScotland, since 2010. Educ. Glasgow University. Previously held a number of senior marketing positions with Guinness in Africa, Europe, the Middle East and North

America; also worked in marketing with Nestlé and Beechams in London; joined VisitScotland from Diageo in 2001; Director of Marketing, VistScotland, 2001-2010, Acting Chief Executive, from June 2010. Awarded the title of Scottish Marketeer of the Year, Scottish Marketing Awards, 2004; Fellow, Institute of Direct Marketing; Fellow and former Chair, Marketing Society in Scotland; OBE for services to tourism, 2005. Address: (b.) VisitScotland, Ocean Point One, 94 Ocean Drive, Edinburgh EH6 6JH.

Rougvie, Alexander, BSc, MA. Director of Continuing Education, University of St. Andrews, 1991-2009 (retired); Admissions consultant in USA, since 2009; b. 17.06.47, Kirkcaldy; m., Ann; 1 s.; 3 d. Educ. Kirkcaldy High School; Heriot-Watt University. Various construction management posts in London and SE, 1970-75; Building Manager, 1975; Circle 33 Housing Trust Ltd., 1979-87; Senior, then Principal Lecturer, Polytechnic of Central London, 1987-91; Continuing Education Coordinator, then Director of Continuing Education, University of St. Andrews. Various Housing Association Committee Memberships, 1984-2004. Publication: "Project Evaluation and Development", 1987. Recreations: gliding; music; travel; DIY; constructive idleness.

Rowallan, Lord (John Polson Cameron), ARICS. Chairman, Lochgoin Covenanters Trust; b. 8.3.47, Glasgow; m., Claire; 2 s.; 2 d; 1 steps.; 1 stepd. Educ. Eton College; Royal Agricultural College. Estate Agent, since 1969; Company Director, since 1989; Commentator, since 1986; Patron, Depression Alliance. Recreations: equestrianism and auctions. Address: (h.) Meiklemosside House, Fenwick, Ayrshire KA3 6AY.
E-mail: john.rowallan@gmail.com

Rowley, Alex, MA (Hons), MSc. MSP (Labour), Mid Scotland and Fife region, since 2016 (Cowdenbeath, 2014-16); Deputy Leader, Scottish Labour Party, since 2015; b. 30.11.63, Dunfermline; 3 d. Educ. St Columba's High School, Dunfermline; Newbattle Abbey College, Dalkeith; Edinburgh University. General Secretary of the Scottish Labour Party, 1998-99; worked as an education official with the TUC and worked for five years as an assistant, election agent and constituency manager to Gordon Brown; first elected to Fife Regional Council in 1990, became Chairman of Finance, later became the first leader of the new Fife Council and Labour Council Group Leader; Labour candidate, 2011 Scottish Parliament election. Address: Scottish Parliament, Edinburgh EH99 1SP.

Rowling, Joanne Kathleen (J.K.), OBE, BA. Writer; b. 31.7.65; m. (1); 1 d.; m. (2); 1 s.; 1 d. Educ. Exeter University. Publications: Harry Potter and the Philosopher's Stone, 1997; Harry Potter and the Chamber of Secrets, 1998; Harry Potter and the Prisoner of Azkaban, 1999; Harry Potter and the Goblet of Fire, 2000; Fantastic Beasts and Where to Find Them, 2001; Quidditch Through The Ages, 2001; Harry Potter and the Order of the Phoenix, 2003; Harry Potter and the Half-Blood Prince, 2005; Harry Potter and the Deathly Hallows, 2007; The Tales of Beedle the Bard, 2008; The Casual Vacancy, 2012; The Cuckoo's Calling (pseudonym: Robert Galbraith), 2013; The Silkworm (pseudonym: Robert Galbraith), 2014; Very Good Lives, 2015; Career of Evil (pseudonym: Robert Galbraith), 2015. Address: The Blair Partnership, PO Box 7828, London W1A 4GE.

Rowlinson, Professor Peter, MA, DPhil. Emeritus Professor of Mathematics, University of Stirling, since 2006; b. 23.10.44, Cambridge; m., Carolyn. Educ.

Cambridgeshire High School; New College, Oxford. University of Stirling: Lecturer in Mathematics, 1969-92, Senior Lecturer in Mathematics, 1992-94, Reader in Mathematics, 1994-96, Professor of Mathematics, 1996-2006. Visiting Associate Professor of Mathematics, California Institute of Technology, 1975-76; President, Edinburgh Mathematical Society, 2003-05. Publications: Eigenspaces of Graphs (Co-author), 1997; Spectral Generalizations of Line Graphs (Co-author), 2004; An Introduction to the Theory of Graph Spectra (Co-author), 2010; journal articles. Address: Institute of Computing Science and Mathematics, University of Stirling, Stirling FK9 4LA; T.-01786 467468.
E-mail: p.rowlinson@stirling.ac.uk

Roxburghe, 10th Duke of (Guy David Innes-Ker), b. 18.11.54; m., 1, Lady Jane Meriel Grosvenor (m. diss.); 2 s.; 1 d.; 2, Virginia Mary Wynn-Williams; 1 s.; 1 d. Educ. Eton; Sandhurst; Magdalene College, Cambridge. Address: (h.) Floors Castle, Kelso TD5 7RW.

Roy, Frank, BA. MP (Labour), Motherwell and Wishaw, 1997-2015; b. 29.8.58, Motherwell; m., Ellen Foy; 1 s.; 1 d. Educ. St Joseph's High School, Motherwell; Our Lady's High School, Motherwell; Motherwell College; Glasgow Caledonian University. Ravenscraig steelworker, 1977-91; PPS to Helen Liddell, Deputy Secretary of State for Scotland, 1998-99; PPS to Dr John Reid, MP, Secretary of State for Scotland, 1999-2001; PPS to Helen Liddell, Secretary of State for Scotland, 2001; Government Whip, 2005-2010.

Roy, Kenneth. Editor, The Scottish Review, since 1995; Chair, Institute of Contemporary Scotland, since 2014 (Director, 2000-2010); Founder, Young Scotland Programme and Young United Kingdom and Ireland Programme; b. 26.3.47, Falkirk; m., Margaret; 2 s. Journalism and occasional publishing, 1962-72; broadcasting, 1972-82; publishing and occasional journalism, 1983-2003; Founder and Publisher, Who's Who in Scotland, 1985-2005. Critic of the Year, Scottish Press Awards, 1990, 1993; Columnist of the Year, British Press Awards, 1994; Past President, Auchinleck Boswell Society; Oliver Brown Award, 2002. Publications include: Travels in a Small Country, 1987; Conversations in a Small Country, 1989; The Closing Headlines (autobiography), 1993; The Invisible Spirit: a life of post-war Scotland, 2013. Address: (b.) Suite 216, Liberator House, Glasgow Prestwick Airport, Prestwick KA9 2PT; T.-01292 473777.
E-mail: admin@scottishreview.net

Roy, Lindsay Allan, CBE, BSc, FRSA. Former MP (Labour), Glenrothes and Central Fife (2008-2015); Headteacher, Kirkcaldy High School, February-November 2008; Rector, Inverkeithing High School, 1989-2008; b. 19.1.49, Perth; m., Irene Elizabeth Patterson; 2 s.; 1 d. Educ. Perth Academy; Edinburgh University. Assistant Rector, Kirkcaldy High School, 1983-86; Depute Rector, Glenwood High School, Glenrothes, 1986-89; Chairman, Modern Studies Association, 1976-79; Chairman, Modern Studies Panel, Scottish Examination Board, 1980-83; Member, Consultative Committee on the Curriculum Central Committee for Social Subjects, 1978-85; Chairman, Higher Still Group Awards Steering Committee, 1996-98; Member, Board of Management, Lauder College, 1998-2006; past President, Headteachers' Association of Scotland; Member, National Qualifications Steering Group, 2003-08.

Royan, Professor Bruce, BA (Hons), MBA, MBCS, FCLIP, FCMI, FRSA, FSA (Scot). Chief Executive,

Concurrent Computing Ltd., since 2002; b. 22.1.47, Luton; m., Ann Elizabeth Wilkins; 1 s.; 1 d. Educ. Dunstable Grammar School; North West Polytechnic; Glasgow University. Systems Development Manager, British Library, 1975-77; Head of Systems, National Library of Scotland, 1977-85; Director, Singapore Integrated Library Automation Service, 1985-88; Principal Consultant, Infologistix Ltd., 1988-98; Director of Information Services and University Librarian, Stirling University, 1989-96; Chief Executive, Scottish Cultural Resources Access Network, 1996-2002; Visiting Professor, School of Creative Industries, Napier University, 1997-2011; Interim Director of Knowledge and Information, The Robert Gordon University, 2004-05. Secretary, Working Party on Access to the National Database, 1980-83; Member, Council, Library Association of Singapore, 1987-88; Convenor, Higher Education IT Directors in Scotland, 1991-93; Executive Chairman, Bath Information and Data Services, 1991-96; Councillor, The Library Association, 1994-99; Chair, National Datasets Steering Group, 1994-96; Board Member, Croydon Libraries Internet Project, 1995-96; Chair, Scottish Collaborative On-demand Publishing Enterprise (SCOPE), 1996-98; Councillor, Institute of Information Scientists, 1997-99; Member, Content Creation Task Group, New Opportunities Fund, 1998; Member, National Grid for Learning Scottish Steering Group, 1998-2003; Chair, UK Metadata for Education Group, 2000-04; Chair, British Council Library and Information Advisory Committee, 2001-03; Member, Culture Online Steering Committee, 2001-03; Director, Virtual Hamilton Palace Trust, 2003-11; Councillor, Chartered Institute of Library and Information Professionals, 2006-11; Chair, Coordinating Council of Audiovisual Archives Associations, 2009; Trustee, The Edinburgh Singers, 2013; Chair, The Edinburgh Singers, 2014-15. Recreations: choral singing, antique maps; travel. Address: (h.) Bowmont Tower, Greenhill Gardens, Edinburgh EH10 4BL.

Royle, Trevor Bridge, MA, FRSE. Author and Journalist; Member, Scottish Government's Commemoration Panel for First World War; Honorary Fellow, School of History, Classics and Archaeology, University of Edinburgh; Honorary Fellow, Association for Scottish Literary Studies; Trustee, Combat Stress (The Veterans Mental Welfare Society); b. 26.1.45, Mysore, India; m., Dr. Hannah Mary Rathbone; 3 s. Educ. Madras College, St. Andrews; Aberdeen University. Editor, William Blackwood & Sons Ltd.; Literature Director, Scottish Arts Council, 1971-79; Presenter for BBC Radio Scotland and BBC World Service, 1980-88; Literary Editor, Scotland on Sunday, 1988-90; Associate Editor, Scotland on Sunday, 1991-97; Associate Editor, Sunday Herald, 1999-2015. Publications: We'll Support You Evermore: The Impertinent Saga of Scottish Fitba' (Co-Editor), 1976; Jock Tamson's Bairns (Editor), 1977; Precipitous City: The Story of Literary Edinburgh, 1980; A Diary of Edinburgh, 1981; Edinburgh, 1982; Death Before Dishonour: The True Story of Fighting Mac, 1982; The Macmillan Companion to Scottish Literature, 1983; James and Jim: The Biography of James Kennaway, 1983; The Kitchener Enigma, 1985; The Best Years of their Lives: The Post-War National Service Experience, 1986; War Report: The War Correspondents' View of Battle from the Crimea to the Falklands, 1987; The Last Days of the Raj, 1989; A Dictionary of Military Quotations, 1989; Anatomy of a Regiment, 1990; In Flanders Fields: Scottish poetry and prose of the First World War, 1990; Glubb Pasha, 1992; Mainstream Companion to Scottish Literature, 1993; Orde Wingate: Irregular Soldier, 1995; Winds of Change, 1996; Scottish War Stories (Editor), 1999; Crimea: The Great Crimean War, 1854–56, 1999; Civil War: the wars of the three kingdoms 1638-1660, 2004; Patton: Old Blood and Guts, 2005; The Flowers Of The Forest: Scotland And The First World War, 2006; The Royal Scots: A Concise History, 2006; The Black Watch: A Concise History, 2006; The Gordon Highlanders: A Concise History, 2007; The Royal Highland Fusiliers: A Concise History, 2007; Queen's Own Highlanders: A Concise History, 2007; The King's Own Scottish Borderers: A Concise History, 2008; The Argyll and Sutherland Highlanders: A Concise History, 2008; The Cameronians: A Concise History (2008); The Road to Bosworth Field: A New History of the Wars of the Roses (2009); Montgomery: Lessons in Leadership from the Soldier's General, 2010; A Time of Tyrants: Scotland and the Second World War, 2011; ed, Isn't All This Bloody? Scottish Writing From The First World War, 2014; Britain's Lost Regiments: The Illustrious Band of Brothers Time Has Forgotten, 2014; Bearskins, Bayonets and Body Armour: Welsh Guards 1915-2015, 2015; radio plays: Magnificat, 1984; Old Alliances, 1985; Foreigners, 1987; Huntingtower, 1988; A Man Flourishing, 1988; The Pavilion on the Links, 1991; The Suicide Club, 1992; Tunes of Glory, 1995; stage play: Buchan of Tweedsmuir, 1991. Recreations: watching rugby football; hill-walking; investigating battlefields. Address: (h.) 6 James Street, Edinburgh EH15 2DS; T.-0131 669 2116.

Ruckley, Professor Charles Vaughan, CBE, MB, ChM, FRCSEdin, FRCPEdin. Emeritus Professor of Vascular Surgery, Edinburgh University; former Consultant Surgeon, Royal Infirmary, Edinburgh; b. 14.5.34, Wallasey; m., Valerie Anne Brooks; 1 s.; 1 d. Educ. Wallasey Grammar School; Edinburgh University. Research Fellow, University of Colorado, 1967-68. Vascular Surgical Society, Great Britain and Ireland: President, 1993-94, Secretary/Treasurer; Chairman, Venous Forum, Royal Society of Medicine, 1997-99; Member, Association of Surgeons of Great Britain and Ireland. Recreations: angling; music; tennis; gardening. Address: 3 Blackbarony Road, Edinburgh EH16 5QP.

Rumbles, Michael John, MSc (Econ), BEd. MSP, North East Scotland region (Liberal Democrat), since 2016, West Aberdeenshire and Kincardine, 1999-2011; b. 10.6.56, South Shields; m., Pauline; 2 s. Educ. St James' School, Hebburn; Durham University; University of Wales. Army Officer, 1979-94; Team Leader, Business Management, Aberdeen College, 1995-99. Convener, Standards Committee, Scottish Parliament, 1999-2003; Liberal Democrat Chief Whip and Business Manager, 2008-2011. Address: Scottish Parliament, Edinburgh EH99 1SP.

Rummery, Professor Kirstein, LLB (Hons), MA, PhD. Professor of Social Policy, University of Stirling, since 2007; b. 12.06.70, London; m., Simon Lippmann; 2 s.; 1 d. Educ. Vienna International School; University of Kent; University of Birmingham. Research Fellow in Social Policy, University of Birmingham, 1992-95; Research Fellow, NPCRDC, University of Manchester, 1995-2002, Lecturer in Social Policy, 2002-05, Senior Lecturer, 2005-07. Member, The Social Policy Association Executive Committee; Member of Board of Directors of Engender. Publications: Author of 'Disability, Citizenship and Community Care', 2002; Co-editor, 'Partnerships, New Labour and the Governance of Welfare', 2002; Co-editor, 'Women And New Labour', 2007; Co-editor, Local Policy Review. Recreations: choral singing; cycling; cooking. Address: (b.) Department of Applied Social Sciences, Colin Bell Building, University of Stirling FK9 4LA; T.-01786-467693; e-mail: kirstein.rummery@stir.ac.uk

Rush, Dr. Christopher, MA (Hons). Writer; b. 23.11.44, St. Monans; m., Patricia Irene Boyd (deceased); 1 s.; 1 d.; re-married Anna Kurkina; 1 d. Educ. Waid Academy; Aberdeen University. Former Teacher, George Watson's College, Edinburgh. Has won six Scottish Arts Council bursaries, two SAC book awards, twice been short-listed for Scottish Book of the Year Award; shortlisted for McVitie Scottish Writer of the Year, 1988; Screenwriter, Venus Peter (based on own book). Publications include: Peace Comes Dropping Slow; A Resurrection of a Kind; A Twelvemonth and A Day; Two Christmas Stories; Into the Ebb; With Sharp Compassion; Venus Peter Saves the Whale; Last Lesson of the Afternoon; To Travel Hopefully: Journal of a Death Not Foretold; Hellfire and Herring; Will; Sex, Lies and Shakespeare; Aunt Epp's Guide For Life; New Words in Classic Guise: An Introduction to the Poetry of Felix Dennis; Collected Poems of Alastair Mackie 1954-1994 ed.; Penelope's Web. Recreation: staying alive. Address: (h.) 107 Dalkeith Road, Edinburgh EH16 5AJ; T.-01333 451229; e-mail: confutatisuk@yahoo.co.uk

Ruskell, Mark Christopher, BSc (Hons), MSc. MSP (Scottish Green), Mid Scotland and Fife, since 2016; b. 14.5.72. Educ. University of Stirling; SAC - University of Aberdeen. Career history: LETS Project Development Worker, Falkirk Voluntary Action Resource Centre, 1997-2001; Community Economic Development Officer, Midlothian Council, 2001-02; Policy and Campaigns Consultant, Organic Targets Bill Steering Group, 2000-03; Project Development Worker, Soil Association Scotland, 2002-03; Member of the Scottish Parliament (Mid-Scotland and Fife region), 2003-07; Marine & Coastal Policy Officer, RSPB Scotland, 2007-08; Director of Communications, Scottish Renewables, 2008-2010; Business Development Manager, GreenEnergyNet.com, 2011; Consultant, Realise Renewables, 2011. Address: Scottish Parliament, Edinburgh EH99 1SP.

Russell, Sir (Alastair) Muir, KCB (2001), FRSE, FInstP. Chairing Member, Judicial Appointments Board for Scotland, since 2008; Chairman, Board of Trustees, Royal Botanic Garden Edinburgh, since 2011; Board Member, National Home Building Council, and Chair of Scottish Committee, since 2012; Chairman, Dunedin Concert Trust, since 2009; Trustee, Glasgow School of Art, since 2009; Trustee, Moredun Research Institute, since 2009; b. 9.1.49; m., Eileen Alison Mackay. Educ. High School of Glasgow; Glasgow University (BSc NatPhil). Joined Scottish Office, 1970; seconded as Secretary to Scottish Development Agency, 1975-76; Assistant Secretary, 1981; Principal Private Secretary to Secretary of State for Scotland, 1981-83; Under Secretary, 1990; seconded to Cabinet Office, 1990-92; Under Secretary (Housing), Scottish Office Environment Department, 1992-95; Deputy Secretary, 1995, Secretary and Head of Department, Scottish Office Agriculture, Environment and Fisheries Department, 1995-98; Permanent Under-Secretary of State, Scottish Office, 1998-99; Permanent Secretary, Scottish Executive, 1999-2003; Principal and Vice-Chancellor, University of Glasgow, 2003-09. Non-Executive Director, Stagecoach Holdings, 1992-95. Council Member, Edinburgh Festival Society, 2004-09. Director, UCAS, 2005-09; Convener, Universities Scotland, 2006-08; Board Member, USS, 2007-09. FRSE, 2000; FInstP, 2003; Hon. LLD, Strathclyde, 2000; DUniv, Glasgow, 2001; Dr HC, Edinburgh 2009; Hon FRCPS (Glasg), 2005. Freeman, City of London 2006. Recreations: music; food; wine. Club: New (Edinburgh).
E-mail: muir.russell@btinternet.com

Russell, Sheriff Albert Muir Galloway, CBE, QC, BA (Oxon), LLB. Sheriff, Grampian, Highland and Islands, at Aberdeen, 1971-91; b. 26.10.25, Edinburgh; m., Margaret Winifred Millar; 2 s.; 2 d. Educ. Edinburgh Academy; Wellington College; Brasenose College, Oxford; Edinburgh University. Lt., Scots Guards, 1944-47; Member, Faculty of Advocates, 1951; Standing Junior Counsel to Board of Trade, Department of Agriculture and Forestry

Commission; QC (Scot), 1965; Vice Chairman, Board of Management, Southern Group of Hospitals, Edinburgh, 1966-70; Governor, Moray House College of Education, 1965-70. Recreations: golf; music. Address: (h.) Tulloch House, 1 Aultbea, Ross-shire IV22 2JB.

Russell, Emeritus Professor Elizabeth Mary, CBE, MD, DSc, DipSocMed, DObstRCOG, FFCM, FRCPGlas, FRCPEdin, MRCGP, FRSE. Emeritus Professor of Social Medicine, Aberdeen University; Hon. Consultant in Public Health Medicine, 1972-2001; b. 27.1.36, Preston; m., Roy Weir (2007). Educ. Marr College, Troon; Glasgow University. General practice until 1964; public health management and social medicine, 1964-72; academic public health and health services research, since 1972. Recreations: gardening; music; voluntary work. Address: (b.) Kilburn, Inchgarth Road, Pitfodels, Aberdeen AB15 9NX; T.-01224 861216; e-mail: e.m.russell@abdn.ac.uk

Russell, Professor Ian Gordon, BEd, PhD. Emeritus Professor, since 2014; Director, Elphinstone Institute, Aberdeen University (1999-2014); b. 17.2.47, Aberdeen; m., Norma; 1 s. Educ. King's School, Ely; Nottingham High School; Sheffield City College of Education; Leeds University. Headteacher, Anston Greenlands School, Rotherham, 1986-99; fieldwork in folklore and ethnology, since 1969; broadcast, made films, lectured, in UK and USA; created archive of Village Carols; published widely on traditional singing, humour, and Christmas carols; Director, Village Carols; Director, Festival of Village Carols; Editor, Folk Music Journal, 1980-93; President, North Atlantic Fiddle Convention. Recreations: singing and playing folk music; walking; Morris dancing; travel. Address: (b.) Elphinstone Institute, Aberdeen University, MacRobert Building, King's College, Aberdeen AB24 5UA; T.-01224 272386.

Russell, Rev. John, MA. Minister, Tillicoultry Parish Church, 1978-2000; b. 29.5.33, Glasgow; m., Sheila Spence; 2 s. Educ. Cathedral School, Bombay; High School of Glasgow; Glasgow University. Licensed by Glasgow Presbytery, 1957; ordained by United Church of Canada, 1959; Assistant Minister: Trinity United Church, Kitchener, Ontario, 1958-60, South Dalziel Church, Motherwell, 1960-62; Minister: Scots Church, Rotterdam, 1963-72, Southend Parish Church, Kintyre, 1972-78; Member of various General Assembly Committees, since 1972; Convener, General Assembly's Committee on Unions and Readjustments, 1987-90; Convener, Parish Reappraisal Committee, 1990-94; Vice Convener, Board of National Mission, 1994-95; Convener, Board of National Mission, 1995-96; Moderator, Presbytery of Stirling, 1993-94; Clerk, Presbytery of Northern Europe, 1967-71; Clerk, Presbytery of Dunkeld and Meigle, 2001. Recreations: travel; reading. Address: Kilblaan, Gladstone Terrace, Birnam, Dunkeld PH8 0DP; T.-01350 728896.

Russell, John Graham, FCIT. Chairman: John G. Russell (Transport) Ltd., since 1969, Fife Warehousing Ltd., since 1988, Carntyne Transport Co. Ltd., since 1970; Director: Alloa Warehousing, since 1988, Impact Holdings UK plc, since 2009; b. Edinburgh; m., Isobel Margaret Hogg; 2 s.; 2 d. Educ. Merchiston Castle School, Edinburgh. Address: (b.) Deanside Road, Hillington, Glasgow G52 4XB; T.-0141 810 8200; e-mail: john.russell@johngrussell.co.uk

Russell, Jonathan. Publishing Director (Regionals), Media Scotland, since 2013; former Editor, The Herald (2010-2012); previously Assistant Editor of the Daily Record and Sunday Mail. Began career as a reporter on the Evening Express in Aberdeen and also worked on weekly newspaper, the Inverurie Advertiser; held several senior editorial roles, including Scottish Editor of the Daily Mirror and Editor of the Paisley Daily Express.

Russell, Laurie James, BSc, MPhil. Chief Executive, The Wise Group, since 2006; b. 8.8.51, Glasgow; m., Pam; 2 s. Educ. Glasgow University. Researcher, Planning Department, Strathclyde Regional Council, 1976-78; Area Co-ordinator, Faifley Initiative, Clydebank, 1978-84; Executive, Chief Executive's Department, Strathclyde Regional Council, 1984-87; PA to Chief Executive, Strathclyde Regional Council, 1987-89; Chief Executive, Strathclyde European Partnership, 1989-2006. Recreations: politics; European issues; music; golf. Address: (b.) The Wise Group, 72 Charlotte Street, Glasgow G1 5DW; T.-0141 314 1461.

Russell, Professor Michael, MA, FRSA. MSP (SNP), Argyll and Bute, since 2011, South of Scotland, 2007-2011 (previously 1999-2003); Cabinet Secretary for Education and Lifelong Learning, 2009-2014; Minister for Culture, External Affairs and the Constitution, February-December, 2009; Minister for Environment, 2007-09; Professor of Scottish Culture and Governance, University of Glasgow, since 2015; b. 9.8.53, Bromley; m. Cathleen Macaskill; 1 s. Educ. Marr College, Troon; Edinburgh University. Creative Producer, Church of Scotland, 1974-77; Director: Cinema Sgire, Comhairle Nan Eilean, 1977-81, Celtic Film and TV Festival, 1981-83; Executive Director, Network Scotland Ltd., 1983-91; Director, Eala Bhan Ltd., 1991-2009; Chief Executive, SNP, 1994-99. Active in various voluntary and arts bodies. Publications: author of 7 books, including a novel, 'The Next Big Thing', 2007. Recreations: cooking; tending my Argyll garden. Address: (h.) Feorlean, Glendaruel, Argyll PA22 3AH.
E-mail: Michael.Russell.msp@scottish.parliament.uk

Russell, Professor Ric William Lockerby, OBE, DA, ARSA, ARIBA, FRIAS. Architect, since 1970; Senior Partner, Nicoll Russell Studios, since 1982; b. 12.8.47, Stockton-on-Tees; m., Irene Hill (divorced); 1 s.; 3 d. Educ. Dundee High School; Duncan of Jordanstone College of Art; University of Dundee. Robbie and Wellwood Architects (Partner, 1977); co-founded Nicoll Russell, 1982; architect and designer responsible for major civic buildings and civil engineering structures throughout Britain; has lectured and tutored at many universities throughout career. Commissioner, Royal Fine Arts Commission for Scotland, 1998-2004; Advisory Board Member, Architecture and Design Scotland, 2004-07, Board Member, 2007-2011; Member, Student Awards Committee, Royal Incorporation of Architects in Scotland, 1993-2005; Member, Housing Awards Panel, Saltire Society, 2000-04; has received seven Royal Institute of British Architects awards and five Civic Trust awards. Recreations: drawing; music; DIY. Address: (b.) Nicoll Russell Studios, 111 King Street, Broughty Ferry, Dundee; T.-01382 778966; e-mail: ric.russell@nrsarchitects.com

Russell, Shendl, DCE. President, Scottish Official Board of Highland Dancing; Head Teacher; b. 29.3.56, Ayr; m., Robert D. Harvey. Educ. Ayr Academy; Craigie College. Scottish Official Board of Highland Dancing: Delegate, South Africa, Australia; former Scottish champion. Recreations: dancing; football; rugby. Address: (h.) 3 Greenside Avenue, Prestwick KA9 2HB; T.-01292 478577; e-mail: shendl@btinternet.com

Russell, Professor William Clelland, BSc, PhD, FRSE. Professor of Biochemistry, University of St. Andrews,

1984-95, now Emeritus Research Professor; b. 9.8.30, Glasgow; m. 1, Dorothy Ada Brown (deceased); 2, Margaret McDougall; 1 s.; 1 d. Educ. Allan Glens' School, Glasgow; University of Glasgow. Chemist, Royal Ordnance Factories, 1955-56; Research Chemist, J&P Coats, Paisley, 1956-59; Research Fellow: Virology Unit, University of Glasgow, 1959-63, Ontario Cancer Institute, Toronto, Canada, 1963-64; staff member, latterly Head of Virology Division, MRC at National Institute for Medical Research, London, 1964-84. Member: MRC Grants Committee, SHHD Biomedical Committee; Chair, Scientists for Labour, 1995-2005. Publications: over 140 scientific papers. Recreations: walking; music. Address: (h.) 84 Bow Butts, Crail, Anstruther KY10 3UT; T.-01333 450614; e-mail: wcr@st-andrews.ac.uk

Rust, James Hamilton, LLB, WS, NP. Partner, Morton Fraser LLP, since 1985; b. 22.7.58, Aberdeen; m., Janet Anne Ruddiman; 1 s.; 1 d. Educ. Aberdeen Grammar School; Loretto School; Aberdeen University. Legal Apprentice and Assistant, Esslemont & Cameron, Aberdeen, 1979-82; Legal Assistant, Morton Fraser & Milligan WS, 1982-85; Clerk, Society of Writers to Her Majesty's Signet; Honorary Consul for Portugal in Edinburgh. Recreations: running; theatre; Scottish Country Dancing; outdoor pursuits. Address: (b.) Quartermile Two, 2 Lister Square, Edinburgh EH3 9GL; T.-0131-247-1013; e-mail: james.rust@morton-fraser.com

Rutherford, Henry Roan, PhD, MSc, BArch, RIBA, FRIAS, MRTPI. Director, Wren Rutherford Austin Smith Lord, since 1997; b. 30.11.46, Dunfermline; m., Alison Moira Peebles; 1 s.; 1 d. Educ. Bell Baxter High School, Cupar; Heriot-Watt University; University of Edinburgh; University of Glasgow. Irvine New Town Corporation: Conservation Officer, 1972, Architect, Housing Group, 1974, Principal Architect (Housing), 1978; Partner, Wren Rutherford Architects, 1997. Awarded Joint Best Architect in Scotland, 1996; three Civic Trust Awards; seven Saltire Society Awards; four RIBA Awards Scotland; four RIAS Awards; Scottish Design Award, 2014. Recreations: sailing; hillwalking. Address: (b.) 296 St Vincent Street, Glasgow G2 5RU; T.-0141 223 8500.

Rutter, John, FRGS. Head Teacher, Inverness High School, since 2014. Educ. Newcastle University; Moray House of Edinburgh. Formerly Year Head and Deputy Head, North Berwick High School. Publications: Higher Geography; Mining, Minerals and Metals; Geography for CSEC; AQA Geography B; IGCSE Geography. Address: Montague Row, Inverness, Inverness-Shire IV3 5DZ; T.-01463 233586.

Ryan, Jack, DipComEd. Promoting 'Value Based' Leadership for Young People and Community Leaders. Chief Executive, Columba 1400, since 2015; former Chief Executive, Crossroads Caring Scotland (1997-2014); b. 9.6.61, Hamilton; m., Janine Barbour; 2 s. Educ. Hamilton Grammar School; Moray House, Edinburgh. Draughtsman, 1978-81; professional musician, 1981-83; Community Musician, Strathclyde Regional Council, 1983-88; Senior Development Officer, Govan Initiative Ltd., 1990-91; Project Manager, CAVOC Motherwell, 1991-92; Director, Govan Community Organisations Council, 1992-96; Lottery Officer, South Lanarkshire Council, 1997. President, Hamilton Rugby Football Club. Recreations: musician; computer programming; running/swimming; youth rugby coach. Address: (b.) Columba 1400, Staffin, Isle of Skye IV51 9JY.

Ryan, Professor Kevin Martin, BSc (Hons), PhD, FSB. Professor, Faculty of Medicine, University of Glasgow, since 2007; Senior Group Leader, Beatson Institute for Cancer Research, Glasgow, since 2007; b. 14.06.70, Stoke-on-Trent; m., Justine Nicola Parrott; 2 s. Educ. Biddulph High School, Staffordshire; University of Liverpool;

University of Glasgow. Pre-Doctoral Fellow, Beatson Institute for Cancer Research, 1995-96; Post-Doctoral Fellow, United States National Cancer Institute, Maryland, USA, 1996-2001; Group Leader and Head, Tumour Cell Death Laboratory, Beatson Institute for Cancer Research, 2001-07. Fellowships and Awards: Cancer Research UK Senior Fellow, 2002-08; European Association for Cancer Research - Certificate of Merit, 2002; Elected Fellow of The Institute of Biology (FIBiol), 2009; Conferred Fellow of The Society of Biology (FSB), 2009; Recipient of the 2010 European Association for Cancer Research 'Cancer Researcher Award'. Awarded the 2012 Tenovus Medal. Recreations: swimming; hill-walking and travel. Address: (b.) Beatson Institute for Cancer Research, Garscube Estate, Switchback Road, Glasgow G61 1BD; T.-0141 330 3655.

Ryder, Jane, MA, WS, FSA Scot. Consultant; Chair, Historic Environment Scotland, since 2015; Board member, Revenue Scotland, since 2015; Deputy Chair, Seafish Industry Authority, 2012-15; Chair, Arts & Business Scotland, 2011-15; Chief Executive, Office of the Scottish Charity Regulator (OSCR), 2006-2011. Educ. St Andrews University. Qualified as a solicitor in both England and Scotland and for 11 years was a partner in a commercial firm in Edinburgh; became Director of the Scottish Museums Council, 1995; appointed by Scottish Ministers in 2003 to establish the Office of the Scottish Charity Regulator (OSCR). Author of various articles and the textbook Professional Conduct for Scottish Solicitors. Appointed by English Ministers as Non Executive Director of Marine Management Organisation (2010). Formerly Chair, Scottish Refugee Council; formerly Vice Chair, Stevenson College of Further Education.
E-mail: jane@janeryder.co.uk

S

Salmond, Alexander Elliot Anderson, MA (Hons). Economist; MP (SNP), Gordon, since 2015, MSP Aberdeenshire East, 2011-16, Gordon, 2007-2011; First Minister of Scotland, 2007-2014; MP, Banff and Buchan, 1987-2010; Leader, Scottish National Party, 1990-2000 and 2004-2014; MSP, Banff and Buchan, 1999-2001; SNP International Affairs and Europe spokesperson in the House of Commons, since 2015; b. 31.12.54, Linlithgow; m., Moira McGlashan. Educ. Linlithgow Academy; St. Andrews University. Vice-President: Federation of Student Nationalists, 1974-77, St. Andrews University SRC, 1977-78; Founder Member, SNP 79 Group, 1979; Assistant Agricultural and Fisheries Economist, DAFS, 1978-80; Economist, Royal Bank of Scotland, 1980-87. Hon. Vice-President, Scottish Centre for Economic and Social Research; former Member, Select Committee on Energy. Address: (b.) 84 North Street, Inverurie, Aberdeenshire AB51 4QX; T.-01467 670070; House of Commons, London SW1A 0AA.

Salter, Professor Donald McGovern, BSc, MBChB, MD, FRCPath, FRCP (Edin). Professor of Osteoarticular Pathology, University of Edinburgh, since 2005; Consultant Histopathologist, Lothian University Hospital Trust; b. 28.02.57, Edinburgh; m., Marleen; 2 s.; 1 d. Educ. Ross High School, Tranent; University of Edinburgh. Lecturer, Pathology, University of Edinburgh, then Senior Lecturer, then Reader. Recreations: golf; gardening; dodging. Address: (b.) Molecular Medicine Centre, Western General Hospital, Crewe Road, Edinburgh.
E-mail: donald.salter@ed.ac.uk

Saltoun, Lady (Flora Marjory). Elected Member, House of Lords, 1999-2014; Chief of the Name of Fraser, since 1979; b. 18.10.30, Edinburgh; 3 d. Educ. St. Mary's School, Wantage.

Salvesen, Alastair Eric Hotson, CBE, MBA, CA, HRSA, FCIM, FCMI, FRSA, FSAS, FRAgS, FRIAS. Chairman, Dawnfresh Seafoods Ltd., since 1983 (Managing Director, 1981-93); Chairman, Edinburgh New Town Cookery School, since 2009; b. 28.7.41; m., Elizabeth Evelyn; 1 s.; 1 d. Educ. Fettes; Cranfield. Chairman: Starfish Ltd., since 1986, Mull of Kintyre Seafoods, since 1988, Silvertrout Ltd, 2004, Dovecot Studios Ltd., since 2001; Director: Archangels Investment Ltd, Praha Investment Holdings Ltd., since 1985, Richmond Foods plc, 1994-2003, New Ingliston Ltd., since 1995, Luing Cattle Society, 1966-99; President, Royal Highland and Agricultural Society of Scotland, 2001-02; Member, Council, Shellfish Association of GB, since 2003; Governor: Fettes College Trust, since 1994 (Deputy Chairman, since 2010), Donaldson Trust, 1997-2009, Compass School, 1994-2009 (Chairman, 1996-2009); Member, Queen's Bodyguard for Scotland (The Royal Company of Archers); Liveryman, Worshipful Company of Fishmongers. Recreations: shooting; archery; farming; forestry; contemporary Scottish art. Address: Whitburgh, Pathhead, Midlothian EH37 5SR; T.-01875 320304; (b.) Dawnfresh Seafoods Ltd., Bothwell Park Industrial Estate, Uddingston, Lanarkshire G71 6LS; T.-01698 810008.

Salvesen, Robin Somervell, FBIM, DL, Chevalier de Dannebrog 1st Class; b. 4.5.35, Edinburgh; m., Sari; 3 s.; 4 d. Educ. Fettes College; Oxford University. The Royal Scots, Queen's Own Nigeria Regiment; TA, 7/9 Bn., The Royal Scots, 8/9 Bn., The Royal Scots 52 Lowland Volunteers; retired Major; Director, shipping companies, A.F. Henry & Macgregor, Christian Salvesen plc; Lloyds Register of Shipping, 1974-87; Chamber of Shipping, 1974-88; British Shipowners Association, 1984-99; Member, Lights Advisory Committee, 1987-2003; Member, East Lothian Council, 1965-68; Royal Danish Consul, 1972-87; Vice Convenor, Daniel Stewarts and Melville College, 1978-80; Governor, Fettes College, 1975-85; Chairman, Leith Nautical College, 1979-88; former Chairman, Association for the Protection of Rural Scotland; President, Edinburgh Area Scouts, 1991-2008; Member, Merchant Company of the City of Edinburgh (Assistant, 1977-80); Elder, Church of Scotland, St Mary's, Haddington; President, South East Region Scotland Scouts, 2008-2015 (retired). Recreation: shooting. Address: Eaglescairnie House, Haddington EH41 4HN.

Sanders, John, BA (Hons), DipCons. Architectural Conservator, since 1988; Simpson & Brown Architects, Edinburgh, since 1989; Buildings Conservation Partner, since 2000; b. 9.3.61; m., Susan. Educ. Central School of Art, London; Heriot Watt University. Assistant on Conservation Projects, Charlewood Curry Partnership, Newcastle-upon-Tyne, 1985-87. Interests in 19th Century Church Architecture. Address: (b.) St. Ninian's Manse, Quayside Street, Edinburgh EH6 6EJ; T.-0131 555 4678; e-mail: jsanders@simpsonandbrown.co.uk

Sanderson of Bowden, Lord (Charles Russell Sanderson), KB, DL. Life Peer; Chairman, Scottish Mortgage and Trust, 1993-2003; Chairman, Hawick Cashmere Co., 1991-2013, Director, since 2013; Chairman, Clydesdale Bank, 1999-2004; President, Royal Highland Agricultural Society, 2002-03; Vice Lord Lieutenant, Roxburgh and Selkirk, 2003-08; Director, Develica Deutschland plc, 2006-08; Director, Accsys plc, 2007-2013; b. 30.4.33, Melrose; m., Frances Elizabeth Macaulay; 1 s.; 1 s. deceased; 2 d. Educ. St. Mary's School, Melrose; Glenalmond College; Bradford University; Scottish College of Textiles. Commissioned, Royal Signals; Partner, Charles P. Sanderson, 1958-87; former Director, Johnston of Elgin, Illingworth Morris, Edinburgh Woollen Mills; former Chairman, Shires Investment PLC, Edinburgh Financial Trust, Scottish Pride Holdings; President, Scottish Conservative and Unionist Association, 1977-79; Chairman, National Union of Conservative and Unionist Associations Executive Committee, 1981-86; Minister of State, Scottish Office, 1987-90; Chairman, Scottish Conservative Party, 1990-93; Chairman, Scottish Peers Association, 1998-2000; Director: United Auctions Ltd., 1993-99, Watson and Philip PLC, 1993-99, Morrison Construction PLC, 1995-2001; Member, Board, Yorkshire Bank and National Australia Bank Europe, 1999-2004; Chairman, Eildon Housing Association, 1976-83; Member, Court, Napier University, 1994-2001; Chairman, Glenalmond Council, 1994-2000; Chairman, St Mary's School, Melrose, 1998-2004; Member, Court, Frameworker Knitters Company, since 2000; Under Warden, 2003-04; Upper Warden, since 2004; Master, 2005-06; Chairman, The Abbotsford Trust, 2008-2015, Board Member, since 2015; DL. Recreations: golf; amateur dramatics; photography; fishing. Address: (h.) Becketts Field, Bowden, Melrose, Roxburgh, TD6 0ST.

Sanderson, William. Farmer; Honorary Treasurer, Royal Highland and Agricultural Society of Scotland, 2005-09, Honorary Vice President, 2009-2010, Chairman, 2002-04; Vice President, Dalkeith Agricultural Society; b. 9.3.38, Lanark; m., Netta; 4 d. Educ. Dalkeith High School. Past Chairman, South Midlothian and Lothians and Peeblesshire Young Farmers Clubs; Past Chairman, Dalkeith Agricultural Society; President, Royal Caledonian Curling

Club, 1984-85; Honorary Life Member, Oxenfoord and Edinburgh Curling Clubs; Past President, Oxenfoord and Edinburgh Curling Clubs; Scottish Curling Champion, 1971 and 1978 (2nd, World Championship, 1971). Recreations: curling; exhibiting livestock. Address: (h.) Blackshiels Farm, Blackshiels, Pathhead, Midlothian; T.-01875 833288.

Sandison, Bruce Macgregor. Writer and Journalist; b. 26.9.38, Edinburgh; m., Dorothy Ann Rhodes; 2 s.; 2 d. Educ. Royal High School, Edinburgh. Commissioned into Royal Army Service Corps, 1956-60; sometime poultry farmer and agricultural contractor; full-time writing, since 1981; Columnist (environment, game fishing, hill-walking), The Herald, The Scotsman; contributor, Tales of the Loch, Sporting Gentleman's Gentleman (series), Radio Scotland, Radio 4, Landward, BBC TV; Founding Chairman, The Salmon Farm Protest Group, 2002. Publications: The Trout Lochs of Scotland; The Sporting Gentleman's Gentleman; Game Fishing in Scotland; The Hillwalker's Guide to Scotland; The Heather Isles; Tales of the Loch; Long Walks with Little People; Trout and Salmon Rivers and Lochs of Scotland; Walk Scotland; Angling Lines; Rivers and Lochs of Scotland; Lies, Damned Lies and Anglers; Sandison's Scotland; Gracious Gentlemen; Secret Lochs and Special Places. Recreations: hill-walking; game fishing; photography; swimming; music; reading; chess; bridge. Address: Hysbackie, Tongue, by Lairg, IV27 4XJ; T.-01847 55 274; e-mail: bsandison@btinternet.com

Sannella, Professor Donald Theodore, BS, MS, PhD, FRSE. Professor of Computer Science, Edinburgh University, since 1998; b. 7.12.56, Boston USA; m., Monika-Jeannette Lekuse; 1 s.; 1 d. Educ. Yale University; University of California at Berkeley; Edinburgh University. Editor-in-Chief, Theoretical Computer Science, since 2000; Director, Contemplate Ltd, since 2009. Address: (b.) Laboratory for Foundations of Computer Science, School of Informatics, Edinburgh University, EH8 9AB; T.-0131-650 5184; e-mail: dts@inf.ed.ac.uk

Sargent, Professor Frank, BSc, PhD. Professor of Bacterial Physiology, University of Dundee, since 2007; b. 4.7.70, Kirkcaldy; m., Tracy Palmer; 2 s. Educ. Auchmuty High School, Glenrothes, Fife; University of Edinburgh; University of Dundee. Postdoctoral researcher: John Innes Centre, Norwich, 1996-98, University of East Anglia, Norwich, 1998-2000; Royal Society University Research Fellow, University of East Anglia, Norwich, 2000-07. The Wain Medal, 2010; The FEBS Young Group Leader Award, 2009; The Colworth Medal, 2007; The Fleming Prize, 2006. Address: (b.) Division of Molecular Microbiology, College of Life Sciences, University of Dundee, Dundee DD1 5EH; T.-01382 386463; e-mail: f.sargent@dundee.ac.uk

Sarwar, Anas. MSP (Labour), Glasgow region, since 2016; MP (Labour), Glasgow Central, 2010-2015; Shadow Minister of State for International Development, 2014-15; Deputy Leader, Scottish Labour Party, 2011-14; b. 14.3.83; m., Furheen; 1 s. Educ. Hutchesons' Grammar School; Glasgow University. Formerly NHS General Dental Practitioner. Former Member of Select Committees on: International Development, Arms Export Controls; former Vice-chair, PLP Departmental Group for International Development; Member, Labour Party, since 1999. Awards: The Sun's "Best New Politician" award, 2009; Politician of the Year award at the British Muslim Awards, 2014; Spirit of Britain award, British Muslum Awards, 2015. Address: Scottish Parliament, Edinburgh EH99 1SP.

Satsangi, Jack (Jyoti), BSc, MBBS, DPhil, FRCP (Edin), FRCP (UK), FMedSci, FRSE. Professor of Gastroenterology, University of Edinburgh, since 2000; Consultant Physician, Western General Hospital, Edinburgh, since 2000; b. 8.5.63, Batley. Educ. Brentwood

School, Essex; St. Thomas's Hospital, London; Worcester College, University of Oxford. University of Oxford: MRC Training Fellow, 1992-96, MRC Clinician Scientist, 1997-2000; Honorary Consultant Physician, John Radcliffe Hospital, Oxford, 1999-2000. Member, Committee, Medical Research Society; Association of Physicians of Great Britain and Ireland. Recreations: tennis; running; saxophone. Address: (b.) Gastrointestinal Unit, Molecular Medicine Centre, Western General Hospital, Edinburgh EH4 2XU; T.-0131 651 1807; e-mail: j.satsangi@ed.ac.uk

Saunders, Professor Alison Marilyn, BA, PhD. Emeritus Professor of French, Aberdeen University; b. 23.12.44, Darlington. Educ. Wimbledon High School GPDST; Durham University. Lectrice, the Sorbonne, 1968-69; Lecturer in French, Aberdeen University, 1970-85; Senior Lecturer in French, 1985-90. Recreations: swimming; gardening; DIY; cooking; antiquarian book-collecting; endurance riding. Address: (h.) 75 Dunbar Street, Old Aberdeen, Aberdeen AB24 3UA; T.-01224 494806.

Saunders, Donald Goodbrand. Poet and Writer, since 1968; b. 16.7.49, Glasgow; m., Anne; 1 s. Educ. McLaren High School, Callander. Writer, mainly of poetry, for 40 years; published four books, as well as contributing to various Scottish and UK periodicals and anthologies; has received three Scottish Arts Council writers' bursaries. Publications include: The Glasgow Diary, 1984; Findrinny, 1990; Sour Gas and Crude, 1999; Libretto of "Knotgrass Elegy", 2001 and book and lyrics of musical "Shenachie", 2006. Address: (h.) 17 Jellicoe Avenue, Gartmore, FK8 3RQ; T.-01877 389 074; e-mail: dongosa@hotmail.co.uk

Saunders, Professor William Philip, BDS, DSc (hc), PhD, FDSRCS(Edin), FDSRCPS(Glas), FDSRCS(Eng), MRD, FHEA, FHKCDS. Emeritus Professor, University of Dundee (Professor of Endodontology, 2000-2013); Dean of Dentistry, 2000-2011; Consultant in Restorative Dentistry, 1988-2013; b. 12.10.48, Carlisle; m., Jennifer Anne; 1 s.; 1 d. Educ. Maidstone Grammar School; Royal Dental Hospital of London. Dental Officer, RAF, 1970-75; general dental practice, 1975-81; Lecturer, Department of Conservative Dentistry, Dundee University, 1981-88; Senior Lecturer in Clinical Practice, Glasgow Dental Hospital and School, 1988-93; Professor in Clinical Dental Practice, Glasgow University, 1993-95, Professor of Endodontology, 1995-2000. Postgraduate Dental Hospital Tutor, Glasgow Dental Hospital, 1992-95; Editor, International Endodontic Journal, 1992-98; President, British Endodontic Society, 1997-98; Chairman, Association of Consultants and Specialists in Restorative Dentistry, 1999-2002; Dental Council, Royal College of Surgeons of Edinburgh, 2000-09 and since 2011, Dean, Dental Faculty, since 2014; Chairman, Speciality Advisory Board in Restorative Dentistry RCSEd, 2006-2012; President, European Society of Endodontology, 2009; Chair, Dental Schools Council, UK, 2008-2011; Recipient, Inaugural Scottish Dental Lifetime Achievement Award, 2012. Publications: papers and chapters in books on endodontology and applied dental materials science. Clubs: Royal Air Force, New (Edinburgh). Recreations: ornithology; natural history; Scottish art; golf. Address: (h.) 139 Glasgow Road, Perth PH2 0LU.

Savege, Jim, BA, PhD. Chief Executive, Aberdeenshire Council, since 2015. Educ. St. Columba's College; Liverpool Polytechnic; University of Sheffield. Director, @Ichemy, 1996-2000; Director & Senior Consultant, International Consulting Group Ltd, 2000-02; HR Shared Service Project Leader, Staffordshire County Council, 2002-03; HR Director, Staffordshire County Council, 2004-

07; Cumbria County Council: Corporate Director, Human Resources, 2007-08, Corporate Director, Organisational Development, 2008-2012, Corporate Director, Environment, 2012-13, Corporate Director, Environment and Community Services, 2013-15. Publications: Proposed Development of Otterburn Military Training Area in Northumberland National Park: A National Perspective, Journal of Environmental Planning and Management, 1995; The future for the defence estate - Changing demands for army training, Brassey's for the Centre for Defence Studies, 1995; Soldiers, Stone Curlews, and SSSI's: Maintaining the Balance, ECOS 18, 68-74, 1997. Address: Woodhill House, Westburn Road, Aberdeen AB16 5GB; T.-08456 081207.

Savidge, Malcolm Kemp, MA (Hons), FRGU. Former UK Vice-President, United Nations Association; MP (Labour), Aberdeen North, 1997-2005; b. 9.5.46, Redhill. Educ. Wallington County Grammar School, Surrey; University of Aberdeen; Aberdeen College of Education. Production/Stock Control and Computer Assistant, Bryans' Electronics Ltd., 1970-71; Mathematics Teacher, Greenwood Dale Secondary School, Nottingham, 1971; Mathematics and Religious and Social Education Teacher, Peterhead Academy, 1972-73; Mathematics Teacher, Kincorth Academy, Aberdeen, 1973-97. Member, Aberdeen City Council, 1980-96: Vice-Chair, Labour Group, 1980-88, Finance Convener, Policy Vice-Convener, Deputy Leader, 1994-96; Governor, Robert Gordon's Institute of Technology, 1980-88; Governor, Aberdeen College of Education, 1980-87; JP, 1984-96; Fellow, Robert Gordon University, 1997. Recreations: exploring life; puzzles; reading; real ale; spectator sport.

Savill, Professor Sir John Stewart, BA, MBChB, PhD, FRCP, FRCPE, FRCSEd (Hon), FASN, FMedSci, FRSE, FRS. Vice Principal and Head, College of Medicine and Veterinary Medicine, University of Edinburgh, since 2002; Chief Executive, Medical Research Council, since 2010; b. 25.4.57, London; m., Barbara; 2 s. Educ. Thames Valley Grammar School; University of Oxford; University of Sheffield. House Surgeon, House Physician and House Officer, Sheffield, 1981-83; Senior House Officer, General Medicine, University Hospital, Nottingham, 1983-84; Rotating Registrar in Renal and General Medicine, Ealing and Hammersmith, 1984-86; MRC Training Fellow and Honorary Senior Registrar, Royal Postgraduate Medical School, 1986-89; Senior Registrar, Renal and General Medicine, Hammersmith Hospital, 1989-90; Wellcome Trust Senior Research Fellow in Clinical Science, and Senior Lecturer, University of London, 1990-93; Professor in Medicine, Head, Division of Renal and Inflammatory Disease, University of Nottingham and Honorary Consultant Physician, University Hospital, Nottingham, 1993-98; Professor of Medicine, 1998-2006, Professor of Experimental Medicine, since 2006 and former Director, MRC/University of Edinburgh Centre for Inflammation Research, 1998-2002, University of Edinburgh; Honorary Consultant Physician, Royal Infirmary of Edinburgh, 1998-2010. Part-time Chief Scientist for the Scottish Government Health Directorates, 2008-2010; Governor, Health Foundation, 2001-2010. Recreations: hockey; rugby; cricket; football; literature. Address: University of Edinburgh, Queen's Medical Research Institute, 47 Little France Crescent, Edinburgh EH16 4TJ; T.-0131 242 9313; e-mail: head.cmvm@ed.ac.uk

Saville, Alan, BA, FSA, MCIfA, FSA Scot. Archaeologist; Senior Curator, National Museums Scotland, 1989-2015; President, Society of Antiquaries of Scotland, 2011-14; Editor, European Journal of Archaeology, 2004-10; President, Bristol and Gloucestershire Archaeological Society, 2009-10; Vice-President, Society of Antiquaries of Scotland, 2003-06; b. 31.12.46, London; m., Annette Carruthers. Educ. Colfe's Grammar School, London; Birmingham University. Archaeological Research Assistant, Department of the Environment, London, 1972-74; Archaeologist, Cheltenham Art Gallery and Museum, 1974-76; Field Officer, Western Archaeological Trust, Bristol, 1976-85; Archaeological Consultant, Cheltenham, 1985-89; President, Council for Scottish Archaeology, 2001-03; Member, Ancient Monuments Board for Scotland, 2001-03. Treasurer, Society of Antiquaries of Scotland, 1992-2000; Chairman, The Lithic Studies Society, 1983-90; Conservation Co-ordinator, The Prehistoric Society, 1989-93; Joint Editor, Transactions of the Bristol and Gloucestershire Archaeological Society, 1983-89. Recent publication: Flint and Stone in the Neolithic Period (editor), 2011. Recreations: book collecting; cinema; listening to blues & soul. Address: 25/5 Warrender Park Road, Edinburgh EH9 1HJ; T.-0131 229 8379.

Sawers, Professor Lesley, MA, PhD. Honorary Professor, Glasgow Caledonian University; formerly Vice Principal and Pro Vice Chancellor, Business and Innovation, Glasgow Caledonian University (2013-2015); Chief Executive, Scottish Council for Development and Industry, 2008-2013. Educ. Glasgow University; Stirling University. Previously held a number of senior posts in the public and private sectors; joined SCDI from Glasgow Chamber of Commerce, where she was Chief Executive; formerly Strategic Communications Advisor to the Board of VisitScotland; formerly Royal Mail Group Director of Scottish Affairs and Chairman of the Royal Mail Group Advisory Board (Scotland); nine years at ScottishPower in a number of senior management roles, and has worked in strategic management consultancy in both London, Europe and North America. Currently holds a number of external directorships, including Non Executive Director, Glasgow City Marketing Bureau, Non Executive, Scottish Environmental Protection Agency; Trustee, Glasgow Life; Trustee, Commonwealth Youth Trust; Ambassador for Edinburgh Royal Military Tattoo; Member of Secretary of State's Business Board. Awarded an Honorary Doctorate from Strathclyde Business School in 2009 and Glasgow Caledonian University in 2012. Address: (b.) Cowcaddens Road, Glasgow G4 0BA; T.-0141 331 8728.

Sawkins, Professor John William, MA (Hons), MSc (Econ), PhD, FHEA. Deputy Principal (Learning and Teaching) and Professor of Economics, Heriot-Watt University; b. 27.10.65, Croydon; m., Morag Easson; 2 s. Educ. Wolfreton School; Edinburgh University; Glasgow University. Lecturer, Department of Economics, University of Aberdeen, 1992-95, Heriot-Watt University, 1995-2001; Senior Lecturer, Heriot-Watt University, 2001-05, Reader, 2005-08, Professor, since 2008, Dean of The University (Arts, Humanities and Social Sciences), 2007-2012, Head of Accountancy, Economics and Finance, 2009-2012, Deputy Principal (Learning and Teaching) since 2012. Member, South East Scotland Water Customer Consultation Panel (Waterwatch Scotland), 2003-2011; Board Member, Consumer Focus Scotland, 2008-2013. Recreations: gardening; music. Address: (b.) George Heriot Wing, Heriot-Watt University, Edinburgh EH14 4AS; T.-0131 4513611; e-mail: j.w.sawkins@hw.ac.uk

Scally, Dr John, BA (Hons). Chief Executive, The National Library of Scotland, since 2014. Educ. University of Strathclyde; University of Cambridge; Aberystwyth University. Curator in the British Antiquarian Division, National Library of Scotland, 1993-2002, Deputy Head of Rare Books, 2002-03; Director of University Collections, University of Edinburgh, 2003-2012, Director of Library & University Collections, 2012-14. Address: National Library of Scotland, George IV Bridge, Edinburgh EH1 1EW; T.-0131 623 3700.

Scanlon, Mary. MSP (Conservative), Highlands and Islands region, 1999-2006 and 2007-2016; former Scottish Conservative and Unionist Party's spokesperson for Education and Lifelong Learning; b. 25.5.47, Dundee.

Schaper, Professor Joachim Ludwig Wilhelm, PhD (Cantab), Habilitation (Tübingen). Professor and Chair in Hebrew, Old Testament and Early Jewish Studies, University of Aberdeen, since 2006, Director of Research, since 2011; b. 19.03.65, Hanover, Germany; m., Dr. Marie-Luise Ehrenschwendtner; 1 d. Educ. Schiller Schule (Hanover, Germany); Universität Tübingen; University of Cambridge, Trinity College. PhD Cambridge, 1993; Habilitation Tübingen, 1999; Universität Tübingen, 1999-2005; Heisenberg-Fellow of The Deutsche Forschungsgemeinschaft, 2002-05; Reader in Old Testament, University of Aberdeen, 2005-06. Recreations: books; travel. Address: (b.) University of Aberdeen, School of Divinity, History and Philosophy, Aberdeen AB24 3UB; T.-01224-272840.
E-mail: j.schaper@abdn.ac.uk

Schlesinger, Professor Philip Ronald, BA, PhD, DrHC, DrHC, FRSE, FRSA, FAcSS. Professor in Cultural Policy, University of Glasgow, since 2007; Deputy Director, CREATe, RCUK Centre for Copyright and New Business Models in the Creative Economy, since 2012; b. 31.8.48, Manchester; m., Sharon Joy Rose; 2 d. Educ. North Manchester Grammar School; Queen's College, Oxford; London School of Economics. University of Greenwich: Lecturer, 1974, Senior Lecturer, 1977, Principal Lecturer, 1981; Head, Division of Sociology, 1981-88, Professor of Sociology, 1987-89; Professor of Film and Media Studies, University of Stirling, 1989-2006; Social Science Research Fellow, Nuffield Foundation, 1982-83; Jean Monnet Fellow, European University Institute, Florence, 1985-86; British-Hispanic Chair of Doctoral Studies, Complutense University of Madrid, 2000-01; Chair, Research Assessment Panel for Communication, Cultural and Media Studies, 1995-96 and 1999-2001; Visiting Professor of Media and Communication, University of Oslo, 1993-2004; Visiting Fellow, Maison des Sciences de l'Homme, Paris, 2002, 2005; Visiting Professor: University of Lugano, 2006-07, Institut d'Études Politiques, Toulouse, 2009, CELSA, Université de Paris-Sorbonne (Paris IV) 2010, London School of Economics, 2010-13 (reappointed from 2013-16), LUISS University, Rome, 2011; Visiting Chair of Communication, University of Salamanca, 2012; Co-Editor, Media, Culture and Society, since 1982; Media Adviser, Know How Fund, 1994-98; Board Member, Scottish Screen, 1997-2004; Board Member, TRC Media, Glasgow, 1998-2008; Member, Film Education Working Group reporting to Department of Culture, Media and Sport, 1998-99; Member, Scottish Advisory Committee of Ofcom, since 2004, Chairman, 2009-2014; Member, Ofcom Content Board, since 2014; Expert Adviser on broadcasting, Scotland Bill Committee, Scottish Parliament, 2012. Publications: Putting "Reality" Together, 1978, 1987; Televising "Terrorism", 1983; Communicating Politics, 1986; Media, Culture and Society, 1986; Los Intelectuales en la Sociedad de la Informacion, 1987; Media, State and Nation, 1991; Women Viewing Violence, 1992; Culture and Power, 1992; Reporting Crime, 1994; European Transformations, 1994; International Media Research, 1997; European Communication Council Report, 1997; Men Viewing Violence, 1998; Consenting Adults?, 2000; Open Scotland?, 2001; Mediated Access, 2003; The SAGE Handbook of Media Research, 2004; The European Union and the Public Sphere, 2007; Curators of Cultural Enterprise, 2015; The Rise and Fall of the UK Film Council, 2015. Recreations: the arts; walking; travel. Address: Centre for Cultural Policy Research, University of Glasgow, Glasgow G12 8QQ; T.-0141 330 5036; e-mail: philip.schlesinger@glasgow.ac.uk

Schlicke, Paul Van Waters, BA, PhD. Honorary Senior Lecturer in English, University of Aberdeen, since 2010, Director of Undergraduate Programmes, 2005-08; b. 21.04.43, Charleston, South Carolina, USA; m., Judith Ross Napier; 2 s.; 1 d. Educ. Gonzaga Preparatory School, Spokane, Washington, USA; Stanford University; University of California, San Diego. Lecturer in English, University of Aberdeen, 1971-89. President: Dickens Society of America, 1994, International Dickens Fellowship, 2003-05; Chairman, Board of Trustees, Charles Dickens Museum, 2005-09. Recreation: road running. Address: (b.) School of Language and Literature, University of Aberdeen, Aberdeen AB24 3UB; T.-01467 643337.
E-mail: p.schlicke@abdn.ac.uk

Schofield, Rev. Melville Frederick, MA. Former Chaplain to Western General and Associated Hospitals, Edinburgh, (retired); b. 3.10.35, Glasgow; m., Christina Skirving Crookston. Educ. Irvine Royal Academy; Dalkeith High School; Edinburgh University and New College. Ordained Assistant, Bathgate High, 1960-61; Minister, Canal Street, Paisley, 1961-67; Minister, Laigh Kirk, Kilmarnock, 1967-88. Former Moderator, Presbytery of Irvine and Kilmarnock; former Moderator, Synod of Ayr; radio and TV broadcaster; Past President, No. 0 Kilmarnock Burns Club. Recreations: international Burns engagements; golf; after-dinner speaking. Address: (h.) 25 Rowantree Grove, Currie, Midlothian, EH14 5AT; T.-0131-449 4745; e-mail: afterate@hotmail.com

Scobie, William Galbraith, MB, ChB, FRCSEdin, FRCSGlas. Former Consultant Paediatric Surgeon, Lothian Health Board, now retired; part-time Senior Lecturer, Department of Clinical Surgery, Edinburgh University, 1971-92; Assistant Director, Edinburgh Postgraduate Board for Medicine, 1986-92; b. 13.10.36, Maybole; m., Elizabeth Caldwell Steel; 1 s.; 1 d. Educ. Carrick Academy, Maybole; Glasgow University. Registrar, General Surgery, Kilmarnock Infirmary; Senior Registrar, Royal Hospital for Sick Children, Glasgow; Senior Registrar, Hospital for Sick Children, London; Senior Paediatric Surgeon, Abu Dhabi, 1980-81. Recreations: fishing; golf; gardening; music. Address: (h.) 133 Caiyside, Fairmilehead, Edinburgh EH10 7HR; T.-0131-445 7404.

Scothorne, Richard Mark, MA, MPhil. Director, Rocket Science UK Ltd.; b. 17.7.53, Glasgow; m., Dr. Sarah Gledhill; 1 s.; 1 d. Educ. Royal Grammar School, Newcastle upon Tyne; St. Catharine's College, Cambridge; Edinburgh University. Various posts in local government, 1977-86; Scottish Director, British Shipbuilders Enterprise Ltd., 1986-87; Economic Development Manager (Depute Director of Planning), Lothian Regional Council, 1987-92; Director, Partners in Economic Development Ltd., 1992-99; Director, Workforce One Ltd., 1999-2001. Specialist Adviser to House of Commons Select Committee on Education and Employment, 1997-2000; Council Member, The Cockburn Association, since 2014. Publication: The Vital Economy: integrating training and enterprise (Co-author), 1990. Recreations: hill-walking; mountain biking; Scottish art and architecture. Address: (b.) Rocket Science, 2 Melville Street, Edinburgh EH3 7NS; T.-0131 226 9292.

Scott, Alastair, BA. Travel writer and author, freelance photographer, broadcaster and Yachtmaster Ocean skipper; b. 19.3.54, Edinburgh; m., Sheena. Educ. Blairmore; Sedbergh; Stirling University. Travelled around the world, 1978-83; wrote three travel books, 1984-87 – Scot Free, A Scot Goes South, A Scot Returns; cycled 5,000 miles in E. Europe, 1987-88; wrote Tracks Across Alaska (800-mile sled dog journey), 1988-90; travelled Scotland, 1993-94, wrote Native Stranger; presented BBC film version of

Native Stranger, 1995; worked on fiction, took up sailing, 1996-2007; solo voyages round Ireland, Faroes & Shetland and became yacht charter skipper. Publications: first novel, Stuffed Lives, published 2004; Salt and Emerald - A Hesitant Solo Voyage Round Ireland, 2008; Eccentric Wealth - The Bulloughs of Rum, 2011. Now working on a children's novel. Recreations: reading; running; sailing; playing concertina. Address: Mill of Kincraigie, Coull, Tarland, Aberdeenshire AB34 4TT; e-mail: frog@alastair-scott.com; web: www.alastair-scott.com

Scott, Professor Alexander, MA, MSc, PhD. Professorial Fellow, Heriot-Watt University, since 1989; b. 7.3.45, Lerwick; m., Anne Elliot; 3 d. Educ. Anderson Educational Institute; Boroughmuir Secondary; Edinburgh University. Research Assistant, Edinburgh University, 1967-70; Research Fellow, Heriot-Watt University, 1970-89; Director, The Polecon Co., 1972-89; External Examiner, CNAA, 1981-85; Member, Joint Working Party on Economics, Scottish Examination Board, 1989-90; Chairman, Southfield Housing Society, 1977-80; Executive Director, Edinburgh Business School, since 1997; Trustee, Edinburgh Quartet, 2000-06; President, Edinburgh Breakfast Rotary Club, 2008-09; External Examiner, Durham University DBA Programme, since 2011. Publications: four books and numerous papers. Recreations: hill-walking; classical guitar; woodworking. Address: (b.) Edinburgh Business School, Heriot-Watt University, Edinburgh; T.-0131-451 3090.

Scott, Andrew. Director of Population Health Improvement, Scottish Government. Address: (b.) St Andrew's House, Regent Road, Edinburgh EH1 3DG.

Scott, Professor Andrew George, BA. Professor of European Union Studies, University of Edinburgh, since 2002; b. 3.10.53, Lanark. Educ. Lanark Grammar School; Heriot-Watt University. Economist, Scottish Office, 1978-79; Lecturer, Department of Economics, Heriot-Watt University, 1979-92; Senior Lecturer, Faculty of Law, University of Edinburgh, 1992-2002. Published widely on economic and political aspects of European integration. Recreations: hillwalking; running; reading; music. Address: (b.) School of Law, University of Edinburgh, Old College, Edinburgh.

Scott, Sheriff Principal Craig Alexander Leslie, QC. Sheriff Principal, Glasgow and Strathkelvin, May 2011. Career: solicitor in 1984, then admitted to the Faculty of Advocates in 1986; from then until 1999 practised as an Advocate, working principally in the areas of reparation, (including medical and professional negligence), defamation, commercial law, property law and administrative law; served as an Advocate Depute, 1994-97; Standing Junior Counsel to the Scottish Office Environment Department, 1994-97, and to the Scottish Office Development Department, 1997-1999; Sheriff of Glasgow and Strathkelvin, 1999-2011; served as a specialist Sheriff in the Commercial Court in Glasgow.
Address: (b.) 1 Carlton Place, Glasgow G5 9DA.

Scott, Eleanor, R., MB, ChB. MSP (Green), Highlands and Islands, 2003-07; b. 23.7.51, Inverness; divorced; 1 s.; 1 d.; partner: Rob Gibson. Educ. Bearsden Academy; University of Glasgow. Junior hospital doctor posts, Inverness, Stirling, Elgin, 1974-78; Trainee, general practice, Nairn, 1979; Community Paediatrician, Highlands, 1980-2003. Has stood for election at all levels, 1990-2001. Recreations: traditional music; gardening. Address: Tir nan Oran, 8 Culcairn Road, Evanton, Ross-shire IV16 9YT; T.-01349 830388; e-mail: eleanorsco@googlemail.com

Scott, Professor Hamish, MA, PhD, FBA, FRHistS, FRSE, FSA Scot. Wardlaw Professor Emeritus of International History, St Andrews University, until 2009; Hon. Senior Research Fellow, University of Glasgow, since 2005; b. 12.7.46, Glasgow. Educ. George Heriot's School, Edinburgh; Edinburgh University; London School of Economics. Lecturer, Birmingham University, 1970-78; joined St Andrews University as Lecturer, 1979. Publications: as author: The Rise of the Great Powers 1648-1815, 1983; British Foreign Policy in the Age of the American Revolution, 1990; The Emergence of the Eastern Powers 1756-1775, 2001; The Birth of a Great Power System 1740-1815, 2006; as editor: Enlightened Absolutism, 1990; The European Nobilities in the Seventeenth and Eighteenth Centuries, 1995; 2nd ed, 2007; Royal and Republican Sovereignty in Early Modern Europe, 1997; Cultures of Power in Europe during the long eighteenth century, 2007; The Oxford Handbook of Early Modern European History, 2 vols., 2015. Recreations: classical music; hill-walking; watching sport. Address: (b.) School of Humanities (History), University of Glasgow, 2 University Gardens, Glasgow G12 8QQ; T.-0141 339 8452; e-mail: Hamish.Scott@glasgow.ac.uk

Scott, Hugh Johnstone, DA, CertEd. Writer; Art tutor, Pitlochry Festival Theatre, 2004-2014; Drawing tutor, Argyll College, 2008-2012; b. Paisley; m., Mary (Margo) Smith Craig Hamilton; 1 s.; 1 d. Educ. Paisley Grammar School; Glasgow School of Art. Various jobs, then art school; art teacher, until 1984; full-time writing since 1984, including Writing Fellow, City of Aberdeen, 1991; Lecturer in Creative Writing, Glasgow University Adult and Continuing Education Department, since 1988, Art Tutor, since 1998; Tutor in Creative Writing; winner, Woman's Realm children's short story competition, 1982; winner, children's category, Whitbread Book of the Year, 1989, for Why Weeps the Brogan?; short-listed, Mcvitie's Prize, 1990; Tutor, Arvon Foundation Ltd., 1994; Writing guru for Writers' Forum magazine, since 2007. Publication: Likely Stories, 2011. Recreations: weight training; exploring England; day-dreaming; reading, of course; painting.

Scott, Ian Edward. Deputy Chief Executive and Director of Change, Scottish Court Service, 1995-2004; m., Maureen Ferrie; 1 s.; 1 d. Educ. Bellahouston Academy. Regional Sheriff Clerk, Lothian and Borders, 1992-95; Sheriff Clerk, Edinburgh, 1992-95; Sheriff Clerk of Chancery, 1992-95; Regional Sheriff Clerk, Glasgow and Strathkelvin, 1996-98; Regional Sheriff Clerk, North Strathclyde, 1997-98; Area Director West, 1998-2001. Hon. Member, Royal Faculty of Procurators, Glasgow. Recreations: amateur astronomy; rugby; making changes. Address: (h.) Meadowbank, Annandale Avenue, Lockerbie; T.-01576 203132.

Scott, James Archibald, CB, LVO, FRSE, FScotVec, MA; b. 5.3.32, Palestine; m., Dr. Elizabeth Agnes Joyce Buchan-Hepburn; 3 s.; 1 d. Educ. Dollar Academy; St. Andrews University; Queen's University of Ontario. RAF Pilot, 1954-56; Commonwealth Relations Office, 1956-65, serving in New Delhi and New York; Scottish Office, 1965; Private Secretary to Secretary of State for Scotland, 1969-71; Secretary, Scottish Education Department, 1984-88; Secretary, Industry Department for Scotland, 1988-91; Chief Executive, Scottish Development Agency, 1991-92; Executive Director, Scottish Financial Enterprise, 1992-95; Director, Scottish Power plc, 1993-96; Director, Dumyat Investment Trust PLC, 1995-2000; Member of Court, Heriot-Watt University, 1995-2001. Chevalier de L'ordre du Mérite. Address: (h.) 38 Queen's Crescent, Edinburgh EH9 2BA; T.-0131-667 8417.
E-mail: james.scott1@blueyonder.co.uk

Scott, James Niall, OBE, LLB; b. 5.4.52, Glasgow; m., Judith; 3 s.; 2 d. Educ. Jordanhill College School; Aberdeen University. External Examiner, Glasgow University Law School, 1990-92; Managing Partner, McGrigor Donald,

1994-97; Chairman, KLegal and McGrigors, 2002-04; Executive Chairman, UK Fisheries Offshore Oil and Gas Legacy Trust Fund Limited; Chairman, Mark Scott Foundation; Managing Director, The Offshore Pollution Liability Association Limited; Director: Scottish Ballet and the Barcapel Foundation Ltd. Recreations: swimming; golf; hill-walking. Address: 66 Langside Drive, Glasgow G43 2ST; T.-0141-637 8759; e-mail: nscottnsbs.org.uk

Scott, James Orrock, FCCA. Board Member, Angus, East of Scotland Housing Association, 1988-2012 (retired); Chairman and Board Member, Northern Housing Company Limited, 2000-2010 (retired); Treasurer, SHARP (Scottish Heart and Arterial Disease Risk Prevention), 1992-2005; b. 13.12.40, Dundee; m., Alva; 1 s. Educ. Grove Academy. Former Senior Partner, Henderson Loggie, Chartered Accountants. Past President, Scottish Branch Executive, Society of Certified Accountants; first President, Scottish Athletics Federation. Recreations: athletics; bowling. Address: (h.) 99 Monifieth Road, Broughty Ferry, Dundee DD5 2SL; T.-01382 731822.

Scott, Janys Margaret, QC, MA (Cantab). Called to bar, 1992, took silk, 2007; b. 28.8.53, Radcliffe; m., Revd Dr Kevin F. Scott; 2 s.; 1 d. Educ. Queen Elizabeth's Girls Grammar School, Barnet; Newnham College, Cambridge. Lecturer in Iraq, 1976-78; Solicitor, Oxford, 1978-86; Solicitor, Edinburgh, 1987-91; Honorary Lecturer, Dundee University, 1989-94. Convener, Scottish Child Law Centre, 1992-97; Chairman, Stepfamily Scotland, 1998-2002; Visiting Bye-Fellow, Newnham College, Cambridge, 2002; Chairman, BAAF Scottish Legal Group, 2004-2010; UK delegate to CCBE Family Law Working Group, since 2012; Chairman, Advocates' Family Law Association, since 2013; appointed Part-time Sheriff, 2005. Publication: Education Law in Scotland, 2003. Address: (b.) Parliament House, Edinburgh EH1 1RF; T.-0131-226 5071.

Scott, John. MSP (Conservative), Ayr, since 2000; Member, Scottish Parliament Corporate Body; Deputy Convener, Petitions Committee; m., Charity (deceased); 1 s.; 1 d. Farming at Balkissock, Ayrshire, since 1973; Founder Director, Ayrshire Country Lamb Ltd., 1988-93; partner in family catering enterprises, 1986-2000; established Ayrshire Farmers' Markets, 1999; Convener, Hill Farming Committee, National Farmers' Union of Scotland, 1993-99; Chairman, Ayrshire and Arran Farming and Wildlife Advisory Group, 1993-99; Chairman, South of Scotland Regional Wool Committee, 1996-2000; JP; Elder, Ballantrae Church; Chairman, Scottish Area Committee, UK Conservative Countryside Forum, 1998-2000; Chairman, Ayrshire Farmers' Market, since 2000; Chairman, Scottish Association of Farmers' Markets, 2001-04; Council Member, Scottish Agricultural Society, 2004; Coopted Regional Adviser on South of Scotland Board, Moredun Foundation, 2004. Recreations: geology; curling; bridge; rugby. Address: (b.) 1 Wellington Square, Ayr KA7 1EN.

Scott, John Andrew Ross. Chairman, NHS Orkney, 2007-2015; Editor, Living Orkney Magazine, since 2008; Editor, Orkney Today, 2003-08; Leader, Scottish Borders Council, 2002-03; Member, since 1995 (Liberal Democrat Scottish Transport Spokesman, 1998-99); Honorary Provost of Hawick, 1999-2002; News Editor, Hawick News, 2001-02; b. 6.5.51, Hawick; 2 s.; 2 d. Educ. Hawick High School. Worked on father's farm, 1966-74; Journalist, Hawick News, 1977-78, Tweeddale Press Group, 1978-2002, Chief Reporter, Southern Reporter, 1986-2000; first SDP Member, Roxburgh District Council (1980-85) and Borders

Regional Council; Chairman, Roxburgh District Licensing Board, 1984-85; first Chairman, Borders Area Party, SDP, 1981-84; Secretary, Roxburgh and Berwickshire Liberal Democrats, 1988-89, Vice Chairman, 1993-94; Chairman, Scottish Association of Direct Labour Organisations Highways Division, 1994-96; Chairman, South East Scotland Transport Partnership, 1998-2003; Chairman, COSLA Road Safety Task Group, 1999-2001; Chairman, South of Scotland Rural Partnership, 2003; Liberal Democrat Candidate, Dumfries, 2001; South of Scotland Liberal Democrat Candidate, 1999 and 2003. Performed in the first Scottish Amateur Dramatic productions of both 'Cats' (2014) and 'Les Miserables' (2015) with Kirkwall Amateur Operatic Society. Rejoined SNP in December 2014. Serving on Ministerial Task Group on Health and Social Care Integration (2013-15); Ministerial Task group on Health Promoting Health Service (2013-15) and the Scottish Public Health Review Group (2015). Publication: Beyond Tweedbank: The case for extending the Borders Rail Link to Hawick, 2004. Recreations: writing; singing; amateur dramatics; walking. Address: (h.) Burnquoy, Weyland Bay, St. Ola, Orkney KW15 1TD; T.-01856 874330; e-mail: johnandwanda@tiscali.co.uk

Scott, John Dominic, QC, Solicitor Advocate, LLB, DipLP. Partner, Capital Defence Lawyers, since 1991; Solicitor-Advocate, since 2001; b. 20.7.64, Glasgow. Educ. Holyrood Secondary School, Glasgow; Glasgow University. Trainee and Assistant, Hughes, Dowdall & Company, Glasgow, 1985-88 (qualified Solicitor, since 1987); joined Gilfedder & McInnes (now Capital Defence Lawyers), Edinburgh, 1988; Member, Executive Committee, Howard League for Penal Reform in Scotland, Convenor, since 2006; Past President, Edinburgh Bar Association; Chair, Scottish Human Rights Centre, 1997-2005; Vice-President (Crime) of Society of Solicitor Advocates, since 2008. Address: (b.) 34 Leith Walk, Edinburgh EH6 5AA; T.-0131-553 4333; e-mail: johndscott@talk21.com

Scott, Sir John Hamilton, KCVO. Farmer; Lord-Lieutenant, Shetland, 1994-2011; Chairman, Woolgrowers of Shetland Ltd.; b. 30.11.36; m., Wendy Ronald; 1 s.; 1 d. President, Shetland NFU, 1976; Nature Conservancy Council Committee for Scotland, 1984-91; N.E. Scotland Board, Scottish Natural Heritage, 1992-97; Chairman, Shetland Crofting, Farming and Wildlife Advisory Group, 1984-94; Chairman: Shetland Arts Trust, 1994-98, Sail Shetland Ltd., 1996-2000, The Belmont Trust, 1996-2011; Trustee, Shetland Charitable Trust, 1994-2011. Club: The Alpine Club. Recreations: hills; music; pruning. Address: (h.) Keldabister Banks, Bressay, Shetland, ZE2 9EL; T.-01595 820281; e-mail: scott.gardie@virgin.net

Scott, John Philip, MA (Cantab), MBA, FCII, FCSI, DL. Chairman, Scottish Mortgage Investment Trust, since 2009. Educ. Cambridge University, INSEAD. Career: former international investment banker who maintains a number of interests in the technology, insurance and investment trust sectors; former executive director of Lazard Brothers & Co., Limited. Chairman of Impax Environmental Markets plc (2014) and of Alpha Insurance Analysts Ltd (2013). Appointed Director, Scottish Mortgage, 2001. Currently Director of various companies, including Martin Currie Pacific Trust plc, JP Morgan Claverhouse Investment Trust plc, Schroder Japan Growth Fund plc, Bluefield Solar Investment Fund Ltd. and Alternative Asset Opportunities PCC Limited. Chairman of Dunedin Income Growth Investment Trust PLC, until May 2012; Senior Independent Director, Xaar plc, 2001-2010; Director, Miller Insurance, 2001-2012; Deputy Chairman of Endace Limited (New Zealand), 2005-2013. Trustee, the Abbotsford Trust. Deputy Lieutenant for Roxburgh, Ettrick and Lauderdale.

Address: (b.) c/o Scottish Mortgage, Calton Square, 1 Greenside Row, Edinburgh EH1 3AN.

Scott, Sir Kenneth Bertram Adam, KCVO, CMG. Extra Equerry to The Queen, since 1996; b. 23.1.31, Belfast; m., 1, Gay Smart (deceased); m., 2, Esme Scott (deceased 2010); 1 s.; 1 d.; 1 step. s. Educ. George Watson's College; Edinburgh University. HM Diplomatic Service, 1954-85; HM Ambassador to Yugoslavia, 1982-85; Assistant Private Secretary/Deputy Private Secretary to The Queen, 1985-96; Acting Chairman, Provisional Election Commission for Bosnia, 1996. Governor, George Watson's College, 1997-2002; Vice-President, Royal Overseas League; Trustee: Edinburgh University Development Trust, Hopetoun House Preservation Trust, 1997-2007. Publications: St. James's Palace: A History, 2010; Lords of Dalkeith, 2014. Recreations: travel; music; golf. Address: (h.) 13 Clinton Road, Edinburgh EH9 2AW; T.-0131-447 5191.

Scott, The Hon. Lady (Margaret E. Scott), QC. Senator of the College of Justice, since 2012. Admitted as a solicitor in 1989 and to the Faculty of Advocates in 1991; became a QC in 2002; has been involved mainly in criminal defence work, specialising in appeals, since 1991; regularly acted as senior counsel from 1995 and from 1996 for a period as an ad hoc Advocate Depute; has been lead counsel in some of the most difficult and serious cases including numerous full bench cases and cases before the Judicial Committee of the Privy Council and United Kingdom Supreme Court, since 2002; appointed as a part-time sheriff in 2002; lead counsel on the Lockerbie appeal, 2007-2009. Address: (b.) Parliament House, Edinburgh EH1 1RQ.

Scott, Michael M., OBE, BSc, DipEd. Self-employed natural history writer, consultant, broadcaster and cruise ship lecturer; b. 10.5.51, Edinburgh; m., Sue Scott. Educ. George Heriot's School, Edinburgh; Madras College, St. Andrews; University of Aberdeen. Awards: O.B.E., 2005 "for services to biodiversity conservation in Scotland"; Planta Europa Silver Leaf, 2007 "for excellent work in European wild plant conservation". Assistant Education Officer, Royal Zoological Society of Scotland, 1974-76; Scottish Field Officer, Wildlife Youth Service, World Wildlife Fund, 1976-80. Radio work includes: Saving Species, Living World, World of the Move, Nature, Litmus Test, MacGregor's Gathering; Scottish Co-ordinator, Plantlife – The Wild Plant Charity, 1989-2004; Chair, Save the Cairngorms Campaign, 1990-94; Editor, Scottish Environment News, 1991-2001; Chair, Scottish Wildlife and Countryside Link, 1995-99; Deputy Chairman, Scottish Natural Heritage, 1999-2005. Publications: Young Oxford Book of Ecology, 1994 (Environment Prize for Children and Young People's Literature, Germany, 2001); Scottish Wild Flowers, 2011; Scottish Wild Flowers Mini Guide, 2012; Mountain Flowers (in press). Cruise ship lecturer for Voyages of Discovery, Fred Olsen Cruise Line, Cruise & Maritime Voyages, Saga, Noble Caledonia, Regent Seven Seas Cruises, Viking Cruises (agent: the P&R Agency, East Sussex). Recreations: natural history; photography; travel; Runrig concerts. Address: Cana, North Strome, Lochcarron, Ross-shire IV54 8YJ; T.-01520 722588; Website: www.mmscott.co.uk
E-mail: michael@mmscott.co.uk

Scott, Major Nigel William, MBA, Dip BA & Couns., MIOD, MCMI. Business Development Consultant, Associate, The Institute of Design Innovation, Glasgow School of Art, since 2012, Head of Coaching, Institute of Directors Scotland, since 2005; Managing Director: Dundern Ltd., since 2002, Munro Greenhouses, since 2007; b. 28.4.59, Wimbledon, Surrey; m., Catherine Joy Macnaughton; 1 s.; 1 d. Educ. Dollar Academy; Royal Military College Sandhurst; Glasgow Polytechnic. Commissioned, Argyll and Sutherland Highlanders (Princess Louise's), 1978; served in Hong Kong, N. Ireland, Cyprus, Falklands, N. America, UK; commanded D Company 3/51 Highland Volunteers (TA), 1990-93; worked in management consultancy: Taylor Clarke Partnership, 1989-91, PE International, 1991-92; Senior Partner, Scott Associates: organisation development, 1993-2003; Strategy Director, The Forward Training Partnership, 1997-98; Director, Dundern Limited: organisation and business development, since 2003. Chair, Kilmaurs Primary School Board, 2002-05; JP East Ayrshire District Court, 2003-05; Member, Board of Management, Audit and HR Committees, Forth Valley College, since 2013; Scottish Amateur Swimming Association Judge. Recreations: gardening; swimming; sailing; DIY; music; reading. Address: (h.) 17 Princes Street, Stirling FK8 1HQ; T.-07785 343130; e-mail: nigel-scott@outlook.com

Scott, Paul Henderson, CMG, MA, MLitt. Honorary Fellow, Glasgow University, since 1996; b. 7.11.20, Edinburgh; m., B.C. Sharpe (divorced 2010) 1 s.; 1 d.; m., Laura Fiorentini. Educ. Royal High School, Edinburgh; Edinburgh University. HM Forces, 1941-47 (Major, RA); HM Diplomatic Service in Foreign Office, Warsaw, La Paz, Havana, Montreal, Vienna, Milan, 1947-80. Convener, Advisory Council for the Arts in Scotland, 1981-97; Rector, Dundee University, 1989-92; Convener, Scottish Centre for Economic and Social Research, 1990-95; Vice-President, Scottish National Party, 1991-97; President, Scottish Centre, International PEN, 1992-97; President, Edinburgh Sir Walter Scott Club, 1996; President, Saltire Society, 1996-2002; Chairman, Edinburgh Robert Louis Stevenson Club, 2006-09. Publications: 1707, The Union of Scotland and England, 1979; Walter Scott and Scotland, 1981; John Galt, 1985; The Age of MacDiarmid (Co-Editor), 1980; In Bed with an Elephant: The Scottish Experience, 1985; A Scottish Postbag (Co-Editor), 1986; The Thinking Nation, 1989; Towards Independence — essays on Scotland, 1991; Andrew Fletcher and the Treaty of Union, 1992; Scotland in Europe: a dialogue with a sceptical friend, 1992; Scotland: a Concise Cultural History (Editor), 1993; Defoe in Edinburgh and Other Papers, 1995; Scotland's Ruine (Co-Editor), 1995; Scotland: An Unwon Cause, 1997; Still in Bed with an Elephant, 1998; The Boasted Advantages, 1999; A Twentieth Century Life, 2002; The Saltoun Papers (Editor), 2003; Scotland Resurgent, 2003; Spirits of the Age (Editor), 2005; The Union of 1707; Why and How, 2006; The Age of Liberation, 2008; The New Scotland, 2008; The Independence Book (Joint Editor), 2008; A Nation Again (Editor), 2011; Scotland: A Creative Past, An Independent Future, 2014. Address: (h.) 33 Drumsheugh Gardens, Edinburgh EH3 7RN; T.-0131-225 1038.

Scott, Primrose Smith, CA. Head of Quality Review, Institute of Chartered Accountants of Scotland, 1999-2002; Senior Partner, The McCabe Partnership, 1987-99; b. 21.9.40, Gorebridge. Educ. Ayr Academy. Trained with Stewart Gilmour, Ayr; qualified as CA 1963; joined Romanes & Munro, Edinburgh, 1964; progressed through manager ranks to Partner, Deloitte Haskins & Sells, 1981-87; set up own practice, Linlithgow, 1987; moved practice to Edinburgh, 1997. Member, Accounts Commission, 1988-92; Non-Executive Director: Dunfermline Building Society, 1990-2005, Northern Venture Trust plc, 1995-2010; Director, Ecosse Unique, since 2004; Institute of Chartered Accountants of Scotland: Member, Council, 1988-95, first Convener, GP Committee, 1990, Vice President, 1992-94, President, 1994-95; Honorary Treasurer, Hospitality Industry Trust Scotland, 1994-2002; Trustee, New Lanark Conservation Trust, 2002-06; Commissioner, Queen Victoria School, Dunblane, 1998-2006; Treasurer: Age Concern Scotland/Age Scotland, 2003-2014, Borders Youth Theatre, 2007-2014; Fellow, SCOTVEC, 1994. Recreation:

walking her dogs. Address: (h.) The Cleugh, Redpath, Earlston TD4 6AD.

Scott, Professor Roger Davidson, BSc, PhD, CPhys, FInstP, FRSE. Personal Professorship, University of Glasgow, 1994; Non-Executive Director, Nuclear Decommissioning Authority, 2004-08; b. 17.12.41, Lerwick; m., Marion McCluckie; 2 s.; 1 d. Educ. Anderson Institute, Lerwick; Edinburgh University. Demonstrator, Edinburgh University, 1965-68; Lecturer, then Depute Director, then Director, SURRC, 1968-98; Recreations: watching football; walking dogs; home maintenance. Address: (h.) 6 Downfield Gardens, Bothwell G71 8UW; T.-01698 854121.

Scott, Roy, DL, JP, OStJ, VMSM, GCLJ, CMLJ, MD, FRCS (Glas), FRCS (Edin), FSA (Scot). Retired Urologist; Honorary Sheriff, South Strathclyde/Dumfries/Galloway; b. 17.7.35, Waterloo, Wishaw; m., Janette J.C.; 1 s.; 2 d. Educ. Wishaw High School; University of Glasgow. House Phys/Surgeon; Captain (Temp. Major), RAMC - Kenya, Aden; Surgical Junior posts, Stobhill/Royal Infirmary Glasgow; Consultant Urologist, Glasgow Royal; Hon. Clinical Senior Lecturer, University of Glasgow; Hon. Lecturer, Strathclyde University; Hon. Member, South Central Section, American Urological Society; Ext. Referee, University of Amman; Past Council Member, British Association Urological Surgeons. Author/Co-Author, several books including The Trades House of Glasgow; Co-Author, 6th/7th Edition, 1st Aid Manual; various articles, Burns Chronicle; Member, Millennium and New Millennium Masters; (Livery Companies) London; Past Chairman, Glassford Trust; Arkansas Traveller. Ex Deacon Inc Tailors; Ex Deacon Convener, Trades House Glasgow; Past-President, Sandyford Burns Club; Hon. Member, Sandyford Burns Club; Chancellor, Order of St. Lazarus (Scotland); Past Hospitaller, Order of St. Lazarus (Scotland); Secretary, Clan Scott Scotland. Recreations: fishing; Burns; gardening; music; boating. Address: (h.) Garrion, 27 Forest View, Kildrum, Cumbernauld G67 2DB. E-mail: roy-janette@blueyonder.co.uk

Scott, Stephen R., LLB, WS. Consultant, Burness Paull LLP, since 2015; Owner, McClure Naismith, 2000-2015; Solicitor, since 1988; b. 16.10.64, Elgin; m., Jane; 1 s. Educ. Elgin Academy; Edinburgh University. McClure Naismith: Assistant, 1993-96, Associate, 1996-2000. Recreation: marathon running.

Scott, Tavish Hamilton, BA (Hons). MSP (Liberal Democrat), Shetland, since 1999; Leader, Scottish Liberal Democrats, 2008-2011; Deputy Minister for Finance, Public Services and Parliamentary Business, Scottish Executive, 2003-05; Minister for Transport, 2005-07; b. 6.5.66, Inverness; 3 s.; 1 d. Educ. Anderson High School, Lerwick; Napier College, Edinburgh (which became Napier University). Research Assistant to Jim Wallace, MP, 1989-90; Press Officer, Scottish Liberal Democrats, 1990-92; Owner/Manager, Keldabister Farm, Bressay, 1992-99; Shetland Islands Councillor, 1994-99; Chairman, Lerwick Harbour Trust, 1997-99. Recreations: football; golf; cinema; reading; current affairs; Up Helly Aa. Address: (b.) 171 Commercial Street, Lerwick ZE1 0HX; T.-01595 690044; e-mail: tavish.scott.msp@scottish.parliament.uk

Scott, William, BSc, MSc, FRPharmS, (Hon) DSc. Former Chief Pharmaceutical Officer, Scottish Government (1992-2015); Honorary Professor, The Robert Gordon University, Aberdeen, since 2004; b. 26.10.49, Bellshill; m., Catherine Muir Gilmour; 1 s.; 1 d. Educ. Wishaw High School; Heriot Watt University; Strathclyde University. Resident Pharmacist, Nottingham City Hospital, 1975-76; Staff Pharmacist, Eastern General Hospital, Edinburgh, 1976-79; Principal Pharmacist, Western General Hospital, Edinburgh, 1979-86; Chief Administrative Pharmaceutical Officer, Tayside Health Board, 1986-90; Deputy Chief Pharmacist, Scottish Office, 1990-92. Honorary Doctorate of Science, Robert Gordon University, 2006; Visiting Professor, Strathclyde University, since 2008; Honorary Doctorate of Science, Strathclyde University, 2009. Recreations: walking; reading.

Scott-Dempster, Robert Andrew, LLB (Hons), WS. Partner, Gillespie Macandrew LLP, since 2003 (Head of Land and Rural Business Department); b. 30.4.67, Reading; m., Camilla; 2 s. Educ. Marlborough College; Edinburgh University. Captain, 1st Battalion The Black Watch, 1990-95; Associate, Murray Beith Murray WS, 1997-2002. Chairman, Scottish Land & Estates Legal and Taxation Committee. Recreations: fishing; golf; climbing/hill walking; biography. Address: (b.) 5 Atholl Crescent, Edinburgh EH3 8EJ; T.-0131 225 1677. E-mail: robert.scott-dempster@gillespiemacandrew.co.uk

Scott Moncrieff, John Kenneth, LLB, WS. Partner, Murray Beith Murray, WS, 1978-2015; b. 9.2.51, Edinburgh; m., Pilla; 1 s.; 2 d. Educ. Marlborough College; Edinburgh University. Bailie of Holyroodhouse and Honorary Consul of Monaco. Board Member and Founding Chair, Cheek by Jowl Theatre Co.; Chair: Scottish Youth Theatre (2013), John Buchan Heritage Museum Trust; Trustee, various charitable trusts and companies. Recreations: football; theatre; hillwalking and writing light verse. Address: 23 Cluny Drive, Edinburgh EH10 6DW; T.-0131-447-1791; e-mail: john.scomo@outlook.com

Scouller, Glen, DA, RGI, RSW. Artist; b. 24.4.50, Glasgow; m., Carol Alison Marsh; 2 d. Educ. Eastbank Academy; Garthamlock Secondary; Glasgow School of Art; Hospitalfield College of Art, Arbroath. RSA Painting Award, 1972; W. O. Hutcheson Prize for Drawing, 1973; travelling scholarship, Greece, 1973; started teaching, Glasgow schools, 1974; part-time tutoring, Glasgow School of Art, 1986-89; Lauder Award, Glasgow Art Club, 1987; Scottish Amicable Award, RGI, 1987; David Cargill Award, RGI, 2006; Residency, L'Association Charles Rennie Mackintosh, Collioure, 2008; Crinan Residency Award, RGI, 2013; elected, RGI, 1989; painting full-time since 1989; elected, RSW, 1997; solo exhibitions: John D. Kelly Gallery, Glasgow, 1977; The Scottish Gallery, Edinburgh, 1980; Fine Art Society, Glasgow, 1985, 1988; Harbour Arts Centre, Irvine, 1986; Fine Art Society, Edinburgh, 1989; Portland Gallery, London, 1989, 1992, 1994, 1998, 2011; Macaulay Gallery, Stenton, 1990, 1993, 1996; French Institute, Edinburgh, 1990; Open Eye Gallery, Edinburgh, 1992, 1994, 1997, 2000, 2002, 2007, 2012, 2014; Roger Billcliffe Gallery, Glasgow, 1992, 1995, 1998, 2003, 2007, 2010, 2015; Everard Read Gallery, Johannesburg, 1997, 2000 (CT), 2001, 2006, 2007, 2008 (CT); Corrymella Scott Gallery, Newcastle-upon-Tyne, 1999; Lemon Street Gallery, Truro, 2002; John Davies Gallery, Moreton-in-Marsh, 2004, 2008; Red Box Gallery, Newcastle upon Tyne, 2005; Henshelwood Gallery, Newcastle upon Tyne, 2005; Thompson's Marylebone, London, 2006; Lemond Gallery, 2011; Inverarity, Glasgow, 2010; Rowallan Castle, Ayrshire, 2012; Gallery 1 at Crinan Hotel, 2014; works in public, corporate and private collections worldwide. Recreations: travel; music; gardening. Address: East Loudounhill Farm, Darvel KA17 0LU; web: www.glenscouller.com E-mail: glen.scouller@btinternet.com

Scullion, Adrienne Clare, MA, PhD, FRSA, FRSE. James Arnott Chair in Drama, University of Glasgow, since 2005; b. Glasgow. Educ. University of Glasgow. Lecturer, Trinity College Dublin, 1992-93; British

Academy Post Doctoral Fellow, University of Glasgow, 1993-96, Lecturer, then Senior Lecturer, 1996-2005. Chair, The Citizens' Theatre, Glasgow; Member of the Board of the National Library of Scotland; Lay member of the Court of Edinburgh Napier University. Address: (b.) School of Culture and Creative Arts, University of Glasgow, Glasgow G12 8QQ; T.0141 330 4677; e-mail: adrienne.scullion@glasgow.ac.uk

Seafield, Earl of; b. 20.3.39, London; m., Leila Refaat (2nd m.); 2 s. Educ. Eton; Cirencester Agricultural College. Recreation: countryside activities. Address: Old Cullen, Cullen, Buckie AB56 4XW; T.-01542 840221.

Sealey, Barry Edward, CBE, BA (Hons) (Cantab), CBIM; b. 3.2.36, Bristol; m., Helen Martyn; 1 s.; 1 d. Educ. Dursley Grammar School; St. John's College, Cambridge. RAF, 1953-55. Joined Christian Salvesen as trainee, 1958; joined Board, Christian Salvesen PLC (responsible for Food Services Division), 1969; appointed Managing Director, 1981, Deputy Chairman and Managing Director, 1987; retired from Christian Salvesen, 1990. Active Business Angel, since 1990, served on numerous company boards. Address: (h.) Flat 5, 2 The Cedars, Edinburgh EH13 0PL. E-mail: bes@morago.co.uk

Searle, Rev. David Charles, MA, DipTh. Retired; Minister of the Church of Scotland, since 1965; Warden, Rutherford House, Edinburgh, 1993-2003; b. 14.11.37, Swansea; m., Lorna Christine Wilson; 2 s.; 1 d. Educ. Arbroath High School; St. Andrews University; London University; Aberdeen University. Teacher, 1961-64; Assistant Minister, St. Nicholas Church, Aberdeen, 1964-65; Minister: Newhills Parish Church, 1965-75, Larbert Old, 1975-85, Hamilton Road Presbyterian Church, Bangor, Co. Down, 1985-93; Contributor, Presbyterian Herald; Editor, Rutherford Journal of Church and Ministry, 1993-2003. Publications: Be Strong in the Lord; Truth and Love in a Sexually Disordered World; The Ten Commandments; Through the Year with William Still; abridged version of Calvin's 'Commentary on Psalms'; Joseph: His Arms Were Made Strong. Recreations: sail-boarding; gardening; hill-walking; stick-making. Address: (h.) 30 Abbey Lane, Grange, Errol PH2 7GB; e-mail: dcs@davidsearle.plus.com

Seaton, Professor Anthony, CBE, BA, MD (Cantab), DSc(hc) Aberdeen, FRCPLond, FRCPEdin, FFOM, FMedSci. Emeritus Professor, Aberdeen University; Hon. Consultant, Institute of Occupational Medicine, Edinburgh, since 2003; b. 20.8.38, London; m., Jillian Margaret Duke; 2 s. Educ. Rossall School, Fleetwood; King's College, Cambridge; Liverpool University. Assistant Professor of Medicine, West Virginia University, 1969-71; Consultant Chest Physician, Cardiff, 1971-77; Director, Institute of Occupational Medicine, Edinburgh, 1978-90; Professor of Environmental and Occupational Medicine, Aberdeen University, 1988-2003; Editor, Thorax, 1977-82; Chairman, Department of Environment Expert Panel on Air Quality Standards, 1991-2002; President, British Thoracic Society, 1999; Member, Department of Health Committee on Medical Aspects of Air Pollution, 1991-2003; Member, Royal Society Working Group on nanoscience, 2003/04; Chairman, Natural Environment Research Council's Research Advisory Committee on Human Health and the Environment, 2006/07; Member, Industrial Injuries Advisory Council, since 2013; Member, EU Scientific Committee on Occupational Exposure Limits, since 2015. Publications: books and papers on occupational and respiratory medicine; essays in Scottish Review. Recreations: keeping fit; opera; painting; sculpture. Address: (h.) 8 Avon Grove, Cramond, Edinburgh, EH4 6RF; T.-031-336 5113.

Seaton, Professor Nigel, BSc (Hons), MSE, PhD. Principal and Vice-Chancellor, Abertay University, since 2012; b. 1960, Falkirk; m.; 3 c. Educ. University of Edinburgh; University of Pennsylvania. Career: worked as a research engineer with Atkins Research and Development and BP, 1986-89; lecturer in chemical engineering at the University of Cambridge and fellow, tutor and Director of Studies in Chemical Engineering and Natural Sciences at Clare College, 1989-97; Visiting Professor, School of Chemical Engineering at Cornell University, 1996-97; Head of the School of Chemical Engineering, becoming Head of the Division of Engineering and then Head of the Institute for Materials and Processes, University of Edinburgh, 1998-2003, Dean of Undergraduate Studies, College of Science and Engineering, then Assistant Principal (Taught Programme Development) and later Vice-Principal (Academic), 2003-08; Deputy Vice-Chancellor (Academic Development), University of Surrey, then Senior Deputy Vice-Chancellor, 2008-2012. Address: Abertay University DD1 1HG.

Seckl, Professor Jonathan Robert, BSc, MB, BS, MRCP(UK), PhD, FRCPE, FMedSci, FRSE. Moncrieff-Arnott Professor of Molecular Medicine, Edinburgh University, since 1997; Professor of Endocrinology, 1996-97; Head, School of Molecular and Clinical Medicine, 2002-03; Director of Research, College of Medicine and Veterinary Medicine, 2005-2012, Executive Dean, since 2010; Vice-Principal (Planning, Resources and Research Policy), since 2012; Chairman, Molecular Medicine Centre, 1996-2001; Member: Scottish Science Advisory Committee, 2004-08, Council of Academy of Medical Sciences, 2009-2011, Council, Society for Endocrinology, since 2011; b. 15.8.56, London; m., Molly; 1 s.; 1 d. Educ. William Ellis School, London; University College Hospital Medical School, London. Sir Jules Thorn Research Fellow in Neuroendocrinology, Charing Cross and Westminster Medical School, 1984-87; Honorary Clinical Assistant, National Hospital for Nervous Diseases, London, 1984-87; Lecturer in Medicine, Edinburgh University, 1987-89; Wellcome Trust/Royal Society of Edinburgh Senior Clinical Research Fellow, 1989-97. Publications: papers on glucocorticoids and their metabolism in stress, cognitive aging and metabolic disorders, as well as developmental programming of disease. Address: (b.) Queen's Medical Research Institute, 47 Little France Crescent, Edinburgh EH16 4TJ; T.-0131-242-6777; e-mail: j.seckl@ed.ac.uk

Secombes, Professor Christopher John, BSc, PhD, DSc (hc), DSc (Aberdeen), FRSB, FRSE. Regius Chair of Natural History, University of Aberdeen, since 2014; Head, Scottish Fish Immunology Research Centre, University of Aberdeen, since 2001; b. 1.4.56, London; m., Karen Ruth; 2 s.; 1 d. Educ. Longdean School, Hemel Hempstead; University of Leeds; University of Hull. Department of Zoology, University of Aberdeen: Lecturer, 1984-91, Senior Lecturer, 1991-97, Professor, 1997, Head of Zoology, 2001-02, Head of Biological Sciences, 2002-2011. President, International Society for Developmental and Comparative Immunology, 2003-06; Adjunct Professor, University of Tromso, 2003-06; Established Chair of Zoology, School of Biological Sciences, University of Aberdeen, 2004-2014. Editor, Fish and Shellfish Immunology; Member, Editorial Board: Veterinary Immunology and Immunopathology, Molecular Immunology. Address: School of Biological Sciences, University of Aberdeen, Zoology Building, Tillydrone Avenue, Aberdeen AB24 2TZ; T.-01224 272872; e-mail: c.secombes@abdn.ac.uk

Sefton, Rev. Henry Reay, MA, BD, STM, PhD. Associate Minister, Kirk of St. Nicholas Uniting, Aberdeen, since

2002; Chaplain, College of St Nicholas, Aberdeen, since 1989; b. 15.1.31, Pitsligo. Educ. Brechin High School; St. Andrews University; Glasgow University; Union Theological Seminary, New York. Assistant Minister, Glasgow Cathedral, 1957-58, St. Margaret's, Knightswood, Glasgow, 1958-61; Acting Chaplain, Hope Waddell Training Institution, Nigeria, 1959; Associate Minister, St. Mark's, Wishaw, 1962; Minister, Newbattle, 1962-66; Assistant Secretary, Church of Scotland Department of Education, 1966-72; Lecturer in Church History, Aberdeen University, 1972-90, Senior Lecturer, 1991-92; Master of Christ's College, Aberdeen, 1982-92; Alexander Robertson Lecturer, Glasgow University, 1995; Coordinator in Christian Studies, Aberdeen University, 1995-97; Moderator, Aberdeen Presbytery, 1982-83, Synod of Grampian, 1991-92; Convener, Church of Scotland Board of Education, 1987-91; Clerk, Aberdeen Presbytery, 1993-95; President: Scottish Church Society, 1988-91, Church Service Society, 1991-93; Chairman, Association of University Teachers (Scotland), 1982-84. Recreations: hill-walking; church architecture; stamp and coin collecting. Address: (h.) 25 Albury Place, Aberdeen, AB11 6TQ; T.- 01224 572305.

Selkirk of Douglas, Rt. Hon. Lord (James Alexander Douglas-Hamilton), PC, QC, MA, LLB. Appointed Life Peer, 1997; MSP (Conservative), Lothians, 1999-2007; MP (Conservative), Edinburgh West, 1974-97; b. 31.7.42, Dungavel House, Strathaven; m., (Priscilla) Susan (Susie) Buchan; 4 s. Educ. Eton; Balliol College, Oxford; Edinburgh University. Officer, TA 6/7 Bn. Cameronians Scottish Rifles, 1961-66, TAVR, 1971-74, Captain in the Cameronian Company of the 2nd Battalion of Lowland Volunteers; Advocate, 1968-74; Councillor, Murrayfield-Cramond, 1972-74; Scottish Conservative Whip, 1977; a Lord Cmnr., HM Treasury, 1979-81, PPS to Malcolm Rifkind MP, at Foreign Office, later as Secretary of State for Scotland, 1983-87; Parliamentary Under Secretary of State: at the Scottish Office for Home Affairs and Environment, 1987-89; for Home Affairs and Environment, 1989-92 (with additional responsibility for local government finance 1989-90, and with additional responsibility for the arts in Scotland, 1990-92); for Education and Housing, Scottish Office, 1992-95; Minister of State for Home Affairs and Health, Scottish Office, 1995-97. Member, Scottish Select Committee Scottish Affairs 1981-83; Honorary Secretary: Conservative Parliamentary Constitutional Committee, Conservative Parliamentary Aviation Committee, 1983-87; Chairman, Scottish Parliamentary All-Party Penal Affairs Committee, 1983; Honorary President, Scottish Amateur Boxing Association, 1975-98; President: Royal Commonwealth Society (Scotland), 1979-87, Scottish National Council of UN Association, 1981-87; Member, Council, National Trust for Scotland, 1977-82; Honorary Air Commodore No. 2 (City of Edinburgh) Maritime Headquarters Unit and President International Rescue Corps, 1995; Honorary Air Commodore No. 603 (City of Edinburgh) Squadron, 2000-2015; President, International Rescue Corps, since 1995; Patron, Hope and Homes for Children (Chairman, Edinburgh Support Group, 2002-07); President, Scottish Veterans Garden City Association Incorporated, since 2003; President, Trefoil House Charity, 2007; Chairman, Scottish Advisory Committee of Skill Force, 2009. Oxford Boxing Blue, 1961; President, Oxford University Conservative Association, 1963; President, Oxford Union, 1964. Publications: Motive For A Mission: The Story Behind Hess's Flight to Britain, 1971; The Air Battle for Malta: The Diaries of a Fighter Pilot, 1981; Roof of the World: Man's First Flight over Everest, 1983; The Truth about Rudolf Hess, 1993; "After You, Prime Minister", 2009. Recreations: golf; debating; history. Address: House of Lords, London SW1A 0PW.

Sellar, William David Hamilton, MVO, BA, LLB, FRHistS. Lord Lyon King of Arms, 2008-2014; Bute Pursuivant of Arms, 2001-08; Islay Herald of Arms Extraordinary, since 2014; b. 27.2.41, Burnside, Glasgow; m., Susan Margaret Sainsbury; 4 s. Educ. Kelvinside Academy; Fettes College; St. Edmund Hall, Oxford; Edinburgh University. Solicitor; Legal Assessor and Depute Clerk of Court, Scottish Land Court, 1967-68; Lecturer, Senior Lecturer, Faculty of Law, University of Edinburgh, 1969-95. Secretary, Company of Scottish History Ltd., 1972-77; Literary Director, The Stair Society, 1979-84; President, Scottish Society for Northern Studies, 1984-87; Member, Ancient Monuments Board, 1991-97; Chairman of Council, Scottish History Society, 1998-2001; Vice-President, Society of Antiquaries of Scotland, 1999-2002; Chairman, Conference of Scottish Medievalists, 2000-03; Honorary President, Scottish Genealogy Society, since 2009. Publications on Scots Law and Legal History, Highland History and Genealogy. Recreations: walking; island hopping; golf. Address: (b.) 6, Eildon Street, Edinburgh EH3 5JU.

Sellers, Professor Susan Catherine, MA, DEA, PhD. Professor of English and Related Literature, St Andrews University, since 1998; b. 7.5.57, Lymington; m., Jeremy Thurlow; 1 s. Educ. British School, Brussels; Sorbonne, Paris. Senior Researcher, Ecole Normale Superieure, Paris, 1989-95; Reader, St Andrews University, 1995-98; Visiting Fellow, New Hall, Cambridge, 1994-95; Invited Fellow, St John's College, Oxford, Summer 1994; Leverhulme Research Fellow and Senior Visiting Scholar, Trinity College, Cambridge, 2001-02. Publications: Writing Differences; Delighting the Heart; Taking Reality by Surprise; Feminist Criticism: Theory and Practice; Language and Sexual Difference; Coming To Writing (translation); Three Steps on the Ladder of Writing (translation); The Semi-Transparent Envelope: Women Writing (Co-author); The Hélène Cixous Reader; Instead of Full Stops; Hélène Cixous: Authorship, Autobiography and Love; The Cambridge Companion to Virginia Woolf (Co-editor); Myth and Fairy Tale in Contemporary Women's Fiction; The Writing Notebooks of Hélène Cixons (Editor). Address: (b.) School of English, University of St. Andrews, Fife, KY16 9AL; T.-01334 462666.

Sempill, 21st Baron (James William Stuart Whitemore Sempill); b. 25.2.49; m.; 1 s.; 1 d. Educ. St Clare's Hall, Oxford. Succeeded to title, 1995; Company Director; contested (Conservative) Edinburgh North and Leith, Scottish Parliamentary election, 1999.

Semple, Colin Gordon, MA, MBChB, FRCP(Glas), FRCP(Ed), FRCP(London), MD. Consultant Physician, Southern General Hospital, Glasgow, since 1988; Honorary Clinical Senior Lecturer, Glasgow University, since 1988; b. 19.3.53, Glasgow; m., Elaine; 1 s.; 1 d. Educ. Loretto School; Brasenose College, Oxford; Glasgow University. General Physician with interest in diabetes and endocrinology and special interest in postgraduate medical education; Associate Postgraduate Dean, 2002-08; Deputy Medical Director, NHS Education Scotland, 2006-08; Chairman, General Medicine Specialist Advisory Committee, 1999-2003; Royal College of Physicians and Surgeons of Glasgow: Member, Council, 1986-90, Deputy Honorary Secretary, 1995-98, Honorary Secretary, 1998-2001, Vice-President, 2005-07, Dean, Faculty of Podiatric Medicine, since 2012. Recreations: golf; gardening; walking; curling.

Semple, David, LLB. Mediator, coach, business adviser; Chairman, Non Intrusive Crossover System Ltd; Chair, Cancer Support Scotland (Tak Tent); formerly Partner and Chairman, Semple Fraser WS; b. 29.12.43, Glasgow; m., Jet; 2 s.; 1 d. Educ. Loretto School; Glasgow University. Partner, Bird Son & Semple, 1968-73; Bird Semple and Crawford Herron, 1973-88; Bird Semple Fyfe Ireland,

1988-90. President, Glasgow Chamber of Commerce, 1996-97; Chairman, Interactive Media Alliance Scotland, 1998-99. Recreations: golf; hill-walking; bagpipes. Address: (b.) 39 Kelvin Court, Great Western Road, Glasgow G12 0AE; T.-0141-3340744; e-mail: david.semple@btinternet.com

Semple, Peter d'Almaine, DL, MD, FRCPGlas, FRCPEdin, FRCPLond. B. 30.10.45, Glasgow; m., Judith Mairi Abercromby; 2 d. Educ. Belmont House; Loretto; Glasgow University. Consultant Physician, Inverclyde Royal Hospital, 1979-2009 (retired); former Postgraduate Medical Tutor, Inverclyde District; Honorary Clinical Senior Lecturer, Glasgow University (retired). Past Chairman, Medical Audit Sub-Committee, Scottish Office; Past President, Greenock and District Faculty of Medicine; Past Chairman, West of Scotland Branch, British Deer Society; Past Director, Medical Audit and Property Convenor, Royal College of Physicians and Surgeons of Glasgow; Deputy Lieutenant, Renfrewshire; Past Chairman, Ardgowan Hospice. Recreations: field sports; gardening. Address: (h.) High Lunderston, Inverkip, PA16 0DU; T.-01475 522342.

Semple, Walter George, BL, DUniv, NP. Solicitor, 1963-2012; b. 7.5.42, Glasgow; m., Dr. Lena Ohrstrom; 3 d. Educ. Belmont House, Glasgow; Loretto School; Glasgow University. President, Glasgow Juridical Society, 1968; Tutor and Lecturer (part-time), Glasgow University, 1970-79; Council Member, Law Society of Scotland, 1976-80 and 2003-2011; Chairman, Scottish Lawyers European Group, 1978-81; Member, Commission Consultative des Barreaux Europeens, 1978-80, 1984-87; President, Association Internationale des Jeunes Avocats, 1983-84; Chairman, Scottish Branch, Institute of Arbitrators, 1989-91; Board Member, Union Internationale des Avocats, 1997-2001; Dean, Royal Faculty of Procurators in Glasgow, 1998-2001; President, Franco Scottish Business Club, 2000-01; Trustee and Treasurer, John Muir Trust, 2007-2013; Chairman, Campbell Lee plc, 2002-07; Council Member, Geological Society of Glasgow, since 2014. Recreations: fishing; skiing; music; geology. Address: (h.) 79 Lancefield Quay, Glasgow G3 8HA.

Senior, Nora. Chair, Scottish Chambers of Commerce, since 2013; President, British Chambers of Commerce, since 2013; b. St. Andrews. Educ. University of Glasgow. Career: established The PR Centre in 1990; Managing Director at Hall Associates, Saatchi & Saatchi's Scottish-based PR consultancy; became Executive Chair, UK Regions and Ireland of global public relations and public affairs consultancy, Weber Shandwick in 2009. Recognised by a number of industry awards including Scottish Businesswoman of the Year (2003); a global 'Stevie' award for Best Woman in Business in Europe, Middle East and Asia; a Scottish Woman of Achievement Award and a Fellow of the Chartered Institute of Public Relations for outstanding contribution to the PR industry in Scotland; non-executive Board member of the National Trust for Scotland; Vice Chair of the Scottish Chamber of Commerce (SCC); a Regional Adviser to the London Stock Exchange; Chair of the Women in Business Group (Edinburgh Chamber of Commerce). Address: Scottish Chambers of Commerce, 30 George Square, Glasgow G2 1EQ; T.-0141 204 8316; e-mail: admin@scottishchambers.org.uk

Sewel, Lord (John Buttifant Sewel), CBE, LLD. Senior Vice-Principal, University of Aberdeen, 2001-04; Parliamentary Under-Secretary of State, Scottish Office, 1997-99; b. 1946; m., Jennifer; 1 s.; 1 d.; 2 step-d. Educ. Hanson Boys' Grammar School, Bradford; Durham University; University College Swansea; Aberdeen University. Councillor, Aberdeen City Council, 1974-84 (Leader of the Council, 1977-80); President, COSLA, 1982-84; Member, Accounts Commission for Scotland, 1987-96; Member, Scottish Constitutional Convention, 1994-95. Research Assistant, Department of Sociology and Anthropology, University College of Wales, Swansea, 1967-69; Aberdeen University, 1969-2004; successively Research Fellow, Lecturer, Senior Lecturer, Professor, Dean, Faculty of Economic and Social Sciences, 1989-94; Vice Principal and Dean, Faculty of Social Sciences and Law, 1995-97, Professor and Vice-Principal, 1999-2001, Senior Vice-Principal, 2001-04; created Peer, 1996; Opposition Spokesperson for Scotland, 1996-97; Parliamentary Under-Secretary of State, Scottish Office (Minister for Agriculture, the Environment and Fisheries), 1997-99; Lords Select Committees: Member, European Union, since 2006, Member, NATO Parliamentary Assembly, since 2005, Chair, NATO Sub-Committee Transatlantic Economic Relations, since 2006; Chair, European Union Sub-Committee D (Environment and Agriculture), since 2007; UK representative to NATO Parliamentary Assembly, 1999-2002 and since 2005. Recreations: hill-walking; skiing; watching cricket. Address: House of Lords, London SW1.

Sewell, Professor John Isaac, PhD, DSc, CEng, FIEE, FIEEE. Emeritus Professor of Electronic Systems, since 2005; Professor of Electronic Systems, Glasgow University, 1985-2005 (Dean, Faculty of Engineering, 1990-93, Member, Court, 2000-04); b. 13.5.42, Kirkby Stephen; m., Ruth Alexandra Baxter; 1 d. Educ. Kirkby Stephen Grammar School; Durham University; Newcastle-upon-Tyne University. Lecturer, Senior Lecturer, Reader, Department of Electronic Engineering, Hull University, 1968-85. Publications: 163 papers. Recreations: swimming; climbing. Member, Council, Baptist Union of Scotland, 2008-2013. Address: (h.) 16 Paterson Place, Bearsden, Glasgow G61 4RU; T.-0141-586 5336. E-mail: Sewellmac@aol.com

Shanks, Duncan Faichney, RSA, RGI, RSW. Artist; b. 30.8.37, Airdrie; m., Una Brown Gordon. Educ. Uddingston Grammar School; Glasgow School of Art. Part-time Lecturer, Glasgow School of Art, until 1979; now full-time painter; one-man shows: Stirling University, Scottish Gallery, Fine Art Society, Talbot Rice Art Gallery, Edinburgh University, Crawford Centre, Maclaurin Art Gallery, Glasgow Art Gallery, Fine Art Society, touring exhibition (Wales); taken part in shows of Scottish painting, London, 1986, Toulouse, Rio de Janeiro, 1985, Wales, 1988; Scottish Arts Council Award; Latimer and MacAulay Prizes, RSA; Torrance Award, Cargill Award, MacFarlane Charitable Trust Award, RGI; May Marshall Brown Award, RSW; The Lord Provost's Prize for painting (GOMA), 1996; tapestry commissioned by Coats Viyella, woven by Edinburgh Tapestry Company, presented to Glasgow Royal Concert Hall, 1991. Recreations: music; gardening.

Shanks, Melvyn D., BSc, DipEd, MInstP, CPhys, SQH. Principal, Belmont House School, since 2006; b. 15.7.62, Glasgow; m., Lynn; 2 s. Educ. The High School of Glasgow; University of Glasgow; University of Strathclyde. Teacher of Physics and Maths, The High School of Glasgow, 1985-90; Belmont House School: Head of Physics, 1990-97, Depute Head, 1997-2005. Recreation: member of the Salvation Army; music; golf; reading. Address: (b.) Belmont House School, Newton Mearns, Glasgow G77 5DU; T.-0141-639-2922. E-mail: admin@belmontschool.co.uk

Shanks, Rev. Norman James, MA, BD, DD; b. 15.7.42, Edinburgh; m., Ruth Osborne Douglas; 2 s.; 1 d. Educ. Stirling High School; St. Andrews University; Edinburgh

University. Scottish Office, 1964-79; Chaplain, Edinburgh University, 1985-88; Lecturer in Practical Theology, Glasgow University, 1988-95; Leader, Iona Community, 1995-2002; Minister, Govan Old Parish Church, Glasgow, 2003-07. Convener, Acts Commission on Justice, Peace, Social and Moral Issues, 1991-95; Chairman, Edinburgh Council of Social Service, 1985-88; Chairman, Secretary of State's Advisory Committee on Travelling People, 1985-88; Convener, Church and Nation Committee, Church of Scotland, 1988-92; Moderator, Glasgow Presbytery, 2002-03; President, Scottish Churches Open College, 2001-03; Member, Broadcasting Council for Scotland, 1988-93; Member, Scottish Constitutional Convention, 1989-97; Central Committee of World Council of Churches, 1998-2006 (Moderator of WCC 9th Assembly Planning Committee, 2003-06); Member of Board of Christian Aid, 2000-05; Member of Greater Glasgow and Clyde Health Board, since 2010; HonDD, Glasgow University, 2005. Recreations: armchair cricket; occasional golf. Address: (h.) 1 Marchmont Terrace, Glasgow G12 9LT; T.-0141-339 4421.

Shanks, Thomas Henry, MBE, MA, LLB. Solicitor (retired); Writer; Honorary Sheriff, Lanark, since 1982; Judge; Chairman, Appeals Service, 1985-2003; b. 22.10.30, Lanark; m., Marjorie A. Rendall; 1 s.; 1 d. (by pr. m.); 3 step s.; 1 step d. Educ. Lanark Grammar School; Glasgow University. Intelligence Corps (National Service), 1954-56. Depute Clerk of Peace, County of Lanark, 1961-74; Chairman, Royal Burgh of Lanark Community Council, 1977-80 and 1983-86; Captain, Lanark Golf Club, 1962 and 2001; President, Lanark Golf Club, since 2014; Lanark Lord Cornet, 1968. Recreations: golf; writing. Address: (h.) 5 Friarsfield Road, Lanark.

Sharkey, Jeffrey. Principal, Royal Conservatoire of Scotland, since 2014. Educ. Manhattan School of Music; Yale University; University of Cambridge. Director of Music, The Purcell School and Head of Academic Music, Wells Cathedral School, 1996-2001; Dean, Cleveland Institute of Music, 2001-06; Director, Peabody Institute, 2006-2014. Founding member of the Pirasti Piano Trio, which recorded with ASV Records in the United Kingdom and toured throughout Europe and the United States; coached chamber music as a faculty member and in master classes and summer festivals; performed with the Baltimore Symphony and collaborated with members of the Cleveland, Orion, and Cavani Quartets. Address: Royal Conservatoire of Scotland, 100 Renfrew Street, Glasgow G2 3DB; T.-0141 332 4101.

Sharp, Paul M., BSc, PhD, MRIA, FRSE, FRS. Alan Robertson Chair of Genetics, University of Edinburgh, since 2007; b. 12.09.57, Heanor. Educ. University of Edinburgh. Lecturer, Associate Professor, Trinity College, University of Dublin, 1982-93; Professor of Genetics, University of Nottingham, 1993-2007. President, Society for Molecular Biology and Evolution, 2008. Address: (b.) Institute of Evolutionary Biology, University of Edinburgh, Kings Buildings, Edinburgh EH9 3FL; T.-0131-651-3684; e-mail: paul.sharp@ed.ac.uk

Sharp, Paula, MA (Cantab). Self Employed Management Consultant, since 1994; Scottish Boundary Commissioner, since 2010; b. 27.09.53, London; m., Dr. Stephen Sharp. Educ. Cheltenham Ladies' College; Girton College, Cambridge. Various Local Government Finance Posts to 1989; Senior Manager, Coopers & Lybrand, 1989-94. Board Member, Link Living/Link Homes, 1995-2005; Board Member, Turning Point Scotland, 1999-2009 (Chair, 2005-07); Board Member, Rock Trust, 2009-2015 (Chair, 2009-2013); Ian Doig Award (2008) for services to CIPFA

in Scotland. Recreations: travel; walking; Gaelic language and culture; music (traditional and classical).

Sharp, Professor Peter Frederick, OBE, BSc, PhD, CPhys, CSci, FInstP, ARCP, FIPEM, FRSE. Emeritus Professor of Medical Physics, University of Aberdeen; b. 13.8.47, Spalding; 2 s. Educ. Spalding Grammar School; Durham University; Aberdeen University. University of Aberdeen: Lecturer in Medical Physics, 1974-83, Senior Lecturer in Medical Physics, 1983-90. Honorary Sheriff, Stonehaven. Publication: Practical Nuclear Medicine (Editor). Address: (b.) Department of Biomedical Physics and Bioengineering, Foresterhill, Aberdeen AB25 2ZD; T.-01224 552499; e-mail: p.sharp@abdn.ac.uk

Sharwood Smith, Professor Michael Anthony, PhD, MA, DipAppLing. Honorary Professorial Fellow, University of Edinburgh; Professor Emeritus, Heriot-Watt University; b. 22.5.42, Cape Town, South Africa; m., Ewa Maria Wróblewska; 2 d. Educ. King's School, Canterbury; St Andrews University; Edinburgh University. English Teacher: Centre Pédagogique Regionale, Montpellier, France; British Centre, Sweden; British Council Senior Lecturer, Adam Mickiewicz University, Poznan, Poland; Senior Lecturer, Utrecht University, Netherlands. Founding Vice-President, European Second Language Association; Honorary Professorial Fellow, Edinburgh University. Publications: over 100 on English linguistics, applied linguistics and second language acquisition; books include: Second Language Learning: Theoretical Foundations, 1994; Founding Editor, Second Language Research journal. Recreations: painting and drawing; music, trumpet and guitar; flight simulation. Address: (b.) Room 4.03 Charteris Land, University of Edinburgh, Old Moray House, Holyrood Road, Edinburgh EH8 8AQ.

Shaw, Rev. Alistair Neil, MA (Hons), BD (Hons), MTh. Minister, St. Paul's Parish Church, Johnstone, since 2003; b. 6.7.53, Kilbarchan; m., Brenda Bruce; 2 d. Educ. Paisley Grammar School; University of Glasgow. Minister: Relief Parish Church, Bourtreehill, Irvine, 1982-88, Laigh Kirk, Kilmarnock, 1988-99, Greenbank Parish Church, Clarkston, Glasgow, 1999-2002. Moderator of Presbytery of Irvine and Kilmarnock, 1995-96; Moderator of Presbytery of Greenock and Paisley, 2009-10. Recreations: foreign travel; ancient history; swimming; cycling; walking. Address: 9 Stanley Drive, Brookfield, Johnstone, Renfrewshire PA5 8UF; T.-01505 320060; e-mail: ans2006@talktalk.net

Shaw, Major General David, CBE, MDA, DipM. Director, Unicorn ARC and AFV Estates; Chairman of Trustees, AF&V Launchpad; Visiting Professor, Aberdeen Business School, since 2010; b. Ceylon (Sri Lanka). Career History: commissioned into the Royal Artillery in 1976; commanded 40 Regiment Royal Artillery (The Lowland Gunners); instructor at the Royal Military Academy at Sandhurst; served in Bosnia in 1996 as the Spokesman and Head of Media Operations for Multi-National Division South West; lecturer on management, procurement and technology on MSc course at the Royal Military College of Science at Shrivenham; Director of Media and Communication for the Army, Headquarters Land Forces, 2007-2009; General Officer Commanding 2nd Division, 2009-2012; Governor, Edinburgh Castle, 2009-2012. Royal Scots Club; Bembridge Sailing Club; former Commodore, Royal Artillery Yacht Club. E-mail: dahshaw@gmail.com

Shaw, Rev. Professor Douglas William David, OBE, MA, LLB, BD, DD (Glasgow and St Andrews). WS. Professor of Divinity, St Andrews University, 1979-91 (Dean, Faculty of Divinity, 1983-86, Principal, St. Mary's College, 1986-92); Minister, Church of Scotland, since 1960; b. 25.6.28, Edinburgh; m., Edinburgh Academy; Loretto; Ashbury

College, Ottawa; St. John's College, Cambridge; Edinburgh University. Practised law as WS (Partner, Davidson and Syme, WS, Edinburgh), 1952-57; Assistant Minister, St. George's West Church, Edinburgh, 1960-63; Official Observer, Second Vatican Council, Rome, 1962; Lecturer in Divinity, Edinburgh University, 1963-79; Principal, New College, and Dean, Faculty of Divinity, Edinburgh, 1973-78; Visiting Fellow, Fitzwilliam College, Cambridge, 1978; Visiting Lecturer, Virginia University, 1979. Publications: Who is God?, 1968; The Dissuaders, 1978, In Divers Manners (Editor), 1990; Dimensions, 1992; Theology in Scotland. Recreation: relaxing. Address: (h.) 4/13 Succoth Court, Edinburgh EH12 6BZ; T.-0131-337 2130; e-mail:DWilliamDShaw@aol.com

Shaw, Rev. Duncan, BD (Hons), MTh. Minister, St. John's, Bathgate, since 1978; b. 10.4.47, Blantyre; m., Margaret S. Moore; 2 s.; 1 d. Educ. St. John's Grammar School, Hamilton; Hamilton Academy; Trinity College, Glasgow University. Assistant Minister, Netherlee Parish Church, Glasgow, 1974-77. Clerk, West Lothian Presbytery, since 1982 (Moderator, 1989-90). Recreations: gardening; travel (in Scotland). Address: St. John's Parish Church Manse, Mid Street, Bathgate, EH48 1QD; T.-Bathgate 653146; e-mail: westlothian@cofscotland.org.uk

Shaw, Jo, BA (Cantab), LenDr (Brussels), LLD (Edin), FRSA, AcSS. Salvesen Chair, European Institutions, University of Edinburgh, since 2005; Dean of Research, College of Humanities and Social Science, 2009-2013; Director, Institute for Advanced Studies in the Humanities, since 2014; Senior Research Fellow, Federal Trust, London, since 2001; b. 17.09.61, Shipley; 1 s. Educ. Bradford Girls' Grammar School; Trinity College, Cambridge. Lecturer in Law, University of Exeter, 1984-90; Senior Lecturer in Law, Keele University, 1990-95; Professor of European Law and Director of The Centre for The Study of Law in Europe, University of Leeds, 1995-2001; Professor of European Law, University of Manchester, 2001-04. Author of many books and papers on European Union Law. Recreations: photography; swimming; walking. Address: (b.) Institute for Advanced Studies in the Humanities, University of Edinburgh, Hope Park Square, Edinburgh EH8 9NW; T.-0131 650 9587; e-mail: jo.shaw@ed.ac.uk

Shaw, Professor Sir John Calman, CBE, KStJ, Dr hc, LLD, BL, FRSE, CA. Former Governor, Bank of Scotland (1999-2001); b. 10.7.32, Perth; m., Shirley Botterill; 3 d. Educ. Strathallan; Edinburgh University. Qualified as Chartered Accountant, 1954; Partner, Graham, Smart & Annan, CA, Edinburgh, latterly Deloitte Haskins & Sells, 1960-1987; President, Institute of Chartered Accountants of Scotland, 1983-84; Johnstone Smith Professor of Accountancy, Glasgow University, 1977-83; Non-Executive Director, Bank of Scotland, 1990-2001, Deputy Governor, 1991-99. Director of various Investment Trusts and other companies (1982-2002); former Trustee, Scottish Science Trust and David Hume Institute; Receiver General, Priory of Scotland of Most Venerable Order of St. John, 1992-2002; Chairman, Scottish Higher Education Funding Council, 1992-98; Board Member, Scottish Enterprise, 1990-98; Deputy Chairman, Edinburgh Festival Society, 1990-2000; Executive Director, Scottish Financial Enterprise, 1986-90, later Chairman, 1995-99; author of various texts and publications on accountancy and corporate governance. Recreations: listening to music; walking; travel. Address: (b.) Tayhill, Brae Street, Dunkeld PH8 0BA.

Shaw, Mark Robert, BA, MA, DPhil, FRES, FRSE. Honorary Research Associate (Department of Natural Sciences), National Museums of Scotland, Keeper of Natural Sciences (formerly Geology and Zoology), 1996-2005; b. 11.5.45, Sutton Coldfield; m., Francesca Dennis Wilkinson; 2 d. Educ. Dartington Hall School; Oriel College, Oxford. Research Assistant (Entomology), Zoology Department, Manchester University, 1973-76; University Research Fellow, Reading University, 1977-80; Assistant Keeper, Department of Natural History, Royal Scottish Museum, 1980-83; Keeper of Natural History, National Museums of Scotland, 1983-96. Recreations: field entomology; family life. Address: (h.) 48 St. Albans Road, Edinburgh, EH9 2LU; T.-0131-667 0577; (b.) National Museums of Scotland, Chambers Street, Edinburgh EH1 1JF; T.-0131-247 4246; e-mail: m.shaw@nms.ac.uk

Shaw, Michael. Group General Counsel, Royal Bank of Scotland, since 2016. Educ. College of Law, London; University of Cambridge. Trainee and Associate Solicitor, Clifford Chance LLP, 1998-92; Associate Solicitor, Herbert Smith, 1997-98; Secretary to the Panel, Takeover Panel, 1996-98; Partner, Herbert Smith, 1997-2009; Deputy Group General Counsel, Barclays, 2009-2015. Address: RBS, Head Office, 36 St Andrew Square, Edinburgh EH2 2AD; T.-0345 724 2424.

Shaw, Neil, BSc, BA (Hons). Field Officer, School Leaders Scotland; Past President, School Leaders Scotland; b. 30.12.53, Airdrie; m., Nan; 1 s.; 1 d. Educ. Airdrie Academy; University of Glasgow. Mathematics Teacher, Caldervale High School, Airdrie, 1977-87; Principal Teacher of Mathematics: Crookston Castle Secondary School, Glasgow, 1987-90, Carluke High School, 1990-93; Assistant Head Teacher, Boclair Academy, Bearsden, 1993-98; Head Teacher: Broxburn Academy, 1998-2002, Boclair Academy, 2002-2013. Recreation: golf (Airdrie Golf Club, New Club St Andrews). E-mail: nshaw@ascl.org.uk

Shaw, Richard Wright, CBE, MA, FRSA. Principal and Vice Chancellor, University of Paisley, 1992-2001; b. 22.9.41, Preston; m., Susan Angela; 2 s. Educ. Lancaster Royal Grammar School; Sidney Sussex College, Cambridge. Assistant Lecturer in Management, then Lecturer in Economics, Leeds University, 1964-69; Lecturer in Economics, then Senior Lecturer, Stirling University, 1969-84; part-time Lecturer, Glasgow University, 1978-79; Visiting Lecturer, Newcastle University, NSW, 1982; Head, Department of Economics, Stirling University, 1982-84; Professor and Head, Department of Economics and Management, Paisley College, 1984-86, Vice Principal, 1986, Principal, 1987-92. Director, Renfrewshire Enterprise, 1992-2000; Member, Scottish Economic Council, 1995-98; Director, Higher Education Careers Service Unit, 1996-2001; Member, Board of Management, Reid Kerr College, 1993-2001; Member, Scottish Business Forum, 1998-99; Convener, Committee of Scottish Higher Education Principals, 1996-98; Member, Independent Review of Higher Education Pay and Conditions, 1998-99; Chairperson, Lead Scotland, 2001-07. Fellow, Scottish Vocational Education Council, since 1995; DUniv (Glasgow), 2001; DUniv (University of the West of Scotland), 2008. Recreations: sketching and painting. Address: (b.) Drumbarns, 18 Old Doune Road, Dunblane FK15 9AG.

Shearer, David James Buchanan, BAcc, CA, FRSA. Chairman: Liberty Living Group, since 2015, Scottish Edge Fund, since 2014, Mouchel Group, 2012-14, Aberdeen New Dawn Investment Trust plc, since 2012; Co-Chairman, Martin Currie (Holdings) Limited, 2012-14; Senior Independent Director, STV Group plc; Non-Executive Director, Mithras Investment Trust plc, since 2007; Senior Independent Director, Renold plc; Superglass Holdings plc, 2007-2012; Scottish Financial Enterprise, 2005-2010; Governor, The Glasgow School of Art, 2004-2010; Chairman, Crest Nicholson plc,

2007-09; Chief Strategic Adviser and Non-Executive Director, City Inn Limited, 2010-2011; Non-Executive Director, HBOS plc, 2004-07; b. 24.3.59, Dumfries; partner, Virginia Braid. Educ. Eastwood High School, Glasgow; Glasgow University; Columbia Business School (Leadership Development Programme). Joined Deloitte & Touche (formerly Touche Ross & Co.), 1979; qualified CA, 1982; Partner, 1988; Partner in charge, Corporate Finance, 1992-99; National Corporate Finance Executive Member, 1992-99; Global Director of Corporate Finance, Deloitte Touche Tohmatsu, 1996-99; Senior Partner, Scotland & Northern Ireland, 1999-2003; UK Board Member, 1999-2003; UK Executive Group Member, 1999-2003. Recreations: heli-skiing; yachting; rugby; golf; art; wine. Address: (b.) Buchanan Shearer & Co Limited, 32 Great Western Terrace Lane, Glasgow G12 9XA; T.-0141 342 4243.
E-mail: djbshearer@btopenworld.com

Shedden, Fred, MA, LLB. Chair, The Centre for Confidence and Well-being, since 2007; Non Executive Director: iomart Group plc, 2000-2011, Murray International Trust plc, since 2000; b. 30.6.44, Edinburgh; m., Irene; 1 s.; 1 d. Educ. Arbroath High School; Aberdeen University. McGrigor Donald: Partner, 1971, Managing Partner, 1985-92, Senior Partner, 1993-2000. Director, Scottish Financial Enterprise, 1989-99; Director, Standard Life Assurance Society, 1992-99; Director, Scottish Metropolitan Property PLC, 1998-2000; Non executive director, Glasgow School of Art, 2002-2010. Address: The Centre for Confidence and Well-being, Suite 403, 111 West George Street, Glasgow G2 1QX; T.-07516 961 800.
E-mail: shedden@madasafish.com

Sheehan, Wendy Anne, LLB, DipLP, NP. Partner, Sheehan Kelsey Oswald Family Law Specialists; Sheriff, Scottish Court Service, since 2005; b. 26.12.68, Glasgow. Educ. St. George's School for Girls; University of Aberdeen. Trainee, Assistant, Associate Solicitor, Russel and Aitken, Solicitors, 1990-96; Associate, Balfour and Manson, Solicitors, 1996-2000; Partner, MHD Solicitors, 2000-06. Former Chair, Couple Counselling Lothian; former Convener, CALM. Author for Butterworths Family Law Service; various published articles on family law. Listed as leading family lawyer in both Chambers and Partners guide to the legal profession and The Legal 500. Address: (b.) Forsyth House, 93 George Street, Edinburgh EH2 3ES; T.-0771-892-1242; e-mail: wendy.sheehan@sko-family.co.uk

Sheldon, David Henry, QC, LLB (Hons), DipLP; b. 22.4.65, Dundee. Educ. High School of Dundee; Aberdeen University. Admitted as Solicitor, 1990; Lecturer in Private Law, Edinburgh University, 1990-98; Associate Dean, Faculty of Law, Edinburgh University, 1994-97; admitted to Faculty of Advocates, 1998; took silk, 2013. Publications: Evidence: Cases and Materials, 1996; Scots Criminal Law, 2nd edition, 1997; The Laws of Scotland: Stair Memorial Encyclopaedia (Contributor); Court of Session Practice (Contributor). Recreations: rock climbing; cycling; music; song; laughter and the love of friends. Address: (b.) Advocates' Library, Parliament House, Edinburgh EH1 1RF; T.-0131-667 2043.

Shepherd, Professor James, BSc, MB, ChB, PhD, FRCPath, FRCP (Glas), FMedSci, FRSE. Emeritus Professor in Vascular Biochemistry, University of Glasgow, since 2006; b. 8.4.44, Motherwell; m., Janet Bulloch Kelly; 1 s.; 1 d. Educ. Hamilton Academy; Glasgow University. Lecturer, Glasgow University: Biochemistry, 1968-72, Pathological Biochemistry, 1972-77; Assistant Professor of Medicine, Baylor College of Medicine, Houston, Texas, 1976-77; Senior Lecturer in Pathological Biochemistry, Glasgow University, 1977-84; Visiting Professor of Medicine, Geneva University, 1984; Director, West of Scotland Coronary Prevention Study; Director, Prospective Study of Pravastatin in the Elderly at Risk; Executive Member, Treating to New Targets Study, 1998-2005; Principal Investigator, Jupiter UK, 2005-08; Chairman, European Atherosclerosis Society, 1993-96; Visiting Professor, The Cleveland Clinic, 1998; author of textbooks and papers on lipoprotein metabolism and heart disease prevention. Address: 17 Barriedale Avenue, Hamilton ML3 9DB.

Shepherd, Robert Horne (Robbie), MBE, MUniv (Aberdeen). Freelance Broadcaster, since 1976, including presenter of BBC Radio Scotland's Take The Floor, since 1981; Journalist and Author, specialising in the Doric language; b. 30.4.36, Dunecht, Aberdeen; m., Agnes Margaret (Esma) (1961); 1 s. Educ. Robert Gordon's College, Aberdeen. Left school at 15 to work in accountant's office, eventually becoming ASCA; management accountant, fish firm, 13 years; self-employed accountant. Hon. President, Friends of Elphinstone Institute, University of Aberdeen; Hon. President, Buchan Heritage Society. Author on Books of the Doric. Received the Hamish Henderson Award for services to Traditional Music and inducted into the Hall of Fame - Scots Trad Music Awards, 2006. Recreations: gardening; traditional arts of Scotland, especially the use of the Doric tongue.

Sheppard, Tommy. MP (SNP), Edinburgh East, since 2015; b. 1959, Coleraine, County Londonderry. Educ. local grammar school in Coleraine; Aberdeen University. Elected Vice President of the NUS (1982-84); worked in the East End of London and in 1986 was elected as a Labour member on Hackney London Borough Council; became Deputy Leader of the Council in 1990; joined Edinburgh District Council in 1994; Assistant General Secretary, Labour Party, 1994-97. Founded The Stand Comedy Club in Edinburgh in 1995; (expanded to include branches in Glasgow and Newcastle upon Tyne and is now one of the largest venues at the Edinburgh Fringe Festival). Edinburgh South organiser of the Yes Scotland campaign in 2012; Member, SNP, since 2014. Member: National Council of the Scottish Independence Convention, Common Weal. Address: House of Commons, London SW1A 0AA.

Sheridan, James. Labour MP, Paisley and Renfrewshire North, 2005-2015, West Renfrewshire, 2001-05; b. 24.11.52, Glasgow; m., Jean; 1 s.; 1 d. Educ. St Pius Secondary School. Trade union official, TGWU, 1999-2000; material handler, 1984-99; TGWU Convenor, Pilkington Optronics, 1985-99. Recreation: keep-fit activities. Address: (h.) 31 Park Glade, Erskine, Renfrewshire PA8 7HH.

Sheridan, Michael. Principal Solicitor, Sheridans, Glasgow, since 1974; Secretary, Scottish Law Agents Society, since 2004; b. 28.3.48, Glasgow; m., Carole; 3 s. Educ. St. Aloysius College, Glasgow; St. Mungo's Academy; University of Glasgow. Solicitor at Dundee and Glasgow, since 1972; College and University Lecturer, 1974-2001; Joint Standing Committee on Legal Education, 1998-2001; First Tier Tribunal Judge, Her Majesty's Courts and Tribunal Service. Recreations: hill walking; cycling; travel. Address: (b.) Scottish Law Agents Society, 166 Buchanan Street, Glasgow G1 2LW; T.-0141 332 3536.
E-mail: secretary@slas.co.uk

Sheridan, Tommy. Co-Convener, Solidarity (Scotland). Educ. University of Stirling; b. 7.3.64, Glasgow; m., Gail. MSP (Solidarity), Glasgow, 2006-07 (Scottish Socialist, 1999-2006). Member, Glasgow City Council, 1992-2003; President, Anti Poll Tax Federation, 1989-92.

Sherriff, Robert Mark, CBE, BA, DL. Stockbroker, since 1960; Chairman, Executive Committee, Erskine Hospital, 2000-05; Chairman, The MacRobert Trust Tarland, 1994-2006; Vice Lord Lieutenant, Stirling: Falkirk, 1995-2011; b. 29.3.36, Kilmacolm; m., Margaret Fraser; 2 s.; 2 d. Educ. Cargilfield; Sedbergh; Trinity College, Cambridge. National Service in the Argyll and Sutherland Highlanders, 1954-56; served with TA from 1956; joined R.C. Greig & Co., Stockbroker, Glasgow, 1959; became a Partner (now Director); former Vice Chairman, Greig Middleton & Co. Ltd., Glasgow; former Director, King & Shaxson Holdings PLC and Gerrard Group PLC, London; former Vice Chairman, Scottish Building Society; retired as Chairman, Highland TAVRA, 1996; Trustee, the Stirling Smith Art Gallery and Museum. Recreations: tennis; golf; shooting; skiing. Address: (h.) The Old Manse, Blairdrummond, by Stirling FK9 4UX.

Shiach, Allan G., BA. Chairman, Macallan-Glenlivet PLC, 1979-96; Chairman, Scottish Film Council, 1991-97; Chairman, Scottish Film Production Fund, 1991-96; Chairman, Scottish Screen, 1996-98; b. Elgin; m., Kathleen Breck; 2 s.; 1 d. Educ. Gordonstoun School; McGill University, Montreal. Writer/Producer, since 1970; Writer/Co-Writer: Don't Look Now, The Girl from Petrovia, Daryl, Joseph Andrews, Castaway, The Witches, Cold Heaven, Regeneration, In Love and War, and other films; Member: Broadcasting Council for Scotland, 1988-91; Member, Council, Scotch Whisky Association, 1984-96; Chairman, Writers' Guild of G.B., 1989-91; Director, Rafford Films, since 1982; Director, Scottish Media Group plc, 1993-2006; Governor, British Film Institute, 1992-98. Hon. Doctorate of Arts, Napier University (June, 2007); Hon. Doctorate Honoris Causa, Aberdeen University (November 2007). Co-author, co-producer, "Priscilla, The Musical", Palace Theatre, London, March 2009-January 2012; also productions in New York, Brazil, Italy etc; co-writer and script consultant on the Norwegian film Kon-Tiki (2012), which was nominated for an Oscar in 2013 in the foreign language category. Visiting Professor, Edinburgh Napier University, since 2015; Freeman, City of London, 1988; e-mail: algscott@aol.com

Shields, Tom, BA. Journalist; b. 9.2.48, Glasgow; 1 s.; 1 d. Educ. Bellarmine Comprehensive; Lourdes Secondary School (no miracle); Strathclyde University. Journalist, Sunday Post; Diary Writer, The Herald, 1979-2002; Columnist, Herald Scotland. Publications: Tom Shields' Diary; Tom Shields Too; Tom Shields Free at Last; Tom Shields Goes Forth; Just the Three Weeks in Provence (Co-author). Recreation: Celtic studies.

Shinton, Philip, MA (Cantab). Chair of College of Teachers, Edinburgh Steiner School, since 2010; Class Teacher, Edinburgh Steiner School, since 1989; b. 24.3.57, Birmingham; m., Dorothy Baird; 1 s.; 2 d. Educ. Solihull School; Jesus College, Cambridge; Emerson College, Sussex. Class Teacher: Elmfield School, Stourbridge, 1987-89, Edinburgh Steiner School, 1989-2012, then Chair of College of Teachers, 2010-2012. Recreations: walking long distance foot paths; birdwatching; gardening. Address: (b.) Edinburgh Steiner School, 60 Spylaw Road, Edinburgh EH10 5BR; T.-0131 337 3410.
E-mail: Philipshinton@tiscali.co.uk

Shinwell, Sir (Maurice) Adrian, Kt, DL, LLB, NP. Solicitor; Senior Partner, Kerr Barrie, Glasgow, since 1991; Deputy Lieutenant, Renfrewshire, 1999-2011; b. 27.2.51; m., Lesley McLean; 2 s.; 1 d. (1 s. deceased). Educ. Hutchesons' Boys' Grammar School; Glasgow University. Admitted Solicitor, 1975; joined Kerr, Barrie & Duncan, 1976; Notary Public, since 1976; Tutor (part-time), Law Faculty, Glasgow University, 1980-84; Solicitor-Mediator, 1994-2004; Director: National Theatre of Scotland, 2007-15, Digital Animations Group plc, 2002-07, St. Leonards School, 2001-2004, Kerr Barrie Nominees Ltd. Scottish

Conservative and Unionist Association: Member, Scottish Council, 1982-98; Chairman, Eastwood Association, 1982-85; Chairman, Cumbernauld and Kilsyth Association, 1989-91; Vice-President, 1989-92; President, 1992-94; Scottish Conservative and Unionist Party: Chairman, Candidates' Board, Member, Scottish Executive and Scottish Council, 1998-2000; Member, Central Advisory Committee on Justices of the Peace, 1996-99; Vice Chairman, Justices of the Peace Advisory Committee, East Renfrewshire, 2000-06. T.-0141-221 6844.

Shirreffs, Jennifer Anne, MBE (2009), DL, CStJ, M.Univ, BSc. Director, Aberdeen and NE Deaf Society, 1984-2009, Chairman, Board of Directors, 1992-2003 and 2008-09; Deputy Lieutenant, City of Aberdeen, since 2005; Burgess of the City of Aberdeen, since 2000; b. 20.1.49, Aberdeen; m., Dr Murdoch J. Shirreffs. Educ. Aberdeen High School for Girls; University of Aberdeen. PA to Rt. Hon. Jo Grimond MP while Rector of Aberdeen University, 1971-72; Co-ordinator, Community Arts Projects, Rowntree Trust, 1972-73. Chairman, Aberdeen Centenary Committee, Royal Scottish Society for Prevention of Cruelty to Children (now Children First), 1983-85; Trustee, Aberdeen Gomel Trust (Aberdeen City Council), since 1990; Vice-Chairman, St. John's Association (Aberdeen) and Order Committee, since 1994 and Chairman, since 2011; Elected Commander of the Order of St John, 2004; Chairman, Friends of Scottish Ballet (Grampian), 1989-2007; Chairman, Trading Company of Scottish Ballet, 2000-07; Director and Chairman, Friends of Aberdeen and NE Scotland Music School, since 1998; Director, Aberdeen Performing Arts running His Majesty's Theatre Music Hall, Lemon Tree and Aberdeen Box Office, 2001-2014; Chairman: HMT Centenary Committee, Music Hall 150th Anniversary Committee; University of Aberdeen: Member, General Council Business Committee, since 1994, Member of University Court, since 2012, Convener, Student Affairs Committee, since 2012, Chairman, Friends of the Elphinstone Institute, since 2006; Member and past president (2005-06) of Rotary Club of Aberdeen St. Machar; Member and past president (2006-07) of the Inner Wheel of Aberdeen St. Machar; Vice President, Bon Accord Ladies' Probus Club (Aberdeen), 2009 and President, 2010. Member of the Torry Trust, 2010-13. Recreations: piano playing (pianist for 66th Aberdeen Company Boys Brigade, since 1963); Boys' Brigade 50 year service medal awarded, 2013; philately; travel and languages; crosswords & sudoku; cooking and entertaining; visual and performing arts and music of all types. Address: (h.) 72 Gray Street, Aberdeen AB10 6JE; T.-01224-321998.
E-mail: jennys72@hotmail.co.uk

Shirreffs, Murdoch John, MB, ChB, DObstRCOG, FRCGP, MFHom. General Medical Practitioner, Gilbert Road Medical Group, Bucksburn, Aberdeen, 1974-2015; Medical Hypnotherapist and Homoeopathic Specialist; Specialist in Charge, NHS Grampian Homeopathy Service; b. 25.5.47, Aberdeen; m., Jennifer McLeod. Educ. Aberdeen Grammar School; Aberdeen University. General Practice Trainer, 1977-99; Secretary, Grampian Division, British Medical Association, 1978-2005; former Member, BMA Scottish Council. Awarded Provost Medal, NE Scotland Faculty, Royal College of General Practitioners, 2012. Past President, North of Scotland Veterans' Hockey Club; Member, Scottish LX (over 60s) Veterans' Hockey Team; Burgess, Guild of City of Aberdeen, since 2001. Recreations: hockey; opera and classical music; big band jazz; DIY; gardening; food and wine; travel. Address: (h.) 72 Gray Street, Aberdeen, AB10 6JE; T.-01224 321998.
E-mail: murdoch_and_jenny_shirreffs@msn.com

Short, Agnes Jean, BA (Hons), MLitt. Writer; b. Bradford, Yorkshire; m., Anthony Short (qv); 3 s.; 2 d. Educ. Bradford Girls' Grammar School; Exeter University; Aberdeen University. Various secretarial, research and teaching jobs, both in UK and abroad; took up writing,

1966; 19 novels, most of which have a Scottish setting; also short stories and radio; Constable Award, 1976. Recreations: dog-walking; whisky-tasting; good food; small hills. Address: (h.) Khantore, Crathie, by Ballater, Aberdeenshire AB35 5TJ.
E-mail: a.short154@btinternet.com

Sibbald, Michael Robert, BA, MBA; b. 30.8.48, Edinburgh; m., Margaret; 2 s.; 1 d. Educ. George Heriot's School; Heriot-Watt University; Glasgow University. Lay Member, Employment Appeals Tribunal, since 2002; Non Executive Director, Whitehall Industry Group, 2004-07; Non Executive Director, Shaw Associates, 2007-11; Non Executive Director, Edinburgh Leisure Ltd, 2008-2014; Member, Advisory Council, Public Concern at Work, 2006-2013; Director, Cessi Holdings Ltd, 2013. Recreations: reading; sports cars; athletics; football; hill walking. Address: (h.) The Long House, Deanfoot Road, West Linton EH46 7DX; T.-01968 660569.

Sibbett, Professor Wilson, CBE, FRS, FRSE, BSc, PhD. Emeritus Professor; Wardlaw Professor of Natural Philosophy, St. Andrews University (Director of Research, 1994-2003, Chairman, Department of Physics and Astronomy, 1985-94); Chair, Scottish Science Advisory Committee, 2002-06; b. 15.3.48, Portglenone, N. Ireland; m., Barbara Anne Brown; 3 d. Educ. Ballymena Technical College; Queen's University, Belfast. Postdoctoral Research Fellow, Blackett Laboratory, Imperial College, London, 1973-76; Lecturer in Physics, then Reader, Imperial College, 1976-85. Fellow: Institute of Physics, Royal Society of Edinburgh, Royal Society (of London). Honorary Degrees: LLD (Dundee), DSc (Trinity College Dublin), DSc (Glasgow), DU (Strathclyde). Recreation: golf. Address: (b.) School of Physics and Astronomy, St. Andrews University, North Haugh, St. Andrews, KY16 9SS; T.-01334 463100.

Siddiqui, Professor Mona, OBE (2011), MA, MIL, PhD, DLitt (Hons), FRSE, FRSA, Hon FRIAS. Professor of Islamic and Interreligious Studies, Assistant Principal for Religion and Society, Divinity School, University of Edinburgh, since 2011; Professor of Islamic Studies and Public Understanding, Glasgow University, 2006-2011; Director, Centre for the Study of Islam, Glasgow University, 1998-2011; Commissioner on the Calman Commission, 2008-09; b. 3.5.63, Karachi, Pakistan; m., Farhaj; 3 s. Educ. Salendine-Nook High School, Huddersfield; Leeds University; Manchester University. Lecturer in Arabic and Islamic Studies: Manchester Metropolitan University, 1989-90, Glasgow Caledonian University, 1993, Glasgow University, 1995. Chair, BBC Scottish Religious Advisory Council, 2005; Member, BBC Central Religious Advisory Council, 2003; Member, World Economic Forum Council on Faith, 2007-09; Contributor, Thought for the Day, BBC Scotland and Radio 4. Three Hon. Degrees: HDLitt (Leics), HD Civil Laws (Huddersfield), DLitt (Wolverhampton); Hon. Doctorate, University of Roehampton, 2014; Debretts 500 Most Influential, January 2014. Awarded OBE for services to interfaith relations, 2011. Recreations: interior decorating; cooking; reading. Address: (b.) Divinity School, University of Edinburgh, New College, Mound Place, Edinburgh EH1 2LX; e-mail: Mona.Siddiqui@ed.ac.uk

Sillars, James. Columnist, The Scotsman; Management consultant; Assistant Secretary-General, Arab-British Chamber of Commerce, 1993-2002; b. 4.10.37, Ayr; m., Margo MacDonald (qv) (deceased); 1 s.; 3 d. Educ. Ayr Academy. Member, Ayr Town Council and Ayr County Council Education Committee, 1960s; Member, Western Regional Hospital Board, 1965-70; Head, Organisation Department, Scottish TUC, 1968-70; MP, South Ayrshire, 1970-79; Co-Founder, Scottish Labour Party, 1976; MP, Glasgow Govan, 1988-92.

Sim, Alastair Elliot, BA (Hons), MA, MPhil, FRSA. Director, Universities Scotland, since 2009; b. 24.8.67, Edinburgh; m., Fiona Parker; 2 s. Educ. Oxford University; University of Delaware; Glasgow University; Queen Margaret University. Civil Servant, Scottish Office/Scottish Government, 1989-2009; Private Secretary to Minister for Agriculture and the Environment, 1992-93; developed policy and legislation on constitutional reform and protection of the natural heritage, 1993-2000 (seconded to European Commission DG - Environment, 1994-95); Senior Civil Service, since 2000; Head of Division, Environment and Rural Affairs, 2000-04; Director of Planning, University of Glasgow (secondment), 2004-06; Director of Policy and Strategy, Scottish Court Service, 2006-09. Publications: Author: Rosslyn Blood, 2004, The Unbelievers, 2009. Recreations: family; writing; cycling; the outdoors. Address: (b.) Universities Scotland, Holyrood Park House, 106 Holyrood Road, Edinburgh EH8 8AS; T.-0131 226 1111.

Sime, Martin, MA. Director and Chief Executive, Scottish Council for Voluntary Organisations, since 1991; b. 23.9.53, Edinburgh. Educ. George Heriot's; St. Andrews University; Edinburgh University. Social and Economic History Researcher, 1976-78; Sheep Farmer, 1978-81; Freelance Researcher, 1982; Project Manager, Sprout Market Garden, 1983-85; Development/Principal Officer (Day Services), Scottish Association for Mental Health, then Director, 1985-91. Recreations: cinema; food; bridge. Address: (b.) Mansfield Traquair Centre, Mansfield Place, Edinburgh EH3 6BB; e-mail: martin.sime@scvo.org.uk

Simmers, Graeme Maxwell, CBE, CA; b. 2.5.35, Glasgow; m., Jennifer M.H. Roxburgh; 2 s.; 2 d. Educ. Glasgow Academy; Loretto School. Qualified CA, 1959; commissioned Royal Marines, 1959-61, Hon. Colonel, Royal Marines Reserve, 2000-06. Former Partner, Kidsons Simmers CA; Chairman, Scottish Highland Hotels Group Ltd., 1972-92; Member, Scottish Tourist Board, 1979-86; Chairman, HCBA (Scotland), 1984-86; Past Chairman, Board of Management, Member of National Executive, BHA; Elder and Treasurer, Killearn Kirk; Governor, Queen's College, Glasgow, 1989-93; Chairman, Scottish Sports Council, 1992-99; Non-Executive Director: Forth Valley Acute Hospitals Trust, 1993-2001, Forth Valley Health Board, 2002-2010; Past Chairman of Governors, Loretto School; Member, Stirling University Court, 2000-2010; 2012 Honorary Degree of Doctor of The University of Stirling; Captain, Royal and Ancient Golf Club of St. Andrews, 2001-02 (Past Chairman, Championship Committee). OBE, 1982. Recreations: rugby; golf; skiing. Address: (h.) 11 Crawford Gardens, St Andrews, Fife KY16 8XG; T.-01334 475519.
E-mail: graeme.simmers@btinternet.com

Simon, Shona M. W., MA, LLB, DipCG, DipLP. President, Employment Tribunals (Scotland), since 2009, Vice President, 2004-09; b. 9.5.60, Greenock; m., Dr. E. J. Simon; 2 s. Educ. Greenock Academy; University of Edinburgh. Careers Adviser, 1984-88; Partner, Mackay Simon, Employment Lawyers, 1993-2002; Equal Opportunities Development Adviser, Scottish Parliament, 2001-02. Publications: joint author, Employment Law (textbook); joint Update Editor, Simon & Taggart: Employment Tribunal Practice in Scotland. Recreations: cooking; reading. Address: (b.) Central Office of Employment Tribunals, The Eagle Building, 215 Bothwell Street, Glasgow G2 7TS.
E-mail: shona.simon@judiciary.gsi.gov.uk

Simpson, Alan Gordon, OBE, DL, MA (Oxon), CEng, MICE. Chairman, Macrobert Arts Centre, since 2015;

Partner, W. A. Fairhurst and Partners, 1989-2009; Chairman, University of Stirling Court, 2007-2015; Chairman, Lake of Menteith Fisheries Ltd, since 2009; Chairman, National Youth Orchestra of Scotland, 1998-2011; b. 15.2.50, Edinburgh; m., Jan; 1 s.; 1 d. Educ. Rugby School; Magdalen College, Oxford. Brian Colquhoun and Partners, 1972-78; W.A. Fairhurst and Partners, 1979-2009; Deputy Lieutenant, Stirling and Falkirk; Chairman, Institution of Civil Engineers Scotland, 2011-2012; Chairman, Glasgow and West of Scotland Branch of the Institution of Civil Engineers, 2006-07; Member, Council, Institution of Civil Engineers, 2000-03. Recreations: music; skiing; archery. Address: (h.) Arntomie, Port of Menteith, by Stirling.

Simpson, Graham. MSP (Scottish Conservative), Central Scotland region, since 2016. Elected Councillor, South Lanarkshire Council in 2007; selected to contest the East Kilbride Constituency in the Scottish Parliament election, 2016. Address: Scottish Parliament, Edinburgh EH99 1SP.

Simpson, Professor Hugh Walter, MB, ChB, MD, PhD, FRCPath, FRCP(Glas). Emeritus Professor; Senior Research Fellow, University Department of Surgery, Glasgow University and Royal Infirmary; Head of Pathology, Glasgow Royal Infirmary, 1984-93; Honorary Visiting Professor, University of Minnesota, since 1970; b. 4.4.31, Ceres Fife; m., Myrtle Emslie (see Myrtle Simpson); 3 s.; 1 d. Educ. Bryanston; Edinburgh University. Leader of numerous expeditions to polar and tropical regions; 4,000 miles sledged in polar regions; awarded Polar Medal, Mungo Park and Pery Medals; Man of the Year, Greenland Radio, 1965; Gold Medal Lecture, Royal College of Surgeons of Edinburgh, 1995; Scientist of the Year Lecture, Little Rock, Arkansas, 1978. Founder Editor, International Journal of Chronobiology; Visiting Scientist, National Institute of Health, Washington, 1978-79. Publications: 164 scientific publications, especially on breast cancer survival. Recreation: skiing. Address: (h.) Farleiter, Kincraig PH21 1NU; T.-01540 651288.
E-mail: h.simpson257@btinternet.com

Simpson, James, OBE, DSc, BArch, FRIAS, RIBA FSAScot. Architect & Conservator; Working Consultant, Simpson & Brown; b.27.07.44, Edinburgh; m. Ann Bunney (1968). Educ. Belhaven Hill; Trinity College Glenalmond; Edinburgh College of Art. Ian G. Lindsay & Ptrs, Edinburgh, 1962-71; Feilden+Mawson, Norwich & Edinburgh, 1972-77; Simpson & Brown, from 1977; Surveyor of the Fabric of York Minster (1993-4); Vice-President, ICOMOS-UK; past Commissioner, RCAHMS; past chairman, Scottish Society for Conservation & Restoration (SSCR); past member: Ancient Monuments Board for Scotland (AMBS), Scottish Conservation Bureau Advisory Panel (SCBAP), Cockburn Association Council, Historic Environment Advisory Council for Scotland (HEACS), Edinburgh World Heritage Trust (EWHT) & Scottish Lime Centre Trust; Building Preservation Trusts: Cockburn Conservation Trust, Scottish Historic Buildings Trust, Mavisbank Trust, Penicuik House Preservation Trust, Scottish Redundant Churches Trust, St Stephen's Playfair Trust, Perth City Market Trust & Orient Trust. Address: (b.) St. Ninian's Manse, Quayside Street, Edinburgh EH6 6EJ; T.-0131 555 4678.

Simpson, Very Rev. James Alexander, BSc (Hons), BD, STM, DD. Chaplain to the Queen in Scotland; Moderator, General Assembly of the Church of Scotland, 1994; b. 9.3.34, Glasgow; m., Helen Gray McCorquodale; 3 s.; 2 d. Educ. Eastwood Secondary School; Glasgow University; Union Seminary, New York. Minister: Grahamston Church, Falkirk, 1960-66, St. John's Renfield, Glasgow, 1966-76;

Minister, Dornoch Cathedral, 1976-97. Publications: There is a time to ....; Marriage Questions Today; Doubts are not Enough; Holy Wit; Laughter Lines; The Master Mind; Dornoch Cathedral; More Holy Wit; Keywords of Faith; All About Christmas; The Laugh Shall Be First; Life, Love and Laughter; A Funny Way of Being Serious; At Our Age; The Magic of Words, 2013. Recreations: golf; photography; writing. Address: Dornoch, Perth Road, Bankfoot, Perthshire PH1 4ED; T.-01738 787710.

Simpson, Rev. James Hamilton, BD, LLB. Minister, The Mount Kirk, 1965-2004; Chairman, Church of Scotland General Trustees, 2003-07; b. 29.6.36, Overtown; m., Moira W. Sellar; 2 s. Educ. Buckhaven High School; Edinburgh University; Glasgow University. Prison Chaplain, Greenock, 1971-81; Hospital Chaplain, Ravenscraig, 1983-2006. Recreations: sea fishing; boating; gardening; touring (especially Iberia). Address: (h.) 82, Harbourside, Kip Village, Inverkip PA16 0BF; T.-01475 520 582; e-mail: jameshsimpson@yahoo.co.uk

Simpson, John. Chief Executive, Our Dynamic Earth, since 1998. Address: Dynamic Earth, Holyrood Road, Edinburgh EH8 8AS; T.-0131 550 7800.

Simpson, Kenneth James, BMSc, MBChB (Hons), MSc, MD, PhD, FRCP(Edin). Senior Lecturer in Hepatology, University of Edinburgh, since 2000; Consultant Physician, Royal Infirmary, Edinburgh, since 1996; b. 11.8.60, Edinburgh; m., Rona; 2 s.; 1 d. Educ. Craigmount High School, Edinburgh; University of Dundee, University of London; University of Edinburgh. House Physician and Surgeon, Ninewells Hospital, Dundee, 1983-84; Senior House Officer, Western Infirmary/Gartnavel General, Glasgow, 1984-86; MRC Clinical Scientist, Clinical Research Centre, Northwick Park, London, 1986-89; Medical Registrar, Guildford and Kings College Liver Unit, 1989-91; Lecturer in Medicine/Senior Registrar, University of Edinburgh, Royal Infirmary, 1991-95; MRC Travelling Fellow, University of Michigan, USA, 1995-96. Publications: contributor, textbooks on hepatology; scientific papers. Recreations: reading crime novels; running. Address: (b) Royal Infirmary of Edinburgh, Old Dalkeith Road, Edinburgh EH16 4SA; T.-0131-536 2248; e-mail: k.simpson@ed.ac.uk

Simpson, Professor Mary, MA, PhD. Professor Emeritus, University of Edinburgh, since 2006; b. 4.12.42, Inverurie; m., Thomas Hardy Simpson; 1 s.; 1 d. Educ. Aberdeen Academy; Aberdeen University. Assistant Experimental Officer, Torry Research Station, Aberdeen, 1959-65; Researcher in Education, then Professor of Educational Research, Northern College, 1976-99; Professor of Classroom Learning, Edinburgh University, 1999-2005. Independent Member, National Educational Development Groups for: Standard Grade, 1983-87, 5-14 Assessment, 1989-92, Higher Still, 1994-97, 5-14 Evaluation Programme, 1991-97. Member, Scottish Consultative Council on the Curriculum, 1991-2000; Director and Chairman, Cornerstone Community Care Ltd., 1979-2000. Address: (h.) 6 Osborne Terrace, Edinburgh EH12 5HG.

Simpson, Myrtle Lillias, DL. Author and Lecturer; former Member, Scottish Sports Council; Past Chairman, Scottish National Ski Council; b. 5.7.31, Aldershot; m., Professor Hugh Simpson (qv); 3 s.; 1 d. Educ. 19 schools (father in Army). Writer/Explorer; author of 12 books, including travel, biography, historical and children's; first woman to ski across Greenland; attempted to ski to North Pole (most northerly point reached by a woman unsupported);

numerous journeys in polar regions on ski or canoe; exploration in China and Peru; Mungo Park Medal, Royal Scottish Geographical Society; Perrie Medal, Ski Club of Great Britain; received the Scottish Award for Excellence in Mountain Culture, 2013; former Editor, Avenue (University of Glasgow magazine). Recreations: climbing; skiing; canoeing; beekeeping. Address: (h.) Farletter, Kincraig, Inverness-shire PH21 1NU; T.-01540 651288.
E-mail: h.simpson257@btinternet.com

Simpson, Philip James Dalrymple, QC, LLB (Hons), LLM, DipLP, CIOT. Advocate, since 2001; Barrister (England and Wales), since 2001; b. 23.2.73, Glasgow; m., Anna Louise Robertson; 1 d.; 1 s. Educ. Bearsden Academy; University of Aberdeen; University of Regensburg; University of Edinburgh. Legal Assistant to the Lord President, 1999-2000; freelance legal translator, 2001-08; called to English Bar (Inner Temple), 2001. Publications: articles on Scots law and legal history. Recreations: opera; chess; European literature. Address: (b.) Advocates Library, Parliament House, Edinburgh EH1 1RF; T.-0131-226 5071.
E-mail: philip.simpson@advocates.org.uk

Simpson, Dr. Richard John, MB ChB, FRCGP, FRCPsych, DSHEC. MSP (Labour), Mid Scotland and Fife, 2007-2016; Shadow Minister for Public Services and Wealth Creation, 2015-16; Shadow Minister for Public Health, 2007-2015; b. 22.10.42, Edinburgh; m., Christine Margaret MacGregor; 2 s. Educ. Perth Academy; Trinity College, Glenalmond; Edinburgh University. Career history: President of Scottish Union of Students; Principal in General Practice; Psychiatrist and Honorary Professor, Stirling University; MSP, Ochil Constituency and Deputy Justice Minister; Consultant Psychiatrist in Addictions. Chair, Council of Management, Strathcarron Hospice; Chair, Medical Group of Scottish BAAF. Publications: 40 peer reviewed medical papers; 3 chapters of books on psychiatry in general practice; benzodiazepines psychology in general practice. Recreations: golf; gardening; classical music.

Sinclair, 18th Lord (Matthew Murray Kennedy St Clair). Director, Saint Property Limited; b. 9.12.68; m., Laura Cicely Coode; 2 s. Succeeded to title, 2004. Address: Knocknalling, St. Johns Town of Dalry, Castle Douglas DG7 3JT; e-mail: enquiries@saintproperty.com

Sinclair, Celia Margaret Lloyd, RGN, DMS, MBA, FCMI. Chief Executive, Coralyn Ltd. Founder and Chairman of the Willow Tea Rooms Charitable Trust, established to safeguard and restore Charles Rennie Macintosh's Willow Tearooms in Sauchiehall Street. Past Chairman of Court, Glasgow Caledonian University; formerly Board Member: Scottish Enterprise; Glasgow Chamber of Commerce; National Board for Nursing, Midwifery and Health Visiting for Scotland; Member: Merchants House, Glasgow; The Western Club, Glasgow; The Glasgow Art Club (Trustee and Vice Chairman of the Building Steering Group for the Club's renovations).
E-mail: celia_sinclair@btconnect.com

Sinclair, Rev. Colin Andrew Macalister, BA (Hons), BD (Hons). Minister, Palmerston Place Church of Scotland, since 1996; b. 16.9.53, Glasgow; m., Ruth Mary Murray; 1 s.; 3 d.; 1 granddaughter. Educ. Glasgow Academy; Stirling University; Edinburgh University. Training Officer, Scripture Union, Zambia, 1974-77; Assistant Minister, Palmerston Place Church of Scotland, Edinburgh, 1980-82; Church of Scotland Minister, Newton on Ayr, 1982-88; General Director, Scripture Union

Scotland, 1988-96. Chair, Scripture Union International Council; Convener, Mission & Discipleship Council, CFS. Publication: A Hitch-Hiker's Guide to the Bible. Recreations: family; reading; sport. Address: (b.) Annan House, 10 Palmerston Place, Edinburgh EH12 5AA.

Sinclair, Rev. David Ian, BSc, BD, PhD, DipSW. Minister, Wellington Church, Glasgow, since 2008; formerly Secretary, Church and Society Council, Church of Scotland (2005-08); b. 23.1.55, Bridge of Allan; m., Elizabeth Mary Jones; 1 s.; 1 d. Educ. High School of Stirling; Aberdeen University; Bristol University; University College, Cardiff; Edinburgh University. President, Student Christian Movement of Britain and Ireland, 1975-76; Social Worker (Community Development), Livingston, 1980-84; Assistant Minister, Dunblane Cathedral, 1987-88; Minister, St Andrews Martyrs, 1990-99, with Boarhills and Dunino, from 1993; Secretary, Church and Nation Committee, Church of Scotland, 1999-2005. Recreations: photography; music; armchair sport. Address: 31 Hughenden Gardens, Glasgow G12 9YH.

Sinclair, Douglas, CBE. Chair, Scotland Committee, Consumer Futures, since 2013; Chair, Consumer Focus Scotland, 2008-2013; Chair, Scottish Consumer Council, 2006-08; Member, Accounts Commission, since 2007; Depute Chair, Accounts Commission, since 2009; b. 28.1.46, Ellon; m., Mairi; 2 d. Educ. Inverness Royal Academy; Edinburgh University. Administrative Assistant, Midlothian CC, 1969-72; Administrative Officer, Barnardo's Scotland, 1972-75; Depute Director of Administration, then Director of Administration, Western Isles Islands Council, 1975-85; Chief Executive, Ross and Cromarty DC, 1985-90; Chief Executive, Central Regional Council, 1990-95; Chief Executive, Convention of Scottish Local Authorities (COSLA), 1995-99; Chief Executive, Fife Council, 1999-2006.

Sinclair, Eric T.A., MA, DipEd. Education Consultant, since 2000; Owner, The School Timetable Company; Non executive member, NHS Grampian Board, since 2015; b. 20.9.48, Edinburgh; m., Johanna Beckley; 3 c. Educ. Bell Baxter High School, Cupar; St. Andrews University; Edinburgh University; Moray House College. Taught, Teacher Training Colleges, Cameroon, Nigeria; Head of English, English High School, Istanbul; Head of English, St Joseph's College, Dumfries; Assistant Rector, Forres Academy; Depute Rector, Bridge of Don Academy; Rector, Kirkwall Grammar School; Rector, Aboyne Academy and Deeside Community Centre, Aberdeenshire. Publication: Man, Dog, Stroke: Musings of a Deeside Whippet and his Master, 2011. Recreations: reading; music; voluntary work for The Stroke Association. Address: (b.) 38 Barclay Park, Aboyne; T.-013398 86899; e-mail: eric@school-timetable.co.uk

Sinclair, Gerard William, LLB (Hons), DipLP, NP. Chief Executive, Scottish Criminal Cases Review Commission, since 2003; b. 24.9.61, Bellshill; m., Helen; 1 s.; 3 d. Educ. Trinity High School, Cambuslang; Strathclyde University. Trainee and Legal Assistant, Ross Harper and Murphy, Glasgow, 1984-88; Senior Partner, Sinclair McCormick and Giusti Martin, Glasgow, 1988-2003. Part-Time Sheriff; former Member, Council, Law Society of Scotland. Address: (b.) 17 Renfield Street, Glasgow G2 5AH; T.-0141 270 7030.

Sinclair, Marion, MA (Hons), MPhil (Publishing), MBA. Chief Executive, Publishing Scotland, since 2008. Educ. University of Glasgow; University of Stirling; University of

Edinburgh. Editorial and Marketing Assistant, Polygon, 1988-90; Editorial Director, Polygon, 1990-97; Lecturer, Publishing Studies, Edinburgh Napier University, 1997-2003; Business Development, Publishing Scotland, 2003-08. Worked in the book publishing sector for 28 years, running a literary press; awarded Sunday Times UK Small Publisher of the Year, and published books appearing on the Booker shortlist and winners of the Saltire Society Book of the Year, McVitie's Prize, The John Llewellyn Rhys prize and the Betty Trask Award. Board Member: Gaelic Books Council, BookSource. Address: Publishing Scotland, Scott House, 10 South St Andrew Street, Edinburgh EH2 2AZ; T.-0131 228 6866.

Sinha, Professor Brajraman Prasad, BSc, Dip. Building Science, PhD, DSc. Professor of Structural Engineering, Edinburgh University, 1999-2002; now Emeritus Professor; b. 20.12.36, Hazipur, India; m., Nageshwari Sinha; 2 s.; 1 d. Educ. Zila School, Monghyr, India; Patna University; Liverpool University; Edinburgh University. Engineering Assistant, Patna University, 1957-59; Assistant Engineer, Bihar Electricity Board, 1959-60; Assistant Engineer, Department of Public Works, Bihar, 1960-63; Design Engineer, 1968-69; Edinburgh University: Demonstrator and Researcher, 1966-68; Research Fellow to Senior Lecturer, 1969-95; Reader, 1995-99; Visiting Professor, Bihar College of Engineering, 1984; Visiting Academic, Santa Catarina Florianopolis, Brazil, since 1991; Visiting Professor, Indian Institute of Science, 2000; Visiting Professor, University of Dresden, 2003, University of Ancona (Italy), 2002; Executive Director, International Masonry Engineering Council for Developing Countries, 1984-2004. Member: Lothian Racial Equality Council, since 1984, Chair, 2004-07; Member, Senate, Edinburgh University, 1984-2002; Chairman, Hindu Temple and Cultural Centre, Edinburgh, 1985-86; President, Indian Arts Council, 1994. Publications: Structural Masonry for Developing Countries (co-ed.), 1992; Re-inforced and Pre-stressed Masonry (contributor), 1989. Recreations: reading; overseas travel; photography; table tennis; writing. Address: (b.) Institute of Infrastructures and Environment, School of Engineering and Electronics, Edinburgh University, Kings' Buildings, Edinburgh EGH9 3JN; T.-0131-650 5726.
E-mail: B.Sinha@ed.ac.uk

Skene, Charles Pirie, OBE, DBA, FBIPP, ARPS, FRSA. Chairman, Skene Group of companies; Visiting Professor of Entrepreneurship, Robert Gordon University; Holder of the Queen's Award for Enterprise Promotion, 2005; b. 30.4.35, Aberdeen; m., Alison; 1 s.; 2 d. Educ. Loretto. Past President of numerous organisations, including Aberdeen Chamber of Commerce and Association of Scottish Chambers of Commerce; Past Chairman: Industry Year 1986, Industry Matters 1987; Donor of the Annual Skene Aberdeen Festival Award, 1976-99; Past Chairman, CBI Education and Training Committee; Chairman, CBI (Scotland) Enterprise Group, 1994-96; Member, Task Force to investigate under-achievement in schools, 1996-97; organised Skene Young Entrepreneur's Award, Scotland, 1986-2002; Member, Scottish Executive's Review of Education for Work and Enterprise Group, 2001-02; endowed Chair of Entrepreneurship, The Robert Gordon University Centre for Entrepreneurship, 2001. Address: (b.) 23 Rubislaw Den North, Aberdeen, AB15 4AL; T.-01224 326221.

Skeoch, Norman (Keith), BA, MA. Chief Executive, Standard Life plc, since 2015; Head of Standard Life Investments, since 2004; b. 11.56; m.; 2 s. Educ. University of Sussex; University of Warwick. Career history: Government Economic Service, 1979-80; James Capel &

Co Limited (HSBC Securities from 1996), 1980-99: International Economist (1980), Chief Economist (1984), Director of Economics and Strategy (1993), Managing Director of International Equities (1998); joined Standard Life Investments in 1999 as Chief Investment Officer, became Director in 2006. Board Member, Financial Reporting Council and the Investment Association. Awarded honorary doctorates from the University of Sussex and Teesside University; worked with government and trade bodies in establishing best practice in stewardship and governance in the wake of the global financial crisis. Fellow of the Society of Business Economists; European Personality of the Year by Funds Europe, 2013. Address: Standard Life House, 30 Lothian Road, Edinburgh EH1 2DH; T.-0131 225 2552.

Skinner, Denzil, MBA. Chair, Essential Edinburgh, since 2011; Partner, Denzil Skinner & Partners LLP, since 2012. Educ. Heriot Watt University. HM Forces, 1977-1988, Commissioned into 16/5 The Queen's Royal Lancers; Director & Company Secretary, Hamilton & Inches, 1989-2010. Address: Essential Edinburgh, 139 George Street, Edinburgh EH2 4JY; T.-0131 220 8580.

Skinner, Simon, MBA. Chief Executive, The National Trust for Scotland, since 2015. Educ. Stirling University. Career history: Director, Marketing and Client Services, Scottish Widows, 1996-2002; Director, Sales and Service, The AA, 2003-2004; Director, Corporate Services, Equitable Life, 2005-09; AEGON Scottish Equitable: Director, Customer Services, 2009-11, Chief Operating Officer, 2011; Chief Executive, AEGON Ireland, 2011-15. Address: The National Trust for Scotland, Wemyss House, 28 Charlotte Square, Edinburgh EH2 4ET; T.-0131 243 9300.

Slater, Professor Peter James Bramwell, BSc, PhD, DSc, FRSB, FRSE. Kennedy Professor of Natural History, St. Andrews University, 1984-2008, Emeritus, since 2008 (Head, School of Biological and Medical Sciences, 1992-97; Dean, Faculty of Science, 1998-2002); b. 26.12.42, Edinburgh; m., Elisabeth Vernon Smith; 2 s. Educ. Edinburgh Academy; Glenalmond; Edinburgh University. Demonstrator in Zoology, Edinburgh University, 1966-68; Lecturer in Biology, Sussex University, 1968-84. Secretary, Association for the Study of Animal Behaviour, 1973-78, President, 1986-89, Medallist, 2000; European Editor, Animal Behaviour, 1979-82; Editor, Advances in the Study of Behavior, 1990-2005. Recreations: walking; ornithology; music. Address: (b.) Vagaland, Stromness, Orkney KW16 3AW; T.-01856 850148.

Slaven, Tracey, BA (Hons) Econ, MBA. Deputy Secretary, Strategic Planning, University of Edinburgh, since 2013; b. 23.04.67, Jarrow; m., Mark Slaven; 3 d. Educ. Hedworthfield Comprehensive, Jarrow; Strathclyde University; Durham University. Economic Assistant, Industry Department for Scotland, 1989-92; Economist and Head of Corporate Planning, Highlands and Islands Enterprise, 1992-2001; Corporate Planning, AWG PLC, 2001-03; Executive Director, Countryside Agency, 2003-05; Deputy Director, Scottish Government, 2005-09; Chief Executive, Student Awards Agency Scotland, 2009-2012; Deputy Director for Higher Education and Learner Support, Scottish Government, 2012-2013. Recreations: reading; time with our children and various animals in very rural community. Address: (b.) Governance and Strategic Planning, Old College, University of Edinburgh, South Bridge, Edinburgh EH8 9YL; T.-0131 650 2132.

Sleeman, Professor Derek Henry, BSc, PhD, FBCS, FRSE. Fellow of European Artificial Intelligence Societies (2004); Emeritus Professor of Computing Science, Aberdeen University; b. 11.1.41, Penzance; m., Margaret G. Rankine; 1 d. Educ. Penzance Grammar School; King's College, London. Secretary, SS AISB, 1979-82; Academic

Co-ordinator, European Network of Excellence in Machine Learning, 1992-95. Publications: 200 technical papers. Recreations: hill and coastal path-walking; photography. Address: (b.) Computing Science Department, King's College, Aberdeen University, Aberdeen AB24 3FX; T.-01224 272288.

Sloan, Brian. Chief Executive, Age Scotland, since 2012; b. 28.12.61, Glasgow; m., Katie; 2 s.; 2 d. Educ. Keil School (Dumbarton); Liverpool Hope University. Bank Officer, Clydesdale Bank, 1980-84; Sales Director, Capital Bank, 1984-2000; Senior Executive, Bank of Scotland, 2000-09; Managing Director, Hotel Connections Ltd, 2009-2010; Business Development: Capital Credit Union, 2010-2011, Young Enterprise Scotland, 2011-2012; Chairman, Age Scotland Enterprises, 2011-2013. Volunteer Panel Member, Children's Hearing System. Recreations: golf (8 handicap); competitive squash player. Address: (b.) Causewayside House, 160 Causewayside, Edinburgh EH9 1PR; T.-07961 083203.
E-mail: brian.sloan@agesscotland.org.uk

Slumbers, Martin, BSc, ACA. Chief Executive and Secretary, Royal and Ancient Golf Club of St Andrews, since 2015; b. 1960, Brighton. Educ. University of Birmingham; Price Waterhouse. Accounting Trainee, PwC, 1981-85; Finance, Salomon Brothers, London, 1985-94; CFO, Salomon Brothers Hong Kong Limited, 1994-97; Finance, Salomon Brothers AG, 1984-98; CFO, Salomon Brothers, UK, 1997-98; Deutsche Bank, London: CFO Global Markets, 1998-2001, COO, 2001-03; Head, Global Business Services, Deutsche Bank, 2003-2013; own business, since 2013. Address: Royal and Ancient Golf Club of St Andrews, Fife KY16 9JD.

Small, Christopher. Writer; b. 15.11.19, London; 3 d. Educ. Dartington Hall; Pembroke College, Oxford. Journalist and miscellaneous writer; Literary Editor and Dramatic Critic, Glasgow Herald, 1955-80. Publications:Ariel Like A Harpy: Shelley, Mary & Frankenstein; The Road to Miniluv: George Orwell, the State & God; The Printed Word. Recreation: gardening. Address: (h.) Park House, Isle of Lismore, Oban, Argyll PA34 5UN; T.-01631 760222.

Small, Emeritus Professor John Rankin, CBE, DLitt, BSc (Econ), FCCA, FCMA. Emeritus Professor, Department of Accountancy and Finance, Heriot-Watt University; b. 28.2.33, Dundee; m., Catherine Wood; 1 s.; 2 d. Educ. Harris Academy; Dundee School of Economics. Industry and commerce; Lecturer, Edinburgh University; Senior Lecturer, Glasgow University. Director of and Consultant to various organisations; President, Association of Chartered Certified Accountants, 1982-83; Vice-Principal, Heriot-Watt University, 1974-78, 1987-90, Deputy Principal, 1990-94. Chairman, Commission for Local Authority Accounts in Scotland, 1983-92; Chairman, National Appeal Panel for Entry to Pharmaceutical Lists (Scotland), 1987-95; Board Member, Scottish Homes, 1993-2002. Recreation: golf. Address: (h.) 39 Caiystane Terrace, Edinburgh EH10 6ST; T.-0131-445 2638.

Small, Stephen J., CQSW. Director, St Andrew's Children's Society Ltd., since 1996; b. 3.11.61, Edinburgh; m., Kay L. Anderson; 1 s.; 2 d. Educ. Holyrood RC High School, Edinburgh; Moray House College of Education. Social Worker, Humberside County Council, 1986-88; Social Worker, Lothian Regional Council (Midlothian District), 1988-95; Senior Social Worker, Director, St Andrew's Children's Society Ltd., since 1995. Address: (b.) 7 John's Place, Leith, Edinburgh EH6 7EL; T.-0131 454 3370; e-mail: ssmall@standrews–children.org.uk

Smart, Ian Stewart, LLB, NP. Past President, Law Society of Scotland; Solicitor, Partner, Ian S. Smart & Co., since 1991; b. 10.9.58, Paisley. Educ. Paisley Grammar School; Glasgow University. Solicitor and then Partner, Ross Harper & Murphy, 1980-91; Council Member, Law Society of Scotland, since 1997. Recreation: St Mirren; Labour Party politics. Address: (b.) 3 Annan House, Cumbernauld G67 1DP; T.-01236 731027.

Smart, John Dalziel Beveridge, CVO. Lord Lieutenant, Kincardineshire, 1999-2007 (retired); b. 12.8.32, Edinburgh; m., Valerie Blaber; 2 s. Educ. Harrow; Administrative Staff College. 2nd Lt., Black Watch (RHR), Korea, 1952; PA to Chief of Staff, 1953. J. & J. Smart (Brechin) Ltd., 1953 (Director, 1954); Director, Don Brothers, Buist & Co. Ltd., 1964 (Managing Director, 1985; retired, 1987). Chairman, British Polyolefin Textiles Association, 1986-97; Member, St. Andrews Management Institute, 1989; Chairman, Scottish American Community Relations Committee, 1990-93; Dean, Guildry of Brechin, 1991-93; DL, Kincardineshire, 1993; Member, Queen's Bodyguard for Scotland, Royal Company of Archers. Recreation: countryside. Address: (h.) Kincardine, 9A The Glebe, Edzell, Brechin DD9 7SZ; T.-01356 648416; e-mail: smart@kincardine9.plus.com

Smethurst, Emeritus Professor Colin, BA, BLitt, MA, Officier Palmes Academiques. Marshall Professor of French, Glasgow University, 1980-98; b. 3.8.37, Bedford; m., Claudine Rozenberg; 2 d. Educ. Slough Grammar School; Keble College, Oxford. Assistant Lecturer, Lecturer, Senior Lecturer in French, Liverpool University, 1962-80. President, Institut Francais d'Ecosse, 1989-96; Secretary, Association of University Professors of French, 1983-87; Visiting Professor, Sorbonne (Paris IV), 1998-99. Publications: Zola: Germinal; Chateaubriand: Atala, René; editions of Balzac novels; Chateaubriand: Ecrits politiques. Address: (h.) 6 Westbourne Crescent, Bearsden G61 4HD.

Smillie, Anne. Chief Executive, Scottish Badminton Union, since 1989; Executive Board Member, Badminton World Federation, 2002-08; Chair, BWF Events Committee, 2007-08; b. 17.8.56, Glasgow. Educ. Victoria Drive Secondary School; Anniesland College. Joined Scottish Badminton Union, 1980; Director of major badminton events, including 1992 European Championships, 1994 World Team Championships, 1997 World Team and Individual Championships, 2007 World Team Badminton Championships. Recreations: music; reading. Address: (h.) 55 Westerton Avenue, Westerton, Glasgow; T.-0141-942 9804.

Smillie, Carol. Television Presenter. Credits include: Wheel of Fortune; The Travel Show; Holiday; The National Lottery Live; Hearts of Gold; Smillie's People; Changing Rooms; Midweek National Lottery Live; Summer Holiday; Star Secrets; Holiday Swaps; Dream Holiday Homes; Postcode Challenge; Strictly Come Dancing; A Brush with Fame; Duke of Edinburgh 80th Birthday.
Web: www.carolsmillie.tv

Smith of Gilmorehill, Baroness (Elizabeth Margaret Smith), MA. Peer, House of Lords, since 1995; Deputy Lieutenant, City of Edinburgh; former Chairman, Edinburgh Festival Fringe Society (1995-2012); Council Member, Russo-British Chamber of Commerce; Governor, English Speaking Union; Trustee, John Smith Memorial Trust; Patron, University of Glasgow 2001 Campaign; b. 4.6.40, Ayr; m., Rt. Hon. John Smith, MP (deceased); 3 d. Educ. Hutchesons Girls Grammar School; Glasgow University. LLD, Glasgow University, 1998. Recreations: family; garden; the arts. Address: (b.) House of Lords, London, SW1A 0PW.

Smith, Agnes Houston, BL. Honorary Sheriff, Dundee, since 1990; b. 27.9.33, Prestwick; m., David Robert Smith; 3 d. Educ. Hutchesons' Girls Grammar School, Glasgow; Glasgow University. Solicitor in Paisley, Edinburgh and Dundee, 1955-92. President, Dundee Society of Glasgow University Graduates; Non-Executive Director, Dundee Healthcare NHS Trust, 1993-99. Recreations: golf; gardening; grannying. Address: (h.) Windyridge, Kellas, by Broughty Ferry DD5 3PQ; T.-01382 350475; e-mail: nancy.smith2@btinternet.com

Smith, Allan Keppie. CBE, DUniv, BSc, FREng, CEng, FIMechE, FWeldI. Chairman, Railcare Ltd., 1995-2001; Managing Director, Facilities Management Division, Babcock International Group PLC, Rosyth Royal Dockyard, until 1997; b. 18.5.32. Joined Army for National Service, 1953; commissioned, REME, 1954; Babcock & Wilcox: joined as Graduate Trainee, 1955; appointed: Industrial Engineering Manager, Renfrew Works, 1965, Production Director, Renfrew Works, 1974, Managing Director, Renfrew and Dumbarton Works, 1976; Managing Director, Babcock Thorn Limited and Chairman, Rosyth Royal Dockyard plc, 1986; Director, Babcock International Group PLC, 1989. Past President, Scottish Engineering; Past Chairman, Council of the Welding Institute; Honorary Doctor, University of Paisley; awarded Institute of Marketing Scottish Marketer of the Year, 1992. Address: (h.) The Forts, Hawes Brae, South Queensferry EH30 9TE; T.-0131-319 1668; e-mail: allanksmith@btinternet.com

Smith, Alyn. Member of the European Parliament for Scotland (SNP), since 2004; b. 1973, Glasgow. Educ. Leeds University; University of Heidelberg; Nottingham Law University; College of Europe in Natolin. Taught English in India and worked with Scotland Europa in Brussels; later moved to London and qualified as a lawyer with commercial law firm Clifford Chance; SNP staff worker in Holyrood, prior to election in 2004. Contested Edinburgh West for the SNP at the 2001 general election and the 2003 Scottish Parliament election. Honorary President of both the youth wings of the SNP, the Young Scots for Independence and the Federation of Student Nationalists, as well as a member of the SNP's National Executive Committee. Full member of the Committee on Agriculture and Rural Development, European Parliament; won the coveted Scottish Farmer Magazine award for "Outstanding Contribution to Scottish Agriculture" at the Highland Show in 2009; alternate member of the Education and Culture Committee in addition to the Constitutional Affairs Committee; full member of the Delegation for relations with the Arabian Peninsula, and also sits as alternate member on the Parliament's Delegation for Relations with Switzerland, Iceland and Norway.
E-mail: alyn.smith@europarl.europa.eu

Smith, The Rt. Hon. Lady (Anne Smith), QC. Senator of the College of Justice in Scotland; b. 1955; m.; 1 s.; 1 d. Educ. Edinburgh University. Admitted, Faculty of Advocates, 1980. Address: Parliament House, Parliament Square, Edinburgh EH1 1RQ.

Smith, Rt. Rev. Brian Arthur. Episcopal Bishop of Edinburgh, 2001-2011; b. 1943; m., Elizabeth Hutchinson; 2 d. Educ. George Heriot's School, Edinburgh; Edinburgh University; Fitzwilliam College, Cambridge; Jesus College, Cambridge; Westcott House, Cambridge. Curate, Cuddesdon, 1972-79; Tutor, Cuddesdon College, Oxford, 1972-75; Ripon College, Cuddesdon: Director of Studies, 1975-78, Senior Tutor, 1978-79; Director of Training, Diocese of Wakefield, 1979-87; Priest-in-Charge, St. John, Halifax, 1979-85; Honorary Canon, Wakefield Cathedral, 1981-87; Archdeacon of Craven, 1987-93; Bishop Suffragan, Tonbridge, 1993-2001. Member, Scotland UNESCO Committee, 2008-2014; Vice-President, Modern Church, since 2009; Director, St Mary's Music School, since 2010; Governor, Loretto School, since 2012; President Emeritus, RMCU, since 2012; Hon. Lecturer, St Augustine Theological School, Botswana, 2013, 2015. Recreations: reading; music; walking; browsing in junk shops. Address: Flat E, 2A Dean Path, Edinburgh EH4 3BA; T.-0131 220 6097.
E-mail: bishopsmith@btinternet.com

Smith, David Bruce Boyter, OBE, Drhc, MA, LLB, FRSA, FInstD. Director and Chief Executive, Dunfermline Building Society, 1987-2001; Vice Chairman, Scottish Opera, 2000-04; Past Chairman, Building Societies Association; b. 11.3.42, St. Andrews; m., Christine Anne; 1 s.; 1 d. Educ. High School, Dunfermline; Edinburgh University. Legal training, Balfour & Manson, Edinburgh; admitted Solicitor, 1968; Solicitor, Standard Life Assurance Co., 1969-73; Dunfermline Building Society: Secretary, 1974-81, General Manager (Admin.), 1981-86, Deputy Chief Executive, 1986. Past Chairman, Northern Association of Building Societies; Vice President, European Mortgage Federation; Chairman, NHBC (Scotland) and Board Member, NHBC (UK), 2004-12; Member, Scottish Conveyancing and Executry Services Board, 1996-2003; Deputy Chairman, Glenrothes Development Corporation, 1990-96; Chairman, Institute of Directors, Scottish Division, 1994-97; Vice Chairman, Scottish Fisheries Museum, 1993-2007; former Vice Chairman of Court and Finance Convener, Edinburgh University; Chairman, University of Edinburgh Investment Committee, 2004-2011; Chairman, Carnegie Dunfermline & Hero Fund Trusts, 2008-2010; Board Member, Carnegie UK Trust, 2002-14; Executive Committee, Carnegie Trust for Universities of Scotland, 2005-2015. Recreations: golf; sailing; the arts.

Smith, Sir David Cecil, Kt, MA, DPhil, FRS, FRSE. Principal and Vice-Chancellor, Edinburgh University, 1987-94; President, Wolfson College, Oxford, 1994-2000; m., Lesley Margaret Mollison Mutch; 2 s.; 1 d. Educ. St. Paul's School, London; Queen's College, Oxford. Browne Research Fellow, Queen's College, Oxford, 1956-59; Harkness Fellow, University of California, Berkeley, 1959-60; University Lecturer, Department of Agriculture, Oxford University, 1960-74; Fellow and Tutor, Wadham College, Oxford, 1964-74; Melville Wills Professor of Botany, Bristol University, 1974-80; Sibthorpian Professor of Rural Economy, Oxford University, 1980-87. President, British Lichen Society, 1972-74; President, British Mycological Society, 1980; President, Society for Experimental Biology, 1983-85; President, Scottish Association for Marine Science, 1993-2000; President, Linnean Society, 2000-03. Publication: The Biology of Symbiosis (Co-author), 1987. Address: 13 Abbotsford Park, Edinburgh EH10 5DZ; T.-0131-446 0230; e-mail: smithsymbiosis@aol.com

Smith, Donald Alexander, MA, PhD. Director, Netherbow Arts Centre, 1983-2001; Curator, John Knox House, since 1989; Director, Scottish Storytelling Centre, 1995-2013; Director, Tracs (Traditional Arts and Culture Scotland), since 2014; b. 15.2.56, Glasgow; m., Alison; 3 s.; 2 d. Educ. Stirling High School; Edinburgh University. Researcher, School of Scottish Studies, 1979-82. Chairperson, Scotland 97 (anniversaries of St. Ninian and St. Columba); Organiser, Scottish Churches Millennium Programme; Chair, Scottish National Theatre Working Party (SAC/Scottish Executive), 2000-01; Chair, Literature Forum for Scotland, 2002-06; Board Member, National Theatre of Scotland, 2004-07; Coordinator, Traditional Arts and Culture Scotland (TRACS), since 2013. Publications: The Scottish Stage, 1994; Edinburgh Old Town Pilgrims'

Way, 1995; John Knox House: Gateway to Edinburgh's Old Town, 1996; Celtic Travellers: Scotland in the Age of the Saints, 1997; History of Scottish Theatre, 1998; Storytelling Scotland: A Nation in Narrative, 2001; A Long Stride Shortens the Road: Poems 1979-2004, 2004; Some to Thorns, Some to Thistles, 2005; The English Spy, 2007; Between Ourselves, 2008; God, the Poet and the Devil: Robert Burns and Religion, 2008; Arthur's Seat: Journeys and Evocations, 2009; Ballad of the Five Marys 2013; Freedom and Faith, 2013; Edinburgh's Old Town: Journeys and Evocations, 2014; Scotland's Democracy Trail, 2014; Pilgrim Guide to Scotland, 2015. Address: (b.) Scottish Storytelling Centre: The Netherbow, 43-45 High Street, Edinburgh EH1 1SR; T.-0131-556 9579.

Smith, Drew. Former MSP (Labour), Glasgow (2011-16). Formerly Spokesperson on Social Justice; formerly Deputy Equalities Spokesperson; formerly Shadow Cabinet Secretary for the Constitution. Studied at the universities of Aberdeen and Glasgow. Worked for Labour at Holyrood and Westminster and as a policy and communications officer in health promotion. Active in the north Glasgow community. Previous Chair, Scottish TUC Young Workers Committee (2008) and Scottish Young Labour (2006); Member, STUC General Council, 2006-2010.

Smith, Elaine A., BA (Hons), DPSM. MSP (Labour), Central Scotland region, since 2016 (Coatbridge and Chryston, 1999-2016); Deputy Presiding Officer, 2011-16; b. 7.5.63, Coatbridge; m., James Vann Smith; 1 s. Educ. St Patrick's School, Coatbridge; Glasgow College; St Andrew's Teacher Training College. Teacher, 1986-87; supply teacher, 1987-88; local government officer, Monklands District Council, 1988-90, Highland Regional Council, 1990-97; Volunteer Development Scotland, 1997-98; supply teacher, 1999. Recreations: family; swimming; reading. Address: (b.) Unit 65, Fountain Business Centre, Coatbridge, Lanarkshire; T.-01236 449122.

Smith, Elaine Constance, BA. Actress; b. 2.8.58, Baillieston; m., Robert Morton; 2 d. Educ. Braidhurst High School, Motherwell; Royal Scottish Academy of Music and Drama; Moray House College of Education. Career: Teacher of Speech and Drama, Firrhill High School, Edinburgh, 1979-82; joined 7:84 Theatre Company, 1982; moved to Wildcat Stage Productions, 1982; since 1986, worked with Borderline Theatre Co., Royal Lyceum, Dundee Rep., Tron Theatre, Traverse, Byre Theatre and Lead in Glasgow and Aberdeen panto; two national tours of Calendar Girls including West End run; co-written and starred in I Dreamed A Dream; TV work includes City Lights, Naked Video, Rab C Nesbitt and 2000 Acres of Sky; original cast member, The Steamie; Film work includes Women Talking Dirty, 16 Years of Alcohol and Nina's Heavenly Delights. Patron, Relationships Scotland, Zero Tolerance, Scottish Youth Theatre, Borderline Theatre and Byre Theatre; Hon. Doctorate, Dundee and Glasgow Universities; BA, Queen Margaret Univ., 2007; Agent: Independent Talent Group, London; Production company with husband (RPM Arts), since 1990. Recreations: swimming; tennis; reading.
Web: www.elainecsmith.com

Smith, Elizabeth Jane, MA (Hons), DipEd. MSP (Conservative), Mid Scotland and Fife, since 2007; Shadow Cabinet Secretary for Education and Skills, since 2016; b. 27.2.60, Edinburgh. Educ. George Watson's College; University of Edinburgh; Moray House College of Education. Teacher of Economics and Modern Studies, George Watson's College, 1983-98; Head of Chairman's Office, Conservative Central Office,

Scotland, 1998-2003; Part Time Teacher and Political Consultant, 2003-07. Fellow Commoner, Corpus Christi College, Cambridge, 1992. Publications: History of George Watson's Ladies' College, 2006; Outdoor Adventures, 2003. Recreations: cricket; hill-walking; photography; travel. Address: (b.) Scottish Parliament, Holyrood Road, Edinburgh EH99 1SP; T.-0131 348 6762.
E-mail: elizabeth.smith.msp@scottish.parliament.uk

Smith, Gordon Duffield. Chief Executive, Scottish Football Association, 2007-10; b. 29.12.54, Kilwinning. Former football player; played for Rangers and Brighton & Hove Albion FC; later worked as a football agent and BBC football pundit.

Smith, Grahame. General Secretary, Scottish Trades Union Congress (STUC), since 2006. Partner, Liz Campbell; 2 s. Educ. Strathclyde University (Honours Degree in Economics and Industrial Relations). Joined STUC as an Assistant Secretary in 1986, Deputy General Secretary, 1996-2006 (heading up the STUC's policy and campaigns department); appointed as a Commissioner for the UK Commission for Employment and Skills (UKCES), 2007; joined the Board of Scottish Enterprise, 2008; joined the Board of Skills Development Scotland, 2014. Recreations: enjoys reading and music and interested in most sports, but particularly football. Address: (b.) STUC, 333 Woodlands Road, Glasgow G3 6NG; T.-0141 337 8100; e-mail: gsmith@stuc.org.uk

Smith, Iain, BA (Hons). Scottish Public Policy Consultant; MSP (Scottish Liberal Democrat), North East Fife, 1999-2011; Deputy Minister for Parliament, Scottish Executive, 1999-2000; Convener, Procedures Committee, Scottish Parliament, 2003-05, Convener, Education Committee, 2005-07, Member, Europe and External Relations Committee, 2007-08; Convener, Economy, Energy and Tourism Committee, 2008-2011; b. 1.5.60, Gateside, Fife. Educ. Bell Baxter High School, Cupar; Newcastle upon Tyne University. Councillor, Fife Council, 1995-99 (Leader of Opposition and Lib Dem Group, 1995-99); Councillor, Fife Regional Council, 1982-95 (Leader of Opposition and Lib Dem Group, 1986-95). Chair, Scottish Liberal Democrat General Election Campaign, 2001 and 2005. Recreations: cinema; travel; reading.

Smith, Professor Ian K., MA, MEd, DipEd. Professor of Education, University of the West of Scotland; Dean of School of Education, University of the West of Scotland, (formerly University of Paisley), 2003-09; Head of School of Education, University of Paisley, 2000-03; b. 28.7.53, Glasgow; m., Aileen; 1 s. Educ. Hutchesons' Boys' Grammar School, Glasgow; University of Glasgow. Teacher of History, Lanark Division, Strathclyde Region, 1976-82; Principal Teacher of History, Dunbarton Division, Strathclyde Region, 1982-89; Staff Development Trainer, Dunbarton Division, 1989; Secondary Assistant Headteacher Posts, including School Co-ordinator TVEI, Dunbarton Division, 1989-92; Senior Lecturer and PGCE (Secondary) Course Co-ordinator, Craigie College of Education (subsequently Faculty of Education, University of Paisley), 1992-2000. Member: SOED National Steering Group on Training for Mentoring, 1994-95; GTCS Working Group on Partnership in Initial Teacher Education, 1996-97; National Working Group on Quality Assurance in Initial Teacher Education, 1999-2002; Scottish Teacher Education Committee, 2000-09 (Chair, 2005-08); Scottish Executive Induction Implementation Group, 2001-07; Scottish Executive National Chartered Teacher Review Group, 2007; General Teaching Council for Scotland, as Universities Scotland Representative, 2001-09; Convener, GTCS Education Committee, 2005-09. Expert consultant for

The Teaching Council, Ireland, 2010, and The Council of Europe/European Union from 2010 (including work at Pan-European level, and in a range of countries, such as Albania, Armenia, Azerbaijan, the Czech Republic and Greece). Editor, Scottish Educational Review, 2011-13. Publications: various books and book chapters, journal articles, conference papers and research reports, including 'Models of Partnership in Programmes of Initial Teacher Education. A Systematic Review Commissioned by the General Teaching Council Scotland' (Co-Author), 2005; Convergence or Divergence? Initial Teacher Education in Scotland and England (Co-Author), 2006 and a range of publications for the Council of Europe, since 2011, eg. "Underpinning Integrity in the Albanian Education System: Compilation of PACA (Project against Corruption in Albania) Outputs" (Co-Author), 2013. Recreations: reading; exercise; travel. Address: (b.) School of Education, University of the West of Scotland, Ayr Campus, University Avenue, Ayr KA8 0SX; T.-01292 886272; e-mail: ian.smith@uws.ac.uk

Smith, Father James. Parish Priest, St Gabriels Parish, Prestonpans, since 2012. Address: St. Martin of Tours Catholic Church, High Street, Tranent EH33 1HJ; T.-01875 610232; e-mail: frjamessmith@gmail.com

Smith, Professor Jeremy John, BA, MPhil, PhD, AKC, FEA, FRSE. Professor of English Philology, Glasgow University, since 2000; b. 18.10.55, Hampton Court; m., Dr Elaine P. Higgleton; 1 d. Educ. Kingston Grammar School, Kingston-upon-Thames; King's College, London; Jesus College, Oxford; Glasgow University. College Lecturer, Keble College, Oxford. 1978-79; Glasgow University: Lecturer, English Language, 1979-90; Senior Lecturer, 1990-96; Reader, 1996-2000. Publications: Older Scots: A Linguistic Reader, 2012; Old English: A Linguistic Introduction, 2009; Sound Change and the History of English, 2007; Introduction to Middle English (Co-author), 2002; New Perspectives on Middle English Texts (ed. with S. Powell), 2000; Essentials of Early English, 1999; Historical Study of English, 1996; English of Chaucer (with M. L. Samuels), 1988. Recreations; hill walking; opera. Address: (b.) Department of English Language, Glasgow University, Glasgow, G12 8QQ; T.-0141-330 5684.

Smith, John, Alexander, OND (Agri). Member, Scottish Land Court, since 2006; Partner, WW Smith and Son (Farmers), since 1978; b. 14.2.59, Cardenden; m., Susan Mary Watson; 3 d. Educ. Dundee High School; North of Scotland College of Agriculture, Craibstone. Member, Scottish Agricultural Wages Board, 1998-2006; Chairman, NFU Scotland Legal and Technical Committee, 2000-05; Director, NFU Scotland, 2000-05; Director, Royal Highland Educational Trust, 2001-06; Chairman, Lantranto Agricultural Crops Industry Group, 2001-06. School Speaker for Royal Highland Educational Trust; Trustee, Fowlis Easter Hall, 1986-2015; Member of Board of Governors, Angus College, 2009-2013; Member, Dundee and Angus Foundation, since 2014. Recreations: curling with Lundie and Auchterhouse Curling Club. Address: (h.) Bridgefield House, Kettins, Blairgowrie, Perthshire PH13 9JJ; T.-01828 628169.

Smith, Rev. John Raymond, MA, BD. Minister, Morningside United Church, Edinburgh, 1998-2013; b. 12.4.47, Dumfries; m., Isabel Jean McKemmie; 3 d. Educ. Dumfries Academy; University of Edinburgh; University of Geneva. Minister, School Wynd Church, Paisley, 1973-82; World Mission Secretary, Congregational Union of Scotland, 1978-86, President, 1988-89; Minister, Oakshaw Trinity Church, Paisley, 1991-98; Moderator, Presbytery of Edinburgh, 2007-08. Convener, Education and Learning Committee, United Reformed Church; Examiner, Royal College of Surgeons, Edinburgh; Member, Intercollegiate Committee for Basic Surgical Examinations. Clubs: Royal Scots, Edinburgh. Recreations: walking; writing; travel; photography. Address: (h.) 25 Whitehaugh Park, Peebles EH45 9DB; T.-01721 724 464; e-mail: office@jrsmith.eu

Smith, Professor Julia Mary Howard, BA, MA (Cantab), DPhil (Oxon), FRSE, FRHistS, FSAScot. Edwards Professor of Medieval History, University of Glasgow, since 2005; b. 29.5.56, Cambridge; m., Hamish Scott. Educ. South Hampstead High School GPDST; Newnham College, Cambridge; Corpus Christi College, Oxford. Temporary Lecturer: Department of History, University of Sheffield (1-year contract), 1981-82; Department of Mediaeval History, University of St Andrews (1-year contract), 1982-93, Department of History, University of Manchester (3-year contract), 1983-86; Department of History, Trinity College, Hartford, CT. USA (1986-90: Assistant Professor, 1990-95: Associate Professor); Reader in Mediaeval History, School of History, University of St Andrews, 1995-2005. Publications include: Province and Empire: Brittany and the Carolingians, 1992; Europe After Rome: A New Cultural History 500-1000, 2005; Early Medieval Rome and the Christian West (Editor), 2000; Gender in the Early Medieval World: East and West 300-900 (Co-Editor), 2004; Cambridge History of Christianity, volume III: AD 600-1100 (Co-Editor), 2008. Recreations: hill walking; chamber music; gardening. Address: (b.) School of Humanities, University of Glasgow, 10 University Gardens, Glasgow G12 8QQ; T.-0141-330-5139. E-mail: julia.smith@glasgow.ac.uk

Smith, Professor Leslie Samuel, BSc, PhD. Professor of Computing Science, University of Stirling, since 2000; b. 3.10.52, Glasgow; m., Brigitte Beck-Woerner. Educ. Allan Glen's School; University of Glasgow. Started programming in 1974, and returned to University to study it properly in 1977; Lecturer, Glasgow University, 1980-83; joined Stirling University after a year as an independent consultant. Member, EPSRC College; Senior Member, IEEE; Member, Acoustical Society of America and Society for Neuroscience. Recreations: playing jazz piano. Address: (b.) Department of Computing Science and Mathematics, University of Stirling, Stirling FK9 4LA; T.-01786 467435; e-mail: lss@cs.stir.ac.uk

Smith, Professor Lorraine Nancy, BScN, MEd, PhD. Emeritus Professor, Glasgow University (Professor of Nursing, 1990-2011, Head of School, 1990-2001), Honorary Senior Research Fellow, since 2012; b. 29.6.49, Ottawa; m., Christopher Murray Smith; 1 s.; 1 d. Educ. University of Ottawa; Manchester University. Appointed, Clinical and Biomedical Research Committee (Scotland), 1992-94; co-opted to National Board of Scotland for Nursing, Midwifery and Health Visiting, 1997-2000; appointed, Clinical Standards Advisory Group (UK), 1994-99; Convenor, Royal College of Nursing Research Society (Scotland), 1999-2005; Chair, Work Group of European Nurse Researchers, 2004-08; Chair, SIGN 118 & 119; RCN Scotland Board Member, 2009-10; Director, St Andrew's Clinics for Children (STACC). Recreations: bridge; golf; sailing. Address: (b.) 5 Huntly Gardens, Glasgow G12 9AS; T.-0141-330 5498; e-mail: lorraine.smith@glasgow.ac.uk

Smith, Margaret, MA. Former MSP (Liberal Democrat), Edinburgh West; b. 1961, Edinburgh; 1 s.; 1 d.; 3 step-sons. Civil partnership, 2006. Educ. Broughton High School; Edinburgh University. Political organiser; Member, City of Edinburgh Council, 1995-99. Recreations: reading; travel.

Smith, Matt, OBE, JP. Non Executive Director, Scottish Water; Commissioner, Scottish Human Rights Commission; Member: Scottish Standards Commission, Employment Appeals Tribunal, North Strathclyde JP Advisory Committee; Director, Irvine Bay Regeneration Company; Director, Unity Enterprise; Executive Member and Hon. Fellow, Scottish Council for Development and Industry; Public Interest Member, ICAS Regulation Board; Member, CIPFA Disciplinary Scheme Committee; former Scottish Secretary, UNISON, 1993-2010 (NALGO, from 1973) and President, STUC, 1999-2000; b. 4.2.52, Irvine; m., Eileen; 1 s.; 1 d. Educ. Stevenston High School; Ardrossan Academy. Served on Commission on Scottish Devolution (Calman); Commission on Local Government and Scottish Parliament (McIntosh). Former Member and Vice Chair, Broadcasting Council for Scotland; Church and Nation Committee, Church of Scotland; Equal Opportunities Commission, Scottish Advisory Committee; Centre for Scottish Public Policy; Scottish Local Government Information Unit; Ayrshire Economic Forum. Lay Advisor, Royal College of Physicians (Edinburgh). Campaign for Scottish Parliament including Constitutional Convention; Vice Chair, Labour for a Scottish Parliament; former Stevenston Burgh Councillor and Dean of Guild; Parliamentary Candidate, Labour, 1979. Recreations: family; travel; music. E-mail: mattsmith52@hotmail.co.uk

Smith, Nigel R. Principal, VoxScot Referendum Consultants, since 2004; Managing Director, David Auld Valves Ltd., 1976-2004; b. 9.6.41, Girvan; m., Jody; 2 s.; 2 d. Educ. Dollar Academy. Staff and management appointments, Bowater Paper, Richard Costain, Rank Hovis McDougall. Member, Executive, Scottish Engineering Employers Association, 1985-90; Member, Broadcasting Council for Scotland, 1986-90; Member, BBC General Advisory Council, 1991-93; Member, Glasgow Development Agency, Strategy Review Panel, 1993-94; Member, Scottish Constitutional Commission, 1993-94; Chairman, Broadcasting for Scotland Campaign, 1993-97; Chairman, Scotland Forward Devolution Yes Campaign, 1997; Member, Bank of England Scottish Consultative Committee, 1993-2003; Chairman, British "No" euro campaign, 2002-04. Recreations: hill-walking; offshore sailing; music; reading, particularly biography. Address: (b.) VoxScot, 2 Crosshouse Road, Campsie Glen, Glasgow G66 7AD; T.-01360 311413.

Smith, Ralph Andrew, QC, LLB, DipLP. Advocate, since 1985; QC, since 1999; b. 22.3.61, Scotland; m., Lucy Moore Inglis; 1 s.; 1 d. Educ. Edinburgh Academy; Kelvinside Academy; Aberdeen University. Junior Counsel to Lord President, 1989-90; Standing Junior Counsel to Department of Environment, 1992-99; Advocate Depute (ad hoc); Deputy Judge, Upper Tribunal (Part Time). 2012. Legal Member, Lands Tribunal for Scotland (Full Time), 2014. Address: (h.) Castlemains, Gifford, East Lothian EH41 4PL.

Smith of Kelvin, Baron (Sir Robert Haldane Smith), CA, FCIBS. Chairman, Scotland Devolution Commission, since 2014; Chancellor, University of Strathclyde, since 2013; Member, Council of Economic Advisors to First Minister of Scotland, since 2007; Chairman, Advisory Group to Scottish Government on young people not in education, employment or training, since 2006; Chairman, Scottish and Southern Energy, since 2005; Non-executive Director: Standard Bank Group, since 2003, Aegon UK Ltd., since 2002, 3i Group plc, since 2004; Member, Judicial Appointments Board for Scotland, since 2002; Chancellor, University of The West of Scotland, since 2003; Regent, Royal College of Surgeons, since 2002; Deputy Chairman, China Britain Business Council, since 2003; b. 8.8.44, Glasgow; m.; 2 d. Educ. Allan Glen's School. Robb

Ferguson & Co., CA, 1963-68; qualified CA, 1968; ICFC (now 3i); Managing Director, National Commercial and Glyns Ltd., 1983-85; General Manager, Corporate Finance Division, Royal Bank of Scotland plc; Managing Director, Charterhouse Development Capital Ltd., and Executive Director, Charterhouse Bank Ltd., 1985-89; Morgan Grenfell Private Equity: CEO, 1989-96, Chairman, 1989-2001; Member, Group Executive Committee, Deutsche Bank, 1996-2000; Chief Executive, Morgan Grenfell Asset Management, 1996-99; Vice Chairman, Deutsche Asset Management, Deutsche Bank AG, 1999-2002; Chairman, The Weir Group plc, 2002-2013. Non-executive Director: Tip Europe plc, 1987-89, Stakis plc, 1997-99 (Chairman, 1998-99), Bank of Scotland plc, 1998-2000, MFI Furniture Group plc, 1987-2000. Member, Financial Services Authority, 1997-2000; Member, Board, Financial Reporting Council, 2001-04; Member, Board of Trustees, British Council, 2002-05; Chairman, FRC Group on Audit Committees Combined Code; Trustee, National Museums of Scotland, 1985-2002 (Chairman, Board of Trustees, 1993-2002); President, British Association of Friends of Museums, 1995-2005; President, Institute of Chartered Accountants of Scotland, 1996-97; Commissioner, Museums and Galleries Commission, 1988-98 (Vice Chairman, 1997-98). Hon. Doctorates, Edinburgh University, 1999, Glasgow University, 2001, Paisley University, 2003. Publication: Managing Your Company's Finances. Address: (b.) 39 Palmerston Place, Edinburgh EH12 5AU; T.-0131-527 6010.

Smith, Sir Robert Hill, Bt. MP (Liberal Democrat), West Aberdeenshire and Kincardine, 1997-2015; b. 15.4.58; m., Fiona Cormack; 3 d. Educ. Merchant Taylors' School, Northwood; University of Aberdeen. Managed family estate; Member, Aberdeenshire Council, 1995-97; Liberal Democrat Spokesman on Transport and the Environment, 1997-99, Scottish Affairs Spokesman, 1999-2001; Member, Scottish Affairs Select Committee, 1999-2001; Liberal Democrat Deputy Chief Whip, 2001-06, Scottish Whip, 1999-2001, Energy Spokesman, 2005-06, Trade and Industry Spokesman, 2005-06; Member: Trade and Industry Select Committee, 2001-05, European Standing Committee A, 2000-01, Procedures Committee, 2001-10, Unopposed Bills (Panel), 2001-10, Standing Orders, 2001-10, Accommodation and Works, 2003-05, International Development, 2007-09; Deputy Shadow Leader of the House, 2007-10. Honorary Vice President, Energy Action Scotland.

Smith, Sarah. Radio and Television reporter with BBC Scotland, since 2014; Scotland Editor of the BBC, since 2016; b. 1968; m., Simon Conway. Educ. University of Glasgow. Began journalistic career as a graduate trainee with BBC Scotland, then BBC Northern Ireland; Assistant producer with BBC Youth Programmes, working on Rough Guide, Rapido and Reportage, 1991-93; news and current affairs, first as assistant producer with the Public Eye and Here & Now programmes; producer for the BBC on Newsnight, Public Eye and Rough Guides; reporter for 2 years on 5 News; the first newsreader on More4 News; Channel 4 News's Washington correspondent, then Business correspondent in 2011. Address: BBC Scotland, 40 Pacific Quay, Glasgow G51 1DA.

Smith, Sarah. University Secretary, University of Edinburgh, since 2013. Educ. Oxford University; Imperial College, London; Harvard Business School. Career: Civil Service, Whitehall and Scottish Government. Address: University of Edinburgh, Room 214, Old College, South Bridge, Edinburgh EH8 9YL; T.-0131 650 2144.

Smith, Shona Houston, LLB (Hons), DipLP, NP. Partner, Balfour and Manson; b. 17.11.66, Glasgow. Admitted, Solicitor, 1991; specialised in family law, since 1993;

Board Member, Scottish Child Law Centre, 1996-99; former Chair and Treasurer of the Family Law Association; former Treasurer, Scottish Collaborative Family Law Group; Treasurer, Family Law Arbitration Group Scotland, since 2011. Address: (b.) 62 Frederick Street, Edinburgh EH2 1LS; T.-0131 200 1238; e-mail: shona.smith@balfour-manson.co.uk

Smith, Emeritus Professor Stanley Desmond, OBE, BSc, PhD, DSc, FRS, FRSE. Emeritus Professor (Professor of Physics, Heriot-Watt University, 1970-96); Founder, Edinburgh Instruments Ltd., 1971, Chairman, 1971-2011; Founder and Chairman, Edinburgh Biosciences Ltd; b. 3.3.31, Bristol; m., Gillian Anne Parish; 1 s.; 1 d. Educ. Cotham Grammar School; Bristol University; Reading University. SSO, RAE, Farnborough, 1956-58; Research Assistant, Department of Meteorology, Imperial College, London, 1958-59; Lecturer, then Reader, Reading University, 1960-70; Head, Department of Physics, Heriot-Watt University, 1970-96. Member: Advisory Council for Applied Research and Development, 1985-87, Advisory Council on Science and Technology, 1987-88, Defence Scientific Advisory Council, 1985-91, SERC Astronomy and Planetary Science and Engineering Boards, 1985-88, Council, Institute of Physics, 1984-87; Chairman, Scottish Optoelectronics Association, 1996-98. Royal Medal, Royal Society of Edinburgh, 2011. Recreations: skiing; mountaineering; golf. Address: (b.) Treetops, 29D Gillespie Road, Edinburgh EH13 0NW; desgillsmith@gmail.com; T.-0131 441 7225; (b.) Edinburgh Biosciences Ltd; T.-01506 429 274; e-mail: des@edinbio.com

Smith, Tommy, DUniv, DMus, DLitt, hon. FRIAS. Musician (tenor saxophone), Educator and Composer; b. 27.4.67, Edinburgh. Won best soloist and best group award, Edinburgh International Jazz Festival, aged 14; recorded his first albums as a leader, aged 15; joined Gary Burton Quintet, 1985-87; signed to Blue Note Records, 1989; won British Jazz Award, 1989; hosted Jazz Types, BBC TV; began recording for Linn Records, 1993; founded Scottish National Jazz Orchestra, 1995; won BT British Jazz Award for Best Ensemble, ScotRail Award for most outstanding group performance, Arts Foundation/Barclays Bank jazz composition fellowship prize, 1996; made youngest-ever Doctor of the University, Heriot-Watt University, 1999; has premiered four original saxophone concertos; Sound of Love album reached No. 20 in American Gavin Jazz Chart; started own record company, 2000; Honorary Fellow, Royal Incorporation of Architects of Scotland and Creative Scotland Award, 2000; Founder, The Tommy Smith Youth Jazz Orchestra, since 2002; Hamlet British Jazz Award for best tenor saxophonist, 2002; received second doctorate, Glasgow Caledonian University; won BBC 'Heart of Jazz' Award, 2008; winner of the Best Woodwind title at the inaugural Scottish Jazz Awards, 2009; Best Educator, Scottish Jazz Awards, 2011; Lord Provost Award for Music, 2009; 26 solo albums; appointed head of jazz, Scotland's first full time jazz course, Royal Conservatoire of Scotland; awarded Professorship, Royal Conservatoire of Scotland, 2010; Best Educator, Scottish Jazz Awards, 2012; Best Album of the year 'KARMA', Scottish Jazz Awards, 2012; received third doctorate, Edinburgh University, 2013; Best Big Band, Scottish Jazz Awards, 2009, 2011; Best Big Band, British Jazz Awards, 2012. Recreations: golf; cooking; poetry; cinema; art & design. Address: (b.) c/o Spartacus Records Ltd., PO Box 3743, Lanark ML11 9WD; e-mail: ts@snjo.co.uk

Smith, Walter, OBE; b. 24.2.48, Lanark. Joined Dundee United, 1966; joined Dumbarton, 1975; rejoined Dundee United, 1977, became Youth coach, then Assistant Manager; appointed coach of Scotland Under 18 team, 1978; became coach of the Under 21 team, then Assistant Manager for the Scotland World Cup team, 1986; joined Rangers in 1986 and became Manager in 1991; won the league in first six full seasons; won the Scottish Cup and League Cup three times each; Manager, Everton, 1998-2002; Assistant to Manchester United in 2004; National Coach, Scottish Football Association, 2004-2007; Manager, Rangers, 2007-2011, Chairman, 2013.

Smith, Professor William Ewen, BSc, DIC, PhD, DSc, FRSC, FRSE. Emeritus Professor of Inorganic Chemistry (Professor from 1987); b. 21.2.41, Glasgow; m., Frances Helen Williamson; 1 s.; 1 d. Educ. Hutchesons' Boys Grammar School; Strathclyde University. Visiting Scientist, Oak Ridge National Laboratory, 1965-67; SERC and ICI Fellow, University College, London, 1967-69; Lecturer, then Reader, then Professor, then Emeritus Professor, Strathclyde University, since 1969; Chief Scientific Officer, Reninshaw Diagnostics Ltd., 2010-2012 (Chief Executive Officer, 2007-2010). Publications: 300 papers and reviews. Recreations: golf; sailing. Address: Department of Pure and Applied Chemistry, Strathclyde University, Glasgow, G1 1XL; T.-0141-552 4400.

Smout, Professor Thomas Christopher, CBE, MA, PhD, FRSE, FSA (Scot), FBA. HM Historiographer in Scotland; b. 19.12.33. Address: Chesterhill, Shore Road, Anstruther, Fife KY10 3DZ; e-mail: christopher@smout.org

Smyth, Colin. MSP (Labour), South Scotland region, since 2016. Career history: worked as a teacher, becoming a Labour party organiser in 2003; General Secretary of the Scottish Labour Party, 2008-2012; elected to Dumfries and Galloway Council in 2007, representing the Nith Ward, re-elected in 2012. Address: Scottish Parliament, Edinburgh EH99 1SP.

Smyth, Professor John Fletcher, MD, FRCPE, FRCP, FRCSE, FRCR, FRSE. Emeritus Professor of Medical Oncology; Assistant Principal, University of Edinburgh, since 2009, Director of Cancer Research Centre, 2002-05; Hon. Director, Cancer Research UK (formerly Imperial Cancer Research Fund) Medical Oncology Unit, now Clinical Cancer Research Centre, 1980-2005; President of the Federation of European Cancer Societies, 2005-07; b. 26.10.45; m., (1) Catherine Ellis; 2 d (marr. diss.); m., (2) Ann Cull; 2 step d. Educ. Bryanston School; Trinity College, Cambridge (BA, 1967, MA, 1971); St. Bartholomews Hospital (MB Chir 1970); MD Cantab, 1976; MSc London, 1975; MRCP, 1973. House Officer posts: St. Bartholomew's Hosp. and RPMS, London, 1970-72; Assistant Lecturer, Dept. of Med. Oncology, St. Bartholomew's Hospital, 1972-73; CRC Research Fellowship, Inst. Cancer Res., 1973-75; MRC Travelling Fellowship, Nat. Cancer Inst., USA, 1975-76; Senior Lecturer, Inst. Cancer Research, 1976-79. Honorary Consultant Physician, Royal Marsden Hospital and Brompton Hospital, 1977-79; Lothian Health Board, 1979-2008; Visiting Professor of Medicine and Associate Director for Medical Research, University of Chicago, 1979; Professor of Medical Oncology, University of Edinburgh, 1979-2008. Member of Council: EORTC, 1990-97; UICC, 1990-94; President, European Society for Medical Oncology, 1991-93; Federation of European Cancer Societies, Treasurer, 1992-97, President 2005-2007. Editor-in-Chief, European Journal of Cancer, 2000-2010; Member, Committee on Safety of Medicines, 1999-2005; Chair, Expert Advisory Group for Haematology & Oncology Commission on Human Medicines, 2006-13; Member, Board of Governors, Bryanston School, 1989-2014. Publications: contributions to various medical and scientific journals on cancer medicine, pharmacology, clinical and experimental cancer therapeutics. Recreations: flying and singing (sometimes simultaneously). Club:

Athenaeum. Address: 18 Inverleith Avenue South, Edinburgh EH3 5QA; T.-0131 552 3775.

Smyth, Professor Noel Frederick, BSc (Hons), PhD. Professor of Nonlinear Waves, University of Edinburgh, since 2009 (Lecturer, since 1990); Professor, University of Wollongong, since 2008; b. 16.5.58, Brisbane, Australia; m., Juliet Elizabeth Smyth; 1 s. Educ. Toowong State High School; University of Queensland; California Institute of Technology. Research Fellow: California Institute of Technology, 1984, University of Melbourne, 1984-86; Research Associate, University of New South Wales, 1986-87; Lecturer, University of Wollongong, 1987-90; University of Edinburgh: Lecturer, 1990-99, Senior Lecturer, 1999-2004, Reader, 2004-09. Librarian, Edinburgh Mathematical Society, 1992-97; Engineering and Physical Sciences Research Council Peer Review College, since 2006. Publications: 115 refereed scientific papers; 4 book chapters. Address: (b.) School of Mathematics, University of Edinburgh, Mayfield Road, Edinburgh EH9 3FD; T.-0131 650 5080; e-mail: n.smyth@ed.ac.uk

Somerville, Shirley-Anne, BA (Hons). MSP (SNP), Dunfermline, since 2016, Lothians, 2007-2011; Minister for Further Education, Higher Education and Science, Scottish Government, since 2016; Deputy Chief Executive, SNP, 2013-16; b. 2.9.74; m., Myles. Educ. Kirkcaldy High School; Strathclyde University; Stirling University. Scottish National Party: Member, since 1990. Contested Edinburgh Central constituency, 2007 Scottish Parliament election. Returned as replacement MSP for Lothians region on 5 September 2007. Trustee and Member of the Scotland Committee, Shelter UK, 2011-16; Director of Communities, Yes Scotland, 2012-13. Address: Scottish Parliament, Edinburgh EH99 1SP.

Sorensen, Alan Kenneth, DL, BD, MTh, DipMin, FSA (Scot). Minister, Wellpark Mid Kirk, Greenock, since 2000; previously in St. Christopher's, Pollok from 1983. Broadcaster, since 1979; b. 16.04.57, Clydebank. Educ. Hutchesons' Boys' Grammar; Glasgow University; Edinburgh University. Sometime gravedigger, musician and comedian; Retail Management prior to Parish Ministry. Appointed Deputy Lieutenant for Renfrewshire, 2014; Church of Scotland's National Advisor on local broadcasting for many years; has received 38 national and international broadcasting awards. Recreations: collecting 60's onwards pop music; family history; studying Scottish castles; enjoying fine wine. Address: (h./b.) 101 Brisbane Street, Greenock PA16 8PA.
E-mail: alan.sorensen@ntlworld.com

Soutar, David, MB, ChB, FRCS(Ed), FRCS(Glas), ChM. Consultant Plastic Surgeon, West of Scotland Regional Plastic Maxillofacial Surgery Unit, 1981-2008; Chairman, Division of Trauma and Related Services, North Glasgow Universities NHS Trust, 2000-06; b. 19.12.47, Arbroath; m., Myra; 2 s.; 1 d. Educ. Ayr Academy; University of Aberdeen. General surgical training, Grampian Health Board; plastic surgery training, Aberdeen, Glasgow, Munich; Honorary Clinical Senior Lecturer, Glasgow University. Member, Council, British Association of Plastic Surgeons, 1988-92, 1994-2002 (President, 2001). Publications: four books; over 30 book chapters; over 70 articles. Recreations: music; gardening.

Souter, Sir Brian, BA. Chairman, Stagecoach Group plc, since 2013 (Chief Executive, 2002-2013, Chairman, 1980-2002); b. 1954; m., Elizabeth McGoldrick; 3 s.; 1 d. Educ. Dundee University; University of Strathclyde. Address: (b.) 10 Dunkeld Road, Perth, PH1 5TW.

Souter, William Alexander, MBChB(Hons), FRCSEd. Consultant Orthopaedic Surgeon, Princess Margaret Rose Orthopaedic Hospital, Edinburgh, 1968-1997; b. 11.5.33, Cupar; m., Kathleen Bruce Georgeson Taylor; 1 s.; 2 d. Educ. Falkirk High School; George Watson's Boys' College, Edinburgh; Medical School, Edinburgh University. Registrar in Hand Surgery, Derbyshire Royal Infirmary, 1964; Senior Registrar, Orthopaedic Department, Edinburgh, 1965-68; Instructor in Orthopaedic Surgery, University of Washington, Seattle, 1967; Honorary Senior Lecturer in Orthopaedics, Edinburgh University, 1977-97; Visiting Professor, Bioengineering Department, Strathclyde University, 1985-88. Member, Council, British Orthopaedic Association, 1986-88 and 1993-95; Member, Council, Royal College of Surgeons of Edinburgh, 1988-98; Inaugural President, British Elbow and Shoulder Society, 1989-90; British Society for Surgery of the Hand: Member, Council, 1977-78, 1992-94, President, 1993; Chairman, Accreditation Committee, Federation of European Societies for Surgery of the Hand, 1992-96; European Rheumatoid Arthritis Surgical Society: Member, Executive Committee, 1979-81 and 1993-2001, President, 1995-99; President, Rheumatoid Arthritis Surgical Society, 1982 and 1998-2000; Honorary Member: British Society for Surgery of the Hand, 2001, Societe Francaise Chirurgie Orthopedique et Traumatologique, 1999, Netherlands Rheumatoid Arthritis Surgical Society, 2001, Spanish Society for Surgery of the Shoulder and Elbow, 1996, European Rheumatoid Arthritis Surgical Society, 2002, British Elbow and Shoulder Society, 2003; International Federation of Societies for Surgery of the Hand (IFSSH) Award: Pioneer of Hand Surgery, 2007. Recreations: gardening; music; hill-walking; photography; golf. Address: (h.) Old Mauricewood Mains, Penicuik, Midlothian EH26 0NJ; T.-01968 672609; e-mail: wsouter@btinternet.com

Southwood, Ann, BA (Hons), DipCG, CertYCW. Principal, Newbattle Abbey College, since 2000; b. 25.5.54, York. Educ. Queen Anne Grammar School, York; Middlesex University. National Development Officer, Scottish Executive, Adult Educational Guidance Initiative Scotland, 1994-98; Adult Guidance Manager, Career Development, Edinburgh and Lothian, 1995-2000. Recreations: music; sport; travel. Address: (b.) Newbattle Road, Dalkeith EH22 3LL; T.-0131 663 1921; e-mail: office@newbattleabbeycollege.ac.uk

Sparks, Professor Leigh, MA, PhD. Professor of Retail Studies, Stirling University, since 1992; Dean, Faculty of Management, 1995-2000; Head, Stirling Graduate School, since 2011; b. 15.2.57, Bridgend, Wales; m., Janice Lewis. Educ. Brynteg C.S.; Christ's College, Cambridge; St. David's University College, Wales. Researcher, Lecturer, Senior Lecturer, Professor, Institute for Retail Studies, Stirling University. Chair, Scotland's Towns Partnership. Recreation: watching sport, especially rugby. Address: (b.) Institute for Retail Studies, Stirling University, Stirling FK9 4LA; T.-01786 467384; e-mail: Leigh.Sparks@stir.ac.uk; web: www.stirlingretail.com

Speakman, Professor John Roger, BSc, PhD, DSc. Professor of Zoology, Aberdeen University, since 1997 (Director, Institute of Biological and Environmental Sciences, 2007-2011); b. 29.11.58, Leigh; m., Mary Magdelene; 1 s.; 1 d. Educ. Leigh Grammar School; Stirling University. Lecturer, 1989, Senior Lecturer, 1993, Reader, 1995, Aberdeen University; Chairman, Aberdeen Centre for Energy Regulation and Obesity, since 1998; Royal Society Leverhulme Senior Research Fellow, 2000. Publication: Body Composition Analysis: A Handbook of Non-Invasive Methods, 2001. Address: (b.) Department of Zoology, Aberdeen University, Aberdeen AB24 2TZ; T.-01224 272879.

Speirs, Alison Jane, BA, DCE, DipSEN. Head Teacher, Cedars School of Excellence, since 1999; Minister, Struthers Memorial Church, Glasgow, since 2004; b. 6.5.53, Motherwell; divorced; 1 s.; 1 d. Educ. Greenock Academy; Jordanhill College; Open University. Primary Teacher, since 1973; Teacher of children with additional support needs, 1991-99; Co-Founder, Cedars School of Excellence in 1999; Member and Youth Leader, Struthers Memorial Group of Churches, since 1986. Publication: Author, "Within These Walls", 2005. Recreations: voluntary work; musical production; reading; poetry. Address: (h.) The Cedars, 44 Ardgowan Street, Greenock PA16 8EL; T.- 01475 727042; e-mail: alison@speirs.org

Spence, Professor Alan, MA. Professor of Creative Writing, University of Aberdeen, Artistic Director, WORD Festival; Writer (poet, playwright, novelist, short-story writer); b. 5.12.47, Glasgow; m., Janani (Margaret). Educ. Allan Glen's School, Glasgow; Glasgow University. Writer in Residence, Glasgow University, 1975-77, Deans Community School, 1978, Traverse Theatre, Edinburgh, 1983, City of Edinburgh, 1986-87, Edinburgh University, 1989-92, Aberdeen University, 1996-2001 (Professor in Creative Writing, since 2001); winner, People's Prize, 1991; Macallan/Scotland on Sunday Short Story competition, 1993; McVitie's Prize, 1996; TMA Drama Award, 1996; Glenfiddich Spirit of Scotland Award, 2006. Publications: poetry: ah!; Glasgow Zen; Seasons of the Heart; Clear Light; Morning Glory; short stories: Its Colours They Are Fine, Stone Garden; novels: The Magic Flute, Way to Go, The Pure Land; Night Boat; plays: Sailmaker; Space Invaders; Changed Days. Recreations: meditation; running; playing flute. Address: 21 Waverley Park, Edinburgh EH8 8ER; T.-0131 661 8403; e-mail: a.spence@abdn.ac.uk

Spence, James William, KFO (Norway), RON (Netherlands), DL (Orkney), BSc, MNI, MICS. Lord-Lieutenant of Orkney, since 2014; Master Mariner, since 1971; Shipbroker, since 1975; Company Director, since 1977; Honorary Sheriff, Grampian Highland and Islands (Kirkwall), since 2000; Vice Lord-Lieutenant (Orkney), 2011-14; b. 19.1.45, St. Ola, Orkney; m., 1, Margaret Paplay Stevenson (deceased); 3 s. (one deceased); 2, Susan Mary Price. Educ. Leith Nautical College, Edinburgh; Robert Gordon's Institute of Technology, Aberdeen; University of Wales, Cardiff. Merchant Navy, 1961-74 (Member, Nautical Institute, 1972, Member, Royal Institute of Navigation, 1971); Micoperi SpA, 1974-75 (Temporary Assistant Site Co-ordinator on Scapa Flow Project); John Jolly (Shipbrokers, Stevedores, Shipping and Forwarding Agents) since 1975 (Manager, 1975, Junior Partner, 1976-77, Proprietor and Managing Director, since 1978, Chairman of the Board, since 2003). Vice-Consul for Norway, 1976, Consul, 1978-2014; Vice-Consul for the Netherlands, 1978-94; Member, Kirkwall Community Council, 1978-82; Member, Orkney Pilotage Committee, 1979-88; Chairman, Kirkwall Port Employers' Association, 1979-87 (Member, since 1975); Chairman, RNLI, Kirkwall Lifeboat Station Branch Committee, 1997-2004 (Station Hon. Secretary, 1987-96, Deputy Launching Authority, 1976-87); Chairman, Pier Arts Centre Trust, 1989-91 (Trustee, 1980-91); Chairman, Association of Honorary Norwegian Consuls in the UK and Ireland, 1993-95. Recreations: oenology; equestrian matters; Orcadian history; vintage motoring. Address: (h.) Alton House, Kirkwall, Orkney KW15 1NA; T.-01856 872268.
E-mail: cc@johnjolly.co.uk
E-mail: bs3920@yahoo.com

Spence, Professor John, OBE, ARCST, BSc, MEng, PhD, DSc, FREng, FRSE, CEng, FIMechE. Professor Emeritus, Strathclyde University, since 2001, Trades House of Glasgow Professor of Mechanics of Materials, 1982-2001; b. 5.11.37, Chapelhall; m., Margaret Gray Hudson; 2 s. Educ. Airdrie Academy; Royal College of Science and Technology; Sheffield University. Engineering apprenticeship, Stewarts & Lloyds (now British Steel Corporation); Senior Engineer, then Head of Stress Analysis, Babcock & Wilcox Research Division; Strathclyde University: Lecturer, 1966, Senior Lecturer, Reader, Professor since 1979, Deputy Principal, Pro-Vice Principal and Vice Principal, 1994-2001; Acting Principal, Bell College, Hamilton, 2004/05. Served on many national committees: President, Institution of Mechanical Engineers, 1998/1999; EPSRC; British Standards Institution; Engineering Professors Council; Engineering Council Senate and BER; Research Assessment Exercise Panel 30 in 1992, 1996 and Chair in 2001; Accreditation Board, Hong Kong Institution of Engineers; Scottish Higher Education Funding Council; Royal Academy of Engineering Council. Awarded OBE in Birthday Honours List in 2008; Chair, Search for Truth Charitable Trust, since 2009. Address: (b.) Cairn O'Mount, 32 Commonhead Street, Airdrie ML6 6NS; e-mail: john.spence@strath.ac.uk

Spencer, Professor Alec P., BA (Hons), MA. Former Director, Rehabilitation and Care, Scottish Prison Service (2001-06); Honorary Professor, School of Applied Social Science, University of Stirling, since 2005; Convener, The Scottish Consortium on Crime and Criminal Justice (SCCCJ); Public Appointments Assessor for Commissioner for Ethical Standards on Public Life in Scotland; Trustee, Lucy Faithfull Foundation; b. 12.3.46, London; m., Joan; 2 s.; 1 d. Educ. Dame Alice Owen School; Keele University. Joined Scottish Prison Service, 1972; Governor, Dungavel, Peterhead, Edinburgh and Glenochil Prisons; Chairman and Founder, Scottish Forum on Prisons and Families, 1990-2000; Chair, Scottish Accreditation Panel for Offender Programmes, 2006-10; Chairman and Member of Board of Directors, INCLUDEM, 2001-10; Chairman, Scottish Association for Study of Offending (SASO), 2006-2011; Adviser, Scottish Parliament, Justice 2 Sub-Committee Inquiry into sexual offenders against children, 2006; Chairman, Dollar Community Council, 1990-93. Publications & Reports: Working with Sex Offenders in Prisons and through Release to the Community, 1999; Prisoner Supervision System, 2000; Review of Future Management of Sex Offenders, 2002; Balancing Risk and Need, 2009. Recreations: music; walking; early Penguin books. Address: Oakburn, 92 The Ness, Dollar, Clackmannanshire FK14 7EB; T.-01259 743044.
E-mail: spencer@oakburn.co.uk

Spens, Michael Colin Barkley, MA. Headmaster, Fettes College, Edinburgh, since 1998; b. 22.9.50, Weybridge; m., Deborah Susan; 1 s.; 2 d. Educ. Marlborough College; Selwyn College, Cambridge. United Biscuits Plc, 1972-74; Radley College, Oxon, 1974-93 (Assistant Master, 1974-93, i/c Careers, 1974-84, Housemaster, 1984-93); Headmaster, Caldicott, Farnham Common, 1993-98. Recreations: golf; running; wood-turning; bridge; geology; mountaineering; electronics. Address: (h.) Headmasters' Lodge, Fettes College, Edinburgh EH4 1QX; T.-0131-311 6701.

Spilg, Walter Gerson Spence, MB, ChB (Hons), FRCPath, FRCPG, FRCPG. Consultant Pathologist, Victoria Infirmary, Glasgow, 1972-99, in Administrative Charge, 1986-99; Honorary Clinical Senior Lecturer, Glasgow University, since 1973; b. 27.10.37, Glasgow; m., Vivien Anne Burns; 1 s.; 2 d. Educ. Hutchesons' Boys' Grammar School, Glasgow; Glasgow University. Registrar in Pathology, Glasgow Royal Infirmary, 1965-68; Senior Registrar in Pathology, Victoria Infirmary, Glasgow, 1968-69; Lecturer in Pathology, Glasgow University (Western Infirmary),

1969-72. Former President, Caledonian Branch, Association of Clinical Pathologists; (Locum) Consultant Pathologist, Wishaw General Hospital, Lanarkshire. Recreation: bridge. Address: (h.) 4B Newton Court, Newton Mearns, Glasgow, G77 5QL; e-mail: walterspilg@aol.com

Spowart, James McInally, FCIBS. Director, Scottish Water, since 2009; b. 19.11.50, Dunfermline; m., Janis Bell Spowart; 2 s. Educ. Beath High School, Cowdenbeath; Edinburgh Chamber of Commerce; Napier University. Founder: Direct Line Financial Services, Standard Life Bank, Intelligent Finance; spent 25 years with Royal Bank of Scotland (prepared the blue print for telephone banking); led a campaign to save HBOS (2008-09). West Lothian Business Man of the Year, 2002; Business Insider Award, 2002. Honorary Doctor of Business, Napier University; Non-executive director of Scottish Water and Commissioner to the Church of Scotland, 2011-12; Chairman of We-evolution (a Church of Scotland run charity). Recreations: golf; reading; swimming. Address: 16 Sarazen Green, Livingston; T.-01506 439988.
E-mail: jimspowart@hotmail.com

Spray, Professor Christopher James, MBE, FRSA, PhD, MA, MCIEEM. Chair of Water Science & Policy, UNESCO Centre for Water Law, Policy and Science, Dundee University, since 2009; NERC Senior Research Fellow, 2015/16; b. 11.7.53, Marlborough; m., Deborah; 3 s. Educ. Marlborough College, Wiltshire; St. John's College, Cambridge; Aberdeen University. Research Fellow in Zoology, Aberdeen University, 1978-84; Anglian Water Authority, Cambridge, 1984-89; National Rivers Authority, Anglian Region, 1989-91; Conservation Manager, then Environment Director, Northumbrian Water Limited, 1991-2004; Director of Environmental Science, Scottish Environment Protection Agency, 2004-09; President, Institute of Ecology and Environmental Management, 2004-06; Trustee, Wildfowl and Wetlands Trust, 2003-09; Trustee, Freshwater Biological Association, 2006-2013, Chair 2010; Council Member, RSPB, 1999-2003; Trustee of British Trust for Ornithology, 2001-03; Director of River Restoration Project, 1995-99; past Chairman of Tweed Forum; past Director, Industry and Nature Conservation Association. Board Member, Heritage Lottery Fund (NE) Committee, 2001-04; Member, Government's Advisory Committee on Releases to the Environment, 1999-2002; Member, England Biodiversity Group, 2002-04, Scotland Biodiversity Group, 2006-09. Recreations: birdwatching; running; conservation; hill walking. Address: (b.) UNESCO Centre for Water Law, Policy and Science, University of Dundee, Dundee DD1 4HN; T.-01382 388362.
E-mail: C.J.Spray@dundee.ac.uk

Spreng, Callum. Managing Director, Spreng & Co Ltd; b. 28.7.61. St. Andrews; m., Lorna Hunter. Educ. Dunfermline High School. Journalist, Dunfermline Press Newspaper Group, 1979-1984; Asst. Editor, SSEB News, SSEB, 1984-1986; various communications roles then Head of Communications, General Accident Fire & Life Assurance Corporation plc, 1986-1998; Communications Director, SMG plc, 1998-2007; Corporate Communications Director, ProStrakan Group plc, 2007-2008. Member, Council, CBI Scotland, 2007-2012. Recreations: golf; classic cars; motorsport. Address: (b.) 155 Albion Street, Glasgow G1 1RU.

Sprent, Professor Janet I., OBE, BSc, ARCS, PhD, DSc, FRSE, HonDAgSci, SLU (Sweden). Emeritus Professor of Plant Biology, Dundee University; Trustee, Royal Botanic Garden Edinburgh, 2007-2015, Research Associate, since 2015; b. 10.1.34, Slough; m., Emeritus Professor Peter Sprent. Educ. Slough High School; Imperial College, London; Tasmania University. Has spent 31 years at Dundee University; research focussed on nitrogen fixing legumes, both tree and crop species; currently involved in international collaboration, mainly in Africa, Australia and Brazil; Dean of Science and Engineering, 1987-89; Deputy Principal of the University, 1995-98. Council Member, NERC, 1991-95; Member, Scottish Higher Education Funding Council, 1992-96; Member, Joint Nature Conservation Committee, 1994-2000; Member, then Chairman, Board of Governors, Macaulay Land Use Research Institute, 1989-2001; Member, Board, Scottish Natural Heritage, 2001-07; Member, Royal Commission on Environmental Pollution, 2002-08; Council Member, Scottish Association for Marine Science, 2003-08; Hon. Research Fellow, James Hutton Institute. Publications: six books and over 200 chapters/papers. Recreations: research; hill-walking. Address: 32 Birkhill Avenue, Wormit, Fife DD6 8PW; T.-01382 541706.

Sprot of Haystoun, Lt.-Col. Aidan Mark, MC, JP. Landowner (Haystoun Estate) and Farmer, since 1965; b. 17.6.19, Lilliesleaf. Educ. Belhaven Hill; Stowe. Commissioned, Royal Scots Greys, 1940; served Palestine, 1941-42, Western Desert, 1942-43, Italy, 1943-44, NW Europe, 1944-45; continued serving with Regiment in Germany until 1952, Libya, Egypt and Jordan, 1952-55, UK, 1955-58, Germany, 1958-62; Adjutant, 1944-45; Commanding Officer, 1959-62; retired, 1962. County Councillor, Peeblesshire, 1963-75; DL (Peeblesshire), 1966-80; Lord Lieutenant, Tweeddale, 1980-94; Member, Queen's Bodyguard for Scotland (Royal Company of Archers), since 1950; County Director, Peeblesshire Branch, Red Cross, 1966-74, Patron, since 1983; Badge of Honour, British Red Cross Society, 1998; County Commissioner, Peeblesshire Scout Association, 1968-73, Chairman, 1975-80, President, 1980-94; President, Borders Area Scout Association, 1994-99; Scout Medal of Merit, 1994; Honorary Secretary, Royal Caledonian Hunt, 1964-74; President, Lowlands of Scotland TA&VRA, 1986-89; President, Lothian Federation of Boys' Clubs, 1989-96, now Hon. Vice-President; Honorary Freeman, Tweeddale District, 1994; Vice-President, Royal Highland and Agricultural Society of Scotland, 1986; Trustee, Royal Scottish Agricultural Benevolent Institution, 1989-98; Member, Church of Scotland Service Chaplains Committee, 1974-82 and 1985-92; Honorary President, Peebles Branch, Royal British Legion Scotland, since 1990; Honorary President, Tweeddale Society, since 1994; Honorary Member, Rotary Club of Peebles, since 1986. Publication: Swifter than Eagles (war memoirs). Recreations: country sports; motor cycle touring. Address: (h.) Crookston, by Peebles, EH45 9JQ; T.-01721 740209.

Sproul-Cran, Robert Scott, MA (Cantab), PhD. Managing Director, Northlight Productions Ltd., since 1991; Project Manager, Voice of My Own (VOMO); b. 14.8.50; m., Elizabeth Ann; 3 s.; 1 d. Educ. Daniel Stewart's College; Pembroke College, Cambridge; Edinburgh University. Trainee, Phillips & Drew, Stockbrokers, London, 1971-72; Announcer, then Head of Presentation, BBC Radio Scotland, 1979-85; Radio Manager, BBC Aberdeen, 1986-90; Scottish Correspondent, BBC Daytime Television, 1990-91; freelance Graphic Designer and Underwater Photographer, since 1976; Director, Scotland the Brand marketing organisation, 2003-04; Chief Executive, Tartan TV Ltd., 2000-07. Winner, Scottish Corporate Communications Award, RTS Award for video graphics; directed "In Search of the Tartan Turban" which was nominated for an RTS award and won a BAFTA in the British Academy Children's Film and Television Awards, 2004; illustrated Maurice Lindsay's Glasgow; exhibited, Aberdeen Artists' annual exhibition; wrote and directed short film 'The Elemental' shown at Edinburgh

International Film Festival, 2009 with completion funding from UK Film Council. Publication: Thicker than Water (novel and screenplay); Schrödinger's Caterpillar (novel). Directed "Marrakech" and 'I Can't Remember Anything' for Treading The Borders theatre company. Created computer graphics for feature film 'The Happy Lands' (Dir: Robert Rae). Recreations: oil painting; windsurfing; sub aqua; playing bad rock guitar. Address: (b.) Northlight Productions Ltd., Hassendeanburn House, Hawick TD9 8RU; T.-01450 870106; web: www.northlight.tv

Spurway, Professor Neil Connell, MA, PhD. Emeritus Professor of Exercise Physiology, University of Glasgow; b. 22.8.36, Bradford; m., Alison Katherine Middleton; 3 s. Educ. The Grammar School, Falmouth, Cornwall; Jesus College, Cambridge University. Assistant, then Lecturer, then Senior Lecturer in Physiology, University of Glasgow, 1963-96, Professor of Exercise Physiology, 1996-2001. Chair, British Association of Sport and Exercise Sciences, 2000-02; Chair, Glasgow University Gifford Lectureships Committee, 1994-98; Member, Exercise Physiology Steering Group, BOA, 1991-2004; President, Royal Philosophical Society of Glasgow, 2003-05; Chair, Science and Religion Forum, 2006-09; Vice-President, European Society for Study of Science and Theology, 2008-2010; President, Scottish Church Theological Society, since 2015. Publications: Humanity, Environment and God; Genetics and Molecular Biology of Muscle Adaptation (Co-Author); Creation and the Abrahamic Faiths; Theology, Evolution and the Mind; Laws of Nature, Laws of God?; many papers and book chapters. Recreations: sailing; skiing; hill walking; philosophy; poetry; theatre; grandchildren. Address: 76 Fergus Drive, Glasgow G20 6AP; T.-0141-946 3336.
E-mail: Neil.Spurway@glasgow.ac.uk

Squire of Rubislaw, Romilly, OStJ, DA, FSAScot, FHSS, FSSA, SHA. Heraldic Artist and Quondam Herald Painter in the Court of the Lord Lyon, Edinburgh, and the Office of the Chief Herald of Ireland, Dublin, since 1983; Heraldic consultant to a number of exiled Royal Houses; b. 3.4.53, Glasgow. Educ. High School of Glasgow; Glasgow School of Art, Jordanhill College. Taught at Seconary School level, 1976-83. Participant in the world's first Heraldic Artists Workshop, Ottawa, Canada, 1996; awarded the "Corel Prize" for excellence in Heraldic Art, 1996; Craft Member, Society of Heraldic Arts, 1999; Grand Officer of the Imperial Order of the Star of Ethiopia, 2000; Board Member and Fellow, Society of Scottish Armigers, USA, 2003. Chairman, The Heraldry Society of Scotland, 2003-08; appointed Deputy Secretary to the Standing Council of Scottish Chiefs, 1990, Hon. Secretary, 2003-2012 (retired); Knight of the Order of the Eagle of Georgia, 2010; Knight of the Imperial Order of St Anne, 2011; Fellow of the Heraldry Society of Scotland, 2011. Publications include: Gem Pocket Tartans; Kings and Queens of Europe and Kings and Queens of Great Britain; The Collins Encyclopedia of the Clans and Families of Scotland; Clans and Tartans. Address: Studio 4, 30 Elbe Street, Leith, Edinburgh EH6 7HW; T.-0131 553 2232; e-mail: romilly.squire@virgin.net

Stacey, Hon. Lady (Valerie Elizabeth), QC, LLB (Hons). Senator of the College of Justice, since 2009; Chairman, Employment Appeal Tribunal, since 2013; Queen's Counsel, since 1999; Vice Dean, Faculty of Advocates, 2004-07; Member, Judicial Appointments Board for Scotland, 2005-07; Member, Sentencing Commission for Scotland, 2003-06; b. 25.5.54, Lanark; m., Andrew; 2 s. Educ. Elgin Academy; Edinburgh University. Solicitor, 1978; Advocate, 1987; Advocate Depute, 1993-96; Standing Junior Counsel, Home Office in Scotland, 1996-99; Temporary Sheriff, 1997-99. Recreation: listening to

music. Address: (b.) Supreme Courts, Parliament House, Parliament Square, Edinburgh EH1 1RQ; T.-0131-225 2590.

Stachura, Professor Peter Desmond, MA, PhD, DLitt (Stirling), FRHistS. Professor of Modern European History and Director, Centre for Research in Polish History, Stirling University, 2000-2009, Director, Research Centre for Modern Polish History, since 2010; Member, Scottish Parliamentary Cross Party Working Group on Poland, 2009-13; Member, Advisory Board of the Kresy-Siberia Foundation, 2010-13; Member of the Editorial Advisory Board of the academic history periodical, Glaukopis (Warsaw); b. 2.8.44, Galashiels; m., Kay Higgins; 1 s., 1 d. Educ. St. Mirin's Academy, Paisley; Glasgow University; East Anglia University. Research Fellow, Institut für Europäische Geschichte, Mainz, Germany, 1970-71; Stirling University: Lecturer in History, 1971-83, Reader, 1983-2002. Chairman (and Founder), The Polish Society, 1996-2013; Editor, Occasional Papers Series, Centre for Research in Polish History, 2001-2010. Major publications: Nazi Youth in the Weimar Republic, 1975; The Weimar Era and Hitler: a critical bibliography, 1977; The Shaping of the Nazi State (Editor), 1978 (reprinted, 2014); The German Youth Movement, 1900-1945, 1981; Gregor Strasser and the Rise of Nazism, 1983 (reprinted, 2014); The Nazi Machtergreifung (Editor), 1983 (reprinted, 2014); Unemployment and the Great Depression in Weimar Germany (Editor), 1986; The Weimar Republic and the Younger Proletariat: an economic and social analysis, 1989; Political Leaders in Weimar Germany: a biographical study, 1992; Themes of Modern Polish History (Editor), 1992; Poland Between the Wars, 1918-1939 (Editor), 1998; Poland in the Twentieth Century, 1999; Perspectives on Polish History (Editor), 2001; The Poles in Britain 1940-2000 (Editor), 2004; Poland, 1918-1945: An Interpretive and Documentary History of the Second Republic, 2004; The Warsaw Rising, 1944 (Editor), 2007; numerous articles in scholarly journals and anthologies in English, German and Polish. Recreations: supporting Celtic FC; discovering Poland; vexillology. Address: (h.) Ashcroft House, Chalton Road, Bridge of Allan, FK9 4EF; T.-01786 832793.
E-mail: pdstachura@yahoo.com

Staff, Alan. Chief Executive, Apex Scotland, since 2010. Educ. Gilberd School, Colchester, Essex; University of East Anglia; Essex University. Career history: Director of Modernisation, Suffolk Mental Health Partnerships NHS Trust, 2002-06; CEO, CrossReach, 2006-09; President, Eurodiaconia, 2007-09. Recreations: performance art; rugby; politics; travel; walking; developing young musicians. Address: (b.) 9 Great Stuart Street, Edinburgh EH3 7TP; T.-0131 220 0130.
E-mail: admin@apexscotland.org.uk

Stafford, Alyson, CBA. Director-General Finance, Scottish Government, since 2010. Joined the Scottish Government as Director of Finance in June 2005. Qualified as a Chartered Accountant in 1992 and her services to the public sector were recognised in 2002 when she received honorary membership of the Chartered Institute of Public Finance Accountants (nominated by CIPFA Scotland). Her career has spanned private, public and central government sectors. She has been at the forefront of change leading strategic, operational and corporate services in the Health Service in England and Scotland as a Chief Executive as well as Director of Finance. Address: (b.) Scottish Government, 3B.99, 3B South, Victoria Quay, Edinburgh EH6 6QQ; T.-0131 244 7341.

Stair, 14th Earl of (John David James Dalrymple); b. 4.9.61, Edinburgh. Army Officer, 1981-86; Land

Owner/Manager, since 1989. Retired Board Member, Dumfries and Galloway Enterprise; Retired Board Member, Scottish Environment Protection Agency, West; Cross Bench Member, House of Lords. Interests: farming; environmental matters. Recreations: all outdoor activities; gardening; flying. Address: (b.) Stair Estates, Sheuchan, Castle Kennedy, Stranraer DG9 8SL; T.-01776 702024.

Stalley, Professor Richard Frank, MA, BPhil. Professorial Research Fellow in Philosophy, Glasgow University, since 2008, Professor of Ancient Philosophy, 1997-2008, Head of Philosophy Department, 1990-93, 2001-04; b. 26.11.42, Leamington; m., Ellen May Ladd; 1 s.; 1 d. Educ. De Aston School; Worcester College, Oxford; Harvard University. Lecturer in Moral Philosophy, Glasgow University, 1968-84; Senior Lecturer in Philosophy, 1984-97. Publications include: An Introduction to Plato's Laws, 1983; Aristotle's Politics, 1995; many articles on ancient philosophy and on Scottish philosophy. Recreations: walking; opera. Address: (h.) 73 Jordanhill Drive, Glasgow G13 1UW; T.-0141 959 2668.

Stanley, Kenneth Alan, LLB (Hons), NP, WS. Solicitor; Senior Partner, Aitken Nairn, WS, Edinburgh, since 2000 (Partner, since 1984); b. 31.7.57, Edinburgh; 2 d. Educ. Boroughmuir High School; University of Edinburgh. Solicitor, 1981; Alston Nairn and Hogg, WS, later with W.G. Leechman, becoming Partner in both firms which amalgamated with Aitken Kinnear to become Aitken Nairn. Recreation: golf. Address: (b.) 7 Abercromby Place, Edinburgh EH3 6LA; T.-0131-556 6644; e-mail: kens@aitkennairn.co.uk

Stannett, Alan Edward, JP, BSc (Hons), ACIArb, MIAgM. Farmer, since 1971; Business Consultant, since 2001; b. 25.9.49, Cambuslang; m., Sharon; 2 s.; 2 d. Educ. Coatbridge High School; University of Glasgow. Agricultural Consultant, Lugg and Gould Ltd, 1971-73; Farm Manager: Riverford Farms, Devon, 1973-76, Harviestoun Estate, Dollar, 1976-84, Buccleuch Estates, Thornhill, 1984-2001; Farmer, Dalgarnock Pigs, Thornhill, since 2001; Managing Director, Cara Consultants Ltd, since 2001. Court Serving Justice of the Peace, since 1988; Chair, Barony College, 2001-09; Member, Scottish Funding Council, since 2007. Board Member, Scotlean Ltd. Recreations: family; rugby; photography. Address: Carronhill, Thornhill, Dumfriesshire DG3 5AZ; T.-01848 331510; e-mail: alan@cara.co.uk

Stansfeld, John Raoul Wilmot, MBE, DL, MA (Oxon), FIFM. Director, Dunninald Estate Ltd., since 1990; b. 15.1.35, London; m., Rosalinde Rachel Buxton; 3 s. Educ. Eton; Christ Church, Oxford. Lt., Gordon Highlanders, 1954-58; Director, Joseph Johnston & Sons Ltd., 1962-2001; Chairman, North Esk District Salmon Fishery Board, 1967-80; Esk Fishery Board Committee, 1980-85; Vice Chairman, Association of Scottish District Salmon Fishery Boards, 1970-85; Director and Chairman, Montrose Chamber of Commerce, 1984-97; Editor, Salmon Net Magazine, 1978-85; Chairman, Scottish Fish Farmers Association, 1970-73; Secretary, Diocese of Brechin, 1968-76. Member, Royal Company of Archers (Queen's Bodyguard for Scotland); Freeman City of London; Liveryman Skinners' Company, 1957. Publications: The Story of Dunninald, 1999; The People's Sculptor: The Life and Art of William Lamb (1893-1951), 2013. Recreations: reading; jigsaw puzzles; trees. Address: (h.) Dunninald, Montrose, Angus DD10 9TD; T.-01674 674842.

Stark, Edi, MA (Hons), ALA. Broadcaster (BBC Radio Scotland), and journalist; b. Edinburgh; m., Gavin Stark; 1 s.; 1 d. Educ. Aberdeen University; RGIT. Community Librarian, Glasgow and Livingston; Northsound Radio, 1980-90. Awards: Two Sony Golds, two Silver and three

Bronzes in categories for best speech programme, best speech broadcaster and best news special. President, Scottish Clinical Skills Network; Honorary Member Aberdeen Artists' Society; Honorary Degree of Master of Aberdeen University, 2009. Lives in Edinburgh. Recreations: conversation; food and drink; travel; reading; contemporary art. Address: (b.) c/o BBC Radio Scotland, The Tun, Holyrood Road, Edinburgh.

Stear, Professor Michael James, BSc, PhD. Professor of Immunogenetics, University of Glasgow, since 1999; b. 31.1.55, London; m., Lynne Carol Stear; 1 s.; 1 d. Educ. Queen Victoria School, Dunblane; University of Aberdeen. BSc (Hons), University of Aberdeen, 1976; PhD, University of Edinburgh, 1980; Research Fellow, Australian National University, 1980-85; Visiting Professor, University of Nebraska-Lincoln, USDA Meat Animal Research Center, 1985-88; Førsteamanuensis, National Veterinary Institute, Oslo, 1989; Senior Research Fellow, then Professor, Glasgow University Veterinary School, from 1990. Address: (b.) Institute of Infection, Immunity and Inflammation, Garscube Estate, University of Glasgow, Bearsden Road, Glasgow G61 1QH; T.-0141-330-5762; e-mail: michael.stear@glasgow.ac.uk

Steedman, Professor Mark, FBA, FRSE, BSc (Hons), PhD. Professor of Cognitive Science, Edinburgh University, since 1998; b. 18.9.46, Middlesex; m., Professor Bonnie Webber. Educ. Watford Boys Grammar School; University of Sussex; Edinburgh University. Research Associate, School of Artificial Intelligence, Edinburgh University, 1969-72; Research Fellow: Edinburgh University, 1972-73, University of Sussex. 1973-76; Lecturer, University of Warwick, 1976-82; Edinburgh University: Lecturer, 1983-86, Reader, 1986-88; University of Pennsylvania: Associate Professor, Computational Linguistics, 1989-92, Professor in Computer and Information Science, 1992-98. Joint Founding Editor, Language and Cognitive Processes, 1984-92; Senior Editor, Cognitive Science, 1997-99; Advisory Editor: Cognition, 1980-2000; Linguistics, 1979-92; Journal of Semantics, since 1985; Language and Cognitive Processes, since 1993. Publications: Surface Structure and Interpretation, Linguistic Inquiry Monograph 30, 1996; The Syntactic Process, 2000; Taking Scope, 2012. Recreations: jazz; hill-climbing. Address: (b.) Informatics, 10 Crichton Street, Edinburgh EH8 9AB; T.-0131-650 4631.

Steedman, Robert Russell, OBE, RSA, RIBA, FRIAS, ALI, DA, MLA. Former Partner, Morris and Steedman, Architects and Landscape Architects (retired); b. 3.1.29, Batu Gajah, Malaysia; m., 1, Susan Scott (m. diss.); 1 s.; 2 d.; 2, Martha Hamilton. Educ. Loretto School; School of Architecture, Edinburgh College of Art; Pennsylvania University. Governor, Edinburgh College of Art, 1974-86; Commissioner, Countryside Commission for Scotland, 1980-88; Chairman, Central Scotland Woodlands Project, 1984-88; Association for the Protection of Rural Scotland Award Panel, 1995-99; elected Associate, Royal Scottish Academy, 1973, Academician, 1979; Council Member, RSA, 1981 (Deputy President, 1982-83, 1999-2000, Secretary, 1983-91); Commissioner, Royal Fine Art Commission for Scotland, 1983-96; Deputy Chairman, 1994-96, former Member, Council, RIAS; Member, Council, National Trust for Scotland, 1999-2006; Trustee, St. Andrews Preservation Trust, 2002-08; Trustee, Falkland Heritage Trust, 2002-2012; nine Civic Trust Awards, 1963-78; British Steel Award, 1971; RIBA Award for Scotland, 1974, 1989; European Heritage Medal, 1975; Association for the Protection of Rural Scotland, 1977, 1989; Borders Region Award, 1984; Honorary Degree, DLitt, University of St. Andrews, 2006; Royal Incorporation of Architects in Scotland (RIAS) Lifetime Achievement Medal, 2009; Scottish Design Awards 2009; Architecture Lifetime Achievement Award; Honorary Degree, DUniv, University of Stirling, 2011. Address: (h.) Muir of Blebo, Blebocraigs, by Cupar, Fife KY15 5UG.

Steel of Aikwood, Rt. Hon. Lord (David Steel), KT, KBE, PC, DL. Non-Executive Director, General Mediterranean Holding S.A. (Luxembourg); Presiding Officer, Scottish Parliament, 1999-2003; MP, Tweeddale, Ettrick and Lauderdale, 1983-97 (Roxburgh, Selkirk and Peebles, 1965-83); Leader, Liberal Party, 1976-88; b. 31.3.38, Kirkcaldy; m., Judith MacGregor; 2 s.; 1 d. Educ. Prince of Wales School, Nairobi; George Watson's College, Edinburgh; Edinburgh University (MA, LLB). Assistant Secretary, Scottish Liberal Party, 1962-64; Interviewer, BBC TV Scotland, 1964-65; Presenter, weekly religious programme, STV, 1966-67, for Granada, 1969, for BBC, 1971-76; Liberal Chief Whip, 1970-75; Sponsor, Private Member's Bill to reform law on abortion, 1966-67; President, Anti-Apartheid Movement of Great Britain, 1966-69; Chairman, Shelter, Scotland, 1969-73; Member, British Council of Churches, 1971-75; Rector, Edinburgh University, 1982-85; Chubb Fellow, Yale, 1987; Hon. DUniv (Stirling), 1991; DLitt, University of Buckingham, 1994; Hon. Doctorate, Heriot Watt University, Edinburgh, 1996; HonLLD, Edinburgh, 1997; HonLLD, Strathclyde, 2000; HonLLD, Aberdeen 2001; HonDr, Open University, 2002; HonLLD, St Andrews, 2003; Hon LLD, Glasgow Caledonian, 2004; Hon LLD, Brunel, 2010; awarded Freedom of Tweeddale, 1988, and Ettrick and Lauderdale, 1990; The Commander's Cross of the Order of Merit (Germany), 1992; Chevalièr du Legion D'Honneur (France), 2003; Knight of the Order of the Thistle, 2004; DL, 1989-2013; contested Central Italy seat, European elections, 1989; President, Liberal International, 1994-96; former Vice President, Countryside Alliance; Visiting Fellow, St Antony's College, Oxford, 2013; Honorary Fellow, Royal College of Obstetricians and Gynaecologists, 2013; Lord High Commissioner, 2003/4. Publications: Boost for the Borders, 1964; Out of Control, 1968; No Entry, 1969; The Liberal Way Forward, 1975; Militant for the Reasonable Man, 1977; High Ground of Politics, 1979; A House Divided, 1980; Border Country (with Judy Steel), 1985; The Time Has Come (with David Owen), 1987; Mary Stuart's Scotland (with Judy Steel), 1987; Against Goliath (autobiography), 1989. Recreations: angling; vintage motoring. Address: (b.) House of Lords, London SW1A 0PW.

Steel, Professor Christopher Michael, BSc, MB, ChB, PhD, DSc, FRCPEdin, FRCPath, FRCSEdin, FRSE, FMedSci. Emeritus Professor in Medical Science, St. Andrews University (Professor, 1994-2004); b. 25.1.40, Buckhaven; m., Dr. Judith Margaret Spratt; 2 s.; 1 d. Educ. Prince of Wales School, Nairobi; George Watson's College, Edinburgh; Edinburgh University. House Physician/House Surgeon/ Resident/Senior House Officer, Edinburgh Teaching Hospitals; Graduate Research Fellow in Medicine, 1968; joined MRC staff, 1971; MRC Travelling Research Fellow, University of Nairobi, 1972-73; Assistant Director, MRC Human Genetics Unit, Edinburgh, 1979. Board Member: Scottish Cancer Foundation, Medical Research Scotland (2004-2010), Association for International Cancer Research; published over 300 scientific papers and book chapters; Member, Government Gene Therapy Advisory Committee, 1994-99. Recreations: golf; skiing; music; theatre. Address: (b.) The Medical School, University of St Andrews, North Haugh, St Andrews KY16 9TF; T.-01334 463599; e-mail: mandjsteel@talktalk.net

Steel, David Robert, OBE, MA, DPhil, FRCP (Edin). Senior Research Fellow (Honorary), University of Aberdeen, since 2009; b. 29.5.48, Oxford; m., Susan Elizabeth Easton; 1 s.; 1 d. Educ. Birkenhead School; Jesus and Nuffield Colleges, Oxford. Lecturer in Public Administration, Exeter University, 1972-84; Assistant Director, National Association of Health Authorities, 1984-86; Secretary, Health Board Chairmen's and General Managers' Groups and SCOTMEG, 1986-90; NHS in Scotland: Director of Corporate Affairs, 1990-95, Head of Health Gain, 1995-99; Chief Executive, Clinical Standards Board for Scotland, 1999-2002; Chief Executive, NHS Quality Improvement Scotland, 2003-09. Address: (h.) 29 Park Road, Edinburgh EH6 4LA.

Steele, Professor Robert James Campbell, BSc, MB, ChB, MD, FRCSEd, FRCSEng, FCSHK, FRCPE. Professor of Surgery, Dundee University, since 1996; b. 5.3.52, Edinburgh; m., Annie Scott Anderson; 1 s.; 2 d. Educ. Daniel Stewart's College, Edinburgh; Edinburgh University. Surgical training, Edinburgh, 1977-85; Lecturer in Surgery, Chinese University of Hong Kong, 1985-86; Lecturer in Surgery, Aberdeen University, 1986-90; Senior Lecturer and Reader in Surgery, Nottingham University, 1990-96. Publications: in breast cancer, gastrointestinal surgery and colorectal cancer. Recreations: music; Scottish country dancing; country sports. Address: (b.) Department of Surgery, Ninewells Hospital, Dundee DD1 9SY; T.-01382 660111; e-mail: r.j.c.steele@dundee.ac.uk

Steer, Christopher Richard, BSc (Hons), MB, ChB, DCH, FRCPE, FRCPCH. Consultant Paediatrician; Lead Clinician; Hon. Senior Lecturer, Department of Child Life and Health, Edinburgh University; Hon. Senior Lecturer, Department of Biomedical Science, St. Andrews University; Hon. Senior Lecturer, Department of Child Life and Health, Dundee University; General Medical Council Examiner and Associate; Principal Regional Examiner, SE Scotland for Royal College of Paediatrics and Child Health; b. 30.5.47, Clearbrook, near Plymouth; m., Patricia Mary Lennox. Educ. St. Olaves and St. Saviours Grammar School, London; Edinburgh University. Fellow, Royal Medical Society. Publications: Textbook of Paediatrics (Contributor); Treatment of Neurological Disorders (Contributor). Recreations: our garden; golf. Address: (b.) Paediatric Unit, Kirkcaldy Acute Hospitals NHS Trust, Victoria Hospital, Kirkcaldy, Fife; T.-01592 643355.

Steiner, Eleanor Margaret, MB, ChB, DPH, MFCM, MRCGP, MICGP, FRSH, FFICS, FFPH. Formerly General Practitioner at Appin and Easdale, formerly Principal in general practice in Perthshire; Executive Member, Scottish Child Law Centre; Medical Member, Disability Appeals Tribunal; Medical Assessor, Social Security Appeals Tribunals; Aeromedical Doctor, St. John International Air Ambulance; Member, SACOT (Scottish Advisory Committee on Telecommunications); Member, DIEL (OFTEL Committee for Advice on Disabled and Elderly); Founder, National Society of Associate GPs; b. 21.5.37, Glasgow; m., Mark Rudie Steiner (qv); 1 s. Educ. Albyn School, Aberdeen; Aberdeen University. Surgical Assistant, Freiburg; worked in hospitals, Switzerland, Canada, USA; Departmental Medical Officer/Senior Medical Officer, Aberdeen City; Organiser, Family Planning Services, Aberdeen; Member, Rubella Working Party; Adviser, Aberdeen Telephone Samaritans; Assistant, Psychiatry, Murray Royal Hospital, Perth; Contributor, Scientific Congress, Institute of Advanced Medical Sciences, Moscow. Recreations: sailing; hill-walking; international contacts. Address: (h.) Atlantic House, Ellenabeich, Isle of Seil, by Oban, Argyll PA34 4RF; T.-01852 300 593.

Steiner, Mark Rudie, LLB, NP. Legal Consultant; former part-time Chairman, Social Security Appeal Tribunal and Disability Appeal Tribunal; former Scottish Representative, Consumers in the European Community Group; Member, Potato Marketing Board Consumer Liaison Committee;

Member, National Pharmaceutical Consultative Committee Working Group on Quality Assurance; m., Dr. Eleanor Steiner, DPH, MFCM, MRCGP, MICGP, FFICS, FFPH; 1 s. Educ. Aberdeen University. Long-time international radio/TV commentator and Foreign Correspondent; Editor, Canadian Broadcasting Corporation, Toronto and Montreal; Editor, Swiss Broadcasting Corporation, Berne; Lecturer on Swiss affairs and advisor to Anglo-Swiss organisations and authorities; international war crimes investigator; Procurator Fiscal in Scotland; Partner and Director of various firms and companies; Past Chairman, Patients Association, Perth Community Relations Council; Delegate, Scottish Council for Racial Equality; neutral observer at various overseas political trials; contributor to various international journals; retired Principal, Goodman Steiner & Co., Defence Lawyers and Notaries in Central Scotland; former Member, Scottish Consumer Council. Publications: Alpine Legends of Switzerland; Nell of the Seas; Nell of The Islands; Boy on a Kite; The Wages of Pleasures and various travel and children's books; Literary Consultant and Editor with Nevis International Books. Visiting Lecturer and public speaker in UK and overseas. Recreations: sailing; developing international exchanges. Address: (h.) Atlantic House, Ellenabeich, Isle of Seil, by Oban, Argyll PA34 4RF; T.-Balvicar 300 593.

Stell, Geoffrey Percival, BA, FSA, FSA Scot. Visiting Lecturer, Edinburgh College of Art, University of Edinburgh; Head of Architecture, Royal Commission on the Ancient and Historical Monuments of Scotland, 1991-2004; b. 21.11.44, Keighley; m., Evelyn Florence Burns; 1 s.; 1 d. Educ. Keighley Boys' Grammar School; Leeds University; Glasgow University. Historic Buildings Investigator, RCAHMS, 1969-91; sometime Chairman, Scottish Vernacular Buildings Working Group; sometime Chairman, Scottish Urban Archaeological Trust; sometime Vice-President, Council for Scottish Archaeology. Publications include: Dumfries and Galloway; Orkney at War, volume 1 (World War I); Monuments of Industry (Co-author); Buildings of St Kilda (Co-author); Loads and Roads in Scotland (Co-editor); The Scottish Medieval Town (Co-editor); Galloway, Land and Lordship (Co-editor); Materials and Traditions in Scottish Building (Co-editor); Scotland's Buildings (Co-editor); Lordship and Architecture in Medieval and Renaissance Scotland (Co-editor). Recreations: gardening; music; travel, particularly in Scotland and France. Address: (h.) Beechmount, Borrowstoun, Bo'ness, West Lothian, EH51 9RS; T.-01506 510366; e-mail: gpstell@gmail.com

Stephen, Rev. Donald Murray, TD, MA, BD, ThM. Minister, Marchmont St. Giles' Parish Church, Edinburgh, 1974-2001; Secretary, Church of Scotland Chaplains' Association, 1991-2007; b. 1.6.36, Dundee; m., Hilda Swan Henriksen (deceased); 2 s.; 1 d; m., 2, Marjorie Roberta Bennet. Educ. Brechin High School; Richmond Grammar School, Yorkshire; Edinburgh University; Princeton Theological Seminary. Assistant Minister, Westover Hills Presbyterian Church, Arkansas, 1962-64; Minister, Kirkoswald, 1964-74; Chaplain, TA, 1965-85 (attached to 4/5 Bn., RSF, 205 Scottish General Hospital, 2nd Bn., 52nd Lowland Volunteers); Convener, Committee on Chaplains to Her Majesty's Forces, General Assembly, 1985-89. Recreations: golf; curling. Address: 10 Hawkhead Crescent, Edinburgh EH16 6LR; T.-0131-658 1216; e-mail: donaldmstephen@gmail.com

Stephen, Sheriff Principal Mhairi Margaret, BA, LLB, QC. President, Sheriff Appeal Court; Sheriff Principal of Lothian and Borders, since May 2011; Sheriff of Lothian & Borders at Edinburgh, 1997-2011; b. 22.1.54, Falkirk. Educ. George Watson's Ladies College; Edinburgh University. Allan McDougall and Co., SSC, 1976-97

(Partner, 1981-1997). Recreations: curling; golf; hillwalking; music. Address: Sheriff Principal's Chambers, Sheriff Court House, 27 Chambers Street, Edinburgh EH1 1LB; T.-0131 225 2525.

Stephen of Lower Deeside in the City of Aberdeen (Baron Nicol Stephen), LLB, DipLP. MSP (Liberal Democrat), Aberdeen South, 1999-2011; Deputy First Minister, and Minister for Enterprise and Lifelong Learning, 2005-07; Deputy Minister for Education and Young People, 2000-03 (Deputy Minister for Enterprise and Lifelong Learning, 1999-2000); Minister for Transport, 2003-05; b. 23.3.60, Aberdeen; m., Caris Doig; 2 s.; 2 d. Educ. Robert Gordon's College, Aberdeen; Aberdeen University; Edinburgh University. Trainee Solicitor, C. & P.H. Chalmers, 1981-83; Solicitor, Milne and Mackinnon, 1983-88; Senior Manager, Touche Ross Corporate Finance, 1988-91; Member, Grampian Regional Council, 1982-92 (Chair, Economic Development, 1986-91); MP, Kincardine and Deeside, 1991-92; Scottish Liberal Democrats: Parliamentary Spokesperson for Small Businesses, 1991-92, Treasurer, 1992-95, Health Spokesperson, 1995-97, Education Spokesperson, 1997-99, Scottish Party Leader, 2005-08; Director, Project Management, management consultancy company, 1992-99; Chairman of the Campaign for Rail Electrification Aberdeen to Edinburgh (CREATE), 1988-92; Director, Grampian Enterprise, 1989-92; Director, Grampian Youth Orchestra. Recreation: golf. Address: (b.) Room 103, Fielden House, House of Lords, London SW10 3SH; e-mail: stephenn@parliament.uk

Stephens, Chris. MP (SNP), Glasgow South West, since 2015; b. 20.3.73, Glasgow. Educ. Trinity High School, Renfrew. Employed by Glasgow City Council, and is a Senior UNISON activist in the city, acting as a lead negotiator, and having represented trade union members on issues such as disability and racial discrimination, occupational pension protection, and on equal pay matters. Member of the SNP's National Executive Committee; Convener of Glasgow Pollok Constituency Association; Secretary of the SNP Trade Union Group. Recreation: proud Partick Thistle supporter and regularly attends matches. Address: House of Commons, London SW1A 0AA.

Stephens, Professor Jonathan Paul, BA (Hons), MMus, PhD, PGCE. Emeritus Professor of Music and Music Education, University of Aberdeen; b. 12.7.51, Redruth, Cornwall; m., Rhona Lucas; 1 s.; 2 d. Educ. Redruth Grammar School; University of Wales, Aberystwyth. Secondary and private teaching, Wales, 1973-77; Lecturer in Music, Hertfordshire College of Higher Education, 1977-82; Lecturer in Music, 1982-84, Co-ordinator for Music Education, 1983-88, Principal Lecturer and Deputy Head of Music, 1984-88, Bretton Hall College of Higher Education; Director of Music (1988-2001) and Head of Aesthetic Education (1991-2001), Northern College, then Aberdeen University, since 2001; Professor in music and music education, since 1993. Chair, ISME Commission for Music in Schools and Teacher Training, 1988-92; Founder Member and British Representative, European Association for Music in Schools, 1990-2000; President, International Research Alliance of Institutions for Music Education, 1997-99; Board Member, ISME, 2000-04; Member, Music in Education Section Committee of Incorporated Society of Musicians (UK), 2002-05 and 2007-09, Warden, 2010-11, Member of Executive Committee and Council, ISM, 2009-2012; Executive Committee of National Association of Youth Orchestras, 2004-2010, Board Member, 2009-2010; Editorial Board of International Journal of Music Education, 2004-2012; compositions have been widely performed; frequent lecturer, music and music education, national and international. Recreations: reading; writing; composing; walking; gardening. Address: (b.) School of Education, University of Aberdeen, MacRobert Building, King's College, Aberdeen AB24 5UA.

Stephenson, Professor Jill, MA, PhD. Professor Emeritus, Modern German History, University of Edinburgh; b. 17.01.44, Edinburgh; m., Dr. R. P. Stephenson (deceased). Educ. George Watson's Ladies' College; University of Edinburgh. Assistant Lecturer in Modern History, University of Glasgow, 1969-70; Lecturer in History, University of Edinburgh, 1970 (Senior Lecturer, 1984, Reader, 1991). Publications: Women in Nazi Society, 1975; The Nazi Organisation of Women, 1981; Women in Nazi Germany, 2001; Hitler's Home Front: Württemberg Under The Nazis, 2006. Recreations: gardening; food and wine; opera. Address: (b.) School of History, Classics and Archaeology, University of Edinburgh, Edinburgh; e-mail: j.stephenson@ed.ac.uk

Stephenson, Professor Roger Henry, BA (Hons), PhD. William Jacks Professor of Modern Languages, Glasgow University, 1998-2008 (rtd); Professor of German by conferment of title, 1994-95; Professor of German Language and Literature, 1995-98; Principal Investigator, AHRC Large Research Project on 'Ernst Cassirer', 2002-07; (Founding) Head, School of Modern Languages and Cultures, Glasgow University, 2000-03; Director, Centre for Intercultural Studies, Glasgow University, 1992-2008; b. 5.11.46, Liverpool; m., Hedy. Educ. Holt High School, Liverpool; University College London. Lecturer, German, Glasgow University, 1972; Fellow, Cornell University, NY, USA, 1979; Glasgow University: Senior Lecturer, German, 1989; Head, German Department, 1990-97; Vice President, UK and Irish Conference, University Teachers of German, 1997-98; President, Scottish Conference, University Teachers of German, 2006-08; Visiting Professor: University of Zurich, 2005, University of Hamburg, 2007. Publications: Goethe's Wisdom Literature, 1983; Goethe's Maximem und Reflexionen, 1986; Goethe's Conception of Knowledge and Science, 1995; (Co-editor) Cultural Studies of the Symbolic, Yearbook, 2000-08; Friedrich Nietzsche and Weimar Classicism, 2005; Studies in Weimar Classicism, 2010; Festschrift, 2011. Professor Emeritus and Professorial Research Fellow, University of Glasgow, since 2008.

Stevely, Professor William Stewart, CBE, BSc, DPhil, DipEd, FRSB. Former Principal and Vice Chancellor, The Robert Gordon University (1997-2005); Professor Emeritus, The Robert Gordon University; Chairman, UCAS, 2001-05 (Member, Board, 2000-05); Convener, Universities Scotland, 2002-04; Board Member, Scottish University for Industry (SUFI), 2004-08; Board Member, Scottish Agricultural College, 2005-08, Vice Chair, 2008-2013; Board Member, Skills Development Scotland, 2008-2010; Chairman, Ayrshire and Arran Health Board, 2006-2011; Council Member, the Open University, 2008-2010, Vice Chair, since 2010; b. 6.4.43, West Kilbride; m., Sheila Anne Stalker; 3 s.; 2 d. Educ. Ardrossan Academy; Glasgow University; Oxford University. Lecturer and Senior Lecturer in Biochemistry, Glasgow University, 1968-88; Professor and Head, Department of Biology, Paisley College, 1988-92; Vice Principal, Paisley University, 1992-97. Member, Scottish Higher Education Funding Council, 1994-97; Member, National Board for Nursing, Midwifery and Health Visiting for Scotland, 1993-2000; Board Member, Quality Assurance Agency for Higher Education, 1998-2002. Address: (h.) 10 Evergreen Estate, Coalhall KA6 6PQ.

Steven, Andrew John Maclean, LLB, PhD, DipLP, NP, WS. Scottish Law Commissioner, since 2011; b. 8.11.72, Banff. Educ. Banff Academy; University of Edinburgh. Admitted as a Solicitor, 1999; Lecturer in Law, University of Edinburgh, 2000, then Senior Lecturer, 2010. Author of numerous publications on Property Law. Address: (b.) Scottish Law Commission, 140 Causewayside, Edinburgh EH9 1PR; T.-0131 668 2131.
E-mail: andrew.steven@ed.ac.uk

Steven, Jim. Head of Education Services, The Highland Council, since 2013. Career: Assistant Head Teacher, Plockton High School; Principal Teacher of Mathematics, Eyemouth High School; Teacher of Mathematics, Fortrose Academy; Invergordon Acdemy: Deputy Head Teacher, then Head Teacher, 1999-2013. Address: The Highland Council, Glenurquhart Road, Inverness IV3 5NX.

Stevenson, Celia Margaret Stirton. Formerly Head of Inward Investment and Communications, Scottish Screen; b. Ballantrae; m., Charles William Forbes Judge; 2 s.; 1 d. Educ. Wellington School, Ayr; Edinburgh College of Art. Interior design business, 1970-80; Reporter/Presenter, West Sound, Ayr, 1981-84; Scottish Television: Reporter/Presenter, 1984-86, Promotions trailer-maker, 1987-89, Head of Programme Planning and Film Acquisition, 1990-95; Director, Scottish Screen Locations Ltd., 1995-97; Director of Locations, Scottish Screen, 1997-98. Board Member, British Film Commission, 1997-2000; Member, Steering Group, UK Film Commission Network, 1996-98. Recreations: cooking; reading; keeping fit; gardening.

Stevenson, Gavin, BSc, CIPFA. Chief Executive, Dumfries and Galloway Council, since 2009, Head of Paid Service for all Council employees; formerly Executive Director of Corporate Services, Perth and Kinross Council. Educ. Edinburgh University. Career History: Director of Audit Scotland; senior roles in the NHS, Department of Social Security, Audit Commission and retail. Address: (b.) Council Offices, English Street, Dumfries DG1 2DD; T.-030 33 33 3000.

Stevenson, Gerda. Actress, Singer, Writer, Book Illustrator, Director; b. 10.4.56, West Linton; m., Aonghas MacNeacail; 1 s. Educ. Peebles High School; Royal Academy of Dramatic Art, London (DDA, Vanbrugh Award). Has performed with 7:84 Theatre Co., Scottish Theatre Company, Royal Lyceum Theatre (Edinburgh), Traverse Theatre, Communicado, Monstrous Regiment, Victoria Theatre (Stoke on Trent), Contact Theatre (Manchester) and with Freefall at Lilian Baylis Theatre, London, and Birmingham Rep; directed Uncle Jesus for Edinburgh Festival Fringe; Assistant Director, Royal Lyceum, on Merchant of Venice and A Doll's House; Founder Member and Director, Stellar Quines Theatre Co.; TV work includes Clay, Smeddum and Greenden, Square Mile of Murder, Grey Granite, Horizon: Battered Baby, The Old Master, Taggart, Dr. Finlay, The Bill; films: The Stamp of Greatness, Tickets to the Zoo, Blue Black Permanent (BAFTA Scotland Best Film Actress Award, 1993), Braveheart; directed short film, An Iobairt, in Gaelic for BBC; extensive radio work includes title roles in Bride of Lammermoor and Catriona; adapted a number of works for radio, including The Heart of Midlothian by Sir Walter Scott for BBC Radio 4 (nominated for a Sony Award in 2008); freelance producer for Radio Scotland; wrote and illustrated children's book, The Candlemaker.

Stevenson, (James Alexander) Stewart. MSP (SNP), Banffshire and Buchan Coast, since 2011 (Banff and Buchan, 2001-2011); Minister for Environment and Climate Change, 2011-2012; Minister for Transport, Infrastructure and Climate Change, 2007-2010; former Shadow Deputy Justice Minister; b. 15.10.46; m., Sandra

Isabel Pirie. Educ. Bell Baxter School, Cupar; Aberdeen University. Director, Technology Innovation, Bank of Scotland, 1969-99. Address: (b.) Unit 8, Burnside Business Centre, Burnside Road, Peterhead AB42 3AW.

Stevenson, Professor Jane Barbara, MA, PhD. Regius Professor of Humanity, University of Aberdeen, since 2007; b. 12.2.59, London; m., Peter Davidson. Educ. Haberdashers' Aske's School for Girls; Newnham College, Cambridge. Drapers' Research Fellow, Pembroke College, Cambridge, 1985-88; Lecturer, Late Antique and Early Medieval History, University of Sheffield, 1988-95; Interdisciplinary Research Fellow (later Reader), University of Warwick, 1995-2000; Reader in Post-Classical Latin, University of Aberdeen, 2000-05, Professor of Latin, 2005-07. Publications: Edward Burra; Women Latin Poets; The Laterculus Malalianus and the School of Archbishop Theodore; Good Women; Astraea. Recreations: cooking; gardening. Address: (b.) Department of History, King's College, University of Aberdeen AB24 JFX; T.-01888 562244; e-mail: j.b.stevenson@abdn.ac.uk

Stevenson, Neil Alan, LLB, MSc. Chief Executive, Scottish Legal Complaints Commission, since 2015; Director of Representation and Professional Support, The Law Society of Scotland, 2009-2015. Educ. Dundee High School; University of Edinburgh; University of Birmingham. Training and Research Officer, NHS Education for Scotland, 2001-04; Deputy Director of Education and Training, The Law Society of Scotland, 2004-07, Head of Strategic Change, 2007-09; Director, Lawcare Ltd, 2006-2015, Trustee, 2006-2015; Trustee and Scottish National Council Member, ESU (Scotland), 2005-2013; Council Member (lay), General Dental Council, since 2009; Director, Scottish Arbitration Centre, 2011-2014. Address: The Stamp Office, 10-14 Waterloo Place, Edinburgh EH1 3EG; T.-0131 201 2130.

Stevenson, Professor Randall, MA, MLitt, FEA. Professor of Twentieth-Century Literature, University of Edinburgh, since 2005; b. 25.6.53, Banff; m., Sarah Carpenter; 2 s.; 1 d. Educ. Hillhead High School, Glasgow; Edinburgh University; Linacre, Oxford. Assistant, then Principal Lecturer in English, Women Teachers' Training College, Birin-Kebbi, NW State Nigeria; Lecturer, then Senior Lecturer, then Reader in English, University of Edinburgh. Publications include: Oxford English Literary History vol. 12, 1960-2000, 2006; Twentieth Century Scottish Drama (Co-Author), 2000; Modernist Fiction, 1998; Scottish Theatre since the Seventies, ed (Co-Author), 1996. Recreations: running; tennis; football; hill walking; astronomy. Address: (b.) Department of English Literature, University of Edinburgh EH8 9JX; T.-0131 650 4288.
E-mail: randall.stevenson@ed.ac.uk

Stevenson, Struan John Stirton. Former MEP for Scotland (1999-2014); b. 4.4.48, Ballantrae; m., Pat Stevenson; 2 s. Educ. Strathallan School; West of Scotland Agricultural College. Conservative Councillor, Kyle and Carrick District Council, 1970-92 (Leader of the Administration, 1986-88); Conservative Group Leader, COSLA, 1986-88; European Parliament: Chairman, Fisheries Committee, 2001-04; Conservative Spokesman on Fisheries and Deputy Spokesman on Agriculture; Vice President, EPP-ED (European People's Party-European Democrats) Group in the European Parliament, 2005-09. Hon. Doctor of Science, State Medical Academy, Kazakhstan, 2000; Honorary Citizen of Semipalatinsk, East Kazakhstan, 2004; Hon. Professor, Sakharim University, Semey, 2007; Awarded Order of 'Shapagat' (Mercy) by President of Kazakhstan, 2007. Publication: 'Crying Forever'- A Nuclear Diary, 2006, Russian Edition, 2007; Stalin's Legacy - The Soviet War on Nature, 2012; "So Much Wind - the Myth of Green Energy", 2013. Recreations:

contemporary art; music; theatre; opera; poetry; hill-walking.

Stewart, A. J. (Ada F. Kay). Playwright and Author; b. 5.3.29, Tottington, Lancashire. Educ. Grammar School, Fleetwood. ATS Scottish Command; first produced play, 1951; repertory actress, 1952-54; BBC TV Staff Writer/Editor/Adaptor, Central Script Section, 1956-59; returned to Scotland, 1959, as stage and TV writer; winner, BBC New Radio Play competition, 1956; The Man from Thermopylae, presented in Festival of Contemporary Drama, Rheydt, West Germany, 1959, as part of Edinburgh International Festival, 1965, and at Masquers' Theatre, Hollywood, 1972; first recipient, Wendy Wood Memorial Grant, 1982; Polish Gold Cross for achievements in literary field. Publications: Falcon - The Autobiography of His Grace, James the 4, King of Scots, 1970; Died 1513-Born 1929 - The Autobiography of A.J. Stewart, 1978; The Man from Thermopylae, 1981. Recreation: work. Address: (h.) 33 Howe Street, Edinburgh EH3 6TF.

Stewart, Alan David, MA (Hons). Regulatory Affairs Manager (Scotland), Ofcom, since 2003; Independent Reviewer, General Teaching Council for Scotland, since 2013; Judicial Panel Member, Scottish Football Association, since 2011; b. 27.7.58, Falkirk; m., Christine; 2 s. Educ. Graeme High School, Falkirk; Glasgow University; Strathclyde University. Assistant Public Relations Officer, Cumbernauld Development Corporation, 1983-86; Press Officer, Strathclyde Regional Council, 1986-92; Principal Officer (Corporate Communications and Marketing), Lothian Regional Council, 1992-94. Recreations: hill-walking; cycling; supporting Falkirk FC. Address: (h.) 12 Heugh Street, Falkirk FK1 5QR.

Stewart, Alexander Donald, BA, LLB, WS; b. 18.6.33, Edinburgh; m., Virginia Mary Washington; 1 s.; 5 d. Educ. Wellington College, Berkshire; Oxford University; Edinburgh University. Retired solicitor. Partner, Moncrieff Warren Paterson, 1963-85, McGrigor Donald, Glasgow, 1985-93; Director, Scottish Amicable Life Assurance Society, 1984-97 (Chairman, 1994-97); Director, Prudential plc, 1997-2004; Chairman, Murray Extra Return Investment Trust, 1998-2005; Chairman, St. Mary's Music School, Edinburgh, 2008-2010; Hon. Consul for Thailand in Scotland. Recreations: music; field sports; curling; rhododendrons. Address: (h.) Ardvorlich, Lochearnhead, Perthshire.

Stewart, Alexander James. MSP (Scottish Conservative), Mid Scotland and Fife region, since 2016. Career history: Councillor for Perth City South; Conservative candidate for Perth and North Perthshire, UK General Election, 2015; Conservative candidate, Clackmannanshire and Dunblane, Scottish Parliament election, 2016. Address: Scottish Parliament, Edinburgh EH99 1SP.

Stewart, Andrew Fleming, LLB (Hons.), QC; b. 12.9.63, Dundee; m., Lesley Katherine Dawson; 2 d. Educ. Perth High School; Edinburgh University. Solicitor: Clifford Chance, London, 1988-90, Tods Murray WS, Edinburgh, 1990-94; Legal Assistant to Lord President, Court of Session, 1994-95; Advocate, since 1996; Tutor, Law Faculty, University of Edinburgh, 1985-88 and since 1990; Lecturer (part-time), Université de Nancy 2, France, since 1993; Standing Junior Counsel, Department of Trade and Industry, 2000-09; Clerk to Examiners, Faculty of Advocates, 2001-03; Clerk of Faculty of Advocates, 2003-09; Advocate Depute, since 2009. Member, Board of Practice and Procedure, Church of Scotland, 2001-05;

Chairman, Scottish Churches Committee, since 2007; Treasurer, Scottish Committee, Franco-British Lawyers Society, 1998-2001; Editor, Session Cases, since 2001. Recreations: golf; music. Address: Advocates Library, Parliament House, Edinburgh EH1 1RF; T.-0131-226 5071.

Stewart, The Hon. Lord (Angus Stewart), QC, BA, LLB. Senator of the College of Justice, since 2010; Queen's Counsel; b. 14.12.46; m., Jennifer Margaret Stewart; 1 d. Educ. Edinburgh Academy; Balliol College, Oxford University; Edinburgh University. Called to the Scottish Bar, 1975; Trustee, National Library of Scotland, 1994-2002; Treasurer, E Boat International Offshore Class Association, since 1994; Keeper of the Advocates Library, 1994-2002; President of the Stewart Society, 2001-04; Senior Advocate Depute, 2005-08; Leading Counsel, Billy Wright Inquiry, NI, 2008-10; Chair, Scottish Council of Law Reporting, 1997-2001; President, Stair Society, since 2013; Honorary Sheriff, Campbeltown, 2014. Address: (b.) Parliament House, Edinburgh EH1 1RQ.

Stewart, Professor Emeritus Averil M., BA, FCOT, TDip, FFCS. Emeritus Professor of Occupational Therapy; Head, Department of Occupational Therapy and Art Therapy, Queen Margaret University College, Edinburgh, 1986-2001; b. 7.4.43, Edinburgh; m., J. Gavin Stewart. Educ. Dunfermline High School. Member, Vice-Chairman and Chairman, Occupational Therapists Board, CPSM, 1980-92; Trustee, Dementia Services Development Centre, 1996-2004; Secretary, Scottish Arctic Club, 1998-2008; volunteer work with the Scottish Wildlife Trust, since 2000. Recreations: wilderness travel; gardening. Address: (h.) 29 Highfield Crescent, Linlithgow EH49 7BG; e-mail: gaveril.stewart@virgin.net

Stewart, David. MSP (Labour), Highlands and Islands, since 2007; MP, Inverness East, Nairn and Lochaber, 1997-2005; Convener of the Scottish Parliament Public Petitions Committee, since 2011; b. 5.5.56; m., Linda. Career history: member of Labour's Executive; Assistant Director for Rural Affairs, Scottish Council for Voluntary Organisations. Formerly member of the Scottish and Work and Pensions Select Committees; Parliamentary Private Secretary to Alistair Darling, Secretary of State for Scotland, 2003-05. Former Chief Whip of the Labour Party in Holyrood. Address: (b.) Scottish Parliament, Edinburgh EH99 1SP.

Stewart, Douglas Fleming, MA, LLB, WS, FSA Scot, FRSSA. Partner, J. & F. Anderson, WS, 1961-92; Solicitor, Crown Estate Scotland, 1970-91; b. 22.5.27, Sydney; m., Catherine Coleman; 2 d. Educ. George Watson's College; Edinburgh University. RAF, 1945-48; Chairman, Commercial Union, Edinburgh Board, 1979-91, and its Scottish Advisory Committee, 1977-97. Member, Edinburgh University General Council Business Committee, 1961-69; Secretary/Treasurer, Stewart Society, 1968-87 (also Hon. Vice-President); Trustee, Church of Scotland Trust (former Chairman); Session Clerk, Braid Church, Edinburgh, 1979-91; President, Watsonian Club, 1989-90; Treasurer of Friends of National Museums of Scotland, 1972-89; Chairman, Comiston Probus Club, 1999; President, Braid Bowling Club, 2003; Royal Overseas League, Edinburgh Committee; Royal Scottish Society of Arts (Science and Technology), Council. Publications: The Story of Braid Church (Co-author); A Lawful Union, the annals of J & F Anderson, WS and Strathern & Blair, WS (Co-author). Recreations: astronomy; bowling; swimming. Address: (h.) Greenhill Court, 98/5 Whitehouse Loan, Edinburgh EH9 1BD; T.-0131-447 4887.

Stewart, George Girdwood, CB, MC, TD, BSc, FICFor, Hon. FLI; b. 12.12.19, Glasgow; m., Shelagh Jean Morven Murray (deceased); 1 s.; 1 d. Educ. Kelvinside Academy, Glasgow; Glasgow University; Edinburgh University. Royal Artillery, 1940-46 (mentioned in Despatches); Forestry Commission: District Officer, 1949-60, Assistant Conservator, 1960-67, Conservator (West Scotland), 1967-69, Commissioner, Forest and Estate Management, 1969-79. Commanding Officer, 278 (Lowland) Field Regiment RA (TA), 1956-59; President, Scottish Ski Club, 1971-75; Vice President, National Ski Federation of Great Britain and Chairman, Alpine Racing Committee, 1975-78; National Trust for Scotland: Member of Council, 1975-79, Representative, Branklyn Garden, 1980-84, Regional Representative, Central and Tayside, 1984-88; Forestry Consultant, 1989-93; Chairman, Scottish Wildlife Trust, 1981-87; Member, Countryside Commission for Scotland, 1981-88; Member, Environment Panel, British Railways Board, 1980-90; Cairngorm Estate Adviser to Highlands and Islands Enterprise, 1988-98; Associate Director, Oakwood Environmental, 1990-2003; Member, Cairngorm Recreation Trust, since 1986; President, Scottish National Ski Council, 1988-94, Hon. Vice-President, 1997-2014; Specialist Adviser to House of Lords Select Committee on EEC Forestry Policy, 1986; National Service to Sport Award, 1995; Member, British Veterans' Tennis Team, Seniors World Team Championships, 1999, 2001, 2002; International Tennis Federation Super Seniors World Individual Championships, 2006 and 2007, Winner Doubles; Fellow, Royal Society of Arts; London Olympics 2012 Torch Bearer. Recreations: skiing; veterans' tennis; studying Scottish painting. Address: (h.) Stormont House, 11 Mansfield Road, Scone, Perth PH2 6SA; T.-01738 551815.

Stewart, Ian James. Editor, The Scotsman, since 2012; Editor, Scotland on Sunday; former Editor, Edinburgh Evening News (2001-04); b. 4.8.60, Kingston-upon-Thames; m., Lesley; 1 s.; 1 d. Educ. Royal High School, Edinburgh; Napier College, Edinburgh. Royal Marines, 1979-82; Nottingham Evening Post, 1986-91; The Scotsman, 1991-98; Scottish Daily Mail, 1998-1999; Scotland on Sunday, 1999-2001. Recreations: mountain biking; reading; shooting; sailing. Address: (b.) Orchard Brae House, 30 Queensferry Road, Edinburgh EH4 2HS; T.-0131 311 7654.

Stewart, James Blythe, MA, LLB, LLB, Advocate; b. 22.4.43, Methil. Educ. Buckhaven High School; University of Edinburgh. Research Assistant, Faculty of Law, University of St. Andrews, 1966-67; Heriot-Watt University: Assistant Lecturer in Law, 1967-69, Lecturer in Law, 1969-76, Senior Lecturer in Law, 1976-98; retired 1998. Historian, East Fife FC. Recreations: football spectating; bowls; golf. Address: (h.) 3 Comely Bank Terrace, Edinburgh EH4 1AT; T.-0131-332 8228.

Stewart, Rev. James Charles, MA, BD, STM, FSA Scot. Minister, Kirk of St. Nicholas, Aberdeen (The City Kirk), 1980-2000; b. 29.3.33, Glasgow. Educ. Glasgow Academy; St. Andrews University; Union Theological Seminary, New York. Assistant Minister, St. John's Kirk of Perth, 1959-64; Minister: St. Andrew's Church, Drumchapel, 1964-74, East Parish Church of St. Nicholas, Aberdeen, 1974-80. Chairman, Aberdeen Endowments Trust, 2002-2010; Honorary President, and Editor of 'The Record', of the Church Service Society; Hon. archivist, Kirk of St. Nicholas. Address: 54 Murray Terrace, Aberdeen AB11 7SB; T.-01224 587071.

Stewart, Lt Col (Retd). Johnny. Lord-Lieutenant for Clackmannanshire, since 2004. Served 22 years in the Scots Guards and is an extra Equerry to the Duke of Kent. Adjutant of the Royal Company of Archers (the Sovereign's Bodyguard in Scotland); Chairman of the Scots Guards Association; formerly Deputy Lord-Lieutenant for Clackmannanshire; runs family farm near Dollar comprising sheep and forestry.

Stewart, Kevin. MSP (SNP), Aberdeen Central, since 2011. Formerly local councillor (13 years); formerly depute leader of Aberdeen city council, having led the SNP group into coalition with the Lib Dems in 2007. Convener of Local Government and Regeneration Committee, also sitting on Welfare Reform Committee and Justice Sub-Committee on Policing. Address: (b.) Third Floor, 27 John Street, Aberdeen AB25 1BT.

Stewart, Rev. Norma Drummond, MA, MEd, DipTh, BD, MTh. Minister, Strathbungo Queen's Park Church, Glasgow, 1979-2000; Locum Tenens, Dennistoun Blackfriars, Glasgow, 2000-06; Part-time Chaplain, Glasgow Royal Infirmary, 2001-06; b. 20.5.36, Glasgow. Educ. Hyndland Secondary School, Glasgow; University of Glasgow; Bible Training Institute, Glasgow; University of London (External); Trinity College, Glasgow; International Christian College, Glasgow; University of Aberdeen; University of Kent. Teacher, Garrioch Secondary School, Glasgow, 1958-62; Missionary, Overseas Missionary Fellowship, West Malaysia, 1965-74; ordained to ministry, Church of Scotland, 1977; occasional Lecturer and Tutor in Old Testament; Participant in Congress on World Evangelisation, Manila, 1989; Member, Council of Christians and Jews. Recreation: Old Testament research; commenced PhD research, 2010. Address: 127 Nether Auldhouse Road, Glasgow G43 2YS; T.-0141 637 6956; e-mail: normadstewart@btinternet.com

Stewart, Norman MacLeod, BL, SSC. Consultant, Allan, Black & McCaskie, Solicitors, Elgin 1997-99, Senior Partner, 1984-97; Chairman, Elgin and Lossiemouth Harbour Board, 1993-2009; President, Law Society of Scotland, 1985-86; b. 2.12.34, Lossiemouth; m., Mary Slater Campbell; 4 d. Educ. Elgin Academy; Edinburgh University. Training and Legal Assistant, Alex. Morison & Co., WS, Edinburgh, 1954-58; Legal Assistant: McLeod, Solicitor, Portsoy, 1958-59, Allan, Black & McCaskie, Solicitors, Elgin, 1959-61 (Partner, 1961-97); Council Member, Law Society of Scotland, 1976-87 (Convener, Public Relations Committee, 1979-81, and Professional Practice Committee, 1981-84). Past President, Elgin Rotary Club; Past Chairman, Moray Crime Prevention Panel; President, Edinburgh University Club of Moray, 1987-89. Recreations: walking; golf; music; Spanish culture. Address: (h.) 25 Saltcoats Gardens, Bellsquarry South, Livingston, West Lothian EH54 9JD; T.-01506 419 439.

Stewart, Patrick Loudon McIain, MBE, LLB, WS. Lord Lieutenant, Argyll and Bute; Stewart Balfour & Sutherland, Solicitors, Campbeltown, Senior Partner, 1982-2000; Secretary, Clyde Fishermen's Association, 1970-2009; Marine Environment Consultant, Scottish Fishermen's Federation, 2009-2014; Honorary Sheriff at Campbeltown; b. 25.7.45, Campbeltown; m., Mary Anne McLellan; 1 s.; 1 d. Educ. Edinburgh Academy; Edinburgh University. Partner, Stewart Balfour & Sutherland, Campbeltown, 1970; former Executive Member, Scottish Fishermen's Federation; former Director, Scottish Fishermen's Organisation Ltd.; A Vice President of The Marine Society & Sea Cadets; Cadet Forces Medal and two clasps. Recreations: walking; reading. Address: 2 Castlehill, Campbeltown, Argyll PA28 6AW; T.-01586 551717.

Stewart, Robert. Headteacher, Biggar High School, since 2011. Formerly Deputy Head Teacher, Lower School, Uddingston Grammar School. Address: Biggar High School, Market Road, Biggar, South Lanarkshire ML12 6FX; T.-01899 222050.

Stewart, Sir Robert Christie, KCVO, CBE, TD; Lord Lieutenant, Clackmannanshire, 1994-2002; b. 3.8.26, Dollar; m., Ann Grizel Cochrane; 3 s.; 2 d. Educ. Eton; University College, Oxford. Lt., Scots Guards, 1944-49; 7th Bn., Argyll and Sutherland Highlanders TA, 1951-66; Lt.-Col., 1963-66; Hon. Col., 1/51 Highland Volunteers, 1972-

75; Landowner; Lord Lieutenant, Kinross-shire, 1966-74; Member, Perth and Kinross County Council, 1953-75; Chairman, Kinross County Council, 1963-73; Chairman and President, Board of Governors, East of Scotland College of Agriculture, 1970-83. Recreations: shooting; golf; the countryside. Address: (h.) Mains of Arndean, by Dollar FK14 7NT; T.-01259 742527.

Stewart, Susan, MA (Hons), PGDip, FRSA, FCIPR. Director, The Open University in Scotland, since 2015; Owner, Susan Stewart Communications, since 2014. Educ. Renfrew High School, University of St Andrews; Smith College; Strathclyde University; Caledonian University. Political Journalist, Scottish Television, 1991-93; Press and Parliamentary Liaison Officer, Strathclyde Regional Council, 1993-95; Head of Media Relations, Glasgow City Council, 1995-98; Depute Head, Press Office, Scottish Executive, 1998-2001; First Secretary, Scottish Affairs, British Embassy, Washington DC, The Scottish Government, 2001-05; Director of Corporate Communications, University of Glasgow, 2005-2012; Director of Communications, Yes Scotland, 2012-2013. Non Executive Board Member, National Health Education for Scotland (NES), since 2015; Board member, Glasgow Film Theatre; former Board member: Glasgow Chamber of Commerce, Barnardos Scotland, Glasgow Arts Festival; founder member, Globalscot Network. Recreations: theatre; opera; reading; politics in all forms; kayaking in the Kyles of Bute. Address: The Open University in Scotland, Jennie Lee House, 10 Drumsheugh Gardens, Edinburgh EH3 7QJ.

Stewartby, Lord (Bernard Harold Ian Halley), RD, FBA, FRSE, PC, Kt, Baron, KStJ, LittD. Retired Banker; b. 10.8.35, London; m., The Hon. Deborah Buchan (qv); 1 s.; 2 d. Educ. Haileybury; Jesus College, Cambridge (Hon. Fellow 1994). Royal Navy (National Service), 1954-56; Director, Brown Shipley and Co. Ltd., Merchant Bankers, 1971-83; MP North Hertfordshire (Conservative), 1974-92; Under-Secretary of State for Defence, 1983; Economic Secretary to the Treasury, 1983-87; Minister of State for the Armed Forces, 1987-88; Deputy Secretary of State, Northern Ireland, 1988-89; Director, Financial Services Authority, 1992-97; Deputy Chairman, Standard Chartered plc, 1993-2004; Deputy Chairman, Amlin plc, 1995-2006; Author, The Scottish Coinage, 1955; English Coins 1180-1551, 2009; President, Sir Halley Stewart Trust, since 2002; President, The Stewart Society, 2007-2010; Chairman, Treasure Valuation Committee, 1996-2001; Medallist, The Royal Numismatic Society, 1996; Hon. Keeper of Medieval Coins, Fitzwilliam Museum Cambridge, since 2008. Recreations: history; tennis. Address: (h.) Broughton Green, Broughton, by Biggar ML12 6HQ.

Stewartby (The Lady), Deborah Charlotte. Honorary Sheriff, Tweeddale, 2008; Non-Executive Director, Scottish Opera, 2000-03; Scottish Ballet, 2000-07; Council Member, John Buchan Society (grand-daughter of John Buchan), since 2001, Chairman, 2006-2010, Vice President, since 2010; b. 19.10.47, London; m., Rt. Hon. Lord Stewartby; 1 s.; 2 d. Senior Researcher, 1974-92 (P.A. of Ian Stewart, MP); Director of Appeals and Public Affairs, Bryson House, Belfast, 1991-98. Governor, Princess Helena College, 1986-99; President, Howard Cottage Society, 1995-2007; Member, Scottish Borders Childrens' Panel, 2004-2009; Scottish Trustee, Barnardo's, 2004-06; Trustee, John Buchan Heritage Museum Trust, since 2010, Vice President, 2015. Recreations: performing arts; gardening. Address: (h.) Broughton Green, Broughton, by Biggar ML12 6HQ.

Stewart-Clark, Sir Jack, Bt. Chairman, Dundas Castle Ltd, since 1999; Member of European Parliament for East Sussex and Kent South, 1979-99; Vice President, European Parliament, 1992-97; b. 17.9.29, West Lothian; m., Lydia Loudon; 1 s.; 4 d. Educ. Eton; Balliol College, Oxford; Harvard Business School. Coldstream Guards, 1948-49; J. & P. Coats, 1952-70 (Managing Director, J. & P. Coats Pakistan, 1961-66); Managing Director, J. A. Carp's Garenfabrieken, 1966-70; Philips Industries, 1970-79 (Managing Director, Philips Electrical Ltd., 1970-74, Pye of Cambridge Ltd., 1974-79). Member, Queen's Bodyguard for Scotland, Royal Company of Archers. Publications: European Competition Law; Drugs Education, It's My Problem as Well. Recreations: golf; photography; music; classic cars. Address: (h.) Dundas Castle, South Queensferry, near Edinburgh, EH30 9SP; T.-0131-331 1114.

Stihler, Catherine Dalling, MA (Hons), MLitt. Member, European Parliament, since 1999; European Parliamentary Labour Party (EPLP) Whip, since 2014; b. 30.7.73, Bellshill; m., David; 1 s. Educ. Coltness High School, Wishaw; St Andrews University. Parliamentary assistant to Ann Begg, 1997-99; elected MEP for Scotland, 1999; President of European Parliament Health Intergroup, 2000-02; EPLP health spokesperson, 1999-2004; Deputy Leader, EPLP, 2004-06. Vice Chair, Internal Market and Consumer Protection Committee, since 2014; Committee member: Internal Market and Consumer Protection; Substitute member: Economic and Monetary Affairs, delegation for relations with Switzerland, Iceland and Norway and to the European Economic Joint Parliamentary Committee; Organisation member: Co-operative Party, Amicus, European Movement, Labour Movement for Europe, RSPB, SERA, European Young Labour, Engender, Campaign for Parliamentary Reform, First Step Forum, Fabian Society, National Childbirth Trust, Socialist Health Association. Publication: Women and the Military (Contributor). Recreations: running marathons; yoga; swimming; music; film; studying languages. Address: (b.) Constituency Office, 25 Church Street, Inverkeithing, Fife KY11 1LG; T.-01383 417799; e-mail: cstihlermep@btconnect.com

Stimson, Professor William Howard, BSc, PhD, CBiol, FSB, FWIF, FIoN, FRSE. Emeritus Professor, Strathclyde University (former Professor of Immunology); Chairman: Alfacyte Ltd., WH Stimson and Associates, Quantilyte Ltd; Director/CSO, Solus Scientific Solutions Ltd.; b. 2.11.43, Liverpool; m., Jean Scott Baird; 1 s.; 1 d. Educ. Prince of Wales School, Nairobi; St. Andrews University. Research Fellow, Department of Obstetrics and Gynaecology, Dundee University, 1970-72; Lecturer, then Senior Lecturer, Biochemistry Department, Strathclyde University, 1973-80. Holder, Glasgow Loving Cup, 1982-83; Member, Editorial Boards, four scientific journals; 207 scientific publications; 34 patents. Recreations: mechanical engineering; walking; golf. Address: (b.) SIPBS, Strathclyde University, Hamnet Building, Glasgow G4 0NR; T.-0141-548 3729.
E-mail: w.h.stimson@strath.ac.uk

Stirling of Garden, Col. Sir James, KCVO, CBE, TD, BA, FRICS. Lord Lieutenant of Stirling and Falkirk, 1983-2005; Chartered Surveyor; b. 8.9.30; m., Fiona; 2 s.; 2 d. Educ. Rugby; Trinity College, Cambridge. Partner, Ryden and Partners, 1962-89; Director, Scottish Widows Life Assurance Society, 1974-96. Chairman, Highland TAVRA, 1981-86, President, 1990-96; Director, Woolwich Building Society, 1975-95; Honorary Sheriff, Stirling, 1996. Prior, Order of St. John, Scotland, 1997-2009; Hon. Doctor, University of Stirling, 2004; Grand Cross of the Order of St.

John, 2004. Address: (h.) Dambrae, Buchlyvie, Stirlingshire.

Stirling, John Boyd, WS. Clerk to HM Society of Writers to the Signet, 2002-08; Solicitor Advocate, since 2005; Partner, Gillespie MacAndrew, since 2005; b. 8.3.68, Glasgow; m., Julie; 2 s. Educ. Glasgow Academy; Edinburgh University. Trainee, W & J Burness WS; Solicitor, Scottish Office, Assistant, then Partner, Bennett and Robertson (which merged with Gillespie MacAndrew). Recreations: fly fishing; wine. Address: (b.) 5 Atholl Crescent, Edinburgh EH3 8EJ; T.-0131 225 1677; e-mail: john.stirling@gillespiemacandrew.co.uk

Stobo, James, CBE, DL, FRAgS. Farmer; Chairman, Moredun Foundation for Animal Health and Welfare, 1994-2000; former Director, New Park Management Ltd.; b. 9.12.34, Lanark; m., Pamela Elizabeth Mary Herriot (deceased); 1 s.; 2 d. Educ. Edinburgh Academy. Farming, since 1951; Past Chairman and President, Scottish Association of Young Farmers Clubs; Member, Home-Grown Cereals Authority, 1971-76; President, National Farmers' Union of Scotland, 1973-74; President, Animal Diseases Research Association, 1980-95; President, Longridge Towers School, since 2000, Chairman of Governors, 1982-2000; Chairman, Scottish Seed Potato Development Council, 1988-95; Director, John Hogarth Ltd., Kelso Mills; Vice-President, Royal Smithfield Club; Trustee, Queen Elizabeth Castle of Mey Trust, 1996-2011; Ex Director, Castle and Gardens of Mey Ltd.; President, Aberdeen-Angus Cattle Society, 2001-02; Deputy Lieutenant, County of Berwick, 1987. Recreation: photography. Address: Nabdean, Berwick-upon-Tweed TD15 1SZ; T.-01289 386224.

Stollery, Professor Peter John, BMus (Hons), MA, PhD, PGCE, FRSA. Professor of Electroacoustic Music and Composition, University of Aberdeen, since 2007, Head of Department of Music, 2006-2010, Head of the School of Education, 2010-2011; b. 24.07.60, Halifax; m., Catherine; 2 s.; 1 d. Educ. Heath Grammar School, Halifax; University of Birmingham. Assistant Teacher of Music, The Judd School, Tonbridge, 1984-89, Head of Music, 1989-91; Lecturer in Music, Northern College, Aberdeen, 1991-2001; University of Aberdeen: Lecturer in Music, 2001-02, Senior Lecturer in Music, 2002-05, Reader in Composition and Electroacoustic Music, 2005-07. Chair of Sound Festival; former Chair, Sonic Arts Network; Board Member: invisiblEARts. Recreations: listening; working with children. Address: (b.) School of Education, University of Aberdeen, MacRobert Building, Aberdeen AB25 5UA; T.-01224 274601.
E-mail: p.stollery@abdn.ac.uk
Website: www.petestollery.com

Stone, Professor David, MD, FRCP, FFPHM, FRCPCH. Emeritus Professor of Paediatric Epidemiology, University of Glasgow, since 2014 (Professor, 2000-2013); b. 13.5.49, Glasgow; 2 s.; 2 d. Educ. High School of Glasgow; Edinburgh University. Trained in general medicine and public health, Glasgow and London; Senior Lecturer in Epidemiology, Ben Gurion University of the Negev, Israel, 1981-85; Senior Lecturer, Glasgow University, 1985-2000, Founding Director, Paediatric Epidemiology and Community Health Unit, Department of Child Health. Recreations: music; dining; current affairs.

Stone, James Hume Walter Miéville, MA, FRSA. MSP (Liberal Democrat), Caithness, Sutherland and Easter Ross, 1999-2011; re-elected to The Highland Council for the Tain and Easter Ross Ward in 2012;

freelance newspaper columnist and broadcaster, since 1991; b. 16.6.54, Edinburgh; m., Flora Kathleen Margaret Armstrong; 1 s.; 2 d. Educ. Tain Royal Academy; Gordonstoun School; St Andrews University. Cleaner, fish-gutter, stores clerk, 1977-81; Assistant Site Administrator/Site Administrator, Bechtel G.B. Ltd., 1981-84; Administration Manager, Odfjell Drilling and Consulting Co. Ltd., 1984-86; Director, Highland Fine Cheeses Ltd., 1986-94; Member, Ross and Cromarty District Council, 1986-96; Member, The Highland Council, 1995-99 (Vice-Chair, Finance). Member, Cromarty Firth Port Authority, 1998-2001; Liberal Democrat Spokesman for: Education and Children, 1999-2000, Highlands and Fishing, 2000-01, Equal Opportunities, 2001-2011, Finance, 2002-2011; Trustee, Tain Museum Trust; Trustee, Tain Guildry Trust; Trustee, Highland Buildings Preservation Trust; Director, The Highland Festival, 1994-2000. Recreations: gardening; reading; music; butterflies and funghi. Address: (b.) Knockbreck House, Tain IV19 1LZ; T.-01862 892 726.

Stone, Rodney, BA, DipRM. Leisure Manager, since 1976; Member, sportscotland Board, since 2011; b. 11.10.51, Belfast; m., Alison; 1 s.; 1 d. Educ. Methodist College Belfast; University of Stirling. Local Authority Recreation Officer: Ayrshire, 1976-78, Cumbernauld, 1978-84, Glasgow, 1984-86; Leisure Centre Manager, Edinburgh, 1986-87; Leisure Services Manager, Midlothian District Council, 1987-95; Head of Leisure and Community Development, Moray Council, 1995-2000; Head of Lifelong Learning and Leisure, Aberdeenshire Council, 2000-2011. Chair, Vocal (Chief Culture and Leisure Officers Association), 1998-2000 and 2007-2010; Secretary, 2001-06; former international athlete. Address: (h.) Tullynessle Steading, Tullynessle, Alford, Aberdeenshire AB33 8QR; T.-019755 62218; e-mail: jarstone@btinternet.com

Stone, Professor Trevor W., BPharm, PhD, DSc, FBPhS, Hon FRCP (Lond). Professor of Pharmacology, Glasgow University, since 1989; co-Director, PharmaLinks, since 2003; b. 7.10.47, Mexborough; m., (1) Anne Corina; divorced; m., (2) L. Gail Darlington. Educ. Mexborough Grammar School; London University; Aberdeen University. Lecturer in Physiology, Aberdeen University, 1970-77; Senior Lecturer/Reader in Neuroscience, then Professor of Neuroscience, London University, 1977-88. Editor-in-Chief, Journal of Receptor, Ligand and Channel Research, since 2008; Editor, British Journal of Pharmacology, 1980-86. Publications: 400 scientific papers and 13 books; Microiontophoresis and Pressure Ejection, 1985; Purines: Basic and Clinical Aspects, 1991; Neuropharmacology, 1995; Pills, Potions and Poisons – How Drugs Work, 2000. Recreations: photography; snooker; music; working. Address: (b.) Neuroscience and Psychology, West Medical Building, Glasgow University, Glasgow G12; T.-0141-330 4481.

Storey, Professor Kate Gillian, BSc (Hons), PhD. Head of Division of Cell and Developmental Biology, University of Dundee, since 2010, Chair of Neural Development, since 2007; b. 27.11.60, London; m., Jonathan Gordon; 1 s.; 1 d. Educ. Parliament Hill School, London; Sussex University; PhD Cambridge University; Harkness Fellowship, University of California at Berkeley, 1987. Lecturer, Deptartment of Human Anatomy and Genetics, 1994-2000; College of Life Sciences, University of Dundee, since 2000. Major Science/Art Exhibition "Primitive Streak", since 1997. Fellow of Society of Biology; Fellow of the Royal Society of Arts; Fellow of the Royal Society of Edinburgh. Recreations: long distance running; beach combing. Address: (b.) College of Life Sciences, University of Dundee, Dow Street, Dundee DD1 5EH; T.-01382 385691; e-mail: k.g.storey@dundee.ac.uk

Stott, Professor David James, MB, ChB, MD(Glas), FRCP(Glas), FRCP(Edin). Professor of Geriatric Medicine, Glasgow University, since 1994; b. 4.6.59, Rugby; m., Shiona; 1 s.; 1 d. Educ. Eastwood High School; Glasgow University. Trained in research methodology, MRC Blood Pressure Unit, 1982-84; Senior Lecturer (Honorary Consultant) in Geriatric Medicine, 1991-94. Recreations: golf; hill-walking; acoustic guitar. Address: (b.) Academic Section of Geriatric Medicine, Glasgow Royal Infirmary G4 0SF; T.-0141-211 4976.

Stove, Thomas William. Convener, Shetland Islands Council, 1999-2003; b. 17.7.35, Sandwick, Shetland; m., Alma; 2 d. Educ. Anderson Education Institute, Lerwick. Owner/Director, Televiradio (Shetland) Ltd., 1966-96; Member, Zetland County Council/Shetland Islands Council, 1970-78; Member, Lerwick Harbour Trust, 1980-96 (Chairman, 1983-96). Trustee, Shetland & Orkney Multiple Sclerosis Research Project. Recreations: boating; walking; classic cars; DIY. Address: (h.) Nordaal, Sandwick, Shetland ZE2 9HP; T.-01950 431434; e-mail: tandastove@btinternet.com

Strachan, Gordon, OBE. Scottish football manager; Manager, Scotland national team, since 2013; b. 9.2.57; m., Lesley Scott; 2 s.; 1 d. Played for Dundee, Aberdeen, Manchester United, Leeds United and Coventry City, as well as the Scotland national team. Managed Coventry City, Southampton, Celtic and Middlesbrough. In club football, played 635 league games, scoring a total of 138 goals, playing 21 of 25 career seasons in either the English or Scottish top-flight. Earned 50 caps in international football, scoring five goals and playing in two FIFA World Cup final tournaments, Spain, 1982 and Mexico, 1986. Retired from playing in 1997 at age 40, setting a Premier League record for an outfield player. FWA Footballer of the Year for the 1990-91 season while at Leeds; also named Manager of the Year in Scotland multiple times by writers and players while at Celtic; inducted into the Scottish Football Hall of Fame in 2007. Analysed football matches for the media, most notably on BBC Sport's Match of the Day 2; works as a regular pundit on ITV's coverage of the FA Cup; official FIFA Ambassador for Scotland, 2006 FIFA World Cup. Address: The Scottish Football Association Ltd, Hampden Park, Glasgow G42 9AY.

Strachan, Professor Sir Hew Francis Anthony, MA, PhD, FRHistS, FRSE, HonDUniv (Paisley) 2005. Lord Lieutenant of Tweeddale, since 2014; Professor, International Relations, University of St Andrews, since 2015; Chichele Professor of the History of War and Fellow, All Souls College, University of Oxford, 2002-2015; Professor of Modern History, Glasgow University, 1992-2001 (Visiting Professor, since 2002); Director, Scottish Centre for War Studies, 1996-2001; Life Fellow, Corpus Christi College, Cambridge, since 1992; b. 1.9.49, Edinburgh; m., Pamela Dorothy Tennant (née Symes); 1 s.; 1 step s.; 2 d.; 1 step d. Educ. Rugby School; Corpus Christi College, Cambridge. Senior Lecturer, Department of War Studies and International Affairs, Royal Military Academy, Sandhurst, 1978-79; Research Fellow, Corpus Christi College, Cambridge, 1975-78; Fellow, Corpus Christi College, since 1979: Tutor for Admissions, 1981-88, Director of Studies in History, 1986-92, Senior Tutor, 1987 and 1989-92. Governor, Rugby School, 1985-2007, and Stowe School, 1990-2002; DL (Tweeddale), 2006-2014; Lord Lieutenant, Tweeddale, since 2014; Commonwealth War Graves Commission, since 2006; Member, Council,

Society for Army Historical Research, 1980-95, Army Records Society, 1990-94, Council, National Army Museum, 1994-2003; Joint Editor, War in History, 1994-2013; Member, Queen's Bodyguard for Scotland (Royal Company of Archers); Brigadier, 2008; Visiting Professor, Royal Norwegian Air Force Academy, since 2000; Trustee, Imperial War Museum, since 2010; Chair, Task Force on the Military Covenant for the Prime Minister, 2010. Publications: British Military Uniforms; History of the Cambridge University Officers Training Corps; European Armies and the Conduct of War; Wellington's Legacy: the Reform of the British Army 1830-54; From Waterloo to Balaclava: Tactics, Technology, and the British Army 1815-1854 (Templer Medal, 1986); The Politics of the British Army (Westminster Medal, 1998); Oxford Illustrated History of the First World War (Editor), 1998; The British Army, Manpower and Society into the 21st Century (Editor), 2000; The First World War Vol. I: To Arms, 2001; The First World War: a new illustrated history, 2003; Big Wars and Small Wars (Editor), 2006; Clausewitz's on War: A Biography, 2007; Clausewitz in the 21st Century (Editor), 2007; The Changing Character of War (Editor), 2011; How Wars End (Editor), 2012; British Generals and Blair's Wars (Editor), 2013; The Direction of War, 2013; numerous articles and reviews. Knighted in the 2013 New Year Honours for services to the Ministry of Defence. Recreations: shooting; rugby football. Address: (h.) Glenhighton, Broughton, Biggar ML12 6JF.

Strang, David, QPM. HM Chief Inspector of Prisons for Scotland, since 2013. Career: Chief Constable of Dumfries and Galloway Constabulary, 2001-07; Chief Constable of Lothian and Borders Police, 2007-2013. Address: HM Prisons Inspectorate, Saughton House, Broomhouse Drive, Edinburgh EH11 3XD; T.-0131 244 8482.

Strang, Gavin Steel, BSc (Hons), DipAgriSci, PhD. MP (Labour), East Edinburgh, 1970-2010; b. 10.7.43, Dundee; m., Bettina Smith; 1 s. Educ. Morrison's Academy, Crieff; Edinburgh University. Parliamentary Under Secretary of State, Department of Energy, February to October, 1974; Parliamentary Secretary, Ministry of Agriculture, 1974-79; Principal Labour Agriculture Spokesman, 1992-97; Cabinet Minister with responsibility for Transport, 1997-98. Recreations: golf; swimming; the countryside.

Strange, Rt. Revd. Mark. Bishop of Moray, Ross & Caithness, since 2007; m., Jane; 3 c. Educ. University of Aberdeen; Lincoln Theological College. Ordained in the Anglican ministry a deacon in 1989 and priest in 1990; first pastoral appointment was as a curate at St Barnabas with Christ Church, Worcester (1989–92), then the Vicar of St Wulfstan's, Warndon, Worcester (1992–98); formerly canon of St Andrew's Cathedral, synod clerk of the diocese, and had a leading role in developing the church's youth network throughout Scotland and organising its annual youth week events; Rector of Holy Trinity Church, Elgin and priest in charge of St Margaret's, Lossiemouth, St Michael's, Dufftown and St Margaret's, Aberlour, 1998-2007. Address: The United Diocese of Moray, Ross and Caithness, 9-11 Kenneth Street, Inverness IV3 5NR; T.-01463 237503.

Strang Steel, Sir (Fiennes) Michael, 3rd Bt, CBE. Former Member, Deer Commission for Scotland (2000-2010); b. 22.2.43; m., Sally Russell; 2 s.; 1 d. Educ. Eton. Retired Major, 17th/21st Lancers, 1962-80. Former Forestry Commissioner; VLL. Address: (h.) Philiphaugh, Selkirk, TD7 5LX.

Strang Steel, Malcolm Graham, BA (Cantab), LLB. Partner, Turcan Connell, WS, 1997-2009; Partner, W. & J. Burness, WS, 1973-97; b. 24.11.46, Selkirk; m., Margaret Philippa Scott; 1 s.; 1 d. Educ. Eton; Trinity College, Cambridge; Edinburgh University. Sometime Chairman, Albyn Housing Society Ltd., Scottish Dyslexia Trust; Secretary: Standing Council of Scottish Chiefs, 1973-83, Scottish Agricultural Arbiters and Valuers Association, 1998-2009; Member, Council, Law Society of Scotland, 1984-90. Recreations: shooting; fishing; tennis; reading. Address: (h.) Greenhead of Arnot, Leslie, Glenrothes KY6 3JQ.

Strathclyde, Lord (Thomas Strathclyde), PC. Leader of the House of Lords, 2010-2013; Chancellor of the Duchy of Lancaster, 2010-2013; Leader of the Opposition, House of Lords, 1998-2010; b. 22.2.60, Glasgow; m., Jane; 3 d. Educ. Wellington College; East Anglia University; University of Aix-en-Provence. Bain Clarkson, Insurance Brokers, 1982-88; Government Whip, 1988; Minister for Tourism, 1989; Minister for Agriculture and Fisheries, Scottish Office, 1990-92; Parliamentary Under Secretary of State, DoE, 1992-93; Minister of State, Department of Trade and Industry, 1993-94; Government Chief Whip, 1994-97; Opposition Chief Whip, 1997-98. Chairman, Strathclyde Commission on Restructuring the Scottish Conservative and Unionist Party, 1997-98. Directorships held: Trafalgar Capital Management Ltd., 2001-2010 (Chairman), Scottish Mortgage Investment Trust plc, 2004-2010, Galena Asset Management Ltd., 2004-2010, Marketform Group Ltd., 2004-2010, Hampden Agencies Ltd., 2008-2010, Trafigura Beheer BV; Adviser to various companies in the UK and internationally; Governor, Wellington College; Board Member, Centre for Policy Studies (CPS). Address: (b.) House of Lords, London SW1; T.-020 7219 3000.

Strathmore and Kinghorne, 19th Earl of (Simon Patrick Bowes-Lyon); b. 18.6.86. Succeeded to title, 2016. First cousin twice removed of Queen Elizabeth II, and a great-great nephew of the late Queen Elizabeth, the Queen Mother. Address: Glamis Castle, Forfar DD8 1QJ.

Straton, Timothy Duncan, TD, CA, CTA. B. 1.10.42, Edinburgh; m., Gladys Margaret George (deceased); 1 s.; 1 d. Educ. Edinburgh Academy. Treasurer, Scottish National War Memorial. Recreations: family; heritage railways; photography; golf; curling; bowls. Address: (h.) 32 Wardie Road, Edinburgh EH5 3LG; T.-0131 552 4062.

Street, Margaret Dobson, MBE, FSA Scot; b. 18.10.20, Hawick; m., Richard Andrew Rutherford Street (deceased); 2 s. Educ. Hawick High School; Alva Academy. Civil Servant, 1938-48; Ministry of Labour and National Service, 1938-47; Ministry of National Insurance (Inspectorate), 1947-48; voluntary work since 1948, apart from freelance writing on household and conservation topics; Honorary Secretary Leith Civic Trust, until 1997, Patron, since 1998; Convener, Friends of North Carr Lightship; Member, North East Fife District Council, North Carr Management Committee; Saltire Society Representative, Council, National Trust for Scotland, 1986-95; Secretary, Mungo Park Commemoration Committee; Trustee, Robert Hurd Memorial Fund; Appeal Convener, Wallace Statue, Lanark; Member, Steering Committee, Brownsbank; Appeal Convener, Wallace Statue, Dryburgh; Vice-Chairman, Saltire Society, 1983-94, Chairman, 1995-97; Saltire Society's Andrew Fletcher of Saltoun Award for services to Scotland, 1992; Honorary Member, Saltire Society, 1997. Recreations: promotion of Scottish cultural activity; conservation. Address: (h.) 115 Trinity Road, Edinburgh; T.-0131-552 2409.

Stringer, Professor Dame Joan Kathleen, DBE, CBE, BA, CertEd, PhD, CCMI, FRSA, FRSE, HonDLitt (Keele). Principal and Vice-Chancellor, Edinburgh Napier

University, 2003-2013; Board Member, Universities and Colleges Employers Association (UCEA), 2001-2010; Board Member, Leadership Foundation for Higher Education (LFHE), 2005-2010; Chair, Education UK Scotland Committee, 2005-2012; Board Member, Universities and Colleges Admissions Service (UCAS), 2009-2013; Board Member, National Theatre of Scotland, since 2009; Member: Executive Committee, Scottish Council Development and Industry, 1998-2013, Council, World Association for Co-operative Education, 1998-2003, Edinburgh International Festival Council, 1999-2005, Scottish Committee, British Council, 2000-2012, Judicial Appointments Board for Scotland, 2002-07; Convenor, Scottish Council for Voluntary Organisations, 2002-07; b. 12.5.48, Stoke on Trent; m., Roel Mali. Educ. Portland House High School, Stoke on Trent; Stoke on Trent College of Art; Keele University. Assistant Principal, Robert Gordon University, 1991-96, having joined as Lecturer, 1980; Principal, Queen Margaret University College, Edinburgh, 1996-2002; Visiting Lecturer, Aberdeen University, 1984-86. Member: Joint University Council for Social and Public Administration, 1982-91, Royal Institute of Public Administration, 1984-91, Management Board, North of Scotland Consortium on Wider Access, 1988-92, Board of Management, Aberdeen College, 1992-96, Grampian Health Board, 1994-96, CVCP Commission on University Career Opportunities, 1995-2001, Scottish Committee, National Committee of Inquiry into Higher Education (The Dearing Committee), 1996-97, Human Fertilisation and Embryology Authority, 1996-99, Secretary of State's Consultative Steering Group and Financial Issues Advisory Group on the Scottish Parliament, 1998-99, Scottish Council for Postgraduate Medical and Dental Education, 1999-2002, Scottish Health Minister's Learning Together Strategy Implementation Group, 2000-01, Scottish European Structural Funds Forum, 2000-02, Department of Health's Working Group on the Modernisation of the SHO, 2000-02, Scottish Nursing and Midwifery Education Council Advisory Group, 2000-01, Institute of Directors, The British Chamber of Commerce; Auditor, Higher Education Quality Council, 1992-95; Commissioner (with responsibility for Scotland), Equal Opportunities Commission, 1995-2001; Chair, Northern Ireland Equality Commission Working Group, 1998-99; Vice Convener, Committee of Scottish Higher Education Principals, 1998-2002; Commissioner, Scottish Election Commission, 1999; Chair, Scottish Executive Strategic Group on Women, 2003; Member, Board: Higher Education Statistics Agency, since 2003, Quality Assurance Agency for Higher Education, 2002-06, Higher Education Careers Services Unit, 2000-05; Convenor, International Committee, Universities Scotland, 2006-2012; Honorary Doctorate 'honoris causa', University of Edinburgh, 2011; Council Member, Institute of Directors, since 2013; Chair, Board of Trustees, Edinburgh City Festival Theatres Trust, since 2013; Non-Executive Director, City Refrigeration Holdings Ltd, since 2013; Non-Executive Director, Grant Property Ltd, since 2013; Council Member, Royal Society of Edinburgh, since 2013; Chair, Board of Directors, Community Integrated Care, since 2014; Senior Education Adviser, British Council, since 2013; Hon. Doctor of the University, Open University, 2014. Publications: contributed articles in field of politics with particular reference to British Public Administration and employment and training policy. Recreations: music (especially opera); gardening; cats.

Strudwick, Major General Mark Jeremy, CBE. Chief Executive, The Prince's Scottish Youth Business Trust, 2000-2012; b. 19.4.45; m. (1), Janet Elizabeth Coleridge Vivers (deceased 2013); 1 s.; 1 d.; m. (2), Susan Jennifer Garrett-Cox (nee Guest); 2 step s.; 1 step d. Educ. St. Edmund's School, Canterbury; Royal Military Academy, Sandhurst. Commissioned, The Royal Scots (The Royal Regiment), 1966 (Colonel, 1995-2005); served UK, BAOR,

Cyprus, Canada, India, Northern Ireland (Despatches twice); Commanded, 1st Bn. The Royal Scots, 1984-87; Instructor, Staff College Camberley, 1987-88; Assistant Chief of Staff, G1/G4 HQ Northern Ireland 1988-90; Higher Command and Staff Course, 1989; Commanded, 3 Infantry Bde., 1990-91; NDC New Delhi, 1992; Deputy Military Secretary, Ministry of Defence, 1993-95; Director of Infantry, 1996-97; ADC to HM The Queen, 1996-97; General Officer Commanding, Army in Scotland, and Governor, Edinburgh Castle, 1997-2000; Colonel Commandant, The Scottish Division, 1997-2000. Member, Royal Company of Archers, Queen's Bodyguard for Scotland, since 1994 (Brigadier 2006); Commodore Infantry Sailing Association, 1997-2000; Her Majesty's Commissioner, Queen Victoria School, Dunblane, 1997-2000; Governor: Royal School, Bath, 1993-2000, Gordonstoun School, 1999-2007; Chairman: Scottish Veterans' Residences, since 2001, Scottish National War Memorial, since 2009; Trustee, Historic Scotland Foundation, since 2001; KStJ, 2015; Prior, Order St John, Scotland, since 2015. Recreations: golf; shooting; fishing; sailing. Address: Scottish Veterans' Residences, 53 Canongate, Edinburgh EH8 8BS.

Struthers, Professor Allan, BSc, MD, FRCP, FESC, FRSE, FMedSci. Professor of Cardiovascular Medicine, Dundee University, since 2000; b. 14.8.52, Glasgow; m., Julia Diggens; 1 s.; 1 d. Educ. Hutchesons' Boys' Grammar School; Glasgow University. Junior posts, Glasgow teaching hospitals, 1977-82; Senior Medical Registrar, Royal Postgraduate Medical School and Hammersmith Hospital, London, 1983-85; Wellcome Senior Lecturer, Department of Clinical Pharmacology, Ninewells Hospital, 1985-92; Professor of Clinical Pharmacology, 1992-2000. Recreations: cycling; walking; travel; opera.

Struthers, Shona. Chief Executive, Colleges Scotland, since 2014. Educ. University of Glasgow; Chartered Institute of Marketing; Chartered Institute of Management Accountants; Manchester Metropolitan University. Business/Product Development Management Accountant, Imperial Chemical Industries, 1988-95; Company Director, Webaspx Ltd, 1998-2001; Board Member, Falkirk Women's Technology Centre, 1995-2005; Finance and Communications Director, Zeneca/Avecia Ltd, 1995-2005; Board Member, Scottish Further Education Unit, 2005-08; Finance & Corporate Services Director/Company Secretary, Snowdon Consulting Ltd/Scottish Further Education, 2007-08; Business Merger Director, Snowdon Consulting Ltd/Scotland's Colleges, 2008-09; Executive Officer Adviser, Snowdon Consulting Ltd/City of Glasgow College, 2010-11; Merger Director, Snowdon Consulting Ltd/Scottish Agricultural College, 2011-12; Strategic Financial Advisor, Snowdon Consulting Ltd/DTZ Consulting, 2006-2013; Director, Snowdon Consulting, 2006-2013; Board Support/CEO Advisor, Snowdon Consulting Ltd/Colleges Scotland, 2011-13; Director of Policy and Public Affairs, Colleges Scotland, 2013-14; Board Member, Forth Valley College, 2008-2014; Acting Chief Executive, Colleges Scotland, 2014. Address: Colleges Scotland, Argyll Court, The Castle Business Park, Stirling FK9 4TY; T.-01786 892000.

Stuart, Jamie; b. 10.9.20, Glasgow; widower; 2 d. Educ. Whitehill School, Glasgow. Flying Officer/Wireless Operator/Air Gunner, RAF, 1941-46; Actor/Social Worker/Evangelist; athlete: Scottish two-miles steeplechase champion, 1948. Publications: A Glasgow Bible; Will I Be Called An Author? The Glasgow Gospel; Auld Testament Tales; Proverbs in the Patter; A Counterblaste to Tobacco; A Scots Gospel; Still Running. Address: (h.) 436 Edinburgh Road, Glasgow G33 2PW; T.-0141-778 2437.

Stuart, John Forester, MA (Cantab). Secretary General, General Synod, Scottish Episcopal Church, since 1996; b. 26.5.59, Broughty Ferry; m., Sally Ann Bell; 2 s. Educ. Dundee High School; Daniel Stewart's and Melville College; Queens' College Cambridge, College of Law, Guildford.Articled Clerk and subsequently Solicitor, Macfarlanes, London, 1982-86; Solicitor and subsequently Partner, J. & F. Anderson, Solicitors, Edinburgh (merged, 1992, to become Anderson Strathern), 1986-96. Recreations: music; walking; astronomy. Address: (b.) 21 Grosvenor Crescent, Edinburgh EH12 5EE; T.-0131-225 6357.

Stuart, Mhairi Ross, MA (Hons). Presenter, Scotland Live, BBC Scotland, since 2006, Presenter, Good Morning Scotland, 1999-2006; b. 8.12.67, Glasgow; m., Roderick Stuart. Educ. Cleveden Secondary School, Glasgow; Glasgow University. BBC, since 1991 (News Trainee/Producer/Presenter). BT Scotland Radio News Broadcaster of the Year, 1999. Recreations: sailing; skiing. Address: (b.) News Room, BBC Scotland, 40 Pacific Quay, Glasgow G51 1DZ.

Sturgeon, David, BL, MLitt. Registrar and Deputy Secretary, Heriot-Watt University, 1967-95; b. 10.12.35, Kilwinning; m., Nancy McDougall; 1 d.; 2 s. Educ. Dalry High School, Ayrshire (Blair Medallist, 1950); Glasgow University. National Service (RASC - War Office), 1957-59; Trainee Actuary, Scottish Widows Fund, 1959-61; Administrative Assistant, Royal College of Science and Technology (later, Strathclyde University), 1961-67. Secretary and Treasurer, Edinburgh Society of Glasgow University Graduates, 1971-2004; Hon. degree, Heriot-Watt University, 1996; Chairman, Dalry (Ayrshire) Burns Club, 2002. Recreations: golf; music (particularly Scottish country dance music). Address: (h.) 10 Dalhousie Road, Eskbank, Midlothian EH22 3AS; T.-0131-663 1059; e-mail: davidsturgeon35@hotmail.com

Sturgeon, Nicola, LLB (Hons), DipLP. MSP (SNP), Glasgow Southside, since 2011, Glasgow Govan, 2007-2011, Glasgow, 1999-2007; First Minister of Scotland, since 2014; b. 19.7.70, Irvine. Educ. Greenwood Academy, Irvine; University of Glasgow. Trainee Solicitor, Glasgow, 1993-95; Solicitor, Stirling, 1995-97; Solicitor, Drumchapel Law Centre, Glasgow, 1997-99; Deputy First Minister, and Cabinet Secretary for Infrastructure, Investment and Cities (with responsibility for Government Strategy and the Constitution), 2012-14. Recreations: reading; theatre. Address: (b.) 627 Pollokshaws Road, Glasgow G41 2QG.

Sturrock, John Garrow, QC, LLB (Hons), LLM, LLD, FRSA, MCIArb. Chief Executive, Core Solutions Group Ltd., since 2004; Queen's Counsel, since 1999; accredited Mediator, since 1996; Door Tenant, Brick Court Chambers, London, since 2013; Director of Training and Education, Faculty of Advocates, 1994-2002; Visiting Professor of Advocacy Skills and Conflict Resolution, Glasgow Graduate School of Law, since 1999; Honorary Degree of Doctor of Laws, Edinburgh Napier University, 2010; Distinguished Fellow, International Academy of Mediators, since 2009; b. 15.4.58, Stirling; m., Fiona Swanson; 2 s.; 1 d. Educ. Stirling High School; Waid Academy, Anstruther; Edinburgh University; University of Pennsylvania. Senior President, Edinburgh University Students' Association, 1980-81; apprentice Solicitor, 1981-83; qualified Solicitor, 1983-84; Harkness Fellow, US, 1984-85; Member, Faculty of Advocates, since 1986; Standing Junior Counsel to Department of Transport in Scotland, 1991-94; Member, Judicial Studies Committee in Scotland, 1997-2004; Member, Joint Standing Committee on Legal Education, 1988-2005. Recreations: family; golf; contemporary music; ships and the sea. Address: (h.) 6 Claverhouse Drive, Edinburgh EH16 6BS; T.-0131-667 8256; (b.) 10 York Place, Edinburgh EH1 3EP; T.-0131 524 8188; e-mail: John.Sturrock@core-solutions.com

Subak-Sharpe, Emeritus Professor John Herbert, CBE, CBiol, FSB, BSc, PhD, FRSE. Professor Emeritus, Glasgow University and Honorary Senior Research Fellow in Virology, since 1994; Professor of Virology, Glasgow University, 1968-94; Honorary Director, MRC Virology Unit, Institute of Virology, Glasgow, 1968-94; b. 14.2.24, Vienna; m., (1953) Barbara Naomi Morris; 2 s.; 1 d. Educ. Humanistisches Gymnasium, Vienna (escaped from Vienna to the UK by Kinder transport, 1939); Birmingham University. Assistant Lecturer in Genetics, Glasgow University, 1954-56; Member, ARC scientific staff, AVRI Pirbright, 1956-61; Visiting Fellow, California Institute of Technology, 1961; Member, MRC Experimental Virus Research Unit scientific staff, Glasgow, 1961-68; Visiting Professor, NIH, Bethesda, 1967-68. Visiting Fellow, Clare Hall, Cambridge, 1986; elected Member (Past Chairman, Course and Workshops Committee), EMBO, since 1969; Trustee (former Secretary and Vice-President), Genetical Society, 1971-99; Member, Genetic Manipulation Advisory Group, 1976-80; Chairman, MRC Training Awards Panel, 1986-89; Member, Governing Body, West of Scotland Oncological Organisation, since 1974, and Governing Body, Animal Virus Research Institute, Pirbright, 1986-88; Member, Scientific Advisory Group of Equine Virology Research Foundation, 1987-98; Member, Medical Research Council Cell Biology and Disorders Board, 1988-92; Biochemical Society CIBA Medal and Prize, 1993. Recreations: travel; bridge. Address: (h.) 63 Kelvin Court, Glasgow G12 0AG; T.-0141-339 1863.

Suckling, Professor Colin James, OBE, BSc, PhD, DSc, CChem, FRSC, FRSA, FRCPS (Glasg), HonFRCS (Edin), FRSE. Freeland Professor of Chemistry, Strathclyde University, since 1984; b. 24.3.47, Birkenhead; m., Catherine Mary Faulkner; 2 s.; 1 d. Educ. Quarry Bank High School, Liverpool; Liverpool University. Lecturer, Department of Pure and Applied Chemistry, Strathclyde University, 1972; Royal Society Smith and Nephew Senior Research Fellow, 1980; Dean, Faculty of Science, 1992-96; Deputy Principal, 1996-98; Pro-Vice Principal, 1998-2000; Vice Principal, 2000-02; Convener, RSE Chemistry Committee, 1989-91; Member of Council, RSE, 1989-92; Member, General Teaching Council, 1993-95; Member, Board: Systems Level Integration Ltd., 1998-2000, Lanarkshire Technology and Innovation Centre, 1998-2000; Governor, Bell College of Technology, 1999-2007; Member of Court, University of Paisley (West of Scotland); Chairman, West of Scotland Schools Orchestra Trust, 2007-2012; Chairman, Scottish Advisory Committee on Distinction Awards, 2003-10; Chairman, Strathclyde Youth Jazz Orchestra Trust; Chairman, Harmony Music Trust; Member, Joint Committee on Higher Surgical Training, 2003-05; Member, Senate of Surgery, 2003-05; Public Partner, Scottish Medicines Consortium; Chairman, Patient and Public Involvement Group, Scottish Medicines Consortium, 2012-15. Royal Society of Chemistry Adrien Albert Prize Lecturer, 2009-10; Nexxus Lifetime Achievement Award, 2011; Indian Society of Chemists and Biologists Gold Medal, 2011; Honorary Life Fellow of Indian Society of Chemists and Biologists, 2015. Publications: Chemistry Through Models (Co-author), 1978; Biological Chemistry (Co-author), 1980; Enzyme Chemistry, Impact and Applications (Co-author), 1984, 1989, 1998; 200 research publications. Recreations: music; horn playing. Address: (b.) Department of Pure and Applied Chemistry, Strathclyde University, 295 Cathedral Street, Glasgow G1 1XL; T.-0141-548 2271. E-mail: c.j.suckling@strath.ac.uk

Summers, Alan Andrew, QC, LLB, BCL. Advocate, since 1994; Treasurer, Faculty of Advocates, since 2012; Special Advocate to UK Government, since 2007; Standing Junior Counsel to Scottish Executive, 2000-05; b. 27.8.64, Bridge of Allan; m., Rosemary Helen Craig; 1 s.; 4 d. Educ. Grove Academy, Broughty Ferry; University of Dundee; St. Catherine's College, University of Oxford. Lecturer, Department of Scots Law, University of Edinburgh; Solicitor. Recreations: spending time with his family; reading. Address: (b.) Advocates Library, Parliament House, Edinburgh EH1 1RF; T.-0131-226 5071; e-mail: Alan.Summers@advocates.org.uk

Summers, John P., OBE, FREHIS, FCIWM. Chairman, Beautiful Perth Charity; former Chief Executive, Keep Scotland Beautiful (1999-2009) (retired); b. 22.12.46, Rhynie; m., Alison; 1 s.; 1 d. Educ. Aberdeen Academy; Napier College, Edinburgh. Environmental Health Officer, Aberdeenshire, 1972-79; Depute Director of Environmental Health, Banff and Buchan District Council, 1979-90; Director of Environmental Health, Moray District Council, 1990-94, Chief Executive, 1994-96; Director of Technical Services, Moray Council, 1996-99. Director of Foundation for Environmental Education (FEE). Recreations: reading; Scottish traditional music. Address: 12 Dryburgh Crescent, Perth PH1 1SF; e-mail: jpsumms@gmail.com

Summers, Sheriff William. Sheriff for Grampian, Highlands and Islands at Banff and Peterhead. Educ. University of Aberdeen. Career: admitted as a Solicitor in 1981 and as a Solicitor Advocate in 2003; accredited by the Law Society of Scotland as a commercial law mediator in 2004; a tutor in civil advocacy, and a civil reporter to the Scottish Legal Aid Board, 1997-2003.

Sutherland, Countess of (Elizabeth Millicent Sutherland). Chief of Clan Sutherland; b. 30.3.21; m., Charles Noel Janson (deceased 2006); 2 s.; 1 s. (deceased); 1 d. Educ. Queen's College, London; abroad. Land Army, 1939-41; Laboratory Technician, Raigmore Hospital, Inverness, and St. Thomas's Hospital, London, 1941-45. Address: (h.) Dunrobin Castle, Sutherland; House of Tongue, Lairg, Sutherland.

Sutherland of Houndwood, Lord (Stewart Ross), KT, FBA, PRSE, MA. Chairman, FROG Education UK, since 2013; President, David Hume Institute, 2005-08; Hon. President, Alzheimer Scotland, since 2002; Chairman, Scottish Care, since 2002; Pro-Chancellor, University of London, 2006-08; Chairman, Associated Board of the Royal Schools of Music, 2006-2012; Member, Editorial Advisory Board, Encyclopedia Britannica, 2005-2011; President, Royal Society of Edinburgh, 2002-05; President, Saltire Society, 2002-05; Provost, Gresham College, London, 2002-08; Chairman, QPA, 2002-05; Principal and Vice-Chancellor, Edinburgh University, 1994-2002; Chairman, Royal Commission on Long-Term Care of the Elderly, 1997-99; b. 25.2.41, Aberdeen; m., Sheena Robertson; 1 s.; 2 d. Educ. Woodside School; Robert Gordon's College; Aberdeen University; Cambridge University. Assistant Lecturer, Philosophy, UCNW, 1965-68; Lecturer, Senior Lecturer, Reader, Stirling University, 1968-77; Professor, Philosophy of Religion, King's College, London, 1977-90 (Vice-Principal, 1981-85, Principal, 1985-90); Vice-Chancellor, London University, 1990-94, and HM Chief Inspector of Schools (England), 1992-94; Visiting Fellow, Australian National University, 1974; Chairman, Brit. Acad. Postgraduate Studentships, 1987-94; Member: Council for Science and Technology, 1993-2000, Hong Kong University Grants Com., 1995-2004, Higher Education Funding Council, England, 1996-2002; Director, NHP, 2001-05; Editor, Religious Studies, 1984-90; Chairman: House of Lords Select Committee on Science and Technology, 2006-09, House of Lords Committee on Affordability of Child Care, 2014-15; Secretary of State's Committee on Appeal Procedures, 1994-96, Royal Institute

of Philosophy, 1988-2006, President, since 2011; President, Society for Study of Theology, 1985, 1986; Prime Warden, Goldsmiths' Company, 2012-2013. Publications: several books and papers. Recreations: jazz; theatre; rough gardening. Address: (b.) House of Lords, Westminster, London SW1A 0PW; e-mail: sutherlands@parliament.uk

Sutherland, Alan D.A., MA (Hons), MBA, MA. Chief Executive, Water Industry Commission for Scotland, since 2005; b. 8.4.62, Glasgow; m., Olga; 1 s.; 1 d. Educ. Eastwood High School; St Andrews University; University of Pennsylvania. Management trainee, Lloyds Bank PLC, 1984-85; Stockbroker, Savory Milln, 1985-86; Robert Fleming & Company, investment bank, 1986-91; Management Consultant, Bain & Company, 1992-97; Managing Director, Wolverine CIS Ltd., 1997-99; Water Industry Commissioner for Scotland, 1999-2005. Recreations: theatre; restaurants; history. Address: (b.) Water Industry Commission for Scotland, Moray House, Forthside Way, Stirling FK8 1QZ. E-mail: enquiries@watercommission.co.uk

Sutherland, David I.M., CBE, MA, MEd, DLitt, DUniv, DPhil, FCCEAM. Chief Executive/Registrar, The General Teaching Council for Scotland, 1985-2001; b. 22.1.38, Wick; m., Janet H. Webster; 2 s. Educ. Aberdeen Grammar School; Aberdeen University; University of Zurich. Teacher of Modern Languages, Aberdeen Grammar School, 1962-66; Lecturer in Education, Stranmillis College of Education, Belfast, 1966-69; Lecturer in Educational Psychology, Craigie College of Education, Ayr, 1969-72; Assistant Director of Education, Sutherland County Council, 1972-75; Divisional Education Officer (Inverness), then Depute Director of Education, Highland Regional Council, 1975-85. Chair, Gordon Cook Foundation. Recreations: golf; walking; theatre; reading. Address: Hazelwood, 5 Bonnington Road, Peebles EH45 9HF; T.-01721 722232. E-mail: disutherland@peebles1.demon.co.uk

Sutherland, Sheriff David Oman, MA, LLB. Sheriff, Wick, Dornoch, Stornoway, Inverness, since 2001; b. 24.8.50, Inverness; m., Jean Diana; 3 s.; 1 d. Educ. Morrisons Academy, Crieff; University of Edinburgh. Balfour and Manson, Edinburgh, 1973-76; Macneill and Critchley, Inverness, 1977-79; Sutherland and Co., Inverness, 1979-2001. Recreations: golf; reading. Address: Sheriff Court House, Bridge Street, Wick; T.-01955 602846.

Sutherland, Elizabeth (Elizabeth Margaret Marshall). Writer; b. 24.8.26, Kemback, Cupar; m., Rev. John D. Marshall; 2 s.; 1 d. Educ. St. Leonard's Girls' School, St. Andrews; Edinburgh University. Social Worker for Scottish Episcopal Church, 1974-80; Curator, Groam House Museum, Rosemarkie, 1982-93; author of: Lent Term (Constable Trophy), 1973, The Seer of Kintail, 1974, Hannah Hereafter (Scottish Arts Council Book Award), 1976, The Eye of God, 1977, The Weeping Tree, 1980, Ravens and Black Rain: The Story of Highland Second Sight, 1985, The Gold Key and The Green Life, 1986; In Search of the Picts, 1994; Guide to the Pictish Stones, 1997; Five Euphemias: Women in Medieval Scotland, 1999; Lydia, Wife of Hugh Miller of Cromarty, 2002; The Bird of Truth, 2006; Boniface, Bishops and Bonfires, 2010; Amendment of Life, 2010; One of the Good Guys, 2011; Spoiled Children, 2012; Of Sinks and Pulpits, 2013; The Great Triduum, 2015. Recreations: Highland history; Gaelic folklore; the Picts. Address: (h.) 17 Mackenzie Terrace, Rosemarkie, Ross-shire IV10 8UH; T.-Fortrose 620924.

Suttie, Ian A. Chairman, First Oil Expro. Career history: qualified as a Chartered Accountant with Deloitte's in Aberdeen; joined I.T.T Consumer Products, at their UK headquarters in Hastings, as Business Planning Manager; spent considerable periods in Brussels at their European headquarters; returned to Aberdeen in 1977 and held commercial positions with 3 drilling contractors before leaving Dan Smedvig as operations manager to join, as M.D., a subsidiary of the fully quoted Petrocon Group Plc; invited to join the Group Board in 1983 and completed a management buy-out of two of the subsidiaries in May 1988; over the next 13 years built the Orwell Group Plc to a turnover of £100M and employees in the excess of 600 operating in 14, fully staffed, international countries; established First Oil Plc, which is now the largest, private, UK owned company producing oil and gas in the North Sea; purchased BSW, based in Lancaster; also owns other mooring service business including Mooring Systems and First Marine Solutions. Recently acquired a Strathclyde University spin out, which has patented 'CoRMaT' tidal turbine technology. Honoured with numerous awards including: Scottish Entrepreneur of the Year in 2001, by Ernst & Young; Grampian Industrialist of the Year in 2002; the Queens Award for Industry - International Trade in 2004; the Spotlight Award at the 2009 Offshore Technology Conference in Houston and the Scottish Business Awards Entrepreneur of the Year in 2011; awarded an Honorary Doctorate by Aberdeen University in 2012. Address: First Oil plc, 1 Queen's Terrace, Aberdeen AB10 1XL; T.-01224 624666.

Swadling, Janet Diana, BA, MBA, FCIS. Acting Chief Executive, Scotland's Rural College (SRUC); b. Luton, Beds; 2 d. Educ. Icknield High School, Luton; Heriot Watt University. Institution of Electrical Engineers, London, 1983-89; The Stock Exchange, 1989-90; North West Kent College, 1990-96; SRUC, formerly SAC (The Scottish Agricultural College), since 1996. Address: (b.) SRUC, West Mains Road, Edinburgh EH9 3JG; T.-0131 535 4200; e-mail: janet.swadling@sruc.ac.uk

Swainson, Charles P., MBChB, FRCPE. Hon. Professor, University of Edinburgh, since 2007; Convener, Business Committee, General Council, University of Edinburgh, since 2012; Consultant Renal Physician, 1981-2010; Medical Director, NHS Lothian, 1998-2010; Medical Director and Vice Chair, Scottish Advisory Committee on Distinction Awards, since 2009; Treasurer, Royal College of Physicians of Edinburgh, since 2011; b. 18.5.48, Gloucester; m., Marie Irwin; 1 s. Educ. St. Edward's School, Cheltenham; Edinburgh University. Senior Lecturer, Christchurch, NZ, 1981-86; Consultant Physician, Royal Infirmary of Edinburgh, 1986-2010. Member, Lothian Children's Panel, 1987-95. Recreations: wine; golf; skiing. Address: (h.) 33 Granby Road, Edinburgh EH16 5NP.

Swan, Iain Ruairidh Cameron, MD, FRCS(Edin). Senior Lecturer in Otolaryngology, Glasgow University, since 1986; Consultant Otologist, MRC Institute of Hearing Research, since 1986; Honorary Consultant Otolaryngologist, Glasgow Royal Infirmary, since 1986; b. 19.5.52, Motherwell; m., Helen Buchanan; 1 s.; 1 d. Educ. Glasgow Academy; Glasgow University. SHO/Registrar, Glasgow, 1978-81; Clinical Research Fellow, MRC Institute of Hearing Research, 1981; Senior Registrar in Otolaryngology, Glasgow, 1981-86; clinical attachment, University of Tubingen, 1984-85. Examiner, Final Fellowship, Royal College of Surgeons of Edinburgh and Royal College of Physicians and Surgeons, Glasgow. Recreations: bridge; opera; mountain biking. Address: (b.) Department of Otolaryngology, Royal Infirmary, Glasgow G31 2ER; T.-0141-211 4695; e-mail: iain@ihr.gla.ac.uk

Swan, Jeanna, DL. Lord-Lieutenant for Berwickshire, since 2014. Formerly a senior partner in a large veterinary practice in the Scottish eastern borders region; trustee of the MacRobert Trust since 2001; formerly Deputy Lord-

Lieutenant for Berwickshire. Member of South Lammermuir riding club; interested in farming and the local community. Address: Scottish Borders Council, Council Headquarters, Newtown St. Boswells, Melrose TD6 0SA; T.-01835 825005.

Swanson, Alexander James Grenville, MB, ChB, FRCS Edin. Consultant Orthopaedic Surgeon, 1980-2001; Honorary Senior Lecturer, University of Dundee, since 2001; b. 18.10.41, Ecclefechan; 2 s. Educ. Dingwall Academy; St. Andrews University. Postgraduate training: St. Andrews, 1967-68, Edinburgh, 1968-69, Glasgow, 1969-70, Edinburgh, 1970-74, Dunfermline, 1974-75; Lecturer, then Senior Lecturer and Honorary Consultant, Dundee University, 1975-83. Recreations: downhill skiing; cross-country skiing; travel. Address: (h.) 9 Roxburgh Terrace, Dundee DD2 1NX.

Swapp, George David, OBE, DL, MA (Hons), DipEd. Deputy Lieutenant, Kincardineshire, 1990-2006; Member Aberdeenshire Council, 1995-2007; b. 25.5.31, Labuan; m., Eva Jane MacNab; 2 s.; 2 d. Educ. Mackie Academy, Stonehaven; Aberdeen University. RAF Staff College, graduate and directing staff, 1965-68; Ministry of Defence (Training Policy), 1971-74 and 1978-80; promoted Wing Commander, 1971; Board Chairman, RAF Officer and Aircrew Selection Centre, 1974-78; Head, RAF Officer Training Establishment, Bracknell, 1980-83; retired from RAF, 1983. Former Member, Grampian Regional Council, 1986-96; Founder Member, Stonehaven Heritage Society; Dunnottar Woodland Park Association. Recreations: hill-walking; local history; travel; geography; protection and enhancement of amenities and woodlands. Address: (h.) 9 Urie Crescent, Stonehaven AB39 2DY; T.-Stonehaven 764124.

Sweeney, Brian Philip, QFSM, MA, FIFireE, HonPhD, DipEFEng. Columnist, Evening Times; formerly Chief Officer and Chief Executive, Strathclyde Fire and Rescue; b. 14.7.61, Glasgow; m., Pamela; 3 s. Educ. Holyrood Academy; University of Coventry; Glasgow Caledonian University. Former Surveyor; joined Strathclyde Fire Brigade, 1981; served in Glasgow and was promoted on three occasions, becoming Station Officer in 1989; promoted to Divisional Commander in 1998, then Director of Operations in 2000, then Deputy Chief in 2003. Member: Institution of Fire Engineers, Chief Fire Officers Association. Recreations: reading and music. Address: Evening Times, 200 Renfield Street, Glasgow G2 3QB.

Sweeney, Jim, MSc, DipYCS, FRSA. Chief Executive, YouthLink Scotland, since 2006; b. 5.6.53; m., Elizabeth; 2 s. Educ. Jordanhill (Diploma in Youth and Community Work); Strathclyde University (Masters Degree). Worked in local government in Lanark and Ayr, including Community Learning & Development Manager, North Lanarkshire, 1996-2006. Current appointments: member of Duke of Edinburgh Scottish Advisory Committee; CLD Standards Council for Scotland, Executive member; Vice Chair of Young Scot and Scotland's Learning Partnership; member of BIG Lottery Expert Advisory Panels for Young Start and Realising Ambition programmes; member of Scottish Leaders Forum; member of National Economic Forum; member of Third Sector Employability Forum; member of National CLD Steering Group and Co-Chair, National Youth Work Strategy Stakeholder Reference Group. Recreations: football; golf; bowling; reading; travel; cooking; music; malt whisky and wine appreciation; public speaking and voluntary work with Mary's Meals. Address: (b.) Rosebery House, 9 Haymarket Terrace, Edinburgh EH12 5EZ; T.-0131 313 2488.
E-mail: jsweeney@youthlinkscotland.org

Sweeney, Professor William John, DRSAM, ARAM. Composer, since 1974; Professor of Music, formerly Head of Department of Music, University of Glasgow; b. 05.01.50, Glasgow; m., Susannah Conway; 1 s.; 1 d. Educ. Knightswood Senior Secondary School; RSAMD; RAM. Teacher of Clarinet and Woodwind, Central Region, 1975-85; Performer, 1973-95, 2010; Lecturer, University of Glasgow, since 1997. National Executive Committee, Musicians Union, 1989-2004; Chair of EC, 2003; BAFTA (Scotland) Award for Best Music, 1997, Creative Scotland Award, 2005, British Composer Award (BASCA/Radio 3), 2011. Recreations: reading; walking; supporting Partick Thistle. Address: (h.) 4 Stonefield Avenue, Glasgow G12 0JF; T.-0141-579-4789.
E-mail: William.Sweeney@glasgow.ac.uk

Swinburne, John. MSP (SSCUP), Central Scotland, 2003-07; former Director, Motherwell Football Club (1999-2015); former Director/Company Secretary, A.D.S. Ltd (2008-2012); b. 4.7.30, Throop, USA; m., Moira Baird; 3 s.; 1 d. Educ. Dalziel High School, Motherwell. Engineer, 1947-77; freelance journalist, 1977-79; Commercial Manager, Motherwell Football Club, 1980-2003; Founder and Leader of the Scottish Senior Citizens Party and the first ever Member of Parliament in the UK representing pensioners. Author of three books on Motherwell F.C; 1st Novel, The Homecoming, published June 2012. Recreation: football. Address: (h.) 65 Derwentwater, East Kilbride G75 8JT; T.-01355 228501; e-mail: john774@btinternet.com

Swingler, Robert James, MD, FRCP (Edin., Lond.) Consultant Neurologist, Department of Neurology, NHS Tayside Acute Services Division, Ninewells Hospital and Medical School, Dundee; b. 4.7.56, London; 1 s.; 3 d. Educ. Wandsworth School; Guy's Hospital, University of London. Lecturer in Neurology, University of Edinburgh, 1987-90; Senior Registrar, Neurology, Dundee Royal Infirmary, 1990-95; MRC Travelling Fellow, Harvard University, 1992-93. Address: (b.) NHS Tayside Acute Services Division, Ninewells Hospital and Medical School, Dundee DD1 9SY; T.-01382 660111.
E-mail: robert.swingler@nhs.net

Swinney, John Ramsay, MA (Hons). MSP (SNP), Perthshire North, since 2011, North Tayside, 1999-2011; Deputy First Minister of Scotland, since 2014; Cabinet Secretary for Education and Skills, since 2016; Cabinet Secretary for Finance, Constitution and Economy, 2007-2016; Shadow Minister for Finance and Public Service Reform, 2005-07; Leader, Scottish National Party, 2000-04; Leader of the Opposition, Scottish Parliament, 2000-04; MP (SNP), North Tayside, 1997-2001; b. 13.4.64, Edinburgh; m., Elizabeth Quigley; 2 s.; 1 d. Educ. Forrester High School, Edinburgh; Edinburgh University. Research Officer, Scottish Coal Project, 1987-88; Senior Managing Consultant, Development Options Ltd., 1998-92; Strategic Planning Principal, Scottish Amicable, 1992-97. SNP Treasury Spokesman, 1995-99; Deputy Leader, Scottish National Party, 1998-2000; Shadow Minister for Enterprise and Lifelong Learning, 1999-2000. Convener, Enterprise and Lifelong Learning Committee (Scottish Parliament), 1999-2000; Convener, European and External Relations Committee, 2004-05. Recreation: hill-walking. Address: (b.) 17-19 Leslie Street, Blairgowrie PH10 6AH; T.-01250 876576.

Swinson, Jo. MP (Liberal Democrat), Dunbartonshire East, 2005-2015; Minister for Employment Relations, Consumer and Postal Affairs, Department for Business, Innovation and Skills, 2012-15; Minister for Women and Equalities, Department of Culture, Media and Sport, 2012-

2015; b. 5.2.80; m., Duncan Hames; 1 s. Educ. Douglas Academy, Milngavie; London School of Economics. Formerly Marketing Manager for a number of companies, latterly the Glasgow-based company SpaceandPeople; helped the company win awards including Best E-Business at the Scottish Winners at the Web Awards, 2003; Chair, Liberal Democrats' Campaign for Gender Balance, 2006-08; Liberal Democrat Shadow Foreign Affairs Minister, 2008-2010; Deputy Leader, Scottish Liberal Democrats, 2011; Parliamentary Private Secretary to: Vince Cable, 2011-2012, Deputy Prime Minister Nick Clegg, 2012. Recreations: running; reading; hiking; ceilidh dancing.

Swinton, Major General Sir John, KCVO, OBE. Lord Lieutenant, Berwickshire, 1989-2000; Queen's Bodyguard for Scotland (Royal Company of Archers), since 1977 (Captain, 2003-07); President, Borders Branch, SSAFA, 1993-2006; Trustee, Scottish National War Memorial, 1988-2009 (Chairman, 1995-2009); President, Berwickshire Civic Society, 1996-2005 (Chairman, 1982-96); Chairman, Berwickshire Recreation Sports Trust, 1997-2005; Trustee, The Scots at War Trust, 1996-2009; Trustee, Berwick Military Tattoo, 1996-2007; Patron, POWER, 1995-2009; b. 21.4.25, London; m., Judith Balfour Killen (deceased); 3 s.; 1 d. Educ. Harrow School. Enlisted Scots Guards, 1943; commissioned, 1944; served NW Europe (twice wounded); Malaya, 1948-51 (Despatches); ADC to Field Marshal Sir William Slim, Governor General of Australia, 1953-54; Regimental Adjutant, Scots Guards, 1960-62; Adjutant, RMA, Sandhurst, 1962-64; comd. 2nd Bn., Scots Guards, 1966-68; Lt.-Col. commanding Scots Guards, 1970-71; Commander, 4th Guards Armoured Brigade, BAOR, 1972-73; Brigadier, Lowlands and Commander, Edinburgh and Glasgow Garrisons, 1975-76; GOC London District and Major General comd. Household Division, 1976-79. Honorary Colonel, 2nd Bn., 52nd Lowland Volunteers, 1983-90; President, Lowland TA & VRA, 1992-96; National Chairman, Royal British Legion Scotland, 1986-89; Coordinator for Scotland, Duke of Edinburgh's Award 25th Anniversary Appeal, 1980 (Honorary Liaison Officer for the Borders, 1983-85); Chairman, Roxburgh and Berwickshire Conservative Association, 1983-85; Chairman, Thirlestane Castle Trust, 1984-90; Trustee, Army Museums Ogilby Trust, 1978-91; Council Member, Commonwealth Ex-Services League, 1984-98; Member, Central Advisory Committee on War Pensions, 1986-89; Chairman, St. Abbs Head National Nature Reserve Joint Management Committee, 1991-98; President, Royal Highland and Agricultural Society of Scotland, 1993-94; President, Berwickshire Naturalists Club, 1996-97; Chairman, Scottish National Motorsport Collection, 1998-2001. Address: (h.) Kimmerghame, Duns, Berwickshire; T.-01361 883277; e-mail: kimmerghame@amserve.com

Swinton, Professor John, PhD, BD, RMN, RNMH. Professor in Practical Theology and Pastoral Care, Aberdeen University, since 1997; Honorary Professor, Centre for Advanced Nursing, Aberdeen University, since 1999; b. 20.10.57; m., Alison; 2 s.; 3 d. Educ. Summerhill Academy, Aberdeen; Aberdeen University. Registered nurse, 1976-90; Aberdeen University, 1990-97; Lecturer in Practical Theology, Glasgow University, 1997. Address: (b.) School of Divinity, Religious Studies and Philosophy, King's College, Old Aberdeen, Aberdeen AB24 3UB; T.-01224 273224.

Swinton, Tilda. Award-winning British actress known for both arthouse and mainstream films; b. 5.11.60, London; partner, Sandro Kopp; 2 c. Educ. Queen's Gate School, London; West Heath Girls' School; Fettes College; New Hall (now known as Murray Edwards College), Cambridge University. Worked with the Traverse Theatre in Edinburgh, starring in Mann ist Mann by Manfred Karge, and the Royal Shakespeare Company, before embarking on a career in film in the mid-1980s; developed a performance/installation live art piece in the Serpentine Gallery, London in 1995 (on display to the public for a week, asleep or apparently so, in a glass case, as a piece of performance art); has appeared in a number of films, including Burn After Reading, The Beach, The Chronicles of Narnia, and was nominated for a Golden Globe for performances in The Deep End and We Need to Talk About Kevin. Won the Academy Award for Best Supporting Actress for her performance in Michael Clayton in 2007.

Sykes, Diana Antoinette, MA (Hons). Director, Fife Contemporary Art & Craft (formerly Crawford Arts Centre), since 1988; b. 12.9.59, Stirling. Educ. Stirling High School; University of St. Andrews; University of Manchester; Sweet Briar College, USA. Chair, Scottish Arts Council Exhibitions Panel, 1995-97; Member, St. Andrews Youth Theatre Board, 1991-2001; Chair, Management Committee, Mobile Projects Association Scotland, 1986-88; Trustee of the Barns-Graham Charitable Trust, 2005-2013; Member of steering group for Off the Rails Arthouse and of Lateral Lab. Recreations: travel; arts and museums and heritage. Address: (b.) FCA & C, The Town Hall, Queen's Gardens, St. Andrews KY16 9TA; T.-01334 474610; e-mail: diana.sykes@fcac.co.uk

Symington, Rev. Alastair Henderson, MA, BD. Minister Emeritus, Troon Old Parish Church; Chaplain to The Queen in Scotland, since 1996; b. 15.4.47, Edinburgh; m., Eileen Margaret Jenkins; 2 d. Educ. Daniel Stewart's College, Edinburgh; Edinburgh University; Tubingen University, West Germany. Assistant Minister, Wellington Church, Glasgow, 1971-72; Chaplain, RAF, 1972-76; Minister: Craiglockhart Parish Church, Edinburgh, 1976-85, New Kilpatrick Parish Church, Bearsden, 1985-98, Troon Old Parish Church, 1998-2012; Locum Minister, Galston Parish Church, since 2013; Convener, Committee on Chaplains to HM Forces, 1989-93; Vice-Convener, Board of Practice and Procedure, 2002-05; Convener, Committee on Presbytery Boundaries, 1999-2004; Moderator, Presbytery of Dumbarton, 1992; Moderator, Presbytery of Ayr, 2012 and 2013. Contributor, Scottish Liturgical Review. Publications: Westminster Church Sermons, 1984; Reader's Digest Family Guide to the Bible (Co-author), 1985; For God's Sake, Ask!, 1993. Recreations: golf; rugby; music; France; wines. Address: 1 Cavendish Place, Troon KA10 6JG; T.-01292 312556; e-mail: revdahs@btinternet.com

Symon, Ken. Editor, Scottish Business Insider, since 2016; Tai Chi Teacher, Rising Spring Tai Chi, since 2012; Founding Director, Symon Media Ltd, since 2009, Managing Director, since 2009. Educ. University of Strathclyde. Career history: Industrial Correspondent, Evening Times, 1988-95; Deputy Editor, The Sunday Times Scotland, 1995-98; Business Editor, The Scotsman, 1998-2000; Owner, Simple Communication, 2000-03; Business Editor, Sunday Herald, 2003-07; Business Development Director, McGarvie Morrison Media, 2007-09; Head of Business Engagement, Better Together Ltd, May 2014-September 2014. Fellow of the Royal Society for the encouragement of Arts, Manufactures and Commerce (RSA). Address: Scottish Business Insider, 7 Castle Street, Edinburgh EH2 3AH; T.-020 7293 3000.
E-mail: editor@insider.co.uk

T

Tait, A. Margaret, MBE, BSc. Vice-President, International Federation of University Women, Geneva; Member, St. Margaret's Chapel Guild, Edinburgh Castle; Member, Egyptology Scotland, Royal Caledonian Horticultural Society and Royal Horticultural Society; Member, British Federation of Women Graduates; Member, Lothian Pharmacy Practice Committee; b. 8.10.44, Edinburgh; m., J. Haldane Tait; 1 d. Educ. George Watson's Ladies' College, Edinburgh; Edinburgh University; Jordanhill College of Education. Former Teacher of Mathematics, Bellahouston Academy, Glasgow; former Member, Lothian Children's Panel; former Honorary Secretary, Scottish Association of Children's Panels; former Chairman, Dean House Children's Home, Edinburgh; Volunteer, Edinburgh Citizens' Advice Bureau; formerly Secretary of State's Nominee to General Teaching Council; former Member, Scottish Legal Aid Board; former Member, Lothian Health Council; former Vice Chairman, Lothian Healthy Volunteers and Student Research Modules Ethics Committee; former General Council Assessor, University of Edinburgh Court. Recreations: golf; horticulture; Spanish; playing bridge. Address: (h.) 6 Ravelston House Park, Edinburgh EH4 3LU; T.-0131-332 6795; e-mail: margarettait@me.com

Tait, Professor Elizabeth Joyce, CBE, FRSE, DUniv (Open), PhD, BSc, FSRA. Director, Innogen Institute, Edinburgh University, since 2014; Director, ESRC Innogen Centre, Edinburgh University, 2002-07; b. 19.02.38, Edinburgh; m., Dr. Alec Tait; 1 s.; 2 d. Educ. Glasgow High School for Girls; Glasgow University; Cambridge University. Career History: Lecturer, then Senior Lecturer, Technology Faculty, Open University; Professor, Environmental and Technology Management, University of Strathclyde; Deputy Director, Research and Advisory Services, Scottish Natural Heritage; Director, Scottish Universities Policy Research and Advice Centre (SUPRA), Edinburgh University. Member: Governing Council, Roslin Institute; UK Department of Health Emerging Sciences and Bioethics Advisory Committee (ESBAC), 2012-14; UK Synthetic Biology Leadership Council; John Innes Centre Science and Impact Advisory Board. Recreations: gardening; hill walking. Address: (b.) Innogen Institute, Old Surgeons Hall, High School Yards, Edinburgh EH1 1LZ; T.-0131 650 9174; e-mail: joyce.tait@ed.ac.uk

Tait, Stuart R., LLB (Hons), DipLP (Aberdeen). Partner, CMS Cameron McKenna LLP, since 2014; Partner, Dundas & Wilson CS LLP, 1995-2014; b. 22.8.63, Edinburgh; divorced; 1 s.; 1 d. Educ. Fettes College, Edinburgh; Aberdeen University. Trained at Dundas & Wilson, 1986-88; Seconded to Linklaters & Paines, London, 1990-91. Member of the Scottish Board, Investment Property Forum. Recreations: swimming; cycling; curling; travel. Address: (b.) Saltire Court, 20 Castle Terrace, Edinburgh EH1 2EN; T.-0131-228 8000; e-mail: stuart.tait@cms-cmck.com

Tait, Rev. Thomas William, MBE, BD, RAFVR (Rtd). Parish Minister, Rattray, Blairgowrie, 1972-97; Corps Chaplain, Royal Air Force Air Cadets (UK), 2002-2010; b. 11.11.31, Dunfermline; m., Irene Pope; 1 s.; 2 d. Educ. Dunfermline High School; St. Colm's College, Edinburgh; Edinburgh University; Christ's College, Aberdeen; Aberdeen University. HQ Staff, Boys' Brigade, 1954-61; Missionary, Church of Scotland, South Arabia, 1962-67; ordained and inducted, 1972; Member, Assembly Council, 1984-88; Chaplain, 2519 (Strathmore) Squadron, Air Training Corps, since 1974; Chaplain, Dundee and Central Scotland Wing, ATC, 1978-96; Principal Chaplain, Scotland and Northern Ireland, Air Training Corps, 1996-2002; awarded Defence Council Letter of Appreciation for Services to Air Cadet Organisation, 1999; Chairman, Blairgowrie Schools Council, 1975-89; Member, Perth and Kinross Health Council, 1980-91 (Chairman, 1984-91); Chairman, Tayside Health Council, 1992-98; Chairman, Blairgowrie and District Branch, Royal British Legion Scotland, 1992-97, and Chaplain, Angus and Perthshire Area, 1994-99; commissioned RAFVR, 1977 (retired Flt. Lt., 1988); Moderator, Dunkeld and Meigle Presbytery, 1978; awarded Lord Lieutenant's Certificate for Meritorious Service to ATC, 1985; Member, Secretary of State's Consultative Panel on Registration of Nursing Homes and Private Hospitals, 1993-97; Member, Tayside Health Board Quality Monitoring Team, 1993-98; Member, Scottish Office Nursing Homes Standards Steering Group, 1994-97; Member, Chaplain's Committee, Air Cadet Council (UK), since 1996; Member, CRAG (Clinical Research and Audit Group), 1997-98; Member, Multi Research Ethics Committee for Scotland, 1997-2001; Convener, Scottish Association of Health Councils, 1997-98; Member, Advocacy Team, State Hospital, Carstairs, 1998-2014; Member, Independent Advocacy Perth & Kinross, since 2014; Member, Air Cadet Council, since 2002; Member, Air Cadet Organisation Management Board, since 2005; appointed a Member of the Most Excellent Order of the British Empire in 2011 for services to the Air Training Corps. Recreations: encouraging others to work in voluntary organisations; swimming; reading; overseas travel. Address: 3 Rosemount Park, Blairgowrie PH10 6TZ; T.-01250 874833; e-mail: tw.tait@virgin.net

Tallach, Rev. James Ross, MB, ChB. Free Presbyterian Minister, Stornoway, since 2009; Assistant Clerk of Synod, since 2006; b. Tighnabruaich, Argyll; m., Mairi McCuish Martin; 2 d. Educ. Nicolson Institute, Stornoway; Aberdeen University. House jobs in surgery, medicine and obstetrics, Inverness, Aberdeen, and Bellshill, 1967-69; Medical Missionary, Mbuma, Zimbabwe, 1969-76; training for ministry, 1976-80; ordained medical missionery, Mbuma, 1980-83. Moderator of Synod, 1996; Clerk to Foreign Mission Committee of F.P. Church, since 1989; Convener, Church Home, Inverness, since 2001; Convener, Training of Ministry Committee, since 2004. Recreations: gardening; walking. Address: Free Presbyterian Manse, 2 Fleming Place, Stornoway, Isle of Lewis HS1 2NH; T.-01851 702501. E-mail: jrtallach@btinternet.com

Tams, Professor Christian Jakob, State Exam (Law), LLM, PhD (Cantab). Professor of International Law, University of Glasgow, since 2008; b. 18.7.73, Hamburg, Germany. Educ. Martino Katharineum; University of Kiel; University of Lyon; University of Cambridge. Assistant Professor, University of Kiel (Germany), 2005-09. Various publications on International Law; member of the Royal Society of Edinburgh Young Academy and of the The German Court of Arbitration for Sport. Recreations: naval fiction; maritime history. Address: University of Glasgow, School of Law, Glasgow G12 8QQ; T.-0141 3305184; e-mail: christian.tams@glasgow.ac.uk

Tanner, Professor (Kathleen) Elizabeth, FRSE, FREng, FBSE, MA, DPhil, FIMMM, FIMechE, CEng, CSci. Professor of Biomedical Materials, University of Glasgow, since 2007; Adjunct (Visiting) Professor of Biomechanics and Biomaterials, Lund University, Sweden, since 1998; b. 20.3.57, Farnham. Educ. Wycombe Abbey; Lady Margaret Hall, Oxford. University of London: Research Assistant, Department of Materials, Queen Mary College, 1983-88; Advanced Research Fellow, Queen Mary and Westfield College, 1988-93, Lecturer, Department of Materials and IRC in Biomedical Materials, 1993-95, Reader in Biomaterials and Biomechanics, Department of Materials and IRC in Biomedical Materials, 1995-98; Co-Head of the Biomechanics Laboratory, Department of Orthopaedics, Lund University, Sweden, 1998-2001; Dean of

Engineering, Queen Mary and Westfield College, University of London, 1999-2000, Professor of Biomedical Materials, Department of Materials, 1998-2007. Founder Member and First President (2000), UK Society for Biomaterials; Secretary of European Society for Biomaterials, 2005-09. Recreations: riding; tennis; cookery; dressmaking. Address: (b.) James Watt South Building, University of Glasgow, Glasgow G12 8QQ; T.- 0141 330 3733; e-mail: elizabeth.tanner@glasgow.ac.uk

Tanner, Susanne Lesley Murning, LLB (Hons), DipLP, MCIArb. Advocate Depute, since 2011; Advocate, since 2000; b. 29.10.74, Stirling; m., David Henderson Tanner; 1 s. Educ. George Watson's College, Edinburgh; Edinburgh University. Solicitor, Burness Solicitors, Edinburgh, 1997-99; Tutor, Criminal Court Practice, University of Edinburgh, since 2008; Lecturer, Evidence, Edinburgh Napier University, since 2006; Assistant on Master's Court, Merchant Company of Edinburgh, since 2004; Governor, Governing Council, George Watson's College, since 2010. Address: (b.) Advocates' Library, Parliament House, Parliament Square, Edinburgh EH1 1RF; T.-0131 226 5071. E-mail: susannetanner@hotmail.com

Tartaglia, Most Rev. Philip, PhB, STD. Archbishop of Glasgow, since 2012; b. 11.1.51, Glasgow. Educ. St. Mungo's Academy, Glasgow; St. Vincent's College, Langbank; St Mary's College, Blairs, near Aberdeen; Pontifical Scots College and the Pontifical Gregorian University in Rome. Ordained priest by Archbishop Thomas Winning in the Church of Our Lady of Good Counsel, Dennistoun on 30 June 1975; moved to Rome in 1976 and later started research for doctorate in Sacred Theology; Acting Vice-Rector, the Scots College in Rome, then Dean of Studies in 1978; obtained STD degree in 1980, then became Assistant priest at Our Lady of Lourdes, Cardonald, while at the same time becoming an extramural lecturer at St. Peter's College, Newlands, Glasgow; appointed lecturer at St. Peter's College in 1981, becoming director of studies in 1983; became Vice-Rector, Chesters College, Bearsden in 1985, then Rector, 1987-93; sent to St. Patrick's, Dumbarton as assistant priest before being appointed parish priest of St Mary's, Duntocher in 1995; returned to seminary as Rector of the Pontifical Scots College, Rome in 2004; Bishop of Paisley, 2005-2012. Address: 196 Clyde Street, Glasgow G1 4JY; T.-0141 226 5898.

Tasker, Moira, MA (Hons), MSc, FRSA. Former Director, The Cockburn Association (The Edinburgh Civic Trust); Chief Executive, Citizens Advice Edinburgh, 2009-2015. Educ. Bell Baxter High School, Cupar, Fife; University of Edinburgh; Heriot-Watt University. Member, Cross Party Group on Volunteering and the Voluntary Sector of Scottish Parliament; Member, Management Committee, The Edinburgh Trust; Member, Management Committee, Scottish Local History Forum. Recreations: travel; Russian culture.

Tate, Professor Austin, BA (Hons), MSc, PhD, CEng, FAAAI, FBCS, FBIS, FREng, FRSE. Director, AIAI (Artificial Intelligence Applications Institute), since 1985; Chair in Knowledge-Based Systems, University of Edinburgh, since 1995; Co-ordinator, Virtual University of Edinburgh (Vue); Co-ordinator for Distance Education; b. 12.5.51, Knottingley, West Yorkshire; m., Margaret Mowbray. Educ. King's School, Pontefract; Lancaster University; Edinburgh University. Address: (b.) AIAI, School of Informatics, University of Edinburgh, Informatics Forum, Crichton Street, Edinburgh EH8 9AB; T.-0131-651 3222.

Tavener, Alan, MA, MSc, ARCO, ARCM, HonARSCM. Artistic Director, Cappella Nova, since 1982; Director of Music, Jordanhill Parish Church, Glasgow; freelance Musical Director and Consultant; Director of Music,

University of Strathclyde, until 2012; b. 22.4.57, Weston-Super-Mare; m., Rebecca Jane Gibson. Educ. City of Bath Boys' School; Brasenose College, Oxford; University of Strathclyde. Conducted several world premieres of choral works and several CDs of early, romantic and contemporary music. Recreations: architecture; Italy; Scottish country dancing; food and drink. T.-0141 552 0634; e-mail: alan.cappella-nova@strath.ac.uk

Tavener, Rebecca Jane. Soprano; Creative Director, Cappella Nova; b. 3.5.58, Trowbridge; m., Alan Tavener. Co-founded Cappella Nova, 1982; Concert Manager, Glasgow University, 1983-89; Founder and Director, Chorus International, 1990-94; founded Canty (medieval vocal ensemble), 1998; launched new early music consortium for Scotland, 1998; launched own recording label, ROTA, 1998. Recreations: Italophilia; retail therapy; gourmandising; reading history books. Address: (h.) 35 Crosbie Street, Glasgow G20 0BQ; T.-(b.) 0141-552 0634; e-mail: cappella.nova@strath.ac.uk

Taylor, Rev. Baker Stephen Covington, BA (Hons), BBS, MA, MDiv, FSA Scot. Minister, Kirk of St. Nicholas Uniting, Aberdeen (The City Church), since 2005; b. 1.12.58, Kountze, Texas, United States; m., The Rev. Gillian R. Trew. Educ. Temple High School; Temple College, Texas; University of Texas; Abilene Christian University; Austin Presbyterian Theological Seminary. Associate Minister, University Avenue Church of Christ, Austin, 1984-85; Lecturer, Abilene Christian University, 1986-89; Minister: Lee Green United Reformed Church, London, 1990-2005, Geddes Place United Reformed Church, Bexleyheath, Kent, 1990-94, Bromley United Reformed Church, Kent, 1994-2005. Chairperson, Friends of The Kirk of St. Nicholas; Governor, Robert Gordon's College; Honorary Chaplain, University of Aberdeen; Admiral, Texas Navy; Associate Member, Iona Community; Church Service Society; Scottish Church Society; Fellow, Society of Antiquaries of Scotland; Burgess of Guild of the City of Aberdeen. Recreations: numismatics; vexillology; Gaelic studies; archaeology. Address: (h.) The Manse, 12 Louisville Avenue, Aberdeen AB15 4TX; T.-01224 314318; e-mail: minister@kirk-of-st-nicholas.org.uk

Taylor, Brian, MA (Hons). Political Editor, BBC Scotland; b. 9.1.55, Dundee; m., Pamela Moira Niven; 2 s. Educ. High School of Dundee; St. Andrews University. Reporter, Press and Journal, Aberdeen, 1977-80; Lobby Correspondent, Thomson Regional Newspapers, Westminster, 1980-85; Reporter, BBC Scotland, Glasgow, 1985-86; Co-Presenter, Left, Right and Centre, BBC Scotland, 1986-88; Political Correspondent, BBC Scotland, 1988-90. DLitt, Napier University; DLitt, Abertay University; LLD, Dundee University. Publications: The Scottish Parliament, 1999; Scotland's Parliament: Triumph and Disaster, 2002. Recreations: golf; theatre. Address: (b.) BBC Scotland, Pacific Quay, Glasgow G51 1DA.

Taylor, Emma. Headteacher, Stromness Academy, since 2015; former Headteacher, Farr High School (2013-15). Address: Stromness Academy, Stromness, Orkney KW16 3JS; T.-01856 850660.

Taylor, Rev. Ian, BSc, MA, LTh, DipEd. Lecturer on music and the arts, broadcaster, opera director; b. 12.10.32, Dundee; m., Joy Coupar, LRAM; 2 s.; 1 d. Educ. Dundee High School; St. Andrews University; Durham University; Sheffield University; Edinburgh University. Teacher, Mathematics Department, Dundee High School; Lecturer in Mathematics, Bretton Hall College of Education; Senior Lecturer in Education, College of Ripon and York St. John; Assistant Minister, St. Giles' Cathedral, Edinburgh; Minister, Abdie & Dunbog and Newburgh, 1983-97; Moderator, Presbytery of St. Andrews, 1995-96; Secretary, History of Education Society, 1968-73; extensive work in adult education (appreciation of music and the arts); Director, Summer Schools in Music, St. Andrews University; numerous courses for St. Andrews, Edinburgh, Cambridge and Hull Universities and WEA; has played principal roles in opera and operetta; Director, Gilbert and Sullivan Society of Edinburgh, 1979-87; Director, Tayside Opera, 1999; compiled Theatre Music Quiz series, Radio Tay; presented own operetta, My Dear Gilbert...My Dear Sullivan, BBC; Writer of revues and documentary plays with music, including Tragic Queen (Mary Queen of Scots), St. Giles' Cathedral, Edinburgh Festival Fringe, 1982, and John Knox (Church of Scotland Video); President, East Neuk of Fife Probus Club, 2007-08. Publications: How to Produce Concert Versions of Gilbert Sullivan; The Gilbert and Sullivan Quiz Book; The Opera Lover's Quiz Book; Maths for Mums and Dads. Address: Lundie Cottage, Arncroach, Fife KY10 2RN; T.-01333 720 222; e-mail: ian.taylor@tesco.net

Taylor, James Alastair, BSc, LLB, LLD. Chairman, The Review into the Expenses and Funding of Civil Litigation in Scotland, 2011-13; Chairman, The Disciplinary Board of The Institute of Chartered Accountants of Scotland; b. 21.2.51, Inverness; m., Lesley Macleod; 2 s. Educ. Nairn Academy; Aberdeen University. Apprenticed to Brander & Cruickshank, Advocates in Aberdeen, 1975-77; apprenticed to, Assistant with, Lefevre & Co., Advocates in Aberdeen, 1977-78; Assistant, later Partner, A.C. Morrison & Richards, Advocates in Aberdeen, 1978-87; Partner and latterly Head of Litigation Department, McGrigor Donald, 1988-98; attained rights of audience in Supreme Courts in Scotland, 1993; Sheriff of Lothian and Borders at Edinburgh, 1998; Sheriff of Glasgow and Strathkelvin, 1999-2005; Sheriff Principal of Glasgow and Strathkelvin at Glasgow, 2005-2011. Designated one of the sheriffs to hear commercial actions, 1999; Member of The Board of The Civil Courts Review, 2007-09; Director of Lodging House Mission, 2002-2012; Visiting Professor of Law, Strathclyde University, 2007-2013. Publications: International Intellectual Property Litigation (Contributor); Sentencing Practice (Contributor); Macphail's Sheriff Court Practice, 3rd Edn (Contributor). Recreations: golf; music; good food and wine.
E-mail: jtaylor210@btinternet.com

Taylor, James Bradley, OBE, FRIN. Chairman of the Board of the Scottish Public Pensions Agency, since 2007; Board Member, Scottish Ballet, 2005-2012; Chair, Scotland's Lighthouse Museum, 2005-2011; IoD Faculty Member, since 2005; Board Member, Eastgate Theatre, 2006-2011; Younger Brother of Trinity House, since 1991; Board Member, Mull of Kintyre Seatours, since 2004; Nautical Assessor to the Court of Session, since 1996; Freeman of the City of London; High Constable of the Port of Leith; Vice President, Royal Institute of Navigation, since 2012, Fellow (FRIN) and Member of Council, since 2009; Chairman, Eastgate Theatre, 2010-2012; b. 12.8.45, Paisley; m., Elizabeth Sherwood. Educ. George Watson's College, Edinburgh; Britannia Royal Naval College; Defence School of Languages; Royal Naval College Greenwich; Royal College of Defence Studies. Chief Executive, Northern Lighthouse Board, 1993-2006; Community Councillor, Eddleston, 1999-2005, and since 2012; Royal Navy, 1963-93; commanded: HM Submarines Grampus, 1974-75; Orpheus, 1975-77; Spartan, 1980-82; HM Ship London, 1989-90; Chief of Staff, Submarine Flotilla, 1990-92; Member, Royal College of Defence Studies, 1992. Recreations: country sports; history; music and dance; classic cars; travel. Address: Stewarton House, Eddleston, Peebles EH45 8PP.

Taylor, Rt. Rev. John Mitchell, MA. Bishop of Glasgow and Galloway, retired 1998; b. 23.5.32, Aberdeen; m., Edna

Elizabeth Maitland; 1 s.; 1 d. Educ. Banff Academy; Aberdeen University; Theological College, Edinburgh. Curate, St. Margaret's, Aberdeen; Rector: Holy Cross, Knightswood, Glasgow, St. Ninian's, Pollokshields, Glasgow, St. John the Evangelist, Dumfries; Canon, St. Mary's Cathedral, Glasgow. Recreations: angling; hill-walking; sketching; music. Address: (h.) 85 Lord Lyell Drive, Kinnordy View, Kirriemuir DD8 4LF.

Taylor, Malcolm John, TD, DL, MA, FRICS. Chartered Surveyor/Land Agent; Director, Bell Ingram; b. 21.11.61, Glasgow; m., Helen McKay; 2 s. Educ. Dumfries Academy; Aberdeen University. Chairman, RICS in Scotland, 2004-05. Recreations: field sports; music; natural history. Address: (b.) Bell Ingram, Manor Street, Forfar; T.-01307 462516.

Taylor, Margie, MSc, MBA, FDSRCSEd, FDSRCPS(Glasg), FFPHM, FFGDP (UK). Chief Dental Officer, Scottish Government; Honorary Senior Lecturer, Glasgow University; Dundee University; b. Edinburgh. Educ. James Gillespie's High School for Girls; Edinburgh University; Heriot-Watt University. Consultant in dental public health, NHS Lanarkshire, 1994-2007; formerly Chief Administrative Dental Officer, Fife Health Board, and Honorary Senior Lecturer, St. Andrews University. Board Member, Health Scotland; Past President, Royal Odonto-Chirurgical Society of Scotland. Address: (b.) Scottish Government, Room IR.08, St. Andrew's House, Regent Road, Edinburgh EH1 3DG.

Taylor, Martin, MBE, DUniv (Paisley). Guitarist/ Composer, since 1972; b. 20.10.56, Harlow, Essex; m., Elizabeth Kirk; 2 s. Educ. Passmores Comprehensive School, Harlow. Self-taught guitarist (began playing aged four); became professional musician at 15, touring UK, Europe and USA; solo recording debut, 1978 (for Wave Records); toured world with Stephane Grappelli, 1979-90; recorded eight solo albums for Linn Records, 1990s, becoming biggest selling British jazz recording artist in the UK; became first British jazz artist to sign recording contract with Sony Jazz (Columbia) in over 30 years; currently tours the world as solo artist and records and composes music for television and film. Founder, Kirkmichael International Guitar Festival; Founder, Guitars for Schools Programme. Best Guitarist, British Jazz Awards, eleven times; Grammy nomination, 1987; Gold Badge of Merit, British Academy of Composers and Songwriters, 1999; Freedom of the City of London, 1998; received the BBC Radio 2 "Heart of Jazz" Award in recognition of his career in music, 2007; presented with a Lifetime Achievement Award from the North Wales Jazz Guitar Festival for his "Contribution to Jazz Guitar Worldwide", 2007; 2010 BBC Folk Awards 'Best Original Composition' nomination; 2010 Doctor of Music (honoris causa), Royal Scottish Academy of Music and Drama (RSAMD). Publication: Kiss and Tell (autobiography), 1999. Recreations: horse racing; horse drawn gypsy wagons; collects vintage and rare American guitars and mandolins.

Taylor, Dr. Mary. Chief Executive, Scottish Federation of Housing Associations, since 2010. Over thirty five years working in the Scottish housing sector; career ranges from a Housing Management Trainee at SSHA to Senior Teaching Fellow at the University of Stirling; worked with committees of various housing associations as well as previously sitting on the Board of the SFHA and Chartered Institute of Housing (CIH) Scotland. Fellow of the Chartered Institute of Housing (CIH). Honorary Fellow of RICS. Membership of the Joint Improvement Partnership Board. Address: (b.) Sutherland House, 149 St Vincent Street, Glasgow G2 5NW.

Taylor, Rt. Rev. Maurice, STD. Bishop Emeritus of Galloway, since 2004; Bishop of Galloway, 1981-2004; b.

5.5.26, Hamilton. Educ. St. Aloysius College, Glasgow; Our Lady's High School, Motherwell; Pontifical Gregorian University, Rome. Royal Army Medical Corps, UK, India, Egypt, 1944-47; Assistant Priest: St. Bartholomew's, Coatbridge, 1951-52, St. Bernadette's, Motherwell, 1954-55; Lecturer, St. Peter's College, Cardross, 1955-65; Rector, Royal Scots College, Spain, 1965-74; Parish Priest, Our Lady of Lourdes, East Kilbride, 1974-81. Vice President, Progressio (formerly Catholic Institute for International Relations). Publications: The Scots College in Spain, 1971; Guatemala, A Bishop's Journey, 1991; El Salvador: Portrait of a Parish, 1992; Opening Our Lives to the Saviour (Co-author), 1995; Listening at the Foot of the Cross (Co-author), 1996; Being a Bishop in Scotland, 2006; It's the Eucharist, Thank God, 2009; Life's Flavour, 2014; What Are They Talking About?, 2015. Address: 41 Overmills Road, Ayr KA7 3LH; T.-01292-285865. Web: www.bishopmauricetaylor.org.uk

Taylor, Peter Cranbourne, MA, CA. Chairman, Scottish National Blood Transfusion Association, 1995-2010; b. 11.8.38, Yeovil; m., Lois Mary; 1s.; 1d Educ. Edinburgh University. Chartered Accountant/Partner: Romanes and Munro, Edinburgh, 1964-74; Deloitte Haskins and Sells, 1974-90; Coopers and Lybrand, 1990-95. Member, Scottish Dental Practice Board, 1991-2001. Recreations: country pursuits. Address: (h.) Totleywells House, Winchburgh, West Lothian EH52 6QJ.

Taylor, Professor Samuel Sorby Brittain, BA, PhD, Officier dans l'Ordre des Palmes Academiques. Professor of French, St. Andrews University, 1977-95, now Professor Emeritus; b. 20.9.30, Dore and Totley, Derbyshire; m., Agnes McCreadie Ewan (deceased 2007); 2 d. Educ. High Storrs Grammar School, Sheffield; Birmingham University; Paris University. Royal Navy, 1956-58 (Sub Lt., RNVR); Personnel Research Officer, Dunlop Rubber Co. ("Sickness-Absence in Rubber Industry"), 1958-60; Research Fellow, Institut et Musee Voltaire, Geneva, 1960-63; St. Andrews University: Lecturer, 1963, Reader, 1972, Professor, 1977, retired, 1995; Chairman, National Council for Modern Languages, 1981-85; Member, Executive Committee, Complete Works of Voltaire, 1970-85; Project Leader, Inter-University French Language Teaching Research and Development Project ("Le Francais en Faculte"/"En fin de compte"), 1980-88; Director, Nuffield Foundation project ("Nuffield French for science students"), 1991-99; Chairman, Scottish Joint Working Party for Standard Grade in Modern Languages, 1982-84; Chairman, St Andrews Green Belt Forum, 2008-2015. Publications: definitive text of Voltaire's Works, 1974; definitive iconography of Voltaire, completed. Recreations: athletics timekeeping; photography; Liberal Democrats; Franco-Scottish Society. St Andrews Preservation Trust. Address: (h.) 11 Irvine Crescent, St. Andrews KY16 8LG; T.-01334 472588; e-mail: ssbt423@btinternet.com

Taylor, Scott, BA (Hons) Marketing. Chief Executive, Advance City Marketing, since 2016; former Chief Executive, Glasgow City Marketing Bureau (2006-2016); b. 20.06.62, Manchester; m., Carol; 1 s.; 1 d. Educ. Clayton High School; University of Strathclyde. Former general manager of three Glasgow city centre hotels, as well as brand manager for two of Forte Hotels' brands; joined Greater Glasgow & Clyde Valley Tourist Board in 1998 as Director-Convention Bureau, later becoming Director of Marketing, encompassing both Leisure and Discretionary Business Tourism; took over as Chief Executive in July 2004, and then established Glasgow City Marketing Bureau (GCMB). Recreations:

travelling; hill walking; mountain biking. Address: Advance City Marketing, 70 West Regent Street, Glasgow G2 2QZ.

Taylor, William James, QC (Scotland), QC (England and Wales), MA, LLB, FRSA. Advocate, since 1971; Barrister, since 1990; b. 13.9.44, Nairn. Educ. Robert Gordon's College, Aberdeen; Aberdeen University. Standing Junior Counsel to DHSS, 1978-79, to Foreign and Commonwealth Office, 1979-86; Temporary Sheriff, 1997-99; Member, Criminal Injuries Compensation Board, 1997-2000; Member, Scottish Criminal Cases Review Commission, 1999-2004. Parliamentary candidate (Labour), West Edinburgh, February and October, 1974; Lothian Regional Councillor, 1973-84 (Secretary, Labour Group); Chairman, COSLA Protective Services Committee; Part-time Sheriff, since 1999; Chairman, Scottish Opera, 2004-07; Past Chairman, Traverse Theatre; previous Board Member, Royal Lyceum Theatre, Edinburgh; Past Chairman, Federation of Scottish Theatres. Recreations: the arts; sailing; skiing; Scottish mountains; restoring a garden. Address: (b.) Parliament House, Parliament Square, Edinburgh EH1 1RF; T.-0131-556 0101; e-mail: qc@wjt.org.uk

Teasdale, Sir Graham Michael, Kt, MB, BS, FRCP, FRCSEdin, FRCSGlas, FRCSLond, FACSHon, FMedSci, FRSE. Professor and Head, Department of Neurosurgery, Glasgow University, 1981-2003; Consultant Neurosurgeon, Institute of Neurological Sciences, Glasgow, 1975-2003; President, Society of British Neurological Surgeons, 2000-02; b. 23.9.40, Spennymoor; m.; 3 s.; 3 d. Educ. Johnston Grammar School, Durham; Durham University. Postgraduate clinical training, Newcastle-upon-Tyne, London and Birmingham, 1963-69; Assistant Lecturer in Anatomy, Glasgow University, 1969-71; specialist training in surgery and neurosurgery, Southern General Hospital, Glasgow, 1971-75; Senior Lecturer, then Reader in Neurosurgery, Glasgow University, 1975-81. President, International Neurotrauma Society, 1993-2000; Chairman, European Brain Injury Consortium, 1995-2003; President, Section of Clinical Neurosciences, Royal Society of Medicine, 1998-99; former President, Royal College of Physicians and Surgeons of Glasgow, 2003-06; Chairman of Board, NHS Quality Improvement Scotland, 2006-10. Address: Duchal Road, Kilmacolm PA13 4AY.

Telfer, Andrew. Joint Senior Partner, Baillie Gifford, since 2012. Address: (b.) Calton Square, 1 Greenside Row, Edinburgh EH1 3AN.

Templeton, Professor Allan, CBE, MBChB, MD (Hons), FRCOG, FRCP, FRCPE, FACOG, FMedSci. Emeritus Professor of Obstetrics and Gynaecology, University of Aberdeen; President, Royal College of Obstetricians and Gynaecologists, 2004-07; Hon. Director, Office for Research and Clinical Audit, RCOG, 2008-2014; b. 28.6.46, Glasgow; m., Gillian Penney; 3 s.; 1 d. Educ. Aberdeen Grammar School; University of Aberdeen. Junior hospital posts, Aberdeen Royal Infirmary; Lecturer, then Senior Lecturer, University of Edinburgh. Former Member, Human Fertilisation and Embryology Authority. Publications: books and scientific papers on human infertility. Recreation: mountains. Address: (b.) Oak Tree Cottage, Lecknasaide, Gairloch IV21 2AP; e-mail: allan.templeton@abdn.ac.uk

Tennant, David. Actor; b. 18.4.71, Bathgate, Lothian. Educ. RSAMD. Acted with the 7:84 Theatre Company; Theatre includes: Touchstone in As You Like It (RSC), 1996, Romeo in Romeo and Juliet (RSC), 2000, Antipholus of Syracuse in Comedy of Errors (RSC), 2000, Jeff in The Lobby Hero (Donmar Warhouse and New Ambassadors), 2002 (nominated Best Actor Laurence Olivier Theatre Awards, 2003); Television includes: Casanova in Casanova 2005, The Doctor in Doctor Who, 2005-2010 (tenth Doctor); Films include: Bright Young Things, 2003, Harry Potter and the Goblet of Fire, 2005. Address: (b.) c/o Independent Talent Group, Oxford House, 76 Oxford Street, London W1D 1BS.

Terry, Sheila M., BSc (SocSci), MBA, DipTRP, DipPL, FRSA. Chartered Town Planner, since 1976; b. 24.10.49, Edinburgh; m., John Terry. Educ. George Watson's Ladies College; Edinburgh University. Pre 1975: various planning posts in Cherwell DC, Northamptonshire County Council and Dunfermline Burgh Council; Senior Planning Officer, Warwick District Council, 1975-79; Assistant Borough Planning Officer and Senior Planning Officer, LB Hillingdon, 1979-88; Head of Planning/Principal Officer (Planning), Stirling District Council, 1988-96; Head of Planning and Transportation, Falkirk Council, 1996-2007. Trustee, New Lanark Trust, since 2008. Recreations: travel; art and architecture; theatre; swimming.

Theodossiou, Professor Ioannis, BSc, MPhil, PhD. Professor, Economics, University of Aberdeen Business School, since 1998; b. 03.07.54, Athens, Greece; m., Eleni Mente-Theodossiou; 1 s.; 1 d. Educ. University of Piraeus (The Graduate School of Industrial Studies of Piraeus); The University of Glasgow. Bank Employee, 1976-81; Tutor in Economics, 1982-86; Teaching Assistant, 1987-88; Teaching Fellow, 1988-90; Lecturer in Economics, 1990-95; Senior Lecturer in Economics, 1995-98; Reader in Economics, 1998. Participated in and coordinated several European Commission funded projects on issues of health inequalities, low pay, well-being and job satisfaction. Fellow, Royal Statistical Society; Member, Council of the Scottish Economic Society. Publications: 'Wage Inflation and the Two Tier Labour Market' (book); edited volumes, chapters in books and research papers in many economic journals. Recreations: motorcycles; hill walking. Address: (b.) University of Aberdeen Business School, Edward Wright Building, Aberdeen AB24 3QY; T.-01224 272183; e-mail: theod@abdn.ac.uk

Thewliss, Alison. MP (SNP), Glasgow Central, since 2015; Shadow SNP Spokesperson (Cities), since 2015; b. 13.9.82; m.; 1 s.; 1 d. Former Glasgow City councillor for the Calton ward (2007-2015). Member, Communities and Local Government Committee, House of Commons, since 2015. Address: House of Commons, London SW1A 0AA.

Thewliss, James, BSc (Hons). Retired Head Teacher, Harris Academy, Dundee (1997-2015); b. 24.4.53, Motherwell; m., Ann White; 1 s.; 1 d. Educ. Dalziel High School, Motherwell; Glasgow University. Geography Teacher, Braidhurst High School, Motherwell, 1976 -85; Principal Teacher, Geography, Perth High School, 1986-89; Assistant Rector, Perth High School, 1989-91; Assistant Head Teacher, Carluke High School, 1991-93; Depute Rector, Wallace High School, Stirling, 1993-97. Vice Convener, General Teaching Council Scotland, 2005-09; President, School Leaders Scotland, 2010-2011. Recreations: supporting Motherwell Football Club; football purist.

Thin, Andrew, BSc (Hons), MBA, DipM. Chairman, Scottish Canals, since 2014; Non Executive Director, Scottish Government, since 2010; Board Member, Children's Hearings Scotland, since 2011; b. 21.1.59, Edinburgh; m., Frances Elizabeth; 1 s.; 1 d. Educ. Glenalmond College; Edinburgh University. Director, James Thin Booksellers, 1985-89; Team Leader, Highlands and Islands Development Board, 1989-91; Chief Executive, Caithness and Sutherland Enterprise, 1991-95. Chairman, John Muir Trust, 1997-2003; Board Member, Crofters Commission, 2001-06; Convener, Cairngorms National Park Authority, 2003-06; Chairman, Scottish Natural Heritage, 2006-2014. Recreations: long-distance running; canoeing; hill-walking. Address: (h.) Wester Auchterflow, by Munlochy, Ross-shire IV8 8PQ; T.-01463 811632; e-mail: andrew.thin@hotmail.co.uk

Thin, David Ainslie, BSc. Chairman, James Thin Ltd., 1992-2002; b. 9.7.33, Edinburgh; m., Elspeth J.M. Scott; 1 s.; 2 d. Educ. Edinburgh Academy; Loretto School; Edinburgh University. James Thin Ltd., 1957-2002; President, Booksellers Association of GB and Ireland, 1976-78; Chairman, Book Tokens Ltd., 1987-95. Recreations: golf; travelling; reading. Address: (h.) Balfour House, 21/1 East Suffolk Park, Edinburgh EH16 5PN; T.- 0131-667 2725.

Thomaneck, Emeritus Professor Jurgen Karl Albert, MEd, Drphil. Professor in German, Aberdeen University, 1992-2001; Aberdeen City Councillor, 1996-2003 (Convener, Education and Leisure Committee, 1999-2003); b. 12.6.41, Germany; m., Guinevere Ronald; 2 d. Educ. Universities of Kiel, Tubingen, Aberdeen. Lecturer in German, Aberdeen University, since 1968. Grampian Regional Councillor, 1984-96; President, Aberdeen Trades Council, 1982-2001; Convenor, Grampian Joint Police Board, 1995-98; Board Member, Grampian Enterprise Ltd., until 1995; President, KIMO UK, 1996-2003; author/editor of 10 books, 15 contributions to books, 30 articles in learned journals, all in German studies. Recreation: football. Address: (h.) 17 Elm Place, Aberdeen AB25 3SN.

Thompson, Professor Alan Eric, MA (Hons), PhD, FRSA, FSA(Scot). Emeritus Professor of the Economics of Government, Heriot-Watt University; b. 16.9.24; m., Mary Heather Long; 3 s.; 1 d. Educ. Kingston-upon-Hull Grammar School; Edinburgh University. Edinburgh University: Assistant in Political Economy, 1952-53, Lecturer in Economics, 1953-59 and 1964-71; Professor of the Economics of Government, Heriot-Watt University, 1972-87; Parliamentary Labour candidate, Galloway, 1950, 1951; MP (Labour), Dunfermline, 1959-64; Member, Royal Fine Art Commission for Scotland, 1975-80; Chairman, Northern Offshore Maritime Resources Study, 1974-83; Governor, Newbattle Abbey College, 1975-85 (Chairman, 1980-83); Member, Local Government Boundaries Commission for Scotland, 1975-80; Member, Scottish Council for Adult Education in HM Forces, 1973-2000; BBC National Governor for Scotland, 1975-79; Governor, Leith Nautical College, 1981-85; Trustee, Bell's Nautical Trust, 1981-85; Parliamentary Adviser, Scottish Pharmaceutical General Council, 1984-2000. Publications: Development of Economic Doctrine (Co-author), 1980; articles in academic journals. Address: (h.) 11 Upper Gray Street, Edinburgh EH9 1SN.

Thompson, Professor Alastair Mark, ALCM, MBChB, MD, FRSCEd. Honorary Professor, University of Dundee; b. 18.11.60. Educ. Boroughmuir High School, Edinburgh; Edinburgh University. Lecturer, University of Edinburgh, 1991-96; Senior Lecturer/Reader, University of Dundee, 1996-2002; Visiting Professor of Surgical Oncology, MD Anderson Cancer Centre, Houston, 2010; Professor of Surgery,

Department of Surgical Oncology, University of Texas. Address: (b.) Dundee Cancer Centre, Ninewells Hospital and Medical School, Dundee DD1 9SY; T.-01382 383223; e-mail: a.m.thompson@dundee.ac.uk

Thompson, Bruce Kevin, MA. Headmaster, Strathallan School, since 2000; b. 14.11.59, Bath; m., Fabienne; 2d. Educ. Newcastle High School; New College, Oxford University. Cheltenham College: Assistant Master, 1983-94; Head of Classics, 1986-94; Assistant Housemaster, 1990-94; Depute Rector, Dollar Academy, 1994-2000. Chairman: Scottish HMC, 2011, Scottish Rugby Council. Recreations: rowing; weight training; music; literature. Address: (b.) Strathallan School, Forgandenny, Perth, PH2 9EG; T.-01738 815000.

Thompson, David George, Dip in Consumer Affairs, MCTSI. Vice President, CTSI, since 2009; MSP (SNP), Skye, Lochaber and Badenoch, 2011-16, Highlands and Islands, 2007-2011; b. 20.9.49, Lossiemouth; m., Veronica; 3 d. Educ. Lossiemouth High Secondary. Trading Standards Officer (TSO), Banff Moray & Nairn CC, 1971-73; Assistant Chief TSO, Ross & Cromarty County Council, 1973-75; Chief TSO, Comhairle nan Eilean Siar, 1975-83; Depute Director of Trading Standards, Highland Regional Council, 1983-86, Director of Trading Standards, 1986-95; Director of Protective Services, Highland Council, 1995-2001. Member of Church of Scotland; Member of GMB. Address: (h.) Balnafettack Farm House, Leachkin Road, Inverness IV3 8NL; T.-01349 864701.

Thompson, Owen. MP (SNP), Midlothian, since 2015; b. 17.3.78. Educ. Beeslack High School, Penicuik; Edinburgh Napier University. Career in Financial Services industry, then elected to Midlothian Council in November 2005 at the Loanhead by-election; re-elected in both 2007 and 2012; became Leader of Midlothian Council in 2013. Recreations: football; rugby; craft beer; films. Address: House of Commons, London SW1A 0AA.

Thompson, Simon, BA (Politics and Economics), MBA. Chief Executive, Chartered Institute of Bankers in Scotland, since 2007. Educ. University of Newcastle-upon-Tyne; University of Edinburgh. Lived and worked in Poland and the Czech Republic from 1994 to 2000, teaching and then managing a series of international education and training businesses; managed the International Accounting Education Standards Board (IAESB), an independent standards-setting board established by the International Federation of Accountants (IFAC), developing and promoting International Education Standards for Professional Accountants; previously worked for the Association of Chartered Certified Accountants (ACCA), establishing ACCA in 25 countries in Central & Eastern Europe, and leading a number of EU and other donor-funded accounting education and reform programmes. Address: (b.) The Chartered Institute of Bankers in Scotland, Drumsheugh House, 38b Drumsheugh Gardens, Edinburgh EH3 7SW; T.-0131 473 7777; e-mail: simon@charteredbanker.com

Thomson, Albert, KCHT, OLJ, CStN, BA, MICPEM, FSA Scot. Senior Project Manager, Stirling Group, since 2014. Educ. The Open University. Police Constable, Aberdeen City Police, 1969-75; Grampian Police: Police Constable, 1975-84, Police Sergeant, 1984-89, Police Inspector, 1989-95, Emergency Planning Officer, 1995-99; Delivery Team Leader, Rubicon Response Limited,

1999-2005; Business Assurance Leader, Petrofac Training, 2004-2010. Address: Stirling Group, Lord Cullen House, Fraser Place, Aberdeen AB25 3UB.

Thomson, Ben. Chairman, The National Galleries of Scotland. Educ. Edinburgh University. Career: started work for Kleinwort Benson in London, then joined Noble Group, the UK investment bank, 1990; Chief Executive of Noble Group, 1997 and became Chairman in 2007, until its merger with Execution Limited in 2010. Chairman: Urbicus Ltd (property debt fund management company), Inverleith LLP (a corporate finance firm), Barrington Stoke (a Scottish publishing company that publishes books for reluctant readers). Non-Executive Director: Fidelity Special Values plc, The Scotch Malt Whisky (Holdings) Ltd. Recreations: enjoys opera and art; former Scottish international athlete, and enjoys most sports, especially skiing and triathlon. Address: (h.) 33 Inverleith Terrace, Edinburgh EH3 5NU.

Thomson, David. Chief Superintendent, Head of Training, Scottish Police College, since 2007; b. 6.4.56, Greenock; m., Denise; 1 s.; 1 d. Educ. Greenock Academy; Glasgow Caledonia University. Quantity Surveyor, 1974-82; Police Constable, Greenock, 1982-89; Police Sergeant, Paisley and Scottish Police College, 1989-94; Police Inspector, Glasgow Southside, 1994-2000; Chief Inspector, Planning, 2000-04; Superintendent, Hamilton, Glasgow City Centre, 2004-07. Home Office Research Award. Recreations: golf; running; music. Address: (b.) Tulliallan Castle, Kincardine, Fife FK10 4BE; T.-01259 73 2154; e-mail: davidbpthomson@hotmail.co.uk

Thomson, David Mark, BA. Artistic Director/joint Chief Executive, Royal Lyceum Theatre, Edinburgh, 2003-2016; b. 26.4.64, Bellshill; 1 s.; 1 d. Educ. Caldervale High School, Airdrie; Strathclyde University. Arts worker, Maryhill Arts Centre, Glasgow; Assistant Director, Theatre Royal, Stratford East, London; Assistant Director, Royal Shakespeare Company; Associate Director, Nottingham Playhouse; Artistic Director, Brunton Theatre, Musselburgh. Author of four professionally produced plays for theatre; Fringe First Award. Recreation: music.

Thomson, Sir (Frederick Douglas) David, Bt, BA. Chairman, S.A. Meacock & Co. Ltd., since 1996; Chairman, The Investment Company plc, since 2004; Member, Royal Company of Archers (Queen's Bodyguard for Scotland); b. 14.2.40, Edinburgh; 2 s.; 1 d. Educ. Eton; University College, Oxford. Recreations: shooting; skiing. Address: (h.) Holylee, Walkerburn, Peeblesshire; T.-07831 355691; e-mail: sirdthomson@holyee.go-plus.net

Thomson, George. Chief Executive, Volunteer Scotland. Address: (b.) Jubilee House, Forthshire Way, Stirling FK8 1QZ; T.-01786 479593.

Thomson, George Buchanan, FCIBS; b. 10.1.24, Glasgow; m. (1), Margaret I. Williams (deceased); (2), Margaret R.H. Campbell (deceased). Educ. Eastwood Secondary School. Joined Union Bank of Scotland, 1940; War Service, 1942-46 with RAF (Navigator, Bomber Command); held various banking appointments, 1947-86; retired as Assistant General Manager (Branch Administration, West), Bank of Scotland; Past President, Institute of Bankers in Scotland; Director and Chairman, Association for the Relief of Incurables; Lately Hon. Treasurer, Scottish Civic Trust; former Convener, Board of

Stewardship and Finance, Church of Scotland; Director, Ian Skelly Holdings Ltd., 1986-89; Director, Clydesdale Development Company, 1988-95; Moderator, Dumbarton Presbytery, Church of Scotland, 2000-01. Recreations: music; reading; church. Address: (h.) 1/3-2 Capelrig Gardens, Newton Mearns, Glasgow G77 6NF.

Thomson, Rev. Iain Urquhart. Minister, Parish of Skene, 1972-2011 (retired); b. 13.12.45, Dundee; m., Christine Freeland; 1 s.; 2 d. Educ. Harris Academy, Dundee; Inverness Royal Academy; Aberdeen University; Christ's College, Aberdeen. Assistant Minister, Castlehill Church, Ayr, 1970-72. Clerk, Presbytery of Gordon, 1988-2000; Clerk and Treasurer, Synod of Grampian Trusts Committee, since 1993; Patron of the Seven Incorporated Trades of Aberdeen, since 2013. Recreations: golf; theatre; gardening. Address: 4 Keirhill Gardens, Westhill, Aberdeenshire AB32 6AZ; T.-01224 746743.
E-mail: ianuthomson@googlemail.com

Thomson, Professor James Alick, MA, PhD. Emeritus Professor of Psychology, Strathclyde University (Professor, since 2000); b. 9.12.51, Inverness; m., Dana O'Dwyer; 1 d. Educ. Inverness Royal Academy; Edinburgh University. Research Scholar, Uppsala University, Sweden, 1973; Post-doctoral Fellow, University of Paris, 1977-78; Strathclyde University: Lecturer, 1979-91, Senior Lecturer, 1992-94, Reader, 1995-99. Publications: The Facts About Child Pedestrian Accidents, 1991; Child Development and the Aims of Road Safety Education (Co-Author), 1996; Child Safety: Problem and Prevention from Pre-School to Adolescence (Co-Author), 1996; Kerbcraft: A Manual for Road Safety Professionals, 1997; Studies in Perception and Action V (Co-Editor), 1999; Crossroads: Smart Strategies for Novice Pedestrians, 2005; 80 scientific articles and government reports. Recreations: rock climbing; hillwalking; mountaineering; photography; travel; Gaelic language and literature. Address: (b.) Department of Psychology, Strathclyde University, 40 George Street, Glasgow G1 1QE; T.-0141-548 2572; e-mail: j.a.thomson@strath.ac.uk

Thomson, Sir John Adam, GCMG; b. 27.4.27, Bieldside, Aberdeen; m., 1, Elizabeth Anne McClure (deceased); 3 s.; 1 d.; 2, Judith Ogden Bullitt. Educ. Aberdeen University; Trinity College, Cambridge. Joined Foreign Office, 1950; seconded to Cabinet Office as Chief of Assessment Staff, 1968-71; Minister and Deputy Permanent Representative, NATO, 1972; Head of UK Delegation, MBFR Exploratory Talks, Vienna, 1973; Assistant Under Secretary for Defence and Disarmament, 1973-76; British High Commissioner in India, 1977-82; British Permanent Representative and Ambassador to UN, 1982-87; Principal Director, 21st Century Trust, 1987-90; Director, ANZ Grindlays, 1987-96; International Adviser, ANZ Grindleys Bank, 1996-98; Chairman, Flemings Emerging Markets Investment Trust, 1990-97; Chairman, Minority Rights Group, 1991-99; Director's Visitor, Institute for Advanced Studies, Princeton, 1995-96. Trustee, National Museums of Scotland, 1990-99; Member, Council, International Institute of Strategic Studies, 1987-96; Trustee, Indian National Trust for Art and Cultural Heritage, 1988-2010; Research Affiliate, MIT, Cambridge, Massachusetts; Foreign Honorary Member, American Academy of Arts and Sciences. Recreations: hill-walking; tennis.

Thomson, Rev. John Morria Arnott, TD, JP, BD, ThM. Church of Scotland Minister (retired); b. 27.02.49, Buckhaven; m., Marlene Jeffrey Logan; 1 s.; 1 d. Educ. Irvine Royal Academy; University of Glasgow; Columbia Theological Seminary, Atlanta, USA. Career: Journalist, Irvine Herald; Executive Officer, Natural Environment Research Council; Admin Officer, Irvine Development Corporation; Assistant Project Co-ordinator, Wiltshire County Council; Minister: Houston and Killellankirk, 1978-88, St Nicholas Parish, Lanark, 1988-2001; Minister,

Hamilton Old Parish Church, 2001-2014. Chaplain, RNR (Clyde Division), 1986-92; Chaplain, TA, 105 Regiment, Royal Artillery, 1992-2005; Justice of the Peace, since 2001. Chaplain, Royal British Legion, Hamilton. Publication: "Can These Bones Live?", 2006. Recreations: sailing; music; writing; travel; history. Address: 8 Skylands Place, Hamilton ML3 8SB; T.-01698 422511; e-mail: jt@john1949.plus.com

Thomson, Professor Joseph McGeachy, LLB, FRSE, FRSA, HonFSALS; b. 6.5.48, Campbeltown. Educ. Keil School, Dumbarton; Edinburgh University. Lecturer in Law, Birmingham University, 1970-74; Lecturer in Laws, King's College, London, 1974-84; Professor of Law, Strathclyde University, 1984-90; Regius Professor of Law, Glasgow University, 1991-2005; Commissioner, Scottish Law Commission, 2000-09; Honorary Sheriff, Campbeltown, 2014. Recreations: bridge; food and wine. Address: (h.) Askomel End, Low Askomil, Campbeltown PA28 6EP; T.-01586 554 930.

Thomson, Ken. Director General for Strategy & External Affairs, Scottish Government; International and Constitution Director. Career history: Private Secretary to Scottish Office Ministers in the early 1990s; involved in work to prepare for devolution in 1997; Principal Private Secretary to the Rt. Hon. Donald Dewar MP MSP, 1997-99; senior lead on constitutional policy, since 2005; other experience includes work in private offices, on public health, managing legislation, on secondment to the Scottish Prison Service and to the financial services sector, and on transport, natural heritage and economic development policy. Address: Scottish Government, St. Andrew's House, Regent Road, Edinburgh EH1 3DG.

Thomson, Lesley, QC, LLB (Hons). Solicitor General for Scotland, since 2011. Twenty five years' experience as a prosecutor, including as District Procurator Fiscal for Selkirk, District Procurator Fiscal for Edinburgh, and interim Area Procurator Fiscal for Lothian & Borders, and led on trial advocacy and deaths investigation within COPFS; appointed Area Procurator Fiscal for Glasgow in May 2008. Acknowledged specialist in the prosecution of serious crime, including organised crime and financial crime, and an expert in the proceeds of crime legislation, having authored a textbook on criminal confiscation. Address: (b.) Crown Office, 25 Chambers Street, Edinburgh.

Thomson, Lesley Ann. Managing Director, Liddell Thomson Management Consultants; Director, Spreng & Co; b. 11.2.59, Glasgow. Member, Entrepreneurial Scotland; Trustee, Dewar Arts Awards; Governor, Glasgow School of Art. Address: (b.) The Herald Building, 155 Albion Street, Glasgow G1 1RU; T.-0141 548 5181.
E-mail: info@liddellthomson.com

Thomson, Malcolm George, QC, LLB. Practice at Scottish Bar, since 1974; Temporary Judge, Court of Session, since 2002; b. 6.4.50, Edinburgh; m. (1), Susan Gordon (m. dissolved); 2 d.; m. (2), Maybel King. Educ. Edinburgh Academy; Edinburgh University. Standing Junior Counsel, Department of Agriculture and Fisheries and Forestry Commission, 1982-87; QC (Scotland), 1987; called to the Bar, Lincoln's Inn, 1991; Chairman, National Health Service Tribunal, Scotland, 1995-2005; Member, Scottish Legal Aid Board, 1998-2006; Editor, Scots Law Times Reports, 1989-99; Scottish Case Editor, Current Law, 1977-97. Recreations: sailing; skiing. Address: (h.)12 Succoth Avenue, Edinburgh EH12 6BT; T.-0131-337 4911.

Thomson, Michelle. MP, Edinburgh West, since 2015 (SNP MP, 2015). Educ. Royal Scottish Academy of Music & Drama. Worked as a professional musician for a number of years; completed an MSc in IT and worked in Financial

Services over 23 years in a variety of senior roles delivering IT and business change; set up small business in property in 2009 and recently spent 2 years of the referendum as Managing Director of Business for Scotland (spoke at over 90 events, took part in high-profile debates and undertook extensive media appearances); SNP Spokesperson for Business, Innovation & Skills, 2015. Address: House of Commons, London SW1A 0AA.

Thomson, Professor Neil Campbell, MBChB, MD, FRCPGlas, FRCPLond. Emeritus Professor, University of Glasgow, since 2011; Professor of Respiratory Medicine, Glasgow University, 2001-2011; b. 3.4.48, Kilmarnock; m., Lorna Jean; 2 s.; 1 d. Educ. Speir's School, Beith; Glasgow University. Junior hospital doctor, Glasgow teaching hospitals, 1972-80; Research Fellow, McMaster University, Hamilton, Ontario, 1980-81; Consultant Respiratory Physician, Western Infirmary & Gartnavel General Hospital, Glasgow, 1982-2011; Honorary Professor, Glasgow University, 1996-2001; Chair, British Lung Foundation Scientific Committee, 2001-2004; Member, Committee on Safety of Medicine, 1999-2001. Publications: Asthma and COPD: Basic Mechanisms and Clinical Management, 2009; Manual of Asthma Management (2nd edition), 2001. Recreations: reading; walking; gardening. Address: (b.) Department of Respiratory Medicine, Gartnavel General Hospital, Glasgow; T.-0141-211 3241.

Thomson, Paul William, BSc (Hons), PhD, DipEd. Rector, Jordanhill School, Glasgow, since 1997; b. 25.7.57, Glasgow; m., Dr. Mary Thomson (deceased); 2 s. Educ. Dollar Academy; University of Glasgow. Teacher of Physics, Boclair Academy, 1983-87; Principal Teacher of Physics, Chryston High School, 1987-90; Assistant Head Teacher, Vale of Leven Academy, 1990-94; Depute Head Teacher, Hermitage Academy, 1994-97. Member, Board, Scottish Examinations Board, 1990-98; Member, SQA Advisory Council, 2003-2010; Member, Board, Scottish Qualifications Authority, since 2010; Winner, Becta 'ICT in Practice Leadership Award', 2006; Convenor, SQA Advisory Council, since 2013; RSE Education Committee, 2008-13; Board member, Cancer Support Scotland. Recreations: tennis; golf. Address: (b.) 45 Chamberlain Road, Glasgow G13 1SP; T.-0141-576 2500.
E-mail: PThomson@jordanhill.glasgow.sch.uk

Thomson, Rev. Peter David, MA, BD. Minister, Comrie with Dundurn, 1978-2004; b. 4.11.41, St. Andrews; m., Margaret Celia Murray; 1 s.; 1 d. Educ. Dundee High School; Edinburgh University; Glasgow University; Tubingen University. Minister, Balmaclellan with Kells, 1968-78; Moderator, Kirkcudbright Presbytery, 1974-75; Convener, Nomination Committee, General Assembly, 1982-85. Chairman, New Galloway and Kells Community Council, 1976-78; Moderator, Perth Presbytery, 1988-89 and 2012-13. Recreations: haphazardly pursued interests in photography, wildlife, music, theology, current affairs. Address: 34 Queen Street, Perth PH2 0EJ.
E-mail: peterthomson208@btinternet.com

Thomson, Professor Richard Ian, MA, DipHistArt (Oxon), MA, PhD, FRSE. Watson Gordon Professor of Fine Art, Edinburgh University, since 1996; Director, Visual Arts Research Institute, Edinburgh, 1999-2004; Trustee, National Galleries of Scotland, 2002-2010; b. 1.3.53, Tenterden; m., Belinda Jane Greaves; 2 s. Educ. Dragon School, Oxford; Shrewsbury School; St. Catherine's College, Oxford; Courtauld Institute of Art, London University. Lecturer/Senior Lecturer/Reader, Manchester University, 1977-96; Curator or Co-Curator of several exhibitions: The Private Degas, 1987, Camille Pissarro: Impressionist Landscape and Rural Labour, 1990, Monet to Matisse, 1994; Seurat and the Bathers, 1997; Theo van Gogh, 1999; Monet: the Seine and the Sea 1878-1883, 2003; Toulouse-Lautrec and Montmartre, 2005; Degas,

Sickert, Toulouse-Lautrec, 2005; Monet, 1840-1926, 2010. Publications: Toulouse-Lautrec, 1977; Seurat, 1985; Degas: The Nudes, 1988; Edgar Degas: Waiting, 1995; Framing France (Editor), 1998; Soil and Stone (Co-Editor), 2003; The Troubled Republic. Visual Culture and Social Debate in France, 1889-1900, 2004. Van Gogh Visiting Fellow, University of Amsterdam (2007); Slade Professor of Fine Art, University of Oxford (2009); Conseil Scientifique, Institut National d'Histoire de l'Art, since 2008; Conseil Scientifique, Musée d'Orsay, since 2010. Recreations: gardening. Address: (b.) History of Art, School of Arts, Culture and Environment, University of Edinburgh, 20 Chambers Street, Edinburgh EH1 1JZ; T.-0131-650 4124.

Thomson, Ross, MA (Hons). MSP (Scottish Conservative), North East Scotland region, since 2016; b. 21.9.87, Aberdeen. Educ. University of Aberdeen. Career history: Coatbridge and Chryston constituency candidate in the Scottish Parliament 2007 elections; Gordon constituency candidate, United Kingdom general election, 2010; elected to Aberdeen City Council at the 2012 Aberdeen City Council election; contested the Aberdeen Donside by-election in 2013; candidate, Aberdeen South and North Kincardine constituency in the 2016 Scottish Parliament election. Address: Scottish Parliament, Edinburgh EH99 1SP.

Thomson, S. Kenneth, MHSM, DipHSM. Chief Executive, Yorkhill NHS Trust, 1997-2000; Conductor, Glasgow Gaelic Musical Association, since 1983; Board Member, National Waiting Times Special Health Board, 2003-09; Lay Member, Employment Tribunals; Lay Member, General Pharmaceutical Council Investigating Committee, since 2007; Chair, Scottish Advisory Committee on Distinction Awards, since 2010; b. 20.8.49, Campbeltown; m., Valerie Ferguson (deceased 2009); 1 s.; 1 d. Educ. Keil School, Dumbarton. Administrative trainee, Scottish Health Service; various administrative and management posts, Glasgow and West of Scotland; Chief Executive, Law Hospital NHS Trust, 1997-2000. National Mod Gold Medallist, 1979. Publication: Slighe an Airgid - 20 Songs for Gaelic Choirs. Inducted into Traditional Music Hall of Fame, 2013; Lay Member, Scottish Social Services Council Committees. Recreations: opera; Gaelic language and culture; theatre; The Archers; swimming; composing and arranging music. Address: (h.) 14 Cleveden Drive, Glasgow G12 0SE; T.-0141-334 7773.

Thomson, William P. L., OBE, MA, MUniv, DipEd; b. 9.5.33, Newmilns; m., Elizabeth Watson; 1 s.; 3 d. Educ. Dundee High School; St. Andrews University. Teacher of History and Geography/Deputy Head Teacher, Anderson High School, Shetland, 1958-71; Rector, Kirkwall Grammar School, Orkney, 1971-91; Historian. Honorary Sheriff. Publications: The Little General and the Rousay Crofters, 1981; Kelp-Making in Orkney, 1983; History of Orkney, 1987; Lord Henry Sinclair's 1492 Rental of Orkney, 1996; New History of Orkney, 2001; Orkney: Land and People, 2008; Orkney Crofters in Crisis, 2013. Address: (h.) South Manse, Burray, Orkney KW17 2SS; T.-01856 731330.

Thorburn, David John, LLB, FCIBS. Former Chief Executive, Clydesdale Bank PLC (2011-2015); b. 9.1.58, Glasgow; m., Maureen. Educ. Hamilton Academy; Glasgow University; Harvard Business School. Clydesdale Bank PLC, 1978-83; TSB Group PLC, 1984-93; Clydesdale Bank PLC, 1993-2015.

Thornhill, Professor Christopher John, BA, MA (Cantab), PhD. Professor of European Political Thought,

Head of Politics, University of Glasgow, since 2006; b. 08.06.66, Shipley, West Yorkshire; 1 s.; 1 d. Educ. Oakbank Grammar School, Keighley; Bradford College; Cambridge University. Lecturer: University of Sussex, 1993-95, King's College London, 1995-2003; Reader, King's College London, 2003-04, Professor, 2004-05. Publications include: Political Theory in Modern Germany, 1999; Karl Jaspers: Politics and Metaphysics, 2002; Niklas Luhmann's Theory of Politics and Law (Co-Author), 2003; German Political Philosophy: The Metaphysics of Law, 2006; A Sociology of Constitutions and State Legitimacy in Historical-Sociological Perspective, 2011. Recreations: classical music; hill-walking; travel; cricket. Address: (b.) Department of Politics, Adam Smith Building, University of Glasgow G12 8RT; T.-0141 330 5076.
E-mail: c.thornhill@lbss.gla.ac.uk

Thornton, Philip John Roger, WS, MA, DipALP, NP. Consultant, Russel and Aitken, Solicitors, since 2012; b. 28.7.47, Prestbury; m., Alexandra Janet Taylor; 2 d. Educ. Manchester Grammar School; Edinburgh University. Solicitor, Russel and Aitken, WS, 1973-75; Partner, Russel and Aitken, 1975-2012. Tutor, Edinburgh University; Examiner, Society of Messengers at Arms and Sheriff Officers; Secretary, Edinburgh Family Planning Trust. Recreations: family holidays; art history; cinema; tennis. Address: (b.) 27 Rutland Square, Edinburgh EH1 2BU; T.-0131 228 5500.

Thurso, 3rd Viscount Rt. Hon. Sir (John Archibald Sinclair), BT, PC. MP (Liberal Democrat), Caithness, Sutherland and Easter Ross, 2001-2015; Spokesman for Business, Innovation and Skills, 2009-2010; b. 10.9.53; m.; 2 s.; 1 d. Educ. Eton. Chairman, Scrabster Harbour, 1997-2001; Non-Executive Director: Lochdhu Hotels, since 1975 (Chairman, since 1995), Sinclair Family Trust, since 1976 (Chairman, since 1995), Thurso Fisheries, since 1979 (Chairman, since 1995); Ulbster Holdings, since 1994 (Chairman, since 1994), Mossimans Ltd., 1998-2002; President, Academy of Food and Wine Service, since 1998; Chair, International Wine and Spirit Competition Ltd, since 1999; Member, Parliamentary Banking Standards Commission, 2012-2013. Address: Thurso East Mains, Thurso.

Tiefenbrun, Ivor Sigmund, MBE. Executive Chairman, Linn Products Ltd., Glasgow; Director, IST Marine Ltd; b. 18.3.46, Glasgow; m., Evelyn Stella Balarksy; 2 s.; 1 d. Educ. Strathbungo Senior Secondary School; Strathclyde University (Sixties dropout). Worked overseas, 1971-73; founded Linn Products, 1973. Chairman, Federation of British Audio, 1983-87; Council Member, Design Council, 1995-98; Founder Member, Entrepreneurial Exchange; Honorary Fellow, Glasgow School of Art, since 1999; Scottish Entrepreneur of the Year, 2001; established registered charity Cure Crohn's Colitis to raise funds for patient centric research into Inflammatory Bowel Disease, 2006. Appointed Visiting Professor at Strathclyde University by the Department of Design, Manufacture and Engineering Management, 2004; inducted to Entrepreneurial Exchange Hall of Fame, 2011; appointed Member of the William Robertson Society, The University of Edinburgh, 2011; appointed Founder Member, Strathclyde University's Academy of Distinguished Entrepreneurs, 2011. Recreations: thinking; music; reading; sailing. Address: (b.) Linn Products Ltd., Glasgow Road, Waterfoot, Eaglesham, Glasgow G76 0EQ; T.-0141-307 7777; e-mail: ivor@linn.co.uk

Tierney, Professor Stephen (Joseph Anthony), LLM (Toronto), LLM (Liverpool), LLB Hons (Glas), DipLP (Edin). Professor of Constitutional Theory, University of Edinburgh, since 2008; Director, Edinburgh Centre for Constitutional Law, since 2009; British Academy Senior Research Fellow, 2008-09; ESRC Senior Research Fellow, 2013-15; b. 11.03.67, Glasgow; m., Ailsa Barbara Henderson; 3 s. Educ. Our Lady of Lourdes Primary, East Kilbride; St. Bride's Secondary, East Kilbride; Universities of Glasgow, Liverpool, Toronto and Edinburgh. Lecturer in Law: University of Hull, 1995-97, Brunel University, 1997-99; University of Edinburgh: Lecturer in Law, 1999-2005, Reader in Law, 2005-08. Publications (books): Nationalism and Globalisation, 2015; Constitutional Referendums: The Theory and Practice of Republican Deliberation, 2012; Europe's Constitutional Mosaic (Co-Author), 2011; Public Law and Politics: The Scope and Limits of Constitutionalism (Co-Author), 2008; Multiculturalism and the Canadian Constitution, 2007; Accommodating Cultural Diversity: Contemporary Issues in Theory and Practice, 2007; Towards an International Legal Community? The Sovereignty of States and the Sovereignty of International Law (Co-Author), 2006; Constitutional Law and National Pluralism, 2004; Accommodating National Identity: New Approaches in International and Domestic Law, 2000. Legal Adviser to the House of Lords Constitution Committee, since 2014; Judicial Appointments Board for Scotland, since 2015; Executive Committee, UK Constitutional Law Association, since 2015; Editor, UK Constitutional Law blog, since 2015; Constitutional Adviser to the Scottish Parliament Referendum Bill Committee, 2013-14; Constitutional Adviser to the Scottish Parliament Scotland Bill Committee, 2011; Editorial Board, European Public Law. Recreations: golf; hill-walking; family recreation. Address: School of Law, University of Edinburgh, Old College, South Bridge, Edinburgh EH8 9YL; T.-0131 650 2070; e-mail: s.tierney@ed.ac.uk

Tilley, Catrin, BSc (Econ), FCMI, MInstF. Partner, More Partnership Fundraising Consultants, since 2012; b. 29.06.55, St. Neots; m., Prof. Rick Maizels; 2 s.; 1 d. Educ. Hinchingbrooke School, Huntingdon; University College London. Head, Fundraising, Membership, Publications, CND London, 1982-88; Assistant Director (Admin), Greenpeace UK, London, 1988-91; Deputy Director, Comic Relief, London, 1992-95; Director of Development and Alumni, University of Edinburgh, 1996-2003. Trustee, UK Institute of Fundraising, 2005-08; Executive Committee, Scottish Institute of Fundraising, 2005-08; Director of External Affairs, National Galleries of Scotland, 2003-2012. Address: (b.) More Partnership, 31 Exchange Street, Dundee DD1 3DJ; T.-0797 101 9226.
E-mail: ctilley@morepartnership.com

Timms, Peter. Former Chairman, David MacBrayne Limited; Chairman: Schroder UK Mid Fund Plc, 2000-2014, Flexible Technology Ltd., since 1981; Non Executive Director, Mount Stuart Trust. Address: (b.) Flexible Technology Trust, Townhead, Rothesay, Isle of Bute PA20 9JH.

Tindall, Benjamin Hemsley, DipSocSci, RIAS, RIBA, FSA (Scot). Principal, Benjamin Tindall Architects, since 1982; b. 21.12.53, Scotland; m., Jill Watson. Educ. University of Edinburgh; University of Pennsylvania. Notable architectural commissions in Edinburgh include, The Queen's Gallery Palace of Holyroodhouse, The Hub, Edinburgh's Festival Centre; Fringe Shop and Offices. Elsewhere, housing on Barra, Melgund Castle, Forfar, An Camas Mòr, Rothiemurchus and projects on Orkney, Jersey, etc (see www.benjamintindallarchitects.co.uk). Elected Trustee for National Trust for Scotland; former Chairman, Sir Patrick Geddes Memorial Trust. Recreations: owner and harbourmaster, Cove, Berwickshire. Address: 17 Victoria Terrace, Edinburgh EH1 2JL; T.-0131 220 3366.

Tobin, Professor Alyson Kim, BSc (Hons), PhD, FSB. Honorary Professor, University of St Andrews, since 2013; Honorary Research Associate, James Hutton Institute, since 2013; Deputy Vice Chancellor, York St John University, since 2013; Dean of The Faculty of Science, University of St Andrews, 2007-2011, Acting Vice-Principal (Learning and Teaching) 2011, Professor in Biology, since 2008; b. 7.9.56, Coventry; m., Tim Tobin; 2 s. Educ. John Cleveland College, Hinckley, Leics; University of Newcastle upon Tyne. Royal Society Alfred Spinks Research Fellow, 1982-87; Royal Society University Research Fellow, 1987-97; Reader in Plant Sciences, University of St Andrews, 1997-2008. Fellow of the Society of Biology, 2010; Council Member, Society of Biology (Scotland Branch), since 2011; Member, International Advisory Board Indus Foundation Indo-American Education Summit, 2013; Executive Committee, UK Deans of Science; Director, Dundee Science Centre Board, since 2010; Plant and Microbial Sciences Committee, Biotechnology and Biological Sciences Research Council, 2002-06; Executive Committee of The Federation of The European Societies of Plant Biology, 2007-09; Member (Scotland Representative), Biosciences Federation Education Committee, 2008-10; Spencer Industrial Arts Trust Scholar, 1978; Plant Science Scotland, Board Member, since 2005; Convener, Plant Metabolism Group, Society for Experimental Biology, 1995-2000; Honorary Research Fellow, Scottish Crops Research Institute, since 2005; Director, St Andrews Botanic Garden Education Trust, 2005-07. Publications: 'Plant Biochemistry' (Co-Author), 2008 and academic journal publications in plant physiology and biochemistry. Recreations: piano; hill walking. Address: (b.) York St John University, Lord Mayor's Walk, York YO31 7EX; T.-01904 876608; e-mail: a.tobin@yorks.ac.uk; School of Biology, Biomolecular Sciences Building, University of St Andrews, St Andrews KY16 9ST.

Todd, Alison, BSc (Hons), DipAppSocSci, HND. Chief Executive, Children 1st, since 2014, Director of Children and Family Services and External Affairs, 2009-2014; b. 21.3.66, Forfar. Educ. Brechin High School; Robert Gordon University; Open University. Various residential care positions, 1993-95; State Support Offficer, Ministry of Defence, 1995-98; Community Development Officer, Ormiston Housing Cooperative, 1998-2001; Centre Manager, Rathbone Charity, 2001; Services Manager, ChildLine Scotland and NorthWest, 2001-06; Assistant Director, NSPCC North of England, 2006-07; North of England Business Workstream Leader (Seconded), NSPCC, 2007-09. Voluntary Experience - Girl Guides Association Rainbow Leader, 1990-93; Homestart Volunteer, 1995-98; Children's Panel Member, 2000-01; Director, Scottish Alliance of Children's Rights, Angus Summer Playscheme. Recreations: reading; walking; overseas holidays. Address: (b.) Children 1st, 83 Whitehouse Loan, Edinburgh EH9 1AT; T.-0131 446 2325.
E-mail: alison.todd@children1st.org.uk

Todd, Maree. MSP (SNP), Highlands and Islands region, since 2016; previously worked as a pharmacist for NHS Highland. Address: Scottish Parliament, Edinburgh EH99 1SP.

Toft, Anthony Douglas, CBE, LVO, BSc, MD, FRCPE, FRCPGlas, FRCPLond, FRCPI, FACP(Hon), FRACP(Hon), FRCSE, FRCPC(Hon), FRCGP(Hon), FFPM (Hon), FFAEM (Hon), FCPS Pakistan (Hon), FCPS Bangladesh (Hon), FAM Singapore (Hon), MAM Malaysia (Hon). Consultant Physician, Royal Infirmary, Edinburgh, 1978-2009; Physician to the Queen in Scotland, 1996-2009; Chief Medical Officer, Scottish Equitable Life Assurance (now Aegon UK), 1987-2015; b. 29.10.44, Perth; m.,

Maureen Darling; 1 s.; 1 d. Educ. Perth Academy; Edinburgh University. President, British Thyroid Association, 1996-99; Chairman, Professional and Linguistic Assessment Board, 1999-2006; President, Royal College of Physicians of Edinburgh, 1991-94; Chairman, Collegiate Members' Committee, Royal College of Physicians of Edinburgh, 1978; Vice-President, Royal College of Physicians, 1989-91; Chairman, Scottish Royal Colleges, 1992-94; Chairman, Joint Committee of Higher Medical Training, 1993-96; Member, Health Appointments Advisory Committee, 1994-2000. Recreations: golf; gardening; collecting Scottish Art. Address: (h.) 41 Hermitage Gardens, Edinburgh EH10 6AZ; T.-0131-447 2221; e-mail: toft41@hotmail.com

Toley, Richard, BA (Hons), MPhil, PGCE. Headmaster, Lathallan School, Johnshaven, since 2009; b. 28.6.71, Kingston-Upon-Thames; m., Indrani; 1 s.; 1 d. Educ. Chatesmore; St David's University College, Lampeter; University of St Andrews; University of Strathclyde. Teacher of History/Classics/Rugby: Merchant Taylors School, Liverpool, 1996-99, Careers Co-ordinator, High School of Dundee, 1999-2004, Teacher of History, Director of Co-Curriculum, 2004-06; Head of Senior School, Lathallan School, 2006-09 (led development of only new Senior Independent School in country); while Headmaster, introduced 'Civilianship Programme from age 5-18 developing 'Confidence Without Arrogance'. Advanced Higher History Setter, 2007-09; made Fellow of Royal Society of Arts, 2012; Board member, SCIS (Scottish Council of Independent Schools), Chairman, Finance and General Purposes Committee, 2014. Recreations: Scottish Provincial Silver, 'Warhammer'; cricket. Address: Brotherton Castle, Johnshaven, Angus DD10 0HN; T.-01561 362220; e-mail: richardtoley@lathallan.org.uk

Tolley, David Anthony, MB, BS (Lond), FRCS, FRCSEdin, FRCPEdin. Consultant Urological Surgeon, Western General Hospital, Edinburgh, since 1980; Honorary Senior Lecturer, Department of Surgery/Urology, Edinburgh University, since 1980; Past President, Royal College of Surgeons of Edinburgh, formerly Treasurer and Director of Standards; formerly President, European Intrarenal Surgery Society, European Association Academic Urologists; b. 29.11.47, Warrington; m., Judith Anne Finn; 3 s.; 1 d. Educ. Manchester Grammar School; Kings College Hospital Medical School, London University. House Surgeon and Physician, Kings College Hospital; Lecturer in Human Morphology, Southampton University; Lecturer in Anatomy and Fulbright Fellow, University of Texas at Houston; Surgical Registrar, Hammersmith and Ealing Hospitals, London; Senior Surgical Registrar (Urology), Kings College Hospital, London; Senior Urological Registrar, Yorkshire Regional Training Scheme. Previously Member: MRC Working Party on Urological Cancer; MRC Working Party on Superficial Bladder Cancer; Editorial Board, British Journal of Urology; Council, British Association of Urological Surgeons; Standing Commitee on Postgraduate Education; Board, Minimal Access Therapy Training Unit Scotland; Education Committee, Royal College of Surgeons of Edinburgh; Member, Specialty Advisory Committee in Urology; former President, British Society for Endourology; Past Chairman, Scottish Urological Oncology Group; formerly Chairman, Specialty Advisory Board in Urology, Royal College of Surgeons of Edinburgh; former Member, Council, Royal College of Surgeons of Edinburgh; formerly Chairman, Section of Endourology, British Association of Urological Surgeons; Examiner, Intercollegiate Board in Urology; Member, Board, European Society for Urotechnology; Member, Editorial Board, Journal of Endourology; Member, Editorial Board, Hungarian Endourology; Honorary Member, Romanian Society for Endourology;

Honorary Member, Romanian Urological Association; Editor, Surgeons' News; Chairman, Quincentenary Board, Royal College of Surgeons Edinburgh. Address: (b.) Murrayfield Hospital, Corstorphine Road, Edinburgh; T.-0131-334 0363.

Tomkins, Professor Adam, LLB (UEA), LLM (Lond), FRSE. MSP (Scottish Conservative), Glasgow, since 2016; Shadow Cabinet Secretary for Communities, Social Security, the Constitution and Equalities, since 2016; John Millar Professor of Public Law, University of Glasgow, since 2003; former Legal Adviser to the House of Lords Select Committee on the Constitution (2009-2015); Adviser to Strathclyde Commission (2013-14); Member, Smith Commission on Scottish Devolution (2014); b. 28.06.69, Newbury; m., Lauren J. Apfel; 3 s.; 1 d. Educ. Gillingham School, Dorset; University of East Anglia; London School of Economics. Career History: Lecturer in Law, King's College London; Fellow and Tutor in Law, St. Catherine's College, Oxford. Publications: Author of: "The Constitution After Scott", 1998; "Public Law", 2003; "Our Republican Constitution", 2005; "European Union Law", 2006; "British Government and The Constitution", 2011. Recreations: whisky; guitar music; football. Address: (b.) School of Law, University of Glasgow, Glasgow G12 8QQ; T.-0141 330 4180. E-mail: adam.tomkins@glasgow.ac.uk

Tomlinson, Professor Alan, MSc, PhD, DSc, FCOptom, FAAO. Professor of Vision Science, Glasgow Caledonian University, since 1992; b. 18.3.44, Bolton; partner, Professor Daphne McCulloch; 1 s. Educ. Lampton Grammar School, North London; Bradford University; Manchester University Institute of Science and Technology. Fellowship, British Optical Association, 1966; Registration, General Optical Council, 1966; Lecturer, Opthalmic Optics: Bradford University, 1967-68; UMIST, 1968-77; Director, Clinical Research, Wesley Jesson Inc, Chicago, USA, 1977-79 and 1983-86; Professor of Optometry: Indiana University, 1980-83, Southern California College of Optometry, 1986-91; Council Member, General Optical Council, 1999-2009; Member, British Universities Committee of Optometry, 1992-2009, Chair, 1997-99; Council Member, College of Optometry (UK), 1994-98; Member, Advisory Committee, American Academy of Optometry, 1993-98. Publications: 140 papers in scientific journals; Complications of Contact Lens Wear, 1992. Recreations: tennis; running; theatre; music. Address: (b.) Vision Science, Department of Life Sciences, Glasgow Caledonian University, City Campus, Glasgow G4 0BA; T.-0141-331 3380.

Tomlinson, Anna, MTheol (Hons) (St Andrews), PGCE, SQH. Head of St Margaret's School for Girls, Aberdeen, since 2014; b. 1.12.74, Preston. Educ. St Aidan's C of E High School; St Andrew's University; Lancaster University; Edinburgh University. Head of Religion and Philosophy, St George's School for Girls, Edinburgh, 1999-2006, Deputy Head, 2006-2014. Recreations: cooking; singing; walking; travel. Address: St Margaret's School for Girls, 17 Albyn Place, Aberdeen AB10 1RU; T.-01224 584466; e-mail: info@st-margaret.aberdeen.sch.uk

Topping, Professor Barry H.V., BSc, PhD, DSc (hc), CEng, CMath, CITP, MBCS, MICE, MIStructE, MIMechE, FIMA. Emeritus Professor, Heriot-Watt University, Edinburgh; Director, Computational Technology Solutions, Stirlingshire; Honorary Professor, University of Pecs, Hungary; b. 14.2.52, Manchester. Educ. Bedford Modern School; City University, London. Lecturer in Civil Engineering, Edinburgh University, 1978-88; Von-Humboldt Research Fellow, Stuttgart University, 1986-87; Senior Lecturer, Heriot-Watt University, 1988-89, Reader, 1989-90, Professor of Structural Engineering, 1990-95, Professor of Computational Mechanics, 1995-2006. Co-Editor, Computers and Structures; Senior Editor, Civil-Comp Conference Series. Address: (b.) Dun Eaglais, Station Brae, Kippen, Stirlingshire FK8 3DY.

Topping, Professor Keith James, BA, MA, PhD, CPsychol, FBPsS. Emeritus Professor, Educational and Social Research, University of Dundee; b. 1.10.47, Stockport; m., Mei; 4 s. Educ. Marple Hall Grammar School; Universities of Sussex, Nottingham and Sheffield. After substantial practice as an educational psychologist for social services, health and education, moved to Dundee in 1992 to establish a training course for eucational psychologists; went on to establish a professional doctorate and become a professor specializing in research on peer learning, parental involvement and behaviour problems. Over 300 publications including over 20 books. Recreation: mountaineering. Address: Nethergate, Dundee DD1 4HN; e-mail: k.j.topping@dundee.ac.uk

Torphichen, 15th Lord (James Andrew Douglas Sandilands); b. 27.8.46; m.; 4 d. Address: Calder House, Mid Calder, West Lothian.

Torrance, David. MSP (SNP), Kirkcaldy, since 2011; b. 13.3.61, Kirkcaldy. Educ. Balwearie High School; Adam Smith College. Employed by British Gas and other companies before going into politics full-time in 2007, working for Chris Harvie MSP. Fife councillor. Assistant District Commissioner, Kirkcaldy Scouts. Address: (b.) Scottish Parliament, Edinburgh EH99 1SP.

Torrance, Very Rev. Professor Iain Richard, TD, MA, BD, DPhil, Hon DD, Hon DTheol, Hon LHD, FRSE. Pro-Chancellor, University of Aberdeen, since 2013; Dean of the Chapel Royal in Scotland, since 2013; Dean of the Order of the Thistle, since 2014; Hon Professor of Early Christian Doctrine and Ethics, University of Edinburgh, since 2013; a Chaplain-in-Ordinary to HM The Queen in Scotland, since 2001; President Emeritus and Professor of Patristics Emeritus, Princeton Theological Seminary, since 2013; Professor in Patristics and Christian Ethics (Emeritus), University of Aberdeen, since 2004; Master of Christ's College, Aberdeen, 2001-04; Moderator, General Assembly, Church of Scotland, 2003-04; Co-Editor, Scottish Journal of Theology, 1982-2015; b. 13.1.49, Aberdeen; m., Morag Ann MacHugh; 1 s.; 1 d. Educ. Edinburgh Academy; Monkton Combe School, Bath; Edinburgh University; St. Andrews University; Oriel College, Oxford University. Minister, Northmavine, Shetland, 1982-85; Lecturer in New Testament and Christian Ethics, Queen's College, Birmingham, 1985-89; Lecturer in New Testament and Patristics, Birmingham University, 1989-93; Aberdeen University: Lecturer, 1993-97, Senior Lecturer in Divinity, 1997-99, Professor in Patristics and Christian Ethics (Personal Chair), 1999-2004, Head, Department of Divinity with Religious Studies, 2000-01, Dean, Faculty of Arts and Divinity, 2001-03; President and Professor of Patristics, Princeton Theological Seminary, 2004-12. Chaplain to the Moderator of the General Assembly, 1976; Member, International Dialogue between the Orthodox and the Reformed Churches, 1992-2012, co-chair since 2005; Member, General Assembly's Panel on Doctrine, 1993-2002; Member, Ethics Committee, Grampian Health Board, 1996-2000; Hon. Secretary, Aberdeen A.U.T., 1995-98, Hon. President, 1998-99; Secretary, Society for the Study of Christian Ethics, 1995-

98; Judge, Templeton (UK) Awards, 1994-99; Templeton Advisory Board, 2008-11; TA Chaplain, 1982-97; ACF Chaplain, 1996-2000; Member, Academie Internationale des Sciences Religieuses, since 1997; Convener, General Assembly's Committee on Chaplains to HM Forces, 1998-2002; Senate Assessor to Aberdeen University Court, 1999-2003; Member, Committee of Highland TAVRA, 1999-2004; Member, QAA's Benchmarking Panel for Degrees in Theology and Religious Studies, 1999-2000; Member of the C-1 Religious Leader Commission, since 2010; Select Preacher, University of Oxford, 2004, University of Aberdeen, 2009, 2013, University of Cambridge, 2016; Convener of General Assembly of Church of Scotland's Theological Forum, since 2013; Trustee, University of Aberdeen Development Trust, since 2013; Free Burgess of the Burgh of Aberdeen, 2004; Friend for Life Award 2004, Equality Network, Scotland; Honorary Doctor of Divinity (St Andrews, 2005; Aberdeen, 2005; Edinburgh, 2012); Honorary Doctor of Theology (Debrecen, 2006); Honorary Doctor of Humane Letters (King Coll, TN, 2007); Corresponding Fellow, Royal Society of Edinburgh, 2007; (converted to FRSE on return to Scotland, 2013); Honorary Distinguished Alumnus, Princeton Theological Seminary, 2012; OStJ, 2015. Publications: Christology after Chalcedon, 1988; Human Genetics: a Christian perspective (Co-Author), 1995; Ethics and the Military Community, 1998; To Glorify God: Essays on Modern Reformed Liturgy (Co-Author), 1999; Bioethics for the New Millennium (Editor), 2000; Oxford Handbook of Systematic Theology (Co-Editor), 2007; Cambridge Dictionary of Christian Theology (Co-Editor), 2011; The Correspondence of Severus and Sergius, 2011. Recreations: historical Scottish culture (buildings, literature, art). Address: (h.) 25 The Causeway, Duddingston Village, Edinburgh EH15 3QA; T.-0131 661 3092.
E-mail: iain.torrance@oriel.oxon.org

Tosh, Murray, MA. MSP (Conservative), West of Scotland, 2003-07, South of Scotland, 1999-2003 (Deputy Presiding Officer, Scottish Parliament, 2001-07); b. 1.9.50, Ayr; m., Christine (deceased); 2 s.; 1 d. Educ. Kilmarnock Academy; Glasgow University; Jordanhill College of Education. Principal Teacher of History, Kilwinning Academy, 1977, Belmont Academy, Ayr, 1984; Councillor, Kyle and Carrick District Council, 1987-96 (Convener of Housing, 1992-96); Chairman, Central Ayrshire Conservative and Unionist Association, 1980-83, Ayr Conservative and Unionist Association, 1985-90. Recreations: hill-walking; reading; watching football and cricket; family history; visiting mediaeval castles; foreign holidays. Address: (h.) 14 Harleyburn Avenue, Melrose, Roxburghshire TD6 9JZ.

Toth, Emeritus Professor Akos George, Dr. Jur., PhD. Professor of Law, Strathclyde University, 1984-2001; Jean Monnet Chair of European Law, 1991-2001; b. 9.2.36, Mezotur, Hungary. Educ. Budapest University; Szeged University; Exeter University. Strathclyde University: Lecturer in Law, 1971-76, Senior Lecturer, 1976-82, Reader, 1982-84; British Academy Research Readership, 1993-95. Publications: Legal Protection of Individuals in the European Communities, 1978; The Oxford Encyclopaedia of European Community Law: Vol. I: 1990, Vol. II: 2005, Vol. III: 2008. Recreations: travel; music; opera; theatre; swimming; walking. Address: (b.) Strathclyde University, Law School, Graham Hills Building, 50 George Street, Glasgow G1 1QE; T.-0141-548 3594; e-mail: toth@strath.ac.uk

Totten, Sheriff William John, LLB (Hons). Sheriff of Glasgow and Strathkelvin, since 1999; b. 11.9.54, Paisley; m., Shirley Ann Morrison; 1 s. Educ. John Neilson Institute, Paisley; Glasgow University. Apprentice, Tindal, Oatts and Rodger, Solicitors, 1977-79; admitted as Solicitor, 1979; Procurator Fiscal Service, 1979-83; Assistant, then Partner, Beltrami and Co., 1983-88; admitted to Faculty of Advocates, 1989; Advocate Depute, 1993-96. Address: (b.) Glasgow Sheriff Court, 1 Carlton Place, Glasgow; T.-0141-429 8888.

Townley, Professor Barbara, BA, MSc, PhD. Professor, Chair of Management, St Andrews University; Director, Institute for Capitalising on Creativity; b. 9.10.54, Manchester. Educ. Worsley Wardley Grammar School; Lancaster University; London School of Economics. Lecturer: Lancaster University, 1983-85, University of Warwick Business School, 1985-90; Professor, Faculty of Business, University of Alberta, Canada, 1990-2000; Chair of Management and Organization, Edinburgh University, 2000-05. Publications: author of four books and many articles on management, organisation, performance measurement. Currently researching the creative industries. Recreation: travel. Address: (b.) Management School, Gateway, North Haugh, University of St Andrews, St Andrews, Fife KY16 9RJ; T.-01334 462808.

Trainor, Professor Sir Richard Hughes, KBE (2010), BA, MA, DPhil, FRHistS, FAcSS, FRSA, FKC. Rector, Exeter College, Oxford, since 2014; Principal and Professor of Social History, King's College London, 2004-2014, Professor Emeritus, since 2014; b. 31.12.48, New Jersey; m., Dr. Marguerite Wright Dupree; 1 s.; 1 d. Educ. Calvert Hall High School, Maryland; Brown University; Princeton University; Merton and Nuffield Colleges, Oxford University. Junior Research Fellow, Wolfson College, Oxford, 1977-79; Lecturer, Balliol College, Oxford, 1978-79; Glasgow University: Lecturer in Economic History, 1979-89, Senior Lecturer in Economic and Social History, 1989-95, Director, Design and Implementation of Software in History Project, 1985-89, Professor of Social History, 1995-2000, Co-Director, Computers in Teaching Initiative Centre for History, 1989-2000, Dean of Social Sciences, 1992-96, Vice-Principal, 1996-2000, Senior Vice-Principal, 1999-2000; Vice-Chancellor and Professor of Social History, Greenwich University, 2000-04. Honorary Fellow, Trinity College of Music, since 2003; Honorary Fellow, Merton College, Oxford, since 2004; Honorary Fellow, Institute of Historical Research, since 2009; Rhodes Scholar; Chair, Advisory Council, Institute of Historical Research, 2004-09; Honorary Secretary, Economic History Society, 1998-2004 and President, since 2013; President, Universities UK, 2007-09; Convener, Steering Group, Universities UK/DfES Review of Student Services, 2002; Member, US/UK Fulbright Commission, 2003-09 and Patron, since 2010; Council Member, Arts and Humanities Research Council, 2006-2011; Member, University of London Board of Trustees, 2009-2013; Joint Editor, Scottish Economic and Social History, 1989-94; Governor, St Paul's School, 2012-14; Governor, Royal Academy of Music, since 2013; Honorary Degrees: University of Kent, 2009 (Doctor of Civil Law); Rosalind Franklin University of Medicine and Science, 2012 (Doctor of Humane Letters); University of Glasgow, 2014 (Doctor of the University); Member of Council, University of Oxford, since 2015; Trustee, Museum of London, since 2014. Publications: Black Country Elites: the exercise of authority in an industrialised area 1830-1900, 1993; University, City and State: the University of Glasgow since 1870 (Joint Author), 2000. Recreations: parenting; observing politics; tennis. Address: (h.) 45 Mitre Road, Glasgow G14 9LE; T.-01865 279605.

Trees, Professor Alexander (Sandy). Chairman, Moredun Research Institute, since 2011. Educ. Edinburgh's Royal

(Dick) School of Veterinary Studies. Has made an enormous contribution to research into livestock health and is internationally recognised for this knowledge of veterinary parasitology; appointed Senior Lecturer, University of Liverpool in 1980, before being appointed Head of the Parasite and Vector Biology Division and then subsequently Dean of Liverpool's Faculty of Veterinary Science, until retirement in 2008. President, Association of Veterinary Teachers and Research Workers, 1996-97; President, Royal College of Veterinary Surgeons, 2009; formerly Council member of the Royal Society of Tropical Medicine and Hygiene; a founding Diplomate of the European Veterinary Parasitology College; Executive Board member, World Association for Veterinary Parasitology. Over 120 scientific papers and numerous presentations at regional, national and international conferences. Address: The Moredun Group, Pentlands Science Park, Bush Loan, Penicuik, Midlothian EH26 0PZ; T.-0131 445 5111.

Trew, Professor Arthur Stewart, BSc, PhD, FRSE, FRSA. Professor of Computational Science, University of Edinburgh, since 2006, Assistant Principal for Computational Science, Deputy Head of the College of Science and Engineering and Head of the School of Physics and Astronomy; b. 20.10.57, Belfast, Northern Ireland; m., Lesley Margaret Trew (nee Smart); 1 s.; 1 d. Educ. Royal Belfast Academical Institution; University of Edinburgh. Computing Officer, University of Edinburgh, 1983-85; Lecturer, Department of Clinical Sciences, Glasgow, 1985-86; Research Fellow, Department of Physics, Edinburgh, 1986-90, Programme Manager, EPCC, 1990-94, Director, EPCC, 1994-2010, Deputy Director, NESC, since 2001. Director, UoE HPCx Ltd. Recreations: running; cycling; hill walking. Address: (b.) School of Physics and Astronomy, University of Edinburgh, James Clerk Maxwell Building, Peter Guthrie Tait Road, King's Buildings, Edinburgh EH9 3FD; T.-0131 650 5025; e-mail: a.s.trew@ed.ac.uk

Trewavas, Professor Anthony James, BSc, PhD, FRS, FRSE, FRSA, FWIF, Academia Europea. Professor, Institute of Plant Molecular Science, Edinburgh University, since 1990; b. 17.6.39, London; m., Valerie; 1 s.; 2 d. Educ. Roan Grammar School; University College, London. Lecturer/Reader, Edinburgh University; Visiting Professor, Universities of Michigan State, Calgary, California (Davis), Bonn, Illinois, North Carolina, National University of Mexico; University of Milan. Publications: 260 scientific papers; three books. Recreations: music (particularly choral); reading. Address: (h.) Old Schoolhouse, Croft Street, Penicuik EH26 9DH; e-mail: Trewavas@ed.ac.uk

Trotter, Alexander Richard, CVO (2013), OStJ, JP, FRSA. Lord Lieutenant of Berwickshire, 2000-2014; Chairman, Thirlestane Castle Trust, 1996-2007; b. 20.2.39, London; m., Julia Henrietta Greenwell; 3 s. Educ. Eton College; City of London Technical College. Royal Scots Greys, 1958-68; Member, Berwickshire County Council, 1969-75 (Chairman, Roads Committee, 1974-75); Manager, Charterhall Estate and Farm, since 1969; Chairman, Meadowhead Ltd. (formerly Mortonhall Park Ltd.), since 1974; Director, Timber Growers' GB Ltd., 1977-82; Vice Chairman, Border Grain Ltd., 1989-2003; Council Member, Scottish Landowners' Federation, 1975-2004 (President, 1996-2001, Chairman, Land Use Committee, 1975-78, Convener, 1982-85); Member, Department of Agriculture Working Party on the Agricultural Holding (Scotland) Legislation, 1981-82; Member, Nature Conservancy Council, and Chairman, Scottish Committee, 1985-90; Member, UK Committee for Euro Year of the Environment, 1986-88; Member, Scottish Tourist Board Graded Holiday Parks Overseeing Committee, 1993-2013; Ensign, Queen's Bodyguard for Scotland (Royal Company of Archers). Recreations: skiing; golf; shooting. Address: Whinkerstones Farm, Duns, Berwickshire TD11 3RE; T.-01890 840210; e-mail: alex@charterhall.net

Trotter, Christopher H. Food Writer/Food Consultant; b. 21.09.57, Aberdeen; m., Caroline; 2 s. Educ. Marlborough College; Oxford Polytechnic. Career: Manager, Chef, Portsonachan Hotel; Founder and Proprietor, "Scotland's Larder", Scottish Food Shop and Demonstration Facility; Founder, Momentum Food Consultancy; Author. Chair, Pioneer Health Foundation; Member, Board of SFAC. Publications: The Scottish Kitchen; Scottish Cooking; The Whole Hog; The Whole Cow. Recreations: squash; tennis; food and drink; walking. Address: Buckthorns House, Upper Largo, Leven KY8 6EA; T.-01333 360 219; e-mail: ct@christophertrotter.co.uk

Troughton, Jamie Michael, DipArch, MA (Cantab), RIBA. Director: Tulliemet Ltd, since 1999, Ristol Ltd., since 2007; b. 8.11.50, Hambleden; m., Sarah Campbell-Preston; 1 s.; 2 d. Educ. Trinity College Cambridge. Qualified Architect, RIBA, 1977; Foster Associates, 1975-78; Richard Rogers and Partners, 1978-82; Founding Partner, Troughton McAslan Architects, 1983; Chairman, John McAslan and Partners, 1996-98; Award winning buildings for British Rail; London Underground; Apple Computers; Yapi Kredi Banksi, Istanbul; Canary Wharf FC3, London. Trustee, National Musuems of Scotland, 2011. Address: Atholl Estates Office, Blair Atholl, Pitlochry PH18 5TH; T.-01796 481355.

Troup, Colin Andrew, DPhil, LLB. Legal Secretary to the Lord Advocate; b. 23.05.61, Glasgow; m., Niamh Mary Hartnett; 2 d.; 1 s. Educ. Dumfries Academy; University of Glasgow; Balliol College, Oxford. Solicitor, Paisner & Co, London, 1991-99; Scottish Executive Solicitor's Office, 1999-2005, 2008-09; Legal Secretary to the Lord Advocate, 2005-08, 2009-. Address: (b.) Lord Advocate's Chambers, 25 Chambers Street, Edinburgh EH1 1LA; T.-0844-561-2000.

Truman, Donald Ernest Samuel, BA, PhD, CBiol, FRSB. Higher Education Consultant; b. 23.10.36, Leicester; m., Kathleen Ramsay; 1 s.; 1 d. Educ. Wyggeston School, Leicester; Clare College, Cambridge. NATO Research Fellow, Wenner-Grenn Institute, Stockholm, 1962-63; MRC Epigenetics Research Group, Edinburgh, 1963-72; Lecturer, Department of Genetics, Edinburgh University, 1972-78; Senior Lecturer, 1978-89, Head of Department, 1984-89, Director of Biology Teaching Unit, 1985-89; Vice-Dean and Vice-Provost, Faculty of Science and Engineering, 1989-98; Assistant Principal, Edinburgh University, 1998-2002; Aneurin Bevan Memorial Fellow, Government of India, 1978; Chairman, Edinburgh Centre for Rural Research, 1993-2002; Member, Council, Scottish Agricultural College, 1995-2002; Director, Edinburgh Technopole Company Ltd., 1996-2002; Member, Board of Directors, Edinburgh Lifelong Learning Partnership, 1999-2002. Publications: The Biochemistry of Cytodifferentiation, 1974; Differentiation in Vitro (Joint Editor), 1982; Stability and Switching in Cellular Differentiation, 1982; Coordinated Regulation of Gene Expression, 1986. Recreations: gardening; books; birds. Address: (h.) 36 Ladysmith Road, Edinburgh EH9 3EU.

Truscott, Ian D., QC, LLB (Hons), LLM, PhD. Solicitor Advocate; Visiting Professor of Law, Strathclyde University, 1998-2010; Part-time

Employment Judge, Employment Tribunal (England and Wales), since 2002; b. 7.11.49, Perth; m., Julia; 4 s. Educ. Perth Academy; Edinburgh University; Leeds University; Strathclyde University. Solicitor, 1973-87; Advocate, 1988-2013; Barrister, 1995-2013; QC, since 1997. Address: (b.) Albany House, 58 Albany Street, Edinburgh EH1 3QH; T.-0131-557-1545.

Tucker, Professor John Barry, BA, MA, PhD, FRSE. Professor Emeritus, University of St. Andrews, since 2006, Professor of Cell Biology, 1990-2006; b. 17.3.41, Arundel; m., Janet Stephen Murray; 2 s. Educ. Queen Elizabeth Grammar School, Atherstone; Peterhouse, Cambridge (State Scholar and Kitchener National Memorial Scholar). Fulbright Travel Scholar and Research Associate, Department of Zoology, Indiana University, 1966-68; SERC Research Fellow, Department of Zoology, Cambridge, 1968-69; Lecturer in Zoology, St. Andrews University, 1969-79 (Chairman, Zoology Department, 1982-84); Reader in Zoology, 1979-90. Member: SERC Advisory Group II, 1977-80, SERC Molecular Biology and Genetics Sub-committee, 1986-89, Editorial Board of Journal of Embryology and Experimental Morphology, 1979-88. Recreations: cycling; hill-walking; astronomy; reluctant gardener. Address: (b.) School of Biology, Bute Building, University of St. Andrews, St. Andrews, Fife KY16 9TS; T.-01334 839596; e-mail: jbt@st-and.ac.uk

Tulloch, William Alexander. Farmer, since 1968; Chairman, NFUS LFA Committee, 2007-2012; North Scotland Area Advisor for Moredun Research Institute; Regional Advisor for NFU Mutual; b. 22.03.52, Aberdeen; m., Madeleine Frances; 1 s.; 1 d. Educ. Disblair Primary; O'Neil Corse Primary; Alford Academy; Clinterty Agricultural College. Formerly active Member of the Young Farmers movement; posts included Secretary; Treasurer and finally Club Chairperson; became Proficiency Test Chairman (3 years); also Secretary/Treasurer for the Cromar and Upper Deeside Ploughing Association. Address: Milton Bank, Corse, Lumphanan, Banchory AB31 4RY; T.-013398 83654; e-mail: tulloch.s@btinternet.com

Turley, Mark John, BSc (Hons), MBA, MCIOH. Director of Housing, City of Edinburgh Council, 1996-2014, Director, Services for Communities, 2006-2014, Executive Director of Housing, 1993-2014; b. 25.6.60, Dudley. Educ. High Arcal Grammar School, Sedgley; Leicester University. Sheffield City Council, 1981-91; Head of Tenant Services, York City Council, 1991-93. Recreations: playing violin and guitar; reading.

Turmeau, Professor William Arthur, CBE, FRSE, Dr. h.c. (Edinburgh University), Doctor of Education (Napier University), BSc, PhD, CEng, FIMechE. Chairman, Scottish Environment Protection Agency, 1995-99; Principal and Vice-Chancellor, Napier University, 1982-94; b. 19.9.29, London; m., Margaret Moar Burnett; 1 d. Educ. Stromness Academy, Orkney; Edinburgh University; Moray House College of Education; Heriot-Watt University. Royal Signals, 1947-49; Research Engineer, Northern Electric Co. Ltd., Montreal, 1952-54; Mechanical Engineer, USAF, Goose Bay, Labrador, 1954-56; Contracts Manager, Godfrey Engineering Co. Ltd., Montreal, 1956-61; Lecturer, Bristo Technical Institute, Edinburgh, 1962-64; Napier College: Lecturer and Senior Lecturer, 1964-68, Head, Department of Mechanical Engineering, 1968-75, Assistant Principal and Dean, Faculty of Technology, 1975-82. Member, IMechE Academic Standards Committee; Vice Chairman, ASH (Scotland). Recreations: modern jazz; Leonardo da Vinci. Address: (h.) 132 Victoria Street, Stromness, Orkney KW16 3BU; T.-01856 850500; e-mail: profwaturmeau@aol.com

Turnbull, The Hon. Lord (Alan). Senator of the College of Justice, since 2006. Address: (b.) Parliament House, 11 Parliament Square, Edinburgh EH1 1RQ.

Turnbull, Wilson Mark, DipArch (with distinction in design), MLA (summa cum laude) (Penn), MBCS, RIBA, FRIAS, FLI. Principal, Mark Turnbull Landscape Architect; Chairman and Director, Turnbull Jeffrey Partnership, Landscape Architects, 1999-2001 (Principal, 1982-98); Chairman and Director, Envision 3D Ltd, since 1999; b. 1.4.43, Edinburgh. Educ. George Watson's; Edinburgh College of Art, School of Architecture; University of Pennsylvania. Assistant Professor of Architecture, University of Southern California, 1970-74; Partner, W.J. Cairns and Partners, Environmental Consultants, 1974-82; Partner, Design Innovations Research, 1976-81; Council Member, Cockburn Association (Edinburgh Civic Trust), 1986-95; Commissioner, Countryside Commission for Scotland, 1988-92; Commissioner, Royal Fine Art Commission for Scotland, 1996-2005; Chairman, Edinburgh Greenbelt Initiative, 1988-91; Director, Edinburgh Greenbelt Trust (the Edinburgh Greenspace Trust, since 2007), since 1991, Vice-Chairman, 1993-2002; Chair, Landscape Institute Scotland, since 2011; Member, Landscape Institute Technical Committee, since 1994, Chair, since 2013; Member, Board of the Landscape Institute, since 2013; Awards: Andrew Grant Travel Scholarships; Edinburgh Corporation Medal for Civic Design; Faculty Medal, Department of Landscape Architecture, University of Pennsylvania; Fulbright Scholarship. Recreation: sailing. Address: (b.) Creag an Tuirc House, Balquhidder, Perthshire FK19 8NY; T.-01877 384 728.

Turner, John. Consultant, The Croft Management Consulting Ltd, since 2015; former Chief Executive, NHS 24 (2008-2015). Career in health service management and leadership, with experience in service delivery management as well as at government level; joined the NHS in 1987 as a National General Management Trainee in England, working in the East Midlands and Yorkshire areas; worked in general and teaching hospitals, as well as in community, mental health, and learning disabilities services; became a Director of the Bassetlaw Hospital and Community Services NHS Trust in Nottinghamshire in 1992; moved to Scotland in 1994 and spent eight years as the Chief Executive of the Community Health NHS Trust, and then the Primary Care NHS Trust, in the Scottish Borders; joined the Scottish Government Health Department in 2003 as Pay Modernisation Director, leading the national implementation of the new General Medical Services contract for GPs, before then taking on the national lead role for the implementation of Agenda for Change (the grading and pay system for NHS staff); former member of the NHS 24 Independent Review Team; Acting Chief Executive of NHS Western Isles, 2007-08. Address: (b.) The Croft, St. Boswells, Melrose, Roxburghshire TD6 0AE.

Turner, John R., MA, HonMA, MusB, FRCO. Organist and Director of Music, Glasgow Cathedral, 1965-2010; Lecturer, Royal Scottish Academy of Music, 1965-2007; Organist, Strathclyde University, 1965-2010; b. Halifax. Educ. Rugby; Jesus College, Cambridge. Recreations: reading; travel. Address: (h.) Binchester, 1 Cathkin Road, Rutherglen, Glasgow G73 4SE; T.-0141-634 7775.

Turner, Professor Kenneth John, BSc, PhD. Emeritus Professor of Computing Science, Stirling University (Professor, 1987-2014); b. 21.2.49, Glasgow; m., Elizabeth Mary Christina; 2 s. Educ. Hutchesons' Boys Grammar School; Glasgow University; Edinburgh University. Data Communications Designer, International Computers Ltd.,

1974-76; Senior Systems Analyst, Central Regional Council, 1976-77; Data Communications Consultant, International Computers Ltd., 1977-87. Recreations: choral singing; craft work; sailing. Address: (b.) Department of Computing Science and Mathematics, Stirling University, Stirling, FK9 4LA; T.-01786 466000.

Tweeddale, 14th Marquis of (Charles David Montagu Hay); b. 6.8.47; succeeded to title, 2005.

Twist, Benjamin. Director, Creative Carbon Scotland; carbon consultant; b. 17.4.62, London; m., Margaret Corr. Educ. Crown Woods Comprehensive School; University of Edinburgh. Freelance Director of Theatre, Music Theatre and Opera throughout Scotland, UK, Europe, North America and New Zealand; Artistic Director of Contact Theatre, Manchester, 1994-98. Member, SAC Capital Committee, 1999-2003; Chair: SAC Capital Committee, 2003-07, SAC Lottery Committee, 2007-10; Member: SAC, 2003-07, Joint Board of SAC and Scottish Screen, 2007-2010; Trustee, The Theatres Trust, 2007-2013, Vice Chair, 2011-13; Chair, Hebrides Ensemble, since 2010. Address: (h.) 39 Rosslyn Crescent, Edinburgh EH6 5AT; e-mail: ben.twist@blueyonder.co.uk

Tyre, The Hon. Lord (Colin Jack Tyre), CBE, LLB, DESU. Senator of the College of Justice, since 2010; b. 17.4.56, Dunoon; m., Elaine Patricia Carlin (deceased); 1 s.; 2 d. Educ. Dunoon Grammar School; Edinburgh University; Universite d'Aix Marseille. Lecturer in Scots Law, Edinburgh University, 1980-83; Tax Editor, CCH Editions Ltd., Bicester, 1983-86; Advocate, 1987-98; QC, 1998-2010; Standing Junior Counsel to Scottish Office Environment Department in planning matters, 1995-98; President, Council of Bars and Law Societies of Europe, 2007; Member, UK Delegation to CCBE, 1999-2004; Head of Delegation, 2004; Scottish Law Commissioner (part-time), 2003-09. Publications: CCH Inheritance Tax Reporter; contributor to Stair Memorial Encyclopaedia; Tax for Litigation Lawyers (Co-Author); Chairman, Board of Governors, Fettes College, Edinburgh, since 2012. Recreations: orienteering; golf; mountain walking; popular music. Address: (b.) Supreme Courts, 11 Parliament Square, Edinburgh EH1 1RQ; T.-0131 225 2595.

U

Uddin, Dr Wali Tasar, MBE, DBA, DLitt. Joint President, European Bangladesh Federation of Commerce & Industry (EBFCI); Hon Consul General of Bangladesh in Scotland, since 2002; b. 17.4.52, Moulvibazar, Bangladesh. Educ. Moulvibazar Govt. HS; Putney College (HNC); m., Syeda; 2 s.; 3 d. Chairman and Chief Executive, Universal Koba Corp Ltd and Britannia Spice Scot Ltd., 2000, also consultant, The Verandah and Lancers Brasserie; established Travel Link Worldwide Ltd.; Chairman and Chief Executive, Frontline International Air Services UK Ltd., 1997; consultant in restaurant and travel trade sectors; Hon Consul General of Bangladesh in Scotland, 1993-98; Chief Co-ordinator, Indian Earthquake Disaster Appeal Fund Scotland, 2001, Chief Co-ordinator, Bangladesh Flood Victim Appeal Fund Scot; Chairman, Bangladesh Br C of C; Founding Director, Edinburgh Mela (Asian Festival) Ltd.; Founder and Chairman, Bangladesh Samity (Association) Edinburgh; Co-ordinator, Expo Bangladesh, 2005; Chairman: Commonwealth Society Edinburgh; Bangladesh Council in Scotland, Scotland Bangladeshi International Humanitarian Trust; Bangla Scot Foundation; Ethnic Enterprise Centre Edinburgh; Director, Edinburgh C of C, 2002; Patron: Bangladesh Cyclone Disaster Appeal Fund; Royal Hospital for Sick Children Edinburgh; Scotland School of Asian Cuisine, Fife College; Director, Sylhet Women's Medical College and Hospital, 2005; Adviser, Atish Dipankar, University of Science and Technology, 2004; Chairman, Advisory Board, University of East London Business School, 2004; former Chairman and Director-General, British Bangladesh Chamber of Commerce in UK; Patron, Lion Children's Hospital, Sylhet, 1997; Trustee: Bangladesh Female Academy, 2004, Shahajalal Mosque Edinburgh; Member, Edinburgh Merchant Co; Board Member, Council for Foreign C of C and Industries; Executive Member, Royal Commonwealth Society, Edinburgh; Young Scot Award, Int Jr C of C, 1992; Lifetime Achievement Award, Asian Jewel Awards, 2006; Outstanding Achievement in catering Award, The British Bangladeshi Who's Who; Curry King Award, Scottish Curry Awards; DBA (hc), Queen Margaret UC, 2000; Hon DLitt, Heriot Watt University, 2007; MInstP; MCMI; FInstSMM. Recreations: supporting Heart of Midlothian FC and the Bangladesh cricket team; football; family; working with the televisual media (ethnic, national and international). Clubs: Rotary International. Address: Universal Koba Corporation Ltd, Britannia Spice Restaurant, 150 Commercial Street, Ocean Drive, Leith, Edinburgh EH6 6LB; e-mail: waliuddin@aol.com
Web: www.britanniaspice.co.uk

Uist, The Hon. Lord (Roderick Macdonald), LLB. Senator of the College of Justice, since 2006; b. 1.2.51. Educ. St Mungo's Academy; University of Glasgow. Career history: admitted to the Faculty of Advocates in 1975; Advocate Depute, 1987-93 (Home Advocate Depute from 1990); appointed Queen's Counsel in 1989; called to the Bar of England and Wales in 1997 (Inner Temple); Legal Chairman of the Pension Appeal Tribunals for Scotland, 1995-2001; Member: Criminal Injuries Compensation Board, 1995-2000, Criminal Injuries Compensation Appeals Panel, 1997-99; Temporary Judge in 2001-06; took the judicial title Lord Uist and sits in the Outer House. Prominent cases presided over include the 2006 trial of three of the race hate murderers of Kriss Donald. Address: Parliament House, 11 Parliament Square, Edinburgh EH1 1RQ.

Ulph, Professor David Tregear, MA, BLitt, FRSA, FRSE. Professor of Economics, University of St. Andrews, since 2006; Director, Scottish Institute for Research in Economics (SIRE,) since 2009; b. 26.10.46, Belshill; m., Elizabeth Margaret; 2 d. Educ. Hutchesons Boys Grammar School; University of Glasgow; University of Oxford. Lecturer in Economics: University of Stirling, 1971-77, University College London, 1977-82; Reader in Economics, University College London, 1982-84; Professor of Economics, University of Bristol, 1984-91, Head of Department of Economics, 1984-87; Professor of Economics, University College London, 1992-2001, Head of Department of Economics, 1992-97, Executive Director, ESRC Centre for Economic Learning and Social Evolution, 1997-2001; Chief Economist and Director of Analysis & Research, Inland Revenue, 2001-04; Chief Economist and Director of Analysis, HM Revenue & Customs, 2004-06. Member: Economic Affairs Committee, ESRC, 1986-88, Research Grants Board, ESRC, 1993-98, Council of European Economic Association, 1991-94, Council of Royal Economic Society, 1995-99; Member of Editorial Board: Review of Economic Studies, 1981-90, Journal of Industrial Economics, 1986-88, European Economic Review, 1991-95. Recreations: bridge; cinema; travel; cooking. Address: (h.) Sealladh Mor, Bankhead Courtyard, Bankhead Farm, Peat Inn, Fife KY15 5LF; T.-01334 840393; e-mail: david@ulph.me.uk

Upton, Emeritus Professor Brian Geoffrey Johnson, BA, MA, DPhil, FRSE, FGS. Emeritus Professor of Petrology, Edinburgh University, since 1999; b. 2.3.33, London; m., Bodil Aalbaek Upton; 2 s.; 1 d. Educ. Reading School; St John's College, Oxford University. Geological Survey of Greenland, 1958-60; Fulbright Fellow, California Institute of Technology, 1961-62; Lecturer, Geology, Edinburgh University, 1962-72; Carnegie Fellow, Geophysical Laboratory, Washington, 1970-71; Edinburgh University: Reader in Geology, 1972-82; Professor of Petrology, 1982-99; Executive Editor, Journal of Petrology, 1983-94; Clough Medallist, Geological Society, Edinburgh, 2001. Recreations: painting; gardening; travel. Address: (b.) Grant Institute, The King's Buildings, James Hutton Road, Edinburgh EH9 3FE; T.-0131 650 5110.

Uren, Neal Gordon, BSc (Hons), MB, ChB, MD (Hons), FRCP, FESC, FACC. Consultant Cardiologist, since 1997; b. 9.11.60, Kirkcaldy; m., Dr. Janet Murray; 2 s.; 1 d. Educ. Balwearie High School, Kirkcaldy; University of Edinburgh. House Officer, Edinburgh, 1984-85; Senior House Officer, Newcastle Teaching Hospitals, 1985-87; Hammersmith Hospital: Cardiology Registrar, 1988-89, Research Registrar, 1990-93; Senior Registrar, Leicester, 1993-97; Interventional Fellow, Stanford University Hospital, USA, 1995-96. Treasurer, British Cardiovascular Intervention Society, 2002-06; Council Member, British Cardiovascular Society, 2006-10; Clinical Director for Cardiac Services, 2011-present. Recreations: golf; bass guitar; travel. Address: Edinburgh Heart Centre, Royal Infirmary, Edinburgh EH16 4SA; T.-0131 242 1046.
E-mail: neal.uren@nhslothian.scot.nhs.uk

U'ren, William Graham, BSc (Hons), DipTP, FRTPI. Town Planning Consultant (semi-retired); Adviser to the Scottish Public Services Ombudsman; Chair, Crichton Trust, Dumfries; Trustee, New Lanark Trust; b. 28.12.46, Glasgow; m., Wendy; 2 d. Educ. Aberdeen Grammar School; Aberdeen University; Strathclyde University. Director of Planning and Technical Services, Clydesdale District Council, 1982-96; Director, Royal Town Planning Institute in Scotland, 1997-2007; Town Planning Consultant, Dundas and Wilson, 2007-2012. Past Chairman, Scottish Society of Directors of Planning; former Member, Scottish Government's Marine Strategy Forum; former Member,

Heritage Lottery Fund Committee for Scotland; former Member, Scottish Cricket Union Committee; Past President, Uddingston Cricket Club; formerly Founder Trustee, Built Environment Forum Scotland; formerly Trustee, Planning Aid for Scotland. Recreations: local history; listening to music; travel; town-twinning; watching cricket and rugby; bird watching; philately. Address: (b.) 'Carseview', 125 Hyndford Road, Lanark ML11 9AU.

Urquhart, Jean. Former MSP (Independent), Highlands and Islands (2012-16) (SNP MSP, 2011-12); b. 17.5.49, West Lothian. Educ. Lindsay High School, Bathgate. Former SNP councillor, Highland Council (2003-2011). Member, RISE - Scotland's Left Alliance, since 2015.

Urquhart, Canon John. Retired Parish Priest (St. Bernadette's, Larbert); Founder and Former Chairman, Diocesan Heritage and Arts Commission; b. 1.7.34, Bowhill, Fife. Educ. St. Ninian's, Bowhill; St. Columba's Cowdenbeath; Blairs College, Aberdeen; Scots College, Spain; St. Andrew's College, Drygrange. Assistant: St. Joseph's, Sighthill, Edinburgh, Our Lady and St. Andrew's, Galashiels; Chaplain, St. Mary's Balnakiel; Parish Priest: St. Paul's, Muirhouse, Edinburgh, St. Margaret's, Dunfermline. Address: 100 Glasgow Road, Falkirk FK1 4HJ; T.-01324 621038.

Urquhart, Linda Hamilton, OBE, LLB, WS. Chairman, Morton Fraser, since 2011; b. 21.9.59, Edinburgh; m., Lord Burns (David S Burns) ; 2 d. Educ. James Gillespie's High School; University of Edinburgh. Trainee Solicitor, Steedman Ramage WS, 1981-83; Morton Fraser: Solicitor, 1983-85, Partner, 1985-2012, Chief Executive, 1999-2011. Board Member, Scottish Enterprise and CBI; Chairman, Investors in People Scotland; Non-Executive Director, Adam & Company and Edinburgh Airport; Member, Edinburgh Business Forum; Trustee, Marie Curie Cancer Care and RSA Foundation; Ambassador, Girlguiding UK; Co-Editor, Greens Property Law Bulletin. Recreations: singing; sailing; walking; skiing; golf. Address: (b.) Quartermile Two, 2 Lister Square, Edinburgh EH3 9GL; T.-0131-247-1020; e-mail: linda.urquhart@morton-fraser.com

Usher, Professor John Richard, BSc (Hons), MSc, PhD, CMATH. Professor of Mathematics, Robert Gordon University, 1998-2001 (retired 2001); b. 12.5.44, London; m., Sheila Mary McKendrick; 1 d. Educ. St. Nicholas Grammar School, London; Hull University; St Andrews University. Lecturer, Mathematics, Teesside Polytechnic, 1970-74; Senior Lecturer, Mathematics, Glasgow College of Technology, 1974-82; Head of School of Mathematics (later School of Computing and Mathematical Sciences), Robert Gordon University, 1983-92; Senior Lecturer, Mathematics, 1992-98; Scottish Branch Committee, IMA: Vice-Chairman, 1983-85, Chairman, 1985-88, Hon. Member, 1988 -89; Member, IMA Council, 1987-90; External examiner for various Universities; Examiner for SCOTEC; Moderator for SCOTVEC; Member, UCAS Scottish Higher Education Mathematical Sciences and Computing Panel; Eucharistic Assistant, St. Ternans, Scottish Episcopal Church, Muchalls. Recreations: reading; walking; theatre-going; concert-going; bridge; croquet. Address: 20 St. Crispin's Road, Newtonhill, Stonehaven, Kincardineshire AB39 3PS.
E-mail: johnandsheilausher@btinternet.com

Usher, Professor Michael Barham, OBE, BSc, PhD, DUniv, CBiol, FRSB, FRES, FRSE. Chief Scientist, Scottish Natural Heritage, 1991-2001, Leverhulme Emeritus Fellow, 2001-03; b. 19.11.41, Old Colwyn; m.,

Kathleen Fionna Munro; 1 s.; 1 d. Educ. Portsmouth Grammar School; Edinburgh University. Lecturer, Senior Lecturer, Reader, Department of Biology, University of York, 1967-91; Adviser on termite research, British Technical Assistance to the Government of Ghana, 1971-73; research in the Antarctic and Sub-Antarctic, 1980-81; Nature Conservancy Council for Scotland and Scottish Natural Heritage, Chief Scientific Adviser/Chief Scientist, 1991-2001; Honorary Professor: in Zoology, University of Aberdeen, in Environmental Science, University of Stirling, in Biological Sciences, University of Edinburgh. Chairman of Group of Experts on European Diploma for Protected Areas, Council of Europe, 2010-13; former Independent Member of the UK's Joint Nature Conservation Committee; Chairman of Trustees of Bumblebee Conservation Trust; former Chairman of Trustees of Forth Naturalist & Historian; former Trustee of Royal Botanic Garden Edinburgh and Woodland Trust; former International Conservation Fellow, Durrell Wildlife Conservation Trust, Jersey. Publications: over 240 scientific papers; 14 books. Recreations: walking; natural history photography; philately. Address: (b.) Biological and Environmental Sciences, School of Natural Sciences, University of Stirling, Stirling FK9 4LA; e-mail: m.b.usher@stir.ac.uk

V

Vance, Dr James. Rector, Culloden Academy, since 2012. Educ. Belfast High School. Principal Teacher of History, then Depute Rector, Banff Academy, 2001-2010; Rector, Golspie High School, 2010-2012. Address: (b.) Keppoch Road, Inverness, Highland IV2 7JZ; T.-01463 790851.

van der Kuyl, Professor Christiaan Richard David, FRSE, BSc (Hons), FRSA, Hon DBA. Chairman, Tayforth Consulting Limited and 4J Studios Limited; CEO, brightsolid Online Innovation Limited, 2007-2013; b. 20.8.69, Dundee. Technology Entrepreneur; Director, Sensation Science Centre, Dundee; Visiting Professor, Digital Entertainment, University of Abertay Dundee; Elected Member, The Council at RSE; Convener, Young Persons Committee, RSE; Member, The Board of The Scottish Institute for Enterprise; Chair, The Development Advisory Board, Napier University; Member, Smith Group; Chairman, Entrepreneurial Exchange. Recreations: playing computer games; music; golf; cycling. Club: New Club. Address: (b.) Tayforth Consulting Limited, Seabraes, Perth Road, Dundee DD1 4LN; T.-01382 341027.

Vannet, Sheriff Alfred Douglas, LLB, FRSA. Sheriff of South Strathclyde, Dumfries and Galloway at Airdrie, 2001-09, now retired but part time; All-Scotland floating Sheriff, 2000-01; Honorary Professorial Teaching Fellow, since 2011 and Senior Tutor in criminal litigation, School of Law, University of Glasgow, since 2010; b. 31.7.49, Dundee; m., Pauline Margaret Renfrew; 1 s.; 1 d. Educ. High School of Dundee; Dundee University. Procurator Fiscal Depute, Dundee; Dundee University. Procurator Fiscal Depute, Dundee, 1976-77; Procurator Fiscal Depute, then Senior Procurator Fiscal Depute, Glasgow, 1977-84; Assistant Solicitor, Crown Office, 1984-90; Deputy Crown Agent, 1990-94; Regional Procurator Fiscal, Grampian, Highland and Islands at Aberdeen, 1994-97; Regional Procurator Fiscal, Glasgow and Strathkelvin, 1997-99. Honorary Member, Royal Faculty of Procurators in Glasgow, since 1997. Recreations: walking; curling. Address: (b.) Airdrie Sheriff Court, Graham Street, Airdrie ML6 6EE. E-mail: sheriff.advannet@scotcourts.gov.uk

Vardy, Professor Alan Edward, BSc, PhD, DSc, DEng, FREng, FRSE, EurIng, CEng, FICE, FASCE, FRSA. Research Professor in Civil Engineering, Dundee University, since 1995; Director, Dundee Tunnel Research, since 1995; b. 6.11.45, Sheffield; m., Susan Janet; 2 s.; 1 d. Educ. High Storrs Grammar School, Sheffield; Leeds University. Lecturer in Civil Engineering, Leeds University, 1972-75; Royal Society Warren Research Fellow, Cambridge University, 1975-79; Dundee University: Professor of Civil Engineering, 1979-95 (Deputy Principal, 1985-89, Vice-Principal, 1988-89); Director, Wolfson Bridge Research Unit, 1980-90; Royal Society/SERC Industrial Fellow, 1990-94; Director, Lightweight Structures Unit, 1998-2004. Address: Kirkton of Abernyte, Perthshire PH14 9SS; T.-01828 686241.

Varty, Professor E. Kenneth C., BA (Hons), PhD, DLitt, Chevalier dans l' Ordre des Palmes Academiques, Chevalier dans l' Ordre des Arts et des Lettres. Professor Emeritus, Glasgow University, since 1990; Life Member, Clare Hall, Cambridge University, since 1984; b. 18.8.27, Derbyshire; m., Hedwig; 2 d. Educ. Bemrose School, Derby; Nottingham University. Assistant Lecturer, then Lecturer, French, University College of N. Staffs, 1953-61; Lecturer/Senior Lecturer, French, Leicester University, 1961-68; Stevenson Professor of French, Glasgow University, 1968-90; Dean, Faculty of Arts, Glasgow University, 1978-81; President, Alliance Française de Glasgow, 1982-89. Publications: Reynard, Renart, Renaert, 1999; Reynard the Fox, 2000. Recreations: travel; art galleries; museums; historic sites etc. Address: (h.) 4 Dundonald Road, Glasgow, G12 9LJ; T.-0141 339 1413.

Veal, Sheriff Kevin Anthony, KSG, KC*HS, LLB. Retired Sheriff (Tayside Central and Fife at Forfar, 1993-2014); b. 16.9.46, Chesterfield; m., Monica Flynn; 2 s.; 2 d. Educ. Lawside Academy, Dundee; St. Andrews University. Partner, Burns Veal and Gillan, Dundee, 1971-93; Legal Aid Reporter, 1978-93; Temporary Sheriff, 1984-93; Tutor, Department of Law, Dundee University, 1978-85; Dean, Faculty of Procurators and Solicitors in Dundee, 1991-93. Musical Director, Cecilian Choir, Dundee, since 1975; Member, University Court, Abertay Dundee, 1998-2009; Member, Council, Sheriffs' Association, 2000-03; Honorary President, Dundee Operatic Society, since 2003; Hon. Fellow, University of Abertay Dundee, 2010. Recreations: organ and classical music; hill-walking.

Vermeulen, Rev. Chris, BTh (Rhodes), MA (Sheffield). Minister, St. Columba's Parish Church, Largs, since 2014; Minister, Orchardhill Parish Church, Giffnock, 2005-14; b. 19.1.61, Vanderbijlpark, South Africa; m., Elaine; 1 s.; 1 d. Educ. Vaal High School, Vanderbijlpark, South Africa; Rhodes University; Sheffield University. Formerly Minister, St. David's Presbyterian Church (Nigel, South Africa); moved to Scotland to study at Glasgow University while still ministering part time in the Falkirk area; called to Barrhead Congregational Church (now part of the United Reformed Church) and served as their minister for 6 years until 2000; moved to Manchester to become Research Fellow, Woodlands Project on a 5 year contract. Vice-Convenor, Glasgow Presbytery Mission Strategy. Co-Founder, the www.emergingchurch.info website; currently serves on the organising committee of the Euro Church Network (www.eurochurch.net); instrumental in bringing the Together in Missions Missional Leadership course to Scotland (www.missionalleadership.org.uk). Publication: "The Church Facing the Future". Address: St. Columba's Parish Church, Gallowgate Street, Largs, Ayrshire KA30 8LX; T.-01475 686212.

Verster, Phil. Managing Director, ScotRail, since 2015. Educ. Stellenbosch University/Universiteit Stellenbosch; Newcastle University; London Business School. Production Director, Bombardier Transportation, 2001-03; Engineering Operations Director, South Eastern Trains, 2003-06; Irish Rail: Chief Mechanical Engineer, 2007-2010, Assistant Chief Executive Officer (Engineering), 2009-2011, Assistant CEO (Engineering) and Deputy CEO, 2011; Route Managing Director, Network Rail, 2011-15. Address: ScotRail, Atrium Court, 50 Waterloo Street, Glasgow G2 6HQ.

Vettese, Raymond John, DipEd, BA (Hons). Teacher and Writer; b. 1.11.50, Arbroath; m., Maureen Elizabeth. Educ. Montrose Academy; Dundee College of Education; Open University. Journalist, Montrose Review, 1968-72; student, 1972-75; barman, 1975-77; factory worker, 1977-78; clerical officer, 1978-85; teacher, since 1985 (supply teacher, 1997-2001); Library Assistant, 2001; Preses, Scots Language Society, 1991-94; William Soutar Fellowship, 1989-90; SAC Bursary, 1999. Publications: Four Scottish Poets, 1985; The Richt Noise, 1988 (Saltire Society Best First Book); A Keen New Air, 1995. Recreations: reading; music; cooking; chess. Address: (h.) 9 Tayock Avenue, Montrose, DD10 9AP; T.-01674 678943.

Vettriano, Jack, OBE; b. 1951, Fife. Painter. Early career in Scottish coalfields; received no formal tuition in art; first submitted works to Royal Scottish Academy, 1988; sell-out solo exhibitions in Edinburgh, London, Hong Kong and New York.

Vickerman, Jill. Scottish Secretary, The British Medical Association (BMA), since 2013. Educ. Edinburgh University. Career: held a number of senior posts with the Scottish Government, including Head of Health Analytical Services, and Senior Economic Statistician in the Office of the Chief Economic Advisor; formerly Policy Director in the quality unit of the Scottish Government's health and social care directorates. Trustee for Erskine Charity for Scottish Veterans. Address: BMA, 14 Queen Street, Edinburgh EH2 1LL; T.-0131 247 3000.

Vickerman, Keith, BSc, PhD, DSc, FLS, FMedSci, FRSE, FRS. Regius Professor of Zoology, Glasgow University, 1984-98; Consultant Expert on Parasitic Diseases, World Health Organisation, 1973-98; b. 21.3.33, Huddersfield; m., Moira Dutton; 1 d. Educ. King James Grammar School, Almondbury; University College, London (Fellow, 1985). Wellcome Lecturer in Protozoology, University College, London, 1958-63; Tropical Research Fellow, Royal Society, 1963-68; Glasgow University: Reader in Zoology, 1968-74; Professor of Zoology, 1974-84, Head, Department of Zoology, 1979-85. Leeuwenhoek Lecturer, Royal Society, 1994; Linnean Society Gold Medal for contributions to science, 1996. Publications: The Protozoa (Co-author), 1967; many papers in scientific and medical journals. Recreations: drawing and painting; gardening. Address: (h.) 16 Mirrlees Drive, Glasgow G12 0SH.

Voss, Jens-Peter. German Consul General in Scotland, since 2015; b. 5.9.53, Hamburg-Harburg; m., Barbara; 2 d. Final exams at school (Abitur), Alexander-von-Humboldt Gymnasium Hamburg-Harburg, 1972; Reserve Officer's Training Federal German Navy (Senior Commander Naval Reserve, rtd.), 1973-75; Studies in Economics and Business Administration, University of Hamburg, 1975-80; In Spierling & Voss Co., metal foundry and general machinery: trainee, assistant to the management, head of commercial department & partner, 1975-81; Preparatory courses for senior diplomatic service, Bonn, 1981-83; Secretary, press and cultural affairs, Embassy Kinshasa/Zaïre, 1983-86; Federal Ministry for Foreign Affairs, Bonn (international scientific and technological co-operation), 1986-89; Secretary (economics), Embassy Copenhagen/Denmark, 1989-92; Counsellor, Head of Trade Promotion Office, Embassy Peking/PR China, 1992-97; Federal Ministry for Foreign Affairs, Head of Special Unit "management modernisation", 1997-2000; Deputy Head of Economics Department, Embassy Rome/Italy, 2000-03; Deputy Head of Economics Department, Embassy Peking, 2003-06; Deputy Head of Mission, Embassy Pyongyang, DPR Korea, 2006-08; Ambassador Extraordinary and Plenipotentiary to the Republic of Haïti, Embassy Port-au-Prince, 2008-2012; Consul General, Shenyang/PR China, 2012-2015. Address: Consulate of the Federal Republic of Germany, 16 Eglinton Crescent, Edinburgh EH12 5DG; T.-0131 337 2323.

Vousden, Karen Heather, CBE, BSc, PhD, FRSE, FRS, FMedSci. Director, Beatson Institute for Cancer Research, since 2002; b. 19.7.57, Gravesend; m., Robert Ludwig; 1 d. Educ. Gravesend School for Girls; Queen Mary College, London University. Head, Human Papillomavirus Group, Ludwig Institute for Cancer Research, St Mary's Hospital, 1987-95; Director, Molecular Virology and Carcinogenesis Laboratory, ABL Basic Research Program, USA, 1995-99; Chief, Regulation of Cell Growth Laboratory, National Cancer Institute, USA, 1999-2002. Recreation: hill-walking. Address; (b.) Beatson Institute for Cancer Research, Garscube Estate, Switchback Road, Bearsden, Glasgow G61 1BD; T.-0141 330 3953.

W

Waddell, Bruce. Formerly Director of Media, The Big Partnership; Editor-in-Chief, Scottish Daily Record and Sunday Mail Ltd, 2009-2011; b. 18.3.59, Bo'ness, West Lothian; m., Catherine; 1 s. Educ. Graeme High School, Falkirk; Napier University. Reporter, Journal and Gazette, Linlithgow, 1977-87; News Sub-editor, The Scottish Sun, 1987-90; Deputy Editor, Sunday Scot, 1991; Marketing Executive, Murray International, 1991-92; Features Sub-editor, The Sun, 1992-93; Deputy Editor, The Scottish Sun, 1993-98; Editor, The Scottish Sun, 1998-2003. Recreations: golf; football; classic cars.

Waddell, John MacLaren Ogilvie, LLB, WS, FRSE. Consultant, Archangel Informal Investment Ltd and Non Executive Director; b. 12.4.56, Inverness; m., Alice Emily Bain; 1 s.; 1 d. Educ. Inverness Royal Academy; George Watson's College; Edinburgh University. Qualified as a Solicitor, 1980. Address: (b.) 20 Rutland Square, Edinburgh EH1 2BB.

Waddell, Moray, BSc(Hons), MSc, CEng, MIEE, MIMechE, MCIBSE, FIoD. Director of Engineering, Northern Lighthouse Board, since 2000; b. 22.3.64, Haddington; m., Susan Joan Tennant; 2 s. Educ. Dunbar Grammar School; Edinburgh University; Glasgow University. Trainee engineer, Property Services Agency; Engineer and Project Manager, Property Services Agency and Ministry of Defence. Recreations: sailing; motor sports. Address: (b.) 84 George Street, Edinburgh, EH2 3DA; T.-0131-473 3100.

Wade, Gillian. Floating Sheriff of Tayside, Central and Fife, since 2015; Head, National Sexual Crimes Unit (NSCU), 2011-13. Career: a solicitor qualified to practise both north and south of the border; specialised in media related matters including defamation, contempt of court and copyright; partner of firms in Glasgow and London; appointed Legal Convenor to the Mental Health Tribunal for Scotland in 2004; appointed an ad hoc Advocate Depute in 2007; assumed a full time post in Crown Office in 2008; joined the NSCU team at its inception in June 2009; appointed a Senior Advocate Depute and Deputy Head of the National Sexual Crimes Unit in 2010. Publications include: Associate Editor, Tolley's Journal of Media law and Practice, 1988-1996; Greens Weekly Digest "The Defamation Act 1996", 1997.

Wade, Professor Nicholas James, BSc, PhD, FRSE. Emeritus Professor of Psychology, Dundee University, since 2009; b. 27.3.42, Retford, Nottinghamshire; m., Christine Whetton; 2 d. Educ. Queen Elizabeth's Grammar School, Mansfield; Edinburgh University; Monash University. Postdoctoral Research Fellow, Max-Planck Institute for Behavioural Physiology, Germany, 1969-70; Lecturer in Psychology, Dundee University, 1970-78, Reader, 1978-91. Publications: The Art and Science of Visual Illusions, 1982; Brewster and Wheatstone on Vision, 1983; Visual Allusions: Pictures of Perception, 1990; Psychologists in Word and Image, 1995; A Natural History of Vision, 1998; Purkinje's Vision: The Dawning of Neuroscience, 2001; Destined for Distinguished Oblivion: The Scientific Vision of William Charles Wells (1757–1817), 2003; Perception and Illusion: Historical Perspectives, 2005; The Moving Tablet of the Eye. The Origins of Modern Eye Movement Research, 2005; Insegne Ambiguë. Percorsi Obliqui tra Storia, Scienza e Arte, da Galileo a Magritte, 2007; Circles: Science, Sense and Symbol, 2007; Giuseppe Moruzzi, Ritratti di uno scienziato, Portraits of a scientist, 2010; Visual Perception: an introduction, 3rd ed, 2013; Galileo's Visions: Piercing the Spheres of the Heavens by Eye and Mind, 2014; Art and Illusionists, 2015. Recreations: golf; cycling. Address: (h.) 36 Norwood, Newport-on-Tay, Fife DD6 8DW; T.-01382 543136; e-mail: n.j.wade@dundee.ac.uk

Wake, Joseph Robert, MA, Officier des Palmes Académiques; b. 16.5.42, Corbridge; 1 s.; 2 d. Educ. Royal Grammar School, Newcastle upon Tyne; Edinburgh University; Moray House College of Education. Teacher, Kirkcaldy High School, 1966-69, St. Modan's High School, Stirling, 1969-71; Principal Teacher of Modern Languages, Grangemouth High School, 1971-72; Head of Central Bureau for Educational Visits and Exchanges in Scotland, 1972-2002; International Education Adviser, British Council Scotland, 2002-07 (retired); active executive member of the Scotland-Russia Institute. Recreations: cricket; philately; Scottish dancing. Address: (h.) 4 Downie Grove, Edinburgh EH12 7AX; T.-0131 334 1523.

Walford, Ian. Director, Museums Galleries Scotland. Career: joined the Civil Service in Whitehall in 1987 before moving to the Scottish Office in Edinburgh in 1993; has been involved in a number of high profile projects, including leading the Scotland Bill team in 1997-98 and heading the first Scottish Cabinet Secretariat in 1999-2000; also involved in leading the planning for Scottish Executive involvement in the G8 summit at Gleneagles in 2005 and setting up Scottish Resilience within the Scottish Government in 2008 to co-ordinate emergency planning and response across Scotland; joined Historic Scotland as Chief Operating Officer in June 2011, appointed Acting Chief Executive in 2012. Address: Museums Galleries Scotland, Waverley Gate, 2-4 Waterloo Place, Edinburgh EH1 3EG; T.-0131 550 4100.

Walker, Audrey R., BA, MCLIP. Librarian, Turcan Connell, since 2006; b. 18.10.57, Glasgow. Educ. Clydebank High School; Robert Gordon University, Aberdeen. Library Assistant, 1975-80; Senior Library Assistant, Telford College, Edinburgh, 1980-84; Assistant Librarian: Scottish Office Library, 1987, Post-Graduate Medical Library, 1988-90, Advocates Library, 1990-94; Librarian, Signet Library, 1994-2006. Honorary Member, CILIP in Scotland, since 2008; Honorary Treasurer, Chartered Institute of Library and Information Professionals in Scotland. Recreations: cycling; reading; gardening; cinema. Address: (b.) Turcan Connell, Princes Exchange, 1 Earl Grey Street, Edinburgh EH3 9EE; T.-0131 228 8111.

Walker, Bill, BSc (Hons), MBA, FCMI, FIET, CEng. MSP (Independent), 2012-2013, (SNP), Dunfermline, 2011-12; Councillor, Fife Council, 2007-2012; m., June; adult children. Educ. Royal High School (Old), Edinburgh; University of Edinburgh; Illinois Institute of Technology, Chicago. Career: 1963-1990: various posts from design engineer to managing director in businesses specialising in medical scanning equipment (Scotland and overseas); 1990-2007: range of positions from sales manager to company director in energy supply and shipbuilding sectors (Scotland and overseas). Political interests: energy; environment; transportation; enterprise and regeneration; Scottish Independence. Recreations: gardening; reading; crosswords; travel; DIY as time permits.

Walker, Professor Brian Robert, BSc, MB, ChB, MD, FRCPE, FRSE. Professor of Endocrinology, University of Edinburgh, since 2001; b. 12.7.63, Glasgow; m., Dr Jane Walker; 2 s. Educ. Glasgow Academy; University of

Edinburgh. University of Edinburgh: MRC Training Fellow, 1990-93, Lecturer in Medicine, 1993-96, British Heart Foundation Senior Research Fellow, 1996-2006. Address: (b.) Endocrinology Unit, Centre for Cardiovascular Science, Queen's Medical Research Institute, 47 Little France Crescent, Edinburgh EH16 4TJ; T.-0131 242 6770; e-mail: B.Walker@ed.ac.uk

Walker, Emeritus Professor David Morrison, OBE, DA, FSA, FSA Scot, FRSE, HFRIAS, Hon. LLD (Dundee), Hon. DLitt (St Andrews). Honorary Professor of Art History, University of St. Andrews, 1994-2001, Emeritus Professor, since 2001; Chief Inspector of Historic Buildings, Scottish Office Environment Department, 1988-93; Manager, Dictionary of Scottish Architects research and database project, 2002-07, Editor, 2007-2012, Consultant Editor, since 2012; b. 31.1.33, Dundee; m., Averil Mary Stewart McIlwraith (deceased); m. (2), Sheila Margaret Mould (2005), MA, MLitt, MCLIP; 1 s. Educ. Morgan Academy, Dundee; Dundee College of Art. Voluntary work for National Buildings Record, Edinburgh, 1952-56; National Service, Royal Engineers, 1956-58; Glasgow Education Authority, 1958-59; Dundee Education Authority, 1959-61; Historic Buildings Branch, Scottish Office: Senior Investigator of Historic Buildings, 1961-76, Principal Investigator of Historic Buildings, 1976-78; Principal Inspector of Historic Buildings, 1978-88. Alice Davis Hitchcock Medallion, 1970; Patron, Society of Architectural Historians of Great Britain, 2008; Europa Nostra Award for Dedicated Service, 2009. Publications: Dundee Nineteenth Century Mansions, 1958; Architecture of Glasgow (Co-author), 1968 (revised and enlarged edition, 1987); Buildings of Scotland: Edinburgh (Co-author), 1984; Dundee: An Illustrated Introduction (Co-author), 1984; St. Andrew's House: an Edinburgh Controversy 1912-1939, 1989; Central Glasgow: an illustrated architectural guide (Co-author), 1989. Address: (h.) 22 Inverleith Row, Edinburgh EH3 5QH.

Walker, Donald George, MA (Hons). Deputy Editor, The Scotsman, Scotland on Sunday and Edinburgh Evening News, since 2015; b. 16.6.68, St. Andrews; 3 s. Educ. Kirkcaldy High School; University of Edinburgh. Trainee journalist, DC Thomson, Dundee, 1991; Reporter, Edinburgh and Lothians Post, 1992-93; Sub-Editor, Daily Mirror, London, 1993-97; Deputy Sports Editor, The Scotsman, 1997-98; Sports Editor, The Scotsman, 1998-2012; Assistant Editor, The Scotsman, 2012-2015. Recreations: football; rugby and East Fife FC.
E-mail: dwalker@scotsman.com

Walker, (Edward) Michael, CBE, FRICS. Chairman, Walker Group (Scotland) Ltd., Westerwood Ltd., and associated companies, since 1986 (Founder, 1969); Chairman, Lothian and Edinburgh Ltd. (LEEL), 1996-2000 (Director, since 1991); b. 12.4.41, Aberdeen; m., Flora Margaret; 2 s.; 1 d. Educ. Aberdeen Grammar School. President, Edinburgh and District Master Builders Association, 1987 and 1996; Past President, Scottish House Builders Association; former Committee Member, NHBC (Scotland) Ltd., 1990-96; former Lord Dean of Guild, City of Edinburgh, 1992-96; Captain of Industry Award, Livingston Industrial and Commercial Association, 1987; Homes for Scotland Industry Achievement Award, 2009. Recreations: skiing; scuba diving; walking; reading. Address: (b.) Walker Group (Scotland) Ltd., Westerwood House, Royston Road, Deans Industrial Estate, Livingston, W. Lothian; T.-01506 413101.

Walker, Gavin Norman, DL, CA. Chairman, Kibble Education and Care Centre; Chairman, Accord Hospice; Chairman, Renfrewshire Sports Charity; Director,

Merchants House of Glasgow; b. 16.03.43, Paisley; m., Alexandra; 1 s. Educ. John Neilson Institution. Partner, Milne, Craig, Chartered Accountants, Paisley, 1973-2001, Senior Partner, 1985-2001 (retired). Member of Court, University of the West of Scotland, 2002-2011, Chair of Audit, 2008-2011; Trustee, Miss Elizabeth Kibble's Trust; Chairman, The Western Club, 2011-12; Deputy Lieutenant for Renfrewshire, 2009. Recreations: golf; curling; fishing. Address: Holmhurst, South Avenue, Paisley PA2 7SP; T.-0141-884-7101.
E-mail: gavin.walker@btinternet.com

Walker, Professor Greg Mapley, BA, PhD, FRHS, FEA, FSA. Regius Professor of Rhetoric and English Literature, University of Edinburgh, since 2010, Masson Professor of English, 2007-10; b. 08.09.59, Coventry; m., Sharon; 2 s. Educ. Horndean School; Southampton University. Career History: British Academy Post-Doctoral Fellow, University of Southampton; Lecturer in English: University of Queensland, University of Buckingham, University of Leicester; Reader, and Professor of English, University of Leicester. Publications: author of books including, Writing Under Tyranny: English Literature and The Henrician Reformation, 2005. Recreations: dog lover; fan of progressive rock music; Nottingham Forest FC. Address: (b.) Department of English Literature, University of Edinburgh, Edinburgh EH8 9LH; T.-0131 650 3049; e-mail: greg.walker@ed.ac.uk

Walker, Rev. Dr James Bernard, MA, BD, DPhil. Chaplain, St. Andrews University, 1993-2011 (retired); Associate Director, Student Services (retired); b. 1946, Malawi; m., Sheila; 3 s. Educ. Hamilton Academy; Edinburgh University; Merton College, Oxford. Church of Scotland Minister: Mid Craigie linked with Wallacetown, Dundee, 1975-78, Old and St. Paul's, Galashiels, 1978-87; Principal, The Queen's College, Birmingham, 1987-93; joined St. Andrews University in 1993. Recreations: hill-walking; tennis; golf.

Walker, Jane, MB, ChB, MRCP, FRCR. Consultant Radiologist, since 1995; b. 12.7.62, West Kirby; m., Brian Walker; 2 s. Educ. Birkenhead High School; Edinburgh University. House and Senior House Officer posts; trained in radiology, Edinburgh; specialised in obstetric and gynaecological radiology. Address: (b.) Ultrasound Department, Simpson Centre for Reproductive Health, Royal Infirmary, 51 Litle France Crescent, Edinburgh EH16 4SA; T.-0131-242 2801.
E-mail: jane.walker@ luht.scot.nhs.uk

Walker, Maria. Director of Education and Children's Services, Aberdeenshire Council, since 2011. Educ. Aberdeenshire. Career History: separate successful careers in both teaching and community work; has held a number of different positions at Strathclyde Regional Council, Tayside Regional Council and Perth & Kinross Council; Depute Director of Education and Children's Services, Perth & Kinross Council, held a number of different roles within education and cultural services, 1996-2011. Address: (b.) Woodhill House, Westburn Road, Aberdeen AB16 5GB; T.-0345 6081208.

Walker, Michael, BSc (Hons), LLB, LLM, DipLP. Senior Legal Officer, Scottish Criminal Cases Review Commission, since 2007; b. 26.04.68, Cumbernauld. Educ. Ardrossan Academy; University of Strathclyde; University of Glasgow. Solicitor in Private Practice; Legal Officer, SCCRC, 2001-07 (Member of the team of Solicitors which reviewed the conviction of Abdelbaset Ali Mohmed Al Megrahi; Junior Legal Officer, SCCRC,

2007-2011. Address: (b.) Portland House, 17 Renfield Street, Glasgow G2 5AH; T.-0141 270 7030; e-mail: mwalker@sccrc.org.uk

Walker, Scott. Chief Executive, NFU Scotland, since 2011. Progressed through a number of roles in NFUS, starting as Commodity Director in 1994; headed up the Union's Policy team as Policy Director, since 2004. Address: NFU Scotland, Head Office, Rural Centre - West Mains, Ingliston, Midlothian EH28 8LT; T.-0131 472 4000.

Walker, Sue, CEng, MIChemE, BSc Hons (Strathclyde). Scottish Chief Commissioner, Girlguiding Scotland, since 2012; b. 22.6.62, Bellshill, Lanarkshire; m., Ken Walker; 2 d.; 1 s. Educ. St Ambrose High School, Coatbridge; Strathclyde University. Chemical Engineer, ExxonMobil, 1983-90, Consultant Engineer, 1997-2001; Process Engineer, BP, Grangemouth, since 2001. Brownie leader, since 1997, Limekilns, Fife. Fife County Commissioner, 2006-2011; Girlguiding Scotland: marketing & communication chair, 2011-2012; Scottish executive member, since 2007. Recreations: ultramarathon running and ultramarathon race support; cooking; baking; reading. Address: (b.) Girlguiding Scotland HQ, 16 Coates Crescent, Edinburgh EH3 7AH; T.-0131 226 4511.

Walker, Professor William Barclay, BSc, MSc. Professor Emeritus of International Relations, University of St. Andrews, Head, School of International Relations, 2003-06; b. 7.12.46, Longforgan; m., Carolyn Scott; 1 s. Educ. Shrewsbury School; Edinburgh University. Design Engineer, Ferranti Ltd., 1970-72; Research Fellow, Science Policy Research Unit, Sussex University, 1974-78; Research Fellow, Royal Institute of International Affairs, 1978-80; Science Policy Research Unit, Sussex University: Senior Fellow, 1981-92, Professorial Fellow and Director of Research, 1993-96; Member, Strategic Research Board, Economic and Social Research Council, 2002-06; Recipient, Leverhulme Trust Research Fellowship, 2008-09; Nobel Institute (Oslo) Visiting Fellowship, 2009. Publications: Plutonium and Highly Enriched Uranium: World Inventories, Capabilities and Policies (Co-author), 1997; Unchartered Waters: The UK, Nuclear Weapons and the Scottish Question (Co-Author), 2001; Weapons of Mass Destruction and International Order, 2004; A Perpetual Menace: Nuclear Weapons and International Order, 2011. Recreations: piano-playing; literature; walking. Address: 41 Upper Gray Street, Edinburgh EH9 1SN; T.-0131 667 8664; e-mail: wbw@st-andrews.ac.uk

Wallace, Anne Maree, MBChB, MScComMed, FFPH, Diploma in Advanced Executive Coaching. Independent coach and mentor; Director of Public Health, NHS Forth Valley, 2008-2013; Non-Executive Director: NHS Health Scotland, since 2009, Food Standards Scotland, since 2015; b. 18.9.55, Edinburgh; m., David Wallace; 2 s.; 1 d. Educ. John Watson's School, Edinburgh; Aberdeen University. Graduated as a doctor in 1978 and completed intitial training in Aberdeen and Falkirk; moved to Edinburgh to train in Public Health Medicine; worked as a Consultant, Public Health Medicine in NHS Lothian until 2000; Deputy Director of Public Health, 2001-04; Interim Director of Public Health, 2004-05; Director of Training in Public Health in Scotland and the lead consultant in the newly formed Scottish Public Health network, 2005-08. Honorary Senior Lecturer, Edinburgh University; qualified advanced executive coach. Recreations: hill walking; cooking. Address: (h.) 33 Malleny Millgate, Balerno, Edinburgh EH14 7AY; T.-0131 449 4310.
E-mail: annemareewallace@gmail.com

Wallace, Archibald Duncan, MB, ChB. Medical Practitioner, Campbeltown, since 1950; Hon. Sheriff of North Strathclyde at Campbeltown, since 1980; b. 4.1.26, Glasgow; m., Rona B. MacLennan; 1 s.; 2 d. Educ. High School of Glasgow; Glasgow University. Sector Medical Officer, Argyll and Clyde Health Board, until 1988; Civilian MO to RAF Machrihanish, until 1988. Past Chairman, Campbeltown Branch, RNLI; RNLI Silver Medal; Past President, Campbeltown Rotary Club; Past Captain, Machrihanish Golf Club. Recreations: golf; gardening. Address: (h.) Lilybank House, Low Askomil, Campbeltown; T.-01586 552658.

Wallace, Claire Denise, BA, PhD. Professor, Sociology, University of Aberdeen, since 2005; President, European Sociological Association, 2007-09; b. 04.12.56, London; m., Dr. Christian Haerpfer. Educ. Walthamstow High School, London; University of Kent. Career History: Research Fellow, University of Kent; Lecturer, University of Plymouth; Visiting Professor, University of Derby; Senior Lecturer in Sociology, University of Lancaster; Head of Sociology, Central European University, Prague; Head of Sociology, Institute for Advanced Studies, Vienna. Vice Pirincipal, Research and Knowledge Exchange, Aberdeen, 2011-2014. Recreations: hill walking; horse riding; music (classical and folk). Address: (b.) University of Aberdeen, Edward Wright Building, Aberdeen AB24 3QY; T.-01224 773137; e-mail: claire.wallace@abdn.ac.uk

Wallace, Colin Russell, ChEHO, FREHIS. Twice Past President, Royal Environmental Health Institute Scotland; former Environmental Health Manager, South Ayrshire Council (1996-2009). Commenced employment with Ayr County Council, 1970; Qualified as a Sanitary Inspector, 1974; Environmental Health Officer, Kyle & Carrick District Council, 1975, Senior Environmental Health Officer, 1985, Principal Environmental Health Officer, 1991. Recreations: music and hi-fi; mountain biking. Address: Royal Environmental Health Institute of Scotland (REHIS), 19 Torphicen Street, Edinburgh EH3 7DH; T.-0131-229-2968.

Wallace, David, BA. Chief Executive, Student Loans Company, since 2015. Educ. Hutchesons' Grammar School; Glasgow Caledonian University. Career history: Manager, Price Waterhouse, 1989-92; Abbey National plc: Finance & Admin Manager, Marketing & Sales, Special Projects Manager, 1992-97, Finance Director, Life Division, 1997-2002, Director, Transformation and Wealth Management & Long Term Savings, 2002-05; Chief Operating Officer for Santander's Insurance and Asset Management Division, 2005; CEO, Response Handling Limited, 2006-09; Director, MacDonald Wallace, 2009-2010; Student Loans Company: Interim Chief Operating Officer, 2010-2011, Deputy CEO and Executive Director for Strategic Development and Change Management, 2011-14, appointed Deputy Chief Executive and Executive Director for Finance, Strategy and Corporate Services in 2014. Governor of Court, Glasgow Caledonian University and Chair of its Finance and General Purpose Committee, since 2007. Founding member of the Scottish Government's Financial Services Advisory Board and its precursor, the Financial Services Strategy group. Recreations: sporting activities; cooking; the 'great outdoors'. Address: Student Loans Company, 100 Bothwell Street, Glasgow, Lanarkshire G2 7JD; T.-0141 306 2000.

Wallace, Professor Heather M., BSc, PhD, FRCPath, FBPharmacolS, FBTS, ERT. Professor of Biochemical Pharmacology and Toxicology, Division of Applied Medicine, University of Aberdeen; b. 10.6.54, Edinburgh; m., Professor R. John Wallace; 1 s.; 1 d. Educ. Hamilton Academy; University of Glasgow; University of Aberdeen. Career: University of Aberdeen:

Postdoctoral Fellow, MRC, 1979-81; CRC, 1981-83; Wellcome Lecturer, 1983; New Blood Lecturer, 1983-91; University Research Fellow, 1991-92; Senior Lecturer, 1991-2013. Recreations: golf; tennis; badminton. Address: (b.) University of Aberdeen, Polwarth Building, Foresterhill, Aberdeen; T.-01224 437956; e-mail: h.m.wallace@abdn.ac.uk

Wallace, Iain Wilson, BSc (Hons), MB, ChB, MBA, FRCGP, DRCOG. Medical Director, NHS Lanarkshire, since 2013; b. 3.3.60; m., Jane; 2 d. Educ. Paisley Grammar School; University of Glasgow; University of Strathclyde. Recreations: travel; eating out; motor racing. Address: (b.) Board HQ, Kirklands Hospital, Fallside Road, Bothwell G71 8BB; e-mail: iain.wallace@lanarkshire.scot.nhs.uk

Wallace, Rev. James, MA, BD. Minister of Peebles: St. Andrews Leckie Church of Scotland, 1983-2011 (retired); NHS Spiritual Care, Chaplain, NHS Borders (retired); b. 8.9.46, Greenock; m., Marjorie; 1 s.; 2 d. Educ. Dunfermline High School; Edinburgh University; New College, Edinburgh. Assistant, Paisley Abbey, 1972-73; Minister of Lochcraig, Church of Scotland, Fife, 1973-83; Part-time Chaplain to Hay Lodge Hospital, 1983-2005. Recreations: rugby; music; reading. Address: 52 Waverley Mills, Innerleithen EH44 6RH; T.-01896 831637.

Wallace of Tankerness, Rt. Hon. Lord (James Robert Wallace), PC, QC, MA (Cantab), LLB (Edinburgh), Hon DLitt (Heriot-Watt), Hon. DUniv (Open), Doctor honoris causa (Edinburgh), 2009. Advocate General for Scotland, 2010-2015; Leader of Liberal Democrat Peers; Deputy Leader of House of Lords, 2013-2015; Created Life Peer, 2007; Hon. Professor, Institute of Petroleum Engineering, Heriot-Watt University, 2007-2010; Chair, Relationships Scotland, 2008-2010; Board of St. Magnus International Festival, 2007-2014; MSP (Liberal Democrat), Orkney, 1999-2007; Deputy First Minister, 1999-2005; Minister for Justice, 1999-2003; Minister for Enterprise and Lifelong Learning, 2003-05; MP (Liberal Democrat, formerly Liberal), Orkney and Shetland, 1983-2001; Leader, Scottish Liberal Democrats, 1992-2005; Advocate, 1979; QC (Scot.), 1997; b. 25.8.54, Annan; m., Rosemary Janet Fraser; 2 d. Educ. Annan Academy; Downing College, Cambridge; Edinburgh University. Called to Scottish Bar, 1979; contested Dumfries, 1979, and South of Scotland Euro Constituency, 1979; Member, Scottish Liberal Party Executive, 1976-85 (Vice-Chairman, Policy, 1982-85); Honorary President, Scottish Young Liberals, 1984-85; Liberal Democrat Spokesman on Fisheries, 1988-97, and on Scotland, 1992-99; jointly awarded Andrew Fletcher Award for services to Scotland, 1998. Publication: New Deal for Rural Scotland (Co-Editor), 1983. Recreations: golf; reading; travelling. Address: (h.) Northwood House, Tankerness, Orkney KW17 2QS; T.-01856 861383. E-mail: wallacej@parliament.uk

Wallace, Cllr Joe. Provost, Midlothian Council, since 2012; represents Penicuik Ward (SNP). Address: (b.) Midlothian House, Buccleuch Street, Dalkeith EH22 1DN; T.-0131 271 3100; e-mail: joe.wallace@midlothian.gov.uk

Wallace, Professor John, CBE (2011), MA, FRSAMD, FRAM, HonRCM, HonLCM, DMus (Aberdeen), DCons (RCS), DLitt (Strathclyde). Principal, Royal Conservatoire of Scotland, 2002-2014; b. 1949, Methilhill. Educ. Buckhaven High School; King's College, Cambridge; York University; Royal Academy of Music. Principal Trumpet, Philharmonia Orchestra, 1976-95; Principal Trumpet, London Sinfonietta, 1987-2001; founded The Wallace Collection (brass ensemble),

1986; Artistic Director of Brass, Royal Academy of Music, 1993-2001; has premiered new works by Peter Maxwell Davies, Harrison Birtwistle, H K Gruber, Malcolm Arnold, James MacMillan, Stuart MacRae, Mark Anthony Turnage and Jonathan Dove. Publication: Companion to Brass Instruments (Co-Editor), 1997; The Trumpet (Co-Author), 2012. Address: 157B Camphill Avenue, Glasgow G41 3DR.

Wallace, Rev. Dr. William Fitch, BDS, BD. Minister, Pulteneytown and Thrumster Church, 1990-2008; Convener, Church of Scotland Board of Ministry, 2002-03; b. 6.10.39, Falkirk; m., Jean Wyness Hill; 1 s.; 3 d. Educ. Allan Glen's School; Glasgow University; Edinburgh University. Minister, Wick St. Andrew's and Thrumster Church, 1974-90; former missionary dentist. Convener, Church of Scotland Board of Social Responsibility, 1993-97. Recreations: family; golf; gardening. Address: Lachlan Cottage, 29 Station Road, Banchory, Aberdeenshire AB31 5XX; T.-01330-822-259. E-mail: williamwallace39@talktalk.net

Wallen, Rob. Principal and Chief Executive, North East Scotland College. Address: (b.) Gallowgate, Aberdeen AB25 1BN; T.-01224 612000.

Walls, Professor Andrew Finlay, OBE, MA, BLitt, DD, FSA Scot. Honorary Professor, Edinburgh University, since 1987; Curator of Collections, Centre for the Study of Christianity in the Non-Western World, 1996-2008; Emeritus Professor, Religious Studies, University of Aberdeen; b. 21.4.28; m., Doreen Mary Harden (deceased, 2009); 1 s.; 1 d.; m., (2) Dr Ingrid Marion Reneau. Librarian, Tyndale House, Cambridge, 1952-57; Lecturer in Theology, Fourah Bay College, Sierra Leone, 1957-62; Head, Department of Religion, University of Nigeria, 1962-65; Aberdeen University: Lecturer in Church History, 1966-69, Senior Lecturer, 1969, first Head, Department of Religious Studies, and Riddoch Lecturer in Comparative Religion, 1970, Reader, 1975, Professor of Religious Studies, 1979-85, Emeritus Professor, 1985; Director, Centre for the Study of Christianity in the Non-Western World, 1982-96; Visiting Professor of World Christianity, Yale University, 1988; Visiting Professor of Ecumenics and Mission, Princeton Theological Seminary, 1997-2001; Monrad Visiting Professor of World Christianity, Harvard University, 2000. Co-opted Member, Aberdeen Education Committee, 1971-74; Aberdeen City Councillor, 1974-80; Convener, Arts and Recreation, COSLA, 1978-80; Chairman, Council for Museums and Galleries in Scotland, 1978-81; Vice-Chairman, Committee of Area Museums Councils, 1980-81; Member, Williams Committee on the future of the national museums, 1979-82; Trustee, National Museum of Antiquities of Scotland, 1982-85; Member, Museums Advisory Board for Scotland, 1984-85; Trustee, National Museums of Scotland, 1985-87; Methodist Preacher; Past Chairman, Disablement Income Group, Scotland; President, British Association for the History of Religions, 1977-80; Editor, Journal of Religion in Africa, 1967-86; Henry Martyn Lectures, Cambridge University, 1988; Margaret Harris Lectures, Dundee University, 1989; Annual Missiology Lecturer, Fuller Theological Seminary, 1996; Burns Lecturer, Otago University, New Zealand, 2000; Lowell Lecturer, Boston University, 2004; Bainton Lecturer, Yale Divinity School, 2004; Co-chair, Yale-Edinburgh Group on the History of the Missionary Movement; Emeritus Professor, Akrofi Christaller Institute, Ghana, since 2003; Professor, History of Mission, Liverpool Hope University, since 2008. Distinguished Career Award, American Society of Church History, 2007. Address: (h.) 58 Stanley Street, Aberdeen AB10 6UR; T.-01224 581929; e-mail: a.f.walls@ed.ac.uk

Walsh, Garry Michael, MSc, PhD, FIMLS. Reader, School of Medicine, University of Aberdeen, since 2004; b. 4.8.57, London; m., Catherine. Educ. St. James' School,

London; Brunel University; London University. Medical Laboratory Scientific Officer, Histocompatability Testing Laboratory, Royal Postgraduate Medical School, London; academic research, Cardiothoracic Institute, Brompton Hospital, London; Visiting Fellow, Allergy Division, National Children's Hospital, Tokyo, Japan; postdoctoral position, University of Oxford; Senior Research Fellow/Honorary Lecturer, later Honorary Senior Lecturer, Department of Medicine and Therapeutics, University of Leciester Medical School; joined Aberdeen University, 1997 as Senior Lecturer. Scientific Advisor, UCB Institute of Allergy, Brussels; Member, MRC Advisory Board; Founding Editor of Therapeutics and Clinical Risk Management; Member of Editorial Board of Clinical and Experimental Allergy. Publications: over 100 papers and review articles in international scientific and medical journals). Recreations: hillwalking; golf; gastronome; motorocycling. Address: Department of Medicine and Therapeutics, Institute of Medical Sciences, University of Aberdeen, Foresterhill, Aberdeen AB25 2ZD; T.-01224 552786; e-mail: g.m.walsh@abdn.ac.uk

Walsh, James Richard. Leader, Argyll and Bute Council; b. 19.12.46; 2 s. Educ. Dunoon Grammar School. Became a member of South Cowal Community Council, 1978; Elected to Argyll & Bute District Council, 1980; Elected to Strathclyde Regional Council, 1982; Leader of Argyll & Bute new Unitary Authority, 1996-99; COSLA Spokesperson on Rural Affairs, 1996-99; Spokesperson for Education, 2001-07. Chair, Duke of Edinburgh Award Group for Argyll & Bute; Trustee of the Cowal Hospice Trust. Recreations: music; sport; reading. Address: (b.) Argyll and Bute Council, Kilmory, Lochgilphead PA31 8RT; T.-01546 604328; e-mail: dick.walsh@argyll-bute.gov.uk

Walsh, Susan. Principal and Chief Executive, Glasgow Clyde College, since 2012. Formerly Principal of Cardonald College Glasgow. Address: Cardonald Campus, 690 Mosspark Drive, Glasgow G52 3AY; T.-0141 272 9000.

Walsh, Professor Timothy Simon, BSc (Hons), MBChB (Hons), FRCP, FRCA, MD, MSc, FFICM. Consultant, Anaesthetics and Intensive Care, Edinburgh Royal Infirmary, since 1999; Professor, University of Edinburgh, since 2006; b. 17.1.64, Redhill, Surrey; m., Claire Doldon; 3 s. Educ. Trinity School, Croydon; University of Edinburgh. Trained in general medicine, anaesthetics and intensive care in South East Scotland; medical officer, rural South Africa, 1989-90; research, Scottish Liver Transplant Unit. Publications: 100 publications in area of critical care, since 2000. Address: Royal Infirmary of Edinburgh, Edinburgh EH16 2SA; T.-0131-536 1000.

Walton, Professor John Christopher, BSc, PhD, DSc, CChem, FRSC, FRSE. Research Professor of Chemistry, St. Andrews University, since 1997; b. 4.12.41, St. Albans; m., Jane Lehman; 1 s.; 1 d. Educ. Watford Grammar School for Boys; Sheffield University. Assistant Lecturer: Queen's College, St. Andrews, 1966-67, Dundee University, 1967-69; Lecturer in Chemistry, United College, St. Andrews, 1969-80; Senior Lecturer, 1980-86, Reader, 1986-96. Elder, Seventh-day Adventist Church. Recreations: music; philosophy. Address: (b.) School of Chemistry, St. Andrews University, St. Andrews, Fife, KY16 9ST; T.-01334 463864; e-mail: jcw@st-andrews.ac.uk

Wannop, Professor Urlan Alistair, OBE, MA, MCD, MRTPI. Emeritus Professor of Urban and Regional Planning, Strathclyde University; b. 16.4.31, Newtown St. Boswells; 1 s.; 1 d. Educ. Aberdeen Grammar School;

Edinburgh University; Liverpool University. Appointments in public and private practice, 1956-68; Team Leader, Coventry-Solihull-Warwickshire Sub-Regional Planning Study, 1968-71; Director, West Central Scotland Plan, 1972-74; Senior Deputy Director of Planning, Strathclyde Regional Council, 1975-81; Professor of Urban and Regional Planning, Strathclyde University, 1981-96. Member, Parliamentary Boundary Commission for Scotland, 1983-98. Address: (h.) 43 Lomond Street, Helensburgh G84 7ES; T.-01436 674622.

Warburton, Mark. Manager, Rangers FC, since 2015; b. 6.9.62, London; m., Liz. Educ. The Latymer School, Edmonton. Youth career: Leicester City, 1977-78; Senior career: Enfield, 1981-85, Boreham Wood, 1985-88; Brentford Manager, 2013-15. Honours: Brentford: Football League One Runner Up: 2013-14 (promotion to second tier), Rangers: Scottish Championship: 2015-16 (second tier), Scottish Challenge Cup: 2015-16; Individual: Football League Championship Manager of the Month: November 2014; Football League One Manager of the Month: December 2013; Football League Team of the Week: 3-9 November 2014; League Managers Association Performance of the Week: 24-30 November 2014; London Manager of the Year, 2015. Address: Rangers FC, Ibrox Stadium, 150 Edmiston Drive, Glasgow G51 2XD; T.-0871 702 1972.

Ward, Professor Sir John Macqueen, CBE, CA, FRSE, FIET, FRSA. Former Resident Director, Scotland and North of England, IBM United Kingdom Ltd; Professor, Heriot Watt University; former Chairman, Scottish Homes; former Chairman, Scottish Enterprise; former Chairman, Dunfermline Building Society; b. 1.8.40, Edinburgh; m., Barbara Macintosh; 1 s.; 3 d. Educ. Edinburgh Academy; Fettes College. Joined IBM UK Ltd. at Greenock plant, 1966; worked in France and UK; appointed European Director of Information Systems, 1975, and Havant Site Director, 1981. Past Chairman: SQA, Macfarlane Group, Queen Margaret University College, Governing Body, Scottish CBI, Scottish Post Office Board, Quality Scotland Foundation, Advisory Scottish Council for Education and Training Targets, Scottish Electronics Forum, Institute of Technology Management; European Assets Trust; former Director, Scottish Business in the Community; former Trustee, National Museums of Scotland; Honorary Doctorate, Napier University, Strathclyde University, Heriot-Watt University, Glasgow Caledonian University; Queen Margaret University College.

Ward, Professor Mark Gordon, BA. Professor of German Language and Literature, Glasgow University, 1997-2011; Head of School of Modern Languages and Cultures, 2008-2010; Principal Examiner, CSYS AH German, since 1987; b. 4.2.51, Hemel Hempstead; m., Janet Helen; 2 s. Educ. Leeds Grammar School; King's College, London University. Tutorial Research Scholar, Bedford College, London University, 1974-75; Lecturer, then Senior Lecturer, Department of German, Glasgow University, 1975-97; Dean, Faculty of Arts, 1995-99; Director of Studies, Crichton Campus, 1999-2007. Publications include: Theodor Storm: Der Schimmelreiter, 1988; Laughter, Comedy and Aesthetics: Kleist's Der Zerbrochne Krug, 1989; Perspectives on German Realism, 1995; Romantic Dreams, 1998; Theodor Storm – Erzählstrategien und Patriarchat, 1999; Borders and Margins, 2006. Recreations: music; gardening; sport. Address: (h.) 8 Crawford Crescent, Uddingston G71 7DP; T.-01698 814078; e-mail: markgward2@yahoo.co.uk

Ward, Maxwell Colin Bernard, MA. Managing Director, The Independent Investment Trust, since 2000; Chairman:

Scottish Equitable Policyholders' Trust, 2004-2010; Director, Aegon UK, 1999-2010; Chairman, Dunedin Income Growth Investment Trust, 2002-06; Director, Foreign and Colonial Investment Trust, 2000-2011; Director, The Edinburgh Investment Trust, since 2011; b. 22.8.49, Sherborne; m., Sarah Marsham; 2 s.; 2 d. Educ. Harrow; St. Catharine's, Cambridge. Baillie Gifford & Co.: Trainee, 1971-75, Partner, 1975-2000. Director: Scottish Equitable Life Assurance Society, 1988-94, Scottish Equitable plc, 1995-99. Recreations: tennis; squash; bridge; country pursuits. Address: (b.) 17 Dublin Street, Edinburgh EH1 3PG; T.-0131 558 9434.

Ward, Michael, MBE. Curator, Grampian Transport Museum, since 1983. Educ. Northampton Grammar School; Lincoln College of Art. Conservator, Bass Museum of Brewing, 1976-1983 (part of a three man team hired to establish the museum to celebrate Bass bi-centenary in 1977). Has collected and collated an extraordinary range of transport items, as well as the almost-complete restoration of a tramcar found buried in an Aberdeenshire field. Address: Grampian Transport Museum, Alford, Aberdeenshire AB33 8AE.

Ward, Rosemary. Director, The Gaelic Books Council - the lead organisation for Gaelic literature in Scotland; Gaelic spokesperson for SCIAF. Address: (b.) The Gaelic Books Council, 32 Mansfield Street, Glasgow G11 5QP; T.-0141 337 6211.

Ward, Thomas, LLB (Hons). Sheriff of North Strathclyde at Dunoon, since 2010; b. 3.4.53, Glasgow; m., Ruth Zegleman; 3 s. Educ. St. Aloysius College, Glasgow; University of Dundee. Partner, Blair and Bryden Solicitors, Greenock, 1980; Part Time Sheriff, 1991-2000; Legal Member, CICAP, 2001; Legal Assessor, GMC, 2002; Part Time Immigration Judge, 2002; Legal Assessor, NMC; Legal Member, PMETB; Part Time Sheriff, 2005. Recreations: walking; watching cricket; visiting France. Address: (b.) Sheriff Court, George Street, Dunoon PA23 8BQ; e-mail: sherifftward@scotcourts.gov.uk

Ward Thompson, Professor Catharine J., PhD, DipLA, BSc, FLI, FRSA. Professor of Landscape Architecture, Director of OPENspace Research Centre and Associate Dean of Research, Knowledge Exchange and Impact, College of Humanities and Social Sciences, University of Edinburgh, since 2011; b. 5.12.52; m., Henry Swift Thompson; 3 c. Educ. Holy Cross Convent, Chalfont St. Peter; Southampton University; Edinburgh University. Landscape Assistant/Landscape Architect/Senior Landscape Architect, 1973-81; Lecturer and Studio Instructor, School of Landscape Architecture, Edinburgh College of Art, 1981-88; Head of School, 1989-2000; Director of Research, Environmental Studies, 2000-02; Research Professor of Landscape Architecture, Edinburgh College of Art, 2002-2011; Consultant, Landscape Design and Research Unit, Heriot-Watt University, 1989-2005; Honorary Professor, University of Edinburgh, 2007-2010. Recreations: dance; gardening. Address: (h.) 11 Douglas Crescent, Edinburgh EH12 5BB; T.-0131-6515827 (work).

Wardrop, James Arneil, OBE, DL, FCIBS, FUniv, FSA Scot, HPAI. Retired Banker; Deputy Lieutenant, Renfrewshire; Honorary President, Accord Hospice (formerly Chairman); Hon. Vice-Patron, Japan Society of Scotland; Hon. President, Paisley Art Institute; b. 19.4.40, Paisley. Educ. John Neilson Institution, Paisley. Joined National Bank of Scotland, by a process of mergers absorbed into Royal Bank of Scotland, Deputy Agent, San Francisco, 1978-81, Manager, International Division, 1981-

94 - Edinburgh and Glasgow; Elder, Paisley Abbey; Hon. Member: Paisley Burns Club, Old Paisley Society; Trustee, SSAFA, Renfrew and Inverclyde; Honorary Vice President, Ferguslie Cricket Club; Hon. President, T.S. Grenville, Sea Cadets, Paisley Unit; Trustee, Miss Kibble's Trust; Director, Incorporated Glasgow Renfrewshire Society; Member, Committee, Scotland's Gardens, Renfrewshire and Inverclyde and National Committee; Member, Renfrewshire Valuation Appeal Panel; Past Deacon, Paisley Hammermen Society; Member of Executive, Paisley District Battalion, the Boys' Brigade; Lately Box Master, Old Weavers Incorporation, Paisley; Member, Church of Scotland Committee for Chaplains to HM Forces. Recreations: country pursuits; gardening; music. Address: (h.) Saint Kevins, Meikleriggs, Paisley PA2 9PT; T.-0141-887 3627.

Wark, Kirsty, BA; b. 1955, Dumfries; m., Alan Clements; 1 s.; 1 d. Educ. Edinburgh University. Joined BBC as radio researcher, 1976; became radio producer, current affairs; produced and presented Seven Days, 1985; then concentrated on presenting (Reporting Scotland; Left, Right and Centre); General Election night coverage, 1987, 1992, 1997; BBC coverage, Scottish Parliamentary elections, 1999; Presenter, Breakfast Time, Edinburgh Nights; Presenter, The Late Show, 1990-93; Presenter, One Foot in the Past, 1993-99; joined Newsnight and Newsnight Review's team of presenters, 1993; Presenter, Restless Nation, Building a Nation; The Kirsty Wark Show; Lives Less Ordinary; Tales from Europe; The Book Quiz (BBC4), 2008; A Question of Genius (BBC2), 2009 and 2010; The Review Show (BBC2), since 2010; The Home Movie Roadshow (BBC2), 2010; Celebrity Masterchef (BBC1), 2010; cameo appearances in: Dr Who (BBC TV), 2007, Spooks (BBC TV), 2009, The I.T. Crowd (Channel 4), 2007, The Amazing Mrs Pritchard (BBC1), 2006; Beyond The Pole (Film), 2009; Party Animals (BBC TV), 2009; The Man Who Collected the World: William Burrell (BBC TV), 2013; Iain Banks: Raw Spirit (BBC TV), 2013; Blurred Lines: The New Battle of The Sexes (BBC TV), 2014; Would I Lie To You (BBC TV), 2014; Scotland's Art Revolution: The Maverick Generation (BBC TV), 2014; The Summer Exhibition: BBC Arts at the Royal Academy (BBC TV), 2014 and 2015; Edinburgh Extra (BBC TV), 2014; General Election, 2015 (BBC TV); Our World: Kidnapped For A Decade (BBC TV), 2015; Manchester International Festival (BBC TV), 2015; BBC Proms (BBC TV), 2015. Journalist of the Year, BAFTA Scotland, 1993; Best TV Presenter award, 1997; Scot of the Year, 1998; Scottish Insider Business Woman of the Year, 2002; Outstanding Contribution to Broadcasting - BAFTA Scotland, 2013; former Council Member, Prince's Trust; Patron, Maggie's Centre; formed production company with husband in 1990. Recreations: family; tennis; swimming; cooking; beach-combing; reading. Address: (b.) Black Pepper Media Ltd., PO Box 26323, Ayr KA7 9AY.
E-mail: info@blackpeppermedia.com
web: www.blackpeppermedia.com

Warner of Craigenmaddie, Gerald, OStJ, MA, FSAScot. Author; contributor to CapX blog (Centre for Policy Studies), since 2014; contributor to Breitbart London blog, since 2014; occasional leader writer, The Sunday Telegraph, since 2009; columnist, Scotland on Sunday, 1997-2014; author, blog 'Is it just me?', The Daily Telegraph, 2008-2010; leader writer, Scottish Daily Mail, 1998-2014; b. 22.3.45. Educ. St. Aloysius' College, Glasgow; Glasgow University. Vice-Chairman, Una Voce (International Latin Mass Federation), Scotland, 1965-66; Administrative Assistant, Glasgow University, 1971-74; author and broadcaster, 1974-89; Diarist (under pseudonym Henry Cockburn), Sunday Times Scotland, 1989-95; columnist, 1992-95; Special Adviser to Secretary of State for Scotland, 1995-97. Council Member, 1745 Association, 1967-70; Member, Scottish Council of Monarchist League,

1969-71; Chairman, The Monday Club – Scotland, 1973-74; Secretary, Conservative Party's Scottish Policy Committee on Education, 1976-77; Parliamentary candidate, Hamilton, October 1974. Knight of Grace and Devotion, Sovereign Military Order of Malta, 1979; Knight, Jure Sanguinis, Sacred Military Constantinian Order of St. George, 1994; Knight of the Order of Merit of St. Joseph of Tuscany, 2005; Knight of the Order of St. Maurice and St. Lazarus, 2005. Publications: Homelands of the Clans, 1980; Being of Sound Mind, 1980; Tales of the Scottish Highlands, 1982; Conquering by Degrees, 1985; The Scottish Tory Party: A History, 1988; The Sacred Military Order of St. Stephen Pope and Martyr, 2005; Scotland's Ten Tomorrows (contributor), 2006; Secret Places, Hidden Sanctuaries (Co-Author), 2009. Recreations: literature; genealogy; Brummelliana. Address: 17 Huntly Gardens, Glasgow G12 9AT.

Warnock, Henry, BSc, CEng, MCIBSE, MIMechE. Director, Henderson Warnock, since 1993; formerly Chairman, Scottish Youth Theatre; b. 14.2.57, Glasgow; m., Felicity. Educ. Allan Glens School, Glasgow; University of Strathclyde. Design Engineer: IDC, Stratford-upon-Avon, DSSR, Glasgow; Senior Design Engineer: Building Design Partnership, Brian Ford Partnership. Director: Theatre Cryptic, Dancebase, Edinburgh. Recreations: travelling; rollerblading; music; film. Address: 38 New City Road, Glasgow G4 9JT; T.-0141-353 2444;
E-mail: hwarnock@hendersonwarnock.com

Warren, Gareth. Principal, Morrison's Academy, Crieff, since 2015. Educ. Watford Grammar School for Boys. Taught chemistry at a number of schools in the UK and gained an international educational perspective on a three-year posting as head of science at an independent school in Bermuda; former Deputy Head Teacher, George Watson's College, Edinburgh (2009-2015). Address: Morrison's Academy, Ferntower Road, Crieff, Perthshire PH7 3AN; T.-01764 653885.

Waterhouse, Lorraine Alice Margaret, BA (Maths/Psych), MSW. Formerly Vice Principal, Equality and Diversity, University of Edinburgh; b. 3.7.49, Toronto, Canada; m., J. D. Waterhouse; 1 s.; 1 d. Educ. St. Michaels, London, Ontario, Canada; University of Western Ontario, London, Canada. Social Worker, Royal Hospital for Sick Children, Dept. of Child and Family Psychiatry, Edinburgh, 1972-76; Lecturer, Social Work (Half-Time), University of Edinburgh, 1976-80; Senior Social Worker (Half-Time), Royal Hospital for Sick Children, Edinburgh, 1976-80; University of Edinburgh: Lecturer, Social Work (Half-Time), 1980-92, Lecturer, Social Policy (Quarter-Time), 1988-94, Senior Lecturer, Social Work (Part-Time), 1992-94, formerly Head of School, Social and Political Studies. Member: Joint University Council (Social Work), 1994-2000, Editorial Board, Journal of Social Work, since 2001, Editorial Board, Journal of Child and Family Social Work, since 1996, Editorial Board, British Journal of Social Work, since 2004; Convenor, Enquire, Children in Scotland, 2000-03; Chair, Individual Employment Complaints Tribunals for Edinburgh City, since 1998.

Waters, Donald Henry, OBE, CA. Director, Scottish Media Group, 1997-2005; Chairman, Scottish and Grampian Television Retirement Benefits Scheme, 1999-2014; Chairman, Caledonian Publishing Pension Fund, (Herald and Evening Times), 1999-2014; Deputy Chairman and Chief Executive, Grampian Television PLC, 1993-97 (Chief Executive and Director, 1987-93); b. 17.12.37, Edinburgh; m., June Leslie Hutchison; 1 s.; 2 d. Educ. George Watson's, Edinburgh; Inverness Royal Academy. Director, John M. Henderson and Co. Ltd., 1971-76;

Grampian Television PLC: Company Secretary, 1976, Director of Finance, 1979; Director: Scottish Television and Grampian Sales Ltd., 1980-97, Moray Firth Radio Ltd., 1982-89, Independent Television Publications Ltd. (TV Times), 1987-90, Cablevision Scotland PLC, 1987-91; Chairman, Celtic Film and Television Association, 1994-96; Vice-Chairman, BAFTA Scotland; Visiting Professor of Film and Media Studies, Stirling University, 1991-95; Chairman, Police Dependant Trust for Grampian, 1992-96; Past Chairman (1984), Royal Northern and University Club, Aberdeen; Chairman, Glenburnie Properties Ltd., 1993-97; Director: Central Scotland Radio Ltd. (Scot FM), 1994-96 (Chairman, 1995-96), GRT Bus Group PLC (now FirstGroup PLC) 1994-96, British Linen Bank Ltd., 1995-99, Bank of Scotland North of Scotland Local Board, 1999-2001, Scottish Post Office Board, 1996-2001, Consignia Advisory Board for Scotland, 2001-03, Johnstons of Elgin Ltd., since 1999, Aberdeen Asset Management PLC, 2000-2011; Member, ITV Council and ITV Broadcast Board, 1987-97; Fellow, Royal Society of Arts; Council Member, CBI Scotland, 1994-2001; Council Member, Cinema and Television Benevolent Fund, 1987-99; Member, Royal Television Society, since 1988; Director, Aberdeen Royal Hospital NHS Trust, 1996-99; Chairman, New Royal Aberdeen Children's Hospital Project Steering Group; Member of Council, Aberdeen Chamber of Commerce, 1996-2003; Governor, Aberdeen University, 1998; Member, Grampian and Islands Family Trust, 1988-2005; Joint Chairman, Grampian Cancer Macmillan Appeal, 1999-2004; Member of Council, SATRO; Burgess of Guild, since 1979 (Assessor, 1997-2002); Director, Blenheim Travel Ltd, 1982-89; Institute of Directors, 1980-2003. Address: (h.) Balquhidder, 141 North Deeside Road, Milltimber, Aberdeen AB13 0JS; T.-Aberdeen 867131; e-mail: donaldwaters@btinternet.com

Watkins, Trevor, BA, PhD, FSA, FSAScot. Emeritus Professor of Near Eastern Prehistory, since 2004; Hon. Professorial Fellow, University of Edinburgh, since 2007; b. 20.2.38, Epsom; m., Antoinette (nee Loughran); 1 s.; 2 d. Educ. Kingston Grammar School; University of Birmingham. Career History: Research Fellow, University of Birmingham; Lecturer in Archaeology, University of Edinburgh, then Senior Lecturer, then Professor. Rhind Lecturer, 2009. Recreations: reading; theatre; classical music; walking. Address: (b.) School of History, Classics & Archaeology, University of Edinburgh EH8 9AG; T.-01383 412083; e-mail: t.watkins@ed.ac.uk

Watson, Alexander Bell, OBE, DL, MA, MEd, FCIM, FSA Scot. Formerly Chairman of Board, NHS Tayside (2007-2015); Chairman, Scottish NHS Board Chairs Group, 2013-14; Member, Scottish Funding Council, 2006-2010; Deputy Lieutenant for Angus, since 2007; Chair of Angus College Board of Management, 2004-09; Chair, Entitlement Card Project Group, Customer First, 2005-09; Chief Executive, Angus Council, 1995-2005 (Chief Executive, Tayside Regional Council, 1995); Honorary Fellow, University of Abertay; b. 20.5.45, Airdrie; m., Jean; 3 s. Educ. Airdrie Academy; Glasgow University; Jordanhill College of Education. Teacher of Classics, Morrison's Academy, Crieff, 1968; Principal Teacher of Classics: Portree High School, 1971, McLaren High School, Callander, 1973; Assistant Director of Education: Central, 1975, Strathclyde, 1983; Senior Depute Director of Education, Central Regional Council, 1986; Director of Education, Tayside Regional Council, 1990-94. President, then General Secretary, Association of Directors of Education in Scotland, 1992-95; Chair, National Co-ordinating Committee on Staff Development of Teachers, 1994-95; Member, Board of Management, Angus College, since 1997; Secretary, Society of Local Authority Chief Executives and Senior Managers (Scotland), 1995-2007; Chair, Scottish Advisory Committee, Duke of Edinburgh's

Award Scheme, 1999-2003; Vice-Chairman, Young Scot, 2002-05, Non-Executive Director, since 2009; Vice-Chairman, Angus College Board of Management, 2003-04. Recreations: music; reading; fishing; Scottish heritage; DIY.

Watson, Alistair Gordon, LLB, DipLP, NP. Sheriff of North Strathclyde at Kilmarnock, since 2007; b. 1.7.59, Dundee; m., Susan; 1 s.; 2 d. Educ. High School of Dundee; University of Dundee. Procurator Fiscal Depute (1984-89); Partner in Cameron Pinkerton & Co, Solicitors, then Watson & Mackay, Solicitors, 1989-98; appointed Scotland's First Public Defender in 1998; Director of Public Defence Solicitors' Office, 1998-2005; All Scotland Floating Sheriff, at North Strathclyde, 2005-07. Recreations: family; photography. Address: (b.) Sheriffs' Chambers, Kilmarnock Sheriff Court, St Marnoch Street, Kilmarnock KA1 1ED.

Watson, Arthur James, RSA, DA. Senior Lecturer, Duncan of Jordanstone College of Art & Design, University of Dundee, since 1996; President, The Royal Scottish Academy, since 2012 (Secretary, 2007-2012); b. 24.06.51, Aberdeen. Educ. Aberdeen Grammar School; Grays School of Art, Aberdeen. Founded Peacock Printmakers, an artists' print workshop, gallery and publisher, 1974. Board Member: WASPS, Friends of The Royal Scottish Academy; Secretary, The Royal Scottish Academy. Recreation: traditional song. Address: (h.) 20 Marine Parade, City Quay, Dundee DD1 3BN; T.-01382 220151; e-mail: a.j.watson@dundee.ac.uk

Watson, Billy. Chief Executive, Scottish Association for Mental Health (SAMH), since 2008. Career history: Hospital Administrator, Stonehouse Hospital, 1992-94; Business Manager, Hairmyres and Stonehouse Hospitals NHS Trust, 1994-99; Regional Manager, RNIB, 1999-2000; Assistant Director, RNIB Scotland, 2000-03, Director, 2003-04; Group Director, RNIB, 2004-08. Address: Scottish Association for Mental Health, Brunswick House, 51 Wilson Street, Glasgow G1 1UZ; T.-0141 530 1000.

Watson, Dave, LLB. Unison Scottish Organiser (Bargaining and Campaigns), since 1999; b. 24.5.56, Liverpool. Educ. Nower Hill High School; Stanmore College; University of Strathclyde. Leisure Management, London Borough Harrow, 1974-79; Organising Assistant, South Wales NALGO; Branch Organiser, Dorset NALGO, 1980-90; Regional Officer, Unison Scotland, 1990-99; Scottish Executive Health Department HR Strategy Implementation Manager (Secondment), 1999-2001. Secretary, Socialist Health Association; Scottish Labour Party Executive; Vice-Chair, Scottish Labour Party, 2007; Secretary, Scottish Trade Union Labour Party (STULP); Chair, Scottish Labour Party, 2008/09. Recreations: military history; golf. Address: (b.) Unison House, 14 West Campbell Street, Glasgow G2 6RX; T.-0845 355 0845; e-mail: d.watson@unison.co.uk

Watson, Professor George Alistair, BSc, MSc, PhD, FIMA, FRSE. Professor Emeritus, Department of Mathematics, Dundee University, since 2008, Professor, 1988-2007; b. 30.9.42, Aberfeldy; m., Hilary Mackay; 1 d. Educ. Breadalbane Academy; Edinburgh University; Australian National University. Demonstrator, Computer Unit, Edinburgh University, 1964-66; Dundee University: Research Fellow, then Lecturer, Mathematics Department, 1969-82; Senior Lecturer, Mathematical Sciences Department, 1982-84; Reader, Department of Mathematics and Computer Science, 1984-88. Recreation: gardening. Address: (h.) Westercraig, 8 Dundee Road, Broughty Ferry,

Dundee DD5 1LY; T.-01382 730204. E-mail: craigievar@btinternet.com

Watson, Gordon. Chief Executive, Loch Lomond & The Trossachs National Park, since 2014; formerly Director of Operations; m.; 2 d. Instrumental in establishing Loch Lomond & The Trossachs National Park, including as a new planning authority; subsequently developed the planning function into a delivery focused operation using innovative approaches and partnership working to attract high quality and sustainable development to the National Park, 1999-2002. Address: (b.) Carrochan Road, Balloch G83 8EG; T.-01389 722600.

Watson, Professor John Francis, BSc, PhD, CEng, FIEE, SMIEEE. Dean, Faculty of Design and Technology, Robert Gordon University, since 2006; b. 3.1.55, Kirkcaldy; m., Patricia; 3 s. Educ. Kirkcaldy High School; Heriot Watt University. Development Engineer, GEC, 1977-81; RGIT: Lecturer, 1981-86, Senior Lecturer, 1986-2003, Head, School of Engineering, 2003-06. Recreations: fly fishing; running and occasionally walking. Address: (b.) Faculty of Design and Technology, Robert Gordon University, Faculty Office, Garthdee Road, Aberdeen AB10 7QB; T.-01224 263500; e-mail: j.f.watson@rgu.ac.uk

Watson of Invergowrie, Lord (Michael Goodall Watson), BA (Hons). Labour Education spokesman in the House of Lords, since 2015; MSP (Labour), Glasgow Cathcart, 1999-2005; Minister for Tourism, Culture and Sport, Scottish Executive, 2001-03; MP (Labour), Glasgow Central, 1989-97; b. 1.5.49, Cambuslang. Address: House of Lords, Westminster, London SW1A 0PW; e-mail: watsonm@parliament.uk

Watson, Norma Anne, OBE, DCE, ACE, NFFC, FEIS, FRSA. Convener, General Teaching Council for Scotland, 1999-2007; Head Teacher, Kirkhill Nursery School, Broxburn, 1983-2007; b. Edinburgh; m., Christopher Simpson Watson. Educ. Broxburn Academy; Moray House College of Education. Vice-Convener, Educational Institute of Scotland Education Committee, 1992-2008; National President of the Educational Institute of Scotland, 1994-95. Recreations: walking; reading. Address: (h.) 7, Queens Road, Broxburn, West Lothian EH52 5QZ.

Watson, Peter, BA, LLB, SSC. Solicitor, PBW Law; b. 22.1.54, Greenock; m., Claire Watson; 2 d. Educ. Eastwood High School, Glasgow; Strathclyde University; Edinburgh University; Scandinavian Maritime Law Institute, Norway; Dundee Petroleum Law Institute. Qualified, 1981; Solicitor to the Supreme Courts; Notary Public; former Temporary Sheriff; Visiting Professor, Law School, University of Strathclyde; Chairman, Yorkhill Children's Foundation; Past President, Society of Solicitor Advocates; Hon. Vice-President and former Chairman, Association of Mediators; Visiting Professor, Nova University, Fort Lauderdale, Florida; Member, Steering Committee, and Negotiator, Piper Alpha Disaster Group; Secretary, Braer Disaster Group; Secretary, Lockerbie Air Disaster Group; former Official Collaborator, International Labour Organisation, Geneva; Member, Criminal Rules Council; Member, Board, Sports Law Centre, Anglia University; Honorary Citizen of Nashville, Tennessee; large media practice based in Glasgow. Publications: Civil Justice System in Britain; Crimes of War – The Antony Gecas Story; The Truth Written in Blood; Dunblane – A Predictable Tragedy; DNA and the Criminal Trial; In Pursuit of Pan Am. Recreations: working out; drinking fine wine; golf. Address: (b.) PBW Law, 18 Woodside Place, Glasgow G3 7QF; T.-0141 439 1990.

Watson, Professor Roderick, MA, PhD, FRSE. Poet; Literary Critic and Writer; Professor Emeritus in English, Stirling University; b. 12.5.43, Aberdeen; m., Celia Hall Mackie; 1 s.; 1 d. Educ. Aberdeen Grammar School;

Aberdeen University; Peterhouse, Cambridge. Lecturer in English, Victoria University, British Columbia, 1965-66; collections of poetry include Trio; True History on the Walls; Into the Blue Wavelengths. Other books include The Penguin Book of the Bicycle, MacDiarmid, The Poetry of Norman MacCaig, The Poetry of Scotland (Editor) and The Literature of Scotland (2 vols); From the Line: Scottish War Poetry 1914-1945. Recreation: cycling; motor cycling; alto saxophone. Address: (h.) 19 Millar Place, Stirling; T.-Stirling 475971; e-mail: rbwatson19@gmail.com

Watt, Alison, OBE. Painter; b. 1965, Greenock. Educ. Glasgow School of Art. Won the John Player Portrait Award; became the youngest artist to be offered a solo exhibition at the Scottish National Gallery of Modern Art, in 2000, with an exhibition called Shift, with 12 huge paintings featuring fabric alone; shortlisted for The Jerwood Painting Prize in 2003; awarded the 2005 ACE (Art+Christianity Enquiry) award for 'a Commissioned Artwork in Ecclesiastical Space'; subsequent project Dark Light was supported by her Creative Scotland Award of 2004 from the Scottish Arts Council; took part in the prestigious Glenfiddich residency in 2005; served as the seventh artist in residence at the National Gallery, London, 2006-2008; youngest artist to present a solo exhibit at The National Gallery. Work is widely exhibited and is held in many prestigious private and public collections including, The Uffizi Gallery, Florence, The National Portrait Gallery, London and The British Council.

Watt, Allan. Director, Prince's Trust - Scotland, since 2013. Educ. University of Oxford. Consultant, Monitor Group, 1987-89; Project Manager and Executive Assistant, Scottish Enterprise, 1989-93; Director of Development, The Wise Group, 1993-2000; Head of Community Investment and Public Affairs, Royal Bank of Scotland, 2000-03; Interim Chief Executive, The Prince's Trust, 2003-04; Head of Group Brand Communication and Employee Communication, Royal Bank of Scotland, 2004-2010, Head of Communication and Marketing, Asia Pacific, 2010-2013. Address: The Prince's Trust - Scotland, Head Office, 6th Floor, Portland House, 17 Renfield Street, Glasgow G2 5AH; T.-0141 204 4409.

Watt, David C., PhD (HC), Adv. DipEd, BA, DPE, CYS. Executive Director, Institute of Directors; Honorary Colonel, RMR Scotland; Ambassador for Prince and Princess of Wales Hospice, Glasgow; Chairman Commonwealth Gymnastics Confederation; author, commentator and contributor; m., Maggie. Board Member: Scottish Sports Futures, British Gymnastics, Fife Sport and Leisure Trust; Honorary President, Scottish Gymnastics and Honorary Vice President, BasketballScotland; former Scottish Partnership Manager, New Millennium Experience Company and Director, Organising Leisure and Leisure Training.com. Address: (b.) 29 Abercromby Place, Edinburgh EH3 6QE; T.-0131 557 5488. Web: iodscotland.com

Watt, Jim, MBE (1980). Co-commentator and analyst, Sky Sports, since 1996; former boxer; b. 18.7.48, Glasgow. Turned professional, 1968; British Lightweight Champion, 1972-73, 1975-77; European Lightweight Champion, 1977-79; World Lightweight Champion, 1979-81; four successful defences of World title; Freedom of Glasgow, 1981.

Watt, John. Chairman of the Parole Board for Scotland, since 2013. Qualified solicitor; career in the Crown Office and Procurator Fiscal Service, latterly serving as area procurator fiscal in Grampian and then in Argyll & Clyde;

extensive experience of managing a large caseload and making decisions in serious and high-profile cases, and of joint working with criminal justice partners such as the courts, police and social work departments. Address: Parole Board for Scotland, Saughton House, Broomhouse Drive, Edinburgh EH11 3XD; T.-0131 244 8373.

Watt, John Alexander, MA (Hons), MA, PhD, OBE. Director of High Life Highland, 2011-2013; Director of New Start Highland, since 2012; Chair, Scottish Land Fund Committee, since 2012; Member, Big Lottery Scotland Committee, since 2013; Director, Kessock Books, since 2014; Director of Strengthening Communities, Highlands and Islands Enterprise, 2003-2012; b. 16.9.51, Dunfermline; m., Hilary Lawson; 1 s.; 1 d. Educ. Inverness Royal Academy; University of Aberdeen; University of Waterloo, Ontario, Canada. Teacher, Chaminade Secondary School, Karonga, Malawi, 1973-74; Tutor, Open University, 1981-82; Highlands and Islands Development Board, 1981-91; Highlands and Islands Enterprise, 1991-2012. Recreations: hill walking; golf; social enterprise development. Address: 23 Broadstone Park, Inverness IV2 3JZ; T.-01463-241252. E-mail: johnawatt@btinternet.com

Watt, Karen, MA, MSc, ACIS. Director of Culture, Europe & External Affairs, Scottish Government, since 2015, Director of External Affairs, 2012-2015, Head of Enterprise and Tourism, 2012 (January-November); Principal Private Secretary to the First Minister of Scotland, 2009-2012; Director of Regulation and Inspection, Communities Scotland, 2003-08; Chief Executive, The Scottish Housing Regulator, 2008-09; b. 5.7.64, Antrim; m., Dr Stephen Watt; 3 s. Educ. Antrim Grammar School; St Andrews University. Department of Social Security, 1987-91; Scottish Homes: Senior Planning Analyst, 1991-96, Performance Auditor, 1996-98, Performance Audit Manager, 1998-2001; Head of Regulatory Policy and Information, Communities Scotland, 2001-03. Address: (b.) 3E 91 Victoria Quay, Leith, Edinburgh EH6 6QQ.

Watt, Maureen. MSP (SNP), Aberdeen South and North Kincardine, since 2011, North East Scotland, 2006-2011; Minister for Public Health, since 2014; Convener of the Infrastructure and Capital Investment Committee, 2011-14; Convener of the Rural Affairs and Environment Committee, 2009-2011; Minister for Schools and Skills, 2007-09; b. 23.6.51, Aberdeen; m. Educ. Keith Grammar School; University of Strathclyde; University of Birmingham. Comprehensive School Teacher, Social Studies, Reading, Berkshire, 1974-76; Personnel Assistant, then Personnel Manager, Deutag Drilling (now KCA Deutag). Daughter of the late Hamish Watt MP (Banffshire), 1974-79; mother of Stuart Donaldson MP (West Aberdeenshire & Kincardine). Address: (b.) Scottish Parliament, Edinburgh EH99 1SP; Constituency Office: 51 Victoria Road, Torry, Aberdeen AB11 9LS.

Watt, Professor Roger, BA (Cantab), PhD, FRSE. Professor of Psychology, Stirling University, since 1988; b. London; m., Helen; 2 s.; 1 d. Educ. St. Olaves School; Downing College, Cambridge. Formerly Scientist, MRC Applied Psychology Unit, Cambridge; expert witness, various including Cullen Inquiry and Ladbroke Grove Rail Crash. 2 books published. Recreation: trumpet player. Address: (b.) Department of Psychology, Stirling University, Stirling FK9 4LA; T.-01786 467640; e-mail: r.j.watt@stirling.ac.uk

Watters, Pat. Chairman, Scottish Fire and Rescue Service, since 2012; President, Convention of Scottish Local Authorities, 2001-2012; b. 4.2.48, Glasgow; m., Marilyn; 1 s.; 1 d. Educ. Our Lady and St Margaret's School. Entered local government, Strathclyde Regional Council, 1982; Vice President, COSLA, 1999-2001; former COSLA Spokesperson for Personnel Resources and local government's Lead Negotiator; Chair, Scottish Strategy

Forum for Local Authority Employees; Vice-Chair, Police Negotiating Board; Chair, PNB Chief Officers Committee; Member, South Lanarkshire Council, since 1995 (Chair of Corporate Resources). Address: (b.) Scottish Fire and Rescue Service Headquarters, 5 Whitefriars Crescent, Perth PH2 0PA; T.-01738 475260.

Watterson, Professor Andrew, BA, PhD, CFIOSH, FCR. Professor of Health, University of Stirling, since 2000; Head of Occupational and Enviromental Health Research Group, since 2000; b. 13.08.48. Lecturer in Health, Southampton University, 1980-92; Head of OSHU, NTU, 1992-94; Head of Department of Health, De Montfort University, Leicester and Professor of Occupational and Environmental Health, 1994-2000. Publications: author of 3 books, 1 edited book, 24 chapters in books, 25 published reports and numerous peer reviewed papers in scientific and medical journals. On editorial boards and civil society organisations dealing with risks and hazards of the agricultural, electronics and fish farming industries; acted as an advisor to the World Health Organization. Main research interests relate to regulation and enforcement, health impact assessments, participatory action research and occupational cancer prevention. Address: (b.) Occupational and Environmental Health Research Group, University of Stirling, Stirling FK9 4LA; e-mail: aew1@stir.ac.uk

Watts, Professor Colin, BSc, DPhil, FRS, FRSE, FMedSci. Professor of Immunobiology, University of Dundee, since 1999; b. 28.4.53, London; m., Susan Mary (nee Light); 1 s.; 2 d. Educ. Friend's School, Saffron Walden; Bristol University; Sussex University. EMBO Long Term Fellow, University of California, Los Angeles, 1980-82; Beit Memorial Fellow, MRC Lab of Molecular Biology, Cambridge, 1982-86; Lecturer, then Reader, Department of Biochemistry, University of Dundee, 1986-99. Tenovus Scotland Margaret Maclellan Prize, 2000; Descartes Prize, European Union, 2002 (shared); Wellcome Trust Molecular and Cell Panel, 1993-96; MRC Training and Career Development Panel, 2005-09; Scientific Advisory Boards, Jenner Institute Vaccine Research, 2001-05; Lister Institute of Preventative Medicine, since 2015; Editorial Boards: Science, Eur. Journal of Immunology, Journal of Cell Biology; Journal of Cell Science. Recreations: music; cities; armchair sport. Address: (b.) Division of Cell Signalling and Immunology, College of Life Sciences, University of Dundee DD1 5EH; T.-01382 384233; e-mail: c.watts@dundee.ac.uk

Way of Plean, George Alexander, OStJ, LLB (Hons), FSAScot, FRSA, NP, SSC, Companion of the Order of Malta, Knight of St Maurice (Italy), Knight of Vila Vicosa (Portugal). Former Hon. Royal Consul of Portugal; Sheriff of Tayside, Central and Fife, since 2009; retired consultant, Beveridge and Kellas; Procurator Fiscal (2003-09), now Falkland Pursuivant Extraordinary, HM Court of The Lord Lyon; b. 22.5.56, Edinburgh; 1 s. Educ. Boroughmuir School; University of Edinburgh; University of Oxford (Pembroke College). Secretary, Standing Council of Scottish Chiefs, 1984-2003; Member, Convention of the Baronage of Scotland; Past President, Society of Solicitors in the Supreme Courts; Member, Council, Law Society of Scotland, 2001-09; Member, Sheriff Court Rules Council, 2007-09; Freeman, City of Glasgow, 1997; Queens Jubilee Medal. Publications: Collins Clans and Family Encyclopaedia (Editor-in-Chief); Homelands of the Clans; Everyday Scots Law; Scottish Clans and Tartans. Recreations: heraldry and orders of chivalry. Address: (b.) Sheriff Court, 6 West Bell Street, Dundee.

Weatherhead, Alexander Stewart, OBE, TD, MA, LLB. Retired Solicitor; formerly Senior Partner, Brechin Tindal Oatts (formerly Tindal Oatts), Solicitors, Glasgow (Partner, 1960-97, Consultant, 1997-98); b. 3.8.31, Edinburgh; m., Harriett Foye; 2 d. Educ. George Watson's College, Edinburgh; Larchfield School, Helensburgh; Glasgow

Academy; Glasgow University. Royal Artillery, 1950-52; TA, 1952; Lt. Col. Commanding 277 (A&SH) Field Regiment, RA (TA), 1965-67, The Lowland Regiment, RA (T), 1967 and Glasgow and Strathclyde Universities OTC, 1970-73; Colonel, 1974; TAVR Colonel, Lowlands (West), 1974-76; ADC (TAVR) to The Queen, 1977-81; Honorary Colonel, Glasgow and Strathclyde Universities OTC, 1982-98; Member, Lowlands RFCA, since 1967, Chairman, 1990-93; Member, Royal Artillery Council for Scotland, 1972 (Vice Chairman, 1996-2001); Council Member, Law Society of Scotland, 1971-84 (Honorary Vice-President, 1983-84); Member, Royal Commission on Legal Services in Scotland, 1976-80; Council Member, Society for Computers and Law, 1973-86, Honorary Member, since 1986 (Chairman, 1981-84); Temporary Sheriff, 1985-92; Member, Royal Faculty of Procurators in Glasgow, since 1960 (Dean, 1991-95, Hon. Member, 1997); Director, Glasgow Chamber of Commerce, 1991-95; Member, Research Ethics Committee, Glasgow Royal Infirmary, 1999-2006; Member, Business Committee General Council, University of Glasgow, 2001-05 and 2007-2011; Member, Medical Research Ethics Committee, Scotland (B), 2005-06; Member, Incorporation of Weavers of Glasgow, since 1949; Commodore, Royal Western Yacht Club, 1995-98. Recreations: sailing; reading; music. Address: (h.) 52 Partickhill Road, Glasgow G11 5AB; T.-0141-334 6277; e-mail: sandywd@aol.com

Weaver, C. Giles H., FCA, MBA. Proprietor, Greywalls Hotel, Gullane, since 1976; b. 4.4.46; m., Rosamund B. Mayhew; 2 s.; 2 d. Educ. Eton College; London Business School. Ernst & Young, 1966-70; London Business School, 1971-73; Jessel Securities/Berry Wiggins, 1973-76; Director, Ivory & Sime plc, 1976-86; Managing Director Pensions, Prudential Portfolio Managers, 1986-90; Murray Johnstone Ltd.: CIO, 1990-93, Managing Director, 1993-99, Chairman, 1999-2000. Trustee, Lutyens Trust; Director: EP Global Trust plc; Past Chair, New Club Edinburgh; Past Deputy Chair, National Galleries of Scotland. Recreations: golf; bridge; skiing; stalking. Address: (b.) Hill Fort House, Drem, East Lothian EH39 5AZ.

Webb, Professor David John, MD, DSc, FRCP, FRSE, FAHA, FESC, FFPM, FMedSci FBPharmacolS, FBHS. President, British Pharmacological Society, since 2016; Christison Professor of Therapeutics and Clinical Pharmacology, University of Edinburgh, since 1995 and Consultant Physician, Lothian University Hospitals NHS Trust, since 1990; b. 1.9.53; m.; 3 s. Educ. Dulwich College (Kent Scholarship), 1964-71; The Royal London Hospital, 1971-76; MB BS, University of London, 1977; MD, University of London, 1990; DSc, University of Edinburgh, 2000; MRCP UK (Royal College of Physicians, London), 1980; FRCP, Edinburgh, 1992; FFPM, UK, 1993; FRCP, London, 1994; FAHA/International Fellowship, American Heart Association, 1998; FMedSci, UK, 1999; FESC, 2001; FRSE, 2004; FBPharmacolS, 2004; FBHS, 2014. House Officer Posts, The Royal London Hospital Scheme, 1977-78; Senior House Officer, Chelmsford Hospitals. 1978-79; Senior House Officer, medical rotational scheme, Stoke Mandeville Hospital, 1979-80; Registrar, medical rotational scheme, Royal London Hospital, 1980-82; Registrar in Medicine, Western Infirmary, Glasgow, 1982-85; MRC Clinical Scientist, MRC BP Unit, Western Infirmary, Glasgow, 1982-85; Lecturer in Clinical Pharmacology, St George's Medical School, London, 1985-89; Senior Registrar in Medicine, St George's Hospital, London, 1985-89; Consultant Physician, Lothian University Hospitals NHS Trust, since 1990; Senior Lecturer in Medicine, University of Edinburgh, 1990-95; Christison Professor of Therapeutics and Clinical Pharmacology, University of Edinburgh, since 1995; Director, Clinical Research Centre (CRC), University of Edinburgh, 1990-96; Head, University Department of Medicine, University of Edinburgh, 1997-

98; Head, Department of Medical Sciences, University of Edinburgh, 1998-2001; Wellcome Trust Research Leave Fellowship, and Leader, Wellcome Trust Cardiovascular Research Initiative (CVRI), University of Edinburgh, 1998-2001; Director of the Education Programme, Wellcome Trust Clinical Research Facility (WTCRF), Edinburgh, since 1998; Convenor, Cardiovascular Interdisciplinary Group, University of Edinburgh, 1999-2000; Head, Centre for Cardiovascular Science (CVS), University of Edinburgh, 2000-04; Chairman, New Drugs Committee (Scottish Medicines Consortium), 2001-05; Executive Committee, British Hypertension Society, 1991-94; British Pharmacological Society: Executive Committee, 1994-98, Clinical Vice-President, 1995-98, Director and Trustee, 1996-99, and 2004, Vice President (Meetings), 2012, President-Elect, 2014, Chairman, Committee of Professors and Heads of Clinical Pharmacology & Therapeutics, 2004-8; Section Committee I, Academy of Medical Sciences, 2000-02; Trustee, High Blood Pressure Foundation, since 1991; Research Director, High Blood Pressure Foundation, since 1993; Councillor, Clinical Division, International Union for Pharmacology (IUPHAR), since 2004; Chairman, Scottish Medicines Consortium, 2005-08; Vice-President, Royal College of Physicians of Edinburgh, 2006-09; Lead - Wellcome Trust Scottish Translational Medicine and Therapeutics Initiative (STMTI), 2008; EACPT, President, 2009; President, Scottish Society of Physicians, 2010; Lead Clin Pharmacol, MRC Scottish Clin Pharmacol and Pathway Programme (SCP3), 2010; Non-Executive Director, MHRA, since 2013; Chair, NIBSC Scientific Advisory Committee, since 2014. Publications: The Molecular Biology & Pharmacology of the Endothelins (Molecular Biology Intelligence Unit Monograph Series), Co-Author, 1995; The Endothelium in Hypertension, ed, Co-Author, 1996; The Year in Therapeutics Vol 1, ed, Co-Author, 2005. Recreations: summer and winter mountaineering; scuba diving; reading late at night. Clubs: Scottish Mountaineering Club; Scottish Malt Whisky Society. Address: (h.) 75 Great King Street, Edinburgh EH3 6RN; e-mail: d.j.webb@ed.ac.uk

Webster, Andrew George, LLB (Hons), DipLP, FRSA. Advocate, since 1992; b. 20.7.67, Wick; m., Sheila Mairead; 2 d. Educ. Wick High School; University of Aberdeen. First Scottish Standing Junior Counsel; Part-time Sheriff; Part-time Chairman, Pension Appeal Tribunal for Scotland; Standing Junior Counsel to: Ministry of Defence (Air Force), 1997-2000, Ministry of Defence, 2000-2012; Legal Assessor: Medical Practitioners Tribunal Service (formerly General Medical Council), since 2010. Address: (b.) Advocates' Library, Parliament House, Edinburgh EH1 1RF; T.-0131-226 5071.

Webster, Jack (John Barron), BEM, DLitt, MUniv. Author and Journalist; b. 8.7.31, Maud, Aberdeenshire; m., Eden Keith; 3 s. Educ. Maud School; Robert Gordon's College, Aberdeen. Reporter, Turriff Advertiser; Reporter/Sub Editor, Aberdeen Press & Journal/Evening Express; Chief Sub-Editor, Scottish Sunday Express; Feature Writer, Scottish Daily Express; Feature Writer, Sunday Standard; Columnist, The Herald. Columnist of the Year, 1996; Speaker of the Year, 1996. Publications: The Dons, 1978; A Grain of Truth, 1981; Gordon Strachan, 1984; Another Grain of Truth, 1988; 'Tis Better to Travel, 1989; Alistair MacLean (biography), 1991; Famous Ships of the Clyde, 1993; The Flying Scots, 1994; The Express Years, 1994; In the Driving Seat, 1996; The Herald Years, 1996; From Dali to Burrell, 1997; Webster's World, 1997; The Reo Stakis Story, 1999; The Auld Hoose: The Story of Robert Gordon's College, 2005; Jack Webster's Aberdeen, 2007; A Final Grain of Truth, 2013; television films: The Roup, 1985; As Time Goes By, 1987; Northern Lights, 1989; Webster Goes West, 1991; John Brown: The Man Who Drew a Legend, 1994; Walking Back to Happiness,

1996; video film: The Glory of Gothenburg, 1993; stage plays: The Life of Grassic Gibbon, 2007; From Dali to Burrell, 2010. Address: (b.) 58 Netherhill Avenue, Glasgow G44 3XG; T.-0141-637 6437.
E-mail: jackwebster637@virginmedia.com

Webster, Professor John Bainbridge, MA, PhD, DD, FRSE. Professor of Divinity, University of St Andrews, since 2013; b. 20.6.55, Mansfield. Educ. Bradford Grammar School; Cambridge University. Chaplain and Tutor, St John's College, Durham, 1982-86; Professor of Systematic Theology, Wycliffe College, University of Toronto, 1986-96; Lady Margaret Professor of Divinity, University of Oxford, 1996-2003; Professor of Systematic Theology, University of St Andrews, 2003-2013. Publications: Eberhard Jungel; Barth's Ethics of Reconciliation; Barth's Moral Theology; Barth; Word and Church; Holiness; Holy Scripture; Confessing God; Barth's Earlier Theology; Domain of the Word; God Without Measure. Address: (b.) St Mary's College, South Street, St Andrews, Fife KY16 9JU.

Webster, Professor Nigel Robert, BSc, MB, ChB, PhD, FRCA, FRCPEdin, FRCSEdin. Professor of Anaesthesia and Intensive Care, Aberdeen University, since 1994; b. 14.6.53, Walsall; divorced; 1 s.; 2 d.; m. (2), Helen Frances Webster. Educ. Edward Shelley High School, Walsall; Leeds University. Member, scientific staff/Consultant, Clinical Research Centre, Northwick Park Hospital, Harrow; Consultant in Anaesthesia and Intensive Care, St. James's University Hospital, Leeds. Address: (b.) Institute of Medical Sciences, Foresterhill, Aberdeen AB25 2ZD; T.-01224 681818.

Webster, Professor Robin Gordon Maclennan, OBE, MA (Cantab), MA (Arch), RIBA, FRIAS, RSA. Emeritus Professor of Architecture, Scott Sutherland School of Architecture, The Robert Gordon University, Aberdeen; Partner, CameronWebster architects, since 2005; Senior Partner, Robin Webster & Associates, Aberdeen, 1984-2004; b. 24.12.39, Glasgow; m., Katherine S. Crichton (deceased); 1 s.; 2 d.; m., Pauline Lawrence, 2012. Educ. Glasgow Academy; Rugby School; St. John's College, Cambridge; University College London. Assistant, Gillespie Kidd & Coia, Architects, Glasgow, 1963-64; National Building Agency, London, 1965-67; Senior Partner, Spence and Webster, Architects, 1972-84; Lecturer, Bartlett School of Architecture, 1969-74; Visiting Lecturer, Washington University, St. Louis, 1975, Cambridge University, 1976-77, and Mackintosh School, Glasgow School of Art, 1978-84. Commissioner, Royal Fine Art Commission for Scotland, 1992-98; Chairman, Alexander Thomson Association, 2011-2013; Secretary, Walmer Crescent Association; Trustee, Glasgow City Heritage Trust, 2007-2012; Trustee, Scottish Stained Glass Symposium; Trustee, House for an Art lover. Recreations: looking and drawing. Address: (h.) 7 Walmer Crescent, Glasgow G51 1AT; T.-0141 330 9898.
E-mail: robin.webster@mac.com

Weir, Viscount (William Kenneth James Weir), BA, Hon. DEng (Glasgow), Hon. FEng. Director, The Weir Group PLC, 1966-99 (Chairman, 1983-99); Director and former Vice-Chairman, St. James' Place Capital plc; Chairman, Balfour Beatty plc, 1996-2003 (Deputy Chairman, 1992-96, Director, since 1977); Chairman, CP Ships Ltd., 2001-04; Director, Canadian Pacific Railway Co., 1989-2004; Chairman, Major British Exporters; b. 9.11.33, Glasgow; m., 1, Diana MacDougall (m. diss.); 1 s.; 1 d.; 2, Jacqueline Mary Marr (m. diss.); 3, Marina Sevastopoulo; 1 s.; 1 d. Educ. Eton; Trinity College, Cambridge. Member, London Advisory Committee,

Hongkong and Shanghai Banking Corporation, 1980-92; Deputy Chairman, Charterhouse J. Rothschild PLC, 1983-85; Member, Court, Bank of England, 1972-84; Co-Chairman, RIT and Northern PLC, 1982-83; Director, 1970, Chairman, 1975-82, Great Northern Investment Trust Ltd.; Member, Scottish Economic Council, 1972-85; Director, British Steel Corporation, 1972-76; Chairman, Patrons of National Galleries of Scotland, 1984-95; Member, Queen's Bodyguard for Scotland (Royal Company of Archers). Recreations: shooting; golf; fishing. Address: (h.) Rodinghead, Mauchline, Ayrshire.

Weir, Michael, LLB. SNP MP, Angus, since 2001; SNP Chief Whip in the House of Commons, since 2015; b. 24.3.57, Arbroath; m., Anne; 2 d. Educ. Arbroath High School; Aberdeen University. Myers and Wills, Montrose, 1979-81; Charles Wood and Son, Kirkcaldy, 1982-83; Myers and Wills, Montrose, 1983-84; J. & D.G. Shiell, Brechin, 1984-2001. Dean of Society of Procurators and Solicitors in Angus, 2001; Member, Speakers Panel. Address: (b.) 16 Brothock Bridge, Arbroath DD11 1NG; T.-01241 874522.

Weir, Sheriff Robert, QC, BA (Hist, Hons), LBE. Sheriff, South Strathclyde, Dumfries and Galloway, since 2016. Educ. Durham University; Dundee University. Admitted as a solicitor in 1991; joined Maclay Murray & Spens as a trainee solicitor in 1992; Solicitor, then Partner, HBM Sayers, 1994-2008; appointed as a Stipendiary Magistrate in 2008; admitted to the Faculty of Advocates in 1995, and practised principally in commercial dispute resolution, with a specialty in maritime law; Advocate Depute, 2005-08 and took silk in 2010; appointed Part Time Sheriff in 2011. Address: Sheriff's Chambers, Sheriff Court House, Wellington Square, Ayr KA7 1EE; T.-01292 292200.

Welch, Dr. Dorothy Ann, BSc, PhD. Deputy Secretary, University of Glasgow, since 2009; b. 1.3.60, Dundee; m., Alan Welch; 1 s.; 1 d. Educ. University of Edinburgh; University of Cambridge. Career History: Lecturer in Chemistry, Heriot-Watt University; Computing Officer, University of Edinburgh; Director of Scottish Wider Access Programme; College Registrar, University of Edinburgh. Address: (b.) University of Glasgow, University Avenue, Glasgow G12 8QQ.
E-mail: dorothy.welch@glasgow.ac.uk

Weller, Professor David Paul, MBBS, MPH, PHD, FRACGP, MRCGP, FAFPHM. Head of School, Clinical Sciences and Community Health, Edinburgh University, James Mackenzie Professor of General Practice, since 2000; b. 21.7.59, Adelaide; m., Dr Belinda Weller; 1 s.; 2 d. Educ. Prince Alfred College, Adelaide; University of Adelaide. Training and working in family medicine, UK and Australia, 1984-90; PhD studies, 1991-94; Senior Lecturer, Department of General Practice, Flinders University of South Australia, 1995-99. Board Member, Lothian Primary Care Trust, Scottish Cancer Foundation. Recreations: running; hill-walking; piano. Address: (h.) 42 Craiglea Drive, Edinburgh EH10 5PF.

Weller, Richard, MD, FRCP (Ed). Senior Lecturer, Dermatology, University of Edinburgh, since 2002; b. 21.7.62, Münster, Germany; m., Dr Julie Gallagher; 1 s.; 1 d. Educ. Malvern College; St. Thomas' Hospital, London University. General medical training, England and Australia, 1987-92; dermatology training: St. John's Institute of Dermatology, London, 1993, Aberdeen Royal Infirmary, 1994-96; Lecturer, Dermatology, Edinburgh Royal Infirmary, 1996-98; Visiting Research Fellow: Immunbiologie Abteilung, HHU, Düsseldorf, 1999,

Department of Surgery, University of Pittsburgh, USA, 2000-01. Recreations: mountaineering; sailing. Address: (h.) 79 Dundas Street, Edinburgh EH3 6SD; e-mail: r.weller@ed.ac.uk

Wells, Carol Ann (Annie). MSP (Scottish Conservative), Glasgow region, since 2016. Food retail manager, for one of the UK's leading brands for the last 12 years; worked in various locations throughout Glasgow. Address: Scottish Parliament, Edinburgh EH99 1SP.

Wells, Margaret Jeffrey, MA, CQSW. Independent Management and Care Consultant, since 2004; former Non Executive Board Member, Scottish Children's Reporter Administration; b. 22.7.55, Berwick-upon-Tweed; m., Tony Wells; 1 s.; 1 d. Educ. Berwickshire High School, Duns; University of Edinburgh; University of Glasgow. Director of Partnership Development and Child Health Commissioner, Lothian NHS Board, 2002-04; Director of Housing and Social Work, Aberdeenshire Council, 1995-2002; Depute Director of Social Work, Grampian Regional Council, 1993-95, Assistant Director of Social Work, 1992-93; District Manager (Dundee West), Tayside Regional Council, Area Fieldwork Manager (Hospitals), 1989-92, Senior Social Worker, Mental Health, Perth & Kinross. Governor, The Robert Gordon University, 2001/02; President, Association of Directors of Social Work, 2000; Social Work adviser to COSLA; Member: Ministerial Joint Futures Group, Mental Health References Group. Recreation: singing. Address: (h. & b.) 22 Comerton Place, Drumoig, Leuchars, St. Andrews, Fife KY10 0NQ; e-mail: margaretwells22@btinternet.com

Wells, Peter William, BVM&S, PhD, MRCVS. Chairman, Moredun Scientific Ltd, since 2008; Chairman, GALVmed, since 2012; b. 23.2.46, Hexham, Northumberland; m., Ceri; 2 s. Educ. Queen Elizabeth Grammar School, Hexham; University of Edinburgh; University of Guelph. Global Head of Research and Development, Novartis Animal Health Inc, 2004-08; Head of Research and Development, Novartis Animal Vaccines, 2000-04; Head of Research and Development Biologicals, Hoechst Roussel Vet, 1995-2000; various roles in Hoechst Animal Health, Hoechst UK, 1980-95; Visiting Scientist, International Laboratory for Research on Animal Diseases, 1978-80; Senior/Principal Veterinary Research Officer, Moredun Institute, 1973-78; Lecturer in Immunology, Royal (Dick) School of Veterinary Studies, 1972-73. Recreations: cycling; walking. Address: (b.) Moredun Scientific Ltd, Pentlands Science Park, Bush Loan, Penicuik, Midlothian EH26 0PZ; T.-0131 445 6206; e-mail: pwells@moredun-scientific.com

Welsh, Andrew Paton, DL, MA (Hons), DipEd, DipFrench (Open). MSP (SNP), Angus, 1999-2011; Member, Scottish Parliament Corporate Body, 1999-2006; Convener, Audit Committee, 1999-2003; Deputy Convener, Local Government and Transport Committee, 2003-04; Member, Scottish Commission for Public Accounts; National Vice-President, SNP, 1987-2004; Deputy Convener, Audit Committee, 2004-07; Convener, Finance Committee, 2007-2011; Member, Audit Committee, 2007-09; MP (SNP), Angus, 1997-2001 (MP, Angus East, 1987-97); b. 19.4.44, Glasgow; m., Sheena Margaret Cannon (see Sheena Margaret Welsh); 1 d. Educ. Govan High School; Glasgow University. Member, Stirling District Council, 1974; MP (SNP), South Angus, 1974-79; SNP Parliamentary Spokesman on Housing, 1974-78 and 1987-2001, Self-Employed and Small Businesses, 1975-79 and 1987-97, Agriculture, 1975-79 and 1987-97, Education, 1997-2001; Parliamentary Chief Whip, 1977-79 and 1987-99; Member, Select Committee on Members' Interests, 1989-92; Member, House of Commons Chairmen's Panel,

1997-2001; Member, Scottish Affairs Committee, 1992-2001; SNP Executive Vice Chairman for Administration, 1979-83, for Local Government, 1984-87; Parliamentary candidate, East Angus, 1983; Member, Church and Nation Committee, Church of Scotland, 1984-85; Member, Dundee University Court, 1984-87; Provost, Angus District Council, 1984-87; Convener, Cross Party Tartan Day Group, 2005-2011; Trustee, National Prayer Breakfast for Scotland, 1999-2011; Member, Scottish Bible Society; Trustee, David Hume Institute, 2011-2015; awarded The Honour of Freeman of Angus by the unanimous vote of Angus Council, September 2012; appointed Deputy Lieutenant of Angus, January 2013. Recreations: music; horse riding; languages. Address: (h.) Montquhir, Carmyllie, Arbroath; T.-01241 860317.

Welsh, Ian, MA (Hons), MA, DPSE, FRSA. Chief Executive, Health and Social Care Alliance Scotland; b. Prestwick; m., Elizabeth; 2 s. Educ. Prestwick Academy; Ayr Academy; University of Glasgow. Former professional footballer, Kilmarnock FC; Teacher (former Deputy Head Teacher, Auchinleck Academy); formerly Director, Human Resources and Public Affairs, Prestwick International Airport; Chief Executive, Kilmarnock FC, 1997-2001. Former Member, Kyle and Carrick District Council, then South Ayrshire Council; former MSP; former Governor, Craigie College of Education; former Chair, North Ayrshire Partnership; former Chair, Scottish Advisory Committee of the Voluntary Sector National Training Organisation. Address: (b.) Venlaw Building, 349 Bath Street, Glasgow G2 4AA; T.-0141 404 0231.

Wend, Prof. Petra, PhD, FRSA, FRSE. Principal and Vice-Chancellor, Queen Margaret University, since 2009; Deputy Vice-Chancellor and Deputy Chief Executive, Oxford Brookes University, 2005-09; b. 21.01.59, Gütersloh, Germany; partner, Professor Philip James; 1 d. Educ. Münster University; University of Leeds. Middlesex Polytechnic, later Middlesex University: Lecturer, Senior Lecturer, then Principal Lecturer, 1989-97; Deputy Head, School of Languages, 1996-97 (Acting Head, 1995); Director of Curriculum, Learning and Quality, 1997-99; University of North London: Dean, Faculty of Humanities and Education, 1999-2002; Pro Vice-Chancellor (Learning and Teaching), 2000-02; Director of Learning, Teaching and Student Affairs, London Metropolitan University, 2002-05; Deputy Vice-Chancellor and Deputy Chief Executive, Oxford Brookes University, 2005-09. Member, Society of Renaissance Studies, since 1991; Member, Commission for Widening Access, since 2015; Chair, National Implementation Board for Teaching Scotland's Future, 2012-2015; Vice-Convener, Universities Scotland, since 2012; Convenor, Universities Scotland Learning and Teaching Committee, 2010-12; Member: QAA Board, QAA Scotland, SDS/SFC Skills Committee, until 2013; Edinburgh Business Leadership Forum, British Council Scotland Advisory Committee, Goodison Group Forum. Publications: The Female Voice: lyrical expression in the writings of the five Italian Renaissance poets, 1994; German Interlanguage, 1996, 2nd edition, 1998; Geschäftsbriefe schnell und sicher formulieren, 2004; contributed articles to learned journals on linguistics and on institutional strategies. Recreations: painting; sport; Arsenal FC (season ticket holder). Address: (b.) Queen Margaret University, Queen Margaret University Drive, Edinburgh EH21 6UU; T.-0131 474 0483; e-mail: pwend@qmu.ac.uk

Wersun, Ana, CSP. Honorary Consul, Republic of Slovenia in Scotland, since 2004; Consultant Physiotherapist, since 1976; b. 30.12.54, Brezice, Slovenia; m., Dr. Alec Wersun; 2 d. Educ. Brezice School; University of Ljubljana. Qualified as a Physiotherapist in Ljubljana, 1976; worked as a Physiotherapist in Slovenia, Switzerland and UK both in The National Health Services and in Private Practice, 1976-2008. Member, Consular Corps, Edinburgh and Leith, since 2004. Honorary Treasurer, Consular Corps of Edinburgh and Leith. Recreations: hill walking; classical music; painting; reading. Address: (h. & b.) 3 Coltbridge Terrace, Edinburgh EH12 6AB; T.-0131-337 5167; e-mail: sloveneconsulate@btinternet.com

West, Denise. Head of Commercial, DC Thomson, since 2014. Commercial Director, Scottish Daily Record and Sunday Mail Ltd, 2000-2013; Managing Director (Scotland and North East), Trinity Mirror, 2012-14. Address: (b.) Lang Stracht, Mastrick, Aberdeen AB15 6DF; T.-01224 690 222.

West, Gary James, MA, PhD. Senior Lecturer in Celtic and Scottish Studies, University of Edinburgh, since 2009; Broadcaster, Presenter, BBC Radio Scotland, since 2003; b. 9.11.66, Aberfeldy. Educ. Pitlochry High School, Breadalbane Academy; University of Edinburgh. Lecturer, Celtic & Scottish Studies, University of Edinburgh, since 1994. Piper and Folk Musician; Member: Ceolbeg, Clan Alba, Hugh MacDiarmids Haircut, Vale of Atholl Pipe Band; toured widely in Europe and North America; regular recording artist; presenter of 'Pipeline', BBC Radio Scotland. Board Member: Creative Scotland, Auchindrain Musuem Trust, Gordon Duncan Memorial Trust; Chair, Traditional Arts and Culture Scotland. Recreations: music; football; golf. Address: (b.) 27 George Square, Edinburgh EH8 9LD; T.-0131 552 7087; e-mail: gary.west@ed.ac.uk

West, Peter William Alan, OBE, DL, MA, DUniv, DPhil; b. 16.3.49, Edinburgh; m. Margaret Clark; 1s; 1d. Educ. Edinburgh Academy; St Andrews University. Administrator, Edinburgh University, 1972-77; Assistant Secretary, Leeds University 1977-83; Deputy Registrar, Strathclyde University, 1983-89, Secretary to the University of Strathclyde, 1990-2010; Chief Operating Officer, Edinburgh College of Art, 2010-2011. Chair, Scotland/Malawi Partnership, 2005-2010; Doctor (honoris causa), University of Rostov-on-Don, Russia; Doctor (honoris causa), University of Malawi; Deputy Lieutenant of the City of Glasgow; Honorary Fellowships of University of Strathclyde and Bell College, Hamilton. Awarded the OBE for services to HE in Scotland and Malawi in the Queen's Birthday Honours, 2006. Scottish Honorary Consul of the Republic of Malawi from 2010. Recreations: reading; drinking wine; supporting the leading football teams of Scotland (Hibernian) and Africa (the Flames of Malawi) through thick and thin. Address: 10 Matilda Road, Glasgow G41 5HL; T.-0141 423 4181.

Whaling, Rev. Professor Frank, BA, MA, PhD, ThD, FSAM, FRAS, FABI, FWLA, FIBA, FICS, FWIA. Emeritus Professor of the Study of Religion, Edinburgh University; Methodist Minister; b. 5.2.34, Pontefract; m., Margaret; 1 s.; 1 d. Educ. Kings School, Pontefract; Christ's College, Cambridge; Wesley House, Cambridge; Harvard University. Methodist Minister, Birmingham Central Hall, 1960-62, Faizabad and Banaras, North India, 1962-66, Eastbourne, 1966-69; Teaching Fellow, Harvard University, 1972-73 (Harvard Doctorate, 1969-73); appointed Lecturer, Study of Religion, Edinburgh University, 1973. Theyer Honor Award, Harvard; Maitland Award, Cambridge; various Reseach Awards; Chair, Scottish Churches China Group, 1985-93; Chair, Edinburgh Inter-Faith Association, 1985-99, President, since 1999; Director, Edinburgh Cancer Help Centre, 1987-91; Chair, Scottish Inter-Faith Symposium, 1987-94; Consultant, World Without Hunger (charity); BBC,

Paulist Press, International Inter-Faith Council; Alistair Hardy Trust; Encyclopedia of World Spirituality (26 vols); Chair, Edinburgh International Centre for World Spiritualities, 1999-2004; Executive Director, Scottish Inter-Faith Council, 2002-05. Council Member, SHAP Working Party on Religion in Education, Religious Education Movement in Scotland. Visiting Lecturer and Professor, USA, China, South Africa, India, England; Hon. Life Fellow, British Association for the Study of Religion; ICS Scot of the Year, 2007. Publications: over 100 papers, over 250 reviews; books written and/or edited: An Approach to Dialogue: Hinduism and Christianity, 1966; The Rise of the Religious Significance of Rama, 1980; John and Charles Wesley, 1981; The World's Religious Traditions: Current Perspectives in Religious Studies, 1984; Contemporary Approaches to the Study of Religion: Vol. I, 1984, Vol. II, 1985; Christian Theology and World Religions, 1986; Religion in Today's World, 1987; Compassion Through Understanding, 1990; Dictionary of Beliefs and Religions, 1992; The World: How It Came Into Being and our Responsibility for It, 1994; Theory and Method in Religious Studies, 1995; Christian Prayer for Today, 2002; Understanding Hinduism, 2009; General Editor: (9 vol) Understanding Faith, since 2002; Understanding the Brahma Kumaris, 2012. Recreations: music; art; sport; inter-faith activities. Address: (h.) 21 Gillespie Road, Edinburgh EH13 0NW; T.-0131-441 2112.

Whatley, Professor Christopher Allan, OBE, BA, PhD, FRHistS, FRSE. Emeritus Professor of Scottish History, Dundee University (Vice-Principal and Head, College of Arts and Social Sciences, 2006-2014, Dean, Faculty of Arts and Social Sciences, 2002-06, Head, Department of History, 1995-2002); b. 29.5.48, Birmingham; 1 s.; 1 d. Educ. Bearsden Academy; Strathclyde University. Lecturer, Ayr College, 1975-79, Dundee University, 1979-88, St. Andrews University, 1988-92, Dundee University, 1992-94; Senior Lecturer, 1994. Editor, Scottish Economic and Social History, 1995-99; Chairman, SCCC Review Group, Scottish History in the Curriculum; Consultant Editor, Scotland's Story; Chair, Scottish Historical Review Trust, 2002-06; Director, Dundee University Press, 2003-2014; Board member, Dundee Repertory Theatre, since 2007; Council member, Royal Society of Edinburgh, 2006-09; Council member, Royal Historical Society, 2009-11; Chairman, Board of Governance, Scottish Institute for Policing Research, 2009-2014. Publications: The Scottish Salt Industry, 1570-1850; Onwards from Osnaburgs: the rise and progress of a Scottish textile company; Bought and Sold for English Gold?: explaining the union of 1707; The Manufacture of Scottish History (Co-editor); The Life and Times of Dundee (Co-author); The Remaking of Juteopolis: Dundee 1891-1991 (Editor); John Galt (Editor); The Industrial Revolution in Scotland; Modern Scottish History, 1707 to the Present (Co-editor); Scottish Society 1707-1830: Beyond Jacobitism, Towards Industrialisation; Victorian Dundee: Image and Realities (Co-editor); The Scots and the Union; The Union of 1707: New Directions (Co-editor); A History of Everyday Life in Scotland, 1600-1800 (Co-editor); Jute No More: Transforming Dundee (Co-editor); The Scots and the Union: Then and Now. Address: (h.) Tayfield Cottage, 51 Main Street, Longforgan, by Dundee DD2 5EW; T.-07972229750; e-mail: c.a.whatley@dundee.ac.uk

Wheater, Professor Roger John, OBE, DUniv, CBiol, FSB, FRSA, FRSGS (Hon), FRZSS (Hon), FRSE. President, Scottish Wildlife Trust, 2006-08; Chairman, National Trust for Scotland, 2000-05; Director, Royal Zoological Society of Scotland, 1972-98; Honorary Professor, Edinburgh University, since 1993; b. 24.11.33, Brighton; m., Jean Ord Troup; 1 s.; 1 d. Educ. Brighton, Hove and Sussex Grammar School; Brighton Technical College. Commissioned, Royal Sussex Regiment, 1953; served Gold Coast Regiment, 1953-54; 4/5th Bn., Royal Sussex Regiment (TA), 1954-56; Colonial Police, Uganda, 1956-61; Chief Warden, Murchison Falls National Park, 1961-70; Director, Uganda National Parks, 1970-72; Member, Co-ordinating Committee, Nuffield Unit of Tropical Animal Ecology; Member, Board of Governors, Mweka College of Wildlife Management, Tanzania; Director, National Park Lodges Ltd.; Member, Uganda National Research Council; Vice Chairman, Uganda Tourist Association; Council Member, 1980-91, and President, 1988-91, International Union of Directors of Zoological Gardens; Chairman, Federation of Zoological Gardens of Great Britain and Ireland, 1993-96; Chairman, Anthropoid Ape Advisory Panel, 1977-91; Member, International Zoo Year Book Editorial Board, 1987-99; President, Association of British Wild Animal Keepers, 1984-99; Chairman, Membership and Licensing Committee, 1984-91; Chairman, Working Party on Zoo Licensing Act, 1981-84; Council Member, Zoological Society of London, 1991-92, 1995-99, 2002-03, Vice President, 1999; Chairman, Whipsnade Wild Animal Park, 1999-2002; Vice-President, World Pheasant Association, since 1994; Trustee, Gorilla Organisation, 1995-2010, Chairman, 2008-2010; Chairman, European Association of Zoos and Aquaria, 1994-97; Member of Council, National Trust for Scotland, 1973-78, and 2000-05, Executive Committee, 1982-87, and 2000-05; Chairman, Cammo Estate Advisory Committee, 1980-95; ESU William Thyne Scholar, 1975; Assessor, Council, Scottish Wildlife Trust, 1973-92; Consultant, World Tourist Organisation (United Nations), 1980-2010; Member, Secretary of State for Scotland's Working Group on Environmental Education, 1990-94; Board Member, Scottish Natural Heritage, 1995-99 (Deputy Chairman, 1997-99); Chairman, Access Forum, 1996-2000; Founder Patron, Dynamic Earth, Trustee, 1999-2012; Patron, Friends of Kailzie Wildlife, since 2012; Member, Strategic Development Fund Panel - Royal Society of Wildlife Trust, 2007-2011; Vice-Chairman, Edinburgh Branch, English Speaking Union, 1977-81; President, Edinburgh Special Mobile Angling Club, 1982-86; President, Cockburn Trout Angling Club, since 1997; Trustee, Tweed Foundation, since 2006; Chairman, Tourism and Environment Forum, 1999-2003; Chairman, Heather Trust, 1999-2002; Deputy Chairman, Zoo Forum, 1999-2002; Vice-President, European Network of National Heritage Organisations, 2000-05; President, Tweeddale Society, since 2007; Chairman, Beaver-Salmonid Group, 2009-2015; President, Innerleithen Probus Club, 2010-2011, Vice President, 2009-2010; Member, Royal Zoological Society of Scotland Board, since 2011. Recreations: country pursuits; painting; gardening. Address: (h.) 17 Kirklands, Innerleithen, Borders EH44 6NA; T.-01896-830403.
E-mail: roger.wheater@btinternet.com

Wheatley, Professor Denys N., BSc, PhD, DSc, MD (h.c. multi), CIBiol, FRSB, FRCPath. Visiting Professor of Physiology, Wayne State Medical School, Detroit; Professor, Semmelweis Medical University, and Odessa Medical University; Foreign Member, Ukrainian Academy of Medical Sciences; Director, "BioMedES" Ltd.; Past President, International Federation for Cell Biology; Chief Scientific Officer, Bio-Cancer Treatments International; formerly at the Dept. of Pathology, University of Aberdeen; b. 18.3.40, Ascot; divorced; 2 d. Educ. Windsor Grammar School; King's College, University of London. Research Fellow, Aberdeen University, 1964-67; MRC Travelling Fellow/USPHS Fellow, 1967-70; 1970 onwards: Lecturer, Senior Lecturer, Reader in Cell Pathology, Aberdeen University. Publications include: Cell Growth and Division; The Centriole: a Central Enigma of Cell Biology; Editor: Theoretical Biology and Medical Modelling, Oncology News; "BipolART: Art and Bipolar Disorder - a Personal Perspective". Recreations: cello; piano; swimming; painting. Address: (h.&b.) Leggat House, Keithhall, Inverurie AB51 0XL; T.-01467-670280.

Wheatley, The Right Hon. Lord (John Francis Wheatley), PC, QC, BL. Senator, College of Justice, 2000-2010 (retired); b. 9.5.41, Edinburgh; m., Bronwen Catherine Fraser; 2 s. Educ. Mount St. Mary's College, Derbyshire; Edinburgh University. Called to Scottish Bar, 1966; Standing Counsel to Scottish Development Department, 1968-74; Advocate Depute, 1974-78; Sheriff, Perthshire and Kinross-shire, at Perth, 1980-98; Temporary High Court Judge, 1992; Sheriff Principal of Tayside Central and Fife, 1998-2000. Member, Parole Board, 2000-03; Chairman, Judicial Studies Committee, 2000-06. Recreations: music; gardening. Address: Braefoot Farmhouse, Fossoway, Kinross-shire.

Wheeler, Professor Simon Jonathan, MA, DPhil, CEng, MICE. Cormack Professor of Civil Engineering, Glasgow University, since 1996; b. 30.4.58, Warlingham, Surrey; m., Noelle Patricia O'Rourke; 1 s.; 2 d. Educ. Whitehaven Grammar School; St. John's College, Cambridge; Balliol College, Oxford. University Lecturer in Soil Mechanics, Queen's University of Belfast, 1984-88; Lecturer in Soil Mechanics, Sheffield University, 1988-92; Lecturer in Civil Engineering, Oxford University, and Fellow of Keble College, Oxford, 1992-95. Recreation: mountaineering. Address: (b.) School of Engineering, Rankine Building, Glasgow G12 8LT; T.-0141-330 5202.

Wheelhouse, Paul. MSP (SNP), South Scotland, since 2011; Minister for Community Safety and Legal Affairs, Scottish Government, 2014-16, Minister for Environment and Climate Change, 2012-14; b. 22.6.70, Northern Ireland. Educ. Stewart's Melville College, Edinburgh; Aberdeen University; Edinburgh University. Worked as an economist with two firms and has acted as a policy adviser to a wide range of public, private and voluntary organisations. Address: (b.) Scottish Parliament, Edinburgh EH99 1SP.

White, Barry. Chief Executive, Scottish Futures Trust, since 2009; Non Executive Director, Scottish Roads Partnership, since 2014. Educ. Belfast Royal Academy; University of Edinburgh. Major, HM Forces (Army) Corps of Royal Engineers, 1987-94; Regional Managing Director, Morrison Construction Group, 1994-2001; Project Director, Partnerships UK, 2001-04; Director, Skanska Infrastructure Development, 2004-07; Managing Director, BAM PPP, 2007-09. Member, Board of Trustees, LAR Housing Trust, since 2015. Address: (b.) 1 St. Colme Street, Edinburgh EH3 6AA.

White, Iain, BSc (Hons), MEd. Principal, Newlands Junior College, since 2014; b. 2.2.54, Greenock; m., Gail. Educ. Greenock High School; Glasgow University. Biology Teacher, then Principal Biology Teacher, Cowdenknowes High School, Greenock, 1977-87; Assistant Rector, Rothesay Academy, 1987-92; Depute Head Teacher, Port Glasgow High School, 1992-94; Head Teacher, Govan High School, Glasgow, 1994-2014. Past Captain, Greenock Golf Club. Recreations: golf; skiing; travel; watching football; Robert Burns; after-dinner speaking; playing the bagpipes. Address: (b.) 6 Inverlair Avenue, Glasgow G43 2HS; T.-0141 212 4477.

White, Sandra. MSP (SNP), Glasgow Kelvin, since 2011, Glasgow, 1999-2011; b. 17.8.51, Glasgow; m.; 3 c. Educ. Garthamlock Secondary School; Glasgow College; Cardonald College. Former SNP councillor in Renfrewshire; Press Officer, William Wallace Society. Served as an SNP Parliamentary group whip in the first parliamentary session and currently sits on the parliament's Public Petitions Committee, and Equal Opportunities Committee. Forged a role as a crusading campaigner and

working MSP while also holding her party's Deputy Social Justice portfolio. Campaigned against closures and downgrading (including a 1,600 signature petition) at the Royal Hospital for Sick Children, Yorkhill and the Queen Mother's Hospital; also campaigned extensively against racism and for better treatment of asylum seekers, including joining an occupation against so-called 'dawn raids'; other campaigns have included the successful attempts to save the 7:84 theatre group from threatened loss of funding by the Scottish Arts Council and involvement in Stop the War Coalition events. High-profile constituency work has included the August 2006 case of an 86-year old widow who was threatened with court by Glasgow Housing Association. Recreations: reading; walking; meeting people. Address: (b.) Scottish Parliament, Edinburgh EH99 1SP.

White, Professor Stephen Leonard, MA, PhD, DPhil, LittD, FRSE, FBA. Bryce Professor of Politics, Glasgow University, since 1991; b. 1.7.45, Dublin; m., Ishbel MacPhie; 1 s. Educ. St. Andrew's College, Dublin; Trinity College, Dublin; Glasgow University; Wolfson College, Oxford. Lecturer in Politics, Glasgow University, 1971-85, Reader, 1985-91. President, British Association for Slavonic and East European Studies, 1994-97; Chief Editor, Journal of Communist Studies and Transition Politics, 1994-2011; Coeditor, Journal of Eurasian Studies, since 2010. Publications include: Political Culture and Soviet Politics, 1979; Britain and the Bolshevik Revolution, 1980; Origins of Detente, 1986; The Bolshevik Poster, 1988; After Gorbachev, 1993; Russia Goes Dry, 1996; How Russia Votes (with others), 1997; Values and Political Change in Postcommunist Europe (with others), 1998; Russia's New Politics, 2000; The Soviet Elite from Lenin to Gorbachev (Co-author), 2000; Putin's Russia and the Enlarged Europe (with others), 2006; Understanding Russian Politics, 2011. Address: (h.) 11 Hamilton Drive, Glasgow G12 8DN; T.-0141-334 9541.

Whitefield, Gavin, CBE, CPFA, DPA. Chief Executive, North Lanarkshire Council, since 2000; b. 7.2.56; m., Grace; 2 d. Educ. Lanark Grammar School; Bell College, Hamilton. Audit Assistant, Exchequer and Audit Department, Civil Service, 1974-76; Clydesdale District Council: Assistant Auditor, 1976-84, Computer Development Officer, 1984-86, Principal Housing Officer (Finance and Administration), 1986-89; Assistant Director of Housing (Finance and Administration), Motherwell District Council, 1989-95; Director of Housing and Property Services, North Lanarkshire Council, 1995-2000. Past Chair, SOLACE Scotland, 2007/08. Recreations: hill-walking; football. Address: (b.) Civic Centre, Windmillhill Street, Motherwell ML1 1AB; T.-01698 302252; e-mail: chief.executive@northlan.gov.uk

Whitefield, Karen. MSP (Labour), Airdrie and Shotts, 1999-2011; b. 8.1.70, Bellshill. Educ. Calderhead High School, Shotts; Glasgow Caledonian University. Civil servant, Benefits Agency, 1991-92; PA to Rachel Squire, MP, 1992-99. Congressional Intern on Capitol Hill, 1990. Recreations: swimming; reading; travel.

Whiteford, Eilidh, MA Hons, MA, PhD. MP (SNP), Banff and Buchan, since 2010; SNP Spokesperson for Work and Pensions, since 2010; b. 24.4.69, Aberdeen; m., Stephen Smith. Educ. Banff Academy; Glasgow University; Guelph University, Ontario. Worked for Allan Macartney MEP, then Ian Hudghton MEP until the 1999 elections; later helped new MSP Irene McGugan establish a constituency office in the first term of the Scottish Parliament; returned to Glasgow University in

1999, lecturing in Scottish Literature and developing access routes into higher education for mature students (in Glasgow University's adult and continuing education department); campaigning role in the voluntary sector as Co-ordinator of the Scottish Carers' Alliance, from 2001; moved to Oxfam (2003), working as a policy adviser and campaigns manager for over six years. Very actively involved in the Make Poverty History campaign in 2005 and helped establish the Scottish Fair Trade Forum. Member, Select Committee on Scottish Affairs, 2010-2015. Recreation: reading. Address: (b.) House of Commons, London SW1A 0AA.

Whitehead, Maire Catherine, BEd; b. 15.12.40, Glasgow; m., Ronald Bryson Whitehead; 1 s.; 2 d. Educ. Notre Dame High School, Glasgow; St. Andrew's College; University of Glasgow. Career History: Assistant Teacher: St. James Secondary School, Paisley, St. Saviour's Primary School, Glasgow, St. Alphonsus Primary School, Glasgow; Assistant Head: St. Luke's Primary School, Glasgow, St. Peter's Primary School, Glasgow; Headteacher, St. Vincent's Primary School, Glasgow; Headteacher, St. Mirin Primary School, Glasgow. Board Member, National Waiting Times Centre; Board Member, National State Hospital; Lay Member, NHS Education for Scotland (NES); former Member, Governance Steering Group, Scotland's Colleges; Trustee, City of Glasgow College Foundation. Recreations: reading; fine dining; debating. Address: (h.) 22 The Oaks, Millholm Road, Glasgow G44 3YQ; T.-0141-637 8597.
E-mail: maire.whitehead@ntlworld.com

Whitehorn, Will, MA Hons (Aberdeen). Chairman, Scottish Exhibition and Conference Centre (SECC), since 2013. Educ. The Edinburgh Academy; University of Aberdeen. Career: Brand Development and Corporate Affairs Director, Virgin Management, 1987-2007, Virgin, 1987-2011; President, Virgin Galactic, 2004-2010; Chairman, next fifteen, 2004-2011. Chair, Transport Systems Catapult Ltd at Technology Strategy Board, since 2013; Chairman, Speed Communications, since 2011; Non Executive Director, Stagecoach Group plc, since 2011; Director, STFC Innovations Limited, since 2010; Director, ILN Media Group, since 2008; Trustee and Board Member, Internews Europe, 2011-2013; Non Executive Director, CA Coutts Holdings, 1999-2005; Fellow at The Royal Aeronautical Society. Address: (b.) Exhibition Way, Glasgow G3 8YW; T.-0141 248 3000.

Whiten, Professor (David) Andrew, BSc, PhD, FBPS, FRSB, FRSE, FBA. Professor of Evolutionary and Developmental Psychology, St. Andrews University, since 1997, Wardlaw Professor of Psychology, since 2000; Royal Society Leverhulme Trust Senior Research Fellow, 2006-07; b. 20.4.48, Grimsby; m., Dr. Susie Challoner; 2 d. Educ. Wintringham School, Grimsby; Sheffield University; Bristol University; Oxford University. Research Fellow, Oxford University, 1972-75; Lecturer, then Reader, St. Andrews University, 1975-97; Director, 'Living Links to Human Evolution' Research Centre (www.living-links.org.uk), since 2008; Visiting Professor, Zurich University, 1992, Emory University, 1996; Delwart International Scientific Prize, 2001; Rivers Memorial Medal, Royal Anthropological Institute of Great Britain and Ireland, 2007; Osman-Hill Medal, Primate Society of Great Britain, 2010; Sir James Black Medal, Royal Society of Edinburgh, 2013; Elected Fellow of the Cognitive Science Society, 2013; Senior Prize and Medal for Public Engagement, Royal Society of Edinburgh, 2014; Hon DSc, Heriot-Watt University, 2015. Publications: see www.st-andrews.ac.uk/profile/aw2. Recreations: painting; walking; wildlife; good-lifing. Address: (b.) School of Psychology

and Neuroscience, St. Andrews University, St. Andrews KY16 9JU; e-mail: a.whiten@st-and.ac.uk

Whitford, Philippa. MP (SNP), Central Ayrshire, since 2015; SNP Health spokesperson in the House of Commons, since 2015; b. 24.12.58, Belfast, Northern Ireland; m., Hans Pieper; 1 s. Educ. Wood Green: St. Angela's Providence Convent Secondary School, London; Douglas Academy, Milngavie; University of Glasgow. Medical volunteer in a UN hospital in Gaza in 1991/92 just after the first Gulf War and during the Intifada; Consultant Breast Cancer Surgeon at Crosshouse Hospital, Kilmarnock for over 18 years; led the development of Scottish Breast Cancer standards to raise the quality of care across Scotland. Address: House of Commons, London SW1A 0AA.

Whitley, Rev. Laurence Arthur Brown, MA, BD, PhD. Minister, Glasgow Cathedral (St Mungo or High), since 2007; Minister, Montrose Old (now Old and St Andrew's) Parish, 1985-2007; (Busby East with West, 1975-85); b. 19.9.49, Port Glasgow; m., Catherine MacLean MacFadyen; 1 s.; 1 d. Educ. Edinburgh Academy; Edinburgh University; St. Andrews University. Assistant Minister, St. Andrews, Dundee, 1974-75. Parliamentary candidate (SNP), Dumfriesshire, February and October, 1974. Publication: A Great Grievance - a history of Scottish lay patronage to 1750. Recreation: hupomonopraxis. Address: (h.) 41 Springfield Road, Bishopbriggs, Glasgow G64 1PL; T.-0141-762-2719.
E-mail: labwhitley@btinternet.com

Whittemore, Professor Colin Trengove, BSc, PhD, DSc, NDA, FRSE. Emeritus Professor; Professor of Agriculture and Rural Economy, Edinburgh University, 1990-2007; Head, Institute of Ecology and Resource Management, Edinburgh University, 1991-2001; Postgraduate Dean, College of Science and Engineering, 2002-07; b. 16.7.42, Chester; m., Chris; 1 s.; 3 d. Educ. Rydal School; Newcastle-upon-Tyne University. Lecturer in Agriculture, Edinburgh University and Head, Animal Production, Advisory and Development, Edinburgh School of Agriculture; Professor of Animal Production, Head, Animal Division, Edinburgh School of Agriculture; Head, Department of Agriculture, Edinburgh University. Sir John Hammond Memorial Prize for scientific contribution to an understanding of nutrition and growth; President, British Society of Animal Science, 1998; Royal Agricultural Society of England Gold Medal for research; Mignini Oscar; David Black Award. Publications: author of over 200 research papers and five text books of animal sciences. Recreations: skiing; riding; writing local agricultural histories. Address: (h.) 17, Fergusson View, West Linton, Peeblesshire EH46 7DJ.

Whittle, Brian. MSP (Scottish Conservative), South Scotland region, since 2016; Chief Executive Officer, Demon Sport, since 2013; b. 26.4.64, Troon. Educ. Marr College; Glasgow University. Athlete, UK Athletics, 1985-96 (won the gold medal in the 4 x 400 metres relay at both the 1986 European Athletics Championships and 1994 European Athletics Championships); Manager, Spence Allan Associates Ltd/Corporate Events Scotland, 1996-98; Director: Catlyst Consulting/Events Ltd, 1998-2000, Ian McLauchlan Associates, 2000-03, PB Events Ltd, 2003-08; Director of Sport, Sports Social Media, 2008-2010; self-employed (special projects), since 2010; Global Head of Business Development, Uniquedoc, since 2013. Contested the 2015 UK general election in the constituency of Kilmarnock and Loudoun for the Conservatives. Address: Scottish Parliament, Edinburgh EH99 1SP.

Whittle, Pamela, CBE. Chair, Scottish Health Council; non-executive Board Member, Healthcare Improvement Scotland; Chair, Greenspace Scotland; Board Member, Stevenson College Edinburgh; President, Royal Caledonian Horticultural Society; Director, Gardening Scotland; b.

30.12.48, Bristol; m., Richard; 1 s. Educ. Monks Park School, Bristol; Sarum St Michael, Salisbury; Open University. Director, Health Improvement, Scottish Government, 2002-08; former non-executive Board Member, NHS Quality Improvement Scotland. Address: (b.) Delta House, 50 West Nile Street, Glasgow G1 2NP; T.-0141 225 6983.
E-mail: pam.whittle@scottishhealthcouncil.org

Whitton, David Forbes. MSP (Labour), Strathkelvin and Bearsden, 2007-2011; b. 22.4.52, Forfar; m., Marilyn; 1 s.; 1 d. Educ. Morgan Academy, Dundee. Journalist, DC Thomson, Dundee, 1970-76; Fife Free Press, Kirkcaldy, 1976-78; Scotsman, Glasgow, 1978-81; Industrial Editor, Daily Record, Glasgow, 1981-86; Presenter, Producer, Head of Public Affairs, Scottish Television, Glasgow, 1986-96; Director, Media House Ltd, Glasgow, 1996-98; Special Adviser to Donald Dewar MSP, First Minister of Scotland, 1998-2000; Managing Director, Whitton PR Ltd, 2000-07. Recreations: golf; music; grandchildren.

Whitty, Niall Richard, MA, LLB, FRSE. Honorary Professor, Edinburgh University School of Law, since 2014; b. 28.10.37, Malaya; m., Elke M.M. Gillis; 3 s.; 1 d. Educ. Morrison's Academy, Crieff; St Andrews University; Edinburgh University. Law apprenticeship, 1963-65; private practice, 1965-66; Member, legal staff, Scottish Office Solicitor's office, 1967-71; legal staff, Scottish Law Commission, 1971-94; Commissioner, Scottish Law Commission, 1995-2000. Visiting Professor, Edinburgh University School of Law, 2000-2014; General Editor, Stair Memorial Encyclopaedia, February 2000-June 2014. Recreations: gardening; piping; legal history. Address: (h.) St Martins, Victoria Road, Haddington EH41 4DJ; T.-0162 082 2234.

Whyte, Iain. General Secretary, Church of Scotland Guild. Address: (b.) 121 George Street, Edinburgh EH2 4YN; T.-0131 225 5722.

Whyte, Professor Iain Boyd, BA, MPhil, MA, PhD, FRSE, FRSA. Professor of Architectural History, Department of Architecture, Edinburgh University, since 1996; b. 6.3.47, Bexley; m., Deborah Smart; 1 s.; 1 d. Educ. St Dunstan's College; Nottingham University; Cornell University; Cambridge University; Leeds University. Lecturer, then Reader, then Professor of Architectural History, Edinburgh University; External Examiner: Courtauld Institute of Art, National University of Singapore, University College London. Getty Scholar, 1989-90; Getty Grant Program Senior Scholar, 1998-2000; Visiting Senior Program Officer, Getty Grant Program, 2002-04; Trustee, National Galleries of Scotland, 1998-2002; Member, Selection Committee, 23rd Council of Europe exhibition, 1995-96; Chair, RIHA (International Association of Research Institutes in the History of Art), since 2010; Samuel H. Kress Professor, Center for Advanced Study in the Visual Arts, National Gallery of Art, Washington, DC, 2015-2016; extensive publications on architectural and art history. Recreations: music; rowing. Address: (b.) Department of Architecture, 20 Chambers Street, Edinburgh EH1 1JZ; T.-0131-650 2322.

Whyte, Rev. James, BD, DipCE. Parish Minister, Fairlie, Ayrshire, 2006-2011 (retired); b. 26.4.46, Glasgow; m., Norma Isabella West; 1 s.; 2 d. Educ. Glasgow; Jordanhill College; Glasgow University. Trained as planning engineer; studied community education (Glasgow and Boston, Mass., USA); Community Organiser with Lamp of Lothian Collegiate Trust, Haddington; Organiser of Community Education, Dumbarton, 1971-73; Assistant Principal Community Education Officer, Renfrew Division, Strathclyde Region, 1973-77; entered ministry, Church of Scotland, 1977; Assistant Minister: Barrhead Arthurlie, 1977-78, St. Marks, Oldhall, Paisley, 1978-80; Minister: Coupar Angus Abbey, 1981-87, Broom, Newton Mearns, 1987-2006. Recreations: gardening; reading. Address: 32 Torburn Avenue, Giffnock, East Renfrewshire G46 7RB; T.-0141 620 3043.

Whyte, Robert, MB, ChB, FRCPsych, DPM. Consultant Psychotherapist, Carswell House, Glasgow, 1979-2000; b. 1.6.41, Edinburgh; m., Susan Frances Milburn; 1 s.; 1 d. Educ. George Heriot's, Edinburgh; St. Andrews University. House Officer in Surgery, Arbroath Infirmary, 1966; House Officer in Medicine, Falkirk and District Royal Infirmary, 1967; Trainee in Psychiatry, Dundee Psychiatric Services, 1967-73; Consultant Psychiatrist, Duke Street Hospital, Glasgow, 1973. Past Chairman, Scottish Association of Psychoanalytical Psychotherapists. Address: (h.) Waverley, 70 East Kilbride Road, Busby, Glasgow G76 8HU; T.-0141-644 1659.

Wickham-Jones, Caroline R., MA, MIFA, FSA, FSA Scot, FFCS. Archaeologist; b. 25.4.55, Middlesborough; 1 s. Educ. Teesside High School; Edinburgh University. Honorary Research Fellow, University of Aberdeen; author and broadcaster with research interests in early (postglacial) settlement of Scotland, submerged archaeology, landscape history, and the preservation of the cultural heritage; Trustee, Caithness Archaeological Trust; former Council Member, National Trust for Scotland; Council Member, Institute of Field Archaeologists, 1986-90; former Secretary, Society of Antiquaries of Scotland; former Trustee, John Muir Trust; Livery Woman of the City of London (Skinners Company). Publications: Scotland's First Settlers; Arthurs Seat and Holyrood Park, a Visitor's Guide; Orkney, an Historical Guide; The Landscape of Scotland, a hidden history; Between the Wind and the Water, World Heritage Orkney; Fear of Farming. Recreations: travel; wilderness walking; socialising. Address: (h.) Cassie, St. Ola, Orkney KW15 1TP.
E-mail: c.wickham-jones@mesolithic.co.uk

Wiercigroch, Professor Marian, MEng, ScD, DSc, CEng, CMath, FIMechE, FIMA, FRSE. Sixth Century Chair in Applied Dynamics and Director, Centre for Applied Dynamics, Aberdeen University; b. 14.7.60, Poland. Educ. Silesian University of Technology, Poland; Aberdeen University. Research Fellow, Aberdeen University, 1990-91; Lecturer, Silesian University of Technology, 1992-93; Senior Fulbright Scholar, University of Delaware, USA, 1994; Lecturer, then Senior Lecturer, then Reader, Aberdeen University, 1994-2002, Professor of Engineering, 2002-06, Sixth Century Chair in Applied Dynamics, since 2006, Director for International Development. Recreations: Alpine skiing; tennis; hill-walking. Address: (b.) Centre for Applied Dynamics Research, School of Engineering, Aberdeen University AB24 3UE.

Wightman, Andy. Writer; MSP (Scottish Green), since 2016; b. Dundee. Educ. University of Aberdeen. Career history: scientist working on renewable energy at the University of Aberdeen; Projects Officer with Central Scotland Countryside Trust; became a self-employed writer and researcher in 1993; contributed to a wide range of debates on land use, land reform, the Crown estate, common good land, local democracy and fiscal reform, over the next 20 years; author of a number of reports on these topics; also served as a Specialist Adviser to the UK Parliament's Scottish Affairs Committee Inquiry on land reform, 2014-2015; coordinator of the Land Action

Scotland campaign; member of the Commission on Local Tax Reform, 2015; Co-founder of Reforesting Scotland, a group dedicated to substantial reforestation. Publications: Who Owns Scotland, 1996; Scotland: land and power. An agenda for land reform, 1999; The Poor Had No Lawyers, 2013. Address: Scottish Parliament, Edinburgh EH99 1SP.

Wightman, John Watt, CVO, CBE, RD, MA, LLB, WS. Chairman, Morton Fraser Partnership, 1988-99; Solicitor to H. M. The Queen in Scotland, 1984-99; Chairman, Craig & Rose PLC, 1993-2000; b. 20.11.33, Leith; m., Isla Macleod; 1 s.; 2 d. Educ. Daniel Stewart's College; St. Andrews University; Edinburgh University. Morton Fraser Partnership, 1960-99 (Partner, then Chairman). Commodore, Royal Naval Reserve, 1982-85; Chairman, Lowland TAVRA, 1992-95; Elder, St. George's West Church; Trustee: Earl Haig Fund for Scotland, 1999-2004, Haig Housing, 1995-2012. Recreations: sailing; fishing; ornithology. Address: 58 Trinity Road, Edinburgh EH5 3HT; T.-0131 551 6128.

Wilcox, Christine Alison, BA (Hons), MCLIP. Librarian, S.S.C. Library, Edinburgh, since 1991; b. 18.7.63, New Zealand; m., Michael Wilcox; 2 s.; 1 d. Educ. South Wilts Grammar School, Salisbury; Manchester Polytechnic Library School. Assistant Librarian, Barlow Lyde and Barlow Gilbert, Solicitors, London, 1984-86; Librarian, Beaumont and Son, Solicitors, London, 1986-89; posting to Bahrain accompanying husband, 1989-91. Secretary, Scottish Law Librarians Group, 1993-95. Publications: Directory of Legal Libraries in Scotland; Union List of Periodical and Law Report Holdings in Scotland. Recreations: needlework; hill-walking. Address: (b.) S.S.C. Library, 11 Parliament Square, Edinburgh EH1 1RF; T.-0131-225 6268; e-mail: christine@ssclibrary.co.uk

Wild, John Robin, JP, BDS, DPD, FDSRCS(Edin), DGDP. Chairman, District Courts Association, 2002-04; Chief Dental Officer, Department of Health, 1997-2000; Consultant in Dental Public Health, NHS Dumfries and Galloway, 2005-07; b. 12.9.41, Scarborough; m., Eleanor Daphne Kerr; 1 s.; 2 d. Educ. Sedbergh School; Edinburgh University; Dundee University. General Dental Practitioner, Scarborough, 1965-71; Dental Officer, East Lothian, 1971-74; Chief Administrative Dental Officer, Borders Health Board, 1974-87; Regional Dental Postgraduate Adviser, S.E. Regional Committee for Postgraduate Medical Education, 1982-87; Deputy Chief Dental Officer, 1987-93, then Chief Dental Officer and Director of Dental Services for the NHS in Scotland, 1993-97, Scottish Office Department of Health; Hon. Senior Lecturer, Dundee Dental School, since 1993; JP for District of Ettrick and Lauderdale, 1982-2001; Past Chairman, Scottish Council, British Dental Association; Vice President, Commonwealth Dental Association, 1997-2003; President, Council of European Chief Dental Officers, 1999-2000; Chairman, Scottish Borders Justices Committee, 2000-05; Member, Judicial Council for Scotland, 2007-09; Member, Disciplinary Pool of Institute and Faculty of Actuaries, since 2001. Recreations: vintage cars (restoration and driving); music; gardening. Address: (h.) Braehead House, St. Boswells, Roxburghshire; T.-01835 823203.

Wilkin, Andrew, BA, MA, MCIL. Senior Lecturer in Italian Studies, University of Strathclyde, 1986-2009; b. 30.5.44, Farnborough; m., Gaynor Carole Gray; 1 s.; 1 d. (also 1 s.; 1 d. by pr. m.). Educ. Royal Naval School, Malta; University of Manchester; Open University. Assistant Lecturer, then Lecturer in Italian Studies, University of Strathclyde, 1967-86; Associate Dean, Faculty of Arts and Social Sciences, 1986-93; Course Director, BA European Studies, 1989-97. Governor, Craigie College of Education,

1985-91; Editor, Tuttitalia, 1992-97; Member, Modern Languages Panel, UCAS Scotland, 1993-2000. Publications: Harrap's Italian Verbs (Compiler), 1990, 2002, 2009; G. Verga, Little Novels of Sicily (Editor), 1973; 25 Years Emancipation? – Women in Switzerland 1971-96 (Co-Editor), 1997. Invested Cavaliere dell'Ordine al Merito della Repubblica Italiana, 1975; Elder, St. David's Memorial Park Church, Kirkintilloch; Vice-Convener, Business Committee, Presbytery of Glasgow. Recreations: travel; reading; Scottish History; supporting Partick Thistle F. C. Address: (h.) 29 Forest Place, Lenzie, Glasgow G66 4UH; T.-0141-777-7607.
E-mail: andrew.wilkin@hotmail.co.uk

Wilkins, Emeritus Professor Malcolm Barrett, BSc, PhD, DSc, AKC, FRSE. Regius Professor of Botany, Glasgow University, 1970-2000, now Emeritus Professor (Dean, Faculty of Science, 1985-88; Member, University Court, 1993-97); b.27.2.33, Cardiff; m., Mary Patricia Maltby; 1 s.; 1 d. (deceased). Educ. Monkton House School, Cardiff; King's College, London University. Lecturer in Botany, King's College, London, 1958-64; Lecturer in Biology, then Professor of Biology, East Anglia University, 1964-67; Professor of Plant Physiology, Nottingham University, 1967-70. Rockefeller Foundation Fellow, Yale University, 1961-62; Corporation Research Fellow, Harvard University, 1962-63; Darwin Lecturer, British Association for the Advancement of Science, 1967; elected Corresponding (Honorary) Member, American Society of Plant Physiologists, 1984; Chairman, Life Science Working Group, European Space Agency, 1987-89; Trustee, Royal Botanic Garden, Edinburgh, 1990-99, Chairman, 1994-99; Vice President, Royal Society of Edinburgh, 1994-97; Member, Advisory Council, Scottish Agricultural College, since 1992. Clubs: Caledonian (London), New (Edinburgh). Recreations: fishing; model engineering. Address: (h.) 5 Hughenden Drive, Glasgow G12 9XS; T.-0141-334 8079.

Wilkinson, Sheriff Alexander Birrell, QC, MA, LLB. Sheriff of Lothian and Borders at Edinburgh, 1996-2001; Sheriff of Glasgow and Strathkelvin at Glasgow, 1991-96; Temporary Judge, Court of Session, 1993-2003; b. 2.2.32, Perth; m., Wendy Imogen Barrett; 1 s.; 1 d. Educ. Perth Academy; St. Andrews University; Edinburgh University. Advocate, 1959; practised at Scottish Bar, 1959-69; Lecturer in Scots Law, Edinburgh University, 1965-69; Sheriff of Stirling, Dunbarton and Clackmannan, at Stirling and Alloa, 1969-72; Professor of Private Law, Dundee University, 1972-86 (Dean, Faculty of Law, 1974-76 and 1986); Sheriff of Tayside, Central and Fife at Falkirk, 1986-91; a Chairman, Industrial Tribunals (Scotland), 1972-86; Chancellor, Dioceses of Brechin, 1982-98, and of Argyll and the Isles, 1985-98, Scottish Episcopal Church; a Director, Scottish Episcopal Church Nominees Ltd., since 2004 and a Trustee of the General Synod of the Scottish Episcopal Church, since 2005; Chairman, Scottish Marriage Guidance Council, 1974-77; Chairman, Legal Services Group, Scottish Association of CAB, 1979-83; President, The Sheriffs' Association, 1997-2000. Publications: Gloag and Henderson's Introduction to the Law of Scotland, 8th and 9th editions (Co-editor); The Scottish Law of Evidence; The Law of Parent and Child in Scotland (Co-author); Macphail's Sheriff Court Practice, 2nd Edition (Contributor); The Legal Systems of Scottish Churches (Contributor). Recreations: collecting books and pictures; reading; travel.

Wilkinson, Carol. Chair, Scottish Children's Reporter Administration, since 2010. Career: held a number of senior posts in local authorities, with responsibility for managing a range of children's services and overseeing child protection work; became Director of Social Work in Falkirk; recently retired from the Scottish Social Services Council (Chief Executive since its creation in 2001). Recently chaired the group set up by the Scottish Government to examine residential child care; former member of Barnardo's Scottish Committee; elected President of the Association of Directors of Social Work in 2001. Address: Head Office: Scottish Children's Reporter Administration, Ochil House, Springkerse Business Park, Stirling FK7 7XE; T.-0300 200 1555.

Wilkinson, Professor John Eric, BSc, MEd, PhD, CPsychol. Professor of Education, Glasgow University, 1998-2009; Deputy Dean, Faculty of Education, 2001-05; Emeritus Professor of Education, since 2009; b. 22.5.44, Lancashire; 2 s.; 1 d. Educ. Accrington Grammar School; St Andrews University; Dundee University; Glasgow University. Assistant Master, Brockehurst Sixth Form College, 1968-70; Research Assistant, Nottingham University, 1970-72; Glasgow University: Lecturer, Education, 1973-91; Senior Lecturer, 1991-98; Head of Department, 1995-99; Professor, University of Taipei, Taiwan, ROC, 2009. Publications: numerous journal articles, a book, and book chapters. Recreations: art collecting; ballet appreciation; swimming. Address: (b.) Department of Early Childhood Education, University of Taipei, West Aiguo Road, Taipei, Taiwan, Republic of China; (h.) Flat 4, 17 Crown Terrace, Glasgow, G12 9ES.
E-mail: jericwilkinson@hotmail.com

Will, James. Non-executive Director, The Scottish Investment Trust PLC, since 2013; Non-executive Director, Herald Investment Trust PLC, since 2015; formerly Chairman, Shepherd and Wedderburn (2010-2014). Address: (b.) Myreside, by Gifford, Haddington, East Lothian EH41 4JA; T.-07794 013211; e-mail: jas_will@btinternet.com

Willetts, Professor Brian Benjamin, MA, PhD, FRSE. Professor Emeritus of Engineering, Aberdeen University; b. 12.6.36, Old Hill; m., Patricia Margaret Jones; 1 s.; 1 d. Educ. King Edward VI School, Stourbridge; Emmanuel College, Cambridge. Assistant Engineer, City of Birmingham, 1959-61; Executive Engineer, Government of Northern Nigeria, 1961-63; Lecturer/Senior Lecturer, Lanchester Polytechnic, 1963-66; Aberdeen University: Lecturer/Senior Lecturer, 1967-85, Professor of Civil Engineering, 1985-2001. Address: (h.) Grove, 24 Broomlands, Kelso, Roxburghshire TD5 7PR; T.-01573 225968.

Williams, Professor Brian Owen, CBE, MD, HonDSc, FRCP. Past President, Royal College of Physicians and Surgeons of Glasgow (2006-2009); retired Consultant Geriatrician; b. 27.02.47, Glasgow; m., Martha; 2 d. Educ. Kings Park Secondary, Glasgow; University of Glasgow. Trained in General Medicine and Geriatric Medicine; President: British Geriatrics Society, 1998-2000, European Union Geriatric Medicine Society, 1998-2000. Honorary Professor, University of Glasgow, since 2007; Chairman, Abbeyfield Society in Scotland, since 2013; Chairman, Board of Governors, Hutchesons' Grammar School, since 2013. Publications: book chapters and original papers on medicine of old age. Recreations: gardening; theatre; literature. Address: (h.) 15 Thorn Drive, High Burnside, Glasgow G73 4RH; T.-0141 634 4480.
E-mail: brianwilliams@gmx.com

Williams, Craig David, MA (Hons), PGDJ. Producer/Director, BBC Scotland Current Affairs; b. 9.8.71, Edinburgh; m., Pauline McLean; 1 s. Educ. Royal High School, Edinburgh; University of Edinburgh; University of Strathclyde. Reporter: Border Telegraph, 1994-95; Radio Borders, 1995-96; Radio Forth, 1996-97; Producer, BBC Scotland News and Current Affairs, 1997-2000; Media Correspondent, Business am, 2000-01; Editor, Newsnight Scotland, BBC, 2001-08; Producer/Director: 'Thatcher and the Scots' 'Panorama: What Happens After Sorry?', 'Holyrood and the Search for Scotland's Soul', 'Panorama: Will the Scots ever be Happy?', 'Power of Scotland', 'Why Didn't Scots Vote Tory?', 'A Church in Crisis?'; 'Who needs Trident?'; 'Portillo on Salmond'; 'The Great Tram Disaster'; 'Getting Scotland to Work'; 'Eric Liddell: A Champion's Life'; 'Who Killed My Son?'; 'Scotched Earth'; 'Peter Higgs: Particle Man'; 'Iain Banks: Raw Spirit'; 'Our Friends in The North'; 'What Women Want'; 'How The Campaign Was Won'; 'The War over Fracking'; 'The Rise of the SNP'; Executive Producer: 'Holyrood: What Went Wrong?', 'Did Your Vote Count?' (BAFTA Scotland winner, 2007). Address: (b.) BBC Scotland, Zone 4.14, 40 Pacific Quay, Glasgow G51 1DA; T.-0141-338 3440.
E-mail: craig.williams@bbc.co.uk

Williams, Professor Jeffrey Graham, BSc, PhD, FRSE. Professor of Developmental Biology, Dundee University, since 1998; Wellcome Trust Principal Research Fellow; b. 5.11.48, Tredegar; m., Dr Natalia Zhukovskaya; 2 s.; 2 d. Educ. Abertillery Grammar School; Kings College, London. Harkness Fellow/Postdoctoral Fellow, MIT (Boston, USA), 1973-75; Staff Scientist, ICRF, 1975-94; Jodrell Professor of Anatomy, UCL, 1994-98. Member, CRC Scientific Committee, 1992-94; Member, MRC Molecular and Cellular Medicine Board, since 1998. Recreations: squash; golf; guitar. Address: (b.) College of Life Sciences, MSI/WTB/JBC Complex, University of Dundee, Dundee DD1 5EH; T.-01382 385823.

Williams, Marion, BEd, BSc (Hons). Director, The Cockburn Association, since 2009. Educ. Highsted Grammar School; Harrow College of Technology & Art; Homerton College; The Open University. Career history: Teacher, Secondary Schools and Village Colleges, 1978-84; Associate Lecturer and Consultant, Scribbles, 1985-93; Regional Development Manager, Red House Books, 1992-95; Head of Religious Studies (maternity cover), Boswell School, 1995-96; Councillor, Braintree District Council, 1995-99; Contract Manager, Learning Services, Essex County Council, 1996-2000; Project Manager, South East Museums Services, 1999-2001; Chair, Braintree NHS Care Trust, 2001-05; Political Advisor, House of Commons, 2001-07; Development Manager, OneCity Trust, 2007-09. Panel Member, Edinburgh Urban Design Panel, since 2009; Executive Committee Member, ICOMOS UK, since 2015. Recreations: football (Newcastle United); hill walking; photography; all things cultural. Address: The Cockburn Association, 55 High Street, Edinburgh EH1 1SR; T.-0131 557 8686.
E-mail: director@cockburnassociation.org.uk

Williams, Professor Morgan Howard, BSc Hons, PhD, DSc, CEng, CITP, FBCS, FRSA. Professor Emeritus, Heriot-Watt University, since 2014 (Professor of Computer Science, 1980-2014, Head of Department, 1980-88 and 2002-03); b. 15.12.44, Durban; m., 1. Jean Doe (marr. diss.), 2 s.; m., 2. Pamela Mason (deceased); m., 3. Margaret Rae Wilson. Educ. Grey High School, Port Elizabeth; Rhodes University, Grahamstown. Physicist in Antarctic Expedition, 1968-69; Rhodes University: Lecturer in Computer Science, 1970-72, Senior Lecturer, 1972-77, Professor and Head of Department, 1977-80; British Council Visiting Researcher, Darwin College, Cambridge, 1974-75. Member, Standing Committee of IUCC, 1984-88;

Member, Committee of Conference of Professors of Computer Science, 1986-88; Member, SERC Systems Engineering Committee, 1992-94; Member, EPSRC IT College, 1995-2005. Address: School of Mathematical and Computer Sciences, Heriot-Watt University, Riccarton, Edinburgh EH14 4AS; T.-0131-451 3430; e-mail: m.h.williams@hw.ac.uk

Williams, Professor Richard A., OBE, FREng, FTSE, FIChemE, FIMMM, FMES, FRSA, BSc (Eng), PhD. Principal and Vice Chancellor, Heriot-Watt University, since 2015; b. 1960, Worcester; m., Jane M. Taylor; 2 c. Educ. The King's School, Worcester; Imperial College London. Trainee graduate metallurgist, Anglo American Corporation in Johannesburg and Welkom, 1979-80; De Beers Industrial Diamonds Research Laboratory, South Africa and Imperial College London (Royal School of Mines), 1982-86; appointed Lecturer in Chemical Engineering, University of Manchester Institute of Science and Technology (now University of Manchester) in 1986; appointed Royal Academy of Engineering-Rio Tinto Professor of Minerals Engineering at the University of Exeter (based at the Camborne School of Mines) in 1993; University of Leeds: appointed as Anglo American plc Professor of Mineral and Process Engineering in 1999 (responsible for developing a new Institute of Particle Science and Engineering, a core development in re-development of chemical engineering at the University within the recently formed School of Process, Materials and Environmental Engineering); Head of the Department of Mining (2001-2003); Director of British Nuclear Fuels Limited (BNFL) Research Alliance at University, responsible for development of new activities in nuclear energy waste processing (2000-2006); foundational Director of a regional Centre for Industrial Collaboration in Particle Science and Technology (2003-2006) and of the Leeds Nanomanufacturing Institute (2004-2010); appointed Pro-Vice-Chancellor (2005) responsible for leadership of enterprise, knowledge transfer and international strategy. Vice-President, Royal Academy of Engineering, 2005-08; inaugurated the EATechnology-Royal Academy Engineering Entrepreneurs Prize; Visiting Professor at the University of New South Wales (UNSW); Director of: Leeds, York and North Yorkshire Chamber of Commerce; Leeds Ventures Limited; Optomo plc (Founder); Industrial Tomography Systems plc (Founder); Structure Vision Ltd (Founder); University of Leeds IP Limited; University of Leeds Consulting Limited; White Rose Technology Limited; University of Leeds Innovations Limited; Dispersia Ltd (Founder) and Medilink (Yorkshire and Humber) Limited. Editor of Minerals Engineering, Advanced Powder Technology, Chemical Engineering Reactional Design, Particle and Particle Systems Characterisation, Particuology, The Chemical Engineering Journal, Nuclear Energy Science and Technology and Recent Patents on Chemical Engineering. Graduate of the Higher Education Academy's Top Management Programme (2007). Recipient of a number of awards and prizes including the Beilby Medal and Prize in 1997; Isambard Kingdom Brunel Lectureship (1998); Noel E. Webster Medal (2001); Royal Academy of Engineering Silver Medal (2003) and The Society of Chemical Industry Research and Development for Society Award (2009). Recreations: industrial history and art. Address: Heriot-Watt University, Edinburgh Campus, Edinburgh EH14 4AS; T.-0131 449 5111.

Williams, Professor Richard John, BA (Hons), MA, PhD. Professor, Contemporary and Visual Cultures, University of Edinburgh; b. 01.06.67, Washington DC, USA; m., Stacy Boldrick; 1 s.; 1 d. Educ. Manchester Grammar School; Goldsmiths College, London; Manchester University. Lecturer in Art and Design, History and Theory, Liverpool John Moores University, 1997-2000; Lecturer/Senior Lecturer in History of Art, University of Edinburgh, since 2000. Publications: Author: 'After Modern Sculpture', 2000; 'The Anxious City', 2004; 'Brazil: Modern Architectures in History', 2009. Recreations: hillwalking; thinking about going hillwalking. Address: (b.) School of Arts, Culture and Environment, University of Edinburgh, Alison House, 12 Nicholson Square, Edinburgh EH8 9DF; T.-0131 650 4122; e-mail: r.j.williams@ed.ac.uk

Williams, Roger Bevan, MBE, DMus, PhD, BMus, FRCO, FTCL, ARCM, PGCE, FGMS. Emeritus Organist, University of Aberdeen; formerly Conductor, Composer, Musician; formerly Master of Chapel and Ceremonial Music and Organist, University of Aberdeen; Head, Music Department, University of Aberdeen, 1988-2006; b. 30.8.43, Swansea; m., Ann Therese Brennan; 1 s.; m., Katherine Ellen Smith; 2 s.; 1 d. Educ. Mirfield Grammar School, Yorkshire; Huddersfield School of Music; University College, Cardiff; Goldsmiths' College, University of London; King's College, Cambridge. Assistant Organist, Holy Trinity Church, Brompton, 1971; Lecturer, 1971, Director, 1973-75, Chiswick Music Centre; Organist, St. Patrick's Church, Soho, 1973; Musical Director, Sacred Heart Church, Wimbledon, 1975; Lecturer, West London Institute, 1975-78; Organist, Our Lady of Victories, Kensington, 1978-97; Lecturer, University of Aberdeen, 1978-88; Chorus Master, SNO Chorus, 1984-88; Harpsichordist, Aberdeen Sinfonietta, since 1988; first recording of Arne's Six Organ Concertos, 1988; Music at Castle Fraser: catalogue, 1995, CDs, 1997; numerous compositions, editions, catalogues of music holdings in North East Scotland. Recreations: board games; cooking; gardening. Address: (h.) The Old Hall, Barthol Chapel, Oldmeldrum, Inverurie AB51 8TD; T.-01651 806634.

Williams, Tommy, JP. Social Worker, since 1980; Member, Renfrewshire Council (Convener of Housing and Community Safety Policy Board); b. 28.8.52, Paisley; m., Margaret; 1 d. Educ. St. Mirin's Academy, Paisley; Notre Dame College of Education, Bearsden. Social Worker, Glasgow; UNISON Convener, Strathclyde Social Work Stewards, 1991-96; Member, Argyll and Clyde Health Board, 2001-06; Member, Greater Glasgow and Clyde Health Board; Chair, Renfrewshire Community Health Partnership; Chair, North Strathclyde Community Justice Authority; Chair, Renfrewshire Leisure Ltd., since 2003; Chair, Paisley and Renfrewshire North Labour Party. Recreation: supporting Celtic. Address: 83 Arkleston Road, Paisley PA1 3TS; T.-0141-887 6465.

Williamson, (Andrew) Peter, MSc, HDip, MHCIMA. Managing Director, NMS Enterprises Ltd., since 2003; Director, Visitor Operations, National Museums Scotland; b. 23.9.63, Edinburgh; m., Jennifer; 2 s.; 1 d. Educ. George Watson's College; Napier University. Walt Disney Company, 1984-85; Sheraton International Hotel Company, 1986-93; Whitbread Hotel Company (Marriott Hotels UK), 1995-2002. Member: Edinburgh Tourism Action Group (ETAG), Unique Venues of Edinburgh (UVE), Institute of Directors (IOD). Recreations: golf; reading; travelling. Address: (b.) National Museums Scotland, Chambers Street, Edinburgh EH1 1JF; T.-0131 247 4365; e-mail: p.williamson@nms.ac.uk

Williamson, Raymond MacLeod, MA, LLB, FRSA, FRSAMD. Lord Dean of Guild of the City of Glasgow, 2013-2015; b. 24.12.42, Glasgow; m., Brenda; 1 s.; 1 d. Educ. High School of Glasgow; Glasgow University. Partner, MacRoberts Solicitors, Glasgow and Edinburgh, 1971-2006; Employment Judge, 2005-2014. Trustee, High School of Glasgow Educational Trust; Vice Chairman, The

High School of Glasgow; Chairman, Westbourne Music; President, Glasgow Art Club, 2009-2012; Director, Merchants House of Glasgow; Trustee, Royal Conservatoire of Scotland Trust and Endowment Trust; Honorary President, Scottish International Piano Competition; Chairman, Royal Scottish National Orchestra, 1985-91; Governor, Royal Scottish Academy of Music and Drama, 1990-2002; Chairman, Children's Music Foundation in Scotland, 1994-2000; Dean, Royal Faculty of Procurators in Glasgow, 2001/04; President, Glasgow High School Club, 2003/04; Honorary President, National Youth Choir of Scotland. Recreation: music. Address: (h.) 11 Islay Drive, Newton Mearns, Glasgow G77 6UD; T.-0141-639 4133.

Wills, Dr. Jonathan, MA, PhD; b. 1947. Shetland journalist, author, broadcaster, political activist, Shetland Councillor (Lerwick South), mariner and wildlife expert; operates a wildlife tourism business around some of Shetland's finest seabird and seal colonies during the summer months. Educ. University of Edinburgh. Career history: first student to be Rector of the University of Edinburgh; Muckle Flugga Lighthouse boatman; Scotland correspondent for The Times; Senior Producer at BBC Radio Shetland, and editor of the Shetland Times, before pioneering the e-media Shetland News; also held a number of public posts and has written books for children. Honorary Warden of the Noss Island National Nature Reserve. Publications: Old Rock - Shetland in pictures; A Place in the Sun: Shetland and Oil, 1991; Innocent Passage: The Wreck of the Tanker Braer, 1993; The Travels of Magnus Pole, Chatto & Windus, 1984; Wilma Widdershins And The Muckle Tree: A Shetland Story, 1991; The Lands of Garth: A short history of Calback Ness, 1978. Address: (b.) Lerwick South Ward, Sundside, Bressay, Shetland ZE2 9ER; T.-07831 217 042.
E-mail: jonathan.wills@shetland.gov.uk

Wilson of Tillyorn, Baron (David Clive Wilson), KT, GCMG, MA (Oxon), PhD, FRSE. Life Peer (1992). President, Royal Society of Edinburgh, 2008-2011; Master of Peterhouse, Cambridge, 2002-08; Chancellor, Aberdeen University, 1997-2013; Deputy Vice-Chancellor, Cambridge University, 2005-08; Member, Council, Glenalmond College, 1994-2005 (Chairman, 2000-05); President, Bhutan Society of the UK, 1998-2008; President, Hong Kong Association and Hong Kong Society, 1994-2012; Registrar, Order of St. Michael and St. George, 2001-2010; Vice-President, Royal Scottish Geographical Society, since 1998; Member, Board, Martin Currie Pacific Trust, 1993-2003; Trustee, Carnegie Trust for the Universities of Scotland, since 2000; Member, Prime Minister's Advisory Committee on Business Appointments, 2000-09 (Chairman, 2008-09); b. 14.2.35, Alloa; m., Natasha Helen Mary Alexander; 2 s. Educ. Trinity College, Glenalmond; Keble College, Oxford. Entered Foreign Service, 1958; Third Secretary, Vientiane, 1959-60; language student, Hong Kong, 1960-62; Second, later First Secretary, Peking, 1963-65; FCO, 1965-68; resigned, 1968; Editor, China Quarterly, 1968-74; Visiting Scholar, Columbia University, New York, 1972; rejoined Diplomatic Service, 1974; Cabinet Office, 1974-77; Political Adviser, Hong Kong, 1977-81; Head, S. European Department, FCO, 1981-84; Assistant Under Secretary of State, FCO, 1984-87; Governor of Hong Kong, 1987-92. Member, Governing Body, School of Oriental and African Studies, 1992-97; Member, Council, CBI Scotland, 1993-2000; Chairman, Scottish and Southern Energy plc (formerly Scottish Hydro Electric), 1993-2000; Chairman, Scottish Committee, British Council, 1993-2002; Trustee, Scotland's Churches Scheme, 1999-2002 and 2008-2015, Vice President, since 2015; Chairman, Scottish Peers Association, 2000-02 (Vice-Chairman, 1998-2000); Chairman, Trustees, National Museums of Scotland, 2002-

06 (Trustee since 1999); Chairman, Council of St. Paul's Cathedral, London, 2009-2015; Lord High Commissioner to the General Assembly of the Church of Scotland, 2010 and 2011; Burgess of Guild, City of Aberdeen, 1990; Hon Fellow, Keble College, Oxford, 1987; Hon Fellow, Peterhouse, Cambridge, 2008; Hon.LLD (Aberdeen); Hon.DLitt (Sydney); Hon.DLitt (Abertay, Dundee); Hon.LLD, Chinese University, Hong Kong; Hon.DLitt (Hong Kong); Hon.Dr*hc* (Edin); KStJ. Recreations: mountaineering; reading. Address: (h.) 64 Great King Street, Edinburgh EH3 6QY.

Wilson, Alan Oliver Arneil, MB, ChB, DPM, FRCPsych, FFCS. Former consultant in private practice, Murrayfield Hospital, Edinburgh (now retired); Member, Executive Group of Board of Directors, and First President, World Association for Psychosocial Rehabilitation; Consultant (in Scotland), Ex-Services Mental Welfare Society; b. 4.1.30, Douglas; m., Dr. Fiona Margaret Davidson; 3 s. Educ. Biggar High School; Edinburgh University. RAMC, 1953-55; psychiatric post, Stobhill General Hospital, Glasgow, and Garlands Hospital, Carlisle, 1955-63; Consultant Psychiatrist and Deputy Physician Superintendent, St. George's Hospital, Morpeth, 1963-77; Consultant Psychiatrist, Bangour Hospitals, 1977-89; former Member, Clinical Teaching Staff, Faculty of Medicine, Edinburgh University; Clinical Lecturer, University of Newcastle upon Tyne. Chairman, Group for Study of Rehabilitation and Community Care, Scottish Division, RCPsych. V.M. Bekhterev Medal awarded by Bekhterev Psychoneurological Research Institute, St. Petersburg; Gálfi Béla Award for services to Hungarian Psychosocial Rehabilitation; Member, Founding Group, Morpeth Northumbrian Gathering; former part-time Hibernian FC footballer. Recreations: golf; music; guitar; blethering; curling. Address: (h.) 1, Croft Wynd, Milnathort, Perth and Kinross KY13 9GH; T.-01577 864477.
E-mail: olly_wilson@btinternet.com

Wilson, Brian, PC, MA (Hons). Director: Celtic plc, since 2005, AMEC Nuclear, since 2005; Chair: Scottish International Land Trust, since 2013; Harris Tweed Hebrides, since 2007, Havana Energy, since 2010, Britain's Energy Coast, 2009-2014; Prime Minister's Special Representative on Overseas Trade, 2003-05; MP (Labour), Cunninghame North, 1987-2005; former Minister for Energy and Industry, Department of Trade and Industry (2001-03); b. 13.12.48, Dunoon; m., Joni Buchanan; 2 s.; 1 d. Educ. Dunoon Grammar School; Dundee University; University College, Cardiff. Journalist; Publisher and Founding Editor, West Highland Free Press; Contributor to The Guardian, Scotsman, etc.; first winner, Nicholas Tomalin Memorial Award for Journalism; contested Ross and Cromarty, Oct., 1974, Inverness, 1979, Western Isles, 1983; front-bench spokesman on Scottish Home Affairs etc., 1988-92, Transport, 1992-94 and 1995-96, Trade and Industry, 1994-95; Minister of State, Scottish Office (Education, Industry and Highland and Islands), 1997-98; Minister for Trade, Department of Trade and Industry, 1998-99; Minister of State for Scotland, 1999-2001; Minister of State, Foreign and Commonwealth Office, 2001; Honorary Fellow, University of Highlands and Islands, 2010; Visiting Professor, Glasgow Caledonian University, since 2008; UK Business Ambassador, since 2012; Institute of Directors UK Global Director of the Year, 2011. Address: Cnoc Na Meinn, 7A Mangersta, Isle of Lewis HS2 9EY.

Wilson, Brian, OBE, LLB. Deputy Chairman, Local Government Boundary Commission for Scotland, 1999-2008; b. 20.2.46, Perth; m., Isobel Esson; 3 d. Educ. Buckie High School; Aberdeen University. Various posts with Marks & Spencer, Banff County Council, Inverness County

Council and Banff and Buchan District Council; Chief Executive, Inverness District Council, 1978-95; Depute Chief Executive, The Highland Council, 1995-98. Recreations: walking; painting; computing; cutting hedges. Address: (h.) 11 Lochardil Place, Inverness IV2 4LN; T.-01463 237454.

Wilson, Campbell. Rector, Peebles High School, since 2011. Formerly Deputy Head, Dumfries High School. Address: Peebles High School, Springwood Road, Peebles, Peeblesshire EH45 9HB; T.-01721 720291.

Wilson, Colin Alexander Megaw, LLB (Hons). First Scottish Parliamentary Counsel, 2006-2012 (retired); b. 4.1.52, Aberdeen; m., Mandy Esca Clay (divorced); 1 s.; 1 d. Educ. High School of Glasgow; Edinburgh University. Admitted as a Solicitor, 1975; Assistant Solicitor, then Partner, Archibald Campbell & Harley, WS, Edinburgh, 1975-79; Assistant Legal Secretary to Lord Advocate, 1979-99, and until 1993 Assistant, then Depute, Parliamentary Draftsman for Scotland; Scottish Parliamentary Counsel, 1993-2006. Recreations: hill-walking; choral singing; family.

Wilson, Corri. MP (SNP), Ayr, Carrick and Cumnock, since 2015. Elected to South Ayrshire council in the 2012 local elections for the ward of Ayr East. Address: House of Commons, London SW1A 0AA.

Wilson, Donald, OStJ, BA (Hons), MSc, TQ (Secondary). Lord Provost and Lord Lieutenant of the City of Edinburgh, since 2012; b. 4.12.59, Selkirk; partner, Elaine Brand; 1 step-s.; 1 step-d. Educ. Galashiels Academy; University of Stirling; The City University, London; Moray House College of Education, Edinburgh. Teacher of Computing, 1984-2012; Adult Education Tutor, 1984-2012; Acting Senior Teacher, ICT, 1997-99; Curriculum Development Officer, ICT, 1999-2001. Labour Councillor, City of Edinburgh Council, since 1999; Bailie of City of Edinburgh, 2007-2012; Member, Board: Edinburgh Technology Transfer Centre, 1999-2012, International Centre for the Mathematical Sciences, since 1999; Chair, Transnational Demos Project, since 2001; Board Member, Edinburgh International Science Festival, since 2007, Chair, 1999-2007, President, since 2012; Board Member, Edinburgh Science Foundation, 1999-2012, Chair, 1999-2007; Chair, Edinburgh Convention Bureaux, 2003-05; Chair, City of Edinburgh Council, Smart City & ICT Sounding Board, 2000-07; Member, Edinburgh & Lothians Tourist Board, 1999-2005, Chair, 2003-05; Chair, Edinburgh & Lothians Area Tourism Partnership, 2005-06; Member, Board, Gorgie City Farm, since 2008; Member, Lothian and Borders Police Board, 2010-2011; Chair and Director, Edinburgh International Festival society, since 2012; Chair and Director, Edinburgh Royal Military Tattoo Ltd, since 2012; Director and Trustee, Our Dynamic Earth Charitable Trust, since 2012; Governor of the Incorporated Trades of Edinburgh, since 2014; Veterans and Armed Forces Champion, since 2012; Volunteering Ambassador, since 2012; Vice President, Shipwrecked Mariners' Society, since 2014. Recreations: film; opera; sci-fi; computers; sudoku; antiques. Address: (b.) City Chambers, High Street, Edinburgh EH1 1YJ; T.-0131 529 4000; e-mail: lord.provost@edinburgh.gov.uk

Wilson, Gerald R., CB, MA, FRSE, DUniv; b. 7.9.39, Edinburgh; m., Margaret (deceased); 1 s.; 1 d. Educ. Holy Cross Academy; Edinburgh University. Assistant Principal, Scottish Home and Health Department, 1961-65; Private Secretary, Minister of State for Scotland, 1965-66; Principal, Scottish Home and Health Department, 1966-72;

Private Secretary to Lord Privy Seal, 1972-74, to Minister of State, Civil Service Department, 1974; Assistant Secretary, Scottish Economic Planning Department, 1974-77; Counsellor, Office of the UK Permanent Representative to the Economic Communities, Brussels, 1977-82; Assistant Secretary, Scottish Office, 1982-84; Under Secretary, Industry Department for Scotland, 1984-88; Secretary, Scottish Office Education and Industry Department, 1988-99, Scottish Executive Enterprise and Lifelong Learning Department, 1999; Special Adviser, Royal Bank of Scotland Group, 2000-09; Member, Court, Strathclyde University, 1999-2012, Vice Convener, 2008-2012; Member, Board: Royal Scottish National Orchestra, 2000-06 (Vice Chairman, since 2002); ICL (Scotland), 2000-02; Chairman, Fairbridge in Scotland, 2006-2011; St Andrew's Children's Society, 2003-2010; Chairman, Scottish European Educational Trust, 2006-2012; Governor, George Watson's College, Edinburgh, 2000-09; Chairman, Scottish Biomedical Foundation Ltd., 1999-2004; Hon. Sec., Friends of the Royal Scottish Academy, since 2009; Treasurer, Royal Society of Edinburgh, since 2012. Recreation: music. Address: (b.) 17/5 Kinnear Road, Edinburgh EH3 5PG.

Wilson, Professor Gordon McAndrew, MA, PhD, FRSA. Chair, Belleisle Conservatory Limited; b. 4.12.39, Glasgow; m., Alison Rosemary Cook; 2 s.; 1 d. Educ. Eastwood Secondary School; Glasgow University; Jordanhill College of Education. Teacher of History and Modern Studies: Eastwood Secondary School, 1963-65, Eastwood High School, 1965-67; Lecturer in Social Studies, Hamilton College of Education, 1967-73 (Head of Department, 1973-81); Principal Lecturer in Inservice Education, then Assistant Principal, Jordanhill College of Education, 1981-88; Principal, Craigie College of Education, 1988-93; Assistant Principal and Director of University Campus Ayr, Paisley University, 1993-99, now Emeritus Professor. Chairman, South Ayrshire Hospitals NHS Trust, 1997-99; Chairman, Ayrshire and Arran Acute Hospitals NHS Trust, 1999-2004; Non-Executive Board Member, NHS Ayrshire and Arran, 1999-2007; President, Ayrshire Chamber of Commerce and Industry, 2002-04; Chair, East Ayrshire Community Health Partnership, 2005-08. Recreations: reading; gardening; walking; music. Address: (h.) 51 Greenfield Avenue, Alloway, Ayr KA7 4NX; T.-01292 443889.

Wilson, Hamish Robert McHattie, CBE, MA (Aberd), MA, PhD (Cantab), FRCGP (Hon). Vice Chair, Healthcare Improvement Scotland, since 2011; Lay Member, Scottish Dental Practice Board, since 2011; b. 19.01.46, Aberdeen; m., Joyce Hossack; 3 d. Educ. Robert Gordon's College, Aberdeen; University of Aberdeen; Emmanuel College, Cambridge. Entered Health Service Administration in 1972; held range of posts with Grampian Health Board including Board Secretary, Unit General Manager, Director of Contracts and Planning, and Director of Primary Care; also Executive Board Member, 1991-99; Head of Primary Care Division, Scottish Executive Health Department, 1999-2006. Member: Scottish Advisory Board of Marie Curie Cancer Care; Lay Member, Assembly of Royal Pharmaceutical Society, since 2013; Independent Governor, Robert Gordon University, since 2015. Recreations: music; theatre; cinema; hellenic studies; family history. Address: (h.) 9 Gordon Road, Aberdeen AB15 7RY; T.-01224 312226; e-mail: hamish.wilson60@btinternet.com

Wilson, Helen Frances, DA, RSW, RGI, PAI. Artist; b. 25.7.54, Paisley; 1 d. Educ. John Neilson High School, Paisley; Glasgow School of Art. Drawings and paintings in public and private collections; awards and prizes include: Cargill Travelling Scholarship (Colonsay and Italy), 1976; First Prize, Scottish Drawing Competition, 1997; elected: RGI, 1984, RSW, 1997 and PAI, 2005. Recreations: watching theatre, ballet, pantomime and people. Address: (h.) 1 Partickhill Road, Glasgow; T.-0141-339 5827. E-mail: helenfwilson@gmail.com

Wilson, Ian Matthew, CB, MA. b. 12.12.26, Edinburgh; m., 1, Anne Chalmers (deceased); 3 s.; 2, Joyce Town (deceased). Educ. George Watson's College; Edinburgh University. Assistant Principal, Scottish Home Department, 1950; Private Secretary to Permanent Under Secretary of State, Scottish Office, 1953-55; Principal, Scottish Home Department, 1955; Assistant Secretary: Scottish Education Department, 1963, Scottish Home and Health Department, 1971; Assistant Under Secretary of State, Scottish Office, 1974-77; Under Secretary, Scottish Education Department, 1977-86; Secretary of Commissions for Scotland, 1987-92. Member, RSAMD Governing Body, 1992-2000; President, University of Edinburgh Graduates' Association, 1995-97; Director, Scottish International Piano Competition, 1997-2004. Address: (h.) 47 Braid Hills Road, Edinburgh EH10 6LD; T.-0131-447 1802.

Wilson, James Wiseman, OBE, OStJ. Director, Barcapel Foundation, since 1970; b. 31.5.33, Glasgow; m., Valerie Grant; 1 s.; 3 d. Educ. Trinity College, Glenalmond; Harvard Business School. Marketing Director, Scottish Animal Products, 1959-63; Sales Director, then Managing Director, then Chairman, Robert Wilson & Sons (1849) Ltd., 1964-85. Trustee, Scottish Civic Trust, 1974-2004 and Chairman, Management Committee, 1984-2004; National Trust for Scotland: Member of Council, 1977-82 and 1984-89, President, Ayrshire Members' Centre; Honorary President, Skelmorlie Golf Club and Irvine Pipe Band; won Aims of Industry Free Enterprise Award (Scotland), 1980. Recreations: golf; backgammon; skiing; bridge; travelling. Address: (h.) The Turret House, Skelmorlie Castle, Skelmorlie, Ayrshire PA17 5EY; T.-01475 521127.

Wilson, Janette Sylvia, LLB, NP. Solicitor of the Church of Scotland and Law Agent to the General Assembly, since 1995; b. 15.1.51, Inverness. Educ. Inverness Royal Academy; Edinburgh University. Law Apprentice, then Assistant, Dundas & Wilson, CS, Edinburgh, 1973-77; Assistant, then Partner, Ross Harper & Murphy, Edinburgh, 1977-81; Depute Solicitor, Church of Scotland, 1981-95. Secretary, Scottish Churches Committee; Member, The Churches Legislation Advisory Service; Secretary, Dr Neil's Garden Trust. Recreations: keeping fit; reading; gardening. Address: (b.) 121 George Street, Edinburgh; T.-0131-225 5722.

Wilson, John. Chief Executive, NHS Fife, 2012-2014 (retired). Educ. degree in public administration, and a Postgraduate Diploma in Health Services Management. Thirty-five years operational experience of hospital management gained in Glasgow, Edinburgh and Fife; held a variety of management posts across Fife; formerly Chief Executive of NHS Fife Operational Division.

Wilson, John G., MA. MSP (Ind), Central Scotland, 2007-2016; Director, Scottish Low Pay Unit, 2001-07; b. 28.11.56, Falkirk; m., Frances M. McGlinchey; 1 d. Educ. Camelon High School; Coatbridge College; Glasgow University. Coachbuilder, 1972-82; Project Co-ordinator, Castlemilk Housing Involvement Project, 1987-94; Director, Glasgow Council of Tenants Associations, 1994-97; The Poverty Alliance: Senior Economic Development Officer, 1998-99, Fieldwork Manager, 1999-2001. Falkirk District Councillor, 1980-82; SNP Parliamentary candidate, Hamilton South, 2001, 2003; Westminster Candidate, 2005, Lanark and Hamilton East; Local Councillor, North Lanarkshire Council, 2007-09. Recreations: Tai Chi; archery; National Trust; Historic Scotland; RSPB; Woodlands Trust; Scottish CND; Member, Scottish Green Party.

Wilson, Dr. Lena, CBE, BA, MBA. Chief Executive, Scottish Enterprise, since 2009, Chief Operating Officer, 2005-09; Chief Executive Officer, Scottish Development International, 2006-2009; b. 13.2.64, Paisley. Educ. St Andrews High School, East Kilbride; Glasgow Caledonian University; Strathclyde University. Production and quality management, electronics industry, 1985-89; Manager, Locate in Scotland, 1989-94; Deputy Chief Executive, Scottish Enterprise Forth Valley, 1994-98; Senior Advisor, World Bank, Washington DC, 1998-2000; Senior Director, Customer Relations, Scottish Enterprise, 2000-05. Member, Financial Services Advisory Board; Board Member, Intertek Group PLC; Ambassador, Prince and Princess of Wales Hospice. Recreations: fitness; the arts; travel; family and friends. Address: (b.) Scottish Enterprise, Atrium Court, 50 Waterloo Street, Glasgow G2 6HQ.

Wilson, Les. Documentary Producer/Director, since 1980; Director, Caledonia TV Ltd., since 1992; b. 17.7.49, Glasgow; m., Adrienne Cochrane (marr. diss., 2006); 2 d.; m., Jenni Minto. Educ. Grove Academy, Broughty Ferry. Trainee Journalist, 1969-70; hippy trail, 1970-71; Reporter, Greenock Telegraph, 1972-73; Reporter, STV, 1973-78; Editor, STV political programme, Ways and Means, 1979-80; Producer/Director, STV, 1981-92. Winner, Celtic Film Festival Award, 1991; BAFTA Scotland and British Telecom Factual/Current Affairs awards, 1997; British Telecom Factual/Current Affairs award, 1998; Scots Independent, Oliver Brown Award, 2013. Publications: Scotland's War (Co-author), 1995; Fire in the Head (a novel), 2010; Islay Voices (Co-editor), 2016. Recreation: Islay – the island, its people, its malts. Address: (b.) 147 Bath Street, Glasgow G2 4SQ; T.-0141-564 9100; e-mail: lwilson@caledonia.tv

Wilson, Professor Lindsay, BA, DipEd, PhD, CPyschol. Professor of Psychology, University of Stirling, since 1998; b. 24.6.51, Aberdeen; m., Jean; 2 s. Educ. Biggar High School; University of Stirling; University of Edinburgh. Research Fellow, Max Planck Institute for Psychiatry, Munich, 1979-80; University of Stirling: Medical Research Council Training Fellow, 1980-83, Lecturer then Senior Lecturer, 1983-98, Head, Department of Psychology, 1995-2001. Recreations: sailing; hillwalking. Address: (b.) Department of Psychology, University of Stirling, Stirling FK9 4LA; T.-01786 467640.

Wilson, Monica Anne, BA, DipPCT. Retired. Former Caledonian Professional Adviser, Effective Practice Unit, Community Justice Services Division, Scottish Government, 2009-2012; Counsellor in Primary Care, 1997-2013; b. 4.3.51, Arundel; m., Keith Stewart ; 1 step-d. Educ. Our Lady of Sion School, Worthing; Stirling University; Edinburgh University; Strathclyde University. Research Assistant, Stirling University, 1975-78; Research Officer, Scottish Consumer Council, 1978-80; Research Fellow, Edinburgh University, 1980-82; Research and Development Officer, Forth Valley Health Board, 1985-89; Joint Co-ordinator, CHANGE Project, 1989-96, Director, CHANGE, 1997-2009. Joint Developer, Caledonian System, accredited by the Scottish Accreditation Panel for Offender Programmes, 2004-2009; Member, Scottish Advisory Panel on Offender Rehabilitation, 2012-2016. Main publication: Men Who Are Violent to Women (Co-Author), 1997. Butler Trust Award, 2009. Recreations: gardening; DIY; sailing; music. Address: (h.) 2 Kirk Brae, Clackmannan FK10 4JW; T.-01259 211 662. E-mail: monica.wilson78@yahoo.co.uk

Wilson, Robert Gordon, BL, LLD. Retired Solicitor; b. 16.4.38, Glasgow; m., Edith M. Hassall; 2 d. Educ. Douglas High School for Boys; Edinburgh University. National Secretary, SNP, 1963-71; MP, Dundee East, 1974-87; Scottish National Party: Chairman and National Convener, 1979-90, Vice-President, 1992-97; Rector, Dundee University, 1983-86; Member, Court,

University of Abertay Dundee, 1992-96; Member, Church and Nation Committee, Church of Scotland, 2000-03; Director, Age Concern Dundee Ltd., 2001-05; Temp. Chairman, Couple Counselling Tayside, 2006; Chairman, Solas (Centre for Public Christianity), 2010-2013; Director, Dundee Citizens Advice Bureau, 2011; Director, Options for Scotland, 2013. Publications: SNP: The Turbulent Years, 1960-90, 2009; Pirates of the Air: The Story of Radio Free Scotland, 2011; Scotland: The Battle for Independence (1990-2014), 2014. Recreations: reading; writing. Address: (h.) 48 Monifieth Road, Dundee DD5 2RX.

Wilson, Roy. General Manager, Pitlochry Festival Theatre, 1961-95, Art Exhibitions Director, 1995-2004; b. St. Andrews. Educ. Burgh School and Madras College, St. Andrews. Proprietor, grocer's business, St. Andrews, 1953-58; Assistant Manager, Pitlochry Festival Theatre, 1958-61. Winner David K. Thomson Award, 1995, in recognition of his contribution to Pitlochry Festival Theatre. Recreations: plays and theatre in general; most forms of classical music, with particular interest in choral singing; listening to records; reading; art and antiques. Address: (h.) Kilrymont, Bruach Lane, Pitlochry, Perthshire PH16 5DG; T.-Pitlochry 472897.

Wilton, Brian, MBE. Managing Director, Tartan Ambassador Ltd, since 2014; Director, Scottish Tartans Authority, since 1995. Educ. English School, Nicosia, Cyprus. Address: Scottish Tartans Authority, Fraser House, Muthill Road, Crieff, Perthshire PH7 3AY.

Windsor, Malcolm L., PhD, FRSC, OBE. Secretary, North Atlantic Salmon Conservation Organization, 1984-2012; Buckland Foundation Professorship, 2014; Independent Reviewer of the EU-New Zealand Research Cooperation Agreement, 2013; b. Bristol; m., Sally; 2 d. Educ. Cotham Grammar School, Bristol; Bristol University. Researcher, University of California, 1965-67; fisheries research, Humber Laboratory, Hull, 1967-75; Fisheries Adviser to Chief Scientist, Ministry of Agriculture and Fisheries, London, 1975-84. Chairman, Duddingston Village Conservation Society and Rutland Square and Street Association. Publication: book on fishery products. Recreations: local conservation work; jazz; walking. Address: (h.) 1 Duddingston House Courtyard, Edinburgh EH15 1JG; T.-0131 661 7707; e-mail: mw@mwindsor.net

Windsor, Col. Rodney Francis Maurice, CBE, DL. Farmer; b. 22.2.25, Redhill; m., Deirdre Chichester (deceased); m. Angela Stainton (deceased); 2 s.; 1 d. Educ. Tonbridge School. Enlisted Royal Armoured Corps, 1943; commissioned The Queen's Bays, 1944-52; Captain, 1949; ADC to CINC and High Commissioner Austria, 1949-50; served in North Irish Horse (TA), 1959-67; Lt. Col. Commanding, 1964-67; Colonel TA N. Ireland, 1967-71; ADC (TA) to HM The Queen, 1970-75; Member, Highland TA Association, 1971-77; Member, Banff and Buchan District Valuation Appeal Committee, 1982-96 (Chairman, 1989-96); Deputy Lieutenant:, Co. Antrim, 1967-97, Aberdeenshire, since 1989; Hon. President, Turiff Branch, Royal British Legion Scotland, since 1997; Member, Aberdeen Committee, Scottish Veterans Garden City Association, since 1993. Recreations: field sports; golf. Address: (h.) The Old Laundry, Byth House, New Byth, Turriff, Aberdeenshire AB53 5XN; T.-01888 544164.

Winn, Professor Philip, BA, PhD. Professor of Neuroscience, Institute of Pharmacy and Biomedical Sciences (SIPBS), University of Strathclyde; Honorary Professor of Psychology, University of St Andrews; b.

31.10.54, Hull; m., Jane E. Burrows; 2 s.; 1 d. Educ. Isleworth Grammar School; University of Hull. Research Scientist, Institute of Neurology, 1979-80; Pinsent-Darwin Student of Mental Pathology, University of Cambridge, 1980-83; Lecturer, Professor, Dean of Science, Vice-Principal (Learning and Teaching), University of St. Andrews, 1984-2009; Deputy Principal (Strategy), University of Strathclyde, 2010-2011. Fellow: Society of Biology, Association for Psychological Science. Address: (b.) SIPBS, 161 Cathedral Street, Glasgow G4 0RE.

Winney, Robin John, MB, ChB, FRCPEdin. Retired Consultant Renal Physician, Edinburgh Royal Infirmary; b. 8.5.44, Dunfermline. Educ. Dunfermline High School; Edinburgh University. Recreations: badminton; curling; golf. Address: (h.) 74 Lanark Road West, Currie, Midlothian EH14 5JZ.
E-mail: robinwinney@btopenworld.com

Winstanley, Charles, TD, JP, MBA, DBA, DL. Chair of the Board, Academy of Medical Royal Colleges, since 2016; Non Executive Director, Scottish Public Pensions Agency, since 2015; Chair, Scottish Police Pension Board, since 2015; Chairman: NHS Lothian, 2007-2013, Edinburgh Leisure, 2010-2015; Member: Tribunals Disciplinary Panel, since 2014, Asylum and Immigration Tribunal, since 2003; Non Executive Director: Ministry of Defence, 2010-2014, Scottish Government, 2010-2013, UK Supreme Court, since 2011; b. 6.3.52, London; m., Columbine (divorced); 1 s.; 1 d. Educ. Wellington College; RMA Sandhurst; Henley Management College. Served 16/5 Lancers and Royal Yeomanry, 1970-93; Justice of the Peace, since 1993; Member, National Consumer Council for Postal Services, 2002-08; Chairman, Norfolk Probation Board, 2001-06; Panel Chairman, General Medical Council, 2000-07; Non Executive Director, Norfolk and Norwich University Hospital Trust, 1999-2006. Deputy Lieutenant, Greater London, since 1997. Recreations: fly fishing; sailing; motorcycling.

Winter, Dr. Mike, FRCGP, FRCPsych. Medical Director, Procurement Commissioning and Facilities SBU, NHS NSS, since 2013; b. 17.06.56, Scotland; m., Margaret; 1 s.; 1 d. Educ. Bathgate Academy; Edinburgh University. General Practitioner, Whitburn, West Lothian, 1987-96; Medical Director: Lanarkshire Healthcare NHS Trust, 1996-99, NHS Lothian Primary Care, 1999-2008, National Services Division, 2008-2013. Board Member, The Vine Trust; Ambassador, Girlguiding Edinburgh. Recreations: cooking; photography; skiing. Address: (b.) Gyle Square, Edinburgh EH12 9EB; T.-0131 275 7023; e-mail: mike.winter@nhs.net

Winter, Robert. Lord-Lieutenant and Lord Provost of Glasgow, 2007-2012; b. 31.03.37, Glasgow; m., Sheena Morgan Duncan; 4 s.; 1 d. Educ. Allan Glen's High School; Strathclyde University; Glasgow University. Director of Social Work, Greenock and Port Glasgow, 1969-75; Strathclyde Regional Council Depute Director of Social Work, 1975-95, then Director of Social Work, 1995-96. Past President, Association of Directors of Social Work, 1980-81; Member, General Council, 1996-2005 (Chairman of Fitness to Practice Panel, until 2007). Member, Greater Glasgow Health Board PCT, 1996-2005; Convener, Risk Management Authority, 2004-08. Recreations: walking; swimming; reading; football.

Winter-Scott, Rosemary, OBE. Executive Director, International Association of Insolvency Regulators. Educ. Durham University. Formerly a senior manager in Training and Enterprise Councils (TECs) in England with policy responsibility for HR and Business Development; Chief Executive of Investors in People Scotland, 1997-2003, then Deputy Director, Learning, Development and Careers, HR Directorate of the Health Department, Scottish Executive, then Deputy Director, Employability and Skills, Lifelong Learning Directorate, Scottish Government, 2004-2009, then undertaking a short term project conducting a strategic review of Learning Connections in Scottish Government; The Accountant in Bankruptcy and Agency Chief Executive, 2009-2015. Board Member, ACE (Association of Chief Executives), since 2010; Convenor/Chair of Jordanhill School Board, 2008-2013. Recognised in the Queen's Birthday Honours list 2014 and awarded Officer of the Order of the British Empire (OBE) for her public service to Insolvency Services in Scotland and voluntary service to education through Jordanhill School. Address: (b.) 1 Pennyburn Road, Kilwinning, Ayrshire KA13 6SA.

Wise, Lady (Morag B. Wise), QC, LLB (Hons), DipLP, LLM. Senator of the College of Justice, since 2013. Educ. University of Aberdeen; McGill University. Became a solicitor in 1989 and joined Morton Fraser LLP; called to the bar in 1993, joining Westwater Advocates, and specialised in family law; Queen's Counsel, since 2005, and was appointed a Temporary Judge of the Court of Session in 2008; Member of the Disciplinary Committee of the Faculty of Advocates, since 2005; Chair of the Advocates' Family Law Association, since 2007, having served as Vice Chair, since 2000. Address: (b.) Parliament House, Edinburgh EH1 1RQ.

Wiseman, Alan William. Director and Chairman, Robert Wiseman Dairies, 1979-2010; National Dairy Council, Scottish Dairy Association; b. 20.8.50, Giffnock. Educ. Duncanrig Senior Secondary School, East Kilbride. Left school to be one of his father's milkmen, 1967; has been a milkman ever since. Scottish Businessman of the Year, 1992; Scottish Business Achievement Award, 1994; Fellow, Royal Agricultural Society. Recreation: golf.

Wishart, Colin Fraser, DA, RIBA, FRIAS, SSA. Chartered Architect; Principal, Freespace Architecture, since 2002; Visiting Teaching Fellow, Duncan of Jordanstone College, University of Dundee, 1997-2008; formerly Honorary Fellow, The School of Arts, Culture and Environment, The University of Edinburgh (appointed 2004); Professional Member, Society of Scottish Artists, since 1990; architectural photographer; b. 20.8.47, Dundee; divorced. Educ. Grove Academy; Duncan of Jordanstone College of Art. Architect, Thoms and Wilkie, Chartered Architects, Dundee, 1972-73; Senior Architect, City of Dundee Corporation, 1973-90; Principal Architect, City of Dundee Council, 1990-96; Partner, Battledown Studio, Natural Architecture, 1996-2002. Past President, Dundee Institute of Architects, since 1988; President, Dundee Institute of Architects, 1986-88; Vice President, Royal Incorporation of Architects in Scotland, 1986-88; RIBA Representative, Architects Registration Council, 1989-96; National Juror, RIBA Awards, 1988. Recreations: photography; fine art; music; poetry. Address: 12 Farm Road, Anstruther, Fife KY10 3ER; T.-01333 310 589; e-mail: colinform@hotmail.co.uk web: www.colinform.co.uk

Wishart, James, BD. Minister of Religion, 1985-2009 (retired); b. 26.12.44, South Ronaldsay, Orkney; m., Helen Donaldson; 1 s.; 1 d. Educ. Kirkwall Grammar School; Aberdeen University. Farming, 1960-80; University, 1980-85. Recreations: photography; European languages; walking. Address: (h.) Upper Westshore, Burray, Orkney KW17 2TE.

Wishart, Professor Jennifer Grant, MA, PhD, FRSE. Professor of Developmental Disabilities in Childhood, University of Edinburgh, since 1998; b. 9.5.48, Dundee; m.,

Thomas Arrol. Educ. Harris Academy, Dundee; University of Edinburgh. Research Psychologist, University of Edinburgh, 1970-95, Reader, 1995-96; first Scottish Chair in Special Education, Moray House Institute of Education, Heriot-Watt University, 1996-98. Research Advisor to Scottish and UK Down's Syndrome Associations and National Down Syndrome Foundation (Canada); funding assessor for national/international government bodies and charities. Peer reviewer for c40 academic journals; c100 papers/chapters in psychology/education/medical journals and interdisciplinary textbooks. Recreations: wine/food; travel; English pointers. Address: 10/13 West Mill Road, Edinburgh EH13 0NX; e-mail: J.Wishart@ed.ac.uk

Wishart, Peter. MP (SNP), Perth and North Perthshire, since 2005, North Tayside, 2001-05; SNP Shadow Leader of the House of Commons, since 2015; Chair, Scottish Affairs Select Committee, since 2015; previously served as the SNP's Westminster Spokesperson for the Constitution, Home Affairs, Culture, Media and Sport, Transport, International Development and Chief Whip; b. 9.3.62; 1 s. Educ. Moray House College of Education. Community worker, 1984-85; musician with Runrig, 1985-2001. Address: (b.) 35 Perth Street, Blairgowrie, Perthshire PH10 6DL; 9 York Place, Perth PH2 8EP.
E-mail: wishartp@parliament.uk

Wishart Ruth, BA (Hons), FRSA. Columnist and Broadcaster; b. Glasgow; m. Rod McLeod (died 2004). Educ. Eastwood Senior Secondary; Open University. Board Member, Creative Scotland; Chair, Dewar Arts Awards. Contact: ruth@kilcreggan.demon.co.uk

Wiszniewski, Adrian, BA (Hons). Artist/Designer; b. 31.3.58, Glasgow; m., Diane Foley; 2 s.; 1 d. Educ. Mackintosh School of Architecture, Glasgow School of Art. Around 40 solo exhibitions throughout the world, since 1983; commissions include: two large paintings for Liverpool Anglican Cathedral 1996, Gallery of Modern Art, Glasgow, 1996, Millennium Tower, Hamilton, 1997-98; work purchased by museums worldwide including Tate Gallery, London and MOMA, New York. New York Design Award for designs of six rugs in collaboration with Edinburgh Tapestry Workshop; has created limited edition books. Recreations: looking at pictures; cinema; family.

Withers, Professor Charles William John, BSc, PhD, FBA, FRSE, FRHistS, FRGS, FRSA, FRSGS, FSA, Member, Academea Europaea. Professor of Historical Geography, Edinburgh University, since 1994; Geographer Royal for Scotland, since 2015; b. 6.12.54, Edinburgh; m., Anne; 2 s.; 1 d. Educ. Daniel Stewart's College, Edinburgh; St. Andrews University; Cambridge University. Publications: author of 17 books, 130 academic articles. Recreations: reading; hill-walking. Address: (b.) Institute of Geography, Edinburgh University, Drummond Street, Edinburgh; T.-0131-650 2559.

Withers, James. Chief Executive, Scotland Food & Drink, since 2011; Chief Executive, NFU Scotland, 2008-2011, Deputy Chief Executive, 2005-08. Address: (b.) Scotland Food & Drink, 3, The Royal Highland Centre, Ingliston, Edinburgh EH28 8NB.

Withers, John Alexander (Jack), FCIL. Writer; b. Glasgow; m., Beate (Bea) Haertel. Educ. North Kelvinside School; Jordanhill College of Education (Youth and Community Diploma). Left school at 14; worked in garage, electrical industry, labouring, National Service, unemployment, razor-blade salesman; long periods abroad, wandering, wondering, working: France, FRG, Italy, Scandinavia, Spain, North Africa; youth worker; freelance writer; ski instructor; librarian; performance poet; Scottish republican and radical; plays for radio, TV, theatre; James Kennoway Screenplay Award (shared); Scottish Arts Council Awards; short stories published in numerous journals in UK, Denmark and West Germany; Editor, Two Tongues — Two Cities; books: Glasgow Limbo, A Real Glasgow Archipelago, Balancing on a Barbed Wire Fence, Hijack. Address: (h.) Flat 2, 6 Kirklee Gate, Glasgow G12 0SZ; e-mail: bea.withers@ntlworld.com

Witney, Eur. Ing. Professor Brian David, BSc, MSc, PhD, NDA, NDAgrE, CEng, CEnv, FIMechE, Hon.FIAgrE, MemASABE. Director, Land Technology Ltd., 1995-2013; Hon. Professor of Agricultural Engineering, Edinburgh University, since 1989; Professor of Terramechanics, Scottish Agricultural College, Edinburgh, 1994-95; b. 8.6.38, Edinburgh; m., Maureen M.I. Donnelly; 1 s.; 2 d. Educ. Daniel Stewart's College, Edinburgh; Edinburgh University; Durham University; Newcastle University. Senior Research Associate, Newcastle upon Tyne University, 1962-66; Research Fellow, US Army Research Office, Duke Univ., 1966-67; Senior Scientific Officer, Military Engineering Experimental Establishment, Christchurch, 1967-70; Head, Agricultural Engineering Department, East of Scotland College of Agriculture, Edinburgh, 1970-86; Director, Scottish Centre of Agricultural Engineering, 1987-95, and Vice-Dean, Scottish Agricultural College, 1990-95. President, Institution of Agricultural Engineers, 1988-90; President, European Society of Agricultural Engineers, 1993-94; Managing Editor, Landwards, 1996-2007; Managing Editor, Land Technology, 1994-96; Editor and Chairman, Editorial Board, Journal of Agricultural Engineering Research, 1998-2001, Biosystems Engineering, 2002-07; Chairman, Douglas Bomford Trust, 1998-2003. EurAgEng Award for services to agricultural engineering, 2000. Publication: Choosing and Using Farm Machines. Address: (h.) 33 South Barnton Avenue, Edinburgh EH4 6AN.

Wolf, Professor Charles Roland, OBE, BSc, PhD, FRSE, FMedSci, FSA, FBTS. Founder and Chief Scientific Officer, CXR Biosciences Ltd., 2001-2012; b. 26.2.49, Sedgefield; m., Helga Loth; 1 s.; 1 d. Educ. Surrey University. Royal Society Fellow, Institute for Physiological Chemistry, University of Saarland, W. Germany 1976-77; Visiting Fellow, National Institute of Environmental Health Sciences, North Carolina, 1977-80; Visiting Scientist, ICI Central Toxicology Laboratories, Macclesfield, 1980-81; Head Scientist, Biochemistry Section, Institute of Toxicology, Mainz, W. Germany, 1981-82; Head, ICRF Molecular Pharmacology Group, Edinburgh University, 1982-92. Gerhard Zbinden Award, 2001. Publications; Molecular Genetics of Drug Resistance (Co-Editor), 1997; numerous scientific papers. Recreations: weaving; piano playing; gardening; hiking; poetry. Address: (b.) Medical Research Institute, Jacqui Wood Cancer Centre, Ninewells Hospital and Medical School, Dundee DD1 9SY; T.-01382 383134.

Wolffe, James, QC. Dean, The Faculty of Advocates, since 2014. Educ. Balliol College, Oxford; University of Edinburgh. Advocate, since 1992; First Standing Junior Counsel to the Scottish Ministers, 2002-07; QC since 2007; Advocate Depute, 2007-2010; Vice-Dean of the Faculty of Advocates, 2013-14. Council member, Justice Scotland; Trustee, The Abbotsford Trust; called to the bar of England & Wales (2013); door tenant at Brick Court Chambers, London. Address: Advocates Library, Parliament House, Edinburgh EH1 1RF; T.-0131 226 5071.

Wolffe, The Hon Lady Wolffe (Sarah Wolffe), QC. Senator of the College of Justice, since 2014; m.; 2 s.

Career: qualified as a solicitor in 1992 and worked at the Bank of Scotland legal department, 1992-93; called to the bar in 1994 and until 2008 practised as a junior counsel, mainly in commercial and public law; standing junior counsel to the Department of Trade and Industry and its successor departments; ad hoc advocate depute, 2007-2014; appointed QC in 2008. As senior counsel, practised mainly in commercial and public law. Chancellor to the Bishop of the Argyll and Isles, 2004-2013; Chancellor to the Bishop of Edinburgh, 2007-2014; MacGillivray, Insurance Law, Scottish contributor to 10th and 11th editions; Mithani, Directors Disqualification, Scottish Editor for 2012 edition; Member: Disciplinary Tribunal of the Faculty of Advocates, 2005-2008, Police Appeals Tribunal, 2013-2014; CCEB Working Group on Insurance Law (appointed expert), 2013-2014; Faculty of Advocate's Law Reform Committee, 2013-2014; Commercial Court Consultative Committee, 2000-2004; Canons Committee of the Scottish Episcopal Church, 1995-98. LLB with Distinction, University of Edinburgh, 1989; DipLP, University of Edinburgh, 1990; BA (Summa Cum Laude, Phi Beta Kappa), Dartmouth College, Hanover, NH, USA, 1984. Clubs: Dairymen's Country Club; Waverley Lawn Tennis, Squash and Sports Club. Scottish Civil Justice Council, Advocate Member, 2014. Emigrated to the United Kingdom in 1987. Address: Judicial Office for Scotland, Parliament House, Edinburgh EH1 1RQ.

Wong, Emeritus Professor Henry H.Y., BSc, PhD, DIC, CEng, FRAeS, DUniv. Emeritus Professor, Department of Aeronautics and Fluid Mechanics, Glasgow University; Senior Research Fellow, since 1987; Adviser to the Guangdong Higher Education Bureau, China, since 1985; Adviser to Glasgow University on Chinese Affairs, since 1986; Chair Professor, Nanjing University of Aeronautics and Astronautics, since 1987; "Concurrent" Professor, National University of Defense Technology, Changsha, since 1989; b. 23.5.22, Hong Kong; m., Joan Anstey; 2 s.; 1 d. Educ. St. Stephen College, Hong Kong; Jiao-Tong University, Shanghai; Imperial College, London; Glasgow University. Assistant Lecturer, Jiao-Tong University, 1947-48; Engineer, Armstrong Siddeley, 1949; Structural Engineer, Hunting Percival Aircraft, 1949-51; Senior Structural Engineer, de Havilland Aircraft, 1952-57; Senior Lecturer, Hatfield Polytechnic, 1957-59; Lecturer, Senior Lecturer, then Reader in Aeronautics and Fluid Mechanics, Glasgow University, from 1960; Economic and Technological Consultant to Shantou Special Economic Zone, China, since 1988. Former Treasurer and Vice-Chairman, Kilmardinny Music Circle; Chairman, Glasgow Summer School, 1979-95; Consulting Editor, Contemporary Who's Who, American Biographical Institute, since 2002; City of Glasgow Lord Provost's Award, 1988. Recreations: reading; music; painting; swimming. Address: (h.) 77 Antonine Road, Bearsden, Glasgow; T.-0141-942 8346.

Wood, Alex, BA (Hons), MLitt, MEd. Genealogical researcher, teacher and writer; b. 17.11.50, Dundee; m., Frances Kinnear; 2 d. Educ. Paisley Grammar School; New University of Ulster; Moray House College of Education; Edinburgh University; Stirling University; Strathclyde University. English Teacher, Craigroyston High School, 1973-75; Community Worker, Pilton Central Association, 1975-77; Remedial Teacher, Craigroyston High School, 1977-79; Principal Teacher, Learning Support, Craigroyston High School, 1979-90; Head of Centre, Millburn, Bathgate, 1990-96; Head Teacher, Kaimes School, 1996-99; Special Schools and Social Inclusion Manager, Edinburgh Education Department, 1999-2000; Principal and Head Teacher, Wester Hailes Education Centre, 2000-2011 (seconded Headteacher, Tynecastle High School, 2008-09). Edinburgh District Councillor, Pilton Ward, 1980-87;

Parliamentary Candidate, Dumfriesshire, 1979 and West Edinburgh, 1984. Recreations: genealogy; reading; running. T.-0775 9898890.
E-mail: alexander.wood@blueyonder.co.uk; web: www.alexwood.org.uk

Wood, Brian James, JP, BSc (Hons), FRSA. Rector, Hazlehead Academy, Aberdeen, 1993-2009 (retired); b. 6.12.49, Banff; m., Doreen A. Petrie; 1 s.; 1 d. Educ. Banff Academy; Aberdeen Academy; Aberdeen University; Aberdeen College of Education. Teacher of Physics, George Heriot's School, Edinburgh, 1972-75; Mackie Academy, 1975-89, latterly as Depute Rector; Rector, Mearns Academy, 1989-93. Deputy Convener of the Board of the Cairngorms National Park Authority; Justice of the Peace, Grampian Highlands and Islands; Honorary Sheriff at Stonehaven; Member, University of Aberdeen Business Committee. Recreations: golf; fishing; reading; local history. Address: (h.) 13 Edinview Gardens, Stonehaven; T.-01569 763888; e-mail: brian.j.wood@btinternet.com

Wood, Fergus, TD. Former Provost of Stirling (2008-2012); Farmer & Co. Director, since 1974; b. 10.09.42, Glasgow; m., Francesca; 2 s.; 1 d. Educ. Trinity College, Glenalmond. Trainee Journalist, Glasgow Herald, 1960-63; Scholarship in Communications, Norway, 1963-65; Journalist, Evening Times, Glasgow, 1965-69; PRO Phillips Phonographic Industries, Holland, 1969-72; Information Officer, Stirling University, 1972-80; Director, Scottish Woollen Industry, 1980-88; MD, Scottish Wool Centre Ltd., Aberfoyle, 1988-2008. Project Director, Scottish Fine Wool Producers, 1998-2005; Major in TA (TD in 1978); TA Service, 1960-90. Recreations: Celtic music (Band Leader, Kinlochard Ceilidh Band; Silver Discs, 2000 and 2003 from music industry). Address: (h.) Ledard Farm, Kinlochard, Stirling FK8 3TL; T.-01877 387219; e-mail: ferg@ceilidh-band.demon.co.uk

Wood, Graham Allan, MBChB, BDS, FDSRCPS, FRCS(Ed), FDSRCS(Ed), FDSRCS(Eng). Interim Professor in Oral Medicine, Royal Hospitals Trust and University of Belfast, since 2011; Consultant Oral and Maxillofacial Surgeon, Southern General Hospital, Glasgow, 1995-2010; Past Vice Dean, Faculty of Dental Surgery, Royal College of Physicians and Surgeons of Glasgow; Honorary Clincial Senior Lecturer, University of Glasgow, since 1995; Clinical Professor, University of Texas, USA, 1990-2000; b. 15.8.46, Glasgow; m., Lindsay Balfour; 1 s.; 1 d. Educ. Hillhead High School, Glasgow; University of Glasgow; University of Dundee. General dental practice, Glasgow, 1968-70; House Officer, Senior House Officer, Registrar, dental specialties, Glasgow Dental Hospital, Glasgow Victoria Infirmary and Canniesburn Hospital, 1970-72; Dental Surgeon, Grenfell Mission, Labrador, Canada, 1972-73; House Officer (plastic surgery), Dundee Royal Infirmary, 1978; Senior Registrar (oral and maxillofacial surgery), North Wales, 1979-83; Consultant, Oral and Maxillofacial Surgeon, North Wales, 1983-95. Fellow, International Association of Oral and Maxillofacial Surgeons; Fellow, British Association of Oral and Maxillofacial Surgeons. Recreations: hillwalking; golf; sailing; skiing. Address: (h.) Cambro, Gryffe Road, Kilmacolm PA13 4BB; T.-01505 873954; e-mail: Graham.Wood@belfasttrust.hscni.net

Wood, Sir Ian Clark, CBE (1982), LLD, BSc, DBA, DTech, CBIM, FCIB, FRSE. Chairman and Chief Executive, John Wood Group PLC, 1967-2006, Chairman, 2007-2012; Chairman, J.W. Holdings, since 1982; Chancellor, Robert Gordon University, since 2004; Chairman, The Wood Foundation; b. 21.7.42, Aberdeen; m., Helen Macrae; 3 s. Educ. Robert Gordon's College,

Aberdeen; Aberdeen University. Joined family business, John Wood & Sons, 1964; Chairman, Scottish Enterprise Board, 1997-2000; Fellow, Royal Society of Arts; Grampian Industrialist of the Year, 1978; Young Scottish Businessman of the Year, 1979; Scottish Free Enterprise Award, 1985; Scottish Business Achievement Award Trust — joint winner, 1992, corporate elite leadership award services category; Hon. LLD, 1984; Hon. DBA, 1998; HonDTech, 2002; Corporate Elite "World Player" Award, 1996; Scottish Business Insider Ambassador for Scotland, 2001; Fellow: Scottish Vocational Educational Council, Scottish Qualifications Authority; Business Achievement Award, Business Insider, 2002; Entrepreneurial Exchange Hall of Fame, 2002; Business Insider/PWC Scotland PLC Awards, CEO of the Year, 2003; Glenfiddich Spirit of Scotland Award for Business, 2003; Entrepreneurial Exchange Philanthropist of the Year, 2008; Inducted into Offshore Energy Centre's Hall of Fame, Houston, 2009; Member, Scottish Sea Fisheries Council, since 2007; awarded Energy Institute's Cadman Medal, 2010; SCDI President's Award, November, 2011; Honorary Doctor of Engineering, Heriot Watt University, 2012; Honorary Doctor of Science, Strathclyde University, 2013; Lifetime Achievement Award, Oil & Gas UK, 2012; American Scottish Foundation's Wallace Award, 2012; Broadwalk UK Chairman of the Year Award, 2012; Royal Society of Edinburgh Royal Medal, 2013; Chairman of Commission of Developing Scotland's Young Workforce; Leader, appointed by UK Government of a Review on maximising UKCS Oil & Gas recovery. Recreations: tennis; family; art. Address: (b.) J W Holdings Ltd, Blenheim House, Fountainhall Road, Aberdeen AB15 4DT; T.-01224 619842.

Wood, Jane Frances. Director of External Affairs for Business in the Community, since 2015; Managing Director of Business in the Community Scotland, since 2015; formerly Chief Executive, Scottish Business in the Community (2009-2015); formerly Chair, Essential Edinburgh; b. 11.4.62, Oxford; m., Christopher Wood; 2 s.; 2 d. Educ. Madras College; Napier University. Marketing Manager, Scottish and Newcastle, 1987-89; Marketing Director, The Guinea Group, 1989-97; Director of Communications, GJW Public Affairs Europe, 1997-99; Head of Corporate Affairs, Alliance Boots, 1999-2009. CBI Scotland Council; Member, First Minister's National Economic Forum; Board Director, Institute of Directors Scotland; Member, Ministerial 20:20 Climate Change Delivery Group. Address: (h.) Port Lodge, 7 High Street, Dunbar, East Lothian EH42 1EA; T.-01368 865265; e-mail: janewood@sbcscot.com

Wood, Professor Robert Anderson, BSc, MB, ChB, FRCPEdin and Glas, FRCSEdin, FRCPsych. Formerly Her Majesty's Inspector of Anatomy for Scotland (2007-2014); Postgraduate Medical Dean and Professor of Clinical Medicine, Aberdeen University, 1992-99; Member, Advocates Discipline Tribunal; b. 26.5.39, Edinburgh; m., Dr. Sheila Pirie; 1 s.; 3 d. Educ. Edinburgh Academy; Edinburgh University. Consultant Physician, Perth Royal Infirmary, 1972-92; Deputy Director of Postgraduate Medical Education, Dundee University, 1985-91; Dean, RCPE, 1992-95, Councillor, 1990-92, Treasurer, 1999-2003, Trustee, since 2004; Director, MDDUS, 2004-09, previously Member of Council, 1992-2004; Member, Harveian Society (President, 1998-99); Member, Tribunal Service Criminal Injuries Compensation Appeals Tribunal, 2000-2011. Member, Royal and Ancient, Blairgowrie, Elie and Craigie Hill golf clubs. Address: (h.) Ballomill House, Abernethy, Perthshire.

Woodroffe, Wing Commander Richard John, MBE. Veolia Water Nevis, since 2007; b. 12.6.50, Newmarket;

m., Elizabeth Clare; 3 s. Educ. Khormaksar, Changi, Rutlish and King Alfred's (Wantage) Grammar Schools; North Berkshire College. Purser Officer, P&O Lines Ltd., 1968; joined RAF, 1971: Pilot Officer, RAF St. Athan, 1972, Deputy Officer Commanding Accounts Flight, RAF Benson, 1973-74, Officer Commanding Personnel Services Flight, RAF Saxa Vord, 1974-75, promoted to Flying Officer, 1974, Operations Wing Adjutant and No. 3 (F) Squadron Intelligence Officer, RAF Germany Harrier Force, 1976-78, promoted to Flight Lieutenant, 1978, Officer Commanding Administration Flight, RAF Saxa Vord, 1979, Aide-de-Camp to Air Officer Commanding-in-Chief, Headquarters RAF Strike Command, 1980-82, Works Services and Airfield Survival Measures Project Officer, RAF Kinloss, 1982-84, promoted to Squadron Leader, 1984, College Secretariat 1 and College Press Liaison Officer, RAF College, Cranwell, 1984-86, Officer Commanding Personnel Management Squadron, RAF Bruggen, 1986-88, promoted to Wing Commander, 1988, assumed command of Administration Wing, RAF Leuchars, Fife, 1988-91, Air Member for Personnel's Management Planner and Briefer, MOD, 1991-93, Chairman of Boards, Officer and Aircrew Selection Centre, Cranwell, then Deputy President, Ground Boards, 1993-96; posted to NATO HQ Allied Forces Central (Brunssum, The Netherlands), 1996-2001; General Secretary, Royal British Legion Scotland, 2001-04; Thames Water Nevis, 2004-07; Trustee, Scottish Veterans' Garden City Association. Recreations: sub-aqua; fishing; flytying; rough shooting; social golf; rugby. Club: The Royal Air Force. Address: 15 Pitreavie Court, Dunfermline, Fife KY11 8UU; T.-01383 749630.

Woods, (Adrien) Charles, MA. Director, Scottish Universities Insight Institute, since 2012; Visiting Professor, University of Strathclyde, European Policies Research Centre; formerly Senior Director, Strategy and Chief Economist, Scottish Enterprise; b. 22.9.55, London. Educ. St. Andrews University. Various posts, Scottish Development Agency, 1981-91; Scottish Enterprise: Director, Policy and Planning, 1991-92, Director, Operations, 1992-94; Chief Executive, Scotland Europa, 1994-97. Recreations: golf; cycling. Address: University of Strathclyde, Collins Building, 21 Richmond Street, Glasgow G1 1XQ; e-mail: charlie.woods3@btinternet.com

Woods, Professor Philip John, BSc, PhD, CPhys, FInstP, FRSE. Professor of Nuclear Physics, Edinburgh University, since 2000, Head of Institute for Physics, 2005-09; b. 25.6.61, Lincoln; m., Colette; 1 s.; 1 d. Educ. City Comprehensive School, Lincoln; Manchester University. Research Fellow, Birmingham University; Lecturer, then Reader, Edinburgh University, 1988-2000. Recreation: overseas travel. Address: (b.) School of Physics and Astronomy, Edinburgh University, Edinburgh EH9 3JZ; T.-0131-650 5283; e-mail: pjw@ph.ed.ac.uk

Woodward, Rob. Chief Executive, STV Group plc. Career history: Managing Partner of Braxton UK, the strategy consulting practice of Deloitte; also led Deloitte Consulting's European TMT group; has specialised in advising TMT companies on strategic and corporate finance issues for the past 20 years; Managing Director, UBS Corporate Finance (worked in both London and New York), latterly co-head of the European Technology Group; joined Channel 4 in 2001 as Managing Director of 4 Ventures and was appointed as Commercial Director in 2002; executive member of the Channel 4 Corporation Board and responsible for Channel 4's commercial focus; served as Commercial Director of Channel 4 Television until 2005; Senior Advisor at LongAcre Partners; joined STV Group plc (formerly SMG plc) in March 2007. Pro-Chancellor,

City University London; Chair, University Council, since 2012, Member of the Council, since 2006, former Deputy Pro-Chancellor; Trustee of the National Endowment for Science, Technology and the Arts (NESTA); sits on the Advisory Board of Criticaleye; formerly a Non-Executive Director of RaceTech Holdings; Council Member, National Youth Theatre. Address: STV Group plc, Pacific Quay, Glasgow G51 1PQ; T.-0141 300 3000.

Woolhouse, Professor Mark Edward John, OBE, MA, MSc, PhD, FRSE, FMEdSci. Chair of Infectious Disease Epidemiology, University of Edinburgh, since 1997; b. 25.4.59, Shrewsbury; m., Dr. Francisca Mutapi; 1 d. Educ. Tiffin School, Kingston, Surrey; New College, University of Oxford; University of York; Queen's University, Canada. Research Fellow: University of Zimbabwe, 1985-86, Imperial College, London, 1986-89, University of Oxford, 1989-97. Recreations: walking; fly-fishing. Address: (b.) Centre for Immunity, Infection and Evolution, University of Edinburgh, Ashworth Laboratories, King's Buildings, Charlotte Auerbach Road, Edinburgh EH9 3FL; T.-0131 650 5456.

Woollins, Professor John Derek, BSc, PhD, FRSE, FRSC, CChem. Professor (Chemistry), since 1999, Vice Principal (Research) and Provost, University of St Andrews; b. 18.8.55, Cleethorpes; m., Alexandra Martha Zoya; 3 s.; 1 d. Educ. Cleethorpes Grammar School; University of East Anglia. University of British Columbia; Michigan State University; Leeds University; Imperial College, London; Professor, Loughborough University. Publications include: (books) Non Metal Rings, Cages, Clusters; Inorganic Experiments; 550 papers. Recreation: travel. Address: (b.) College Gate, North Street, St Andrews KY16 9AJ.

Woolman, The Hon. Lord (Stephen Woolman), Hon LLD. Senator of the College of Justice in Scotland, since 2008; Advocate, since 1987; b. 16.5.53, Edinburgh; m., Dr Helen Mackinnon; 2 d. Educ. George Heriot's School; Aberdeen University. Lecturer in Law, Edinburgh University, 1978-87; QC, 1998; Advocate Depute, 1999-2002; Deputy Chairman, Boundary Commission for Scotland, since 2009; Chairman of Council, St George's School for Girls, since 2011. Publication: Contract (4th edition), 2010. Keeper of the Advocates Library, 2004-08. Recreation: cinema. Address: (b.) Parliament House, Edinburgh EH1 1RF.

Wooton, Professor Ian, MA, MA, MPhil, PhD, FRSA. Professor of Economics, Strathclyde University, since 2003; Research Fellow, Centre for Economic Policy Research, London, since 1994; Fellow, CESifo Research Network, Munich, since 2006; b. 4.4.57, Kirkcaldy; 1 s.; 1 d.; Partner, Andrew Sawers. Educ. Kirkcaldy High School; St. Andrews University; Columbia University, New York. Associate Professor of Economics, University of Western Ontario, London, Canada, 1982-95; Bonar-Macfie Professor of Economics, Glasgow University, 1995-2003. Recreations: travel; architecture. Address: (b.) Department of Economics, Strathclyde Business School, University of Strathclyde, 199 Cathedral Street, Glasgow G4 0QU; T.-0141 548 3580; (h.) Flat 3/1, 26 Belhaven Terrace West, Glasgow G12 0UL; T.-0141-357 3708; e-mail: ian.wooton@strath.ac.uk

Wotherspoon, James Robert Edwards, DL, WS, LLB. Senior Partner, Macandrew & Jenkins WS; Deputy Lieutenant, Inverness; b. 17.3.55, Inverness; m., Mairi Fleming (nee Stewart); 2 s.; 1 d. Educ. Loretto School, Musselburgh; University of Aberdeen. LLB, Aberdeen;

Apprenticeship, Patrick & James, WS, Edinburgh; joined MacAndrew & Jenkins, WS, Inverness in 1979. Honorary Norwegian Consul; Deputy Lieutenant and Clerk to The Lieutenacy Inverness, Lochaber, Badenoch and Strathspey. Recreations: golf; tennis; sailing; stalking; shooting; fishing. Address: (b.) 5 Drummond Street, Inverness IV1 1QF; T.-01463 723500.
E-mail: james@macandrewjenkins.co.uk

Wright, Andrew Paul Kilding, OBE, BArch, RIBA, PPRIAS, FRSA, FSA Scot, FFCS. Chartered Architect and Heritage Consultant; Partner, Law & Dunbar-Nasmith, 1981-2001; b. 11.2.47, Walsall; m., Jean Patricia; 1 s.; 2 d. Educ. Queen Mary's Grammar School, Walsall; Liverpool University School of Architecture. Practising architect, since 1972; President, Inverness Architectural Association, 1986-88; External Examiner, Robert Gordon University, 1990-2003; Council, Royal Institute of British Architects, 1988-94 and 1995-97; President, Royal Incorporation of Architects in Scotland, 1995-97 (Member, Council, RIAS, 1985-94, 1995-99); Diocesan Architect, Diocese of Moray, Ross and Caithness, 1989-98; Consultant Architect to National Trust for Scotland for Mar Lodge Estate, 1995-99; Board Director, Glasgow 1999 Festival Company, 1996-2003; Member, Ancient Monuments Board for Scotland, 1996-2003; Commissioner, Royal Fine Art Commission for Scotland, 1997-2005; Hon. Adviser, Scottish Redundant Churches Trust, since 1996; Member, Church of Scotland Committee on Artistic Matters, 1999-2005; Trustee, Clan MacKenzie Charitable Trust, since 1998; Architectural Adviser, Holyrood Progress Group, Scottish Parliament, 2000-04; Conservation Adviser to Highland Historic Buildings Trust, since 2001; Conservation Advisory Panel to Hopetoun House Preservation Trust, 1997-2007; Member, Historic Environment Advisory Council for Scotland, 2003-09, Vice-Chair, 2003-06; Member, National Trust for Scotland Conservation Committee, 2007-2011; Trustee, Scottish Lime Centre Trust, since 2011; Member, Post Completion Advisory Group, Holyrood Building Project, 2004-06; Trustee: Cawdor Maintenance Trust, since 2010, Cawdor Heritage Charity, since 2010; Member, Historic Scotland Advisory Committee, since 2012; Member, Historic Scotland/RCAHMS Transition Advisory Board, 2013-15; Trustee, Knockando Woolmill Trust, since 2015. Recreations: music; railway history; fishing. Address: (b.) 16 Moy House Court, Forres IV36 2NZ; T.-01309 676655.

Wright, Bill, RSW, RGI, PAI, DA. Painter; b. 1.9.31, Glasgow; m., Anne Elizabeth; 3 d. Educ. Hyndland Secondary School; Glasgow School of Art. Work in several public and private collections in Norway, USA, Germany, Switzerland, Sarajavo, Saudi Arabia, Belgium; included in exhibitions in Wales, Poland, Germany, Norway, Yugoslavia, Netherlands; elected: RSW, 1977, RGI, 1990, PAI, 1995; formerly Adviser in Art, Strathclyde Regional Council; formerly Lecturer, Scottish Arts Council; Erstwhile President, Scottish Artists Benevolent Society. Recreations: opera; gardening; lobster fishing. Address: (h.) 16 Craigendoran Avenue, Helensburgh G84 7AZ; T.-01436 672886.

Wright, Professor Crispin James Garth, MA, PhD, FBA, BPhil, DLitt, FRSE. Director, Northern Institute of Philosophy, University of Aberdeen, since 2009; Professor of Logic and Metaphysics, St. Andrews University, 1978-2009; Leverhulme Personal Research Professor, 1998-2003; Bishop Wardlaw Professor, since 1997; Global Distinguished Professor, New York University, since 2002; b. 21.12.42, Bagshot, Surrey; m., Catherine; 2 s. Educ. Birkenhead School; Trinity College, Cambridge. Junior Research Fellow, Trinity College, Oxford, 1967-69; Fellow/Research Fellow, All Souls College, Oxford, 1969-78. Publications: Wittgenstein on the Foundations of Mathematics, 1980; Frege's Conception of Numbers as Objects, 1983; Realism, Meaning and Truth, 1986; Truth and Objectivity, 1992; The Reason's Proper Study (Co-author), 2001; Saving the Differences, 2003. Recreations: mountaineering; gardening; travel. Address: (b.) Northern Institute of Philosophy, University of Aberdeen, Old Brewery, High Street, Aberdeen AB24 3UB.

Wright, Rev. David Livingston, MA, BD, FFCS. Minister of Religion, Church of Scotland, since 1957; b. 18.5.30, Aberdeen; m., Margaret Brown; 1 d.; 2 s. Educ. Robert Gordon's College, Aberdeen; King's College, Aberdeen University. Organist and choirmaster, 1946-54; RAMC, 1949-51; Choirmaster of Youth for Christ, 1951-55; Minister: Cockenzie Chalmers Memorial, 1957-64, Forfar Lowson Memorial, 1964-71, Hawick Old, 1971-85, linked with Teviothead, 1972, Stornoway St Columba's Old Parish, 1985-98 and RAF chaplain. Former Moderator, Jedburgh and Lewis Presbyteries; convenor of Business Superintendance and World Mission committees; former Chairman, Scottish Reformation Society and National Church Association. Publications: reviews, articles, books - The Word Must Take Priority; The Way Forward for the Kirk; The Meaning of the Lord's Day; Reformed Book of Common Order (Contributor); Reformed and Evangelical (Editor); The Difference Christ Makes; Preaching the Word. Recreations: Cardiactive group; walking the dog; reading; playing piano and organ. Address: (h.) 84 Wyvis Drive, Nairn IV12 4TP; T.-01667 451613.

Wright, Professor Eric George, BSc, PhD, FRSB, FRCPath, FRSE. Professor of Experimental Haematology, University of Dundee (Emeritus, since 2010); b. 11.1.49, Wolverhampton. Educ. Wolverhampton Grammar School; Sussex University. Manchester University. WHO Research Fellow, Sloan Kettering Cancer Center, New York; Research Fellow, Paterson Institute for Cancer Research, Manchester; Lecturer in Cellular Pathology, University of St. Andrews; senior scientific positions, Medical Research Council Radiation and Genome Stability Unit, Harwell; Honorary Professor, Brunel University, University of Reading; Fellow of the Higher Education Academy, 2007; Fellow of the British Institute of Radiology, 2007. David Anderson-Berry Medal, Royal Society of Edinburgh, 1999; Weiss Medal of the Association for Radiation Research, 2007; Bacq Alexander Award of the European Radiation Research Society, 2008; Sylvanus Thompson Medal of the British Institute of Radiology; Member, UK Department of Health Committee on Medical Effects of Radiation in the Environment, 1996-2007; Member of Steering Committee, Academic Clinical Oncology and Radiobiology Research Network, 2005-09. Publications: 200 scientific papers. Recreations: music; gardening; hillwalking. Address: (h.) Willowhill, Forgan, Newport on Tay, Fife DD6 8RA; e-mail: e.g.wright@dundee.ac.uk

Wright, George Gordon. Publisher and Photographer; b. 25.6.42, Edinburgh; m., Carmen Ilie; 1 s. Educ. Darroch Secondary School; Heriot Watt College. Started publishing as a hobby, 1969; left printing trade, 1973, to develop own publishing company; founder Member, Scottish General Publishers Association; Past Chairman, Scottish Young Publishers Society; Oliver Brown Award, 1994; Secretary/Treasurer, 200 Burns Club, since 1991. Photographic Exhibitions: The Netherbow, 1979; National Library of Scotland, 2001. Publications: MacDiarmid: An Illustrated Biography, 1977; A Guide to the Royal Mile, 1979; Orkney From Old Photographs, 1981; A Guide to Holyrood Park and Arthur's Seat, 1987; E-book for the iPad from iTunes: 'A Great Idea at the Time' (Memoirs of a Scottish Photographer and Publisher), Vol. I. Growing Up in Edinburgh, 2013, Vol. II. A Precarious Occupation, 2015, Vol. III. Winners and Losers, 2015, Vol. IV. Highlights and Lowlights, 2015; The Dunedin Amateur Weight-Lifting Club, Edinburgh, 1932-1970. Recreations: history of Edinburgh; photography; jazz. Address: (h.) 25 Mayfield Road, Edinburgh EH9 2NQ; T.-0131-667 1300.

Wright, Rev. Kenyon Edward, CBE, MA, BA, MTh, DLitt. President, Constitutional Commission; Consultant on Justice and Peace to ACTS (Action of Churches Together in Scotland); Canon Emeritus and Companion of the Order of the Cross of Nails, Coventry Cathedral; Fellow, Scottish Council (Development and Industry); b. 31.8.32, Paisley; m., Betty Robinson; 3 d. Educ. Paisley Grammar School; Glasgow University; Cambridge University. Missionary in India, 1955-70; Director, Ecumenical Social and Industrial Institute, Durgapur, India, 1963-70; Director, Urban Ministry, Coventry Cathedral, 1970-74; Canon Residentiary and Director of International Ministry, Coventry Cathedral, 1974-81; General Secretary, Scottish Churches Council and Director, Scottish Churches House, 1981-90; Chair, Executive, Scottish Constitutional Convention, 1989-99; Member, Consultative Steering Group on the Scottish Parliament. Recreations: reading; walking; travel; living life to the full. Address: 1 Churchill Close, Ettington, Stratford CV37 7SP; T.-01789-740356. E-mail: kenyonwright@aol.com

Wright, Malcolm Robert, OBE, FRCGP, FRCPE, FRSA, Honorary Doctor, Paisley University, CIHSM. Chief Executive, NHS Grampian, since 2014; Chief Executive, NHS Education for Scotland, 2004-2014; b. 1.9.57, Blyth; 1 s.; 1 d. Educ. Kings School, Tynemouth; Penicuik High School. Hospital Manager, Great Ormond Street, London, 1989-92; Unit General Manager, Lothian Health Board, 1992-94; Chief Executive, Edinburgh and Sick Children's NHS Trust, 1994-99; Chief Executive, Dumfries and Galloway Acute and Maternity Hospitals NHS Trust, 1999-2001; Chief Executive, Dumfries and Galloway Health Board, 2001-04; Chair, Ministerial and Young People's Health Support Group, since 2000. Recreations: cycling; reading; theatre; opera; classical music; outdoor activity. Address: (b.) NHS Grampian, Summerfield House, 2 Eday Road, Aberdeen AB15 6RE.

Wright, Professor Robert Edward, BA, MA, PhD, FRSA, FFCS, ILTM, AcSS. Professor of Economics, University of Strathclyde, since 2005; b. 28.4.58, Trenton, Ontario, Canada. Educ. Trenton High School; University of Western Ontario; University of Stockholm; INED, Paris; University of Michigan. Research Fellow, Birkbeck College, London University, 1987; Lecturer/Senior Lecturer in Economics, University of Glasgow, 1991-95; Professor of Economics, University of Stirling, 1995-2005. Recreation: mountaineering. Address: (b.) Department of Economics, Sir William Duncan Building, 130 Rottenrow, Glasgow G4 0GE; T.-0141 548 3861.

Wright, Timothy Edward, BA. Chief Executive, Edinburgh University Press, since 1998; b. 17.2.60; m., Michaela Hoskier; 2 s.; 2 d. Educ. St. Edmund's School, Canterbury; Sunderland Polytechnic. Longman Publishing Group: European Sales Manager, 1984-90, International Sales Director, 1990-94; Sales and Marketing Director, Churchill Livingstone Publishers, 1994-98; Council Member, UK Publishers Association, 2007-2010; Chairman, Independent Publishers Guild, 2006-08 (Director, since 2001); Member: Book Development Council of Publishers Association, 1994-98, Scottish Arts Council Arts Project Committee, 1999-2002, International Board, Publishers Association, 2002-07, Council Academic and Professional Publishers; Vice Chairman, Book Trade Charity, since 2009. Recreations: shooting; cricket; classical music. Clubs: MCC, Farmers'. Address: Shrubhill, Dunblane, Perthshire FK15 9PA.

Wyke, John Anthony, MA, PhD, VetMB, HonFRCVS, FRSE, FMedSci. Emeritus Professor and Honorary Fellow, Glasgow University; b. 5.4.42, Cleethorpes. Educ. Dulwich College; Cambridge University; Glasgow University; London University. Leukemia Society of America Fellow, Universities of Washington and Southern California, 1970-72; Staff Scientist, Imperial Cancer Research Fund, 1972-85; Assistant Director of Research, 1985-87; Director, Beatson Institute for Cancer Research, 1987-2002; Director, Scottish Cancer Foundation, since 2002 (Chairman, 2002-2010); Director, Association for International Cancer Research, since 2003; Member of Council, Royal Veterinary College, 2008-2012; Trustee, RSE Scotland Foundation, since 2012. Address: (h.) 6 Ledcameroch Road, Bearsden, Glasgow G61 4AA.
E-mail: johnwyke@hotmail.co.uk

Wyllie, Andrew, CBE, FREng, MBA, BSc, CEng, FICE, CCMI. Chief Executive, Costain Group plc, since 2005; Non Executive Director, Scottish Water, since 2009; Vice President, Institution of Civil Engineers, since 2015; b. 24.12.62, Romford; m., Jane Morag Hudson; 1 d. Educ. Dunfermline High School; University of Strathclyde; London Business School. Taylor Woodrow, 1984-2005; Managing Director, Taylor Woodrow Construction Ltd., 2001-05. Fellow: British American Project, 2003, Institute of Directors; Member, CBI Construction Council. T.-01628 842444; e-mail: andrew.wyllie@costain.com

Wyllie, Gordon Malcolm, MStJ, LLB, DUniv (Glasgow), FSA Scot, NP, TEP, FFCS, WS. Former Partner, Bird Semple (2012-2014); former Partner, Biggart Baillie LLP, Solicitors (1980-2012); b. Newton Mearns. Educ. Dunoon Grammar School; Glasgow University. Clerk to General Commissioners of Inland Revenue, Glasgow North and South Divisions (1990-2009); Honorary Treasurer, Edinburgh Summer School in Ancient Greek, 1975-99; Director, Bailford Trustees Ltd.; Chairman, Britannia Panopticon Music Hall Trust, 1997-2005; Convener, Scottish Grant-Making Trusts Group, 2006-2010; Regional Chairman, Action Medical Research; Member, Council, Friends at the End, 2000-02; Chairman, Edinburgh Subscription Ball Committee; Freeman of Glasgow; Burgess of Edinburgh; Deacon, Incorporation of Hammermen of Edinburgh, 1996-99; Preses, Grand Antiquity Society of Glasgow, 2000-01; Boxmaster, Convenery of Trades of Edinburgh, 2000-03; Deacon Convener, Trades of Edinburgh, 2003-06; Clerk to the Trades House of Glasgow, 1987-2004; Governor, Trades Maiden Hospital of Edinburgh; Chairman, Edinburgh West End Community Council, since 2005; Deacon, Inc. of Bonnetmakers and Dyers of Edinburgh, 2003-09; wrote Scottish contribution to International Bar Association's International Dictionary of Succession Terms; Elder, Church of Scotland, since 2005; Member, Trusts and Succession Committee of the Law Society of Scotland, since 2005 (Chairman, since 2011) and the European Commission's Group of Experts on Succession and Wills in the EU, 2005-08. Recreations: music; history and the arts generally; country walks; foreign travel.

Wyllie, Very Rev. Dr. Hugh Rutherford, MA, Hon.DD (Aberdeen), FCIBS. Minister, Old Parish Church of Hamilton, 1981-2000; Moderator, General Assembly of the Church of Scotland, 1992-93; Lay Member, Scottish Executive's Working Party, General Medical Practitioners,

2000-02; b. 11.10.34, Glasgow; m., Eileen E. Cameron, MA; 2 d. Educ. Shawlands Academy; Hutchesons' Grammar School, Glasgow. Union Bank of Scotland, 1951-53; RAF, 1953-55; Glasgow University, 1956-62; Assistant Minister, Glasgow Cathedral, 1962-65; Minister, Dunbeth Church, Coatbridge, 1965-72; Minister, Cathcart South Church, Glasgow, 1972-81; Moderator, Presbytery of Hamilton, 1989-90, Convener, Business Committee, 1991-95; President, Hamilton Burns Club, 1990; founder, Hamilton Centre for Information for the Unemployed, 1983; introduced Dial-a-Fact on drugs and alcohol, 1986; established Hamilton Church History Project, 1984-87; Convener, General Assembly's Stewardship and Budget Committee, 1978-83; Convener, Stewardship and Finance Board, 1983-86; Convener, Assembly Council, 1987-91; Member, Board of Nomination to Church Chairs, 1985-91 and 1993-99; Member, General Assembly's Board of Practice and Procedure, 1991-95; Member, Board of Communication, 1999-2003; Non-Executive Director, Lanarkshire Health Care NHS Trust, 1995-99, Vice-Chairman, 1996-99; Trustee, Lanarkshire Primary Care NHS Trust, 1999-2001; Dr William Barclay Memorial Lecturer, 1994; admitted as Hon. Freeman, District of Hamilton, 1992; elected Member, Council, Scout Association, 1993-2003; Master, Hamilton Hospital, 1982-2000; Chaplain: Royal British Legion, Hamilton, 1981-2001, Lanarkshire Burma Star Association, 1983-2001, Q Division, Strathclyde Police, 1984-2001; George and Thomas Hutcheson Award, 2002. Recreations: gardening; DIY. Address: 18 Chantinghall Road, Hamilton ML3 8NP.

Wyllie, James Hogarth, BA, MA. Reader in International Relations, and Director of the MSc Strategic Studies Degree Programme, Aberdeen University; b. 7.3.51, Dumfries; m., Claire Helen Beaton; 2 s. Educ. Sanquhar Academy; Dumfries Academy; Stirling University; Lancaster University. Research Officer, Ministry of Defence, 1974-75; Tutor in Politics, Durham University, 1975-77; Lecturer in Politics, University of East Anglia, 1977-79; freelance journalism; frequent current affairs comment and analysis, BBC Radio; Commonwealth Fellow, University of Calgary, 1988; International Affairs Analyst, Grampian Television, 1989-94; Specialist Correspondent, Jane's Intelligence Review, 1992-98. Publications: Influence of British Arms; European Security in the Nuclear Age; Economist Pocket Guide to Defence (Co-author); International Politics since 1945 (Contributor); European Security in the New Political Environment. Address: (b.) Department of Politics and International Relations, Aberdeen University, Aberdeen AB24 3QY; T.-01224 272725.
E-mail: j.h.wyllie@abdn.ac.uk

Wynd, Andrew H. D., MBE, MIOD. Chief Executive, Scottish Spina Bifida Association. Address: (b.) The Dan Young Building, 6 Craighalbert Way, Cumbernauld, Glasgow G68 0LS; T.-01236 794500.
E-mail: chiefexec@ssba.org.uk

Y

Yarrow, Sir Eric Grant, MBE, DL, CEng, MRINA, FRSE. Chairman, Clydesdale Bank PLC, 1985-91 (Director, since 1962); Director, National Australia Bank Ltd., 1987-91; b. 23.4.20, Glasgow; m., 1, Rosemary Ann Young (deceased); 1 s. (deceased); 2, Annette Elizabeth Francoise Steven (m. diss.); 3 s.; 3, Joan Botting; 3 step d. Educ. Marlborough College; Glasgow University. Served engineering apprenticeship, G. & J. Weir, 1938-39; Royal Engineers, 1939-45; served Burma, 1942-45 (Major, RE, 1945); Yarrow & Co. Ltd. (later Yarrow PLC): Assistant Manager, 1946, Director, 1948, Managing Director, 1958-67, Chairman, 1962-85, President, 1985-87; Director, Standard Life Assurance Company, 1958-91; Chairman, Princess Louise Scottish Hospital, Erskine, 1980-86, Hon. President, since 1986; President, Scottish Convalescent Home for Children, 1957-70; Council Member, Royal Institution of Naval Architects, since 1957 (Vice President, 1965, Honorary Vice President, 1972); Member, General Committee, Lloyd's Register of Shipping, 1960-89; Deacon, Incorporation of Hammermen in Glasgow, 1961-62; Chairman, Yarrow (Shipbuilders) Ltd., 1962-79; Officer (Brother), Order of St. John, since 1965; Deputy Lieutenant, County of Renfrewshire, 1970-96; Prime Warden, Worshipful Company of Shipwrights, 1970-71; Council Member, Institute of Directors, 1983-90; President, Smeatonian Society of Civil Engineers, 1983-84; President, The Marlburian Club, 1984; Vice President, Royal Highland and Agricultural Society for Scotland, 1990. Address: (h.) Craigrowan, Kilmacolm PA13 4PD; T.-01505 872067.

Yeates, Damien. Chief Executive, Skills Development Scotland, since 2008. Over 16 years' experience in economic and social initiatives in Glasgow; previously Chief Executive of the Scottish University for Industry and the Govan Initiative; initiated a number of very successful programmes to promote skills and lifelong learning, including the establishment of the Digital Media Academy, the Community Technology Academy Network and the Blended Learning of Construction Skills (BLOCS) programme. Previously held directorships of the Scottish Urban Regeneration Forum and Realizations International Ltd. Address: (b.) 150 Broomielaw, Atlantic Quay, Glasgow G2 8LU.

Yellowlees, Lesley Jane, CBE, FRSC, FInstP, BSc, PhD, FRSE. Vice-Principal and Head of the College of Science & Engineering, University of Edinburgh, since 2011; President, Royal Society of Chemistry, 2012-2014; b. 31.8.53, London; m., Peter Yellowlees; 1 s.; 1 d. Educ. St Hilary's School, Edinburgh; University of Edinburgh. University of Edinburgh: Senior Lecturer, 1992, Reader, 1998, Personal Chair in Inorganic Electrochemistry, 2005-2010, Head of the School of Chemistry, 2005-2010. Royal Society of Chemistry Council; IUPAC 2011 Distinguished woman in Chemistry; DSc Heriot-Watt University. Recreations: cooking; entertaining; reading; walking. Address: (b.) College of Science & Engineering Office, University of Edinburgh, Weir Building, The King's Buildings, West Mains Road, Edinburgh EH9 3BF; T.-0131 650 5754; e-mail: l.j.yellowlees@ed.ac.uk

Young, Professor Archie, BSc, MBChB, MD, FRCP (Glas), FRCP (Lond), FRCP (Edin). Professor Emeritus, University of Edinburgh; b. 19.9.46, Glasgow; 1 s.; 1 d. Educ. High School of Glasgow. Training posts, Glasgow, London, Oxford; Consultant/Honorary Consultant posts: Oxford Rehabilitation Research Unit, University of Oxford, Royal Free Hospital and Medical School, London; Professor of Geriatric Medicine, Royal Free Hospital Medical School, then University of Edinburgh (retired 2007). Recreations: physical. Address: 45 Polton Road, Lasswade, Midlothian.

Young, Chick. Football Correspondent, BBC Television and Radio, since 1988; b. 4.5.51, Glasgow. Educ. Glasgow High School; Bellahouston Academy, Glasgow. Daily Record, 1969-72; Carrick Herald, Girvan, 1972; Irvine Herald, 1972-73; Charles Buchan's Football Monthly, London, 1973-74; Editor, Scottish Football magazine, 1974-75; Scottish Daily News, 1975; Scottish Daily Express, 1976; Evening Times, Glasgow, 1977-88; Radio Clyde, 1977-95; BBC, since 1988; Sunday People, 1988-89; Scotland on Sunday, 1989-91; Columnist, Daily Star, since 1996; Columnist, Daily Express, since 2004; Columnist, BBC website, since 2002; Columnist, Paisley Daily Express, since 2012. Fraser Award, Young Journalist of the Year, 1973; British Provincial Sports Journalist of the Year, 1987; Sony Award, British Sports Broadcaster of the Year (Bronze), 1997; Scottish Sports Journalist of the Year Runner-up, 1997 and 2002; RTS Provincial Sports Reporter of the Year, 2000. Publications: Rebirth of the Blues; Mo. Address: (b.) BBC TV Sport, 40 Pacific Quay, Glasgow G51 1DA; e-mail: chick.young@bbc.co.uk

Young, Jill. Chief Executive, National Waiting Times Centre Board. Address: (b.) Golden Jubilee National Hospital, Beardmore Street, Clydebank G81 4HX.

Young, John Maclennan, OBE. Farmer, since 1949; Hon. Sheriff, Grampian, Highlands and Islands, since 1995; JP for Caithness, 1970-99; b. 6.6.33, Thurso. Educ. Thurso Miller Academy. Member, Caithness County Council, 1961-75 (Chairman, Housing Committee, 1968-73, Chairman, Planning Committee, 1973-75); Member, Highland Regional Council, 1974-90 (Chairman, Roads and Transport Committee, 1978-90); Provost of Caithness, 1995-99; Member, Caithness District Council, 1974-96 (Convener of the Council, 1974-96); Member, The Highland Council, 1995-99; President, Caithness Area Executive Commitee, NFU of Scotland, 1963 and 1964; Chairman, Scrabster Harbour Trust, 2001-03; Chairman, Wick Airport Consultative Committee, 1990-2002. Address: (b.) Sordale, Halkirk, Caithness KW12 6XB; T.-01847 831228.

Young, Lesslie. Chief Executive, Epilespy Scotland. Address: Head Office, 48 Govan Road, Glasgow G51 1JL; T.-0141 427 4911.

Young, Mark Richard, BSc, PhD, FRES, FSBiol, CBiol. Emeritus Senior Lecturer, Aberdeen University; b. 27.10.48, Worcester; m., Jennifer Elizabeth Tully; 1 s.; 1 d. Educ. Kings School, Worcester; Birmingham University. Lecturer, Aberdeen University, 1973-89; Director of Teaching, School of Biological Sciences, 2004-2011; Academic Director, Centre for Learning and Teaching, 2007-2011. Member, North Board, Scottish Environment Protection Agency, 1996-2002; Member, Advisory Committee on SSSIs, 1998-2008. Recreations: natural history; walking; ball sports; visiting Hebridean islands. Address: (b.) School of Biological Sciences, University of Aberdeen, Oceanlab, Newburgh AB41 6AA; T.-01224 274420; e-mail: m.young@abdn.ac.uk

Young, Meriel, BA, PGDipM, MCIM. Director, Promote A Route, since 2007; Board Member, Loch Lomond and The Trossachs National Park Authority, 2002-2010; b. 10.01.73, Oban; m., Tim Hall; 2 s.; 1 d.

Educ. Oban High School; Heriot Watt University. Self-employed consultant and chartered marketer specialising in recreational and environmental management, communications and education; broad experience in project management across the public and private sector in community greenspace planning, urban forestry, transport and health policy; previously employed by City of Edinburgh Council (City Development), 1999-2003, and Woodland Trust Scotland, 1997-99; early freelance activities included running a day trips business, lecturing on environmental education and interpretation, and forestry contracting. Member of Central Scotland Regional Forestry Forum (FCS). Recreations: hillwalking; running; cycling; kayaking; sailing; yoga; travel; music; art. Address: 4 Kirkliston Road, South Queensferry, Edinburgh EH30 9LT.

Young, Rona Macdonald, BD, DipEd. Minister of Ayr: St Quivox Church, 2009-2015 (retired); Minister of Crosshouse Parish Church, 1991-2001; Minister of New Cumnock Parish Church, 2001-09 (Church returned to Full Status in 2004); b. 4.5.50, Giffnock, Glasgow; m., Thomas C. Young; 2 d.; 2 grandsons. Educ. Marr College, Troon; Craigie College, Ayr; Glasgow University. Primary School Teacher, Bentinck Primary, Kilmarnock, 1971-75; Minister of Crosshouse Parish Church, 1991-2001 (Church returned to Full Status in 1996). Recreation: reading. Address: (h.) 16 Macintyre Road, Prestwick, Ayrshire KA9 1BE; T.-01292 471982.

Young, Professor Stephen, BCom, MSc. Emeritus Professor, Adam Smith Business School, University of Glasgow (retired 2014); b. 20.8.44, Berwick upon Tweed; 1 s.; 1 d. Educ. Berwick Grammar School; Liverpool University; Newcastle University. Economist, Government of Tanzania, 1966-68; Head, International Economics, Milk Marketing Board, 1969-73; Lecturer/Senior Lecturer, Paisley College of Technology, 1973-79; Senior Lecturer/Professor, Strathclyde University, 1980-2005, and Head of Department of Marketing, 1992-96. Recreations: mountaineering (Munroist 3410); cycling; travelling; writing. Address: (h.) 42 Brierie Gardens, Crosslee, Johnstone PA6 7BZ; T.-01505 615554; e-mail: younstephen@gmail.com

Young, Sheriff Principal Sir Stephen Stewart Templeton, QC, 3rd Bt. Sheriff Principal of Grampian, Highland and Islands, 2001-2012; b. 24.5.47; m.; 2 s. Educ. Rugby; Trinity College, Oxford; Edinburgh University. Sheriff, Glasgow and Strathkelvin, 1984; Sheriff of North Strathclyde at Greenock, 1984-2001.

Young, William Smith Geates, LLB (Hons), NP. Chairman, Brechin Tindal Oatts; b. 21.12.55, Girvan; m., Margot Glanville Jones. Educ. Girvan Academy; Glasgow University. Joined Tindal Oatts & Rodger, 1978; admitted Solicitor, 1980; Managing Partner, Tindal Oatts, 1993; Managing Partner, Brechin Tindal Oatts, 1997-2008. SFA Class 1 Referee List, 1990-2005; FIFA List of International Linesmen, 1992, 1993; FIFA List of International Referees, 1994-2000; SFA Referee Committee, since 2009; UEFA Referee Observer, since 2010. Recreations: football; golf; after-dinner speaking. Address: (b.) 48 St. Vincent Street, Glasgow G2 5HS; T.-0141-221 8012.
E-mail: wsgy@bto.co.uk

Younger, Sir John (David) Bingham, KCVO. Lord-Lieutenant of Tweeddale, 1994-2014; b. 20.5.39, Doune; m., Anne Rosaleen Logan (deceased, 2012); 1 s.; 2 d. Educ. Eton College; Royal Military Academy, Sandhurst. Argyll and Sutherland Highlanders, 1957-69; Scottish and Newcastle Breweries, 1969-79; Founder and Managing Director, Broughton Brewery Ltd., 1979-95; Director, Broughton Ales, 1995-96. Deputy Lieutenant, Tweeddale, 1987, Vice Lord-Lieutenant, 1992. Chairman, Board of Governors, Belhaven Hill School Trust, 1988; Chairman, Scottish Borders Tourist Board, 1989; Member, A&SH Regimental Trust and Committee, 1985-96; Member, Queen's Bodyguard for Scotland (Royal Company of Archers) since 1969, Secretary, 1993-2007, Brigadier, 2002, Ensign, 2010; Vice President, RHASS, 1994; River Tweed Commissioner, 2002; President: Lowland Reserve Forces and Cadets Association, 2006-2014, SSAFA Forces Help (Borders), since 2006, Peebles County Cricket Club, since 2006; Chairman, Bowmen Ltd, since 2008; Director, Eastgate Theatre and Arts Centre, Peebles, since 2014. Recreation: the countryside. Address: (h.) Glenkirk, Broughton, Peeblesshire ML12 6JF; T.-01899 830570.

Younger, Professor Paul, DL, FREng, FRSE, FGS, FIChemE, FICE. British hydrogeologist, environmental engineer and writer; Rankine Chair of Engineering and Professor of Energy Engineering, School of Engineering, University of Glasgow, since 2012; b. 1.11.62. Educ. Newcastle University; Oklahoma State University. Chair, SustaiNE, 2010-11; Director, Newcastle Institute for Research on Sustainability, Newcastle University, 2010-12. Director of four companies engaged in the water and energy sectors, including Non-Executive Technical Director of CluffGeothermal; Chair of the Global Scientific Committee of the Planet Earth Institute. Publications: Mine Water: Hydrology, Pollution, Remediation, 2002; Water - all that matters, 2012; published more than 250 papers in the international peer-reviewed literature. Address: Systems, Power & Energy Group, James Watt South Building, Room 623c, University of Glasgow, Glasgow G12 8QQ; T.-0141 330 5042; e-mail: paul.younger@glasgow.ac.uk

Younger, Susan Emma, LLB, DipLP, WS, NP. Chief Executive, Cairn Mhor Childcare Partnership Ltd, since 2015; formerly Partner and Head of Banking, Morton Fraser (2002-2015); b. 12.4.64, Morpeth; m., Michael Younger; 3 d. Educ. St. Margarets, Newington, Edinburgh; Aberdeen University. Traineeship, Bonar Mackenzie, 1987-89; Assistant, Shepherd and Wedderburn, 1989-90; Associate, Anderson Strathern, 1990-2002. Tutor for Professional Competency Course for WS Society; Lay Member, Chartered Institute of Bankers. Recreations: skiing; cooking; piano and my 3 beautiful children. Address: (b.) 8, Pentland House, Saltire Centre, Glenrothes KY6 2AH; T.-01592 631031.
e-mail: susan.younger@cairnmhor.org

Youngson, Professor George Gray, CBE, MB, ChB, PhD, FRCSEdin. Consultant Surgeon, Royal Aberdeen Children's Hospital, 1985-2010 (retired); Emeritus Professor of Paediatric Surgery, Aberdeen University, since 2010; b. 13.5.49, Glasgow; m., Sandra Jean Lister; 1 s.; 2 d. Educ. Buckhaven High School; Aberdeen University. House Officer to Professor George Smith, 1973; Research Fellow, 1975; Registrar in General Surgery, 1975-77; Senior Resident in Cardiac and Thoracic Surgery, University Hospital, London, Ontario, 1979; Lecturer in Clinical Surgery, Aberdeen University, 1981; Clinical Fellow, Paediatric Surgery, Hospital for Sick Children, Toronto, 1983; Lecturer in Surgical Paediatrics and Transplantation, Aberdeen University, 1984; Vice President and Member of Council, Royal College of Surgeons of Edinburgh, 2009-2012. Recreations: sport (tennis, golf and squash); music (piobaireachd, guitar). Address: (h.) Birken Lodge, Bieldside, Aberdeen.

Yousaf, Humza. MSP (SNP), Glasgow Pollok, since 2016 (Glasgow region, 2011-16); Minister for Transport and the Islands, since 2016; Minister for Europe and International Development, 2014-16, Minister for External Affairs and International Development, 2012-14; b. 7.4.85. Active in the SNP and Glasgow politics since his teens. Graduated from Glasgow University in 2007 with a degree in politics. Has worked for Alex Salmond as a parliamentary researcher and later at party HQ; also worked with the late Bashir Ahmed MSP as a parliamentary researcher. Media spokesperson for Islamic Relief Scotland. Address: (b.) Scottish Parliament, Edinburgh EH99 1SP.

Z

Zealley, Helen Elizabeth, OBE, MD, FRCPE, FFPH. Former Non-Executive Member, Scottish Environment Protection Agency (2006-2013); former Non-Executive Member, Central Scotland Green Network Board (2011-13); Chief Administrative Medical Officer and Director of Public Health, Lothian Health Board, 1988-2000; Honorary Senior Lecturer, Edinburgh University, 1988-2000; b. 10.6.40; m., Dr. Andrew Zealley (qv) (deceased); 1 s.; 1 d. Educ. St. Albans High School; Edinburgh University. Former Member, Council, Royal College of Physicians, Edinburgh; former Member, Board, Faculty of Public Health Medicine; former Vice President, MedAct; former Member, Court, Edinburgh University; former Trustee, Waverley Care (2001-2014); Hon. Fellow, Scottish Environment LINK, since 2011. Recreations: family and home; sailing; skiing. Address: (b.) 12 Tipperlinn Road, Edinburgh EH10 5ET; T.-0131-447 5545.

Zhou, Professor Wuzong, BSc, PhD. Professor in Chemistry, University of St Andrews, since 2010; b. 25.04.56, Hangzhou, China; m., Chuan Gao; 1 s.; 1 d. Educ. Fudan University, Shanghai; University of Cambridge. University of Cambridge: Postdoctoral Research Assistant, 1987-88, Research Fellow, Queens' College, 1987-90, Research Associate, 1988-93, Assistant Director of Research, 1993-98; Reader in Chemistry, University of St Andrews, 1999-2010. Recreation: reading. Address: (b.) School of Chemistry, University of St Andrews, St Andrews KY16 9ST; T.-01334 467276; e-mail: wzhou@st-andrews.ac.uk